TV Times FILM & VIDEO GUIDE

1998

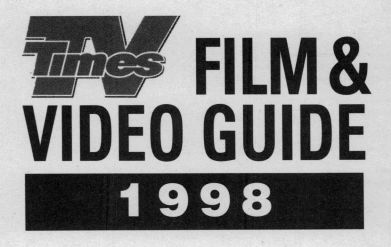

FILM & VIDEO GUIDE

TV Times

1998

David Quinlan

B.T. Batsford Ltd London

© David Quinlan 1997
First published 1997

Typset by Bernie Cavender Design & Greenwood Graphics Publishing
and printed by Mackays of Chatham plc

Published by B.T. Batsford Ltd
583 Fulham Road, London SW6 5BY

A CIP catalogue for this book is
available from the British Library

ISBN 0 7134 8284 2

Introduction

Welcome to the fourth edition of the family-friendly *TVTimes Film and Video Guide* which comprises a collection of more than 6,000 reviews from the *TVTimes* archive, together with assessments of many recent films yet to appear on television or even video.

As before, we have kept the reviews mainly to major US and British film to obtain a greater coverage of these markets, particularly in terms of the last 10 years. Thus you will find few continental films, silent movies or TV movies, although some may have crept in.

Reviews often have to be shortened in *TVTimes*, according to how many films are being shown on all channels in a particular week. But most appear here in their full versions (the writer's cut). Any lists of films that readers would like to see included in future editions of this book will be most welcome, and can be sent to me c/o the publishers.

Ratings

The rating system corresponds closely to the five-star grading that has been used in *TVTimes* since the beginning of 1995. It equates approximately as follows, with one minor addition:

★★★★★ Unmissable
★★★★ Very good
★★★ Good in parts
★★ Watchable
★ Missable

You may also occasionally encounter the term **R.B.** This stands for 'Really Bad' or, if you prefer, 'Rock Bottom'. Don't say that we haven't warned you about the very few films that get this rating!

Video

A ⓥ indicates that the film is available to buy and/or rent on video. Availability may vary as some films are bound to be withdrawn in the months that follow the book's publication.

Family Viewing

The family viewing guide symbols that appear by the films titles translate as follows:

⊙ Suitable for children to watch alone
○ Family fare
◑ Elements of sex, violence, bad language or adult themes may make the film unsuitable for youngsters to watch
● Adults only

Dates/Running Times

Dates of films should correspond with those on the credits of the movie, and running times indicate the original length of the film. Please bear in mind that films run one minute in every 25 shorter on television and video than they do in the cinema.

Alternative Titles

Aka (also known as) denotes any alternative titles by which the film may be known.

The majority of the film reviews here were written by me, but there are also pieces by *TVTimes* writers of past years, as well as by my present colleagues Diana Hall, Judith Jacobs (whose video reviews have made another valuable contribution to this edition), Steven Bunney and Kevin Wilson.

Whether your tastes run to *High Noon* and *The Grapes of Wrath*, or *Toy Story* and *Sense and Sensibility*, you should find most of your personal favourites in the pages that follow. Happy viewing!

David Quinlan
Addington, 1997

A

Abandon Ship ○
(aka: Seven Waves Away)
1957, UK, 100 mins, b/w
Dir: Richard Sale
Stars: Tyrone Power, Mai Zetterling, Lloyd Nolan, Stephen Boyd
Rating: ★★★

Gripping sea adventure where survivors from a sunken luxury liner crowd a small boat commanded by Tyrone Power. A telling portrait of courage in adversity; not for the squeamish.

ABBA the Movie ○ Ⓥ
1977, Sweden/Australia, 95 mins, colour
Dir: Lasse Hallstrom
Stars: Anni-Frid Lyngstad, Agnetha Faltskog, Benny Andersson, Bjorn Ulvaeus
Rating: ★★★

If the first half of this concert film-cum-musical portrait doesn't tell you why the Swedish group ABBA became the biggest world pop stars since The Beatles, then nothing will. Photogenic, melodious, happy and professional, the quartet is all of these. Its two girls are both strong singers and the lyrics of their songs, too few of which can be heard here, are highly original. Somewhere around the middle of the film, though, things start to go a bit wrong. Blame a too-loud soundtrack (which you can turn down a bit on TV!), the monotonously slender plot, and the lack of insight into the group without which an otherwise glorious finale can't quite take wing.

Abbott and Costello Go to Mars ○
1953, US, 76 mins, b/w
Dir: Charles Lamont
Stars: Bud Abbott, Lou Costello, Mari Blanchard
Rating: ★

Actually, they go to Venus, so somebody slipped up somewhere. The habitants of that far-off planet turn out to be the Miss Universe beauties, though they're armed to the shoulders. The team was past its sell-by date by now and this is one of their least tolerable ventures.

Abbott and Costello in the Foreign Legion ☉
1950, US, 80 mins, b/w
Dir: Charles Lamont
Stars: Bud Abbott, Lou Costello, Patricia Medina
Rating: ★★

A hundred lashes to the slapdash scripters who made this one of the weaker entries in the Abbott and Costello comedy career. Bud and Lou are beaux of the desert and the jests are enough to make a camel blush. Still, Patricia Medina sparkles behind her yashmak and a good collection of bad guys includes Walter Slezak, Douglass Dumbrille, Marc Lawrence and Tor Johnson. On second thoughts, failure with a cast like that deserves a thousand lashes.

Abbott and Costello Meet Captain Kidd ☉
1952, US, 70 mins, colour
Dir: Charles Lamont
Stars: Bud Abbott, Lou Costello, Charles Laughton, Leif Erickson
Rating: ★★

This was Bud Abbott's pet project – but he never thought he'd get Charles Laughton to agree to do it. 'I never have been able to do a double-take,' Laughton explained. 'If I do a picture with Lou Costello, I can learn.' Laughton hams it up in style in a historical romp that's fun rather than funny. One of the few films made in the rather bizarre Supercinecolor.

Abbott and Costello Meet Dr Jekyll and Mr Hyde ○
1953, US, 77 mins, b/w
Dir: Charles Lamont
Stars: Bud Abbott, Lou Costello, Boris Karloff
Rating: ★★

This slapstick comedy was one of a series in which Abbott and Costello met every Hollywood monster from Dracula to the Mummy. In this adventure-comedy-horror, they're American policemen in London at the turn of the century, hindering British bobbies in their attempts to solve the 'mad beast' murders. One critic remarked that the make-up and cameraman's tricks were clever, but the worst monsters were some of the jokes in the script. Be that as it may, parents should be reminded that, thanks to Boris Karloff's performance as Jekyll and Hyde, the film originally had an 'X' certificate. On the other hand, that was more than 40 years ago.

Abbott and Costello Meet Frankenstein ○
1948, US, 83 mins, b/w
Dir: Charles Barton
Stars: Bud Abbott, Lou Costello, Bela Lugosi, Lon Chaney Jr
Rating: ★★★★

In 1948, Universal decided to end its 20-year horror series with a bang. Abbott and Costello, its top box-office stars, would be pitted against all the monsters. The title, of course, is a misnomer. Bud and Lou meet everybody but Frankenstein. At least the British distributors called it *Abbott and Costello Meet the Ghosts*. Lon Chaney Jr is again Lawrence Talbot the Wolf Man, while Bela Lugosi plays Dracula for the first time since 1930. Efforts were made to persuade Boris Karloff to return as Frankenstein's monster, but they were unsuccessful. So Glenn Strange, former Western villain who had played the creature before, was again encased in monster make-up. There's even a guest 'appearance' from the Invisible Man. The result is alarmingly successful, with chills and cackles coming in balanced proportions.

Abbott and Costello Meet the Invisible Man ☉
1951, US, 82 mins, b/w
Dir: Charles Lamont
Stars: Bud Abbott, Lou Costello, Nancy Guild, Adele Jergens
Rating: ★★★

This is one of the best of several films that veteran Hollywood director Charles Lamont made with the comedy team of Bud Abbott and Lou Costello. A lot of intelligent fun is had with the invisibility gimmick, especially in a hilarious boxing match in which tubby Lou Costello has more than a little invisible help. His opponent is John Day, a good-looking ex-boxer turned actor, who found himself back in the ring several times during his film career! Incidentally, Abbott and Costello almost never played characters actually called Bud and Lou – but they do here.

Abbott and Costello Meet the Keystone Cops ☉
(aka: Abbott and Costello Meet the Keystone Kops)
1954, US, 79 mins, b/w
Dir: Charles Lamont
Stars: Bud Abbott, Lou Costello, Mack Sennett, Lynn Bari
Rating: ★★★

Certainly the best Abbott and Costello comedy of the Fifties, if only because

A

such genuine slapstick men as Mack Sennett, Heinie Conklin, Hank Mann and Roscoe Ates are around to provide atmosphere and a little fun. The film is set in 1912, and the heroine is Lynn Bari, who had a 20-year Hollywood career and was once described as 'the Paulette Goddard of the B-picture'. Most of the jokes here are pretty tired, and the film's not really funny until the final chase, which really whips up the pace.

Abbott and Costello Meet the Killer Boris Karloff ⊙

1949, US, 84 mins, b/w
Dir: Charles T Barton
Stars: Bud Abbott, Lou Costello, Boris Karloff
Rating: ★

More mayhem and comedy capers from Bud and Lou who were in the process of meeting all the famous film 'frighteners' when this murder lark was made. Having just co-starred with Lon Chaney Jr and Bela Lugosi, to say nothing of the Invisible Man, the boys now had as guest star the master chiller himself. Karloff plays an evil old Indian (the turbaned variety), who chases little Lou through the Lost Caverns in a hair-raising climax. Overall, though, it's a lukewarm and lacklustre dose of chuckles and chills.

Abbott and Costello Meet the Mummy ⊙

1955, US, 79 mins, b/w
Dir: Charles Lamont
Stars: Bud Abbott, Lou Costello, Marie Windsor
Rating: ★★

The only screen monster that Bud Abbott and Lou Costello hadn't previously met gets a grip on them in this typical A and C comedy. Marie Windsor, raven-haired actress from the Forties and Fifties who never got the parts her talents deserved, plays the villainess to the hilt, in the finest Gale Sondergaard tradition. The humour is tried and true, but by and large the lads are in fair form, Costello in particular making the most of a scene where a medallion is slipped into his food.

ABC Murders, The

See: The Alphabet Murders

Abliene Town ○

1946, US, 89 mins, b/w
Dir: Edwin L Marin
Stars: Randolph Scott, Ann Dvorak,

Edgar Buchanan, Lloyd Bridges
Rating: ★★★

Tough-skinned, fast-moving Western – the first of a whole run of Randolph Scott action films made by director Edwin L Marin, a series that was stopped short by Marin's early death in 1951. Rhonda Fleming, who had made her debut in another Scott Western, *In Old Oklahoma,* three years earlier, was upped to the second female lead in this one, below Ann Dvorak who has a Marlene Dietrich-style role as a singing saloon queen. Based on Ernest Haycox's novel *Trail Town.*

Abominable Dr Phibes, The ● ⓥ

1971, UK, 93 mins, colour
Dir: Robert Fuest
Stars: Vincent Price, Joseph Cotten, Virginia North
Rating: ★★★★

Spoof horror piece with delightful Thirties' decor, a series of grisly deaths and a plot about a disfigured madman (Vincent Price) who, from the depths of his grandiose mansion, vows to kill the 10-man surgical team 'responsible' for the death of his wife. Phibes' massive cinema organ, which graces the beginning and the end, is rather splendid and, as the dead wife he keeps preserved, you may just recognise the delectable Caroline Munro, later a star of such action spectaculars as *The Golden Voyage of Sinbad.*

About Last Night... ● ⓥ

1986, US, 113 mins, colour
Dir: Edward Zwick
Stars: Rob Lowe, Demi Moore, James Belushi
Rating: ★

No surprises here: boy meets girl, boy beds girl, girl moves in, boy fights with girl, girl moves out, boy gets girl. Rob Lowe and Demi Moore bare a lot of body in the cause of simulated passion but the dialogue, although it has moments of truth, tends to the raucous and doesn't convey much real tenderness. Acting honours go to plainish Elizabeth Perkins and plumpish James Belushi, who both sketch in deftly the qualities that make them loners. Just a word about that fake snow in the winter scenes, you guys: it was *terrible.*

About Mrs Leslie ○

1954, US, 104 mins, b/w
Dir: Daniel Mann
Stars: Shirley Booth, Robert Ryan, Marjie Millar, Alex Nicol
Rating: ★★★

That highly watchable actress Shirley Booth, who notched up an Academy Award for her performance in *Come Back, Little Sheba,* actually gets a chance to look a little glamorous in this downbeat love story. She plays a woman who runs a rather ordinary boarding house but treasures memories of a middle-age love affair. Robert Ryan gives a fine performance as the world-weary aircraft designer lost in the history of the American Civil War, who becomes Booth's part-time lover. The film's tightly written sentiments and absorbing drama are admirably suited for transference to the TV screen.

Above Suspicion ○

1943, US, 90 mins, b/w
Dir: Richard Thorpe
Stars: Joan Crawford, Fred MacMurray, Basil Rathbone
Rating: ★★★

A fast-moving comedy-thriller made when tales of espionage and adventure were all the rage (even Hitchcock joined in with *Foreign Correspondent* and *Saboteur*). This one is crammed with brash, flag-waving Hollywood dialogue (mostly for Fred MacMurray) and enough twists to keep any mystery fan guessing until the last reel.

Above the Law ● ⓥ (aka Nico)

1988, US, 99 mins, colour
Dir: Andrew Davis
Stars: Steven Seagal, Sharon Stone, Henry Silva, Pam Grier, Thalmus Rasasula
Rating: ★★

Steven Seagal's debut is a numbingly violent thriller that offers us gratuitous blood and bone for the sake of a gasp from the audience. Seagal is a cop who, naturally, doesn't so much arrest his suspects as take them apart at the seams. He bulldozes his way into something big that involves master hit-men and a senatorial assassination at the end of the line, upsets authority – 'Nico,' whispers his wife (Sharon Stone), 'why is the CIA calling you at two in the morning?' – and finally demolishes the entire china shop. Dislikeable characters throughout make it hard to want to stick around and see what happens to them and the film is dull in between its bursts (or should I say, spurts) of violent action.

Above the Rim ● ⓥ

1994, US, 97 mins, colour
Dir: Jeff Pollack

Stars: Duane Martin, Leon, Tupac Shakur, David Bailey, Tonya Pinkins, Marion Wayans
Rating: ★★★

This basketball morality tale takes a while to get into, but eventually scores a few points both above and below the rim. A high school star, Kyle (Duane Martin), hot-headed and selfish, clearly needs a steadying influence other than that of his mother. Along comes Shep (Leon), a former star who blew his own career after feeling responsible for the death of his friend, and now takes a job at Kyle's school as a security cop. Thanks to Shep's negative attitude, though, Kyle looks more likely to end up in the clutches of the local crime lord (Tupac Shakur) who just happens to be Shep's brother. All of this interrelates satisfactorily if somewhat predictably – apart from the unexpected violence of the ending – and provides a pointed lesson in how to avoid the lower strata of ghetto life provided, of course, you have the talent. None of the performances are less than convincing and there's some lovely colour photography.

Above Us the Waves ○ Ⓥ
1955, UK, 99 mins, b/w
Dir: Ralph Thomas
Stars: John Mills, John Gregson, Donald Sinden
Rating: ★★★

One of director Ralph Thomas's best films, this is also among the most exciting he ever made. It's the true-to-life story of an assault by midget submarines on a giant German battleship that threatened Allied shipping during World War Two. The photography by Ernest Seward is praiseworthy, and the climax will have even non-war film fans on the edges of their seats.

Absence of Malice ◑ Ⓥ
1981, US, 116 mins, colour
Dir: Sydney Pollack
Stars: Paul Newman, Sally Field, Bob Balaban, Melinda Dillon
Rating: ★★★★

Paul Newman is close to his best here as an innocent man whose life is virtually wrecked – because hotheads at the DA's office believe he *may* be someone who could help crack a months-old investigation into the disappearance of a prominent union leader. So the news of his possible complicity is leaked to a hard-headed newsgirl (Sally Field) who duly splashes it all over the front page. Subsequent developments lead almost inevitably to tragedy before Newman,

by now romantically involved with the contrite reporter, decides to get his own back. Although the ways and means of this are not presented in quite the hard-hitting manner they might be, it's nice to see the bad guys get their come-uppance at the end. Bob Balaban's coldly sneaky investigator also catches the eye in a smooth and thought-provoking entertainment.

Absent-Minded Professor, The ⊙ Ⓥ
1961, US, 97 mins, b/w
Dir: Robert Stevenson
Stars: Fred MacMurray, Nancy Olson, Keenan Wynn
Rating: ★★★★

A riotous comedy from the Disney stable, made by the studio's best director, Robert Stevenson, who did *Mary Poppins* for them three years later. Fred MacMurray, as the prof of the title, accidentally invents a rubbery substance that makes things fly. Things from then on happen at breakneck speed, with some very funny chase sequences and wonderful comic support from James Westerfield as a continually bewildered cop, and from Keenan Wynn, making the first of several appearances in Disney comedies as the crooked financier Alonzo Hawk, a role he was still playing as late as 1974 in *Herbie Rides Again*. One of the funniest scenes of all in this film involves Wynn bounding, uncontrollably up and down on his lawn. Wynn's real-life father Ed is very droll as the local fire chief.

Absolute Beginners ◑ Ⓥ
1986, UK, 107 mins, colour
Dir: Julien Temple
Stars: David Bowie, Patsy Kensit, Eddie O'Connell, James Fox
Rating: ★★★

Certainly the biggest British musical in a couple of decades, and not half as bad as some critics avowed. Julien Temple's film re-creates the summer of 1958 when 'teenagers started' and so, he contends, did modern Britain, with all its racial warts and sores. It's a pity the film doesn't have the courage to go all the way with its approach of the first 15 minutes which vividly evokes nostalgia for the environments of Soho and Notting Hill in a slightly surrealistic and kaleidoscopic way, creating its atmosphere through a flurry of images, off-camera lines and surreptitiously prowling cameras. The clean exhilaration of all this, however, is sullied not only by the Notting Hill riots that form

the climax but by a sub-plot (involving heroine Patsy Kensit) straight out of a British pop musical of the Sixties.

Absolute Power ● Ⓥ
1997, US, 121 mins, colour
Dir: Clint Eastwood
Stars: Eastwood, Gene Hackman, Ed Harris, Laura Linney, Scott Glenn, Judy Davis
Rating: ★★★

Expertly made and satisfyingly entertaining, if progressively less likely, this is yet another thriller that shows us the American president up to his neck in chicanery. Master burglar Luther (Eastwood), retired for many years, plans one last job: to rob a rich presidential supporter (E G Marshall), currently away from his vast mansion. He's trapped in the vault by the arrival of the owner's wife (Melora Hardin) and her latest lover, the Prez (Hackman). Murder ensues, witnessed by Luther through a two-way mirror. At first intending to flee the country, Luther's turned around by the Prez's crocodile tears on TV for the bereaved man. And when secret servicemen target Luther's daughter (Linney), the old maestro really moves into action. In spite of the strong cast, Eastwood, who even composed some of the music, dominates this film as the laid-back thief. You're on his side to such a degree as to even swallow developments in the last reel that border on the incredible.

Abyss, The ◑ Ⓥ
1989, US, 134 mins, colour
Dir: James Cameron
Stars: Ed Harris, Mary Elizabeth Mastrantonio, Michael Biehn
Rating:★★★

'He's losing it,' cry the crew of the stranded 'submersible' as skipper Ed Harris starts babbling at about 12,000 feet down, while diving to disarm a nuclear warhead. The film, too, starts to lose it at about this point, after a fine first two hours whose urgency and excitement is what James Cameron, who made *Aliens* and the *Terminator* films, is all about. But the whole 'alien' involvement in the later stages could conveniently have been ditched into the abyss of the title, to say nothing of the money the producers could have saved on special effects. Cameron is also responsible for a script that disintegrates when asked to express human emotion , but which drives the drama along in fine style as long as the action is strong and virile. The excitement in

A

the main body of the film is super-charged, with racing tracking shots and an agonising resuscitation scene adding to the tension. Mary Elizabeth Mastrantonio is along for the dive as Harris's estranged scientist wife, and Cameron favourite Michael Biehn enjoys himself as the naval lieutenant who 'loses it' in style and prepares to blow up nothing less than the entire world.

Accident ◐ ⓥ
1967, UK, 105 mins, colour
Dir: Joseph Losey
Stars: Dirk Bogarde, Stanley Baker, Jacqueline Sassard, Michael York
Rating: ★★

Casts and credits came no more fashionable in 1967 than in this flashback drama, which caused highbrow critics to reach for such adjectives as 'elliptical', 'seminal' and 'schematic' in describing director Joseph Losey's approach to the story of three men involved with the same woman. The script by Harold Pinter, from the novel by Nicholas Mosley (both of whom play cameo roles in the film), breaks down the characters' thoughts, actions and motives to clearly reveal their personalities. There are skilful portraits from Dirk Bogarde, Stanley Baker, Michael York and Vivien Merchant. Only Jacqueline Sassard as the girl at the centre of things seems to fall below this level of excellence.

Accidental Hero ◐ ⓥ
(aka: Hero)
1992, US, 117 mins, colour
Dir: Stephen Frears
Stars: Dustin Hoffman, Geena Davis, Andy Garcia, Chevy Chase, Joan Cusack
Rating: ★★★★

Petty thief Dustin Hoffman, about to go to prison for receiving stolen property, saves 54 people from a burning plane, but his homeless pal Andy Garcia takes the credit – and the one million dollars that goes with it. Previously unwilling to step into the limelight, Hoffman belatedly tries to grab the glory (despite having robbed the people he was rescuing). But, as is traditionally the case in this kind of social comedy, the fates conspire against him, and under the guidance of survivor and crusading reporter Gale Gayley (a super-sexy performance by Geena Davis) and her scoop-hungry editor (Chevy Chase, unbilled and unwigged), Garcia becomes a national celebrity. What's more he's a nice

guy (who starts doing good deeds) and Hoffman isn't – so hasn't justice been done? Well, you'll know the answers to that. The spirit of Frank Capra lives in this modern-day story quite rightly given an old-fashioned (save the language) treatment. After you've shed a tear or two, the film neatly sends you off with a laugh in the final scene. All the performances are good.

Accidental Tourist, The ◐ ⓥ
1988, US, 121 mins, colour
Dir: Lawrence Kasdan
Stars: William Hurt, Kathleen Turner, Geena Davis, Bill Pullman, Ed Begley Jr
Rating: ★★

Acted with great care, this is a long, drawn-out and sometimes boring romantic drama. William Hurt is the central character, a tour-book writer and walking iceberg who has become zombiefied since the death of his only son a year earlier. No wonder wife Kathleen Turner wants to leave this member of an extremely eccentric family who play weird card games and never answer the phone. For some reason, dog trainer Geena Davis is attracted to Hurt, setting up the triangular motif that dominates the film. You can't think that either woman is getting much of a bargain and the path to Hurt's choice between them is not exactly fun. Davis's performance, though, is a knockout and won her an Oscar.

Accused, The ○
1948, US, 101 mins, b/w
Dir: William Dieterle
Stars: Loretta Young, Wendell Corey
Rating: ★★★

A taut psychological thriller with some pretty complex characters as well as moments of suspense and a good story. Director William Dieterle presents it all with confident visual flair, and compels attention as the varying characters approach their dates with destiny. Loretta Young handles an unusual part well, but Wendell Corey's role is the most interesting in the film.

Accused, The ◐ ⓥ
1988, US, 111 mins, colour
Dir: Jonathan Kaplan
Stars: Jodie Foster, Kelly McGillis
Rating: ★★★★★

Jodie Foster deservedly won an Oscar in this brutal, uncompromising drama about the battle to prosecute onlookers at a gang rape after the actual attackers

get off on reduced charges. Foster couldn't be better as the far-from squeaky-clean victim, betrayed by the justice system, who fights her corner is like an alleycat. The film itself is a real time-bomb of a drama that provides both graphic, unpalatable food for thought and excellent courtroom dramatics, especially when attorney Kelly McGillis, mortified by her failure to represent Foster to the best of her ability, fights for self-redemption under threat of dismissal from her firm. McGillis is driven on by the realisation that, in the unlikely event of her prosecuting the jeering crowd successfully, the original rapists will be forced to serve the full term of the light five-year sentence they had been given and have their crime reclassified from 'reckless endangerment' to rape. Powerful, hyper-emotive stuff and engrossing entertainment too.

Ace in the Hole ○ ⓥ
(aka: The Big Carnival)
1951, US, 112 mins, b/w
Dir: Billy Wilder
Stars: Kirk Douglas, Jan Sterling, Robert Arthur
Rating: ★★★★★

An expertly turned out study of a brutal sensation monger – produced, directed and partly written by Billy Wilder. Although the story may leave a sour taste, it is packed with tension, high drama and first-rate acting. Kirk Douglas offers another of his callous, hard-driving portrayals as the ruthless reporter out to make a sensation from the story of a man trapped by a rock fall. Jan Sterling is subtly sluttish and sullen as the trapped man's wife. Repulsive as the leading character is, you may be even more appalled by the dreadful crowd which congregates around the scene, full of glee at being in on a cheap thrill, as a man's tragedy is quickly turned into a circus.

Aces High ○ ⓥ
1976, UK, 114 mins, colour
Dir: Jack Gold
Stars: Malcolm McDowell, Christopher Plummer, Simon Ward, Peter Firth
Rating: ★★

R C Sherriff's classic play about life in the trenches during World War One, *Journey's End*, was reworked as a drama of fliers in the Royal Flying Corps by screenwriter Howard Barker. Fine aerial sequences (directed by Derek Cracknell) but the dramatics on the ground soar rather less and the characters tend towards cliché.

Ace Ventura, Pet Detective
◐ ⓥ
1993, US, 86 mins, colour
Dir: Tom Shadyac
Stars: Jim Carrey, Sean Young,
Courteney Cox
Rating: ★★★

Although it has only one or two big laughs, this is quite a jolly lowbrow jape, with a neat central idea and Jim Carrey mugging madly in the title role. Missing animals are this hunter's bag all right, although naturally he's an ace at the formula stuff as well. After solving the mystery of a missing shih-tzu dog, Ace is hired to investigate the poolnapping of a dapper dolphin who's the ball-playing mascot of the local Miami football team. Ace soon gets in the hair of lady lieutenant Einhorn (Sean Young) as well as the bed of the dolphin's PR girl (Courteney Cox). There are one or two pleasant incidentals: the menagerie Ace keeps at his apartment disappears at the mere sound of the landlord; and he drives his car sideways as a result of an earlier fracas with another petnapper. No, Ace won't bore you and you might even get a chuckle or two – especially at Carrey's dead-on impersonation of Sean Connery as James Bond.

Ace Ventura: When Nature Calls ◐
1995, US, 97 mins, colour
Dir: Steve Oedekerk
Stars: Jim Carrey, Simon Callow, Ian McNeice, Maynard Eziashi
Rating: ★★★

This son of *Carry On Up the Jungle* is a broad but often funny sequel to the original, with Jim Carrey's 'pet detective' called to investigate the theft of a sacred white bat that may mean tribal warfare if it's not recovered. Even pottier, then, than the last one, but Carrey and director Oedekerk know how to make this crude material work. Only Carrey could make a mass spitting scene funny. And only Carrey could ride to the rescue at the end on an ostrich and do it with such aplomb. The star is, admittedly even more OTT than necessary, but his fans will still love it.

Across the Great Divide ⊙ ⓥ
1977, US, 101 mins, colour
Dir: Stewart Raffill
Stars: Robert Logan, Heather Rattray
Rating: ★★★★★

If you've forgotten how much fun films used to be, take a look at this, the best of the *Wilderness Family*-style adventures. Director Stewart Raffill has taken his own story, of how two children, a teenage girl and a boy about 10, trek across the American wilderness to Oregon over desolate plain and icy mountain, with the help of a roguish frontier gambler, and has told it clearly and strongly, with never a drop in pace and barely a concession to sentimentality. There isn't even a hint of a romance between the gambler and the girl, who is allowed to be entirely her own character. The animal footage is fabulous, as deer and lioncubs romp with the children and a bear convincingly menaces the gambler, who hides in a beaver's lodge as the tenant exits hastily by the back door. Robert Logan, in his best screen performance, is almost faultless as the gambler: the charm never seems forced and the ending promises no guarantee of his redemption. Heather Rattray, too, is excellent as Holly: one of those rare sub-teen portrayals whose strength and truth she is unlikely to equal.

Across the Pacific ○
1942, US, 99 mins, b/w
Dir: John Huston
Stars: Humphrey Bogart, Mary Astor, Sydney Greenstreet
Rating:★★

A rugged action thriller from the same team – star Humphrey Bogart, director, John Huston – that had just made *The Maltese Falcon*. Bogart's role in many ways foreshadows the world-weary adventurer – also called Rick – that he played in his next film, *Casablanca*.

Across the Wide Missouri ○
1951, US, 78 mins, colour
Dir: William A Wellman
Stars: Clark Gable, Ricardo Montalban, Maria Elena Marques
Rating: ★★

Unusual Western, oddly reminiscent Of Oliver Reed's The *Trap*. Clark Gable, radiating sincerity, gives one of his best performances as the rugged trapper, and Maria Elena Marques, who only made one other Hollywood film, is enchanting as the girl.

Action in the North Atlantic ○
1943, US, 127 mins, b/w
Dir: Lloyd Bacon
Stars: Humphrey Bogart, Raymond Massey, Alan Hale
Rating: ★★★

And the action is everything in this all-guns-firing Warner Brothers tribute to the American marines. Excellent battle scenes involving submarines and surface vessels and fine performances. It is outside Humphrey Bogart's usual metier, but he gives a rugged portrayal that complements the inner steel of Raymond Massey as his captain. And there's a peach of a performance from that perennial Hollywood blonde, Iris Adrian, here seen as Alan Hale's domineering wife.

Acts of Love ● ⓥ
aka: Carried Away
1995, US, 113 mins, colour
Dir: Bruno Barreto
Stars: Dennis Hopper, Amy Irving, Amy Locane, Julie Harris
Rating: RB

If you believe this, you'll believe anything. Down on the farm, gammy-legged Hopper looks after his dying mother (Harris) and teaches at the local school, while conducting an on-off affair with a nearby widow (Irving) whom he loved as a boy. Flaxen-haired city girl Locane joins his class, stables her horse in his barn and in no time at all has seduced him by stripping to her assets in his hayloft. Just the kind of guy she'd go for, right? Well, Locane's character *is* a couple of jacks short of a full deck, but that won't stop you feeling ill-at-ease with the whole thing, not to mention the full-frontal nudity of oldies Hopper and Irving and the strange mix of nostalgia values and rural four-letter dialogue. Hopper and Locane are not good. Irving and Harris are better, but not good enough to rescue a leaky old ship that might as well call in the salvage crew after the first reel.

Act of Violence ○
1948, US, 92 mins, b/w
Dir: Fred Zimmemann
Stars: Van Heflin, Robert Ryan, Jane Leigh, Mary Astor, Phyllis Thaxter
Rating: ★★★

This thriller bursts into action without so much as a single credit appearing on the screen (they're left to the end). Commonplace, nowadays, but when director Fred Zinnemann pulled the stunt in an effort to hold the audience's interest from start to finish, it was regarded as something of an innovation – and a welcome one at that. Originally, Gregory Peck and Humphrey Bogart were set to play the roles finally filled by Heflin and Ryan.

A

Adam's Rib ○

1949, US, 100 mins, b/w
Dir: George Cukor
Stars: Spencer Tracy, Katharine
Hepburn, Judy Holliday, Tom Ewell,
David Wayne
Rating: ★★★★

Spencer Tracy and Katharine
Hepburn are in sparkling form as
lawyers whose marriage comes under
strain when they find themselves on
opposing sides in court, but they face
stiff opposition from Judy Holliday as
the lady accused of shooting her husband. Strong support, too, from Tom
Ewell as the man winged by Holliday's
shot and David Wayne as a songwriter
with none-too honourable designs on
Hepburn. George Cukor has the comedy under perfect control.

Addams Family, The ① ⓥ

1991, US, 101 mins, colour
Dir: Barry Sonnenfeld
Stars: Anjelica Huston, Raul Julia,
Christopher Lloyd, Christina Ricci
Rating: ★★

This living horror comic (from the famous newspaper strip and subsequent
TV series) looks great. Doubtless its
cobwebs are the finest money can buy.
Here is the familiar gallery of ghouls
led by Morticia, a symphony in black,
white and blood-red, matriarch to a
gothic family whose pet is Thing, a
severed hand. And yet something is
missing. It's flair, imagination, or
whatever magic ingredient is needed to
make the Addamses (if they'll pardon
the expression) spring to life. A dance
sequence at a party almost does it, but
most of the characters stubbornly stay
cardboard comic cut-outs.
Honourable exceptions are
Christopher Lloyd as long-lost brother
Fester, a shaven demon with a wonderful idiot grin; and Christina Ricci as
the Addams daughter, a perfectly
poker-faced malevolent child.

Addams Family Values ○ ⓥ

1993, US, 92 mins, colour
Dir: Barry Sonnenfeld
Stars: Anjelica Huston, Raul Julia,
Christopher Lloyd, Joan Cusack, Carol
Kane
Rating: ★★

More of the same, only less. The gleefully ghoulish Addamses are back,
with Morticia (Anjelica Huston) having a baby and Fester (Christopher
Lloyd) in love with the Black Widow
(Joan Cusack), a notorious husband-
killer posing as the Addamses' new
nanny. Like Cusack's initially amus-

ing performance, the whole thing
wears thin in quite a short time, with
few really funny lines to keep it going.
Huston has almost nothing to do and
she and Raul Julia (as her husband) get
little room for improvisation under
Barry Sonnenfeld's head-on direction.
Lloyd does what he can with Fester,
grinning idiotically again (visually he's
perfect) and pining for love. 'Some
day,' he's told, 'you'll meet someone
very special ... someone who won't
press charges.'

Addicted to Love ○ ⓥ

1997, US, 100 mins, colkour
Dir: Griffin Dunne
Stars: Meg Ryan, Matthew Broderick,
Kelly Preston, Tcheky Karyo
Rating: ★★

There are a few quiet sniggers in this
lightest of romantic comedies, whose
fragile plot would probably collapse at
the touch of a finger. Astronomer
Broderick loses teacher girlfriend
Preston to the lure of New York where
she is soon shacked up with French
restaurateur Karyo. Spying on her
from the derelict building opposite
which he also makes his home,
Broederick is soon joined by Karyo's
jilted mistress (Ryan). It isn't long
before they have launched a series of
schemes with the aim of splitting the
couple up and reuniting with their
former mates. Unexpected
consequences arise (says the synopsis).
Well, no, actually entirely expected
consequences arise and the getting
there is largely dull (the pair's plots are
annoying rather than amusing), save
for a few funny moments towads the
end. Karyo, though too old for his
role, at least gives the thing a bit of
spark.

Admirable Crichton, The ○

(aka: Paradise Lagoon)
1957, UK, 93 mins, colour
Dir: Lewis Gilbert
Stars: Kenneth More, Diane Cilento,
Cecil Parker, Sally Ann Howes, Martita
Hunt, Jack Watling
Rating: ★★★

Director Lewis Gilbert took a break
from making such distinguished war
films as *Reach for the Sky* and *Carve Her
Name with Pride* to create J M Barrie's
famous comedy story about a noble
family marooned on a desert island.
Kenneth More enjoys himself immensely as the butler who gradually
but inevitably takes over. Cecil Parker
offers splendidly pompous support as

Lord Loam and Diane Cilento is delightful as Tweeny.

Adolf Hitler – My Part In His Downfall ○

1972, UK, 102 mins, colour
Dir: Norman Cohen
Stars: Jim Dale, Bill Maynard, Spike
Milligan, Windsor Davies, Arthur Lowe
Rating: ★★

This film version of Spike Milligan's
best-selling account of his wartime
army days is a funny-sad black comedy enriched by the comic talents of
Bill Maynard, Windsor Davies and
Arthur Lowe. Jim Dale makes a brave
try at playing Spike, even though he's
clearly too old for the part, but Spike
himself steals the show playing his
own father. Although the film undergoes some changes of mood, the
underlying wit of the original sees it
through.

Adventure ○

1945, US, 125 mins, b/w
Dir: Victor Fleming
Stars: Clark Gable, Greer Garson, Joan
Blondell
Rating: ★★

This was Clark Gable's first film after
war service and the publicity ran:
'Gable's back and Garson's got him!'
Gable plays a tough sailor who falls for
a staid librarian: both he and Greer
Garson were then among America's
top 10 moneymakers at the box office.
The film rounded off a notable 10
years for director Victor Fleming – a
decade in which he directed such films
as *Captains Courageous*, *Dr Jekyll and Mr
Hyde* and *The Wizard of Oz*, as well as
Gone With the Wind, for which he won
an Oscar. This one's humdrum by his
standards.

Adventure of Sherlock Holmes' Smarter Brother, The ○ ⓥ

1975, UK, 91 mins, colour
Dir: Gene Wilder
Stars: Gene Wilder, Madeline Kahn,
Marty Feldman
Rating: ★★

Gene Wilder made his name as a
funny man in Mel Brooks' films, and
his first film as star-director turns out
to be a typically Brooksian curate's egg
of a helter-skelter farce, fussily set in
Victorian times, but with some nice
scenes involving Roy Kinnear. These
are mostly played for laughs, but include one piece of calculated
excitement which really stirs the blood,
as he and Wilder swing at each other

with giant-sized boot and glove from the tops of speeding carriages.

Adventures in Babysitting
See: A Night on the Town

Adventures of Baron Munchausen, The ○ ⓥ
1988, UK, 131 mins, colour
Dir: Terry Gilliam
Stars: John Neville, Eric Idle, Sarah Polley, Uma Thurman, Ray D Tutto (Robin Williams)
Rating: ★★

This fantasy adventure is a work of considerable visual imagination, but not a little tedium too – very much like the good baron's stories themselves. You'll remember that he was the tall tale-teller from the past who assured his listeners that he had visited the Moon (and bested its king), visited the inside of the volcano of the gods (and fallen for Venus) and been swallowed into the belly of a gigantic whale – each time accompanied by his faithful companions, a strong man, a dwarf who can blow men over and an idiot whose feet move faster than sound. All of these tales are woven into the film's central story, the siege of a mythical European town by a Turkish army whose caliph is after Munchausen's head. The film succeeds in fits and starts, but its \ screenplay is couched in much too high-flown terms, and the ending doesn't play fair, even by its own standards. A feast for the eyes, then, but a mixed blessing for the mind.

Adventures of Buckaroo Banzai Across the Eighth Dimension, The ○ ⓥ
1984, US, 102 mins, colour
Dir: W D Richter
Stars: Peter Weller, John Lithgow, Ellen Barkin, Jeff Goldblum, Christopher Lloyd
Rating: ★

A Marvel comic book hero-type film that shows even less regard for its audience than for logic. Familiar elements are thrown into the 'plot' in haphazard fashion by director W D Richter (who would do better even later), while neuro-surgeon super-hero Banzai, played uncharismatically by Peter Weller, takes on aliens from outer space who want to ...well, who knows or cares... something to do with an overthruster that can take you through mountains ... I think. Matt Clark, at that time a welcome character star with his disgruntled, hangdog looks, plays the senator who tries to

keep track of it all, while John Lithgow as the villain looks as though he enjoyed himself rather more than I did. Great cast, though, and brilliant Metrocolor photography by Fred Koenekamp. The ending threatens a sequel that mercifully never happened.

Adventures of Bullwhip Griffin, The ○ ⓥ
1965, US, 110 mins, colour
Dir: James Neilson
Stars: Roddy McDowall, Suzanne Pleshette, Karl Malden
Rating: ★★★

This Disney adventure caper was the film in which Tony Hancock was to have made his Hollywood debut. But the deal fell through and Hancock's role as a down-at-heel actor with a treasure map was taken over by Richard Haydn. Roddy McDowall gives one of his sprightlier performances as the 1890 Bostonian butler at large in the Far West, where he achieves an accidental reputation as a prizefighter. The script makes clever use of the material it parodies and Karl Malden is an amiably shifty villain.

Adventures of Don Juan ○ ⓥ
(aka: The New Adventures of Don Juan)
1948, US, 110 mins, colour
Dir: Vincent Sherman
Stars: Errol Flynn, Viveca Lindfors, Robert Douglas, Raymond Burr, Alan Hale, Ann Rutherford
Rating: ★★★★

Flynn's final glorious fling. This was the last major swashbuckler mounted by Warner Brothers for its superstar of sword and swagger, Errol Flynn. Richly costumed in splendid Technicolor, the film is no masterpiece, but made with immense confidence by director Vincent Sherman and so crammed with action there hardly seems to be a sequence that doesn't begin or end with a fight. Flynn is still very nearly at his most deft and agile, and finds a worthy fencing adversary in the British actor Robert Douglas as the treacherous Duc de Lorca. Viveca Lindfors is forthright as the queen who, like Bette Davis before her, secretly loves her champion, while Romney Brent as King Philip seems to have an idea this is a subtle picture: he's too good for the role. It was, alas, all downhill for Flynn after this. But, with the mass battle royal at the end, and the final romantic gesture for the fadeout, he

certainly gave his fans something to remember him by.

Adventures of Huckleberry Finn, The ○
1939, US, 91 mins, b/w
Dir: Richard Thorpe
Stars: Mickey Rooney, Walter Connolly, William Frawley
Rating: ★★

Solidly entertaining MGM version of the Mark Twain classic, with Mickey Rooney giving a breezy but controlled account of the title role. The scene-stealing characters, though, are two Mississippi conmen, delightfully played in this version by Walter Connolly and William Frawley.

Adventures of Marco Polo, The ○ ⓥ
1938, US, 100 mins, b/w
Dir: Archie Mayo
Stars: Gary Cooper, Sigrid Gurie, Basil Rathbone
Rating: ★★★

Don't expect historical accuracy from this light-hearted epic which casts an understandably uneasy-looking Gary Cooper as the famed 13th-century Venetian explorer. The producer, Samuel Goldwyn, was more concerned with offering lavish entertainment than factual information and he succeeded, with a cast of some 5,000, headed by Cooper, Basil Rathbone (who replaced originally cast John Carradine as the villain of the piece) and Sigrid Gurie, billed in the advertising for the film as having been 'discovered by Samuel Goldwyn in Norway'. In fact, by the time the picture was released, it had been discovered that Gurie hailed from the rather less exotic land of Brooklyn. Director Archie Mayo (who replaced John Cromwell after a few days) sees to it that the pageant moves at a lively clip. Look out for Lana Turner in her sixth film, making a short appearance as a slave girl.

Adventures of Mark Twain, The ⊙ ⓥ
1944, US, 130 mins, b/w
Dir: Irving Rapper
Stars: Fredric March, Alexis Smith
Rating: ★★★

Well-acted and entertaining, if a bit rambling, this lavish biography of Mark Twain and his adventurous life has picturesque black and white photography by Sol Polito who shot many of Errol Flynn's earlier films. The plot as a whole fails to grip, but does have a number of felicitous moments and the

A

riverboat scenes are splendid. Fredric March's Twain is on the dull side.

Adventures of Mark Twain, The ⊙ ⓥ

1985, US, 86 mins, colour
Dir: Will Vinton
Voice star: James Whitmore
Rating: ★★★

Ever seen an entire feature film made in moving plasticene? You could be in for a pleasant surprise. This labour of love, peppered with the wit and wisdom of Mark Twain, is a sight more imaginative and entertaining than some live-action films. It supposes that Twain, born and dying in the years of Halley's Comet, builds a fantastic flying machine from which he hopes to be engulfed in the flaming comet that he believes gave birth to him. With him on the voyage go several of his most famous fictional characters – Tom Sawyer, Huckleberry Finn, Becky Thatcher and Homer, the famous jumping frog. On board they discover a mysterious door, which admits them to numerous Twain characters and stories. A space Satan is chillingly frightening, the story of Adam and Eve touching and amusing; there's even a sequence on varying kinds of heaven. 'Is there a Heaven or a Hell?' muses Twain. 'I wouldn't like to express an opinion. I have friends in both places.'

Adventures of Milo and Otis, The ⊙

(Koneko Monogatari)
1986, Japan, 80 mins, colour
Dir: Masanori Hata
Stars: Narrated by Dudley Moore
Rating: ★★★★

You won't believe some of the scenes in this amazing animal adventure with great appeal for kids – especially a dog riding through the sea on a giant turtle, and the same dog pulling a cat out of a pit on the end of a rope. Encounters between the cat and a snake, the cat and a deer and the cat and an owl, or the cat sitting on a pig, are commonplace by comparison. Reminiscent of *The Incredible Journey*, this Japanese film (with English narration by Dudley Moore) relates the adventures of a pugdog, Otis, and a ginger cat, Milo, when they stray from their farm, after the cat has been washed down-river in a wooden box.

Adventures of Pinocchio, The ⊙ ⓥ

1996, UK/Fr/Ger/Cz/US, 94 mins, colour
Dir: Steve Barron

Stars: Martin Landau, Geneviève Bujold, Udo Kier, Bebe Neuwirth
Rating: ★★★

At its best this is an enchanting live-action version of Carlo Collodi's well-loved story about the little wooden puppet who is given the chance to become a real boy. Martin Landau follows his Oscar tour-de-force in *Ed Wood* with another wonderful creation in Geppetto, the puppet's maker – a sad, weather-beaten old woodcarver whose dreams of having a son seem dashed when Pinocchio falls into the hands of evil showman Lorenzini (Udo Kier). The supporting cast of this colourful pantomime features enthusiastic comic turns from Dawn French, Griff Rhys Jones, John Sessions and Bebe Neuwirth, while, in Pinocchio himself, Jim Henson's Creature Workshop has created a pine hero who is truly lovable. Good fun, especially for children.

Adventures of Priscilla Queen of the Desert, The ① ⓥ

1994, Australia, 103 mins, colour
Dir: Stephan Elliott
Stars: Terence Stamp, Hugo Weaving, Guy Pearce, Bill Hunter, Sarah Chadwick, Mark Holmes
Rating: ★★★★

Two drag queens and an ageing transsexual bitching their way through the Australian Outback aboard a near clapped-out bus named Priscilla sounds pretty weird. And the finished film is. But wonderfully weird, fabulously flamboyant and decidedly deviant it is too. To be fair, the plot is basically a one-joke affair, with the outrageous lead characters having to cope with prejudice and derision in a succession of one-track dead end towns. But it is undeniably infectious. Terence Stamp is a revelation as the transsexual Bernadette, a former showgirl. And Guy Pearce (best-known as Mike in TV soap *Neighbours*) is a scream as Adam, the loud-mouthed but fey Sydney muscle boy who is a sensation in sequins and slingbacks, especially when teetering on top of the bus sitting inside a 20-foot high stiletto-heeled shoe, 50 feet of sliver lamé material flowing behind him and miming to grand opera. With a succession of eye-popping visuals and provocative song-and-dance routines to Village People, Lena Horne and Abba, *Priscilla* is a genuine one-off comic event.

Adventures of Quentin Durward, The ○

(aka: Quentin Durward)
1955, UK, 101 mins, colour
Dir: Richard Thorpe
Stars: Robert Taylor, Kay Kendall, Robert Morley
Rating: ★★★★

The third in a splendid trilogy of films which Robert Taylor made for MGM in England (the others were *Ivanhoe* and *The Knights of the Round Table*). This one has a fast pace, splendid Technicolor photography and an exciting confrontation in a bell tower as its climax.

Adventures of Robin Hood, The ⊙ ⓥ

1938, US, 102 mins, colour
Dir: Michael Curtiz
Stars: Errol Flynn, Olivia de Havilland, Basil Rathbone, Claude Rains
Rating: ★★★★

Forget Kevin Costner, forget Richard Greene, Errol Flynn is the definitive bandit of Sherwood Forest in this, the Robin Hood film by which all others should be judged. All the elements that go to make a classic film are here: perfect casting, lots of vigorous action, a strong story and rousing music by Erich Wolfgang Korngold. Flynn is perfectly cast as Robin, Olivia de Havilland is a winsome Maid Marian, Claude Rains is a delightfully rascally King John and Basil Rathbone sneers as only he can as the evil Guy of Gisbourne. Even the most minor of supporting roles is well scripted and observed. Director Michael Curtiz, a master of action and adventure films, pulled out all the stops with this one. It confirmed Flynn as the cinema's greatest swashbuckling hero and no-one to this day has bettered him. Much against the studio's wishes, he did all his own stunts, including the classic swordfight with Rathbone, complete with huge dancing shadows.

Adventures of Sadie, The

See: Our Girl Friday

Adventures of Sherlock Holmes, The ○

1939, US, 83 mins, b/w
Dir: Alfred Werker
Stars: Basil Rathbone, Nigel Bruce, Ida Lupino
Rating: ★★★

To a generation of cinemagoers, Basil Rathbone *was* Sherlock Holmes. Tall, supercilious and ascetic, he fitted the role as surely as a Savile Row deerstalker fitted the character. And Nigel Bruce, another British actor, made a superb bumbling, stumbling Watson. In this, the second of their film adventures together, they encounter Holmes' arch-enemy Moriarty, splendidly portrayed by a third British actor, the sepulchral-toned George Zucco.

Adventures of Tartu, The ○
(aka: Tartu)
1943, UK, 103 mins, b/w
Dir: Harold S Bucquet
Stars: Robert Donat, Valerie Hobson, Walter Rilla, Glynis Johns
Rating: ★★★

Robert Donat's smart performance gives a lift to this familiar, but carefully, briskly made wartime thriller. Donat plays Capt Stevenson, linguist, chemical engineer and explosives expert, with a panache that would have done credit to James Bond. Whether smoothing the lapel of his over-padded suit, passing his hand over a headful of waves that could be plotted on graph paper, or simply bursting into action, Donat fits the part of the debonair Stevenson like a glove. There's also a heart-rending performance from Glynis Johns, then only 19, as a badly frightened young girl whose patriotism drives her to deeds of desperate courage.

Adventures of Tom Sawyer, The ⊙
1938, US, 78 mins, colour
Dir: Norman Taurog
Stars: Tommy Kelly, Jacky Moran, May Robson
Rating: ★★★

The original Selznick classic, with Tommy Kelly and Ann Gillis making sparky leads and Victor Jory frightening as the villainous Injun Joe. It moves fluently from one incident to another and is always most attractive to look at, thanks to the art direction of William Cameron Menzies (who two years earlier had directed *Things to Come*) and the photography of another Oscar winner, James Wong Howe. Howe's colour camerawork brings a nightmare quality to the film's most exciting scenes – in a graveyard and a network of caverns.

Adventuress, The
See: I See a Dark Stranger

Affair In Trinidad ○
1952, US, 98 mins, b/w
Dir: Vincent Sherman

Stars: Rita Hayworth, Glenn Ford
Rating: ★★

Echoes of *Gilda*, but, alas, only echoes, in this 'comeback' vehicle prepared for Rita Hayworth by her studio Columbia after her four years away (she married and divorced Aly Khan), along the lines of her past successes there. Leading man Glenn Ford is back, as is chubby character player Steven Geray, but the handling no longer has the confidence to carry such a tuppence-coloured plot. Rita sings a couple of numbers, 'Trinidad' and 'I've Been Kissed Before', but the fires that burned so bright in *Gilda* are noticeably lower here.

Affair to Remember, An ○
1957, US, 115 mins, colour
Dir: Leo McCarey
Stars: Cary Grant, Deborah Kerr, Richard Denning
Rating: ★★

A four-handkerchief remake of the classic weepie which originally saw the light of day in 1939 as *Love Affair*, with Irene Dunne. A couple fall in love and make a tryst for six months later on top of the Empire State Building to see if their feelings have changed. Elegantly steered on its tearful way by the performances of the stars and Leo McCarey, who also made the original and won an Oscar for its screenplay. Remade again in 1994 with Warren Beatty, under the original title. For all the talent involved, this is on the dull side.

Affair with a Stranger ○
1953, US, 89 mins, b/w
Dir: Roy Rowland
Stars: Jean Simmons, Victor Mature
Rating: ★★

A mediocre dose of suds and tears about an item in a gossip column that sets of a chain reaction among the friends of a writer (Victor Mature) and his wife (Jean Simmons, sold short by Hollywood again). It's directed with no great style by Roy Rowland.

Afraid of the Dark ●
1991, UK, 91 mins, colour
Dir: Mark Peploe
Stars: Ben Keyworth, Fanny Ardant, James Fox, Paul McGann, Clare Holman, Robert Stephens
Rating: ★

For all those who love a good anti-climax, director Peploe has a whole string of them ready for you in this psychological chiller-drama. Young

Lucas (Ben Keyworth) is going blind and needs a sight-saving operation. He is also going out of his tiny little mind and fearsomely jealous of the new baby his blind mother (Fanny Ardant) is about to have. Meanwhile, a slasher is stalking the district cutting the faces of blind people. Lucas, a born peeper, steals a telescope and starts seeing fragments of murder. His blind sister seems about to fall victim to the killer. But wait ... all is not what it seems, as Peploe gives us the first of several 'But waits... ' which only end when the final credits roll before what seems to have been set up as the final chill. It's slightly stiffly performed by a cast who seem to have been instructed to act as enigmatically as possible.

African Fury
See: Cry, the Beloved Country

African Queen, The ○
1951, US/UK, 105 mins, colour
Dir: John Huston
Stars: Katharine Hepburn, Humphrey Bogart, Robert Morley
Rating: ★★★★★

Not-to-be-missed John Huston film made on location under testing conditions. Humphrey Bogart at last won the Oscar he deserved, for his portrayal of the dissolute, vulgar and cowardly riverboat captain who is persuaded to take a stern lady missionary on a dangerous voyage down African rivers in World War One to try to sink a German gunboat. Richly characterised, it's a thoroughly enjoyable film. Katharine Hepburn was also nominated for an Academy Award for her portrayal of the rasp-tongued spinster who gradually develops mellower feelings towards her rugged, alcohol-soaked companion.

African Rage
See: Tigers Don't Cry

Africa Screams ⊙
1949, US, 79 mins, b/w
Dir: Charles Barton
Stars: Bud Abbott, Lou Costello, Hillary Brooke
Rating: ★★

Bud Abbott and Lou Costello are up to no good in the jungles of Africa in this underrated comedy. Famous lion tamers Frank Buck (inspiration for the series *Bring 'Em Back Alive*) and Clyde Beatty join in the mayhem alongside one-time 'Stooges' Shemp Howard and Joe Besser. Howard was actually physically sick in the studio tank at

A

United Artists (standing in for a swirling jungle river) during production. Real-life heavyweight prizefighters, the Baer brothers, Max and Buddy, add muscle as the formidable Hillary Brooke's henchmen.

Africa Texas Style ☉

1967, US, 106 mins, colour
Dir: Andrew Marton
Stars: Hugh O'Brian, John Mills, Tom Nardini, Nigel Green, Adrienne Corri
Rating: ★★

A likeable animal adventure with good performances from John Mills (the central figure in the film's best sequence, when he demonstrates the lie of the land instead of controlling his plane) and Tom Nardini. The action is thunderingly well shot by director Andrew Marton and his unit, and one skirmish with a dyspeptic rhinoceros is especially engaging. There's a fleeting appearance, as a girl at an airport, by Hayley Mills.

After Dark, My Sweet ○

1990, US, 111 mins, colour
Dir: James Foley
Stars: Jason Patric, Rachel Ward, Bruce Dern, George Dickerson
Rating: ★★

If it had been 30 minutes shorter and had a different director and leading actress, this doomy *film noir* could have been a cracker. That might sound drastic, but there was a lot of potential here if a tighter overall grip had been exercised on the project, which emerges as an occasionally fascinating but too often slow and soporific suspenser. Jason Patric is pretty good as the no-hoper who forms the axis of the plot: an ex-boxer escaped from a psychiatric hospital only to wander into a bizarre plot to kidnap the diabetic son of rich parents. Bruce Dern is always watchable as the ex-cop who dreams up the scheme, but Rachel Ward is less than adequate as the seductive alcoholic who draws Patric into the plot. The story – the title has no relevance whatsoever – is nicely rounded off, but by that time you may have lost interest, which is frankly a real shame. Jane Greer, where are you when we need you most?

After Hours ◐ ⓥ

1985, US, 97 mins, colour
Dir: Martin Scorsese
Stars: Griffin Dunne, Rosanna Arquette, Verna Bloom, Linda Fiorentino, Teri Garr
Rating: ★★

A comedy that proves that ace director Martin Scorsese is not at his best in lighter mood. The idea is great: cuddly Griffin Dunne, a taller version of Dudley Moore, goes chasing after a girl downtown and lurches from disaster to disaster in a series of events that somehow contrive to interlock. The chill and still of the early hours on deserted city streets seem to seep into the bones of the plot, which staggers on in staccato fashion, amusing us with its developments (Cheech and Chong are actually funny!) but muffling them in Scorsese's execution.

After the Fox ○

1966, UK/Italy, 103 mins, colour
Dir: Vittorio De Sica
Stars: Peter Sellers, Victor Mature, Britt Ekland, Martin Balsam
Rating: ★★

For those who like to see Peter Sellers in a number of disguises, this Vittorio De Sica-directed comedy should be a beanfeast. Mainly, Sellers plays an Italian master crook who foils the police with a series of wild schemes. The opening sequence – a gallery of the world's most inept criminals – gets the film off with a bang. Thereafter, this is a mild comedy whose good ideas mostly fire on only one cylinder, and whose director and cast seem largely not up to be on the same comedy wavelength as the star. Still, Victor Mature sends up his own film image nicely as a fading screen idol and Martin Balsam scores as his agent.

Against All Odds ● ⓥ

1984, US, 128 mins, colour
Dir: Taylor Hackford
Stars: Jeff Bridges, Rachel Ward, James Woods, Alex Karras, Richard Widmark
Rating: ★★

A loose remake of the 1947 Robert Mitchum thriller *Out of the Past* (shown in Britain as *Build My Gallows High*). Not at all bad on the whole, laced with contemporary sex and violence as well as miles of footage of lovely Mexican beaches and a final shoot-out (a long time coming) that's like the gangster equivalent of a Sergio Leone Western. Veteran Richard Widmark easily steals the acting honours from Jeff Bridges, underplaying, James Woods, overplaying, and Rachel Ward, hardly playing at all. The music provides the intensity the offbeat drama badly needs elsewhere. Jane Greer and Paul Valentine, co-stars in the Mitchum original, make cameo appearances here.

Against the Wind ○

1947, UK, 96 mins, b/w
Dir: Charles Crichton
Stars: Simone Signoret, Robert Beatty, Jack Warner, Gordon Jackson
Rating: ★★★

Charles Crichton directed this Ealing spy thriller. Jack Warner is untypically cast as a traitor working alongside British and Belgian agents who are sent to France to work with the resistance. Simone Signoret makes her British film debut, and Robert Beatty and a host of character actors play out their roles in the forces with varying conviction. Exciting if sometimes implausible.

Agent 8¾

See: Hot Enough for June

Age of Consent ◐

1969, Australia, 103 mins, colour
Dir: Michael Powell
Stars: James Mason, Helen Mirren
Rating: ★★★

Michael Powell's Australian idyll in which Helen Mirren, nude and nubile, raised the temperatures of cinema-going males the world over, but subsequently decided to go back to the sterner stuff of the Royal Shakespeare Company, for whom she made a remarkable Lady Macbeth. James Mason still manages to register well as the artist trying to find himself and there are some breathtaking locations on and around the Great Barrier Reef.

Age of Innocence, The ○

1993, US, 139 mins, colour
Dir: Martin Scorsese
Stars: Michelle Pfeiffer, Daniel Day-Lewis, Winona Ryder, Geraldine Chaplin, Richard E Grant, Jonathan Pryce
Rating: ★★★

An amazingly elegant, exquisitely made period romance, paced in stately but never tedious style, and marred (considerably) only by its complete inability to surprise. In fashionable New York of the 1870s, Archer (Daniel Day-Lewis), a handsome young lawyer, is to be married to beautiful, impeccably mannered airhead May (Winona Ryder), but falls in love with the intelligent and ever-so-slightly dangerous Countess Olenska (Michelle Pfeiffer), who has a messy marriage behind her and is advised to avoid a divorce action which would offend the closed New York society which has, with mixed enthusiasms, taken her back. Given the bulwark of this initial setback, the writers contrive to thwart the would-be lovers' happiness at every remaining step of the story, to an irritating degree. The performances are excellent, though: Pfeiffer has come a long way since her early days and this is as good as anything she's done. Even so, she doesn't entirely overshadow Ryder, who is truly admirable in a difficult subordinate role. Certainly a film to win the impeccable taste award of its year.

Agnes of God ○ ⓥ
1985, US, 98 mins, colour
Dir: Norman Jewison
Stars: Jane Fonda, Anne Bancroft, Meg Tilly
Rating: ★★★

A sort of ecclesiastical whodunnit about a young novitiate nun who seems to have strangled the baby no-one knew she was having, and the investigative psychiatrist determined to find out the truth. Meg Tilly is the nun, Jane Fonda the shrink, and Anne Bancroft the hip-talking Mother Superior who tries to come between them: all are excellent. The ending is logically the only possible one, but can't help but lend a sense of anti-climax to an otherwise absorbing adult tale that almost entirely escapes its stage origins.

Agony and the Ecstasy, The ○
1965, US, 140 mins, colour
Dir: Carol Reed
Stars: Charlton Heston, Rex Harrison, Diane Cilento
Rating: ★★

Carol Reed's careful study of the painter Michelangelo and his work on the Sistine Chapel. Rex Harrison is unexpectedly good as the warrior Pope who all too often opposes the painter's ideas, while Charlton Heston, though physically completely miscast, is surprisingly good as the artist. The first half is dreadfully uninteresting, but there's much more human development in the second, even though Harrison gets some pretty trite dialogue from Philip Dunne's script, which has him saying, on viewing the finished ceiling, 'This work is so much greater than both of us,' when what he reputedly said was, 'Sprinkle a little gold paint on it – it will make it look much better.' Although there are one or two moving moments, this is, on the whole, a missed opportunity.

Aguirre: Wrath of God ◐
(Aguirre, der Zorn Gottes)
1972, West Germany, 95 mins, colour
Dir: Werner Herzog
Stars: Klaus Kinski, Ruy Guerra
Rating: ★★★★

Chilling, hypnotic adventure down the Amazon river with Klaus Kinski getting madder by the second as he and his raft-borne team of conquistadors search for the Inca city of El Dorado. West German director Werner Herzog hits every nerve-end right on the button, showing Hollywood just how to do it in terms of tension as the Spaniards get whittled down one by one by headhunting Indians.

A-Haunting We Will Go ⊙
1942, US, 68 mins, 67W
Dir: Alfred Werker
Stars: Stan Laurel, Oliver Hardy
Rating: ★★

Laurel and Hardy are assigned to deliver a coffin – which has a live gangster inside. One of their later films, made away from the auspices of Hal Roach with whom they had worked for so long. Henry Morgan and Elisha Cook Jr are gangsters.

Air America ◐ ⓥ
1990, US, 112 mins, colour
Dir: Roger Spottiswoode
Stars: Mel Gibson, Robert Downey Jr, Nancy Travis, Lane Smith
Rating: ★★

Perhaps the noisiest film of its year, if not the easiest to follow (not unconnected aspects perhaps), this is the story of a CIA-backed US air company in 1969 Laos, running food to the villagers and drugs and guns for the local warlord to help him fight against the communists. The motto of the pilots is 'Anything, anywhere, anytime'. Gene (Mel Gibson) is storing a nest-egg of guns for his imminent retirement. Billy (Robert Downey Jr) is the newcomer, regarded as a maverick in America but a greenhorn in Laos. Their hair-raising flights together – and separately – form the core of the story, which is one long succession of explosions, crash-landings, drunken sprees and shouted conversations. The climax is heavily contrived but balanced by some witty captions at the very end dealing with the ultimate fates of the various characters involved.

Air Force ○
1943, US, 145 mins, b/w
Dir: Howard Hawks
Stars: John Garfield, Gig Young, Arthur Kennedy, Charles Drake, John Ridgely, Harry Carey
Rating: ★★★

If you can ignore the flag-waving American sentiment and occasional truculence, and concentrate on its action sequences and effective quieter moments, this Howard Hawks production is a hell of a war film. John Garfield, John Ridgely (a character player in a rare leading role) and Harry Carey give fiercely well-defined portrayals of men under stress. And plum-nosed George Tobias, who starred in *Captains of the Clouds,* is aloft again, though you may wince at his victorious yell of 'Fried Jap going down', a rare lapse in Dudley Nichols' purposeful and believable screenplay. Hawks' direction is masterly in its pace, economy and power.

Air Force One ◐ ⓥ
1997, US, 123 mins, colour
Dir: Wolfgang Petersen
Stars: Harrison Ford, Gary Oldman,. Glenn Close, William H Macy, Xander Berkeley, Wendy Crewson, Liesel Matthews
Rating: ★★

That pillar of integrity Harrison Ford finally ascends to the US presidency in the most flag-waving American film since the end of World War Two. Very silly and often unintentionally funny, the ridiculous plot poses the idea of the president's plane being hijacked by radical Russian rebels to achieve the release of a Kazakhstan despot the Americans and Russians conspired to capture. Given the choice of escaping the hail of gunfire in an emergency escape pod, Ford stays on board. 'Let's not forget,' growls a brasshat back home, 'he's a former Medal of Honor winner. This man knows how to fight.' (Applause). And so he does, knocking off terrorists in the bowels of the plane. Ford, Oldman (the villain), Close (the vice-prez) and others do what they can with these pantomime characters, but they're all hostage to a risible script. Lots of excitement, though, well-staged.

Airbeads ○
1994, US, 92 mins, colour
Dir: Michael Lehmann
Stars: Brendan Fraser, Steve Buscemi, Amy Locane, Nina Siemasko, Joe Mantegna
Rating: ★

The title pretty well tells you what to expect from this featherweight teen comedy with just a few smiles, about a trio of rock musicians who accidentally take a pop radio station hostage in

A

their bid to get their new song played on the airwaves. By the sound of what we hear at the end, it wasn't worth it. Most often the film mistakes violence for humour and hasn't too many places to go after setting up its central situation. Brendan Fraser is an unconvincing rocker, a world that the furtive Steve Buscemi, usually seen as a bad guy, seems to occupy with more ease. Amy Locane and Nina Siemasko are appropriately air-headed as the two tight-busted blondes in attendance, and Joe Mantegna slums it with some panache as the station's DJ.

Airplane O

1980, US, 86 mins, colour
Dir: David Zucker
Stars: Robert Hays, Julie Hagerty, Lloyd Bridges, Peter Graves, Leslie Nielsen, Robert Stack
Rating:★★★

The spoof of disaster movies that set millions rocking with laughter, thanks to an inventive script and wonderfully poker-faced playing by a starstrewn cast. Loosely based on an Arthur Hailey novel originally filmed as *Zero Hour!*

Airplane II – The Sequel O

1982, US, 85 mins, colour
Dir: Ken Finkleman
Stars: Robert Hays, Julie Hagerty, Lloyd Bridges, Chuck Connors, William Shatner, Peter Graves
Rating: ★★★

Those *Airport* spoofers are at it again, with Robert Hays once more (barely) at the controls, this time of a disaster-bound space shuttle headed for the moon. Keep an eye on what's going on in the background of the scenes: it's often funnier than what's happening up front. We especially liked the poster with an aged boxer, advertising *Rocky XX VIII*.

Airport O Ⓥ

1969, US, 137 mins, colour
Dir: George Seaton
Stars: Burt Lancaster, Dean Martin, Jacqueline Bisset, Jean Seberg, George Kennedy, Helen Hayes
Rating: ★★★

The prototype airborne disaster movie of modern times, with Burt Lancaster and Dean Martin at the controls, Van Heflin as the man with the bomb, George Kennedy making the first of his several appearances in such films and Helen Hayes taking an Oscar as a little old lady on board.

Airport 1975 O

1974, US, 106 mins, colour
Dir: Jack Smight
Stars: Charlton Heston, Karen Black, George Kennedy
Rating: ★★★

The second in the series of airborne suspensers derived from the Arthur Hailey bestseller gives us another star-studded cast facing death in the skies as stewardess Karen Black finds herself in charge of a crippled airliner and ever reliable Charlton Heston flies to the rescue. Director Jack Smight racks up the tension comendably and, among those strapped into their seats and exhibiting varying degrees of aplomb and hysteria, are Gloria Swanson, playing herself, the regulation nuns, Helen Reddy and Martha Scott, Myrna Loy, Sid Caesar and Linda (*The Exorcist*) Blair.

Airport '80... Ⓒ

(aka: The Concorde – Airport '79)
1979, US, 123 mins, colour
Dir: David Lowell Rich
Stars: Alain Delon, Susan Blakely, Robert Wagner, Sylvia Kristel, George Kennedy, Eddie Albert
Rating: ★★

Airport meets James Bond, and the result is very superior hokum. As the *Concorde* takes off, the second thread of the plot is already in motion. Power-mad Robert Wagner, who runs a missile plant, has been caught selling arms to the bad guys of the world, and his reporter-mistress Susan Blakely is the girl with the evidence. And what is she travelling on? That's right! 'It's still amazing to me, only three and a half hours ago we were in Paris,' muses Capt Alain Delon just before Wagner launches an attack missile against the plane. The plot then develops into Tom and Jerry stuff, and one can visualise Wagner jumping up and down with rage as each new attempt fails. 'I'd love to see what my horoscope said for the morning,' yells co-pilot George Kennedy (simply running away with the film) as he banks to avoid two of Wagner's fighter planes. The dialogue is hilarious, the photography magnificent, the pace unflagging.

Airport '77 O

(aka: Airport III)
1977, US, 113 mins, colour
Dir: Jerry Jameson
Stars: Jack Lemmon, Lee Grant, George Kennedy, James Stewart, Joseph Cotten, Olivia de Havilland, Brenda

Vaccaro
Rating: ★★

After two *Airplane!* spoofs, it's hard to take any of the four *Airport* films seriously for a minute. This third entry has a novel idea at its core – a plane surviving a crash with an oil rig and having to be rescued from the sea bed before it is crushed by water pressure but its passenger list is the usual motley crew of deadbeats and adulterers. The crash and subsequent rescue bid are well handled, but the tension would have been all the greater had the script made you care about any of the victims. Christopher Lee does the honourable thing in the mould of Oates of the Arctic and takes an early bath. The rest of the cast look as though they wish they'd done the same!

Airport III

See: Airport '77

Aladdin O Ⓥ

1992, US, 91 mins, colour
Dir: John Musker, Ron Clements
Voice stars: Robin Williams, Scott Weinger, Linda Larkin, Jonathan Freeman
Rating: ★★★★

More from modern Disneyland, a kaleidoscope of adventures that's always doing the unexpected – blink and you miss a visual joke – and makes Robin Williams the star voice of the piece as a show-off, non-stop genie of the lamp, who does everything but say 'Good Morning, Baghdad!' 'Getting kinda fond of you,' he confides to Aladdin at one point, ' . . . not that I want to pick out curtains.' Set in an eastern city where the traders sell Dead Sea tupperware, the film is full of semi-adult humour that's bound to please parents, as much as the story, visual delights and animal supporting characters (including a performing monkey who sounds like Donald Duck) will please the children. On the musical front, the Menken-Ashman score is on the thin side, its big number, 'Brand New World', sounding very much like a mixture of ballads from the duo's previous *Beauty and the Beast* and *The Little Mermaid*. A small quibble at a big, colourful show that's more consistently entertaining than any pantomime.

Alamo, The O

1960, US, 193 mins, colour
Dir. John Wayne
Stars: John Wayne, Richard Widmark,

Laurence Harvey, Frankie Avalon, Richard Boone, Linda Cristal
Rating. ★★

John Wayne's first film as director and star, an epic Western about the state of Texas' fight for independence, is a troubled affair. Wearing one expression – that of a man with a $12 million budget weighing heavy on his conscience – his character of Davy Crockett spouts endless pompous and gratuitous homilies to a better way of life. It's not until the rip-roaring, crushing climax of total massacre that the film comes alive at all.

Alamo Bay ◯
1985, US, 98 mins, colour
Dir: Louis Malle
Stars: Ed Harris, Amy Madigan, Ho Nguyen, Donald Moffat
Rating: ★★

There's a Western struggling to get out of this present-day account of Texas redneck shrimp fishermen and their conflict with the Vietnamese boat people whose determination to earn a living invades their territorial waters. It leads not only to outright warfare but also to the Texans' enlistment of the Ku Klux Klan. The film has some fresh and valid social statements to make and it puts them across forcibly, even if the script fails to raise the events above the level of routine drama which, while interesting, lacks dramatic punch. Ed Harris, and real-life wife Amy Madigan give dour, downbeat performances that probably reflect the bitterness involved, but fail to do much for the film itself.

Albert RN ◯
(aka: Break to Freedom)
1955, UK, 88 mins, b/w
Dir: Lewis Gilbert
Stars: Anthony Steel, Jack Warner, Robert Beatty, Anton Diffring
Rating: ★★

One of a long line of good British 'escape' films, started by *The Wooden Horse*, and carried on by such gems as *The Colditz Story* and *Danger Within*. PoWs create a dummy – the Albert RN of the title – as a cover up for an absentee prisoner.

Alexander the Great ◯
1956, US, 141 mins, colour
Dir: Robert Rossen
Stars: Richard Burton, Fredric March, Claire Bloom, Harry Andrews, Stanley Baker
Rating: ★★★

A much underrated epic, with stunningly staged battle scenes, Richard Burton at his stormy best and a script that keeps sentiment (if not philosophy) to the minimum. The overall cast is remarkable, the 'middle order' players including Harry Andrews, Stanley Baker, Peter Cushing, Niall MacGinnis, Michael Hordern, Peter Wyngarde, Helmut Dantine and that delightful French actress Dannielle Darrieux.

Alfie ● ⓥ
1966, UK, 114 mins, colour
Dir: Lewis Gilbert
Stars: Michael Caine, Shelley Winters, Millicent Martin, Julia Foster, Jane Asher, Shirley Anne Field
Rating: ★★★

Bill Naughton wrote the screen adaptation of his own highly successful stage play and the result was one of the British cinema's biggest comedy hits of the mid-Sixties. Michael Caine scores as the totally amoral anti-hero who remains engaging and likeable, a girlchaser de-luxe. And there's a remarkable supporting cast in which the females – especially Vivien Merchant – are all very good.

Alf's Button Afloat ☉
1938, UK, 89 mins, b/w
Dir: Marcel Varnel
Stars: Bud Flanagan, Chesney Allen, Alistair Sim
Rating: ★★★

There had already been a couple of versions of W A Darlington's famous farce (one featuring Anton Dolin and the Royal Ballet!) before the Crazy Gang got hold of it and made it their own. They play six buskers serving in the Marines. They discover a magic button which, when rubbed, produces a genie (magnificently played by Alastair Sim) who tends to *stripe* everything pink.

Alias Bulldog Drummond
See: Bulldog Jack

Alias Jesse James ☉
1959, US, 92 mins, colour
Dir: Norman Z McLeod
Stars: Bob Hope, Rhonda Fleming, Wendell Corey
Rating: ★★★

The last of Bob Hope's really funny comedies, pitching him once again into *Paleface* territory as an inept insurance man who sells a policy to Jesse James. 'Ain't a-Hankerin'' is a cute novelty song in the best 'Buttons and Bows'

tradition, and it's nicely delivered by Hope and leading lady Rhonda Fleming. The action and fun still come fast and furious. Stay tuned for the ending in which Hope receives a few unexpected helping hands when besieged by outlaw gunmen.

Alice ◐ ⓥ
1990, US, 105 mins, colour
Dir: Woody Allen
Stars: Mia Farrow, Joe Mantegna, William Hurt, Judy Davis, Cybill Shepherd, Alec Baldwin
Rating: ★★

Another Woody Allen film that will delight his fans and further irritate those who can't stand his work. Mia Farrow has the Woody-type role (and the Woody-type dialogue) as the mousy, well-to-do housewife who starts a whole new cycle in her life when she suddenly experiences an attraction to another man (Joe Mantegna) and visits Dr Yang (a last screen role for character actor Keye Luke), discovering his marvellous potions, one of which can make her invisible. Using her new-found 'gift', she soon finds out what a slimebag her husband (William Hurt) is – which the rest of us could see from the start – and discovers herself in the process. All this is told in typically Allen style, with some brilliantly witty lines (though not enough), much overlapping dialogue (monotonous after a while) and a plot that's fun but gets a bit too silly towards the end. Farrow is excellent.

Alice Doesn't Live Here Anymore ◐ ⓥ
1974, US, 113 mins, colour
Dir: Martin Scorsese
Stars: Ellen Burstyn, Kris Kristofferson, Billy Green Bush, Diane Ladd, Harvey Keitel
Rating: ★★★★★

Seldom was an Academy Award more deserved than that won by Ellen Burstyn, who gives one of the cinema's great female performances as the attractive if dumpy widow who falteringly sets out to make a new life for herself and her 11-year-old son after her husband dies in an accident. Although Burstyn dominates the film, the action that swirls around her is crammed with laughs and truths that deserve almost equal praise. Alice enjoys a unique, just-right relationship with her son. 'Don't look back,' she tells him, as they leave their old home, 'or you might turn into a pillar of shit.'

A

Alice's four-letter words are so rare that they're a delightful part of the wry, anything goes humour that keeps her afloat on the bilge of the world. Robert Getchell's screenplay never opts entirely for the soft centre, and Scorsese's direction rightly and sensibly just pays homage to it, seeing that it gets its full justice. A completely original screen classic.

Alice in Wonderland ○
1951, US, 75 mins, colour
Dir: Hamilton Luske, Wilfred Jackson
Rating: ★★★★

This Disney adaption of Lewis Carroll's classic children's story was miserably underrated in its time, mainly by people who objected to the studio's 'Americanisation' of the story's characters. In fact, the Disney animation team is on top form, especially with the Caterpillar, the Cheshire Cat, the March Hare, the Mad Hatter and Bill the Lizard. And the Queen of Hearts is a formidable adversary in best Peggy Mount style. Besides the dreamy title number, the catchy songs include 'I'm Late' and 'A Very Merry Unbirthday to You'.

Alice's Restaurant ◑
1969, US, 111 mins, colour
Dir: Arthur Penn
Stars: Arlo Guthrie, Pat Quinn
Rating: ★★★★

Kaleidoscopic, attractive patchwork of a ruin about the early life of singer Arlo Guthrie, son of the legendary Woody Guthrie. The deconsecrated church at which Arlo and his hippie friends gather has real atmosphere, there are some funny and touching moments, catchy theme music by Arlo himself and an outstanding performance by Pat Quinn as Alice.

Alien ● Ⓥ
1979, US, 117 mins, colour
Dir: Ridley Scott
Stars: Tom Skerritt, Sigourney Weaver, Ian Holm, John Hurt, Harry Dean Stanton, Veronica Cartwright
Rating: ★★★

A silly but very exciting slice of science-fiction – it broke box office records all over the world – about a monster from another planet loose aboard a spaceship, devouring the crew one by one. Directed with force if not finesse by Ridley Scott, it has a performance by Sigourney Weaver as Lt Ripley that could and should have made her a star. She was little seen for a while but went on to make the

sequel, *Aliens, Working Girl* and *Gorillas in the Mist*. The hardware is imposing, and the alien itself mostly horrifyingly convincing, although the film's vein of foolishness persists in scenes of characters creeping around alone in search of the ship's cat when they're all too aware that the alien may be slithering around waiting.

Alien Nation ● Ⓥ
1988, US, 94 mins, colour
Dir: Graham Baker
Stars: James Caan, Mandy Patinkin, Terence Stamp
Rating: ★★★

A science-fiction thriller that welds an old plot to a new concept. Cops, drug dealers, the old cop with the new partner – you could see this story every night on the box. What gives it the scifi twist is that it's set in the future. A few years previously, a vast shipload of aliens has landed in America, and its occupants, vaguely human in appearance, have been assimilated into the general population. In effect, they have taken the place of blacks as ghetto-dwellers, living in a kind of unholy Toontown amid the slag of the city. When a veteran cop (James Caan) sees his partner killed by alien hitmen, revenge drives him to volunteer for the job nobody wants – partner to America's first alien detective (Mandy Patinkin). The film mistakenly underplays the alien factor in its search for the plot and a spectacular climax. Even so, it remains edgily exciting: pretty good entertainment in a minor key.

Aliens ● Ⓥ
1986, US, 137 mins, colour
Dir: James Cameron
Stars: Sigourney Weaver, Michael Biehn, Carrie Henn, Lance Henriksen, Paul Reiser
Rating: ★★★★★

Flight Officer Ripley (Sigourney Weaver, repeating her role from *Alien*) is the living proof that, when the going gets tough, the tough get going. Somehow, after 57 years in hyper space (she hasn't changed a bit), she's induced to go back to the alien planet where it all started. The aliens have taken over from human colonists and a little girl's the sole survivor. And Weaver's Ripley really gets the bit between her teeth when the kid's in danger. Like the bad guys who incur Clint Eastwood's wrath when they mess with his dog, you know the aliens are in deep trouble when the girl disap-

pears. You can almost hear John Wayne shouting: 'Fill your hands, you sons of a bitch', as Ripley charges to the rescue armed with what seems like half her spaceship's arsenal. It's a tremendous part for any actress, and Weaver responds by bruisingly giving it all she's got. She's helped in the impact she makes by the fact that the film has 300 per cent more action than its predecessor once it gets going and 100 per cent more logic. Crisis follows crisis as director James Cameron hammers away at your nerve-ends. Aliens to the left of you, aliens to the right of you: it never lets up.

Alien 3 ● Ⓥ
1992, US/UK, 115 mins, colour
Dir: David Fincher
Stars: Sigourney Weaver, Charles Dance, Charles S Dutton, Brian Glover, Lance Henriksen
Rating: ★★

Too much talk and not enough action cripple this muddled third segment of the *Alien* saga. Sigourney Weaver, in the least of her three performances in these films, is still Lt Ripley, cast adrift from her homebound vessel by an alien intruder, and the only human survivor of a subsequent crash on to a prison planet whose few inhabitants are the shaven-headed scum of the galaxy and have no weapons. The alien, regenerating itself via a dog, is soon scuttling into slobbery, heavy-headed, tombstone-toothed action. Similar in structure to the first film, with people creeping around in the dark after an unknown force, the film has too many scenes with the prisoners shouting obscenities about their condition, and not enough cohesion in its story which moves, when at all, in fits and starts. There is less of a sense of evil, and more of a simpler science-fiction menace.

Alive and Kicking ● Ⓥ
aka: Indian Summer
1996, UK, 98 mins, colour
Dir: Nancy Meckler
Stars: Jason Flemyng, Antony Sher, Dorothy Tutin, Anthony Higgins, Bill Nighy, Diane Paris
Rating: ★★★

For once a film's publicity is right: this is, on the whole, a tender, humorous and passionate story of a gay ballet dancer living with AIDS. It certainly catches the heady emotion both of a gay relationship under the shadow of death, and the performance of a ballet that may be the dancer's last. Jason

Flemyng has never been better nor more charismatic than as the dancer, and there are notable contributions from Antony Sher as his therapist lover, Dorothy Tutin as the slightly dotty founder of the ballet, Anthony Higgins as Flemyng's mentor, and Philip Voss as a ballet master and Tutin's ex. A pity the Sher character is supposed to be 30, though. Mr Sher has many fine qualities, but looking 30, alas, was by this time no longer one of them.

Al Jennings of Oklahoma ○
1951, US, 79 mins, colour
Dir: Ray Nazarro
Stars: Dan Duryea, Gale Storm, Dick Foran
Rating: ★★★

This colourful Western followed hard on those which glorified the exploits of the James Brothers and the Younger Brothers. It tries to do the same thing for Al Jennings, played by Dan Duryea in one of his two 'true life' adventure roles of the late Forties (the other being *Black Bart – Highwayman*). This too is about brothers, Al and Frank Jennings, lawyers gone to the bad who eventually tired of the outdoor life and were said to have lived to a ripe old age.

All About Eve ○ ⓥ
1950, US, 138 mins, b/w
Dir: Joseph L Mankiewicz
Stars: Bette Davis, Anne Baxter, George Sanders, Gary Merrill
Rating: ★★★★★

Bette Davis received her eighth Academy Award nomination in 16 years for this brilliant dissection of Broadway life. Anne Baxter, magnificently hateful as the insidious Eve (you want to jump into the screen and throttle her before she does any more damage), was also nominated for an Oscar. Twelve further 'nods' to the Academy board made the film the most Oscar-nominated picture in history. It actually won six: Best Picture, Best Director (Joseph L Mankiewicz), Best Script (Mankiewicz again), Best Supporting Actor (George Sanders), Best Sound and Best Costume Design. All this, and Marilyn Monroe in an eye-catching supporting role. Barbara Bates, as a new 'Eve', is also worthy of note in a film laced with razor-sharp acting and caustic, witty phrases.

All at Sea
See: Barnacle Bill

All Creatures Great and Small ○
1974, US/UK, 92 mins, colour
Dir: Claude Whatham
Stars: Simon Ward, Anthony Hopkins, Lisa Harrow, Freddie Jones
Rating: ★★★

An enjoyable little trifle (except for those squeamish about things happening to animals) as newly qualified vet Simon Ward comes to work at a Yorkshire practice where he very soon learns the facts of country life. Acting honours are wholly stolen by Anthony Hopkins as Ward's senior partner, who is exactly as one would imagine a country doctor or vet to be, jiggling his pipe noisily between his teeth, brushing recalcitrant hair away from his eyes, or trying desperately to remember to do his accounts, Hopkins makes this inconsequential film entirely his own.

Allegheny Uprising
See: The First Rebel

All Hands on Deck ○
1961, US, 98 mins, colour
Dir: Norman Taurog
Stars: Pat Boone, Dennis O'Keefe, Barbara Eden, Buddy Hackett
Rating: ★★

An energetic musical romp with a plot that wouldn't disgrace a Marx Brothers film. Pat Boone has the Zeppo role as the romantic lead (and sings some Ray Evans-Jay Livingston songs), while Buddy Hackett and a turkey called Owasso lead the farceurs. There's also a pelican, an egg, a newshen and an admiral, none of whom, in the best tradition of farce, are supposed to encounter one another. Snappy editing by Frederick Y Smith keeps it moving pretty well.

All I Desire ○
1953, US, 79 mins, b/w
Dir: Douglas Sirk
Stars: Barbara Stanwyck, Richard Carlson
Rating: ★★

Barbara Stanwyck is perfectly cast as a strong but tormented woman who reluctantly returns to her hometown years after a bitter divorce. She dominates the tear-stained plot but, under Douglas Sirk's sensitive direction, Universal starlets Marcia Henderson and Lod Nelson do their best screen work as her contrasting daughters; Lyle Bettger is also distinctive as the merchant who fancies the returning prodigal.

Alligator ● ⓥ
1980, US, 94 mins, colour
Dir: Lewis Teague
Stars: Robert Forster, Robin Riker, Henry Silva, Dean Jagger
Rating: ★★★★

A cross between *Jaws* and *Them!*, with a 40-foot alligator loose in the sewers of Chicago. If anyone so much as sets foot in these murky waters, it's snap! crackle! pop! and out come bits of body to the surface, to the consternation of detective Robert Forster and pretty herpetologist Robin Riker, whose own pet alligator was flushed down the loo by her father 10 years before (yes, you've guessed it). Ramon, for such is our scaly slayer's name, munches up pretty well all the cast before the end, including Henry Silva, enjoying himself as a big game hunter who tries to bring his methods to the backstreets of Chicago. Altogether this is a film of some style, with all the expected storm-drain excitements and a personable hero and heroine in the beleaguered Forster and the piquant Riker.

Alligator Named Daisy, An ○
1955, UK, 88 mins, colour
Dir: J Lee Thompson
Stars: Donald Sinden, Diana Dors, Margaret Rutherford, Jean Carson
Rating: ★★

Enjoyable frolic (though its song-and-dance routines aren't up to much) with a brilliant cast headed by Donald Sinden, Diana Dors and Margaret Rutherford, plus a winsome alligator for good measure.

All I Want for Christmas ⊙ ⓥ
1992, US, 92 mins, colour
Dir: Robert Lieberman
Stars: Harley Jane Kozak, Jamey Sheridan, Thora Birch, Ethan Randall, Leslie Nielsen, Lauren Bacall
Rating: ★★

Film suitable for children to watch alone are rare birds these days outside of Disney's cartoon features, so it's as well that the personal charm of little Thora Birch just about keeps this cardboard cracker from sinking in its own saccharine. Christmas is coming, and all seven-year-old Hallie (Birch) wants is for her divorced parents to reunite. To this end, she enlists the help of her brother (Ethan Randall) and his pals, who hatch an elaborate plan. There's lots of artificial heart in this family film, plus Lauren Bacall (as the kids' granny) and Leslie Nielsen as guest stars. It you enjoy watching preco-

A

cious children work their manipulative wiles, while the film-makers try to do the same thing with your emotions, this could be for you, even if it's really as empty as a stocking on Christmas Eve.

All Night Long ◑

1981, US, 89 mins, colour
Dir: Jean-Claude Tramont
Stars: Barbra Streisand, Gene Hackman, Diane Ladd, Dennis Quaid
Rating: ★★★

This is quite a nice little comedy in its gently quirky way. Gene Hackman is a middle-aged, minor executive who can't take being trodden on any more, and throws a chair out of the (closed) window. His marriage follows it when he falls in love with his son's mistress (Barbra Streisand), the nutty nymphomaniac wife of his cousin. Hackman's demotion to nightstore manager results in some amusing encounters with shoplifters and assorted felons and there are elements of *The Graduate* in there somewhere. Hackman is very good in a rare comedy role.

All of Me ◑ ⓥ

1984, US, 93 mins, colour
Dir: Carl Reiner
Stars: Steve Martin, Lily Tomlin, Victoria Tennant
Rating: ★★★

A madcap, crazy comedy about a wealthy woman's soul trapped by mistake after her death in the body of her oddball lawyer (Steve Martin). In the hands of Martin's oftime collaborator and director Carl Reiner the action moves swiftly through the usual uneasy blend of side-splitting visual gags and juvenile vulgarity. Martin, a comic actor who is at his best with physical comedy, has rarely been funnier on film. He delivers a tour-de-force performance as the legal eagle who has to battle constantly with the very vocal soul of crotchety millionairess Lily Tomlin, over everything from going to the toilet to sex. Although it seems unbearably silly at first, its sense of humour creeps up on you.

All Quiet on the Western Front ◯ ⓥ

1930, US, 130 mins, b/w
Dir: Lewis Milestone
Stars: Lew Ayres, Louis Wolheim
Rating: ★★★★★

The doyen of sound war films, this is a vivid and consistently involving version of Erich Maria Remarque's famous pacifist novel about the progressive disillusionment of young German soldiers (and one in particular) during World War One. The ending is now one of the movies' immortal moments and Academy Awards went to the picture itself, and to director Lewis Milestone.

All That Heaven Allows ◯

1955, US, 89 mins, colour
Dir: Douglas Sirk
Stars: Jane Wyman, Rock Hudson
Rating: ★★

A follow-up for the stars, Jane Wyman and Rock Hudson, and director Douglas Sirk to their hit with *Magnificent Obsession*, this romantic weepie looks very artificial today, like a woman's magazine story of the Fifties sprung to life. But the lush Technicolor photography of Russell Metty still looks as good now as it did then.

All That Jazz ● ⓥ

1979, US, 123 mins, colour
Dir: Bob Fosse
Stars: Roy Scheider, Jessica Lange, Ann Reinking, Leland Palmer, John Lithgow, Keith Gordon
Rating: ★★★★

Bob Fosse's acerbic musical, red in tooth and claw, has a lot to offer in one way or another, not least Roy Scheider as you have never seen him before: singing, jumping, clowning, being allowed to react a lot visually and generally to dominate a film in such a way as he's rarely had elsewhere. The film itself is quasi-autobiographical in that it deals with a dance director who suffers a heart attack, but Fosse has only used his own experiences as a starting point for a dazzling display of cinematic pyrotechnics that resemble one of those fragmented patterns you see at the bottom of a kaleidoscope. It's almost impossible to realise such a project without being self-indulgent at one stage or another or making the occasional miscalculation (the open-heart surgery at the end is massively difficult to watch) but it's entertaining, imaginative and, at its highpoints, thrilling stuff. The girls all excel in the dance numbers, which have the exhilaration of Fosse's all-out sweatgland-bursting snap without ever becoming ragged.

All the Brothers Were Valiant ◯

1953, US, 101 mins, colour
Dir: Richard Thorpe

Stars: Robert Taylor, Stewart Granger, Ann Blyth, Betta St John, Keenan Wynn
Rating: ★★

This rousing sea adventure was one of the most colourful films that MGM ever made. A trio of rather stuffy leading performances (Robert Taylor, Stewart Granger, Ann Blyth) is amply compensated by an amazing in-depth cast, and some full-blooded action scenes. The ending-comes over as a trifle unlikely, but all in all it's a well-plotted yarn, based on a book by Ben Ames Williams.

All the King's Men ◯

1949, US, 109 mins, b/w
Dir: Robert Rossen
Stars: Broderick Crawford, Joanne Dru, John Ireland, John Derek, Mercedes McCambridge
Rating: ★★★★

Hard-hitting, true-life dramas come no stronger than this story of the rise and fall of a power-hungry politician. Robert Penn Warren's novel, inspired by ruthless, corrupt Louisiana state governor Huey Long, has been brilliantly realised as a film by screenwriter Robert Rossen, who also directed. It won the best picture Oscar in its year, as well as best actor for burly Broderick Crawford (who captures the ambitious 'Willie Stark' to the last shady scowl) and best supporting actress for Mercedes McCambridge on her film debut. A raw, shocking portrait of the misuse of power.

All the Marbles

See: The California Dolls

All the President's Men ◯ ⓥ

1976, US, 138 mins, colour
Dir: Alan J Pakula
Stars: Dustin Hoffman, Robert Redford, Jack Warden, Martin Balsam, Hal Holbrook, Jason Robards
Rating: ★★★★

Director Alan J Pakula shapes this gripping story of the Watergate scandals with his usual emphasis on urban paranoia. The star charisma of Dustin Hoffman and Robert Redford, as *Washington Post* journalists Woodward and Bernstein, never detracts from the considerable documentary detail which, despite its many excellences, would have been better with a more audible dialogue track, less murky photography and a clearer introduction of the characters concerned. The acting, however, is a treat.

All the Right Moves ◑ ⓥ
1983, US, 91 mins, colour
Dir: Michael Chapman
Stars: Tom Cruise, Lea Thompson
Rating: ★★★

An excellent youth-oriented film which, thanks to its theme of American football, was undeservedly denied a screening over here on its first appearance. Former cinematographer Michael Chapman made an impressive directorial debut, and Tom Cruise took another stride towards superstardom as the high school senior struggling to escape the environment of a depressed steel town. A gritty script by Michael Kane gives Cruise ample opportunities to demonstrate his growing range as an actor, especially in scenes with Charles Cioffi as his father, and with Craig T Nelson, giving a superb performance as the hard-nosed coach who wants the big time as much as Cruise.

All Through the Night ○
1942, US, 107 mins, b/w
Dir: Vincent Sherman
Stars: Humphrey Bogart, Conrad Veidt, Kaaren Verne, Peter Lorre
Rating: ★★

A light-hearted, rough-and-tumble wartime thriller, with Humphrey Bogart rooting out a nest of spies. There is rather too much comedy relief from Frank McHugh, but a simply marvellous supporting cast that includes Conrad Veidt, Peter Lorre, William Demarest, Judith Anderson, Jackie Gleason, Wallace Ford, Jane Darwell, Barton MacLane and Phil Silvers.

Almost an Angel ○ ⓥ
1990, US, 95 mins, colour
Dir: John Cornell
Stars: Paul Hogan, Elias Koteas, Linda Kozlowski
Rating: ★★

This comedy about a criminal who believes he has been saved from death by God to become a worker of good deeds has a few nice set pieces and quite a few smart one-liners, but it could have been a whole lot better. The film leans heavily on star Paul Hogan's easygoing charm and it's a credit to Hogan's persona that it works as well as it does. Believing himself charmed, Hogan gets into all sorts of scrapes knowing nothing can happen to him. Not a bad film, and Hogan fans will enjoy seeing their hero again but one does get the sneaking suspicion that he peaked early with *Crocodile Dundee*.

Along Came Jones ○
1945, US, 90 mins, b/w
Dir: Stuart Heisler
Stars: Gary Cooper, Loretta Young, William Demarest, Dan Duryea
Rating: ★★

Enjoyable Western about a mild-mannered cowpoke who impersonates a notorious badman – with dire consequences. Nunnally Johnson's screenplay has a strong vein of humour which enables Gary Cooper and Dan Duryea to enjoy themselves hugely as goodie and baddie respectively.

Along the Great Divide ○
1950, US, 88 mins, colour
Dir: Raoul Walsh
Stars: Kirk Douglas, Virginia Mayo, John Agar, Walter Brennan
Rating: ★★★

Blazing colour photography (by Sid Hickox), an unusual detective element to the plot, a spectacular desert backdrop and storm, and a hard-driving performance by Kirk Douglas are the key factors that lift this Warners Western above the ordinary. Direction is in the capable hands of Raoul Walsh, who ensures that the pace is surprisingly good and the action scenes hit hard.

Alphabet Murders, The ○
(aka: The ABC Murders)
1966, UK, 93 mins, b/w
Dir: Frank Tashlin
Stars: Tony Randall, Anita Ekberg, Robert Morley
Rating: ★★

Having completed their quartet of Miss Marple thrillers, MGM turned their attention to Agatha Christie's other famous detective, Hercule Poirot. Here he investigates a series of murders whose victims initials are AA, BB and so forth. Madcap comedy expert Frank Tashlin seemed an odd choice to direct Dame Agatha's famous story of suspense and sudden death. But he had a good ally in Tony Randall who, despite previously being best known as a light comedian, proved a natural for the part of Poirot.

Altered States ● ⓥ
1980, US, 102 mins, colour
Dir: Ken Russell
Stars: William Hurt, Blair Brown
Rating: ★★

The Jekyll and Hyde story brought up to date. Jekyll (William Hurt) is now Jessop, a scientist; Hyde, the hairy other self he releases when dabbling in secret potions prepared by South American medicine men from lizards, human blood and psychedelic mushrooms. This psychological twaddle is dressed up in pounding, eye-hurting, top-of-the-pops style by Ken Russell, who seems to have told his cast to jabber their dialogue so fast that the audience won't have time to take in all its latent absurdities. Russell certainly drums the shock value home at a good 95 per cent, with the aid of some superb special effects. But the ending, spectacular though it is, finally reveals this as a film with nowhere to go.

Alvarez Kelly ○
1966, US, 116 mins, colour
Dir: Edward Dmytryk
Stars: William Holden, Richard Widmark, Janice Rule
Rating: ★★

Based on a true incident during the American Civil War when a vast herd of cattle see-sawed between equally hungry opposing forces, this Western packs plenty of colourful action.William Holden and Richard Widmark play vigorously in the leads, but are out-acted by Patrick O'Neal, as an egotistic Union commander, and Richard Rust, as a leering Confederate sergeant. The best moment comes, when one side digs a massive tunnel towards the cattle, only to come, in an unnerving moment, face to face with the enemy underground. Director Edward Dmytryk quite rightly likes this bizarre confrontation and lets his camera linger on the scene. The theme song is a bit of a hoot.

Always ○ ⓥ
1989, US, 122 mins, colour
Dir: Steven Spielberg
Stars: Richard Dreyfuss, Holly Hunter, Audrey Hepburn, John Goodman, Brad Johnson
Rating: ★★

You could call this pretty dopey romance, about an airborne fire-fighter who dies and goes to Heaven (a remake of 1943's *A Guy Named Joe*), a pancake landing from whizzbang director Steven Spielberg. Thank goodness it picks up in the last half hour; otherwise there could have been wreckage strewn everywhere. The problem is, of course, the script, which is partly responsible (but only partly) for making the film seem so wrongly cast. Although the dialogue gives him a bumpy ride throughout, Richard Dreyfuss keeps control pretty well

A

most of the time as the daredevil pilot who takes one too many risks and leaves his flying-controller girlfriend (a strident Holly Hunter) grief-stricken on the ground. Up in the firefighters' heaven, though, guardian angel Audrey Hepburn tells Dreyfuss to get back down there and straighten Hunter's life out. And so he does. Most of the cast are better actors than you'd guess from watching this. But the fire-fighter scenes are spot-on, even though some of the footage is 'pinched' from a real forest blaze.

Amadeus ❶ Ⓥ

1984, US, 158 mins, colour
Dir: Milos Forman
Stars: F Murray Abraham, Tom Hulce, Elizabeth Berridge, Simon Callow
Rating: ★★★★

This eight-Oscar film spotlights the clash of wills in 18th-century Vienna between two composers: Mozart (Tom Hulce), a vulgar, licentious popinjay with a hyena laugh, but kissed with genius, and Salieri (F Murray Abraham), the court composer whose work Mozart mocks and who, even while he plots his tormentor's destruction, is tortured himself by the knowledge that Mozart is the greatest composer he has ever heard. Looking at the story through Salieri's envy-green eyes is a clever ploy by writer Peter Shaffer and one that works. Mozart is so awful, so much a crass vulgarian, that our instinctive wish is for him to get what he deserves – obscurity. Like Salieri, however, we are pulled both ways by the beauty of his music, so that Shaffer compels us to follow developments attentively to their horrifying conclusion. Salieri is played in masterly style throughout by Abraham (winning one of the film's Academy Awards), conveying inner feelings by eyes, mouth or gesture rather than words. Even so, the film is almost stolen by Jeffrey Jones, six-inch-thick but inch-perfect as the emperor.

Amarcord ●

1973, Italy/France, 123 mins, colour
Dir: Federico Fellini
Stars: Puppela Maggio, Magali Noel
Rating: ★★

Director Federico Fellini's award-winner is a grab-bag of fragmentary boyhood memories: crude pranks at school; the death of the mother; the first encounter with sex. The best episode concerns a loony uncle who climbs to the top of an enormous tree and won't come down. All in all,

though, even with such moments of pictorial beauty as a huge liner looming up through the fog, ablaze with light, and despite its Academy Award as best foreign film, this project is likely to prove less than gripping for today's average viewer.

Amazing Dr Clitterhouse, The ○

1938, US, 87 mins, b/w
Dir: Anatole Litvak
Stars: Edward G Robinson, Claire Trevor, Humphrey Bogart
Rating: ★★★

A consistently enjoyable pre-war Warners gangster romp, with Edward G Robinson and Humphrey Bogart as hero and villain, just as they had been in the studio's *Bullets or Ballots*. Robinson plays a criminologist who joins a gang of thieves (headed by Bogart as a character called Rocks) to study the criminal mind. Claire Trevor oozes class in the female lead and the supporting cast is positively stuffed with familiar faces – and one familiar voice. Needing a good speaker for the voice of an unseen radio announcer, the studio picked on one of their young contract players: Ronald Reagan.

Amazing Mr Beecham, The

See: The Chiltern Hundreds

Amazing Mr Blunden, The ○

1972, UK, 98 mins, colour
Dir: Lionel Jeffries
Stars: Laurence Naismith, Lynne Frederick, Garry Miller, Diana Dors
Rating: ★★★★

Lionel Jeffries' second venture into direction: although not as overwhelmingly popular as his first film, *The Railway Children*, this is every bit as good. The remarkably self-assured performance by Lynne Frederick, as the elder of two children involved with ghosts from a century before, is better than anything else in either film.

Amazing Mr Forrest, The

See: The Gang's All Here [1939]

Amazing Mrs Holliday, The ○

1943, US, 96 mins, b/w
Dir: Bruce Manning
Stars: Deanna Durbin, Edmond O'Brien, Barry Fitzgerald
Rating: ★★

Deanna Durbin goes to war in a film that starts off looking like a forerunner

to *The Inn of the Sixth Happiness*. A pity the plot didn't stay in the Far East, for it gets sillier as it goes along, leaving Durbin's lovely song interludes as the main interest.

Amazon Women on the Moon ❶ Ⓥ

1986, US, 81 mins, colour
Dir: Joe Dante, Carl Gottlieb, John Landis, Robert K Weiss, Peter Horton
Stars: Rosanna Arquette, Steve Guttenberg, Michelle Pfeiffer, Carrie Fisher, Griffin Dunne
Rating: ★★

Don't be too attracted by the cast: this is a quite often mildly amusing, but rarely hilarious compendium of comedy sketches in the still-current American 'rude' vein, punctuated by a black-and-white take-off of an old science-fiction movie that probably looked funnier in its original form. A class cast which, besides the above, includes Sybil Danning, Andrew Dice Clay, Ralph Bellamy, Steve Forrest, Kelly Preston, Arsenio Hall, Ed Begley Jr and (briefly) hulking veteran Mike Mazurki, at least keeps boredom at bay in the main.

Ambassador, The ○

1984, US, 90 mins, colour
Dir: J Lee Thompson
Stars: Robert Mitchum, Ellen Burstyn, Rock Hudson
Rating: ★★★

This political thriller retains a hint of topicality in its Middle East crisis setting. Robert Mitchum plays the title role with monumental calm; he's the US ambassador to Israel, caught in the middle of the fierce conflict between Zionist and extremist Palestinian factions. His determined efforts to seek a solution to the fighting are somewhat complicated by his wife's affair with a high-ranking PLO official. Veteran British directory Lee Thompson efficiently glosses over the plot's implausible moments and the scenes between Mitchum and Ellen Burstyn (as his wife) possess adult wit and real-istic weariness.

Ambassador's Daughter, The ○

1956, US, 106 mins, colour
Dir: Norman Krasna
Stars: Olivia de Havilland, John Forsythe, Myrna Loy, Adolphe Menjou
Rating: ★★

Pleasant comedy of mistaken identity, whose chief charms lay in allowing Olivia de Havilland, Myrna Loy and

Adolphe Menjou to make screen comebacks. Romantic froth.

Ambush ○
1949, US, 89 mins, b/w
Dir: Sam Wood
Stars: Robert Taylor, John Hodiak, Arlene Dahl, Jean Hagen, Don Taylor
Rating: ★★

This looks like an ordinary Western on the surface – until one takes a closer look at its credentials. The director is Sam Wood, one of MGM's most experienced men, and the screenplay is by Marguerite Roberts, who wrote John Wayne's Oscar-winning Western, *True Grit*. Robert Taylor plays impassively as the Cavalry scout hero, but there's a dynamic, throat-clutching action climax that may make you jump.

Ambush at Tomahawk Gap ○
1953, US, 73 mins, colour
Dir: Fred F Sears
Stars: John Derek, John Hodiak, Maria Elena Marques, David Brian, Ray Teal
Rating: ★★★

Remarkably rough, tough, gripping and well-characterised Western about four desperadoes, with an Indian girl in tow, hunting for buried gold. Its script was attentive enough to character to attract several star players to act in it. John Hodiak and Maria Elena Marques had co-starred before – with Clark Gable in *Across the Wide Missouri* – and here, as there, they give tough, realistic portrayals.

Ambush Bay ○
1966, US, 109 mins, colour
Dir: Ron Winston
Stars: Hugh O'Brian, Mickey Rooney, James Mitchum, Tisa Chang
Rating: ★★

Explosive action film about a group of Marines on a top secret mission in the Far East during World War Two. Mickey Rooney is in typically pugnacious form as a tough little sergeant.

American Anthem ○
(aka: Take It Easy)
1986, US, 101 mins, colour
Dir: Albert Magnoli
Stars: Mitch Gaylord, Janet Jones, Michael Pataki
Rating: RB

There can't be too many films featuring Olympic gymnasts and, if this is anything to judge by, there may not be too many more. Mitch Gaylord is, for

an athlete, a reasonable actor but the mistakes lie in a) asking him to play a gymnast and b) saddling him with a perfectly ludicrous script that must have come out of the Ark. Does Gaylord bring off the quadruple wotsit at the end? Will his unloving dad make a last-minute appearance at the event? Can a duck swim?

American Buffalo ●
1996, US, 90 mins, colour
Dir: Michael Corrente
Stars: Dustin Hoffman, Dennis Franz, Sean Nelson
Rating: RB

Did we miss something here? Like a plot? This is a well-acted version of David Mamet's three-handed play, but you may be hard-put to fathom what any of it means, even though (or perhaps because) its characters never use one word where eight will do. Franz is a ghetto junk dealer and Hoffman his seemingly unemployed acquaintance (friend would be too strong a word here) who joins him and three others in a weekly game of poker where the rest may or may not be cheating. The synopsis tells us that the two men, and perhaps their black teenager 'gofer' (Nelson) are planning some sort of robbery, although you'd be pushed to glean that from the film. Hoffman appears to be playing both ends against the middle, and the two men rant and swear a lot in a meaningless sort of way. The end comes to no definite conclusion except that Hoffman has wrecked Franz's shop in a fit of temper. We thought they should have stuck to poker.

American Flyers ◑ ⓥ
1985, US, 114 mins, colour
Dir: John Badham
Stars: Kevin Costner, David Grant, Rae Dawn Chong
Rating: ★★

Made before he hit the big time in The *Untouchables*, this cycling drama about two brothers who untangle their mixed emotions as they compete in a gruelling race, has a striking performance by Kevin Costner. But, ultimately, the film makes too many big statements and attempts to career in too many directions. It's not a patch on screenwriter Steve Tesich's earlier cycle movie, *Breaking Away*, which managed to keep all its themes and ideas in proportion. The women's roles in particular are hopelessly underwritten.

American Friends ○ ⓥ
1991, UK, 96 mins, colour
Dir: Tristram Powell
Stars: Michael Palin, Connie Booth, Trini Alvarado, Alfred Molina
Rating: ★★★

Based on a fragment from the diary of Michael Palin's great-great-grandfather, this is an unexpected film from the former Monty Python star: a gentle, leisurely romantic anecdote with moments of comedy and wry observation, and a final delicate balance between tragedy and happiness. it's performed in rather studied style by Palin himself as the academic, and by Connie Booth and Trini Alvarado as aunt and niece, the 'American friends' he meets on holiday in the Alps, who both fall in love with him. Pleasant and watchable, even if it doesn't make us feel much for the characters, the film abounds in delicious satirical studies of Oxford dons. The screenplay, by Palin and director Tristram Powell, is literate and even has its poetic moments. Somehow, though, it remains inconsequential, a vignette of depth but no weight and, in the end, of curiosity value only.

American Gigolo ● ⓥ
1980, US, 117 mins, colour
Dir: Paul Schrader
Stars: Richard Gere, Lauren Hutton, Hector Elizondo, Nina Van Pailandt, Bill Duke
Rating: ★★★★

Another strong, dark social thriller from Paul Schrader, writer of *Taxi Driver*, *Rolling Thunder* and *The Hardcore Life*. The environment is redolent of Raymond Chandler, while the constant night-time scenes of Richard Gere driving around poor and rich areas of a coastal city to grating, doomy music (by Giorgio Moroder) remind us that we're not that far removed from *Taxi Driver* itself. Gere's 'hero' is the all-American cowboy made good: he pleases rich women for rich rewards. Where he comes unstuck – in a typical Schrader touch – is in accepting an 'unusual' assignment, one that leads to his being framed for murder. Although the film rather loses its grip in the last two reels this is, on the whole, an impressive piece of work. Gere copes quite well with a difficult role even if his dialogue is sometimes a bit difficult to hear.

American Graffiti ○ ⓥ
1973, US, 110 mins, colour
Dir: George Lucas

A

Stars: Richard Dreyfuss, Ron Howard, Paul Le Mat, Charles Martin Smith
Rating: ★★★

Part-financed by Francis Ford Coppola, and written and directed by George Lucas, this is the high school nostalgia classic which, made while Americans were still dying in Vietnam, looks back towards the rock 'n' roll, juke-box, drive-in and soda-fountain America of the not-so-distant past. It's a film about rebels without causes and the pop culture of the early 60s. A winner.

American Guerilla In the Philippines, An ○ ⓥ
(aka: I Shall Return)
1950, US, 105 mins, colour
Dir: Fritz Lang
Stars: Tyrone Power, Micheline Presle, Tom Ewell, Jack Elam
Rating: ★★

Noisy but vaguely dull Hollywood war film with a taciturn performance by Tyrone Power in the lead. There are eye-catching portrayals from Tom Ewell and Jack Elam, but it's a strange film to come from German expatriate Fritz Lang. British title (they obviously didn't approve of such Yankee flag-waving!): *I Shall Return*.

American Heart ● ⓥ
1992, US, 114 mins, colour
Dir: Martin Bell
Stars: Jeff Bridges, Edward Furlong
Rating: ★

You've seen more depressing films than this, but not many. Jeff Bridges is fresh out of jail and reunited with his 14-year-old son (Edward Furlong). Their accommodation is grubby and the landlady dubious about their ability to pay. Still, Bridges gets a job as a window-cleaner and the kid has to enrol in school. It's the filmmakers rather than society who decree these people have no chance. Happy endings were well out of style when this was made, so Bridges loses all his earnings to a vengeful ex-partner-in-crime and the kid is soon consorting with junkies, pushers, strippers and hookers. It gets so that you can't wait for Bridges to go back to crime so that you can all go home. It takes nearly two hours, though, and in all that time not one of the performers reaches our emotions.

American In Paris, An ☉ ⓥ
1951, US, 115 mins, colour
Dir: Vincente Minnelli
Stars: Gene Kelly, Leslie Caron, Oscar Levant
Rating: ★★★★

Vincente Minnelli's enchanting musical raised standards to a new level, with Gene Kelly and Leslie Caron forming a brilliant dancing partnership. Minnelli's direction was full of vivid, imaginative touches. And George Gershwin's music was the perfect background for a Paris which really sprang to life. The film won eight Oscars, including one for best picture; one for story and screenplay (by Alan Jay Lerner); and a special award to Kelly for his superb choreography, topped by his number with the kids and the final 'ballet'.

American President, The
◑ ⓥ
1995, US, 113 mins, colour
Dir: Rob Reiner
Stars: Michael Douglas, Annette Bening, Martin Sheen, Michael J Fox, Richard Dreyfuss, Samantha Mathis
Rating: ★★★

A slightly more serious version of the sort of stuff Spencer Tracy and Katharine Hepburn were making 40 years before, this posits the not-too-likely but lightly entertaining question of what the effect on day-to-day US government might be if a widower president were to fall in love. What adds some spice to the formula is that the woman (Annette Bening) for whom the President (Michael Douglas) falls is a political lobbyist with a flag-burning background. A star-laden supporting cast gives the proper weight to some effective dialogue in the story of the fall in the President's popularity when the liaison is discovered. Douglas and Bening are both as believable as the script allows, which means not quite, although you'll enjoy being in their company, and Bening catches well the innate warmth and outward aggression of the woman who finds her unique situation predictably too tough to handle.

American Tail, An ☉
1986, US, 80 mins, colour
Dir: Don Bluth
Voice stars: Dom DeLuise, Madeline Kahn, Nehemiah Persoff, Christopher Plummer
Rating: ★★★★

This faintly off-beat cartoon feature outpointed anything the rival Disney studio had produced since *The Jungle Book* almost 20 years earlier. There certainly can't be many animated features that would dare start their story in 1885 Russia. Beneath the Moscowitz family, fleeing repression to start a new life in America, live the Mousekewitzes, fleeing their own oppression to the States because they think, in the words of the film's catchiest song 'There are no cats in America'! The grim voyage of the immigrants is nicely caught by the animators without any recourse to over-sombre detail. The Mousekewitz son, Fievel, is washed overboard, arrives in America in a bottle and sets out to find his family. From here on, the film slips into slightly more routine cat-and-mouse stuff but there are two or three excellent characters, including a calculating cockroach; Henri le Pigeon, busy decorating the Statue of Liberty; and a fat orange cat (voiced by Dom DeLuise) who's vegetarian (apart from the occasional fish), a thicko and a softie and becomes Fievel's friend.

American Way, The ◑
(aka: Riders of the Storm)
1986, US, 105 mins, colour
Dir: Maurice Phillips
Stars: Dennis Hopper, Michael J Pollard, Eugene Lipinski, James Aubrey
Rating: ★★

'Boy, there's some incredibly weird people out there,' exclaims skipper Dennis Hopper as he leads his crew of spaced-out Vietnam veterans, manning a pirate TV station aboard an old bomber plane. Among his men are Michael J Pollard as the resident electronics wizard, dodging all the missiles an enraged US military can launch, and an oriental sitting astride a massive bomb. And these are the quieter members of a crew that soon becomes dedicated to blocking the nomination of one Willa Westinghouse, a presidendal candidate planning to start another war somewhere, somehow. This is a bitter black comedy constantly battling to shrug off an ordinary plot and working best when it succeeds. Hopper and Pollard offer their familiar 'eccentric' characterisations, but the central 'surprise' of the plot is rather obvious throughout.

American Werewolf in London, An ●　ⓥ
1981, UK, 103 mins, colour
Dir: John Landis
Stars: David Naughton, Griffin Dunne, Jenny Agutter, John Woodvine
Rating: ★★

A joky horror film that's even funnier than it thinks it is. David Naughton and Griffin Dunne are two Americans adrift on English country moors until they come across The Slaughtered Lamb, an inn where the Hammer Bit Part Union clam up like camels in a sandstorm when asked about the five-pointed star on the wall. 'Beware the moon, lads,' warns purse-lipped Brian Glover, 'and stick to the road.' Oohaah, lads. But of course they leave the road and wander blithely across the moors in the thrashing rain (are we actually supposed to *believe* this?), where they say a few four-letter words as they're in for an adult rating anyway for having their throats torn out in the next scene. Naughton survives (!) and, before bedding Nurse Jenny Agutter, has a visitation from his dead friend. Dr Woodvine pooh-poohs all this. 'If there were a monster roaming around the north of England, we'd have seen it on the telly,' he protests. How right. Not like *News at Ten* to miss out on anything like that. Imagine Trevor McDonald's eyebrows. There's a lot more of this before Naughton metamorphises in a really impressive scene and eats up half the population of London.

Amityville Horror, The ● Ⓥ
1979, US, 117 mins, colour
Dir: Stuart Rosenberg
Stars: James Brolin, Margot Kidder, Rod Steiger, Don Stroud
Rating: ★★★★

This film carries a unique disclaimer that 'certain events and characters have been altered to heighten dramatic effect'. It forms a disturbing coda to an allegedly true story about a house haunted by victims and killer from a previous mass murder there, and by evil spirits from a long-distant (Red Indian) past. It certainly is most persuasively done, with James Brolin and Margot Kidder suitably fraught as the young couple who do well to stay three weeks in a neighbourhood where thunder and lightning are the order of the night – quite apart from what oozes through the boards of their home.

Amityville II: The Possession ● Ⓥ
1982, US, 104 mins, colour
Dir: Damiano Damiani
Stars: Burt Young, James Olson, Rutanya Aida
Rating: ★★

The now-familiar ride up the dark stairways of a haunted house to meet whatever horrors the special effects ex-

perts can dream up. Although not stated anywhere in this film, this is, in fact, a prequel to *The Amityville Horror* dealing with events that (might have) happened before that film. Demonic possession is soon in the air, especially when slobby father Burt Young tells a visitor: 'This is my first-born, Sonny. He hasn't been feeling well lately'. Unsympathetic characters give us plenty of chance to cheer for the demons.

Amityville 4: The Evil Escapes Ⓞ Ⓥ
1989, US, 100 mins, colour
Dir: Sandor Stern
Stars: Patty Duke, Jane Wyatt
Rating: ★★

The fourth of six films to date about the possessed house in Amityville comes up with the pretty dotty idea of having the evil of the Amityville house 'transmigrate' into a peculiar-looking lamp – something which can be transferred from house to house and from family to family, thereby giving prospective Amityville film-makers as many angles as they could wish, and condemning audiences to interminable variations on a theme. At least we can consider ourself brighter than the beleaguered family here. Finding her pet parrot done to a turn in the toaster oven, Alice (Jane Wyatt) blames herself for leaving the bird's cage open, never wondering how the bird managed to incinerate itself.

Amongst Friends ● Ⓥ
1993, US, 88 mins, colour
Dir: Rob Weiss
Stars: Steve Parlavecchio, Joseph Lindsay, Mira Sorvino
Rating: ★★

Three teenage boys from well-to-do families enjoy a privileged childhood in Long Island. But, instead of going on to high school and sedate suburban lives, they turn to crime. This is a rather jerkily-paced story of twenty-something gangsters who fall out over the inevitable girl, but it does throw up a couple of charismatic performers in Steve Parlavecchio (who looks like James Dean) and Joseph Lindsay (who looks like Rob Lowe). Mira Sorvino is a good-looking and appealing heroine. Not always as interesting as it gets in the last half-hour, the film does exercise a certain fascination as its (clichéd) storyline approaches the inevitable confrontational conclusion.

Amorous Adventures of Moll Flanders, The Ⓞ
1965, UK, 126 mins, colour
Dir: Terence Young
Stars: Kim Novak, Richard Johnson, Angela Lansbury, George Sanders, Leo McKern, Vittorio De Sica
Rating: ★★

A film much after the style of *Tom Jones*, with bags of colour and incident. Kim Novak is the female Tom, chased around every bedchamber in London town. Although Hugh Griffith, memorable in *Tom Jones*, is here also, this time as a prison governor, the film misses some of the lip-smacking period relish with which the earlier film (and the age) so distinguished itself.

Amorous Prawn, The Ⓞ
(aka: The Amorous Mr Prawn)
1962, UK, 89 mins, b/w
Dir: Anthony Kimmins
Stars: Ian Carmichael, Joan Greenwood, Cecil Parker, Dennis Price
Rating: ★★

A film adaptation of the riotously successful stage farce about an army headquarters that gets turned into a luxury hotel. And the screen version has a cast more starry than almost any stage play could hope to muster. It was directed by the redoubtable Anthon Kimmins, who had made almost all George Formby's smash hit comedies.

Amsterdamned ● Ⓥ
1987, Holland, 113 mins, colour
Dir: Dick Maas
Stars: Huub Stapel, Monique van de Ven
Rating: ★★

This facile but fast-paced Dutch film is a kind of Creature from the Black Canal. 'There's something fishy going on here,' mutters one character early on, just before being disembowelled by the Demon Diver. How right he is. Nothing clever about what follows, either, just a speedy mix of commercial elements that includes cuties dangling their toes from lilos in the deadly waters and the inevitable speedboat chase towards the end. Connoisseurs of subtitling, as well as bosses of the well-known fast-food chain, will be delighted to see a 'McDonalds' translated as 'top quality beef'.

Anaconda ● Ⓥ
1997, US, 89 mins, colour
Dir: Luis Llosa
Stars: Jennifer Lopez, Ice Cube, John Voight, Jonathan Hyde, Eric Stoltz, Kari Wohrer
Rating: ★★★

A

There haven't been many giant snake movies and perhaps predictably this one turns out to be a mixture of turgidity and frenzied excitement. The anaconda attack effects, though, are simply sensational, well worth waiting for and amply compensate for the sluggish voyage down the Amazon that precedes them. Otherwise it's formula stuff, in that people are unrealistically antagonistic towards one another, and that characters – and snakes – you'd assumed to have been killed return inevitably from watery graves. But it's the execution of the action that takes the breath away, especially one shot of the pipeline-sized anaconda swooping down on a man attempting to escape its jaws by diving off the top of a waterfall. The widescreen process on display here is presumably SlitherScope.

Anastasia O
1956, US, 105 mins, colour
Dir: Anatole Litvak
Stars: Ingrid Bergman, Yul Brynner, Helen Hayes, Akim Tamiroff, Martita Hunt, Felix Aylmer
Rating: ★★★★

The film in which Ingrid Berginan returned to Hollywood and won an Oscar all in one swoop. However, she is out-acted by that dowager duchess of actresses, Helen Hayes, in a good strong story about an attempt to pass off a young woman as the surviving daughter of the last Czar of Russia.

Anatomy of a Murder O
1959, US, 160 mins, b/w
Dir: Otto Preminger
Stars: James Stewart, Lee Remick, Ben Gazzara, Arthur O'Connell, Eve Arden
Rating: ★★★★

Otto Preminger's highly watchable courtroom drama, with James Stewart as the slow-talking lawyer picking his way determinedly through a tangle of rape and murder. It was explosive stuff in its time, with most of the controversy centring on the scenes in which the prosecution (a striking early appearance by George C Scott) is trying to establish that Lee Remick was not raped at all, but only too willing. There are two fine supporting performances from Arthur O'Connell and Eve Arden as Stewart's dog-eared assistant and wisecracking secretary, both creating characters that are instantly likeable.

Anchors Aweigh ⊙ Ⓥ
1945, US, 140 mins, colour
Dir: George Sidney

Stars: Gene Kelly, Frank Sinatra, Kathryn Grayson
Rating: ★★★★

This lively and colourful musical was a triumph for Gene Kelly and made him a major star at MGM. He and Frank Sinatra are two sailors on leave in Hollywood and Kelly is chasing Kathryn Grayson, an aspiring singer. The plot's pretty thin, but that doesn't matter: the songs, written by Jule Styne and Sammy Cahn, are great and Kelly's dancing is spectacular. A particular high point is a routine he does with cartoon mouse Jerry (of Tom and Jerry fame). Beautifully done and highly entertaining. Kelly, who did all the choreography, really put his mark on this musical, and it shows.

Anderson Tapes, The ◑ Ⓥ
1971, US, 98 mins, colour
Dir: Sidney Lumet
Stars: Sean Connery, Dyan Cannon, Martin Balsam, Alan King, Ralph Meeker, Christopher Walken
Rating: ★★★

Despite its heavy undertones of satire, irony and social comment, this entertaining film from Sidney Lumet is basically a 'caper' thriller. Sean Connery gives a fine study of bullet-headed aggressiveness as a professional safe-cracker who is as far removed from James Bond as it's possible to imagine. Still, he does have a bedmate worthy of 007 in the sinuous shape of Dyan Cannon, and the robbery itself provides a thrilling, if black-edged, climax.

And God Created Woman ●
1956, France, 92 mins, colour
Dir: Roger Vadim
Stars: Brigitte Bardot, Curt Jurgens, Jean-Louis Trintignant
Rating: ★★

Roger Vadim's first film as a director created quite a stir when it first arrived in Britain in 1957, on account of its sexiness and its exploitation of the physical charms of a semi-nude Brigitte Bardot. It was cut by four minutes from the original version, and clearly exception was taken to the title which was changed in Britain to *And Woman ... Was Created* – evidently to keep God out of it. When the film was reissued there in 1967, it was under the proper title and with a couple of deleted minutes restored.

And God Created Woman ● Ⓥ
1988, US, 94 mins, colour
Dir: Roger Vadim

Stars: Rebecca DeMornay, Vincent Spano, Frank Langella, Donovan Leitch, Judith Chapman
Rating: ★★

Roger Vadim returns to the title if not the story of his greatest hit with Brigitte Bardot but the best you can say is that there have been worse Vadim films in the past couple of decades. Rebecca DeMornay and Vincent Spano do help as the couple who undergo a marriage of convenience to get her out of jail. Frank Langella is the gubernatorial candidate who keeps a friendly eye on her progress and you can pretty well guess the rest, given that Vadim is such a romantic at heart. DeMornay does take her clothes off, but for all that it's a naive, innocent, almost primitive film. Quite entertaining, if you're really stuck with nothing to do for an hour and a half.

... And Justice for All ◑ Ⓥ
1979, US, 117 mins, colour
Dir: Norman Jewison
Stars: Al Pacino, Jack Warden, John Forsythe, Christine Lahti, Sam Levene, Craig T Nelson
Rating: ★

Difficult-to-like black satire with an unattractive central performance by Al Pacino, who's supposed to be the only sane lawyer in a legal world gone mad. His judges include one who lets off robbers and rapists with probation, another with a suicide complex during recesses (a wildly overdone performance from Jack Warden) and a third, an ultra-hardliner (John Forsythe doing his best with a ludicrous role) who comes up himself for rape and assault. Pacino's own cases seem doomed to tragedy: two of his clients are sent unnecessarily to jail through no fault of his own; one hangs himself, the other takes hostages and is shot. If this is comedy, it is of the very blackest kind. But director Jewison ensures that it's far too overblown to succeed as comedy or drama. The pace is leaden, mainly because individual scenes are time and again stretched beyond breaking point, but without fleshing out any of the background. Everyone shouts a lot.

And Now for Something Completely Different O
1971, UK, 89 mins, colour
Dir: Ian MacNaughton
Stars: Graham Chapman, John Cleese, Terry Gilliam, Michael Palin, Eric Idle, Terry Jones
Rating: ★★

Early Monty Python film intended for the US market, which explains the fact that most of the sketches had appeared in the UK TV series. John Cleese enjoys his classic encounter with a pet-shop owner over a distinctly deceased parrot.

And Now the Screaming Starts! ● Ⓥ

1973, UK, 87 mins, colour
Dir: Roy Ward Baker
Stars: Peter Cushing, Stephanie Beacham, Herbert Lom, Patrick Magee, Ian Ogilvy
Rating: ★★

Family curses and malevolent ghosts make up the brew for this grisly horror film, which becomes pretty sinister towards the end. Denys Coop's remarkably skilled camerawork is rather negated by strange colour, as putrescent-looking as the severed hand which hovers on the edges of the film.

And Now Tomorrow ○

1944, US, 86 mins, b/w
Dir: Irving Pichel
Stars: Alan Ladd, Loretta Young, Susan Hayward
Rating: ★★

Hollywood works in mysterious ways and thus Raymond Chandler, esteemed author of hard-boiled detective fiction, was assigned by Paramount to co-script this romantic drama from Rachel Field's sentimental bestseller. Spirited playing from Loretta Young and Susan Hayward as warring sisters, the more stolid Alan Ladd and Barry Sullivan completing the romantic quadrangle.

Androcles and the Lion ☉

1952, US, 98 mins, b/w
Dir: Chester Erskine
Stars: Jean Simmons, Alan Young, Victor Mature, Robert Newton, Elsa Lanchester
Rating: ★★

Gabriel Pascal had made an impression with his British-made film adaptations of plays by George Bernard Shaw, above all *Pygmalion*. But *Androcles and the Lion* is a trifle heavy-handed where a lighter touch is required and perhaps because of one or two instances of debatable casting. Nevertheless, it is reasonably faithful to the original and does contain some good performances by its star-studded cast. Victor Mature, as the captain, took over the role which was to have been played by James Donald who dropped out of the cast.

Android ○

1982, US, 80 mins, colour
Dir: Aaron Lipstadt
Stars: Klaus Kinski, Brie Howard, Don Opper, Kendra Kirchner
Rating: ★★★

A unique combination of elements from *Frankenstein*, *Metropolis* and Frank Capra films sparks this science fiction film, the best new movie from a first-time director (Aaron Lipstadt) since John Carpenter burst on the cinema scene with *Dark Star*. Klaus Kinski is the mad doctor to the life (though even he may not be quite what he seems) while Don Opper (who also co-scripted) will bring a tear to your eye as the android Max – especially when tentatively trying to make a date with a female fugitive who has invaded his space station. You'll be hoping that this robot hero can, like Pinocchio, 'beat the system'!

Andromeda Strain, The ○

1970, US, 127 mins, colour
Dir: Robert Wise
Stars: Arthur Hill, James Olson, Kate Reid
Rating: ★★

The combination of writer Nelson Gidding and director Robert Wise has often been at its best in providing chills and thrills. Together they made *The Haunting* and *Audrey Rose*. This science fiction yarn hits hard in the eerie beginning and in the hair-raising climax. The ending, in fact, is worthy of a James Bond film: you'll perch on the very edge of the armchair as James Olson fights against time (assailed by poison gas and deadly laser beams) to disarm a self-destruct device before it can trigger itself off.

And Soon the Darkness ◐

1970, UK, 98 mins, colour
Dir: Robert Fuest
Stars: Pamela Franklin, Michele Dotrice, Sandor Eles
Rating: ★★

Carrying uncomfortable contemporary resonance, this is a rather protracted chiller from the pen of Brian Clemens, which seems to take a long time to get around to its suspenseful final reel. At least, however, the script succeeds in keeping you guessing as to the identity of the pervert pursuing two pretty English nurses cycling in France, which is what it has seemed determined at all costs to do.

And Then There Were None ○

(aka: Ten Little Niggers)
1945, US, 98 mins, b/w
Dir: Rene Clair
Stars: Barry Fitzgerald, Louis Hayward, Walter Huston, June Duprez, C Aubrey Smith, Roland Young
Rating: ★★★★★

Rene Clair's atmospheric version of Agatha Christie's classic thriller is one of the best mystery films you are ever likely to see, as well as being one of the creepiest – thanks to Clair's edgy direction and Charles Previn's doom-filled music. If you haven't seen the ending coming, you will find it quite shattering. And the beginning, with the cast travelling to the unknown island on a storm-swept boat, is a masterpiece of mood-setting. Among those meeting ingenious deaths are Sir C Aubrey Smith, Richard Haydn, Roland Young and Mischa Auer. Forget other versions – this is the one to watch.

Angel ○

1937, US, 91 mins, b/w
Dir: Ernst Lubitsch
Stars: Marlene Dietrich, Herbert Marshall, Melvyn Douglas
Rating: ★★★

This Marlene Dietrich film has a dash of polish and sophistication given to a risqué, romantic comedy by that old master of the genre, Ernst Lubitsch. The title song by Frederick Hollander and Leo Robin sets the mood for a light fantastic Parisian romp in which Dietrich wears a wardrobe of clothes that few other actresses would, or could, get away with.

Angel ● Ⓥ

1982, UK, 90 mins, colour
Dir: Neil Jordan
Stars: Stephen Rea, Alan Devlin, Veronica Quilligan, Honor Heffernan, Marie Kean, Ray McAnally
Rating: ★★★

Although set in Ireland this film is more of a contemporary black thriller than a comment on the latter-day Irish troubles. Stephen Rea, as the musician who swaps his saxophone for a submachine gun to avenge the dance hall murder of two acquaintances, is firmly in the tradition of lone-wolf heroes established by Alan Ladd in Hollywood 40 years earlier. And Chris Menges' imaginative photography exactly matches the mood of the film. It was a formidable cinematic debut for Sligo-born Neil Jordan, both as writer and

A

director – a slice of Raymond Chandler, if you like, within a particularly abrasive and desperate Irish context.

Angel Face ○

1952, US, 91 mins, b/w
Dir: Otto Preminger
Stars: Robert Mitchum, Jean Simmons, Mona Freeman, Herbert Marshall
Rating: ★★★

This moody and rather unsettling RKO *noir* thriller looks as though it were written with studio contractees Jane Greer or Faith Domergue in mind. But Greer had just left the studio and, when Jean Simmons arrived from England, studio boss Howard Hughes, after months of not knowing what to do with her, gave her the disturbed murderess in *Angel Face*. Icily effective she is too, ensnaring poor Robert Mitchum who was at one time or another the fall guy for pretty well all the studio's formidable stock of femmes fatales.

Angel Heart ● ⓥ

1987, US, 113 mins, colour
Dir: Alan Parker
Stars: Mickey Rourke, Robert De Niro, Charlotte Rampling
Rating: ★★★

A surrealist detective story or a modern reworking of an old legend? Alan Parker's powerful thriller certainly has bags of style and it flaunts it too. You get lots of clues along the way as to what it's all about, amid a welter of blood and voodoo, but they may not be enough unless you have your wits about you. Mickey Rourke gives a startled, shuffling performance as a seedy private eye in 1955 whose precarious living has earned him little apart from a permanent designer stubble. Summoned by the mysterious Louis Cyphre (smoothly played by Robert De Niro), he is commanded, money no object, to find an obscure crooner, Johnny Favorite, who vanished in 1943 after being injured in the war. Every contact he talks to seems to end up dead, but gradually the fantastic truth begins to dawn ... Thumped along by doomy music, the film treads a bloody path to its inexorable conclusion, against menacing backgrounds that sometimes seem to have a life of their own. It's something a little different for strong stomachs.

Angel in Exile ○

1948, US, 90 mins, b/w
Dir: Allan Dwan
Stars: John Carroll, Adele Mara
Rating: ★★★

This unusual, well-handled movie melodrama was made by Republic when they were trying hard to build themselves up as realistic rivals to the major Hollywood studios. It's a modest but effective semi-Western about a bad man who undergoes a change of heart when hailed as a miracle man by Mexican peasants. The assured direction is from the experienced hands of Allan Dwan. Adele Mara's fiery Raquel catches the eye.

Angels and Insects ● ⓥ

1995, UK, 117 mins, colour
Dir: Philip Haas
Stars: Mark Rylance, Patsy Kensit, Jeremy Kemp, Kristin Scott Thomas
Rating: ★

A pretentious take on a spooky story in which everyone speaks in deliberate tones. Ultimately, Philip Haas' adaptation of A S Byatt's novella promises very much more than it delivers. Mark Rylance, in an incredibly stilted performance that has nothing to do with real life, is the explorer and naturalist drawn like a moth to the flame of Eugenie (pallid Patsy Kensit), the daughter of a rich amateur insect collector (Jeremy Kemp) who has invited him to stay. To his amazement, the naturalist, who has little in common with Kensit, finds her keen to marry him. Allowed only into her bedroom to breed, he finds himself in a few years the father of whole collection of siblings as pasty as their ancestors. If all this seems to be leading to some horrific discovery, don't expect anything too startling from the plot as drawn out (long drawn out) here. There are two good performances, from Saskia Wickham and Kristin Scott Thomas, but not much substance for a running time this long. Not for people who dislike watching ants, either.

Angels in the Outfield ○ ⓥ

(aka: Angels)
1994, US, 102 mins, colour
Dir: William Dear
Stars: Danny Glover, Christopher Lloyd, Brenda Fricker, Tony Danza, Ben Johnson, Jay O Sanders
Rating: ★★

The 1951 original of this baseball fantasy-comedy was fairly sentimental although pretty funny in parts too. In this version, the sugar has clearly liquefied into syrup for an audience that plainly isn't expected to bring any expectations of subtlety and imagination with them. The grumpy middle-aged manager has changed from white Paul Douglas to black Danny Glover, the kid who sees angels helping the ragged team who suddenly start winning has changed sex from girl to boy, and the plot now serves up more corn than you'll see on the floor of a cinema after the performance. The only characters to survive their wade through this well of treacle are Christopher Lloyd as wild-eyed Al the Angel and Jay O Sanders as the splendidly detestable radio commentator who's rooting for the team to fail (keep going, Jay, we're on your side). Few heartstrings remain unplucked in the ensuing melee.

Angels One Five ○ ⓥ

1951, UK, 98 mins, b/w
Dir: George More O'Ferrall
Stars: Jack Hawkins, Michael Denison, John Gregson, Dulcie Gray
Rating: ★★

This much-praised film tribute to 'The Few' received no greater acclaim than from Group Captain Douglas Bader, legless air ace of the Battle of Britain. 'I went to see it with my tongue in my cheek,' Bader commented. 'I came out amazed. I could not fault it.' Moving and authentic, if not in the same class as *The Way to the Stars*, the film is set on a Royal Air Force base in the summer of 1940. With their roles here, Jack Hawkins and John Gregson took giant strides towards stardom. Seen today, though, the film's upper-crust accents (and attitudes) hurt it badly, and it has too little action.

Angel Street

See: Gaslight

Angels with Dirty Faces ○ ⓥ

1938, US, 97 mins, b/w
Dir: Michael Curtiz
Stars: James Cagney, Pat O'Brien, Humphrey Bogart, Ann Sheridan
Rating: ★★★★

Three of Warners 'big five' gangster stars (the other two were George Raft and Edward G Robinson) came together in this classic of the genre. James Cagney and Pat O'Brien, in their familiar roles of likeable gangster and priest respectively, are the boys from the slums who grow up on opposite sides of the law. Humphrey Bogart has his usual part, too, as a humourless crook with whom Cagney is clearly destined to fall out. Add Ann Sheridan, bursting to stardom as the girl involved, and the Dead End Kids (later, among other things, the Bowery Boys) as the little toughs with whom Cagney and O'Brien have different ways of dealing, and the mixture is irresistible, encapsulating the whole spectrum of Warners thrillers and crime dramas of the Thirties in one potent dose.

Angie ● ⓥ
1994, US, 107 mins, colour
Dir: Martha Coolidge
Stars: Geena Davis, Stephen Rea, James Gandolfini, Aida Turturro, Philip Bosco, Jenny O'Hara
Rating: ★★★

Feisty working girl Angie Scacciapensieri (Geena Davis) lives with her boyfriend Vinnie (James Gandolfini) in a close-knit Brooklyn community. She gets pregnant and, on the verge of marriage, sets off to find meaning in her life. The best scenes are the earlier ones, including the hilarious birth; the worst come as the movie runs downhill towards its manipulatively weepy ending. Stephen Rea is predictably underused as the Irish lawyer for whom Angie falls, but Davis holds together the moments of high drama and hysterical comedy with great gusto. Director Martha Coolidge clearly wants to steer her film towards a more serious, substantial and meaningful last reel, but, lightly scripted by co-producer Todd Graff, the story only entertains, in fits and starts, on a superficial level throughout.

Angry Silence, The ○
1959, UK, 95 mins, b/w
Dir: Guy Green
Stars: Richard Attenborough, Pier Angeli, Michael Craig
Rating: ★★★★★

One of the great post-war films: a poignant, moving and extremely penetrating portrait of the pressure, both physical and mental, put upon a man who refuses to strike, by members of his union. Richard Attenborough is hauntingly true as the 'blackleg', Pier Angeli delicate and moving as his wife – her best screen work since *Somebody Up There Likes Me*. It can't have pleased the unions or the militants, but nonetheless much of it remains engraved in the mind – especially Brian Bedford's repellent bully and Alfred Burke's magnificent dog-eared and hateful Communist organiser. Easily director Guy Green's most memorable film.

Angus ① ⓥ
1995, US, 90 mins, colour
Dir: Patrick Read Johnson
Stars: Charlie Talbert, George C Scott, Ariana Richards, Kathy Bates, Rita Moreno, James Van Der Beck
Rating: ★★

Pretty much par for the Hollywood college course, this is the story of a fat kid bullied by the school smart Alecks but good at football and science and secretly pining for the school cheerleader queen. Handed the title of Winter Prom King as an embarrassment, Angus – you'll win no prizes for guessing – comes through and wins the maiden's heart. Charlie Talbert is believable enough as Angus, who at least has the satisfaction of breaking the chief bad boy's nose at various stages of the action, but Kathy Bates is severely under-used as his mother and George C Scott is uneasily cast as the ever-sleepy gramps about to marry a woman in her twenties.

Animal Crackers ⊙ ⓥ
1930, US, 98 mins, b/w
Dir: Victor Heerman
Stars: Groucho Marx, Harpo Marx, Chico Marx, Zeppo Marx, Margaret Dumont, Lillian Roth
Rating: ★★★★

The film in which Groucho sings 'Hooray for Captain Spaulding' and Harpo turns out to have stolen half the house when forced to open his capacious raincoat. Yes, The (four) Marx Brothers in full flow, with Groucho propositioning the incomparable Margaret Dumont by rolling up his trouser leg and then going down on the other knee. The plot has something to do with a stolen painting but don't let it bother you; it certainly doesn't seem to bother the four stars.

Animal Farm ○
1955, UK, 72 mins, colour
Dir: Joy Batchelor
Rating: ★★★★

Still Britain's best feature cartoon: a brilliantly animated, strongly dramatic version of George Orwell's classic allegory. The makers can even be excused for altering the ending in the cause of dramatic effect. Extraordinary voice work by Maurice Denham as all the animals. A few comic episodes are justifiably inserted to lighten the strong and sombre tone of the whole.

Anna ① ⓥ
1986, US, 95 mins, colour
Dir: Yurek Bogayevicz

Stars: Sally Kirkland, Paulina Porizkova, Robert Fields, Stefan Schnabel, Larry Pine
Rating: ★★

A more modern-day cousin of *All About Eve*: Sally Kirkland's Oscar-nominated title role sees her convincingly playing a Czech film star who can find no work in America after escaping her homeland to follow a director-husband who no longer wants anything to do with her. Getting a $200-a-week understudy role in an off-Broadway show enables her to take under her wing the waiflike Paulina Porizkova as Krystyna, a teenage Czech refugee who, with teeth capped and face made up, proves to look just like Audrey Hepburn. Krystyna soon attracts the attention of showbiz scouts Anna meets in her quest for work and, when the older woman offers her protégée her identity and her life, Krystyna takes her up on it. Good performances and an interesting milieu should add up to a class movie here, but somehow the piece fails to entertain, even though the director shies away from a seemingly inevitable tragic ending.

Anna and the King of Siam ⊙
1946, US, 128 mins, b/w
Dir: John Cromwell
Stars: Irene Dunne, Rex Harrison, Linda Darnell, Lee J Cobb, Gale Sondergaard
Rating: ★★★

A film unlike any Hollywood had made before, this romantic drama was such a success on its appearance in 1946 that, inside 10 years, Rodgers and Hammerstein had produced smash-hit stage and screen musical versions of the story. The film is a songless but charming and very moving version of the story of Anna Owens and her friendship with the King of Siam.

Anna Christie ○
1930, US, 90 mins, b/w
Dir: Clarence Brown
Stars: Greta Garbo, Charles Bickford, Marie Dressler
Rating: ★★

'Give me a whisky, with ginger ale on the side – and don't be stingy, baby'. Imagine that in a gruff Swedish accent, and you have Greta Garbo's first words for the screen, in the morality drama for which MGM proudly announced: 'Garbo speaks!' *Anna Christie*, which is taken from Eugene O'Neill's play, has Garbo in less sophisticated mood as a

A

prostitute trying to start life afresh in a fishing community. Her deep-felt (not to say deep-voiced) performance gives the hackneyed venture some validity. Veteran actress Marie Dressler also made the most of her big emotional moments to set herself up with a wonderful last few years at MGM in the twilight of her career. The film's a must for collectors of a complete Garbo catalogue of superior screen suffering.

Anna Karenina ○ ⓥ

1947, UK, 123 mins, b/w
Dir: Julien Duvivier
Stars: Vivien Leigh, Ralph Richardson, Kieron Moore
Rating: ★★

Julien Duvivier's elegant but rather stuffy version of Tolstoy's novel, immortalised in two film versions by Garbo (*Love* in 1927 and, the more famous *Anna Karenina* in 1935). Vivien Leigh makes a wistful doomed heroine and Ralph Richardson is in cuttingly splendid form as her cuckolded husband. Attention to detail in costumes and settings is immaculate, and the camerawork of distinguished French cinematographer Henri Alekan achieves some fine effects in black and white. It did not, however, restore the fortunes of its producer, Alexander Korda, to their pre-war glory.

Anna Karenina ○

1935, US, 95 mins, b/w
Dir: Clarence Brown
Stars: Greta Garbo, Fredric March, Freddie Bartholomew, Basil Rathbone, Maureen O'Sullivan
Rating: ★★★

Beautifully crafted MGM version of Tolstoy's famous novel of illicit romance at the court of Russia in the 19th century. A haunting portrayal by Greta Garbo in the title role and a piercing performance by Basil Rathbone as her husband are the things that stand out in the foreground of one's memory, against the backcloth of some distinguished black and white photography.

Anne of the Indies ○

1951, US, 81 mins, colour
Dir: Jacques Tourneur
Stars: Jean Peters, Louis Jourdan, Debra Paget, Herbert Marshall
Rating: ★★★

Jean Peters, sadly lost to the screen when she married millionaire-recluse Howard Hughes, cuts a dashing figure as the lady buccaneer in this rousing action movie. Talented director Jacques Tourneur packs in enough action for half-a-dozen pirate films.

Anne of the Thousand Days ○ ⓥ

1969, US, 145 mins, colour
Dir: Charles Jarrott
Stars: Richard Burton, Genevieve Bujold, Irene Papas, Anthony Quayle, Michael Hordern
Rating: ★★★

This sumptuous costume drama won Oscar nominations for best picture, best actor (Richard Burton as Henry VIII) and best actress (Genevieve Bujold as Anne Boleyn). In the event it clinched only one Academy Award that year – the one for costume design. Engrossing, well-crafted drama, even if Burton was to have unfair competition in the Henry VIII stakes a couple of years later from Sidney James in *Carry On Henry*!

Annie ○ ⓥ

1982, US, 128 mins, colour
Dir: John Huston
Stars: Albert Finney, Carol Burnett, Aileen Quinn, Tim Curry
Rating: ★★

A huge-scale musical that starts tremendously well, but goes relentlessly downhill. Quite why veteran director John Huston allowed himself to be wooed to direct it as his first (and last) musical we shall never know. Just one of the giant sweet sets cost a million dollars, and that kind of expenditure was carried through into the stunning costumes (by Theoni V Aldredge) and big production numbers. Albert Finney shaved his head as munitions millionaire Daddy Warbucks, Aileen Quinn (chosen after a nationwide talent search) is a touch too cute as the moppet of the title, and Carol Burnett steals the show as gin-swigging orphanage crone Miss Hannigan. The highlights are the showstopping numbers 'Hard Knock Life for Us' and 'Tomorrow'.

Annie Get Your Gun ⊙

1950, US, 107 mins, colour
Dir: George Sidney
Stars: Betty Hutton, Howard Keel, Louis Calhern, J Carrol Naish, Edward Arnold, Keenan Wynn
Rating: ★★★

Blockbuster musical Western about a lady sharpshooter. Betty Hutton took over the role of Annie Oakley, to which Judy Garland had been assigned before falling ill, and turned it into a

personal triumph. She and her co-star Howard Keel put over Irving Berlin's lively songs in great style.

Annie Hall ○ ⓥ

1977, US, 94 mins, colour
Dir: Woody Allen
Stars: Woody Allen, Diane Keaton, Tony Roberts, Carol Kane, Paul Simon
Rating: ★★★

Woody Allen's first commercial success and his fourth collaboration with his then-girlfriend, Diane Keaton. It's easy to speculate that it was also his most autobiographical to date, with the theme of the main character living in a house built under a rollercoaster followed through into his later *Radio Days*. This assured comedy deals with the shifting sands of a new relationship. The Oscar voters were impressed and awarded the film statuettes for Best Picture, Director and Screenplay (co-written by Allen with his regular collaborator, Marshall Brickman). Sigourney Weaver fans should keep their eyes peeled for her brief debut film appearance as Woody's date outside a cinema.

Annie Oakley ○

1935, US, 88 mins, b/w
Dir: George Stevens
Stars: Barbara Stanwyck, Preston Foster, Melvyn Douglas, Moroni Olsen
Rating: ★★★

The historical story, more or less, of the lady later immortalised in *Annie Get Your Gun*, Barbara Stanwyck was surely born to play the spunky sharpshooter character of Annie Oakley. George Stevens presents her story as a bumper bundle of comedy, romance and Wild West stuntwork. Lively semi-Western with good dialogue, this love story was one of Stevens's earliest successes, made when Stanwyck was at the height of her early career.

Ann Vickers ○

1933, US, 73 mins, b/w
Dir: John Cromwell
Stars: Irene Dunne, Walter Huston
Rating: ★

Almost a pocket version of Sinclair Lewis' novel, with Irene Dunne breathlessly chasing from affair to affair, pregnancy to pregnancy, while becoming a prominent social worker and industrial reformer, and all in the space of 73 minutes. Doctor friend Edna May Oliver has it about right when she says that 'Ann's going to make the world over if it takes her all

We'd like your thoughts...

TV Times Film and Video Guide

Thank you for purchasing this book. We hope you enjoy it. While you're reading the book you can use this card as a bookmark. Then, we'd like your comments so we can continue to publish books which will interest our readers. Please fill out this card and return it to us.

Your reaction to this book:

_____

_____

Where did you buy this book?

_____

Your profession:

_____

Name: _____ Mr/Mrs/Ms/Miss/Dr Other:

Address: _____

Postcode: _____ Country: _____

E-Mail Address: _____

☐ From time to time we are approached by other companies for the rental of our database.
If you would prefer not to have your details passed to such companies, please tick box.

http://www.batsford.com

b

winter.' RKO proclaimed that the picture would 'inflame the nation like a purifying fire'. Alas, these were the strait-laced Thirties and all the film did was burn the studio's fingers.

Another Country ● Ⓥ

1984, UK, 90 mins, colour
Dir: Marek Kanievska
Stars: Rupert Everett, Colin Firth, Anna Massey, Betsy Brantley, Cary Elwes, Michael Jenn
Rating: ★★

Based on the true-life story of Guy Burgess, this is a study of homosexuality at a public school in the Thirties and how persecution led ultimately to one of the young men involved defecting to the Russians from the Diplomatic Corps. The ritual of public school life is hideously well observed, even if the story's grip is hardly vicelike. Rupert Everett is exceptionally good as the languorous 'Bennett' who flouts school conventions to his eventual cost.

Another 48 Hrs ● Ⓥ

1990, US, 95 mins, colour
Dir: Walter Hill
Stars: Eddie Murphy, Nick Nolte, Brion James, Kevin Tighe, Ed O'Ross
Rating: ★★

Sequels to smash-hit films really should have something better than this to offer the paying public. This is an utterly routine slam-bang action comedy packed with familiar and predictable scenes and elements culled from dozens of similar films. The shoot-out in the strip club, the flight down the fire escape, the villain discovered with a naked woman, the saloon-bar brawl, the crooked cops – absolutely no prizes for guessing the identity of Mr Big the Ice-Man – and virtually no wisecracking lines from Eddie Murphy and Nick Nolte, who just take the money and run. Directed in tired but efficient style by Walter Hill, this would be completely dismissed without its star names.

Another Man, Another Chance ○

(aka: Another Man, Another Woman)
1977, France/US, 132 mins, colour
Dir: Claude Lelouch
Stars: James Caan, Genevieve Bujold, Francis Huster
Rating: ★★

Another of French director Claude Lelouch's finally-they-met convergent romances, this time set in the old west. In this picturesque setting a French immigrant (Genevieve Bujold) is destined

to meet a veterinarian, played by James Caan. Going through the tragedies that bring this about would give away too much of the plot; suffice to say that the film has quite an amount of charm, if perhaps not quite enough to see it through its lengthy running time. Caan fans will enjoy the sight of their hero doing some unexpected things, such as playing billiards on horseback, and feeding (and changing) a baby. They may object though, to the director's insistence on shooting everything through a yellow lens to convey a sense of period, a device that proves rather trying to the eyes.

Another Man's Poison ○

1951, UK, 89 mins, b/w
Dir: Irving Rapper
Stars: Bette Davis, Gary Merrill, Anthony Steel
Rating: ★★

The lightning flashes match those in Bette Davis's eyes as she laughs in the face of death in this all-stops-out melodrama about a woman with a penchant for poisoning those who get in her way. Directed by Irving Rapper, who made some of Bette's most notable successes, including *Now, Voyager*.

Another Stakeout ○ Ⓥ

1993, US, 109 mins, colour
Dir: John Badham
Stars: Richard Dreyfuss, Emilio Estevez, Rosie O'Donnell, Madeleine Stowe
Rating: ★

There's lots of shouting and very little plot in this unbearably tedious sequel to the entertaining original. Embarrassments and misunderstandings far outweigh the action in this story and, although Richard Dreyfuss and Emilio Estevez are back on duty (minus their moustaches), it just goes to show what a difference a well-constructed script will make to a movie. Rosie O'Donnell is squirmingly strident as the assistant D.A. who sets up the stakeout to find a missing witness, and only Cathy Moriarty as the witness does anything to contribute to the film, although Madeleine Stowe (unwisely) reprises her role, unbilled (wisely) as Dreyfuss' love. And can you believe Miguel Ferrer failing to pick up his 'accidental' Las Vegas jackpot at the beginning of the film? No way: even hit-men gotta live.

Another Time, Another Place ○

1958, US, 98 mins, b/w
Dir: Lewis Allen

Stars: Lana Turner, Barry Sullivan, Sean Connery, Glynis Johns
Rating: ★★

A love story which gave Sean Connery (in a pre-James Bond role) his first real chance in a big star part. He was chosen by the leading lady herself, Lana Turner. Connery seized the opportunity to show his worth, and the American actress had no regrets about her choice. Would that the film itself possessed the same conviction.

Another Woman ❶ Ⓥ

1988, US, 81 mins, colour
Dir: Woody Allen
Stars: Gena Rowlands, Mia Farrow, Ian Holm, Blythe Danner, Gene Hackman, Martha Plimpton
Rating: ★★

Impeccably acted, though sometimes as dry and dusty as an old Latin primer, Woody Allen's Bergmanesque drama is basically *Scrooge* for highbrows. Gena Rowlands is the college professor who, reaching 50, sets to work on a new book at her hideaway writing flat (we should all afford such luxuries), where she begins to hear voices through the ventilation, ostensibly from the psychiatrists next door. The problems of a pregnant woman (Mia Farrow) on the couch there mirror her own. She begins to see herself in a different light, more as others see her. Are the voices ghostly, or are they really there? By the end, they have helped Rowlands cast off the old and bring on the new. Allen's writing here is often perceptive (if occasionally shallow), but certainly for minority audiences only. Mainline moviegoers may agree with the character half-way through who says that: 'We've talked this to death'.

Another You ● Ⓥ

1991, US, 98 mins, colour
Dir: Maurice Phillips
Stars: Gene Wilder, Richard Pryor, Mercedes Ruehl, Stephen Lang, Vanessa Williams, Kevin Pollak
Rating: ★

The in-and-out partnership of Gene Wilder and Richard Pryor has come a long way down from the dizzy heights of *Silver Streak* and hits a new low with this formula farce about a small-timer conman (Pryor) enlisted to look after a mental patient and pathological liar (Wilder) as part of his punishment of community service. Staunch fibbing ensues in a zany but wafer-thin plot that soon sees the duo in deep trouble in more ways than one. Pryor piles up

A

the wisecracks, albeit in subdued style (symptoms of his real-life illness are all too evident), while Wilder twitches nervously as only he can. A wince-worthy comedy for devoted fans of the two stars only-

Any Number Can Play ○
1949, US, 112 mins, b/w
Dir: Mervyn LeRoy
Stars: Clark Gable, Alexis Smith, Wendell Corey, Audrey Totter
Rating:★★

Clark Gable is at his debonair best here as an honest gambler. It's just as well, as this is a lacklustre drama by his own demanding standards. Even the cast doesn't have a polished MGM look about it, except for the presence in the supporting cast of Frank Morgan (his last film role) and Mary Astor. Mervyn LeRoy does keep it moving well, and Richard Brooks' slightly off-beat dialogue occasionally rises above a sloppy sub-plot that threatens to swamp the film.

Anything Can Happen ○
1952, US, 107 mins, b/w
Dir: George Seaton
Stars: Jose Ferrer, Kim Hunter
Rating:★★

In complete contrast to his memorable roles as Toulouse-Lautrec in *Moulin Rouge* and Cyrano de Bergerac in the film of that name, Jose Ferrer here starred in an amusingly off-beat if over-sentimental film about the adventures of a Georgian emigré (Georgia in Russia, that is) in the great United States of America. Ferrer's portrayal is fresh, vital and entertaining, carrying off every comic situation with irresistible verve. He is supported by a rich array of ethnic 'types', including Nuri Bey, a Turk, played by plump-cheeked Kurt Kasznar; Ferrer's uncle, a successful chef, portrayed by snake-eyed Oscar Beregi; and, best of all, the formidable Natasha Lytess.

Anything Goes ○
1956, US, 106 mins, colour
Dir: Robert Lewis
Stars: Bing Crosby, Donald O'Connor, Mitzi Gaynor, Jeanmaire
Rating:★★

Lively and very colourful musical in which Bing Crosby sets up what must be an all-time record: he played the same part that he had played in the first version of the film 20 years earlier! At that time Ethel Merman filled the part now sparklingly played by Mitzi Gaynor. Cole Porter wrote the

score that includes what was an over-whelming hit of the Thirties – the title song. Too many flat spots, though: the original's still better. Director Robert Lewis' only film.

Any Wednesday ○
1966, US, 109 mins, colour
Dir: Robert Ellis Miller
Stars: Jane Fonda, Jason Robards, Dean Jones, Rosemary Murphy, Ann Prentiss
Rating:★★★★

One of the great fun films of the Sixties, and in its original uncut form, as opposed to the mutilated version which appeared in this country's cinemas as *Bachelor Girl Apartment*. It's a warm, wise and witty adaptation of Muriel Resnik's hit stage play, scripted by the author herself. Good performances from all the principals, and from Ann Prentiss, sister of Paula, as a too-bright secretary. And there's a memorably hilarious sequence as the three stars and Rosemary Murphy (as Jason Robards' wife) play word games in Robards' car.

Any Which Way You Can ◑ ▽
1980, US, 116 mins, colour
Dir: Buddy Van Horn
Stars: Clint Eastwood, Sondra Locke, Geoffrey Lewis, Ruth Gordon
Rating:★★

This zany romp is a shade more agreeable and entertaining than its predecessor *Every Which Way But Loose*. The best thing is that the streak of malice carried by the earlier film has been largely ironed out, leaving us with the antics of Clyde the orangutan, some crude but sometimes quite effective gags and a bruising bare-knuckle fight at the end. William Smith is a personable opponent for Clint Eastwood, whose fans will lap it up.

Anzio ○ ⓥ
(aka: Battle for Ando)
1967, Italy, 117 mins, colour
Dir: Edward Dmytryk
Stars: Robert Mitchum, Arthur Kennedy, Peter Falk, Robert Ryan, Earl Holliman, Mark Damon
Rating:★★★

A big Italian-American co-production based on the famous Wynford Vaughan-Thomas book on the subject and how decisions were allegedly taken in 1944 that cost thousands of Allied lives. The screenplay takes an hour or so to get down to brass tacks but then enlivens the film with a dan-

gerous pasage through a minefield and a sharp shootout between snipers before the moral is brought home (and not overstated either).

Apache ○
1954, US, 91 mins, colour
Dir: Robert Aldrich
Stars: Burt Lancaster, Jean Peters, John McIntire, Charles Buchinsky (Bronson)
Rating:★★

Much-heralded but unexceptional Western with Burt Lancaster playing a blue-eyed Indian as the last of the great Apache warriors. The approach is too reverent, perhaps because the story is solidly based on fact. Nonetheless there are exciting and suspenseful moments and good acting from Jean Peters as Lancaster's squaw.

Apache Rifles ○
1964, US, 92 mins, colour.
Dir: William H Witney
Stars: Audie Murphy, Michael Dante, Linda Lawson
Rating: ★★

A latter-day Audie Murphy Western that goes great guns for several reels and loses its original fire only in the last half an hour. For 60 minutes or so, it's a handsome Cavalry Western, with blue and yellow uniforms dashing everywhere, some really bad white miners, and Indian-hating Murphy being converted to peace-loving ways by the most beautiful white missionary ever to tread desert. Some early shots, both indoor and outdoor, are remarkably well composed by director William H Witney. Action is bang on target. And there's some nice, slack-jawed villainy from L Q Jones. But this Audie Murphy sure was a hard man to kill in his Westerns. Here, he gets an Indian lance smack-dab through the chest and he's back on duty 'three weeks later' with his arm in a sling.

Apache Uprising ○
1966, US, 90 mins, colour
Dir: R G Springsteen
Stars: Rory Calhoun, Corinne Calvet, John Russell, Lon Chaney Jr, DeForest Kelley
Rating: ★★

Indian arrows fly again in this Sixties' action film that's a treasury of stars from the past. Johnny Mack Brown, husky cowboy actor who once starred with Greta Garbo, turns up as the sheriff. And there's a nostalgic reunion for Richard Arlen and Jean Parker, who co-starred in a number of adventures in the Forties.

Apartment, The ○ Ⓥ

1960, US, 125 mins, b/w
Dir: Billy Wilder
Stars: Jack Lemmon, Shirley MacLaine,
Fred MacMurray, Ray Walston, Edie
Adams, Jack Kruschen
Rating: ★★★★★

Whether fast-talking his way out of a
tight situation, straining spaghetti
through a tennis racket, or saving
Shirley MacLaine from a suicide attempt, Jack Lemmon is totally
watchable throughout this black-edged
romantic comedy from Billy Wilder.
It won five Academy Awards, including best film, and clocked up
numerous other nominations, including acting awards for Lemmon,
MacLaine and Jack Kruschen as
Lemmon's doctor neighbour.

Apartment for Peggy ○

1948, US, 99 mins, colour
Dir: George Seaton
Stars: Jeanne Crain, William Holden,
Edmund Gwenn
Rating: ★★★

Old-timer Edmund Gwenn scoops up
the acting honours in this warm, sentimental comedy about an old university
professor, contemplating a quiet suicide, who is given new interest in life
through the problems of two young
students who move into his attic.
Plump-cheeked Gene Lockhart is almost as good as another professor, and
Jeanne Crain quite charming as the girl.

Apocalypse Now ● Ⓥ

1979, US, 150 mins, colour
Dir: Francis Coppola
Stars: Marlon Brando, Robert Duvall,
Martin Sheen, Frederic Forrest, Dennis
Hopper, Harrison Ford
Rating: ★★★

Many thought this would be the
Vietnam film to end them all.
Unfortunately it isn't, in any sense.
Parts of this long film, though, are so
brilliant – the opening sequences are
stunningly atmospheric – that you long
for a better whole. Vittorio Storraro's
amazing colour photography shows
the Far Eastern landscape in far greater
clarity than you would have thought
possible. And Martin Sheen's
voiceover narration a la Humphrey
Bogart is another successful ingredient
of the film. But, in spite of its impact,
its sound and its fury, the movie is also
often slow and pretentious. Its action
throws in every possible atrocity to
shock the viewer: in words as well as
pictures Francis Ford Coppola plays
heavily for effect. Marlon Brando's

renegade Colonel – Sheen's attempts
to assassinate him form the hub of the
story – cannot be despatched with a
bullet, but must be hacked to pieces
with a machete to symbolise the simultaneous slaughter of a sacrificial bull.
Coppola does attempt to balance his elements with injections of some
horrifically black humour, including a
superbly choreographed attack by helicopters to the music of 'Ride of the
Valkyrie'. In the end, though, the
stage-manager in him wins, while the
director loses.

Apollo 13 ○ Ⓥ

1995, US, 140 mins, colour
Dir: Ron Howard
Stars: Tom Hanks, Kevin Bacon, Bill
Paxton, Ed Harris, Gary Sinise, Kathleen
Quinlan
Rating: ★★★★

'Houston, we've got a problem.' With
these matter-of-fact words, there started an epic space rescue saga that
proves every bit as gripping in this film
reconstruction as it did in real life.
Three astronauts, one a last-minute replacement, were headed for the Moon
when an explosion tore away part of
their ship, causing them to lose power,
oxygen and guidance. A massive rescue operation, using the minimum
equipment the spacecraft had left, was
mounted by a NASA HQ almost as
much in the dark as the astronauts. The
performances here are all A1: Tom
Hanks, Kevin Bacon and Bill Paxton
as the crew, Ed Harris as Mission
Control, Kathleen Quinlan as Hanks'
wife and Gary Sinise as the astronaut
whose last-minute defection (through
contact with measles) proved a blessing in disguise when he was able to
bring his expertise to parts of the rescue mission. To the untutored eye,
technical details all seem fine. And,
despite its length, the story moves
crushingly along, allowing almost no
respite from its tension.

Apple Dumpling Gang, The ○

1974, US, 100 mins, colour
Dir: Norman Tokar
Stars: Bill Bixby, Susan Clark, Don
Knotts, Tim Conway
Rating: ★★★

Although this Western comedy doesn't
quite fire on all six-shooters, it's the
best Disney romp since *Snowball Express*
two years earlier. Susan Clark, more
usually seen in ladylike roles, revels in
her unexpected casting as Dusty, part-
time stagecoach owner and full-time

wildcat, who becomes involved with a
footloose gambler (Bill Bixby), three
orphan kids (the gang of the title), two
incompetent oudaws (Don Knotts,
Tim Conway) and a gang of despera-
dos headed by Slim Pickens. There's
also the grizzled, melancholy Harry
Morgan as the sheriff, who gets the
film's best line when he tells Knotts
and Conway: 'With you two, it's always 'attempted' robbery!'

Apple Dumpling Gang Rides Again, The ○

1979, US, 88 mins, colour
Dir: Vincent McEveety
Stars: Tim Conway, Don Knotts, Tim
Matheson
Rating: ★★

A broad Western farce from Disney,
full of comic character actors who can
be relied on to go over the top, like
Jack Elam (as Big Mac), Kenneth Mars
(as Woolly Bill) and Ruth Buzzi (as
Tough Kate). Fish-eyed Don Knotts is
rather funnier than his partner Tim
Conway, but kids will enjoy the simple
slapstick and the uncomplicated storyline and cheer as our goofy heroes ride
off into the sagebrush sunset.

Appointment in Honduras ○

1953, US, 79 mins, colour
Dir: Jacques Tourneur
Stars: Glenn Ford, Ann Sheridan,
Zachary Scott
Rating: ★★

Colourful thrills in Central America,
brimming with revolutionary fervour
at the turn of the century. The action,
handsomely shot in Technicolor by
Joseph Biroc, reinforces a novelettish
story of an affair between one of the
protagonists and the wife of an acquaintance. Strong performances by
Glenn Ford and Ann Sheridan
counter-balance the clichés in the
script, but Zachary Scott is wasted in
the role of the husband.

Appointment In London ○

1952, UK, 96 mins, b/w
Dir: Philip Leacock
Stars: Dirk Bogarde, Dinah Sheridan, Bill
Kerr, Bryan Forbes, Ian Hunter
Rating: ★★★

A war film which does for Bomber
Command what *Angels One Five* did for
the Spitfire boys – and does it just as
well. Director Philip Leacock makes an
excellent job of depicting the strain and
stress that the bomber crews had to endure. The climactic raid is about the
best thing of its kind seen on screen to
that date, thanks partly to the bomber

A

experts who were attached to the production unit, assigned the task of giving advice at every stage. Dirk Bogarde gives one of the best of his early performances as the young wing commander on the verge of cracking up.

Appointment with Danger ○

1949, US, 89 mins, b/w
Dir: Lewis Allen
Stars: Alan Ladd, Phyllis Calvert, Paul Stewart, Jan Sterling, Henry Morgan
Rating: ★★

At the height of her film career in Britain, Phyllis Calvert went to Hollywood to star with Alan Ladd in this Paramount thriller. The film, though not completely successful, has some crisp, tough dialogue, as well as an early appearance by Jack Webb, as a hired killer. It was three years before Webb began his famous *Dragnet* series on TV, and he was beginning to make a name for himself in prominent supporting roles, mostly as cunning, chicken-hearted crooks. Paul Stewart, that slim, steely-eyed purveyor of menace, plays his boss.

Appointment with Death ◐

1988, US, 108 mins, colour
Dir: Michael Winner
Stars: Peter Ustinov, Lauren Bacall, Carrie Fisher, John Gielgud
Rating: ★

Peter Ustinov stars once more as ace Belgian detective 'Hercuool Pwarow', as he pronounces it, but neither he nor glitz can lift the picture from an impression of little more than a routine whodunit. Michael Winner's direction is only lacklustre, the script and characterisations bland and there simply are not enough murders to sustain the interest of even the most avid Agatha Christie fan. Christie stories somehow induce even the best of actors to stand around stiffly and give stilted performances, as if they felt their chief function in the film was to behave suspiciously by sounding vaguely unconvincing. Piper Laurie, though miscast as the ogress bumped off in the midst of the Palestinian desert, does have her moments.

Appointment with Venus ○

(aka: Island Rescue)
1951, UK, 89 mins, b/w
Dir: Ralph Thomas
Stars: David Niven, Glynis Johns, Kenneth More
Rating: ★★★

A delightful comedy, directed by Ralph Thomas, which has nothing to do with space opera but centres on a prize cow. It was scripted by Nicholas Phipps, who had earlier worked on some of the famous Anna Neagle romances of the Forties.

April Fools, The ○

1969, US, 95 mins, colour
Dir: Stuart Rosenberg
Stars: Jack Lemmon, Catherine Deneuve, Peter Lawford, Jack Weston, Myrna Loy, Charles Boyer
Rating: ★★

Catherine Deneuve's international ventures have been consistently less successful than her films in her native France, and she's out of luck again with this forced and unbelievable romantic comedy that also suffers from being particularly modish, which dates it rather badly. A tremendous cast, though, is still worth watching, including Jack Lemmon, as professional and funny as ever, Myrna Loy, Charles Boyer, Sally Kellerman, Melinda Dillon, Peter Lawford, Jack Weston and Harvey Korman.

April In Paris ⊙ ⓥ

1952, US, 101 mins, colour
Dir: David Butler
Stars: Doris Day, Ray Bolger, Claude Dauphin
Rating: ★★★

Frothy, light and witty musical romp. Doris Day and Ray Bolger don't exactly go together like Laurel and Hardy, but they do strike sparks in the film's best musical sequence, a riotous song-and-dance session in the galley of an ocean liner. Day sings the title number and several more, while Bolger's effortless dancing (as a romantic leading man he's a strain) is a delight.

April Showers ○

1948, US, 94 mins, b/w
Dir: James V Kern
Stars: Jack Carson, Ann Sothern, Robert Alda, S Z Sakall
Rating: ★★

Typical Hollywood musical backstage drama of the Forties. Jack Carson and Ann Sothern lend their likeable personalities to the leading roles, and there are plenty of tunes from the era depicted (1912) to set you humming. Shot in black and white for reasons known only to the studio.

Arabesque ○

1966, US, 105 mins, colour
Dir: Stanley Donen
Stars: Gregory Peck, Sophia Loren, Alan Badel, Kieron Moore
Rating: ★★★

From the opening credits, it's plain that director Stanley Donen is prepared to resort to all the tricks in the cinematic trade to make this as as rivetting a thriller as his earlier *Charade*. Donen's enthusiasm for making the best of his material lends pace and sustained interest to a rather fatuous tale about a university rofessor involved in sinister goings-on around a Middle East oil state. Gregory Peck is amusingly bewildered, if surprisingly tough, as the professor and Sophia Loren provides the glamorous mystery element in the plot. Perhaps the biggest mystery is how she manages to change her Dior dresses (sometimes in the same sequence) at a rate bordering on the miraculous. Good (but not that good), it makes relaxing entertainment.

Arabian Adventure ⊙

1979, UK, 98 mins, colour
Dir: Kevin Connor
Stars: Christopher Lee, Oliver Tobias, Emma Samms, Mickey Rooney
Rating: ★★

The Thief of Baghdad this isn't, but director Kevin Connor's movie is nonetheless a star-spangled exotic adventure complete with handsome prince, beautiful princess, a magic carpet and all manner of evil schemers and mechanical monsters, lavishly mounted and well photographed. Christopher Lee is suitably formidable as the dictator, Oliver Tobias makes a handsome prince, Mickey Rooney scurries and gibbers as the guardian of the sacred rose and beetle-browed Milo O'Shea glowers purposefully as the dictator's double-dealing minion.

Arabian Nights ⊙

1942, US, 86 mins, colour
Dir: John Rawlins
Stars: Jon Hall, Maria Montez, Leif Erickson, Sabu, John Qualen, Turhan Bey
Rating: ★★

Universal's follow-up to *Ali Baba and the Forty Thieves* finds the studio less happy with their control of early Technicolor. The crowd and pitched-battle scenes are elaborate, but messy because director John Rawlins seems to have no proper control over colour contrasts (or crowds). The cast is full of fascinating people, including Leif Erickson and Thomas Gomez as the bad guys, Norwegian character actor John Qualen as Aladdin (!) and comedy stars Shemp Howard (later one of

The Three Stooges) and Billy Gilbert in character roles.

Arachnophobia ◐ ⓥ
1990, US, 106 mins, colour
Dir: Frank Marshall
Stars: Jeff Daniels, Harley Jane Kozak, John Goodman, Julian Sands
Rating: ★★★

This is not the film to see if you're scared of spiders. In fact its disadvantage as a chiller is that it's nothing *but* spiders. One scene of spider scares may prove memorable in a story, but a complete film of them proves a touch monotonous. On the whole, though, this is a tense and exciting (if humourless) movie, especially at the end, when chief arachnophobe Jeff Daniels has to tackle the lethal insects in their lair. The spiders have a little help here from the special effects department, but it all makes for a thrilling final tableau. On the debit side, the film is dully scripted and directed with rather too much camera movement by Frank Marshall. There's also lots of low-angle shots of people hanging around waiting to get bitten by spiders, but good performances – especially from Daniels and from Harley Jane Kozak as his wife. John Goodman pops in towards the end as an insect exterminator with 'Bug-B-Ware' embroidered on his cap.

Arise My Love ○
1940, US, 113 mins, b/w
Dir: Mitchell Leisen
Stars: Claudette Colbert, Ray Milland, Walter Abel
Rating: ★★★

Claudette Colbert is elegantly at home in this freewheeling comedy-thriller. Splendidly directed by Mitchell Leisen, the film treads a delicate path between love, humour and war with considerable success. Charles Brackett and Billy Wilder sprinkle some sparkling lines in their script, several of them going to Walter Abel as the heroine's editor, who has his celebrated speech about not being happy at all.

Aristocats, The ☉ ⓥ
1970, US, 78 mins, colour
Dir: Wolfgang Reitherman
Voice Stars: Eva Gabor, Phil Harris, Sterling Holloway, Hermione Baddeley, Scatman Crothers, Maurice Chevalier
Rating: ★★★★

This enchanting cartoon is one of the most tuneful Disney ever made. Eva Gabor, foreshadowing her mice in *The Rescuers*, lends her delightful voice to the heroine, Duchess, who, with her three kittens, is left a vast sum of money in early 20th-century Paris. Her late employer's butler is next in line for the fortune should anything happen to the cats. Catchy songs, hilarious chases and delightful musical interludes. And don't forget – everybody wants to be a cat...

Armed and Dangerous ◐ ⓥ
1986, US, 88 mins, colour
Dir: Mark L Lester
Stars: John Candy, Eugene Levy, Meg Ryan, Robert Loggia
Rating: ★★

Roly-poly US comedy actor John Candy always seemed too big for the material Hollywood provided him with. His films, notably *Uncle Buck*, *The Great Outdoors* and *Who's Harry Crumb?*, were usually little more than a series of chases and misunderstandings as his character blundered from one disaster to another, usually in a variety of outlandish male and female disguises. The formula is much the same here, with Candy as a sacked cop confronting the Mafia almost singlehandedly. The most outrageous scene has him trussed up in a blue tuxedo with a ruffled shirt that makes his enormous bulk look like a wrapped Christmas present.

Army of Darkness: The Medieval Dead ● ⓥ
1992, US, 89 mins, colour
Dir: Sam Raimi
Stars: Bruce Campbell, Embeth Davidtz, Marcus Gilbert, Ian Abercrombie
Rating: ★★

More literally a horror comic sprung to life than any episode of a *Creepshow* film, this is the third film in director Sam Raimi's *Evil Dead* trilogy. This time, the medieval dead rise (and ride) as Bruce Campbell's Ash, sucked back in time to the 13th century, fails to recite the sacred words correctly in his quest for the Necronomicon (Book of the Dead) and raises all the old bones in the graveyard. Crudely acted and scripted, but with some invention and visual splendours, the film isn't actually as good as its excellent trailer makes it look. Still fans of such games as Demonworld, Dungeons and Dragons and Heroquest should relish this, while film buffs will groan at the dialogue and its delivery and congratulate themselves on spotting Bridget Fonda, who appears very briefly at the start.

Around the World in 80 Days ☉ ⓥ
1956, US, 167 mins, colour
Dir: Michael Anderson
Stars: David Niven, Robert Newton, Cantinflas, Shirley MacLaine, Charles Boyer, Ronald Colman
Rating: ★★★

Mike Todd's glistening film adaptation of Jules Verne's famous extravaganza was overwhelmingly voted Best Picture at the 1956 Oscars ceremony. The screenplay, music and photography also took Academy Awards. More than 40 guest stars appear in cameo roles, and Robert Newton takes his last film role as the intrepid Inspector Fix. Still sporadically entertaining today, but way too long.

Arouse and Beware
See: The Man from Dakota

Arrival, The ◐ ⓥ
1996, US, 119 mins, colour
Dir: David N Twohy
Stars: Charlie Sheen, Lindsay Crouse, Teri Polo, Ron Silver
Rating: ★★★

A neat sci-fi thriller on the 'We are not alone' theme. Charlie Sheen is unusually cast as a nerdy-looking scientist who picks up a signal which he is convinced comes from outer space. Despite obstruction from his superiors, Sheen discovers that not only is he right, but that the signal is being returned by aliens already living on Earth... A tense thriller develops, well-paced in spite of its length, with some good (and some pretty cheesy) special effects, as Sheen finds himself drawn deep into the Mexican jungle to get to the root of a plot that involves colonisation and global warming. Ron Silver is effective in the bad guy role he found himself typecast in during the 1990s, while Lindsay Crouse is also on board as a climatologist who believes Sheen when no one else does.

Arrowhead ○
1953, US, 105 mins, colour
Dir: Charles Marquis Warren
Stars: Charlton Heston, Jack Palance, Katy Jurado, Brian Keith
Rating: ★★

A vigorous, well-photographed Cavalry versus Indians Western, climaxed by one of the best hand-to-hand fights ever seen on film, between Charlton Heston and Jack Palance, who give intense, muscle-rippling performances. *Arrowhead* was written and directed by Charles Marquis Warren,

A

who has written many fine Western novels, including *Only the Valiant*.

Arthur ◐ Ⓥ

1980, US, 97 mins, colour
Dir: Steve Gordon
Stars: Dudley Moore, Liza Minnelli, John Gielgud, Geraldine Fitzgerald, Jill Eikenberry
Rating: ★★★★

John Gielgud won an Oscar and Dudley Moore was nominated for one in this side-splitting comedy about a tiny, near-40, cosseted billionaire whose drunken, girl-laden life is menaced by a family who threaten to cut him off without a penny unless he marries a socially acceptable milk-and-water heiress. Heiress's father is a self-made homicidal maniac who will put a knife through Arthur if he doesn't sway up to the altar. So what's the poor little chap, who loves a sassy shoplifter, to do? The answer makes for a comedy that gleams with wisecracks. Moore perfectly captures a state of permanent inebriation, while Gielgud plainly relishes the butler whose tongue rolls deliciously round rude insults that belie his primness.

Arthur 2: On the Rocks Ⓥ

1988, US, 113 mins, colour
Dir: Bud Yorkin
Stars: Dudley Moore, Liza Minnelli, John Gielgud, Geraldine Fitzgerald, Jack Gifford
Rating: ★★

We'll say this for Dudley Moore's Arthur: it's nice to see him again, but he was a lot more fun when he was filthy rich. Not that there aren't quite a few fun moments in this sequel, but its real problem is that none of it is even remotely believable. It's not the situations and development, however. Characters themselves change quite suddenly, without the slightest justification. When we first meet Arthur, he's still rich, perennially tipsy and married to his Linda (still Liza Minnelli, who's the best thing in the film when she's allowed to be). Then his ex-fiancée's dad does a deal (one of the film's many weak plotlines) which leaves Arthur penniless. 'Don't you feel a little relieved?' asks Liza. 'Yes,' gulps Dudley. 'Relieved of 750 million dollars.' Does Arthur take it all lying down? You bet. Face down in the gutter of life, until the ghost of his dead butler (John Gielgud) comes down to sort him out. Then Arthur does battle with his enemies in a finale that's just as unconvincing as everything else in the film.

Article 99 ● Ⓥ

1991, US, 96 mins, colour
Dir: Howard Deutch
Stars: Ray Liotta, Kiefer Sutherland, Kathy Baker, Lea Thompson, Forest Whitaker, Eli Wallach
Rating: ★★★

Let's hear a cheer one more time for the good guys against harsh and self-serving authorities. And, despite a story that runs along as bumpily as a hospital trolley, the urge to watch the underdogs win sees this one through an emotive conclusion. A slightly more serious sideshoot of *M*A*S*H* and *The Hospital*, the story centres on a forces veterans hospital where patients, if they can get treatment at all, are shunted out before they are ready, thanks to reams of red tape that bind all but the most maverick members of state, led by rebel surgeon Ray Liotta, a constant thorn in the side of administrator John Mahoney, who runs the hospital to his convenience and profit rather than those of the patients. Enter Kiefer Sutherland as the new surgeon on the block, add a dash of romance behind those operating doors, cap it all off with a mutiny after Liotta is framed and suspended and you have a surefire recipe that leaves you wishing the film had picked up its pace, and the body of its plot, a bit earlier on. Never mind, its heart (ouch, a reminder that there are some gruesome ops here) is in the right place.

Artists and Models ⊙

1955, US, 109 mins, colour
Dir: Frank Tashlin
Stars: Dean Martin, Jerry Lewis, Shirley MacLaine, Dorothy Malone
Rating: ★★★

The zany touch of writer-director Frank Tashlin, responsible for some of Hollywood's most side-splitting comedies in the 1946-66 period, is stamped all over this Dean Martin and Jerry Lewis extravaganza. Lewis excels as the nincompoop whose dreams are used by cartoonist Martin for adventure ideas. The supporting cast glitters with talent, including Eddie Mayehoff, superior stooge of so many Martin and Lewis romps, Shirley MacLaine (then right at the start of her career), Anita Ekberg, Jack Elam, Dorothy Malone, Kathleen Freeman and Eva Gabor.

Ashanti ◐ Ⓥ

1979, US, 117 mins, colour
Dir: Richard Fleischer
Stars: Michael Caine, Peter Ustinov, Beverly Johnson, Omar Sharif, Rex Harrison
Rating: ★

Top model Beverly Johnson made her screen debut as Michael Caine's wife in this pot-boiler about African slave-traders. Peter Ustinov and Omar Sharif go through familiar characterisations as the villains, while Rex Harrison and William Holden have little more than cameo roles. The action is in the safe hands of veteran director Richard Fleischer, and fans of vintage film will identify the swarthily portly figure of Eric Pohlmann in one of his last film performances.

Ash Wednesday ◐

1973, US, 90 mins, colour
Dir: Larry Peerce
Stars: Elizabeth Taylor, Henry Fonda, Helmut Berger, Keith Baxter
Rating: ★

A film for the very rich. With a subtler script, it could well have been made 40 years earlier with tremendous success. Elizabeth Taylor is the woman who undergoes cosmetic surgery – the operation scenes are dauntingly painful. Henry Fonda is her husband, and he behaves like a man who knows he's fighting a losing battle with the script, but is still determined to act everyone off the screen. He does.

Ask a Policeman ⊙

1939, UK, 82 mins, b/w
Dir: Marcel Vamel
Stars: Will Hay, Graham Moffatt, Moore Marriott
Rating: ★★★

It's an idyllic life for Sgt Dudfoot, Albert and Harbottle (Will Hay, Graham Moffatt and Moore Marriott). They are the three policemen charged with protecting the village of Turnbotham Round from crime. But there hasn't been a crime for ten years. Pressure from the Chief Constable forces them to try to drum up a bit of business. Although it's showing its age a bit now, this delightfully dotty comedy is from Will Hay's best period and is still good for a chuckle or two.

As Long as They're Happy ○

1955, UK, 91 mins, colour
Dir: J Lee Thompson
Stars: Jack Buchanan, Janette Scott, Jean Carson
Rating: ★★★

Made at a time when the major British studios, Rank and Associated-British, were spreading their musical wings and tentatively imitating Hollywood, this is a good-natured romp with tuneful songs and vigorous choreography. Jean Carson and Janette Scott give vivacious performances, while Jack Buchanan as their harassed father (he had also starred in the stage version) is as suave and debonair as ever. Guest stars include Diana Dors and Norman Wisdom and the frolics (satirising the escapades of a 'crying' crooner) are nicely photographed in Eastman Colour by Gilbert Taylor.

Asphalt Jungle, The ○ ⓥ
1950, US, 112 mins, b/w
Dir: John Huston
Stars: Sterling Hayden, Louis Calhern, Sam Jaffe, Jean Hagen
Rating: ★★★★

John Huston's classic crime caper is a taut, realistic thriller that concentrates on the intricate plotting of a jewel robbery and the subsequent undoing of the thieves. First-rate roles for Sterling Hayden, Louis Calhern and Sam Jaffe are rewarded with performances to match. Marilyn Monroe makes an impression in a small but showy 'bit'. Remade three times and copied countless others, the film remains a model of its kind.

Asphyx, The ●
1973, UK, 99 mins, colour
Dir: Peter Newbrook
Stars: Robert Powell, Robert Stephens, Jane Lapotaire
Rating: ★

Although it features such distinguished British performers as Robert Powell, Robert Stephens and Jane Lapotaire, this horror film about a man who tries to trap the spirit of death does take some following, even by the standards of this extravagant genre. The beginning, with its glimpses into Victorian 'psychological research', is fascinating.

Assassin, The
See: Venetian Bird

Assassin, The ● ⓥ
(aka: Point of No Return)
1993, US, 108 mins, colour
Dir: John Badham
Stars: Bridget Fonda, Gabriel Byrne, Dermot Mulroney, Anne Bancroft, Harvey Keitel, Miguel Ferrer
Rating: ★★★★

Slightly better than the French original, this remake of La Femme Nikita has much the same vices and virtues. It starts strongly, sags in the middle, but fires on all cylinders again in the last

reel. In the Hollywood version, it's thin-lipped Bridget Fonda as a more acceptably vulnerable 'heroine', a criminal junkie who kills a policeman in a drug induced haze during a narcotics raid shoot-out between her cohorts and the police. Sentenced to death, and seemingly executed, she wakes up to find herself locked away but targeted for a secret government programme that trains assassins to melt into the world, and carry out their occasional assignments at the ring of a telephone. Fonda is on the money in the training sequences, but the mid-section, which has her falling for photographer Dermot Mulroney, is not only soppy but three-quarters redundant. Byrne is solid, though, as the 'trainer' who develops a sneaking regard (and desire) for his protegée. Harvey Keitel makes a brief guest appearance at the end as the 'cleaner' called in to eliminate everyone when Fonda's toughest job goes awry.

Assassination Bureau, The ○
1968, UK, 110 mins, colour
Dir: Basil Dearden
Stars: Oliver Reed, Diana Rigg, Telly Savalas, Curt Jurgens
Rating: ★★★

This is a pleasingly idiotic, mildly funny comedy-thriller about the attempts of an inept group of assassins to murder their own boss back in 1906. Diana Rigg, in her first big cinema role, plays a militant feminist reporter out to scoop the world. Brilliant writer Wolf Mankowitz added some biting dialogue to the original screenplay which was written by the film's producer, Michael Relph. Basically it's a welcome attempt to hark back to the Ealing style of somewhat sly comedy, and certainly Oliver Reed's witty perfonnance in the lead suggests that you shouldn't believe a word of it.

Assassins ● ⓥ
1995, US, 125 mins, colour
Dir: Richard Donner
Stars: Sylvester Stallone, Antonio Banderas, Julianne Moore
Rating: ★★

Old Hollywood star Victor Mature was a much better actor than most of his critics allowed. Here, Sylvester Stallone offers the sort of monolithic, by-the-numbers performance that Mature was often accused of giving but rarely did. Tired of killing people for a living, Stallone plans to get out after 'one last job'. We all know that

this sort of pension plan can lead to no end of complications and before you can say Lee Harvey Oswald, rival hitman Antonio Banderas has moved in on Sly's golden handshake, a two million dollar contract. Banderas has fun with his long-haired psychopath, treating it a bit like a dry run for his next slaughterhouse, Desperado. Poor old Stallone, though, doesn't look as if he's having much fun at all. He flexes specs rather than pecs, and even keeps his shirt on; alas the acting techniques have been left at home in the hall on this one. Director Richard Donner supplies suitably computer-style guidance of the ensuing action, in a film that blows many people away and kicks the hell out of credibility.

Assault ◐
1970, UK, 91 mins, colour
Dir: Sidney Hayers
Stars: Suzy Kendall, Frank Finlay, Lesley-Anne Down, Freddie Jones
Rating: ★★★

The hunt for a maniac who is raping and killing schoolgirls is the harsh subject of this grim detection drama with a well-concealed surprise ending. Frank Finlay plays the investigating police superintendent and Suzy Kendall is the schoolteacher who places her own life in jeopardy in an attempt to uncover the identity of the murderer. The film was made by Stanley Hayers, a specialist in thrillers and chillers, who makes suspenseful use of the camera-as-murderer technique.

Assault on a Queen ○
1966, US, 106 mins, colour
Dir: Jack Donohue
Stars: Frank Sinatra, Tony Franciosa, Virna Lisi
Rating: ★

This sloppy adventure film about a group of hijackers who aim to hold up the Queen Mary on the high seas is an unusual movie to come from the pen of Rod Serling, who wrote Seven Days in May and Planet of the Apes. Here Serling settles for pure escapist entertainment, without a hidden meaning in sight. Alas, the results resemble a Crosby-Hope-Lamour Road film without the laughs. Frank Sinatra, Virna Lisi and Tony Franciosa do little more than go through the motions in this tired enterprise.

Assault on Precinct 13 ● ⓥ
1976, US, 90 mins, colour
Dir: John Carpenter
Stars: Austin Stoker, Laurie Zimmer,

A

Darwin Joston
Rating: ★★★★

A super-tense story of a siege directed by John Carpenter, who later made *Halloween, The Fog* and *The Thing,* but whose first hit this was. There's just no let-up in this well-written film about a police station in a ghetto district which finds itself surrounded by gangs of heavily armed youths. The attackers have sworn blood vengeance on the killer of one of their members, now inside the station. The catch is that the station, due for demolition, is manned only by a skeleton staff. Carpenter milks the maximum suspense from the subsequent attempts by the police and their prisoners to escape or survive. Thanks to drily humorous dialogue, all the characters come across as real and human, eliciting our sympathy in their desperate attempts to avoid seemingly inevitable ends.

Assignment K ○

1967, UK, 97 mins, colour
Dir: Val Guest
Stars: Stephen Boyd, Camilla Sparv, Leo McKern, Michael Redgrave
Rating: ★★

Routine British espionage thriller from the prolific hand of writer/director Val Guest. Leads Stephen Boyd and Camilla Sparv play with only marginal interest, and the sparks only fly from the supporting players, notably Leo McKern, Michael Redgrave and John Alderton. Crisp Technicolor camerawork by Ken Hodges, who makes the most out of the film's interesting variety of locations.

Assisi Underground, The ○ Ⓥ

1984, US, 115 mins, colour
Dir: Alexander Ramati
Stars: Ben Cross, James Mason, Irene Papas, Maximilian Schell, Karl-Heinz Hackl
Rating: ★★

Brilliantly photographed in colour by Giuseppe Rotunno, this is in some ways a bigger-scale version of the 1960 British film *Conspiracy of Hearts,* in that it deals with the efforts of the religious communities in Italian towns in World War Two to help Jewish refugees escape from the Nazis. The treatment is resolutely superficial, but Ben Cross, James Mason (in his last film) and especially German actor Karl-Heinz Hackl do their best to make the characters spring to life.

Associate, The ○ Ⓥ

1996, US, 110 mins, colour
Dir: Daniel Petrie
Stars: Whoopi Goldberg, Dianne Wiest, Tim Daly, Eli Wallach, Bebe Neuwirth, Austin Pendleton
Rating: ★★★

Whoopi Goldberg made too many films for her own good in the mid 1990s but at least this gimmicky comedy, though overlong, is one of the better ones. Unable to make own way in man-driven Wall Street, Whoopi finds herself sidelined by wolfish associate Daly, who not only steals her promotion, but leaves her in the cold. It's perhaps not surprising Whoopi gets shafted, since she looks more like a bag lady than a corporate raider, but she's determined to fight back. Inventing a white male partner, and investing in her ex-colleague's dowdy PA (Wiest), Whoopi puts the world to rights and the worms to flight – until she has to produce her sleeping partner. This is the cue for some amazing prosthetics that make her look like Rod Steiger, but also a passage where the film is at its slowest and most squirm-worthy. There's a fun last reel, though, even if it's a long time getting there, and a great part for Wiest as the mouse that roars.

Astonished Heart, The ○

1949, UK, 89 mins, b/w
Dir: Antony Darnborough, Terence Fisher
Stars: Noel Coward, Celia Johnson, Margaret Leighton
Rating: ★★

If you don't like this unusually literate romantic comedy, it should be easy to find a scapegoat. For Noel Coward not only stars in it, he also wrote the screenplay and composed the background music into the bargain. It was in fact the last film of which the Master was really in charge. But it looks dreary and dated today.

Asylum ●

1972, UK, 92 mins, colour
Dir: Roy Ward Baker
Stars: Robert Powell, Charlotte Rampling, Peter Cushing, Britt Ekland, Patrick Magee, Herbert Lom
Rating: ★★★★

Compilation horror movies from Amicus Films abounded in the British cinema of the Sixties and Seventies, but this is about the best – and has suitably sombre performances from Robert Powell and Patrick Magee at its centre, a framework story more chillingly effective than in any other Amicus film. The direction by Roy Ward Baker is calculated to be bad news for anyone trying to give up biting their nails; and a good cast, including Herbert Lom (in fine form as a maker of living dolls), Peter Cushing and Charlotte Rampling, gives their director grim-faced support. Excellent colour work and lighting effects by Denys Coop also play a prominent role in evoking the horror.

At Close Range ● Ⓥ

1985, US, 115 mins, colour
Dir: James Foley
Stars: Sean Penn, Christopher Walken, Mary Stuart Masterson, Millie Perkins, Christopher Penn, Candy Clark
Rating: ★

Brat-packer Sean Penn's promising career looked set to take off with this violent, downbeat father/son drama. And the script presented Penn for once with a well-drawn character, a rough kid drawn towards a world of violence by his murdering crook of a father (yet another chilling, smiling psychopath from Christopher Walken), but held teetering on the edge by his love for a spunky 16-year-old girl (a rare tiresome performance from Mary Stuart Masterson). The bad news is partly the jerky direction of James Foley, partly dialogue which seems to have been subjected to some primitive form of recording, with Tennessee accents an additional problem. Instead of letting the situations speak for themselves, Foley has his actors laboriously spell things out, so some scenes seem to go on for an eternity. It is, in short, a film that one way or another sorely tries our patience.

At Gunpoint ○

(aka: Gunpoint)
1955, US, 81 mins, colour
Dir: Alfred Werker
Stars: Fred MacMurray, Dorothy Malone, Walter Brennan, Tommy Rettig
Rating: ★★★

One of several sturdy Westerns Fred MacMurray made in the Fifties. This one bristles with the tension engendered by the casting of MacMurray as a mild storekeeper whose accidental shooting of a bank robber makes him the town outcast when the outlaw's gang threatens to come back and take revenge. Excellent support from Walter Brennan, Dorothy Malone, surly Skip Homeier and little Tommy Pettig. Rich pastures for Western fans.

Atlantic City ◐ ⓥ
(aka: Atlantic City USA)
1980, France/Canada, 104 mins, colour
Dir: Louis Malle
Stars: Burt Lancaster, Susan Sarandon, Michel Piccoli
Rating: ★★

Louis Malle's drama about small-time crooks with big-time dreams finds the director on foreign soil, but still getting fine performances from his actors, who include Burt Lancaster, splendidly cast as the ageing gangster, Susan Sarandon and Michel Piccoli. Despite winning five Oscar nominations, including Best Actor (Lancaster), Best Actress (the delightful Sarandon), Best Director and Best Picture, the movie emerged from the year's Oscar ceremonies empty-handed and, in spite of its carefully conceived style and deeply etched portraits, it does leave a faintly unpleasant aftertaste.

Atlantic City ○
1944, US, 87 mins, b/w
Dir: Ray McCarey
Stars: Brad Taylor, Constance Moore
Rating: ★★★

Hollywood musicals were never more popular than with wartime audiences, and 36 of them were made in 1944 alone. Many, like this one, used slim storylines and forgettable leading players, but boosted their chances at the box-office by injecting 'guest spots' from well-known singers and musicians of the day. Those featured here included Paul Whiteman and his orchestra, Louis Armstrong and his orchestra, Jerry Colonna, Buck and Bubbles, Dorothy Dandridge and Belle Baker.

Atlantis, the Lost Continent ⊙
1961, US, 90 mins, colour
Dir: George Pal
Stars: Anthony Hall, Joyce Taylor, John Dall
Rating: ★

A lurid and cheap-looking George Pal mythical fantasy. For John Dall (here the villain) it was a long way down from Hitchcock's Rope of 12 years earlier, in which he was one of the murderers. The dialogue is as stiff as the scenery.

At Long Last Love ○
1975, US, 118 mins, colour
Dir: Peter Bogdanovich
Stars: Burt Reynolds, Cybill Shepherd, Madeline Kahn
Rating: ★

Peter Bogdanovich's tribute to the Fred-and-Ginger musicals of the Thirties follows Hollywood's then current theory of hiring actors who can sing and dance a bit rather than singers and dancers who can act a bit. And Burt Reynolds, Cybill Shepherd, Madeline Kahn and Duilio Del Prete all show some nice touches – especially when they let themselves go a little. For all that, they remain actors in unfamiliar guise, all of their deficiences exposed by the glaring spotlight of the cinema. But the Cole Porter score to this scatty romp is pure delight.

At Play in the Fields of the Lord ● ⓥ
1991, US, 187 mins, colour
Dir: Hector Babenco
Stars: Tom Berenger, Daryl Hannah, Kathy Bates, Aidan Quinn, John Lithgow, Tom Waits
Rating: ★★

Hollywood was going green in a big way in the early Nineties, but this contribution to the cycle is about as weird and studied as you might expect from director Hector Babenco, who made Kiss of the Spider Woman. A visually stunning drama about the fate of a tribe of Amazonian Indians, Babenco's film follows their destruction through the well-meaning but deadly interference of a group of American missionaries and a half Cheyenne Indian (Tom Berenger, down in the jungle yet again) who decides to go native and live in their community. A thoughtful but massively overlong epic which does pick up considerably towards the end to help drive its message home.

At Sword's Point
See: Sons of the Musketeers

Attack! ○
1956, US, 107 mins, b/w
Dir: Robert Aldrich
Stars: Jack Palance, Eddie Albert, Lee Marvin, Robert Strauss, Richard Jaeckel
Rating: ★★★

A look at the cast suggests that this tough, bitter war drama is another Dirty Dozen. And it has the same director – Robert Aldrich. There the similarity ends. Attack! is a war film so frank and un-American that when it was shown at the Venice festival, a US ambassador walked out in protest. Eddie Albert dominates the film with a tremendously impressive performance as the cowardly captain, even over Jack Palance's snarling ferocity as the revengeful lieutenant.

Attack of the 50ft Woman ◐
1958, US, 72 mins, b/w
Dir: Nathan Hertz
Stars: Allison Hayes, William Hudson
Rating: ★

Never mind the quality – see the height! Bizarre science-fiction nonsense which appears on many all-time worst film lists, with Allison Hayes as neurotic Nancy who meets a giant alien in the desert. Having pinched her priceless diamond, the monster makes her radioactive, which causes her to grow and grow and eventually go on the rampage.

Attack of the 50ft Woman ◐ ⓥ
1993, US, 89 mins, colour
Dir: Christopher Guest
Stars: Daryl Hannah, Daniel Baldwin, Frances Fisher, William Windom
Rating: ★

The star of Splash and Roxanne lands her first truly 'big' role in this fair remake of the famously awful Fifties sci-fi fantasy. Mild-mannered Nancy (Daryl Hannah) has a close encounter with a UFO in the desert, grows to gigantic proportions and goes on the rampage – for revenge on her twotiming husband (Daniel Baldwin). Much attention is paid to lovingly recapturing the spirit of the 1958 original, with harsh lighting, wooden direction and gently mocking low-budget effects. An enjoyable enough fantasy yarn that gives new meaning to the expression 'tall tale'. Unfortunately, though, Hannah, usually well at home in primitive roles, is almost as terrible as Allison Hayes was in the 1958 version.

At the Circus ⊙
1939, US, 87 mins, b/w
Dir: Edward Buzzell
Stars: Groucho Marx, Chico Marx, Harpo Marx, Margaret Dumont, Eve Arden
Rating: ★★★

The film in which Groucho Marx, as J Cheever Loophole, sang 'Lydia the Tattooed Lady' long before it was immortalised by the Muppets. He also woos statuesque Margaret Dumont for the penultimate time. 'That night,' he tells her, 'I drank champagne from your slipper – two quarts. It would have held more but you were wearing inner soles.' Memorable moments include the search of the strongman's apartment, ending in a snowstorm of feathers, and the finale, with an entire orchestra being towed out to sea still playing the Prelude to Act III of Wagner's Lohengrin.

A

At the Earth's Core ○ ⓥ
1976, UK, 90 mins, colour
Dir: Kevin Connor
Stars: Doug McClure, Peter Cushing, Caroline Munro
Rating: ★★★

Another ripping yarn from the makers of *The Land That Time Forgot* and *The People That Time Forgot* which, like them, is based on a novel by Edgar Rice Burroughs. Here the burrowing is done by Peter Cushing's splendid 'iron mole' and more conventional muscle is supplied by the amiable hero, Doug McClure. Cushing steals the film with a hugely enjoyable performance as an absent minded Professor Challenger-like scientist who is delighted to be at the centre of the earth and cheerfully unaware of the dangers surrounding him. While the special effects are sometimes shaky and most of the monsters are all too clearly men in rubber suits, the zest of the performances and Kevin Connor's brisk direction make for a light-hearted slice of adventure hokum.

Attila the Nun ○
1955, Italy/France, 83 mins, colour
Dir: Pietro Francisci
Stars: Anthony Quinn, Sophia Loren
Rating: ★★

With a cast of Hollywood (Anthony Quinn, Eduardo Ciannelli), Italian (Sophia Loren, Ettore Manni), French (Henri Vidal, Claude Laydu) and Greek (Irene Papas) players, producers Carlo Ponti and Dino De Laurentiis were heavily reliant on the dubbing for the international version of this, one of their first big epics. The 'cast of thousands' of fur-clad extras looks impressive thundering across the screen and Quinn plays the title role, according to one contemporary reviewer, 'with simple, uncomplicated vigour'.

At War with the Army ⊙
1950, US, 100 mins, b/w
Dir: Hal Walker
Stars: Dean Martin, Jerry Lewis, Polly Bergen, Mike Kellin
Rating: ★

Paramount's first solo vehicle for Dean Martin and Jerry Lewis set them on a fabulous seven-year roll of film success before they went their separate ways. Their stereotypes were already established: Martin the smooth-talking girlchaser, Lewis as what, in today's parlance, would be called the nerd. Not their most wonderful: there are still some rough edges, but a few mild-

ly funny comedy routines in the stagy and stodgy whole. The film's big song hit was 'The Navy Gets the Gravy and the Army Gets the Beans'.

Audrey Rose ● ⓥ
1977, US, 113 mins, colour
Dir: Robert Wise
Stars: Marsha Mason, Anthony Hopkins, John Beck
Rating: ★★★

Be prepared for two highly charged hours with this gripping drama about a 12-year-old girl called Ivy who's possessed by the soul of another (Audrey Rose of the title) who died the moment Ivy was born. It's one of those films about children that is definitely not for young viewers. The possessed girl is most convincingly played by a young lady called Susan Swift, and her agonised parents by Marsha Mason and John Beck. A pivotal role goes to Britain's Anthony Hopkins as the dead girl's distraught father who insists on communicating with his daughter through Ivy.

August ○
1995, UK, 89 mins, colour
Dir: Anthony Hopkins
Stars: Anthony Hopkins, Kate Burton, Leslie Phillips, [Gawn] Grainger, Rhian Morgan
Rating: ★

'You and I are so tedious, Ieuan, because we're such boring people,' one of the characters tells Anthony Hopkins during his adaptation of Chekhov's *Uncle Vanya*, set in a country house in the Welsh hills of decades ago, where the occupants are slowly stagnating. The arrival of Hopkins' dead sister's husband (Phillips) and his new wife (Burton) should stir things up a bit and so it does – but in the wrong way. Hopkins and his plain-Jane niece (Morgan), once happy with their dryasdust life, become discontented, he drunken and despairing, she finding her obsession with the local doctor having to be confronted. It sounds a reasonable formula for drama, but not in this version, which just lies and dies in the Welsh sunshine. This is as miserable a film as you could (not) wish to encounter, and Phillips' final complaint – 'This house is a nightmare, a living Welsh hell,' is likely to fall on few deaf ears.

Auntie Mame ○
1958, US, 143 mins, colour
Dir: Morton DaCosta
Stars: Rosalind Russell, Forrest Tucker,

Coral Browne
Rating: ★★★

Re-creating her smash Broadway performance as Auntie Mame, the highclass Bohemian, Rosalind Russell won the fourth and last Best Actress Oscar nomination of her career. She was a hit all over again as big-spending society hostess Mame Dennis, who believes that 'Life is a banquet – and most poor suckers are starving to death'. Not even the Depression that wipes out her fortune can depress Mame for long. Infinitely superior to *Mame*, the musical remake, with Lucille Ball and Bea Arthur, this film was tailor-made for Miss Russell's talents and she delivers 110 per cent.

Aunt Julia and the Scriptwriter ① ⓥ
(aka: Tune In Tomorrow)
1990, US, 107 mins, colour
Dir: Jon Amiel
Stars: Peter Falk, Barbara Hershey, Keanu Reeves, Patricia Clarkson, Bill McCutcheon
Rating: ★★★

This is for sure no ordinary film. Set in 1951, in the world of radio, its combination of romance, lunacy and bittersweet humour centres on Pedro (Peter Falk), a brilliant, controversial soap-opera writer, who feeds on the intrigues of those about him, and creates ratings and havoc at the same rime. His number one target for material at the VIXBU station in New Orleans is rookie newswriter Martin (Keanu Reeves) and his infatuation for his – sort of – Aunt Julia, 15 years his senior (Barbara Hershey, at 43 passing for 36 with years to spare). The soap opera that results on radio, riddled with incest, hatred of rats and persecution of Albanians, is ludicrous enough to be fun, although it wears a bit thin towards the end when the whole enterprise threatens to turn sour. Falk frequently verges on being the whole show, but Hershey and Reeves are good enough to make you care about their romance.

Austin Powers – International Man of Mystery ① ⓥ
1997, US, 94 mins, colour
Dir: Jay Roach
Stars: Mike Myers, Elizabeth Hurley, Robert Wagner, Michael York
Rating: ★

A hapless, witless parody of James Bond movies, made 20 years too late. Despite a bright start, it proves to be a very, very basic satire of the sort you might see at the end of a TV special. Nothing special about this, though, and least of all in a cast of non-actors headed by Myers and Hurley. Wow! Fab! Groovey! Not! Seriously folks, this is so awful that, unless you fancy a below-average 'Carry On' style film, you'd be better off having 40 winks.

Author! Author! O
1982, US, 110 mins, colour
Dir: Arthur Hiller
Stars: Al Pacino, Dyan Cannon, Tuesday Weld, Alan King
Rating: ★★

A marriage-go-round comedy about a Broadway playwright (Al Pacino) trying to tie up all the loose ends of two failed marriages, cope with various troublesome offspring and deliver urgently needed re-writes for his latest play. It seeks to dig deeper than Neil Simon, whose territory this clearly is, but emerges as a bland confection. It is left to the sparkling playing of Dyan Cannon and Tuesday Weld, as the women in his life, to give the film a vitality that's sadly missing in the script.

Autumn Sonata O
1978, Sweden, 97 mins, colour
Dir: Ingmar Bergman
Stars: Ingrid Bergman, Liv Ullmann
Rating: ★★★

The great Ingrid Bergman deliberately made this first collaboration with her distinguished namesake, director Ingmar Bergman, her last work for the cinema. In it, she plays a pianist whose almost total absence on concert tours has left her daughter (Liv Ullmann) an emotional cripple. When the prodigal mother returns after the death of her lost lover, Ullmann lets her have it in a verbal battering that goes on all through the night. This grim, unrelenting tirade is harrowingly well enacted by the two stars. It's sad that two people with so much in common refuse to stop looking for a fight with each other, especially the daughter – and the film may strike chords in our own lives that we'd rather leave unstruck. But, as a portrait of two fine actresses digging deep into their own emotional resources to play their parts, it has rarely been bettered.

Avalanche O
1978, US, 91 mins, colour
Dir: Corey Allen
Stars: Rock Hudson, Mia Farrow
Rating: ★

As disaster movies go, this one is pretty disastrous – although the avalanche scene at the end is a triumph of editing over matter. A number of major stars battle gamely against prevailing wintry conditions. And they all read the script?

Avalanche Express O
1979, US, 88 mins, colour
Dir: Mark Robson
Stars: Robert Shaw, Lee Marvin, Linda Evans, Maximilian Schell, Horst Buchholz
Rating: ★★★

The late Mark Robson – he died just before this film was finished and it was completed by Monte Hellman – must have thought he was back at his old studio, RKO, in its final mid-Fifties years while making *Avalanche Express*. For this fast and frenetic thriller has all the hallmarks of the colourful SuperScope 'cheapies' that the studio churned out in its bid to survive. A top Russian defector must be got to America by transcontinental express for no other apparent reason than it makes for an incident-filled story. It's what used to be called a cloak-and-dagger: the train exteriors, as the express rushes through night-time, snowbound country, arouse some atmosphere, the regulation shootouts provide some routine excitement and the avalanche scenes are quite spectacular. The acting is barely serviceable, and Robert Shaw stridently overplays but Jack Cardiff's thoughtful colour photography is a delight to the eye, and adds to the enjoyment of the film.

Avalon O ⓥ
1990, US, 122 mins, colour
Dir: Barry Levinson
Stars: Aidan Quinn, Kevin Pollack, Lou Jacobi, Armin Mueller-Stahi, Elizabeth Perkins, Joan Plowright
Rating: ★★★★

Director Barry Levinson has set most of his semi-autobiographical films (including the earlier *Diner* and *Tin Men*) in Baltimore, the city where he grew up. This, his most epic story to date, traces an immigrant family's history over more than 50 years and charts the disintegration of the family unit alongside the growth in television. It's a long, meandering film in which every human emotion is milked to great effect. Some sections do work better than others, but as a whole, it is an impressive achievement. The best scenes are undoubtedly the huge, raucous and often shrill family gatherings. Most of the actors were little known but they live and breathe Levinson's colourful characters, with the more familiar figure of Joan Plowright a standout as the intrusive mother hen figure.

Avanti! ❶
1972, US, 144 mins, colour
Dir: Billy Wilder
Stars: Jack Lemmon, Juliet Mills
Rating: ★★★

Billy Wilder's last completely successful comedy, *Avanti!* neatly combines the two halves of Jack Lemmon's screen persona – frenzied young comic and angst-ridden middle-aged man – in the story of a dyspeptic millionaire seduced by continental sunshine, his late father's lifestyle and the charms of Juliet Mills. She's never been better, more attractive or more relaxed than in this fun-filled comedy whose only problem is a touch of overlength.

Awakenings ❶ ⓥ
1990, US, 117 mins, colour
Dir: Penny Marshall
Stars: Robert De Niro, Robin Williams, Julie Kavner, John Heard, Penelope Ann Miller, Max Von Sydow
Rating: ★★★★

In 1969, under a new treatment, a dozen patients who had been catatonic since surviving encephalitis 30 to 40 years earlier, were revived temporarily by a caring doctor and a new drug. This heartwarming and heartbreaking film is their story. It focuses on the first patient to be 'awakened' – Leonard, miraculously and agonizingly re-created by Robert De Niro. Dramatically, the film is hampered by the fact that its high-point, the 'reawakening' itself, occurs half-way through the story and the downbeat aspects set in from then on. But there is still much to admire and touch the emotions throughout the film. Robin Williams captures exactly the withdrawn nature of the neurologist who finds it easier to communicate with a catatonic patient than with his fellow man. Julie Kavner, as his faithful nurse, and John Heard as the sceptical chief of medicine, are also excellent, and there are painfully poignant portraits from many of those playing the other patients, whose reflex reactions to things being thrown at them first alert Williams and his staff that there is still a functioning mind inside the helpless body.

Away All Boats! O
1956, US, 118 mins, colour
Dir: Joseph Pevney
Stars: Jeff Chandler, George Nader,

A

Julie Adams
Rating: ★★

Universal-International made mainly double-feature fodder for the mass market in the Fifties, but this was one of their most prestigious projects, based on a best-selling book by Kenneth M Dodson and featuring half the studio's contract stars. But the studio was so used to making colourful, shallow entertainments at this period that *Away All Boats!* comes out as much like any other assembly-line action film, under the uninspired direction of Joseph Pevney. Jeff Chandler is well cast as the aloof naval commander trying to weld his inexperienced crew into a fighting unit, and the supporting cast is pretty interesting, including George Nader, David Janssen, Julie Adams, Richard Boone, Keith Andes, ex-Tarzan Lex Barker and future Tarzan Jock Mahoney.

Awfully Big Adventure, An
● ⓥ
1995, UK, 110 mins, colour
Dir: Mike Newell
Stars: Georgina Cates, Hugh Grant, Alan Rickman, Peter Firth, Alun Armstrong, Prunella Scales
Rating: ★★

A miserable, mean-spirited film drained of any sense of joy in the world it portrays. Georgina Cates plays the impressionable Liverpool 16-year-old in 1947 who has ambition but no virtue in any sense. Hugh Grant is the monocled, boy-baiting boss of a local theatre company who, for some reason not apparent on screen, gives her a job. From what follows, it seems unlikely Georgina would last a week, let alone a season. But she hangs on long enough for the nearly-famous P J O'Hara (Alan Rickman) to return to the company and make advances to her, attracted perhaps by her heroic chest since she has no discernible personality. After one kiss, the foolish virgin throws herself on the bed and pulls up her skirts. There's a twist or two in the tail of all this, but they're just as glum as all the rest and tragedy looms for practically the entire cast at the end. Grant, Rickman and Peter Firth (as the stage manager still carrying a torch for Grant) do their best to flesh out these grey and unpleasant people.

Awful Truth, The ○
1937, US, 92 mins, b/w
Dir: Leo McCarey
Stars: Cary Grant, Irene Dunne, Ralph

Belamy, Alex D'Arcy
Rating: ★★★★

A very funny romantic comedy. Screenwriter Vina Delmar, with assistance from director Leo McCarey himself, took a 15-year-old stage farce and brought it up as fresh as paint. Cary Grant and Irene Dunne play with pleasure and consummate timing as the divorcing couple who are clearly going to survive any amount of madcap antics and hair's-breadth escapes from embarrassment to get back together in the end. As those who nearly come between them, Ralph Bellamy and Molly Lamont, the latter an English actress who never quite made Hollywood stardom, play difficult roles with considerable panache.

AWOL
See: Lionheart

Babe ⊙ ⓥ
1995, Australia, 92 mins, colour
Dir: Chris Noonan
Stars: James Cromwell, Magda Szubanski
Voice stars: Christine Cavanaugh, Miriam Margolyes, Hugo Weaving, Roscoe Lee Browne
Rating: ★★★★★

Pigs generally have had a lean time of it in the movies. *Babe* however, re-dresses the balance. It's a witty, stylish, beautifully-crafted charmer set on a fairy-tale Australian farm. Babe is a runty piglet won at a country fair by a ruddy-cheeked farmer. The trouble with Babe is that he isn't willing to settle for his destiny – the dinner table – and so learns to do a sheepdog's job instead. If you think this sounds just for kids, then think again. *Babe* is quite simply the most original comedy for years. And did we mention that Babe talks? And the rest of the barnyard animals, too, all in perfect English with tiny lips quivering in a way not seen since the days of talking horse *Mr Ed* on TV. *Babe* is a clever, seamless mix of real animals and animatronics from the Henson Creature Features workshop. It's a grade A slice of ham in anyone's books and you'll be rooting for Babe to come through in the sheepdog trials at the end.

Babe, The ○ ⓥ
1992, US, 115 mins, colour
Dir: Arthur Hiller
Stars: John Goodman, Kelly McGillis, Bruce Boxleitner, J C Quinn, Trini Alvarado, Peter Donat
Rating: ★ ★ ★

George Herman 'Babe' Ruth is one of America's greatest sporting legends, a burly baseball hero who also has a passion for wine, women and food. Thankfully this old-fashioned but gritty biopic (which never saw the light of day in British cinemas) doesn't completely whitewash the off-field life of the great man. *Roseanne* star John Goodman fills out every inch of the big basher, truculently dominating the film, and, thanks to great make-up, is a dead ringer for the Babe too. Kelly McGillis is quietly competent as Ruth's second wife. You don't have to be a complete baseball nut to enjoy this film but it does help. For that kind of fan, at least, *The Babe* hits a home run.

Babes In Arms ☉
1939, US, 93 mins, b/w
Dir: Busby Berkeley
Stars: Mickey Rooney, Judy Garland
Rating: ★★★

This is probably the original 'Hey kids, let's put on a show' musical. Mickey Rooney and Judy Garland star in a fast and furious piece of fun based rather loosely on the original Rodgers and Hart stage show of the same name. Rooney dominates the whole picture; he's five feet of pure energy and eagerness. To a generation brought up on how to be cool and laconic, such in-your-face cheerfulness can doubtless be deeply irritating. Still, there's no denying the lad's talent and energy. The exuberance of the whole thing is infectious, with Busby Berkeley weaving his directorial magic to create a box office smash.

Babes In Toyland ☉ ⓥ
(aka March of the Wooden Soldiers)
1934, US, 73 mins, b/w
Dir: Charles Rogers
Stars: Stan Laurel, Oliver Hardy,
Charlotte Henry
Rating: ★★★★

This magical fantasy was said to have been one of Oliver Hardy's favourite films; he and Stan portray Dum and Dee, who work at the toy factory, and Charlotte Henry, who plays Bo-Peep, was also Alice in the original film of *Alice in Wonderland*. The toytown settings are quite fantastic, and the land of the famous bogeymen, who live down a well, is a really imaginative creation, without being too frightening for today's tough-guy kids – who will also appreciate the excitement of the final battle between the hairy bogeymen and Stan's army of life-size toy soldiers.

Babes In Toyland ☉
1961, US, 105 mins, colour
Dir: Jack Donohue
Stars: Ray Bolger, Tommy Sands,
Annette Funicello
Rating: ★★

Though it's not as good as the Laurel and Hardy original (what could be?) of Victor Herbert's fairytale operetta, there were few brighter, more colourful films in the whole of the decade than this Disney version. Henry Calvin and Gene Sheldon take Stan and Ollie's roles, Tommy Sands and Annette Funicello (here billed as

'Annette') are attractive leads with decent singing voices, and Ray Bolger makes one of his infrequent film appearances as the villainous Barnaby. The camera trickery is ahead of its time and the toy soldiers' attack at the end gives splendid value. Bland, perhaps, but never dull.

Babes on Broadway ☉
1941, US, 118 mins, b/w
Dir: Busby Berkeley
Stars: Mickey Rooney, Judy Garland,
Richard Quine, Fay Bainter
Rating: ★★★

This was to have been a three-star musical, but 20th Century-Fox wouldn't loan Shirley Temple to MGM as the third prong of this Judy Garland-Mickey Rooney fiesta and so a fascinating idea never materialised. Virginia Weidler takes the female role, Garland and Rooney prove they can keep the show afloat by themselves and the songs include 'FDRJones' and the Oscar-nominated 'How About You?' It was an immensely popular film with its wartime public.

Baby Boom ○ ⓥ
1987, US, 103 mins, colour
Dir: Charles Shyer
Stars: Diane Keaton, Harold Ramis, Sam
Shepard, Sam Wanamaker, James
Spader
Rating: ★★★★

One of the warmest, least complicated and most likeable of Diane Keaton's performances. She has never looked better, either, than here, playing a fearsome businesswoman nicknamed 'The Tiger Lady', who is all at sea when suddenly lumbered with her dead cousin's baby. Survive a first half hour that's alternately daft and embarrassing, in fact, and you're in for a treat. Just when the film seems about to become sloppy and sentimental in the second half, it really picks up its skirts and flies, just as Keaton does from the city. Usurped at work by a young pretender (James Spader at his smarmiest), she high-tails it for the hills, buying a mansion in the country that proves, behind its lovely facade, to be as rot-ridden as the one Tom Hanks bought in *The Money Pit*. Subsequent developments are not only very enjoyable, but quite in keeping with the character's abilities as a dynamic business lady. Sunny and funny.

Baby Doll ● ⓥ
1956, US, 114 mins, b/w
Dir: Elia Kazan

Stars: Carroll Baker, Karl Malden, Eli
Wallach, Mildred Dunnock
Rating: ★★★

When this explosive and provocative drama was first released in the mid-Fifties, *Time* magazine claimed it as 'just possibly the dirtiest American picture ever legally exhibited' and the Catholic Legion of Decency condemned it for 'dwelling upon carnal suggestiveness'. Compared to Hollywood's sexual excesses of later times, that condemnation now looks a little OTT, but there is still no denying the power of some of the sexual imagery here, particularly a torrid love scene on a swing. Without one kiss exchanged between Carroll Baker and Eli Wallach, there is more heat coming off the screen than from a roaring coal fire. The Oscar-nominated screenplay was adapted for the screen by Tennessee Williams, and rarely has the American Deep South been portrayed as more depressing or sleazy. The film also garnered an Oscar nomination for star Baker (in only her second film) as the under-age and over-developed wife who stirs the sexual embers in wily Sicilian Wallach.

Baby Face ○
1933, US, 70 mins, b/w
Dir: Alfred E Green
Stars: Barbara Stanwyck, George Brent,
Donald Cook
Rating: ★★★

Super-fast essay on how to succeed in business by pure sexual smoulder, as Barbara Stanwyck vamps her way from the bottom of a firm to the top via every seducible male employee. The notorious Hays Code threw a fit at it all this, and Warners had to shoot a new ending giving Stanwyck a reformatory change of heart before the censor would allow it a certificate. George Brent and a young John Wayne are two of 'Baby Face's' hypnotised victims.

Baby Face Nelson ◐
1957, US, 85 mins, b/w
Dir: Don Siegel
Stars: Mickey Rooney, Carolyn Jones,
Cedric Hardwicke
Rating: ★★★

A harsh, uncompromising gangster film featuring a Mickey Rooney far removed from his MGM musical days. Snarling defiance and bile, Rooney dominates a cheap-looking but action-packed movie whose tasty cast also includes Carolyn Jones, Sir Cedric Hardwicke, Elisha Cook Jr, Leo

B

Gordon, Ted de Corsia, John Hoyt, Jack Elam, Emile Meyer, Lisa Davis (as the 'lady in red') and Anthony Caruso. Don Siegel directs in his toughest vein.

Baby, It's You ●

1982, US, 105 mins, colour
Dir: John Sayles
Stars: Rosanna Arquette, Vincent Spano
Rating: ★★

Back in the days when Rosanna Arquette was still making decent movies, she joined a whole crowd of young actors who would soon become better known in this flavoursome period piece about high-school lovers who go together like oil and water. Although sharp in its observation of (young) human behaviour, the film's raucous, high-throttle approach becomes tiresome towards the end and it doesn't quite fulfil its initial promise. When interest in the story flags, though, you can while away the time spotting people like Tracy Pollan, Fisher Stevens, Caroline Aaron, Matthew Modine, Robert Downey Jr and Robin Johnson. Arquette and Vincent Spano are both excellent in the leading roles.

Baby on Board ○ Ⓥ

1992, US, 95 mins, colour
Dir: Frankie Schaeffer
Stars: Judge Reinhold, Carol Kane, Geza Kovacs
Rating: ★

Judge Peinhold, who must be one of the poorest choosers of scripts in Hollywood history, strikes out again with this romantic caper thriller featuring curly Carol Kane as Maria, a widow on the run from the Mafia, along with her charmingly precocious four-year-old daughter. The likeable Reinhold is Ernie, the luckless cab driver sucked into the feud. The rest of the movie consists more or less of one long chase scene, and will be okay for undemanding families who like this sort of thing, although occasionally a bit violent for sensitive toddlers. In fact, if you've ever wondered what New York looks like as seen from inside a cab at high speed then this is the movie for you.

Baby's Day Out ○ Ⓥ

1994, US, 98 mins, colour
Dir: Patrick Read Johnson
Stars: Joe Mantegna, Lara Flynn Boyle, Joe Pantoliano, Brian Haley, Cynthia Nixon, Fred Dalton Thompson
Rating: ★★

Read the words 'A John Hughes Production' and you know what to expect. And the *Home Alone* creator doesn't disappoint. It's another variation on his 'innocent kids triumph over naughty adults' theme, the kid here being a mere nine-month-old. So, if you're in a silly mood, it could be even funnier when Baby Bink, played by two of the most good-natured and adorable twins you're ever likely to see, is kidnapped by a trio of inept crooks led by Joe Mantegna, gets lost on the streets of Chicago, and comes home safe at the end of the day. You hold your breath as Baby, thanks to some clever trick photography, performs some amazing, death-defying stunts, and you'll wince (both at the script and the pratfalls) as Mantegna and his bumbling crew suffer slapstick injury after injury in their attempts to relocate the missing baby and claim the ransom from Bink's rich parents. Quite violent for younger viewers, it's predictable but still amusing at times.

Baby - Secret of the Lost Legend ①

1985, US, 95 mins, colour
Dir: B W L Norton
Stars: William Katt, Sean Young, Patrick McGoohan
Rating: ★

This overly cute, muddily coloured dinosaur picture about a young American couple rescuing a new-born prehistoric animal from the African rain forest suffers from lurching violently in tone. It would have been perfect family fare but for semi-nudity and implied lovemaking between the two leads, William Katt and Sean Young. Katt comes off better in the acting stakes, but both have an uphill struggle with the unconvincing models. Patrick McGoohan, making a rare film appearance, is a suitably evil foil.

Bachelor Knight ○
(aka: The Bachelor and the Bobby Soxer)

1947, US, 95 mins, b/w
Dir: Irving Reis
Stars: Cary Grant, Myrna Loy, Shirley Temple, Rudy Vallee
Rating: ★★★★★

Screamingly funny comedy, superbly structured and scripted by Sidney Sheldon, with the incomparable Cary Grant at the top of his form as a 40-ish lecturer forced to squire the young girl who has a crush on him, to the extent of competing for her with her younger admirers. Myrna Loy – who has the

famous 'man of power' running dialogue with Grant – Rudy Vallee, Shirley Temple, Ray Collins and Harry Davenport all play with pleasure. Scenes at an athletics meeting and a nightclub table are just riotous. Enjoy.

Bachelor of Hearts ○

1958, UK, 100 mins, colour
Dir: Wolf Rilla
Stars: Hardy Kruger, Sylvia Syms, Ronald Lewis
Rating: ★★

A pleasant, sunny, incident-filled romantic comedy of university life, this film brought Hardy Kruger back to Britain after his runaway success here as the escaped prisoner-of-war in *The One That Got Away*. The supporting cast is packed with stars-to-be, including Barbara Steele (the 'queen of horror') in her first role.

Bachelor Party ● Ⓥ

1984, US, 90 mins, colour
Dir: Neal Israel
Stars: Tom Hanks, Tawny Kitaen
Rating: ★

A very lowbrow comedy somewhat enhanced by the presence of Tom Hanks as the happy-go-lucky guy whose decision to get married provides the momentum for the action. If you loved *Porky's* and *National Lampoon's Animal House*, then you should like this one. The easily offended, however, should approach with caution.

Backbeat ● Ⓥ

1994, UK, 100 mins, colour
Dir: Iain Softley
Stars: Sheryl Lee, Stephen Dorff, Ian Hart
Rating: ★★★

I always thought of Pete Best as the fifth Beatle, but before Best, or at least at the same time, there was Stuart Sutcliffe. Torn between his desire to paint and his love of music, Sutcliffe also had an uncertain relationship with John Lennon, and an affair with the enigmatic Kirchherr during the band's Hamburg days that brought the frictions within the group to a head. The impressions of real people seem spot-on here, but there's a certain lack of chemistry between leads Sheryl Lee (as Kirchherr) and Stephen Dorff (as Sutcliffe) that prevents you becoming too involved with their problems. It's left to Ian Hart to steal the show as Lennon. The Beatles' music, as ever, is great, and director Iain Softley moves the story along fast enough to keep all but the odd patch of tedium at bay.

Backdraft ● Ⓥ

1991, US, 131 mins, colour
Dir: Ron Howard
Stars: Kurt Russell, William Baldwin, Robert De Niro, Donald Sutherland, Jennifer Jason Leigh, Scott Glenn, Rebecca DeMornay
Rating: ★★

Although it's long, drawn-out and often spectacular, this is no *Towering Inferno*. Unintelligible dialogue, sometimes indistinct, sometimes drowned out by the fires or the music, renders the complex arson plot virtually incomprehensible. William Baldwin mumbles huskily like a man talking through a mouthful of apple; the rest of a distinguished cast falls victim to Ron Howard's poor direction and the general soundtrack noise. Only Donald Sutherland, as a jailbird who is to fire what Anthony Hopkins is to murder in *The Silence of the Lambs*, really stamps his authority on the role. The fire scenes are superb, with special effects going off all over the place, and the backdrafts (freak fireballs) claiming their victims like something out of a horror film. Take along a heat shield and a hearing aid.

Back from Eternity ○

1956, US, 97 mins, b/w
Dir: John Farrow
Stars: Robert Ryan, Anita Ekberg, Rod Steiger, Phyllis Kirk, Gene Barry
Rating: ★★

This adventure is the familiar chestnut about a plane crash landing in the jungle and the survivors having to fight off natives to survive. The crippled plane is repaired but will only carry five of the passengers to safety! It was familiar to director/producer John Farrow, too, who first used the story 17 years earlier in *Five Came Back*. Despite a bigger budget and therefore better production values, this version doesn't eclipse the original. Nevertheless, it's quite exciting and has strong performances by Robert Ryan, Rod Steiger, Phyllis Kirk and Gene Barry.

Background to Danger ○

1943, US, 80 mins, b/w
Dir: Raoul Walsh
Stars: George Raft, Sydney Greenstreet, Peter Lorre, Brenda Marshall
Rating: ★★★

This very fast-moving Warners wartime espionage drama gets through

a mighty lot of plot in its actual 80-minute running time, with hero George Raft having to extract himself from one tricky situation after another. Raft (for the Americans), Sydney Greenstreet (for the Germans) and Peter Lorre (for the Russians) are all after the same envelope which contains details of a phoney plan along similar lines to *The Man Who Never Was*. Lovely Brenda Marshall is the heroine, but a much sharper image is registered by the Danish-born actress Osa Massen, who performs much the same function in the plot as the mystery woman at the start of *The 39 Steps*.

Backlash ○

1956, US, 84 mins, colour
Dir: John Sturges
Stars: Richard Widmark, Donna Reed
Rating: ★★★

Set in the wilds of Arizona, this tough John Sturges Western, about a gunman out to find his father's killer, includes good helpings of hard-riding outlaws, Apache raiders, duels to the death and range warfare. The plot is unusually well worked-out for a Western, and contains one or two first-rate surprises in the closing reel. 'If they ever get around to giving Oscars for the busiest Western of the year,' remarked one contemporary critic, 'this one would be a certain winner'.

Back Room Boy ☉

1942, UK, 82 mins, b/w
Dir: Herbert Mason
Stars: Arthur Askey, Googie Withers, Moore Marriott, Graham Moffatt
Rating: ★★

It became the standard thing for Britain's top radio comics to tilt with the Nazis on screen in wartime, and this Arthur Askey farce is no exception. He's packed off to the Scottish coast after scrambling the BBC news 'pips'. Those institutions of British comedy films of the era, wheezy Moore Marriott and tubby Graham Moffatt, add to the fun.

Back to Bataan ○ Ⓥ

1945, US, 97 mins, b/w
Dir: Edward Dmytryk
Stars: John Wayne, Anthony Quinn, Beulah Bondi
Rating: ★★★

Big John Wayne takes on the japs, aided by Anthony Quinn and a small army of Filipino resistance fighters in this rousing action saga. The Japanese army has overrun the Philippines, sending General MacArthur packing,

promising to return. Meanwhile it's down to the Duke to hold the fort. The Japanese are all evil and nasty and there's a fair bit of flag-waving, but that was just what was needed when the film was made. Director Edward Dmytryk handles it all (especially the battle scenes) with vigour and flair. Wayne's character is based on a real-life American who fought with the resistance movement. It may not be a classic, but this is an exciting and well made war epic.

Back to School ◐ Ⓥ

1986, US, 96 mins, colour
Dir: Alan Metter
Stars: Rodney Dangerfield, Sally Kellerman
Rating: ★★★

An outrageous gag-a-minute comedy that's the most successful cinema showcase to date for oversized American comic Rodney Dangerfield. He's the millionaire owner of the Tall and Fat chain of discount clothes stores, who enrols at his son's school as a (very) mature student by greasing the palm of the education authorities. The comedy rarely rises above the belt 'Maybe you can help me straighten out my Longfellow,' he asks a blonde student in his English class – but despite the clichéd characters, it's hard not to laugh along at the humour arising from the ridiculous scenario. Sally Kellerman is particularly good as the hands-on literature teacher who recites Dylan Thomas with breathless perfection and teaches in the same seductive way.

Back to the Beach ○ Ⓥ

1987, US, 92 mins, colour
Dir: Lyndail Hobbs
Stars: Frankie Avalon, Annette Funicello, Lori Loughlin, Connie Stevens, Don Adams, Edd Byrnes, Pee-wee Herman
Rating: ★★★

This lampoon of the beach party movies of the Sixties, complete with Annette Funicello (hardly changed at all), Connie Stevens and Frankie Avalon (changed but looking incredibly good) is such a sweetie of a film and such fun for most of the time that you can forgive its shortcomings (it's a shade lacking in directorial professionalism). Frankie bores everyone with his surfing stories, Annette confesses she always wanted to be the bad girl, and everything is much as it was way back when, with Annette leading beachniks in a musical number, numbing her teenage son with peanut butter sandwiches and holding a pyjama party when she's down in the dumps. Possibly funniest of all is the teenage son everyone hates and whose head Avalon uses as a battering ram to break down a door.

Back to the Future ○ ⓥ
1985, US, 115 mins, colour
Dir: Robert Zemeckis
Stars: Michael J Fox, Christopher Lloyd, Lea Thompson, Crispin Glover, Thomas F Wilson
Rating: ★★★★

The collision of past, present and future has long fascinated Hollywood, and here's a time-travel movie that not only gets golden boy Steven Spielberg's seal of approval (he's executive producer), but has spawned two sequels. The youthful Michael J Fox puts his good looks to good use as teenager Marty McFly, who travels from 1985 back to 1955 in a time machine made from a DeLorean car. While in the past, he accidentally stops his parents from meeting and falling in love, with dire consequences for his own future. How Marty patches up the history he has changed is shown in complex but thoroughly entertaining fashion by director Robert Zemeckis, and the year 1955 is re-created with nostalgia and humour. Christopher Lloyd stands out with an exceptionally zany performance as Dr Emmett Brown, the eccentric inventor of the DeLorean time machine, in an ingenious and ultimately charming time-travel jaunt.

Back to the Future Part II
○ ⓥ
1989, US, 107 mins, colour
Dir: Robert Zemeckis
Stars: Michael J Fox, Christopher Lloyd, Lea Thompson, Thomas F Wilson, Elisabeth Shue
Rating: ★★

The biggest box-office hit of 1985, *Back to the Future* was an exhilarating switchback of a movie that zipped along between thrills and comedy and deserved every bit of its enormous success. The sequel, unfortunately, is more steamroller than roller-coaster, relentlessly grinding its way from one putative cliff-hanger to the next with little variation of pace and no time at all for the quirky characterisation that made the first film a delight.

Back to the Future Part III
⊙ ⓥ
1990, US, 112 mins, colour
Dir: Robert Zemeckis

Stars: Michael J Fox, Christopher Lloyd, Mary Steenburgen, Lea Thompson, Thomas F Wilson, Elisabeth Shue
Rating: ★★★★★

It's quite a journey. And for once the publicity is right. They have saved the best for last. Zemeckis' adventures of Marty McFly (Michael J Fox) in a Western setting of 1885 move like the DeLorean time machine of Doc, Brown (Christopher Lloyd). That is to say, like a thunderbolt, with flames burning up the edges of the film. When Marty discovers the doctor's name on a tombstone – shot in the back in 1885 – he has to go back in time to stop it happening. Adopting the name Clint Eastwood, McFly jets back from 1955 to 1885, where he evades an Indian charge and finds the good doctor reluctant to come back since he's fallen in love with schoolteacher Clara, with whom he shares a love of science and Jules Verne. Mary Steenburgen, terrific in the part, was presumably chosen for her experience in time-travel in *Time after Time*! Things move very fast indeed from then on, proceeding to a traditional gun duel in Main Street which happens to coincide with the time for our heroes' journey back to the future. Zemeckis constantly plays amusing variations on Western traditions and wraps things up tidily at the end.

Bad and the Beautiful, The
○ ⓥ
1952, US, 118 mins, b/w
Dir: Vincente Minnelli
Stars: Lana Turner, Kirk Douglas, Walter Pidgeon, Dick Powell, Barry Sullivan, Gloria Grahame
Rating: ★★★

Hollywood stabs itself in the back (with the help of some of its biggest stars) in this dark and penetrating look at the fluctuating fortunes of an egomaniac mogul, played with silky power by Kirk Douglas. Gloria Grahame won a best supporting actress Oscar as an ambitious wife. Although the film was not as popular as it might have been, probably because of its theme, Charles Schnee's screenplay is full of insight and biting humour and deservedly made him another of the film's Oscar winners. Much better than the same director's later stab at Hollywood, *Two Weeks in Another Town*.

Bad Behaviour ● ⓥ
1992, UK, 103 mins, colour
Dir: Les Blair

Stars: Stephen Rea, Sinead Cusack, Philip Jackson, Phil Daniels, Saira Todd
Rating: ★★★★

Gently amusing, this is an improvised film and really quite nicely so, about a mild crisis in the state of a modern marriage of two Irish people (Stephen Rea, Sinead Cusack) living in London's semi-fashionable Kentish Town. Most centrally, it concerns the arrival in their life of a wheeler-dealer shark (Philip Jackson), forever on his mobile phone, offering them advice on the builders to get for their bathroom renovation, and then charging them for it. The builders turn out to be twins (both played by Phil Daniels) who create a barrage of noise that plays havoc with Rea's neighbours. On and off Cusack is also beset by: their two children; a deserted and slightly loopy wife with all the troubles in the world; a chatty but empty friend; and various relatives of the above. All of the performances are good, with a nice natural feel, but pride of place undoubtedly goes to Jackson's Howard, with a meaningless phrase for every occasion, a predatory air and a tendency to turn nasty at the hint of non-payment of one of his specious bills. Fun.

Bad Boys ● ⓥ
1995, US, 118 mins, colour
Dir: Michael Bay
.Stars: Will Smith, Martin Lawrence, Téa Leoni, Tcheky Karyo, Theresa Randle, Marc Macaulay
Rating: ★★★

A box-office blaster from the *Beverly Hills Cop* school of film-making. This time we get two black cops for the price of one – one of whom (Will Smith) doesn't act much and the other of whom (Martin Lawrence) acts rather too much for comfort. Although a crowd pleaser for its action scenes, the film has too much interplay and too little plot: 'You're startin' to get on my goddam nerves,' says Lawrence at one point, and he's not kidding. Still, Leoni is a (white) heroine straight from the front cover of a fashion magazine and, just when you've started to nod off at the heroes' incessant rattle, a first-rate shootout comes along to liven you up again. Two mysteries: who is the second girl to be killed and what has she to do with the plot, and why do the villains kidnap the vital witness at the end instead of killing her off? Answers, please, on postcards only.

Bad Company ◐

1972, US, 92 mins, colour
Dir: Robert Benton
Stars: Jeff Bridges, Barry Brown, John Savage
Rating: ★★★

Charming, likeable American Civil War drama with a clutch of personable performances from the ragamuffin bunch of youngsters on the run from Union Army conscription. Barry Brown is amusingly prim as the small town boy who joins forces with Jeff Bridges' ramshackle group of runaways, while David Huddleston's bearlike presence as outlaw Big Joe Simmons casts a menacing shadow over the autumnal landscapes, lovingly photographed by Gordon Willis. An immensely assured work from first-time director Robert Benton (who went on to make *Kramer vs Kramer* and *Places in the Heart*).

Bad Day at Black Rock ○

1954, US, 81 mins, colour
Dir: John Sturges
Stars: Spencer Tracy, Robert Ryan, Anne Francis, Dean Jagger, Walter Brennan
Rating: ★★★

Too much talk and too little action slows down this 'modern' Western, although the material is good – and very original – and the situations at times crackle with suspense. There are convincing performances from some of Hollywood's best actors, including Spencer Tracy as the one-armed war veteran coming to a township that seems to be nursing a guilty secret.

Bad For Each Other ○

1953, US, 83 mins, b/w
Dir: Irving Rapper
Stars: Charlton Heston, Lizabeth Scott
Rating: ★★

Here's medicine and romance again proving a bad mix for the doctor, just as they did in *The Citadel* and *Green Fingers*. Charlton Heston and sultry Lizabeth Scott (as the girl who's no good for him) had been teamed before on his first major film, *Dark City*. This film's not very good though. Nobody looks as though they're having a good time and neither does the audience.

Bad Girls ◐ ⓥ

1994, US, 98 mins, colour
Dir: Jonathan Kaplan
Stars: Madeleine Stowe, Andie MacDowell, Drew Barrymore, Mary

Stuart Masterson
Rating: ★★★

They're bad all right, in every sense of the word. When Cody (Madeleine Stowe), a honky tonk harlot (the film's description) shoots a customer to protect one of her girls, in this sometimes rousing Western, her three hookers save her from the hangman's noose and all four go on the run together. Cody's idea is to reclaim the $12,000 she has saved in the bank. At the bank, though, the girls are tracked down by lawmen at the same time as Kid Jarrett (James Russo), an old adversary of Cody's, robs the bank – and Cody. The rest of the action more or less concerns the girls' efforts to get back the cash, leading to too many slow scenes. But there's a terrific gunfight at the end, as the girls finally take on the outlaws. Dialogue's mostly ludicrous, but any script that comes up with the line 'Pick it up, put it in, die like a man,' can't be all bad. Drew Barrymore puts in some terrific riding and steals the film; Stowe is also fine.

Bad Influence ● ⓥ

1990, US, 102 mins, colour
Dir: Curtis Hanson
Stars: James Spader, Rob Lowe, Lisa Zane, Kathleen Wilhoite
Rating: ★★

More 'sex, lies and videotape' for James Spader in this satanic sideshoot from *Strangers on a Train*. Spader plays a brainy computer boffin, anxious both for a top job and a way out of getting hitched to a beautiful and wealthy socialite. When he runs into evil thrillseeker Alex (played by Rob Lowe, looking much more mature than in his Brat Pack days), Spader sees a man who makes things happen by his own rules. Lowe soon gets him what he wants – but the price is sky-high and soul-deep. The acting of the leading duo is good but the writing isn't always worthy of their efforts in this interesting but flawed little shocker.

Badlands ● ⓥ

1973, US, 94 mins, colour
Dir: Terrence Malick
Stars: Martin Sheen, Sissy Spacek, Warren Oates
Rating: ★★★

This grim drama about a couple who go on a murderous spree across the midwest of America, killing ten innocent people, is based on a true incident and has become something of a cult classic. Debut director/writer Terrence Malick gave early starring roles to

Martin Sheen and Sissy Spacek. Sheen is the vengeful and socially maladjusted Kit and Spacek is his mindless teenaged girlfriend Holly. Warren Oates makes a strong impression as Holly's father, but he ends up as Kit's first victim. Despite fine portrayals, the main characters are totally unlikeable, which means you watch as a fascinated observer without becoming involved with them or their motives. The film is visually impressive but ultimately depressing.

Bad Lieutenant ● ⓥ

1992, US, 98 mins, colour
Dir: Abel Ferrara
Stars: Harvey Keitel, Frankie Thorn, Victor Argo
Rating: ★

You've heard of feelgood films: here's a feelbad one. Director Abel Ferrara's study of a totally corrupt cop contains almost every adult certificate element you could think of. Drugs and needles of all kinds, the rape of a nun, prostitution, three-in-a-room brothel frolics, brutal murders and sexual humiliation. Despite (or perhaps because of) all this, it remains practically unwatchable. Harvey Keitel gives a performance of typically fierce intensity, as the cop headed straight for hell, but briefly sidetracked both by the nun's rape, which gnaws at his Catholic guts, and by a world baseball series that stands to win him a fortune. There's no let-up here, as Ferrara's prowling camera brings every element of the film down to street level and below; and it's all too much, turning the audience off instead of on to the problems illustrated in the film.

Bad Man of Brimstone ○

1938, US, 90 mins, b/w
Dir: J Walter Ruben
Stars: Wallace Beery, Virginia Bruce, Dennis O'Keefe, Bruce Cabot
Rating:

Beefy, swaggering Wallace Beery was still a big noise at MGM (he had won an Oscar earlier in the decade for *The Champ*) when he made this rugged comedy-Western that the studio hoped might emulate the success of *Viva Villa!*. If only more trouble had been . taken with the script, the studio might have had a top-grade Western on its hands.

Bad Man's River ○

1972, Spain/Italy, 90 mins, colour
Dir: Gene Martin
Stars: Lee Van Cleef, James Mason,

B

Gina Lollobrigida
Rating: ★

Although Lee Van Cleef was doubtless pleased to get away from a run of grim Western killers, he and his co-stars, Gina Lollobrigida and James Mason, seem ill-at-ease with the vein of comedy that runs rather too close to the surface of this Spanish-Italian action romp. Screenwriters Gene Martin and Philip Yordan keep their plot writhing like a snake with every variety of cross and double-cross they can lay their pens on, but the odds are that you won't believe a word of it.

Bad News Bears, The ○

1976, US, 100 mins, colour
Dir: Michael Ritchie
Stars: Walter Matthau, Tatum O'Neal, Vic Morrow
Rating: ★★★

Wonderfully likeable and entertaining feelgood movie about a team of ragamuffin, semi-delinquent, abrasive kids somehow licked into shape as a baseball team by grouchy old Walter Matthau. Marvellous script by Bill Lancaster hits home in all the right places without you even noticing your emotions are being ruthlessly manipulated. The baseball action is exciting, there are lots of funny lines and Tatum O'Neal as the team's girl star has never been better. Two sequels were made in the hope that lightning might strike twice. They just struck out instead

Bad Timing ●

(aka: Bad Timing: A Sensual Obsession)
1979, US, 135 mins, colour
Dir: Nicolas Roeg
Stars: Art Garfunkel, Theresa Russell, Harvey Keitel, Denholm Elliott
Rating: ★★★★

In the creation of Alex Linden, director Nicolas Roeg and his screenwriter Yale Udoff have come up with a psychopath to set alongside Norman Bates in *Psycho*. At the start, the story runs like a suicide attempt by a girl after a tiff with her boyfriend. But gradually, horrifyingly, Roeg prises the relationship apart until you realise the truth. One can't go further into the plot without touching on the final nasty twists to a very unpalatable if well-made story. Theresa Russell, here coming over as a kind of young Gloria Grahame, is very good as the girl. But actor-singer Art Garfunkel is only barely equal to the demands of her analyst lover.

Ball of Fire ○

1941, US, 111 mins, b/w
Dir: Howard Hawks
Stars: Gary Cooper, Barbara Stanwyck, Oscar Homolka, Dana Andrews, Dan Duryea
Rating: ★★★

A sparkling Billy Wilder-Charles Brackett script provides Barbara Stanwyck with a rare comedy glamour role as showgirl Sugarpuss O'Shea in an amusing and inventive modern reworking of the Snow White theme. Howard Hawks, usually found making action film, is the director, displaying an unexpectedly deft comedy touch. And some of the early Forties slang is as fascinating as it is baffling. Producer Samuel Goldwyn, never one to waste good material, revamped the whole thing a few years later as a vehicle for Danny Kaye called *A Song Is Born*.

Balto ⊙ Ⓥ

1995, US, 78 mins, colour
Dir: Simon Wells
Voice stars: Kevin Bacon, Bob Hoskins, Bridget Fonda, Phil Collins
Rating: ★★★★

One of the few cartoons of the nineties to really challenge the Disney studio in animation, effectiveness and all-round storytelling. Balto is a crossbreed husky who lives in the frozen wastes of Alaska. Desperate to be accepted by the other (pure-bred) huskies, Balto gets the chance to prove his worth when a vital shipment of medicine goes astray in a blizzard. Adventure, comedy and suspense combine thereafter to produce an enthralling animated feature. Kevin Bacon and Bob Hoskins excel as, respectively, the voices of Balto and Boris, a cantankerous goose.

Bambi ⊙ Ⓥ

1942, US, 69 mins, colour
Dir: David Hand
Rating: ★★★★★

One of Walt Disney's most enduring classics, only released on video in 1994. A brilliant depiction of forest life, the changing seasons and weather conditions (notably leading to the exquisitely animated song 'Little April Shower'), it's a heart-warming and sometimes heart-rending tale of a young fawn growing up in the forest and his friendship with an equally young rabbit and skunk. Superbly realised action scenes and sometimes witty dialogue combine to give the film an overwhelming appeal, with

Thumper the ground-drumming rabbit unexpectedly proving the star of the show. Tinies should have an adult standing by for their reactions to the fate of Bambi's mother. Made with great dignity, the film is still an altogether enchanting experience.

Bananas ◑ Ⓥ

1971, US, 82 mins, colour
Dir: Woody Allen
Stars: Woody Allen, Louise Lasser
Rating: ★★

Hilarity slips into vulgarity rather too often in this typically in-and-out early Woody Allen comedy which embroils the little man in a South American revolution. Like the revolutionaries, the gags fire off in all directions – there are spoof TV commercials and even a *Battleship Potemkin* joke for buffs. Jacob Morales has many of the best moments as the rebel leader especially when, drunk with power, he declares Swedish to be the new national language. Woody's life as a human guinea pig at the start of the film is funny enough to make you wish there were more of it, but you'll have to keep your eyes peeled to spot Sylvester Stallone (in his second film) as a hoodlum.

Bandit of Sherwood Forest, The ⊙

1946, US, 87 mins, colour
Dir: Henry Levin
Stars: Cornel Wilde, Anita Louise, Esmond, Edgar Buchanan, George Macready
Rating: ★★

A kind of *Twenty Years After*, Sherwood Forest style, and actually based on a novel called *Son of Robin Hood*. Following in the footsteps of such distinguished Old Sherwoodians as Douglas Fairbanks and Errol Flynn, Cornel Wilde cuts a dashing figure as Hood's scion in this spectacular adventure film. It was one of the few to take advantage of Wilde's real-life prowess as an international fencer.

Bandit of Zhobe, The ○

1959, UK, 81 mins, colour
Dir: John Gilling
Stars: Victor Mature, Anne Aubrey, Anthony Newley
Rating: ★★

A fiery 19th-century adventure yarn that makes little sense but bulges with action that keeps coming at you. It's one of several exotic action films made in Britain in the Fifties with such Hollywood stars as Victor Mature (as here) and Robert Taylor.

Band of Angels ○

1957, US, 127 mins, colour
Dir: Raoul Walsh
Stars: Clark Gable, Yvonne De Carlo,
Sidney Poitier
Rating: ★★

This big, expensive action film, adapted from a best-seller by Robert Penn Warren, tended to acquire the reputation of a poor man's *Gone With the Wind*, set as it is in the southern states at the time of the American Civil War, and with Gable as its star. Acting honours, however, are stolen by Sidney Poitier as a rebellious negro overseer. Lucien Ballard's WarnerColor photography sets off the action in handsome fashion, especially in a chase scene through swamplands. Overall, though, it's a disappointing epic that lacks sparkle.

Bandolero ○

1968, US, 106 mins, colour
Dir: Andrew V McLaglen
Stars: James Stewart, Dean Martin,
Raquel Welch, George Kennedy
Rating: ★★★★

It's remarkable that all Andrew McLaglen's best Westerns have been made with James Stewart as star. Stewart's integrity, plus a gritty performance from Dean Martin and striking colour photography, go a long way to making *Bandolero!* above average as a fiery adventure yarn. All the action is well staged, especially the opening rescue of Martin and his gang from the hangman (a bouquet to Guy Raymond who believes that there is 'nothing worse than a sloppy hanging') and film fans will recognise Jack Mahoney, once the Range Rider and Tarzan, as a rancher who gets killed off in the first reel.

Band Waggon ⊙

1939, UK, 85 mins, b/w
Dir: Marcel Varnel
Stars: Arthur Askey, Richard Murdoch,
Pat Kirkwood
Rating: ★★★

A rare chance to catch up on the version of radio's first-ever comedy series, which won enormous popularity in its time. Arthur Askey and Richard Murdoch are once again to be discovered in their flat on the roof of Broadcasting House, but the nearness of war demanded that in the film they get involved with spies as well. The radio show itself, broadcast on Sunday evenings, was so popular in late Thirties Britain that it was said church services were cancelled because of it.

Band Wagon, The ⊙ ⓥ

1953, US, 112 mins, colour
Dir: Vincente Minnelli.
Stars: Fred Astaire, Cyd Charisse, Jack
Buchanan, Oscar Levant
Rating: ★★★★

With the line, 'Gosh, with all this raw talent around, why can't us kids get together and put ourselves on a show,' this musical is a sophisticated tribute to all the innocent backstage musicals that preceded it. Twenty years after Fred Astaire made his debut in *Dancing Lady*, this film gave him perhaps his best role in one of the best movies of his career, as a fading Hollywood musical star persuaded to make a comeback. Cyd Charisse (in her first starring role and dubbed for vocals by India Adams) plays a ballet dancer picked to partner Fred in a stage show, and Ava Gardner makes a guest appearance. Out of all the film's songs, only one was new – 'That's Entertainment', written in just 30 minutes by Arthur Schwartz and Howard Dietz.

Bang the Drum Slowly ○

1973, US, 97 mins, colour
Dir: John Hancock
Stars: Michael Moriarty, Robert De Niro,
Vincent Gardenia
Rating: ★★★

This is the best of four good films made by the American director John Hancock (the others are *Let's Scare Jessica to Death, California Dreaming*, and *Baby Blue Marine)*, none of which have been widely seen on this side of the Atlantic. The reason here is fairly obvious, for the theme is baseball. But the playing of Michael Moriarty and Robert De Niro sweeps aside all sentiment attached to the theme of a dying baseball player, makes the most of the script's moments of abrasive humour and generally raises the film far above the average weepie.

Banjo on My Knee ○

1936, US, 95 mins, b/w
Dir: John Cromwell
Stars: Barbara Stanwyck, Joel McCrea,
Walter Brennan
Rating: ★★★

This rather delightful musical works well despite having very few musical stars in it! Down the cast there's Tony Martin (billed as Anthony) and Buddy Ebsen (a pretty fair hoofer in his younger days). But the two stars, Barbara Stanwyck and Joel McCrea, weren't obvious musical material. Stanwyck sings surprisingly well – surprising that is until you realise she

started off as a song and dance girl in the Ziegfeld Follies. The story, about McCrea going on the run after killing a man, is of little consequence, so don't worry too much about it. just enjoy the film for what it is – a lightweight piece of fun, with some very entertaining individual scenes. Stanwyck fans will love watching her letting her hair down.

Bank Detective, The
See: The Bank Dick

Bank Dick, The ⊙
(aka: The Bank Detective)
1940, US, 74 mins, b/w
Dir: Edward Cline
Stars: W C Fields, Cora Witherspoon,
Una Merkel, Grady Sutton
Rating: ★★★

W C Fields' last comedy classic in which he emerges from the mass henpecking of a family of females to become the hero of his local town. Fields' screenplay, written under the pseudonym of Mahatma Kane Jeeves, is a happy amalgam of themes and characters from other, earlier Fieldsian romps – including the hat that won't go on the Fields head for the very good reason that he's lifting it in the air with his own cane.

Bank Holiday ○

1938, UK, 86 mins, b/w
Dir: Carol Reed
Stars: Margaret Lockwood, Hugh
Williams, John Lodge
Rating: ★★★

This was director Carol Reed's first big success, starring Margaret Lockwood, who had appeared for him in *Midshipman Easy*. Here she plays a nurse who is poignantly torn between two men. Hers is just one of the stories which, in similar fashion to the later *Holiday Camp*, capture a long-gone era of the British middle- and working-classes on holiday. Strangely, Kathleen Harrison plays a cockney mum in both films.

Barabbas ○

1961, Italy/US, 134 mins, colour
Dir: Richard Fleischer
Stars: Anthony Quinn, Silvana Mangano,
Arthur Kennedy, Jack Palance
Rating: ★★★

Sombre Italian-American epic with a good deal to recommend it thanks to a thoughtful performance by Anthony Quinn as the man set free when Jesus was crucified and to a quality script by Christopher Fry. There's also a fero-

B

cious piece of over-acting from Jack Palance as a sadistic gladiator.

Barb Wire ● Ⓥ
1996, US, 98 mins, colour
Dir: David Hogan
Stars: Pamela Anderson Lee, Temuera Morrison, Victoria Rowell, Jack Noseworthy, Xander Berkeley, Steve Railsback
Rating: ★

The big bid for stardom by pneumatic five-minute wonder Pamela Anderson Lee has her looking like Brigitte Bardot in a comic-strip rip-off of *Casablanca* set in 2017. Unfortunately she still acts like Pamela Anderson Lee. A second Civil War has left America in chaos. In Steel Harbor, one of its most dangerous places, tough, leather-clad mercenary Barb Wire (that's Pambo) runs the Hammerhead bar. Soon she's involved in the hunt for the special contact lenses that can fool the retinal scanners used by the armed forces. Lots of nasty action follows, with the star having mixed fortunes with a string of Schwarzenegger-style one-liners in the midst of the mayhem. The trouble is that she's just not as likeable as Arnie; with him, we laugh with the hero and his impossible feats – here we're laughing at the heroine and her unlikely antics.

Barbarella ● Ⓥ
1967, France/Italy, 98 mins, colour
Dir: Roger Vadim
Stars: Jane Fonda, John Phillip Law, David Hemmings, Anita Pallenberg, Milo O'Shea
Rating: ★★

The film that Jane Fonda is reputedly least fond of - it portrays her as a space maiden and general sex object, a far cry from the liberated ladies she portrays today. It's enjoyable, though, with John Phillip Law – in films since childhood – as the winged hero.

Barbarian and the Geisha, The ○ Ⓥ
1958, US, 105 mins, colour
Dir: John Huston
Stars: John Wayne, Eiko Ando, Sam Jaffe
Rating: ★★

John Huston's pictorially beautiful film about the first American ambassador to Japan, a role for which John Wayne seems odd casting. A curio.

Barbarosa ○
1981, US, 90 mins, colour
Dir: Fred Schepisi
Stars: Willie Nelson, Gary Busey, Isela Vega, Gilbert Roland
Rating: ★★★

A Western by the Australian director Fred Schepisi. This saga of revenge and banditry in the old West makes effective landscape use of Rio Grande scenery and Western singer Willie Nelson (in the ride part of a notorious outlaw), with Gary Busey (who made such an early hit in *The Buddy Holly Story*) as a Texan of German descent who becomes his partner in robbery and pillage. Lots of action.

Barbary Coast ○
1935, US, 91 mins, b/w
Dir: Howard Hawks
Stars: Edward G Robinson, Miriam Hopkins, Joel McCrea
Rating: ★★★

Ben Hecht and Charles MacArthur wrote Edward G Robinson a rich 'rascal' role for this rip-roaring epic of the San Francisco waterfront in the 1850s, which cast him as a kind of gold rush equivalent of Little Caesar. When a society swell ignores him, Robinson snarls: 'I'll fix him – and that horseface he calls his wife!'

Barbary Coast Gent ○
1944, US, 87 mins, b/w
Dir: Roy Del Ruth
Stars: Wallace Beery, Binnie Barnes, John Carradine, Noah Beery Jr
Rating: ★★

Big Wallace Beery blusters his way through another of the rough and ready comedy adventures that he made with such regularity for MGM. Despite a good supporting cast in this tall tale of a Western bandit trying to go straight, Beery's really the whole show.

Barcelona ◑ Ⓥ
1994, US, 101 mins, colour
Dir: Whit Stillman
Stars: Taylor Nichols, Chris Eigeman, Tushka Bergen, Mira Sorvino, Thomas Gibson
Rating: ★★★

This is like a mellow kind of Woody Allen film, only with New York Wasp humour replacing New York Jewish. Ted (Taylor Nichols) is the Woody figure, a salesman working in post-Franco Barcelona, who receives an unwelcome visit from his obnoxious, ever-cadging, ever-meddling cousin Fred (Chris Eigeman), now in the US navy. Ted reminds Fred of the maxim that guests, like fish, 'tend to stink on

the third day', but the whiff of mutual dislike is in the air long before that. Ted has just decided he's into homely girls, but ends up with a glamorous one, a situation soon ruined by Fred's ill-meaning intervention. Things don't develop quite as you'd expect, however. And, though sometimes self-consciously smart and, in rare moments, even tedious, the film is full of droll humour and remains a civilised pleasure to be with to the end. The atmosphere and excitement of Barcelona as a city are splendidly caught.

Barefoot Contessa, The ○ Ⓥ
1954, US, 128 mins, colour
Dir: Joseph L Mankiewicz
Stars: Humphrey Bogart, Ava Gardner, Edmond O'Brien, Marius Goring, Rossano Brazzi
Rating: ★★

A star-studded if rather stolid drama about a stunning Spanish gipsy dancer and her rise and fall in the dizzy world of stardom. Humphrey Bogart is at his most world-weary as a disillusioned, cynical Hollywood writer, but it was Edmond O'Brien's portrayal of a loudmouthed press agent that took the acting honours and won him an Academy Award. Writer-director Joseph L Mankiewicz, who had already won Oscars for *A Letter for Three Wives* and the even more highly esteemed *All About Eve*, faltered somewhat on the script of this one, which is rather over-sardonic in tone.

Barefoot In the Park ○ Ⓥ
1967, US, 105 mins, colour
Dir: Gene Saks
Stars: Robert Redford, Jane Fonda, Charles Boyer, Mildred Natwick
Rating: ★★★★

A spicy, dry and often hilariously scripted comedy about two honeymooners. It achieves both warm, human relationships, and comic lines that are set against one another with precision balance, never overloading the laughs, but rattling them out at a consistent pace. 'I think I'm going to be a lousy wife,' Jane Fonda tells Robert Redford at the door of their honeymoon hotel. 'But I'm very sexy.' After six days and nights, he's convinced. 'I have to go to work,' he gasps, staggering out on the seventh. I don't do this for a living.' Alas in their new flat (top floor) comes the dawn. The radiator won't radiate, the bed (to Jane's horror) fails to arrive for the first night and snow comes through the skylight. It's a film cocktail that never fails to sparkle

Barfly ● ⓥ
1987, US, 100 mins, colour
Dir: Barbet Schroeder
Stars: Mickey Rourke, Faye Dunaway,
Alice Krige, J C Quinn
Rating: ★★

This is a vignettes-from-the-early-life-
the-writer-type movie. You know,
you've seen 'em: the writer getting all
nostalgic about his slum beginings in
garret rooms, and the rich characters
of the poor people he knew. *Barfly*
plays a variation on this theme in that
it homes in on the slurred, blurred
lives of downtown alcoholics, frequent-
ing cheap bars whenever and wherever
they can get cheap credit. Mickey
Rourke, coming on like a male Mae
West, gives another of his low-life, de-
signer-stubble studies as the writer.
Faye Dunaway is good, too, as the
slightly higher-class lush who takes
him under her wing and occasionally
beats his brains out. He takes on the
bartender (Sylvester Stallone's brother
Frank) in a nightly brawl, and his
seedy, smelly lifestyle is captured by
the director down to the last peeling
flap on the wallpaper. Some of this is
entertaining, some indulgent, some
merely tedious.

Barkleys of Broadway, The
○ ⓥ
1949, US, 105 mins, colour
Dir: Charles Walters
Stars: Fred Astaire, Ginger Rogers,
Oscar Levant, Billie Burke
Rating: ★★★

Let's face it, any film with Fred and
Ginger above the titles has got to be
good. Add a screenplay by Adolph
Green and Berry Comden, music by
Harry Warren and Ira Gershwin, and
Oscar Levant third billed and this
should be a classic. But it isn't. This
tale of a dancing couple who split because she wants to be a serious actress
starts well and ends well, but loses its
way in the middle. Ginger was
brought in to renew the partnership
that had lapsed for a decade when
first choice Judy Garland backed out
due to illness. Whatever its shortcomings, Fred and Ginger together
again were ample compensations, as
were Fred singing 'They Can't Take
That Away From Me' and Oscar
doing his own version of 'Sabre
Dance'.

Barnacle Bill ☉
(aka: All at Sea)
1957, UK, 87 mins, b/w
Dir: Charles Frend

Stars: Alec Guinness, Irene Browne
Rating: ★★★

This rib-tickling comedy film – although muted by Ealing standards –
was the last collaboration from the
fantastically successful team of Ealing
Studios and Alec Guinness. And
Guinness' talents for comedy and disguise were rarely better displayed
than in a witty story that pokes fun at
local government and other institutions. Playing Captain Ambrose, who
has the sea in his blood but is the
world's worst sailor, Guinness also
portrays the hero's six ancestors, all
of whom die hilariously heroic naval
deaths.

**Barretts of Wimpole Street,
The** ○
1934, US, 109 mins, b/w
Dir: Sidney Franklin
Stars: Norma Shearer, Charles
Laughton, Fredric March, Maureen
O'Sullivan
Rating: ★★★

A well-acted, slightly staid, but handsomely produced version of the
romance between Elizabeth Barrett
and Robert Browning under the eagle
eye of her martinet father. Norma
Shearer was never better cast than as
Elizabeth and consequently gives her
finest film performance, even though
she is only one year younger than
Charles Laughton, who gives a striking portrayal of the intractable Mr
Barrett. Fredric March is poorly cast
as Browning, but struggles hard to
make something of the role. Director
Sidney Franklin must have had a great
affection for this most romantic of true
stories: 23 years later he remade it for
the same studio, this time with Jennifer
Jones and Bill Travers.

Barricade ○
1950, US, 75 mins, colour
Dir: Peter Godfrey
Stars: Ruth Roman, Dane Clark,
Raymond Massey:
Rating: ★★

A gripping little Technicolor thriller
with plenty of action. Raymond
Massey, so expert a villain, here plays
a character so evil that few will forget
him. The plot, a landbound remake of
The Sea Wolf, is unusual and takes several unexpected turnings.

Barton Fink ● ⓥ
1991, US, 117 mins, colour
Dir: Joel Coen
Stars: John Turturro, John Goodman,
Judy Davis, Michael Lerner, John

Mahoney, Jon Polito
Rating: ★★

An interesting black joke from the
Coen brothers, who gave us *Raising
Arizona* and *Miller's Crossing*. Here they
dump a much-lauded young Jewish
playwright (John Turturro) into the
entertainment-oriented Hollywood of
1941. But the film's not only a satire
of life in a poverty row studio of the
war years, but a dark little number
about Fink's run-down hotel, whose
wallpaper peels obscenely in the heat
from cardboard-thin walls, and whose
only inhabitants are a red-eyed bellboy
(Steve Buscemi, clearly auditioning for
Renfield in Coppola's *Dracula)* and an
aged liftman who never says anything
but the number of the floor. Here
Fink meets writer's block, as well as a
moose of a man (John Goodman) in
the room next door. He's also due to
encounter violent death, a towering inferno and, maybe, a head in a hatbox.
It's a black comedy that doesn't actually give you much to laugh about, just a
shade too clever and perverse for its
own good.

Basic Instinct ● ⓥ
1992, US, 128 mins, colour
Dir: Paul Verhoeven
Stars: Michael Douglas, Sharon Stone,
George Dzundza, Jeanne Tripplehorn,
Denis Arnt, Leilani Sarelle
Rating: ★★

Credit director Paul Verhoeven with a
keen cinematic brain. He only has
about 70 minutes of plot here, so he
packs it (cynics might say pads it) with
gory murders, hot sex scenes, death
defying car chases and lots of lovely
California scenery. The result may be
flaky tripe, but it goes out and grabs
you from the start. The curtain rises
on a violent love scene involving a
sumptuously built blonde (whose body
doesn't quite resemble any one of the
three main suspects) who pounds up
and down on her lover, ties his hands
to the bed posts and pounds up and
down on his head with an ice-pick.
Gets your attention, right? Enter detective Michael Douglas who interviews
the victim's mistress (Sharon Stone), a
foul-mouthed, done-it-all millionaire
authoress who's just written a book detailing just such a murder. Double
bluff? Maybe. But you won't need
two guesses to forecast Douglas falling
heavily for his shapely suspect. You
may not even be sure who dunnit at
the end, for the film is pretty good
when it remembers to concentrate on
the plot. Douglas, Stone and Co snap,

B

snarl, smoulder, smooch and keep straight faces in the cause of melodrama.

Basil The Great Mouse Detective

See: The Great Mouse Detective

Basquiat ● Ⓥ

1996, US 106 mins, colour
Dir: Julian Schnabel
Stars: Jeffrey Wright, Benicio Del Toro, Gary Oldman, Parker Posey, David Bowie
Rating: ★

Star-studded but stagnant, this is a terminally slow portrait of the Haitian/American painter Jean-Paul Basquiat whose graffiti-style paintings won him the friendship of the rich and famous and covers of national magazines, before his almost inevitable death from an overdose of heroin at the age of 27. Jeffrey Wright languidly re-creates Basquiat, who seemingly couldn't be bothered to be civil to people most of the time, and just painted what he felt. Artist-director Schnabel's treatment certainly brings us no closer to unravelling the secret of Basquiat's genius. David Bowie (perfect as Andy Warhol), Willem Dafoe, Tatum O'Neal, Parker Posey, Dennis Hopper, Gary Oldman, Christopher Walken and Courtney Love flit in and out: none gives a bad performance. But the torpor attached to the painter's personality as shown here somehow seems to affect the whole film.

Bataan ○

1943, US, 114 mins, b/w
Dir: Tay Garnett
Stars: Robert Taylor, George Murphy, Thomas Mitchell
Rating: ★★

A big money-maker and immensely popular in its time, this war film now looks sadly dated with its studio jungles and *10 Little Niggers* plot, as American soldiers defending a Pacific island go off and do silly things so that they keep the plot rolling by getting killed off one by one. In 1943 this was inspiring stuff, and there are still occasional excitements, even though Robert Taylor looks miscast as the sergeant left in charge when the patrol's officer is killed.

Bathing Beauty ○

1944, US, 101 mins, colour
Dir: George Sidney
Stars: Red Skelton, Esther Williams
Rating: ★★

'Hollywood's Mermaid' Esther Williams was launched to stardom in this elaborate aquatic extravaganza. The plot hardly held water, but escapist entertainment was the name of the game and MGM had picked a winner in the form of the champion swimmer who looked just dreamy in a swimsuit and peachy in glorious Technicolor. Good trouper that he is, Red Skelton provides some great comedy, including tripping tutu-clad into a ballet class. Director George Sidney and choreographer John Murray Anderson have a field day with the aquatic climax that mixes fire and water to the strains of Strauss's 'Blue Danube' waltz.

Batman ☉ Ⓥ

1966, US, 105 mins, colour
Dir: Leslie H Martinson
Stars: Adam West, Burt Ward, Burgess Meredith, Lee Meriwether, Cesar Romero, Frank Gorshin
Rating: ★★

Colourful film based on the famous television series. Fine fun for children (and perhaps some adults!), with a great performance from Burgess Meredith who squawks splendidly as The Penguin, waddling rings round his fellow villains.

Batman ◑ Ⓥ

1989, US, 126 mins, colour
Dir: Tim Burton
Stars: Michael Keaton, Jack Nicholson, Kim Basinger, Robert Wuhl, Pat Hingle, Billy Dee Williams
Rating: ★★★

This dark and *film noir*-influenced update of the comic-strip hero smashed records left, right and centre. Jack Nicholson's bravura performance as The Joker, with his grotesque acid scarred clown face and green hair, takes top honours even if his camp becomes too high before the end. Michael Keaton struggles manfully to bring a human personality to the man in the rubber suit, but it really is The Joker's show. The special effects are good, the fight scenes are well done and the Batmobile's pretty impressive, too. There's an almost gothic look to Gotham City at night (like something out of *Metropolis*) and the final confrontation with The Joker atop a skyscraper provides a fitting climax. And remember, the phrase of the season was: 'Never rub another man's rhubarb!'

Batman and Robin ○ Ⓥ

1997, US, 125 mins, colour
Dir: Joel Schumacher
Stars: Arnold Schwarzenegger, George Clooney, Chris O'Donnell, Uma Thurman, Alicia Silverstone, Michael Gough
Rating: ★★★

This pleasing addition to the series gives us a new heroine in Batgirl (Alicia Silverstone), two new villains in Mr Freeze (Arnold Schwarzenegger) and Poison Ivy (Uma Thurman, stealing the show with her Mae West impersonation) and even a new Batman in *ER*'s George Clooney. He slips easily into the traditional cape and that painful-looking Batsuit, while Arnie tries to freeze Gotham City and Uma plans a takeover of the world by plants. Awesome sets don't quite dominate the amusing characters here, but the film is hit by occasional pretensions beyond its comic-strip status, some dodgy model work and a few patches almost as ponderous as Arnie in his ice-suit. Good fun, though, with lots of high-velocity action: fans will have few grumbles.

Batman Forever ○ Ⓥ

1995, US, 122 mins, colour
Dir: Joel Schumacher
Stars: Val Kilmer, Nicole Kidman, Jim Carrey, Tommy Lee Jones, Chris O'Donnell
Rating: ★★★

For a change it's the acting rather than the action that makes the third screen adventure of Gotham's dark knight worthwhile. Val Kilmer is much better cast as Batman than was Michael Keaton – he even gets the emotionless voice right – while Tommy Lee Jones and Jim Carrey act their fiendish socks off as his evil, not to say deranged opponents, Two Face and The Riddler. And, if Chris O'Donnell seems wrong for Robin, then Nicole Kidman and Drew Barrymore provide more personable female support than old pointy ears has had to date. Even manservant Michael Gough gets in on the act more than usual, emerging as a personality in his own right. A circus sequence at the beginning provides the punchiest of the visual thrills, too many of the combat sequences lacking cohesion and definition, setting off routine explosions and punch-ups which don't help the progression of a scene. No, it's personalities rather than power that see this one through, and Kilmer even gets to crack wise. 'Why, doctor' he tells the predatory Kidman, 'Are you trying to get under my cape?'

Batman Returns ◑ ⓥ
1992, US, 127 mins, colour
Dir: Tim Burton
Stars: Michael Keaton, Danny DeVito, Michelle Pfeiffer, Christopher Walken, Michael Gough
Rating: ★★

Amazing in conception, with sets reminiscent of German expressionist movies of the Twenties and Thirties Batman's joust with The Penguin, Catwoman and Max Schreck is rather less in execution and effect. There's not much story to speak of, resulting in the film falling victim to its own set design. And animal rights protesters are likely to be up in arms at the apparent cruelty to whole hordes of penguins. Michael Keaton's Batman is even more taciturn than before, leading you to wonder from Christopher Walken's Schreck whether he might not have made a better stab at the role. Walken is a businessman who has been sucking Gotham dry, and 'kills' secretary Michelle Pfeiffer (more fun when she's being ditzy) who is revived by cats and somehow transformed into Catwoman. She and DeVito as the penguin certainly look their roles and emote fiercely; even so, the film's darkness works against it where the action is concerned, and you may be looking at your bat watches long before the end.

Batteries Not Included ⊙ ⓥ
1987, US, 105 mins, colour
Dir: Matthew Robbins
Stars: Hume Cronyn, Jessica Tandy, Frank McRae, Elizabeth Pena
Rating: ★★★★

Elderly apartment owners are hiding out in fear from developers' enforcers with baseball bats. It looks like a case for the A-Team. But wait. The B-Team is at hand, in the form of tiny, living spaceships from a galaxy far, far away. And, after being befriended by old Hume Cronyn and his fellow-fogeys, the aliens will do *anything* to help. This is a very silly film of great charm, whose most engaging scenes are those in which the aliens help Cronyn to make a fresh go of his cafe. Though little girls may shed a tear at the appropriate moments, it's perfect viewing for the very young, and a refreshing tonic for the rest of us.

Battle Beneath the Earth ○
1967, UK, 92 mins, colour
Dir: Montgomery Tully
Stars: Viviane Ventura, Kerwin Mathews
Rating: ★

Don't look now but those fiendish Chinese are burrowing under the Pacific with their atom bombs again. 'My God, they're everywhere,' says the Allied supreme commander. Never fear, sir, Professors Kerwin Mathews and Viviane Ventura, in unzipped red boiler suit, will soon put an end to the devils. And so they do, in a film that qualifies for the term 'fantastic' in every sense of the word.

Battle Beyond the Stars ○
1980, US/Japan, 104 mins, colour
Dir: Jimmy T Murakami
Stars: Richard Thomas, Robert Vaughn, George Peppard, John Saxon
Rating: ★★★

A cheeky, colourful science-fiction remake of *The Magnificent Seven,* with Robert Vaughn, looking no different 20 years on, actually returning to his original task as one of the avenging septet. The rest of the space seven include George Peppard as an intergalactic cowboy and Richard Thomas, once John-Boy of *The Waltons.* Effects are well up to the new par established by such blockbusters as *Star Wars,* and there are some ingenious touches (though not quite enough) like the severed arm that carries on a life of its own. Heroine Darlanne Fluegel is rather put in the shade by the magnificent Sybil Danning as the Valkyrie warrior St Exmin.

Battle Circus ○
1953, US, 90 mins, b/w
Dir: Richard Brooks
Stars: Humphrey Bogart, June Allyson, Keenan Wynn, Robert Keith
Rating: ★★★

This Korean War story brings together the sweet and the sour: hard-shelled Humphrey Bogart as a cynical major and girl-next-door June Allyson as the nursing officer who loves him. Bogey and Juney go together like chalk and cheese, but even so the film has its moments, thanks to Richard Brooks' direction, which is superior to his script.

Battle Cry ○
1954, US, 149 mins, colour
Dir: Raoul Walsh
Stars: Van Heflin, Aldo Ray, Tab Hunter, Nancy Olson, Dorothy Malone
Rating: ★★

A long slog through the loves of US Marines en route to battle in World War Two, scripted by Leon M Uris from his own massive novel. The ladies come off best. Anne Francis and Nancy Olson exude warmth, and Dorothy Malone appears in a dry run for the series of fading blondes that would culminate in her Academy Award for *Written on the Wind.*

Battle for Anzio
(See: Anzio)

Battle for the Planet of the Apes ○ ⓥ
1973, US, 92 mins, colour
Dir: J Lee Thompson
Stars: Roddy McDowall, Claude Akins
Rating: ★★

John Huston's distinctive features prove to be recognisable even under John Chambers' marvellous ape make-up in this, the 'final chapter' of the Apes saga that had begun five years earlier. Much of its force and originality is now blurred but Roddy McDowall's strong performance – he plays here the son of the character he first created – provides the sturdy central pivot the film sorely needs.

Battleground ○
1949, US, 118 mins, colour
Dir: William Wellman
Stars: Van Johnson, John Hodiak, Ricardo Montalban
Rating: ★★★

War-film fans will like this vivid action film about the Battle of the Bulge, and of American troops fighting against huge odds towards the end of World War Two in Europe. The strong vein of humour is very welcome, and director William Wellman loses no chance to make real human beings out of the characters on the battlefield. He is helped by a talented supporting cast that includes Ricardo Montalban, Richard Jaeckel, Jerome Courtland, Marshall Thompson, Don Taylor, James Whitmore, Denise Darcel, Leon Ames and James Arness.

Battle Hymn ○
1957, US, 108 mins, colour
Dir: Douglas Sirk
Stars: Rock Hudson, Dan Duryea, Anna Kashfi
Rating: ★★★

Rock Hudson's third modern-day adventure in the East (the others were *Spiral Road* and *Thunder of the Gods*) is an exciting and sometimes moving story of a chaplain whose wartime bravery earns him a string of honours. The strong supporting cast includes veteran bad man Dan Duryea, doing well in a rare sympathetic role as Hudson's army sergeant companion.

B

Battle of Britain ○ ⓥ

1969, UK, 131 mins, colour
Dir: Guy Hamilton
Stars: Michael Caine, Kenneth More,
Laurence Olivier, Susannah York, Robert
Shaw, Christopher Plummer
Rating: ★★

Reverential, all-star treatment of the famous period of conflict which turned
the tide of World War Two. The film
comes spectacularly alive in the skies,
even though the dialogue remains
rooted to the tarmac: watch out for the
exchange between Ralph Richardson
(British minister) and Curt Jurgens
(German baron) which is particularly
priceless. Michael Caine is excellent at
the head of the all-star cast. On the
whole, though, a doomed venture,
made at the wrong time.

Battle of Midway, The ○ ⓥ

(aka: Midway)
1976, US, 130 mins, colour
Dir: Jack Smight
Stars: Charlton Heston, Henry Fonda,
James Coburn, Glenn Ford
Rating: ★★

Some of the drama and impact of the
mighty World War Two naval battle
still emerges from under the weight of
a star-studded cast in this blockbuster
spectacular which mingles actual
wartime footage, sterling star performances and soap-opera subplots.
Originally released in Sensurround,
the film is now kinder to the eardrums,
and will allow you to concentrate on
spotting the many stars – including
Magnum's Tom Selleck – in minor
roles.

Battle of Powder River

See: Tomahawk

Battle of the Bulge ○ ⓥ

1965, US, 163 mins, colour
Dir: Ken Annakin
Stars: Henry Fonda, Robert Shaw,
Robert Shaw, Dana Andrews, George
Montgomery, Ty Hardin
Rating: ★★★★

Blockbuster war film about the
Germans' last serious attempt to win
the war by making a determined thrust
with an army of Tiger tanks in order
to gain time to build enough jet planes
to blast the Allies out of the sky.
Robert Shaw is the fanatical tank commander, blue eyes blazing, Henry
Fonda earnest and true as the
American officer who pin-points the
coming attack and finds the tanks' vital
attacking position by gliding through

fog in a reconnaissance plane. In the
supporting cast James MacArthur
catches well the transformation from
boy-to-man as the young lieutenant
who's the sole survivor of a machine-
gun massacre of prisoners; and George
Montgomery is particularly noteworthy as a battle-hungry sergeant.
Technicolor photography by Jack
Hildyard is fresh and clear. And the
American sense of humour is ever present, never more so than when Fonda
and pilot are gliding through the fog.
'We'll pick up a landmark,' says
Fonda. 'Sure,' replies the pilot, 'We'll
pick up a landmark – right in the kisser.' It's nice to think war was like that
as well.

Battle of the River Plate, The ○

(aka: Pursuit of the Graf Spee)
1956, UK, 115 mins, colour
Dir: Michael Powell, Emeric Pressburger
Stars: John Gregson, Anthony Quayle,
Peter Finch, Ian Hunter, Jack Gwillim,
Bernard Lee
Rating: ★★★

A Royal Command Performance film
which aroused a certain amount of criticism from those who thought that the
war movie was too outdated a genre in
1956 to set before a queen. Anthony
Quayle is the man to watch for acting
honours in this excellently made story
of how the British finally caught up
with the German battleship *Graf Spee*.

Battle of the Sexes, The ○

1960, UK, 83 mins, b/w
Dir: Charles Crichton
Stars: Peter Sellers, Robert Morley,
Constance Cummings
Rating: ★★★★

A very funny, often brilliant comedy,
which raises laughs by pitting Scots
canniness (personified by Peter Sellers)
against American efficiency, embodied
by Constance Cummings. Sellers has
rarely been more insidiously hilarious,
and Robert Morley, wearing what
must be one of the biggest kilts ever
made, makes his tweed magnate boss a
fine figure of pompous fun. The stars
are supported in the ensuing shenanigans by some of Scotland's finest
character players of the period

Battle of the V1 ○

(aka: V1)
1958, UK, 109 mins, b/w
Dir: Vernon Sewell
Stars: Michael Rennie, Patricia Medina,
Milly Vitale, David Knight
Rating: ★★

A factually-based wartime drama made
by the veteran and prolific British director Vernon Sewell. Michael Rennie
and David Knight immerse themselves
completely in a thrilling quantity of
cloak-and-dagger work in the story of
a hunt, helped by the Polish underground, for one of Hitler's deadliest
secret weapons, the VI rocket. Actual
shots of Royal Air Force bombing raids
heighten the atmosphere of realism.

Battlestar Galactica ○ ⓥ

1978, US, 125 mins, colour
Dir: Richard A Colla
Stars: Lorne Greene, Richard L Hatch,
Dirk Benedict, Ray Milland, Ed Begley
Jr, John Colicos
Rating: ★★

Television's answer to *Star Wars*, made
for more than $10 million by
Universal in an attempt to emulate
rival 20th Century-Fox's cinema success. Lorne Greene is an intergalactic
Moses, leading a band of fugitives
from across space to a promised land –
Earth. It's more or less a reworking of
Wagon Train, with deadly robots (the
Cylons) substituting for hostile
Indians. All good fun, and the effects
are above par, but several shots – in
particular the launching of fighter jets
– seem to be repeated endlessly.

Battle Stations ○

1956, US, 81 mins, b/w
Dir: Lewis Seiler
Stars: John Lund, William Bendix, Keefe
Brasselle, Richard Boone
Rating: ★★

A rather unusual war film about
frayed relationships aboard a 'ghost'
US aircraft carrier, which the Japanese
believe (wrongly) they have sunk.
Director Lewis Seiler came to films via
a flurry of silent Westerns in the early
1920s. But his penchant for war films
soon made itself apparent. *Air Circus*
was his first big one, in 1928, and his
best, the superb *Guadalcanal Diary*, appeared in 1943.

Battle Taxi ○

1955, US, 82 mins, b/w
Dir: Herbert L Strock
Stars: Sterling Hayden, Arthur Franz,
Marshall Thompson
Rating: ★★

An all-male war adventure about the
work of the US helicopter rescue service during the Korean conflict. The
action involves some magnificent
stunts with helicopters, and
Hollywood stunt pilots had to take
some genuinely alarming risks.

Bat 21 ● ⓥ
1988, US, 105 mins, colour
Dir: Peter Markle
Stars: Gene Hackman, Danny Glover,
Jerry Reed
Rating: ★★★★★

This has to be the first Vietnam film to
get the balance right between the old-
style combat movie and the *Platoon*
bloodbath. And it mixes rugged action
and dialogue with continuous suspense. It laments the loss of life and
the agony involved, without losing
sight of the continuation of its exciting
storyline or of the necessities of war.
Lovers of action, compassionate
thinkers and pacifists will all find satisfaction here. On top of that, the true
story of a Lieutenant-Colonel (Gene
Hackman) stranded deep in Viet-Cong
territory with knowledge vital to the
enemy, and his friendship through
radio with the reconnaissance pilot
(Danny Glover) who becomes determined to save him, works on all levels.
The actors are terrific, the action exciting and unsparing and the script rarely
puts a foot wrong. Poignant vignettes
punctuate the tension without breaking
it. Good? As Glover would say, that's
a copy!

Beachcomber, The ○
1954, UK, 90 mins, colour
Dir: Muriel Box
Stars: Glynis Johns, Robert Newton,
Donald Sinden, Paul Rogers, Donald
Pleasence
Rating: ★★★

Robert Newton is beautifully cast as
Somerset Maugham's drunken South
Seas vagabond, the Honourable Ted.
This part was first played by Charles
Laughton in the 1938 film *Vessel of
Wrath* in which Newton, strangely, had
a supporting role. Glynis Johns proves
more than a match as the missionary
who first loathes him, then loves him.

Beaches ● ⓥ
1988, US, 123 mins, colour
Dir: Garry Marshall
Stars: Bette Midler, Barbara Hershey,
John Heard, Spalding Gray, Lainie
Kazan
Rating: ★★★★★

There hasn't been a double-girl bawler
like this since *Old Acquaintance*. Two
11-year-old girls from disparate backgrounds meet accidentally on a holiday
beach and form a bond of exceptional
friendship that somehow holds, in spite
of long periods apart and occasional
blazing rows, down the years, through

to a tremendous weepie climax you
will need at least two handkerchiefs to
even see. Mary Agnes Donoghuey's
script, as adept at funny one-liners –
the film isn't all tears – as at dramatic
confrontations, pulls all the right emotional strings, and Bette Midler and
Barbara Hershey, both first-rate, give it
full value. Generally it's Hershey's
character who has the crises in life and
the ebullient Midler who's always on
hand with a well-padded shoulder.
Besides the stars, mention should be
made of little Mayim Bialik - who's an
11 year-old Midler to the life - and
Marcie Leeds. Basically, though, this
is just a terrific script that makes you
realise the value of friendship. There
aren't too many of those around.

Beach Party ☉
1964, US, 101 mins, colour
Dir: William Asher
Stars: Bob Cummings, Dorothy Malone,
Frankie Avalon, Annette Funicello
Rating: ★★★

This teenage surfing comedy musical,
about a group of holidaying youngsters 'studied' by a professor and his
glamorous assistant, is great fun.
Director William Asher swings it along
nicely on a slender story and a few
songs, and the performances he gets
from his actors are uniformly good.
The hit of the show is undoubtedly
Harvey Lembeck's Eric Von Zipper,
the leader of a motorcycle gang, for
whom things somehow just won't go
right. Watch out for a surprise, unbilled guest star right at the end.

Bear Island ● ⓥ
1979, UK/Canada, 118 mins, colour
Dir: Don Sharp
Stars: Donald Sutherland, Vanessa
Redgrave, Richard Widmark, Christopher
Lee, Lloyd Bridges
Rating: ★★

The usual Alistair MacLean combination of exciting action, rugged far-flung
locations, foolish dialogue and positive
performances, the exception here being
Vanessa Redgrave, whose Norwegian
accent makes her sound like Inspector
Clouseau. The Arctic settings, beautifully photographed by Ian Hume, give
the highly coloured adventure an additional boost and Don Sharp, who
made the sizzling speedboat sequence
in another MacLean inspired film,
Puppet on a Chain, this time offers us a
snowboat chase guaranteed to warm
the iciest blood.

**Beast from 20,000 Fathoms,
The** ●
1953, US, 80 mins, b/w
Dir: Eugene Lourie
Stars: Paul Christian, Paula Raymond,
Cecil Kellaway, Lee Van Cleef
Rating: ★★

A science fiction adventure, based on a
tale by Ray Bradbury, about a gigantic
monster, this has some fine special effects from Ray Harryhausen, and an
early featured role for Lee Van Cleef,
who's allowed to take a pot shot at the
creature loose in the city. Many of the
sets in the film were built at enormous
expense - only to be quickly destroyed
as part of the plot.

Beast of the City ○
1932, US, 87 mins, b/w
Dir: Charles Brabin
Stars: Walter Huston, Jean Harlow,
Wallace Ford, Jean Hersholt, Mickey
Rooney
Rating: ★★★

Strong gangster drama which was one
of the first films to tell the crime battle
from the policeman's point of view.
Jean Harlow is at her best as the
blonde who tempts the police chief's
brother (Wallace Ford) off the straight
and narrow, and the film ends, as one
contemporary reviewer put it, 'in the
biggest massacre in years.'

Beasts of Marseilles, The
See: Seven Thunders

**Beast with Five Fingers,
The** ●
1946, US, 88 mins, b/w
Dir: Curt Siodmak
Stars: Peter Lorre, Robert Aida, Andrea
King
Rating: ★★★

William Fryer Harvey's classic story of
the macabre is brought to the screen,
with Peter Lorre giving an eye-popping, memorable performance as the
man haunted by the beast of the title (a
severed hand with a life of its own).
Directed with a bravura touch by
Robert Florey (he made his first great
horror film, *The Murders in the Rue
Morgue*, back in 1932), endowing the
scary proceedings with a unique nightmare quality.

Beat Street ●
1984, US, 107 mins, colour
Dir: Stan Lathan
Stars: Rae Dawn Chong, Guy Davis, Jon
Chardiet, Leon W Grant
Rating: ★★★★

B

Or: Street Beat. For this emotive musical, centred on the shortlived breakdancing craze, takes us right down to street level. Here are ghettoes that look like ghettoes, subways that look like subways and housing conditions made to appear genuinely cramped – both a disgrace to humanity and a credit to those who rise above them. And, despite its story thread of lovers from different sides of the tracks, this is a film totally lacking in pretentiousness; rarely does it go over the top. Semi-allegorical elements are woven with surprising grace into the fabric of a beat musical, and give it an emotive bite not seen in this kind of entertainment since *West Side Story*. The rap music, with its easy-to-hear jive talk, is well done by the performers, while its characters, and certainly the lower-life ones, seem real and not contrived and the climax will bring tears to your eyes as well as taps to your toes. Grab this beat: it makes *Flashdance* seem like a damp squib.

Beat the Devil ○
1953, US/UK, 100 mins, b/w
Dir: John Huston
Stars: Humphrey Bogart, Gina Lollobrigida, Peter Lorre, Jennifer Jones, Robert Morley
Rating: ★★★

This offbeat comedy-thriller may be the strangest of the several films made together by Humphrey Bogart and John Huston. With its African setting and curious mix of ill-assorted people, it's always a treat to look at, but sometimes odd to listen to. Huston's script (co-written with the somewhat eccentric Truman Capote) is full of peculiar asides and little in-jokes. Of the splendidly cosmopolitan cast, Gina Lollobrigida looks the most uncomfortable and Peter Lorre comes off the best. His expressive face and courtly manner with dialogue provide many quiet chuckles in an erratically entertaining film.

Beavis and Butt-Head Do America ◐ ⓥ
1996, US, 81 mins, colour
Dir: Mike Judge
Voices: Mike Judge, Robert Stack, Cloris Leachman, Eric Bogosian
Rating: ★

B & B are a coarser teen version of The Stupids. With their minds unable to focus beyond sex and TV, the blinkered bunglers wander grossly through life offending as many people as possible with their simple, scatologi-

cal fun. Subtlety's out of style here, folks, as B & B become involved with a guy who wants his wife offed in Vegas. Interpreting 'do' as 'have sex with', our heroes eagerly grab the hit-men's assignment and become involved in a nationwide hunt after they come into possession of some gizmo that could wipe out the world. Leaving a trail of death, destruction and disgusting acts behind them, B & B evade the best efforts of the FBI to collar them, raising everything but a smile along the way. Fans of the spotty slugs will enjoy it; others may find The Three Stooges masters of slapstick by comparison. Robert Stack's voice smoothly supplies the only amusing lines as an FBI chief with an obsession for full cavity searches.

Beau Brummell ○
1954, US/UK, 111 mins, colour
Dir: Curtis Bernhardt
Stars: Stewart Granger, Elizabeth Taylor, Peter Ustinov, Robert Morley, James Donald
Rating: ★★★★

One of the most colourful and convincing slices of history that MGM ever produced, *Beau Brummell* inevitably courted controversy when it was chosen as the Royal Command Performance film of its year. But the Regency atmosphere is marvellously well caught in this portrait of the scandalous Brummell (Stewart Granger) leader of fashion in his day, spendthrift and scoundrel. The impact of the film is heightened by the magnificent performance of Peter Ustinov as the Prince of Wales. The actor reveals the prince as a man not to be laughed at, but sympathised with. Together, he and Granger make the final scene a moving movie moment. And Elizabeth Taylor, portraying Lady Patricia, never looked more beautiful, under the loving gaze of Oswald Morris's colour camera.

Beau Geste ○
1939, US, 114 mins, b/w
Dir: William A Wellman
Stars: Gary Cooper, Ray Milland, Robert Preston, Susan Hayward, Brian Donlevy, J Carrol Naish
Rating: ★★★

Like Robert Mitchum, Gary Cooper had a deceptively lazy delivery that endeared him to millions, although he had a gentler style than Mitchum, and there was nearly always a twinkle of humour behind the eyes. Here he is Beau (of course) in the best screen ver-

sion of P C Wren's classic yarn of three brothers who join the Foreign Legion. The climax at the fort littered with dead men gave rise to a thousand comedy skits, and Brian Donlevy gave one of his most memorable screen portrayals as the scarred and sadistic sergeant.

Beau James ○
1957, US, 107 mins, colour
Dir: Melville Shavelson
Stars: Bob Hope, Vera Miles, Paul Douglas, Alexis Smith
Rating: ★★★

Quite a pleasant excursion into romantic nostalgia, made at a time when Bob Hope was trying to widen the range of his appeal. The drama lacks bite, but the period atmosphere has a melancholy charm and there are some bright guest spots.

Beautiful Blonde from Bashful Bend, The ○
1949, US, 77 mins, colour
Dir: Preston Sturges
Stars: Betty Grable, Cesar Romero, Rudy Vallee, Olga San Juan, Sterling Holloway
Rating: ★★

The last of a long string of comedy hits that made their writer-director, Preston Sturges, something of a cult figure in the film world. This story of a lady sharpshooter might have been merrier with another Betty (Hutton) in the lead but a supporting cast to delight all vintage-film fans includes Margaret Hamilton (the green-faced witch from *The Wizard of Oz*), Sterling Holloway, Olga San Juan, and three stars of 1930s two-reeler comedies: Hugh Herbert, El Brendel and Chester Conklin. Sturges fortunes were well on the wane by this time, and critics slammed the film. By most directors' standards, however, it remains a pretty enjoyable romp.

Beautiful Girls ● ⓥ
1996, US, 113 mins, colour
Dir: Ted Demme
Stars: Matt Dillon, Timothy Hutton, Mira Sorvino, Uma Thurman, Lauren Holly, Rosie O'Donnell, Annabeth Gish
Rating: ★★★★

Of all the films about diners, singles, camaraderie and groups of twentysomethings staring the big three-O in the face, this is one of the best. Its small-town atmosphere is convincing, and nearly all the characters have become flesh and blood before the end of the film. It's tough, though, to see

Dillon cheating on Sorvino for a fling with Holly and, with all due respect, one would have thought the girl's roles better cast the other way round. Making commitments, settling down, that's what the theme is all about – although you wonder whether some of these prematurely middle-aged people will ever achieve these goals. Scott Rosenberg's screenplay is full of telling little lines – in one cute reference to *The Wizard of Oz*, Hutton is reminded that he should 'never let a woman behind the curtain, to see the little old man working the levers' – and contains a gem of a role for 13-year-old Natalie Portman, to which this talented actress does full justice.

Beauty and the Beast ⊙ Ⓥ
1991, US, 85 mins, colour
Dir: Gary Trousdale, Kirk Wise
Voice stars: Paige O'Hara, Robby Benson, Jerry Orbach, Angela Lansbury, Jo Anne Worley
Rating: ★★★★★

A classic Disney cartoon feature, very much in the tradition of *Sleeping Beauty*, but with slightly more wit and innovation in the minor characters, and with 'big' Broadway-style songs rather than 'novelty' numbers. Beauty is not *too* beautiful and the Beast not *too* beastly, but even so they're outshone by the servants at the Beast's castle, all of whom have been turned into things like clocks, candlesticks, wardrobes and teapots. Hit of the show is undoubtedly a Chevalier-style candelabra called Lumiere, who also leads off the most enjoyable musical number, when all the utensils launch into a Ziegfeld Follies routine while inviting Beauty to 'Be Our Guest'. But the film is also poignant, scary, exciting and invigorating when it needs to be. And remember, in the words of the clock: 'If it ain't Baroque, don't fix it!'

Beauty Jungle, The ○
(aka: Contest Girl)
1963, UK, 114 mins, colour
Dir: Val Guest
Stars: Janette Scott, Ian Hendry, Ronald Fraser, Edmund Purdom
Rating: ★★

Val Guest's eminently watchable portrait of the in-fighting behind the plastic smiles and pneumatic busts of the beauty contest world. Janette Scott is the no-claws-barred beauty queen and Ian Hendry is as excellent as ever as the manager who moulds her to his ideal.

Because of Him ⊙
1945, US, 88 mins, b/w
Dir: Richard Wallace
Stars: Deanna Durbin, Charles Laughton, Franchot Tone
Rating: ★★★

This musical, pleasantly centred on a series of amusing absurdities, isn't quite up to the standard of Deanna Durbin and Charles Laughton's previous venture together, *It Started with Eve*, four years earlier. But Deanna's millions of fans will enjoy her singing 'Danny Boy' and Laughton steals the show as a conceited stage star. Franchot Tone, too, as a Broadway playwright, shows a fine sense of the ridiculous.

Because You're Mine ○
1952, US, 103 mins, colour
Dir: Alexander Hall
Stars: Mario Lanza, Doretta Morrow, James Whitmore
Rating: ★★

Mario Lanza (alias Alfred Cocozza from Philadelphia) got a new co-star in the curvy Doretta Morrow (alias Doretta Marano from Brooklyn) in the fourth of his musicals for MGM, which saw the real beginning of the weight problems (he had shed almost four stones, rather too much, since *The Great Caruso*) that would help to undermine his sensational film career. Here he anticipated Elvis Presley eight years later by playing a popular singer drafted to the army. Besides the title song, the hits included 'Be My Love' (revised from *The Toast of New Orleans*), 'All the Things You Are' and Lanza's own smash rendition of 'The Lord's Prayer'. Seven years later he was dead, from a heart attack after yet another crash diet. It was the lovely Morrow's only film and she, too, was not destined for a long life, dying from cancer aged 42.

Becket ○
1966, US/UK, 148 mins. colour
Dir: Peter Glenville
Stars: Richard Burton, Peter O'Toole, John Gielgud, Donald Wolfit, Martita Hunt
Rating: ★★★★

Superior entertainment in a powerful story of the friendship-turned-sour between Henry II (a flamboyant, eye-catching performance by Peter O'Toole) and his one-time fellow adventurer Thomas Becket. British director Peter Glenville splashes the exciting slice of history convincingly across his colour canvas. And the dialogue is studded with sparkling

phrases. One particularly remembers Becket's description of the shedding of his worldly goods as 'the clumsy gesture of a spiritual gatecrasher.'

Becoming Colette ● Ⓥ
1991, US, 93 mins, colour
Dir: Danny Huston
Stars: Klaus Maria Brandauer, Mathilda May, Virginia Madsen, Paul Rhys, Jean-Pierre Aumont, John Van Dreelen
Rating: ★

A disappointingly cheap and tawdry version of how the best-selling authoress Colette (who wrote *Gigi*) learned about lust, life and lewdness in late 19th-century Paris. Star Klaus Maria Brandauer chews the scenery as well as his dialogue, while director Danny Huston unashamedly makes the most of the formidable figures of his two female stars, the Caron-like Mathilda May and the lascivious-looking Virginia Madsen, by getting their clothes off in two-way (two ways) and three-way sex scenes. Shame on you Danny Huston: father John would not have approved, we're sure, of this meretricious piece, whose sole saving graces are its atmosphere and (bogus) Paris settings. Madsen and May do look luscious, but never sound quite convinced about the lines they're saying. They are, however, better than most of the cast.

Bedazzled ❶
1967, UK, 107 mins, colour
Dir: Stanley Donen
Stars: Peter Cook, Dudley Moore, Eleanor Bron, Raquel Welch, Barry Humphries
Rating: ★★

After their success on British TV, this was Peter Cook and Dudley Moore's biggest attempt to break into the world of mainline film comedy. But the most successful sequence in this story of a little man (Dud) who sells his soul to the Devil (Pete) in return for seven wishes, is the 'leaping nuns', itself a direct transference from television. And, despite several tries later at re-teaming, both of these funny men proved most successful with solo ventures. Raquel Welch puts in a guest appearance here as one of the seven deadly sins. Yes, she's Lust.

Bedelia ○
1946, UK, 90 mins, b/w
Dir: Lance Comfort
Stars: Margaret Lockwood, Ian Hunter, Barry K Barnes, Anne Crawford
Rating: ★★

B

Margaret Lockwood proved in such epics as *The Wicked Lady* and *The Man in Grey* that she could bring an immaculate polish to the parts of evil women. She does it once more in this tale of a bewitching murderess who disposes of one husband after another for their insurance money.

Bedford Incident, The ○ ⓥ

1965, US, 105 mins, b/w
Dir: James B Harris
Stars: Richard Widmark, Sidney Poitier, James MacArthur, Martin Balsam
Rating: ★★★

James Poe, best known for his adaptations of Tennessee Williams' plays for the screen (*Cat on a Hot Tin Roof, Summer and Smoke*), here contributes a concise, brittle screenplay which does a lot to build up the tension in the story of an American nuclear warship tracking a Russian atomic submarine, as both steer an uneasy course through icebergs off the coast of Greenland. Richard Widmark is superb as the insanely patriotic warship skipper who takes his men to the limits of their endurance and his country to the brink of war.

Bedknobs and Broomsticks ⊙

1971, US, 117 mins, colour
Dir: Robert Stevenson
Stars: Angela Lansbury, David Tomlinson, Roddy McDowall, Sam Jaffe, Bruce Forsyth
Rating: ★★★

Disney follow-up to *Mary Poppins,* with some enchanting cartoon segments (directed by Ward Kimball) inserted into its live-action story about a trio of evacuee children who undergo some remarkable adventures in 1940 with the assistance of a down-to-earth witch (personably portrayed by *Murder She Wrote*'s Angela Lansbury). The undersea sequences, with their accompanying song – 'Bobbing Along on the Bottom of the Beautiful Briny Sea' – will delight younger viewers. It was artfully reissued by Disney with the selling line 'You'll believe a woman can fly!'

Bedlam ●

1946, US, 80 mins, b/w
Dir: Mark Robson
Stars: Boris Karloff, Anna Lee
Rating: ★★

Addicts of the macabre should on no account miss this. The last of the famous Val Lewton/RKO horror classics of the Forties, this has a fine sense of period atmosphere, filling one with revulsion for the conditions in which unfortunate asylum inmates are forced to exist. Anna Lee gives one of her best performances as the intrepid heroine.

Bed of Roses ○ ⓥ

1996, US, 86 mins, colour
Dir: Michael Goldenberg
Stars: Christian Slater, Mary Stuart Masterson, Pamela Segall
Rating: ★★

You really want to cheer for a good old-fashioned romantic movie like this one: the trouble is, though, that it's just too Mills & Boonish for its own good. Christian Slater's a florist (thus the title) smitten with smooth, smart merchant banker Mary Stuart Masterson; she has problems, though, that means the path to true love will be anything but the bed of roses of the title. The stars are both good, if not perhaps as charismatic as you would expect; but these are underwritten roles that never make the deep cut into your emotions that this sort of thing requires if we're to sniffle at the inevitable happy ending. In support, Pamela Segall shines as Masterson's lacking-in-social-graces friend.

Bedroom Window, The ● ⓥ

1987, US, 115 mins, colour
Dir: Curtis Hanson
Stars: Steve Guttenberg, Elizabeth McGovern, Isabelle Huppert, Paul Shenar
Rating: ★★★

A silly but entertaining thriller which follows some unexpected paths to reach a familiar chase-and-rescue, trap-the-killer climax. Steve Guttenberg fairly convincingly takes a change of pace as the yuppie executive whose affair with the boss's wife (Isabelle Huppert, not very good) leads them to the edge of a whirlpool of circumstance when, just after sex, she witnesses a psycho attacking a young girl (Elizabeth McGovern). Knowing she can't tell the police because of their affair, Guttenberg volunteers to be the witness; when, through a hazardous chain of events, Guttenberg himself becomes a suspect, Huppert refuses to come to his aid. Although it gets nowhere near Hitchcock's black logic, the film's hook of suspense works well enough to keep us snapping at the bait until an undeniably tense and exciting climax, worked out in fairly formula fashion by director Curtis Hanson. Not even Hitch, though, could have helped McGovern, otherwise solid,

bring off a bar-room sequence in which she has to 'lure' the killer into following her.

Bedtime for Bonzo ⊙

1951, US, 83 mins, b/w
Dir: Norman Taurog
Stars: Ronald Reagan, Diana Lynn, Walter Slezak
Rating: ★★

Ronald Reagan stars in a bright comedy that's often cited as the lowpoint of his career, presumably on the grounds that it teamed him with a chimp. But it's certainly better than one or two other films he made at this time, and shows him to be a relaxed comedy player undeterred by the inevitability of being upstaged by an animal. Diana Lynn is a delightful heroine and the chimpanzee (who died tragically in a fire soon after the film had been completed) is hilarious.

Bedtime Story ○

1941, US, 85 mins, b/w
Dir: Alexander Hall
Stars: Fredric March, Loretta Young, Robert Benchley
Rating: ★★★

A sparkling, racy romantic comedy with the accent on laughs, made by director Alexander Hall hard on the heels of his classic fantasy-farce, *Here Comes Mr Jordan.* Wittily scripted by Richard Flournoy, who cut his writing teeth on the earliest (and best) of the *Blondie* comedies, the plot's developments keep stars Fredric March and Loretta Young on their toes – just as well since they're confronted by a battery of supporting scene-stealers, including Eve Arden, Robert Benchley, Helen Westley and Joyce Compton. And, thanks in part to Joseph Walker's top-grade photography, Loretta has never looked lovelier.

Bedtime Story ○

1964, US, 99 mins, colour
Dir: Ralph Levy
Stars: Marlon Brando, David Niven, Shirley Jones
Rating: ★★★

'But isn't there a name for men who get money from women?', says David Niven to Marlon Brando in this smoothly crafted entertainment. 'Yeah,' replies Brando. 'Smart!' Both men are confidence tricksters – in very different circles, Niven being an upper-crust devil – but Brando's upstart learns fast. Soon the rivals are battling it out for the rogues' kingdom of the Riviera. Both Brando and Niven give excellent performances in this polished, pleasant comedy that's enjoyable without being uproarious and shot in terrific Technicolor. Remade in 1988 with Steve Martin and Michael Caine, as *Dirty Rotten Scoundrels*.

Beethoven ○ ⓥ

1992, US, 87 mins, colour
Dir: Brian Levant
Stars: Charles Grodin, Bonnie Hunt, Stanley Tucci, Dean Jones, Oliver Platt, David Duchovny
Rating: ★★

If you love oversized, slobbering pooches then this mutt comedy will be right up your kennel. The title character is a 185lb Saint Bernard dog. Stolen as a puppy, he stumbles into the lives of the Newton family – much to the annoyance of father (Charles Grodin). The human cast, a pretty good one by the standards of this sort of romp, all contribute well, but even so are constantly upstaged by their massive fourlegged co-star. Good, clean family fun, thank goodness, with a particularly good role for Dean Jones, well at home in Disney-style romps in his days as a star but here enjoying himself hugely as the villain.

Beethoven's 2nd ○ ⓥ

1993, US, 89 mins, colour
Dir: Rod Daniel
Stars: Charles Grodin, Bonnie Hunt, Debi Mazar
Rating: ★

A pretty basic doggy comedy with a bit of plot-pinching from *101 Dalmatians*. Beethoven the Saint Bernard falls in love with Missy, a lady dog owned by the monstrous Regina, and subsequently (after a lot of romantic music and twosome shots) has four puppies which the children of Beethoven's reluctant master (Charles Grodin) hide in the basement. Since the family is broke, it would seem to be easier to sell the pups. But no. Even father agrees to keep them, thus setting the rest of the plot in motion in which Regina (Debi Mazar), in true Cruella De Vil style, decides to get the profit-making litter for herself. The rest of the story is very simple fun that will keep young children amused while dad does a crossword. Best scene: Beethoven pulling down half a holiday cabin (thus saving his teenage mistress from rape) and dowsing its partying occupants in the adjoining lake.

Beetlejuice ① ⓥ

1988, US, 92 mins, colour
Dir: Tim Burton
Stars: Alec Baldwin, Geena Davis, Michael Keaton, Jeffrey Jones, Winona Ryder, Sylvia Sidney
Rating: ★★★

Tim Burton's unstructured but visually delightful live-action cartoon provides Mchael Keaton, looking like Ken Dodd after an accident, with a nonstar-billed but definitely star part as the raucous and repulsive 'bio-exorciser' Betelgeuse, who can only be contacted when his name is pronounced (correctly) three consecutive times. Among those who feel the need to contact him are Mr and Mrs Maitland (Alec Baldwin and Geena Davis), newly-deads who are confined to a living hell in their own home which is being destroyed by its obnoxious new owners, a city couple with a daughter (Winona Ryder) majoring in weirdness. Burton's quirky vision of the afterlife springs into life only when the grotesque Keaton's on screen. But, although it needed to be a bit sharper, this witches' brew is still free and easy fun.

Before and After ● ⓥ

1995, US, 108 mins, colour
Dir: Barbet Schroeder
Stars: Meryl Streep, Liam Neeson Edward Furlong, Alfred Molina, John Heard
Rating: ★

It isn't often you'll see a mainline film with such stars as Meryl Streep and Liam Neeson that turns out as badly as this. A family is thrown into turmoil when their son's girlfriend is killed and the boy takes flight, leaving bloodstained clothes and tools in the back of his car. This is certainly a viable dramatic situation, but writer Ted Tally has totally failed to construct a watchable story around it. What really happened is made clear after an hour, leaving the film with nowhere to go, despite the writer's efforts to make the protagonists tell different stories. You keep thinking there must be something more to this, some twist, but in the end there isn't. The framework of the plot, such as it is, leaves Barbet Schroeder's clumsy direction no room to create dramatic tension. What attracted the stars to the script as written can only be guessed; but their strained performances, as it tries very unconvincingly to make them wrangle, are evidence of their problems. Static, halting, dull and dismal.

Before Sunrise ● ⓥ

1995, US, 101 mins, colour
Dir: Richard Linklater
Stars: Ethan Hawke, Julie Delpy
Rating: ★

Not at all like director Richard Linklater's previous films *Slacker* and *Dazed and Confused,* but unfortunately just as tedious. It's hard to see how anyone thought this story could work in this day and age and certainly with writing of such poor quality. A French student meets an American student on a train and stops off with him in Vienna, where they wander around falling in love. Julie Delpy, as the girl, is an actress of some charm; but opposite her she has Ethan Hawke, an actor of limited expression and no charm at all. In any case, both of them are soon bested by the banality of the dialogue. 'Why is it,' asks Hawke, 'that a dog sleeping in the sun is beautiful, but a guy trying to get money out of a bank in the street looks like a moron?' Ah, there's depth for you. And this lad's no fool. 'That's the Danube over there,' says Delpy. 'Ah,' says Hawke, quick as a flash, 'that's the river, right?' When he tells us, though that he's 'sick of myself because I'm with myself all the time', he does at least have us on his side.

Before Winter Comes ①

1968, UK, 102 mins, colour
Dir: J Lee Thompson
Stars: David Niven, Topol, Anna Karina, John Hurt, Anthony Quayle
Rating: ★

One of the films that Israeli star Topol made on the strength of his stage success (later repeated in the film version) in *Fiddler on the Roof*. Here he plays a kind of jack-of-all-trades at a camp for displaced persons in Austria just after World War Two. Pretty Technicolor photography by Gilbert Taylor almost compensates for the non-emergence of any positive storyline, and there's a good performance by John Hurt as an eager but inexperienced junior officer.

Beggar's Opera, The ○

1952, UK, 94 mins, colour
Dir: Peter Brook
Stars: Laurence Olivier, Stanley Holloway, George Devine, Dorothy Tutin
Rating: ★★★

John Gay's colourful musical play eventually begot the memorable *Threepenny Opera*. But here's the original version of the story of the scoundrel awaiting execution, and the women who create his lifeline.

B

Laurence Olivier (as Macbeth) and Stanley Holloway sing their own songs, the rest of the cast is superbly dubbed by operatic experts. Vivid, vigorous and stimulating, if perhaps never quite true cinema. Brilliant Technicolor photography by Guy Green, who could always be relied on for a first-class job, and a small early role for Kenneth Williams.

Beguiled, The ❶ ⓥ

1970, US, 109 mins, colour
Dir: Don Siegel
Stars: Clint Eastwood, Geraldine Page, Elizabeth Hartman
Rating: ★★★

'Guess you're drying up like the rest of us women round here,' murmurs the housekeeper to the milkless cow - a comment which encapsulates the content of this, perhaps the strangest yet most spellbinding film that the *Dirty Harry* combination of Clint Eastwood and director Don Siegel ever made. Ostensibly a close-knit drama with a background of the American Civil War, the story soon develops into a kind of full blooded Southern states melodrama, smouldering with suppressed passions, at which Geraldine Page excels. Once again she's a fading Southern belle, brooding over the past, and here in charge of a seminary for young ladies which is turned into a hotbed of intrigue with the arrival of a wounded Unionist soldier who soon reveals his opportunist nature.

Behemoth the Sea Monster ❶
(aka: The Giant Behemoth)

1959, UK, 70 mins, colour
Dir: Eugene Lourie, Douglas Hickox
Stars: Gene Evans, Andre Morell, Leigh Madison
Rating: ★★

Monster-from-the-depths film co-directed by Eugene Lourie – once production designer for director Jean Renoir – and Douglas Hickox. Hickox, then only 30, later made *Sitting Target* and *Brannigan* with John Wayne. Brisk, punchy and good of its kind.

Behind the Mask ○

1958, UK, 99 mins, colour
Dir: Brian Desmond Hurst
Stars: Michael Redgrave, Tony Britton, Cari Mohner
Rating: ★★

Vanessa Redgrave made a low-key screen debut in this serious-minded hospital drama made as a vehicle for her distinguished father, Michael Redgrave, who plays a wealthy, deeply caring surgeon constantly at odds with dispassionate associates. Brian Desmond Hurst's busy direction keeps our interest going, and there's sharp Eastman Colour photography along those white corridors by the Oscar-winning Robert Krasker.

Behold a Pale Horse ❶

1964, US, 118 mins, b/w
Dir: Fred Zinnemann
Stars: Gregory Peck, Anthony Quinn, Omar Sharif
Rating: ★

Made just after *Lawrence of Arabia,* in which Omar Sharif scored a great personal success, this very slow adventure film has him as a priest caught between an ex-guerilla leader and the police chief who has sworn to catch him. The director is the distinguished Fred Zinnemann, and the journey on film before the adversaries finally clash, though long, is often pictorially beautiful. But, in the acting clash, the stars are all put in the shade by Raymond Pellegrin's portrait of an informer – drawn to the life.

Being There ○ ⓥ

1979, US, 130 mins, colour
Dir: Hal Ashby
Stars: Peter Sellers, Shirley MacLaine, Melvyn Douglas, Jack Warden, Richard Basehart
Rating: ★★

If you like comedies of embarrassment, then this simple-minded black farce will delight you. Peter Sellers was nominated for an Academy Award as the illiterate middle-aged gardener who, in a few days, moves from a sheltered existence through a ludicrously improbable series of misunderstandings to candidacy for the United States presidency. But it was Melvyn Douglas who took the film's Oscar as his benefactor.

Believers, The ● ⓥ

1987, US, 113 mins, colour
Dir: John Schlesinger
Stars: Martin Sheen, Helen Shaver, Robert Loggia, Harris Yulin, Jimmy Smits
Rating: ★

An unfortunate title for a nasty voodoo chiller full of improbabilities and implausibilities. A pity, for a lot of it is excitingly made by director John Schlesinger; it is events rather than script that torpedo this one amidships. A good cast does its best to lend credibility to the story of a psychotherapist

(Martin Sheen) who has lost his wife in an accident in the home and moves with his small son (engagingly played by Harley Cross) to another city where he finds that boys are being slaughtered in the cause of some obscure and evil sideshoot of a tribal religion. Sheen, Helen Shaver, Robert Loggia and others have undoubtedly registered better elsewhere, even though they give *The Believers* all that their director could ask.

Bell, Book and Candle ○

1958, US, 103 mins, colour
Dir: Richard Quine
Stars: James Stewart, Kim Novak, Jack Lemmon, Hermione Gingold, Elsa Lanchester
Rating: ★★★

This delightful witchcraft comedy is fun all the way and allows James Stewart, Jack Lemmon and Kim Novak to let their hair down in no uncertain fashion, Lemmon in particular having a great time as an impish warlock. The film is almost stolen from all of them by a talented Siamese cat called Pyewacket.

Bell Bottom George ○

1943, UK, 97 mins, b/w
Dir: Marcel Varnel
Stars: George Formby
Rating: ★

George Formby's film career was dipping into decline when he made this wartime caper which has three scriptwriters trying to think up new things for the lad from Lancashire to do. Comedy expert Marcel Varnel makes the most of what they devise and George sings the title song and 'Swim Little Fish' among others.

Belle de Jour ● ⓥ

1967, France/Italy, 100 mins, colour
Dir: Luis Buñuel
Stars: Catherine Deneuve, Jean Sorel, Michel Piccoli
Rating: ★★★

A surrealistic voyage into the mind of a bored, wealthy housewife (Catherine Deneuve) who leads the double life of afternoon prostitution. Director Luis Buñuel blends memory, fantasy and reality seamlessly, and it is never certain if what is seen is reality or fantasy. An exquisite and spellbinding film whose moral tone (Buñuel refuses to judge his character's actions) shocked Mary Whitehouse and her supporters into a vocal campaign on its first TV screening.

Belle of New York, The ⊙

1952, US, 82 mins, colour
Dir: Charles Walters
Stars: Fred Astaire, Vera-Ellen, Marjorie Main, Keenan Wynn
Rating: ★★★

A lighter-than-air MGM period musical with Vera-Ellen as the nimble Fred's leading lady. An attractive score by Harry Warren and Johnny Mercer includes 'Seeing's Believing' (well-named, since the stars literally dance on air to it) and one that became something of an Astaire trademark, 'I Wanna Be a Dancin' Man'. Alice Pearce, who scored such a hit in another MGM musical, *On the Town* (as Gene Kelly's wallflower date), raises more laughs here as a sassy Salvation Army girl.

Belle of the Nineties ○

1934, US, 73 mins, b/w
Dir: Leo McCarey
Stars: Mae West, Roger Pryor, John Mack Brown
Rating: ★★

Mae West in full flood (or, at least, in as full a flood as contemporary censorship allowed) in a typical vehicle scripted by her and thus giving her the chance to use all her co-stars as stooges off whom to bounce her memorable one-liners. If her screenplay owes more to vaudeville melodramas than anything else, it does allow her to sing 'My Old Flame', 'American Beauty' and 'Troubled Waters', with Duke Ellington's Orchestra in nifty support. Roger Pryor and Johnny Mack Brown are among those caught up in the whirlwind from the West and director Leo McCarey knows what he is doing.

Belles of St Trinian's, The ⊙

1954, UK, 91 mins, b/w
Dir: Frank Launder
Stars: Alastair Sim, Joyce Grenfell, George Cole, Hermione Baddeley
Rating: ★★★

The first and best of the crazy comedies devoted to the merry, madcap, mayhem-bent misses of St Trinian's School, created by cartoonist Ronald Searle. Alastair Sim, helped by witty dialogue that one can almost see him savour, is a riot in the dual roles of a headmistress of dubious honesty and her brother, a bookmaker of even more dubious morals.

Belle Starr ○ ⓥ

1941, US, 87 mins, colour
Dir: Irving Cummings
Stars: Gene Tierney, Randolph Scott, Dana Andrews, John Sheppard, Elizabeth Patterson
Rating: ★★★

Back in the days when the Technicolor Western was big and broad, they made films like the original *Belle Starr*. Ernest Palmer and Ray Rennahan's colour photography is as lush as it comes, the action is just sufficient and doesn't intrude on the well-handled love interest. Gene Tierney, always at her best as tough cookies, is just right as the gun-toting heroine, while Randolph Scott would have to wait more than 15 years for comparable hard-hitting roles. This certainly arouses an unusual amount of emotion for a film of its kind, with its excellent story and superior supporting performances from Dana Andrews, John Sheppard (later Shepperd Strudwick) and Louise Beavers.

Bell for Adano, A ○

1945, US, 104 mins, b/w
Dir: Henry King
Stars: Gene Tierney, John Hodiak, William Bendix, Richard Conte
Rating: ★★★

John Hodiak never realised his full potential in Hollywood films - except in the leading role of this touching, human account of an American army unit in charge of a small Italian town during World War Two. The many characters are vividly coloured in, and Henry King's sensitive direction is in tune with his subject throughout.

Bellman and True ● ⓥ

1987, UK, 122 mins, colour
Dir: Richard Loncraine
Stars: Bernard Hill, Derek Newark, Kieran O'Brien, Richard Hope, Frances Tomelty, Ken Bones
Rating: ★★

Deliberately doomy and tortuously long (with lots of shots of people in rooms thinking), this is a crime film with distinct ambitions in the direction of stature. The lugubrious Bernard Hill can scarcely raise a smile as the alcoholic computer gadgets expert reluctantly drawn into a big-time caper of increasing complexity. The first half of the film concerns his entrapment (via the stepson who lives with him, running from lodging to lodging), the second the planning and execution of the raid (on a major holding bank) itself. There's too little of such crustily amusing dialogue as the gang boss (Derek Newark) employs with his tunnellers ('Thanks lads. If you hurry you might just catch the last tube') and

just too much gloom and doom. The slow motion at the beginning is maddening although it does set the film's stately pace in which the bursts of action towards the end come as a welcome relief.

Bells Are Ringing ○

1960, US, 127 mins, colour
Dir: Vincente Minnelli
Stars: Judy Holliday, Dean Martin, Fred Clark
Rating: ★★

This musical-comedy spree was the last film made by Judy Holliday before she died of throat cancer a few years later. Here she's her usual dizzy self as a girl who runs a telephone answering service and gets involved in the lives of her customers. The voice she falls in love with belongs to Dean Martin. A lengthy and slow-moving piece in this form, it was originally a stage hit for Judy and was adapted for the screen by Betty Comden and Adolph Green, who wrote the play with Jule Styne. Some fun, with some good songs, too, including 'Just in Time' and 'The Party's Over', even if the script hasn't quite the wit or invention to carry the show.

Bells of St Mary's, The ○ ⓥ

1945, US, 126 mins, b/w
Dir: Leo McCarey
Stars: Bing Crosby, Ingrid Bergman, Henry Travers, Ruth Donnelly, Rhys Williams
Rating: ★★★

Bing Crosby stars again as Father O'Malley in a sequel to *Going My Way*, for which he had won an Oscar in the previous year. Both films, which are among his best-remembered, blend pathos and humour with perfect professionalism. Here he teams delightfully with Ingrid Bergman, who plays a nun running a school on a shoestring. The title song, sung by Bing, was a huge hit at the time, and the film was at the top of the box-office for its year.

Belly of an Architect, The ●

1987, UK/Italy, 118 mins, colour
Dir: Peter Greenaway
Stars: Brian Dennehy, Chloe Webb
Rating: ★★

After years of contributing memorable supporting performances to a wide variety of films, heavyweight American character actor Brian Dennehy achieved star status in this art-house work from Peter Greenaway, director of *The Draughtsman's Contract*. Dennehy

B

is the architect of the title, mounting a prestigious exhibition in Rome but obsessed by intestinal problems which may, or may not, be phantom symptoms parallelling his much younger wife's pregnancy. Despite Dennehy's imposing presence and the excellent use of ravishing Roman locations, the film fails to engage the emotions because of the director's typically cool approach and his reluctance to confront the drama head-on.

Beloved Infidel ○
1959, US, 123 mins, colour
Dir: Henry King
Stars: Gregory Peck, Deborah Kerr, Eddie Albert, Philip Ober
Rating: ★

F Scott Fitzgerald, on whose novel the films of *The Great Gatsby* were based, gets the Hollywood biopic treatment in this hand tearjerker. Directed in a curiously tired fashion by Henry King, who has such excellent films as *Wait 'Til the Sun Shines, Nellie, In Old Chicago, The Gunfighter, Twelve O'Clock High* (the last two with Gregory Peck) and *Carousel* to his credit.

Ben ●
1972, US, 95 mins, colour
Dir: Phil Karlson
Stars: Lee Harcourt Montgomery, Joseph Campanella
Rating: ★★★

Restored to the big city by night - the surroundings in which he has always worked best – director Phil Karlson made a belated return to something like form with this no-frills, no-nonsense sequel to *Willard*, relating the further adventures of Ben, the rat who walked by himself. The pursuit of Ben by police through the city's storm drains could, in fact, just as easily be a manhunt as a rat-hunt. Karlson directs his action – and its integral if familiar elements of harassed policeman, sympathetic child who befriends rat, and fast-talking, cynical reporter – with a brusque intensity against sombre, low-key settings, building steadily to the fiery climax.

Bend of the River
See: Where the River Bends

Beneath the Planet of the Apes ● ⓥ
1970, US, 95 mins, colour
Dir: Ted Post
Stars: James Franciscus, Charlton Heston, Kim Hunter
Rating: ★★★

Although it lacks the impact of the actual premise of the original *Planet of the Apes,* this first sequel is in many ways more exciting and visually stylish than the original, with a good script and some particularly suspenseful and striking scenes in the overgrown ruins of what was once the New York subway. James Franciscus takes over the reins of the principal role from Charlton Heston, who makes a crucial cameo appearance towards the end of the film. This is, incidentally, the only Ape film in which Roddy McDowall does not appear. His role as Cornelius is here played by David Watson.

Beneath the Twelve-Mile Reef ○
1953, US, 102 mins, colour
Dir: Robert D Webb
Stars: Robert Wagner, Terry Moore, Richard Boone, Gilbert Roland, J Carrol Naish, Peter Graves
Rating: ★★

The vogue for underwater photography was still at its height when director Robert D Webb decided to dip below the waves for this swimsuited love story. Robert Wagner and Terry Moore (female) are the children of rival families of Greek sponge fishermen and the fleets' constant quarrelling provides the cue for plenty of underwater adventure, all stunningly well photographed with the Florida coastline standing in amazingly well for Greece. The cameraman's achievements reach their peak in a fierce underwater fight at the climax of the film, as two young divers battle each other and the ocean kelp that threatens to strangle them.

Benefit of the Doubt ●
1992, US, 89 mins, colour
Dir: Jonathan Heap
Stars: Donald Sutherland, Amy Irving
Rating: RB

A lethally silly thriller that gets worse as it goes on. We all know that softly spoken, chillingly smiling Donald Sutherland is a bad guy who has done 22 years for killing his wife and, presently released, aims to revenge himself on the now 34-year-old daughter (Amy Irving) who put him away. The film's job is to make us believe that Irving and her 10-year-old son could be so taken in as to restore her father to their lives, believing him innocent. It fails miserably – especially as Sutherland is never sympathetic, and soon starts bumping off other people in Irving's life. Performances are

not good and the movie was bad for Irving's faltering career; have a good laugh towards the end – it's the only emotion you'll be able to summon up. Badly directed by Jonathan Heap, whose action is so unconvincing as to rob proceedings of any menace.

Bengal Brigade ○
(aka: Bengal Rifles)
1954, US, 87 mins, colour
Dir: Laslo Benedek
Stars: Rock Hudson, Arlene Dahl, Ursula Thiess, Dan O'Herlihy, Torin Thatcher
Rating: ★★

This adventure story was an unusual subject for Laslo Benedek to direct, so soon after making Marlon Brando's *The Wild One.* One suspects he saw more nuances in Hall Hunter's original novel than Universal-International envisaged in the finished film, which they saw as just a Rock Hudson action adventure. Hudson plays with some sensitivity the young man court-martialled in India in 1856, for disobeying a superior's order – even though his action led to the capture of a rebel-held fort. Arlene Dahl and Ursula Thiess are merely decorative, but there are strong performances from Dan O'Herlihy and Torin Thatcher as two other officers.

Bengal Rifles
See: Bengal Brigade

Ben-Hur ○ ⓥ
1959, US, 212 mins, colour
Dir: William Wyler
Stars: Charlton Heston, Jack Hawkins, Stephen Boyd, Haya Harareet, Hugh Griffith, Sam Jaffe
Rating: ★★★★★

Despite the spectacular success of such action set-pieces as the chariot race, you may find that it is the moving moments that remain the most permanent memories of William Wyler's truly magnificent film of the hoary old story by General Lew Wallace, which was filmed several times in silent days, but hadn't been remade since 1926. The dialogue (restructured by Christopher Fry from Karl Tunberg's original screenplay), photography and direction combine to cast a potent spell – movie magic, indeed, completely overwhelming one's resistance to the Victorian-style sentiments of the original material. Charlton Heston is a tower of strength, as always, but perhaps has never before or since expressed so eloquently the dignity of the human spirit, surviving the impossible. Haya Harareet is tender and true as Esther, Stephen Boyd sharply and magnetically evil as Messala. 11 Oscars: Best Picture, director, actor (Heston), supporting actor (Hugh Griffith), colour photography, costume design, music (by Miklos Rozsa), art direction, editing, sound effects and sound recording.

Benji ⊙
1974, US, 86 mins, colour
Dir: Joe Camp
Stars: Edgar Buchanan, Peter Breck, Patsy Garrett
Rating: ★★★

A doggie film for youngsters, much along the lines of the *Lassie* movies of the Forties. Benji (a very talented dog actor) is a mongrel stray who becomes a hero after two children to whom he's attached succumb to kidnappers Although there's rather too much slow motion in the film, the kidnap section of its story engenders an amount of tension and should prove thrilling for younger viewers.

Benji the Hunted ⊙
1987, US, 88 mins, colour
Dir: Joe Camp
Stars: Frank Inn, Red.Steagall
Rating: ★★★★

Humans get pushed well into the background in the fourth adventure of filmland's most popular pooch since *Lassie*. Benji is obviously superbly-trained and many of his stunts are truly amazing, during a story that has him shipwrecked and caring for an orphan brood of cougar cubs. There's a big bad wolf and mercifully a minimum of script as Benji's usual director, Joe Camp, tells the story almost entirely without people or dialogue. Fascinating, colourful stuff and so cleanly shot in the wilds of Washington and Oregon that you can almost smell the country air.

Benny & Joon ◑ Ⓥ
1993, US, 98 mins, colour
Dir: Jeremiah Chechik
Stars: Johnny Depp, Mary Stuart Masterson, Aidan Quinn, Julianne Moore
Rating: ★★★

This romance is offbeat all right, but pretty sad too: its lovers don't stand a chance of anything permanent in the world. Joon (Juniper) – Mary Stuart Masterson – is a mentally unbalanced (?schizophrenic) young woman living, on the edge of tantrums and in the care of her brother Benny (Aidan Quinn) who has just lost their latest housekeep-

er to one of Joon's fits. Into their lives comes Sam (Johnny Depp), a semi-literate simpleton who dresses like Buster Keaton, has an intimate mastery of silent-film comedy technique and toasts bread with a steam iron. Joon falls heavily: Benny throws Sam out. The lovers run away but Joon is overcome by noises in her head and ends up in a psychiatric hospital. There's a happy ending– of sorts. Delicately played by its leading trio, but especially by Aidan Quinn in the most difficult of the three roles, this is an admirable, but unenjoyable and pretty despairing film.

Benny Goodman Story, The ○
1955, US, 117 mins, colour
Dir: Valentine Davies
Stars: Steve Allen, Donna Reed
Rating: ★★★★

Bright, lively musical biopic, confidently made by Universal-International hard on the heels of its success with *The Glenn Miller Story*. Steve Allen is no James Stewart, it's true, but the film is riddled with jazz greats, including Kid Ory, Lionel Hampton, Martha Tilton and Gene Krupa. Donna Reed gets a chance to show her warmer side as Goodman's wife and oozes charm but the music makes the film; it includes clarinet solos dubbed by Goodman himself.

Bernadette ⊙
1987, France, 118 mins, colour
Dir: Jean Delannoy
Stars: Sydney Penny, Jean-Marc Bory, Michel Simonnet, Roland Lesaffre
Rating: ★★★

A solid, sincere version of the 19th century visions of Bernadette at Lourdes, told in an affecting but straightforward manner and, almost unbelievably, with scarcely a tedious moment. Credit this to the storytelling skills of director Jean Delannoy and to the hypnotic performance of teenage American actress Sydney Penny, who avoids all temptations to embellish her role to its detriment, yet shows sufficient feeling to make us believe in Bernadette as a person. The results are likely to bring more than one lump to the throat before Bernadette's tale is told.

Berserk ◑
1967, UK, 96 mins, colour
Dir: Jim O'Connolly
Stars: Joan Crawford, Ty Hardin, Diana Dors, Michael Gough
Rating: ★★

La Crawford queens it in style over a series of grisly murders at a circus. Red herrings abound, and, like Superintendent Robert Hardy, you may have a little trouble in spotting the killer.

Bert Rigby, You're a Fool ◑
1989, US, 94 mins, colour
Dir: Carl Reiner
Stars: Robert Lindsay, Anne Bancroft, Corbin Bernsen, Robbie Coltrane
Rating: ★★

Rather uneasily dedicated to Gene Kelly, this is a ramshackle comedy-musical with a ragbag of ingredients that just don't hang together. Everything in this film seems to be operating at half-cock, with the exception of its leading man, the sparkling Robert Lindsay, who gets some chance, though not enough, to demonstrate the song-and-dance talents that took him to stardom on the London and New York stages in *Me and My Girl*. Lindsay's a miner who dreams of stardom and turning his tatty British north country bingo hall into a glittering palace of entertainment. His subsequent misadventures on the road and then in California raise a few smiles, but are pretty rough-and-ready stuff, a criticism that could never be levelled at the elegant Mr L, doing his imitations of Keaton, Chaplin, Astaire and Kelly with uncanny style.

Best Defense ◑ Ⓥ
1984, US, 94 mins, colour
Dir: Willard Huyck
Stars: Dudley Moore, Eddie Murphy, Kate Capshaw, George Dzundza, Helen Shaver
Rating: ★

Dudley Moore teamed with Eddie Murphy sounds a mouth-watering prospect, but in fact the Murphy sequences were added on at a later date to try and save a not-very-funny slapstick comedy. Dudley is an engineer working on America's new Supertank who gets involved with industrial spies and Eddie comes in as the luckless lieutenant who has to field-test the new weapon, managing to get lost behind enemy lines in the middle of a war. One of Dud's duds which not even Murphy at his most strident and frenetic can rescue.

Best Friends ○
1982, US, 116 mins, colour
Dir: Norrnan Jewison
Stars: Burt Reynolds, Goldie Hawn, Jessica Tandy, Barnard Hughes
Rating: ★★

B

There are a few good laughs in this rather muffled comedy of marital discord, most of them provided by the interplay between Goldie Hawn and Burt Reynolds as two live-together screenwriters who decide on (his) impulse to get married. A honeymoon spent at her and his parents' homes – his mother tucks him up in a single bed at night and asks him if he'd like her to leave the light on – is such a total disaster that it seems the marriage is wrecked. Finally torrential storms wreck their apartment and wash away his car. 'That's not fair', wails Reynolds. 'That's heaven relieving itself on my bed'. What else can happen? Only a contrived happy ending, that's what.

Best Little Whorehouse In Texas, The ◐ ⓥ
1982, US, 110 mins, colour
Dir: Colin Higgins
Stars: Burt Reynolds, Dolly Parton, Dom DeLuise, Charles Durning
Rating: ★★

A zingy little musical stretched out rather uncomfortably over two hours with a couple of hummable songs and hardly enough plot to cover a whorehouse customer's embarrassment in a police raid. Like June, Dolly Parton is bustin' out all over as the madame of a bordello, established in 1910 and happily accepted by the local county, which suddenly becomes the centre of a morals storm. Burt Reynolds gets the chance to sing a zippy duet with Dolly ('Sneakin' Around') as the sheriff who shares her bed and turns a blind eye to the others all around him. And bulky Charles Durning enjoys a few blithe musical moments as the state governor who enjoys 'side-stepping' and sitting on a fence of his own skilful making.

Best Man, The ○
1964, US, 104 mins, b/w
Dir: Franklin Schaffner
Stars: Henry Fonda, Cliff Robertson, Edie Adams, Kevin McCarthy
Rating: ★★★★

If you would bet that it was impossible to make a thrilling drama out of an American presidential nomination campaign, this biting film would see you losing your money. As the contrasting candidates, Henry Fonda and Cliff Robertson both slip quickly into their characters, and there's a wealth of supporting talent, notably Kevin McCarthy as Fonda's agent, veteran Lee Tracy in an acid performance as

the retiring president, and humorist Shelley Berman in a telling little role. The film is excellently lit by cameraman Haskell Wexler, and director Franklin Schaffner keeps a right grip on the flow of the action, right up to one of the most surprising surprise endings you are likely to encounter.

Best of Enemies, The ○ ⓥ
1962, UK/Italy, 104 mins, colour
Dir: Guy Hamilton
Stars: David Niven, Alberto Sordi, Michael Wilding, Harry Andrews
Rating: ★★

An elegantly sardonic comedy about the wartime prison-camp friendship between two officers from opposing sides - one British, one Italian. The British acting contingent is a stalwart one: beside David Niven and Michael Wilding, there are Harry Andrews, promoted from his normal sergeant-major to captain, Ronald Fraser and Bernard Cribbins.

Best of Everything, The ○
1959, US, 122 mins, colour
Dir: Jean Negulesco
Stars: Hope Lange, Robert Evans, Joan Crawford, Stephen Boyd, Diane Baker, Brian Aherne, Louis Jourdan
Rating: ★★★

Slick, opulent and overly complex, this soap-opera has no less than six stories going on at once. That's the nub of the problem: with too little time for deep characterisation everyone ends up as just thumbnail sketches. It's sad to see Joan Crawford billed fifth, but she relishes every minute of her role as an embittered typing-pool scourge. The theme song, sung by Johnny Mathis, won an Oscar nomination for Alfred Newman and Sammy Cahn.

Best of the Badmen ○
1951, US, 84 mins, colour
Dir: Wiliam D Russell
Stars: Robert Ryan, Claire Trevor, Robert Preston, Walter Brennan, Bruce Cabot
Rating: ★★

Too much jaw-jaw and not enough war-war hamper this Western that proves to be yet another post-Civil War story featuring the James Brothers and Younger Brothers. Though it shows signs of promise in its opening scenes, it doesn't rise too far above stereotyped mediocrity thereafter, in spite of a first-rate cast that includes Robert Ryan, Robert Preston, Claire Trevor and Walter Brennan, with Lawrence Tierney mak-

ing a fierce Jesse James. First-class Technicolor photography, too (by the great Edward Cronjager), of the burnished brand so seldom seen today. There's some witty dialogue for Brennan and Bruce Cabot, and another smiling Western villain for Preston, to go with those he played in *Blood on the Moon* and *Whispering Smith*.

Best of the Best ◐ ⓥ
1989, US, 100 mins, colour
Dir: Bob Radler
Stars: Eric Roberts, Christopher Penn, Sally Kirkland, James Earl Jones, Louise Fletcher
Rating: ★

You've seen this chop-socky film before, but the surprising thing about it is that, despite an all-star cast, with seven Oscar nominations between them, it's just as badly acted as any Jean-Claude Van Damme film. 'Yes, but what about your shoulder?', asks Eric Roberts' mum (Louise Fletcher with nothing to do) when he's chosen for the American team against Korea. Well, that's his part of the plot taken care of. Philip Rhee's brother was killed by the Korean he's fighting, so that's the usual revenge motif accounted for. Sally Kirkland and James Earl Jones (who comes closest, but not that close, to coping with the risible dialogue) are the coaches as Roberts goes emotionally way over the top with the help of a screenplay that pulls every clichéd weepie string in the book. The fights are good, but with all these minus factors who cares?

Best of Times, The ◐ ⓥ
1986, US, 103 mins, colour
Dir: Roger Spottiswoode
Stars: Robin Williams, Kurt Russell, Pamela Reed, Holly Palance, M Emmet Walsh, Margaret Whitton
Rating: ★★★

Haunted by his failure to catch a ball that would have given his college a football victory over neighbouring giants, Robin Williams manoeuvres a restaging of the entire game in this affectionate comedy about small-town life and ambitions gone sour. Though it's a film whose appeal to the gut emotions wins through in the end, its leading characters (Williams, Kurt Russell) do get a bit tiresome at times and are more than matched by the warmly sexy Holly Palance and chirpily spicy Pamela Reed who play their loving but long-suffering wives. At times, it's a trudge towards the big game at the end, but it proves to be worth it.

Best Seller ● ⓥ

1987, US, 110 mins, colour
Dir: John Flynn
Stars: James Woods, Brian Dennehy,
Victoria Tennant
Rating: ★★

James Woods, he of the flick-knife
cheekbones and bullet-hole eyes, gets
another chance to play a man you'll
love to hate in this well-begun but
spottily developed thriller. Woods is a
discarded hitman who, with the help of
a cop (Brian Dennehy) who writes
bestsellers, aims to nail the magnate for
whom he eliminated business rivals.
Dennehy is as tough as ever as the
cop, but it's Woods's film. Like the
similar Henry Silva two decades before, it's to his credit that you get a jolt
of guilty pleasure from watching him
dispatch his victims. The ending, incidentally, depends heavily on the
contrivance of a teenage girl hostage
leaving a safe place against orders, and
then running down a stairway where
she can see a killer at bay!

Best Shot ❶ ⓥ
(aka: Hoosiers)

1986, US, 115 mins, colour
Dir: David Anspaugh
Stars: Gene Hackman, Barbara Hershey,
Dennis Hopper
Rating: ★★★★

It's not often that sports films challenge
for a five-star rating, but this one
comes mighty close. Only an over-the-
top last few minutes from the script
and a surfeit of slow-motion that stops
the adrenaline flowing cost David
Anspaugh's basketball hymn-to-the-un-
derdog a gold medal. Otherwise, folks
(to home in on the film's own tone),
this is a real topnotcher which does all
the right things by its familiar elements. And it has the inestimable
Gene Hackman, as the long-banned
sports coach called back from pasture
by an old friend, the headmaster of
tiny Hickory High. Everying goes
wrong at first: firebrand Hackman
kicks one player off his already small
squad, upsets the acting coach and gets
himself thrown off the touch-bench for
yelling at the referee. Last year's star
refuses to play, and one of the team's
fathers (Dennis Hopper, Oscar-nominated), an ex-basketball coach, turns
out to be the town drunk. You could
jot down some of the subsequent developments before you see them but,
thanks to some crafty editing and sensible camera coverage of Hackman's
fevered touchline participation, fore-
knowledge won't stop you getting to

your feet to cheer the Hickory team
on. The performances are wholeheart-
ed and team members nicely
individualised. Best shot is right.

Best Things In Life Are Free, The ○

1956, US, 99 mins, colour
Dir: Michael Curtiz
Stars: Gordon MacRae, Dan Dailey,
Ernest Borgnine, Sheree North
Rating: ★★★★

Sheree North's vitality-packed dancing,
to 'The Black Bottom' and 'The Birth
of the Blues', steals the spotlight from
stars Gordon MacRae, Dan Dailey
and Ernest Borgnine in this gaily-
coloured and enjoyable musical biopic
of the songwriters De Sylva, Brown
and Henderson. Forget the plot, although Tony Galento is fun as a
Kansas City gangster, and concentrate
on a score (put across with panache by
choreographer Rod Alexander and
veteran director Michael Curtiz) that
includes 'Button Up Your Overcoat',
'Sonny Boy', 'Sunny Side Up', 'Broken
Hearted', 'If I Had a Talking Picture
of You' and many more. Songpacked?
You've got it. But the fashion for musicals was fading fast, and this was to
be MacRae's last film of any note.

Best Years of Our Lives, The ○

1946, US, 175 mins, b/w
Dir: William Wyler
Stars: Myrna Loy, Fredric March, Dana
Andrews, Teresa Wright, Harold Russell
Rating: ★★★★

William Wyler's powerful story of
American servicemen returning from
World War Two and fighting to adjust to civilian life. It was a box office
colossus and won Academy Awards
for Sam Goldwyn (as producer), director William Wyler, star Fredric
March, and handless war veteran
Harold Russell. Myrna Loy, never
nominated for an Oscar in a long and
distinguished Hollywood career, was
unjustly neglected here.

Betrayal from the East ○

1945, US, 83 mins, b/w
Dir: William Burke
Stars: Lee Tracy, Nancy Kelly
Rating: ★★

A typical WW2 gung-ho story of love
and honour that is pure fiction but has
the ring of authenticity thanks to seri-
ous-toned narration and an epilogue
by Drew Pearson. The former GI
who gives his all in the defence of the
Panama Canal is played by Lee Tracy,

nominated for an Oscar for his role in
The Best Man in the Sixties.

Betrayed ○
(aka: When Strangers Marry)

1944, US, 67 mins, b/w
Dir: William Castle
Stars: Kim Hunter, Dean Jagger, Robert
Mitchum, Neil Hamilton
Rating: ★★★

This black little drama wastes not a
second of its running time and is far
superior to the horror films for which
its director, William Castle, later became better known. Kim Hunter,
Dean Jagger and Robert Mitchum are
all very effective as the three points of
a deadly triangle.

Betrayed ○

1953, US, 108 mins, colour
Dir: Gottfried Reinhardt
Stars: Clark Gable, Lana Turner, Victor
Mature, Louis Calhern
Rating: ★★

Clark Gable was looking tired and
jaded when he made this rather lacklustre action drama of the wartime
Dutch resistance movement, threatened by a mysterious traitor. It was
shot mostly on location in Holland, far
from his usual stamping grounds.
Victor Mature takes what acting honours are going, as a resistance leader
with a mother fixation.

Betrayed ● ⓥ

1988, US, 127 mins, colour
Dir: Costa-Gavras
Stars: Debra Winger, Tom Berenger,
John Heard, Betsy Blair, John Mahoney
Rating: ★★

Strong and scary stuff, this tough romantic thriller becomes progressively
less believable as the plot goes along.
Debra Winger plays another of her
wry loners as a Department of Justice
agent sent to investigate a Mid-West
widower farmer (Tom Berenger), suspected of carrying out a contract
killing. In so doing, she not only falls
in love with him but uncovers a vast
nest of rats in the shape of an Aryan
supremacy movement akin to the Ku
Klux Klan, with a network of agents
all over America. Solid performances;
a pity about that credibility gap.

Betsy's Wedding ❶ ⓥ

1990, US, 94 mins, colour
Dir: Alan Alda
Stars: Alan Alda, Molly Ringwald, Ally
Sheedy, Joe Pesci, Madeline Kahn, Joey
Bishop, Anthony LaPaglia
Rating: ★★★

B

There hasn't been so much flimsy fun spun round a film marriage since Bette Davis's *Wedding Breakfast*. Alan Alda is the harassed father, determined to stage a grand affair for daughter Molly Ringwald, even though all she wants is a quiet affair at and after the registry office. Strange man Alda. He has wild dreams which end with him wrestling with, or trying to throttle his hapless wife (Madeline Kahn). But then his whole family, a traditional American mix of Jews and Italians, is a little mad. Ringwald is at a fashion design college and wears clothes that make her look, as her future in-laws term it, 'like an explosion in a dress factory'. Second daughter Ally Sheedy is a cop. 'So glad you brought your gun,' remarks mother, 'you never know who's going to break in.' She falls for the dim gangster offspring of daddy's shady business associate (Burt Young). There's lots of gently wisecracking dialogue, courtesy Alda himself, before Betsy is finally married off in a second-class tent (provided by Young) that is rapidly succumbing to a rainstorm of tropical proportions.

Better Off Dead ◐ Ⓥ
1985, US, 97 mins, colour
Dir: Savage Steve Holland
Stars: John Cusack, David Ogden Stiers, Kim Darby, Diane Franklin
Rating: ★★

Although admittedly nutty – almost like a strip from *Mad* magazine come to life - this is a mostly gross and wickedly unfunny teenage comedy that runs like a dream sequence from some other film. John Cusack comes on like a vague teenage second cousin to Woody Allen as the youth who tries to get over the loss of his girlfriend to the school ski champ, while his mother wears reindeer heads at Christmas and serves up green goo for dinner. His father scuttles in and out in his aardvark coat trying to mend windows broken by the paper boy and his little brother constructs laser beams from cereal packets and studies how to build your own space shuttle from household items (he does it in the end). The trouble is that this manic brew's constituents are too heavily underlined to be funny, and its overdrawn characters asked to mug to an alarming degree. But Diane Franklin has impish charm as the French girl who helps Cusack forget and the film grows on you a little as it goes on.

Betty Blue ● Ⓥ
(aka: 37°le Matin)
1986, France, 120 mins, colour
Dir: Jean-Jacques Beineix
Stars: Béatrice Dalle, Jean-Hugues Anglade, Consuelo de Haviland
Rating: ★★★★

Imagine a Bardot film for the Eighties from the man who made *Diva*, then streak it with tinges of Gallic low-life, *Love Story* and the Marx Brothers. You probably still haven't caught the flavour (which is everything) but it's the best we can do! Out by the sea in a setting that could only be in the south of France, a would-be writer and presently general handyman lives in a bungalow on stilts and gets involved with Betty (then-newcomer Béatrice Dalle), who engages in a passionate and uninhibited affair before burning his bungalow down in a gentle hint to him to pursue his writing ambitions in Paris. It isn't long in Paris before poor BB starts getting those strange headaches and the last thread of the plot begins to unravel. Young Dalle, then only 21, a looker with great gappy teeth, jutting lower lip and provocative figure (the wardrobe mistress couldn't have been over-employed on this one) handles her big scenes well towards the end. The film itself is gorgeous to look at, nicely paced and hauntingly scored. A curiosity rather than a masterpiece, but one from a director whose sense of cinema never seems less than at one with his subject.

Between Two Women ○
1944, US, 83 mins, b/w
Dir: Willis Goldbeck
Stars: Lionel Barrymore, Van Johnson
Rating: ★★

Handsome doctor Randall Adams (Van Johnson), called 'Red' in this episode of the Gillespie series, is torn between the charms of wealthy Marilyn Maxwell and ailing Gloria DeHaven. Johnson had become a major star at MGM in the war years, and this was his farewell to Blair Hospital after four films there.

Between Two Worlds ○
1944, US, 112 mins, b/w
Dir: Edward A Blatt
Stars: John Garfield, Paul Henreid, Sydney Greenstreet, Eleanor Parker
Rating: ★★★

The Warner Brothers repertory company is present in something approaching full strength (although it was a pity no room could be found for Peter Lorre) in this doughtily cast version of Sutton Vane's play *Outward Bound*, in which a shipload of dead or dying souls travels between limbo and eternity. Sydney Greenstreet is in his usual formidable form as the 'examiner', (who decides who goes to Heaven and Hell), but John Garfield has so little to do that he hardly justifies his top billing over Paul Henreid and Eleanor Parker, who provide the main thrust of the story as a refugee couple hovering between suicide and redemption.

Beverly Hillbillies, The ◐ Ⓥ
1993, US, 93 mins, colour
Dir: Penelope Spheeris
Stars: Jim Varney, Cloris Leachman, Erika Eleniak, Dabney Coleman, Lily Tomlin, Lea Thompson
Rating: ★★

Fans of one of the best-loved US TV sitcoms of the Sixties won't want to miss this big-budget remake. But they may be disappointed. For, while the one-joke story of a family of hicks from the sticks striking oil and moving to Beverly Hills, thoroughly discomfiting society there, worked brilliantly for half an hour each week, this extended format lacks the punch and pace needed to sustain it past three times that length. Even so, some of it is so silly you can't help laughing and Lily Tomlin has a fine old time as prim (but frequently baffled) secretary Miss Hathaway. Lots of corny knockabout comedy then, plus a cameo by Buddy Ebsen, the original TV Jed in the role taken here by Jim Varney.

Beverly Hills Cop ● Ⓥ
1984, US, 105 mins, colour
Dir: Martin Brest
Stars: Eddie Murphy, Judge Reinhold, Lisa Eilbacher, John Ashton, Ronny Cox, Steven Berkoff
Rating: ★★★

Eddie Murphy's biggest hit, and the one that confirmed his position as a top international star. He fires on all cylinders here, as a tough Detroit cop who decides to track down the man responsible for the murder of an admittedly shady friend. The trail leads to Beverly Hills where Murphy makes friends and enemies and wreaks havoc on the way. He's fast, flip, flash and ahead of the game.

Beverly Hills Cop II ● Ⓥ
1987, US, 102 mins, colour
Dir: Tony Scott
Stars: Eddie Murphy, Judge Reinhold, Jurgen Prochnow, John Ashton, Ronny

Cox, Brigitte Neilsen
Rating: ★★★

This second crime caper for Eddie Murphy's Axel Foley keeps up the standard set by the first, providing fast and furious adult entertainment. Although Murphy's fast talking steals most of the big laughs, Judge Reinhold, as his seemingly-gentle sidekick who proves to have developed a Rambo complex, also makes the most of his opportunities. Villainess Brigitte Nielsen orders her adversaries to 'Eat the floor!' in one of the many memorable lines (screenplay by Larry Ferguson and Warren Skaaren) from perhaps the most-quoted film of the Eighties.

Beverly Hills Cop III ● Ⓥ

1994, US, 104 mins, colour
Dir: John Landis
Stars: Eddie Murphy, Judge Reinhold, Hector Elizondo, John Saxon, Theresa Randle, Alan Young, Stephen McHattie
Rating: ★★★

Eddie Murphy's back one more time as streetsmart Detroit detective Axel Foley in an underrated sequel that deserved to restore the flagging fortunes of its star to a greater degree than it did. After his boss is gunned down, Axel tracks the killer to a California theme park. The fish-out-of-water formula is a bit well-worn, but there's enough action and laughs to satisfy, with director John Landis surprisingly scoring highest marks on the action front. The excellent cast includes a bonus in the reappearance of the manic Bronson Pinchot (from the original *Cop* film) as Serge, this time supplying the ultimate personal survival weapon complete with microwave and CD player!

Beyond a Reasonable Doubt ○ Ⓥ

1956, US, 80 mins, b/w
Dir: Fritz Lang
Stars: Dana Andrews, Joan Fontaine, Sidney Blackmer
Rating: ★★

One of director Fritz Lang's last Hollywood films, this twisty thriller has improved with age, although it still doesn't grip as it should. Dana Andrews is well cast in a role originally intended for Joseph Cotten, but Joan Fontaine seems a little long in the tooth as his fiancee, in a role that called for more sparkle.

Beyond the Blue Horizon ⊙

1942, US, 76 mins, colour
Dir: Alfred Santell
Stars: Dorothy Lamour, Richard Denning, Jack Haley, Patricia Morison
Rating: ★★

Dorothy Lamour was so popular as the maiden bursting into sarong in wartime South Seas adventures that Paramount was actually encouraged to splash out with Technicolor on such tropical escapades as *Aloma of the South Seas*, *Typhoon* and *Rainbow Island*. Dorothy swims with a tiger, ambles with an ape, and tangles (in more ways than one) with jungle boy Richard Denning. The familiar flat features of Abner Biberman (who later turned director on similar spectacular fare) crop up as one of the natives. There's a welcome tongue-in-cheek tone to the proceedings, and cinematographer Charles Boyle at least justifies the studio's outlay on colour.

Beyond the Forest ○

1949, US, 96 mins, b/w
Dir: King Vidor
Stars: Bette Davis, Joseph Cotten, David Brian, Ruth Roman
Rating: ★★★

Supposedly the film that led to the final break between Bette Davis and Warner Brothers, this melodrama, cleverly described by one critic as 'fiercely trashy', looks a whole lot better today. Directed by King Vidor with one eye on symbolism and another on the intensity of the Davis performance, it has a European feel, tensions and innuendoes galore, a classic Davis line in 'What a dump!' and a sensational ending. Davis fans will love it.

Beyond the Limit

See: The Honorary Consul

Beyond the Poseidon Adventure ○

1979, US, 122 mins, colour
Dir: Irwin Allen
Stars: Michael Caine, Sally Field, Telly Savalas, Peter Boyle, Jack Warden, Karl Malden
Rating: ★★

Like its predecessor, this disaster epic is very well acted and excitingly shot. Michael Caine and the perky Sally Field both give their best performances for some time and there are respectable showings from Karl Malden, Shirley Jones and Telly Savalas. There the resemblance to the earlier film, alas, ends. For the script (though written by the capable Nelson Gidding) and situations are really so silly as to make further comparisons

futile. The action, though, is all one would expect from producer-director Irwin Allen, and the film will prove rewarding for undemanding adventure fans.

Beyond Therapy ●

1986, US/France, 93 mins, colour
Dir: Robert Altman
Stars: Julie Hagerty, Jeff Goldblum, Glenda Jackson, Tom Conti, Genevieve Page, Christopher Guest
Rating: ★

Perhaps director Robert Altman should himself have taken to the psychiatrist's couch after this adults-only version of *The Goon Show*. All of its characters are burblingly bonkers, from the therapists themselves to the several flakebrains pouring out disconnected thoughts in their consulting-rooms. Yet even with a starry cast, a fair share of funny one-liners and a nice music score by Gabriel Yared, Altman has managed to turn their comic capers into a painfully boring film. The elegance of the cast and their costumes contrasts uneasily enough with the often foul-mouthed dialogue but the film's chief stumbling block is its director's lack of timing. So used to meaningful drama, Altman stamps a ponderous touch all over the gossamer thread of this thinking man's porno comedy.

Beyond the Stars ○ Ⓥ

1989, US, 88 mins, colour
Dir: David Saperstein
Stars: Martin Sheen, Christian Slater, Sharon Stone, Robert Foxworth
Rating: ★★★

The James Dean-like Christian Slater plays rocket-mad teenager Eric Michael who, after launching a home-built, miniature rocket that causes damage at school, gets punished by being sent to stay with his father, who now lives with a girlfriend. While lonely Eric kicks his heels in the new community, he discovers that one of its inhabitants just happens to be his all-time hero – ex-astronaut Andrews (Martin Sheen), now an alcoholic near-hermit. As Eric and his new girlfriend (Maryam D'Abo) piece together the mystery of Andrews' bitterness and the secret of his long-ago trip to the moon, there unravels a quality small-town drama with a strong message for peace. F Murray Abraham has a small but dynamic role as a whale-watching fanatic, and Sheen gives a touching performance as the peace-seeking space hero. For the curious, there's also

B

Sharon Stone, as Slater's possible future mother-in-law!

B F's Daughter ○
(aka: Polly Fulton)
1948, US, 108 mins, b/w
Dir: Robert Z Leonard
Stars: Barbara Stanwyck, Van Heflin, Charles Coburn, Richard Hart
Rating: ★★★

A typically tempestuous role for La Stanwyck as the headstrong daughter of a tycoon. Not surprisingly, the British distributors didn't think much of the title (B F doesn't carry the same double-meaning in America). So the film was rechristened *Polly Fulton* for its British release. The men in Polly's life are played by Van Heflin, as a stubborn young political economist, and Richard Hart, as a stuffy socialite who becomes a war hero.

Bhaji on the Beach ● ⓥ
1993, UK, 101 mins, colour
Dir: Gurinder Chadha
Stars: Kim Vithana, Jimmi Harkishin, Sarita Khajuria, Mo Sesay, Lalita Ahmed, Zohra Segal
Rating: ★

Distasteful, rather unpleasant account, filled with jarring bad language, of an Asian women's club's day trip to Blackpool. The middle-aged dreamer becomes involved with a concert-party lothario; the runaway wife is tracked down by her husband and his violent brother; two teenagers flirt with the lads; a pregnant would-be graduate thinks of an abortion when rejected by her boyfriend; and the elderly member of the party becomes involved in a stage routine with male strippers. There's an ugly white-brown confrontation at an M6 service stop and generally not much that's nice happens to characters that you feel on the whole deserve to be treated with more dignity. Asian communities protested and it's not hard to see why.

Bhowani Junction ○
1956, US/UK, 110 mins, colour
Dir: George Cukor
Stars: Ava Gardner, Stewart Granger, Bill Travers
Rating: ★★

Filmed on location in Pakistan, this screen translation of John Masters' meaty novel of unrest, violence and love in pre-independence India gave Ava Gardner and her co-stars a strenuous time. Ava was trampled on by more than 100 native extras, then bruised and shaken in a staged fight

with a soldier. Years later, she declared it 'the toughest film I ever worked on'.

Bible ... in the Beginning, The ○
1966, US/Italy, 174 mins, colour
Dir: John Huston
Stars: Michael Parks, Richard Harris, George C Scott, Ava Gardner, Stephen Boyd, John Huston
Rating: ★

The retelling of the whole of the *Old Testament* by a number of famous directors – the original idea of this project – predictably proved too daunting a task, and John Huston was eventually entrusted with simply telling the story up to Abraham and Isaac. He also plays Noah in the film's best episode, which comes complete with an impressive flood sequence.

Bicycle Thieves ○ ⓥ
1948, Italy, 90 mins, b/w
Dir: Vittorio De Sica
Stars: Lamberto Maggiorani, Enzo Staiola, Lianella Carell
Rating: ★★★★★

Delicate, moving, post-war Italian film, with a director (Vittorio de Sica) right at his peak, and an entrancing performance from the urchin Enzo Staiola. An honest, beautifully told story of the search by a workman and his little son for a stolen bicycle that is life or death to their family, this is a film of rare humanity that took an Academy Award in its year.

Biddy ○
1983, UK, 86 mins, colour
Dir: Christine Edzard
Stars: Celia Bannerman
Rating: ★★★

The obverse side of *Mary Poppins* – the story of a real Victorian nursemaid whose microcosmic world hides what her constant chatter reveals – a vivid imagination that seeks escape in literary flights of fancy to vary her well-ordered life. Celia Bannerman gives a perfectly controlled portrait of this caring, yet in a way frustrated soul. In this quiet, leisurely, but engrossing film (provided you give it time to come to terms with you) she ends up in a room stuffed - almost horrifyingly full of memories - but with her essential essence distilled into those whose lives she has helped to form. Christine Edzard's direction of her own script tracks and sometimes traps this fascinating character in her own, tightly packed doll's house exis-

tence, forever forsaking the projection of self.

Big ○ ⓥ
1988, US, 102 mins, colour
Dir: Penny Marshall
Stars: Tom Hanks, Elizabeth Perkins, Robert Loggia, John Heard
Rating: ★★★

The most successful in the rash of age-reversal comedies that assailed us in the late 80s. Two-thirds genuine fun and one-third slightly squirmy embarrassment, the film has a couple of truly delightful scenes, where the boy-turned-man (Tom Hanks, nominated for an Oscar) makes his adult acquaintances behave like children again. Other situations are standard for the course, including the heroine (the personable Elizabeth Perkins), who inevitably falls for the hero's boyish charm, and the adult business protagonists who are confounded by his innocence.

Bigamist, The ○
1953, US, 83 mins, b/w
Dir: Ida Lupino
Stars: Edmond O'Brien, Joan Fontaine, Ida Lupino
Rating: ★★★

Edmond O'Brien, who had become stuck in a series of Westerns and low-budget crime stories at this stage in his Hollywood career, eagerly seized upon the meaty acting opportunities offered by Collier Young's script in this story of a salesman with wives in each of two neighbouring American cities. Young's then-wife, actress Ida Lupino, directs the film as well as playing one of the women involved. And she brings out all the poignancy of the situation, as well as providing it with a vital backbone of credibility.

Big Blue, The ◑ ⓥ
1988, France/US, 110 mins, colour
Dir: Luc Besson
Stars: Rosanna Arquette, Jean-Marc Barr, Jean Reno, Paul Shenar, Griffin Dunne
Rating: ★

There sure is a lot of the big blue (sea, that is) in this story of the lifelong rivalry between two deep-sea divers. The tragic ending is obvious always and pretty silly at that. Still, Rosanna Arquette is as engagingly buck-toothed and shapely as ever and does a pretty good level best to hold it all together for nigh on two hours. She gets little help from Jean-Marc Barr as the haunted diver who just wants to go off and play with the dolphins, and Griffin Dunne is in all too briefly as her New York boss. With locations in Greece, Sicily, New York, Peru and the French Riviera, this film may make you long for a holiday in more ways than one.

Big Broadcast of 1936, The ○
1935, US, 97 mins, b/w
Dir: Norman Taurog
Stars: Jack Oakie, George Burns, Gracie Allen, Bing Crosby, Ethel Merman
Rating: ★★

This sequel to the 1932 film *The Big Broadcast*, which had George Burns and Gracie Allen as radio station owners, sees them this time as potty inventors, while Jack Oakie is the radio station man to whom they try to sell crazy ideas about 'radio eyes'. As with all the series, it's a kaleidoscope of unconnected speciality turns, somehow kept in some kind of shape by director Norman Taurog. Highlights include a comedy sketch by Mary Boland and Charlie Ruggles, the stunning dancing of the Nicholas Brothers, and Ethel Merman singing 'It's the Animal in Me', to the accompaniment of a troupe of dancing elephants. This number was deleted from *We're Not Dressing* the previous year, but happily resurrected here.

Big Broadcast of 1938, The ○
1938, US, 90 mins, b/w
Dir: Mitchell Leisen
Stars: W C Fields, Bob Hope, Martha Raye, Dorothy Lamour, Shirley Ross, Lynne Overman
Rating: ★★

The American showbusiness paper *Variety* once offered $10,000 to anyone who could fathom the plot of this all-star extravaganza, typical of many such offerings from Hollywood studios in the Thirties. Bonuses here include W C Fields in a dual role as bumbling brothers and doing his classic billiards routine; and Bob Hope and Shirley Ross with the original version of the song that became Hope's theme tune 'Thanks for the Memory'. That plot, incidentally, has something to do with sabotage on a race across the Atlantic between two giant liners. As far as we know, no one has ever collected the $10,000.

Big Bus, The ○
1976, US, 85 mins, colour
Dir: James Frawley
Stars: Joseph Bologna, Stockard

Channing, John Beck, Ned Beatty, Jose Ferrer
Rating: ★★★★

Fancy a ride? This one is quite a laugh. The driver (Joseph Bologna) of the monster bus in this spoof disaster epic is under suspicion of once having eaten 116 passengers (his co-driver was responsible). New co-driver Shoulders (John Beck) suffers blackouts at high speed. The villain (Stuart Margolin), intent on sabotaging bus HQ, turns the lights out so that he can flash his torch. There are a lot more characters; these are only the sane ones. Although this journey runs out of ideas before the end, even its asides and background lines are funny while it still has a full head of steam. Satires on scenes and climaxes from a dozen other films are crammed into it. It's *Hellzapoppin* on wheels.

Big Business ○ Ⓥ
1988, US, 97 mins, colour
Dir: Jim Abrahams
Stars: Bette Midler, Lily Tomlin, Fred Ward, Edward Herrmann
Rating: ★★★

There's some brilliant trickcamera-work in the later stages of this fairly funny farce as one mismatched set of Bette Midler-Lily Tomlin twins bumps into the other. The story goes like this: the girls are muddled at birth when the millionaire father of one twinset is forced to buy the town of Jupiter Hollow to get his wife into its hospital. Thirty years later, predatory big businesswoman Bette 'A' and daffy-dilly sister Lily 'A' are set to close down the industry they've inherited in Jupiter Hollow, while the two Hollow residents, strong-willed Lily 'B' and starry-eyed sister Bette 'B', set out from the cornfields to stop them! The film doesn't waste much time at all and sets up some good gags on the side, including the tramp outside the Waldorf Hotel who keeps seeing double. Director Abrahams' deft touch keeps the helter-skelter of changing partners – baffling husbands, boyfriends, lovers and colleagues alike – from becoming tiresome. And the trickwork when the foursome meets in the ladies' loo is worth the price of admission alone.

Big Carnival, The
See: Ace in the Hole

Big Chill, The ● Ⓥ
1983, US, 115 mins, colour
Dir: Lawrence Kasdan

Stars: Tom Berenger, Glenn Close, Jeff Goldblum, William Hurt, JoBeth Williams, Kevin Kline
Rating: ★★★

This is a film with many nice touches, human moments and fragments of natural comic dialogue. Eight people reunite for the funeral of one of their friends from a close-knit group of a few years back when their set-the-world-to-rights fervour burned more brightly. Glenn Close, William Hurt and Meg Tilly give stand-out performances in an excellent star cast. The dead friend was originally played by Kevin Costner in flashback scenes, but his role ended up on the cutting-room floor.

Big Circus, The ○
1959, US, 109 mins, colour
Dir: Joseph M Newman
Stars: Victor Mature, Rhonda Fleming, Red Buttons, Vincent Price
Rating: ★★

One of the semi-blockbusters made by minor studio Allied Artists (formerly Monogram) when trying to break into the better-quality market in the 1950s. Irwin Allen, later a king of disaster movies, is the power behind this one, and there are a few disasters for circus owner Victor Mature (well cast for once although improbably called Hank Whirling!) to overcome. A good cast of semi-star names includes Peter Lorre as a clown.

Big Clock, The ○
1947, US, 95 mins, b/w
Dir: John Farrow
Stars: Ray Milland, Charles Laughton, Maureen O'Sullivan, George Macready
Rating: ★★★★★

Terrific thriller full of memorable scenes and images. Charles Laughton scores as the megalomaniac publisher whose strange speech pattern reflects the giant clock of the title in the lobby of his headquarters. Laughton's wife Elsa Lanchester is treasurable as an extremely talented but totally zany painter with a string of ex-husbands. Ray Milland and Maureen O'Sullivan are also good as the hero and heroine caught up in a web of violence and jealousy, and George Macready contributes another of his hissable snakes-in-the-grass. Director John Farrow tops it off with an exciting chase climax. Vaguely remade in 1987 as *No Way Out.*

B

Big Combo, The ◑ Ⓥ

1954, US, 90 mins, b/w
Dir: Joseph Lewis
Stars: Cornel Wilde, Richard Conte, Brian Donlevy, Jean Wallace
Rating: ★★★

It comes as something of a surprise to find that this tough low-budget crime thriller was made in the mid-Fifties, since it has all the hallmarks of the archetypal Forties *film noir* – laconic dialogue, a pervading sense of fatalism, flawed characters who are trapped in hells of their own making and perverse (for the time) sexuality. All of which are to be expected, however, from director Joseph Lewis, one of the best (and most underrated) exponents of 'B' feature film-making in the Forties. Here he is very well served by the lowkey monochrome cinematography of John Alton and his key actors, Cornel Wilde, Richard Conte, Brian Donlevy and Jean Wallace, while Lee Van Cleef and Earl Holliman contribute chilling cameos as a couple of sadistic hoods.

Big Country, The ○ Ⓥ

1958, US, 165 mins, colour
Dir: William Wyler
Stars: Gregory Peck, Jean Simmons, Carroll Baker, Charlton Heston, Burl Ives, Charles Bickford
Rating: ★★★

The sweeping music, by Jerome Moross, is the thing most people remember today from this big-scale Western, which marked Gregory Peck's debut as a producer. This story of an easterner out West cost $3 million to make, and took five months to film. One of its highlights is a desperate fight, in mud and murk, between those two big men of the screen, Peck and Charlton Heston. But Jean Simmons gives the outstanding performance as a schoolteacher caught in the centre of a land dispute, between two embittered old ranchers (played to the hilt by Burl Ives – winning an Oscar – and Charles Bickford). Miss Simmons has a ranch and – equally importantly – the water which is coveted by her neighbours. William Wyler directs with a suitable sense of occasion.

Big Deal at Dodge City ○

(aka: A Big Hand for the Little Lady)
1966, US, 95 mins, colour
Dir: Fielder Cook
Stars: Henry Fonda, Joanne Woodward, Jason Robards, Kevin McCarthy
Rating: ★★★★

A different, absorbing and richly rewarding Western about a huge game of poker (actually played at Laredo, whatever the title says). The character played with distinction by Joanne Woodward assumes considerable importance towards the climax – besides accounting for the movie's original title, *A Big Hand for the Little Lady* – and the twist ending is devastating.

Big Easy, The

1986, US, 108 mins, colour
Dir: Jim McBride
Stars: Dennis Quaid, Ellen Barkin, Ned Beatty, John Goodman
Rating: ★★★

Dennis Quaid is the tough detective and Ellen Barkin the even tougher assisstant district attorney in this wel-paced and slightly different thriller. The steamy New Orleans backdrop adds colour to the drama of murder, drugs and police corruption, making this an absorbing watch. Quaid is very good as the cool detective and Barkin rises above her stereotyped straight-laced legal eagle character to produce a performance of real passion. Although the story may not be startlingly original, dirctor Jim McBride packages it into a fast-moving and stylish thriller.

Bigfoot and the Hendersons ○ Ⓥ

(aka: Harry and the Hendersons)
1987, US, 110 mins, colour
Dir: William Dear
Stars: John Lithgow, Melinda Dillon
Rating: ★★★

The sweet and sentimental story of how a yeti-type creature comes to live with an ordinary family in suburban Seattle and how it teaches them the lessons of love and peace. Reminiscent at times of *E. T.* (and, in fact, co-produced by an uncredited Steven Spielberg), it's full of amusing, touching images - like the gentle Bigfoot mourning the death of a mink stole and the family roast, and burying them in a shallow grave. Bigfoot's excellent creature effects, by award-winning make-up expert Rick Baker, were Oscar-nominated.

Biggest Bank Robbery, The ○

(aka: A Nightingale Sang In Berkeley Square)
1980, UK, 95 mins, colour
Dir: Ralph Thomas
Stars: Richard Jordan, David Niven, Gloria Grahame, Elke Sommer
Rating: ★★

The Thomas brothers, Ralph and Gerald, did much over several decades to keep us laughing with the highlysuccessful *Doctor* and *Carry On* films. Ralph Thomas stayed with comedy for this robbery caper. David Niven plays a ruthless leader of a big London gang Hollywood's Gloria Grahame appears as a semi-retired American musical comedy star, and glamorous Elke Sommer is splendidly cast as a bank manager's sexy secretary.

Big Girls Don't Cry... They Get Even

See: Stepkids

Biggles ○ Ⓥ

1986, UK, 108 mins, colour
Dir: John Hough
Stars: Neil Dickson, Alex Hyde-White, Fiona Hutchinson
Rating: ★

The much-loved World War One heroics of Biggles, the pilot from Captain W E Johns' series of books, are updated to 1986 Manhattan via a timetravel gimmick. Neil Dickson as Biggles is the best thing in a so-so film that hardly plays fair with fans of the original. A huskier, younger version of Peter O'Toole, he has a genteel streak that conceals the viciousness required in war. But the big drawback is Alex Hyde-White as his time-travelling American buddy, whose acting is as wooden as a Stalag vaulting horse. A bold idea ruined in the execution.

Big Hand for the Little Lady, A

See: Big Deal in Dodge City

Big Heart, The

See: Miracle on 34th Street

Big Heat, The ◑ Ⓥ

1953, US, 90 mins, b/w
Dir: Fritz Lang
Stars: Glenn Ford, Gloria Grahame, Lee Marvin, Jocelyn Brando
Rating: ★★★★

A classic *film noir*, decorated by director Fritz Lang's stylish handling of what could have been a routine cops-and robbers story and by stunning monochrome camerawork from Charles Lang Jr. Glenn Ford gives a strong, concentrated performance as a policeman but it is Lee Marvin – crystallising his villainous screen image – who sears into the memory as he throws scalding coffee into Gloria Grahame's face.

Big House USA ◐
1955, US, 82 mins, b/w
Dir: Howard W Koch
Stars: Broderick Crawford, Ralph Meeker
Rating: ★★

Tough thriller about five men determined to break out of jail. Cast also includes such regular 'heavies' as Lon Chaney Jnr, William Talman and Charles Bronson. Some searing sequences in this one, blackly violent for its time.

Big Jake ○ ⓥ
1971, US, 110 mins, colour
Dir: George Sherman
Stars: John Wayne, Richard Boone, Maureen O'Hara, Patrick Wayne, Bruce Cabot
Rating: ★★

John Wayne corralled old friends, family and regular associates to help make this kidnap Western, but it's a major disappointment. Fashionable violence has been tacked on to a familiar story of a rugged father overcoming hostility with his sons to nail the bad guys, and a mediocre script doesn't help matters. Maureen O'Hara sets the tone as Wayne's wife, who calls on his help when their grandson is grabbed and held for ransom by raiders. 'It will require an extremely harsh and unpleasant kind of man to deal with,' she says, as the camera cuts to a gigantic close-up of The Duke, squinting down the barrel of a gun. Directed in pedestrian fashion by George Sherman.

Big Jim McLain ○
1953, US, 76 mins, b/w
Dir: Edward Ludwig
Stars: John Wayne, Nancy Olson, James Arness, Alan Napier
Rating: ★

John Wayne, that most patriotic of Americans, put up the money for this film himself, as it was among the first to point out the 'dangers' of the Communist menace to the Americans in their own outposts. It's the rough, tough story of a US special agent's attempts to expose a nest of Communist agents in Hawaii. Fists fly faster than the dialogue as Big Jim – that's Wayne – tracks the Commies down. But even Big John is dwarfed by James Arness, who plays his assistant. Wayne, at 6ft 4in, was three inches shorter. Nancy Olson, that prettiest of Fifties heroines, calms Wayne's brow for the film's few tender moments.

Big Knife, The ◐
1955, US, 110 mins, b/w
Dir: Robert Aldrich
Stars: Jack Palance, Ida Lupino, Wendell Corey, Shelley Winters, Jean Hagen, Rod Steiger
Rating: ★★★

Based on Clifford Odets' claustrophobic play, this systematic carve-up job on Hollywood caused quite a sensation when it burst on the film scene. Director Robert Aldrich was always a bit of a maverick and here he clinically dissects the star-building machine, producing a bitterly tawdry portrait of the movie world's capital. The man in the spotlight is Charlie Castle (Jack Palance, so tense you expect him to literally explode), a top box-office star who leads a tormented, drink-sodden private life. The acting is rivetingly powerful, particularly from a disturbingly blond Rod Steiger, Wendell Corey (as Steiger's sinister hatchet-man) and, as one of Charlie's few remaining friends, Wesley Addy.

Big Land, The ○
(aka: Stampeded!)
1956, US, 92 mins, colour
Dir: Gordon Douglas
Stars: Alan Ladd, Virginia Mayo, Edmond O'Brien
Rating: ★★

Known in Britain as *Stampeded!*, this latter-day Alan Ladd Western packs plenty of action, has some good action from Edmond O'Brien, and introduces Ladd's own son David in a supporting role. Some faces from the Forties in lesser roles include Julie Bishop and Don Castle.

Big Man, The ● ⓥ
1990, UK, 119 mins, colour
Dir: David Leland
Stars: Liam Neeson, Joanne Whalley-Kilmer, Ian Bannen, Billy Connolly
Rating: ★★

A tough British drama about an ex-miner, jailed during the great mine strike, and now out of work, who accepts the offer of a bare-knuckle fight from a shady businessman. This, incidentally, seems rather an odd reason for his wife to leave him. It takes an awful long time for the fight to come about and this, despite the surface brutality, is, like the rest of the film's fistfights, not exactly convincing, the punches visibly missing. However, the make-up of beaten boxers is agonisingly, excruciatingly good, and there are dogged, personable performances from Liam Neeson, Joanne Whalley-Kilmer,

Ian Bannen and Billy Connolly. The doom-laden atmosphere, too, is quite well achieved by director David Leland.

Big Night ● ⓥ
1995, US, 106 mins, colour
Dirs: Stanley Tucci, Campbell Scott
Stars: Stanley Tucci, Minnie Driver, Ian Holm, Isabella Rossellini, Michael Shalhoub
Rating: ★★

Flavoursome but slow, this – a bit like the cooking on offer at the failing Italian restaurant owned by immigrant brothers Tucci and Shalhoub in the Fifties. Their fortunes contrast sadly with the gaudy Italian restaurant across the way run by Holm, who is giving the customers what they want at inflated prices. Holm plans to finish the brothers off with a spurious promise of getting a famous musician Louis Prima and His Band to come to their restaurant – knowing they will invest their remaining savings in the banquet. It works, of course, and *Big Night* is mainly about a glorious night of food served only to neighbourhood drunks and hangers-on. It's hard to feel sympathy for Tucci, as he not only lacks the passion to save himself, but is also bonking Holm's mistress (Rossellini) unknown to his girlfriend (Driver). This is altogether a small, intricate film in the *Marty* tradition, but it lacks any pace or rhythm and has a downbeat and aimless ending that leaves the viewer less than satisfied.

Big Noise, The ☉
1944, US, 74 mins, b/w
Dir: Malcolm St Clair
Stars: Stan Laurel, Oliver Hardy
Rating: ★★

One of Laurel and Hardy's last comedies, this one has some inventive ideas, but was rather hampered by studio insistence on using old Stan-and-Ollie routines without any new variations. The duo's fans may spot a small appearance by Edgar Dearing who was the hopping-mad motorcycle cop in their classic *Two Tars*. Here, he's a ... motorcycle cop.

Big Picture, The ◐ ⓥ
1988, US, 100 mins, colour
Dir: Christopher Guest
Stars: Kevin Bacon, Emily Longstreth, Jennifer Jason Leigh, Michael McKean
Rating: ★★

At least the constant appearances of famous guest stars will keep you from dropping off in this story of a film

B

school prize winner who soon loses his sense of values in Tinseltown. Unable to make up its mind whether to be a satire, an out-and-out comedy or a morality tale, the film ends up as the kind of bastardised entertainment to which the young film-maker himself (Kevin Bacon) falls victim. In Hollywood he agrees to make any changes to his script in order to make a start, ditches his girlfriend for a starlet, gets an effete agent and neglects those who have his best interests at heart. It's as difficult to feel much sympathy for him as it is to give the film of his dreams any chance of success. Still, Martin Short is hilarious as the agent, and J T Walsh as unctuous as ever as a mogul with a penchant for lesbian angles. You may also spot, if you're quick, Eddie Albert, Elliott Gould, Roddy McDowall, Stephen Collins. June Lockhart and John Cleese. Alas, they've all been in bigger and better pictures.

Big Red One, The ◐ ⓥ
1980, US, 113 mins, colour
Dir: Sam Fuller
Stars: Lee Marvin, Mark Hamill, Robert Carradine, Bobby DiCicco, Stephane Audran, Kelly Ward
Rating: ★★★★

After remaining inactive for nearly a decade, cult writer-director Samuel Fuller came up with, despite its Eighties blood and guts, a film that is curiously old-fashioned. It's not a bad idea to follow the fortunes of four GIs, who seem to have charmed lives while bodies crash to the ground all around them, through North Africa, Sicily, Belgium, Czechoslovakia and Germany itself. Their sergeant is Lee Marvin, a relic from World War One, haunted by memories, and with a full circle tightening around his neck as the story moves towards the end of the war and his nemesis. Marvin is at his most restrained and the other soldiers, led by Mark Hamill, are all good, if insufficiently well drawn. The film gains strength as it goes on and some of its set pieces, especially a shoot-out in a home for the insane, are tactfully handled and quite memorably done.

Big Shot, The ○
1942, US, 82 mins, b/w
Dir: Lewis Seiler
Stars: Humphrey Bogart, Irene Manning
Rating: ★★★

Interesting and rare Humphrey Bogart gangster film, one of the first following his breakthrough to big stardom with

The Maltese Falcon and *High Sierra*. A weaker than usual supporting cast means that Bogart is virtually the whole show as the ex-big shot trapped by his own reputation after he has decided to opt out of a major robbery which could land him with a life sentence. The film, especially in its action sequences, is largely well handled by Lewis Seiler.

Big Show, The ○
1960, US, 113 mins, colour
Dir: James B Clark
Stars: Esther Williams, Cliff Robertson, Robert Vaughn
Rating: ★★

Circus sagas petered out after the Sixties and this was one of the last big ones. Esther Williams in her last film – a rare role as a dramatic actress – was teamed with two up-and-coming stars, Cliff Robertson and Robert Vaughn, who play brothers at their father's circus. Director James B Clark shows all the old Hollywood skill at tightening the tension on tightrope and trapeze, in a story which runs oddly parallel to the Biblical tale of Joseph and his Brethren. An unusual item is a troupe of performing polar bears, which also has a vital part to play in the story.

Big Sky, The ○
1952, US, 122 mins, b/w
Dir: Howard Hawks
Stars: Kirk Douglas, Dewey Martin
Rating: ★★

After a dynamic start to his movie career, Kirk Douglas suffered his first major flops in 1952 with two Westerns, *The Big Trees* and *The Big Sky*. *The Big Sky* is certainly the more ambitious of the two, originally premiered at two hours 20 minutes, but later cut to just over two hours. Even at the shorter length, it's still a leisurely saga that badly needs Technicolor and a lot more action to give gusto to its story of three Kentuckian frontiersmen at the turn of the 19th century. Jim Davis, later Jock Ewing in *Dallas*, plays a villain, one-film wonder Elizabeth Threatt is striking as an Indian princess, Dimitri Tiomkin contributed a typically haunting score, and the scenery (largely shot in Grand Teton National Park) is imposing even in black and white.

Big Sleep, The ○ ⓥ
1946, US, 114 mins, b/w
Dir: Howard Hawks
Stars: Humphrey Bogart, Lauren Bacall, John Ridgely, Martha Vickers, Dorothy

Malone
Rating: ★★★★

The archetypal private eye thriller, with Humphrey Bogart, as Philip Marlowe, trying to unravel a plot so fiendish that even the writers and director didn't understand all of it, whilst bandying words with Lauren Bacall in some of the raciest exchanges that ever got past the censors in the immediate post-war years. A supporting cast to treasure includes Elisha Cook Jr with another of his little guys who are life's losers, former Western star Bob Steele as a cold-blooded killer and a bespectacled Dorothy Malone as a bookstore proprietress keen to show Bogart her complete stock. The plot thunders along and, like Bogart, barely seems to stop for breath between one confrontation and another.

Big Sleep, The ◐
1978, UK, 95 mins, colour
Dir: Michael Winner
Stars: Robert Mitchum, Sarah Miles, Richard Boone, Candy Clark, Joan Collins, Edward Fox
Rating: ★

Raymond Chandler's tangled web of deception, murder and blackmail - immortalised in the 1946 Humphrey Bogart version – is here unhappily transferred by director Michael Winner to an English seaside setting. Star Robert Mitchum is an unusually elegant Philip Marlowe, while James Stewart and Joan Collins are the best of a supporting cast that also includes Candy Clark, Sarah Miles, Richard Boone, Edward Fox (spectacularly miscast as a shady bookie), John Mills, Oliver Reed and Richard Todd.

Big Steal, The ○
1949, US, 72 mins, b/w
Dir: Don Siegel
Stars: Robert Mitchum, Jane Greer, William Bendix, Ramon Novarro
Rating: ★★

Don Siegel made this hectic comedy thriller early in his career, after winning Oscars for his first two films. The accent is on the thrills, as the plot soon develops into one chase after another. Robert Mitchum and William Bendix are amusingly well matched in the leading roles.

Big Store, The ☉
1941, US, 80 mins, b/w
Dir: Charles Reisner
Stars: Groucho Marx, Chico Marx, Harpo Marx, Tony Martin, Virginia Grey
Rating: ★★★

This film, the last of the five the Marx Brothers made for MGM, has them as store detectives, headed by Groucho in an incredibly moth-eaten fur coat. The best scene comes early on, with Groucho entertaining Margaret Dumont in his office, despite clouds of smoke emanating from his desk. The slapstick finale is uncharacteristic, but pretty funny nonetheless. Also the film in which Tony Martin made a big hit singing 'Tenement Symphony'.

Big Street, The ○

1942, US, 88 mins, b/w
Dir: Irving Reis
Stars: Lucille Ball, Henry Fonda, Agnes Moorehead, Barton MacLane, Eugene Pallette, Sam Levene
Rating: ★★

Based on Damon Runyon's story *Little Pinks*, this morality tale set in Runyon's famous world of guys and dolls offered a big chance to Lucille Ball, who grabbed all her opportunities as the grasping Gloria who remains spoiled and self-centred even when tragedy strikes her down. They gave Lucy a quality leading man too, and it's just a pity that Henry Fonda is so badly miscast as the 'busboy' who worships Lucy's glitzy singer from afar. Director Irving Reis conjures up a climax that has few parallels in the art of making an audience cry.

Big Top Pee-wee ○

1988, US, 86 mins, colour
Dir: Randal Kleiser
Stars: Pee-wee Herman, Kris Kristofferson, Valeria Golino, Penelope Ann Miller
Rating: ★

Paul Reubens' Pee-wee Herman is certainly an odd-looking creation. Dressed in a suit several sizes too small, and sporting a white face and silly walk and voice, he's one of America's top children's entertainers. His first feature film, *Pee-wee's Big Adventure*, was a monster hit, but this overblown sequel was a damp squib. The Pee-wee bubble had burst.

Big Town, The ● ⓥ

1987, US, 109 mins, colour
Dir: Ben Bolt
Stars: Matt Dillon, Tommy Lee Jones, Diane Lane, Tom Skerritt, Bruce Dern, Suzy Amis, Lee Grant
Rating: ★

This is the cinematic equivalent of a dime novel. It has the whiff of Mickey Spillane about it, although even Spillane would have disowned plot developments that ignore all logic. Matt Dillon plays the ace dice player who arrives in Chicago to become an 'arm', coming under the wing of gambling entrepreneurs Bruce Dern and Lee Grant and becoming involved with sweet, child-tied Suzy Amis and sassy stripper Diane Lane, married to the crooked gambler (Tommy Lee Jones, with hair raked back) he has just taken for $14,000. 'You think I can make it in Chicago?' he asks his mentor. No contest. There's a simple-minded subplot of sorts which involves Dern's thirst for revenge on the gambler who blinded him years before and who has a small red heart tattooed on his right wrist. Gee, wonder if they'll ever find him? Dillon strikes poses, Tom Skerritt lends his wry charm to a too-brief part and Don Lake scores as a very nervous dice salesman. It isn't boring, but that's about all you can say.

Big Trees, The ○

1952, US, 89 mins, colour
Dir: Felix Feist
Stars: Kirk Douglas, Eve Miller, Patrice Wymore
Rating: ★★

Made three times before, in 1919, 1927 and 1938 (under the title *Valley of the Giants*), this action yarn was revamped by Warner Brothers as a vehicle for Kirk Douglas. He's excellent as an unscrupulous charmer and the vigorous action is sharply captured in Technicolor by Bert Glennon. The plot is skilfully constructed and the dialogue boasts a welcome vein of humour. But it lacks the driving force a top director might have given it.

Big Trouble In Little China ● ⓥ

1986, US, 100 mins, colour
Dir: John Carpenter
Stars: Kurt Russell, Kim Cattrall, Dennis Dun, James Hong
Rating: ★★

The title could easily refer to the final state of director John Carpenter's spoof of an *Indiana Jones*-style adventure that manages to misfire on most cylinders, even while boasting some spectacular action and inventive fantasy sequences. Kurt Russell does a reprise of the John Wayne accent that served him so well in *Escape from New York*, but looks faintly harassed, as well he might, as a philosophising CB trucker, played as a cross between a swaggering Wayne, adventurous Harrison Ford and wacky Bill Murray.

Virtually every Asian actor in Hollywood appears to have been signed up for this story of kidnap and Triad gangs, crossed with a black fantasy about a seven-foot tall Chinese magician controlling an evil empire deep beneath San Francisco's Chinatown district. Carpenter has more success composing the music for the film which is rousing stuff. Easy entertainment, but disappointingly thin.

Bill & Ted's Bogus Journey ○ ⓥ

1991, US, 93 mins, colour
Dir: Peter Hewitt
Stars: Keanu Reeves, Alex Winter, William Sadler, Joss Ackland
Rating: ★★★

At the Bill and Ted University in the 27th century (motto: Party On, Dudes), there's trouble afoot. Science students dressed like citizens of Oz are devastated by the arrival of wicked superbrain Joss Ackland who has created robot Bill-and-Teds to go back in time to destroy their predecessors. Far out man! If you haven't seen *Bill and Ted's Excellent Adventure*, you're lost from now on, as Bill and Ted (still Alex Winter, doubling as his own granny, and Keanu Reeves) are bumped off by their metal doubles, and end up in a quite bodaciously imaginative Hell, where they encounter Devil-Dude and Death-Dude. Their one chance of returning is to beat the Grim Reaper, who has never lost, at a game. Naturally Death (William Sadler) expects this to be something like chess. But Bill and Ted choose Battleships! This is no great movie, but definitely a cult in the making: good fun and non-heinous to boot. Party on!

Bill & Ted's Excellent Adventure ○ ⓥ

1988, US, 91 mins, colour
Dir: Stephen Herek
Stars: Keanu Reeves, Alex Winter, George Carlin, Bernie Caseie
Rating: ★★★

Though it takes time to warm to, this fantasy comedy is just daft enough to be engaging. Bill and Ted are two 17-year-olds whose minds are more on music than schooling. So much so that they're in danger of failing a vital history course, which will get Ted sent off to military academy and break up their band. This, for reasons best known to the Guardians of the Future, is not on. So they enable Bill and Ted to travel back through time in a telephone box

B

(someone's seen *Doctor Who*), where they collect a series of historical figures who'll help them through the exam. Keanu Reeves and Alex Winter are well into the spirit of the thing as scapegrace Bill and Ted and, after seeing their excellent (well, moderately amusing) adventures, you may never want to pronounce Socrates any other way than 'Sew-crayts'.

Billion Dollar Brain ◑

1967, UK, 111 mins, colour
Dir: Ken Russell
Stars: Michael Caine, Karl Malden, Francoise Dorleac
Rating: ★★

This is Ken Russell's Harry Palmer spy thriller with its memorable icebound climax. Among the villains of the piece: the dependable Karl Malden and blustering Ed Begley, who clearly relishes his role as a mad general. Yet another famous figure in the cast is Oscar Homolka, that gruff, wickedly humorous, always immensely enjoyable character actor who was first seen in Palmer-land in *Funeral in Berlin*, again with Michael Caine, a year earlier.

Billy Bathgate ● ⓥ

1991, US, 106 mins, colour
Dir: Robert Benton
Stars: Dustin Hoffman, Nicole Kidman, Loren Dean, Bruce Willis
Rating: ★★★

Taken from the best-seller by E L Doctorow, and with a tightly written screenplay by playwright Tom Stoppard, this compelling exploration of the world of 1930s gangsters centres on the activities of murderous mobster Dutch Schultz (edgily played by Dustin Hoffman). The story is told as seen through the eyes of young Billy Bathgate (Loren Dean), an opportunist street kid who, seduced by the glamour of power, money and the life of crime, works his way up to become one of Dutch's most trusted flunkies. A grim and glossy drama from director Robert (*Kramer vs Kramer*) Benton, *Billy Bathgate* captures well the seedy gangster underworld atmosphere but, while the eyes can feast on lush period detail and lavish, expensive-looking sets, there is ultimately not enough story to absorb the mind.

Billy Budd ○

1962, US/UK, 112 mins, b/w
Dir: Peter Ustinov
Stars: Peter Ustinov, Robert Ryan, Melvyn Douglas, Terence Stamp, Ronald

Lewis, David McCallum
Rating: ★★★

Fine performances distinguish this solid version of Herman Melville's stern allegory of good versus evil on board a British navy ship in 1797, headed by Terence Stamp's Oscar-nominated portrayal of the naive and incorruptible seaman whose clash with sadistic master-at-arms Robert Ryan ends in tragedy. Peter Ustinov co-wrote the screenplay with Robert Rossen and stars as Captain Vere. While his direction is somewhat unambitious (the focus is more often than not on his players in a manner more suited to television than to the cinema), there is no denying the film's cumulative power.

Billy Liar! ○

1963, UK, 96 mins, b/w
Dir: John Schlesinger
Stars: Tom Courtenay, Julie Christie, Wilfred Pickles, Mona Washbourne
Rating: ★★★

This 'kitchen-sink' answer to *The Secret Life of Walter Mitty* provides a welcome comedy role for Tom Courtenay as the young north countryman who lives entirely in a dream world. He has strong competition, though, from the female contingent, especially Mona Washbourne as his down-to-earth mum, Julie Christie, well in character as his 'dream' girl and Helen Fraser, charming in an irksome role. The superb photography by Denys Coop includes one marvellous shot of a runner on the skyline.

Billy Madison ◑ ⓥ

1995, US, 89 mins, colour
Dir: Tamra Davis
Stars: Adam Sandler, Bridgette Anderson, Darren McGavin
Rating: ★

This American 'idiot' lowbrow comedy is just so stupid you have to be amused every now and then. Talentwise, though, its 'gormless' star, Adam Sandler, is a long way short of Jim Carrey or – to find a more direct forebear – Jerry Lewis, of whose childlike appeal he has very little. Playing the deliberately oafish son of a millionaire, Sandler finds he has to pass each (previously failed) grade in high school in two weeks if he is to take over dad's business. Of course, there's a rival even more obnoxious than Billy for the post of chief exec, and the incredibly beautiful 3rd-grade teacher for whom Billy falls. Much of the comedy is clumsy or objectionable or both and,

although there are inspired moments, they're swept away on a tidal wave of stunningly-unfunny toilet-inspired humour. The end product makes *Back to School* look a comedy classic. But then if you liked that, you'll get the occasional smile from this.

Billy Rose's Diamond Horseshoe ○ ⓥ

(aka: Diamond Horseshoe)
1945, US, 104 mins, colour
Dir: George Seaton
Stars: Betty Grable, Dick Haymes, Phil Silvers
Rating: ★★★★

Betty Grable's fans will be delighted by her vivacious performance (even Grable-haters will find her livelier than usual) in this dazzling, very expensive looking musical which has a lively script full of unforced humour, some tuneful songs and both Dick Haymes and Phil Silvers at their best. The most popular number was 'The More I See You', but the score also includes 'You'll Never Know', 'Let Me Call You Sweetheart', 'Aba Daba Honeymoon' (featuring guest star Willie Solar) and 'Melancholy Baby'. Choreographer Hermes Pan makes the most of his chances to interrupt the action by staging some swinging dance routines, especially 'Cooking Up a Show'. Even the fomula plot is so persuasively done as to bring a lump to the throat of the unwary towards the end.

Billy Rose's Jumbo

See: Jumbo

Billy the Kid ○

1940, US, 95 mins, colour
Dir: David Miller
Stars: Robert Taylor, Brian Donlevy, Ian Hunter, Mary Howard
Rating: ★★

The West's most famous outlaw has been dead since 1881, but the filmmakers won't let him lie down. Since 1930 he has been reincarnated by actors ranging from Wallace Beery to Paul Newman. This production was an entirely different kettle of fish. Based on a novel giving a fairly romantic account of the outlaw, it stars Robert Taylor. Action fans will find there's no shortage of gunplay.

Billy the Kid and the Green Baize Vampire ●

1985, UK, 93 mins, colour
Dir: Alan Clark
Stars: Phil Daniels, Alun Armstrong,

Louise Gold
Rating: ★★

The streetwise British film of the Eighties collides head-on with the pop video, and the result is a musical about a Cockney snooker superstar who takes on a world champion whose vampiric aspect must surely be based on Ray Reardon! The music sounds great, the singers are good and the staging imaginative within an obviously limited budget. What a pity the orchestral backing is so deafening that you can't hear too many of the words in the songs so vital in a film like this where the songs not only tell practically the whole story, but provide the atmosphere as well. Daniels and Armstrong demonstrate some mighty potting power which must have taken a lot of practice.

Biloxi Blues ◐ ⓥ
1987, US, 106 mins, colour
Dir: Mike Nichols
Stars: Matthew Broderick, Christopher Walken, Penelope Ann Miller
Rating: ★★★

The second part of playwright Neil Simon's autobiographical trilogy, this relates with candour and ripe service humour, but above all with affection, Simon's months of training at an army boot camp in Mississippi for a war that was over before he could get to it. Matthew Broderick is just right as the young Simon, but Christopher Walken is a shade too emotional (if interesting) as the eccentric sergeant with a plate in his head who drills his platoon to distraction. Though well told, this ends up very much the standard recruit-training yarn, even if it is infused with Simon's unique humour, often surprisingly well delivered in Broderick's narrative to the story.

Bingo ○ ⓥ
1991, US, 87 mins, colour
Dir: Matthew Robbins
Stars: Cindy Williams, David Rasche, Robert J Steinmiller, David French, Kurt Fuller
Rating: ★

After Benji, but before there was Beethoven, along came Bingo. He wasn't nearly as successful as the other two, and little wonder. An unbelievably resourceful collie dog in the Lassie mould, Bingo runs away from mistreatment in a circus and straight into the heart of a young boy. Then the boy's footballer father gets transferred, Bingo is left behind – but he decides to travel across country to be reunited with his young friend. Someone has obviously seen *Lassie Come Home* and *The Incredible Journey* here, and easily-moved children may be weeping buckets at the end of this facile frolic. No sequels, though: not so much bow-wow as bow out.

Bird ● ⓥ
1988, US, 160 mins, colour
Dir: Clint Eastwood
Stars: Forest Whitaker, Diane Venora, Michael Zelniker
Rating: ★★★

'Male, about 65' is said to have been the medical report on the death of jazz musician Charlie 'Bird' Parker. Parker was in fact 34, a big man, but a hulk as full of drugs and drink as he could lay hands on. Director Clint Eastwood's account of his career, told in flashback fashion, is a caring film that tells us Parker was a gentle, genial giant, blessed with a musical genius that kept sparking his career even when he could hardly stay on his feet long enough to fulfil an engagement. Forest Whitaker and Diane Venora live the roles of Parker and his wife Chan to a remarkable degree, but the film drifts on too long and is very darkly photographed. No matter, there's always the music – Bird's own amazingly complex jazz renditions of standards still take some beating today.

Birdcage, The ● ⓥ
1996, US, 119 mins, colour
Dir: Mike Nichols
Stars: Robin Williams, Nathan Lane, Gene Hackman, Dianne Wiest, Dan Futterman, Calista Flockhart
Rating: ★★★

This new version of the French comedy classic *La Cage aux Folles* works well enough in fits and starts and must rate as one of the fizzier Hollywood remakes of Gallic hits. This time round it's Robin Williams and Nathan Lane as the gay couple who encounter a mid-life crisis when Williams' 'straight' son (from a one-off heterosexual experience) decides to get married. The bride-to-be is the daughter of a pro-morals senator (Gene Hackman) whose colleague has just died in bed with an under-age black prostitute! While Hackman and wife Dianne Wiest are en route to the flat above Williams' gay night-spot to vet their prospective 'in-laws', crowds of TV news crews are only a pace behind. Much funnier when it gets cracking on the ensuing dinner party – Hank Azaria is priceless as the prancing houseboy who has to turn butter/chef – the film suffers heavily from the modern pitfall of overlength. Williams' funny-but-harmless personality is perfect for the snarlingly harassed 'husband' and Hackman in drag at the end is less convincing than you might imagine.

Bird Man of Alcatraz ○ ⓥ
1962, US, 148 mins, b/w
Dir: John Frankenheimer
Stars: Burt Lancaster, Karl Malden, Thelma Ritter, Neville Brand, Telly Savalas, Edmond O'Brien
Rating: ★★★★★

The now famous story of Robert Stroud, the 'life' prisoner who took up the study of birds, and became a leading authority on the subject, makes a memorable and moving film which Burt Lancaster himself considered among his finest, alongside *Sweet Smell of Success*. Lancaster's Stroud is a moving portrait of a man who suddenly finds hope in an unexpected quarter, and there's a good performance from Neville Brand as the warder who befriends him.

Bird on a Wire ◐ ⓥ
1990, US, 110 mins, colour
Dir: John Badham
Stars: Mel Gibson, Goldie Hawn, David Carradine, Bill Duke, Joan Severance
Rating: ★★

For a mainline megastar movie, this is uncomfortably unconvincing. Ruthlessly formulaic, predictable and empty-headed, it raises very little chemistry between Mel Gibson and Goldie Hawn, whose hearts don't seem to be in it, and completely wastes David Carradine as the villain, not giving him a single decent scene. Nothing somehow seems real, and we never quite figure out why Mel is on the run after spending 15 years as a relocated witness (equally difficult to work out the reason for this in the first place). The final shootout in a zoo begins very promisingly but goes on too long.

Birds, The ◐ ⓥ
1963, US, 118 mins, colour
Dir: Alfred Hitchcock
Stars: Rod Taylor, Tippi Hedren, Suzanne Pleshette, Jessica Tandy
Rating: ★★★★

Alfred Hitchcock's sensational version of the Daphne Du Maurier story has the same key elements as his previous film *Psycho:* suspense, horror and tremendous impact. Thanks to skilful direction and almost flawless special ef-

B

fects, this tale of birds turning against humans and attacking them in multitudes is chillingly effective. Tippi Hedren responds perfectly to the demands of her director, and her performance is matched by Suzanne Pleshette's glowing, bitter-sweet portrayal of the local schoolteacher, still in love with hero Rod Taylor. Jessica Tandy adds another keenly-etched character, but the outstanding memory from this savage film is still the evil of the birds themselves. The final scenes are grimly magnetic, frighteningly foreboding.

Birds and the Bees, The ○
1956, US, 94 mins, colour
Dir: Norman Taurog
Stars: George Gobel, Mitzi Gaynor, David Niven
Rating: ★★★

A charming remake, fizzingly photographed in Technicolor, of Preston Sturges' famous comedy film *The Lady Eve*, about a naive young man who is conned by a trio of card sharps aboard a luxury liner. The song-and-dance interludes between the buzzy George Gobel and vivacious Mitzi Gaynor (presumably the bee and the bird) are quite delightful.

Birdy ● ⓥ
1984, US, 120 mins, colour
Dir: Alan Parker
Stars: Matthew Modine, Nicolas Cage, John Harkins, Karen Young, Bruno Kirby
Rating: ★★

For such a highly rated film this proves to be rather dull when you actually come to see it. You can appreciate, though, the commercial factors that hyped up Alan Parker's movie about a youth who becomes obsessed by birds (the feathered variety) and the idea that he has to fly. This doesn't look too possible, especially as he's kept in a schizophrenically silent condition in an army hospital after his experiences in Vietnam. It's well-acted, especially by Nicolas Cage as Birdy's buddy, a sensitive performance worthy of the Oscar nomination it didn't get. But the story simply hasn't the dramatic strength to sustain its slim theme towards its impending, yet ever-elusive (anti) climax. Parker directs with attention to the more exploitable aspects around the film's perimeters.

Birthday Present, The ○
1957, UK, 100 mins, b/w
Dir: Pat Jackson
Stars: Tony Britton, Sylvia Syms, Jack Watling
Rating: ★★

Small-scale but neatly-scripted, well-acted and effective drama about a man whose life is almost ruined through his attempt to smuggle a watch through customs. There are no big stars, but the performances are solid.

Bishop's Wife, The ○
1947, US, 130 mins, b/w
Dir: Henry Koster
Stars: Cary Grant, Loretta Young, David Niven, Monty Woolley
Rating: ★★★

Hollywood magic (in more ways than one) at its sentimental best. Cary Grant is in wonderful form as the freewheeling, ice-skating angel sent down from Heaven to put a few decent people back on the road to happiness from which they seem to have stumbled. Although, with its snow-covered ending, it should ideally be seen at Christmas, the film is perfect entertainment at any time.

Bite the Bullet ○
1975, US, 131 mins, colour
Dir: Richard Brooks
Stars: Gene Hackman, James Coburn, Candice Bergen, Ben Johnson
Rating: ★★★★

Director Richard Brooks makes sure that this story of an endurance race on horseback across south-west America in 1908 keeps going at a gallop, crammed with action and incident. For once, Gene Hackman, as the sensitive man who loves horses more than he wants to win the race, seems slightly at sea – perhaps at having to express so much humanity in one soul. But James Coburn and Candice Bergen sit more easily in the saddle. Menacing actor Paul Stewart, familiar from such Hollywood films as *The Window* and *Champion*, makes a welcome appearance as the man behind the race. The best performance of all, though, comes from craggy, Oscar-winning character star Ben Johnson, as the veteran rider of the group. He has a magnificent final scene that tops anything else in this hell-for-leather film.

Bitter Harvest ◑
1963, UK, 96 mins, colour
Dir: Peter Graham Scott
Stars: Janet Munro, John Stride, Anne Cunningham, Alan Badel
Rating: ★★★

Ted Willis wrote this haunting little parable about a country girl who moves to London, and discards true love in favour of what she thinks are the bright, inviting lights. Janet Munro makes one feel genuinely sorry for this silly but tragic figure.

Bitter Moon ●
1992, US/France, 135 mins, colour
Dir: Roman Polanski
Stars: Peter Coyote, Emmanuelle Seignier, Hugh Grant, Kristin Scott Thomas
Rating: RB

'I say chaps, Nigel and Fiona are in trouble. Taking this cruise to Istanbul on their seventh anniversary, they were bally well accosted by this deviant American cripple and his nymphomaniac wife. Dashed bad luck, or what? If only Nigel hadn't said, 'It's bad for an old married couple to be seen together all the time,' it might never have happened. This chap told his whole bally life story; bally tedious it was, too, but poor old Nigel was besotted by his wife, don't you see, so he had to stay and listen to the whole load of poppycock!' If you insist on doing the same as poor old Nigel, at least you'll be able to build up a treasury of ludicrous lines from what must be Roman Polanski's worst film. Top of the dunghill is probably disabled Peter Coyote's estimation of his then-mistress (Emmanuelle Seignier): 'I loved her too. But our credit was running out. We were headed for sexual bankruptcy.'

Bitter Victory ○
1957, France, 82 mins, b/w
Dir: Nicholas Ray
Stars: Richard Burton, Curt Jurgens, Ruth Roman
Rating: ★★

Nicholas Ray's bleak war film about retribution that turns sour in the desert. As with most Ray films, this one split the critics, though most gave a thumbs down to Ray's efforts to enliven what is basically a tedious combination of war and romance, topheavy with dialogue and stock characters. Richard Burton, Curt Jurgens and Ruth Roman labour mightily to make something of the affair; among those miscast in support are Alfred Burke (as a major) and Christopher Lee (as a sergeant), roles you would have thought better cast the other way round.

Black Angel ○
1946, US, 80 mins, b/w
Dir: Roy William Neill

Stars: Dan Duryea, June Vincent, Peter Lorre, Broderick Crawford, Wallace Ford
Rating: ★★★

This was director Roy William Neill's last film before his early death at 60. Neill was the man responsible for most of Universal's Sherlock Holmes films with Basil Rathbone. Here he creates a splendidly grating atmosphere for a doomy story about an alcoholic searching for his wife's killer in order to clear an innocent man. Dan Duryea remains compellingly watchable in this role and, although Peter Lorre is rather wasted as a slug-like nightclub-manager, the heroine is played by the fascinating June Vincent, a silky blonde who never quite made it in Hollywood, but who here gives full value to such smoochy songs as 'Heartbreak' and 'Time Will Tell'.

Black Arrow, The
(aka: The Black Arrow Strikes)
1948, US, 76 mins, b/w
Dir: Gordon Douglas
Stars: Louis Hayward, Janet Blair
Rating: ★★★

Based on Robert Louis Stevenson's famous adventure novel. Louis Hayward, although a little old for for the part, makes a dashing hero, while George Macready is an excellent malevolent Sir Daniel. The ending is somewhat changed but exciting nonetheless, and Charles Lawton's sparkling photography is another factor in the film's favour. Good entertainment for children of all ages.

Black Bart ○
(aka: Black Bart – Highwayman)
1948, US, 80 mins, colour
Dir: George Sherman
Stars: Yvonne De Carlo, Dan Duryea
Rating: ★ ★ ★

This colourful Western was made at a time when Dan Duryea was getting most of his best roles. He plays a holdup bandit who falls in love with the famous entertainer Lola Montez. Frank Lovejoy and John McIntire make film early film appearances.

Blackbeard's Ghost ○ ⓥ
1967, US, 107 mins, colour
Dir: Robert Stevenson
Stars: Peter Ustinov, Suzanne Pleshette, Dean Jones
Rating: ★★★★

The Walt Disney studio at its most inventive and amusing, with all sorts of fun being had from the invisibility of Blackbeard the Pirate's ghost as he helps athletes and gamblers alike past the winning post. Peter Ustinov enjoys himself engagingly in the title role, Dean Jones is a likeably harassed hero, and heroine Suzanne Pleshette also has her moments, especially when she's winning at a casino and refuses to quit while she's ahead.

Blackbeard the Pirate ⊙
1952, US, 100 mins, colour
Dir: Raoul Walsh
Stars: Robert Newton, Linda Darnell, Keith Andes, William Bendix
Rating: ★★

Rolling his eyes wildly, and charging up and down the deck like a bearded Bligh, Robert Newton revels in this, his second pirate picture, following his immortal portrayal of Long John Silver two years before.

Black Beauty ○ ⓥ
1971, UK, 106 mins, colour
Dir: James Hill
Stars: Mark Lester, Walter Slezak, Peter Lee Lawrence, Ursula Glas, Patrick Mower
Rating: ★★

James Hill, director of such beguiling animal stories as *Born Free, An Elephant Called Slowly* and *The Belstone Fox*, here wove an appealing adventure story from Anna Sewell's novel about a black horse that undergoes various hardships, moving from one owner to another. Then-popular child star Mark Lester tugs at the heartstrings in the lead.

Blackboard Jungle ⓝ
1955, US, 101 mins, b/w
Dir: Richard Brooks
Stars: Glenn Ford, Anne Francis, Sidney Poitier, Vic Morrow, Louis Calhern, Margaret Hayes
Rating: ★★★★

Nominated for four Oscars but coming away empty-handed on the night, this uncompromising drama about race and violent confrontation in the classroom propelled Richard Brooks to the front rank of American directors. It also marked the screen debut of Vic Morrow as a sadistic troublemaker, and gave a huge boost to Sidney Poitier's meteoric rise as Hollywood's leading black actor. The film was something of a landmark, being the first in Hollywood to feature rock music, with Bill Haley's 'Rock Around the Clock' playing over the opening credits.

Black Castle, The ○
1952, US, 81 mins, b/w
Dir: Nathan Juran
Stars: Richard Greene, Boris Karloff, Paula Corday
Rating: ★★

Paula Corday, the heroine of this cloak and dagger adventure, began her career in such films as *The Body Snatcher* – also with Boris Karloff. It's strange to find Karloff cast as a goodie, in this tale of an evil Austrian nobleman who roams the catacombs of his cavernous castle, where he holds his lovely wife against her will. But Stephen McNally, as the callous count and Lon Chaney, as his hulking bodyguard, have a high old time dispensing the sneers and the scowls. Richard Greene is every bit as dashing a hero as fans of his would expect.

Black Cat, The ⓝ
(aka: House of Doom)
1934, US, 65 mins, b/w
Dir: Edgar G Ulmer
Stars: Boris Karloff, Bela Lugosi
Rating: ★★★

Boris Karloff and Bela Lugosi gave two of their best performances in this strong horror film with effectively bizarre settings, in which both were rather cast against type. Karloff plays a suave and ruthless devil-worshipper without a sympathetic bone in his body, while Lugosi's a basically kindly but vengeance-obsessed doctor. Incidentally the film has virtually nothing in common with the Edgar Allan Poe short story on which it is supposedly based.

Black Cat, The ⓝ
1941, US, 70 mins, b/w
Dir: Albert S Rogell
Stars: Basil Rathbone, Broderick Crawford, Bela Lugosi, Gale Sondergaard
Rating: ★

This horror whodunit is a disappointment, especially as it boasts a rare gathering of ghoulish character stars, including Basil Rathbone, Bela Lugosi and Gale Sondergaard. Gladys Cooper, Anne Gwynne and Alan Ladd – in one of his last roles before stardom – look perturbed, possibly by the comedy antics of Hugh Herbert and Broderick Crawford, which dissipate too many of the chills.

Black Cauldron, The, ○ ⓥ
1985, US, 80 mins, colour
Dir: Ted Berman, Richard Rich
Voice stars: Grant Bardsley, Susan Sheridan, John Byner, John Hurt
Rating: ★★★

B

The Disney contribution to the sword-and-sorcery cycle turns out to be an artful combination of Disney and Tolkien, but with no truly memorable characters to turn it into an animation classic. Some of the peripheral characters, indeed, like the cat at the beginning, recoiling in horror from the proffered slops, and the dogs and dragons whose prey forever eludes their slavering jaws by a width of cloth, could do with expansion into major characters in the plot. Based (very freely) on a series of books by Lloyd Alexander, the plot tells of an oracular pig (a rather wet character) whose vision is required by the evil Horned King to find the location of the Black Cauldron. But the teenage pig-keeper, Taran, is determined that no such thing will happen. Packed with plot, the film, although a bit too spooky in parts for little ones, will delight six- to twelve-year-olds appreciative of a bit more bite.

Black Dakotas, The O
1954, US, 64 mins, colour
Dir: Ray Nazarro
Stars: Gary Merrill, Wanda Hendrix, John Bromfield, Noah Beery Jr
Rating: ★

Well-photographed Western that packs more action into its hour's running time than many films of twice its length. Would that the acting and screenplay had the same strength.

Black Fury O
1935, US, 92 mins, b/w
Dir: Michael Curtiz
Stars: Paul Muni, Karen Morley, William Gargan, Barton MacLane
Rating: ★★★

This hard-hitting tale of industrial action and brutal strike-breaking in a Pennsylvania mining town was pretty tough stuff in its day and indeed is still tense and watchable today. It's dominated by Paul Muni's powerful central performance as the striking miner whose colleague is killed by thug Barton MacLane. Muni captures MacLane and barricades himself and his prisoner inside the mine – becoming a nationwide news story. Long before Robert De Niro, Muni would go to great lengths to research a part. For this film he worked for weeks with miners, learning their job, accents and mannerisms. The results were worth the effort and gave Muni another portrayal to add to an impressive collection of fine roles. He also had gritty support from MacLane, J Carrol Naish and John Qualen.

Black Hand O
1950, US, 93 mins, b/w
Dir: Richard Thorpe
Stars: Gene Kelly, J Carrol Naish
Rating: ★★

Even though he doesn't dance a step, Gene Kelly still treads nimbly through this story of one man's vendetta against the Mafia. Nowadays, no doubt, it would have a tragic ending. But even so, it didn't do too well at the box-office in its day. Perhaps MGM would have improved its chances by changing the title to that of Kelly's character: Johnny Columbo.

Black Hole, The O ⓥ
1979, US, 97 mins, colour
Dir: Gary Nelson
Stars: Maximilian Schell, Anthony Perkins, Robert Forster, Yvette Mimieux, Joseph Bottoms, Ernest Borgnine
Rating: ★★

Robust, robotic space opera, even if the story is compounded of familiar motifs from a variety of fantasy and science-fiction favourites. Even the central figure belongs to the familiar mad scientist school of villains. In respect of its robots and its space-travel hardware, it's something of a cousin to *Star Wars*, though it lacks that film's sheer panache. But there's plenty going on most of the time and no doubt all space-minded youngsters will revel in it.

Black Horse Canyon ⊙
1954, US, 81 mins, colour
Dir: Jesse Hibbs
Stars: Joel McCrea, Mari Blanchard
Rating: ★★

The story of various people trying to capture a magnificent black stallion. Not so much a Western, more of an alfresco adventure, this refreshingly different film gave Joel McCrea one of the best of his later roles as the worldly-wise drifter who helps a hot-headed ranch girl (the fiery Mari Blanchard, never better) to capture the stallion. Murvyn Vye and Bill Williams scowl effectively as the bad guys.

Black Jack O
1979, UK, 110 mins, colour
Dir: Ken Loach
Stars: Stephen Hirst, Louise Cooper, Jean Franval
Rating: ★★

Vaguely reminiscent of the Tommy Steele vehicle *Where's Jack?*, this period adventure (set in 1750) marked a considerable departure for British director Ken Loach, whose previous credits included *Kes* and *Family Life*. The narrative is stylised with some skill, but some of the performances are less than persuasive (the fact that the film carries no script credit may have a bearing) and the accents are variable. But the film certainly is colourful.

Black Knight, The O
1953, UK, 85 mins, colour
Dir: Tay Garnett
Stars: Alan Ladd, Peter Cushing, Patricia Medina
Rating: ★

Third, last and very much worst of a trio of action films that Alan Ladd made in Britain in the early Fifties. This frightful foray into early English history is set in Arthurian times, with Ladd, as a swordmaker out to avenge his dead master, given such dialogue as: 'Lemme speak, sire. You gotta lissen. England's gonna be invaded.' The battle scenes are impressively organised, but it's not enough.

Black Legion O
1936, US, 83 mins, b/w
Dir: Archie Mayo
Stars: Humphrey Bogart, Ann Sheridan, Erin O'Brien-Moore, Dick Foran
Rating: ★★

One of Humphrey Bogart's earliest bona-fide roles and he's terrific, even if the ending of this Ku Klux Klan drama is never totally convincing. But there are some quite grim and frightening sequences in what was a bold film for its time.

Black Magic O
1949, US, 105 mins, b/w
Dir: Gregory Ratoff
Stars: Orson Welles, Nancy Guild, Akim Tamiroff
Rating: ★

Orson Welles, an enthusiastic conjuror in his own right, must have been greatly attracted to the role of Cagliostro, 18th century magician, mesmerist and general all-round scoundrel. Unfortunately, Welles, encouraged by an over-ripe script, clambers all over the role and just about spits out the pieces as well. The film certainly has its own florid atmosphere and pretty Nancy Guild, who made too few films, is effective in a dual role.

Blackmail O ⓥ
1929, UK, 78 mins, b/w
Dir: Alfred Hitchcock
Stars: Anny Ondra (voice: Joan Barry),

John Longden, Sara Allgood
Rating: ★★★

Britain's first part-talkie directed by Alfred Hitchcock (who makes his usual small appearance, this time on a tube train), is still amazingly hypnotic to watch today, with several sequences that remain genuinely striking. The amosphere reeks with the feeling that something nasty is going to happen any second, a sign that Hitchcock's expertise at tightening tension was already building up. Future directors Ronald Neame and Michael Powell were clapper boy and stills cameraman respectively on this landmark thriller.

Blackmail ○ ⓥ
1939, US, 90 mins, b/w
Dir: H C Potter
Stars: Edward G Robinson, Ruth Hussey, Guinn Williams
Rating: ★★

A rarely seen but serviceable Edward G Robinson thriller which carries echoes of *I Am a Fugitive from a Chain Gang*, the classic realist drama from Robinson's old studio, Warner Bros. This was made over at MGM and there's a certain lack of toughness in the script and supporting cast, although Edward G comfortably snarls his way through hell and high water as he is framed, sentenced to a chain gang, escapes, is blackmailed, jailed again, and brings the plot to a fiery conclusion.

Black Narcissus ○
1946, UK, 100 mins, colour
Dir: Michael Powell, Emeric Pressburger
Stars: Deborah Kerr, Sabu, David Farrar, Jean Simmons, Flora Robson
Rating: ★★★★★

Ravishingly photographed in Technicolor, this is an unusual but palpable hit from the Powell and Pressburger team, masters of the offbeat, who shot it in between making *A Matter of Life and Death* and *The Red Shoes*. Deborah Kerr heads the group of nuns who are overtaken by worldly pleasures that shatter their lives at a remote convent in lush Himalayan jungles. Kathleen Byron, as another of the nuns, gives a brilliant portrayal of approaching madness.

Black Orchid, The ○
1958, US, 95 mins, b/w
Dir: Martin Ritt
Stars: Sophia Loren, Anthony Quinn, Mark Richman, Ina Balin
Rating: ★★★

The first of Anthony Quinn's 'European' roles leading up to his triumph five years later in *Zorba the Creek*. In this unexpectedly tender love story he plays an Italian wooing a gangster's widow. The film also established Sophia Loren's claim as an actress of some worth and paved the way for her Oscar-winning triumph three years later in *Two Women*.

Blackout
See: Contraband

Black Rain ● ⓥ
1989, US, 125 mins, colour
Dir: Ridley Scott
Stars: Michael Douglas, Andy Garcia, Kate Capshaw, Ken Takakura
Rating: ★★

Despite its Japanese background (very picturesquely shot) and high level of violence, this is a routine crime thriller with a gun-barrel-load of familiar ingredients. Michael Douglas, looking wearier and older, is the slightly crooked, rule-bending cop sent to Japan with an oriental master crook captured in America. No prizes for guessing what happens at Tokyo Airport, nor any of the plot's other developments, given that Andy Garcia is Douglas's happy-go-lucky, honest partner, Ken Takakura the Japanese associate reluctant to go out on a limb for Douglas, and Kate Capshaw the club hostess who tells him to leave town. The only twist in the tale lies in the methods Douglas finally employs to get close to his quarry, leading to a chase climax in which another motorcycle is conveniently parked next to the one stolen by the bad guy. Yusaka Matsuda makes rather a good job of the lithe, sneering villain.

Black Rainbow ● ⓥ
1989, US, 101 mins, colour
Dir: Mike Hodges
Stars: Rosanna Arquette, Jason Robards, Tom Hulce
Rating: ★★

Not content with being an okay if overlong straight thriller about a medium who finds herself seeing deaths – a theme used before, although not all that often – *Black Rainbow* finally makes it through to the supernatural proper in the last reel. This aspect seems rather 'tacked on' and not entirely relevant to the main theme of a moderately written but well acted and directed thriller, with some doomy *film noir* music by John Scott to back its trance of death. Rosanna Arquette's

childlike voluptuousness is quite effective as the visionary in white who suddenly starts foreseeing events of urest black. The variable Jason Robards is for once on form as her father, who doesn't believe a word of it, and Tom Hulce somewhat caught between the two as the reporter on the scent of a decidedly unusual story.

Black Robe ● ⓥ
1991, Canada, 100 mins, colour
Dir: Bruce Beresford
Stars: Lothaire Bluteau, Aden Young, Sandrine Holt, August Schellenberg
Rating: ★★

This beautifully-photographed Canadian film is a cross between *The Mission* and *Dances With Wolves* – a sort of *Dances With Moose*, perhaps. Those films showed how to portray early communion with native inhabitants as exciting, enthralling cinema. Beresford's film, while shimmering to look at and earnest of intent, shows how all too easy it is to bore your audience stiff with the same subject matter. There's lots of mud and snow and the atmosphere of primitivism is quite well caught. Only occasionally, however, does the story catch fire: a scene in which Lothaire Bluteau as the Jesuit priest (the black robe of the title) translates writing for native Indians who have never seen it is one of the few to generate genuine warmth and interest, and afford brief amusement.

Black Room, The ◑ ⓥ
1935, US, 67 mins, b/w
Dir: Roy William Neill
Stars: Boris Karloff, Marian Marsh
Rating: ★★

A period chiller with Boris Karloff on the rampage as twin brothers, in the first of numerous films he made for Columbia after his big successes at Universal in the early Thirties. A gruesomely spectacular climax and imaginative direction by Roy William Neill, who made many of Basil Rathbone's Sherlock Holmes films.

Black Rose, The ○
1950, US/UK, 120 mins, colour
Dir: Henry Hathaway
Stars: Tyrone Power, Orson Welles, Jack Hawkins, Cecile Aubry, Michael Rennie, Herbert Lom
Rating: ★★★

Spectacular adventure with outstanding colour photography by Jack Cardiff. At the helm here is Hollywood veteran Henry Hathaway, imperiously putting his imposing cast

B

through its paces in an enjoyably fanciful Far Eastern saga. Tyrone Power and Jack Hawkins are solidly teamed as the adventuresome friends falling foul of Orson Welles' Mongol chieftain.

Black Sheep ① ⓥ

1996, US, 86 mins, colour
Dir: Penelope Spheeris
Stars: Chris Farley, David Spade, Tim Matheson, Christine Ebersole, Gary Busey
Rating ★★

A crude and basic although not offensive comedy starring cuddly Chris Farley as the clumsy sibling of a would-be senatorial candidate (Tim Matheson) – a disaster magnet if ever there were one. 'I'm not a brother, I'm an embarrassment,' he howls in anguish – and so he is, so much so that attempts to hide him in the country result only in further humiliation on the front pages of local newspapers. A bit like Margaret Thatcher's relationship with John Major around the same time, although, unlike Lady T, Chris does come good in the end. Harmless but hardly hilarious. Farley's sidekick David Spade is scarcely in it.

Black Sheep of Whitehall, The ⊙

1941, UK, 80 mins, b/w
Dir: Basil Dearden
Stars: Will Hay, John Mills, Basil Sydney, Felix Aylmer
Rating: ★★★

This is the Will Hay comedy that has the ferociously fast and funny motorcycle and sidecar chase as its climax, with Hay and John Mills on the bike, to which is attached a bath chair with an aged professor aboard. Partly done by back projection, of course, but the children should fall off the armchairs laughing. Hay plays a bumbling professor who thwarts a dastardly Nazi plot.

Black Shield of Falworth, The ○

1954, US, 100 mins, colour
Dir: Rudolph Maté
Stars: Tony Curtis, Janet Leigh, Daniel O'Herlihy, Barbara Rush
Rating: ★★★

Exuberant, spectacular Hollywood version of Merrie England, filled with battling bodies, wonderful mangling of the English language by Tony Curtis and attractive supporting performances by Daniel O'Herlihy, Barbara Rush and Herbert Marshall. Janet Leigh is a

stunning heroine and the whole fast-moving thing has an invigorating comic-strip vitality running through it. Hang your brain in the hall, sit back and let this one flow over you.

Black Spurs ○

1965, US, 81 mins, colour
Dir: R G Springsteen
Stars: Rory Calhoun, Terry Moore, Scott Brady, Linda Darnell
Rating: ★

A ragged Western about a crisis in the life of an embittered bounty hunter, this features the last screen appearance of Linda Darnell. A few weeks later, she was killed in a fire. It's all decked out with one of those rousing Western theme songs. And fans of vintage film stars will recognise Bruce Cabot, Lon Chaney Jr, Richard Arlen and James Best in the supporting cast.

Black Stallion, The ○

1979, US, 117 mins, colour
Dir: Carroll Ballard
Stars: Mickey Rooney, Kelly Reno, Teri Garr
Rating: ★★★

A 1941 children's classic (by Walter Farley) about a boy's adventures with his Arabian horse from shipwreck to racing championship. Beautifully filmed by director Carroll Ballard and photographer Caleb Deschanel for Francis Coppola's Zoetrope studios, with Kelly Reno as the admirable hero. Mickey Rooney turns in a lovely, restrained performance as a wise old horse trainer. It gets a bit slow in patches, but remains stunningly shot throughout. The brilliant opening sequences contain material that may be distressing to sensitive younger children.

Black Sunday ①

1976, US, 140 mins, colour
Dir: John Frankenheimer
Stars: Robert Shaw, Bruce Dern, Marthe Keller
Rating: ★★

This is an over-expanded 50-minute story, but director John Frankenheimer keeps the tension massively high throughout the last fifth of a chilling tale of a Black September-style plot to wipe out 80,000 Americans at the Super Bowl. Robert Shaw, Bruce Dern, Marthe Keller and Fritz Weaver all stand up well as personalities against the action.

Black Swan, The ⊙

1942, US, 85 mins, colour
Dir: Henry King

Stars: Tyrone Power, Maureen O'Hara, Laird Cregar, George Sanders, Anthony Quinn
Rating: ★★★

Spirited pirate fare, made in rousing Technicolor. George Sanders doesn't seem too happy as the red-bearded villain and can't offer Tyrone Power, whose good looks and swordsmanship were both at their peak, much competition in the swashbuckling stakes. More stylish villainy is provided by a black-patched Anthony Quinn, the stoutly suave Laird Cregar and oily sophisticate George Zucco.

Black Tent, The ○

1956, UK, 93 mins, colour
Dir: Brian Desmond Hurst
Stars: Anthony Steel, Donald Sinden, Andre Morell, Donald Pleasence
Rating: ★★

Exotic adventure yarn from the Rank factory, with Anthony Steel as the British officer who joins the bedouin during the African campaign and marries the sheikh's daughter. Pleasantly shot romantic drama, all very stiff upper lip.

Black Widow ○

1955, US, 95 mins, colour
Dir: Nunnally Johnson
Stars: Van Heflin, Ginger Rogers, Gene Tierney, George Raft
Rating: ★★

Flashback thriller that turns out to be a faintly uninteresting whodunnit. Van Heflin is first-rate as the Broadway producer trying to prove he didn't murder the girl found dead in his flat. Nunnally Johnson's witty script keeps things buzzing – despite some unexpectedly poor performances.

Black Widow ① ⓥ

1987, US, 103 mins, colour
Dir: Bob Rafelson
Stars: Debra Winger, Theresa Russell, Dennis Hopper, Sami Frey, Nicol Williamson, Diane Ladd
Rating: ★★★

It's refreshing these days to find a thriller with so much plot, although this one is a bit too complex for its own good, even if it does just enough to keep you engrossed to the end. The admirable Debra Winger has a tough time coping with the difficult role of the workaholic Department of Justice investigator whose beady brains detect a link between the seemingly natural deaths of wealthy middle-aged men. No-one is prepared to follow up her suspicions, but naturally she's right or we wouldn't have a film. Doing the matching, catching and dispatching is the picture's other female star, Theresa Russell, as the black widow of the title. Like the spider, you see, she mates and she kills. The investigator's Achilles heel is that she envies her suspect's lifestyle, and even becomes involved with one of the husbands-to-be. These weaknesses make the character oddly dislikeable. We can never quite take to her, any more than viewers may take to a film which asks them to do so much of the spadework themselves.

Black Windmill, The ⓒ
1974, UK, 106 mins, colour
Dir: Don Siegel
Stars: Michael Caine, Joseph O'Conor, Donald Pleasence, John Vernon
Rating: ★★

This espionage thriller is slick and craftsmanlike but runs along familiar lines and is packed with such veterans of the genre as John Vernon, Donald Pleasence, Clive Revill and Joss Ackland. Michael Caine, as usual, gives full value as the intelligence agent whose pursuit of gun runners ultimately threatens his own family. But the film remains uncharacteristic of its distinguished director, Don Siegel, who also made *Dirty Harry* and *The Shootist*.

Black Zoo ⓒ
1963, US, 88 mins, colour
Dir: Robert Gordon
Stars: Michael Gough, Jeanne Cooper, Rod Lauren, Virginia Grey
Rating: ★★

Michael Gough's only starring American film is a horror story which casts him as a carnival owner who uses his big cats to kill his enemies, a situation used 30 years previously in *Murders in the Zoo*. This version includes some chilly set-pieces. In the supporting cast you will find Jerome Cowan and Elisha Cook Jr who on the face of it do not seem to have much in common. But vintage film-fans will remember that Cowan played Sam Spade's murdered partner, and Cook did his memorable portrait of the would-be tough gunman, both in John Huston's 1941 classic *The Maltese Falcon*.

Blade Runner ⓒ Ⓥ
1982, US, 130 mins, colour
Dir: Ridley Scott
Stars: Harrison Ford, Rutger Hauer, Sean Young, Edward James Olmos, M Emmet Walsh, Daryl Hannah
Rating.: ★★

The special effects and sets of this 21st century detective yarn are brilliant, even if the storyline takes some following. If you aren't lost after the first 15 minutes, you score high marks on the genius IQ computer bank file. Harrison Ford is the monosyllabic hero hunting down deadly replicants (human duplications) amid breathtaking visuals that even surpass those in director Ridley Scott's previous film *Alien*.

Blade Runner – The Director's Cut ⓒ Ⓥ
1992, US, 117 mins, colour
Dir: Ridley Scott
Stars: Harrison Ford, Rutger Hauer, Sean Young, Edward James Olmos, M Emmet Walsh, Daryl Hannah
Rating: ★★★★

Preview audiences for this futuristic *film noir* classic in 1982 were confused by its storyline of a former cop in the next century tracking down mutinous replicants who have escaped to Earth from space. Executives at Warners had what they thought was the perfect answer: get British director Ridley Scott to re-edit certain sequences, add an upbeat ending and a hard-boiled voiceover from star Harrison Ford to explain the actions and motivation of his character. Almost a decade later, Scott was given the chance to look again at the film, and the result here is the cut he would have preferred to be released originally. And it marks the elevation of a flawed cult film to true classic status. Out goes the much maligned narration and the silly ending and the film now flows better with a moody and languid pace and its groundbreaking score by Vangelis tinkered with to awesome effect.

Blame it on Rio ⓒ Ⓥ
1983, US, 100 mins, colour
Dir: Stanley Donen
Stars: Michael Caine, Joseph Bologna, Michelle Johnson, Demi Moore, Valerie Harper
Rating: ★★★

A rarity: a sex comedy that at times is both sexy and funny – though not, you should be warned, all of the time. At least Stanley Donen's cameras catch the authentic Brazilian atmosphere, as Michael Caine and Joseph Bologna, both with marriage problems, go for a tropic holiday with their daughters and Caine embarks on an affair with his friend's (very nubile) 'little girl'. Much of what follows is quite funny, particularly when Bologna finds out but

proves to have an amorous secret of his own. Caine and Bologna play the shenanigans in commendably relaxed style and, while Michelle Johnson can't act for toffee, she certainly is an apple of a dish: must be why Caine falls in love with her! Even in the less showy role, though, you'd have put your money on Demi Moore for stardom out of the two girls involved.

Blame it on the Bellboy ⓒ Ⓥ
1991, UK, 78 mins, colour
Dir: Mark Herman
Stars: Dudley Moore, Bryan Brown, Richard Griffiths, Patsy Kensit, Alison Steadman, Penelope Wilton
Rating: ★★

Just a moderately amusing comedy of mistaken identity, this, but at least you can't accuse it of being too long. Picturesquely set in Venice, it all stems from the confusion surrounding the names Horton, Orton and Lawton, three guests at a hotel. One (Dudley Moore) is there to buy a villa, the second (Bryan Brown) is a hired assassin and the third (tubby Richard Griffiths) a north country mayor out for a dirty weekend. All the expected complications with sex and gangsters ensue, but the dialogue has its occasionally happy moments: 'You don't meet many people when you're an assassin', growls Brown to Penelope Wilton, who's there for a blind date with Griffiths. Neatly constructed and wound up by first-time director Mark Herman, the script mixes titters and tedium in about equal proportions. Of the cast, Wilton steals the show as the spinster whose toothy exterior conceals a spine of steel.

Blanche Fury ○
1948, UK, 95 mins, colour
Dir: Marc Allegret
Stars: Valerie Hobson, Stewart Granger, Walter Fitzgerald, Michael Gough, Maurice Denham
Rating: ★★★

A lavish slice of gloom and doom, set in period, wonderfully photographed in Technicolor by Guy Green and Geoffrey Unsworth (both Oscar-winners) and altogether typical of Rank's splash-out policy of post-war years which nearly bankrupted the company. The story is pure melodrama, a sort of *Jane Eyre* meets *The Gypsy and the Gentleman,* with passions running high up at t'hall. But Valerie Hobson never looked lovelier or more alluring under the smouldering direction of Frenchman Marc Allegret.

B

Blank Check
See: Blank Cheque

Blank Cheque O Ⓥ
(aka: Blank Check)
1994, US, 94 mins, colour
Dir: Rupert Wainwright
Stars: Brian Bonsall, Karen Duffy, Miguel
Ferrer, Michael Lerner
Rating: ★★

For much of its running time, this is a
good example of how not to make an
entertaining film about an 11-year-old
boy accidentally coming into a million-
dollar fortune in stolen money. The
naive treatment by first-time director
Rupert Wainwright ensures that many
of the more interesting gags are
thrown away, as Preston (Brian
Bonsall), the Cinderella of his family,
proceeds to spend his way through the
million in less than a week. And
Pseuds Corner specialists will have a
field day in his relationship with bank
teller/FBI agent Karen Duffy, to whom
he gives a good time while she's pursuing the million and the crook (Miguel
Ferrer) who stole it - especially as
Preston plans to woo her if she's still
available when he's 18. But Michael
Lerner is amusing as the crooked bank
president who advises Ferrer after a
week's fruitless pursuit that it 'might
be easier to steal another million dollars' and you're left regretting the
catalogue of missed opportunities in
what might have been, and almost still
is, a nice little film.

Blaze O Ⓥ
1989, US, 121 mins, colour
Dir: Ron Shelton
Stars: Paul Newman, Lolita Davidovich,
Jerry Hardin
Rating: ★★

If shot as a TV movie, this freewheeling biopic would probably have been
called *The Governor and the Strip Queen*,
and passed on the sex scenes. Here it's
recrafted as a vehicle for its star (Paul
Newman with a quiff) and provides,
with a top-notch production, quite
good if somewhat protracted entertainment. Senator Earl K Long (an actorly
portrait by Newman), first seen declaring 'I have a weakness for
tough-willed, iron-minded, independent women with big hooters', gets all
of that and more in Blaze Starr (red-
haired Lolita Davidovich, good if not
outstanding), a girl from a backwoods
family who has become top cat at a
plush New Orleans strip joint. She
also loves him, in her own way, and
the scandal of their affair rocks the

governor's seat in more ways than
one. Interesting rather than great, this
hasn't the sort of script that makes for
great cinema, but should still provide
Newman fans with much to admire.

Blazing Saddles ❶ Ⓥ
1974, US, 90 mins, colour
Dir: Mel Brooks
Stars: Cleavon Little, Gene Wilder, Slim
Pickens, David Huddleston, Mel Brooks,
Madeline Kahn
Rating: ★★★

Arguably Mel Brooks' funniest film,
Blazing Saddles is without doubt his
most successful. Daft situations, zany
sight gags and a smattering of toilet humour are thrown together to lampoon
every Western you've ever seen.
Cleavon Little plays a black sheriff
sent to protect a small town from land
developers. Of course, he's not exactly welcomed with open arms and his
only ally is the lone prisoner in his
new jail (Gene Wilder). The gags
come thick and fast like the pellets
from a scattergun. It's all extremely
silly, but great fun even if you've seen
it before. Interesting footnote: for
many years this spoof was the highest-
grossing Western ever, until *Dances
With Wolves* comfortably overtook it.

Bless This House O
1972, UK, 89 mins, colour
Dir: Gerald Thomas
Stars: Sidney James, Diana Coupland,
Terry Scott, June Whitfield
Rating: ★★

Or, to be more precise, *Bless This House
meets Happy Ever After*, as the Abbots'
new neighbours prove to be none
other than Terry Scott and June
Whitfield. Scott's old sparring partner
Bill Maynard is also in the cast, and
regular *Carry On* director Gerald
Thomas is at the helm of a series of familiar slapstick scenes involving fire,
water and DIY decorating.

Blind Alley O
1939, US, 75 mins, b/w
Dir: Charles Vidor
Stars: Chester Morris, Ralph Bellamy,
Ann Dvorak, Melville Cooper
Rating: ★★★

A skillful *film noir* with shades of *The
Desperate Hours* as a group of escaped
convicts hold a family hostage. An
above-par offering from German-born
director Charles Vidor, who was also
responsible for that evergreen of
Hollywood erotica, *Gilda*. It's a taut
story (scripted by three writers based
in turn on a hit play) with great moody

black and white photography. It was
remade as *The Dark Past*, starring
William Holden, in 1948.

Blind Corner O
1963, UK, 76 mins, b/w
Dir: Lance Comfort
Stars: William Sylvester, Barbara
Shelley, Elizabeth Shepherd
Rating: ★★★

A minor British thriller but an above
average one, thanks to a tight script
and William Sylvester's performance
as a blind man in danger. Barbara
Shelley is in fine form too, given a
chance for once to play a sexy dramatic lady instead of her usual frightened
(or frightening) Hammer heroine.

Blind Date O
1959, UK, 95 mins, b/w
Dir: Joseph Losey
Stars: Stanley Baker, Hardy Kruger,
Micheline Presle, Gordon Jackson
Rating: ★★★

Intriguing, if slightly obtuse, suspense
thriller which proved a big boost to director Joseph Losey's career in Britain
after he had been blacklisted in his native America by the Un-American
Activities Committee. Intelligent, sardonic dialogue, a skilful dovetailing of
flashbacks and present action, and a
clever performance by Stanley Baker
as a class-conscious policeman bitter
about his own status and the corruption he knows exists in the Force,
overcome the improbabilities of the
plot to make the film a big success by
its own unambitious standards.

Blind Date ❶ Ⓥ
1987, US, 93 mins, colour
Dir: Blake Edwards
Stars: Kim Basinger, Bruce Willis, John
Larroquette
Rating: ★★

Some date! Nebbish third-grade businessman Bruce Willis, a scruffy
workaholic failure desperate for a date
at a big do, accepts his brother's offer
of Nadia (Kim Basinger), a shy southern belle who mustn't be allowed to
drink. So what does he do? Right!
The man clearly hasn't seen any
Gremlins films. What's more, he buys a
bottle of champagne to take the girl
along to the recording studio where he
used to play guitar. Is this credible or
what? Moreover, this opening sequence underlines the film's whole
basic problem. Comedy like this urgently needs to be rooted in reality.
But *Blind Date* is so totally unbelievable
from start to finish that it just isn't

funny. A witty script would help, but this one is pretty moderate, and it's only when director Blake Edwards manages to string a set of sight gags together towards the end that the film shows signs of breaking out of its laughter vacuum.

Blind Fury ● Ⓥ

1989, US, 87 mins, colour
Dir: Phillip Noyce
Stars: Rutger Hauer, Terrance O'Quinn, Brandon Call, Lisa Blount, Meg Foster
Rating: ★★★

This is a chop-their-limbs-off action film but, to its credit, it's one that tries hard, and often successfully, to keep a sense of humour running through its mayhem. Rutger Hauer is the blind Vietnam vet with quite impossible prowess with a sword, handed an equally impossible assignment in escorting a nine-year-old boy to his father. The boy's also wanted by Nevada gangsters who have just killed his mother and need the boy to force his chemist father (Terrance O'Quinn) into the drugs business. Director Phlip Noyce keeps the action-packed journey as lively as you could wish and sword firmly in cheek. Two of the villains are called Lyle and Tector (after the brothers in *The Wild Bunch*) and the gangsters' secret weapon at the end turns out to be master screen swordsman Sho Kosugi. 'I'm gonna put that blind man in a wheelchair,' grinds Tector. No chance!

Blind Terror ❶ Ⓥ

(aka: See No Evil)
1971, UK, 89 mins, colour
Dir: Richard Fleischer
Stars: Mia Farrow, Robin Bailey, Dorothy Alison, Paul Nicholas
Rating: ★★★★★

A virtuoso performance by Mia Farrow, and powerhouse direction by Richard Fleischer, makes this spiral staircase-type thriller (blind girl menaced by unknown killer) one of the best of its kind. Fleischer's gradual build-up of the tension is an object lesson on how to make this kind of suspense work to the maximum effect. Farrow's delicate, sympathetic and later agonising performance remains one of the best of her career to date.

Blink ● Ⓥ

1994, US, 106 mins, colour
Dir: Michael Apted
Stars: Madeleine Stowe, Aidan Quinn, Bruce A Young
Rating: ★★

This is the one about the cop who falls in love with a beautiful witness to murder and tries to protect her from the killer. The formula stuff is given a twist by making the witness (Madeleine Stowe) the recipient of newly grafted eyes following 20 years of blindness. This leads to 'perceptual delay', which means that objects that are blurred to her now can crop up before her eyes, crystal-clear, 24 hours after. Strung out beyond its story, the plot takes too long to get going, although Stowe's unexpected visions make for some jumpy moments to begin with. Although the actress herself is remarkably good, she has too much shouting, screaming and romancing to do in scenes that interrelate her with cop Aidan Quinn, whose behaviour, like hers, is none too logical at times.

Bliss ● Ⓥ

1985, Australia, 111 mins, colour
Dir: Ray Lawrence
Stars: Barry Otto, Lynette Curran, Miles Buchanan, Helen Jones, Gia Carides
Rating: ★★

A black fantasy that blends rule-bending ideas with box-office elements in a crude, outrageous, often repulsive mix that at the same time offers a sentimental overview of a story that moves in zigzag fashion towards a happy ending. Harry (Barry Otto) is a fortyish ad executive with a comely, but faithless wife. Their snooty son and buxom daughter are both steeped in drugs and perversion. Affable enough in himself, Harry suffers a heart attack and 'dies' for four minutes before a prolonged spell in hospital and open heart surgery. Afterwards, he becomes convinced he sees visions of hell and resolves to purify his soul. His family have him locked away, but not before he has met Honey (Helen Jones), a hooker from the outback and all-round child of nature; their destinies become inextricably involved, even after Henry is freed from the asylum and falls prey to the great demon Advertising again. The ending takes the film into the realms of green fable rather than black farce. A definite oddity.

Bliss of Mrs Blossom, The ○

1968, UK, 93 mins, colour
Dir: Joseph McGrath
Stars: Shirley MacLaine, Richard Attenborough, James Booth, Freddie Jones, Willie Rushton, Bob Monkhouse
Rating: ★★★★

There's a high percentage of fun in this crazy comedy about a wife (Shirley MacLaine) whose lover (James Booth) came to mend her sewing machine, stayed for four years and now lives in the attic. Her husband (Richard Attenborough) is a bra-manufacturer (known as Orpheus in the Undieworld) whose ambitions to invent an expanding bra come to grief in spectacular fashion. Director Joseph McGrath converts the lives of these people – played with beautifully straight faces by the trio of stars – into a kaleidoscope of colour, noise and fun, in a superb series of visual jokes. Not least of these is Freddie Jones' acutely comic detective, and Bob Monkhouse puts in an appearance as a maniac psychiatrist. Only in the last 15 minutes does the fun flag.

Blithe Spirit ○ Ⓥ

1945, UK, 96 mins, colour
Dir: David Lean
Stars: Rex Harrison, Constance Cummings, Kay Hammond
Rating: ★★★★

Another happy Noel Coward/David Lean collaboration to follow their success with *In Which We Serve* and *This Happy Breed*. Superbly shot in Technicolor by Ronald Neame, it gave the honey-voiced Kay Hammond one of her best film roles, as the ghost of Rex Harrison's late wife, who turns up to haunt his new bride. Margaret Rutherford also scores heavily as an eccentric medium.

Blob, The ● Ⓥ

1988, US, 95 mins, colour
Dir: Chuck Russell
Stars: Shawnee Smith, Kevin Dillon, Donovan Leitch, Jeffrey DeMunn, Candy Clark, Joe Seneca
Rating: ★★★★

A rip-roaring remake of the 1958 cult classic. Treasures of that film are preserved here: for example, the amoebic green mass exploding through the cinema screen (while the audience is watching a slasher film). But *The Blob* is much more than that: director Chuck Russell uses ominous camera angles, grating music, misty woods, silent streets or swirling sewers to create genuine areas of apprehension. And the random killing of sympathetic characters as well as nasty ones leads to some unusual switches of focus in the plot. In the end it's left to the feisty heroine (Shawnee Smith in an absolute gift of a part into which she throws everything) to take on the mon-

B

ster in much the same death-staring way that Sigourney Weaver tackles her foes in *Aliens*.

Blockade ○
1938, US, 85 mins, b/w
Dir: William Dieterle
Stars: Madeleine Carroll, Henry Fonda, Leo Carrillo
Rating: ★★★

Banned in some American cities in its day since, although it doesn't take sides, it is unmistakeably set against the background of the Spanish Civil War, *Blockade* can be seen today as an exciting action film with well organised crowd and battle scenes. Much of the dialogue for the film was supplied (uncredited) by the novelist James M Cain, who wrote *The Postman Always Rings Twice*.

Block-Heads ⊙
1938, US, 60 mins, b/w
Dir: John G Blystone
Stars: Stan Laurel, Oliver Hardy, Patricia Ellis
Rating: ★★★★

One of the last great Laurel and Hardy feature comedies, made before a change of studio two years later hastened their decline. There are some splendid scenes of typical Stan-inspired cataclysmic disaster, two of which leave Ollie firstly buried up to his neck in sand and then ditto, in the remains of his own garage. Some of the dialogue exchanges are held in great affection by aficionados, and justifiably so.

Blonde Fist ● Ⓥ
1991, UK, 102 mins, colour
Dir: Frank Clarke
Stars: Margi Clarke, Carroll Baker
Rating: ★

No wonder the British film industry all but died out at the time if this inane comedy was the best we could come up with. The omens were certainly good, with the writing chores in the capable hands of Frank Clarke, who penned *Letter to Brezhnev*, and the starring role, of a working class woman making good with her fists as a female boxer, going to his sister, the pneumatic blonde bombshell Margi Clarke. But thanks to Frank Clarke's own ponderous direction and a script that proves not so much intelligent and humorous as a patronising fairytale of working-class life, it sinks quickly into a domestic drama comprising an endless stream of unfunny one-liners delivered at a snail's pace. It's also

particularly sad to see Carroll Baker taking part in such mindless drivel.

Blonde Venus ○
1932, US, 97 mins, b/w
Dir: Josef von Sternberg
Stars: Marlene Dietrich, Herbert Marshall, Cary Grant
Rating: ★★★

A star vehicle for the moody and magnetic Marlene Dietrich, here shimmeringly photographed by Bert Glennon. It's a fairly daft story, a melodrama of love and jealousy, in which producer-director Josef von Sternberg foists upon Dietrich the chance to sing 'Hot Voodoo' in a gorilla suit (how many actresses can count that among their golden opportunities?). A bizarre mixture of campy excess and soapy drama.

Blondie ⊙
1938, US, 68 mins, b/w
Dir: Frank R Strayer
Stars: Penny Singleton, Arthur Lake, Gene Lockhart, Ann Doran
Rating: ★★

With Penny Singleton and Arthur Lake perfectly cast as the bothered and bewildered Bumsteads of Chic Young's strip cartoon, this film marked the beginning of one of the longest movie series in Hollywood history. The *Blondie* films ran from 1938 to 1950 and their millions of fans watched Larry Simms (as Baby Dumpling) stay and grow up with the series. Daisy, the incorrigible dog, and Mr Beasley, the long suffering madman (played by prolific character actor Irving Bacon), were other regulars during the early years of a series which kept its popularity to the end.

Blood Alley ○
1955, US, 115 mins, colour
Dir: William Wellman
Stars: John Wayne, Lauren Bacall, Paul Fix, Mike Mazurki, Anita Ekberg
Rating: ★★

John Wayne as a seafaring soldier of fortune. Having already disposed of all unfriendly Japanese in the Second World War, this marked the start of Wayne's new campaign against any Orientals with Communist leanings. Only Wayne could get away with a line like this ... Lauren Bacall asks him in one scene why he killed a Chinese soldier. He replies: 'Seemed like a good idea.'

Blood and Sand ○ Ⓥ
1941, US, 123 mins, colour
Dir: Rouben Mamoulian

Stars: Tyrone Power, Linda Darnell, Rita Hayworth, Anthony Quinn, John Carradine
Rating: ★★★

Tyrone Power followed in the fancy footwork of Rudolph Valentino with this lavish remake of the silent star's 1922 classic saga of a matador's rise from rags to riches to retribution and won himself quite a few critical ears and tails in the process. For it, he was reunited with Linda Darnell (in the last of their four films together) and director Rouben Mamoulian, who had put Power through his paces in *The Mark of Zorro*. The role of the second female lead finally went to Rita Hayworth who made a fine, sensuous job of it and came near to stealing the picture from Power with a steamy (for the time) tango with Anthony Quinn. Mamoulian's sumptuous direction was attractively complemented by the Oscar-winning cinematography of Ernest Palmer and Ray Rennahan.

Blood and Wine ● Ⓥ
1996, US, 110 mins, colour
Dir: Bob Rafelson
Stars: Jack Nicholson, Jennifer Lopez, Stephen Dorff, Michael Caine, Judy Davis
Rating: ★

Director Rafelson's tale of a stolen necklace is a thriller without thrills. Jack Nicholson struggles badly as the thief, but Michael Caine is better as his lethally coughing English associate, and Judy Davis even better still, but too little seen as Nicholson's cuckolded wife. Alas, characters' motivations remain unclear as Davis and son Stephen Dorff make off (accidentally) with the jewels after she has beaten Nicholson to a pulp in self-defence. Unfortunately that's by no means the end of this tedious and unpleasant film that will leave you needing a) a bath and b) a holiday.

Blood Beach ●
1980, US, 90 mins, colour
Dir: Jeffrey Bloom
Stars: David Huffman, Mariana Hill, John Saxon
Rating: ★★★★

Jack Arnold, who made *The Creature from the Black Lagoon* and *The Incredible Shrinking Man*, would have been proud of this one. People are getting sucked through the sand like nobody's business in Southern California. 'Just when you know it's safe to go into the water,' growls police chief John Saxon, 'you can't get to it!' Something's under there all right and the creature's no anti-climax when it appears at the end: a sort of giant octopus without tentacles, but with an extended Venus fly trap mounted on top. Ugh! Intelligence gapes from every pore of this monster movie, and director Jeffrey Bloom builds suspense uncomfortably well as his camera lurks at a distance like some prowling predator. Bloom cleverly uses an sorts of little things to build up the atmosphere of menace and you can sense the stuffy stench of the monster's lair when it's finally invaded. Individual performances are almost all good: a group of interesting actors obviously sniffed a solid script and a marketable product.

Blood from the Mummy's Tomb ●
1971, UK, 87 mins, colour
Dir: Seth Holt
Stars: Andrew Keir, Valerie Leon, James Villiers
Rating: ★★

One of Hammer's most striking horror films, directed by the talented Seth Holt, who died before it was finished. Holt (and Michael Carreras, who completed the film) revive the old story of the mummy's revenge on those who have defiled its tomb and make it seem chillingly fresh. And the imposing Valerie Leon, in by far her best role, makes the most of her chances in the dual roles of Egyptian queen of darkness and professor's daughter.

Bloodline ◐
(aka: Sidney Sheldon's Bloodline)
1979, US, 116 mins, colour
Dir: Terence Young
Stars: Audrey Hepburn, Ben Gazzara, James Mason, Omar Sharif
Rating: ★

Frantically overheated thriller from Harold Robbins country, with Audrey Hepburn continuing her screen comeback as the heiress to 'an international pharmaceutical empire' desperately dodging various attempts on her life.

Blood Money ◐
(aka: Requiem for a Heavyweight)
1962, US, 100 mins, b/w
Dir: Ralph Nelson
Stars: Anthony Quinn, Jackie Gleason, Mickey Rooney, Julie Harris
Rating: ★★★

Gripping, tragic story of a fading boxer. Quinn is painfully real as the boxer, Mountain Rivera, and strong support comes from Mickey Rooney, Jackie Gleason and Harry Bellaver.

Appearing as one of Mountain's opponents: a 21-year-old Cassius Clay, before he himself became World Heavyweight Champion.

Blood Oath ● ⓥ
(aka: Prisoners of the Sun)
1990, Australia, 108 mins, colour
Dir: Stephen Wallace
Stars: Bryan Brown, George Takei, Jason Donovan, Tetsu Watanabe
Rating: ★★★

A sturdy combination of 'blood island' prison-camp film and court-martial drama, this war atrocities story, based on real facts, runs along familiar lines, but grips most of the way through. Bryan Brown, who once portrayed the victim of a court-martial in *Breaker Morant,* is the prosecuting officer who must try to convict Japanese officers from the island where 300 Australian soldiers have been found butchered and buried. But he has no witnesses, no evidence and defendants who merely insist that no massacres ever took place. In the end, a breakthrough comes, though it provides neither side with much satisfaction. Well put together, the film throws up an interesting new actress in Canadian born Aussie Deborah Unger.

Blood of the Vampire ●
1958, UK, 85 mins, colour
Dir: Henry Cass
Stars: Donald Wolfit, Barbara Shelley, Vincent Ball
Rating: ★★

This gory horror film, played with enormous enthusiasm by a cast led by Donald Wolfit, is not, for once, a Hammer film, although it was scripted by Jimmy Sangster, who was to become a Hammer stalwart for more than a decade. Full-blooded support from Victor Maddern as a one-eyed hunchback and from the first lady of British horror, Barbara Shelley. The excellent colour photography is the work of co-producer Monty Berman.

Blood on My Hands
See: Kiss the Blood Off My Hands

Blood on Satan's Claw ●
(aka: Satan's Skin)
1971, UK, 93 mins, colour
Dir: Piers Haggard
Stars: Patrick Wymark, Linda Hayden, Barry Andrews, Michele Dotrice
Rating: ★★

This very shuddery horror film is a demon offspring from *Children of the Damned* out of Vincent Price's *Witch-*

finder-General. Some very nasty things happen to Simon Williams, remembered as James Bellamy from *Upstairs, Downstairs.* And Linda Hayden gives her best screen performance as the leader of the devil children behind some gruesome goings-on in a 17th century village.

Blood on the Arrow ○
1964, US, 91 mins, colour
Dir: Sidney Salkow
Stars: Dale Robertson, Martha Hyer, Wendell Corey
Rating: ★

Dale Robertson is the strong silent hero of this fast-paced but poorly scripted Western, in which he out-draws what looks like the slowest gunfighter in the west. Martha Hyer is a traditional heroine in long, blonde tresses and off-the-shoulder blouse, while two of the villains are Ted de Corsia and Elisha Cook Jr, two familiar faces from Hollywood crime films of the Forties and Fifties.

Blood on the Moon ○
1948, US, 88 mins, b/w
Dir: Robert Wise
Stars: Robert Mitchum, Barbara Bel Geddes, Robert Preston, Walter Brennan
Rating: ★★★★

Excellent dark Western, sturdily directed by Robert Wise, and featuring a strong performance by Robert Mitchum in the middle of a great period for him at RKO that also included *Crossfire* and *Build My Gallows High. A* fight in a darkened bar-room is only one of numerous memorable moments from this most powerful and atmospheric of post-war Westerns, to which Robert Preston, Barbara Bel Geddes, Phyllis Thaxter and Walter Brennan all make striking contributions.

Blood on the Sun ○ ⓥ
1945, US, 98 mins, b/w
Dir: Frank Lloyd
Stars: James Cagney, Sylvia Sidney, Wallace Ford, Robert Armstrong
Rating: ★★★

Never-say-die James Cagney battles fiendish orientals plotting world domination in 1928, with the help of beautiful double agent Sylvia Sidney appearing in her first film for four years. Premier Tanaka (ironically also the name of a Japanese Prime Minister) was a real-life bad guy who allied with war lords and industrialists to further his own ends. Also suffering the slit-eyed treatment as villainous Col Tojo is burly Robert Armstrong,

B

memorable as Denham in *King Kong, Son of Kong* and *Mighty Joe Young.*

Blood Red ⚈ Ⓥ

1988, US, 91 mins, colour
Dir: Peter Masterson
Stars: Eric Roberts, Giancarlo Giannini, Dennis Hopper, Burt Young, Susan Anspach, Michael Madsen
Rating: **RB**

You've heard of spaghetti action films, now meet the vino Western. Sicilian immigrants to old California are muscled off their vineyards by railroad bully-boys, who murder the leader of the farmers' resistance. His son Marco (Eric Roberts, in plunging neckline and posy leather trousers) takes to the hills as a galloping avenger, cutting down his enemies one by one. Hollywood used to be able to make this kind of thing standing on its head, but alas no more. This is not so much *The Mark of Zorro* as *The Snore of Marco*, with drippy romantic interludes in between bursts of inconclusive action. Under Peter Masterson's direction, an all-too-distinguished cast rises to new heights of ineptitude. Pick of this curdled vintage of over-acting is Dennis Hopper's railroad boss, a role for which the actor was extremely unwise to attempt an Irish accent. Julia Roberts, in her first film, has only about three lines, which she may remember as three too many.

Blood Simple ⚈ Ⓥ

1983, US, 96 mins, colour
Dir: Joel Coen
Stars: John Getz, Frances McDormand, M Emmet Walsh, Dan Hedaya
Rating: ★★★★

A real *film noir* for the Eighties. There probably hasn't been a thriller as minimal as this since *Detour* in 1945. But director Joel Coen, making an impact with his very first film, has taken the accepted elements of adulterous couple, vengeful, dislikeable husband and corruptible private eye and moved them slowly and deliberately towards their own destinies. Blood is black, fear and agony are real. You may doze off in the exposition, but you'll sure as hell stay awake for the climax, as the story moves inexorably towards its pre-planned conclusion. M Emmet Walsh, after years of tiny and largely unrewarding roles, is brilliant as the wholly seedy Texas private eye whose perfect crime turns sour. An impressive first feature, if a shade too calculated to make the topmost bracket.

Bloodsport ⚈ Ⓥ

1987, US, 92 mins, colour
Dir: Newt Arnold
Stars: Jean-Claude Van Damme, Leah Ayres, Bolo Young, Donald Gibb, Forest Whitaker
Rating: ★

Or, more appropriately, *Bloodspurt.* The kind of movie that made you wonder where the industry was going, it takes us back 15 years to the kung fu rage, only with more blood and bone. People are getting killed out there, but Frank Dux (Jean-Claude Van Damme) wants to become world karate champion. There are a lot of preliminary bouts which really waste our time, since we know that Dux will fight and annihilate Chong Li, a Korean who flexes big pectorals a lot, in the final reel. The direction lacks intelligence, the acting lacks talent. And what is Forest Whitaker, the big black actor from *Bird* and *The Crying Game,* doing in all this? Only he could tell us.

Bloody Mama ⚈

1969, US, 90 mins, colour
Dir: Roger Corman
Stars: Shelley Winters, Don Stroud, Robert De Niro, Bruce Dern, Pat Hingle
Rating: ★★★

One of the last films to date to be directed by Roger Corman (who made the 'Edgar Allan Poe' horror films of the Sixties), this is a kind of second cousin to *Bonnie and Clyde,* except that there are no redeeming features about the appalling Ma Barker (Shelley Winters) and her brood of homicidal sons, which includes Robert De Niro in one of his earliest roles. A violent, unpleasant story that captures the right primitive backwoods feel.

Blossoms in the Dust ☉

1941, US, 99 mins, colour
Dir: Mervyn LeRoy
Stars: Greer Garson, Walter Pidgeon
Rating: ★★★

The first film (it's about orphan children) that Greer Garson and Walter Pidgeon made together started a box office bonanza unseen at MGM since the peak years of Jeanette MacDonald and Nelson Eddy. The studio teamed them together seven more times in the next 12 years – years that included such highly praised hits as *Madame Curie* and *Mrs Miniver.*

Blowing Wild ○

1953, US, 90 mins, b/w
Dir: Philip Yordan
Stars: Gary Cooper, Barbara Stanwyck,

Anthony Quinn, Ruth Roman, Ward Bond
Rating: ★★

Even with the writing talents of Philip Yordan, the star power of Gary Cooper, Barbara Stanwyck, Anthony Quinn and Ruth Roman, and one of those rolling ballads by Frankie Laine ('Marina mine – set me free. Free from black gold; our love never can be'), this drama of desire in the oil-fields of Mexico in the 1930s fails to strike many sparks. Stanwyck has the most interesting character and the film could do with more of her. But there's some (literally) dynamite action towards the end.

Blown Away ⚈ Ⓥ

1994, US, 120 mins, colour
Dir: Stephen Hopkins
Stars: Jeff Bridges, Tommy Lee Jones, Lloyd Bridges, Suzy Amis, Forest Whitaker
Rating: ★★

If you want to see a truly average mad bomber movie, set your time switch on this one. Chock full of false alarms – which switch will detonate the next bomb? – and shamelessly manipulating its audience, the film gives us Jeff Bridges as the former Irish terrorist now on the right side of the law as a crack member of the Boston bomb squad, versus Tommy Lee Jones as the unreformed bomber who escapes from prison in Ireland and picks off Bridges' squad and friends one by one. But then the plot, such as it is, functions only as a kind of underpinning to a parade of cat-and-mouse scenes, as Bridges conveniently just fails to suss out devices in time to save his colleagues and friends. At least Jones doesn't come back from the dead at the end (one's as happy to see the back of his bogus Irish accent). Otherwise, though tightly enough edited, this is filmmaking by numbers - or should it be clicks?

Blow Out ⚈ Ⓥ

1981, US, 108 mins, colour
Dir: Brian De Palma
Stars: John Travolta, Nancy Allen, John Lithgow, Dennis Franz
Rating: ★★★

John Travolta is a movie sound man who discovers that a car tyre blowout on a bridge was really a gunshot, followed by the car going over the side. He gamely rescues a prostitute in the car with a male politician (a neat flip of the Chappaquiddick scandal) and then his troubles start! Director Brian De

Palma split the critics with this homage to Hitchcock. The opening scenes are a nice tongue-in-cheek indication of the shocks that are to follow.

Blow Up ● Ⓥ

1966, UK, 110 mins, colour
Dir: Michelangelo Antonioni
Stars: David Hemmings, Vanessa Redgrave, Sarah Miles, Peter Bowles, Verushka, Jane Birkin
Rating: ★★★

Michelangelo Antonio's much-discussed film about a trendy photographer who comes to believe he may have photographed a murder. The boldly sexual role played by Vanessa Redgrave, the exuberant nude sequence involving a group of young models, and the music score, which combined rock and modern-jazz idioms, were all among the factors that contributed to the film's success. How you interpret its story is part of the fascination.

Blue Angel, The ◑ Ⓥ

1930, Germany, 102 mins, b/w
Dir: Josef von Sternberg
Stars: Emil Jannings, Marlene Dietrich
Rating: ★★★★

The Marlene Dietrich classic about a middle-aged professor who becomes infatuated with a nightclub singer. Shot in an atmosphere of stifling sexuality, the film is still one of the most harrowing depictions of human degradation on record. Dietrich's appearance as Lola-Lola, in sheer stockings, silk topper, high heels and garter belt, remains one of the unshatterable images of cinema history. The film made her a world star, and she went to Hollywood later in the year. In the English language version of the film, it's interesting to compare Dietrich's rather guttural English with the seductive, all-purpose continental accent she soon developed in Hollywood.

Blue in the Face ● Ⓥ

1995, US, 88 mins, colour
Dirs: Wayne Wang, Paul Auster
Stars: Harvey Keitel, Mel Gorham, Jared Harris, Giancarlo Esposito, Madonna, Michael J Fox, Lily Tomlin
Rating: ★★★★

A companion piece to the same directors' Smoke, this further slice of New York life again stars Harvey Keitel as the Brooklyn cigar store manager around whom the film is built. As he recalls the events of one crazy summer, a series of sketches and monologues

takes place, interrupted by musical interludes, archive footage and off-the-wall cameos by Roseanne, Lou Reed, Madonna, Michael J Fox and more. This may not sound too structured and it isn't. But, though it's mainly improvised, the film is also sharp and witty and fascinatingly ramshackle, creating a memorable and joyous celebration of Brooklyn life.

Bluebeard ●

1972, US/Italy, 125 mins, colour
Dir: Edward Dmytryk
Stars: Richard Burton, Raquel Welch
Rating: ★

This is what I suppose you could call high Gothic camp, with Richard Burton not as the Landru or Gilles de Retz of history but, would you credit it, a fictitious Austrian aristocrat with a blue-tinged beard, who does away with six wives, sundry hangers-on and a cat. All his brides, being played by some of the world's loveliest actresses, try to use their shapely wiles to turn our hero on. But he, sterile soul, remains singularly aloof, apart from struggling with some unspeakable dialogue. The results are fine, perhaps, for girl-starved males, but Burton fans are likely to find themselves demanding more in the way of drama.

Bluebeard's Eighth Wife ○

1938, US, 85 mins, b/w
Dir: Ernst Lubitsch
Stars: Claudette Colbert, Gary Cooper, David Niven, Edward Everett Horton
Rating: ★★★

Gary Cooper, who had previously starred for Ernst Lubitsch, master director of naughty-but-nice comedies, in Design for Living, is perfect casting for this later Lubitsch romp, as a millionaire who can handle money but not wives. Claudette Colbert is the girl who aims to be his eighth (but not last: she's after his alimony) wife, and there's astringent support from David Niven, Edward Everett Horton and Warren Hymer, plus Franklin Pangborn in his typecast but delightful running role of the snooty manager.

Bluebeard's 10 Honeymoons ○

1960, UK, 93 mins, b/w
Dir: W Lee Wilder
Stars: George Sanders, Corinne Calvet, Patricia Roc, Jean Kent
Rating: ★★

Unlike the Richard Burton film, this chiller really is based on the case of Henri 'Bluebeard' Landru, the murder-

ous monsieur who disposed of 10 wives. Among those getting the final curtain call from suave George Sanders are Greta Gynt, Maxine Audley, Corinne Calvet and Jean Kent.

Blue Bird, The ⊙

1940, US, 80 mins, colour
Dir: Walter Lang
Stars: Shirley Temple, Johnny Russell, Gale Sondergaard, Eddie Collins
Rating: ★★

This much-neglected fantasy was Shirley Temple's present from 20th Century-Fox for their not allowing her to do The Wizard of Oz. Like Judy Garland in that film, Shirley also sets out on an incredible journey - to find the bluebird of happiness, searching for it in the past, the future and the Land of Luxury. The photography and art direction perfectly capture the sometimes quite creepy mood of Maeterlinck's original fairy-tale play, and Gale Sondergaard as a cat and Eddie Collins as a dog offer first-class class, if faintly sinister, supporting contributions. Bits, though, are just too twee.

Blue Chips ● Ⓥ

1994, US, 108 mins, colour
Dir: William Friedkin
Stars: Nick Nolte, Mary McDonnell, J T Walsh, Shaquille O'Neal, Louis Gossett
Rating: ★

An intimate knowledge of the rules of basketball might help you a little here; but not much. This is a fairly uninteresting sports drama about the 'buying' of star students for university teams, with an over-the-top performance from Nick Nolte as the true-blue coach who sinks to corruption in order to assemble a winning team. J T Walsh is his usual loathsome self as the brains behind the bribes, and Mary McDonnell uncharacteristically damp as Nolte's supportive ex-wife. Basketball fans may be encouraged to go along by the presence of several junior greats (including the mighty Shaquille O'Neal) as members of Nolte's squad, and all of them prove serviceable actors. For the rest of us, though, there's little to cheer for here. Give us Beau Chumps any day.

Blue Dahlia, The ○

1945, US, 99 mins, b/w
Dir: George Marshall
Stars: Alan Ladd, Veronica Lake, William Bendix, Howard da Silva
Rating: ★★★★

B

The last great Forties crime film to star Alan Ladd and Veronica Lake - creatures of the Hollywood night. And what music they made together. This one also has war veteran William Bendix complaining about the 'monkey music' in his head, a lean and laconic screenplay by Raymond Chandler, and a rare fat part for that lugubrious character actor Will Wright, here as a hotel detective. They reshot the original ending – now the odds are you'll never guess 'who-dunnit'.

Blue Gardenia, The ○

1953, US, 90 mins, b/w
Dir: Fritz Lang
Stars: Anne Baxter, Richard Conte, Ann Sothern, Raymond Burr, Nat 'King' Cole
Rating: ★★★

Solid Fritz Lang-directed thriller released in the same year as his classic *The Big Heat*. The characters are riddled with neuroses and blunder through a world of glossy nightspots and sudden death, all photographed evocatively in light and shade by the high priest of *film noir* cameramen, Nicholas Musuraca. His best effects come with rain-streaked windows – and a murder reflected in the shards of a shattered mirror. Lang's tracking shots that harry the characters emphasise their entrapment in circumstances largely of their own making, especially Norah, plaintively played by Anne Baxter, who believes she may have killed a man who attacked her.

Blue Hawaii ⊙ ⓥ

1961, US, 103 mins, colour
Dir: Norman Taurog
Stars: Elvis Presley, Joan Blackman, Nancy Walters, Angela Lansbury
Rating: ★★

Angela Lansbury has always excelled at playing characters much older than herself – here she was only 10 years older than Elvis Presley but was picked to play his mother! This picture-postcard romp is little more than an Hawaiian tourist board film, padded out with 14 songs from the King, including the title song, first crooned by Bing Crosby in the 1937 film *Waikiki Wedding*. As lightweight as a lei, but it all looks splendid in Panavision and Technicolor.

Blue Heat ● ⓥ

(aka: The Last of the Finest)
1990, US, 106 mins, colour
Dir: John MacKenzie
Stars: Brian Dennehy, Joe Pantoliano,

Jeff Fahey, Bill Paxton
Rating: ★★★

The city's finest are after a drugs bust again, and this time it's a big one. Nationwide, in fact. It's the involvement of the US government that lends an edge to this well-made but basically routine tale of four cops who turn vigilante when one is killed and their leader thrown off the force - while in pursuit of said druglords. The cops are quite nicely drawn by the star quartet, there's a lot of pseudo-smart dialogue, action in which the bullets fly thicker than the four-letter words and an ironic subplot in which the super-honest cops are tempted to head for Mexico when they come into possession of $23 million worth of tainted money. Overall, though, it's a by-the-numbers job.

Blue Ice ● ⓥ

1992, UK, 106 mins, colour
Dir: Russell Mulcahy
Stars: Michael Caine, Sean Young
Rating: ★

Former MI6 agent Harry Anders (Michael Caine in a Harry Palmer type character 25 years on) just wants a quiet life running a backstreets jazz club. The trouble with Harry is that intrigue and murder dogs his every move. When beautiful American Stacy (Sean Young) prangs his prize car, Harry finds himself plunged back into the world of espionage. It's a shallow thriller but with a stylish feel, thanks to the stunning visuals conjured up by *Highlander* director Mulcahy. Silly dialogue, though, finally sinks it.

Blue Jean Cop ● ⓥ

(aka: Shakedown)
1988, US, 90 mins, colour
Dir: James Glickenhaus
Stars: Peter Weller, Sam Elliott, Patricia Charbonneau
Rating: ★★★

A fast-moving thriller where actions speak louder than words. That's just as well, since director James Glickenhaus has filled the soundtrack with so much background noise that 30 per cent of the dialogue flies by before you can grasp it. It takes about 20 minutes before you accept this in the spirit that it doesn't matter. Then you can settle down to a rough, tough, spectacularly action-packed story that's not to be taken at all seriously. *Robocop's* Peter Weller is a legal aid lawyer who teams up with shaggy undercover cop Sam Elliott, to prove a disreputable client innocent of murder

– and clear up police corruption and a city-wide drugs ring for good measure. The girls involved are nothing much, but both Weller and Elliott bring a little more to their dialogue than other actors might have done, and that's to their credit. Action is certainly in the 'terrific' league, especially a shootout in Times Square that careers on to a crash in New York harbour.

Blue Juice ● ⓥ

1995, UK, 96 mins, colour
Dir: Carl Prechezer,
Stars: Sean Pertwee, Catherine Zeta Jones, Ewan McGregor
Rating: ★

Surfing movies never were strong on storylines, relying on the massive waves for their impact. Director Carl Prechezer just barely scrapes a plot out of this dated British straggler in the genre about a surfer who, nearing 30, has to decide between his girlfriend and those big blue waves. Quite a lot of clumsy comedy is injected in an attempt to enliven the project, but poor performances (Catherine Zeta Jones' is about the best) are so thick on the ground it's difficult to raise any interest in the outcome. Most unconvincing throughout: almost like a 'Carry On' film trying to retain credibility in its characters as well as raising a smile.

Blue Lagoon, The ○

1949, UK, 103 mins, colour
Dir: Frank Launder
Stars: Jean Simmons, Donald Houston
Rating: ★★★

Spectacular, colourful adventure film, adapted much more effectively than the 1980 remake – from H de Vere Stacpoole's famous novel of the same title, about two children facing the perils of nature on a desert island. The director of the stunning Technicolor photography – the film was shot on location in Fiji – was a young cameraman called Geoffrey Unsworth, who many years later was to win an Academy Award for *Cabaret*.

Blue Lamp, The ○ ⓥ

1949, UK, 84 mins, b/w
Dir: Basil Dearden
Stars: Jack Warner, Jimmy Hanley, Dirk Bogarde, Robert Flemyng
Rating: ★★★

A now classic slice of British post-war cinema realism from Ealing Studios, with Jack Warner creating the character of kindly copper George Dixon that was to serve him so well. He made some 430 episodes of *Dixon of*

Dock Green for television between 1955 and 1976, when he finally hung up his truncheon and retired. Other plus factors include a truculent young Dirk Bogarde as the villain, glimpses of actual police work and an exciting factual account of a murder hunt.

Blue Max, The ◐ Ⓥ
1966, US, 156 mins, colour
Dir: John Guillermin
Stars: George Peppard, James Mason, Ursula Andress, Jeremy Kemp
Rating: ★★

This isn't war, but it certainly is entertainment. With that proviso safely out of the way, one can definitely award a medal to director John Guillermin (later to make the *Towering Inferno*) and his cameraman on as riveting, bloody and thoroughly convincing series of World War One aerial dogfights as you are ever likely to see – to which a throbbing music score by Jerry Goldsmith gives additional excitement. Perhaps Guillermin's utter concentration on the aerial drama explains why his ground scenes are so unworthy in comparison. But James Mason does manage to make an impression as the suavely convincing Count Von Klugerman and Jeremy Kemp has one of his best film roles as his ruthless pilot nephew.

Blue Murder at St Trinian's ☉
1957, UK, 85 mins, b/w
Dir: Frank Launder
Stars: Terry-Thomas, George Cole, Joyce Grenfell, Lionel Jeffries
Rating: ★★★★

The little horrors of this infamous school give way to the nubile nymphets of the sixth form in this further catalogue of the girls' farcical adventures. The school song at the start is especially funny, and the beauty leading the girls into one catastrophe after another really is Sabrina. It's a pity that such talented and funny people as Terry Thomas and Joyce Grenfell have so little to do, but Lionel Jeffries waltzes away with the comedy honours. Alastair Sim appears briefly at the beginning of affairs as the imprisoned Miss Fritton.

Blues Brothers, The ● Ⓥ
1980, US, 135 mins, colour
Dir: John Landis
Stars: John Belushi, Dan Aykroyd, James Brown, Ray Charles, Carrie Fisher, Aretha Franklin
Rating: ★★

One of the highest-grossing films of all time in America (although its cost was astronomical). A cataclysmic orgy of noise and destruction, it saw tubby John Belushi and big Dan Aykroyd shoot to stardom as the adult Abbott and Costello of the Eighties. Alas, two years later Belushi was dead, from an accidental overdose of drugs.

Blue Steel ● Ⓥ
1989, US, 103 mins, colour
Dir: Kathryn Bigelow
Stars: Jamie Lee Curtis, Ron Silver, Clancy Brown, Elizabeth Pena
Rating: ★

The role of a cop fighting to find a serial killer in the city would seem tailor-made for Jamie Lee Curtis' tough-tender personality. Sadly, the character is helplessly adrift in a ludicrous psychothriller that needs at least four (equally silly) climaxes before it can stagger to a conclusion. Badly scripted, packed with giggle-prone dialogue and events that go on too long and just hold up the story, the film's stuck from the start with the audience knowing who the killer is.

Blue Thunder ● Ⓥ
1982, US, 108 mins, colour
Dir: John Badham
Stars: Roy Scheider, Malcolm McDowell, Warren Oates, Candy Clark, Daniel Stern
Rating: ★★★★

Director John Badham comes up trumps here: this is a good helicopter action thriller and no messing about. Maverick police chopper flier Roy Scheider gets a new assignment to fly an ultra-sophisticated, fully-armed helicopter to be used in emergency riot control. When the man in overall charge of the project (Malcolm McDowell) turns out to be Scheider's old nemesis from 'Nam (Oh! Those headaches again!), you know he's in trouble. You also know he's going to find out something that isn't good for him, that everyone around him is liable to be killed, and that he'll end up aboard Blue Thunder taking on the bad guys single-handed: but that's half the fun. Apart from the subsequent action being in the top bracket, the script is also a winner, giving out with some nice laconic lines.

Blue Tiger ● Ⓥ
1994, US, 84 mins, colour
Dir: Norberto Barba
Stars: Virginia Madsen, Toru Nakamura, Dean Hallo, Ryu Ishibashi, Harry Dean Stanton
Rating: ★

A modest thriller about the activities of the Yakuza (Japanese Mafia), which swallow up the life of single Mum Virginia Madsen when her small son is killed in a gangland shootout. She sets out for revenge in a series of unlikely developments involving the revealing of blue tigers tattooed on the chests of oriental men. For some fairly obscure reason (unless it's for the producers to get her clothes off), Madsen has most of her body tattooed with a red tiger by an alcoholic tattoo artist – a role that proves a cruel waste of Harry Dean Stanton's talent – in a film that has lots of brutally violent action, but absolutely no likeable characters.

Blue Velvet ● Ⓥ
1986, US, 120 mins, colour
Dir: David Lynch
Stars: Kyle MacLachlan, Isabella Rossellini, Dennis Hopper, Laura Dern, Dean Stockwell
Rating: ★★

David Lynch's nightmare thriller lurches uncertainly between *film noir* and film bizarre. Even so, it certainly commands attention. It's reminiscent of one of those 'drug gang', darkly coloured movies of the late Sixties that the British censor would never pass, a feeling underlined by the presence of Dean Stockwell and Dennis Hopper, survivors from just that cycle of film. Here they hover dangerously on the edges of a story which centres on Kyle MacLachlan (Lynch's *Twin Peaks* star), whose gruesome discovery of a human car in a field leads him to a sensual Italian torch singer (Isabella Rossellini). MacLachlan is suitably mesmerised as the youth, while Hopper and Rossellini charge with frenzied abandon at their psychosexual deviates.

Blume In Love ◐
1973, US, 117 mins, colour
Dir: Paul Mazursky
Stars: George Segal, Susan Anspach, Kris Kristofferson, Shelley Winters, Marsha Mason
Rating: ★★★

One of the wryest, most individual adult comedies to emerge from Hollywood in the Seventies. George Segal's hangdog expression and harassed humour are perfectly suited to the character of Blume, a lawyer much beset by life and especially by passionate memories of the ex-wife who threw him out on his ear after he had a fling with his secretary. Segal himself has

B

never been better. But there are also outstanding contributions from Marsha Mason (just before she hit stardom) as his mistress and Shelley Winters as a plump matron. Director Paul Mazursky's sardonic and perceptive script makes the characters much more likeable than those in his previous hit *Bob & Carol & Ted & Alice*. This time, the humour is both warmer and more biting. It goes on too long, though.

Bob & Carol & Ted & Alice ①
1969, US, 105 mins, colour
Dir: Paul Mazursky
Stars: Natalie Wood, Robert Culp, Elliott Gould, Dyan Cannon
Rating: ★ ★

Highly influential sex comedy which, under the direction of Paul Mazursky, was a tremendous hit at the box-office tills, and made stars out of Elliott Gould and the plastic Dyan Cannon. Especially noteworthy for the brilliant opening helicopter shots of a car making its way to the mountain hideaway where the group talk-in ensues, and the much-publicised four-in-a-bed sequence at the end. It was also very nice to see the delectable Natalie Wood back on the screen after an absence of three years. Dated, though.

Bobo, The ○
1967, UK, 105 mins, colour
Dir: Robert Parrish
Stars: Peter Sellers, Britt Ekland, Rossano Brazzi, Adolfo Celi
Rating: ★★

One of two comedies that then-married Peter Sellers and Britt Ekland made together casts him as a singing matador, and her as a famous courtesan whom he must conquer in order to assure his future as a troubador. Hattie Jacques, John Wells and Ferdy Mayne brighten up the supporting cast, although director Robert Parrish seems to be trying hard to give the impression that he wasn't really cut out to be making Sellers comedies.

Bob Roberts ① ⓥ
1992, US, 103 mins, colour
Dir: Tim Robbins
Stars: Tim Robbins, Giancarlo Esposito, Ray Wise, Susan Sarandon, Alan Rickman
Rating: ★★★

Writer-director-star Tim Robbins almost gives us a telling political satire but not quite. As played by the imposingly bland 6ft 5in Robbins, Bob

Roberts is a singer who would be senator. And the story shows him and his cronies as fiendishly clever manipulators of the public in their quest for power. Despite his clean-cut, Kennedy-style image, Roberts is clearly a sham, with a murky past involving drugs and the exploitation of housing for the poor – well up to the dirty tricks of the political scene that will put the opposition out of the running. We can see it; but Joe Public worships him, and the coup de grace in Roberts' campaign is a fake assassination attempt, with his chief journalistic opponent as the fall guy. The result, though still frightening, isn't as tight or hard-hitting as it might have been, even though the film's heart is in the right place – firmly on its sleeve.

Bob, Son of Battle
See: Thunder in the Valley

Body and Soul ○
1947, US, 104 mins, b/w
Dir: Robert Rossen
Stars: John Garfield, Lilli Palmer, Anne Revere, Canada Lee
Rating: ★★★

A classic story of corruption in boxing, many of whose participants were to fall foul of the House Un-American Activities Committee within the ensuing few years. John Garfield has a perfect role as the pugilistic protagonist who becomes involved with crime and corruption in his quest to box his way out of his ghetto environment. Unsentimental in approach and almost impressionistic in treatment, the film had many imitators but few peers.

Body Double ● ⓥ
1984, US, 109 mins, colour
Dir: Brian De Palma
Stars: Craig Wasson, Gregg Henry, Melanie Griffith, Deborah Shelton
Rating: ★★

A second-rate actor, played by Craig Wasson, witnesses a brutal slaying, but can he trust the evidence of his own eyes? This suspense thriller from Brian De Palma is a violent and voyeuristic re-working of Hitchcock's *Rear Window* and *Vertigo*. An interesting frisson is supplied by the casting (as a porn star) of Melanie Griffith, the daughter of one of Hitchcock's favourite blondes, Tippi Hedren, star of *Marnie* and *The Birds*.

Bodyguard, The ● ⓥ
1992, US, 124 mins, colour
Dir: Mick Jackson

Stars: Kevin Costner, Whitney Houston, Gary Kemp
Rating: ★★

Kevin Costner has a lot on his plate here. Not only must he protect a singer/actress (Whitney Houston) from a threatening-letter writer and an unknown hit-man, he also has to contend with an entire supporting cast whose acting is at best moderate. The ordinary dialogue does no one any favours, either, but director Mick Jackson stages some tense action scenes when the plot is allowed to follow its natural course. Costner comes over as a cross between Steve McQueen and Gary Cooper in a movie that sorely needs his star presence. Houston sings distinctively.

Body Heat ● ⓥ
1981, US, 113 mins, colour
Dir: Lawrence Kasdan
Stars: William Hurt, Kathleen Turner, Richard Crenna, Ted Danson, Mickey Rourke
Rating: ★★★★

A real *film noir* for the Eighties. Writer-director Lawrence Kasdan has fired the ashes of *Double Indemnity* and fashioned a new wife-and-lover-plot-to-kill-husband story that has only that basic situation in common with its carnal forefather. The twists and triple twists that follow the actual murder are ingenious in the extreme. As the lovers and with the liberty adult certificates give today, Wilham Hurt and Kathleen Turner genuinely capture the idea of an overriding passion that outstrips all other moral considerations. At the back of it all is the motif of heat: a fire, a fryer in a cafe and, of course, the weather and the love/lust affair. The dialogue between Hurt and Turner is terse, loaded and beautifully delivered by the stars. As for the director, he's made the kind of film where nothing is superfluous and the clue to the denouement might pass by in a trice under your very nose.

Body of Evidence ● ⓥ
1993, US, 100 mins, colour
Dir: Uli Edel
Stars: Madonna, Willem Dafoe, Anne Archer, Joe Mantegna, Jurgen Prochnow, Julianne Moore
Rating: ★

It's not often that Hollywood blows it with a courtroom thriller, but the trouble here is that the body of evidence isn't substantial enough to fill an episode of *L.A. Law*. If only it had as many curves as its star Madonna (dramatic actress – not!), the daft dialogue wouldn't matter too much. As it is, the lack of plot is only underlined by the slowness of a film in which the story is irrelevant to sex scenes that are supposedly daring, but in fact pretty much as boring as the rest of the movie. Madonna's a 'gallery owner' (!) who seduces men with weak hearts who fall so heavily for her intense style of lovemaking that they write her into their wills. The plot, such as it is, doesn't hang together for a moment, but you'll probably be too busy trying to stay awake to think about it. A lot of good people are involved: Willem Dafoe, Joe Mantegna, Anne Archer, Julianne Moore and Frank Langella, and have very little to do but spotlight the star (whose performance is inferior to any of theirs), take the money and run. It's a bit of a trial.

Body Snatcher, The ◐
1945, US, 77 mins, b/w
Dir: Robert Wise
Stars: Boris Karloff, Henry Daniell, Bela Lugosi
Rating: ★★★

Carefully made horror film, with bravura high-spots, about an Edinburgh doctor in 1832 forced to employ a grave robber to continue his work. Henry Daniell is excellent as the doctor and the climactic ride along rain-lashed highways is a splendidly eye-popping piece of cinema.

Body Snatchers ● Ⓥ
1993, US, 84 mins, colour
Dir: Abel Ferrara
Stars: Gabrielle Anwar, Billy Wirth, Meg Tilly, Forest Whitaker, Terry Kinney
Rating: ★★

An apocalyptic update of *Invasion of the Body Snatchers*, with no Kevin McCarthy, but most other elements intact. The aliens are now shown to need some time to take over the bodies of humans and substitute them with blank replicas, via invasion by tendrils from the pods which bend people to their will. Director Abel Ferrara, in a switch from his usual mean-streets beat, cunningly casts a set of fairly blank-looking actors, so that the deceptions may be more chillingly accomplished. Once more, two survivors escape at the end, but with nowhere to go. Slow to start, it certainly has its moments near the end and is, if nothing else, a dire warning not to go to sleep in the bath. Meg Tilly, in and out of alienation, gives the best performance. Not a patch on

the original, but not a waste of your time either.

Boeing Boeing ○
1965, US/UK, 102 mins, colour
Dir: John Rich
Stars: Tony Curtis, Jerry Lewis, Dany Saval, Suzanna Leigh, Thelma Ritter
Rating: ★★

A creaky stage play, about two bachelors trying to keep various air stewardess girlfriends apart in the face of the arrival of faster Boeing jet planes, is transformed into a creaky film. But the frantic playing of Tony Curtis and Jerry Lewis, dispensing double-takes with disarming energy, at least papers over the cracks. The Parisian location of Curtis' bachelor flat is conjured up via several fuzzy exterior shots and a pseudo-Maurice Chevalier voice-over. But despite all the frantic attempts at deception, why does Curtis have different bedrooms for each of his three fiancées?

Bofors Gun, The ●
1968, UK, 106 mins, colour
Dir: Jack Gold
Stars: Nicol Williamson, Ian Holm
Rating: ★★

Director Jack Gold made an impressive feature film debut with this compelling drama which charts the brutalizing effects of military life through the experiences of seven soldiers who are given the futile task of guarding an obsolete World War Two Bofors anti-craft gun at a British army camp in Germany in 1954. His skill with actors was superbly demonstrated: showy roles went to David Warner and, in particular, Nicol Williamson, but the contributions from a near-perfect cast, which includes Ian Holm, Peter Vaughan, John Thaw and Richard O'Callaghan, are similarly well-performed. And National Service survivors will get a special identification with the situation! The film however, gets far too oppressive towards the end and will be no one's idea of light entertainment.

Boiling Point ● Ⓥ
1993, US, 93 mins, colour
Dir: James B Harris
Stars: Wesley Snipes, Dennis Hopper, Valerie Perrine, Viggo Mortensen
Rating: ★★★

An odd choice of title for a strange, off-beat, low-key crime thriller in which neither the heroes nor the villains exactly ooze menace. These are by and large people making the best of a short

straw on either side of the law. Their plans for the future are short-term and without much prospect. Wesley Snipes is the cop who is near quitting after shedding both a partner and a wife; Dennis Hopper is the longtime loser hoping that the acquisition of a cold-blooded hitman partner (Viggo Mortensen) will give him a last chance of reconciliation with his wife (Valerie Perrine) and comfortable retirement. The paths of the men cross several times – a gents loo, a coffee-stall, a dance floor – without them realising it. At the end, as a sop to Hollywood happy endings, law and order prevail. Too downbeat to be exciting, the film's fascination is in its mood, and in the background of the dance hall – tiny lives played out in slow tempo.

Bolero ●
1934, US, 83 mins, b/w
Dir: Wesley Ruggles
Stars: George Raft, Carole Lombard, Frances Drake, Ray Milland
Rating: ★★

Despite a general critical thumbs-down, this dance-drama was so popular with the public that stars George Raft (who started his career as a dancer) and Carole Lombard were rushed into a follow-up called *Rumba*. Added attractions include famous fan-dancer Sally Rand, a fiery performance from Frances Drake as one of Raft's partners, Ray Milland (here billed as Raymond) five years before *French Without Tears*, and top-notch art direction and costume design. Never mind the story – watch the terrific dance routines.

Bombsite Stolen
See: Cottage to Let

Bond Street ○
1948, UK, 108 mins, b/w
Dir: Gordon Parry
Stars: Jean Kent, Roland Young, Kathleen Harrison, Derek Farr
Rating: ★★

The first of the 'portmanteau' films made by playwright Terence Rattigan with writer/producer Anatole de Grunwald. These would later become very grand and include *The VIPs* and *The Yellow Rolls Royce*. There's already a touch of class in the setting for this one, whose events revolve round the preparations for a posh wedding. And a veritable pot-boiler it proves: there's a crisis at the dressmakers, blackmail at the invisible menders and murder at the jewellers. The script is pretty vari-

B

able in quality, but a good cast – Jean Kent, Roland Young, Kathleen Harrison, Derek Farr, Hazel Court, Ronald Howard, Patricia Plunkett, Kenneth Griffith – gives the vehicle the surface gloss it needs.

Bonjour Tristesse ○
1957, UK, 93 mins, colour
Dir: Otto Preminger
Stars: David Niven, Deborah Kerr, Jean Seberg
Rating: ★★

This ostensibly stylish melodrama set on the French Riviera is about a rakish Frenchman who falls for a repressed American beauty, an affair which has tragic consequences. In tow is his 17-year-old daughter who seems to be turning into a chip off the old block. Superficial is a good word to describe this whole picture and credibility isn't helped by the unfortunate casting. David Niven is as perfectly English as ever as the Parisian womaniser and Jean Seberg is totally unconvincing as his daughter. Deborah Kerr tries her best as the tragic Anne, but even she is hampered by a poor script.

Bonnie and Clyde ◐ Ⓥ
1967, US, 108 mins, colour
Dir: Arthur Penn
Stars: Warren Beatty, Faye Dunaway, Michael J Pollard, Gene Hackman, Estelle Parsons
Rating: ★★★★

One of the most exciting discoveries of its time. Director Arthur Penn shows all the dirt, sweat and above all desperation of the trade – outlawry – whose members lived by the very ends of shreds of nerves, knowing that death, sudden and painful, was never further away than a knock on a shuttered door in the night. The disreputable, edgy, unreal atmosphere of the times and the disregard for the life that still remains precious is very well conveyed, with Warren Beatty keeping a tight grip on the moody Clyde, who robs banks (and kills as a result of it) only because he knows no other way of life. But the real find of the film was Faye Dunaway, giving a slow-burning fusebox of a performance as Bonnie, with one stand-out moment – mistily photographed against a yellow cornfield – when she realises she can never go back to her old life.

Bonnie Prince Charlie ○
1948, UK, 113 mins, colour
Dir: Anthony Kimmins
Stars: David Niven, Margaret Leighton,

Jack Hawkins, Finfay Currie
Rating: ★★

British film spectacular about the Young Pretender and the rising of '45. It boasts fine colour photography, in many cases in the actual locations where Charles' adventures and battles took place. David Niven takes the title role – an unusual piece of casting and one that, in the opinion of many, didn't work too well. Hardly the fault of this versatile actor, just that in this role he was somewhat out of his element. And the film's stately pace didn't help him, either.

Bonnie Scotland ☉
1935, US, 80 mins, b/w
Dir: James W Horne
Stars: Stan Laurel, Oliver Hardy, June Lang, Jimmy Finlayson
Rating: ★★★

One of the most delightful of Stan Laurel and Oliver Hardy's vintage comedies from their golden Thirties period. This one includes some hilarious tomfoolery in Scotland (where Stan travels from America only to discover he has inherited not a fortune but a set of bagpipes) and India, as well as one of their famous dance routines. This one evolves from an order by their sergeant (the pop-eyed Jimmy Finlayson) to pick up a mass of litter with spikes – an operation which L and H gradually transform into an impromptu soft-shoe shuffle. The film also includes the classic scene where Stan, hopelessly out of time on the march, gradually transfers his own step to the entire squad.

Boomerang ○
1946, US, 88 mins, b/w
Dir: Elia Kazan
Stars: Dana Andrews, Jane Wyatt, Lee J Cobb, Arthur Kennedy
Rating: ★★★★

Dana Andrews, an actor very much in the forefront of 20th Century-Fox's realist dramas, is in crisp, hard-hitting form in this true-life story as the politically ambitious attorney who is unconvinced of the guilt of a vagrant who has 'confessed' to the broad-daylight murder of a priest. The location filming, night-time shots and the fine details of the attorney's battle to establish the validity of his case all serve to give the film a unique grip.

Boomerang ● Ⓥ
1992, US, 116 mins, colour
Dir: Reginald Hudlin
Stars: Eddie Murphy, Robin Givens,

Halle Berry, Grace Jones, Eartha Kitt
Rating: ★★

There aren't many good things in this Eddie Murphy equivalent of a Rock Hudson-Doris Day comedy, set in the fashion world and with photography dedicated to the worship of one E Murphy. The wittily barbed exchanges between Hudson and Day (and Tony Randall) are replaced with four-letter words and a dinner party scene rife with references to sex, one that ends with the parents of a prospective boyfriend having sex in the bathroom for an hour. Funny, huh? It's as glossy as those comedies of yesteryear, but without any of the finesse. So who expects finesse in an Eddie Murphy film? Halle Berry is an attractive heroine, but all in all this was another step on the slope downwards for this particular five-minute wonder.

Boom Town ○
1940, US, 120 mins, b/w
Dir: Jack Conway
Stars: Clark Gable, Spencer Tracy, Claudette Colbert, Hedy Lamarr
Rating: ★★

Clark Gable and Spencer Tracy pal up and break up, and get rich and go broke so many times in this oil-drilling saga that it's hard to keep track. But, while Gable and Tracy got dirty making it, the film itself cleaned up at the box-office. It was the last of what Tracy called 'my three Gable pictures' (the others being *San Francisco* and *Test Pilot*). The two men got along well, but Tracy reckoned enough was enough, and never conceded top billing for a major role again.

Boost, The ● Ⓥ
1988, US, 100 mins, colour
Dir: Harold Becker
Stars: James Woods, Sean Young, Steven Hill
Rating: ★★

If you had to cast one actor as a hyper-tense, high-flying salesman with a quick temper and a vulnerability to cocaine, it would have to be James Woods. And Woods it is, in this cautionary tale about the effects of demon drugs. Its melodramatic, over-the-top approach explains why it lay on the shelf for two years before a cinema release. Woods gives his usual 100 percent and Sean Young has some appealing, vulnerable moments as his wife, but they never come across as real people in this sad and harrowing but rarely affecting story. Woods is such an unsympathetic character to begin with, and gives such an unvarying performance, that sympathy is hard to muster and he and Young lack that vital spark of warmth that would make their plight easier to reach out to.

Border, The ●
1980, US, 107 mins, colour
Dir: Christopher Leitch
Stars: Telly Savalas, Danny De La Paz, Eddie Albert
Rating: ★★

This is a hard-hitting action film highlighting the unlawful smuggling of cheap Mexican labour across the Mexican/American border. It attempts to expose the corrupt element in the American border police (here in the form of a Commander played by screen veteran Eddie Albert) that lets traffickers get away with it. Telly Savalas stars as a very different lawman from the lollipop-sucking crook-seeker he portrayed in *Kojak*; he's a rugged US patrolman whose refusal of bribery has led to his transfer from the city to the no-man's-land which separates Mexico and the United States.

Border, The ●
1981, US, 108 mins, colour
Dir: Tony Richardson
Stars: Jack Nicholson, Harvey Keitel, Valerie Perrine, Warren Oates
Rating: ★★

Far from his famous Sixties films *Tom Jones* and *The Charge of the Light Brigade*, British director Tony Richardson casts a suitably severe eye on the serious problem of illegal immigration on the Texas-Mexico border. Heading a first-rate cast, Jack Nicholson is reckless enough to appear with a dangerously receding hairline and a hint of a potbelly as the former cop who refuses to become involved in the wholesale corruption rife amongst his fellow border patrolmen. Even so, his character is no saint and it's hard to care too deeply about the fates of these unfortunate people trapped in the brutally depicted squalor of a Tex-Mex hell.

Border Incident ○
1949, US, 92 mins, b/w
Dir: Anthony Mann
Stars: Ricardo Montalban, George Murphy, Howard da Silva
Rating: ★★★

This tight-knit crime film, the forerunner of many others about 'wetbacks' – illegal immigrants scuttling across the border from Mexico to the United States – is similar in structure to another good thriller also directed by Anthony Mann: *T-Men*. One particular death scene is most uncompromising for the 1940s, and tension is kept on high throughout by the director and his formidable cast.

Borderline ◑
1980, US, 104 mins, colour
Dir: Jerrold Freedman
Stars: Charles Bronson, Bruno Kirby, Ed Harris
Rating: ★★

Another variation on what used to be called a social-conscience thriller, showing Hollywood's concern at the traffickers in human cargo who operate along the US-Mexico border. Charles Bronson is in trenchant form as the border patrolman out to put a stop to it, while the charismatic and later star-billed Ed Harris makes his first major film appearance as the villain. Bulky Wilford Brimley also scores in a supporting role.

Border River ○
1954, US, 80 mins, colour
Dir: George Sherman
Stars: Joel McCrea, Yvonne De Carlo, Pedro Armendariz
Rating: ★★★

A rugged 'A' class Western, set in the time of the American Civil War, with Joel McCrea battling Pedro Armendariz for Yvonne De Carlo and a fortune in arms, all in aid of the Confederacy. There's plenty of tough action, with McCrea continuing his image as the quietly spoken but grimly determined man whom it's dangerous to double-cross. Miss De Carlo puts personality into the heroine, while fine Mexican actor Armendariz makes as greasy and smiling a villain as any Western fan could possibly want. An excellent climactic fight between him and McCrea in quicksand territory must have left both men needing a bath.

Bordertown ○
1934, US, 80 mins, b/w
Dir: Archie Mayo
Stars: Bette Davis, Paul Muni, Margaret Lindsay, Robert Barrat, Eugene Pallette
Rating: ★★★

Paul Muni received top billing but the dramatic garlands were easily snatched from him by Bette Davis, who gave a spirited, no-holds-barred performance as the wife of border town casino owner Eugene Pallette whom she murders to clear the way for her amorous pursuit of Muni. She succeeds, too, in overcoming Archie Mayo's somewhat flabby direction. The film served as the basis for 1940's *They Drive By Night*, with Ida Lupino in the reworked Davis role.

Born Free ☉
1965, UK, 95 mins, colour
Dir: James Hill
Stars: Virginia McKenna, Bill Travers
Rating: ★★★★★

If you thought that animal weepies had had their day when Lassie retired, then pad along and have a good cry at this one, magnificently transferred to the screen from Joy Adamson's best-selling story of Elsa the lioness. Big bonuses, apart from the lions themselves, are the clear, sunny Technicolor photography, John Barry's marvellous wide-open spaces music, and the near-miraculous way that stars Virginia McKenna and Bill Travers romp as to the manner born with the three lionesses who play Elsa at various stages of her growth, as the Adamsons rear Elsa from a cub after her mother has been killed. Otherwise, when the music rises to a crescendo, and Elsa strikes again at the heart by being happy, or playful, or naughty, or beaten in a fight, you'll be quite lost. Only hardened animal-haters will avoid blubbering almost all the way through.

Born on the Fourth of July ● ⓥ
1989, US, 145 mins, colour
Dir: Oliver Stone
Stars: Tom Cruise, Bryan Larkin, Raymond J Barry, Kyra Sedgwick, Willem Dafoe
Rating: ★★

No wonder Tom Cruise's Vietnam veteran finds it hard to come to terms with himself on his return to civilian life in this harrowing film that leaves absolutely no visceral aspect of his physical and mental plight unstated. He's not only gunned down a village fun of women and babies, but one of his own men as well. Shot up himself, his spine severed, he makes desperate efforts to walk again, but then suffers a terrible accident that leaves him a paraplegic for life. How he comes to a sort of peace takes a grossly overlong 145 minutes, which includes all kinds of unnecessary scenes and parts of scenes – a tragedy that such an emotive subect should drain itself in such a self-destructive way. This one-note descent into a private hell puts an immense strain on our innate sympathy

B

for the character, even though Cruise (Oscar-nominated) is pretty nearly as good as the circumstances will allow. It's full of director Stone's oft-vented bile at the Vietnam conflict; but that alone isn't enough to make a great movie.

Born to Dance ○

1936, US, 108 mins, b/w
Dir: Roy Del Ruth
Stars: Eleanor Powell, James Stewart, Virginia Bruce, Una Merkel
Rating: ★★★

Eleanor Powell, perhaps the most positive, confident and devastating female dancer the screen ever saw, became a star with this Cole Porter/MGM musical whose score includes 'Easy to Love', 'I've Got You Under My Skin' and the spectacular climactic number 'Swingin' the Jinx Away'. James Stewart sings (just about) as her co-star, almost as embarrassing a musical experience for him as his appearance on skates in *Ice Follies of 1939*.

Born to Kill
See: Lady of Deceit

Born Yesterday ○

1950, US, 103 mins, b/w
Dir: George Cukor
Stars: Judy Holliday, William Holden, Broderick Crawford
Rating: ★★★★

The punchy protagonists in this film adaptation of the stage comedy success turn it into a boxing match played out with words, wit and wisdom instead of fists. Judy Holliday's brilliant performance as the seemingly dumb blonde won her an Academy Award and set her up for a run of bright comedies at the studio (Columbia) through the Fifties. Broderick Crawford is also delightful as the shady tycoon (whose mistress she is) who determines to 'educate' her, to his cost.

Born Yesterday ○ ⓥ

1993, US, 101 mins, colour
Dir: Luis Mandoki
Stars: Melanie Griffith, Don Johnson, John Goodman, Edward Herrmann
Rating: ★★

The film fan's tendency is to resist a remake of a classic. And indeed, the first 40 minutes of this one gives us every cause. The old magic exercises its spell in the last hour, even in diluted form, so that we cheer once again for bimbo mistress Billie Dawn, as she 'gets learning' and turns the tables on her gangster lover. Melanie Griffith is

ideally cast as the hapless showgirl taught the facts of American life by journalist Don Johnson, but the lighting is unflattering to her, so that she looks too old for the role. Have a look, then wait for the Judy Holliday version to come around: this is the real class.

Bostonians, The ○ ⓥ

1984, UK, 122 mins, colour
Dir: James Ivory
Stars: Christopher Reeve, Vanessa Redgrave, Madeline Potter, Jessica Tandy
Rating: ★★

After filming Henry James's *The Europeans*, it was perhaps natural for the prolific producer-director team of Ismail Merchant and James Ivory to tackle his anti-feminist tract, The *Bostonians*. It's an uneven affair that manages to take all the fire out of its central fight over a young and impressionable girl by a handsome smooth-talking lawyer (Christopher Reeve) and a spinster (Vanessa Redgrave) who makes her promise never to marry. Reeve fails to exorcise the ghost of Superman in the central role, but richer pickings are to be had in the supporting roles, notably Jessica Tandy's feminist pensioner Miss Birdseye and Linda Hunt's Dr Prance. As expected the period and social detail is overwhelmingly good and the photography of Walter Lassally exquisite. But *The Bostonians* is really little more than a catalogue of lost opportunities.

Botany Bay ○

1952, US, 90 mins, colour
Dir: John Farrow
Stars: Alan Ladd, James Mason, Patricia Medina, Cedric Hardwicke
Rating: ★★

Rugged and exciting if only skin-deep adventure film, splendidly shot in colour, about a cargo-load of convicts bound for Australia's Botany Bay. It is adapted from the novel by Charles Nordhoff and James Norman Hall, who wrote *Mutiny on the Bounty*. Director John Farrow's sea sequences are stirring, the action is tough and uncompromising, and James Mason's performance as Gilbert, sadistic captain of the convict ship, is impeccable.

Both Ends of the Candle ○
(aka: The Helen Morgan Story)

1957, US, 118 mins, b/w
Dir: Michael Curtiz
Stars: Ann Blyth, Paul Newman, Richard

Carlson, Gene Evans
Rating: ★★

Another Hollywood biopic, the genre at which they were so good, and a real breakaway for Ann Blyth, used almost exclusively in 'sweet' parts throughout her career. Here cast in a really meaty part as Helen Morgan, disturbed and disturbing torch singer of the late 1920s and early 1930s, Miss Blyth's attempt to convey the complexities of the character is a brave try. And the free-for-all atmosphere of roaring Chicago is well captured by Oscar-winning director Michael Curtiz. Miss Blyth's singing voice was ironically too operatic for the role, and her songs were 'ghosted' by Gogi Grant.

Both Sides of the Law
See: Street Corner

Bottoms Up! ○

1959, UK, 89 mins, b/w
Dir: Mario Zampi
Stars: Jimmy Edwards, Arthur Howard, Martita Hunt, Sydney Tafler, Vanda Hudson
Rating: ★

A full-blown film version of the radio and TV series 'Whack-O!', with Jimmy Edwards blustering away splendidly as the school head whose accountant is turf rather than chartered. Arthur Howard is the dithering deputy head, Pettigrew, and Vanda Hudson makes a delectable matron. The plot, which shouldn't be paid too much attention, is something about an oriental prince coming to the school as a pupil.

Bound ● ⓥ

1996, US, 118 mins, colour
Dirs: The Wachowski Brothers
Stars: Jennifer Tilly, Gina Gershon, Joe Pantoliano
Rating: ★★★★

Terrific dark thriller with echoes of the early work of the Coen Brothers – strange as this, too, is made by a fraternal team, the Wachowskis. A hot lesbian love affair between mobster's mistress Tilly and ex-con Gershon leads to the girls planning to lift the $2 million in Mafia money currently being guarded by the Mob's launderer, who also happens to be the bisexual Tilly's paramour. Someone has already paid the ultimate price for attempting to make off with the loot, but the girls' clever scheme to get away with it goes well until Tilly makes an unwise phone call... Lots of dark blood flows in this skilfully interlocking, deliciously amoral take, mostly shot in a few rooms, but all the more suspenseful for that. Gershon and Tilly are well contrasted, Pantoliano excellent as the money minder and all the Mafiosos carry real menace. A bit long though, especially towards the end.

Bound for Glory ○
1976, US, 146 mins, colour
Dir: Hal Ashby
Stars: David Carradine, Ronny Cox, Melinda Dillon
Rating: ★★★

The story of homespun philosopher-singer-guitarist Woody Guthrie and his travels during the Depression years of the 1930s. David Carradine does well (and performs all his own songs) in the leading role, and the film's compositions – especially of a dust-storm or a 'squatters' camp in the rain – are often impressive. But the story is rather too long and tends to be repetitive. Robert Getchell's screenplay comes as something of a disappointment after the heights of *Alice Doesn't Live Here Anymore*. Still, director Hal Ashby does show a remarkable feel for time and place.

Bounty, The ◐ ⓥ
1984, New Zealand, 133 mins, colour
Dir: Roger Donaldson
Stars: Mel Gibson, Anthony Hopkins, Laurence Olivier, Edward Fox, Daniel Day Lewis, Bernard Hill
Rating: ★★

This third version of the classic story of mutiny and betrayal is a competent if uninspired adventure yarn. In a revisionist version that sets out to put the record straight, Anthony Hopkins' Captain Bligh bears little relation to Charles Laughton's earlier strutting, arrogant monster. And Mel Gibson's Fletcher Christian is portrayed less as a champion of the underdog than as an unreliable friend who prefers to go native with a coloured wife than do his duty and return with the ship to England. Beautiful to look at and with another typically haunting score in the *Chariots of Fire* mould from Vangelis, *The Bounty* suffers from problems of structure and climax that come two thirds of the way through, leaving it adrift with the horizon too distant. Daniel Day Lewis and Liam Neeson have supporting roles.

Bout de Souffle, A
See: Breathless [1959]

Bowery, The ○
1933, US, 90 mins, b/w
Dir: Raoul Walsh
Stars: Wallace Beery, George Raft, Jackie Cooper, Fay Wray, Pert Kelton
Rating: ★★★

One of the first films to break away from the stagy studio confines, and portray the people, streets and characters of the city. Big, gruff Wallace Beery and little, pouty-mouthed Jackie Cooper were already big box-office together when director Raoul Walsh teamed them with slit-eyed George Raft and lovely Fay Wray in this bruising story of life in New York's East Side. The (real-life) names of the two leading characters – Steve Brodie and Chuck Connors – were both adopted by Hollywood actors in later years. The vigour of the direction placed the film well ahead of its time, and its portrait of the poorer quarter of New York in the 1890s fairly teems with life. Watch out for a super performance from feisty Pert Kelton as Beery's saloon soubrette girlfriend.

Boxing Helena ● ⓥ
1993, US, 105 mins, colour
Dir: Jennifer Lynch
Stars: Julian Sands, Sherilyn Fenn, Bill Paxton, Kurtwood Smith, Art Garfunkel
Rating: ★

An obsessive surgeon (Julian Sands) decides to amputate the arms and legs of the object of desire (Sherilyn Fenn) and keep her in a box in the living room. This would-be shocker proves that debutante director Jennifer Lynch possesses none of the weird genius of father David, of *Twin Peaks* fame. Some unintentionally hilarious dialogue and inept performances make this suitable viewing only for conoisseurs of truly bad movies.

Boy, Did I Get a Wrong Number! ○
1966, US, 97 mins, colour
Dir: George Marshall
Stars: Bob Hope, Elke Sommer, Phyllis Diller
Rating: ★★★

Here is Bob Hope, brighter, funnier and a lot less sentimental than in some of his early Sixties films, as an estate agent accidentally involved with a runaway actress. Hope's scriptwriters, too, are back to something like their old form. 'Coffee?', he asks his son. 'You want to stay awake in class?' In addition to glamorous Elke Sommer is a bubble bath queen, there are two more dotty females around in the

shape of Phyllis Diller as Hope's maniacal maid and squeaky-voiced Joyce Jameson as the telephone operator who gives Hope the original wrong number. The plot and dialogue are just the kind that used to have Hope fans rolling in the aisles in the Forties and everything culminates in a frantic freeway chase in which Hope starts off being chased by three police cars but finishes up by following them.

Boy from Oklahoma, The ○
1953, US, 88 mins, colour
Dir: Michael Curtiz
Stars: Will Rogers Jr, Nancy Olson, Lon Chaney Jr, Anthony Caruso
Rating: ★★★

After his tremendous success as his rope-twirling, comedian father in *The Story of Will Rogers*, Warners put young Will Rogers Jr straight into this gentle, amusing, fast-paced Western. He gets good support from sunny Nancy Olson as a fiery lass called Katie Brannigan who's handier with a gun than the hero.

Boy on a Dolphin ○ ⓥ
1957, US, 111 mins, colour
Dir: Jean Negulesco
Stars: Alan Ladd, Sophia Loren, Clifton Webb
Rating: ★★

A plot about sunken treasure is the flimsy excuse for a brilliant travelogue around the isles of Greece and the contours of Sophia Loren. Alan Ladd is an unlikely archaeologist, the diving scenes are picturesque, and Clifton Webb (for once the bad guy) puts across his lines with his customary astringency. He plays a character called Mr Parmalee. A little in-joke: Parmalee was Webb's middle name.

Boys ● ⓥ
1995, US, 86 mins, colour
Dir: Stacy Cochran
Stars: Winona Ryder, Lukas Haas, Skeet Ulrich, John C Reilly, Chris Cooper, Jessica Harper
Rating: ★★

This rites of passage/mystery drama is rather undercut by the fact that its protagonists, Haas and Ryder, look about the same age, when the story should be about a teenage college student falling for an older woman. The fact that the stars are the right ages for their roles only makes the miscasting worse, an aspect with which the usually reliable Ryder, in particular, finds it difficult to cope, as she searches in vain for a way to portray a vampish 25-

B

year-old. The plot's mystery slant, in fact, proves rather more interesting: Ryder is found lying in a field, unable to move after being thrown from a horse, and cared for by Haas, who takes her to his school room. It seems that something rather more sinister happened to the heroine the night before the fateful ride, although the explanation, when it comes, isn't quite as dramatic as we might have expected. The upbeat ending will at least send you to bed in a good mood.

Boys, The O
1962, UK, 123 mins, b/w
Dir: Sidney Furie
Stars: Richard Todd, Robert Morley
Rating: ★★★

A courtroom whodunnit which poses the question: are we all inclined to pre-judge people because of the way they look and dress, especially when they're members of the younger generation? Good, tense, well-constructed stuff.

Boys from Brazil, The ❶ Ⓥ
1978, US, 123 mins, colour
Dir: Franklin J Schaffner
Stars: Gregory Peck, Laurence Olivier, James Mason, Steve Guttenberg, Denholm Elliott, Uta Hagen
Rating: ★★

Ira Levin's compulsively readable book about Nazi resurgence in South America is turned into a film which tends to underline its latent absurdities. It contains excellent visuals by French photographer Henry Decae and good supporting portrayals by Lilli Palmer and Denholm Elliott, outsmarting the three principals, Gregory Peck, Laurence Olivier and James Mason, all of whom seem rather uneasily cast.

Boy from Mercury, The O Ⓥ
1996, UK/Eire/France, 87 mins, colour
Dir: Martin Duffy
Stars: James Hickey, Rita Tushingham, Tom Courtenay, Hugh O'Conor
Rating: ★★★

A gentle and largely successful evocation of an Irish childhood in the late 1950s. Young Harry (Hickey) falls foul of the school bully, watches agog the exploits of Flash Gordon at Saturday morning pictures, bonds with his dog Max, takes enforced visits to his father's grave, and entertains his brother's child-minding girlfriend rather more than his older sibling. In the privacy of his bedroom, he communicates with the Mercurians by flashing his torch at their spaceship – actually a plane passing in the night.

Less welcome companions are his martinet schoolmaster and rather disreputable 'uncle' Tony (Courtenay) who seems to be winning a toehold in the affections of Mum (Tushingham). He also makes friends with a 'rich boy' whose parents seem to live in another world – of indoor toilets and coloured loo paper. Seldom has childhood been more expertly brought back to life.

Boys in Brown O
1949, UK, 85 mins, b/w
Dir: Montgomery Tully
Stars: Jack Warner, Richard Attenborough, Dirk Bogarde, Michael Medwin, Jimmy Hanley, Alfie Bass
Rating: ★★★

A film about Borstal Boys which broke new ground when it was first released (hard to believe now that it was then considered daring) and provides the film buff with intriguing glimpses of stars when they were young. Here are Dirk Bogarde and Richard Attenborough, still playing juvenile delinquents in their late twenties. And Jimmy Hanley doing the same at 32! As the governor, Jack Warner epitomises considerate authority as thoroughly as he had represented the kindlier arm of the law in *The Blue Lamp*.

Boys Town O
1938, US, 96 mins, b/w
Dir: Norman Taurog
Stars: Spencer Tracy, Mickey Rooney, Henry Hull, Leslie Fenton
Rating: ★★★

Said to have been Louis B Mayer's favourite film, this true-ish story is blazingly effective sentiment, with Spencer Tracy winning his second consecutive Oscar, this time as the priest who founded a sanctuary for wayward boys. He and Mickey Rooney were among the world's five most popular stars at the time and the public flocked to see the film. But Tracy decided that the Academy Award he had won (which had in any case, been erroneously inscribed to 'Dick Tracy'!) really belonged to the real-life Flanagan. He sent it along to the priest with a new inscription that read 'To Father Edward J Flanagan, whose great human qualities, kindly simplicity and inspiring courage were strong enough to shine through my humble effort: Spencer Tracy.'

Boys Will Be Boys ☉ Ⓥ
1935, UK, 75 mins, b/w
Dir: William Beaudine

Stars: Will Hay, Gordon Harker, Jimmy Hanley, Claude Dampier
Rating: ★★★

Will Hay really hit his film stride in this school comedy, in which he appears for the first time in a feature film in his famous characterisation of a down-at-heel and distinctly inefficient schoolmaster. Hay himself helped write the screenplay, from characters created by J B Morton, alias 'Beachcomber'. How the famous Dorking necklace enters the story, and how it gets inside the ball to be used as the famous Narkoverian rugby match makes for a wildly hilarious conclusion. Several plot elements from *Boys Will Be Boys* turned up again years later in *Blue Murder at St Trinian's*.

Boy 10 Feet Tall, A
See: Sammy Going South

Boy Who Could Fly, The O
1986, US, 114 mins, colour
Dir: Nick Castle
Stars: Lucy Deakins, Jay Underwood, Bonnie Bedelia, Fred Savage, Fred Gwynne, Louise Fletcher
Rating: ★★★

A well-intentioned film that tackles the subjects of mental illness and suicide head-on. But for much of its running time, it's pretty heavy going. Lucy Deakins as a new girl in town and Jay Underwood, as her neighbour, a mute, autistic boy who dreams of flying, handle their difficult roles with amazing grace, but they have an uphill battle with sombre material. The supporting cast of well-known faces, including Colleen Dewhurst as a sympathetic teacher, Fred Gwynne as the boy's alcoholic uncle, and Louise Fletcher as a soft-spoken psychiatrist, all turn in terrific portrayals.

Boy Who Had Everything, The ❶
1984, Australia, 94 mins, colour
Dir: Stephen Wallace
Stars: Jason Connery, Diane Cilento, Laura Williams, Lewis Fitz-Gerald, Ian Gilmour
Rating: ★★

Jason Connery's first star role came in this penetrating look at the childish and almost barbaric rites that apparently still existed in Australia in 1965 for unfortunate first-year 'freshers' at some universities and colleges of further education. Certainly a more dislikeable set of characters in any film would be tough to find. It's not easy to understand anyone surviving three whole terms under their jurisdiction. The trouble is that, given this premise, the film never seems to go anywhere, especially in not sending Jason off to Vietnam, when the plot keeps dropping hints that that's what's most likely to happen. Connery has a definite raw-boned charisma and proves a most convincing runner in some of the most realistic race sequences yet.

Boyz N the Hood ● Ⓥ

1991, US, 111 mins, colour
Dir: John Singleton
Stars: Cuba Gooding Jr, Larry Fishburne, Ice Cube, Nia Long, Angela Bassett
Rating: ★★★★

Amid so much that's dross and inconsequential in this genre, it's good to find a film that's so relevant to modern living. To be accurate, black modern living in the poor quarter of L.A: where children grow up (if they grow up) trying to concentrate on their homework against background noises of police helicopters patrolling the district and the machine-gun fire of rival neighbourhood gangs exchanging mutual murder. If the outcome of this particular story is fairly predictable, that's not to deny the strength in its telling – an amazing first-time effort from its 23-year-old director. His portrait of growing up comes across as real and affects us all.

Brady Bunch Movie, The ● Ⓥ

1995, US, 98 mins, colour
Dir: Betty Thomas
Stars: Shelley Long, Gary Cole, Michael McKean, Jean Smart, Henriette Mantel, David Graf
Rating: ★★

First cousins to The Stupids, the Bradys are gaudily-clad, head-in-clouds relics from the Sixties, who confound people with their guilelessness. Irresistible or deeply irritating according to your mood and/or your kinship with the original TV series. The crackerbarrel philosophy of Father (Gary Cole) is especially hard to bear in this one. The unheralded sequel (see *A Very Brady Sequel*) is actually much better.

Brain Smasher ● Ⓥ

1993, US, 88 mins, colour
Dir: Albert Pyun
Stars: Andrew Dice Clay, Teri Hatcher, Brion James, Tim Thomerson, Charles Rocket, Nicholas Guest
Rating: ★★★

Subtitled *A Love Story* in case you mistake it for a horror movie, this is a wild adventure with martial arts stunts and action. There are plenty of laughs, too, mostly courtesy of comedian Andrew Dice Clay, who stars as a bouncer known as the Brain Smasher. His chance meeting with a supermodel (Teri Hatcher) and their adventures fleeing from a gang of Chinese fighting monks who seek the ultimate power (yes, really) make for a most engaging, tongue-in-cheek caper.

Brainstorm ○

1965, US, 114 mins, b/w
Dir: William Conrad
Stars: Jeffrey Hunter, Anne Francis, Dana Andrews, Viveca Lindfors
Rating: ★★

William *(Cannon)* Conrad directed this thriller about a man caught in a series of violent events that seem to be fashioned to drive him out of his mind. The actors try hard, but the plot takes some swallowing.

Brainstorm ◐ Ⓥ

1983, US, 106 mins, colour
Dir: Douglas Trumbull
Stars: Christopher Walken, Natalie Wood, Louise Fletcher, Cliff Robertson
Rating: ★★

Completed with difficulty after the death of one of its stars, Natalie Wood, in a drowning tragedy, Douglas Trumbull's sci-fi drama has at least the core of an interesting idea, successfully carried out in spasms, and most notably so the nearer it approaches the realms of the straight thriller. Wood, Christopher Walken, Louise Fletcher and others are working on a project which enables brain waves to be transferred from one head to another, so that ultimately 'experiences' can be recorded. The government soon has its beady eyes on the project for its armed forces and when Fletcher dies from a heart attack (which she 'records' on tape) it's up to Walken and Wood to destroy the programme before the warmongers can put it to use. At times, the film is exciting, tense and amusing in turn. But not, alas, all of the time.

Bramble Bush, The ○

1960, US, 105 mins, colour
Dir: Daniel Petrie
Stars: Richard Burton, Barbara Rush, Jack Carson, Angie Dickinson
Rating: ★★

Emotion-charged drama, with Richard Burton adding weight to a *Peyton Place*-type story of a young doctor faced with a crisis of principles through his love for a married woman. This was Burton's first American film after his success in *Look Back in Anger,* and he lent authority to a difficult role. The story is taken from Charles Mergendahl's best-seller.

Bram Stoker's Dracula ● Ⓥ

1992, US/UK, 123 mins, colour
Dir: Francis Ford Coppola
Stars: Gary Oldman, Winona Ryder, Anthony Hopkins, Keanu Reeves, Tom Waits, Richard E Grant
Rating: ★★

An Oscar winner for costume design and nominated for production design, this new version of the vampire legend flaunts its sense of style with some justification, the opening sequence showing Dracula's origins being particularly breathtaking. The scenes in Edwardian England are pretty good too, and Gary Oldman's count proves an evil and convincing seducer, making this one of the sexiest Draculas in memory. There's lots of blood-letting, too, but what is missing is any sense of fear or real horror. The down side includes Anthony Hopkins' unexpectedly camp performance as Van Helsing and Keanu Reeves' embarrassing attempt at an English accent. Chuckles and creeps here, then, but nary a chill.

Branded ○

1950, US, 94 mins, colour
Dir: Rudolph Maté
Stars: Alan Ladd, Mona Freeman, Charles Bickford
Rating: ★★

A fairly gripping Western from Alan Ladd and Paramount to follow their first, *Whispering Smith.* 'They call me Choya,' says Ladd in this one, and proves to be as tough as his name: as someone obligingly explains in the course of the action, choya is Spanish for cactus. When asked if he has any friends, this impassive hombre replies, through gritted teeth: 'My guns'. This is fair stuff for Western fans, with as complex a plot as you could expect in a horse-opera, the prettiest of heroines in feisty Mona Freeman and lots of exciting action up and down the picturesque valley of the Rio Grande. Veteran actors Charles Bickford and Tom Tully give the stars solid support.

Brandy for the Parson ○

1951, UK, 79 mins, b/w
Dir: John Eldridge
Stars: James Donald, Kenneth More, Jean Lodge
Rating: ★★

B

Amiable Ealing-style comedy. James Donald and Jean Lodge find themselves inadvertently involved with smuggler Kenneth More, whose bright and breezy performance gave him another leg up the ladder to stardom. A large roster of familiar character actors decorate the edges of the movie, among them Alfie Bass, Charles Hawtrey, Reginald Beckwith and the almost inevitable Sam Kydd. Director John Eldridge's pacing is leisurely but he displays an attractive narrative style and makes excellent use of some well chosen locations.

Brannigan ○ ⓥ

1975, UK, 111 mins, colour
Dir: Douglas Hickox
Stars: John Wayne, Richard Attenborough, Judy Geeson, Mel Ferrer
Rating: ★★★

The British director of this tough crime drama, Douglas Hickox, was quoted at the time as saying that he 'just wanted to make a John Wayne movie'. Well, he did it. Even more old-fashioned than the star's previous police drama, *McQ, Brannigan* is also more fun. Hickox was an expert at blazing action scenes and his style and Wayne's dovetail perfectly. The script doesn't exactly match other departments, but it has its moments, mainly in the reactions of Britishers ridden roughshod over by Wayne's Chicago cop. 'I was only here for the beer,' protests a bowler-hatted type after being punched three times in a superb London pub brawl. And another, horrified at Wayne's commandeering of his car and 'flying' it over an opening Tower Bridge, protests: 'I waited a year for delivery.'

Brasher Doubloon, The

See: The High Window

Brassed Off ◖ ⓥ

1996, UK, 105 mins, colour
Dir: Mark Herman
Stars: Tara Fitzgerald, Ewan McGregor, Pete Postlethwaite, Stephen Tompkinson
Rating: ★★★

'I know there's a spot of bother at pit,' says brass band leader Postlethwaite, coughing another lungful of coal dust into his handkerchief. 'But this is something separate. This is music. And it's music that matters.' There's no cosy, Ealing-style comedy here though: it's 1992 and pits all over the country are closing. The government are the bad guys and the film lets you know it, even if you can understand the majority of miners going for £23,000

redundancy and a lifetime of freedom from pneumoconiosis, as against the downside of an uncertain future. 'If this lot were seals or whales,' Postlethwaite tells a massed audience at the national brass band finals, 'You'd all be up in arms.' You suspect that the issue wasn't quite as straightforward as that, but it is to this angry film, which strikes a good many grace notes before overplaying its hand at the end. Shot in very good colour which for once doesn't make Yorkshire look grim and grey.

Bravados, The ◖ ⓥ

1958, US, 98 mins, colour
Dir: Henry King
Stars: Gregory Peck, Joan Collins, Stephen Boyd, Albert Salmi
Rating: ★★★

The credentials of this tough Western are first-rate: written by the prolific Philip Yordan, from a novel by that fine western writer Frank O'Rourke, and directed by Henry King, one of the best of Hollywood's veteran directors (he began in early silent days). Here, King sustains the tensions, aroused by Gregory Peck's crazed hunt for the bandits who murdered his wife, at a remarkable pitch.

Brave Don't Cry, The ○

1952, UK, 90 mins, b/w
Dir: Philip Leacock
Stars: John Gregson, Meg Buchanan, John Rae, Fulton Mackay
Rating: ★★★

This stark, harrowing and suspense-packed story of a group of miners trapped down a Scottish pit was based on a real-life disaster (at Knockshinnoch) and produced by the famous director of documentaries John Grierson. It was one of the biggest successes of the short-lived British state-backed film company, Group Three Productions, and is flawlessly acted by a cast who were then all virtually unknown. Its people are full of character, the dialogue crackles with the wit and courage of men facing death, and the rescue attempts will leave many fingernails in shreds. A sincere and moving film.

Braveheart ● ⓥ

1995, US/UK, 177 mins, colour
Dir: Mel Gibson
Stars: Mel Gibson, Sophie Marceau, Patrick McGoohan, Catherine McCormack, Brendan Gleeson, James Cosmo
Rating: ★★★★★

A truly epic film about the life of 13th century Scottish rebel leader William Wallace (Mel Gibson) and his fight for freedom for his homeland from the English king Edward Longshanks (Patrick McGoohan). Brilliantly directed by its star, the film starts at a leisurely pace. But, once the fighting starts, it carries the viewer along at the the speed of a rollercoaster, with battle following battle and some of the most bloody and gruesome hand-to-hand fighting ever captured on film. These combat scenes are certainly spectacular affairs and Gibson displays masterful control of sequences involving thousands of extras. The script delves deeply into the politics of the period, with English and Scottish nobles switching allegiances with frightening regularity for financial reward. A major triumph for all concerned, but especially Gibson, who gives a rousing central performance as the charismatic blue-faced leader with more than a hint of the spirit of Spartacus running through his veins.

Brazil ● ⓥ

1985, UK/US, 142 mins, colour
Dir: Terry Gilliam
Stars: Jonathan Pryce, Robert De Niro, Michael Palin, Bob Hoskins, Kim Greist, Ian Holm
Rating: ★★★

Director Terry Gilliam's film is clearly influenced by his work as director and animator with the Monty Python team, even if it is perhaps rather more than a Pythonesque version of *1984*. The net result too is more of an entertainment than the Orwell tale, if only because the terror is leavened with streaks of surrealist humour and because Sam (Jonathan Pryce) does have his moments of triumph on the way to inevitable doom at the hands of the State. Working at Information Retrieval, Sam is a faceless cipher who dreams of flying through the sky as a bird, rescuing his ideal girl. Then she materialises, in the form of subversive Jill (Kim Greist) who's wanted by the State. While his private world (and his flat) is disintegrating, save for his friendship with an outlawed, crusading heating engineer (Robert De Niro), Sam's infatuation with Jill and his determination to save her leads him down nightmare corridors from which there's no escape. If it seems long at times, the action, when it does come, is fast and furious.

Breaker Morant ❶ Ⓥ
1979, Australia, 107 mins, colour
Dir: Bruce Beresford
Stars: Edward Woodward, Jack
Thompson, Bryan Brown
Rating: ★★★

This is the true story of three
Australian soldiers put on trumped-up
court martial charges for political reasons during the Boer War. Edward
Woodward is effective in the title role,
one of the accused, and Jack
Thompson gives a powerful performance as his defence lawyer. The
action scenes in the first third of the
film are well done and the courtroom
scenes that follow are tense. Writer/di-
rector Bruce Beresford builds a
powerful drama that will have you raging against injustice.

Breakfast at Tiffany's ○ Ⓥ
1961, US, 106 mins, colour
Dir: Blake Edwards
Stars: Audrey Hepburn, George
Peppard, Mickey Rooney, Patricia Neal,
Buddy Ebsen, Martin Balsam
Rating: ★★★★★

One of the great film successes of the
Sixties, containing possibly the best
performance of Audrey Hepburn's career. Warm-hearted, tragic and
extraordinarily funny in turn, this bitter-sweet, scatterbrained entertainment
pulls pretty well every emotional
string. The wandering spirit of this
wonderful, invigorating picture is enchantingly captured by Hepburn, at
her wistful best, and George Peppard:
their offbeat romance makes director
Blake Edwards' castings seem perfection. Among other highlights:
Hepburn, as the kooky Holly
Golightly, using her own voice to sing
'Moon River' (which won an Oscar for
the best song); the final chase in the
rain after the beloved Cat; and the
fresh and delightfully relaxed scene in
the jeweller's shop. Mickey Rooney,
John McGiver (as the deadpan jewellery salesman) and Buddy Ebsen also
score well; but this is Hepburn's show.

Breakfast Club, The ● Ⓥ
1984, US, 97 mins, colour
Dir: John Hughes
Stars: Emilio Estevez, Judd Nelson,
Molly Ringwald, Ally Sheedy, Anthony
Michael Hall, Paul Gleason
Rating: ★★

This dialogue film about five angry
young people trapped in an all-day detention at an American high school
reaches high but only gets so-so far.
There are times when the character

piece almost catches fire, though, mostly in the humorous shafts that cut
through the social barriers dividing the
characters. But ultimately the film
proves too facile, merely reflecting
commonplace attitudes and opting for
a tidy, cop-out ending with the boys
getting the girls they've been angled
away from all along. Too much bad
language and shouting, underlined by
over-emotional playing – compensation, perhaps, for the inconsistency of
the characters.

Breakheart Pass ○ Ⓥ
1975, US, 90 mins, colour
Dir: Tom Gries
Stars: Charles Bronson, Ben Johnson,
Jill Ireland, Richard Crenna, Charles
Durning
Rating: ★★★★

A rare and consistently enjoyable combination of Western and whodunnit,
set aboard a train carrying vital medicine in 1873. People on the train start
dying mysteriously, one by one. The
obvious suspect is Charles Bronson, as
a killer under arrest. Fans of this sort
of plot will know that's too easy, but
the problem is that, as soon as someone comes under suspicion, he gets
bumped off. Director Tom Gries and
his experienced second-unit aide
Yakima Canutt keep the action tumbling across the screen. Cameraman
Lucien Ballard shines when he's given
the chance and the train itself is magnificent, charging along to some of the
best film music Jerry Goldsmith has
written.

Breaking Away ○
1979, US, 100 mins, colour
Dir: Peter Yates
Stars: Dennis Christopher, Dennis
Quaid, Daniel Stern, Barbara Barrie
Rating: ★★★★

This engaging film was, perhaps surprisingly and less than predictably, a
success. Fundamentally, it's about
four teenagers in Indiana who are, for
various reasons, uncertain of their fu-
tures after they leave high school. But
the development and the film's treatment make it far more entertaining
than the basic material might suggest.
In addition, a largely unfamiliar but accomplished cast make it the more
convincing. Foremost among the players are Barbara Barrie (deservedly
nominated for an Oscar) and Paul
Dooley as the bewildered parents of
Dennis Christopher, a youngster who
yearns to be an Italian bicycle racing
champion and speaks in pidgin Italian

to boot. Peter Yates' direction and the
film itself were also nominated for
Academy Awards, although in the end
its only major Oscar was for Steve
Tesich's screenplay.

Breaking In ● Ⓥ
1989, US, 94 mins, colour
Dir: Bill Forsyth
Stars: Burt Reynolds, Casey Siemaszko,
Sheila Kelley, Albert Salmi
Rating: ★★

A gentle, almost inconsequential crime
comedy-thriller about a young burglar's brief but fruitful apprenticeship
in the hands of an old pro. Burt
Reynolds is faintly uneasy as the sexagenarian safecracker, a part to which
he does bring a certain faded charm as
well as a new toupee that permits him
to look slightly thin on top – but carefully coiffed, as would befit a man
meticulous about both his appearance
and his felonious profession. Scottish
director Bill Forsyth certainly brings a
fresh approach to American crime: the
action, such as it is, is hardly dynamic
and the emphasis decidedly on character. Unfortunately, neither Reynolds
nor Casey Siemaszko, as Reynolds' apprentice safecracker, really live their
parts, and the more down-to-earth impression is made by L.A. Law's Sheila
Kelley as Siemaszko's prostitute girlfriend.

Breaking Point, The ○
1951, US, 97 mins, b/w
Dir: Michael Curtiz
Stars: John Garfield, Patricia Neal,
Phyllis Thaxter
Rating: ★★

This is one of three Hollywood versions of Ernest Hemingway's To Have
and to Have Not. The others are the
Humphrey Bogart film of the same
name, and Audie Murphy's The Gun
Runners. This one has taciturn John
Garfield in the lead. Director Michael
Curtiz charges it with as much tension
as he can muster.

Breaking the Sound Barrier
See: The Sound Barrier

Breaking the Waves ● Ⓥ
1996, UK/Fr/Den/Iceland, 158 mins,
colour
Dir: Lars Von Trier
Stars: Emily Watson, Stellan Starsgård,
Katrin Cartlidge, Jean-Marc Barr, Udo
Kier, Adrian Rawlins
Rating: ★★

This epic tragedy is not so much a picture of misery as a whole pitcher of

B

misery. Bess, a girl from a primitively religious Scottish community in the 1970s, is, to put it mildly, mentally fragile. But she is inherently good and has a deal of fey charm, thus winning the heart of rugged oil-rigger Jan (Starsgård) who marries her, to the horror of the elders. The rest of the film is a catalogue of woes. Jan is paralysed in an accident and encourages Bess to make love to other men and tell him about it. Watson is touching, even brilliant, as the naïve Bess, but the film's problem is director Von Trier, who clearly sees it as a masterpiece and contributes grainy, colour-drained, out-of-focus camerawork, lengthy 'chapter headings', an inordinate running time and a symbolic ending. Pretentious is the word, while the plot is plainly ridiculous and – Watson apart – not too well acted.

Break in the Circle O
1955, UK, 92 mins, colour
Dir: Val Guest
Stars: Forrest Tucker, Eva Bartok,
Marius Goring, Eric Pohlmann
Rating: ★★★

A neatly plotted spy yarn with an abundance of shady characters, kidnappings, gunfire, fisticuffs and heroics. Forrest Tucker is a rugged hero and Eva Bartok a provocative heroine. Val Guest's workmanlike handling of his own script and Walter Harvey's appropriately low-key Eastman Colour photography make this a cut above most British thick-ear thrillers of its time.

Breakout ☾
1975, US, 96 mins, colour
Dir: Tom Gries
Stars: Charles Bronson, Robert Duvall,
Jill Ireland, John Huston, Randy Quaid,
Sheree North
Rating: ★★

The producers of this thriller use a foreword to tell us that the prison escape method shown in the film has actually been used. At least that serves to scotch one of the many implausibilities in their story, which gets by on its exciting action sequences and a rich variety of supporting characters. Hard to tell at times, in fact, whether director Tom Gries is playing it all in light-hearted vein, although the bloody events of the last few reels seem to contradict the theory, and the escape itself is full of tension. But a key part of the action involves Randy Quaid convincing prison guards that he's a girl. Mr

Quaid is about six-feet-five and weighs 200 pounds!

Break to Freedom
See: Albert RN

Breathless ● ⓥ
(aka: A Bout de Souffle)
1959, France, 90 mins, b/w
Dir: Jean-Luc Godard
Stars: Jean-Paul Belmondo, Jean
Seberg Rating: ★★★★

Director Jean-Luc Godard's debut film was a trend-setter and the hit of the 1959 Cannes Film Festival. Jean-Paul Belmondo, in his first major film success, plays a casually ruthless and amoral small-time crook who, en route to Paris in a stolen car, shoots and kills a traffic cop. Keeping just one step ahead of the law, he meets up with his American girlfriend (Jean Seberg) in Paris and suggests a trip to Italy. But he has two problems: she doesn't really want to go and he has no money. Belmondo's persona as a Gallic Bogart is entirely intentional, even down to mimicking some of Bogie's gestures, as Godard made the film as a homage to American gangster films. Belmondo's character is the most colourful and well-rounded in the film, while Seberg's is rather thin and insubstantial. The film jumps from scene to scene, giving it pace and mirroring the erratic ways of Belmondo's character.

Breathless ● ⓥ
1983, US, 101 mins, colour
Dir: Jim McBride
Stars: Richard Gere, Valerie Kaprisky
Rating: ★

The camera-worship of Richard Gere reached new heights with a full-frontal shower scene in this vulgarisation of the classic French thriller A Bout de Souffle. The original film, directed by Jean-Luc Godard and written by François Truffaut, was a landmark of the French New Wave for its style and direct-to-camera monologues. But it was a mistake to transfer the story of a cop-killing amoral punk to Los Angeles and making Gere's kinetic character a self-obsessed loser hooked on Jerry Lee Lewis music and Silver Surfer comics. Naked for most of the time, semi-naked for the rest, constantly snapping fingers and forever stopping by any available mirror to wiggle his hips and preen, Gere ends up irritating rather than sympathetic.

Breed Apart, A ☾
1984, US, 101 mins, colour
Dir: Philippe Mora
Stars: Rutger Hauer, Kathleen Turner,
Powers Boothe
Rating: ★

Shot in North Carolina, this conservation drama – centring on a recluse's battle to protect the eggs of a rare eagle on the island where he lives – is absolutely stunning to look at. But the plot is strictly for the birds. Cool, blond, deep-voiced Rutger Hauer takes a break from cold-eyed killers to play the independent-minded conservationist. But he, Powers Boothe (familiar to TV viewers as Philip Marlowe) and that feisty actress Kathleen Turner, also a fictional detective, the V I Warshawski of film and radio fame, cannot do anything to sustain this thin and disjointed story.

Brewster's Millions ☉
1945, US, 84 mins, b/w
Dir: Allan Dwan
Stars: Dennis O'Keefe, Helen Walker,
June Havoc
Rating: ★★

Perennial farce about a man who can't get rid of his millions. It's interesting to look at this, one of the more successful renditions of the theme in the five attempts to date. After a slow beginning, director Allan Dwan takes it along at a rampaging pace, with amusing performances from Eddie 'Rochester' Anderson and Mischa Auer in the supporting cast.

Brewster's Millions O ⓥ
1985, US, 97 mins, colour
Dir: Walter Hill
Stars: Richard Pryor, John Candy,
Lonette McKee
Rating: ★

This oft-filmed story of a man who must spend several millions of dollars to inherit several million more always seems a tedious tale, and certainly doesn't improve in this uneventful reworking for Richard Pryor, directed in lacklustre fashion by Walter Hill.

Bribe, The O
1948, US, 105 mins, b/w
Dir: Robert Z Leonard
Stars: Robert Taylor, Ava Gardner,
Vincent Price, Charles Laughton, John
Hodiak
Rating: ★★

Director Robert Z Leonard, king of lightness and brightness at MGM for 30 years, seems an unusual choice to direct what amounts to a *film noir* although, as one would expect from the studio, this is a glossier example than usual. Leonard dresses it up in swirling mists, mirror images and rain-streaked windows. Robert Taylor seems not entirely at his ease as the drug-busting agent besotted by femme fatale Ava Gardner, but Charles Laughton and Vincent Price as the villains revel in their surroundings.

Bride, The ●
1985, US, 119 mins, colour
Dir: Franc Roddam
Stars: Sting, Jennifer Beals, Anthony Higgins, Clancy Brown, David Rappaport, Geraldine Page
Rating: ★

A trite and flat remake of the Boris Karloff/Elsa Lanchester *Bride of Frankenstein*. It's not helped by having two of the least animated actors – pop singer Sting as Dr Frankenstein and Jennifer Beals as his gauze-wrapped creation – in the leading roles. It's left for an electrifying scene in which a cat crosses Beals' path and the girl snarls back like a lion to suggest the sort of punch the rest of the film so badly lacks. At the end of the day, dwarf actor David Rappaport steals the film from the principals.

Bride Came C.O.D., The ○
1941, US, 92 mins, b/w
Dir: William Keighley
Stars: James Cagney, Bette Davis, Stuart Erwin, Jack Carson, Eugene Pallette, George Tobias
Rating: ★★

The unlikely team of James Cagney and Bette Davis in a comedy that could just as well have been called *Headstrong Heiress*. Miss Davis works hard, but is plainly not at home in comedy and after this and The *Man Who Came To Dinner*, returned to the headier realms of melodrama. It's left to Cagney and Jack Carson, reunited from *The Strawberry Blonde*, to raise the laughs in a comedy that's consistently amusing without ever becoming uproarious.

Bride of Frankenstein ◐
1935, US, 75 mins, b/w
Dir: James Whale
Stars: Boris Karloff, Colin Clive, Elsa Lanchester, Ernest Thesinger
Rating: ★★★★★

Without doubt the best of all the Universal horror films, in which Frankenstein creates a bride for the monster, with tragic results. Director

James Whale tells the story swiftly and incisively, with fluid camerawork, elegant settings, clever lighting and some weirdly effective theme music. In this film Boris Karloff's monster reaches full flower. Scenes of his friendship with a blind hermit, and his being chained up for the townsfolk to ogle, provide genuinely moving moments. The plot also introduces Dr Praetorious, who forces Frankenstein to collaborate in his schemes. As played by Ernest Thesiger (with intense relish), Praetorious is a masterly portrait of madness. He lives in a draughty castle, full of endless stairs, tending the miniature beings he has 'bottled' away (a splendid piece of trick photography) and swigging gin, which he also uses to calm the monster. Spot if you can Walter Brennan and John Carradine among the villagers.

Brides of Dracula ●
1960, UK, 85 mins, colour
Dir: Terence Fisher
Stars: Peter Cushing, Yvonne Monlaur, David Peel, Martita Hunt
Rating: ★★

A follow-up to the highly successful remake of Bram Stoker's classic vampire story. Peter Cushing is again Van Helsing and David Peel as handsome a villain as one could wish. The finale is splendidly staged against the flapping sails of a windmill.

Bridge, The ● ⓥ
1991, UK, 110 mins, colour
Dir: Syd Macartney
Stars: Saskia Reeves, David O'Hara, Anthony Higgins, Rosemary Harris, Joss Ackland
Rating: ★★

Vaguely in *Lady Chatterley's Lover* country, this is a very prettily set story of a repressed Victorian mother of 29 or so who falls madly, passionately in love with an artist on his annual Suffolk holiday, and he with her. Saskia Reeves pants attractively and inevitably sheds all her clothes as the lovers consummate their mutual lust in the artist's beach hut (cor!). Alas, hubby (Anthony Higgins) returns, tells her that he can 'forgive everything, Isobel, except melodrama', and it ends in tears or, in the artist's case, the painting of his greatest work. Joss Ackland has too little to do, although he does it well, but the couple themselves, Reeves and David O'Hara (with glum countenance and Sean Connery voice), do very little to gain your sympathy at their ultimate betrayal.

Bridge at Remagen, The ○
1968, US, 116 mins, colour
Dir: John Guillermin
Stars: George Segal, Robert Vaughn, Ben Gazzara, Bradford Dillman, E G Marshall, Peter Van Eyck
Rating: ★★

Talented director John Guillermin shows the facility for explosive action scenes that carried him through *The Blue Max* and *The Towering Inferno*. A virile cast, including George Segal, Ben Gazzara, Robert Vaughn and Bradford Dillman, grits its teeth and gives the film its all. This war film has a routine plot, but crisp photography and tense action scenes more than compensate.

Bridge on the River Kwai, The ○ ⓥ
1957, UK, 161 mins, colour
Dir: David Lean
Stars: William Holden, Alec Guinness, Jack Hawkins, Sessue Hayakawa
Rating: ★★★★

Anti-war classic starring Alec Guinness as a British officer who raises the morale of his captured regiment in a PoW camp in Burma by building a bridge but in doing so is unwittingly helping the Japanese war effort. William Holden is the American escapee who returns to destroy the bridge. An intelligent, ironic and deeply stirring film, directed on an epic scale by David Lean. Based on the novel by Pierre Boulle, who was credited for the screenplay in the place of blacklisted writers Carl Foreman and Michael Wilson. The film won Oscars for Best Picture, Director, Actor (Alec Guinness), Script, Photography (Jack Hildyard) and Music (Malcolm Arnold).

Bridges at Toko-Ri, The ○
1954, US, 103 mins, colour
Dir: Mark Robson
Stars: William Holden, Fredric March, Grace Kelly, Mickey Rooney
Rating: ★★★

A war film of the type Hollywood does so well. Packed with incident and spectacular flying scenes, it's the story of a pilot who is reluctant to fly on a near-impossible mission. This tricky decision is tied up with a touching love story that may have you reaching for a handkerchief before the end. In an excellent cast, which helps make this a superior production of its kind, Mickey Rooney stands out with his brave-as-a-bantam portrait of a helicopter rescue pilot.

B

Bridges of Madison County, The ◑ Ⓥ

1995, US, 135 mins, colour
Dir: Clint Eastwood
Stars: Clint Eastwood, Meryl Streep,
Annie Corley, Victor Slezak, Jim Hainie
Rating: ★★

Grand, all-consuming passion is always difficult to put across on screen and, valiantly though Climt Eastwood and Meryl Streep try here, they don't have the material to enable them to do it. The result is a long and quite frequently boring film adaptation of a florid best-seller. Streep is particularly ill-served by the dialogue, resulting in one of her least convincing performances, as the Italian-born Iowa ranch wife who enjoys an idyllic few days with Eastwood's travelling photographer, who proves to be the overwhelming love of her life. The dialogue is less unkind to Eastwood, who rewards it by directing like a sleepwalker. Giggles were scarcely repressed by the London preview audience, although there are one or two poignant moments towards the end, and it should be added that a girl in the row behind me was quite audibly in floods of tears throughout. *Brief Encounter*, however, this is not.

Bridge Too Far, A ◑ Ⓥ

1977, UK, 175 mins, colour
Dir: Richard Attenborough
Stars: Dirk Bogarde, Sean Connery,
Robert Redford, James Caan, Michael
Caine, Edward Fox, Gene Hackman
Rating: ★★★

Richard Attenborough's re-creation of the Second World War Arnhem landings and their aftermath is almost exactly the long blockbuster action film one would have expected from the director of *Oh! What a Lovely War* and *Young Winston*. The preamble is lengthy and the action and special effects are ruthlessly efficient. One tank battle early on vividly expresses the violence of war, although the lesson is needlessly rubbed home in later sequences. But the really impressive performances come from Edward Fox (as Lt.-General Horrocks) and Sean Connery (as Major-General Urquhart) – and from Frank Grimes in a minor role.

Brief Encounter ◯ Ⓥ

1945, UK, 86 mins, b/w
Dir: David Lean
Stars: Celia Johnson, Trevor Howard,
Stanley Holloway, Joyce Carey
Rating: ★★★★★

Amazingly atmospheric, touchingly understated love story adapted by Noël Coward and others from Coward's play *Still Life*. Married Celia Johnson meets a young doctor (Trevor Howard) on her weekly shopping trip to town, and their friendship gradually turns to a love that they know has no future. Director David Lean never puts a foot wrong, neither do the actors, the agony of their frustrated feelings etched on their faces for all to see. Brilliantly photographed by Robert Krasker, especially in the railway scenes, and deft supporting playing from Stanley Holloway, Joyce Carey, Cyril Raymond and young Margaret Barton. The final scene involving Johnson is particularly poignant and speaks volumes with almost no dialogue.

Brigadoon ◯ Ⓥ

1954, US, 108 mins, colour
Dir: Vincente Minnelli
Stars: Gene Kelly, Van Johnson, Cyd
Charisse
Rating: ★★

Audiences for big screen musicals were waning when MGM put this production of Lerner and Loewe's stage hit before the cameras. Even so, it was a fatal mistake to penny-pinch on this one and shoot it entirely in the studio on artificial-looking sets that only emphasised its stagebound origins. Director Vincente Minnelli also experienced difficulty with filling the rectangular frame in his first encounter with CinemaScope. As for the cast, Cyd Charisse moves exquisitely but Gene Kelly is uncharacteristically sluggish in yet another of his more whimsical roles. In all, the film offers disappointingly few pleasures except for the most ardent fan of the pretty if bland score.

Brigand, The ◯

1952, US, 92 mins, colour
Dir: Phil Karlson
Stars: Anthony Dexter, Anthony Quinn,
Jody Lawrance, Gale Robbins
Rating: ★★★

Swashbuckling adventure film, handsomely mounted in Technicolor, and with more than a few echoes of *The Prisoner of Zenda*. Anthony Dexter, the debonair leading man whose previous film had been the starring role in *Valentino*, plays the dual role of king and commoner and shows a neat touch in the swordplay. But he's no match at acting for Anthony Quinn, who smoothly walks off with the film as the villain.

Brigand of Kandabar, The ◯

1965, UK, 81 mins, colour
Dir: John Gilling
Stars: Ronald Lewis, Oliver Reed,
Yvonne Romain
Rating: ★★★

Rally round the flag, men. Those dastardly tribesmen are killing our chaps at the Khyber Pass again. Here at least is a film which makes no bones about its intentions. It's more or less one long round of battles, duels and skirmishes. And some of the battle scenes are pretty good, too. Oliver Reed overacts like mad as a fierce native chieftain.

Brigham Young ◯

1940, US, 114 mins, b/w
Dir: Henry Hathaway
Stars: Tyrone Power, Linda Darnell,
Dean Jagger, Brian Donlevy, Jane
Darwell, John Carradine
Rating: ★★★

Big-scale depiction of the Mormons' epic trek from Illinois to their new home state, Utah. Dean Jagger is forthright in the title role, but has to concede top billing to the romantic leads, Tyrone Power and Linda Darnell. They don't, however, match his fire in a performance that revived his own career but couldn't, alas, make this stirring film a box-office success.

Bright Eyes ☉

1934, US, 83 mins, b/w
Dir: David Butler
Stars: Shirley Temple, James Dunn,
Jane Darwell
Rating: ★★★

Shirley Temple got her first solo billing above the title in this sentimental drama in which she plays the orphan daughter of a pilot, and brings joy into the life of an old man who doesn't believe in Father Christmas. Sounds gooey, but it's actually enchanting stuff, thanks to Shirley's own talented, down-to-earth approach to the story. She also sings 'On the Good Ship Lollipop'.

Bright Leaf ◯

1950, US, 110 mins, b/w
Dir: Michael Curtiz
Stars: Gary Cooper, Lauren Bacall,
Patricia Neal, Jack Carson, Donald Crisp
Rating: ★★

A rare unsympathetic role for Gary Cooper in this highly dramatic film about a ruthlessly ambitious man determined to monopolise the American tobacco industry. Cooper does well, and Karl Freund's black-and-white photography admirably captures the turn of the century feel. But the film's best performance comes from Patricia Neal, as the girl who marries the tobacco tycoon to exact a bitter-sweet revenge.

Bright Lights, Big City ● Ⓥ

1988, US, 103 mins, colour
Dir: James Bridges
Stars: Michael J Fox, Kiefer Sutherland, Phoebe Cates, Swoosie Kurtz, Frances Sternhagen
Rating: ★★

Though it's good to see Michael Fox attempting something different and deeper, this film is certainly not much fun. To be sure, it's a downbeat subject – a young New Yorker drowning in drugs and depression – but it never really goes anywhere. None of its few plot lines develop into anything substantial. Dramas of character need strong writing to grip the attention, and here the script is only average: Fox's personality holds it together for a while, but none of the other younger cast members is very effective, and the girls, Phoebe Cates, Tracy Pollan (soon to become Mrs Fox in real life) and Swoosie Kurtz, don't amount to much at all. Jason Robards is more tolerable as a boozy veteran researcher with Fox's firm, and Dianne Wiest acts her socks off as Fox's dying mother. But, in a film that doesn't affect our emotions, she's fighting a lost cause.

Brighton Beach Memoirs ◐ Ⓥ

1986, US, 108 mins, colour
Dir: Gene Saks
Stars: Blythe Danner, Bob Dishy, Jonathan Silverman
Rating: ★★.

It's hard to believe that this Neil Simon story won the New York Drama Critics' award as the best new play of 1983. All the more discredit to director Gene Saks for making such a dull film out of it. It's partly based on Simon's own life but, since Jonathan Silverman is actually rather obnoxious as the Simon character, there's nothing very endearing or nostalgic about the piece. It concentrates almost entirely on the boy's leering introduction to sex and misses out on the simple emotional appeal that should be the cornerstone of such fare. The entire cast is unmemorable.

Brighton Rock ○ Ⓥ

(aka: Young Scarface)
1947, UK, 91 mins, b/w
Dir: John Boulting
Stars: Richard Attenborough, Hermione Baddeley, William Hartnell, Carol Marsh
Rating: ★★★★

Richard Attenborough was almost always unexpectedly good when asked to portray menace and he's very good indeed in this story of a psychotic petty hoodlum at large in post-war Brighton. Sordid for its time, but strong, tense and realistic, with good support for the star from William Hartnell, Carol Marsh, Nigel Stock, Alan Wheadey and especially Hermione Baddeley as a raddled end-of-pier entertainer. Graham Greene's novel is intelligently adapted for the screen by Greene himself and Terence Rattigan, a formidable writing duo that supplies crisp, threatening, unpleasant dialogue.

Bringing Up Baby ☉

1938, US, 102 mins, b/w
Dir: Howard Hawks
Stars: Cary Grant, Katharine Hepburn, May Robson
Rating: ★★★★

A delightful screwball comedy of the very best vintage, with Cary Grant and Katharine Hepburn on glittering form: he a mild-mannered, orderly paleontologist painstakingly reconstructing a priceless dinosaur skeleton, she a batty heiress with a wilful dog (the one and only Asta from the *Thin Man* series) who grabs a vital bone from Grant's masterpiece. 'Baby' is another troublesome animal in Hepburn's possession: a Brazilian leopard. Glorious chaos ensues from the encounter between scientist and heiress, the dialogue sparkles and director Howard Hawks presides over the whirling insanity with evident glee. There are also wonderful contributions from the support cast, in particular Charles Ruggles as Major Applegate, May Robson as Aunt Elizabeth and Fritz Feld as the psychiatrist.

Bring On the Night ◐ Ⓥ

1985, UK, 97 mins, colour
Dir: Michael Apted
Stars: Sting, Omar Hakim, Darryl Jones, Kenny Kirkland, Trudie Styler, Miles Copeland
Rating: ★★★

If you're a fan of the particular brand of rockjazz played by Sting's ensemble here, there's no doubt you're in for a feast of it with this film, as well as an informative insight into the weeks of rehearsal that lead to a single concert performance. We're less sure that

you'll want to watch the graphic filming of Sting's baby, but shut your eyes if you don't fancy that sort of thing and just listen to the music – as well as a few wild moments of pleasure in the interviews given by the extremely talented black American musicians who make up the band. To his credit, Sting fits in with these like a glove – another tribute to long hours of rehearsal.

Britannia Hospital ● Ⓥ

1982, UK, 105 mins, colour
Dir: Lindsay Anderson
Stars: Malcolm McDowell, Leonard Rossiter, Joan Plowright, Robin Askwith, Fulton Mackay, Alan Bates
Rating: ★★

Director Lindsay Anderson's first film in eight years is a bitter, black and bloody satire on hospitals, unions, snobbery, spare-part surgery and society itself: indeed, anything within its reach. Anger drips from its jaws like the blood from the stitches of the composite creature mad surgeon Graham Crowden hopes to unveil to visiting royalty. Malcolm McDowell again returns to the role of Mick Travis (previously seen in Anderson's *If...* and *O Lucky Man!*), now an investigative reporter seeking to unmask the 'Frankenstein' surgeon. Leonard Rossiter is the senior hospital administrator who will stop at nothing (even murder) to see that the royal visit goes ahead. Meanwhile, demonstrators gather outside the hospital gates, and the whole unstable brew explodes in a final reel that ultimately lapses into pretentiousness.

Broadcast News ◐ Ⓥ

1987, US, 131 mins, colour
Dir: James L Brooks
Stars: William Hurt, Albert Brooks, Holly Hunter, Joan Cusack, Lois Chiles, Jack Nicholson
Rating: ★★★

This immensely entertaining comedy-romance set in the Washington bureau of a TV news network has three excellent, Oscar-nominated performances from William Hurt, Albert Brooks and Holly Hunter as the central triangle of characters. All the daily drama of a hectic newsroom is there – last-minute changes, missing tapes, large egos and difficult bosses. William Hurt is exactly right as the charming, although actually rather vulnerable ex-sportscaster whose ability to succeed without the requisite brain-power is a source of huge irritation to Holly Hunter's workaholic TV producer, convincingly

B

torn between the professional and the personal life. And Albert Brooks is perfect as the best friend (who of course harbours deeper affections for Hunter's character). In the end, the satire takes second place to the romance, but it is a story that has a refreshingly realistic conclusion.

Broadway Danny Rose ⓘ ⓥ

1984, US, 84 mins, b/w
Dir: Woody Allen
Stars: Woody Allen, Mia Farrow, Nick Apollo Forte, Milton Berle
Rating: ★★★

A quirky Woody Allen film in which the comedy is of a gentle variety. Allen both directs and stars as Danny Rose, a theatrical manager with a collection of no-hope acts. His luck changes when an overweight singer comes into fashion again thanks to a nostalgia boom. But he has Mafia connections – and Danny's involvement with his mistress Tina (Mia Farrow, brilliant if almost unrecognisable in a ridiculous bubble wig) lands him in hot water. It's the by-now-familiar Allen theme of a loser triumphing against unbelievable adversity, but the little maestro brings it up fresh and funny. Most hilarious scene: Allen and Farrow running through a warehouse storing gas containers that when hit by their pursuers' bullets, leave everyone with high-pitched voices.

Broadway Melody of 1936, The ○

1935, US, 110 mins, b/w
Dir: Roy Del Ruth
Stars: Jack Benny, Eleanor Powell, Robert Taylor, Buddy Ebsen
Rating: ★★★

Second and best of this series of musical comedies, with Jack Benny on top form as a waspish Broadway theatre critic. Eleanor Powell has never danced better and a very young Robert Taylor was never lovelier! The Arthur Freed-Nacio Herb Brown songs include 'You Are My Lucky Star' and 'Broadway Rhythm'.

Broadway Melody of 1938 ○

1937, US, 110 mins, b/w
Dir: Roy Del Ruth
Stars: Robert Taylor, Eleanor Powell, George Murphy, Judy Garland
Rating: ★★

Eleanor Powell's dazzling dancing is the most eye-catching thing in this typical MGM musical from the late Thirties. The juvenile leads are a gangling Buddy Ebsen (long before Davy

Crockett or Barnaby Jones) and Judy Garland, making her first big impact with her famous 'Dear Mr Gable' song.

Broadway Melody of 1940 ○

1940, US, 102 mins, b/w
Dir: Norman Taurog
Stars: Fred Astaire, Eleanor Powell, George Murphy, Frank Morgan
Rating: ★★★

The last of the *Broadway Melody* series of musicals from MGM has the wonderful Eleanor Powell (billed at the time as 'the world's greatest tap dancer') partnered by none other than Fred Astaire in a thinnish story of an aspiring dance duo (Astaire and George Murphy) aiming for stage stardom. Powell and Astaire should have been absolute dance dynamite, but the chemistry doesn't always quite fizz. However, this is a minor quibble when the film is scored by Cole Porter and there are such wonderful numbers as the glittering 'Begin the Beguine', 'I've Got My Eyes on You' and the great shipboard number featuring Powell, 'I Am the Captain'.

Broken Arrow ○

1950, US, 93 mins, colour
Dir: Delmer Daves
Stars: James Stewart, Jeff Chandler, Debra Paget
Rating: ★★★

This exciting and moving Western, beautifully shot in Technicolor, was a landmark film in Hollywood history. For the first time since silent days, the Red Indian was depicted as a human being, rather than a brute savage merely in the film to bite the dust at the hands of the US Cavalry. It was adapted from a big social-consience novel by Elliott Arnold, and marked the first step out West for director Delmer Daves after a series of thrillers. James Stewart's sincerity gives stature to the role of the frontier scout who tries to keep the peace. Jeff Chandler made his name with his strong and dignified portrait of the famous Indian chief Cochise, whom he would play in two further films – *Battle at Apache Pass* and *Taza, Son of Cochise*.

Broken Arrow ● ⓥ

1996, US, 108 mins, colour
Dir: John Woo
Stars: John Travolta, Christian Slater, Samantha Mathis, Delroy Lindo, Frank Whaley, Kurtwood Smith
Rating: ★★

Hang your minds in the foyer (or hall) and enjoy the non-stop action in this

ballistic thriller about a rogue USAF officer (John Travolta) who steals two nuclear missiles and holds the nation to ransom. However, he fails to dispatch his co-pilot (Christian Slater) as planned: Slater manages to eject into the desert – and thereby hangs the rest of the tale. We seem to remember Steven Seagal scotched one of these hare-brained schemes a couple of years earlier, and here Slater proves almost as troublesome to the bad guys, especially when he teams up with park ranger Samantha Mathis (with an inexhaustible supply of bullets and lipstick). The action just keeps on coming here, from truck fights, train fights and mid-air fights to hair-raising flights through a copper mine. That's a good thing, as the action is the only thing John Woo is directing well. Travolta does what he can with a part that offers him nothing, Slater is unmemorable. The rest of the acting is all as unimpressive as the action is explosive.

Broken Hearts and Noses

See: Crimewave

Broken Journey ○

1947, UK, 89 mins, b/w
Dir: Ken Annakin
Stars: Phyllis Calvert, James Donald, Margot Grahame, Francis L Sullivan
Rating: ★★

A British entry to the aircraft-crashed-in-the-middle-of-nowhere stakes. Mostly par for the crash course, but with Sonia Holm and Grey Blake forming a touching relationship as a nurse and her iron-lung patient.

Broken Lance ○ ⓥ

1954, US, 96 mins, colour
Dir: Edward Dmytryk
Stars: Spencer Tracy, Robert Wagner, Jean Peters, Richard Widmark, Katy Jurado, Earl Holliman
Rating: ★★★★

A magnificent performance by a white-haired Spencer Tracy dominates everything else in this strong Fox Western remake of the Edward G Robinson drama *House of Strangers* with echoes of King Lear for good measure. Only Katy Jurado, as Tracy's 'woman', even gets near to the star's crackling sincerity and abrasive authority in spite of a supporting cast that includes Richard Widmark, Robert Wagner, Hugh O'Brian, Earl Holliman (as Tracy's sons) and Jean Peters. Philip Yordan, who wrote the screenplay for the Robinson original, was rather oddly given an Oscar for 'best motion picture story' on *Broken Lance*. Good roughhouse duel at the end, but spectacular Cinemascope scenery will be a bit lost on TV.

Bronco Billy ◑ Ⓥ
1980, US, 119 mins, colour
Dir: Clint Eastwood
Stars: Clint Eastwood, Sondra Locke, Geoffrey Lewis, Scatman Crothers, Sam Bottoms
Rating: ★★★

A holiday for the Clint Eastwood gang from all that heavy stuff like *Dirty Harry* and *The Gauntlet*. It tries entertainingly to mix the Eastwood Western myth, straitjacketed into a modern rodeo show, with a Thirties' screwball comedy that might well have been called *Footloose Heiress*. The film's heart is certainly in the right place and there are some good moments along the trail, especially when the rodeo's motley crew, including two native Americans, visit a mental institution (an inmate of which happens to be Lewis, sent there for the 'murder' of his disappeared wife). The chief physician tells them: 'You can take your meals with the staff or the patients, whichever you feel most comfortable with.'

Bronx Tale, A ● Ⓥ
1993, US, 122 mins, colour
Dir: Robert De Niro
Stars: Robert De Niro, Chazz Palminteri, Lillo Brancato
Ratinj: ★★★★

Somewhere between *GoodFellas*, *Grease* and *West Side Story*, Robert De Niro's directorial debut is full of Bronx flavour that even overcomes its lack of excitement and pace. If you can survive its torrent of bad language, there's a lot to savour in this story of a Bronx boy who worships a lethal gangster, played with charm by Chazz Palminteri (who also wrote it), despite the efforts of the boy's father (De Niro) to keep him on the straight and narrow. In spite of the gangster's viciousness and ruthlessness, he's also like a father to the boy, restricting him to sideline activities, not allowing him to become a gun-toting hoodlum 'like me' and even offering some laconic advice on his love life. Joe Pesci turns up in a cameo role, one of many colourful characters who include Mush, a losing gambler so abysmal that 'the racecourse touts gave him tickets already torn up'.

Brother Orchid ⊙
1940, US, 91 mins, b/w
Dir: Lloyd Bacon
Stars: Edward G Robinson, Humphrey Bogart, Ann Sothern, Dorald Crisp
Rating: ★★★★

Possibly the most charming crime comedy ever made. Edward G Robinson is perfect as the racketeer, forever looking for 'the real class', who seeks refuge in a monastery when shot in a gang war. Humphrey Bogart is a wonderful snarling villain and Ann Sothern delightful as Robinson's long-suffering moll. If you're looking for 'the real class' in Warner gangster classics, this is it.

Brothers-in-Law ○
1956, UK, 94 mins, b/w
Dir: Roy Boulting
Stars: Richard Attenborough, Ian Carmichael, Terry-Thomas
Rating: ★★★

The Boulting brothers strike at the legal profession in the second of their successful comedy series of the Fifties. Ian Carmichael is fine as the embryo barrister for whom no case is open and shut.

Browning Version, The ● Ⓥ
1951, UK, 90 mins, b/w
Dir: Anthony Asquith
Stars: Michael Redgrave, Jean Kent, Wilfrid Hyde White, Bill Travers
Rating: ★★★

One of the 'prestige' British productions of its time, this is a fine film version of Terence Rattigan's stage play of marital discord against a background of school life. Michael Redgrave gave one of the best screen performances of his career as the hapless schoolmaster whose loveless existence and professional humiliation have given him a defensive armour of coldness and even, at times, brutality. How this armour is pierced makes for dramatic entertainment. There are good performances, too, from Jean Kent as the cold-blooded wife, Nigel Patrick as her science-master lover, and Wilfrid Hyde White somewhat untypically cast as the headmaster.

Browning Version, The ● Ⓥ
1994, UK, 100 mins, colour
Dir: Mike Figgis
Stars: Albert Finney, Greta Scacchi, Matthew Modine, Julian Sands
Rating: ★★

The famous Terence Rattigan play updated (ie with four-letter words) to the

modern era. Now, under writer Ronald Harwood's guidance, it no longer seems to develop and build as it once did. By using strong language, and skimping on character, Harwood fails to supply the literate underpinning required to make us sympathise with the unpopular public school, teacher (Albert Finney) being put out to grass. Not that there is anything wrong with the performances here, especially those of Greta Scacchi, as his faithless, bitchy wife, and of Finney himself – a towering portrayal of a wasted life, even if the screenplay now makes him more likeable from the start than Rattigan intended. Colour photography is excellent: a cut in class above most other things in the film.

Brubaker ● Ⓥ
1980, US, 130 mins, colour
Dir: Stuart Rosenberg
Stars: Robert Redford, Yaphet Kotto, Jane Alexander, Murray Hamilton, Morgan Freeman
Rating: ★★★★

An old-fashioned but hearteningly entertaining prison film, with Robert Redford winning new haloes as the crusading prison governor determined to reform the vilest and most violent jail farm in the whole of the US. Naturally, there are those for him and those agin, and thereby hangs the nub of the tale. If Redford is sometimes too good to be true, this does sustain audience sympathy throughout, and ensures that the final scene is as moving as it is intended to be. Jane Alexander offers another of her strong human portrayals.

Brute Force ◑
1947, US, 96 mins, b/w
Dir: Jules Dassin
Stars: Burt Lancaster, Hume Cronyn, Charles Bickford, Yvonne De Carlo
Rating: ★★★★

A brilliant, blackly violent expose of the worst kind of American prison life. Writer (later director) Richard Brooks and director Jules Dassin rarely did better work than in this unrelenting portrait of sadistic guards driving their captives to a desperate attempted breakout. Stand-out performances from Burt Lancaster, Hume Cronyn Howard Duff, Whit Bissell and John Hoyt.

Buccaneer, The ○
1958, US, 121 mins, colour
Dir: Anthony Quinn
Stars: Yul Brynner, Claire Bloom,

B

Charlton Heston, Charles Boyer, Inger Stevens
Rating: ★★★★

Cecil B DeMille's last film – he died while it was being made. His long-time associate Henry Wilcoxon took over as producer, and the direction of the film went to actor Anthony Quinn, who made such a good job of this splendid adventure yarn that one wonders why it was the only film he directed. A number of interesting items emerged from the $2 million epic. But the most newsworthy was a humble hairpiece, described as a 'sensitive blend of Bonaparte, Presley and a well-kept Irish setter'. Why was the hair so important? It adorned the most famous bald plate in the world – that of Yul Brynner. Among the cast, Claire Bloom wields a spirited sword as a tough-talking pirate girl. The battle scenes – DeMille hired 12,000 extras – are immense.

Buchanan Rides Alone ○
1958, US, 78 mins, colour
Dir: Budd Boetticher
Stars: Randolph Scott, Craig Stevens Jennifer Holden
Rating: ★★

Randolph Scott takes on almost an entire town in this example of director Budd Boetticher's tough, individual and highly rated Westerns of the 1950s. The bad guys department is, as usual, a happy hunting ground for spotters of those familiar figures who never turn up their toes. Here they include stout, menacing Barry Kelley, the angular and shifty L Q Jones and big, blustering Peter Whitney. The settings at times seem a little cramped, but the colour photography is razor sharp and the plot and dialogue need no alibis.

Buck and the Preacher ○
1971, US, 102 mins, colour
Dir: Sidney Poitier
Stars: Sidney Poitier, Harry Belafonte, Ruby Dee
Rating: ★★

Sidney Poitier starred in and directed this lively Western, giving it all the traditional elements of entertainment shootouts, ambushes, battles with Indians and the like – while at the same time inserting a smattering of accusatory comment on the ill-treatment of Negroes 'whose graves are as unmarked as their place in history'. Poitier the actor seems content to stand back and let the limelight fall on Harry Belafonte's showy performance.

The idea of having the Indians come to the rescue of the wagon train besieged by outlaws is a gem.

Buck Privates ⊙
(aka: Rookies)
1941, US, 84 mins, b/w
Dir: Arthur Lubin
Stars: Bud Abbott, Lou Costello, Jane Frazee
Rating: ★★

Although Bud Abbott and Lou Costello were nominally billed third and fourth on the cast list, this army comedy was their first starring vehicle. It's loud, lively and one of their better films, and the fact that they aren't on screen all of the time means that they don't have to strain to pull in the laughs. In the supporting cast are Nat Pendleton, here a dumb sergeant instead of his usual dumb police officer, and Shemp Howard, later to become one of The Three Stooges. Jane Frazee is a breezy heroine, and the Andrews Sisters sing 'Boogie Woogie Bugle Boy from Company B'.

Buck Rogers in the 25th Century ○ ⓥ
1979, US, 89 mins, colour
Dir: Daniel Hailer
Stars: Gil Gerard, Erin Gray, Pamela Hensley
Rating: ★★★

Enter the sci-hero with the James Bond sense of humour. This film, originally intended as the pilot for the TV series, but subsequently shown in the cinemas, may be more loony than moony. But at least it's a lot more fun than the po-faced *Battlestar Galactica* films, especially with the deft playing of Gil Gerard at the helm. And he has two sexy leading ladies in Pamela Hensley as the villainous enemy princess, and Erin Gray as the earth commander whose icy exterior soon melts under Buck's offbeat charm. Sometimes the film's audacity overreaches itself, as where Buck 'teaches' a 25th-century musician 20th-century music – the lesson is far too peremptory to convince. But mostly its approach (propositioned by the glamorous Erin, Buck confesses that after 500 years in space, he isn't quite ready for that kind of action) comes as a breath of fresh air in the force field.

Bud Abbott and Lou Costello in Hollywood ○
1945, US, 80 mins, b/w
Dir: S Sylvan Simon
Stars: Bud Abbott, Lou Costello, Jean

Porter
Rating: ★★★

One of Abbott and Costello's funniest comedies, with inspired direction from S Sylvan Simon and a riotous roller-coaster ride for the climax. The setting provides MGM with the opportunity for guest appearances by such studio contract players of the time as Lucille Ball, little Jackie 'Butch' Jenkins, Preston Foster and 'Rags' Ragland.

Buddy, Buddy ① ⓥ
1981, US, 96 mins, colour
Dir: Billy Wilder
Stars: Jack Lemmon, Walter Matthau, Paula Prentiss, Klaus Kinski
Rating: ★

The saddest episode in Billy Wilder's glittering career, *Buddy, Buddy* shows the full extent of the 20-year decline in the standards of the Austrian-born director and his regular collaborator, writer I A L Diamond, from the dizzy heights of *Sabrina* and *The Apartment* to little more than a mass of crass ideas, poor timing and four-letter words. This is an attempt at a re-run of *The Odd Couple* by teaming Jack Lemmon and Walter Matthau as, respectively, a jilted husband intent on committing suicide and a professional hitman unlucky enough to have an adjoining hotel room. But the material is almost nonexistent and it's left to the mugging of the stars to carry the sorry affair.

Buddy Holly Story, The ○ ⓥ
1978, US, 113 mins, colour
Dir: Steve Rash
Stars: Gary Busey, Don Stroud, Charles Martin Smith, Maria Richwine
Rating: ★★★★

More shots in the arm like this were what biopics needed in the 1970s. This really is a remarkable recreation of a singer whose skill with music placed him in the same category as The Beatles a few years later. The film benefits from the fact that the stars, Gary Busey (as Buddy), Don Stroud and Charlie Martin Smith not only look like Holly and The Crickets, but sound like them, generating all their own excitement on stage. And their performances are very good, too. The story is fluently told and, if one could have wished for more of the romantic ballads that, sung in Holly's highly individual manner, were such a significant part of his output, the whole film is so much better than you might imagine, that this is a minor grumble.

Buffalo Bill ○

1944, US, 90 mins, colour
Dir: William Wellman
Stars: Joel McCrea, Maureen O'Hara
Rating: ★★★

There are some simply tremendous scenes of hundreds of animals on the move in this crowd-pleasing, dust-rousing, spectacularly colourful account of the noted frontier scout and buffalo hunter's life. Factually something of a disgrace, but emotionally right on the mark, the film has one of Joel McCrea's most solid performances in the title role. Director William Wellman, who drives the film along in fine style, wanted to portray the old Westerner in more truthful, critical light, but studio boss Darryl F Zanuck insisted on preserving the myth of a great hero, down to a sentimental, beautifully staged ending. Zanuck was right.

Buffalo Bill and the Indians ① ⓥ

1976, US, 120 mins, colour
Dir: Robert Altman
Stars: Paul Newman, Joel Grey, Burt Lancaster
Rating: ★

Robert Altman's exposure of the great western hero as a fraud was given a rough ride by many critics though it's made with the director's customary flourish and dark humour. Tedious.

Buffy the Vampire Slayer ① ⓥ

1992, US, 86 mins, colour
Dir: Fran Rubel Kuzui
Stars: Kristy Swanson, Donald Sutherland, Rutger Hauer, Luke Perry
Rating: ★★

Somewhere between *Prom Night* and *Dracula* without any real sense of menace, this vampire comedy fails on most counts. Buffy (Kristy Swanson), a high school cheerleader, is the latest in a centuries-old line of nubile vampire-slayers trained by a mystery man (Donald Sutherland) who comes to call. At first, thanks to Sutherland's sober and delicately balanced performance, this works quite well, as Buffy moves from boy-mad airhead to vampire-mad airhead, even if the chunky, busty Swanson is only barely up to the high kicks and seems to get a considerable assist in the stuntwork and gymnastics. The vampires, however, are relentlessly comic, with fancy-dress fangs never conveying the idea of an endangered heroine.

Bug ①

1975, US, 101 mins, colour
Dir: Jeannot Szwarc
Stars: Bradford Dillman, Joanna Miles, Richard Gilliland, Patty McCormack
Rating: ★★★

A nasty and, at least at first, believable horror film in which fire-making insects erupt from cracks in the ground after an earthquake. Even then, things might have been relatively okay, had not potty professor Bradford Dillman (there's always one) decided to meddle in things best left alone. The story developments get less credible later on, but there are some disgustingly good special effects and neat direction of the human stars by Jeannot Szwarc.

Bugles in the Afternoon ○

1952, US, 85 mins, colour
Dir: Roy Rowland
Stars: Ray Milland, Hugh Marlowe, Forrest Tucker, Barton MacLane, Helena Carter
Rating: ★★

Rousing Warner Bros. Western with a central character called Kern Shafter (they don't make up names like that any more) who re-enlists in the Cavalry after being dishonourably discharged. Ray Milland is suitably impassive as the wronged cavalryman, and the encounters between white man and Indian are among the most exciting action scenes ever shot. George Reeves, screen portrayer of Superman, appears as Lt Smith.

Bugs Bunny/Road Runner Movie, The ⊙

1979, US, 92 mins, colour
Dir: Chuck Jones, Phil Monroe
Rating: ★★★

The lunacy's pretty non-stop in this feature-length compilation of animation director Chuck Jones' best Warner cartoons. Bugs battles with Martians (well, er, just one, actually) and Daffy Duck tries to prove he's the Errol Flynn of Duckdom. Meanwhile, Wile E Coyote is still trying to make a meal of the Road Runner using a wild collection of highly unlikely and uniformly unsuccessful traps. Great fun for kids of all ages.

Bugsy ● ⓥ

1991, US, 135 mins, colour
Dir: Barry Levinson
Stars: Warren Beatty, Annette Bening, Harvey Keitel, Ben Kingsley, Elliott Gould, Joe Mantegna
Rating: ★★

Bugsy Siegel was a gangster as dangerous as he was debonair. In the Hollywood of the early Forties, he saw himself as a patriot – and maybe a star. He also had a dream: to build a gambling casino in Las Vegas that would create a city. This film attempts to tell the story of that dream, and Bugsy's obsessive relationship with good time girl Virginia Hill. At the same time, it cannot escape the criminal origins of its story; and it lacks the urgency of the best gangster films, despite Warren Beatty's dynamic portrayal of Siegel, a man who could ooze charm and be subject to savage fits of anger in the same hour. Ida Lupino-lookalike Annette Bening does solid work as Virginia, as do Ben Kingsley as Bugsy's partner and an overweight Elliott Gould as a squealer. Long, stylish and sombre, it prowls on towards an end that even those who don't know the history of this true story will see coming.

Bugsy Malone ○ ⓥ

1976, UK, 93 mins, colour
Dir: Alan Parker
Stars: Scott Baio, Jodie Foster, Dexter Fletcher, Bonnie Langford
Rating: ★★★

The first big-screen impact by Alan Parker is a gangster movie pastiche, a world populated by children masquerading as mobsters and molls, who 'drive' pedal cars and where the deadliest weapon to hand is a gun that fires 'splurge' bullets that resemble custard pie mix. Future household names to look for include Scott Baio as the hero, Jodie Foster as the speakeasy vamp, Dexter Fletcher as the aptly named Baby Face, and Bonnie Langford (billed as Bonita) as a would-be child singing star. Foster was furious when her big number 'My Name is Tallulah', was dubbed by a professional singer.

Bulldog Breed, The ○

1960, UK, 97 mins, b/w
Dir: Robert Asher
Stars: Norman Wisdom, Edward Chapman, Ian Hunter, David Lodge
Rating: ★★

Norman Wisdom joins the navy and is volunteered for rocket duty as Britain's first astronaut. Even though (or perhaps because) he co-wrote the script himself, this simple sea-going comedy is not one of the little man's better efforts by any means, and he retorts to vigorous mugging and slapstick to keep the film afloat. Still, there is the odd funny moment.

B

Bulldog Drummond ○

1929, US, 86 mins, b/w
Dir: F Richard Jones
Stars: Ronald Colman, Joan Bennett,
Lilyan Tashman, Claud Allister
Rating: ★★

Sapper's famous gentleman adventurer
was featured in silent pictures, but this
was the first talkie about the redoubtable Bulldog Drummond. To
this day, Ronald Colman's account of
the title role (which he repeated five
years later in *Bulldog Drummond Strikes
Back*) is considered by many to be unsurpassed. Among incidental pleasures
is the comic relief supplied by Claud
Allister, doing his 'Silly Englishman'
act as Algy. And the role of the heroine received spirited playing from the
19-year-old Joan Bennett, whose first
success this was.

Bulldog Jack ○

(aka: Alias Bulldog Drummond)
1935, UK, 72 mins, b/w
Dir: Walter Forde
Stars: Jack Hulbert, Ralph Richardson,
Fay Wray
Rating: ★★★

Chills and chuckles galore as Jack
Hulbert (aided by the beautiful Fay
Wray of *King Kong* fame) takes the
place of the injured Bulldog
Drummond on the chase after the
Morelle gang of dastardly jewel
thieves. Splendid climax in London's
Underground system.

Bull Durham ● ⓥ

1988, US, 108 mins, colour
Dir: Ron Shelton
Stars: Kevin Costner, Susan Sarandon,
Tim Robbins
Rating: ★★

Susan Sarandon's squirrel eyes and
wild performance steal all the attention
going (even from Kevin Costner and
Tim Robbins) in this exceptionally
foul-mouthed baseball drama, 20 per
cent of which you won't understand,
and a further 20 per cent of which disappears down a muffled sound track.
Still, the colour photography is just
fine, and there are moments when the
film's attempted bittersweet feel does
come across, as old pro Costner (looking faintly like Paul Newman in this
one) eventually gets a hot-headed
young pitcher (Robbins) to do as he's
told – and become a major league star.
And then there's always Sarandon as
the film's axis, a baseball-mad local
lady who picks a likely new player to
shack up with every season – until
Costner, who wants her himself, tells

Robbins he'll lose his lucky streak unless he lays off sex. 'This is the
darndest thing,' wails Sarandon in consequence. 'The Durham Bulls can't
lose and I can't get laid.' She's a delight.

Bullet for a Badman ○

1964, US, 80 mins, colour
Dir: R G Springsteen
Stars: Audie Murphy, Darren McGavin,
Ruta Lee
Rating: ★★

One of the last of the long series of
Westerns Audie Murphy made at the
Universal studios. The Eastman
Colour photography by Joseph Biroc is
a cut above the routine and the supporting cast as strong as ever in these
rousing little films. The players here
include Ruta Lee, George Tobias,
Alan Hale Jr, Skip Homeier, Edward
C Platt and, as Murphy's principal
protagonist, Darren McGavin, the latter giving a particularly forceful
performance.

Bullet for Joey, A ○

1955, US, 85 mins, b/w
Dir: Lewis Allen
Stars: Edward G Robinson, George Raft,
Audrey Totter
Rating: ★★★

A throwback to Hollywood's golden
era, with two great gangster stars in
one film, which is about a plot to kidnap a scientist. Such old crime
stalwarts as George Dolenz, Peter Van
Eyck and Kaaren Verne add to the
Forties feel.

Bullets or Ballots ○ ⓥ

1936, US, 81 mins, b/w
Dir: William Keighley
Stars: Edward G Robinson, Humphrey
Bogart, Joan Blondell, Barton MacLane
Rating: ★★★★

One of the best of the Warner
Brothers racketeering dramas of the
Thirties, with Edward G Robinson
and Humphrey Bogart snapping and
snarling at each other in a series of
confrontations that end in a memorable shoot-out, vividly staged by
cameraman Hal Mohr and director
William Keighley. Bogart employs
some memorable pieces of dramatic
'business' to show himself to be a
thinking actor, and outshine fellow-
baddie Barton MacLane.

Bullets Over Broadway ◑ ⓥ

1994, US, 105 mins, colour
Dir: Woody Allen
Stars: John Cusack, Dianne Wiest,

Chazz Palminteri, Jennifer Tilly, Mary-
Louise Parker, Tracey Ullman
Rating: ★★

A very disappointing Woody Allen
comedy with everyone straining for effect and almost no laughs at all. These
Roaring Twenties characters are almost all irritating or silly or both and
pretty well the only interesting one is
Chazz Palminteri as the gangster's hit-
man who turns out to be an unsung
genius and rewrites playwright John
Cusack's work to success. And even
he has to come to a disappointingly
conventional end. The chief letdown
here is the dialogue, only admittedly,
co-written by Woody, who seems to
have almost entirely lost his ear for
funny one-liners and the way neurotic
people really speak. These bullets may
be fizzing over Broadway, but they
have a spent quality which flattens
their impact. Dianne Wiest, as a
Swanson-type star, somehow made
this fools' gold seem like the real thing
and won an Oscar in the process.

Bullitt ○ ⓥ

1968, US, 106 mins, colour
Dir: Peter Yates
Stars: Steve McQueen, Robert Vaughn,
Jacqueline Bisset, Don Gordon, Robert
Duvall
Rating: ★★★★

Besides being a taut suspense drama in
its own right, *Bullitt* possesses the now
legendary car chase through the streets
and hills of San Francisco that opened
up a whole new box-office bonanza for
producers of crime thrillers. Philip
D'Antoni, who produced *Bullitt*, hit the
jackpot again three years later in similar vein with *The French Connection*,
which has a classic chase sequence of
its own. In the title role Steve
McQueen's charismatic, hard-hitting
performance established him as the
world's number one pin-up, while
Jacqueline Bisset's strikingly warm portrayal of his girlfriend made the
English girl a top Hollywood star. As
for the plot, suffice to say that it will
keep you guessing right up to the end.

Bullseye! ◑ ⓥ

1990, UK, 90 mins, colour
Dir: Michael Winner
Stars: Michael Caine, Roger Moore,
Sally Kirkland, Deborah Barrymore
Rating: RB

As a comedy, this doesn't even hit the
dartboard. Michael Caine and Roger
Moore play unscrupulous scientists
and their doubles, two British con
men. The resultant chase between the

four over a nuclear fusion formula for producing cheap energy is handled heavily by the director – but the chief culprit is the script, something without which Moore in particular can't operate. Some of it is nearly passable, but not quite, and Caine's American accent as the 'bad' double is atrocious. Guest appearances by Jenny Seagrove, John Cleese, Alexandra Pigg and Patsy Kensit, but all to little avail in this numbingly unfunny and occasionally unpalatable experience.

Bullwhip O
1958, US, 80 mins, colour
Dir: Harmon Jones
Stars: Guy Madison, Rhonda Fleming, James Griffith
Rating: ★★

Hardly as vigorous as the title implies, this is rather a slow romantic Western with Guy Madison ideally cast as the laconic westerner who escapes the hangman by agreeing to an arranged marriage with firebrand (or, at least, she's meant to be) Rhonda Fleming. James Griffith makes a highly original villain with a nice line in humour, but he's given too little to do. Pleasant if uninspired entertainment at a jog-trot.

Bunny Lake Is Missing O
1965, UK, 107 mins, b/w
Dir: Otto Preminger
Stars: Laurence Olivier, Carol Lynley, Keir Dullea, Noel Coward, Martita Hunt, Finlay Currie
Rating: ★★★★

A thriller that really thrills. Bunny Lake is a little American girl alleged to have disappeared on a visit to London. The problem the police, led by a puzzled Laurence Olivier, soon face is: does the child really exist? John and Penelope Mortimer's screenplay is full of pleasing incidentals which happily bring in Finlay Currie as a surgeon at a macabre dolls' hospital, Martita Hunt as an old lady who records children's fantasies, and Noël Coward as a boozy old intellectual with a vast collection of sadistic-looking objets d'art.

Buona Sera, Mrs Campbell O
1968, US, 113 mins, colour
Dir: Melvin Frank
Stars: Gina Lollobrigida, Phil Silvers, Telly Savalas, Shelley Winters
Rating: ★★★

Unexpectedly delightful comedy about an Italian housewife (Gina Lollobrigida) whose life of ease at the

expense of three Americans, all of whom assume they fathered her wartime child, is threatened by an Air Force reunion. The screenplay by Melvin Frank, Denis Norden and Sheldon Keller is full of funny fines and a good cast includes Lee Grant, Peter Lawford and Janet Margolin.

'burbs, The O Ⓥ
1988, US, 103 mins, colour
Dir: Joe Dante
Stars: Tom Hanks, Bruce Dern, Carrie Fisher, Rick Ducommun, Corey Feldman, Henry Gibson
Rating: ★★★

A bizarre comedy in which assorted American suburbanites (thus the title) become obsessed with the idea that a family of mad scientists has moved in across the road. From being occupied with nothing more unlawful than neighbours' dogs pooping on their lawns, Ray (Tom Hanks), Art (Rick Ducommun) and all-American ex-Vietnam psycho Mack (Bruce Dern) find themselves drawn to the mysterious old house on the corner, where the Klopeks have moved in. Hanks, seemingly perfectly cast in everything he does, has just the right width of manic streak in this comedy of edges, in which everything is just a little bit larger (or more eccentric) than it would be in real life. Funny, in its observation of the 'burbs' various foibles, yet at the same rime you have the feeling that Dana Olsen's screenplay is saying that this comedy could have been a tragedy had our heroes been wrong about the Klopeks. There are barbs in these 'burbs.

Burning Hills, The O
1956, US, 94 mins, colour
Dir: Stuart Heisler
Stars: Tab Hunter, Natalie Wood, Skip Homeier
Rating: ★★

A rather naive 'pop' Western about a ruthless cattle baron and a young man trying to avenge his brother's death. It features the then-hot romantic duo Tab Hunter and Natalie Wood as the couple who manage to fall in love in spite of the violence around them. Pay Teal, so often the sheriff in Westerns, gets a meatier role on the other side of the law. He's the cattle baron.

Burning Secret O
1988, UK/US, 105 mins, colour
Dir: Andrew Birkin
Stars: Klaus Maria Brandauer, Faye Dunaway, David Eberts, Ian Richardson,

John Nettleton
Rating: ★★★

Andrew Birkin's first film (his second was *The Cement Garden* (1993) adapts a short story by Stefan Zweig (who also wrote *Letter From An Unknown Woman* which was superbly filmed in 1948 by Max Ophuls) with great sensitivity and adroitness. Faye Dunaway is both coolly stylish and yet passionate, as befits a woman on the brink of a love affair. By contrast, Klaus Maria Brandauer brings a touch of menace to his charming Lothario character to great effect. The production, filmed entirely on freezing-looking locations in Prague and Marienbad, is lush and suitably atmospheric. This is old-fashioned melodrama, brought off to a T: definitely a double tissue job.

Burnt Offerings C
1976, US, 115 mins, colour
Dir: Dan Curtis
Stars: Karen Black, Oliver Reed, Bette Davis, Lee Montgomery, Burgess Meredith
Rating: ★★

A predecessor of *The Amityville Horror*, about a house (and a ghost upstairs?) which takes possession of its inhabitants. Director Dan Curtis' skilful direction helps disguise the basic silliness of the affair, and adds effectiveness to some of the shock set-pieces, notably a sequence in a swimming pool. Karen Black is quite good as the possessed wife, especially when she becomes involved in the inevitable *Psycho*-style twist at the end, but the rest of the players – Oliver Reed, Bette Davis and Burgess Meredith in particular – have far too high a time for the film's own good.

Burn, Witch, Burn
See: Night of the Eagle

Business As Usual
1987, UK, 90 mins, colour
Dir: Lezli-An Barrett
Stars: Glenda Jackson, John Thaw, Cathy Tyson, Eamon Boland, Buki Armstrong
Rating: ★

A film with its heart on its sleeve. Its heart is notably with right-wing radical causes. And, in exploring themes raised by its story of sexual harassment at work, it flies the flag for militancy as a surefire method for achieving justice. Scenes of police brutality may be gratuitous, but they are certainly not foreign to the ideals of debutant feminist director Lezli-An Barrett if this is anything to judge by.

B

But her film is so far over the top, in spite of caring performances from Glenda Jackson and John Thaw, that it soon forfeits any claim to credibility.

Busman's Honeymoon ○
(aka: Haunted Honeymoon)
1940, UK, 95 mins, b/w
Dir: Arthur B Woods
Stars: Robert Montgomery, Constance Cummings, Leslie Banks
Rating: ★★★

MGM described this Lord Peter Wimsey whodunnit as 'a love story with detective interruptions'. Americans Robert Montgomery and Constance Cummings aroused some national ire when cast as such an essentially British couple as Lord Peter and his bride. But they acquitted themselves well enough, even though some of their thunder was stolen by a colourful supporting cast that includes a glum Robert Newton and Sir Seymour Hicks as a resourceful butler.

Bus Stop ○ ⓥ
1956, US, 96 mins, colour
Dir: Joshua Logan
Stars: Marilyn Monroe, Don Murray, Arthur O'Connell, Betty Field. Eileen Heckart, Hope Lange
Rating: ★★★★

Always on the brink of embarrassment, but never quite falling in, this film-with-a-heart was one of the best sentimental wallows of its year. Marilyn Monroe, so awkward in some scenes, can be infuriatingly just as brilliant in others. Don Murray is perfect as the gauche young cowboy who pursues Monroe's world-weary singing southern belle during his one-day trip to the city for the annual rodeo. Even so, both are out-scored by Arthur O'Connell as a hoary old cowpoke on the sidelines.

Buster ● ⓥ
1988, UK, 102 mins, colour
Dir: David Green
Stars: Phil Collins, Julie Walters, Larry Lamb, Stephanie Lawrence
Rating: ★★★

A glamorised treatment, in a comedy-drama setting, of the great train robber Buster Edwards. Phil Collins is unexpectedly good as Buster, but Julie Walters as his wife, although she delivers a lively performance, never quite escapes her own image. Despite a few dead patches, the film's content grips the attention through to its conclusion; the robbery itself is handled in low-key fashion, and the film glosses over the less savoury aspects of the £2million

crime which pitched Edwards and 14 others into the headlines in 1963. Though the story hasn't quite enough dramatic structure to sustain its length, the dialogue is a constant help. 'Hardly bleedin' Clacton, is it?' mutters Buster's partner Bruce Reynolds, as he and Edwards swat tropical flies in Acapulco. 'If we was in Clacton', snarls Buster, 'we'd get some TCP from the chemist's'.

Busting ●
1973, US, 92 mins, colour
Dir: Peter Hyams
Stars: Elliott Gould, Robert Blake
Rating: ★★★★

A fast, tough, funny thriller about two unconventional cops, personably played by Robert Blake and Elliott Gould before they fell from grace with cinema audiences: this was a last high-point for both of them for quite a while. Director Peter Hyams drives it along in fine, clean, confident style, with some tremendous chase sequences, including a hair-raising pursuit in a supermarket. Good hard-nut jokes, strong action, clear-cut characters and a bleak but atmospheric city feel: great entertainment value from Hyams in his first cinema feature.

Butch and Sundance, The Early Days ○
1979, US, 110 mins, colour
Dir: Richard Lester
Stars: William Katt, Tom Berenger, Jeff Corey, Brian Dennehy
Rating: ★★

Given his success with the Musketeer films, Richard Lester was perhaps the obvious director to entrust with this 'prequel' to the famous Oscar-winning *Butch Cassidy and the Sundance Kid*. Once again, Lester's amusingly inventive touches are everywhere, although his handling of the overall pace is less sure. Tom Berenger and William Katt, the two young actors who play the roles created by Paul Newman and Robert Redford, do well enough, with Katt particularly engaging as Sundance, even looking at times just like a younger version of Redford himself. The dialogue lacks the witty spark of the original but the action comes in dynamic bursts, with Brian Dennehy making a fearsome O C Hanks, forever trying to drill our heroes full of holes.

Butch Cassidy and The Sundance Kid ○ ⓥ
1969, US, 112 mins, colour
Dir: George Roy Hill

Stars: Paul Newman, Robert Redford, Katharine Ross, Strother Martin, Jeff Corey, Cloris Leachman
Rating: ★★★★★

Perhaps the greatest Western of the Sixties and certainly the most likeable, with Paul Newman and Robert Redford at their most charismatic as the eponymous outlaws. The dialogue shines with constant wit, the action is spot-on, the photography Conrad Hall's best-ever. Even the supporting players are beautifully drawn: Katharine Ross as Etta, Strother Martin as Percy, Henry Jones as the bike salesman, Timothy Scott as News Carver (forever searching for a mention of himself in the gang's exploits) and a glimpse of the young Sam Elliott (years later to marry Ms Ross) as a card player. Academy Awards for screenplay, cinematography, music score and the song 'Raindrops Keep Fallin' on My Head'. And it still looks good more than 25 years on.

Butcher's Wife, The ◑ ⓥ
1991, US, 107 mins, colour
Dir: Terry Hughes
Stars: Demi Moore, Jeff Daniels, George Dzundza, Mary Steenburgen, Frances McDormand
Rating: ★★★

It's always a vibrant surprise when players you've been watching for years as dramatic talents suddenly blossom forth as singers. Such is the case here with the Oscar-winning Mary Steenburgen who, with a supporting role in this feelgood film, proves herself a blues singer of grace, warmth and talent. She's one of the characters within a few blocks who come under the influence of Marina (Demi Moore), a clairvoyant from a lighthouse, who has moved to the neighbourhood because she felt fated to marry Leo (George Dzundza), a butcher as plump as his loin chops. That's part of a greater destiny for Marina, involving Leo, Dr Tremor (Jeff Daniels), a psychiatrist who feels 'uncomfortable' being called a shrink, his aggressive girlfriend (Margaret Colin), Grace (Frances McDormand), a neurotic clothes-shop assistant, and others whose lives Marina touches and enriches. Steenburgen has the best lines as well as the best songs. 'I'm looking,' she tells McDormand, 'for something dowdy and plain.' It's a romantic fantasy that's never juvenile, and, for her fey and fetching Cassandra of the tenements, Moore might well have been Oscar-nominated had not this nice little film been a flop at the box-office.

But Not For Me ○
1958, US, 105 mins, b/w
Dir: Walter Lang
Stars: Clark Gable, Carroll Baker, Lilli Palmer
Rating: ★★★

This was something of a landmark in comedy films. For the first rime, Clark Gable, the uncrowned king of Hollywood, allowed people to poke fun at his age – and got the bird from the bird he fancied. He plays an ageing Broadway wolf who makes a last pass only to find that he's got a better knowledge of plays than of playing around with women. Lilli Palmer is gorgeous, Carroll Baker rather lost.

Buttercup Chain, The ◐
1970, UK, 95 mins, colour
Dir: Robert Ellis Miller
Stars: Hywel Bennett, Leigh Taylor-Young, Jane Asher, Sven-Bertil Taube
Rating: ★★

The sights, sense, colours and atmosphere of a long, sun-filled summer have rarely been better captured than by the ravishing Technicolor photography of Douglas Slocombe in this sex fantasy about two loving couples. The four young leading players, Hywel Bennett, Jane Asher, Leigh Taylor-Young and Sven-Bertil Taube, all do well, and Clive Revill is also very good as a 'kind and unexpected' millionaire in love with Ms Taylor-Young. The music score, by Richard Rodney Bennett, gives the film an extra-special lift.

Butterfield 8 ◐
1960, US, 108 mins, colour
Dir: Daniel Mann
Stars: Elizabeth Taylor, Laurence Harvey, Eddie Fisher, Dina Merrill
Rating: ★★

Elizabeth Taylor won her first Oscar for her performance as the nymphomaniac Gloria Wandrous in this glossy romantic drama based on John O'Hara's bestselling novel. In its time it was something of a trend-setter as regards its frank, outspoken dialogue, plus just a dash of semi-nudity. Director Daniel Mann gave it plenty of oldstyle Hollywood sophistication as well. Some saw Liz Taylor's Oscar as a sympathy award for having just missed after being nominated in the previous three years. But her portrayal of the self-destructive Gloria is never less than compulsively watchable.

Butterflies Are Free ◐
1972, US, 104 mins, colour
Dir: Milton Katselas
Stars: Goldie Hawn, Edward Albert, Paul Michael Glaser, Eileen Heckart
Rating: ★★

The delightful Goldie Hawn here plays a free-living girl who guides a restricted young blind man (played by Edward Albert, real-life son of Eddie Albert) to his freedom. Eileen Heckart won an Academy Award (best supporting actress) for her wasp-tongued portrayal of the hero's over-protective mother.

Bye Bye Birdie ○
1963, US, 112 mins, colour
Dir: George Sidney
Stars: Janet Leigh, Dick Van Dyke, Ann-Margret, Maureen Stapleton
Rating: ★★★

This lively musical about a pop idol called up for service in the Army is shamelessly aimed at Elvis Presley and casts some sharp satirical shafts in that direction. Janet Leigh, struggling under the handicap of a black wig, still manages to outshine rival Ann-Margret. But the film is completely stolen by tombstone-toothed Paul Lynde, superbly harassed as the father of the smalltown girl on whom the idol has chosen to bestow his last civilian kiss.

Bye Bye Love ◐ ⓥ
1995, US, 105 mins, colour
Dir: Sam Weisman
Stars: Matthew Modine, Paul Reiser, Randy Quaid, Janeane Garofalo, Lindsay Crouse, Ed Flanders
Rating: ★★★

Just amusingly enough written to keep you watching, this patchwork of setpiece scenes is a sometimes perceptive, sometimes funny and not too often tedious look at three recently divorced fathers in charge of their kids for the weekend. Matthew Modine is the flirt who ends up with three prospective conquests for the evening, all bearing culinary gifts. If only they'd arrived at different times. Randy Quaid is the star of the show as the angry Vic, who demolishes the porch which now houses the lounging form of his ex-wife's new lover and would like to do the same to the local talk radio's divorce doctor – a Christmas-present-wrapped part for actor-director Rob Reiner. 'You get married today,' says the radio doctor, 'you stand less chance of staying together than surviving a shark attack.' Not quite true, perhaps, but a nice one-liner.

By Hook or By Crook
See: I Dood It

By the Light of the Silvery Moon ☉
1953, US, 101 mins, colour
Dir: David Butler
Stars: Doris Day, Gordon MacRae, Leon Ames, Rosemary de Camp
Rating: ★★★

Doris Day back in tomboy mood, in a sequel to the earlier On Moonlight Bay. It looks a bit more dated now than the average Warners/Day musical, but still the small-town atmosphere is nicely built up, and supporting players Leon Ames, Mary Wickes and Rosemary deCamp, all repeating their assignments from the earlier film, are a pleasure to watch. Besides the title number, songs include 'Ain't We Got Fun', 'Be My Little Baby Bumble Bee' and (in the brightest production number) 'King Chanticleer'.

By the Sword ◐ ⓥ
1991, US, 91 mins, colour
Dir: Jeremy Paul Kagan
Stars: Eric Roberts, F Murray Abraham
Rating: ★

Fencing films have not exactly been plentiful and this one shows you why. Errol Flynn and Basil Rathbone may have thrilled us to the core in The Adventures of Robin Hood, but there's little excitement to be had in the training of fencers for Olympic glory. And a dire script is no help. 'How,' asks one female student of another, 'do you seriously expect to find a man where guys play with long, pointy objects?' And, having had his advances rejected, a male fencer complains, 'I was just being myself,' to which the girl comes back with the devastating riposte, 'Why don't you try being someone else for a change?' Touché! F Murray Abraham is the old janitor who's an ace from years gone by, but seems to do little cleaning apart from ineffectually flicking a feather duster.

B

C

Cable Guy, The ◐ ⓥ
1996, US, 97 mins, colour
Dir: Ben Stiller
Stars: Jim Carrey, Matthew Broderick,
Leslie Mann, George Segal, Diane Baker,
Eric Roberts
Rating: ★★★

This nightmare comedy is something a
bit different from Carrey – and he
brings it off too. The Cable Guy is the
TV man from Hell. With friends like
this, no-one needs enemies. Just a few
words of encouragement from Steven
(Broderick) are enough to condemn
him. Carrey's Cable Guy battens on to
him like a barnacle. Denied love and
affection in a TV-drenched childhood,
this lisping leech tries to buy them by
installing all the latest gadgets in the
homes of his 'preferred customers'.
Getting rid of this grinning spectre is
another matter: Hell hath no fury like a
Cable Guy scorned. And rejection always brings retribution: a fact
underlined by an ending that rounds
things off exactly in the mood the film
establishes and keeps. Carrey and
Broderick couldn't do more to make
this work; and Janèane Garofalo has
fun in a cameo as a waitress at a medieval club where Broderick finds
himself jousting against a gleeful
Carrey for his very life.

Cabaret ◐ ⓥ
1972, US, 128 mins, colour
Dir: Bob Fosse
Stars: Liza Minnelli, Michael York, Joeil
Grey, Marisa Berenson
Rating: ★★★

The musical sequences are razor-sharp
under ex-dancer Bob Fosse's direction in
this hugely successful film version of
John Kander and Fred Ebb's throat-gripping, adrenalin-charging stage show.
While singing and dancing, at least, Liza
Minnelli, as Sally Bowles, and Joel Grey
as the painted emcee of Berlin's Kit Kat
Klub of the Thirties, give the performances of their lives, and it was no
surprise when they and Fosse collected
three of the film's eight Academy
Awards. Dramatically, the film is often
unsure of itself, but its dynamic, often
devastating songs carry the day.

Cactus ◐
1986, Australia, 96 mins, b/w
Dir: Paul Cox

Stars: Isabelle Huppert, Robert Menzies
Rating: ★★

This romantic drama is a challenging
piece of work from Dutch-born Paul
Cox, one of Australia's most innovative directors, with French actress
Isabelle Huppert giving a typically
strong performance as the
Frenchwoman escaping a bad marriage
and, while staying with friends in
Australia, partially blinded in a car accident. Her guilt-ridden friends
introduce her to a neighbour, Robert, a
shy, spiky individual who has been
blind since birth and is a cactus fanatic.
The two find friendship and eventually
more. The many quirky asides and peripheral characters tend to get in the
way of the narrative, but there's fine
camerawork by Yuri Sokol, and the
soundtrack is full of fascinating, eerie
noises from the Australian bush.

Cactus Flower ○ ⓥ
1969, US, 103 mins, colour
Dir: Gene Saks
Stars: Ingrid Bergman, Walter Matthau,
Goldie Hawn, Rick Lenz
Rating: ★★★★

Despite the cynicism inevitable in approaching such a romantic story these
days, you'll find that this adaptation of
a stage success is wise, witty and altogether welcome. Ingrid Bergman is a
delight as the staid secretary (blooming
rarely, like the cactus) who is at one
time unkindly described as 'sort of like
a large Band-Aid'. And Goldie Hawn,
as her rival for Walter Matthau, won
an Oscar in this, only her second film
appearance.

Cactus Jack ○
(aka: The Villain)
1979, US, 89 mins, colour
Dir: Hal Needham
Stars: Kirk Douglas, Ann-Margret, Arnold
Schwarzenegger
Rating: ★

This comic Western is a sort of live-action equivalent of the cartoon series
featuring The Road Runner and his
disaster-prone adversary Wile E
Coyote. Here it's Kirk Douglas as the
inept outlaw of the title whose attempts
to stop the hero (Arnold
Schwarzenegger) and heroine (Ann-
Margret) from getting some vital cash
to its destination only rebound on himself. Paul Lynde and Robert Tessier
score as two Indians called Anxious
Elk and Nervous Beaver, while the director of the farcical mayhem is
comedy-action specialist Hal Needham.
One could do without his attempts to

'lift' the comedy with quick-motion sequences when one would have thought
editing skills would have sufficed.

Caddyshack ◐
1980, US, 95 mins, colour
Dir: Harold Ramis
Stars: Chevy Chase, Rodney
Dangerfield, Bill Murray
Rating: ★★★

This zany, low-brow, knockabout comedy is fast-moving, juvenile and in the
worst possible taste. In other words,
it's a hoot! Its comic chaos centres on a
golf club upon which boorish, tasteless
Rodney Dangerfield descends. Ted
Knight is the snobbish club captain,
Chevy Chase its insincerely modest
golf pro and Bill Murray the grounds-
man obsessed with ridding the course
of gophers. The woefully underused
Dangerfield is wonderful as the kind of
person right-thinking people run and
hide from – the kind you always find
yourself sitting next to on a long air
flight. The most humorously disgusting scene is where the club pool is
emptied because a floating chocolate
bar is assumed to be something quite
different!

Cadillac Man ● ⓥ
1990, US, 98 mins, colour
Dir: Roger Donaldson
Stars: Robin Williams, Tim Robbins,
Annabella Sciorra, Pamela Reed, Elaine
Stritch, Lori Petty
Rating: ★★★

Would you buy a car from Joey
Walsh? Joey (Robin Williams) is
banking that you will, especially as he
owes $20,000 to gangsters, has
promised his ex-wife $500 a month for
his daughter's education, has two mistresses (at least) and gets two days to
sell 12 cars or lose his job. All of
Joey's troubles disappear, though,
from the moment a new one crashes
right through the window of his showroom in the shape of bemused,
enraged Larry (Tim Robbins), wielding a machine-gun and with half a ton
of explosives strapped to his bike.
Larry is convinced that half the showroom staff has been having his wife (a
secretary there) and it's Joey (ironically
one of the few who hasn't) who becomes the front-man in a nationwide
hostage drama. Although the film is
occasionally heavy-handed and sometimes wearing (a lot of people shout at
each other a lot of the time), you can
forgive it a lot for tying up its plot
threads so neatly at the end after a
splendid last reel. Williams oozes fake

charm – which is just what the character (and situation) demands.

Caesar and Cleopatra ○ Ⓥ
1945, UK, 138 mins, colour
Dir: Gabriel Pascal
Stars: Vivien Leigh, Claude Rains, Flora Robson, Stewart Granger
Rating: ★★

Stunning Technicolor photography by four of the best in the business Freddie Young, Jack Cardiff, Robert Krasker and Jack Hildyard – and a moody performance by Flora Robson are the main bonuses to this leisurely, expensive adaption of Shaw's play. Britain's costliest film at the time it was made, it failed to persuade cinemagoers to see it. Imposing sets, lavish costumes and stars by the handful failed to disguise the ponderous nature of Gabriel Pascal's direction, although Claude Rains' wonderful, civilised Caesar is pretty well director-proof. Viven Leigh could have been the perfect Cleopatra had she been induced to produce a livelier performance.

Caged Ⓓ
1950, US, 96 mins, b/w
Dir: John Cromwell
Stars: Eleanor Parker, Agnes Moorehead, Jan Sterling
Rating: ★★★

The transformation of a young, essentially innocent girl into a self-assured but embittered woman is depicted with perceptive realism, in this story of a sweet, innocent young girl who is sent to prison for unwittingly being involved in a bank robbery. There, brutal treatment by a sadistic wardress (played by 6ft 2in, 16st Hope Emerson, who was Oscar-nominated) and the evil influence of other inmates, turns her into a hard-boiled, brassy woman. Eleanor Parker, devoid of make-up and wearing only an old dress of Shirley Temple's plus prison overalls, was also nominated for an Oscar for her vivid, painful performance as the girl who endures everything from loneliness to having her hair shorn off.

Cage of Gold ○
1950, UK, 83 mins, b/w
Dir: Basil Dearden
Stars: Jean Simmons, David Farrar, James Donald, Madeleine Lebeau, Herbert Lom, Bernard Lee
Rating: ★★

This romantic thriller was one of the last films Jean Simmons made in England before going off to Hollywood, and her class shows, in

comparison with the rest of the cast. Good location shots of Paris and a strong whodunnit plot when Simmons is suspected of bumping off a blackmailer.

Cahill, United States Marshal Ⓓ Ⓥ
1973, US, 103 mins, colour
Dir: Andrew V McLaglen
Stars: John Wayne, George Kennedy, Gary Grimes, Neville Brand
Rating: ★★★

If an award were to be given for the most underrated John Wayne Western of post-war years, there's no doubt that *Cahill* would get our vote. In some ways it is a companion film to the previous year's *The Cowboys*, which also involved Wayne with children. In this case the boys are his character's own two sons (the elder of whom is Gary Grimes, the teenager from *Summer of '42*), two wild minors who become involved in robbery and murder. Wayne has to round up the 'galoots' responsible, to help the boys out of what becomes a very scary scrape, and the results make thundering entertainment. The action is slightly stylised – an unusual departure for the director, Andrew V McLaglen – with George Kennedy in one of his meatiest roles as the villain who might well have stepped straight out of theatrical high melodrama. And you'll love both the thunder and lightning finale and the performances of Neville Brand as Wayne's half-breed friend.

Caine Mutiny, The ○ Ⓥ
1954, US, 125 mins, colour
Dir: Edward Dmytryk
Stars: Humphrey Bogart, Jose Ferrer, Van Johnson, Fred MacMurray, Robert Francis, Lee Marvin
Rating: ★★★★

You'll end up liking none of the characters in this famous sea story, in which Humphrey Bogart received an Oscar nomination as the unbalanced, ball-bearing-clicking Captain Queeg, mutinied against, then finally destroyed in the memorable climactic courtroom scene. Tremendous Technicolor photography by Franz Planer complements Stanley Roberts' bitter, corrosive screenplay which takes its characters apart and pares them down to their rawest emotions. There are worthy contributions from Robert Francis (killed shortly afterwards in an air crash), Fred MacMurray, always at his best when being sneaky, Jose Ferrer, scathing but with a glimpse of compas-

sion as a lawyer, E G Marshall, Lee Marvin and Claude Akins. But it's Bogart you'll remember.

Cairo ○
1963, UK, 91 mins, b/w
Dir: Wolf Rilla
Stars: George Sanders, Richard Johnson, Eric Pohlmann
Rating: ★★

A workmanlike if a trifle mechanical re-hash of John Huston's *The Asphalt Jungle*. It's neat and well-characterised, with the role of the mastermind (formerly played by Sam Jaffe) now tailored to measure exactly up to George Sanders' inimitable brand of insolent charm.

Cairo Road ○
1950, UK, 95 mins, b/w
Dir: David Macdonald
Stars: Eric Portman, Laurence Harvey
Rating: ★★★

A grim, documentary-style production which spotlights the efforts of Cairo's police chief (Eric Portman) and his (sometimes too) eager assistant (played with inappropriately poker-faced coolness by Laurernce Harvey) in laying traps for drugs traffickers along Egypt's frontiers. Many of the actors who became familiar playing suspicious characters in British films of the Fifties, including Marne Maitland, Harold Lang, Karel Stepanek, Gregoire 'Coco' Aslan and Abraham Sofaer, make early screen appearances. The Middle Eastern feel is well maintained by direction that otherwise keeps to the rudimentary. A perceptive performance by Portman stands head and shoulders above the rest of the cast.

Cal Ⓓ Ⓥ
1984, UK, 102 mins, colour
Dir: Pat O'Connor
Stars: Helen Mirren, John Lynch, Donal McCann, John Cavanagh, Ray McAnally
Rating: ★★

Although this well-made British film is ostensibly about the Irish Question, the only question most viewers are likely to find themselves asking is how long it will take mournful, guilt-obsessed John Lynch to get into farm widow Helen Mirren's bed. He drove the car, you see, for the assassin who killed her husband, and thereby hangs the irony. Outside this central issue, the film paints a probably justifiably bleak view of Belfast in the Eighties' troubles. Alas, it can offer no answer, only at best a cry of anguish in an abrasively-scripted film which remains watchable

C

even if all concerned seem to be having a thoroughly miserable time.

Calamity Jane ○ ⓥ
1953, US, 100 mins, colour
Dir: David Butler
Stars: Doris Day, Howard Keel, Philip Carey, Dick Wesson, Allyn McLerie
Rating: ★★★★★

From the opening shots of Doris Day singing 'Whipcrackaway' on top of the Deadwood stagecoach, this film is pure delight. Calamity Jane sets out to show that anything a man can do, she can do better. Only Wild Bill Hickok, played by Howard Keel, seems unimpressed. It takes a whole string of songs and dances before Jane can convince him that under her tough exterior there is a woman's heart that is his for the asking. Breeze-fresh and full of get-up-and-go, the film contains one of the best original scores ever written for the screen, the hit song from which, 'Secret Love' won in Academy Award.

Calamity Jane and Sam Bass ○
1949, US, 85 mins, colour
Dir: George Sherman
Stars: Yvonne De Carlo, Howard Duff, Lloyd Bridges
Rating: ★★

Yvonne De Carlo was given a chance to break away from her sultry Eastern image with this portrait of the famous frontier wildcat. And she certainly puts plenty of fire into the role. A cast full of Hollywood stalwarts includes Lloyd Bridges, Marc Lawrence, Milburn Stone and, as Jim Murphy, Norman Lloyd, best remembered as the man who fell from the Statue of Liberty at the end of Hitchcock's *Saboteur*.

Calcutta ○
1945, US, 83 mins, b/w
Dir: John Farrow
Stars: Alan Ladd, Gail Russell, William Bendix, June Duprez
Rating: ★★★

Shot in 1945 when its star, Alan Ladd, was still at the peak of his laconic powers, this dark thriller, eventually released in 1947, has a Chandleresque screenplay by Seton I Miller that brims with memorable man-woman exchanges between Ladd and Gail Russell, who's a little too soft for a role that needed a Donna Reed, a Ruth Roman or even a Hedy Lamarr. Reliable support comes from Ladd's ofttime co-star William Bendix (they're hunting the killers of their partner), and the villains are as sneaky as can be.

And remember (as Ladd has cause to): 'Man who trust woman walks on duckweed over pond'.

California Conquest ○
1952, US, 79 mins, colour
Dir: Lew Landers
Stars: Cornel Wilde, Teresa Wright, Alfonso Bedoya
Rating: ★★

This Western about Spanish Californians trying to escape the yoke of Mexican rule was made by Lew Landers, one of Hollywood's most prolific directors. Its fast pace can be attributed to Landers' training in the Thirties, when he began with such horror 'quickies' as *The Raven*, subsequently turning out scores of horror, action and adventure films, not one of them over 80 minutes in length. *California Conquest* is, at 79 minutes, his longest film and, like the rest of them, moves along like an express train.

California Dolls, The ◖
(aka: ... All the Marbles)
1981, US, 115 mins, colour
Dir: Robert Aldrich
Stars: Peter Falk, Vicki Frederick, Laurene Landon, Burt Young, Richard Jaeckel
Rating: ★★★

Robert Aldrich's bleakly humorous survival movie transfers Peter Falk from a crumpled mac to a crumbling Cadillac as he ferries his two-girl wrestling team around some of the less attractive venues of America's industrial Mid-West, their goal being the tacky neon glitter of Reno, where the climactic championship is held. *California Dolls* turned out to be Aldrich's last film, and the familiar cynicism is all there: life is a violent arena where your protective layers are ripped to shreds. Peter Falk is on top form as the seedy wheeler-dealer promoter and you don't have to be a wrestling fan to enjoy the film, which is extremely funny at times. The final wrestling bout will have you on the edge of your seat.

California Holiday ○ ⓥ
(aka: Spinout)
1966, US, 93 mins, colour
Dir: Norman Taurog
Stars: Elvis Presley, Shelley Fabares, Deborah Walley
Rating: ★★

Some fizzy songs and a cracking motor race are the highlights of this Elvis Presley musical produced by Joe Pastemak. Dodie Marshall's hip-waving dancer is the best of the quartet of

curvy cuties surrounding the star, while such stalwart veterans as Cecil Kellaway, Una Merkel and Carl Betz bring up the rear.

California Man ◖ ⓥ
(aka: Encino Man)
1992, US, 89 mins, colour
Dir: Les Mayfield
Stars: Sean Astin, Brandon Farley, Pauly Shore, Megan Ward, Mariette Hartley, Richard Masur
Rating: ★★

An unexpected summer hit in America in 1992, this Disney romp is just like the kind of novelty teen comedy the studio was making 20 years ago. In fact, substitute Brandon Farley here for Jan-Michael Vincent and this could almost be a reworking of *The World's Greatest Athlete*. Sean Astin plays a chubby teenager, striking out with the girls and victimised by the school bully. While excavating for a swimming pool, he finds a caveman frozen in ice 12 feet below the ground. 'Link' is soon the hit of Astin's school, where he masquerades as an Estonian and helps him win the heart of the school prom queen (Megan Ward). All this is pepped up a bit (but not much) by Pauly Shore's mumblespeak as Astin's zombie-like friend. Don't see this expecting anything new or meaningful.

California Split ◖
1974, US, 108 mins, colour
Dir: Robert Altman
Stars: George Segal, Elliott Gould, Ann Prentiss, Gwen Welles
Rating: ★★

There are some very funny lines in this Robert Altman film about two compulsive gamblers who will bet on anything. Perhaps one can forgive the fact that the gambling scenes themselves generate little tension, as this was presumably not the director's primary intention. He concentrates more on overlapping dialogue, an improvised air and individual performances. Ann Prentiss and Gwen Welles as a couple of pushy but sympathetic hookers, with whom the boys become involved, are a treat.

California Suite ○ ⓥ
1978, US, 103 mins, colour
Dir: Herbert Ross
Stars: Alan Alda, Michael Caine, Jane Fonda, Maggie Smith, Walter Matthau, Richard Pryor, Bill Cosby
Rating: ★★★

The famous Beverly Hills Hotel in Los Angeles is the setting for this omnibus-type film of several stories. Written by Neil Simon, it is much in the Simon mould with a delicious blend of comedy and touches of straight drama. Among the star cast are Maggie Smith, as a British actress who has been nominated for an Academy Award (she actually won an Oscar for this film!), Michael Caine, as her antiques-dealer husband, Walter Matthau, as a businessman from Philadelphia, Jane Fonda, as a wisecracking divorcee from New York, Alan Alda, as her screenwriter ex-husband, and Bill Cosby and Richard Pryor as two Chicago doctors who are close friends.

Call Harry Crown ◑
(aka: 99 44/100% Dead)
1974, US, 98 mins, colour
Dir: John Frankenheimer
Stars: Richard Harris, Edmond O'Brien, Ann Turkel, Bradford Dillman, Chuck Connors
Rating: ★★★

A smooth and not too serious thriller about a gang war and the gunman (Richard Harris) who is called in to end it.. Ann Turkel and Kathrine Baumann are pretty newcomers with splendidly impressive figures. There are some good shoot-ups for the undemanding and a personable villain (Chuck Connors) with a hook hand – and other attachments – to be bested. It moves, it amuses and it entertains. Director John Frankenheimer steers the mayhem along like a well-oiled and happily-tuned motor.

Calling Bulldog Drummond ○
1951, UK, 80 mins, b/w
Dir: Victor Saville
Stars: Walter Pidgeon, Margaret Leighton, Robert Beatty, Peggy Evans, David Tomlinson
Rating: ★★

Sapper's famous fictional detective has been seen in films for over 50 years. Here he's played by Walter Pidgeon, but acting honours go to Margaret Leighton as an attractive and resourceful policewoman. David Tomlinson is ideally cast as Bulldog's sidekick Algy. Silly plot, though.

Call Me ●
1987, US, 96 mins, colour
Dir: Sollace Mitchell
Stars: Patricia Charbonneau, Patti D'Arbanville, Sam Freed, Stephen McHattie, Steve Buscemi, David Strathairn
Rating: ★★

This may be the first movie in which the hero is an obscene phone caller. Anna (Patricia Charbonneau), mistakenly thinking the caller's her boyfriend, goes to a sleazy bar to meet 'him' and witnesses a murder there. As the murderer's a cop, she's not sure what to do, and gradually finds her only solace in the seductive voice on the other end of the line. It's an interesting concept, but the execution of it is only mediocre and the film's enthusiasni for 'dirty talk' rather overwhelms the central story thread. Still, if you pay *Call Me* a visit, you may never view oranges in quite the same light again . .

Call Me Bwana ⊙
1963, UK, 103 mins, colour
Dir: Gordon Douglas
Stars: Bob Hope, Anita Ekberg, Edie Adams, Lionel Jeffries
Rating: ★★

Gleefully scatty Bob Hope comedy – one of the last reasonably good ones he made – which finds our hero well at home tossing out wisecracks to the natives in the depths of the African jungle. Lionel Jeffries helps to keep it rolling zanily along.

Call Me Genius
See: The Rebel

Call Me Madam ○
1953, US, 117 mins, colour
Dir: Walter Lang
Stars: Ethel Merman, Donald O'Connor, Vera-Ellen, George Sanders
Rating: ★★★

The best thing about this rather flat Irving Berlin musical was that it brought Ethel Merman back to Hollywood for a leading role for the first time since the Thirties. You'll get restless between the musical numbers, but these are almost all outstanding, from the dancing of Vera-Ellen and Donald O'Connor to such songs as 'It's A Lovely Day Today', 'You're just In Love', 'The Best Thing For You', 'Hostess with the Mostest' and 'International Rag'.

Call Me Mister ○
1951, US, 95 mins, colour
Dir: Lloyd Bacon
Stars: Betty Grable, Dan Dailey, Danny Thomas, Dale Robertson
Rating: ★★★

This pleasing musical reunited master choreographer Busby Berkeley and director Lloyd Bacon for the first time since their smash hit of 1933, *42nd Street*. It's not in the same class as that masterpiece, but Betty Grable and Dan Dailey are on good form as the leads, she an entertainer working in Japan during the Korean War, he her GI husband, separated from her but trying to win her back by getting himself posted to the same army camp. No prizes for guessing the outcome, but along the way there are lots of laughs and Berkeley creates some likeable dance routines, particularly the title number for Grable and Dailey. Danny Thomas and Dale Robertson are also given chances as contrasting suitors who both have an eye on Betty. A pretty fair show.

Call Northside 777 ○
1947, US, 111 mins, b/w
Dir: Henry Hathaway
Stars: James Stewart, Richard Conte, Lee J Cobb, Helen Walker
Rating: ★★★★★

Documentary-style thriller based on the actual case of a reporter who ferreted around until he found out the truth about a 12-year-old murder case. Absorbing every step of the way thanks to Henry Hathaway's pacy direction of an incident-filled script and another very fine perfomance from James Stewart – right up to the final agonising attempts to prove the innocence of the man sent down for a murder he didn't do. Fine cinema.

Camelot ○ ⓥ
1967, UK, 178 mins, colour
Dir: Joshua Logan
Stars: Richard Harris, Vanessa Redgrave, Franco Nero, David Hemmings, Lionel Jeffries
Rating: ★★

This mediocre musical is really a technician's triumph: the music and lyrics, by Frederick Loewe and Alan Jay Lerner, the photography of Richard Kline, and John Truscott's costume designs are all very pleasing indeed. Of the perfomances, that of Richard Harris – who also does his own singing – stands out with his forthright and sympathetic King Arthur. But Vanessa Redgrave, perhaps not beautiful enough from the start, is not a notable success as Guinevere. The score includes 'If Ever I Would leave You', 'C'est Moi' and 'Camelot'.

Campbell's Kingdom ○
1957, UK, 100 mins, colour
Dir: Ralph Thomas
Stars: Dirk Bogarde, Stanley Baker, Michael Craig, Barbara Murray, James Robertson Justice
Rating: ★★★

C

Creditable British attempt to make a rousing adventure story in the best Hollywood tradition, based on a novel by Hammond Innes. Dirk Bogarde is a forthright hero, but Stanley Baker steals the film by making Morgan a truly villainous figure. The Eastman Colour photography of mountain locations is most attractive, and Ralph Thomas's direction gives the movie plenty of pace and urgency. The film's only weak point is its script, which has more than its share of silly lines. Once it moves into action, however, it's a different picture altogether.

Canadian Bacon ○ ⓥ

1995, US/Can, 91 mins, colour
Dir: Michael Moore
Stars: Alan Alda, John Candy, Rhea Perlman, Kevin Pollak, Kevin J O'Connor, Rip Torn
Rating: ★

Desperate stuff, this, full of stars who should have known better, but ending up as a sort of transatlantic equivalent of *Whoops Apocalypse*. Give *Roger & Me* director Michael Moore a story about the US declaring war on Canada to increase the President's rating among hawks, and you might seem to have laughter guaranteed. A lot of talented people jumped to the wrong conclusion here, forgetting that Moore had never actually made a fictional feature film. Even Dan Aykroyd and James Belushi crop up in guest roles, but humour is nuked from the word Go, and the film's only funny line comes in the closing credits: 'No Canadians were harmed during the making of this film' – we thought we'd save you the trouble of sitting through the rest. Rip Torn deserves some kind of *Star Trek* medal for boldly going further over the top than any man before.

Canadian Pacific ○

1949, US, 95 mins, colour
Dir: Edwin L Marin
Stars: Randolph Scott, Jane Wyatt, Victor Jory, Nancy Olson
Rating: ★★

A tired old Western plot, about bad hats out to stop the building of the railroad, is given a lift by the performances in this action adventure, especially those of Jane Wyatt, as an intrepid frontier doctor, and Nancy Olson, spirited in her screen debut as a tomboy French-Canadian. It's hard to believe that craggy old Randolph Scott could be fancied by both of these feisty young females, but Hollywood Westerns do tend to ignore normal

logic. Nicely shot in Cinecolor, partly on location in the Canadian Rockies, although the colour work falls down when it leaves the countryside. A bit on the long side, but that allows room for snarling Victor Jory to properly etch one of his rasping-voiced villains. J Carrol Naish is the (very expendable) comic relief.

Canadians, The ○

1961, US, 85 mins, colour
Dir: Burt Kennedy
Stars: Robert Ryan, John Dehner, Torin Thatcher
Rating: ★★

Movies about those Mounties who always get their man have been few and far between. Here's an exciting manhunt story written and directed by Burt Kennedy, later to become one of America's foremost directors of Westerns. Robert Ryan, incidentally, played a Mountie in his first film – De Mille's *North West Mounted Police*.

Can Can ○

1960, US, 131 mins, colour
Dir: Walter Lang
Stars: Frank Sinatra, Shirley MacLaine, Maurice Chevalier, Louis Jourdan, Juliet Prowse
Rating: ★

Less Ooo-La-La than Oh! No! No! Just how 20th Century-Fox allowed the hit Broadway musical to transfer to the screen as an unmitigated bore is a tragedy of the modern film musical. It had everything going for it – an all-star cast, fantastic Cole Porter songs, including 'C'est Magnifique', 'Let's Do It' and 'It's All Right With Me', and great dance numbers – but ended up with ponderous direction, dull performances and a tiresome screenplay. Even the dance numbers struck a wrong note, posing the question: just why did the can-can prove so scandalous? Shirley MacLaine's brassy central performance as the cafe owner facing prosecution for allowing the dance to be staged illegally, is strictly one-dimensional.

Candleshoe ⊙

1977, UK, 101 mins, colour
Dir: Norman Tokar
Stars: David Niven, Helen Hayes, Jodie Foster, Leo McKern
Rating: ★★★

Disney rarely missed with its British films and this is another winner. Jodie Foster is the tough American 14-year-old whom a crooked detective plans to foist off as the heiress to an English fortune. Naturally, once in England,

Jodie's cynical exterior soon breaks down to reveal a heart of pure Disney, especially when the marchioness (Helen Hayes) proves all but broke and the butler (David Niven) appears in a number of disguises to help keep up appearances. Things develop well from here, with some lovely photography of the English countryside not allowed to interfere with a rattling good pace. The film is splendidly edited, presentably written in faintly *Just William* vein by David Swift and Rosemary Anne Sisson, and has some charming child performers.

Candy ●

1968, US/Italy, 115 mins, colour
Dir: Christian Marquand
Stars: Marlon Brando, Richard Burton, James Coburn, Walter Matthau, Charles Aznavour, Ewa Aulin
Rating: ★

The famous (and famously bad) comedy saga about a nubile nymphet who gives herself to mankind for any amount of charitable reasons. Marlon Brando and Walter Matthau offer amusing evidence that they are good enough to surmount any number of deficiencies in a script.

Candyman ● ⓥ

1992, US, 101 mins, colour
Dir: Bernard Rose
Stars: Virginia Madsen, Tony Todd, Xander Berkeley, Kasi Lemmons, Vanessa Williams
Rating: ★★★★

A good modern horror film, full of guts and gore, but scary enough to make you fight shy of the bathroom cabinet mirror before you go to bed. Virginia Madsen again demonstrates her amazing range in an anguished role far from her sometime glamour image. She's a mature student who opens up a particularly disgusting can of worms when she calls up the vast black phantom known as Candyman who guts his victims, well, from ear to there. British director Bernard Rose ensures there are not too many uncalled-for giggles in the blood-soaked but (by the standards of the genre) logical developments that follow. A sequel, *Candyman 2: Farewell to the Flesh*, is not in the same class.

Cannonball

See: Carquake

Cannonball Run, The ○ ⓥ

1980, US, 95 mins, colour
Dir: Hal Needham
Stars: Burt Reynolds, Dom DeLuise,

Farrah Fawcett, Roger Moore, Dean
Martin, Sammy Davis Jr
Rating: ★

An amazingly star-studded cast, Burt
Reynolds' then-popularity and a continuing catalogue of chaotic car chases
were presumably the ingredients that
pulled the American public in, and (in
its own country at least) made this embarrassingly witless comedy a huge
box-office success. Encouraged by its
success, Reynolds made far too many
similar smash-em-up-on-the-road romps
in the next decade, hastening the decline of his film career.

Cannonball Run II ○ ⓥ
1983, US, 108 mins, colour
Dir: Hal Needham
Stars: Burt Reynolds, Dom DeLuise,
Dean Martin, Sammy Davis Jr, Telly
Savalas, Shirley MacLaine
Rating: ★★

Even more daft than its less-than-illus-
trious predecessor, this car chase
caper is knee-deep in second-rate stars
and some surprising appearances
from some first-rate stars (Frank
Sinatra, Dean Martin and Sammy
Davis Jr for example). Amiable Burt
Reynolds has a thoroughly enjoyable
time doing his good ole boy act again
(as in previous *Cannonball* and *Smokey
and the Bandit* movies) as one of the
host of ill-assorted drivers who dash
at highly illegal speeds across
America. The best thing in the film is
Dom DeLuise who, as the schizo-
phrenic Victor, turns in moments of
stress into tubby superhero Captain
Chaos!

Cannon for Cordoba ○
1970, US, 104 mins, colour
Dir: Paul Wendkos
Stars: George Peppard, Raf Vallone
Rating: ★★

Also known as *Dragon Master,* this is a
pretty average Western, notable only
for beautiful on-location filming in
Spain. George Peppard is an intelligence captain called upon to quell a
marauding band of Mexican outlaws.
Look out for the late Pete Duel (of *Alias
Smith and Jones* fame). Elmer
Bernstein's stirring music adds to the
atmosphere.

Can't Buy Me Love ◑
1987, US, 94 mins, colour
Dir: Steve Rash
Stars: Patrick Dempsey, Amanda
Peterson, Courtney Gains, Seth Green
Rating: ★★★

High school nerd Patrick Dempsey
sees a way to buy himself into popularity (with the money he's saved for a
telescope) when the obscure object of
his desires, cheerleader queen Cindy
(Amanda Peterson), desperately needs
$1,000 to replace a ruined dress she's
'borrowed' from her mother. He loans
her the money in return for her dating
him for a month. She's beginning to
fall for him at the end of the period, but
the poor sap is too blinded by the 'stardom' she's given him to see it. Around
about here, the plot isn't too logical.
But, although the film is overly simplistic and paints a pretty appalling picture
of American girlhood at every turn, the
two young leads involve us sufficiently
in their lives to make us feel irritated
and angry with them when they blow
it.

Canterbury Tale, A ○ ⓥ
1944, UK, 124 mins, b/w
Dir: Michael Powell
Stars: Eric Portman, Sheila Sim
Rating: ★★

And a bizarre tale this is too, mystical
and alienating even by that often brilliant director Michael Powell's
standards. A dangerous crank is on
the loose in a southern English village
in wartime, pouring glue on local girls'
hair when they go out at night.
Photographer Erwin Hillier contrives
to catch the atmosphere of the Engish
countryside in summer in black and
white – no mean feat – while there are
early career appearances by Dennis
Price and Sheila Sim, both to rise to
prominence in post-war British cinema.
Long and languorous, this strange kettle of fish finally drifts away into its
own heat haze.

Canterville Ghost, The ○
1943, US, 96 mins, b/w
Dir: Jules Dassin
Stars: Charles Laughton, Margaret
O'Brien, Robert Young, William Gargan,
Rags Ragland, Peter Lawford
Rating: ★★★

An absolutely charming piece of film
whimsy about a tired old ghost who is
doomed to roam his ancestral home
until one of his descendants performs a
deed brave enough to lift the curse of
cowardice from his family. With
Charles Laughton in top comedy form
as the ghost, and the delightfully unsugary Margaret O'Brien – even
making a passing attempt at an English
accent! – as the little girl who befriends
him, it's a rich piece of escapist entertainment.

Can't Help Singing ○
1944, US, 89 mins, colour
Dir: Frank Ryan
Stars: Deanna Durbin, Robert Paige,
Akim Tamiroff
Rating: ★★

Three Hollywood foreigners, Akim
Tamiroff, Leonid Kinskey and
Thomas Gomez, help enliven this
Forties' musical, which offers Deanna
Durbin out west, and in Technicolor
too. The Jerome Kern songs include
'More and More', which was nominat-
ed for an Academy Award.

Can't Stop the Music ○
1980, US, 124 mins, colour
Dir: Nancy Walker
Stars: Valerie Perrine, Steve
Guttenberg, Bruce Jenner, Tammy
Grimes, June Havoc, Jack Weston
Rating: ★★

Curiously old-fashioned youth musical
featuring the Village People and their
massive hit 'YMCA'. Grisly rehash of
the 'Let's put on a show' plotline, all
high-spirited noise, lights, slogans,
movement and dazzle. All of the acting, though, is rather strained.

Canyon Crossroads ○
1955, US, 83 mins, b/w
Dir: Alfred Werker
Stars: Richard Basehart, Phyllis Kirk,
Stephen Elliott
Rating: ★★★

A modern-style Western concerning
the quest for uranium, this is as much
an adventure thriller as a horse opera.
Phyllis Kirk, that slimmest and prettiest
of Fifties' heroines, and Richard
Basehart both mould characters one
cares about.

Canyon Pass ○
(aka: Raton Pass)
1950, US, 84 mins, b/w
Dir: Edwin L Marin
Stars: Dennis Morgan, Patricia Neal,
Steve Cochran
Rating: ★★

Oscar-winning actress Patricia Neal
enioys herself hugely as a bad girl in
this off-beat Western. The film whips
up a fair ration of excitement, even
though Warner Bros. didn't rate it
highly enough to splash out on
Technicolor. But then Miss Neal always seemed at her best in black and
white.

Canyon Passage ○
1946, US, 92 mins, colour
Dir: Jacques Tourneur

C

Stars: Dana Andrews, Susan Hayward, Brian Donlevy, Lloyd Bridges, Patricia Roc, Andy Devine
Rating: ★★★

A full-blooded Western with some spectacular action and scenery, strikingly shot in colour. There's a pulsating battle against Indians, and a fist-fight between Dana Andrews and Ward Bond that took days to shoot. Hoagy Carmichael, that ubiquitous piano player of the Forties, appears as a top-hatted character aptly named Linnet, chirping one or two tuneful melodies that include the memorable and catchy 'Buttermilk Sky'.

Cape Fear ◐ Ⓥ
1962, US, 106 mins, b/w
Dir: J Lee Thompson
Stars: Gregory Peck, Robert Mitchum, Polly Bergen, Martin Balsam, Lori Martin, Telly Savalas
Rating: ★★★★

Robert Mitchum can be frighteningly evil when he puts his mind to it and the two best examples are *The Night of the Hunter* and this tense and chilling thriller. He plays Max Cady, a psychopath recently released from prison. He's after the man who put him there, lawyer Sam Bowden (Gregory Peck). Cady terrorises the family in various ways, but is smart enough to keep the law at arm's length. Eventually, Bowden realises he'll have to deal with Cady himself. Mitchum is grimly realistic, Peck powerful as the family man backed into a corner and there are excellent supporting performances from Polly Bergen, Martin Balsam and Telly Savalas in a very early role. Striking black and white photography heightens the sense of menace and J Lee Thompson's direction doesn't allow the tension to slacken for a moment.

Cape Fear ● Ⓥ
1991, US, 128 mins, colour
Dir: Martin Scorsese
Stars: Robert De Niro, Nick Nolte, Jessica Lange, Juliette Lewis, Joe Don Baker, Illeana Douglas
Rating: ★★★

Max Cady (Robert De Niro) is a maniac with a mission. And he's harder to kill than The Terminator. Max walks through fire, water and brutal beatings to exact his revenge on the lawyer (Nick Nolte) who suppressed evidence that would have saved him from 14 years in jail – because of the intense brutality of the rape of which Cady was guilty. Now Cady's back, to teach the lawyer and his family 'something

about loss'. Like their dog, the lawyer's friend, their maid and the detective they hire. He traps the daughter, menaces the wife. And finally catches up with the whole family on a houseboat in a storm. Even nastier than the 1962 version, but not quite as good.

Capricorn One ○
1978, US, 128 mins, colour
Dir: Peter Hyams
Stars: Elliott Gould, James Brolin, Brenda Vaccaro, Sam Waterston, O J Simpson, Hal Holbrook
Rating: ★★★★★

This pounding action drama is completely original, but many of its situations are worked by director Peter Hyams in tried and trusted Hollywood fashion. Elliott Gould stars as the reporter who gets wind of the fact that the first manned mission to Mars may be a giant hoax. James Brolin leads the trio of astronauts who are told that their families' lives depend on their co-operation. You could virtually write the plot developments yourself from then on, but they're shunted along with such verve by Hyams that you won't much care, especially in a nerve-crunching last 20 minutes as Brolin and Gould desperately flee from the baddies, with the help of a telling guest appearance from Telly Savalas as a crop-duster pilot.

Captain America ○ Ⓥ
1989, US, 95 mins, colour
Dir: Albert Pyun
Stars: Matt Salinger, Ned Beatty, Scott Paulin
Rating: ★★★

Rising from the dead just when the world really needs a superhero, Captain America returns to save the day in this fast-moving comic-book saga. The *Marvel* comic hero is played with just the right level of humour and two-dimensional gravitas by Matt Salinger. Scott Paulin enjoys himself being irredeemably evil as the villain, The Red Skull, and there's a strong supporting cast that includes Ned Beatty, Ronny Cox, Melinda Dillon and Michael Nouri. It's all pure hokum, of course, but entirely in the spirit of the comics and enormous fun.

Captain Apache ○
1971, US/Spain, 94 mins, colour
Dir: Alexander Singer
Stars: Lee Van Cleef, Carroll Baker, Stuart Whitman
Rating: ★★

A Western made in the Continental style, this stars Lee Van Cleef in the title role of an Indian serving with US Army Intelligence. Captain Apache's assignment is to track down the killer of an Indian Commissioner named Collier, whose dying words were mysterious and enigmatic – 'April morning'. Van Cleef is no stranger to this type of film, since he rose to major fame during the vogue for 'spaghetti Westerns'. Less usually, in this Western, he is heard as a vocalist in a couple of songs.

Captain Blood ○ Ⓥ
1935, US, 119 mins, b/w
Dir: Michael Curtiz
Stars: Errol Flynn, Olivia de Havilland, Basil Rathbone, Lionel Atwill, Guy Kibbee
Rating: ★★★★

The film in which Tasmanian-born Errol Flynn, following just a couple of small Hollywood roles, burst upon the world as a new star. (Britain's Robert Donat had been unable to accept the part of swashbuckling doctor Peter Blood.) The action scenes are choreographed with a surge and unity of which even Busby Berkeley would have been proud. Stirring stuff.

Captain Boycott ○
1947, UK, 93 mins, b/w
Dir: Frank Launder
Stars: Stewart Granger, Cecil Parker, Alastair Sim, Mervyn Johns
Rating: ★★★

This lusty historical drama has plenty of pace and punch, as well as integrity, in its story of how badly landowners treated their tenant farmers in the Ireland of the 19th century. Stewart Granger revels in his hero's role; and Robert Donat's brief and uncredited guest appearance leaves one gasping for more.

Captain Caution ○
1940, US, 85 mins, b/w
Dir: Richard Wallace
Stars: Victor Mature, Louise Platt, Leo Carrillo, Bruce Cabot
Rating: ★★

The 'hunk' legend about Victor Mature started around this film, which gave the beefcake star his first major leading role as a husk-y man of action on the seven seas in the early 19th century. His leading lady in this fastmoving period piece is pretty Louise Platt, whose spirited character is in marked contrast to her weepy wife in John Ford's *Stagecoach*.

Captain Clegg
See: Night Creatures

Captain Eddie ○
1945, US, 107 mins, b/w
Dir: Lloyd Bacon
Stars: Fred MacMurray, Lloyd Nolan, Charles Bickford
Rating: ★★

A gently nostalgic look at the life of American air ace Captain Eddie Rickenbacker. The action spans a quarter of a century as Rickenbacker, marooned at sea after being shot down in World War Two, looks back at his life. Fred MacMurray gets sympathetic support from Thomas Mitchell, Charles Bickford and James Gleason, while a young Richard Conte can be seen as one of Rickenbacker's shipmates in distress.

Captain from Castile ○
1947, US, 140 mins, colour
Dir: Henry King
Stars: Tyrone Power, Jean Peters, Cesar Romero, Lee J Cobb, John Sutton
Rating: ★★★

A spectacular adventure film which introduced the fiery Jean Peters to the screen, this slice of 16th-century history was among the first of its kind to be made largely on location. Ostensibly a story of a Spanish adventurer, played by Tyrone Power, it is mainly concerned with Hernan Cortez and his conquest of the Aztec Empire. Lots of duels and battle scenes should please the action fans, and the colour photography by Charles Clarke and Arthur Arling is clarity itself.

Captain Horatio Hornblower RN ○
1951, UK, 117 mins, colour
Dir: Raoul Walsh
Stars: Gregory Peck, Virginia Mayo, Robert Beatty, James Robertson Justice, Stanley Baker
Rating: ★★★

The brightest bits of three C S Forester novels rolled into one omnibus edition of thrills. The awesome battle scenes in this rousing seafaring epic of the Napoleonic Wars were among the most expensive ever shot in Britain. But the dialogue scenes often run aground. Robert Beatty steals the honours as Peck's second-in-command.

Captain January ⊙
1936, US, 75 mins, b/w
Dir: David Butler
Stars: Shirley Temple, Guy Kibbee, Slim Summerville, June Lang
Rating: ★★★

This Shirley Temple film finds the most famous child star looked after by a lighthousekeeper. Authorities, of course, break into their idyll, giving rise to one of Shirley's best remembered lines: 'Cap! Cap! Cap! I don't want to go!' It's not all tears though. Shirley finds time to dance a step or two, and sing 'Early Bird', 'At the Codfish Ball' and 'The Right Somebody to Love'.

Captain Kronos – Vampire Hunter ●
1972, UK, 91 mins, colour
Dir: Brian Clemens
Stars: Horst Janson, Caroline Munro, Ian Hendry
Rating: ★★★

Not at all typical of Hammer's output, this atmospheric fantasy chiller comes from the fertile brain of writer Brian Clemens, who on this occasion sat in the director's chair as well. The camera is at times both narrator and predator, as the hero, a sort of Gothic Superman, stalks or is stalked by his prey. And there are good roles for Horst Janson, as Kronos, John Cater, John Carson, Ian Hendry and the fetching Caroline Munro.

Captain Nemo and the Underwater City ⊙
1968, UK, 106 mins, colour
Dir: James Hill
Stars: Robert Ryan, Chuck Connors, Nanette Newman
Rating: ★★

Silly but enjoyable schoolboy adventure with some fine sets inside the submarine *Nautilus* and an exciting undersea battle against a giant squid. Britain's Bill Fraser and Kenneth Connor provide light relief as a pair of not-too-clever gun-runners. Robert Ryan, Chuck Connors, Nanette Newman and Luciana Paluzzi have to grit their teeth, clench their jaws and play it for real.

Captain Pirate ⊙
(aka: Captain Blood, Fugitive)
1952, US, 85 mins, colour
Dir: Ralph Murphy
Stars: Louis Hayward, Patricia Medina, John Sutton, Ted de Corsia
Rating: ★★★

Plenty of action and swordplay in the sequel to *The Fortunes of Captain Blood*, with Louis Hayward, one of the best swordsmen Hollywood (well, actually South Africa) ever produced, making the fencing seem easy in the title role. His gossamer touch with a line and smooth personality, adds a lot more of the character than exists in the script. Patricia Medina once again partners him – as indeed she did in several other films – while Malu Gatica, as a tavern singer, has a pleasing voice and attractive enough personality to make one wonder why she wasn't seen more often in films. The fine Technicolor photography by Charles Lawson Jr helps to make this, despite a scrappy start, a good action package, full of battles of all kinds.

Captain Ron ◖ Ⓥ
1992, US, 100 mins, colour
Dir: Thom Eberhardt
Stars: Kurt Russell, Martin Short, Mary Kay Place, Benjamin Salisbury, J A Preston
Rating: ★★

A colourful and largely inoffensive Disney romp starring the manic Martin Short as an executive who inherits a yacht, decides to take the family on the trip of a lifetime, then makes the mistake of hiring Captain Ron (Kurt Russell) to skipper the boat. Russell, unexpectedly handed the comic role instead of his co-star, steals every scene with his dime-store impersonation of Robert Newton, as the drunken, one-eyed lecher with dubious nautical skills and no sense of direction. But, while the film cruises for laughs, the outcome is more a series of soggy comic adventures set within a Caribbean travelogue. Like Russell's next film, *Tombstone*, though, this was an unexpected box-office success in the States.

Captains Courageous ○ Ⓥ
1937, US, 115 mins, b/w
Dir: Victor Fleming
Stars: Spencer Tracy, Freddie Bartholomew, Melvyn Douglas, Lionel Barrymore, Mickey Rooney
Rating: ★★★★

The original, and certainly the best version of Rudyard Kipling's famous story about the spoiled rich kid who learns about the real values of life when he falls (literally) into the hands of a group of earthy Portuguese fishermen. Spencer Tracy claimed the first of what was to be two consecutive Academy Awards as one of the fishermen, and Freddie Bartholomew is the boy. A heart-breaking ending ensures there won't be too many dry eyes in your sitting-rooms.

C

Captain Sindbad O
1963, US/West Germany, 85 mins, colour
Dir: Byron Haskin
Stars: Guy Williams, Heidi Bruhl, Pedro Armendariz
Rating: ★★★★

American director Byron Haskin, who made *The War of the Worlds*, shot this spellbinding film in Bavaria with a largely British cast. It has a cyclone, a tidal wave, a wizard with a pet ocelot, a superb nine-headed monster – and even dancing girls. The Technicolor photography is jewel-bright and the only sad note is that the great Mexican actor Pedro Armendariz died shortly after completing his role as the villain.

Captains of the Clouds O
1942, US, 125 mins, colour
Dir: Michael Curtiz
Stars: James Cagney, Dennis Morgan, Alan Hale, Brenda Marshall
Rating: ★★

An at-times inspiring story of the Royal Canadian Air Force, full of fascinating technical detail, and with James Cagney, fresh from his Oscar for *Yankee Doodle Dandy*. Cagney is in fine form as the irresponsible 'bush pilot' who steals his best friend's girl but, in true Hollywood fashion, shows his true worth when lives are in danger. All a bit melodramatic, perhaps, for today's tastes, but the director (the formidable Michael Curtiz) creates some good action scenes, and there's richly rounded support from Alan Hale, George Tobias and Reginald Gardiner. It's all topped off with the vividly attractive Technicolor which typified the period.

Captain's Paradise, The O Ⓥ
1953, UK, 89 mins, b/w
Dir: Anthony Kimmins
Stars: Atec Guinness, Yvonne De Carlo, Celia Johnson
Rating: ★★★

Very popular comedy from the Fifties with a gentle touch of Ealing about it (although it was made by Alexander Korda's London Films) and a witty script co-written by actor-author Nicholas Phipps, who also penned himself a part in the film and frolics. He provides a very seaworthy vehicle for Alec Guinness, as a steamer captain with a wife on either side of the Mediterranean. In North Africa, there's exotic dancer Yvonne De Carlo, who yearns to be a conventional housewife; in Gibraltar, prim Celia Johnson secretly wants to kick over the traces. Captain Guinness, steaming contentedly back and forth between the two, gets his comeuppance in the end, of course, but not before you've had a chance to enjoy the cruise.

Captain's Table, The O
1958, UK, 89 mins, colour
Dir: Jack Lee
Stars: John Gregson, Peggy Cummins, Donald Sinden, Reginald Beckwith, Nadia Gray
Rating: ★★★

Jack Lee is such a recognised director of rugged action (*A Town Like Alice*, *Robbery Under Arms*) that it comes as a surprise to find him at the helm of this pleasant little comedy about a skipper who steps from a grimy steamer to the bridge of a luxury liner.

Captive City, The O
1952, US, 91 mins, b/w
Dir: Robert Wise
Stars: John Forsythe, Joan Camden, Harold J Kennedy
Rating: ★★★

John Forsythe, later trapped in the profitable mediocrity of *Dynasty*, had his first major role in this taut, torn-from-the-headlines thriller, and gave a strong and convincing performance as the crusading newspaper editor fighting small-town corruption. At least two contemporary critics compared him to Henry Fonda. Director Robert Wise maintains excellent suspense and employs the deep focus camera of his cinematographer, Lee Garmes, to considerable dramatic effect.

Captive Heart, The O
1946, UK, 108 mins, b/w
Dir: Basil Dearden
Stars: Michael Redgrave, Rachel Kempson, Mervyn Johns, Jack Warner, Basil Radford, Gordon Jackson
Rating: ★★★

A moving drama about a group of PoWs, their life in captivity and the lives of their loved ones back home. The settings cannot be faulted: all the camp scenes were shot at Marlag Milag Nord, in Germany, only six weeks after it was liberated from the Nazis. Nor does the script lack realism. One of the co-writers, Guy Morgan, was a Marlag inmate. Michael Redgrave plays a Czech officer who has assumed a dead Briton's identity to escape the Nazis. And Jimmy Hanley is excellent, among a battery of familiar British actors, as Private Matthews, a cockney wide boy who keeps up his friends' spirits with his stories of girls he has known.

Car, The ●
1976, US, 98 mins, colour
Dir: Elliot Silverstein
Stars: James Brolin, Kathleen Lloyd, John Marley
Rating: ★★

A combination of *Duel*, *Jaws* and *The Exorcist* as a demon car goes on the rampage. The theme was originally surveyed more tightly in a *Twilight Zone* episode and later reprised with some impact by director John Carpenter with Stephen King's *Christine*.

Caravaggio ● Ⓥ
1986, UK, 97 mins, colour
Dir: Derek Jarman
Stars: Nigel Terry, Sean Bean, Tilda Swinton
Rating: ★★★

Considering that one might describe maverick filmmaker Derek Jarman and the Italian artist Michelangelo Caravaggio as blood-brothers almost 400 years apart, it always seemed that Jarman was the ideal director to film the painter s tortured life story. As Caravaggio painted portraits of young men with his brushes, so Jarman does with his camera – skilfully aided by the colourwork of cinematographer Gabriel Beristain. Of the merits of the film's anachronistic content, one is less sure, but there are measured portrayals in the required vein by Nigel Terry, Sean Bean and Tilda Swinton.

Caravan O
1946, UK, 122 mins, b/w
Dir: Arthur Crabtree
Stars: Stewart Granger, Anne Crawford, Jean Kent
Rating: ★★

Those who like romantic novels will probably enjoy this period drama with Stewart Granger. Here is in his customary handsome hero guise, with Dennis Price as the dastardly villain and – a surprising bit of casting – Robert Helpmann, at the time best known as a dancer, playing a gentleman's gentleman. Granger loves a beauty called Oriana, but after an abortive attempt on his life engineered by his rival, he loses his memory and marries a gypsy girl who has nursed him back to health. Florid escapism from Gainsborough which kept people's spirits up amid the austerities of post-war Britain.

Caravans O
1978, US, 123 mins, colour
Dir: James Fargo
Stars: Anthony Quinn, Michael Sarrazin,

Jennifer O'Neill, Christopher Lee, Joseph Cotten
Rating: ★★★

An unusual adventure story, set in the Middle East in 1948 and concerning an American emissary (Michael Sarrazin) sent to find a senator's daughter (Jennifer O'Neill). After unsuccessfully marrying a native army officer, she has joined a nomadic caravan travelling across the desert. Douglas Slocombe's photography and Mike Batt's distinctive music are the real stars of this film, which also features Anthony Quinn as a kind of Zorba the Sheik. Apart from varying blue and grey skies over a desert ghost town, in fact, Slocombe's glowing colour work is well up to his usual high standards. The size of the drama is not sufficient to make this a great film but it remains in many ways an exhilarating, fascinating experience.

Caravan to Vaccares ○
1974, UK/France, 98 mins, colour
Dir: Geoffrey Reeve
Stars: Charlotte Rampling, David Birney, Michael Lonsdale, Michael Bryant
Rating: ★★

Alistair MacLean adventure romp which leans heavily on its action, the colour of its (Spanish) settings and the ultra-cool performances of David Birney and Charlotte Rampling. Geoffrey Reeve's direction is mechanically efficient.

Carbine Williams ○
1952, US, 91 mins, b/w
Dir: Richard Thorpe
Stars: James Stewart, Jean Hagen, Wendell Corey
Rating: ★★

By British standards American jails seem to be extraordinarily tough, Yet, paradoxically, prisoners in the US are occasionally afforded facilities they would never get over here. An example of this is the case of Robert Stroud, the *Bird Man of Alcatraz*. He was allowed all the books and equipment he needed to become an expert on birds while he was serving a life sentence. And here is the case of David Marshall Williams who, while serving 30 years for manslaughter, was allowed to make a revolutionary type of gun. His story is authentic in almost every detail, for the real-life Williams worked on the film as a technical adviser, Playing the film Williams, James Stewart gives a predictably sturdy, sincere perfomance.

Carbon Copy ◑
1981, US, 90 mins, colour
Dir: Michael Schultz
Stars: George Segal, Susan Saint James, Jack Warden, Denzel Washington
Rating: ★★

Although this comedy about a white businessman who finds he has a black son is embarrassing at times, there are moments when it is unexpectedly and uncommonly funny. For this, we can thank not just the shafts of wit in Stanley Shapiro's violently variable script, but especially the star, George Segal. He reacts with superb timing and an immense range of facial grimaces as the hen-pecked, boss-pecked executive whose offspring (a young Denzel Washington) descends on him from the 20-year past.

Card, The ○
(aka: The Promoter)
1952, UK, 91 mins, b/w
Dir: Ronald Neame
Stars: Alec Guinness, Petula Clark, Glynis Johns, Valerie Hobson
Rating: ★★★★

Made at a time when Alec Guinness could do no wrong in the British cinema, this is a cleverly commercial adaption of Arnold *(Clayhanger)* Bennett's Potteries novel about a poor-born opportunist who becomes mayor of his local town. Many fine little individual scenes build up to make an enchanting whole. Guinness has never been better, and Glynis Johns, Valerie Hobson and Petula Clark are finely contrasted as the ladies in his life.

Cardboard Cavalier ○
1948, UK, 95 mins, b/w
Dir: Walter Forde
Stars: Sid Field, Margaret Lockwood
Rating: ★★

This British farce, set in the days of Cavaliers and Roundheads, was popular comedian Sid Field's third and last film. Two years later he died at the age of 46. Margaret Lockwood enjoys herself as Nell Gwynne, and Field's trusty sidekick Jerry Desmonde is on hand to play Col Lovelace to Field's barrowboy hero, who rejoices in the name of Sidcup Buttermeadow (get it?). Pretty mild fun, but better than Field's other two attempts at screen stardom.

Cardinal Richelieu ○
1935, US, 83 mins, b/w
Dir: Rowland V Lee
Stars: George Arliss, Maureen O'Sullivan,

Edward Arnold, Cesar Romero
Rating: ★★

Briskly-paced account of Cardinal Richelieu's intrigues at the court of King Louis XIII. George Arliss dominates the film in the title role, bringing out different shades of the Cardinal's character with considerable skill. Photographer J Peverall Marley and director Rowland V Lee combine to give the film a lavish and authentic period facade.

Care Bears Movie, The ⊙
1985, US, 75 mins, colour
Dir: Arna Selznick
Rating: ★

Candy floss philosophy and pretty pastel colours dominate this cartoon adventure with the animated soft-toy teddies. Harry Dean Stanton and Mickey Rooney are among those lending their voices to a story designed for a very young audience.

Career ○
1959, US, 105 mins, b/w
Dir: Joseph Anthony
Stars: Dean Martin, Anthony Franciosa, Shirley MacLaine, Carolyn Jones
Rating: ★★★

A sombre, bitter account of a young actor's fight to reach the top, and of a cynical producer who tramples over everyone in sight. The well-constructed script is by James Lee, who wrote the original play. The best perfonnance comes from the sharp-faced Carolyn Jones as a talent agent who's all brightness on the outside, and shrieking loneliness within.

Carefree ○
1938, US, 85 mins, b/w
Dir: Mark Sandrich
Stars: Fred Astaire, Ginger Rogers, Ralph Bellamy, Luella Gear, Jack Carson, Hattie McDaniel
Rating: ★★★

The shortest and perhaps least popular of the ten Fred Astaire-Ginger Rogers musicals, this was an attempt to combine a Howard Hawks-type wacky comedy with music and dancing. But it failed to ignite the box office and the duo slipped out of the list of ten top box office draws – a list they had topped just two years earlier. It was Astaire's idea to play a psychiatrist ('shrinks' were as popular then in Hollywood as now) but RKO was experiencing severe financial difficulties so the film has a penny-pinching look. Ginger was badly photographed and

C

the public felt cheated by the lack of big budget spectacular numbers. The highlight is when they dance 'The Yam'.

Cargo of Innocents ○
(aka: Stand by for Action!)
1943, US, 109 mins, b/w
Dir: Robert Z Leonard
Stars: Robert Taylor, Charles Laughton, Brian Donlevy, Walter Brennan
Rating: ★★

Salty, dramatic American World War Two action drama, set almost entirely aboard an old, but still combat-worthy warship. The story is a bit of a paradox: a rather crass war yarn containing a few well-filmed battle-sequences. The object, apparently, is to show that the wartime US Navy was composed of spoilt playboys, as portrayed by Robert Taylor, as well as tough, hard-working commanders of the type played by Brian Donlevy. Taylor and Donlevy are at daggers drawn until their ship picks up a lifeboat packed with women and babies and becomes a floating nursery-cum-maternity unit. Watching over all this with a fiery but friendly eye is a senior officer played by Charles Laughton. There's some good below-decks humour, but too many lulls between the action.

Cargo to Capetown ○
1951, US, 80 mins, b/w
Dir: Earl McEvoy
Stars: Broderick Crawford, John Ireland, Ellen Drew, Edgar Buchanan, Ted de Corsia
Rating: ★★

This tough thriller about trouble aboard an oil tanker was the follow-up for its two stars, John Ireland and Broderick Crawford, to their Oscar-winning success *All the King's Men*. In *Cargo to Capetown*, Crawford again gets the chance to pull out all the acting stops as a rugged engineer. The action, rough and raw, compares in ferocity with some of today's western films. Highlights include a hurricane at sea, and a tremendous fist-fight between the two principals.

Carlito's Way ● ⓥ
1993, US, 145 mins, colour
Dir: Brian De Palma
Stars: Al Pacino, Sean Penn, Penelope Ann Miller, Viggo Mortensen, John Leguizamo
Rating: ★★

Stars Al Pacino and director Brian De Palma are on numbingly familiar ground here with this real grind of a movie about a legendary gangster de-

termined to go straight after being released from a long stretch in prison. The odds are well against him, of course, just as the odds are long against our finding any originality in such a theme. The results are predictably violent and depressing but what saves the film is its acting: Pacino, surely more deserving of an Oscar here than for his overrated performance in *Scent of a Woman*, is quite riveting as this doomed and tormented man. But even so he is matched by an almost unrecognisable Sean Penn as a slimy, frizzy-haired Jewish lawyer mesmerised by the criminal world.

Carlton-Browne of the F.O. ○ ⓥ
(aka: Man In a Cocked Hat)
1958, UK, 88 mins, b/w
Dir: Roy Boulting
Stars: Terry-Thomas, Peter Sellers, Luciana Paluzzi, Thorley Walters, Ian Bannen
Rating: ★★★★

Sometimes explosively funny Boulting Brothers satire on the diplomatic service, with Peter Sellers scoring as the oily prime-minister of an unnamed eastern Mediterranean country, and Terry-Thomas ideally cast as the hapless diplomat who achieves a 'brilliant series of disasters'.

Carla's Song ● ⓥ
1996, UK, 127 mins, colour
Dir: Ken Loach
Stars: Robert Carlyle, Oyanka Cabezas, Scott Glenn
Rating: ★★★

A Glasgow bus driver falls in love with a Nicaraguan refugee and, saving her from suicide, goes with her to Nicaragua to lay the ghosts of her violent past. Despite Carlyle's busman being a rather unsympathetic character, the first half of Ken Loach's film is a quite touching, offbeat love story, culminating in the lovers fleeing to Loch Lomond, where, after an idyllic picnic, the weather turns surly and the bus they've taken there gets stuck in the mud. The Nicaragua half is the longer and the poorer for it. It's difficult to see why Carla (Cabezas) can't be taken to her former lover straight away, as she is fully aware of the state of his injuries in the war between Contras and Sandanistas. Reunions between old friends add nothing to the narrative, but there are one or two bursts of action and an entirely appropriate ending that returns poignancy to the tale.

Carmen Jones ○
1954, US, 105 mins, colour
Dir: Otto Preminger
Stars: Dorothy Dandridge, Harry Belafonte, Olga James
Rating: ★★★★

Full of ringing tunes and emotive power, *Carmen Jones* was a triumphant filming by Otto Preminger of Oscar Hammerstein's all-black Broadway adaption of Bizet's *Carmen*. It seems a shame that Dorothy Dandridge and Harry Belafonte, both reputable singers, were not allowed to use their own voices, but their performances are right on the ball and the songs are excitingly staged – particularly 'That's Love' (originally 'Habanera') and 'Stand Up and Fight Until You Hear the Bell' (from the 'Toreador's Song'). The dynamic Pearl Bailey as Frankie enjoys her finest film hour.

Carnal Knowledge ❶ ⓥ
1971, US, 96 mins, colour
Dir: Mike Nichols
Stars: Jack Nicholson, Candice Bergen, Art Garfunkel, Ann-Margret, Cynthia O'Neal, Rita Moreno
Rating: ★★★★

The cynical undertones director Mike Nichols hinted at in *The Graduate* are fully matured in this thought-provoking study of the developing sexual attitudes of two men, from their student days to middle-age, celebrated at the time of its release for its sexual frankness in language and gesture. A fine performance, as you would expect, comes from Jack Nicholson as the maverick, uncaring bachelor; less expected at the time was the warmth and emotion projected by Ann-Margret, hitherto just a sexy musical-comedy star, as the girl whose voluptuous sexuality brings her only despair. She was deservedly nominated for an Academy Award as best supporting actress and was unlucky to lose to one of the best-ever performances in that category: Cloris Leachman's in *The Last Picture Show*.

Carnival ○
1946, UK, 93 mins, b/w
Dir: Stanley Haynes
Stars: Sally Gray, Michael Wilding, Bernard Miles, Stanley Holloway, Jean Kent
Rating: ★★

Heavily tragic melodrama based on Compton Mackenzie's famous novel. Sally Gray, one of the loveliest and most durable of British actresses through the Thirties and Forties, plays the ballet dancer heroine, in the late 19th century, who treads the steady downhill slope after her lover deserts her. The prolific Eric Maschwitz adapted Mackenzie's book and the result raised a good few tears in its time. The supporting cast includes those two formidable doyennes of the English cinema, Nancy Price and Catherine Lacey, as well as several up-and-coming young actresses, including Jean Kent, Brenda Bruce and Hazel Court.

Carnival Story ○

1954, US, 90 mins, colour
Dir: Kurt Neumann
Stars: Anne Baxter, Steve Cochran, Lyle Bettger, George Nader
Rating: ★★★

Lurid tale of circus chicanery chiefly notable for offering a rare sympathetic role to that excellent movie villain Lyle Bettger. He's very good and so is Anne Baxter as the fellow high-wire star he marries. Their efforts, and those of Steve Cochran as an oily carnival barker, make this a colourful melodrama with a tang of realism. And the love scenes are handled with rare feeling and conviction for a Hollywood film of the early Fifties. The melodrama that accompanies them sometimes becomes as taut as a high-wire braced to the point of snapping, with the innate danger of the character's occupations adding a tingle to the emotional suspense.

Carousel ○ Ⓥ

1956, US, 123 mins, colour
Dir: Henry King
Stars: Gordon MacRae, Shirley Jones, Cameron Mitchell, Gene Lockhart
Rating: ★★★★

Full of warmth and colour, and some of the most lilting music Oscar Hammierstein ever wrote, this is an almost totally successful version of the stage smash. Gordon MacRae and Shirley Jones, the sweethearts from *Oklahoma!* are fortuitously re-teamed as Billy Bigelow, the irresponsible fairground barker, and Julie Jordan. Frank Sinatra had been cast as Billy, but he dropped out when he found he had to shoot all the scenes twice, once in widescreen and once in normal ratio. MacRae was rushed into the role and produced the perfomance of a lifetime. So did Barbara Ruick, as the girl who falls for fisherman Mr Snow, and Cameron Mitchell is also excellent as the rascally Jigger. Both Ruick and Mitchell sing remarkably well, and indeed one of the bonuses of this

particular musical is that all of the players do their own singing. And what songs! Look almost anywhere in this score and you'll find a hit: 'If I Loved You', 'My Boy Bill', 'June is Busting Out All Over', 'A Real Nice Clambake', 'When I Marry Mr Snow', 'When the Children Are Asleep', 'What's the Use of Wondrin' and, 'You'll Never Walk Alone'.

Carpetbaggers, The ○

1964, US, 150 mins, colour
Dir: Edward Dmytryk
Stars: George Peppard, Alan Ladd, Bob Cummings, Martha Hyer, Carroll Baker
Rating: ★★★

One of the earliest adaptations of a Harold Robbins novel for the big screen. Despite patches of silly dialogue and sub-standard technical qualities, the film makes good entertainment through the sheer weight of its production, by the expanse of its subject – Hollywood between the two world wars – the magnitude of its story, and its insight into those roaring free-for-all days when everything and everybody was there for the taking. It's one of those films where the (anti) hero's hair gets greyer as the story progresses, but his stony expression never changes. Carroll Baker is truly awful as the glamorous star drinking her way to oblivion but Alan Ladd is impressive in his last film, and Bob Cummings even better, giving the performance of the film as a glib, slimy ten-percenter.

Carquake ○
(aka: Cannonball)

1976, US, 93 mins, colour
Dir: Paul Bartel
Stars: David Carradine, Bill McKinney, Veronica Hamel
Rating: ★★

A film for action fans about the ultimate car race across America. There are no rules and all the contestants are out to win the $100,000 prize at any cost – including life itself. From the moment the drivers rev their engines, the action is practically relentless: skids, swerves, smashes and crashes. Famous film director Roger Corman has a small role as the District Attorney, and an even stranger piece of casting has *Hill Street Blues* favourite Veronica Hamel as a voracious contestant.

Carrie ○

1952, US, 120 mins, b/w
Dir: William Wyler
Stars: Laurence Olivier, Jennifer Jones, Miriam Hopkins, Eddie Albert, Basil

Ruysdael, Ray Teal
Rating: ★★★★

Based on a famous first novel by Theodore Dreiser which was banned at the beginning of the century for being too daring, this is the tragic story of a young girl corrupted by big city life. Reminiscent of *The Blue Angel*, it is given remarkable depth and poignancy by the acting of Jennifer Jones as the girl, Miriam Hopkins and, in particular, Laurence Olivier. Director William Wyler's streets of Chicago at the turn of the century are teeming with life. And he also captures the atmosphere of the intangible moral code that hovers over, and dominates, the entire film. Olivier's once-prosperous restaurant manager, willing to go to any lengths for the young girl he loves although he is already married, is a pitiable creature portrayed with restraint and understanding. It's as fine a performance as he ever contributed to the cinema, and ensures that the final scenes are deeply moving.

Carrie ● Ⓥ

1976, US, 94 mins, colour
Dir: Brian De Palma
Stars: Sissy Spacek, Piper Laurie, John Travolta, Amy Irving, William Katt, Nancy Allen
Rating: ★★

Thunderously overwrought piece of Grand Guignol horror from the modern master of bloodstained mayhem, Brian De Palma. It stars sensitive actress Sissy Spacek who gives an anguished performance as the high-school girl whose sheltered upbringing (by a religious fanatic mother) has in no way prepared her to deal with the supernormal gift of telekinesis. Piper Laurie was nominated for an Academy Award for her performance as the mother, and John Travolta is also in there somewhere among the guts and gore. If you succeed in surviving the ensuing blood-feast, be prepared for the ending, which is one of the great shocks of the cinema.

Carrington ● Ⓥ

1995, UK, 120 mins, colour
Dir: Christopher Hampton
Stars: Emma Thompson, Jonathan Pryce, Steven Waddington, Rufus Sewell, Samuel West, Penelope Wilton
Rating: ★★★

A one-of-a-kind story – about the relationship between Dora Carrington (Emma Thompson), a mannish but heterosexual painter who always referred to herself by her surname, and

C

Lytton Strachey (Jonathan Pryce), the homosexual writer and historian with whom she lived, on and off, for 17 years. The two unconventional figures are intensely drawn to one another, Lytton, to his amazement, almost (but not quite) to the point of heterosexual love. An army officer (Steven Waddington) comes into their lives, whom Carrington marries so as not to break up their (understated) menage à trois. As a marriage, it is less successful than their friendship, but all of Lytton and Dora's affairs fade away, leaving them alone again. Pryce seems punctilious perfection as the bearded Lytton; Thompson has a few uncertain moments, but generally does a difficult role well. Samuel West appears the best of the actors portraying their various lovers; period detail is immaculately caught.

Carrington VC ○
(aka: Court Martial)
1954, UK, 106 mins, b/w
Dir: Anthony Asquith
Stars: David Niven, Margaret Leighton, Allan Cuthbertson, Laurence Naismith, Clive Morton, Noelle Middleton
Rating: ★★★

David Niven gives a fine central performance as a highly decorated army officer wrongly brought up on three court-martial charges in an absorbing drama which transferred successfully from stage to celluloid. Allan Cuthbertson is effective as the jealous superior officer who trumps up the charges and Margaret Leighton is shrewish as the wife who stabs Carrington, metaphorically, in the back. The courtroom scenes are tense and filled with sharp, terse dialogue. Director Anthony Asquith extracts top perfomances from the cast and creates a powerful drama from Carrington's crisis.

Carry On Abroad ○ Ⓥ
1972, UK, 89 mins, colour
Dir: Gerald Thomas
Stars: Sidney James, Kenneth Williams, Charles Hawtrey, Joan Sims, Kenneth Connor, Bernard Bresslaw
Rating: ★★

One of the strongest casts ever put together for a Seventies Carry On comedy – it includes Sidney James, Kenneth Williams, Charles Hawtrey, Joan Sims, Kenneth Connor, Bernard Bresslaw, Barbara Windsor and Hattie Jacques – sallies forth to the island of Elsbels for a week of fun, games and double-entendres. There are some

amusing jibes at the expense of catch-penny Mediterranean hotels.

Carry On Admiral ○ Ⓥ
(aka: The Ship Was Loaded)
1957, UK, 82 mins, b/w
Dir: Val Guest
Stars: David Tomlinson, Peggy Cummins, Ronald Shiner, Joan Sims
Rating: ★★

Not, in fact, one of the Carry On series (it just preceded the first of them) but in the more restrained vein of farce to which fans of David Tomlinson had become accustomed in the Fifties. Much of the hilarity in this navy lark stems from the performance of A E Matthews, then 87, as a muddled old admiral.

Carry On Again Doctor ○ Ⓥ
1969, UK, 88 mins, colour
Dir: Gerald Thomas
Stars: Kenneth Williams, Sidney James, Barbara Windsor, Charles Hawtrey, Joan Sims, Jim Dale
Rating: ★★

Subtitled The Bowels Are Ringing, this medicinal mayhem offers Sid James as a Pacific island hospital orderly with a harem of wives. Despite the fact that they have not been among the best in the series, the hospital farces proved the most popular of the Carry Ons.

Carry On Behind ○ Ⓥ
1975, UK, 90 mins, colour
Dir: Gerald Thomas
Stars: Elke Sommer, Kenneth Williams, Joan Sims, Kenneth Connor
Rating: ★★

The team had already done Carry on Camping, so this later romp, set on a caravan site, has as good a title as any. And guest star Elke Sommer's archaeological Ninotchka is a real and unexpected bonus. 'Vot is called de place,' she asks Kenneth Williams (as the stuffy Professor Crump) 'vere Roman soldiers are vor drinking and vor women and...' 'The NAAFI?,' suggests Williams hopefully. And her delightfully fractured English even manages to make such old lines as 'Iz bleeding terrible' sound funny.

Carry On Cabby ○ Ⓥ
1963, UK, 92 mins, b/w
Dir: Gerald Thomas
Stars: Sidney James, Hattie Jacques, Kenneth Connor, Charles Hawtrey, Esma Cannon, Liz Fraser
Rating: ★★

One of the few Carry On films without the redoubtable Kenneth Williams in

the cast. A lively entry in the famous series, this story of a fleet of taxis driven by glamorous cabbies managed to raise more chuckles than either of its immediate predecessors (Carry On Regardless and Carry On Cruising) and heralded an upsurge in the standard of Carry Ons that was to continue over the next three or four years.

Carry On Camping ○ Ⓥ
1968, UK, 88 mins, colour
Dir: Gerald Thomas
Stars: Sidney James, Kenneth Williams, Joan Sims, Terry Scott, Peter Butterworth, Dilys Laye
Rating: ★★

An appropriate title if ever there were one. But the cast had to work hard to keep their spirits up this time, as the film was made not in the sunniest weeks of the summer but in a field adjacent to Pinewood Studios during a particularly wet week in November. The publicists made much mileage out of the notable keep-fit sequence in which Barbara Windsor's bikini top flies off during one of the more vigorous physical jerks. The supporting cast is full of all the best Carry On people, including Joan Sims, Terry Scott, Peter Butterworth, Dilys Laye and Bernard Bresslaw, plus Kenneth Williams' old sparring partner from Beyond Our Ken – Betty Marsden.

Carry On Cleo ○ Ⓥ
1964, UK, 90 mins, colour
Dir: Gerald Thomas
Stars: Sidney James, Amanda Barrie, Kenneth Williams, Kenneth Connor, Joan Sims, Charles Hawtrey
Rating: ★★★

Encouraged by Cleopatra, the Carry On team go back in time creating corn in Egypt and Rome ('Equality or Bust' state the Women's Lib placards: 'Blimus' cries Sid James). Lively playing; one of the best. Relish Kenneth Williams as Caesar, whether feeling queasy en voyage ('Just a little sic in transit, Gloria') or being stabbed by conspirators ('Infamy! Infamy! They've all got it in for me!').

Carry On Columbus ○ Ⓥ
1992, UK, 91 mins, colour
Dir: Gerald Thomas
Stars: Jim Dale, Bernard Cribbins, Julian Clary, Rik Mayall, Larry Miller
Rating: ★

A dire latecomer to the 'Carry On' series, this clumsy costume caper only has Jim Dale (as Columbus) from the old gang, and extravagant mugging from Rik Mayall, Julian Clary (foolishly asked to imitate Kenneth Williams), Alexei Sayle and others from the newer BBC2-type brigade. Early promise from King Ferdinand (Leslie Phillips) – 'What makes you think he's up to it?' – and Queen Isabella June Whitfield) – 'I have seen his testimonials' – is soon dissipated on a sea voyage in which vapidity vies with vacuity as Columbus discovers America with nary a joke in sight. Larry Miller as the Indian chief raises a few half-smiles towards the end, but Williams, Sid James, Barbara Windsor, Charles Hawtrey and Joan Sims are sadly missed. Frankie Howerd, who died before he could begin his role, was well out of it: not even the slave girls are attractive.

Carry On Constable ○ Ⓥ
1960, UK, 86 mins, b/w
Dir: Gerald Thomas
Stars: Sidney James, Kenneth Connor, Kenneth Williams, Hattie Jacques, Eric Barker, Shirley Eaton
Rating: ★★

Farce in the force in this early entrant to the *Carry On* series, with the British bobby painted a bluer shade of blue in a cheerful series of vignettes. Such stalwarts as Eric Barker, Terence Longdon, Hattie Jacques and Irene Handl loom up in support, but funniest of all are Sidney James as the station sergeant and Joan Sims as WPC Passworthy.

Carry On Cowboy ○ Ⓥ
1965, UK, 95 mins, colour
Dir: Gerald Thomas
Stars: Sidney James, Kenneth Williams, Jim Dale, Charles Hawtrey, Joan Sims, Angela Douglas
Rating: ★★★

The big bad Rumpo Kid (Sid James) has taken over Stodge City in the wild west, so the mayor (Kenneth Williams) sends for someone to clean up the town. Unfortunately, the state sends Marshall P Nutt (Jim Dale), who is really a sanitary inspector! The usual asinine antics you would expect from the *Carry On* team, with the lowbrow laughs coming thick and fast. By no means the best of the series as some people seem to think, but good for a few near-the-knuckle chuckles. For instance, Sid James complaining about peace negotiations with the Indians: 'First it's peace on, then it's peace off!' Twas ever thus.

Carry On Cruising ○ Ⓥ
1962, UK, 85 mins, colour
Dir: Gerald Thomas

Stars: Sidney James, Kenneth Williams, Liz Fraser, Kenneth Connor, Dilys Laye, Lance Percival
Rating: ★★

The first of the series to be made in colour, which means that the ocean waves are as blue as the jokes. Skippered by Sidney James, the men all have their eyes on the main chance, while the girls all have their eyes on the men. Very moderate.

Carry On Dick ○ Ⓥ
1974, UK, 89 mins, colour
Dir: Gerald Thomas
Stars: Sidney James, Kenneth Williams, Barbara Windsor, Hattie Jacques, Bernard Bresslaw, Joan Sims
Rating: ★★★

Perhaps the last of the really funny *Carry Ons*, almost inevitably in period costume, as were all the best in this comedy series, and with the invaluable Sidney James in the dual role of Dick Turpin and the Reverend Mr Flasher.

Carry On Doctor ○ Ⓥ
1968, UK, 90 mins, colour
Dir: Gerald Thomas
Stars: Sidney James, Frankie Howerd, Kenneth Williams, Jim Dale, Barbara Windsor, Charles Hawtrey
Rating: ★★

Probably the best of the four *Carry On* visits to a hospital, subtitled 'a bed-panorama of hospital life'. Jim Dale and Anita Harris bring a touch of freshness to the time-honoured, highly farcical situations.

Carry On – Don't Lose Your Head ○ Ⓥ
1966, UK, 90 mins, colour
Dir: Gerald Thomas
Stars: Sidney James, Kenneth Williams, Joan Sims, Dany Robin, Peter Butterworth, Jim Dale
Rating: ★★★

Ribald revolution romp from the *Carry On* gang. The Scarlet Pimpernel becomes the Black Fingernail; and such names as Rodney Ffing and Citizen Bidet give rise to predictable but much-relished jokes.

Carry on Emmannuelle ❶ Ⓥ
1978, UK, 85 mins, colour
Dir: Gerald Thomas
Stars: Suzanne Danielle, Kenneth Williams, Kenneth Connor, Jack Douglas
Rating: ★

Despite its leering lewdness and heavy reliance on the word 'up' the laughs, this does represent a small step *up* from

the depths of *Carry On England*. Its few moments of genuine humour are unfortunately nearly all in the first reel. But it's good to see Kenneth Williams in full flow (bringing the house down with 'I can't straighten anything; I'm completely bent') and new girl Suzanne Danielle tries hard (another overworked *Carry On* word), affecting an interesting French accent. If only it weren't so sloppily paced and edited, in fact, this might be a great deal funnier.

Carry On: Follow That Camel ○ Ⓥ
1967, UK, 90 mins, colour
Dir: Gerald Thomas
Stars: Kenneth Williams, Phil Silvers, Jim Dale, Charles Hawtrey, Anita Harris, Peter Gilmore
Rating: ★★★

Jim Dale is Bertram Oliphant West (B.O. to his friends), while such names as Sergeant Nocker and Captain Le Pice give rise to predictable double-entendres from the other ranks, and the gang gaily mix up *Morocco* with *Beau Geste* in this sledgehammer satire on all Foreign Legion adventure films. Phil Silvers' conniving sergeant is Bilko in all but name. And Anita Harris is personable enough as Corktip (you'll remember Claudette Colbert played Cigarette in *Under Two Flags*) to make one wonder why she didn't earn more than two *Carry On* roles.

Carry On Henry ○ Ⓥ
1971, UK, 89 mins, colour
Dir: Gerald Thomas
Stars: Sidney James, Kenneth Williams, Joan Sims, Barbara Windsor, Charles Hawtrey, Terry Scott
Rating: ★★★

Sid James enjoys himself hugely as Henry VIII, a role that – in comedy at any rate – he might have been born to play. Richly costumed and inventively scripted, this is one of the most enjoyable of the Seventies *Carry Ons*. A running gag about Charles Hawtrey undergoing various forms of torture to make him sign a document is particularly funny.

Carry On Jack ○ Ⓥ
(aka: Carry On Venus)
1964, UK, 85 mins, colour
Dir: Gerald Thomas
Stars: Bernard Cribbins, Kenneth Williams, Juliet Mills, Donald Houston
Rating: ★★

The first *Carry On* comedy in period costume, this nautical jaunt is an amalgam of skits on *Mutiny on the Bounty* and

C

Billy Budd. This one certainly has its moments, especially in an early scene involving Jim Dale and Ian Wilson as 'carriers' and in a sequence where the ship's cannon backfires on Bernard Cribbins, Charles Hawtrey and Percy Herbert. No Sidney James, Joan Sims, Kenneth Connor, Barbara Windsor or Hattie Jacques this time around, but Kenneth Williams, for once given a character to work on, has some pricelessly funny moments as the inappropriately named Captain Fearless.

Carry On Loving ○ ⓥ
1970, UK, 90 mins, colour
Dir: Gerald Thomas
Stars: Sidney James, Kenneth Williams, Charles Hawtrey, Joan Sims, Hattie Jacques, Terry Scott
Rating: ★

Little more than warmed-over 'double entendres' from earlier films, delivered by a cast of regulars past their sell-by date. The subject may be sex, set around the antics of the Wedded Bliss Marriage Agency, but there's no danger of anyone actually getting down to the real thing. This one is strictly for die-hard fans.

Carry On Matron ○ ⓥ
1972, UK, 89 mins, colour
Dir: Gerald Thomas
Stars: Sidney James, Kenneth Williams, Hattie Jacques, Charles Hawtrey, Barbara Windsor, Terry Scott
Rating: ★★

Another series of low jinks in hospital wards filled with characters that could only have come from a *Carry On* film, to follow in the footsteps of *Carry On Nurse* and *Carry On Doctor.*

Carry On Nurse ○ ⓥ
1959, UK, 85 mins, b/w
Dir: Gerald Thomas
Stars: Kenneth Connor, Kenneth Williams, Shirley Eaton, Joan Sims, Charles Hawtrey, Leslie Phillips
Rating: ★★

The second of the famous comedy series, and the first of several *Carry Ons* to be set in a hospital. Bedpan jokes are almost as overworked as the nurses, who are continually fending off the advances of the patients. The usual repertory company of stalwarts is joined by Leslie Phillips, Joan Hickson and Shirley Eaton.

Carry On Regardless ○ ⓥ
1961, UK, 85 mins, b/w
Dir: Gerald Thomas

Stars: Sidney James, Kenneth Connor, Charles Hawtrey, Joan Sims, Kenneth Williams, Liz Fraser
Rating: ★

A series of farcical episodes, rather than one story, make up this, the fifth in the *Carry On* series. Our friends form a 'Helping Hands' agency, and predictably chaos ensues five times over, with extra help from that queen of ditherers, Esma Cannon.

Carry On Screaming ○ ⓥ
1966, UK, 95 mins, colour
Dir: Gerald Thomas
Stars: Harry H Corbett, Kenneth Williams, Jim Dale, Fenella Fielding, Peter Butterworth, Joan Sims
Rating: ★★★★

This horror comic proves to be one of the *Carry On* gang's finest hours. Even the worst of its corny jokes take on a new amusement in a turn-of-the-century setting and a mock horror story. And the *Carry On* stock company is perfectly cast and in irrepressible form: Jim Dale as the dithering Potter, doing a little impromptu jig in bare feet during a police investigation; Fenella Fielding as Valeria, with alabaster cleavage and a face straight from a chalk quarry; Peter Butterworth, plump and droll as Sgt Harry H Corbett's assistant; Joan Sims, in fine fettle as Corbett's harridan wife; and Kenneth Williams as the mad, reincarnated Dr Watt, who has one final glorious moment as he falls into his own cauldron. Best scene: when Corbett comes home transformed into a wolfman, and Sims is too busy nagging him to notice the difference.

Carry On Sergeant
1959, UK, 80 mins, b/w
Dir: Gerald Thomas
Stars: William Hartnell, Bob Monkhouse, Shirley Eaton, Eric Barker, Dora Bryan
Rating: ★★

This was the one that started it all, back in 1958. A low-budget comedy about the army, it rang the box-office bell with such vigour that a sequel had to follow. And a sequel to that.

Carry On Spying ○ ⓥ
1964, UK, 85 mins, b/w
Dir: Gerald Thomas
Stars: Kenneth Williams, Barbara Windsor, Bernard Cribbins, Charles Hawtrey, Eric Pohlmann, Erie Barker
Rating: ★★

Many of the *Carry On* regulars were missing for this sub-Bond caper, although bubbly Barbara Windsor makes a welcome addition to the gang

in this, her first *Carry On* film. The pace is faster than before, but the whole enterprise is totally lacking in subtlety, something the series surprised us all by occasionally providing in subsequent outings. The last of the series in black-and-white.

Carry On Teacher ○ ⓥ
1959, UK, 86 mins, b/w
Dir: Gerald Thomas
Stars: Ted Ray, Kenneth Connor, Kenneth Williams, Joan Sims, Charles Hawtrey, Hattie Jacques
Rating: ★★

Third in the famous series, with Ted Ray showing how good he might have been as a second Will Hay. Here he's an acting headmaster hoping to move on to better things. But with a staff that includes Kenneth Williams, Kenneth Connor, and Charles Hawtrey, it's a pound to a pinch of itching powder it will end in disaster.

Carry On Up the Jungle ○ ⓥ
1970, UK, 89 mins, colour
Dir: Gerald Thomas
Stars: Frankie Howerd, Sidney James, Charles Hawtrey, Joan Sims, Terry Scott, Kenneth Connor
Rating: ★★★

The *Carry On* gang revert to the period costume in which their antics always seem funniest: here they are in darkest Africa, circa 1900, searching for the rare Oozulum bird. Jacki Piper, Valerie Leon and Edwina Carroll are the birds of a different feather. Terry Scott plays Jungle Boy. Kenneth Williams is the only member of the original gang not on parade, but Frankie Howerd, as a professor rejoicing in the name of Inigo Tinkle, is a more than adequate replacement. The jungle jokes come as thick and fast as the Pinewood undergrowth, through which strides Bernard Bresslaw as Upsidasi, perhaps the least likely native warrior on record.

Carry On Up the Khyber ○ ⓥ
1968, UK, 85 mins, colour
Dir: Gerald Thomas
Stars: Sidney James, Kenneth Williams, Charles Hawtrey, Roy Castle, Joan Sims, Bernard Bresslaw
Rating: ★★★

One of the highpoints of the *Carry On* films, with the series' only classic sequence – the dinner-party at the Governor's residence which continues despite the fact that the place is under siege from hostile tribesmen and the ceiling is falling in on the meal. Sid James cackles while Kenneth Williams as the Khasi of Kalabar burns to undermine both Sid and his protectors, the Third Foot and Mouth regiment. Bernard Bresslaw looms large in the background as native chief Bungdit Din. Vintage stuff.

Carry On Venus
See: Carry On Jack

Carson City ○
1952, US, 87 mins, colour
Dir: André De Toth
Stars: Randolph Scott, Raymond Massey, Lucille Norman, Richard Webb
Rating: ★★★

A definitely upper-class Randolph Scott Western, this was well received when it first appeared, not least for Raymond Massey's sneering, leering perfomance as Big Jack Davis, as cultured as he is treacherous, given equally to popping champagne corks and shooting adversaries in the back. Scott is a sturdy hero and singer Lucille Norman a pallid heroine (as well she might be without a note to sing). The first film in WarnerColor.

Cars That Ate Paris, The ◐
1974, Australia, 91 mins, colour
Dir: Peter Weir
Stars: John Meillon, Melissa Jaffer, Terry Camilleri
Rating: ★★

Dirctor Peter Weir's monstrous fantasy is set not in Paris, France, but Paris, Australia, where the townsfolk lay traps for unwary night-time motorists. The good people of Paris 'treat' the survivors of the resulting crashes and make their living from the pickings from the wrecks. A good idea, uncertainly acted by its Australian cast, but full of inventive touches.

Carve Her Name with Pride ○ Ⓥ
1958, UK, 119 mins, b/w
Dir: Lewis Gilbert
Stars: Virginia McKenna, Paul Scofield, Jack Warner, Billie Whitelaw
Rating: ★★★★

Inspiring, moving and exciting account of the wartime heroism of Violette Szabo, with a vivid account of her commando-type training, and solid performances from Paul Scofield, Jack Warner, Virginia McKenna and Billie Whitelaw.

Casablanca ○ Ⓥ
1942, US, 102 mins, b/w
Dir: Michael Curtiz
Stars: Humphrey Bogart, Ingrid Bergman, Paul Henreid, Claude Rains, Sydney Greenstreet, Conrad Veidt
Rating: ★★★★★

You must remember this: perhaps Hollywood's best-loved movie. Warners wanted Ronald Reagan and Ann Sheridan for the leads; what they got was Humphrey Bogart, Ingrid Bergman and imortality. Director Michael Curtiz, who brilliantly caught *Casablanca*'s raffish atmosphere in a Hollywood studio, won an Oscar. And the film itself was voted Best Picture. It's so much Bogart and Bergman's film that you tend to forget that Claude Rains, Paul Henreid, Conrad Veidt, Sydney Greenstreet and Peter Lorre were in it too. They're all gone now, but you get the feeling that somewhere in the great cinema in the sky, Rick's Cafe Americain is still open for business.

Casanova Brown ○
1944, US, 92 mins, b/w
Dir: Sam Wood
Stars: Gary Cooper, Teresa Wright, Frank Morgan
Rating: ★★

Frank Morgan, the crusty character actor who won lasting fame as the Wizard of Oz in the Judy Garland classic, only made two films away from his home lot at MGM between 1937 and his death in 1949. This richly humorous production from RKO Radio was one of them. It offers viewers a rare treat of seeing Gary Cooper holding a baby. Not only holding it, but changing it, feeding it and generally doting on it like any proud father. Cooper, in fact, shows a real flair for comedy – especially in the scene where he accidentally burns down his in-laws' glossy magazine-type home. Sam Wood, another refugee from MGM, directs with relish.

Casanova's Big Night ⊙
1953, US, 86 mins, colour
Dir: Norman Z McLeod
Stars: Bob Hope, Joan Fontaine, Basil Rathbone, Vincent Price, John Carradine, Lon Chaney Jr, Audrey Daiton
Rating: ★★★

Inspired, extravagant nonsense in the steps of Bob Hope's many other costume frolics. The novel setting of Venice in the 18th century gives him all sorts of opportunities for gags – as when he dips his finger in the Venetian waters, sniffs and remarks: 'Ah, must be Canal Number Five.' This dithering, disarming romp has Hope forced to impersonate the great lover

Casanova. The supporting cast which, including Basil Rathbone, Vincent Price, Lon Chaney and John Carradine, looks like a horror film director's dream, cunningly amplify the star's comedy by taking themselves and their roles in deadly earnest. Stay tuned for the ending in which Hope rebels against Paramount's idea that his character be given the chop.

Casbah ○
1948, US, 94 mins, b/w
Dir: John Berry
Stars: Yvonne De Carlo, Tony Martin, Marta Toren, Peter Lorre
Rating: ★★

The classic Charles Boyer-Hedy Lamarr romantic adventure *Algiers* itself based on a French original, is uncomfortably revamped as a musical in this version. Despite the fact that the songs are tolerable in an Arabian Nights sort of way, and Tony Martin sings them well, it's the plot elements which work the best. And, although Martin can be hardly anyone's idea of the romantic thief Pepé Le Moko, Peter Lorre is excellent as the wily inspector determined to bring him to book.

Casino ● Ⓥ
1995, 177 mins, colour
Dir: Martin Scorsese
Stars: Robert De Niro, Sharon Stone, Joe Pesci, James Woods, Kevin Pollak, Don Rickles
Rating: ★★★★★

Director Martin Scorsese returns with actors Robert De Niro and Joe Pesci in tow to the gangster theme that served them so well in *GoodFellas*. This time, De Niro is a small-time Mafia hood and successful gambler who rises to the top in the world of Las Vegas gambling houses, but who is brought down by the actions of his drug-addicted wife (Sharon Stone) and psychotic best friend (who else but Pesci?). With a film that's epic in scale and painted on a huge canvas in flashy brushstrokes, Scorsese turns in a breathtaking tale of money, sex, greed, twisted loyalties and naked ambition. And it's ultra-violent. But the highpoint of the film is the transformation of Sharon Stone from beautiful bimbo to award-winning actress of great, untapped talent. Her performance here is nothing short of miraculous. The camerawork is dazzling, the sets and costumes spot-on. Highly recommended. But not for those faint of heart or stomach.

C

Casino de Paree
See: Go into Your Dance

Casino Royale ○ Ⓥ
1967, UK, 150 mins, colour
Dir: John Huston, Ken Hughes, Robert Parrish, Joe McGrath, Val Guest
Stars: David Niven, Peter Sellers, Ursula Andress, Woody Allen, Barbara Bouchet
Rating:★★

This spoof on the James Bond films is a colourful lark, though very dated in its shiny Sixties pop-art way. Still, the all-star cast is fun, with Woody Allen as Jimmy Bond and Barbara Bouchet as a beautiful Moneypenny. You'll find that there are several James Bonds and '007s' in the film, including Peter Sellers, David Niven, Daliah Lavi and Ursula Andress.

Casper ○ Ⓥ
1995, US, 100 mins, colour
Dir: Brad Silberling
Stars: Bill Pullman, Christina Ricci, Cathy Moriarty, Eric Idle, Amy Brenneman
Rating: ★★★

A pleasant and exceptionally well-designed fantasy/comedy which robs TV's famous friendly ghost of some of his innocence in the name of hi-tech Nineties effects. The film zips along for the first half-hour or so and, though it gets a bit wearing once its novelty appeal has gone, it reasserts its sense of pace and invention in a riotous finale. Here, Casper is the ghost of a 12-year-old boy haunting a vast castle just inherited by Cruella de Vil-type Cathy Moriarty who, with inept henchman Eric Idle, suspects there's treasure on the site. Enter exorciser Bill Pullman (Dan Aykroyd having fled the premises) whose career dealing with 'the living impaired' is just a cover for his attempts to get in touch with his dead wife 'on the other side'. Pullman, with disbelieving daughter Christina Ricci in tow, is hired by Moriarty to 'out' the ghost: he finds himself not only dealing with lovable Casper, but his three gross uncle-ghosts who have no intention of vacating the premises. Sufficient FX fun ensues to entertain youngsters most of the time. Brief guest appearances by Mel Gibson, Clint Eastwood and Rodney Dangerfield add to the fun.

Cassandra Crossing, The ○
1976, US, 129 mins, colour
Dir: George Pan Cosmatos
Stars: Sophia Loren, Richard Harris, Ava Gardner, Burt Lancaster, Martin Sheen
Rating: ★★★★

Disaster strikes again! This time it's plague on board the Trans-Continental Express in a film that moves always with a sense of urgency. The script runs the full gamut of Hollywood clichés, but parts of the journey are tremendously exciting. The plague is carried by a saboteur trying to escape his pursuers. Of course, there are convenient babies, children, food, dogs, and drinking water for him to touch before he expires, transmitting the disease (maybe) to an assortment of typical Hollywood characters. A sinister note is provided by the Intelligence colonel (a very serious Birt Lancaster) who may be out to re-route the whole plague-ridden train to disaster. It's all immense hokum, of course, but done with great dash and panache, with some pulsating action. The director is the Greek George Pan Cosmatos, who keeps the suspense well on the rails.

Cass Timberlane ○
1947, US, 119 mins, b/w
Dir: George Sidney
Stars: Spencer Tracy, Lana Turner, Zachary Scott, Mary Astor, Tom Drake, Albert Dekker
Rating: ★★

A sincere adaptation from a Sinclair Lewis novel, about a respectable midwestern judge who marries a beautiful but immature bride and has trouble keeping pace with her youth. Solid, if uninspired. The usual commanding performance from Spencer Tracy.

Cast a Dark Shadow ○
1955, UK, 82 mins, b/w
Dir: Lewis Gilbert
Stars: Margaret Lockwood, Dirk Bogarde, Kay Walsh, Kathleen Harrison, Mona Washbourne
Rating: ★★★

This shivery thriller with a touch of graveyard humour came too late to revive Margaret Lockwood's fading film career, and she marched off to success in other fields. Actually, she gives her best performance in some years as the razor-tongued ex-barmaid in danger of being murdered for her money by shady young fortune-hunter Dirk Bogarde. Ten years earlier it was more likely to have been Lockwood doing the killing off!

Cast a Giant Shadow ○
1966, US, 141 mins, colour
Dir: Melville Shaveison
Stars: Kirk Douglas, Senta Berger, Angie Dickinson, John Wayne, Frank Sinatra,

Yul Brynner
Rating: ★★

Big action film (with the famous line: 'This has got to be the biggest blow-up since falsies!') stars Kirk Douglas as the daredevil soldier of fortune who's in every military action ('I knew they wouldn't start D-Day without you,' says his wife, and they don't), culminating in the Israeli War of 1948. Douglas is rather disappointing, but there's a warmly glowing portrait of the 'war widow' from Angie Dickinson, and the ending, with its cleverly underplayed sentiment, is the most moving moment in the film.

Cast a Long Shadow ○
1958, US, 82 mins, colour
Dir: Thomas Carr
Stars: Audie Murphy, Terry Moore, John Dehner, James Best
Rating: ★★

America's most decorated Second World War serviceman, Audie Murphy, is the star of this unusual Western. Unusual, because it shows that even in the Wild West illegitimacy was regarded as a stigma. The film doesn't harp too much upon the subject, however. Guns blaze to good effect and there's a splendid cattle stampede.

Castaway ● Ⓥ
1986, UK, 117 mins, colour
Dir: Nicolas Roeg
Stars: Oliver Reed, Amanda Donohoe, Georgina Hale
Rating: ★★

Guys, if you advertised in the classified columns for a 'wife' to accompany you for a year on a deserted tropical island and Amanda Donohoe replied and said 'yes', it would presumably sound like real paradise. Girls, if you went along with the above scheme, planned a year out of your life and then found out you were to be paired with a bellicose chauvinist in the shape of burly Oliver Reed, how would you feel? This is the scenario created by Nicolas Roeg as he stylishly commits Lucy Irvine's soapy best-seller to the screen. As these two disparate characters struggle to adapt to the rigours of living in 'paradise', let alone coping with each other, the fragile bond of mutual dependence soon begins to fray. Roeg's treatment of this latter-day Robinson Crusoe story is full of luscious imagery and a preoccupation with shape, surrealism and symbolism which perhaps only the director can fully understand. Reed is as resistible as he's probably supposed to be but, handed a thankless task by the screenwriter, Donohoe almost makes a winning character out of her castaway.

Castle Keep ◐

1969, US, 107 mins, colour
Dir: Sydney Pollack
Stars: Burt Lancaster, Peter Falk, Patrick O'Neal, Bruce Dern, Jean-Pierre Aumont
Rating: ★★★

This film is certainly off the beaten track, as one might expect from its source – a very bizarre novel by William Eastlake that hovers between fantasy and reality. Burt Lancaster plays the one-eyed American major who billets his few remaining men at an Ardennes castle filled with priceless art treasures. It is also in the direct line of the German advance. The ensuing proceedings add up to distinctive entertainment and, in case you should be thinking this might be a war film without battles, there are skirmishes throughout and a really colossal holocaust at the end, when the Germans throw everything at the castle and its occupants.

Castle on the Hudson ○

(aka: Years Without Days)
1940, US, 77 mins, b/w
Dir: Anatole Litvak
Stars: John Garfield, Ann Sheridan, Pat O'Brien, Burgess Meredith, Jerome Cowan
Rating: ★★★

The castle of the title is no romantic pile, but the tough jail 'up the river' known as 'Sing Sing'. This is in fact a re-working of the Spencer Tracy film *20,000 Years in Sing Sing*, based on the book of the same title by real-life Sing Sing warden Lewis Lawes. John Garfield's portrayal of the wisecracking crook added to his growing list of chip-on-the-shoulder rebel roles, while Ann Sheridan provides a strong portrayal of resilient girlfriend Kay (and proves a far better gangster's moll than Bette Davis in the 1933 movie). Pat O'Brien is excellent as the sympathetic warden in charge of Garfield and Burgess Meredith attacks with gusto his role as the leader of a breakout. It's all directed with pace by Anatole Litvak.

Casualties of War ● ⓥ

1989, US, 113 mins, colour
Dir: Brian De Palma
Stars: Michael J Fox, Sean Penn, Don Harvey, Sam Robards
Rating: ★★★

The approach of this Vietnam drama, about the deliberate rape and murder of a local girl by four US servicemen while a fifth stood helplessly by, seems unimpeachable, its heart undoubtedly in the right place. Sean Penn and Michael J Fox are uncommonly well cast as the brutish sergeant (who leads the rape) and the conscience-stricken PFC and both do the roles impassioned justice. However, you wouldn't expect De Palma to understate anything and he doesn't (except perhaps the rape itself); in many places the drama suffers from directorial overkill. And the ending, striving to satisfy its audience, is far too pat. But it's a strong piece of film-making, filled with the restless camerawork for which its director is noted, and which finds its niche in the hurly-burly desperation of jungle warfare.

Cat and the Canary, The ◐ ⓥ

1978, US, 98 mins, colour
Dir: Radley Metzger
Stars: Honor Blackman, Edward Fox, Michael Callan, Wendy Hiller
Rating: ★★

This is a decent enough remake of the old Bob Hope comedy-chiller about an heiress in peril in a creepy old house. It has a good cast too: Honor Blackman, Edward Fox, Michael Callan, Peter McEnery, Wendy Hiller, Olivia Hussey, Carol Lynley and Wilfrid Hyde White. An entertaining blend of gasps and chuckles, mildly recommended if you haven't seen the original.

Cat and the Canary, The ○

1939, US, 72 mins, b/w
Dir: Elliott Nugent
Stars: Bob Hope, Paulette Goddard, John Beal, Gale Sondergaard
Rating: ★★★★

From Bob Hope's best period (1939-48), this is the classic comedy-chiller that really gave his career a very big boost. One of the earliest of 'old dark house' mysteries, first filmed in 1927, it is tailored here to Hope's brightest comedy style, although his wisecracks seem just a pace away from panic as a shadowy killer stalks his victims around an old mansion in the swamps. In the first of several films with Hope, Paulette Goddard proves herself an ideal spirited-but-frightened heroine. Commented one contemporary American reviewer: 'Miss Goddard's screams would put a traffic snarl in Times Square'. Made before in a rarely-seen silent version of 1927.

Cat Ballou ○ ⓥ

1965, US, 96 mins, colour
Dir: Elliot Silverstein

Stars: Jane Fonda, Lee Marvin, Michael Callan, Tom Nardini, Nat' King' Cole
Rating: ★★★★

Pleasurable spoof Western about a shy young college miss who tilts her pretty nose at outlawry after her father has been killed by a hired gunfighter. Her 'gang' consists of two pusillanimous outlaws who never fire guns on principle, and an all-American Indian. 'It's no use blaming me,' he keeps saying, 'for what the Indians did to Custer.' But the Ballou band is not complete. And its real centrepiece is Kid Shelleen, as drunk a gunman as ever fell off his horse. The Kid turns out to be a glorious character study which won an Oscar for Lee Marvin. Not a lurch, not a sway, not a whisky-soaked blotch on the face are missed in Marvin's performance. 'Your eyes,' exclaims the Indian, they're all bloodshot.' Growls Marvin: 'You oughta see them from my side.'

Cat Chaser ● ⓥ

1989, US, 90 mins, colour
Dir: Abel Ferrara
Stars: Peter Weller, Kelly McGillis, Charles Durning, Frederic Forrest, Juan Hernandez
Rating: ★★

This does the job as a violent thriller, but it hasn't half the subtlety its first ten minutes promise, running more like Hank Jansen than Elmore Leonard, on whose crime novel the film is based. Kelly McGillis obviously fancied some sort of cathartic experience after *The Accused*. Here she seems happy just to show off her body as the wayward wife of De Boya, an ex-secret policeman in Latin America, a woman only too eager to resume an affair with her former lover George (Peter Weller). He's an ex-Marine who now owns a Florida hotel where the clientele are outnumbered by the staff. Other characters are involved in all this, all of them with an eye to the $2 million De Boya is said to have stashed away. But they are rootlessly written people, given more substance than the screenplay deserves by the actors, especially Charles Durning, Frederic Forrest and Juan Hernandez.

Catch Me a Spy ○

1971, US, 94 mins, colour
Dir: Dick Clement
Stars: Kirk Douglas, Marlène Jobert, Trevor Howard, Tom Courtenay, Patrick Mower
Rating: ★★

C

Writer-director Dick Clement and actor Tom Courtenay, who combined to such good effect on *Otley*, are together again in a not dissimilar but less effective spy comedy-thriller. Clement and his long-time collaborator Ian La Frenais have fashioned an ingenious plot, full of nice little comic flashes, with double agents everywhere and the hero and heroine dodging spies in Scotland in a manner reminiscent of *The 39 Steps*. Kirk Douglas and the appealing Marlene Jobert both offer attractive performances, but it's sad to see Trevor Howard wasted in an unworthy role and, for all its merits, the caper is never quite credible.

Catch-22 ● Ⓥ

1970, US, 115 mins, colour
Dir: Mike Nichols
Stars: Alan Arkin, Martin Balsam, Paula Prentiss, Jon Voight, Richard Benjamin, Art Garfunkel
Rating: ★★★

Joseph Heller's stunning and surreal black comedy about services life in World War Two is a novel that could never really be transferred to the screen and satisfy its thousands of devotees. That said, Buck Henry's screen adaptation, while inevitably having to leave out characters and favourite incidents, is a remarkable piece of work which largely succeeds in capturing the spirit of the original while hardly sticking to the letter. And Mike Nichols' direction is clever enough to bring out both the humour and the bitterness, focusing on Alan Arkin's impressive Captain Yossarian and a lavish array of lesser characters.

Catered Affair, The ○

(aka: Wedding Breakfast)
1956, US, 93 mins, b/w
Dir: Richard Brooks
Stars: Bette Davis, Ernest Borgnine, Debbie Reynolds, Barry Fitzgerald, Rod Taylor
Rating: ★★★★

After the success of *Marty,* film-makers rushed to the work of writer Paddy Chayefsky. This story is another of his looks at the lower strata of American life. Ernest Borgnine and Bette Davis play a Bronx couple whose quiet life runs into all sorts of troubled waters when their daughter (Debbie Reynolds) decides to get married. Borgnine gives a subdued performance that's just right.

Cat from Outer Space, The ☉

1978, US, 103 mins, colour
Dir: Norman Tokar
Stars: Ken Berry, Sandy Duncan, Harry Morgan
Rating: ★★★

Lots of winningly realised fun and games in this Disney comedy, a sort of close encounter of the furred kind as the alien moggy of the title foils a space-energy spy plot with the help of the powers that emanate from his illuminated collar. The film benefits enormously from the relationship between the wise-cracking (talking) cat and the eccentric doctor (sympathetically played by Ken Berry) who becomes his sidekick. Roddy McDowall is rather too far over the top as the bad guy.

Catlow ◐

1971, Spain, 101 mins, colour
Dir: Sam Wanamaker
Stars: Yul Brynner, Richard Crenna, Daliah Lavi, Leonard Nimoy
Rating: ★

A dull Western from the pen of Louis L'Amour, the author of *Hondo*. Like the star's Sabata Westerns, this was filmed in Spain, with some splendid scenery getting the full treatment from Ted Scaife's Metrocolor camerawork. Daliah Lavi is a spitfire bandit girl in the finest Raquel Welch tradition, but too little is seen of Leonard (Mr Spock) Nimoy as the bounty killer: it hardly seemed worth the trek back from the stars for this role.

Cat on a Hot Tin Roof ○ Ⓥ

1958, US, 108 mins, colour
Dir: Richard Brooks
Stars: Elizabeth Taylor, Paul Newman, Burl Ives, Jack Carson, Judith Anderson
Rating: ★★★★

A favourite critical complaint is that Hollywood 'emasculated ' the endings of Tennessee Williams works such as this one and *Sweet Bird of Youth*. But that certainly will not spoil your enjoyment of this powerful film. And while the original Williams themes and climaxes would be acceptable screen fare by today's standards, whether the average member of the public would rather see them this way is another thing. In this case, the theme that has been 'toned down' is homosexuality and the alcoholism of Brick (Paul Newman), who prefers the bottle to his lovely wife (a glowingly beautiful Elizabeth Taylor), is played up accordingly. But the important thing is that the spirit and highly charged atmosphere of the original have

been retained. Burl Ives repeats his stage triumph as the dying Big Daddy, and the strong performances of Newman and Miss Taylor were rewarded with Academy Award nominations. But no one tops Jack Carson's brilliant supporting portrayal of the sneaky Gooper – a masterly piece of acting.

Cat People ◐

1942, US, 73 mins, b/w
Dir: Jacques Tourneur
Stars: Simone Simon, Kent Smith
Rating: ★★★★

The film that started a great cycle of fantasy-horror films in the mid-Forties. It became famous as the first film not to show its monster, and to prove that the power of suggestion was just as likely to scare the daylights out of an audience as actually seeing some fiendish creation. Brilliantly photographed and recommended – but not for the nervous.

Cat People ● Ⓥ

1982, US, 118 mins, colour
Dir: Paul Schrader
Stars: Nastassia Kinski, Malcolm McDowell, John Heard, Annette O'Toole, Ed Begley Jr, John Larroquette
Rating: ★★

Alas, poor RKO classic of 1942, we knew you well. Director Paul Schrader substitutes blood, gore and viscera for shape, shadow and unknown menace in this updated version. Both leading ladies are required to appear in the nude, and four-letter words are spat as frequently as hatred from the dripping jaws of the panthers into which the central brother-and-sister characters are wont to turn. Special effects, though, are fairly minimal and the script steers an uneasy course just this side of risibility. Nastassia Kinski is occasionally quite effective as the chief catwoman, but John Heard's talent is barely glimpsed as the zookeeper who loves her not from afar but far too near for safety.

Cat's Eye ◐ Ⓥ

1984, US, 90 mins, colour
Dir: Lewis Teague
Stars: James Woods, Alan King, Drew Barrymore, Kenneth McMillan
Rating: ★★★

In contrast to other chillers by Stephen King, this fantasy from the King brain is on the light-hearted side and rather fun. Drew Barrymore is quite likeable as the girl whose telepathic call for help alerts a stray cat that she's in danger, and causes it to use up quite a percentage of its nine lives, with the *pièce de resistance* coming as the cat does battle with an evil troll threatening to steal Drew's breath away. The trick work involved is good enough to draw the viewer into the fray, and the cat actors are intelligently deployed at all times.

Cattle Annie and Little Britches ○

1979, US, 95 mins, colour
Dir: Lamont Johnson
Stars: Burt Lancaster, John Savage, Rod Steiger, Scott Glenn, Amanda Plummer, Diane Lane
Rating: ★★

It should be pointed out that burly Burt Lancaster plays neither of the title roles in this pleasant, slightly spoof action Western. It refers to the two teenage tearaway girls who batten themselves on to his tattered bandit gang in the 1890s, and inspire them to hit the outlaw trail again.

Cattle Drive ○

1950, US, 77 mins, colour
Dir: Kurt Neumann
Stars: Joel McCrea, Dean Stockwell, Chill Wills
Rating: ★★

Photographed in beautiful colour, this pleasing Western has a vigorous performance from the young Dean Stockwell – as a spoiled teenager along on a huge cattle drive – whose enthusiasm spurs Joel McCrea to one of the best of his latter-day performances as the old hand who teaches him about life and the tricks of the trail.

Cattle King

See: Guns of Wyoming

Cattle Queen of Montana ○

1955, US, 88 mins, colour
Dir: Allan Dwan
Stars: Barbara Stanwyck, Ronald Reagan, Gene Evans, Jack Elam
Rating: ★★

A presentable Western with marvellous Technicolor photography by John Alton. Barbara Stanwyck does well as, unusually, a nice, uncomplicated lady with the super name of Sierra Nevada Jones, and Ronald Reagan is for once ideal as the mysterious gunfighter with whom she falls in love. The story is of a higher than usual calibre for a horse opera and the scenery really superb. The gutsy Stanwyck as usual did her own stuntwork, so impressing the local Blackfoot Indians that they named her Princess Many Victories and made her an honorary member of the tribe.

Caught ○

1948, US, 88 mins, b/w
Dir: Max Ophuls
Stars: James Mason, Barbara Bel Geddes, Robert Ryan
Rating: ★★

This sometimes tense morality tale about a shop girl who believes that marrying a rich man is the route to happiness too often lapses into tiresome soap opera that proves a waste of a good cast. Barbara Bel Geddes is the girl, Robert Ryan the neurotic millionaire she marries and James Mason (in his first American film) is the young, intelligent doctor she falls for. It all ends better for the heroine than she deserves, but not without a fair bit of pointless angst in between and no small amount of scene-stealing competition between the stars. On the whole it's stylish but also slow-moving and depressing: you can't help feeling Bel Geddes deserves all the suffering for being so damn silly in the first place.

Caught in the Draft ⊙

1941, US, 82 mins, b/w
Dir: David Butler
Stars: Bob Hope, Dorothy Lamour, Eddie Bracken
Rating: ★★★

Now one of the rarest of Bob Hope's comedy films, this contemporary romp finds the great man in good form as a movie hero who's such a coward in real life that he'll 'jump when someone, cracks their knuckles'. While in pursuit of Dorothy Lamour he finds himself in the army, and thereby hangs the title and the fun. Panicky little Eddie Bracken made some of his first strides towards the top at Paramount as the star's minion who finds himself also enlisting.

Cavalcade ○

1933, UK, 120 mins, b/w
Dir: Frank Lloyd
Stars: Diana Wynyard, Clive Brook Herbert Mundin, Una O'Connor
Rating: ★★★

Noel Coward's down-through-the-years family saga lifted almost bodily from the London stage (Fox even imported a genuine London taxi) and the winner of three Oscars, including best picture and a best director trophy for Frank Lloyd, whose second Academy Award it was. His standing began to slip soon after *Mutiny on the Bounty* two years later and he is little remembered today.

Cease Fire ● ⓥ

1985, US, 97 mins, colour
Dir: David Nutter
Stars: Don Johnson, Lisa Blount, Robert F Lyons, Chris Noel, Richard Chaves
Rating: ★★★

Director David Nutter's only major film to date is a moving account of mid-Eighties America that's interesting on two counts. One, in that it's a very serious look at the recurrent nightmares that haunted the lives of the country's Vietnam veterans and two, in that it takes two players whose looks might otherwise limit them, and really gives them a chance to act. Neither Don Johnson nor Lisa Blount lets their director down. Their anguished performances in a key scene almost rival those of Jane Fonda and Jon Voight in *Coming Home*. The film itself is slow to take a grip on you, but its sincerity shines through.

Ceiling Zero ○

1935, US, 95 mins, b/w
Dir: Howard Hawks
Stars: James Cagney, Pat O'Brien, June Travis, Stuart Erwin, Barton MacLane
Rating: ★★

An interesting film concerning World War One aviators who find it hard to come down from their combative 'high' and settle again to civilian life. This one carries its own charge of tension, plus a clever and complex performance by James Cagney and an intelligent and effective portrayal by Isabel Jewell in a difficult minor role. Director Howard Hawks brings both excitement and realism to his shooting and editing of the flying scenes.

Cemetery Club, The ① ⓥ

1993, US, 106 mins, colour
Dir: Bill Duke
Stars: Ellen Burstyn, Olympia Dukakis, Diane Ladd, Danny Aiello, Lainie Kazan, Christina Ricci
Rating: ★★

'You're never too old to have some fun' is the message of this gentle romantic comedy. Our feisty, fiftysomething heroines (Olympia Dukakis, Ellen Burstyn and Diane Ladd), a trio of grey-haired, sharp-tongued Jewish widows (strange that the casting director should choose three non-Jewish actresses for these roles), meet each week to visit the graves of their husbands – until the day a stranger (Danny Aiello) appears at the cemetery. There's lots of *Golden Girls*-type squabbles in this one, with the quality cast rolling waspish tongues

C

round some acid-sharp lines. Burstyn is wonderful in the side of the movie that becomes a touching sweet-natured romance, but some of the other performances are too self-indulgent at times.

Century ● Ⓥ
1993, UK, 112 mins, colour
Dir: Stephen Poliakoff
Stars: Charles Dance, Miranda Richardson, Clive Owen, Robert Stephens, Liza Walker, Joan Hickson
Rating: ★★

A bizarre, pretentious but sometimes quite absorbing arthouse movie which mixes its period medical drama with a dash of romance, and tops it off with some beautiful photography and a loving evocation of an era long past. At the turn of the century when much medicine was still considered quackery, Paul Reisner (Clive Owen) emerges as the star pupil of the mysterious Prof Mandry (Charles Dance). But Reisner lands in big trouble when he falls in love with Clara (Miranda Richardson), a laboratory assistant with a mysterious past. The performances here are suitably enigmatic, but, under Stephen Poliakoff's arty direction, the film annoyingly takes a long time getting nowhere fast.

Chad Hanna ○
1940, US, 86 mins, colour
Dir: Henry King
Stars: Henry Fonda, Dorothy Lamour, Linda Darnell, Guy Kibbee
Rating: ★★

Pretty unusual for a Hollywood film of its time, this is a heated romantic melodrama set against a travelling circus in the 1840s. It almost works, but not quite, despite the right touch of nostalgic affection by director Henry King and vivid Technicolor photography by Ernest Palmer.

Chains of Gold ● Ⓥ
1990, US, 94 mins, colour
Dir: Rod Holcomb
Stars: John Travolta, Marilu Henner, Bernie Casey, Hector Elizondo
Rating: ★★

In between episodes in the *Look Who's Talking* comedy saga, John Travolta ventured into *Miami Vice* territory, but the territory and change of pace don't altogether suit him. Playing an idealistic social worker and ex-alcoholic, he becomes involved with a vicious Florida crack gang through his efforts to rescue a 13-year-old boy from a life of crime. The gang itself has a whole army of such boys, supplying crack to

the nation. And the penalty for defection is, naturally, death. Travolta swears a lot, sweats a lot and goes without a shave, but can't convince us that all this is quite his cup of tea, especially the serial-like developments that leave him dangling over a pit of alligators. Although based on true events and people, which puts its heart firmly in the right place, the slack treatment the film gets makes it definitely a second-class citizen in the genre.

Chain Reaction ○ Ⓥ
1996, US, 106 mins, colour
Dir: Andrew Davis
Stars: Keanu Reaves, Morgan Freeman, Rachel Weisz, Fred Ward, Brian Cox, Joanna Cassidy
Rating: ★★★

There's lots of action in this espionage thriller if you don't mind not being able to follow the plot. Keanu Reeves gets back into the kind of thriller in which his fans will pay to see him, as a research worker on a project to harness hydrogen for clean energy. No sooner has the project reached fruition than mysterious figures move in on its headquarters, murder the project's associate leader and make off with certain specifications, as the lab blows up behind them. Unfortunately, these are useless without the 'frequencies' that control them – and guess who has those? Right! The plot gets pottier, so don't worry about it. Just enjoy the action set-pieces which include some hair-raising stuff on a dividing bridge and a desperate battle in an unoccupied house. Keanu runs forever; but laconic Morgan Freeman walks away with the film.

Chalk Garden, The ○
1964, UK, 106 mins, colour
Dir: Ronald Neame
Stars: Hayley Mills, Deborah Kerr, John Mills, Edith Evans, Felix Aylmer
Rating: ★★

Someone – most likely Ross Hunter, expert producer of Hollywood 'glossies' – has put a soft centre of sticky sentimentality in the bitter almonds of Enid Bagnold's play about a teenage girl who lives in a world of lies because she lacks love and understanding. As the girl, Hayley Mills gestures a lot but sounds unconvinced by the dialogue. Edith Evans gives a brilliant portrayal of the possessive old lady with no more ability to give love to the girl than life to the plants in her garden of chalk. It's a performance as impressive in close-up as it is at long range.

Deborah Kerr and John Mills round out the cast.

Challenge, The ●
1982, US, 112 mins, colour
Dir: John Frankenheimer
Stars: Scott Glenn, Toshiro Mifune
Rating: ★★

Director John Frankenheimer tries to combine the action of a chop-socky film with the scale and spirit off Kurosawa epic and falls heavily between the two stools. Scott Glenn is well in character as the cynical back-streets battler who foolishly accepts an obviously murky assignment to take two ancient swords back to Japan and in no time at all has been beaten up, knifed and left for dead. With dialogue that sounds as if it comes from a sword-and-sandal movie of 30 years earlier, action is clearly called for to save the day, and it's sharply done, too, though the spurts of it are rather too sparsely spaced. But you'll enjoy the devastating final battle, which appears to do no good at all to the Kyoto Conference Centre, let alone the actors who get bits of them sliced all over it.

Chamber of Horrors ◐
1966, US, 121 mins, colour
Dir: Hy Averback
Stars: Patrick O'Neal, Cesare Danova, Laura Devon, Patrice Wymore
Rating: ★★

A dose of Rue Morguery, set in Maryland of the 1890s where a madman is on the loose. Watch for the 'fear flasher' and the 'horror horn' which enable one to take evasive action at the film's 'four supreme fright points', as suggested by the original publicity. Patrick O'Neal has a field day as the madman, humming softly to himself while he screws an axe blade onto his hook hand while contemplating his next victim. There's also a special guest star. You'll have to be sharp to catch him, as he's on screen for all of two and a half seconds.

Chamber, The ● Ⓥ
1996, US, 111 mins, colour
Dir: James Foley
Stars: Chris O'Donnell, Gene Hackman, Faye Dunaway, Lela Rochon, Richard Bradford, Robert Prosky
Rating: ★

Just where this John Grisham story is going and what's its dramatic point, perhaps only Grisham could tell us. After an explosive opening, the story limps along in desultory fashion and pretty much fizzles out at the end. An old Ku Klux Klan activist (Hackman) sits in Death Row awaiting execution for a bombing years before that cost the lives of twin boys. His lawyer grandson (O'Donnell), whose father committed suicide and whose aunt (Dunaway) is an alcoholic, arrives to fight the case. There are leads which fail to come to any climax and the finding of a co-conspirator that's no revelation since we haven't seen the man before. O'Donnell is weak and unconvincing in a part that looks like a Tom Cruise reject. It's a poor role, but O'Donnell brings nothing to it. And it's never clear (like many things here) quite what game the governor's playing. The results are, kindly, not very interesting. Hackman does his best as the dead man walking, but Dunaway overacts as his daughter.

Champ, The O Ⓥ

1979, US, 123 mins, colour
Dir: Franco Zeffirelli
Stars: Jon Voight, Faye Dunaway, Ricky Schroder, Jack Warden, Arthur Hill, Joan Blondell
Rating: ★

Those in charge of the casting for this updated version of MGM's classic Oscar-winning sudser deserve a nifty right uppercut. Never for one moment does Faye Dunaway gain our sympathy for her efforts to get a larger share of the boy whom she deserted seven years before, nor is Jon Voight anyone's idea of an ageing ex-world champion boxer who has looked after the kid since she left. Voight mugs frantically as the champ – at least it's a performance in the Wallace Beery tradition. And we can say the same for Ricky Schroder as his son. Dunaway struggles Ms-fully with a part that just isn't hers. But none of them can do anything about the pace, and the film bobs and weaves like a punch-drunk punk until it falls asleep on its feet. Get your fellow viewer to wake you up at the end in time for the final fight – it's well worth a look.

Champagne Charlie O

1944, US, 100 mins, b/w
Dir: Alberto Cavalcanti
Stars: Tommy Trinder, Stanley Holloway, Jean Kent
Rating: ★★★★

Described at the time as 'one of the best musical-comedies made in this country to date', this boisterous and invigorating period piece recreates (impressively, considering wartime exigencies) gaslit London of the 1860s for

its farcical story of the 'drinking song' rivalry of two of the foremost music-hall personalities of the day – roles in which Tommy Trinder and Stanley Holloway prove perfectly cast.

Champagne for Caesar O

1950, US, 99 mins, b/w
Dir: Richard Whorf
Stars: Ronald Colman, Celeste Holm, Vincent Price
Rating: ★★★

Mad but fun, this is a delightfully idiotic Hollywood comedy that was badly handled by its studio, adored by the critics and shunned by the public. Ronald Colman, as the unemployed genius seeking to win a fortune on a radio quiz (for reasons of revenge, not personal gain), shows himself a farceur with the lightest of touches, while Vincent Price is a wild-eyed delight as the nasty 'soap magnate' forever going into one of his 'trances'. And Caesar? He's a parrot who happens to like champagne, and he's voiced by Mel Blanc of Bugs Bunny fame. It's a sustained squawk that's full of fizz from beginning to end.

Champion O

1949, US, 99 mins, b/w
Dir: Mark Robson
Stars: Kirk Douglas, Marilyn Maxwell, Arthur Kennedy
Rating: ★★★★★

Kirk Douglas slugged his way to fame in this gruelling boxing story that was not overtaken for face-smashing realism until *Raging Bull* came along years later. Douglas delivers a knock-out *tour-de-force* performance as a ruthless, merciless, sadistic man who destroys anything or anyone who stands in the way of his ambition. It shocked audiences of the day and still retains that power today. Douglas seized the role gladly after being shown Carl Foreman's blistering script and he was promised top billing. It was the wisest decision of his early career, turning him into an overnight sensation and earning him a Best Actor Oscar nomination to boot. Arthur Kennedy is also superb as Douglas's trusting, loving brother while Ruth Roman, in one of her earliest roles, is utterly captivating as the victimised wife.

Champions O Ⓥ

1983, UK, 115 mins, colour
Dir: John Irvin
Stars: John Hurt, Edward Woodward, Jan Francis, Ben Johnson, Peter Barkworth, Kirstie Alley
Rating: ★★★

It's difficult to be as thrilled by a winner when you know the outcome, but you just have to cheer for Bob Champion, the jockey who was not only cured of the cancer which, without treatment, would have killed him in months, but went on to win the Grand National on a horse which, a few months before, had nearly been put down after snapping a tendon. John Hurt is perhaps a little too expert at anguish (there are times when he looks like a dying crow) to be cast as Champion but, apart from a few obvious doubles in the Grand National, he does a splendid job in and out of the saddle. Champion himself obviously insisted that the film should not show him as a saint; and so it presents his weaknesses and vices along with his strengths and virtues. Jan Francis is all warmth and sympathy as the girl who chases and catches him.

Chance Meeting

See: The Young Lovers

Chances Are O Ⓥ

1989, US, 108 mins, colour
Dir: Emile Ardolino
Stars: Cybill Shepherd, Robert Downey Jr, Ryan O'Neal, Mary Stuart Masterson, Christopher McDonald
Rating: ★★

In this fantasy Cybill Shepherd's dead husband comes back to Earth in the (much younger) shape of Robert Downey Jr, who initially remembers nothing of his previous life. Romantic complications ensue because Shepherd's daughter (Mary Stuart Masterson) fancies Downey and Ryan O'Neal carries a torch for Shepherd. By the generally high standards of such whimsy, this film is highly improbable mainly because you don't believe in the characters, or the situations in which they find themselves, even though the treatment remains quite winningly sweet-natured throughout. Downey tries hard with what he's given and occasionally rises above it, but the rest of the cast copes less well with the uphill struggle.

Changeling, The ●

1979, US, 107 mins, colour
Dir: Peter Medak
Stars: George C Scott, Trish Van Devere, Melvyn Douglas, John Colicos
Rating: ★★★★★

A very superior example of the haunted-house thriller, whose horrors are never (well, only in flashback) seen. There's the obligatory dire warning, of

C

course, from a member of the historical society that sold George C Scott the house in question after his wife and daughter have been killed in an accident. 'That house isn't fit to live in,' she hisses. 'It doesn't want people.' People, unfortunately, are just what it does want, and Mr Scott in particular, his own loss making him a potent force for spirits to communicate with. The ghost lurks in narrow, confined spaces and age-old cobwebbed rooms, and director Peter Medak's camera tracks relentlessly through these claustrophobic environs like an invader in some old and murky painting stirred almost to life. The result is quite the most frightening film since *The Haunting*, much aided by the supernaturalistic portrayal of the star. Scenes at the end involving a wheelchair may crunch you right into your armchair. Most horror films these days are not for the squeamish. *The Changeling* is old-fashioned in that respect: it's not for the nervous.

Chant of Jimmie Blacksmith, The ● ⓥ

1978, Australia, 124 mins, colour
Dir: Fred Schepisi
Stars: Tommy Lewis, Freddy Reynolds
Rating: ★★★★

A very violent true story about an Australian half-breed at the turn of the century who, ill-treated beyond belief by a succession of white masters, went berserk and killed two of the families that had caused him so much pain. Fred Schepisi's film of these events is beautifully composed and skilfully made, even if it doesn't entirely avoid dull spots and is sometimes hard to follow. Tommy Lewis is extraordinarily naturalistic as the much-abused Jimmie, and there are other good performances from Freddy Reynolds as his blood brother, and from Angela Punch as his ever-suffering wife.

Chaplin ◐ ⓥ

1992, US, 158 mins, colour
Dir: Richard Attenborough
Stars: Robert Downey Jr, Kevin Kline, Dan Aykroyd, Marisa Tomei, Anthony Hopkins, Geraldine Chaplin
Rating: ★★

Long and caring, the outcome of Richard Attenborough's ambitious biography of Charlie Chaplin was perhaps inevitable: bits of film history dully stuck together with famous actors striking poses as other famous actors but no real life, not even from Robert Downey Jr's carefully considered and visually very good Chaplin. Slowly the

Chaplin history unfolds: its facts are interesting, but their presentation sadly lacks the persuasive qualities necessary to attract us to them. Although beautifully dressed and set and professionally made, this remains a pageant rather than a picture and could signal the end of such ambitious biopics for some time to come.

Charade ○ ⓥ

1963, US, 114 mins, colour
Dir: Stanley Donen
Stars: Cary Grant, Audrey Hepburn, Walter Matthau, James Coburn, George Kennedy
Rating: ★★★★

Thrillers like *Charade* lean heavily on character and directorial flair to make them work, and seldom has one worked better than this. Stanley Donen – previously best-known for his Gene Kelly musicals – doesn't miss a trick in keeping the action moving at a furious rate, spinning madly from one red herring to another, disclosure upon disclosure Sometimes he goes for deadpan comedy, at others his camera is trained all out for thrills. But the two never clash – *Charade* is constantly intriguing, with its combination of wit and directness. And when thrills it really is a seat-gripper. One scene especially, a rooftop fight between Cary Grant and George Kennedy, is skilfully exciting. And a tracking shot of a villain firing at the hero through a forest of marble pillars is coolly calculated to set the pulses racing.

Charge at Feather River, The ○

1953, US, 96 mins, colour
Dir: Gordon Douglas
Stars: Guy Madison, Frank Lovejoy Helen Westcott, Vera Miles
Rating: ★★★

Arrows to the left of you, arrows to the right of you. And if you weren't careful, you might have got one in the eye when you first saw this personable action film, for it was originally released in 3-D. Guy Madison and Frank Lovejoy make forthright leads while the supporting cast is full of gritty humour – notably from Dick Wesson, a 'Scat' comedian who should gone further in films. As the girls kidnapped by Indians, both Helen Westcott and Vera Miles prove more than mere ciphers in the story. Max Steiner's music skilfully underscores some of the best action scenes that director Gordon Douglas ever shot.

Charge is Murder, The ○

(aka: Twilight of Honor)
1964, US, 116 mins, b/w
Dir: Boris Sagal
Stars: Richard Chamberlain, Claude Rains, Joan Blackman, Nick Adams
Rating: ★★

Richard Chamberlain's first big film role after his success as *Dr Kildare* casts him as a knight-in-armour lawyer defending a young hothead (Nick Adams) accused of murdering his wife's lover. As the wayward teenage wife, Joey Heatherton gives off strong echoes of the early Marilyn Monroe; while veteran Claude Rains scores as a wise and witty legal eagle on the hero's side. Veteran cowboy star Pat Buttram (remember him as Gene Autry's partner in countless minor Westerns?) has a most unusual role, giving him a chance to reveal genuine ability beneath that homely grin.

Charge of the Light Brigade, The ○

1936, US, 115 mins, b/w
Dir: Michael Curtiz
Stars: Errol Flynn, Olivia de Havilland, Patric Knowles, Donald Crisp, David Niven
Rating: ★★★

This legendary Hollywood epic has little to do with historical fact and everything to do with thrilling action featuring legendary swashbuckler Errol Flynn. The picture has everything: glamour, excitement, romance (with Olivia de Havilland – Flynn's romantic partner in many an adventure), incredibly realistic battle scenes and some breathtaking stunts. Director Michael Curtiz keeps the whole thing moving at breakneck speed – regardless of the suffering of either human or animal. In fact, Flynn said that this film was 'the toughest picture I ever made'. If you want to know what actually happened at Balaclava, you should refer to Tony Richardson's meticulously researched 1968 version, but it's not half as exciting.

Charge of the Light Brigade, The ○ ⓥ

1968, UK, 141 mins, colour
Dir: Tony Richardson
Stars: Trevor Howard, Vanessa Redgrave, David Hemmings
Rating: ★★★

The Michael Curtiz/Errol Flynn version of the fatuous suicidal charge was an almost impossible act to follow but director Tony Richardson's version of the events is an engrossing, if not vigorously exciting film. For a start, he sticks to the facts of the battle and the events that led up to it, something Hollywood didn't bother to do. Having said that, those facts are tinged by Richardson's inevitable knock at British imperialism and the arrogance of the upper classes, but given the period this seems fair comment. Acting honours go to John Gielgud as Lord Raglan and Trevor Howard as Lord Cardigan, although there are uniformly fine performances from a gallery of British acting talent. If you want gungho thrills and adventure, stick with Errol; if you want to feel that history is being relived, this is the version to watch.

Chariots of Fire ○ Ⓥ
1981, UK, 120 mins, colour
Dir: Hugh Hudson
Stars: Ben Cross, Ian Charleson, Nigel Havers, Alice Krige, Ian Holm, John Gielgud
Rating: ★★★★★

Winner of four Academy Awards and nominated for four others, this stirring story of the battle between two Olympic runners from different social and ethnic backgrounds hit an unexpected box-office bullseye. Director Hugh Hudson had a solid background in shooting commercials, but this was his auspicious feature film debut. John Gielgud and Lindsay Anderson had wonderful cameos as anti-semitic Cambridge officials, but many considered that Ian Holm, as a professorial coach, was robbed of his best supporting actor Oscar when it was awarded to Gielgud for *Arthur*. Patriotic flag-waving, pretty photography and a memorable score by Vangelis.

Charley Moon ☉
1956, UK, 92 mins, colour
Dir: Guy Hamilton
Stars: Max Bygraves, Dennis Price, Shirley Eaton
Rating: ★★

This British showbusiness musical from the Fifties, directed by Guy Hamilton, is often phoney and frequently embarrassing, with a poor script and cardboard characters. However, there are redeeming features: Max Bygraves, who is thoroughly likeable in the title role of the ex-national serviceman who goes into variety and, reluctantly leaving his less talented friend Harold behind, leaps up the ladder to stardom; a good cast – Dennis Price (as Harold), Shirley Eaton, Michael Medwin, Eric Sykes and Bill Fraser among them; one good song –

'Out of Town'; and some nice photography by the distinguished Jack Hildyard.

Charley's Aunt ○
1941, US, 81 mins, b/w
Dir: George Seaton
Stars: Jack Benny, Anne Baxter, Kay Francis, James Ellison, Laird Cregar, Edmund Gwenn
Rating: ★★★

Jack Benny enjoys one of his finest screen hours in this rollicking, fast-paced version of Brandon Thomas's oft-filmed play. Playing with enthusiasm, and romping crazily along his laughter route as an over-aged Oxford undergraduate in 1890, forced to masquerade as a rich Brazilian lady, Benny takes the fullest advantage of the chance to handle a straight farcical assignment without recourse to his radio retinue of writing wisecrackers. A marvellous supporting cast includes one or two players on the brink of Hollywood stardom.

Charley's Big-Hearted Aunt ○
1940, UK, 76 mins, b/w
Dir: Walter Forde
Stars: Arthur Askey, Richard Murdoch, Phyllis Calvert, Graham Moffatt
Rating: ★★

Brandon Thomas's famous farce about an undergraduate forced to invent, and imitate, a South American aunt was re-tailored to the talents of the two stars, on the strength of their great success in the hit radio series *Band Waggon*. Stalwarts of the British comedy film, between 1935 and 1945, plump Graham Moffatt and doddery Moore Marriott, are on hand to add to the fun, and the heroine is Phyllis Calvert, who was appearing in her second film.

Charley Varrick ◐
1973, US, 111 mins, colour
Dir: Don Siegel
Stars: Walter Matthau, Joe Don Baker, Felicia Farr, Andy Robinson, Sheree North
Rating: ★★★

This highly-rated Don Siegel-directed thriller pulled off the rare double of delighting critics and public alike. Walter Matthau – how pleasurable to see him break away from comedy for a change – brings his own laconic brand of charm to Charley Varrick, a small-time bank robber who suddenly and, to him unexpectedly, hits it big to the tune of more than $750,000. The drawback is it's Mafia money, and

Charley and his young partner soon have a syndicate hit-man on their trail. Matthau's gift with throwaway lines is too good to be wasted altogether and Siegel ensures that humour isn't completely neglected. And the minor characters are all fully rounded people, from Joe Don Baker's fastidious killer (faintly reminiscent of Richard Widmark in *Kiss of Death*) called Molly, through Marjorie Bennett's eccentric old dear ('that's mine: an obscene call, I expect') to Sheree North's blackmailing nymphomaniac photographer.

Charlotte's Web ☉
1972, US, 85 mins, colour
Dir: Charles A Nichols, Iwao Takamoto
Rating: ★★★

A feature cartoon of some charm chronicling the adventures of a pig, Wilbur, and his friend Charlotte the spider, whose magic web-weaving not only saves him from being chopped into streaky bacon, but makes him famous throughout the land. The scene-stealer is a rat called Templeton, voiced by Paul Lynde, who has all the best lines.

Charly ○ Ⓥ
1968, US, 106 mins, colour
Dir: Ralph Nelson
Stars: Cliff Robertson, Claire Bloom, Leon Janney
Rating: ★★★

Too much science, like crime, it seems, doesn't pay. Thus Charly, a moron converted to near-genius by a brain operation, finds he must revert in a short time to his former self. Meanwhile, he has fallen in love with the teacher who has set the cycle in motion. Although director Ralph Nelson's treatment of this tricky theme verges on the pedestrian, first-rate performances by Cliff Robertson and Claire Bloom bring out all the heartbreak and frustration involved and turn the film into a near-classic of its kind. Robertson won an Best Actor Oscar for his portrayal, and the film was an unexpected winner with the public as well.

Chase, The ◐
1966, US, 135 mins, colour
Dir: Arthur Penn
Stars: Marlon Brando, Jane Fonda, Robert Redford, Angie Dickinson
Rating: ★★

Arthur Penn, who later made *Bonnie and Clyde* and *Little Big Man*, treads a gory, brutal path in this high-powered look at the warped, evil inhabitants of an American town, and the comparatively clean convict on the run they

C

seek to destroy. Although basically unbelievable, the film remains utterly holding throughout, extremely well made and quite beautifully photographed in colour, especially in one scene where an escaped prisoner runs across an irrigated field at sunset. The acting is often very good, particularly from James Fox, getting an amazingly natural American accent for a British actor. Action is over-bloody.

Chase, The ● ⓥ
1994, US, 89 mins, colour
Dir: Adam Rifkin
Stars: Charlie Sheen, Kristy Swanson
Rating: ★★

There are some good moments but lots of chances missed in this action comedy which at least lives up to its title by spending 95 per cent of its footage on one car chase. Charlie Sheen, convicted of an armed robbery he was nowhere near, flees from justice, is unluckily trapped by two local cops and grabs the nearest bystander (Kristy Swanson) as hostage, finding out later that she's the daughter of the richest man in the state. The chase starts well with lots of incident, but really needs to sustain the serio-comic mayhem on the freeway at a blood-surging rate if it's to carry us along for the ride. Nor do we believe for a moment kidnapper and hostage making love at the wheel at 80 miles an hour after she has fallen for his innocence – quite apart from it putting the brake on the thrills and spills. Given the stop-go pace, credibility takes a back seat long before the end, despite a personable performance by Sheen himself. You might also spot a guest shot from Cary Elwes as a newscaster to whom spontaneity is a complete stranger.

Chase a Crooked Shadow ◑
1957, UK, 87 mins, b/w
Dir: Michael Anderson
Stars: Anne Baxter, Richard Todd, Herbert Lom
Rating: ★★★★

Probably director Michael Anderson's best film, this is one of those marvellous Fifties mysteries in which nothing and no-one is quite what they seem. You may have a hard time sorting out the plot twists before the final solution arrives, especially as Anderson and stars Anne Baxter, Richard Todd and Herbert Lom do their best to mislead you at every twist and turn.

Chato's Land ●
1971, US/Spain, 100 mins, colour
Dir: Michael Winner

Stars: Charles Bronson, Jack Palance, Richard Basehart, James Whitmore
Rating: ★

An excessively unpleasant Western on a revenge theme, with Charles Bronson as the half-Apache stalking the posse who are supposed to be hunting him, after they rape his woman and burn his friend. One of Bronson's victims is knifed in the neck, another scalped, a third lassoed with a rattlesnake and a fourth clubbed to death with a rock. Gratuitous violence is certainly not to be sniffed at by director Michael Winner but, to his credit, he does get veteran bad guy Jack Palance to give his best performance in a while as the ex-confederate officer who leads the posse.

Chattahoochee ● ⓥ
1989, US, 97 mins, colour
Dir: Mick Jackson
Stars: Gary Oldman, Dennis Hopper, Frances McDormand, Pamela Reed, Ned Beatty
Rating: ★★

Disregard the upbeat-sounding title. This is a grim and harrowing docudrama, slowly steered along by its director, about the horrendous treatment of inmates at an institution for the criminally insane. Gary Oldman is just fine (as is his – localised – American accent) as Emmett, a Korean War veteran who is sent to Chattahoochee after going berserk and shooting up the neighbourhood. Gradually coming to his senses inside, he befriends another patient (Dennis Hopper) and begins a furtive campaign of letters to his sister (Pamela Reed) to try to get publicity on the weekly bearings and torture to which the inmates have to submit at the hands of sadistic guards. It's horrifying to realise that something out of medieval times could still exist as recently as 1955 (Emmett didn't get out until 1959). But the film perhaps over-emphasises these conditions, making the catalogue of filth and ill-treatment too much for the eye.

Cheap Detective, The ○
1978, US, 92 mins, colour
Dir: Robert Moore
Stars: Peter Falk, James Coco, Louise Fletcher, John Houseman, Nicol Williamson, Dom DeLuise
Rating: ★★

Everybody thinks they can do a parody of Humphrey Bogart movies and writer Neil Simon is no exception. But the magic of the original material is strong and resists in stubborn style, making this no more than a mild and genial parody of both *Casablanca* and

The Maltese Falcon. Peter Falk lays on the Bogey stuff as thick as treacle, and a formidable cast contributes some good laughs along the way, not least John Houseman who settles well into the Sydney Greenstreet tradition.

Cheaper by the Dozen ○
1950, US, 85 mins, colour
Dir: Walter Lang
Stars: Clifton Webb, Jeanne Crain, Myrna Loy, Edgar Buchanan
Rating: ★★★★

Warm, tender, human and funny and very much along the lines of the famous *Life With Father* (although this is even better), this is the real-life story, set in 1921, of an eccentric time and motion expert, his 12 children and his Victorian-style household run with all the precision of his office. First-rate performances by Clifton Webb and Myrna Loy as father and mother shine like jewels in the midst of Leon Shamroy's glowing colour photography. Few cameramen were as adept at capturing the nostalgic glow of a time gone by. *Cheaper by the Dozen* was so popular that it gave rise to a sequel two years later, *Belles on Their Toes,* again with Myrna Loy.

Checking Out ◑
1989, US, 98 mins, colour
Dir: David Leland
Stars: Jeff Daniels, Melanie Mayron, Michael Tucker, Ann Magnuson
Rating: ★

A lightweight black comedy about the American obsession with death, which was examined decades earlier with sharper and funnier humour in *Send Me No Flowers*. This is a couple of good chuckles, but is mostly pretty weak. Jeff Daniels takes the Rock Hudson part as the young executive who sees his best friend keel over with a heart attack and panics himself into thinking he's about to follow suit. Covering himself with more tubes and plastic than a hospital operating theatre, he can no longer think about making love to his wife, getting on with his job or taking care of his children: he is preoccupied with 'checking out'. Daniels lacks the controlled panic of the hypochondriac and director David Leland over-paces it all, injecting it with shots from wide-angle lenses to emphasise its surreal and comic qualities. Chances are you'll fall asleep before Daniels comes to his senses.

Cheers for Miss Bishop ○
1941, US, 95 mins, b/w
Dir: Tay Garnett

Stars: Martha Scott, William Gargan, Edmund Gwenn, Sterling Holloway, Sidney Blackmer
Rating: ★★★

Martha Scott has to age 50 years in this nicely directed chronicle of a schoolma'am's life. It comes out as a sort of *Goodbye Miss Chips*, strong on the atmosphere of a small mid-western town in the late 19th century, and with excellent music by Edward Ward (who was nominated for an Oscar) and photography by Hal Mohr.

Cheyenne Social Club, The ◐
1973, US, 103 mins, colour
Dir: Gene Kelly
Stars: James Stewart, Henry Fonda, Shirley Jones, Sue Ane Langdon
Rating: ★★★

A comedy-Western of great charm, mainly because of its two stars. James Stewart and Henry Fonda are the two wandering cowboys who rub their hands in glee at the prospect of inheriting The Cheyenne Social Club, and then rub their heads in despair as they discover the truth – that the Club is the town's bordello. There's some nice exchanges of dialogue between Stewart and Fonda, especially during their long trek to Cheyenne, but director Gene Kelly flexes fewer muscles than he perhaps should to make this gentle entertainment more dynamic.

Chicago Joe and the Showgirl ◐ Ⓥ
1989, UK, 103 mins, colour
Dir: Bernard Rose
Stars: Kiefer Sutherland, Emily Lloyd, Patsy Kensit, Keith Allen, Liz Fraser, Alexandra Pigg
Rating: ★★

An almost surrealistic treatment of a grim and fascinating real-life murder case. It could have worked too, but severe script problems and a rare dud performance from Emily Lloyd are damaging minus factors that undermine director Bernard Rose's imagination at every turn. The dialogue is studded with lines that either raise a nervous titter or simply don't advance the drama. And Lloyd's impish portrayal of the showgirl who eggs on an American soldier to murder never captures the vicious, unbalanced nature you expect to see in a character who is clearly meant to revel in the blood and guts of it all. The baby-faced Kiefer Sutherland is convincing by comparison as the gang-connected lieutenant who may not be what he

seems; and Patsy Kensit even better as his English rose on the side.

Chief Crazy Horse ○
(aka: Valley of Fury)
1955, US, 88 mins, colour
Dir: George Sherman
Stars: Victor Mature, Suzan Ball, John Lund, Ray Danton, Dennis Weaver
Rating: ★★

Director George Sherman holds one's interest in this Western, which tells the story of one of the greatest Indian chiefs and his ultimately doomed alliance with the white man. The large cast includes David Janssen, in the days before he became one of television's busiest actors.

Children of a Lesser God ◐
1986, US, 110 mins, colour
Dir: Randa Haines
Stars: William Hurt, Marlee Matlin, Piper Laurie, Philip Bosco
Rating: ★★★

Although it struggles a bit when William Hurt has to 'verbalise' deaf-mute co-star Marlee Matlin's dialogue, this is otherwise a throat-grippingly successful love story of a distinctly unconventional nature. Matlin's wonderfully expressive face enables her to give a performance that won her an Academy Award, while Hurt and Piper Laurie (who plays Matlin's mother) were also nominated for Oscars. Based on the equally triumphant play, this film version benefits from sensitive direction by Randa Haines that brings out both the comic and tragic aspects of the affair between teacher Hurt and his 'special pupil' and from glistening Metrocolor photography of the coldly beautiful Canadian landscape by John Seale.

Children of the Corn ● Ⓥ
1984, US, 93 mins, colour
Dir: Fritz Kiersch
Stars: Peter Horton, Linda Hamilton, John Franklin, R G Armstrong
Rating: ★★

This expansion of a short story by ace horror writer Stephen King calls for a firm suspension of logic on the part of its audience and plants its mayhem on familiar ground. Somewhere in Nebraska, a band of psychotic children have killed all adults and established a religious community worshipping a mysterious deity of the corn fields. You'll cull some chills and nervous chuckles from subsequent goings-on which carry echoes of *The Dark Secret of Harvest Home* and *The Wicker Man*. The real star of the film is Craig Stearns' art

direction, which suggests a hidden evil around every corner.

Children's Hour, The ◐
(aka: The Loudest Whisper)
1961, US, 107 mins, b/w
Dir: William Wyler
Stars: Audrey Hepburn, Shirley MacLaine, James Garner, Miriam Hopkins, Fay Bainter
Rating: ★★★★★

The relaxation of censorship codes meant that Hollywood could really do justice to Lillian Hellman's famous play about the effects that a child's malicious whispers about two teachers' alleged lesbian relationship have on the lives of the people concerned. And, with William Wyler at the helm (he'd directed a watered-down version, *These Three*, nearly 30 years earlier), a superb film resulted. Five Oscar nominations resulted in nothing from a film industry still slightly sensitive about giving awards to films with such themes. Audrey Hepburn is excellent and Shirley MacLaine unbearably touching. The moving ending is perfectly handled by the director.

Child's Play ● Ⓥ
1988, US, 91 mins, colour
Dir: Tom Holland
Stars: Catherine Hicks, Chris Sarandon, Brad Dourif, Alex Vincent
Rating: ★

Horror films almost always ask us to suspend our disbelief for the chills to bite. But here's a would-be chiller that's just too silly for that to happen. A crazed killer, with some belief in occult powers, transfers his soul to the body of a doll before he dies. Quite why the doll doesn't come to life before it's bought by a child's mother from a tramp is only one of the mysteries of this film but, under the name of Chuckie, he then sets out to revenge himself on the partner who betrayed him and the cop who gunned him down. There's actually more to the plot, but it's even more preposterous, culminating in the doll gradually becoming human, thus giving the heroes a chance to kill it. Director Tom Holland finally brings this lame nag home via several false climaxes as it staggers towards the 90-minute mark. Chuckie's worth a chuckle here: no more. Better, though, than the sequels that followed.

Chiltern Hundreds, The ○
(aka: The Amazing Mr Beecham)
1949, UK, 84 mins, b/w

C

Dir: John Paddy Carstairs
Stars: Cecil Parker, A E Matthews, David Tomlinson, Lana Morris
Rating: ★★★

A classic film comedy with an Ealing touch, about a young viscount (David Tomlinson) who attempts to get out of service in the Army and marry his American fiancee by announcing that he is standing as a candidate for Parliament. There's a rich characterisation from A E Matthews as Lord Lister and a brief glimpse of Anthony Steel as an adjutant.

China Girl ● Ⓥ

1987, US, 90 mins, colour
Dir: Abel Ferrara
Stars: James Russo, Richard Panebianco, Sari Chang, David Caruso, Russell Wong
Rating: ★

This ludicrously overpumped melodrama emerges as a pop promo video cross between *The Godfather* and *East Side Story*. Young lovers from the opposite sides of the Chinese-Italian tracks meet meltingly at one of those ghetto discos where everybody seems to wear vests, and are promptly engulfed in gang warfare whose hotheaded elements are supposed to be kept in check by their own side. The characters do little but scream and shout at each other, beat each other with heavy metal or blast each other bloodily with heavier artillery. However viciously beaten, though, they all get up and run away when the cops arrive. Director Ferrara tops it off with overdone lighting effects and portentous close-ups of inanimate objects. His film, very slow for its running time, is dedicated to the people of Chinatown and Little Italy, but we should think they'd want to give it back.

China Seas ○

1935, US, 90 mins, b/w
Dir: Tay Garnett
Stars: Clark Gable, Jean Harlow, Wallace Beery, Rosalind Russell, Robert Benchley, Akim Tamiroff
Rating: ★★★

The stars are an entertainment in themselves in this rousing romantic adventure with Cap'n Clark Gable trying to hang on to his cargo of gold against China Seas Pirates, as well as dealing with contrasting women on board. Film-maker, traveller and sometime round-the-world yachtsman Tay Garnett directs with a good sense of atmosphere and locale. The sea scenes are rousingly done, and such big names

as Gable, Jean Harlow, Wallace Beery, Rosalind Russell, Robert Benchley and Akim Tamiroff all catch the eye. Acting honours, however, go to veteran MGM star Lewis Stone.

China Syndrome, The ◐ Ⓥ

1979, US, 122 mins, colour
Dir: James Bridges
Stars: Jane Fonda, Jack Lemmon, Michael Douglas, Scott Brady, Jame Hampton
Rating: ★★★

What went wrong at the nuclear power plant? What caused the 'second shudder' when a valve stuck and a crisis occurred? Chief technician Jack Lemmon, radical photographer Michael Douglas and TV reporter Jane Fonda are determined to find out. The ensuing developments form a social conscience thriller along the lines of a nuclear *Coma*. Even if you have difficulty in following what's going on, the tension propels the story along by itself and the climax, although contrived and drawn out, is unbearably suspenseful.

Chinatown ● Ⓥ

1974, US, 131 mins, colour
Dir: Roman Polanski
Stars: Jack Nicholson, Faye Dunaway, John Huston, Perry Lopez, John Hillerman, Diane Ladd
Rating: ★★★

Roman Polanski's tough, downbeat contribution to the private eye thriller cycle. Jack Nicholson brings his own brand of cynical integrity to the role of a small-time detective in Los Angeles, 1937, who takes on a small matrimonial case, only to find it inevitably escalating into something that involves corruption on a city-wide scale. Polanski keeps his film scrupulously in period, not only in looks, but the way it's made as a whole, the only concessions to the Seventies being the rugged dialogue, and some fringe violence – our hero has his nose slit to warn him off. Watch out for the director himself in a small but memorable role as the vicious, knife-wielding hood. And John Huston brings his own brand unique of affable corruption to the role of a millionaire with much to hide.

Chisum ○ Ⓥ

1970, US, 110 mins, colour
Dir: Andrew V McLaglen
Stars: John Wayne, Forrest Tucker, Ben Johnson, Bruce Cabot, Christopher George, Richard Jaeckel
Rating: ★★

All action but not much heart, this is a routine latter-day John Wayne Western in which women hardly get a look in. Sideline attractions include rousing music by Dominic Frontiere (with the title song by Merle Haggard) and more Hollywood Western veterans than we have space to list! But a sense of danger is missing, robbing the film of any edge, even though it's set in the 1870s against the complex and fascinating history of the Lincoln County wars.

Chitty Chitty Bang Bang ⊙ Ⓥ

1968, US/UK, 145 mins, colour
Dir: Ken Hughes
Stars: Dick Van Dyke, Sally Ann Howes, Lionel Jeffries, Gert Frobe, Anna Quayle, Benny Hill
Rating: ★★

A rather weak British musical despite being produced by the James Bond team, co-scripted by Roald Dahl, and based on a collection of stories by Ian Fleming. It includes such familiar 007 faces as Desmond Llewellyn and Gert Frobe, but in contrast to the James Bond films, the special effects are wobbly and the score a hit and miss affair. The story is a sugar-coated piece of whimsy about an amazing vintage car – a 'fine four-fendered friend' to chirpy Dick Van Dyke and two precocious kids – that can take to water or the air with the greatest of ease. The best thing about the film are the amazing sets and the bizarre mechanical contraptions of Rowland Emmett, especially the sausage and egg machine. In the human cast, Frobe and Anna Quayle make the most of their roles as villains.

Choirboys, The ●

1977, US, 119 mins, colour
Dir: Robert Aldrich
Stars: Charles Durning, Louis Gossett Jr, Perry King, Randy Quaid, James Woods, Don Stroud
Rating: ★★

Imagine turning over a stone in some dark corner of the *Hill Street Blues* precinct, and what crawls from underneath might well be the 'choirboys'. The title refers to ten maverick policemen on night duty in Los Angeles; and, from the start, shock, horror and melodrama run rampant as some of Hollywood's most abrasive modern 'tough guy' actors, including Charles Durning, Burt Young, James Woods, Don Stroud, Robert Webber, Louis Gossett, Perry King and Randy Quaid, lend their talents to a series of darkly eccentric character studies.

Chorus Line, A ◐
1985, US, 111 mins, colour
Dir: Richard Attenborough
Stars: Michael Douglas, Terrence Mann,
Alyson Reed
Rating: ★★

They should have got Bob Fosse to re-make this one. Instead, they hired Britain's Oscar-winning Richard Attenborough, who had never made a musical before and the result is, well, just unexciting. Attenborough takes the show that set the stage alight and, in this curiously flat version, dampens its spirit. Talented directors often miss out on the sheer adrenalin-pumping verve of a hit musical – think of John Huston and *Annie* – and, in the treat-ment here, the performances seem oddly muffled. The success of the in-sipid Cassie (Alyson Reed) is even less fair than in the stage show; frankly she's a bit of a pain. In the show's big number, 'What I Did for Love', the camera angles make you fear more for her safety in high heels on a high iron stairway than attentive to the lyrics of the song.

Chorus of Disapproval, A
○ Ⓥ
1988, UK, 100 mins, colour
Dir: Michael Winner
Stars: Anthony Hopkins, Jeremy Irons,
Richard Briers, Patsy Kensit, Jenny
Seagrove, Sylvia Syms
Rating: ★★★

Any seaside rep would give its eye teeth to have a company like this: Jeremy Irons, Jenny Seagrove, Patsy Kensit, Richard Briers, Gareth Hunt, Prunella Scales, Lionel Jeffries, Sylvia Syms and Alexandra Pigg. The com-pany's director is none other than Anthony Hopkins, sporting an impec-cable Welsh accent (as well he might) in this adaptation of Alan Ayckbourn's play which, under Michael Winner's direction, provides pretty good fun and proves, perhaps, that Winner's real tal-ent lies in comedy. Hopkins is superb as the little Welsh Hitler, Irons vastly amusing as the shy Yorkshire widower turned local Lothario. But no-one can take the film away from Prunella Scales as Hopkins' pudding's wife, having a late, late fling with Irons. Occasionally, the film's characters grow too large for life, but overall the writer and direc-tor's affection for the subject shines through. No great movie, but very British and Winner's best effort in ages.

Chosen, The
See: Holocaust 2000

Christine ● Ⓥ
1983, US, 111 mins, colour
Dir: John Carpenter
Stars: John Stockwell, Alexandra Paul,
Harry Dean Stanton, Robert Prosky,
Christine Belford, Keith Gordon
Rating: ★★★

This is the one about the demon car and it may make you wary of walking the streets at night. Christine is a beau-ty all right. Red as the devil, all gleaming chrome and dazzling head-lamps, playing tunes on the radio to express her thoughts. But woe betide anyone who comes between her and her young master Arnie. This is a film that believes strongly in action, and its scenario never misses a chance to aim for the lowest common denominator. But, after a longish period of delineat-ing Arnie's many enemies that Christine will eventually take to the grinder's, there are few dull spots in the film's lengthy running time, although the final duel between Christine and the excavator doesn't have quite the variation of excitement that it might have done. Arnie is well played by Keith Gordon, who splendidly creates two quite separate characters.

Christmas Carol, A
See: Scrooge [1951]

Christmas Holiday ○
1944, US, 92 mins, b/w
Dir: Robert Siodmak
Stars: Deanna Durbin, Gene Kelly,
Richard Whorf, Gale Sondergaard
Rating: ★★★

With a title like this, and Gene Kelly co-starring with Deanna Durbin, this has to be, you would think, a warm and happy musical. Well you would be wrong, especially with director Robert Siodmak, king of Forties' *film noir*, at the helm, working from a source novel by Somerset Maugham. Kelly is excellent as the smooth rotten apple obsessed with Durbin's cabaret singer. Pretty unusual.

Christmas In Connecticut ○
1945, US, 101 mins, b/w
Dir: Peter Godfrey
Stars: Barbara Stanwyck, Dennis
Morgan, Sydney Greenstreet, Reginald
Gardiner, S Z Sakall, Una O'Connor
Rating: ★★

A nostalgic if corny treat. Barbara Stanwyck is the lady with the double life – the chic spinster newspaper columnist who, when ordered by her boss to entertain a war hero at Christmas with her family at home on a Connecticut farm, must then rustle up aforementioned family and home. 'I don't have a farm,' she admits from her New York apartment. 'I don't even have a window box!' And thereby hangs the comic thread of this festive fable.

Christmas In July ☉
1940, US, 67 mins, b/w
Dir: Preston Sturges
Stars: Dick Powell, Ellen Drew, Raymond
Walburn, Al Bridge, William Demarest
Rating: ★★★

Ace comedy writer-director Preston Sturges may have got the germ of the idea for this fun-feast from The Three Stooges' short *Healthy, Wealthy and Dumb*. There, of course, the resemblance ends. This is a joyously scripted, helter-skelter, occasionally talky but by-and-large hilar-ious tale of a man who thinks he's won a fortune in a competition and proceeds to go on the spending spree to end them all. Dick Powell took further steps away from his image as a song-and-dance man, while such Sturges regulars as Raymond Walburn, William Demarest and Franklin Pangborn provide charac-teristic support.

Christmas Martian, The ○
1971, Canada, 63 mins, colour
Dir: Bernard Gosselin
Rating: ★★★

Charming Canadian film about two small children who befriend a Martian stranded in the snow, and help him mend his spaceship. Shades of *E.T.*

Christmas Story, A ☉ Ⓥ
1983, US, 98 mins, colour
Dir: Bob Clark
Stars: Melinda Dillon, Darren McGavin,
Peter Billingsley
Rating: ★★★★

Director Bob Clark, best known for his offensive, juvenile sex comedies *Porky's* and *Porky's II: The Next Day*, turned in quite a sweet festive family film here. Set around the misadventures of an American family in the 1940s as Christmas approaches, its cast is won-derful (especially Darren McGavin as a father battling with a smoke-belching furnace) and the laughs come non-stop, in wry, very American fashion. A clas-sic of its kind.

Christmas Tree, The ○
1969, US, 110 mins, colour
Dir: Terence Young
Stars: William Holden, Virna Lisi, Brook
Fuller
Rating: ★

C

Terence Young, who made several of the James Bond action films, got right away from all that when he wrote and directed this king-sized weepie about a young boy dying from radiation poisoning. The child acquires two tame wolves to ease him through his dying days, and they're very appealing. The script, however, could have been stiffened by draining away some of its unnecessary sentiment.

Christopher Columbus O
1948, UK, 104 mins, colour
Dir: David Macdonald
Stars: Fredric March, Francis L Sullivan, Florence Eldridge, Kathleen Ryan, Derek Bond, Felix Aylmer
Rating: ★★

A lavishly-mounted, British-made account of Columbus' efforts in the late 15th century to prove that the world is round. There's too much talk and not enough action until near the end, but sterling performances come from Fredric March, Derek Bond, Felix Aylmer and that 200-pound master of menace, Francis L Sullivan. This Technicolor epic fared no better at the box-office than the two financial flops made of the Columbus story in more recent times.

Christopher Columbus: The Discovery O ⓥ
1992, US, 121 mins, colour
Dir: John Glen
Stars: George Corraface, Rachel Ward, Marlon Brando, Robert Davi, Tom Selleck, Catherine Zeta Jones
Rating: ★★

Halfway between a history lesson and a Sinbad film, this harks back to the days when Hollywood sailed the seven seas every other week. Never dull, John Glen's film hurtles through history at a rate of knots. Marlon Brando mumbles in his finest Fifties' fashion as Torquemada. A grumpy Tom Selleck gets a laugh just by coming on in a crown as the Spanish king. A girlish Rachel Ward is Queen Isabella and George Corraface flashes his teeth a lot as Columbus, going through such violent mood and personality changes (one minute dashing adventurer, the next ranting zealot) as to make you think there must have been more of the film than appears in this version. Rather more credibility is lent by Oliver Cotton (CC's right-hand-man), Nigel Terry (a scowling bad guy) and Robert Davi as CC's fellow-captain; Davi's last line is worth staying in your seats for.

Chuka O
1967, US/UK, 105 mins, colour
Dir: Gordon Douglas
Stars: Rod Taylor, Ernest Borgnine, John Mills, Luciana Paluzzi, Louis Hayward
Rating: ★★

An intense, if rather slow-moving Western. The ever-reliable suspense of impending Indian attack on a fort becomes stronger as the climax of the film draws near.

Chump at Oxford, A ⊙
1940, US, 63 mins, b/w
Dir: Alfred Goulding
Stars: Stan Laurel, Oliver Hardy
Rating: ★★★★

In 1940 Laurel and Hardy returned to producer Hal Roach, with whom they'd made their best films, for two short features, *A Chump at Oxford* and *Saps at Sea*. A burlesque on *A Yank at Oxford*, this joyous comedy finds the boys given the chance of an Oxford education after foiling a gang of bank robbers. But they soon become the butt of endless practical jokes from a gang of bullies led by Peter Cushing, in one of his earliest screen roles. The material is delightful in both sections and even touching at the end. Certainly the last great Laurel and Hardy comedy.

Cimarron O
1960, US, 142 mins, colour
Dir: Anthony Mann
Stars: Glenn Ford, Maria Schell
Rating: ★★

This is another case of a remake being a pale shadow of the original. The 1931 version had a huge budget, thousands of extras and won a trio of Oscars and although it looks a bit dated now, it's still a better film than this one. Set around the time of the Oklahoma land rush: Glenn Ford is the homesteader who, cheated out of his land, becomes sheriff of a new town and also runs the local newspaper. Despite a strong cast that includes Ford, Maria Schell, Anne Baxter, Russ Tamblyn and Vic Morrow and direction from Anthony Mann, this is a formula cowboy film that does little justice to the original novel.

Cimarron Kid, The O
1951, US, 83 mins, colour
Dir: Budd Boetticher
Stars: Audie Murphy, James Best, Yvette Dugay, Hugh O'Brian
Rating: ★★

The story of Bill Doolin and the Daltons - one of the most exciting true

tales in Western history - has been filmed several times, notably with Randolph Scott in 1949. Alas, in real life Doolin came to a less happy end than the one depicted here. Not one of director Budd Boetticher's best westerns, but there is some efficiently staged excitement and blazing Technicolor photography.

Cincinnati Kid, The O ⓥ
1966, US, 113 mins, colour
Dir: Norman Jewison
Stars: Steve McQueen, Edward G Robinson, Ann-Margret, Karl Malden, Tuesday Weld, Joan Blondell
Rating: ★★★

If you're a card-playing fanatic, or a gambler of any kind, this Thirties' drama will probably wind up your nerves, bring all your sweat glands into action, rivet you to the screen and give you no end of enjoyment. Despite the starry cast, though, the human element to the drama is largely missing. The atmosphere is there, but seems to have gone stale on us. The actors do their best without really shining, but director Norman Jewison, who does keep the action moving at a steady clip, seems to have no overall hold on his subject, giving us no theme to get involved with. Steve McQueen is the poker-playing kid, but he gets a raw deal from the script. Cutting a few more aces are Tuesday Weld (as McQueen's quiet country mistress) and Joan Blondell, while Edward G Robinson lords over all in more ways than one as 'The Man', whom McQueen has to beat to get to the top of the red-hot poker tree. The final game between them is worth anybody's stake to an armchair view.

Cinderella ⊙ ⓥ
1950, US, 75 mins, colour
Dir: Wilfred Jackson, Hamilton Luske, Clyde Geronimi
Voice stars: Ilene Woods, William Phipps, Eleanor Sudley, Verna Felton
Rating: ★★★

Too many human characters and not enough of Disney's delightful animals are the downside to this generally enjoyable Disney version of the fairytale classic. Never mind, every time the mice Gus and Jacques and the ferocious cat Lucifer hold centre stage, the film blazes into fire. And there's a toe-tapping score that includes the title song and the famous 'Bibbidi-Bobbidi-Boo'. The wicked stepmother and two repulsive ugly sisters (complete with Olive Oyl-type arms and legs, and huge feet) are well up to the Disney tradition for formidable female villains. What was it that Uncle Walt had against women?

Cinderfella ☉ ⓥ

1960, US, 91 mins, colour
Dir: Frank Tashlin
Stars: Jerry Lewis, Anna Maria Alberghetti, Ed Wynn, Henry Silva
Rating: ★★

Colourful Jerry Lewis pantomime romp, with Jerry as a male Cinders, and a dazzling princess, beautifully played and sung by Anna Maria Alberghetti. Henry Silva also scores as Fella's polo-playing stepbrother, but the comedy routines are sometimes overdone to the verge of tedium. Providing the music at the ball: Count Basie and his band. You'll probably get tired of this, though, long before midnight comes.

Circle of Deception ○

1960, UK, 100 mins, b/w
Dir: Jack Lee
Stars: Bradford Dillman, Suzy Parker, Harry Andrews, Robert Stephens
Rating: ★★

An agonisingly intense performance from Bradford Dillman as an Allied officer captured by the Gestapo in France and subjected to unedifying interrogation techniques highlights this tense drama. Director Jack Lee sacrifices some of the suspense by using a flashback framework but the ironic ending is worth waiting for.

Circle of Friends ◑ ⓥ

1995, UK, 102 mins, colour
Dir: Pat O'Connor
Stars: Minnie Driver, Chris O'Donnell, Colin Firth, Geraldine O'Rawe, Saffron Burrows, Alan Cumming
Rating: ★★★

Readers of the book on which this pleasant film is somewhat shakily based should be told that screenwriter Andrew Davies has one or two quite different fates in store for the characters than those originally envisaged by author Maeve Binchy. The results unnecessarily romanticise the original, which took a more jaded and shaded view of life in an Irish village and nearby Dublin University. In this version, the 'circle of friends' described by Binchy is reduced to the central trio of Irish girls who have been chums since childhood. A polyglot cast of British, American and Irish actors achieve a commendable unity of Irish accents, with Minnie Driver amazingly good in the pivotal role of Benny,

Alan Cumming splendidly slimy as her home-town suitor and Chris O'Donnell convincingly charismatic as the school sports hero for whom she falls. Good performances, then, but trite material with which Colin Firth in particular fails to cope without some embarrassment.

Circus, The ☉

1928, US, 72 mins, b/w
Dir: Charles Chaplin
Stars: Charlie Chaplin, Merna Kennedy
Rating: ★★★

Although this Charlie Chaplin film has some joyous comedy moments along the way, its pathos undoubtedly works less well than in previous Chaplin classics, such as *The Kid*. Nonetheless, the industry felt moved to offer Chaplin a special Oscar that year 'for versatility and genius in writing, directing and producing *The Circus*'. Chaplin himself, as the tramp who becomes a star clown, is still in vintage form, but there is no Mack Swain or Eric Campbell for him to play against, and the supporting cast is undeniably weaker than in many of his films.

Circus of Horrors ●

1960, UK, 91 mins, colour
Dir: Sidney Hayers
Stars: Anton Diffring, Yvonne Monlaur, Erika Remberg, Jane Hylton, Donald Pleasence, Conrad Phillips
Rating: ★★

There's a whole parade of lovely young actresses for power-mad Anton Diffring to bump off at his circus, when they get a bit grumpy at their billing on the big top marquee, in this lively shocker. These unlikely circus stars include Vanda Hudson, Erika Remberg, Yvonne Romain and Yvonne Monlaur. The gorilla gets Donald Pleasence and, indeed, there can't be many of the cast left by the time policemen Conrad Phillips and Jack Gwillim close in on Diffring in an exciting last reel.

Circus World

See: The Magnificent Showman

Cisco Pike ●

1972, US, 94 mins, colour
Dir: Bill L Norton
Stars: Kris Kristofferson, Karen Black, Gene Hackman, Harry Dean Stanton
Rating: ★★★

This gripping thriller earned an 'X' certificate from the British film censor on release in 1972 thanks to its drug-related theme and hero who's a drug pusher. Kris Kristofferson – in a role that reflects in some ways his own per-

sonality – is a singer/songwriter whose star faded with the end of the swinging Sixties. At the barrel of a gun he is forced back into the drugs scene by the bitter cop (Gene Hackman) who once arrested him, and now wants a personal pension to cushion his retirement from the force.

Citadel, The ○

1938, UK, 110 mins, b/w
Dir: King Vidor
Stars: Robert Donat, Rosalind Russell, Ralph Richardson, Rex Harrison, Emlyn Williams, Francis L Sullivan
Rating: ★★★★

Star Robert Donat, director King Vidor and the film itself were all nominated for Academy Awards. In the event, the only major award taken by this fine version of A J Cronin's medical saga was the New York Film Critics' award for best film. Extremely well adapted by a bevy of screenwriters, who included co-star Emlyn Williams, the film grips and entertains throughout, frequently touching the emotions with its skilful dialogue and persuasive direction. Ralph Richardson gives a memorable portrayal of Donat's stalwart friend, Denny, in a story peppered effectively with mini-climaxes.

Citizen Kane ○ ⓥ

1941, US, 119 mins, b/w
Dir: Orson Welles
Stars: Orson Welles, Joseph Cotten, Ray Collins, Everett Sloane, Dorothy Comingore
Rating: ★★★★★

Still on most critics' lists of the best ten films ever made, Orson Welles' towering, brilliantly edited and hypnotically entertaining jigsaw of a film is a trailblazing masterpiece that advanced the cinema by light years. Full of scenes that could be shown on their own and have the same impact, the film uses settings, light and shade (and, unusually, ceilings on its sets), to achieve realism and mood. Despite critical raves, the industry treated the movie, which surveys the rise and fall of a newspaper magnate, with considerable indifference. They gave it only one Academy Award (for the screenplay) and ignored Gregg Toland's wonderful, innovative deep-focus photography. You'll find a journey through the gates of Xanadu brings fresh rewards with each visit.

Citizens Band ○
(aka: Handle With Care)

1977, US, 100 mins, colour
Dir: Jonathan Demme

C

Stars: Paul Le Mat, Candy Clark
Rating: ★★★★★

Director Jonathan Demme has been
feted in recent years for *Married to the
Mob* and *The Silence of the Lambs*, but this
early comedy equals anything he's ever
done. Reminiscent of the films of
Frank Capra with its multitude of characters and incident, and wonderfully
emotive ending, it gives the underrated
and versatile Paul Le Mat his best role
to date as the small-town guy who tries
to hold several threads of his life together while trying to cope with wildcat
broadcasters threatening to wreck his
emergency rescue service. Demme directs with a great feeling of affection for
his characters, creating the kind of film
which leaves you with a warm feeling
at the end.

City Beneath the Sea ○

1953, US, 87 mins, colour
Dir: Budd Boetticher
Stars: Robert Ryan, Mala Powers,
Anthony Quinn, Suzan Ball
Rating: ★★

This potboiler stars Robert Ryan and
Anthony Quinn as rival deep sea
divers on the hunt for treasure in the
sunken city of Port Royal. The action
bubbles along and is enlivened by an
undersea earthquake, but is strictly studio conveyor-belt fodder.

City Beneath the Sea (1971)

See: One Hour to Domesday

City for Conquest ○

1940, US, 101 mins, b/w
Dir: Anatole Litvak
Stars: James Cagney, Ann Sheridan,
Frank Craven, Donald Crisp, Arthur
Kennedy, George Tobias
Rating: ★★★

A typical James Cagney role as (to
quote the publicity) 'a slum newsboy
who rises to fame by the power of his
chunky fists, in a city peopled with
hoodlums, frustrated do-gooders and a
few geniuses.' Actually, it's a bit more
sentimental than that, with Cagney sacrificing everything to help his brainy
brother. This role is played by Arthur
Kennedy (in his first film), foreshadowing his classic portrayal of Kirk
Douglas' brother in *Champion* nine
years later. The supporting cast is full
of surprises, from a slick-haired
Anthony Quinn, through character star
Blanche Yurka, to Elia Kazan, who
went on to become an Oscar-winning
director. The whole film is immensely
entertaining.

City Hall ● Ⓥ

1996, US, 110 mins, colour
Dir: Harold Becker
Stars: Al Pacino, John Cusack, Bridget
Fonda, Danny Aiello, Tony Franciosa
Rating: ★★★

Crime thriller specialist Harold Becker
examines corruption in high places in
this all too convincing look at life on
the line in New York. But, although
his film remains engrossing and entertaining, it never quite punches with the
weight that could have put it in the top
class. No surprise, either, as to the
identity of the chief culprit in the affair,
which will be obvious to hardened
crime fans soon after the film gets into
its stride. The beginning is excellent:
the catalyst to the action that follows,
as a policeman and drug-dealer gun
each other down in a rainswept street,
and a child gets caught in the crossfire.
Mayor Al Pacino and deputy mayor
John Cusack are sidetracked from poli-
ticking, and drawn into the affair, in
which a concealed probation report
that led to the dealer being on the
streets (he came from a Mafia family)
proves to be merely the juice escaping
from a very messy can of worms.
Good dialogue and intriguing in-fighting just see this one through.

City Heat ● Ⓥ

1984, US, 97 mins, colour
Dir: Richard Benjamin
Stars: Clint Eastwood, Burt Reynolds,
Jane Alexander, Madeline Kahn, Rip
Torn, Richard Roundtree
Rating: ★★★

A crime romp within whose framework
Clint Eastwood and Burt Reynolds can
exercise their familiar film characters.
The word 'framework' just about sums
up the plot, which is set in the early
1930s and concerns the demise of private eye Reynolds' partner and the
subsequent battle by Reynolds and cop
Eastwood (his former police colleague)
to corner the two gang leaders involved. Reynolds displays his agility,
Eastwood walks down Main Street in
the open while others fire at him from
cover, there's a lot of fairly inconsequential gunfire and a running gag
about a suitcase loaded with dynamite,
and it's all pretty enjoyable. Just don't
expect any surprises.

City Is Dark, The ○

(aka: Crime Wave)
1954, US, 74 mins, b/w
Dir: André De Toth
Stars: Gene Nelson, Sterling Hayden,
Phyllis Kirk, Ted De Corsia, Charles

Bronson
Rating: ★★★

Tough little *film noir* from Warner
Brothers, grittily directed by Andre de
Toth and full of Hollywood's shadiest
underworld types, including Jay
Novello, Ted De Corsia, James Bell,
Timothy Carey and Charles Bronson
(billed as Charles Buchinsky). Gene
Nelson, best known as a dancer, turns
in a decent job of straight acting, and
Phyllis Kirk is attractively plucky as his
wife. You may have trouble following
detective Sterling Hayden's dialogue, as
he talks with a toothpick in his mouth
for most of the film!

City Jungle, The ○

(aka: The Young Philadelphians)
1959, US, 136 mins, b/w
Dir: Vincent Sherman
Stars: Paul Newman, Barbara Rush,
Alexis Smith, Brian Keith, Robert Vaughn
Rating: ★★★

A much better title for a movie that
started life as *The Young Philadelphians*.
Paul Newman gives another of his intense, exhilarating performances as the
young legal eagle on the make. Just
how his alcoholic lawyer in *The Verdict*
might have started out) and he gets
sensitive support from lovely Barbara
Rush. The friend he defends on a
murder charge is played by Robert
(*Man from UNCLE*) Vaughn who gives
an outstanding performance that won
him an Oscar nomination.

City Lights ⊙ Ⓥ

1931, US, 85 mins, b/w
Dir: Charles Chaplin
Stars: Charlie Chaplin, Virginia Cherrill,
Florence Lee
Rating: ★★★★

Charlie Chaplin didn't always achieve
the difficult double of successful comedy and successful pathos for which he
often strove, but this film, released
silent after almost three years in the
making, was a triumph for him on both
fronts. His scenes with the blind flower
girl are genuinely touching, and the sequence in the boxing ring one of the
most hilarious in all Chaplin's distinguished contributions to the cinema.

City of Bad Men ○

1953, US, 82 mins, colour
Dir: Harmon Jones
Stars: Jeanne Crain, Dale Robertson,
Richard Boone, Lloyd Bridges
Rating: ★★

Large-scale, off-beat Western about
gangs planning to run off with the pro-

ceeds from the Fitzsimmons-Corbett heavyweight fight. John Day, the young actor who plays Corbett, was well used to sparring for the cameras. He also 'fought' Kirk Douglas in *Champion* and Tony Curtis in *The Square Jungle*. This is ambitious but lacks inspiration and there's no central drive in the script.

City of Industry ● Ⓥ
1996, US, 97 mins, colour
Dir: John Irvin
Stars: Harvey Keitel, Stephen Dorff, Famke Janssen, Timothy Hutton, Wade Dominguez, Dana Barron
Rating: ★★

Thieves fall out. Same old same old. This specimen, though, is very dark, full of merciless men, plus a well-achieved and over-riding feeling of heat, even in the hours of darkness within which most of the action takes place. Keitel plays a retired criminal, living in wealthy anonymity, but called out of retirement to help his younger brother (Hutton) in one last heist. Jorge (Dominguez) and cocky young wheel-man Skip (Dorff) make up the gang, who bring off a million-dollar jewel robbery. Dorff, already resolved to take the lot, shoots Dominguez and Hutton, but a wounded Keitel escapes. With the help of Dominguez's widow (Janssen), he tracks Dorff down. Straightforward, doomy, bloody, hard-nut stuff this, in which no one answers questions straight away: pregnant pauses, sleaze and violence rule. Keitel is well at home in these surroundings and doesn't have to smile – though he's entitled to when Dorff shoots his own remaining henchman to go clear with the boodle.

City of Joy ○ Ⓥ
1992, UK/US/India, 134 mins, colour
Dir: Roland Joffe
Stars: Patrick Swayze, Pauline Collins, Art Malik, Shabana Azmi, Om Puri
Rating: ★★★★★

Director Roland Joffe scores an emotional bullseye with this far-away movie. Poor as they are, the peasants of Calcutta are still oppressed by a local godfather, who controls their work and takes their protection money. Newly arrived in the City of Joy, one of the slum villages where the poor live, is Hassan Pal (Om Puri), who becomes a rickshaw driver to provide for his family. Then there is Dr Max (Patrick Swayze), an American surgeon on the run from personal ghosts and disasters on the operating table. In spite of his

intentions of not becoming involved, Max, after initial rough handling from the godfather's vicious son and his thugs, soon finds himself drawn to the problems of the local clinic run by Sister Joan (a plumply reassuring Pauline Collins). Though necessarily simplistic, the film brings home something of the poverty of the city, and Swayze is good enough to overcome his somewhat uneasy casting. The native contingent is notably fine, with Puri eliciting sympathy for the tubercular rickshaw man, Shabana Azmi warmly dignified as his wife and Art Malik as a really despicable villain who cuts people up with razor blades. A winner.

City of Lost Children, The ● Ⓥ
1995, France, 112 mins, colour
Dir: Jean-Pierre Jeunet, Marc Caro
Stars: Ron Perlman, Judith Vittet, Daniel Emilfork
Rating: ★★

A dark fantasy majoring in weirdness, this is gross, grotesque and gruesome in turns, with moments of charm and fascination. Far too long, though, for its content – its intermediate stages may send you to sleep before things begin to hot up towards the end. On an oilrig in the sea, mad scientist Daniel Emilfork and his Lilliputian mother, assisted by the six clone images of his former partner, whom he consigned to the depths in a fight, kidnaps children to steal their dreams and stop his premature ageing. Pitted against him are One (Ron Perlman from TV's *Beauty and the Beast*), whose tiny brother is one of the stolen, and Miette (Judith Vittet), the wharfside waif who leads the kids plotting to get their friends back. Then there are the evil Siamese twin sisters, the deadly automatic flea, the mad deep-sea diver and other characters, all of whose function seems chiefly to be as weird as possible. Fantasy fans may like some or all of this, others will struggle to understand the half of it.

City Slickers ● Ⓥ
1991, US, 114 mins, colour
Dir: Ron Underwood
Stars: Billy Crystal, Daniel Stern, Bruno Kirby, Patricia Wettig, Helen Slater, Jack Palance
Rating: ★★★★

Though it has lots of funny lines, this is basically a poignant and sometimes exciting story about three urban workhacks, each basically dissatisfied with his life who, at the age of 39

apiece, take a two-week 'holiday' together on an arranged cattle drive. Almost all of the subsequent developments work well, and so do the guys – Billy Crystal, Daniel Stern and Bruno Kirby – though the picture is stolen from all of them by the Oscar-winning performance of Jack Palance as the veteran trail boss who (literally) teaches them the ropes. Great colour photography along the trail by Dean Semler and a climax that will have you cheering for the city cowboys, wraps up this unusual but rewarding entertainment package.

City Slickers: The Legend of Curly's Gold ● Ⓥ
1994, US, 110 mins, colour
Dir: Paul Weiland
Stars: Billy Crystal, Jack Palance, Daniel Stern, Jon Lovitz, David Paymer, Patricia Wettig
Rating: ★★★

Quite jolly, if still very much a sequel, this canyon caper takes up the story of city slicker Billy Crystal at a time when, on the eve of his 40th birthday, he's having nightmares about having buried Jack Palance's trail boss (from the first film) alive. Discovering a treasure map in the hat Palance gave him, Crystal not unnaturally sets out to find the million dollars in gold that Palance's daddy is alleged to have stolen from the Western Pacific Railroad in 1908. Taking (intentionally) his friend Phil (Daniel Stern) and (unintentionally) his own gabby brother (Jon Lovitz), Crystal hits the trail. Of course there are bad guys, stampedes, hazardous passages, and Palance again – a touch over the top this time as his own twin brother – also after the gold. The story doesn't hang together too well if you think about it, but enough wisecracks rattle around the marvellous scenery for you not to dwell on the cracks in the plot.

City Streets ☉
1931, US, 82 mins, b/w
Dir: Rouben Mamoulian
Stars: Gary Cooper, Sylvia Sidney, Paul Lukas, William Boyd, Guy Kibbee
Rating: ★★★

Although its characters are killers and bootleggers, this innovative film is not so much a crime drama as a romance with gangster embellishments. And, though there are ten killings in the film, the audience isn't actually shown one of them. Today's directors, obsessed with graphic violence, would have a fit, but in 1931 Rouben Mamoulian was

C

more concerned with the overall style of the film, using the symbolism of various kinds of bars to stress the plight of the trapped central characters. Gary Cooper is well at home as the taciturn sharpshooter, but he's matched by Sylvia Sidney, in her first major film role, as the pathetic yet resolute Nan. Paul Lukas is miscast as the gang leader (George Bancroft would have been better) but plump Guy Kibbee triumphantly overcomes casting against type as a mob killer.

Clairvoyant, The ○

1935, UK, 73 mins, b/w
Dir: Maurice Elvey
Stars: Claude Rains, Fay Wray, Mary Clare, Felix Aylmer
Rating: ★★★

Claude Rains and Fay Wray came to England (where British-born Rains had been a stage actor long before he tried his luck in Hollywood) to make this unusual and absorbing drama. Rains plays a fake clairvoyant called Maximus, who tours the halls with his wife as 'stooge' in the audience, then suddenly finds he has a real gift for foretelling the future. This is fine as long as he is forecasting Derby winners, but threatens to wreck his life when he foresees accidents and disasters. Rains gives a masterly performance, which carries the film through its slower patches to reach a most exciting underground climax.

Clan of the Cave Bear, The ● ⓥ

1985, US, 99 mins, colour
Dir: Michael Chapman
Stars: Daryl Hannah, James Remar, Pamela Reed, Thomas G Waites, Curtis Armstrong
Rating: ★★★

A hefty blow for cavegirl's lib is struck by this film of Jean M Auel's monster bestseller. And, even as you giggle at some of the subtitles imposed on the Neanderthal dialogue, you'll be rooting for Daryl Hannah to come through in the end. She's one of the 'Others', a blonde Cro-Magnon orphan adopted by the regressive Neanderthals, and a pretty wimpish six-year-old who grows up rather unbelievably to be tall and leggy Daryl. Forced to submit by the tribe's embryo leader Brond, who likes nothing if not his own way, Daryl bears his child but at the same time secretly learns the hunting arts forbidden to women – which gets her expelled even after her slingshot saves a child from the jaws of a wolf. Resourcefully

surviving the winter to the astonishment of the tribe, she is granted the title 'Woman Who Hunts'. This, as you can imagine, goes down like a lead balloon with Brond, and you know that a day of reckoning will have to come. Nicely pitched between the erotic fantasy of *One Million Years BC* and the ultra-realism of *Quest for Fire,* it's thoroughly enjoyable.

Clara's Heart ● ⓥ

1988, US, 108 mins, colour
Dir: Robert Mulligan
Stars: Whoopi Goldberg, Michael Ontkean, Kathleen Quinlan, Neil Patrick Harris, Spalding Gray
Rating: ★★★

A real tearjerker with Whoopi Goldberg as a Jamaican maid with a big heart who comes to look after a 12-year-old American boy. His baby sister has just died and this finally cracks apart his parents' faltering marriage. Whoopi, with an immaculate Jamaican accent, teaches him all about life and how to grow up, in a story that makes for a very slow and cumbersome journey towards understanding. Clara the maid also has a dark secret which seems to take forever to come tumbling out of the closet. Nonetheless, there are some telling moments. Whoopi is well on form and Neil Patrick Harris very good as the boy. An emotionally powerful ending provides us with a rather better memory of the film than its overall pace perhaps deserves.

Clarence, the Cross-eyed Lion ⊙

1965, US, 98 mins, colour
Dir: Andrew Marton
Stars: Marshall Thompson, Betsy Drake, Richard Haydn
Rating: ★★★

Charming animal adventure featuring the stars of the television series *Daktari.* The director is Andrew Marton, who should be well at home with animals and the jungle – he was the man who directed the sensational second-unit action scenes in the 1951 version of *King Solomon's Mines.* Betsy Drake, the personable actress who was at one time married to Cary Grant, plays an anthropologist.

Clash of the Titans ○ ⓥ

1981, UK, 118 mins, colour
Dir: Desmond Davis
Stars: Laurence Olivier, Harry Hamlin, Judi Bowker
Rating: ★★

Some formidable acting talents were notably under-employed in this visually spectacular fantasy based on the Greek legend of Perseus, the mortal son of the god Zeus. Laurence Olivier, Claire Bloom, Maggie Smith, Burgess Meredith and Sian Phillips are an impressive group of acting heavyweights but they are let down by a lightweight, nay featherweight, script. Harry (*L.A. Law*) Hamlin makes a handsome Perseus and Judi Bowker a winsome Andromeda, but they are overshadowed by pretty much the rest of the cast. Mind you, everyone is overshadowed by the special effects, created by that master of the grand illusion Ray Harryhausen. These are what make the film worth watching.

Class ●

1983, US, 98 mins, colour
Dir: Lewis John Carlino
Stars: Jacqueline Bisset, Rob Lowe, Andrew McCarthy
Rating: ★

Overloaded with sex scenes and bad language, this is one of those million-to-one scenarios in which unlikelihood is piled on improbability – well-enough made by director Lewis John Carlino but never communicating in genuine emotional terms. Andrew McCarthy is a virginal student who just happens to be picked up by stunning Jacqueline Bisset (exceptionally unlikely in view of the character's looks) who just happens to be filthy rich roommate Rob Lowe's discontented mother. Coincidences continue to pile up in a comedy that has some class (courtesy Bisset) but no credibility at all. Writers Jim Kouf and David Greenwalt do give us a few very funny lines, but it isn't nearly enough.

Class Action ● ⓥ

1990, US, 109 mins, colour
Dir: Michael Apted
Stars: Gene Hackman, Mary Elizabeth Mastrantonio, Colin Friels, Larry Fishburne, Donald Moffatt
Rating: ★★★★

Another successful Hollywood courtroom drama, solid all the way, but familiar in construction apart from the fact that the cross-bench protagonists are a father (Gene Hackman) and daughter (Mary Elizabeth Mastrantonio). No matter how often you tell it, though, the triumph of good over evil works with an audience as jury every time you try the case. All you need is a decent script (and this is more than that) and the little detail that unhinges the bad guys towards the end. In this instance, Hackman's the idealistic lawyer whose courtroom triumphs have to be set against his failure as a family man, a failure that has alienated his daughter, now a smart corporate counsel. The case over which they clash concerns deaths caused by a faulty car, and entails such time-honoured elements as the records that go back years, double-dealing behind the scenes and – no surprise! – the final surprise witness. It's expertly handled by director Michael Apted and a classy cast. Pay up for this action and you won't be suing for your money back.

Clean and Sober ● Ⓥ

1988, US, 125 mins, colour
Dir: Glenn Gordon Caron
Stars: Michael Keaton, Kathy Baker, Morgan Freeman, M Emmet Walsh, Claudia Christian, Brian Benben
Rating: ★★★

This well-written, involving drama of drug and alcohol addiction is a little overlong but illuminated by its actors and their personalities. Not as downbeat as you might expect, it features a whole cluster of telling portrayals, from Michael Keaton (who went straight from the drugs clinic here to the asylum of *The Dream Team*), Kathy Baker, Morgan Freeman and M Emmet Walsh (his best in years). There are no dud performances in this film. Baker, in particular, is heart-rending. A bit heavy on expletives, perhaps, but in a film with so much anger to expend, it's perhaps understandable.

Clean Slate ① Ⓥ

1994, US, 107 mins, colour
Dir: Mick Jackson
Stars: Dana Carvey, Valeria Golino, Michael Gambon, James Earl Jones, Kevin Pollak, Barkley
Rating: ★

A misbegotten comedy vehicle for Dana Carvey, the less funny half of the Wayne-and-Garth duo from *Wayne's World*. Dana's a private eye in a plot that might even have worked a bit better played straight, but is pretty much a non-starter on any level. Carvey's character's problem is that each morning he forgets what's gone the day before. There are echoes of *Groundhog Day* in this but, alas, only echoes. A talented dog called Barkley keeps proceedings afloat for the first few minutes: his character has a 'depth perception' problem which tends to lead to him sailing wide of his targets. Make the most of Barkley, though, as he's the

only good thing in the film. The chief crime here is the running time.

Clear and Present Danger ① Ⓥ

1994, US, 143 mins, colour
Dir: Phillip Noyce
Stars: Harrison Ford, Willem Dafoe, Anne Archer, James Earl Jones, Donald Moffat, Thora Birch
Rating: ★★★★

'Truth needs a soldier' trumpets the publicity. And it certainly finds one in Harrison Ford's Jack Ryan, who takes on the whole US government hierarchy up to the President himself in this follow-up to *Patriot Games*. After the disclosure that a close friend was involved with Colombian drug cartels, the President sanctions a covert operation against the drug barons by sending crack soldiers into the country under the command of mercenary Willem Dafoe. The President's aides, smoothly feathering their own nests over the affair, ensure that CIA man Ryan is the only one not in the know: he thinks he's still after Colombian connections to the dead man's money. He's soon involved, though, and the government wishes he weren't as Ryan dodges death and destruction in his search for the truth. A good story here, with sides clearly drawn, and lots of gun-rattling action and emotional involvement, especially when Ryan and colleagues are trapped by machine-gunners in a network of narrow streets. Henry Czerny and Harris Yulin are just right as the hissable heavies back at the White House.

Cleopatra ○ Ⓥ

1963, US, 243 mins, colour
Dir: Joseph L Mankiewicz
Stars: Elizabeth Taylor, Richard Burton, Rex Harrison, Roddy McDowall, Martin Landau, Hume Cronyn
Rating: ★★

The casting of Hollywood's most glamorous couple of the day as famous lovers Antony and Cleopatra must have seemed a dream ticket for 20th Century-Fox. But not even Elizabeth Taylor and Richard Burton could make this turkey fly. It was a $43 million yawn-inducing slice of indigestible history. One critic of the day hilariously summed up the gaudy, opulent mess as: 'Elizabeth Taylor is the first Cleopatra to sail down the Nile to Las Vegas.'

Cleopatra ○

1934, US, 101 mins, b/w
Dir: Cecil B DeMille

Stars: Claudette Colbert, Warren William, Henry Wilcoxon
Rating: ★★★

The sumptuous spectacle, especially the scenes aboard Cleopatra's barge, dwarfs everything else in this Cecil B DeMille version of the Antony and Cleopatra saga, which has the considerable advantage of being less than half the length of the disastrous Elizabeth Taylor epic of almost 30 years later. A minxish Cleo is created by Claudette Colbert, the French-born Hollywood star.

Client, The ● Ⓥ

1994, US, 121 mins, colour
Dir: Joel Schumacher
Stars: Susan Sarandon, Tommy Lee Jones, Brad Renfro, Anthony LaPaglia, J T Walsh, Anthony Edwards
Rating: ★★

A slackly started suspense yam that seems to take a long time getting anywhere. To the objective viewer, it appears that the 11-year-old boy at the centre of things could have saved us all a couple of hours by spilling the beans to police about a Mafia lawyer who shot himself after telling the boy things the DA would like to hear. But since he hates authority almost as much as he fears the Mob, the boy elects to keep quiet. This is where ex-alcoholic lady lawyer Reggie Love (Susan Sarandon) comes in, and we get a semblance of a story, as Mafia hitmen try first to frighten, then silence the kid before he can tell the FBI where a certain body is hidden. The ensuing drama, though, never ready bites, despite the good tries offered by Sarandon, by Tommy Lee Jones as a power-seeking DA, and by Will Patton as a snidey cop. The script errs by failing to make Sarandon as sympathetic as she should be.

Cliffhanger ① Ⓥ

1993, US, 112 mins, colour
Dir: Renny Harlin
Stars: Sylvester Stallone, John Lithgow, Janine Turner, Michael Rooker, Ralph Waite, Craig Fairbrass
Rating: ★★★

From its dizzying opening thrills, as a girl climber plunges to her death when a mountain rescue goes wrong, this action film delivers on adventure if not logic. Months later, Sylvester Stallone, who may have been at fault, has quit the rescue service when a crisis occurs. Unknown to him, it involves desperate criminals whose mid-air hijack has gone wrong, leaving them crashed in the snow in bad weather, with suitcases

C

containing millions somewhere on the mountain. 'If you don't do this now,' yells Stallone's girl Janine Turner 'you re gonna be stuck on a ledge for the rest of your life.' Well, a man can't turn his back on that kind of cliché, and Sly's soon up there battling evil mastermind John Lithgow and his gang. Lithgow tries to look viciously invincible, but shoots his trustiest ally in the back for no good reason, fails to kill the good guys when he should and lets a hostage go without collecting the ransom first! Lots of fraying ropes, fingertip holds, avalanches and collapsing bridges. Hang on! – to everything but your thinking cap.

Clock, The
See: Under the Clock

Clockers ● Ⓥ
1995, US, 128 mins, colour
Dir: Spike Lee
Stars: Mekhi Pfifer, Harvey Keitel, Delroy Lindo, Isaiah Washington, John Turturro
Rating: ★★★

Although this film about urban backstreets crime proves ultimately worthwhile, it takes a *long* time to get going. Basically a murder mystery of the what-really-happened variety, the script cunningly turns our conceptions of its characters upside down at the end, although it isn't really clear how some of them get away with their crimes. Chief among the ghetto layabouts and drug dealers on show here is Strike (Mekhi Pfifer) whose gentler side is represented by his giant train set. When the local crack king orders him to make a hit, however, it's his straight arrow brother who takes the rap. Aggressive local cop Harvey Keitel is determined to set the record straight and so he does, but perhaps not quite in the way he imagines when he first gets the case. Director and cowriter Spike Lee has much too much peripheral non-action going on here, spinning the film out beyond the hour mark before it gets down to the meat. Street-level performances give the in-your-face quality the director requires.

Clockwise ○ Ⓥ
1985, UK, 97 mins, colour
Dir: Christopher Morahan
Stars: John Cleese, Alison Steadman, Penelope Wilton, Stephen Moore, Joan Hickson
Rating: ★★★

It was a long wait to see John Cleese in his final starring role for the cinema but worth it. Cleese, with his Hitler mous-

tache, grasshopper run and madman's eyes, is on top manic form as the punctilious headmaster of a mixed comprehensive from whose basilisk gaze no miscreant or misdemeanour escapes. Chosen to chair a headmasters' conference, he sets off cross-country by train. Betrayed by Basil Fawlty's favourite word— 'Right!' – he has a convoluted conversation with a ticket collector that results in him missing his connection – the prelude to a pattern of disasters that build to a patchwork quilt catastrophe of giant proportions. The ensuing escapades evoke about the number of laughs you might expect from an average *Fawlty Towers* – still not bad for a 90 minute movie, if not quite Cleese at full throttle. Funniest scenes: Cleese vandalising a phone box in a paroxysm of Fawlty fury; and Cleese kicking a car stuck in a field only to fall in the mud himself.

Clockwork Mice ● Ⓥ
1994, UK, 104 mins, colour
Dir: Vadim Jean
Stars: Ian Hart, Catherine Russell, Ruaidhri Conroy, Art Malik, John Alderton
Rating: ★★★

An impressive British drama from *Leon the Pig Farmer* co-director Vadim Jean. Ian Hart plays Steve, an idealistic young teacher at a special needs school who manages to win over most of his pupils, but faces problems with one particular destructive boy, Conrad James (Ruaidhri Conroy). However, through a mutual love of cross-country running, Steve finally finds a way to break through Conrad's shell. Newcomer Conroy is terrific as the moody teenager, and the scenes between troubled pupil and caring teacher work well. The supporting cast includes a host of familiar TV faces, including John Alderton, James Bolam, Art Malik and Nigel Planer as the other teachers.

Close Encounters of the Third Kind ○ Ⓥ
1977, US, 127 mins, colour
Dir: Steven Spielberg
Stars: Richard Dreyfuss, Francois Truffaut, Teri Garr, Melinda Dillon, Bob Balaban
Rating: ★★★★

For those who happen not to know, a close encounter of the third kind is defined as actual contact with the occupants on an Unidentified Flying Object. Set mainly in an Indiana town (though some sequences take place as far afield as India), Steven Spielberg's

dazzling film is a story of ordinary people confronted by the extraordinary. The film is especially outstanding tor the staggering and imaginative special effects of its spectacular concluding scenes.

Close My Eyes ● Ⓥ
1991, UK, 108 mins, colour
Dir: Stephen Poliakoff
Stars: Clive Owen, Saskia Reeves, Alan Rickman
Rating: ★★

The once-taboo theme of sex between a brother and sister is tackled at fun tilt by director Stephen Pollakoff in a film that's a visual stunner, yet awkward in its portrayal of human relationships, and hampered by two central performances, by Saskia Reeves and Clive Owen, that aren't terribly good. So, while the exchanges between the two are making the audience shuffle and occasionally giggle, it's the happenings and characters in the margins of the film that prove most interesting. The hangdog-looking Alan Rickman is right on the money as Reeves' cuckolded husband and the events involving Owen's AIDS-infected boss (Karl Johnson) are touching and notably well contrived. And, while the naked flesh of our illicit lovers lurches off screen for another breather, Poliakoff finds time to capture the unique qualities of a particularly hot summer in the English countryside.

Close to Eden ◑ Ⓥ
(aka: A Stranger Among Us)
1992, US, 111 mins, colour
Dir: Sidney Lumet
Stars: Melanie Griffith, Eric Thal, Tracy Pollan, John Pankow, Mia Sara
Rating: ★★

For most of us, Hasidic Jewry is a closed world, so Sidney Lumet's window on to a warm, loving if totally tradition-bound community is more than welcome. Unfortunately, there's rather too much concentration on the Hasidic world and too little on the plot, leaving cop Emily Eden (Melanie Griffith) to make her final breathless deductions even as she's finally failing to seduce the Hasidic Ariel (Eric Thal) from his intended bride. There are a few good thrills, but a few titters too, as the miscast but gallant Griffith (in a role for which Debra Winger would have been better suited) pursues the murderer of a Hasidic diamond dealer. Andrzej Bartkowiak's photography makes an excellent contrast between the enclosed Hasidic world – browns and golds – and the bleak red-white-and-blue brightness of the outside world.

Clown, The ○

1952, US, 92 mins, b/w
Dir: Robert Z Leonard
Stars: Red Skelton, Jane Greer, Tim Considine
Rating: ★★

All screen comics seem to want to play for pathos at some stage of their career, and here it was Red Skelton's turn to go for Pagliacci, with moderate success, as a drunken has-been who once toplined in the Ziegfeld Follies. Jane Greer plays his divorced wife with feeling, and Tim Considine is charmingly natural as his adoring son, but otherwise the film suffers from a weak supporting cast and the feeling that Skelton's studio, MGM, weren't convinced that the film would make any money. As it happens, they were right, and Skelton's film career slipped into decline. Watch out for Charles Bronson as a dice player.

Clue ◑

1985, US, 90 mins, colour
Dir: Jonathan Lynn
Stars: Eileen Brennan, Tim Curry, Madeline Kahn, Christopher Lloyd, Michael McKean, Lesley Ann Warren
Rating: ★

Despite all the frantic running around and shouting (principally from Tim Curry as a hyperactive butler), this comedy murder-mystery doesn't amount to much. Inspired by the game 'Cluedo' – known in the US as 'Clue' – it is in fact a pale imitation of the earlier and more satisfying sleuthing spoof *Murder By Death*. Christopher Lloyd, since a star in the *Back to the Future* films, is a suitably eccentric Professor Plum. There were three different endings shot, each identifying a different killer, but this British print has only one, which is enough.

Clueless ◑ Ⓥ

1995, US, 98 mins, colour
Dir: Amy Heckerling
Stars: Alicia Silverstone, Dan Hedaya, Stacey Dash, Brittany Murphy, Wallace Shawn
Rating: ★★

The mid-Nineties take on the US teenage scene, this is quite fun for 40 minutes or so, but decreasingly less so once the heroine (Alicia Silverstone) gets clued in to puppy love. This airheaded rich girl is the envy of her set. 'The columns of my house,' she coos, 'date all the way back to 1972,' and you tremble for her future, and that of

the country. Never mind, she's always ready with a cutting riposte. 'Do you know what time it is?' barks corporate lawyer daddy (Dan Hedaya) after one particularly late distress call. Alicia pouts and furrows her brow. 'Watches don't really go with my outfit, daddy,' she says. There's no comeback to that.

Cluny Brown ○

1946, US, 100 mins, b/w
Dir: Ernst Lubitsch
Stars: Jennifer Jones, Charles Boyer, Peter Lawford, Reginald Owen, C Aubrey Smith
Rating: ★★★

Jennifer Jones gives one of her most delightful performances in this, the last great Ernst Lubitsch comedy: he died a year later aged only 55. Miss Jones plays a plumber's niece following in the footsteps of her uncle. She meets a penniless Czech boffin (Charles Boyer) in 1938 London and together they make some amusing assaults on the English caste system. Richard Haydn steals the film as a stuttering village chemist, but there's also excellent character work from Una O'Connor, Ernest Cossart, Reginald Owen and C Aubrey Smith.

Coal Miner's Daughter ○

1980, US, 119 mins, colour
Dir: Michael Apted
Stars: Sissy Spacek, Tommy Lee Jones, Beverly D'Angelo, Levon Helm
Rating: ★★★★★

Sissy Spacek's southern accent, singing voice and admirable naturalistic acting all merit ten out of ten in this moving musical biopic about Loretta Lynn, a poor-born Tennessee girl who married at 13, had seven children and became America's number one female Country and Western star. Sissy deservedly scooped the year's Best Actress Oscar from under the noses of more fancied nominees. The direction of Britain's Michael Apted is exemplary in its feel for time and place, and Tommy Lee Jones provides fine support as Lynn's unfeeling husband, the driving force behind her fortunes. If the film glosses over some of the less savoury aspects of the true story – drugs, nervous breakdowns etc – the treatment is in keeping with Spacek's wholesome portrait of the singing mum. She can be our number one lady of Country and Western any day.

Coast of Skeletons ◑

1964, UK/South Africa, 90 mins, colour
Dir: Robert Lynn

Stars: Richard Todd, Dale Robertson, Marianne Koch
Rating: ★★

The first of two films that Richard Todd made in the character of investigator Harry Sanders. The photography, both underwater and along the coastline of South-West Africa (now Namibia), is remarkably clear and there's an explosive climax.

Coast to Coast ○

1980, US, 90 mins, colour
Dir: Joseph Sargent
Stars: Dyan Cannon, Robert Blake
Rating: ★★★

The basic idea of this picture is so good that it would be a hell of a film if it fired on all cylinders all of the time. Dyan Cannon is its driving force as a wife who escapes from the asylum to which her grasping husband has had her committed to avoid an expensive divorce. She teams up with a trucker (Robert Blake) who has problems of his own and plans to turn her in for the husband's reward money. Zany incidentals liven up the story as it rolls along the highway, and both leads seem to be doing all their own stuntwork. It looks hairy enough to give the film that little extra boost.

Cobra ● Ⓥ

1986, US, 87 mins, colour
Dir: George Pan Cosmatos
Stars: Sylvester Stallone, Brigitte Nielsen, Reni Santoni
Rating: ★★

Comic-book stuff about the modern American equivalent of a sect of Kaliworshippers, hell-bent on creating a new world by chopping up nubile young things with axes and switchknives – which seems a strange way to achieve such ambitions. Still, if crime is a disease then Marion Cobretti (Sylvester Stallone), a lone-wolf cop who chews long matches, is the self-proclaimed cure. He's a member of the Zombie Squad, a group for which Stallone's performance here eminently qualifies him, who track down and exterminate 'psychos' (Norman Bates beware). He locates a vital witness, and then has to protect her from the efforts of the bad guys. The villains are encouraged to overact, which they do without much flair, save for Lee Garlington, a dead ringer for Stockard Channing, as the pawky policewoman secretly in league with the killers.

C

Cobweb, The ○

1955, US, 135 mins, colour
Dir: Vincente Minnelli
Stars: Richard Widmark, Lauren Bacall,
Charles Boyer, Gloria Grahame, Lillian
Gish, John Kerr
Rating: ★★

A sombre story of rising tension between patients and administration at an American psychiatric clinic. A strange film to come from ex-director of musicals, Vincente Minnelli – although he gets a splendid performance from veteran Lillian Gish, unusually cast as an old battleaxe. The cast-list is a treasure-house of experienced Hollywood performers, from the smooth charm of Charles Boyer as a psychiatrist, to the mature loveliness of Fay Wray – of *King Kong* fame – as his wife.

Coca Cola Kid, The ● Ⓥ

1984, Australia, 94 mins, colour
Dir: Dusan Makaveyev
Stars: Eric Roberts, Greta Scacchi, Bill
Kerr, Chris Haywood, Kris McQuade
Rating: ★★★

If you want to see a truly nutty film, this is probably about as close these days as you'll get. Imagine a sort of Ealing plot, with Goonish humour and adult trimmings, and you're only within hailing distance of what's a typical film from its director. Two very photogenic leads, Eric Roberts and Greta Scacchi, who also give decent performances, provide the sexual spark to a wild tale of an American whiz-kid coca-cola salesman out to rope in the last diehard fizz-making independent (Bill Kerr) from the Australian outback. As usual in a Makaveyev film you get all the trimmings, which means every exploitative angle he can lay his hands on – in the case of the delectable Scacchi, she of the challenging gaze, there are quite a number – diced with his own form of devilish satire. Bill Kerr adds another to his gallery of character portrayals as the outback independent, although it's not too clear what happens to him at the end.

Cockleshell Heroes ○ Ⓥ

1955, UK, 94 mins, colour
Dir: Jose Ferrer
Stars: Jose Ferrer, Trevor Howard, Dora
Bryan, Anthony Newley, David Lodge
Rating: ★★★

A rattling good war film on an unusual theme: the blowing-up of enemy battleships by a highly-trained group of men in cockleshell canoes. It was one of the first British war films to be made in Technicolor, and the photography is first-rate, as are the performances of Jose Ferrer (who also directed), Trevor Howard and then-newcomer Percy Herbert. The training of the men is even more entertaining than the raid itself.

Cocktail ● Ⓥ

1988, US, 103 mins, colour
Dir: Roger Donaldson
Stars: Tom Cruise, Bryan Brown,
Elisabeth Shue, Laurence Luckinbill,
Kelly Lynch
Rating: ★★

A lightweight concoction about an ex-Army buddy who becomes the hottest thing behind a Manhattan bar. And despite the weak and derivative material, Cruise's ear-to-ear grin still managed to light up the box office to the tune of $80 million. The storyline, which has him tutored in the art of pouring the niftiest cocktails in the sexiest fashion by craggy Bryan Brown and then fighting each other over pulling the same girls, is nothing more than an excuse for displaying acres of flesh. Look closely for goose-pimples and blue lips in Cruise's waterfall seduction of Elisabeth Shue – the water was freezing.

Cocktails in the Kitchen

See: For Better, For Worse

Cocoanuts, The ⊙

1929, US, 89 mins, b/w
Dir: Robert Florey
Stars: Groucho Marx, Harpo Marx, Chico
Marx, Zeppo Marx, Margaret Dumont
Rating: ★★★

'Just think, tonight, when the moon is sneaking around the clouds, I'll be sneaking around you ... Oh, I can see you now ... You and the moon ... You wear a necktie so I'll know you.' Yes, it's Groucho Marx, propositioning the galleon-like Margaret Dumont in the Marx Brothers' earliest released film comedy. Groucho's the manager of a Florida hotel devoid of guests, or much else. The telephone rings. Groucho picks it up. 'Ice water in room 412?' he asks. 'Where did you get it?'

Cocoon ○ Ⓥ

1985, US, 117 mins, colour
Dir: Ron Howard
Stars: Don Ameche, Jessica Tandy,
Steve Guttenberg, Hume Cronyn, Brian
Dennehy, Wilford Brimley
Rating: ★★★

A heartwarming and very unusual fantasy about an alien spacecraft that returns to earth after an absence of 10,000 years (the visitors seem to live more or less forever) to pick up 20 crewmen they left in 'pods' at the bottom of the sea centuries before. They take them to a deserted swimming pool, failing to realise that the lifeforce with which they energise the water to revive their comrades is in turn rejuvenating three old fogeys from a nearby retirement home who bathe there every day. All this takes rather a long while to get going, and one could do with more of the hot-blooded antics of the elderly trio and the women who share their secret. That said, Don Ameche, Hume Cronyn and Wilford Brimley (who, at 50, had to be set for another 20 years of crusty old men) have very winning ways, and their ladies, Jessica Tandy (the real-life Mrs Cronyn), Gwen Verdon and Maureen Stapleton, are not far behind. You'll especially enjoy Ameche's demonstration of breakdancing!

Cocoon: the Return ○ Ⓥ

1988, US, 130 mins, colour
Dir: Daniel Petrie
Stars: Don Ameche, Wilford Brimley,
Courteney Cox, Hume Cronyn, Steve
Guttenberg, Jessica Tandy
Rating: ★★

All the old cast is back for this lesser sequel to *Cocoon*, in which the old stagers made young by alien contact return to planet Earth with predictably dramatic consequences. The first hour or so is fairly tedious, but the latter stages are pretty good with some affecting moments, especially the scene where Hume Cronyn visits injured wife Jessica Tandy in hospital. Their poignant portrayals make this second trip just about worthwhile.

Codename Wildgeese ◐

1984, US/West Germany, 101 mins,
colour
Dir: Anthony M Dawson
Stars: Lewis Collins, Lee Van Cleef,
Ernest Borgnine, Mimsy Farmer, Klaus
Kinski
Rating: ★★

A sort of *Dirty Dozen* meets *The Wild Geese*, with an international cast on a mission to destroy an opium depot deep in the jungles of Thailand. Lewis Collins, Ernest Borgnine and Lee Van Cleef assume the required grim expressions, Klaus Kinski is dubbed into Oxford English and thousands of oriental stuntmen bite honourable dust.

Code of Silence ○ Ⓥ

1985, UK, 101 mins, colour
Dir: Andrew Davis

Stars: Chuck Norris, Henry Silva, Bert Remsen, Molly Hagen, Dennis Farina
Rating: ★★

This Chuck Norris film could just as easily have been called 'A Force of One', if Chuck and his cohorts hadn't already used it for a previous fist-feast. The Bronson-style plot involves the poker-faced Norris obliterating the South American branch of the Mafia (led by Henry Silva) single-handed after they have kidnapped the innocent daughter of a stateside mobster. If it's only action you want, the movie should satisfy in its 18-certificate way, and there's even an attempt at a story in the sub-plot of the corrupt policeman for whom Norris refuses to cover. But all the bone-crunching mayhem and Chicago location shooting can't disguise the fact that director Andrew Davis is padding his film in *Miami Vice* style to reach its feature length.

Cold Comfort Farm ○ Ⓥ
1995, UK, 100 mins, colour
Dir: John Schlesinger
Stars: Kate Beckinsale, Rufus Sewell, Ian McKellen, Eileen Atkins, Sheila Burrell, Joanna Lumley
Rating: ★★★★

A frisky film version of Stella Gibbons' rural comic classic. Cool, clever Flora Poste, orphaned at 21, decides to stay with relatives at Cold Comfort Farm. Within its squalid depths, she finds gloom and doom only occasionally interrupted by rural revelry and lays in the hay, mainly courtesy of dark and brooding Seth (Sewell), youngest of the eccentric Starkadders who sweat, slave, moan and groan under the iron rule of Aunt Ada Doom, who saw 'something nasty in the woodshed' as a child and hasn't left her bedroom for decades, save for biannual 'countings' to make sure her snivelling and servile family is still there. Flora sets about reforming all of them and, being the head prefect sort she is, polishes off the job in no time. It's a delicious pastiche of rural romances all the way from Jane Austin to Thomas Hardy. No great weight to it, like Beckinsale's portrayal of Flora – but both film and performance are, in their lightly witty way, about right.

Cold Feet ◑
1989, US, 94 mins, colour
Dir: Robert Dornhelm
Stars: Keith Carradine, Sally Kirkland, Tom Waits, Bill Pullman, Rip Torn
Rating: ★★

This quirky comedy, dipped in various shades of grey and black (with a dash

of red for the blood it spills), is off the beaten track in more ways than one. For a start, it's set in the wilds of Montana. That's where crooked Monte (Keith Carradine) heads, with a fortune in emeralds hidden inside the horse he's riding, having ditched his associates, demented psycho Tom Waits and voracious blonde Sally Kirkland. Carradine's destination is the ranch of his brother (Bill Pullman), where he aims to – well, it's never clear what Monte aims to do 'ceptin' he never gits around to doin' it. Meanwhile, the gruesome twosome pursue some. And one of the twists to this strange, beautifully-photographed film is that Waits is a real psycho who actually kills people. Full of half-funny comic touches and off-kilter dialogue.

Colditz Story, The ○ Ⓥ
1954, UK, 97 mins, b/w
Dir: Guy Hamilton
Stars: John Mills, Eric Portman, Christopher Rhodes, Lionel Jeffries, Bryan Forbes, Ian Carmichael
Rating: ★★★

The British really couldn't go wrong with prisoner-of-war escape stories in the early Fifties. And this one, a first major success for its young director, Paris-born Guy Hamilton, is firmly in the tradition of *The Wooden Horse*. Episodic, but personably acted by all concerned, especially Eric Portman as the senior officer.

Cold Sweat ◑
1970, France/Italy, 94 mins, colour
Dir: Terence Young
Stars: Charles Bronson, Liv Ullmann, James Mason, Jill Ireland
Rating: ★★

Terence Young, who directed the Bond films *Dr No, From Russia with Love* and *Thunderball,* made this thriller on location in France. The script does not do justice to the tension of the original novel – *Ride the Nightmare* by Richard Matheson, himself a prolific screenplay-writer – but Charles Bronson does all that can be expected of him, and Liv Ullmann's anguished performance as his wife will reward her legions of fans.

Cold Turkey ○
1970, US, 101 mins, colour
Dir: Norman Lear
Stars: Dick Van Dyke, Pippa Scott, Bob Newhart, Edward Everett Horton, Vincent Gardenia, Jean Stapleton
Rating: ★★

A bit of a curate's egg is this satirical comedy aimed at American middle-

class attitudes. It stars Dick Van Dyke in a strange role as the self-seeking small-town reverend seizing the chance to get his town's name on the map when Edward Everett Horton's tobacco king offers a $25 million prize to any town that can give up smoking for 30 days. Bob Newhart is the oily publicity executive responsible for the stunt and there is a succession of entertaining character turns from a good cast: all human life is there down to the minutest (sometimes fairly unpleasant!) detail.

Colonel Blimp
See: The Life and Death of Colonel Blimp

Colonel Chabert, Le ◑ Ⓥ
1994, France, 111 mins, colour
Dir: Yves Angelo
Stars: Gérard Depardieu, Fanny Ardant, Fabrice Luchini, Romane Bohringer
Rating: ★★★

Although not without dull patches, this is on the whole an absorbing account of Honoré de Balzac's tale of a French officer, presumed dead in the Napoleonic Wars, who returns home after countless impoverishments and humiliations. Looming out of the murk like some Gallic Scrooge, Gerard Depardieu is formidable in this role, discovering that his wife (Fanny Ardant) has remained with his wealth, but stands to lose her ambitious new husband if Chabert is declared alive. What will Chabert, having convinced an astute lawyer (his wife's) of his authenticity, settle for – if anything. That's the nub of this carefully composed story of power, ambition and torment. The unspoken friendship between Chabert and the lawyer with a rat-trap mind (Fabrice Luchini) is nicely sketched in but never overstated.

Colorado Territory ○
1949, US, 94 mins, b/w
Dir: Raoul Walsh
Stars: Joel McCrea, Virginia Mayo, John Archer, Dorothy Malone, Henry Hull
Rating: ★★★★

A cracking Western remake of *High Sierra,* with Joel McCrea lending a granite authority to the Humphrey Bogart role as the outlaw escaped from prison who dreams of one last holdup. Director Raoul Walsh, who also made the original, supplies an atmosphere heavy with tension, and writers John Twist and Edmund H North back his efforts with intelligent dialogue. They draw their characters with hard-etched but not unsympathetic lines. The

C

rugged scenery is beautifully captured by Sid Hickox, a Western specialist.

Color of Money, The ● Ⓥ

1986, US, 119 mins, colour
Dir: Martin Scorsese
Stars: Paul Newman, Tom Cruise, Mary Elizabeth Mastrantonio, Helen Shaver, John Turturro, Bill Cobbs
Rating: ★★★

'Fast Eddie' Felson is back – and playing pool again. That's the good news, and fans of the sport and Paul Newman, who won a long-delayed Oscar for his role, will revel in this sequel to *The Hustler*. Richard Price's hard-boiled, if not too well structured screenplay concentrates this time on the sporting angles, by-passing the tragic drama of the original. Newman is superb, while Tom Cruise, as the young pool hustler he takes under his wing, hasn't much to do but 'strut his stuff', though he does it with great confidence. Martin Scorsese directs with polish and a feel for the right angle at the right time, while the snooker itself is effectively choreographed, both stars potting their set-up shots with masterly aplomb.

Color of Night ● Ⓥ

1994, US, 122 mins, colour
Dir: Richard Rush
Stars: Bruce Willis, Jane March, Lance Henriksen, Brad Dourif, Lesley Ann Warren, Ruben Blades
Rating: ★★

Bruce Willis is a psychiatrist ready to throw in the towel after an already-suicidal patient throws herself out of a high window. Fleeing to a fellow shrink, Willis finds himself smack dab in the middle of a murder mystery. As the victim (Scott Bakula) has a mysterious girlfriend we never see, a house rigged like a fortress, a quintet of weird patients and is trailed around by creepy music, it's odds-on he's not destined to see the second reel. And so it proves, with Willis beset by nightmares, the local police chief (Ruben Blades) who seems to be a one-man band, and a mysterious girl who, being Jane March, the 'sinner from Pinner', wears no underwear and seduces him in the pool. Although March's line 'I'm a struggling actress' drew a giggle from the audience, she's really no worse than the rest of this all-too-distinguished cast. Occasionally effective as a thriller, the film is unrelentingly nasty and earns no marks as a whodunnit: the killer is glaringly obvious from their first appearance on screen.

Color Purple, The ◑ Ⓥ

1985, US, 152 mins, colour
Dir: Steven Spielberg
Stars: Danny Glover, Whoopi Goldberg, Margaret Avery, Oprah Winfrey
Rating: ★★★

This manipulative mixture of familiar elements from *Roots* and similar dramas is what you might call a six-handkerchief movie. It does go on a long time, but a lot of it works very well, even if you resent director Steven Spielberg, in a big Oscar try, allowing you to see him pull the strings while you sit there trying to restrain a tear. Whoopi Goldberg gives a moving performance as the girl who goes through more trials and perils than a silent serial heroine (Desreta Jackson, who plays the younger Celie, is also very good). Oprah Winfrey and Danny Glover make early marks, too, and the film was nominated for 11 Academy Awards. When it came to the ceremonies, though, the Academy saw right through Spielberg's intentions, and didn't give it one.

Colors ● Ⓥ

1988, US, 121 mins, colour
Dir: Dennis Hopper
Stars: Sean Penn, Robert Duvall, Maria Conchita Alonso, Randy Brooks
Rating: ★★

Or: *Hill Street Blues* with an adult certificate. This realist thriller about the police's attempted crack-down on ghetto gang warfare even has Trinidad Silva as one of the gang heads, a function he performed similarly as Jesus on *Hill Street*. That series perhaps first made the outside world aware of the armed street gangs – Bloods and Royals and the like – bossing the backstreets of cities like Los Angeles. Dennis Hopper turns this situation into a slam-bang action film with dramatic shootouts that recall gangster films of the Thirties. Robert Duvall is the wily veteran cop and Sean Penn his cocky, aggressive young partner. Their relationship follows a predictable pattern down to the final scene, but then this, unlike *Hill Street Blues,* is a movie where actions always speak louder than words.

Colt 45 ○

1950, US, 74 mins, colour
Dir: Edwin L Marin
Stars: Randolph Scott, Zachary Scott, Ruth Roman, Lloyd Bridges
Rating: ★★★

This lively Western, distinguished by the forthright playing of the two Scotts,

Randolph and Zachary, as goodie and baddie, is an 'A' feature horse-opera in every respect except its brief running-time. The conflict between the two men roars across the western plains – and the pace of the action, tightly edited, never drops. Coincidence note: Ian MacDonald plays a Westerner called Miller, just as he does (to even greater effect) in the Western classic *High Noon*.

Column South ○

1953, US, 85 mins, colour
Dir: Frederick De Cordova
Stars: Audie Murphy, Joan Evans, Robert Sterling
Rating: ★★

A Western made at the height of Audie Murphy's career with Universal-International. It features an unusual role for Robert Sterling, as a bigoted cavalry captain. It's unusual because Sterling was, for many years, one of Hollywood's best 'good guys'.

Coma ◑ Ⓥ

1977, US, 113 mins, colour
Dir: Michael Crichton
Stars: Genevieve Bujold, Michael Douglas, Elizabeth Ashley, Rip Torn, Richard Widmark, Lois Chiles
Rating: ★★★★

There hasn't been a heroine like Genevieve Bujold's Sue Wheeler in quite a while. In fact the intrepid detective had seemed a theme of the past until *Coma* came along. It gets revived with a vengeance in this story of a doctor who uncovers a racket in spare-part surgery at her own hospital. The perils of Pauline subsequently have nothing on our Sue: scaling to dizzy heights up air shafts; being pursued at length by a hired killer, on whom she ultimately turns the tables in gruesome fashion; beating off security guards and fleeing through a sinister institute; clambering along ventilation systems above a kaleidoscope of dangling corpses; clinging to the top of a speeding ambulance; until finally cornered by the big villain, who turns out to be none other than: but ah! That would be going too far. Would that the script were less comatose stuff. Fortunately, the action prevails and makes this film for most of its running time a real gripper. Bujold's exploits are such that, under the circumstances, co-stars Michael Douglas and company can only stand and gasp.

Comancheros, The ○ Ⓥ

1961, US, 107 mins, b/w
Dir: Michael Curtiz

Stars: John Wayne, Stuart Whitman, Ina Balin, Lee Marvin
Rating: ★★★

John Wayne in action – and how! The explosive action scenes are the best things about this rumbustious Western, as one would expect from the Hungarian-born director Michael Curtiz, whose last film this was. Wayne, of course, remains largely impervious to direction. For the rest, Lee Marvin makes a fine swaggering, half-scalped bad guy but disappears all too soon.

Comanche Station ○
1960, US, 74 mins, colour
Dir: Budd Boetticher
Stars: Randolph Scott, Nancy Gates, Claude Akins, Skip Homeier
Rating: ★★

A typically tough Randolph Scott Western from his later years in films, directed by Budd Boetticher, with whom he made several films in the Fifties. Nancy Gates is a pretty heroine and no mean actress, while character villainy is in the capable hands of a trio of excellent 'uglies', Claude Akins, Skip Homeier and Richard Rust.

Come and Get It ○
1936, US, 99 mins, b/w
Dir: William Wyler
Stars: Edward Arnold, Joel McCrea, Frances Farmer, Walter Brennan
Rating: ★★

Another epic drama from the works of Edna Ferber, whose massive novels proved irresistible film fodder to the Hollywood of the Thirties. Frances Farmer does her best screen work in a dual role, Joel McCrea is a stalwart hero and Walter Brennan took the first of his three 'best supporting actor', Oscars as a Swedish immigrant. Magnificent scenery amid the forests of Wisconsin is filmed with documentary clarity.

Come Back, Little Sheba ○
1952, US, 99 mins, b/w
Dir: Daniel Mann
Stars: Burt Lancaster, Shirley Booth, Terry Moore, Richard Jaeckel
Rating: ★★★

It's a tribute to the talents of director, Daniel Mann (who also directed the hit play) and his veteran Hollywood screenwriter Ketti (real name: Katherine) Frings that such a seemingly unattractive subject should prove so engrossing throughout. Credit, too, the performances, notably Shirley Booth,

the distinguished stage actress winning an Oscar in her first film, as the drudge, Burt Lancaster, in one of the first of his quieter performances, as her alcoholic husband, Terry Moore (also Oscar-nominated) and Richard Jaeckel. Little Sheba, by the way, who never does come back, is the leading character's lost dog.

Come Back to the 5 & Dime Jimmy Dean, Jimmy Dean ● Ⓥ
1982, US, 105 mins, colour
Dir: Robert Altman
Stars: Cher, Sandy Dennis, Karen Black, Sudie Bond, Marta Heflin, Kathy Bates
Rating: ★★

Half-a-dozen middle-aged women gather for the 20th anniversary meeting of a rather seedy James Dean remembrance club in a small Texas town. True to form in this kind of thing, skeletons are soon cascading from cupboards as decades-old lies are stripped away to reveal less palatable truths beneath. Although the film can't quite escape its stage origins, it's very skilfully made by director Robert Altman, especially where the past is reflected in a huge mirror behind the bar of the 5 & Dime store. Sandy Dennis twitches in her familiar bird-like style as the frump who says her son is James Dean's, Cher is quite affecting as the fading belle of the town and Karen Black suitably enigmatic as an at-first-unrecognised stranger. Most impressive of all, however, is Marta Heflin's understated portrait of the pregnant mother-of-six who is happy with her lot.

Come Blow Your Horn ○
1962, US, 112 mins, colour
Dir: Bud Yorkin
Stars: Frank Sinatra, Lee J Cobb, Tony Bill, Barbara Rush
Rating: ★★

Frank Sinatra revels in the witticisms of this very Jewish comedy – and watch for *Bonanza's* Dan Blocker, very funny in the cameo role of an irate Texan. On the whole, though, a slightly disappointing version of the Neil Simon play.

Comedians, The ○
1967, US/Bermuda/France, 160 mins, colour
Dir: Peter Glenville
Stars: Richard Burton, Elizabeth Taylor, Alec Guinness, Peter Ustinov, Lillian Gish, Cicely Tyson
Rating: ★★

Graham Greene's famous story, adapted for the cinema by Greene himself, about a group of people in strife-torn Haiti, all of whom find that they have, in modern parlance, to make some sort of commitment. The story suffers from the central casting of Richard Burton and Elizabeth Taylor, who are essentially 'stars', but Alec Guinness is particularly good as the strange Major Jones – just as much at home in Greene-land here as he had been eight years earlier in *Our Man in Havana*. Lillian Gish and Paul Ford are consistently enjoyable as archetypal innocent Americans abroad, caught up in events beyond their ken.

Comedy of Terrors ● Ⓥ
1963, US, 85 mins, colour
Dir: Jacques Tourneur
Stars: Vincent Price, Boris Karloff, Peter Lorre, Basil Rathbone, Joe E Brown
Rating: ★★★★

Perhaps the most successful horror-farce ever made, this gleeful gallery of ghoulishness is a delight from start to finish. In the depths of a cobwebbed funeral parlour lurk two lugubrious undertakers, Waldo (Vincent Price) and his frog-like underling Felix (Peter Lorre). Waldo's chalky-white father-in-law (Boris Karloff) is also there, aged about 100 by the look of him, but refusing to die off and leave Price the business, in spite of the fact that the medicine bottle Price gives him has a skull and crossbones on it. To add to Price's problems, business is so bad that he and Lorre have to go out and boost trade by helping a few of the sicklier local residents to meet their maker. A black comedy, rich in pace, invention and atmosphere: Price, Lorre and Basil Rathbone (as their landlord) play to the audience in glorious fashion. And Karloff's Aged Parent is the funniest thing around.

Come Fill the Cup ○
1952, US, 113 mins, b/w
Dir: Gordon Douglas
Stars: James Cagney, Phyllis Thaxter, Raymond Massey, Gig Young, James Gleason, Sheldon Leonard
Rating: ★★★

An untypical James Cagney film in that the human dynamo has a battle with the bottle before he starts tangling with gangsters. Cagney's sustained brilliance gives this tough, raw story of a newspaperman who crashes his way back to the top, after drinking costs him his job and girlfriend, some of the kick of the classic film about alcohol-

C

ism *The Lost Weekend.* James Gleason and Gig Young are also strong in support.

Come Next Spring ○
1955, US, 92 mins, colour
Dir: R G Springsteen
Stars: Ann Sheridan, Steve Cochran, Walter Brennan, Sherry Jackson
Rating: ★★★

A sentimental rural drama that no-one at Republic Studios expected to amount to much, although its script had attracted Ann Sheridan, Steve Cochran, Sonny Tufts, Walter Brennan and Edgar Buchanan. When it came out, word of mouth soon spread about the 'nice little picture' that had resulted, and the studio found itself with a nice little profit on its hands. The events of the movie seem so real, in fact, that they make its appealing storyline seem almost dull. Miss Sheridan gives her best performance in ages in a down-to-earth role; Cochran is a gallant second as the errant husband that now returns to their farm seemingly a changed man. Great care was obviously taken in the making of this movie, and it pays off. Even Trucolor seems muted in this very pleasing yarn.

Come On George! ⊙
1939, UK, 88 mins, b/w
Dir: Anthony Kimmins
Stars: George Formby, Pat Kirkwood, Joss Ambler, Ronald Shiner
Rating: ★★★

Formby in rollicking form as a lad who longs to be a jockey, and naturally ends up by climbing aboard the fiercest racehorse that ever broke a rider's collar-bone. He also finds time for several songs in his inimitable style.

Comes a Horseman ◖ ⓥ
1978, US, 113 mins, colour
Dir: Alan J Pakula
Stars: James Caan, Jane Fonda, Jason Robards, Richard Farnsworth
Rating: ★★★★

A romantic Western directed (by Alan J Pakula) and photographed (by Gordon Willis) with a real feel for time and period – the ranchland of Montana in 1945. It's an elaborate but persuasive treatment of a familiar theme. Jane Fonda holds it together with another magnificent performance as the rancher fighting to make it on her own and not have to sell out to the local cattle baron (Jason Robards), whose affair with her as a girl had been the death of her father. James Caan is effective as the 'horseman' who proves her one helper

and the blazing climax, in which they and Robards are involved, brings an interesting film to a highly satisfactory conclusion.

Come See the Paradise ● ⓥ
1990, US, 131 mins, colour
Dir: Alan Parker
Stars: Dennis Quaid, Tamlyn Tomita, Sab Shimono, Pruitt Taylor Vince
Rating: ★★★

The 'rounding up' of Japanese-Americans who were herded together in US confinement camps was one of the war's most scandalous injustices. Only in recent times has compensation for the surviving victims been agreed. Alan Parker's story about this ignoble episode in American history, and the mixed marriage caught up in it, runs a bit like a glowingly photographed TV mini-series, but nonetheless has some fine moments. These chiefly stem from the loving relationship between Lily (Tamlyn Tomita) daughter of a Japanese, and Jack (Dennis Quaid), an Irish-American forever in trouble for helping strikers in one form or another. Historically, the film will be an eye-opener for those of us who were hardly aware such a side to World War Two existed: understandable but still deplorable. As a story, the film is pretty long and slow in the telling: its best moments tend to be spaced too far apart for the comfort of constant attention.

Come September ○
1961, US, 112 mins, colour
Dir: Robert Mulligan
Stars: Rock Hudson, Gina Lollobrigida, Sandra Dee, Bobby Darin, Walter Slezak
Rating: ★★

When he wasn't being a rugged hero, Rock Hudson could turn a very effective hand at light comedy and produced some very enjoyable romps during the Sixties. *Come September* is not one of his more memorable efforts, but it's not his fault. Blame falls on the lack of a witty script and indifferent support from Bobby Darin and Sandra Dee. Gina Lollobrigida, on the other hand, gives as good a performance as her part allows. It's a farce about Hudson's villa in Italy being used as a guest house while he isn't there. The film's problem is that it tries to be witty and sophisticated, which it isn't.

Come to the Stable ○
1949, US, 94 mins, b/w
Dir: Henry Koster
Stars: Loretta Young, Celeste Holm, Hugh Marlowe, Elsa Lanchester, Thomas

Gomez
Rating: ★★★

Nuns, churches, Christmas: all the best ingredients of the Hollywood tearjerker are included in this likeable, if head-in-the-clouds story of two nuns from France trying to raise a large sum of money in America. Heart-warming stuff, so delicately and charmingly played by Loretta Young and Celeste Holm (especially good as a nun who turns out to be a whizz at tennis), that they were both nominated for Academy Awards. Thomas Gomez is a riot as the Italian-bred Brooklyn gangster the nuns wind round their little fingers.

Comfort and Joy ○ ⓥ
1984, UK, 115 mins, colour
Dir: Bill Forsyth
Stars: Bill Paterson, Eleanor David, Clare Grogan, Alex Norton, Patrick Malahide, Rikki Fulton
Rating: ★★

A mellow comedy-drama from director Bill Forsyth, about a local radio deejay (Bill Paterson), who has little time to feel sorry for himself over his girlfriend walking out when he becomes involved in an 'ice-cream war' on the streets of Glasgow. The anecdote is sweet but lacks spice – exactly the ingredient for which the rival ice-cream 'families' are looking. Forsyth's cameras close in on the homely face of Paterson for their best effects, and he's equal to the test.

Comic, The ◖
1969, US, 90 mins, colour
Dir: Carl Reiner
Stars: Dick Van Dyke, Michele Lee, Mickey Rooney, Cornel Wilde, Carl Reiner
Rating: ★★★

Surprisingly denied a theatrical release in Britain, this is a fine tragicomic look at the life of a silent screen comedian with a self-destructive ego, beautifully played by Dick Van Dyke whose film character is a fascinating amalgam of several real-life movie mirth-makers. Also first rate are Mickey Rooney, Cornel Wilde and Michele Lee, with Pert Kelton scoring strongly in a vignette role. The recreation of silent films is excellently done and the Hollywood atmosphere of the times seems so authentic that one can almost smell the excitement.

Coming Home ● ⓥ
1978, US, 121 mins, colour
Dir: Hal Ashby
Stars: Jane Fonda, Jon Voight, Bruce

Dern, Robert Ginty, Penelope Milford, Robert Carradine
Rating: ★★★

Jane Fonda, Jon Voight and Bruce Dern is a pretty high-powered acting trio by anyone's standards, and their superior performances dominate this story of a Vietnam officer's wife who falls in love with a paraplegic just returned from the war. Despite the acting – especially by Fonda and Voight, who both won Academy Awards – this is essentially an old plot in new dressing. It's high-class Vietnam soap opera, in fact, with few surprises. One wonders if the heavy use of four-letter words in the script might have been more effective if confined to Voight's final speech which, as he drifts helplessly into a state of anguish, represents the high point of the actor's career to date.

Coming to America ● ⓥ
1988, US, 116 mins, colour
Dir: John Landis
Stars: Eddie Murphy, James Earl Jones, Arsenio Hall, John Amos
Rating: ★★★

Almost every black actor in Hollywood seems to appear in this rude but funny Eddie Murphy comedy about an African prince who travels to the Queens district of New York – where else? – to find a bride. It's directed by John Landis, who steered Murphy to success in *Trading Places*. The adult script is peppered with risqué one-liners and there's some nudity. But by far the greatest fun is to be had trying to spot the different characters played by Murphy and Arsenio Hall. The make-up disguises are by Rick Baker, who won an Oscar for the special effects in Landis's *An American Werewolf in London*, and the best has Murphy as an elderly white Jew.

Command, The ○
1954, US, 94 mins, colour
Dir: David Butler
Stars: Guy Madison, Joan Weldon, James Whitmore
Rating: ★★★

An action-packed Western in which a Cavalry officer is saddled with the dangerous assignment of steering a wagon train through hostile Indian territory. This was the first CinemaScope Western, and the first 'scope film of any kind from Warner Brothers, a studio previously committed to the 3-D process. Not surprisingly, they threw everything but the kitchen sink into *The Command* – not forgetting the

panoramic shots that showed the new process off to its best effect. Guy Madison was one of the most popular Western stars at the time (he had also starred in the first 3-D Western, *The Charge at Feather River*), and he and James Whitmore both give splendidly forthright performances.

Command Decision ○
1948, US, 112 mins, b/w
Dir: Sam Wood
Stars: Clark Gable, Walter Pidgeon, Van Johnson, Brian Donlevy, Charles Bickford, John Hodiak
Rating: ★★★

Clark Gable, Walter Pidgeon and Van Johnson have the plum roles in this grim-faced but fascinating study of the emotions of top brass who, faced with the choice of sacrificing a few lives to save many, elect to send American air crews to their deaths. With its all-male cast and a script bristling with cynicism and irony, the film was hailed by critics as the first serious Hollywood attempt at a thinking man's World War Two film. The film's moments of humour are very welcome.

Commando ● ⓥ
1985, US, 95 mins, colour
Dir: Mark L Lester
Stars: Arnold Schwarzenegger, Rae Dawn Chong, Dan Hedaya
Rating: ★★

If violent action is your favourite thing in films, then come on down. There is probably more per square foot of it here then in any other film. The mayhem is largely wrought by mighty Arnold Schwarzenegger (the film opens on a close-up of his biceps) who never delivers one blow or bullet where three will do. To set off this human H-bomb, the film-makers fall back on the old story of the quiet strong-man stung into action by a threat to something he loves – in this case his young daughter. To get her back, Arnie's army consists of himself and a stewardess (Rae Dawn Chong) he hijacks into helping him – but it's more than enough for the bad guys, most of whom are Arnie's size just to even the odds a little. Arnie just straps on his arsenal and it's all over bar the shooting, not to mention the throat-cutting, limb-hacking and head-chopping, with the most spectacular death of all reserved for the chief villain, who fails to shoot our hero when he has the chance. As many clichés are turned over as bodies and at one stage one of the bad guys even says: 'Take her below!'

Commitments, The ● ⓥ
1991, US/UK, 118 mins, colour
Dir: Alan Parker
Stars: Robert Arkins, Angeline Ball, Maria Doyle, Bronagh Gallagher, Andrew Strong
Rating: ★★★

Like other factual or fictional stories of bands on the rise, Alan Parker's film gets a tremendous boost from the dynamic performance of its songs by the motley crew of actors and musicians who make up Dublin's The Commitments – 'Saviours of Soul'. You could quite happily watch this well-drilled, adrenaline-throbbing lot all night, and maybe the film would be even more enjoyable if you did. Parker's script piles contrivance on contrivance to make the story go the way he wants, and you can still hardly believe the band breaking up at the end when in reality they'd be high on success. The whole constant four-letter wrangling among the band, in fact, gets a bit wearing, although the script contains a good quota of smile-inducing lines. 'The piano's me granny's,' explains the latest recruit. 'She doesn't know I took it. But she doesn't use the front room very often.' Such occasional gems, the authentic Dublin backstreets feel and the music – this band would be a hit anywhere – make this gig worth a visit.

Communion ◑ ⓥ
1989, US, 105 mins, colour
Dir: Philippe Mora
Stars: Christopher Walken, Lindsay Crouse, Frances Sternhagen, Andreas Katsulas
Rating: ★★

A literate, intelligent and delicate (but not completely successful) 'true life' story of an American writer who really did see little blue men from outer space and eventually found other people who had seen exactly the same creatures (including his own son). Christopher Walken's performance as the writer is remarkable, and Lindsay Crouse is almost as good as his wife. The dialogue has a strange, improvised quality which only intermittently comes off and the film tells its interesting story at rather too great a length. The end product needs patience but makes mainly absorbing viewing for the discerning. Not your average dose of gore, slime and schlock, that's for sure.

C

Company of Wolves, The
① ⊙
1984, UK, 96 mins, colour
Dir: Neil Jordan
Stars: Angela Lansbury, David Warner, Sarah Patterson, Stephen Rea, Tusse Silberg, Graham Crowden
Rating: ★★

A bold fantasy horror tale from director Neil Jordan (it could hardly be more different from his previous *Angel*) that crosses *Legend of the Werewolf* with *Red Riding Hood*. That it fails by the highest standards of its kind is perhaps due to an inconsistent pace that is sometimes as torpid as the bizarre, almost medieval background music and because not all the acting matches that of Angela Lansbury's Granny in quality, as she fills the heroine's head with grim stories of wolves and is doomed, as in the fairy tale, to come to a sticky end. The special effects are gruesomely vivid, and the film is uncommonly successful at creating a fairytale horror environment inhabited by wolves, snakes, polecats, owls, and toads, hopping, prowling and slithering round the crooked houses of the forest.

Compromising Positions ○
1985, US, 98 mins, colour
Dir: Frank Perry
Stars: Susan Sarandon, Raul Julia, Edward Herrmann, Judith Ivey, Mary Beth Hurt, Joe Mantegna
Rating: ★★★

A pleasant surprise: an old-fashioned comedy-thriller-whodunnit whose comic overtones gradually give way to the plot in as painless a way as possible. A lothario dentist in a wealthy area is bumped off. The heroine, an ex-journalist and mother-of-two to whom he had made the standard passing pass, finds her inquisitive nose twitching when several of her friends turn out to have been involved with the victim. In this role, which may look at first glance like a Goldie Hawn reject, Susan Sarandon gave one of 1985's best performances – and that's not easy in this kind of lightweight entertainment. Whether wisecracking, vulnerable, can't-leave-it-alone curious or sick-to-the-stomach brave, Sarandon uses her wide eyes and expressive face to get it just right in a highly intelligent performance.

Compulsion ①
1959, US, 103 mins, b/w
Dir: Richard Fleischer
Stars: Orson Welles, Dean Stockwell, Bradford Dillman
Rating: ★★★★

Although the names have been changed, this is a fairly faithful telling of the infamous Loeb and Leopold case, in which two wealthy college students were brought to trial for the murder of a colleague in 1924. Dean Stockwell and Bradford Dillman are excellent as the two utterly amoral killers but they are overshadowed by Orson Welles, who gives a grandstanding bravura performance as their defence lawyer. It's a tense and absorbing drama and full of suspense even for those familiar with the case and its outcome. The courtroom scenes, especially, are electrifying.

Computer Wore Tennis Shoes, The ⊙
1969, US, 91 mins, colour
Dir: Robert Butler
Stars: Kurt Russell, Cesar Romero, Joe Flynn
Rating: ★★

High Jinks at Medfield College, where, under the auspices of the Disney Studios, various madcap technical and medical misadventures flourished during the late Sixties and early Seventies. Several of these romps starred the studios' perennial juvenile lead, Kurt Russell, who later went on to adult stardom. The studio's touch for screwball comedy was beginning to fade at this time, but the entertainment is amiable enough, especially in the knockabout finale. Cesar Romero and Richard Bakalyan, as the crooks, and Joe Flynn and William Schallert, as the academics, run acting rings round their younger co-stars.

Comrades ①
1987, UK, 178 mins, colour
Dir: Bill Douglas
Stars: William Gaminara, Robin Soans, Imelda Staunton, Philip Davis, Keith Allen, John Hargreaves
Rating: ★★

Long stretches without dialogue. Lingering close-ups of faces and objects. Carefully composed images. An impeccable attention to period detail. Mud and grime. A passionate care for the oppression of the poor. Yes, this story of the Tolpuddle Martyrs and their adventures after deportation to Australia is British film-making at its most concerned. The first half of this epic seems at times wilfully deliberate to the point that it's hard to keep one's attention on what is (sometimes not) going on. Once in Australia the film picks up, both in pace and incident and gains strength from the charismatic performance of John Hargreaves as a convict. Pretty good ensemble playing from little-known players as the Martyrs; and some ripe cameos from such familiar actors as Michael Hordern, James Fox, Barbara Windsor, Freddie Jones, Vanessa Redgrave and Robert Stephens.

Comrade X ○
1940, US, 87 mins, b/w
Dir: King Vidor
Stars: Clark Gable, Hedy Lamarr, Oskar Homolka, Felix Bressart, Eve Arden
Rating: ★★★

Fast and funny farce, made by MGM on the heels of *Ninotchka*, with a racy script by Ben Hecht and Charles McArthur, who wrote *The Front Page*. Like that, this has a newspaperman hero, played at the double by Clark Gable, who is faced with the problem of getting the world's most glamorous tram-driver, Hedy Lamarr, out of her native Russia. The fact that Hedy doesn't want to go is the least of his problems. Director King Vidor keeps it going at the pace of a runaway tram and the chase climax is hilarious. Good satire, good fun.

Con Air ● ⊙
1997, US, 110 mins, colour
Dir: Simon West
Stars: Nicolas Cage, John Cusack, John Malkovich, Ving Rhames, Steve Buscemi, Rachel Ticotin
Rating: ★★★★

We've seen the one about crooks taking over the plane that's just transporting them to justice several times in recent years. But this powerhouse of a film, full of the most explosive action imaginable, gives a whole new adrenalin rush to the old idea. The worst criminals in America are being flown to a new super-secure prison. 'I hope this goes smoothly,' mutters one agent '...all those monsters on one plane.' Hah! Caught in the middle of the ensuing carnage is Poe (a pumped-up Nicolas Cage, as a macho version of James Stewart), a paroled ex-soldier who works from within the plane to bring the escapees to justice. Sensational editing will have you clenching your fists with tension, even though things get a shade too silly at the end.

Conan the Barbarian ① ⊙
1981, US, 129 mins, colour
Dir: John Milius
Stars: Arnold Schwarzenegger, James Earl Jones, Max Von Sydow
Rating: ★★

Grim, taciturn and monosyllabic, big Arnold Schwarzenegger is perfectly cast as Robert E Howard's classic fantasy hero. An unsubtle tale of blood, death and revenge set in a mythical primitive age, this film holds to the spirit of the original stories without actually drawing directly on any of them. Arnie (thankfully) says very little, but then he isn't really expected to. What is slightly surprising is that an intelligent actor like James Earl Jones should chose to play the baddie in such sword-and-sandal hokum.

Conan the Destroyer ○ Ⓥ
1984, US, 103 mins, colour
Dir: Richard Fleischer
Stars: Arnold Schwarzenegger, Grace Jones, Wilt Chamberlain, Mako, Sarah Douglas, Olivia D'Abo
Rating: ★★

This *Conan* sequel is a sort of comicstrip adventure with the accent on the comic. 'Back to the crypt' is a typical sample of its dialogue, and the acting is rudimentary to say the least. Unfortunately comedy needs talent and there's very little evidence of much of that in front of these cameras, although Grace Jones does at least perform with enthusiasm as a formidable female warrior. So, in the end, we're left with the action which, thanks to the professionalism of veteran director Richard Fleischer, is, although formula stuff, brilliantly presented and edited to offer the maximum impact. Further *Conan* sequels were threatened, but Arnold Schwarzenegger, who here has fun with a drunk scene, moved on to subtler stuff.

Concierge, The
See: For Love or Money

Concorde – Airport '80, The
See: Airport '79

Concrete Jungle, The
See: The Criminal

Condorman ⊙
1981, UK, 90 mins, colour
Dir: Charles Jarrott
Stars: Michael Crawford, Oliver Reed, Barbara Carrera
Rating: ★★★

In enlivening this action-comedy from the Disney studio, Michael Crawford reminds us how much he has been missed since he defected to theatre and TV. He's a cartoonist (with a convincing American accent) who gets the chance to play his own creation, Condorman,

when the CIA hires him to bring back doe-eyed defector Barbara Carrera from Russia. The action is efficient throughout, especially in a speedboat battle in which the Condorcraft with its laser gun takes on the KGB's five black boats with their machine guns.

Cone of Silence ○
(aka: Trouble in the Sky)
1960, UK, 92 mins, b/w
Dir: Charles Frend
Stars: Michael Craig, Bernard Lee, Peter Cushing, Elizabeth Seal, George Sanders, Andrew Jackson
Rating: ★★

Buckle your seat-belts for a sweat-inducing slice of airborne suspense. Undervalued character actor Bernard Lee (best known as 'M' in the early Bond films) is here thrust into the spotlight usually reserved for stars. He's a pilot under pressure, a careful, steady type who inexplicably starts crashing planes. The manufacturers are far from pleased and all-too eager to lay the blame at his feet. To give the story extra impetus, a couple of nasty sorts are thrown in: George Sanders as a snide executive and Peter Cushing as a pompous pilot.

Coney Island ⊙
1943, US, 96 mins, colour
Dir: Walter Lang
Stars: Betty Grable, George Montgomery, Cesar Romero, Phil Silvers
Rating: ★★★

Just the sort of colourful, tune-filled tonic of which wartime audiences were in so much need, this confirmed peaches-and-cream Betty Grable's reputation as Fox's biggest musical star. As well as such oldies as 'Pretty Baby', 'Cuddle Up a Little Closer' and 'Put Your Arms Around Me Honey', Betty warbles songs by Ralph Rainger (killed in an air crash while the film was being made) and Leo Robin that include 'Take It from There' and 'Lulu from Louisville'. Perhaps the acting is as over-bright as the colour, but Walter Lang's direction, the multitude of songs and the choreography of the famous Hermes Pan (who stages a splendid finale with 'There's Danger in a Dance') swing it along with all the gaiety of the fairground of the title. The studio and star were so fond of the film that they actually reworked it only seven years later under the title *Wabash Avenue*.

Confession ○
1937, US, 90 mins, b/w
Dir: Joe May

Stars: Kay Francis, Ian Hunter, Basil Rathbone, Jane Bryan, Donald Crisp
Rating: ★★★

Although it's set in Warsaw, the actors all speak perfect English in this tearjerking drama that calls for a full box of tissues to get through the highly emotional storyline. Kay Francis is well cast as a cabaret singer who kills a philandering concert pianist when she learns he's been performing with her daughter. A top-notch cast – and special attention is paid to the film's musical content.

Confessions of a Nazi Spy ○
1939, US, 102 mins, b/w
Dir: Anatole Litvak
Stars: Edward G Robinson, George Sanders, Paul Lukas, Lya Lys
Rating: ★★★

Edward G Robinson is in quietly authoritative mood in this well-paced, fascinating story of the bid by American G-men to break up a worldwide Nazi spy ring. Director Anatole Litvak's sober approach is reminiscent of the surge of documentary-style thrillers which began some six years later with *The House on 92nd Street*. Here, he draws especially good performances from Robinson himself and from Paul Lukas as a propaganda agent.

Confidential Agent ○
1945, US, 122 mins, b/w
Dir: Herman Shumlin
Stars: Charles Boyer, Lauren Bacall, Wanda Hendrix, Katina Paxinou, Peter Lorre, George Coulouris
Rating: ★★★

Written by Robert Buckner, a man responsible, as writer-producer, for some of Hollywood's most polished and persuasive action films, *Confidential Agent* is typical of the many black thrillers turned out by Warners in the Forties – exciting and splendidly paced. Charles Boyer does well in a role that sounds as if it were written for Humphrey Bogart. And Buckner's adaptation of Graham Greene's novel grips throughout.

Confidentially Connie ○
1953, US, 74 mins, b/w
Dir: Edward Buzzell
Stars: Janet Leigh, Van Johnson, Louis Calhern, Walter Slezak, Gene Lockhart
Rating: ★★

This MGM second-feature is a bright, light and lively frolic about the efforts of an expectant mum to satisfy her craving for prime steak. Bubbly Janet

C

Leigh makes the most of her material as Connie and bluff Louis Calhern is at the top of his form is her cantankerous Texas father-in-law. Very good, too, is Gene Lockhart as the college dean who regards dinners given to him by promotion-seeking staff as one of the perks of his office.

Confidential Report ○ ⓥ
(aka: Mr Arkadin)
1955, UK, 99 mins, b/w
Dir: Orson Welles
Stars: Orson Welles, Michael Redgrave, Akim Tamiroff, Patricia Medina, Paola Mori, Robert Arden
Rating: ★★

Orson Welles' first film since *Othello*, three years earlier, has a complicated flashback structure reminiscent of *Citizen Kane* and a leading character who's the mythical figure of a dominating financier, again with shades of Welles' *Kane*. *Confidential Report* was filmed in Spain and bears all the Welles trademarks – tilted camera angles, heavy atmospheric shots, overlapping dialogue. But as a result of a low budget and some pretty amateurish acting, the film rarely touches base with reality.

Confirm or Deny ○
1941, US, 78 mins, b/w
Dir: Archie Mayo
Stars: Don Ameche, Joan Bennett, Roddy McDowall, Arthur Shields
Rating: ★★

Set in wartime London, this romantic drama has some quite realistic scenes of the Blitz, but otherwise proves largely uninteresting. Don Ameche is not entirely at home as the American correspondent, although more so than is Joan Bennett as the teletype operator at the Ministry of Information who falls for him. The supporting cast, though, includes a very young Roddy McDowall and that delightful comic character actor Eric Blore, more familiar to buffs for his regular appearances in Fred Astaire and Ginger Rogers musicals.

Conflict ○ ⓥ
1945, US, 86 mins, b/w
Dir: Curtis Bernhardt
Stars: Humphrey Bogart, Sydney Greenstreet, Alexis Smith, Charles Drake, Rose Hobart
Rating: ★★★

It's fascinating to see Humphrey Bogart and Sydney Greenstreet cast against type – as a man who wants to kill his wife and the psychiatrist who tries to trap him respectively. The casting, and

the performances that result, give a whole new edge to a stock movie plot. Director Curtis Bernhardt – aided by the menacingly dark cinematography of Merritt Gerstad – displays intelligent use of a mobile camera to add shivers to the thrills.

Conflict of Wings ⊙
(aka: Fuss Over Feathers)
1954, UK, 84 mins, colour
Dir: John Eldridge
Stars: John Gregson, Muriel Pavlow, Kieron Moore
Rating: ★★★

This story of a battle between villagers and the RAF over a bird sanctuary is extremely well thought out by screenplay writers Don Sharp and John Pudney, has a string of likeable performances headed by John Gregson and Muriel Pavlow and the bonus of delightful Eastman Colour photography by Arthur Grant and Martin Curtis. A credit mark to all concerned.

Congo Crossing ○
1956, US, 85 mins, colour
Dir: Joseph Pevney
Stars: George Nader, Virginia Mayo, Peter Lorre
Rating: ★

A colourful and unusual adventure story with some picturesque settings. *Congo Crossing* was Peter Lorre's third film on his comeback to the screen after a five-year absence brought on mainly by illness. He returned weightier, but more astringent than ever. Alas, his is about the only enthusiastic performance from a tired-looking cast that also includes Virginia Mayo and George Nader.

Connecticut Yankee in King Arthur's Court, A ⊙
1949, US, 106 mins, colour
Dir: Tay Garnett
Stars: Bing Crosby, Rhonda Fleming, William Bendix, Sir Cedric Hardwicke, Henry Wilcoxon
Rating: ★★★★

This remake of Mark Twain's fantasy that had once provided a hit role for Will Rogers is perfectly tailored to Bing Crosby's laid-back charm. Peppered with inventive incident and photographed so ravishingly in colour by Ray Rennahan that you almost forget Rhonda Fleming can't act, the film also has attractive characters and a winning score by James Van Heusen and Johnny Burke. Pick of the songs is the immortal 'Busy Doin' Nothin' which, shared by Crosby with such unlikely

vocalists as William Bendix and Sir Cedric Hardwicke, became one of the Old Groaner's most enduring hits.

Connecting Rooms ○
1969, UK, 99 mins, colour
Dir: Franklin Gollings
Stars: Bette Davis, Michael Redgrave, Alexis Kanner, Kay Walsh
Rating: ★★

An old-fashioned story of love blooming in middle-age, set against a background of pop music and student riots. Michael Redgrave is quite touching as the unwanted and unemployed school-teacher who rents a room next to Bette Davis, as a seedy cellist. Somewhat underrated.

Conqueror Worm, The
See: Witchfinder-General

Conquest of Cochise ○
1953, US, 70 mins, colour
Dir: William Castle
Stars: Robert Stack, John Hodiak, Joy Page
Rating: ★★

Briskly-told, plainly-acted Western, pleasantly shot in colour and set against some stunning scenery. The many strings to the plot are quickly gathered up, and tied securely during director William Castle's rousing finale. Better casting would have made this a grade 'A' horse opera.

Conquest of Space ○
1955, US, 81 mins, colour
Dir: Byron Haskin
Stars: Walter Brooke, Eric Fleming, Mickey Shaughnessy
Rating: ★★★

First-rate acting from the entire cast enlivens this now-dated but fun story of a trip to Mars. The Martian landscapes weren't too brilliant even then, but the action sequences are good and the film doesn't have a single dud performance. One of the first large-scale, documentary-style space films, it was one of several famous special effects sagas produced by George Pal for Paramount in the Fifties. The first or these was *Destination Moon* which appeared in 1950. *When Worlds Collide* followed in 1951, and Pal's version of H G Wells' *War of the Worlds* in 1953: all three won Oscars.

Conquest of the Planet of the Apes ○ ⓥ
1972, US, 95 mins, colour
Dir: J Lee Thompson
Stars: Roddy McDowall, Don Murray,

Ricardo Montalban, Natalie Trundy
Rating: ★★★

The fourth episode of the Apes saga, full of sound and fury, providing a field day for the colour cameras of Bruce Surtees, who did such a good job on *The Outlaw Josey Wales*. Here, he makes colour by De Luxe seem more vivid than ever before, especially in the final fierce battle between apes and men, when the screen is filled with flickering, flaming reds, yellows and browns. Although various elements of the plot strain credibility to the limit – would you believe a circus owner who champions animal emancipation, or that apes could really be trained to do such sophisticated things as filing and cooking in the next 20 years? – Roddy McDowall is again on hand as Caesar to sustain our interest and anticipation.

Consenting Adults ● ⓥ
1992, US, 95 mins, colour
Dir: Alan J Pakula
Stars: Kevin Kline, Mary Elizabeth Mastrantonio, Kevin Spacey, Rebecca Miller, Forest Whitaker, E G Marshall
Rating: ★★

Kevin Kline and Mary Elizabeth Mastrantonio are reunited from *The January Man* for this urban thriller about a wife-swapping weekend which ends in murder. Unfortunately, director Alan Pakula can't decide if he is shooting a straightforward drama or a thriller. That, combined with cavernous leaps of logic and no sense of the passage of time in the script leaves the film sinking under the weight of its own absurdities. The cast are all pretty good, with Kevin Spacey on top form as the new psychopath on the block. It may not make much sense, but at least Alan J Pakula keeps any blood-letting to a low level.

Conspiracy of Hearts ○
1960, UK, 110 mins, b/w
Dir: Ralph Thomas
Stars: Lilli Palmer, Sylvia Syms, Yvonne Mitchell
Rating: ★★

A wartime escape story with a difference, about a group of nuns who help Jewish children to escape from Italy and Nazi persecution. The villains are rather theatrical, but Ernest Steward's vivid black-and-white photography makes the most of the escape sequences, which contain some tense, exciting and moving moments. The best performance comes from Megs Jenkins, who also makes by far the most convincing nun.

Conspiracy Theory ● ⓥ
1997, US, 136 mins, colour
Dir: Richard Donner
Stars: Mel Gibson, Julia Roberts, Patrick Stewart
Rating: ★★★

Although developments in this paranoia thriller get increasingly unlikely towards the end, its offbeat fascination rarely ceases to grip. Crackpot cabbie Jerry (Mel Gibson) is suspicious of everything. He sees sinister signs all around. His doors are quadruple-locked. Behind them, in his rat-trap flat, he pieces together copy for his 'Conspiracy Theory' handout leaflets. He believes NASA is plotting to kill the president. By night he spies on lawyer Alice (Julia Roberts), badgering her by day with ideas about multiple conspiracies. And yet, somewhere, it seems, jabbering Jerry may have hit a nerve. Men cosh and kidnap him. Drugged and brainwashed, he makes a crazy escape in a wheelchair. For 100 minutes this is fascinating stuff: what the hell *is* going on? Alas, once the plot's secret is out things get dafter by the minute. But, for Gibson's hurt, hunted haunted hero, it remains a thriller to reckon with.

Constant Husband, The ○
19515, UK, 88 mins, colour
Dir: Sidney Gilliat
Stars: Rex Harrison, Kay Kendall, Margaret Leighton
Rating: ★★★

Sparkling Launder and Gilliat comedy about a man who has lost his memory, then finds he's the perfect husband six times over. Cecil Parker and George Cole are excellent in their wittily-written roles as a psychiatrist and a tempestuous Italian, respectively. It's bright, saucy and at times a riot.

Consuming Passions ◐
1988, US, 98 mins, colour
Dir: Giles Foster
Stars: Tyler Butterworth, Vanessa Redgrave, Jonathan Pryce, Sammi Davis, Prunella Scales
Rating: ★★★

The equivalent of a minor Ealing comedy, Eighties style. Ian Littleton, played by tiny Tyler Butterworth as a cross between Norman Wisdom and Ian Carmichael, enrols at Chumley's Chocolate Factory with little hope of success as he has two left everything. Little hope that is until he accidentally plummets three workmen on a trestle into a giant chocolate vat, which devours them noisily within seconds. Sacked on the spot, Ian's reinstated when it's discovered that people hate the chox being marketed by whizzkid Jonathan Pryce and love the new variety. 'Quite unusual,' offers one tester. 'Got a lot of body in it.' Toss in (but, please, not the chocolate vat) Vanessa Redgrave enjoying herself immensely as the predatory Maltese widow of a 'victim' – a veritable falcon of a woman who sinks her talons into Ian for all she can get – and you have a surefire recipe for a tasty black comedy morsel.

Contact ○ ⓥ
1997, US, 147 mins, colour
Dir: Robert Zemeckis
Stars: Jodie Foster, Matthew McConaughey, James Woods, Tom Skerritt, Angela Bassett, David Morse
Rating: ★★

A long and scholarly science-fiction film, sometimes over-sentimental and too often uninvolving, but with some inspired (and inspiring) passages. Foster is the obsessed astronomer who seems to have spent her whole life – from childhood as an advanced radio ham – searching for contact with those 'out here', at first on the airwaves, but with adulthood, in outer space. Too long, unfortunately, elapses before she makes 'contact' and is helped by a genius billionaire (John Hurt) to unravel cryptic alien formulae. The film really picks up a gear about here with some wonderful moments, although the digital addition of President Clinton into several scenes is a mistake and evokes only giggles: an actor should have played this role. Foster is mostly exceptionally good, especially when blasting through megaspace. Errors are made in the last reel, though, that result in our interest draining away.

Contest Girl
See: The Beauty Jungle

Contraband ○
(aka: Blackout)
1940, UK, 92 mins, b/w
Dir: Michael Powell
Stars: Conrad Veidt, Valerie Hobson, Esmond Knight
Rating: ★★★

Conrad Veidt plays a Danish sea captain who finds himself unwittingly involved in a British spy ring in this fast-moving and enjoyable thriller directed by Michael Powell. Veidt is brilliant in the central role, although after seeing him so often as the nasty Nazi Major Strasser in *Casablanca*, it's

C

hard to accept him as a goodie. There are also good performances from Valerie Hobson and Esmond Knight.

Contraband Spain

1956, UK, 82 mins, colour
Dir: Lawrence Huntington
Stars: Richard Greene, Michael Denison, Anouk Aimee
Rating: ★

It makes a change to see Richard Greene casting aside his swashbuckling gear, and here he and Michael Denison, as a British customs officer (Greene's an FBI agent), have a busy time following a tortuous trail of smuggling, blackmail and general skulduggery along the Franco-Spanish border. The beautiful Anouk Aimee is rather wasted in the midst of such thick-ear thrills. The action often drags and the supporting cast is poor.

Conversation, The ◑

1974, US, 113 mins, colour
Dir: Francis Ford Coppola
Stars: Gene Hackman, John Cazale
Rating: ★★★★

Shattering revelations can often be the garland round the neck of the well-made thriller. But when they occur in five-second flashbacks, you'd better be sharp to keep up. To say more would be going unfairly into the ingenious plot of this Francis Ford Coppola film, which features Gene Hackman as a professional eavesdropper haunted by the time his 'bugging' cost the lives of three people and terrified that it's happening again. Hackman is excellent as the 'tapper', and the mood of his loneliness and isolation is well established. But don't blink during the last reel. A pre-stardom Teri Garr and Harrison Ford appear in minor roles.

Convicted ○

1950, US, 91 mins, b/w
Dir: Henry Levin
Stars: Glenn Ford, Broderick Crawford, Dorothy Malone, Ed Begley
Rating: ★★★

Enticing vintage film about prison life, featuring a really splendid cast. Glenn Ford has the hero's part as a man sent to prison for a killing, accidental of course, as any film of Ford's will assume. Broderick Crawford plays the prison governor and Millard Mitchell gives one of his inimitable character portrayals as a 'con'.

Convict 99 ☉

1938, UK, 91 mins, b/w
Dir: Marcel Varnel

Stars: Will Hay, Moore Marriott, Graham Moffatt, Googie Withers
Rating: ★★★★

Another relishable British Thirties comedy classic, with Will Hay as a prison governor who turns his cells into homes from home, complete with armchairs, electric fires, radios and curtains. For once, bewhiskered Moore Marriott steals the show from under Hay's pince-nez, as a would-be escapee called Jerry the Mole, forever tunnelling his way to nowhere. Hay's other constant cohort, tubby Graham Moffatt, is also on hand in this richly funny comedy.

Convoy ○

1978, UK, 110 mins, colour
Dir: Sam Peckinpah
Stars: Kris Kristofferson, Ali MacGraw, Ernest Borgnine, Burt Young
Rating: ★★

A Western with trucks instead of gunmen, Sam Peckinpah's film works well on and off, but could have done with the overall drive of the C W McCall record on which it's based. Peckinpah gives Kris Kristofferson little chance to endow the major character, Rubber Duck (leader of a convoy of trucks running for Mexico after a fracas with police), with the charisma of which he's capable. The movie certainly has its moments; the problem is that they all belong, as it were, to different films. It also has some nice lines. A film of contrasting pleasures and annoyances, then, and, being a Peckinpah vehicle, one that's also peppered with slow motion.

Coogan's Bluff ◑ ⊽

1968, US, 94 mins, colour
Dir: Don Siegel
Stars: Clint Eastwood, Lee J Cobb, Susan Clark, Tisha Sterling, Don Stroud
Rating: ★★★

This rough-and-tumble Clint Eastwood cop thriller, containing some really excitingly-shot chase sequences, can be seen now as a kind of dry run for Dennis Weaver's famous *McCloud* series on TV. Don Stroud is outstanding as Eastwood's quarry, and Tisha Sterling also shines in the strong supporting cast. Good action fare.

Cookie ● ⊽

1989, US, 98 mins, colour
Dir: Susan Seidelman
Stars: Peter Falk, Dianne Wiest, Emily Lloyd, Jerry Lewis
Rating: ★

Take a dozen surefire box-office elements, cast Peter Falk as a wily Mafioso, Emily Lloyd as his streetwise daughter by mistress Dianne Wiest, Brenda Vaccaro as his raucous wife and sundry other talented players, and what do you get? You get a turkey, that's what! The script isn't too bad, so you have to lay most of the blame at the feet of director Susan Seidelman, who did wonders with similar material in *Smithereens* and *Desperately Seeking Susan,* but here displays little sense of the timing or pacing needed for a good comedy. This has only one pace and we're here to tell you it's not fast. Falk and Lloyd at least emerge with decent performances that left their reputations relatively unscathed.

Cook, the Thief, His Wife and Her Lover, The ● ⊽

1989, UK/France,.120 mins, colour
Dir: Peter Greenaway
Stars: Richard Bohringer, Michael Gambon, Helen Mirren, Alan Howard, Tim Roth, Gary Olsen
Rating: ★★

Trust director Peter Greenaway, who made *The Draughtsman's Contract* and *Drowning by Numbers,* to produce a film that was at once the most stylish and repellent of its year. Vulgarity is the keynote and no opportunity is missed to underline it, from the continuous sex and violence, to the crass opulence of the restaurant where it all takes place. Michael Gambon, who in real life and not this Restoration equivalent of the Eighties, would be guaranteed to empty for weeks any restaurant at which he ate, is a disgusting gangster who 'dines' at the Hollandais (which he owns) with his much-beaten wife (Helen Mirren). When she spies a bookseller (Alan Howard) across the vomit on the red plush, it's lust at first sight. When Gambon finds out, the film finally fulfils its promise of something to offend everyone. Michael Nyman's score is his best to date, Greenaway takes it all full-tilt and head-on and Mirren and Howard, who have to perform most of their scenes in the nude, give service above and beyond the call of duty. Don't eat anything for 24 hours before you see it.

Cool Hand Luke ◑ ⊽

1967, US, 126 mins, colour
Dir: Stuart Rosenberg
Stars: Paul Newman, George Kennedy, J D Cannon, Strother Martin, Jo Van Fleet, Dennis Hopper
Rating: ★★★★

Stuart Rosenberg's deservedly popular film has Paul Newman ideally cast as the carefree guy sentenced to two years on a chain gang. He becomes known as Cool Hand Luke because of his devil-may-care attitude and determination to escape. Grittily acted (George Kennedy won an Oscar as another prisoner) and powerfully made, the film also became famous for its phrase, 'Put him in the Box' – the diabolical sentence for prisoners who have incurred the wrath of the guards. Watch also for the memorable egg-eating sequence. Strother Martin, who plays the brutal captain, later rose to co-star status.

Cool Runnings ○ ⓥ
1993, US, 99 mins, colour
Dir: Jon Turteltaub
Stars: Leon, Doug E Doug, John Candy
Rating: ★★

A modest, old-fashioned, one-joke film about the first Jamaican bobsled team to compete in the Olympic Games. The script does its best to jazz the subject up, and there are a few (doubtless fictitious) spanners in the works before the team – consisting of a pushcart champion and three sprinters who fell in the Olympic trials – makes it on to the ice of the Winter Olympics. Coach John Candy does everything but implore his guys to win one for the Gipper, and although the ending is a bit of an anticlimax, the odds are that you'll be in there cheering and crying for the troupe from the tropics.

Cool World ☽ ⓥ
1992, US, 102 mins, colour
Dir: Ralph Bakshi
Stars: Gabriel Byrne, Kim Basinger, Brad Pitt
Rating: ★★

The British certificate (12) really said it all for this mixture of live-action and animation that falls between two stools. Despite strong language it isn't really an adult attraction and the language and sexual references make it not at all suitable for younger children. Once again, though, the actors do yeoman service in the cause of cartoon fun, especially Kim Basinger as the curvy embodiment of Holli Would, a 'doodle' who longs to be real and 'experience it all'. Gabriel Byrne is the cartoonist who finds himself trapped in his own creation and Brad Pitt the other sort of human inhabitant of a world where, apart from one or two main characters, the animation is fluid and skilful but uninteresting.

Cop ● ⓥ
1987, US, 110 mins, colour
Dir: James B Harris
Stars: James Woods, Lesley Ann Warren, Charles Durning
Rating: ★★

You've got to hand it to James Woods. You can't take your eyes off this lethal actor, even in a mediocre movie like this crime thriller, which runs like a Clint Eastwood reject of a few years carrier. No matter: Woods dead-set in pursuit of the bad guys is still a fearsome sight. With tender moments he's less secure, though he's on his own with this dialogue. Spitting out four-letter words like spent bullets and slitting his eyes in search of any clue, Woods is the last man you'd care to have on your tail, as a maverick cop who can't even be dragged off the scent by his superiors after getting wind of a serial killer who inflicts appalling injuries on his victims. Even though Eastwood and Charles Bronson have been down these mean and blood-soaked streets before, Woods, as a man who does nothing by half measures, makes them his own. The film's implicit anti-feminism may restrict the numbers of those who respond to it.

Copacabana ☉
1947, US, 91 mins, b/w
Dir: Alfred E Green
Stars: Groucho Marx, Carmen Miranda, Steve Cochran
Rating: ★★

The very idea of teaming Groucho Marx with Carmen Miranda makes the mouth water, but don't expect too much from this moth-eaten, very cheap-looking black-and-white comedy-musical, which has both funsters straining for laughs as they strive to carry the show on their own shoulders without a decent script to support them. A few light chuckles, but overall about as mangy as the legendary lover of Groucho's memoirs.

Cop & 1/2 ○ ⓥ
1993, US, 93 mins, colour
Dir: Henry Winkler
Stars: Burt Reynolds, Norman D Golden II, Ray Sharkey, Ruby Dee
Rating: ★

Burt Reynolds' biggest hit in years, though it's no better than most of his woeful output since 1980. It's a knowingly performed, strenuously overplayed comedy about a veteran cop (Reynolds) forced to take an eight-year-old black kid (Norman D Golden II) on shift with him in order to prise

out information the boy has on a drugs deal. The kid wants to be a cop and his price for the info is a stint on patrol. Henry Winkler's direction of their subsequent encounters with the crooks encourages his cast to overact and their larger-than-life performances consequently lack any conviction. The stupid comic criminals are a completely outmoded conception, and sad, in view of the fact that some of them, notably Ray Sharkey (whose last film this was), and Marc Macaulay, are obviously capable of genuine menace.

Copper Canyon ○
1950, US, 83 mins, colour
Dir: Jonathan Latimer
Stars: Ray Milland, Hedy Lamarr, Macdonald Carey, Mona Freeman, Harry Carey Jr
Rating: ★★

Star Ray Milland has described this Western – which boasts some magnificent colour photography – as one of the films he most enjoyed making. He plays a trick-sharpshooter who may or may not be a famous gunman. As an expert horseman and marksman, Milland was at home on the Hollywood range, despite this being only his second Western in 57 films. And none of the ten top stuntmen hired for the production was required to stand in for him in the man-sized rough-and-tumble action sequences.

Copycat ● ⓥ
1996, US, 123 mins, colour
Dir: Jon Amiel
Stars: Sigourney Weaver, Holly Hunter, Dermot Mulroney, William McNamara, Will Patton, Harry Connick Jr
Rating: ★★

Even by 1990s standards this serial killer thriller is particularly nasty, so much so that you almost expect Hannibal Lecter to be called in to assist the cops, rather than Sigourney Weaver's criminal psychologist, nearly hanged, drawn and quartered by a madman herself and now mortally afraid to venture out of her apartment. Director Jon Amiel's camera dwells lingeringly on sadistic details as the killer copies famous murders of the past, corpse for corpse and cut for cut. Not much entertainment value in this, although the director gives us lots of scary creepings in the dark as Holly Hunter and partner Dermot Mulroney seek out Weaver's help and then have to try (and of course fail) to protect her from the killer's attentions. Weaver, sometimes overacting, finally does grab

C

our sympathies at the end – which contains one very clever shock, but Hunter, miscast, gives another annoying performance. Will Patton, as her cop ex-lover unreasonably jealous of Mulroney, offers the film's best portrayal by a country mile.

Cornered ○
1945, US, 102 mins, b/w
Dir: Edward Dmytryk
Stars: Dick Powell, Walter Slezak, Luther Adler, Micheline Cheirel
Rating: ★★★★

This high-tension *film noir* is one of Edward Dmytryk's best pictures. Dick Powell's tough guy hero is the equal of his Philip Marlowe in *Farewell, My Lovely* – adept at quick action and cynical dialogue, but romantic enough to cry at the memory of his dead first wife. After several writers had had a go at the script, John Paxton, who wrote Powell's version of *Farewell, My Lovely,* was called in, and did a brilliant job of tightening the whole film up, adding suspense and action scenes to create a *noir* spy classic. Thoroughly decadent studies of villainy from Walter Slezak, Luther Adler and Steven Geray add to the flavour.

Corn Is Green, The ○
1945, US, 118 mins, b/w
Dir: Irving Rapper
Stars: Bette Davis, John Dall, Nigel Bruce, Joan Lorring
Rating: ★★★

Irving Rapper, who directed Bette Davis on two of her other great Forties hits, *Now, Voyager* and *Deception,* assists her to give another telling performance in this fine adaptation of Emlyn Williams' famous play. Welsh actor Rhys Williams who plays Mr Jones, also acted as technical adviser on the film.

Corn Is Green, The ○
1979, US, 93 mins, colour
Dir: George Cukor
Stars: Katharine Hepburn, Ian Saynor, Bill Fraser, Anna Massey
Rating: ★★

In her tenth (and final) teaming with veteran Hollywood director George Cukor, Katharine Hepburn gives a typically proud performance as the devoted teacher in a small Welsh mining town, coming to terms with the school's solitary gifted pupil. Here, the lush location photography is a mite too swish, emphasing the sentimental side of the story. And, while Miss Hepburn's acting is always worth

watching, Ian Saynor struggles to make much of an impression as her talented protegé.

Corridors of Blood ◐
1958, UK, 95 mins, b/w
Dir: Robert Day
Stars: Boris Karloff, Betta St John, Christopher Lee, Finlay Currie
Rating: ★★★

This film laudably brought back Boris Karloff to films after three years' retirement and gave him a far more interesting part to play than the ones that had driven him away in the early Fifties. It's grisly but literate, an interesting period horror thriller, highlighted by Karloff's own compassionate performance as the surgeon who becomes a drug addict when he experiments on himself in bids to find an anaesthetic. Christopher Lee and Francis de Wolff enjoy themselves thoroughly as two evil bodysnatchers called Resurrection Joe and Black Ben. The title refers to the primitive conditions that existed in hospitals at the time.

Corrina, Corrina ○ ⓥ
1994, US, 114 mins, colour
Dir: Jessie Nelson
Stars: Whoopi Goldberg, Ray Liotta, Tina Majorino, Wendy Crewson, Larry Miller, Don Ameche
Rating: ★

An incredibly schmaltzy story of the impossible romance between the newly-widowed father (Ray Liotta) of a five-year-old girl and the black divorcee (Whoopi Goldberg) he hires as a housekeeper. The parade of child-minding candidates he rejects at the beginning of the film is frankly, like the rest of the story, pretty ridiculous. But fortunately Tina Majorino, as the little girl, is, like Whoopi, a real charmer and just about stops us giving up on the whole damned thing. A good supporting cast is embarrassingly wasted.

Corsican Brothers, The ○
1941, US, 111 mins, b/w
Dir: Gregory Ratoff
Stars: Douglas Fairbanks Jr, Ruth Warrick, Akim Tamiroff, J Carrol Naish
Rating: ★★★

Surprisingly, this lively costume adventure was the first sound version of Alexandre Dumas' famous swashbuckling tale. Twin brothers seek revenge on an evil nobleman (a plum role for swarthy Akim Tamiroff) who has wiped out their family. Director Gregory Ratoff, more familiar in char-

acter roles as excitable foreigners, sets a hot pace throughout, and gets excellent performances from fellow character players Tamiroff, J Carrol Naish and H B Warner, as well as from Douglas Fairbanks Jr as the twins of the title.

Cottage to Let ○
(aka: Bombsight Stolen)
1941, UK, 90 mins, b/w
Dir: Anthony Asquith
Stars: Leslie Banks, John Mills, Alastair Sim, Carla Lehmann, George Cole
Rating: ★★★

Anthony Asquith's vigorous comedy-thriller, about Nazi agents on the loose in Scotland, is a splendid piece of fiction of its time. George Cole makes his screen debut at the age of 16 as a cockney evacuee; John Mills is chillingly cast against type as the leading Nazi; and there are striking climactic scenes at an old mill and a carnival hall of mirrors.

Cotton Club, The ◐ ⓥ
1984, US, 127 mins, colour
Dir: Francis Coppola
Stars: Richard Gere, Gregory Hines, Diane Lane, Bob Hoskins, Nicolas Cage
Rating: ★★★

Cornet player Richard Gere finds himself caught in the middle of mobster rivalry in the 1920s in Francis Coppola's stylish gangster film. He gets a job in Harlem's famous Cotton Club, run by gangland overlord Owney Madden (Bob Hoskins), while his brother gets a job as Dutch Schultz's bodyguard. Threads of three different stories intertwine to reach an exciting climax, involving dancer Gregory Hines, Gere, Dutch Schultz (James Remar) and Hoskins. The film looks great and, despite a script that is a little too bumpy, keeps on the boil right to the end. Hoskins and sidekick Fred Gwynne are excellent as is Gregory Hines, who dances up a storm with his brother Maurice. In fact the only problem is Gere, whose performance is flat and uninteresting. He apparently did all his own cornet solos for the film. Maybe he should have concentrated on the acting rather than blowing his own trumpet.

Couch Trip, The ◐
1988, US, 98 mins, colour
Dir: Michael Ritchie
Stars: Dan Aykroyd, Walter Matthau, Charles Grodin, Donna Dixon
Rating: ★★

Remember the remarks about the lunatics taking over the asylum? What about the saying: 'Physician heal thy-self.' And of course you've heard the story about the imposter who makes a bigger success of his role than the man whose personality he's stolen. All three familiar themes are rolled into one story in this solo vehicle for Dan Aykroyd as the escaped mental patient who ends up taking over the practice (and radio show) of a Beverly Hills psychiatrist (Charles Grodin in a typical role) who is himself headed for the couch. (C)rude in the modern American man-ner, the film moves along well, and is good for a few chuckles, notably at the end when one of Aykroyd's patients (a bogus cleric played by Walter Matthau) climbs on to the top of the famous 'Hollywood' sign and threatens to jump off. 'How does this reflect on your treatment of him,' a reporter asks Aykroyd. 'Badly,' he replies. 'But maybe he won't live to tell about it.'

Countdown ○
1967, US, 101 mins, colour
Dir: Robert Altman
Stars: James Caan, Robert Duvall, Joanna Moore
Rating: ★★★

The three major talents connected with this science-fiction thriller were all on the threshold of hugely successful ca-reers. James Caan and Robert Duvall went on to appear together in Francis Coppola's *The Godfather* and Sam Peckinpah's *Killer Elite*, while director Robert Altman went on to his own fame. An exciting space saga with a bone-crushing last reel that will leave you breathless, *Countdown* is most un-characteristic of its director and the ethereal qualities of his later work.

Counterfeit Killer, The ○
1968, US, 95 mins, colour
Dir: Josef Leytes
Stars: Jack Lord, Shirley Knight
Rating: ★★

Hawaii Five-O's Jack Lord has a rough time as an undercover man in this thriller about a ring of counterfeiters. He's shot at, beaten up and thrown in jail for two months – and that's just for openers. To be seen in cameo roles are Charles Drake, Oscar-winning actress Mercedes McCambridge and angular, menacing L Q Jones.

Counterfeit Traitor, The ○
1962, US, 140 mins, colour
Dir: George Seaton
Stars: William Holden, Lilli Palmer, Hugh Griffith, Eva Dahlbeck
Rating: ★★★

Long but frequently fascinating – and sometimes agonisingly suspenseful – true-life espionage story about a busi-nessman who lives dangerously as a double agent for the Allies during World War Two. There's a tremen-dous performance from classic beauty Lilli Palmer, still haunting here in her late Forties.

Countess Dracula ● ⓥ
1970, UK, 94 mins, colour
Dir: Peter Sasdy
Stars: Ingrid Pitt, Nigel Green, Lesley-Anne Down
Rating: ★★

Director Peter Sasdy and star Ingrid Pitt combine well here to suggest the air of total corruption that pervades the castle of the Hungarian countess who bathes in the blood of virgins to preserve her youth. Ken Talbot's rich photography should provide a test of how your colour television copes with varying shades of red. Indeed, in retrospect the film seems to have been all browns, reds and golds, indicating director and cine-matographer's determination to paint a portrait of decay that could have come from the canvasses of Goya. A lot of the supporting acting is of variable quali-ty, but time and again Miss Pitt pulls it all together with her fierce portrait of a bitter woman's determination to hang on to an unexpected, if grisly, new lease of life at all costs.

Count Five and Die ○
1957, UK, 92 mins, b/w
Dir: Victor Vicas
Stars: Jeffrey Hunter, Nigel Patrick, Anne-Marie Duringer
Rating: ★★★

The Franco-Russian director Victor Vicas only made a handful of films, of which this tense war drama and the contrasting *The Wayward Bus* are the best. Here he builds the suspense with terse assurance towards a strikingly shot climax. The convincing espionage fiction is helped by a strong star trio: Jeffrey Hunter's stolid, gullible American is neatly contrasted with Nigel Patrick's jaunty, quick-witted major in charge – not personality traits that one would readily associate with the actors – and the suspected radio op-erator of Anne-Marie Duringer, a West German actress little seen in English-speaking films.

Count of Monte Cristo, The ○
1934, US, 119 mins, b/w
Dir: Rowland V Lee

Stars: Robert Donat, Elissa Landi, Louis Calhern, Sidney Blackmer
Rating: ★★★★

Still the outstanding version of Dumas' classic tale of revenge for unjust impri-sonment. It's a notable director's triumph for Rowland V Lee, who made outstanding use of black and white throughout the Thirties, a period in which he also made *Zoo in Budapest*, *Son of Frankenstein* and *Tower of London*. Here he creates a Chateau d'If with dungeons so dingy, dusty and dirty that they almost make you cough.

Country Girl, The ○
1954, US, 104 mins, b/w
Dir: George Seaton
Stars: Bing Crosby, Grace Kelly, William Holden
Rating: ★★★★

Bing Crosby, in a rare dramatic role, gives the finest performance of his screen career as Frank Elgin, a middle-aged Broadway has-been. This tremendously powerful and moving film version of Clifford Odets' play won Oscars for Grace Kelly, as Best Actress, and writer-director George Seaton, for Best Screenplay. Bing was ironically only nominated for an Oscar, having won the award for a much lesser perfor-mance ten years earlier in *Going My Way*.

Count the Hours ○
(aka: Every Minute Counts)
1953, US, 74 mins, b/w
Dir: Don Siegel
Stars: Teresa Wright, Macdonald Carey
Rating: ★★

Despite an indifferent script and un-even acting, director Don Siegel makes this low-budget RKO thriller quite a tense and exciting drama. Macdonald Carey plays a lawyer who risks private life and career in a race against time to prove the innocence of a man due to be condemned to death. Carey's authori-tative in the role and Teresa Wright works hard as the troubled and hysteri-cal wife of the man so close to execution. But it's Siegel's skills that keep the pot boiling and it's the film's pace that carries it through, in spite of its deficiencies.

Count Yorga, Vampire ●
1970, US, 91 mins, colour
Dir: Bob Kelljan
Stars: Robert Quarry, Michael Murphy, Roger Perry
Rating: ★★★★

The film that pumped new blood into the vampire cycle, if only for a while.

C

A succession of highly effective and sometimes very gruesome shock moments – the sight of the vampire count rushing at the screen as if from nowhere is really very scary – is capped by the shock twist in the final few feet of film. Director Bob Kelljan, a former actor, made nothing better than this rough-hewn contemporary version of the ancient legend.

Count Your Blessings ○
1959, US, 102 mins, colour
Dir: Jean Negulesco
Stars: Deborah Kerr, Rossano Brazzi, Maurice Chevalier, Patricia Medina
Rating: ★★

Jean Negulesco, one of Hollywood's most romantically minded directors, made this melodrama that's faintly reminiscent of another Deborah Kerr film, *Perfect Strangers* (1946). Again, Deborah plays a wartime bride who finds difficulty in adjusting to post-war married life, in this case with Rossano Brazzi. Martin Stephens, the minor menace from *The Innocents* and *Children of the Damned*, contributes an amusing portrayal of the boy who tries to keep his parents' marriage where he thinks it belongs – on the rocks.

Courage Mountain ○ Ⓥ
1989, UK, 98 mins, colour
Dir: Christopher Leitch
Stars: Juliette Caton, Charlie Sheen, Leslie Caron
Rating: ★★★

Three yodels for this spirited sequel to earlier Heidi adventures in which Heidi is a teenager whose days at boarding school prove all too short when the boots of war stomp all over the school and she is thrown into an orphanage. Escaping with four tremulous companions, she faces the same means of escape as Julie Andrews in *The Sound of Music* – over the Alps. When Heidi's grandfather (Jan Rubes) bids her goodbye with the line: 'The mountain is inside you. It will always be there,' we fear the worst. But the adventure that follows proves quite strong and stirring, even if it can't quite make up its mind between the Shirley Temple approach and 1989 realism. But there are some good bits, especially the flight over the mountains and a horrendous orphanage which rivals the one from *The Wolves of Willoughby Chase*.

Courage of Kavik, the Wolf Dog, ○
1978, Canada/US, 90 mins, colour
Dir: Peter Carter

Stars: Ronny Cox, John Ireland, Linda Sorenson, John Candy
Rating: ★★

This is the sort of animal adventure story, shot in glorious colour and packed with incident, that has been popular with children since the days of Lassie. The hero is a sled-race dog called Kavik who is bought by a wealthy man for exhibition purposes. Kavik will have none of his new owner, however, and embarks on a 2,000-mile journey to rejoin the boy who saved his life. Keep a handkerchief handy for the end.

Courage of Lassie ⊙
1946, US, 93 mins, colour
Dir: Fred M Wilcox
Stars: Lassie, Elizabeth Taylo, Tom Drake, Frank Morgan
Rating: ★★★

One of the best investments MGM ever made was to pay five dollars for a collie dog in the early 1940s. The dog, of course, was Lassie, and the success of *Lassie Come Home* and *Son of Lassie* meant there just had to be a third film. Throughout the film, the shaggy hero, who becomes a war hero but has problems on his return, is referred to as Bill. But such was the box-office pull of Lassie that the studio insisted the name remain in the title of the picture.

Courage Under Fire ◐ Ⓥ
1996, US, 115 mins, colour
Dir: Edward Zwick
Stars: Denzel Washington, Meg Ryan, Lou Diamond Phillips, Michael Moriarty, Matt Damon, Scott Glenn
Rating: ★★★★★

Director Zwick, who gave us *Glory*, scores again with another story of war, this time a much more modern one set in the Gulf. Washington, still trying to live with himself and an army cover-up after he blew up a US tank by mistake in night time battle, is asked to validate the posthumous claims of a dead helicopter pilot to a Medal of Honor. At first, the only unusual aspect of the case is that the pilot was a woman (Ryan). The worrying discrepancies start to spring up in the stories of her surviving crew. Under pressure, one dubs her a hero, the other a coward. The resolution couldn't be more moving, agonising or dramatically satisfying. There's a first-rate performance by Phillips as the man who seemingly hated Ryan, and the film is only marred by some over-emphatic supporting acting. Finally, though, it says a great deal about the

different kinds of courage needed to survive.

Courier, The ● Ⓥ
1987, Ireland, 85 mins, colour
Dir: Joe Lee, Frank Deasy
Stars: Gabriel Byrne, Ian Bannen, Cait O'Riordan, Padraig O'Loingsigh, Patrick Bergin
Rating: ★★★

This is Dublin imitating Hollywood circa 1948. No bad thing, either, even on as low a budget as this. As a thriller, it's ultra-simplistic, but faster-paced than many, with hardly a dull moment. Padraig O'Loingsigh and Cait O'Riordan are personable leads with talent to spare, while Gabriel Byrne provides what Hollywood would call the marquee attraction as a sadistic drugs dealer who enforces loyalty with violence, rewards treachery with death and seems to spread his evil shadow over half the city. When the hero's girl's brother becomes Byrne's latest victim, the scene is set for a naive but seemingly effective vendetta which has the heroine justifiably asking her lover if he thinks he's Clint Eastwood. Frank Deasy and Joe Lee certainly know how to direct a film though, and their story is full of terse and suspenseful sequences, with Ian Bannen contributing a grumpy, rat-trap policeman only half a jump behind the villain.

Court Jester, The ⊙ Ⓥ
1955, US, 101 mins, colour
Dir: Melvin Frank
Stars: Danny Kaye, Glynis Johns, Basil Rathbone, Angela Lansbury
Rating: ★★★★★

Magnificent, madcap, medieval romp with Danny Kaye at the top of his form whether performing one of his tongue-twisting songs or fighting a duel with villainous Basil Rathbone. Best of all: the sequence where Kaye is forced to joust with the most fearsome knight in the land (wonderfully well played by by burly Robert Middleton). One of them will have to drink from a tankard which contains a poison pellet, but each has trouble remembering whether it is in 'the chalice from the palace, the flagon with the dragon, or the vessel with the pestle'. Undiluted joy: easily Kaye's best film.

Court Martial
See: Carrington VC

Court-Martial of Billy Mitchell, The ○
(aka: One Man Mutiny)
1955, US, 100 mins, colour
Dir: Otto Preminger
Stars: Gary Cooper, Charles Bickford,
Ralph Bellamy, Rod Steiger, Elizabeth
Montgomery
Rating: ★★★

A fine, blazing courtroom drama, with
Gary Cooper as the visionary and
much-maligned Billy Mitchell who
stood trial in 1925 in secret for bucking
the Army and fighting for a separate Air
Force, as well as correctly predicting
that one day the US would have to fight
Japan. But even 'Coop' is acted off the
screen by Rod Steiger as a truly hateful
prosecutor. Although he only makes a
late appearance in the film, Steiger's
ruthless portrayal makes a powerful impact on the proceedings. The film's
script, good but not that good, was a
surprising choice as an Oscar nominee.

Courtneys of Curzon Street, The ○
1947, UK, 120 mins, b/w
Dir: Herbert Wilcox
Stars: Anna Neagle, Michael Wilding,
Gladys Young, Coral Browne
Rating: ★★★

Very successful through-the-years saga
whose sentiments never ring false.
Anna Neagle plays the maid who marries her aristocratic employer. It was
her second success in a row opposite
Michael Wilding (a late choice for her
leading man in the previous year's
Piccadilly Incident) and established them
as Britain's leading post-war romantic
team.

Courtship of Eddie's Father, The ○
1963, US, 117 mins, colour
Dir: Vincente Minnelli
Stars: Glenn Ford, Shirley Jones, Stella
Stevens, Dina Merrill
Rating: ★★★

Director Vincente Minnelli had the
right light touch for this bright, entertaining comedy-drama about a little
boy trying to pick his widower dad a
new wife. The boy is played with
charm by Ron Howard, later a top
Hollywood director.

Cousins ◑ Ⓥ
1989, US, 110 mins, colour
Dir: Joel Schumacher
Stars: Ted Danson, Isabella Rossellini,
Sean Young, William Petersen, Lloyd
Bridges
Rating: ★★★★

A lushly romantic Hollywood adaptation of the French hit *Cousin Cousine*.
There are no surprises in the plot, so
director Joel Schumacher opts for
sweepingly lyrical music with a touch
of the Italian, and for making immensely nice, sympathetic characters out of
dance master Ted Danson and legal
secretary Isabella Rossellini, both of
whose marital partners (Sean Young,
William Petersen) bed anything in sight
at the droop of an eyelid. When Ted's
dad (Lloyd Bridges) tells Isabella that
his son is 'a failure in everything but
life,' you know Ted's a nice guy. The
central relationship is nicely developed
over a period of months, leaving you in
no doubt as to the outcome, but things
do go on rather a long time, even if
some balance is struck by the insertion
of some funny wisecracks. Rossellini,
looking amazingly like her mother
Ingrid Bergman in certain shots, gives a
skilfully diffident portrayal, but is given
a run for her money by tall Sean
Young, who manages to make
Danson's wife both flighty and dislikeable, but full of personality and odd
redeeming features too.

Cover Girl ⊙ Ⓥ
1944, US, 100 mins, colour
Dir: Charles Vidor
Stars: Rita Hayworth, Gene Kelly, Phil
Silvers, Lee Bowman, Otto Kruger
Rating: ★★★★

Flushed with the success of two musicals teaming their biggest star, Rita
Hayworth, with Fred Astaire,
Columbia decided to mount a really
major musical for her. When they
took a chance on little-proved MGM
contract dancer Gene Kelly as her co-
star, the studio hit the jackpot. Kelly
brought his friend Stanley Donen from
MGM with him as co-choreographer
and the two men worked out a routine
that foreshadowed all their innovative
work together over the next ten years.
This was the 'alter ego' dance that
Kelly performs with his mirror image
(which turns into his conscience) in a
store window. Stunningly costumed
and shot in Technicolor, the film also
has a hit score by Jerome Kern and Ira
Gershwin that includes 'The Show
Must Go On', 'Who's Complaining',
'Make Way For Tomorrow'and 'Long
Ago and Far Away'. Hayworth, Kelly
and Phil Silvers are all on top form and
the dances have an irresistible sweep
and vitality.

Cowboy ○
1958, US, 90 mins, colour
Dir: Delmer Daves

Stars: Glenn Ford, Jack Lemmon, Brian
Donlevy, Anna Kashfi, Richard Jaeckel
Rating: ★★★

This genial Western is based on the
true experiences of Frank Harris, who
found that the lure of life on the range
was too strong to ignore. Jack Lemmon
considers it one of his favourite films
and certainly his comedy-flecked study
of a raw novice on a cattle drive is
most attractive. 'Raw' is the word, for
Lemmon, who's no horsemen, claims
he had to have his saddle-soreness
cured by local anointment with whisky
by the unit wranglers! Glenn Ford is
impressive as the leathery cattleman
who accepts Harris into partnership
and then proceeds to teach him the
business the hard way. Delmer Daves'
direction achieves a happy balance of
action and quizzical humour.

Cowboy and the Girl, The
See: Lady Takes a Chance

Cowboys, The ◑ Ⓥ
1972, US, 128 mins, colour
Dir: Mark Rydell
Stars: John Wayne, Roscoe Lee Browne,
Colleen Dewhurst, Bruce Dern
Rating: ★★★

Still unmistakeably a legendary figure
of the west, even when wet-nursing an
entire crew of sub-teenagers on a cattle
drive, John Wayne's image remains impervious to the over-sentimentality
inherent in this project. He strides
through the story like a dinosaur that
has triumphantly survived its own era.

Cowboy Way, The ◑ Ⓥ
1994, US, 110 mins, colour
Dir: Gregg Champion
Stars: Woody Harrelson, Kiefer
Sutherland, Cara Buono, Dylan
McDermott, Ernie Hudson
Rating: ★★★

Although slow to start, this rowdy
thriller is quite fun once it gets going, as
rodeo riding rivals Woody Harrelson
and Kiefer Sutherland hit the big city in
search of a Cuban-born friend who, unknown to them, has been murdered by
profiteers who have enslaved his immigrant daughter at their sewing
sweatshop. Pretty silly, of course, as
you can predict your heroes riding
through the city traffic with as much accuracy as you can see them roping the
bad guys – but enjoyable if you're in
the right frame of mind. Harrelson is
about right as the bone-headed, woman-
charming, debt-welshing half of the duo
and Sutherland okay as his sobersides
sidekick.

C

Crackers O
1984, US, 92 mins, colour
Dir: Louis Malle
Stars: Donald Sutherland, Jack Warden, Sean Penn
Rating: ★

You can have a great cast (Donald Sutherland, Jack Warden, Sean Penn) and a good director (Louis Malle) and an idea that worked well before (*Big Deal on Madonna Street*) and still end up with a stinker. Supposedly an 'off-beat comedy caper', this certainly misses every beat it can. Its criminals may be inept, but even so they're yards ahead of the script and direction! A gang of deadbeats decides to rob the big safe in the local pawn shop, owned by legendary meanie Jack Warden. That's it, really. With a tight script and a bit of pace, it could have been fun, guys. As it is, this must be one that everyone involved would prefer to forget. You would be wise to do the same.

Crack in the Mirror O
1960, US, 97 mins, b/w
Dir: Richard Fleischer
Stars: Orson Welles, Juliette Greco, Bradford Dillman
Rating: ★★

Orson Welles, Juliette Greco and Bradford Dillman all play dual roles in this Paris-based, ingenious thriller-drama with a courtroom climax. Dillman, the young actor with a mean look (though in an appropriate part he can be just as pleasant), had co-starred with Welles before in another powerful courtroom drama called *Compulsion*.

Craft, The ● Ⓥ
1996, US, 101 mins, colour
Dir: Andrew Fleming
Stars: Robin Tunney, Fairuza Balk, Neve Campbell, Rachel True, Helen Shaver, Skeet Ulrich, Assumpta Serna
Rating: ★★★

Good of its kind if you like tales of teenage witchery, this feisty special effects scarer focuses on four high-school girls majoring in weirdness. Just as an addict might move from soft to hard drugs, this quirky quartet moves from dabbling in the occult to the real thing, invoking demons to wreak revenge on their enemies. A couple of deaths later it's all too much for the girl with the most natural powers (Tunney). She wants out but the others won't let her, particularly chief witchette Balk, a veritable gorgon of a goth who's aiming to drive the defector to suicide. A few tart lines mark this one out as better than most of its kind. The fearsome four-

some is really the whole show, and everyone else pales by comparison.

Craig's Wife O
1936, US, 75 mins, b/w
Dir: Dorothy Arzner
Stars: Rosalind Russell, John Boles, Billie Burke, Jane Darwell
Rating: ★★

This was the film that established Rosalind Russell-both as an actress of forcefulness and substance, and as a name above the title. When Dorothy Arzner, Hollywood's foremost woman director of the Thirties, undertook to make a fresh film of George Kelly's play about a fastidious wife who alienates all those around her, she insisted that Columbia borrow Russell from MGM for the title role. Russell did not let her down, giving a performance of icy dominance. The role of Mrs Craig's walked-over husband cried out for a dull actor, and it certainly got one in John Boles, who performed similar services in other 'women's pictures' (such as *Stella Dallas* and *Back Street*) during the course of the decade.

Crash ●
1996, Can, 98 mins, colour
Dir: David Cronenberg
Stars: James Spader, Holly Hunter, Elias Koteas, Deborah Unger, Rosanna Arquette, Peter MacNeil
Rating: ★★

You'll likely as not want to crash out of this alienating story from a director who seemingly doesn't like making anything if it isn't controversial. This may work for Michael Douglas, but director Cronenberg strikes out again with this thoroughly unpleasant film about people obsessed with sex who, through a bizarre scientific researcher from a hospital, achieve new 'highs' through a fetish for car accidents and bodily injuries. This in turn leads them to a group that likes to re-create famous automobile accidents, including those that ended the lives of James Dean and Jayne Mansfield. As in most of the director's films, visceral details are as nasty as they come. And the dialogue is often difficult to hear, not surprising as the actors seem most of the time to be speaking in whispers.

Crash Dive O
1943, US, 105 mins, colour
Dir: Archie Mayo
Stars: Tyrone Power, Dana Andrews, Anne Baxter, James Gleason, Henry Morgan
Rating: ★★

One of these super-efficient American war films from the Forties. This one has the bonus of Oscar-winning actress Anne Baxter is the girl loved by two naval officers serving aboard the same submarine. Good action, skilfully shot in colour by master cameraman Leon Shamroy, who had three Academy Awards to his name by 1945.

Crash of Silence, The
See: Mandy

Crazy House
See: The House in Nightmare Park

Crazy People ❶ Ⓥ
1990, US, 93 mins, colour
Dir: Tony Bill
Stars: Dudley Moore, Darryl Hannah, Paul Reiser, Mercedes Ruehl, J T Walsh, David Paymer
Rating: ★★★

Slight, silly, but quite engaging, this is a sideshoot of *The Dream Team*. Here, though, the field of the team is not adventure but advertising, as inmates of an asylum design best-selling ads by trying an amazing new concept: honesty. Spearheading their efforts is Emory (Dudley Moore), a frazzled ad executive who got institutionalised after thinking up original posters along the same lines. Within a week, thanks to his campaigns being distributed by accident, his firm is trying to get him out again or, failing that, employing him and his fellow jaybirds from art therapy class as an advertising unit, It all explodes, of course, when everyone gets too greedy. But, this being that kind of film, there's a happy ending, as well as one or two quite sharp barbs of satire along the way. The actual ads themselves are by and large too lewd to commit to print but they, like the film, are good black comedy fun.

Creature from the Black Lagoon, The ❶
1955, US, 79 mins, b/w
Dir: Jack Arnold
Stars: Richard Carlson, Julie Adams
Rating: ★★

This horror shocker created quite a stir when it first came out, and the initial appearance of its monster – one scaly claw clutching at the shore on emergence from the water – is a splendid piece of stage-management by director Jack Arnold. Julie Adams, in unscientific brief shorts, is a screaming heroine in the most vulnerable tradition of Fay Wray.

Creeping Flesh, The ●

1972, UK, 88 mins, colour
Dir: Freddie Francis
Stars: Peter Cushing, Christopher Lee
Rating: ★★★★

This impressive Tigon horror movie is very much a return in class and style to the early Hammer films. Peter Cushing plays the scientist with a skeleton in the cupboard (his mad ex-wife) as well is one on the slab, the remains of a giant prehistoric man which develops new flesh when water drops on the bones. A great deal of scientific mumbojumbo is handled with sufficient flair to keep us from pondering its latent absurdities. But the film's real secret lies in its style, never flashy, but knitting together its complicated plot with considerable skill. Cushing's customary cultured performance looks even better in a strong storyline, while Lorna Heilbron is excellent as the repressed daughter to whom he administers an 'anti-evil' serum with perhaps inevitable results.

Creeping Unknown, The

See: The Quatermass Experiment

Creepshow ● ⓥ

1981, US, 120 mins, colour
Dir: George A Romero
Stars: Hal Holbrook, Adrienne Barbeau, Leslie Nielsen, Ted Danson, Ed Harris
Rating: ★★

This collaboration between one of America's greatest horror directors (George A Romero of *The Night of the Living Dead* fame) and top horror novelist Stephen King promises much with its five stories-in-one format. But despite supplying shocks in all the right places, it leaves you thinking 'so what?' at the end. King himself turns up in *The Lonesome Death of Jordy Verrill* episode, but his appearance only emphasises that he should stick to what he does best. Watch for early appearances by Ed Harris and Ted Danson. A lot better, incidentally, than *Creepshow 2*.

Creepshow 2 ● ⓥ

1987, US, 90 mins, colour
Dir: Michael Gornick
Stars: Lois Chiles, George Kennedy, Dorothy Lamour, Tom Savini, Page Hannah, Stephen King
Rating: ★

Only three stories for comic-book horror fans in this second compendium of creepies – and all of them good for more chuckles than chills under the direction of Michael Gornick, who was well-advised to stick to his career as a

cinematographer after this. The third, concerning a hit-and-run victim who comes back to haunt his killer, has the best of George A Romero's dialogue and the best performance (Lois Chiles), but simply doesn't know how to round off its story with any ending other than the sickeningly conventional. Gornick's direction has no idea of how to shock an audience other than with head-on or overt horror; it's almost as sad as the appearance of a much-aged Dorothy Lamour in episode one.

Crime and Punishment ○

1935, US, 88 mins, b/w
Dir: Josef von Sternberg
Stars: Peter Lorre, Edward Arnold, Marian Marsh, Tala Birell
Rating: ★★★

One of the most interesting films made by the fascinating, bug-eyed, Hungarian-born Hollywood star Peter Lorre – a cold but strangely compelling version of Dostoevsky's novel. Predictably, and even with Josef von Sternberg in the director's chair, the film's writers kicked out most of the psychological undertones of the original, making Lorre's murderer's descent into guilt-ridden anguish rather too peremptory for total belief. Both von Sternberg and Lorre, however, had carefully read the original book and their interpretation, if confined by the demands of melodrama, is full of masterly touches and unexpected flashes of sardonic humour.

Crime of Passion ○

1956, US, 86 mins, b/w
Dir: Gerd Oswald
Stars: Barbara Stanwyck, Sterling Hayden, Raymond Burr, Fay Wray
Rating: ★★

Barbara Stanwyck, queen of movie melodrama, is in her element in this dramatic story of a wife who will stop at nothing – even murder – to further her husband's career. Although she dominates the film, her thunder is almost stolen at times by Fay Wray, giving a compellingly understated portrayal.

Crimes and Misdemeanors ◐ ⓥ

1989, US, 104 mins, colour
Dir: Woody Allen
Stars: Martin Landau, Woody Allen, Mia Farrow, Anjelica Huston, Alan Alda, Claire Bloom
Rating: ★★★

One of Woody Allen's better movies, this blends his three themes – comedy,

drama and personal angst – in almost as seamless a way as in *Hannah and Her Sisters*. As in *Hannah*, the action is bathed in a golden glow. But there's nothing golden about the predicament of Judah (Martin Landau), faced with a neurotic, quasi-blackmailing mistress (Anjelica Huston) and a gangster brother (Jerry Orbach) who offers him the devil's way out of the mess. Allen himself stars in the film's second plot, as a twitchy documentary film-maker whose marriage is falling apart. In a well-worked ending, the two leading characters only meet each other at a wedding in the final scene, where everything is resolved not as in a Hollywood happy ending, but as it might be in real life. Though a little top heavy with philosophical talk, the film and its doomy mood are lightened by some typical Woody one-liners.

Crimes of Passion ● ⓥ

1984, US, 115 mins, colour
Dir: Ken Russell
Stars: Kathleen Turner, Anthony Perkins, John Laughlin, Annie Potts, Bruce Davison
Rating: ★★★

Originally called *China Blue,* a rather better title, this is a heady psychothriller from Ken Russell, dripping with strong dialogue and graphic sex and photographed almost entirely in pastel neon shades. Anthony Perkins, entering into the gaudy spirit of the thing with total commitment, superbly dominates the film as the Peeping Tom priest who haunts the strip joints of the city and alternately longs to save or have (using fevered epithets that amalgamate the Bible and the gutter) a ritzy prostitute called China Blue (Kathleen Turner), who's a better actress in the bedroom than most Hollywood starlets on screen. Enter unhappily married Bobby (John Laughlin), sent to spy on CB in her daytime capacity of draughtsperson for a garment film, and the scene is ultimately set for a *Klute*-type finale. The direction makes the most of what the film has and the raunchy music thickens its atmosphere; but it's Perkins' frenzied strength that gives this hemlock cocktail its lethal kick.

Crimes of the Heart ◐ ⓥ

1986, US, 105 mins, colour
Dir: Bruce Beresford
Stars: Diane Keaton, Jessica Lange, Sissy Spacek, Sam Shepard, Tess Harper
Rating: ★★

C

Diane Keaton, Sissy Spacek and Jessica Lange in the same film seems too good to be true. And so, in a way, it proves. Even though the ladies are all as luminous as you'd expect (as three sisters living on the edge of madness with an inheritance of same), this anecdote is far too slight for the talents involved. The sisters, all eccentric and subject to violent outbursts in which they hardly know what they are doing, are brought together again by the terminal illness of their grandfather (Hurd Hatfield: Dorian Gray trying in vain to look ancient), but more urgently by the fact that the youngest, Babe (Sissy Spacek), has just shot her husband close to death. Occasionally too dull even for these three to redeem, the film is glowingly, if fairly gloomily shot in colour by Dante Spinotti, and has some felicitous comic moments, mostly from Spacek.

Crime Time ● Ⓥ

1996, UK, 120 mins, colour
Dir: George Sluizer
Stars: Stephen Baldwin, Sadie Frost, Pete Postlethwaite, Karen Black, Geraldine Chaplin, James Faulkner
Rating: ★

A bad 'B' crime movie about an out-of-work actor (Baldwin) whose portrayal of a serial killer (Postlethwaite) on a television crime programme shoots him into the public eye. He begins to identify with the killer – who removes an eye and a stocking from his female victims. When the killer is injured and stops his deadly handiwork, the actor, increasingly unhinged, finds himself out of work, unless... Interesting idea for late-night gore fiends and criminal psychologists, but numbingly overlong and less than professionally done. The players, particularly Sadie Frost, need more help from their director than they seem to be getting here. The once-great Karen Black is awful in an all-too-showy supporting role.

Crimewave ◐

(aka: Broken Hearts and Noses)
1985, US, 85 mins, colour
Dir: Sam Raimi
Stars: Brion James, Louise Lasser, Sheree J Wilson, Paul Smith
Rating: ★

Sam Raimi, who made *The Evil Dead* trilogy, and maverick film makers Joel and Ethan Coen combine their talents here to make a comedy. And it's terrible. Stick to the serious stuff, boys. Raimi and the Coens reveal themselves here as admirers of The Three Stooges, whose poke-in-the-eye direct style of

comedy is yoked to a would-be *Airplane* of *film noir*, about two 'exterminators' (Paul Smith and Biron James) on a robbery and killing spree. The result? Didn't we tell you already? It's terrible! Unless you fancy a good sleep, stay away. The timing is crashing, the actors contort their faces desperately to try and make something of it and, to their credit, in the last 10 minutes they almost do.

Crime Wave

See: The City Is Dark

Criminal, The ●

(aka: The Concrete Jungle)
1960, UK, 97 mins, b/w
Dir: Joseph Losey
Stars: Stanley Baker, Sam Wanamaker, Margit Saad, Patrick Magee, Jill Bennett
Rating: ★★★

Stanley Baker's rugged performance and a really top-notch supporting cast make this thriller live up to its reputation as one of the toughest films ever made in Britain. Joseph Losey's direction is fast-paced and uncompromising, and the action is raw, shocking in parts, always compelling. And be prepared for a script (by Alun Owen) that takes a hard look at Britain's prison system.

Criminal Law ● Ⓥ

1988, US, 118 mins, colour
Dir: Martin Campbell
Stars: Gary Oldman, Kevin Bacon, Karen Young, Joe Doe Baker, Tess Harper
Rating: ★★

Not half as bad as its two-year wait for a cinema release might suggest, this serial killer thriller is overlong and rather sonorously presented. It does, however, have good performances from Kevin Bacon as the criminal and Gary Oldman as the law, a very smart legal eagle who gets Bacon off the hook on an especially grisly murder/rape/mutilation charge, only to realise that a) Bacon's guilty b) he's gleefully killing to some kind of rote and c) is toying with Oldman by asking him to represent him again. There's some eye-closing suspense, and good support from Karen Young and Elizabeth Shepherd, but the film comes close to being silly at times and lets its last scene go on too long. With this cast and a good story (not the same as a good script!) it could have been excellent. One imagines the two leading actors could just as easily have played each other's roles, but no doubt both enjoyed the change of pace.

Criminals

See: Once Upon a Crime

Crimson Cult

See: Curse of the Crimson Altar

Crimson Pirate, The ○

1952, UK, 100 mins, colour
Dir: Robert Siodmak
Stars: Burt Lancaster, Nick Cravat, Eva Bartok, Torin Thatcher
Rating: ★★★

Burt Lancaster made this British swashbuckler in the midst of his man-of-action period that also included *The Flame and the Arrow*. This adventure story is played relentlessly tongue-in-cheek; a burlesque, in fact, with Lancaster poking fun at his own acrobatic ability, ably assisted by little, bearded Nick Cravat, in real life his former circus partner. Good colour photography by Otto Heller and loads of battles at sea complement skilful direction by Robert Siodmak. Christopher Lee has a small role and gets to fight a duel with the star.

Crimson Tide ● Ⓥ

1995, US, 116 mins, colour
Dir: Tony Scott
Stars: Gene Hackman, Denzel Washington, George Dzundza
Rating: ★★★

Boy, are the men of the United States submarine *Alabama* in trouble. They're not only on full nuclear alert, and in possession of an incomplete message regarding the launch of their missiles against Russia, but there's mutiny, and counter-mutiny, aboard their own vessel. The captain (Gene Hackman) is a by-the-book professional seaman, which makes his (unlawful) decision to relieve his new exec (Denzel Washington) of his duties after a pre-nuclear shouting match all the more surprising. Washington's subsequent successful assumption of command and confinement of Hackman to his quarters seems even more bizarre. Never mind, logic isn't a necessary ingredient in films like this: driven thunderously along by director Tony Scott, its suspense really bites and its undersea action hammers home the thrills. And, before the deep-sea tension starts to rise, there are some fine shots of the submarine above water, puffing like a grampus as it plunges through and then beneath the waves.

Cripple Creek ○

1952, US, 77 mins, colour
Dir: Ray Nazarro

Stars: George Montgomery, Karin Booth, Jerome Courtland, Richard Egan
Rating: ★★

One of a whole posse of Technicolor Westerns George Montgomery made at Columbia in the early Fifties, all of them chock-full with action and gunplay, and setting a rousing pace from the opening scenes. Some interesting names cropped up in the supporting casts of these vigorous movies, and here there's William Bishop, Richard Egan, Don Porter and John Dehner to back up the stars in a story of two federal agents working undercover to bring to book a big gang of bullion raiders.

Crisis ○
1950, US, 95 mins, b/w
Dir: Richard Brooks
Stars: Cary Grant, Jose Ferrer, Paula Raymond, Signe Hasso, Ramon Novarro, Gilbert Roland
Rating: ★★

An often tense Richard Brooks film, set in one of those South American republics where the government could change at any second and a rifle barrel peers from every corner. Cary Grant is unusually cast as the surgeon held hostage so that he can operate on the current dictator, a very similar situation to that found in *State Secret*, which was being made in Britain at more or less the same time. Two Hollywood veterans from the Latin lover bracket, Antonio Moreno and Ramon Novarro, make valuable contributions to the suspense, and the riot scenes are spectacularly staged. The pace is a bit stately at times away from the action scenes.

Criss Cross ○
1948, US, 87 mins, b/w
Dir: Robert Siodmak
Stars: Burt Lancaster, Yvonne De Carlo, Dan Duryea
Rating: ★★★★

Another moody, doom-laden crime thriller from the Forties directed by Robert Siodmak, who made the brilliant 1945 version of *The Spiral Staircase*. The American-born, German-raised Siodmak came to Hollywood in the war years and, throughout the Forties, created his own world of dark action films, a world of night, of desperation, of menace, of murder and of despair. Most of those elements are present in *Criss Cross*, a rarely-seen but classic example of *film noir*. Burt Lancaster, all sub-surface menace, rarely allows himself a smile as the man whose obsession

with his ex-wife (a well-cast Yvonne De Carlo) drags him ever deeper into a mire of secrecy and crime. Dan Duryea is a splendidly flashy villain and Tony Curtis makes his film debut in a tiny role as a young gigolo.

CrissCross ● ⓥ
1992, US, 101 mins, colour
Dir: Chris Menges
Stars: Goldie Hawn, Keith Carradine, Arliss Howard, J C Quinn, James Gammon, Steve Buscemi
Rating: ★

For all of those who can't believe there's a Goldie Hawn film that wasn't worth releasing, here's the proof. Goldie makes another stab at serious drama here, following the rather more successful *Deceived*. But this shallow story of a woman's struggle in the Sixties to make a better life for herself and her 12-year-old son is slow and oversaturated with melodrama. The plot sees Hawn taking a job as a stripper to make ends meet after her soldier husband (Keith Carradine), a mixed-up Vietnam vet, has left her for life in a monastery. Even Goldie's fiercest fans will have to fight to enjoy this one or, for that matter, to even stay awake.

Critical Condition ● ⓥ
1986, US, 100 mins, colour
Dir: Michael Apted
Stars: Richard Pryor, Rachel Ticotin, Ruben Blades, Joe Mantegna
Rating: ★

The talents of comedian Richard Pryor are wasted in this supposedly madcap mixture of medical mayhem, as are those of director Michael Apted. Writers Denis and John Hamill are to blame for a script that even Pryor's comic gifts can't salvage. All in all, there's too much going on to too little comic effect. Apted hasn't had too many flops in a distinguished career, but this was certainly one of them.

Critters ◑ ⓥ
1986, US, 86 mins, colour
Dir: Stephen Herek
Stars: Dee Wallace Stone, M Emmet Walsh, Billy Green Bush
Rating: ★★

A group of aliens escape from a prison in space and ends up causing chaos in Kansas. Looking like oversized hairballs, the Krites (hence critters) are no real danger to mankind, although the bounty hunters sent to catch or destroy them are a bit heavy-handed. All done with tongues firmly in cheeks, *Critters* is enjoyable enough, if ultimately rather

predictable. A fun idea is having translations of the critters' gobbledegook chattering coming up as subtitles in colloquial English.

Crocodile Dundee ○ ⓥ
1986, Australia, 102 mins, colour
Dir: Peter Faiman
Stars: Paul Hogan, Linda Kozlowski, John Meillon
Rating: ★★★

A pleasant surprise and no mistake. Expect a broad, vulgar farce from Aussie comic Paul Hogan on his major film debut? Think again, cobber. Hogan projects an endearing image as a tall tale-telling outback man whose flip chat cloaks a tough and experienced hide. To be sure, there are many funny lines – but always within the context of the story. The first half of the film is taken almost straight, with a streak of quirky, natural wit, as Dundee shows an inquisitive American reporter (Linda Kozlowski) the wild regions where he had a (much-embroidered) narrow escape from a crocodile. His subsequent exploits in New York are more predictable and less relaxed, but still enjoyable. Kozlowski, with her Esther Rantzen looks and Jane Fonda voice, is perfectly cast as the amorous scribe, and Hogan's subtle, inch-perfect underplaying is a revelation.

Crocodile Dundee II ○ ⓥ
1988, Australia, 111 mins, colour
Dir: John Cornell
Stars: Paul Hogan, Linda Kozlowski, John Meillon
Rating: ★★

A largely disappointing sequel to the original box office smash, with Aussie charmer Paul Hogan again as Mick 'Crocodile' Dundee, so called because of his infamous battle with a giant croc. Hogan's real-life partner, Linda Kozlowski, is still the heroine and still helpless, and it's left to Hogan as the irreverent, amiable Aussie to carry the movie on his charisma alone.

Cromwell ○ ⓥ
1970, UK, 141 mins, colour
Dir: Ken Hughes
Stars: Richard Harris, Alec Guinness, Robert Morley, Dorothy Tutin, Frank Finlay, Timothy Dalton
Rating: ★★

Some folk have said that Oliver Cromwell was the last person to enter Parliament with honourable intentions. They might be right. But here we see a rather laboured and grinding version of

C

his rise to puritanical power, directed by Ken Hughes, who had made such a good historical job of *The Trials of Oscar Wilde* in 1960. The Lord Protector and pretender to the throne vacated by Charles I (Alec Guinness) is played by Richard Harris who does a splendid job in convincing us that, perhaps, Cromwell was just a pretender.

Crooks and Coronets ○
(aka: Sophie's Place)
1969, UK, 120 mins, colour
Dir: Jim O'Connolly
Stars: Telly Savalas, Edith Evans, Warren Oates, Cesar Romero
Rating: ★★

Kojak is a crook! Well, at any rate, before his famous cop characterisation was thought of, Telly Savalas came to Britain to make this daft comedy about some American crooks trying to rob an English stately home. At times, the pace is as sedate as the English aristocracy portrayed: but the magnificently lunatic climax is worth waiting for, as crooks fall out on the final assault on Great Friars, and are finally repulsed by a concerted counter-attack involving crossbows, a lion, and Edith Evans at the controls of a vintage German plane. It has to be said that Dame Edith has no trouble in beating the Americans at the acting game, either.

Crooks Anonymous ○
1962, UK, 87 mins, b/w
Dir: Ken Annakin
Stars: Leslie Phillips, Stanley Baxter, Wilfrid Hyde White, Julie Christie
Rating: ★★

A quite amusing comedy, one of a successful series from producers Julian Wintle and Leslie Parkyn, which gave Julie Christie her first starring role in pictures. Brisk direction by Ken Annakin carries the film triumphantly through its stickier patches.

Cross Creek ○ ⓥ
1983, US, 122 mins, colour
Dir: Martin Ritt
Stars: Mary Steenburgen, Rip Torn, Peter Coyote, Alfre Woodard
Rating: ★★★★

Definitely an old-fashioned film, and very nearly an exceptional one. Director Martin Ritt goes back to the Deep South he lovingly surveyed in *Sounder* and *Conrack* and digs up a true story about a 30-year-old failed woman writer, Marjorie Kinnan Rawlings, who, in 1928, left her husband and went to live in an obscure part of the Florida Everglades to continue writing

her 'Gothic romances'. Inevitably the lives of the dirt-poor people of the Creek became her life and she began to write about them instead. Her memoir, *Cross Creek,* was published in 1942 and, ironically, the weakest parts of this warm and gentle film are where her actual words are used. When Ritt relies on the screenplay written for him by Dalene Young, the movie is often a real heartbreaker. Not a lot happens to Marjorie in Cross Creek, yet you are never bored. And the performance of Mary Steenburgen as Marjorie, shamefully ignored in the Oscar race that year, is exactly the blend of femininity and strength that the role requires.

Crossfire ○
1947, US, 85 mins, b/w
Dir: Edward Dmytryk
Stars: Robert Young, Robert Mitchum, Robert Ryan, Gloria Grahame, Sam Levene
Rating: ★★★★

Probably Edward Dmytryk's best film, and a milestone in the history of the American crime thriller. The script, by John Paxton and Richard Brooks, from Brooks' own novel *The Brick Foxhole,* was so adult, hard-hitting and entertaining at the same time, that it opened the door for a whole series of superior racial prejudice films. The three Roberts, Mitchum, Young and Ryan, are all excellent, with top honours perhaps going to Ryan, in this story of the murder of a Jewish ex-GI well played by Sam Levene. A young Gloria Grahame made such a striking impression in this film that she was nominated for an Academy Award.

Crossing Delancey ○
1988, US, 97 mins, colour
Dir: Joan Micklin Silver
Stars: Amy Irving, Peter Riegert, Reizl Bozyk, Jeroen Krabbé, Sylvia Miles
Rating: ★★★

A Jewish *Moonstruck,* though not quite as good. It's a romance of embarrassing moments, with Amy Irving as the bookstore girl from uptown horrified to find herself the victim of old-style matchmaking with Sam the pickleman from downtown. There are some pleasant patches in subsequent developments, with the dry-humoured Peter Riegert deservedly getting all the best lines as Sam: a beautifully understated performance. Irving is competent-plus as the girl and, if a few unlikely plot acrobatics towards the end rather rob the film of its climactic emotional impact, the odds are that you'll still be hoping

Irving makes the 'right' decisions before the curtain comes down on the story.

Crossing Guard, The ● ⓥ
1995, US, 114 mins, colour
Dir: Sean Penn
Stars: Jack Nicholson, David Morse, Anjelica Huston, Robin Wright, Piper Laurie, Richard Bradford, John Savage
Rating: ★★★

Guilty of overkill on more than one occasion, this sombre drama still manages to draw an agonised performance from Jack Nicholson that ranks with his best. It's the long and at times dreary story of two men trying to come to terms with the death of a child in a hit-and-run accident: Nicholson is the father, drowning his sorrow in drink, Morse the driver, sent to prison, but still not at peace with himself on his release: Nicholson sees that release simply as a chance to get even. Although some points are thumped home with a sledgehammer, it's redeemed by the acting. Piper Laurie and Richard Bradford put in good, concerned work as Morse's parents, and Anjelica Huston is quite exceptional as Nicholson's bile-filled ex-wife. Their performances raise the drama to heights that director Penn's own screenplay doesn't really justify. Not one, though, to cheer you up.

Cross of Iron ● ⓥ
1977, UK/West Germany, 119 mins, colour
Dir: Sam Peckinpah
Stars: James Coburn, James Mason, Maximilian Schell, Senta Berger, David Warner
Rating: ★★★

This grim war film set during the German army's disastrous Russian campaign in 1943 is a more thoughtful film than director Sam Peckinpah's usual fare, although it's still up to his usual bloody and violent standard. It not only deals with the German/Russian battle, but with the conflict between an arrogant Prussian officer (Maximilian Schell) and a more pragmatic, battle-weary sergeant (James Coburn). As a story of men suffering the pressures of war, the film has a worthy air, but harsh realism stops it being an enjoyable film, even though at times it is admittedly engrossing. Schell fills the role of the upper class officer well, but Coburn seems less at ease with the intelligent, philosophical but tough sergeant.

Crossplot ○

1969, UK, 92 mins, colour
Dir: Alvin Rakoff
Stars: Roger Moore, Martha Hyer, Alexis
Kanner, Francis Matthews, Bernard Lee
Rating: ★★

Roger Moore and Bernard Lee are
ironically cast as an advertising executive (innocently entangled in an
assassination attempt) and his client in
this thriller, four years before they met
again as James Bond and his boss 'M'.
Apart from its tense finale, the plot is
commonplace, but there's some nice
Eastman Colour photography of
London locations by Brendan J
Stafford a veteran (and one time director) of films whose career went back to
the earliest days of British sound
cinema.

Crossroads ◑

1986, US, 96 mins, colour
Dir: Walter Hill
Stars: Ralph Macchio, Joe Seneca, Jami
Gertz
Rating: ★★

For anyone except the most die-hard
traditional blues aficionado, the music
is the thread that holds this film together. Ralph Macchio, seen in the *Karate
Kid* role, of which this is a sort of musical version, is a brilliant young
musician who finds Willie, an aged survivor of the blues era, and takes him
on the road back to the Mississippi
delta, where he and other blues legends
had lived and played. This could have
been a more intelligent film, but for the
fact that it obviously wanted to keep
Karate Kid fans watching. Nevertheless,
it remains an entertaining tale. Joe
Seneca is enjoyable as Willie and
Macchio, as the 'lightnin' kid', looks a
convincing guitarist. And there are
some satisfying slices of old-time philosophy. 'Blues,' explains Seneca to his
young travelling companion, 'ain't
nothin' but a good man feelin' bad.'
The only slightly jarring note is
Eugene's climactic guitar duel with a
heavy metal player which doesn't have
much to do with the blues.

Crow, The ● Ⓥ

1994, US, 110 mins, colour
Dir: Alex Proyas
Stars: Brandon Lee, Michael Wincott,
Ernie Hudson, Jon Polito
Rating: ★★

The sad thing about this impressively
staged comic-strip action movie in the
ultra-violent mould, as far as being a
tribute to its deceased star, is that Lee's
presence doesn't actually add anything
to it. His part could be played by
Dolph Lundgren or any other action
star without changing the impact of the
film. As it is, Lee is rock star Eric
Draven, who meets a violent death on
the eve of his wedding and returns
from the grave a year later to wreak
vengeance on those who also raped
and killed his bride-to-be.
Accompanied by the crow that has
brought his soul back to earth, he sets
about an orgy of death and destruction.
The result is a bit like one of director
Michael Winner's bloodbaths of the
Seventies with a horror-film slant, although overhead travelling shots of the
dark city, whether set ablaze by arson-
ists on Devil's Night (Hallowe'en Eve),
or rising sullenly from the ground, are
undeniably impressive. The crow's
good too.

Crowded Sky, The ○

1960, US, 104 mins, colour
Dir: Joseph Pevney
Stars: Dana Andrews, Efrem Zimbalist Jr,
Rhonda Fleming, Anne Francis, Keenan
Wynn
Rating: ★★

This nail-biting story may remind some
viewers of John Wayne's *The High and
the Mighty*, to which, especially with its
star-studded cast, it bears a more than
coincidental resemblance. Suspenseful
if superficial, it matches the dramatic
talents of old TV favourite Efrem
Zimbalist Jr against those of the more
screen-seasoned Dana Andrews.
Rhonda Fleming, Anne Francis, John
Kerr and Keenan Wynn are among
others gripping their seats for the
bumpy ride ahead.

Crowd Roars, The ○

1932, US, 85 mins, b/w
Dir: Howard Hawks
Stars: James Cagney, Joan Blondell, Eric
Linden, Ann Dvorak, Guy Kibbee, Frank
McHugh
Rating: ★★

James Cagney is in the typical form of
his early years as a cocky and aggressive racing-driver. This was how the
public were beginning to want to see
him, and Warners lost no time in supplying him with a brisk number of
appropriate star vehicles. Eric Linden
scores as his younger brother, and Joan
Blondell and Ann Dvorak are strong as
the girls in their life. Some good racing
locations were shot for the movie,
which turned up again when Warners
remade the film as *Indianapolis Speedway*
in 1939.

Crowd Roars, The ○

1938, US, 92 mins, b/w
Dir: Richard Thorpe
Stars: Robert Taylor, Edward Arnold,
Maureen O'Sullivan, Frank Morgan,
William Gargan, Jane Wyman
Rating: ★★

Robert Taylor trained hard for his role
in this solid, typical Hollywood boxing
film, and it shows in the fights in the
ring. It also cost him a broken finger,
but the star felt it was worth it to help
him escape the pretty-boy label with
which he had been tagged after co-starring with Greta Garbo in *Camille*.

Cruel Sea, The ○ Ⓥ

1952, UK, 120 mins, b/w
Dir: Charles Frend
Stars: Jack Hawkins, Denholm Sinden,
John Stratton, Denholm Elliott, Virginia
McKenna, Stanley Baker
Rating: ★★★★★

A grimly realistic account, given in
semi-documentary fashion, of the Battle
of the Atlantic and of a corvette's crew
who found that their worst enemy was
the sea. Ealing Studios' brilliant adaptation of the famous Nicholas
Monsarrat novel was the film which
turned Jack Hawkins, Donald Sinden,
Stanley Baker and Virginia McKenna
into stars. It was Sinden's major screen
debut and he turned in what still ranks
as the finest performance of his career.
To meet the demands of early Fifties'
cinema, Ealing were forced to bowd-
lerise the book in many respects, yet, to
their great credit, emerged with a first-
rate film. It's dignified, thoughtful and
always exciting to look at. It has moments of high tension and nervy
anxiety, as when the ship ploughs
through survivors in its determination
to sink the enemy or presents itself as a
sitting target in the full glare of a burning tanker. And the suspense is
constantly accentuated by the pips of
the asdic apparatus pinging on the
soundtrack with menacing melody, a
harbinger of imminent danger. At the
centre of everything is Jack Hawkins'
portrait of the skipper, intense, authoritative, tautly controlled yet not
unemotional.

Crucible, The ◑ Ⓥ

1996, US, 124 mins, colour
Dir: Nicholas Hytner
Stars: Daniel Day-Lewis, Winona Ryder,
Paul Scofield, Joan Allen, Bruce Davison,
Rob Campbell
Rating: ★★

Winsome wench Winona Ryder desires dashing Daniel Day-Lewis in this

C

serious slice of 17th-century sex and sorcery. Only trouble: he has a wife (played by Joan Allen, who gives the film's most considered performance by a country mile). As Dan's former lover, Winona feels she has a right, and so drinks a charm to see Joan off for good. Lots of intensity, shouting and breast-beating follow before gaunt Paul Scofield – who better to play a puritanical elder or witchfinder-general? – pronounces sentence on those who practise witchery-pokery to achieve their aims in life. Day-Lewis is so arrogant you can't feel any sympathy for his eventual predicament; mud and tedium prevail in a film that never escapes its stage origins.

Cruisin' Down the River ○

1952, US, 80 mins, colour
Dir: Richard Quine
Stars: Dick Haymes, Billy Daniels, Audrey Totter, Cecil Kellaway
Rating: ★★

One of the Blake Edwards-Richard Quine musicals of the Fifties that bulged with music and colour, and were all the better for their brevity. This is one of their few early musicals not to star Frankie Laine, but it does have Billy Daniels, with his old black magic on board a riverboat that crooning gambler Dick Haymes wants to turn into a floating night-club. Undemanding entertainment all the way.

Cry-Baby ① ⓥ

1990, US, 85 mins, colour
Dir: John Waters
Stars: Johnny Depp, Amy Locane, Ricki Lake, Kim McGuire, Polly Bergen, Iggy Pop
Rating: ★★★

Cult director John Waters makes another foray into mainline cinema with this pastiche of Fifties rock'n'rebel movies, which is great fun up to a point, with more than a touch of the old Waters outrageousness. About 50 percent of it is wonderful, while the other half, especially when the songs go on a bit, only serves to remind us how awful some of the original movies were. The colour is exactly the right shade of garishness, the direction is as snappy as hell and the supporting cast of grotesques a mine of half-forgotten faces from every decade. Stars Johnny Depp and Amy Locane have fun as the boy from The Drapes and the girl from The Squares whose hormone-driven love affair sparks the film. At 85 minutes of ghoulish glee, the film just about

manages not to outstay its welcome. Kim McGuire is a notable addition to the Waters gallery of gargoyles as an awful Drape woman who even scares convicts watching *The Creature from the Black Lagoon*.

Cry for Happy ○

1961, US, 110 mins, colour
Dir: George Marshall
Stars: Glenn Ford, Donald O'Connor
Rating: ★★

The promising combination of Irving Brecher, who wrote for the Marx Brothers on *At the Circus* and *Go West*, and director George Marshall, who worked with Bob Hope, W C Fields and Martin and Lewis, doesn't quite deliver the goods in this *Teahouse of the August Moon*-style comedy about a group of US combat cameraman at large in a geisha house. Still, it's good-natured fun, with Glenn Ford giving an uncharacteristically relaxed performance in the lead role.

Cry Freedom ① ⓥ

1987, UK, 157 mins, colour
Dir: Richard Attenborough
Stars: Kevin Kline, Penelope Wilton, Denzel Washington, John Hargreaves, John Thaw
Rating: ★★★

Although wordy and occasionally long-winded, Richard Atteborough's film about doomed South African activist Steve Biko (a role that consolidated stardom for Denzel Washington) is, on the whole, a very eloquent cry for freedom. And, despite a running time that seems profligate, the story keeps moving at quite a good pace as it changes from an exposé to a combination of tear-jerker and escape movie. It's in the escape section at the end that the director makes his only really false step, inserting flashbacks into a flight from authority that seriously undercut the emotional impact of the climax. Elsewhere, Attenborough is content to let the events speak for themselves and they do so with sickening effect. And, although the South African law enforcers are portrayed as one-dimensional brutes, this does give the film a necessary balance. There are charismatic performances from Washington and from John Hargreaves as the Australian reporter friend of central character Donald Woods (Kevin Kline).

Cry Havoc ○

1943, US, 97 mins, b/w
Dir: Richard Thorpe

Stars: Margaret Sullavan, Joan Blondell, Ann Sothern, Fay Bainter, Marsha Hunt
Rating: ★★★

Hollywood wartime heroism of the feminine variety, as a bunch of volunteer nurses at a Pacific base hospital stand by their patients while the Japanese close in. Margaret Sullavan dominates the film in a role originally planned for Joan Crawford, but having the similar Ann Sothern and Joan Blondell in the same film (and sometimes side by side) proves to be a little too much of a good thing.

Crying Freeman ● ⓥ

1996, US/Jap, 100 mins, colour
Dir: Christophe Gans
Stars: Mark Dacascos, Julie Condra, Byron Mann, Rae Dawn Chong, Tcheky Karyo, Mako
Rating: ★★★

As a combination of comic-book hero and kung fu/yakuza thriller, this is a pretty good film for fans of adult comic-strip action. Taking itself seriously, keeping the action flowing and largely avoiding high-flown or unintentionally funny dialogue – 'Someone is going to pay for the massacre of those 16 Chinese in the soya factory' is about the only duff line – it tells the story of a near-invincible mixed-race assassin pledging allegiance to a Chinese dragon society and knocking off mobsters and witnesses all over the world. A beautiful girl (Condra) the hit-man (Dacascos) can't kill triggers off a whole internecine war involving rival crime societies, crooked cops and a wonderful Lady Macbeth figure (Yoko Shimada) with ambitions to control the whole shebang. Director Gans mixes huge close-ups with sharply lensed 'death' scenes in which the action is always about to explode.

Crying Game, The ● ⓥ

1992, UK, 108 mins, colour
Dir: Neil Jordan
Stars: Stephen Rea, Forest Whitaker, Miranda Richardson, Jaye Davidson, Adrian Dunbar, Jim Broadbent
Rating: ★★

The IRA thriller gets a few new twists here, but ironically it's the twists that fragment the film until it falls apart. Things start strongly: black British soldier (Hollywood's Forest Whitaker with a fair London accent) is captured by IRA men Stephen Rea, Adrian Dunbar and Miranda Richardson, and held hostage. Subsequent developments, after Rea and Whitaker became almost-friends, hit home hard and it's only when Rea tracks down Whitaker's girlfriend (Jaye Davidson) in London that the film starts to go to pieces. It's not only in the relationship between Rea and Davidson that credibility takes a beating, but in several other key plot developments, to which director Neil Jordan's own dialogue can't lend conviction. Rea looks miserable about people of different sexes throwing themselves at him, as well he might, and there are some strange wobbles in the lighting towards the end as well as in the script. Richardson is fine and her Belfast accent sounds right. Davidson is almost convincing but (despite the Oscar nomination) not quite.

Cry In the Dark, A ◐ ⓥ

1988, Australia, 121 mins, colour
Dir: Fred Schepisi
Stars: Meryl Streep, Sam Neill, Bruce Myles, Nick Tate, Charles Tingwell
Rating: ★★★

The facts behind Australia's Lindy Chamberlain case are so extraordinary that they easily survive director Fred Schepisi's laborious treatment, to provide a movie that sticks in the mind and should set you arguing for weeks. It seems unbelievable, given the total lack of proof, not to mention motive, weapon or body, that any jury could have convicted Chamberlain of the murder of her baby daughter. Yet, just a few years ago this is exactly what took place. Camping at night, Lindy heard the baby cry and returned to her tent to glimpse a dingo fleeing and her baby gone. Meryl Streep (whose Australian accent sounds fine to the untutored ear) and Sam Neill are certainly good as the distraught parents, and the film finally does good emotive work at the end, even if it's a long haul. But the final question you'll be asking is not how good a film this is, but how could this happen?

Cry In the Night, A ◐

1956, US, 75 mins, b/w
Dir: Frank Tuttle
Stars: Natalie Wood, Edmond O'Brien, Brian Donlevy, Raymond Burr
Rating: ★★

Great idea, great stars and some suspense in this story of a kidnapping. A pity Natalie Wood was no torn-skirt temptress here at 18, but there's fine black-and-white night photography, and a super psychotic performance from Raymond Burr, reminiscent of his work in *Rear Window*.

Cry of the Banshee ◐

1970, UK, 87 mins, colour
Dir: Gordon Hessler
Stars: Vincent Price, Elisabeth Bergner, Patrick Mower
Rating: ★★

Thirties' screen star Elisabeth Bergner made a comeback to the screen in this beautifully photographed (John Coquillon using colour by Movielab) horror film, as the high priestess of a coven in 16th century England, who summons up an avenging spirit to destroy her enemies. The ending is likely to both surprise and shock.

Cry Terror ○

1958, US, 96 mins, b/w
Dir: Andrew L Stone
Stars: James Mason, Rod Steiger, Inger Stevens, Angie Dickinson, Jack Klugman
Rating: ★★★★

Eye-catching performances by the trio of 'baddies' – Rod Steiger, Angie Dickinson and Jack Klugman – steal the honours in this tightly-paced, tension-laden tale of a family held hostage by a psychopath planning an extortion coup. Inger Stevens is also good as James Mason's wife, while director Andrew L Stone makes a fine job of cramming on the suspense.

Cry, the Beloved Country ○ ⓥ

(aka: African Fury)
1951, UK, 96 mins, b/w
Dir: Zoltan Korda
Stars: Canada Lee, Sidney Poitier, Joyce Carey, Charles Carson
Rating: ★★★

Zoltan Korda, one of the three famous Korda brothers (the others were Alexander and Vincent), always shot his movies in far-off exotic locations, evoking a strong sense of period and locale. They could also often be counted upon to have a secondary meaning and give an audience food for thought on their way home. This drama, filmed in South Africa, was no exception. The film scores highly because of its attention to detail and it keeps undue sentiment at bay.

Culpepper Cattle Co, The ◐

1972, US, 92 mins, colour
Dir: Dick Richards
Stars: Gary Grimes, Billy Green Bush, Bo Hopkins
Rating: ★★

Another tough-talking Western that tries to show America's wild days as they were. It was the debut of director

Dick Richards, who subsequently made *Farewell My Lovely* and *March or Die*, both of which displayed a similar obsession for de-glamourising familiar film genres. Here the grime and gore are counter-balanced by the director's treatment as, helped by the photography, he contrived to bring something of the quality of old sepia photographs to his view of the west. Although the film never quite seems sure of what it wants to do – it starts off as a poetic treatment of a cattle drive and ends in the style of *The Magnificent Seven* – interest in its developments is sustained by the performances of the four tough cowboys who befriend greenhorn Gary Grimes on the drive – Luke Askew, Bo Hopkins, Wayne Sutherlin and especially Geoffrey Lewis as Russ Caldwell.

Curly Sue ○ ⓥ

1991, US, 101 mins, colour
Dir: John Hughes
Stars: James Belushi, Alisan Porter, Kelly Lynch, John Getz, Fred Dalton Thompson
Rating: ★★

Just to prove that occasionally they do make 'em like they used to, here's a sort of Shirley Temple film for the Nineties. Although the formula never really works in today's terms, the movie was a big popular hit which must prove something. Bill Dance (James Belushi) and his cute but sassy nine-year-old sidekick Curly Sue (Alisan Porter) are hoboes. When Bill is hit by a car driven by Kelly Lynch, as an attorney as wealthy as she's beautiful and intense, things start looking up for our footloose, four-flushing friends. Down-to-earth playing by Belushi and Porter (as engaging a moppet as the cinema's thrown up in quite a while) stop this from oozing pure saccharine even if it never engages our emotions.

Curly Top ○

1935, US, 75 mins, b/w
Dir: Irving Cummings
Stars: Shirley Temple, John Boles, Rochelle Hudson, Jane Darwell
Rating: ★★★

Shirley Temple attempts to bring sweetness and light to an orphanage, much to the displeasure of the grumpy superintendent, played by pop-eyed Rafaela Ottiano. This is the one in which Shirley has a pony and a pet duck, and sings 'Animal Crackers in My Soup', one of her greatest hits.

C

Curse of Frankenstein, The ●

1957, UK, 83 mins, colour
Dir: Terence Fisher
Stars: Peter Cushing, Christopher Lee
Rating: ★★★

Contemporary critics pursed their lips and were shocked at the full-frontal gore and spare-part surgery in this gaudy shocker but audiences had no such lily-livered inhibitions and flocked to see the bold, bad Baron and his do-it-yourself creature in vivid colour for the first time. Terence Fisher's unflinching depiction of horror and his skill as a storyteller established him as the best post-war maker of screen chillers, made international stars of Peter Cushing (in his first outing as *Frankenstein*) and Christopher Lee, in his one-and-only appearance as the Creature.

Curse of the Cat People, The ◐

1944, US, 70 mins, b/w
Dir: Robert Wise
Stars: Simone Simon, Kent Smith, Jane Randolph
Rating: ★★★

An indirect sequel to *Cat People* and, amazingly, just as good. Ann Carter gives a quite unnerving performance as the little girl who lives in a nightmare world of her own imagination. This chilling continuation of the story of the Smiths was the first directorial assignment for Robert Wise, hitherto an editor (on such films as *Citizen Kane*). Later he made a number of significant films and won two Academy Awards.

Curse of the Crimson Altar ●

(aka: Crimson Cult)
1968, UK, 88 mins, colour
Dir: Vernon Sewell
Stars: Boris Karloff, Christopher Lee, Barbara Steele, Rupert Davies
Rating: ★★

With such a superb cast, this should have been the horror film to end them all. It isn't quite – perhaps too many ghouls spoil the broth. Still, this witchcraft thriller contains some lurid shock moments, very sexy love scenes, and commendable underplaying from Boris Karloff, whizzing about in a wheelchair, in one of his last major films. The raven-haired Barbara Steele, the 'queen of horror films', is rather wasted in a smallish part of a long-dead witch.

Curse of the Demon

See: Night of the Demon

Curse of the Fly, The ●

1964, UK, 86 mins, b/w
Dir: Don Sharp
Stars: Brian Donlevy, Carole Gray
Rating: ★★

This British film completed the 'fly' trilogy about a family's obsession with the transference of matter through space, the first two with Vincent Price. Price's mantle as senior member of the family is here assumed by screen veteran Brian Donlevy, on his third visit to post-war Britain following *The Quatermass Experiment* and *Quatermass II*. Carole Gray is startlingly effective as the heroine.

Curse of the Mummy's Tomb, The ● Ⓥ

1964, UK, 80 mins, colour
Dir: Michael Carreras
Stars: Terence Morgan, Ronald Howard, Fred Clark, Jeanne Roland
Rating: ★

The beat of the cloth-wrapped feet sounds again, this time along the cobblestones of fog-enshrouded Victorian London. 'See where he goes,' cries Inspector John Paul to his men, after the mummy has committed murder in the drawing room before their eyes, 'but keep your distance.' Too true. Indeed, fans of the traditional B-grade horror film are likely to be happy all round, as the madman cries, 'Kill Her!' to the monster, while the scantily clad heroine lies draped picturesquely across a block of stone. A Hammer horror in more ways than one.

Curse of the Werewolf ●

1961, UK, 92 mins, colour
Dir: Terence Fisher
Stars: Oliver Reed, Yvonne Romain, Clifford Evans, Anthony Dawson
Rating: ★★

Hammer's fourth 'original copy', after their versions of the Frankenstein, Dracula and Mummy sagas. Guy Endore's novel *The Werewolf of Paris* was an obvious source of material, and Hammer producer Anthony Hinds, using his pseudonym of John Elder, provided a very serviceable screenplay from it, giving full rein to director Terence Fisher's natural talent for period flavour and a well-knit storyline. The role of the werewolf was difficult to cast. But the choice finally fell on an unknown young actor who had been confined to playing minor bullies. His name was Oliver Reed.

Curtain Call at Cactus Creek ○

(aka: Take the Stage)
1950, US, 86 mins, colour
Dir: Charles Lamont
Stars: Donald O'Connor, Gale Storm, Vincent Price, Walter Brennan
Rating: ★★★

This Western comedy is a kind of sideshoot from W C Fields' famous comedy, *The Old Fashioned Way*, in that it deals with a travelling repertory company in 19th century America, with an awful old ham (in this case played by Vincent Price, who thoroughly enjoys himself) as its leading player. Three-time Oscar-winner Walter Brennan is also in good form as the hoary old outlaw who joins the troupe, while Donald O'Connor and the improbably-named Gale Storm (real name: Josephine Cottle) keep the flag flying for the younger generation.

Curtain Up! ○

1952, UK, 82 mins, b/w
Dir: Ralph Smart
Stars: Margaret Rutherford, Robert Morley, Kay Kendall
Rating: ★★

The man financing the repertory company has an aunt. The aunt has written a play. And the company has to put it on. A situation tailor-made for the talents of Margaret Rutherford (as the aunt) and Robert Morley (as the company's director) whose performances give an immense boost to this film version of a stage farce. The stars make the most of the witty lines in the screenplay, while Dame Margaret's real-life husband, Stringer Davis, has a small supporting role.

Custer of the West ○

1966, US/Spain, 140 mins, colour
Dir: Robert Siodmak
Stars: Robert Shaw, Mary Ure, Robert Ryan, Jeffrey Hunter, Ty Hardin
Rating: ★★

Shot mainly in Spain, this epic Western was the last major film from Robert Siodmak, the American-born, German-trained director who made his name in Hollywood with a clutch of powerful thrillers that included *Phantom Lady*, *The Spiral Staircase* and *The Killers*. With the help of Robert Shaw's vivid portrayal of Custer, Siodmak keeps the action here rolling at a thunderingly good pace considering the film's length. Among the rest or the cast, Robert Ryan scores well as a gold-hungry deserter. It provides plenty of colourful adventure from a runaway train and the shooting of treacherous rapids, leading inevitably to the famous Custer's 'last stand'.

CutThroat Island ◐ ⓥ

1995, US, 123 mins, colour
Dir: Renny Harlin
Stars: Geena Davis, Matthew Modine, Frank Langella, Harris Yulin, Maury Chaykin, Patrick Malahide
Rating: ★★★★

Yo-ho for this underrated epic – a 17th-century female pirate adventure yarn. But then this tongue in cheek, high-seas demolition derby is everything you would expect from the director of *Die Hard 2* and *Cliffhanger*. Geena Davis (Mrs Harlin) is Morgan Adams, a ridiculously buxom pirate who fails to save the life of her father at the hands of her blackhearted brother (Frank Langella, gloriously chewing the scenery) and then decides to beat Langella to the legendary CutThroat Island and find the treasure her father buried there. Her main problem is the map revealing the location has been divided into three pieces. She only has the first, etched on her father's scalp. Almost everything from entire ships to Jamaican sea ports are destroyed along the way in a series of spectacular stunts that will take your breath away. Small children will be entranced by the antics of Morgan's pet monkey, but may be frightened by some bloody action sequences. Ardent feminists will cheer Geena's acrobatic exploits throughout.

Cutting Edge, The ○ ⓥ

1992, US, 101 mins, colour
Dir: Paul Michael Glaser
Stars: D B Sweeney, Moira Kelly, Roy Dotrice, Dwier Brown, Terry O'Quinn
Rating: ★

This is a wondrously bad film about ice pairs skating, with a script and situations that seem to have been stitched together from bad movies of 60 years ago. The chances are that you'll enjoy every minute of this even while spluttering uncontrollably into your coke or coffee as ex-ice hockey star D B Sweeney and 'ice queen' Moira Kelly feud their way to the world pairs championships and into each other's arms. 'For 20 years I've been working on this,' exclaims their Russian coach Roy Dotrice), describing the 'Panicenko' movement that you know they'll refuse to do and then bring off at the last. Everyone except Sweeney and Kelly is excruciatingly bad, small wonder spouting lines that crash like lead pucks on to the ice. Puerile, silly and very enjoyable.

Cyrano de Bergerac ○ ⓥ

1990, France, 138 mins, colour
Dir: Jean-Paul Rappeneau
Stars: Gerard Depardieu, Jacques Weber, Anne Brochet
Rating: ★★★★

This French film of Rostand's classic play was highly successful and deservedly so, as it has everything – wit, drama, unrequited love and lots of swashbuckling action. Gerard Depardieu fills the role of the swaggering chevalier with the prominent proboscis with lusty vigour. He also manages to convey Cyrano's self-conscious insecurities because of his love for Roxane (luminously portrayed by Anne Brochet). The balcony love scene is wittily done, as is the sequence in which Cyrano creates a fracas in a theatre, and the final scene is poignant in the extreme. The film looks spectacular. Even the subtitles aren't the usual irritating necessity, and they're also well-written – not suprising as they were the work of novelist Anthony Burgess.

D

Da

1988, US, 102 mins, colour
Dir: Matt Clark
Stars: Barnard Hughes, Martin Sheen, William Hickey, Doreen Hepburn, Hugh O'Conor
Rating: ★★

Despite the occasional abrasiveness of its protagonists, this is a sweet-natured picture about memories, and about the relationship down the years between a talented Irish boy and the father who seemed unruffled by time (or much else) and rooted in the past. Unfortunately sweetness and nostalgia, like the film, only grip in fits and starts, but it is acted to perfection by Martin Sheen as the son who went to America and by Barnard Hughes as the blustery old man who stayed in Ireland and whose ghost comes to make its peace after his own funeral. This leads to often humorous flashbacks to the past, highlighted by attempts to drown the family dog, and by the old man's ruining his son's big chance with the local floozy.

Dad ○ ⓥ

1989, US, 116 mins, colour
Dir: Gary David Goldberg
Stars: Jack Lemmon, Ted Danson, Olympia Dukakis, Kathy Baker, Kevin Spacey, Ethan Hawke
Rating: ★★

This is an actors' showcase, and Jack Lemmon, with the help of prosthetic makeup that's a touch over the top (do many 78-year-old Americans actually look about 90?), does everything anyone could to make this story of senility and belated filial concern just as gutwrenching as possible. He's already proved himself a wow at this sort of thing and does so again here. And, although the film is virtually a two-hander between Lemmon and Ted Danson as his son, it's full of good performances and emotive moments. Alas, the story itself seems to reach an end several times, only to go off at a tangent, until it finally seems about four hours long. The makers might argue that life's a bit like that – just one damn thing after another – but it doesn't make for very fluent entertainment in a film whose highpoints all seem to occur in the middle. The best section is the part where Danson rehabilitates

D

Lemmon after the latter's suffocating wife has had a heart attack. It's downhill from here on, but, if you cry easily at the movies, you'll cry a lot at this one.

Daddy Long Legs ○
1955, US, 126 mins, colour
Dir: Jean Negulesco
Stars: Fred Astaire, Leslie Caron, Terry Moore, Thelma Ritter, Fred Clark
Rating: ★★★

When an irresistible force meets an old immovable object then, to quote Fred Astaire in this musical's Oscar-nominated song, 'Something s Gotta Give'. And what gives here is entertainment of the most elegant and sophisticated variety, especially when Astaire and Leslie Caron get anywhere near the dance floor. She's a waif without means, he's a man without a wife, and the twain shall eventually meet via a delightfully convoluted plot which has Fred 'adopting' Leslie to pay for her education in America. The world's most graceful old fogey gets hep with 'The Sluefoot' and Mlle Caron makes a charming partner.

Dakota Incident ○
1956, US, 88 mins, colour
Dir: Lewis R Foster
Stars: Linda Darnell, Dale Robertson, John Lund, Ward Bond
Rating: ★★

A Western that only springs to life in its periodic bursts of full-blooded action. Even a good cast that, in cricketing terms, bats right down to number 11, can do little with Frederic Louis Fox's stodgy dialogue; to add insult to injury they get killed one by one as the plot casts them as stranded stagecoach passsengers at the mercy of rampaging Indians. Oscar-winning photographer Ernest Haller, though, is to be congratulated on making the Trucolor process for once acceptable.

Dallas ○
1950, US, 94 mins, colour
Dir: Stuart Heisler
Stars: Gary Cooper, Ruth Roman, Raymond Massey, Steve Cochran
Rating: ★★

A typical Gary Cooper Western with the tall, tanned and taciturn cowboy providing the firepower and fighting capability of a modem regiment as he wages a lone battle against carpetbaggers. The climax, in which he duels with Raymond Massey, is a spellbinder. Overall, though, competent rather than inspired.

Damage ● ⓥ
1992, UK, 111 mins, colour
Dir: Louis Malle
Stars: Jeremy Irons, Juliette Binoche, Rupert Graves, Miranda Richardson, Ian Bannen, Leslie Caron
Rating: ★

A slow, grim, melodramatic and strangely unemotional portrait of the decay caused by obsessive love. Jeremy Irons plays an up-and-coming government minister who falls hopelessly and passionately in love with his son's girlfriend (Juliette Binoche), a young woman happy both to supply his needs and remain engaged to his son. Tragedy inevitably strikes, and viewers so inclined can stay to watch the destruction of the lives of nearly all those involved. Irons' and particularly Binoche's hearts don't seem to be in this; but you may well feel the same way in rather less time. The valuable Miranda Richardson gives the only good performance in the film as Irons' discarded wife.

Dam Busters, The ○ ⓥ
1954, UK, 125 mins, b/w
Dir: Michael Anderson
Stars: Richard Todd, Michael Redgrave, Ursula Jeans, Derek Farr
Rating: ★★★★

Inspired film-making from a British film industry still brimming with confidence before the bubble burst in the late Fifties. Michael Redgrave is superb as the scientist who invents the famous 'bouncing bomb' and Richard Todd at his best as the squadron-leader picked to lead the team that delivers it to the German dams it must destroy. The tremendously popular march theme by Eric Coates became a standard for all brass bands.

Dames ○
1934, US, 90 mins, b/w
Dir: Ray Enright
Stars: Joan Blondell, Dick Powell, Ruby Keeler, ZaSu Pitts, Guy Kibbee
Rating: ★★★

The 'gold-digger'-style musicals never had the strongest of stories and depended on their songs and Busby Berkeley dance routines to bring in the paying public. This plot must be the thinnest of all but within its gossamer framework are housed such classic numbers as 'The Girl at the Ironing Board', 'When You Were a Smile on Your Mother's Lips' and 'I Only Have Eyes for You', in which jigsaw puzzle pieces on dancing girls' backs form a giant portrait of Ruby Keeler.

Damien – Omen II ● ⓥ
1978, US, 107 mins, colour
Dir: Don Taylor
Stars: William Holden, Lee Grant, Jonathan Scott-Taylor
Rating: ★★

The only drawback to the splendidly-made Omen films is that the good guys so seldom even look like winning. Thus the results of their encounters with Damien are such a foregone conclusion that the chief excitement lies in seeing what new and spectacular deaths can be dreamt up by the special effects wizards. The most dazzling effect here involves slicing a man in two. Meanwhile Jonathan Scott-Taylor does very nicely as the teenage Damien (son of the Devil, you'll remember) and seems to dispatch some new victim every few seconds of the film. It's all frighteningly entertaining, if predictable.

Damnation Alley ○
1977, US, 91 mins, colour
Dir: Jack Smight
Stars: Jan-Michael Vincent, George Peppard, Dominique Sanda
Rating: ★★

This science-fiction thriller gets off to a spectacular start with the world ravaged by a searing nuclear holocaust. Of course, the dangers are not over for a band of intrepid Americans who set out across their country in search of a small pocket of civilisation thought to have survived the horror. Tidal waves, ceaseless storms and other freak weather conditions, allied with such fearsome threats as giant scorpions and carnivorous cockroaches, are just some of the hazards in their way. As an imaginative, action-filled adventure yarn, it has some splendid moments, even if the script is not up to the scale of the story.

Damned Don't Cry, The ○
1950, US, 100 mins, b/w
Dir: Vincent Sherman
Stars: Joan Crawford, David Brian, Steve Cochran, Kent Smith
Rating: ★★

A typical Joan Crawford crime vehicle, allowing her to run the gamut from laughter to tears, from poverty to power, and pitching her up to her mink in crime and corruption. Her fans will love every melodramatic minute. A young Richard Egan appears as her husband in the opening scenes.

Damn the Defiant
See: HMS Defiant

Dance Hall ○
1950, UK, 90 mins, b/w
Dir: Charles Crichton
Stars: Natasha Parry, Jane Hylton, Diana
Dors, Petula Clark
Rating: ★★

Ealing Studios took a look at another
British tradition – the palais de danse –
with a film whose conventional, relatively shapeless story uses the local
palais as a background to examine the
experiences of a quartet of factory girls
who spend their evenings searching for
relaxation and excitement. You might
notice the same extras in scene after
scene, but nostalgia is well catered for
by Geraldo and His Orchestra and Ted
Heath and His Music.

Dance Little Lady ○
1954, UK, 105 mins, colour
Dir: Val Guest
Stars: Terence Morgan, Mai Zetterling,
Guy Rolfe, Mandy Miller
Rating: ★★

Terence Morgan makes the best impression, as a sponger as smooth as he
is nasty, in this ballet-orientated story,
tailored to the talents of Britain's then
screen wonder child, Mandy Miller. It
bases its appeal on its blend of small-girl
sentiment, highly coloured melodramatics and ballet (the dance ensembles are
very well done). Mai Zetterling and
Guy Rolfe provide rather limp support
to Mandy's undeniable charm, but the
story's fiery climax is most effective.

Dance of the Vampires ◑
(aka: The Fearless Vampire Killers)
1967, UK, 110 mins, colour
Dir: Roman Polanski
Stars: Jack MacGowran, Roman
Polanski, Sharon Tate, Ferdy Mayne,
Alfie Bass
Rating: ★★★

Perhaps Polanski's most bizarre film –
a spoof horror movie that turns out to
be more horror than spoof. Alfie Bass
is very funny as a Jewish vampire for
whom a crucifix holds no fear. 'Boy,'
he cries, advancing on a maiden shield-
ing herself with a cross, 'have you got
the wrong vampire!'

Dances with Wolves ◑ ⓥ
1990, US, 185 mins, colour
Dir: Kevin Costner
Stars: Kevin Costner, Mary McDonnell,
Graham Greene, Rodney A Grant
Rating: ★★★★★

It's rare that a film lives up to its rave
reviews, but Kevin Costner's debut as
director does just that. He plays

Dunbar, an American lieutenant of the
1860s who escapes the horror of the
Civil War (and, narrowly, the amputa-
tion of his foot) to live in peace and
tranquillity in the far frontier. Here, at
his outpost, and by no real design of
his own, he comes to befriend, then
live among the local Sioux Indians.
Overcoming initial hostility, he learns
their language, fights for them and falls
in love with a white woman captured
by them as a child. In one of the film's
most telling snatches of dialogue,
Dunbar records that he has 'never
known people so eager to laugh, so
close as a family, so dedicated to each
other. The only word is harmony.'
Shadows close across this harmony and
happiness before the end but no matter: Dunbar has had his day in the sun.
He also makes the acquaintance of a
timber wolf which becomes almost
tame; his playful game with the animal
earns him his Indian name: Dances
with Wolves. Costner's film really has
everything: action, emotion, romance,
laughter and an insight, admittedly superficial, into a half-lost culture. A
remarkable first movie.

Dance with a Stranger ● ⓥ
1984, UK, 101 mins, colour
Dir: Mike Newell
Stars: Rupert Everett, Miranda
Richardson, Ian Holm, Stratford Johns,
Joanne Whalley
Rating: ★★★

Stylish, biting retelling of the story of
Ruth Ellis, the last woman to be
hanged in Britain, shot in appropriately
harsh colours by Peter Hannan.
Though one can understand filmmakers' obsession with Ellis, first played 28
years earlier by Diana Dors in *Yield to
the Night*, the events of the case are perilously close to the monotonous for the
sustainment of the a full-length movie.
One row, reconciliation, love-making
session or beating between Ellis and
her lover are, after all, very much like
another, despite the excellent performances of Miranda Richardson (who
conjures up a remarkable physical resemblance) and Rupert Everett. Ian
Holm offers his customary skilled support as Ruth's oft-rejected older suitor,
and Stratford Johns also scores in a role
far removed from his old image as
Chief Inspector Barlow. The film's finally a narrow victory for style over
content.

Dancing Lady ○
1933, US, 95 mins, b/w
Dir: Robert Z Leonard
Stars: Joan Crawford, Clark Gable,

Franchot Tone
Rating: ★★★

You wouldn't usually associate Clark
Gable and Joan Crawford with musicals, but here they have plenty of classy
support to help carry the score of this
back-stage saga of a poor-born but honest dancer (Crawford!) struggling to
make it to Broadway without compromising her ideals. Fred Astaire makes
his feature debut with a couple of
dance routines.

Dancing with Crime ○
1946, UK, 83 mins, b/w
Dir: John Paddy Carstairs
Stars: Richard Attenborough, Sheila Sim,
Barry K Barnes
Rating: ★★

A crime thriller about two Army mates
who become involved with a criminal
gang operating from a dance hall. The
action moves briskly, and the film provides some fascinating insights into the
British way of relaxation in the immediate post-war years. Bill Rowbotham,
who plays hero Richard Attenborough's
friend, later became better known as Bill
Owen. Watch out for a brief appearance by Dirk Bogarde as a policeman –
his first acting role in films.

Dancing Years, The ○
1949, UK, 96 mins, colour
Dir: Harold French
Stars: Dennis Price, Patricia Dainton,
Gisèle Preville, Olive Gilbert
Rating: ★★

Pleasant, lightweight Ivor Novello musical about a poor young pianist who
becomes a famous composer. Elegant
playing from Dennis Price complements some fine singing by Olive
Gilbert and Martin Ross.

Dangerous Corner ○
1935, US, 65 mins, b/w
Dir: Phil Rosen
Stars: Melvyn Douglas, Virginia Bruce
Rating: ★★

This murder thriller is based on a successful stage play by J B Priestley and
rather shows up its theatrical origins.
Some overnight bonds are stolen and
the principal suspect apparently commits suicide. Despite its stagebound
limitations, sound performances, from
Melvyn Douglas, Conrad Nagel and
Virginia Bruce and an interesting plot
create a mystery that's a little different.

Dangerous Crossing ○
1953, US, 76 mins, b/w
Dir: Joseph M Newman

D

Stars: Jeanne Crain, Michael Rennie
Rating: ★★

A suspense thriller about a frightened bride whose husband disappears on their honeymoon voyage. Adapted by Leo Townsend from a story by master mystery writer John Dickson Carr, the plot of this one is guaranteed to keep you guessing to the very end.

Dangerous Ground ● Ⓥ
1997, S Afr, 91 mins, colour
Dir: Darrell James Roodt
Stars: Ice Cube, Elizabeth Hurley, Ving Rhames
Rating: RB

Director Roodt has made some good films about South Africa, but this certainly isn't one of them. If we say that Elizabeth Hurley's South African accent is about the best thing in the movie, you'll get the drift. US rap star Ice Cube stars in this story of fraternal revenge, as the black American on a flying visit to the Cape for his father's funeral. But his younger brother has disappeared, up to his neck in debt to a Jo'burg kingpin of crime (Ving Rhames). 'This whole trip is just stressin' me the f*** out,' mutters Cube, before deciding on putting the country to rights. 'Drugs had taken over from Apartheid,' he complains in voice-over narration. 'And it was up to me to stop it.' And so he does, adopting a more relaxed attitude to local customs at the same time. 'When the time came to sacrifice the goat,' he asserts, 'I didn't hesitate!' Performances are bad, dialogue worse, pacing non-existent. Return to sender.

Dangerous Liaisons ● Ⓥ
1988, US, 120 mins, colour
Dir: Stephen Frears
Stars: Glenn Close, John Malkovich, Michelle Pfeiffer, Swoosie Kurtz, Uma Thurman
Rating: ★★★

British director Stephen Frears' first American film is an elegant portrayal of the jaded decadence of the 18th century French aristocracy on the eve of the French Revolution. The film is based on Christopher Hampton's acclaimed stage version of Choderlos de Laclos' novel *Les Liaisons Dangereuses*, a scandalous success when it first appeared in 1782. The story concerns two aristocratic libertines, played by Glenn Close and John Malkovich, who embark on a cruel intrigue to spread corruption and dismay around them wherever they can. Michelle Pfeiffer plays a devout and faithful bourgeois wife who be-

comes one of their victims. Without being absurdly anachronistic, the cast bring an immediacy and modernity to their roles that reveals the depth of feeling that exists beneath the powdered wigs and elegan language.

Dangerous Minds ● Ⓥ
1995, US, 106 mins, colour
Dir: John N Smith
Stars: Michelle Pfeiffer, George Dzundza, Courtney B Vance
Rating: ★★★

If not quite in the *Stand and Deliver* bracket, this true story of the turning-round of a ghetto classroom by an attractive ex-Marine turned teacher strikes most of the right emotional chords. A confident leap into the mainstream by Canadian director John N Smith, after numerous well-praised but out-of-the-way films, the film gives Michelle Pfeiffer a showcase role as tough-enough LouAnne, who tames a class of smart but rebellious teenagers and turns them into achievers. Smith's unobtrusive but persuasive direction and Pfeiffer's laid-back performance underline the futility of violence and crime in such an environment and, in a film that's upbeat without being mawkish, send us home cheering for the good guys.

Dangerous Mission ○
1954, US, 75 mins, colour
Dir: Louis King
Stars: Victor Mature, Piper Laurie, William Bendix, Vincent Price
Rating: ★★

This adventure thriller really had everything going for it: a dazzling snowbound setting, Technicolor photography and a strong cast that includes Victor Mature, Piper Laurie, William Bendix and Vincent Price, though they prove *film noir* people adrift in these outdoor locales. That said, it must be added that director Louis King overplays his hand a bit on the thrills quite needlessly. And shame on the scriptwriters for giving the talented Piper Laurie so little to do.

Dangerous Moonlight ○
(aka: Suicide Squadron)
1941, US, 95 mins, b/w
Dir: Brian Desmond Hurst
Stars: Anton Walbrook, Sally Gray
Rating: ★★★

The romantic film drama that sent Richard Addinsell's 'Warsaw Concerto' soaring into the wartime pop charts. It's a splendidly-acted story of a Polish pianist who joins the Royal Air Force to

avenge himself on the country that has ravaged his own native land. Tight direction, excellent aerial combat scenes.

Dangerous When Wet ○
1953, US, 90 mins, colour
Dir: Charles Walters
Stars: Esther Williams, Fernando Lamas, Jack Carson
Rating: ★★★

Director Charles Walters was a former dancer and dance director who made too few films on his own. Almost all of his solo work behind the camera was good, resulting in some of the happiest and most heart-warming musicals of the Forties, Fifties and Sixties. Unsurprisingly, then, this is one of Esther Williams' best aqua-musicals, with the star as a reluctant Channel swimmer who falls in love with a French nobleman (Fernando Lamas, in real life her husband-to-be). A sequence combining live-action with some inventive animation, in which Esther swims with Tom and Jerry, is quite delightful, and Jack Carson, Charlotte Greenwood and Donna Corcoran all score well in a strong supporting cast. The title is so perfect for an Esther Williams movie that they must have thought of it before they made the picture.

Dangerous Woman, A ● Ⓥ
1993, US, 107 mins, colour
Dir: Stephen Gyllenhaal
Stars: Debra Winger, Gabriel Byrne, Barbara Hershey, David Strathairn
Rating: ★

Sometimes good actors see a story that's a little different and sniff a masterpiece in the making. All too often, alas, they're wrong, and so it proves in this rather fey story about a slightly-retarded 30-year-old who lives with an aunt six years older, whose husband has died. Debra Winger is just marvellous as the girl who can't lie but, against the naivety of the dialogue and the sluggishness of the direction, she's fighting a lost cause. Gabriel Byrne's a bore as the boozy Irish handyman who becomes sexually involved with both women, but Barbara Hershey just about keeps the giggles at bay in a thankless role as the glamorous aunt. Connoisseurs of bad dialogue will have a field day here and, to be fair to him, Byrne gets the worst of it. 'Sometimes we have to tell lies to get at the truth' or 'You're a wonder, like a primitive thing that's never been spoiled. You might as well live in a glass cocoon' would defeat a string of Oscar-winners.

Not even the wonderful Winger can save this one.

Danger Route ○

1967, UK, 92 mins, colour
Dir: Seth Holt
Stars: Richard Johnson, Carol Lynley, Barbara Bouchet
Rating: ★★

Richard Johnson gets four leading ladies – Carol Lynley, Barbara Bouchet, Sylvia Syms and Diana Dors – for the price of one in this thriller about a government hit man who wants to give it all up. Of course, his bosses won't let him and thereby hangs a routine but exciting tale.

Danger Within ○

1958, UK, 101 mins, b/w
Dir: Don Chaffey
Stars: Richard Todd, Michael Wilding, Richard Attenborough, Bernard Lee
Rating: ★★★

A whodunnit with a difference, in the style of *Stalag 17*. Can you spot the traitor in the PoW camp before Col Richard Todd and his investigators? Todd is cast as the head of the Escape Committee, and Bernard Lee has one of his best roles as senior British officer in the camp. Dennis Price also scores as a captain whose interest centres on his forthcoming presentation of *Hamlet* at the camp theatre.

Danny the Champion of the World ⊙

1989, UK, 94 mins, colour
Dir: Gavin Millar
Stars: Jeremy Irons, Samuel Irons, Robbie Coltrane, Jean Marsh
Rating: ★★★

The heroes and villains are engagingly whiter than white and blacker than black in this charming adaptation of Roald Dahl's story about a father and son (real-life father and son Jeremy and Samuel Irons) who hold out against scheming landgrabbers. Robbie Coltrane and Jean Marsh score well as the obnoxious developer and the child welfare agent. Master Irons is a real charmer, and the beautiful colour photography lends a warm glow to this winning tale.

Dante's Inferno ○

1935, US, 88 mins, b/w
Dir: Harry Lachman
Stars: Spencer Tracy, Claire Trevor
Rating: ★★★

This heady concoction is one of Hollywood's more remarkable 'folies de grandeur' in which Spencer Tracy's power-hungry carnival man, evil streaming from his maniacal eyes, vies for attention with the inferno itself. This is the fairground sideshow to end them all: a monstrous pit of hell entered through the belly of a giant figure of Satan, and littered with infernal paintings and tableaux. Rita Hayworth has (under her real name, Rita Cansino) a supporting role in this remarkable cinematic curiosity which climaxes in a spectacular sequence set on board a floating casino.

Dante's Peak ◑ Ⓥ

1996, US, 108 mins, colour
Dir: Roger Donaldson
Stars: Pierce Brosnan, Linda Hamilton, Charles Hallahan, Grant Heslov
Rating: ★★

They should have thrown the script into the volcano that dominates this master-blaster disaster epic with million-dollar special effects. No one will believe Pierce Brosnan's warnings of imminent volcanic eruption (does this sound like *Jaws*?), so he takes a long time bonding with local mayor Linda Hamilton (bizarre coincidence: the mayor in *Jaws* was played by Murray Hamilton) before an explosive last 40 minutes mercifully engulfs the plot as well as the countryside. Eye-opening spectacle combines with well-marshalled narrow escapes to make bits towards the end edge-of-seat stuff. Alas, lots of foolish dialogue ensures that the problems of these two people don't amount to a hill of beans compared to the mountain of lava cascading towards them.

Darby O'Gill and the Little People ⊙

1958, UK, 93 mins, colour
Dir: Robert Stevenson
Stars: Jimmy O'Dea, Sean Connery, Janet Munro, Albert Sharpe, Kieron Moore
Rating: ★★★

Although this vigorous Disney fantasy-lays on its Oirish blarney with a trowel, the special effects are far ahead of their time and director Robert Stevenson rampages through the incident-filled plot in the smartest possible order. Jimmy O'Dea is totally beguiling as the king of the leprechauns, while Sean Connery and Kieron Moore make a virile hero and villain.

Daring Game ○

1968, US, 100 mins, colour
Dir: Laslo Benedek

Stars: Lloyd Bridges, Joan Blackman
Rating: ★★

This typical Sixties pot-boiler has Lloyd Bridges back in *Sea Hunt* territory as the leader of a team of scuba divers out to rescue a professor held captive by revolutionaries. Fair.

Dark Angel ● Ⓥ

1990, US, 92 mins, colour
Dir: Craig R Baxley
Stars: Dolph Lundgren, Brian Benben, Betsy Brantley, Matthias Hues, Michael J Pollard
Rating: ★★★

Or: Drug Dealer from Outer Space. With the help of modern technology, the results are nasty but quite fun, with massive Dolph Lundgren amusingly teamed with tiny Brian Benben as an FBI man who would surely have failed the physical. Alien Hues, already 6ft 6in without his build-up shoes, lumbers around killing his victims with a razor sharp compact disc, or extracting bodily fluids from them to form an inter-galactic drug. He's pursued not only by earthly cop Lundgren but by an alien law-enforcer who looks even more ghastly than him. The aliens also have flame-guns that almost never hit people, but blow up things just behind them. Director Craig R. Baxley, who also made *Action Jackson*, knows how to stage this kind of thing all right, and makes sure we hardly have time to pause for breath or to consider how silly it all is. The result is what you might call a blast.

Dark Angel, The ○

1935, US, 110 mins, b/w
Dir: Sidney Franklin
Stars: Fredric March, Merle Oberon, Herbert Marshall, Janet Beecher
Rating: ★★★

This revival of a silent film weepie has Merle Oberon and Fredric March sensitively portraying the woman and man torn apart by war, he being posted missing and she marrying another. A polished script by Lillian Hellman and Mordaunt Shairp gives the stars every assistance in ensuring you'll need a handkerchief or two for the later stages of the film.

Dark Avenger, The ○
(aka: The Warriors)

1955, UK, 85 mins, colour
Dir: Henry Levin
Stars: Errol Flynn, Joanne Dru, Peter Finch, Yvonne Furneaux, Michael Hordern
Rating: ★★

D

Just about the last cinematic buckle Errol Flynn ever swashed. Made only four years before Flynn's death in 1959, this is a dashing costume piece about an audacious English prince who foils a dastardly French plot to keep France for the French. Peter Finch is a fine, cruel villain.

Dark City ()

1950, US, 88 mins, b/wr
Dir: William Dieterle
Stars: Charlton Heston, Lizabeth Scott, Dean Jagger, Viveca Lindfors, Ed Begley
Rating: ★★★

The high-tension thriller which introduced to the screen a Bogart-style newcomer in Charlton Heston who, for his own protection, would probably have been glad of one of the suits of armour he was to wear in his later films. Also starring are the *Dragnet* team of Jack Webb and Henry Morgan, and there's a gem of a performance from Ed Begley as a bookie with ulcers, plus a poignant portrayal from Don DeFore.

Dark Command ○

1940, US, 92 mins, b/w
Dir: Raoul Walsh
Stars: John Wayne, Claire Trevor, Roy Rogers, Walter Pidgeon
Rating: ★★

After *Stagecoach,* Republic Studios swiftly realised it had a major new star in John Wayne on its hands and immediately mounted a special vehicle for him, in what turned out to be the Studio's most expensive film to date. The darkly photographed story proved to be the familiar one of 'Bloody' Bill Cantrell and his post-Civil War raiders. Possibly hoping for the emergence of a second Wayne in quick succession, Republic cast their young cowboy star Roy Rogers as his younger brother but Rogers, though a popular Western hero for another 12 years, proved not to quite have the stature for big-budget films.

Dark Corner, The ○

1946, US, 98 mins, b/w
Dir: Henry Hathaway
Stars: Mark Stevens, Lucille Ball, Clifton Webb, William Bendix
Rating: ★★★★

The dark corner in the title of this archetypal Hollywood *film noir* of the Forties represents the predicament of the hero (a private eye just out of jail after being framed), who is just as surely alienated from the world as the returning ex-servicemen in *The Best*

Years of Our Lives, released the same year. His insecurity is underlined when it seems someone is trying to frame him anew. 'I'm backed up in a dark corner,' mutters Mark Stevens as the detective, 'and I don't know who's hitting me.' All this and William Bendix as the mysterious White Suit, Clifton Webb as a cultured vulture, claustrophobic direction by Henry Hathaway, and brilliantly shaded photography by Joe MacDonald. What more could any self-respecting fan of the genre want?

Dark Crystal, The ○ ⓥ

1982, US, 94 mins, colour
Dir: Frank Oz
Rating: ★★★

Jim Henson and his Muppet workshops caught everyone hopping with this brilliantly detailed and ultra-dark children's fantasy that was a million miles removed from the primary coloured brilliance of *The Muppet Show*. No Kermit or Miss Piggy in this universe, just monstrous flesh-eating Skeksis and their counterparts, the Mystics. They battle over possession of the shattered Dark Crystal, which will give ultimate power to the holder, unless it is restored to its rightful resting place. A young Gelfling has the task of saving the planet, but he's a real wimp and no mistake. A warning for children under 10: just like the best Disney good-versus-evil tale, the dark side is here represented by the sort of distressing creatures that could cause nightmares.

Darker than Amber ○

1970, US, 96 mins, colour
Dir: Robert Clouse
Stars: Rod Taylor, Suzy Kendall, Theodore Bikel, Jane Russell
Rating: ★★

Films and TV movies have made several attempts at capturing the world of John McDonald's houseboat-bound detective Travis McGee. This is as good as any, with striking location photography in Florida and the Caribbean, rugged Rod Taylor as McGee, and some excellent cameos from the supporting cast, notably Anna Capri, and Janet MacLachlan, plus terrifyingly authentic performances of vicious thugs from William Smith and Robert Phillips.

Dark Eyes ① ⓥ

1987, Italy, 117 mins, colour
Dir: Nikita Mikhalkov
Stars: Marcello Mastroianni, Silvana

Mangano, Marthe Keller, Elena Sofonova
Rating: ★★★

Lush music by Francis Lai announces a return by Marcello Mastroianni to *Sunflower* country. In an unquenchably romantic piece, based mostly on Chekhov's *Lady With a Little Dog,* Mastroianni makes dazzling use of his entire repertoire as a working-class Romeo seduced by riches into a life of opulent idleness within an increasingly barren marriage. Until he conquers the 'lady with a little dog', a Russian woman who falls in love with him but flees back to her husband in Moscow. It's one of those films full of scenes that conjure up old paintings, in many of which you can feel an atmosphere of sunshine, or heavy mists, or simply sumptuous emptiness. Despite some stretches that touch tedium, the director's skill keeps the piece alive until the (you guessed it) romantic ending.

Dark Eyes of London, The ①

1939, UK, 76 mins, b/w
Dir: Walter Summers
Stars: Bela Lugosi, Hugh Williams, Greta Gynt
Rating: ★★★

Hollywood chillmonger Bela Lugosi, the original Dracula, crossed the Atlantic to net an 'H' certificate for this British thriller about a series of gruesome murders. Based on a story by prolific purveyor of suspense Edgar Wallace, it boasts several creepy characters – but none so awesome as Lugosi's sinister Dr Orloff. Although the film came out in 1939, sharp eyes will notice that all its references (newspapers etc) are to 1936. A mystery perhaps, deeper than the one in the film.

Darkman ● ⓥ

1990, US, 95 mins, colour
Dir: Sam Raimi
Stars: Liam Neeson, Frances McDormand, Colin Friels, Larry Drake
Rating: ★

An unintentionally laughable modern sex clone of *Phantom of the Opera,* directed by Sam Raimi (of *Evil Dead* fame) on a wing and a prayer, with a little help from an unseen organist in the background. You'd never guess the four stars were all fine players from their painful efforts to bring any credibility to a non-script that Raimi and four other people cobbled together from old clichés, clattering banalities and fragments of better films. Liam Neeson is the scientist ready to perfect artificial skin that can be used as a mask. He's almost there (cue cliché: 'I can feel it. God, I can almost taste it.') when horribly disfigured in his laboratory by thugs hired to get a document he may have in his possession. The rest of the plot doesn't take much guessing. Congratulate Aussie Friels on his American accent, marvel at how different Larry Drake is from his retard on *LA Law*, spot *Evil Dead* star Bruce Campbell in a cameo, and Jenny Agutter unbilled, wince at the poor process work, and you've seen it, done it. Find something better to do.

Dark Mirror, The ○
1946, US, 85 mins, b/w
Dir: Robert Siodmak
Stars: Olivia de Havilland, Lew Ayres, Thomas Mitchell, Richard Long
Rating: ★★★

Fine actress Olivia de Havilland gives a tour-de-force performance as identical twin sisters, one of whom is a murderess, in this complex, *film noir*-style psychological thriller, directed from Nunnally Johnson's script by Robert Siodmak the year after his best film, *The Spiral Staircase*. The special effects by Devereaux Jennings and Paul Lerpae are brilliantly done, enabling de Havilland to play opposite herself and appear totally convincing as two people. It has a satisfactorily upbeat ending, but de Havilland said of her roles: 'The technical problems involved in playing a dual role were extremely difficult to solve, and that horrible Terry I had to play haunts me today.'

Dark Obsession
See: Diamond Skulls

Dark Page, The
See: Scandal Sheet

Dark Passage ○ ⓥ
1947, US, 106 mins, b/w
Dir: Delmer Daves
Stars: Humphrey Bogart, Lauren Bacall, Bruce Bennett, Agnes Moorehead
Rating: ★★★

Humphrey Bogart is an escaped convict, wrongly jailed for the murder of his wife in this gripping and unusual thriller. For the first 40 minutes you don't see the star, only hear his voice – the camera sees through his eyes: a neat cinematic trick that was used to equally good effect a year later in *Lady in the Lake*. It's only after Bogart has plastic surgery that the camera turns on his 'new' face. Lauren Bacall is as cool as ever as the girl who hides him from

the authorities, but Agnes Moorehead, given an unusually glamorous role, overacts shrilly. The Bogart/Bacall scenes are a delight, though, even if they are underplayed compared to those they shared in *To Have and to Have Not*. It's a good yarn with enough twists and turns to keep you guessing.

Dark Victory ○ ⓥ
1939, US, 100 mins, b/w
Dir: Edmund Goulding
Stars: Bette Davis, George Brent, Humphrey Bogart, Geraldine Fitzgerald, Ronald Reagan
Rating: ★★★

A very superior soap opera which might almost have won its star, Bette Davis, her third Academy Award: she was nominated but lost to Vivien Leigh's Scarlett O'Hara in *Gone With the Wind*. This story of a society woman dying from a brain tumour but offered a brief chance of happiness, was lovingly directed by Edmund Goulding.

Dark Waters ○
1944, US, 90 mins, b/w
Dir: André De Toth
Stars: Merle Oberon, Franchot Tone, Thomas Mitchell, Fay Bainter
Rating: ★★★★

Deep in the bayou someone is menacing Merle Oberon, trying to drive her out of her mind, in this notable study in fear. John Qualen, Thomas Mitchell, Elisha Cook and Fay Bainter make a formidably grotesque quartet of conspirators and the stage management of the swampland scenes at night is splendid. Watch it in the dark to appreciate its full power.

Dark Wind, The ● ⓥ
1991, US, 112 mins, colour
Dir: Errol Morris
Stars: Lou Diamond Phillips, Gary Farmer, Fred Ward, Guy Boyd
Rating: ★★

This may be the first native American *film noir*. Slow to get going, this murky, desert murder thriller has an unfathomable plot, and Lou Diamond Phillips as Jim Chee, a Navajo policeman who finds his dead-end assignment unexpectedly enlivened by mysterious happenings in the night. A light aircraft is seemingly misguided into crashing. The pilot dies. A passenger is shot. A note is left in his mouth about a deal. And maybe a third party makes off. Investigating a local burglary which may in some way be connected, Chee finds himself warned off by his chief (Fred Ward) and roughed up by an FBI

man (Guy Boyd) who seems to think Chee knows where the plane's vanished cargo went. When he thinks about it, Phillips does know too. Exciting towards the end, this is slightly pretentious stuff, with soporific narration by Phillips, who's otherwise okay.

Darling ①
1965, UK, 125 mins, b/w
Dir: John Schlesinger
Stars: Dirk Bogarde, Julie Christie, Laurence Harvey
Rating: ★★

The film that won Julie Christie an Oscar and established her as the spirit of the swinging Sixties now looks very outmoded. Even at the time it seemed crammed with clever-clever chat and 'in' dialogue, though the acting from Miss Christie was so brilliant it hardly appeared to matter. Time, however, has fortified the remark of one contemporary critic who observed that: 'The characters aren't noticeably of the sort whom one might actually meet.' Christie, though, is still magnetic in her best screen performance as the girl who, trapped in a gilded cage of her own charms, drifts from one man to another gaining what she fondly calls 'experience'. It isn't difficult to see that this little social moth is destined to get her wings burned in the end.

Darling Lili ○
1969, US, 136 mins, colour
Dir: Blake Edwards
Stars: Julie Andrews, Rock Hudson, Jeremy Kemp
Rating: ★★★

Rather underrated at the time of its initial release, when both Julie Andrews and Rock Hudson were beginning to lose their box-office magic, this is an entertaining war spoof with some tuneful music and Julie enjoying herself as a German spy. A bit long, but always good fun.

D'Artagnan's Daughter ①
1994, France, 136 mins, colour
Dir: Bertrand Tavernier
Stars: Sophie Marceau, Philippe Noiret, Nils Tavernier, Claude Rich
Rating: ★★

Too much non-productive, plot-stopping chat slows up this French swashbuckler which is too larkish even to be tongue-in-cheek, and lacks real vigour. And, in true Gallic style, leading lady Sophie Marceau is required to bare her breasts almost as often as her rapier. For a novice nun, she picks up fencing remarkably quickly too, as she

D

helps her father (Philippe Noiret) and his aged musketeers to foil a plot involving the poisoning of the young king at his coronation. Dingy settings seem contrary to the spirit of the lighthearted proceedings, although Marceau, Noiret and their cohorts look good enough with the sword to convincingly dispatch a few of their opponents on the sparse occasions when the film actually condescends to burst into action.

D.A.R.Y.L ○ Ⓥ
1985, US, 99 mins, colour
Dir: Simon Wincer
Stars: Barret Oliver, Mary Beth Hurt, Michael McKean, Colleen Camp, Josef Sommer, Kathryn Walker
Rating: ★★★

This lively fantasy adventure about a robot boy, the product of artificial insemination and a computerised brain is just like a Disney film of the Fifties with the addition of computers and scientific hardware. Escaping into the outside world with the help of a sympathetic and soon-despatched scientist, Daryl (nicely played by Barret Oliver) soon lands in the laps of foster parents Mary Beth Hurt and Michael McKean. Their fondness for such a well-behaved boy is somewhat tempered by the fact that he doesn't seem to need their friendship and is ultra-good at everything from maths to baseball. Australian director Simon Wincer makes sure that the obvious possibilities of all this are as enjoyable as they should be, before science intervenes to retrieve its youthful project, and the film is able to slip a gear into the obvious, but equally enjoyable chase sequences for its final 20 minutes. Filmmaking by numbers, perhaps, but none the worse for that.

Date with Judy, A ○
1948, US, 113 mins, colour
Dir: Richard Thorpe
Stars: Jane Powell, Wallace Beery, Elizabeth Taylor, Robert Stack, Carmen Miranda
Rating: ★★★

An MGM 'teen swing' musical that's the perfect mirror of its time, with teenagers bopping away to the music of Xavier Cugat and his Orchestra, and veteran screen tough-guy Wallace Beery doing an incredible rumba with Carmen Miranda. Elizabeth Taylor's singing voice is not, alas, her own, but Jane Powell's is, and she uses it delightfully.

Daughter of Rosie O'Grady, The ☉
1950, US, 104 mins, colour
Dir: David Butler
Stars: June Haver, Gordon MacRae, Gene Nelson, Debbie Reynolds
Rating: ★★

A switch of studios for the O'Grady family. Rosie O'Grady's original exploits in *Sweet Rosie O'Grady* were made at 20th Century-Fox, but, although one-time Fox contractee June Haver replaces another Fox blonde musical star, Betty Grable, as leading lady, this sequel was made over at Warner Brothers. Haver gets formula Warners backing from Gordon MacRae, S Z Sakall, Debbie Reynolds and Gene Nelson (whose dancing steals the show) and there's a good selection of turn-of-the-century melodies.

Daughters Courageous ○
1939, US, 102 mins, b/w
Dir: Michael Curtiz
Stars: Claude Rains, John Garfield, Jeffrey Lynn, Fay Bainter, Priscilla Lane
Rating: ★★★

Something of a rehash of the previous year's *Four Daughters*, again with John Garfield, Claude Rains, the Lane sisters and Gale Page providing enough sincerity to cut through the sentiment. It couldn't be a sequel – as Garfield's character had been killed off at the end of the previous film (which itself would be remade in 1955 as *Young at Heart*). The film became known for a while for Garfield's novel approach to courting Priscilla Lane, eyeing her up and down and then saying 'Wanna buy me a beer?'

Dave ◑ Ⓥ
1993, US, 110 mins, colour
Dir: Ivan Reitman
Stars: Kevin Kline, Sigourney Weaver, Frank Langella, Ben Kingsley, Charles Grodin, Ving Rhames
Rating: ★★★★★

Director Ivan Reitman lives up to his name by getting everything right in this triumphant treatment of the old dual identity theme. Gary Ross's magic screenplay never puts a foot wrong in its development of the story of a presidential impersonator Dave (Kevin Kline) who runs a temp agency one moment, and the White House the next. Dave's ascendancy to the Oval office is the brainchild of chief of staff Frank Langella, who seems to have the nation's interests at heart when Dave's double, the Prez himself, has a stroke while bedding a White House secretary. The vice-president (Ben Kingsley) apparently has a screw loose, so it's Dave for the hot seat. It soon turns out that Langella's the second

biggest crook around after the old president, and has had Kingsley put out of the way on an eastern tour to further his plans to inherit the presidency for himself. It won't surprise you to find that things don't work out the way the bad guys expect, but you'll get constant pleasure from the way it's done.

David and Bathsheba ○
1951, US, 111 mins, colour
Dir: Henry King
Stars: Gregory Peck, Susan Hayward, Raymond Massey, Kieron Moore, James Robertson Justice
Rating: ★★

Good crowd scenes and costumes compensate for some casting weaknesses in this Hollywood slice of the Bible. But Gregory Peck is fine as King David, and Leon Shamroy's colour photography is another plus factor. King Saul is played by silent screen star Francis X Bushman (at the age of 68). Bushman is best remembered as the evil Messala in Fred Niblo's great 1925 silent version of *Ben Hur*.

David Copperfield ☉ Ⓥ
1934, US, 130 mins, b/w
Dir: George Cukor
Stars: W C Fields, Freddie Bartholomew, Lionel Barrymore, Frank Lawton, Edna May Oliver, Roland Young
Rating: ★★★★

This masterfully cast version of the Dickens classic remained the best example of the author's work on screen until the post-war British versions of *Great Expectations* and *Oliver Twist*. W C Fields (replacing an uneasily-cast Charles Laughton), Roland Young, Basil Rathbone and Edna May Oliver might have been born to play the roles of Micawber, Uriah Heep, Murdstone and Aunt Betsey Trotwood. Fields especially is quite brilliant and the young British actor Freddie Bartholomew is extremely appealing as the boy David. Co-screenwriter Hugh Walpole also plays a small cameo role as a cleric.

David Copperfield ○
1970, UK, 110 mins, colour
Dir: Delbert Mann
Stars: Robin Phillips, Susan Hampshire, Laurence Olivier, Edith Evans, Michael Redgrave, Ralph Richardson
Rating: ★★

Originally produced for American TV, but shown in cinemas here, this is the most star-studded version of Dickens' famous novel yet made, with such stalwarts as Laurence Olivier and Richard

Attenborough in minor roles. The most welcome performances come from Ralph Richardson (Micawber) and Edith Evans' definitive portrayal of Aunt Betsey Trotwood.

Davy ⊙
1957, UK, 85 mins, colour
Dir: Michael Relph
Stars: Harry Secombe, Bill Owen, Adele Leigh, Ron Randell, Susan Shaw, Alexander Knox
Rating: ★★

William Rose, who scripted entertainment is as diverse as *Genevieve* and *Guess Who's Coming to Dinner?*, wrote this comedy-musical as Harry Secombe's first big feature film. Secombe sings well, especially in company with Adele Leigh, and Joan Sims and Liz Fraser can be glimpsed as waitresses. Pretty corny, though.

Davy Crockett and the River Pirates ⊙
1955, US, 81 mins, colour
Dir: Norman Foster
Stars: Fess Parker, Buddy Ebsen
Rating: ★★

Second Davy Crockett film is, like the first, spun together from two TV shows but none the worse for it. Vigorous, colourful fun, packed with action, including a tremendous free-for-all on board a sinking keel boat. Fess Parker again dons the coonskin cap as a virile Crockett.

Davy Crockett – King of the Wild Frontier ⊙
1954, US, 93 mins, colour
Dir: Norman Foster
Stars: Fess Parker, Buddy Ebsen
Rating: ★★★

Originally conceived as episodes for a television series, the Crockett project was quickly converted to a feature film (with a sequel to follow) when the Disney studio saw what a winner it had on its hands. Fess Parker, a taciturn, slow-spoken actor with only minor film appearances to his credit, became a national figure with his presentation of the intrepid frontier scout as a powerful, determined figure, with a welcome wry wit. The action is presented in short, sharp episodes as colourful and explicit as a comic-book story. A handsome, vigorous adventure.

Dawn at Socorro ○
1954, US, 79 mins, colour
Dir: George Sherman
Stars: Rory Calhoun, Piper Laurie, David Brian, Alex Nicol, Edgar Buchanan,

Kathleen Hughes
Rating: ★★

Big, dramatic Western on the theme of the ace gunslinger who tries to hang up his holsters. Action and direction constantly come to the rescue of a rather poor screenplay (from which Piper Laurie suffers most), and the final shoot-out is staged with some imagination by director George Sherman.

Dawning, The ○ ⓥ
1988, UK, 97 mins, colour
Dir: Robert Knights
Stars: Anthony Hopkins, Rebecca Pidgeon, Jean Simmons, Trevor Howard, Hugh Grant
Rating: ★★★

Not a popular film in Britain in its time, dealing as it does with the gunning down of British officers by Irish terrorists, albeit in 1920. It is, however, a good one, photographed in crystal-clear colour and solidly crafted. Although not always gripping, it's well acted by a distinguished cast, plus Rebecca Pidgeon as the 18-year-old girl who befriends fugitive terrorist Anthony Hopkins. She certainly needed to have more talent than most actresses of her age, although in subsequent years her career has not progressed as it might have done. Jean Simmons has a telling tipsy scene which she confesses to have been 'happy, calm and useless most of my life'.

Dawn Patrol, The ○
1938, US, 103 mins, b/w
Dir: Edmund Goulding
Stars: Errol Flynn, David Niven, Basil Rathbone, Barry Fitzgerald
Rating: ★★★★

This WWI aviation drama, directed by Edmund Goulding, puts over its anti-war message with considerable skill. A remake of Howard Hawks' 1930 version, it uses much of that film's aerial footage. Errol Flynn and David Niven are very good indeed in the roles taken in the original by Richard Barthelmess and Douglas Fairbanks Jr; and Basil Rathbone, playing the commander of a Royal Flying Corps squadron in 1914 France, gives one of his finest performances. Tony Gaudio's fine monochrome cinematography is exemplary.

Day at the Races, ⊙ ⓥ
1937, US, 107 mins, b/w
Dir: Sam Wood
Stars: Groucho Marx, Chico Marx, Harpo Marx, Maureen O'Sullivan, Allan Jones, Margaret Dumont
Rating: ★★★

Vintage Marx Brothers comedy in which a failing sanatorium hires Dr Hackenbush (Groucho) to restore its flagging fortunes. Alas, Groucho is a horse doctor and sees no reason to change his treatments. 'The last patient I gave one of these,' he leers, brandishing an enormous pill, 'won the Kentucky Derby.' Groucho pursues Margaret Dumont – 'Marry me and I'll never look at any other horse'; Chico is devoted to Maureen O'Sullivan – 'If she wants a Hackenabush, she's gonna get a Hackenabush'; and Harpo plays Pied Piper with an enchanting group of black children (who include Dorothy Dandridge). All this and the 'tutsy frutsy' ice cream routine too.

Daydreamer, The ⊙
1966, US, 98 mins, colour
Dir: Jules Bass
Stars: Cyril Ritchard, Paul O'Keefe
Rating: ★★★

Charming Hans Christian Andersen musical which combines live action with puppet animation, with very entertaining results. The 'voice cast' includes such well-known film names as Boris Karloff, Tallulah Bankhead, Burl Ives, Hayley Mills and Terry-Thomas.

Day of the Badman ○
1958, US, 81 mins, colour
Dir: Harry Keller
Stars: Fred MacMurray, Joan Weldon, John Ericson, Robert Middleton
Rating: ★★

Well-acted, skilfully mounted but unexciting Western, with Fred MacMurray turning in yet another reliably good performance as the frontier judge who loses his girlfriend to a coward. Oily Robert Middleton is the villain.

Day of the Dolphin, The ○ ⓥ
1973, US, 104 mins, colour
Dir: Mike Nichols
Stars: George C Scott, Trish Van Devere, Paul Sorvino
Rating: ★ ★

Despite George C Scott's convincing portrayal of a marine biologist, this is a cumbersome mixture of science-fiction, spy thriller and heavy-handed comedy. The political misuse of talking dolphins seems an odd choice of subject for writer Buck Henry and director Mike Nichols (the team responsible for *The Graduate* and *Catch-22*) and the film comes alive only in the underwater sequences, superbly photographed by William A Fraker.

D

Day of the Evil Gun ○

1968, US, 93 mins, colour
Dir: Jerry Thorpe
Stars: Glenn Ford, Arthur Kennedy, Dean Jagger
Rating: ★★

Downbeat Western about two men, in love with the same woman, forced to band together when she is kidnapped by Indians. Glenn Ford and Arthur Kennedy build up a tense relationship, and a stout supporting cast includes Dean Jagger and John Anderson.

Day of the Jackal, The ① Ⓥ

1973, UK/France, 142 mins, colour
Dir: Fred Zinnemann
Stars: Edward Fox, Michael Lonsdale, Alan Badel, Tony Britton, Cyril Cusack, Delphine Seyrig
Rating: ★★★★

Director Fred Zinnemann's otherwise excellent and highly successful version of Frederick Forsyth's best-selling novel has just two intrinsic weaknesses. One is that the leading character, an ace assassin, is so passionless that any audience would have difficulty in identifying with him (despite Edward Fox's fine performance) through his many hair-raising adventures. The other is that the ultimate outcome is inevitable, since the assassin's target is General de Gaulle. Zinnemann's strategy is to counter these deficiencies by cramming his plot with as much incident as possible to keep it buzzing. Thus the police manhunt for the jackal is counterpointed by his own immaculate and sometimes frighteningly unemotional preparations. And the director's final triumph is that the climax really will have you on the edge of your seat, forgetting even that the target must survive. Fox's authoritative portrayal is solidly backed by an international cast, in which Franco-British actor Michael Lonsdale is outstanding as his chief pursuer.

Day of the Locust, The ●

1974, US, 145 mins, colour
Dir: John Schlesinger
Stars: Donald Sutherland, Karen Black, Burgess Meredith, William Atherton, Geraldine Page
Rating: ★★

A daddy longlegs of a film, sprawling all over its story of life at the wrong end of Hollywood in the late Thirties, and finally finding its *raison d'etre* in a long and bloody riot scene at the end. William Atherton, then a fresh-faced newcomer, has the role on which all the action turns, as the young sketch artist who moves in with an old vaudevillian turned drunken salesman (Burgess Meredith) and his silly, virginal daughter (Karen Black). Director John Schlesinger lovingly recreates the period (as he was to do with *Yanks*), much of it in soft focus, intending to lend a glow of nostalgia to this adaptation of the bestseller by Nathanael West, but neglecting the most important element of all: discipline.

Day of the Triffids, The ①

1962, UK, 95 mins, colour
Dir: Steve Sekely
Stars: Howard Keel, Kieron Moore, Janette Scott
Rating: ★★

John Wyndham's powerful, doomy novels, mainly about human beings caught up in events outside their natural experience, have translated better on the whole to radio than to the visual media. This is one of the best known of his stories and the only surprise was that no one had filmed it before (it was written in 1946). The director is Hungarian Steve Sekely, who made many low-budget thrillers in the Hollywood of the Forties. This is probably his best film, with some quite frightening sequences.

Daylight ○ Ⓥ

1996, US, 114 mins, colour
Dir: Rob Cohen
Stars: Sylvester Stallone, Amy Brenneman, Claire Bloom, Viggo Mortensen, Stan Shaw, Rosemary Forsyth
Rating: ★★★

An improbable but exciting sort of Lowering Inferno, as a massive explosion in a freeway under the Hudson River kills hundreds and traps a small group of survivors facing fire and flood in a tunnel now blocked at both ends. Disgraced ex-emergency services chief Kit (inevitably Stallone, the king of action redemption) is a taxi-driver on the scene and figures out a hazardous way to reach those entombed. This involves an extremely unlikely sequence with Stallone dropping through slowed-up giant steel fans before they get back to warp speed. Once down there, he finds an elderly couple, a group of convicts, a dog, the obligatory heroine (Brenneman) and a tunnel security man. No nuns this time round. You don't need a slide rule to figure out there'll be a few casualties on the way to eventual escape, but special effects work overtime with fearsome flames, avalanches of mud and water and showers of sparks to keep the tension hopping.

Days of Heaven ○ Ⓥ

1978, US, 95 mins, colour
Dir: Terrence Malick
Stars: Richard Gere, Brooke Adams, Sam Shepard, Linda Manz
Rating: ★★

A ravishingly shot (by Nestor Almendros) story of immigrants to the Texas Panhandle in 1916. Director Terrence Malick really captures the feeling of time and place, although he fails to build up the story's relationships well enough to sustain his own obvious ambitions, despite charismatic acting by Richard Gere, Linda Manz and Sam Shepard. But it was no surprise on Oscar night when Almendros stepped up to receive his well-deserved Academy Award.

Days of Thunder ① Ⓥ

1990, US, 107 mins, colour
Dir: Tony Scott
Stars: Tom Cruise, Nicole Kidman, Robert Duvall, Randy Quaid, Michael Rooker, Cary Elwes
Rating: ★★

Or: Top Car. This noisy popcorn movie has the same director (Tony Scott) and star (Tom Cruise) as the mindless mega-hit *Top Gun* but, instead of jets, our ears are assaulted by the roar of stock car engines. This is a peculiarly American form of racing where it seems the object is to push the other driver into the wall and where the race is stopped every few minutes for fresh tyres, with the drivers resuming the race in the same positions. Developments on the track remain predictable (down to the final freeze frame), but somewhat less than credible, as cocky young driver Cruise sets out to grab his share of stock car glory. Cruise's rivals include another 'iceman' in cool Russ (Cary Elwes) and Rowdy (Michael Rooker), a bozo who crashes, giving Cruise the one good line: 'Any surgery around his brain is bound to be minor.'

Days of Wine and Roses ①

1962, US, 117 mins, b/w
Dir: Blake Edwards
Stars: Jack Lemmon, Lee Remick, Charles Bickford, Jack Klugman
Rating: ★★★

The title song, sung by Andy Williams, earned an Oscar, but lent a rather misleading rosy glow to this study of alcoholism that was very direct and uncompromising (and almost unpalatable) for its time. Jack Lemmon, then still best known for his comic roles, and Lee Remick are uncomfortably convincing as the couple on a downward spiral into oblivion.

Day the Earth Caught Fire, The ◐

1961, UK, 99 mins, b/w
Dir: Val Guest
Stars: Janet Munro, Leo McKern, Edward Judd
Rating: ★★★★

Unbearably tense and uncomfortably realistic science-fiction thriller, directed (and co-written) by Val Guest in the middle of his most productive period. Guest builds his suspense flawlessly, as the population of Europe wilts under tropical temperatures-plus, and two diligent journalists uncover alarming reasons behind it all. Well worth stopping in for. Spot, if you can, the young Michael Caine as a policeman.

Day the Earth Stood Still, The ○ ⓥ

1951, US, 90 mins, b/w
Dir: Robert Wise
Stars: Michael Rennie, Patricia Neal, Hugh Marlowe, Sam Jaffe
Rating: ★★★★

As relevant now as on the day of its release, this landmark science-fiction film delivers its anti-nuclear message with dignity and restraint. Edmund H North's literate script is performed beautifully by an excellent cast led by Michael Rennie as the Christ-like alien, and Patricia Neal, enormously affecting as the proprietress of the boarding house in which Rennie seeks shelter. There's much else to savour in this Hollywood classic, from Robert Wise's superbly controlled direction and Bernard Herrmann's haunting score to the imposing presence of Rennie's giant robot companion Gort.

Dazed and Confused ● ⓥ

1993, US, 95 mins, colour
Dir: Richard Linklater
Stars: Jason London, Milla Jovovich, Michelle Burke, Joey Lauren Adams, Wiley Wiggins
Rating: ★

US high school life '76 style – 'Say man you got a joint?' – in which you keep waiting for something awful to happen to one of the end-of-year tearaways who specialize in destroying neighbourhood property. Alas, it never does. It's the kind of film in which characters say things like 'No one kills a senior year pal – 'specially if they're starting

quarterback'. Not much relevance for audiences outside America? You got it. Writer-director Richard Linklater's facile approach grabs a few easy laughs here and there, particularly via a pot-smoking Puerto Rican. At least one of the characters has it right when he says, 'If these are the best days of my life, remind me to kill myself'.

Dead, The ○ ⓥ

1987, UK, 82 mins, colour
Dir: John Huston
Stars: Anjelica Huston, Donal McCann, Dan O'Herlihy, Donal Donnelly, Marie Kean
Rating: ★★★

John Huston's last film could be termed an Irish indulgence. But it gives us a chance to hear some of James Joyce's most penetrating prose, spoken by people who know what it's all about. Thus Anjelica Huston and Donal McCann give full value, and get our total attention, from their big speeches at the end, while allowing Donal Donnelly (taking over Jack MacGowran's niche as the dishevelled Irishman) and Dan O'Herlihy to steal the major part of the film as the drunken revellers at an annual Dublin feast at the home of spinster sisters in the winter of 1904. Despite occasional sags, the piece remains a little hymn to nostalgic memories, and a fitting climax to the cinematic career of such an avowed Hibernophile.

Dead Again ● ⓥ

1991, US, 105 mins, colour
Dir: Kenneth Branagh
Stars: Kenneth Branagh, Emma Thompson, Andy Garcia, Derek Jacobi, Hanna Schygulla
Rating: ★

For those who have their doubts about Kenneth Branagh's talents, this ludicrous thriller provides further ammunition. To start with, the title should have a question mark after it. Is Emma Thompson really going to meet the same fate at the end of this life as she did in the last? She's an amnesiac given into the charge of detective Mike Church (Branagh) and seems to be having nightmares about her past life. Hypnotist Derek Jacobi appears from nowhere to take her back into a past that involves a composer murdering his wife with scissors, a scenario that Branagh soon establishes happened 40 years before. It gets a lot sillier, with Andy Garcia's old-age makeup a real hoot.

Dead Bang ● ⓥ

1989, US, 108 mins, colour
Dir: John Frankenheimer
Stars: Don Johnson, Penelope Ann Miller, William Forsythe, Bob Balaban
Rating: ★★

It's always a flaw of the James Bond movies that the bad guys never kill 007 off when they have him dead to rights. The flaw becomes a gaping hole in this otherwise proficient thriller. The villains – American white supremists who gun everyone else down in the blink of an eye, have hero Don Johnson looking down a gun barrel on several separate occasions, but they never pull the trigger. Johnson himself, a man who transforms his face when he smiles, is well at home as an LA cop, battling alcoholism and summonses from his ex-wife, who rides roughshod over prissier associates when he becomes involved in a case of cop-killing that escalates into an inter-state hunt. The film's 'surprise' at the end should be guessed at an early stage by fans of these hard-boiled thrillers, though they'll be highly satisfied by the vividly staged underground shootout.

Dead Calm ● ⓥ

1988, Australia, 96 mins, colour
Dir: Phillip Noyce
Stars: Sam Neill, Nicole Kidman, Billy Zane
Rating: ★★★★

Director Phillip Noyce takes three actors, two boats, a dog and an ocean and conjures up some spine-tingling suspense and plenty of shocks. Events take a turn for the worse when Sam Neill and Nicole Kidman encounter psychopath Billy Zane while in the middle of the Pacific Ocean. The happily married couple get separated and the unstable young killer sets to work terrorizing Kidman on her yacht. True, there are several moments that defy belief, when Kidman could escape her ordeal, but Noyce does a good job of keeping the pace and tension cranked up. Terrific.

Dead Can't Lie, The ● ⓥ

(aka: Gotham)
1988, US, 97 mins, colour
Dir: Lloyd Fonvielle
Stars: Tommy Lee Jones, Virginia Madsen, Colin Bruce, Frederic Forrest
Rating: ★★★

This modern *film noir* is strange, almost ludicrous, but one of a kind and that's for sure. Tommy Lee Jones is a run-down private eye who's hired by a (literally) haunted man to find the

D

ghost of his dead wife (she's been trailing him) and buy her off with the jewels he stole from her grave. At least, I think this is what happens. No mistaking what happens when Jones meets steamy Virginia Madsen and can't believe she's a ghost. The poor sap falls heavily. Then he finds out the truth, but is it the whole truth? Although you may not understand it all, there's lots of emotional power in the exchanges between Jones and the voluptuous Madsen – shot by the director in tight, glossy closeup (it was originally made for cable TV) with dark backgrounds. 'And you had the best of her,' she whispers, 'all the best of her.' But does he? Even though this one loses its drive three-quarters of the way through, it remains different. And Jones and Madsen *are* both good.

Dead Cert ○
1974, UK, 99 mins, colour
Dir: Tony Richardson
Stars: Scott Antony, Judi Dench, Michael Williams
Rating: ★

The career of British director Tony Richardson went off the boil after early success with *The Entertainer, Look Back in Anger, A Taste of Honey, The Loneliness of the Long-Distance Runner* and *Tom Jones*, for which he won a well-deserved Oscar in 1963. This murder-thriller set against the world of horseracing came a decade later and is decidedly inferior work. Despite the fact that the film is based on a cracking good novel by Dick Francis and the production team went to the trouble of staging its own Grand National race, it is a plodding affair that lurches from drama to crisis instead of building momentum to a gripping climax.

Dead End ○
1937, US, 93 mins, b/w
Dir: William Wyler
Stars: Joel McCrea, Sylvia Sidney, Humphrey Bogart
Rating: ★★★

William Wyler's strong film about ghetto life in the America of the Thirties is rather obviously studio-set, but sparks to life with the appearance of Humphrey Bogart as a gangster who's a hero to the local youngsters, a group of teenagers who later made films as the Dead End Kids, the East Side Kids and the Bowery Boys.

Deadfall ◐
1968, UK, 120 mins, colour
Dir: Bryan Forbes
Stars: Michael Caine, Giovanna Ralli, Eric Portman, Nanette Newman
Rating: ★★

Michael Caine is a master jewel thief in this stop-go thriller. Best sequence: Caine bringing off a daring cat burglary at great risk to life and limb, intercut with clips from the concert attended by the owners of the house he is robbing. Otherwise, the thrills are undernourished.

Deadlier Than the Male ○
1966, UK, 101 mins, colour
Dir: Ralph Thomas
Stars: Richard Johnson, Elke Sommer, Sylva Koscina, Nigel Green
Rating: ★★

Bulldog Drummond updated to the Bond era. Richard Johnson makes a brave attempt to keep up with Sapper's original concept of the character, amid a mass of hardly-clad girls and exploding gadgets. Drummond has two formidable female adversaries in the shapes of Elke Sommer and Sylva Koscina in a violent thriller whose best moments come in a human chess game between Drummond and his arch-enemy Petersen, played in sinister style by Nigel Green.

Deadline – USA ● ⓥ
(aka: Deadline)
1952, US, 87 mins, b/w
Dir: Richard Brooks
Stars: Humphrey Bogart, Kim Hunter, Ethel Barrymore, Ed Begley, Paul Stewart, John Doucette
Rating: ★★★

You can almost smell the ink on the printing presses in this gripping newspaper drama about an embattled editor (a superbly cast Humphrey Bogart) and his fight to stop the sale of his beloved paper and at the same time expose a crime boss. Among a superb supporting cast, Martin Gabel is fascinating as the Capone-style Mafia boss, belching out evil incarnate. Ethel Barrymore, meanwhile, stamps her authority on the pivotal role of the noble and tough newspaper-owning widow, Mrs Garrison, trying to resist the efforts of her spendthrift daughters (Fay Baker, Joyce MacKenzie) who want the sale to go through to support their lifestyle. Bogart has a great last line.

Deadly Advice ● ⓥ
1993, UK, 97 mins, colour
Dir: Mandie Fletcher
Stars: Jane Horrocks, Brenda Fricker, Imelda Staunton, John Mills, Edward Woodward, Billie Whitelaw
Rating: ★★

A mildly amusing black comedy about a repressed Welsh librarian (didn't Peter Sellers once play one of those?) who, rebelling against her nearest and dearest, receives help in bumping them off from the ghosts of some of Britain's most famous murderers. Jane Horrocks, fast developing into a latter-day Rita Tushingham, plays this lethal lady, beset at the outset by an impossibly puritan mother (Brenda Fricker), who even drags her out of the local pub at lunchtime (what she's doing there herself is anyone's guess). Mummy clearly has to go and, though Jane's asthmatic, secretly scarlet sister (Imelda Staunton) helps her dump the corpse in the river, she's soon jealous of the attention her bisexual Chippendale boyfriend is giving Jane, and threatens to turn her in ... Where will it all end? Horrocks is quite beguiling and Ian Abbey (the only convincing Welsh accent) excellent as the male stripper. But it's rather a raucous film with little room for subtlety. Not bad, though, in a sub-Ealing manner.

Deadly Affair, The ◐
1966, UK, 107 mins, colour
Dir: Sidney Lumet
Stars: James Mason, Simone Signoret, Harriet Andersson, Maximilian Schell
Rating: ★★★★★

Downbeat but totally absorbing espionage drama in typical John Le Carré style. The impressive low-key photography of Freddie Young sets the mood of bleakness, blackness and danger into which hard-pressed security agent James Mason must probe. He's out to break an espionage ring that lies behind a murder that most people thought was suicide. Director Sidney Lumet offers set pieces of nail-biting excitement.

Deadly Game, The
See: Third Party Risk

Deadly Is the Female
See: Gun Crazy

Deadly Pursuit ◐
(aka: Shoot to Kill)
1988, US, 110 mins, colour
Dir: Roger Spottiswoode
Stars: Sidney Poitier, Tom Berenger, Kirstie Alley
Rating: ★★★

A picturesquely-shot chase thriller that runs like a high-class TV movie. A maniac has mercilessly killed a ransom victim after his demands have been met, and must be tracked down by a city-wise law enforcer (Sidney Poitier) and a mountain guide (Tom Berenger). Meanwhile the killer, identity unknown, joins an adventure tour planning to seize its guide (Kirstie Alley) and force her to take him to Canada. Packed with as much taut action as the plot will allow, but let down by silly situations, the film draws gasps and giggles in about equal number. Poitier, looking scarcely older on his return to acting after 10 years away, gives a majestic performance as the obsessed FBI agent. And the script does have a few much-appreciated amusing lines. 'Maybe we could give it some food,' mutters Poitier, as he and Berenger face a grizzly bear up in the mountains. Berenger gives him a quick but withering glance. 'We *are* the food,' he replies.

Dead Man ● Ⓥ

1996, US, 121 mins, b/w
Dir: Jim Jarmusch
Stars: Johnny Depp, Gary Farmer, Mili Avital, Lance Henriksen, Alfred Molina, Gabriel Byrne, Robert Mitchum
Rating: ★

A weird but not wonderful black-and-white western, ponderously paced throughout. Johnny Depp, doing his Buster Keaton act again, is William Blake, an easterner out west who, finding the job promised to him as an accountant has been filled weeks before, takes up with a flower seller (Mili Avital), has to shoot her ex (Gabriel Byrne) and wanders lonely as a cloud, and about as useful, through an overbrightly shot western landscape. Along the way he acquires, in the company of an American Indian called Nobody (Gary Farmer), a quite unexpected reputation as a killer and desperado. In years to come, Byrne, John Hurt (overacting dreadfully), Lance Henriksen and Alfred Molina may come to wonder what they were doing in such pretentious, semi-surrealist tosh. Neil Young's clangorous music may drive you nuts long before Depp's final fate is settled. Not good.

Dead Man Walking ● Ⓥ

1995, US, 120 mins, colour
Dir: Tim Robbins
Stars: Susan Sarandon, Sean Penn, Robert Prosky, Clancy Brown, Raymond J Barry, R Lee Ermey, Scott Wilson
Rating: ★★

Despite wonderful performances by Susan Sarandon (winning an Oscar)

and Sean Penn (Oscar-nominated) it must be admitted that this story about the death-cell friendship between a nun and a convicted killer and rapist is something of an ordeal. There's no letup from the prison environment, which contributes much to the doomy atmosphere of a film that you could recommend whole-heartedly for its acting, but hardly at all in terms of an evening's entertainment. Penn does finally find God, but you may find the arms of Morpheus rather sooner.

Dead Men Don't Wear Plaid ○ Ⓥ

1982, US, 95 mins, b/w
Dir: Carl Reiner
Stars: Steve Martin, Rachel Ward, Reni Santoni, Carl Reiner
Rating: ★★★★★

This supremely funny and inventive parody of the *film noir* thrillers of the Forties has a gimmick: director Carl Reiner has edited into his story a series of carefully chosen chps from Hollywood films of the period. Steve Martin (never before as likeable as this) is the detective trying to solve what must be the most baffling case any Chandleresque private eye can have faced. Around every corner of the twisted trail await (literally) Alan Ladd, Bette Davis, James Cagney, Barbara Stanwyck and more. The plot vaguely concerns Nazis on a South American island but don't listen to a word of it. Wallow instead in the splendid pastiche music by Miklos Rosza, the costumes of Edith Head (her last film work) and the use of Humphrey Bogart as the hero's confidant and leg-man. Rachel Ward has bags of class as femme fatale Juliet and the script displays a delightfully zany sense of humour. A real sweetie.

Dead of Night ◐

1945, UK, 95 mins, b/w
Dir: Alberto Cavalcanti, Robert Hamer, Basil Dearden, Charles Crichton
Stars: Mervyn Johns, Michael Redgrave, Googie Withers, Sally Ann Howes
Rating: ★★★★★

Mervyn Johns' finest film: a must for chiller addicts and still revered as the greatest piece of ghost-story telling ever to come from the British cinema. Its *pièce de resistance* is the final story, in which Michael Redgrave unnervingly plays a ventriloquist who appears to be exchanging personalities with his demonic dummy, Hugo. But the final scene is, in its unsettling way, more frightening than any of the tales told

to Johns by the inhabitants of a dark old cottage, most of which reach shattering climaxes thanks to knife-edge direction by Robert Hamer, Basil Dearden and Alberto Cavalcanti. The story directed by Charles Crichton, intended as comic relief, is somewhat less successful.

Dead or Alive ◐

1968, Italy/US, 89 mins, colour
Dir: Franco Giraldi
Stars: Alex Cord, Robert Ryan, Arthur Kennedy, Nicoletta Macchiavelli
Rating: ★★★

This spaghetti Western is better than most, and certainly better-paced than the 'Dollars' films it followed. The ending might be rather too bitterly ironic for most tastes, but Alex Cord gives one of his best performances as the bounty hunter, and the whole thing has a downbeat flavour which suits its mood very well.

Dead Poets Society ○ Ⓥ

1989, US, 126 mins, colour
Dir: Peter Weir
Stars: Robin Williams, Robert Sean Leonard, Ethan Hawke, Josh Charles, Norman Lloyd, Lara Flynn Boyle
Rating: ★★★

Undermined by a series of improbabilities, this is a nonetheless often emotive film showcasing the considerable talents of Robin Williams as an innovative and eccentric English teacher arriving at a stuffy and expensive public school in Vermont. Indeed so extraordinary and incendiary are his methods – his subject is life, the English is incidental – that you wonder how teacher and school ever accepted each other in the first place. Nor is it easy for us to accept parents who react to their son's brilliance on stage by packing him off to a military academy. An unlikely story, though you may think Williams' engaging personality sufficiently forceful to put it across. The performances are uniformly good, from Williams and his septet of poetry students to Norman Lloyd as the martinet headmaster who seeks to protect not the truth but the good name of the school.

Dead Pool, The ● Ⓥ

1988, US, 91 mins, colour
Dir: Buddy Van Horn
Stars: Clint Eastwood, Patricia Clarkson, Liam Neeson
Rating: ★★★

A lively thriller in the 'Dirty Harry' series, spotlighting Clint Eastwood's fifth

D

canter in the role. Crisply edited, it's the old story of a killer with a list (of victims). Under Buddy Van Horn's best direction to date, it comes up pretty fresh, and Jim Carrey makes a brief but showy appearance at the start as a rock star. The one stand-out scene that'll have you on the edge of your seat comes when the killer sends a bomb onto the streets of San Francisco strapped to a remote control toy car.

Dead Presidents ● ⓥ

1995, US, 119 mins, colour
Dir: Hughes Brothers
Cast: Larenz Tate, Keith David, Rose Jackson, Chris Tucker, Freddy Rodriguez, N'Bushe Wright
Rating: ★★

The drifting of black Americans into crime after their return from the war in Vietnam forms the core of this sometimes explosively exciting, but progressively alienating action thriller. Our sympathy is increasingly demanded for characters who become unfortunately less sympathetic as the story goes on. The early Vietnam sequences are vivid and uncompromisingly real, but the story becomes grindingly routine after the main characters return to America and, in spite of good performances, our minds progressively disengage, with the ending coming as nothing near the poignant tragedy that the directors obviously intended. Great trailer: don't let it fool you. The 'dead presidents', by the way, refers to the used currency our 'heroes' plan to steal in the film's climax.

Dead Reckoning ○

1946, US, 97 mins, b/w
Dir: John Cromwell
Stars: Humphrey Bogart, Lizabeth Scott
Rating: ★★★

One of Humphrey Bogart's more successful ventures outside the walls of Warner Studios, not least because it gave him a strong vis-a-vis in the sultry shape of Lizabeth Scott (on loan from across the way at Paramount). Investigating the disappearance of an army pal, Bogart's character becomes both the hunter and the hunted as director John Cromwell creates a web of intrigue seen through low-key lighting and unusual camera angles. Both the characters and the plot are tough and tender at the same time, in this too-seldom-seen thriller.

Dead Ringers ● ⓥ

1988, Canada, 118 mins, colour
Dir: David Cronenberg
Stars: Jeremy Irons, Genevieve Bujold,

Heidi von Palleske
Rating: ★

Preposterous, humourless psycho-horror (supposedly based on a true story) from director David Cronenberg that represents a sad come-down for the Canadian schlock-horror director after the dizzy heights of *The Fly*. Although well-performed in a dual role by Jeremy Irons, who stands alone in keeping unintentional mirth at bay for three-quarters of the plot, the film's unconvincing script and lack of light and shade eventually does for it more effectively than could be managed by either of Irons' twin surgeons, the battier of whom (by a whisker) craves to create steel implements for operating on mutant women (really!). Few will care about the fates of any of the characters involved in this ludicrous and deeply unpleasant farrago.

Dead Zone, The ● ⓥ

1983, US, 90 mins, colour
Dir: David Cronenberg
Stars: Christopher Walken, Brook Adams, Tom Skerritt, Herbert Lom, Anthony Zerbe, Martin Sheen
Rating: ★★★

Christopher Walken is a car crash victim who wakes from a five-year coma to find that he has strange psychic powers and can see into the future, in this gripping psychological thriller based on Stephen King's best-selling novel. By simply touching hands with someone, he can see their fate and this ability helps him rescue a child from a burning house and solve a series of murders. But then he realises he has the power to change the future. When he presses palms with cynical politician Martin Sheen, he realises Sheen, as president of the US, is capable of pushing the button. Without doubt, this is the most faithful screen adaptation of a King story. Having said that, it gets bogged down a bit in the middle with the murder mystery, but picks up again in the final third and there's a nice twist at the climax.

Dear Brigitte ... ○

1965, US, 100 mins, colour
Dir: Henry Koster
Stars: James Stewart, Glynis Johns, Fabian, Billy Mumy, Brigitte Bardot
Rating: ★★

Made by James Stewart in his 'family comedy' period of the early Sixties, this farce, about a literary-minded professor with a mathematical genius called Erasmus for a son, has a few screamingly funny moments. Best of these is

when Erasmus, asked to divide one prodigious number by another, solemnly pronounces that it won't go. Nothing daunted, the scientists feed the problem into their computer which gets a nasty case of the tilts.

Dear Heart ○

1965, US, 114 mins, b/w
Dir: Delbert Mann
Stars: Glenn Ford, Geraldine Page, Angela Lansbury
Rating: ★★★

Warm, old-fashioned, genuine sort of film, about two middle-aged people who almost miss their chance of happiness together, because time has sapped their confidence in love, and made them want to settle for security. Glenn Ford and Geraldine Page play it so well together that, even though we've seen it all before, the old story still works. The old-time atmosphere is heightened by the appearance of Alice Pearce, memorable as the toothy spinster miss with the braying voice in *On the Town*. In *Dear Heart* she plays ... a spinster miss.

Dear Mr Prohack ○

1949, UK, 91 mins, b/w
Dir: Thornton Freeland
Stars: Cecil Parker, Hermione Baddeley, Glynis Johns, Dirk Bogarde, Sheila Sim
Rating: ★★

An adaptation of a story by Arnold Bennett, this comedy features Cecil Parker in one of his best performances as a Treasury official who comes into a fortune, but has less success with his own finances than those of the nation. The supporting cast is very strong, but the amusing central situation gradually wears thin.

Dear Murderer ○

1947, UK, 94 mins, b/w
Dir: Arthur Crabtree
Stars: Eric Portman, Greta Gynt, Dennis Price, Maxwell Reed, Jack Warner
Rating: ★★★

What a revelation Oslo-born blonde glamour girl Greta Gynt was in this complex and grim crime melodrama from the Gainsborough studio. And her thrilling performance as a footloose wife whose lovers pay the ultimate price at the hands of her husband was more than matched by Eric Portman as her jealous, murderous spouse. In fact, every one of the unpleasant characters get their just deserts in the intelligent script by the ever-reliable team of Muriel and Sydney Box and Peter Rogers.

Dear Wife ○

1949, US, 87 mins, b/w
Dir: Richard Haydn
Stars: William Holden, Joan Caulfield,
Mona Freeman, Edward Arnold, Billy De
Wolfe
Rating: ★★

Continuing the lighthearted saga of
Bill and his Ruth, begun in an earlier
film, *Dear Ruth* (and continued later in
Dear Brat). Here, as in the later film,
the spotlight is on Ruth's tomboy
teenage sister Miriam, played by pretty
Mona Freeman. What a change of
pace this was for William Holden.
The following year he started a film
dead, shot and drowned, in a swimming-pool, in *Sunset Boulevard*.

Death and the Maiden ● ⓥ

1994, UK/US, 104 mins, colour
Dir: Roman Polanski
Stars: Sigourney Weaver, Ben Kingsley,
Stuart Wilson
Rating: ★

A massive hit on stage, this three-han-
der about a South American woman
haunted by memories of her torture at
the hands of an oppressive regime
seems slow to develop on screen and
has little chance of escaping its stage
origins. Sigourney Weaver and Ben
Kingsley deliver strong performances,
but it all drones on a bit and you long
for something to be resolved, as the
woman (Weaver) holds hostage the
man (Kingsley) she believes responsible for her past humiliation, no
physical details of which are spared
the audience. Stuart Wilson is slightly
less effective as the woman's husband
and the action teeters on the brink of
an anti-climax at the end. Parents
should be advised that this contains
extreme bad language, violence, nudity and graphic accounts of physical
torture.

Death at Broadcasting House ○

1934, UK, 71 mins, b/w
Dir: Reginald Denham
Stars: Ian Hunter, Austin Trevor, Jack
Hawkins
Rating: ★★★

Advanced photography techniques
help make the studios of the BBC appropriately sinister as ham actor
Donald Wolfit 'gets his' in this early
British whodunnit with a starry list of
suspects and intriguing glimpses of
popular radio personalities of the
time. You're unlikely to spot the
killer.

Death Becomes Her ◐ ⓥ

1992, US, 103 mins, colour
Dir: Robert Zemeckis
Stars: Meryl Streep, Goldie Hawn, Bruce
Willis, Isabella Rossellini
Rating: ★★★

A triumph of prosthetic, state-of-the-art
effects over a *Man from UNCLE*-style
plot, this is the story of a potion that restores eternal youth – at a price (in
more ways than one). Meryl Streep is
every inch the glamour-puss Broadway
star, who feels age gripping her by the
throat when she sees dowdy Goldie
Hawn (from whom she had stolen plastic surgeon Bruce Willis) looking
exquisite at 50. Offered The Potion,
the dispirited and dilapidated Meryl
coughs up and becomes young again.
But Goldie, having re-entered the picture, is intent on enlisting Willis, now
sunk to embalming, into her plan to
bump the long-hated Meryl off. This is
a cue for a whole barrage of special effects which have already started when
Goldie blows up to 20 stone after
Willis has deserted her. Heads swivel
on bodies, limbs stick out at awkward
angles but still function, and – in an FX
man's masterstroke – a see-through
hole can be made in the middle of a
body. The pace is a bit slow sometimes for a comedy, but there's always
the next effect to look forward to.

Death Hunt ◐

1981, US, 97 mins, colour
Dir: Peter Hunt
Stars: Charles Bronson, Lee Marvin,
Angie Dickinson, Carl Weathers, Ed
Lauter
Rating: ★★

A glacial Western, with Charles
Bronson as the man on the run across
the Arctic and Lee Marvin as the battle-
weary Mountie who always get his
man. Various stereotypes around
them are quite well presented by director Peter Hunt to spice the plot.
There's Angie Dickinson as the woman
who turns up for little apparent reason
except to wait for Marvin; Carl
Weathers – Apollo Creed from the
Rocky films – as the Mountie's (obviously expendable) right-hand man; Ed
Lauter, smiling and sneering in the
same gesture as the real bad guy responsible for Bronson's plight; and
Andrew Stevens as the obligatory rookie constable undergoing his baptism of
fire.

Death in Venice ◐ ⓥ

1971, Italy, 130 mins, colour
Dir: Luchino Visconti

Stars: Dirk Bogarde, Silvana Mangano,
Bjorn Andresen, Marisa Berenson
Rating: ★★★

This elegant and beautiful story about
an ageing composer's unrequited passion for a young boy, set against the
crumbling decadence of pre-Great War
Venice, has a dark side, with the threat
of disease cutting through the city. It
also has a very fine central performance from Dirk Bogarde, whose
obsession with the 14-year-old boy and
the embodiment of beauty he represents, threatens to overwhelm him.
Director Luchino Visconti has lovingly
transferred Thomas Mann's haunting
novel to the screen but although visually stunning, it is ultimately rather
empty. Nevertheless, the film has
much to commend it and will amply reward those patient enough to accept
the story's slow unfolding.

Death on the Nile ○ ⓥ

1978, UK, 140 mins, colour
Dir: John Guillermin
Stars: Peter Ustinov, Bette Davis, David
Niven, Mia Farrow, Angela Lansbury,
Maggie Smith
Rating: ★★★

It was to be expected after the success
of Murder on the Orient Express that the
same production team would launch a
whole series of sleuthing films based on
Agatha Christie stories. And the setting could not be grander than the
temples and pyramids of the Nile,
where love, lust, revenge and murder
sit well with centuries-old curses and
mysticism. Peter Ustinov takes over
from Albert Finney as the rotund
Belgian detective, Hercule Poirot, but
the case of murder aboard a Nile cruise
ship doesn't tax his 'little grey cells' too
much. This overlong film will, however, tax your patience as the final scenes
are taken up with endless re-runs of the
crime from the viewpoint of everyone
on board. Even so, there are a number
of individual performances to enjoy,
notably those of Mia Farrow, Bette
Davis, Angela Lansbury and (especially) Maggie Smith.

Death Race 2000 ◐ ⓥ

1975, US, 90 mins, colour
Dir: Paul Bartel
Stars: David Carradine, Simone Griffeth,
Sylvester Stallone
Rating: ★★

A truly anarchic, blow-them-all-to-bits
fantasy caper that fires on all cylinders
except the script. The cars are hot, the
acting's not, though you may enjoy a
pre-Rocky Sylvester Stallone as a com-

D

petitor called Machine Gun Joe Viterbo. The violence of the action leaves the Road Runner and Wile E Coyote with more than a little to answer for.

Death Ship ●

1979, Canada, 90 mins, colour
Dir: Alvin Rakoff
Stars: George Kennedy, Richard Crenna, Nick Mancuso, Sally Ann Howes
Rating: ★

The characters in this ingenious horror film do such silly things that your sympathies may well be with the mysterious black ship (with a lifeforce of its own) that seems to be trying to bump them off. A star studded cast seems to do its best to manoeuvre its members into situations least likely to ensure their survival. It's a familiar Hollywood horror framework, although in this case both film and director (Alvin Rakoff) are Canadian.

Death Takes a Holiday ○

1934, US, 78 mins, b/w
Dir: Mitchell Leisen
Stars: Fredric March, Evelyn Venable, Guy Standing, Gail Patrick
Rating: ★★★

An absorbing, well-played film drama based on a play by Italian Alberto Casella. Fredric March is outstanding as Prince Sirki, alias Death. It is stylish and dreamlike, but a bit slow even in its brief running time.

Deathtrap ◐ Ⓥ

1982, US/UK, 112 mins, colour
Dir: Sidney Lumet
Stars: Michael Caine, Christopher Reeve, Dyan Cannon
Rating: ★★★★

Even an improvement on the long-running play, this spine-chilling charade has good performances from Dyan Cannon, Christopher Reeve and especially Michael Caine, as the once wildly popular playwright fallen on hard times whose eyes light up when he receives a superb new play from in untried writer through the post. From here on in the plot merely trifles with its audience, deliberately changing course so often that you are finally unprepared to accept anything at face value and conditioned to expect the unexpected. No plot of one of the protagonists can be certain of success, no corpse guaranteed dead. It is, of course, all too far-fetched to have anything to do with real life, but simply what the French call a *divertissement;* very ingeniously writer Jay Presson Allen (from Ira Levin's play) has diverted us too.

Death Wheelers, The

See: Psychomania

Death Wish ● Ⓥ

1974, US, 94 mins, colour
Dir: Michael Winner
Stars: Charles Bronson, Hope Lange, Vincent Gardenia
Rating: ★★★

It's getting so that a mugger's not safe on the streets of New York any more. Especially so when Charles Bronson is the one-man vigilante committee who cuts the city's hoodlum population down to size after three of them have killed his wife (Hope Lange) and reduced his daughter (Kathleen Tolan) to a living vegetable. A variable script is heftily combatted by skilful action scenes and good night-time photography on city streets. It's certainly exciting, though the morality may be questionable, even in this day and age. The public were clearly on the vigilante's side, and made the film a big hit: small wonder that Bronson subsequently made four further *Death Wish* films, all of them inferior.

Death Wish 2 ● Ⓥ

1981, US, 93 mins, colour
Dir: Michael Winner
Stars: Charles Bronson, Jill Ireland, Vincent Gardenia
Rating: ★

Nothing succeeds like excess, it seems, as Charles Bronson reprises his role as the vigilante architect, bumping off every mugger in sight in Los Angeles, having already laid waste to the ungodly in New York in the first of the crime thrillers, which Michael Winner also directed. And with a cast list that contains such characters as Stomper, Punkcut and Cutter it's very much the recipe as before (and after).

Death Wish 3 ● Ⓥ

1985, UK, 90 mins, colour
Dir: Michael Winner
Stars: Charles Bronson, Deborah Raffin, Ed Lauter, Gavan O'Herlihy, Martin Balsam, John Gabriel
Rating: ★★

Entertaining and at the same time frighteningly predictive. When Michael Winner shot this third *Death Wish* film on the streets of Lambeth (although it's set in New York), could he have foreseen the Brixton riots that followed soon afterwards? And could this story of street violence happen here? Happily Charles Bronson as the lone vigilante is here to wipe the teenage punks and their leaders off the face of

the streets. 'Who is this man? We need him!' gasps an elderly resident, as the impassive Bronson unloads a missile-launcher. The star's minimalist acting offers proof that life begins at 65; Deborah Raffin is the romantic interest who's clearly expendable in every way.

Death Wish 4: The Crackdown ● Ⓥ

1987, US, 96 mins, colour
Dir: J Lee Thompson
Stars: Charles Bronson, Kay Lenz, John P Ryan, Perry Lopez
Rating: RB

Once a vigilante, always a vigilante. Charles Bronson is wheeled out again (not quite yet in his bathchair) as the righter of wrongs, this time wiping out half the drug dealers in Los Angeles. More a case of *Death Wish Fulfilment*. With veteran J Lee Thompson at the helm, you might expect this episode to herald a slight upsurge in the series. Instead the film, apart from action scenes, which are mechanically efficient, is a complete and utter disaster, a woeful script driving some of its actors to desperate lengths. As the two detectives tracking Bronson, Soon Teck-Oh and George Dickerson seem to be competing for the worst supporting actor of the year award. Bronson himself contributes very little, apart from knocking people out with ridiculous ease.

Decadence ● Ⓥ

1993, UK, 95 mins, colour
Dir: Steven Berkoff
Stars: Steven Berkoff, Joan Collins
Rating: RB

A so-called black comedy in which writer-director-star Steven Berkoff spews up bile against the aristocratic ruling classes in an attack far more vituperative and wider of the mark than anything you've seen in *Spitting Image*. No bodily function is left unturned, few scenes of (rhyming!) dialogue fail to contain offensive language or suggestions of the most foul behaviour imaginable. Joan Collins joins the 'fun' by spitting out more four-letter words than you'd find on the pages of one of her sister Jackie's books. Just as well Mary Whitehouse had retired: this coarse course on sledgehammer satire would have finished her off. Let's see them try to edit this odious offering for TV.

Deceived ◐ Ⓥ

1991, US, 105 mins, colour
Dir: Damian Harris
Stars: Goldie Hawn, John Heard, Ashley

Peldon, Robin Bartlett, Amy Wright
Rating: ★★★

As the title implies, this is Goldie Hawn in dramatic vein. A well-made thriller with an iffy script, especially towards the end when it often contributes the wrong line at the wrong moment, it casts Goldie as a businesswoman who becomes involved through a quirk of fate with Jack (John Heard), whom she marries. Six years into the marriage, little unexplained events, like her husband being seen in New York when he said he was going to Boston, cast doubts in her mind. After an old museum curator is murdered, and Jack killed in a car crash, it becomes apparent to Goldie that her husband was leading some kind of double life. A devious criminal, perhaps, but, thanks to that script, a very careless one, leaving incriminating evidence around all over the place. When it. comes to keeping the suspense hopping, though, closing mysteriously in on people and objects and frightening the audience almost as much as Goldie, director Damian Harris proves himself an expert. Hawn and Heard are good when the script allows them to be, but it's the scenes without dialogue where this film is at its considerable best.

Deceivers, The ◑ ⓥ
1988, UK, 103 mins, colour
Dir: Nicholas Meyer
Stars: Pierce Brosnan, Saeed Jaffrey, Shashi Kapoor, Helena Michell, Keith Michell
Rating: ★★★

Boasting a cast packed with real Indian actors, it's guaranteed that this lavish update on *The Stranglers of Bombay* will carry a ruthlessly authentic touch. Mixing the vogue for portraits of colonialism with a horrific if rousing true-life adventure, the film tells one more time the story of the T'huggee cult. Followers of the devil goddess Kah, they throttled and robbed rich travellers and buried the bodies of their victims. Much in the mould of *The Four Feathers* (our hero browns up and travels as a T'huggee to crack the cult), the plot stretches credulity at times, especially when the 'sugar gourd' of Kali is supposed to infuse our upright hero (Pierce Brosnan) with a lust for blood. But Brosnan is no mean actor as well as prime beefcake, and he pulls the story through in good style to its bloody conclusion. Shashi Kapoor and Saeed Jaffrey offer variations on their familiar (in this case murderous) rascals.

Deception ○ ⓥ
1947, US, 112 mins, b/w
Dir: Irving Rapper
Stars: Bette Davis, Paul Henreid, Claude Rains
Rating: ★★★★

A remarkable example of how to transform a trite story from within by sheer force of acting personality. Paul Henreid, Claude Rains and Bette Davis, three of Warners' glittering stock company of stars, never earned their keep more than on this screenplay, which perhaps would never have got off the ground in today's cinematic climate. The result was such absorbing entertainment that, as one contemporary critic put it: 'I wouldn't have missed it for the world.'

Decision at Sundown ○
1959, US, 77 mins, colour
Dir: Budd Boetticher
Stars: Randolph Scott, John Carroll, Karen Steele
Rating: ★★

Another of the Westerns Randolph Scott made with director Budd Boetticher, which is rather hampered by its small-town setting. Scott plays a man who comes a-looking for the hombre who caused the death of his wife, only to have his vengeful ideals compromised by finding that she was worthless. Very much an adult Western, with Scott splendidly grim in the lead, and full of little incidentals which mark it as a thinking man's action film.

Decision Before Dawn ○
1951, US, 119 mins, b/w
Dir: Anatole Litvak
Stars: Richard Basehart, Oskar Werner, Hildegarde Neff, Gary Merrill
Rating: ★★★

Many cinemagoers think of Oskar Werner's screen career beginning with *Jules et Jim* and then going on to such English-speaking films as *Ship of Fools* and *Interlude*. But here's a film that proves the baby-faced Werner was giving excellent performances before Jules and Jim were thought of. Here he is on screen almost all of the time as Happy, a German prisoner of war who agrees to spy against his own country for the Allies. And a very fine job he makes of it, too, creating a likeable and sympathetic character with whom one lives through a series of hairsbreadth escapes on a dangerous mission. The excitement is well sustained by director Anatole Litvak, and the climax very moving.

Decline and Fall ◑
(aka: Decline and Fall of a Birdwatcher)
1968, UK, 113 mins, colour
Dir: John Krish
Stars: Colin Blakely, Robert Harris, Leo McKern, Robin Phillips
Rating: ★★

This bizarre adaptation of Evelyn Waugh's famous novel comes across as a sort of upper crust *Lucky Jim*. It involves the unlikely expulsion from Oxford of a theological student (Robin Phillips, then a bright new face). His subsequent innocent decline into nefarious misdoings ends in his being sent to prison as a white slave trafficker. A misfire this, but with some dazzling vignettes by Donald Sinden (one of the best performances of his career), Donald Wolfit and Colin Blakely.

Decoy (1962)
See: Mystery Submarine

Deep, The ◑ ⓥ
1977, US, 123 mins, colour
Dir: Peter Yates
Stars: Robert Shaw, Jacqueline Bisset, Nick Nolte, Eli Wallach, Lou Gossett Jr
Rating: ★★

Although rightly compared unfavourably to *Jaws* when it first appeared, this film is lively, spirited and at times rather frightening light entertainment. Part-scripted by Peter Benchley, the author of *Jaws*, and based on another of his seagoing novels, it's again an adventure in which the ocean depths figure prominently, although this time guarding sunken treasure. Robert Shaw plays a rugged ocean-wise recluse who is also a treasure-hunter – and lighthouse-keeper. The personable Eli Wallach scores as an old seadog. The action is plentiful, with undersea excitement, a battle with a giant moray eel – in a terrifying sequence – and even an element of voodoo.

Deep Cover ● ⓥ
1992, US, 112 mins, colour
Dir: Bill Duke
Stars: Larry Fishburne, Jeff Goldblum, Victoria Dillard, Charles Martin Smith, Gregory Sierra
Rating: ★★★

There are some good sequences in this backstreets thriller which allies elements of an old-fashioned *film noir* (the undercover, cut-off cop; the deep, monotone narration) to a more modern, if familiar story about said cop's attempts to bust a nationwide narcotics organisation. Naturally he becomes dazzled by

D

the ease of his new life as a drug dealer (his father was a criminal junkie) and, kept largely in the dark by superiors themselves at the mercy of government whim, sinks deeper into the life of the underworld. The dialogue between dope-dealers who never seem to trust each other has the ring of truth and the story is incisively told by director Bill Duke, who made *A Rage in Harlem*. Larry Fishburne rightly allows himself few smiles as the cop who's never quite on top of his own destiny, while Jeff Goldblum is pretty well on the mark as the dope-dealing big-time lawyer whose life and mind hover on the brink of explosive violence.

Deep In My Heart ○
1954, US, 132 mins, colour
Dir: Stanley Donen
Stars: Jose Ferrer, Merle Oberon, Walter Pidgeon, Paul Henreid
Rating: ★★★

There are any number of reasons why you should put up with the cardboard storyline of this MGM biopic about Sigmund Romberg. But the foremost has to be Jose Ferrer's side-splitting, 15-minute musical comedy burlesque buried in the soggy depths of this mammoth musical. The skit is a takeoff of all the old cliché-ridden operettas you've ever suffered through. It's the fastest, cleverest thing in the film. And there are some sizzling numbers from an array of guest stars, notably 'I Love to Go Swimmin' with Women', by Gene Kelly and his brother Fred. And Cyd Charisse, dancing 'One Alone' in form-fitting white satin, gives the old number a whole new vibrancy. For the rest, it's the mixture as before in Hollywood musical biographies: poverty, struggle, success, failure, and final triumph. Opera star Helen Traubel makes a hit every time she appears.

Deep in the Heart
See: Handgun

Deep Six, The ○
1957, US, 106 mins, colour
Dir: Rudolph Maté
Stars: Alan Ladd, Dianne Foster, William Bendix, Keenan Wynn, James Whitmore
Rating: ★★

It's surprising to find tough-guy Alan Ladd cast as a reluctant hero. But here he's a Quaker serving on a destroyer in World War Two. Director Rudolph Maté, a former cameraman, ensures that the action is lively, especially in the climactic raid on a Japanese-held island. Canadian Dianne Foster has the soli-

tary female role, and the cast also includes Ladd's old Paramount punching partner, William Bendix.

Deep Valley ○
1947, US, 104 mins, b/w
Dir: Jean Negulesco
Stars: Ida Lupino, Dane Clark, Fay Bainter, Henry Hull
Rating: ★★★

This film suffered in its day after being unfavourably compared with *High Sierra*. Ida Lupino gives a superb performance as the repressed farm girl finding love (at least temporarily) with an escaped prisoner. And director Jean Negulesco (*How to Marry a Millionaire*, *Three Coins in the Fountain*) was helped greatly by location shooting in Big Sur and Big Bear due to a strike at the Warners studio. The tragic ending, alas, is obvious from the start.

Deer Hunter, The ● ⓥ
1978, US, 183 mins, colour
Dir: Michael Cimino
Stars: Robert De Niro, John Cazale, John Savage, Christopher Walken, Meryl Streep, George Dzundza
Rating: ★★★★★

A richly detailed, angry picture, for many 'the' Vietnam war film , but one that also deals with such subjects as American small-town life, rites of passage, love and death in a way that haunts the memory. Director Michael Cimino trained as an architect and he has constructed *The Deer Hunter* like a mighty building where every stone has a function: here every frame has a tale to tell. He extracted convincing portrayals from Robert De Niro, John Cazale and John Savage and a marvellous dominating performance from Christopher Walken, which established his star status and won him an Oscar. Other Academy Awards included Best Picture and Best Editor for Peter Zinner and Cimino. Meryl Streep, in one of her earliest roles, plays the girl who turns from Walken to De Niro in the numbingly poignant later stages of the film.

Defence of the Realm ◐ ⓥ
1985, UK, 96 mins, colour
Dir: David Drury
Stars: Greta Scacchi, Gabriel Byrne, Denholm Elliott, Ian Bannen, Bill Paterson, Robbie Coltrane
Rating: ★★★

This is a British political thriller which not only entertains, but also kicks against the governmental establishment of the 1980s. Ambitious newsman

Nick Mullen, played by then-newcomer Gabriel Byrne, latches onto a Profumoesque exposé, and a prominent Labour MP (Ian Bannen) resigns. There's a story bigger than Watergate ripe for the writing but can Mullen survive to tell the tale? Director David Drury keeps the plot on a tight rein. In the acting stakes the excellent Byrne is edged out by Denholm Elliott as a dandruffed, alcoholic war-horse of the newsroom (he won a BAFTA award for his work).

Defending Your Life ○ ⓥ
1991, US, 114 mins, colour
Dir: Albert Brooks
Stars: Albert Brooks, Meryl Streep, Rip Torn, Lee Grant, Buck Henry, Shirley MacLaine
Rating: ★

The cinema hasn't had too much luck with fantasy in recent times, and this film about death is on the whole pretty turgid stuff that only, if you'll pardon the expression, comes to life at the end. Albert Brooks, you see, is dead, and the story is about his 'processing' in Judgement City to see whether he goes on to a higher place, or back to earth to try again. This sort of thing always sounds good on paper, but Brooks barely gives it a chance, wearing too many hats as star, director (the biggest mistake) and writer. The segments with Meryl Streep (we should all meet Meryl in Heaven) are the best but the scenes of Brooks' 'trial', with Rip Torn and Lee Grant as the opposing lawyers, are almost completely unsuccessful, with too little tightness in the telling. The emotive ending works pretty well, but it's almost too late: Brooks has already squeezed all but the last gasp of life out of his 'fantastic' project.

Defenseless ● ⓥ
1992, US, 104 mins, colour
Dir: Martin Campbell
Stars: Barbara Hershey, Sam Shepard, Mary Beth Hurt, J T Walsh, Jay O Sanders, Sheree North
Rating: ★★

Here's yet another hot-shot lady lawyer having an affair with one of her clients. It was never like this on *LA Law!* Still, not many legal eagles are as finely feathered as Barbara Hershey, but she's up to her gorgeous beak in trouble when she becomes involved with a man accused of involvement in a porno racket. She thinks he is innocent, you see – but we know better. Or do we? At any rate, when the shady suitor turns up stiffer than yesterday's British

Rail sandwich, nosy copper Sam Shepard is sent to investigate. There are few surprises from here on as the murder mystery plot attempts to thicken – but the quality acting of the cast, notably, from Hershey and from Mary Beth Hurt in, for her, an offbeat role, ensures that this at least hits the par for the courtroom thriller course.

Defiant Ones, The ○ ⓥ
1958, US, 96 mins, b/w
Dir: Stanley Kramer
Stars: Tony Curtis, Sidney Poitier
Rating: ★★★★

One of the earliest and best films on racial intolerance, this tale of two convicts on the run planted Sidney Poitier firmly at the top as the only big negro box-office star since Paul Robeson. It also gave Tony Curtis another chance to break away from his beefcake image, and confirmed the promise as a serious actor that he had shown in *Sweet Smell of Success*. Brilliantly directed by Stanley Kramer, whose constant switching between pursuers and pursued gives the piece an insistent rhythm, the film won well-deserved Academy Awards for its screenplay (by Nathan E Douglas and Harold Jacob Smith) and the dazzling black-and-white photography of Sam Leavitt.

Delicate Delinquent, The ⊙
1956, US, 101 mins, b/w
Dir: Don McGuire
Stars: Jerry Lewis, Darren McGavin, Martha Hyer
Rating: ★★★

This uneven but largely winning spoof on the then-Hollywood vogue for juvenile delinquent films was Jerry Lewis's first feature film without regular partner Dean Martin. In fact, the role of the cop assigned to keep an eye on Lewis's shy and cowardly janitor who is mistaken for a hoodlum was actually written for Martin, but went in the end to Darren McGavin. It's an agreeable mix of social satire and knockabout comedy, and even its sentiment works quite well. The studio was taking no chances on Lewis as a solo attraction, and made the film on the cheap in black-and-white. In the event, they needn't have worried.

Delirious ○ ⓥ
1990, US, 95 mins, colour
Dir: Tom Mankiewicz
Stars: John Candy, Mariel Hemingway, Emma Samms, Raymond Burr, Jerry Orbach
Rating: ★★★

An engagingly silly John Candy comedy about a TV scriptwriter who has an accident and falls into his own daily soap. The nice thing is that he finds he can control developments in the serial by typing them in his dreams, contrary to the real-life wishes of the guy who's been called in to rewrite his stuff. You'll like, too, the idea of Robert Wagner turning up as an unwanted guest star – 'But you're Robert Wagner, you don't do daytime soap,' Candy tells the bemused actor, who is supposed to be in character, just before Wagner blasts him with a shotgun for sending him to Cleveland. Candy exercises his own brand of personal charm and, if the comedy basically isn't up to much, and falls apart at the end, it's mainly thanks to the star that it proves at least a useful antidote to those daytime office blues.

Deliverance ● ⓥ
1972, US, 109 mins, colour
Dir: John Boorman
Stars: Jon Voight, Burt Reynolds, Ned Beatty, Ronny Cox, Billy McKinney
Rating: ★★★

This harsh, brutal adventure story with hints of significance divided the critics when first shown, but undoubtedly established the international reputation of its director, John Boorman, who received one of the film's several Oscar nominations. Burt Reynolds and Jon Voight did all their own dangerous stuntwork riding the rapids, as two of the four central characters, businessmen on a survival-against-nature holiday. They soon find that nature isn't all they have to combat, and thereby hang some of the film's less savoury aspects. The final image is as haunting as it is unexpected, and may disturb your dreams.

Delta Force, The ◑ ⓥ
1986, US, 129 mins, colour
Dir: Menahem Golan
Stars: Chuck Norris, Lee Marvin, Martin Balsam, George Kennedy
Rating: ★★

After a career as a solo attraction, Chuck Norris joined the all-star brigade in this prolonged hijack thriller, which pits America's Delta Force – a cross between the Marines and Britain's SAS – against Arab terrorists and their hostages aboard a Boeing 707. Both Robert Forster and David Menaham are realistically menacing as the hijackers and it's their acting that catches the eye rather than the stars – Chuck, as an independent

major called in for this vital mission, and a tired-looking Lee Marvin. The action – when it comes – is right out of James Bond's textbook, especially Chuck's motorcycle with its anti-rocket launchers. But, though you admire Chuck for doing almost all his own stunts, no plus factors can conceal the fact that this film is achingly overlong.

Delta Force 2 ● ⓥ
1990, US, 111 mins, colour
Dir: Aaron Norris
Stars: Chuck Norris, Billy Drago
Rating: ★★

Chuck Norris plays the US colonel who leads an American SAS-style unit into action against Latin American drug barons. His brother Aaron directs. It's an all-action drama that calls on Chuck's famed skills as a stuntman rather than on any in-depth acting. There's some humour in the *Dirty Harry* vein, the hint of a question about America's rights ('If America accuses us of being a nation of drug pushers, then we accuse America of being a nation of drug addicts,' says the fictional Latin-American president) and tons of explosive action.

Demetrius and the Gladiators ○ ⓥ
1954, US, 101 mins, colour
Dir: Delmer Daves
Stars: Victor Mature, Susan Hayward, Michael Rennie, Anne Bancroft
Rating: ★★

A sequel to Fox's first big CinemaScope success *The Robe,* with Victor Mature again as Demetrius, the Greek who is given charge of the robe of Christ at the Crucifixion. There are some good battles in the arena – when the stars are not doing battle with the script.

Demolition Man ● ⓥ
1993, US, 114 mins, colour
Dir: Marco Brambilia
Stars: Sylvester Stallone, Wesley Snipes, Sandra Bullock, Nigel Hawthorne
Rating: ★★★

A real blast of an action comedy largely set in 2032, when nightmare psycho Simon Phoenix (Wesley Snipes) breaks out after 30 years frozen in the CryoPenitentiary and proceeds to terrorise the good people of San Angeles (as LA has become), which has outlawed nicotine, caffeine, fluid transfer activities (sex) and violations of verbal morality (swearing) and has no defence against such a man. None, that is, except Sgt John Spartan (Sylvester Stallone), similarly frozen 30 years be-

D

fore for being a cop who threw away the rule book and cost lives. Dominated by its amazing special effects and searing action, the film still finds room for a quite witty script which Snipes handles rather better than Stallone, although in most other respects they're well-matched in a ruthlessly entertaining bombshell of a film which squarely hits its target.

Dennis the Menace ○ ⓥ
(aka: Dennis)
1993, US, 97 mins, colour
Dir: Nick Castle
Stars: Mason Gamble, Walter Matthau, Joan Plowright, Christopher Lloyd
Rating: ★

This is a laugh and a half. Well, about half a laugh actually. I think it came when villain Christopher Lloyd coughed after being set on fire and smoke poured out of his mouth. Yes, that must have been it. There's nothing wrong with the premise here: an angelic-looking but awful five-year-old kid torments his elderly neighbour and can't resist touching things that lead to escalating disaster. The two themes join forces when the elderly couple-next-door (Walter Matthau and Joan Plowright) agree to look after the little monster (Mason Gamble) while his parents are away. Under the treatment of director Nick Castle, however, this becomes a clodhopping affair that's never in touch with reality and is mostly unbearable to watch. The director seems to have little idea how to create comedy that will actually get you laughing. Oh well, it is at least wonderfully well shot in glowing Technicolor, and half a laugh is better than none.

Dentist in the Chair ○
1960, UK, 84 mins, b/w
Dir: Don Chaffey
Stars: Bob Monkhouse, Peggy Cummins, Kenneth Connor, Eric Barker
Rating: ★★

There must be a twist in the British sense of humour, when film-makers have turned out so many broad comedies with a medical background; this farce (and the following entry) about dentistry are guaranteed to make your ribs ache rather than your gums; Peggy Cummins, as pretty as ever, is the young student who makes patients forget all about their pains and dentists' drills.

Dentist on the Job ○
(aka: Get on with It)
1961, UK, 88 mins, b/w

Dir: C M Pennington-Richards
Stars: Bob Monkhouse, Kenneth Connor
Rating: ★★

You'll give that white, white smile to those blue, blue jokes in this Carry On-style farce. Star Bob Monkhouse also had a hand in the script (one of his fellow-writers was Hazel Adair, original co-ordinator of *Crossroads*). And such experienced exponents of farce as Charles Hawtrey, Kenneth Connor, Eric Barker and Richard Wattis need no laughing gas to help them out.

Dentist, The ● ⓥ
1996, US, 95 mins, colour
Dir: Brian Yuzna
Stars: Corbin Bernsen, Molly Hagan
Rating: ★★

Hounded by the IRS and confronted with his wife's infidelity, dentist Alan Feinstone cracks. Avenging himself on his wife by taking all her teeth out, he speeds off to his surgery, where his patients are in for a hairy day. 'Nothing is free of decay,' he mutters. 'It can only lead to rot, filth and corruption.' What happens when the man from the IRS arrives is perhaps best left to your imagination. Suffice it to say that a balding Corbin Bernsen brings a new meaning to malpractice in the title role of this horror film, quite conventional by the standards of director Yuzna, more used to offering us mega-budget, mega-bucket effects and gore. Bernsen gleefully extracts what he can from the role. Molly Hagan is the best of the maidens menaced in (and by) his surgery.

Denver and Rio Grande ○
1952, US, 89 mins, colour
Dir: Jerry Hopper
Stars: Edmond O'Brien, Laura Elliott, Sterling Hayden, Dean Jagger
Rating: ★★★

One of the rousing outdoor adventures that producers William Pine and William Thomas made with such regularity at Paramount in the Fifties. This one is a Western with fine Technicolor photography, good villains (especially Lyle Bettger) and a really spectacular head-on train crash.

Desert Attack
See: Ice Cold in Alex

Desert Bloom ◑ ⓥ
1985, US, 106 mins, colour
Dir: Eugene Corr
Stars: Jon Voight, JoBeth Williams, Annabeth Gish, Ellen Barkin
Rating: ★★★

An intelligent family drama observing the story of a girl's growing pains in an emotionally deprived and politically warped environment, set in Las Vegas in 1950. Jon Voight plays a World War II veteran devoted more to his short-wave radio and military rumours than he is to his family. Stupidly compensating for feelings of inadequacy and impotency, he mistreats his stepdaughters, takes to the bottle and makes a play for his wife's sexually provocative sister – nicely played by Ellen Barkin. But the focus is on the family's teenage daughter, glowingly captured by Annabeth Gish, who is also the film's narrator. Altogether a powerful drama.

Desert Fox, The
See: Rommel - Desert Fox

Desert Hawk, The ○
1950, US, 77 mins, colour
Dir: Frederick De Cordova
Stars: Yvonne De Carlo, Richard Greene, George Macready, Jackie Gleason, Rock Hudson
Rating: ★★

A capital cast graced this Oriental extravaganza, the kind which Universal were adept at making. Indeed, these sword and sandal pictures were practically a studio speciality. Great fun, if you have a taste for such colourful escapist entertainment. Rock Hudson has a supporting role.

Desert Hearts ◑ ⓥ
1985, US, 93 mins, colour
Dir: Donna Deitch
Stars: Helen Shaver, Patricia Charbonneau, Audra Lindley
Rating: ★★★

There are some scorching scenes in this first feature from Donna Deitch (who also plays a tiny role in the film as a Hungarian gambler). The opening is reminiscent of the 1939 Hollywood classic *The Women*, as would-be divorcees stay at a ranch near Reno waiting for their 'freedom' to come through. But Deitch's mind is on more searching issues, and the film soon develops into a love affair between two of the women there. Sound film-making and excellent acting from the leading players (Helen Shaver, Patricia Charbonneau, Audra Lindley) ensures the film touches the emotions, even though it makes little concession in terms of costume to the late 1950s setting.

Desert Mice ○
1959, UK, 82 mins, b/w
Dir: Michael Relph

Stars: Alfred Marks, Sidney James, Dora Bryan, Marius Goring
Rating: ★★

An entertaining double-edged tribute to ENSA – the bands of gallant entertainers who, during World War Two, travelled around entertaining British armed forces. Here the mobile entertainers are headed by an enjoyable roster of familiar British character actors, including Sid James, Dora Bryan, Reginald Beckwith, Irene Handl and Dick Bentley.

Desert Patrol
See: Sea of Sand

Desert Rats, The ○ ⓥ
1953, US, 88 mins, b/w
Dir: Robert Wise
Stars: Richard Burton, Robert Newton, James Mason, Robert Douglas, Chips Rafferty
Rating: ★★★★

This reconstruction of a phase in the battle for Tobruk ranks as one of the best and most realistic of Fifties Hollywood war films. And its acting brings the desert conflict vividly to life. Richard Burton gives the most sensitive of his early performances as the harsh, disciplinarian officer sent to bring order to a raw division of Australian troops fighting a desperate rearguard action against overwhelming odds. And Robert Newton is at his most disciplined and persuasive as an alcoholic schoolmaster turned reluctant soldier.

Desert Song, The ○ ⓥ
1953, US, 110 mins, colour
Dir: Bruce Humberstone
Stars: Kathryn Grayson, Gordon MacRae, Steve Cochran, Raymond Massey, Dick Wesson
Rating: ★★

Third screen version of Sigmund Romberg's melodious desert musical, awash with action and colour, and with the original score practically intact. Leading songsters Kathryn Grayson and Gordon MacRae seem so ill-at-ease with their roles that such attractive performers as Dick Wesson, Allyn McLerie (reunited from *Calamity Jane*) and Raymond Massey have no difficulty in diverting one's attention throughout.

Design for Living ○
1933, US, 90 mins, b/w
Dir: Ernst Lubitsch
Stars: Gary Cooper, Fredric March, Miriam Hopkins, Edward Everett Horton,

Franklin Pangborn
Rating: ★★★

Delightfully described by one reviewer as 'chic fluff', this is a light and witty adaptation for the screen of the Noel Coward play about two men who find a free-spirited girl moving in to make a platonic menage-a-trois to ensure that they fulfil their respective artistic potentials. Although writer Ben Hecht had to remove most of Coward's sexual sting from the dialogue, he admirably preserved the general feel of the piece, and Hans Dreier's art direction is in a class by itself.

Desire ○
1936, US, 96 mins, b/w
Dir: Frank Borzage
Stars: Marlene Dietrich, Gary Cooper
Rating: ★★★

Marlene Dietrich never looked lovelier than in this elegant romantic drama in which she plays a glamorous jewel thief and sings 'Awake in a Dream'. Gary Cooper's innocent abroad is a perfect foil for her worldly wisdom and there are confident character studies from Akim Tamiroff and William Frawley.

Desiree ○ ⓥ
1954, US, 110 mins, colour
Dir: Henry Koster
Stars: Marlon Brando, Jean Simmons, Merle Oberon, Michael Rennie
Rating: ★

A lavish but ultimately disappointing historical drama detailing the tangled love life of Napoleon Bonaparte. Marlon Brando never wanted to play the emperor but owed Fox a movie and so reluctantly agreed to add star power to the overblown soap opera. His performance is the only good thing about the finished product.

Desire Me ○
1947, US, 91 mins, b/w
Dir: Jack Conway
Stars: Greer Garson, Robert Mitchum, Richard Hart, George Zucco
Rating: ★★

Rather misleading title for this Greer Garson melodrama, about a man who leaves his friend to die when they escape from a PoW camp, then heightens the crime by trying to seduce his friend's wife. Of Miss Garson's two leading men, Robert Mitchum was to go on to a star career. But the unfortunate Richard Hart died four years later, aged 35.

Desire Under the Elms ○
1958, US, 114 mins, b/w
Dir: Delbert Mann
Stars: Sophia Loren, Anthony Perkins, Burl Ives
Rating: ★★

The screenplay of this brooding drama, adapted from Eugene O'Neill's play, is by Irwin Shaw, who wrote *The Young Lions*. Sophia Loren infuses the story with her own brand of sexual smoulder; also in the cast, in a supporting role, is Pernell Roberts, who was for many years Adam Cartwright in the popular *Bonanza* series.

Despair ○
1978, West Germany/France, 119 mins, colour
Dir: Rainer Werner Fassbinder
Stars: Dirk Bogarde, Andrea Ferreol
Rating: ★★

After a good start, in which the cutting wit of Tom Stoppard's screenplay is heard at its best, director Rainer Werner Fassbinder exerts an increasingly heavy hand on this screen version of Vladimir Nabokov's delicate fantasy about a German chocolate manufacturer on the brink of madness. Playing another of Nabokov's double-named characters (like James Mason's Humbert Humbert in *Lolita*), Dirk Bogarde gives a civilised and credible portrait of paranoia as Hermann Hermann. It's a fascinating failure.

Desperado ●
1995, US, 103 mins, colour
Dir: Robert Rodriguez
Stars: Antonio Banderas, Joaquim de Almeida, Salma Hayek, Steve Buscemi, Cheech Marin
Rating: ★★★

'Bless me, father,' mutters Banderas, 'for I have just killed quite a few men.' For all those who bemoan the passing of the spaghetti western, here's a straggler for the Nineties. Not so much a fistful of dollars, here, though, as a fistful of pesetas, with swarthily sweating Banderas and his guitar-case full of guns demolishing an entire town in the cause of revenge Down Mexico Way. Behind every bar lurks a menacing face: verily this must be the most lawless town in all Mehico. They're all cannon fodder, though, for the whirling, plunging, twisting Banderas, whose real mission is to gun down the local drug lord. Only pausing to bed the sultry bookseller (stunning Salma Hayek) and befriend the local street urchin, Banderas mows down baddies by the dozen before calling in a couple

D

of similarly inclined friends, which is only to show off guitar cases that fire rockets, since it's obvious Banderas can take on the whole town by himself.

Desperadoes, The ○

1943, US, 85 mins, colour
Dir: Charles Vidor
Stars: Randolph Scott, Glenn Ford, Claire Trevor, Evelyn Keyes
Rating: ★

Glenn Ford completed this Western just before leaving Hollywood to join the US Marines. Here he's a gunfighter framed for murder and he certainly managed to put in a lot of target practice for the real thing. The film, based on a novel by Max Brand, is packed with gun-battles and fist-fights, but its plot is terribly hackneyed. Ford understandably seems to have his mind on other things and Randolph Scott has hardly anything to do. Evelyn Keyes lacks her usual fire and Claire Trevor can do little with the same brassy character she's played a dozen times before. Only Edgar Buchanan, as the heroine's rascally father, and burly Guinn Williams can infuse any real life into it.

Desperados, The ●

1969, UK/Spain, 90 mins, colour
Dir: Henry Levin
Stars: Vince Edwards, Jack Palance, George Maharis, Sylvia Syms
Rating: ★

American Civil War (and after) adventure drama with grim-faced Vince Edwards unable to escape his murderous past, despite the (at one time) topless charms of Sylvia Syms. Nice restrained performance from Neville Brand, but Jack Palance goes over the top. There's lots of explosive, tough action in this Spanish-made western, whose violence is all too much.

Desperate Hours, The ○

1955, US, 113 mins, b/w
Dir: William Wyler
Stars: Humphrey Bogart, Fredric March, Arthur Kennedy, Martha Scott, Gig Young
Rating: ★★★★

In the early Fifties, Humphrey Bogart's tough-guy characters were generally a bit soft-hearted. But on the release of this film version of a successful play, the word went round: Bogey's back. So he was. And deadlier than ever as the leader of a trio of escaped criminals holed up in a.private house. The result is a taut, suspenseful thriller, made with a marvellous cast and all the power and expertise at director William Wyler's command. It never looks like a play

and the last reel is gripping, exciting, explosive stuff with a memorable confrontation between Bogart and Fredric March.

Desperate Hours ● ⓥ

1990, US, 105 mins, colour
Dir: Michael Cimino
Stars: Mickey Rourke, Anthony Hopkins, Mimi Rogers, Kelly Lynch, Shawnee Smith
Rating: ★★★

Not as good as the Bogart original, this new, slightly opened-out version of Joseph Hayes' play still generates enough action and emotion to make it work. Mickey Rourke has the Bogart role as the psychopath who, in this adaptation, seduces his leggy lawyer (Kelly Lynch: all lawyers should look like this) and, with her help, sets up an escape from custody that sees him first team up with two confederates, then hole up at a private house. Holding the occupants – Anthony Hopkins, his estranged wife Mimi Rogers and their two children, a foul-mouthed teenager (Shawnee Smith) and a querulous kid (Danny Garrett) – as terrified hostages, Rourke waits for Hopkins to collect enough money from the bank to help him make a getaway. If you've seen the original, you'll know what happens in the end, but, though it's pitched on too hysterical a level (with the screeching music score joining in), the acting and Michael Cimino's furious-paced direction just about keep the old stager going.

Desperately Seeking Susan ◑ ⓥ

1985, US, 104 mins, colour
Dir: Susan Seidelman
Stars: Rosanna Arquette, Aidan Quinn, Madonna, Robert Joy, Laurie Metcalf
Rating: ★★

A gaudy, trendy, comic jumble which caught the imagination of the public in '85, but is beginning to date. It gave a boost to the careers of Rosanna Arquette and Madonna that neither was quite able to sustain in the following years. Really amusing at first, the film becomes wearisome (and seemingly louder!) as it goes on: Arquette takes centre stage as a bored suburban wife who, drawn to free-living Madonna's lifestyle, ends up switching identities with her after a crack on the head brings on a severe case of amnesia. This gives director Susan Seidelman all the plot complications she could possibly wish, yet somehow she fails to make the most of them, relying on the photogenic and attractive leading trio

to keep the movie going as long as they do. You'll be entertained, but don't expect too much.

Desperate Moment ○

1953, UK, 88 mins, b/w
Dir: Compton Bennett
Stars: Dirk Bogarde, Mai Zetterling, Philip Friend, Albert Lieven
Rating: ★★

Made at a time when Dirk Bogarde seemed to be forever playing men on the run, this Rank product again casts him as a fugitive, fighting to right past wrongs. The plot lacks tension and takes some believing too, but Bogarde and Mai Zetterling make the most of their roles, and the authentic post-war Berlin settings give the chase an atmosphere of chilling urgency when the dialogue and situations allow.

Desperate Siege

See: Rawhide

Destination Gobi ○

1952, US, 91 mins, colour
Dir: Robert Wise
Stars: Richard Widmark, Don Taylor, Murvyn Vye
Rating: ★★★

Gutsy American war film about a marathon trek through the Gobi desert by a small US naval detachment. Well directed by Robert Wise, who never lets the interest sag. Richard Widmark's sound acting gives the film authority and he's backed by an excellent cast that includes Earl Holliman in his screen debut. The plot packs good-humoured excitement with the laughs in the right places; and Charles G Clarke's Technicolor photography is highly commendable.

Destination Inner Space ◑

1966, US, 83 mins, colour
Dir: Francis D Lyon
Stars: Scott Brady, Sheree North, Gary Merrill, John Howard
Rating: ★★

Diving belle Sheree North and a rather splendid amphibian monster compete for attention in this fast and lively piece of underwater science-fiction, which passes 83 minutes away in no time. The thing, about whose menacing attentions the scientists look surprisingly unconcerned, is as imaginative as it is many-splendoured, with a blue-mottled scaly body, iridescent red and orange fins, and comb-like attachments. And the underwater photography (by Brick Marquard) is clarity itself – seldom has Eastman Colour looked so attractive.

Destination Tokyo ○ Ⓥ

1943, US, 135 mins, b/w
Dir: Delmer Daves
Stars: Cary Grant, John Garfield, John Ridgely, Dane Clark
Rating: ★★★

This good war film was the first movie directed by Delmer Daves, who subsequently turned out such films as *Dark Passage, Broken Arrow* and *3:10 to Yuma.* Here he is lucky in having the immense presence of Cary Grant as the commander of a submarine, the crew of which is full of familiar faces; among them are John Garfield, Dane Clark, John Forsythe and Robert Hutton.

Destroyer ○

1942, US, 99 mins, b/w
Dir: William A Seiter
Stars: Edward G Robinson, Glenn Ford, Marguerite Chapman
Rating: ★★

Wartime action film about a ship's crew who have as many battles among themselves as they do with the enemy. Watch for fast-talking little Hollywood tough guy, Leo Gorcey. As Seaman Sarecky, he plays one of his few roles outside his character of Slip, leader of the Bowery Boys.

Destry ○

1954, US, 96 mins, colour
Dir: George Marshall
Stars: Audie Murphy, Thomas Mitchell, Mari Blanchard, Lyle Bettger, Lori Nelson, Wallace Ford
Rating: ★★★

Remake of the famous James Stewart Western classic, with Audie Murphy ideally cast as the milksop cowboy who cleans up a town. George Marshall directed two versions of this classic action yarn and this one comes (a respectable) second, despite its ace cast.

Destry Rides Again ○

1939, US, 94 mins, b/w
Dir: George Marshall
Stars: Marlene Dietrich, James Stewart, Charles Winninger, Mischa Auer, Brian Donlevy
Rating: ★★★★

After *Angel* in 1937, Marlene Dietrich was labelled 'box-office poison' by American exhibitors but her lively performance as the hard-boiled saloon girl in this broad, brawling and bawdy Western turned her film career around and made her a hot property again, as well as allowing her to show a delicious flair for comedy. Fortunately for filmgoers, she won the part of Frenchy

from Universal's original choice, Paulette Goddard. The merry mixture of action and comedy never flags under George Marshall's spirited direction and the casting of James Stewart as the mild but crusading sheriff was inspired.

Detective, The ●

1968, US, 114 mins, colour
Dir: Gordon Douglas
Stars: Frank Sinatra, Lee Remick, Ralph Meeker, Jacqueline Bisset, Jack Klugman
Rating: ★★★★

Ignore the awkwardness of the first 20 minutes; this is a film that builds up as it goes along and, for all its brutality and brutally lurid depiction of homosexuality, one that is based on real values. As a thriller, it is superbly constructed (although rather well less written in parts) and directed with great single-mindedness by Hollywood veteran Gordon Douglas. It's the best work of his career. The acting, too, is excellent, particularly from Frank Sinatra, those world-weary eyes never put to greater effect, and from Lee Remick as his sad nymphomaniac wife. Their scenes together carry a genuine emotional charge, making this high-class adult entertainment.

Detective, The

See: Father Brown

Devil and Miss Jones, The ○

1941, US, 97 mins, b/w
Dir: Sam Wood
Stars: Jean Arthur, Robert Cummings, Charles Coburn, Edmund Gwenn, S Z Sakall, Spring Byington
Rating: ★★★★

Eccentric millionaire Charles Coburn goes undercover to find out how the workers in one of his department stores tick in this delightful comedy. Shopgirl Jean Arthur takes pity on him when he is transferred by the harsh store management to the shoe department. Obviously, Coburn sees the error of his selfish ways, the store managers get their come-uppance and everyone else lives happily ever after. Director Sam Wood keeps the comedy sparkling and Arthur makes the most of her central role. Not to be outdone, Coburn, Spring Byington and Robert Cummings all put in fine, fun performances. Hugely enjoyable.

Devil at 4 O'Clock, The ○

1961, US, 126 mins, colour
Dir: Mervyn LeRoy
Stars: Spencer Tracy, Frank Sinatra,

Kerwin Matthews, Jean-Pierre Aumont
Rating: ★★★★★

Frank Sinatra and Spencer Tracy have a battle royal for acting honours in this story of a Pacific island threatened by volcanic eruption. The characters are reminiscent of Graham Greene's. Most of the film was made on location in Hawaii, but the volcanic explosion was shot in California. The 'island' you see in the blast was really a 200-foot long, 45-foot high pile of landscaped mud, filled with explosive. Of such common clay are movie miracles made!

Devil Dogs of the Air ○

1935, US, 86 mins, b/w
Dir: Lloyd Bacon
Stars: James Cagney, Pat O'Brien, Margaret Lindsay, Frank McHugh
Rating: ★★

Hardly back in the hangar after *Ceiling Zero,* made the same year, James Cagney and Pat O'Brien take to the skies again in this all-flags-waving tribute to the US Marine Flying Corps. As usual, Cagney is the cocky guy who needles everyone else, but proves his worth in the end, O'Brien his slightly stuffy friend who makes him see the light. Somehow the two actors, great personal friends, managed to sustain these images to the benefit of the boxoffice, throughout the Thirties. In this action film, there's some superb stunt flying to back the cornball plot, and memorable special effects. Plenty of humour in the script helps too, with Frank McHugh getting one of the best of his many comedy relief roles.

Devil in a Blue Dress ● Ⓥ

1995, US, 102 mins, colour
Dir: Carl Franklin
Stars: Denzel Washington, Jennifer Beals, Don Cheadle, Tom Sizemore
Rating: ★★★★★

A *film noir* with a black hero is a pretty ironic concept but, after showing promise with *One False Move,* director Carl Franklin hits the jackpot here. There's not one false move in this film from start to finish: Franklin has reproduced a pulp fiction detective flick of the post-war years to perfection. And in Denzel Washington he finds the ideal actor to play 'Easy' Rawlins, a war hero who has bought his own home, but finds his lifestyle on the line when he loses his job. An ex-boxer of dubious repute who runs a bar Easy frequents puts him in touch with the blue-jowled, shady-looking Albright (Tom Sizemore) who offers Easy 100 dollars to locate the vanished girlfriend

D

(Jennifer Beals) of a politician. That's all – but that's not all, of course, as Easy's first contact ends up dead the same night he sees her. The plot, though difficult to penetrate, is simple enough, and its peripheral characters are all amazingly well drawn, notably Mouse (Don Cheadle), a trigger-happy friend of Easy's from out of town, called in to help our increasingly desperate and angry hero.

Devil on Horseback ○
1954, UK, 89 mins, b/w
Dir: Cyril Frankel
Stars: Googie Withers, John McCallum, Jeremy Spenser
Rating: ★★

Husband and wife team Googie Withers and John McCallum star in this film about a boy jockey (Jeremy Spenser) whose head swells along with his list of winners. The racing scenes make exciting viewing.

Devil's Brigade, The ○
1968, US, 126 mins, colour
Dir: Andrew V McLagien
Stars: William Holden, Cliff Robertson, Vince Edwards, Claude Akins, Richard Jaeckel, Dana Andrews, Michael Rennie
Rating: ★★

Noisy, flag-waving, relentlessly routine all-action sideshoot from *The Dirty Dozen*, with William Holden leading the troop of misfits who find themselves in Italy after training for combat in Norway. An immense all-star cast is largely wasted.

Devil's Canyon ○
1953, US, 88 mins, colour
Dir: Alfred Werker
Stars: Dale Robertson, Virginia Mayo, Stephen McNally, Arthur Hunnicutt
Rating: ★★

This grim Western has a pretty extraordinary cast, but no more remarkable than the plot and screenplay, both of which are hard to swallow, especially when captured bandit queen Virginia Mayo is assigned to an all-male prison. Despite the fact that you might be tempted to term the result 'She's Working Her Way Back to Prison', the actual depiction of life in jail seems depressingly accurate, apart from Mayo's presence, and Nicholas Musuraca's sombre lighting keeps Technicolor well under control. Best scene: grizzled Arthur Hunnicutt's hilarious account of the poker game with his mother-in-law that led to his 99-year sentence.

Devil's Disciple, The ○
1959, UK, 83 mins, b/w
Dir: Guy Hamilton
Stars: Burt Lancaster, Kirk Douglas, Laurence Olivier, Janette Scott
Rating: ★★★

Burr Lancaster and Kirk Douglas star in a real blockbuster based on George Bernard Shaw's play about the American War of Independence. The excellence of the action is equalled by the dialogue, Laurence Olivier, in particular, having a wonderful time spouting caustic witticisms as the strutting, sneering, smirking General Burgoyne. Might have been even more rousing (and earned a lot more money) if they'd shot in colour.

Devil's Doorway ○
1950, US, 84 mins, b/w
Dir: Anthony Mann
Stars: Robert Taylor, Louis Calhern, Paula Raymond, Marshall Thompson
Rating: ★★★

By the time this film appeared, Robert Taylor was thoroughly launched into the Westerns that were to dominate his later years at MGM. The unusual thing about *Devil's Doorway* is that he plays not a gunfighter but a full-blooded Shoshone Indian who owns rich grassland coveted by the white man. The first of a notable series of Westerns for director Anthony Mann.

Devils of Darkness ●
1964, UK, 90 mins, colour
Dir: Lance Comfort
Stars: William Sylvester, Tracy Reed, Hubert Noel
Rating: ★★

There are plenty of lovely actresses for vampire Hubert Noel to get his teeth into in this horror film including South African leading lady Carole Gray, who starred with Cliff Richard in *The Young Ones,* Tracy Reed, Diana Decker and Rona Anderson, heroine of Fifties' British thrillers.

Devil's Own, The ● Ⓥ
1997, US, 107 mins, colour
Dir: Alan J Pakula
Stars: Harrison Ford, Brad Pitt, Margaret Colin, Treat Williams, Natascha McElhone
Rating: ★★

Unevenly paced and less than riveting throughout, this action thriller is almost saved by honest-to-goodness, 100 per cent performances by stars Ford, Pitt and Colin. Beginning with a highly improbable house-to-street shoot-out

between the IRA and the British army in Belfast, the plot progresses in only marginally more likely fashion. Frankie (Pitt), fleeing Ireland with funds to buy Stinger missiles in America, re-locates as the basement lodger of New York cop O'Meara (Ford). If this had happened in real life, the IRA would have bought their missiles and sailed off home, but needs of intrigue entail a falling-out with the supplier (Williams) and subsequent action that blows the terrorists' cover. The script is couched for effect rather than realism and offers up a badly-acted Brit intelligence officer who speaks in dated dialogue from films 20 years ago. Action, too, is shade below the top level. Pitt's Irish accent sounds authentic – more than you can say for the story.

Diabolique ● Ⓥ
1996, US, 107 mins, colour
Dir: Jeremiah Chechik
Stars: Sharon Stone, Isabelle Adjani, Chazz Palminteri, Kathy Bates, Shirley Knight, Spalding Gray
Rating: ★

Hammy acting hampered further by clunky dialogue and ham-fisted direction manages to take all the creeps and suspense out of a creepy suspense classic. The French version made audiences cringe in fear when it came out in 1955. This one will only evoke cringes of a different kind. Cruel headmaster Palminteri is dispatched by his faint-hearted (literally) wife (Adjani) and much put-upon mistress (Stone). Or is he? Has he returned from the dead to haunt them? Not content with whisking away every shred of subtlety from the original, the remake completely wrecks itself by revising the ending, presumably so not to spoil Sharon Stone's image too much. Even if you haven't seen the original, this is one to avoid.

Diagnosis: Murder ○
1974, UK, 95 mins, colour
Dir: Sidney Hayers
Stars: Christopher Lee, Jon Finch, Judy Geeson
Rating: ★★

World-famous for his portrayal of Dracula, Christopher Lee is still in sinister vein in this thriller. The film tries to vary its familiar plot – husband out to bump off wife so that he can marry attractive mistress – by making the wife (Dilys Hamlett) unusually resourceful, and the inspector on the case (Jon Finch) a surly, oddball character with problems of his own.

Dial M for Murder O ⓥ
1954, US, 105 mins, colour
Dir: Alfred Hitchcock
Stars: Ray Milland, Grace Kelly, Robert Cummings
Rating: ★★★★

Jumpy, suspenseful Alfred Hitchcock thriller, with Grace Kelly as a woman convicted of murdering a man who broke into her house, and Ray Milland as the husband who had paid the man to kill her. Most of the suspense in this, one of Hitchcock's most famous films, falls into the will-he-won't-he, edge-of-the-seat variety, Will she escape the hangman? Will he ever give himself away? It doesn't look like it. But the inspector (John Williams) has a breathtaking trick up his sleeve. Milland is suitably impassive, Miss Kelly suitably frightened-out-of-her-wits. Robert Cummings has the role of the wife's best friend, and Anthony Dawson is impressively sinister as the public school black sheep who will do anything for money.

Dial 999 O
(aka: The Way Out)
1955, UK, 87 mins, b/w
Dir: Montgomery Tully
Stars: Gene Nelson, Mona Freeman, John Bentley, Michael Goodliffe
Rating: ★★★★

A gem of a thriller, one of the best co-features British studios ever made. Director Montgomery Tully keeps the action moving and the tension as tight as a bowstring. Gene Nelson, the ex-dancer from *Oklahoma!*, gives his finest acting performance as a man on the run. And a self-effacing portrayal from Michael Goodliffe provides first-rate support.

Diamond Head O
1963, US, 107 mins, colour
Dir: Guy Green
Stars: Charlton Heston, Yvette Mimieux, George Chakiris, France Nuyen
Rating: ★★

Charlton Heston gets plenty of meat into which to sink his acting teeth in this film – as the ruthless head of a modern agricultural dynasty in Hawaii, whose self-righteous attitude conceals the skeletons in his own cupboard. Director Guy Green gets an unexpectedly fine and sensitive portrayal from France Nuyen as Heston's half-caste mistress. The developments, though, are pure soap-opera.

Diamond Horseshoe
See: Billy Rose's Diamond Horseshoe

Diamonds O
1975, US/Israel, 101 mins, colour
Dir: Menahem Golan
Stars: Robert Shaw, Richard Roundtree, Barbara Seagull, Shelley Winters
Rating: ★★

The trouble with 'caper' films is that it always takes a long time to get round to the main event (the robbery itself) and the supporting bouts tend to be of lesser interest. Such is the case here, in which it's Robert Shaw and Richard Roundtree who go clambering through ventilators and across ceilings to steal a fortune in jewels. The actual robbery sequence, when it comes, is likely to keep most viewers near the edges of their seats.

Diamonds Are Forever O ⓥ
1971, UK, 119 mins, colour
Dir: Guy Hamilton
Stars: Sean Connery, Jill St John, Charles Gray, Lana Wood, Bruce Cabot
Rating: ★★★

One of Sean Connery's best films as James Bond. This is a sparkling action adventure, pocked only by a few doubles-entendres so dubious that only Connery, purring like a sated leopard, could handle them. Guy Hamilton's stylish direction exudes confidence and he is brilliantly backed by the crystal-clear photography of Ted Moore (equalled by the second unit camerawork of Harold Wellman). The action set-pieces really deliver the goods, and Jill St John proves both sexy and endearingly goofy as the heroine. Lana Wood, sister of Natalie, is another of the female decorations.

Diamond Skulls ● ⓥ
(aka: Dark Obsession)
1989, UK, 87 mins, colour
Dir: Nick Broomfield
Stars: Gabriel Byrne, Amanda Donohoe, Michael Hordern, Judy Parfitt, Sadie Frost
Rating: ★★

There's not much to this one, although if you like pretty actresses with no clothes on there's quite a bit of that. Gabriel Byrne is the distinctly unstable nobleman tortured by the past peccadilloes of a wife (Amanda Donohoe) who now appears to be trying to stay faithful. Driving home in one of his preoccupied states, after a military reunion, he runs over a girl who turns out to be the cook at another noble household. The sensitive member of the party (Douglas Hodge), horrified by the revelation that the girl lived 17 hours after Byrne's evil influential friend (Struan Rodger) insisted she was dead, suffers almost as many crises of conscience as the noble Byrne. You may not have trouble guessing the rest, and the acting is just okay (save for Michael Hordern who's marvellously roguish as Byrne's doddering father). The flimsy story, which never quite makes up its mind what kind of movie it wants to be, at least has the decency not to outstay its welcome.

Diamonds on Wheels ⊙
1972, UK, 85 mins, colour
Dir: Jerome Courtland
Stars: Patrick Allen, Peter Firth
Rating: ★★

Perfect entertainment for children, this is Disney's equivalent of a Children's Film Foundation thriller. Peter Firth made his screen debut as the leader of a trio of teenagers unaware that their rally car contains a fortune in stolen diamonds. The resultant thrills and spills are directed with supreme efficiency by former Hollywood actor Jerome Courtland.

Diane O
1955, US, 110 mins, colour
Dir: David Miller
Stars: Lana Turner, Roger Moore, Pedro Armendariz, Cedric Hardwicke, Marisa Pavan
Rating: ★★

A richly costumed prowl down the 16th-century corridors of power at the French court, with Lana Turner as the scheming femme fatale Diane de Poitiers. Christopher Isherwood wrote the script, and a formidable supporting cast includes Torin Thatcher, Taina Elg, Geoffrey Toone, John Lupton and Henry Daniell. Stiffish, though.

Diary of a Chambermaid, The O
1946, US, 86 mins, b/w
Dir: Jean Renoir
Stars: Paulette Goddard, Burgess Meredith, Francis Lederer, Hurd Hatfield, Judith Anderson
Rating: ★★★

Paulette Goddard goes blonde and gives one of her best film performances as a vixenish 19th-century French chambermaid in this unsettling screen version of the famous novel by Octave Mirbeau. The script was by co-star Burgess Meredith, then Goddard's husband. It's not at all like most post-war Hollywood offerings, which is what you might expect from the work of famous French director Jean Renoir.

D

Diary of a Madman ●

1963, US, 95 mins, colour
Dir: Reginald Le Borg
Stars: Vincent Price, Nancy Kovack,
Elaine Devry
Rating: ★

Vincent Price fans, but few others, will
get good value from this grisly horror
film about demonic possession. Price is
possessed by the Horla which shines a
green filter in his eyes and makes him
do the most terrible things which he
knows little about: only a trail of blood
that would make a bloodhound turn
and run in sheer disbelief leads Price
up to the attic. There's even a gory
daub on the banisters to make sure he
doesn't lose his way where he finds the
head of one his victims neatly tucked
away. Despite Price's enthusiasm as
the involuntary madman, Reginald Le
Borg's direction is styleless and shows a
total lack of imagination. The many
conversational close-ups, for example,
only go to make the dialogual scenes
more tedious. It's comic-strip horror at
its worst.

Dick Tracy ● Ⓥ

1990, US, 103 mins, colour
Dir: Warren Beatty
Stars: Warren Beatty, Al Pacino,
Madonna, Dustin Hoffman, Mandy
Patinkin, Dick Van Dyke
Rating: ★★★

This comic-strip sprung to life would
make a wow of a stage musical.
There's so much music in the film,
mostly from Madonna and Mandy
Patinkin, that the storyline seems like a
series of dramatic interruptions. if it
lacks emotive impact, that's the effect of
the makers' own intentions in brilliantly
constructing the film as a comic-book
sprung to life. The bad guys all have
exaggerated features (a shade too much
so) and they and the reporters and police all wear different coloured coats to
correspond to the drawings in the original Dick Tracy police detective strip, so
faithfully recreated here. Still, we can
appreciate the performance of Warren
Beatty, an admirable Tracy, Madonna,
doing her best screen work to date as a
singing siren, and especially Al Pacino,
perfectly cast as the ranting Big Boy
Caprice, looking like a caricaturist's impression of Sylvester Stallone.

Die, Die, My Darling

See: Fanatic

Die Hard ● Ⓥ

1988, US, 131 mins, colour
Dir: John McTiernan

Stars: Bruce Willis, Bonnie Bedelia, Alan
Rickman, Alexander Godunov, Reginald
VelJohnson, Paul Gleason
Rating: ★★★★★

This is some spectacular action film and
you'd better believe it. Director John
McTiernan and his technicians fairly
blast the screen apart after a group of
highly trained ex-terrorists hijack a vast
company building at Christmas with
even vaster sums of money in its vaults.
Would you believe $640 million?
Don't stop to count it: you won't have
time. Enter lone wolf cop Bruce Willis,
whose wife is a terrorist hostage. He
becomes a one-man army, fighting desperately to bring help and stay alive.
Although he tears the building to shreds
doing it, this is no Stallone or
Schwarzenegger cutting down the baddies with ease. Willis barely escapes the
bad guys time and again. He's
scratched, scorched, shot, stunned,
strangled, throws himself down lift
shafts or the side of the building and
finds time to make friends with a street
cop (Reginald VelJohnson) down below
on a two-way radio. The bad guys are
brimful of menace, the story throws in
some unexpected twists and the action
is explosive, painful and dynamically
staged. You'll wince at Willis picking
glass out of his feet in an eye-shutting
scene and be too shell-shocked to guess
the final piece of action before it comes.

Die Hard 2 ● Ⓥ

1990, US, 118 mins, colour
Dir: Renny Harlin
Stars: Bruce Willis, Bonnie Bedelia,
William Atherton, Franco Nero, William
Sadler, Reginald VelJohnson
Rating: ★★★★

Even if it takes a while getting up a
head of steam, and lacks the claustrophobic dynamism of *Die Hard*, this is
still a powerhouse action thriller, with
Bruce Willis again as John McClane,
'the wrong guy in the wrong place at
the wrong time'. The wrong place this
time is an airport paralysed by terrorists who will resort even to causing the
crash of passenger planes to free a
Central American dictator (Franco
Nero) on his way to the US to face
drug charges. One of the planes hovering over the airport contains Willis'
wife (Bonnie Bedelia), not that he has
much time to think of her as he tackles
hostile airport police (led by Dennis
Franz), a SWAT squad and an army
special missions force, not to mention
the terrorists. Once again Willis bears
a charmed life, even making like James
Bond when he takes to a motor-bike on

ice treads. The dialogue's not important (just as well since you often can't
hear it): no, the action's the thing and
the second half contains enough of it to
send fans of the first film home happy.

Die Hard With a Vengeance ● Ⓥ

1995, US, 128 mins, colour
Dir: John McTiernan
Stars: Bruce Willis, Jeremy Irons, Samuel
L Jackson, Colleen Camp, Graham
Greene
Rating: ★★★

Bruce Willis is back in that dirty old
vest again, but he loses a bit of humanity as well as blood in this story, which
reveals all too clearly the writers' desperation in trying to come up with a
third-time round caper. The only
things that are really new are some annoying hand-held camerawork, and
Willis excitingly fleeing from bursting
dam waters rushing at him down an
underground tunnel. The best the
writers can come up with for a plot has
Jeremy Irons, as the brother of the bad
guy Willis killed in the first film, planting a series of massive bombs across
New York – seemingly as part of a plan
to get Willis, to avenge his brother, but
actually the decoy for a venture that
would have gladdened dead brother's
heart. Samuel L Jackson is along for
the black audience as a shopkeeper
hauled in on Willis' cross-city crusade,
but neither is allowed much chance to
make us smile in their adversity, with
dialogue you often can't hear. Lots of
violent action, though, including a spectacular subway crash.

Die Monster Die ● Ⓥ

(aka: Monster of Terror)
1965, UK, 80 mins, colour
Dir: Daniel Haller
Stars: Boris Karloff, Nick Adams, Suzan
Farmer
Rating: ★★

This Grand Guignol chiller is based on
a story by master horror writer H P
Lovecraft, called *The Colour Out of Space*.
It's one of only a handful of films (another is *The Dunwich Horror*, also based
on a Lovecraft story) to have been directed by Daniel Haller, who was art
director on all of Roger Corman's
Edgar Allan Poe stories made in
America in the Sixties. Disappointingly
routine.

Digby – the Biggest Dog in the World ○

1973, UK, 88 mins, colour
Dir: Joseph McGrath

Stars: Jim Dale, Spike Milligan, Angela
Douglas, Milo O'Shea, Dinsdale Landen,
Victor Spinetti
Rating: ★★

This shaggy comedy romp is about an
old English sheepdog who grows to
enormous size after drinking a new
super-growth chemical by mistake. It's
good to see such a truly family film,
even though children might not appreciate all of its funniest moments, such
as most of Spike Milligan's dialogue
(the great man is well on form as a mad
doctor) or the scene in which Jim Dale
learns how to eat in a transport cafe
with a knife, fork and spoon chained to
the table.

Diggstown
See: Midnight Sting

Dillinger ○ ⓥ
1944, US, 100 mins, b/w
Dir: Max Nosseck
Stars: Lawrence Tierney, Edmund Lowe,
Anne Jeffreys, Elisha Cook Jr
Rating: ★★★

This sombre reconstruction of the rise
and fall of America's one-time public
enemy number one dates from the
Forties when, unlike the Thirties, few
first-rate gangster movies were being
made. This harsh and atmospheric
look at the famous gangster's career is
a happy exception, its bullet-strewn
edges being decorated by such stalwarts of racketeer romps as Elisha
Cook Jnr, Eduardo Ciannelli and Marc
Lawrence. It also brought Lawrence
Tierney, real-life brother of Scott
Brady, fame in the title role.

Dillinger
1973, US, 107 mins, colour
Dir: John Milius
Stars: Warren Oates, Ben Johnson,
Michelle Phillips, Cloris Leachman, Harry
Dean Stanton, Richard Dreyfuss
Rating: ★★★

The first film made by the American
director John Milius, whose subsequent
output has included *The Wind and The
Lion* and *Conan the Barbarian*. Milius
pushes along his bullet-strewn narrative
in the best *Untouchables* style, graphically
illustrating the violence and self-glorifi-
cation that bubbles beneath his
characters on both sides of the legal
fence. The acting is first-rate, with exception of a wild performance by
Richard Dreyfuss (as Baby Face
Nelson) which provides little hint of the
Oscar-winning splendours to come in
his career. The tailpiece will hit you
hard.

Dime Box
See: Kid Blue

Dimples ○
1935, US, 78 mins, b/w
Dir: William A Seiter
Stars: Shirley Temple, Frank Morgan
Rating: ★★★

Another Civil War setting for little
Shirley Temple in a plot which teams
her with lovable Frank Morgan as her
grandfather. Shirley plays a street entertainer, which gives her a chance to
sing 'Picture Me Without You', 'He
Was a Dandy', 'What Did the Blue Jay
Say?' and 'Dixie Anna'. The last reel
won't leave a dry eye in the sitting-
room.

Diner ● ⓥ
1982, US, 110 mins, colour
Dir: Barry Levinson
Stars: Daniel Stern, Steve Guttenberg,
Mickey Rourke, Kevin Bacon, Ellen
Barkin, Michael Tucker
Rating: ★★★

This nostalgia-and-reminiscence piece is
a well-observed and affectionate portrait of American youth in 1959, and in
particular of five guys in their early 20s
who still hang out at the same riverside
diner they've sat in for years, even
though one of them is now married.
Of these sharply contrasted characters,
the standouts are Boogie (Mickey
Rourke), who tries to make his own
rules but finds life's not like that, and
Fenwick (Kevin Bacon), an embittered
loner who drinks too much, has
dropped out of college and is brighter
than he would care to admit to any of
his friends. The fabric of the picture
(written as well as directed by Barry
Levinson) results in a portrait rather
than a story, but one that's frequently
rewarding. The Metrocolor photography of Peter Sova is spot-on and the
use of contemporary pop music on the
soundtrack provides the final nostalgic
glow.

Dingaka ○
1964, South Africa, 98 mins, colour
Dir: Jamie Uys
Stars: Stanley Baker, Juliet Prowse, Ken
Gampu
Rating: ★★

An unusual adventure film, made in
South Africa, about a tribesman who
has to venture into a big city that bewil-
ders him, in order to exact revenge.
The first 40 minutes of the film have
such good, atmospheric moments, with
brown figures swarming across the
screen, that it seems almost like a folk-

odyssey, or fable with a documentary
flavour, doing for the African something similar to the most subjective of
the pre-Black Power Southern
American Negro stories. Bertha Egnos'
special tribal songs, and Basil Gray's
music, together with Jamie Uys' sympathetic direction, go a long way
towards achieving this. And Ken
Gampu brings great strength and dignity to the African who must avenge the
death of his wife, even if it means slaying a local witch doctor.

Dinner at Eight ○ ⓥ
1933, US, 113 mins, b/w
Dir: George Cukor
Stars: Marie Dressler, John Barrymore,
Wallace Beery, Jean Harlow, Lionel
Barrymore, Lee Tracy
Rating: ★★★★

A star-studded portmanteau picture,
made with supreme confidence by director George Cukor at an MGM
riding high in the early Thirties.
Cinemagoers got full value from the
performances of John Barrymore, foreshadowing his own last years as a
fading, alcoholic matinee idol; from
Lionel Barrymore, wheezing convincingly as the shipping magnate whose
fortune and health alike are ailing;
from Jean Harlow and Wallace Beery
as a feuding nouveau riche couple;
from Edmund Lowe as the caring doctor trying to back out of his affair with
Harlow; from Billie Burke as Lionel
Barrymore's selfish, fluttering wife; and
from the great Marie Dressler as a
stage star on hard times. There's even
the classic device of film fiction, the key
character (in this case two) who never
appears. And the closing duologue between Harlow and Dressler is still an
exchange to relish.

Diplomatic Courier ○
1952, US, 98 mins, b/w
Dir: Henry Hathaway
Stars: Tyrone Power, Patricia Neal,
Stephen McNally, Hildegarde Neff, Karl
Malden
Rating: ★★★

First class espionage thriller that is liable to put a little strain on your
nervous system. Tyrone Power is the
American agent dodging danger behind
the Iron Curtain, and, with the help of
crisply natural dialogue, Patricia Neal
and Hildegarde Neff put personality
into the female roles. Spot Lee Marvin
in a small role as a military policeman.
The film was the latest (and in fact the
last) in a line of actuality thrillers from
director Henry Hathaway, all made at

D

20th Century-Fox and including such classics as *The House on 92nd Street, 13 Rue Madeleine, Kiss of Death, Call Northside 777* and *Fourteen Hours,* all made between 1945 and 1951. In this one, the sense of constant danger is heightened by Lucien Ballard's heavily shadowed photography.

Dirigible O
1931, US, 93 mins, b/w
Dir: Frank Capra
Stars: Fay Wray, Jack Holt, Ralph Graves
Rating: ★★

A rare treat for lovers both of Frank Capra films and of the work of the queen of screen screamers, Fay Wray. Its action sequences still look exciting today, even if the dialogue scenes are static and boring. Look hard at the snow scenes in this story of early aviators battling to make it to the South Pole. The film was actually shot at the height of summer and the actors, sweating in fur parkas, are being bombarded by wind machines blowing bleached cornflakes into their faces in 90-degree heat. The film itself launched both Capra and his studio, Columbia, into the big time, there to stay.

Dirty Dancing ● Ⓥ
1987, US, 96 mins, colour
Dir: Emile Ardolino
Stars: Patrick Swayze, Jennifer Grey, Jerry Orbach
Rating: ★★★

This extraordinarily successful film, which rocketed Patrick Swayze to stardom – he dances with grace and also sings one of the soundtrack's songs – is like an adult version of a pop musical from the mid-Sixties. The amazing thing is that, although its dated script and illogical plot hurt the film badly, a great deal of it still works. The dancing's good and so is the music, and even the script has odd lines that hit home, as when Max (Jack Weston), the ageing proprietor of the film's glamorous holiday camp, confesses on closing night that he feels 'like it's all slipping away'. The dialogue does, however, also contain Swayze's classic exclamation: 'Nobody leaves Baby in the corner!'

Dirty Dingus Magee O
1970, US, 90 mins, colour
Dir: Burt Kennedy
Stars: Frank Sinatra, George Kennedy, Anne Jackson, Jack Elam
Rating: ★

A woeful slapstick Western from Burt Kennedy full of embarrassingly mis-

fired scenes, although Jack Elam contributes an amusing cameo as a would-be fearsome western outlaw, John Wesley Hardin. The supporting cast is full of faces from Kennedy's own little stock company of excellent character players, including John Dehner, Henry Jones, Don 'Red' Barry, Harry Carey Jr, Kathleen Freeman and Paul Fix. Sinatra tries to sink himself into the role of the grubby, unscrupulous small-time outlaw of the title – although, quite honestly, it isn't his scene.

Dirty Dozen, The ◑ Ⓥ
1967, US, 150 mins, colour
Dir: Robert Aldrich
Stars: Lee Marvin, Ernest Borgnine, Robert Ryan, Charles Bronson, John Cassavetes, Telly Savalas
Rating: ★★★

A rugged World War Two actioner about a team of GI murderers and thugs given the stark choice of the firing squad or a suicide mission to wipe out Hitler's top generals. If the mission is a success it will lead to their release from military custody with a clean slate. It's a typical vehicle from director Robert Aldrich, filled with frantic action sequences, and bucket-loads of explosive action and violence. The acting is uniformly good, with John Cassavetes and Lee Marvin especially deserving of a mention in dispatches.

Dirty Harry ◑ Ⓥ
1971, US, 103 mins, colour
Dir: Don Siegel
Stars: Clint Eastwood, Harry Guardino, Reni Santoni, John Vernon, Andy Robinson
Rating: ★★★

All tough and violent cop thrillers today, both good and bad, have a common ancestor, *Dirty Harry.* Harry Callahan (Clint Eastwood) strides grimly through San Francisco in pursuit of a psychopath, paying little heed to the formal niceties of the law. So little heed, in fact, that when he catches him, the killer is soon released again, thanks to Harry's unorthodox arrest procedure. Knowing the killer will strike again, Harry is soon back on his tail. Panned for being too violent and amoral by some critics when it was released, it pales by comparison with some present-day offerings. Eastwood is tall and taciturn in this modern-dress Western – his Magnum .44 pistol doing most of his talking for him. Andy Robinson is marvellous as the gibbering maniacal psychopath.

Whatever your reservations about Harry's methods, one look at the killer and you know whose side you're on.

Dirty Knights' Work
See: Trial by Combat

Dirty Rotten Scoundrels O Ⓥ
1988, US, 110 mins, colour
Dir: Frank Oz
Stars: Steve Martin, Michael Caine, Glenne Headly, Anton Rodgers, Barbara Harris
Rating: ★★★

This cheerful comedy about confidence tricksters at large on the French Riviera is an ingenious remake of the 1963 film *Bedtime Story.* Suave Lawrence Jamieson (Michael Caine in the David Niven role) is the one who has it all: silver-rinsed American matriarchs with enough money to walk lopsided are easy prey and supply him with that to which he has become accustomed: wealth. Freddy Benton (Steve Martin in the Marlon Brando part) isn't yet in that league. All that he lacks is class. After a brush with Lawrence, Freddy decides that this is the man to teach him. Lawrence's price is to hand Freddy a humiliating role as his idiot brother and do him out of any share in the profits while grooming him for superstar stardom. There are some gleaming barbs in the duel of wits that follows, with touches of Tom and Jerry supplied by Martin's lunatic sense of humour – especially funny as the idiot. Both stars, in fact, are very good, laughs come at regular intervals, the script is almost too sophisticated to contain a swear-word (good grief!) and you may be surprised at how it all turns out. A highly civilised comedy.

Dirty Weekend ● Ⓥ
1992, UK, 102 mins, colour
Dir: Michael Winner
Stars: Lia Williams, David McCallum, Rufus Sewell, Michael Cule
Rating: RB

Director Michael Winner attempts a female *Death Wish,* and the result is a deeply, deeply unattractive, even despicable movie. Lia Williams, a distinguished stage actress, makes a conspicuously inauspicious starring film debut as Bella, who falls victim in turn to a contemptuously faithless lover and a Peeping Tom heavy breather across the way from her Brighton flat. She decides she has 'had enough', flips, and does the peeper in with a hammer. Acquiring a knife and a gun, she dons a tight-fitting dress and goes out in search of perverts anonymous, which she finds swarming around Brighton like flies. Swatting them dead, and polishing off a mass murderer while strolling along the pier, she moves on to some other town. Ludicrous and thoroughly distasteful, this is clumsily directed and inexcusably violent exploitation without any redeeming features.

Disclosure ● ⓥ
1994, US, 128 mins, colour
Dir: Barry Levinson
Stars: Michael Douglas, Demi Moore, Donald Sutherland, Rosemary Forsyth
Rating: ★★★

Like many Michael Douglas films this is a calculating mix of highly provocative elements with a crowd-pleasing progression of plot. As Tom, a key employee at a computer firm, Douglas is passed over for a top job and finds his new boss is Demi Moore, with whom he shared a lengthy and torrid relationship before he met his wife. Invited up to Moore's suite, he finds her descending voraciously on him in search of sexual satisfaction. Accused of sexual harassment the next day, he countersues, only to find Moore stacking the evidence against him with the connivance of everyone from wolfish MD Donald Sutherland down. He gets himself a smart lawyer 'who'd change her name to TV listings to get it in the paper'. But computer messages from 'A Friend' warn him that the affair will not be over even if he wins on the harassment charge. Full of graphic sexual detail, virtual reality technology and key developments in the storyline, the film craftily throws something to everyone, notably in its handling of the ending. Douglas and Moore are entirely competent while Sutherland bulges with odious charm.

Dishonored Lady ○
1947, US, 85 mins, b/w
Dir: Robert Stevenson
Stars: Hedy Lamarr, John Loder, Dennis O'Keefe, William Lundigan
Rating: ★

Director Robert Stevenson blotted an honourable Hollywood record – all the way from *Jane Eyre* to *Mary Poppins* – with his soporific treatment of what sounded like an interesting story until you saw it. If it had been more sharply done, it could have been a suspenseful psychological thriller with elements of murder and blackmail thrown in.

Disorderly Orderly, The ⊙
1963, US, 89 mins, colour
Dir: Frank Tashlin
Stars: Jerry Lewis, Glenda Farrell, Everett Sloane
Rating: ★★★

One of Jerry Lewis' funniest solo comedies, in which the unexpected is always happening. Take the scene where Jerry comes charging down the hospital corridor with a trolleyful of laundry bags. In the other direction, a doctor, carrying two glasses balanced on a tray. You close your eyes and wait for the crash. When you open them again, nothing has happened. Jerry has missed him. Kathleen Freeman makes a splendid comic foil as the horse-faced nurse who has to put up with Jerry's frantic antics.

Disorganized Crime ①
1989, US, 101 mins, colour
Dir: Jim Kouf
Stars: Hoyt Axton, Corbin Bernsen, Ruben Blades, Fred Gwynne, Ed O'Neill, Lou Diamond Phillips
Rating: ★★

Laughs are a bit thin on the ground in this weak crime comedy unless you are the sort of person who can cope with ill-timed slapstick and finds people swearing at each other funny for the sake of watching an admittedly excellent cast. For the rest of us, it's sad to see so many talented players wasted on a dumb cops 'n' robbers chase film. Hoyt Axton, Fred Gwynne, Lou Diamond Phillips, Ruben Blades, Ed O'Neill and Corbin Bernsen try hard, but without a script worthy of the name, it's all largely down to vigorous mugging in the hopes of raising a smile.

Distant Drums ○
1951, US, 101 mins, colour
Dir: Raoul Walsh
Stars: Gary Cooper, Mari Aldon, Richard Webb, Ray Teal, Arthur Hunnicutt
Rating: ★★

Fairly straightforward cowboys versus Indians Western, except that the setting is the Florida everglades. Director Raoul Walsh makes the most of the plentiful action scenes, the familiar bearded features and coonskin hat of Arthur Hunnicutt are prominent and former ballerina Mari Aldon makes an impressive debut as a girl rescued from Redskin captivity.

Distant Trumpet, A ○
1964, US, 116 mins, colour
Dir: Raoul Walsh
Stars: Troy Donahue, Suzanne Pleshette,

James Gregory
Rating: ★★

This Cavalry vs Indians horse opera has noble intentions, as the Indians are seen as real people and a negotiated peace ends the film. Nevertheless, it still ends up treating the subject in rather one-dimensional 'cowboys 'n' Injuns' fashion. This isn't helped much by a colourless hero (Troy Donahue as Lt Matt Hazard!) and a rather irrelevant love interest (Suzanne Pleshette). Still it's a fairly good yarn and the battle scenes between cavalry and Indians are exciting and well-staged. There's some rousing cavalry music by Max Steiner, good villainy from Claude Akins and spirited direction by veteran action man Raoul Walsh to help the threadbare story along.

Distant Voices, Still Lives ① ⓥ
1988, UK, 85 mins, colour
Dir: Terence Davies
Stars: Freda Dowie, Peter Postlethwaite, Angela Walsh
Rating: ★★★

Director Terence Davies, arguably one of the most ambitious and most painstaking craftsmen at work in British films of the Eighties and Nineties, has turned personal memories of his family upbringing in Liverpool of the Forties and Fifties into a remarkable debut feature that won plaudits wherever it was shown. Christenings, weddings and a funeral are the highlights for a family dominated by a brutal patriarch, who turns the lives of his wife and children into a bleak, endless nightmare. 'Some of my family have seen the film. It opened up a lot of wounds and they cried,' says Davies. 'But my mother said, 'He's told the truth,' which I have.' It's actually two films in one, with *Still Lives* shot two years after *Distant Voices*, with the same cast but different technicians. But they run together as a seamless labour of love.

Distinguished Gentleman, The ① ⓥ
1992, US, 112 mins, colour
Dir: Jonathan Lynn
Stars: Eddie Murphy, Victoria Rowell, Joe Don Baker, Lane Smith, Kevin McCarthy, James Garner
Rating: ★★★

Quite a jolly if inconsequential vehicle for Eddie Murphy as a con-man elected to Congress where he finds himself, natch, perfectly at home. Lane Smith's impersonation of Richard Nixon (his

D

character name actually is Dick, and much is made of it) is equally in its natural setting as the big white self-serving shark on whose major committee Murphy soon contrives to get – with the intention of pocketing as many back-handers as possible in the shortest time. Alas it's not long before a pretty face (Victoria Rowell) and a good cause (cancer in children) steady Eddie, and he rounds on the rogues responsible (headed by Smith) with a 'sting' in the tail of the film. The ending really sums up the enterprise: at the final wisecrack, Rowell reacts while Murphy just mugs to the camera. They'll make a black Bob Hope of him yet.

Divided Heart, The ○
1954, UK, 89 mins, b/w
Dir: Charles Crichton
Stars: Cornell Borchers, Yvonne Mitchell, Armin Dahlen, Michel Ray
Rating: ★★★

Yvonne Mitchell won a British Academy Award for her role as a Yugoslavian mother fighting to get back her son from foster-parents. Another of the Academy's awards – for the Best Foreign Actress – went to Berlin-born Cornell Borchers, who plays the boy's foster-mother. The actor who will have many people reaching for their handkerchiefs is dark-eyed Michel Ray, who plays the boy pathetically torn between two worlds.

Divine Madness ① ⓥ
1980, US, 95 mins, colour
Dir: Michael Ritchie
Stars: Bette Midler
Rating: ★★★

Bette Midler is almost at full throttle in this film record of the singer's sensational, perpetual motion stage show. For those who have been to the Moon and don't know, the divine Ms M on stage is a sort of non-stop Lenny Bruce, telling the foulest possible jokes in between singing soulful, but gutsy ballads. The woman is so outrageous you wonder what she can possibly do next. Then she does it!

Dixie ○
1943, US, 89 mins, colour
Dir: A Edward Sutherland
Stars: Bing Crosby, Dorothy Lamour, Marjorie Reynolds
Rating: ★★★

Bing Crosby looks even more doleful than usual in blackface in this potted biography of showman Dan Emmett, who is credited with the idea of starting black-and-white minstrel shows. But there's a dash of liveliness about the climax, which purports to show how Dixie was born. Bing also sings 'Sunday, Monday or Always' and 'I'm from Missouri', but co-star Dorothy Lamour doesn't sing a note. Shame on you, Paramount.

D.O.A. ○
1950, US, 83 mins, b/w
Dir: Rudolph Maté
Stars: Edmond O'Brien, Pamela Britton, Luther Adler, Neville Brand, Beverly Campbell
Rating: ★★★

Loosely remade with Dennis Quaid and Meg Ryan, this is a typically morose Hollywood *film noir* of the postwar years, shot mostly at night, and featuring a pugnacious performance by Edmond O'Brien as the man who, poisoned by unknown hands, has only a short time to find his own murderer. Screen debuts for Neville Brand, very effective as a psychotic thug, and Beverly Garland, here billed as Beverly Campbell. Not quite as good as its reputation, this is, all the same, pretty hypnotic stuff with spurts of quite savage action.

D.O.A. ● ⓥ
1988, US, 100 mins, colour
Dir: Rocky Morton, Annabel Jankel
Stars: Dennis Quaid, Meg Ryan, Charlotte Rampling, Daniel Stern
Rating: ★★★

'Drop dead,' says Meg Ryan to Dennis Quaid in the course of this thriller. Poor guy – that's just what he's in the process of doing, trying to find his own killer after falling victim to a slow-acting poison. So what's it all about, Dennis? The answers would still run like the remake of an old *film noir* (which this is), even without the black-and-white 'bookends' that top and tail the film. The side of the plot that involves Charlotte Rampling is, without giving too much away, much more interesting than the part that pops its head up at the end, almost as if to confound the viewer for presuming to beat Quaid to the answers. Quaid himself, coming on here like a combination Jack Nicholson and Alan Ladd, is really pretty good and Ryan just great as the student who reluctantly helps Prof Quaid root out the truth. Directors Rocky Morton and Annabel Jankel fill the screen with too many unnecessary shots, but the thriller aspects of the film are well handled.

Doc Hollywood ① ⓥ
1991, US, 105 mins, colour
Dir: Michael Caton-Jones
Stars: Michael J Fox, Julie Warner, Woody Harrelson, George Hamilton, Bridget Fonda
Rating: ★★

A throwback to Forties-style stories has to be something special to make it in today's Schwarzenegger, sci-fi-oriented film world. This nothing-much-happens number certainly isn't that. Michael J Fox is the brash city doctor headed to Los Angeles for a career in plastic surgery, but sidelined into a small country town, Grady, en route. That's where he crashes his car, has to do 32 hours community service as a doctor, and falls for the local ambulance driver (Julie Warner). There's not enough of Fox's involvement with the locals to make an emotive story out of all this, and it remains a lightweight, faintly unbelievable tale.

Doc Savage – The Man of Bronze ○
1975, US, 100 mins, colour
Dir: Michael Anderson
Stars: Ron Ely, Paul Gleason
Rating: ★★

This rather too unambitious cartoon-style adventure, light on action and special effects, was one of the few box-office misses for films based on comic-strip heroes. A cross between Superman and Indiana Jones, the mighty Doc Savage first appeared in 1933 in a monthly comic strip magazine created by Lester Dent, who wrote under the pen name of Kenneth Robeson. The film is set in 1936, and any parody is affectionately offered, almost as a reverence to the character involved. Subtleties in the treatment, however, are notably lacking, and the sequel promised at the end of the movie never arrived.

Doctor, The ① ⓥ
1991, US, 123 mins, colour
Dir: Randa Haines
Stars: William Hurt, Christine Lahti, Elizabeth Perkins, Mandy Patinkin, Adam Arkin, Charlie Korsmo
Rating: ★★

It's debatable if William Hurt was good casting for the central role of this film about a doctor who gets cancer. It gets so you care little more about his character at the end than you did at the start – indeed, he doesn't seem to have changed that much. Supposedly a meeting with a dying cancer patient (Elizabeth Perkins) softens his outlook on life, turning him into more of a human being who cares about his fellows. But on Hurt, it doesn't show. Much more accessible is Christine Lahti as his wife. It's not a particularly good, nor consistent role, but Lahti enriches it with sincerity and warmth. Otherwise, the pace is slow and the heart only occasionally uplifted. Those who dislike seeing surgery on screen are given plenty of opportunity to look the other way.

Doctor at Large ○
1957, UK, 104 mins, colour
Dir: Ralph Thomas
Stars: Dirk Bogarde, Muriel Pavlow, Donald Sinden, James Robertson Justice, Shirley Eaton
Rating: ★★

Third in the series of *Doctor* comedy films gives Dirk Bogarde a piquant new partner in Muriel Pavlow (re-introduced from the first film), and still manages to raise quite a few genuine laughs from its corny catalogue of venerable medical jokes.

Doctor at Sea ○
1955, UK, 93 mins, colour
Dir: Ralph Thomas
Stars: Dirk Bogarde, Brigitte Bardot, James Robertson Justice, Maurice Denham
Rating: ★★★★

Actually an improvement on its predecessor, *Doctor in the House*, with a long succession of amusing moments as one crazy situation after another rings the bell. Especially the final, glorious shipboard chaos that ensues when the captain mixes whisky with nerve pills. Dirk Bogarde is a likeable hero and his leading lady is none other than Brigitte Bardot, complete with the famous shower scene and most attractive French-accented English. James Robertson Justice fares even better as the martinet ship's captain than as the irascible surgeon Sir Lancelot Spratt in the previous film, but the outstanding contribution in the supporting cast comes from Maurice Denham, who's in tremendous form. If ever there were a laugh on the ocean wave, this is it.

Doctor Blood's Coffin ◐
1961, UK, 92 mins, colour
Dir: Sidney J Furie
Stars: Kieron Moore, Hazel Court, Ian Hunter
Rating: ★

A grisly blend of horror and science fiction, as strange disappearances terrorise the inhabitants of a small Cornish vil-

lage. The director is the young Canadian Sidney J Furie who went on to make *Southwest to Sonora*, *The Ipcress File* and *Lady Sings the Blues*. This one's pretty bad though.

Doctor Dolittle ○ Ⓥ
1968, US/UK, 144 mins, colour
Dir: Richard Fleischer
Stars: Rex Harrison, Samantha Eggar, Anthony Newley, Richard Attenborough
Rating: ★★

A simplistic musical version of Hugh Lofting's tales of the eccentric doctor who talks to animals. Rex Harrison's splendid Dolittle owes a fair amount to his Prof Higgins from *My Fair Lady*. There's also Anthony Newley, really letting a jaunty cockney tenor rip as Matt, and Richard Attenborough's brief appearance as a circus owner.

Doctor in Clover ○ Ⓥ
1966, UK, 101 mins, colour
Dir: Ralph Thomas
Stars: Leslie Phillips, James Robertson Justice, Shirley Anne Field, Joan Sims, John Fraser
Rating: ★★★

It seems that in the Fifties and Sixties, as fast as Richard Gordon wrote a new *Doctor* comedy book, Rank had Jack Davies fashion a screenplay from it. Apart from the usual crop of medical jokes to try to make some less modest part of the anatomy sound like something else, Davies' script shows a nice line in invention. Hilarious scenes include Joan Sims trying to give patient Arthur Haynes a blanket bath (in which it looks as though she had a hard task keeping a straight face) and Leslie Phillips going Mod in Carnaby Street as part of a rejuvenation treatment. Phillips releasing laughing gas is also funny.

Doctor in Distress ○ Ⓥ
1963, UK, 102 mins, colour
Dir: Ralph Thomas
Stars: Dirk Bogarde, Samantha Eggar, James Robertson Justice, Mylene Demongeot, Barbara Murray, Donald Houston
Rating: ★★

After Michael Craig had donned the white overall for the fourth *Doctor* comedy, to follow *Doctor in the House*, *Doctor at Sea* and *Doctor at Large*, the Rank Organisation pressed Dirk Bogarde back into service for this entry into the series, which plays more or less as series of revue sketches. Most of the old crew are back, including Bogarde and James Robertson Justice – both in more

than usually amorous mood – and Donald Houston. The most effective scene is a marvellous send-up of a film producer and his glamorous star, by Leo McKern and Jill Adams.

Doctor in Love ○ Ⓥ
1960, UK, 97 mins, colour
Dir: Ralph Thomas
Stars: Michael Craig, Virginia Maskell, Leslie Phillips, James Robertson Justice, Reginald Beckwith
Rating: ★★

More leaves from Richard Gordon's comic casebook, this time with the accent on girls, who include Virginia Maskell, Carole Lesley, Joan Sims, Liz Fraser and Fenella Fielding. Leslie Phillips is his usual foxy self as one of the two young doctors pursuing them.

Doctor in the House ○ Ⓥ
1954, UK, 91 mins, colour
Dir: Ralph Thomas
Stars: Dirk Bogarde, Muriel Pavlow, Kenneth More, Donald Sinden, Donald Houston, Kay Kendall, James Robertson Justice
Rating: ★★★

The rumbustious hospital comedy which introduced the beer-swilling, rugger-playing, women-chasing students of Richard Gordon's best-selling book. This renowned, joke-a-minute British comedy film was the first of the popular *Doctor* series. And few, one fancies, would argue that it wasn't one of the best. In its vastly amusing tale of medical students at a large hospital, Dirk Bogarde and Kenneth More both give engaging performances, and James Robertson Justice, as Sir Lancelot, created his medical autocrat role for the first time. Also featured, though all too briefly, was the delightful Kay Kendall, fresh from her triumph and trumpet-playing in that other British comedy success of the period, *Genevieve*. The gags are as numerous as they are funny, including one at the point where Sir Lancelot suddenly shoots a question at the otherwise preoccupied Simon (Bogarde): 'What's the bleeding time?'

Doctor in Trouble ○ Ⓥ
1970, UK, 90 mins, colour
Dir: Ralph Thomas
Stars: Leslie Phillips, Harry Secombe, Angela Scoular, Irene Handl, Robert Morley, James Robertson Justice
Rating: ★★

Leslie Phillips' doctor is in trouble, all right, in the last to date of the famous comedy series. In the course of an ocean voyage, he falls in the water,

D

loses his trousers, has to dress up as a woman and nearly gets hanged, drawn and quartered by a breeches-buoy.

Doctor Rhythm ○

1938, US, 80 mins, b/w
Dir: Frank Tuttle
Stars: Bing Crosby, Mary Carlisle, Beatrice Lillie
Rating: ★★★

For some reason this wasn't very popular in its time, but it has worn better than most of Bing Crosby's Paramount musicals of the Thirties. There are hummable songs, a pleasingly idiotic story (originally from O Henry) about a vet hired as a bodyguard, Andy Devine and Sterling Holloway competing in degrees of hoarseness – and the incomparable Beatrice Lillie almost at her most eccentric. All this and a scene-stealing parrot too.

Doctor's Dilemma, The ○

1959, UK, 99 mins, colour
Dir: Anthony Asquith
Stars: Leslie Caron, Dirk Bogarde, Alastair Sim, Robert Morley, Felix Aylmer, Michael Gwynn
Rating: ★★★

Colourful MGM film based on George Bernard Shaw's medical spoof about an unscrupulous artist in bad health, his devoted wife and the doctors she calls in. It's an unusual performance from Dirk Bogarde as the patient – considering he made his name as a doctor in the *Doctor* series. And it's an unusual one, too, from Leslie Caron as the wife – since the role was originally written for an older woman.

Doctor Zhivago ○ Ⓥ

1965, US/UK, 192 mins, colour
Dir: David Lean
Stars: Omar Sharif, Julie Christie, Tom Courtenay, Geraldine Chaplin, Rod Steiger, Alec Guinness
Rating: ★★★★

Omar Sharif's face, bleak as the steppes; the desperation of those on a long, doom-laden train journey across the plains to the Urals; the last idyll in the midst of snowbound landscapes for Sharif and Julie Christie; a charge across ice and snow-sodden trenches in wartime; and guerilla warriors mowing down a group of white-clad youths in a field of golden corn. These are the images which haunt you from David Lean's lyrical, five-Oscar treatment of Boris Pasternak's epic novel of strife and love in early 20th century Russia.

Dodge City ○ Ⓥ

1939, US, 104 mins, colour
Dir: Michael Curtiz
Stars: Errol Flynn, Olivia de Havilland, Ann Sheridan, Bruce Cabot, Frank McHugh, Alan Hale
Rating: ★★★

Vintage Warner Brothers Western which reunites Errol Flynn with Olivia de Havilland, his co-star in the other Thirties action classics, *Captain Blood* and *The Adventures of Robin Hood.* Michael Curtiz, the Hungarian-born director who became one of Hollywood's top men at filming bloodstirring action, made all three. There's a wonderful bar-room brawl, an immense feeling of wide-open spaces and brilliant marshalling of crowd scenes, as well as glowing photography in soft, rich early Technicolor by Sol Polito and Ray Rennahan.

Dodsworth ○

1936, US, 101 mins, b/w
Dir: William Wyler
Stars: Walter Huston, Ruth Chatterton, Paul Lukas, Mary Astor, David Niven
Rating: ★★★★★

This affecting film of Sinclair Lewis' novel was one of director William Wyler's first major triumphs. Walter Huston is marvellous as the businessman who retires early and takes an extended holiday in Europe with his selfish wife. And you'll be praying that he makes the right decisions in the end. David Niven and John Payne feature in minor roles.

Dog Day Afternoon ● Ⓥ

1975, US, 130 mins, colour
Dir: Sidney Lumet
Stars: Al Pacino, John Cazale, Charles Durning, Chris Sarandon, Carol Kane, Lance Henriksen
Rating: ★★

There's a lot to admire in this account of an attempted bank heist by two inept young robbers and their subsequent attempts to get away despite the cordon of police surrounding them. The acting is excellent, at least on the surface; Frank Pierson's screenplay won an Oscar and the film is beautifully made by director Sidney Lumet with some stunning overhead shots. It's meant, I think, as a funny-sad black comedy, although most of its humour comes from its characters swearing repeatedly, which does wear thin after a while. The two robbers, although given full value by Al Pacino and John Cazale, also prove tiresome, unsympathetic people, and only in the last 20

minutes is any tension or excitement engendered by their plight. Most of it is too grating or abrasive to entertain and non-Pacino fans may be restless throughout.

Dog's Life, A ○

1918, US, 30 mins, b/w
Dir: Charles Chaplin
Stars: Charlie Chaplin, Edna Purviance
Rating: ★★★

Charlie Chaplin in his most famous guise – the little tramp – and an appealing dog called Scraps. How can we resist such a combination? The best sequences involve man and dog working together to scrounge food – an early example of the moral: united we stand, divided we fall. This, one of the longest of Charlie's early films, was his first 'Million Dollar' release and bore his autograph at the beginning, together with the legend: 'None genuine without this signature!'

Dogs of War, The ● Ⓥ

1980, US, 113 mins, colour
Dir: John Irvin
Stars: Christopher Walken, Tom Berenger, Colin Blakely, JoBeth Williams
Rating: ★★

Director John Irvin certainly gets to grips with Frederick Forsyth's bestseller about mercenaries in Africa although, despite some explosively effective action sequences, the film is perhaps a shade too dispassionate to set the pulses racing. Christopher Walken is a charismatic lead and there's a very good supporting performance from Colin Blakely.

Dolly Sisters, The ○

1945, US, 114 mins, colour
Dir: Irving Cummings
Stars: Betty Grable, John Payne, June Haver, S Z Sakall, Reginald Gardiner
Rating: ★★★

There shouldn't be a dry eye in the house at the end of this epic, song-filled musical which kept wartime audiences enraptured. Betty Grable and June Haver display four of the best legs in the business as the real-life sisters of the title, and prove they can both milk a sentimental song for its maximum effect. John Payne, in the last of his musical roles opposite Fox's singing blondes (Grable, Haver and Alice Faye), has his thunder largely stolen by the performing seal with which he is forced to share the spotlight in one scene. Irving Cummings directs with affection.

Dolores Claiborne ◑ ⓥ
1995, US, 131 mins, colour
Dir: Taylor Hackford
Stars: Kathy Bates, Jennifer Jason Leigh, David Strathairn, John C Reilly, Eric Bogosian, Christopher Plummer
Rating: ★★★

Although this isn't the greatest of mystery dramas, Kathy Bates and Jennifer Jason Leigh do their reputations no harm with their solid performances as a traumatised mother and daughter. As the film opens, Bates is battling with her aged employer (Judy Parfitt) who falls down the stairs to her death. Local sheriff Christopher Plummer, convinced that Bates lured her slimy husband (David Strathairn) to his death in a disused well years before, is determined to get her for murder this time, especially as Bates was caught with a rolling pin in her hand. Enter Leigh, who hasn't seen her mother for 15 years and seems to have good reason to hate her. If the story structure here is good, the dialogue is on less firm ground, Parfitt in particular being ill-served by Tony Gilroy's adaptation of a Stephen King novel. But Bates and Leigh have an intensity that keeps you watching to the end to find out if she dunnit and why.

Dominick and Eugene
See: Nicky and Gino

Dominique ◑
1978, UK, 100 mins, colour
Dir: Michael Anderson
Stars: Cliff Robertson, Jean Simmons, Jenny Agutter
Rating: ★★

Faintly reminiscent of *Diabolique* (alias *The Fiends*), this is also rather (a long way) after director Michael Anderson's previous entry in the baffling-thriller field, *Chase a Crooked Shadow*, made 20 years previously. Jean Simmons makes a welcome reappearance as the lady who may be the victim of a terror campaign by her husband, or may even be the perpetrator. A distinguished supporting cast includes Jenny Agutter, Simon Ward, Judy Geeson, Flora Robson, Ron Moody, Jack Warner and Michael Jayston.

Domino Principle, The ◑
(aka: The Domino Killings)
1977, US, 100 mins, colour
Dir: Stanley Kramer
Stars: Gene Hackman, Candice Bergen, Richard Widmark, Mickey Rooney, Eli Wallach
Rating: ★★

Presumably the title has something to do with the escalation of events in this predictable thriller. Gene Hackman is the convict sprung by 'them' in order to carry out a special assignment, which is cloaked in mystery, although hardened thriller fans should have little trouble in guessing pretty well what's going on. Richard Widmark contributes the best portrayal in a distinguished cast, and Mickey Rooney offers his customarily pugnacious performance.

Donnie Brasco ● ⓥ
1997, US, 126 mins, colour
Dir: Mike Newell
Stars: Al Pacino, Johnny Depp, Michael Madsen, Anne Heche
Rating: ★★★

Rock-hard crime thriller on a familiar theme: FBI man infiltrates the Mob in the hope of bringing gangsters to justice. With Depp as the cop in deep, and Pacino as his pal and mentor, this works well as an action drama. Its philosophy and motives are less clear-cut. What is the script suggesting by giving Depp daughters called Sherry, Kerry and Terry, or by making him turn turtle on his ideals? Although Depp has been befriended by Pacino, he also sees the man kill and maim and knows him for what he is. So we're surprised when Depp goes home long enough to hit his wife and say: 'I'm not like them. I am them. All these years being the guy in the white hat. And fer what? Fer nuthin.' The puzzling nature of the character isn't helped by Depp's impassivity. Pacino though gives a stunning performance that allows us to see every facet of the man passed over for high Mob office in favour of the thuggish Madsen. Good, sometimes gruesome entertainment: its action strikes home hammer-hard.

Donovan's Brain ○
1953, US, 83 mins, b/w
Dir: Felix Feist
Stars: Lew Ayres, Nancy Davis, Gene Evans, Steve Brodie
Rating: ★★★

Second screen re-working of Curt Siodmak's science-fiction shocker about a scientist's attempt to keep a brain alive, which backfires when it starts to control the scientist. Thanks mainly to Lew Ayres' electrifying acting in a Jekyll-and-Hyde role, the turn preserves all the psychological tension of the original.

Donovan's Reef ○
1963, US, 105 mins, colour
Dir: John Ford
Stars: John Wayne, Lee Marvin, Jack Warden, Dorothy Lamour, Elizabeth Allen, Cesar Romero
Rating: ★★

John Wayne and his favourite director John Ford swap the wide open spaces of the prairie for the wide open spaces of a Pacific island in this sprawling, brawling adventure story that's packed with many Ford regulars such as Edgar Buchanan and Mike Mazurki. Heroes John Wayne and Lee Marvin are two mighty tough guys who would break a beer bottle at an angry word. The acting class is supplied by Jack Warden as a doctor, and by Elizabeth Allen as his blue-stocking daughter. Watch for the amusing continuity slip when she falls in the sea with stockings on, and emerges bare-legged.

Don't Bother to Knock ◑
1952, US, 76 mins, b/w
Dir: Roy Baker
Stars: Marilyn Monroe, Richard Widmark, Anne Bancroft
Rating: ★★

Richard Widmark doesn't appear as happy in this stop-go chiller as in most of his post-war films for Fox, but then he has high-powered female co-stars Marilyn Monroe and Anne Bancroft both intent on making early impressions. Good, no; interesting, certainly.

Don't Bother to Knock ◑
(aka: Why Bother to Knock?)
1961, UK, 89 mins, colour
Dir: Cyril Frankel
Stars: Richard Todd, Elke Sommer, June Thorburn, Nicole Maurey
Rating: ★★

Richard Todd's first film venture as an independent producer sees him as an amorous travel agent on a laugh-and-mishap-filled tour of Europe. Veteran Judith Anderson – so memorable as Mrs Danvers in *Rebecca* – easily takes the acting honours. It's an uneasy role for Todd, and stopped his glittering run of success in its tracks.

Don't Drink the Water ○
1969, US, 100 mins, colour
Dir: Howard Morris
Stars: Jackie Gleason, Estelle Parsons
Rating: ★★

Woody Allen's stage play adapted to the talents of portly Jackie Gleason in a comedy film that never reached British shores. Gleason plays a Jewish caterer

D

who, accused of spying in a Communist country, takes refuge with his family in the American embassy. Former comic supporting actor Howard Morris is the director.

Don't Ever Leave Me ○

1948, UK, 85 mins, b/w
Dir: Arthur Crabtree
Stars: Jimmy Hanley, Petula Clark
Rating: ★★

This largely laughless comedy about the kidnapping of a teenage girl is remarkable for its parade of stars past and present. Besides those in the bigger roles, watch for fleeting appearances from Anthony Steel, Patricia Dainton and Dandy Nichols. Petula Clark – in the days when her public still thought of her as an impish schoolgirl – plays the all-too-willing kidnap victim, while with Hugh Sinclair, Anthony Newley, Barbara Murray, Brenda Bruce, Sandra Dorne and Maurice Denham offer sound support.

Don't Just Lie There, Say Something! ◐

1973, UK, 91 mins, colour
Dir: Bob Kellett
Stars: Brian Rix, Leslie Phillips, Joan Sims, Joanna Lumley
Rating: ★

A mere glance at the title and the three stars (Brian Rix, Leslie Phillips and Joan Sims) is sufficient to indicate the brand of entertainment – lively, saucy, broad, clothes-losing capers in the British tradition. It's based on the successful stage farce by Michael Pertwee who also wrote the screenplay for this much less successful film.

Don't Look Now ● ⓥ

1973, UK, 110 mins, colour
Dir: Nicolas Roeg
Stars: Donald Sutherland, Julie Christie
Rating: ★★★

You'll either love or hate this supernatural Daphne du Maurier tale made even more inscrutable by director Nicolas Roeg. The Baxters (Donald Sutherland and Julie Christie) travel to Venice after the accidental death of their young daughter. They become involved with two odd sisters, one of whom is a psychic and claims she can help them contact their daughter. Nothing is what it seems in this strange film, which, with Roeg's fine camerawork and the Venice location, is stunning to watch. Sutherland and Christie give intense performances, but if you demand a logical plot with an equally logical conclusion, you will find

this film irritating. If you let its surreal magic seduce you, you'll understand why it has a strong cult following.

Don't Make Waves ○

1967, US, 96 mins, colour
Dir: Alexander Mackendrick
Stars: Tony Curtis, Claudia Cardinale, Robert Webber, Sharon Tate
Rating: ★

An unhappy experience in Hollywood for ace British comedy director Alexander Mackendrick, who had made such gems as *Whisky Galore!*, *The Man in the White Suit* and *The Ladykillers*. Mackendrick had hit it big on a previous visit to America to make *Sweet Smell of Success*. But this time he found himself saddled with two stars in Tony Curtis and Claudia Cardinale whose lustre on the international scene was beginning to wane, and a script much inferior to the material on which he'd been able to work previously. Studio interference rendered the results even less to the director's liking and the comedy was further hacked about in Britain, where it barely surfaced as a second feature. An unfortunate end to a distinguished directorial career.

Don't Take it to Heart ○

1944, UK, 91 mins, b/w
Dir: Jeffrey Dell
Stars: Richard Greene, Edward Rigby, Patricia Medina
Rating: ★★★

Richard Greene made a couple of good films in his native England after being invalided out of the war and before returning to Hollywood. This ghost comedy co-stars him with then-wife Patricia Medina and is worthy of comparison with *The Ghost Goes West* and *The Canterville Ghost*. Jeffrey Dell's direction gives the ingenious story many little embellishments that mark it out as way above average in the fantasy field.

Don't Tell Mom the Babysitter's Dead ◐ ⓥ

1991, US, 105 mins, colour
Dir: Stephen Herek
Stars: Christina Applegate, Joanna Cassidy, John Getz, Josh Charles, Conceta Tomei
Rating: ★★

The title betrays only one of the many chances that this not-bad comedy misses. Five kids, left behind when their mother goes on holiday to Australia for two months, get a sadistic old witch to look after them and the household while she's away. Straight away though, the writers make the minder

drop dead, and pitch us right into another kind of film. Head daughter Christina has to get a job to support the family (the minder has been buried with the housekeeping). Faking a CV, she falls on her cute blonde Sandra Dee-type feet when given an executive assistant's job with a clothing company Now if Tina were to use her teenage know-how to make her way in the company, this would be all right. But she doesn't do that for another hour, and in the meantime we get a sappy plot about teenage romance and the junior members of the family stealing thousands from the firm's petty cash Tina has borrowed for groceries (as if she'd take the whole cashbox home!). The last half hour contains some quite bright moments, until Mom comes home to spoil everything before the film has reached any sort of climax.

Doomed Cargo

See: Seven Sinners

Doomwatch ◐

1972, UK, 92 mins, colour
Dir: Peter Sasdy
Stars: Ian Bannen, Judy Geeson
Rating: ★★

A chiller based on the famous TV series which made a star of Robert Powell before his character was killed off. In this adventure, series regulars John Paul, Simon Oates and Jean Trend take a back seat while guest stars Ian Bannen and Judy Geeson investigate strange happenings on a far-flung island.

Doors, The ● ⓥ

1991, US, 141 mins, colour
Dir: Oliver Stone
Stars: Val Kilmer, Meg Ryan, Kevin Dillon, Kyle MacLachlan, Frank Whaley, Kathleen Quinlan
Rating: ★★

Director Oliver Stone turns his uncompromising gaze on the self destruction of a rock star. The Adonis-like (well, to begin with) Jim Morrison of The Doors died aged 28 and, if this account of his later life is to be relied on, the only wonder is that he lived that long. Deeply into drugs and booze, he was barely ever in his right mind, yet found time to write poetry and poetic lyrics to songs as well. As played by Val Kilmer here, Jim was a born exhibitionist with a death wish. 'Death turns you on?' asks his long-suffering girlfriend (Meg Ryan, ditzier than usual). 'Life,' he tells her, 'hurts a lot more. When you die, the pain is over.' This is one of the few coherent conversations between a cast of characters who become tiresome long before the film is over. Stone's movie is wonderfully well put together, but we never get to know Jim, or any of the others involved. Kilmer works tremendously hard, but it's difficult to care about a character with so few redeeming features.

Door to Door ○
1984, US, 88 mins, colour
Dir: Patrick Bailey
Stars: Ron Leibman, Arliss Howard
Rating: ★★★

This offbeat crime comedy rolls along at a steady lick and boasts a powerful central performance from Ron Leibman as a glib, smooth-talking travelling salesman whose sideline in con tricks puts him at odds with the law. Only Arliss Howard fails to shine as the no-hoper Leibman takes under his wing to learn the art of getting one's foot in the door and keeping it there.

Double Bunk ○
1961, UK, 92 mins, b/w
Dir: C M Pennington-Richards
Stars: Ian Carmichael, Janette Scott, Sidney James, Liz Fraser, Dennis Price
Rating: ★★★

This naval lark was Sid James' last film before becoming one of the *Carry On* team. There are some nice bits of comic business on the voyage and some familiar names in the distinguished supporting cast. All told, an enjoyable comedy entertainment of the kind that British studios used to do so well.

Double Confession ○
1950, UK, 85 mins, b/w
Dir: Ken Annakin
Stars: Derek Farr, Joan Hopkins, Peter Lorre, William Hartnell
Rating: ★★

Director Ken Annakin showed in an earlier film, *Holiday Camp,* that he liked to be beside the seaside. But, in this crime drama that proves almost impossible to follow, he makes the resort of 'Seagate' appear a very sinister place indeed. The whodunnit plot benefits enormously from Peter Lorre's almost apologetic menace.

Double Impact ● Ⓥ
1991, US, 118 mins, colour
Dir: Sheldon Lettich
Stars: Jean-Claude Van Damme, Alonna Shaw, Geoffrey Lewis, Alan Scarfe
Rating: ★★

If you fancy two Jean-Claude Van Dammes for the price of one (and it isn't worth more), you may get both a smile and a thrill from this bone-crunching action yarn about twin brothers who are separated as babies when their parents are murdered by Chinese mobsters. Watching Jean-Claude trying to sketch out two different characters, though, is quite a hoot, and director Sheldon Lettich certainly shows a flair for action as well as convincingly presenting us with two Van Dammes on screen at the same time.

Double Indemnity ○
1944, US, 106 mins, b/w
Dir: Billy Wilder
Stars: Barbara Stanwyck, Fred MacMurray, Edward G Robinson
Rating: ★★★★★

This excellent crime thriller, enveloped in an atmosphere of doom and tightly directed by Billy Wilder, has now become a classic of its kind. It's incisively written and impeccably structured by Wilder and Raymond Chandler from the novel by James M Cain. Barbara Stanwyck creates her most magnetic femme fatale as the smouldering blonde who seduces insurance man Fred MacMurray into murdering her husband. Her entrance down a stairway is one of the great moments of sexual attraction in the cinema.

Double Life, A ○
1947, US, 103 mins, b/w
Dir: George Cukor
Stars: Ronald Colman, Signe Hasso, Edmond O'Brien, Shelley Winters, Ray Collins, Philip Loeb
Rating: ★★★★

A terrific film from the opening frame to closing credits, this was Shelley Winters' first film break after a success on the stage, and it established her as a star. Ronald Colman stars as a gifted stage actor whose despair and murderous moods come from playing the lead in *Othello.* Winters is a buxom, sultry waitress, who is attracted to the married thespian, but soon discovers his propensity for violence. Colman's performance is absolutely riveting and deservedly won an Oscar.

Double Man, The ○
1967, US, 105 mins, colour
Dir: Franklin J Schaffner
Stars: Yul Brynner, Britt Ekland, Clive Revill, Anton Diffring
Rating: ★★★

Which Yul Brynner is which? That's the key to this ingenious and thoroughly

absorbing espionage thriller. The twists and turns of the plot, based on Henry S Maxfield's *Legacy of a Spy,* reward close watching, and lead to an exciting ski-lift climax, in which Brynner's clever performance reaches its suspenseful height. Even Britt Ekland is more mobile than usual and makes a likeable leading lady.

Double X ● ◑
aka: Double X: The Name Of The Game
1992, UK, 95 mins, colour
Dir: Shani S Grewal
Stars: Norman Wisdom, Gemma Craven, William Katt, Simon Ward, Bernard Hill
Rating: RB

Consistently through the years, in spite of its efforts to improve its image, the British cinema has been dogged by inept, wooden thrillers that make you laugh (and inwardly cringe). Since the early Fifties, fading film presences have been tempted to appear in these. The lineup here includes Norman Wisdom as a safecracker, Bernard Hill imitating Peter Sellers as an Irish gangster, Simon Ward (trying to look nasty) and, of course, the visiting American 'star', in this case William Katt, who has grown up to look like Sterling Hayden. Deeply unpleasant in theme, the film tries to earn its adult certificate with a short scene of torture, but comes nowhere near. What hurts it more are its smug characterisations, the slaps in the face that are no more than pats, the unconvincing gunplay and actors who lurch through their roles like performers on stage at your local church play. Laughable.

Down and Out In Beverly Hills ● Ⓥ
1986, US, 103 mins, colour
Dir: Paul Mazursky
Stars: Nick Nolte, Bette Midler, Richard Dreyfuss, Little Richard, Elizabeth Pena
Rating: ★★

Hugely successful Hollywood comedy based (yet again) on a French original, this time the 1932 classic *Boudu Sauvé des Eaux.* It totally revived the star careers of Richard Dreyfuss and Bette Midler, although the film is stolen from both of them by a dog called Mike. Not all that good, though.

Down Argentine Way ○
1940, US, 94 mins, colour
Dir: Irving Cummings
Stars: Betty Grable, Don Ameche, Carmen Miranda, J Carrol Naish
Rating: ★★

This was the film that launched 20th Century-Fox's dazzlingly coloured se-

D

ries of musicals, often with vivid and imaginative choreography, that ran throughout the 1940s. The films paired any two from Alice Faye, Don Ameche, Betty Grable and John Payne, and this one stars Ameche with Grable (who actually replaced Faye when the latter went down with appendicitis). Carmen Miranda, of the whirling skirts, fruit-compote hats and delightfully fractured English, was also a part of the Fox musical scene and had a big hit here with 'South American Way'. Other musical highlights are a sizzling dance speciality from The Nicholas Brothers and an amusing novelty number, 'Sing to Your Senorita', from Charlotte Greenwood and Leonid Kinsley.

Downhill Racer ○
1969, US, 101 mins, colour
Dir: Michael Ritchie
Stars: Robert Redford, Gene Hackman, Camilia Sparv
Rating: ★★★

Interesting and at times exciting story of a poor-born ski-ace trying to win an Olympic gold. The film has excellent colour photography on and off the ski slopes. Robert Redford not only set up the production company for the film, but did most of the dangerous downhill racing himself.

Down Three Dark Streets ○
1954, US, 85 mins, b/w
Dir: Arnold Laven
Stars: Broderick Crawford, Ruth Roman, Martha Hyer, Marisa Pavan
Rating: ★★★

Good thriller which holds together three story threads well and maintains its factual approach throughout. Broderick Crawford is first rate as the FBI agent investigating a colleague's death and director Arnold Laven keeps things tense, compact and plausible.

Down Went McGinty
See: The Great McGinty

Dracula ●
1931, US, 84 mins, b/w
Dir: Tod Browning
Stars: Bela Lugosi, Edward Van Sloan, Dwight Frye, Helen Chandler
Rating: ★★★★

Tod Browning's original and sometimes very sinister story of a vengeful vampire. The opening sequence is still a brilliant example of how to make the flesh creep, photographed in black and white, always a horror film's best asset. For sheer flesh-creeping nastiness, the

settings of the count's homes in England and Transylvania has only been equalled in Browning's own *Mark of the Vampire*, made five years later. Lugosi is a forbidding character as Dracula – but the outstanding performance comes from Dwight Frye, as Dracula's dupe. Cinema has few scenes to equal the first sight of his madness, standing gibbering in a ship filled with dead men.

Dracula ●
1979, US/UK, 109 mins, colour
Dir: John Badham
Stars: Frank Langella, Laurence Olivier, Donald Pleasence, Kate Nelligan, Trevor Eve
Rating: ★

Abandon ship! Drac is back. And Frank Langella is visually a perfect Count Dracula in this over-styled re-telling of the Bram Stoker original. He is more than a match for Trevor Eve's sheepish Jonathan Harker, Laurence Olivier's ripely sliced Van Helsing and Donald Pleasence's familiar wild-eyed doctor. Director John Badham seems more conscious in achieving striking visuals (sometimes very good – as in the sequence where a vampire girl is encountered underground) than in getting his technical details right: a victim's bitemarks appear on the opposite side to the bite, and a vampire reflects not in a mirror but does in water. A major disappointment.

Dracula ●
1973, US, 100 mins, colour
Dir: Dan Curtis
Stars: Jack Palance, Simon Ward, Penelope Horner
Rating: ★★★

Director Dan Curtis clearly has a yearning to make a great horror film out of Bram Stoker's classic novel. The brilliant opening scenes declare his ambition. Mists rise from a black Transylvanian lake, like the memory of some faded and forgotten painting. A pack of great dogs, ownerless, pounds helter-skelter along the dim lakeside and through the dark pines that line it. But words soon take over from images and Richard Matheson's screenplay is uncharacteristically flabby. Jack Palance restrains himself commendably from over-acting as the Count, but just misses on the menace. Penelope Horner's Mina is the one first-class performance: deep and penetrating.

Dracula ●
(aka: The Horror of Dracula)
1958, UK, 82 mins, colour

Dir: Terence Fisher
Stars: Peter Cushing, Christopher Lee, Melissa Stribling, Michael Gough
Rating: ★★★★

Hammer's original vampire film, an excellent adaptation of Bram Stoker's classic book. Plush, glossy, but above all scarifying, with a devastatingly effective climax whose special effects were much imitated in subsequent years. Christopher Lee is definitely intimidating in the title role and the film is directed by Terence Fisher with drive and great single-mindedness. Many sequels followed, all with Lee as Dracula, but none of them are half as good as this one.

Dracula [1993]
See: Bram Stoker's Dracula

Dracula AD 1972 ● Ⓥ
1972, UK, 100 mins, colour
Dir: Alan Gibson
Stars: Christopher Lee, Peter Cushing, Stephanie Beacham
Rating: ★

The old Hammer vampire legend sits rather uneasily in modern tinies, the dialogue suggesting that the studio had half-decided to play this one for laughs. But the final confrontation between Peter Cushing and Christoper Lee is a good one, and there is an above-average line-up of beauties for Dracula to bite.

Dracula Dead and Loving It ● Ⓥ
1996, US, 89 mins, colour
Dir: Mel Brooks
Stars: Leslie Nielsen, Mel Brooks, Amy Yasbeck, Lysette Anthony, Peter MacNicol
Rating: ★★

It took Mel Brooks 21 years to progress from Young Frankenstein to Old Dracula. But, far from being a ruthless satirical dissection of the legend, this proves to be more of a straight re-telling of the story with a few comic twists. Not enough, though, to make us cackle with ghoulish glee. Funniest moment of not very many: when Dracula (Nielsen) is dancing with Mina (Yasbeck) at the grand ball, the crafty Van Helsing (Brooks himself) rips a curtain away from a vast mirror to reveal that the vampire casts no reflection. 'Hmm,' remarks a guest. 'She's doing quite well without him, isn't she?' Nielsen at least plays it straight, as do most of the cast, Anthony putting most life (after death) into her role as Lucy. Anne Bancroft, the real-life Mrs Brooks, does a brief and scarcely necessary cameo as a gypsy woman. Yes, Dracula's still dead but the odds are that you won't be loving it.

Dracula Has Risen from the Grave ● ⓥ

1968, UK, 92 mins, colour
Dir: Freddie Francis
Stars: Christopher Lee, Rupert Davies, Veronica Carlson
Rating: ★★

Dracula's tears of blood are the most original touch in this film. However, director Freddie Francis manages to stage one or two nice tableaux amid the gore.

Dracula – Prince of Darkness ● ⓥ

1965, UK, 90 mins, colour
Dir: Terence Fisher
Stars: Christopher Lee, Barbara Shelley, Andrew Keir, Francis Matthews
Rating: ★★

The first sequel to the fine original Hammer *Dracula* suffers from a less credible basic premise, and heroes and heroines so silly that it's difficult to sympathise with their plight. Never mind, Christopher Lee is as hissingly horrifying as ever as the master of darkness. It's not until the film is over that you realise he hardly has a word to say. A minor annoyance is provided by the crossed swords at Dracula's castle. You would have thought the Count would not have allowed anything in the shape of a cross in his domain.

Dracula Prisoner of Frankenstein ●

1972, UK/Spain, 90 mins, colour
Dir: Jesus Franco
Stars: Dennis Price, Howard Vernon, Mary Francis
Rating: ★

Spanish director Jesus Franco took a break from making sex romps to stitch together this horror film that's reminiscent of the tail-end of the Hollywood horrors of the Forties, when all the monsters were thrown together in one ghoulish pot-pourri. Just like that, Franco mixes together all the standard ingredients of the genre, and comes up with a pretty indigestible brew. Vampires are out for blood, the monster drags his feet, the werewolf looks miserable, winds howl, hinges creak and candles flicker (although Frankenstein seems to have plenty of electricity for his laboratory). Britain's

Dennis Price has the leading role, in one of his last films.

Dracula's Daughter ●

1936, US, 70 mins, b/w
Dir: Lambert Hillyer
Stars: Otto Kruger, Gloria Holden, Marguerite Churchill
Rating: ★★★

The best of the subsequent Universal Dracula series by some way, tenuously adapted from Bram Stoker's short story. Lambert Hillyer, a director whose experience stretches back to the early silent days, keeps a very firm grip on the clammy atmosphere, and the two ladies are absolutely splendid. Marguerite Churchill makes a pretty and resourceful heroine, while London-born Gloria Holden creates a real figure of pity as the countess afflicted with the curse of the vampire.

Dragnet ○ ⓥ

1987, US, 106 mins, colour
Dir: Tom Mankiewicz
Stars: Dan Aykroyd, Tom Hanks, Christopher Plummer, Harry Morgan
Rating: ★★

If they'd stuck to the style of the beginning, this pastiche on the old TV cop series of the Fifties might have been a gem. It's still enjoyable old-fashioned entertainment, even if it does give way too soon to a plot that looks like a throw off from the *Our Man Flint* or *Matt Helm* series. Dan Aykroyd is the modern-day nephew of the now-deceased Joe Friday, immortalised on TV by Jack Webb; like his uncle he goes strictly by the book. Tom Hanks completes the star pairing as Friday's new partner, a maverick who gradually assumes some of Friday's identity. Aykroyd is suitably stolid, throwing his lighter moments into amusing relief, in what was his best work before *Driving Miss Daisy*. Director Tom Mankiewicz, who should have taken this performance as his keystone, has been quoted as saying, 'I believe good comedy should have a base in realism.' Right you are Tom: a pity you didn't apply the maxim here.

Dragonheart ● ⓥ

1996, US/UK, 103 mins, colour
Dir: Rob Cohen
Stars: Dennis Quaid, David Thewlis, Pete Postlethwaite, Dina Meyer, Julie Christie, voice of Sean Connery
Rating: ★★★★

Shot entirely in Slovakia, this fantasy adventure features the most personable dragon (voiced by Sean Connery) since

Disney drew a cartoon version of this mythical beast some 50 years ago. And the idea of a dragonslayer (Quaid) teaming up with the (very last) dragon he's stalking is pretty novel in itself. Adding poignancy to the exciting action is the fact that the dragon once gave half its heart to the (now gone to the bad) king to save his life. If the ruler now dies, so does the dragon. Robust action sequences mix easily with some unusually clever dialogue for Connery's dragon which, not surprisingly, steals the show.

Dragon Seed ○

1944, UK, 145 mins, b/w
Dir: Jack Conway, Harold S Bucquet
Stars: Katharine Hepburn, Walter Huston, Akim Tamiroff, Turhan Bey, Aline MacMahon, Hurd Hatfield
Rating: ★★★

An interesting effort to follow the success of writer Pearl S Buck's The *Good Earth* (which won two Oscars when filmed in 1937). Two screenwriters, Marguerite Roberts and Jane Murfin, toiled mightily to compress another vast Buck novel about China into something under two and a half hours actual running time, but it still seems a bit unwieldy, even when controlled by two directors. Katharine Hepburn, emoting fiercely with eyelids taped down, is always worth watching, however, especially in the film's extraordinary final tableau. Walter Huston, Akim Tamiroff and particularly Agnes Moorehead also do good work.

Dragonslayer ●

1981, US, 108 mins, colour
Dir: Matthew Robbins
Stars: Peter MacNicol, Caitlin Clarke, Ralph Richardson, John Hallam, Peter Eyre, Albert Salmi
Rating: ★★★★

This exciting and inventively executed medieval adventure is one of the best of the sword-and-sorcery films, with a really tremendous dragon, imaginative scenery and special effects that are well up to par. Ralph Richardson is as richly relishable as ever as the master sorcerer whom the villagers hope will rid them of the aged but ill-tempered dragon Vermithrax Pejorative, to whom they have to sacrifice a village virgin every now and then to appease his ire. Few actors would make a better wizard than Richardson, but he is dispatched all too soon, leaving the job of dragon-slaying in the inexperienced hands of his apprentice (Peter MacNicol) with the help of the militant village youth leader (Caitlin Clarke)

D

who turns out to be a girl hiding from the virgin lottery carried out whenever the dragon plays up. Subsequent scenes inside the dragon's rocky domain have exactly the right feel. There's fire on the water, and you can almost smell the stench of the dragon and its brood.

Dragon, The Bruce Lee Story ❶ Ⓥ

1993, US, 121 mins, colour
Dir: Rob Cohen
Stars: Jason Scott Lee, Lauren Holly, Robert Wagner, Nancy Kwan
Rating: ★★

A biography that looks almost as ludicrous as any of its star's films, *Dragon* still works quite well as entertainment. And there are some chilly overtones involving Lee's son Brandon, killed earlier that year while filming, as the movie dwells at length on the nightmare 'demons' that pursued both father and son. Scenes where Lee is attacked by restaurant staff wielding kitchen choppers may give rise to more laughs than thrills. Jason Scott Lee and Lauren Holly catch Lee and his wife well enough, and Rob Cohen's direction keeps the film moving at a pace that (apart from a very slow credit sequence) keeps us occupied without stretching our minds.

Dragonwyck ○

1946, US, 103 mins, b/w
Dir: Joseph L Mankiewicz
Stars: Gene Tierney, Vincent Price, Walter Huston, Glenn Langan, Anne Revere, Jessica Tandy
Rating: ★★★

Vincent Price's career as a merchant of menace really began to take off from 1946, in *Dragonwyck* and, to a lesser extent, *Shock,* in which he played a mad doctor. *Dragonwyck,* Joseph L Mankiewicz's first film as director (he also wrote the script from Anya Seton's novel), is an elegant chiller atmospherically set in an 1840s mansion wherein Price lurks down the years, trying to get rid of various wives. He's terrific, and Gene Tierney is beautiful as the newest endangered wife.

Dragoon Wells Massacre ○

1957, US, 88 mins, colour
Dir: Harold Schuster
Stars: Dennis O'Keefe, Barry Sullivan, Mona Freeman, Katy Jurado
Rating: ★★★

Exciting and moving by turns, this Western about a wagon train trying to survive in Apache territory is an action

film with heart that finds outdoor adventure specialist Harold Schuster back to his best form. Its script by Warren Douglas (a former minor Hollywood star who also plays a supporting role) creates real people and attracted a good cast – Dennis O'Keefe, Barry Sullivan, Katy Jurado, Mona Freeman, Jack Elam (for once a sympathetic figure), Sebastian Cabot and more. Terrific photography by William Clothier, both in close-up and long shot, makes the most of the colour by De Luxe. A serious, exciting and emotionally effective example of its kind.

Draughtsman's Contract, The ❶

1982, UK, 103 mins, colour
Dir: Peter Greenaway
Stars: Anthony Higgins, Janet Suzman, Anne Louise Lambert
Rating: ★★

A fascinating – if not perhaps 'easy' film – which became one of London's biggest box-office hits, and was the third film made by director Peter Greenaway. Greenaway himself has described it in these terms: 'It's a very literate film; the dialogue has been very carefully worked out for puns and conceits. The whole thing is an elaborate charade, a conceit, which the 17th century enjoyed doing.' You may enjoy seeing it if you're the patient kind.

Dr Crippen ❶

1962, UK, 98 mins, b/w
Dir: Robert Lynn
Stars: Donald Pleasence, Coral Browne, Samantha Eggar
Rating: ★★★

Although the film is overlong, Donald Pleasence is never less than compelling in the title role of this account of a notorious Edwardian murderer. A slow, sincere reconstruction of the famous murder case of 1910, it sets out to prove that Crippen killed his wife only by accident – although you may find writer Leigh Vance's version less than convincing. Coral Browne conveys well the mixed feelings of Crippen's coarse, but pitifully love-craving wife, while Samantha Eggar gives one of her best performances as Crippen's young mistress Ethel, giving the role depth and sensitivity, and fully exploring the gamut of the girl's emotions. Nicolas Roeg's black-and-white photography is very atmospheric.

Dr Cyclops ○

1940, US, 75 mins, colour
Dir: Ernest B Schoedsack

Stars: Albert Dekker, Janice Logan, Thomas Coley
Rating: ★★★

A mad scientist, conducting bizarre experiments in deepest Brazil, shrinks former colleagues and leaves them to struggle against now-gigantic insects, birds and small animals. Albert Dekker is splendidly sinister as the scientist, and there are some suspenseful shock moments, notably the group's efforts to train a rifle on their sleeping tormentor, and the nail-biting climax. Directed by Ernest B Schoedsack, co-director of *King Kong.*

Dreamboat ○

1952, US, 83 mins, b/w
Dir: Claude Binyon
Stars: Clifton Webb, Ginger Rogers, Jeffrey Hunter, Anne Francis
Rating: ★★★

A riotous comedy film about a crusty college professor whose students discover he was once an idolised silent movie star. There are some riotous glimpses of silent films Clifton Webb and Ginger Rogers' characters are supposed to have made, as well as a hilarious scene from one of Webb's Forties' films, *Sitting Pretty.* Sheer joy, with Fred Clark and Elsa Lanchester given acidly witty supporting roles by director Claude Binyon's sparkling script.

Dreamchild ❶

1985, UK, 94 mins, colour
Dir: Gavin Millar
Stars: Coral Browne, Peter Gallagher, Ian Holm, Jane Asher
Rating: ★★

An ambitious and gimmicky exploration of the relationship between the Rev Charles L Dodgson (aka Lewis Carroll) and the little girl who inspired him to write *Alice's Adventures in Wonderlattd.* The film, directed by Gavin Millar, sets out with the idea that Dodgson was unnaturally attracted to under-age girls. But the presentation is clumsy, involving several long, lustful gazes between Ian Holm as Dodgson and newcomer Amelia Shankley as Alice. An amusing diversion is created by grotesque caricatures of characters from the Wonderland story, produced by Jim Henson's Muppet workshops and voiced by Alan Bennett, Julie Walters and Fulton Mackay.

Dream Demon ● Ⓥ

1988, UK, 89 mins, colour
Dir: Harley Cokliss

Stars: Jemma Redgrave, Kathleen
Wilhoite, Jimmy Nail, Timothy Spall,
Annabelle Lanyon
Rating: ★★★

A pretty scary this-house-possessed
horror film, hampered by an unconvincing central performance (from
Jemma Redgrave) and unbelievable
characters, but conceptually fairly interesting. Bride-to-be Redgrave moves
into a rented house on the run-up to
her wedding and immediately starts experiencing the most horrendous
nightmares that not only strike you as
convincing, but tell her the truth about
her fiancé and bring her face-to-face
with the horrific past of the house itself.
She's joined by Jenny (Kathleen
Wilhoite – very good), an American
who feels she may once have lived
there. Together the girls confront a
dream demon that may destroy them
both. Take a friend to this one, excitingly thought out by director Harley
Cokliss who has perhaps retained some
of his own more livid nightmares and
incorporated them in the story. Seat-
clutching stuff.

Dream Lover ● ⓥ
1993, US, 103 mins, colour
Dir: Nicholas Kazan
Stars: James Spader, Mädchen Amick
Rating: ★★

This is pretty offbeat, if not as tight or
taut or effective as it might be. James
Spader, typecast as the yuppie who has
it all, divorces his first wife and runs
slap into wide-eyed brunette Mädchen
Amick, who swiftly becomes Mrs
Spader No 2. But when she says, 'Just
because I'm half-way pretty, guys look
into my eyes and think they know me,'
you suspect there's something afoot.
Spader finds she's changed her name
and divorced herself from her parents.
Still, he's willing to forget this, and they
have two children together. But then
she starts getting smoochy phone calls,
and there are those unspecified bills
from the Hotel Chanticleer. It's all a
diabolical plot, of course, and not many
of its later developments hold water.
Even so, Spader takes centre stage
rather well, which is more than can be
said for his vacuous leading lady. And
the ending is neatly worked out, even if
you can't agree with the conclusions
Spader draws from it. Hitchcock might
have made us believe more of it.

Dream Team, The ❶ ⓥ
1989, US, 113 mins, colour
Dir: Howard Zieff
Stars: Michael Keaton, Christopher

Lloyd, Peter Boyle, Stephen Furst,
Lorraine Bracco, Dennis Boutsikaris
Rating: ★★★★

Any film that comes up with an idea
that's fairly new after nearly a century
of the cinema deserves some kudos. *The
Dream Team* deserves even more for
eventually overcoming our apprehen-
sions and making us laugh at its four
escaped psychiatric patients who are accidentally left adrift in the New York.
'It's great to be young and in-sane,'
gasps Michael Keaton as they set out to
see a ball game. But he and his three
comrades have to 'sane up' pretty fast if
they're to rescue their psychiatrist
(Dennis Boutsikaris) from the murderous intentions of two crooked cops
(Philip Bosco, James Remar). Slow to
hit its stride, and initially often as sad as
you'd expect, the film gains momentum
with the unwinding of the mainspring
of its plot and proves frequently funny
in its closing stages. Keaton is aces as
the short-fused Billy: he ought to make
more of this kind of fun.

Dream Wife ○
1952, US, 101 mins, b/w
Dir: Sidney Sheldon
Stars: Cary Grant, Deborah Kerr, Walter
Pidgeon, Betta St John
Rating: ★

Cary Grant is given another opportunity to exercise his inimitable flair for
comedy in this fluffy number. And
he's perfectly in command of his role as
a rather bewildered suitor in a
woman's world. The dialogue and situations are occasionally fresh and
funny, but the plot goes on too long for
its own good. It showed at the time
that Hollywood could still weave gossamer fancies – but not without
straining more than a little.

Dr Ehrlich's Magic Bullet ❶
1940, US, 103 mins, b/w
Dir: William Dieterle
Stars: Edward G Robinson, Ruth Gordon,
Otto Kruger, Donald Crisp, Maria
Ouspenskaya, Montagu Love
Rating: ★★★

One of the best of the Warner medical
biographies, with Edward G Robinson
as the 19th century German chemical
genius who eventually invented a cure
for syphilis. Despite the tricky subject,
this makes compelling, well-written
drama, with Robinson outstanding in
the title role.

Dressed to Kill ○
1946, US, 70 mins, b/w
Dir: Roy William Neill

Stars: Basil Rathbone, Nigel Bruce,
Patricia Morison
Rating: ★★

Basil Rathbone cracks his last case in
the long Universal series, appropriately
known in Britain as *Sherlock Holmes and
the Secret Code,* and about stolen bank
plates. One-time opera star Patricia
Morison has the female lead.

Dressed to Kill ● ⓥ
1980, US, 100 mins, colour
Dir: Brian De Palma
Stars: Michael Caine, Angie Dickinson,
Nancy Allen, Keith Gordon, Dennis Franz
Rating: ★★

A highly exploitative suspense story,
recognisably from the blood-spattered
hands of director Brian De Palma.
This is perhaps his most blatant
homage to Hitchcock (and especially
Psycho), though the master might shift
uneasily in his grave at the long drawn-
out tension, the flashy sex scenes and
the four-letter words used for shock effect. Michael Caine, Angie Dickinson
and Nancy Allen do sterling service
above and beyond the call to keep the
frenzied farrago ticking over. The mechanics of suspense are worked quite
well by the director and may frighten
the easily scared quite badly.

Dresser, The ❶ ⓥ
1983, UK, 118 mins, colour
Dir: Peter Yates
Stars: Albert Finney, Tom Courtenay,
Edward Fox, Zena Walker, Michael
Gough
Rating: ★★

Suitably theatrical performances by
Albert Finney and Tom Courtenay
(both inexplicably nominated for
Oscars) adorn this bludgeoning tragi-
comedy about the relationship between
an ageing, temperamental, married
knight of the theatre and his devoted
gay dresser. The Finney character is
rather obviously modelled on Donald
Wolfit but, since both he and the dresser are patently unsympathetic, such
minor felicities as the film has – including a wonderful scene where half the
cast of the play attempt to produce a
backstage tempest for Finney's King
Lear – go largely unappreciated in the
face of the repetitive haranguing between the two men. Both of them are
roundly out-acted by Eileen Atkins as
the thin-lipped stage manager.

Dressmaker, The ● ⓥ
1988, UK, 92 mins,-colour
Dir: Jim O'Brien
Stars: Jane Horrocks, Joan Plowright,

D

Billie Whitelaw
Rating: ★★

The British cinema of the late Eighties seemed too often to be rooted in the past, and here's another *Hope and Glory* meets *Yanks* set in the wartime years. With its multiplicity of period trimmings, it looks, to use the vernacular of the Liverpool where its rather grim story is set, 'dead expensive'. It's also a fairly good job of work all round. Jane Horrocks is Rita, a slightly repressed teenager looked after by two aunts (Joan Plowright, Billie Whitelaw) and soon pitched into an encounter with an American soldier who wants what wartime Yanks were supposed to want. When she slaps him off regretfully he turns to her fun-loving Aunt Billie instead. Capable, careful performances etch themselves into a reasonably interesting portrait of the times, authentic to almost the last detail – although I'd like to know what the coin was that Rita is given to buy forty 2 1/2d stamps.

Driftwood ● Ⓥ
1996, Ire, 100 mins, colour
Dir: Ronan O'Leary
Stars: James Spader, Anne Brochet, Barry McGovern, Anna Massey
Rating: ★★

There are echoes of *Misery* and *Psycho* in this odd, uninvolving piece about obsessive love in a remote place. When a man (Spader), suffering from a broken leg as well as amnesia, is washed ashore, it's the answer to a maiden's prayer for batty Sarah (a miscast Brochet) who has lived there, lonely, loveless and debt-ridden, since her mother's death two years ago, and now has only her sculptures in wood for company – apart from holding conversations with her mother's corpse, Convincing the man that he's on an uninhabited island, Sarah soon draws him into her bed. What with the nearby presence of a lecherous old storekeeper (McGovern), the impending tragic end is so obvious that the makers have to resort to a slightly supernormal twist to achieve any sense of surprise. This minor piece of gothic erotica supposedly cost £5 million to make, though from what's on screen it's difficult to see how.

Drive a Crooked Road ○
1954, US, 82 mins, b/w
Dir: Richard Quine
Stars: Mickey Rooney, Dianne Foster, Kevin McCarthy
Rating: ★★

This role, as a cocky little mechanic who becomes involved in murder, marked another step towards recognition as a straight actor for pint-sized Mickey Rooney, star of many musicals and comedies of the early Forties. A year later, Rooney was being acclaimed for his fine performance in the war film, *The Bold and the Brave*.

Driver, The ○ Ⓥ
(aka: Driver)
1978, US, 91 mins, colour
Dir: Walter Hill
Stars: Ryan O'Neal, Bruce Dern, Isabelle Adjani, Ronee Blakely
Rating: ★★★

This effective modern *film noir* crime drama stars Ryan O'Neal as a professional getaway driver and Bruce Dern as the obsessive detective determined to catch him. The fact that none of the characters in the film have proper names (they're only The Driver, The Detective, The Connection, etc) give it a disconnected existential feel and an air of mystery it otherwise wouldn't have. Dern takes the acting honours although O'Neal makes his taciturn character quite believeable. Director writer Walter Hill directs with pace and style to make this a crime film that's interesting and slightly different. The best scene is where O'Neal takes a carload of crooks who doubt his ability on a high-speed run around an underground car park, deliberately using pillars and walls to rip off parts of their car as he goes.

Driving Miss Daisy ○ Ⓥ
1989, US, 99 mins, colour
Dir: Bruce Beresford
Stars: Morgan Freeman, Jessica Tandy, Dan Aykroyd, Patti Lupone
Rating: ★★★★

It's really hard to see anyone disliking this sweet-natured, if sharp-tongued story of a 70-year-old southern American Jewish lady (Jessica Tandy, winning an Oscar), forced by her son (Dan Aykroyd) to take on a black chauffeur (Morgan Freeman) after she can no longer be trusted behind her own wheel. This is 1948 and the winds of change are only beginning to blow through the magnolias outside her Georgia mansion. The movie (also an Oscar winner) gently probes the demeaning position of blacks in the south, but only in so far as it fits writer Alfred Uhry's policy of education by an entertaining kind of persuasion. What's more important is the relationship between the three main characters,

and this is carefully, flawlessly sketched in by Tandy, Freeman and Aykroyd, the latter quietly effective in a different kind of assignment from his comedy roles.

Dr Jekyll and Mr Hyde ◐
1931, US, 98 mins, b/w
Dir: Rouben Mamoulian
Stars: Fredric March, Miriam Hopkins
Rating: ★★★★

This is still the best version by far of Robert Louis Stevenson's macabre story, in which Fredric March deservedly won an Oscar for his terrifying portrayal of the Victorian doctor who develops a sinister double personality. Directed by Rouben Maniou[l]ian, the film is a powerfully imaginative piece, full of symbolism and spine-chilling atmosphere. The opening scene in which Jekyll goes to the lecture theatre and the audience has its first view of March remains a classic of cinematography, while the transformations from Jekyll to Hyde and back again were achieved in one take by the inspired use of makeup and coloured filters. March's chilling, unforgettable performance proved that he was well capable of far, far more than light comedy roles.

Dr Jekyll and Mr Hyde ◐
1941, US, 120 mins, b/w
Dir: Victor Fleming
Stars: Spencer Tracy, Ingrid Bergman, Lana Turner
Rating: ★★

Fredric March's Oscar for the 1931 version of the classic horror tale has undeservedly overshadowed Spencer Tracy's performance in this early Forties remake. Using a minimum of make-up, Tracy achieves the maximum in horror in the transformation scenes with a combination of lighting and facial expression. At first set to play the roles in reverse, Ingrid Bergman and Lana Turner decided to play the bad and good girl respectively. But their decision was ill-advised – even to beat typecasting – for each had much more to offer the other role.

Dr Jekyll and Ms Hyde ● Ⓥ
1995, US, 88 mins, colour
Dir: David Price
Stars: Sean Young, Tim Daly, Harvey Fierstein, Stephen Tobolowsky, Polly Bergen, Robert Wuhl
Rating: RB

When the best bits of the film are all in the trailer, and the trader's embarrassingly bad, you're really in trouble. This is a totally misbegotten and completely unfunny take on the Stevenson horror classic that makes Hammer's *Doctor Jekyll and Sister Hyde* of 20-odd years ago seem like an unsurpassed masterpiece. 'You look as though you need something long and stiff,' is about the script's best joke, advice you may well heed after tottering out of this one. The entire cast is in desperate straits here, and deserves your sympathy, if perhaps not your support. At least the film comes up with a unique credit at the end – for 'Poodle vocal stylings'. There's no answer to that.

Dr Jekyll and Sister Hyde ●
1971, UK, 94 mins, colour
Dir: Roy Ward Baker
Stars: Martine Beswick, Ralph Bates, Gerald Sim
Rating: ★★★★

A ridiculous idea, you might think, to travesty Stevenson's old chiller classic by turning Mr Hyde (and Dr Jekyll) into a woman. Strangely, though, the notion results in one of the best films to come out of Hammer studios since their peak period some ten years earlier. Director Roy Ward Baker turns in his best work in years and combines with Technicolor cameraman Norman Warwick to make the film visually magnetic in its own way. Martine Beswick makes a fetching Sister Hyde, positively radiating evil, and the transformation sequences are above average for this sort of thing.

Dr No ○ ⓥ
1962, UK, 111 mins, colour
Dir: Terence Young
Stars: Sean Connery, Ursula Andress, Joseph Wiseman, Jack Lord, Bernard Lee
Rating: ★★★★

First, fastest and best of the James Bond films. Sean Connery is an agile, handsome and sardonic hero, Ursula Andress still the most delectable Bondswoman on record. The action moves swiftly enough to cover the holes in the plot, and the humour is of a standard not maintained in some of the later Bond extravaganzas. This is the one, to refresh your memory, in which Bond meets the gorgeous Honey is singed by a flamethrower, tickled by a tarantula, dogged by bloodhounds, grilled by some electric fencing, drugged by coffee, swamped by seawater and nearly atomised in a nuclear pile.

Drop Dead, Darling ○
(aka: Arrivederci Baby!)
1966, UK, 105 mins, colour
Dir: Ken Hughes
Stars: Tony Curtis, Rosanna Schiaffino, Lionel Jeffries, Nancy Kwan
Rating: ★★

At times sparkling black comedy about a confidence trickster who marries, then murders, for money. There's one delightfully audacious sequence in which Tony Curtis appears as a young teenager, complete with lollipop and velvet shorts. Curtis skates happily over the thin ice of this idea, to make it an inspiration. There are too many flat spots, but some very funny moments are topped by the last words of Fenella Fielding, which are worth waiting to hear.

Drop Zone ● ⓥ
1994, US, 105 mins, colour
Dir: John Badham
Stars: Wesley Snipes, Yancy Butler, Gary Busey
Rating: ★

The mindless action film *par excellence*, a combination of skydiving, hijack thriller and robbery caper, and a long way down for star Wesley Snipes in the acting stakes: this makes *Passenger 57* look like an action masterpiece. You're not likely to have a clue what's going on as the film drifts anonymously past your eyes. Gary Busey, like Snipes, is criminally wasted as yet another grinning villain. Others contribute little and least of all personality – to the whoosh-slam-bang proceedings. A grim comedown for director John Badham compared to such aerial seat-grippers as *Blue Thunder*. Dub this one *Flop Zone*.

Drowning by Numbers ● ⓥ
1988, UK, 118 mins, colour
Dir: Peter Greenaway
Stars: Joan Plowright, Juliet Stevenson, Joely Richardson, Bernard Hill
Rating: ★★

A series of 'moving paintings' that depicts three women from the same family who all drown their husbands. As a black comedy, this is a great idea by maverick British director Peter Greenaway, but he lingers too long in the telling of the tale, and gives it too little substance. Not that the whole thing doesn't have a certain consistency. The coroner (Bernard Hill), who fancies all three women and lies about the watery deaths, has a 13-year-old son who numbers deaths, animal and human, fires off fireworks for every

victim and has such a yen for the 'skipping girl' that he circumcises himself for her. All very contrived and artificial, the film gradually sheds its tedium as it develops. Cinematographer Sacha Vierney's colour images – the fashionable word is 'painterly' – should have been worth an Oscar nomination. An intellectual farce, the film fascinates throughout without actually raising a smile.

Drowning Pool, The ◑
1975, US, 108 mins, colour
Dir: Stuart Rosenberg
Stars: Paul Newman, Joanne Woodward, Anthony Franciosa, Murray Hamilton, Gail Strickland, Melanie Griffith
Rating: ★★

A lively follow-up to *The Moving Target*, in which Paul Newman first played detective Lew Harper. It's a woman who hires Harper again (in this case played by Newman's wife Joanne Woodward) and he's soon up to his shoulder-holster in a lethal tangle that's murkier than the bayou in which his client's mother (Coral Browne) is soon found floating. Director Stuart Rosenberg, after a slowish start, sticks to a brisk telling of the basic story. The dialogue is tough, but the acting (apart from Newman and Richard Jaeckel as a bullet-headed cop) mannered and not too convincing. Newman himself, though, is a huge consolation. Some of his individual scenes, in which he displays a subtly quirky sense of humour, make wonderfully successful conversation pieces. He alone emerges from *The Drowning Pool* dripping with credit.

Dr Phibes Rises Again ●
1972, UK, 89 mins, colour
Dir: Robert Fuest
Stars: Vincent Price, Robert Quarry, Peter Cushing
Rating: ★★

Robert Quarry, alias Count Yorga, takes over from Joseph Cotten as the new adversary for a Dr Phibes reactivated by fresh blood to replace the embalming fluid which has preserved him since his last adventure. This time the sense of the ludicrous is not used so well to the film's own advantage, although there is a good quota of splendidly ingenious deaths, topped by Hugh Griffith being flung overboard from a liner in a giant gin bottle.

D

Dr Socrates ○

1935, US, 74 mins, b/w
Dir: William Dieterle
Stars: Paul Muni, Ann Dvorak, Barton
MacLane, Ralph Bellamy
Rating: ★★★

Paul Muni, taking the title role of a
small-town doctor forced to treat a
wounded gangster, here worked for the
first time with director William
Dieterle. It's Muni's performance that
keeps you watching.

Dr Strangelove ○ ⓥ

Or: How I Learned to Stop Worrying
and Love the Bomb
1963, US, 93 mins, b/w
Dir: Stanley Kubrick
Stars: Peter Sellers, George C Scott,
Sterling Hayden, Keenan Wynn, Slim
Pickens, James Earl Jones
Rating: ★★★

With the possible exception of *2001:
A Space Odyssey*, this is probably the
most famous of the relatively infrequent but always original films
produced by the controversial and
highly individual director Stanley
Kubrick. A black comedy on a nuclear theme, it has the inimitable Peter
Sellers triumphant in a trio of roles
(notably as Strangelove, the scientist
whose artificial arm repeatedly makes
a Heil Hitler sign as an involuntary reflex action) and an impressive
supporting cast which includes
Keenan Wynn. Sellers and Wynn
share what is the film's funniest scene,
involving a telephone call to an
American President.

Dr Syn ○

1937, UK, 81 mins, b/w
Dir: Roy William Neill
Stars: George Arliss, Margaret
Lockwood, John Loder
Rating: ★★★

Russell Thorndike's famous adventure
novel about the smuggling clergyman
at large in the 19th century was filmed
almost simultaneously by Hammer as
Captain Clegg and by Disney (with Peter
Cushing and Patrick McGoohan respectively) in the early Sixties. This is
the first version and just as exciting and
well-handled as any, weakened only by
the central casting of aristocratic
George Arliss as Dr Syn.

Dr Syn Alias the
Scarecrow ○

1963, UK, 93 mins, colour
Dir: James Neilson
Stars: Patrick McGoohan, George Cole,
Tony Britton, Geoffrey Keen, Kay Walsh,

Patrick Wymark
Rating: ★★★

A rip-roaring, fast-paced, *Boy's Own*-
style smuggling adventure from the
Disney studio. Patrick McGoohan is
ideally cast as the imperturbable vicar,
who is also the Scarecrow, the Robin
Hood-style leader of the smugglers. A
hand-picked cast of convincing ruffians
backs him splendidly, especially
George Cole as the sexton. The story
constantly grips, and there are several
moments of real tension, particularly a
jailbreak, where McGoohan's knife-
edge playing and the taut direction of
James Nielson do much to tighten the
audience stranglehold. The
Scarecrow's mask is a splendid
Hammer-style creation; it, and one or
two other jumpy moments, make the
film perhaps just a little scary for
young children.

Dr Terror's House of
Horrors ●

1964, UK, 98 mins, colour
Dir: Freddie Francis
Stars: Peter Cushing, Christopher Lee,
Roy Castle, Donald Sutherland
Rating: ★★

Taking its cue from the popular portmanteau style of *Dead of Night* some 20
years previously, this was the first of
Amicus' successful series of horror
story compendiums. The five segments – featuring were wolves,
vampires, voodoo, killer vines and a
re-working of *The Beast with Five Fingers*
– are of varying quality, but there's no
doubting the authentic creepiness of
the opening and closing sequences.
These are dominated by Peter
Cushing's genuinely sinister Dr
Sandor Schreck, a dealer of death
through his set of Tarot cards. Max
Adrian has fun as a vampire and, in
the same episode, a youthful Donald
Sutherland makes one of his first film
appearances.

Drugstore Cowboy ● ⓥ

1989, US, 101 mins, colour
Dir: Gus Van Sant
Stars: Matt Dillon, Kelly Lynch, James Le
Gros, Heather Graham, James Remar
Rating: ★★★

Quite skilfully made, apparently on a
low budget, this rough-edged drama is
a kind of *Bonnie and Clyde* of the drug
generation. There's even an allusion
to not wanting to end up like Bonnie
and Clyde in a recurring song. Matt
Dillon (as 'Bad' Bobby Hughes) and
Kelly Lynch are young marrieds who,
with two confederates, rob drug stores

for their own fixes and supply to others. As Dillon's quite effective
narrative explains it: 'We were just trying to stay high.' But the cops pursue,
death rears its head and it all has to
stop, for Dillon at least. 'I'm a junkie,'
he says with resigned regretfulness. 'I
liked the whole lifestyle. But it didn't
pay off.' The film's nicely old-fashioned in construction and Dillon
reminiscent of the gangsters of earlier
film eras, with his paranoias about the
mention of pets or hats on the bed.
He gives his best performance in several years. The film's no masterpiece,
but its effective little sermon does stick
in the mind.

Drum, The ○

(aka: Drums)
1938, UK, 96 mins, colour
Dir: Zoltan Korda
Stars: Sabu, Roger Livesey, Valerie
Hobson, Raymond Massey, Francis L
Sullivan
Rating: ★★★

Rip-roaring adventure yarn about the
British in India struggling to prevent
rebel tribesmen from usurping a young
prince's throne. The battle scenes are
extraordinarily well done, and the
Technicolor photography takes the
breath away. As the little prince, Sabu
followed solidly on his success in
Elephant Boy; and the suavity and presence of Raymond Massey gives much
power to the villainous Ghul. Our
favourite line comes from the sergeant-
major instructing his men on how to
behave at a Mohammedan party: 'It
doesn't matter what the entertainment
is, snakes or stomach-wiggling or what-
not. I want to see a look of rapture on
every face.'

Drum Beat ○

1954, US, 107 mins, colour
Dir: Delmer Daves
Stars: Alan Ladd, Audrey Dalton, Marisa
Pavan, Robert Keith, Charles Bronson,
Warner Anderson
Rating: ★★

Tough-guy star Charles Bronson enjoyed one of his first big roles in this
Western, as a vicious renegade Indian
terrorising the west in the late 19th
century. Bronson, who had just
changed his name (from his real one,
Charles Buchinski), makes the most of
his part as the formidable Captain
Jack, overshadowing Alan Ladd, playing in his first big Western since *Shane*.
Director Delmer Daves' stern direction
helps make the most of spectacular ambush and battle scenes, and J Peverell

Marley's Warnercolor photography broke away from the conventional chocolate-box hues to drape the Western backdrop convincingly in golds and browns.

Drum Crazy ○
(aka: The Gene Krupa Story)
1960, US, 101 mins, b/w
Dir: Don Weis
Stars: Sal Mineo, Susan Kohner, James Darren, Yvonne Craig
Rating: ★★

This biography of the late, great jazz drummer Gene Krupa should have been the big breakthrough for Sal Mineo. But he didn't quite make it. Perhaps he was still too young, at 21, and too slight of stature to sustain stardom beyond a teenage rave. A pity: he really has the joint jumping with a keenly-observed copy of the Krupa style, with backing from such real-life jazz greats as Shelly Manne, Loring 'Red' Nichols, Buddy Lester, Bobby Troup and Anita O'Day.

Drums Along the Mohawk ○
1939, US, 103 mins, colour
Dir: John Ford
Stars: Claudette Colbert, Henry Fonda, Edna May Oliver, Arthur Shields, Ward Bond, John Carradine
Rating: ★★★

One of John Ford's early Western successes, this 'pioneers versus Indians' adventure romance has some remarkable colour photography by Bert Glennon, the expected scenes of Redskin siege and pioneer hardship, Claudette Colbert keeping her upper lip prettily stiff, and Henry Fonda's famous marathon footslog through an Indian gauntlet. Solid, cunningly crafted entertainment.

Dr X ◑
1932, US, 82 mins, colour
Dir: Michael Curtiz
Stars: Lionel Atwill, Fay Wray, Lee Tracy
Rating: ★★★

A splendid essay into the macabre from the same team – director Michael Curtiz, stars Lionel Atwill and Fay Wray and the Warner Studio – that made the classic *The Mystery of the Wax Museum*. Only the unwelcome intrusion of a fast-talking reporter, annoyingly played by Lee Tracy, mars the sinister atmosphere of this creepy thriller about a full-moon murderer who strangles his victims with something that seems too powerful to be a normal human arm. Curtiz's cultured direction has bags of flair and doesn't

miss a trick. Wray is as touchingly vulnerable as ever as Dr X's daughter. Made in two-colour Technicolor but normally shown on TV in black and white.

Dry Rot ○
1956, UK, 87 mins, b/w
Dir: Maurice Elvey
Stars: Ronald Shiner, Brian Rix, Sidney James, Michael Shepley, Joan Sims, Peggy Mount
Rating: ★★

A formidable cast of farceurs has a wild time in this film adaptation of the famous Whitehall comedy hit about three itinerant bookmakers trying to earn an honest – well, almost honest – living. Heather Sears makes her screen debut and the charms of Shirley Ann Field can be very briefly glimpsed as a waitress at the Three Frogs Cafe. But Peggy Mount sweeps all else before her in a relatively short, but devastating appearance as the indomitable Sergeant Fire.

Dry White Season, A ● Ⓥ
1989, US, 107 mins, colour
Dir: Euzhan Palcy
Stars: Donald Sutherland, Winston Ntshona, Jurgen Prochnow, Janet Suzman, Marlon Brando, Susan Sarandon
Rating: ★★★

Richard Attenborough's *Cry Freedom* spawned a whole batch of films about South African atrocities, and here's another. Once again, there's the caring white man (Donald Sutherland) who gradually comes to realise the full horror of the apartheid regime (the film is set in 1976) and there's a showy role for Marlon Brando as the Orson Welles-like lawyer who tears government witnesses to pieces at an inquest on a murdered black, knowing that it won't make a jot of difference. 'Justice and law could be described as distant cousins,' he tells Sutherland. 'And, here in South Africa, they're not on speaking terms at all.' It's all well-made and depressingly familiar, easily arousing our resentment and anger, although the upbeat ending is not only highly fanciful but would surely carry horrendous consequences for all concerned. The acting is quite good, if with rather passing attempts at local accents by some prominent members of the cast.

Duck Soup ☉
1933, US, 68 mins, b/w
Dir: Leo McCarey

Stars: Groucho Marx, Harpo Marx, Chico Marx, Zeppo Marx, Margaret Dumont, Louis Calhern
Rating: ★★★★

A Marx Brothers classic in which Groucho plays Rufus T Firefly and asks Margaret Dumont for a lock of her hair, adding: 'I'm letting you off lightly – I was going to ask for the whole wig.' Groucho (he plays the president of the postage-stamp republic of Freedonia) also has a miraculous scene in which Harpo plays his mirror image. Instead of feeling to see if the mirror were there – the obvious step Groucho tries to outwit Harpo by making sudden movements, in a sequence which becomes a memorable example of the Marxes' comic invention.

Duck, You Sucker
See: A Fistful of Dynamite

Duel ○ Ⓥ
1971, US, 91 mins, colour
Dir: Steven Spielberg
Stars: Dennis Weaver
Rating: ★★★★

Originally made for television, this classic chase-and-suspense thriller was the first film to be directed by Steven Spielberg. The prolific Dennis Weaver gives one of his very best performances as a driver who is at first harried and eventually terrified by a huge truck, the face of whose driver he cannot see. Spielberg maintains the whole nightmare situation at fever pitch.

Duel at Diablo ◑
1965, US, 103 mins, colour
Dir: Ralph Nelson
Stars: James Garner, Sidney Poitier, Bibi Andersson, Dennis Weaver, Bill Travers
Rating: ★★★★

Cavalry-and-Indians Westerns were thin on the ground in the Sixties and this one must have come as an oasis of red meat and strong drink to fans of the genre. James Garner is much more effective here, as a memory-haunted squaw-widower, than in his lighter roles. Even so, he is unable to prevent Sidney Poitier from running away with the film as a sharp-dressing horse-breaker. The beginning is fine, with bold helicopter work over two lone figures in scrub country, and Ralph Nelson's direction keeps things going at a remorselessly good clip. The action itself is blood-and-thunder at its best. Seldom can arrows have thudded more convincingly into their victims. The picture is rounded off by

D

Neal Hefti's unusual, stirring music, really just a series of chords strung together, but haunting in its way.

Duel In the Jungle ○
1954, UK, 101 mins, colour
Dir: George Marshall
Stars: Dana Andrews, Jeanne Crain, David Farrar
Rating: ★★

On safari in darkest Africa, gorgeous Jeanne Crain, in spite of the help of Dana Andrews, has a pretty tough time trying to escape the clutches of treacherous David Farrar. Much publicised at the time of making – Miss Crain's 'diary' was serialised in the magazine *Picturegoer* – but the excitement that seemed inherent in the script never quite comes across.

Duel in the Sun ○ ⓥ
1946, US, 130 mins, colour
Dir: King Vidor
Stars: Jennifer Jones, Gregory Peck, Joseph Cotten, Lionel Barrymore, Lillian Gish, Walter Huston
Rating: ★★

David O Selznick spent almost $5 million on this epic Western (starring his wife Jennifer Jones as a half-breed spitfire called Pearl), more than his outlay for *Gone With the Wind*. But the controversy the film aroused – US religious organisations protested about the lack of morals and the amount of blood spilled – ensured it of box-office if not critical success. Stars Jones, Gregory Peck and Joseph Cotten (untypically cast as bad and good brothers respectively) are backed by Lillian Gish, Walter Huston, Lionel Barrymore, Herbert Marshall, Otto Kruger and Charles Bickford.

Duellists, The ● ⓥ
1977, UK, 101 mins, colour
Dir: Ridley Scott
Stars: Keith Carradine, Harvey Keitel, Cristina Raines, Edward Fox, Robert Stephens, Albert Finney
Rating: ★★

A tragi-comedy about the hate-love-hate relationship between two French officers in Napoleonic times, one of whom persists in fighting duels with the other over some obscure quarrel for the best part of 20 years. It's almost a 'ripping yarn', and director, Ridley Scott, of *Alien* fame, seems not to know quite what to do with it, except to make it almost absurdly beautiful, as if he had decided to settle for a bid for the best photography Oscar and let the theme of the story

settle its own course. As a result, the duel scenes are quite dwarfed by the (sometimes bleak) beauty of the landscapes. A decided oddity.

Duffy ○
1968, US/UK, 101 mins, colour
Dir: Robert Parrish
Stars: James Coburn, James Mason, Susannah York, James Fox
Rating: ★★

Caper film in which twist piles on twist as four eccentric adventurers plan to relieve a millionaire of his money. John Alderton shines in a supporting role. And the plot has a strong twist to its tail. But still, it's oddly arid.

Dulcimer Street
See: London Belongs to Me

Dumb & Dumber ● ⓥ
1994, US, 106 mins, colour
Dir: Peter Farrelly
Stars: Jim Carrey, Jeff Daniels, Lauren Holly, Teri Garr, Charles Rocket
Rating: ★★

Third major outing for the charismatic Jim Carrey casts him as Lloyd Christmas, a Jerry Lewis-type dimwit with a dream – to open his own worm farm and call it 'I Got Worms'. One day, Lloyd finds a briefcase and persuades his equally thick pal Harry (Jeff Daniels) to head to Colorado and return the case to its rightful and beautiful owner Mary (Lauren Holly). But being dumb – and Harry being even dumber – the pair don't realise that the case contains ransom money to release Mary's kidnapped husband. So, all along the road to Colorado, the unsuspecting pair, in dog-trainer Harry's flea-infested van, the outside of which looks like a sheepdog, is pursued both by kidnappers and cops. It's a lowbrow comedy of many amusing moments rather than consistent rib-tickling fun, and strongly tailored to Carrey's particular clowning talents. Disappointing compared to Carrey's previous efforts in *Ace Ventura* and *The Mask*, but a huge hit with the public.

Dumbo ⊙ ⓥ
1941, US, 64 mins, colour
Dir: Ben Sharpsteen
Rating: ★★★★★

Brief but memorable Walt Disney feature cartoon about the little circus elephant whose ears were so big that he could fly. Full of vivid, colourful animation and memorable characters, including some wonderful crows. The

score includes the Oscar-nominated 'Baby Mine' as well as 'Pink Elephants on Parade' (the centre of an imaginative nightmare sequence) and (sung by the crows) 'When I See an Elephant Fly'.

Dune ● ⓥ
1984, US, 140 mins, colour
Dir: David Lynch
Stars: Francesca Annis, Brad Dourif, Kyle MacLachlan, Sian Phillips, Sting, Max von Sydow
Rating: ★★

A triumph of visual imagination, but a mishmash of storytelling, *Dune*, from the marvellous Frank Herbert novel, is cast in bold strokes. As might be expected from the director David Lynch, the monstrosities are amazing (especially the sandworms, and the Supreme Being, a cross between a giant millipede and a maggot), and dwelt upon with some relish. But you'll need your thinking caps on to follow the plot, and even who is doing what to whom. As for the opening narration by Virginia Madsen, as the princess, which is meant to explain it all, it makes less sense than a tongue-twisting monologue.

Dunkirk ○
1958, UK, 135 mins, b/w
Dir: Leslie Norman
Stars: John Mills, Richard Attenborough, Bernard Lee, Robert Urquhart
Rating: ★★

One of the last films from Ealing Studios: a graphic reconstruction of the famous Allied retreat from the advancing Nazis in 1940. It was also one of the most expensive films Ealing had ever made, and it certainly has its excitement, while failing, apart from the beach evacuation, to provide anything that one hadn't seen before. There's the procession of refugees, the officer who sacrifices himself for the men, the wounded soldier who has to be left behind by his comrades: familiar types and situations all. Extremely well and carefully made in every detail. Of the actors, however, only Bernard Lee really gets his character to spring to life, in a highly sympathetic performance.

Dust Be My Destiny ○
1939, US, 88 mins, b/w
Dir: Lewis Seiler
Stars: John Garfield, Priscilla Lane, Alan Hale, Frank McHugh
Rating: ★★★

Good-looking John Garfield was on familiar ground in this story of an ex-prisoner working on a farm and suspected of murdering the mean-minded boss. Here, he gives a punchy, convincing performance. Pretty Priscilla Lane, as the boss's daughter, is miscast, but there are some fine character performances from Alan Hale as a truth-seeking newspaper editor, Charley Grapewin (best-known for his Grandpa Joad in *The Grapes of Wrath* in 1940) as a sympathetic brakeman, and Moroni Olsen as an idealistic defence attorney. Although the film was among director Lewis Seiler's most profitable, it's a shame that the script did not quite do justice to the fine cast.

Dying Young ① ⓥ

1991, US, 111 mins, colour
Dir: Joel Schumacher
Stars: Julia Roberts, Campbell Scott, Vincent D'Onofrio, Colleen Dewhurst, Ellen Burstyn
Rating: ★

Without Julia Roberts as star, there isn't much doubt that this maudlin tearjerker would have died in its infancy at the box-office. There's not much even the 'Pretty Woman' can do with this unconvincing tale of a leukemia victim who hires the least qualified of the applicants as his nurse just because she's attractive. There's a lot of tealeaf-gazing thereafter by one of the characters but you don't need a crystal ball to guess the (few) subsequent developments of a film that gets more embarrassing and tedious by the minute. Director Joel Schumacher piles on the agony until it's so over the top you have to laugh. Julia gives her all, but the dialogue and general approach is too much. Opposite her, Campbell Scott has so little light and shade in his performance that he might have walked off the set of *Thunderbirds*. We all like a good cry but this is ridiculous.

Dynamite Man from Glory Jail ○

(aka: Fools' Parade)
1971, US, 95 mins, colour
Dir: Andrew V McLaglen
Stars: James Stewart, Anne Baxter, George Kennedy, Kurt Russell
Rating: ★★★

This differs from other Andrew McLaglen-directed Westerns in that it's set in 1935. Yet it still manages to retain more of the elements of a Western than those of a thriller.

Mattie Appleyard, the grizzled ex-convict determined to claim his $25,000 prison savings against all the odds (the money is in the bank of the town that just outlawed him), is a part tailor-made for the sincerity and quiet heroism that James Stewart projected so well throughout his career. In many ways, the character he created, with variations, in several Frank Capra films, comes to terms with Seventies cinema in *Dynamite Man* – bloody but unbowed.

Each Dawn I Die ○ ⓥ

1939, US, 85 mins, b/w
Dir: William Keighley
Stars: James Cagney, George Raft, Jane Bryan, George Bancroft, Victor Jory
Rating: ★★★★

Hard-hitting, if progressively less likely Warners prison drama, which gave James Cagney plenty of acting opportunities as the reporter framed for manslaughter when he gets too close to the crooked activities of the district attorney – played with splendidly sinister scowl by Victor Jory. Inside prison walls, Cagney soon gains the support of kingpin hoodlum George Raft by proving he's an okay guy and from then on the plot moves predictably if always entertainingly to its action-packed conclusion. Grumpy-looking John Wray also deserves a mention, as the meanest guard in the prison.

Eagle Has Landed, The ① ⓥ

1976, UK, 117 mins, colour
Dir: John Sturges
Stars: Michael Caine, Donald Sutherland, Robert Duvall, Jenny Agutter, Donald Pleasence, Anthony Quayle
Rating: ★★

Tom Mankiewicz's spotty adaptation of Jack Higgins' best-selling novel lands somewhere between *Where Eagles Dare* and *The Dirty Dozen*, except that the protagonists are a group of Nazi infiltrators bent on kidnapping Winston Churchill. The action sequences (although late in coming) are first-rate in the capable hands of director John Sturges. The two best performances – hardly surprising as the stars (Michael Caine, Donald Sutherland, Robert Duvall, Jenny Agutter) get the worst lines from Mankiewicz's variable script – come from Jean Marsh (as a German secret agent) and John Standing (as the parish priest).

Eagle's Wing ①

1978, UK, 111 mins, colour
Dir: Anthony Harvey
Stars: Martin Sheen, Sam Waterston, Harvey Keitel, Stephane Audran, Caroline Langrishe
Rating: ★★

A Western about endurance. Shot in Mexico by British director Anthony

E

Harvey the film carries a feeling of primitive times, accentuated by the burnished colour photography of Billy Williams. Martin Sheen and Sam Waterston are impressive as the principal protagonists, each striving to prove that there is nothing more likely to make an ultimate winner than a bad loser.

Earl Carroll Vanities O

1945, US, 91 mins, b/w
Dir: Joseph Santley
Stars: Dennis O'Keefe, Constance Moore, Eve Arden, Otto Kruger
Rating: ★★

A feather-brained musical, but lavish by Republic Studios' yardsticks, with some great music from Woody Herman and his boys and a hit song, 'Endlessly', sung here by Constance Moore, which was to become a standard. Eve Arden is on hand to make with the wisecracks against settings that, typical of Republic, have a faintly hand-me-down look.

Early Bird, The ⊙

1965, UK, 95 mins, colour
Dir: Robert Asher
Stars: Norman Wisdom, Edward Chapman, Jerry Desmonde
Rating: ★★

Norman Wisdom was hitting new depths with each film at the end of his film career with Rank, and here his tedious antics as a little milkman fighting against a big dairy just never get off the ground. The situations send telegrams in advance. The jokes are elaborately staged – and look it. The only original slapstick moment comes when Norman gets taken for a ride by a runaway power-mower.

Earth Girls Are Easy O ⓥ

1988, US, 100 mins, colour
Dir: Julien Temple
Stars: Geena Davis, Jeff Goldblum, Damon Wayans, Julie Brown, Jim Carrey, Michael McKean
Rating: ★★

This typically glitzy musical farce from Julien *Absolute Beginners* Temple is a throwback to the Sixties, when all blondes were bimbos and beach bunnies fawned around smirking surfers. Add a visit from a spacecraft and you have a sort of *Beach Blanket Alien*. For at least an hour the tackiness, although intentional, is just overwhelming. It does get a bit better towards the end, though, thanks largely to the sympathetic efforts of Jeff Goldblum (mysteriously billed fourth in the begin-

ning credits) and then-wife Geena Davis, a six-foot, liquid-lipped charmer who was already proving herself too good for this sort of thing.

Earthquake O

1974, US, 129 mins, colour
Dir: Mark Robson
Stars: Charlton Heston, Ava Gardner George Kennedy, Lorne Greene, Barry Sullivan, Richard Roundtree
Rating: ★★

One of the biggest disaster epics on record. It provides escapist entertainment on a vast scale with Los Angeles reduced to rubble as buildings sway, crack, totter and tumble and a giant dam threatens to crack and release billions of gallons of water into an already devastated countryside. Small wonder the brilliant visual effects by Frank Brendel, Albert Whitlock and Glen Robinson won one of the film's two Academy Awards. Watch for Walter Matthau's guest shot as a drunk; and marvel at Charlton Heston's skill and authority in a routine role, whether saving his wife from yet another suicide attempt or fearlessly risking death among the debris.

Easter Parade ⊙ ⓥ

1948, US, 110 mins, colour
Dir: Charles Walters
Stars: Judy Garland, Fred Astaire, Peter Lawford, Ann Miller, Jules Munshin
Rating: ★★★★

One of the most famous of all the celebrated MGM musicals, this was originally to have starred Gene Kelly. But Kelly had an accident that broke his ankle and Fred Astaire was persuaded to come out of early retirement and take over the role. It turned out to be a lucky 'break' for Fred as the result, which includes the famous 'drum' dance and the 'Couple of Swells' duet with Judy Garland, was one of his biggest ever hits.

East of Eden O ⓥ

1955, US, 115 mins, colour
Dir: Elia Kazan
Stars: Julie Harris, James Dean, Raymond Massey, Burt Ives
Rating: ★★★★

Based on the powerful, brooding novel by the late Nobel Prize-winning author John Steinbeck, this sombre and moving story of rivalry between two brothers provided the now legendary James Dean with his first major and still most highly regarded acting role. Jo Van Fleet, playing his mysterious mother, won an Oscar.

East of Piccadilly O

(aka: The Strangler)
1940, UK, 79 mins, b/w
Dir: Harold Huth
Stars: Sebastian Shaw, Judy Campbell, Niall MacGinnis
Rating: ★★

Or: the case of the nylon stocking murders. This wartime British thriller, a densely atmospheric murder mystery, comes with good writing credits. The script was co-written by bestselling authoress Lesley Storm, and by J Lee Thompson, later to become a distinguished director (of such films as *Tiger Bay*). Silent screen idol Henry Edwards has a supporting role.

East of Sudan O

1964, UK, 84 mins, colour
Dir: Nathan Juran
Stars: Anthony Quayle, Sylvia Syms, Jenny Agutter
Rating: ★

Adventure story set in the Sudan late last century, with Anthony Quayle as a forthright soldier of fortune trying to steer a party of battle survivors to safety and the cast often playing against filmed backgrounds. A 12-year-old Jenny Agutter plays a native girl. If you think you've seen some of the more spectacular scenes somewhere else, you re right. The 'extra' footage is from the 1939 version of *The Four Feathers*. Alas, despite the addition of such spectacle, the film itself never matches the excitement of its opening few scenes.

East of Sumatra O

1953, US, 85 mins, colour
Dir: Budd Boetticher
Stars: Jeff Chandler, Anthony Quinn, Suzan Ball, Marilyn Maxwell
Rating: ★★

It was while filming this action film, set on a Pacific island and about a mining engineer in conflict with the islanders, that the tragic Suzan Ball sustained the leg injury that was eventually to end her life aged 22. The director is Budd Boetticher, who has since become a cult figure, and the tense climax is a fight with machetes and flaming torches.

East Side, West Side O

1949, US, 108 mins, b/w
Dir: Mervyn LeRoy
Stars: Barbara Stanwyck, James Mason, Van Heflin, Ava Gardner
Rating: ★★

Glossy emotional drama, with a big star cast, and some interesting side slants on

American high society. Half-way through, the film belatedly develops into a fast-moving murder thriller. James Mason stars as a playboy whose world is the New York 'smart set'. He is torn between the attractions of his West Side mistress, Isabel, and his wife, Jessie, a pillar of the fashionable East Side. Fans of Ava Gardner should be warned that the lady gets bumped off quite early on. But there's a fierce and unusual fist-fight between Van Heflin and six-foot actress Beverly Michaels. And Oscar-winning actress Gale Sondergaard, in her last screen performance for a long while (a brush with the Un-American Activities Comunittee signalled an early end to that major career), icily dominates every scene in which she appears. Often too stodgy though.

Easy Living O
1937, US, 86 mins, b/w
Dir: Mitchell Leisen
Stars: Jean Arthur, Edward Arnold, Ray Milland, Luis Albemi
Rating: ★★★

This screwball romantic comedy wasn't much liked by some contemporary critics but now stands as a classic of the genre. With Preston Sturges scripting and Mitchell Leisen directing, the mood is one of elegant lunacy as a fur coat flung from a window changes Jean Arthur's life.

Easy Money O
1947, UK, 94 mins, b/w
Dir: Bernard Knowles
Stars: Jack Warner, Petula Clark, Dennis Price, Greta Gynt
Rating: ★★

The British became very fond of multiple story films in the Forties – *Dead of Night*, *The Wallet*, *Holiday Camp* and the Maugham complications all spring to mind – but the vogue was killed off rather quickly by the advent of half-hour stories on television. This one is about the effect on four people, from varying walks of life, of a massive win on the pools.

Easy Rider ● ⓥ
1969, US, 94 mins, colour
Dir: Dennis Hopper
Stars: Peter Fonda, Dennis Hopper, Jack Nicholson, Karen Black, Robert Walker, Luana Anders
Rating: ★★★★

The famous counter-culture action drama starring Peter Fonda, Dennis Hopper and Jack Nicholson and featuring a great rock soundtrack. Bikers Captain America and Billy score a co-

caine deal in LA and set off across the States to the Mardi Gras in New Orleans. Along the way they encounter hostility and bigotry, but they find a kindred spirit in disillusioned, alcoholic lawyer George Hanson when they share a night with him in jail ... Nicholson (Oscar nominated) shot to belated stardom as the lawyer and the film, although bleak and abrasive, will stay with you long after its final tragedies unfold.

Easy to Love O
1953, US, 95 mins, colour
Dir: Charles Walters
Stars: Esther Williams, Van Johnson, Tony Martin, John Bromfield
Rating: ★★★

Not much plot here – Esther Williams loves Van Johnson but he doesn't seem to notice her, so she has an affair with her swimming instructor, hoping Van will get jealous – but that shouldn't stop you enjoying this very tuneful (and colourful!) MGM musical. Esther is given plenty of opportunities to display her aquatic abilities and the musical numbers are spectacularly staged by veteran choreographer Busby Berkeley. The film's climax is the classic number involving dozens of motorboats towing dozens of skiers.

Easy to Wed O
1946, US, 110 mins, colour
Dir: Edward Buzzell
Stars: Van Johnson, Esther Williams, Lucille Ball, Keenan Wynn
Rating: ★★★

Lucille Ball and Keenan Wynn give show-stopping performances in this zany remake of the classic comedy *Libelled Lady*, with Esther Williams doing a minimum of swimming as the heiress who sues a newspaper for $2 million. Director Edward Buzzell was also responsible for a couple of Marx Brothers comedies.

Eating Raoul ❶
1982, US, 83 mins, colour
Dir: Paul Bartel
Stars: Paul Bartel, Mary Woronov, Robert Beltran
Rating: ★★★

A wild black comedy about a penurious couple who raise the money to buy a restaurant by murdering the perverts they lure into their house via the sex-ad columns. 'Do you think we could buy another frying pan?' the wife (Mary Woronov) asks her husband (Paul Bartel, who also directed the film). 'I'm getting a little squeamish about using

the one we use to kill people.' It's an uneven film (just not black enough perhaps) and its three leading players strangely all look like other people: Paul Bartel resembles British TV personality Clement Freud, Mary Woronov is like Sally Kellerman, and Robert Beltran (as Raoul) like Erik Estrada of *CHiPS* fame. Buck Henry comes on for a funny turn as a lascivious loan company manager called Leech.

Eat My Dust! O
1976, US, 90 mins, colour
Dir: Charles Griffith
Stars: Ron Howard, Christopher Norris
Rating: ★

Hang on tight for this scriptless dust-rouser about two youngsters with a passion for speed – which develops into one long car chase. Star Ron Howard, a former child player, has since turned director with success.

Echoes of a Summer O
1975, US, 98 mins, colour
Dir: Don Taylor
Stars: Richard Harris, Jodie Foster, Lois Nettleton
Rating: ★★

It must have been every actor's greatest dread in the Seventies to be cast in a film with Jodie Foster, then a precocious bundle of young talent. And imagine Jodie playing a girl with only a short time to live. Well, that's just what she does in this beautifully photographed weepie. She makes all her adult co-stars seem shallow by her mature understanding of the role and consequent understated performance which goes a long way towards taking the stickiness out of the sentiment.

Eddie ❶ ⓥ
1996, US, 101 mins, colour
Dir: Steve Rash
Stars: Whoopi Goldberg, Frank Langella, Dennis Farina, Richard Jenkins, Lisa Ann Walker
Rating: ★

Another 'dreams come true' sports movie, relying heavily on Whoopi Goldberg to get it through the hoop. She's Eddie, a basketball-mad fan of the New York Knicks who, by fluke and coincidence, finds herself the team's coach. We've been here before, of course, with Goldie Hawn in *Wildcats* and others, but the expected giggles and the adrenalin surge when the team finally comes good are in extremely short supply here, no thanks to Steve Rash's jerky direction and a faceless script that needed more pezazz.

E

Whoopi as always gives it her best shot, but she needs a more naturally sympathetic character than she's got here to soar to victory.

Eddie Cantor Story, The ○
1953, US, 116 mins, colour
Dir: Alfred E Green
Stars: Keefe Brasselle, Marilyn Erskine, Aline MacMahon, Will Rogers Jr
Rating: ★★

Despite having the same director (Alfred E Green) as *The Jolson Story*, this similar biopic on another of America's best-loved entertainers was nowhere near as successful with the public. If Keefe Brasselle's Cantor doesn't quite have the warmth of personality that Larry Parks brought to Jolson, the production is on a similar lavish scale and the famous Cantor songs and routines are present in strength. The script, though, is totally lacking in flair.

Eddy Duchin Story, The ○
1956, US, 123 mins, colour
Dir: George Sidney
Stars: Tyrone Power, Kim Novak, Victoria Shaw, James Whitmore, Rex Thompson
Rating: ★★★

A musical tearbath about the triumph-and-tragedy life of American pianist Eddy Duchin. The film was a great personal success for Tyrone Power, whose fingering to the playing of Carmen Cavallaro is first-rate. The film is a little too over-emotional to make the topmost bracket, but Kim Novak acts with a very sure touch as Duchin's wife, and Australian actress Victoria Shaw, schoolgirl-awkward in ordinary scenes, is surprisingly powerful in the dramatic ones. James Whitmore provides solid support.

Edge of Darkness ○
1943, US, 124 mins, b/w
Dir: Lewis Milestone
Stars: Errol Flynn, Ann Sheridan, Walter Huston, Judith Anderson, Helmut Dantine, Ruth Gordon
Rating: ★★★

Pretty downbeat for a Hollywood war film of 1943, this story of the resistance in Norway has a subdued and credible performance from Errol Flynn, even if his star presence in some ways hampers the film. With an opening uncannily reminiscent of *Beau Geste*, the movie carries remarkable intensity at times.

Edge of Doom ○
(aka: Stronger than Fear)
1950, US, 99 mins, b/w
Dir: Mark Robson
Stars: Dana Andrews, Farley Granger, Joan Evans, Robert Keith
Rating: ★★

Adapted from Catholic author Leo Brady's prizewinning novel, this sombre and over-pious film examines the perverted thinking of a tormented youth nagged by the problems of poverty and a sense of guilt over the death of his pious mother. The consequences make for a powerful murder story with religious and psychological overtones. The darkly handsome Farley Granger broods convincingly as the mixed-up kid and gaunt Robert Keith scores as a detective out to trap a killer.

Edge of Eternity ○
1959, US, 80 mins, colour
Dir: Don Siegel
Stars: Cornel Wilde, Victoria Shaw, Edgar Buchanan, Mickey Shaughnessy, Jack Elam
Rating: ★★

Don Siegel, who went on to make *Dirty Harry*, was already making colour crime thrillers like *Edge of Eternity* on location before most people had started to think about it. The location in this case is awesome – in and around the Grand Canyon – and Siegel uses it spectacularly in the climactic fist-fight, which takes place in a mining bucket hundreds of feet above ground level. Cornel Wilde has the Clint Eastwood-type role as the tough-talking sheriff out to solve the case.

Edge of the City ○
(aka: A Man Is Ten Feet Tall)
1957, US, 85 mins, b/w
Dir: Martin Ritt
Stars: John Cassavetes, Sidney Poitier, Jack Warden, Kathleen Maguire
Rating: ★★★★

Edge of the City was a landmark film in the careers of stars John Cassavetes and Sidney Poitier and director Martin Ritt. A punchy, dramatic *On the Waterfront*-style exposé of both American union racketeering and working-class racial prejudice in the mid-Fifties, the film has a towering performance by Poitier, and others that fit the story like gloves. If you've seen this moralising kind of film before – excellent though this example is – you'll be able to predict the finish easily enough. But it still makes mighty powerful entertainment. The only thing that seems dated is the intrusive background score.

Edison, The Man ○
1940, US, 107 mins, b/w
Dir: Clarence Brown
Stars: Spencer Tracy, Rita Johnson, Lynne Overman, Charles Coburn
Rating: ★★★

Solid, worthy follow-up to *Young Tom Edison*. Spencer Tracy is ideal as the adult Edison, and Rita Johnson, an actress who seldom got the breaks she deserved, enjoys her finest film hour as his wife – even though a temptation to alter the facts to suit the drama isn't always resisted.

Educating Rita ① Ⓥ
1983, UK, 110 mins, colour
Dir: Lewis Gilbert
Stars: Michael Caine, Julie Walters, Michael Williams, Maureen Lipman
Rating: ★★★★

As a lower-class British housewife hungering for an education, Julie Walters launched herself into the acting limelight, winning the Best Actress BAFTA Award and a Golden Globe in this surprisingly winning film version of Willy Russell's stage play. The story concerns a 26-year-old peroxide-blonde hairdresser who gets a drunken Oxford don for a tutor when she comes to open university to better herself. Michael Caine as the don also won a BAFTA award, although the film almost loses its way in his character's disillusionment, not only with life, but with the 'new woman' he seems to have created. In the end, the story reasserts itself, thanks to a climax that's just right without being overtly happy and to extremely attractive performances by the two stars in virtually the only roles of any stature in the whole film.

Edward My Son ○
1949, UK, 112 mins, b/w
Dir: George Cukor
Stars: Spencer Tracy, Deborah Kerr, Ian Hunter, James Donald
Rating: ★★★

Towering performances from the stars in the drama of a man who is spurred by the birth of his son to elevate himself from obscurity to peerage, losing all his friends along the way. Based on the hit play by Robert Morley and Noel Langley, in which the son never actually appears, this was MGM's first production in Britain after World War II. The great George Cukor was brought from Hollywood to direct, and Deborah Kerr came back to star as the wife, two years after leaving England for America.

Edward Scissorhands ◐ Ⓥ

1990, US, 107 mins, colour
Dir: Tim Burton
Stars: Johnny Depp, Winona Ryder,
Dianne Wiest, Kathy Baker, Vincent
Price, Alan Arkin
Rating: ★★★

Director Tim Burton, of *Batman* and
Beetlejuice fame, is obviously destined to
become a master of the dark fairytale.
Once upon a time … there was an
everyday American town, with a
spooky hilltop castle just around the
corner. There lived Vincent Price,
alias The Inventor, and he made a
man, Edward (Johnny Depp), but died
before his creation could be completed,
leaving the hapless Edward with long
scissor blades for hands. Burton's film
takes up the story when Edward is discovered by the local Avon lady
(Dianne Wiest), falls in love with her
daughter (Winona Ryder) and becomes the rage of the neighbourhood.
Edward snips and snaps away happily,
creating horrendous haircuts, grotesque
gardens and brighter, better poodles.
Ere long, alas, with the inevitability of
all good fairytales, Edward's hands
(with which he can also unpick locks)
get him into trouble. An enormous
amount of vision and invention (not to
mention expense) has gone into the
staging of this story; and, if it hasn't
quite the stature to measure up to the
likes of Frankenstein, Depp is every
inch the pitiable creature at the mercy
of how his dead creator has left him.

Ed Wood ◐ Ⓥ

1994, US, 124 mins, b/w
Dir: Tim Burton
Stars: Johnny Depp, Patricia Arquette,
Martin Landau, Sarah Jessica Parker,
Jeffrey Jones, Bill Murray
Rating: ★★★★

Most major studios refused to back this
hilarious film about one of
Hollywood's worst-ever directors. It
wasn't the fact that Ed Wood Jr, responsible for such truly terrible films as
Glen or Glenda? and *Plan 9 from Outer
Space*, was a cross-dresser who loved to
wear angora sweaters on set. It was because director Tim Burton wanted to
shoot it in black and white. He stuck
to his guns and the results fully vindi-
cate his stand, adding period feel to the
sweet-tempered biopic. Johnny Depp
delivers one of his finest and most in-
depth performances as Wood, a
director who shot most of his epics in a
matter of days on home movie budgets
and with casts of Hollywood misfits.
These characters are where Burton's

elaborate tribute is at its strongest.
Martin Landau is astonishing (rightly
winning a clutch of best supporting
actor awards) as horror king Bela
Lugosi, addicted in old age to mor-
phine and living in squalor. All in all,
an offbeat film that, instead of revelling
in a life of abject failure, desperation
and trashiness, celebrates it with great
visual style and panache.

Egg and I, The ☉

1947, US, 104 mins, b/w
Dir: Chester Erskine
Stars: Claudette Colbert, Fred
MacMurray, Marjorie Main, Percy Kilbride
Rating: ★★★

A sunny, funny fizz-bang comedy.
Claudette Colbert and Fred
MacMurray work well together as
newly-weds up to their necks in trouble
on a poultry farm, but the film is more
memorable for introducing Ma and Pa
Kettle (Majorie Main and Percy
Kilbride), a pair of raucous rurals who
went on to feature in nine spin-off films.

Egyptian, The ○

1954, US, 139 mins, colour
Dir: Michael Curtiz
Stars: Edmund Purdom, Jean Simmons,
Michael Wilding, Victor Mature, Gene
Tierney, Peter Ustinov
Rating: ★★

Michael Curtiz's superb control of the
crowd scenes, and Leon Shamroy's
breathtaking colour photography, ensure that the spectacle saves this
Hollywood slice of ancient history.
Edmund Purdom takes the title role,
and Peter Ustinov is excellent as
Kaptah, his rascally servant. The story
– set in Thebes, 1300 BC – tells of two
men, a medical student called Sinuhe
(played well by Purdom, despite some
overlong speeches) and a low-born military cadet, Horemheb (played in let's
rip-up-the-scenery fashion by Victor
Mature – his best line is 'More wine,
you waddling toad!') and their adventures after they rescue the Pharaoh of
Egypt from a lion. The cast is mightier
than the film.

Eiger Sanction, The ◐ Ⓥ

1975, US, 125 mins, colour
Dir: Clint Eastwood
Stars: Clint Eastwood, George Kennedy,
Vonetta McGee
Rating: ★

Lovers of mountain climbing are in
for a rare treat here, for the story is
about an assassin who has to carry out
his mission on one of three climbers
with whom he shares an expedition to

the perilous north face of the Eiger
mountain in Switzerland. Lovers of
the thriller are not in for such a good
deal, as the story takes a long and slippery road up to the obvious
conclusion. Clint Eastwood provides
the star power (and direction); rare
acting quality comes from Jack
Cassidy as a gay, treacherous spy.
Another Alpine disaster.

18 Again! ○ Ⓥ

1988, US, 100 mins, colour
Dir: Paul Flaherty
Stars: George Burns, Charlie Schlatter,
Jennifer Runyon, Tony Roberts
Rating: ★★

Yet another rejuvenation comedy, but
a pretty affable one at that, with young
Charlie Schlatter doing a very good impression of how George Burns would
have been at 18. when he and the cigar-
puffing old reprobate switch bodies
during a car crash. Since the title is the
reversal of numerals on a birthday cake
and Burns was actually 91 or so at the
time, maybe *19 Again* would have been
a more appropriate title! But that
would have taken our hero beyond the
age of high school, where all the fun
takes place. Burns himself gets the
rough end of the deal with some smut-
tily shoddy lines, while young Schlatter
laps up the best of the situations, sway-
ing, smiling and stooping in the best
Burns fashion as he outwits enemies
who have previously flattened him
mentally and physically. Though the
film doesn't escape embarrassment,
there are some good performances
around here, notably from Schlatter,
Tony Roberts as his downtrodden dad
and Anthony Starke as the class bully.
Generically speaking, the son who's
about a foot shorter than his father
seems about as likely as *18 Again!* itself.

Eight Iron Men ○

1952, US, 80 mins, b/w
Dir: Edward Dmytryk
Stars: Bonar Colleano, Lee Marvin,
Arthur Franz, Richard Kiley
Rating: ★★★

The credentials of this war film are as
high as they come: the producer is
Stanley Kramer and the director
Edward Dmytryk. It's about an eight-
man squad, trapped in a ruined house
by enemy machine-gun fire. Outside,
another of their number lies pinned
down in a shell-hole. Tension predictably rises rapidly between the men.
Bonar Colleano makes a splendid job
of his one and only Hollywood role, as
the cocky Collucci, and his characteri-

E

sation dominates the film. His dreams of a pin-up girl (Mary Castle) provide refreshing breaks of charm and humour in the sombre if exciting tale.

Eight Men Out ◑ ⓥ
1988, US, 120 mins, colour
Dir: John Sayles
Stars: John Cusack, John Mahoney, Charlie Sheen, D B Sweeney, Christopher Lloyd, David Strathairn
Rating: ★★

Although painstakingly reconstructed by writer-director John Sayles, this ends up as a dullish depiction of baseball's biggest scandal – the 'fix' of the World Series by the Chicago White Sox in 1919. Underpaid by their money-grabbing owner, who welshed on every promise, the ringleaders were easy prey for the gamblers and mobsters who brought financial incentive to bear, then proved just as unreliable as the players' bosses when it came to paying up. Some good actors, notably John Cusack, D B Sweeney, Charlie Sheen, David Strathairn and Michael Lerner, as crime kingpin Arnold Rothstein, couldn't be bettered. But Sayles' treatment is far too slow. The period is observed to the last detail, although the dialogue ('Way to go, Joe!') strikes a few anachronistic notes.

Eight O'Clock Walk ○
1953, UK, 87 mins, b/w
Dir: Lance Comfort
Stars: Richard Attenborough, Cathy O'Donnell, Derek Farr
Rating: ★★

Almost a reprise for Richard Attenborough of his role in *London Belongs to Me*. Again he's a working-class lad involved in the murder of a girl, and again he faces the gallows. Attenborough tries to look harassed, but he's been through it all before. Cathy O'Donnell is very sympathetic as his young wife and Derek Farr and Ian Hunter ooze authority as rival counsels on the case.

Eight on the Run ○
(aka: Eight on the Lam)
1967, US, 106 mins, colour
Dir: George Marshall
Stars: Bob Hope, Shirley Eaton, Jill St John, Phyllis Diller
Rating: ★★

This spasmodically funny comedy about a widower with seven children (and a very large dog) marked something of a return to form for its star after such early-Sixties disasters as *A Global Affair* and *I'll Take Sweden*.

Veteran director George Marshall – who had directed Hope seven times before – maintains a frenzied pace.

84 Charing Cross Road ○ ⓥ
1986, US, 97 mins, colour
Dir: David Jones
Stars: Anne Bancroft, Anthony Hopkins, Judi Dench, Mercedes Ruehl
Rating: ★★★

An unusual and delightful film, *84 Charing Cross Road* gave Anne Bancroft one of her most memorable roles. She plays Helene Hanff, a New York book collector and Anglophile. She starts up a correspondence with Frank Doel (Anthony Hopkins), who works in an antiquarian bookshop in London. The film, based on a true story, spans 20 years of their written friendship. Despite the closeness generated by their letters the two never met, which, perhaps, is the ultimate sadness of the film. Hopkins plays the undemonstrative Doel with his usual understated skill, but has to take second place to Bancroft. Beautifully constructed, this gentle but absorbing drama shows its theatrical origins and does at times seem a little static, but still, it's a joy to watch.

80,000 Suspects ○
1963, UK, 113 mins, b/w
Dir: Val Guest
Stars: Richard Johnson, Claire Bloom, Cyril Cusack
Rating: ★★★

Thriller about an epidemic which threatens to sweep across a big city. Yolande Donlan, wife of the film's director, Val Guest, has a key role in the story and she's very good.

El Cid ○ ⓥ
1962, US, 184 mins, colour
Dir: Anthony Mann
Stars: Charlton Heston, Sophia Loren, John Fraser, Raf Vallone
Rating: ★★★★

You'll be impressed by the sweep and grandeur of this dignified epic, inevitably with Charlton Heston as the legendary 'lord' of 11th century Spain who, after being exiled from the Spanish courts, leads his followers to rid the country of the Moors, before riding into history. It's in the quieter moments – times of passion and tragedy – that *El Cid* is at its best and here Heston and Sophia Loren, giving a superb, warmly real performance as his wife, register really well as heroic characters. Fitting nicely into supporting roles are Raf Vallone, John Fraser,

Herbert Lom and Gary Raymond, although Genevieve Page is rather a weak link as a heartless queen. The photography is superb and only the muddled quality of the battle scenes keeps this from the top rank of first-rate epics of the screen.

El Condor ◑
1970, US, 102 mins, colour
Dir: John Guillermin
Stars: Jim Brown, Lee Van Cleef
Rating: ★★

Slow Western set against some mightily imposing scenery. Heroes Jim Brown and Lee Van Cleef, both after a fortune in gold hidden in a far-off fortress, were hot in films at the time though, like the spaghetti Western this resembles, not for long. One critic remarked that leading lady Mariana Hill looked good even with her clothes on, which is sexist, but especially apt: she never gave a more striking performance.

El Dorado ○
1967, US, 127 mins, colour
Dir: Howard Hawks
Stars: John Wayne, Robert Mitchum, James Caan, Arthur Hunnicutt, Ed Asner
Rating: ★★★★

Action abounds in this colourful Western whose characters are happily two sizes larger than life. The film is uproarious, lively and has character, swagger and style. Shoot-outs occur at regular intervals, and for no special reason, although one particular gun battle in a chapel is worth anyone's money. Stitched into the mayhem is a series of running gags guaranteed to break down the fiercest anti-Western resistance. Great stuff from director Howard Hawks.

Electric Dreams ○ ⓥ
1984, US, 97 mins, colour
Dir: Steve Barron
Stars: Lenny Von Dohlen, Virginia Madsen, Maxwell Caulfield, Bud Cort
Rating: ★★★

The story of the computer that develops human tendencies and tries to dominate its master is by now a familiar one and usually has a tragic ending. But, since this is a musical, or at least nearly one, it's a sure bet that the ending will be (literally) on an upbeat note – and, in this case, a good thing too. Lenny Van Dohlen is Miles, a bespectacled architect who buys a computer to wake him up in the morning and finds it does a lot more besides, apart from, through an initial mistype, calling him Moles. He falls in love with the

Emperor Waltz, The O

1948, US, 106 mins, colour
Dir: Billy Wilder
Stars: Bing Crosby, Joan Fontaine,
Roland Culver
Rating: ★★

Quite what the most abrasive of black
comedy directors, Billy Wilder, was
doing making the more romantic type
of Bing Crosby musical is one of the
mysteries of the age. Although Victor
Young's background music was nominated for an Academy Award, this
frothy Viennese frippery, revolving
around a phonograph salesman of
1901, remains a strange choice for
Crosby, Wilder, Joan Fontaine and all
concerned. Brutal fights; wonderful on
location photography by Joseph Biroc.

Empire of the Ants ●

1977, US, 90 mins, colour
Dir: Bert I Gordon
Stars: Joan Collins, Robert Lansing
Rating: ★

It's Joan Collins – no mean maneater
herself on the screen – versus a colony
of giant ants in this science-fiction
thriller. It's based (rather remotely) on
the famous H G Wells story. A good
laugh.

Empire of the Sun ◐ Ⓥ

1987, US, 152 mins, colour
Dir: Steven Spielberg
Stars: Christian Bale, John Malkovich,
Miranda Richardson, Nigel Havers, Joe
Pantoliano, Leslie Phillips
Rating: ★★★

Steven Spielberg sometimes appears obsessed with telling his stories from a
child's point of view. Here it's newcomer Christian Bale as an 11-year-old
boy separated from his parents and
having to survive an internment camp
after the Japanese invade China during
World War Two. There's no denying
the power of the amazing set pieces (especially the evacuation of Shanghai) in
this adaptation of the epic J G Ballard
novel, but on a human level, the film is
less happy. John Malkovich's opportunistic *King Rat* type threatens to
become a fully developed character but
never follows through. There's a
strong British contingent – including
Paul McGann in an early role – but it's
Bale who takes most of the attention.
His flight through swamp scrub outside
the prison camp in which he spends
most of his time is one of the film's few
highlights.

Empire State ● Ⓥ

1987, UK, 104 mins, colour
Dir: Ron Peck
Stars: Ian Sears, Emily Bolton, Ray
McAnally, Cathryn Harrison, Martin
Landau
Rating: ★

Reminiscent of a British exploitation
film of 20 years earlier – dozens of characters, strobe lighting and a pop
soundtrack, all in search of a plot.
Pretty well every element an adult certificate could encompass is here – but no
comprehensible narrative. Something
seems to be going on at the Empire
State, a gleaming nightclub with dolly
hostesses upstairs and a gay bar downstairs – though we never really find out
what. Still, the film has style and energy
in its fruitless search for content and
charismatic performances from Ray
McAnally as the State's proprietor and
Lee Drysdale as a crisp young rent boy
on the make. A bareknuckle fight at the
end, though, is unforgivably violent.

Empire Strikes Back, The O Ⓥ

1980, US, 124 mins, colour
Dir: Irvin Kershner
Stars: Harrison Ford, Mark Hamill, Carrie
Fisher, Billy Dee Williams, Alec Guinness
Rating: ★★★

Second in the *Star Wars* trilogy. A masterpiece of special effects, it punctuates
a tortuous storyline with bursts of swift
and violent action. Mark Hamill, looking as though he really believed in it
all, is back as Luke Skywalker, and romance blossoms between Leia (Carrie
Fisher) and Han Solo (Harrison Ford).
Although the awesome ice-planet Hoth
is put to insufficient use, the swamp
planet, with its weird little maharishi-
type inhabitant (courtesy of
Muppet-maker Frank Oz), makes up
for it with fronds, gloom, mists and
hidden horrors, all beautifully keyed in
brown, green and grey.

Enchanted April O Ⓥ

1991, UK, 99 mins, colour
Dir: Mike Newell
Stars: Miranda Richardson, Joan
Plowright, Josie Lawrence, Michael
Kitchen, Jim Broadbent, Alfred Molina
Rating: ★★

An archetypal British made-for-televi-
sion movie – high on period detail and
genteel to a point that makes one long
for something really dramatic to happen
and interrupt the almost incessant dialogue. Not that Peter (*The Ruling Class*)
Barnes' dialogue is bad. Much of it has
the air of a pretty good parody of the

kind of Edwardian play that delighted
middle-class matinees – polished, safe
and, above all, not too witty. The performances, too, are exactly what one
would expect, with the honours going
to Jim Broadbent's not-quite-as-boring-
as-he-seems husband. It's always a
pleasure to see Joan Plowright deliver
yet another variation on her now beautifully polished Beryl Reid impression
(this one won her an Oscar nomination); and Polly Walker is right on
target with her cool society vamp.

Enchanted Cottage, The O

1945, US, 92 mins, b/w
Dir: John Cromwell
Stars: Dorothy McGuire, Robert Young
Rating: ★★

Robert Young plays a disfigured and
embittered World War One veteran
and Dorothy McGuire is the plain girl
with whom he finds true love in this incurably romantic story. They move
into a secluded cottage which has been
the venue for dozens of honeymooners,
all of whom have found happiness. A
small miracle happens: Young's disfigurement disappears and McGuire
becomes a beautiful young woman ...
Despite a fine script from De Witt
Bodeen and Herman J Mankiewicz and
intelligent direction from John
Cromwell, this looks a good deal less
impressive today than when it first appeared, with very mannered acting and
developments that, even given 'fantastic' licence, just aren't believable. Still,
its heart is in the right place and it does
offer sentiment without sentimentality.

Enchantment O

1948, US, 101 mins, b/w
Dir: Irving Reis
Stars: David Niven, Teresa Wright,
Farley Granger
Rating: ★★★

An unashamedly romantic story about
a stately London house and the. people
who live – or have lived – in it. A typically lavish Sam Goldwyn production,
it employs an interesting flashback
technique, and the camerawork is outstanding. The screenplay by John
Patrick and direction by the underrated
Irving Reis both skilfully add to the
film's effectiveness as a weepie of class
and charm.

Encino Man
See California Man

Encore O

1951, UK, 88 mins, b/w
Dir: Pat Jackson

E

Stars: Nigel Patrick, Roland Culver, Kay Walsh, Glynis Johns

Rating: ★★★

Dramatisations of three more Somerset Maugham stories, this time introduced by the author himself. This was chronologically the third and last of the popular British compilation films from Maugham's works. A splendid British cast does the drily effective tales full justice, with Kay Walsh especially delightful in one episode as a chatterbox spinster.

Enemies, A Love Story ●

1989, US, 120 mins, colour

Dir: Paul Mazursky

Stars: Ron Silver, Anjelica Huston, Lena Olin, Margaret Sophie Stein

Rating: ★★

No wonder Ron Silver wanders through this carnal, Jewish-slanted tragi-comedy looking dazed, like Zeppo in a Marx Brothers film. Three wives yet he has – all of them pursuing him, or going round the bend, or both. You can almost hear the man muttering to himself as he turns his collar up against the snow in some Bronx backstreet of 1949, where the cameraman always has a sepia filter over his lens. *Enemies* takes a bit of getting into, but it has some rare, ripe moments in its second half, especially when two of the wives meet. Silver seems numbed by it all, as well he might. Anjelica Huston, Lena Olin and Margaret Sophie Stein are all great as the women. The meal they serve up, is overlong, but it does have some tasty moments.

Enemy Below, The ○

1957, US, 98 mins, colour

Dir: Dick Powell

Stars: Robert Mitchum, Curt Jurgens, Theodore Bikel, David Hedison

Rating: ★★★

German actor Curt Jurgens made his first major mark on the international film scene in this surprisingly tough and tense World War Two submarine chase drama, directed by former film star Dick Powell. Jurgens and Robert Mitchum are a beautifully balanced match as the skippers who gradually come to respect each other, and Harold Rosson's Technicolor photography vividly captures the claustrophobic undersea tension.

Enemy from Space ●

See: Quatermass II

Enemy Mine ○ ⓥ

1985, US, 108 mins, colour

Dir: Wolfgang Petersen

Stars: Dennis Quaid, Louis Gossett Jr, Brion James

Rating: ★★★

Dennis Quaid and Louis Gossett Jr (the latter unrecognisable under mountains of latex) as earthman and alien creature forgetting their differences to survive an inhospitable planet together. Everything about this film is spectacularly larger than life; the video version has a bonus of an extra 15 minutes of footage cut from the version seen in British cinemas, adding several key quieter moments and making the ending more comprehensible.

Enforcer, The ○ ⓥ

(aka: Murder Inc)

1950, US, 87 mins, b/w

Dir: Bretaigne Windust

Stars: Humphrey Bogart, Zero Mostel, Ted De Corsia, Everett Stoane

Rating: ★★★★

One of the most gruelling of even Humphrey Bogart's gangster films. Faint-hearts should be warned that there are killings galore – murder by knife, by razor, by pick axe – all done with horrific but hypnotic realism. Gripping entertainment in semi-documentary style. The stars are backed by a host of good character studies, plus a script by Martin Rackin, and photography by Robert Burks, that add impact to the action.

Enforcer, The ● ⓥ

1976, US, 95 mins, colour

Dir: James Fargo

Stars: Clint Eastwood, Harry Guardino, Bradford Dillman, John Mitchum, Tyne Daly

Rating: ★★★

Clint Eastwood returns as unorthodox *Dirty* Harry Callahan, in trouble as usual with his superiors because of his methods that tend to succeed but leave a pile of corpses in his wake. Here, in a complex story by Sterling Silliphant and Dean Reisner, he ends up with a female partner, well played by Tyne Daly, alias Lacey of *Cagney and Lacey*. Plenty of vivid action from first-time director James Fargo, while Eastwood has the character down to a 'T' and there is excellent use of locations.

England Made Me ○

1972, UK, 100 mins, colour

Dir: Peter Duffell

Stars: Peter Finch, Michael York,

Hildegarde Neil, Michael Hordern

Rating: ★★★

Another of Peter Finch's towering performances, this time as a German industrialist, determined to preserve his mid-Thirties' empire at all costs. The costs may include marriage to the English girl (Hildegarde Neil, a shade too dispassionate) who is his strong right arm, and the possible dispatch of her worthless brother (Michael York) for whom she nurses an incestuous desire. Based on a novel by Graham Greene, this is stern and uncompromising stuff. But Michael Hordern contributes an amusing cameo as a penniless, seedy reporter, and Michael York turned in his best screen work to date.

English Patient, The ● ⓥ

1996, US/UK, 166 mins, colour

Dir: Anthony Minghella

Stars: Ralph Fiennes, Kristin Scott Thomas, Juliette Binoche, Willem Dafoe, Naveen Andrews, Colin Firth

Rating: ★★★

No wonder this epic of the Egyptian desert just before and during World War Two took so many acting awards around the world. Its performances are finely crafted with loving care. Fiennes, as the horrifyingly burnt 'patient' around whom the story revolves, Binoche and Scott Thomas are first-rate, but then so is the whole cast. At 166 minutes, though, it does go on a bit. Debit director Minghella here: he's obviously marvellous with actors, but his screenplay never uses one word where several will do. So the film's flawless performances, stunning use of desert scenery and perfectly serviceable romantic tragedy are constantly undercut by a lack of pace and rhythm: people are made to enter and exit as if in a play – but the scene rarely moves forward fluidly after they do. Still Minghella does write one memorable line for Fiennes surely destined for screen immortality. Remorseful over their affair, he tells married Scott Thomas: 'Every night, I cut out my heart. But in the morning it was full again.' Aaah.

Englishman Who Went Up a Hill but Came Down a Mountain, The ○ ⓥ

1995, UK, 99 mins, colour

Dir: Chris Monger

Stars: Hugh Grant, Tara Fitzgerald, Colm Meaney, Kenneth Griffith, Ian McNeice

Rating: ★★

This mild comedy set in 1917 Wales is much in the mould established by

Ealing Studios' rivals in the 1950s: gentle stuff in which the wily locals invariably outwitted the city gents who had come to do something dastardly to the local environment. Hugh Grant and Ian McNeice are map makers come to measure a village landmark, to declare it to be a mountain (over 1000 feet) or a hill. When the incline is found to be 984 feet high, the villagers are up in arms and decide to elevate it to mountainhood by piling earth on its summit. Even the fire-breathing vicar (Kenneth Griffith) allows them to work on Sunday in an attempt to finish the task. There are some amusing moments here, but far too many leisurely ones as well. Grant is very much Grant, while Tara Fitzgerald, who for once keeps her clothes on, is quite charming as the love interest and sports a splendidly natural-sounding Welsh accent. Most of the rest of the acting is on the theatrical side.

Enid Is Sleeping
See: Over Her Dead Body

Ensign Pulver ○
1964, US, 104 mins, colour
Dir: Joshua Logan
Stars: Robert Walker, Burl Ives, Walter Matthau, Millie Perkins
Rating: ★★

Noted US film-maker Joshua Logan directed and co-wrote this ramshackle follow-up to his famous *Mister Roberts*. Robert Walker takes over the title role, which had won Jack Lemmon an Oscar, but he lacks the maniacal edginess that made Lemmon's Pulver so funny. The film, in fact, is more noteworthy for its cast, little-known then, of whom many went on to stardom: Walter Matthau, Diana Sands, James Farentino, Larry Hagman, James Coco and Jack Nicholson among them. Burl Ives brings an amusing irascibility to The Captain which almost fills the gap left by James Cagney's departure from the role.

Entertainer, The ◐
1960, UK, 97 mins, b/w
Dir: Tony Richardson
Stars: Laurence Olivier, Brenda de Banzie, Joan Plowright, Alan Bates, Roger Livesey, Albert Finney
Rating: ★★★

Archie Rice, seedy seaside entertainer who is a failure in his career and as a man, is another in the memorable gallery of dramatic creations that only a Laurence Olivier could have brought so compellingly to life. He repeats his stage triumph in John Osborne's play alongside a terrific cast including wife, Joan Plowright, plus Roger Livesey, Brenda de Banzie, Alan Bates, Shirley Ann Field, Albert Finney, Thora Hird, and Daniel Massey. Years after seeing the film, his grotesque smile and dead eyes remain vivid in the memory.

Entertaining Mr Sloane ●
1969, UK, 94 mins, colour
Dir: Douglas Hickox
Stars: Beryl Reid, Peter McEnery, Harry Andrews
Rating: ★★

A spasmodically successful adaptation of the Joe Orton play that makes a virtue of bad taste, but gets tedious before the end. Beryl Reid is unforgettable as a middle-aged, frumpy spinster minus her false teeth and dressed in a see-through baby-doll nightie – trying to seduce young lodger Mr Sloane (a lean and muscular Peter McEnery, oozing sexual menace out of every pore). And Harry Andrews is every inch her predatory, seedy spiv brother, who wants to satisfy his own carnal lust with the blond stud he elevates to his leather-clad chauffeur. Douglas Hickox – at long last given the chance to shine at the helm of a full-length feature after years as an assistant director – has the measure of Orton's sourly outrageous humour, and is helped greatly by ttle gaudy, multi-coloured Gothic cemetery lodge set.

Enter the Dragon ● ⊚
1973, US, 97 mins, colour
Dir: Robert Clouse
Stars: Bruce Lee, John Saxon, Ahna Capri, Angela Mao
Rating: ★★

Bruce Lee's biggest international venture is a bit like a Universal B-picture of the Forties – on a million-dollar budget. Lee cleans up the white Slave/narcotics market on an offshore Chinese island, and he and co-star John Saxon polish off hundreds of kung-fu experts just before the US helicopter fleet arrives. Bits of the action are hysterically funny and bits of it – especially a pursuit through a maze of mirrors – are quite exciting. Personality-wise, honours go to little Angela Mao (a hapkido black belt champion) as Lee's sister, as demure as she is devastating.

Equinox ◐ ⊚
1992, Canada, 103 mins, colour
Dir: Alan Rudolph
Stars: Matthew Modine, Lara Flynn Boyle, Fred Ward, Tyra Ferrell, Marisa Tomei, M Emmet Walsh
Rating: ★★★

A fascinating movie with a disappointing ending. It's a kind of surrealist *film noir* which opens with a destitute old woman dying on the street. From a letter found on her, morgue attendant Tyra Ferrell begins to piece together the story of twin sons she gave away for adoption. Both have grown up to look like Matthew Modine; both hover dangerously on the edge of sanity. One is a mass of insecurities and strange aggression. The other is a gangster whose barely controlled violence brings him to the attention of a local crime kingpin. Stunningly well constructed, and studded with apposite lines: 'My whole life seems to be taking place without me in it,' declares the baffled 'good' Modine, the film almost ascends the peaks of perfection before falling headlong into the pit of an 'I don't how to end this, so let's close with a stunningly enigmatic shot' ending. Pity.

Equus ◐ ⊚
1977, UK, 132 mins, colour
Dir: Sidney Lumet
Stars: Richard Burton, Peter Firth, Colin Blakely, Jenny Agutter, Joan Plowright, Harry Andrews
Rating: ★★

This strange story was one of its decade's most magnetic stage plays. In this long film version all the cracks show, even though the wallpapering of director Sidney Lumet is as expert as can be. Richard Burton has one of the most demanding parts of his later years as the psychiatrist who has to find out why a strange youth (Peter Firth) blinded six horses. Firth is excellent, easily besting a distinguished supporting cast, most of whom give actorly performances whose mechanics show all too near the surface. Hokum at heart, the story is exceptionally well done in places, especially in some of the scenes between psychiatrist and patient.

Eraser ● ⊚
1996, US, 117 mins, colour
Dir: Charles Russell
Stars: Arnold Schwarzenegger, Vanessa Williams, James Caan, James Coburn, Robert Pastorelli, Andy Romano
Rating: ★★★

Though it won't go down in the annals as your – or even Arnie's – best movie, this is a good action film for fans, with the heavy artillery department working overtime. Our hero is the ace enforcer for the US witness protection programme. He sees to it that they stay

E

protected against all comers before their identities are erased. The film opens on a Mafia witness about to be torched by the Mob before Arnie roars to the rescue: in a nice touch the character reappears later in a key role, by which time Arnie is deeply embroiled in guarding the only witness in a high-profile case of selling arms to foreign mercenaries. The heavy-duty action that follows provides a megablast of mayhem, with laser 'nail guns' in the forefront. Somehow, though, the whole central set-up fails to convince. James Caan's character's defection is never satisfactorily explained and characters are thrust arbitrarily into situations of danger without much forethought or logic.

Erik the Viking ○ ⓥ
1989, UK, 108 mins, colour
Dir: Terry Jones
Stars: Tim Robbins, Mickey Rooney, Eartha Kitt, Terry Jones, John Cleese
Rating: ★

Monty Python meets Sinbad the Sailor without the laughs. Fashionably photographed, mainly in brown and white, this is the scattershot story of how Erik attempted to end the Age of Warfare by besting the dragon of the North Sea, blowing the Horn Resounding in the legendary island of Hy-Brasil (Atlantis), awakening the gods and getting them to release the sun that has been swallowed by Fenrir the wolf. Sounds fun, doesn't it? Alas, although there are a few chuckles (mainly provided by the dry delivery of John Cleese as villainous Halfdan the Black), the vehicle proves as unwieldy as a Viking sword, as cumbersome as the Viking clothing and as ramshackle as a Viking hut. Performances range from exaggerated to hysterical. And just what is Tim Robbins doing starring in this?

Ernest Saves Christmas ○
1988, US, 88 mins, colour
Dir: John Cherry
Stars: Jim Varney
Rating: ★★★

This was the second of (to date) seven big screen adventures featuring well-meaning disaster Ernest P Worrell, a sort of American version of Mr Bean. After 151 years, Santa's magic powers are dimming and he wants to pass the torch on to a kindly but down-on-his-luck TV host, whose show has just been cancelled. Naturally, bungling Ernest gets involved with disastrous results, but all ends happily for Christmas Eve.

Errand Boy, The ⊙ ⓥ
1961, US, 92 mins, b/w
Dir: Jerry Lewis
Stars: Jerry Lewis, Brian Donlevy, Dick Wesson
Rating: ★★★

A wacky, way-out comedy, written and directed by its star, Jerry Lewis, with Jerry's home studio, Paramount, seeing service as the Paramutual Pictures of the story. The long string of gags that ensues rather lacks discipline, but it's good-natured fun, and the stars of the then-popular TV Western series *Bonanza* pop up in guest appearances.

Escapade ○
1955, UK, 88 mins, b/w
Dir: Philip Leacock
Stars: John Mills, Yvonne Mitchell, Alastair Sim
Rating: ★★

Delightful, relaxed performances from John Mills, Yvonne Mitchell and Alastair Sim in a sensitive comedy-drama about a father obsessed with his campaign for world peace, while his three sons are up to some strange tricks at their boarding school.

Escapade In Japan ○
1957, US, 95 mins, colour
Dir: Arthur Lubin
Stars: Teresa Wright, Cameron Mitchell, Jon Provost, Philip Ober
Rating: ★★

Japan has never been more lovingly presented, nor better photographed than in this Technicolor treat about two little boys who, surviving a plane crash, decide to trek to Tokyo on their own. Cameron Mitchell and Teresa Wright are just perfect as the anguished parents who try to track them down. The film is full of incidental pleasures, not least the boys' hilarious visit to a geisha house, leading to a tense climax with the kids at risk. Clint Eastwood has a tiny role.

Escape ○
1940, US, 104 mins, b/w
Dir: Mervyn LeRoy
Stars: Robert Taylor, Norma Shearer, Conrad Veidt
Rating: ★★★

A thriller set in pre-war Germany about a young American artist (Robert Taylor) desperately trying to rescue his sick mother from a concentration camp. It was one of the first Hollywood attempts to show what life was like in Germany in the early days of the Nazi regime, and captures well the fearful atmosphere in a country where people are polite – but speak only in generalities.

Escape by Night ○
1952, UK, 79 mins, b/w
Dir: John Gilling
Stars: Bonar Colleano, Sidney James, Andrew Ray, Ted Ray, Simone Silva
Rating: ★★

It's hard to think of the loveable wise-cracking Sid James as a screen villain but his role here as a vicious gangster was his big break in the cinema world. Andrew Ray, still riding high on his success as *The Mudlark, is* featured with his real-life father Ted playing, for the only time in a film, his on-screen dad as well.

Escape from Alcatraz ① ⓥ
1979, US, 112 mins, colour
Dir: Don Siegel
Stars: Clint Eastwood, Patrick McGoohan, Fred Ward, Roberts Blossom
Rating: ★★★★

A solid, old-fashioned prison movie, still a Clint Eastwood film for all that it's based on fact, but refreshingly free from excessive violence and four-letter words. Familiar elements of the genre – the prison gang leader, the martinet warden, the eventual break – are smoothly integrated with a downbeat approach that eschews making heroes out of the quartet of inmates bent on escape. Director Don Siegel is clearly having little truck with sideline issues and indeed, with a movie already running around two hours, he has little call for them. His actors, Eastwood included, sink themselves entirely in their roles, all problems are (perhaps too obviously) eased aside for the final bid for freedom and few of those who see the film are likely to find it below their expectations.

Escape from Fort Bravo ○
1953, US, 98 mins, colour
Dir: John Sturges
Stars: William Holden, Eleanor Parker, John Forsythe, William Demarest
Rating: ★★★

Vigorous, he-man Cavalry Western, forcefully directed by the redoubtable John Sturges, who also made *The Magnificent Seven.* Slow-moving at the start, the story works up to a tense climax when the principal characters are trapped by Indians. Good acting all round from a cast headed by Wilham Holden and John Forsythe.

Escape from LA ● ⓥ
1996, US, 100 mins, colour
Dir: John Carpenter

Stars: Kurt Russell, Stacey Keach, Cliff Robertson, Steve Buscemi, Valeria Golino, Peter Fonda
Rating: ★

Admire only the production design from this otherwise cheesy sequel to *Escape from New York*, a ragbag of routine action sequences cribbed from other people's movies. It's 2013 and LA, ripped from America by an earthquake, is a desolate island where the scum of the earth are sent to rot. The US President's daughter has absconded with a black box that can 'shut down' the planet, and ended up in LA. Renegade adventurer Snake Plissken (Russell) is injected with a slow-killing poison to ensure his return, and sent out to get the box and kill the girl. Once he gets there, the visuals impress, but the rest is tired retreads of things we've seen before, notably the gladiatorial arena where combatants are assigned impossible tasks which no one has ever performed (Snake, of course, obliges). A stellar cast can do little with a banal and basic script, which it took three people, including Russell, to write. Take your own escape route: don't bother.

Escape from New York 🌓 Ⓥ
1981, US, 95 mins, colour
Dir: John Carpenter
Stars: Kurt Russell, Lee Van Cleef, Ernest Borgnine, Donald Pleasence, Isaac Hayes, Harry Dean Stanton
Rating: ★★★

A stylish, extravagant and deliberately eye-catching John Carpenter enterprise set in 1997 on Manhattan island, the whole of which is walled in to create one vast prison to which very bad boys are consigned for the rest of their lives. When the US president crash lands thare, a master thief (played by Kurt Russell with a Clint Eastwood whisper) is given 24 hours to earn an amnesty by getting him out. His exciting and often fearsome adventures in the attempt form the body of the story. One scene of a boxing ring turned into a gladiatorial area is really imaginative both in conception and execution, as Russell and a massive opponent battle with spiked clubs.

Escape from the Planet of the Apes ○ Ⓥ
1971, US, 98 mins, colour
Dir: Don Taylor
Stars: Roddy McDowall, Kim Hunter, Bradford Dillman
Rating: ★★★

Not so much a sequel to the second film in the series, more a neat and inge-

nious re-working of Pierre Boulle's original premise. Here, the apes make off from their incinerated planet (it blew up at the end of *Beneath the Planet of the Apes*) in Charlton Heston's original spacecraft, to land in modern America. Bradford Dillman gives a superb performance as Dr Dixon, while Roddy McDowall and Kim Hunter are excellent as usual under the clever simian make-up. One of the best of the Apes movies – and it moves well all the way.

Escape Route ○
(aka: I'll Get You)
1952, UK, 79 mins, b/w
Dir: Peter Graham Scott
Stars: George Raft, Sally Gray, Clifford Evans
Rating: ★★

George Raft's second British film casts him as an FBI agent tracking down the brains behind a huge kidnapping ring. Playing the brains: Clifford Evans, once famous in TV's *The Power Game*. It's pretty slow, but the climax is a terrific running fight through a riverside wharf.

Escape to Happiness
See: Intermezzo

Escape to Victory ○
1981, US/UK, 111 mins, colour
Dir: John Huston
Stars: Sylvester Stallone, Michael Caine, Pele, Bobby Moore, Max Von Sydow, Daniel Massey
Rating: ★

A really excruciating PoW camp escape film, so artificially contrived as to be only a pace ahead of a sketch from a variety show. The idea is that a team of footballing prisoners will take on the might of the Reich, win and escape at the same time. Takes some believing, doesn't it? Lots of famous soccer stars are in the cast, plus Sylvester Stallone in goal: one can hardly believe John Huston directed this, but he did. Bad luck John: you were the one who needed to escape.

Escape to Witch Mountain ○
1974, US, 74 mins, colour
Dir: John Hough
Stars: Eddie Albert, Ray Milland, Donald Pleasence
Rating: ★★

This Disney sci fi spree may leave the less demanding child agog. The two children, Kim Richards and Ike Eisenmann, are excellent. But the last half-hour cheats them of their triumph

by playing their adventures for laughs rather than thrills.

Esther Waters ○
1948, UK, 109 mins, b/w
Dir: Ian Dalrymple
Stars: Kathleen Ryan, Dirk Bogarde, Fay Compton
Rating: ★★

Gloom and doom became for some reason fashionable in British films of the post-war years, and in this 19th century weepie Kathleen Ryan suffers spectacularly as a servant-girl who falls for a ne'er-do-well and pays for it down the years. The rascal is played by Dirk Bogarde at a time when his career was full of such shady, shallow characters.

Eternally Yours ○
1939, US, 95 mins, b/w
Dir: Tay Garnett
Stars: Loretta Young, David Niven, Broderick Crawford
Rating: ★★

Loretta Young deserts the more dependable charms of her society boyfriend Broderick Crawford for charismatic magician David Niven, but comes to have second thoughts about her decision in this interesting drama, typical of Hollywood's output at this period. A really strong supporting cast includes such hardened scene-stealers as ZaSu Pitts, Billie Burke, C Aubrey Smith and Eve Arden.

E.T. The Extra -Terrestrial ⊙ Ⓥ
1982, US, 115 mins, colour
Dir: Steven Spielberg
Stars: Dee Wallace, Peter Coyote, Henry Thomas, Drew Barrymore, Robert MacNaughton, C Thomas Howell
Rating: ★★★★

The most successful family film of all time, perhaps the most succesful film Walt Disney never made. Combining elements of *Peter Pan* and *The Bible*, director Steven Spielberg weaves a highly manipulative spell in his story of a little lost alien that is sure not to leave a dry eye in the house. Perhaps it was this sense of brazen manipulation or just sheer jealousy at its monstrous box office success that led to its Oscars haul being restricted to technical awards for visual and audio effects, sound, and for John Williams' sweeping score. E.T's voice is supposedly by Debra Winger. Cute fun.

Eureka ● Ⓥ
1982, UK/US, 129 mins, colour
Dir: Nicolas Roeg

E

Stars: Gene Hackman, Theresa Russell, Rutger Hauer, Jane Lapotaire
Rating: ★★

A sort of *Citizen Kane* on ice. Gene Hackman is (in flashback) a man who makes a fortune in Yukon gold, keeps a strange stone with a shape on it, and is finally beset by gangsters in the Caribbean. Sounds hard to follow? You've got it. But Nicolas Roeg's puzzle piece is also beautifully scored, skilfully shot and made deliberately in fragments, like the facets of a diamond showing a previously hidden face with a change of light.

Even Cowgirls Get the Blues ● Ⓥ
1993, US, 106 mins, colour
Dir: Gus Van Sant Jr
Stars: Uma Thurman, John Hurt, Rain Phoenix, Angie Dickinson
Rating: ★

This tedious film is like a flower power comedy of 25 years ago. Sissy (Uma Thurman), born with abnormally long thumbs, becomes a professional hitch-hiker, ends up at the Rubber Rose Ranch, a distinctly kinky establishment currently in danger of being taken over by the lesbian cowgirls who hover about its fringes. Sissy falls heavily for the leader, Bonanza Jellybean (Rain Phoenix – hard to know which name is sillier), consults The Chink (Pat Morita), a wise man from the hills who guards a giant clockworks in a cave, and helps the cowgirls in their fight to breed a flock of whooping cranes. A cross between any number of movies from the late Sixties, this is the kind of film where characters look at each other through a hole in a piece of toast and a string quartet plays in a field. As you'll have gathered the thumb total of this foolish frolic is not very much.

Evening Star, The ① Ⓥ
1996, US, 128 mins, colour
Dir: Robert Harling
Stars: Shirley MacLaine, Bill Paxton, Miranda Richardson, Juliette Lewis, Jack Nicholson, Ben Johnson
Rating: ★★

There are a number of good lines and wise words in this sequel to *Terms of Endearment*, and one breathtaking scene when a brief breeze tells MacLaine a friend has died. Alas, moments of merit are not enough by themselves to sustain a film of this length, and writer Harling, of *Steel Magnolias* fame, should have left the directorial duties to someone who knew how. Too many sticky and stiff scenes result from handling

that, unlike the writing, lacks finesse. He even allows the film to drift on five minutes too long. Time has passed and MacLaine, instead of arguing with her now-dead daughter, is at loggerheads with her sex-crazy teenage granddaughter (Lewis). 'You spray this house with happiness repellent,' Lewis yells with some justification, before leaving home with her latest boyfriend. Cue for granny to zoom into an affair with her therapist (a sadly misjudged performance by Paxton). Fragmentary from then on, the film's lifted at the end by Nicholson's cameo.

Evergreen ○ Ⓥ
1934, UK, 91 mins, b/w
Dir: Victor Saville
Stars: Jessie Matthews, Sonnie Hale
Rating: ★★★★

This enchanting musical was Jessie Matthews' greatest popular success, opening up the possibility of a Hollywood career although, for personal reasons, she chose to remain in Britain. Playing mother-and-daughter stars of London's theatreland, Jessie, dazzlingly photographed by Glenn MacWilliams, sings 'Over My Shoulder', 'Dancing on the Ceiling' and more. The high-key lighting is reminiscent of the Astaire-Rogers musicals being made at the time on the other side of the Atlantic.

Everybody Does It ○
1949, US, 98 mins, b/w
Dir: Edmund Goulding
Stars: Paul Douglas, Celeste Holm, Linda Darnell
Rating: ★★★★

This vintage Hollywood comedy was lighter fare than usual for director Edmund Goulding, more often associated with such serious drama as the Bette Davis vehicles *Dark Victory*, *The Old Maid* and *The Great Lie*. Beetle-browed comedian Paul Douglas is boring businessman Leonard Borland, keen to promote wife Celeste Holm's operatic career – until her debut bombs and glamorous soprano Linda Darnell discovers that he has a splendid baritone voice himself. Douglas is a very amiable buffoon, Holm plays wittily (and sings prettily) and Darnell is fine as the catalyst for potential domestic disaster. Contemporary critics sniffed, but when audiences reached for their handkerchiefs, it was to dry the tears of laughter from their eyes.

Everbody's All American
See: When I Fall in Love

Everybody Sing ○
1937, US, 80 mins, b/w
Dir: Edwin L Marin
Stars: Judy Garland, Allan Jones, Fanny Brice, Reginald Owen, Billie Burke, Reginald Gardner
Rating: ★★★

Although this was one of MGM's shorter-length musicals, they still managed to squeeze in a dozen songs, showcase a young Judy Garland, give Fanny Brice the chance to do her famous 'Baby Snooks' routine and get Allan Jones on to share the singing.

Everyone Says I Love You ① Ⓥ
1996, US, 91 mins, colour
Dir: Woody Allen
Stars: Woody Allen, Goldie Hawn, Alan Alda, Julia Roberts, Edward Norton, Drew Barrymore
Rating: ★★

A sad day for musicals. Woody Allen fans may smile indulgently at this fey attempt to create a musical in which almost none of the cast can sing, but it provides only embarrassment and fidgety bottoms for the rest of us. Some of the vocalising attempts here are so painful that one can only boggle at how bad Drew Barrymore's singing must have been for her to end up dubbed. Woody as usual rows gamely and occasionally wise-crackingly through a sea of his own neuroses while he attempts to woo and win Julia Roberts as the girl of his dreams. Then there's the problems of his extended family, not to mention the 'mad dog' killer that Woody's ex-wife (Goldie Hawn) has befriended in prison and taken into her home on his departure from clink. The songs are all gorgeous standards and even survive some of the assaults on their lyrics.

Every Girl Should Be Married ○
1948, US, 85 mins, b/w
Dir: Don Hartman
Stars: Cary Grant, Betsy Drake, Franchot Tone, Diana Lynn
Rating: ★★

Model Betsy Drake took most of the best reviews for this mild comedy in which she made her acting debut, complete with bubbly voice and cue-jumping delivery. A year later she married her co-star Cary Grant (she was the third of his four wives). Some of the lines are certainly funny, but the confection is overcooked by director Don Hartman.

Every Home Should Have One ◐
(aka: Think Dirty)
1971, UK, 94 mins, colour
Dir: Jim Clark
Stars: Marty Feldman, Judy Cornwell, Shelley Berman, Julie Ege, Patrick Cargill
Rating: ★

This was Marty Feldman's first starring role after an appearance in Richard Lester's The *Bed Sitting Room* (1969) and the smutty script (by Feldman, Barry Took and Denis Norden) gives him plenty of opportunities to display his frenetic brand of Jerry Lewis-style mugging. Dim.

Every Minute Counts
See: Count the Hours

Everything You Always Wanted to Know About Sex, But Were Afraid to Ask ● ⓥ
1972, US, 85 mins, colour
Dir: Woody Allen
Stars: Woody Allen, John Carradine, Anthony Quayle, Lynn Redgrave, Burt Reynolds, Gene Wilder
Rating: ★★★

Although parts of this seven-episode romp are admittedly too crude to be funny, with Woody Allen at the reins in his zaniest mood, you know you're in for a good few laughs. The best of the stories are the first, second and last, the opener being about a court jester (Woody) who tries to seduce the Queen (Lynn Redgrave). Alas, the poor fool gets his hand stuck in the Queen's chastity belt, which enables Mr Allen to go around for the rest of the scene with his hand clasped to Miss Redgrave's bottom (yes, he did write the script). Best line, by the jester about the prowess of the King (Anthony Quayle): 'He's the only man I know who can swim the moat length-wise.' In the second yarn, Gene Wilder is just superb as a doctor who falls in love with a sheep, while the last story (in which Burt Reynolds joins Woody) imagines all parts of the male body are populated by little men, and studies their reactions as they prepare for making love. For most of the way, an enjoyably rude jape.

Every Which Way But Loose ◐ ⓥ
1978, US, 114 mins, colour
Dir: James Fargo
Stars: Clint Eastwood, Sondra Locke, Geoffrey Lewis, Beverly D'Angelo, Ruth Gordon
Rating: ★

This is a very loose-limbed comedy of mayhem which its star Clint Eastwood (who also directed) intends no-one to take seriously. An orang-utan called Clyde steals practically every scene. It's so like an old biker movie of the Sixties, though, that you practically expect Peter Fonda and Dennis Hopper to wander in at any minute. The story and the characters are really too silly even by the standards of this kind of romp, and the film's disparate elements hardly ever begin to gel. It still pulled 'em in at the box-office, though, and Eastwood's personal share of the profits was said to be more than $15 million. No wonder he made a sequel, *Any Which Way You Can*.

Evil Dead, The ● ⓥ
1983, US, 85 mins, colour
Dir: Sam Raimi
Stars: Bruce Campbell, Ellen Sandweiss, Betsy Baker, Hal Delrich, Sarah York
Rating: ★★★

This sensationally scary film from Sam Raimi cleaned up at the world's box-offices, returning vast profits on its $400,000 budget. Five young people seek shelter in a remote abandoned woodland cabin – and find pretty well everything except shelter. Following the discovery of an ancient Book of the Dead, they're soon being possessed by dormant woodland demons in *10 Little Niggers* style, giving rise to some special effects that are pretty breathtaking on such a low budget. Raimi's trademark black humour is already in evidence at this early stage of his career, and he's greatly aided by the moody photography of Tim Philo and Joshua M Becker which suggests the menacing presence of the lurking demons even when they can't be seen. For those who demand rivers of gore, this one has that too; a bit of everything, in fact, and all done well.

Evil Dead II ● ⓥ
1987, US, 85 mins, colour
Dir: Sam Raimi
Stars: Bruce Campbell, Sarah Berry, Dan Hicks, Kassie Wesley
Rating: ★★

Good clean fun for those horror fans who demand nothing more than a welter of blood, swivelling zombies and non-stop action and don't ask for a story that makes any kind of sense. It's all, as the dialogue demonstrates, tongue-in-cheek (well, chainsaw-in-cheek anyway) and director Sam Raimi probably has it about right when he claims that 'we're just trying to give the audience a good time'. As for the rest,

Denise Bixler is far too dishy and talented to get killed in the first reel and the rest of the cast give it all they've got which isn't terribly much but suffices for the occasion. That cabin in the woods is still infested with evil spirits and you may find their gruesome antics growing on you as the film goes on.

Evil Under the Sun ○ ⓥ
1981, UK, 115 mins, colour
Dir: Guy Hamilton
Stars: Peter Ustinov, Jane Birkin, Colin Blakely, James Mason, Maggie Smith, Roddy McDowall
Rating: ★★

There's another cast-to-treasure in this follow-up to the same producers' *Death on the Nile*. If only the film lived up to the accumulated talents of Peter Ustinov, Maggie Smith, Roddy McDowall, James Mason, Diana Rigg, Colin Blakely and the rest. Alas, too often director Guy Hamilton seems to let the plot almost go to sleep under the Adriatic sun of the title. However, the opening sequence is an excellent piece of scene-setting, and the pairing of Maggie Smith and Diana Rigg provides some delightfully bitchy moments.

Evita ◐ ⓥ
1996, UK, 133 mins, colour
Dir: Alan Parker
Stars: Madonna, Antonio Banderas, Jonathan Pryce, Jimmy Nail
Rating: ★★★

Despite the hype, *Evita* never was the greatest of stage musicals. The film, even with the performance of Madonna's career in a role she was born to play, and (too many) stunningly orchestrated crowd scenes, can't improve it that much. There's almost no dialogue and, in between high-points, things do seem to be droning on and on. The songs are glorious, but the narrative is bloated and repetitive: the film begins blindingly well, but only sustains this inspiration and momentum for the first half hour. As you can see, a film of pros and cons. Madonna fans shouldn't miss it: for others, buying the CD may be the wiser option.

Excalibur ● ⓥ
1981, UK, 140 mins, colour
Dir: John Boorman
Stars: Nigel Terry, Helen Mirren, Nicholas Clay, Nicol Williamson, Cherie Lunghi
Rating: ★★

Director John Boorman ambitiously romps through the entire Arthurian legend – from possession of the sword Excalibur by Uther Pendragon to the

E

death of his son, King Arthur – in this gigantic slice of blood and sorcery which is not for the fainthearted. The result is almost always the handsomest of films to behold. Dramatically, it has its moments, too, even if it never quite achieves that monstrously difficult blend of grandeur and madness for which it strives. The battle scenes hold all the excitement and gore that modern wizardry will allow, but Boorman's quieter visual effects can bring gasps to the throat – and giggles, as in Helen Mirren's battle armour, which might well be authentic but seems to have strayed in from *Fire Maidens from Outer Space*.

Executive Decision ● Ⓥ

1996, US, 132 mins, colour
Dir: Stuart Baird
Stars: Kurt Russell, Halle Berry, John Leguizamo, David Suchet, Oliver Platt, Steven Seagal
Rating: ★★★

An action film where Steven Seagal dies after the first 20 minutes? Two years earlier, it would have been unthinkable, but how the mighty fall. Seagal, star of such brutal knuckle busters as *Under Siege*, literally takes a dive in this brisk *Die Hard*-style thriller, and cinema audiences in the US cheered him on his way. The action takes place aboard a commercial plane packed with innocent travellers. Also aboard are a group of Islamic terrorists and enough deadly nerve gas to kill everyone from New York to Washington. The film's pièce de resistance is the invasion of the plane by a group of US agents who gain entry by flying under and connecting two planes together by a sort of tunnel. As gripping as this sequence is, the rest of the film is a bit of a muddle in which actions definitely speak louder than the risible dialogue handed to star Kurt Russell, as an anti-terrorist pen-pusher who finds himself in the forefront of the action.

Executive Suite ○

1954, US, 104 mins, b/w
Dir: Robert Wise
Stars: William Holden, June Allyson, Fredric March, Barbara Stanwyck, Walter Pidgeon, Shelley Winters
Rating: ★★★

One of those all-star films stemming from massive bestselling books, a genre of which Hollywood became particularly fond in the mid-Fifties. The world of big business becomes a battleground when a company chairman dies without naming his successor. The conflict between those fighting over the position is developed with good character insight, their ambitions, dislikes and individual foibles presented with a distinctly human touch. Punchy performances all round, especially from William Holden, Dean Jagger, Barbara Stanwyck and Nina Foch.

Exodus ○

1960, US, 220 mins, colour
Dir: Otto Preminger
Stars: Paul Newman, Eva Marie Saint, Ralph Richardson, Peter Lawford, Lee J Cobb, Sal Mineo
Rating: ★★

Otto Preminger's version of Leon Uris' vast novel about the birth of modern Israel split critics and public alike. Paul Newman radiates sincerity as the young Israeli leader; scenes of the refugees escaping their Cyprus detention centre are the most suspenseful in the film; and Ernest Gold's stirring score won an Oscar. Humorist Mort Sahl implored at the preview, as the film entered its fourth hour: 'Otto, let my people go!'

Exorcist III, The ● Ⓥ

1990, US, 109 mins, colour
Dir: William Peter Blatty
Stars: George C Scott, Brad Dourif, Jason Miller, Nicol Williamson, Viveca Lindfors
Rating: ★★

He's back! The devil, that is, in a Linda Blair-less sequel to the original, in which poor dead priest Jason Miller from the first film is resurrected and tossed in a lunatic asylum, wrapped round the body and mind of a serial killer. When the 'Gemini' killings start all over again, an incredulous George C Scott, as a police lieutenant involved in both cases, has to try to root out the truth – and the cure. The story begins well, with the horror element being lightened by the joky relationship between Scott and Ed Flanders, as the kind of priest who tells a sinner 'God loves you, everyone else thinks you're an asshole.' But as soon as Flanders is killed, the film begins to flounder in a welter of demonic talk, occasionally alleviated by the odd very effective shock moment.

Experiment In Terror

See: The Grip of Fear

Explorers ○ Ⓥ

1985, US, 109 mins, colour
Dir: Joe Dante

Stars: River Phoenix, Ethan Hawke, Jason Presson, Amanda Peterson
Rating: ★★★

This rather odd but interesting little picture is a cross between a teen angst film and a sci-fi adventure. In the beginning, three young friends, a dreamer, an egghead and a misfit, decide to build their own spacecraft. This is mixed in with the usual schoolroom antics, bullies versus nerds, puppy love and parental troubles for the egghead. The big switch comes when they actually succeed in making a working spacecraft and set off for other worlds. Not a rip-roaring *Star Wars* adventure, but a quirky and entertaining tale told well by director Joe Dante. Ethan Hawke, River Phoenix and Jason Presson have fun as the teenage astronauts.

Expresso Bongo ◑ Ⓥ

1959, UK, 111 mins, b/w
Dir: Val Guest
Stars: Laurence Harvey, Sylvia Syms, Cliff Richard, Yolande Donlan
Rating: ★

A film adaptation of the satirical musical that revolves around Soho and its thriving coffee bars in the late Fifties. The movie's main problem is that it never makes up its mind in which direction it's supposed to be travelling and ends up as an earthy, happy-go-lucky ramble. Laurence Harvey hams the part of the get-rich-quick agent splendidly, but Sylvia Syms seems ill-at-ease as his stripper girlfriend.

Extreme Measures

1996, US, 118 mins, colour
Dir: Michael Apted
Stars: Hugh Grant, Gene Hackman, Sarah Jessica Parker, David Morse, Bill Nunn, Debra Monk
Rating: ★★★

A slick medical thriller that owes a lot to *Coma*, and more than it deserves to Gene Hackman, whose portrait of a misguided-but-mad scientist might have caused Boris Karloff to mutter: 'Just a little less, Gene'. Even so, director Michael Apted screws the maximum suspense from a story that, apart from the occasional medical slip, intrigues almost all the way. The script could perhaps have done with more humour, but Hugh Grant's floppy-haired doctor would add a touch of class even to *ER* and Sarah Jessica Parker is a spirited heroine.

Extreme Prejudice ◑ Ⓥ

1987, US, 104 mins, colour
Dir: Walter Hill

Stars: Nick Nolte, Powers Boothe, Michael Ironside, Maria Conchita Alonso, Rip Tom, Clancy Brown
Rating: ★★

Shunned by the cinemagoing public for two decades, the Western has re-grouped its forces and emerged in other guises. The modern action thriller, with its constant chases, killings and shootouts, provides an ideal cover and, with its 'Tex-Mex' border setting, and a Texas ranger hero in Nick Nolte, director Walter Hill's film comes closer to the old Hollywood shoot-em-ups. There are even the two old friends, now on opposite sides of the law, who must shoot it out in the end. Ostensibly, though, this is a thriller about six soldiers of fortune, all official-ly listed as dead, who home in on the border town where Nolte is having a tough time keeping the lid on the drugs trade run by his old chum Powers Boothe. Even with some crazy dia-logue, Boothe has no problem walking off with the film, the action itself is for-mula stuff, and lots of extras, as well as most of the cast, bite the adobe dust. They sure have it tough down Mexico way.

Eye for an Eye, An ● Ⓥ
1981, US, 106 mins, colour
Dir: Steve Carver
Stars: Chuck Norris, Christopher Lee, Richard Roundtree
Rating: ★★

The plot is no great strain on the brain – Martial Arts expert Chuck Norris (with a little help from his friends) takes on wicked Christopher Lee and his henchmen and demolishes them. But the movie is an expertly crafted piece of kung foolery designed to show-case former world karate champion Chuck, and director Steve Carver – a graduate of the New World School of exploitation film-making – displays a good eye for high-kicking action. He even succeeds in making the usually monolithic Mr Norris look dramatical-ly quite lively.

Eye for an Eye, An ● Ⓥ
1996, US, 101 mins, colour
Dir: John Schlesinger
Stars: Sally Field, Kiefer Sutherland, Ed Harris, Joe Mantegna, Beverly D'Angelo
Rating: ★★

Director John Schlesinger has an emo-tive subject here, but his low-key treatment fails to make the most of the potential suspense and terror that should be part of the territory. Sally Field is happily settled with second hus-band Ed Harris, plus a daughter from each of her marriages. Then the older girl, at home alone preparing for a party, is raped and murdered by an in-truder. Police identify the assailant (Kiefer Sutherland) but he gets off on a legal technicality. At first intent on per-sonal revenge, Field is warned off by an FBI agent working undercover to root out vigilante elements in selfhelp groups. But when the police fail to act on information she supplies on a sec-ond woman the killer is stalking, and the woman ultimately suffers the same fate as her daughter, Field grits her lit-tle teeth and sets a vengeance plan in motion. Routinely competent in a TV movie way, the film benefits from its star cast, but is unlikely to linger in your memory.

Eye of the Cat ● Ⓥ
1969, US, 102 mins, colour
Dir: David Lowell Rich
Stars: Michael Sarrazin, Gayle Hunnicutt, Eleanor Parker
Rating: ★★

Bizarre shocker about devious plotting in a house full of felines. Eleanor Parker enjoys herself in another crip-ple-in-a-wheelchair role but it's the cats, full of silky menace, who steal this off-beat thriller.

Eyes In the Night ○
1942, US, 80 mins, b/w
Dir: Fred Zinnemann
Stars: Edward Arnold, Ann Harding, Donna Reed, Stephen McNally
Rating: ★★

This off-beat thriller about a blind de-tective trying to outwit a gang of spies was one of director Fred Zinnemann's earliest assignments, and provided an out-of-character role for Edward Arnold as the detective. Fans of vin-tage films will have a field day, recognising such stars as Steven Geray, Allen Jenkins, Reginald Denny, Barry Nelson, Milburn Stone and Mantan Moreland. The elegant Ann Harding seemed here to have stepped into mother roles too quickly but the lead-ing character's dog steals the show anyway.

Eyes of Laura Mars ● Ⓥ
1978, US, 104 mins, colour
Dir: Irvin Kershner
Stars: Faye Dunaway, Tommy Lee Jones, Brad Dourif, René Auberjonois, Raul Julia
Rating: ★★★

An old-fashioned creepie, rather un-worthy of its Oscar-winning star, Faye Dunaway, although its murders are di-rected with a lot of flair by Irvin Kershner. Miss Dunaway plays a rather way-out fashion photographer who finds herself seeing the murders of her friends as they happen, via some nightmarish second sight. The plot needs her visions to pep it all up, but for an hour or so it careers along nasti-ly but nicely. Whodunnit fans should be able to spot the killer.

Eyewitness ◐ Ⓥ
(aka: Sudden Terror)
1970, UK, 95 mins, colour
Dir: John Hough
Stars: Mark Lester, Lionel Jeffries, Susan George, Jeremy Kemp
Rating: ★★★★

A breathlessly exciting thriller along the lines of the story of the boy who cried wolf. Mark Lester is the boy on a strife-torn Mediterranean island who witnesses a murder – then tries to get people to believe it while the murderer closes in on him. John Hough's furious direction in the final chase sequence will leave you gasping.

Eyewitness ○
1956, UK, 82 mins, b/w
Dir: Muriel Box
Stars: Donald Sinden, Muriel Pavlow, Michael Craig, Belinda Lee
Rating: ★★

This pursuit thriller made a nice change of pace for Muriel Pavlow after a series of milk-and-water roles, al-though the role of a girl who witnesses murder and goes on the run for the rest of the film didn't really suit her. There's a fine performance, though, from Nigel Stock, who acts everyone else off the screen as an unwilling, deaf safebreaker. The story has too many threads but provides some excitement.

E

F

Fabulous Baker Boys, The
● ⓥ
1989, US, 113 mins, colour
Dir: Steve Kloves
Stars: Jeff Bridges, Michelle Pfeiffer,
Beau Bridges, Jennifer Tilly
Rating: ★★★

No-one who has seen this romantic comedy can ever forget the sight of Michelle Pfeiffer in a blazing red dress crawling all over the top of a piano and crooning 'Makin'Whoopee'. She's pure dynamite in a role that takes full advantage of her natural singing talent and casts her as the saviour of a dying lounge saloon double act, played with great knowing charm by real-life brothers Jeff and Beau Bridges. You know where the story is heading after the initial set-up, but thanks to spot-on performances and a stellar script, the getting-there is most enjoyable.

Face Behind the Mask, The ○
1941, US, 69 mins, b/w
Dir: Robert Florey
Stars: Peter Lorre, Evelyn Keyes, Don Beddoe
Rating: ★★★

Peter Lorre in a rare appearance as a man of his own nationality, Hungarian. This is about a man who, his face horribly disfigured in a fire, becomes a criminal mastermind beneath a rubber mask. Lorre wore no actual mask for the role, only chalk-white make-up and strips of tape to help him immobilise part of his features. Said Lorre: 'If an actor can't make his body do what he wants it to do, he isn't an actor. If he feels he needs mounds of make-up to create an illusion, he's a mere impressionist.' The scene where he first removes the bandages and sees his fire-ravaged face is genuinely harrowing.

Face In the Crowd, A ○
1957, US, 126 mins, b/w
Dir: Elia Kazan
Stars: Andy Griffith, Patricia Neal, Anthony Franciosa, Walter Matthau, Lee Remick
Rating: ★★★★

A powerful drama about media exploitation. Andy (Matlock) Griffith is Lonesome Rhodes, a drunken down-and-out with a guitar and a wry sense of humour who is discovered by reporter Patricia Neal. He is given his own radio show and within weeks is the station's main asset. A move to television and national stardom soon follows. But the power and influence of stardom begin to corrupt and Rhodes becomes involved with a right-wing political group. Griffith gives a powerful performance in this, his first film, and never quite reached these heights again. It was also the debut film for Lee Remick, who plays the cheerleader Rhodes marries.

Face of a Fugitive ○
1958, US, 81 mins, colour
Dir: Paul Wendkos
Stars: Fred MacMurray, Lin McCarthy, Dorothy Green, James Coburn
Rating: ★★★★

This film is small-scale, originally released as a second-feature, but one contemporary critic remarked that this taut Western, about a man running from his past, is 'worth going almost any distance to see.' Director Paul Wendkos puts impact into every scene right from the start. The credits unfold over a sketch of the wanted man. Across the face, one bar after another appears, creating a prison motif which is repeated throughout the film, with barred foregrounds, ruined buildings, a fence, an iron bedstead. With rare economy and truth, the powerful script refuses to be side-tracked into extraneous action, and sticks to its theme of the redemption of a man. Lin McCarthy is especially impressive as the green but fanatically fair sheriff. And Fred MacMurray creates a memorable figure as the fugitive.

Faces ⓥ ◐
1968, US, 130 mins, b/w
Dir: John Cassavetes
Stars: John Marley, Gena Rowlands, Lynn Carlin
Rating: ★★★

Although one of his best films, this is still very typical of director John Cassavetes' work. It deals with a very human and essentially ordinary problem (in this case a 14-year marriage that has gone stale), much of the acting is improvised and the feel almost documentary. The acting is very good. Also typical were the rave reviews the critics gave it and the lukewarm response from the public. John Marley and Lynn Carlin play the couple who look elsewhere for love: he with a prostitute (Gena Rowlands), she with an old beatnik (Seymour Cassel). Although it has its flat spots the film is ultimately rewarding for those who stick with it.

Fahrenheit 451 ○
1966, UK, 111 mins, colour
Dir: Francois Truffaut
Stars: Julie Christie, Oskar Werner, Cyril Cusack, Anton Diffring
Rating: ★★★★

Underrated science-fiction film adapted from Ray Bradbury's novel. Set in a book-burning society of the future, it has haunting performances from Julie Christie and Oskar Werner and delicate colour photography by Nicolas Roeg, who was soon to become one of the major directors of the British cinema.

Fail Safe ○
1964, US, 111 mins, b/w
Dir: Sidney Lumet
Stars: Henry Fonda, Walther Matthau, Frank Overton, Dan O'Herlihy, Larry Hagman
Rating: ★★★

The straight version of *Dr Strangelove*, tautly handled by Sidney Lumet, is a tension-fraught vision of a nightmare coming true. The film didn't receive its true recognition at the time, as *Strangelove*, which treated similar subject matter – nuclear war – as black comedy, had just been released. Henry Fonda offers another of his authoritative Americans, in the form of the President, and only Fritz Weaver's performance is over the top in a sober supporting cast. You'll sweat as the bombers keep on going towards Moscow: director Lumet ensures it's a masterly if leisurely lesson in suspense.

Fair Wind to Java ○
1953, US, 92 mins, colour
Dir: Joseph Kane
Stars: Fred MacMurray, Vera Ralston, Robert Douglas, Victor McLaglen
Rating: ★★

Somewhere in the gulf between Joseph Conrad and Douglas Fairbanks comes this lushly coloured adventure yarn, one of a fistful of bigger-budgeted adventures from the pinchpenny Republic Studio in the Fifties. It could be better (and a lot worse) than it is, with lots of brawn (Fred MaMurray, Victor McLaglen, Buddy Baer), a better-than-usual performance from Vera Ralston (the studio boss's wife) as a Javanese dancer and a typically sneaky swashbuckling villain from Britain's Robert Douglas. Awful backdrops, good volcanic eruption, credibility kept easily at arm's length. Rainy-day fare.

Falcon and the Co-eds, The ○

1943, US, 67 mins, b/w
Dir: William Clemens
Stars: Tom Conway, Jean Brooks Rating:
★★★

Not until James Bond films surfaced was a screen sleuth surrounded by so many beautiful women as Tom Conway in this above-average *Falcon* murder thriller. Quite creepy in places, too – not surprising considering the script is largely the work of Ardel Wray, who worked on some of the Val Lewton chillers.

Falcon and the Snowman, The ● Ⓥ

1984, US, 130 mins, colour
Dir: John Schlesinger
Stars: Timothy Hutton, Sean Penn, David Suchet, Lori Singer
Rating: ★★

British director John Schlesinger's career has been uneven to say the least since his Oscar-winning triumph with *Midnight Cowboy*. Most of his films have tended to be disappointments, and this falls into that category. Routine, clichéd and ponderous, it's a spy story that offers no motivation for its real-life characters, two former altar boy childhood friends who end up spying against America for the Russians. Timothy Hutton and Sean Penn (in one of the best performances of his career) go through the required motions as a spy centre worker and a junkie drug dealer respectively, who both end up passing on top secrets.

Falcon In Hollywood, The ○

1944, US, 65 mins, b/w
Dir: Gordon Douglas
Stars: Tom Conway, Barbara Hale
Rating: ★★

RKO cheated on the budget of this one – it's a murder mystery set in a film studio! That super blonde Veda Ann Borg scores heavily as a wisecracking taxi-driver.

Falcon in Mexico, The ○

1944, US, 70 mins, b/w
Dir: William Berke
Stars: Tom Conway, Mona Maris
Rating: ★★

The Falcon heads south to solve a mystery involving the emergence of new paintings from a supposedly dead artist, giving RKO the opportunity to add flavour to the backgrounds by using some of Orson Welles' footage from his documentary *It's All True*.

Tom Conway's sleuth looks ill-at-ease on unfamiliar ground; leading lady Martha MacVicar had a second career under the name Martha Vickers.

Falcon in San Francisco, The ○

1945, US, 66 mins, b/w
Dir: Joseph H Lewis
Stars: Tom Conway, Rita Corday
Rating: ★★

Director Joseph H Lewis was renowned for his classy 'B' movie thrillers, but he's batting on a sticky wicket here thanks to a sub-standard script which hinted that the *Falcon* series was reaching its sell-by date. Good locations and a bright child actor (Sharyn Moffett) are the only plus factors in this story of smuggling.

Falcon Strikes Back, The ○

1943, US, 65 mins, b/w
Dir: Edward Dmytryk
Stars: Tom Conway, Harriet Hilliard
Rating: ★★★

A much-used style of title for the great detectives of novel and film, most of whom 'struck back' in their time. This adventure of the Falcon was directed by Edward Dmytryk (a young director on his way to the top) whose subsequent career would be hampered by the Communist witchhunts.

Fallen Angel ○

1945, US, 97 mins, b/w
Dir: Otto Preminger
Stars: Dana Andrews, Alice Faye, Linda Darnell, Charles Bickford, Anne Revere, Bruce Cabot
Rating: ★★

This dark thriller was a follow-up for director Otto Preminger to his tremendously successful *Laura*. It suffers by comparison, but time has lent it qualities of its own. The direction of the scenes in the cafe is particularly interesting, as it seems that Preminger is trying to lend sinister shafts to the narrative. Alice Faye is not really comfortable in these black surroundings, but the other members of an excellent cast all seem well at home: Dana Andrews as the con-man involved with two girls, one fair, one dark; Linda Darnell, as the sluttish Stella; and Bruce Cabot, Charles Bickford, Percy Kilbride and John Carradine as assorted bystanders and suspects in an eventual murder. There's even an oft-repeated theme song – 'Slowly' which echoes the one in *Laura*.

Fallen Idol, The ○

1948, UK, 94 mins, b/w
Dir: Carol Reed
Stars: Ralph Richardson, Michele Morgan, Bobby Henrey, Jack Hawkins, Dora Bryan
Rating: ★★★★

One of Carol Reed's most subtly engrossing films, showing great understanding of character, and made in the middle of his best period (the movies he made on either side were *Odd Man Out* and *The Third Man*). Bobby Henrey responds perfectly to the demands of his director as the lonely little boy at a foreign embassy in London, who tries to protect his friend the butler (a magnetic and very sympathetic portrayal by Ralph Richardson) when the man is suspected of murder.

Falling Down ● Ⓥ

1993, US, 115 mins, colour
Dir: Joel Schumacher
Stars: Michael Douglas, Robert Duvall, Barbara Hershey, Rachel Ticotin, Frederic Forrest, Tuesday Weld, Lane Smith
Rating: ★★★

Michael Douglas gives a gripping performance as a man pushed beyond his limits in this unnerving drama set in the sweltering heat of LA's urban jungle. It begins when a shopkeeper refuses law-abiding citizen Douglas a simple request. Suddenly, Douglas snaps – and off he storms on a one-man crusade to crush the bullies and bureaucrats whom he feels are standing in his way. Robert Duvall is charismatic as the cop who, about to retire, finds himself on the trail of this white collar vigilante but, for those who feel the iron claw of inner-city stress, it's Douglas's sad and misguided anti-hero who remains the abiding memory from this powerful if somewhat pointless film.

Falling in Love ○ Ⓥ

1984, US, 107 mins, colour
Dir: Ulu Grosbard
Stars: Meryl Streep, Robert De Niro
Rating: ★★★

Robert De Niro in a romantic drama is as rare as a white Christmas, but his pairing here with Meryl Streep, as commuters who fall in love on their daily trip to Manhattan, is an unexpected delight. True, there are many coincidences for cynical viewers and New York's station platforms have never looked cleaner. But lovers of pulp fiction and anyone who harks

F

back to the golden Douglas Sirk days of 1950s Hollywood melodrama, will be weeping uncontrollably.

Fall of the House of Usher, The ● ⓥ
1960, US, 85 mins, colour
Dir: Roger Corman
Stars: Vincent Price, Mark Damon, Myrna Fahey
Rating: ★★★

A beautiful young girl's suitor comes to ask for her hand in marriage and meets her strange and gloomy older brother. Only then does the horror begin. This is the first of director Roger Corman's films based on Edgar Allan Poe's Gothic stories and an impressive start to the series. Vincent Price is in gloriously obsessed form as the doomed brother and exudes menace and apprehension in just the right quantities. Is he dangerous or merely eccentric? The photography is marvellous and the whole production is a delight for fans of Gothic horror.

Fall of the Roman Empire, The ○ ⓥ
1964, US, 173 mins, colour
Dir: Anthony Mann
Stars: Sophia Loren, Stephen Boyd, Alec Guinness, James Mason, Christopher Plummer, Omar Sharif
Rating: ★★★★

With its bleak settings and towering central story, which dwarfed personal relationships, it was inevitable that *Roman Empire* should emerge as a director's and photographer's film, rather than relying on acting for its impact. Robert Krasker's hard-edged photography brings an added magnetism to such scenes as a chariot race, a wintry funeral, a lovers' tryst and a savage pitched battle in a cave. Sophia Loren, in the film's only substantial female role, looks stunning throughout, especially in one overhead shot of her sprawled on a couch in a flimsy, hyacinth-pink gown. Mann's handling of the tumultuous crowd scenes constantly makes one aware that this important period of history is being filmed with the care, and on the scale, it deserves. Despite the scale of the action, there are several performances to admire, too – especially from Alec Guinness as the warm, wise, dying Marcus Aurellus, gentle but firm, the last of the great Roman emperors.

Fall Time ● ⓥ
1994, US, 88 mins, colour
Dir: Paul Warner

Stars: Mickey Rourke, Stephen Baldwin, Sheryl Lee, David Arquette, Jason London
Rating: ★

A grim, grisly, but hardly gripping thriller about three teenagers from macho homes who stage a fake shooting for a thrill, then find themselves caught up in a real-life bank robbery. Two of them dump a 'body' in their boot, only to find it's not their friend but the accomplice of the real robber. Recovering, he takes them prisoner. Meanwhile, the third teen has been captured by the chief robber (Mickey Rourke) who forces him to take part in the robbery instead of his partner, taking as a hostage the female cashier who should be the third member of the original gang but doesn't seem to be. You'll be quite glad to see most of these dislikeable people bumped off – in the final bloodbath – if only to get your own back for wasting your time on the whole tedious affair.

False Witness ❶
(aka: Zigzag)
1970, US, 105 mins, colour
Dir: Richard A Colla
Stars: George Kennedy, Anne Jackson, Eli Wallach
Rating: ★★★

We've seen this one before, even though this version plays an interesting variation on a well-worn theme. Facing death, a man launches an ingenious scheme to provide for his wife, involving, in this case, framing himself for an unsolved murder. Naturally, he's miraculously cured, and faces the horrendous task of escaping the fate he's prepared for himself. Nicely nervy performances by George Kennedy, Eli Wallach and Anne Jackson make this a good bet in the suspense stakes.

Fame Is the Spur ○
1947, UK, 116 mins, b/w
Dir: Roy Boulting
Stars: Michael Redgrave, Rosamund John, Bernard Miles, Carla Lehmann
Rating: ★★★

Although pretty engrossing stuff, this was not quite the great movie it might have been considering its credentials. The source novel, said to have been based on the career of Ramsey MacDonald, is by Howard Spring, and the screenplay written by Nigel Balchin. Michael Redgrave gives his usual strong, thoughtful performance as the politician whose quest for fame gradually alienates him from his ideals and friends alike, but Roy Boulting's

direction perhaps just lacks the power to stir the blood. Skilful film-making though, and a major British film of its time.

Family Affair, A ○
1937, US, 69 mins, b/w
Dir: George B Seitz
Stars: Lionel Barrymore, Spring Byington, Cecilia Parker, Eric Linden, Mickey Rooney
Rating: ★★★

Little did MGM know that this small-scale comedy would turn into an absolute goldmine known as the Andy Hardy series. The Hardy films – portraits of American small-town life in the pre-war and wartime years – made big money for the studio, principally on the popularity of Mickey Rooney, who played the Hardys' youngest son, always in and out of girl trouble. Within two years, Rooney would be America's most popular film star.

Family Business ❶ ⓥ
1989, US, 110 mins, colour
Dir: Sidney Lumet
Stars: Sean Connery, Dustin Hoffman, Matthew Broderick, Rosana DeSoto
Rating: ★★★

Pretty risky business, actually, in that the family tradition here through three generations is crime. Sean Connery, Dustin Hoffman and Matthew Broderick represent the generations involved, all three going on an exciting heist when the grandson feels he has to prove himself in the family way. It's quite enjoyable, although fairly lightweight by the standards of the talents involved, including director Sidney Lumet. And it's difficult to sympathise with the film's moral point of view. Still, Connery is at his roguish best as the grandpa and Broderick does well as the young sprig. Hoffman seems miscast as Broderick's dad, letting Connery steal all the best moments in the film.

Family Jewels, The ⊙
1965, US, 95 mins, colour
Dir: Jerry Lewis
Stars: Jerry Lewis, Donna Butterworth, Sebastian Cabot, Robert Strauss
Rating: ★★

Watch out folks – Jerry Lewis is directing himself again, and that means half the usual quota of laughs. Even so, this comedy gets off to a bright start, with the first ten minutes containing some very good visual gags, plus the always useful scene where the apparently inept hero clears the table after taking on the biggest hustler in the poolroom. It all makes pretty good entertainment for children, with plenty of bright colour, and simple, straightforward humour, coupled with the fact that the central character (Donna Butterworth) is a 12-year-old girl. When her father dies, she has to decide which of her six uncles is to be her legal guardian. The uncles, all dotty, of course, are all played by Lewis, who also appears as the family chauffeur.

Family Plot ○ ⓥ
1976, US, 120 mins, colour
Dir: Alfred Hitchcock
Stars: Karen Black, Bruce Dern, Barbara Harris, William Devane
Rating: ★★★

Hitchcock's last film is perhaps lightweight Hitch, but still an entertaining comedy-thriller in which the Master gets more chance than usual to display his sense of humour. Classic Hitchcock situations abound in the story of a fake spiritualist (Barbara Harris) and her cabbie lover (Bruce Dern) who are out to find the long-lost illegitimate nephew of a millionairess who wants to leave him all her money. It's not giving too much of the plot away to say that the nephew turns out to be a notorious kidnapper (William Devane). Trails cross, uncross and cross again in a typical Hitchcock finale. The stars all give good performances, while remaining subservient to the director's demands on the plot and especially such set pieces as a car chase and a funeral. There's even some serviceable suspense at the end.

Family Way, The ❶
1966, UK, 110 mins, colour
Dir: Roy Boulting
Stars: Hayley Mills, Hywel Bennett, John Mills
Rating: ★★★

John Mills turns the tables on daughter Hayley – who walked away with their earlier film *Tiger Bay* – by stealing every scene in which he appears in this story of a north country wedding and a young couple frustrated by the proximity of their in-laws. His is a fully rounded portrayal of an old-school working man, well in the tradition of his other provincial portrayals in *Hobson's Choice* and the underrated *The History of Mr Polly*. It's also a performance that touches the heart, as do those of Hywel Bennett (in his screen debut) and Hayley Mills as the newly-weds.

Fan, The ● ⓥ
1996, US, 114 mins, colour
Dir: Tony Scott
Stars: Robert De Niro, Wesley Snipes, Ellen Barkin, John Leguizamo, Benicio Del Toro
Rating: ★★

The psycho Robert De Niro made his own in *Taxi Driver* and *Cape Fear* has spiralled out of control, as he plays an obsessed baseball fan who sees murder as the way to get his favourite player (Wesley Snipes) back in the team. When Snipes proves understandably ungrateful, De Niro kidnaps the star's son. If you think this is unlikely, it gets sillier, and Snipes is so odious you half hope that stalker De Niro will actually get him. It's all an overwrought, underdone suspense thriller with too little drama to justify the length. While *Top Gun* director Tony Scott puts a high gloss on the slam-bang proceedings, this can't atone for the film's lack of substance.

Fanatic ❶
(aka: Die, Die, My Darling)
1964, UK, 97 mins, colour
Dir: Silvio Narizzano
Stars: Tallulah Bankhead, Stefanie Powers, Peter Vaughan, Yootha Joyce, Donald Sutherland
Rating: ★★

This fearsome dose of Grand Guignol from the house of Hammer horror features Tallulah Bankhead, in her last screen role, playing with all stops out as a religious fanatic who imprisons her dead son's fiancée – to the accompaniment of a screenplay by Richard Matheson, who wrote almost all the film adaptations of Edgar Allan Poe's work. One little annoyance: why does the fanatic leave the girl with a convenient ashtray in her attic prison, when she is a professed hater of smoking?

Fancy Pants ⊙
1950, US, 88 mins, colour
Dir: George Marshall
Stars: Bob Hope, Lucille Ball, Bruce Cabot
Rating: ★★★

Bob Hope reverts to almost pure Mack Sennett slapstick in this riotous, glowingly Technicolored comedy, a hectic remake of *Ruggles of Red Cap* that pokes fun at everything from Westerns to English gentlemen. Hope plays Humphrey, an actor hired to pose as an English butler by an adventurer who wants to marry Agatha, daughter of the wealthy Floud family. Agatha's social-climbing mother is so impressed

that she drags Humphrey back west to teach the tearaway Agatha how to be a proper Eastern lady. Songs by Jay Livingston and Ray Evans and a vivacious performance by Ball round off a bright package.

Fandango ○
1984, US, 91 mins, colour
Dir: Kevin Reynolds
Stars: Kevin Costner, Judd Nelson, Elizabeth Daily
Rating: ★★

This was the film in which Kevin Costner first showed star quality – but then he had ended up on the cutting-room floor in his previous two parts. Here he provides dynamic presence at the heart of this rites-of-passage picture set in 1971 when the Vietnam war and the draft were still looming large in students' lives. The rest of the good cast are up to the material's demands if not having the same assured confidence with the script as Costner.

Fanny ○
1960, US, 133 mins, colour
Dir: Joshua Logan
Stars: Leslie Caron, Maurice Chevalier, Charles Boyer, Horst Buchholz
Rating: ★★★

The bistros and fish stalls of the old Marseilles waterfront were the setting for Marcel Pagnol's salty 1930s trilogy (memorably filmed in France at the time) about Fanny, César, Panisse and the other characters of the ancient Mediterranean port. Director Joshua Logan has taken his cameras back to the old haunts to tell the story once more, with feeling. Jack Cardiff's photography gives a glossy rinse to the old city. Leslie Caron gives a poignant performance as the girl who falls in love with a sailor (Horst Buchholz), then finds, after he has gone away to sea, that she is expecting his baby. Maurice Chevalier is touchingly true as the old man who marries the girl for the sake of the child.

Fanny by Gaslight ○
1944, UK, 108 mins, b/w
Dir: Anthony Asquith
Stars: Phyllis Calvert, James Mason, Wilfrid Lawson, Stewart Granger
Rating: ★★★

The Gainsborough Lady, who inclined her head so charmingly from the company's trademark, never smiled more radiantly than in the early Forties when, at their Shepherd's Bush and Islington studios, Gainsborough produced a crop of box-office winners.

F

With the advantage of a good script adapted from Michael Sadleir's novel and direction by Anthony Asquith, *Fanny by Gaslight* proved to be one of Gainsborough's best. And as the evil Lord Manderstoke, James Mason contributed one of his 'villainous cad' parts.

Fantasia O Ⓥ

1940, US, 117 mins, colour
Dir: Samuel Armstrong, James Algar, Bill Roberts, Paul Satterfield, Hamilton Luske, Jim Handley, Ford Beebe, T Hee, Norman Ferguson, Wilfred Jackson
Rating: ★★★★★

Probably the best and most imaginative Disney cartoon feast ever set before an audience. Eight pieces of music are set to cartoon images to create a wonderland of magic and charm; once entered, you are completely under its spell for close to two hours. Some of the colour work is still amazing today and so brilliant are the cartoons that it often seems that the music has been synchronised to the picture and not vice versa. All eight segments are excellent, but outstanding are the 'Nutcracker Suite' (the dance of the toadstools is a comic highlight never to be forgotten), 'The Rite of Spring' (a brilliantly impressionistic vision of the Dark Ages), Beethoven's 'Pastoral Symphony' (sentimental but possibly the most delightful of all) and 'A Night on a Bare Mountain' (a scary, eerie and lurid interpretation of Mussorgsky). All this, and, Mickey Mouse as 'The Sorcerer's Apprentice' too. Such stuff as dreams are made of – outlasting the years.

Fantastic Voyage O

1966, US, 100 mins, colour
Dir: Richard Fleischer
Stars: Stephen Boyd, Raquel Welch, Edmond O'Brien, Donald Pleasence, Arthur Kennedy
Rating: ★★

Fantastic is the word for it as five scientists are shrunk to pinpoint size and injected into the vein of a genius to try and save his life. The special effects are weirdly beautiful, and the same could be said for Raquel Welch in her first big starring role. The plot gets progressively sillier.

Far and Away ◑ Ⓥ

1992, US, 140 mins, colour
Dir: Ron Howard
Stars: Tom Cruise, Nicole Kidman, Thomas Gibson, Robert Prosky, Barbara Babcock
Rating: ★★★

There hadn't been such a sprawlingly old-fashioned romantic melodrama as this in quite a while. Tom Cruise, with an Irish accent good enough to pass muster unless you're Irish, is the son of a poor dirt farmer in 1890s western Ireland. Swearing vengeance for the death of his father and the burning of their home, he somehow ends up with the daughter (Nicole Kidman) of his sworn enemy finding that she is as eager to escape her environment as he is. They get to America posing as brother and sister, lodging in what turns out to be a brothel, where there is, but naturally, only one room for the both of them. Cruise takes out his frustrated love for her by earning money as an unorthodox boxer, but their unspoken affection proves their undoing and a tragedy or two ensues, before the story sweeps to a gloriously corny and excitingly shot finish in the midst of the great Oklahoma land rush of 1903. The film teems with detail in a relatively unobtrusive manner, in the fashion of films from a much earlier time.

Far Country, The O

1954, US, 95 mins, colour
Dir: Anthony Mann
Stars: James Stewart, Ruth Roman, Corinne Calvet, Walter Brennan
Rating: ★★★

A rip-snorting Technicolor Western from the middle of director Anthony Mann's best period of work. Stars James Stewart and Ruth Roman have to give second-best to Walter Brennan (another of his grizzled Westerners), Corinne Calvet as a winsome French-Canadian spitfire and John McIntire as the top-hatted villain. Solid value for fans of both Stewart and the Western.

Farewell Again O

(aka: Troopship)
1937, UK, 81 mins, b/w
Dir: Tim Whelan
Stars: Leslie Banks, Flora Robson, Robert Newton
Rating: ★★★

Absorbing, well-directed British film which has worn remarkably well and remains well worth a view as the archetypal a-few-hours-ashore style drama. The photography – James Wong Howe, Hans Schneeburger and Wilkie Cooper all worked on the film – is first-rate, while director Tim Whelan pulls disparate elements together with consummate skill to create a richly human film.

Farewell, My Lovely ◑

1975, US, 95 mins, colour
Dir: Dick Richards
Stars: Robert Mitchum, Charlotte Rampling, John Ireland, Sylvia Miles, Jack O'Halloran, Anthony Zerbe
Rating: ★★★

The best of the more modern recreations of Forties' detective thrillers, and only a pace behind the Dick Powell original. Robert Mitchum is a serviceable Marlowe, even at 57, and lovers of the atmospheric thick-ear thriller won't complain about the action. Charlotte Rampling does quite a good imitation of Lauren Bacall as the society siren, handling the best of the throwaway dialogue with dry aplomb. And there's an early screen role for Sylvester Stallone as one of the bad guys. Director Dick Richards, whose best film this is, prowls his cameras menacingly through some marvellously seedy neo-Forties settings.

Farewell, My Lovely O

(aka: Murder, My Sweet)
1945, US, 95 mins, b/w
Dir: Edward Dmytryk
Stars: Dick Powell, Claire Trevor, Anne Shirley, Otto Kruger, Mike Mazurki
Rating: ★★★★

With one bound, Dick Powell leapt from baby-faced singer to tough-guy superstar in this remarkably faithful adaptation of Raymond Chandler's hard-boiled thriller. He plays detective Philip Marlowe, and chronicles his involvement with the massive Moose Malloy's search for his ex-girlfriend Velma, whose identity remains a mystery until near the end. Full of very punchy scenes (often aided by camera trickery) and an atmosphere of menace, the film has dry, laconic acting by Powell. The movie's eye-opening centrepiece is Marlowe's imprisonment in a terrifying clinic, from whence, though drugged to the eyeballs, he eventually manages to escape, producing the classic piece of self-advice: 'Okay Marlowe, you're a tough guy, you've been sapped twice, choked, beaten silly with a gun, shot in the arm until you're as crazy as a couple of waltzing mice. Now let's see you do something really tough – like putting your pants on!' Chandler was so grateful to writer John Paxton for retaining the structure, flavour and much of the dialogue of the original novel that he wrote him a personal letter of thanks.

Farewell to Arms, A ○ Ⓥ
1957, US, 150 mins, colour
Dir: Charles Vidor
Stars: Rock Hudson, Jennifer Jones,
Vittorio De Sica, Mercedes McCambridge
Rating: ★★

This epic combination of weepie and
World War One action film was first
brought to the screen in 1932 with
Helen Hayes and Gary Cooper. This
version encompasses much more of
Ernest Hemingway's novel and boasts
a steady and occasionally inspired performance by Rock Hudson that ranks
among his best. Jennifer Jones is rather
less successful as the nurse with whom
he falls in love, but the war scenes, including a colossal snowbound retreat
reminiscent of Vidor's *War and Peace,*
have a quite breathtaking impact.

Farewell to the King ◐ Ⓥ
1988, UK, 117 mins, colour
Dir: John Milius
Stars: Nick Nolte, Nigel Havers, James
Fox, Frank McRae
Rating: ★★★★

There's a lot of the spirit of Joseph
Conrad in this wartime adventure. Set
(and shot) in Borneo, it catches the
imagination in much the same way as
Conrad's flavoursome stories of wan-
derings and adventures in the Far East.
Nick Nolte is impressive as Learoyd,
an American deserter who becomes
king of a Bornean tribe, and has much
in common with Conrad's *Lord Jim.*
Both stories contain blood brothers of
different races, action in the jungle and
a narrator who lives through at least
part of the story, played in this case by
Nigel Havers, giving his best film performance as the botanist turned officer
whose mission is to enlist the jungle
tribes for the fight against the Japanese.
Some of the consequent battle scenes
amid monsoon conditions are vividly,
imaginatively staged.

Far from the Madding Crowd ○
1967, UK, 169 mins, colour
Dir: John Schlesinger
Stars: Julie Christie, Terence Stamp,
Peter Finch, Alan Bates
Rating: ★★★

Although never in quite the same
league as Roman Polanski's *Tess,* John
Schlesinger's attempt at confining the
lush, sweeping narrative of Thomas
Hardy to the screen is a worthy one.
As the central character, Bathsheba
Everdene, Julie Christie is in imperious
form – a strongly independent soul on
the surface, but a victim of Hardy's ob-

sessions with the fallibility of man and
the cruel hand of fate underneath. The
film is worth watching for Miss
Christie alone. The three men vying
for her hand in marriage are played by
an impressive trio – Alan Bates, Peter
Finch and Terence Stamp, with Finch
just edging out the others in the acting
stakes.

Fargo ● Ⓥ
1996, US, 97 mins, colour
Dir: Joel Coen
Stars: Frances McDormand, William H
Macy, Steve Buscemi, Harve Presnell,
Peter Stormare
Rating: ★★★

A grim black comedy based on one of
those bizarre sequences of events
where petty crime leads to mass murder. Desperate for money, which he
will not get from his wife's millionaire
father, Jerry (William H Macy) hires,
through a friend, two evil-tempered,
short-fused gunmen (Steve Buscemi,
Peter Stormare) to kidnap his own wife
for a million dollar ransom, leading
them to believe it's only a small proportion of that sum. Just about everything
goes wrong, leading the crooks to leave
a swathe of bloody murders behind
them. Then the millionaire (Harve
Presnell) refuses to give Macy the
money and insists on delivering it himself. Fortunately the lady chief of
police (Frances McDormand), although
six months pregnant, is very much
more astute than her staff, and is soon
on the trail of the truth. A fascinating
mixture of gore and giggles, not without its dull patches, this has an ace
performance by McDormand, and
some very off-kilter dialogue.
Staggering in with a bullet through the
neck, Buscemi grimaces at his colleague. 'You should see the other guy,'
he growls.

Far Horizons, The ○
1955, US, 108 mins, colour
Dir: Rudolph Maté
Stars: Charlton Heston, Fred MacMurray,
Donna Reed, Barbara Hale, William
Demarest
Rating: ★★

Jump into your canoe for a refresher
course in early American history.
Opening up the west wasn't all done in
covered wagons; sometimes they took
to the boats. A splashing time is had
by all in this colourful 'dramatisation'
of classroom history, which was the
biggest film ever produced by the ac-
tion-minded unit of producers William
Pine and William Thomas. The script

hits a few rocks and shallow passages,
but there's enough action to keep the
going good. Charlton Heston and
Fred MacMurray keep stiff jaws as the
waterborne pioneers Lewis and Clark.

Farmer Takes a Wife, The ○
1953, US, 81 mins, colour
Dir: Henry Levin
Stars: Betty Grable, Dale Robertson,
Thelma Ritter, John Carroll
Rating: ★★★

The blonde hair and million-dollar legs
of Betty Grable – the idol of and sex
symbol for the GIs of World War Two
– can be seen in this breeze-fresh musical version of a much earlier film, with
eight good tunes pepping up the plot.
Thelma Ritter has a good comedy role.
Betty's heyday, though, was clearly
over: in Britain, the film was released
as a second-feature.

Far North ◐ Ⓥ
1988, US, 89 mins, colour
Dir: Sam Shepard
Stars: Jessica Lange, Charles Durning,
Tess Harper, Donald Moffat, Patricia
Arquette
Rating: RB

Well might the makers of this farrago
thank the North American Loon Fund.
Only they perhaps would have been
loony enough to believe they could
make any money from a story that revolves entirely around a
not-quite-all-there family that can't
make up its mind whether or not to
shoot a horse. Personally, we'd have
shot writer-director Sam Shepard instead, especially for giving us so many
dingy shots of trees to pad his film out
to an interminable hour and a half. He
gets strident performances from Jessica
Lange, Charles Durning, Tess Harper
and Patricia Arquette, though he does
give them dialogue that never manages
to sound like things people would really say.

Far Off Place, A ○ Ⓥ
1993, US, 105 mins, colour
Dir: Mikael Salomon
Stars: Reese Witherspoon, Ethan
Randall, Maximilian Schell, Jack
Thompson, Robert Burke
Rating: ★★★

Although probably a bit too graphic at
times for young children, and certainly
red in tooth and claw, this is a superbly
shot, old-fashioned Disney adventure
that will please teenagers and pre-teens
of a stern disposition. Nonnie (Reese
Witherspoon), a game warden's daughter, and Harry (Ethan Randall), a

F

visitor from the city, are two teenagers living on an African wildlife reserve. A brutal attack by a gang of ivory poachers leaves the kids orphaned and as the only witnesses to the murders of their parents, they are forced to flee into the barren Kalahari Desert. There they face hunger, exhaustion, sandstorms and wild animals, with the killers all the while hot on their trail. The trek's a shade on the slow side, but pictorial qualities compensate, the acting is staunch, and the elephants steal the show.

Fashions of 1934 ○
(aka: Fashions)
1934, US, 78 mins, b/w
Dir: William Dieterle
Stars: William Powell, Bette Davis, Frank McHugh, Verree Teasdale
Rating: ★★★

One doesn't expect much from Hollywood films with titles like this, but the presence of William Powell, as a dapper con-man, and Bette Davis, a devious designer, alerts you to the fact that there may be more than a parade of gowns on display here. And so it proves. An accompanying story of industrial chicanery is decked out with dance spectacle from Busby Berkeley, a witty script that allows room for a rollicking performance from Verree Teasdale as a fake duchess, a lively story and sophisticated good humour. Powell is at his most debonair, and even Frank McHugh is more bearable than usual as an enterprising photographer who carries a miniature camera in the handle of his cane.

Fast and Furious ○
1939, US, 70 mins, b/w
Dir: Busby Berkeley
Stars: Franchot Tone, Ann Sothern, Lee Bowman, Ruth Hussey
Rating: ★★★

One of several Hollywood comedy-mysteries spun around the sleuthing exploits of husband and wife team Joel and Garda Sloane (played here by Franchot Tone and Ann Sothern), whose wisecracks and light touch made their adventures obvious rivals to the *The Thin Man* series. Busby Berkeley directs without a sum number in sight although he does have a bevy of beauty contestants as part of the murder-strewn plot.

Fast and Loose ○
1939, US, 80 mins, b/w
Dir: Edwin L Marin
Stars: Robert Montgomery, Rosalind

Russell, Ralph Morgan
Rating: ★★

There are lots of good actors to bolster one's enjoyment of this otherwise routine romantic mystery thriller from the MGM stable. Robert Montgomery (in training for his next role as Lord Peter Wimsey) and Rosalind Russell are bright leads and the supporting cast is full of those familiar faces to whom one could never quite put the name.

Fast and Loose ○
1954, UK, 75 mins, b/w
Dir: Gordon Parry
Stars: Stanley Holloway, Kay Kendall, Brian Reece
Rating: ★

A romping bedroom farce of Whitehall proportions. Ben Travers, who wrote many of the Whitehall successes in the Thirties, actually worked on the screenplay of this film, which is an inferior remake of the 1934 version of his play *A Cuckoo in the Nest*.

Fast Company ○
1938, US, 75 mins, b/w
Dir: Edward Buzzell
Stars: Melvyn Douglas, Florence Rice, Louis Calhern
Rating: ★★

Comedy mystery featuring the sleuthing book experts from *Fast and Loose*, Joel and Garda Sloane. Here they're played by Melvyn Douglas (the best Joel) and Florence Rice. The best Garda, Ann Sothern, didn't come along until the third adventure, *Fast and Furious*. Nostalgia fans will catch their breath at a list of suspects that includes some of Hollywood's most distinctive character actors of the day, Louis Calhern, Shepperd Strudwick, Dwight Frye, Douglass Dumbrille, Thurston Hall, George Zucco and Horace MacMahon among them.

Fastest Gun Alive, The ○
1956, US, 85 mins, b/w
Dir: Russell Rouse
Stars: Glenn Ford, Broderick Crawford, Jeanne Crain, Russ Tamblyn, Leif Erickson
Rating: ★★

A workmanlike, if not too inspired, airing for what must be one of the oldest Western plots around – the gunman who tries to retire but has to face yet another fast gun to whom the word has somehow got around. Director Russell Rouse ensures that the following events keep one guessing until the end of the last reel. Glenn Ford gives an edgy,

carefully considered performance as the man whose prowess with a gun hangs over him like the Sword of Damocles, but the most powerful portrayal comes from Broderick Crawford, as the man hunting him.

Fast Lady, The ○
1962, UK, 95 mins, colour
Dir: Ken Annakin
Stars: James Robertson Justice, Stanley Baxter, Leslie Phillips, Julie Christie
Rating: ★★★

The same team's follow-up to the hilarious success of *Very Important Person* and *Crooks Anonymous*. The fast lady of the title is not, as one might imagine, Julie Christie – here playing her first big role in a colour film – but a souped-up car.

Fatal Attraction ● ⊙
1987, US, 120 mins, colour
Dir: Adrian Lyne
Stars: Michael Douglas, Glenn Close, Anne Archer, Fred Gwynne
Rating: ★★★

A rollercoaster thriller about a one-night stand that goes hideously wrong. Feminists were up in arms about the portrayal of the spurned lover (Glenn Close) who sets out to ruin married Michael Douglas 'happy' home life. On a more superficial level, it's a cracking good white-knuckle ride, with plenty of shocks and heart-stopping moments, several of which are annoyingly telegraphed well ahead. The much-imitated ending would be more at home in a *Rambo* film, and the unreleased alternative 'suicide' ending for Japan, that implies Douglas will be charged with murder because his fingerprints are found on a knife used two-thirds of the way through the film, would have been an improvement. None of this fazed the paying public, who made the film an enormous popular hit.

Fat City ◐
1972, US, 100 mins, colour
Dir: John Huston
Stars: Stacy Keach, Jeff Bridges, Susan Tyrrell, Candy Clark
Rating: ★★★★

John Huston's best film of the Seventies. The film's theme song, 'Help me Make it Through the Night', composed and sung by Kris Kristofferson, is immensely appropriate, as the film is all about making it through the night and day – getting a foothold on life, and coming to terms with failure. Stacy Keach and Jeff Bridges give career-best performances as two boxers in whom hope springs eternal, but leads, inevitably, to their continual disillusionment. And that much underrated and underused actress Susan Tyrrell gives a haunting performance as the sad Oma, using a voice that sounds thoroughly soaked in a mixture of gin and tears. Conrad Hall's photography rightly emphasises the non-existent glamour of the lower reaches of the boxing profession.

Father Brown ○
(aka: The Detective)
1954, UK, 90 mins, b/w
Dir: Robert Hamer
Stars: Alec Guinness, Joan Greenwood, Peter Finch, Cecil Parker, Bernard Lee, Sidney James
Rating: ★★★★

This stylish comedy-thriller is probably director Robert Hamer's most successful film apart from *Kind Hearts and Coronets*, and it reunited him with Alec Guinness. Guinness cleverly gets under the skin of G K Chesterton's priest-detective; his scenes with Peter Finch's suave master criminal Flambeau are a delight. In the course of the story Hamer veers from high suspense, through near-melodrama to light comedy and, with the invaluable help of Guinness, he masters them all.

Father Came Too ○
1963, UK, 93 mins, colour
Dir: Peter Graham Scott
Stars: Stanley Baxter, Leslie Phillips, James Robertson Justice, Sally Smith
Rating: ★★

A comedy from the *Fast Lady* team that starts off promisingly with a Scotsman worrying about the size of the tip his bride has given the chambermaid on their honeymoon, before it trails off into a series of music-hall jokes about how not to decorate a house. People put their feet in paint buckets, get their faces painted when they open doors, fall through floorboards, tread on wallpaper they are about to put up, and generally behave in similar fashion to circus clowns. Stanley Baxter is the harassed husband, Sally Smith a dishy bride.

Father Goose ○ ⓥ
1964, US, 116 mins, colour
Dir Ralph Nelson
Stars: Cary Grant, Leslie Caron, Trevor Howard, Jack Good
Rating: ★★★

Thank goodness for Cary Grant. He makes this naive family comedy seem at times the quintessence of wit, play-

ing a sockless, unshaven, whisky-swilling beachcomber in the Pacific during World War Two. He's blackmailed into spying for the Allies by wily old officer Trevor Howard, who reveals the whereabouts of a bottle of whisky hidden on Grant's island for every snippet of information sent. What Grant doesn't bargain for are teacher Leslie Caron and her seven schoolgirl charges who get cast away on the island with him. As long as Grant has the upper hand in his running battle with the flock of females, the film remains funny. When it's the other way round, it's frequently embarrassing, thanks to a heavy performance by Caron that almost sinks the ship.

Father Hood ◑ ⓥ
1993, US, 95 mins, colour
Dir: Darrell James Roodt
Stars: Patrick Swayze, Sabrina Lloyd, Halle Berry, Michael Ironside, Diane Ladd, Adrienne Barbeau
Rating: ★★

Small-time criminal Jack Charles (Patrick Swayze) is saddled with being a dad when his daughter Kelly (Sabrina Lloyd) runs away from her miserable foster home. Jack is forced to take Kelly and her brother (Brian Bonsall) on the run in this action-packed but largely comical cross-country chase. Screen idol Swayze does well as the tough hoodlum with the soft centre and some decent laughs help offset the ever-lurking sentimentality in a story which could do with just a little bit more bite and believability.

Father of the Bride ○ ⓥ
1950, US, 93 mins, b/w
Dir: Vincente Minnelli
Stars: Spencer Tracy, Joan Bennett, Elizabeth Taylor, Russ Tamblyn, Don Taylor
Rating: ★★★★

Famous comedy about the many crises leading up to an impending marriage. Spencer Tracy is superb as the harassed father, and there are some lovely set-piece comedy scenes. Elizabeth Taylor (at 17) and Rusty (Russ) Tamblyn (at 15) are his daughter and son. Great fun, which led to a sequel – *Father's Little Dividend* – with Tracy again as the star. Joan Bennett plays the heartily domestic mother.

Father of the Bride ○ ⓥ
1991, US, 105 mins, colour
Dir: Charles Shyer
Stars: Steve Martin, Diane Keaton,

Kimberly Williams, Martin Short
Rating: ★★★

This glossy, slightly ruder remake of the Spencer Tracy-Joan Bennett classic is not far short of the original in warmth and humour, with Steve Martin superb as the doting father who careers off the rails at the news of his beloved daughter's impending wedding. The script hardly makes the most of Diane Keaton's talents as his wife, though, and Kimberly Williams not unexpectedly lacks Elizabeth Taylor's beauty and glow. Martin Short scores in a smartly written cameo role, and the whole makes ideal, well-paced entertainment for reasonably broadminded families.

Father of the Bride Part II
○ ⓥ
1995, US, 107 mins, colour
Dir: Charles Shyer
Stars: Steve Martin, Diane Keaton, Martin Short, Kimberly Williams
Rating: ★

A distressingly flat sequel in which almost nothing happens except Steve Martin going gooey in turn over daughter, wife, home and babies – as both daughter and wife prove to be expecting at the same time. Warmth and generosity don't sit well with a Martin character, but here the old wild and crazy lion is painfully tamed, managing only a few snarls of defiance before succumbing entirely to an unbearably sticky and sentimental script. As to his problems, well, they don't amount to a hill of beans, since a man who can afford to buy back his own palatial home at an excess of $100,000, build a baby extension out of *Ideal Home* and hold a huge double baby shower obviously has enough money to make us all want to go out and rob a bank. The film still has Diane Keaton's charm going for it; she alone emerges from this lumpen glucose mess with any credit.

Fathers' Day ○ ⓥ
1997, US, 99 mins, colour
Dir: Ivan Reitman
Stars: Robin Williams, Billy Crystal, Nastassja Kinski, Julia-Louis Dreyfus, Bruce Greenwood, Mel Gibson
Rating: ★★★

One-liner chuckles come consistently in this amiable canter for Crystal and Williams as lawyer and failed writer respectively, both suckered by an old flame (Kinski) into hunting for her missing teenage son on the grounds that one of them might be his real father. Crystal's a smart cookie on his

F

third marriage whose skill in head-buttting comes in handy in the quest, but Williams has the sharper moments as the would-be-suicide who 'teaches English as a third language at the Jewish community centre'. Also on the trail is Kinski's husband (Greenwood) who gets trapped in a crashed portaloo in a ditch... but no, you don't want to know about that one. Crystal and Williams team cheerily enough in this underrated comedy. 'You know Lou Gehrig,' says Crystal. 'The baseball player! He died of Lou Gehrig's disease.' Williams' eyes widen. 'Gee,' he gasps, 'what are the odds on that?'"

Father's Doing Fine ○
1952, UK, 83 mins, colour
Dir: Henry Cass
Stars: Richard Attenborough, Heather Thatcher, Diane Hart
Rating: ★★★

A boisterous British comedy about a scatterbrained widow, her four equally dotty daughters, various offspring, and a life full of trouble and strife. There are more entrances and exits than in a Brian Rix farce and great fun is had by all, especially Richard Attenborough as the expectant father of one of the daughters.

Father's Little Dividend ○
1951, US, 82 mins, b/w
Dir: Vincente Minnelli
Stars: Spencer Tracy, Joan Bennett, Elizabeth Taylor, Russ Tamblyn, Don Taylor
Rating: ★★★

For once a sequel that's almost as good as the original. This is a sparkling comedy follow-up to *Father of the Bride*, with the same cast, writers and director. Spencer Tracy is magnificent, at first loathing the idea of grandfatherhood, then doting on the baby when it does arrive, even though it erupts in floods of tears whenever he gets near it. A model of how to make a superbly constructed, constantly funny situation comedy.

Fathom ○
1967, UK, 99 mins, colour
Dir: Leslie H Martinson
Stars: Raquel Welch, Anthony Franciosa, Ronald Fraser, Richard Briers
Rating: ★★

Spy spoof, with Raquel Welch as a sky diver involved with an enigmatic Englishman and a Scot who claims to be a top security chief. Top-dressing from director Leslie Martinson (though

not, fortunately, for Miss Welch) includes some remarkable colour effects.

Fat Man and Little Boy
See: Shadow Makers

Favour, the Watch and the Very Big Fish, The ○ ⓥ
1991, UK/France, 89 mins, colour
Dir: Ben Lewin
Stars: Bob Hoskins, Jeff Goldblum, Natasha Richardson, Angela Pleasence, Jean-Pierre Cassel
Rating: ★

A surreal, stylised comedy that has some attractive elements, but one major fault: apart from one or two isolated moments, it just isn't funny. Bob Hoskins is Louis, a photographer of staged religious scenes who, through a favour to a friend, becomes involved with Sybil (Natasha Richardson), who runs a beauty parlour and doubles as a voice-over actress for porno movies. She in turn tells him about her affair with a glum pianist (Jeff Goldblum), whom she drove to madness and violence when seduced by a demon violinist. The pianist emerges from jail to be grabbed by Louis who wants him to pose as Jesus in a series of tableaux. Director Ben Lewin signals the few funny moments heavily.

FBI Story, The ○
1958, US, 149 mins, colour
Dir: Mervyn LeRoy
Stars: James Stewart, Vera Miles, Murray Hamilton, Larry Pennell, Nick Adams
Rating: ★★★

The last crime story directed by Mervyn LeRoy, and made at Warners, scene of such great LeRoy successes as *Little Caesar*, *Five Star Final* and *I Am a Fugitive from a Chain Gang*. It rambles a bit from time to time, but James Stewart is a pillar of strength and integrity, and enough ammunition is expended in numerous thrill-a-minute segments about famous gangsters to make the average *Untouchables* story appear sedate by comparison.

Fear ● ⓥ
1996, US, 96 mins, colour
Dir: James Foley
Stars: Mark Wahlberg, Reese Witherspoon, William Petersen, Amy Brenneman, Alyssa Milano
Rating: ★

Apart from some crudely manipulated but quite effective suspense terror at the end, this is almost a disaster. Nubile teenager Witherspoon, teetering off to school in full warpaint, boobs

hanging out of her mini, is clearly not destined for a long virginity. What father Petersen is doing allowing this can only be imagined, but unsurprisingly the entire family is soon in the clutches of the date from hell, a soft-voiced psycho (Wahlberg), whom Reese meets hanging out with his wild-eyed mates at the local pool hall. She thinks she sees a gentler side to him, but it's only a cover for the rages that surface whenever he sees her with anyone he considers threatening. Once she gets the picture, Reese tries to cast him aside. Too late, too late, and the scene is set for one of those confrontational setpieces at which Hollywood excels – although the villain shooting his own henchmen is one cliché too many even for this heap of unconvincing contrivances.

Fear Inside, The ● ⓥ
1991, US, 115 mins, colour
Dir: Leon Ichaso
Stars: Christine Lahti, Dylan McDermott, Jennifer Rubin, David Ackroyd, Thomas Ian Nicholas
Rating: ★★

For three-quarters of its running time at any rate, this is a psychological thriller that's better than most. Pretty unpleasant most of the time, it features another good performance by Christine Lahti, as the lady trapped in her own home by agoraphobia, not to mention a psychopathic robber (Dylan McDermott) and his seemingly nice-as-pie killer girlfriend (Jennifer Rubin). Credibly etched characters rack up the tension in an often jumpy, scary thriller that unfortunately becomes increasingly unlikely and illogical in the last couple of reels. Extensive use of blue filters may prove a bit of an eyestrain here.

Fear Is the Key ○ ⓥ
1972, UK, 108 mins, colour
Dir: Michael Tuchner
Stars: Barry Newman, Suzy Kendall, John Vernon, Ray McAnally
Rating: ★★★

During the 20-minute, no-holds-barred car chase that opens the thriller, it seems that Barry Newman is still carrying on the duel with death that he started in his previous film, *Vanishing Point*. In the event, *Fear Is the Key* proves to be a cleverly-plotted, helter-skelter, Alistair MacLean thriller, ideally suited to Newman's own high pressure, short-fuse style of acting. Here he's cast as a man out for revenge on those who killed his wife, child and brother, and his hard-driving portrayal of the obsessed Talbot carries the film excitingly through to an equally thrilling climax, 400 feet down on the seabed. In the featured cast, watch out for Ben Kingsley.

Fearless ● Ⓥ
1993, US, 122 mins, colour
Dir: Peter Weir
Stars: Jeff Bridges, Rosie Perez, Tom Hulce, Isabella Rossellini, John Turturro
Rating: ★

Director Peter Weir has made some impressive films in his time, but this isn't one of them. Jeff Bridges plays the survivor of an air crash who now has no fear of dying and gets up everyone's nose with his bizarre attitudes on his return to the living. It might be a bit more interesting if Bridges were a ghost but alas it's just a form of PCS (Post-crash shock) and, though helpless to help himself, he does aid a fellow survivor (Rosie Perez) to come to terms with the loss of her baby. Such arrant nonsense needs to be a good deal faster of foot to be of interest and this turns out instead to be a deeply irritating (not to mention slow and boring) film which Weir's mystic, doomy treatment and Bridges' dishevelled mumbling do little to enliven. Perez was mysteriously Oscar-nominated for this, although much of her dialogue is unintelligible.

Fearless Vampire Killers, The
See: Dance of the Vampires

Fedora ○
1978, West Germany, 115 mins, colour
Dir: Billy Wilder
Stars: Marthe Keller, William Holden, Jose Ferrer, Hildegarde Knef, Frances Sternhagen
Rating: ★★

Billy Wilder's stately puzzle picture co-written with his old partner-in-crime I A L Diamond and adapted from a short story by former actor Tom Tryon. Why should a seemingly age-less actress throw herself under a train for no apparent reason? You may well guess most of the answers before the end, but the fascination lies in the picture's sheer style, its contemplation of celebrity and its portrait of people trapped within their own images.

Feds ◐
1988, US, 91 mins, colour
Dir: Dan Goldberg
Stars: Rebecca DeMornay, Mary Gross, Ken Marshall
Rating: ★

This film's executive producer, Ivan Reitman, has delivered some of Hollywood's greatest comedy hits as a director, including *Ghost Busters, Kindergarten Cop, Twins* and *Dave*. But this was a rare dud. Rebecca DeMornay and Mary Gross are the un-happy twosome enduring numerous vulgar jokes and considerable humilia-tion at the hands of male recruits at the FBI's training school. It's basically a re-hash of ideas and gags that were already looking exceedingly ropey from the *Police Academy* films and *Private Benjamin*. There isn't an original idea or gag in Len Blum and Dan Goldberg's transparent screenplay.

Feeling Minnesota ● Ⓥ
1996, US, 99 mins, colour
Dir: Steve Baigelman
Stars: Keanu Reeves, Cameron Diaz, Vincent D'Onofrio, Delroy Lindo, Courtney Love, Tuesday Weld, Dan Aykroyd
Rating: ★★

It's hard to know exactly where they went wrong with this attractively cast drama of alienation that turns into a road movie with a rainbow ending. But perhaps one of the film's problems is that it's attractively cast. Keanu Reeves can do light comedy and light action, but he's all at sea in this story, as Jjaks (any film with a leading charac-ter called Jjaks is in trouble to begin with), fresh out of prison and back in town for his brother's wedding. He's seduced by the bride (Diaz) who was being forced into the marriage by local gangsters and they run away together. The improbabilities start piling up from here on in as small-town deprivation is ditched in favour of an escapist love story, the film finally falling heavily be-tween a good many stools. Even so, it's better than the trailer for the movie, which seems contrived to make you not want to see it.

Fellow Traveller ◑ Ⓥ
1989, UK, 97 mins, colour
Dir: Philip Saville
Stars: Ron Silver, Imogen Stubbs, Hart Bochner, Daniel J Travanti
Rating: ★★★

If there's an entertaining way of look-ing at the late Forties' Communist witchhunts and their effect on those artists pulled into their web, chewed over and spat out into oblivion, then writer Michael Eaton comes close to it here. Ron Silver plays a blacklisted writer, an ex-Communist sympathiser forced to flee America *sans famille*. In Britain, he does pretty well for himself, quickly sliding into the bed of his best friend's ex-mistress (Imogen Stubbs) and getting a job as a writer (under a pseudonym) on TV's *Robin Hood*. But old ghosts return to haunt him. The back-and-forth flashback structure works to surprising effect, the settings are well in period, be it 1943, 1947 or 1954 and the performances, especially Daniel J Travanti's, flesh out the char-acters nicely. The *Robin Hood* interludes look very much like the real thing, with Silver's vengeful bile for past wrongs occasionally spilling out amusingly in scenes that will never see the light of screen.

Female Perversions ●
1996, US, 110 mins, colour
Dir: Susan Streitfeld
Stars: Tilda Swinton, Amy Madigan, Karen Sillas, Paulina Porizkova, Clancy Brown, Frances Fisher
Rating: ★

A lot of well-known players seen to think there's a feature film in this, but there isn't. Eve (Tilda Swinton in her first American film) is a smart, but faintly flaky lawyer about to come up for a judgeship. Her sex life is fuzzy at the borders – she takes male and fe-male lovers without seeming to notice the difference – but Eve is a straight arrow compared to most of the other females in the film, notably her shoplift-ing sister (Amy Madigan) and the women who share the boarding house to which Eve comes to get her sister out of her latest scrape. There's The Recurring Dream, lots of nudity (porn mogul Zalman King was executive pro-ducer and this is just as odd as his other ventures into 'class') and a series of barely significant events that come, like the famous old radio show, to no definite conclusion. Be more positive: give it a miss.

Feminine Touch, The ○
1956, UK, 91 mins, colour
Dir: Pat Jackson
Stars: George Baker, Belinda Lee, Delphi Lawrence, Adrienne Corri
Rating: ★★

Sir Michael Balcon tries to do for the nursing profession what he had done for the policeman with *The Blue Lamp*. It's a sympathetic look at the lives and loves of five trainee nurses. Mostly credible, too, though it's doubtful you would find five such attractive girls at the same hospital, a factor which tends to draw out the soap opera qualities lurking in the script. A very young

F

George Baker provides a surgical shoulder to cry on.

FernGully: The Last Rainforest ☉ ⓥ
1992, US, 76 mins, colour
Dir: Bill Kroyer
Voice stars: Tim Curry, Samantha Mathis, Christian Slater, Robin Williams, Jonathan Ward, Grace Zabriskie, Cheech Marin, Tommy Chong
Rating: ★★★

An ecologically friendly cartoon feature that's clean, green (very) and on your screen. The families of FernGully are horrified to learn that humans are near with their leveller: one of the humans, Zak, an Australian student (with an American accent) helping the tree-fellers, is accidentally instrumental in releasing Hexxus, evil spirit of the woods, from his tree prison. Shrunk to fairy size by the precocious Crysta, Zak helps the fairies try to fight both Hexxus and the leveller. Helping and hindering in the fight is Batty Koda (distinctively voiced by Robin Williams), a bat escaped from laboratory experiments (yes, all ecological protest is here). Lively enough when Batty and Hexxus are around, the film also has a successful line in humour – a singing iguana is good fun – but could do with rather more of it.

Ferris Bueller's Day Off ◖ ⓥ
1986, US, 103 mins, colour
Dir: John Hughes
Stars: Matthew Broderick, Alan Ruck, Mia Sara, Jennifer Grey
Rating: ★★★

A teenage comedy demonstrating the great lengths to which the irrepressible Ferris (Matthew Broderick) will go to in order to hoodwink his parents and high school principal into thinking he's sick, when, in fact, all he wants to do is play truant for a day. Irreverent attitude, cast sassiness, tons of rock music and all the other expected ingredients are present and as always, teen film maestro John Hughes presents his teenagers' feeling of superiority to adults as being totally justified. In the adult camp, there's a pricelessly funny performance from Jeffrey Jones as the high school principal, driven nearly out of his mind in his frustrated pursuit of Ferris.

Ferry to Hong Kong ◯
1958, UK, 113 mins, colour
Dir: Lewis Gilbert
Stars: Curt Jurgens, Orson Welles, Sylvia Syms
Rating: ★★

An adventure story offering a personality clash between Orson Welles and Curt Jurgens, as well as providing some very attractive and exotic shots of the mysterious Far East. Filmed on location at a cost of half a million pounds, it represented one of the first attempts by British film-makers to rival the opulent escapism that Hollywood was providing.

Fever Pitch ● ⓥ
1996, UK, 105 mins, colour
Dir: David Evans
Stars: Colin Firth, Ruth Gemmell, Neil Pearson, Ken Stott, Holly Aird, Stephen Rea
Rating: ★★

This is a laddish, serio-comic attempt to examine the fanaticism of the British soccer fan. The re-living of a classic sporting event, however, is always a dangerous thing, since the live magic of the moment can't be recaptured – and the build-up to this one pitches us into the midst of some pretty uninteresting people. Paul (Firth), a football-mad teacher, awaits the climax of the 1989 season, with Liverpool and Arsenal battling for the League Championship. When maths teacher Sarah (Gemmell) asks him to stay the night after nary so much as a date, it's hardly surprising he gets her pregnant. This only momentarily defects his thoughts from the matter in hand: a match more vital than any Sarah might have in mind. Slips abound: Sarah never looks remotely pregnant, and even suggests they go on holiday together on 8 October. Not only is this in the football season, but in the school term as well!

Few Good Men, A ◖ ⓥ
1992, US, 138 mins, colour
Dir: Rob Reiner
Stars: Tom Cruise, Jack Nicholson, Demi Moore, Kiefer Sutherland, Kevin Bacon, Kevin Pollak
Rating: ★★★★

This predictable but powerful courtroom drama is fuelled by the high-octane performances of Tom Cruise and Jack Nicholson, brandishing charisma as well as their acting credentials, as two men on opposite sides of the military fence. 'Why would a lawyer with nine months experience and a record of plea bargaining get a murder case?' muses naval lieutenant Cruise. 'Perhaps so it never sees the inside of a courtroom.' A marine has died after being attacked by two fellow marines; ostensibly, it's a

homicidal plot. But Cruise sniffs a Code Red, a rather harsher equivalent of public school ragging. Alas, Cruise and hot-headed co-counsel Demi Moore's investigation soon falls foul of the rocks patrolled by the great white shark, Col Jack Nicholson himself. You'll know the outcome, of course, but be happy to stay the course and welcome it with a cheer when it comes.

ffolkes
See: North Sea Hijack

Fiddler on the Roof ◯ ⓥ
1971, US, 180 mins, colour
Dir: Norman Jewison
Stars: Topol, Norma Crane, Leonard Frey
Rating: ★★★

Topol's star quality doesn't burn quite so bright in this film version of the overwhelming musical success as it had in the original stage version, but it's still impossible to see anyone else in the role of the Jewish milkman with five marriageable daughters. Often rousing in its score, the film is less effective once the music stops, and goes on rather a long time. It's still well worth a look, though, if only for Topol's inspired performance of the big hit number 'If I Were a Rich Man'. Director Norman Jewison's treatment of the piece is perhaps over-ambitious, as underlined by Oswald Morris' sombre photography, full of browns and golds, which surprisingly won him an Oscar although not really among his best work.

Fiddlers Three ◯
1944, UK, 88 mins, b/w
Dir: Harry Watt
Stars: Tommy Trinder, Frances Day, Sonnie Hale
Rating: ★★

The idea of most British comedy films of the early Forties was to provide an escapist cure for the wartime blues. And this British sideshoot from Eddie Cantor's *Roman Scandals* certainly fitted the bill. Bright spark Diana Decker made her screen debut at the age of 17.

Field, The ◖ ⓥ
1990, UK, 110 mins, colour
Dir: Jim Sheridan
Stars: Richard Harris, John Hurt, Tom Berenger, Sean Bean, Frances Tomelty, Brenda Fricker
Rating: ★★★

Harris reaffirms his qualities as a great actor in this deep, very Irish tragedy from writer/director Sheridan. After decades of unworthy roles, Harris triumphs here as a weathered farmer who has for ten years nurtured with loving care a field leased to him by a widow from whom he hopes to buy. Unknown to him, his son Bean is, with the connivance of the village idiot (Hurt), up to all sorts of tricks to drive the widow out. Although the story's plot twists take some swallowing, Sheridan's direction is expert, especially in the climatic action sequence. And there's always Harris, looking like Hemingway's Old Man of the Sea ought to look, and towering over his fellows.

Field of Dreams ○ ⓥ

1989, US, 106 mins, colour
Dir: Phil Alden Robinson
Stars: Kevin Costner, Amy Madigan, James Earl Jones, Ray Liotta, Burt Lancaster, Gaby Hoffmann
Rating: ★★★★★

This very winning fantasy is certainly one of a kind. Kevin Costner is an Iowa farmer, alienated from his baseball-mad father as a teenager, who hears voices that tell him to build a baseball field (at the cost of half his corn) in which a ghost team of legendary outlawed players then appears. Further voices drive him to locate a self-exiled author (James Earl Jones) and an obscure doctor (Burt Lancaster) who missed playing major league baseball by a whisker. The result is a bizarre movie but one which frequently touches the emotions in the manner of the finest Hollywood 'moonshine'. The film's endearing qualities are boosted by the wholesome performances. You may think it's dumb to begin with but if you're any sort of romantic, you'll soon be won over by its magic. Frank Capra would have approved.

Fiendish Plot of Dr Fu Manchu, The ○

1980, UK, 108 mins, colour
Dir: Piers Haggard
Stars: Peter Sellers, Helen Mirren, David Tomlinson
Rating: ★★

This is a typical latter-day film from Peter Sellers in that it's fun without actually being very funny (apart from the appearance of a clockwork tarantula) painless enough and probably closer to pure Goonery than Sellers had been for some time. If they could have added Spike Milligan as Nayland Smith's aged servant (played here by John le Mesurier), Harry Secombe as the keeper of the Crown Jewels, forced to take a

cure for obesity (John Sharp), and Michael Bentine as the lunatic Harley Street specialist in elephants (Clement Harari) you could have had a sentimental reunion. Sellers acquits himself quite well as Nayland Smith and Fu Manchu while Simon Williams is funny in support as a man from the ministry who is wet – usually in more ways than one. Helen Mirren adopts a stage cockney accent as the policewoman engaged to track Fu Manchu down in this pleasant lightweight lunacy.

Fierce Creatures ❶ ⓥ

1997, UK, 98 mins, colour
Dirs: Robert Young, Fred Schepisi
Stars: John Cleese, Jamie Lee Curtis, Kevin Kline, Michael Palin, Robert Lindsay, Carey Lowell
Rating: ★★

Not so much a follow-up to *A Fish Called Wanda* as a sort of *Carry On Up the Zoo*. An Anzac tycoon (Kline) takes over an English zoo, putting ex-army man Cleese in charge, with the task of increasing takings by 20 per cent. Cleese decrees that the zoo shall contain only fierce animals, which is the cue for the keepers (including Lowell, Lindsay, Ronnie Corbett and an intensely annoying Palin as non-stop talker Bugsy) to present even the most docile of their charges as savage creatures to save their skins. Even worse than Cleese is the tycoon's American son (also Kline) who, with his curvaceous assistant (Curtis) in tow, soon turns the zoo into a sort of sponsored version of a holiday camp. There's lots of leery, laboured humour here, but not much that actually makes you laugh. Most of the jokes centre on sex and other bodily functions – you can just bet that the zoo's cuter keepers will end up in their underwear and they do. It's formula farce.

Fifth Avenue Girl ○

1939, US, 79 mins, b/w
Dir: Gregory La Cava
Stars: Ginger Rogers, Walter Connolly
Rating: ★★

Ginger Rogers was the tops in musicals with Fred Astaire, but she lit no fires on her own until the early Forties. Top screwball comedy director Gregory La Cava was hired to boost the chances of this comedy about a workless girl hired to pose as a gold-digger, but he couldn't do much with its tiresome plot. Tim Holt steps down from the saddle to play the rich boy for whom Miss Rogers falls.

Fifth Element

1997, France/US/UK, 127 mins, colour
Dir: Luc Besson
Stars: Bruce Willis, Gary Oldman, Milla Jovovich, Ian Holm, Luke Perry, Lee Evans
Rating: ★★★★

Bruce Willis' latest blockbuster is a rip-roaring futuristic adventure battle to save Earth. Every 5,000 years a door opens up between our universe and another dimension, where a dark force waits to extinguish all life and light. Willis plays a 23rd-century New York taxi driver who finds he's the last chance for mankind when a beautiful half-naked woman (model Milla Jovovich) crashes through the roof of his flying cab. She is LeeLoo, the Fifth Element, a supreme being who holds the key to defeating the darkness. It's thrilling stuff, with eye-popping special effects and jaw-dropping sets, plus suitably tongue-in-cheekacting. Gary Oldman is a hilarious redneck Texan villain and Ian Holmes is delightfully eccentric as a priest safeguarding ancient secrets, while Chris Tucker is a riot of noise and colour as Bruce's exotic drag queen sidekick. Great fun is guaranteed.

Fifth Musketeer, The ○

1978, US, 106 mins, colour
Dir: Ken Annakin
Stars: Beau Bridges, Sylvia Kristel, Ursula Andress, Cornel Wilde, Lloyd Bridges, Jose Ferrer
Rating: ★★

Yet another re-telling of Dumas' famous story *The Man in the Iron Mask*, with lavish production values, full-blooded fight sequences, two of the world's most beautiful actresses and a fascinating sense of romantic heroics. Beau Bridges proves more effective than one might expect in the dual role of the French king and his twin brother, while Jack Cardiff's lush Eastman Colour photography and Rex Harrison's engagingly crafty Colbert are other plus factors.

55 Days at Peking ○ ⓥ

1962, US/UK, 154 mins, colour
Dir: Nicholas Ray
Stars: Charlton Heston, Ava Gardner, David Niven, Flora Robson, John Ireland
Rating: ★★★

Some time, there is a great film to be made about the Boxer Rebellion, that strange and violent piece of history when the embassies of five countries held out for 55 days against thousands of vicious Chinese Boxer

F

warriors in the siege of Peking. Visually, and as far as exciting action can take it, this goes a long way to being that film. As a spectacle, it's fine value for money. Too much so-so dialogue slows it down, but every time that second-unit director Andrew Marton takes over from Nicholas Ray, the picture springs to life with eye-catching action.

52 Pick Up ● Ⓥ
1986, US, 108 mins, colour
Dir: John Frankenheimer
Stars: Roy Scheider, Ann-Margret, Kelly Preston, John Glover, Vanity, Robert Trebor
Rating: ★★★

Very nasty but pretty effective, this shows just what can happen when a man takes a step out of line. Roy Schelder is the tough-talking, self-made businessman, seduced into an affair by a nubile blonde as a prelude to blackmail. When he gives the crooks a figurative V sign, they steal his gun and clothing and kill the girl. Scheider, who has already swallowed his pride to tell his wife (Ann-Margret) everything, now has to track down the blackmailers to tell them that, despite a prospering business, he only currently has $52,000 (thus the title) to his name. From here on in, it's a game of bloody cat and mouse played to a violent end. Scheider grits his teeth and convinces throughout, while John Glover has a dream of a role in early Richard Widmark style as the photographer who runs the blackmail racket.

Fighter Squadron ○
1948, US, 96 mins, colour
Dir: Raoul Walsh
Stars: Edmond O'Brien, Robert Stack, Tom D'Andrea, Henry Hull
Rating: ★★★

Under the vigorous direction of Raoul Walsh, an exciting, red-blooded action film has been woven around the grim realities of war in this stirring account of US fighter pilots battling the Luftwaffe in 1943-4. Edmond O'Brien is the commander of a small squadron, becoming grounded (like the script), while in the skies the thrilling music of Max Steiner takes over, providing a pounding accompaniment to dogfights, strafings, explosions and bomb raids, all awesomely well shot in Technicolor by Syd Wilcox and Wilfred M Kline. Rock Hudson is alleged to have required 38 takes before completing his one scene in this, his first film!

Fighting Back ○
1982, Australia, 98 mins, colour
Dir: Michael Caulfield
Stars: Lewis Fitz-Gerald, Paul Smith, Kris McQuade
Rating: ★★

A distant Australian relative of *The Miracle Worker,* as a dedicated teacher tries to win friendship of a violent and deeply disturbed 13-year-old boy, at the risk of the hatred of his fellow teachers and finally even his job. A bit unremitting in its punishing portrait of a difficult relationship, and ruthlessly cute in its depiction of happier times (teacher and boy on a camping canoeing holiday). But still there are times when the film cuts right to the heart. The acting is generally competent and, in the case of Kris McQuade as the boy's mother, rather more.

Fighting Man of the Plains ○
1949, US, 94 mins, colour
Dir: Edwin L Marin
Stars: Randolph Scott, Jane Nigh, Victor Jory, Bill Williams
Rating: ★★★

This 'A' class Western was one of three made by star Randolph Scott for 20th Century-Fox when they were toying with the idea of using the cheap Cinecolor process for their major outdoor features. Treacherous looking Victor Jory was in all three; usually Jory played waistcoated villains, but here he heads a fine supporting cast as a gambler who befriends Scott (an outlaw posing as a marshal) and helps him when he can. Dale Robertson got his first major role with the studio here as Jesse James, who has a short but key role to play in the action. Jane Nigh and Joan Taylor are weak as the women involved, but Barry Kelley and Bill Williams strongly supply tight-lipped and smiling villainy respectively.

Fighting Prince of Donegal, The ○
1966, UK, 104 mins, colour
Dir: Michael O'Herlihy
Stars: Peter McEnery, Susan Hampshire, Gordon Jackson
Rating: ★

With its cardboard castle and script that will have you chuckling at every other line, this is a 'penny dreadful' Disney historical epic, squarely aimed at children. Some of the performances are better than the film deserves, notably from Peter McEnery in the title role, and from Gordon Jackson, cast successfully against type as a smirking villain. But director Michael O'Herlihy

makes the mistake of reckoning sheer noise is a substitute for pace and action.

Fighting 69th, The ○ Ⓥ
1940, US, 90 mins, b/w
Dir: William Keighley
Stars: James Cagney, Pat O'Brien, George Brent, Alan Hale, Frank McHugh
Rating: ★★

With the advent of war in Europe, the Warners stars who had been busy shooting it out in city streets suddenly presented a united front against a common enemy. James Cagney, Pat O'Brien and George Brent were all piled in to *The Fighting 69th,* the studio's biggest war film to that date, about a World War One regiment also known as 'The Fighting Irish'. Its two most famous scions, both portrayed here, were the poet Joyce Kilmer and the priest Father Duffy, whose statue stands in Times Square. 'I don't go that Holy Joe stuff,' snarls braggart Cagney to pious Pat at the beginning of the film. He does before the end. though, like all good Hollywood heroes should. There's action a-plenty and a supporting cast that, as in so many Warners films, is worth its weight in gold.

Fighting Sullivans, The ○
(aka: The Sullivans)
1944, US, 111 mins, b/w
Dir: Lloyd Bacon
Stars: Anne Baxter, Thomas Mitchell
Rating: ★★★

Pretty well all the right emotional strings were pulled by this wartime flagwaver about five brothers, devoted to one another, who broke all the rules by getting postings together on the same naval cruiser. Casting of virtually unknown actors as the brothers is a great help, and Thomas Mitchell offers another well-judged performance as the boys' father.

Figures in a Landscape ◐
1970, UK, 110 mins, colour
Dir: Joseph Losey
Stars: Robert Shaw, Malcolm McDowell
Rating: ★

Allegory is the name of the game in this desiccated thriller, in which two fugitives flee a nameless force across a nameless country. The ruggedness of the action, and Robert Shaw's abrasive performance (he also wrote the script) almost save it from boredom.

File of the Golden Goose, The ○
1969, UK, 102 mins, colour
Dir: Sam Wanamaker

Stars: Yul Brynner, Charles Gray, Edward Woodward, John Barrie
Rating: ★★

The performances of Yul Brynner and Edward Woodward distinguish this B-feature thriller in A-feature dressing about American and British undercover men after a counterfeiting ring. Charles Gray offers another of his hedonistic villains; Karel Stepanek and Walter Gotell clamp their jaws and look grim; and Graham Crowden is successfully cast against type as a sadistic killer inseparable from his umbrella knife.

File on Thelma Jordon, The ○
(aka: Thelma Jordon)
1949, US, 100 mins, b/w
Dir: Robert Siodmak
Stars: Barbara Stanwyck, Wendell Corey, Paul Kelly
Rating: ★★★

Another chance for Barbara Stanwyck to show that she could play the poor little bad girl just as well as Bette Davis or Joan Crawford. As the brittle and beautiful femme fatale with husky voice and gleaming lips, La Stanwyck had no equal. Here, as usual, she's involved in murder, in a movie that's slow on pace, but has bags of atmosphere and style.

Filofax ◐ Ⓥ
(aka: Taking Care of Business)
1990, US, 107 mins, colour
Dir: Arthur Hiller
Stars: James Belushi, Charles Grodin, Anne DeSalvo, Loryn Locklin, Veronica Hamel, Mako
Rating: ★★★

If you dislike 'nice' films, this is not for you. A variant on *Trading Places,* it casts (equally happily) James Belushi as a convict who escapes from prison to see a baseball game, and Charles Grodin as the workaholic ad salesman into whose hands his Filofax falls. Grodin gets mugged and then thrown in jail, which is fortunate for Belushi who has taken over Grodin's lifestyle for an ad-pitch weekend, sinfully beating a powerful could-be client (Mako) at tennis, bedding the boss's daughter, and wining and dining in Grodin's best white suit. Grodin learns a lot, Belushi falls on his feet and everything is neatly tied up with a happy ending. Belushi and Grodin don't put a foot wrong, unlike Hector Elizondo, who overdoes his caricature of Belushi's hated warden. Veronica Hamel makes the most of her few chances as Grodin's wife.

Final Analysis ● Ⓥ
1992, US, 124 mins, colour
Dir: Phil Joanou
Stars: Richard Gere, Kim Basinger, Uma Thurman, Eric Roberts, Paul Guilfoyle
Rating: ★★★

This Hitchcock-style thriller has more twists than the steps of the lighthouse where, once it's introduced into the story, you just know the principal protagonists will end up. Once psychiatrist Richard Gere has taken on Uma Thurman as a disturbed patient, and been introduced to her seductive sister (Kim Basinger), the story continually dodges this way and that. You're never quite certain who's plotting what, or which combination of the characters is on which side of the law. Ignore some fairly foolish goings-on in the courtroom and throw yourself headlong into this intoxicating brew, shot through with flashes of lightning and screechingly scored in the Bernard Herrmann manner by George Fenton. Basinger makes as luscious a femme fatale as anyone could wish and her acting has improved by miles from earlier days. A polished, excitingly paced piece of *film noir.*

Final Combination ● Ⓥ
1993, US, 93 mins, colour
Dir: Nigel Dick
Stars: Michael Madsen, Lisa Bonet, Gary Stretch
Rating: RB

A real grade Z movie this, in every sense, the kind of film that has no business going anywhere but straight to video. God knows what the title means, but the story has bimbo-happy cop Michael Madsen trying to track down a boxing serial killer (Gary Stretch) with the help of a reporter (Lisa Bonet) who's the first girl in ages not to actually lie down immediately before the cop's monolithic advances. Madsen is no second Kirk Douglas here, nor even William Bendix, but he's a lot better than Bonet and Stretch in what must be one of the worst-performed movies in quite a while. And, true to form, the serial killer escapes death only to come back for a final confrontation with the detective when you or I would be half-way to another continent.

Final Conflict, The
See Omen III – The Final Conflict

Final Countdown, The ○
1980, US, 104 mins, colour
Dir: Don Taylor

Stars: Kirk Douglas, Martin Sheen, Katharine Ross, James Farentino, Charles Durning
Rating: ★★★

It can hardly be said that this is a science-fiction film. But for the foundation of its story it does borrow from a stock science-fiction theme, for it is essentially of the 'time travel' variety. An American aircraft carrier on routine duty in the Pacific encounters a storm of unprecedented violence. When it's all over, captain and crew find themselves back in time the day before the Japanese attack Pearl Harbor. The subsequent story developments are ingeniously worked out with sufficient logic to make them convincing and compelling. Quite an unusual, fascinating movie.

Finders Keepers ⊙
1966, UK, 94 mins, colour
Dir: Sidney Hayers
Stars: Cliff Richard, Viviane Ventura, Robert Morley, Peggy Mount
Rating: ★★

For this musical comedy with a Spanish setting, a big search was made to find an actress to play the Spanish girl who falls for Cliff. The quest ended with the choice of 21-year-old Viviane Ventura, who was born in London, but spoke Spanish fluently. Here she sings a lively duet with Cliff, called 'Paella'. Peggy Mount and Robert Morley ('for £10,000, I'd walk naked down Horse Guards Parade') provide formidable comedy support for the stars.

Finders Keepers ◐
1984, US, 96 mins, colour
Dir: Richard Lester
Stars: Michael O'Keefe, Beverly D'Angelo, Louis Gossett Jr., David Wayne, Brian Dennehy, Jim Carrey
Rating: ★★

A light and agreeable train romp which starts really well, but ultimately fails as a film because, for all the energy with which director Richard Lester invests it, it simply isn't funny. Most of the unnecessary four-letter words in the script of this frenzied froth go to Beverly D'Angelo, so it's much to her credit that she's still the best thing in a film which defies the efforts of such experienced players as David Wayne, Ed Lauter, Brian Dennehy, Pamela Stephenson and Louis Gossett to get a laugh. Harmless enough, but totally lacking in comic distinction.

Find the Lady ○
1976, Canada, 79 mins, colour
Dir: John Trent

F

Stars: Lawrence Dane, John Candy,
Peter Cook, Dick Emery
Rating: ★

A lot of bright comic stars from various
countries got themselves involved in
this ramshackle romp about a bizarre
kidnap. Big John Candy, later a popular star of Hollywood comedies, made
his major screen debut in a crazy mis-
adventure never shown in cinemas
outside its native Canada.

Fine and Dandy
See: The West Point Story

Fine Madness, A ◗
1966, US, 104 mins, colour
Dir: Irvin Kershner
Stars: Sean Connery, Joanne Woodward,
Jean Seberg, Patrick O'Neal
Rating: ★★★★

A nine-tenths hilarious comedy, with a
few sinister undertones, about an
amorous out-of-work poet called
Samson Shillitoe (Sean Connery), who
falls foul of one of his mistresses' husbands. Good performances from
Joanne Woodward, screamingly funny
as the poet's long-suffering and amusingly belligerent wife, and Sue Ane
Langdon, as the chattiest of his 'victims', highlight this pleasing
entertainment. Patrick O'Neal's satirical portrait of a psychiatrist is
frighteningly droll until he catches
Connery in the steam-bath with his
wife (O'Neal's, that is) and consigns
him to a gruesome brain operation –
performed by a dotty scientist, played
in best Peter Sellers style by Clive
Revill.

Fine Romance, A ◗ Ⓥ
(aka: Tchin Tchin; A Touch of
Adultery)
1992, US/Italy, 83 mins, colour
Dir: Gene Saks
Stars: Julie Andrews, Marcello
Mastroianni, Ian Fitzgibbon, Jean-Pierre
Castaldi, Maria Machado
Rating: ★

A romantic comedy that echoes the
style of continental movies from the
Sixties, but lacks their class and joie-de-
vivre. Unimaginative casting doesn't
help, either, with Marcello Mastroianni
as Cesareo, the archetypal incurably romantic Italian, and Julie Andrews as
Pamela, a prim English rose. The pair
discover they have both been jilted and
romance blossoms between them as
they set out to retrieve their errant
spouses. Andrews, here in her late
fifties, still looks fabulous, and the Paris
settings are a delight. Gene Saks'

heavy-handed direction at least keeps
proceedings short enough to justify
Andrews fans taking a look.

Finest Hour, The ● Ⓥ
1991, US, 110 mins, colour
Dir: Shimon Dotan
Stars: Rob Lowe, Gale Hansen, Tracy
Griffith, Eb Lottimer
Rating: ★★

What does it take to be a hero?
Apparently, a spindly moustache, a
crew cut, a sleepy look and a good casting agent. Rob Lowe stars as a tough
raw recruit who becomes a SEAL – a
member of the elite US navy commando fighting force – in this cheapie
cash-in action thriller set during the
Gulf War. Despite the shallowness of
the main characters, there are some
fine *Top Gun*-style heroics and an un-
dercurrent of rivalry in love and war.
If only it didn't go on so long.

Fingers at the Window ○
1942, US, 80 mins, b/w
Dir: Charles Lederer
Stars: Lew Ayres, Basil Rathbone,
Laraine Day
Rating: ★★★

Neat and highly professional
Hollywood crime thriller of its time,
splendidly edited, with Lew Ayres giving good value to the role of the
unemployed actor caught up in a deception which could cost him his life.

Finian's Rainbow ○ Ⓥ
1968, US, 140 mins, colour
Dir: Francis Ford Coppola
Stars: Fred Astaire, Petula Clark, Tommy
Steele, Keenan Wynn
Rating: ★★★

Directed by Francis Ford Coppola this
charming, colourful (fine Technicolor
camerawork by Philip Lathrop) and at
times bitingly satirical musical first saw
light of day on stage in 1947, a peak period for the American musical.
Coppola's casting gambles all come off.
Fred Astaire is lovable but never fey as
Finian, the Irish wanderer; Petula
Clark (in the role created on Broadway
by Ella Logan, aunt of Jimmy) is fresh
and charming as his daughter; and
Tommy Steele funny and tuneful as
Og the leprechaun. The songs include
'Old Devil Moon'.

Fireball 500 ◗
1966, US, 92 mins, colour
Dir: William Asher
Stars: Frankie Avalon, Annette Funicello,
Fabian, Chill Wills
Rating: ★★

Despite a spectacular fight and some
hair-raising scenes of stock-car racing,
this is pretty tough, chewy meat, showing the Frankie Avalon-Annette
Funicello team away from the beach
and near the end of the road. There
are some sexy love scenes, not, of
course, involving Annette, but Frankie,
who harder and more professional than
before, prefers a blonde who husks:
'I'm getting restless. You know how I
am when I'm restless.' Good action,
bad script? Right on.

Fire Birds
See: Wings of the Apache

Firecreek ◗
1968, US, 104 mins, colour
Dir: Vincent McEveety
Stars: James Stewart, Henry Fonda,
Inger Stevens, Gary Lockwood, Dean
Jagger, Jack Elam
Rating: ★★★★

Enjoyable, old-style Western with
James Stewart as the mild-mannered
farmer-cum-sheriff whose resolute core
slowly but surely comes to the surface
when five tough and vicious marauders
invade his town. Vincent McEveety's
direction is especially effective in the
pulsating *High Noon*-style climax and
the Technicolor photography exemplary, particularly in a nighttime scene
at a bizarre 'wake'. The performances
of Stewart – radiating sincerity and determination – and Henry Fonda, as the
tormented outlaw leader, lift a basically
ordinary action yarn right out of the
rut.

Fire Down Below ○
1957, UK, 116 mins, colour
Dir: Robert Parrish
Stars: Rita Hayworth, Robert Mitchum,
Jack Lemmon, Herbert Lom, Bernard
Lee, Anthony Newley
Rating: ★★

Although not quite as explosive as its
advance notices had proclaimed, the
teaming of Rita Hayworth, Robert
Mitchum and Jack Lemmon gives this
strange triangular melodrama quite a
powerful kick. Lemmon comes off
best, two years after his Academy
Award for *Mr Roberts,* as a young
Caribbean fisherman who becomes
consumed with hatred after falling out
with his partner (Mitchum) over a mystery woman (Hayworth) whom
Mitchum seems to regard with contempt. The most exciting part of the
film comes when Lemmon is trapped
by a girder in the bow of a sinking
Greek tramp steamer. The title song,

quite a hit in its time, is scorched through by Shirley Bassey.

Firefox ◐ ⓥ

1982, US, 131 mins, colour
Dir: Clint Eastwood
Stars: Clint Eastwood, Freddie Jones, David Huffman, Warren Clarke
Rating: ★

Clint Eastwood takes a cold war espionage story that could have been knocking around 30 years ago and, as well as directing, lends his own abrasive personality to the leading role. He plays a Vietnam-haunted US pilot (a part that would have been perfectly suited to Errol Flynn) called on to sneak the Russians' latest top-secret aircraft from under their very noses. Every step of the way, the assignment becomes progressively less likely. Eastwood's British supporting cast labour mightily with their Russian accents and the special effects involved in showing the high-speed Firefox planes in action are often pretty good. Overall, though, this is Eastwood's slackest job in quite a while, with barely enough action, unconvincing fistfights and stodgily directed dialogue scenes that stretch the film away past the two-hour mark.

Fire Maidens from Outer Space ○

1956, UK, 80 mins, b/w
Dir: Cy Roth
Stars: Anthony Dexter, Susan Shaw
Rating: **RB**

Five space scientists in a tinpot craft land on Jupiter's 13th moon to find it inhabited by girls in mini-togas in this supremely daft, if mildly entertaining British sci-fi romp. One of the cinema's great bad films of all time, and another step on the long road down for Hollywood's Anthony Dexter, who had started his career in the title role of *Valentino*.

Firm, The ● ⓥ

1993, US, 155 mins, colour
Dir: Sydney Pollack
Stars: Tom Cruise, Gene Hackman, Jeanne Tripplehorn, Holly Hunter, Hal Holbrook, Ed Harris
Rating: ★★

This is one of those get-yourself-out-of-this thrillers that Hollywood adores. Tom Cruise is the hotshot young lawyer just out of Harvard who signs up with a plush Tennessee law firm that provides him with a house, a car and a small fortune. Unfortunately it also offers him a prison cell: the Firm is

the principal state legislator for the Mafia and no one ever leaves it. Not alive, at any rate. Cruise is contacted by FBI agent Ed Harris and told: 'Your life, as you know it, is over.' A witness protection programme is offered. Of course, his career will be finished, and the Firm will almost certainly find him and kill him. In any case, they have a blackmail hold on him, with photos of a fleeting affair they can show his wife. So there's no way out. But hold on there, guys: this is a Tom Cruise film. A pretty slow Tom Cruise film at that, although the Hitchcock-style last 30 minutes is just about worth waiting for. A pity we didn't manage to mention Gene Hackman in all this, as Hackman gives the best performance in the movie by some way as a cynical co-lawyer.

First a Girl ○ ⓥ

1935, UK, 94 mins, b/w
Dir: Victor Saville
Stars: Jessie Matthews, Sonnie Hale, Griffith Jones, Anna Lee
Rating: ★★★

This enchanting musical took the public (if not the critics) by storm, and proved Jessie Matthews' second most successful after *Evergreen*. The story is the original of the Eighties' Julie Andrews movie *Victor/Victoria*, with Jessie, as a girl impersonating a boy impersonating a girl, never sexier and singing 'Everything's in Rhythm with My Heart' and 'Say the Word and I'm Yours'. The finale, a sequence set in a gigantic bird cage, is quite extraordinary, although the reality was less exotic. The cage, 40 feet high, was built in open fields at Northolt in North London and filmed between two and five in the morning, while 52 chorus girls in feathers perched all over the bars. If Jessie looks doubtful in one or two shots, it's probably because her perch was 30 feet up!

First Blood ● ⓥ

1982, US, 93 mins, colour
Dir: Ted Kotcheff
Stars: Sylvester Stallone, Richard Crenna, Brian Dennehy, David Caruso
Rating: ★★★

An excitingly made blood-and-thunder film that pits a wronged Vietnam veteran against the redneck police force of a small mid-west town. Sylvester Stallone plays the muscular Medal of Honor winner picked up for vagrancy on the slightest of pretences by sheriff Brian Dennehy, and subsequently beaten and humiliated by his deputy,

before the inevitable happens: he goes berserk, escapes and takes to the wooded and rocky local countryside. From then on, it's only a question of spinning the film out as Stallone first picks off the pursuing posse one by one, then escapes from being trapped in a mine and comes lookin' for Dennehy and blasting apart practically his whole town. Pretty nearly the action film of its year, this gives its audience what they want: continual, violent and fluid action with a hero it's easy to identify with. The best scenes are probably those in the mine, where Stallone fights off a cave of rats to reach freedom.

First Deadly Sin, The ●

1980, US, 112 mins, colour
Dir: Brian Hutton
Stars: Frank Sinatra, Faye Dunaway, Brenda Vaccaro, James Whitmore
Rating: ★★

If you're squeamish about operations, prepare to close your eyes to the opening sequence of this city-streets thriller, which brings Frank Sinatra half-way between his own film *The Detective and* such vigilante cop thrillers as *10 to Midnight*. The screenplay is fatally flawed by a sub-plot which has Sinatra mooning over his dying wife (Faye Dunaway) and works best when he gets down to the main business of tracking down a particularly unpleasant psychopathic killer. A stalking pursuit around the flapping cellophane tunnels of a building site is splendidly staged by director Brian Hutton, while at police headquarters acting honours are solidly snaffled by doughty veteran James Whitmore as a pathologist. Sinatra himself looks a bit old but then so might anyone who had to read some of these lines.

First Do No Harm ◐ ⓥ

1996, US, 90 mins, colour
Dir: Jim Abrahams
Stars: Meryl Streep, Fred Ward, Margo Martindale, Seth Adkins
Rating: ★★★

A quality production for those who like their films inspired by real events, this true 'against-the-odds' style drama stars Streep as the mother of an epileptic boy who is prescribed a series of drugs, and suffers seemingly irreversible side effects. The star gives her usual excellent performance as the feisty mum who opposes the medical profession to try a 'miracle' diet that she feels could save the life of her son, touchingly well played by Seth Adkins. With its long, hard look at the horrors suffered by all

F

the family, this film, originally made for TV, proves very disturbing but ultimately uplifting, especially as some of the roles are played by former epileptics, who have been drug- and seizure-free for some years since following the 'ketogenic' diet.

First Great Train Robbery, The ◑

1978, US, 108 mins, colour
Dir: Michael Crichton
Stars: Sean Connery, Donald Sutherland, Lesley-Anne Down, Wayne Sleep, Michael Elphick
Rating: ★★★

Train robberies have provided a basic story ingredient for many a motion picture but where this one differs is that it is set in 1855. The film is rich in Victorian period detail, but it's the action that counts, in which respect the robbery sequence is effectively done. A bearded Sean Connery stars as the gentleman crook whose interest in perpetrating the robbery is more particularly a matter of fascination with crime. Donald Sutherland has a splendid character part as his accomplice. Good entertainment for anyone who enjoys a film in 'caper' style.

First Love ○

1939, US, 84 mins, b/w
Dir: Henry Koster
Stars: Deanna Durbin, Helen Parrish, Robert Stack
Rating: ★★★

Deanna Durbin goes to the ball in this romantic musical – but is warned she must leave by midnight. But there's a midnight kiss and she has to flee, dropping a slipper on the stairway. So, as you can see, this is very much a Cinderella-like affair – and absolutely intentionally so. It's fun of charm and frothily directed by Henry Koster, always a dab hand at this sort of thing. It's the film in which Deanna's songs include the bit 'Amapola' and in which she received her first screen kiss – from Robert Stack.

First Men in the Moon ○

1964, UK, 99 mins, colour
Dir: Nathan Juran
Stars: Edward Judd, Lionel Jeffries, Martha Hyer
Rating: ★★★

Entertaining H G Wells yarn about a moon expedition in 1899, led by a professor who has invented a substance which defies gravity. Exciting special effects by Dynamation wizard Ray

Harryhausen, who creates the Selenites, complement a super performance by Lionel Jeffries as the professor – all sudden ups and downs, snuffles and flashes of illuminating thought. The space vehicle comes equipped with all mod cons – even including its own livestock.

First Monday In October ◑

1981, US, 99 mins, colour
Dir: Ronald Neame
Stars: Jill Clayburgh, Walter Matthau, Jan Sterling, Barnard Hughes
Rating: ★★★

A comedy-drama that's sometimes caustic, sometimes likeable and sometimes as dry as the law books over which Jill Clayburgh and Walter Matthau wrangle. She's the first woman judge to be appointed to the American Supreme Court, he, naturally, is the recalcitrant rebel who opposes her but finally falls for her charm. The film seems a little short, but the stars play the limited situations wonderfully well together.

First Power, The ● ⓥ

1990, US, 96 mins, colour
Dir: Robert Resnikoff
Stars: Lou Diamond Phillips, Tracy Griffith, Jeff Kober, Mykel T Williamson
Rating: ★★

A silly and far-fetched but quite suspenseful chiller on the now-familiar theme of a serial killer's spirit returning after execution to possess the bodies of others and continue his killing spree. Lou Diamond Phillips is quite good as the detective who at first thinks he's going out of his mind, then follows a bloody trail with the help of beautiful red-haired psychic Tracy Griffith, real-life half-sister of Melanie. The action keeps the plot hopping, and it's well-orchestrated throughout by director Robert Resnikoff – though the final scene is unnecessary and stretches the whole plot too far.

First Rebel, The ○ ⓥ

(aka: Allegheny Uprising)
1939, US, 81 mins, b/w
Dir: William A Seiter
Stars: John Wayne, Claire Trevor
Rating: ★★

After the success of *Stagecoach*, RKO hurriedly put their new cowboy star John Wayne and his leading lady Claire Trevor in other Western action dramas. This saga, set in an America still under British rule, has Wayne battling against Brian Donlevy, who is selling guns to the Indians, and George Sanders, a

tyrannical British officer. A good cast, then, and plenty of action too. Not a bad film, but not a memorable one, either, in spite of its offbeat setting.

First Travelling Saleslady, The ○

1956, US, 92 mins, colour
Dir: Arthur Lubin
Stars: Ginger Rogers, Carol Channing, Barry Nelson, James Arness, Clint Eastwood
Rating: ★

Ginger Rogers and Carol Charming go west to sell barbed wire to ranchers in this lightweight comedy Western, one of the last films Rogers made for RKO. Both ladies appear to be having fun, but it's all pretty forgettable really. The only point of interest for the film buff is that Miss Channing's tall Texan boyfriend is played by Chnt Eastwood! Even taller James Arness is also around, in one of his comparatively few big-screen roles; he had to be content with remaining the Clint Eastwood of the little screen.

First Wives Club, The ○ ⓥ

1996, US, 102 mins, colour
Dir: Hugh Wilson
Stars: Goldie Hawn, Bette Midler, Diane Keaton, Sarah Jessica Parker, Maggie Smith, Stockard Channing
Rating: ★★★★

'Don't get even, darlinks,' advises Ivana Trump. 'Just get everything.' And Midler, Hawn and Keaton, deserted by their husbands for younger women, prove there's life in the old bitches yet: revenge begins at 45. Thus the downtrodden Diane, vodka-sodden Goldie and blinkered Bette get tough, get sober and get even to get their own back on their errant swains. Even though there's a socko supporting cast packed with stars, these middle-aged Mata Haris are almost inevitably the whole deal, with Keaton in particular proving herself an outstanding physical clown, especially in moments of high panic when the trio gets trapped trying to get the goods on one of the guys. It's fun nearly all the way and, if it could have been even funnier, that's a small quibble. Stay tuned for the girl's song at the end: it's pretty sensational.

First Yank into Tokyo ○

(aka: Mask of Fury)
1945, US, 82 mins, b/w
Dir: Gordon Douglas
Stars: Tom Neal, Barbara Hale, Richard Loo
Rating: ★★

RKO cashed in on the end of the war by adding newsreel footage to the end of this spy film, re-shaping its plot to involve the atomic bomb, and extending its running time to bring it up to 'A' feature level. It all looks a bit ludicrous today, save for Richard Loo's considered portrait of the Japanese officer who's quickly on to the fact that the 'oriental' hero (made to look that way with plastic surgery) is an American he used to know. The British understandably baulked at the flagwaving title and intelligently called the film *Mask of Fury*.

Fish Called Wanda, A ● Ⓥ
1988, UK, 108 mins, colour
Dir: Charles Crichton
Stars: John Cleese, Jamie Lee Curtis, Kevin Kline, Michael Palin, Tom Georgeson, Maria Aitken
Rating: ★★★★

Monty Python meets Ealing comedy when a stuffy London barrister becomes involved with a double-crossing gang of jewel thieves. Writer-star John Cleese plays straight-man to the comic antics of Jamie Lee Curtis's coolly calculating vamp Wanda, Michael Palin's stuttering pet-lover and Oscar-winning Kevin Kline's dim-witted ex-CIA agent in this funny frolic. Veteran Ealing director Charles Crichton handles the farce with aplomb and keeps the plot rattling along at a fair lick.

Fisher King, The ● Ⓥ
1991, US, 137 mins, colour
Dir: Terry Gilliam
Stars: Robin Williams, Jeff Bridges, Amanda Plummer, Mercedes Ruehi
Rating: ★★★★

A stylish and visionary emotional fantasy from director Terry Gilliam, this entwines the sorry life of former cult deejay Jack Lucas (Jeff Bridges) with that of former history professor Parry (Robin Williams) who has become a vagrant in the big city. How these two lost souls discover salvation and the meaning of life through each other makes an excellent lark movie that merges moments of deep melodrama with sudden shafts of happiness. A real treat, with a career-best performance from Mercedes Ruehl as Bridges' girlfriend that won her the Oscar as best supporting actress.

F.I.S.T. ○
1978, US, 145 mins, colour
Dir: Norman Jewison
Stars: Sylvester Stallone, Rod Steiger, Peter Boyle, Melinda Dillon, David

Huffman
Rating: ★★★

A sort of trucking version of *The Godfather*, this was one of Sylvester Stallone's first big efforts to strike out on his own after the success of *Rocky*. He co-wrote the screenplay of this turbulent if rather overlong drama, in which he plays an angry young workless man in late 1930s Chicago who becomes involved with thuggery in his efforts to help set up a workers' union. The moral of absolute power corrupting absolutely is a familiar one. but director Norman Jewison finds genuine excitement in the nocturnal clashes between strikers and company men, and real charm in Stallone's courtship of his Lithuanian wife-to-be (the invaluable Melinda Dillon) which recalls his scenes with Talia Shire in *Rocky*.

Fistful of Dollars, A ◑ Ⓥ
1964, Italy, 96 mins, colour
Dir: Sergio Leone
Stars: Clint Eastwood, Marianne Koch
Rating: ★★

The impact of the action in this trailblazing adventure film opened the floodgates for the huge numbers of spaghetti Westerns that made fortunes for their producers in the Sixties and early Seventies. This one made an international star out of Clint Eastwood, up to then best-known for his running role in the TV series *Rawhide*. Eastwood doesn't have a lot to say, but then the most famous Western screen heroes rarely did. Dramatically staged shoot-outs occur on and off throughout a plot that's mainly cribbed from the Japanese samurai action classic *Yojimbo*.

Fistful of Dynamite, A ◑
(aka: Duck, You Sucker)
1972, Italy, 150 mins, colour
Dir: Sergio Leone
Stars: Rod Steiger, James Coburn
Rating: ★★★

This wham-bam, rip-roaring adventure yarn set in revolutionary Mexico is lively fun, providing you don't examine the plot too closely and forgive the somewhat eccentric casting (Rod Steiger is a Mexican bandit, James Coburn an Irish explosives expert). In fact the American title of the film, *Duck, You Sucker*, accurately sums up the flavour of this tortilla Western. Sergio Leone, who directed all of Clint Eastwood's classic spaghetti Westerns, is at the helm and there's a much greater sense of broad humour. Steiger and Coburn seem to enjoy themselves immensely, Coburn flashing a devilishly

pearly grin that's equal to Burt Lancaster at his best. Fast-moving, noisy action stuff.

Fitzwilly Strikes Back ○
1967, US, 102 mins, colour
Dir: Delbert Mann
Stars: Dick Van Dyke, Barbara Feldon, Edith Evans
Rating: ★★★

Not a sequel, curiously enough, but the very same film that was known in America simply as *Fitzwilly*. Dick Van Dyke is the butler who has to organise a Christmas Eve robbery in order to rescue his employer's ailing fortunes. Edith Evans is in splendid dowager form, looking like some Ruritanian Queen Mother who has inadvertently wandered into the staff pantry during celebrations and is now doing her best to pretend that she's not really there at all.

Five Angles on Murder
See: The Woman in Question

5 Branded Women ○
1960, Italy/US, 106 mins, b/w
Dir: Martin Ritt
Stars: Silvana Mangano, Van Heflin Vera Miles, Barbara Bel Geddes, Jeanne Moreau, Richard Basehart
Rating: ★★

A tough but less than magnetic film about five girl guerillas in Yugoslavia, during World War Two. The star line-up of actresses all give strong performances, almost eclipsing their male co-stars. The quintet of branded women (they actually have their hair shaved off for having had relations with Nazi soldiers: and the actresses really had to undergo just that indignity, although they all look rather striking) is completed by Carla Gravina, then only 20, who became a major star in her native Italy.

Five Came Back ○
1939, US, 75 mins, b/w
Dir: John Farrow
Stars: Chester Morris, Lucille Ball, C Aubrey Smith, John Carradine
Rating: ★★★

This film about a small plane load of passengers crashing in South American jungle and threatened by headhunters was an unexpected big success and a boost for the career of its director, John Farrow. Its plot (the writing credits are distinguished to say the least) still carries some suspense, even if the eventual survivors are arranged in highly contrived fashion.

F

Five Card Stud ◐

1968, US, 100 mins, colour
Dir: Henry Hathaway
Stars: Dean Martin, Robert Mitchum,
Inger Stevens, Roddy McDowall, Yaphet
Kotto
Rating: ★ ★ ★

A Western for Agatha Christie fans.
Director Henry Hathaway takes a firm
grip on the tension from the opening
card game, that engenders a lynching,
and never lets up – as the card players
are killed one by one by a mysterious
assassin. Robert Mitchum is perhaps
larger than life as a gun-toting preacher,
but Dean Martin is extremely good as
the reluctant 'hero' and strong supporting work comes from Inger Stevens,
Yaphet Kotto and Bill Fletcher.
Excellent Technicolor photography ties
up a first-rate thriller package.

Five Corners ● ⓥ

1987, US, 93 mins, colour
Dir: Tony Bill
Stars: Jodie Foster, Tim Robbins, Todd
Graff, John Turturro, Elizabeth Berridge
Rating: ★

Set in 1964, this oddity could, apart
from its four-letter words, have been
made then too. The whole enterprise
seems old-fashioned, its disparate elements coming across with curiously
muffled effect, and its social sentiments
getting swamped by a routine plot
about the local psycho coming home
from the pen and kidnapping the
Bronx belle, given the gamest of tries
by Jodie Foster. Not that the plot helps
her much: it certainly isn't too likely,
for instance, that she would keep an appointment with a homicidal maniac by
a deserted swimming-pool at midnight.
But then none of the characters here is
any too bright. Some of the dialogue is
ludicrous, and some plain peculiar,
while the supporting acting ranges
from the eccentric to the bemused.
The two penguins in the plot, though,
are nice, and deeply talented.

Five Days One Summer ◐

1982, US, 108 mins, colour
Dir: Fred Zinnemann
Stars: Sean Connery, Betsy Brantley,
Lambert Wilson
Rating: ★

The last film to come from the distinguished Austrian-born director Fred
Zinnemann boasts superb location
cinematography by Giuseppe
Rotunno, which adds dimension to
the story of the romance in the Alps
between middle-aged Scottish doctor
Sean Connery and Betsy Brantley,

with emotional (and otherwise) intervention by guide Lambert Wilson.
Solidly crafted in the tradition of
movies from a more leisurely age of
moviemaking, but slow going and
very predictable.

Five Easy Pieces ○ ⓥ

1970, US, 98 mins, colour
Dir: Bob Rafelson
Stars: Jack Nicholson, Susan Anspach,
Karen Black
Rating: ★ ★ ★

Cult study of American alienation and
one of the few US films to explore the
question of class distinctions.
Brilliantly acted by Jack Nicholson as
the self-tormenting drifter who's in
flight from middle-class rectitude and
responsibility. 'I move around a lot,' he
tells his paralysed father, 'not because
I'm looking for anything but to get
away from things that go bad if I stay.
Auspicious beginnings.' The film
earned Academy Award nominations
for Best Film, Script (Adrien Joyce),
Actor (Nicholson) and Actress (Karen
Black).

Five Finger Exercise ○

1962, US, 109 mins, b/w
Dir: Daniel Mann
Stars: Rosalind Russell, Jack Hawkins,
Maximilian Schell, Richard Beymer
Rating: ★ ★

Emotionally charged drama, based on
Peter Shaffer's successful play, about a
warring family for whom a young
German tutor acts as an explosive catalyst. Director Daniel Mann came to
films from Broadway, and was responsible for both stage and screen versions
of *Come Back Little Sheba* and *The Rose
Tattoo.*

Five Fingers ○

1952, US, 105 mins, b/w
Dir: Joseph L Mankiewicz
Stars: James Mason, Danielle Darrieux,
Michael Rennie
Rating: ★ ★ ★

A thriller that's as smooth and steely
James Mason's central performance as
the embassy valet who stole Allied secrets for the Nazis. Director Joseph L
Mankiewicz masterminds the documentary approach that had already
distinguished a number of Fox realist
thrillers in post-war years. The result
is a tension-filled winner all the way.

Five Golden Hours ○

1960, UK/Italy, 90 mins, b/w
Dir: Mario Zampi
Stars: Ernie Kovacs, Cyd Charisse,

George Sanders, Kay Hammond
Rating: ★ ★

Off-beat but clumsy comedy about a
professional mourner and con-man
who has the wool pulled over his eyes
by a beautiful widow. Watch for the
captivating Kay Hammond, star of
Blithe Spirit.

Five Graves to Cairo ○

1943, US, 96 mins, b/w
Dir: Billy Wilder
Stars: Franchot Tone, Erich von
Stroheim, Anne Baxter, Akim Tamiroff
Rating: ★ ★ ★ ★

This highly successful wartime adventure gave Erich von Stroheim one or
his most famous roles (as Rommel) and
confirmed Austrian-born Billy Wilder's
standing in Hollywood following his
initial success there the previous year
with *The Major and the Minor.* He also
collaborated on the script with Charles
Brackett. It contains a strong vein of
humour , as well as lots of action and
suspense.

Five Heartbeats, The ● ⓥ

1991, US, 120 mins, colour
Dir: Robert Townsend
Stars: Michael Wright, Harry J Lennix,
Leon, Robert Townsend, Tico Wells,
Diahann Carroll
Rating: ★ ★

Although it makes a change from
today's black crime movies, this is a
long and sometimes incoherent account
of the rise and fall of a black pop
group, which starts up in 1965. A
good-looking film, it charts the group's
progression from small-time to big-
time, along the way falling into the
clutches of a shady shark who owns a
record company, and losing the lead
singer to a combination of drugs and
booze. Besides overlength, the film suffers from the fact that its leading
characters (and their women) are insufficiently defined – apart from its
lyricist, played by Robert Townsend,
who also directed the film. Chuck
Patterson is good as the manager and
it's nice to see Harold Nicholas, once of
the dazzling dancing Nicholas Brothers,
as the group's aged choreographer.

Five Million Miles to Earth

(See: Quatermass and the Pit)

Five Pennies, The ○

1959, US, 117 mins, colour
Dir: Melville Shavelson
Stars: Danny Kaye, Barbara Bel Geddes,
Louis Armstrong
Rating: ★ ★ ★

Danny Kaye tackles something akin to a straight acting role in this sentiment-based tribute to jazzman Red Nichols, whose traumatic private life was a natural for Hollywood treatment. Barbara Bel Geddes gives sympathetic support as Nichols' wife and several jazz greats are also in the film, including Louis Armstrong, whose duets with Kaye are the highspots of the film.

Five Star Final ○
1931, US, 89 mins, b/w
Dir: Mervyn LeRoy
Stars: Edward G Robinson, Marian Marsh, H B Warner, Aline MacMahon, Boris Karloff
Rating: ★★★★

A scathing indictment of sensationalist journalism that pulls no punches on its way to an uncompromising ending. Edward G Robinson, who had just scored his first big film success with *Little Caesar*, creates a real character as a fast-talking big city editor. He gets strong support from Aline MacMahon, as a staunch secretary, and Boris Karloff, as an odious unfrocked minister who now wheedles his way into people's confidence to get scandal material for the paper. Preview audiences found Karloff's character, T Vernon Isopod, so effectively repulsive that they complained about his being allowed to live!

5 Steps to Danger ○
1955, US, 80 mins, b/w
Dir: Henry S Kesler
Stars: Sterling Hayden, Ruth Roman
Rating: ★★★

Made towards the end of the Communist spy-scare era in America, this well-knit drama dwells less on the Red Menace than its predecessors, and more on action, suspense and intrigue. Ruth Roman and Sterling Hayden keep the plot moving well along its well-worn but very twisting road. And Werner Klemperer – later the familiar Colonel Klink from *Hogan's Heroes* – gives a good study in villainy, in the days before he became known as a funnyman. The story is a tangle of Hitchcockian proportions.

5,000 Fingers of Dr T, The ⊙
1953, US, 88 mins, colour
Dir: Roy Rowland
Stars: Hans Conried, Tommy Rettig, Peter Lind Hayes, Mary Healy
Rating: ★★★

A wild fantasy musical, so far ahead of its time that the distributors completely mishandled it, making it a flop at the

box-office. The fingers in the title belong to the 500 boys imprisoned in the castle of the fiendish Dr T, condemned to play 500 pianos to eternity. Amazing Technicolor photography by Franz Planer, some pleasant songs and a 'dungeon ballet' that's a gem of imaginative thought and execution. Eccentric character star Hans Conried has himself a ball as Dr T, the piano teacher who becomes the subject of the youthful hero's nightmare visions.

Five Weeks In a Balloon ⊙
1962, US, 101 mins, colour
Dir: Irwin Allen
Stars: Red Buttons, Peter Lorre, Barbara Eden, Cedric Hardwicke, Fabian, Richard Haydn
Rating: ★★

Based on a novel by Jules Verne, this is a colourful, star-studded adventure story about a balloon expedition to Africa in the 19th century. Director and co-writer Irwin Allen's treatment is deliberately comic and fills the old vehicle with enough laughing gas to lift it clear off the ground. Children can goggle while adults giggle, and both will enjoy the antics of the balloon and of a chimp called Duchess, as well as Peter Lorre's throwaway line in sinister jokes, and plump Billy Gilbert's apoplectic slapstick.

Fixed Bayonets! ○
1951, US, 93 mins, b/w
Dir: Samuel Fuller
Stars: Richard Basehart, Gene Evans, Michael O'Shea, Richard Hylton
Rating: ★★★

Another in a long line of gritty war films directed by Samuel Fuller, running through 30 years from *Steel Helmet* to *The Big Red One*. Fuller's handling of the situation where a platoon is pinned down in a cave brings little relief from the pressures they are under, dispenses almost entirely with humour, and concentrates on the stress, mental and physical, that the soldiers face. Good performances from a cast headed by Richard Basehart, Gene Evans and Michael O'Shea. James Dean has a tiny role.

Flame and the Arrow, The ○
1950, US, 88 mins, colour
Dir: Jacques Tourneur
Stars: Burt Lancaster, Virginia Mayo, Robert Douglas
Rating: ★★★★

This brilliant adventure film established Burt Lancaster as the natural successor to Errol Flynn in Warner

Brothers' swashbucklers. It also strengthened his credentials as a leading man and not just another tough guy; from then on he began to get a much wider range of roles. Recouping several times its original cost to the surprise of the studio (it was the 11th biggest grossing film in the world for the year), the film found underrated director Jacques Tourneur re-using sets from Flynn's *Adventures of Don Juan* in a joyous and action-filled story of derring-do in medieval Lombardy. Lancaster, teamed with his ex-circus partner Nick Cravat, does almost all his own stunts. Britain's Robert Douglas, once a national fencing champion, provides handsome, personable villainy.

Flame in the Streets ○
1961, UK, 93 mins, colour
Dir: Roy Baker
Stars: John Mills, Sylvia Syms
Rating: ★★★

Ted Willis wrote this sincere early screen look at the colour problem with the versatile John Mills as the 'liberal' unionist who finds his values called into question when his daughter falls for a young black man. There's an exciting Guy Fawkes night climax.

Flame of Araby ○
1951, US, 77 mins, colour
Dir: Charles Lamont
Stars: Jeff Chandler, Maureen O'Hara, Richard Egan, Susan Cabot
Rating: ★★

At one time, Universal was a studio quite noted for its Eastern or Oriental action-adventure extravaganzas. This one was made at a time when the grey-haired Jeff Chandler had won considerable popularity. And what better co-star could there have been than the fiery, red-haired Maureen O'Hara, one of the best swashbuckleresses in the business.

Flame of the Barbary Coast ○
1945, US, 97 mins, b/w
Dir: Joseph Kane
Stars: John Wayne, Ann Dvorak
Rating: ★★

A standard Republic 'gambling saloon' Western. The studio at least gave their regular action man, John Wayne, a decent leading lady in spitfire Ann Dvorak, and threw in the San Francisco earthquake for good measure. But an uncharacteristically slack script by Borden Chase hurts the film's efforts in other departments. A good

F

supporting cast includes Virginia Grey, Joseph Schildkraut, William Frawley, Adele Mara (on her way up at the studio), Paul Fix and Marc Lawrence.

Flame Over India
See: North West Frontier

Flaming Feather ○
1951, US, 78 mins, colour
Dir: Ray Enright
Stars: Sterling Hayden, Forrest Tucker, Barbara Rush, Richard Arlen, Victor Jory
Rating: ★★

A lively Technicolor Western about outlaw-led renegade Indians, directed by Ray Enright, a man who knew Hollywood from top to bottom. He made this film soon after finishing a string of westerns with Randolf Scott.

Flamingo Road ○
1949, US, 94 mins, b/w
Dir: Michael Curtiz
Stars: Joan Crawford, Zachary Scott, David Brian, Sydney Greenstreet, Pierre Watkin, Virginia Huston
Rating: ★★★

Joan Crawford, although a little long in the tooth to be a cooch dancer, gave one of the best of her post-war performances here, most notably in scenes she shares with hulking Sydney Greenstreet. He plays a tyrannical sheriff who frames Crawford's dancer/waitress on a prostitution charge when he considers she stands in the way of his political progress. Their exchanges smoulder with hate, overshadowing even grim-faced David Brian and sneering Zachary Scott, the latter playing yet another charming yet callous weakling. Good, solid, welltold melodrama with a script re-written at Crawford's demand and some nice, oppressive small-town atmosphere.

Flaming Star ○ ⓥ
1960, US, 92 mins, colour
Dir: Don Siegel
Stars: Elvis Presley, Steve Forrest, Barbara Eden, Dolores Del Rio
Rating: ★★★

Certainly a candidate for Elvis Presley's best film, virtually songless and made a couple of years before his film career started to slide into interchangeable milk-and-water musicals. A Western with echoes of classic tragedy, it's drivingly well directed by Don Siegel, who achieves some scenes of great beauty and others of stunning excitement, the two elements combining in the initial attack by Indians on a farmhouse. For once, the frontier land

looks vast, inhospitable and just as it should. But they should have reshot the bungled ending.

Flashback ●
1990, US, 105 mins, colour
Dir: Franco Amurri
Stars: Dennis Hopper, Kiefer Sutherland
Rating: ★★★

Flawed but underrated action comedy which works extremely well for the fist hour but then begins to go off the rails. Until then, though, there are some sparkling exchanges of dialogue between Dennis Hopper, as the ex-hippie hero now being escorted to justice, and Kiefer Sutherland, as his young FBI captor. Hopper gently guys his own image, and Sutherland is in particularly sharp form at the beginning of the story: scenes between them on a train are the best in the film. There are also some nice comic moments later on, notably a sequence involving a Christmas tree. Once Sutherland's own hippie background comes into play, though, the film is never the same force.

Flashdance ① ⓥ
1983, US, 96 mins, colour
Dir: Adrian Lyne
Stars: Jennifer Beals, Michael Nouri, Lilia Skala
Rating: ★★

With a soundtrack that sounds like a *Fame* sequel, a stream of tough dialogue, sensational disco choreography and a story about a girl who's a welder by day and a club dancer by night, this film rang the bell with the hardcore teen trade in a big way in spite of its absurdities. How unlikely that Jennifer Beals' boyfriend would anonymously arrange for her dreamed-of ballet audition, and then spill the beans! Then the whole thing is about half as close to life *as Saturday Night Fever,* but it has toe-tapping music and some emotive moments, like the impossibly happy ending, that work in spite of everything.

Flash Gordon ○ ⓥ
1980, US, 115 mins, colour
Dir: Mike Hodges
Stars: Sam J Jones, Melody Anderson, Topol, Max Von Sydow, Brian Blessed
Rating: ★★

Everything about this lavish film version of Alex Raymond's 1930s' comic strip is OTT, but especially Danilo Donati's impressive sets and a pounding rock score by Queen. Former American footballer and *Playgirl* magazine centrefold Sam J Jones is a rather bland Flash, but Max

Von Sydow relishes every moment of his role as Ming the Merciless, plotting nothing less than world domination. Among the wealth of British talent in the supporting roles, look out for Robbie Coltrane (in his first feature film) as a man at the airport.

Flashpoint ① ⓥ
1985, US, 94 mins, colour
Dir: William Tannen
Stars: Kris Kristofferson, Treat Williams, Rip Torn, Tess Harper, Kevin Conway
Rating: ★

This action film with a vein of mystery threatens early on to settle down into being a lively thriller, but never really follows through. The source of the $800,000 found on a 20-year-dead corpse by two border patrolmen (Kris Kristofferson, Treat Williams) is fairly obvious from the beginning, but the film spells it out for you at the end in case you missed it. Tess Harper is, as usual, wasted, while Rip Torn overacts grindingly as the senior patrolman who helps our heroes in their investigations. William Tannen's direction is too flat to be much help, but then he doesn't have a lot to work on from the start.

Flatliners ● ⓥ
1990, US, 114 mins, colour
Dir: Joel Schumacher
Stars: Kiefer Sutherland, Julia Roberts, Kevin Bacon, William Baldwin, Oliver Platt, Kimberly Scott
Rating: ★★

Don't expect to learn too much about life after death from this horror-ish story of a quintet of medical students who take it in turns to stay 'dead' for as long as possible. In spite of the stylish presentation, starry cast and two-hour running time, the result is a pile of old cobblers that will remind old-time film buffs and late horror show fans of some of those doomed medical ventures of the black and white Forties when zombies walked and ghoulies talked. Contrary to the film's publicity about the visions of briefly dead people brought back to life, what happens to our heroes here is that they are haunted by images from the past, which return in the present. Despite good performances from the cast, it gets more preposterous by the reel.

Fled ● ⓥ
Dir: Kevin Hooks
Stars: Laurence Fishburne, Stephen Baldwin, Salma Hayek, Will Patton, Robert Hooks
Rating: ★

Arch dialogue and tired plotting sink this pursuit action thriller that could be dubbed De Fightin' Ones, so often do Baldwin and Fishburne try to beat the daylights out of one another as chained convicts on the run. You may spend more time laughing than thrilling at some ludicrous supporting acting, and writing that makes fools even out of such a good featured player as Will Patton. Baldwin and Fishburne break loose from a chain gang but it's a set-up by government agents who have their eyes on a disc that could condemn a South American narcotics kingpin. Guns blast, our heroes bear charmed lives, Fishburne ridiculously finds time to fall for Salma Hayek, and there's even the obligatory sequence in a strip joint. If you can believe a computer hacker like Baldwin could have a glamorous stripper girl-friend, then you'll believe anything in this moth-ridden thriller.

Fleet's In, The ○
1942, US, 93 mins, b/w
Dir: Victor Schertzinger
Stars: Dorothy Lamour, William Holden, Eddie Bracken, Betty Hutton
Rating: ★★

Zesty wartime musical with a string of Johnny Mercer hits including 'I Remember You', 'Somebody Else's Moon' and 'Tangerine'. Rather too much of minor dancers, comics and vocalists and not quite enough room for an all-star cast which, besides Dorothy Lamour, William Holden and Eddie Bracken, includes Betty Hutton and Cass Daley, both making bombshell film debuts. Jimmy Dorsey and His Band are also in there fighting for footage.

Flesh and Blood ● Ⓥ
1985, US/Holland, 126 mins, colour
Dir: Paul Verhoeven
Stars: Rutger Hauer, Jennifer Jason Leigh, Tom Burlinson, Susan Tyrrell, Brion James, Bruno Kirby
Rating: ★

Pity Rutger Hauer in this 10th-century mud-and-guts epic. I mean, here he is, a medieval rogue, thrown down a castle well, up to the neck in contaminated water, fireballs overhead, plague in the courtyard, a vengeful army outside and the only man who can rescue him chained to a wall. And what happens? It starts raining, that's what. At that point, you have to accept that it's one of those days and reach for your glass of Guinness or Hamlet cigar – if you could light it. Never mind, there's

heaps of rape and pillage in this hideous but sometimes hilarious visceral variety show, performed with over-the-top relish by its motley cast. 'Agnes, are you all right?' bellows her swain, besieging the castle to retrieve her from rascally Rutger's clutches. 'Yes,' shrieks the damsel, jumping up and down. 'Having a good time!'

Flesh and Bone ● Ⓥ
1993, US, 126 mins, colour
Dir: Steve Kloves
Stars: Dennis Quaid, Meg Ryan, James Caan, Gwyneth Paltrow
Rating: ★★

Not quite what those going for a Quaid-Ryan-Caan movie probably have in mind, this is a grim, slow but occasionally absorbing retribution drama set on the desolate Texas plains. Thirty years before the main action, a farming family takes in a 'mute' boy found wandering in their yard, unaware that he's the front man for his thieving father (James Caan), for whom he unlocks the door. The usual procedure is that the victims are sound asleep, but this night things go wrong and tragedy ensues: the family, with the exception of the baby, is slaughtered. Decades later the boy (now Dennis Quaid), not surprisingly taciturn and withdrawn, ekes out a living filling slot machines: the father has disappeared. By accident, Quaid becomes involved with a girl (Meg Ryan) who... but no, you don't have to be a crystal-gazer to see the rest of the story, nor Caan's re-emergence in it. In the end the plot develops into a conventional thriller, even if at times it has seemed to be thinking it's something deeper. Caan and Gwyneth Paltrow steal the show as the baddies; there's no sign at all of the trademark Quaid smile.

Flesh and Fantasy ○
1943, US, 94 mins, b/w
Dir: Julien Duvivier
Stars: Edward G Robinson, Charles Boyer, Barbara Stanwyck, Betty Field, Robert Cummings, Thomas Mitchell
Rating: ★★★

A high-class trilogy of macabre tales, directed by Frenchman Julien Duvivier during his enforced wartime stay in Hollywood. The choicest of the trio involves Edward G Robinson as an attorney who scoffs at palmist Thomas Mitchell's prediction that the attorney's about to commit a murder. It's based on Oscar Wilde's classic story *Lord Arthur Savile's Crime*.

Fletch ○ Ⓥ
1985, US, 96 mins, colour
Dir: Michael Ritchie
Stars: Chevy Chase, Joe Don Baker, Dana Wheeler-Nicholson, Tim Matheson, Geena Davis
Rating: ★★★★

An exceptionally enjoyable comedy *film noir* for which star Chevy Chase is ideally suited. Scriptwriter Andrew Bergman obviously has a weakness for Bob Hope films and the result of his collaboration with Chase and director Michael Ritchie is a sort of 'My Favourite Reporter', except that Chase's character is no coward, even if he does always seem to be on the spot or on the run. He's supercool reporter Irwin ('Don't call me Irwin') Fletcher; on the trail of a drugs ring, he finds that his comparatively low-profile seashore hangout is the key to some very big men in drugs trafficking, when one of them hires Fletch the beach bum as an assassin. None of this need be taken any more seriously than in any Hope romp of the Forties, but Chase is ever ready with a wisecrack in the tightest of corners and you'll chuckle happily throughout.

Fletch Lives ○ Ⓥ
1989, US, 95 mins, colour
Dir: Michael Ritchie
Stars: Chevy Chase, Julianne Phillips, Hal Holbrook, Cleavon Little, R Lee Ermey
Rating: ★

Much anticipated after the initial success of *Fletch*, this was a dismal disappointment, a lifeless sequel drained of every vital sign. The clichéd characters are so cardboard they could topple over at the touch of a finger, and the plot runs like an indifferent episode of the old TV series *Moonlighting*. The identity of the villain must be 1989's worst kept secret and dunce's caps will be passed around for failing to pick him out. Chase sleepwalks through it and the occasional flashes of graveyard humour comes across as hearty but forced and laboured, and his impersonations are unimpressive. An early scene in which Fletch sings 'Zippedee-Doo-Dah' with cartoon characters is quite endearingly tacky, but it's all downhill from then on.

Flight of the Doves ○
1971, UK, 97 mins, colour
Dir: Ralph Nelson
Stars: Ron Moody, Jack Wild, Dorothy McGuire, Stanley Holloway
Rating: ★★★

F

After presumably purging his system with *Soldier Blue*, director Ralph Nelson turned his talents completely in the opposite direction with this whimsical Irish fancy about two children (Jack Wild and the tiny, very appealing Helen Raye) searching for their equivalent of the crock of gold at the end of the rainbow. Photographed in pretty, postcard colours by Harry Waxman, the film has a song or two from Dana, and gives Ron Moody full scope for his flair for impersonations as the children's wicked Uncle Hawk.

Flight of the Intruder ◑ Ⓥ
1991, US, 113 mins, colour
Dir: John Milius
Stars: Danny Glover, Willem Dafoe, Brad Johnson, Rosanna Arquette
Rating: ★

'The most boring Vietnam war movie since *The Green Berets*,' said *Variety* of this unpleasant story about bored US pilots. Frustrated by the lack of action during the 1972 peace talks, one of their number decides on a private mission to wipe out the People's Resistance Park in Hanoi. The film's only redeeming feature is the raid itself On the ground, though, things look extremely static. Principal roles are played by Danny Glover, as the tough-talking commander, Willem Dafoe as a veteran flier and Brad Johnson as an ace pilot. Rosanna Arquette and Tom Sizemore are also in a good cast: presumably they did all read the script.

Flight of the Navigator ○ Ⓥ
1986, US, 89 mins, colour
Dir: Randal Kleiser
Stars: Joey Cramer, Veronica Cartwright, Cliff De Young, Sarah Jessica Parker
Rating: ★★★

An engaging, if minor chunk of science-fantasy from the Disney studio. Despite a promising beginning, with a boy recovering from an accident to find strangers living at his home (could be anything, but in fact he's lost eight years from his life without himself ageing), the film simply can't follow through with enough incident. The boy has been (in 1978) on a mission to a distant planet, one of whose ships now (in 1986) needs his help. This leads the film into a brief section of its greatest charm, as the boy examines the specimens of alien life the spaceship has gathered from various planets, including a moving sludge of mud (with a cold) that eats anything. Parents of teenies should be aware that, despite

the original 'U' certificate, the film does contain mild bad language. More to the point, they may wonder about people (in the film) who let children of eight and 12 wander home through woods in the dark.

Flight of the Phoenix, The ○
1965, US, 149 mins, colour
Dir: Robert Aldrich
Stars: James Stewart, Richard Attenborough, Peter Finch
Rating: ★★★★

An ingenious variation on the Hollywood plot of the 'plane that crashes in the middle of nowhere'. In a high class acting battle, Richard Attenborough's navigator descended from RAF officer to near-alcoholic, wins the narrowest of points verdicts over James Stewart's stubborn, veteran pilot. An outrageous piece of casting against character comes off in Dan Duryea's mincing, bespectacled Standish; and Ian Bannen, too, finds plenty to get his teeth into as a Scots engineer with a rasping wit. A good, entertaining film that packs quite a grip and offers a nail-biting climax.

Flight of the White Stallion
See: Miracle of the White Stallions

Flight to Tangier ○
1953, US, 90 mins, colour
Dir: Charles Marquis Warren
Stars: Joan Fontaine, Jack Palance, Corinne Calvet, Robert Douglas
Rating: ★★

This mystery thriller packed with action features one of the longest chase sequences ever filmed. Art director Hal Pereira is to be congratulated for capturing the sleazy atmosphere of Tangier without ever moving out of Hollywood. He turned the entire Paramount Studio into a facsimile of the city, complete with winding alleys and grubby bars. A pity the stars did not 'front' his work with more inspired performances.

Film-Flam Man, The ○
(aka: One Born Every Minute)
1967, US, 115 mins, colour
Dir: Irvin Kershner
Stars: George C Scott, Michael Sarrazin, Sue Lyon
Rating: ★★★★★

A crazy character comedy that remains one of the most delightful films George C Scott has ever made. Almost buried under make-up, he's a rascally old con-man called Mordecai who takes an army deserter (Michael Sarrazin) under

his wing and makes him his apprentice. Some of their con-tricks together are very funny and there's a marvellous, town-wrecking car chase staged by director Irvin Kershner and his veteran second-unit director Yakima Canutt. The screenplay, which helps the fun fairly whiz along, was provided by British comedy king William Rose (whose credits date back to *Genevieve* and *The Ladykillers*). Here Rose provides choice supporting roles for Harry Morgan and Albert Salmi as the sheriff and his deputy, forever one frustrating step behind the two 'flim-flam' men. Altogether a refreshing and likeable dose of laughter.

Flintstones, The ⊙ Ⓥ
1994, US, 91 mins, colour
Dir: Brian Levant
Stars: John Goodman, Elizabeth Perkins, Rick Moranis, Rosie O'Donnell, Kyle MacLachlan, Elizabeth Taylor, Halle Berry
Rating: ★★★

It's certainly fascinating to see the well-loved cartoons of our childhood spring so colourfully to life. Sets, costumes and special effects are fabulous – the town of Bedrock, two million years BC, is amusingly realised – and the fun and humour of the original cartoons is charmingly recaptured, with visual puns galore, plenty of wise-cracks and rib-tickling slapstick antics from John Goodman, who was born to yell 'Yabba Dabba Doo!' Elizabeth Perkins as Wilma and Jack Moranis and Rosie O'Donnell as neighbours Barney and Betty Rubble are also nicely in character. The skeletal story, though, does rather let things down. Fred becomes a pawn of his scheming boss (Kyle MacLachlan), but finds fame and fortune while his old pal Barney grows poorer as a result. Thank goodness for incidental fun and imaginative effects, which, with its big nostalgia value, make this enjoyable for adults and kids.

Flipper ⊙
1963, US, 87 mins, colour
Dir: James B Clark
Stars: Chuck Connors, Luke Halpin
Rating: ★★★

This wildlife adventure about a boy and his pet dolphin is highly recommended for young children. The script is intelligent, and director James B Clark has a real feel for the Florida Keys locations, wonderfully well captured in colour. Remade in 1996.

Flipper ⊙ Ⓥ

1996, US, 96 mins, colour
Dir: Alan Shapiro
Stars: Paul Hogan, Elijah Wood, Chelsea
Field, Isaac Hayes, Jonathan Banks,
Jason Fuchs
Rating: ★★

Perhaps a little violent for very young
children, this is an amiable revival of
the 1960s' television series, with a
1990s ecological angle. Elijah Wood
plays a surly teenager who visits his
seadog uncle (Paul Hogan), makes
friends with an orphaned dolphin and
discovers that bad guys are polluting
the seas. It's a formula story, but
Hogan is good as the ex-hippie uncle
and the underwater photography is impressive. No comic villains in this one,
either: the main villain is an unpleasant
and menacing as in any adult thriller –
and he may scare the tinies a bit too.
Otherwise, great for five to 11-year-
olds, if a bit of a slog for their parents.

Flipper and the Pirates ⊙
(aka Flipper's New Adventure)

1964, US, 103 mins, colour
Dir: Leon Benson
Stars: Luke Halpin, Pamela Franklin
Rating: ★★

The second screen adventure of the
dolphin who became a superstar of
Sixties' television. Small children who
liked the first film can here enjoy
Flipper defeating a rather harmless trio
of convicts who hold a prim English
family to ransom. And co-star Luke
Halpin seems to be genuinely fond of
his dolphin friend, which will add to
the realism of the thing for youngsters.
As for Flipper himself, he's acquired
one or two new tricks – like butting his
enemies in the midriff to knock them
cold.

Flirting With Disaster ● Ⓥ

1996, US, 92 mins, colour
Dir: David O Russell
Stars: Ben Stiller, Patricia Arquette, Téa
Leoni, Alan Alda, Lily Tomlin, George
Segal, Mary Tyler Moore
Rating: ★★

A jolly if rude little frolic about dys-
functional couples which doesn't
always escape tedium, but bowls along
in a good-natured, anarchical way until
its couples all end up more or less
where they started. These searches for
one's real parents are fraught with danger in movies, as Woody Allen proved
in *Mighty Aphrodite*, and almost always
end in the unexpected. Despite its scattershot success rate, this one has a
brilliant cast, including Arquette and

Leoni as the girls vying for unknown
Stiller's favours, Alda and Tomlin as
the hophead parents he's only too glad
to escape from and, funniest of all,
Moore and Segal as the squabbling,
neurotic foster-parents who step right
out of their league when they try to follow Stiller on his quest. Despite nice
bits, though, the piece doesn't quite
manage to build up to the fine frenzy of
comic chaos it might have done.

Floods of Fear ○

1958, UK, 84 mins, b/w
Dir: Charles Crichton
Stars: Howard Keel, Anne Heywood, Cyril
Cusack, Harry H Corbett
Rating: ★★★

Singer Howard Keel came to Britain
after a run of Hollywood musicals to
play a strong straight role as an escaped convict in this rugged and
uncompromising thriller. Director
Charles Crichton charges his atmosphere with latent violence as two
prisoners and a warder in charge of
them are trapped by floods at an isolated house whose only other occupant is
an attractive woman. Characters are
drawn with bold, sharply defined lines
(Crichton himself wrote the screenplay, from a novel by John and Ward
Hopkins) and the forthright portraits
of the star quartet grip audience attention throughout.

Florian ○

1940, US, 91 mins, b/w
Dir: Edwin L Marin
Stars: Robert Young, Helen Gilbert,
Charles Coburn, Lee Bowman
Rating: ★★

If you saw *Miracle of the White Stallions*,
then you'll know all about the famous
white Lippizan horses from the Spanish
riding stables in Vienna. Florian is one
of those, a regal stallion of first-rate intelligence who virtually has to carry
this whole film on his broad white
shoulders. Ballerina Irina Baronova is
the only other member of the cast to really get a look in. Despite her brilliant
dancing, and the presence of co-stars
Robert Young and Charles Coburn,
it's Florian's show.

Flowers In the Attic ● Ⓥ

1987, US, 92 mins, colour
Dir: Jeffrey Bloom
Stars: Louise Fletcher, Victoria Tennant,
Kristy Swanson, Jeb Stuart Adams
Rating: RB

Author Virginia Andrews must have
spun around on her royalties at the
sight of what the cinema has done to

her bestselling book. Writer-director
Jeffrey Bloom has turned her engrossing chiller (based on fact) into
something that seems utterly preposterous. Bloom's flat, flairless direction
and the poor performances he extracts
from his players, together with his own
hysterical script, ensure that giggles of
derision far outweigh any suspense
from the first reel onwards. Even as
Victorian melodrama along *East Lynne*
lines, you would be hard put to swallow this tale of four children,
impoverished by their father's death,
who are taken by their mother
(Victoria Tennant) to the mansion of
her invalid father and locked away in
an attic lest grandad should get to
know of them. Character names like
Corrine, Bart and Cory hardly add to
the quickly disintegrating reality of the
whole miserable enterprise.

Fluke ○ Ⓥ

1995, US, 96 mins, colour
Dir: Carlo Carlei
Stars: Matthew Modine, Nancy Travis,
Eric Stoltz, Max Pomeranc, Ron Perlman,
Jon Polito, voice of Samuel L Jackson
Rating: ★★★

A charming film version of James
Herbert's novel about a man reincarnated as a dog, marred only by
over-sentimentality towards the end.
Killed in a car shunt with his best
friend (Stoltz), Thomas (Modine)
wakes up again as a retriever cross
named Fluke. A streetwise hound
called Rumbo (raspingly well voiced by
Samuel L Jackson) gens him into the
doggy rules of life, before Fluke, who
has vague memories of a former life,
decides, like Lassie, to go home.
Although the film never loses its appeal, director Carlei tends to go for the
easily drawn tear towards the end,
when the dog is helping his young master (and former son) to get over the
death of his father. All performances
are good, especially from Pomeranc (
the kid previously seen in *Searching for
Bobby Fischer*) and the dog, a real-life retriever TV star named Comet, who
had to be roughed up a bit to look like
a mongrel.

Fly Away Home ○ Ⓥ

1996, Can/US, 105 mins, colour
Dir: Carroll Ballard
Stars: Anna Paquin, Jeff Daniels, Dana
Delany
Rating: ★★★★

Inspirational pictures of a skein of
geese following a powered glider
shaped like a goose will have you

F

reaching for the handkerchiefs in the stunningly shot, well-realised weepie about a teenage girl (Paquin), who loses her mother in a New Zealand car crash and goes to live with her father half-way across the world in the wilds of Canada. Here her love for life is rekindled when she 'adopts' a clutch of goose eggs, all of which hatch to provide her with a ready-made family of 16 goslings. Crunch time comes when the geese should fly south – and face having their wings clipped by the authorities if they don't. Thus the glidoplane, invention of the girl's father (Daniels) who must teach her to fly as she's the only one the geese will follow. Paquin isn't especially good as the girl, but no matter: when the film takes to the skies, our spirits soar with it, as the geese head off on an emotive migratory journey.

Fly, The ● Ⓥ

1958, US, 95 mins, colour
Dir: Kurt Neumann
Stars: Al Hedison, Patricia Owens, Herbert Marshall, Vincent Price
Rating: ★★★

Despite the fact that the premise for this film is patently ridiculous (and indeed biologically impossible), it's fun and frightening in equal measure. Scientist André (Al Hedison) invents a matter transfer machine, but when he personally test drives it, a fly gets trapped in the chamber with him. At the other end, he comes out with an enormous fly's head, and the fly has his. Patricia Owens as his wife and Vincent Price as his brother deal with the problem in their own ways (say no more!). Gleefully gruesome, this film has become something of a cult classic.

Fly, The ● Ⓥ

1986, US, 100 mins, colour
Dir: David Cronenberg
Stars: Jeff Goldblum, Geena Davis, John Getz, Joy Boushel
Rating: ★★★★

Although its horrors get rather too much to take towards the end, this is an immensely superior remake of the 1958 horror classic about a scientist who tries to transport human matter from one machine to another, but gets his genes mixed with those of a fly accidentally locked in the teleportation machine with him. In his finest screen performance, Jeff Goldblum creates one of the most pitiable figures of the horror genre since Boris Karloff's creature in the Frankenstein films, even upstaging the Oscar-winning makeup

effects by Chris Walas and Stephan Dupuis. Geena Davis, who was soon to be Mrs Goldblum for a while, is excellent as the reporter he falls for, one of several characters who engage our emotions by seeming to be real people. Well worth a look, this, even if you have to peep through your fingers at times.

Fly II, The ● Ⓥ

1989, US, 105 mins, colour
Dir: Chris Walas
Stars: Eric Stoltz, Daphne Zuniga, John Getz
Rating: ★★

A jolly cauldron of fly vomit and no mistake. The script – especially one unintentionally funny scene – is nowhere near the calibre of its ancestor, but this horror film does have some touching moments, lots of action and excitement and a passable stag-beetle monster, which is what you get if you cross a man and a fly. Eric Stoltz follows up his malformed teenager in *Mask* with another heavy-duty makeup job.

Flying Deuces, The ⊙

1939, US, 67 mins, b/w
Dir: Edward Sutherland
Stars: Oliver Hardy, Stan Laurel, Jean Parker
Rating: ★★★

Laurel and Hardy return to the Foreign Legion, where they scored such a success in an earlier film *Beau Chumps*. They even have the same actor, Charles Middleton, playing the fort commander. And there's another of their charming song and dance numbers, this time joining the fort band in a rendition of 'Shine On, Harvest Moon'.

Flying Down to Rio ○ Ⓥ

1933, US, 85 mins, b/w
Dir: Thornton Freeland
Stars: Dolores Del Rio, Gene Raymond, Raul Roulien, Fred Astaire, Ginger Rogers
Rating: ★★★

With this musical Fred Astaire and Ginger Rogers set RKO back on the road to solvency. It was their first screen teaming, and the result was pure Hollywood magic, packed with extraordinary dance numbers and unforgettable tunes. Bland Gene Raymond and exotic Dolores Del Rio were the nominal stars, but the public mainly flocked to see Astaire and Rogers doing the carioca. Everything about the production was lavish, from its stunning art deco sets to its armies

of chorus girls, sometimes even on the wings of planes!

Flying Leathernecks ○ Ⓥ

1951, US, 102 mins, colour
Dir: Nicholas Ray
Stars: John Wayne, Robert Ryan, Don Taylor, Janis Carter
Rating: ★★

A Howard Hughes war spectacular, made with the co-operation of the US Marines, which probably accounts for the brilliance of the photography of the Guadalcanal aerial dogfights, superbly captured in sharp, bright Technicolor which today's colour processors never seem able to reproduce. John Wayne and Robert Ryan are the officers whose inevitable feud ranges from the wartime Pacific to peacetime America, and grizzled veteran Jay C Flippen provides stalwart support.

Flying Tigers ○ Ⓥ

1942, US, 100 mins, b/w
Dir: David Miller
Stars: John Wayne, John Carroll, Anna Lee
Rating: ★★★

Rousing wartime propaganda that helped bolster the American spirit. It was the Republic studio's salute to the all American Volunteer Group flying for China and Chiang Kai-Shek (long before Pearl Harbor) who received $500 for every Japanese plane shot down. John Wayne, in the first of his many war films, is the leader of one squadron of carefree pilots, and he displays a soft heart beneath the tough, blustering exterior. The film displays all the clichés that were becoming commonplace in Hollywood aerial combat film, including frequent shots of Japanese pilots dying horrible deaths in graphic close-up, bullets smashing through the canopies of their planes, and exploding in their faces, blood pouring from their mouths and eyes.

Fog, The ● Ⓥ

1979, US, 90 mins, colour
Dir: John Carpenter
Stars: Adrienne Barbeau, Hal Holbrook, Janet Leigh, Jamie Lee Curtis
Rating: ★★

A splendid idea for a horror film turns out, in this treatment, to be ripe old sub-Roger Corman hokum about long-dead leper seamen returning to avenge themselves on the town that robbed them of their gold these 100 years before. The approach is very obvious, crushing the inventive theme beneath a ship load of standard horror clichés.

But the ladies, Adrienne Barbeau, Jamie Lee Curtis and Janet Leigh, are all worthwhile.

Fog
See: A Study in Terror

Fog Over Frisco ○
1934, US, 68 mins, b/w
Dir: William Dieterle
Stars: Bette Davis, Donald Woods, Margaret Lindsay, Lyle Talbot
Rating: ★★

Never mind the complex plot, which crams incident upon incident into the short running time. What makes this thriller a real treat is William Dieterle's frenetically fast direction which employs just about every trick in the cinematic book – dissolves, wipes and fades and the kind of editing that makes Richard Lester look like a sleepwalker. If there had been an Oscar for sheer speed, Dieterle would have won, hands down.

Folks! ● ⓥ
1992, US, 109 mins, colour
Dir: Ted Kotcheff
Stars: Tom Selleck, Don Ameche, Anne Jackson, Michael Murphy, Christine Ebersole
Rating: ★

Tom Selleck's film career took a nose-dive here; nor is it the kind of sign-off Don Ameche would have wished in films. Comedies come no blacker or harder (and not much worse, either) than this tale of the chaos caused when hapless Jon (Selleck) invites his parents to live with him because his father (Ameche) is suffering from senile dementia. Everyone suffers from then on, the audience especially, as, in the first half of the film, Selleck loses various parts of his anatomy to an assortment of slapstick accidents. The second half features Selleck trying to find ways to end the lives of his parents, at their request. Euthanasia would be a good solution to the whole film, a totally tasteless frolic that may invoke a few uncomfortable giggles.

Follow a Star ○
1959, UK, 103 mins, b/w
Dir: Robert Asher
Stars: Norman Wisdom, June Laverick
Rating: ★★

This Norman Wisdom comedy is on the maudlin side, with the unnecessary addition of a handicapped girlfriend for the star. But the supporting cast is one to treasure, with Jerry Desmonde,

Richard Wattis, Charles Gray, Dick Emery and John le Mesurier in its ranks. The main theme is more or less borrowed from *Singin' in the Rain*.

Follow Me, Boys! ⊙
1966, US, 130 mins, colour
Dir: Norman Tokar
Stars: Fred MacMurray, Vera Miles, Lillian Gish, Charlie Ruggles
Rating: ★★★★

This Disney saga doesn't dazzle you with cleverness; it has moments when charm tips over into nausea and it slows towards the end. Yet this was one of the nicest films of its year. With no megastar names and a spun-out piece of Americana to work with, the set-up can't have looked promising. Yet the actors rise to the occasion, the direction (by Norman Tokar) is care itself, the small-town atmosphere is never lost, and the corn becomes sweet, warm and human. Fred MacMurray, a tower of acting quality here, gives one of his best performances as the footloose musician who drops off at a tiny mid-West town because he has an eye for the banker's daughter (Vera Miles) and stays not only to marry her, but becomes the town's first scoutmaster and, of course, one of its best-loved citizens. Tokar sparks the film's slower second half with a couple of fine, throat-lumping scenes, including one in which MacMurray, who has always wanted to be a lawyer, defends an elderly lady (Lillian Gish) on a charge of insanity.

Follow That Dream ○ ⓥ
1962, US, 105 mins, colour
Dir.Gordon Douglas
Stars: Elvis Presley, Anne Helm, Arthur O'Connell, Joanna Moore
Rating: ★★★

One of Elvis Presley's brightest films, this is an amusing comedy about a family of hillbillies. Tuneful songs, too.

Follow That Horse! ○
1959, UK, 80 mins, b/w
Dir: Alan Bromly
Stars: David Tomlinson, Mary Peach, Cecil Parker
Rating: ★★

A chance to savour one of the last of David Tomlinson's famous silly-ass characterisations for the cinema, here as a civil servant on the trail of a horse that has swallowed a top-secret microfilm. And there's also an opportunity to admire the permanently perplexed Cecil Parker.

Follow the Fleet ○
1936, US, 110 mins, b/w
Dir: Mark Sandrich
Stars: Fred Astaire, Ginger Rogers, Randolph Scott, Harriet Hilliard, Betty Grable
Rating: ★★

A much overrated Fred Astaire musical, a couple of notches below *Top Hat* which it followed for RKO. Astaire and Ginger Rogers dance up a storm but Randolph Scott and Harriet Hilliard are woefully miscast as the film's comedy stars. Irving Berlin, who loved to write for Astaire more than any other singer, provides the toe-tapping tunes, including the classic 'Let's Face the Music and Dance'.

Folly to be Wise ○
1952, UK, 91 mins, b/w
Dir: Frank Launder
Stars: Alastair Sim, Roland Culver, Elizabeth Allan
Rating: ★★★

The delightful talent of Alastair Sim helps glue together this film version of a James Bridie comedy play. Sim's a chaplain chairing a brains trust that turns into a catalogue of sexual scandal. Some of the other performances are amusing too, with Janet Brown making a rare appearance, and George Cole popping in as guest star.

Food of the Gods, The ◑
1976, US, 88 mins, colour
Dir: Bert I Gordon
Stars: Ida Lupino, Ralph Meeker, Marjoe Gortner, Pamela Franklin
Rating: ★

A pretty messy horror film whose special effects vary from wobbly to excellent as a farmload of monster animals goes on the rampage thanks to the food of the title, originally invented by H G Wells. The dialogue is treasurable for addicts of such late-night fare. 'Giant rats! Awful giant rats,' screeches Ida Lupino, running from her farm. 'But we're looking for Mr Skinner,' says her companion unimpressed. Britain's Pamela Franklin weighs in as the inevitable imperilled heroine. 'Why do you work for me?' asks industrialist Ralph Meeker. 'Well,' she muses, 'jobs for female bacteriologists are just not that easy to find.'

Fool for Love ◑
1985, US, 106 mins, colour
Dir: Robert Altman
Stars: Sam Shepard, Kim Basinger, Harry

F

Dean Stanton, Randy Quaid
Rating: ★

Writer-star Sam Shepard's deliberately enigmatic play still runs like a play, in spite of direction by Robert Altman that alternately opens things out and focuses rightly on the drama. A grubby ranch in the New Mexico desert is run by Harry Dean Stanton, who may be father both to Kim Basinger, who works there, and Sam Shepard, who has come to win her back after past infidelities. Or then again, this may all be just a figment of their imaginations, told by all three to Kim's suitor Randy Quaid. The cast is good – Stanton, in particular, is always worth watching – but the piece itself is slow, symbolic and empty.

Fools of Fortune ◐

1990, UK, 109 mins, colour
Dir: Pat O'Connor
Stars: Mary Elizabeth Mastrantonio, Iain Glen, Julie Christie, Michael Kitchen
Rating: ★★

The Irish countryside is the real star of this slow historical saga that tends to melodrama. The Irish war of independence is the spark that destroys a family and kindles an unlikely love story. Iain Glen plays a profoundly tortured soul who seeks retribution on the British army soldiers who murdered his family in rural Ireland. His performance is genuinely moving, as is that of Julie Christie as his mother, who relishes every minute of her descent into depression and alcoholism. American Mary Elizabeth Mastrantonio is a surprising choice as the young English woman who helps Glen's character through his troubles, but her English accent is impeccable.

Fools' Parade

See: Dynamite Man from Glory Jail

Footlight Parade ○ ⓥ

1933, US, 100 mins, b/w
Dir: Busby Berkeley
Stars: James Cagney, Joan Blondell, Ruby Keeler, Dick Powell, Guy Kibbee
Rating: ★★★★

This James Cagney film is notable for two reasons. Not only does it present the usually tough star in light vein, tripping the light fantastic, but it's also one of the best examples of one of those wonderful Warner Brothers musicals with numbers by Busby Berkeley. It has four big production numbers. You have to be patient, though, because three of them don't come until the last half-hour. But when they do come, the

wait has been worthwhile. The best is the fantastic 'By a Waterfall' in which scores of shapely girls go through their paces (or strokes) in a gigantic swimming pool. Another number, 'Shanghai Lil', gives Cagney the chance to do a dance as a sailor enamoured of an oriental girl (Ruby Keeler). The third, 'Honeymoon Hotel', presents Dick Powell distracted on his wedding night by a bevy of beautiful brides.

Footlight Serenade ○

1942, US, 80 mins, b/w
Dir: Gregory Ratoff
Stars: Betty Grable, John Payne, Victor Mature, Jane Wyman
Rating: ★★

Victor Mature's third film in a row opposite Betty Grable, which casts him as a boxer making a career in showbiz and her as the chorus girl who takes over from the leading lady and becomes a star. A familiar, cosy musical framework, steered on its predictable but entertaining way by the Russian-born director (and character actor) Gregory Ratoff, who was improbably put in charge of several Fox musicals from the 1942-47 period. A quality supporting cast includes Phil Silvers, June Lang, Jane Wyman and James Gleason. Mysteriously made in black and white, as opposed to the gaudy Technicolor Fox used for most of their Forties' musicals.

Footloose ○ ⓥ

1984, US, 107 mins, colour
Dir: Herbert Ross
Stars: Kevin Bacon, Lori Singer, John Lithgow, Dianne Wiest, Christopher Penn, Sarah Jessica Parker
Rating: ★★

Disco dancing dug back into the rock 'n' roll era for this silly old plot, which runs like a cross between *Saturday Night Fever, Rock Around the Clock* and *Rebel Without a Cause*. Actually, the story of the town that bans music goes back 50 years or more, although it wouldn't seem today to have a place outside farce or comic opera. Young Ren (Kevin Bacon) finds himself a rebel without applause when he comes to the 'redneck' town of Boford where the good ol' boys have banned dancing and parties and all that awful teenage stuff. The local preacher (John Lithgow, who tries every which way to make something of the part) breathes fire and brimstone over the local congregation to such an extent that they're soon burning half the books in the local library. 'It's not that we don't talk,' he

tells his wife (Dianne Wiest, in another performance that smacks of desperation). 'It's just that people sometimes run out of things to say.' It's hard to believe the average teenager will watch all this without falling about.

Footsteps in the Dark ○

1941, US, 96 mins, b/w
Dir: Lloyd Bacon
Stars: Errol Flynn, Brenda Marshall, Ralph Bellamy, Alan Hale
Rating: ★★

A pretty unusual assignment for Errol Flynn, who's given a break from swashbucklers, as a mystery story writer dabbling in amateur detective work. Director Lloyd Bacon keeps it going nicely and there are scene-stealing supporting roles for Lee Patrick and William Frawley, only two of many familiar Hollywood characters from the period in the cast of this lightweight but polished piece of fun.

Footsteps in the Fog ○

1955, UK, 90 mins, colour
Dir: Arthur Lubin
Stars: Stewart Granger, Jean Simmons, Bill Travers, Belinda Lee
Rating: ★★★

The then-married Grangers returned to England from Hollywood to make this throwback to thrillers of the Thirties and Forties, with characters padding around in the pea-soupers trying to bump each other off. Jean Simmons gets the better of the acting duel as a minx of a maid who blackmails her murdering employer into making her first his housekeeper, then his wife. The Technicolor photography is quite excellent.

For a Few Dollars More ◐

1965, Italy, 130 mins, colour
Dir: Sergio Leone
Stars: Clint Eastwood, Lee Van Cleef, Klaus Kinski
Rating: ★★

The second in Clint Eastwood's alternately violent and ponderous Western trilogy, memorable for the scenes in which he and Lee Van Cleef shoot off each other's hats, and where Van Cleef strikes a match on Klaus Kinski's neck.

For Better, For Worse ○

(aka: Cocktails In the Kitchen)
1954, UK, 84 mins, colour
Dir: J Lee Thompson
Stars: Dirk Bogarde, Susan Stephen, Cecil Parker, Dennis Price
Rating: ★★★★

Arthur Watkyn's famous stage success has proved successful material for drama societies up and down the land – but still comes up like new in this bright little film version. Delightful performances from both Dirk Bogarde and Susan Stephen as the would-be happy couple, helped by a full compliment of British character comedians, ensure a fistful of chuckles. The simple plotline is packed full of amusing incident in this warm, human and charmingly funny domestic comedy dressed up as fresh as paint by Guy Green's Eastman Colour camerawork.

Forbidden O

1932, US, 83 mins, b/w
Dir: Frank Capra
Stars: Barbara Stanwyck, Adolphe Menjou, Ralph Bellamy, Dorothy Peterson, Henry Armetta
Rating: ★★

Sensitive, touching performances by Adolphe Menjou and Barbara Stanwyck lift this tragedy-laden romantic drama, more typical of such Thirties weepies as *Back Street* than the average Frank Capra film. Not that Capra doesn't do a highly professional job on what he himself described as a '99.44% soap opera', especially in an understated scene in which the leading players engage in mock romantic dialogue while wearing Halloween masks.

Forbidden Planet O ⓥ

1956, US, 98 mins, colour
Dir: Fred M Wilcox
Stars: Walter Pidgeon, Anne Francis, Leslie Nielsen
Rating: ★★★

A science-fiction thriller that later became a cult classic. The climax is frighteningly well done, Leslie Nielsen keeps a straighter face than in any of his *Naked Gun* comedies, and the film's 'inhuman' star, Robby the Robot, proved so popular that MGM brought him back for a second appearance, in another fantasy, *The Invisible Boy*. Walter Pidgeon and Anne Francis head the human cast. Looks a bit creaky today.

Force of Arms O

1951, US, 100 mins, b/w
Dir: Michael Curtiz
Stars: William Holden, Frank Lovejoy, Nancy Olson, Gene Evans
Rating: ★★

Wartime love story enlivened by the injection of some fierce combat scenes. The dour William Holden and the ultra-pretty Nancy Olson were one of the most popular romantic teams of the early Fifties. Paramount had already teamed them three times, and they co-star again in this story of an infantry sergeant who falls in love with a WAC officer.

Force 10 from Navarone O ⓥ

1978, UK, 118 mins, colour
Dir: Guy Hamilton
Stars: Robert Shaw, Harrison Ford, Edward Fox, Barbara Bach, Franco Nero, Richard Kiel
Rating: ★★

Those *Guns of Navarone* saboteurs are at it again in this lively adventure film, trying to blow up a dam to stop the Germans 'cutting Yugoslavia in half'. The dialogue's a lot like that example and, with everyone saying 'the place is crawling with Krauts', it could well be a film of 20 years earlier. Still, there's Edward Fox around, doing splendid work as ever-so-British demolitions expert Miller (the part created by David Niven). What an incorrigible scene-stealer the man is! In comparison, Robert Shaw doesn't quite come across with his usual crackling fire, while Harrison Ford seems to be trying to imitate John Wayne. One expects him to shout 'shape up or ship out' at any moment. The action and special effects are good enough to satisfy most fans of the genre, but the scriptwriters are the real saboteurs of this expedition.

Foreign Affair, A O

1948, US, 116 mins, b/w
Dir: Billy Wilder
Stars: Jean Arthur, Marlene Dietrich, John Lund, Millard Mitchell
Rating: ★★★

Amusing Billy Wilder comedy, given a slightly rough edge by its war-torn Berlin backgrounds. Jean Arthur and Marlene Dietrich spar delightfully; John Lund had about his last decent movie role as the man in the middle. As scabrously funny as all the best Wilder comedies (though less vicious than its contemporary reputation) the film also contains some delightful musical interludes, including Jean Arthur's 'Iowa State' song and two from Dietrich entitled 'Black Market' and 'Ruins of Berlin'. Millard Mitchell supplies some spiky wit at the head of the supporting cast.

Foreign Body O

1986, UK, 111 mins, colour
Dir: Ronald Neame
Stars: Victor Banerjee, Warren Mitchell,

Geraldine McEwan, Denis Quilley
Rating: ★

An oddity that unsurprisingly never found its public, this is like a Fifties' comedy caught in a time capsule and whisked three decades on. Victor Banerjee, all Asiatic earnestness, is the ever-smiling Calcutta refugee who comes to England and progresses from bus conductor to bogus Harley Street doctor in a remarkably short time. He becomes wildly successful and pretty girls flock for consultations. There's a lot of non-contact sex of the kind seen in old Norman Wisdom and Dirk Bogarde comedies, and even the old chestnut of boiling milk symbolising Banerjee's rising passion. A beautiful Indian girl called Sinitta Renet who's briefly in the film at the start knocks spots off the English competition (even Amanda Donohoe), who were all presumably numbed by having read a script which contains no laughs at all. However, Ken Howard's music is delightful and the whole prescription would probably have gone down quite well (minus nudity) in 1954.

Foreign Correspondent O

1940, US, 119 mins, b/w
Dir: Alfred Hitchcock
Stars: Joel McCrea, Laraine Day, Herbert Marshall, George Sanders, Edmund Gwenn
Rating: ★★★★

Alfred Hitchcock's plea to America to join the war, under the cover of a thriller about a reporter's bid to smash an espionage ring. It's memorable for the scene in a windmill where Joel McCrea's coat gets caught in moving machinery; Edmund Gwenn as a chillingly matter-of-fact assassin; and the drama of a crashing aeroplane, filmed head-on by the director, who ingeniously put his cameras inside the cabin. There was a transparency screen on the other side and, behind the screen, a huge water tank, which burst apart (and through the screen, and into the cabin) at the touch of a button. Hitchcock himself makes his usual fleeting guest appearance.

Foreign Intrigue O

1956, US/Italy, 97 mins, colour
Dir: Sheldon Reynolds
Stars: Robert Mitchum, Genevieve Page, Ingrid Thulin
Rating: ★★★

Strange to find a crime film of the mid-Fifties in colour, although the Eastman Colour photography of Vienna and Stockholm is extremely pleasing. It's a

F

fast-paced thriller with press agent Robert Mitchum forever loping down alleys and shadowy byways trying to unravel an espionage mystery well knit together by writer-director Sheldon Reynolds, a radio specialist who only made two or three films. Ingrid Thulin, soon to become one of director Ingmar Bergman's favourite actresses, is seen in an early role as the dishy blonde in love with our lazy-lidded hero.

Foreman Went to France, The O
(aka: Somewhere In France)
1942, UK, 87 mins, b/w
Dir: Charles Frend
Stars: Clifford Evans, Constance Cummings, Tommy Trinder, Robert Morley, Gordon Jackson
Rating: ★★★

An exciting re-creation of the incredible exploit of a civilian who went to France in 1940 to recover top-secret machinery in danger of falling into the hands of the advancing Germans. Humour, purveyed in the face of adversity by the wisecracking Tommy Trinder, provides a nice balance to the heroic adventures of the 'foreman', played in forthright fashion by Clifford Evans. Based on a real-life character called Melbourne Johns, to whom the film is dedicated.

Forever Amber O
1947, US, 140 mins, colour
Dir: Otto Preminger
Stars: Linda Darnell, Cornel Wilde, Richard Greene, George Sanders, Jessica Tandy, Anne Revere
Rating: ★★

Hollywood gave this historical inelodrama an elaborate treatment, but inevitably bowdlerised Kathleen Winsor's runaway bestseller of sex and swashbuckling, the forerunner of a thousand coffee-table epics in similar vein. Britain's Peggy Cummins was first picked to play the infamous Amber St Clair, but was later dropped from the film in favour of Hollywood's sultry Linda Darnell.

Forever and a Day O
1943, US, 104 mins, b/w
Dir: René Clair, Edmund Goulding, Cedric Hardwicke, Frank Lloyd, Victor Saville, Robert Stevenson, Herbert Wilcox
Stars: Merle Oberon, Anna Neagle, Ray Milland, Claude Rains, Ida Lupino, Gladys Cooper, C Aubrey Smith
Rating: ★★★

More than 100 stars of their day gave their services free for this film, the profit being shared between urgently needed cash for Britain's war effort and America's National Foundation for Infantile Paralysis. No less than 21 famous scriptwriters worked on the film, a blockbuster epic of English family life through 140 years. The tremendous cast includes every British-born actor in Hollywood at the time. One of them was Sir Cedric Hardwicke who shared the directing with six other famous names of the cinema and, in company with Buster Keaton, provides the most joyous scene in the film – a delicious few moments as two plumbers who try to instal a bathtub.

Forever Female O
1954, US, 94 mins, b/w
Dir: Irving Rapper
Stars: William Holden, Ginger Rogers, Paul Douglas, Pat Crowley
Rating: ★★★★

Biting comedy about an ageing actress fighting against both Old Father Time and competition from a young and peppy actress. As the youngster, 20 year-old Pat Crowley offers a sparkling performance in her first film role. Ginger Rogers gives an observant, beautifully calculated portrayal of the doyenne star, and all concerned revel in the acidly witty script by Oscar-winning writers Julius J and Phillip G Epstein.

Forever Young O O Ⓥ
1992, US, 102 mins, colour
Dir: Steve Miner
Stars: Mel Gibson, Jamie Lee Curtis, Isabel Glasser, Elijah Wood
Rating: ★★★

A quintuple handkerchief movie, this silly but wildly engaging romance works because Mel Gibson and Isabel Glasser really do give a feeling of total love as he roars across the skies testing new fighter planes in 1939. Before he can pluck up the courage to propose, a road accident takes her out of his life for ever, into a permanent coma. Utterly shattered, Gibson volunteers for a cryogenic experience, to be frozen for a year. He wakes up 50 years later, seemingly no older. Somehow he catapults out of the clutches of a disbelieving military, and into the life of a divorcee nurse (Jamie Lee Curtis, whose son (Elijah Wood) released him from his ice prison. How Gibson sorts out Curtis' and Wood's problems as well as his own (which includes fits in which he begins to age) make up the

bulk of the story which may provide a titter or two, and certainly a tear or two before a finale which may creep up on you unawares.

Forget Paris O Ⓥ
1995, US, 101 mins, colour
Dir: Billy Crystal
Stars: Billy Crystal, Debra Winger, Joe Mantegna, Cynthia Stevenson, William Hickey
Rating: ★★★

Here's a romantic comedy that works hard at being both comic and romantic. The comedy's often on firm ground, with more than a dozen smart lines. The romance is less secure, with Debra Winger playing off Billy Crystal gamely, but rather less naturally than did Meg Ryan in When Harry Met Sally ... Finally, it's a film that, like Crystal and Winger with their marriage, tries perhaps a little too hard to please. He's a basketball referee – cue for some nice reaction lines between diminutive Crystal and skyscraper players – she's an airline official he meets in Paris when her company loses his father's body there en route to burial. She's separated and vulnerable; he can't stop joking. He charms. She falls. They marry. But the cold light of the USA brings not only wildly conflicting schedules and an inability to conceive, but a permanent visit from her doddering father (William Hickey, stealing the show). A recipe for disaster? You got it. Like their relationship, the film wears thin at times – but there's always the next set of Crystal wisecracks round the corner.

For Keeps?
See: Maybe Baby

For Love or Money O Ⓥ
(aka: The Concierge)
1993, US, 94 mins, colour
Dir: Barry Sonnenfeld
Stars: Michael J Fox, Gabrielle Anwar, Anthony Higgins
Rating: ★

Black marks to the film that starts off with a great idea and then ditches it after the first reel. Michael J Fox is the concierge (day manager) at a swish hotel, and he's a wheeler-dealer who can do anything for anyone. He bargains outside the premises with street traders for theatre tickets, and has his own cut-price shop where (after he takes his cut) hotel customers can save hundreds of dollars. There are dozens of stories to be told here, but unfortunately the film jettisons almost all of them after the first 15 minutes in favour of by far the soppiest: Fox, who's saving all his fat tips to buy his own hotel, falls for perfume assistant/singer Gabrielle Anwar, who just happens to be the mistress of the heartless shark (Anthony Higgins) who's agreed to bankroll Fox for the rest of his hotel. The film then devotes 90% of its running time to the increasingly drippy situation of Fox organising Anwar and Higgins' love life while falling ever deeper for the girl but trying to keep his mind on the money. Fox is good in his know-it-all guise but less strong on sincerity.

For Me and My Gal O
(aka: For Me and My Girl)
1942, US, 104 mins, b/w
Dir: Busby Berkeley
Stars: Judy Garland, Gene Kelly, George Murphy, Marta Eggert, Richard Quine, Keenan Wynn
Rating: ★★★

The Harry Palmer who's the central character in this wartime musical has nothing to do with Michael Caine, but did provide a film debut for a 30-year-old Broadway musical star called Gene Kelly. And what company he found himself in – Judy Garland, George Murphy and director Busby Berkeley. Although the plot of the film is pure Hollywood cornball, the public were really grabbed by its patriotic fervour, and made it a big hit for MGM, setting Kelly up for a fabulous career at the studio. The songs come at you in dozens. but among the more memorable are 'Oh, You Beautiful Doll', 'After You've Gone', 'Ballin' the Jack' and the Garland-Kelly duet on the title song.

Formula, The O
1980, US, 115 mins, colour
Dir: John G Avildsen
Stars: George C Scott, Marlon Brando, Marthe Keller, John Gielgud
Rating: ★★

It's hard to work out what attracted two actors who were then two of the world's top stars to appear in a film whose script is its weakest link. Formula is right, in fact, for this is a standard high-finance thriller whose roots cross with those of *Marathon Man* and countless others where implications are worldwide and stretch up to men at the top of skyscrapers, whose power the hero cannot break. It starts well as a police investigation thriller, but the trite screenplay soon takes its grip. Marlon Brando has to resort to a

weird bag of tricks to enliven a stereotyped villain who could have been played by any efficient Hollywood character star. Little remains of the rest apart from another limp performance by Marthe Keller and a series of 'Suspicious' minor characters who are bumped offin sequence, presumably for bad acting. George C Scott's frayed veteran cop is the strongest element in a film whose excitements are all too deliberate, and there's good work too from Calvin Jung as his Oriental sidekick.

Forrest Gump ❶ ⓥ
1994, US, 142 mins, colour
Dir: Robert Zemeckis
Stars: Tom Hanks, Gary Sinise, Robin Wright, Sally Field
Rating: ★★★

Interesting and decidedly different, this multi-Oscar-winning survey of 30 years of American history through the eyes of a simple man (another virtuoso role for Tom Hanks) never quite pulls off a mixture of tragedy and fantasy that only occasionally blends into a whole. While the girl he loves (Robin Wright) succumbs to the drug culture, and his lieutenant in Vietnam (Gary Sinise) has his legs blown off, Forrest survives with mind (he has an IQ of only 75) and body virtually unscathed. While almost everyone he touches seems to die, Forrest himself meets Elvis and sundry presidents on the way to accidentally becoming a millionaire through shrimp fishing and computers. Moving moments are always counterbalanced by violent ones: even the ending is sad, though life goes on. Perhaps the film is saying that life is a tragedy we have to live. Hanks couldn't be better as Forrest, yet, like the film, he rarely touches our hearts.

Forsyte Saga, The
See: That Forsyte Woman

Fort Algiers O
1953, US, 78 mins, b/w
Dir: Lesley Selander
Stars: Yvonne De Carlo, Carlos Thompson, Raymond Burr, Leif Erickson
Rating: ★★

This was the action film for which Yvonne De Carlo brought Argentinian matinee idol Carlos Thompson to Hollywood. Raymond Burr is a turbanned villain, and some of the battle scenes are genuine – fighting between French Legionnaires and Arab tribesmen was filmed by a location unit in North Africa.

Fort Apache O ⓥ
1947, US, 127 mins, b/w
Dir: John Ford
Stars: John Wayne, Henry Fonda, Shirley Temple, John Agar, Pedro Armendariz, Victor McLaglen
Rating: ★★★★

Fort Apache was the first of Ford's unofficial trilogy of Cavalry Westerns – the others were *She Wore a Yellow Ribbon* and *Rio Grande*. It possesses all the sweep, grandeur and action of an age long past. John Wayne gives one of his best performances of his long career, although Henry Fonda's stubborn, Custer-like commander is the more interesting role.

Fort Apache the Bronx ❶
1981, US, 123 mins, colour
Dir: Daniel Petrie
Stars: Paul Newman, Edward Asner, Danny Aiello, Ken Wahl, Rachel Ticotin
Rating: ★★

If you had to pick the archetypal, average American cop movie of the Eighties, this would be a likely candidate. Set your story in a tough neighbourhood, throw in an assortment of pimps, pushers and hookers, add a veteran cop and his young partner, toss in the disciplinarian new chief of the station and a story thread involving murder and you have the quintessential formula. The film never rises above the sum total of those ingredients, although Paul Newman and Ken Wahl work quite well together as the partners, and Rachel Ticotin gives an interesting performance as the nurse with whom Newman becomes involved. The ending is inevitably part-tragic and part-hopeful, cut to formula just like the rest.

Fort Dobbs O
1958, US, 90 mins, b/w
Dir: Gordon Douglas
Stars: Clint Walker, Virginia Mayo, Brian Keith, Richard Eyer
Rating: ★★

Clint Walker, of *Cheyenne* fame, gets into trouble through changing clothes with another man. Clint is in fine form in this vigorous Western, looking as gigantic as ever, riding what appear to be Shetland ponies, roughing it with Indians and white men alike and winning the heart of Virginia Mayo.

For the Boys ❶ ⓥ
1991, US, 146 mins, colour
Dir: Mark Rydell
Stars: Bette Midler, James Caan, George Segal, Patrick O'Neal, Christopher

F

Rydell, Arye Gross
Rating: ★★

There's too little patter, singing and dancing in this Bette Midler vehicle which casts the dynamo dame as an entertainer who, through her partnership with another, finds herself frequently involved in taking part in shows 'for the boys' at war. It begins well – the first 30 minutes are hugely enjoyable – but grows increasingly heavy as it (and the wars) go on. It might have been better, in fact, if the scenario had just been limited to one war, the Second World, which would still have afforded enough tragedy and reality – the loss of Midler's husband, the bloody introduction of the touring troupe to real war – to spice the mixture up without making it too lumpy. As it is, the old age make-up that results from making this a 50-year saga merely makes Caan and Midler (who never really suggest, on stage, a legendary partnership) look like troglodytes. The ending touches the right emotional chords for audiences still with the characters after such a long haul.

For the First Time ○
1959, US, 97 mins, colour
Dir: Rudolph Maté
Stars: Mario Lanza, Johanna von Koczian, Zsa Zsa Gabor
Rating: ★★

This Mario Lanza extravaganza moves from mawkish romance through Technicolor European travelogue to maudlin sentimentality. He plays a famous tenor who falls in love with a deaf girl while on the Isle of Capri. But she won't tie the knot until her deafness is cured and she can hear him sing. Mario's fund-raising concert tour is the excuse for the travelogue bit and for him to sing a lot of songs – from operatic arias to one about a pineapple! The climactic scene where she hears him singing 'Ave Maria' surrounded by a chorus of nuns will either have you dewy-eyed or reaching for the nearest strong brown paper bag. Sadly for his millions of fans, it was Lanza's last film. A short while after this film was completed he died of a heart attack at the early age of 38.

For the Love of Benji! ⊙
1977, US, 84 mins, colour
Dir: Joe Camp
Stars: Peter Bowles, Bridget Armstrong, Patsy Garrett
Rating: ★★★

More antics with the scruffy canine who made his debut in *Benji*. This romp, in which Benji goes to Greece, was an enormous success in America, where it grossed over $5 million. Britain's Peter Bowles and Hollywood's Ed Nelson (once Dr Rossi in *Peyton Place)* are among those being upstaged by our furry friend.

For the Love of Mary ○
1948, US, 90 mins, b/w
Dir: Frederick De Cordova
Stars: Deanna Durbin, Edmond O'Brien, Don Taylor, Jeffrey Lynn
Rating: ★★

Deanna Durbin's last film, a light-weight romance which casts her as a White House switchboard operator whose romantic problems have to be sorted out by no less than the President! Songs include 'Moonlight Bay', 'I'll Take You Home Again Kathleen', 'On the Wings of a Song' and 'Let Me Call You Sweetheart'.

For Them That Trespass ○
1949, UK, 95 mins, b/w
Dir: Alberto Cavalcanti
Stars: Richard Todd, Stephen Murray, Patricia Plunkett
Rating: ★★

Richard Todd and Patricia Plunkett (playing yet again a girl who tries to clear a falsely accused man) made their screen debuts in this gripping movie drama which has a lot of high feeling and style, although it is hampered by some stagey-looking sets, particularly when the camera moves inside a 'London pub'. Also, the Cockneys are just a bit too Cockney.

Fort Osage ⊙
1952, US, 72 mins, colour
Dir: Lesley Selander
Stars: Rod Cameron, Jane Nigh, Douglas Kennedy, John Ridgely
Rating: ★★★

Minor but rousing entertaimnent, with the West as wild you could wish. There's a forthright performance in the lead by Rod Cameron, a loping six-footer in the Gary Cooper tradition, and a satisfying free-for-all climax that leaves the sagebrush carpeted with corpses. A vivid, action-packed adventure in above-par Cinecolor, this is a real winner from the unheralded Monogram stable.

Fortress ● Ⓥ
1993, US/Australia, 93 mins, colour
Dir: Stuart Gordon
Stars: Christopher Lambert, Loryn Locklin, Kurtwood Smith, Lincoln Kilpatrick, Jeffrey Combs, Vernon Wells
Rating: ★★

A grimly intense big-budget sci-fi thriller, high on adventure and gory action, which could have done with a stronger performance than Christopher Lambert's in the lead. He's ex-soldier John Brennick, imprisoned in a high-tech, high-security super-jail after his wife gets pregnant in an over-populated Big Brother-type world. Prisoners are implanted with a pain-inflicting 'intestinator' set to explode in their stomachs if they step out of line. Charming. And there's plenty of sadistic torture before Lambert discovers his wife is still alive and makes a bid for freedom. A nightmare for the nervous, then, a feast for futuristic action fans, who will know the outcome reels before it comes. None of the plot makes much sense.

Fortune, The ◐
1974, US, 85 mins, colour
Dir: Mike Nichols
Stars: Stockard Channing, Jack Nicholson, Warren Beatty
Rating: ★★

It has to be said that the piquant Stockard Charming deserves the top billing she gets at the end of this comedy of kidnap and murder. For her own unforced clowning is a clear winner over the heavily stylised performances of her co-stars. Miss Charming plays a spirited heiress who runs away with a married rogue (Warren Beatty) and also becomes involved with his embezzling friend (Jack Nicholson). Once she has discovered that their interest in her is more pecuniary than romantic, the hapless pair start a series of bungled attempts to bump her off. The fun that follows really calls for the snappy treatment of Richard Lester or the biting wit of Billy Wilder. Mike Nichols, who made *The Graduate,* settles for a modern variant on the screwball comedy films of the Thirties.

Fortune Hunter, The
See: The Outcast

Fortune Is a Woman ○
(aka: She Played with Fire)
1956, UK, 95 mins, b/w
Dir: Sidney Gilliat
Stars: Jack Hawkins, Arlene Dahl, Dennis Price, Ian Hunter
Rating: ★★★

This Launder-Gilliat thriller really has the lot: a story in which there's a chain reaction of blackmail, forgery, fraud and murder. Good old Jack Hawkins, as usual, makes you believe that it's all happening. And Hollywood's Arlene

Dahl, coolly enigmatic, was never better cast.

Fort Worth ○
1951, US, 80 mins, colour
Dir: Edwin L Marin
Stars: Randolph Scott, David Brian, Phyllis Thaxter
Rating: ★★

Veteran Western star Randolph Scott once again proves that his characters are hard men to kill or double-cross in this bullet-a-minute Western about outlaws trying to hold up the progress of a railroad. David Brian is ideally suited to the role of the hero's friend who may or may not be on the side of law and order.

Forty Carats ○
1973, US, 110 mins, colour
Dir: Milton Katselas
Stars: Liv Ullmann, Edward Albert, Gene Kelly, Billy 'Green' Bush, Binnie Barnes
Rating: ★

A jaded comedy film from the stage success by the authors of *Cactus Flower*. Liv Ullmann, unlike Ingrid Bergman in the earlier film, has little talent for this sort of light romantic romp, and comes a distant fourth in the female acting stakes, behind Binnie Barnes (wife of the film's producer, Mike Frankovitch), Nancy Walker and the sparkling young actress Deborah Raffin, who has done nothing better since.

48 Hours
See: Went the Day Well?

48 Hrs ● ⓥ
1982, US, 97 mins, colour
Dir: Walter Hill
Stars: Nick Nolte, Eddie Murphy, Annette O'Toole, Frank McRae, James Remar
Rating: ★★

Overheated police thriller with some sensational deep-driving music. It teams a white redneck cop (Nick Nolte) with a hip black convict (Eddie Murphy) in the manhunt for the team that has blown away two careless policemen. The action has some good moments, especially towards the end, and Murphy's swaggering performance made him a movie megastar.

49th Parallel ○
(aka: The Invaders)
1941, UK, 123 mins, b/w
Dir: Michael Powell
Stars: Leslie Howard, Raymond Massey, Laurence Olivier, Anton Walbrook, Glynis Johns, Eric Portman
Rating: ★★

A very patriotic and slightly unreal war film which was the top moneymaker in British cinemas in 1942. Michael Powell's direction skilfully skirts the obvious to create an out-of-the-rut propaganda thriller. Leslie Howard, Laurence Olivier, Eric Portman, Anton Walbrook and Glynis Johns all do their bit for the war effort, and there's a forthright, telling performance from Raymond Massey near the end.

Forty Pounds of Trouble ○
1962, US, 106 mins, colour
Dir: Norman Jewison
Stars: Tony Curtis, Suzanne Pleshette, Phil Silvers, Stubby Kaye, Kevin McCarthy
Rating: ★★

This comedy is bright enough and has a sweet moppet star in Claire Wilcox, but with all the talent involved and a director like Norman Jewison, we might have been entitled to expect something extra-special. Still, the casino and Disneyland backgrounds couldn't be more colourful, and that cast really is tasty: Tony Curtis, Suzanne Pleshette, Kevin McCarthy, Mary Murphy, Stubby Kaye and funny bits from Larry Storch, Howard Morris, Edward Andrews and especially Phil Silvers, on all too briefly as Curtis' boss at the casino.

42nd Street ◐ ⓥ
1932, US, 86 mins, b/w
Dir: Lloyd Bacon
Stars: Warner Baxter, Bebe Daniels, George Brent, Ruby Keeler
Rating: ★★★★

The film that totally revived the popularity of the musical, with the archetypal story of the producer struggling to put on a show and the chorus girl who goes out there and becomes a star when the leading lady crashes out just before the show. The action smoothly integrates the story with the dances (masterminded by Busby Berkeley) and songs – which include '42nd Street', 'Shuffle Off to Buffalo', 'Young and Healthy' and 'You're Getting to be a Habit with Me'. Ginger Rogers is sheer joy as a chorus girl called Anytime Annie ('The only time she said no, she didn't hear the question').

For Whom the Bell Tolls ○
1943, US, 160 mins, colour
Dir: Sam Wood
Stars: Gary Cooper, Ingrid Bergman, Akim Tamiroff
Rating: ★★★

An effective if not totally memorable film version of Ernest Hemingway's adventure set during the Spanish Civil War. Hemingway himself felt all along that Gary Cooper and Ingrid Bergman were the right actors to portray Jordan and Maria. And when the film was released the critics reserved special praise for the performances of Bergman and Katina Paxinou, who played the guerilla leader's woman. You can also admire the rich warmth of the Technicolor photography, and keep your eyes peeled for Yvonne De Carlo, who has a tiny part in a crowd scene.

For Your Eyes Only ○ ⓥ
1981, UK, 127 mins, colour
Dir: John Glen
Stars: Roger Moore, Carole Bouquet, Topol, Jill Bennett, Lois Maxwell, Lynn-Holly Johnson
Rating: ★★★

The 12th 007 epic is a near non-stop series of stunts and smart special effects which rarely gave Roger Moore – or the audience – time to take breath in between bouts of action and suspense. Bernard Lee, who had been Bond's boss 'M' since 1962's *Dr No*, died before his scenes could be filmed, leaving Lois Maxwell as Miss Moneypenny the sole survivor of all 12 movies. Janet Brown and John Wells provide wicked cameos of Margaret and Denis Thatcher.

Foul Play ◐ ⓥ
1978, US, 112 mins, colour
Dir: Colin Higgins
Stars: Goldie Hawn, Chevy Chase, Burgess Meredith, Dudley Moore, Rachel Roberts, Brian Dennehy
Rating: ★★★

Full of delicious absurdities, this is a comedy-thriller in the *Charade* tradition, with wide-eyed Goldie Hawn who plays a librarian (the thought of Goldie as a librarian is amusing in itself) who finds herself pursued across town for no apparent reason by assassins called Stiltskin and Scarface. Television comedian Chevy Chase made his breakthrough to big-time Hollywood stardom in the co-starring role, while Dudley Moore came to the attention of American audiences for the first time as a star comic actor, with his manic portrait of a sex-starved Englishman who can't wait to put his plush swinger's apartment to good use. Of the other actors, only veteran villain Marc Lawrence, looking more like a deadly snake than ever, plays it light enough to catch the mood intended by director

F

Colin Higgins, who also made Gene Wilder's *Silver Streak*.

Four Desperate Men
See: The Siege of Pinchgut

Four Faces West ○
(They Passed This Way)
1947, US, 92 mins, b/w
Dir: Alfred E Green
Stars: Joel McCrea, Frances Dee, Charles Bickford, Joseph Calleia
Rating: ★★★

There's another case for Pat Garrett in this Western, just to prove he did something else with his life apart from chasing Billy the Kid all over the landscape. The story, though, is well off the beaten trail, with thoughtful performances from Joel McCrea, Frances Dee (real-life husband and wife), Charles Bickford (as Garrett), Joseph Calleia and, as another sheriff, William Conrad, already a bulky presence even at this early stage of his career.

Four Feathers, The ○ ⓥ
1978, UK, 95 mins, colour
Dir: Don Sharp
Stars: Beau Bridges, Robert Powell, Jane Seymour
Rating: ★★★

The part of Jack Durrance in A E W Mason's storming saga of action and self-redemption in the heat of North Africa at the turn of the century is traditionally the juiciest in this bloodraising story. In 1939 Ralph Richardson eclipsed all other versions of the part in a magnificent performance, and Laurence Harvey's tortured, if less forceful, Durrance stole *Storm Over the Nile*, the routine remake of 1955. So it's no surprise that Robert Powell walks away with the honours in this latest production of the tale. Jane Seymour is excellent as the heroine, her convincing, high-spirited performance besting such past Ethne's as Fay Wray, June Duprez and Mary Ure.

Four Feathers, The ○ ⓥ
1939, UK, 130 mins, colour
Dir: Zoltan Korda
Stars: John Clements, Ralph Richardson, C Aubrey Smith, June Duprez
Rating: ★★★★★

One of the finest ever British action films, concerning the efforts of a turn-of-the-century Englishman to disprove his cowardice, against a backcloth of Kitchener's war with the Arabs. Magnificent Technicolor photography by Osmond Borrodaile and Georges Perinal and an awe-inspiring perfor-

mance by Ralph Richardson, as the hero's friend, especially when blinded and lost in the heat of the desert. A pulsating adventure yarn.

Four for Texas ○
1963, US, 124 mins, colour
Dir: Robert Aldrich
Stars: Frank Sinatra, Dean Martin, Anita Ekberg, Ursula Andress, Charles Bronson, Victor Buono
Rating: ★★

Another contribution from the Frank Sinatra clan, following hard on the heels of *Ocean's Eleven* and *Sergeants Three*. In this sometimes lively comedy-Western, sharply shot in Technicolor, Sinatra and Dean Martin play a couple of lovable crooks who make a last-ditch alliance to defeat even bigger crooks than themselves. The opening scenes are excellent: a stagecoach manned by Sinatra and Martin beats off bandits before crashing spectacularly into the dust. Unfortunately, only the ending comes up to this standard thereafter. Robert Aldrich directs the slight story at tortoise pace, and receives two performances of statuesque immobility from Ursula Andress and Anita Ekberg.

Four Girls in Town ○
1956, US, 85 mins, colour
Dir: Jack Sher
Stars: George Nader, Julie Adams, Marianne Cook, Eisa Martinelli, Gia Scala
Rating: ★★★★

This Universal-International vehicle for four of its prettiest starlets provides a fascinating behind-the-scenes look at the studio itself. Of the girls, Marianne Cook (who had to change her name from Koch) provides the warmest personality. Alex North contributes one of his lushest and most melodic scores and the studio's top star, Rock Hudson, pops in to make a guest appearance.

Four Guns to the Border ○
1954, US, 85 mins, colour
Dir: Richard Carlson
Stars: Rory Calhoun, Walter Brennan, Colleen Miller, George Nader, Nina Foch
Rating: ★★★

One of a long series of action-packed double-features made at Universal-International Studios in the Fifties – films which made stars out of Rock Hudson, Tony Curtis and Audie Murphy besides the stars of this Western, Rory Calhoun and George Nader. *Four Guns to the Border* was directed by another actor, Richard

Carlson. Jay Silverheels, who plays a half-breed outlaw, was better known for his role as Tonto in the long-running *Lone Ranger* series.

Four Jills In a Jeep ○
1944, US, 89 mins, b/w
Dir: William A Seiter
Stars: Carole Landis, Kay Francis, Martha Raye, Mitzi Mayfair, Phil Silvers, Dick Haymes
Rating: ★★

A fascinating look at USO tour groups, through the eyes of four showbiz ladies who actually made such a trip, and made palatable for wartime audiences by 20th Century-Fox presenting the story in the guise of a musical. The girls, including Kay Francis and Martha Raye, play themselves, and there are singing guest appearances by Betty Grable, Alice Faye and Carmen Miranda. Grable sings 'Cuddle Up a Little Closer' with a million GIs just dying for the chance. Black-and-white lends the film a feel of contemporary reality.

Four Men and a Prayer ○
1938, US, 85 mins, b/w
Dir: John Ford
Stars: Loretta Young, Richard Greene, George Sanders, David Niven, C Aubrey Smith
Rating: ★★

One of John Ford's most vigorous films, this splashy production about four brothers trying to clear their father's name after a massacre in India gave a major movie debut role to a 19-year-old English actor as a raw as his name: Richard Greene. Forthright in the part, alongside such established names as David Niven and George Sanders, Greene went on to a 15-year Hollywood career, before becoming famous the world over as television's *Robin Hood*. Good moments but overall pretty sticky.

Four Musketeers: The Revenge of Milady, The ○
1974, UK, 105 mins, colour
Dir: Richard Lester
Stars: Oliver Reed, Raquel Welch, Richard Chamberlain, Michael York, Faye Dunaway, Frank Finlay
Rating: ★★★

The fun of *The Three Musketeers* is overturned to reveal the darker, more serious side of the coin in this sequel. But the action is still all dazzling stuff, from an epic sword battle in a nunnery to an eye-stunning duel on ice. Faye Dunaway, as the evil Milady, and

Oliver Reed as Athos, playing a more prominent part in the plot in this sequel, are both in dominant form. The sweeping last 15 minutes and the triumphant ending almost make you forget that this is just a notch below the previous film in sheer *joie de vivre*.

Four Seasons, The ○
1981, US, 107 mins, colour
Dir: Alan Alda
Stars: Alan Alda, Carol Burnett, Len Cariou, Sandy Dennis, Rita Moreno, Jack Weston
Rating: ★★★

The policy of the Hollywood superstars these days seems to be to alternate the films they really want to make with the movies they do for money. But *The Four Seasons* is a film in which Alan Alda, as star, screen-writer and director, believed in passionately. He must have been overjoyed when the film proved not only a critical success, but also a financial one. It's a comic but credible and lovingly-photographed portrait of three couples who take their holidays together, but who find the artificiality of their companionship cracking when one of the husbands decides on divorce. Though leisurely in development, the film has a certain charm, and Bess Armstrong, as the 'new' wife who proves the very slim end of the wedge, makes a strong impression.

Fourteen Hours ○
1951, US, 92 mins, b/w
Dir: Henry Hathaway
Stars: Paul Douglas, Richard Basehart, Barbara Bel Geddes, Agnes Moorehead, Robert Keith, Debra Paget
Rating: ★★★★

Although it rather simplifies the issues at stake, this suspense thriller sustains remarkably well for over 90 minutes its central situation of a man threatening to jump off a ledge on a high building. A formidable cast includes Richard Basehart as the disturbed man, Paul Douglas, Agnes Moorehead (in a typically fierce role), Robert Keith, Barbara Bel Geddes, Debra Paget, Jeffrey Hunter, Howard da Silva, Frank Faylen and – in her screen debut – Grace Kelly.

1492: The Conquest of Paradise ① ⓥ
1992, US/UK/France/Spain, 145 mins, colour
Dir: Ridley Scott
Stars: Gérard Depardieu, Sigourney Weaver, Armand Assante, Frank

Langella, Loren Dean, Fernando Rey
Rating: ★★

This was the third of three Christopher Columbus films released in the summer of 1992 to mark the 500th anniversary of the explorer's discovery of America. Although it was definitely a case of saving the best until last, even this spectacularly mounted version is a deeply flawed film, not least in the way of pacing. Backed by millions of dollars from the Spanish government, it features French superstar Gérard Depardieu, visually in commanding form but mangling the English language a shade too far as Columbus, and director Ridley Scott delivering some stunning action visuals in his own distinctive style. But the acting honours are stolen from all and sundry by Michael Wincott, playing the blackest, most sadistic villain seen in a major film for many a long day.

Fourth Protocol, The ① ⓥ
1987, UK, 119 mins, colour
Dir: John Mackenzie
Stars: Michael Caine, Pierce Brosnan, Ned Beatty, Joanna Cassidy, Ray McAnally, Ian Richardson
Rating: ★★★

If you're expecting one of those ever-so-grim cold war thrillers where you could rustle a newspaper and miss a vital part of the plot, then go no further. If you like preposterous, well-acted, well-staged espionage yarns with big treatment, then this will be right up your pre-perestroika street. The two central characters are spy-catcher Michael Caine and crack KGB officer Pierce Brosnan (later to be cast as James Bond!). Brosnan is to assemble a nuclear bomb in Britain from parts smuggled through customs (so much for bringing in too many bottles of wine). Caine is out to stop him. Throw in the sultry Joanna Cassidy as a colonel who's never so much as sipped a pink gin, and you're in for a lively evening.

Four Weddings and a Funeral ● ⓥ
1993, UK, 117 mins, colour
Dir: Mike Newell
Stars: Hugh Grant, Andie MacDowell, Simon Callow, James Fleet, Corin Redgrave, Rowan Atkinson
Rating: ★★★

A Boulting Brothers comedy brought up to date with bad language – hero Hugh Grant always swears several times in moments of crisis – and enough richly funny lines to sustain us

through a rollicking 85 minutes. Unfortunately, the film runs rather more than 30 minutes longer than that, so it's not as uproarious as it might be. A comedy of embarrassments, indiscretions and missed chances, it stars Grant (never better) as a sort of foul-mouthed Bertie Wooster always turning up late for friends' weddings, but avoiding one of his own. His friend Tom (James Fleet) disapproves. 'It worked for my parents,' he says, '… apart from the divorce.' The best of the dialogue here's a bit like that: a seemingly sincere line twisted by an endpiece that makes it funny. And the plot allows room for a funny turn by Rowan Atkinson as an inexperienced priest who refers to the Father, Son and Holy Goat. Good performances from an enthusiastic cast, especially Simon Callow as a bachelor gay whose life is as vivid as his waistcoats.

Fox, The ●
1968, US, 110 mins, colour
Dir: Mark Rydell
Stars: Anne Heywood, Sandy Dennis, Keir Dullea
Rating: ★★★

Mark Rydell created quite a stir on his directorial debut with this very erotic account of two women living together on a farm, whose lesbian-inclined rapport is shattered by the arrival of a sharp, tough young man. Full of symbolism, with a very strong and sexy performance by Anne Heywood, and outstanding colour photography.

Fox and the Hound, The ⊙ ⓥ
1981, US, 83 mins, colour
Dir: Art Berman, Ted Berman, Richard Rich
Voice Stars: Kurt Russell, Mickey Rooney, Pearl Bailey, Jack Albertson, Sandy Duncan, Pat Buttram, John McIntire
Rating: ★★★★

The Disney boys go back to their roots with this *Bambi*-like cartoon about a tame fox-cub and a hound-pup who play together when young, but must grow up to be enemies. Excessive cuteness occasionally intrudes into these early scenes, but you'll do well not to choke up when Widow Tweed (beautifully voiced by Jeanette Nolan) has to say goodbye to her fox, now fully grown, or at the final four-way battle involving fox, hound, hunter and grizzly bear. Lest this should all sound too serious, let's add that comedy isn't neglected, proving most successful in the scenes involving a sparrow and wood-

F

pecker's fruitless quest for dinner in the shape of a devious caterpillar. The animation is excellent throughout, especially in the forest scenes, the action sequences are exciting, and the foxes really do look like foxes, unlike those in Disney's previous *Robin Hood*. The weakest element is the score, so anonymous as to be redundant.

Foxhole In Cairo ○
1960, UK, 80 mins, b/w
Dir: John Moxey
Stars: James Robertson Justice, Adrian Hoven, Peter Van Eyck, Albert Lieven, Fenella Fielding
Rating: ★★

British thriller about German agents detailed to get hold of the British plans for the counter-attack in the Libyan desert. Albert Lieven's Rommel is nicely played if underwritten, and Michael Caine makes an early film appearance as Weber.

Fragment of Fear ◐
1971, UK, 95 mins, colour
Dir: Richard C Sarafian
Stars: David Hemmings, Gayle Hunnicutt, Roland Culver, Daniel Massey
Rating: ★★

This psychological thriller is as fascinating a jigsaw puzzle as the screen has ever presented: only the ending may disappoint you. David Hemmings is fine as the baffled ex-drug addict hero. And there are enigmatic performances from such distinguished players as Dame Flora Robson, Roland Culver, Arthur Lowe, Yootha Joyce, Daniel Massey, Wilfred Hyde White and Mona Washbourne.

Framed ○
(aka: Paula)
1947, US, 82 mins, b/w
Dir: Richard Wallace
Stars: Glenn Ford, Janis Carter, Barry Sullivan, Edgar Buchanan, Karen Morley
Rating: ★★★

Glacial blonde Janis Carter was always at her best as cool, calculating channers, and here is one of her most deadly. Paula (her character) was also the British title of the film, and Miss Carter certainly holds centre stage in a magnetic portrayal of a girl whose goal is money and who certainly wouldn't dream of not casually murdering anyone who stood in her way.

Frances ● ⓥ
1982, US, 140 mins, colour
Dir: Graeme Clifford
Stars: Jessica Lange, Kim Stanley, Sam Shepard
Rating: ★★★

This is a grim and unrelenting biopic of beautiful Hollywood star Frances Farmer, all the more distressing because the horrific incidents featured are true. Jessica Lange really suffers in the title role, getting drunk, being raped and assaulted in a mental hospital (where she's been committed by her hateful, overbearing mother), and finally ending up undergoing a brain operation that ruins her life for ever. Not exactly a jolly night's entertainment, but a solidly crafted drama all the same. Look fast for Kevin Costner as a character in an alley. He has one line.

Francis ⊙
1950, US, 90 mins, b/w
Dir: Arthur Lubin
Stars: Donald O'Connor, Patricia Medina, ZaSu Pitts, Ray Collins, John McIntire
Rating: ★★

Bright, brash farce that, with its sundry sequels, and together with the Ma and Pa Kettle series, kept Universal Studios afloat from 1949 to the late Fifties by taking enormous amounts of money on very low budgets. Francis was a talking mule and his master was Donald O'Connor (after Mickey Rooney, always a poor decision-maker, had turned the job down), who only quit the series after six escapades because the mule was getting more fan-mail than him. In this first romp, the girl is Patricia Medina, while the voice of the mule is supplied by croaky Chill Wills, who carried on this asinine chore for the rest of the series. The films all date pretty badly and look a good deal more tiresome now than they did then. Tony Curtis has a 'bit' in this one.

Frankenstein ◐
1931, US, 71 mins, b/w
Dir: James Whale
Stars: Boris Karloff, Colin Clive, Mae Clarke, John Boles
Rating: ★★★

James Whale's bizarre but almost poetic version of the most famous horror story of all. Notable among its best parts are the opening grave-snatching scene, with Frankenstein and the hunchback lurking behind silhouetted railings at a funeral; and the confrontation between the monster and a little girl which, with its tragic aftermath, remains a little masterpiece. The final hunt for the monster is frighteningly well realised, and Boris Karloff's pitiable creature, to reach full flower in

the sequel, *Bride of Frankenstein*, remains one of the screen's most remarkable creations.

Frankenstein and the Monster from Hell ●
1973, UK, 99 mins, colour
Dir: Terence Fisher
Stars: Peter Cushing, Shane Briant, Madeline Smith
Rating: ★

'Ah, kidneys. Delicious.' It must be Baron Frankenstein, and it is. The country is recognisably Hammer-land. The Baron (Peter Cushing) has secreted a new creature in the depths of the asylum at which he is resident doctor. Alas, the monster David Prowse, later Darth Vader in *Star Wars)* takes a turn for the nurse (Madeline Smith) which proves his undoing. The quality of Terence Fisher's direction slows the Hammer decline in this one, but the script is a touch too tongue-in-cheek, and the playing matches it.

Frankenstein Meets the Wolf Man ◐
1943, US, 73 mins, b/w
Dir: Roy William Neill
Stars: Lon Chaney Jr, Ilona Massey, Bela Lugosi
Rating: ★★

With the death of Ludwig Frankenstein in *The Ghost of Frankenstein*, the Frankenstein series proper ended. But the public demanded more horror – and more monsters per film. So the Wolf Man, created two years previously by Lon Chancy Jr, was brought into the Frankenstein saga. Chaney, being strongly identified with the Wolf Man, was thus no longer available to portray the Monster. The death of Ygor in *Ghost* left Bela Lugosi free to have a stab at the part. Both his interpretation and the film are a definite step down for the series.

Frankenstein Must Be Destroyed ● ⓥ
1969, UK, 97 mins, colour
Dir: Terence Fisher
Stars: Peter Cushing, Veronica Carlson, Freddie Jones, Simon Ward
Rating: ★★

First discovered under a skull-like mask, chasing after a burglar through dismembered bodies after scything off a passer-by's head, the bad baron is up to his old tricks again. Well, not quite it's brain transplants that are uppermost in his mind this time. Things go predictably from then on (although Freddie Jones creates a pitiable creature) and everything ends in the inevitable conflagration.

Frankenstein Unbound ● ⓥ
1990, US, 87 mins, colour
Dir: Roger Corman
Stars: John Hurt, Raul Julia, Bridget Fonda, Jason Patric, Michael Hutchence, Nick Brimble
Rating: ★★

John Hurt plays a 21st century scientist, working on an implosion ray that will make its target disappear: no mess, no radiation. But there are side effects and, before Hurt can work to correct them, one 'side effect', a pulsating cloud that opens the door to time, seizes him and whisks him to the early 19th century, where he meets Byron and Shelley and realises to his horror that Mary Shelley drew her inspiration for *Frankenstein* from life. The creature is still terrorising the countryside but, this being a 1990 film, the call for gore demands that he rip the hearts out of his victims or, at the very least, decapitate them. These effects are dwelt on with some relish by the director, rather undercutting his visual achievements at other parts of the film, especially the icebound climax. Some of the traditional elements, though – like the electrical storm over the castle as Frankenstein prepares the monster's bride – are still intact.

Frankie and Johnny ○ ⓥ
1966, US, 87 mins, colour
Dir: Frederick De Cordova
Stars: Elvis Presley, Donna Douglas
Rating: ★★

Elvis Presley stars as a singing gambler on a Mississippi riverboat, presumably around the turn of the century, in an adaptation of the story of the classic song, with the ending altered so that Presley won't bite the dust. Brightly shot in Technicolor, with Donna Douglas (once of *The Beverly Hillbillies*) a personable female lead, and some amusing hamming by Sue Ane Langdon and Joyce Jameson.

Frankie & Johnny ○ ⓥ
1991, US, 118 mins, colour
Dir: Garry Marshall
Stars: Al Pacino, Michelle Pfeiffer, Hector Elizondo, Kate Nelligan
Rating: ★★

There are no big surprises in this story of a short-order cook falling for a lonely waitress at the fast-food joint where they both work. Just enjoy the pleasure of watching first-rate actors working away like mad to sink themselves into their roles. Johnny's been bad, but not that bad: after all he's Al Pacino. And how could he resist Frankie, particularly as she's played by Michelle Pfeiffer? There's some nice fooling around with their ages and their pasts, and director Garry Marshall decorates it with a bit of busy funny stuff going on half in the background. Pfeiffer's far too attractive for her role, though she's good, especially in her big breakdown scene. Pacino's sincere but never quite lovable. Kate Nelligan, usually so cool, makes a real but convincing switch as Pfeiffer's tarty colleague. It's smooth, over-easy entertainment, even if it doesn't have too much real heart.

Frantic ● ⓥ
1988, US, 120 mins, colour
Dir: Roman Polanski
Stars: Harrison Ford, Emmanuelle Seigner, John Mahoney
Rating: ★★

Star Harrison Ford and director Roman Polanski suffered a rare misfire with this dreary thriller which, with its collection of oily foreigners and seedy settings, is reminiscent of one of those old British 'B' crime films done on an expensive budget. Ford, very low-key in this one, is the surgeon whose wife disappears on a trip to Paris. The stale brew that follows is full of swarthy Arabs, entrepreneurs with carnations in their buttonholes, bodies in empty rooms and a 'McGuffin' in the form of an atomic detonator. Disappointing.

Fraternally Yours
See: Sons of the Desert

Frauds ○ ⓥ
1992, Australia, 94 mins, colour
Dir: Stephan Elliott
Stars: Phil Collins, Hugo Weaving, Josephine Byrnes
Rating: ★

A combination of *Toys* and *An Inspector Calls*, if that's possible, this is an expensive looking surreal black comedy. Housewife Josephine Byrnes kills a burglar, only to discover he's her husband's friend and best man. Enter a weird insurance man (Phil Collins), who tumbles that hubby (Hugo Weaving) and friend planned an insurance scam that went wrong. Now Collins plans to bleed the couple dry. To fight back, they have to beard him in his toy-laden, gadget-ridden lair. All about games and people who never grow up, this could have been a fascinating movie in hands other than those of debutant director Stephan Elliott. But the audience has to be gripped by the throat from the beginning by this sort of thing: here your inclination in the first hour is to nod off waiting for the nitty-gritty to get going. Weird but by no means wonderful, the result is a colourful, oddball misfire.

Fraulein Doktor ◐
1968, UK/Italy, 102 mins, colour
Dir: Alberto Lattuada
Stars: Suzy Kendall, Kenneth More, Capucine, James Booth
Rating: ★★★

Suzy Kendall's biggest role, as a German spy during World War One, and she's good enough to make one wonder why her career didn't catch fire more than it did. Period atmosphere is nicely captured by director Alberto Lattuada and his colour cameraman Luigi Kuveiller. A poison gas attack and graphic trench warfare are notable among some grippingly effective set pieces.

Freaks ●
1932, US, 64 mins, b/w
Dir: Tod Browning
Stars: Wallace Ford, Leila Hyams, Olga Baclanova
Rating: ★★★★

Banned for 30 years, this horror classic remains largely undiluted by time. Once the mainspring of its plot swings into action, the atmosphere gradually clouds over with evil, reaching a climax as circus freaks crawl through mud clutching knives on a dark and stormy night. This scene is all the more effective for being revealed only in flashes of lightning by the director Tod Browning, whose direction of the freaks is quite brilliant, arousing our pity as well as our horror.

Freaky Friday ☉
1976, US, 100 mins, colour
Dir: Gary Nelson
Stars: Jodie Foster, Barbara Harris, John Astin
Rating: ★★★

Jodie Foster takes a Disney holiday from heavy dramatics in this comic forerunner of such recent successes as *Vice Versa* and *Big*. The complications from her swapping identities with mum Barbara Harris are happily endless (and endlessly happy), and there is some mild fun here, especially in a car chase at the end. The Disney process work is as abysmal as ever, but the sunny personalities of the two leading

F

actresses see the project through with charm to spare.

Freddie as F.R.O.7. ⊙
1992, UK, 90 mins, colour
Dir: Jon Acevski
Voice stars: Ben Kingsley, Jenny Agutter, Brian Blessed, Sir Michael Hordern
Rating: ★

Everybody's doing it these days – making cartoon features, that is. This one, with its largely disconnected story, and clod-hopping sense of humour, is one step up from Saturday morning TV fare, with a French frog hero (yes, he did used to be a prince), a busty chop-socky heroine and a villainess who spends most of her time transformed into a snake. Most of the voicing is surprisingly clumsy, although Ben Kingsley's Freddie is acceptable enough, even if he does have trouble with the word camouflage (which, surely, is French), but the goodies are too po-faced, the sentiment too sickly and the songs not integrated with the story. Excruciating for adults, acceptable enough for small children.

Freddy's Dead: The Final Nightmare ● Ⓥ
1991, US, 90 mins, colour
Dir: Rachel Talalay
Stars: Robert Englund, Lisa Zane, Yaphet Kotto
Rating: ★★

Gone for good? Some hopes! At any rate this sixth dice (and slice) with the fiendish Freddy is a jolly horror romp that reveals Freddy's reasons for revenge and ties everything up neatly at the end. Robert Englund gives it his best shot as the scarred child murderer who haunts the dreams of his victims, now after the last surviving teenager from Springwood, scene of the original Elm Street. He hopes that the youth will lead him to his nearest and dearest – the child that was taken away from him after his guilt was discovered. Effects, gory and otherwise, are adequately done, though they don't look too expensive, and Freddy is permitted a nice last line by way of a curtain call.

Freedom Radio ○
(aka: A Voice in the Night)
1941, UK, 95 mins, b/w
Dir: Anthony Asquith
Stars: Clive Brook, Diana Wynyard, Raymond Huntley, Derek Farr
Rating: ★★★

Since eight people worked on the script of this wartime morale-booster, it's surprising it turned out so well. But it is

gripping, strongly-cast and more subtle than most propaganda thrillers of its time. Clive Brook is convincing as the anti-Nazi Austrian doctor who founds the radio of the title, there's an early chance for Derek Farr as his comrade, and film buffs may spot Katie Johnson, later to win fame in *The Ladykillers* but here, 13 years earlier, already in granny roles!

Freejack ◑ Ⓥ
1992, US, 111 mins, colour
Dir: Geoff Murphy
Stars: Emilio Estevez, Mick Jagger, Rene Russo, Anthony Hopkins, Amanda Plummer
Rating: ★★

Although its chases are spectacular and its futuristic settings have all the trimmings, this science-fiction thriller needs beefier actors, in more ways than one, than Emilio Estevez and Rene Russo as its leads. And the dialogue trips up every time it tries to step outside the strict boundaries of the action genre. Estevez is a racing-driver snatched at the moment of his death by a dying force, years in the future, which intends to swap his mind for its own. There's something shaky in the logic of all this if you think about it; so, maintaining a crunching pace, director Geoff Murphy hopes you won't have time to do so while you concentrate on Estevez's escape into the America of 2009, his flight from the armed guards intent on recapturing him and his battle to identify the man behind it all. The intentional thrills mix in with the unintentional chuckles in this vivid but uneasy blaster.

Free Willy ⊙ Ⓥ
1993, US, 111 mins, colour
Dir: Simon Wincer
Stars: Jason James Richter, Lori Petty, Jayne Atkinson, Michael Madsen, August Schellenberg
Rating: ★★★

There have been films about freeing marine creatures before, but few as successful as this, which builds to an exhilarating climax that will have you cheering or crying or both. Jason James Richter is the embryo juvenile delinquent sentenced to the American equivalent of community service for vandalising a marine amusement park. Doing 'time' at the park, the boy becomes attached to Willy, a killer whale and the park's star turn. When the boy learns that the owner plans to sacrifice Willy for the sake of some hefty insurance, there's only one decision he

can make. Never over-sentimental, the film has more backbone than similar ventures would have done in past years and the whale (and his animatronic stand-ins) is a real scene-stealer. Warm, human and gutsy; good entertainment for intelligent children and families alike. Two sequels to date.

French Connection, The ● Ⓥ
1971, US, 104 mins, colour
Dir: William Friedkin
Stars: Gene Hackman, Fernando Rey, Roy Scheider, Tony LoBianco
Rating: ★★★★

Much imitated but rarely bettered, this fast-paced documentary-style thriller took Oscars for best film, actor (Gene Hackman), director (William Friedkin), screenplay (Ernest Tidyman), and editing (Jerry Greenberg). Greenberg's skill is superbly evident in the film's most exciting – and copied – sequence, a race between policeman Hackman's car and an overhead train carrying an escaping killer. Roy Scheider matches Hackman scene for scene as one of the cops involved in busting a multi-million-dollar drug-smuggling racket in New York. Fine location shooting and muscular dialogue add to the overall impact. The two real-life cops on whom the leading characters are based, Eddie Egan and Sonny Grosso, both have supporting roles.

French Connection II ◑ Ⓥ
(aka: French Connection No. 2)
1975, US, 119 mins, colour
Dir: John Frankenheimer
Stars: Gene Hackman, Fernando Rey, Bernard Fresson
Rating: ★★★★

Although slow in the exposition, this thriller ultimately rates even better than the first *The French Connection* film, full of action and working up to some great individual scenes, as when American cop Gene Hackman, drying out after being doped by the narcotics ring he's chasing in Marseilles, gets drunk on cognac and has a hilarious conversation with his French opposite number about baseball and boxing. It's tough, but superior adult entertainment, with Hackman so good that it's hard to tell whether the rest of the film is routine or as riveting as he makes it seem. Even though the plot is hard to believe, the set-pieces are superbly staged and the action hard and violent. The chase leaves Hackman literally breathless and could do the same for you.

Frenchie ○

1950, US, 81 mins, colour
Dir: Louis King
Stars: Joel McCrea, Shelley Winters, Elsa Lanchester, Paul Kelly, Marie Windsor, John Russell
Rating: ★★

Vivid Western, with Joel McCrea standing small chance against such female opposition as Shelley Winters (a gamblin' gal out to avenge the death of her father), Elsa Lanchester and the delicious Marie Windsor. Some of Shelley's dialogue sounds as though it were written for Mae West; and there's a first-class bar-room brawl, no claws barred, between those two fiery ladies of films, Winters and Windsor.

French Kiss ❶ Ⓥ

1995, US, 110 mins, colour
Dir: Lawrence Kasdan
Stars: Kevin Kline, Meg Ryan, Timothy Hutton, Susan Anieh, Jean Reno
Rating: ★★

Star Kevin Kline could be excused for thinking director Lawrence Kasdan owes him a hit after so many mediocre movies together, but this isn't it. Originally called *Paris Match,* a more stylish title that reflects very much what's gone wrong with the film: it's all effect and no style. The two-dimensional characters (it would be nice to warm to these people, but the script ensures we never do) are headed by Meg Ryan, who takes cuteness one layer too far as the girl whose pursuit of an errant fiancé (Timothy Hutton) leads to her unwitting involvement in diamond smuggling. The smuggler is Kline, trying out a number of continental accents, but never quite settling on one. He and Ryan keep striking 'lovable' poses, but actually succeed in avoiding lovability altogether. This fiercely arch screwball romantic comedy could do with a few genuine nuts as well, to prevent it flying apart.

French Lieutenant's Woman, The ❶ Ⓥ

1981, UK, 123 mins, colour
Dir: Karel Reisz
Stars: Jeremy Irons, Meryl Streep, David Warner, Leo McKern, Charlotte Mitchell
Rating: ★★★

There's a romantic magic about times past that gives a lift to long-ago love affairs such as this even before they've begun. And the image of Meryl Streep watching the waves pound in at Lyme Regis with a haunted look in her eyes remains one of the most potent and enduring images from the cinema of the Eighties. Forever looking out to sea for the French lieutenant who abandoned her, Streep is bewitching in the title role, and her English accent is impeccable. The only drawback is that the modern story that frames the main action doesn't have the same strength as the central tale.

French Line, The ○

1953, US, 102 mins, colour
Dir: Lloyd Bacon
Stars: Jane Russell, Gilbert Roland, Arthur Hunnicutt
Rating: ★★★

Jane Russell's musical-comedy variations on Loos-living – *Gentlemen Prefer Blondes* and *Gentlemen Marry Brunettes* were based on shows by Anita Loos, and the film version of the latter was conscripted by Anita's niece Mary – continued with *The French Line,* also co-written by Mary Loos (with Richard Sale). Considered pretty saucy in its day, the film had four minutes snipped out of Jane's bubble-bath and finale routines but is now shown in its original version. Made in 3D, it's a boisterous, entertaining and amusing semi-musical in which Mary McCarty as Jane's friend nearly (but not quite) steals the star's thunder. Kim Novak is in the chorus.

Frenchman's Creek ○

1944, US, 112 mins, colour
Dir: Mitchell Leisen
Stars: Joan Fontaine, Arturo de Cordova, Basil Rathbone, Nigel Bruce
Rating: ★★

Bolstered by its production values – the Technicolor is brilliant, the Victor Young score one of his best – if not by the script and acting, this lavish adaptation of a Daphne du Maurier story about a highborn lady who falls for a French pirate was said to have cost more than $3 million. Even so, its colourful escapism ensured it made a profit. Mitchell Leisen, whose speciality in direction was romantic comedy, was perhaps not the ideal director, but he gets a classy supporting performance from Basil Rathbone that steals the film.

French Mistress, A ○ Ⓥ

1960, UK, 98 mins, b/w
Dir: Roy Boulting
Stars: Cecil Parker, James Robertson Justice, Ian Bannen, Agnes Laurent
Rating: ★★★

Delectable French star Agnes Laurent made a couple of sparky comedies in Britain, this one for the Boulting Brothers as a French teacher who shatters the calm of an all-male school. The attractive young mistress from France parades on the tennis court in the shortest of shorts, displays her bikini at the school swimming pool and captures the heart of the headmaster's son. The headmaster is played by Cecil Parker with a splendid display of blustering pomposity. The fun runs down a little after the first hour, which contains some very amusing moments. You may recognise a very short-haired Michael Crawford as one of boys.

Frenzy ●

1972, UK, 120 mins, colour
Dir: Alfred Hitchcock
Stars: Jon Finch, Barry Foster, Anna Massey, Alec McCowen, Vivien Merchant
Rating: ★★★★

Vintage Hitchcock, filled with the Master's touches, and marking a satisfying return to form after late Sixties lapses, as a killer roams round London strangling women with his old school tie and our (tarnished) hero has a tough time clearing himself of suspicion. Anthony Shaffer's script provides Hitch with all he could want in the way of suspense and black comedy and, in a uniformly excellent cast, Barry Foster and Alec McCowen (as a wife-ridden policeman) stand out. In his first British film for many years, Hitchcock uses London locations to great effect, particularly in the Covent Garden scenes: after watching Barry Foster wrestling with a corpse buried in a sack of potatoes, you might not be able to look a spud in the eye for some time.

Fresh Horses ❶

1988, US, 103 mins, colour
Dir: David Anspaugh
Stars: Molly Ringwald, Andrew McCarthy, Patti D'Arbanville, Ben Stiller
Rating: ★★★

One of those sudden-love, will-he-won't-he hang on to her? romances at which Hollywood has been adept since the silent days. This one keeps you guessing right up to the last few seconds as to whether the central couple will end up together. Molly Ringwald, once again the gal from the wrong side of the tracks, and Andrew McCarthy, once again the college boy with everything, may not be the very brightest of the old Brat Pack, but here prove charismatic and thoughtful enough to carry the old framework over for a touchdown, and raise a tear or two along the way. The dialogue has the occasional hiccup – 'Listen to him. He's a fifth-year senior'

F

– but is mostly sensible, even if it makes McCarthy's character the original Doubting Thomas. At the slightest hint of the scarlet in Ringwald's past he's ready to walk out: some great love. Under the circumstances, it's to the credit of the two leading players that you care to the end.

Freshman, The ○ Ⓥ
1990, US, 102 mins, colour
Dir: Andrew Bergman
Stars: Matthew Broderick, Marlon Brando, Bruno Kirby, Penelope Ann Miller, Paul Benedict, Maximilian Schell
Rating: ★★★

Brando skates! Yes, Hollywood's heavyweight maverick genius takes to the ice like a moving waxwork of *The Godfather* in this pleasant comedy that runs like a classic American short story complete with laconic background narration by Brando's co-star Matthew Broderick. There was once a running gag in the US stage production of *Arsenic and Old Lace* about an escapee (played by Boris Karloff) enraged to be told that he looked like Boris Karloff! It's repeated here, as characters are always about to tell Brando's influential 'importer' that he reminds them of the Godfather, but never quite spit it out. How Broderick comes to New York to study, comes into possession of a rare komodo dragon, falls into the clutches of the Mafia and ends up at a gourmet banquet where the guests pay $350,000 a head, is related with the dry humour of such vintage American story-tellers as O Henry and James Thurber. Brando's a delight, even when you can't hear all the words, in this inconsequential but flavoursome little entertainment.

Friday the Thirteenth ○
1933, UK, 85 mins, b/w
Dir: Victor Saville
Stars: Sonnie Hale, Jessie Matthews, Emlyn Williams
Rating: ★★★

Not the more recent multi-murder bloodbath, but a successful early omnibus film which utilised most of the best British cinema talent of the time. Jessie Matthews, Edmund Gwenn and Ralph Richardson are particularly pleasing.

Frieda ○
1947, UK, 97 mins, b/w
Dir: Basil Dearden
Stars: David Farrar, Mai Zetterling, Glynis Johns, Flora Robson
Rating: ★★★

Swedish star Mai Zetterling made an outstanding impression with her haunting performance in this, her English-speaking debut. The film itself is a powerful drama from Ealing Studios just before they embarked on their famous series of comedies. The theme – a German girl married to an Englishman suffers the hostility of his family – was very relevant to the times. And the intelligent screenplay aims some well-timed darts at bigotry and race hatred.

Fried Green Tomatoes at the Whistle Stop Cafe ◐ Ⓥ
(aka: Fried Green Tomatoes)
1991, US, 130 mins, colour
Dir: Jon Avnet
Stars: Kathy Bates, Jessica Tandy, Mary Stuart Masterson, Mary-Louise Parker, Cicely Tyson
Rating: ★★★★

Southern States nostalgia is on the menu here, as well as the eponymous tomatoes. But for once the story is well enough told to grip the attention for almost all of what's a very long film. Kathy Bates plays a middle-ageing Alabama housewife whose encounter with elderly Ninny (Jessica Tandy) during a visit to an old folks' home unlocks the door to a lifetime of memories. We meet Idgie (Mary Stuart Masterson), a tomboy whose beloved brother is killed by a train, whose friendship is hard-won by his last girlfriend and who, after the girls go into partnership at the Whistle Stop Cafe, ends up accused of murder. There are rather a lot of breaks from here on, for Tandy to reveal various bits of the story, which is a pity as the framing story is much weaker than Idgie's own saga, which is filmed in warmer, deeper colours to underline the difference. Tandy and Bates do as well as they can, but the film really belongs to the two younger actresses, Mary-Louise Parker being particularly good as the much-loved, much-abused, inherently good Ruth.

Friendly Persuasion ○
1956, US, 139 mins, colour
Dir: William Wyler
Stars: Gary Cooper, Dorothy McGuire, Anthony Perkins, Marjorie Main
Rating: ★★★★★

Probably the best film ever to come out of a minor Hollywood studio (Allied Artists), *Friendly Persuasion* is the story of a Quaker family caught up in the American Civil War. Director William Wyler captures a tender mood which

pervades the whole film, and totally catches up the audience in the family's problems. The De Luxe Colour photography is glowingly good, and the climax very moving.

Fright ●
1971, UK, 87 mins, colour
Dir: Peter Collinson
Stars: Honor Blackman, Susan George, George Cole, Dennis Waterman
Rating: ★★

Susan George's fine study in mounting hysteria is responsible for the edgy moments in this slightly nasty chiller. It concerns a homicidal psychotic (a wild performance by Ian Bannen) who returns to his family mansion to stalk the babysitter, while his wife is out for the evening. Director Peter Collinson piles on the suspense with a none-too-steady hand, but Miss George, cardigan asunder and eyes awry, really sustains the horror hokum at fever pitch.

Frighteners, The ● Ⓥ
1996, NZ, 110 mins, colour
Dir: Peter Jackson
Stars: Michael J Fox, Trini Alvarado, Jake Busey, Dee Wallace Stone, Peter Dobson, John Astin
Rating: ★★★★

This thunderingly paced horror comic proves that fright fans can still find original fare. While psychic investigator Fox plies his trade with the help of friendly spooks that only he can see, something distinctly unfriendly is causing an epidemic of heart attacks among the good people of Fairwater – and most of the victims seem to be connected to Fox. Meanwhile Dr Lynskey (Alvarado) whose slobbish husband is about to become victim 37, investigates a 'mad woman' (Stone), whose ghoulishly grinning boyfriend (Busey) murdered 12 people before going to the electric chair. And Fox sees visions of the 'soul collector', a cowled figure swooping over the town on some new victim, even as he himself comes under suspicion. All these plot threads and more are neatly tied together in a story that, in an unreal way, and with characters straight out of *Twin Peaks*, makes perfect sense. Special effects are right on the mark, as walls, mirrors and ceilings bulge, the dead rise and ectoplasmic masses seep away in search of escape.

Fright Night ● Ⓥ
1985, US, 105 mins, colour
Dir: Tom Holland
Stars: Chris Sarandon, Roddy McDowall,

William Ragsdale, Traci Lin
Rating: ★★★★

A vampire movie that for once breaks fresh earth. Naturally, no-one will believe Charley (William Ragsdale) when he tells them that a Count Dracula type (Chris Sarandon) has moved into the spooky mansion next door and is seducing and murdering nubile maidens there. Well, would *you*? The miracle – and certainly the making of the film – is that Roddy McDowall, host of a late, late TV horror show, *does* come along to Hell House, lured by a $500 bait proffered by Charley's girlfriend, who happens to look like the vampire's long-lost love. McDowall wanders around in a state of total disbelief until he happens to notice Sarandon casts no reflection in a glass. From that moment, a confrontation is inevitable, and it's an exciting one at that, with special effects from the team who enlivened *Ghost Busters*. Sarandon is every inch the smoothly savage vampire, but the film's masterstroke is the casting of McDowall as the quivering questor. He provides the human element that adds the blood and guts to the acid bite of the effects men's work.

Fright Night II ● ⓥ
1988, US, 104 mins, colour
Dir: Tommy Lee Wallace
Stars: Roddy McDowall, William Ragsdale, Traci Lin, Julie Carmen
Rating: ★★★

The *Fright Night* gang are back and boy are they in trouble. Roddy McDowall is locked in a psychiatric hospital, William Ragsdale has been bitten and kidnapped by the chief lady vampire and Traci Lin is trapped with a vampire doctor next to a lonely railroad. Can they get themselves out of this? Fans needn't worry – worse is to come. This sequel is pretty lively once it gets going after a slow start. No wonder McDowall wanted to repeat his role as the horror-film telehost forced to turn genuine vampire-killer. It's his best opportunity for years, and he's aces in it. Lin's as nubile an intrepid heroine as the genre's thrown up in ages and Jonathan Fries, as a goofy vampire-cum-werewolf, is the best of the baddies. Special makeup drips the requisite grot, goo and gore, but isn't overused. Not quite as good (or scary) as the original, this is nonetheless a spirited creep into the crypt.

Frogmen, The ○
1951, US, 96 mins, b/w
Dir: Lloyd Bacon

Stars: Richard Widmark, Gary Merrill, Dana Andrews, Jeffrey Hunter, Robert Wagner, Jack Warden
Rating: ★★★

Richard Widmark in one of his typically tough all-action film roles of the early Fifties. As in *Red Skies of Montana, Halls of Montezuma, Destination Gobi* and *Hell and High Water*, Widmark plays an unpopular commander – this time of an underwater demolition team in World War Two. John Tucker Battle's virile screenplay finds no time for ladies, and the supporting cast includes Warren Stevens, Harvey Lembeck and William Bishop.

Frogs ①
1972, US, 91 mins, colour
Dir: George McCowan
Stars: Ray Milland, Sam Elliott, Joan Van Ark
Rating: ★★★

A very stylish and superior horror film. The air of menace hangs as heavily over proceedings as the atmosphere over the swamplands mansion in which Ray Milland and company find themselves under siege from a slimy army of frogs, toads, lizards, snakes, alligators, salamanders and even leeches. Skilful direction by George McCowan – which makes the most of a sharply satirical script and weaves the animal footage into the rest with complete conviction – complements some especially good night-time camerawork by Mario Tosi. There's a startling soundtrack, too, which comes up with a terrifying cacophony of rustling, slithering, hissing and croaking. The final scene, in which one character gets croaked by his attackers, is a masterpiece of montage.

From Beyond ● ⓥ
1986, US, 85 mins, colour
Dir: Stuart Gordon
Stars: Jeffrey Combs, Barbara Crampton, Ken Foree, Ted Sorel
Rating: RB

From the guys who gave you *Re-Animator*, this is a humourless and truly tacky horror film that relies entirely on yucky special effects for its impact. Plus a 'resonator' which acts as a sexual stimulant and the professor who turns the heroine into a lip-smacking bondage slave. Alas, she is neither sexy enough nor actress enough to add spice to this messy story of brain-eating fishes created by some Frankenstein machine. Simply monstrous: one would suggest feeding it to its fish if it had enough intelligence to interest them.

From Beyond the Grave ●
1973, UK, 98 mins, colour
Dir: Kevin Connor
Stars: Peter Cushing, David Warner, Donald Pleasence, Ian Bannen, Diana Dors
Rating: ★★

Another quartet of horror stories from the gore-minded boys at Amicus Films. There's too many corpses and too little chilling atmosphere, but the second episode is good, with father and daughter Donald and Angela Pleasence complementing each other well as a sinister match seller and his daughter. Put an apron on to catch the blood at the end of this story.

From Dusk Till Dawn ● ⓥ
1995, US, 107 mins, colour
Dir: Robert Rodriguez
Stars: Harvey Keitel, George Clooney, Juliette Lewis, Salma Hayek, Quentin Tarantino, Fred Williamson
Rating: ★★★

A thrashingly exciting crime-and-vampire story that almost never slackens its pace, while not taking itself seriously for a minute. Corpses drop faster than four-letter words in Quentin Tarantino's all-action screenplay: a pity Tarantino also casts himself as one of the principal characters, but his lack of thespian ability isn't too much of a drag this time around. He and Clooney are the notorious Gecko brothers. Clooney's a tough thief who'll kill at the twitch of an adversary, Tarantino a complete psycho and rapist who'll kill for no reason at all. If the first half of the film is a blast, it's tame compared to the second as the Geckos, fleeing from the law with a hostage family, rendezvous in Mexico at a night-club which proves to be a massive nest of vampires. Mass battle is soon joined in a film that gets more outrageous by the minute. Blood-hounds will love it.

From Hell to Texas ①
(aka: Manhunt)
1957, US, 100 mins, colour
Dir: Henry Hathaway
Stars: Don Murray, Diane Varsi, Chill Wills, Dennis Hopper
Rating: ★★★

Director Henry Hathaway did a useful job on this convincing Western, previously shown in Britain as *Manhunt*. But he had a good list of players, all typecast but to great effect: R G Armstrong in typical fire-eating form as the vengeful rancher gunning for innocent Don Murray; Dennis Hopper as Armstrong's wild son; Rudolfo Acosta

F

as a crafty Mexican and hoarse-voiced Chill Wills, bringing his own brand of homespun charm to the role of the heroine's father.

From Here to Eternity ○ ⓥ
1953, US, 118 mins, b/w
Dir: Fred Zinnemann
Stars: Burt Lancaster, Montgomery Clift, Deborah Kerr, Donna Reed, Frank Sinatra, Ernest Borgnine
Rating: ★★★★

Its eight Oscars, its scorching love scenes between Burt Lancaster and Deborah Kerr and its raw, shocking portrayal of the oppressions and torments of American army life at the time of Pearl Harbor made this film a sure box-office hit. It also remade Frank Sinatra's career when he won one of the Oscars. Donna Reed (another Oscar-winner), Montgomery Clift, Ernest Borgnine (memorable as the sadistic sergeant who goes gunning for Sinatra), Claude Akins, Mickey Shaughnessy and Jack Warden all snapped up their chances.

From Noon Till Three ○
1975, US, 95 mins, colour
Dir: Frank D Gilroy
Stars: Charles Bronson, Jill Ireland
Rating: ★★

Strange is certainly the word for this black action fantasy romance starring Charles Bronson – although Bronson adventure fans may well not know what to make of this one. No synopsis could convey the flavour of a film that almost creates its own genre and even might have done so with Cary Grant and Irene Dunne in the roles taken by Bronson and his wife Jill Ireland.

From Russia with Love ○ ⓥ
1963, UK, 118 mins, colour
Dir: Terence Young
Stars: Sean Connery, Daniela Bianchi, Pedro Armendariz, Lotte Lenya, Robert Shaw, Bernard Lee
Rating: ★★★

This, the second in chronological order of the James Bond films, differs appreciably from its predecessor *Dr No* as regards pacing. With the same director and the same scriptwriters, the production team clearly learnt a lot from making *Dr No*, and subsequent 007 adventures were to concentrate on action-packed incident. *From Russia With Love* goes at at a spanking pace, beginning with a splendid opening sequence and the now famous credit titles presented on the curves of a belly dancer. Then it's a matter of one high-

light, spectacle or thrill after another, with helicopters, trains, cars and speedboats figuring in some of the fast action. It was, too, the start of the vogue for gadgetry and sundry unorthodox lethal devices, ranging from venom-coated knives to exploding suitcases.

From the Mixed-Up Files of Mrs Basil E Frankweiler
See: The Hideaways

From the Terrace ○
1960, US, 144 mins, colour
Dir: Mark Robson
Stars: Paul Newman, Joanne Woodward, Myrna Loy, Ina Balin, Leon Ames, Felix Aylmer
Rating: ★★

This sprawling love story straddles big business, a family at war and a marriage made in hell, and marked the third screen collaboration between Paul Newman and his wife Joanne Woodward. It was an attempt to reassemble the commercial elements of *Peyton Place,* an earlier hit for the same director, Mark Robson, but it is a glutinous, plodding affair. Woodward comes off best in the acting stakes with a portrait of a soulless, physically frustrated society girl, glinting as sharply as the tiara she appears to reserve for wearing solely in taxis. But in comparison, Newman displays only an inflexible, glum boorishness.

From This Day Forward ○
1946, US, 95 mins, b/w
Dir: John Berry
Stars: Joan Fontaine, Mark Stevens, Rosemary DeCamp, Henry Morgan, Arline Judge, Bobby Driscoll
Rating: ★★

Post-war RKO was no longer the glamour studio it had been in the Thirties and its films reflected that. There were hopes that *From This Day Forward* would make an important contribution to the contemporary problem of soldiers struggling with re-adjustment to civilian life, but not only did the film prove to be more of a flashback romantic drama than a social statement, but also woefully miscast the vaguely aristocratic Joan Fontaine as a Bronx tenement housewife. Chubby-cheeked little Bobby Driscoll, soon to rise to major moppet stardom, steals every scene he's in as Timmy.

Front, The ◑ ⓥ
1976, US, 95 mins, colour
Dir: Martin Ritt

Stars: Woody Allen, Zero Mostel, Michael Murphy, Andrea Marcovicci
Rating: ★★

One of the most vicious forms of blacklisting in the cinema's history was the list compiled by the House UnAmerican Activities Committee in the years following the war. It put thousands of actors, writers, directors and technicians who were alleged to have had connections with communism in trouble, in prison, or just plain out-of-work. Star Woody Allen takes a straight role although fragments of the Allen comedy persona keep breaking in, like Hyde occasionally getting the better of Jekyll – as a man who 'fronts' for three blacklisted writers, that is, they all work under his name. It may give you quite an insight into the incredible things that went on. Zero Mostel gives his best performance in many a day as an actor who finds even nightclub fees cut in half after suspicion clouds his horizon.

Front Page Story ○
1953, UK, 99 mins, b/w
Dir: Jay Lewis
Stars: Jack Hawkins, Elizabeth Allen, Eva Bartok, Derek Farr
Rating: ★★★

One of Britain's better newspaper dramas, this absorbing film benefits from two outstanding performances – from the experienced Jack Hawkins as the news editor, and 10-year-old Jenny Jones as the brave, bossy eldest of a bunch of cockney children. Hawkins in a rare towering rage he's a sight to behold – is given reliable support from a convincing team of newspaper types: Derek Farr, as the editor's treacherous assistant; Michael Goodliffe, the office idealist; and Walter Fitzgerald as an alcoholic reporter assigned to a story of an atomic spy. Elizabeth Allan gives an appealing study of Hawkins' wife, and Eva Bartok brings sincere pathos to the role of a woman accused of murdering her dying husband. The office atmosphere is, for its time, remarkably plausible, in this solid slice of human drama.

Frozen Assets ◑ ⓥ
1992, US, 96 mins, colour
Dir: George Miller
Stars: Shelley Long, Corbin Bernsen, Larry Miller, Matt Clark, Gerrit Graham
Rating: ★

Shelley Long strikes out again in a writhingly embarrassing comedy whose very subject should have warned her off. Corbin Bernsen –

whose real-life mother, Jeanne Cooper, has a cameo role – plays a chauvinistic corporate yuppie who gets transferred to a small-town bank. Long is the feminist head of the business which, to Bernsen's horror, turns out to be a *sperm* bank! Is all this believable or what? The corny plot in which Bernsen clinches a mega-deal to sell 5,000 phials and, in a desperate attempt to attract depositors, hosts a 'Stud of the Year' contest, is lost among the allegedly comic *doubles entendres*. Still, the romantics among us who are still watching this after an hour and a half needn't worry – there's a nappy ending.

Frozen Limits, The O

1939, UK, 84 mins, b/w
Dir: Marcel Varnel
Stars: Bud Flanagan, Chesney Allen
Rating: ★★★

One of several zany farces made by Bud Flanagan and his colleagues in the Crazy Gang in the late Thirties and early Forties. Most of them, like this one, which has the gang organising a new gold rush in the Yukon, were written by Marriott Edgar and Val Guest. Edgar wrote many of Stanley Holloway's famous monologues, including those about Albert and Sam, while Guest went on to become a director. Here the familiar face of Bernard Lee turns up as, of all things, a Western badman called Dangerous Bill McGrew!

Fugitive, The O

1947, US, 104 mins, b/w
Dir: John Ford
Stars: Henry Fonda, Dolores Del Rio, Pedro Armendariz, J Carrol Naish, Robert Armstrong
Rating: ★★★

Director John Ford never tired over the years of telling Henry Fonda that his starring role here of a saintly priest, hunted in a south-of-the-border country that has outlawed the clergy, was the best performance of his career. Fonda is truly riveting and compelling in a film (based on a Graham Greene novel) that sits nicely as a companion piece to Ford's chilling *The Informer*, yet another tale of personal betrayal and challenged morality.

Fugitive, The ◑ Ⓥ

1993, US, 127 mins, colour
Dir: Andrew Davis
Stars: Harrison Ford, Tommy Lee Jones, Jeroen Krabbé, Joe Pantoliano
Rating: ★★★

He's back after 30 years – and still on the run. The massively popular TV series of the mid-Sixties exploded into a big screen adventure nearly three decades later, with Harrison Ford every bit as doggedly glum (and every bit as elusive) as David Jannsen was in the original. He has good reason too: arriving home to find himself battling a one-armed intruder who has shot and clubbed his wife, Dr Richard Kimble is soon accused and convicted of her murder. Inheriting an escape bid by other prisoners also on the way to Death Row, Kimble continues to evade pursuing police by a hairs-breadth as he tries to trace the real killer. This being a big-screen epic, the writers concoct a complex plot behind the one-armed man's break-in as well. None of this, though, stops dynamic Tommy Lee Jones, as the deputy marshall on Ford's trail, from stealing the film from under the star's nose and winning an Oscar. The film has just enough action to sustain its momentum, and its only real fault is that the eventual bad guy *looks* villainous from the start, rather robbing the story of its element of surprise.

Fugitive Kind, The O

1959, US, 135 mins, b/w
Dir: Sidney Lumet
Stars: Marlon Brando, Anna Magnani, Joanne Woodward
Rating: ★★

One of the strongest of all Tennessee Williams' works, *The Fugitive Kind*, based on his play *Orpheus Descending*, is reduced to elements overheated with everything except real emotions. A tempestuous performance by Anna Magnani in the female lead doesn't really save it.

Full House

See: 0 Henry's Full House

Full Metal Jacket ● Ⓥ

1987, UK, 115 mins, colour
Dir: Stanley Kubrick
Stars: Matthew Modine, Lee Ermey, Adam Baldwin, Vincent D'Onofrio, Arliss Howard
Rating: ★★

The only surprise about this very average Vietnam war film is that it took Stanley Kubrick more than a year to make. The story falls into two halves, both familiar staples of military films. The training (in this case particularly hard) of a group of Marine recruits and the combat action, in a slightly stylised and sanitised Vietnam which, as befits

the English locations, seems devoid of jungle, but full of glowing skies and shattered villages and towns. The feeling of these scenes is faintly unreal. More realistic, indeed the best thing about the film, is the drill sergeant, although as the actor, Lee Ermey, is an ex-drill NCO himself, his dialogue is presumably ripped from experience in all its crude but often amusing colour. Of course there's a closing homily on what it all means but even *Platoon* had that; the Americans, it seems, can't resist trying to make some sense out of the whole messy business.

Full Moon In Blue Water ● Ⓥ

1988, US, 94 mins, colour
Dir: Peter Masterson
Stars: Gene Hackman, Teri Garr, Burgess Meredith, Elias Koteas
Rating: ★★

This is a 'chamber piece', the kind of film actors love to do but nobody pays to see. With fewer than 10 characters and virtually a single location, this off-centre comedy-drama is set in the obscure Blue Water Grill, where the owner (Gene Hackman), dolefully watching home movies of his dead wife, is sinking into debts, back taxes and self-pity. He has a girlfriend (Teri Garr), who's more of a concubine, and a dim-witted assistant (Elias Koteas) who looks after his senile, wheelchair-bound father-in-law (Burgess Meredith). Of course, Hackman should marry Garr and accept her savings and a partnership, but then we wouldn't have a movie, so we must watch as businessmen, knowing his land will soon be a goldmine, exert a devious squeeze to make him sell the Blue Water at a rock-bottom price. Garr is excellent as the 36-year-old still living with her mother, but Hackman can't seem to put a consistent character together in this one.

Full of Life O

1956, US, 91 mins, b/w
Dir: Richard Quine
Stars: Judy Holliday, Richard Conte
Rating: ★★

Likeable and well-scripted comedy about a rather dizzy pregnant blonde (Judy Holliday in good form) and her misadventures after she and her husband move in with his Italian father-in-law, a tremendous performance by plump Italian comedian Salvatore Baccaloni. In the end, though, it falls between comedy, drama and embarrassment.

F

Fun and Fancy Free ⊙
1947, US, 73 mins, colour
Dir: Jack Kinney, Bill Roberts, Hamilton Luske
Rating: ★★★

Fun it is, but slightly disappointing too, for a major Disney cartoon that occupies its second half with a version of *Jack and the Beanstalk* that casts Mickey Mouse, Donald Duck and Goofy as the heroes. The first of the two stories (framed by cartoon/live action involving Jiminy Cricket from *Pinocchio* with ventriloquist Edgar Bergen) is a charming but very slight affair about a little performing bear who escapes from a circus. The beanstalk bit is by far the best, with Mickey, Donald and Goofy amusing outside their normal environment and plump comedian Billy Gilbert supplying the voice of Willie the Giant. The animation in this sequence is first-class, particularly when our intrepid trio is wending its way through the jungle of the giant's garden.

Funeral in Berlin ◖
1967, UK, 100 mins, colour
Dir: Guy Hamilton
Stars: Michael Caine, Paul Hubschmid, Oscar Homolka, Eva Renzi
Rating: ★★★

The second screen adventure of cockney spy Harry Palmer, the creation of author Len Deighton. Michael Caine again brings a grudging, rebellious charm to the character, but Evan Jones' screenplay lacks the wealth of finely observed detail that made his first appearance (in *The Ipcress File*) such a welcome antithesis from super-human Bondage. The Russian intelligence officer in charge of the Berlin Wall security (Oscar Homolka in fine, spitting form) makes it known that he is planning to defect and Palmer's assignment is warily to check the authenticity of the rumour. Hugh Burden steals the acting honours as Hallam of the Foreign Office.

Funny About Love ◖
1990, US, 100 mins, colour
Dir: Leonard Nimoy
Stars: Gene Wilder, Christine Lahti, Mary Stuart Masterson, Robert Prosky, Anne Jackson
Rating: ★

When even such good actresses as Christine Lahti and Mary Stuart Masterson can't do anything with a script that's meant to be a warm, funny and occasionally sad look at romance and heartbreak, you know you're in

trouble. You're even worse off, though, when you have Gene Wilder, trying too hard as the impossible-to-live-with cartoonist whose second fling at marriage (with a lady chef) turns into an excruciatingly embarrassing obsession about having a baby. Wilder jokes a lot in between outbursts of hysteria, and does James Cagney impressions, but none of it is amusing, or even touching, when it should be.

Funny Bones ◖
1995, UK, 128 mins, colour
Dir: Peter Chelsom
Stars: Oliver Platt, Jerry Lewis, Leslie Caron, Lee Evans, Oliver Reed, Freddy Davies
Rating: ★★★

If you thought director Chelsom's previous film, *Hear My Song*, was a shade peculiar, wait till you see this one – a one-of-a-kind movie about comedians that has some genuinely funny moments and a lot of very dark ones too: comedy that continually threatens to turn into tragedy and vice versa. In Hollywood, bulky Oliver Platt is the father-haunted son of ace comic Jerry Lewis. Fleeing to the Blackpool (England) of his childhood, he hopes to find some of the material that inspired his father. Instead, he discovers his seemingly half-witted half-brother (Lee Evans), a genuine comic genius, and the other members of the family from whom Lewis stole the material that made him a star. What follows is akin to Punch and Judy in its shades of violence, menace and fun. Evans steals the show as the Norman Wisdom-style clown seemingly sidelined for ever after killing a man in the circus ring. Asked to choose the odd one out between avarice, greed, envy and kindness, Evans selects 'and'...

Funny Face ○ ⓥ
1956, US, 103 mins, colour
Dir: Stanley Donen
Stars: Audrey Hepburn, Fred Astaire Kay Thompson, Robert Flemyng
Rating: ★★★★

A delightful musical that was never given its due when it first appeared. The elfin Audrey Hepburn combined with Fred Astaire, still a Peter Pan of the dance floor at 57, to happily revitalise an enchanting pre-war Gershwin musical romance about a photographer who takes a thin, bookish girl to Paris and transforms her looks and personality. If you need to be reminded that Fred was still the best musical comedy dancer in the business, watch his bull-

fighting routine in 'Let's Kiss and Make-Up', and his timing as he talks his way through the songs, especially the title number. One unexpected pleasure: the real voice of Miss Hepburn (who didn't sing for herself in *My Fair Lady*) making a throat-catching vocal dream out of 'How Long Has This Been Going On?' She also dances divinely, providing Astaire with another gamine partner to follow Leslie Caron from *Daddy Long Legs*.

Funny Girl ○ ⓥ
1968, US, 169 mins, colour
Dir: William Wyler
Stars: Barbra Streisand, Omar Sharif, Kay Medford, Anne Francis, Walter Pidgeon
Rating: ★★★★

This musical biography of unique singer-comedienne Fanny Brice goes on a bit too long, but still made a stunning debut for singer Barbra Streisand, who tied for that year's Best Actress Oscar with Katharine Hepburn. At her best when being goofily funny, Streisand has some memorable songs in this one, including 'Second Hand Rose', 'Funny Girl', 'People', 'My Man', 'I'd Rather Be Blue' and 'Don't Rain on My Parade'.

Funny Lady ○ ⓥ
1975, US, 138 mins, colour
Dir: Herbert Ross
Stars: Barbra Streisand, James Caan, Roddy McDowall, Omar Sharif, Ben Vereen
Rating: ★★★

A musical that continues the story of entertainer Fanny Brice, begun in *Funny Girl*. Barbra Streisand is so right for this role it's amazing, but the film is also illuminated by co-stars James Caan, excellent as the shambling showman Billy Rose, and Roddy McDowall, making a lot out of not very much screen time as Fanny's asexual acolyte.

Funny Thing Happened on the Way to the Forum, A ○ ⓥ
1966, UK, 99 mins, colour
Dir: Richard Lester
Stars: Michael Crawford, Phil Silvers Zero Mostel, Michael Hordern, Buster Keaton, Jack Gilford
Rating: ★★★

The comic talents of five decades are pooled in this helter-skelter musical about capers in ancient Rome, directed by Richard Lester, following his two memorable Beatles films and the equally popular *The Knack*. Buster Keaton, deservedly, has the funniest scene in the film. Keaton died soon after this film was completed and it was released after his death.

Fun with Dick and Jane ◐
1976, US, 95 mins, colour
Dir: Ted Kotcheff
Stars: Jane Fonda, George Segal, Ed McMahon
Rating: ★★★

Dick (George Segal) is a spend-spend-spend aerospace engineer who suddenly finds himself all spent when he is fired. Before they know it, and as soon as word is got around, he and his modish wife (Jane Fonda) are up to their neck in debt. Their ultimate solution is accidental but simple: they turn to crime. A scene where Segal tries to rob a drugstore and ends up being sold packets of contraceptives is really funny. So is the end of a sequence where they hold up a restaurant. The first half of the film is too stylised for its own good, but when Segal, Fonda and a swagbagful of imposters are allowed to take over, we really do have fun with Dick and Jane.

Funeral, The ● ⓥ
1996, US, 99 mins, colour
Dir: Abel Ferrara
Stars: Christopher Walken, Annabella Sciorra, Christopher Penn, Isabella Rossellini, Benicio del Toro, Vincent Gallo
Rating: ★★

An unremitting dark gangster movie where even the blood is black and humour is permitted not even a flicker. The problem with Ferrara's unsmiling film, which is about as friendly as the end of a gun barrel, is that it hasn't a structure to justify the grandiose Hamlet-like tableau of its conclusion. It is, if you like, a one-act film. A Little Italy gangster of the 1930s is shot dead. His brother vows vengeance. The rest is about loaded conversations, bullying macho men, easy women, waiting wives, sweat and cordite, before everything ends in a blast of gunfire. Although it does achieve a dark, stifling feeling of danger and imminent death, the film moves sluggishly and frankly you'd have more fun at a real funeral. Walken, as the older brother, gives his standard death's-head performance, enlightened only by the dispensation of his own philosophy before shooting a victim: 'If I do something wrong, it's because God didn't give me the grace to do something right.'

Furies, The ○
1950, US, 109 mins, b/w
Dir: Anthony Mann
Stars: Barbara Stanwyck, Wendell Corey, Walter Huston, Judith Anderson, Gilbert Roland
Rating: ★★★

Barbara Stanwyk, one of the grandes dames of the cinema, in a typical Stanwyck role. As the headstrong daughter of an equally iron-willed rancher, she falls in love with the son of his worst enemy. A tribute to her durability that she could still be convincing (and do all her own riding and stunting) in roles such as this, at the age of 43. A tigerish supporting cast includes Walter Huston, Judith Anderson, Thomas Gomez, Beulah Bondi, Wallace Ford, Wendell Corey and Blanche Yurka, but they all have to give best to Stanwyck in the end.

Further Up the Creek ○
1958, UK, 91 mins, b/w
Dir: Val Guest
Stars: David Tomlinson, Frankie Howerd, Shirley Eaton, Thora Hird
Rating: ★★

Nautical comedy romp not quite on a par with its predecessor, *Up the Creek*. Thora Hird strikes a welcome aggressive note to the soggy affair, but Peter Sellers is sadly missed. Also featured are Frankie Howerd and Shirley Eaton, who both played comedy in similar vein in *Carry On* films.

Fury ○
1936, US, 89 mins, b/w
Dir: Fritz Lang
Stars: Spencer Tracy, Sylvia Sidney, Walter Abel, Bruce Cabot, Walter Brennan
Rating: ★★★★

Fritz Lang's first American film is a savage and bitter indictment of mob violence, with a performance of fierce and sometimes brooding intensity by Spencer Tracy as the innocent man trapped in jail by a lynch mob baying for his blood. Still timely today.

Fuss Over Feathers
See: Conflict of Wings

Future Cop
See: Trancers

Futureworld ○
1976, US, 104 mins, colour
Dir: Richard T Heffron
Stars: Peter Fonda, Blythe Danner,

Arthur Hill, Yul Brynner
Rating: ★★★

Westworld was a distinctive science-fiction film, full of edginess and shock moments, about a pleasure palace gone wrong. While this sequel is on a similar lavish scale, with a dazzling array of sets, its content is on a more serial-like level. Even so, it remains exciting in parts, the mechanical marvels are admirably amusing and Peter Fonda and Blythe Danner (as a heroine called Socks) acquit themselves capably in the leading roles. There's a rather touching sub-plot about a faceless robot that has to be left behind when its human partner tries to escape.

F/X – Murder by Illusion ◐ ⓥ
1985, US, 103 mins, colour
Dir: Robert Mandel
Stars: Bryan Brown, Brian Dennehy, Diane Venora, Cliff De Young, Mason Adams
Rating: ★★

A nice idea this: a film special effects ace (Bryan Brown) is recruited by US intelligence to stage a fake assassination and help protect a criminal witness. The scheme seems to go wrong and the 'FX' man goes on the run from police and assassins alike. The set pieces here are often ingenious, but at base this is a highly unlikely yarn whose characters remain remarkably dislikeable probably due both to Robert Mandel's untutored direction and a pedestrian script which somehow contrives to just miss the way real people might speak. The best performance is from Cliff De Young as a government agent whose smile is as ready and shallow as it is treacherous. But even the effects aren't all that special.

F/X 2 – The Deadly Art of Illusion ◐ ⓥ
1991, US, 104 mins, colour
Dir: Richard Franklin
Stars: Bryan Brown, Brian Dennehy, Rachel Ticotin, Joanna Gleason, Philip Bosco
Rating: ★★

This sequel to *F/X* starts off as a dark thriller but evolves into something far more casual and lightweight. Bryan Brown is back as Rollie Tyler, the film special-effects man who now specialises only in high-tech toys, such as a clown whose movements obey its owners. He's helped by his wife's ex-husband, a cop, to help with illusory effects on a stakeout. Naturally it all goes wrong, the cop is killed unexpectedly by a second, unknown criminal, and Rollie

F

becomes involved with the case. The first 20 minutes are gripping stuff, but credibility is soon as illusory as Rollie's bag of tricks, and the denouement of the plot looks more like something from a James Bond film, or a caper thriller from the Sixties. By the end, no-one, least of all Brian Dennehy as a policeman turned private eye, seems to be taking it too seriously. Pity.

G

Gaby ○
1958, US, 97 mins, colour
Dir: Curtis Bernhardt
Stars: Leslie Caron, John Kerr, Cedric Hardwicke, Taina Elg
Rating: ★★

Second remake of the classic weepie *Waterloo Bridge*, about a wartime love affair. Former ballerinas Leslie Caron and Taina Elg take over the parts played in former versions by Mae Clarke and Bette Davis (1931) and Vivien Leigh and Virginia Field (1940). The ending's different, but it's still a decent cry.

Gaiety George ○
1946, UK, 98 mins, b/w
Dir: George King
Stars: Richard Greene, Ann Todd, Leni Lynn
Rating: ★★

This British musical, hardly seen since its initial appearance in post-war years, is really not at all bad, capturing much of the spirit of the era (London in the 1890s) in a biopic about an Irish-born showman of the times, and his up-and-down fortunes. American songstress Leni Lynn, a pretty little thing who made several sentimental musicals in Britain in the Forties, sings beautifully and there's an early role for the equally attractive Hazel Court.

Gallant Hours, The ○ Ⓥ
1959, US, 115 mins, b/w
Dir: Robert Montgomery
Stars: James Cagney, Dennis Weaver, Richard Jaeckel, Carl Benton Reid
Rating: ★★★

Although it has a shortage of battle scenes, this tense war drama about the battle for dominance of the Guadalcanal Canal is a fine, well-realised drama. This is largely due to James Cagney's impressive performance as Fleet Admiral 'Bull' Halsey, the man who masterminded the battle against the Japanese Admiral Yamamoto's fleet. An absorbing film that contains one of Cagney's finest portrayals.

Gallipoli ◑ Ⓥ
1981, AUS, 111 mins, colour
Dir: Peter Weir

Stars: Mel Gibson, Mark Lee, Bill Kerr, Robert Grubb, Bill Hunter
Rating: ★★★

Certainly one of the most internationally popular of Eighties Australian movies, this much acclaimed account of the doomed Anzac World War One campaign turned out to be the passport to Hollywood for its director, Peter Weir. Powerful and moving, it's nonetheless a fashionably made and predictably ended film. Mel Gibson and Mark Lee play two champion runners, one from the country, the other from the city, who join forces on a countrywide trek to join the Australian Light Horse and fight at Gallipoli. Some of the film's best moments come in its humorous lines. There's the army doctor who, according to his sergeant, 'has had it all and cured it all'. And there's the outback prospector, who, told about the war with the Turks by our two young heroes – 'If we don't stop them there, they could end up here,' they tell him – offers them a withering glance. 'Yes mate,' he drawls, 'and they're welcome to it.'

Gal who Took the West, The ○
1949, US, 84 mins, colour
Dir: Frederick De Cordova
Stars: Yvonne De Carlo, Scott Brady, Charles Coburn, John Russell
Rating: ★★

Yvonne De Carlo queens it over a vigorous Western that casts her as an actress out west, entertaining the cowboy masses in the wilds of Arizona. Veteran actor Charles Coburn takes the honours with another in his rich gallery of character portrayals. And cameraman William Daniels deserves a special mention for his photography.

Gambit ○
1966, US, 109 mins, colour
Dir: Ronald Neame
Stars: Shirley MacLaine, Michael Caine, Herbert Lom
Rating: ★★★★

Even though it leans heavily on *Topkapi* for inspiration, this is one of the tautest edge-of-seat thrillers the Sixties produced. The film starts with a robbery as it would be if the plan went off to perfection – so we know that it won't. Strangely, that doesn't take the edge away from the suspense. Ronald Neame's direction frays away the nerves, the cutting is commendable and the storyline keeps giving out with another twist to wind us back to fingernail level. Shirley MacLaine is delicious as the girl who slides between bars like a gymnastic eel.

Gambler, The ●
1974, US, 111 mins, colour
Dir: Karel Reisz
Stars: James Caan, Lauren Hutton, Paul Sorvino
Rating: ★

A grim and uncompromising account of a man who can't stop gambling even when he has won back what he lost and brought it home. James Caan brings a tightly-compressed fervour to the title role, but Karel Reisz' static direction unexpectedly fails to recognise the cinematic possibilities offered by the subject, and the story lacks the incident to sustain its length. Morris Carnovsky, best remembered as the bad guy in Humphrey Bogart's *Dead Reckoning*, makes one of his rare film appearances (as Caan's grandfather) since his Hollywood blacklisting in 1950. Unpalatable.

Gambler from Natchez, The ○
1954, US, 88 mins, colour
Dir: Henry Levin
Stars: Dale Robertson, Debra Paget, Thomas Gomez, Kevin McCarthy
Rating: ★

Twentieth Century-Fox were trying to build Dale Robertson into a big star at the time this large-scale action film was made. After watching his stolid performance here, it's easy to see why he didn't quite make the Clark Gable grade in the end. There are far more colourful portrayals from the beautiful Debra Paget, from Thomas Gomez, from Kevin McCarthy as a slyly treacherous villain and from the giant black actor Woody Strode. Director Henry Levin throws in bags of local colour in this story of a gambling vendetta in the American South of the 1840s. Alas, it's still dull.

Gandhi ○ ⓥ
1982, UK, 188 mins, colour
Dir: Richard Attenborough
Stars: Ben Kingsley, Candice Bergen, Edward Fox, John Gielgud, Trevor Howard, John Mills, Martin Sheen
Rating: ★★★★★

Richard Attenborough's best film to date as director proves that he is capable of touching the heart as well as stirring the senses, and deservedly won an Oscar, as did Ben Kingsley: his portrayal of India's supreme man of peace is a stunning example of the master character actor's art. Even across more

than three hours, this saga of 55 years' history is inevitably choppy in places, but to the untutored eye at least it seems that nothing essential has been missed. The atmosphere of India itself is captured all too well in all its splendour and poverty and the Indians, at least, involved in the story emerge as real characters. There are one or two small patches of mild tedium, but many more sequences that stir the imagination, blood and emotions, as a whole panoply of a life dedicated to peace and justice sweeps across the screen. All in all, a staggering achievement.

Gang's All Here, The ○
(aka: The Amazing Mr Forrest)
1939, UK, 77 mins, b/w
Dir: Thornton Freeland
Stars: Jack Buchanan, Googie Withers
Rating: ★★★

Not the Busby Berkeley musical of the same name, but the second of two British Thirties' comedy-thrillers made by debonair Jack Buchanan in the character of John Forrest. In this later adventure, he has become a retired insurance investigator, with Googie Withers in the role of his wife, created in the first film by Buchanan's oft-time stage partner, Elsie Randolph. A stunning supporting cast includes British comedy specialists Syd Walker, Ronald Shiner and Robb Wilton, plus such American stars as Edward Everett Horton (again in his worried penguin act), Jack La Rue and Otto Kruger. The result, not surprisingly, was a box-office hit.

Gang's All Here, The ○
(aka: The Girls He Left Behind)
1943, US, 103 mins, colour
Dir: Busby Berkeley
Stars: Alice Faye, Carmen Miranda, James Ellison
Rating: ★★★

A later Busby Berkeley musical in Technicolor. It's the one with Carmen Miranda (and a parade of bananas) singing and dancing 'The Lady in the Tutti Frutti Hat'. Carmen, in fact, steals the show with some wonderful minced English ('I am spillink ze cat out of ze beans'), though it's also worth watching Charlotte Greenwood's high kicks, and looking out for up-and-coming Fox stars Sheila Ryan, June Haver and Jeanne Crain. Vulgar, colourful, tuneful and almost a complete delight.

Gangster, The ○
1947, US, 84 mins, b/w
Dir: Gordon Wiles

Stars: Barry Sullivan, Belita, Joan Lorring, Akim Tamiroff
Rating: ★★★

A rather curious *film noir*, this, with a gangster looking back on and agonising over his life of crime. Barry Sullivan plays the curiously-named Shubunka, a mobster who has fought his way from petty thief to gang boss. Now at the top, he loses interest in everything but his girl Nancy (Belita), uncaring that rival mobster Cornell (Sheldon Leonard) is closing in on him. The film has an intellectual angle to it not usually associated with gangster films, and was critically well received. Now the playing of Sullivan, Akim Tamiroff and John Ireland looks a bit mannered and the whole thing comes across as very stagey. Nevertheless it's something different and a must for students of the genre.

Garbo Talks ○
1984, US, 103 mins, colour
Dir: Sidney Lumet
Stars: Anne Bancroft, Ron Silver, Carrie Fisher, Hermione Gingold
Rating: ★

Not one of Sidney Lumet's most successful films, this off-beat comedy has its moments, even if it suffers from an excess of cuteness. But the central idea is a delightful one, the cast is tremendous, and Anne Bancroft is at her endearing best as the ageing eccentric forever in search of the elusive and reclusive Greta Garbo.

Garden of Allah, The ○
1936, US, 80 mins, colour
Dir: Richard Boleslawski
Stars: Marlene Dietrich, Charles Boyer, Basil Rathbone, C Aubrey Smith
Rating: ★★★

Ravishingly shot in early Technicolor by W Howard Green and Hal Rossen, this is one of Hollywood's most lushly romantic films. Marlene Dietrich's exotic adventuress, riding off into the desert with a man who turns out to be a monk who has deserted his monastery, is almost matched by the extraordinary Austrian actress Tilly Losch, whom one critic described as: 'In her bizarre costume . . . an embodiment of lust and decadence!' The film established Charles Boyer's reputation as a romantic lover of the screen.

Garden of Evil ○
1954, US, 100 mins, colour
Dir: Henry Hathaway
Stars: Gary Cooper, Susan Hayward,

G

Richard Widmark, Hugh Marlowe
Rating: ★★

Leisurely, at times tense and exciting Western whose storyline follows well-trodden trails. It's considerably boosted by the three stars, Gary Cooper, Susan Hayward and Richard Widmark, who add stature to the routine plot about a disparate group of men rescuing the husband of the woman travelling with them, and then being pursued by vengeful Indians. No prizes for guessing in which order the characters get killed off.

Gardens of Stone ◑ ⓥ
1987, US, 111 mins, colour
Dir: Francis Coppola
Stars: James Caan, Anjelica Huston, James Earl Jones, D B Sweeney, Dean Stockwell, Mary Stuart Masterson
Rating: ★★

The title refers to the tombstones of US soldiers buried at Arlington Cemetery in this impressively-cast but very slightly dull and strangely uninvolving film about a couple of unusually human sergeant-majors and their youthful charges at the Arlington base. There are good portrayals from all the older players, particularly Anjelica Huston (in a rare sympathetic role) and Lonette McKee, and from the much younger Mary Stuart Masterson, whose real-life parents play her family in the film. The central weakness is an uncharismatic performance from D B Sweeney in the film's pivotal role of young soldier Jackie Willow. It's not bad, with the odd effective emotional moment, but hardly the last word on any of the varying genres it touches.

Gas, Food – Lodging ◑ ⓥ
1991, US, 102 mins, colour
Dir: Allison Anders
Stars: Brooke Adams, Ione Skye, Fairuza Balk, James Brolin, Donovan Leitch
Rating: ★★★

Growing up fast in the New Mexico desert town of Laramie are the two teenage daughters of caravan dweller Brooke Adams, long ago deserted by her husband. The oldest (Ione Skye) has sex with any boy that'll have her, the younger, Shade (Fairuza Balk), still has her dreams, mostly lived through the films shown at a local Mexican-speaking cinema. Older sister falls for an English rock collector who leaves her pregnant, Shade hitches up with a local Mexican boy and mother finds someone at last after years alone. Not

much to all this, but it's shot on location with a sense of real camera movement by Allison Anders. Although the too-long screenplay leaves lengthy stretches of dullness that may account for the inattentive viewer, the performances are caring, especially from the wide-awake Balk, seen not so many years before as Dorothy in Disney's *Return to Oz*.

Gaslight ○ ⓥ
(aka: The Murder in Thornton Square)
1944, US, 114 mins, b/w
Dir: George Cukor
Stars: Charles Boyer, Ingrid Bergman, Joseph Cotten
Rating: ★★★

Charming but evil Charles Boyer pushes his wealthy new wife Ingrid Bergman towards madness while searching for her long dead aunt's jewels in this glossy Hollywood melodrama. It's a remake of the 1940 Anton Walbrook/Diana Wynyard film that MGM mogul Louis B Meyer tried to destroy! Luckily for us, the (better) British version survived. Despite an Oscar-winning performance from Bergman, a fine debut portrayal of a flirty chambermaid by an 18-year-old Angela Lansbury and a lavish production under the direction of George Cukor, this remake fails to convey the air of menace that seeped through the original. Nevertheless it's a good film: it just had a very hard act to follow.

Gaslight ○
(aka: Angel Street)
1939, UK, 88 mins, b/w
Dir: Thorold Dickinson
Stars: Anton Walbrook, Diana Wynyard
Rating: ★★★★

Chilling first version of the famous mystery thriller, remade four years later by Hollywood with Ingrid Bergman and Charles Boyer. In this earlier British film, with Diana Wynyard and Anton Walbrook in the leading roles, director Thorold Dickinson achieves an atmosphere alive with menace. Draw the curtains and keep out the light to put yourself in the right mood to be scared.

Gator ◑
1976, US, 111 mins, colour
Dir: Burt Reynolds
Stars: Burt Reynolds, Jack Weston, Lauren Hutton
Rating: ★★★

The most significant thing about this vigorous thriller is that it marked the directorial debut of its star, Burt

Reynolds. All through the film it is evident that Reynolds is trying to do a little something different with each scene. Sometimes he can't prevent the plot becoming bogged down in its own routineness, and the violence of the climax only just survives its juxtaposition with the previous humour, as characters we have come to like get brutally killed off. But the action scenes are first class, and Reynolds gets uniformly good performances from his actors: Jack Weston, stealing the film as a plump and faintly incompetent federal agent; Lauren Hutton, a cool, gaptoothed heroine; Jerry Reed, a country and western singer who lends real menace and evil to the rather cardboard vice king; Alice Ghostley as a cranky social crusader with a passion for cats; and by no means least, from himself. *Gator* chalked up a bright start for its budding director which he hasn't followed through enough.

Gauntlet, The ● ⓥ
1977, US, 108 mins, colour
Dir: Clint Eastwood
Stars: Clint Eastwood, Sondra Locke, Pat Hingle, William Prince
Rating: ★

If Clint Eastwood, again directing himself, wanted to prove that he could make a film tougher, uglier, faster-moving and more explosive than any other modern director of thrillers, then he did a pretty good job with *The Gauntlet*. Right from the start, with Eastwood a (rather unconvincing) drunken cop sent to shepherd a (female) witness back for a trial, to the deliberately ludicrous finale, in which the pair defy what seems like half the hardware in America, this is a slam-bang bloodbath aimed squarely at the box-office.

Gay Desperado, The ○
1936, US, 86 mins, b/w
Dir: Rouben Mamoulian
Stars: Nino Martini, Ida Lupino, Leo Carrillo
Rating: ★★★

This delightful comedy musical directed by Rouben Mamoulian was designed as a vehicle for opera star Nino Martini and has a pretty preposterous plot: crazy Mexican bandido models himself on American screen gangsters and decides to satisfy his love of music by kidnapping a famous tenor. He also manages to gather up heiress Ida Lupino on his first hold-up (more by luck than judgement). The songs – very operatic – are very lovely (although Mischa Auer, in a priceless shot, plainly doesn't think so) but slow up the wonderful comic 'business' going on, particularly Leo Carrillo's hilarious Hispanic. The film looks glorious as well, with great sweeping views of the landscape and bandidos in the swirling dust, of cacti and buildings encrusted with crenellations. Magnifico amigo!

Gay Divorcee, The ○ ⓥ
(aka: The Gay Divorce)
1934, US, 107 mins, b/w
Dir: Mark Sandrich
Stars: Fred Astaire, Ginger Rogers
Rating: ★★★★★

Fred Astaire's West End stage hit *The Gay Divorce* became *The Gay Divorcee* on screen because the censor ruled that divorce was no laughing matter. The story is just as fragile as ever but Astaire and Ginger Rogers dance up a storm, including a delightfully lengthy and complex sequence to the Oscar-winning 'The Continental'. The only song remaining from the original Cole Porter score was the immortal 'Night and Day'. Audiences flocked to see it and it turned the two stars into household names overnight.

Gay Impostors, The
See: Gold Diggers in Paris

Gazebo, The ○
1959, US, 100 mins, b/w
Dir: George Marshall
Stars: Glenn Ford, Debbie Reynolds, Cari Reiner, John McGiver
Rating: ★★★

A hit and miss but mostly delightful black comedy with Debbie Reynolds as a Broadway star whose husband is being blackmailed over a series of nude pictures from her cash-strapped past. He decides to bump off the villain and bury him under a piece of garden furniture, but he kills the wrong man. It's pretty amusing, well-directed fluff, although only when the murder is being planned is the film really funny. Based on a play by Alec Coppel, one of the film's highlights is Reynolds' rendition of 'Something Called Love'.

Geisha Boy, The ⊙
1958, US, 98 mins, colour
Dir: Frank Tashlin
Stars: Jerry Lewis, Marie MacDonald, Barton MacLane, Suzanne Pleshette
Rating: ★★★

Wild Jerry Lewis comedy, full of rib-tickling touches thanks to the direction of Frank Tashlin, a former cartoonist. It was Suzanne Pleshette's first film, and Marie 'The Body' McDonald's last, as a film star involved with Jerry, who plays a third-rate magician. The jokes all work well, especially the one involving hard-nosed major Barton MacLane, who can't wait for his own funeral because he loves hearing 'Taps'.

Gene Krupa Story, The
See: Drum Crazy

General, The ⊙
1926, US, 74 mins, b/w
Dir: Clyde Bruckman
Stars: Buster Keaton, Marion Mack
Rating: ★★★★★

Universally accepted as one of Buster Keaton's greatest feature films, this is based on a book called *The Great Locomotive Chase*, filmed under that title 30 years later by the Disney organisation. It's an action comedy with as many thrills as comic spills and lots of sight gags to embellish a fast-paced story based on true-life incidents in the American Civil War.

Generation
See: A Time for Giving

Genevieve ⊙
1953, UK, 86 mins, colour
Dir: Henry Cornelius
Stars: John Gregson, Dinah Sheridan, Kenneth More, Kay Kendall
Rating: ★★★★

'I'll show them how to play the plumpet.' With such an unlikely line did Kay Kendall shoot to stardom – something that should have happened much earlier – in this richly enjoyable comedy spun round the veteran car run to Brighton. It also made a star of Kenneth More and is greatly helped on its way by a gently funny and beautifully-knit screenplay from that king of comedy, William Rose. Ravishingly shot in colour by Christopher Challis, the film has memorable harmonica music by Larry Adler.

Genghis Khan ○ ⓥ
1965, US, 120 mins, colour
Dir: Henry Levin
Stars: Omar Sharif, Stephen Boyd, James Mason, Françoise Dorléac
Rating: ★★★★

One of the best of the crop of epics produced in the mid-Sixties. Unlike some, it makes no attempt to hang out its story, and keeps the screen brimful of action. The colour photography is exemplary, reaching a peak in the moving final scene. And director Henry Levin tells the full-blooded adventure story with dash, taste and a feel for real human beings.

Gentle Giant ○
1967, US, 93 mins, colour
Dir: James Neilson
Stars: Dennis Weaver, Vera Miles, Ralph Meeker
Rating: ★★★

Harmless, well-photographed story of the friendship between a boy and a bear. Dennis Weaver lends his customary authority to the role of the boy's father, but the principal interest for film fans will lie in the appearance of Huntz Hall, once famous as the gormless Satch in the Bowery comedy films.

Gentleman Jim ○ ⓥ
1942, US, 104 mins, b/w
Dir: Raoul Walsh
Stars: Errol Flynn, Alexis Smith, Jack Carson, Alan Hale, John Loder, Ward Bond
Rating: ★★★

Errol Flynn got the chance to display his physique and give a robust performance in the fictionalised biography of prize-fighter 'Gentleman Jim' Corbett who became the first heavyweight champion of the world under the Marquis of Queensberry rules. The film is played as much for comedy as drama, put over in particular by Jack Carson. The fight scenes are well staged by director Raoul Walsh and first-rate art direction adds to the impact of the movie.

Gentleman's Agreement ○ ⓥ
1947, US, 118 mins, b/w
Dir: Elia Kazan
Stars: Gregory Peck, Dorothy McGuire, John Garfield, Celeste Holm, Anne Revere, Dean Stockwell
Rating: ★★★

Winner of three Oscars and nominated for several more, this is Elia Kazan's clinical dissection of anti-Semitism in America. The direction (Kazan won one of the three Academy Awards) is tautly strung from beginning to end, and the sequence of events joined together with such skill and dramatic cohesion as to make each new development, and the final outcome, totally absorbing. Despite sincere performances from Gregory Peck and Dorothy McGuire, the outstanding portrayals lie in the

G

supporting cast, notably from Celeste Holm (another Oscar-winner), June Havoc, Albert Dekker and Anne Revere.

Gentlemen Prefer Blondes ○ ⓥ
1954, US, 91 mins, colour
Dir: Howard Hawks
Stars: Jane Russell, Marilyn Monroe, Charles Coburn
Rating: ★★★★

How they got Jane Russell and Marilyn Monroe together to make this breeze-fresh comedy is one of the wonders of the age. It contains three of Marilyn's best numbers – 'Bye, Bye, Baby', 'Two Little Girls from Little Rock' and 'Diamonds Are a Girl's Best Friend' – and the girls sing wonderfully well together. Tommy Noonan, as the son of a millionaire infatuated with one of the girls, and George Winslow, the little boy with the foghorn voice, are the pick of a supporting cast, the rest of which is eclipsed by the stars. Howard Hawks directs with verve and the result is a champagne cocktail that could well have been called *Gold Diggers of 1954*. The wit and the humour are all there. Vastly enjoyable.

George in Civvy Street ○
1946, UK, 79 mins, b/w
Dir: Marcel Varnel
Stars: George Formby, Rosalyn Boulter, Ronald Shiner
Rating: ★★

The partnership of music hall favourite George Formby and director Marcel Varnel (who also turned out the best of the Will Hay and Arthur Askey comedies) was looking distinctly jaded after six movies in a row. And despite a formidable array of four new writers, this stale comedy about pub rivalry ended Formby's screen career on a low note.

George Raft Story, The
See: Spin of a Coin

Georgy Girl ① ⓥ
1966, UK, 100 mins, b/w
Dir: Silvio Narrizano
Stars: Lynn Redgrave, James Mason, Alan Bates, Charlotte Rampling
Rating: ★★★★

That attractive actress Lynn Redgrave is both *raison d'être* and chief delight in this story of a tall, solid, 'glumpy' 22-year-old dancing teacher whom nobody loves. With its strange ending, which throws Georgy out of character, and its lack of any real ob-

jective, the film has a certain emptiness that even Lynn Redgrave's agonising, unbelievably close-to-life portrait of lumbering loneliness can't quite fill. Its most effective scenes are those in which she rather pathetically makes fun of her parents and, best of all, conducts a Joyce Grenfell-style dance class for children, complete with a gorgeous range of grunts, groans and gurgles.

Geronimo ○
1962, US, 101 mins, colour
Dir: Arnold Laven
Stars: Chuck Connors, Kamala Devi
Rating: ★★

Hatchet-faced Chuck Connors presides impassively over this actionful slice of Indian history. Connors' real-life wife, Kamala Devi, plays the beautiful Apache girl who loves the warrior chief. The cast also includes Adam West, alias television's Batman, and Denver Pyle. The action moves briskly along and the night-time colour photography is impressive.

Geronimo ① ⓥ
1993, US, 116 mins, colour
Dir: Walter Hill
Stars: Wes Studi, Jason Patric, Gene Hackman, Robert Duvall, Rodney A Grant, Kevin Tighe
Rating: ★★★

Beautifully filmed and intelligently told, if slow and stately most of the way, this is the true story of events leading to the eventual surrender of the great Apache warrior of the title. Notable in the excellent cast are the impassive Wes Studi as the fearless Geronimo, Gene Hackman, in rich form as the general whose task it is to bring Geronimo in under the US government's imposed Reservation system, and Jason Patric as the young Cavalry officer sympathetic to the Apache. In this worthy if deliberate Western, white men really do speak with forked tongues, and we can only watch with shame.

Getaway, The ① ⓥ
1972, US, 122 mins, colour
Dir: Sam Peckinpah
Stars: Steve McQueen, Ali MacGraw, Ben Johnson, Sally Struthers, Slim Pickens
Rating: ★★★

Steely-eyed Steve McQueen gives a memorably glowering performance as the ex-con mastermind behind a ruthlessly efficient bank heist in Sam Peckinpah's typically violent crime caper. Although Ali MacGraw's vacu-

ous performance as McQueen's wife is a bit of a liability, there are enough colourful characters in the supporting cast to compensate. Particularly good are Al Lettieri as a treacherous hit-man and Bo Hopkins as his trigger-happy apprentice.

Getaway, The ● ⓥ
1994, US, 110 mins, colour
Dir: Roger Donaldson
Stars: Alec Baldwin, Kim Basinger, Michael Madsen, James Woods, Jennifer Tilly, Richard Farnsworth
Rating: ★★

Gun-blasting violence and graphic sex enliven an otherwise tiresome thriller about a freelance bank robber and general Mr Fixit (Alec Baldwin) who gets double-crossed more times than a British taxpayer in his efforts to pull one last heist, so that he and his gorgeous accomplice and wife (Kim Basinger) can retire in luxury. Baldwin is pretty anonymous in the old Steve McQueen role, James Woods is shunted out of the plot before he has much chance to shine, and Michael Madsen is an unkempt and unpersonable villain. Basinger, however, is much better than her partner and she and Jennifer Tilly (a vet's wife who gets hooked on the pursuing Madsen) are more interesting bodies than those mown down by the gunfire. Veteran Richard Farnsworth scores in a little cameo right at the end, about the only time Donaldson's direction seems not to be on automatic pilot.

Get Carter ● ⓥ
1971, UK, 112 mins, colour
Dir: Mike Hodges
Stars: Michael Caine, Ian Hendry, Britt Ekland, John Osborne
Rating: ★★★

The influx of directors from television brought a new harsh realism to the British cinema of the late Sixties and early Seventies – especially to the world of the crime thriller, of which this film and *Villain* are prime examples. No principles, morals or good guys exist in these bleak portraits of underworld warfare. Michael Caine's Carter is as nasty as the rest of the racketeers portrayed here. If we sympathise with him, it is only because he is one man against the mob; the same sympathy received by Clint Eastwood, perhaps, in his efforts to earn a few dollars more. The chilly Newcastle settings are splendidly captured by Wolfgang Suschitzky's steely

Metrocolor photography, and both Caine and Ian Hendry are in cutting form.

Get on with It

See: Dentist on the Job

Get Shorty ●

1995, US, 105 mins, colour
Dir: Barry Sonnenfeld
Stars: John Travolta, Gene Hackman, Danny DeVito, Rene Russo, Dennis Farina, Bette Midler
Rating: ★★

This mild satire on Hollywood movie-making has its moments, though you may not be able to think of too many after it's over. John Travolta is Chili, the unflappable, film-mad loan shark dispatched to Tinseltown to collect money owed by Z-movie mogul Harry Zimm (Gene Hackman) who makes films about slime creatures and is shacked up with ageing film siren Karen (Rene Russo). Other elements become involved in both offering Harry money and trying to get it from him, as he tries to make the 're-spectable' film of his dreams – and Chili pitches in with his own film idea, which happens to be the one we're watching. It all gets a bit tiresome here and there, although Travolta is smoothly amusing as the enforcer who's always a step ahead of those in the way, and even persuades diminutive superstar Martin Weir (Danny DeVito) to star in his movie. The dialogue's mostly ho-hum but does contain a few gems. 'I once asked a literary agent,' says Hackman, 'what kind of writing paid best. He said: "Ransom notes."'

Getting Even with Dad ○

1994, US, 108 mins, colour
Dir: Howard Deutch
Stars: Macaulay Culkin, Ted Danson, Glenne Headly, Saul Rubinek, Hector Elizondo, Kathleen Wilhoite
Rating: ★★

Ted Danson expands his handsome but dim charmer from TV's *Cheers* to play a handsome but dim (and with a ponytail) petty crook saddled with looking after his 11-year-old son (Macaulay Culkin) on the eve of a big robbery. Pesky kid Culkin sees a way to blackmail his father into paying for all his years of neglect, and so the fun (such as it is) begins. Little Mac sorely irritates Danson in the movie, and will strain the patience of many viewers too, in a light-hearted but heavy-handed farce mainly for the kids. This is,

in fact, a big sit for small bottoms, which only occasionally achieves the kind of impish fun to which Miles Goodman's bright score hints that it aspires throughout.

Getting It Right ●

1989, UK, 102 mins, colour
Dir: Randal Kleiser
Stars: Jesse Birdsall, Helena Bonham Carter, Peter Cook, John Gielgud, Lynn Redgrave
Rating: ★★★

There are some sharp performances in this throwback to Sixties British cinema, notably from Helena Bonham Carter as a sad and lonely spaced-out teenage aristocrat and Lynn Redgrave as an equally sad and lonely 45-year-old who fears the dark and craves companionship. Hero Jesse Birdsall is sad and lonely, too, in his way. A 31-year-old hairdresser who lives with his parents (but isn't gay), he's only concerned with getting it right – difficult when he's painfully shy with girls. Birdsall is perhaps a shade too diffident as the hero to whom everything starts to happen at once. But this is a pleasant comedy with the right feel about its settings, and some wickedly funny lines. Chances are you'll get a warm feeling when Jesse does eventually get it right.

Getting of Wisdom, The ○

1977, Australia, 101 mins, colour
Dir: Bruce Beresford
Stars: Susannah Fowle, Barry Humphries, Hilary Ryan
Rating: ★★★

Australian Bruce Beresford, now a major director on the international scene, scored his first big international success with this beautifully made and astutely observed story of the stultifying existence undergone by teenage girl students at an exclusive ladies' college in late 19th-century Melbourne. Not that Beresford's film is ever dull. Susannah Fowle, as the plain-Jane heroine who learns more about gamesmanship and cheating than wisdom itself, keeps the plot sparking with her escapades in and out of the classroom and on the sports field. Sometimes things are over-emphasised, one of Beresford's faults in earlier films, but ironed out from this point in his career. Barry Humphries' stentorian portrait of the headmaster, for example, is over-the-top but a model of tact compared to his work in earlier Beresford films.

Gettysburg ● ⓥ

1993, US, 252 mins, colour
Dir: Ronald F Maxwell
Stars: Tom Berenger, Martin Sheen, Jeff Daniels, C Thomas Howell, Sam Elliott
Rating: ★★

Grotesquely overlong, but with thrilling battle scenes, the first two hours of this mammoth account of the crucial battle of the American Civil War are so slow and sleep-inducing you may be inclined to leave before the good bits start. At least half of this speechifying beginning, in which characters speak stiltedly, could usefully be lost. The first half, however, culminates in a magnificent battle sequence on a wooded, mist-en-shrouded hillside, in which the intense performance of Jeff Daniels, exactly right as a scared but determined Union commander, really comes into its own. The second half of the movie is routine battle stuff, full of 'if onlys' and futile charges. A monumental undertaking all told, but with results that too seldom touch the emotions.

Ghost ● ⓥ

1990, US, 127 mins, colour
Dir: Jerry Zucker
Stars: Patrick Swayze, Demi Moore, Tony Goldwyn, Whoopi Goldberg
Rating: ★★★

It's hard to imagine virile, very-much-alive Patrick Swayze as a ghost. But that's what he becomes when shot by a mugger while walking home with lover Demi Moore. Swayze can't figure why he's been left to roam the earth, but it doesn't take him long to work out that he's there for a purpose and that's to protect Demi from those who had his killing rigged to look like a casual shoot-and-run affair. This isn't too easy (as Demi can't see or hear him and he can't move objects) until he latches on to a psychic (Whoopi Goldberg) and takes lessons in telekinesis from subway ghost Vincent Schiavelli. This could have made a first-rate offbeat romantic thriller (and even more money); for the reason it's only effective in patches, look no further than the running time, far too much of which is spent in pseudo-erotic moonings. Never mind, enjoy the thriller plot (though the villain isn't difficult to spot), the special effects and Goldberg's lively, Oscar-winning performance.

Ghost and Mr Chicken, The ⊙

1966, US, 90 mins, colour
Dir: Alan Rafkin

G

Stars: Don Knotts, Joan Staley
Rating: ★★

'Nervous' American comedian Don Knotts never really caught on outside America, despite having made several films, starting with an hilarious debut as the shoe salesman in Doris Day's *Move Over Darling*. Here, he's a timid reporter assigned to spending a night in a haunted house.

Ghost and Mrs Muir, The ○ Ⓥ

1947, US, 104 mins, b/w
Dir: Joseph L Mankiewicz
Stars: Gene Tierney, Rex Harrison, George Sanders, Edna Best, Natalie Wood
Rating: ★★★★

A charming piece of whimsy about a beautiful but impoverished widow helped to fight grasping relations by the ghost of a rascally old sea-dog. The film is beautifully made and consistently entertaining, besides boasting an eye-catching performance by Natalie Wood, then only eight, as the widow's daughter. The moving climax is just right.

Ghost Breakers, The ○

1940, US, 85 mins, b/w
Dir: George Marshall
Stars: Bob Hope, Paulette Goddard, Paul Lukas, Richard Carlson, Anthony Quinn
Rating: ★★★★

A follow-up to the success of co-stars Bob Hope and Paulette Goddard in *The Cat and the Canary* that both tickles the ribs and chills the spine. Directed at a rattling pace by George Marshall brimming with confidence after his success the previous year with *Destry Rides Again*, the film bristles with wisecracks and mixes its chuckles and creepy bits with a facility rarely seen in this genre. Look fast for a young Robert Ryan as an intern near the start of the film.

Ghost Busters ○ Ⓥ

1984, US, 105 mins, colour
Dir: Ivan Reitman
Stars: Bill Murray, Dan Aykroyd, Sigourney Weaver, Harold Ramis, Rick Moranis, Ernie Hudson
Rating: ★★★

This modestly scary supernatural comedy, with some very funny individual lines and moments of visual hilarity thrown in, quite unexpectedly took the box-offices of the world by storm. Bill Murray, Dan Aykroyd and Harold Ramis play three university boffins

who become private exorcisers after their college facility is whipped from under them. After a slow start, business picks up, which isn't surprising as Doomsday itself appears to be at hand. Special effects in the apocalyptic finale are well up to par and admirably counterbalanced by the humour which is *National Lampoon* pleasantly tamed, and delivered with perfect deadpan timing, especially by the laconic Bill Murray. Ivan Reitman's direction is fairly sharp, only occasionally failing to drive the capers along at quite a wild enough speed.

Ghostbusters II ○ Ⓥ

1989, US, 99 mins, colour
Dir: Ivan Reitman
Stars: Bill Murray, Dan Aykroyd, Sigourney Weaver, Harold Ramis, Rick Moranis, Ernie Hudson
Rating: ★★★

Five years have passed and the ghost-busting exorcisers have fallen on hard times. Two of them (Dan Aykroyd, Ernie Hudson) are reduced to entertaining at children's parties. But help is at hand, in the form of a medieval madman who escapes from a painting and terrorises the city. All the cast from the first film (that means Bill Murray, Sigourney Weaver, Harold Ramis, Rick Moranis and sundry minor players) are reunited for this snappy sequel, which provides a serviceable, if highly unlikely dose of spooky fun. The special effects are perhaps not quite so spectacular as in the original, but this one does have a mobile Statue of Liberty to help clean up the bad guys, and a good sprinkling of laconic lines, of which, as usual, Murray makes the most in his deadpan fashion. A bit scary for younger children.

Ghost Catchers ○

1944, US, 68 mins, b/w
Dir: Edward F Cline
Stars: Ole Olsen, Chic Johnson, Leo Carrillo, Lon Chaney Jr, Gloria Jean, Andy Devine
Rating: ★★

Although it has some spooky moments, notably early on, and some funny ones too, this Olsen and Johnson comedy rather wastes its talented cast and shows that, with the success of Abbott and Costello, Universal was beginning to lose interest in the team. Ironically Olsen and Johnson get in a crack about the Abbott and Costello picture *Hold That Ghost* in one scene of a plot which also makes room for singers Gloria Jean,

Ella Mae Morse and Morton Downey and actor-bandleader Kirby Grant. Spot the drummer in Grant's band: it's Mel Tormé.

Ghost Dad ○ Ⓥ

1990, US, 84 mins, colour
Dir: Sidney Poitier
Stars: Bill Cosby, Kimberly Russell
Rating: ★

Sidney Poitier teamed up to direct his old mate Bill Cosby on film for the third time in this lacklustre ghost comedy. Cosby is a family man who dies in a car crash but survives on earth as a spirit. The story outlives his demise 10 minutes into the film, but not for long and soon does a disappearing act of its own. There are plenty of laughs from the special effects as ghostly Cosby tries to tie up one last business deal to provide for his grieving family's future, but once the invisibility gag has been played a couple of times, the novelty wears off. Poitier directs with vitality and verve, but he's badly served by the tedious script.

Ghost and the Darkness, The ● Ⓥ

1996, US/S Afr, 110 mins, colour
Dir: Stephen Hopkins
Stars: Val Kilmer, Michael Douglas, John Kani, Tom Wilkinson, Bernard Hill
Rating: ★★★

Africa 1896: two lions, hunting together for sport rather than food, almost put paid to the East African Railroad by the simple expedient of eating scores of its workers. The British engineer in charge of building a bridge there (Kilmer) is eventually joined by a famous white hunter (Douglas), but the legendary lions survive to kill and kill again on a mixture of luck and cunning. The result, at its best, is a handsome adventure story with a frenziedly exciting last reel: the downside is that there's lot of hanging around waiting for the lions to come and the plot quickly develops into coyote and road runner stuff as the beasts contemptuously evade all traps set for them. Kilmer is excellent with his complex mixture of calm, bravado and uncertainty. But Douglas is a touch too wild-eyed as a sort of Cactus Jack of the African plains.

Ghost Goes West, The ○

1935, UK, 85 mins, b/w
Dir: René Clair
Stars: Robert Donat, Jean Parker, Eugene Pallette, Elsa Lanchester
Rating: ★★★★

Charming, amusing and eminently watchable ghost comedy, directed at a spanking pace by René Clair. Robert Donat plays both the Scottish hero and his ghostly double, and Jean Parker is quite delightful as the American girl with whom he falls in love. The Scottish scenes are atmospherically romantic – quite an achievement for a Frenchman who had never been north of the border. But Harold Rosson's elegant black-and-white photography undoubtedly helped him out a lot.

Ghost of Frankenstein, The ◐

1942, US, 68 mins, b/w
Dir: Erle C Kenton
Stars: Lon Chaney Jr, Cedric Hardwicke, Bela Lugosi, Lionel Atwill
Rating: ★★★

The son also rises, in this case the bold, bad Baron's second son Cedric Hardwicke, continuing his dad's pioneering work with the best of intentions, only to be sabotaged by evil Lionel Atwill and crazy Bela Lugosi, repeating his role from *Son of Frankenstein*. Lon Chaney Jr takes over from Boris Karloff as the Creature in this sadly underrated film – the best of the Universal series after *Bride of Frankenstein*. Director Erle C Kenton, who ten years before had made the Charles Laughton horror classic *Island of Lost Souls*, creates some really chilling moments, especially when Ygor (Lugosi) is reborn within the Creature.

Ghost of St Michael's, The ○

1941, UK, 82 mins, b/w
Dir: Marcel Varnel
Stars: Will Hay, Charles Hawtrey
Rating: ★★★

Will Hay's last film in his famous role of the disreputable schoolmaster, this time in a comedy about a school evacuated to a sinister castle in wartime. Things go bump in the night and successive headmasters keep getting bumped off in a successful chiller comedy that gives Hay some hilarious tomfoolery with his schoolboys, as well as a very compatible new teammate in moon-faced Claude Hulbert.

Ghost Story ●

1981, US, 110 mins, colour
Dir: John Irwin
Stars: Fred Astaire, Mervyn Douglas, Douglas Fairbanks Jr, John Houseman
Rating: ★★★

A formidable quartet of veteran actors – Fred Astaire, Melvyn Douglas, Douglas Fairbanks Jr and John

Houseman – is assembled for this story of a vengeful ghost. The plot has more loose ends than apparitions, which is going some, but the four old smoothies, Astaire especially, see it through.

Ghost Train, The ○

1941, UK, 85 mins, b/w
Dir: Walter Forde
Stars: Arthur Askey, Richard Murdoch, Kathleen Harrison
Rating: ★★★

The third film version of Arnold Ridley's famous play about a group of passengers stranded at a small and sinister rural railway station. It's loaded with chuckles, chills and tailored to the talents of its stars, Arthur Askey and Richard Murdoch.

Ghosts of Mississippi ○ Ⓥ

(aka: Ghosts from the Past)
1996, US, 131 mins, colour
Dir: Rob Reiner
Stars: Alec Baldwin, Whoopi Goldberg, James Wood, Craig T Nelson, Virginia Madsen
Rating: ★★★

This is a memorably emotive subject, but full justice has not quite been done to it here. In 1963, a black Civil Rights leader was shot and killed on his own doorstep by a white racist (Woods), who was freed after two successive all-white juries failed to agree. 25 years later, new findings came to light, and the case was re-prosecuted by a determined assistant DA (Baldwin) and his at-first dubious boss (Nelson). It takes Baldwin a long time to win Nelson over. He loses his wife (Madsen) in the process and only gets the breakthrough after finally gaining the confidence of the victim's widow (Goldberg). The latter seems miscast and her evidence at the hearing unnecessary – we have already seen the crime. There's also some clunky dialogue, especially for Baldwin, and the film as a whole lacks dramatic force. There's times, though, and thank goodness for them, when its message does get across. Thanks to the facts, you'll stay in there for the verdict.

Ghoul, The ◐

1933, UK, 79 mins, b/w
Dir: T Hayes Hunter
Stars: Boris Karloff, Cedric Hardwicke, Ernest Thesiger, Dorothy Hyson
Rating: ★★

Having left England as an unknown nearly a quarter of a decade before, Boris Karloff was welcomed back with

a fanfare of trumpets for his first British starring role, a chiller piece specifically prepared with him in mind. Although visually stylish, the film has a cramped look that suggests a surprisingly low budget, and keeps it below the level of Karloff's best Thirties' work. But the photography, by Gunther Krampf, and make-up, by Heinrich Heitfield, is certainly on a par with his work for Universal. Cedric Hardwicke scores nicely as a conniving solicitor and Ralph Richardson makes his film debut.

Giant ○ Ⓥ

1956, US, 197 mins, colour
Dir: George Stevens
Stars: Elizabeth Taylor, Rock Hudson, James Dean
Rating: ★★★★

Rock Hudson and James Dean were both nominated for an Oscar, in this sprawling, towering adaptation of Edna Ferber's novel of cattle and oil barons. The publicity described the film as 'bigger than Texas itself' and director George Stevens, who did win an Oscar, was able to endow the film with a wealth of personal detail. He also took a courageous stand over the exploitation of Mexican workers. The first two-thirds of the film are stirring stuff, but its grip relaxes rather too much towards the end, and Dean (whose last film this was before his death in a car crash) grapples rather unsteadily with his character once it has progressed to middle age.

GI Blues ○ Ⓥ

1960, US, 100 mins, colour
Dir: Norman Taurog
Stars: Elvis Presley, Juliet Prowse, Robert Ivers, Leticia Roman, James Douglas, Sigrid Maier
Rating: ★★★

Elvis Presley's first film back in Civvy Street after military service is a bright and breezy affair. He's a tank commander in Germany who makes a $300 bet with his army buddies that he can bed icy night club singer Juliet Prowse. Along the way, Elvis churns out such hits as 'Blue Suede Shoes' and 'Wooden Heart' but the script is strictly sub-standard fare, little more than a series of numbers loosely strung around a trite and thin plot.

Gideon of Scotland Yard ○

(aka: Gideon's Day)
1958, UK, 91 mins, colour
Dir: John Ford
Stars: Jack Hawkins, Dianne Foster,

G

Anna Lee, Anna Massey
Rating: ★★★

An incident-packed account of life at Scotland Yard, driving home the point that a policeman's lot is not a happy one. A pleasing addition to the ranks of genteel crime thrillers. Homely fun, stocked with British stalwarts, touched with wry humour. Directed, astonishingly, by John Ford.

Gidget ○
1959, US, 105 mins, colour
Dir: Paul Wendkos
Stars: Sandra Dee, James Darren, Cliff Robertson
Rating: ★★

Happy-go-lucky Sandra Dee became the role model of countless teenage girls in the 1950s. In this beach comedy that led to a slew of sequels and TV movies, she's Gidget (nickname for 'girl midget'), who falls in love with James Darren during a summer of sun and fun. The best of the series, but that's not saying very much!

Gift Horse, The ○
(aka: Glory at Sea)
1952, UK, 100 mins, b/w
Dir: Compton Bennett
Stars: Trevor Howard, Richard Attenborough, Joan Rice, Sonny Tufts
Rating: ★★★

The British seldom went wrong with war films, and this fine piece of craftmanship is in the tradition of *In Which We Serve*. It tells of an old destroyer – given by the Americans to the British navy – that's just about ready for the junkyard, its martinet skipper (Trevor Howard, excellent), its crew and the difficulties they overcome to weld a fighting partnership. Supporting roles are solidly well-acted by a cast that includes Richard Attenborough, glamour girl Joan Rice and American star Sonny Tufts, making his first film for three years.

Gigi ○ ⓥ
1958, US, 119 mins, colour
Dir: Vincente Minnelli
Stars: Leslie Caron, Maurice Chevalier, Louis Jourdan, Hermione Gingold, Eva Gabor
Rating: ★★★★★

Delightful musical that took nine Academy Awards, equalling the record set by *Gone With the Wind*. Maurice Chevalier, as the old man with a twinkle in his eye for 'leetle girls', got a special Oscar 'for his contribution to the world of entertainment for more

than half a century'. Among other award-winners were Vincente Minnelli for his direction, Cecil Beaton (costume design), Andre Previn (score), and Lerner and Loewe for their songs and lyrics. Miss Caron sang and danced in effortless fashion as the heroine of the turn-of-the-century story, which was based on a tale by Colette.

G.I. Jane ● ⓥ
1997, US, 125 mins, colour
Dir: Ridley Scott
Stars: Demi Moore, Viggo Mortensen, Anne Bancroft, Scott Wilson
Rating: ★★★★

Although it goes over the top at the end in the way Hollywood just can't seem to resist, this is an adrenalin-surging action film with some interesting undertones of political chicanery. Already passed over for acting service in the Gulf War, Lt Jordan O' Neil (Moore), a triathlon champ, marksman and all-round smart egg, finds herself selected as a guinea pig – the first woman to train to become a Navy SEAL, in a gruelling, rib-cracking, three-month training course. Sixty per cent dropout: for Jordan, as the posters remind us failure is not an option. You'll be stunned at the savage physical beatings the trainees suffer in a part of the country where it always seems to be raining – but Moore, ideally cast for once, does make you believe she might get through. Director Scott's savage editing technique makes the training scenes pulse with movement. And stand by to gasp when tough company sergeant Mortensen cracks his own broken nose back in joint.

Gilda ○ ⓥ
1946, US, 110 mins, b/w
Dir: Charles Vidor
Stars: Rita Hayworth, Glenn Ford, George Macready, Joseph Calleia
Rating: ★★★★

Of all the femmes fatales of the Forties, Rita Hayworth's Gilda is perhaps the most vivid in the memory. First seen sitting on a bed, tossing back her long tawny hair, every man's image of the immediate post-war sex symbol par excellence, she glides sinuously through a story of deceit, danger and ambition for power. The ambition is that of her husband, magnetically played by George Macready, a scarred death's head of a man who runs a sumptuous gambling casino in Buenos Aires, and aims to become the world's most pow-

erful tycoon. The fly in the ointment is Johnny (Glenn Ford), the tycoon's junior partner, who was once Gilda's lover. Director Charles Vidor had worked with all three principal actors in previous films, and here he uses them as a team to produce an atmosphere loaded with eroticism and menace. Macready's white house, a sort of Gatsby mansion gone to the devil, is, with the gambling casino it contains, an art director's dream. But it's Hayworth you'll remember, in the film that made her *the* siren: whether singing 'Put the Blame on Mame, Boys' or stripping off long black gloves in an unforgettable night-club scene.

Girl Can't Help It, The ○ ⓥ
1956, US, 95 mins, colour
Dir: Frank Tashlin
Stars: Tom Ewell, Jayne Mansfield, Edmond O'Brien, Henry Jones
Rating: ★★★

Full of visual gags, as you'd expect from director Frank Tashlin, this good-natured comedy-musical full of harmlessly dubious humour has Tom Ewell as the out-of-work press agent trying to make voluptuous, but dumb, Jayne Mansfield into a star and thereby justify his engagement to over-the-hill gangster Edmond O'Brien. In the event, the film did make Mansfield a star, albeit not for long; it also preserved on celluloid forever no less than 14 rock 'n' rollers of the period.

Girl Crazy ⊙
1943, US, 95 mins, b/w
Dir: Norman Taurog
Stars: Mickey Rooney, Judy Garland; 'Rags' Ragland, June Allyson
Rating: ★★★★

Of all the Mickey Rooney-Judy Garland musicals made at MGM, this is the most fully realised: And hardly surprising with a score by George and Ira Gershwin that includes 'But Not for Me', 'I Got Rhythm', 'Embraceable You' and 'Fascinatin' Rhythm' and the marvellously-staged (by Charles Walters) 'Bidin' My Time'. All this, plus a finale masterminded by Busby Berkeley, who was originally set to direct the entire film. The story is tediously familiar – Rooney's a bad boy but comes good in the end – but the stars perform with enough energy for half a dozen musicals.

Girl Happy ○ ⓥ
1965, US, 96 mins, colour
Dir: Boris Sagal

Stars: Elvis Presley, Shelley Fabares
Rating: ★★★

One of Elvis' liveliest and funniest offerings. He plays a musician who finds himself chaperon to a vivacious teenage girl. The tunes – including 'Girl Happy', 'Do The Clam', 'Puppet on a String', 'She's Evil' and 'Do Not Disturb' – nearly all have that something extra; and Shelley Fabares is a cute little package who can even survive a sunset kiss. When she finds Elvis has been squiring her on orders, she gets drunk and starts doing a striptease in a local nightclub. Elvis saves her, and his U certificate, in the nick of time. Mary Arm Mobley, a former Miss America, is also sparky in support.

Girl in Room 17, The
See: Vice Squad

Girl in the Headlines ○
(aka: The Model Murder Case)
1963, UK, 93 mins, b/w
Dir: Michael Truman
Stars: Ian Hendry, Ronald Fraser
Rating: ★★★

Thriller fans can play spot-the-killer while film fans play spot-the-face in this cleverly plotted thriller with a gallery of 'second-line' stars to make up the suspects. Among those on Inspector Ian Hendry's list are Kieron Moore, Peter Arne, Jane Asher, Rosalie Crutchley, Patrick Holt, Zena Walker, James Villiers and Robert Harris. It's based on a novel called *The Nose On My Face* by another well known actor, Laurence Payne. Hendry and Fraser are in fine form as the two policemen on the case, and dominate the film.

Girl in the Picture, The ◑
1985, UK, 85 mins, colour
Dir: Cary Parker
Stars: John Gordon Sinclair, Irina Brook, David McCay, Gregor Fisher
Rating: ★★

We're back in the country mapped out by director Bill Forsyth in this Glasgow-set romantic comedy which is, if you like, *Gregory's Girl* five years on. John Gordon Sinclair gives young photographer Alan very much Gregory's character in this story in which he finds, like Judy Garland's Dorothy, that happiness may lie in your own backyard all the time. Sinclair can do wonders with words like 'Good', 'Great' and 'Nice' and his picaresque adventures in search of the girl of his dreams have a certain charm

and are sometimes wryly funny in their observation of life as it is. It must also be admitted, though, that the film is much too slow and that Cary Parker's script and direction, though often wittily observant, aren't quite good enough to overcome that handicap altogether.

Girl In the Red Velvet Swing, The ○ ⓥ
1955, US, 109 mins, colour
Dir: Richard Fleischer
Stars: Ray Milland, Joan Collins, Farley Granger
Rating: ★★★★

Here's an excellent film that relies more on the skills of its director, writers, photograper and designer for its impact than on the acting abilities of its stars. This is a first-class reconstruction by writers Walter Reisch and Charles Brackett of a cause celebre that rocked America just after the turn of the century. Joan Collins, acting with more depth than she had shown in British films, Ray Milland, and Farley Granger, giving his best performance since *Strangers on a Train*, provide the three points of an explosive eternal triangle which inevitably ends in murder. Polished direction by Richard Fleischer.

Girl on Approval ○
1962, UK, 75 mins, b/w
Dir: Charles Frend
Stars: Rachel Roberts, James Maxwell, Annette Whiteley
Rating: ★★★

A penetrating low-budget film about the problems of being foster-parents to a 14-year-old girl angry with the world. Rachel Roberts, just after her triumph in *Saturday Night and Sunday Morning*, gives another fine performance in a very different role, as the suburban mum who finds her marriage under severe strain as she and her husband try to cope with – and love – their rebellious foster-daughter. Under Charles Frend's caring direction, the film pulls all the right emotional strings, as well as making you think.

Girl Rush, The ○
1955, US, 85 mins, colour
Dir: Robert Pirosh
Stars: Rosalind Russell, Fernando Lamas, Eddie Albert, Gloria de Haven
Rating: ★★

Scatterbrained musical comedy about a woman who inherits a share in a tumbledown Las Vegas hotel, and plans to

turn it into a glittering nightclub. Rosalind Russell is enthusiasm itself, Fernando Lamas works hard at being the Latin lover, and Gloria de Haven shows again what a superb dancing star she could have been, if her kind of musical hadn't gone out of style.

Girls at Sea ○
1958, UK, 80 mins, colour
Dir: Gilbert Gunn
Stars: Guy Rolfe, Ronald Shiner, Alan White
Rating: ★

Locked doors, complex explanations, young women dashing around in their nightwear – in fact, all the usual ingredients of farce are the order of the day in this creaky adaptation of the play *The Middle Watch*. Plunging headlong into the fun are Daniel Massey as a gauche lieutenant and, very briefly, old Alf Garnett himself, Warren Mitchell as Arthur. Watch for Ian Holm in his film debut.

Girls He Left Behind, The
See: The Gang's All Here [1943]

Girls Just Want to Have Fun ○
1985, US, 87 mins, colour
Dir: Alan Metter
Stars: Sarah Jessica Parker, Lee Montgomery, Helen Hunt, Jonathan Silverman, Ed Lauter, Shannen Doherty
Rating: ★★★

Quite tolerable as teen movies go, with a fair sprinkling of funny lines, *Girls* is way above the class average for this kind of thing, even though the music numbers are, as ever, graced with ear-splitting sound. Leads Sarah Jessica Parker and Lee Montgomery, both former child players, are personable as the couple from different sides of the tracks who are paired together as dancers for the big contest. They impress as people rather more than as dancers, an area in which glamorous villainess Holly Gagnier looks a bit better than they do.

Girls of Pleasure Island, The ○
1953, US, 95 mins, colour
Dir: F Hugh Herbert
Stars: Leo Genn, Don Taytor, Audrey Dalton, Gene Barry
Rating: ★★★★

Sentimental Hollywood sob-stuff at its very best, superbly scripted by F Hugh Herbert, who wrings the last tear out of a heart-rending ending. Fine acting from Audrey Dalton and

G

Don Taylor brings these characters to life; and watch out in the supporting cast for Elsa Lanchester, giving us another in her catalogue of delightfully dotty females.

Give My Regards to Broad Street ○
1984, UK, 108 mins, colour
Dir: Peter Webb
Stars: Paul McCartney, Bryan Brown, Ringo Starr, Barbara Bach
Rating: ★★

Closer in spirit to The Beatles' own whimsical excesses in their 1967 *Magical Mystery Tour* TV film than the irreverent wit of the features they made with Richard Lester, Paul McCartney's big budget extravaganza is engagingly old-fashioned in outlook. The flimsy story line is subordinate to its artful selection of songs made famous by The Beatles and McCartney's own group, Wings. Ralph Richardson, in his last screen role, appears in an enigmatic cameo.

Give My Regards to Broadway ○
1948, US, 95 mins, colour
Dir: Lloyd Bacon
Stars: Dan Dailey, Charles Winninger, Nancy Guild, Charlie Ruggles
Rating: ★★★

Dan Dailey taps a relaxed dancing path through this pleasant musical about the dying days of vaudeville, and sings several standards, including the title song. Proceedings are additionally brightened both by screen veterans Charles Winninger and Sig Ruman, and by three of the loveliest aspiring actresses of the time, Nancy Guild, Barbara Lawrence and Jane Nigh.

Gladiator, The ● ⓥ
1992, US, 101 mins, colour
Dir: Rowdy Herrington
Stars: James Marshall, Cuba Gooding Jr, Brian Dennehy, Robert Loggia, Ossie Davis, John Heard
Rating: ★★

A brutal backstreets boxing picture, with all the ingredients beloved of cinematic filmgoers down the years. The crooked promoter (Brian Dennehy) who blackmails our young hero (James Marshall) into staying in the (illegal) ring. The dirty fighter who blinds and kills Marshall's best friend. The loyal girlfriend, the promoter's moll, the feckless father, the promoter's hustler and the friend (Cuba Gooding Jr, mysteriously billed above Marshall) who

must be fought and maybe killed in the ring. They're all here, residents from Hollywood's boxing hall of fame, with the twist that the promoter is an ex-light heavyweight champ who himself provides the final opponent when our hero makes his bid to break free and seek a college education. Not a punching cliché fails to land. As you reel out of the cinema, the producers hope you may be too punch-drunk to remember where you've seen it all before.

Glass Bottom Boat, The ○
1966, US, 110 mins, colour
Dir: Frank Tashlin
Stars: Doris Day, Rod Taylor, Arthur Godfrey
Rating: ★★★★

Inventive, rib-tickling comedy about a girl who is chased by spies for secrets from the space laboratory where she works. Director Frank Tashlin brings a lunatic quality to his visual jokes. One remembers with particular affection Doris Day's vacuum cleaner: it looks like a dog and springs from its 'kennel' with alarming rapidity whenever a scrap of litter hits its beloved floor.

Glass Key, The ◉
1942, US, 85 mins, b/w
Dir: Stuart Heisler
Stars: Alan Ladd, Veronica Lake, Brian Donlevy, William Bendix
Rating: ★★★★

Tough, busy thriller in which a shady politician's sidekick just about keeps his boss out of trouble at some damage to life and limb. Jonathan Latimer's dialogue is memorably hard-boiled. William Bendix steals the show as a brutal heavy.

Glass Menagerie, The ○
1987, US, 130 mins, colour
Dir: Paul Newman
Stars: Joanne Woodward, John Malkovich, Karen Allen
Rating: ★★★

Paul Newman wisely doesn't attempt to 'open up' Tennessee Williams' claustrophobic one-set play about a family suffering from its own delusions. Except for an occasional visit to the fire escape or a nearby tenement, the action is confined to the Wingfield family's apartment. The biggest surprise in the top-notch cast is Karen Allen, still best known as Harrison Ford's feisty sidekick in *Raiders of the Lost Ark*. Her interpretation of Laura, Tom's shy crippled sister, lifts Newman's adaptation from the catego-

ry of well-meaning to memorable. Occasionally he will focus too long on things, but these are small irritations.

Glass Web, The ○
1953, US, 82 mins, b/w
Dir: Jack Arnold
Stars: Edward G Robinson, John Forsythe, Marcia Henderson, Richard Denning, Kathleeen Hughes
Rating: ★★★

Creepy, brisk, tightly knit thriller, in which the web is a frame-up for murder and the glass that of the television screen. Originally released as a second-feature to Norman Wisdom's first comedy, *The Glass Web* is much better than that would indicate. Ruthlessly professional acting from Edward G Robinson and John Forsythe, and compelling direction by Jack Arnold ensure that the suspense never sags.

Gleaming the Cube ○ ⓥ
1988, US, 104 mins, colour
Dir: Graeme Clifford
Stars: Christian Slater, Steven Bauer, Min Luong, Micole Mercurio
Rating: ★★

This ho-hum thriller about a teenager out to revenge his brother's killing is taken slightly away from the ordinary by its skateboarding theme and by the involvement of its city's Vietnamese community. That said, the results are at least 20 minutes too long, with skateboarding and other slowing-down elements continually sidetracking the main plot. Full of incidents seemingly put in just to make striking moments in the plot – what teenager would really turn up half-way through his brother's funeral? – it's presentably acted, with Christian Slater parading an early variant on his 'alienated' personality, but tests the patience long before the end.

Glengarry Glen Ross ● ⓥ
1992, US, 100 mins, colour
Dir: James Foley
Stars: Al Pacino, Jack Lemmon, Alec Baldwin, Alan Arkin, Ed Harris, Jonathan Pryce
Rating: ★★

With this adaptation of his own exceptionally foul-mouthed play, writer David Mamet attempts to make a giant-sized drama out of an anecdote about little men with little problems. Only the presence of an all-star cast saves the film version from being a complete grind to watch. Al Pacino, Jack Lemmon, Ed Harris and Alan Arkin are life-soured, short-fused real estate salesman given impossible 'leads' by their head office, with the threat of being fired if they don't sell property. Did anyone ever operate like this? Even if they did, it just seems so unlikely that you get almost as testy about the idea as the characters, one of whom is driven to break into his own office and steal 'good' leads that lie locked in a safe. It all seems pretty potty, but at least the actors give it 100 per cent spit and bile. Everything these characters do is a spiel, but, try as they might, even these driven salesmen can't sell this monotonous movie.

Glenn Miller Story, The ○ ⓥ
1954, US, 116 mins, colour
Dir: Anthony Mann
Stars: James Stewart, June Allyson
Rating: ★★★★

One of the best and most enduring musical biographies ever to come out of Hollywood, packed to the gills with a clutch of hit tunes, from 'Little Brown Jug', 'Chattanooga Choo Choo' and 'In the Mood' to 'String of Pearls' and 'Pennsylvania 6-5000'. Not surprisingly, it was one of the top box office hits of the year. James Stewart looks every inch the trombonist who scrimped and saved and hocked his instrument over the years to make it as a big band composer. Pretty June Allyson had her best role in years as Miller's wife – although she does look younger in the tear-jerking final scenes than the start of the film, set 20 years previously. An added bonus are the appearances of Louis Armstrong and Gene Krupa, blowing up a storm in a Harlem night club scene.

Glimmer Man, The ● ⓥ
1996, US, 92 mins, colour
Dir: John Gray
Stars: Steven Seagal, Keenen Ivory Wayans, Bob Gunton, Brian Cox
Rating: ★

A backward step here for Seagal to the kind of film he was making at the beginning of the decade. Despite the strained attempts at buddy-buddy humour between Seagal and Wayans as mismatched law enforcers, this is a nasty film with few redeeming qualities in which our heroes investigate a series of ritualistic killings in which the victims are crucified against the walls of their homes. Despite the fact that the Ku Klux Klan would appear the obvious suspects, Steve soon cottons on to the fact that the Russian Mafia has something to do with it all. Heads

crack and bones rattle (or was it the other way round?) as our too, too solid hero, this time stiffer and more humourless than ever, finally gets his men. Wayans, clearly a better actor than his material, suffers nobly – as indeed will those who manage to sit through the film.

Glory ① ⓥ
1989, US, 122 mins, colour
Dir: Edward Zwick
Stars: Matthew Broderick, Denzel Washington, Cary Elwes, Morgan Freeman, Cliff DeYoung
Rating: ★★★★★

A stirring war Western with some savage and striking battle scenes, this is the story of the first black regiment to fight for the Union during the American Civil War. Its young white commander, at first reluctant to be hard on his rag-tag troops, later sees that he has to be tough before he can be comradely and generous and eventually win the love of his men. This difficult role, an introverted young man determined not to flinch from duty or from leading his men into battle, is skilfully handled by Matthew Broderick in one of his best performances. Other soldiers are perhaps cut to type, but resourcefully drawn, notably by Morgan Freeman, a gravedigger who becomes a sergeant-major, by Cary Elwes as Broderick's second-in-command, and by Denzel Washington as a black racist, whose performance won him an Oscar.

Glory Alley ○
1952, US, 77 mins, b/w
Dir: Raoul Walsh
Stars: Leslie Caron, Ralph Meeker, Gilbert Roland, Louis Armstrong
Rating: ★★

A good deal of good jazz decorates this story about a disgraced former boxer who finds renewed public glory as a Korean War hero. Louis Amstrong as the boxer's faithful trainer is like a double dose of fresh air each time he put in an appearance. And Leslie Caron appears in one of the earliest of her wholly dramatic roles. Tough-guy Ralph Meeker's the boxer. If the action scenes are the most convincing in the film, it should come as no surprise to film fans who know the work of the director Raoul Walsh, here spending an unaccustomed few weeks with MGM after working more than half his prolific career for Warner Brothers. No-one had more talent at shooting hard-hitting action than Walsh.

Glory at Sea
See: The Gift Horse

Glory Brigade, The ○
1953, US, 82 mins, b/w
Dir: Robert D Webb
Stars: Victor Mature, Lee Marvin, Richard Egan
Rating: ★★

This hard man's, Samuel Fuller-type war film was in fact directed by Robert D Webb, who gets strong performances from Victor Mature, Lee Marvin and Alexander Scourby, and keeps his action going at a fast pace, telling a good story in under 90 minutes. Outstanding black and white photography by Lucien Ballard and not a girl in sight! Good stuff for fans of Hollywood war movies, but don't expect too much subtlety.

Glory Guys, The ○
1965, US, 112 mins, colour
Dir: Arnold Laven
Stars: Tom Tryon, Harve Presnell, Senta Berger, James Caan
Rating: ★★★★

One of the best examples of the Cavalry-and-Indians Westerns from the Sixties, this Sam Peckinpah-inspired, Arnold Laven-directed adventure film, full of action, colour, a gutsy music score and firm characterisation, is a story about the Cavalry as a master, rather than about individual people. Tom Tryon is a rugged hero, and there are well-grafted portrayals from Michael Anderson Jr, Slim Pickens, James Caan (as a garrulous Irishman) and Peter Breck. As the frontier scout, Harve Presnell's magnetically sincere acting exudes the quiet authority and natural casual humour that makes one instantly identify with the character. A cohesive, gripping, anti-war Western, with brilliant colour photography by veteran cinematographer James Wong Howe.

G Men ①
1935, US, 85 mins, b/w
Dir: William Keighley
Stars: James Cagney, Ann Dvorak, Robert Armstrong, Margaret Lindsay, Lloyd Nolan, Barton MacLane
Rating: ★★★★

Once again in the fore of Warners' thriller trends, James Cagney forsakes his famous gangster roles to play an equally dedicated 'G-Man' (Federal Government agent) hunting down public enemies. The film is constructed in swift, staccato scenes by Seton I Miller and directed at a cracking pace by William Keighley.

G

Godfather, The ● ⓥ

1971, US, 175 mins, colour
Dir: Francis Ford Coppola
Stars: Marion Brando, Al Pacino, James Caan, Diane Keaton
Rating: ★★★★★

The first part of Fancis Ford Coppola's Mafia trilogy is, perhaps, the ultimate modern Hollywood gangster opus. All the lead characters are sensational, but the enduring image is of Marlon Brando as the lethal, rasping Godfather of the central New York Mafia family, his cheeks stuffed with cotton wool and his throat jammed with colloquialisms. Although the film is really the story of Brando's college-educated son, played by Al Pacino, it was Brando who won the second Oscar of his career. The film also took Academy Awards for screenplay and as best picture. Darkly brilliant.

Godfather Part II, The ● ⓥ

1974, US, 200 mins, colour
Dir: Francis Ford Coppola
Stars: Al Pacino, Robert Duvall, Diane Keaton, Robert De Niro
Rating: ★★★★★

An even more satisfying film than its much-lauded predecessor, this was the first sequel ever to win a Best Film Oscar – the same as the original film. Al Pacino is in commanding form as the head of the Corleone Mafia family, following the death of godfather Marlon Brando, but he is given a run for his money in an at first confusing sub-plot from Robert De Niro, who plays Brando's character as a young man, revealing his entry into crime from his arrival in America as a penni-less immigrant. There is death and bloodshed by the bucketful, directed with an unmistakable flourish by Francis Ford Coppola, who in all three *Godfather* films juxtaposes the most stunning execution scenes with the calm and serenity of Church cere-monies, such as weddings, christenings and confirmations. The acting is flaw-less, particularly from De Niro, who even beat his acting teacher, Lee Strasberg, to an Oscar; and it's impos-sible not to be swept along by the exhilarating twists and turns of the plot.

Godfather Part III, The ● ⓥ

1990, US, 161 mins, colour
Dir: Francis Ford Coppola
Stars: Al Pacino, Diane Keaton, Talia Shire, Andy Garcia, Eli Wallach, Bridget Fonda
Rating: ★★

Parts I and II were long, but brilliant cinema. Part III, alas, is just long and very slow. Directorial flair and acting charisma are notably absent from this chapter (presumably the last), which deals more or less with a single episode in the later life of Michael Corleone (still Al Pacino). His bastard nephew (the faceless Andy Garcia) falls in love with Michael's daughter (Sofia Coppola) and sets in motion a chain of events which drags Michael back down from semi-respectability into high-pro-file gang wars and even the assassination of the Pope. Pacino, look-ing like a sawn-off Stallone, also sports a Brando hoarseness which detracts from the magnetism of the performance. Shire is the personification of evil as Pacino's sister, but Keaton now seems out of place as his wife. There's no dy-namism in Coppola's direction and the story shuffles along like a Sicilian peas-ant leading a donkey. After more than two-and-a-half hours, you echo Pacino's lament when he asks, 'Where the hell does it end?'

God's Little Acre ◑

1958, US, 110 mins, b/w
Dir: Anthony Mann
Stars: Robert Ryan, Tina Louise, Aldo Ray, Jack Lord, Buddy Hackett, Vic Morrow
Rating: ★★★

Anthony Mann's earthy film adapta-tion of Erskine Caldwell's novel started a whole rash of inferior imita-tions after its appearance. Robert Ryan, long one of Hollywood's most underrated actors, gets right under the skin of the grizzled, free-living Ty Ty Walden, the Georgia farmer who be-lieves he has gold hidden on his land. Aldo Ray and Tina Louise perspire with passion: nobody smiles much.

Godspell ○

1973, US, 103 mins, colour
Dir: David Greene
Stars: Victor Garber, David Haskell, Lynne Thigpen, Katie Hanley
Rating: ★★

Although it has the original Broadway cast aboard, this musical based on the Gospel according to St Matthew never quite bridges the gap between stage and screen. But the cast's vivacity is sometimes infectious, and the score in-cludes 'Day By Day' (the show's big hit), 'Turn Back, O Man', 'All Good Gifts' and 'Beautiful City'. Updated parables include a version of The Prodigal Son illustrated by clips from silent films.

Go for a Take ○

1972, UK, 90 mins, colour
Dir: Harry Booth
Stars: Reg Varney, Norman Rossington, Sue Lloyd, Dennis Price
Rating: ★★

An above-average British comedy of its time, *Go for a Take* runs very much along the lines of a Norman Wisdom romp, giving rubber-faced Reg Varney the opportunity to run amok through a film studio as submarine officer, vam-pire victim, knight, gunman, prisoner, waiter, Tarzan and Viking warrior. It makes clean and pleasant comedy, al-though the apparent budget and shooting restrictions imposed on the film force its star from time to time into some desperate mugging that only his fans and younger children will find funny.

Going in Style ○

1979, US, 96 mins, colour
Dir: Martin Brest
Stars: George Burns, Art Carney
Rating: ★★★

Superb work by the three elderly stars (George Burns, Lee Strasberg and Art Carney) as a trio of old codgers who execute a bank robbery to relieve bore-dom, ensures that this comedy does indeed go in style. Also good are Charles Hallahan and Pamela Payton Wright as the young couple who even-tually end up with the loot.

Going My Way ○

1944, US, 126 mins, b/w
Dir: Leo McCarey
Stars: Bing Crosby, Barry Fitzgerald, Rise Stevens
Rating: ★★★

Leo McCarey's film about a down-to-earth priest who alters the lives of those around him seemed to skate more skilfully around its sentiment than it does to the more jaded view of today. But Bing Crosby was certainly rarely better, Barry Fitzgerald's older priest added a much-needed vein of saltiness, and the film swept all before it at the Academy Awards of its year: Oscars for best film, best director (McCarey), best actor (Crosby), best supporting actor (Fitzgerald) and three more, including one for its hit song, 'Swingin' on a Star'. A huge popular success. A sequel had to follow and it did: *The Bells of St Mary's*.

Goin' South ◑

1978, US, 109 mins, colour
Dir: Jack Nicholson
Stars: Jack Nicholson, Mary

Steenburgen, John Belushi
Rating: ★★★

Although unusual in quality, this
Western plays a variation on a familiar
theme: the rough-hewn man who goes
to work for a fiercely independent
woman and ends up on her side, not
to mention in her bed. The variation
here is that our 'hero' is an especially
disreputable outlaw (Jack Nicholson,
who also directed) saved from the
hangman's noose by a marriage of
convenience to Mary Steenburgen,
who works a useless goldmine (look
out, here comes the plot) left to her by
her father. Nicholson the director
does just fine, but Nicholson the actor
suffers from the strain of split responsibilities, his usual well-modulated
performance often going over the top,
leaving the film relying on the very appealing performance of Steenburgen to
keep our sympathy and the story
going.

Go Into Your Dance ○
(aka: Casino de Paree)
1935, US, 85 mins, b/w
Dir: Archie Mayo
Stars: Al Jolson, Ruby Keeler, Helen
Morgan, Glenda Farrell, Barton
MacLane, Akim Tamiroff
Rating: ★★

The only screen teaming of Al Jolson
and his then-wife Ruby Keeler, heavy
on histrionics and notable chiefly for a
Harry Warren-Al Dubin score (the
composers also appear briefly on
screen together) that includes 'About a
Quarter to Nine' (reprised in *The Jolson
Story*), 'She's a Latin from Manhattan'
and (sung by Helen Morgan) 'The
Little Things You Used to Do'.

Gold ○
1974, UK, 124 mins, colour
Dir: Peter Hunt
Stars: Roger Moore, Susannah York,
Ray Milland, Bradford Dillman
Rating: ★★

This action film starts like a sizzler,
pitching you headlong into a dramatic
story about treachery in high places
which rebounds on those in low places
– condemning hundreds of gold-min-
ers to a watery grave. Roger Moore is
the husky hero, immaculate in matching denims, white or blue. Susannah
York is the husky-voiced heroine who
conclusively out-acts an otherwise all-
male cast. Away from its pulsating
action scenes down the mine, the film
has less substance to offer. But director Peter Hunt knows all about thrills.
He's less successful in a scene in which

Moore and Miss York take a bath together, where both stars seem to be
struggling hard to repress a fit of the
giggles.

Gold Diggers in Paris ○
(aka: The Gay Imposters)
1938, US, 100 mins, b/w
Dir: Ray Enright
Stars: Rudy Vallee, Rosemary Lane,
Hugh Herbert, Allen Jenkins
Rating: ★★★

Fifth and last in the Warner *Gold
Diggers* series, which had started nine
years earlier; this one is distinctly light
on plot, but saved as usual by the
Busby Berkeley musical numbers despite the fact that the great dance
director was by now working on a severely restricted budget. Rudy Vallee
at the height of his radio fame still
failed to make the transition to screen
stardom, but there's a vintage score by
Johnny Mercer, Al Dubin and Harry
Warren.

Gold Diggers of 1933 ○
1933, US, 96 mins, b/w
Dir: Mervyn LeRoy
Stars: Warren William, Joan Blondell
Rating: ★★★★★

Opening with the stunning number
'We're in the Money', with Ginger
Rogers (as Fay Fortune!) clad from
head to toe in silver dollars, this
Depression musical scores in every department and proved that when it came
to staging dance numbers, Busby
Berkeley was peerless. Warners dusted
off the 1929 play *Gold Diggers* of
Broadway for the storyline but it was
the song and dance numbers that make
this film so memorable today. From
the silhouetted (but clearly nude)
dancers of 'Pettin' in the Park' to 60 vi-
olin-playing chorines in 'The Shadow
Waltz' and the emotional climax, 'My
Forgotten Man', which boasted 150 extras playing soldiers back from World
War One with no hope of employment,
the numbers boasted an atmosphere
and personality all their own.

Gold Diggers of 1935 ○ ⓥ
1935, US, 95 mins, b/w
Dir: Busby Berkeley
Stars: Dick Powell, Adolphe Menjou,
Gloria Stuart, Wini Shaw, Glenda Farrell
Rating: ★★★★

There's not a lot of plot in this
Warners musical, but director Busby
Berkeley pulls out all the stops on the
choreography – culminating in the sensational 'Lullaby of Broadway', which
remained his own personal favourite

among all the numbers he staged for
screen musicals. Look closely at the
56 moving miniature pianos in one
scene and see if you can spot the 56
men who are concealed beneath them.

Gold Diggers of 1937 ○
1936, US, 101 mins, b/w
Dir: Lloyd Bacon
Stars: Dick Powell, Joan Blondell, Victor
Moore, Glenda Farrell
Rating: ★★★

This musical continued the fabulous
Gold Diggers series, although perhaps
the lustre was just beginning to dim.
Joan Blondell is back partnering Dick
Powell and they are the 'good guys' in
this quite substantial story of an insurance fraud that does not quite turn out
as planned. But of course it's all just
an excuse for the lavish song and
dance numbers. *42nd Street* director
Lloyd Bacon here achieves attractive
performances from the two stars and
some delightful comedy from Victor
Moore (as the elderly Broadway producer) and Glenda Farrell (as the
gold-digger who pursues him) while
choreographer Busby Berkeley provided some more of his stunning
production numbers notably 'Let's Put
Our Heads Together', featuring 50
couples in huge rocking chairs, and a
fabulous finale involving 70 young
ladies marching across a glossy floor to
Al Dubin and Harry Warren's 'All's
Fair in Love and War'.

Gold in the Streets ● ⓥ
1996, UK, 98 mins, colour
Dir: Elizabeth Gill
Stars: Jared Harris, Aiden Gillen, Ian
Hart, Kevin Geery, James Belushi
Rating: ★

A borderline-tedious film about Irish
immigrants in New York City. One
(Hart) is clearly doomed. Another
(Harris) is saving for his own restaurant back home, but fails to go when
he's doshed up. A third (Aiden Gillen)
gets in with a rich girl, and the newcomer (Geery) is plainly destined for a
humdrum existence amidst New
York's Irish colony. No *Circle of Friends*
here: the problems of these people
don't amount to a hill of beans, and
you'd be an eedjit to get involved.

Golden Blade, The ⊙
1953, US, 80 mins, colour
Dir: Nathan Juran
Stars: Rock Hudson, Piper Laurie,
George Macready, Kathleen Hughes,
Gene Evans
Rating: ★★

G

Arabian Nights adventure, with brisk action and a story about a magic sword. Rock Hudson and Piper Laurie try not to look embarrassed: both, though, were soon to move on to better things.

Golden Boy ○

1939, US, 99 mins, b/w
Dir: Rouben Mamoulian
Stars: William Holden, Barbara Stanwyck, Adolphe Menjou
Rating: ★★★

Boxing gloves or a violinist's bow? That's the choice facing poor Joe in this Thirties drama from the play by Clifford Odets. The film made a star of the young William Holden, as the hero torn between two talents – boxing and music. Much feted in its day, but its lack of genuine emotive appeal has dated it.

Golden Child, The ① ⓥ

1986, US, 93 mins, colour
Dir: Michael Ritchie
Stars: Eddie Murphy, Charles Dance, Charlotte Lewis
Rating: ★★★

Much maligned but actually far more enjoyable than some Eddie Murphy ventures, this unashamed *Indiana Jones* style hokum casts Murphy as a childfinder called to Tibet to find the child of the title, capable of bringing peace to the earth, but now kidnapped by evil forces. Charles Dance will doubtless want to forget his role as the villain, but the proceedings are colourful, action-packed, inventive and punched along at powerhouse pace by director Michael Ritchie. With his usually salty language restricted by the need to make a 'family' entertainment, Murphy is actually quite likeable!

GoldenEye ① ⓥ

1995, UK, 130 mins, colour
Dir: Martin Campbell
Stars: Pierce Brosnan, Izabella Scorupco, Sean Bean, Famke Janssen, Judi Dench, Robbie Coltrane
Rating: ★★★

'You know the name. You know the number,' boomed the publicity for the 1995 model 007 adventure. How very true. Same old Bond. His 'new' adventure is a cross between a high-tech Cold War thriller and *Dr No*. Not *that* high-tech, though: Bond still has his fast car (here a BMW) equipped with rocket launchers and the like. Not that we ever see them in action. Well, seen it all before really – a bit like the film. Pierce Brosnan is a middling Bond: un-

like his famous vodka martini, he's rarely shaken *or* stirred – but may grow into the part if given the chance. The girls are both good – the Rossellini-like Izabella Scorupco as the hapless computer scientist caught up in it all, and Famke Janssen as the orgasmic Xenia Onatopp (!) to.whom every danger is a thrill. There are amusing scenes with Desmond Llewelyn as gadget-man Q and Judi Dench as a teenager-ridden M and the action is all well shot. Sean Bean is a formula villain who has dozens of easy chances to shoot Bond dead and ignores all of them.

Goldengirl ○

1979, US, 104 mins, colour
Dir: Joseph Sargent
Stars: Susan Anton, James Coburn, Robert Culp, Leslie Caron
Rating: ★

An athletics soap-opera! Susan Anton's *Goldengirl* of the title is skyscraper-tall, blonde, stunningly good-looking and not a natural athlete. Anton rises nicely to what acting challenges the script provides, but is clearly less at home on the running track, most of these scenes relying on clever editing and camera angles to suggest her rivals are getting thrashed. She does, however, prove herself a singer of more than usual promise with her rendition of the film's theme tune. Alas for such American wish fulfilment, the story was overtaken by events, with the United States boycotting the Moscow Olympics at which the climax is set.

Golden Girl ○

1951, US, 108 mins, colour
Dir: Lloyd Bacon
Stars: Mitzi Gaynor, Dale Robertson, Dennis Day, James Barton
Rating: ★★★★

Mitzi Gaynor turns in her best screen performance as an aspiring music-hall star in post-Civil War years in this entertaining period mixture of music, action and sentiment. Lloyd Bacon, who directed most of the Thirties' musicals choreographed by Busby Berkeley, pulls out all his best tricks. If you cry easily at films, beware the ending of this one. The dazzling Technicolor photography is by Charles G Clarke.

Golden Hawk, The ⊙

1952, US, 84 mins, colour
Dir: Sidney Salkow
Stars: Rhonda Fleming, Sterling Hayden, Helena Carter, John Sutton
Rating: ★★

A swashbuckling tale of swordfights and sea battles – the type no longer made in Hollywood, but exhilarating to watch. Dazzlingly photographed in Technicolor, it has two exceptionally photogenic leading ladies in Rhonda Fleming and Helena Carter. Clean-cut heroics, anachronistic script and handsomely roguish villainy from John Sutton.

Golden Mistress, The ○

1954, US, 83 mins, colour
Dir: Joel Judge
Stars: John Agar, Rosemarie Bowe, Abner Biberman
Rating: ★★★

Thrill-a-minute adventure story about a hunt for treasure in the jungles of Haiti, and a threat of voodoo vengeance after a golden idol is stolen. Shot entirely in Haiti, this yarn boasts some of the most striking scenery ever recorded on film. Add a hunt for treasure, gooseflesh-provoking voodoo ceremonies and fights with horrific-looking tribesmen and you have a film well worth viewing. Soon after completing it, sultry leading lady Rosemarie Bowe married Robert Stack and retired. They're still married. The film was directed by featured player Abner Biberman under the pseudonym Joel Judge.

Golden Rendezvous ○

1977, US, 103 mins, colour
Dir: Ashley Lazarus
Stars: Richard Harris, Ann Turkel, David Janssen
Rating: ★★★

Another adaptation from Alistair MacLean and a good slice of hokum too. Not much of it makes any sense but the pace never stops. The story is set aboard a ship peopled with characters so cardboard they could fall over at a touch: the intrepid first officer (Richard Harris), the mystery woman (Ann Turkel) who won't talk, the tycoon (David Janssen) who drinks too much, the captain (Robert Flemyng) whose lip juts with determination, the faded blonde (Dorothy Malone), the gambler (Burgess Meredith) with a foolproof system, the good doctor (Gordon Jackson) who won't take arms (but naturally does). The list is as long as a yardarm, with Michael Howard scoring briefly as a steward who gets killed off early on – for scene-stealing, one presumes. On the technical side, cameraman Ken Higgins turns in a first-rate job in this hugely enjoyable film.

Golden Salamander O
1949, UK, 87 mins, b/w
Dir: Ronald Neame
Stars: Trevor Howard, Anouk Aimée,
Herbert Lom, Jacques Sernas
Rating: ★★★

Out-of-the-rut British adventure story
based on a tale by Victor Canning,
which keeps you guessing until the last
scenes. The direction by ex-camera-
man Ronald Neame is swift and
brilliant. The film marked the introduction to British films of the beautiful
French actress Anouk, later Anouk
Aimée. She was just 17 at the time,
and critics in this country raved about
her looks and her acting ability. Slow
to get going, but quite exciting towards
the end.

Golden Virgin
See: The Story of Esther Costello

Golden Voyage of Sinbad, The O ⓥ
1973, UK, 104 mins, colour
Dir: Gordon Hessler
Stars: John Phillip Law, Caroline Munro,
Tom Baker
Rating: ★★★

Special effects wizard Ray Harryhausen
here returned to the scene of his first
great triumph. For it was in *The 7th
Voyage of Sinbad* 15 years earlier that his
process of Dynamation first opened its
magic box of tricks to an eager paying
public. In this later venture,
Harryhausen's famous stop-motion
techniques enable Sinbad to fight a
gryphon, a centaur, a six-armed goddess (each arm bearing a sword) and
various other weird and wonderful opponents. Caroline Munro is an
eye-catching heroine, even if she has little more to do than cower in the face of
some new horror. Sinbad's human opponent is played by Tom Baker, just
before he became TV's Dr Who.

Goldfinger O ⓥ
1964, UK, 111 mins, colour
Dir: Guy Hamilton
Stars: Sean Connery, Honor Blackman,
Gert Frobe, Shirley Eaton
Rating: ★★★

Another Bond cliffhanger (or in this
case, cobalt bomb-hanger), with agent
007 taking on Auric Goldfinger, a master criminal who plans to plunder the
American gold reserves in Fort Knox.
Screenwriters Paul Dehn and Richard
Maibaum miss out on none of the
thrills of Ian Fleming's book. At the
same time they endow Bond with a
sense of humour that Fleming never

gave him. Sean Connery revels in this,
enjoying himself much more as a sort
of super-Saint than in the parts that are
pure Pearl White. German actor Gert
Frobe burst into international film
recognition with the title role, while
wrestler Harold Sakata enjoys fleeting
screen fame by making the Korean
Odd-job a villain fraught with menace.
Another star is the Bond-mobile, in this
case a 'modified' Aston Martin which
has a radar screen and an oil slick, and
fires machine guns to boot.

Gold of the Seven Saints O
1961, US, 89 mins, colour
Dir: Gordon Douglas
Stars: Clint Walker, Roger Moore
Rating: ★★

Two trappers find gold – and an outlaw team hard on their heels. Clint
Walker and Roger Moore are strong in
stature in these roles, if not in histrionic
abilities. The film was made in temperatures of between 100 and 120 degrees.
But the magnificent scenery – the
Arches National Monument with its
fantastic rock formations, the dramatic
Colorado River and the mountains –
made it all worthwhile.

Gold Rush, The ⊙
1925, US, 70 mins, b/w
Dir: Charles Chaplin
Stars: Charlie Chaplin, Georgia Hale,
Mack Swain
Rating: ★★★★★

Surely the funniest of Chaplin's feature films, this sublime saga of the
frozen North has the side-splitting,
beautifully worked-out scene in which
a starving Chaplin and Mack Swain
make a Thanksgiving feast out of one
of Chaplin's boots. Later, a crazed
Swain tries to eat Chaplin himself, seeing him as a gigantic chicken. And the
scene where their cabin totters on the
edge of a precipice is milked for all the
laughs it's worth, and then some
more. The film was mostly shot high
in the Sierra Nevadas at a cost of close
to a million dollars but made a mint.
Chaplin later said that it was the one
by which he would most like to be remembered.

Goldwyn Follies, The O
1938, US, 120 mins, colour
Dir: George Marshall
Stars: Adolphe Menjou, Vera Zorina, Ritz
Brothers
Rating: ★★

You can dip in almost anywhere in this
frantic compendium of comedy, dancing, ballet and song and pull out

something worth watching, from the riotous routines of the Ritz Brothers
(always at their best when not asked to
carry a film on their own shoulders) to
Alan Ladd as an audition singer (he
doesn't get the job). Ventriloquist
Edgar Bergen turns up with the treasurable Charlie McCarthy (Bergen was
never the most brilliant of 'vents', but
McCarthy was so memorable a doll it
didn't matter) and comedian Bobby
Clark makes his first film appearance
since the suicide of his long-time partner, Paul McCullough, two years
earlier. Highlight of it all is probably
the Ritzes' maniac version of 'Serenade
to a Fish'.

Go Naked in the World O
1961, US, 100 mins, colour
Dir: Ranald MacDougall
Stars: Gina Lollobrigida, Anthony
Franciosa, Ernest Borgnine
Rating: ★

An overheated and ultimately foolish
melodrama with Nick (Anthony
Franciosa) discovering that the girl he
has fallen in love with (Gina
Lollobrigida) is a prostitute. The fact
that this piece of information is gleefully imparted to him by his domineering
father doesn't help. So he leaves her;
then he begs her to marry him; then
they go to Mexico; then Nick's dad
begs her to marry Nick. Yes, really.
As you can see, the plot soon parts
company with reality. This wouldn't
be so bad if the film had wit, humour
or style, but it's static and unimaginative. La Lollo looks gorgeous (of
course), but that's about it and
Franciosa seems about to emote himself
into an early grave. Ernest Borgnine
plays with the relish of a man determined at least to enjoy himself if he
absolutely has to appear in tosh like
this.

Gone to Earth
See: The Wild Heart

Gone With the Wind O ⓥ
1939, US, 220 mins, colour
Dir: Victor Fleming
Stars: Clark Gable, Vivien Leigh, Olivia
de Havilland, Leslie Howard, Thomas
Mitchell, Hattie McDaniel
Rating: ★★★★

Although Hollywood's greatest epic,
this is a film of memorable moments,
rather than an outstanding whole. But
the war scenes are magnificently impressive and the burning of Atlanta –
handled by production designer
William Cameron Menzies – a brilliant

G

sequence by any standards. The performance of a lifetime from Vivien Leigh, pulsating with passion, was rightly rewarded with one of the film's nine Academy Awards.

Goodbye Charlie ○
1964, US, 116 mins, colour
Dir: Vincente Minnelli
Stars: Tony Curtis, Debbie Reynolds, Pat Boone, Walter Matthau
Rating: ★★

A zany film comedy about a Romeo who turns into an equally amorous Juliet! The director is the Oscar-winning Vincente Minnelli, who made such happy movies as *Gigi* and *Bells Are Ringing*; here he gets a stand-out performance from Walter Matthau, whose Sir Leopold is a comic creation of which Peter Sellers would have been proud.

Goodbye, Columbus ◐
1969, US, 105 mins, colour
Dir: Larry Peerce
Stars: Richard Benjamin, Ali MacGraw, Jack Klugman
Rating: ★★★

Immensely successful, modish bittersweet romance, filled with dislikeable characters and superbly scripted by Arnold Schulman from Philip Roth's biting portrait of a successful suburban Jewish family. Watch for Michael Nouri, since the leading man of *Flashdance*, Jaclyn (here billed as Jackie) Smith as a model and a guest appearance from director Larry Peerce's opera singer father Jan Peerce. But the honours are stolen from everyone by Michael Meyers as heroine Ali MacGraw's brother.

Goodbye Girl, The ◐ Ⓥ
1977, US, 110 mins, colour
Dir: Herbert Ross
Stars: Richard Dreyfuss, Marsha Mason, Quinn Cummings, Paul Benedict
Rating: ★★★★

If you fancy both a good cry and a happy time, this is the film for you. Full of Neil Simon's wisest and wittiest dialogue, it's the story of an emotional divorcee (Marsha Mason) who's been 'duped' by two men, but still crumbles at the thought of living alone – alone, that is, except for her 10-year-old daughter (Quinn Cummings) with whom she shares an amusingly abrasive relationship. Enter out-of-work actor Elliott (Richard Dreyfuss) who seems to have first claim on their apartment and the three are thrown together by 'one of God's little jests'. They get

on each other's nerves at first, but, well ... it's an old-fashioned sort of film. If it perhaps lacks the warmth and spontaneity of the very best cat-and-dog encounters of the past, then be thankful for the frequent Simon gems, as when Dreyfuss, who won an Oscar, is thrown out of his own flat at first sight, and has to call up his tenant in the pouring rain. '873-5261,' he screeches in desperation. 'It's a flooded booth on 7th Avenue.'

Goodbye Mr Chips! ○
1939, US, 114 mins, b/w
Dir: Sam Wood
Stars: Robert Donat, Greer Garson, Paul Henreid, John Mills
Rating: ★★★★★

James Hilton's novel of a schoolmaster's life was sentimentalised for pre-war audiences, but brilliantly knit together by director Sam Wood, and memorably acted by Robert Donat (as Chips) whose performance won an Academy Award, succeeding againt such competition as Clark Gable in *Gone With the Wind*. The last few minutes are guaranteed to move even the hardest of hearts.

Goodbye Mr Chips ○
1969, UK, 151 mins, colour
Dir: Herbert Ross
Stars: Peter O'Toole, Petula Clark, Michael Redgrave
Rating: ★★

To remake a much-loved film and one that had such a powerful central performance seems an act of madness. To then turn it into a musical just accentuates the lunacy. The best advice to anyone who loves the 1939 Robert Donat version is: watch something else. The story has been messed about with, the music is limp and the songs are instantly forgettable. They even changed Mr Chips' Christian name from Charles to Arthur (Why? What's the point?). To be fair, Peter O'Toole is an engaging Mr Chips (but ignore his singing!) and it seems a shame his talents are largely wasted here. Petula Clark does a fair job as his wife, but Greer Garson she isn't.

Goodbye My Fancy ○
1951, US, 104 mins, b/w
Dir: Vincent Sherman
Stars: Joan Crawford, Robert Young, Frank Lovejoy, Eve Arden
Rating: ★★★

One for the romantics – although this off-beat love story has a bright line in humour, too. Joan Crawford is partic-

ularly good as a lady politician who picks up on old romance while digging up a juicy scandal or two at her old college at the same time. It's a slick comedy-drama which, with its talk of academic liberty and the importance of free education, should please the student community. Eve Arden, the comedienne whose acid wisecracks saved some Forties comedies, had no need to perform a rescue act in this one. Not with Joan Crawford around.

Good Companions, The ○
1957, UK, 104 mins, colour
Dir: J Lee Thompson
Stars: Eric Portman, Celia Johnson, Janette Scott, John Fraser
Rating: ★★★★

This 1957 film of J B Priestley's famous back-stage story was made 25 years after the Matthews-Gielgud original. The tuneful score includes six songs with lyrics by Paddy Roberts, and the remarkable cast will keep star-spotters busy. And, if Janette Scott is certainly no Jessie Matthews, her verve and enthusiasm, together with the sympathetic playing of the entire cast, more than make amends, as she and Paddy Stone dance up a storm while Celia Johnson and Eric Portman, backstage, make off with the acting honours. Excellent colour photography and fairly fizzy direction from J Lee Thompson.

Good Day for a Hanging ○
1958, US, 85 mins, colour
Dir: Nathan Juran
Stars: Fred MacMurray, Robert Vaughn, Maggie Hayes, James Drury
Rating: ★★

Dramatic, well-characterised Western, dealing with the relationship between a dedicated, but very human law officer, and a young ex-convict, in whom the lawman is continually trying to seek out good. Robert Vaughn made one of his first big impressions as the ex-convict, snarling his way to a memorable portrayal. Fred MacMurray is also impressive as the unpopular marshal.

Good Die Young, The ○
1954, UK, 94 mins, b/w
Dir: Lewis Gilbert
Stars: Laurence Harvey, Margaret Leighton, Gloria Grahame, Richard Basehart, Joan Collins
Rating: ★★

The women fare best in this all-star robbery thriller, whose grip would be tighter if only its basic situation were more believable. Gloria Grahame does her good-time girl act once again to perfection, while Joan Collins scores in an unexpectedly quiet role as a pregnant young wife. Freda Jackson's compelling study of selfishness, René Ray's loyal wife (whose brother loses her husband's savings and drives him to crime) and Margaret Leighton's poised sophisticate all make off with the goods while the men (led by Laurence Harvey, Stanley Baker and John Ireland) remain shadowy figures.

Good Earth, The ○
1937, US, 138 mins, b/w
Dir: Sidney Franklin
Stars: Paul Muni, Luise Rainer, Walter Connolly
Rating: ★★★★

Luise Rainer's portrayal of the indomitable wife of a Chinese peasant made her the first actress to win two Academy Awards (following her success in the previous year in *The Great Ziegfeld*) in this dogged MGM adaptation of Pearl Buck's vast best-selling novel. Fame was not to last for the Austrian actress, however, and she was out of Hollywood in just a few more years. Another Oscar went to distinguished cinematographer Karl Freund, for his work on the storm, the famine and the locust sequence, which remains a timeless classic in miniature.

Good Father, The ◑ Ⓥ
1986, UK, 86 mins, colour
Dir: Mike Newell
Stars: Anthony Hopkins, Jim Broadbent, Harriet Walter, Simon Callow, Joanne Whalley
Rating: ★★

This is almost like a throwback to those abrasive Nicol Williamson films of the late Sixties, right down to the girl who rips off her top at one of those boring swinging parties that surely never were. This time it's the admirable Anthony Hopkins in the Williamson role, and it would be hard to find a character more embittered or full of suppressed rage than Bill Hooper, who has left his wife and young son for a reason that does not become apparent (even to Bill) until towards the end of the film. He finds himself channelling his anger into a friend's fight for the custody of his own child, whisked away from him by his lesbian wife. As the friend, Jim Broadbent gives the best performance in the film. Joanne Whalley and Harriet Walter are also good as the mistress and wife in Hooper's life, but

the film finally ends in the middle with Bill unable to decide what to do.

GoodFellas ● Ⓥ
1990, US, 143 mins, colour
Dir: Martin Scorsese
Stars: Robert De Niro, Ray Liotta, Joe Pesci, Lorraine Bracco, Paul Sorvino
Rating: ★★★

Robert De Niro back where he shows up best – in the world of guns and godfathers. Faster-talking than the average Mafia saga, this also has a blackly comic edge. Otherwise, the familiar elements of the genre are all violently and gratingly in place. Ray Liotta is Henry Hill, a war baby who grows up with gangsters and dreams only of being one. He makes dangerous friends like Jimmy the Gent (De Niro) and Tommy DeVito (Joe Pesci), a frighteningly unpredictable hitman who only stops talking for long enough to shoot someone over some (often imagined) insult. These are all 'wiseguys' or 'goodfellas', but Henry's world of glittering nightclubs and easy cheating on his wife (Lorraine Bracco) starts to slide downhill after one of Jimmy and Tommy's maniac fits of fury results in a senseless death of far-reaching consequences. The film's a mite oppressive and certainly too long: you get the sense of having lived with gangsters, all right, but they all talk the same way in the same harsh, metallic voices, brown men with an aura of death hanging about them. Perfectly acted, though, especially by Liotta, De Niro and Oscar-winning Pesci, whose deliberately one-key performances make their characters seem all the more dangerous.

Good Guys and the Bad Guys, The ○
1969 US, 90 mins, colour
Dir: Burt Kennedy
Stars: Robert Mitchum, George Kennedy, David Carradine, Tina Louise
Rating: ★★

Burt Kennedy became an erratic director after the highpoint of *Support Your Local Sheriff!*, but this is one of his better spoof Westerns. Robert Mitchum and George Kennedy score nicely off each other as the bad guys combining to tackle an even worse guy (David Carradine, sneering stonily in the days before *Kung Fu*).

Good Guys Wear Black ◑ Ⓥ
1977, US, 96 mins, colour
Dir: Ted Post
Stars: Chuck Norris, Anne Archer, James

Franciscus
Rating: ★

A stillborn thriller about a group of Vietnam veterans, once an elite squad of assassins who were set up by a traitor. Now, in California five years later, the survivors are being bumped off in Agatha Christie fashion. The plot is quite preposterous and plays at times like a very old American 'B' movie. Chuck Norris acts mostly with his feet but even so is preferable to the rest of an all-too-distinguished cast, of whom Anne Archer especially is (as she later proved) capable of much better work. The suspense sequences, although picturesquely shot on a variety of locations, have all the tension of sago pudding.

Good Humor Man, The ⊙
1950, US, 79 mins, b/w
Dir: Lloyd Bacon
Stars: Jack Carson, Lola Albright, Jean Wallace
Rating: ★★★★★

One of several amusing postwar comedies to tandem the talents of zany young writer Frank Tashlin (later to become a director himself) and veteran Hollywood director Lloyd Bacon. Others were *Innocence Is Bliss*, *The Affairs of Sally* and *Kill the Umpire*, but this is probably the funniest of the lot. Jack Carson excels himself as an ice-cream salesman unwillingly involved with murder and a disappearing corpse. A scream from start to finish, this crams in enough laughs to leave you breathless.

Good Man In Africa, A ● Ⓥ
1993, US/UK, 94 mins, colour
Dir: Bruce Beresford
Stars: Colin Friels, Joanne Whalley-Kilmer, Sean Connery, Louis Gossett Jr, Diana Rigg, John Lithgow
Rating: ★

A terminally tedious anecdote (and that's all it is) about a British diplomat in Africa (played by Australian Colin Friels!), happily in bed with corruption in all quarters, but reawakened to moral values by an incorruptible Scottish doctor (Sean Connery). Saddled with a stroppy African mistress, Friels also has to cope with the advances of Joanne Whalley-Kilmer and Diana Rigg as the wives respectively of the crooked prospective president (Louis Gossett Jr) and the equally crooked chargé d'affaires (John Lithgow with an outrageously exaggerated English accent). A lot of talent goes to waste in this incoherent and in-

G

conclusive tale which starts in nonde-script fashion and goes nowhere slowly.

Good Morning, Boys! ⊙
1936, UK, 79 mins, b/w
Dir: Marcel Varnel
Stars: Will Hay, Graham Moffatt, Lilli Palmer, Martita Hunt
Rating: ★★★

One of Will Hay's earliest film appear-ances in his famous character of a seedy schoolmaster. The cast includes the famous fat boy, Graham Moffatt, a young Charles Hawtrey and Hay's own son, Will Jr, as an unholy trio of schoolboys, as well as Lilli Palmer, also at the beginning of her career, as a kind of Mata Hari. Peter Godfrey, who plays Cliquot, later went on to Hollywood and became a successful di-rector of Warner thriller films. The story, written by Hay himself (and re-made 16 years later with Ronald Shiner as *Top of the Form*) concerns a gang of thieves planning to steal the Mona Lisa.

Good Morning, Vietnam ● ⓥ
1987, US, 120 mins, colour
Dir: Barry Levinson
Stars: Robin Williams, Forest Whitaker, Tung Thanh Trah, Bruno Kirby, J T Walsh
Rating: ★★★

After a handful of films that really did-n't exploit his manic comic talents, Robin Williams exploded on to the screen and made this film a scatological one-man show. He plays a crazy over-the-top army DJ let loose at the armed forces radio station in Vietnam during the 1960s. Director Barry Levinson gave Williams his head, so much of the dialogue was either changed or ad-libbed by the comedian to suit his own style and persona. The result is stream-of-consciousness lunacy and wicked one-liners delivered with ma-chine-gun rapidity, and it earned Williams an Oscar nomination. It's only after the film has finished that you realise that there's very little storyline. But that doesn't matter; it's immensely enjoyable even if, ultimately, it's much ado about nothing.

Good Neighbour Sam ○
1964, US, 130 mins, colour
Dir: David Swift
Stars: Jack Lemmon, Romy Schneider, Edward G Robinson
Rating: ★★★

There's nothing better for a good situa-tion comedy than complications. And this lively film has plenty of those. Jack

Lemmon plays an advertising executive who has to live with his wife's best friend, so that the friend can inherit a fortune. Have you followed the plot so far? Some of the comedy is an embar-rassing misfire. But it gets funnier as it goes along. Lemmon's expertise is con-stantly breathing new life into the film. And there's a very funny running joke about a cigarette advertising film that keeps going wrong.

Good News ○
1947, US, 95 mins, colour
Dir: Charles Walters
Stars: June Allyson, Peter Lawford, Patricia Marshall, Mel Tormé
Rating: ★★★

Dance director Charles Walters made an impressive step up to the director's chair in a college-swing musical whose scarcely believable plot (especially the casting of ever-so-refined Peter Lawford as a brainless football hero) was boosted to the skies by a knockout De Sylva-Brown-Henderson score in which almost every number was a hit: 'Just Imagine', 'Lucky in Love', 'Good News', 'Ladies' Man', 'The Best Things in Life Are Free' and particular-ly the spirited final ensemble 'Varsity Drag', performed with truly infectious joie-de-vivre by Lawford (one of his most likeable screen performances) and especially by fizzy leading lady June Allyson. The pair also combine on 'The French Lesson', an ingenious song written for the film by Betty Comden, Adolph Green and Roger Edens. Filmed before in 1930, but not half as well.

Good, the Bad and the Ugly, The ○
1966, Italy, 186 mins, colour
Dir: Sergio Leone
Stars: Clint Eastwood, Lee Van Cleef, Eli Wallach
Rating: ★★★

The third and last Sergio Leone/Clint Eastwood Western and arguably the best. It's long and rambling but always interesting and has a powerful trio of stars in Eastwood, Eli Wallach and Lee Van Cleef. They're all on the trail of a hoard of gold and they cross, double cross and cheat each other right up to the tense and exciting climax – a three-cornered shoot-out in a cemetery. A sprawling tale set during the American Civil War, the film looks very impres-sive (it was Leone's biggest-budget film at that time). Eastwood is the grim man with no name again but he's posi-tively angelic compared to the ugly,

grasping and amoral Wallach and the cold and sadistic Van Cleef.

Good Time Girl ○
1948, UK, 93 mins, b/w
Dir: David Macdonald
Stars: Jean Kent, Dennis Price, Griffith Jones, Herbert Lom
Rating: ★★★

Jean Kent's striking performance as the reform school refugee in this convinc-ing and very successful British 'social conscience' thriller (based on a true story) got her typed in a kind of role she found hard to escape. Once hailed as one of Britain's most promising di-rectors, David Macdonald disappointed in postwar times, but this is one of his best from the period.

Good Wife, The ● ⓥ
(aka: The Umbrella Woman)
1986, Australia, 97 mins, colour
Dir: Ken Cameron
Stars: Rachel Ward, Bryan Brown, Sam Neill
Rating: ★

A very bizarre kettle of fish and no mis-take. A story of sexual obsession in the Australian outback of 1939, it provides a change of step for husband-and-wife co-stars Rachel Ward and Bryan Brown. She plays the wife trying to es-cape her mother's reputation as a scarlet woman. He's the timber cutter she marries and who inexplicably re-leases her repressed passions by allowing his younger brother to make love to her. Ward has a stab at an Australian accent, Brown tries to subli-mate his macho image and Sam Neill is so oily as the man who comes between them that you wonder why women are so attracted to him. It's unkind to sug-gest these roles are outside the range of these actors, since any star trio would struggle to make sense of them. Professionally directed, though, and beautifully photographed, technical credits that cannot make this overheat-ed melodrama seem any less unlikely than it does.

Goofy Movie, A ⊙ ⓥ
1995, US, 78 mins colour
Dir: Kevin Lima
Voice stars: Bill Farmer, Jason Marsden, Jim Cummings, Kellie Martin, Wallace Shawn, Jo Anne Worley
Rating: ★★

Goofy never was my favourite among Walt Disney cartoon stars and he does-n't improve his reputation here. The lack of well-known voice stars should warn you that this is an indifferent animated feature by Disney standards, with the charmless Goofy depicted as a single father bringing up an adolescent son, Max, who's even more annoying than he is. Max is a tiresome, self-pitying brat and so at least we're on Goofy's side when, fed up with the kid whingeing on about underprivileged upbringing and unrequited love for schoolmate Roxanne, he takes Max off for some male bonding on a fishing trip. The best sequence comes when the quarrelling pair visit a poor man's Disneyland in the shape of Lester's Possum Park. Otherwise, this 'new' Goofy is just the same old idiot with the silly laugh. Here, though, time has passed him by, and even pre-school children may find little to cheer.

Goonies, The ○ Ⓥ
1985, US, 111 mins, colour
Dir: Richard Donner
Stars: Sean Astin, Josh Brolin, Corey Feldman, Ke Huy Quan
Rating: ★★

Full of good ideas, if ultimately something of a likeable mess, this is an adventure story in the Spielberg tradition about a group of kids who hit on a labyrinth of underground tunnels and chambers while trying to find a centuries-old pirate treasure. The sets look like leftovers from an *Indiana Jones* movie, but provide plenty of jumpy moments, as the kids battle against ancient pirate booby traps, as well as a trio of rather too comic crooks, led by Anne Ramsey, later famous as the momma they couldn't throw from the train. You may need an interpreter for some of the children's dialogue, but the action speaks for itself – and there's lots of it. Juvenile honours go to the endearing fat boy of Jeff Cohen, especially when he's blurting out the foul deeds of his past after being forced by Ramsey to 'tell everything'.

Goose Steps Out, The ○
1942, UK, 79 mins, b/w
Dir: Will Hay, Basil Dearden
Stars: Will Hay, Frank Pettingell, Charles Hawtrey, Peter Ustinov, Anne Firth
Rating: ★★

Good, fast fun, as comedian Will Hay (in a dual role as a schoolmaster and a German spy!) is parachuted into wartime Germany. Patchy by Hay's standards, though, with rather too much attention paid to the flag-waving plot.

Gorgo ◐
1960, UK, 78 mins, colour
Dir: Eugene Lourie

Stars: Bill Travers, William Sylvester
Rating: ★★★

Good special effects fantasy film as a mother monster comes charging up the Thames to rescue her offspring, which has been captured by mankind. In its own category, this is certainly a moving and well-handled variation of a familiar theme.

Gorgon, The ●
1964, UK, 83 mins, colour
Dir: Terence Fisher
Stars: Peter Cushing, Christopher Lee, Barbara Shelley
Rating: ★★

Horror specialists Hammer had already ploughed their way through a redoubtable array of vampires, mummies and spare-part creatures by the time they came to this chiller about a snake-haired Medusa, the very sight of whom turns her victims to stone. Peter Cushing and Christopher Lee are bravely cast against type – Cushing as a resoundingly sinister and suspicious doctor, Lee as a sympathetic professor. Director Terence Fisher races through the action while investing the film with a sense of brooding menace. One poor character turns to stone and even loses his hair – which is what comes, perhaps, of actors wearing wigs.

Gorilla at Large ◑
1954, US, 84 mins, colour
Dir: Harmon Jones
Stars: Anne Bancroft, Cameron Mitchell, Charlotte Austin, Lee J Cobb, Lee Marvin, Raymond Burr
Rating: ★★

Formidable cast in carnival murder thriller originally made in 3-D. Oscar-winning Miss Bancroft upstages all but the 'gorilla', although Marvin has a few nice dry lines as a sardonic policeman.

Gorillas in the Mist ◑ Ⓥ
1988, US, 124 mins, colour
Dir: Michael Apted
Stars: Sigourney Weaver, Bryan Brown, Julie Harris
Rating: ★★★★

The amazing story of Dian Fossey, an intrepid American woman who studied, befriended and protected mountain gorillas in the wilds of Africa, doesn't have too many faults. Overlength and a slight over-emphasis on Fossey's affair with a wildlife photographer are two of them, but they are far outweighed by its virtues. Sigourney Weaver is perfectly cast as Fossey; you could imagine no more suitable actress

to portray a dominant woman who fiercely defends (from poachers) property she regards as her own. The story is full of drama, and she takes charge of it from the start. Bryan Brown, Julie Harris and Iain Cuthbertson (as her initial mentor) offer decent support, but the film is essentially Weaver and the gorillas; they come out as both winning and winners and there's an emotional and inspiring ending.

Gorky Park ● Ⓥ
1983, US, 128 mins, colour
Dir: Michael Apted
Stars: William Hurt, Lee Marvin, Brian Dennehy, Joanna Pacula
Rating: ★★★

It certainly is an interesting idea to set a murder investigation in Moscow, where the KGB convolutions run deeper than if the CIA were involved in the States. Three bodies are discovered in Gorky Park, buried in snow with their faces, fingerprints and teeth stripped away. Nevertheless, the city's chief investigator (William Hurt) soon gets on the scent of a conspiracy which predictably involves those in high places, although the workings of the plot remain absorbing and the ending is exhilaratingly right. Hurt is on the mark as the top cop, and Lee Marvin characteristically baccy-spittin' forceful as a visiting American with an interest in sables. Quite a good two hours' worth, although strung out too far. Don't expect a masterpiece and you'll enjoy it.

Go Tell the Spartans ●
1977, US, 114 mins, colour
Dir: Ted Post
Stars: Burt Lancaster, Craig Wasson, Marc Singer
Rating: ★★

A very tough Vietnam war film made by director Ted Post, who has made his movie in the form of a 'patrol' drama, much beloved by makers of Hollywood Westerns and war films and revived so successfully by Oliver Stone in his Oscar winning *Platoon*. Burt Lancaster is in typically uncompromising form as the veteran major and the predictably bloody ending reflects the bitterness and disillusion felt by most Americans as the war came to an end.

Gotham
See: The Dead Can't Lie

Gothic ● Ⓥ
1986, UK, 87 mins, colour
Dir: Ken Russell

G

Stars: Gabriel Byrne, Natasha
Richardson, Julian Sands, Miriam Cyr,
Timothy Spall
Rating: ★

To frighten us, to fire our imagination,
a nightmare must seem totally real.
Ken Russell's tall (and expensive-looking) tale of Shelley, Byron and their
ladies conjuring up demons of the
mind all through a stormy night is
quite plainly such arrant nonsense, like
a pretentious surrealist painting come
to life, that it never raises more than
the occasional visual shudder at some
grisly detail. We're bombarded in fact
with so many horrific images, each intended to offend the sensibilities and
revolt the eyes, that the director never
gives the central idea the chance to
grip. The cast do their best, though in
the case of Julian Sands and Natasha
Richardson, that isn't terribly good.
No, this is no living nightmare. More
like *Monty Python's Life of Byron.*

Go to Blazes ○

1962, UK, 84 mins, colour
Dir: Michael Truman
Stars: Dave King, Robert Morley, Maggie
Smith, Daniel Massey
Rating: ★★★

Fast and funny comedy about three
crooks with a fire engine as their getaway car. The cast is packed with
talent, right down to the minor roles,
and includes Daniel Massey, Dennis
Price, Coral Browne, Norman
Rossington, Miles Malleson, Wilfrid
Lawson, Finlay Currie, Arthur Lowe,
David Lodge, James Hayter, John le
Mesurier and Derek Nimmo! Judging
by this, Dave King should have made
more films.

Go West ⊙

1925, US, 70 mins, b/w
Dir: Buster Keaton
Stars: Buster Keaton
Rating: ★★★

Buster Keaton's sixth feature-length
comedy provides him with one of his
more unusual leading ladies, a jersey
cow named Brown Eyes, who Keaton
himself trained for her screen debut.
Here the bovine beauty vies for the
star's affections with the rancher's
daughter Kathleen Myers in one of the
Wild West's odder romantic triangles,
but as usual, love takes a back seat to
Keaton's splendid roster of gags as he
proves to be the greenest greenhorn
ever to hit the Arizona trail. Roscoe
'Fatty' Arbuckle, by then exiled from
Hollywood after a sex scandal, makes a
bizarre appearance in drag.

Go West ⊙ ⓥ

1940, US, 81 mins, b/w
Dir: Edward Buzzell
Stars: Groucho Marx, Chico Marx, Harpo
Marx, John Carroll
Rating: ★★★

'Brake! The brake!' yelps Chico in the
helter-skelter train-bound finale to this
busy comedy lark. Smiling, Harpo
obliges by snapping the brake in two
and throwing it off the train. It's this
fast, furious and riotous visual finish
that children will find funniest, while
Marx purists will go for the scene at the
start where 'greenhorns' Chico and
Harpo take 'sharpster' Groucho to the
cleaners with the help of a dollar bill on
a piece of string.

Grace of My Heart ● ⓥ

1996, US, 115 mins, colour
Dir: Allison Anders
Cast: Illeana Douglas, Matt Dillon, Eric
Stoltz, John Turturro, Bruce Davison
Rating: ★★

Director Anders has a great idea here
for a film about 12 years in the life of
a woman (Douglas) whose singing talent is sublimated to her drive to write
songs – even if it means other people
sing them. For the first hour this
looks like a winner – with Douglas
deriving her inspirations from
poignant true-life situations other
writers daren't touch. Then it gets
lost in a morass of men and failed
marriages, culminating in the most tedious segment of all when Douglas
falls for a rock musician (Dillon),
whose mental control slips along with
his career. All this hippie stuff (the
film ends in 1970) never did a film
much good in its own time, and so it
proves again here. Douglas is winning, then wearing, but time and
again the music rights the ship: alas, it
capsizes once too often.

Graduate, The ① ⓥ

1967, US, 105 mins, colour
Dir: Mike Nichols
Stars: Dustin Hoffman, Anne Bancroft,
Katharine Ross, William Daniels, Murray
Hamilton
Rating: ★★★★★

Fast, funny, landmark sex comedy driven along with irresistible verve by
Mike Nichols, whose Academy Award
as best director was amazingly the only
Oscar that the film won. Spot-on performances from Dustin Hoffman, Anne
Bancroft and Katharine Ross, superbly
sympathetic song score from Simon
and Garfunkel and an agonising,
cliffhanging ending. Look fast to spot a

tiny cameo from Richard Dreyfuss in
this great entertainment.

Grand Canyon ● ⓥ

1991, US, 134 mins, colour
Dir: Lawrence Kasdan
Stars: Danny Glover, Kevin Kline, Steve
Martin, Mary McDonnell, Mary-Louise
Parker, Alfre Woodard
Rating: ★★

This moody study of American angst
scratches the surfaces of several of the
malaises of American society, but, like
its characters, strikes poses rather than
attitudes. Helicopters pound overhead,
patrolling the city and especially the
'hood; everywhere is the evidence of
bad things coming down. Mack (Kevin
Kline), a lawyer, is rescued from a gang
of street thugs by Simon (Danny
Glover) and feels he must see him again
to thank him and maybe do something
for him. Claire (Mary McDonnell),
Mack's wife, finds an abandoned baby
and is filled with a desire to adopt it.
Simon's sister lives in fear in the bullet-
riddled 'hood, while her son runs with
its young gangs. Mack's filmmaker
friend (Steve Martin) is shot in the thigh
by a mugger after his watch. All of
these people, Glover excepted, seem a
little unhinged. The outlook is bleak.
But director Lawrence Kasdan opts for
a happy ending and a theory that sometimes things come out right. Finally the
film seems to have fewer teeth even
than something like *Hill Street Blues.*
Good performances, though, notably
from McDonnell, and a few smartly
funny lines.

Grand Central Murder ○

1942, US, 73 mins, b/w
Dir: S Sylvan Simon
Stars: Van Heflin, Cecilia Parker, Sam
Levene, Tom Conway
Rating: ★★★

Private eye Rocky Custer, under suspicion for murder, retaliates by taking on
the case himself. Tight, fast, hard-hitting thriller that's a lot better than it
sounds, if a bit cluttered, and very
strongly cast for a 'B' movie. Van
Heflin makes a brashly gritty impression as the hero, and the killer is
difficult to spot.

Grand Prix ○

1966, US, 180 mins, colour
Dir: John Frankenheimer
Stars: James Garner, Eva Marie Saint,
Yves Montand, Toshiro Mifune
Rating: ★★

The highlight of this motor-racing
drama about the lives and loves of dri-

vers on the European racing circuit is undoubtedly a spectacular crash with one car driving up a cliff and another plunging into the sea. But, even with romantic and domestic interludes away from the track, the film remains stuck firmly in bottom gear. James Garner and the international cast do what they can with the pulp-fiction roles, but their thunder is stolen by the sea of cars flying along at 100mph, with their engines growling like tigers.

Grand Tour: Disaster In Time
See: Timescape

Grandview USA ● Ⓥ
1984, US, 97 mins, colour
Dir: Randal Kleiser
Stars: Jamie Lee Curtis, C Thomas Howell, Patrick Swayze, Jennifer Jason Leigh, Troy Donahue
Rating: ★★

A tough little drama revolving around a demolition derby and teenagers' attempts to prove themselves their own people away from parental influence. The cast is full of such stars-to-be as Patrick Swayze, C Thomas Howell, Jennifer Jason Leigh, Jamie Lee Curtis and real-life brother and sister Joan and John Cusack. Fair.

Grapes of Wrath, The ○ Ⓥ
1940, US, 128 mins, b/w
Dir: John Ford
Stars: Henry Fonda, Jane Darwell, John Carradine
Rating: ★★★★★

Compelling, atmospheric story of a migratory family, their struggle to reach California after leaving their Oklahoma dustbowl homes, and the misfortunes that befall them when they arrive at their destination. Full of memorable moments, the film has magnificent performances from Henry Fonda and John Carradine. But it was another noteworthy portrayal, by Jane Darwell as the mother of the family, that won an Academy Award. Director John Ford also took an Oscar for his sensitive handling of a timeless classic, whose ending has haunted filmgoers down the years.

Graveyard Shift ●
1990, US, 87 mins, colour
Dir: Ralph S Singleton
Stars: David Andrews, Kelly Wolf, Stephen Macht, Brad Dourif
Rating: ★★

Though slow to develop and mostly composed of people creeping around after rats, this is rather a jolly horror film about a giant bat (with tentacles

for good measure) that occupies the area beneath an old mill and the adjacent graveyard. When the bullying, lecherous foreman, played with relish, a Vincent Price gleam and a vaguely fake Scottish accent by Stephen Macht, decides to clean out the old basement, the time has come for the sound of bat on bone. The Tom Berenger-like David Andrews is the strong and silent hero, and Brad Dourif steals all his scenes as the exterminator who declares himself to be 'not one of your wheedling types Bruce Dern plays' before disappearing all too soon from the action. It's old-fashioned stuff that horror fans should enjoy.

Gray Lady Down ○
1978, US, 111 mins, colour
Dir: David Greene
Stars: Charlton Heston, David Carradine
Rating: ★★★

When the crew of a damaged submarine in a film say, 'We'll be all right for a day and a half', and the captain replies, 'We won't be down here that long', you can bet your last fathom they're in trouble. With Charlton Heston at the conning-tower, the producers obviously figured out that this film had to be an epic of some sort. So they made it an epic of suspense. There are some tellingly harrowing moments, and the film is quite exceptionally well made. Christopher Reeve makes his screen debut as one of the rescuers.

Grease ○ Ⓥ
1978, US, 110 mins, colour
Dir: Randal Kleiser
Stars: John Travolta, Olivia Newton-John, Stockard Channing, Jeff Conaway
Rating: ★★★

The story is trite, the dialogue equally so, but it's hard not to like this bouncy pastiche of Fifties teen musicals. All the predictable elements are here (young love, macho posing, hot rod racing and rock 'n' roll), but they're mixed to perfection. John Travolta is great as the high school tough who has a fling with nice Olivia Newton-John on holiday, but is embarrassed when she turns up at his school. Olivia is fine, too, as squeaky-clean Sandy. The songs are good – in fact, as many people bought the soundtrack album as watched the film – and the production numbers really swing along.

Grease 2 ○ Ⓥ
1982, US, 115 mins, colour
Dir: Patricia Birch

Stars: Michelle Pfeiffer, Maxwell Caulflied
Rating: ★

A young and energetic cast attempt to recreate the box-office gold of the John Travolta/Olivia Newton-John Fifties musical, but choreographer and director Patricia Birch merely slips up on a slick of her own making. Where the original film had the high-school hero posing as an athlete to win a new girl's affections, here it is a new (English) boy at school posing as a black-clad biker to win over the heroine. British actor Maxwell Caulfield is not known for being animated on screen, preferring petulance and pouting to creating believable characters with any depth. Michelle Pfeiffer must cringe in her stilettoes when she looks back on this early embarrassment. Fans of Fifties movies should enjoy spotting blasts from the past Tab Hunter, Connie Stevens and Eve Arden.

Great Balloon Adventure, The ☉
(aka: Olly Olly Oxen Free)
1978, US, 89 mins, colour
Dir: Richard A Colla
Stars: Katharine Hepburn, Kevin McKenzie, Dennis Dimster
Rating: ★★

Katharine Hepburn enjoys herself as an old junk dealer in this refreshing and invigorating tale about two young boys who want to construct their own hot-air balloon. Kate slums it in style, and there's also a wonderful shaggy dog who shares the aerial adventures with this unlikely trio.

Great Balls of Fire! ◑ Ⓥ
1989, US, 102 mins, colour
Dir: Jim McBride
Stars: Dennis Quaid, Winona Ryder
Rating: ★★

Rock 'n' roller Jerry Lee Lewis was the wild man of Fifties rock, so you would expect a film about his life to be pretty over-the-top, too. And so it is, but unfortunately Dennis Quaid's manic portrayal does the singer little justice – and is the driving force behind a very superficial film. The movie focuses on a brief part of the man's career and how his marriage to his 13-year-old cousin Myra Gale (Winona Ryder) dented it irreparably. Quaid plays the part as if he's performing on stage all the time. Surely, whatever his faults, Lewis is a man of greater depth than this. On the plus side, the scenes of Jerry Lee in concert are well done and exciting but they only serve to show how awful the rest of the film is.

G

Great Caruso, The ○

1950, US, 109 mins, colour
Dir: Richard Thorpe
Stars: Mario Lanza, Ann Blyth
Rating: ★★★★

The greatest hit of Mario Lanza's career, and one of MGM's biggest financial successes, this most cunningly crafted of all 'highbrow' musicals netted the studio close to five million dollars. The screenplay predictably played around with the truth, glossing over Caruso's first wife and going straight on to Ann Blyth as his second, but the running time was so full of music that the plot scarcely mattered. Despite the presence of arias from the works of Verdi, Puccini and Rossini, the film's biggest hits were 'The Loveliest Night of the Year' (first sung by Blyth to Lanza at a dance), 'Because' and the Bach/Gounot 'Ave Maria'. The tumultuous ending left not a dry eye in the house.

Great Catherine ○

1968, UK, 98 mins, colour
Dir: Gordon Flemyng
Stars: Peter O'Toole, Jeanne Moreau
Rating: ★

Lifeless and laughless, this is a would-be comic extension of Shaw's playlet about the amorous adventures of Catherine the Great of Russia and an English officer. The supporting cast includes Zero Mostel, Jack Hawkins and Akim Tamiroff.

Great Day in the Morning ○

1955, US, 87 mins, colour
Dir: Jacques Tourneur
Stars: Robert Stack, Virginia Mayo, Ruth Roman, Raymond Burr
Rating: ★★★

This pre-Civil War Western is definitely superior of its kind. Its hero is another of those tough guys with big hearts, but in this case he's more real than most, and the strongly-written characterisation of this man is what allows Robert Stack to dominate the film against some fierce acting competition. There are good performances from Ruth Roman, Raymond Burr (as a villain called Jumbo Means) and Leo Gordon, but heroine Virginia Mayo, despite top billing, displays little of the fire her character needs. Thanks to cinematographer William Snyder, colour and photography are both excellent and the story has quite a few original twists.

Great Dictator, The ○ Ⓥ

1940, US, 129 mins, b/w
Dir: Charles Chaplin
Stars: Charlie Chaplin, Paulette Goddard, Jack Oakie, Reginald Gardiner
Rating: ★★★

Charlie Chaplin's satire on the Axis leaders was said to have so incensed Adolf Hitler that he thrust the little man to the top of his 'death list' after his proposed conquest of America. Hitler can't have exactly been pleased by the funny performances of Chaplin's co-stars, Jack Oakie as Napaloni (Mussolini), Henry Daniell as Garbitsch (Goebbels) and Billy Gilbert as Herring (Goering). Funniest scene is the one in which Chaplin and Oakie each tries to keep his head higher than the other in revolving barber's chairs.

Great Escape, The ○ Ⓥ

1963, US, 173 mins, colour
Dir: John Sturges
Stars: Steve McQueen, James Garner, Richard Attenborough, James Donald, Charles Bronson, Donald Pleasence
Rating: ★★★★

For its first 90 minutes, this is a truly great example of the POW film. By comparison, its second half is merely exciting. The screenplay, cuttingly well written by James Clavell and W R Burnett from Paul Brickhill's book, has all the bite of the best prison-camp humour and heartbreak too, especially when the first intricate escape tunnel, which has taken weeks to build, is discovered by the Germans. Although it perhaps lacks the emotional involvement to put it in the topmost class, *The Great Escape* still has much to offer in the way of thrills and entertainment. Of the many first-class actors taking part, the three who make the most impact are Steve McQueen as Hilts, who chalks up his 20th escape bid in the course of the film; John Leyton as Willie, the tunneller; and James Donald, giving an immaculate performance as the British commanding officer.

Greatest Show on Earth, The ○ Ⓥ

1952, US, 153 mins, colour
Dir: Cecil B DeMille
Stars: Cornel Wilde, Betty Hutton, Charlton Heston, Dorothy Lamour, James Stewart, Gloria Grahame
Rating: ★★★

Cecil B DeMille's circus blockbuster: it won an Academy Award as the best film of its year, and boasts a spectacular train crash besides thrills in the ring.

Best performances come from James Stewart, as the clown on the run from his past, and Lyle Bettger, as the insanely jealous Klaus. On the glamour side, it's nice to see Betty Hutton and Dorothy Lamour together again. Both had been stalwarts of Paramount pictures for some years.

Great Expectations ○ Ⓥ

1946, UK, 118 mins, b/w
Dir: David Lean
Stars: John Mills, Valerie Hobson, Bernard Miles, Alec Guinness, Jean Simmons
Rating: ★★★★★

Director David Lean turned Charles Dickens's novel into a lavish but unostentatious screen masterpiece that has stood up well to the passage of time. Thanks for this is due, in no small way, to John Mills and Jean Simmons. Alec Guinness made his major screen debut in this film as the toffee-nosed Herbert Pocket and injected some dateless humour into his role. His finest moment comes when he challenges John Mills to a fight. Alec prances around like a ballet dancer. Very showy. But it is John who does all the scoring. The film also contains several pretty frightening sequences, the worst being that in which Finlay Currie, playing the convict Magwitch, jumps out of an eerie churchyard and grabs young Pip.

Great Gatsby, The ◑ Ⓥ

1974, US, 146 mins, colour
Dir: Jack Clayton
Stars: Robert Redford, Mia Farrow, Bruce Dern, Karen Black, Scott Wilson, Sam Waterston
Rating: ★★

About every 25 years the cinema takes it into its head to have a go at Scott Fitzgerald's almost unfilmable story about the mysterious millionaire living in his Long Island mansion, staring out at the Sound and looking destiny enigmatically in the face. Successive generations of bland charmers Warner Baxter in 1926, Alan Ladd in 1949 and Robert Redford here – have attempted the title role. The direction and production design perfectly capture the flavour of the post-World War One period in which the film is set. But they also tend to make the film so rarefied as to squeeze the life force out of it, setting the excellent supporting performances of Karen Black, Bruce Dern, Sam Waterston and Scott Wilson in isolation rather than as part of a whole. You'll also spot Howard Da Silva, who was in the 1949 version before being blacklisted for alleged Communist connections.

Great Gatsby, The ○
1949, US, 90 mins, b/w
Dir: Elliott Nugent
Stars: Alan Ladd, Betty Field, Macdonald Carey, Ruth Hussey, Shelley Winters, Barry Sullivan
Rating: ★★★★

Second and best of the three film versions of F Scott Fitzgerald's famous story of a wealthy socialite gangster un-done by love of a worthless woman. Errol Flynn wanted the title role, but it went to Alan Ladd, who was exactly right for it, and gave a sharply-shaded performance, probably his best. Betty Field doesn't seem so well-cast as Daisy (Susan Hayward, perhaps?), but there's a whole string of interesting supporting performances from Macdonald Carey, Shelley Winters, Barry Sullivan, Ed Begley, Carole Mathews, Henry Hull and Elisha Cook Jr. Together with Ladd, they infuse the picture with real life and they keep the viewer on nerve-edge hoping the story will turn away from an impending tragic ending. Only the film's relatively small scale and lack of ambition push it down from the top level.

Great Guns ☉ ⓥ
1941, US, 74 mins, b/w
Dir: Monty Banks
Stars: Stan Laurel, Oliver Hardy
Rating: ★★

This is the first and best of Laurel and Hardy's films after they left Hal Roach and found control of their material rapidly running away from them. Watch out for Alan Ladd in a tiny part as a soldier buying gum in a store. A year later he was to become a star.

Great Locomotive Chase, The ○
1956, US, 86 mins, colour
Dir: Francis D Lyon
Stars: Fess Parker, Jeffrey Hunter
Rating: ★★★

A good but not outstanding Western thriller from Walt Disney, based on the same story that inspired Buster Keaton's *The General.* Although the characters are never as clear-cut as they might be, the action moves along swift-ly and the Technicolor photography is splendid, Fess Parker is appropriately rugged, but co-star Jeffrey Hunter has a less happy time on the acting front. Still, it's pretty rousing stuff for the younger viewer.

Great Manhunt, The
See: State Secret

Great McGinty, The ○
(aka: Down Went McGinty)
1940, US, 83 mins, b/w
Dir: Preston Sturges
Stars: Brian Donlevy, Muriel Angelus, Akim Tamiroff, William Demarest
Rating: ★★★★

The film started director Preston Sturges' brief but giddy ascent to the ranks of cinema's immortals. A screen-writer with Paramount (after eventful early years as an inventor), Sturges of-fered the studio one of his scripts for 10 dollars on condition that they let him direct it himself. The result was this bitingly satirical comedy about a bird-brained down-and-out (Brian Donlevy) who rises to a governorship thanks to quirks of fate. Full of wonderful mo-ments and a marvellous ending.

Great Mouse Detective, The ☉ ⓥ
(aka: Basil The Great Mouse Detective)
1986, US, 75 mins, colour
Dir: John Musker
Voice stars: Vincent Price, Val Bettin, Barrie Ingham, Candy Candido, Alan Young, Shani Wallis
Rating: ★★★

Lesser Disney: It's the broadness and crudeness of its outlines and general animation that betray this as no more than a mildly enjoyable diversion from the studio. Its good scenes are really limited to two or three – a toyshop bat-tle and a waterfront dive among them – and, of the three musical numbers, only one shows the signs of due care and attention that would soon return to the studio. This is 'Let Me Be Good to You', which could have come straight out of *Chicago* and, raunchily voiced by Melissa Manchester as a mouse chanteuse, momentarily transports pro-ceedings to a more lively dimension. Vincent Price enjoys himself much as one might expect as the arch-fiend Ratigan, a murine relative of Dr Phibes, and some additional fun is af-forded by the mouse queen, target of Ratigan's plot, who looks at the peg-legged bat Fidget dressed in yeoman's uniform and asks, 'Have you been with us long?'

Great Muppet Caper, The ☉ ⓥ
1981, UK, 95 mins, colour
Dir: Jim Henson
Stars: Charles Grodin, Diana Rigg, John Cleese, Robert Morley, Peter Ustinov,

Jack Warden
Rating: ★★★★

'Look, Dad, it's a bear.' 'No dear, it's a frog. Bears wear hats.' The muppets are hardly ever as bad as they might be and here they go on a spoof jewel caper with a full quota of asides to the audi-ence and spoofs of movie legend. Miss Piggy takes part in a (rather good) take-off of an Esther Williams water ballet and a Busby Berkeley dance routine, Kermit and Fozzie pose as twins to foil the villains, and Charles Grodin is splendidly po-faced as the rascally brother of heroine Diana Rigg, falling in love with Miss Piggy with heart-rending sincerity. There are longueurs, of course, but also continuous re-minders of an original humour at work. 'You know,' confides Fozzie to Kermit at a sleazy hotel, 'I may be mis-taken, but the bellhops look like rats.' 'Humph,' says the proprietor, over-hearing, 'you should see the chambermaids.'

Great Outdoors, The ○ ⓥ
1988, US, 90 mins, colour
Dir: Howard Deutch
Stars: Dan Aykroyd, John Candy
Rating: ★★

John Hughes, the writer of *Home Alone*, whose box-office takings made it the biggest comedy money-spinner of all time, has had more hits than misses in his career. There are a few good belly laughs in this caper about a family holi-day going disastrously wrong and the pairing of Dan Aykroyd (always better when playing an unsympathetic charac-ter) and John Candy works well, but the material is on the whole depressing-ly threadbare. Fans of up-and-coming star Annette Bening will recognise her in one of her earliest roles, as Aykroyd's pampered wife.

Great Santini, The ☾
1979, US, 111 mins, colour
Dir: Lewis John Carlino
Stars: Robert Duvall, Blythe Danner, Michael O'Keefe
Rating: ★★

Not exactly a run-of-the-mill film to come across these days, this story of a wildcat Marine Flying Corps colonel and his much put-upon family, with whom he shares a strident and some-times amusing love-loathe relationship. Director Lewis John Carlino (who also wrote the film) hasn't the know-how to extract the skilful performances, espe-cially from the youngsters, that the film needs, although one warms to the ugly daughter (Lisa Jane Persky) who, des-

G

perate for her macho father's attention, tells him she is pregnant by a cross-eyed negro pacifist.

Great Scout and Cathouse Thursday, The ◐

1976, US, 102 mins, colour
Dir: Don Taylor
Stars: Lee Marvin, Oliver Reed, Robert Culp, Elizabeth Ashley, Kay Lenz
Rating: ★

Careering comedy-Western with pantomime performances from Lee Marvin and Oliver Reed as bedraggled Westerner and overweight Indian respectively. The plot's situations come up with some nice ideas, especially Robert Culp's refusal to pay a ransom for his wife because he doesn't want her back, although director Don Taylor's treatment of them is not exactly subtle.

Great St Trinian's Train Robbery, The ○ ⓥ

1965, UK, 94 mins, colour
Dir: Sidney Gilliat
Stars: Frankie Howerd, Dora Bryan, George Cole, Reg Varney
Rating: ★★

St Trinian's listed as an ancient monument. Three hundred of its pupils awarded the MBE ('It's a diabolical liberty,' declares Beatle Ringo in a newspaper headline). Yes, those teenage tigresses are back, thwarting a gang of thieves led by Frankie Howerd and the voice of Stratford Johns. The fun is kept lively, and a little dialogue between Howerd and Leon Thau (as a Pakistani railwayman) towards the end is priceless.

Great Waldo Pepper, The ○ ⓥ

1975, US, 108 mins, colour
Dir: George Roy Hill
Stars: Robert Redford, Bo Svenson, Susan Sarandon
Rating: ★★★

Written by William Goldman, Oscar winner for *Butch Cassidy and the Sundance Kid*, this elegiac homage to World War One fliers who became barnstorming aerial stunt men in the Twenties reunited Robert Redford with George Roy Hill, director of his two hits *Butch Cassidy* and *The Sting*. Redford, as the disillusioned pilot reduced to defying death in an air circus, gives one of his best, least self-admiring performances and Susan Sarandon, as always, is superb. Stunning flying scenes and an intelligent screenplay are major assets.

Great Waltz, The ○

1938, US, 103 mins, b/w
Dir: Julien Duvivier
Stars: Luise Rainer, Fernand Gravet, Miliza Korjus, Lionel Atwill
Rating: ★★★★

One of Hollywood's best reach-for-your-handkerchief biopics of great composers, in this case Johann Strauss. Never mind the story, feel the treatment: the film is full of the splendour of Strauss' lilting music, and the roaring spirit of the times, with French director Julien Duvivier achieving a bewitching blend of music and pictures. Crowd sequences and production numbers are thrillingly well organised and really stir the emotions. Double Oscar-winner Luise Rainer acts quite exquisitely as Strauss' devoted wife; Miliza Korjus sings brilliantly as the opera star he later falls in love with; Fernand Gravet makes Strauss believable both as a musical genius and a flesh-and-blood person.

Great Waltz, The ○

1972, US, 150 mins, colour
Dir: Andrew L Stone
Stars: Horst Buchholz, Mary Costa, Nigel Patrick
Rating: ★★

This great piece of schmaltz is an over-colourful musical biopic of the Viennese composer Johann ('Blue Danube') Strauss Jr. It stars a highly energetic Horst Buchholz as the composer who became the 'Waltz King' despite the efforts of his father Johann Sr (probably best known for 'The Radetsky March') to prevent him from pursuing a musical career. The story is okay while the conflict between tempestuous Johann Sr and eager young Johann lasts. But after dad's demise, we are swept off into an indigestible whirl of chocolate-box romance and champagne-soaked parties – a sort of *Come Dancing* gone mad, with dialogue straight out of a second-feature Western. But then there is the music – 'The Blue Danube' (of course), the 'Tritsch-Tratsch Polka' and 'Thunder and Lightning' are just part of a generous selection. Shame you can't turn the vision off and leave the sound on!

Great White Hype, The ● ⓥ

1996, US, 90 mins, colour
Dir: Reginald Hudlin
Stars: Samuel L Jackson, Jeff Goldblum, Jon Lovitz, Corbin Bernsen, Salli Richardson, Peter Berg, Cheech Marin
Rating: ★★

Occasionally amusing boxing satire starring a very lively Samuel L Jackson as Reverend Sultan, a flamboyant promoter who tries to revive waning interest in the noble sport of fisticuffs – and his own flagging fortunes – by luring a white contender into the all black heavyweight scene. Peter Berg has some funny moments as the earnest but dim challenger, Damon Wayans camps it up as the reigning champ and Jeff Goldblum has too little to do as a journalist working to expose Sultan's scams. Despite its heavyweight cast, it's sloppily paced, and ultimately too lightweight to be a knockout in the comedy-satire class.

Great Ziegfeld, The ○

1936, US, 176 mins, b/w
Dir: Robert Z Leonard
Stars: William Powell, Myrna Loy, Luise Rainer, Frank Morgan
Rating: ★★★★

This is a skilfully structured, extravagantly mounted look at the career of showman Florenz Ziegfeld (astutely played by William Powell) who gave his name to the Ziegfeld Follies. Luise Rainer's sympathetic portrait of Anna Held was rewarded with an Oscar, while the climax may have been remembered by Orson Welles when he came to make *Citizen Kane*. The singer on the revolving staircase in one of the biggest musical numbers will be recognised by some as Dennis Morgan, then still appearing under his real name, Stanley Morner. Strangely, he doesn't use his own (very respectable) singing voice. The tones that issue from his lips, singing about a pretty girl being like a melody, are those of Allan Jones. The film won the Academy Award for Best Film.

Greedy ◐ ⓥ

1994, US, 113 mins, colour
Dir: Jonathan Lynn
Stars: Michael J Fox, Kirk Douglas, Nancy Travis, Olivia D'Abo, Ed Begley Jr, Jonathan Lynn
Rating: RB

A deadeningly over-performed comedy about a group of grasping relatives all willing to go to any lengths to get their hands on the $25 million scrap metal fortune of their elderly wheel-chaired Uncle Joe (Kirk Douglas). All, that is, except failed pro bowler Danny (Michael J Fox), who isn't interested until the relatives drag him into the act. They're super-worried about the old man's nubile 'nurse' (Olivia D'Abo) whom they're afraid will inherit the lot.

We never do find out if Olivia is after the old guy's money, but she's such a bad actress no one will care. Under director Jonathan Lynn's far from gentle persuasion, a whole cast of seasoned pros go further over the top than in a TV variety sketch: interest bites the dust quicker here than in almost any film in living memory. Nancy Travis alone plays it all straight.

Green Berets, The ○ Ⓥ
1968, US, 141 mins, colour
Dir: Ray Kellogg, John Wayne
Stars: John Wayne, David Janssen, Jim Hutton, Aldo Ray, Raymond St Jacques
Rating: ★★★

John Wayne's pro-America-in-Vietnam film is a fine piece of entertainment if one ignores the flag-waving and concentrates on it purely as an escapist war movie. Wayne also had a hand in the direction and his son Patrick had a featured role. In a small role: a then little-known comedian called Richard Pryor.

Green Card ◑ Ⓥ
1990, US, 107 mins, colour
Dir: Peter Weir
Stars: Gérard Depardieu, Andie MacDowell, Bebe Neuwirth, Robert Prosky
Rating: ★★★★

Gérard Depardieu plays a Frenchman in America who enters into a marriage of convenience with horticulturist Andie MacDowell to obtain the precious Green Card that will enable him to stay in the country. She in turn can claim a marvellous apartment with refectory/greenhouse attached that is only available to married couples. They part as strangers, and everything is fine until immigration decides to investigate in depth. In an enforced weekend together, Depardieu and MacDowell discover what the rest of us have guessed·from reel one: but that's romantic cinema for you. Very nicely done, all the same, with dialogue that smacks sweetly of ad-libbing, the same attention to supporting roles as in *Pretty Woman*, and an inspired sequence where the 'happy' couple invents a series of honeymoon snapshots. Depardieu adapts very well to the subtleties of English-speaking comedy, and even submits to some ribbing about his weight.

Green Dolphin Street ○
1947, US, 155 mins, b/w
Dir: Victor Saville
Stars: Lana Turner, Van Heflin, Donna

Reed, Richard Hart
Rating: ★★

The great New Zealand earthquake of 1855 was devastatingly recreated for this story of a young couple in the Antipodes. British director Victor Saville used the Hollywood studio and the Californian redwood forests to film trees being tossed into the air; geysers spouting water and mud; houses collapsing and a mountain splitting down the middle. Even Lana Turner gets her hair mussed: nothing is missed in the cause of realism. But the rest is too often plodding and tedious.

Green Fire ○
1955, US, 95 mins, colour
Dir: Andrew Marton
Stars: Stewart Granger, Grace Kelly, Paul Douglas, John Ericson
Rating: ★★

A colourful film about romance, adventure and emerald mining in the Colombian jungles of South America – surely one of the most unusual settings in film history. During location filming in Colombia, Stewart Granger, Grace Kelly and others lived aboard a huge barge moored in a river. When the river suddenly went into spate, the barge broke loose and was drifting at speed down the river when the natives in canoes rescued the stars. Definitely not in the (soggy) script.

Green For Danger
1946, UK, 91 mins, b/w
Dir: Sidney Gilliat
Stars: Alastair Sim, Trevor Howard, Leo Genn, Sally Gray, Rosamund John
Rating: ★★★★

A really creepy thriller based on Christianna Brand's novel of foul play afoot in a wartime emergency hospital. Alastair Sim is in prime form as the inspector on the case, providing a welcome vein of comedy running through the suspense. All the nurses go round looking suitably shivery and apprehensive (with good cause) and the photography makes the maximum use of the dark and mysterious to heighten tension. The title? A man dies on the operating table, because carbon monoxide cylinders (painted green) are substituted for those containing oxygen. Too scary for young children.

Greengage Summer, The ○
(aka: Loss of Innocence)
1961, UK, 99 mins, colour
Dir: Lewis Gilbert
Stars: Kenneth More, Susannah York, Danielle Darrieux, Jane Asher, Maurice

Denham
Rating: ★★★★

A strange and most appealing film about the pains of growing up. Susannah York shines in her first demanding role in the cinema, as one of four youngsters stranded in France. And the colour photography of the French countryside is quite breathtaking. There's a very welcome appearance by the talented French star Danielle Darrieux, and the young Jane Asher is minxishly effective as Miss York's sister.

Green Grass of Wyoming ○
1948, US, 89 mins, colour
Dir: Louis King
Stars: Peggy Cummins, Charles Coburn, Lloyd Nolan, Robert Arthur
Rating: ★★★

Dog-fever in the Hollywood of the Forties, after MGM had struck it rich with Lassie, was quickly followed by horse-fever. A colt called Flicka spearheaded a host of vigorous, colourful outdoor adventure stories, guaranteed to thrill animal lovers and wring a tear from the most hardened animal-hater. *My Friend Flicka*, *The Red Pony*, *Black Beauty* and *Thunderhead*, *Son of Flicka* were offspring of the idea. *Green Grass of Wyoming*, a sort of sequel to the last of these, is a folksy Western with some exciting trotting scenes towards the end.

Green Grow the Rushes ○
1950, UK, 80 mins, b/w
Dir: Derek Twist
Stars: Richard Burton, Honor Blackman, Roger Livesey
Rating: ★★★

Inspired by the success of *Whisky Galore!*, British filmmakers turned out so many similar comedies in the next few years that it seemed the entire English coast must be a seething nest of rum-runners and smugglers. The scene here is the Kent marsh country and the spirit in question is brandy. Although its brand of whimsy is rather far behind Ealing Studios, *Green Grow the Rushes* has amusing performances by Roger Livesey as Captain Biddle and Harcourt Williams as a chairman of the Bench.

Green Hell ○
1940, US, 87 mins, b/w
Dir: James Whale
Stars: Douglas Fairbanks Jr, Joan Bennett, George Sanders, Alan Hale, George Bancroft, Vincent Price
Rating: ★★

G

A prime cast in one of the last films from the original master of the American sound horror film, British-born James Whale. Here he turned in an oddity among adventure stories, with Douglas Fairbanks Jr, Joan Bennett, George Sanders, Alan Hale, George Bancroft and Vincent Price all emoting madly in the depths of the South American jungle. The screenplay is by double Oscar-winner Frances Marion.

Green Man, The ○
1956, UK, 80 mins, b/w
Dir: Robert Day
Stars: Alastair Sim, George Cole, Terry Thomas, Jill Adams
Rating: ★★★

A happy comedy film about a hired assassin – Alastair Sim – determined to bump off an inept politician (Raymond Huntley) who has come to a country inn for an illicit weekend. Sim's performance – especially when the character is seen in flashback, committing youthful assassinations – reminds one now much subtlety the British comedy film has lost in the past few decades, and how scandalously underused Sim remained. This is written by the old and reliable firm of Frank Launder and Sidney Gilliat.

Gregory's Girl ○ Ⓥ
1980, UK, 91 mins, b/w
Dir: Bill Forsyth
Stars: John Gordon Sinclair, Dee Hepburn, Jake D'Arcy, Clare Grogan
Rating: ★★★★

The freshest and funniest school comedy from Britain since It's *Great to be Young* 25 years earlier. The soccer team of an unnamed Scottish school is in trouble. 'Hear they were awarded a corner last week,' says a spectator at their latest debacle, 'and took a lap of honour.' But wait. There's a new star on the horizon. Her name is Dorothy (Dee Hepburn). She's beautiful. And deadly (with a futba' that is). The deposed striker Gregory (John Gordon Sinclair), demoted to goalie, falls heavily for her. In between his attempts to come to terms with this hopeless infatuation, the film is fiercely funny about school life ... and so true you have to laugh. The two leads are both very good, but the film is stolen by tiny Allison Forster as Gregory's wiser-than-he sister – all of 10 years old.

Gremlins ○ Ⓥ
1984, US, 106 mins, colour
Dir: Joe Dante

Stars: Zach Galligan, Phoebe Cates, Hoyt Axton, Frances Lee McCain
Rating: ★★★★★

Basically a children's film with horrific overtones, this is a vastly entertaining fantasy, directed by Joe (*InnerSpace*) Dante, who doesn't miss a trick from the moody opening in Chinatown when Papa (Hoyt Axton, whose narration and performance are both spot-on) buys a mogwai there. An endearing cross between a chihuahua and a bat-eared fox, the mogwai must not, Axton is told, be exposed to bright light, have water dropped on it or be fed after midnight. Of course, you don't need me to tell you that Axton and his family rapidly do all three, ending up with a whole pack of man-eating, three-feet high, slavering gremlins who, besides people, eat everything in sight, stop the traffic, smoke and gamble in the local bars and enjoy a showing of *Snow White and the Seven Dwarfs*. The trick-work and technical skill involved in all this is immense, and the humour, sentiment, excitement and horror, although all pretty basic, are blended as well as one could reasonably expect. The highlight of the fun and grisly games is undoubtedly the ingenious scene in which Axton's wife disposes of several death-bent gremlins with the aid of kitchen contrivances.

Gremlins 2: The New Batch ◐ Ⓥ
1990, US, 107 mins, colour
Dir: Joe Dante
Stars: Zach Galligan, Phoebe Cates, John Glover, Robert Prosky, Christopher Lee
Rating: ★★★

They're back and hyped to the hilt: singing, dancing, eating and even taking over the cinema. Everything is thrown into this one – from old-time 'B' stars like Kathleen Freeman, Dick Miller and Kenneth Tobey, to getting Daffy Duck to top and tail the movie. It's just as well, as the laughs and thrills are rather fewer this time around: Old Wing (Keye Luke) dies and Gizmo the mogwai, on the loose again, is soon doused with water and gives rise to the puffball creatures that quickly metamorphose into cackling, scaly, bat-eared, fang-baring gremlins. Some of them even take over the laboratory where mad scientist Christopher Lee is conducting all sorts of experiments. 'All a man wants,' he grumbles, 'are some fresh germs.' The gremlins he gets are fresh all right, enough to swallow all his potions and turn into

anything from a talking gremlin-about-town to a monstrous cross between gremlin and spider.

Grey Fox, The ○
1982, Canada, 91 mins, colour
Dir: Phillip Borsos
Stars: Richard Farnsworth, Jackie Burroughs
Rating: ★★★★★

This old-fashioned Western about an old-fashioned Westerner – the true-life character Bill Miner who robbed stagecoaches for 18 years, before serving 26 years for doing it – is well-nigh flawless of its type. The film takes up Miner's story when he's released from prison in 1901 at 60. After an abortive two years trying to scratch a living, he turns to robbing trains instead of stages. Richard Farnsworth, a veteran Western stuntman turned featured player, makes the most of the role of a lifetime as Miner, with a reflective performance that stamps his own slow-burning and humorous personality on the character he's playing. He has admirable assistance from John Hunter's perfectly poised script which never overstates or supplies unnecessary embellishment, but always manages to catch the perfect phrase to fit the scene.

Greyfriars Bobby ☉
1961, UK, 91 mins, colour
Dir: Don Chaffey
Stars: Donald Crisp, Laurence Naismith, Kay Walsh, Andrew Cruickshank, Gordon Jackson
Rating: ★★★

The Disney version, to be taken with a wee drop of scotch, about the 19th century Edinburgh dog who kept a long and lonely vigil by his master's grave until he passed into legend. Donald Crisp, a hardened veteran of several *Lassie* films, is at his crusty best, and the film is cannily set and wonderfully well shot in Technicolor. Have a handkerchief at the ready.

Greystoke – The Legend of Tarzan, Lord of the Apes ◐ Ⓥ
1984, US, 130 mins, colour
Dir: Hugh Hudson
Stars: Ralph Richardson, Ian Holm, Christopher Lambert, Andie MacDowell, James Fox, Cheryl Campbell
Rating: ★★★

As probably befits a movie that cost $33 million and took eight years to get to the screen, production on this mammoth Tarzan epic was a fraught affair.

After casting fashion model and acting newcomer Andie MacDowell as Tarzan's girlfriend Jane, director Hugh Hudson took her voice off the soundtrack and had all her lines redubbed by Glenn Close. To her undying credit, MacDowell bounced back a couple of years later to become one of Hollywood's brightest young stars. Beautifully shot and impeccably acted, the film's main plus is that it sticks closer to the original Edgar Rice Burroughs' novel than all the previous chest-thumping, vine-swinging Hollywood versions. But for all that, it's a dramatically uneven picture. The feat half works best, with the boy Tarzan being raised by a family of cute apes, and is on less sure ground when adult Tarzan (Christopher Lambert) is brought back to Edwardian England.

Gifters, The ●
1990, US, 110 mins, colour
Dir: Stephen Frears
Stars: Anjelica Huston, John Cusack, Annette Bening
Rating: ★★

Con artist Roy Dillon (John Cusack) has a good front for his small-time but successful activities and an attractive girlfriend (Annette Bening) in tow. Everything is fine until his mother (Anjelica Huston) shows up. She tries to come between him and his girl but all the while the Mob is after her. Despite sound performances from all the principals, this film is less satisfying than the novel by Jim Thompson upon which it is based. It's all a little uneven until all the pieces start coming together towards the end. Half the problem, perhaps, is that the characters don't really command our sympathy, making it difficult to care for or about them.

Grigsby
See: The Last Grenade

Grip of Fear, The ◐
(aka: Experiment in Terror)
1962, US, 122 mins, b/w
Dir: Blake Edwards
Stars: Glenn Ford, Lee Remick, Stefanie Powers, Ross Martin
Rating: ★★★

Hitchcock-style thriller tautly turned out by director Blake Edwards. Here, he coaxes a nicely-timed performance from the young Lee Remick as a cashier menaced by a frightened, wheezy killer (a solid start to Ross Martin's film career) who is out to rob her bank. Stefanie Powers is also very good as Remick's younger sister.

There's a tense climax, in a stadium, to a film that's full of edgy moments.

Grip of the Strangler ◐
(aka: The Haunted Strangler)
1958, UK, 79 mins, b/w
Dir: Robert Day
Stars: Boris Karloff, Jean Kent, Elizabeth Allan
Rating: ★★

This literate horror thriller brought Boris Karloff back to British films after more than 20 years away. For the occasion, screenwriter Jan Read contributed a fascinating plot that involves a novelist investigating an old murder case. There's a splendidly atmospheric ending (heightened by Lionel Banes' vivid black-and-white photography), with Karloff in a graveyard, unravelling the mystery at last to his own cost.

Groundhog Day ○ ⓥ
1992, US, 103 mins, colour
Dir: Harold Ramis
Stars: Bill Murray, Andie MacDowell, Chris Elliot, Stephen Tobolowsky
Rating: ★★★

Imagine how you would feel if you woke up at 6am and every day was the same. Well yes, okay, we all feel that way. But for Bill Murray, a self-centred TV weatherman sullenly enduring his fourth annual visit to Punxsutawney on Feb 2 (Groundhog Day), every day from now on really is the same. He's trapped in a 24-hour timelock in which most events – apart from those he affects – are exactly the same. At first, as each 'new' day dawns, Murray is angry, desperate to escape. He confides in his producer (Andie MacDowell) but naturally on the 'next' day their conversation never happened. Nor can he get her into bed, despite learning, day after day, all her whims and fancies. Passing through the 'I can do anything' stage, and past several days of committing suicide in different ways, Murray finally decides on a life of good deeds. Get the picture? So far, so sweet, but all this is inevitably, well, repetitive, so despite a few good laughs, necessity often gets the better of invention. In spurts, though, it's quirky fun in vaguely old-fashioned style.

Grosse Pointe Blank
1997, US, 107 mins, colour
Dir: George Armitage
Stars: John Cusack, Minnie Driver, Dan Aykroyd, Joan Cusack
Rating: ★★

This black comedy comes with a big cult reputation. In the event, it proves to be not as smart as it thinks it is. John Cusack, Minnie Driver (working very hard) and Dan Aykroyd are all better than their material in this story of a hit-man who goes to his high school 10-year reunion and looks up his old girlfriend while on a job in his home town. Things begin promisingly, with a wacky performance from the star's sister, Joan Cusack, as his Girl Friday, but then the film loses momentum. Gun action falls between the convining and the comic, and in the end the film just doesn't quite work. Disappointing.

Group, The ◐
1966, US, 152 mins, colour
Dir: Sidney Lumet
Stars: Candice Bergen, Joan Hackett, Elizabeth Hartman, Shirley Knight
Rating: ★★

This story of the lives of eight college girls from 1933 to 1939, is a pretty strong brew – with its elements of lesbianism, insanity, drunkenness, war, frigidity, death, beating-up and problems over contraception. The best episode is the lightest, as Polly puts up with the harmless and rather jolly eccentricities of her fat old father, who plays cunningly upon the fact that he is supposed to be mad. The fashions are fascinating, and the director, of course, is Sidney Lumet. But can you remember the rest of the group? They were Jessica Walter, Kathleen Widdoes, Joanna Pettet and (most difficult) Mary Robin-Redd.

Grotesque, The ● ⓥ
1995, UK, 98 mins, colour
Dir: John-Paul Davidson
Stars: Alan Bates, Theresa Russell, Sting, Len Headey, James Fleet, John Mills
Rating: ★

A sort of cross between *The Remains of the Day*, *The Servant* and Edgar Allan Poe, and one that doesn't begin to work, hitting a much too farcical note from the first frame. 'George always gives us a good strong ham,' says one of the characters in this East Lynne-with-maggots, a comment that might apply to an all-too-distinguished cast that also includes Jim Carter, Steven Mackintosh and Anna Massey. It's executive producer Trudie Styler, though, who gives the film's best performance – not a difficult feat admittedly. She alone strikes the right note in this *Gormengast* for, well,

G

grotesques. Director Davidson's documentaries about Amazon Indians are rather more impressive than his uninspired handling of this mock-Gothic farrago.

Grumpy Old Men ◑ ⓥ
1993, US, 100 mins, colour
Dir: Donald Petrie
Stars: Jack Lemmon, Walter Matthau, Ann-Margret, Burgess Meredith, Daryl Hannah, Kevin Pollak
Rating: ★★★

Despite a serious credibility deficiency, this is an undeniably lovable, rude (but not too rude) comedy with some very funny outtakes at the end that are guaranteed to send you off in a good mood. Ripely, if enjoyably over-acted by its largely veteran cast, the film topstars those old sparring partners Jack Lemmon and Walter Matthau as two widowed old codgers whose feud and mutual insults seem as perpetual as the snow that clamps down on their Minnesota town. Lemmon and Matthau enjoy themselves exchanging verbal and occasionally physical blows, setting traps for each other, torpedoing the other's TV and depositing dead fish in each other's cars.

Guadalcanal Diary ○
1943, US, 100 mins, b/w
Dir: Lewis Seiler
Stars: Preston Foster, Lloyd Nolan, William Bendix, Richard Conte, Anthony Quinn
Rating: ★★★★

One of the best American films about the Pacific conflict in World War Two. Very patriotic, but immensely exciting, firmly characterised, and in places, very moving too. Richard Jaeckel, the little blond tough guy whose screen credits extended through 25 years to *The Dirty Dozen*, was working as a delivery boy in the 20th Century-Fox mail room when spotted, and signed for the role of Baby Marine. He was almost 17.

Guardian, The ●
1990, US, 90 mins, colour
Dir: William Friedkin
Stars: Jenny Seagrove, Dwier Brown, Carey Lowell, Brad Hall, Miguel Ferrer
Rating: ★

Although very well made, even by today's horror film standards, this is an extremely silly story, dragged out interminably to feature-length, about the spirit of an ancient tree which takes life in the form of a woman and steals newborn babies (in the guise of a child-minder) to feed to the tree.

There's only enough material here for a half-hour *Twilight Zone* episode, and even experienced director Friedkin, who made *The Exorcist*, is pushed to keep our attention for more than a few minutes at a time before he can get cracking on the last-reel climax. Still, the cast plays it straight and gives all they've got and the story does give a new slant to the old phrase: 'The baby slept like a log'.

Guarding Tess ◑ ⓥ
1994, US, 96 mins, colour
Dir: Hugh Wilson
Stars: Shirley MacLaine, Nicolas Cage, Austin Pendleton, Edward Albert, James Rebhorn, Richard Griffiths
Rating: ★★★

Cantankerous is not the word for former US First Lady Tess Carlisle (Shirley MacLaine). Infuriating and impossible would be nearer the mark. Beloved of Americans, her eccentricities and provocative behaviour make her unbearable to live with. So secret service agent Doug Chesnik (Nicolas Cage) can't believe it when he requests him for another year of protection duty after three years of hell in her company. She drives Doug and his fellow-agents wild with ridiculous requests and oddball excursions, followed by a call to the President if the agents dare raise a whisper of protest. Naturally, although this is amusing enough (if a little tedious at times), there has to be a dramatic point – and, sure enough, a real crisis comes in the life of widow Carlisle, to which Doug may be the only answer. MacLaine is perfect casting as the expert in put downs who turns every situation to her own advantage. Cage starts stickily, but grows into the role.

Guess Who's Coming to Dinner ○ ⓥ
1967, US, 112 mins, colour
Dir: Stanley Kramer
Stars: Spencer Tracy, Katharine Hepburn, Sidney Poitier
Rating: ★★★

Intrinsically facile film about the dilemma facing the parents of a white girl wanting to marry a black man but lifted onto an altogether higher plane by the magical acting (their last film together) of Katharine Hepburn and Spencer Tracy, the latter having a superbly delivered closing speech that will bring tears to your eyes. Miss Hepburn took the third of her four best actress awards, and William Rose was also given an Oscar for his screenplay.

Guide for the Married Man, A ◑
1967, US, 91 mins, colour
Dir: Gene Kelly
Stars: Walter Matthau, Inger Stevens, Robert Morse
Rating: ★★★

Star-studded joke of a film directed by Gene Kelly, which surveys 'case histories' as an experienced adulterer (Robert Morse) teaches the art of cheating in marriage. Inger Stevens is too delicious a wife to ever dream of cheating on, but you'll have fun recognising the visitors from Hollywood's A-Z, who include Lucille Ball, Jack Benny, Sid Caesar, Jeffrey Hunter, Jayne Mansfield, Phil Silvers and Terry-Thomas.

Guilty As Sin ● ⓥ
1993, US, 107 mins, colour
Dir: Sidney Lumet
Stars: Rebecca DeMornay, Don Johnson, Jack Warden
Rating: ★★

This okay thriller has good performances from Rebecca DeMornay and Don Johnson, both of which deserve rather better than this adequate but fairly humdrum script. Johnson in particular, oozing evil, does his best screen work in some time as a manipulative womaniser and maybe murderer who lights on DeMornay's high-flying lawyer to defend him on a charge of killing his wife. DeMornay's character, in fact, is the big weakness here. When Johnson says that 'You're not as tough or as smart as I thought you were,' he's right. She's illogical too but maybe we should give her the benefit of the doubt and say that, in the face of Johnson's prime evil, her logic flew out of the window. Later developments could well raise a few gasps from the nervously inclined, but most viewers have no problems keeping two paces ahead of the plot.

Guilty by Suspicion ◑ ⓥ
1990, US, 106 mins, colour
Dir: Irwin Winkler
Stars: Robert De Niro, Annette Bening, George Wendt, Sam Wanamaker, Martin Scorsese
Rating: ★★★

Hollywood's conscience showing again – and very effectively, too, even if there can't be many filmgoers now unaware of the infamous activities of the communist witch-hunters of the postwar period, or the debilitating effects they had on the film industry. Robert De

Niro plays a director whose attendance at a couple of communist meetings in the late Thirties – he was thrown out for arguing too much – jeopardises his whole career 12 years later. He finds himself blacklisted, blocked from working at even the smallest studio. The story is slight and seems to have nowhere much to go – indeed it comes to a stop rather than ends – but the performances make it watchable throughout; Annette Bening is admirable as the ex-wife to whom De Niro finds himself forced to turn.

Guinea Pig, The O
1948, UK, 97 mins, b/w
Dir: Roy Boulting
Stars: Richard Attenborough, Sheila Sim, Bernard Miles
Rating: ★★★

No one today could get away with casting a 25-year-old actor as a 14-year-old schoolboy, but Richard Attenborough's interpretation of the role here is so sensitive that there were te complaints when this film was released. The traumatic times of the elementary schoolboy sent to a public school as part of an education experiment provide touching, sometimes harrowing and often thought-provoking entertainment.

Gumball Rally, The O Ⓥ
1976, US, 105 mins, colour
Dir: Chuck Bail
Stars: Michael Sarrazin, Gary Busey, Normann Burton
Rating: ★★

Here's the forerunner of all those *Cannonball Run* films, a painless panorama of pandemonium about an illegal car race across America. One or two performances even outshine the hardware, notably Tricia O'Neil, a curvy contestant with a fine range of facial expressions, and Harvey Jason as a manic Hungarian aboard a seemingly indestructible motor-cycle.

Gumshoe ◑ Ⓥ
1972, UK, 85 mins, colour
Dir: Stephen Frears
Stars: Albert Finney, Billie Whitelaw, Frank Finlay, Janice Rule
Rating: ★★★★

The opening music (by Tim Rice and Andrew Lloyd Webber, the *Evita* men) and credit titles are both superbly evocative of those Forties' detective thrillers which *Gumshoe* seeks to gently spoof and, at the same time, raise a respectful hat. Director Stephen Frears never loses this mood, from the mo-

ment one first meets Eddie Ginley (a marvellous performance by Albert Finney), a small-time bingo caller and an even smaller-time private eye who dreams of being Humphrey Bogart, Elvis Presley and Dashiell Hammett rolled into one. His subsequent adventures on the trail of the Fat Man will delight any film fan with an affection for the kind of film whose atmosphere *Gumshoe* conjures up. All through the story (cleverly written and constructed by Neville Smith) characters play along with Eddie's fantasies of greatness partly because they know him, but partly because they find it difficult to resist. You'll find *Gumshoe* hard to resist too.

Gun Crazy O
(aka: Deadly is the Female)
1950, US, 87 mins, b/w
Dir: Joseph H Lewis
Stars: John Dall, Peggy Cummins
Rating: ★★★★

A moody minor masterpiece about a couple obsessed both with firearms and each other, and their inevitable flight from the law. Extremely well made, this is one 'cult' classic that justifies its reputation. Director Joseph H Lewis chooses all the right angles for his impact and never puts a foot wrong. Peggy Cummins (she frighteningly ecstatic at the thrill of the crime) and John Dall give their best film performances by a country mile. Certainly to be mentioned in the same breath as *Bonnie and Clyde*.

Guncrazy ● Ⓥ
1992, US, 93 mins, colour
Dir: Tamra Davis
Stars: Drew Barrymore, James LeGros, Billy Drago
Rating: ★★★

Part love story, part thriller and part comedy, this is the *Bonnie and Clyde*-style story of two juvenile misfits on the run. He (James LeGros) is an ex-killer on parole, she (Drew Barrymore, all grown up after *E. T.*) is a poor, mixed-up teenager in a dead-end town. They share an obsession with guns and a passion for each other – and a background of murder soon develops. Barrymore does well with her character, a bored, sluttish 16-year-old who, desperate to be loved, starts corresponding with a prisoner (LeGros) and so begins a long-distance love affair. A touching study of loneliness and doomed love. Despite the modern adult themes, it's almost like an old-fashioned, good-quality B-movie.

Gunfight at Comanche Creek O
1963, US, 90 mins, colour
Dir: Frank McDonald
Stars: Audie Murphy, Colleen Miller
Rating: ★

Audie Murphy gets two heroines for the price of one in this grim-faced but lacklustre Western in which intrepid Audie takes on a whole gang of outlaws. The two girls, Colleen Miller (like Murphy, a refugee from Universal-International) and Susan Seaforth, both make the acting sparks fly. Ben Cooper is the best of the baddies.

Gunfight at Dodge City, The O
1958, US, 81 mins, colour
Dir: Joseph M Newman
Stars: Joel McCrea, Julie Adams, John McIntire, Nancy Gates
Rating: ★★★

Better-than-average Western with Joel McCrea as the famous gunman and gambler Bat Masterson. Nancy Gates must have been used to the character, having previously played opposite a different Bat (George Montgomery) in the Western *Masterson of Kansas*.

Gunfight at the OK Corral O
1956, US, 122 mins, colour
Dir: John Sturges
Stars: Burt Lancaster, Kirk Douglas, Rhonda Fleming, John Ireland, Jo Van Fleet, Earl Holliman
Rating: ★★★

Hollywood's obsession with the battle between the Earps and the Clantons at Tombstone's OK Corral in 1881 reached perhaps its peak (before the 1994 revamps) in this action film that pitched in most of the cinema's best bad guys against Burt Lancaster, earnest but excellent as Wyatt Earp, and Kirk Douglas, more flamboyant but just as good as Doc Holliday. It's amazing, in fact, that so many good actors – such excellent villains as Lyle Bettger, Jack Elam, Lee Van Cleef, Frank Faylen and Ted de Corsia among them – should consent to appear in what amount to very small roles. The lion's share of the acting meat deservedly goes to the Oscar-winning Jo Van Fleet, usually cast as characters much older than herself, who is allowed a rare touch of glamour as Holliday's mistress Kate Fisher. There is, in addition, Frankie Laine's catchy theme song, and the equally famous roaring climax. if you're a Western fan, you can't go far wrong with this.

G

Gunfighter, The ○
1950, US, 84 mins, b/w
Dir: Henry King
Stars: Gregory Peck, Helen Westcott,
Millard Mitchell, Karl Malden
Rating:★★★★

Classic, humourless Western, with
Gregory Peck (in a role originally
sought by John Wayne) as the gunfighter trying (and inevitably failing) to
run away from his past. It carries a
surprising feeling of authenticity for a
Western of this period and there are
good supporting portrayals from
Millard Mitchell, Karl Malden and (as
two gun-happy punks) Richard Jaeckel
and Skip Homeier. Studio executives
at 20th Century-Fox are said to have
blamed the film's indifferent box-office
performance on the fact that Peck wore
a moustache!

Gun for a Coward ○
1956, US, 88 min, colour
Dir: Abner Biberman
Stars: Fred MacMurray, Jeffrey Hunter,
Dean Stockwell, Janice Rule
Rating: ★★

The stars play three brothers in this
strange, but entertaining Western, one
of a clutch of decent horse-operas made
by MacMurray in the late Fifties.
Here, all three are outscored by a
peach of a performance from Chill
Wills, as Loving.

Gun Fury ○
1953, US, 83 mins, colour
Dir: Raoul Walsh
Stars: Rock Hudson, Donna Reed, Phil
Carey, Roberta Haynes
Rating: ★★★

Veteran director Raoul Walsh ensured
plenty of action and strong performances in this 'A' class Western with a
formidable cast. Rock Hudson and
Donna Reed are certainly a notch
above the conventional Western leads,
and the bad guys include Phil Carey,
Lee Marvin, Leo Gordon (very effective in a semi-sympathetic role) and
Neville Brand.

Gunga Din ○ ⓥ
1939, US, 117 mins, b/w
Dir: George Stevens
Stars: Cary Grant, Douglas Fairbanks Jr,
Victor McLagen, Joan Fontaine, Sam
Jaffe
Rating: ★★★★★

RKO's hugely entertaining North-
West Frontier spectacular, with
stalwart sergeants three Cary Grant,
Victor McLaglen and Douglas

Fairbanks Jr on top form. One of the
most stirring and exciting action films
ever made, with some wonderful ban-
tering dialogue, a heart-rending ending
and a performance by Sam Jaffe in the
title role that all but steals the show.
Ace entertainment.

Gung Ho ●
1986, US, 105 mins, colour
Dir: Ron Howard
Stars: Michael Keaton, Mimi Rogers,
Gedde Watanabe
Rating: ★★★

Michael Keaton is at the centre of a
bad case of culture clash when a
Japanese company reopens a car plant
in Pennsylvania and runs it the way
they would back home. Oddly, it's the
American factory workers who come
off worse here, portrayed largely as a
bunch of lazy and inefficient backslid-
ers. The Japanese work ethic means
hard work and pride in their job. If all
this sounds a little serious, don't be
alarmed – it's a fast-moving comedy
that provides a good deal of fun.
Keaton, in zany mood, dominates, but
Gedde Watanabe, as the young
Japanese executive in charge of the
plant, is also very good.

Gun Glory ○
1957, US, 89 mins, colour
Dir: Roy Rowland
Stars: Stewart Granger, Rhonda Fleming
Rating: ★★

Although he was tops at Britain's box-
office during the Forties, it took
Hollywood and a whole posse of
Westerns and other action films to turn
Stewart Granger into an international
star. This drama – about a gunfighter
trying to settle down to ranch fife – is
one of the least exciting, although it's
based on Phillip Yordan's novel *Man of
the West*. The theme song is sung by
Burl Ives.

Gun Hawk, The ○
1963, US, 92 mins, colour
Dir: Edward Ludwig
Stars: Rory Calhoun, Rod Cameron, Rod
Lauren, Ruta Lee
Rating: ★★★

Uneven, but at times quite splendid
Western about a dying gunfighter and
the young man whom he is determined
to steer clear of the outlaw trail. Rory
Calhoun, not the sort one usually associates with great acting, gives a
performance of almost Brando-like intensity as the bandit. The dialogue
written for him seems particularly apposite to the character, with humour,

pathos and the inner workings of the
mind carefully interwoven. Jo Heims'
screenplay rises to greatness by
Western standards in the closing stages.

Gun in Betty Lou's Handbag, The ● ⓥ
1992, US, 89 mins, colour
Dir: Allan Moyle
Stars: Penelope Ann Miller, Eric Thal,
Alfre Woodard, William Forsythe, Cathy
Moriarty, Julianne Moore, Xander
Berkeley
Rating: ★★

Great title, good supporting cast: if
only the two stars had the charm required to carry the rest. Betty Lou
(Penelope Ann Miller) is a meek and
mousy librarian lady with a policeman
husband (Eric Thal) who ignores her, a
boss who bullies her and friends who
think that she's just plain dull (on this
showing, they've got a point). To grab
their attention, she confesses to a murder she didn't commit – and, instantly,
shy Betty Lou becomes a national
celebrity. In the tradition of the best
screwball farces things soon go hopelessly wrong, and the result is a sweet,
if ultimately bland comedy romp.

Gunn ○
1966, US, 94 mins, colour
Dir: Blake Edwards
Stars: Craig Stevens, Laura Devon
Rating: ★★

There's plenty of action in this detective yarn, based on the TV series *Peter
Gunn*, which was created by the director of the film, Blake Edwards.
Edwards also co-wrote the screenplay
with William Peter Blatty, who later
turned his pen to *The Exorcist*.

Gunpoint
See: At Gunpoint

Gun Runner, The ○
(aka: Santiago)
1956, US, 92 mins, colour
Dir: Gordon Douglas
Stars: Alan Ladd, Rossana Podesta,
Lloyd Nolan, Chill Wills
Rating: ★★★

One of Alan Ladd's last big films, an
adventure story casting him as an ex-
military man running guns from Cuba
to Florida during Cuba's war of independence. Stiff direction of the
dialogue by Gordon Douglas is balanced by some tense action scenes.

Gun Runners, The ○
1958, US, 83 mins, b/w
Dir: Don Siegel

Stars: Audie Murphy, Patricia Owens, Eddie Albert, Everett Sloane
Rating: ★★

Don Siegel-directed third screen version of Ernest Hemingway's *To Have and Have Not*, with Audie Murphy as the man who gets involved in gunrunning to Cuba. It's perhaps the most faithful of the three to the spirit of the book, with plenty of action and a supporting cast which guarantees interest, including the baby-faced Richard Jaeckel, thin-lipped Everett Sloane and Jack Elam, taking a well-earned breather from Western shoot-outs.

Guns at Batasi ○
1964, UK, 103 mins, b/w
Dir: John Guillermin
Stars: Richard Attenborough, Jack Hawkins, Mia Farrow, Flora Robson
Rating: ★★★

Richard Attenborough draws the regimental sergeant-major to life in this action drama of unrest in an emergent African state. 'On the parade ground a tyrant, in a hot spot a hero' – for once, the publicity said it all. John Leyton, a former pop singer, does well as the juvenile lead, although his haircut wouldn't do for the Army in 1964.

Guns in the Afternoon ○
(aka: Ride the High Country)
1961, US, 93 mins, colour
Dir: Sam Peckinpah
Stars: Randolph Scott, Joel McCrea, Mariette Hartley, Edgar Buchanan, Warren Oates
Rating: ★★★★★

Director Sam Peckinpah was responsible for some of the most exciting gun duels and shoot-outs ever seen on the screen. This Western remains his best film, despite the notoriety of his later, blood-spattered work. And it includes a final gunfight as fierce and fine as anything the Western has given us. From the opening shot, the adrenaline is flowing, but Peckinpah doesn't short-change on the low-key details that give the proceedings a genuine whiff of life. Joel McCrea and Randolph Scott (whose last film this was before retiring on a fortune estimated at between 50 and 100 million dollars) give career-best performances as two ex-lawmen at loggerheads over a consignment of gold.

Gunsmoke ○
1953, US, 79 mins, colour
Dir: Nathan Juran
Stars: Audie Murphy, Susan Cabot, Paul Kelly, Charles Drake, Jack Kelly
Rating: ★★

Nothing to do with James Amess and his famous Western hero Matt Dillon, who starred in the TV series of the same name, but a spirited Technicolor horse-opera about a hired gun (Audie Murphy) who changes sides in a range war. Directed by Nathan Juran, the film also features Murphy's real-life friend, Charles Drake, and pretty, raven-haired Susan Cabot, whose operatic singing voice was never put to use during her Hollywood film career.

Guns of Darkness ○
1962, UK, 95 mins, b/w
Dir: Anthony Asquith
Stars: Leslie Caron, David Niven, James Robertson Justice
Rating: ★★

Anthony Asquith was an odd choice to direct this adventure story, which has a colourful backcloth of revolution in Central America. The script is by John Mortimer, who had written the film adaptation of *The Innocents* the previous year. For this source, Mortimer had a best seller called *Act of Mercy* by Francis Clifford, whose *The Naked Runner* has also been filmed. Both books deal with ordinary businessmen caught up in high adventure. The atmospheric photography of Robert Krasker is especially effective during a tense battle for life in a sinister swamp.

Guns of Fort Petticoat, The ○
1958, US, 82 mins, colour
Dir: George Marshall
Stars: Audie Murphy, Kathryn Grant, Hope Emerson, Jeff Donnell
Rating: ★★★

Better-than-average Western, directed by George Marshall, who made *Destry Rides Again* and *When the Daltons Rode*. Excitement mounts in the closing stages as the women (who have to defend a cavalry fort while their menfolk are away) begin to fall one by one, and the Indians threaten to overwhelm them.

Guns of Navarone, The ○ Ⓥ
1961, US/UK, 157 mins, colour
Dir: J Lee Thompson
Stars: Gregory Peck, David Niven, Anthony Quinn, Anthony Quayle, Stanley Baker
Rating: ★★★

This blazing adventure yarn pulled the public into cinemas in droves when it was first released. There are fights and nail-biting action scenes galore as six saboteurs scale massive cliffs in a daring attempt to destroy two enormous German guns pointed firmly in the direction of Allied shipping. Almost overloaded with stars, the cast also includes Irene Papas, Gia Scala, James Darren and Richard Harris.

Guns of the Magnificent Seven ○
1968, US, 106 mins, colour
Dir: Paul Wendkos
Stars: George Kennedy, Monte Markham, Joe Don Baker
Rating: ★★★

Next to the original, this is the best of the *Seven* films. Despite the familiar framework of the plot, director Paul Wendkos, whose work remains undervalued in this country, actually manages to raise some fresh excitement from the old story of the septet of gunfighters riding to the rescue of yet another group of downtrodden Mexicans. George Kennedy's unexpectedly lithe and forceful performance as Chris is a great help and holds the film together when it looks as though it might disintegrate after a promising start, as did other follow-ups in the series. Antonio Macasoli's sharp DeLuxe Colour photography helps highlight the action in the thrilling climax, and the gunfighters themselves are quite well defined.

Guns of the Timberland ○
1959, US, 91 mins, colour
Dir: Robert D Webb
Stars: Alan Ladd, Jeanne Crain, Gilbert Roland, Lyle Bettger
Rating: ★★

Jeanne Crain, Hollywood's sweetest teenager in the Forties, played rather a lot of bad girls in her later films, and this Western proves no exception. Rivalling her in the villainy stakes is husky-voiced Lyle Bettger, who for once does not bite the dust – one of the few original touches in this busy story of timber-men at loggerheads. Alan Ladd and Gilbert Roland play the logging partners who fall out with predictably tragic results but more fire is provided by Miss Crain and by Noah Beery Jr. Pop singer Frankie Avalon makes his acting debut.

Guns of Wyoming ○
(aka: Cattle King)
1963, US, 88 mins, colour
Dir: Tay Garnett
Stars: Robert Taylor, Joan Caulfield
Rating: ★★

Latter-day Robert Taylor Western, pleasantly shot in Metrocolor, which casts him as Sam Brassfield, owner of a giant cattle ranch (the American title of

G

the film is, in fact, *Cattle King*). It's nice to see powder-puff blonde Joan Caulfield, again, and the villain – once the hero's best friend – provides a plum role for one of the screen's best oily badmen, Robert Middleton. Overall, though, this is a mighty slow ride through familiar pastures.

Guy Named Joe, A ○
1943, US, 120 mins, b/w
Dir: Victor Fleming
Stars: Spencer Tracy, Van Johnson, Irene Dunne
Rating: ★★

A draggy action-fantasy with Spencer Tracy's sincerity its major asset as an airman who, after getting killed, looks after the fortunes of his fellows. The supporting cast of MGM reliables includes Ward Bond, Lionel Barrymore, Henry O'Neill, Barry Nelson, James Gleason and Don DeFore. Right down the list, without a swimming pool in sight, there's the lovely Esther Williams. Remade by Steven Spielberg in 1989 as *Always*.

Guys and Dolls ○
1955, US, 150 mins, colour
Dir: Joseph L Mankiewicz
Stars: Marlon Brando, Jean Simmons, Frank Sinatra, Vivian Blaine
Rating: ★★★

Samuel Goldwyn's film version of the famous musical about the gambler who falls for the Salvation Army girl retains only Vivian Blaine from the original Broadway stars and she obliges by stealing every scene she is in. The individual song hit is undoubtedly Stubby Kaye with 'Sit Down, You're Rockin' the Boat'. Controversial choices Marlon Brando and Jean Simmons were all right on the night, but it's all a bit wearing.

Gypsy ○
1962, US, 149 mins, colour
Dir: Mervyn Le Roy
Stars: Rosalind Russell, Natalie Wood, Karl Malden
Rating: ★★★★

Rosalind Russell played the stage mother to end them all in this richly entertaining musical about her two daughters, who became actress June Havoc and strip queen Gypsy Rose Lee. The Stephen Sondheim-Jule Stein score includes 'Everything's Coming Up Roses', 'Together Wherever We Go', 'Small World' and 'Let Me Entertain You'. Russell does her own singing, while Natalie Wood (as Rose) is dubbed.

Gypsy ○ ⓥ
1993, US, 142 mins, colour
Dir: Emile Ardolino
Stars: Bette Midler, Peter Riegert, Cynthia Gibb, Ed Asner
Rating: ★★★

A musical in this day and age? Whatever next? Extremely colourful, and with warmth and affection in many of its performances, this is nevertheless a slightly strained version of the old chestnut, difficult to relax with. Bette Midler might have been born to play the part of the stage mother who, frustrated in her own desires for stardom, pushes her two untalented daughters into vaudeville. Midler really gets her teeth into the role of Mama Rose and, though her singing is sometimes not at its best, she enjoys some inspired moments on the acting front. Peter Riegert is quietly excellent as the agent who loves her, and Cynthia Gibb entirely competent as Louise in a role that gives its actress little chance to shine. The songs are melodic, and one includes the classic line: 'Soon this bum'll be Beau Brummell'. Rhymes like that are worth waiting to hear.

Gypsy and the Gentleman, The ○
1957, UK, 107 mins, colour
Dir: Joseph Losey
Stars: Melina Mercouri, Keith Michell, Patrick McGoohan
Rating: ★★

By coincidence, this barnstorming melodrama, about a beautiful gypsy causing the downfall of a philandering rake, was the third film in the careers of both Keith Michell (looking a little overweight) and scenery-chewing Greek actress Melina Mercouri (looking ravishing and playing the foot stomping spitfire for all she was worth). Michell and Mercouri do well to rise above the somewhat silly story, and a big plus is cinematographer Jack Hildyard's striking use of Eastman Colour stock, which manages to evoke both the quality and look of old sporting prints in the numerous exterior scenes.

Gypsy Colt ☉
1954, US, 72 mins, colour
Dir: Andrew Marton
Stars: Donna Corcoran, Ward Bond, Frances Dee
Rating: ★★★

A nice little remake of *Lassie Come Home*, using a horse in the story instead of a dog. Young Donna Corcoran was never more appealing, while Ward

Bond and Frances Dee are believable country folk as her parents. Andrew Marton moves the story smoothly along to a tear-stained conclusion, while the American outdoors is warmly, richly captured in Harold Lipstein's Ansco Color photography. A rock solid MGM family film.

Gypsy Girl
See: Sky West and Crooked

Gypsy Moths, The ❶
1969, US, 110 mins, colour
Dir: John Frankenheimer
Stars: Burt Lancaster, Deborah Kerr, Gene Hackman, Bonnie Bedelia, Scott Wilson, Sheree North
Rating: ★★★

Ebullient director John Frankenheimer and tough-guy star Burt Lancaster continued their association in this tale of three free-fall parachutists. Lancaster and Deborah Kerr renew their on-screen passion of *From Here to Eternity* but Gene Hackman quietly steals this disturbing and – at times – suspenseful film.

Hackers ◑ Ⓥ
1996, US, 104 mins, colour
Dir: Iain Softley
Stars: Angeline Jolie, Fisher Stevens, Lorraine Bracco, Jonny Lee Miller
Rating: ★★

One line – 'Hackers of the world, unite' – sums up the sentiments of this computer-age thriller. Director Iain Softley asks us to sympathise with those who penetrate the world's computer systems and maybe infect them, against those who do the same thing for their own personal gain. A fine difference, you might think, and one which non-computer buffs (are there any left out there?) will find hard to deal with. Computer effects here are dazzling if repetitive, even if the technical side of the plot will defeat any layman hands down. Performances are generally unattractive, although only Lorraine Bracco's is actually less than competent. The implications of it all are suitably frightening and bring into question the right of the computer to dominate the entire business world. 'Manual back-up?' snarls the chief bad guy (Fisher Stevens), 'there *is* no manual back-up!'

Hail the Conquering Hero ○
1944, US, 101 mins, b/w
Dir: Preston Sturges
Stars: Eddie Bracken, Ella Raines, William Demarest
Rating: ★★★

Writer-director Preston Sturges savagely swipes at some of America's most sacred cows – including small-town politics, patriotism and mother-love – in a classic comedy that contains some of his most sustained satire. It was his last totally effective film and it marked the high spot in the movie career of star Eddie Bracken whose shy, bumbling persona was ideal as a vehicle for Sturges' attacks. Here, he's rejected for army service, then hides out while the townsfolk believe him to be a hero in battle and prepare a triumphal return.

Hairspray ◑ Ⓥ
1988, US, 96 mins, colour
Dir: John Waters
Stars: Ricki Lake, Divine, Debbie Harry, Sonny Bono
Rating: ★★★

Like film-maker John Waters' other comedy *Cry-Baby*, this is an engagingly affectionate spoof of teen movies of the Fifties and Sixties that also draws on the director's own memories of the period. Marvellously tacky stuff, with Waters himself as a deranged psychiatrist, Pia Zadora in a cameo role, and Ricki Lake a total delight as the happily overweight teenage heroine who buys her clothes at the Hefty Hideaway dress shop.

Half Angel ○
1951, US, 77 mins, colour
Dir: Richard Sale
Stars: Loretta Young, Joseph Cotten
Rating: ★★

This romantic comedy about a girl with a split personality would probably be treated today as a sex comedy, and all the poorer for it. The evergreen Loretta Young – who started her career at 15 by answering a studio call intended for her sister – sparkles as the girl.

Half a Sixpence ⊙
1967, UK, 148 mins, colour
Dir: George Sidney
Stars: Tommy Steele, Julia Foster
Rating: ★★★

Until it runs out of steam towards the end, this enjoyable adaptation of H G Wells's novel is a flash-bang-wallop of a picture, all sweep and verve, with Tommy Steele and Julia Foster giving run-for-years performances in the leading roles. The song-and-dance routines have the explosive build-up of a combined fireworks display.

Half Moon Street ● ○
1986, US, 90 mins, colour
Dir: Bob Swaim
Stars: Sigourney Weaver, Michael Caine
Rating: RB

A monstrosity filled with dialogue that has an unreal ring, and a cast that sound as though they're acting 99 per cent of the time. Sigourney Weaver, who is, with Michael Caine, one of the only two actors most people will recognise, is disturbed by her living conditions – she invites the landlord in to mend the plumbing while she's in the bath – and her low pay at a research institute. 'How do you manage on £150 a week?' she asks her upper-class twit colleague. 'I don't,' he replies. 'My parents own a small merchant bank.' Not having such essentials to fall back on, Sigourney joins an escort agency, wining, dining and bedding men at a rate sufficient to set her up in luxury in about a fort-

night. That's where Came comes in. He's a political 'fixer' who becomes interested in Siggy for herself. 'Don't put walls around me, Sam,' she warns. 'China was full of walls. I'm sick of them.' Still he goes ahead and the lurking camera, and music indicates that Someone Is Watching It All. Thereafter, the script never disappoints in its utter predictability.

Hallelujah Trail, The ○ Ⓥ
1965, US, 167 mins, colour
Dir: John Sturges
Stars: Burt Lancaster, Lee Remick, Jim Hutton, Donald Pleasence, Brian Keith
Rating: ★★★

A gloriously entertaining comedy-Western about the battle for a wagon train-load of whisky bound for Colorado. The Indians – only one of the factions after the liquor – get all the best dialogue, and all the funniest visual gags. These include one scene where the Indians huddle terrified within a circle of wagons while the Cavalry ride whooping round them. There's a superb climax, and good-humoured playing from Burt Lancaster, Donald Pleasence and Brian Keith. Only Lee Remick is ill-served by her dialogue as the leader of a band of temperance women.

Halloween ● Ⓥ
1978, US, 93 mins, colour
Dir: John Carpenter
Stars: Donald Pleasence, Jamie Lee Curtis, Nancy Loomis, P J Soles
Rating: ★★★

Jamie Lee Curtis, daughter of Tony Curtis and Janet Leigh, made an auspicious film debut in this shocker, in which a killer back from 15 years in the asylum stalks a trio of teenage girls with heavy breath and hand-held camera, and takes a heck of a while to get about his gory business. Director John Carpenter wracks up the suspense to breaking point thanks to ingenious use of tight-tracked camera shots around the rooms of a house. It spawned a clutch of sequels and bare-faced imitators but none was a patch on this spine-tingler.

Halloween II ● Ⓥ
1981, US, 92 mins, colour
Dir: Rick Rosenthal
Stars: Jamie Lee Curtis, Donald Pleasence
Rating: ★★

The masked maniac from John Carpenter's stalk-and-slash classic is still on the loose and terrorising scream

H

queen Jamie Lee Curtis once more. Co-scripted by Carpenter himself, but directed by Rick Rosenthal, the film picks up the action on the same night the original film ended.

Halloween III: Season of the Witch ●
1983, US, 98 mins, colour
Dir: Tommy Lee Wallace
Stars: Dan O'Herlihy, Tom Atkins, Stacey Nelkin
Rating: ★★

Quite a nice little horror story idea even if it's nothing to do with Halloween or any of its other sequels. Something nasty is happening at America's Shamrock Halloween Masks factory, where all the staff are Irish, and it's all due to come to a head (!) on pumpkin night. Genial evil genius Dan O'Herlihy is clearly plotting something foul with the aid of men in blue suits whom he has perhaps picked up as seconds at *Futureworld*. It all degenerates into standard grisly horror before the end, although you may also wonder why O'Herlihy couldn't content himself with just making a fortune from his factory. Three more sequels to the original story have followed since.

Halls of Montezuma ○
1950, US, 113 mins, colour
Dir: Lewis Milestone
Stars: Richard Widmark, Jack Palance, Karl Malden, Robert Wagner
Rating: ★★★

An uncharacteristic war film from Lewis Milestone in that it's all flag-waving, glory-glory and martial music in the background. One expects quieter, grimmer stuff from the man who made *All Quiet on the Western Front* and *Pork Chop Hill*. It's powerfully acted by a strong cast which, besides stars Richard Widmark, Jack Palance, Karl Malden and Robert Wagner, includes Reginald Gardiner in a rare dramatic role – Skip Homeier, Neville Brand and Richard Boone plus Jack (*Dragnet*) Webb as a war correspondent.

Hamburger Hill ● Ⓥ
1987, US, 108 mins, colour
Dir: John Irvin
Stars: Anthony Barile, Michael Patrick Boatman, Don Cheadle, Dylan McDermott, Tim Quill, Steven Weber
Rating: ★★

The futility of war is again writ large before our eyes in this graphic Vietnam drama about a 10-day siege by US airborne troops (the 'Screaming Eagles') of a hill that no one really cared about

and which was forgotten once the battle was over. In writer Jim Carabatsos and director John Irvin's account of the battle, though, it seems to take us far too long to get to know the personalities involved. The film gathers pace in the last half hour, with the final assault, but by then its impetus is all but gone. Having said that, some individual scenes are nicely composed by any measure, and the ensemble performances are goodish while lacking in the individual charisma this kind of enterprise demands. The message is once again painfully driven home, however.

Hamlet ○ Ⓥ
1948, UK, 142 mins, b/w
Dir: Laurence Olivier
Stars: Laurence Olivier, Jean Simmons, Eileen Herlie, Basil Sydney
Rating: ★★★★

Laurence Olivier's film of the Shakespeare tragedy (cut by some two hours from the original's four and a half hours running time) was the second of his screen adaptations of the Bard's plays and the first wholly British picture to win the Best Film Oscar. The star's fascinating interpretation of the role of the moody Dane was controversially received but always compelling, earning him the Oscar for Best Actor. There were Oscars, too, for the art direction and costumes. As director, Olivier made dramatic use of Desmond Dickinson's atmospheric monochrome cinematography.

Hamlet ○ Ⓥ
1990, UK, 133 mins, colour
Dir: Franco Zeffirelli
Stars: Mel Gibson, Glenn Close, Alan Bates, Paul Scofield, Ian Holm, Helena Bonham Carter
Rating: ★★★

Zeffirelli's version of Shakespeare's most famous play chalks quite clearly the line between what attracts in the cinema and the theatre. Think of the cast here: Paul Scofield (as the ghost), Alan Bates (as Claudius), Ian Holm (as Polonius), plus the casting coups of Glenn Close as the queen and Mel Gibson as Hamlet. Theatregoers would pay a fortune to see them. Yet cinema-goers, fed on a diet of special effects, might well pass by on the other side of the road. True, the film actually is a thing of rags and patches. There are too many boring bits in the first half, but Zeffirelli picks it up half-way through and keeps it galloping along to its corpse-strewn finale. Gibson's good, especially in the key speeches, but occa-

sionally falters when trying to lend too much lightness to the role. Close is perfect casting as the double-dealing Queen. Helena Bonham Carter is visually flawless as Ophelia but her reading of the dialogue leaves something to be desired. But it's got to be worth the price of admission, hasn't it, to hear Mad Mel recite 'To Be or Not to Be'? You'd better believe it.

Hamlet ◑ Ⓥ
1996, UK, 242 mins, colour
Dir: Kenneth Branagh
Stars: Branagh, Kate Winslet, Derek Jacobi, Julie Christie, Richard Briers, Timothy Spall, Charlton Heston, Robin Williams, Billy Crystal
Rating: ★★★

After ducking and weaving the slings and arrows of outrageous fortune with such offbeat Hamlets as Nicol Williamson and Mel Gibson in the past few decades, Bard-basher Branagh sees to it that we go the full 15 rounds with the gloomy Dane in this full-text, four-hour version of Shakespeare's play. Sometimes sumptuous to look at, this is undeniably a long slog, but given the full Monty by Branagh (naturally playing Hamlet himself), Winslet (no bloodless Ophelia this) and Briers, whose Polonius is such that you feel that if you looked up craftiness in the dictionary, a picture of Briers in costume would be there. And, every time the film drags, its extraordinary cast relieves the tedium in one fashion or another: Heston and Williams (rather good), Gérard Depardieu and Jack Lemmon (all at sea), plus John Mills, Judi Dench, John Gielgud and Richard Attenborough with scarcely a line between them.

Hammersmith Is Out ◑
1972, US, 108 mins, colour
Dir: Peter Ustinov
Stars: Elizabeth Taylor, Richard Burton, Beau Bridges
Rating: ★

One of Peter Ustinov's rare forays as a film director, in a bizarre story about an escaped madman who improbably becomes an all-powerful magnate. The script's shafts of wit are at their sharpest during the scenes in the asylum itself, while the supporting cast includes Ustinov himself, John Schuck, Leon Ames and that former gangster movie star, George Raft.

Hammett ◑
1982, US, 100 mins, colour
Dir: Wim Wenders

Stars: Frederic Forrest, Peter Boyle, Marilu Henner, Elisha Cook
Rating: ★★★

First scripted in 1976, shot in 1980 and reputedly largely reshot the following year by Francis Coppola, Wim *Paris Texas* Wenders' first American film still turns out to be a stylistic treat. Frederic Forrest is superb as famed author Dashiell Hammett who gets caught up in a real-life *film noir* mystery. The Thirties' studio look is beautifully and authentically re-created and the sordid story of blackmail and murder grips to the end. Crime cultists will realise that several elements of the storyline appear in Hammett's later books.

Handful of Dust, A ○ Ⓥ
1988, UK, 118 mins, colour
Dir: Charles Sturridge
Stars: James Wilby, Kristin Scott Thomas, Rupert Graves, Alec Guinness
Rating: ★★★

Evelyn Waugh's tragi-comic dissection of the indolent aristocracy in pre-war England is brought to the screen with all the loving attention to period detail one might expect from Charles Sturridge, the director of the epic *Brideshead Revisited* series. In comparison, this is a chamber piece, brilliantly acted by its talented young leads James Wilby as the kindly but dull cuckold, Rupert Graves as his smarmy upstart rival and, best of all, Kristin Scott Thomas as the adulterous wife who more than hold their own, in illustrious company, against a string of eye-catching performances (Judi Dench, for example, won a Best Supporting Actress BAFTA award). The stately pacing works in the film's favour, lending resonance to a story which has too many unsympathetic characters for its own good.

Handgun ● Ⓥ
(aka: Deep in the Heart)
1982, US, 100 mins, colour
Dir: Tony Garnett
Stars: Karen Young, Clayton Day
Rating: ★★★★

Films about rape and the woman's attempts to fight back, pioneered by TV movies, gained momentum in the cinema of the Eighties, reaching a spectacular climax with *The Accused*. In this cleverly commercialised example, perky teacher Karen Young, hurt by a previous involvement, says 'No' to gun-crazy Texas boyfriend Clayton Day, following three dates and a sumptuous meal in his flat. Enraged, the macho man forces himself on her – and

changes her life. Advised against prosecution, she takes up arms literally by becoming a crack sharpshooter. The final duel scene at the end is especially effective, not least as you just can't guess who's going to win. Young is very good in the two 'personalities' of her character: you can really believe in her both as a vulnerable girl and an ice-cool killer.

Handle With Care (1977)
See: Citizens Band

Hands Across the Table ○
1935, US, 76 mins, b/w
Dir: Mitchell Leisen
Stars: Carole Lombard, Fred MacMurray, Ralph Bellamy
Rating: ★★★

One of the best examples of the brittle, pseudo-cynical style of Hollywood comedy of the 1934–1936 period, which led to the 'screwball' comedies, of the end of the decade. Carole Lombard sparkles in a screenplay that steers perfectly the difficult course between reality, humour and sentimentality. Said one contemporary critic: 'The story is as slender as a young willow, but before the film comes to an end a bat has been made out of it which sends almost everything to the boundary.'

Hands of the Ripper ●
1971, UK, 85 mins, colour
Dir: Peter Sasdy
Stars: Angharad Rees, Eric Porter, Jane Merrow, Dora Bryan
Rating: ★★★

A sort of Hammer horror version of *Marnie*, with more people getting impaled on a greater variety of sharp weapons than in *Friday the 13th* and its sequels put together. Interesting pale colour photography, good performances and a nice period feel help counter-balance the disappointingly routine development of the plot.

Hand that Rocks the Cradle, The ● Ⓥ
1992, US, 110 mins, colour
Dir: Curtis Hanson
Stars: Annabella Sciorra, Rebecca DeMornay, Matt McCoy, Ernie Hudson, Julianne Moore
Rating: ★★★

Although it has its share of silly moments, this suspense thriller is well enough made to score points most of the time. When pregnant mum Clare (Annabella Sciorra) exposes her hospital doctor as a groper (and other

women join in), he blows his brains out. His own pregnant wife (Rebecca DeMornay) has a miscarriage. Months later, DeMornay shows up at the Sciorra household offering her services as a nanny. She breast-feeds the baby, alienating it from its mother. When the retarded handyman (Ernie Hudson) becomes suspicious, she has him tagged as a child-molester and dismissed. Sister-in-law rumbles her too, but is quickly dispatched in a trap originally set for Sciorra. Soon the scene is set for a climactic night of terror Hollywood can stage-manage standing on its head. DeMornay is icy as the vengeful widow, outshining Sciorra, who does as well as she can with the wife, and Matt McCoy, who has the thankless role of the husband.

Hang 'Em High ● Ⓥ
1967, US, 114 mins, colour
Dir: Ted Post
Stars: Clint Eastwood, Inger Stevens, Ed Begley
Rating: ★★★

This was Clint Eastwood's first starring role in an American Western following his phenomenal success in Italy. It is a bitter film, an uneven one, and sometimes quite as violent as its Italian counterparts. But it's more deserving of serious consideration as a movie than Eastwood's work with Italian director Sergio Leone, not least for the fine, burnished colour photography of Leonard South and Richard Kline, and for an extraordinary supporting cast.

Hanging Tree, The ○
1958, US, 106 mins, colour
Dir: Delmer Daves
Stars: Gary Cooper, Maria Schell, Karl Malden, George C Scott
Rating: ★★

A typically brooding performance from Gary Cooper dominates this Western, directed with a keen eye for detail by Delmer Daves. Set in an unruly Montana gold mining township, the drama unfolds with carefully sustained suspense sequences. A strong supporting cast includes Karl Malden, King Donovan and, best of all, George C Scott, enjoying himself immensely as a phoney faith-healer.

Hangin' with the Homeboys ● Ⓥ
1991, US, 88 mins, colour
Dir: Joseph B Vasquez
Stars: Doug E Doug, Mario Joyner, John Leguizamo
Rating: ★★★

H

A night on the town with four Bronx buddies, two black, two Puerto Rican. Although the film runs out of steam even before its shortish running time is up, there are some funny lines around and a chuckle or two, as one or two of the 'homeboys' learn a thing or two about the future. Comedian Doug E Doug is particularly good as the initially amusing, but finally pitiable Workshy Willie who sees everything as racist. As he tells the (black) employment clerk; 'You're doing this to me because I'm black, right?' Tom's a black actor who finds out that acting is a steadier girlfriend than some women. Of the Puerto Ricans, Vinny's a compulsive womaniser who's never learnt, Johnny a pretty boy shop assistant who really ought to be thinking about going to college. Before you tire of their escapades you'll get enough smiles to justify your money.

Hangman, The ○
1958, US, 86 mins, b/w
Dir: Michael Curtiz
Stars: Robert Taylor, Fess Parker, Jack Lord, Tina Louise
Rating: ★★

A low-key, well-made Western from Oscar-winning director Michael Curtiz. Robert Taylor puts on his sternist face as the embittered lawman whose sobriquet provides the film's title and Jack Lord, later to star in *Hawaii Five-O*, has a featured role.

Hangman's Knot ○
1953, US, 81 mins, colour
Dir: Roy Huggins
Stars: Randolph Scott, Donna Reed, Richard Denning, Lee Marvin, Claude Jarman Jr
Rating: ★★★

Post-Civil War Western with an absolutely cracking cast, including three Oscar-winners: Donna Reed, Lee Marvin (in one of his earliest roles) and Claude Jarman Jr. Although the action is largely confined to four walls, there's plenty of it, and the fight between Marvin and upright Confederate major Randolph Scott is a corker. Despite its familiar plot, in fact, this carefully made Western is well worth watching. Another plus factor: it has spot-on Technicolor photography by master lensman Charles Lawton Jr.

Hangmen Also Die ○
1943, US, 131 mins, b/w
Dir: Fritz Lang
Stars: Brian Donlevy, Anna Lee, Walter Brennan, Gene Lockhart, Dennis O'Keefe
Rating: ★★★

Fritz Lang's fiercely anti-Nazi suspense film about the aftermath of the assassination of Reinhardt Heydrich, 'Hitler's hangman', in Czechoslovakia. It has no really big star names, but there are outstanding performances from Gene Lockhart, Alexander Granach, Walter Brennan, Anna Lee and Tonio Selwart. James Wong Howe again demonstrates his mastery of black and white photography and the film, though long, is always gripping in the telling and never outstays its welcome.

Hangover Square ○
1945, US, 77 mins, b/w
Dir: John Brahm
Stars: Laird Cregar, Linda Darnell, George Sanders
Rating: ★★★

That embryo Sydney Greenstreet, Laird Cregar, lumbers deliciously through his last film role before a crash diet – he aspired to romantic leading roles – killed him at just 28. The mists through which Cregar drifts before some new nefarious deed fortunately blur much of the 1903 Chelsea background which, architecturally and geographically, is typically wide of the Hollywood mark. Otherwise, this is a super dose of gaslit Grand Guignol. An early score by the prolific composer Bernard Herrmann, later to work for Alfred Hitchcock, screeches its own warnings to viewers already rendered apprehensive by Cregar's powerful, subtle and moving rendition of a role that could have drawn audience giggles in the hands of a lesser actor. An exuberant amalgam of murder, arson and music, with a spectacular, if overloaded, climax.

Hannah and Her Sisters ◑ ⓥ
1986, US, 103 mins, colour
Dir: Woody Allen
Stars: Woody Allen, Michael Caine, Mia Farrow, Carrie Fisher, Barbara Hershey, Dianne Wiest
Rating: ★★★★

Another of Woody Allen's funny-sad slices of life with all its complications and anxieties. Abounding in warmth and humour, it marked a forward step from the relative failure and disappointments of Woody's *Interiors* and *Stardust Memories*. Here he returned in triple Oscar-winning form with a delicate romantic portrait of the tensions within family life. With more than a passing nod to Chekhov and *King Lear*, it's the story of three sisters whose upper class lives are interlinked over a two-year period. Allen is in top form as Mia Farrow's hypochondriac ex-husband, but it was Michael Caine who won the Best Supporting Actor Oscar, as the agent who secretly lusts after his wife's sexy sister, played by Barbara Hershey, and Dianne Wiest the Best Supporting Actress as a poor woman who is always busy but has nothing to show for it.

Hanna's War ●
1988, US, 148 mins, colour
Dir: Menahem Golan
Stars: Maruschka Detmers, Anthony Andrews, David Warner, Donald Pleasence, Ellen Burstyn
Rating: ★★

The Golan-Globus answer to *Carve Her Name with Pride*. That hit film, though, was made in 1958 and 30 years on the stories of such war heroines as Violette Szabo and, here, the young Hungarian writer Hanna Senesh seem, especially when told at such length, more appropriate to the format of a mini-series. Menahem Golan's film gets off to a pretty sticky start and only succeeds in spasms. Maruschka Detmers is quite good as Hanna but, like the film, it's a variable performance that's not always totally convincing. Even more up and down is Anthony Andrews as her RAF instructor, with a Scottish accent that mostly stays, but occasionally goes altogether. David Warner and Donald Pleasence, mournfully and myopically respectively, parade their familiar baddies. Action scenes are okay, but too few and far between.

Hannibal ○
1959, Italy, 103 mins, colour
Dir: Carlo Ludovico
Stars: Victor Mature, Rita Gam
Rating: ★

Italo-American action spectacle which loses no chance to spread its battle scenes all over the canvas of its screen, but doesn't convince for a minute as far as the dialogue is concerned. Victor Mature is ideally cast in the title role. No white elephant at the box-office, though: it made a mint.

Hannibal Brooks ○
1968, UK, 102 mins, colour
Dir: Michael Winner
Stars: Oliver Reed, Michael J Pollard
Rating: ★★★★

World War Two adventure that veers skilfully between comedy and drama as British POW Oliver Reed attempts to cross the Alps on the back of an elephant he's liberated from Munich Zoo. Snub-nosed American Michael J Pollard provides comic support and the elephant wins all hearts in the emotive ending.

Hannie Caulder ◑
1971, US, 85 mins, colour
Dir: Burt Kennedy
Stars: Raquel Welch, Robert Culp, Ernest Borgnine, Strother Martin, Jack Elam, Diana Dors
Rating: ★

With Raquel Welch as a female Clint Eastwood clad only in poncho and gunbelt, Ernest Borgnine, Jack Elam and Strother Martin virtually eating the scenery as the villains, and Robert Culp as a sardonic bounty hunter, this Western seemed to have it made. But its story, though riddled with fierce action, just never seems to get going. Stephen Boyd makes an unbilled appearance as a mysterious character called The Preacher and bizarre guest spots by Christopher Lee and Diana Dors heighten the air of unreality.

Hanover Street ◑ ⓥ
1979, US, 108 mins, colour
Dir: Peter Hyams
Stars: Harrison Ford, Lesley-Anne Down, Christopher Plummer, Alec McCowen, Richard Masur, Patsy Kensit
Rating: ★★

Some effective and quite erotic love scenes add to the poignancy of Peter Hyams' attempt to make a *Brief Encounter*-style love story in a war-torn setting. But the passions and attitudes that made such movies are long gone, and their spirit proves too elusive for Hyams to grasp. Faced with such odds, Harrison Ford and Lesley-Anne Down (both of whose hairstyles make only a passing acknowledgement to the Forties) are not equal to the demands placed upon them. In the supporting cast, Michael Sacks, as the pilot's hero navigator, impresses most, while the exciting last 20 minutes underline the fact that Hyams' true vocation – he also made *Busting* and *Capricorn One* – is for fast-moving chase-and-action sequences.

Hans Christian Andersen ◑ ⓥ
1952, US, 120 mins, colour
Dir: Charles Vidor
Stars: Danny Kaye, Farley Granger, Zizi Jeanmaire
Rating: ★★★★

It's a pity about the simple-minded story to this 'fairy-tale' about the great

Danish storyteller, but never mind. You'll still enjoy Danny Kaye's gentle charm and one of the most tuneful scores that Frank Loesser ever wrote: 'The Ugly Duckling', 'Inchworm', 'I'm Hans Christian Andersen', 'The Emperor's New Clothes', 'Thumbelina', 'No Two People' and more – every one a hit. Pure magic.

Happiest Days of Your Life, The ⊙
1950, UK, 81 mins, b/w
Dir: Frank Launder
Stars: Alastair Sim, Margaret Rutherford, Joyce Grenfell
Rating: ★★★★★

No two players were ever more happily teamed than Alastair Sim and Margaret Rutherford in this riotous comedy about a boys' school forced to share its buildings with a girls' school. Dame Margaret quivers indignantly, while Sim dithers delightfully at each new crisis. Joyce Grenfell as the 'Jolly hockey sticks' games mistress adds to the fun. Richly characterised, frantically paced and very funny.

Happiest Millionaire, The ⊙
1967, US, 165 mins, colour
Dir: Norman Tokar
Stars: Fred MacMurray, Tommy Steele, Greer Garson, Geraldine Page
Rating: ★★★

Light, colourful, amusing Disney offering about an eccentric 1916 Boston household. The Sherman brothers contribute their best score outside *Mary Poppins* (it includes 'Fortuosity', 'Watch Your Footwork' and 'What's Wrong with That?') and the well-plotted script never deviates from the proven Disney formula of entertainment pure and simple. Tommy Steele is almost as engaging as the family's toothy Irish butler as a scene-stealing alligator, and doyenne actresses Geraldine Page and Gladys Cooper enjoy themselves with their caustic duet about the social graces. Lesley Ann Warren makes her screen debut.

Happy Ever After ⊙ ⓥ
(aka: Tonight's the Night)
1954, UK, 87 mins, colour
Dir: Mario Zampi
Stars: David Niven, Yvonne De Carlo, A E Matthews, Barry Fitzgerald, Michael Shepley, George Cole
Rating: ★★★★

Another comedy feather in the cap of director Mario Zampi is this rollicking, riotous romp about the new squire of an Irish village, and the locals' attempts

to bump him off. Some of the sequences are really side-splitting, George Cole is especially funny as the village idiot and the film is superbly shot in Technicolor. Niven, A E Matthews, Barry Fitzgerald and Michael Shepley all help speed this drop of Irish fun along at a rattling pace.

Happy Gilmore ◑ ⓥ
1996, US, 92 mins, colour
Dir: Dennis Dugan
Stars: Adam Sandler, Christopher McDonald, Julie Bowen, Frances Bay, Carl Weathers, Richard Kiel
Rating: ★★

This is better than Sandler's previous comedy, *Billy Madison*, although not by that much. But there are a few lunatic laughs in its story of an ice-hockey player subject to violent outbursts. Happy has little talent other than a powerhouse shot and is famous mainly as the only player ever to take off a skate and stab an opponent with it. When he takes to golf, however, he finds he can out-drive all the other players – but his putting is hopeless. How Happy learns to putt on the crazy golf course, presents his manager (Weathers) with the head of the alligator that once bit off his hand and saves Grandma's house from the bad guys bring a few bright moments to this idiot's delight that combines *Tin Cup* with *Dumb & Dumber*.

Happy Go Lovely ○
1950, UK, 97 mins, colour
Dir: Bruce Humberstone
Stars: David Niven, Vera-Ellen, Cesar Romero, Bobby Howes
Rating: ★★★

Lightweight, amusing piece of musical candyfloss made as a semi-official contribution to the Festival of Britain. The plot is no *War and Peace* but it has some good dialogue from the very competent Val Guest and some very fine song and dance routines. Let down by the lack of cinema techniques and natural locales, it is lifted again by the performances of its US-imported stars. Based on a Thirties British musical called *Paradise for Two*.

Happy Is the Bride! ⊙
1957, UK, 85 mins, b/w
Dir: Roy Boulting
Stars: Ian Carmichael, Janette Scott, Cecil Parker
Rating: ★★★

Delightful and highly amusing domestic comedy (a remake of *Quiet Wedding*), directed and part-scripted by Roy

H

Boulting. The fun centres on the trials and tribulations of a young engaged couple whose wedding arrangements become increasingly complicated and almost drive them to despair.

Happy Landing ○
1937, US, 102 mins, b/w
Dir: Roy Del Ruth
Stars: Sonja Henie, Don Ameche, Ethel Merman, Cesar Romero
Rating: ★★

Fortuitous would be the word, rather than happy, for the landing that triggers off the action in this ice-musical, particularly seeing that Don Ameche and Cesar Romero contrive to land their Paris-bound plane just a few skating rinks from Sonja Henie's home in Norway. Subsequent proceedings include Ethel Merman belting out a couple of songs and a extraordinary galvanic tap-dance number by The Condos Brothers called 'War Dance of the Wooden Indians'.

Happy Thieves, The ○
1962, US, 88 mins, b/w
Dir: George Marshall
Stars: Rex Harrison, Rita Hayworth
Rating: ★★

The teaming of Rita Hayworth and Rex Harrison suggests light comedy of the Forties. But this is an up-to-date Sixties frolic about two elegant art thieves – a colourful caper through castles, casinos and conspiracies. An unusual film to come from veteran director George Marshall, more at home with Bob Hope comedies (he made seven) or such classic Westerns as *Destry Rides Again* and *When the Daltons Rode*.

Happytimes
See: The Inspector General

Hard Contract ◑
1969, US, 106 mins, colour
Dir: S Lee Pogostin
Stars: James Coburn, Lee Remick, Lilli Palmer, Burgess Meredith, Patrick Magee, Sterling Hayden
Rating: ★★

In this rather deliberately paced thriller, James Coburn stars as John Cunningham, an enigmatic American hired killer. The film is as much a morality play under its cover of murder thriller, and as such fails to be consistently involving, although certainly there are some good bursts of action. The cast includes Trevor Howard's widow Helen Cherry and the later star-billed Karen Black.

Hard Day's Night, A ⊙ Ⓥ
1964, UK, 85 mins, b/w
Dir: Richard Lester
Stars: John Lennon, Paul McCartney, George Harrison, Ringo Starr, Wilfred Brambell, Norman Rossington
Rating: ★★★★

The Beatles make like Merseybeat Marx Brothers (with a touch of Mack Sennett) in this distinguished debut feature with an enjoyable line in witty lunacy. All four flopheads show a deft touch with a throwaway joke, and examples of the boys' wry sense of humour are legion. Interviewer: 'How did you find America?' John: 'Left after Greenland.' Interviewer: 'What do you call that hairstyle?' George: 'Arthur.' With Richard Lester directing at an 80-mile-an-hour pace and a sharp script by Alun Owen, this is a very funny and entertaining film. Its two best sequences are a wacky, wild fling as the Beatles escape from it all for a few minutes in a field; and a chaotic press conference. It almost goes without saying that the songs are all very good too.

Harder They Fall, The ○ Ⓥ
1956, US, 109 mins, b/w
Dir: Mark Robson
Stars: Humphrey Bogart, Rod Steiger, Jan Sterling, Mike Lane
Rating: ★★★★

One of the most scathing indictments of boxing in film history, this rugged, almost merciless profile of the game featured Humphrey Bogart in his last role. It was one of his most memorable parts, as a once scrupulous sports reporter who has fallen on hard times, but he was already dying of cancer and the tough shooting schedule exhausted him. He also encountered difficulty acting with co-star Rod Steiger, as a manipulative Mob boss, who insisted on Method acting. By underplaying, though, Bogart steals the show, and his scene in a car with boxer Mike Lane towards the end remains one of the most emotive moments in Fifties' films.

Hard, Fast and Beautiful ○
1951, US, 79 mins, b/w
Dir: Ida Lupino
Stars: Claire Trevor, Sally Forrest
Rating: ★★★

Ida Lupino directs this unusual melodrama revolving around the cut and thrust of the tennis world. Claire Trevor is on top form as the grasping mother pushing her daughter up the championship ladder.

Hard Man, The ○
1957, US, 80 mins, colour
Dir: George Sherman
Stars: Guy Madison, Valerie French, Lorne Greene
Rating: ★★

Very tough Western scripted by Leo Katcher from his own hard-hitting novel. Guy Madison is the Texas Ranger who believes in bringing more of 'em back dead than alive while Lorne Greene, TV's Ben Cartwright from *Bonanza*, expertly handles the role of an embittered cattle king.

Hard Target ● Ⓥ
1993, US, 95 mins, colour
Dir: John Woo
Stars: Jean-Claude Van Damme, Yancy Butler, Lance Henriksen, Wilford Brimley
Rating: ★★

Yet another Jean-Claude Van Damme bloodbath, with a little more style than most (though not much), courtesy of Hong Kong director John Woo. Once again, Van Damme is wise enough to surround himself with actors no better than he is (especially heroine Yancy Butler), though he throws himself into the action with a will, demonstrating that one can always dodge a speeding bullet with sideways or upwards leaps, something the bad guys always neglect to do. Down in New Orleans, there's a police strike on, and men are being hunted for money, on 'safaris' organised by crazy Lance Henriksen. He's really the only member of the cast who can act, but this doesn't bother Van Damme who only has to share the final wordless confrontation with him anyway. Our hero is hunted through streets, bayous and old deserted buildings, but it makes no difference: with one bound he's free. Hard target? Make that impossible.

Hard Times
See: The Streetfighter

Hard Way, The ○
1942, US, 109 mins, b/w
Dir: Vincent Sherman
Stars: Ida Lupino, Dennis Morgan, Joan Leslie, Jack Carson
Rating: ★★★★

One of the most neglected of the great Warner Brothers melodramas of the Forties. Ida Lupino was at the peak of her form, and dominates the story as the strong-willed poor-born woman who sees her chance of a new lifestyle by maximising the limited show business talent of her younger sister, riding roughshod over the feelings of all who stand in their way. Lupino won the New York Film Critics award for that year as best actress, but amazingly was not even nominated for an Oscar. Equally surprising, her meaty role had been turned down by Bette Davis. Five years later, with her career faltering, Davis would have given her eye-teeth for the role. As one of those trodden on by Lupino, Jack Carson again demonstrates his ability to poignantly play good-hearted guys with sensitive feelings.

Hard Way, The ❶ Ⓥ
1991, US, 111 mins, colour
Dir: John Badham
Stars: Michael J Fox, James Woods, Stephen Lang, Annabella Sciorra, LL Cool J
Rating: ★★★

Take a friendless cop with some kind of a death wish, on the trail of a serial killer and unable to attract women. 'Maybe it's something about my personality,' he surmises. Then take an egotistical, sawn-off movie star who has no idea about real life, but wants to make a film 'without a goddamn Roman numeral in it'. Nick Lang (Fox) wants real police experience to help him with a new role, and John Moss (Woods) is the man he chooses to provide it. Stunts and chases abound in the ensuing developments of a film that might have been better but remains enjoyable for all that. Fox has a good time (including a running gag about his looking like Nick Lang, only shorter); Woods is as OTT in comedy as he is in drama and just as entertaining.

Harem Holiday ⊙ Ⓥ
(aka: Harum Scarum)
1965, US, 86 mins, colour
Dir: Gene Nelson
Stars: Elvis Presley, Mary Ann Mobley, Fran Jeffries, Michael Ansara
Rating: ★★

Elvis Presley goes east (well, at any rate, as far as the Hollywood Hills) in a colourful comedy-musical about a pop singer kidnapped by a sheikh. Mary Ann Mobley, a one-time Miss America, is the heroine, and the score includes such desert-pop hybrids as 'It's Kismet', 'If You Love a Mirage', 'Go East Young Man' and 'Desert Serenade'. It is directed by former dancing star Gene Nelson, who brings a balletic quality to scenes of karate combat.

Harlem Nights ● Ⓥ
1989, US, 119 mins, colour
Dir: Eddie Murphy
Stars: Eddie Murphy, Richard Pryor
Rating: ★

Eddie Murphy had reached the 'can do no wrong' stage of his career when he produced, directed and wrote this foul-mouthed disaster of a film – proving that he could do wrong and in a big way. Murphy's idea of wry wit and humour is a seemingly constant stream of invective and profanity and the derivative story (a cross between *The Sting* and *The Cotton Club*) holds no surprises. However much his vanity may tell him otherwise, Murphy doesn't showcase his own particular talents as well as other directors and writers have and this film also wastes the considerable comic talents of Richard Pryor and Redd Foxx. If this film has any redeeming virtues they're completely lost under the frantic mugging of the cast.

Harlequin ❶
1980, Aus, 96 mins, colour
Dir: Simon Wincer
Stars: Robert Powell, David Hemmings, Carmen Duncan, Broderick Crawford
Rating: ★★★

An enjoyable science-fiction tall tale about a faith healer and a political plot in Australia. The characters' names suggest a parallel with the Rasputin story but, while the protagonist retains his hypnotic and healing qualities, the plot veers away into something more devious. Robert Powell, blue eyes shining, is every bit as charismatic as the makers could wish as the 'healer' who infiltrates the home of a senator whose child has leukaemia, although, after his arrival, he behaves more like Dracula than Rasputin. David Hemmings keeps rather too low a profile as a senator, but Carmen Duncan is extraordinary as his wife, and Broderick Crawford most effective as the weasel in the political woodpile. It develops ultimately into a paranoid thriller, whose special effects occasionally wobble, but whose other elements remain tight, tense and intriguing throughout.

Harold and Maude ●
1971, US, 92 mins, colour
Dir: Hal Ashby
Stars: Ruth Gordon, Bud Cort, Vivian Pickles, Cyril Cusack
Rating: ★★★

This extremely black comedy about the relationship between a death-obsessed young man and an elderly woman is often very funny and has something to offend almost everyone. The youth's series of staged suicides is particularly amusing, especially when dismissed by his harridan of a mother, who finds him hanging himself from the ceiling of his room and remarks, 'I suppose you think that's very funny.' It's one of a kind.

Harper ❶
(aka: The Moving Target)
1966, US, 121 mins, colour
Dir: Jack Smight
Stars: Paul Newman, Lauren Bacall, Julie Harris, Janet Leigh, Robert Wagner
Rating: ★★★

Paul Newman in a private-eye thriller that was Hollywood's own tribute to those superb Bogart thrillers of the Forties. Newman plays the seedy, tough detective Lew Harper who is, as William Goldman's screenplay succinctly puts it, 'hired by a bitch to find scum'. The 'scum' is a missing millionaire, although his wife (played by Bogart's widow, Lauren Bacall) doesn't seem too upset when warned that he may already be dead. So who's the kidnapper? The flashy playboy (Robert Webber)? The chauffeur who seems to live above his means (Robert Wagner) the drug-addicted pianist (Julie Harris) or a film star who 'got fat' (Shelley Winters)? Or is it all of them? Not above suspicion are Harper's own estranged wife (Janet Leigh) and his lawyer friend (Arthur Hill). As might be expected from such a cast list, this is rather a thing of bits and pieces. But Newman and Bacall really strike sparks off each other in their too-few scenes together.

Harriet Craig ○
1950, US, 94 mins, b/w
Dir: Vincent Sherman
Stars: Joan Crawford, Wendell Corey
Rating: ★★★

Joan Crawford was coming to the end of her sequence of black dramas after winning an Oscar for *Mildred Pierce* in 1945, when she made this one about a ruthlessly ambitious woman – a remake of the 1936 film *Craig's Wife*. Wendell Corey was an excellent foil for queens of the screen, fresh as he was from playing opposite Barbara Stanwyck (in *The Furies* and *The File on Thelma Jordon*) and Crawford is right on the money in the title role.

Harriet the Spy ⊙ Ⓥ
1996, US, 102 mins, colour
Dir: Bronwen Hughes
Stars: Michelle Trachtenberg, Rosie O'Donnell, Gregory Smith, Vanessa Lee Chester, Eartha Kitt
Rating: ★

H

Strictly a time-passer for undemanding kids, this has a child star who's just about as annoying as her name as the smug 11-year-old who spies on her classmates and unfortunately fights back after getting a come-uppance which few will fail to agree is richly deserved. Rosie O'Donnell has some fun as Harriet's mentor Ol' Golly, but otherwise this is largely squirm territory, full of sayings that are meant to be wise but come across as meaningless. The original novel on which it's based was funny and magical and witty, all qualities that this film lacks in abundance.

Harry and Son ◑
1984, US, 117 mins, colour
Dir: Paul Newman
Stars: Paul Newman, Robby Benson, Ellen Barkin, Wilford Brimley, Joanne Woodward
Rating: ★★

A young, virtually unknown actor called Tom Cruise was originally lined up to play Paul Newman's son in this angst-ridden family drama. Robby Benson took the role instead and years later, when Newman had won his first Oscar alongside Cruise in *The Color of Money*, Newman joked: 'Boy did I save you from that one!' Directed, co-produced and co-written by Newman, *Harry and Son* is an underdeveloped hodgepodge that never makes up its mind what it wants to be. Newman is a widower who faces a crossroads in his life. He can either throw in the towel or make a fresh start. The tragedy of the thing is that he goes nowhere. His real-life wife, Joanna Woodward, pops up as an eccentric neighbour, but the overriding sense is of a waste of talent all round.

Harry and the Hendersons
See: Bigfoot and the Hendersons

Harry and Walter Go to New York ○
1976, US, 123 mins, colour
Dir: Mark Rydell
Stars: James Caan, Michael Caine, Elliott Gould, Diane Keaton, Lesley Ann Warren, Charles Durning
Rating: ★

A magnificent cast – James Caan, Michael Caine, Elliott Gould, Diane Keaton, Lesley Ann Warren, Charles Durning and Burt Young – and a talented director, Mark Rydell, are along for the ride in this colourful comedy about two vaudeville comedians and would-be bank robbers in and out of jail in 19th-century America.

Unfortunately, thanks to a disappointingly pallid script, almost none of it works.

Harry Black and the Tiger ○
(aka: Harry Black)
1958, UK, 107 mins, colour
Dir: Hugo Fregonese
Stars: Stewart Granger, Barbara Rush, Anthony Steel, Kamala Devi
Rating: ★★★★

Jungle adventure of superior quality. Excellent colour photography and a cracking climax are bonus attractions to this story of a white hunter in India, a role that sits easily on Stewart Granger's shoulders. Anthony Steel gives one of his best performances as the figure from Black's past, a weakling who now turns up with his wife, while I S Johar is brilliant as Black's Indian helper.

Harum Scarum
See: Harem Holiday

Harvey ⊙ Ⓥ
1950, US, 100 mins, b/w
Dir: Henry Koster
Stars: James Stewart, Josephine Hull, Charles Drake, Peggy Dow
Rating: ★★★★

The smash-hit comedy that provided scores of impersonators with their standard James Stewart impression, as he totters drunkenly home in the company of a six-foot white rabbit (the Harvey of the title) which only he can see. Stewart's in marvellous form, but the film's acting Oscar went to little Josephine Hull, who plays his dithering sister.

Harvey Girls, The ⊙
1946, US, 101 mins, colour
Dir: George Sidney
Stars: Judy Garland, Ray Bolger, John Hodiak, Angela Lansbury, Cyd Charisse, Marjorie Main
Rating: ★★★★

A happy, colourful musical show which reunites Judy Garland with Ray Bolger (who played the scarecrow in *The Wizard of Oz*) and contains such toe-tapping tunes as 'Honky-Tonk' and the big show-stopper 'On the Atcheson, Topeka and Santa Fe'. There's also a memorable wistful trio, 'It's a Great Big World', sung and danced by Garland, Cyd Charisse and Virginia O'Brien and some rousing action scenes, especially towards the end. Angela Lansbury is a delight as a decadent dance-hall hostess.

Has Anybody Seen My Gal ⊙
1952, US, 92 mins, colour
Dir: Douglas Sirk
Stars: Piper Laurie, Charles Coburn, Rock Hudson, Lynn Bari
Rating: ★★★★

A delightful comedy with music, set in the late Twenties and directed by Douglas Sirk before he made a different kind of reputation with such weepies as *Magnificent Obsession* and *Imitation of Life*. The romantic duo of a youthful Piper Laurie and Rock Hudson is irresistible, but even so it's really Charles Coburn who is not only at the centre of things, but also steals the film. Bright, diverting and warm-hearted entertainment, with a fleeting appearance by future superstar James Dean as a youth who orders a complicated ice cream special.

Hasty Heart, The ○
1949, UK, 107 mins, b/w
Dir: Vincent Sherman
Stars: Richard Todd, Ronald Reagan, Patricia Neal
Rating: ★★★★

A great old tear-jerker with a fine performance from Richard Todd as the taciturn Scot in a Burmese war hospital who, unbeknown to him at first, has only a short time to live. It set Todd up for a 15-year career as a major cinema star.

Hatari! ○
1962, US, 159 mins, colour
Dir: Howard Hawks
Stars: John Wayne, Elsa Martinelli, Hardy Kruger
Rating: ★★★

Not surprisingly Howard Hawks, the director with whom John Wayne made *Red River*, *Rio Bravo*, *El Dorado* and *Rio Lobo*, injected much of the spirit of the Western into this big, sprawling drama of a group of big game trappers pursuing their African quarries in Landrovers. Wayne even wears a stetson to heighten the comparison. Hardy Kruger, the German actor so memorable in *The One That Got Away*, gives a deft portrayal of the racing driver whose skill returns to him when he gets behind the wheel of a jeep, and Michele Girardon is notable as a girl called Brandy. Hawks crams in some exciting scenes of animals on the run.

Hatter's Castle ○
1941, UK, 102 mins, b/w
Dir: Lance Comfort
Stars: Robert Newton, Deborah Kerr,

James Mason, Emlyn Williams
Rating: ★★★★

Although not bearing too great a resemblance to the A J Cronin novel on which it's based (most notably in the telescoping together of two of the main characters to make one), this story of a tyrannical Scottish businessman provided an acting tour-de-force for Robert Newton (as the almost-mad hatter of the title) that confirmed his newly won place at the forefront of British cinema.

Haunted ● ⓥ
1995, UK, 110 mins, colour
Dir: Lewis Gilbert
Stars: Aidan Quinn, Anthony Andrews, John Gielgud, Kate Beckinsale, Anna Massey
Rating: ★★

Pianos that play by themselves. Fires that spring up from nowhere. Housekeepers who 'see things'. Ah yes, we've been here before, in Hammer's later years. Indeed, in its way, this film is a ghost of things past itself. Not too well acted, true, but then these things never were. Now, as then, there are almost, but not quite convincing performances, from the visiting American star (Aidan Quinn), the English rose heroine (Kate Beckinsale) and an arch British supporting cast. This one, though, does have an extra touch of class in the (? spectral) form of John Gielgud who at 91 can still give the best performance in the film. And there's some in-your-face sex and nudity, just to remind us that this is 1995 and not some phantom from 30 years before. It packs enough intrigue and dodges along the corridors of its story to hold the interest, too, as Dr Quinn tries to unravel the secret 'haunted' English ancestral estate that seems to be driving Nanny Tess (Anna Massey) out of her mind. Not especially good, but professionally done.

Haunted Honeymoon ○
1986, US, 82 mins, colour
Dir: Gene Wilder
Stars: Gene Wilder, Gilda Radner, Dom DeLuise, Jonathan Pryce, Paul L Smith, Peter Vaughn
Rating: ★

This frantic comedy-chiller saw the last film appearance together of star-director Gene Wilder and real-life wife, comedienne Gilda Radner, who died from cancer in 1989. It's a send-up of old thunderstorm mystery film, but relentlessly overplayed. The main character, who has irrational fears that someone plans to cure him by literally

scaring him to death, spends the entire story in his spooky ancestral home. The cast mug and scream enthusiastically, but the film only manages a few chuckles rather than belly laughs. Wilder's direction is brimming with good ideas, though his pacing is erratic and the chills catch the eye but not the throat. The vital difference between this and the similar Bob Hope classic *The Cat and the Canary* is the lack of feeling that any of it is for real. Only little Ann Way, as the fierce maid-of-all-trades, seems to have come from the old dark houses we used to know.

Haunted Honeymoon
See: Busman's Honeymoon (1940)

Haunted Palace, The ● ⓥ
1964, US, 85 mins, colour
Dir: Roger Corman
Stars: Vincent Price, Debra Paget, Lon Chaney Jr
Rating: ★★★

Roger Corman's film, inspired by the stories of Edgar Allan Poe, leaves behind the light-heartedness of *The Raven* and returns to a sinister world of flickering candles, shadowy corridors and coffins whose inhabitants seem destined not to rest in peace. Vincent Price gives one of his most controlled performances as the man possessed by the evil spirit of his ancestor, and the final few feet contain a shock that will chill you to the bone. The colour photography by Floyd Crosby, shrill music composed by the redoubtable Les Baxter and restrained supporting performances all add to the sense of underlying horror. That frightened little man of the screen, Elisha Cook Jr, adds being burned alive to his gallery of film deaths.

Haunted Strangler, The
See: The Grip of the Strangler

Haunted Summer ●
1988, US, 115 mins, colour
Dir: Ivan Passer
Stars: Philip Anglim, Laura Dern, Alice Krige, Eric Stoltz, Alex Winter
Rating: ★

This story of Shelley and Byron is pretty (thanks to photographer Giuseppe Rotunno) and pretty boring too. Ken Russell made a hash of the same story in *Gothic* and here the only spark of interest in Ivan Passer's tedious treatment lies in how long it will take Byron (Anglim) to get Mary Shelley (Krige) into bed. The answer's 110 of the film's 115 minutes. The actors spout

epigrams and strike poses. Bloodless and gutless, the film just lies there in the Swiss sunshine. Ironically, its most interesting scenes are the closest it gets to the Russell treatment, as the protagonists are visited (in a cavern, in an opium-induced haze) by the monster of their worst nightmares.

Haunting, The ●
1963, UK, 112 mins, b/w
Dir: Robert Wise
Stars: Julie Harris, Claire Bloom, Richard Johnson, Russ Tamblyn, Lois Maxwell, Fay Compton
Rating: ★★★★★

A young American, and three psychic research experts, come to investigate an allegedly haunted house that he has inherited. Faint hearts may not be up to this truly frightening ghost story about a house that was 'born bad' and claims the souls of those who enter it. The film's great strength lies in the fact that the 'thing' is never seen; and the infrared camerawork makes the walls of the house – 'leprous' one of the characters call them – seem almost alive, and brings the horror right out of the screen. Director Robert Wise sets electricity crackling into the audience with a hair-raising opening, and rarely lets the chilling temperature rise. Julie Harris and Claire Bloom are both excellent, striking the right note of hysteria, and clinging together most convincingly when – well, whatever it is – is thundering its anger outside their bedroom door. Tamblyn's performance gradually gains authority and reaches a climax on the last line. And, just when the suspense seems to be slackening, a beautiful study of evil by Rosalie Crutchley sends the shivers racing down our spines again.

Havana ◗ ⓥ
1991, US, 145 mins, colour
Dir: Sydney Pollack
Stars: Robert Redford, Lena Olin, Raul Julia, Alan Arkin
Rating: ★★

Robert Redford is a gambler looking for a big win in the dying days of Batista's Cuba and Lena Olin is the wealthy and married woman he falls for in this overlong drama which seems to be an attempt to make a *Casablanca* for the Nineties. Redford's seventh collaboration with director Sydney Pollack is arguably the team's least successful, especially compared with their previous outing – *Out of Africa*. It looks good and the feel of Cuba during the build-up to Castro's successful bid for

H

power is well realised. But Redford seems too world-weary and disinterested and at 145 minutes, the film is far too long. There are compensations, though, with fine supporting performances from Alan Arkin, Tomas Milan, Mark Rydell and an unbilled Raul Julia. Tighter editing, though, would have made a much more interesting film.

Having Wonderful Time ○
1938, US, 71 mins, b/w
Dir: Alfred Santell
Stars: Ginger Rogers, Douglas Fairbanks Jr, Peggy Conklin, Lucille Ball, Red Skelton
Rating: ★★★

A warmly human and richly amusing kind of American version of *Holiday Camp*. Miss Rogers strings it together in her most vivacious form: from the point where she backgammons a wealthy playboy to sleep, the film's humour really starts to take off. In the supporting cast are Red Skelton, making his debut and doing his famous 'doughnut dunking' routine; Ann Miller; Eve Arden; Allan 'Rocky' Lane, who later became a cowboy star; and Lee Bowman and Jack Carson, both especially good as two of Ginger's suitors whose luck is out.

Hawaii ○
1966, US, 155 mins, colour
Dir: George Roy Hill
Stars: Julie Andrews, Max Von Sydow, Richard Harris, Gene Hackman
Rating: ★★★★

A rarity – a literate epic that also has plenty of action, and is a joy to look at. Dalton Trumbo and Daniel Taradash, who wrote the screenplay of this massive adventure story, have taken James A Michener's enormous novel, and compressed it into compact, intelligent scenes. Max Von Sydow excels as the bigoted minister sent to Hawaii in the 19th century to convert the natives: his portrayal clearly delineates the alternating torment and authority of a man unable to communicate his emotions. Julie Andrews hasn't quite the weight for the role of the consumptive wife who keeps him going through his darkest hours, but makes a game stab at it. While, talking of weight, there's a captivating performance from Jocelyn La Garde as the native ruler. Gene Hackman can be spotted in a minor role. You'll have to concentrate harder to pick up Bette Midler as a seasick bride.

Hawk, The ● ⓥ
1992, UK, 86 mins, colour
Dir: David Hayman
Stars: Helen Mirren, George Costigan, Rosemary Leach, Owen Teale
Rating: ★★★

A gritty, keep-'em-guessing mystery with TV's *Prime Suspect* star Helen Mirren emoting strongly (perhaps a shade too strongly at times) in the central role of suburban housewife Annie Marsh. A casual remark by Annie's husband (George Costigan) leads her to believe that he could be the perpetrator of a series of horrific local murders. But Annie has a history of mental illness and, before long, we are wondering if she's imagining the whole thing. A thoroughly convincing and beautifully crafted British thriller that only fails to stem its credibility gaps towards the end, though the wall of belief just about holds firm through to the unlikely, but highly satisfying ending.

Hawk the Slayer ◑ ⓥ
1980, UK, 93 mins, colour
Dir: Terry Marcel
Stars: Jack Palance, John Terry, Annette Crosbie, Cheryl Campbell, Bernard Bresslaw, Catriona MacColl
Rating: ★

You might have thought that such mediaeval romps had died the death when Universal lost its International. But lo! they live, in this ripely sliced chunk of swords, sandals and sorcery. In a land of swirling mists, a motley crew of Equity reservists rides at the shoulder of heroic Hawk (John Terry) through an orange-skied landscape to Ennio Morricone-style music adapted for rustic flute. They hope to bring peace to the land; but Terrible Jack Palance is a law unto himself as Voltan the Unbelievable wearing a scowl that would intimidate Giant Haystacks, as he over-and-out-acts an understandably cowed crew of minions, and guards his visage with a semi-visor lest his black acne be revealed before the final reel. Methinks there's a vein of satire to all this and that references to 'legions of darkness making savage cuts to the country' are merely veiled jibes at the British Government.

Hawmps! ☉
1976, US, 120 mins, colour
Dir: Joe Camp
Stars: James Hampton, Christopher Connelly, Slim Pickens
Rating: ★★

An elongated comic version of a remarkably nutty little chapter in U S

history already filmed (as a straightforward action film) 20 years earlier as *Camels West*. It deals with a brief but doomed attempt by the U S government just before the outbreak of the Civil War to introduce camels as a substitute for horses for the U S Cavalry in desert conditions. The expected slapstick involving Cavalrymen and their new mounts is followed by a hilarious race between camels and horses, in which wall-eyed Western veteran Jack Elam comes on for a splendid comic turn as the bad hat who tries to sabotage the race. Fellow film Westerners Slim Pickens and Denver Pyle are also along for the bumpy ride, and children will adore a baby camel, Valentine.

Head above Water ● ⓥ
1996, US, 92 mins, colour
Dir: Jim Wilson
Stars: Harvey Keitel, Craig Sheffer, Cameron Diaz, Billy Zane
Rating: ★

Cameron Diaz's burgeoning star career hit a bump with this excruciating failed comedy on the seemingly doomed theme of trying to get rid of a dead body. To be fair, hers is the only halfway decent performance, with Harvey Keitel atrociously over-playing and Craig Sheffer all at sea as the third point in the triangle after Billy Zane (hardly in it) bites the dust in the first few reels of the film, prompting each of the other three to suspect their fellows of bumping him off. Settings are picturesque, but the treatment is leaden in this unlikely and almost unwatchable farrago.

Head Over Heels ○
(aka: Chilly Scenes of Winter)
1979, US, 97 mins, colour
Dir: Joan Micklin Silver
Stars: John Heard, Mary Beth Hurt, Peter Riegert, Kenneth McMillan, Griffin Dunne, Gloria Grahame
Rating: ★★

Director Micklin Silver has written a nice screenplay for this serious comedy-romance, full of natural sounding dialogue that's amusing without being ostentatious. With such a foundation, a film like this should entertain and tug at the heartstrings at the same time. But although it does that at times, there are patches of tedium too. As the obsessive wooer at the centre of things, Heard, combines the cynical-romantic approach of George Segal with the dry delivery of Dustin Hoffman, to register more strongly than he has in any other part. But there are too many self-effacing performances in the cast to give the romance that cutting edge that bites on the emotions. Gloria Grahame fans from the Forties and Fifties will be amused to see that she looks – just like Gloria Grahame. Hasn't changed a bit. Alas, it was to be one of her last film roles.

Hear My Song ● ⓥ
1991, UK, 105 mins, colour
Dir: Peter Chelsom
Stars: Ned Beatty, Adrian Dunbar, David McCallum, Tara Fitzgerald, Shirley Anne Field, William Hootkins
Rating: ★★★★

Chances are you'll be humming the songs of Josef Locke after you leave this one. Locke? Ask your parents. He was an Irish tenor who ruled the halls for nigh on 20 years in post-war times until he had to flee the country on tax evasion charges. Around this brief thread, writer-director Peter Chelsom has woven a decidedly different sort of film. Rotund American actor Ned Beatty enjoys his finest hour since *Deliverance* as Locke, sought by seedy young Irish-born impresario Micky O'Neill (Adrian Dunbar) on a trip back across the sea to Ireland. O'Neill, pressed by creditors at his nightclub, has tried to pass off a Locke impersonator, to the humiliation of his girlfriend's mother (Shirley Anne Field) who shared an affair with Locke 25 years before. Now Micky must make amends, but finding Locke, never mind persuading him back to England and the vengeful arms of the law (David McCallum), proves a tricky thing. The film sags a bit around halfway, and degenerates into farce at the end, but its heart, definitely in the right place, sees it through. Beatty, unlike some of the cast, never overplays. Field, in her late Fifties, is still ravishing.

Hear No Evil ◗ ⓥ
1993, US, 99 mins, colour
Dir: Robert Greenwald
Stars: Mariee Matlin, D B Sweeney, Martin Sheen
Rating: ★★

A peculiar little thriller, okay video fare for the most part, which casts deaf actress Marlee Madin as the girl in danger after a friend steals a priceless coin and hides it in her apartment. Matlin soon finds both a masked killer and crooked police (led by Martin Sheen) on her heels. The pace of the story is sort of stop-go, not surprising when you consider that parts of it are padded out with scenery and soundtrack music and parts of it are almost elliptical, as if little bits of the plot were missing, causing the action to move unnecessarily quickly from one scene to another. Matlin and D B Sweeney (he obviously qualifying in gloom as the Stephen Rea of the Nineties Hollywood scene) are adequate, Sheen quite interesting as a bad guy for once, though his role ends too tamely. Not bad.

Heart and Souls ○ ⓥ
1993, US, 104 mins, colour
Dir: Ron Underwood
Stars: Robert Downey Jr, Charles Grodin, Kyra Sedgwick, Tom Sizemore, Alfre Woodard
Rating: ★★★

An initially iffy but often effective fantasy that pulls relentlessly at our emotions in its later stages. Four people, each with things in life to do, are killed, along with the driver of their bus, whose gaze strays too long on a courting couple in the car speeding alongside. Also caught in the impact.is a pregnant mother, whose baby, born there and then, finds himself with four guardian angels, as the dead people are 'missed' in the pick-up for Heaven. So is he there to help the lost souls achieve their ambitions? Or are they there to help him achieve his? Director Ron Underwood's answer is a bit of both in a film that largely endears itself, but occasionally embarrasses when the spirits step into Robert Downey Jr, as the grown boy, and take over his body. A string of good performances here, from Charles Grodin, Kyra Sedgwick, Tom Sizemore and Alfre Woodard as the quaint quartet, David Paymer as the bus driver and Elisabeth Shue. Only Downey himself seems less than at ease with it all.

Heartbreakers ● ⓥ
1984, US, 98 mins, colour
Dir: Bobby Roth
Stars: Peter Coyote, Nick Mancuso, Max Gail, Carole Laure, Carol Wayne, Kathryn Harrold
Rating: ★★★

On the surface an erotic comedy-drama, this is at heart a serious little number about two macho men adopting different stances to life, but both groping for some kind of meaning to it all which they find impossible to grasp. Peter Coyote and Nick Mancuso, two talented actors who deserved higherprofile careers, are both up to the emotional intricacies and subtleties of all this, although it's a pity that both have to play such unsympathetic characters – men who wallow in self-pity and seem unwilling or unable to assert a pattern of stability in their lives. James Laurenson enjoys himself as the effete owner of a fashionable art gallery and, in so doing, comes across as about the most real character in the film. The girls remain little more than sexy ciphers in a story whose uneasy undertones you may find too unsettling for enjoyment. It's basically a film about insecurity and that may strike too loud a chord in many people's lives.

Heartbreak Kid, The ◗ ⓥ
1972, US, 106 mins, colour
Dir: Elaine May
Stars: Charles Grodin, Cybill Shepherd, Jeannie Berlin
Rating: ★★★★

This Neil Simon script is fun all through – in a biting kind of way. Charles Grodin (who's hardly seemed to age in the last 25 years) has the title role as Lenny, who deserts his talkative Jewish bride of a few days to pursue a beautiful blonde (Cybill Shepherd) from Florida to Minnesota, just stopping off long enough on the way to get a quickie divorce. Lenny's wild fantasies deceive everyone but Shepherd's hard-headed father (Eddie Albert). By the end, though, the point has been well and truly made that Lenny isn't likely to be satisfied with anything for more than a few days at a time. Grodin is unnervingly accurate as the self-seeking hero and Jeannie Berlin brilliant as the bartered bride. Good entertainment.

Heartbreak Ridge ● ⓥ
1986, US, 130 mins, colour
Dir: Clint Eastwood
Stars: Clint Eastwood, Marsha Mason, Everett McGill, Moses Gunn, Bo Svenson
Rating: ★

Clint Eastwood was always destined to be John Wayne's heir when it came to upholding the American macho myth. As director and star of this drama about the Marines' invasion of Grenada, he turned in the most gung-ho Marine Corps movie since *The Duke's Sands of Iwo Jima*. Clint is a barking sergeant, cajoling and wet-nursing young recruits into battle readiness. It's thin material that appears to run even longer than the invasion itself, but then Hollywood was obviously pushed to find a recent confrontation that the Americans had actually won.

Heartburn ◗ ⓥ
1986, US, log mins, colour
Dir: Mike Nichols

H

Stars: Meryl Streep, Jack Nicholson, Jeff Daniels, Maureen Stapleton, Stockard Channing, Richard Masur
Rating: ★★

Hollywood heavyweights Jack Nicholson and Meryl Streep make this lightweight comedy about marriage and infidelity perhaps more enjoyable than it deserves. After a whirlwind romance, political journalist Mark (Nicholson) proposes to food writer Rachel (Streep). But the marriage doesn't seem made in heaven when she suspects he is playing away... There's nothing here we haven't seen before, but thanks to the charisma of the stars and assured and well-observed direction by Mike Nichols it's an enjoyable if rather predictable journey.

Heart Condition ● ⓥ
1989, US, 103 mins, colour
Dir: James D Parriott
Stars: Bob Hoskins, Denzel Washington, Chloe Webb
Rating: ★★

Bob Hoskins must be used to acting with someone who isn't there. First a white cartoon rabbit, now a black ghost, in the form of a criminal lawyer whose heart he has. Hoskins is a cop who's had a heart attack, Denzel Washington the lawyer who wants him to solve a murder – his. Result: an okay movie, but one that doesn't exactly grip the attention throughout. Hoskins gives his familiar blustering, perspiring, hard-cursing performance; Washington is less effective than in some of his roles; and Chloe Webb is negligible as the girl they both love. When Hoskins is 'transformed' with the help of Washington's money, it's amusing that – even with hand-tailored suits and a toupee – he still looks the same old Hoskins.

Heart Is a Lonely Hunter, The ○
1968, US, 125 mins, colour
Dir: Robert Ellis Miller
Stars: Alan Arkin, Sondra Locke, Stacy Keach, Cicely Tyson
Rating: ★★★★

Alan Arkin gives a deeply felt performance here as a deaf mute who moves to a small southern town to be near a similarly affected friend who has been put in a nearby institution. Taking a room in a family home, he has a positive effect on the lives around him but does not cure his own loneliness. This is a brave attempt to bring Carson McCullers' moving and sensitive book to the screen. Brave, but not entirely

successful, as the film tries to cover too much ground and most of the characters, save for Arkin's, are thinly sketched. His performance is the force that moves the story and makes it worth watching. He will surely touch your hearts towards the end.

Heart Like a Wheel ○
1983, US, 110 mins, colour
Dir: Jonathan Kaplan
Stars: Beau Bridges, Bonnie Bedelia, Leo Rossi, Hoyt Axton
Rating: ★★★

Despite a small (but devoted) following in this country, drag racing is a peculiarly American sport. This film, therefore, which is a biopic of the first woman drag-racing champion Shirley Muldowney, may not at first glance appeal. Nevertheless it's a good solid drama and the racing sequences are loud and exciting, once you've figured out what's going on. Muldowney's private life didn't run on the smooth tarmac her racing career did, so there's plenty of off-track drama, too. Bonnie Bedelia fills the starring role so well it's surprising it didn't give her career the boost it deserved. Beau Bridges is also effective as the man she turns to after her divorce. 'Pedal to the metal,' good buddy!

Heat ● ⓥ
1995, US, 170 mins, colour
Dir: Michael Mann
Stars: Al Pacino, Robert De Niro, Val Kilmer, Jon Voight, Tom Sizemore, Amy Brenneman
Rating: ★★★

There's the makings here of a classic confrontational crime drama in the modern manner and the actors with which to tell it. However, although the results are still good enough to satisfy the average fan of Al Pacino and Robert De Niro, the running time is a mighty weight for the film to carry on its shoulders and, in between bursts of savage action, its pace is sometimes ponderous. Pacino is the cop, De Niro the criminal, each dedicated to his own profession, each doomed to a life of loneliness and self-denial. Each is a gladiatorial predator, and there isn't room in the same arena for both of them. The story concentrates heavily on these two, and it's De Niro who comes across as marginally the more sympathetic and three-dimensional. The plot structure has (doubtless intended) echoes of Greek tragedy, but many of its action scenes are needlessly protracted. Worth seeing, though, for

its best scenes, one of which has De Niro and Pacino discussing their not dissimilar philosophies over a cup of coffee.

Heat and Dust ❶ ⓥ
1982, UK, 133 mins, colour
Dir: James Ivory
Stars: Julie Christie, Christopher Cazenove, Greta Scacchi, Julian Glover, Susan Fleetwood, Shashi Kapoor
Rating: ★★★

Director James Ivory's vivid evocation of the sights, sounds and feel of India in the Twenties and the Eighties is every bit as assured as the more expensive visits to the sub-continent in *The Jewel in the Crown* and *A Passage to India*. And, in many ways, it's rather better, less like a tourist guide to the country. One of the most enjoyable of the Merchant-Ivory films.

Heathers ● ⓥ
1989, US, 102 mins, colour
Dir: Michael Lehmann
Stars: Winona Ryder, Christian Slater, Shannen Doherty, Lisanne Falk
Rating: ★★★

Now there's weird, very weird and major weird. But *Heathers*, described by its makers as a teenage black comedy, is mega-weird, for at least 90 minutes that is, before descending to conventionality (by its own standards) in the final reel. There's a queen bitch clique at Westerburg High in Ohio and three of its four members are called Heather. They talk in a language all their own and show no mercy to intruders. The fourth member is Veronica (Winona Ryder) who, rapidly becoming disillusioned with the Heathers, is offered a way out in the form of smiling J D (Christian Slater), whose easy grin hides a psychotic nature and whose plans to 'kill' one of the Heathers and a couple of school bullies with 'fake' frightening schemes prove to Veronica's horror to be all too real. Most of the characters, especially the parents, seem to have stepped from surreal paintings, and provide a bizarre backdrop to the stunning performance of Ryder. Slater, too, is most interesting as the martini-voiced J D, a worthy successor to Norman Bates.

Heaven & Earth ● ⓥ
1993, US, 140 mins, colour
Dir: Oliver Stone
Stars: Tommy Lee Jones, Hiep Thi Le, Joan Chen, Haing S Ngor, Debbie Reynolds
Rating: ★★

The conclusion of Oliver Stone's Vietnam trilogy, following *Platoon* and *Born on the 4th of July*, tells of one woman's horrifying experiences during and after the Vietnam war. Newcomer Hiep Thi Le gives the central role all she's got and the presence of Tommy Lee Jones as the US soldier who falls in love with her, with tragic consequences, adds star quality. They're both terrific, but defeated by the moralising mediocrity of Stone's material. Thus the true story is dramatic but uninvolving, making it harrowing to watch and hard to enjoy.

Heaven Can Wait ○
1943, US, 112 mins, colour
Dir: Ernst Lubitsch
Stars: Don Ameche, Gene Tierney, Charles Coburn, Marjorie Main
Rating: ★★★★

Not the early version of the Warren Beatty film of the same title (that was 1941's *Here Comes Mr Jordan*), but a highly original romantic comedy, this was the great director Ernst Lubitsch's last film classic. Don Ameche is suavely tongue in cheek as the late Lothario telling Satan his sins to engineer himself into the 'Lower Regions' and Gene Tierney gorgeous as his much-beset wife.

Heaven Can Wait ○
1978, US, 100 mins, colour
Dir: Buck Henry, Warren Beatty
Stars: Warren Beatty, Julie Christie, James Mason, Jack Warden, Charles Grodin, Dyan Cannon
Rating: ★★★★★

It is to the great credit of Warren Beatty (showing a delicate touch as a star, producer, co-writer and co-director) that this remake of a classic fantasy film from the Forties is every bit as memorable as the original. Beatty (as the athlete 'taken' too soon by Heaven), Julie Christie (as the girl he falls for but can't keep), James Mason (his best in ages), Jack Warden and Charles Grodin are all first-rate. But the film is almost stolen by (Oscar-nominated) Dyan Cannon as a tycoon's faithless wife.

Heaven Knows, Mr Allison ○
1957, US, 100 mins, colour
Dir: John Huston
Stars: Deborah Kerr, Robert Mitchum
Rating: ★★★★

Deborah Kerr's favourite film and one of John Huston's best, a sort of sideshoot from his own *The African Queen*. Instead of a missionary and a riverboat skipper, Huston gives us a nun and a tough US Marine (Robert Mitchum (perfectly cast), shipwrecked on a Pacific island during World War Two. Virtually a duologue between the two, with lots of action, adventure and drama to hold the interest. Huston's film has moments of high pathos, excitement and tenderness, all in superb settings, as the director and his photographer (the great Oswald Morris) skilfully convey the humid, lush atmosphere of a small tropical island that might be a paradise in other circumstances. The tensions between Kerr and Mitchum are cleverly written and their performances are first-class.

Heavenly Creatures ● Ⓥ
1994, New Zealand, 99 mins, colour
Dir: Peter Jackson
Stars: Kate Winslet, Melanie Lynskey, Sarah Peirse, Diana Kent
Rating: ★★★★

Examinations of real-life murder cases are often fascinating, and this story of two schoolgirls in 1954 New Zealand who plotted to kill the mother of one, in an effort to stay together, is well up with the field, and in a different class (in every respect) to director Peter Jackson's previous work. At first glance, Juliet (Kate Winslet) and Pauline (Melanie Lynskey) have little in common. Juliet is blonde, English, extrovert and considers herself above her teachers and classmates. Pauline is a dark, brooding and uncommunicative New Zealander. But both girls have had afflictions that have caused them suffering – Juliet still has TB and Pauline a slightly gammy leg – and both are highly intelligent dreamers. Jackson seems to get the mood precisely here, with the aid of some imaginative fantasy sequences and stunning overhead shots in woods. The girls are not only exactly right (apparently they closely resemble the originals) but can act as well.

Heavens Above! ◑
1963, UK, 118 mins, b/w
Dir: John Boulting
Stars: Peter Sellers, Eric Sykes, Bernard Miles, Irene Handl, Miriam Karlin
Rating: ★★

After the hilarious goings-on of *Private's Progress*, *Brothers-in-Law* and *Lucky Jim*, this scathing satire about a prison chaplain sent by mistake to the living of a snooty country parish was quite a departure for the Boulting Brothers. One wonders whether snobbery in church people, even if it exists to the extent shown here, is of the same outward kind. But no matter. Eric Sykes, Irene Handl, Miriam Karlin and Roy Kinnear are splendidly scurrilous as the gipsy family to whom Peter Sellers' vicar unwisely opens his home.

Heaven's Gate ◑ Ⓥ
1980, US, 219 mins, colour
Dir: Michael Cimino
Stars: Kris Kristofferson, Christopher Walken, Isabelle Huppert, Sam Waterston, John Hurt, Jeff Bridges
Rating: ★

After scooping five Oscars for *The Deer Hunter*, this next film from writer/director Michael Cimino was eagerly awaited. Budgeted at $7.5 million, it ballooned out of control to $36 million, almost bankrupted its studio and was an unmitigated disaster. It was later shown in Britain in a shorter format. Ravishingly shot in luminous Technicolor by Vilmos Zsigmond, it is basically a Western about the conflict between immigrant settlers and the ruthless empire builders who want them eliminated. What it seriously lacks is an understandable storyline, and that's its ultimate undoing.

Heaven's Prisoners ● Ⓥ
1995, US, 132 mins, colour
Dir: Phil Joanou
Stars: Alec Baldwin, Mary Stuart Masterson, Eric Roberts, Teri Hatcher, Kelly Lynch
Rating: ★★

At least this long, slow crime melodrama isn't as bad as some films set in the Bayou swamplands, and its bursts of action are routinely well handled by director Phil Joanou, even if their gun blasting, mouth-bloodying violence becomes monotonous. Executive producer Alec Baldwin gives himself lots of close-ups, one bead of sweat running photogenically down his left profile, as the hero, an ex-cop and ex-alcoholic who somehow gets involved with big-time local crime (headed by Eric Roberts with plaited hair) after saving an illegal Spanish immigrant tot from a plane crash. Kelly Lynch as his wife gets killed off early on, which is a shame as she's giving the only decent performance. Teri Hatcher has a little fun with the bad girl, but the usually reliable Mary Stuart Masterson is just awful (and wildly miscast) as the stripper who gives Baldwin his initial lead when he pokes his nose into things that would have been better left alone.

H

Heels ○
1937, UK, 90 mins, b/w
Dir: Sonnie Hale
Stars: Jessie Matthews, Louis Borell, Robert Flemyng
Rating: ★★★

Although this airy musical was popular enough in its day, it does in retrospect mark the beginning of the downswing in star Jessie Matthews' career. For the first time in the major part of her run of success as Britain's foremost musical star, Matthews was without the talents of the incomparable director Victor Saville. This time the man behind the camera is her own husband Sonnie Hale and, although it's the best of Hale's three efforts for her, Saville's light touch and innate elegance are already beginning to be missed. Still, Jessie is a delight, as always, and her numbers include 'Head Over Heels in Love', 'May I Have the Next Romance with You?' and 'Looking Around Corners for You'.

Heidi ⊙
1937, US, 88 mins, b/w
Dir: Allan Dwan
Stars: Shirley Temple, Jean Hersholt, Arthur Treacher, Helen Westley
Rating: ★★★

Shirley Temple celebrated her ninth birthday on the set of this cute but unsugary Hollywood version of Johanna Spyri's children's classic about a little Swiss girl living with her grandfather. It was Shirley's third consecutive year as top box-office attraction in America.

Heiress, The ☾
1949, US, 115 mins, b/w
Dir: William Wyler
Stars: Olivia De Havilland, Montgomery Clift, Ralph Richardson, Miriam Hopkins
Rating: ★★★★★

In post-war years, Olivia de Havilland won an Oscar for *To Each His Own* and was further nominated for *The Snake Pit*. But *The Heiress*, which won her a second Oscar, directed by William Wyler in studiously stylish fashion, is surely Olivia's finest hour. Your heart will go out to her as the dowdy spinster Catherine Sloper and, like her, you'll probably never be quite sure as to whether or not handsome young Montgomery Clift is genuinely in love with her or just a fortune-hunter out for her money. De Havilland was never more poignant, Clift never more charismatic. The ending, splendidly acted and stage-managed, is a real hammer blow at the emotions – and exactly right into the bargain.

He Laughed Last ○
1956, US, 77 mins, colour
Dir: Blake Edwards
Stars: Frankie Laine, Anthony Dexter, Lucy Marlow, Richard Long
Rating: ★★★

This Damon Runyon-style comedy, with songs from Frankie Laine, was one of several bright and breezy films (most featuring Laine) made by Blake Edwards before he moved on to such films as *The Pink Panther* and *Breakfast at Tiffany's*. Lucy Marlow sparkles as a chorus girl who inherits a gangster's millions, and character actor Jesse White steals the happy show as gangster Max, tough as a plank – and twice as thick.

Helen Morgan Story
See: Both Ends of the Candle

Helen of Troy ○
1955, US/UK, 118 mins, colour
Dir: Robert Wise
Stars: Rossana Podesta, Jack Sernas, Cedric Hardwicke, Stanley Baker
Rating: ★★

Director Robert Wise (he made *West Side Story*) picked two of the Continent's brightest young stars, Rossana Podesta and Jacques (here Jack) Sernas to play the lovers in this spectacular story of the Trojan War and what led up to it. Down in a minor role, he cast a teenage actress called Brigitte Bardot. But from the moment the cameras rolled at the studios in Rome, the film was in trouble – trouble that almost ended in it being scrapped. Accidents put more than 200 extras in hospital. There was a switch of directors mid-film and a £400,000 fire. After all this hell in Troy, the results were only fair to middling.

Hell and High Water ○
1954, US, 103 mins, colour
Dir: Samuel Fuller
Stars: Richard Widmark, Bella Darvi, Cameron Mitchell, David Wayne
Rating: ★★★★

Pure entertainment from Samuel Fuller, better known as director of such exploitation as *Shock Corridor* and *The Naked Kiss*. Non-stop excitement in a story about a submarine on a secret mission in the Arctic Circle, with an explosive climax as two submarines stalk each other through the depths – one intent on ramming the other.

Hell Below Zero ○ ⓥ
1954, UK, 90 mins, colour
Dir: Mark Robson
Stars: Alan Ladd, Joan Tetzei, Basil Sydney, Stanley Baker, Jill Bennett
Rating: ★★★

Exciting action film, set in the Antarctic, and directed at a cracking pace by Mark Robson. Jill Bennett just has time to take the acting honours as a cool Scandinavian blonde, who's also the skipper of a whaler. A fight with axes between Alan Ladd and Stanley Baker on an ice-floe is the highlight of this adventure yarn, which is based on a popular novel by Hammond Innes called *The White South*, cleverly adapted to the screen by Alec Coppel and Max Trell. Storms at sea are convincingly realistic, and another acting performance that earns full marks is that of Niall MacGinnis as a drunken ship's doctor. Fans of screen escapism will be happy with this one.

Hell Bent for Glory ○
(aka Lafayette Escadrille)
1957, US, 93 mins, b/w
Dir: William A Wellman
Stars: Tab Hunter, Etchika Choureau
Rating: ★★

Director William Wellman, who made such aviation classics as *Wings* (the first Oscar winning film, in 1927), *Men With Wings* and *The High and the Mighty*, continued his romance with the air in this account of his own World War One flying memoirs. Two of the young aviators are played by up-and-coming David Janssen and Clint Eastwood, and Wellman's own son Bill has a featured role.

Hellbound: Hellraiser II ● ⓥ
1989, UK, 96 mins, colour
Dir: Tony Randel
Stars: Clare Higgins, Ashley Laurence, Kenneth Cranham, Ingrid Boorman
Rating: ★★

They're fiddling with that puzzle box again and addicts of gory horror films will be delighted to know that the results are even more disgusting (if less entertaining) than the first time around. What's missing, of course, is the originality of the first film, the second instalment more or less recycling elements, only more so. It does add a mad doctor (Kenneth Cranham), who gives the whole enterprise a whiff of the classic B-movies of the 1940s. 'What is today's agenda?', he snarls. Ah yes, evisceration.' Ashley Laurence and Ingrid Boorman scream with conviction; Clare Higgins comes back (gorily) from the dead as the Lady Macbeth figure; there's a magic mirror and references to Snow White and excellent, imaginative sets – and a baffling ending. Needless to add, this is totally unsuitable for children!

Hell Divers ○

1931, US, 113 mins, b/w
Dir: George Hill
Stars: Wallace Beery, Clark Gable, Dorothy Jordan
Rating: ★★★

Reminiscent of some of Wallace Beery's later Forties vehicles in its rough-and-ready boisterousness, this lively if overlong action film teams puffing Beery with a Clark Gable on the very edge of top stardom. The girl they're fighting over is pretty Dorothy Jordan, one of MGM's most popular leading ladies from the early Thirties, who was lost to the screen when she married explorer and *King Kong* co-director Merian C Cooper.

Hell Drivers ○

1957, UK, 108 mins, b/w
Dir: Cy Endfield
Stars: Stanley Baker, Peggy Cummins, Herbert Lom, Patrick McGoohan
Rating: ★★★

Rough, tough, no emotions barred story of daredevil lorry drivers who seem scarcely to pause for breath between the end of one fight and the beginning of another in their bid to make a fortune in their high-speed vehicles. The love scenes have, courtesy of Stanley Baker and Peggy Cummins, more bite than in most British films of the time, while Herbert Lom, cast for once in a sympathetic role, gives a likeable performance as Gino. Patrick McGoohan has a tremendous time as the brutally villainous Red. Sean Connery and Sidney James have supporting roles.

Heller in Pink Tights ○

1960, US, 100 mins, colour
Dir: George Cukor
Stars: Sophia Loren, Anthony Quinn, Eileen Heckart, Ramon Novarro, Margaret O'Brien, Steve Forrest
Rating: ★★★

Old-time idols Edmund Lowe and Ramon Novarro prop up the cast of this unusual Western based on Louis L'Amour's novel, *Heller with a Gun.* Sympathetically directed by George Cukor, it features a bewigged Sophia Loren as the leading actress of a travelling rep company in the old West. The action includes amusing extracts from the plays (including *La Belle Hélène*) in the company's repertoire. By and large, though, the stars are uneasily

cast, and the results are curiously tedious.

Hellfighters ○ Ⓥ

1969, US, 120 mins, colour
Dir: Andrew V McLaglen
Stars: John Wayne, Katharine Ross, Jim Hutton, Vera Miles, Bruce Cabot
Rating: ★★★

Apart from the subject – red-suited firefighters quell large-scale oil and gas blazes all over the world – this is a typical John Wayne, move-it-along, take-it-or-leave-it movie – full of brawls, battles and blunt staccato dialogue, with a redundant love interest. Fragmentary but entertaining, it's based on the career of 'Red' Adair.

Hellfire Club, The ○

1960, UK, 93 mins, colour
Dir: Robert S Baker
Stars: Keith Michell, Adrienne Corri, Peter Cushing
Rating: ★★

A hoary old melodrama in the Gainsborough tradition, played with enthusiasm and humour by most of the cast – commendably so in view of the tired nature of the whole Victorian enterprise. The background is interesting, although the activities of the infamous Hellfire Club seem rather jaded by today's standards. Especially sprightly performances by Keith Michell (good guy), Peter Arne (bad guy) and Adrienne Corri (bad girl) keep it going.

Hell in Korea

See: A Hill in Korea

Hell is a City ◐

1959, UK, 100 mins, b/w
Dir: Val Guest
Stars: Stanley Baker, John Crawford, Donald Pleasence, Billie Whitelaw
Rating: ★★★

The tense, hard-hitting story of a city-wide manhunt. Stanley Baker is the hard-bitten cop in this kitchen-sink British thriller which makes no attempt to pull its punches or glamorise its characters. One of the finest performances is given by the city of Manchester. Its real-life buildings and settings – smoky pubs, back alleys, a Sunday-morning meeting of gamblers on a slag-heap – give the film a great deal of grim authenticity.

Hell is for Heroes! ◐

1962, US, 90 mins, b/w
Dir: Don Siegel
Stars: Steve McQueen, Fess Parker,

Bobby Darin, James Coburn, Nick Adams, Harry Guardino
Rating: ★★★

Tough, uncompromising war film from Don Siegel with a magnetic performance from Steve McQueen as the professional soldier who enjoys killing for its own sake.

Hello Again ○ Ⓥ

1987, US, 96 mins, colour
Dir: Frank Perry
Stars: Shelley Long, Gabriel Byrne, Corbin Bernsen, Judith Ivey, Sela Ward
Rating: ★★

A not-so-hot first solo comedy vehicle for Shelley Long as a woman who is brought back from the dead by an occult incantation. Most of the comedy before and after death stems from the fact that her character has two left feet and Long is skilful in seeming to get entangled with things without meaning it. In other respects, however, things are less happy; ickily scripted and raucously directed, the film's performances seem unrelaxed. Gabriel Byrne and Corbin Bernsen are both uneasily cast, and the rest of the players are rather below par. One of Long's better vehicles, though, from an unrewarding film career.

Hello, Dolly! ○ Ⓥ

1969, US, 140 mins, colour
Dir: Gene Kelly
Stars: Barbra Streisand, Walter Matthau, Michael Crawford, Louis Armstrong
Rating: ★★★

Hollywood's last multi-million dollar musical in the grand tradition boasts lavish production design, splendid choreography by Michael Kidd and, of course, the clarion-voiced Barbra Streisand as matchmaker Dolly Levi. She was really too young for the role, played variously on stage by Mary Martin, Ginger Rogers, Pearl Bailey, Dora Bryan and, improbably, by Danny La Rue. But she was certainly in fine voice, making more of the songs by Jerry Herman than did Herman himself. Michael Crawford acquits himself commendably as a song-and-dance man under Gene Kelly's direction.

Hell on Frisco Bay ○

1955, US, 98 mins, colour
Dir: Frank Tuttle
Stars: Alan Ladd, Edward G Robinson, Joanne Dru, Paul Stewart, William Demarest
Rating: ★★

H

Though the cast would place this crime thriller a good 10 years earlier, it was one of Warners' first big CinemaScope films, based on a splendid novel by William P McGivern called *The Darkest Hour*. However, under the direction of Frank Tuttle, who made Alan Ladd's first big hit *This Gun for Hire*, the main performances lack any depth, although there are excellent supporting portrayals from Paul Stewart as Robinson's battered sidekick, and Fay Wray, the frightened heroine of so many Thirties' horror films, as Stewart's high-toned mistress. Rod Taylor and Jayne Mansfield have minor roles. Shot in very poor Warnercolor.

Hellraiser ● Ⓥ

1987, UK, 92 mins, colour
Dir: Clive Barker
Stars: Andrew Robinson, Clare Higgins, Ashley Lawrence, Sean Chapman
Rating: ★★★

The advice proffered to TV quiz contestants of yore – 'Open the box!' – would be well unheeded by the protagonists of this horror film which, as gore/slime/maggots/rending-flesh feasts go, is distinctly above average. 'Every drop of blood you spill puts new flesh on my bones,' groans the reviving monster to his besotted female accomplice. Now where have we heard that before? Never mind, this is good stuff of its kind, well edited and directed by its writer Clive Barker, about a man who seems to have made several pacts with the Devil before going into one of those Chinese dens seen at the beginning of *Gremlins*. Here he gets a mysterious box which comes apart and, when locked into a certain formation, can call forth skinhead beings from another dimension. Clare Higgins makes a splendid Lady Macbeth figure as the wife doing her slimy lover's bidding.

Hell's Angels ○

1930, US, 127 mins, b/w
Dir: Howard Hughes
Stars: Jean Harlow, Ben Lyon, James Hall
Rating: ★★★

The classic World War One flying spectacular. The romantic element is the weakest in the movie, although Jean Harlow, in her first major film triumph, does her best to enliven it, especially when informing an understandably hypnotised Ben Lyon that she is 'just going to change into something more comfortable'. The scenes of aerial combat have hardly dated at all, remaining absorbing and exciting, especially a dogfight between RAF and German planes, a sequence which lasts for almost half an hour.

Hellzapoppin' ☉

1941, US, 84 mins, b/w
Dir: H C Potter
Stars: Ole Olsen, Chick Johnson, Mischa Auer, Martha Raye, Jane Frazee, Robert Paige
Rating: ★★★★

Hollywood's craziest comedy this side of the Marx Brothers, only originally less madcap than the long-running stage show on which it was based. It revived the dormant cinema careers of Ole Olsen and Chic Johnson. The projectionist (Shemp Howard of Three Stooges fame) tries to run the film while arguing with his girlfriend and the stars have to step out of it and remonstrate with him. A woman with a potted plant wanders through the movie looking for Mr Jones; a love song is interrupted for a card asking Stinky Miller to go home; a mad private eye (Hugh Herbert) keeps addressing the audience. These are only some of the saner moments in a unique Hollywood experience, directed in freewheeling fashion by H C Potter.

Help! ☉ Ⓥ

1965, UK, 92 mins, colour
Dir: Richard Lester
Stars: John Lennon, Paul McCartney, Ringo Starr, George Harrison, Leo McKern, Eleanor Bron
Rating: ★★★★★

The second Beatles feature turned out to be a latter-day Goon Show with music. Although wholly sublimated to director Richard Lester's zany, flyaway comedy technique, the boys work with a will and great sense of fun at carrying out the gags the script had devised for them. After getting the story – a little thing about a sacrificial ring that ends up on one of Ringo's fingers – out of the way, the laughs come thick and fast. Lester's cutting and editing are models of timing, making things move along at a cracking pace, right up to the final glorious melee on the seashore with the ring passing frantically from one finger to another. And a sequence which starts with Eleanor Bron (an eastern princess on the Beatles' side) whistling a snatch of Beethoven's Ninth to save Ringo from a music-loving tiger, and ends with practically the whole country singing the symphony, is a classic example of the sustained comedy gag – worthy of Laurel and Hardy at something near their best. A shame that the Beatles' career in this sort of film ended here.

Henry V ○ Ⓥ

1944, UK, 137 mins, colour
Dir: Laurence Olivier
Stars: Laurence Olivier, Robert Newton, Renée Asherson, Esmond Knight, Leo Genn, Felix Aylmer
Rating: ★★★★★

Rousing and patriotic at a time when the English spirit needed lifting, Laurence Olivier's first stab at putting the bard on film was an artistic and commercial success. It also proved to be a stirring panoply of comedy, patriotic speeches and some enthrallingly original battle scenes. And it had the cream of the British stage in large and small roles. And not just the legitimate stage – music hall comic George Robey had a cameo role. Olivier starred, directed and had a hand in the screen adaptation, tasks Kenneth Branagh took on when he remade the film in 1989. Marvellous stuff and a tough act to follow.

Henry V ○ Ⓥ

1989, UK, 137 mins, colour
Dir: Kenneth Branagh
Stars: Kenneth Branagh, Derek Jacobi, Simon Shepherd, Robbie Coltrane, Judi Dench, Emma Thompson
Rating: ★★★

A pity this version of Shakespeare's play doesn't grab us from the word go, like Laurence Olivier's in 1944. The comparison between the two is won and lost in those first few scenes. And the night before Agincourt seems to last an eternity, before the film picks up with the battle itself. This is staged with pace and imagination as well as mud and blood by director-star-adapter Kenneth Branagh, as is the pleasing endpiece dealing briefly but amusingly with the courtship of the French princess (Emma Thomson with a convincing accent) by the English king, with the assistance of Geraldine McEwan as a chaperon direct from the French quarter of Tilling. But the pace of earlier scenes seems slow and the low-life characters merely dull and objectionable, rather than colourful and full of life. A purist's *Henry*, perhaps, it serves to remind us how stunning, sweeping and daring was Olivier's film, making this a commoner in faint pursuit of a king.

Henry VIII and His Six Wives ○

1972, UK, 125 mins, colour
Dir: Waris Hussein

Stars: Keith Michell, Charlotte Rampling, Jane Asher, Lynne Frederick, Donald Pleasence
Rating: ★★★

There's pomp but no pomposity in this spin-off from the TV series *The Six Wives of Henry VIII*. As the change of title implies, this condensed version concentrates more on Keith Michell's splendid portrayal of Henry. From the array of wives, Charlotte Rampling's Anne Boleyn and Lynne Frederick as Catherine Howard shine the brightest.

Her Alibi ○ ⓥ
1989, US, 94 mins, colour
Dir: Bruce Beresford
Stars: Tom Selleck, Paulina Porizkova, William Daniels, James Farentino
Rating: ★★

Lightweight comedy fluff with Selleck in a Burt Reynolds-type role as a thriller writer whose claim to have modelled his suave fictitious sleuth upon himself is as empty as his typewriter since his wife left him four years before. Then Porizkova, a mysterious Romanian with a willowy figure and melting eyes, walks into a courtroom accused of murder and Selleck sniffs a story. Giving her an alibi, he takes her to his country house, lusts after her from afar, and writes a new novel based on the developing case, worrying all the time that's she's going to stick a knife in him. 'You fell in love with a murderess,' accuse his family. 'It's tough to meet girls these days,' he grumbles apologetically. Selleck tries hard with the grouchy charm, Porizkova is lovely (though raw as an actress) and William Daniels deservedly get the best lines as Selleck's nagging agent.

He Ran All the Way ○
1951, US, 77 mins, b/w
Dir: John Berry
Stars: John Garfield, Shelley Winters, Wallace Ford
Rating: ★★★

John Garfield gives a haunting study of the hunted killer in this crime drama, charged with a burning intensity by director John Berry and his players. Garfield's portrayal of the cold and callous Nick was the last portrait in his cinematic gallery of men on the run: a year later he died, at 39.

Herbie Goes Bananas ⊙
1980, US, 100 mins, colour
Dir: Vincent McEveety
Stars: Cloris Leachman, Charles Martin Smith, John Vernon
Rating: ★

A mild, harmless lark about the car with a mind of its own, which will look (a bit) better on TV than it did in cinemas. The local scenery is lovely, and, though the human cast is charmless, Herbie the Volkswagen makes up for them. The film's funniest line (from Harvey Korman) must almost have robbed it of its 'U' certificate! But it was worth keeping, as it's about the only laugh there is for mums and dads.

Herbie Goes to Monte Carlo ⊙
1977, US, 105 mins, colour
Dir: Vincent McEveety
Stars: Dean Jones, Don Knotts, Julie Sommars
Rating: ★★

The third 'Love Bug' adventure finds Dean Jones back in the driving seat as Herbie becomes involved with the Monte Carlo Rally and a stolen diamond. Jones is as good as ever, but director Vincent McEveety's poor pacing shows up his performance less well than before. Roy Kinnear is one of the comic villains, while Herbie himself falls for a lady Lancia.

Herbie Rides Again ⊙
1974, US, 88 mins, colour
Dir: Robert Stevenson
Stars: Helen Hayes, Ken Berry, Stefanie Powers, Keenan Wynn
Rating: ★★★

Almost equally successful sequel to the Disney studio's *The Love Bug*, with Herbie the Volkswagen (and a few of his friends) taking on a ruthless property developer, played for all the part's worth by Keenan Wynn. Helen Hayes and Stefanie Powers personably lead the rest of the humans, but it's Herbie's show.

Here Comes Mr Jordan ○
1941, US, 93 mins, b/w
Dir: Alexander Hall
Stars: Robert Montgomery, Claude Rains, Evelyn Keyes, Edward Everett Horton
Rating: ★★★★★

Delightfully droll fantasy about a man sent to heaven before his time that was an unexpected critical and commercial success in its day and won two Academy Awards for its story and screenplay. Director Alexander Hall never made anything so good again, but this was remade to surprisingly delightful effect in 1978 as *Heaven Can Wait*. Edward Everett Horton steals the show in this version as the dithering heavenly messenger 7013.

Here Comes the Groom ⊙
1951, US, 113 mins, b/w
Dir: Frank Capra
Stars: Bing Crosby, Jane Wyman, Alexis Smith, Franchot Tone
Rating: ★★★

Here's a chance to re-evaluate one of Frank Capra's later films, starring Bing Crosby. It mixes sentiment, comedy and songs, the hit number in this one being 'In the Cool, Cool, Cool of the Evening' by Hoagy Carmichael and Johnny Mercer, which won an Academy Award. Also popular was 'Misto Cristofo Columbo' which Bing sings on a plane, accompanied by numerous guest 'passengers', including Louis Armstrong, Cass Daley, Phil Harris and Dorothy Lamour.

Here Come the Girls ⊙
1953, US, 78 mins, colour
Dir: Claude Binyon
Stars: Bob Hope, Tony Martin, Arlene Dahl, Rosemary Clooney
Rating: ★★★

A bright, amusing, likeable Bob Hope comedy-musical. With three co-stars (Tony Martin, Rosemary Clooney and Arlene Dahl), a short running time and several songs to get through, it's not surprising that Hope is given too little scope for his own brand of 'cowardly comedy' in this story of the 'world's oldest chorus boy' on the run from a killer called Jack the Slasher. Playing Jack, and heading a cast of stalwart character players, is scowling Robert Strauss, the actor who won fame in his underwear as Animal in *Stalag 17*. Hope shares a really zippy duet with the delightful Clooney called 'You Got Class'. Stay tuned for the closing Hope crack in an ending which leaves him literally up in the air!

Her Jungle Love ○
1938, US, 81 mins, colour
Dir: George Archainbaud
Stars: Dorothy Lamour, Ray Milland, Lynne Overman, J Carrol Naish
Rating: ★★

Dorothy Lamour was already well launched into her career as the star bursting into sarong when she made this tropical adventure about a jungle girl believed by the natives to be a goddess. Directed by George Archainbaud, who had been in Hollywood since the early silent days, and rather sadly ended his career making Gene Autry Westerns. Here, he is in splendid control of such attractions as a typhoon, a tidal wave and an earthquake.

H

Hero

See: Accidental Hero

Hero at Large ○ ⓥ

1980, US, 98 mins, colour
Dir: Martin Davidson
Stars: John Ritter, Anne Archer, Kevin McCarthy
Rating: ★★

Out-of-work actor Steve Nichols (John Ritter) earns rent money by making public appearances as comic book hero Captain Avenger. On the way home from an appearance (and still in costume) he foils a corner store hold-up, making everyone think there really is a Captain Avenger. Lightweight fun, with the underrated Ritter skimming merrily over the clichés. Anne (*Fatal Attraction*) Archer, in an early role, plays his girlfriend. Kevin McCarthy enjoys himself as one of the bad guys and a young Kevin Bacon can be glimpsed briefly in the supporting cast. It's engaging enough, but too simple-minded for complete success.

Heroes of Telemark, The ○ ⓥ

1965, UK, 131 mins, colour
Dir: Anthony Mann
Stars: Kirk Douglas, Richard Harris, Ulla Jacobsson, Michael Redgrave, Anton Diffring, Eric Porter
Rating: ★★

A Second World War blockbuster that could be best described as *Operation Crossbow* on skis. It's in the action, sharp and telling when it comes, that the film's strength lies. The 'heroes' are lucky in fact that their dialogue is kept to a minimum, for most of it is sub-standard. The photography on the other hand is never less than excellent, from snowy nocturnal landscapes, beautifully captured, to red lamplight reflected in the Germans' helmets. Unfortunately, its crystal clarity tends to heighten the effect of comic-strip war which the film often seems to do its best to give – an effect which is happily shattered in the last 15 minutes with a climactic sequence aboard a sabotaged ship, in which the suspense is really killing; Douglas organises a desperate 'game' to see which child can put a life jacket on first, as the floating deathtrap beneath them nears explosion point. Richard Harris gives the best acting performance, and Jennifer Hilary's touching portrayal makes one of the minor roles spring vividly to life.

He Said, She Said ◖ ⓥ

1991, US, 104 mins, colour
Dir: Ken Kwapis, Marisa Silver
Stars: Kevin Bacon, Elizabeth Perkins, Anthony LaPaglia, Sharon Stone
Rating: ★★★

A sweet-natured romantic comedy in the old style, with nice old-fashioned music by Miles Goodman, but just not quite enough bite to take it into the super-hit class. Elizabeth Perkins and Kevin Bacon are rival columnists for a newspaper. Their competition for a leader column results in them being paired up in opposition. Newsprint leads to television, and in no time at all, they're debating topical subjects with each other on local TV. Of course, they also fall in love, but he's reluctant to commit, and that's where the two directors, Ken Kwapis and Marisa Silver, come in, each showing the course of the romance from their own sex's point of view. Most of it works, although some of it is merely repetitive. Perkins is adorable; Bacon, although miscast, gets by.

He Walked By Night ○

1948, US, 79 mins, b/w
Dir: Anthony Mann, Alfred Werker
Stars: Richard Basehart, Scott Brady, Jack Webb, Roy Roberts
Rating: ★★★

Although this atmospheric noir thriller is credited to Alfred Werker, a lot of it was directed, uncredited, by Anthony Mann, who had already made some striking thrillers, including *T-Men* and *Raw Deal* for the same studio, Eagle Lion. Richard Basehart made a big impact as the killer whose only friend is a dog.

He Who Rides a Tiger ○

1965, UK, 103 mins, b/w
Dir: Charles Crichton
Stars: Tom Bell, Judi Dench, Paul Rogers, Kay Walsh
Rating: ★★★★

Superlative acting by Tom Bell and Judi Dench, and skilful treatment by director Charles Crichton made this film an unexpected winner. Bell plays an habitual criminal whose story springs to vivid life under Crichton's taut direction, aided by photography from John von Kotze that's a treat to watch, and astute editing by Jack Harris and John Smith that never lets our eyes drop from the screen. Sideline highlights include some charming reactions from orphanage children, with whom Bell really does seem at home, and a realistically staged fight between Bell

and Edina Ronay that rivals the no-claws-barred scrap from *The Pumpkin Eater*. The film's only weakness is an improbable twist near the end when the police get on to Bell's biggest robbery. Otherwise it's excellent, compact entertainment.

Hey! Hey! USA ⊙

1938, UK, 92 mins, b/w
Dir: Marcel Varnel
Stars: Will Hay, Edgar Kennedy
Rating: ★★★

The incomparable Will Hay reprises his splendidly shifty Dr Benjamin Twist character (the incompetent headmaster of St Michael's) in this breezy British comedy set in a quaintly observed America full of gun-toting gangsters. Comic stalwart Edgar Kennedy provides slow-burning support under the direction of Marcel Varnel, the dapper Frenchman who made most of Hay's biggest successes.

Hickey & Boggs ◖

1972, US, 111 mins, colour
Dir: Robert Culp
Stars: Bill Cosby, Robert Culp
Rating: ★★★

Fans of Bill Cosby and Robert Culp from the hit comedy-thriller TV series *I Spy* were probably quite surprised to discover their favourites teamed in this Seventies *film noir* in which two shabby private eyes are hired to find a missing girl and find themselves caught up in bloody mayhem. Tautly directed by Culp himself, the hard-hitting results marked one of the first appearances on the movie scene of Walter Hill, here as a writer, but later to become a director of such similar blue-collar thrillers as *48 Hrs*, *Extreme Prejudice*, *Red Heat*, and *Trespass*.

Hidden Agenda ● ⓥ

1990, UK, 108 mins, colour
Dir: Ken Loach
Stars: Frances McDormand, Brian Cox, Brad Dourif, Mai Zetterling
Rating: ★★★

Ken Loach's political thriller hunted a British distributor for some time, and no wonder. For this Cannes Festival prizewinner is a very hot potato indeed. There's a distinctly anti-British and pro-IRA flavour to its powderkeg plot, which concerns the killing of an American lawyer (Brad Dourif, who formed part of an international team investigating infringements of civil liberties in Northern Ireland. A senior British detective (Brian Cox), sent to investigate the death, uncovers a past

CIA plot to dump Edward Heath as prime minister, discredit Harold Wilson and wreck Labour's chances of winning the following election. But publishing his findings, despite the help of the IRA and the dead man's fiancée (Frances McDormand), is another matter. Loach describes the film as 'an important story that wasn't being told'. After the subsequent spate of miscarriages of justice, who is to say where fiction ends and the truth begins?

Hidden Eye, The O
1945, US, 70 mins, b/w
Dir: Richard Whorf
Stars: Edward Arnold, Frances Rafferty
Rating: ★★

Portly Edward Arnold made his second appearance as the blind detective Duncan Maclain (created by novelist Baynard Kendrick) in this competent MGM second-feature with a twisty plot and a list of suspects that includes such shifty Hollywood character actors as Ray Collins, Byron Foulger, Morris Ankrum and Jack Lambert. Friday the dog, Arnold's 'seeing eye', is a real scene-stealer once again.

Hidden Room, The
See: Obsession [1948]

Hideaway ● Ⓥ
1995, US, 105 mins, colour
Dir: Brett Leonard
Stars: Jeff Goldblum, Christine Lahti, Alfred Molina, Alicia Silverstone, Rae Dawn Chong, Jeremy Sisto
Rating: ★

Director Leonard's previous film *The Lawnmower Man* had amazing virtual realty effects and an interesting if flawed story. This one has great special effects too, but bad everything else. Jeff Goldblum and Christine Lahti, one of whose daughters died in a road accident, get into a smash themselves, after which he is brought back from the dead by Dr Alfred Molina, who is clearly one of those scientists who dabble in things best left alone. 'He may seem different to you,' Molina warns Lahti. Too true. Goldblum is locked into the mind of a mass murderer who has also been brought back from the dead. Now he's after Goldblum's other daughter and only Goldblum, whose character is appropriately called Hatch, can stop him. What follows is almost unbearably nasty and crammed full with as many adult-certificate elements as even this kind of movie will take. 'Some souls choose only to live for a short time,' drones psychic Rae Dawn

Chong (in a worthless part). Would that the film did the same. It seems to go on for ever – even to a scene after the credits.

Hideaways, The O
(aka: From the Mixed-Up Files of Mrs Basil E Frankweiler)
1973, US, 105 mins, colour
Dir: Fielder Cook
Stars: Ingrid Bergman, Sally Prager, Richard Mulligan, George Rose
Rating: ★★

A low-key fable about two bored American kids and their encounters with an eccentric recluse – a bizarre role for Ingrid Bergman in one of her last films, playing a woman about 15 years older than herself. Highly suitable for children, although the younger ones will find it has too little action and too many stretches of tedium.

High and Dry
See: The Maggie

High Anxiety O Ⓥ
1977, US, 94 mins, colour
Dir: Mel Brooks
Stars: Mel Brooks, Madeline Kahn, Cloris Leachman, Harvey Korman
Rating: ★★

This comic homage to Alfred Hitchcock is, like all of Mel Brooks' film, simply bubbling with ideas. More's the pity, then, that Brooks takes it all above and beyond its subtler comic possibilities. Under Brooks' own direction, he and the rest of his cast go high over the top together.

High Barbaree O
1947, US, 91 mins, b/w
Dir: Jack Conway
Stars: Van Johnson, June Allyson, Thomas Mitchell
Rating: ★

Van Johnson and June Allyson were a hugely popular MGM romantic team who appeared in almost as many films together as Greer Garson and Walter Pidgeon. Johnson had been among the three most popular stars in the world for 1945 and 1946, but *High Barbaree* signalled the beginning of his decline. The story sounds promising – an airman, shot down in World War Two, makes, with a wounded companion, for an island he remembers from boyhood stories – but becomes ponderous in the telling. There isn't much anyone can have done with this script, but Johnson isn't the world's most interesting actor. Small wonder fellow-flier Cameron Mitchell seems to be failing:

Johnson is boring him (and us) to death with a rambling account of his life.

High Commissioner, The
See: Nobody Runs Forever

Higher Learning ● Ⓥ
1995, US, 128 mins, colour
Dir: John Singleton
Stars: Kristy Swanson, Ice Cube, Jennifer Connelly, Omar Epps, Tyra Banks
Rating: ★

Black power against white supremacists. Rape. Suicide. Mass murder. Just another day at an American university. The director is John Singleton, of *Boyz N the Hood* fame, but this school story has none of that film's power. Its characters are ludicrously overdrawn and you almost wish the sniper who decimates the student bodies at the end would cut down whingeing Kristy Swanson, torn between her efforts for peace, to get the money for her course and to choose between heterosexual and gay lovers. 'Without struggle, there is no progress,' intones Professor Laurence Fishburne sonorously. Not much evidence of either here, both on the racial and filmic fronts.

High Heels ● Ⓥ
1991, Spain, 114 mins, colour
Dir: Pedro Almodovar
Stars: Victoda Abril, Marisa Paredes, Miguel Bosé
Rating: ★★

Is it a black comedy? Is it an offbeat romance? Is it a murder thriller? Or an intimate drama about the relationship between a mother and a daughter down the years? This film from the fashionable Spanish director Pedro Almodovar is certainly his least boring so far – and will definitely keep you guessing to the end, even if it does go on a bit. And you can't wholly dislike a film where the female jailblock inmates go into a dance number while confessed murderess Victoria Abril awaits her fate.

Highlander ◐ Ⓥ
1986, UK, 111 mins, colour
Dir: Russell Mulcahy
Stars: Christopher Lambert, Sean Connery, Roxanne Hart, Clancy Brown, Beatie Edney
Rating: ★★

Thanks to an indecisive and cliché-ridden script, this ambitious fantasy thriller emerges as a very curious film indeed. 'I've been alive for four and half centuries,' groans MacLeod (Christopher Lambert), one of the 'im-

H

mortals' seeking 'the prize'. 'Well,' shrugs the heroine (Roxanne Hart), unfazed. 'Everyone's got their problems.' True, true, but this film has a multitude of them. There are some well-staged duels from a director with a strong pictorial sense, and some noisy songs by Queen, before we get to the final clash between MacLeod and his deadly enemy The Kurgan. Special effects are often impressive. Two sequels to date.

Highly Dangerous ○
1950, UK, 85 mins, b/w
Dir: Roy Baker
Stars: Margaret Lockwood, Dane Clark, Marius Goring, Naunton Wayne
Rating: ★★

A beautiful woman, a tough newspaperman, a sinister police chief and a box of deadly bugs all add up to a fast-moving thriller. Equality for women is one thing, but it really does't stretch to someone like Margaret Lockwood being sent by our government to a Middle East country to probe the use of germs in warfare. One doesn't fancy her chances overmuch, even with the help of Dane Clark, a newspaper reporter, whose interest in Margaret is probably something more than insects. Still less would we bet on her success when we meet the menacing State Police Chief, played with a glint by Marius Goring. But Margaret dreams up a scheme so wildly impossible that it has to be seen to be believed. And oddly enough, it comes off, which brightly rounds out this unabashed hokum.

High Noon ○ ⓥ
1952, US, 85 mins, b/w
Dir: Fred Zinnemann
Stars: Gary Cooper, Grace Kelly, Thomas Mitchell, Lloyd Bridges, Katy Jurado, Otto Kruger
Rating: ★★★★★

Fred Zinnemann's now-classic Western, with its can't-miss ingredients of love, loyalty, duty and guns in the afternoon. Gary Cooper, at his grimmest and best, swept aside all opposition for the Best Actor Oscar, and the film won three other Academy Awards, including one for the famous title song, written by Ned Washington and Dimitri Tiomkin, and sung by Tex Ritter, which both sweeps along and intensifies the drama. Thomas Mitchell, Grace Kelly and Katy Jurado also make notable contributions, while one of the villains is the later-famous Lee Van Cleef, who has the film's striking opening image all to himself.

High Plains Drifter ○ ⓥ
1972, US, 105 mins, colour
Dir: Clint Eastwood
Stars: Clint Eastwood, Verna Bloom, Billy Curtis
Rating: ★★

Clint Eastwood's second outing as a director-star is a leisurely Western revenge story which pays homage to Sergio Leone – the director who contributed most to Eastwood's early career as an actor. As in the Leone 'Dollar' trilogy, Eastwood is an unidentified stranger who rides menacingly into a frontier town and exerts a God-like power over it, having been hired by its citizens to protect them against vengeful outlaws. Orchestrating plots and counter-plots, the stranger deals ruthlessly with the town's corrupt hierarchy and provides the story with an eerie, surrealistic climax. Alongside Eastwood's characteristically laconic performance, midget actor Billy Curtis is a great foil as Mordecai Fortune. Moody, self-conscious and off-beat.

High Sierra ○ ⓥ
1941, US, 96 mins, b/w
Dir Raoul Walsh
Stars: Humphrey Bogart, Ida Lupino, Arthur Kennedy, Joan Leslie
Rating: ★★★★

Hold-up man Roy Earle is out of prison and in need of money, so goes back to what he does best and pulls a robbery job. But he is identified and has to go on the run. Earle is personified by Humphrey Bogart at his bad guy best (seizing his first major role for six years after it had been rejected by several other Warner stars) before *Casablanca* made him a romantic hero, although even here he has a soft centre. The film's action is slowed somewhat by the scenes in which he befriends a hillbilly couple and their handicapped granddaughter (the soft centre bits), but the climax in the Sierra mountains of the title is the stuff of which film legends are made. Ida Lupino is the girl who falls for him and Henry Travers is delightfully folksy as the hillbilly grandpa.

High School High ◑ ⓥ
1996, US, 86 mins, colour
Dir: Hart Bochner
Stars: Jon Lovitz, Tia Carrere, Louise Fletcher, Mekhi Pfiffer
Rating: ★

Zucker Brothers completists – David produced and co-wrote this one – might get a few mild yocks from this gross-out spoof of *Dangerous Minds*-style

school stories where an idealistic teacher (here Lovitz) comes to a ghetto high school and makes the difference. The sort of school where they staple the daily supply of condoms to the sex advice handout and where the best excuse for being late is 'the bell rang before I got here', it has a bat-wielding principal (Fletcher) who, like most heads in such films, is clearly up to no good and would like to get rid of the hapless Lovitz, especially when his unorthodox methods show signs of working. On his side is Fletcher's gorgeous PA (Carrere), who only seems to have one dress to wear, even after she gets it soaked and torn in a fight with a student. There are a few mildly effective bits, but mostly the writers throw in something to offend every ethnic, religious or sexual minority in a desperate bid for laughs.

High Society ○ ⓥ
1956, US, 107 mins, colour
Dir: Charles Walters
Stars: Bing Crosby, Frank Sinatra, Grace Kelly, Celeste Holm, John Lund, Louis Armstrong, Louis Calhern
Rating: ★★★

This musical remake of the Oscar-winning *The Philadelphia Story* united Bing Crosby and Frank Sinatra, the two top singers of their era. And what a memorable occasion it was. An abrasive script by John Patrick was complemented by a score that included 'True Love', 'Who Wants to Be a Millionaire?', 'Now You Has Jazz' and a show-stopping Crosby-Sinatra duet called 'Did You Evah?' But it's Louis 'Satchmo' Armstrong who steals this elegant show.

High Spirits ◑
1988, UK, 97 mins, colour
Dir: Neil Jordan
Stars: Peter O'Toole, Daryl Hannah, Steve Guttenberg, Beverly D'Angelo, Liam Neeson, Ray McAnally
Rating: ★★

An amiable Irish ghost comedy with a few giggles and a personable cast. It's a little low on incident, perhaps, but the sheer glee of the enterprise makes up for some of its shortcomings, which include an over-reliance on repetitious tracking shots by director Neil Jordan. At Castle Plunkett hotel, the rooms are guestless, the debts are endless and the good Lord Plunkett (Peter O'Toole) is legless, and at the end of his tether, when he gets the idea of a few ghosts to drum up trade. A coachload of Americans arrives, but the ghost night is a disaster, and doom beckons Lord Peter again before the real castle ghosts, led by Ray McAnally, decide to bale him out. Generally, the idea, like most ghost comedies, sounds funnier than it is. But you'll find it lively enough (and brief enough) to get by with a smile.

High Tide at Noon ○

1957, UK, 111 mins, b/w
Dir: Philip Leacock
Stars: Betta St John, William Sylvester, Michael Craig, Patrick McGoohan
Rating: ★★

Packed with incident and magnificent scenery, this love story with a difference, set among fisherfolk, took director Philip Leacock back to Nova Scotia, scene of his earlier triumph, *The Kidnappers*. Its top-notch cast includes many of Britain's best young hopefuls of the time, including Michael Craig, Jill Dixon, Patrick McGoohan and Susan Beaumont. Appealing performances by Betta St John and William Sylvester in the leading roles are more than a match for a variable script. It's so fresh that you can almost catch a whiff of the sea air even if that, like the characters, remains at a tantalising distance.

High Time ○

1960, US, 103 mins, colour
Dir: Blake Edwards
Stars: Bing Crosby, Nicole Maurey, Tuesday Weld, Fabian, Richard Beymer
Rating: ★★

Here's a question to baffle the buffs. What has Bing Crosby got in conunon with Rodney Dangerfield? Answer: they both starred in versions of the same plot about a middle-aged millionaire deciding to embark on a belated college education. This is Crosby's film (Dangerfield's, 26 years later, was called *Back to School*) and the Old Crooner throws himself into the farce with a will, singing a couple of songs, perfectly timing his laughs, and even appearing in drag.

High Vermilion

See: Silver City

Highway Patrolman ● Ⓥ

1991, Mexico, 101 mins, colour
Dir: Alex Cox
Stars: Roberto Sosa, Bruno Bichir, Vanessa Bauche, Pedro Armendariz Jr, Jorge Russek, Zaide Silvia Guttieriez
Rating: ★★

This study in moral decay is a borderline-interesting story of a 'patrullero' in Mexico. He starts off full of bright hope, but is quickly suckered into marriage, learns the hard truth about patrolling the road, takes up with a prostitute and slips into a pattern of everyday evils where bribes are the norm – accepted simply because he needs the money. The violent death of his best friend triggers off the final third of the film, as the patrolman seeks some kind of revenge on the drug smugglers who did it. Some of the desperation of the patrullero's work and the country are caught: this and such sideline issues as the hero's rejection by his father, and his attempted – and futile – rehabilitation of the prostitute just about hold the interest for most of the way.

Highway to Hell ●

1991, US, 94 mins, colour
Dir: Ate De Jong
Stars: Chad Lowe, Kristy Swanson, Patrick Bergin, Richard Farnsworth
Rating: ★★

There's lots of action going on in this horror fantasy, but not much of it strikes the same kind of note. Chad Lowe and girlfriend Kristy Swanson, eloping to Las Vegas, decide to take a back road. In less time than it takes to yawn, Lowe duly pulls over, and Swanson is bagged by Hellcop (using two severed hands for handcuffs) who carts her off to Hell. Given advice by Farnsworth, Lowe follows on, and finds himself on a sort of yellow brick road, where references to Oz mix uneasily with a group of bikers, repulsive monsters, cardboard sets, people who explode into nothingness when shot, glimpses of the real Hell and an enigmatic figure called Beezle (Patrick Bergin). Bergin lends the film such much-needed charisma. Lowe displays enthusiasm but not much else. Swanson looks great but doesn't act much. It isn't dull but, frequently miscalculating the right tone, doesn't pull you along with the story either.

High Wind in Jamaica, A ○

1965, UK, 104 mins, colour
Dir: Alexander Mackendrick
Stars: Anthony Quinn, James Coburn, Dennis Price, Gert Frobe, Lila Kedrova, Nigel Davenport
Rating: ★★★★★

Lusty, gutsy yarn of a disreputable group of pirates who become the very unwilling custodians of several spirited children. The flap of sail, the creak of boards and Douglas Slocombe's magnificent colour camerawork make the voyage so believable that you can almost taste the salt: and Deborah Baxter's portrayal is the finest piece of child acting since Hayley Mills in *Tiger Bay*. It's a film one doesn't want to end. Alexander Mackendrick had the knack of getting fine work from children, as he showed in *The Maggie* and *Sammy Going South*. Together, he and his technicians have made an almost classic sea story.

High Window, The ○

(aka: The Brasher Doubloon)
11947, US, 72 mins, b/w
Dir: John Brahm
Stars: George Montgomery, Nancy Guild, Conrad Janis, Fritz Kortner
Rating: ★★

A dip into the world of Raymond Chandler's famous detective Philip Marlowe, full of shifty faces, weak-chinned rich boys and two-timing lovelies. A few liberties have been taken with the original, most notably with the key event, and both George Montgomery and Marlowe look unhappy with that moustache. Still, the story's grip remains considerable, and young Nancy Guild is a heroine in the best Bacall mould.

Hilda Crane ○

1956, US, 87 mins, colour
Dir: Philip Dunne
Stars: Jean Simmons, Guy Madison, Jean-Pierre Aumont
Rating: ★★

Tears and more tears, as Jean Simmons stumbles from one broken marriage to another in her search for happiness. Turgid emotional melodrama with minimal support for a star who deserves better. Still, at least it isn't long.

Hill, The ◑

1965, UK, 122 mins, b/w
Dir: Sidney Lumet
Stars: Sean Connery, Harry Andrews, Ian Bannen, Ian Hendry, Michael Redgrave
Rating: ★★★★

A hard, tough story of life in a military stockade that makes gripping viewing. Although its dialogue is often difficult to grasp, this powerful film leaves one with an indelible impression of pn'mldve violence, for men's emotions have rarely been ripped as raw on screen. Sean Connery broke right away from the Bond image as the bullet-headed ex-sergeant-major who leads the ultimate revolt against authority. Ian Hendry's sneering sergeant is also a splendid piece of character work. Sidney Lumet's determined direction ensures that no punches are pulled.

H

Hill In Korea, A ○
(aka: Hell In Korea)
1956, UK, 81 mins, b/w
Dir: Julian Amyes
Stars: George Baker, Harry Andrews, Stanley Baker, Michael Medwin, Stephen Boyd
Rating ★★★

Goodish British war film about the Korean conflict. George Baker gives a very carefully observed portrait of the national-service officer, and there's some excellent black-and-white photography. In retrospect, however, the chief interest lies in the sweat-anctblood supporting roles – Starliey Baker as Col Ryker, Stephen Boyd as Pte Sims, Robert Shaw as L Cpl Hedge and – in his first film – Michael Caine as Pte Lockyer.

Hill's Angels ⊙
(aka: The North Avenue Irregulars)
1978, US, 99 mins, colour
Dir: Bruce Bilson
Stars: Edward Herrmann, Barbara Harris, Cloris Leachman
Rating: ★★

A pleasant enough Disney comedy that starts well but soon reverts to formula, and even includes the standard obh tory car pile-up finale. The quality cast seems rather wasted in this chichéd story of a new priest in town who tries to unite the local women to form a crack crime-fighting unit.

Hills of Home, The ⊙
(aka: Master of Lassie)
1948, US, 97 mins, colour
Dir: Fred M Wilcox
Stars: Edmund Gwenn, Donald Crisp, Janet Leigh, Tom Drake
Rating: ★★★

Edmund Gwenn as the Scottish doctor manages to outshine even Lassie, his co-star, here in one of her best scripts, which saddles her with a psychological fear of water. How this is eventually overcome will leave few dry eyes in the house. Gwenn and Donald Crisp exude cosy crustiness, while Janet Leigh, in her early contract days with MGM, is as pretty a heroine as you could wish for. Wonderful Technicolor photography of the rolling Scottish (actually Californian) countryside by Charles Schoenbaum.

Hindenburg, The ○
1975, US, 130 mins, colour
Dir: Robert Wise
Stars: George C Scott, Anne Bancroft, William Atherton, Roy Thinnes, Gig Young, Burgess Meredith
Rating: ★

The fascinating idea that the 1937 *Hindenburg* disaster might have been an act of sabotage is rather overwhelmed by an all-star cast and a *Grand Hotel*-style plot structure. Burgess Meredith and Rene Auberjonois are good enough as a couple of cardsharps to merit more screen time.

Hired Hand, The ◐
1971, US, 93 mins, colour
Dir: Peter Fonda
Stars: Peter Fonda, Warren Oates, Verna Bloom
Rating: ★★★

Although slow to start, this thinking man's Western about a cowboy's eternal longings for the wide open prairie has a splendid script by British writer Alan Sharp that comes into its own once the film gets under way. The acting, especially from Vema Bloom who blazes sincerity as the very real, much-put-upon wife, is first class. Peter Fonda's own performance, in fact, is rather better than his direction, which is perhaps the weakest element in this unusual and often rewarding film.

Hireling, The ◐
1973, US, 103 mins, colour
Dir: Alan Bridges
Stars: Robert Shaw, Sarah Miles
Rating: ★★

Another screen adaptation from the work of L P Hartley, who wrote *The Go-Between*. Although the glowing, muted colour photography (Michael Reed) and sumptuous production design (Natasha Kroll) are the equal of the earlier film, they tend to overdominate things here, with the consequence that *The Hireling* is a less cleanly striking film than its predecessor. Sarah Miles gives another of her careful studies of repressed sexuality, but co-star Robert Shaw is never quite at ease as the chauffeur who sets his peaked cap at her, flouting all of the social conventions.

His Butler's Sister ⊙
1943, US, 88 mins, b/w
Dir: Frank Borzage
Stars: Deanna Durbin, Franchot Tone, Pat O'Brien
Rating: ★★★

Breezy is the word for this much-requested Deanna Durbin musical which seems to be the favourite of many of her fans. The sparkling songthrush sings a bar or two of Puccini, plus the popular songs 'While You're Away' and 'Spirit of the Moment' and a medley of 'Russian' ditties. This has probably the best supporting cast of any Durbin musical, including an on-form Pat O'Brien and Franchot Tone, plus such delightful 'below stairs' types as Sig Arno, Akim Tamiroff, Hans Conried, Frank Jenks, Franklin Pangborn and Alan Mowbray.

His Excellency ○
1951, UK, 80 mins, b/w
Dir: Robert Hamer
Stars: Eric Portman, Cecil Parker, Susan Stephen, Helen Cherry
Rating: ★★

This disappointing and rather condescending drama spotlights the dilemmas which must face many good trade unionists who suddenly find themselves controlling the destinies of their fellow-workers. Eric Portman plays the central character – an ex-docker who finds himself governor of a strife-torn West Indian island. Popular, though: another success for Ealing Studios at the box-office.

His Girl Friday ○
1940, US, 89 mins, b/w
Dir: Howard Hawks
Stars: Cary Grant, Rosalind Russell, Ralph Bellamy, Gene Lockhart, John Qualen
Rating: ★★★★

Howard Hawks' rip-roaring remake of the classic newspaper comedy *The Front Page*, with the pivotal role assigned to a woman (Rosalind Russell) instead of a man. Charles Lederer's brilliantly tart script gives her and Cary Grant (as her managing editor and ex-husband) some memorable exchanges as Hawks overlaps scenes and dialogue to carry the black farce along at helterskelter speed. Certainly the kind of film they can't make anymore, as Billy Wilder found when he tried to film the original with a great cast but only moderate success in 1974. Meanwhile, don't miss this classic version.

His Majesty O'Keefe ○
1953, UK, 92 mins, colour
Dir: Byron Haskin
Stars: Burt Lancaster, Joan Rice, Andre Morell, Abraham Sofaer
Rating: ★★

The scenic qualities of the film are rather better than the disjointed plot in this high adventure made during star Burt Lancaster's 'athletic action' period. Stunningly set against Hong Kong and Fijian backgrounds, the story concerns

Cap'n Lancaster's attempts to make a fortune out of pearls, copra or anything else he can lay his hands on, when he's not fighting bands of pirates. Andre Morell is excellent as a disgruntled German trader; Abraham Sofaer scores as a friendly medicine man.

History Is Made at Night ○
1937, US, 93 mins, b/w
Dir: Frank Borzage
Stars: Jean Arthur, Charles Boyer, Colin Clive, Leo Carrillo
Rating: ★★★

Strange mixture of romance, comedy-thriller and high drama, with an excellent sequence of disaster at sea near the end. It's primarily a vehicle for that delightful actress Jean Arthur, and she makes the most of her chances as an unhappily married lady who finds herself at the centre of a baffling and violent series of events in Paris. Charles Boyer is his usual elegant self, and shows a lighter touch than usual, in his interpretation of the man with whom she becomes romantically involved during the very intricate plot.

History of Mr Polly, The ⊙
1949, UK, 94 mins, b/w
Dir: Anthony Pelissier
Stars: John Mills, Sally Ann Howes, Finlay Currie, Edward Chapman, Megs Jenkins
Rating: ★★★★

This vision of H G Wells' classic story of a little man's fight to be free of his wretched life was produced by its star, John Mills, and has immense charm. The original author would surely have been delighted with the performances of Mills, Megs Jenkins, Betty Ann Davies and Finlay Currie, and Desmond Dickinson's sunny photography exactly catches the leisurely pace and atmosphere of British rural life. Wells' ingenious plot, crammed with incident, is treated remarkably faithfully by director Anthony Pelissier's screenplay, with a fire sequence and the final riverside battle between Mills and Currie coming out as the highlights. A memorable British success.

History of the World Part I ● ⓥ
1981, US, 92 mins, colour
Dir: Mel Brooks
Stars: Mel Brooks, Dom DeLuise, Madeline Kahn, Harvey Korman
Rating: ★

'You Romans have a god for everything,' says Comicus (Mel Brooks),' except premature ejaculation. But I

hear that's coming quickly.' You may not credit it, but this is the verbal highpoint of this Brooks gathering of historical excreta, to use a term of which he himself would approve: it's all downhill from there on. Brooks goes at it all with a will, leering at the camera, writing dozens of jokes about bodily functions and constructing whole scenes round single punchlines. He looks as though he's having a tremendous time and, if crude sledgehammer comedies are your bag, you may too. It makes a *Carry On* film resemble a tapestry of wit and understatement.

Hit, The ●
1984, UK, 98 mins, colour
Dir: Stephen Frears
Stars: John Hurt, Tim Roth, Laura Del Sol, Terence Stamp
Rating: ★★

Bleakly dramatic suspense film about a 'squealer' (Stamp) who flees to Spain but finds that retribution eventually catches up with him. The dialogue is frequently amusing and the action red in tooth and claw. The delicious Laura del Sol is the girl improbably hauled along for a desert trek, giving rise to some lovely burnished photography of Spanish landscapes.

Hitcher, The ● ⓥ
1986, US, 97 mins, colour
Dir: Robert Harmon
Stars: C Thomas Howell, Rutger Hauer, Jennifer Jason Leigh, Jeffrey DeMunn
Rating: ★★

Both a road movie and a battle between good and evil, *The Hitcher* is thus a direct descendant from *Duel*. A psycho killer, Ryder (Rutger Hauer), who murders the drivers with whom he hitches lifts, seems to decide that teenager Jim (C Thomas Howell) is the man to end his torment. 'Stop me,' he grates, with a knife to Jim's cheek. When Jim's answer is to propel Ryder from the car, his nightmare begins. Ryder kills more hapless motorists, crimes for which Jim is eventually arrested and jailed. Always grim, unpleasant and visceral, the film is sometimes exciting as well. Howell delineates very well his desperate descent from normal teenager to hyped-up hunter, while Hauer does what he can to make his psycho memorable. The chase sequences are done with all the efficiency and damage we've come to expect from modern Hollywood. It isn't quite the nailbiter *Duel* was (and has a less logical

ending too) but it won't bore you either.

Hitler – The Last Ten Days ● ⓥ
1973, UK, 108 mins, colour
Dir: Ennio De Concini
Stars: Alec Guinness, Simon Ward, Adolfo Celi, Diane Cilento, Eric Porter
Rating: ★★

A flawless British cast, with a few distinguished Continental additions, act out the Fuhrer's last few tortured days in his underground bunker against a Berlin background of burnished browns and flickering reds, superbly captured by the Technicolor cameras of Ennio Guarnieri. Alec Guinness' portrayal in the title role is the perfection one would expect, at least on the surface, although the persuasive qualities of his performance are too often undermined by the uncertainties in the screenplay (based on Gerhardt Boldt's book *The Last Days of the Chancellery*) which never seems sure of its purpose.

Hit the Ice ⊙
1943, US, 82 mins, b/w
Dir: Charles Lamont
Stars: Bud Abbott, Lou Costello, Ginny Simms, Patric Knowles, Elyse Knox, Marc Lawrence
Rating: ★★

Bud and Lou as wartime American papparazzi caught up with a gang of crooks while trying to snap some newspaper pictures; their great ice-skating rink routine is here, as is Sheldon Leonard who later gave up acting to become one of the most successful producers in American TV.

H M Pulham Esq ○
1941, US, 120 mins, b/w
Dir: King Vidor
Stars: Hedy Lamarr, Robert Young, Ruth Hussey, Charles Coburn, Van Heflin, Leif Erickson
Rating: ★★★★

The best of Robert Young's earlier work, starring him as a staid Bostonian businessman looking back on the one magic period of his dull and respectable life. Hedy Lamarr has never been better, or looked lovelier, as the one fine fling of his youth. Here she finally gave the lie to those of her detractors who said that she couldn't act. Director King Vidor's adaptation (with Elizabeth Hill) of John P Marquand's fine novel glows with warmth, wit and wisdom. Sara Haden and Fay Holden take a vacation from the Hardy family series to play character parts, and you

H

may also spot singer John Raitt and star-to-be Ava Gardner in very tiny roles.

HMS Defiant ○
(aka: Damn the Defiant)
1962, UK, 101 mins, colour
Dir: Lewis Gilbert
Stars: Alec Guinness, Dirk Bogarde, Anthony Quayle, Tom Bell, Maurice Denham
Rating: ★★★

A distinguished cast of British actors take to the sea for a spectacular tale of a British ship sailing against Napoleon. Action and mutiny abound, and director Lewis Gilbert makes a splendid job of capturing the period atmosphere. Fine characterisations from a talented cast – Dirk Bogarde has a field day as the sadistic First Lieutenant – ensure engrossing and exciting entertainment.

Hobson's Choice ○
1953, UK, 120 mins, b/w
Dir: David Lean
Stars: Charles Laughton, John Mills
Rating: ★★★★

The great British actor Charles Laughton produced another of his memorable, over-the-top tyrants in David Lean's splendid adaptation of Harold Brighouse's 1915 domestic comedy that gave the British language a metaphor. This Captain Bligh of the bootmaking trade is, of course, eventually outdone and Laughton is almost out-acted by fair-haired, slightly matronly Brenda de Banzie, who gives her all (and became a star as a result) as the tough as old-boots Maggie, a determined Lancashire lass who turns the tables on her despotic dad by marrying John Mills' wonderfully wimpish boothand and using his craftsmanship as a secret weapon in the family war. Lean is in Dickens mode with this carefully set and directed piece, which has some superb photography by Lean regular Jack Hildyard – a particularly memorable scene being where Laughton lumbers through a series of puddles in pursuit of the moon's reflection.

Hockey Night ○
1984, Canada, 77 mins, colour
Dir: Paul Shapiro
Stars: Megan Fellows, Rick Moranis, Sean McCann, Gail Youngs
Rating: ★★

A likeable, if not exceptional, Canathan film about a teenage girl, who, hockeymad, determines to make the boys' team in her new home town when she finds there's no girls' team around.

Megan Fellows is spunky as the girl goalie and the leading man is Rick Moranis, later to feature in *Ghostbusters, Honey, I Shrunk the Kids* and *The Flintstones*.

Hocus Pocus ○ ⓥ
1993, US, 97 mins, colour
Dir: Kenny Ortega
Stars: Bette Midler, Sarah Jessica Parker, Kathy Najimy, Omri Katz, Vinessa Shaw
Rating: ★★★

Burnt at the stake by most critics, this jolly and juicy slice of witchery-pokery proves less than half as black as its reputation. Its cauldron bubbles with funny lines and sensationally good special effects and – eye of newt! – it has Bette Midler looking like a *Spitting Image* puppet of herself as the leader of a trio of Connecticut witches who return from the dead 300 years on, thanks to stupid teenager Max lighting the black candle at the museum that was once their home. If they can breathe in enough souls of children, the witches will live forever. The ending goes too far into sentiment, but Sarah Jessica Parker and Kathy Najimy are right on the mark as the other witches: highlight of the action is their acting as raddled Ronettes to Bette's singing sorceress when the trio invades the local hop.

Hoffa ● ⓥ
1992, US, 140 mins, colour
Dir: Danny DeVito
Stars: Jack Nicholson, Danny DeVito, Armand Assante, J T Walsh, Kevin Anderson, Robert Prosky
Rating: ★★

A tough-talking American blue-collar drama about Jimmy Hoffa, a legendary union leader who jumped into bed with the Mafia early in his career and was eventually to pay for that with his life. Although impressively staged and set – especially in the major action sequences involving strikes by Hoffa's Teamsters – by director Danny DeVito (who also plays a key role), the film is surprisingly dully written by David Mamet. The lack of colour in the words is accentuated by the one-note performance of Jack Nicholson as Hoffa, even though this might reflect the man in real life. Mamet's scenario also gives little sense of the varying times in which the film is set, several years obviously having passed on occasions. Together with dialogue that tends to the repetitive, it leads to your attention wandering

from time to time. The inherent fascination of the subject just about carries it through; but, like a hot air balloon, *Hoffa* looks good, feels good, but hasn't much inside.

Holcroft Covenant, The ● ⓥ
1985, UK, 112 mins, colour
Dir: John Frankenheimer
Stars: Michael Caine, Anthony Andrews, Victoria Tennant, Lilli Palmer
Rating: ★

When three distinguished screenwriters have a go at the same best-selling novel and the result is a clumsy mess, you have to wonder what went wrong. As it is, the words that Edward Anhalt, George Axelrod and John Hopkins have provided make this film version of Robert Ludlum's race-along book run like a dubbed English version of the continental spy thrillers from two decades earlier. Thanks to a marvellously relaxed portrayal by Michael Caine, laughter is more or less kept at bay for about half an hour. But soon such lines as 'What a brilliant way to hide – just become a world-famous public figure' and 'You drive to Geneva taking the back roads – I'll take the train' stumble distressingly over one another. Anthony Andrews gives the impression that his performance might look quite good with different dialogue, but the dual purpose of Victoria Tennant's role is quite beyond her.

Hold That Blonde ○
1945, US, 76 mins, b/w
Dir: George Marshall
Stars: Eddie Bracken, Veronica Lake, Albert Dekker, George Zucco
Rating: ★★

Veronica Lake was never quite the same force without the peek-a-boo hairstyle that she was forced to change when 'peek-a-boo' factory girls started catching the style in machinery, and her studio, Paramount, began to lose interest in her, pitching her into comedy roles that didn't suit her slinky style. Here she's mismatched with firecracker Eddie Bracken in the story of a kleptomaniac who tries to reform a professional lady thief Director George Marshall made several Bob Hope films, and this fast-moving farce is much like them.

Hold That Co-ed ○
(aka: Hold That Girl)
1938, US, 80 mins, b/w
Dir: George Marshall
Stars: John Barrymore, George Murphy,

Marjorie Weaver, Joan Davis
Rating: ★★★

John Barrymore had one of the best roles of his later career as a scheming politician out to be elected to the US Senate and using state funds to finance a college football team as part of his campaign strategy. He makes the most – and sometimes more – of every scene in which he appears, leaving the song and dance chores in this satirical comedy-musical to George Murphy. Joan Davis almost steals the film as a goal-kicking lady footballer in a movie that cheerfully celebrates those two all-consuming American passions – politics and sport.

Hold That Ghost! ○
1941, US, 82 mins, b/w
Dir: Arthur Lubin
Stars: Bud Abbott, Lou Costello, Joan Davis, Mischa Auer, Evelyn Ankers, Richard Carlson
Rating: ★★★

Chuckle as you chill to the first of Abbott and Costello's many encounters with things that went bump in the night. This one was made soon after their initial impact on the cinemagoing public when Universal, their studio, was working its newest star team overtime. Bud and Lou find themselves in a haunted house and the laughs (and dead bodies) come thick and fast, with a great supporting cast working hard. Universal ditched the original ending, where Bud and Lou are running a health farm when a dead body (from the haunted house) falls into the room as they ring for dinner, in favour of a grand musical finale. At least they did leave in Lou's famous 'flickering candle' routine.

Hold That Girl
See: Hold That Co-ed

Hole In the Head, A ○
1959, US, 120 mins, colour
Dir: Frank Capra
Stars: Frank Sinatra, Edward G Robinson, Eleanor Parker
Rating: ★★

Comedy-cum-drama about a good-time Charlie who suddenly finds that he is in danger of losing his most prized possession, his son. Directed by two-time Oscar winner Frank Capra, the film contains two big song hits from its star, Frank Sinatra: 'High Hopes' and 'All My Tomorrows'. The film, though, seems to have a hole in its heart, just not having the emotional pull that it should.

Holiday Camp ○
1947, UK, 97 mins, b/w
Dir: Ken Annakin
Stars: Flora Robson, Dennis Price, Jack Warner, Kathleen Harrison, Hazel Court, Jimmy Hanley
Rating: ★★

This entertaining portrait of the British enjoying themselves in the immediate post-war years started a flood of similar portmanteau' films, and Jack Warner and Kathleen Harrison scored such immense personal successes that a series was made around the Huggetts, the Cockney characters they play. The setting now seems a world away.

Holiday for Lovers ○
1959, US, 103 mins, colour
Dir: Henry Levin
Stars: Clifton Webb, Jane Wyman, Paul Henreid, Carol Lynley
Rating: ★★

Clifton Webb actually contrives to make some fairly tired humour sound like waspish wit in this fiesta of a romp that takes Webb, Jane Wyman and their two daughters to South America. Not that there's much suggestion that they actually went there, as the lovely footage of Brazil and Peru sits uneasily behind the actors superimposed against it. Spanish dancer Jose Greco fires things up towards the end with a terrific speciality number.

Holiday Inn ☉ Ⓥ
1942, US, 101 mins, b/w
Dir: Mark Sandrich
Stars: Bing Crosby, Fred Astaire, Virginia Daie, Marjorie Reynolds
Rating: ★★★

This Irving Berlin musical was directed by Mark Sandrich, who made many of the best Astaire-Rogers musicals of the Thirties. The score includes 'Easter Parade', 'White Christmas' and 'Be Careful, It's My Heart'. Not much of a plot, but with Bing Crosby singing and Fred Astaire dancing, who needs such niceties?

Holiday on the Buses ○
1973, UK, 83 mins, colour
Dir: Bryan Izzard
Stars: Reg Varney, Queenie Watts, Arthur Mullard
Rating: ★

Stan Butler (Reg Varney) and the gang go to a holiday camp in Wales where Stan blows up the toilet and sewage system. While Stan and Jack (Bob Grant) salvage a few cuties from the camp, the indispensable Queenie Watts

and Arthur Mullard salvage a few laughs from the script.

Hollow Reed ●
1995, UK, 104 mins, colour
Dir: Angela Pope
Stars: Joely Richardson, Martin Donovan, Jason Flemyng, Ian Hart
Rating: ★★★

Strong for its first hour, this child abuse/custody drama rather loses its way towards the end instead of gathering power. Little Ollie (sad-eyed Sam Bould) is being beaten by the lover (Flemyng) of his mother (Richardson). But the boy refuses to tell his father (Donovan) whose own position is complicated by the fact that he has recently 'come out' and now lives with his gay lover (Hart). So far, so gripping. But subsequent courtroom scenes are rather melodramatically written, and overplayed. And the resolution of the tale is curiously unsatisfactory – probably like real life, but dramatically underfed. Good performances from Donovan, Richardson and the boy. Flemyng and Hart, although not bad, are less convincing.

Hollow Triumph ○
(aka: The Scar)
1948, US, 80 mins, b/w
Dir: Steve Sekely
Stars: Paul Henreid, Joan Bennett
Rating: ★★★★

Paul Henreid plays a dual role as a crook on the run and his psychologist double in this well-paced and beautifully shot piece of *film noir*. The crook kills the doc to assume his identity only to find the medic had a guilty secret of his own . . . Henreid, famed for his role as freedom fighter Victor Laszlo in *Casablanca*, not only starred in but also produced this tense thriller with a twist in its tail. Joan Bennett gives earnest support as the girl embroiled in the criminal's scheme. A rarely seen and unjustly overlooked entry in the genre.

Holly and the Ivy, The ○
1952, UK, 83 mins, b/w
Dir: George More O'Ferrall
Stars: Ralph Richardson, Margaret Leighton, Celia Johnson, John Gregson, Denholm Elliott
Rating: ★★★★

This adaptation of Wynyard Brown's play about a country cleric at Christmas and the resolution of his own life and those of his three children strikes all the right emotional notes and is acted with great understatement and feeling for character, especially by

H

Ralph Richardson (as the clergyman) and Celia Johnson and Margaret Leighton as his daughters.

Hollywood Canteen ○
1944, US, 124 mins, b/w
Dir: Delmer Daves
Stars: Robert Hutton, Joan Leslie, Bette Davis, John Garfield, Sydney Greenstreet, Joan Crawford
Rating: ★★★

They don't – and indeed can't – make 'em like this any more. Warner Brothers had already had one smash wartime hit with *Stage Door Canteen*, a star-studded musical compendium, and aimed to repeat the trick with this similar project, spun round an eggshell-thin plot about a young soldier who dreams of meeting his favourite film star. Just as well she turns out to be Joan Leslie, who was under contract to the studio. Pretty well the whole Warner roster is on parade (with the exception of Humphrey Bogart), and any film that has a violin duct of 'The Bee' from Joseph Sziged and Jack Benny has to be worth watching.

Hollywood Cavalcade ○
1939, US, 96 mins, colour
Dir: Irving Cummings
Stars: Alice Faye, Don Ameche, Buster Keaton, Ben Turpin, Chester Conklin
Rating: ★★★

A thinly disguised biography of Mabel Normand and Mack Sennett, this film is also a potted history of Hollywood silent films, funniest in its silent comedy scenes. Buster Keaton appears as himself and several of the original Keystone Cops are on hand to join in the fun. Alice Faye throws herself with a will into slapstick scenes that seem primarily designed to get her wet and show off her figure. After all that physical effort, she was probably not best pleased when her three songs (including the hit 'Whispering') were cut from the film – although the plot still slows down a lot in its later stages. Wonderful Fox Technicolor as usual, especially in the interior scenes.

Hollywood Hotel ○
1937, US, 109 mins, b/w
Dir: Busby Berkeley
Stars: Dick Powell, Rosemary Lane, Lola Lane, Hugh Herbert, Glenda Farrell
Rating: ★★★

This lively musical is memorable for its celebrated song 'Hooray for Hollywood' which immediately became the movie capital's rousing theme song. Ronald Reagan does an unbilled

cameo as a radio announcer, and other stars glimpsed briefly include Carole Landis (as a hat check girl) and Susan Hayward (as a starlet sitting at a table). Gossip columnist Louella Parsons plays herself. It was the last of the cycle of Warner musicals that had started with *42nd Street*. Once more Busby Berkeley was at the helm.

Hollywood or Bust ○
1956, US, 95 mins, colour
Dir: Frank Tashlin
Stars: Dean Martin, Jerry Lewis, Anita Ekberg, Pat Crowley
Rating: ★★

Hollywood was courtesy of Paramount and Anita Ekberg – playing herself – supplied the bust for the last of the Dean Martin-Jerry Lewis comedies that had begun with *My Friend Irma* in 1949. Fun and foolery on the road to Los Angeles, with director Frank Tashlin (with whom Lewis would make some of his best solo films) keeping the pace brisk and disguising the fact that Dean and Jerry's double act had practically disintegrated and the stars weren't speaking to each other off screen.

Holocaust 2000 ◐
(aka: The Chosen)
1977, UK/Italy, 105 mins, colour
Dir: Alberto De Martino
Stars: Kirk Douglas, Simon Ward

Rating: ★★

Never mind the plot – a heady combination of *The AntiChrist* and *The Omen*, plus a few extra supernatural trimmings thrown in for good effect. There's plenty to hold your attention in this enjoyably awful film, including Kirk Douglas taking on the Devil, and Simon Ward dressed in white, named 'Angel' but turning out to be something rather nasty, along with a supporting cast that includes a wasted Virginia McKenna, Geoffrey Keen, Anthony Quayle and Alexander Knox. Some lively special effects add to the fun and Alberto de Martino stirs up his brew of hocus pocus with a commendably straight face.

Holy Matrimony ○
1943, US, 87 mins, b/w
Dir: John Stahl
Stars: Gracie Fields, Monty Woolley, Laird Cregar
Rating: ★★★★

A thoroughly enjoyable comedy based on Arnold Bennett's witty novel – about a shy artist, who, horrified by the fame a knighthood brings, 'kills himself

off', switches identities with his dead butler, marries and becomes involved in a public scandal. Easily the best of Gracie Fields' Hollywood ven-tures, blending well with an on-form Monty Woolley as the painter, and receiving rollicking support from a whole battery of the Forties' best character comedi-ans.

Holy Matrimony ○
1994, US, 93 mins, colour
Dir: Leonard Nimoy
Stars: Patricia Arquette, Joseph Gordon Levitt, John Schuck
Rating: ★

A pretty silly comedy-drama about a buxom blonde who finds herself married to a 12-year-old boy. Busty Patricia Arquette is the fairground showgirl who, tired of posing as a cross between Marilyn Monroe and Aunt Sally at a sideshow, allows her boyfriend to talk her into helping him lift the night's takings. When he flees back to his home, a religious community of Hutterite farmers, hides the money, and then gets killed in a car crash, Arquette's on her own. Or not quite. Having married boyfriend to stay in the community, she now finds herself threatened with expulsion – unless she accepts the marriage proposal which Hutterite law compels his 12-year-old brother to offer. A crooked FBI agent is also after the cash, and the rest of the film concerns Arquette's battles with the law, her tiny husband and her own conscience, in pursuit of the loot. A better script might have wrung both fun and poignancy out of this situation, but there are few laughs or tears on offer here. Performances are okay.

Hombre ○
1966, US, 111 mins, colour
Dir: Martin Ritt
Stars: Paul Newman, Fredric March, Richard Boone, Diane Cilento
Rating: ★★★

Director Martin Ritt's third film with Paul Newman, following *Hud* and *The Outrage*, this rugged Western has superb opening scenes. The stagecoach passengers gather together in a waiting-room so dry and dusty it almost makes one cough. Villain Richard Boone's entrance is a tremendous piece of histrionics, each syllable having a satisfying ring, culminating in his facing-down of a would-be passenger who's insulted him, merely by the use of a reflective pause followed by 'What'd you say?' Newman gets to grips with the enigmatic title role, Diane Cilento scores heavily as the too often loved-and-let-down Jessie, and Fredric March grapples gallantly with the cardboard part of an embezzling Indian agent.

Home Alone ○ ⓥ

1990, US, 100 mins, colour
Dir: Chris Columbus
Stars: Macaulay Culkin, Joe Pesci, Daniel Stern, John Heard, Catherine O'Hara, John Candy
Rating: ★★★

Eighty minutes of medium amusement, capped by a side-splitting last 20 minutes, raising several of the biggest cinema laughs in ages: the formula for a box-office blaster from prolific writer John Hughes. And he just about gets away with the unlikely premise that triggers the story. After all, how do you adequately explain an eight-year-old boy being left alone by his parents when they fly off on a Christmas holiday to Paris? Well, you give his parents five kids, add brother-in-law's six, leave Kevin the sleeping victim of a 'head count' that accidentally takes in the kid next door, top it off with a desperate run for the airport, with the kids in third class and the adults in first class, and hope the viewer will believe it. After this, the story veers uneasily between France and America until burglars Joe Pesci and Daniel Stern come on to the scene to liven things up. Getting wise to their plans, Kevin decides to defend his home. How he does so leads to a series of violent jokes that make it no mere coincidence that a shaven-headed Pesci looks like a refugee from The Three Stooges. Be patient and, like Kevin, you'll have fun.

Home Alone 2 – Lost In New York ○ ⓥ

1992, US, 120 mins, colour
Dir: Chris Columbus
Stars: Macaulay Culkin, Joe Pesci, Daniel Stern, Catherine O'Hara, John Heard, Tim Curry, Brenda Fricker, Eddie Bracken
Rating: ★★

A repeat of the hugely successful *Home Alone* formula, except that, instead of being left at home when his family flies off on its Christmas holidays, young Kevin (Macaulay Culkin) takes the wrong plane – and gets stranded in New York. There, he encounters again the two bumbling burglars from the first film (Joe Pesci and Daniel Stern) and, with lots of slapstick comedy and yelps of 'Yikes!', it's up to Kevin to save the day with his homemade army assault course of obstacles again. Not so

much a sequel, more of an action replay but even more violent than the original – so perhaps a little too much for very small eyes. Britain's Brenda Fricker scores as a New York pigeon lady.

Home at Seven ○

(aka: Murder on Monday)
1952, UK, 82 mins, b/w
Dir: Ralph Richardson
Stars: Ralph Richardson, Margaret Leighton, Jack Hawkins
Rating: ★★★

A suspenseful adaptation of R C Sherriff's successful stage play, this makes dramatic enough mystery entertainment, thanks appreciably to its good cast. It stars Ralph Richardson, who also directed in an intense and painstaking fashion that makes you regret that it remained his only work in the latter capacity. It's difficult to believe that the film was made on virtually a shoestring budget and in only 15 days. The film's commendably tight and brief too, giving the viewer short, sharp scenes that make the plot intriguing every step of the way.

Homeboy ● ⓥ

1988, US, 112 mins, colour
Dir: Michael Seresin
Stars: Mickey Rourke, Debra Feuer, Christopher Walken, Thomas Quinn, Ruben Blades
Rating: ★★★

This was Mickey Rourke's pet project, a boxing picture about a pug who's over the hill and so punchdrunk he's liable to die in the ring. The film's a bit slow, its pace rather emphasised by Eric Clapton's doomy guitar score (taken on its own, moodily fine) but with individual scenes nicely realised. Rourke, Debra Feuer (the fairground girl he falls for) and Christopher Walken – the small-time smoothie who tries to suck Rourke into crime – are all well in character, and the final boxing match is not for the squeamish. There's plenty of guts in this film in more ways than one.

Home for the Holidays ◐ ⓥ

1995, US 103 mins, colour
Dir: Jodie Foster
Stars: Holly Hunter, Robert Downey Jr, Anne Bancroft, Charles Durning, Dylan McDermott, Geraldine Chaplin
Rating: ★★

Nightmare family reunion is on the menu here, of the kind that almost never happens in real life. Smart lines and family secrets are on the side plates

to the Thanksgiving turkey, as a representative family, consisting of single-mum daughter (Hunter), gay son (Downey) and stay-in-the-small-town married daughter (Cynthia Stevenson) converge with or without partners on the home of chain-smoking mum (Bancroft) and overweight dad (Durning) who's *compos mentis* in all respects except cutting the turkey with a knife. Everyone behaves unbelievably indecorously and Stevenson and husband Steve Guttenberg predictably storm out. Hunter falls headlong for Downey's (non-gay) companion (McDermott) and everything ends in a haze of happiness. Just like real life. Not.

Home of Our Own, A ○ ⓥ

1992, US, 100 mins, colour
Dir: Tony Bill
Stars: Kathy Bates, Edward Furlong, Soon Teck-Oh, Tony Campisi
Rating: ★★★

A big family weepie about a big family. The 'Lacey tribe', Mom (Kathy Bates) and six kids, pull up roots in Los Angeles and end up in the wilds of Idaho, where they take a half-built house and, with a promise of work for the man who owns the land, make it their own. The resulting catalogue of hardships and tiny triumphs is nicely constructed, and only lacks that certain touch of class that the best Hollywood family pictures have. Performances are competent, especially so from Soon Teck-Oh as the oriental owner of the site, and Bates' real-life husband Tony Campisi makes a rare film appearance as the man who courts, then clouts her.

Home Sweet Homicide

See: What a Carve-Up!

Homeward Bound: The Incredible Journey ⊙ ⓥ

1992, US, 84 mins, colour
Dir: Duwayne Dunham
Voice Stars: Michael J Fox, Sally Field, Don Ameche
Rating: ★★★

Disney have dug up their Sixties family hit, *The Incredible Journey*, and given it a Nineties gloss in the style of *Look Who's Talking*. Three family pets face the perils of open, wild country in their character-forming quest to be reunited with their human beings: Shadow is a venerable golden retriever (voiced with suitable gravitas by Don Ameche), Sassy a well-named long-haired Himalayan cat (voiced by Sally Field) and Chance (voiced by Michael J Fox),

H

a bouncy young American boxer, who also acts as narrator. The story is very much from the animals' point of view, with some witty dialogue and asides. As you would expect, there are some large doses of sentimentality and the humans are doomed to remain mere cyphers. But it's a charmer for all that, beautifully shot in Oregon.

Homicidal ●
1961, US, 87 mins, b/w
Dir: William Castle
Stars: Patricia Breslin, Glenn Corbett, Jean Arless
Rating: ★★

This is the film in which director William Castle, the self-styled 'showman of shock', introduced the 'fright break'. This was an interval of one minute, which allowed the audience time to get out of the cinema before the most frightening scene. In this chiller about a girl in peril from a person unknown, Castle moved away from the more obvious *The House on Haunted Hill* and closer to the territory explored by Hitchcock in *Psycho*, employing variations on the same kinds of suspense devices.

Homicide ● ⓥ
1991, US, 102 mins, colour
Dir: David Mamet
Stars: Joe Mantegna, William H Macy, Rebecca Pidgeon, Ving Rhames, Natalija Nogulich
Rating: ★★★

A slow, sad, low-key, cleverly put-together police detective story, with Joe Mantegna as the Jewish cop who considers himself expendable and an outsider; so he is ready meat for a group of Jewish activists when their organisation crops up in a murder case he's almost accidentally assigned to. The sombre classical music background tends to make you think this is about anti-Semitism. But writer-director David Mamet is too cunning to leave it at that, and that proves merely a cloak for the real story – of how easily men can be manipulated and ruined by their own backgrounds. If only Mamet the writer had assigned somebody to direct who could have upped the pace, this might have been a little classic.

L'Homme de Rio
See: That Man from Rio

Honey, I Blew Up the Kid
⊙ ⓥ
1993, US, 89 mins, colour
Dir: Randal Kleiser

Stars: Rick Moranis, Marcia Strassman, Robert Oliveri, Lloyd Bridges, Gregory Sierra
Rating: ★★★

The Disney formula works like a charm in this occasionally clumsy but consistently likeable sequel to *Honey, I Shrunk the Kids*. Rick Moranis again plays the scatty inventor who this time accidentally subjects his two-year-old son to the effects of a matter-expanding machine. The toddler (played by twins Joshua and Daniel Shalikar) is impishly cute even as a naughty 50-footer, and the scenes where he rampages through Las Vegas are hilarious. A good old-fashioned family frolic whose tendency to get a bit repetitive and tiresome towards the end won't worry the kidlet audience at which it's aimed.

Honey, I Shrunk the Kids
⊙ ⓥ
1989, US, 93 mins, colour
Dir: Joe Johnston
Stars: Rick Moranis, Matt Frewer, Marcia Strassman, Kristine Sutherland
Rating: ★★★★

Every now and again Hollywood produces an 'incredible shrinking people' film, and this hugely successful comedy is as much fun as any of them. Rick Moranis' personable performance makes a sturdy centre for the high jinks here as the scientist dad whose children accidentally turn his experimental ray gun on themselves, and shrink to microscopic size, soon finding themselves in the garden, where they encounter all the usual perils beloved of such films. This one's well-paced though, with one or two outstandingly funny scenes, pretty good trickwork and sparkling Technicolor photography.

Honeymoon Hotel ○
1964, US, 89 mins, colour
Dir: Henry Levin
Stars: Robert Goulet, Robert Morse, Nancy Kwan, Jill St John
Rating: ★★★★

Peppy Robert Morse gives a non-stop, Jerry Lewis-style performance in this racy comedy that even sees the statuesque Robert Goulet unbending at times. Morse has many of the Lewis qualities, including a little-boy-lost attitude that makes him instantly likable. There's also a Jack Lemmon-ish quality to his delivery of a funny line. One dance-comedy scene between him and Nancy Kwan has no real part in the film, but is so good that it obviously had to stay. The comedy shows a remarkably delicate touch in risqué

humour, and all its sex jokes are funny. It also gives Keenan Wynn a part that really allows him to spread his deft comedy talents liberally around him.

Honeymoon in Vegas ❶ ⓥ
1992, US, 96 mins, colour
Dir: Andrew Bergman
Stars: Nicolas Cage, James Caan, Sarah Jessica Parker, Pat Morita, Peter Boyle, Anne Bancroft
Rating: ★★★

It's one of those situations that used to be tailor-made for Hollywood screwball farce. Jack (Nicolas Cage) goes to Vegas with his current squeeze Betsy (Sarah Jessica Parker). Once in the neon city, however, Jack falls prey to millionaire gambler James Caan, who's gobsmacked by Parker's being the image of his dead wife. Taking a still dallying Cage for $65,000 in a poker game, Caan announces the price for the debt is Betsy's spending the weekend with him. The rest of the film concerns Caan's wooing of her in Hawaii and Cage's hot if penniless pursuit. This is all quite light and not unenjoyable, but the film's problems lie with its casting. Cage shouts and sweats a lot; Caan's portrayal is too broad and lacking in charm: you don't really want Parker (who herself oozes curves rather than charisma) to end up with either of these guys. The film does literally spread its wings, though, in a lunatic climax that involves 34 Flying Elvises skydiving on Las Vegas.

Honeymoon Machine, The ○
1961, US, 92 mins, colour
Dir: Richard Thorpe
Stars: Steve McQueen, Brigid Bazlen, Jim Hutton, Paula Prentiss
Rating: ★★★

Sieve McQueen again shows (as he did in *The Reivers*) what a dab hand he could be at comedy, in this zany romp about two sailors who get their hands on an electronic brain, and plan to win a fortune with it, at gambling casinos. On the distaff side, the treacle-voiced Paula Prentiss adds immeasurably to the fun, as does veteran Dean Jagger in a rare comedy film role.

Honeysuckle Rose ○ ⓥ
1980, US, 119 mins, colour
Dir: Jerry Schatzberg
Stars: Willie Nelson, Dyan Cannon, Amy Irving, Slim Pickens
Rating: ★★

With all due respect to the pleasant Amy Irving, it's hard to believe that anyone in his right mind would risk his marriage to the dynamic Dyan Cannon for a fling with her – even if the man in question is an ageing country-and-western singer (Willie Nelson) and Amy's his guitarist on the road. Miss Cannon is tremendous – easily the best thing in the film, in fact – and one can't help thinking that things might have worked better as a whole if Nelson's wife had been played by someone less sensational to look at. It's hard to see what either woman could see in this plain, greying, long-haired, hard-drinking man, although his reedily strong, unusual singing voice gives him a certain magnetism. Still, the music clangs melodically away and veteran character actor Slim Pickens wheezes around happily in the background.

Honky Tonk ○

1941, US, 100 mins, b/w
Dir: Jack Conway
Stars: Clark Gable, Lana Turner, Frank Morgan, Claire Trevor
Rating: ★★

The first screen meeting of Clark Gable and Lana Turner is a lively, glossy, MGM drama that might well have been called *The Con-Man and the Lady*. Gable apart, the film is almost an index of the actresses who played those-hearted slinky blonde temptresses hard of the Forties. Lana Turner, Claire Trevor and Veda Ann Borg are all here. Albert Dekker is a splendidly nasty villain, and Turner's father is played with witty afability by that old MGM stalwart Frank Morgan. The story assumes epic proportions towards the end, giving Lana a chance to show the talent for emotive acting that she had already revealed in *Ziegfeld Girl*.

Honkytonk Man ○ Ⓥ

1982, US, 122 mins, colour
Dir Clint Eastwood
Stars: Clint Eastwood, Kyle Eastwood, John McIntire
Rating: ★★★

Unfairly ignored at the box-office (presumably because audiences would only accept Clint Eastwood with a magnum in his hand, gunning down all and sundry), this is a charming tragi-comedy with a subtle variation by Eastwood on the kind of redneck character usually played by Burt Reynolds. And as director, he is as generous as ever towards his co-stars, in particularly getting a sharp and sensitive portrayal from his real-life son Kyle, here cast as his hero-worshipping nephew. By no means a typical Eastwood vehicle, but satisfying enough if overlong.

Honolulu ○

1939, US, 83 mins, b/w
Dir: Edward Buzzell
Stars: Robert Young, Eleanor Powell, George Burns, Gracie Allen, Rita Johnson, Ruth Hussey
Rating: ★★

This MGM musical has a plot as ramshackle as a grass hut. The compensations, however, are dazzling. George Burns and Gracie Allen tie everyone in verbal knots, and Eleanor Powell storms to glory in the dance routines, which include a brilliant hula number. Harry Warren and Gus Kahn wrote the score, which includes Gracie Allen doing a Mae West on 'The Leader Doesn't Like Music'.

Honorary Consul, The ● Ⓥ

(aka: Beyond the Limit)
1983, US, 104 mins, colour
Dir: John Mackenzie
Stars: Michael Caine, Richard Gere, Bob Hoskins
Rating: ★★★

Graham Greene's novels have often made absorbing entertainment and this is no exception, despite some improbabilities in the plot development, particularly towards the end. Richard Gere, with a fairly odd English accent that baulks at 'a's, plays the young doctor working around the Argentine-Paraguay border who allows himself to become involved in two equally dangerous games: aiding revolutionaries (who he thinks may help him find his missing father) and having a passionate affair with the glamorous young wife of the boozy British consul. Gere's battles with his accent permits those wily old birds Michael Caine (as the consul) and Bob Hoskins (as the Argentine chief of police) to sneak off with the acting honours.

Hoodlum Empire ○

1952, US, 95 mins, b/w
Dir: Joseph Kane
Stars: Brian Donlevy, Claire Trevor, Forrest Tucker, Vera Ralston, Luther Adler, John Russell
Rating: ★★★

A cold-blooded crime thriller featuring many of Hollywood's best gangster actors of the time, made in the pseudo-documentary style pioneered by 20th Century-Fox in post-war years. An unusual film to come from Republic who, like director Joseph Kane, were more used to turning out rousing adventure movies supposedly set in exotic locations.

Hoodlum Priest, The ○

1961, US, 101 mins, b/w
Dir: Irvin Kershner
Stars: Don Murray, Larry Gates, Keir Dullea
Rating: ★★★

Honest and gripping study of a young priest's attempts to save a delinquent youth from his own tragic destiny. Looked on by the critics as a 'sleeper' a low-budget film of surprising quality, this drama gave Keir Dullea, later to star in *2001: A Space Odyssey*, his first motion picture role.

Hook ○ Ⓥ

1991, US, 140 mins, colour
Dir: Steven Spielberg
Stars: Dustin Hoffman, Robin Williams, Julia Roberts, Bob Hoskins, Maggie Smith, Charlie Korsmo
Rating: ★★

You might guess it would take this Steven Spielberg fantasy a long time to get going and it does. But 100 minutes? That's how long it takes fortyish businessman Robin Williams to remember that he was once Peter Pan and get cracking into the core of the plot. Then there's some fun to be had, if of a somewhat heavy-handed variety, as Peter fights to free his children from the clutches of the evil Hook. Strenuously over-scored, over-dressed and over-populated, the film is for the most part a musical without the songs, parading its sets like carnival attractions. Dustin Hoffman makes quite a droll Hook, but Williams seems ill at ease and Bob Hoskins, Maggie Smith, Julia Roberts and others get little chance to shine. Yes, the top dressing's here in abundance, but there's too little spring in the step of this particular Peter Pan.

Hooper ○

1978, US, 100 mins, colour
Dir: Hal Needham
Stars: Burt Reynolds, Jan-Michael Vincent, Sally Field, Brian Keith
Rating: ★★★

A light-hearted look (with serious undertones) at the life of an ageing Hollywood stuntman. Although the stuntmen do their stuff in ripsnorting style, the script lacks the insight and invention to give it the stature to rise above a formula action film. Burt Reynolds turns on the casual charm in the title role, and is involved in the film's best sequence – where Hooper rides alone round the corral outside his ranch-house at night.

H

Hoosiers

See: Best Shot

Hope and Glory ◐ ⓥ

1987, UK, 113 mins, colour

Dir: John Boorman

Stars: Sarah Miles, David Hayman, Derrick O'Connor, Susan Wooldridge, Sammi Davis, Ian Bannen

Rating: ★★★

A slight but often flavoursome recollection of a wartime childhood, John Boorman's memoir is not a portrait of the working classes battling through the Blitz, rather a picture of the lower middle classes in their suburban semis. Sometimes it rings horrendously true, at others it doesn't seem at all the bombsite childhood of contemporary documentaries. The sight of a 15-year-old dancing round celebrating the house down the road being on fire might be a vignette from Boonnan's boyhood, but is still likely to cause a few raised eyebrows. Still, the gangs of boys are well-drawn, as is the grandfather figure, played with relish by Ian Bannen, who all but steals the film. Boorman's own dialogue provides some good chuckles, and there's a rollicking portrait of an absolute monster of a teacher from Barbara Pierson.

Hopscotch ○ ⓥ

1980, US, 104 mins, colour

Dir: Ronald Neame

Stars: Walter Matthau, Glenda Jackson, Ned Beatty

Rating: ★★★★

Enjoyable, inconsequential stuff with Walter Matthau, in the sort of role Cary Grant once claimed as his own, in complete control as America's ace secret service agent who decides to get his own back on the bull-headed bosses who relegated him to a desk job. The merry dance he leads them across the world is always enjoyable and contains several pleasant performances, not least from Matthau himself but also from Glenda Jackson (even if her dialogue is less acid than one might wish), Sam Waterston (as the admiring agent who pursues Matthau), Ned Beatty (as his perspiring, constantly ill-tempered chief) and, in a much smaller role, Jacqueline Hyde as a gabby estate agent. Although the fun game of cat and mouse never reaches the sublime heights of comedy, one would be quite happy for it to go on a lot longer.

Horn Blows at Midnight, The ☉

1945, US, 80 mins, b/w

Dir: Raoul Walsh

Stars: Jack Benny, Alexis Smith, Allyn Joslyn, Dolores Moran, Guy Kibbee, Reginald Gardiner

Rating: ★★★

This is a comedy-fantasy which Jack Benny always joked about on his radio and TV shows in the same way that Ben Lyon referred disparagingly to *Hell's Angels*. Not nearly as bad as Benny always pretended, it's an enjoyable entertainment with a wonderful comic supporting cast that includes Reginald Gardiner, Guy Kibbee, Margaret Dumont, Allyn Joslyn, Mike Mazurki and – best of all – snooty Franklin Pangborn as a hot-and-bothered hotel detective.

Hornets' Nest ◑

1969, US, 110 mins, colour

Dir: Phil Karlson

Stars: Rock Hudson, Sylva Koscina

Rating: ★★

There's a moral here somewhere about the futility of war and its eitect n children, but it's all lost amid a welter of blood-letting and admittedly well-staged action scenes, as Captain Rock Hudson leads a little army of war orphans in World War Two Italy. Hudson gets another Continental leading lady in the sultry Sylva Koscina (a rather unlikely German doctor) to follow Leslie Caron and Claudia Cardinale in previous films, but the mixture of accents and acting styles – the cast includes American, British, Italian, French, German and Yugoslav players – is a bit disconcerting. The kids' leader is well played by Mark Colleano, son of Bonar Colleano, once a favourite face in British films.

Horror Express ●

1972, UK/Spain, 88 mins, colour

Dir: Gene Martin

Stars: Christopher Lee, Peter Cushing, Telly Savalas

Rating: ★★★★

There's something very nasty aboard the train thundering its way across snowscapes in this turn-of-the-century chiller, very good indeed by the rather low standards set in this genre in recent years. Peter Cushing, Christopher Lee and Telly Savalas are on hand to give horror enthusiasts an additional frisson of satisfaction.

Horror of Dracula

See: Dracula [1958]

Horse Feathers ☉ ⓥ

1932, US, 69 mins, b/w

Dir: Norman Z McLeod

Stars: Groucho Marx, Harpo Marx, Chico Marx, Zeppo Marx, Thelma Todd

Rating: ★★★★★

Sheer Marx Brothers mania: Chico helps to run a speakeasy; Harpo catches a dog-catcher; Groucho takes over a college and gives a lecture on the human body that is pure Ronnie Barker. All this and a riotous football match for the finale. Remember – the password is 'Swordfish'.

Horsemen, The ○

1970, US, 109 mins, colour

Dir: John Frankenheimer

Stars: Omar Sharif, Leigh Taylor-Young, Jack Palance

Rating: ★★

This drama of the wide open spaces of Afghanistan is an unusual film for director John Frankenheimer, more at home with thrillers (*The Manchurian Candidate, French Connection II*) or studies of small-town Americana (*All Fall Down, The Gypsy Moths*). Omar Sharif is a proud Afghan rider whose failure in a crucial contest forces him to set out on an epic journey across hazardous terrain in order to redeem himself. Although it never quite breaks free of its own pageantry, *The Horsemen* has some very striking and sometimes savage sequences, notably one in which riders battle each other with whips. Claude Renoir's highly competent colour photography conveys well the primitive power of such barbaric rites.

Horse's Mouth, The

See: The Oracle

Horse Soldiers, The ○ ⓥ

1959, US, 120 mins, colour

Dir: John Ford

Stars: John Wayne, William Holden, Constance Towers, Anna Lee

Rating: ★★

A typical John Ford Western, moderate by the great man's standards, but with splendid scenery and an explosive conflict between two big men – John Wayne as a tough colonel and William Holden as the army surgeon who disagrees with his methods. In supporting roles, two interesting Gibsons. There's Althea, one-time Wimbledon tennis champion, in her only film role, and old-time cowboy star Hoot. And those reliable Western character actors, Strother Martin and Denver Pyle, play two disreputable deserters. Some effective action scenes are topped by a frighteningly well realised street siege.

Horse Without a Head, The ☉

1963, UK, 89 mins, colour
Dir: Don Chaffey
Stars: Jean-Pierre Aumont, Herbert Lom, Leo McKern, Pamela Franklin
Rating: ★★★

A delightful film for children, all pitched on the same note of light but exciting comedy-thriller and full of marvellously inept and humorous crook characters. Leo McKern has a field day as a roguish pedlar whose plans to participate in a great train robbery are constantly at risk at the hands of a gang of children. Riotous climax in a disused novelty factory and excellent colour photography by Paul Beeson.

Hospital, The ●

1971, US, 103 mins, colour
Dir: Arthur Hiller
Stars: George C Scott, Diana Rigg, Barnard Hughes, Nancy Marchand
Rating: ★★★

Mordant black comedy starring Oscar-nominated George C Scott as the harassed chief of a large New York hospital, beset by disasters at work and in his private life. Paddy Chayefsky's sardonic, often hysterically funny script won an Oscar. Filmed on location at New York's Metropolitan Hospital where the crew took over two floors of a newly completed wing.

Hostile Hostages ● ⓥ

(aka: The Ref)
1994, US, 94 mins, colour
Dir: Ted Demme
Stars: Denis Leary, Judy Davis, Kevin Spacey, Glynis Johns, Raymond J Barry, Richard Bright
Rating: ★★★★

A wonderfully abrasive seasonal comedy – but funny viewing at any time of year – starring Denis Leary as Gus, a highly-strung burglar who, following a bungled robbery, takes two hostages (Judy Pavis, Kevin Spacey) and holes up in their home. Gus realises his mistake when the couple – whose marriage is on the rocks – start bickering about absolutely everything. And, with their loathsome relatives about to arrive for Christmas, Gus is trapped in a nightmare somewhere between the devil and the deep blue sea. Enormously entertaining, if you can take the film's constant verbal assault on your ears. The easily offended are advised to steer clear.

Hot Blood ○

1956, US, 85 mins, colour
Dir: Nicholas Ray
Stars: Jane Russell, Cornel Wilde, Luther Adler, Joseph Calleia
Rating: ★★

Director Nicholas Ray, who made this film just before *Rebel Without a Cause*, looks into the cause of modern American gipsies, whom he calls the 'original good-time Charlies', because, he feels, they wander about without taking on any real responsibilities. For star Cornel Wilde, *Hot Blood* was one of the last of his 'Hollywood' films as a dashingly romantic leading man. This one, however, is not as hot as the title suggests.

Hotel ○

1967, US, 124 mins, colour
Dir: Richard Quine
Stars: Rod Taylor, Karl Malden, Melvyn Douglas, Merle Oberon, Richard Conte
Rating: ★★★

Hollywood can do this sort of thing standing on its head. It's the story of various stories played out on the several floors of a luxury hotel, and upstairs in boardroom and penthouse suite a struggle for the control of the hotel is reaching its crucial moments. Only Quincy Jones' inapt score drags proceedings down to ground level. There are some very good performances: Rod Taylor, as the endearingly upright and shrewd young manager; Melvyn Douglas as the owner, grumbling about skyscrapers that threaten to obscure his view; Kevin McCarthy as an all-devouring tycoon with his own personal version of the Lord's Prayer; and especially Karl Malden as Keycase, the sneak thief who is here, there and everywhere, chuckling gleefully to himself and loping along the corridors like Groucho Marx.

Hotel Berlin ○

1945, US, 98 mins, b/w
Dir: Peter Godfrey
Stars: Helmut Dantine, Andrea King, Raymond Massey, Peter Lorre
Rating: ★★

If Bogart and Bacall had done the leading roles, this could have been a top-notch movie. As it is, what seems like half the Warner Brothers repertory company puts in some tremendous work in support of second-string stars Helmut Dantine and Andrea King. Particularly vivid performances come from Raymond Massey, Peter Lorre, George Coulouris, Henry Daniell and Steve Geray. From a novel by Vicki

Baum, who seemed to have a thing about such settings: she also wrote *Grand Hotel.*

Hotel New Hampshire, The ● ⓥ

1984, US, 110 mins, colour
Dir: Tony Richardson
Stars: Rob Lowe, Jodie Foster, Beau Bridges, Nastassja Kinski, Matthew Modine
Rating: ★★★

Considered by many to be Tony Richardson's best film since *Tom Jones*, this is a Herculean adaptation of John Irving's extraordinary novel surveying life, love and death through the eyes of an eccentric American family. A stunning cast includes Rob Lowe and Jodie Foster as a brother and sister with an unhealthy fascination for each other, Matthew Modine in a dual role, Beau Bridges as the idealistic father and Nastassja Kinski as a girl who spends her life inside a bear suit. Adult audiences with a taste for the bizarre will find this black tale exerts a strange fascination that makes it one of a kind. Joely Richardson appears ever so briefly as a waitress.

Hotel Paradiso ○

1966, UK, 96 mins, colour
Dir: Peter Glenville
Stars: Alec Guinness, Gina Lollobrigida, Robert Morley, Peggy Mount
Rating: ★

Skittish cinema version of Feydeau's farce, with Alec Guinness skipping lightly through the kind of role he was already playing with practised ease (and rather better dialogue) in the early Fifties. The fun takes a while to get going, but when it does, the ins and cuts of the different characters through hotel bedrooms are amusing enough. Watch out for scene-stealing Leonard Rossiter as a police inspector.

Hotel Sahara ○

1951, UK, 96 mins, b/w
Dir: Ken Annakin
Stars: David Tomlinson, Yvonne De Carlo, Peter Ustinov, Roland Culver
Rating: ★★★

This amusing trifle was one of several bright films that Hollywood star Yvonne De Carlo made in Britain in the early Fifties. Although the idea – an exotic wartime desert hotel switching its loyalties according to the forces occupying it – is rather more amusing than the execution, there are two very funny performances: by David Tomlinson as a stiff upper-lipped

H

English officer called Puffin, and by the inimitable Peter Ustinov as the ever-panicking proprietor of the hotel.

Hot Enough for June ○
(aka: Agent 8 3/4)
1963, UK, 98 mins, colour
Dir: Ralph Thomas
Stars: Dirk Bogarde, Sylva Koscina, Robert Morley, Leo McKern, John le Mesurier
Rating: ★★

A satirical spy thriller that fails to make the most of its opportunities, with Dirk Bogarde playing a reluctant spy behind the Iron Curtain, and sharing a steamy love scene with sultry Sylva Koscina, who gives the whole film a lift every time she appears. The most suspenseful moments come, so to speak, at the last knockings, with Bogarde beating at the door of his embassy at six in the morning, and the secret police closing in. But there's a lot of irrelevant travelling around Prague before the chase hots up. Bogarde gives his usual polished performance, and Robert Morley is given some opportunity to demonstrate his mastery of irony. Overall, *Hot Enough* is just about lukewarm.

Hot Millions ○
1968, UK, 106 mins, colour
Dir: Eric Till
Stars: Peter Ustinov, Maggie Smith, Karl Malden, Bob Newhart, Robert Morley, Cesar Romero
Rating: ★★★★

Three delightful people who all make too few films – Peter Ustinov, Bob Newhart and Maggie Smith – combine in the frequently hilarious story of an embezzler who sets out to outwit a massive computer. The script – by Ustinov and Ira Wallach – crackles with dry wit, and Newhart and Karl Malden are almost as funny as the star while playing two executives called Gnatpole and Klemper, who must also be confounded by the embezzler. Newhart, in particular, is a delight as the sneaky Gnatpole, always trying to prove something against Ustinov, but never quite able to succeed. And Robert Morley, too, is ideally cast as the real computer expert (impersonated by Ustinov who sends his rival off on a wild butterfly chase to South America).

Hot Property
See: Take Me High

Hot Pursuit ◐ Ⓥ
1987, US, 93 mins, colour
Dir: Steven Lisberger

Stars: John Cusack, Robert Loggia, Wendy Gazelle
Rating: ★★

This lightweight comedy is a cross between a teen movie and a road film, with student John Cusack rushing to catch up with his girlfriend and her family who are off on what for him should be a dream holiday. It's all pretty silly, really but young Mr Cusack gives an engaging performance which makes it worth sticking with. Having said that, it's not as good as Cusack's earlier and superficially simiular comedy *The Sure Thing*. The story is set at a fast pace by director Steven Lisberger, who tends to ride quite well over the plot bumps along the way.

Hot Rock, The ○
(aka: Now to Steal a Diamond in Four Uneasy Lessons)
1972, US, 105 mins, colour
Dir: Peter Yates
Stars: Robert Redford, George Segal, Zero Mostel
Rating: ★★★

British-born director Peter Yates had already made such a reputation directing top stars in big films that he really couldn't go wrong with Robert Redford *and* George Segal in a glossy comedy-thriller about a robbery that does keep going wrong. Although William Goldman's script is not one of his best (or most stylish), there are all sorts of compensations from the actors. Redford engagingly spoofs his own image as.the ice-cool (but inwardly ulcer-prone) robber-in-chief, Ron Leibman is very funny as Murch, who claims he can 'drive anything' and William Redfield contributes a marvellous cameo as the harassed, paranoid police lieutenant. Yates makes ingenious use of his New York surroundings, coming up with all sorts of new locations and new angles on old locations.

Hot Shots! ◐ Ⓥ
1991, US, 85 mins, colour
Dir: Jim Abrahams
Stars: Charlie Sheen, Cary Elwes, Valeria Golino, Lloyd Bridges, Kevin Dunn, Kristy Swanson
Rating: ★★★

A genial *Top Gun* spoof from the *Airplane!* guys. Lloyd Bridges is along for the flight again, as an admiral whose body has almost completely been replaced by spare parts, while Charlie Sheen has the Cruise role as 'Topper' Harley who, though suffering from Paternal Conflict Syndrome,

knows that 'All my life I've wanted to fly. Bomb stuff. Shoot people down.' The unit psychiatrist (Valeria Golino) is a sculpting equestrian for whom Sheen falls 'like a blind roofer'. She also has a 'sizzling stomach' he can fry eggs on. There's a dastardly villain (played by once-incorruptible Efrem Zimbalist Jr), some (very mild) spoofs of other movies and an Indian called Dances with Bikers. But Sheen will come through. 'After all,' he pronounces, producing a little box. 'I've got my father's eyes.' It's the kind of film that even offers you recipes (presumably to be cooked on Golino's tum) with the credits.

Hot Shots! Part Deux ◐ Ⓥ
1993, US, 89 mins, colour
Dir: Jim Abrahams
Stars: Charlie Sheen, Valeria Golino, Lloyd Bridges, Brenda Bakke, Richard Crenna, Miguel Ferrer
Rating: ★★

Well, it's not as funny, as Part Un, and that's for sure. But there are so many attempted gags in this Hollywood spoof that some of them are bound to hit your particular funny bone. 'Topper' Harley (Charlie Sheen) is back, sent in by a demented US president (Lloyd Bridges) to get the men who went in to get the men taken captive by Iraq. Sheen, all beefed up as Rambo the second, keeps a straight face throughout, although Valeria Golino has the best lines, delivered beautifully deadpan. It seems that she is shot at the climax, but no: her lucky Topper charm has stopped the bullet. 'My God,' says Sheen, 'I thought you were – .' 'Gabriela Sabatini?' she replies. Yes, I know, it happens all the time.' There are subtle jokes (though not many), background jokes and lavatorial jokes (lots of these) non-stop to the final credits that assure us that 'Prosthetic animals were used where necessary.' They're pot shots rather than hot shots, but comedy fans are guaranteed a chuckle or two.

Hot Spell ○
1958, US, 86 mins, b/w
Dir: Daniel Mann
Stars: Shirley Booth, Anthony Quinn, Shirley MacLaine
Rating: ★★

Shirley Booth, that arch-portrayer of put-upon women (remember her in *Come Back, Little Sheba?*), turns up acting trumps again as a middle-aged wife who suddenly fmds her husband is contemplating running off with a girl in her twenties. Director Daniel Mann does an admirable job of catching the sultry and oppressive atmosphere of a small Louisiana town; and the three Oscar-winners in the cast (Miss Booth, Anthony Quinn and Eileen Heckart) are given sterling competition by Shirley MacLaine (pert and likeable as Miss Booth's romantic daughter), Earl Holliman, Jody Lawrance and Warren Stevens.

Hot Spot, The ● Ⓥ
1990, US, 130 mins, colour
Dir: Dennis Hopper
Stars: Don Johnson, Virginia Madsen, Jennifer Connelly, Charles Martin Smith, William Sadler
Rating: ★★★

A slow and steamy modern version of a *film noir* – and, despite its too-long running time, quite an effective one at that. Don Johnson is Harry, who drifts into a small Texas town ostensibly looking for work, gets it as a car salesman and promptly becomes involved with two gorgeous women, his boss's predatory wife and the demure 19-year-old receptionist at the showroom. Even when the wife horrifies Harry by suggesting something might happen to aggravate her hubby's weak heart, we can see that things might have worked out well for Harry. But there's one thing we haven't told you: Harry is a travelling bank robber. And this is about to complicate his life no end. Johnson's surly charisma is just right for this role, while both the girls, in different ways, ooze sexual.come-hither. The atmosphere created is so tangibly fascinating, that you hardly realise the story doesn't have much action (apart from the sexual kind). Nice ending, too: apt but not too downbeat. A winner, but only on points.

Hot Spot
See: I Wake Up Screaming

Houdini ○
1953, US, 106 mins, colour
Dir: George Marshall
Stars: Tony Curtis, Janet Leigh, Torin Thatcher, Angela Clarke
Rating: ★★

A vivid account of the life of Harry Houdini, the famous escapologist. It's the film Tony Curtis rates as his 'personal' picture. 'The one I would gladly do for nothing' he said while it was being made. Curtis was a natural for the part: he'd always been interested in magic and illusions and bore a passing resemblance to Houdini himself. The

highlights of this earnest biography are Houdini's escape from an 'impregnable' Scotland Yard jail, his arrest in Germany as a fraud and his acquittal after a courtroom demonstration of his techniques. Another good trick was getting Janet Leigh, then Mrs Curtis, to play Mrs Houdini.

Hound of the Baskervilles, The ○
1939, US, 80 mins, b/w
Dir: Sidney Lanfield
Stars: Richard Greene, Basil Rathbone, Nigel Bruce, Lionel Atwill, John Carradine
Rating: ★★★

Sherlock Holmes found his finest interpreter in the skeletal shape of coolly calculating Basil Rathbone in this splendidly atmospheric version of Conan Doyle's most famous story. Mists swirl, hounds bay, bodies go bump in the night and the game's afoot. 'You surely don't believe in that ridiculous hound legend?' protests Richard Greene, which disqualifies his character from any further sympathy. With Nigel Bruce as Dr Watson, Rathbone went on to gallop through 13 further Holmes adventures.

Hound of the Baskervilles, The ①
1959, UK, 84 mins, colour
Dir: Terence Fisher
Stars: Peter Cushing, André Morell, Christopher Lee, Marla Landi
Rating: ★★

Hammer horror meets Sir Arthur Conan Doyle. And with Peter Cushing as Sherlock Holmes, the scene is well and truly set for a chilling film version of the most famous Baker Street mystery of all. The scenes on the moors, as the famous hound bays his way towards another killing, are Just what Hammer's top director, Terence Fisher, ordered.

Hound of the Baskervilles, The ①
1977, UK, 84 mins, colour
Dir: Paul Morrissey
Stars: Peter Cook, Dudley Moore, Joan Greenwood
Rating: ★

Peter Cook and Dudley Moore's own version of Sherlock Holmes' most famous adventure, full of rusty old jokes and frenziedly acted by an all-too-distinguished cast. The direction is almost non-existent, allowing Messrs Cook and Moore to run riot over the plot as well as the Devon moors. But one running gag involving Denholm Elliott's

chihuahua is screamingly funny if only by dint of sheer persistence, and cleverly sustained to keep you chuckling for minutes.

Hour of Glory
See: The Small Back Room

Hour of the Gun ○
1967, US, 109 mins, colour
Dir: John Sturges
Stars: James Garner, Jason Robards Jr, Robert Ryan
Rating: ★★

One of the many films about the Earp brothers and Doc Holliday, this was made by John Sturges, one of Hollywood's best directors of Westerns. His record includes *Gunfight at the OK Corral*, whose story this film continues. Jon Voight can be seen in one of his earliest screen roles. There's a surging beginning, but the film's adrenalin gradually drains away.

Hour of the Pig, The ● Ⓥ
1993, UK, 117 mins, colour
Dir: Leslie Megahey
Stars: Colin Firth, Ian Holm, Amina Annabi, Donald Pleasence, Nicol Williamson, Lysette Anthony
Rating: ★★★

Bawdy, Breughelesque and bizarre, this is a good-looking, well-constructed black drama that crosses a medieval mystery with portraits of ignorance and fear. The setting is rural 15th century France. A dry lawyer (Colin Firth) finds himself in a society where witches are still burnt at the stake, evil and superstition are kings, women drop their chemises at the merest hint of interest and an animal can be tried and condemned on the same charges as a human. Watchable and well-considered performances by Firth, Ian Holm, Donald Pleasence, Nicol Williamson and Lysette Anthony make this an interesting companion to films like *The Name of the Rose*. The squalor of medieval life is convincingly portrayed, while never getting in the way of the plot.

House ● Ⓥ
1986, US, 93 mins, colour
Dir: Steve Miner
Stars: William Katt, George Wendt, Richard Moll, Kay Lenz
Rating: ★★

Successful but highly derivative horror film about a man who seems to have inherited a house full of demons. William Katt is the man with a monster in every closet. Kay Lenz is wasted in the too-brief role of his estranged wife.

H

House Arrest ○ Ⓥ

1995, US, 109 mins, colour
Dir: Harry Winer
Stars: Jamie Lee Curtis, Kevin Pollak, Ray Walston, Jennifer Tilly, Kyle Howard, Jennifer Love Hewitt
Rating: ★★

A wacky comedy about two kids who lock their warring parents (Curtis, Pollak) in the (well-lit and decorated) cellar of their home in the hope it will bring them to their senses. And so it does. No, we didn't believe it either, especially when other kids catch on to the idea and bring their bickering parents along too. This develops into a kind of upstairs-downstairs situation, which gets a bit more tolerable towards the end, but doesn't seem to have an audience. Good cast, though, including Walston, Tilly and that little gremlin Wallace Shawn, who at least makes us smile when he asks his wife: 'Why do I owe you child support? You've got the kids!' Kyle Howard and Jennifer Love Hewitt are attractive teenage leads as two of the leading instigators of the plot.

House II: The Second Story ◐ Ⓥ

1987, US, 88 mins, colour
Dir: Ethan Wiley
Stars: Arye Gross, Jonathan Stark, Royal Dano
Rating: ★★★

You can't believe this was the film the producers of *House* expected when they asked Ethan Wiley, who scripted it, to write and direct a sequel. You can forget about the guts and gore, because this is a horror comedy, with the emphasis on the latter – somewhat after the style of old Vincent Price films like *The Raven*, but much more zany.

Houseboat ○

1958, US, 110 mins, colour
Dir: Melville Shavelson
Stars: Cary Grant, Sophia Loren, Martha Hyer
Rating: ★★★

Sophia Loren's first Hollywood comedy was this winsome fable about a widower who falls for the Italian girl who looks after his three children. With Cary Grant as the widower, it's guaranteed to skate skilfully over the stickier patches.

House by the River ○

1950, US, 95 mins, b/w
Dir: Fritz Lang
Stars: Louis Hayward, Lee Bowman,

Jane Wyatt
Rating: ★★★

In a story that may send a shiver or two up your spine, Louis Hayward accidentally kills his housemaid while trying to seduce her, then tries to blame her death on his brother. When his wife discovers the truth, he has to consider killing them both. This seemingly improbable melodrama is given a stylistic lift by the fact that it was directed by Fritz Lang, who makes the whole thing visually moody and intriguing. Stilted acting by Hayward, Lee Bowman and Jane Wyatt stops this thriller being any more than interesting, the film's undeniable style not disguising a lack of content. Keep tuned, though, for a chilling, eye-opening ending that will have video viewers freezing frames to see how the director did it.

House Calls ○

1978, US, 98 mins, colour
Dir: Howard Zieff
Stars: Walter Matthau, Glenda Jackson, Art Carney, Richard Benjamin
Rating: ★★★

This romantic comedy is very much in the Seventies style, and, thanks to the skills of Walter Matthau and Glenda Jackson, you'll laugh out loud at some parts of this story of a widowed doctor wooing a salty but lovable divorcee. And Art Carney is a scream as the head of surgery at Matthau's hospital. The funny bits, though, aren't strung together well enough to make a successful whole. The film attempts to be endearing, but only succeeds in spurts.

House in Nightmare Park, The ◐

(aka: Crazy House)
1973, UK, 95 mins, colour
Dir: Peter Sykes
Stars: Frankie Howerd, Ray Milland, Hugh Burden, Kenneth Griffith, Rosalie Crutchley
Rating: ★★★

It's just one darned thing after another for our hapless hero in this delightfully old-fashioned comedy thriller. Frankie Howerd revels in the chance to mix chuckles with chills as a fifth-rate entertainer invited out to a gloomy mansion by a weird collection of aristocrats. Things seem to go bump in the night with hectic regularity on his arrival, and it isn't long before bodies begin to follow them. The proceedings are decked up in good style by director Peter Sykes, who stages his more gasp-provoking moments with considerable expertise. But the giggles hold their

own in the midst of the mayhem. One look at Howerd's crabbed expression is likely to have you falling about. In the centre of a film such as this, he's invaluable. There's a hair-raising scene in a snake-pit, and other developments it wouldn't be fair to reveal.

Housekeeping ○

1987, US, 116 mins, colour
Dir: Bill Forsyth
Stars: Christine Lahti, Sara Walker, Andrea Burchill
Rating: ★★

As a change of pace from his Scottish comedies, director Bill Forsyth made this affectionate memoir of a girl's Canadian childhood, spent in the care – if that's the word – of an eccentric slattern of an aunt, who seems previously to have been some kind of hobo, and keeps crackers in her pockets for the runaway children who live in the frosty woods. The seasons are caught so well that we can almost smell and feel woodsmoke and winter chill. But the film is long and slow for its content, and only occasionally achieves the poignancy for which it strives. It lacks the charismatic spark that the original casting of Diane Keaton might have given it: Christine Lahti is a fine actress, but altogether too down-to-earth for this flaky character. The two girls, Sara Walker and Andrea Burchill, are entirely adequate without having quite the appeal to make their emotions ours.

House of Angels ● Ⓥ

1992, Sweden, 121 mins, colour
Dir Colin Nutley
Stars: Helena Bergstrom, Rikard Wolff, Ernst Gunther, Per Oscarsson
Rating: ★★

A Swedish manor house and the surrounding forest, much coveted by local fartners and businessmen, is left by her grandfather to a nightclub entertainer (Helena Bergstrom) of somewhat shady background. Together with her equally shady cohort, a devil-eyed fellow-entertainer with stubble and earrings, she arrives, leather-clad on a motor bike, to claim the inheritance – and tongues soon start wagging in the small village that adjoins the manor. Although ensuing developments do go on a bit, there is charm and perception in equal proportions as director Colin Nutley details the self-righteousness and prejudice among people who are often more perverted than the newcomers they talk about behind their hands.

House of Bamboo O
1954, US, 102 mins, colour
Dir: Samuel Fuller
Stars: Robert Ryan, Robert Stack,
Cameron Mitchell, Shirley Yamaguchi,
Brad Dexter
Rating: ★★

Twentieth Century-Fox went east to
make this detective thriller – not to
Hong Kong, but Japan, where some
interesting backdrops make a welcome change from those of New
York, Chicago or San Francisco.
Robert Ryan delivers a cold, passionless and precise portrait of a greedy
killer. Director Samuel Fuller went
on to become something of a 'cult'
discovery.

House of Cards ◐ Ⓥ
1993, US, 109 mins, colour
Dir: Michael Lessac
Stars: Kathleen Turner, Tommy Lee
Jones, Asha Menina, Shiloh Strong, Anne
Pitoniak, Esther Rolle
Rating: ★★

Kathleen Turner is not at her best in
this 'problem' drama that plays more
in the style of a TV movie. She takes
the role of a newly widowed mother
who cannot acknowledge the fact that
her six-year-old daughter may be autistic. Admittedly her character is
underwritten, but someone of Turner's
calibre should have been able to do
more with it. However, the film improves in the scenes focusing on the
child. Little Asha Menina manages to
convey an uncanny unworldliness,
which writer/director Michael Lessac
presents clearly and compellingly.
And Tommy Lee Jones is on good, unusually quiet form as the child
psychiatrist involved.

House of Dracula ◐
1945, US, 67 mins, b/w
Dir: Eric C Kenton
Stars: Lon Chaney Jr, John Carradine,
Onslow Stevens, Glenn Strange
Rating: ★★

All the monsters get together for the
last in the Universal series, before they
met Abbott and Costello. The director
of this shocker is Erle C Kenton, who
directed innumerable horror films for
the studio, including *The Ghost Of
Frankenstein*, *House Of Frankenstein* and
The Cat Creeps.

House of Frankenstein ◐
1944, US, 71 mins, b/w
Dir: Eric C Kenton
Stars: Boris Karloff, John Carradine, Lon
Chaney Jr, J Carrol Naish, Lionet Atwill,

George Zucco
Rating: ★★

By the time this contribution to the
Universal horror series came out,
Hollywood audiences were no longer
content with one monster, or even
two. The producers reasoned that
three monsters, a mad scientist and a
hunchback should prove enough for
even the most avid horror fan. They
also threw in every available actor
with a reputation in the genre. Not
surprisingly things fuse here, there and
everywhere in more ways than one.
And it's rather unnerving to see Boris
Karloff as the scientist working on the
creature (now portrayed by ex-cowboy
Glenn Strange) that Karloff had made
immortal 15 years earlier.

House of Fright
See: The Two Faces of Dr Jekyll

House of Games ● Ⓥ
1987, US, 102 mins, colour
Dir: David Mamet
Stars: Lindsay Crouse, Joe Mantegna,
Mike Nussbaum, J T Walsh
Rating: ★★★★

Fancy a psychological up-market version of *The Sting*? Then come with
writer-director David Mamet to the
con-man's kingdom, in a sleazy corner
of the city, called the *House of Games*.
Psychiatrist Lindsay Crouse enters its
portals, to become enmeshed in a
world where the swiftness of the lip de-
ceives the ear. You, the viewer, may
think yourself a step ahead of her, but
be careful, as master-puppeteer Mamet
is inclined to change the rules as he
goes along. Clever it is, and fun too,
with appropriately strange, stylised
performances by players who seem almost under hypnosis.

House of Numbers O
1957, US, 92 mins, b/w
Dir: Russell Rouse
Stars: Jack Palance, Barbara Lang,
Harold J Stone
Rating: ★★

Much of this MGM production was
filmed in San Quentin prison. And
director Russell Rouse's search for realism did not end there, for he
persuaded the authorities to allow
him to use the prison warders and
some of the inmates as 'extras'. It's a
stark prison drama with Jack Palance
giving a tougher-than-tough performance as a homicidal maniac – and
playing the killer's brother in a softer
key.

House of Rothschild, The O
1933, US, 95 mins, b/w
Dir: Alfred Werker
Stars: George Arliss, Boris Karloff,
Loretta Young, Robert Young, C Aubrey
Smith
Rating: ★★★

A lavish historical drama with George
Arliss – who won an Oscar in 1930 for
his portrayal of Disraeli – giving an excellent account of himself in the dual
role of patriarch Mayer Rothschild and
his son Nathan. The screenplay, by director-to-be Nunnally Johnson, makes
for compelling viewing and Alfred
Werker's workmanlike direction gets
the most out of it and out of his strong
cast. Loretta Young is excellent as
Arliss' daughter, Robert Young is sympathetic as her suitor and Boris Karloff,
three years after his surge to stardom
as the monster in *Frankenstein*, provides
a highly enjoyable study in suave villainy. The last few minutes of this film
are in colour.

House of Secrets O
1956, UK, 95 mins, colour
Dir: Guy Green
Stars: Michael Craig, Julia Arnall, Brenda
de Banzie, David Kossoff
Rating: ★★★

Enjoyed by critics and cinemagoers
alike, this exciting crime drama about a
gang of counterfeiters made a star of
Michael Craig, a former extra who had
been confined to minor roles. Craig
punches well, and shaped up as a star
with all the attack, confidence and
charm of a British Robert Mitchum.
American actress Barbara Bates, whose
career would soon be ended by ill-
health, is a pleasant heroine: she and
Austrian-born Julia Arnall bring a welcome touch of warmth to the
slam-bang thick-ear thrills. And that
fine character actress Brenda de Banzie
revels in her casting as the mysterious
and menacing Madame Ballu.

House of Strangers O
1949, US, 101 mins, b/w
Dir: Joseph L Mankiewicz
Stars: Edward G Robinson, Susan
Hayward, Richard Conte, Efrem Zimbalist
Jr, Luther Adler, Paul Valentine
Rating: ★★★★

Dynamic drama, told in the flashback
form much favoured at the time,
about a father's suffocating influence
on his several sons. The style of the
film makes it seem a sort of *I
Remember Papa*, but there's nothing
very kindly about the character so
vividly etched by Edward G

H

Robinson. Richard Conte and Luther Adler are effectively contrasted as the principal sons, and there are early screen appearances for Efrem Zimbalist Jr and Debra Paget. The studio, Fox, remade the film five years later as a Western, *Broken Lance*.

House of the Long Shadows ●

1982, UK, 101 mins, colour
Dir: Pete Walker
Stars: Vincent Price, Peter Cushing, Christopher Lee, Desi Arnaz Jr, John Carradine, Julie Peasgood
Rating: ★★

Take care how you rate this one: it will throw all your judgments back in your face in the last reel. An American author (Desi Arnaz Jr) is sent to an isolated Welsh manor by his publisher (Richard Todd) to win a bet that he can write a book in 24 hours. The manor is alive with mystery, not to mention two caretakers (cadaverous John Carradine and glaze-eyed Sheila Keith), Vincent Price in a red bow-tie, Christopher Lee looking bad-tempered and Peter Cushing posturing madly. But remember, nothing in this old ghouls' reunion is what it seems, not even the story or the history behind the story. At the end two 'normal' twists are followed by two 'super-normal' twists and even a twist tailpiece, which is something of an anti-climax since by this time, we're conditioned to expect anything. 'Ah, piano wire,' muses Price, inspecting the throttled body of Ms Keith. 'He must have heard her sing.' We, too, have heard her sing ...

House of the Seven Hawks, The ○

1959, US, 100 mins, b/w
Dir: Richard Thorpe
Stars: Robert Taylor, Nicole Maurey, Linda Christian, Donald Wolfit
Rating: ★★

A thriller based on a Victor Canning novel which contains enough red herrings to fill a creel. Unfortunately, all these complications only bog the film down so that, despite its team of stars, it never rises much above the ordinary. Robert Taylor and Linda Christian are the leads, but the biggest surprise in this film is David Kossoff's role. Usually cast as the mildest and most inoffensive of men, he plays Wilhelm Dekker who, from his first appearance on the screen, is obviously up to no good.

House of the Spirits, The ● Ⓥ

1993, US/Germany/Denmark/Portugal, 147 mins, colour
Dir: Bille August
Stars: Jeremy Irons, Meryl Streep, Glenn Close, Winona Ryder, Antonio Banderas
Rating: ★

Here's ammunition for those who say that foreign directors these days shouldn't be allowed to make anything without subtitles. Bille August's *Best Intentions* was a deserved international success, but best intentions are not enough when it comes to this massive screen adaptation of Isabel Allende's epic novel. Rarely has 147 minutes seemed longer and the ironic thing is, in this telling of Allende's saga, there seems hardly enough plot for an hour and a half. Meryl Streep is the fey spirit who can move objects and foresee the future; she marries hopeful miner Jeremy Irons, attempting a downright peculiar accent. Somewhere in this is Glenn Close as Irons' sister, yearning after both her brother and his bride, but clearly auditioning for the role of Mrs Danvers in the sequel to *Rebecca*. Most of the lines are delivered by the actors as if in a trance and the film never reaches the epic scale to which it aspires.

House of Wax ◐

1953, US, 88 mins, colour
Dir: André De Toth
Stars: Vincent Price, Frank Lovejoy, Phyllis Kirk, Carolyn Jones, Charles Bronson
Rating: ★★★

Warner Brothers moved fast to cash in on the short-lived Fifties boom in 3-D films, remaking their 1933 chiller *Mystery of the Wax Museum* in under two weeks and cleaning up at the box office in the process. It retains most of its power, even when it's shown 'flat', due in great measure to Vincent Price's gleefully horrid performance as the mad wax museum proprietor who uses real bodies as a basis for his immobile exhibits. Phyllis Kirk makes an attractive heroine with a nice line in screams, Charles Bronson puts in an early screen appearance, here billed as Charles Buchinski, and most wondrous of all, the film was directed by André de Toth who, because he had only one eye, was unable to see in three dimensions!

House on Carroll Street, The ◐ Ⓥ

1987, US, 101 mins, colour
Dir: Peter Yates

Stars: Kelly McGillis, Jeff Daniels, Mandy Patinkin, Jessica Tandy
Rating: ★★★

A decent looking thriller set in 1951 which actually achieves the effect of looking as if it were made at that time. Nothing much wrong with that, although the excitements and characters come across as a shade dated. Kelly McGillis is strong in the central role of a girl who finds that the senate witch-hunter probing her for Communist-affiliated activities is actually the power behind a rather more sinister plot to introduce illegal refugees into America by giving them the identities of dead men. Peter Yates' direction of these nefarious events brings one much in mind of Hitchcock and, although the Master would have hastened the pace here and there, this is a very respectable job of work, with a nicely balanced plot in which characters make logical moves, bursts of action and a typical suspense-film climax in and around (and above) a huge railway station.

House on Haunted Hill ◐

1958, US, 76 mins, b/w
Dir: William Castle
Stars: Vincent Price, Carol Ohmart, Richard Long, Elisha Cook
Rating: ★★

Horror producer/director William Castle was well known for introducing gimmicks in the auditoria of cinemas showing his films. For this haunted house chiller he arranged for a full-size skeleton to 'leap' from the screen and descend on cinemagoers along a hidden wire – a gimmick dubbed 'emergo'. But word soon got around about the stunt and the skeleton was pelted with food and boxes from the concession kiosk each time it appeared. It's silly but good fun as Vincent Price arranges shocks for his house guests while his wife arranges to have him shot as an 'accident'. There are even a couple of genuine chills among the floating sheets and banging windows.

House on 92nd Street, The ○

1945, US, 84 mins, b/w
Dir: Henry Hathaway
Stars: William Eythe, Lloyd Nolan, Signe Hasso, Gene Lockhart
Rating: ★★★★

This drama about a Nazi spy ring was one of the best thrillers that Hollywood ever made. Taut, tense, intricate and really suspenseful, with a superb climax, it set the fashion for a whole host of imitations. Advanced camera techniques, allied to a clever mystery plot, and a brisk, semi-documentary approach by director Henry Hathaway, produced a film worthy of Hitchcock at his best.

House Party ● Ⓥ
1990, US, 104 mins, colour
Dir: Reginald Hudlin
Stars: Christopher Reid, Christopher Martin, Robin Harris
Rating: ★

If this is black American teenage life, show us the door marked Exit. In downtown Blaxville, USA, a party is only a flop if the loo gets clogged or one of the partygoers ends in jail. A guy ain't got a prayer if he can't talk the lingo and a girl only respects a man if he asks her if she's on the pill before he pins her to the bed. Modern black music can be served well, as *Beat Street* showed. But *House Party* is too concerned with its own image to tool its scenario towards some kind of entertainment. The only scene to break through the generations and amuse us all is when the scrawny hero desperately tries to rap-talk his way out of a cellblock gang bang. Better, though, than the two sequels.

Housesitter ○ Ⓥ
1992, US, 102 mins, colour
Dir: Frank Oz
Stars: Steve Martin, Goldie Hawn, Dana Delany, Julie Harris
Rating: ★★

Not exactly the blast of laughter you'd expect from a teaming of Steve Martin and Goldie Hawn, this is an inconsequential romantic comedy that's good for a few chuckles but rather more yawns. Martin's a stuck-in-a-rut architect whose girlfriend (Dana Delany) turns him and his dream house down. Rebounding to a one-night stand with waitress Hawn, Martin arrives at the (empty) house one day to find that Hawn has moved in, having convinced his parents and the whole town that they're married. Martin and Hawn never convince you of their attraction for one another here, and you keep thinking he should marry Delany until the script makes her turn around into a bit of a bitch.

House That Dripped Blood, The ●
1970, UK, 101 mins, colour
Dir: Peter Duffell
Stars: Peter Cushing, Christopher Lee,

Ingrid Pitt
Rating: ★★

Talented director Peter Duffell creates some good shock moments during this quartet of horror stories from the pen of Robert (*Psycho*) Bloch. Ingrid Pitt is in fine, fang-baring form with another of her vampire ladies, and the house rich, dark and filled with shadows – is quite a character in itself. But the most chilling story is the third, with Chloe Franks (the teenage heroine of Disney's *Escape from the Dark*) as a devil-child more genuinely evil than anything out of *The Innocents*. The sombre and brooding atmosphere here is a welcome contrast to the comic-book horror of the other episodes.

Hoverbug, The ☉
1970, UK, 57 mins, colour
Dir: Jan Darnley-Smith
Stars: Jill Riddick, John Trayhorn, Arthur Howard
Rating: ★★★

Dick Brewster and his sister Jenny build a hovercraft to enter in a race, but it keeps falling apart. Luckily, Mr Watt, an eccentric inventor, has invented a high-powered glue, but is it the answer to their problems? An entertaining children's comedy, with the hovercraft race itself as an exciting climax. The Hoverbug of the title is a whimsical, Heath-Robinson-style creation. Character actor Arthur Howard enjoys himself as the dotty Mr Watt, and Jill Riddick and John Trayhorn are delightfully natural as Dick and Jenny.

Howards End ○ Ⓥ
1991, UK, 142 mins, colour
Dir: James Ivory
Stars: Anthony Hopkins, Vanessa Redgrave, Helena Bonham Carter, Emma Thompson, James Wilby, Samuel West
Rating: ★★★★

The most successful adaptation of an E M Forster novel to date, and the best Merchant-Ivory film in quite a while. Vigorously shot and immaculately set, the story starts in 1910 and is related in terms of some feisty dialogue by Ruth Prawer Jhabvala, intelligent stuff that sounds like the conversation of real people. Given this impetus, the players rise to the occasion. Anthony Hopkins' excellence under such circumstances tends to be taken for granted, but Emma Thompson and Helena Bonham Carter are both better than one could possibly have imagined, and James Wilby, clearly relishing playing a nasty piece of work, is a more

effective actor than heretofore. Tony Pierce Roberts' mobile camera work makes the most of the settings, too, from the countryside, through St Pancras Station, to the dusty, cavernous offices of an insurance company. Thompson's subsequent Oscar was richly deserved.

Howard the Duck ○
(aka: Howard ... A New Breed of Hero)
1986, US, 110 mins, colour
Dir: Willard Huyck
Stars: Lea Thompson, Jeffrey Jones, Tim Robbins
Rating: RB

First shown as *Howard the Duck*, but soon dubbed 'Howard the Turkey', this tiresome and embarrassing fantasy adventure proved that *Star Wars* creator George Lucas didn't always have his finger on the pulse of popular taste. it was retitled *Howard ... a New Breed of Hero* in Britain, presumably to disguise the fact that the star is a duck! Based on the adventures of a Marvel Comics character, it laid an egg that, far from being golden, cost Universal Studios millions.

How Green Was My Valley ○ Ⓥ
1941, US, 118 mins, b/w
Dir: John Ford
Stars: Walter Pidgeon, Maureen O'Hara, Donald Crisp, Roddy McDowall, Barry Fitzgerald, Anna Lee
Rating: ★★★★★

Award-winning John Ford tearjerker about life in a Welsh mining village at the end of the 19th century. Beautiful performances by Donald Crisp, Sara Allgood, Roddy McDowall and Barry Fitzgerald produce the maximum impact, especially in the climactic scenes. The Welsh village set, designed by Nathan Juran and Richard Day, is one of the best ever constructed in Hollywood, and turned up in several other films in subsequent years. Juran and Day deservedly took one of the production's many Oscars, which also included awards for Best Film (against strong competition) and Best Director.

How I Won the War ◑
1967, UK, 110 mins, colour
Dir: Richard Lester
Stars: Michael Crawford, John Lennon, Roy Kinnear, Lee Montague
Rating: ★★★

Richard Lester's surrealistic comedy about a small group of soldiers in World War Two is as black a film as you would ever wish to see in colour.

H

The initial 20 minutes are hilarious in Goon Show style, with satire lurking somewhere to the rear, but the film soon develops into a bloodstrewn, charnel-house allegory about unnecessary blood-letting and blatant disregard for human life. The platoon of eight soldiers are, you may think, merely symbols. Six are expendable players in the 'game' of war. The seventh (Michael Crawford) may be Everyman. The eighth (Jack MacGowran) is, in my interpretation, Death. For all its underlying seriousness, the film contains glimpses of humour throughout the mayhem. Funniest of all is Michael Hordern's veteran campaigner, forever referring to 'the wily Pathan'.

Howling, The ● Ⓥ

1980, US, 91 mins, colour
Dir: Joe Dante
Stars: Dee Wallace, Patrick Macnee, Dennis Dugan
Rating: ★★★

The special make-up effects by Rick Baker, later to amaze us on *An American Werewolf in London* and other modern horror film, give an extra dimension to this fang-in-cheek werewolf chiller in which many of the character names are those of directors associated with cinematic terror. Patrick Macnee has a field day as the psychologist involved in dangerous research into werewolves (it must have been almost like playing a villain from *The Avengers*), while ubiquitous character actor Dick Miller crops up as Walter Paisley, whom he originally created in *A Bucket of Blood*. Five sequels followed, none of them anywhere near as much fun as this.

How Sweet It Is! ○

1968, US, 99 mins, colour
Dir: Jerry Paris
Stars: James Garner, Debbie Reynolds, Maurice Ronet
Rating: ★★★

This film springs a rare surprise: a Hollywood comedy about the generation gap that is actually very funny. Every character has a personality of its own. Only the sex jokes are sometimes clumsy. James Garner, friendly with his teenage son like never before (while Mum Debbie Reynolds is fending off the advances of a Riviera playboy), even takes to wearing his offspring's hippie neck-charm. The hotel clerk is horrified. 'It symbolises love and peace,' snarls Garner. 'Y'wanna make something of it?'

How the West Was Won ○ Ⓥ

1962, US, 162 mins, colour
Dir: John Ford, George Marshall
Stars: James Stewart, Henry Fonda, Gregory Peck, Debbie Reynolds, Richard Widmark, John Wayne
Rating: ★★★

The American West has a mighty and turbulent history, some of which is told, in story and folk song, in this epic movie, originally in Cinerama and photographed in gorgeous Metrocolor, which is somewhat dampened down in transition to wide screen – though some early scenes still rate with the best of the West. The storyline is inevitably somewhat bitty: the Civil War is the shortest section and the weakest, and somewhere or other there's a pocket version of every Western you ever saw. Not many of the actors have a chance to register (and certainly not Henry Fonda under a yard of beard), but Debbie Reynolds, surprisingly, is supreme here in a performance that epitomises the spirit of the early West at least as Hollywood saw it.

How to Commit Marriage ○

1969, US, 95 mins, colour
Dir: Norman Panama
Stars: Bob Hope, Jane Wyman, Jackie Gleason
Rating: ★★

Bob Hope and the modern scene never did mix. His comedy technique belonged essentially to a world of fiendish oriental spies, mad doctors and anything that exposed a yellow streak running up the centre of his back. Thus it's not surprising that the most successful parts of this latter-day Hope comedy are his exchanges with fellow veteran Jackie Gleason as an alcoholic impresario. ('Your breath,' Hope tells him, 'could start the windmill on an old Dutch painting') and the occasionally very funny visual gags, especially the ending. Less successful are interludes with Hope as hippie or mystic, invading the world of his teenage daughter, who has decided to live with her fiancé, when her parents decide to divorce.

How to Get Ahead in Advertising ● Ⓥ

1988, UK, 98 mins, colour
Dir: Bruce Robinson
Stars: Richard E Grant, Rachel Ward, Richard Johnson
Rating: ★★

A black horror-comic that might have emanated from Ealing Studios had they still been going 30 years on. Obsessed with the pressure of coming up with an advertising campaign for a boil cream, ad exec Bagley (Richard E Grant) freaks out. Himself having a boil, he imagines it having life (and voice) of its own, representing the Hyde in him to his own Jekyll. Eventually the boil takes over ... or did it all really happen? We'll never know because the film leaves us in no-man's-land. Grant never quite sounds as though he believes in all this, even with such prime lines as 'My grandfather was caught molesting a wallaby in Sydney Zoo in 1919. He put his hand in its pouch. . .' Rachel Ward is okay as his long-suffering wife but, despite some good laughs, the film doesn't quite have the consistency, pace or bite to grip our attention (and funny-bone) throughout.

How to Make an American Quilt ◐ Ⓥ

1995, US, 116 mins, colour
Dir: Jocelyn Moorhouse
Stars: Winona Ryder, Anne Bancroft, Ellen Burstyn, Jean Simmons, Alfre Woodard, Esther Rolle
Rating: ★

Despite its all-star female cast, this is a lengthy and tedious film about a group of women gathered round a giant quilt, and how the love affairs of their corporate pasts influence the present-day heart flutterings of flighty Pitt (Winona Ryder) who still finds time for a hot affair with a local boy in the orange grove before committing herself to her true love. There's probably a moral in there somewhere, but for the life of us we couldn't figure out what it was. For the rest of it, Anne Bancroft, Esther Rolle, Ellen Burstyn, Jean Simmons and Alfre Woodard look wise and sort their lives out in the process of the film. Two of Ryder's *Little Women* sisters, Samantha Mathis and Claire Danes, play quilters when young. It's meant as an uplifting experience but emerges more of a drag: long too.

How to Marry a Millionaire ○ Ⓥ

1953, US, 95 mins, colour
Dir: Jean Negulesco
Stars: Marilyn Monroe, Betty Grable, Lauren Bacall, David Wayne, Rory Calhoun, William Powell
Rating: ★★★

A familiar story of a trio of gold-diggers on the prowl in New York, this was the second CinemaScope feature. The three huntresses are attractively played by Betty Grable, Marilyn Monroe, who makes myopia entertaining, and Lauren Bacall, who has all the best lines and delivers them stylishly. The film has more good humour, perhaps, than real wit, but director Jean Negulesco makes it all very pleasing to watch, with William Powell scoring for the men.

How to Murder a Rich Uncle ○
1957, UK, 80 mins, b/w
Dir: Nigel Patrick
Stars: Nigel Patrick, Charles Coburn, Wendy Hiller
Rating: ★★

Things going bump in the night are mostly the bodies resulting from bungled attempts to kill off old Uncle George in this British comedy of terrors. Michael Caine can be glimpsed carrying people around and uttering an occasional grunt; and that lovable little old lady, Katie Johnson, gives a rib-tickling performance as one of Uncle George's relatives. But stardom, which had found her suddenly with *The Ladykillers*, was not to last for long. She died later the same year at the age of 78.

How to Murder Your Wife ○ ⓥ
1964, US, 118 mins, colour
Dir: Richard Quine
Stars: Jack Lemmon, Virna Lisi, Terry-Thomas, Claire Trevor
Rating: ★★

Eddie Mayehoff, a jovial gent with black button eyes, steals what laughs there are going from under the noses of such experienced comedy stars as Jack Lemmon and Terry-Thomas in this black comedy. Unfortunately, like Lemmon, fed on a diet of pasta by an unwanted wife, it gets progressively more heavy. And if you had a wife as tiresome as Virna Lisi, you might want to drop her into a cement mixer, too.

How to Steal a Diamond in Four Uneasy Lessons
See: The Hot Rock

How to Steal a Million ○
1966, US, 120 mins, colour
Dir: William Wyler
Stars: Audrey Hepburn, Peter O'Toole, Eli Wallach, Hugh Griffith, Charles Boyer
Rating: ★★★

Elegant Audrey Hepburn delivers the goods in more ways than one in this comedy about an attempt to steal a priceless statue.This girl is such fun to watch – the voice, the face are ever-changing, completely individual. And it's not so much what Givenchy clothes

do for Audrey as what she does for Givenchy. There's a sly joke about Givenchy, in fact, during the sleek proceedings, the piece de resistance of which is the robbery itself, in which Topkapi-like safety precautions have to be overcome. Three French matinee idols of the Thirties – Charles Boyer, Fernand Gravet and Marcel Dalio appear in supporting roles, each in his 60s, but all as debonair as ever. And a fat comedian called Moustache is very funny as a museum guard.

How to Succeed In Business Without Really Trying ○
1967, US, 121 mins, colour
Dir: David Swift
Stars: Robert Morse, Michele Lee, Rudy Vallee
Rating: ★★★★

Bright, colourful, zestful musical in the best Hollywood traditions. Robert Morse is most engaging as the young man who starts off in the post-room of a big firm, and succeeds so well that the executives eventually have to band together to stop him getting higher. Michele Lee is entrancing as the girlfriend who watches over him, and sings beautifully, especially in 'I Believe in You'. It's a crime that she was seen so seldom in films. Individual numbers are vividly staged with a zip only seen since in *Cabaret*. The gutsy score, organised, garish colour and fluid, physical camerawork all pay tribute to the heyday of the American musical.

Hucksters, The ○
1947, US, 115 mins, b/w
Dir: Jack Conway
Stars: Clark Gable, Deborah Kerr, Sydney Greenstreet, Ava Gardner
Rating: ★★★

Slick, sophisticated satire aimed squarely at the con-men and sharks of he immediate post-war American advertising world. Clark Gable is at his suave, fast-talking best as brash Vic Norman, who takes New York's ad world by storm – then finds rough weather brewing when he clashes with a sadistic soap magnate, played to dictatorial perfection by Sydney Greenstreet. It was Deborah Kerr's first Hollywood film, but it was Ava Gardner who most boosted her Hollywood stock, displaying a gift for satirical comedy which few suspected she possessed.

Hud ○
1963, US, 112 mins, b/w
Dir: Martin Ritt
Stars: Paul Newman, Patricia Neal,

Melvyn Douglas, Brandon de Wilde
Rating: ★★★★

Martin Ritt's brilliant 'modern Western'. Paul Newman dominates the film as Hud, 'the man with the barbed wire soul', while Patricia Neal's sensitive portrayal as Alma won her an Academy Award. Other Oscars went to Melvyn Douglas as Best Supporting Actor, and to veteran cinematographer James Wong Howe (his second Academy Award) for his fine black-and-white camerawork. Director Ritt keeps a firm grip on the absorbing story about an amoral tearaway (Paul Newman) and the clash of old and new ideas on a huge Texas cattle ranch. Newman was also nominated for an Academy Award for his uncompromising portrayal.

Hudson Hawk ● ⓥ
1991, US, 97 mins, colour
Dir: Michael Lehmann
Stars: Bruce Willis, Andie MacDowell, Danny Aiello, James Coburn, Richard E Grant, David Caruso
Rating: ★★

Wisecracking Hudson Hawk (Bruce Willis) is a cool cat burglar trying to go straight. But some incredibly over-the-top villains are insisting on his crooked help. And so begins a whole set of Keystone Kops-style slapstick adventures, in which Hawk brings off a series of daring art heists that bring back memories of *How to Steal a Million*, *Topkapi* and *Gambit*. This one isn't half as well written as any of those but fast-moving (if completely incoherent) with a few of the Willis wisecracks coming off here and there. Willis places his tongue rather too obviously in his cheek, and the result is glossy but irritatingly overblown entertainment.

Hudsucker Proxy, The ○ ⓥ
1994, US, 111 mins, colour
Dir: Joel Coen
Stars: Tim Robbins, Jennifer Jason Leigh, Paul Newman, Charles Duming
Rating: ★★

A doomed attempt to combine a 1984-style story with a Capra fantasy such as *Meet John Doe* or *Mr Deeds Goes to Town*. It's 1958, and the deeds of this particular long fellow (6ft 5in Tim Robbins with his hair curled upwards) revolve around the Hudsucker company, whose founder (Charles Durning, later to reappear as an angel) has just jumped from the 54th floor. Numskull Tim is hired by vice-prez Paul Newman to be prez so that shares will plummet faster than Durning and the

H

board can buy them for peanuts. Alas, he subsequently invents the hula hoop and shares soar ... so how does he end up contemplating the same leap as Durning? Chances are you won't care a lot, since none of this is rooted in reality. The film's script just can't resist the easy gag – the Hudsucker company advertises vacancies as 'low pay, long hours' – or silly *bon mot*: other vacancies Robbins sees advertised include goat herd and card shark. Get out on that ledge lads: you blew it.

Human Comedy, The ○
1943, US, 117 mins, b/w
Dir: Clarence Brown
Stars: Mickey Rooney, Frank Morgan, Marsha Hunt
Rating: ★★★

This was the favourite film of MGM mogul Louis B Mayer. Its story of an American town during World War II reduced the great man to tears whenever he read it. It contains what many regard as Mickey Rooney's finest screen performance, as the town telegram boy, who has the unenviable task of delivering messages on the days when a telegram can only mean that someone has been wounded or killed in action overseas. But his thunder is stolen whenever up-and-coming child star Jackie 'Butch' Jenkins appears on screen. In the hands of Greta Garbo's regular director, Clarence Brown, *The Human Comedy* emerged as a sentimental celebration of the American way of life.

Human Factor, The ◐
1975, UK/Italy, 96 mins, colour
Dir: Edward Dmytryk
Stars: George Kennedy, John Mills, Rita Tushingham
Rating: ★★★

This vendetta thriller is Edward Dmytryk's best piece of direction in his later years. George Kennedy, full of menace, is articularly good as the man who seeks out a terrorist group in Italy after his wife and children have been killed there.

Human Factor, The ◐
1979, UK, 114 mins, colour
Dir: Otto Preminger
Stars: Richard Attenborough, John Gielgud, Derek Jacobi, Robert Morley, Ann Todd, Nicol Williamson
Rating: ★★

The prospect of Tom Stoppard adapting a Graham Greene novel promises more than film actually offers, though darkly ironic tale of Foreign Office treason still throws up delights: Richard

Attenborough's comic introduction to Maltesers, for example, or the spectacle of fate catching the characters in a pincer grip. Director Otto Preminger's acting discovery, Iman, is perhaps an acquired taste, but the bulk of the cast is pleasantly familiar in this interesting if slow drama. Preminger's direction tends to lack passion, robbing what should be a moving story of some of the human factor of the title – no fault of the formidable Nicol Williamson, who is billed eighth in alphabetical order, but quite clearly has the central part.

Humoresque ○
1947, US, 120 mins, b/w
Dir: Jean Negulesco
Stars: Joan Crawford, John Garfield
Rating: ★★★

A black romantic drama, typical of Hollywood in the mid-Forties, about a wealthy woman who falls for a musician. Joan Crawford makes the most of some pretty good dialogue, written by Clifford Odets and Zachary Gold. As with the contemporary Bette Davis film *Deception*, direction and music sequences are, like the performances impeccable. To ensure absolute perfection visually, a real violinist's arm was passed through an opening in co-star John Garfield's jacket, the special effects men's magic concealing the deception.

Hunchback of Notre Dame, The ○ Ⓥ
1939, US, 117 mins, b/w
Dir: William Dieterle
Stars: Charles Laughton, Maureen O'Hara, Edmond O'Brien, Cedric Hardwicke
Rating: ★★★★★

Superb, compelling version of Victor Hugo's famous tale. Charles Laughton's pity-inspiring, ugly-but-moving portrait of the hunchback is one of the screen's most fantastic achievements, and he dominates the film, despite stiff competition from Cedric Hardwicke, as the tight-lipped Prefet de Paris. And there's a neat little cameo, too, from Walter Hampden as the king. The action scenes are fine (and teem with staggering detail), the photography excellent. One of the most memorable movies Hollywood ever made.

Hunchback of Notre Dame, The ⊙ Ⓥ
1996, US, 91 mins, colour
Dirs: Gary Trousdale, Kirk Wise
Voice Stars: Tom Hulce, Kevin Kline,

Demi Moore, Jason Alexander, Tony Jay, Mary Wickes
Rating: ★★★★

Rejoicing in the finding of another spectacular Gothic building, Notre Dame cathedral, to follow their castle in *Beauty and the Beast*, directors Trousdale and Wise create an animated version of Victor Hugo's classic that's almost as poignant as Charles Laughton's live-action version and certainly as exciting. The first 10 minutes, which contain superbly mobile pieces of scene-setting and story-opening, as well as the best song, are the equal of *Beauty*. The rest only reaches that Oscar-nominated standard in spots and the film rather lacks non-human characters, although there are three splendid cathedral gargoyles called Victor, Hugo and Laverne. Animation is awesome, if, like the action, quite dark and passionate by Disney standards, recalling the more frightening sections of *Fantasia*. Tom Hulce's voice sensitively elicits sympathy for Quasimodo in his unrequited love for the gypsy Esmeralda.

Hunger, The ● Ⓥ
1983, US, 99 mins, colour
Dir: Tony Scott
Stars: Catherine Deneuve, David Bowie, Susan Sarandon
Rating: ★★

In the hands of former TV commercials director Tony Scott, Catherine Deneuve is quite the sexiest bloodsucker ever to grace the screen. Her character has been around since the time of the pharaohs, while her partner in crime, David Bowie, is only 200 years old. But everything about this vampire story – dubbed 'chic trash' by the American critics – looks a million dollars thanks to elaborate art direction and shooting in permanently smoky rooms, creating a visual feast of light, colour and shadow. But where some Hammer vampire films took nudity no further than plunging cleavages, Susan Sarandon has to endure an explicit lesbian shower attack by Deneuve. The story tends towards silliness rather than creating a mood of terror, and the nonstop blood-letting appears excessive in the extreme.

Hungry Hill ○
1946, UK, 109 mins, b/w
Dir: Brian Desmond Hurst
Stars: Margaret Lockwood, Cecil Parker
Rating: ★★

Daphne du Maurier helped write the script of this long and often engrossing film version of her own epic novel about a long-standing, bitter feud between two Irish families. The film also gave early screen chances to several promising young players, among them Michael Denison, Siobhan McKenna, Dermot Walsh, Dan O'Herlihy and Jean Simmons.

Hunted O
(aka: The Stranger in Between)
1952, UK, 84 mins, b/w
Dir: Charles Crichton
Stars: Dirk Bogarde, Kay Walsh, Elizabeth Sellars, Jon Whiteley
Rating: ★★★

Suspenseful and decidedly different thriller. Dirk Bogarde has one of the best of his early screen roles as a murderer on the run – but no one really stands a chance against the brilliant performance of seven-year-old Jon Whiteley, later to win more laurels in *The Kidnappers*. Jon plays a little boy who runs away from home and meets up with a killer. The strange and fascinating relationship that springs up between the two fugitives makes compelling viewing.

Hunter, The ❶ Ⓥ
1980, US, 95 mins, colour
Dir: Buzz Kulik
Stars: Steve McQueen, Eli Wallach, Kathryn Harrold
Rating: ★★

Steve McQueen's last film is a likeable enough thriller that casts him as a true-life modern-day bounty hunter (the real Ralph Thorson makes a cameo appearance as a bartender) with a hankering after the old ways ('New things are no good,' he says). The action scenes are blazingly well presented by director Buzz Kulik, even if the plot has, as one contemporary critic put it, 'holes that Hannibal could have driven elephants through'. A sub-plot with Kathryn Harrold as the hero's pregnant girlfriend could comfortably have been dispensed with, leaving McQueen as his fans would like to remember him, as the man of constant action. The best sequence in the film takes McQueen to Chicago for the pursuit of a much-wanted fugitive.

Hunters, The O
1958, US, 108 mins, colour
Dir: Dick Powell
Stars: Robert Mitchum, Robert Wagner, Richard Egan, May Britt
Rating: ★★

Nothing very relaxing about this strong, taut and noise-filled story of a special jet fighter squadron on a secret mission during the Korean War. Director Dick Powell – the former song-and-dance and tough guy star – inserts a backbone of steel into this strong action film, which boasts some spectacular flying sequences breathtakingly captured in colour. Robert Mitchum is thoroughly convincing as the squadron's leader. Dialogue is less believable.

Hunt for Red October, The O Ⓥ
1990, US, 135 mins, colour
Dir: John McTiernan
Stars: Sean Connery, Alec Baldwin, Scott Glenn, Sam Neill, James Earl Jones, Richard Jordan
Rating: ★★

There's no snap in submarine suspense films any more. Time was when you could have heard a ping! drop as the metal warriors stalked each other beneath the surface. Now the nuclear leviathans are so huge (and John McTiernan's direction so slow) that it's no longer just galleons that are stately. Not even Sean Connery can salvage this waterlogged plot as a Russian sub skipper planning to defect (or is he with a fistful of nuclear weapons aboard his prototype vessel. The Russians, naturally not wanting to lose such a prize, let the Americans think that Connery is a madman about to blow the US apart. All of this cruises through many a doldrum until, thank goodness, a saboteur crops up at the end on the Russian sub and we get an exciting chase and shootout, after one or two minor members of the crew have been gunned down, perhaps for bad acting. For underwater suspense freaks only.

Hurricane, The O
1937, US, 110 mins, b/w
Dir: John Ford
Stars: Dorothy Lamour, Jon Hall, Mary Astor, Raymond Massey
Rating: ★★★

At the then-hefty cost of two million dollars, producer Samuel Goldwyn spared little expence in putting the best-selling novel by Charles Nordhoff and James Norman Hall (authors of *Mutiny On The Bounty*) up there on the screen. Director John Ford and special effects chief James Basevi gave him a devastating hurricane for climax, this sequence alone taking 400,000 dollars out of the movie's budget. Basevi would undoubtedly have won an Academy Award for his work but the special effects Oscar didn't come into being until

two years later. Dorothy Lamour sings 'Moon Over Manukura' to solidify her growing reputation as the maiden bursting into sarong.

Hurricane Smith O
1952, US, 89 mins, colour
Dir: Jerry Hopper
Stars: John Ireland, Yvonne De Carlo, James Craig, Lyle Bettger
Rating: ★★★

Glorious piece of escapism, all action and colour, about a group of thieves and soldiers of fortune who search for sunken treasure in the South Seas. Typical of the Pine-Thomas adventure films made at Paramount in the Forties and Fifties, but better than most, with a sturdy cast that includes John Ireland, Forrest Tucker, Yvonne de Carlo, James Craig, Richard Arlen and Lyle Bettger. Not to be confused with 1941 and 1991 films with the same title. Oddly the 1952 film was based on a novel called *Hurricane Williams*!

Hurry Sundown ❶
1967, US, 146 mins, colour
Dir: Otto Preminger
Stars: Michael Caine, Jane Fonda, John Phillip Law, Faye Dunaway, Burgess Meredith
Rating: ★

A laughable tale of racial bigotry that marked a low point in the career of director Otto Preminger. Despite a top-drawer cast, it is sunk by many factors, among them Michael Caine's inept attempt at an American Deep South accent, a tediously slow first hour and a crazy guns-blazing finale that suggests a pantomime version of Greek tragedy.

Husbands and Wives ❶ Ⓥ
1992, US, 107 mins, colour
Dir: Woody Allen
Stars: Woody Allen, Mia Farrow, Blythe Danner, Liam Neeson, Judy Davis, Juliette Lewis
Rating: ★★

As you'd expect, Mia Farrow and Woody Allen's last film together is way too close for comfort. A funny-sad look at the rocky state of marriage, it makes you laugh and smile wryly from time to time, but also gets on your nerves a bit, with characters repeating the same lines several times over (like in life, sure, but does this make it better?). And the bewildering hand-held camera will surely give you eye strain. Woody tells Mia that he has 'always had this penchant for kamikaze women'. She retorts that, 'You use sex to express every emotion

H

except love'. This is far from the ideal goofy romanticism of their first film *A Midsummer Night's Sex Comedy*, and their parting at the end, and Woody's falling for (but declining) a 20-year-old girl, express, more than anywhere else, lives played out on screen over an 11-year period. Good supporting performances from Judy Davis, typically abrasive, Juliette Lewis (as Allen's younger flight of fancy) and especially Lysette Anthony, amazingly good as the astrological bimbo who takes up with one of the splitting husbands.

Hush... Hush, Sweet Charlotte ● ⓥ
1964, US, 133 mins, b/w
Dir: Robert Aldrich
Stars: Bette Davis, Olivia de Havilland, Joseph Cotten, Agnes Moorehead, Cecil Kellaway, Mary Astor
Rating: ★★★★

A splendidly macabre film thriller (the same director's follow-up to *What Ever Happened to Baby Jane?*) that commits viewers to sit chewing their fingernails for more than two hours. Bette Davis and Olivia de Havilland are admirably enigmatic; and Agnes Moorehead, too, makes an indelible mark on the film as the weird house-keeper. She was Oscar-nominated. Watch for Bruce Dern (as the murder victim at the start) and George Kennedy, both taking early film roles.

Hustle ●
1975, US, 120 mins, colour
Dir: Robert Aldrich
Stars: Burt Reynolds, Catherine Deneuve, Ben Johnson, Eddie Albert
Rating: ★

Not exactly a film that celebrates the finer qualities of the American cinema. In fact, Burt Reynolds' performance as the cynical police lieutenant at the centre of the story is the only saving grace of this routine, facile police thriller in which director Robert Aldrich never misses a chance to emphasise the sordid and the unnecessary. Catherine Deneuve, Eddie Albert, Ernest Borgnine and Ben Johnson are also involved, none of them to any great effect, with Johnson offering one of the few poor performances he has ever given. At the foot of the cast, a young Robert Englund, later Freddy Krueger in the *Elm Street* films, makes one of his earliest appearances, as a hold-up man.

Hustler, The ◐ ⓥ
1961, US, 135 mins, b/w
Dir: Robert Rossen

Stars: Paul Newman, Jackie Gleason, Piper Laurie, George C Scott, Murray Hamilton
Rating: ★★★★

A grim, tragic drama in a low key, but terribly gripping, uplifting and moving in spite of the terrible personal tragedies it unfolds. And it has three magnetically lifelike performances. Paul Newman, as the young pool player determined to beat the great Minnesota Fats (Jackie Gleason at his most phlegmatic) is remarkably compelling, an all-too-vulnerable blue-eyed bombshell who draws one with him wherever he goes. Less expected, judging by her Universal frivolities of the Fifties, is the brilliant portrayal by Piper Laurie of the crippled girl, desperate for a love that is more than ephemeral, and suicidal when she facts to obtain it. Completing a dynamic trio of real people is George C Scott's incisive, keen-edged performance as Newman's hawk-cruel, relentless manager. The final scene between Newman and Scott is a masterpiece in smouldering, if inert, intensity.

I Accuse! ○
1957, UK, 99 mins, b/w
Dir: Jose Ferrer
Stars: Jose Ferrer, Anton Walbrook, Viveca Lindfors, Emlyn Williams
Rating: ★★

L'Affaire Dreyfus was one of the most notorious scandals in the whole of French history and this film is one of several that have dealt with the subject. Jose Ferrer directed and took – with distinction – the central role of the Jewish-French army officer Alfred Dreyfus, convicted of treason on a trumped-up charge. With a screenplay by Gore Vidal, the result is a carefully detailed reconstruction of events that is honest, if sometimes a little too cold. However, some of the courtroom scenes are compelling.

I Am a Camera ○
1955, UK, 98 mins, b/w
Dir: Henry Cornelius
Stars: Julie Harris, Laurence Harvey, Shelley Winters
Rating: ★★

Kaleidoscopic, atmospheric, but rather irritating nostalgia piece from the stories of Christopher Isherwood, later remade in musical form as *Cabaret*. Successfully creating a portrait of a nation falling into moral decay, the film has its grim moments, but there's also a lot to laugh about, especially in the sequences featuring the determinedly amoral Sally Bowles, played close to the edge of tragedy by America's Julie Harris.

I Am a Fugitive from a Chain Gang ○
1932, US, 93 mins, b/w
Dir: Mervyn LeRoy
Stars: Paul Muni, Glenda Farrell, Helen Vinson, Preston Foster
Rating: ★★★★★

This harrowing prison drama caused great controversy when it was released in 1932, based as it was on the true-bfe memoirs of Robert E Burns. Warner Brothers, the only studio brave enough to take on such dramas, created a classic, elements of which have been freely borrowed by other film-makers ever since. Paul Muni gives a powerhouse central performance as the innocent man sentenced to 10 years hard labour. He escapes and starts to re-build his life, but is betrayed by his shrewish wife. Persuaded he will be pardoned if he gives himself up, he goes back to the prison only to suffer brutally at the hands of the warders and have his sentence increased. The grim realism of *Chain Gang* (which was echoed in the later *Black Fury*) was at variance with the escapism offered by other Hollywood studios in the 1930s and, unlike *Black Fury*, it was a great critical and commercial success.

I Am the Law ○

1938, US, 83 mins, b/w
Dir: Alexander Hall
Stars: Edward G Robinson, Otto Kruger, John Beal, Wendy Barrie
Rating: ★★★

Edward G Robinson is on the right side of the law for once (he even dances!) in a story of a crusading law professor who sets out to expose racketeers operating in his city. Surprisingly from Columbia rather than Robinson's home studio, Warners, the plot is familiar stuff, but smoothly done and plausibly written by the prolific Jo Swerling.

I Believe in You ○

1952, UK, 91 mins, b/w
Dir: Basil Dearden
Stars: Cecil Parker, Celia Johnson, Joan Collins, Godfrey Tearle, Laurence Harvey
Rating: ★★★

Ace comedy studio Ealing went dramatic in this very popular film about the work of probation officers. Ealing were able to make much publicity mileage out of the fact that the film gave early chances to two young hopefuls – Joan Collins and Laurence Harvey. They, and Harry Fowler, are perfectly cast as a trio of young people in trouble, as are Cecil Parker and Celia Johnson as the probation officers. Despite the rather cosy view of probation work, the characters and situation spring to life and grip the attention throughout, the performances making us care about the fates of the characters. Cleverly made by director Basil Dearden, who also had a hand in the script.

Ice Cold in Alex ○ ⓥ

(aka: Desert Attack)
1958, UK, 129 mins, b/w
Dir: J Lee Thompson
Stars: John Mills, Sylvia Syms, Anthony Quayle, Harry Andrews
Rating: ★★★

Long but gripping war film, surprisingly based on true events. Much mileage was gained at the time by scenes of John Mills unbuttoning his stiff upper lip to do the same with nurse Sylvia Syms in the desert, but in fact the film's appeal leans more on the emotions and suspense stirred by the interrelationship of all four main characters, as they dice with death at the hands of Germans, minefields and sandstorms and dream of ice-cold beer in Alexandria.

Iceland ○

(aka: Katina)
1942, US, 79 mins, b/w
Dir: Bruce Humberstone
Stars: Sonja Henie, John Payne, Jack Oakie, Osa Massen
Rating: ★★

Wartime flag-waving and such tunes as 'Let's Bring New Glory to Old Glory' rather date this Sonja Henie ice-musical, although the star's Hawaiian hula routine is a hit, and the score does also include 'There Will Never Be Another You', 'It's a Lovers' Knot' and 'You Can't Say No to a Soldier', perhaps not the best advice for singing co-star Joan Merrill to give to the girls back home. John Payne and Jack Oakie, so often Alice Faye's co-stars, do good back-up work here for the star, with Sammy Kaye and His Band providing an enthusiastic backdrop.

Ice Palace ○

1960, US, 143 mins, colour
Dir: Vincent Sherman
Stars: Richard Burton, Robert Ryan, Martha Hyer, Carolyn Jones
Rating: ★★

Edna Ferber's doorstep-sized novel, one of the first of the blockbusters, here filmed with Burton and Ryan as the two fishery tycoons slugging it out during Alaska's struggle to become a state of the Union. Burton comes up with a Welsh-American accent and some minor James Cagney impressions, but it's never convincing.

Ice Pirates, The ○

1984, US, 94 mins, colour
Dir: Stewart Raffill
Stars: Robert Urich, Mary Crosby, Anjelica Huston
Rating: ★★

This spoof on the *Star Wars* type of sci-fi spectacular suffers from an appallingly low budget that doesn't allow the special effects to be all that special. Robert (*Spenser for Hire*) Ulrch is our firm-jawed hero, a pirate who deals in the future's most precious commodity – water. The adventure starts when he agrees to help Mary Crosby, whose lost father has reportedly found a huge supply of water. It's a sort of low-buck *Robin Hood* of the spaceways and providing you can accept the low production values, okay. Your kids will love it, so set the video recorder. Anjelica Huston has one of her pre-stardom roles in this one.

Ice Station Zebra ○ ⓥ

1968, US, 148 mins, colour
Dir: John Sturges
Stars: Rock Hudson, Ernest Borgnine, Patrick McGoohan, Jim Brown
Rating: ★★★

Intrigue and adventure come in equal measure in this exciting adaptation of Alastair MacLean's Arctic thriller. Rock Hudson stars as the leader of a submarine expedition to trace a downed Soviet satellite which contains photos of sensitive US and Russian missile sites. But the sub is damaged and it is clear there's a traitor on board. Is it Russian defector Ernest Borgnine US captain Jim Brown or British naval officer Patrick McGoohan? Things come to a head when they reach Ice Station Zebra, a weather station in the frozen wastes, only to find everyone there has been killed. Muscular playing by all the principals coupled with excellent photography and special effects make this a thrilling yarn even if the plot and counter-plot isn't up to John Le Carré standards. Possibly a little violent for younger children.

I Confess ○ ⓥ

1953, US, 94 mins, b/w
Dir: Alfred Hitchcock
Stars: Montgomery Clift, Anne Baxter, Brian Aherne, Karl Malden, O E Hasse
Rating: ★★★

A rather slower than usual slice of suspense from Alfred Hitchcock, though the climax may still take you by surprise. The central situation isn't new: a murderer confesses to a priest and then refuses to give himself up to the police. But it's given intensity by the performances of Karl Malden as a detective, and O E Hasse, as the refugee who confesses to the crime. More sober portrayals from Montgomery Clift (as the priest), Anne Baxter and Brian Aherne. Hitchcock himself makes his customary appearance. Whereabouts? Just watch the skyline!

I

I Could Go on Singing ○
1963, UK, 100 mins, colour
Dir: Ronald Neame
Stars: Judy Garland, Dirk Bogarde
Rating: ★★★

The critics clapped after a preview of this film, principally because of an emotional bomb of a performance by Judy Garland, cast in a role which sadly reflected her own life. Dirk Bogarde offers sympathetic support. The rest is nothing special, but Garland's singing is.

i.d. ● ⓥ
1994, UK, 110 mins, colour
Dir: Philip Davis
Stars: Reece Dinsdale, Saskia Reeves, Sean Pertwee, Richard Graham
Rating: ★★

There haven't been many films about football hooliganism: this is a genuine attempt to capture the rush of adrenalin and glorification of violence that drives the soccer thug to kill and maim his fellow fan. And, for the first half, as it were it goes well. Four policemen go undercover to crack a core hooligan ring and the worse rackets that may lie behind it. One of them, John (Reece Dinsdale) becomes overpowered by the seething violence around him until it takes over his life and he is transformed into what he was hunting. Once there's the suspicion the undercover squad may be rumbled, the film's grip starts to slide away, and it becomes progressively less convincing. Dinsdale's policeman scores best in his moments of high violence but his times of flagellating self-pity are good only for a giggle. Sean Pertwee is nobody's idea of a thug leader and Richard Graham, as Dinsdale's partner, is hardly less unlikely. Both men are too tidy and over-age to convince. Saskia Reeves is fine as the local barmaid, even if she inevitably takes her clothes off in the course of the action, but senior policemen are rather less credible.

I'd Climb the Highest Mountain ○
1951, US, 89 mins, colour
Dir: Henry King
Stars: Susan Hayward, William Lundigan
Rating: ★★★

This story of a travelling preacher in the early 1900s provided William Lundigan with his biggest movie role. A strapping, fair-haired six-footer, Lundigan came up the hard way – supporting roles in the late Thirties, war service, B-picture leads from the mid-Forties. Here he's treated to a first-rate

supporting cast that includes Alexander Knox, Lynn Bari, Barbara Bates and Gene Lockhart.

Idiot's Delight ○
1939, US, 105 mins, b/w
Dir: Clarence Brown
Stars: Clark Gable, Norma Shearer, Edward Arnold, Charles Coburn, Burgess Meredith
Rating: ★★★

Nothing is more delightful in this thoughtful adaptation of his own pacifist play by Robert Sherwood than the sight of old jug-ears himself, Clark Gable, singing and dancing as the front-man for a six-girl dance team. Although softened for the screen, Sherwood's Pulitzer Prize-winning work still has enough bite to expose the idiocy and pointlessness of militarism while keeping our interest in its story of two of life's failures from the more obscure corners of show business. Good supporting performances from Charles Coburn and Laura Hope Crews (later that year to play Aunt Pittypat in *Gone With the Wind*), but it's Gable's deliberately awful entertainer that you'll remember.

I Don't Care Girl, The ○
1953, US, 78 mins, colour
Dir: Lloyd Bacon
Stars: Mitzi Gaynor, Bob Graham, David Wayne, Oscar Levant
Rating: ★★

The sparkling Mitzi Gaynor series of musicals for 20th Century-Fox *Bloodhounds of Broadway*, *Golden Girl* and *Down Among the Sheltering Palms* were others – didn't quite make her into the star they should have. This one is a snappy, colourful biography of torch singer Eva Tanguay, and its only faults are that it's too short at only 78 minutes, and has a weak leading man in Bob Graham. Oscar Levant tickles the ivories in his own droll style, and Miss Gaynor is enchanting in the title role.

I Dood It ⊙
(aka: By Hook or By Crook)
1943, US, 102 mins, b/w
Dir: Vincente Minnelli
Stars: Red Skelton, Eleanor Powell, John Hodiak, Lena Horne
Rating: ★★

A loose adaptation of Buster Keaton's silent classic *Spite Marriage*, the film is just a lengthy vehicle for the clowning of Red Skelton and the dance artistry of Eleanor Powell, whose climactic number, 'Swinging the Jinx Away',

looks suspiciously like the big routine from her earlier hit 'Born to Dance'. Vincente Minnelli (his second film as director) inherited the movie from other hands, and got the most from the musical greats in the cast, who also include Lena Horne and Jimmy Dorsey and His Orchestra.

If ... ● ⓥ
1968, UK, 111 mins, colour
Dir: Lindsay Anderson
Stars: Malcolm McDowell, David Wood, Christine Noonan, Richard Warwick
Rating: ★★★★

Lindsay Anderson's weird but powerful indictment of the public school system (and the country as a whole?) made a star of Malcolm McDowell in a role he recreated, a few years on, in the same director's *O Lucky Man!* and again for Anderson in *Britannia Hospital*. Here he plays a sixth form boy in whose mind symbolism and fantasy gradually take over from reality, as they do in the film, the first half of which is a kind of up-dated *Tom Brown's Schooldays*, with public school ritual being observed down to the last hideous Stone-Age detail.

If He Hollers, Let Him Go! ◐
1968, US, 106 mins, colour
Dir: Charles Martin
Stars: Dana Wynter, Raymond St Jacques, Kevin McCarthy, Barbara McNair, Arthur O'Connell, John Russell
Rating: ★

Kevin McCarthy and Dana Wynter, the stars of the brilliant science-fiction classic *Invasion of the Body Snatchers* in 1956, were reunited in this intricately plotted thriller with a racialist slant. Lightning, alas, doesn't strike twice for them, and film fans will find most interest in the appearance of two handsome ex-stars, John Russell and James Craig, as a sheriff and police chief respectively.

If I Had a Million ⊙
1932, US, 88 mins, b/w
Dir: Norman Taurog, Stephen Roberts, Norman McLeod, James Cruze, William A Seiter, H Bruce Humberstone
Stars: Charles Laughton, W C Fields, Gary Cooper, Charlie Ruggles, George Raft, Jack Oakie
Rating: ★★★★

Paramount pumped the considerable might of their roster of stars and directors into this bitter-sweet (mostly sweet) compilation of stories about people who unexpectedly come into a million dollars apiece. The Charles

Laughton and W C Fields stories are delightful and you'll spot Gary Cooper, George Raft, Jack Oakie, Charles Ruggles, Frances Dee, Mary Boland and many more familiar star faces from the early Thirties.

If I Were King ○
1938, US, 97 mins, b/w
Dir: Frank Lloyd
Stars: Ronald Colman, Frances Dee, Basil Rathbone, Ellen Drew
Rating: ★★★

One of Ronald Colman's least-seen films, although it's by no means unattractive and, chronologically speaking, follows two of his greatest hits, *Lost Horizon* and *The Prisoner of Zenda*. It's a remake of John Barrymore's 1927 film *The Beloved Rogue* and casts Colman as François Villlon, the 15th-century French adventurer and poet. The star underlines his reputation as a swashbuckler in the action scenes, while only Colman's velvet tones could get away so well with speaking lines in verse. An almost unrecognisable Basil Rathbone matches him line for line as the sly King Louis XI. In later years, the story would be made into a musical as *The Vagabond King*.

If Winter Comes ○
1947, US, 105 mins, b/w
Dir: Victor Saville
Stars: Deborah Kerr, Walter Pidgeon, Janet Leigh, Angela Lansbury, Binnie Barnes
Rating: ★★

Lucky Walter Pidgeon is surrounded by female co-stars (headed by Deborah Kerr), who no doubt helped to cheer him up while making this sombre story of a publisher accused of driving a young girl to suicide. Lots of acting class in the supporting cast which includes Dame May Whitty, Angela Lansbury, Binnie Barnes, Janet Leigh, Virginia Keiley and Rene Ray.

I Know Where I'm Going! ○ Ⓥ
1945, UK, 91 mins, b/w
Dir: Michael Powell, Emeric Pressburger
Stars: Wendy Hiller, Roger Livesey, Pamela Brown, Petula Clark, Finlay Currie
Rating: ★★★★

There are some very odd things about this romantic drama, as you might expect from the unconventional filmmaking team of Michael Powell and Emeric Pressburger. Their script abounds in wit, charm and eccentric characters. Most of these are female,

including Wendy Hiller, terrific as the heroine who thinks she knows where she's going, Catherine Lacey, Petula Clark and particularly Pamela Brown who gets a gem of a role as a decidedly individual Scots lassie. Nicely shot on location in the Scottish islands: cameraman Erwin Hiller somehow makes it look as atmospheric in black-and-white as it undoubtedly would have been in colour.

I Like it Like That ●
1994, US, 110 mins, colour
Dir: Darrell Martin
Stars: Lauren Velez, Jon Seda, Griffin Dunne
Rating: ★★

Black/Latino marrieds Lisette and Chino have a great sex life and three kids, so something obviously has to happen to split them up so that they can get back together by the climax. That something turns out to be a blackout that throws Chino into jail when he tries to take advantage of looters by taking a stereo. The predictable plot developments that follow contain a few amusing moments, especially when the marrieds compare their respective affairs – hers a couple of lines, his a couple of pages – but pretty wearing most of the time in spite of a star turn by *West Side Story* Oscar-winner Rita Moreno as the world's first Puerto Rican Jewish mother. *Molto* swearing and screeching will wear your sympathies pretty thin by the end.

I'll Be Seeing You ○
1944, US, 83 mins, b/w
Dir: William Dieterle
Stars: Ginger Rogers, Joseph Cotten, Shirley Temple
Rating: ★★★

This polished weepie could hardly fail to be a success: Shirley Temple was making her first picture as a teenager after a fabulous career as Hollywood's top child star; Ginger Rogers, too, had a string of successes behind her as a dramatic actress (including the Oscar-winning *Kitty Foyle*) after the great Astaire-Rogers musicals of the Thirties. Rogers skilfully understates her role as a woman convict falling in love (with Joseph Cotten) while on parole, and ensures audience sympathy every step of the tear-stained way.

I'll Be Your Sweetheart ○
1945, UK, 104 mins, b/w
Dir: Val Guest
Stars: Margaret Lockwood, Vic Oliver,

Michael Rennie, Peter Graves
Rating: ★★★

A British musical on a theme much favoured by Hollywood – the lives of writers of popular songs – in this case three of them, at the turn of the century, named Le Brunn, Kahn and Kelly: an unlikely-sounding trio. On a more serious note, the plot also concerns the fight to establish copyright and crush private publishers. Vic Oliver, that Jack Benny of the British halls, plays Kahn. Bewhiskered Moore Marriott, so often a figure of fun in British farces, typically with Will Hay, portrays the tragic figure of Le Brunn. Margaret Lockwood's role, as a songstress of the music-halls, gives her a chance to sing such favourites as 'The Honeysuckle and the Bee', 'Oh, Mr Porter', 'Little Wooden Hut' and 'Sooner or Later'.

Illegal ○
1955, US, 88 mins, b/w
Dir: Lewis Allen
Stars: Edward G Robinson, Nina Foch, Albert Dekker, Hugh Marlowe, Jayne Mansfield, DeForest Kelley
Rating: ★★★

There s an early glimpse of a 22-year-old Jayne Mansfield as the surprise witness in this remake of a 1932 gangster courtroom drama originally filmed as *The Mouthpiece*, and then remade in 1940 as *The Man Who Talked Too Much*. Warners did all three versions, and this marked Edward G Robinson's return to their studio after years away. Tough, no-nonsense stuff, but lacking the vital drive of the star's Thirties vehicles.

I'll Get You
See: Escape Route

I'll Get You for This ○
(aka: Lucky Nick Cain)
1951, UK, 83 mins, b/w
Dir: Joseph M Newman
Stars: George Raft, Coleen Gray
Rating: ★★

George Raft, more usually seen as a denizen of dark corners of the underworld, looks somewhat ill-at-ease in the open-air Italian locations of this James Hadley Chase thriller which casts him as an American gambler (hence the film's alternative title, *Lucky Nick Cain*) who gets involved with a counterfeit gang. Enzo Staiola, the little boy from *Bicycle Thieves*, is a lovable urchin, helping Raft round up the gang while effortlessly stealing scenes from under his nose.

I

Ill-Met by Moonlight ○
(aka: Night Ambush)
1956, UK, 100 mins, b/w
Dir: Michael Powell, Emeric Pressburger
Stars: Dirk Bogarde, Marius Goring,
David Oxley, Cyril Cusack
Rating: ★★★

Slightly different from the usual run of
war films, this British-made adventure
has Dirk Bogarde as one of the British
officers who engineer the wartime kidnapping of a German general (Marius
Goring) who commands 30,000 enemy
paratroopers in Crete. The film's
strong vein of humour doesn't stop it
whipping up plenty of excitement. It's
a true story.

I'll Never Forget What's 'is Name ◐
1967, UK, 99 mins, colour
Dir: Michael Winner
Stars: Orson Welles, Oliver Reed, Carol
White, Wendy Craig
Rating: ★★★

With its jump-cut pacing and frenetic
camera motion, Michael Winner's savage satire on the swinging Sixties in
general and the advertising industry in
particular is clearly a film of its time.
But even if it does show its age, it's
true to say that Peter Draper's acerbic
script offers plenty of wicked insights
amidst the visual confusion. Most of
the best lines are grabbed greedily by
Orson Welles' towering advertising
chief who tries to bully Oliver Reed's
resentful whizzkid into working for
him again. Carol White and Wendy
Craig are touchingly vulnerable as
prim secretary and ignored wife, and
the climactic 'award-winning commercial' is a cleverly constructed
monument to appalling taste.

Illustrated Man, The ◐
1969, US, 103 mins, colour
Dir: Jack Smight
Stars: Rod Steiger, Claire Bloom
Rating: ★★

A brave, and to some degree a successful attempt to transfer the imaginative
fantasy of Ray Bradbury to the screen.
Although not quite fulfilling the
promise of its early scenes, it is by any
standards a strange and compelling
film, with a powerful virtuoso performance by Rod Steiger as the man
entirely covered with beautiful tattoos,
apart from one bare patch.

I Love Melvin ⊙
1952, US, 77 mins, colour
Dir: Don Weis
Stars: Donald O'Connor, Debbie

Reynolds, Una Merkel, Richard
Anderson
Rating: ★★

A minor but fresh and enjoyable
MGM musical, with good tunes, an
entertaining and, for once, original
story, and bouncy performances from
Debbie Reynolds and Donald
O'Connor, two of the youngest veterans (then 20 and 27 respectively) on
the MGM lot. The characters are all
likeable and well-drawn and the
Technicolor photography by expert
Hollywood cameraman Harold
Rosson decorates the settings in gay,
springlike colours. For such a short
running time, it's strange that some of
the film is so lacking in pace – a black
mark to director Don Weis. But its
people are such a pleasure to be with,
that that's easily forgiven.

I Love My Wife ◐
1970, US, 95 mins, colour
Dir: Mel Stewart
Stars: Elliott Gould, Brenda Vaccaro
Rating: ★★

A sex-orientated comedy that varies
from the serious to the satirical, and
from whiplash comedy to flaccid farce.
How anyone could leave the delicious
Brenda Vaccaro, even with her hair in
curlers, for the plastic Angel
Tompkins, is quite beyond me. The
script (by Robert Kaufman) does best
with its incidental lines. One remembers especially Elliott Gould's *cri de
coeur* as his wife and mother-in-law do
battle around him: 'I have three weeks
to live – four if I stay in bed.'

I Love Trouble ○ ⓥ
1994, US, 123 mins, colour
Dir: Charles Shyer
Stars: Julia Roberts, Nick Nolte, Saul
Rubinek, Robert Loggia
Rating: ★★

Although Julia Roberts and Nick Nolte
have charm to spare, this throwback to
comedy-thrillers of the Sixties never
quite hits the mark. There's a microfilm, of course, and the bad guys want
it. What they don't bargain for is that
the rail crash they caused to cloak the
microfilm holder's murder is about to
develop into a battlefield between two
reporters, each determined to root out
the truth. While the newshounds are
inevitably cracking the case and falling
in love, there's some mildly amusing
banter between them, some serviceable
suspense scenes and the inevitable
shootout at the end. Director Charles
Shyer has seen *Charade*, *Arabesque* and
the like, but, despite 'wipes' from scene

to scene, he hasn't quite got the pace
right. Roberts is close to being Audrey
Hepburn and Nolte within hailing distance of Cary Grant, even if the scene
where they ogle each other through
the keyhole of an adjoining door
would have been beneath Hepburn
and Grant's dignity.

I Love You Again ○
1940, US, 110 mins, b/w
Dir: W S Van Dyke II
Stars: William Powell, Myrna Loy
Rating: ★★★

This delightful romantic comedy reunited William Powell, Myrna Loy
and eirector W S Van Dyke II but was
in a different vein from their classic
Thin Man series together. Loy is about
to divorce respectable, deadly dull
Powell when an accident unlocks him
from nine years of amnesia and reveals
a raffish Lothario with distinctly criminal tendencies. Highly entertaining
confusion results, directed at a rattling
pace by Van Dyke from a bubbly
script spiced with some choice exchanges: Powell to Loy, 'You turn my
head.' Loy's retort, 'I've often wished I
could turn your head – on a spit over
a slow fire.' The performances sparkle
and Gene Ruggiero's editing keeps the
film moving at a perfect pace.

I Love You, Alice B Toklas ◐
1968, US, 93 mins, colour
Dir: Hy Averback
Stars: Peter Sellers, Jo Van Fleet, Leigh
Taylor-Young, Joyce Van Patten
Rating: ★★★

Spasmodic Peter Sellers comedy in
which he plays a businessman inducted into the world of 'pot' parties by an
attractive young hippie girl who bakes
him Marijuana cookies. Joyce Van
Patten is hilarious as Sellers' crow-
voiced fiancée.

I Love You to Death ◐
1990, US, 97 mins, colour
Dir: Lawrence Kasdan
Stars: Kevin Kline, Tracey Ullman, Joan
Plowright, William Hurt, Keanu Reeves,
River Phoenix
Rating: ★★

Quirky, slow and as strange as the
true-life case on which it's based, this is
a star-studded study of a philandering,
food-loving Italian (Kevin Kline) and
the wife (Tracey Ullman) and mother-
in-law (Joan Plowright) who decide to
do away with him. Stir in Piver
Phoenix as their helper, William Hurt
and Keanu Reeves as stoned-out amateur assassins and unbilled Phoebe

Cates (Kline's real-life wife) and you have a mixture that tickles the ribs but never produces a lethal dose of laughter. The succession of failed attempts on Kline's life should be absolutely hilarious, but the comedy is often too dark and/or flatly directed to be really funny.

I'm All Right, Jack ○ Ⓥ
1959, UK, 105 mins, b/w
Dir: John Boulting
Stars: Ian Carmichael, Peter Sellers, Terry-Thomas, Richard Attenborough, Dennis Price, Margaret Rutherford
Rating: ★★★

The Boulting Brothers' greatest hit – an anarchic swipe at trade unions and their bosses. It contains Peter Sellers' first unsympathetic portrayal, as the bigoted shop steward, and proved a tremendous box-office hit. A bit too serious and direct for its own good at times, but delightful performances from Ian Carmichael, Terry-Thomas, Irene Handl, and especially Liz Fraser as Cynthia Kite, the rave of the shop floor, who sets her cap at Carmichael.

I Married a Witch ○ Ⓥ
1942, US, 76 mins, b/w
Dir: René Clair
Stars: Fredric March, Veronica Lake, Robert Benchley, Susan Hayward, Cecil Kellaway, Elizabeth Patterson
Rating: ★★★★

French director René Claire made several delightful films during his enforced World War Two stay in Hollywood, and this is among the most fondly remembered. Veronica Lake (never better) and Cecil Kellaway play two 300-year-old sorcerers who come back to plague the life out of the politician (Fredric March) descended from the man who originally had them burned. Kellaway, as the prototype of leprechauns, ghosts, angels and all kinds of benevolent spirits human and inhuman he was to play through the Forties, is a joy as the old sorcerer who looks forward with glee to burning down the town's hotel and goes wild with fury when shrunk and trapped inside a bottle. Robert Benchley, the Hollywood humourist so popular in short films, is almost as good as the amiable doctor quite baffled by it all. Inventive, innovative filmmaking.

Imitation General ○
1958, US, 88 mins, colour
Dir: George Marshall
Stars: Glenn Ford, Red Buttons, Taina

Eig, Dean Jones
Rating: ★★

Veteran director George Marshall (he made *Destry Rides Again*) maintains a fast pace in this war comedy-drama about a sergeant who decides to 'promote' himself to general. Dean Jones, later a regular star of comedies from the Disney studio, is seen to advantage as a zestful corporal.

Imitation of Life ○
1959, US, 124 mins, colour
Dir: Douglas Sirk
Stars: Lana Turner, John Gavin, Dan O'Herlihy, Sandra Dee
Rating: ★★

Glossily presented but wholly unpersuasive. Lana Turner suffers in sable but her character, like the screenplay's appeal to our emotions, is almost entirely synthetic. Director Douglas Sirk does tremendous work under the circumstances and it was largely thanks to his efforts that the film was one of the top moneymakers of its year. A remake of the equally tear-soaked 1934 original with Claudette Colbert, which involved you more in its characters.

Immaculate Conception ● Ⓥ
1991, UK, 120 mins, colour
Dir: Jamil Dehlavi
Stars: James Wilby, Melissa Leo, Shabana Azmi, Zia Mohyeddin
Rating: ★★

This culture-clash drama is as dry and arid as the acting of Merchant-Ivory favourite James Wilby at its core. He is a wildlife conservationist married to a Jewish-American daughter of a US Senator and living in 1988 Pakistan. The couple are so desperate for a child of their own that they visit a eunuch-run shrine reputed to have a cure for infertility. But things take a rum turn when they're slipped the local equivalent of a Mickey Finn ... Director Jamil Dehlavi tries to place this story within the context of political upheaval and conflict. But despite the best intentions, it emerges as a fairly indigestible curate's egg.

Immortal Sergeant, The ○
1943, US, 91 mins, b/w
Dir: John M Stahl
Stars: Henry Fonda, Maureen O'Hara, Thomas Mitchell
Rating: ★★

Although not much liked by its star Henry Fonda ('It was a silly picture,' he told an interviewer testily. 'You

wanna hear the plot? I won the war single-handed!'), this is actually quite a poetic war film (set in North Africa), as one might have expected from that great romantic director John M Stahl, who had previously made such classic weepies as *Back Street*, *Magnificent Obsession* and *Imitation Life*. Not only do the film's emotive elements work well, but Lamar Trotti's screenplay supplies plenty of action too.

I'm No Angel ○
1933, US, 84 mins, b/w
Dir: Wesley Ruggles
Stars: Mae West, Cary Grant, Edward Arnold
Rating: ★★★★

The film in which Mae West really twisted the censor by the tail, as well as consolidating her first big success in *She Done Him Wrong*. She was never allowed quite the same freedom of dialogue (written by herself) after this, but meantime, there are many aphorisms to treasure as Mae plays a carnival dancer who tames lions – and men – as a sideline. 'I like sophisticated men to take me out,' she tells young society swell Kent Taylor. 'I'm not really sophisticated,' he tells her. Growls Mae. 'You're not really out yet, either.' And that's really her in the lions' cage, to the complete dismay of the film's producers, who went purple with anxiety at the thought of their high-priced star in the big cats' dangerous company.

I, Mobster ◐
1958, US, 80 mins, b/w
Dir: Roger Corman
Stars: Steve Cochran, Lita Milan, Robert Strauss, Grant Withers
Rating: ★★★

A typically zestful film from director Roger Corman from the period when he was one of the most prolific (37 movies in 10 years) and best makers of low-budget exploitation pictures largely aimed at the young drive-in cinema audience. Here he revives the kind of gangster opus popular in the Thirties, executing it with pace and narrative drive and drawing from Steve Cochran in the title role one of his best later portrayals.

I, Monster ●
1970, UK, 75 mins, colour
Dir: Stephen Weeks
Stars: Christopher Lee, Peter Cushing, Richard Hurndall
Rating: ★★

Director Stephen Weeks was one of two young British film-makers to

I

emerge in the horror field in the late Sixties (the other, Michael Reeves, died at 25). This was Weeks' second film – at the age of 22 – and it turns out to be a very intelligent and largely faithful reworking of *Dr Jekyll and Mr Hyde*. Christopher Lee gives one of his best performances in one of the best parts that the cinema of terror has offered him in a 30-year career. His portrayal and the director's very authentic-seeming Victorian settings, full of amusingly bizarre bric-a-brac, are both much in contrast to the lurid approach taken by most latter-day film makers to Stevenson's famous double-identity chiller. Tedious at times, though.

Impact ○
1949, US, 111 mins, b/w
Dir: Arthur Lubin
Stars: Brian Donlevy, Ella Raines, Charles Coburn, Helen Walker
Rating: ★★★

Very long and twisty thriller with a biting performance from the underrated Helen Walker, offering us another of her waspish wives, and stealing the distaff honours from the silky Ella Raines. Good background music and an ingenious plot boost this tale of a man who finds himself declared dead in mistake for the person who tried to kill him.

Importance of Being Earnest, The ○ ⓥ
1952, UK, 95 mins, colour
Dir: Anthony Asquith
Stars: Michael Redgrave, Michael Denison, Edith Evans, Dorothy Tutin, Margaret Rutherford, Joan Greenwood
Rating: ★★★★

Oscar Wilde's timeless comic stage satire about the efforts of two men-about-town to get hitched was given top drawer treatment by director Anthony Asquith. He cast Michael Redgrave (who had given one of his finest performances the previous year in Asquith's *The Browning Version*) as one of the suitors, but it is Edith Evans' dragon of a Lady Bracknell who dominates the film. Her indignant cry of '...a handbag?' entered screen history as one of the all-time classic lines and her performance still ranks as the one against which all future interpretations of the role are measured. Even Margaret Rutherford's quivering Miss Prism has to give her best.

Impossible Years, The ○
1968, UK, 92 mins, colour
Dir: Michael Gordon

Stars: David Niven, Lola Albright
Rating: RB

This film comedy is based on the Bob Fisher-Arthur Marx play which ran on Broadway for three years. The jokes are chiefly about virginity, and poor David Niven, saddled with an awful teenage daughter, and faced with such lines as 'Look, pumpkin, if you flunk gym, you won't graduate' retreats behind a bemused expression. Faring better are that warm actress Lola Albright, as his wife, and likeable Chad Everett, as a young professor at the girl's school. Cristina Ferrare is highly resistible as the pumpkin involved, in this nudging, all-too-knowing sex farce.

Impromptu ◑ ⓥ
1990, UK, 107 mins, colour
Dir: James Lapine
Stars: Judy Davis, Hugh Grant, Mandy Patinkin, Bernadette Peters, Emma Thompson, Julian Sands
Rating: ★★

A capable international cast attempts the nearly impossible task of carrying off a light comedy about the relationship between George Sand, Chopin and other artists, writers and musicians in 19th-century Paris. A good try, too, although you have the uneasy feeling that some of the giggles are unsought and that not all the cast is playing on the same level. Judy Davis does a wicked impression of Glenda Jackson playing George Sand; Emma Thompson enjoys herself voraciously in a supporting but immensely showy part; Julian Sands almost attempts a foreign accent as Liszt; Bernadette Peters is occasionally embarrassing but sometimes very funny as his wife. Anton Rodgers restrains himself (just) from playing it as Restoration farce. Hugh Grant smiles shyly a lot as Chopin. Some of the dialogue is smartly written and you'll get a few chuckles for sure though you may find it difficult afterwards to describe what kind of film it was.

Impulse ●
1984, US, 99 mins, colour
Dir: Graham Baker
Stars: Meg Tilly, Tim Matheson, Hume Cronyn
Rating: ★

A very nasty chiller about a town where people are blowing their brains out but not dying. Confused, malevolent and definitely not for the squeamish, this could have been interesting if director Graham Baker, who

made *Alien Nation*, had not chosen to go so far over the top. The delicate talents of Meg Tilly are wasted as the heroine.

Impulse ○
1954, UK, 80 mins, b/w
Dir: Charles De La Tour
Stars: Arthur Kennedy, Constance Smith, Joy Shelton
Rating: ★★

One of two thrillers that the Hollywood actor Arthur Kennedy made in this country (the other was the Agatha Christie mystery *Murder She Said!*) this casts him as an estate agent in a sleepy Sussex town whose association with a shady lady tips him from the straight and narrow. An ordinary thriller, but it keeps you guessing, and Kennedy's presence seems to have inspired some pretty good performances.

Impulse ●
1990, US, 108 mins, colour
Dir: Sondra Locke
Stars: Theresa Russell, Jeff Fahey
Rating: ★★★

Despite solid performances from Theresa Russell, Jeff Fahey and George Dzundza, this thriller relies too heavily on coincidences for its plot twists and, with every startling development, its grip on believability weakens. Russell is an undercover cop whose life and career seem to be going nowhere. When her car breaks down on the way home, on impulse she goes into a bar and picks up a man who is subsequently murdered in his apartment while she is in the bathroom. Would you believe it: he just happened to be a witness she and her department were searching for. It's a hell of a long shot, even more improbable when you would think the police would have circulated a photo of him and that Russell would have seen it. The scenario may be poor, but the story is rattled along at a fair pace.

Inadmissible Evidence ◑
1968, UK, 96 mins, b/w
Dir: Anthony Page
Stars: Nicol Williamson, Jill Bennett, Peter Sallis
Rating: ★★★

An agonisingly accurate and painful portrait of a man whose life is in a hopeless mess. Nicol Williamson is wretchedly riveting as the faded legal eagle whose sex drive is like a death wish. Even if you don't care about the character, you can't deny the power of the performance. Based on John Osborne's biting stage play (in which Williamson again took the leading role), this is a tense, strongly dramatic film, with good work from Eleanor Fazan, Jill Bennett and Gillian Hills as three of the ladies in Williamson's tangled life. Lindsay Anderson appears in a cameo role, as a barrister.

In a Lonely Place O
1950, US, 93 mins, b/w
Dir: Nicholas Ray
Stars: Humphrey Bogart, Gloria Grahame, Frank Lovejoy
Rating: ★★★★

One of Humphrey Bogart's most underrated movies. Bogart plays a scriptwriter whose violent temperament makes him a prime suspect when the body of a girl is found shortly after she had left his apartment. He also has a brittle and faintly bizarre affair with the woman (Gloria Grahame) who provides him with a much-needed alibi. Bogart had wanted his wife Lauren Bacall to play the role, but Warners, who still had her under contract, refused. As it is, he still gives one of his most remarkable and intense performances.

Incendiary Blonde O
1945, US, 113 mins, colour
Dir: George Marshall
Stars: Betty Hutton, Arturo de Cordova, Charles Ruggles, Albert Dekker, Barry Fitzgerald
Rating: ★★★

There can't be many more colourful showbusiness stories than that of 'Texas' Guinan, an American nightclub entertainer who packed more incident into her 48 years than many would have done in twice the time. Betty Hutton gives a typical all-stops-out performance as the gal who was queen of the rodeo, nightclubs, Broadway and even the underworld.

In Cold Blood O
1967, US, 128 mins, b/w
Dir: Richard Brooks
Stars: Scott Wilson, Robert Blake
Rating: ★★★

In Cold Blood, Truman Capote's non-fiction novel-like account about two Kansas killers, is a probing, sensitive, tasteful, balanced and suspenseful documentary-drama. Heading the competent cast are Robert Blake and Scott Wilson, bearing a striking resemblance to the now-dead Kansas drifters who, in the course of a burglary on 15 November 1959, murdered four of a

family. John Forsythe plays the chief investigator who broke the case.

In Country ● Ⓥ
1989, US, 115 mins, colour
Dir: Ted Kotcheff
Stars: Bruce Willis, Emily Lloyd, Joan Allen, Kevin Anderson
Rating: ★★★

More American self-flagellation about Vietnam. This underrated film, though, is engagingly framed in the form of a weepie, with Britain's Emily Lloyd quirkily playing the nubile Kentucky teenager trying to find out more about the father who was killed in the war. Lloyd's certainly an actress to watch, whether or not you approve of her style. And the scenes between her and Bruce Willis (as her uncle) towards the end really hit home as he fills her in on what the war was truly like. Willis is almost unrecognisable – hair lightened and slicked back greasily, droop moustache and underlip beard – in a real character performance that ups his acting stock. This is a peculiarly American problem, but rather more of the deep emotions involved filter through here than is usual; it gets close to the nub of things but remains clear-headed throughout.

Incredible Journey, The ☉ Ⓥ
1963, US, 80 mins, colour
Dir: Fletcher Markle
Stars: Emile Genest, John Drainie, Tommy Tweed, Sandra Scott
Rating: ★★★

The things done by the three animal stars of this exciting Disney adventure would put even Lassie to shame. All in all, Sheila Burnford's book about a retriever, an old bull terrier and a Siamese cat who trek 300 miles together to return home across mountain, river and forest was a sitter for the Disney album. I hope that dog-lovers will forgive me if I say that Tao, the cat, is the real star of film. For one thing, he has more to do than the two dogs. He fights a bear and a lynx (not at the same time!), is swept away in a raging torrent (and survives), and rescues the two dogs when they are locked up by a friendly trapper who thinks he's doing them a good turn. If only the humans and their dialogue were not so gooey, this would be a wonderful film all the way through. Remade in 1993.

Incredible Mr Limpet, The ☉
1963, US, 102 mins, colour
Dir: Arthur Lubin

Stars: Don Knotts, Carole Cook, Jack Weston
Rating: ★★★

Delightful comedy-cartoon-musical about a man who wants to become a fish. The songs are tuneful, the comedy warmly amusing, and the cartoon creates a memorable character in a hermit crab with swivelling eyeballs. The human actors, the boggle-eyed Knotts, tubby Jack Weston, Larry Keating as an apoplectic admiral, and especially Carole Cook as a Shelley Winters-style wife, are all very likeable, creating believable characters that add to the film's charm.

Incredible Shrinking Man, The ●
1957, US, 81 mins, b/w
Dir: Jack Arnold
Stars: Grant Williams, Randy Stuart, April Kent
Rating: ★★★★

This classic science-fiction film has a compelling and literate script (from his novel) by Richard Matheson, sustained direction from Jack Arnold, excellent effects by Clifford Stine and really imaginative art direction by Alexander Golitzen and Robert Clatworthy. The fight between tiny Grant Williams and a spider is still a genuine chiller.

Incredible Shrinking Woman, The ☉
1981, US, 88 mins, colour
Dir: Joel Schumacher
Stars: Lily Tomlin, Charles Grodin, Ned Beatty, Henry Gibson
Rating: ★★★

Universal's new sideshoot from its own 1957 classic *The Incredible Shrinking Man* is mainly for laughs. The same schoolboy enthusiasm for the project is still there, though, and special effects score neatly as Lily Tomlin shrinks towards nothingness. The entire project has a light touch that never allows sentimentality or drama to put a damper on the fun.

Indecent Proposal ● Ⓥ
1992, US, 117 mins, colour
Dir: Adrian Lyne
Stars: Robert Redford, Demi Moore, Woody Harrelson, Seymour Cassel, Billy Connolly
Rating: ★★

This is *Honeymoon in Vegas* without the laughs. Another couple heavily in debt: another billionaire with an eye for the wife. Here the twist is that the rich man (Robert Redford) offers the poor man (Woody Harrelson) a million dollars for one night with his wife (Demi Moore). The couple vow to agree and forget it ever happened. No problems, huh? Well, soon this totally devoted couple is at each other's throats, he yelling that he doesn't trust her any more, and suspecting she's been sleeping with Redford all the time. Convincing? Well, hang on to the edge of that credibility chasm: worse is to follow. The casting, however, sustains you through the rest. Redford turns on the charm, Moore walks around showing off her formidable bust, and Harrelson looks crestfallen and morose even when he's not supposed to be. Two of them end up together but you wouldn't give a plugged nickel for the relationship's survival. Hollywood tripe, this, glossily dished up. The 34 Flying Elvises are sadly missed.

Indiana Jones and the Last Crusade ○ ⓥ
1989, US, 127 mins, colour
Dir: Steven Spielberg
Stars: Harrison Ford, Sean Connery, Denholm Elliott, Alison Doody, John Rhys-Davies, River Phoenix
Rating: ★★★★

Villains in fezzes and Nazis after the Holy Grail. It could only be Indiana Jones (or Monty Python) and it is. Steven Spielberg had to have his arm twisted to cast Sean Connery as the crusty but benign father of Indiana Jones in this third – and many consider finest – of his action-packed adventures. After all, there are only 12 years separating him and Indy star Harrison Ford. But the casting was inspired, with Ford and Connery sparking off each other and the latter engaging in amusing sexual one-upmanship and a string of patronising putdowns. The Nazi villains are less comical and more menacing this time round – Indiana ('just there with a bullwhip to keep the world at bay') even comes face to face with Hitler – and the action set pieces are once again stunningly mounted. Preposterous, exciting and dynamically staged, it's perfect entertainment for all the family.

Indiana Jones and the Temple of Doom ○ ⓥ
1984, US, 118 mins, colour
Dir: Steven Spielberg
Stars: Harrison Ford, Kate Capshaw, Ke Huy Kwan
Rating: ★★

Improbable is hardly the word for this billion-dollar 'B' movie which resurrects the spirit of Mr Moto from Thirties films, but adds an air of artificiality more appropriate to a James Bond movie to which, with its massive sets and thousands of yelling extras, this bears more than a passing resemblance. Highlights of the action include the opening sequence in the Obi-Wan (get it?) nightclub, a duel on a collapsed rope ladder and a running gun battle on mining buckets careering along a kind of underground scenic railway that seems to run for miles. Everything is contrived for its effect on the audience and, although some scenes are not for squeamish kids, one can't help imagining that Crosby, Hope and Lamour are hiding round the next boulder.

Independence Day ○ ⓥ
1996, US, 147 mins, colour
Dir: Roland Emmerich
Stars: Will Smith, Bill Pullman, Jeff Goldblum, Mary McDonnell, Randy Quaid, Robert Loggia, Brent Spiner
Rating: ★★★★

Remember those aliens that invaded our screens in the Fifties, in old films like *Earth Versus the Flying Saucers*? Well they make a spectacular comeback here – on a mega-million-dollar budget. Lifeless characters, effects that vary from cheesy to breathtaking and impossible jingoism are all on show here as America, with a little help from stereotypes around the world, puts paid to the power-hungry invaders. Very silly, but tremendously enjoyable stuff, with adrenalin-rushing action which will have you cheering for the world's forces, led by Smith, Pullman and Goldblum, and booing that nasty mother-ship from outer space. One really scary moment among all the glitz occurs during an alien autopsy, so get ready to shut your eyes if you don't want to see the result...

Indiscreet ○ ⓥ
1958, UK, 100 mins, colour
Dir: Stanley Donen
Stars: Cary Grant, Ingrid Bergman, Cecil Parker, Phyllis Calvert, David Kossoff, Megs Jenkins
Rating: ★★★★

Entertaining and glossy, this frothy romantic comedy makes a shaky start but builds to a glorious final reel at the same pace as Cary Grant and Ingrid Bergman's relationship. A rarity in that the film is actually better than the play it was based on (with Norman

Krasna adapting his own play, *Kind Sir*), its only real surprise was to reveal how deft a comedienne Bergman could be. It's a crying shame she was not offered more opportunity during her career to exploit this talent to the full.

Informer, The ⓓ
1935, US, 91 mins, b/w
Dir: John Ford
Stars: Victor McLaglen, Heather Angel, Una O'Connor, Wallace Ford
Rating: ★★★

Teeming with danger-fraught life and with its angry action spilling across the screen, this stylised examination of the human soul, as seen through the Irish 'Troubles' of the 1920s, was so effectively, chillingly made by director John Ford that his Oscar for best director was only one of several the film won. Ford was so knocked out by the performance of Victor McLaglen (which also took an Academy Award) in the title role that he employed the ugly but lovable veteran actor for the rest of his career. Superb photography by Joseph August suggests menace around every cobbled Dublin corner.

Informers, The ⓓ
1963, UK, 104 mins, b/w
Dir: Ken Annakin
Stars: Nigel Patrick, Frank Finlay, Margaret Whiting, Colin Blakely
Rating: ★★

Quite vicious for its time, this is a crime thriller with a familiar plot, a story of coppers' narks, big bank raids and the detective (Nigel Patrick) who, framed by crooks, vows to bring them to book and clear his name while out on bail. Unfortunately, we are asked to believe that his friendly superior and daughter's godfather (Harry Andrews) could be so taken in by a faked picture and money planted in our hero's house as to say, 'I helped make you – now I'll break you!' Still Patrick is always worth watching, there's a fine free-for-all at the end and Frank Finlay, as the chief crook, gives the best performance in the film.

In Harm's Way ○
1965, US, 167 mins, b/w
Dir: Otto Preminger
Stars: John Wayne, Kirk Douglas, Patricia Neal, Tom Tryon, Paula Prentiss, Henry Fonda
Rating: ★★★

Otto Preminger's epic war film about the Japanese devastation of Pearl Harbor, and the initial stages of the American fight back. The first half is at its best when the action is fiercest, but dwells too much on personal relationships. The second half is very much better, with Hollywood showing just how good it is at the war film. In a lengthy cast – it includes Patrick O'Neal, Franchot Tone and Stanley Holloway – John Wayne gives one of his best performances for some while, as a forceful admiral. Other particularly thoughtful portrayals come from Dana Andrews, Paula Prentiss and Burgess Meredith. Kirk Douglas seems slightly out of character as the bitter officer who dashes off on a convenient suicide mission after a young girl he has raped has taken her own life. But that action, from Pearl Harbor to the Pacific front line, packs a powerful punch.

Inherit the Wind ○
1960, US, 127 mins, b/w
Dir: Stanley Kramer
Stars: Spencer Tracy, Fredric March, Florence Eldridge, Gene Kelly
Rating: ★★★

Stanley Kramer's powerful drama, based on the true incident in which a schoolteacher faced prosecution for lecturing on Darwin's Theory of Evolution in America's Deep South. Spencer Tracy and Fredric March are well matched as the courtroom antagonists. Kramer makes an enthralling spectacle of the courtroom fireworks that take place between these giants of the cinema. Gene Kelly lurks, danceless, on the sidelines as a reporter.

In-Laws, The ○
1979, US, 103 mins, colour
Dir: Arthur Hiller
Stars: Peter Falk, Alan Arkin, Richard Libertini, Penny Peyser, Ed Begley Jr
Rating: ★★★

Peter Falk and Alan Arkin co-star in made-to-measure roles in this zany comedy. Arkin plays a New York dentist and family man who is about to meet his prospective son-in-law's parents for the first time. Little does he suspect that the father, Vince, quite unbeknown to anyone else, is an agent for the CIA. It's all too much for an unadventurous dentist! Arkin plays with what has been termed his 'brand of sub-hysterical panic' but many might well feel that, not for the first time, it's Falk who runs away with the entire film.

In Like Flint ○
1967, US, 114 mins, colour
Dir: Gordon Douglas

Stars: James Coburn, Lee J Cobb, Jean Hale, Andrew Duggan, Anna Lee
Rating: ★

If you like thrillers crammed to overflowing with pretty girls, this spy spoof does its best to please. James Coburn goes through his familiar motions of being Derek Flint, mechanical spy, in athletic style but the absence of any contact with reality, or the hero being in any real danger, brings it down to Batman level. Lee J Cobb, in a performance which includes a classic piece of drag, contributes a tinge of acting respect to the cocksure, cartoon-style charade.

I]n Love and War ◑ ⓥ
1996, UK, 126 mins, colour
Dir: Richard Attenborough
Stars: Sandra Bullock, Chris O'Donnell, MacKenzie Astin, Margot Steinberg, Emilio Bonucci
Rating: ★★

A big, skilfully constructed yet curiously passionless World War One romance featuring O'Donnell as the 18-year-old writer Ernest Hemingway, and Bullock as the Red Cross nurse in her mid-twenties who proves to be the great love of his love. War scenes are skilfully handled, but the central romance obstinately refuses to spark to life: O'Donnell seems to have more of a crush on Bullock than a grand passion, while she seems driven more by desire to look after him than fall into his arms. The episodic story has its touching moments and some impressive ones too, but overall you may feel that Hemingway himself related the history of this romance to rather greater effect in his own novel *A Farewell to Arms*.

In Name Only ○
1939, US, 100 mins, b/w
Dir: John Cromwell
Stars: Cary Grant, Carole Lombard, Kay Francis, Charles Coburn
Rating: ★★★

Cary Grant and Carole Loinbard co-starring might lead you to expect something on the lighter side. But no. This is no zany comedy, rather a sombre drama about a frustrated marriage, though well made and handled with taste by director John Cromwell. Kay Francis gleams with venom as Grant's wife.

Inner Circle, The ◑ ⓥ
(aka: The Projectionist)
1992, US, 134 mins, colour
Dir: Andrei Konchalovsky

Stars: Tom Hulce, Lolita Davidovich, Bob Hoskins, Bess Meyer
Rating: ★★

A long, grim drama that comes at you head-on, set in Stalin's Russia and based on a true story. Tom Hulce is earnest but rather annoying as Ivan, a young cinema projectionist who is taken from his home one night by the KGB, and whisked to the inner sancrum of Soviet power where, thanks to Stalin's love of films, he becomes the Kremlin's private projectionist. Torn between his love for his hero, addiction to his new-found power, loyalty to his wife (Lolita Davidovich) and fear for his life, Ivan eventually has some terrible decisions to make. On-location filming here helps produce some spectacular individual scenes but the acting lacks subtlety with Bob Hoskins going spectacularly over the top as Beria.

InnerSpace ○ ⓥ
1987, US, 119 mins, colour
Dir: Joe Dante
Stars: Dennis Quaid, Martin Short, Meg Ryan, Vernon Wells, Fiona Lewis, Kevin McCarthy
Rating: ★★★★★

Remember the 1966 fantasy *Fantastic Voyage* in which a group of miniaturised scientists were injected into the bloodstream of a human being? Here the vivid imagination of director Joe Dante and his writing team creates brilliant entertainment from a sideshoot of that idea. Hard-drinking naval lieutenant Dennis Quaid is the only one crazy enough to be the guinea pig in a privately financed experiment to inject him into a rabbit. Enter the bad guys, and the chief scientist goes on the run with Quaid and capsule inside a syringe, which he ends up injecting into the backside of ineffectual hypochondriac Martin Short. The rest of this very entertaining film, which seamlessly blends science-fiction, comedy and thrills, involves Quaid contacting Short through the inner ear and trying to keep him clear of immediate extermination by the villains. Quaid and Short both deliver socko performances; and big Vernon Wells has a Jack Palance style menace as the deadly one-armed assassin with an engaging assortment of fake 'hands'.

Innocence is Bliss ☉
(aka: Miss Grant Takes Richmond)
1949, US, 87 mins, b/w
Dir: Lloyd Bacon
Stars: Lucille Ball, William Holden, Janis

I

Carter, James Gleason
Rating: ★★★

Lucille Ball is at her funniest in this wild farce as a dimwit secretary with William Holden as her bookmaker who's having trouble with the syndicate. They land up promoting low cost housing for the homeless when Ball thinks she's working for an estate agent. It bears a startling resemblance to the tales of Damon Runyon – the gambler with the heart of gold, the gal who's smarter than she looks, the characters who hang out with the bookie. Holden had, up to now, been known as a dramatic actor, but here displays a talent for comedy. He holds his own against seasoned veterans like James Gleason and Frank McHugh.

Innocent, The ● Ⓥ

1993, Germany/US, 107 mins, colour
Dir: John Schlesinger
Stars: Isabella Rossellini, Anthony Hopkins, Campbell Scott, Ronald Nitzsche, Hart Bochner
Rating: ★★

As the Berlin Wall comes down, ageing Leonard (Campbell Scott) reflects upon his long-ago love for Maria (Isabella Rossellini), a German girl he met while working on a top-secret British project during the Cold War. John Schlesinger's film is an often engrossing tale of espionage and forgotten love, even if you feel it's missing the sense of passionate drama for which the director was aiming. Anthony Hopkins' accent is on the strained side as the US officer keeping an eye on Leonard, but Jeremy Sinden gives a good account of Scott's commanding officer, and Dietrich Lollmann's lowering colour photography makes East Berlin a menacing additional star of the film.

Innocent Blood ● Ⓥ

1992, US, 115 mins, colour
Dir: John Landis
Stars: Anne Parillaud, Anthony LaPaglia, Robert Loggia, Don Rickles
Rating: ★★

Round up the usual special ejects suspects, there's another vampire movie in town. Though John Landis's modern stab at the dead is strictly fang-in-cheek, it throws in all the adult elements horror and video fans will enjoy: glowing eyes, gouts of blood, gorged throats, the dead come to life, topless dancers, a touch of vaguely kinky sex and enough four-letter words to make a vampire blush. Marie (Anne Parillaud) is the new lady bloodsucker on the block, but she only chomps on the bad guys. Since this is Mob territory and she likes to eat Italian, there's no lack of titbits. After dinner, she blows off the meal's head with a shotgun to ensure he doesn't roam the streets after death (and dark). Marie's problems come when she a) fails to behead mobster kingpin Sal the Shark (Robert Loggia) and b) falls in lust with a good cop (Anthony LaPaglia). The question is: can she resist sinking her teeth into his neck before he's sunk his teeth into the hunt for the crazed Sal? Formula stuff, but fans will lap it up, complete with clips from old vampire movies.

Innocent Bystanders ◑

1972, UK, 111 mins, colour
Dir: Peter Collinson
Stars: Stanley Baker, Geraldine Chaplin, Donald Pleasence, Dana Andrews
Rating: ★

Stanley Baker's last major film, this is in the vein of the long list of hard, tough thrillers that established his rugged screen personality. Written by James Mitchell, the film – with its espionage theme and its confusing plot of double-cross – and triple-cross – could well be an extension of Mitchell's famous TV series *Callan*, the leading character here being a top British agent whose nerve has allegedly gone. Although the colour photography often seems as bleached as the desert settings, director Peter Collinson makes his way briskly through the complicated storyline.

Innocent Man, An ● Ⓥ

1989, US, 114 mins, colour
Dir: Peter Yates
Stars: Tom Selleck, F Murray Abraham, Lalla Robins, David Rasche
Rating: ★★

They could have called this prison drama-cum-revenge thriller *Each Dawn I Die* if Cagney hadn't 'nicked' the title 50 years before. Not that things have changed all that much, apart from the language. Selleck is an ordinary guy framed by two bent vice cops after they bust into his house by mistake and shoot him. Unlikely it all is, but no more so than in Cagney's day when, like Tom, Jimmy was dragged off to serve six years screaming his innocence. In prison, 'shivs' are passed around to do unwanted convicts in, and Selleck has to learn to stand up for himself, with the help of veteran con F Murray Abraham, before getting out in one piece, on parole, to seek a desperate (and again unlikely) revenge on the cops who are still – foolishly – harassing him and his wife. Not a very good movie, as you may have gathered, but certainly quite a watchable one, thanks to its gallery of familiar elements entertainingly put together. Oh yes, and Selleck even does '90 days in the hole', emerging with a stubble and a slight cough.

Innocents, The ◐

1961, UK, 99 mins, b/w
Dir: Jack Clayton
Stars: Deborah Kerr, Michael Redgrave, Peter Wyngarde, Megs Jenkins
Rating: ★★★★★

Jack Clayton's constantly eerie and finally terrifying version of Henry James's *The Turn of the Screw*. Consistent performances by Deborah Kerr and Megs Jenkins, and a briefly powerful one by Peter Wyngarde are nicely counter-balanced by Martin Stephens and Pamela Franklin, perfectly in character as the other-worldly children. Preferably not one to watch alone. And hold tight for the shattering climax.

Innocent Sleep, The ● Ⓥ

1996, UK, 110 mins, colour
Dir: Scott Michell
Stars: Rupert Graves, Annabella Sciorra, Franco Nero, Michael Gambon, John Hannah
Rating: ★★★

One of the better thrillers of its year, with director Scott Michell making a confident feature-film debut in a sleek, forceful crime drama that belies its low budget. A young homeless drunk (Rupert Graves) witnesses the ritual hanging of a prominent Italian banker. He tries to shake his befuddled mind into doing something about it, but it seems that everywhere he turns for help, people are involved in the killing. There are good chase scenes, and performances from all concerned that bring the characters to life or, in the case of Michael Gambon, who is encouraged into Dickensian over-acting, rather larger than life. But, although the elements of his plot are mostly retreads of familiar situations, Michell strings them together to make tense, exciting fare.

Inn of the Sixth Happiness, The ○

1958, US/UK, 151 mins, colour
Dir: Mark Robson
Stars: Ingrid Bergman, Curt Jurgens,

Robert Donat
Rating: ★★★★

A moving story of a lady missionary in China. The film is made more touching by being the last in which the splendid Robert Donat was to appear: he died shortly after completing it, and his performance, fine though it is, is sometimes painful to watch.

In Old California ○
1942, US, 89 mins, b/w
Dir: William McGann
Stars: John Wayne, Binnie Barnes
Rating: ★★

Routine, rather dingy-looking John Wayne Western from Republic, made at a time when the studio should have been doing rather better by their biggest star, following his leap to fame in *Stagecoach*. Wayne as a pharmacist takes some swallowing in this yarn, but he is soon dishing out bullets rather than pellets and pills, as florid Albert Dekker, an excellent villain, tries to ride roughshod over the law at the time of the Gold Rush. Edgar Kennedy and Patsy Kelly supply some predictably over-the-top light relief.

In Old Chicago ○
1938, US, 95 mins, b/w
Dir: Henry King
Stars: Tyrone Power, Alice Faye, Don Ameche, Alice Brady, Brian Donlevy, Andy Devine
Rating: ★★★

Fox's Darryl F Zanuck had wanted Clark Gable and Jean Harlow for the leading roles in this classic Thirties disaster movie but had to settle for Tyrone Power and Alice Faye. The story of rivalry between brothers and Power's romantic entanglement with Faye may be strictly routine but it serves well enough to showcase the still stunning burning of Chicago in 1871. The fire itself was staged on Fox's back lot where it burned for three days under the direction of H Bruce Humberstone. The rest of the film was helmed competently by Henry King and Alice Brady, playing the owner of the cow that started the blaze, won a Best Supporting Oscar.

In Old Oklahoma
See: War of the Wildcats

In Search of Gregory ❿
1969, UK, 90 mins, colour
Dir: Peter Wood
Stars: Julie Christie, Michael Sarrazin, John Hurt, Adolfo Celi
Rating: ★★

Weird little film about a girl in pursuit of a young man she has never met, but by whose description she has been magnetically intrigued. There are some good individual scenes, including a spectacular game of 'autoball', but they don't fit together in quite the way that a cinematic jigsaw should. A good supporting cast is headed by Roland Culver.

In Search of the Castaways ⊙
1961, US/UK, 100 mins, colour
Dir: Robert Stevenson
Stars: Maurice Chevalier, Hayley Mills, George Sanders, Wilfrid Hyde White
Rating: ★★★

An absolutely spiffing time is had by all when this jolly Jules Verne adventure from Disney gets going, and once it does it hardly ever lets up. Pinewood stands in nobly for South America, and ice caverns, giant trees, waterspouts and volcanic eruptions are all convincingly re-created there. Hayley Mills, still fresh and exuberant in her early days with the studio, Maurice Chevalier and the rest all give the impression of enjoying the grand, if occasionally perilous adventure and Paul Beeson's crystal-clear Technicolor photography puts an added sparkle on the thrills. Beeson even finds a touch of poetry in a tableau of four horses rearing in panic against the steel grey of a gathering storm.

Inside Daisy Clover ○ ⓥ
1965, US, 128 mins, colour
Dir: Robert Mulligan
Stars: Natalie Wood, Christopher Plummer, Robert Redford
Rating: ★★

A searching Hollywood self-examination: the drama of a talented teenage singing star almost destroyed by the studio system, its standards and its demands. Director Robert Mulligan, who made *To Kill a Mockingbird* and *Summer of '42*, conducts us chillingly through Daisy's life, from success to disillusionment to rebellion. Natalie Wood gives one of her best performances, and Robert Redford is seen in an early film role as the star she marries. The screenplay tends to hover around the grave of the Hollywood of 1936 without ever getting out its shovel and really digging in.

Inside Moves ○
1980, US, 113 mins, colour
Dir: Richard Donner
Stars: John Savage, David Morse, Diana

Searwid, Amy Wright
Rating: ★★

Here's a film scripted by the husband and wife team of Valerie Curtin and Barry Levinson (who also wrote *Best Friends*). It takes the characters who converge in a bar and follows their fortunes. In Max's Bar, however, the denizens are life's mental and physical misfits. Still, the characters are colourful, appealing and amusing and their hearts, like that of the film, are certainly in the right place. It marks one of the rare screen appearances of real-life double amputee Harold Russell, who won an Oscar in 1946 for *The Best Years of Our Lives*.

Insignificance ●
1985, UK, 105 mins, colour
Dir: Nicolas Roeg
Stars: Michael Emil, Theresa Russell, Tony Curtis
Rating: ★★★

Don't be fooled by the character names in Nicolas Roeg's well-received, ironic and thought-provoking comedy drama. They may be called 'The Professor', 'The Actress', 'The Senator' and 'The Ballplayer' but screenplay and performances – particularly that of Theresa Russell who is seen standing over a subway grating while a gust of air blows her dress above her knees make it quite clear who the protagonists really are – Albert Einstein, Marilyn Monroe, Senator Joseph McCarthy and Joe Di Maggio. Terry Johnson, ingeniously adapting his play for the screen, comes up with a fascinating proposition. The famous four meet in a New York hotel room one night in 1954 during which, among many strange delights, Monroe explains the Theory of Relativity to Einstein! Roeg has always been an ambitious filmmaker. Here subject and style are smartly integrated.

In Society ⊙
1944, US, 74 mins, b/w
Dir: Jean Yarbrough
Stars: Bud Abbott, Lou Costello, Kirby Grant, Ann Gillis
Rating: ★★

A typically frantic Forties vehicle for the slapstick talents of Bud Abbott and Lou Costello casts them as a couple of incompetent plumbers who run amok in a posh mansion. Highlights include the flooding of the bathroom, Lou out of control during a fox hunt and a wild climactic chase with the daffy duo pursuing villain Thomas Gomez in a fire engine. Director Jean Yarbrough, who

I

put Bud and Lou through their comic paces in five features, handles the caper with brisk aplomb, even though some of their antics look little more than embarrassing now.

Inspector, The
See: Lisa

Inspector Clouseau ○ ⓥ
1968, UK, 92 mins, colour
Dir: Bud Yorkin
Stars: Alan Arkin, Delia Boccardo, Frank Finlay
Rating: ★

Alan Arkin took over from Peter Sellers for this one comedy, chronicling the further adventures of the world's worst Sureté detective, called in to circumvent a robbery. The British supporting cast puts in some stout cameos, but Sellers proves a hard act to follow. Clumsy capers.

Inspector General, The ⊙
(aka: Happytimes)
1949, US, 102 mins, colour
Dir: Henry Koster
Stars: Danny Kaye, Barbara Bates, Walter Slezak, Elsa Lanchester
Rating: ★★★

Nikolai Gogol's play doesn't do badly as a vehicle for Danny Kaye, the Goldwyn gloss, some good quips and ditties and a colourful supporting cast making it brighter than it ever seemed on stage. Barbara Bates is a pretty heroine and Walter Slezak supremely oily as Kaye's sometime confidant.

Inspector Hornleigh ○
1938, UK, 87 mins, b/w
Dir: Eugene Forde
Stars: Gordon Harker, Alastair Sim
Rating: ★★★

The first of three popular British comedy-thrillers based on a successful radio series of the immediate pre-war days. Gordon Harker and Alastair Sim who, one imagines, could just as well have tackled each other's roles, are wonderfully well teamed as the inspector and sergeant on the trail of the men who stole the Chancellor of the Exchequer's bag! The results are a bit wordy but very entertaining. Followed by *Inspector Hornleigh on Holiday* and *Inspector Hornleigh Goes to It*: all three are well worth catching for Sim and Harker fans.

Interiors ❶
1978, US, 93 mins, colour
Dir: Woody Allen
Stars: Richard Jordan, Diane Keaton,

Geraldine Page, Sam Waterston
Rating: ★★

Described by some critics as Woody Allen's attempt to make a film in the style of Ingmar Bergman, this heavily-stylised tale of inter-familial bickering does finally get around to showing us the kind of film it might have been all along. As soon as dumpy, abrasive Maureen Stapleton steps on to the scene, as the new bride-to-be of the father of the film's three sisters, the movie not only tightens up, but brightens up, taking its cue from the colour of her dress. She gives the over-intense events a new dimension, a different ingredient against which the other characters – all as neurotic as each other – can play. The performance was rightly rewarded with an Academy Award nomination for best supporting actress, an award she actually won three years later for *Reds*.

Interlude ❶
1968, UK, 113 mins, colour
Dir: Kevin Billington
Stars: Oskar Werner, Barbara Ferris, Virginia Maskell, Donald Sutherland, John Cleese
Rating: ★★

Justifiably high hopes were held for Barbara Ferris at the time of this skilful love story, and it's rather sad that she never made a complete breakthrough to stardom. Here she matches that excellent actor Oskar Werner emotion for emotion in a well photographed, if bleak, look at the affair between a young girl reporter and a famous conductor. Shafts of lunatic humour break up the sentimental moments, and John Cleese has a few deliciously acid lines as a public relations man.

Intermezzo ○ ⓥ
(aka: Escape to Happiness)
1939, US, 69 mins, b/w
Dir: Gregory Ratoff
Stars: Ingrid Bergman, Leslie Howard, Edna Best, John Halliday
Rating: ★★★

This Hollywood remake of Ingrid Bergman's sixth Swedish picture (also called *Intermezzo*) made her an international star. Playing a young pianist involved in an adulterous affair with violinist Leslie Howard, she garnered rave reviews, including one from Britain's Graham Greene who wrote of a 'performance which doesn't give the effect of acting at all but of living'. Impeccable black and white photography by Gregg Toland, and Oscar-nominated musical direction by

Lou Forbes. One of the briefest Hollywood superhits on record.

Internal Affairs ● ⓥ
1990, US, 117 mins, colour
Dir: Mike Figgis
Stars: Richard Gere, Andy Garcia, Nancy Travis, William Baldwin, Annabella Sciorra
Rating: ★★

Gere's brilliant performance as a very crooked cop who has no hesitation in getting people killed fires this otherwise overlong, overdone and directorially very flashy thriller. Taciturn Andy Garcia plays the newcomer to Internal Affairs (the cops' department that investigates cops) whose examination of one corrupt policeman, a former buddy, leads him to an obsession with the buddy's boss (Richard Gere). Garcia has a strange and unbelievable marriage with Nancy Travis that degenerates into abuse and foul-mouthed screaming matches at the drop of a few late nights. No wonder Gere finds it easy to drive a wedge between them, although it's hard to see why he eventually presses the self-destruct button by meddling in Garcia's private life. This is all long, slow and spun out by its director from a straight action film to one with pretensions its plot and dialogue can't sustain. But it's kept alive by the spark of Gere's understated but lethal menace.

International Lady ○
1941, US, 100 mins, b/w
Dir: Tim Whelan
Stars: George Brent, Ilona Massey, Basil Rathbone, George Zucco, Gene Lockhart
Rating: ★★

Typical fast-moving, middle-budget American espionage thriller of the war years. George Brent and Basil Rathbone are well matched as the American and British agents on the track of a spy ring. In a small role: Clayton Moore, later to win TV fame as *The Lone Ranger*.

International Velvet ○
1978, UK, 127 mins, colour
Dir: Bryan Forbes
Stars: Tatum O'Neal, Nanette Newman, Christopher Plummer, Anthony Hopkins
Rating: ★★

There was a 34-year wait for a sequel to the Elizabeth Taylor children's classic *National Velvet*, and after sitting through more than two hours of this inferior soap opera, you'll be wishing director/screenwriter Bryan Forbes had kept his hands off the story. Forbes' real-life wife, Nanette Newman, plays the grown-up Velvet character, now living in England, and looking after an orphaned American niece (Tatum O'Neal). Distrust and animosity on the part of the girl soon melt away when they discover a mutual love of horses. But the film is marred by supremely banal dialogue, matched only by the direction.

Interpol ○
(aka: Pickup Alley)
1957, UK, 92 mins, b/w
Dir: John Gilling
Stars: Victor Mature, Trevor Howard, Anita Ekberg
Rating: ★★

Hollywood's original Mr Beefcake, Victor Mature, frowns and glowers his way through this story about an international crime chase, while Britain's Trevor Howard quietly acts him off the screen. Howard leads the police a merry dance (and runs rings round his fellow stars) as the villain.

Intersection ● ⓥ
1994, US, 99 mins, colour
Dir: Mark Rydell
Stars: Richard Gere, Sharon Stone, Lolita Davidovich, Martin Landau, Jenny Morrison
Rating: ★★

Richard Gere is torn between two women in this remake of a 1970 French film which opens, as does this, with the leading character hovering between life and death after a car crash. What happens between that and the final resolution is just barely interesting in a high-gloss kind of way. Gere turns on the charm, but occasionally goes over the top. Sharon Stone and Lolita Davidovich give it their best shot as the women involved, but they're not quite up to touching our emotions with their problems. Pretty 14-year-old Jenny Morrison makes a promising debut as Gere's daughter and old-stager Martin Landau gets the best bit of dialogue in the film when he tells Gere to get on with things and make a decision between estranged wife (Stone) and new lover (Davidovich). Real life, though, is kept resolutely at bay.

Interview with the Vampire ● ⓥ
1994, US, 138 mins, colour
Dir: Neil Jordan
Stars: Tom Cruise, Brad Pitt, Kirsten Dunst, Antonio Banderas, Christian

Slater, Stephen Rea
Rating: ★★

A sometimes stylish but very nasty horror film, stuffed with more modern matinee idols than pints of blood. Brad Pitt is the 'vampire with a human soul' who, tired of life after his wife and child have died in 18th-century Louisiana, is vampirised by Lestat (Tom Cruise), a merciless and sardonic bloodsucker who fancies a companion. Reluctant to drink human blood, Pitt takes to a diet of rats and chickens before Cruise tempts him with an 11-year-old girl (Kirsten Dunst) who in turn become's Pitt's companion through the decades – and spells trouble for Cruise. Some great and gruesome special effects and an orgy of blood-letting – at times the film seems to be little else – will compensate horror fans for the somewhat stately pace of the piece. But they will be disappointed by the joky ending; the filmmakers have a fine climax in modern America only to throw it away on a silly coda.

Intimate Relations ● ⓥ
1995, UK, 99 mins, colour
Dir: Philip Goodhew
Stars: Julie Walters, Rupert Graves, Matthew Walker, Lisa Sadler, Holly Aird, Les Dennis
Rating: RB

You'd say this was really silly if it weren't based on a true-life murder case. As it is, this is still a dispiriting film to come from Britain in the 1990s – desperately fashionable in its depiction of fair-isle pullover sex behind drawn curtains, frantically modish in its depiction of the participants in this squalid slice of crime history, and desperately with-it in its black (blue collar) humour. Graves is the lodger of dubious background who finds himself in an uncomfortable *ménage á trois* when his landlady (Walters), whose husband is disabled, jumps into bed with him and brings her 13-year-old daughter with her. From here on in, this combustible situation simmers interminably before the inevitable – and clumsily staged – outpouring of violence at the end. The cast give faceless performances in the kind of thing Harold Pinter was doing (much better) 30 years ago.

In the Bleak Midwinter ● ⓥ
1995, UK, 98 mins, b/w
Dir: Kenneth Branagh
Stars: Michael Maloney, Joan Collins, Richard Briers, Jennifer Saunders, Julia

Sawalha, John Sessions
Rating: ★

A chamber piece from Kenneth Branagh (who doesn't appear) about a group of mismatched actors and drop-outs staging a bizarre version of Shakespeare's *Hamlet* in a disused church. Alas, the end result is very self-indulgent, with more than passing similarities to *An Awfully Big Adventure*, which came out the same year. Branagh's film-making efforts here soon degenerate into little more than a lot of verbal sniping and sulking. On the acting front, veteran Richard Briers is on the ball as aged has-been Henry, aghast at the thought of Queen Gertrude being played by a pantomime dame (John Sessions). The situation also gives him one of the best lines in a threadbare collection of luvvie injokes. 'Gertrude' he cries in horror, 'was not written as a shirt-lifter!'

In the Doghouse ○
1961, UK, 84 mins, b/w
Dir: Michael Pertwee
Stars: Leslie Phillips, Peggy Cummins, Hattie Jacques
Rating: ★★

Fast and furious *Carry On*-style comedy about the misadventures of a hapless vet. It was pretty Peggy Cummins' last film to date in a career which stretched back to a debut as a teenager in the Thirties.

In the French Style ◑
1963, US, 105 mins, b/w
Dir: Robert Parrish
Stars: Jean Seberg, Stanley Baker
Rating: ★★★

This touching, involving Anglo-French drama, about a girl called Christina fruitlessly in search of love, is remembered as the film in which Miss Seberg finally obliterated memories of her disastrous film debut in Saint Joan with a haunting performance that brilliantly reflects Christina in all her moods.

In the Good Old Summertime ⊙
1949, US, 115 mins, colour
Dir: Robert Z Leonard
Stars: Judy Garland, Van Johnson, S Z Sakall, Buster Keaton
Rating: ★★★

A musical remake of the 1940 romance *The Shop Around The Corner*, with the location switched from Vienna to Chicago. Judy Garland is virtually the whole show and the songs include, be-

I

sides the title number 'I Don't Care', 'Merry Christmas', 'Put Your Arms Around Me Honey' and 'Wait 'Til the Sun Shines, Nellie'. The three-year-old tot who appears with Judy and Van Johnson at the end of the picture is Judy's daughter Liza Minnelli.

In the Heat of the Night ❶ ⓥ
1967, US, 109 mins, colour
Dir: Norman Jewison
Stars: Sidney Poitier, Rod Steiger, Warren Oates, Lee Grant, Scott Wilson, Larry Gates
Rating: ★★★★

This essentially simple whodunnit is raised far above the norm, thanks to a racially-charged sub-plot and powerful acting from Sidney Poitier and Rod Steiger. Woven together with tension and drama by director Norman jewison, *In the Heat of the Night* scooped five Oscars. Big city policeman Virgil Tibbs (Poltier) comes up against a wall of prejudice when he tries to help bigoted but canny Police Chief Gillespie (Steiger) solve a murder case in a small Southern town. Tibbs finds he has to come to terms with his own prejudices as well as those of the people around him, which adds another dimension to the film. Steiger won an Oscar for Best Actor, while Poitier went on to reprise the role of Tibbs in two fohowups – *They Call Me MISTER Tibbs!* and *The Organisation*. This was the original and best, though, and the intervening years haven't dated it.

In the Line of Fire ● ⓥ
1993, US, 127 mins, colour
Dir: Wolfgang Petersen
Stars: Clint Eastwood, John Malkovich, Rene Russo, Dylan McDermott, Gary Cole
Rating: ★★★

Clint Eastwood's back in smart-suited action, though as Frank Horrigan rather than Harry Callahan, and sensibly playing on his advancing years to add a few frayed edges to the character. Frank's a secret service man, a dinosaur from the Kennedy era, and now 'the only active agent who ever lost a president'. When a psycho assassin (John Malkovich) homes in on the current president, Frank demands back into the protection racket. Trouble is, jogging alongside the president's car, he now has problems keeping up. However, the assassin, realising that Frank was around at the Kennedy killing, begins a cat-and-mouse game with him, taunting him with the failures of his past life. When

one of Clint's buddies gets shot in pursuit of the villain, the old-timer grits his teeth and you know the bad guy's in trouble. Despite a suspensefully edited ending, the film's a tad long, and efficient rather than exciting, especially in its treatment of a rooftop chase, which doesn't make the blood race the way it should.

In the Mouth of Madness ● ⓥ
1994, US, 95 mins, colour
Dir: John Carpenter
Stars: Sam Neill, Julie Carmen, Jürgen Prochnow, Charlton Heston, John Glover
Rating: ★

Gooey, gucky monsters with fangs and tentacles and flicky tongues are looking distinctly past their sell-by date in John Carpenter's dose of small-town horror. Sam Neill is the insurance investigator who is asked to trace Sutter Cane, America's vanished number one best-selling author, whose horror novels affect people in a way that triggers violence. Taking with him publishing assistant Julie Carmen, Neill sets off for the seemingly non-existent town of Hobb's End, which he reaches through what seems like a time tunnel between fact and fiction. Or maybe ... but no ... this is all too silly for words, alas, and none of it seems to have any logic or connection with reality, as all the best chillers have. It's ridiculous, for example, that Neill should work out the way to Hobb's End by arranging sections of the covers of Cane's books. And, if civilization has retreated into pockets of resistance at the end, who is showing a film Neill enters a cinema to watch?

In the Name of the Father ● ⓥ
1993, UK, 133 mins, colour
Dir: Jim Sheridan
Stars: Daniel Day-Lewis, Pete Postlethwaite, Emma Thompson, Corin Redgrave
Rating: ★★★

Considering it concerns one of the major miscarriages of justice this century – the wrongful conviction of the Guildford Four – it's a pity this isn't a more dramatically gripping film. Your attention may wander more than once en route to its explosive conclusion. The facts, of course, speak for themselves. Thanks to police suppression of defence evidence, not only were the Four, led by Gerry Conlon (Daniel Day-Lewis) sentenced to 30-year terms for the bombing of a Guildford pub in

1974, but Conlon's father, resolutely played by Pete Postlethwaite, served several years of a 12-year term before dying in prison. Against this background, director Jim Sheridan makes something of the father-son relationship but very little of the passing years in jail which, despite a few explosive incidents, convey boredom rather than suspense. The formidable Emma Thompson (barely in the film at all till near the end) seems miscast, and her final courtroom scenes rushed and misjudged, as the defence counsel who finally seized on the vital piece of evidence that won the Four their freedom. Day-Lewis does all you could expect as Conlon, and the film does make you wonder how many such miscarriages lurk in the darker corners of the British legal system.

In the Navy ☉
1941, US, 85 mins, b/w
Dir: Arthur Lubin
Stars: Bud Abbott, Lou Costello, Dick Powell, The Andrews Sisters
Rating: ★★★

A pretty funny Abbott and Costello comedy, which gives them a chance to include one or two of their best stage routines, including 'the old shell game', performed here with lemons. Not quite sure at this time of their new stars' pulling power, Universal asked Dick Powell to co-star to boost the film's box-office prospects (which, as it turned out, needed very little boosting). Powell was given a couple of songs and so were The Andrews Sisters, in what proved to be a breezy romp that stands the test of time better than most of the comedians' films.

In the Nick ☉
1960, US, 105 mins, b/w
Dir: Ken Hughes
Stars: Anthony Newley, Anne Aubrey, Ian Hendry, Harry Andrews, Bernie Winters, James Booth
Rating: ★★

Anthony Newley as a prison psychiatrist, with whom a gangster's moll falls in love. Quite a bright comedy with attractive characters and a script that's largely warm and witty. Sort of a sequel to *Jazzboat*, this has its embarrassing moments, but a believable villain in Ian Hendry.

In This Our Life ☉
1942, US, 101 mins, b/w
Dir: John Huston
Stars: Bette Davis, Olivia de Havilland, George Brent, Dennis Morgan, Charles

Coburn, Hattie McDaniel
Rating: ★★★★

Only crusty old Charles Coburn proves a match for Bette Davis (both in the story and the acting department) as she rampages over the rest of the cast in this lurid melodrama about a self-willed hussy who ruins everyone's life including her own. 'There's a demon within Bette,' observed director John Huston afterwards, 'and I let the demon go on this one.'

Into the Night ❶ Ⓥ
1985, US, 115 mins, colour
Dir: John Landis
Stars: Jeff Goldblum, Michelle Pfeiffer, Richard Farnsworth, Irene Papas, Paul Mazursky, David Bowie
Rating: ★★★

A foray into the madness of insomnia, directed by John Landis. The underrated Jeff Goldblum is perfectly cast as the insomniac who becomes involved with damsel-in-distress Michelle Pfeiffer – and much more besides. The starry line-up also features David Bowie, Dan Aykroyd and Richard Farnsworth, as well as cameos from a host of Hollywood directors. The wonderful bluesy soundtrack features BB King. A delight for film buffs, blues fans and insomniacs alike.

Into the West ○ Ⓥ
1992, UK/Ireland, 102 mins, colour
Dir: Mike Newell
Stars: Gabriel Byrne, Ellen Barkin, Brendon Gleeson, David Kelly
Rating: ★★★

Partly a tale about a boy and a horse, partly an allegory, and partly a story of finding yourself and leaving the past behind, this liltingly scored Irish movie has a good deal of charm, even if its pace, like that of the horse (white of course) varies from a trot to a gallop. The horse appears on the seashore, attaches itself to Grandpa Riley and clearly has a mission in life. Cottoning on to Riley's eight-year-old grandson Ossie, it settles into the family high-rise with Ossie's cool, protective older brother Tito and their father (Gabriel Byrne), an ex-traveller who has tried to settle to city life since the death of his wife and now lurches between odd jobs and the bottle. The horse's jumping prowess brings it to the attention of Byrne's arch-enemy, the local (crooked) police inspector, who sees to it that the horse ends up in the hands of an equally corrupt businessman. The film goes a bit precious on us in an over-sentimental ending, but inci-

dentals along the way – especially when boys and horse break into a cinema and watch a Western eating popcorn more than make up for it.

Intrigue ○
1947, US, 90 mins, b/w
Dir: Edwin L Marin
Stars: George Raft, June Havoc, Tom Tully, Helena Carter
Rating: ★

Far from the days of Far Eastern settings heavy with atmosphere, this Shanghai-set thriller is a good representative of Hollywood on its way down from the golden era of the late Thirties and early Forties. George Raft, too, was past his prime as a box-office attraction, and shambles through this story of smuggling and chicanery. Jane Havoc does what she can with a 'dragon lady' sort of role, Helena Carter is a pretty if petulant heroine and the script, which runs like a newspaper comic strip, is a collection of oriental clichés almost as tired as the star. Director Edwin L Marin made some good Randolph Scott Westerns, but he can't do much with this.

Intruder, The ○
1953, UK, 84 mins, b/w
Dir: Guy Hamilton
Stars: Jack Hawkins, Dennis Price, Michael Medwin, George Cole
Rating: ★★★

Two films for the price of one: a wartime action adventure and a suspense drama, as ex-colonel Jack Hawkins hunts out old comrades in a bid to find out why one of them has turned to crime. Director Guy Hamilton, then just starting on a distinguished career, makes it all work well on both levels. Hawkins, too, gets well inside both the 'past' and 'present' personalities of the leading character. Michael Medwin gives just about his best film performance as the corporal turned criminal.

Intruder In the Dust ○
1949, US, 87 mins, b/w
Dir: Clarence Brown
Stars: David Brian, Juano Hernandez, Claude Jarman Jr, Porter Hall
Rating: ★★★★

This adaptation of a William Faulkner novel is in low-key mode throughout, but holds up well both as a study of racial prejudice and as a murder thriller. The white teenager who tries to clear his elderly black friend (played with great dignity by Juano Hernandez) is portrayed by Claude

Jarman Jr, one of the most appealing of Hollywood's child stars, who won a special Academy Award after his performance in *The Yearling* in 1946.

Invaders, The
See: 49th Parallel

Invaders from Mars ○
1953, US, 78 mins, colour
Dir: William Cameron Menzies
Stars: Arthur Franz, Helena Carter, Jimmy Hunt, Leif Erickson
Rating: ★★★

Although it aroused no great attention in its day, this garish, oddball science-fiction film has attained cult stature with the passing of the years. The Cinecolor process forces director/production designer William Cameron Menzies to adopt a green-and-gold colour scheme which gives the film a distinctive, almost muddy look appropriate in particular to the sub-sandpit settings where the Martians carry on their fiendish work. The story is told from the view of a boy, played by Jimmy Hunt, who appeared as a police chief in the (inferior) remake 33 years later.

Invasion of the Body Snatchers ● Ⓥ
1978, US, 111 mins, colour
Dir: Philip Kaufman
Stars: Donald Sutherland, Brooke Adams, Leonard Nimoy, Veronica Cartwright, Jeff Goldblum, Kevin McCarthy
Rating: ★★★

Although it coarsens the original classic 1956 version of the story, this remake of the chilling tale of alien possession is still a good thriller in its own right. Director Philip Kaufman pays homage to the first version of the yarn (in which a weird form of plant life descends on earth and takes over human beings when they fall asleep) not only in his use of the director (Don Siegel) and star (Kevin McCarthy) of the original in cameo roles, but by his use of angled shadow, reminiscent of Forties and Fifties films. Kaufman shows real skill in the way that everyday things are made to carry a sense of menace. And, for all its running length, this film moves along at an unflaggingly exciting pace. The ending carries a considerable shock charge. Further remake (*Body Snatchers*) in 1993.

Invasion of the Body Snatchers ❶ Ⓥ
1956, US, 80 mins, b/w
Dir: Don Siegel

I

Stars: Kevin McCarthy, Dana Wynter, Larry Gates
Rating: ★★★★

Lovers of the chiller-thriller should on no account miss this remarkable science fiction film, which achieved tremendous and unexpected success on its first appearance. Fantasy is presented in its most terrifying form. There are no monsters – only the inhabitants of a small American town, their minds, wills and bodies 'taken over' by a weird form of life from outer space. Director Don Siegel brought an entirely new approach to the horror field. He proved himself master of the chilly clutch at the base of one's spine.

Investigation of Murder, An

See: The Laughing Policeman

Invisible Man, The ○

1933, US, 71 mins, b/w
Dir: James Whale
Stars: Claude Rains, Gloria Stuart, Henry Travers, William Harrigan
Rating: ★★★

Fine Hollywood version of H G Wells's story about the man whose invisibility creates havoc in an English village. The film made a star out of English-born actor Claude Rains, even though his face is not seen until near the end of the film. But he quickly developed into one of Hollywood's most incisive character stars, and was nominated four times for Oscars (shamefully without winning once) as best supporting actor.

Invisible Ray, The ◐

1936, US, 81 mins, b/w
Dir: Lambert Hillyer
Stars: Boris Karloff, Bela Lugosi, Frances Drake, Frank Lawton
Rating: ★★★

This story of a scientist poisoned by radioactive ore, whose touch will kill after a daily antidote has worn off, was one of several grim yarns on which Boris Karloff and Bela Lugosi got together in the Thirties. Well directed by Lambert Hillyer, who made the underrated *Dracula's Daughter* in the same year as this picture.

Invisible Stripes ○

1939, US, 82 mins, b/w
Dir: Lloyd Bacon
Stars: George Raft, William Holden, Humphrey Bogart, Jane Bryan
Rating: ★★★

Seldom-seen (but good), strongly cast prison/crime story based on yet anoth-er book by Warden Lewis E Lawes, seemingly author of the source material for half the prison films in Hollywood's history. Humphrey Bogart's Chuck Martin is clearly related to his Baby Face Martin in *Dead End*, as he's still snapping, snarling and doing the things Bogey did all the time before he became a movie hero. Newcomer William Holden strengthened the cast even more when Warners cast him as ex-con George Raft's kid brother, but Britain's Flora Robson is uneasily cast as their ma. In-joke: when Bogart and moll Lee Patrick are seen leaving a film, it's *You Can't Get Away With Murder*. Not only is the title prophetic to this plot, but it starred Bogart and was based on yet another book by Lawes!

Invitation to a Gunfighter ○

1964, US, 92 mins, colour
Dir: Richard Wilson
Stars: Yul Brynner, George Segal, Janice Rule, Pat Hingle
Rating: ★★

George Segal got his first leading role in this serious Western about a Union town which hires a notorious gunfighter to get rid of its only surviving Rebel homesteader at the end of the American Civil War. Segal is very good as the dogged Reb, while Brynner's role is more or less a continuation of his Chris in the *Magnificent Seven* films.

In Which We Serve ○ ⓥ

1942, UK, 110 mins, b/w
Dir: David Lean, Noel Coward
Stars: Noel Coward, John Mills, Bernard Miles, Celia Johnson, Richard Attenborough, Michael Wilding
Rating: ★★★★

Needing a co-director, Noel Coward gave David Lean his first chance behind the cameras on this inspiring, expertly-scripted war drama. The first British film to depict a naval war in all its grim reality, it proved the country's top moneymaker in the year of its release. Coward himself gave his best screen performance in the lead, and revived the film career of the young John Mills by casting him as Shorty Blake. After Coward and Lean watched the finished film together, Coward turned to Lean and told him: 'Well, dear boy, from now on you can take anything I write and make a film of it.'

Ipcress File, The ○ ⓥ

1965, UK, 109 mins, colour
Dir:, Sidney J Furie

Stars: Michael Caine, Nigel Green, Guy Doleman
Rating: ★★★★

This gruelling spy drama captured the imagination of the public to such a degree that star Michael Caine went on to star in two other (weaker) films about Len Deighton's Cockney crook turned secret agent Harry Palmer. Caine's anti-hero Palmer is a delightful creation, complete with thick spectacles, even thicker London accent, and a taste for Mozart and good food. The film was a huge international success for director Sidney J Furie.

I.Q. ○ ⓥ

1994, US, 100 mins, colour
Dir: Fred Schepisi
Stars: Tim Robbins, Meg Ryan, Walter Matthau, Stephen Fry
Rating: ★

What if Einstein's niece were to fall for a garage mechanic and Einstein colluded with the young man to make him appear a genius? Even if you cast Walter Matthau as Einstein, Meg Ryan as the niece and Tim Robbins as the mechanic, you get a tedious movie, that's what! Robbins' Honest Joe charm is pretty resistible in this one, Ryan wears harsh makeup that makes her look like Doris Day, and Matthau looks as though he's done it all before. But Fred Schepisi's clodhopping direction is the chief culprit in turning this romantic comedy into an indigestible lump that feels heavier than an overcooked pud, giving Stephen Fry, as the unwanted suitor, a Hollywood debut we're sure he'd rather forget.

I Remember Mama ○

1948, US, 134 mins, b/w
Dir: George Stevens
Stars: Irene Dunne, Barbara Bel Geddes, Oscar Homolka, Philip Dorn
Rating: ★★★★★

George Stevens' classic blend of humour and sentiment in the story of a Norwegian family, headed by a wise and indomitable mother, and their sometimes happy, sometimes tragic, always very human experiences, in San Francisco in 1910. Irene Dunne gives one of the best performances of her career (her Norwegian accent sounds impeccable) as Mama, while Oscar Homolka, as a bombastic uncle, creates minor havoc by his mere presence. The long running time is typical of Stevens' meticulous direction, where each scene is milked for every last drop of wonderful sentiment. This time it's justified.

Irma La Douce ①

1963, US, 146 mins, colour
Dir: Billy Wilder
Stars: Jack Lemmon, Shirley MacLaine, Lou Jacobi
Rating: ★★

Fairytale-style comedy which begins with a bang, and ends with a superbly-handled wedding scene, with the bride about to have a baby at any minute. Director Billy Wilder has taken the hit stage musical about a gendarme who falls for a prostitute, stripped it of his songs, and turned it into a pleasant, likeable comedy, with performances from Jack Lemmon and Shirley MacLaine (so memorable together in *The Apartment*) that are every bit as good as one might expect. Too long though; the songs instead of some of the dramatic padding might have made a difference.

Iron Eagle ① ⓥ

1986, US, 119 mins, colour
Dir: Sidney J Furie
Stars: Louis Gossett Jr, Jason Gedrick, David Suchet, Tim Thomerson
Rating: ★★★

Leave logic behind and enjoy the surging action scenes in this gung-ho adventure film about a group of American fighter pilots attempting a perilous hostage rescue somewhere in the Middle East. The dialogue is mainly moronic, but the stars at least look as though they believe in what they're doing and the aerial dogfights really set the adrenalin and blood bubbling. David Suchet is a caricature villain, but then most of this story could have sprung straight from a comic-strip.

Iron Eagle II ① ⓥ

1988, Canada, 101 mins, colour
Dir: Sidney J Furie
Stars: Louis Gossett Jr, Mark Humphrey, Stuart Margolin
Rating: ★★★

Naive and flag-waving, this is a very old-fashioned Hollywood-style 'war' film, with aerial action that edges out anything in *Top Gun*. The simplistic story of bomber pilots aiming to blow up an (unnamed) Arab nuclear base is given a novel tweak by mixing in a team of American and Russian pilots to do the job. And so they do, in spectacular fashion, making this gung-ho action pic a very exciting 20th-century version of *Star Wars* as the pilots, by now maverick after discovering a high-up plot to sabotage the mission by assembling 'Dirty Dozen' misfits,

home in on the missile base. Competent performances are, under the circumstances, all this international co-production requires. Two more sequels followed.

Iron Glove, The ○

1954, US, 77 mins, colour
Dir: William Castle
Stars: Robert Stack, Richard Stapley, Ursula Thiess
Rating: ★★

Swashbuckling adventure based on a true event in 17th-century history, when an adventurer called Charles Wogan was hired to protect the future bride of James, the Old Pretender, on a hazardous journey.

Iron Man, The ○

1951, US, 82 mins, b/w
Dir: Joseph Pevney
Stars: Jeff Chandler, Evelyn Keyes, Stephen McNally, Rock Hudson
Rating: ★★

Third screen version of the vigorous boxing novel of the same name by W R Burnett, who also wrote *Little Caesar*. Jeff Chandler is suitably unrelenting as the miner who turns killer in the boxing ring, and there are good performances from Evelyn Keyes as his girl, Rock Hudson as the friend he ultimately has to fight, and Jim Backus as a sportswriter. The ring scenes are pretty authentic for their day, and director Joseph Pevney keeps the reliable old story going at a good clip.

Iron Maze ● ⓥ

1991, US, 101 mins, colour
Dir: Hiroaki Yoshida
Stars: Jeff Fahey, Bridget Fonda, Hiroaki Murakami, J T Walsh
Rating: ★★

A turgid triangle running along *noir* lines, this is a drawn-out thriller comprising different accounts of an attempted murder – pretty obviously derived from the Japanese classic *Rashomon*. It isn't difficult to figure out the culprit, more difficult to figure out the attraction of moody bellboy Jeff Fahey for Bridget Fonda, the slight, plain American wife of the Japanese tycoon who's building an amusement park in the industrial town where Fahey used to work at the giant steel mill, now closed down. The atmosphere of the town's hopelessness is well established, but the unfolding of the slim plotline is slow and seems to take forever to reach its conclusion. J T Walsh, in a bigger role than usual, does a good turn as the local sheriff.

Iron Mistress, The ○

1952, US, 108 mins, colour
Dir: Gordon Douglas
Stars: Alan Ladd, Virginia Mayo, Joseph Calleia, Phyllis Kirk
Rating: ★★

Colourful adventure story which offers a sometimes exciting if often fanciful portrait of American Western folk hero Jim Bowie, who invented the Bowie knife. The performances are a bit colourless, so the action is everything, especially when Bowie (Alan Ladd), armed only with a knife, takes on a swordsman in a darkened room.

Iron Petticoat, The ○ ⓥ

1956, UK, 96 mins, colour
Dir: Ralph Thomas
Stars: Bob Hope, Katharine Hepburn, James Robertson Justice, Robert Helpmann
Rating: ★★★

A sort of satirical *Ninotchka* refashioned as a Bob Hope comedy. Hope's brilliant comedy barbs are matched by Katharine Hepburn's acid wit. The script is by Ben Hecht, an Academy Award winner as far back as 1928.

Ironweed ● ⓥ

1987, US, 144 mins, colour
Dir: Hector Babenco
Stars: Jack Nicholson, Meryl Streep, Carroll Baker
Rating: ★★★

Despite two towering central performances from Jack Nicholson and Meryl Streep (reunited after the previous year's *Heartburn*), *Ironweed* was a partial disappointment. Dubbed 'a film without an audience' by one critic, it's a low life story set among the street bunis of Manhattan during the great Depression, and based on a Pulitzer Prize-winning novel about a vagrant trying to get back into the society he dropped out of years earlier. Singer-turned-actor Tom Waits gives probably the film's most textured performance, which perfectly conveys the life he's sacrificed. But it's a slow and grimy journey that'll leave you wanting a bath.

Irreconcilable Differences ①

1984, US, 113 mins, colour
Dir: Charles Shyer
Stars: Ryan O'Neal, Shelley Long, Drew Barrymore, Sam Wanamaker, Sharon Stone
Rating: ★★

Any movie is going to have problems recovering from an opening scene in which a (fairly obnoxious) nine-year-old child tells the judge: 'I wanna divorce my parents.' There are times, though, when this attempted screwball romantic drama gives it a fair go, thanks mainly to the efforts of Shelley Long as one half of the warring couple. The plot is full of nostalgia for older (and, alas, better) movies, within whose framework such a story might once have worked if our emotions had been engaged. But we aren't meant to take this one seriously, are we, especially with embryo film director Ryan O'Neal (as Long's other half making a musical version of *Gone With the Wind* that goes over the top in every respect and must have been too horrendous in the first place to even contemplate? But the final courtroom 'tear-jerk', to say nothing of the slanging-match interludes, suggests that maybe this look at the spoilt rich who deserve a second chance represents the world at large and that we should coo in sympathy. Not in this day and age.

Isadora ●

1968, US, 152 mins, colour
Dir: Karel Reisz
Stars: Vanessa Redgrave, James Fox, Jason Robards
Rating: ★★

This biopic does try to convey the flavour of an exceptional woman born wildly out of her time. Isadora was a free spirit, a dancer, and, if you like, a turn-of-the-century hippie. She believed in free expression and free love, and possessed an incredible magnetism which the film somehow fails to bring across, even given the benefit of Vanessa Redgrave's skilful and suitably extravagant interpretation of the title role. As a study of the lives and times of some of the more unusual inhabitants of English, French, Russian and American society in the Edwardian era, however, the narrative remains gripping throughout its lengthy running time, originally more than three hours, but cut for subsequent general consumption. Jason Robards is terrific as Singer of the sewing maching family (by whom Isadora has a child) in one of the film's more amusing interludes.

I See a Dark Stranger ○ ⓥ

(aka: The Adventuress)
1946, UK, 111 mins, b/w
Dir: Frank Launder
Stars: Deborah Kerr, Trevor Howard, Raymond Huntley, Kathleen Harrison, David Tomlinson
Rating: ★★★★

Excellent wartime drama with a multiplicity of incident and some fascinating characters. Deborah Kerr is bewitching as the adventuress who, keen to join the IRA, becomes the pawn of Nazis instead. The writer-director team of Frank Launder and Sidney Gilliat concocted, with the aid of Wolfgang Wilhelm and actor Liam Redmond (who also plays a major part in the film) one of their cleverest and most incisive scripts.

I See Ice ☉

1938, UK, 81 mins, b/w
Dir: Anthony Kimmins
Stars: George Formby, Kay Walsh
Rating: ★★★★

Wigan's cheeky comic George Formby became one of Britain's top box-office film stars in the Thirties. Here, he's on top form as a photographer who falls for a skater, lands himself in prison and ends up refereeing an ice hockey match. Uproarious, fast-moving comedy on and off the ice.

I Shall Return

See: An American Guerilla in the Philippines

Ishtar ○ ⓥ

1987, US, 107 mins, colour
Dir: Elaine May
Stars: Warren Beatty, Dustin Hoffman, Isabelle Adjani, Charles Grodin
Rating: ★★

Is it a road movie? Is it a sharp, witty comedy? Or is it a total turkey? Only a handful of films have been bad-mouthed by the movie industry , prior to release, to the extent of *Ishtar*. It deserves a kinder look; director Elaine May is a true original and she coaxes performances of real, touching humour from the unlikely pairing of Dustin Hoffman and Warren Beatty. They play a pair of down-and-out songwriters who end up in a North African revolution (they actually did write one of the songs they perform: 'Half Hour Song'). Forget the gossip – remember the *Road* comedies and enjoy it!

Island at the Top of the World, The ☉

1974, US, 93 mins, colour
Dir: Robert Stevenson
Stars: Donald Sinden, David Hartman
Rating: ★★

A ripping adventure yarn in the best Victorian tradition, with only wobbly process work letting it down. When the son of an English lord goes missing on an expedition to the Arctic, his fa-

ther is determined to find him, despite only having a curious map carved on whalebone and a rather cryptic entry in a ship's journal. The adventure's the thing in this *Boy's Own Paper* saga, and there's plenty of that.

Island in the Sun ○

1957, US, 119 mins, colour
Dir: Robert Rossen
Stars: James Mason, Joan Fontaine, Dorothy Dandridge, Michael Rennie, Joan Collins, Harry Belafonte
Rating: ★★

Made on location in the sun-soaked Caribbean, this film portrayed one of the first black-white love affairs on screen. James Mason gives a fine performance as the weak, half-white and eventually homicidal son of a plantation owner, and is on record as saying it was one of the films he most enjoyed making. Generally, though, the all-star cast, perhaps sapped by the sunshine, is lacking in inspiration.

Island of Dr Moreau, The ●

1977, US, 95 mins, colour
Dir: Don Taylor
Stars: Burt Lancaster, Michael York, Barbara Carrera, Richard Basehart
Rating: ★★★

This later version of the H G Wells story, splendidly made in 1932 as *Island of Lost Souls*, has some superbly melodramatic dialogue and provides the screen with a splendid dose of grisly hokum, directed by Don Taylor at a pace that kills disbelief. You'll long remember mad scientist Burt Lancaster telling the victims of his experiments that 'He who breaks the law goes back to the House of Pain!'. 'I sleep better here,' mutters Nigel Davenport, in another vintage exchange. 'Not well, but better.'

Island of Dr Moreau, The ● ⓥ

1996, US, 95 mins, colour
Dir: John Frankenheimer
Stars: Marlon Brando, Val Kilmer, David Thewlis, Fairuza Balk, Ron Perlman, William Hootkins
Rating: ★★

It's third time unlucky for this version of H G Wells' chilling fantasy about a scientist playing mix 'n' match with animals and humans in his Pacific island laboratory. Marlon Brando is outrageously over the top in the title role, but his gross and shamelessly camp madman at least has more life than Val Kilmer's morose drifter, slinking sullenly through the undergrowth. And

David Thewlis walks through his role as the hapless shipwreck victim trapped on the island, There's plenty of animal snarling and growling, not to mention pouncing, but so little suspense that the film is not in the slightest bit scary, merely gruesome. Creature effects are okay if, like the film, unmemorable.

Island of the Lost ⊙

1968, US, 91 mins, colour
Dir: Ricou Browning, Richard Carlson
Stars: Richard Greene, Luke Halpin
Rating: ★★

Richard Carlson and Ricou Browning, who starred as scientist and monster in *The Creature from the Black Lagoon*, obviously developed a taste for watery weirdies. They are screenplay writer and co-director, respectively, on this adventure story about a voyage in search of uncharted islands. Richard Greene, in real life an enthusiastic yachtsman, proved an ideal choice for the role of the barquentine skipper who encounters not only undersea perils but carnivorous ostriches and sabre-toothed wolves.

Island Rescue

See: Appointment with Venus

Isn't Life Wonderful! ⊙

1953, UK, 83 mins, colour
Dir: Harold French
Stars: Cecil Parker, Eileen Herlie, Donald Wolfit, Dianne Foster
Rating: ★★★

Comedy of a gentle order, in a charming romp about an Edwardian family. One of the funniest sequences is that in which father, adamantly refusing advice or assistance, nearly kills himself trying to uncrate and assemble a bicycle. And another delightful piece of comedy is the railway trip which mother treats as a terrifying adventure. No big stars in this film, which makes it an unexpected treat.

I Take This Woman ○

1940, US, 97 mins, b/w
Dir: W S Van Dyke II
Stars: Spencer Tracy, Hedy Lamarr, Kent Taylor, Laraine Day
Rating: ★★

This MGM romantic epic about a dedicated doctor who marries a glamour girl took so long to complete (Spencer Tracy, tired of reshooting scene after scene, went off and made another film in the middle) that the trade dubbed it *I Retake This Woman*. What eventually emerged is a routine soap opera, some-

what after the fashion of *The Citadel*, but enlivened by the presence of Tracy, Hedy Lamarr, Jack Carson and Laraine Day.

Italian Job, The ○ ⓥ

1969, UK, 100 mins, colour
Dir: Peter Collinson
Stars: Michael Caine, Noel Coward, Benny Hill, Raf Vallone, Rossano Brazzi
Rating: ★★★

Despite the talents of Michael Caine, Noel Coward and Benny Hill, the cars are the stars of this action-comedy in which Coward's the mastermind who, from inside a prison cell, organises the theft of four million dollars worth of gold bullion. Michael Caine is the leader of a gang of comic crooks who carry out his plans. But it's the getaway chase that you'll remember rather than the robbery itself. It's brilliantly staged by director Peter Collinson, his second-unit director Phillip Wrestler, and a team of stunt drivers known as L'Equipe Remy Julienne. Together, they turn three Mini Coopers into acrobats and contortionists. One car jumps rooftops, while others career through sewers, arcades filled with diners, churches, stairways and other places that cars just aren't supposed to go. Skidding, scudding, screeching and scorching their tyres, they steal the show entirely, leaving scores of pursuing vehicles wrecked in their wake.

It All Came True ○

1940, US, 97 mins, b/w
Dir: Lewis Seiler
Stars: Humphrey Bogart, Ann Sheridan, Jeffrey Lynn, ZaSu Pitts
Rating: ★★

Warners' gangster comedies looked funnier when they came out, juxtaposed to the studio's own crime films, than they do now. Here it's Humphrey Bogart going for Damon Runyon-style comedy as a gangster who, hiding out in a theatrical boarding house, becomes swept up in the atmosphere of the thing and even suggests turning it into a nightclub to solve everyone's financial problems. Sounds great, but the treatment here doesn't have the courage of the Bogart character's convictions and the script lacks real wit. Still, the atmosphere is jolly and seven songs make the movie feel at times almost like a musical.

It Always Rains on Sunday ○

1947, UK, 92 mins, b/w
Dir: Robert Hamer

Stars: Googie Withers, Jack Warner, John McCallum, Jimmy Hanley
Rating: ★★★★

Well and truly installed n the cinema's Hall of Fame, this grimly gripping film flew in the vanguard of a revolution in the British cinema. For the first time, Ealing Studios took cameras out and about, into the city's back streets, and filmed their actors against markets, pubs and slums, alleyways and dock wharfs that were really there. The result was a brilliant new approach to the crime thriller – paralleled at the same time in America by *The Naked City*. The actors slip into their parts like gloves, and the story of a man on the run, who has a way with women, assumes a semi-factual approach that adds to its power and excitement.

It Came from Beneath the Sea ○

1954, US, 80 mins, b/w
Dir: Robert Gordon
Stars: Faith Domergue, Kenneth Tobey
Rating: ★★

Ray Harryhausen, later to become responsible for the Dynamation process used in so many films, including the Sinbad adventures, got his second solo assignment on this science-fiction thriller about a giant octopus that goes on the rampage in San Francisco harbour. And it's an impressive creation. The creature is supposed to have been driven from the depths of the ocean by H-bomb experiments. Almost as impressive to watch is sultry Faith Domergue, once a Howard Hughes protégé at RKO, and as unlikely a scientist as ever was.

It Came from Outer Space ○

1953, US, 81 mins, b/w
Dir: Jack Arnold
Stars: Richard Carlson, Barbara Rush
Rating: ★★★

This tense science-fiction thriller – originally made for 3-D – has common assets with other films of its genre produced at Universal-International in the Fifties: a generous budget, a capable director (Jack Arnold, who made *Tarantula!* and *The Incredible Shrinking Man*) and some excellent source material, in this case a novel by Ray Bradbury. Arnold conducts the chills with a fine sense of mounting suspense and danger.

It Could Happen to You ○ ⓥ

1994, US, 101 mins, colour
Dir: Andrew Bergman

Stars: Bridget Fonda, Nicolas Cage,
Rosie Perez, Wendell Pierce, Seymour
Cassel, Red Buttons
Rating: ★★

Nicolas Cage and Bridget Fonda are
too-good-to-be-true characters in this
romantic fantasy, which never takes itself seriously enough to touch our
emotions, remaining candy-floss fare.
Cage is a cop and all-round-do-gooder
who buys his virago of a wife (the intensely annoying Rosie Perez) a ticket
in the New York State Lottery. Fonda
is a coffee-shop waitress to whom
Cage, stuck for a tip, offers half of his
lottery ticket. Naturally it wins, or we
wouldn't have a story. Cage, true to
his saintly character, sticks to his word
and his wife is furious. The script expects that we'll want Cage and Fonda
to end up together here, but it isn't
that easy to root for characters as sac-
charine-sweet as these. And the scene
where Perez and Cage, divorcing, get
together to divide up the spoils, is
treated almost like vaudeville farce. In
the end, it just about works in its fairy-
tale fashion.

It Couldn't Happen Here ① Ⓥ

1987, UK, 87 mins, colour
Dir: Jack Bond
Stars: Pet Shop Boys, Joss Ackland,
Barbara Windsor
Rating: ★

Loved the music, but shame about the
Pet Shop Boys' only film venture to
date, which is no more than a series of
videos – and a mixed bunch at that –
masquerading as a movie. Such choreography as there is in the dozen or so
musical numbers is mediocre at best.
So to the songs: moody, well-written
stuff with backgrounds that show great
care and invention and are very interesting musically speaking, some of the
most original sounds to emerge from
the pop world since the Sixties. Pet
Shop Boys fans will watch it anyway,
but generally one's advice to the guys
is to stick to the albums: emphasising
their own moroseness hardly lends
sparks to the laboured seaside postcard
charades here.

It Happened in Brooklyn ◯

1947, US, 105 mins, b/w
Dir: Richard Whorf
Stars: Frank Sinatra, Kathryn Grayson,
Peter Lawford, Jimmy Durante, Gloria
Grahame
Rating: ★★

A dispute with Technicolor laborato-
ries led to this MGM musical being

filmed in black-and-white instead of
the usual lavish colour. Frank
Sinatra's best showing as an actor in
the early stages of his career, it also
had a first-rate Jule Styne-Sammy
Cahn score that includes 'Time After
Time', 'I Believe', 'It's the Same Old
Dream' and a smash-hit duet by
Sinatra and veteran Jimmy Durante,
'The Song's Gotta Come from the
Heart'. Gloda Grahame also scored
an early success as the nurse who vies
with singing teacher Kathryn Grayson
for Sinatra's affections.

It Happened One Night ◯ Ⓥ

1934, US, 105 mins, b/w
Dir: Frank Capra
Stars: Clark Gable, Claudette Colbert,
Walter Connolly, Roscoe Karns,
Jameson Thomas, Alan Hale
Rating: ★★★★

A delightful freewheeling comedy that
took the critics by surprise and subsequently became the first film to win all
five major Oscars (film, director, actor,
actress, screenplay), a feat rarely repeated since. The cross-country
journey of Claudette Colbert and
Clark Gable, she on the run from an
arranged marriage, he on the lookout
for a scoop, is still fresh, funny and enchantingly coated with sexual
smoulder.

It Happened on 5th Avenue ◯

1947, US, 115 mins, b/w
Dir: Roy Del Ruth
Stars: Victor Moore, Ann Harding
Rating: ★★

Millionaire Charlie Ruggles allows
hobo Victor Moore to live in his plush
New York apartment while he winters
in Carolina. As you might imagine,
Moore has a high old time, filling the
place with friends and visitors. But
two of those visitors are Ruggles and
his daughter (Ann Harding) – heavily
disguised ... This musical comedy
wears out its welcome eventually, but
it's good-natured entertainment and
the music's fun, too.

It Happened to Jane ◯

(aka: That Jane from Maine)
1959, US, 98 mins, colour
Dir: Richard Quine
Stars: Doris Day, Jack Lemmon, Ernie
Kovacs, Steve Forrest
Rating: ★★★★

A fast-moving comedy with Doris Day
as a small-town lobster-dealer who has
a cargo ruined by the railway and is
determined to get her own back.

Beautiful colour photography and a furious finale involving trains,
complement the likeable portrayals of
Ms Day, Jack Lemmon and the
apoplectic Ernie Kovacs, to make this
one of the most enjoyable comedies in
many a long day.

It Happened Tomorrow ◯

1944, US, 84 mins, b/w
Dir: René Clair
Stars: Dick Powell, Linda Darnell, Jack
Oakie, John Philliber
Rating: ★★★★

French director René Clair made several excellent films during his enforced
wartime stay in Hollywood, but none
more delightful than this fantasy about
a turn-of-the-century reporter. Dick
Powell, just building a new career after
saying goodbye to musicals, plays the
newsman who understandably can't
believe it when he meets an old man
who gives him newspapers that 'foretell' events of the immediate future.
Clair gets everything right, and the result is a film of much amusement and
charm.

It Takes Two ◯ Ⓥ

1995, US, 101 mins, colour
Dir: Andy Tennant
Stars: Kirstie Alley, Steve Guttenberg,
Ashley Olsen, Emma-Kate Olsen, Philip
Bosco, Jane Sibbett
Rating: ★

Nine-year-old 'identical strangers' bring
together the two people they love.
Didn't this sort of thing used to be fun?
Not any more and, although there are
a few laughs in this one – mostly from
the affectionate playing of wily veteran
character actor Philip Bosco as a down-
to-earth butler – it isn't enough to
validate the picture. The Olsen twins
are popular on American TV, but they
don't impress overmuch here, although
Emma-Kate is better than sister Ashley
by quite a large margin. But the director Andy Tennant lacks the confidence
to make it work, while Steve
Guttenberg and Kirstie Alley have the
slightly hunted look of actors who
know they're batting on a sticky wicket. Polish, precision timing and better
editing would all help. But the basic
truth is probably that this kind of simple fun has, sadly, had its day.

It's a Gift ◯

1934, US, 73 mins, b/w
Dir: Norman Z McLeod
Stars: W C Fields, Kathleen Howard,
Baby LeRoy, Jean Rouverol
Rating: ★★★★★

An almost undiluted flask of W C Fields – one of the great man's finest comedies, casting him as a small-town shopkeeper beset by wife, family and customers alike. A whole barrage of masterly scenes includes the sequence where the blind man destroys Fields' shop with a few injudicious waves of his white cane; and the 'sleeping porch' segment where Baby LeRoy obligingly drops grapes into Fields' mouth ('Shades of Bacchus!' Fields gasps), but follows them with an ice pick.

It's Always Fair Weather ○

1955, US, 101 mins, colour
Dir: Stanley Donen
Stars: Gene Kelly, Dan Dailey, Cyd Charisse, Dolores Gray
Rating: ★★★

Back on the town, three war buddies meet up again ten years after VJ day in this vigorous Comden and Green musical. Excellent dancing from Gene Kelly, Dan Dailey and choreographer Michael Kidd; plenty of first rate numbers including the famous 'dustbin dance'. Good use of wide screen may be lost on television.

It's a Mad, Mad, Mad, Mad World ○ Ⓥ

1963, US, 192 mins, colour
Dir: Stanley Kramer
Stars: Spencer Tracy, Milton Berle, Sid Caesar, Mickey Rooney, Ethel Merman, Phil Silvers, Buddy Hackett
Rating: ★★

You can't keep all the people laughing all the time for three hours. But, to its eternal credit, this marathon comedy chase film does have a darned good try. And there are laughs galore in its giant story of 10 people (including Spencer Tracy, Mickey Rooney, Terry-Thomas and Phil Silvers) all after a case of thousand-dollar bills hidden in a certain area 'under a big W'. The bank robber, Jimmy Durante, gives them this enigmatic clue after they have seen his car crash off a mountain road. As he dies, he kicks a large bucket down the mountainside. It's that kind of film. Among those flashing across the screen in fleeting appearances, you may recognise Jerry Lewis, Buster Keaton, Leo Gorcey (without the Bowery Boys), Joe E Brown, Jack Benny and The Three Stooges.

It's a Wonderful Life ○ Ⓥ

1946, US, 125 mins, b/w
Dir: Frank Capra

Stars: James Stewart, Donna Reed, Lionel Barrymore, Thomas Mitchell, Henry Travers, Gloria Grahame
Rating: ★★★★★

This is Oscar-winning director Frank Capra's finest film and could justifiably lay claim to being one of the best movies ever made. It's both a summation of Capra's own career and a peak of achievement for a gentler kind of American cinema which was to fade in post-war years and disappear altogether with the harshness and violence of modern times. James Stewart is at his best as the man asked by an angel to reflect on his life when he contemplates suicide. But it's in the amazing depth of character and incident, all immaculately conceived and executed, that the film scores most heavily. The ending is a real tearjerker and, if you don't agree with Capra that life is really like this, then you might go along with his sentiments that it ought to be.

It's a Wonderful World ○

1956, UK, 89 mins, colour
Dir: Val Guest
Stars: Terence Morgan, George Cole, Kathleen Harrison, Mylene Nicole
Rating: ★★★

A rare British comedy-musical, focussing on the efforts of two impoverished songwriters to break into the world of pop music. Ted Heath and his Music supply most of the melody in this bright film, which extracts every laugh possible from odd-ball landladies, teenage pop fans, highbrow music critics and Tin Pan Alley in general. George Cole is on good form as the scatterbrained half of the writing duo, there's a good dream sequence, and there's also some tuneful songs from Mylene Nicole, who became better known in films under her real name of Mylene Demongeot.

It's a Wonderful World ○

1939, US, 86 mins, b/w
Dir: W S Van Dyke II
Stars: Claudette Colbert, James Stewart, Guy Kibbee, Frances Drake
Rating: ★★★

A big welcome for this screwball comedy. A combination of It Happened One Night and The 39 Steps, with Claudette Colbert as a runaway poetess and James Stewart as the man just running – from the law. Very funny, thanks to a pacy, witty script from Ben Hecht and Herman J Mankiewicz. The inspired story they concocted makes room for several of Hollywood's best

character actors, with even Nat Pendleton and Edgar Kennedy funnier than usual as a couple of comic cops in hot pursuit of Colbert and Stewart.

It's Great to be Young ⊙

1956, UK, 90 mins, colour
Dir: Cyril Frankel
Stars: John Mills, Cecil Parker
Rating: ★★★★

An exuberant comedy-musical, richly shot in Technicolor by Gilbert Taylor and full of fun and youthful bounce. Though made in Britain, it's reminiscent of the Judy Garland-Mickey Rooney let's-put-on-a-show films at MGM in the early Forties. John Mills is in tremendous form as the unorthodox school music master whose sacking provokes a revolution and, with its tuneful score, the film was a hit with critics and public alike. Top songs: 'Marching Strings' and 'You Are My First Love', with Ruby Murray providing Dorothy Bromily's singing voice.

It Should Happen to You ○

1953, US, 100 mins, b/w
Dir: George Cukor
Stars: Judy Holliday, Peter Lawford, Jack Lemmon
Rating: ★★★

Breezy romantic comedy featuring a delightful performance by Judy Holliday as an unemployed model who changes her life by advertising herself from a huge billboard overlooking New York's Columbus Circle. Jack Lemmon makes his film debut and you may spot Constance Bennett and Wendy Barric as panel game members, as well as John Saxon (another film debut) as a boy on a park bench.

It Shouldn't Happen to a Vet ○

1976, UK, 94 mins, colour
Dir: Eric Till
Stars: John Alderton, Colin Blakely, Lisa Harrow
Rating: ★★★

Another pleasant canter through the laughs and heartbreaks of a country vet in 1938. It's a sequel to All Creatures Great and Small, but with John Alderton as the vet and Colin Blakely as his senior partner instead of the previous stars. Neither alteration does any harm, with the result that this romp, additionally enhanced by the distinguished Yorkshire Moor photography of Arthur Ibbetson, is a slight improvement on its predecessor. The delicious Lisa Harrow is again the vet's wife, and supporting parts are on the whole well-drawn, although the county fair proves something of an anti-climax. It's good lightweight fare.

It's Love Again ○
1936, UK, 83 mins, b/w
Dir: Victor Saville
Stars: Jessie Matthews, Robert Young, Sonnie Haie
Rating: ★★★★

The last, and critically most successful of five films made by Britain's top Thirties' musical star, Jessie Matthews, with her favourite director Victor Saville. Jessie sings and dances vivaciously in costumes that seem sometimes amazingly scanty for the time, and does her famous imitation of Mrs Smythe-Smythe, a legendary huntress from the east. Robert Young was brought over from Hollywood to give the film some clout in America, and the Sam Coslow-Harry Woods songs include 'It's Love Again' and 'Gotta Dance My Way to Heaven'. The last highpoint of Jessie's career.

It's Love I'm After ○
1937, US, 90 mins, b/w
Dir: Archie L Mayo
Stars: Leslie Howard, Bette Davis, Olivia de Havilland
Rating: ★★

A rare romantic comedy for the great Bette Davis, this film re-teams her with Leslie Howard after their success together in *The Petrified Forest*. Davis and Howard play feuding Broadway stars, with Olivia de Havilland forming the third point of the embattled triangle as the heiress who develops a crush on Howard's tarnished matinée idol. Casey Robinson's script is full of barbed wisecracks and wry-faced Eric Blore almost steals the show as (inevitably) a gentleman's gentleman.

It's Magic ⊙
(aka: Romance on the High Seas)
1948, US, 100 mins, colour
Dir: Michael Curtiz
Stars: Jack Carson, Janis Paige, Don DeFore, Doris Day
Rating: ★★★

The film that launched the career of Doris Day. She was fourth billed here and only got the role as a last-minute replacement for Berry Hutton. But 26-year-old Doris was the hit of the film, and cornered the market in successive freckle-faced girl-next-door roles in light musicals and dramas. Her big musical numbers, 'It's Magic' and Put

'em in a Box, Tie 'em with a Ribbon and Throw 'em in the Deep Blue Sea', became king-sized hits in the dance halls. Little more than a series of tired romantic situations, the story is pepped up with snappy songs and choreography from Busby Berkeley, who returned specially to Warners studio to create the dance sequences.

It's My Party ●
1995, US, 110 mins, colour
Dir: Randal Kleiser
Stars: Eric Roberts, Gregory Harrison, Lee Grant, Marlee Matlin, Roddy McDowall, George Segal
Rating: ★★★★

A mega-weepie about the last hours of a man dying from AIDS. Nick Stark (Eric Roberts), though, means to go with dignity and a smile. Given just a few days to live, he decides on a night, day and night party, before ending his life with a massive dose of pills. His friends and family, even his long-unseen father (George Segal) all rally round. All that's missing is the long-time lover (Gregory Harrison) who left him a year before. Several hitherto bland talents reveal unsuspected depths in this fine film, from the gently understated direction of Kleiser, to career-best portrayals from Roberts and Harrison, Roberts especially redeeming years of over-the-top performances with a tightly reined-in portrait of a man who faces death with calm, grim gallows humour, 'What are you doing tomorrow?' he asks a friend. 'Nothing,' he's told. Roberts smiles. 'Neither am I,' he says.

It's Never Too Late ○
1956, US, 95 mins, colour
Dir: Michael McCarthy
Stars: Phyllis Calvert, Patrick Barr
Rating: ★★

Bright and breezy family comedy with Phylis Calvert, as the part-time author and full-time mum who suddenly has celebrity status thrust upon her, heading an accomplished cast of farceurs. Director Michael McCarthy keeps the amusing action bubbling over but does little to conceal the piece's stage origins.

It's Not Cricket ⊙
1948, UK, 77 mins, b/w
Dir: Roy Rich
Stars: Basil Radford, Naunton Wayne, Susan Shaw
Rating: ★★★

Basil Radford and Naunton Wayne not for once as their most famous char-

acters, Charters and Caldicott, but as bumbling private eyes Bright and Early. This is a consistently funny comedy which owes much to an amusing performance by Maurice Denham as a ubiquitous German spy and has a riotous climax.

It's Only Money ⊙
1962, US, 84 mins, b/w
Dir: Frank Tashlin
Stars: Jerry Lewis, Zachary Scott
Rating: ★★★

Better than usual Lewis comedy (perhaps because it's directed by Frank Tashlin), which casts Jerry as the unknowing heir to a fortune. Look out for 'The Attack of the Lawn Mowers': it's one of the funniest visual sequences in any Lewis comedy.

It Started In Naples ○
1960, US, 100 mins, colour
Dir: Melville Shavelson
Stars: Clark Gable, Sophia Loren, Vittorio de Sica
Rating: ★★★★

Sophia Loren as a fiery cabaret entertainer in a charming comedy about a hardened 10-year-old Italian waif torn between her and a stiff American uncle. Easily the best comedy Sophia made for Hollywood – perhaps because she felt at home in Naples and its environs. The scenery – especially the harbour settings – is gloriously shot in colour, and there's a likeable performance by a little Italian boy called Manetto. Even Clark Gable, who tended to give rather staid performances in his later years, seems to unbend in the Neapolitan sunshine, to make this an altogether pleasurable experience. But it's Sophia's show. Just watching her flamenco dancing makes it worthwhile.

It Started with Eve ○
1941, US, 90 mins, b/w
Dir: Henry Koster
Stars: Deanna Durbin, Charles Laughton, Robert Cummings
Rating: ★★★★

The captivating Deanna Durbin gets a chance to display a nice sense of comedy, and trills as prettily as ever, in this zany comedy, which was probably the zenith of her career. The story casts Charles Laughton as the millionaire head of a somewhat eccentric family.

Ivanhoe ○ Ⓥ
1952, UK, 107 mins, colour
Dir: Richard Thorpe
Stars: Robert Taylor, Elizabeth Taylor,

Joan Fontaine, George Sanders, Emlyn Williams, Robert Douglas
Rating: ★★★★

All three of Robert Taylor's forays into English legend – the others were *Knights of the Round Table* and *Quentin Durward* – proved notable successes and this lively adaptation of Sir Walter Scott's novel by Noel Langley was the first. Taylor plays Wilfrid of Ivanhoe as a kind of Robin Hood in armour, doing his best to humiliate Prince John and his lieutenants – in this case George Sanders and Robert Douglas, later to take opposite sides in *King Richard and the Crusaders* – while waiting for King Richard to return from the Crusades. The jousting and other action scenes are magnificently handled.

Ivory Hunter

See: Where No Vultures Fly

Ivy ○

1947, US, 99 mins, b/w
Dir: Sam Wood
Stars: Joan Fontaine, Herbert Marshall, Patric Knowles, Cedric Hardwicke
Rating: ★★★

Joan Fontaine escaped her customary casting as a delicate damsel to play an Edwardian poisoness in this melodrama. Director Sam Wood endows the London settings with a nicely sinister atmosphere and the suspense is splendidly sustained. Wood had a classy ally in producer/production designer William Cameron Menzies, who strengthened the mediocre script with some splendid art direction and set design.

I Wake Up Screaming ○ ⓥ

(aka: Hot Spot)
1941, US, 82 mins, b/w
Dir: H Bruce Humberstone
Stars: Betty Grable, Victor Mature, Laird Cregar, Carole Landis
Rating: ★★★

One of Betty Grable's few non-musical roles of the war years, this thriller was remade 12 years later as *Vicki*. An early *film noir*, broodingly photographed by the talented Edward Cronjager, it allows room for rich character studies from burly Laird Cregar as an obsessive detective, Elisha Cook Jr as a twitchy liftboy, and suave Alan Mowbray as a big-headed ham actor. The sense of threat surrounding the 'framed' hero (another serviceable performance from the undervalued Victor Mature) is very well sustained.

I Walk Alone ○

1947, US, 98 mins, b/w
Dir: Byron Haskin
Stars: Burt Lancaster, Kirk Douglas, Lizabeth Scott, Wendell Corey
Rating: ★★★

Burt Lancaster and Kirk Douglas were both at the beginning of their star careers when this grim, tough crime thriller was made. The plot is reminiscent of a couple of Cagney-Bogart vehicles of the late Thirties. And the action flows with a will.

I Walked with a Zombie ⓓ

1943, US, 66 mins, b/w
Dir: Jacques Tourneur
Stars: Tom Conway, Frances Dee, James Ellison
Rating: ★★★

Much better than its title would indicate, this beautifully made drama is a sort of Haitian voodoo offshoot of *Jane Eyre*. A little on the slow side, it nonetheless remained talented director Jacques Tourneur's favourite film, mainly becuse of its poetic qualities. It's very moody and sometimes quite chilly, with a commendably firm central performance by Frances Dee.

I Walk the Line ⓓ

1970, US, 95 mins, colour
Dir: John Frankenheimer
Stars: Gregory Peck, Tuesday Weld, Estelle Parsons, Ralph Meeker, Charles Durning
Rating: ★★

There's another magnetic performance from that underrated actress Tuesday Weld in this tale of moonshine whiskey runners and small-town scandal in America's Deep South. Nine songs by Johnny Cash provide a musical commentary on the hopeless passion of middle-aged sheriff Gregory Peck for Miss Weld's mountain girl.

I Want to Live! ⓓ

1958, US, 120 mins, b/w
Dir: Robert Wise
Stars: Susan Hayward, Simon Oakland
Rating: ★★★★

Harrowing, very compelling dramatisation of the famous Barbara Graham case, with Susan Hayward giving an all-stops-out performance as the woman sentenced to the electric chair. Her showing won her an Academy Award, an honour she had just missed for her equally gripping portrayal of singer Lillian Roth three years earlier in *I'll Cry Tomorrow*.

I Want You ○

1951, US, 102 mins, b/w
Dir: Mark Robson
Stars: Dorothy McGuire, Dana Andrews, Farley Granger, Peggy Dow
Rating: ★★★

Nostalgically atmospheric slice of Americana, spotlighting the problems of small-town families whose menfolk are called away to (the Korean) war. Solid performances from Dorothy McGuire, Dana Andrews, Farley Granger and Peggy Dow.

I Was a Male War Bride ○

(aka: You Can't Sleep Here)
1949, US, 105 mins, b/w
Dir: Howard Hawks
Stars: Cary Grant, Ann Sheridan, Marion Marshall, Randy Stuart
Rating: ★★★★

Director Howard Hawks continued his successful theme of a series of abrasive battles-of-the-sexes between two people eventually destined to fall in love, begun in *Twentieth Century*, *Bringing Up Baby*, *His Girl Friday*, *Ball of Fire* and *To Have and Have Not*. Ann Sheridan carries on splendidly in the tradition of Carole Lombard, Katharine Hepburn and Lauren Bacall, giving an unexpectedly sparkling performance as the American WAC lieutenant detailed to act as interpreter for a male chauvinist French officer, smoothly played by Cary Grant at his deftest. The series of misadventures suffered by the couple, on the way to an inn where Ann sees to it that Cary sleeps with the chickens, makes rollicking entertainment.

I Was Monty's Double ○ ⓥ

(aka: Monty's Double)
1958, UK, 95 mins, b/w
Dir: John Guillermin
Stars: John Mills, Cecil Parker, Michael Hordern, Marius Goring
Rating: ★★★

A fascinating account of how an actor, M E Clifton-James (who plays himself in the film) passed as General Montgomery in an attempt to make the Germans believe that the invasion of Europe would come from North Africa. This amazing deception actually made Hitler hold a Panzer division in the South of France. The screenplay, a compact and compelling piece of work, was written by Bryan Forbes. The only point in his scenario which may annoy students of history is the fictional attempted kidnapping of 'Monty' by the Germans. The real

I

ending was more amusing: James (he had been seconded from an Army office) returned to his base and was arrested as a deserter!

I Wonder Who's Kissing Her Now ⊙

1947, US, 104 mins, colour
Dir: Lloyd Bacon
Stars: June Haver, Mark Stevens, Martha Stewart, Reginald Gardiner, Gene Nelson
Rating: ★★★★

There's a certain freshness and verve that, added to its backstage insights and ultra-tuneful score, give this turn-of-the-century musical biopic the edge over many of its competitors. Hermes Pan's vaudeville routines carry an authentic smack of yesteryear and Ernest Palmer's Technicolor photography is as clear as crystal. The subject is a real-life composer called Joe Howard, breezily played by Mark Stevens, who like his predecessor in musicals at 20th Century-Fox, John Payne, later made his name in tough-guy roles. Here Stevens teams well with vivacious blonde June Haver (although his singing voice was dubbed by Buddy Clark) and their numbers together are charming.

Jabberwocky ◑ ⓥ

1977, UK, 105 mins, colour
Dir: Terry Gilliam
Stars: Michael Palin, Harry H Corbett, Max Wall, John le Mesurier, Warren Mitchell
Rating: ★★

You may or may not find Terry Gilliam's medieval monster mayhem for the Monty Pythons a funny film, but it certainly is messy. It's full of people relieving themselves, flagellating themselves, rolling in mud or worse, fountaining blood and being chopped or chewed to pieces. Ugh! Amid all the grime and gore, it must be admitted, lurks (as well as the jabberwock) the occasional snigger, mostly from Max Wall as King Bruno the Questionable. Gilliam's pictorial flair, however, was never seen to better advantage. Castles are silhouetted against sunsets, boats paddle silkily across stagnant, misty lakes, and the princess tiptoes towards the dazed hero (Michael Palin) through a flutter of nuns' handkerchiefs.

Jack ◯ ⓥ

1996, US, 113 mins, colour
Dir: Francis Ford Coppola
Stars: Robin Williams, Diane Lane, Jennifer Lopez, Bill Cosby
Rating: ★★

Rapid ageing usually forms part of a horror film. Here, it provides a showcase for Robin Williams as a 10-year-old boy embarrassingly trapped inside a 40-year-old body. We too are embarrassed at the situations into which the adult-looking Williams is forced at school but he, like the film, comes good in a triumphant finale when, as a 17-year-old graduate looking 68, he tells parents and fellow-students that his life has been brilliant and spectacular. Love him or loathe him, Williams is virtually the whole show, although Diane Lane is unexpectedly good as his spirited mother.

Jack Ahoy ⊙

1934, UK, 82 mins, b/w
Dir: Walter Forde
Stars: Jack Hulbert, Nancy O'Neil, Alfred Drayton
Rating: ★★★

Long thought to be a lost film, this breezy if makeshift comedy features jolly Jack Hulbert as the latest in a long line of inept sailors. Naturally, this being a Jack Hulbert film, our hero gets to dance a hornpipe. He also accidentally terrorises the admiral to such an extent that that worthy, held hostage in the Far East and confronted by a rescuing Jack, tells him, 'Get out of here at once. If you don't I'll call the bandits!' The film has one big hit song, 'The Hat's on the Side of My Head', which it flogs remorselessly, and a rather limp leading lady in Nancy O'Neil, who is out-sparkled by a too-little-used Tamara Desni as an exotic spy. Surprisingly rough and ready at times, the film has an energetic performance by Hulbert and some nice throwaway lines for those prepared to wait.

Jack & Sarah ◑ ⓥ

1995, UK, 104 mins, colour
Dir: Tim Sullivan
Stars: Richard E Grant, Samantha Mathis, Ian McKellen, Judi Dench, Cherie Lunghi, Eileen Atkins
Rating: ★★★

Apart from the swear-words, this is an old-fashioned cute-baby comedy that could almost have been made 50 years before. Jack's wife (Imogen Stubbs, briefly impressive) dies in childbirth, leaving distraught Jack (Richard E Grant) to go off on a month's drunken bender, before returning to a siege of grandparents who decide that literally handing him the baby will sort him out. As it does. Sort of. Appalled by a succession of tyrannical applicants for nanny, and reluctantly weakening to the advances of his partner (Cherie Lunghi) at work, Jack clutches at straws and hires a friendly American waitress (Samantha Mathis) who has just lost her job. Now you can write the rest of the story as easily as director Tim Sullivan. Grant lacks likeability and Mathis charm, but there are juicy roles for Ian McKellen, as a tramp Grant takes on as a manservant and Eileen Atkins and Judi Dench as the doting grans. 'Do let us in, darling', huffs Dench impatiently, turning up unannounced. 'The neighbours will think we're Jehovah's Witnesses.'

Jack and the Beanstalk ⊙

1952, US, 78 mins, colour
Dir: Jean Yarbrough
Stars: Bud Abbott, Lou Costello, Dorothy Ford, Buddy Baer
Rating: ★★★

Don't expect too much from this Abbott and Costello pantomime. The team seems out of its element, even though the film does contain some of its most hilarious slapstick chases. One could do without the prince and princess and their songs too. Still the giant and his tall housekeeper are fun, as are the singing harp and the hen that lays the golden eggs. Begins in black and white, then bursts into SuperCinecolor when Jack (Lou) climbs the beanstalk into Cloudland.

Jack McCall, Desperado ○

1953, US, 76 mins, colour
Dir: Sidney Salkow
Stars: George Montgomery, Angela Stevens
Rating: ★★★

One of a whole corral-full of Westerns which George Montgomery made for Columbia in the Fifties. This one tinkers with history a bit – Jack McCall is shown to be not so bad a guy, and doesn't actually shoot Wild Bill Hickok in the back – but the action is fast and furious and western fans won't complain.

Jacknife ● Ⓥ

1988, US, 120 mins, colour
Dir: David Jones
Stars: Robert De Niro, Ed Harris, Kathy Baker, Charles Dutton, Loudon Wainwright IIII
Rating: ★★★

This is the type of romance that could at any moment tip over into tragedy. Robert De Niro stars as a Vietnam veteran who decides to take his wartime buddy (Ed Harris) on a fishing trip. An unlikely affair springs up between De Niro and Harris's sister (Kathy Baker) but is threatened by Harris, whose visions of Vietnam still torment him. Fine portrayals from the stars give the film a warmth it doesn't always deserve.

Jackpot, The ⊙

1950, US, 87 mins, b/w
Dir: Walter Lang
Stars: James Stewart, Barbara Hale, James Gleason, Fred Clark
Rating: ★★★★

One of the funniest Hollywood light comedies since the glossy, brittle romps of the late Thirties. The scene where Stewart gets stuck on the stairs, while trying to get to the phone and claim a huge quiz prize, matches anything he ever did in the world of comic cinema. The supporting cast is studded with rib-tickling performances, from old

comedy hands Fred Clark and James Gleason, to a 12-year-old Natalie Wood as Stewart's precocious daughter. Stewart himself suffers exquisite agonies, especially when the prizes turn up, a white elephant every one. After all, what does one do with a giant steer carcass, or a three-year supply of frozen food (all at once)? To say nothing of the embarrassment inflicted by a twee interior decorator (superbly snooty Alan Mowbray) or an artist (glamorous Patricia Medina) commissioned to paint Stewart's portrait. The resulting chaos is hilarious.

Jack's the Boy ○

1932, UK, 89 mins, b/w
Dir: Walter Forde
Stars: Jack Hulbert, Cicely Courtneidge, Winifred Shotter
Rating: ★★★★

This toe-tapping musical comedy-thriller, swung along at a fine pace by Walter Forde (who had directed the star in the previous year's *The Ghost Train*), was probably Jack Hulbert's greatest popular success. The plot's a simple comedy stand-by (the hapless son of a high-up policeman determines to follow in the steps of his father's size twelves), but Hulbert's cheerful energy and the likeable fooling of his real-life wife Cicely Courtneidge (here in a character role as a rambunctious old nurse) give it a style and rhythm all its own.

Jack the Bear ◑ Ⓥ

1993, US, 101 mins, colour
Dir: Marshall Herskovitz
Stars: Danny DeVito, Robert J Steinmiller, Gary Sinise, Reese Witherspoon, Bert Remsen
Rating: ★★

There aren't many degrees of light and shade in this pretty miserable little piece about a 10-year-old boy's first traumatic year in a new home after the death of his mother – a pretty jolting experience in itself as she died in a car crash after storming out in a row. The theme is lightened a little by the fact that the father (Danny DeVito) of the boy and his three-year-old brother is the black-lipped host of a late-night horror show on TV, and is always 'on' for the local kids. What little comedy there is, however, is soon firmly squashed under the heel of tragedy. The father is drinking heavily to forget, and the family falls out with the local Nazi (Gary Sinise) and pays the penalty when he finds ways to blacken their lives. Just occasionally the feeling of a

community is captured, and there's a tensely exciting bit towards the end when the older boy is threatened with extinction at the hands of the bad guy. Not terribly involving though: the cast probably sheds more tears in this one than the audience will.

Jack the Giant Killer ⊙

1962, US, 94 mins, colour
Dir: Nathan Juran
Stars: Kerwin Mathews, Judi Meredith, Torin Thatcher, Don Beddoe
Rating: ★★★

More movie magic to delight (and in some scenes frighten) the children, from a wizard of special effects called Howard Anderson, whose work compares favourably with that of Ray Harryhausen. Kerwin Mathews, previously seen as Gulliver and Sinbad in Harryhausen films, battles various monsters conjured up by a wicked magician. Veteran character actor Don Beddoe is pure delight as the perverse Imp of the Bottle.

Jack the Ripper ◑

1958, UK, 85 mins, b/w
Dir: Robert S Baker
Stars: Lee Patterson, Eddie Byrne
Rating: ★★

To turn the story of Jack the Ripper into a routine chiller is to do it an injustice. This film is guilty. Taken simply as a police thriller, it's quite enjoyable, although some of the plot's shortcomings show through. The period atmosphere is quite well captured and the murders are effective and realistic without being unacceptably horrific. The vivid black-and-white photography is a plus factor.

Jacob's Ladder ● Ⓥ

1990, US, 113 mins, colour
Dir: Adrian Lyne
Stars: Tim Robbins, Elizabeth Pena, Danny Aiello, Matt Craven, Patricia Kalember, Macaulay Culkin
Rating: ★★★

With a screenplay by Bruce Joel Rubin, subsequently to turn director with *Ghost*, this is, for nine-tenths of the way, a brilliantly constructed psychological thriller about a Vietnam veteran (Tim Robbins) who is suffering a series of horrific hallucinations. Struggling to hold on to his sanity, he finds that several of his old war buddies are experiencing similar illusions ... which may have something to do with a mysterious experiment performed in Vietnam. Don't let anyone tell you the surprise ending, especially as it pretty

J

well wrecks the entire film. Robbins is first-rate as the tortured Jacob but Macaulay Culkin is rather annoying in a key supporting role.

Jacqueline ○
1956, UK, 93 mins, b/w
Dir: Roy Baker
Stars: John Gregson, Kathleen Ryan, Richard O'Sullivan
Rating: ★★★

Comedy-drama-weepie about a happy-go-lucky Irishman whose fear of heights drives him to drink and disgrace, especially in the eyes of his children. These prove to be two enchanting moppets, in the forms of Jacqueline Ryan (in the title role) and Richard O'Sullivan. It's a likeable little drama with earnest performances and atmospheric background detail.

Jade ● Ⓥ
1995, US, 95 mins, colour
Dir: William Friedkin
Stars: David Caruso, Linda Fiorentino, Michael Biehn, Chazz Palminteri, Kevin Tighe, Richard Crenna
Rating: ★★

With Joe Eszterhaus as writer here, we know what to expect: a grungy adult certificate thriller with its mind on sex rather than the plot. And this might be a good one, were it better paced and actually led somewhere. The ending is, although partially explanatory, also inconclusive and leaves the viewer less than satisfied. David Caruso, Linda Fiorentino, Chazz Palminteri and a good cast give it their best shot, but these are not rewarding roles from a writer unconcerned with characterisation, interrelationships or progression of plot. The film opens with a (not seen) spectacular murder, as in Eszterhaus' *Basic Instinct*. A philandering millionaire is hatcheted and skinned. The trail leads Asst DA Corelli (Caruso) to a high-class call-girl, the mysterious Jade, as well as to the state governor. Witnesses get bumped off, although by whom and why is never quite clear. Great music by James Horner and terrific dark colour photography by Andrzej Bartkowiak sets the right mood for a *film noir*, but the fascination with the characters that the genre demands is singularly missing.

Jagged Edge ● Ⓥ
1985, US, 108 mins, colour
Dir: Richard Marquand
Stars: Jeff Bridges, Glenn Close, Peter Coyote, Robert Loggia, Leigh Taylor-

Young
Rating: ★★★★

A tough-talking, clever courtroom thriller of the kind that Hollywood seems to produce every two or three years. Just whether any lawyer would get as involved with her client as Glenn Close does with Jeff Bridges during this messy murder trial is open to conjecture. No matter, such indelicacies never used to bother us when we were cheering on Perry Mason as he closed in on the killer at the end, and neither should they here. Despite the fashionable sex, violence and bad language, this is a satisfyingly old-fashioned sort of film, although avid fans of the genre should guess the solution to its ingenious plot at least a reel before the end. None of the characters is very sympathetic, but all of them are well drawn (which is more important here) – especially by Close, Peter Coyote as the shady DA, Robert Loggia as a foul-mouthed investigator and Marshall Colt as a tennis-club stud.

Jailbirds
See: Pardon Us

Jailbreakers ● Ⓥ
1994, US, 79 mins, colour
Dir: William Friedkin
Stars: Shannen Doherty, Antonio Sabato Jr, Vince Edwards, Adrienne Barbeau, Adrien Brody
Rating: ★★★★

This is a tough, nasty, even vicious little number (originally made for cable TV) with a really devastating kick in the tail and an excellent role for Shannen Doherty, once of *Beverly Hills 90210*. She's a high school cheerleader who falls heavily for the motorcycle boy who rides back into town trailing a criminal record behind him. One mean, even psychotic dude, he's soon back in jail after their fateful fling but, as the title indicates, not for long. There are echoes of *Pretty Poison* here, in a film that has no surplus footage, and actually does capture some of the feel of the better drive-in movies of the late Fifties. Nice to see director Friedkin back on form with this raw little piece after so many disappointments. Doherty's a real eye-opener here, with Sabato almost as good as the lad in leathers.

Jailhouse Rock ○ Ⓥ
1957, US, 96 mins, b/w
Dir: Richard Thorpe
Stars: Elvis Presley, Judy Tyler, Dean

Jones, Mickey Shaughnessy
Rating: ★★

Elvis rocks, rolls and stands on other people's blue suede shoes in this, his third film, as a rebel hero who comes out of prison to become (what else?) a pop idol. The Presley pelvis (and larynx) work overtime on such numbers as 'Treat Me Nice', 'Jailhouse Rock' and 'You're So Square'; but for the tragic Judy Tyler, it was her second and last film. Shortly after completing it she was killed in a car crash.

Jake Speed ○
1986, US, 100 mins, colour
Dir: Andrew Lane
Stars: Wayne Crawford, Dennis Christopher, John Hurt
Rating: ★

There have been plenty of films about comic-book heroes, but *Jake Speed* rings the changes in that it's about one that many of its other characters don't believe exists. Only Grandpa thinks that pulp-novel hero Jake is the man to prise his daughter from the grip of white-slave traders. No sooner has he voiced his thoughts than his other grand-daughter (leggy Karen Kopins) finds Jake (Wayne Crawford) and his side-kick (Dennis Christopher) on her doorstep with some hare-brained scheme to rescue her sister. So it's off to Africa where John Hurt entertains us with a broad, revue-sketch villain who takes 'great pride in never having lived up to anything' and where there's more action than in the last 20 minutes of a Schwarzenegger film. It's a nice idea that, with a lot of careful development and witty dialogue, might have been an unexpected delight. The fact that it doesn't begin to work on this level is largely the fault of Crawford himself, who co-scripted (heavily) and isn't really handsome or personable enough to play the hero.

Jamaica Inn ○
1939, UK, 108 mins, b/w
Dir: Alfred Hitchcock
Stars: Charles Laughton, Maureen O'Hara, Robert Newton, Leslie Banks, Emlyn Williams
Rating: ★★★

Villain Charles Laughton and hero Robert Newton had co-starred the previous year, in *Vessel of Wrath*, a Laughton role which Newton himself would play years later in *The Beachcomber*. And his Long John Silver doubtless owed something to Laughton's leering Captain Kidd. An array of British character actors is on hand to help them with full-blooded performances in this swaggering yarn. The results are a trifle lurid, but the film has plenty of thrills.

James and the Giant Peach ☉ Ⓥ

1996, UK/US, 79 mins, colour
Dir: Henry Selick
Stars: Paul Terry, Joanna Lumley, Miriam Margolyes
Voice Stars: Susan Sarandon, Richard Dreyfuss, David Thewlis, Simon Callow

Rating: ★★★

Roald Dahl's children's stories are usually good fun in film form and this mixture of stylised live-action and (mostly) stop-motion animation is no exception. James (Terry) is an English orphan (from about 50 years ago by the look of the costumes) at the mercy of his slatternly aunts Sponge and Spiker, in which Margolyes and Lumley are both absolutely splendid. Then a huge peach grows in their wilderness garden and, while the aunts exhibit it to tourists, James escapes into its centre, swiftly encountering a group of bugs who have grown to human size along with the magically-expanding fruit. So begins a journey of wonder as James and his multi-legged crew reach the ocean, head for New York, and do battle with a mechanical shark, skeleton pirates and a storm disguised as a rhino. A bit slow to start but fun all the way after that, and a miraculous encapsulation of the book's spirit.

Jane Eyre ○

1944, US, 96 mins, b/w
Dir: Robert Stevenson
Stars: Orson Welles, Joan Fontaine, Henry Daniell, Margaret O'Brien
Rating: ★★★★

Despite Robert Stevenson's name as director on the credits, the influence of Orson Welles seems everywhere in this classic RKO version of Charlotte Brontë's broodingly romantic novel, in which Welles also co-stars as Mr Rochester. The early scenes in the monstrous Lowood are particularly effective, thanks in no little part to Peggy Ann Garner's plucky portrait of young Jane, and Elizabeth Taylor's heart-rending account of her doomed companion, Helen. Following the arrival of Jane (now played by a rather too diffident Joan Fontaine) at Thornfield, however, thunder and lightning – and Orson Welles – take over.

Jane Eyre ○ Ⓥ

1996, UK/It/Fr, 112 mins, colour
Dir: Franco Zeffirelli
Stars: William Hurt, Charlotte Gainsbourg, Geraldine Chaplin, John Wood, Elle McPherson, Joan Plowright, Anna Paquin
Rating: ★★

Successive renditions of the Brontë classic have tried to surpass the old Orson Welles version, but none has come close. This is a decent try, somewhat lacking in passion and atmosphere, but not to be sniffed at either. French actress Gainsbourg is certainly plain enough for Jane, although the effort of putting on a (good) English accent probably drains what personality she might have brought to the performance. In any case, the Oscar-winning Anna Paquin is so good as the young Jane that you want her to grow up and play the adult part. Everything else, including Hurt's Mr Rochester, is adequate but scarcely more, and Billie Whitelaw, complete with ghastly grin as Grace Poole, has clearly taken over from Rosalie Crutchley as the gloom and doom lady of the British cinema.

January Man, The ●

1989, US, 97 mins, colour
Dir: Pat O'Connor
Stars: Kevin Kline, Mary Elizabeth Mastrantonio, Susan Sarandon, Rod Steiger, Harvey Keitel
Rating: ★★

This film doesn't quite know whether it's supposed to be a thriller, a comedy or a comedy thriller. So it never quite manages to be any of these things. Disgraced policeman Nick Starkey is brought back to the force by his brother (the police commissioner) to track down a serial killer. The fact that Nick was once involved with his brother's wife and proceeds to have an affair with the Mayor of New York's daughter tends to interfere with the main thrust of the plot and slow things down quite a bit. Still, despite the fact that this is a notably flawed and distinctly odd film, it's still quite fun, thanks to good performances from a seriously heavyweight cast – especially Kevin Kline and Rod Steiger, in a wonderfully OTT, scenery-chewing, upstaging role complete with hideous, ill-fitting curly wig.

Jason and the Argonauts ○ Ⓥ

1963, UK, 104 mins, colour
Dir: Don Chaffe

Stars: Todd Armstrong, Nancy Kovack
Rating: ★★★

The DynaMation man, Ray Harryhausen, is associate producer on this mythological romp, and that means special effects run not. During his quest for the Golden Fleece, Jason has to combat a giant iron man, whose only weakness is his heel; winged she-devils; and a seven-headed hydra (this battle is the highlight of the film). In *The 7th Voyage of Sinbad*, Harryhausen produced a sword-fighting skeleton. Here, we have a whole army of them for Jason and his men to fight at the climax.

Jason's Lyric ● Ⓥ

1994, US, 119 mins, colour
Dir: Doug McHenry
Stars: Allen Payne, Jada Pinkett, Bokeem Woodbine, Treach, Suzzanne Douglas, Forest Whitaker
Rating: ★★

This is the good brother/bad brother storyline, allied to the theme of crime and the Grim Reaper combining to ruin lives based in the 'hood. Clichés abound – 'He died in the war; they just didn't bury him' – and the ingredients are all familiar: gang violence, despairing mother, the naked love scene in a field of flowers, the bank robbery, and even the final revelation of how the hero's father (Forest Whitaker) actually met his death. Depressingly predictable, just like the fates of its characters, although the film is decently made and has a heroine in Jada Pinkett who doesn't overact and has a pleasant personality into the bargain.

Jassy ○

1947, UK, 102 mins, colour
Dir: Bernard Knowles
Stars: Margaret Lockwood, Patricia Roc, Dennis Price, Basil Sydney
Rating: ★★

A turbulent Technicolor tale from Gainsborough Pictures, with excellent production values, well photographed by Geoffrey Unsworth who went on to win an Oscar for *Cabaret*. The director, Bernard Knowles, was also once a cinematographer and had already directed Margaret Lockwood twice in films when he made this moody (but not good) Mallens-style melodrama which cast the star as a fiery gipsy.

Jaws ○ Ⓥ

1975, US, 125 mins, colour
Dir: Steven Spielberg
Stars: Roy Scheider, Robert Shaw, Richard Dreyfuss, Lorraine Gary, Murray

J

Hamilton
Rating: ★★★★

This monster success attacked the box-offices of the world with the same suddenness and ferocity with which the white killer shark of its title descends on the unsuspecting holidaymakers of an American beach paradise. The famous early sequence of the naked girl bather being eaten alive by the shark sets the tone for the swathe of blood and limbs that spreads across this nail-bitingly exciting story. Author Peter Benchley has a cameo as a journalist. Winner of Oscars for John Williams's score, editing and sound. Some of the shark violence may turn younger viewers a little green at the gills.

Jaws 2 ◐ ⓥ
1978, US, 115 mins, colour
Dir: Jeannot Szwarc
Stars: Roy Scheider, Murray Hamilton, Lorraine Gary
Rating: ★★★

No one who thrilled to *Jaws* will want to miss this, although by the time it surfaced in cinemas three years after *Jaws*, shark adventures were two-a-penny and new ways of getting rid of a great white shark were running along similar lines to means of dispatching Dracula: you think up a new one with each succeeding sequel. Roy Scheider again gives a good performance as the police chief. Once more the citizens, again led by Murray Hamilton as the Mayor, won't believe him about the shark menace and even go as far as firing him. Director Jeannot Szwarc packs in as many teasing shots of swimmers taken from below the surface as the plot will decently allow before Scheider and the shark come to their showdown.

Jaws 3 ○ ⓥ
1983, US, 99 mins, colour
Dir: Joe Alves
Stars: Dennis Quaid, Bess Armstrong, Simon MacCorkindale, Louis Gossett Jr, Lea Thompson
Rating: ★★

The story, by Guerdon Trueblood, is so the credits tell us – suggested by the novel *Jaws* by Peter Benchley. Which is about as far as the similarity between this shark shocker and the two previous films goes, even though co-scenarist Carl Gottlieb did work on the script of Steven Spielberg's original film. Instead, the action here takes place in Florida (not Amity Island) but there is still a great white shark or two ready to snap their teeth at a cast that includes Dennis Quaid, Bess

Armstrong and Britain's Simon MacCorkindale and P H Moriarty. The movie was originally shown in cinemas in 3-D so be prepared for sharks coming straight for the screen.

Jaws 4: The Revenge ◐ ⓥ
1987, US, 100 mins, colour
Dir: Joseph Sargent
Stars: Michael Caine, Lorraine Gary, Lance Guest, Mario Van Peebles, Karen Young
Rating: ★

Sean Brody, son of the police chief in the original *Jaws*, is attacked and killed by a great white shark. His mother is convinced the shark has a grudge against her family and looks to her other son Michael, a marine biologist in the Bahamas, for help. The shark follows! The first film was tense, exciting and credible, but by this time the series had gone soft in the head. How can Ellen Brody (Lorraine Gary) imagine a fish can hold a grudge? How did it find out that she was going to the Bahamas? Even assuming you swallow all this, the fish itself is so obviously foam rubber it doesn't exactly exude the kind of menace that keeps you on the edge of your seat. In what one can only assume was a moment of madness, weakness or financial necessity, Michael Caine consented to appear in this waterlogged slog as a dissolute gambler.

Jazzboat ○
1959, UK, 96 mins, b/w
Dir: Ken Hughes
Stars: Anthony Newley, Anne Aubrey, James Booth, David Lodge
Rating: ★★

This madcap musical comedy was made hot on the heels of *Idol on Parade*, the film which shot Anthony Newley into the pop charts (with 'I've Waited So Long') and enabled him to carve out a whole new career. But, apart from one number, 'Somebody to Love', this film concentrates on Newley's comedy talents, casting him as an electrician who pretends to be a big-time crook – and naturally gets mixed up with the real thing. There's quite a bit of dazzling dancing, though, choreographed by the ubiquitous Lionel Blair, whose sister, Joyce, plays Newley's girlfriend, and madcap humour from Bernie Winters as a crook called Mugsy the jinx. It was successful enough to give rise to a sequel, *In the Nick*.

Jazz Singer, The ○
1953, US, 107 mins, colour
Dir: Michael Curtiz

Stars: Danny Thomas, Peggy Lee, Mildred Dunnock
Rating: ★★

Colourful re-make by Warner Brothers of the classic early 'talkie' starring Al Jolson. Danny Thomas assumes the Jolson part of a Jewish boy torn between showbusiness and religion. The tunes, including the catchy 'This is a Very Special Day', are put across well, especially by Peggy Lee. The period has been brought up to date, and the hero is a returned veteran of the Korean War. Thomas plays him with plenty of personality, although his eccentric talent for telling a downbeat yarn is hardly exploited.

Jazz Singer, The ○ ⓥ
1980, US, 115 mins, colour
Dir: Richard Fleischer
Stars: Neil Diamond, Lucie Arnaz, Laurence Olivier, Catlin Adams, Paul Nicholas, James Booth
Rating: ★

The trouble with this new version of the old chestnut is that it's still *The Jazz Singer*. This never was a very good story, and it was a grave error for talented singer Neil Diamond to choose such an antiquated view of Jewish life in America for his screen debut. Give the piece one credit, though: it's only when you listen to Diamond singing in the synagogue that you realise what a good vocalist he really is. Otherwise, the backings all too often drown his throaty tones. As an actor, the taciturn Diamond is almost inevitably outshone by the multi-talented Lucie Arnaz, but more than holds his own with Laurence Olivier's comic-book impression of his whining cantor father.

Jean de Florette ○ ⓥ
1986, France, 122 mins, colour
Dir: Claude Berri
Stars: Gerard Depardieu, Yves Montand, Daniel Auteuil, Elisabeth Depardieu
Rating: ★★★★

The first of a stunning double act of films (the sequel, *Manon des Sources*, is almost as good) shot simultaneously at a cost of $17 million (a French record) about life in a Provençal village in the 1920s. Showered with awards, this first film is about the deceit and skul-duggery involved in the fight for a fertile piece of land and the efforts of two farmers to ruin their neighbour. The cast cannot be faulted (Gerard Depardieu, as a simple hunchback, has his real-life wife, Elisabeth, as his screen partner) and the photography is rich with the warmth of a French countryside in summer. Highly recommended.

Jefferson In Paris ● Ⓥ

1995, US, 139 mins, colour
Dir: James Ivory
Stars: Nick Nolte, Greta Scacchi, Simon Callow, Gwyneth Paltrow, James Earl Jones, Thandie Newton
Rating: ★★

Nick Nolte has done far, far better things than this lavish costume drama set in France just prior to the 1789 Revolution, when Jefferson, later to be US president, was an ambassador in Paris. But the script fails to put his character, or the turbulence of 1770s France, across with sufficient force. Yes. Jefferson still owned slaves; yes, he refused to allow his adored daughter (Gwyneth Paltrow, excellent) to become a nun. But these issues are handled superficially, sidestepped in favour of the muted romance between widower Jefferson and the beautiful Maria (Greta Scacchi), wife of a British artist (Simon Callow, doing another of his bouncy bumblers). And then we have the arrival of young slave Sally (charmingly played by Thandie Newton)... whom we know will bear Jefferson several children. Costumes are gorgeous, attention to period detail impeccable: otherwise the film never does justice to its fascinating subject.

Jeffrey ● Ⓥ

1994, US, 92 mins, colour
Dir: Christopher Ashley
Stars: Steven Weber, Patrick Stewart, Michael T Weiss, Sigourney Weaver, Olympia Dukakis
Rating: ★★★

Although it's much more accessible to mainstream audiences than many gay film and has a good share of gay funny lines, *Jeffrey* never quite knows whether it wants to be a romantic comedy or something more thoughtful. Things start brightly: Jeffrey (Steven Weber), after a succession of weird and wonderful partners, is off sex – and suffering. Wandering around, he gets (mildly) knocked over by a car and is tended by Mother Teresa. 'She looked great,' he remarks. 'Oh please,' chides his friend, 'she's had work done.' Enter Patrick Stewart, walking slyly off with the film as an interior designer in love with a dancer from *Cats*, and taking command of the film until the script undoes his best efforts at the end. The AIDS thing finally scuppers the film from the midway point, destroying its mood until the movie doesn't seem to have a con-

sistent mood at all. The dialogue still fizzes with the occasional fey firework, but, by the end, it's all but sputtered out.

Jennie

See: Portrait of Jennie

Jennifer Eight ● Ⓥ

1992, US, 129 mins, colour
Dir: Bruce Robinson
Stars: Andy Garcia, Uma Thurman, Kathy Baker, Lance Henriksen, John Malkovich
Rating: ★★

For the first 45 minutes, this threatens to be a good serial-killer thriller – but it just doesn't stick to the matter in hand. It spends too much time instead on the romance between burnt-out detective Andy Garcia and beautiful blind girl Uma Thurman – and on Thurman's character in particular – when it should be developing the main thread of its story about a psycho killer who has murdered and cut up eight blind girls (so Garcia insists) and is preparing to strike again. An interrogation sequence involving John Malkovich, who is given an excessive proportion of his pound of flesh as guest star, goes on much too long, and the result of all this is that a potentially tight 90-minute thriller is stretched out to well over two hours. The beginning, though, is excellent – a rain-soaked hunt for a grisly needle in a haystack of garbage – and the last 10 minutes are compulsive stuff.

Jeremiah Johnson ○ Ⓥ

1972, US, 107 mins, colour
Dir: Sydney Pollack
Stars: Robert Redford, Will Geer
Rating: ★★★

The actor-director team of Robert Redford and Sydney Pollack scores again with this spectacularly shot yarn of a mountain trapper and his adventures near the America-Canada border in the 1950s. Episodic in structure, the film is kept constantly interesting by its director who fills the screen with colourful little anecdotes – like the discovery of Hatchet Jack, frozen dead in the mountains, his last will and testament round his neck ('I, Hatchet Jack, being of sound mind and both legs broke'); or an eerie journey through an Indian burial ground. Stunning snowscapes lend the action a primitive grandeur.

Jerry Maguire ● Ⓥ

1996, US, 138 mins, colour
Dir: Cameron Crowe

Stars: Tom Cruise, Renee Zellweger, Cuba Gooding Jr, Bonnie Hunt, Jonathan Lipnicki, Kelly Preston
Rating: ★★★

The tremendous emotional build at the end of this drama of a man looking for the better part of himself, coupled with a great Tom Cruise speech, will send you home feeling great. And that's fine and dandy. But it shouldn't obscure the fact that this is an unnecessarily long film with too little incident for its length, and that not all of director Crowe's dialogue is of the same quality as his final scenes. That said, Cruise, Zellweger and especially Gooding give generously of themselves in a bid to grip you to the story of a sports agent who finds himself jobless, friendless and with but a single client after he tells colleagues the unpalatable truth about their profession. Hunt, as Zellweger's snoopy sister, and Regina King, as Gooding's wife, are also excellent in a fine ensemble cast that includes a delightfully un-cute, bespectacled kid in Lipnicki, who, as widow Zellweger's little son, will win as many hearts as the stars.

Jersey Girl ● Ⓥ

1992, US, 95 mins, colour
Dir: David Burton Morris
Stars: Jami Gertz, Dylan McDermott, Sheryl Lee
Rating: ★★

If you fancy a straightforward version of a story you've seen a couple of hundred times before, there's nothing particularly wrong with this one. Toby (Jami Gertz), from across the river in downtown New Jersey, longs for something better. Finding the man of her dreams (Dylan McDermott) in uptown New York, she pursues him relentlessly, survives getting him to crash his car and finally persuades him to date her. But he's eventually sucked back into his high-flying job and the society girlfriend (Sheryl Lee) with whom he'd had a tiff. But, McDermott being originally a downtown guy himself, and this being a Cinderella story, you don't need to flex your mental muscles to guess the ending. McDermott comes the Richard Gere act a bit heavy but Gertz, even though she's perhaps even more strident than she's meant to be, is winning enough to see it through. Easily pleased romantics will like it.

Jesse James ○

1939, US, 106 mins, colour
Dir: Henry King
Stars: Tyrone Power, Henry Fonda,

J

Nancy Kelly, Randolph Scott, Brian Donlevy, John Carradine
Rating: ★★★

First-rate, big-scale, splendidly directed (by Henry King) Western about the lawless career of the most famous outlaw of them all. There's a glimpse of Lon Chaney Jr just before he made his name in *Of Mice and Men*, and a look at Randolph Scott when he was still playing supporting roles in top films. Tyrone Power's portrayal of Jesse James is remarkably similar in looks and mannerisms to that of Christopher Jones in the television series 30 years later.

Jesus Christ Superstar ○ Ⓥ
1973, US, 107 mins, colour
Dir: Norman Jewison
Stars: Ted Neeley, Carl Anderson, Yvonne Elliman, Barry Dennen
Rating: ★★

Norman Jewison's brash big-screen version of the hit stage musical, which relates the last days of Christ from the viewpoint of Judas Iscariot (a powerhouse performance by Carl Anderson). Good use is made of the desert locations, but the treatment, complete with a camp Herod and military tanks, will not be everyone's religious cup of woe.

Jet Pilot ○
1950, US, 112 mins, colour
Dir: Josef Von Sternberg
Stars: John Wayne, Janet Leigh, Jay C Flippen, Paul Fix
Rating: ★

Directed under duress by Josef von Sternberg, this film was held up for seven years before being finally released in 1957. With its comic-strip dialogue and one-dimensional heroics, it would sit well with Hollywood's more recent spate of 'Red-baiting' films. Janet Leigh is a cutie-pie Russian spy, while John Wayne shambles through the action with a permanent amiable grin. The flying scenes are flashily spectacular.

Jet Storm ○
1959, UK, 86 mins, b/w
Dir: Cy Endfield
Stars: Richard Attenborough, George Rose, Hermione Baddeley, Mai Zetterling, Diane Cilento, Stanley Baker
Rating: ★★

Arch-Goon Harry Secombe makes an effective appearance in a fairly straight dramatic role in this mid-air bomb-in-plane drama with some moments of tension, although not enough.

Secombe joins an all-star cast that includes Stanley Baker, Diane Cilento, Mal Zetterling, Elizabeth Sellars, Marty Wilde and show business personalities Bernard Braden and Barbara Kelly. Richard Attenborough gives another impassioned performance of a disturbed man, following his work in *The Man Upstairs*.

Jewel of the Nile, The ○ Ⓥ
1985, US, 104 mins, colour
Dir: Lewis Teague
Stars: Michael Douglas, Kathleen Turner, Danny DeVito
Rating: ★★★

In some ways better than its predecessor *Romancing the Stone* (perhaps because it takes its villains more seriously), this is an enjoyable if never blood-surging romp that takes up the story of its two main characters six months after *Romancing*. In no time at all, Joan (Kathleen Turner) is in the middle of a desert war, with Jack (Michael Douglas) riding to the rescue. There are some good action sequences thereafter (especially a lengthy one on a fast-moving train) with both stars doing a lot of their own stuntwork, something that adds to the excitement. Turner and Douglas both ooze charisma and, in their relationship, strike all the right emotional sparks off each other. Danny DeVito, as their diminutive pursuer, is seen to rather better advantage than in the first film.

Jezebel ○ Ⓥ
1938, US, 104 mins, b/w
Dir: William Wyler
Stars: Bette Davis, Henry Fonda, George Brent, Margaret Lindsay, Donald Crisp, Fay Bainter
Rating: ★★★

Bette Davis won her second Oscar for her performance as a wilful Southern belle in this handsomely mounted melodrama which Warner Bros gave to the star as a consolation prize for not getting the coveted role of Scarlett O'Hara in *Gone With the Wind*. Another Oscar, for best supporting actress, went to Fay Bainter as Davis' sympathetic aunt. Director William Wyler, borrowed from Samuel Goldwyn for the picture, does an excellent job although even he cannot make Davis' last-reel redemption through love convincing.

JFK ● Ⓥ
1991, US, 191 mins, colour
Dir: Oliver Stone
Stars: Kevin Costner, Sissy Spacek, Tommy Lee Jones, Gary Oldman, John

Candy, Kevin Bacon, Jack Lemmon
Rating: ★★★

Fascinating historically, persuasive and probably correct theoretically, but flawed dramatically, this account of New Orleans attorney Jim Garrison's pursuit of the Kennedy assassins raises the question as to why no-one has filmed it (been allowed to?) before. Far from the powerful document it might have been, the film still grips almost throughout because of the subject, and Garrison's examination and exploration of it. Even director Oliver Stone's pretentious beginning and endpiece can't deny the enormity of the tragedy and its consequences. Kevin Costner is not at his best as Garrison, seeming tired and lacking in conviction. And Sissy Spacek is poorly cast as his nagging wife, a part calling for a less sympathetic actress. The only thoroughly believable performance comes from Jack Lemmon as a private eye reluctant to turn informant even for the little he knows. No matter: the facts win out here. The deaths of many of those involved, including several key witnesses; the suppression or ignoring of evidence by others. A horror film it is for sure but there's not a monster in sight, at least not of the conventional kind.

Jigsaw ◑
1962, UK, 107 mins, b/w
Dir: Val Guest
Stars: Jack Warner, Ronald Lewis, Yolande Donlan
Rating: ★★★★

From the moment director Val Guest's black-and-white camera zooms into a dark, open window, in sinister style, you are drawn chillingly into one of the most compulsive British murder thrillers in years. Jack Warner and Ronald Lewis really live the parts of the dogged investigators, and worthy contributions from Moira Redmond, John le Mesurier (in a rare dramatic role) and Michael Goodliffe.

Jingle All The Way ○ Ⓥ
1996, US, 89 mins, colour
Dir: Brian Levant
Stars: Arnold Schwarzenegger, Sinbad, Rita Wilson, Phil Hartman
Rating: ★

Completely unbelievable and right over the top, this is a high-decibel comedy of violence for those who like seeing reindeer punched out and department stores wrecked by rampaging mobs. At the centre of this maelstrom of mayhem is TurboMan, a toy which stressed-out businessman Schwarzenegger has promised his son for Christmas but has forgotten to buy. Right from the beginning his quest to make amends bears no relation to reality, from the moment the smiling store manager taunts the hordes waiting for the shop to open, then allows them to trample him underfoot. And a running gag about Arnold always falling foul of the same cop fails miserably to work. If only we could sympathise with anyone here, the film might provide some fun. Schwarzenegger is all at sea in this, but even so he is better than an alleged actor called Sinbad who plays his chief rival, or Phil Hartman as the smarmy divorcé next door who coverts Rita Wilson as Arnie's wife.

Jimmy Reardon ●
(aka: A Night In the Life of Jimmy Reardon)
1987, US, 92 mins, colour
Dir: William Richert
Stars: River Phoenix, Ann Magnuson, Meredith Salenger, Ione Skye, Louanne, Paul Koslo
Rating: ★

This 'teenage rebel' film for the Eighties has a magazine cover cast but no likeable people. Director William Richert's own script endows his characters with no commendable facets, allowing them only to sulk and scowl through the story of a working-class 17-year-old who has a rich girl on the hook but can't resist bonking everything else in sight while she keeps him waiting. Only Ann Magnuson, deservedly second-billed, as a Mrs Robinson of the blue-collar belt, brings any warmth and wistfulness to this would-be nostalgic tale. River Phoenix, playing like Mickey Rourke on heat, gives the worst performance of his too-brief career.

Jitterbugs ☉
1943, US, 74 mins, b/w
Dir: Malcolm St Clair
Stars: Stan Laurel, Oliver Hardy, Vivian Blaine, Bob Bailey
Rating: ★★

Another of Laurel and Hardy's Forties' comedies, in the years when they had switched without success from the Hal Roach Studio to MGM and 20th Century-Fox. As in *Way Out West*, they are out to protect the heroine (here Vivian Blaine) from the bad guy (splendid Douglas Fowley). Stan gets to dress up in drag, and Ollie has a nice Southern-style courtship scene with Lee Patrick. The trick ending is a 'gas'!

Joe Dakota ○
1957, US, 79 mins, colour
Dir: Richard Bartlett
Stars: Jock Mahoney, Luana Patten, Charles McGraw
Rating: ★★★

Mystery Western with an excellent story and some neat twists. Even though the direction is too slow, the plot is always intriguing enough to hold the interest. Former Disney child star Luana Patten has the leading feminine role and she's gorgeous. The supporting cast is bolstered by such good 'bad guys' as Charles McGraw, Claude Akins, Anthony Caruso and Lee Van Cleef.

Joe Kidd ◐
1973, US, 88 mins, colour
Dir: John Sturges
Stars: Clint Eastwood, Robert Duvall, John Saxon
Rating: ★★★

A strikingly handsome locomotive steals the attention from such hard men of the screen as Clint Eastwood, Robert Duvall, John Saxon and Don Stroud in this typical Eastwood kill-them-all-and-come-back-alone Western. It's directed for once not by Eastwood himself but by the redoubtable John Sturges.

Joe Macbeth ○
1955, UK, 90 mins, b/w
Dir: Ken Hughes
Stars: Paul Douglas, Ruth Roman, Bonar Colleano, Sidney James
Rating: ★★★

A blood-chilling modern gangster version of Shakespeare's play. Philip Yordan's screenplay is a bit arty at times, but retains the flavour of the original – and its moral: that power feeds upon itself, ultimately bringing self-destruction. Strong direction by Ken Hughes, powerful portrayals by Paul Douglas and especially Ruth Roman as Lady (here Lily) Macbeth. Sidney James, in an offbeat role as Banky (Banquo), is also good.

Joe Versus the Volcano ○ ⓥ
1990, US, 100 mins, colour
Dir: John Patrick Shanley
Stars: Tom Hanks, Meg Ryan, Robert Stack, Lloyd Bridges
Rating: ★★

This peculiar number almost never gets going, save for a few moments of high amusement towards the end. It does, however, have Tom Hanks and Meg Ryan enjoying themselves, which is just as well, as some of their stardust rubs off on the rest of the film. The idea is great: it's just the execution and pacing that drags it down. Hanks is a no-hoper stuck in a dead-end job with American Panascope, 'home of the rectal probe'. When an expensive doctor (Robert Stack) tells him he has a brain cloud, which is rare, spreading and limits his future to about six months, Hanks is easy prey to a hare-brained scheme that involves him sailing to a Pacific island and jumping into a volcano. There's a lovely sight gag involving two gongs on the island, but too few snappy lines and too little incident in the story development.

Joe's Apartment ◐ ⓥ
1996, US, 77 mins, colour
Dir: John Payson
Stars: Jerry O'Connell, Megan Ward, Jim Sterling, Don Ho, Robert Vaughn, David Huddleston
Rating: ★★★

Give a little crawlspace to this rough-edged but very original comedy that will appeal to the *Wayne's World* brigade. A naïve Iowa boy, Joe (Jerry O'Connell), arrives in New York where the only apartment he can find is overrun by cockroaches – 50,000 of them! The 'roaches like Joe – we know that because they can sing, talk and dance and they tell us so – and, to keep Joe happy, they set about dispensing with various baddies out to steal the apartment, and help him win the girl of his dreams. Tucked between some pretty skin-crawling sequences there are Busby Berkeley-style dance routines by the 'roaches and songs about garbage in the moonlight and sewer surfing. Wacky, zany and completely off the wall.

Joey Boy ○
1965, UK, 91 mins, b/w
Dir: Frank Launder
Stars: Harry H Corbett, Stanley Baxter, Reg Varney
Rating: ★★

This wartime comedy about a wide boy who enjoys a profitable time in the army is a rather disappointing effort. Doubly so when one realises the usually-reliable Frank Launder is responsible for both the direction and the script. In the title role, Harry H Corbett tries his hardest with what he's given, but what passes for huniour here is lowbrow and predictable. Also working hard to no worthwhile effect are Stanley Baxter, Bill Fraser, Reg Varney, Lance Percival and Derek Nimmo. There are some bright moments, but not nearly enough to make up for the many dull ones.

Johnny Apollo O
1940, US, 93 mins, b/w
Dir: Henry Hathaway
Stars: Tyrone Power, Dorothy Lamour, Edward Arnold, Lloyd Nolan
Rating: ★★★

Tyrone Power and Dorothy Lamour slipped away from swords and sarongs for this gangster and prison escape drama. It's fairly untypical of its studio (20th Century-Fox) at the time but, thanks to Henry Hathaway's firm direction, it's fast-moving and acceptable crime fare, with an outstanding performance from portly Edward Arnold. He shows he can handle a sympathetic role as well as dispense sneers as power-hungry villains.

Johnny Belinda O
1948, US, 103 mins, b/w
Dir: Jean Negulesco
Stars: Jane Wyman, Lew Ayres, Charles Bickford, Stephen McNally
Rating: ★★★★

Jane Wyman transformed her career with her portrayal of the deaf-mute girl and the depiction of her hard, and later tragic life in a coastal Nova Scotia fishing-farming community. The Academy Award she won for best actress set her up for a whole run of superior soap-operas that became known as The Wyman Weepies.

Johnny Come Lately O Ⓥ
(aka: Johnny Vagabond)
1943, US, 97 mins, b/w
Dir: William K Howard
Stars: James Cagney, Grace George, Marjorie Main, Hattie McDaniel
Rating: ★★

One of James Cagney's most unusual films. He plays a wanderer who comes to the aid of a newspaper proprietress (stage actress Grace George in her only film) being terrorised by the town's crooked boss. A little gunplay is thrown in to keep Cagney's Thirties' fans happy, but otherwise it's a mild character drama which doesn't quite fire on all cylinders.

Johnny Cool O
1964, US, 103 mins, b/w
Dir: William Asher
Stars: Henry Silva, Elizabeth Montgomery, Sammy Davis Jr
Rating: ★★

This drama of a Sicilian assassin didn't shoot that excellent villain Henry Silva

into the star bracket. Perhaps he was too cold and matter-of-fact, although that didn't hurt Alan Ladd in *This Gun for Hire*. Strong supporting cast includes Telly Savalas as a crime tsar.

Johnny Dangerously Ⓓ Ⓥ
1984, US, 90 mins, colour
Dir: Amy Heckerling
Stars: Michael Keaton, Marilu Henner
Rating: ★★

You can forgive this gangster comedy its flat spots and lapses into bad taste because the funny bits really are very funny. Too bad that there aren't enough of them. Michael Keaton plays the title role, a lad who turns to crime to pay his hypochondriac mother's medical bills. His life of crime keeps mum in pills and puts his kid brother through law school. A starry cast that includes Peter Boyle, Marilu Henner, Dom DeLuise, Griffin Dunne, Ray Walston and Danny DeVito works hard to keep things going but what could have been a delightful spoof on all those Warner Bros gangster films of the Thirties and Forties falls flat too often. Still, the gags there are are worth waiting for.

Johnny Eager O
1942, US, 107 mins, b/w
Dir: Mervyn Le Roy
Stars: Robert Taylor, Lana Turner, Van Heflin
Rating: ★★★

An offbeat gangster thriller with a top-notch cast and an Oscar-winning performance from Van Heflin. Robert Taylor plays the villain of the title, shrugging off his usual good-guy image to play a baddie with convincing nastiness. It is one of his finest roles, although given extra depth by the terrific acting of Heflin as his alcoholic friend. The 'Sweater Girl', Lana Turner, smoulders with sensuality – so much so that Taylor was drawn to her romantically in real life. MGM's publicity campaign made the most of their torrid on- and off-screen romance and they took out an ad which read 'TNT – Taylor 'n' Turner – Together, They're Terrific'.

Johnny Frenchman O
1945, UK, 111 mins, b/w
Dir: Charles Frend
Stars: Francoise Rosay, Tom Walls, Patricia Roc
Rating: ★★★

Charming and very convincing story of the rivalry between Breton and Cornish fisherfolk, which benefitted

considerably from location filming in Cornwall. The action includes a terrific fist fight between Ralph Michael and Paul Dupuis. And if you think the French accents are authentic, they should be. The film makers borrowed French refugees from the wartime hostilities to people some of the scenes.

Johnny Guitar O
1953, US, 110 mins, colour
Dir: Nicholas Ray
Stars: Joan Crawford, Sterling Hayden, Scott Brady, Mercedes McCambridge, Ward Bond, Ernest Borgnine
Rating: ★★★★

A really heady Western, rife with symbolism and unusually boasting female protagonists. Joan Crawford's up there running the local gambling saloon, and psychotic cattle baron (or should it be baroness?) Mercedes McCambridge wants her run out of town or hanged, whichever can be arranged the sooner. Everybody has the hots for someone else in this film; even Trucolor has never looked hotter than under Harry Stradling Jr's cameras. Crawford and McCambridge give strong, almost vicious performances; not surprisingly they didn't get on, and director Nicholas Ray eventually had to shoot their scenes together separately. This is a one-of-a-kind Western. Only the minor *The Woman They Almost Lynched* even comes close.

Johnny Handsome ● Ⓥ
1989, US, 94 mins, colour
Dir: Walter Hill
Stars: Mickey Rourke, Ellen Barkin, Elizabeth McGovern, Morgan Freeman, Forest Whitaker, Lance Henriksen
Rating: ★★★

Here's a good old gangster flick in the modern manner. Director Walter Hill does his best job for some time on this story of a facially deformed robber (Mickey Rourke) double-crossed by fellow thieves Ellen Barkin and Lance Henriksen, who kill Johnny's partners and make off with the loot. Near death after an attack by convicts hired by Henriksen, Johnny is offered a new face by plastic surgeon Forest Whitaker if he'll go straight. All this is taken with a pinch of salt by detective A Z Drones (Morgan Freeman) and by the audience, who know that Johnny Gruesome turned Handsome is hellbent on revenge. Fast-moving and undemanding, the film is full of viciously dynamic action scenes and strong performances from all those mentioned. Elizabeth McGovern even manages to put punch and character into the role of the nice girl who almost keeps Johnny on the straight and narrow.

Johnny in the Clouds
See: The Way to the Stars

Johnny Mnemonic ● ⓥ
1995, US, 96 mins, colour
Dir: Robert Longo
Stars: Keanu Reeves, Dina Meyer, Dolph Lundgren, Ice-T, Henry Rollins, Barbara Sukowa
Rating: ★

Action and effects are Nineties-dynamic in this futuristic fantasy about couriers who wander dangerously through world information networks with vital data implanted in their brains. The risks are interception by enemy agents or overloading of the brain cells. No chance of the latter for the viewer in this inanely written, ineptly acted, chop socky-style yarn. In fact, when Johnny (Keanu Reeves) gasps 'I'm a dead man if I don't get this out of my head,' he might have been referring to the script, much of whose dialogue could have been written for an old-time serial. Imploring the gods for a few of the creature comforts he misses, Keanu could perhaps have thrown in a request for an acting refresher course. When the most polished performance in this definitely heinous adventure comes from rapper Ice-T, you know your movie's in trouble. Cast Dolph Lundgren in a character role as a fire-breathing (and lethal) preacher and you've surely given up the ghost. But then director Robert Longo encourages everyone to over-emote in a cybernetic caper you'll want to download from your mind as soon as possible.

Johnny O'Clock ○
1946, US, 95 mins, b/w
Dir: Robert Rossen
Stars: Dick Powell, Lee J Cobb, Evelyn Keyes, Ellen Drew
Rating: ★★

It's a great title but otherwise this is one of Dick Powell's less interesting tough-guy roles, even though he and director Robert Rossen give the film a style that the typically shoddy Columbia production never approaches. Despite Powell's performance and a decent supporting cast that includes Jeff Chandler as a gunman in one of his first roles, the film never really engages your emotions and a sense of danger is noticeably lacking.

Johnny Reno ○
1965, US, 83 mins, colour
Dir: R G Springsteen
Stars: Dana Andrews, Jane Russell, Lyle Bettger
Rating: ★

It's reunion night at the old corral. The marshal with the chip on his shoulder is Dana Andrews. The crooked mayor is that meanest of villains, Lyle Bettger. The sheriff, simple but honest, is Lon Chaney Jr. The upright townsman is John Agar, hero of a dozen Western sagas. The young cowpuncher framed for murder is Tom Drake, once Judy Garland's trolley-bound beau in *Meet Me in St Louis*. And who's the gal in the saloon, swathed in crinoline? It can't be. Not after all these years. But it is. Jane Russell. Add Richard Arlen and Robert Lowery, and raise your glasses to the creaking cowboys' club.

Johnny Suede ● ⓥ
1991, US/Switzerland, 95 mins, colour
Dir: Tom DiCillo
Stars: Brad Pitt, Catherine Keener, Calvin Levels, Tina Louise
Rating: ★

About the only original thing in this slice of minimalist cinema, filmed mostly in the corners of rooms, is the hero's mega-high bouffant hairdo. Otherwise, there are sparks in the dialogue and in the songs – 'I want to meet a model who's only got one name,' sings the hero (Brad Pitt), who idolises Sixties pop star Ricky Nelson – but not enough to suggest the film is going to build the cult reputation some critics thought. There must be better ways of spending even tiny budgets than having the hero encounter a few women, walk along a few streets, ride a few tube trains, amble around with his hand in his knickers, and arrive back at the point he started from. Lots of swearing though for those who like that kind of thing.

Johnny Tremain ☉
1957, US, 81 mins, colour
Dir: Robert Stevenson
Stars: Hal Stalmaster, Luana Patten, Sebastian Cabot, Richard Beymer
Rating: ★★★

This colourful adventure is Walt Disney's version of the start of the American Revolution as seen through the eyes of the title character. Johnny Tremain (Hal Stalmaster) embraces the revolutionary cause after suffering the rough edge of British justice when he is wrongly accused of theft. He joins the

Sons of Liberty and takes part in the infamous (from our point of view) Boston Tea Party. Director Robert Stevenson (English, surprisingly enough) doesn't ignore the history but neither does he allow it to stop this being a ripping adventure yarn of appeal to all ages.

Johnny Vagabond
See: Johnny Come Lately

Joker Is Wild, The ○
1957, US, 127 mins, b/w
Dir: Charles Vidor
Stars: Frank Sinatra, Mitzi Gaynor, Jeanne Crain, Eddie Albert
Rating: ★★★

Solidly entertaining biopic of American nightclub entertainer Joe E Lewis, who started out in the Prohibition Twenties as a singer. After a gangster's razor put paid to any dreams of stardom in that direction, the bitter and disillusioned Lewis began an entirely new career as a sourly wisecracking comedian. Frank Sinatra gives a dramatic performance of total conviction in this demanding role, supported by a trio of lovely ladies in Mitzi Gaynor, Beverly Garland and Jeanne Crain. He also finds time to sing *All the Way* and *Chicago*.

Jokers, The ○
1966, UK, 126 mins, colour
Dir: Michael Winner
Stars: Michael Crawford, Oliver Reed, Harry Andrews, Daniel Massey
Rating: ★★★

Made in the middle of director Michael Winner's most fruitful period, long before he got bogged down in cool crime dramas with Charles Bronson, this is a thoroughly engaging comedy-thriller about two young rogues who hatch a plan to steal the Crown jewels – and then give them back. The first part of the plan goes like clockwork. Michael Crawford and Oliver Reed are perfect as the amateur thieves.

Jolly Bad Fellow, A ◑
(aka: They All Died Laughing)
1964, UK, 94 mins, b/w
Dir: Don Chaffey
Stars: Janet Munro, Maxine Audley
Rating: ★★★

A black comedy in the Ealing manner, whose sometimes witty script, by Donald Taylor and Robert Hamer, casts Leo (Rumpole of the Bailey) McKern as a university don – thus the title – who proceeds to work his way to a fellowship award by eliminating those

J

who stand in his way, after he discovers a poison that leaves no trace. Maxine Audley is most appealing as his wife, but Janet Munro seems miscast as the don's seductive laboratory assistant. The title of the original novel, by C E Vulliamy, is also fun: *Don Among the Dead Men*.

Jolson Sings Again O Ⓥ

1949, US, 93 mins, colour
Dir: Henry Levin
Stars: Larry Parks, Barbara Hale, William Demarest
Rating: ★★★

The successor to *The Jolson Story* surprisingly turned out to be every bit as vivid, colourful, lively and entertaining as the original. Larry Parks once again mimes skilfully to Jolson's singing and Barbara Hale is warmth itself as his new wife. A multitude of songs includes 'Manuny', 'Swanee', 'Toot-Toot-Tootsie', 'Dixie', 'Carolina in the Morning' and 'Sonny Boy'.

Jolson Story, The O Ⓥ

1946, US, 128 mins, colour
Dir: Alfred E Green
Stars: Larry Parks, Evelyn Keyes, William Demarest
Rating: ★★★

This story of Al Jolson's rise to fame was Columbia's biggest money spinner at that time and made a star of Larry Parks, even though Jolson himself provided the singing voice and did the long-shot dances. The musical sequences were directed by Joseph H Lewis, who made a name for himself among film fans for his fine handling of low-budget material in the Forties and Fifties.

Joseph Andrews ●

1976, UK, 98 mins, colour
Dir: Tony Richardson
Stars: Ann-Margret, Peter Firth, Michael Hordern, Beryl Reid, Jim Dale, Natalie Ogle
Rating: ★

Director Tony Richardson returns to the vein he mined so successfully in *Tom Jones*. Although this later costume romp cannot measure up to its illustrious Oscar-winning predecessor, it does have some very funny scenes. Much of it, though, has a tired feeling.

Josh and S.A.M. O Ⓥ

1993, US, 97 mins, colour
Dir: Billy Weber
Stars: Jacob Tierney, Noah Fleiss, Martha Plimpton, Stephen Tobolowsky,

Chris Penn
Rating. ★

Divided between divorced parents and feeling unwanted by both, 12-year-old Josh convinces his younger brother Sam that he has been 'programmed' by the Pentagon. After hearing at an airport stop between parents that their mother has remarried and thinking they've killed a man who menaced them, the boys run away together. A pretty slim premise on which to hang a road movie and indeed this is a pretty slim road movie at that, only barely interesting and tending to repetition. Jacob Tierney and Noah Fleiss are competent young actors, but none too charismatic and there's no emotional pull for the audience in staying around to see what happens to them. Martha Plimpton, Chris Penn and Udo Kier are some of the too-few people along the way, but only Stephen Tobolowsky as the boys' father creates a character who seems to have a life outside the movie.

Journey Back to Oz ⊙

1971, US, 90 mins, colour
Dir: Hal Sutherland
Voice Stars: Liza Minnelli, Mickey Rooney, Ethel Merman
Rating: ★★★

Nostalgia, nostalgia everywhere in this cartoon sequel to *The Wizard of Oz*. Based on L Frank Baum's own first sequel to his children's classic, it adds Dorothy to the plot of that and gives her the voice of Liza Minnelli, daughter of Judy Garland, the original Dorothy. Just for good measure, Margaret Hamilton, the original Wicked Witch, voices Aunt Em, and Mickey Rooney, Judy Garland's favourite dancing partner in films – they made nine together – provides the voice of the Scarecrow. Virtually completed in 1964, but tinkered around with for years before eventual release.

Journey of Natty Gann, The O Ⓥ

1985, US, 101 mins, colour
Dir: Jeremy Kagan
Stars: Meredith Salenger, John Cusack, Ray Wise, Scatman Crothers
Rating: ★★★★★

There's a return to the old values of the Disney studio here with the story of a 14-year-old girl who, tough as any boy, runs away from Depression-gripped Chicago to join her father, who has gone to Washington. She is befriended by a half-breed dog she calls Wolf and by a young drifter (John

Cusack) for whom she feels the first stirrings of love. There's only one way to play Natty successfully, by going in there and giving it all you've got. Young Meredith Salenger does just that: she's never been as effective since. Director Jeremy Kagan conjures up an unfailing, exciting sense of period in creating the best family film the Disney people had turned out in more than a decade.

Journey to the Centre of the Earth O Ⓥ

1959, US, 110 mins, colour
Dir: Henry Levin
Stars: Pat Boone, James Mason, Arlene Dahl, Diane Baker
Rating: ★★★

This spectacular adaptation of the Jules Verne adventure yarn is great fun, and was nominated for four Academy Awards, including special effects, art direction and set decoration. Highlights of the journey include prehistoric reptiles, a magnetic storm and a terrifying earthquake.

Joy Luck Club, The ● Ⓥ

1993, US, 139 mins, colour
Dir: Wayne Wang
Stars: Tamlyn Tomita, Kieu Chinh, France Nuyen, Tsai Chin, Lisa Lu, Andrew McCarthy
Rating: ★★★

A very well acted and presented story of Chinese-American life and the chequered histories that lead to the formation of a family network. But – and here comes the downside – it's also a story which makes it very difficult to keep track of its various threads. These are all enthralling and beautifully done – but not quite memorably enough so that we can keep a grip on its overall pattern. What with four daughters in America and their mothers in China and sometimes their mothers' mothers, it's hard to remember who has done what or had what done to them, and that deficiency strikes at the humanity so vital to the film's appeal. Still, nostalgia buffs will get a kick out of seeing Sixties stars France Nuyen, Lisa Lu, Tsai Chin and Kieu Chinh all delivering first-rate performances under Wayne Wang's direction.

Juarez O

1939, US, 132 mins, b/w
Dir: William Dieterle
Stars: Paul Muni, Bette Davis, Claude Rains, John Garfield, Donald Crisp
Rating: ★★

Everything about this mammoth historical epic was on a big scale; from the 1,000 extras and 54 massive sets – including 12 villages, four cities, and various castles and palaces – to the 3,000 bars of music composed by Erich Wolfgang Korngold. For all that (or perhaps because of it) the whiff of real life escapes it. Paul Muni is almost unrecognisable under tons of make-up as Mexican leader Benito Pablo Juarez, and Bette Davis goes to town as the unbalanced Empress Carlotta, offering a stone-faced tour-de-force of madness personified.

Jubal ○
1956, US, 101 mins, colour
Dir. Delmer Daves
Stars: Glenn Ford, Ernest Borgnine, Rod Steiger, Charles Bronson
Rating: ★★★

Very tough Western, with a performance of integrity, depth and sincerity by Glenn Ford as Jubal, the cowhand who drifts into trouble with the boss's foreman and the boss's wife. A year later, Ford and director Delmer Daves combined again – on the classic Western, *3.10 to Yuma*. This film has a formidable combination of talent in its three leading players, of whom Rod Steiger, perhaps, has the plum role as a cowhand with a lemon-sour nature and a sadistic streak. The story is a strong one, and the picture is beautifully located against a background of Montana mountains.

Judge Dredd ● Ⓥ
1995, UK, 95 mins, colour
Dir: Danny Cannon
Stars: Sylvester Stallone, Diane Lane, Armand Assante, Jurgen Prochnow, Max Von Sydow
Rating: ★★★

Fast and furious futuristic fun, with echoes of *Things to Come* and *Metropolis*. Although its acting will win no Oscars, this is a visually imaginative action fantasy whose praiseworthy production design creates a ghetto city rising to orange skies around which craft buzz like hornets and mosquitoes, miraculously never crashing into one another. The rule of law is administered by 'judges' on motor-bikes. Following an arrest they are judge, jury and sometimes executioner, as they fight to control the block riots that are overrunning the city. Most feared of all, natch, is Judge Dredd (Sylvester Stallone), an artificially created judge who recognises nothing but the law. But there are elements who want him out of the way to

bring the city under their own control, and his genetically contrived evil brother (Armand Assante), soon released from his life imprisonment, seems the ideal tool to bring about their ends. There's a smashing airborne chase on flying motor-bikes and lots of massive baddies for Dredd to beat after he has been framed and escaped back to Mega City One.

Jude ● Ⓥ
1996, UK, 123 mins, colour
Dir: Michael Winterbottom
Stars: Christopher Eccleston, Kate Winslet, Liam Cunningham, Rachel Griffiths, June Whitfield
Rating: ★★

If there is an audience out there for a film as miserable and dispiriting as this, they are sure to appreciate some impassioned acting from Eccleston as Jude, a 19th-century farm boy determined to better himself, Winslet as the forward-thinking cousin who bewitches him, Cunningham as the teacher she marries, and Griffiths as the country girl who ensnares Jude into marriage. Small wonder no one has tried to film this novel before. As well as being controversial for its time, it's depressing and deeply tragic. And it's doubtful whether Thomas Hardy wrote in quite so many raunchy love scenes. However, Winslet, Eccleston and Griffiths are all attractive in the nude as well as darned good actors, in a film which needs all the life and colour it can find to inject into a world where, especially when things are going wrong, it seems to be forever raining.

Judgment at Nuremberg ○
1961, US, 190 mins, b/w
Dir: Stanley Kramer
Stars: Spencer Tracy, Burt Lancaster, Richard Widmark, Marlene Dietrich, Maximilian Schell, Judy Garland
Rating: ★★★

A graphic account of the Nuremberg Trials, in which members of the German judiciary were brought to book in the immediate post-war period. For his impassioned portrayal of the defending counsel, Maximilian Schell took an Academy Award as the year's best actor – but Spencer Tracy, Burt Lancaster and Co are also superb.

Judith ○
1965, US, 109 mins, colour
Dir: Daniel Mann
Stars: Sophia Loren, Peter Finch, Jack Hawkins
Rating: ★

A moderately exciting drama set in strife-torn Israel in 1947. Sophia Loren looks eye-popping in sweater and short shorts but has little meaty acting to do as a Jewess determined to kill her ex-Nazi husband. As a British officer, Jack Hawkins skilfully moulds the most sympathetic character.

Juggernaut ○
1974, UK, 105 mins, colour
Dir: Richard Lester
Stars: Richard Harris, Omar Sharif, Anthony Hopkins, David Hemmings, Ian Holm
Rating: ★★★

This large-scale, water-bound thriller raises a fair amount of tension on its theme of seven bombs planted aboard a luxury liner. Richard Harris leads the team of men assigned to defuse them in the teeth of a howling gale while, back in England, Supt Anthony Hopkins, whose wife is aboard and whose son inadvertently costs two lives, races desperately to track down Juggernaut, the mad bomber. But Roy Kinnear steals the film as the ship's social director – a memorably comic supporting portrayal. David Hemmings is also excellent and the suspense is good if not super-tense. A sub-plot involving Shirley Knight and Omar Sharif (as the ship's Captain) is so negligible as to be simply not worthwhile.

Julia ◑
1977, US, 118 mins, colour
Dir: Fred Zinnemann
Stars: Jane Fonda, Vanessa Redgrave, Jason Robards, Maximilian Schell, Hal Holbrook
Rating: ★★★

This award-winning film is sensitive, atmospheric and often suspenseful. It recounts some early adventures in the life of American playwright Lillian Hellman (Jane Fonda), notably those concerning her childhood friend Julia, who became involved in resistance against the Nazis in the Thirties. Their story is painstakingly retold by director Fred Zinnemann, with assistance from one of the world's best colour cameramen, Douglas Slocombe. Vanessa Redgrave is exceptionally good as Julia, and certainly better than anyone could have expected in a part which creeps so uncomfortably close to her own political feelings. Jason Robards is a treat as Lillian's companion Dashiell Hammett – right back to his best form. Both performances were rightly rewarded with Academy Awards. In the supporting

J

cast, you can see a future Oscar-winner, Meryl Streep, in her first film role.

Julia Has Two Lovers ● Ⓥ

1990, US, 91 mins, colour
Dir. Bashar Shbib
Stars: Daphna Kastner, David Duchovny
Rating: ★

You could almost close your eyes and treat this story of seduction by phone as a radio play. Not that that would make its story any more believable. Julia (Daphna Kastner) is about to marry a man she doesn't love when along comes the voice of Daniel (David Duchovny) who specialises in making obscene phone calls to women to see if he can seduce them. He finds a willing participant in Julia and soon enough is knocking on her door and tumbling her into bed, only to have his lifestyle exposed by one of his previous conquests. There's very little to all of this save for the conversations: the budget apparently ran to about $25 and all of the acting apart from the leading players would discredit your local amateur dramatic society. Duchovny, though, has a lazy, laid-back charm.

Julie Ⓞ

1957, US, 99 mins, b/w
Dir: Andrew Stone
Stars: Doris Day, Louis Jourdan, Barry Sullivan, Frank Lovejoy
Rating: ★★

This overheated tale of a young widow who remarries, only to find that her new husband is a homicidal maniac, marked the beginning of Doris Day's complete breakaway from musicals, and her appointments with fear that continued with *Midnight Lace*. It was made by Andrew Stone, then a young director specialising in high-tension thrillers shot on location.

Julius Caesar Ⓞ Ⓥ

1953, US, 120 mins, b/w
Dir: Joseph L Mankiewicz
Stars: Marlon Brando, James Mason, John Gielgud, Edmond O'Brien, Greer Garson, Deborah Kerr
Rating: ★★★★

One of Hollywood's most prestigious Shakespearean productions, with an electrifying performance by Marlon Brando as Mark Antony, this is definitely the best film version available of the famous play. There are memorable performances from John Gielgud as Cassius and Edmond O'Brien as Casca, and the film's wealth of expert character-drawing extends right down to the minor roles, one of which is

played by Edmund Purdom. Directed with imagination by Joseph L Mankiewicz, the film proved that the public would go for Shakespeare if the impact was strong and the performances attractive enough.

Julius Caesar Ⓞ

1970, US, 117 mins, colour
Dir: Stuart Burge
Stars: Charlton Heston, John Gielgud, Diana Rigg, Jason Robards, Richard Chamberlain, Christopher Lee
Rating: ★★

Charlton Heston stars in this not too well-known version – at any rate in comparison with the more famous Marlon Brando film of Shakespeare's play – made in Britain but with a few top American stars in leading roles somewhat at variance with an array of notable British acting talent. Jason Robards in particular seems ill-at-ease in the role of Brutus, but lovers of Shakespeare and good performances will find much that is rewarding. Robert Vaughn makes a superbly sneaky Casca.

Jumanji Ⓞ Ⓥ

1995, US, 102 mins, colour
Dir: Joe Johnston
Stars: Robin Williams, Bonnie Hunt, Kirsten Dunst, Jonathan Hyde, Bradley Pierce
Rating: ★★★

The idea of people getting sucked into a bizarre board game that becomes a battle for life itself might seem a natural for a horror film. But director Joe Johnston, who made *Honey, I Shrunk the Kids*, opts for the fantasy-adventure-comedy route, with Robin Williams as the man trapped inside the game's invisible jungle for 26 years. After a slow first half-hour, Johnston and Williams have quite a lot of fun with the idea, as two kids at Williams' old home start playing the game and release the 'prisoner', plus a whole jungle-full of wild life, on to an unsuspecting town. Each throw of the dice produces a horde of natural dangers which, though entertaining, is patently absurd, as the (computerised) carnivorous plants, raging rhinos, man-sized mosquitos and leaping lions appear from out of the blue and not out of the game. Never mind, the plot's various ends are neatly tied at the end and its moral tidily driven home. Not for easily frightened tots: others will love it.

Jumbo Ⓞ

(aka: Billy Rose's Jumbo)
1962, US, 125 mins, colour
Dir: Charles Walters
Stars: Doris Day, Stephen Boyd, Jimmy Durante, Martha Raye, Dean Jagger
Rating: ★★★

Pleasantly entertaining musical, Doris's Day's last, about the rivalry between two circuses. The musical numbers are attractively staged, as one would expect with a combination of director Charles Walters and second-unit director Busby Berkeley, who between them have made some of Hollywood's most invigorating musical entertainments. Nice, too, to see old-timers Martha Raye and Jimmy Durante in action again, even if one wishes the script gave the them more into which to sink their teeth.

Jumping Jacks ☉

1952, US, 96 mins, b/w
Dir: Norman Taurog
Stars: Dean Martin, Jerry Lewis
Rating: ★★★

Having created havoc in the Army (*At War With the Army*) and the Navy (*Sailor Beware*), Dean Martin and Jerry Lewis set about destroying the airborne infantry in this story of two song-and-dance men drafted into the paratroopers. Robert Strauss is a delight as the ferocious sergeant who deals summarily with Jerry's request to tuck him up in bed at night. Mona Freeman is a resourceful and feminine heroine; and the film is quite a lot of fun.

Jumpin' Jack Flash ◑ Ⓥ

1986, US, 120 mins, colour
Dir: Penny Marshall
Stars: Whoopi Goldberg, Jonathan Pryce, Jim Belushi, Carol Kane, Annie Potts
Rating: ★★★

The follow-up vehicle to Whoopi Goldberg's Oscar-nominated performance in Steven Spielberg's *The Color Purple* marked a dramatic change of pace and one more akin to her wacky, wisecracking, alternative comedy persona. An uneven comedy spy thriller, its main problem is that Whoopi's character, a hapless bank clerk who receives messages from a British spy trapped behind the Iron Curtain, is just too small for her personality. And Penny Marshall (later to make *Big*, but here in her debut as a director) was unable (or unwilling) to keep her star's wilder excesses in check. But there are still some comic gems, notably the scenes where Whoopi gatecrashes a ball at the British Embassy in New York by impersonating Diana Ross, and when her dress gets caught in an office shredder.

Jungle Book ☉
1942, US, 109 mins, colour
Dir: Zoltan Korda
Stars: Sabu, Joseph Calleia, Rosemary
DeCamp, John Qualen
Rating: ★★★

After a number of successful films in
Britain, teenage Indian star Sabu went
to Hollywood with Alexander and
Zoltan Korda to complete *The Thief of
Bagdad* and stayed with them to make
this colourful adaptation of Kipling's
classic tales. Because it tries to combine too many of the original tales the
film tends to be a little muddled in
places, but the sweep of the action and
the fascination of the animals carries us
through. Like many films of the period, it looks nothing like the real India
but perhaps what it should look like,
according to Hollywood. The film
makes vivid entertainment.

Jungle Book, The ☉ ⓥ
1967, US, 78 mins, colour
Dir: Wolfgang Reitherman
Voice Stars: Phil Harris, Sebastian Cabot,
George Sanders, Louis Prima, Bruce
Reitherman
Rating: ★★★★

Coming up mint-fresh at each reissue,
Disney's jazzed-up Kipling is brimming
with marvellous characters: Baloo the
bear, King Louie of the Apes, Colonel
Hathi the elephant and Kaa the snake
remaining triumphantly individual.
And the whole film, apart from one or
two very small dud patches, goes with
a swing. Best of all is Shere Khan the
tiger, but probably only because he's
voiced by the stiffly threatening tones
of George Sanders. No actor's voice,
surely, was ever more suited to a cartoon role. Only the quartet of
Liverpudlian vultures are at all dated,
although even they retain their inher-
ent-appeal. The Sherman Brothers'
tuneful score – 'King of the Swingers',
'The Bare Necessities' and more – ensures that this one remains the king of
the swingin' cartoons.

Jungle Fever ● ⓥ
1991, US, 132 mins, colour
Dir: Spike Lee
Stars: Wesley Snipes, Annabella Sciorra,
Spike Lee, John Turturro, Anthony Quinn
Rating: ★

Man, this is long and heavy, and it really lays it on you like Spike Lee thinks it
is. After delightful credits, pegged to
street signs, and a stylish opening, this
movie seems to go on for hours and
hours. A savage film that sometimes
resembles a silent, it's a mess of drugs,

adultery, violence and murder and you
re never quite sure that its characters'
motivations are what Lee thinks they
are. The film's racist attitudes will sit
uneasily with some audiences, and its
characters – or, rather, caricatures,
rarely ring true. Subplots abound, if
you can follow them, as the dialogue is
screeched at ear-splitting level and
seems to consist mostly of hysterically
shouted four-letter words. If this is the
fever, man, hand us the antidote.

Jungle Fighters
See: The Long and the Short and the Tall

Junior ○ ⓥ
1994, US, 109 mins, colour
Dir: Ivan Reitman
Stars: Arnold Schwarzenegger, Danny
DeVito, Emma Thompson, Frank
Langella
Rating: ★★★

Put Arnold Schwarzenegger, Danny
DeVito and Emma Thompson together
in the same film and you just have to
get fun. Make Arnold pregnant as well
and you have a film that's not only extremely silly but also very amusing at
times. And, surprisingly, it's DeVito
who gets pushed to one side while
Schwarzenegger and Emma steal most
of the laughs. Arnie and Danny are
dedicated scientists whose fertility project is cancelled by nasty lab supervisor
Frank Langella. Danny gets the idea of
progressing from chimps to impregnat-
ing Arnie – described at the start as a
man with 'all the warmth and charm of
a wall-eyed pike' – with an egg from
the lab. The catch is that the egg belongs, in every sense, to Professor
Emma, whose own project has taken
over the scientists' former premises.
Arnie comes over all broody and decides to keep the baby. If you think
this is idiotic, you should see the rest,
including the giant dressing up as a
woman for a spell at a posh pre-natal
centre. Lots of the kind of humorous
situations you'd expect are carried off
with aplomb by the stars.

Junior Bonner ◐ ⓥ
1972, US, 105 mins, colour
Dir. Sam Peckinpah
Stars: Steve McQueen, Robert Preston,
Ida Lupino
Rating: ★★★

A much quieter film than usual from
Straw Dogs and *Bring Me the Head of
Alfredo Garcia* director Sam Peckinpah
with Steve McQueen in excellent form
as a rodeo rider who comes to realise
that he can't go home on the range

again. There's a lot to recommend in
this study of a fish out of water, a man
searching in a changing world for values that have long since disappeared.
The rodeo footage is pretty exciting
and Jerry Fielding's music is spot-on.

Jurassic Park ◑ ⓥ
1993, US, 126 mins, colour
Dir: Steven Spielberg
Stars: Sam Neill, Laura Dern, Jeff
Goldblum, Richard Attenborough, Bob
Peck, Martin Ferrero
Rating: ★★★

After a long and slow lead-in period,
Steven Spielberg's dinosaur thriller explodes into the kind of action we've all
been waiting for, as the genetically engineered prehistoric animals go berserk
after a renegade employee conveniently
turns off all the electric fences penning
them in, on their island home. It's at
this stage that 90 per cent of the
Jurassic Park staff seem to disappear,
leaving only the principals to flee the
predators and try to turn the current
back on. But you can ignore the plot,
such as it is, since not much of it makes
any sort of sense you can grasp. Sam
Neill and Laura Dern, along with kids
Ariana Richards and Joseph Mazzello,
give vigorous physical performances
dodging the dinos, while Richard
Attenborough (as the park's curator)
and Jeff Goldblum offer rather actorly
portrayals on the fringe of things. The
dinosaurs themselves, of course, are the
real stars, and they're marvellous – terrifyingly awesome and almost totally
convincing. Enough to make even
E.T. phone home.

Juror, The ● ⓥ
1996, US, 115 mins, colour
Dir: Brian Gibson
Stars: Demi Moore, Alec Baldwin,
Lindsay Crouse, Tony Lo Bianco, Joseph
Gordon-Levitt, Anne Heche
Rating: ★

A jurywoman sitting on a hot murder
trial finds herself and her son intimidat-
ed by the hitman who actually
committed the murders for which his
Mafia boss finds himself on trial.
Mostly tedium results from this situation in a doomily conducted plot that
only bursts into life in the last half-
hour. Director Brian Gibson doesn't
muster the dramatic tension he might.
Whispering Alec Baldwin and throaty
Demi Moore at least make themselves
intelligible, which is more than can be
said for newcomer Anne Heche as the
heroine's doctor friend who inevitably
falls victim to Baldwin's silky psychotic

menace, in one of the movie's many non-surprises.

Just Around the Corner ⊙
1938, US, 71 mins, b/w
Dir: Irving Cummings
Stars: Shirley Temple, Charles Farrell, Joan Davis
Rating: ★★★

Shirley Temple chirps her way through a typical Temple musical weepic, set in the Depression. This one contains what is probably her best production number in films – 'I Love to Walk in the Rain'. A good time for vintage-film fans: they can spot wide-mouthed comedienne Joan Davis, black dancer Bill 'Bojangles' Robinson, perfect-mannered, prissy Franklin Pangborn, and veteran vaudevillian Bert Lahr – to win everlasting fame a year later as The Cowardly Lion in *The Wizard of Oz.*

Just Ask for Diamond ○
1988, UK, 94 mins, colour
Dir: Stephen Bayly
Stars: Dursley McLinden, Colin Dale, Susannah York
Rating: ★★

The most inexplicable thing about this spoof *film noir* was the decision to drop the evocative title of screenwriter Adam Horowitz's novel, *The Falcon's Malteser*. But this was just one of a series of absurd misjudgements which mar this potentially entertaining children's film. The world of dark shadows and corruption could have been more convincingly realised and the humour might have been sharper too. Only a few early comic moments and Susannah York as the drink-sodden Lauren Bacardi make any impression.

Just Between Friends ◐
1986, US, 105 mins, colour
Dir: Allan Burns
Stars: Mary Tyler Moore, Christine Lahti, Ted Danson, Sam Waterston
Rating: ★★

This mega-weepie about the friendship between a wife and a mistress (not knowing at first who the other is) is heavy going at first, but gathers strength from the performances of Mary Tyler Moore and Christine Lahti, both perfectly cast. Later developments are not wholly believable, but these two powerhouse performers see it through.

Just For You ○
1952, US, 104 mins, colour
Dir: Elliott Nugent

Stars: Bing Crosby, Jane Wyman, Ethel Barrymore, Natalie Wood
Rating: ★★★

Pleasant musical about a composer, who doesn't spend enough time with his motherless son and daughter. Some splendid mountain scenery, able scene-stealing from a 13-year-old Natalie Wood as the daughter, tuneful songs and colourful dance sequences. There's also Ethel Barrymore, who dominates every scene in which she appears, and will leave you breathless with admiration, as the super-sophisticated headmistress of a superior girls' finishing school.

Just Like a Woman ● ⊙
1992, UK, 109 mins, colour
Dir: Christopher Monger
Stars: Julie Walters, Adrian Pasdar, Paul Freeman
Rating: ★

Someone, somewhere, is due to write another good film soon for that most deserving of actresses, Julie Walters. But this isn't it. The sad thing about this whole, awful mess is that Julie is quite good, even affecting in it. Dreadfully mishandled so as to suggest appalling visual conflicts between the heterosexual transvestite and the effeminate way in which Adrian Pasdar, groping desperately, plays him, it's the story of a businessman who likes dressing up in women's clothes and the landlady who falls for him anyway. One of the problems with all this is that Pasdar never looks like anything but a man, which would be all right in a docu-drama about transvestism, but makes embarrassing nonsense of a plot-line in which he's required to pass muster as a woman for all sorts of reasons.

Just My Luck ⊙ ⓥ
1957, UK, 80 mins, b/w
Dir: John Paddy Carstairs
Stars: Norman Wisdom, Jill Dixon, Margaret Rutherford, Leslie Phillips
Rating: ★★★

Norman Wisdom's luck was just beginning to turn in the late Fifties, but this is still one of his better comedies, even if (or perhaps because) it's not tailored to his specific talents. Splendid support from Margaret Rutherford, Leslie Phillips, Edward Chapman and Joan Sims; the obligatory nice girl is Jill Dixon. The support cast is full of familiar faces from British films of the period: Sam Kydd scowls darkly, Michael Ward dithers, Bill Fraser splutters, and that's Marianne Stone serving behind the tea bar.

Just William ⊙
1939, UK, 69 mins, b/w
Dir: Graham Cutts
Stars: Dicky Lupino, Jenny Laird, Fred Emney, Basil Radford
Rating: ★★

The first attempt to bring Richmal Crompton's infamous ragged rascal of a schoolboy to the screen. Likeable and good fun, the film makes the mistake that all 'William' films made, by trying to drag in too much of a 'thriller' plot to the exclusion of the plethora of little incidents that made the books so readable. Dicky Lupino, from the famous acting family, makes a spirited William, and his cohort Ginger is played by a wide-eyed Roddy McDowall, who would soon achieve far greater stardom in Hollywood.

Just William's Luck ⊙
1947, UK, 92 mins, b/w
Dir: Val Guest
Stars: William Graham, Garry Marsh, Brian Roper, A E Matthews
Rating: ★★

First of two films made in the Forties featuring the scruffy schoolboy hero of Richmal Crompton's best-selling stories. Adapted from several *Just William* tales, it's a lively romp with a jolly knockabout climax in a house that William and his gang of 'outaws' are trying to haunt.

K

Kaleidoscope ○

1966, UK, 104 mins, colour
Dir: Jack Smight
Stars: Warren Beatty, Susannah York, Clive Revill, Murray Melvin
Rating: ★★★

Jack Smight's feisty romantic thriller (with 'Swinging Sixties' trimmings) about a clever gambler. He's also found out as a clever cheat, hence his inability to refuse a police request to help trap a narcotics smuggler (icily played by Eric Porter). A fun film, with Warren Beatty and Susannah York sharing star billing and Clive Revill quite splendid as an unorthodox and faintly sinister Scotland Yard man. By far the funniest scene is that in which Revill and his assistant (Murray Melvin) play cards (for matchsticks) with a pack that they know to be marked. Revill asserts his authority by using a microscope to look at the backs of Melvin's cards and still succeeds in losing.

Kalifornia ● ⓥ

1993, US, 118 mins, colour
Dir: Dominic Sena
Stars: Brad Pitt, Juliette Lewis, David Duchovny, Michelle Forbes
Rating: ★★

Any film with a leading character called Early Grayce has to be pretentious, allegorical, or both. This one also develops into an efficient bloodbath thriller in its last 40 minutes or so, but it's a long and languorous overture to this particular crescendo. David Duchovny plays stymied writer Brian, who has a fascination with serial killers, out of which he thinks he can create a bestseller by visiting the sites of their slaughter across America. His girlfriend (Michelle Forbes), who hopes to have her pornographic pictures accepted as art, goes along to do the illustrations. Unfortunately they take, as fuel-sharing travel companions, real multiple killer Early (Brad Pitt, in yet another attempt to escape his pretty-boy looks) and his feeble-minded mistress (Juliette Lewis). Pitt is genuinely menacing, but the strongest performance comes from Forbes in the least showy role.

Kama Sutra: A Tale of Love ● ⓥ

1996, Ind/UK, 114 mins, colour
Dir: Mira Nair

Stars: Indira Varma, Sarita Choudhury, Naveen Andrews, Ramon Tikaram, Rekha
Rating: ★★

Indian erotica – its sentiments as simple as in Sabu's day. Yes, those bright turbans and opulent places are back, but welded to such a display of flesh as never was seen in Hollywood's account of the Arabian Nights. Two girls are raised as childhood friends and rivals. One (Choudhury) ensnares a king (Andrews) but he falls for the other (Varma) at first sight, and she gives herself to him on his wedding night. Thrown out on her ear, Varma goes for strapping sculptor Tikaram while, back at the palace, Choudhury shies away from sexual contact, and Andrews sinks into an opium-induced haze and a sea of concubines. All might have been well had not Tikaram decided Varma puts him off his stroke. She becomes Andrew's chief courtesan and tragedy beckons. It's clear director Nair means all this as a feminist tract, but it hardly comes across that way. Soft-porn sex mingles with the fairy-tale elements and they make, like Choudhury and her king, uneasy bedfellows.

Kangaroo ○

1952, US, 84 mins, colour
Dir: Lewis Milestone
Stars: Maureen O'Hara, Peter Lawford, Richard Boone, Chips Rafferty
Rating: ★★★

Photographed in blazing Technicolor by Charles G Clarke, this is an exciting, unusual and consistently dramatic action-adventure set in Australian pioneering days. The narrative rivets the interest, Finlay Currie and Maureen O'Hara contribute forthright performances as father and daughter ranchers, and Richard Boone's Gamble is an excellent study of cynical opportunism. Fresh, lively entertainment.

Kansas City Confidential

See: The Secret Four

Kansas City ● ⓥ

1995, US/Fr, 115 mins, colour
Dir: Robert Altman
Stars: Jennifer Jason Leigh, Harry Belafonte, Miranda Richardson, Dermot Mulroney, Steve Buscemi, Michael Murphy
Rating: ★★★

Really irritating performances by Leigh and Richardson in the central roles of this rambling and sometimes repellent road movie means that the music, great

jazz stuff, is the real star here – which is perhaps what director Altman, a jazz devotee, intended in the first place. Blondie (Leigh) kidnaps politician's wife Richardson with some harebrained idea of exerting pressure on gangster Belafonte (who plays a character called Seldom Seen) to release Leigh's husband (Mulroney), to whom Belafonte is about to do something awful. Altman's customary skill at tying disparate threads of a plot together seems to have deserted him here, but Kansas City in the midst of the Depression is splendidly evoked, with modern jazz greats taking the roles of musicians of the time. If only you cared about some of these characters in the way you do about the music.

Kansas Pacific ○

1952, US, 73 mins, colour
Dir: Ray Nazarro
Stars: Sterling Hayden, Eve Miller, Barton MacLane, Douglas Fowley
Rating: ★★

If trains fascinate you, then this vigorous Western has plenty to offer. The actors, headed by Sterling Hayden, aren't too well served by the dialogue, but the story's action shots pull it through. Director Ray Nazarro, an experienced hand at Westerns, ensures that this film has enough vitality and incident to keep the audience hooked throughout.

Karate Kid, The ◗ ⓥ

1984, US, 127 mins, colour
Dir: John G Avildsen
Stars: Ralph Macchio, Noriyuki 'Pat' Morita, Elisabeth Shue
Rating: ★★★★

After Rocky, it's Rocky Junior. Director John G Avildsen has taken the same basic elements that made his boxing film such a success and cunningly crafted them to a seven-stone-weakling-style yarn about Danny (Ralph Macchio), a 15-year-old whose meagre karate training is of no use against the local motorcycle gang, whose leader (the ex of the girl Danny fancies) doubles up as the school bully. As he and his friends are members of the 'no mercy' local karate school, Danny's education is proving a painful one until he meets Mr Miyagi, the repair man at his flats, who proves, not unexpectedly, to be a karate expert and helps Danny train for the local championships. And guess who he meets in the final? Still, it all works very well, and will please younger audiences especially. Attractive Elisabeth Shue seems a trifle mature for our teenage hero, but the film is in any case stolen by veteran 'Pat' Morita as Miyagi, who makes the most of the film's good lines.

Karate Kid Part II, The ○ Ⓥ
1986, US, 113 mins, colour
Dir: John G Avildsen
Stars: Ralph Macchio, Noriyuki 'Pat' Morita, Tamlyn Tomita
Rating: ★★

The success of *The Karate Kid* meant there had to be a sequel – and here it is. As follow-ups go, this is a serviceable one, although it hardly eclipses the orginal. Danny (Ralph Macchio) again takes on the bad guys aided by his wise old tutor Miyagi ('Pat' Morita). The action then changes when the couple go to Miyagi's native Okinawa and Danny becomes involved in a duel. The balance between comforting familiarity and the new is struck fairly well and Morita obviously enjoys himself as he quotes pearls of eastern wisdom, like 'Best way to avoid punch – no be there!' There's a good storm sequence near the end, by which time you may be grateful for any touch of originality in such recycled twaddle.

Karate Kid III ○ Ⓥ
1989, US, 111 mins, colour
Dir: John G Avildsen
Stars: Ralph Macchio, Noriyuki 'Pat' Morita, Robyn Lively
Rating: ★

The relative failure of *Karate Kid Part II* should have taught its producers a thing or two. But no. This comicbook-style second sequel gives us another challenge, another girlfriend and another fight at the end that proves a complete anti-climax. The villains from the first *Karate Kid* (plus a bigger villain) swear vengeance on 'that old dojo and the punk kid' (that's still 'Pat' Morita and a now slightly overweight Ralph Macchio). 'I'm gonna make them suffer for what they did to you,' swears villain number one. 'And suffer. And suffer. You know what the kid's gonna learn from me? Fear in his mind. And pain in his body.' All of which pain and suffering can be undergone by viewers subjecting themselves to this seven-stone weakling of a film.

Katina
See: Iceland

Keep 'Em Flying ☉
1941, US, 86 mins, b/w
Dir: Arthur Lubin

Stars: Bud Abbott, Lou Costello, Martha Raye, Dick Foran
Rating: ★★

Bud Abbott and Lou Costello, having given the Army (*Buck Privates*) and the Navy (*In the Navy*) a slapstick going-over, turned their attentions to the Air Force in this typical Forties farce. Martha Raye steals the film as twins, as well as singing a popular wartime hit called 'Pig Foot Pete'. The film cleaned up at the box-office and Bud and Lou found themselves the top box-office attractions in America by the end of the year.

Keeper of the Flame ○
1942, US, 100 mins, b/w
Dir: George Cukor
Stars: Spencer Tracy, Katharine Hepburn, Richard Whorf
Rating: ★★

The second Katharine Hepburn-Spencer Tracy film, and a very serious affair compared with the gaiety of their first, *Woman of the Year*. This is a straight dramatic story about famous people with feet of clay and has been justly neglected in favour of the comedies the famous pair made together. Glum.

Keep Fit ☉
1937, UK, 82 mins, b/w
Dir: Anthony Kimmins
Stars: George Formby, Kay Walsh
Rating: ★★★

Comedian George Formby, still at his most popular when this comedy was made, plays a naive young barber who gets involved in a high-standard gymnastics competition to try and win the love of a glamorous manicurist. Guy Middleton, as Hector, George's rival in love, is a comic bounder in the finest Terry-Thomas tradition. It's a bouncy, confidently made comedy that's fun throughout and pretty hilarious in its boxing-ring conclusion.

Kelly and Me ☉
1957, US, 86 mins, colour
Dir: Robert Z Leonard
Stars: Van Johnson, Piper Laurie, Martha Hyer, Onslow Stevens
Rating: ★★

Bright little musical about an untalented showman and the white alsatian who transforms his career. Mild, but colourful and enjoyable within its self-set limits. The dog, of course, outshines everyone, though that's not too difficult with most of this cast.

Kelly's Heroes ⬤ Ⓥ
1970, US, 143 mins, colour
Dir: Brian G Hutton
Stars: Clint Eastwood, Telly Savalas, Don Rickles, Carroll O'Connor, Donald Sutherland
Rating: ★★★★

Troy Kennedy Martin's script neatly integrates the humour and the action as five American soldiers decide that there's more to World War Two than killing and being killed: instead they opt to steal 14,000 bars of gold from a bank in Occupied France. There's plenty of action, filmed with the co-operation of the Yugoslav Army, culminating in a head-on battle between six tanks in a small village. To quote a character played by Telly Savalas: 'That ain't an army, it's a circus!' A scene that apes Eastwood's own spaghetti Western showdowns is both unexpected and hilariously funny.

Key Largo ○ Ⓥ
1948, US, 101 mins, b/w
Dir: John Huston
Stars: Humphrey Bogart, Edward G Robinson, Lauren Bacall
Rating: ★★★★

Under John Huston's skilful direction, Richard Brooks' adaptation of Maxwell Anderson's stage success proves cinematic enough not to look like a play and bristles with tension. The chemistry between Humphrey Bogart and Lauren Bacall is as cogent as ever as hotel occupants virtually held hostage by gangsters, but it's the bad guys, notably snarling Edward G Robinson, back to his hateful best, and Claire Trevor, boozing and brazening her way to an Oscar as his mistress, who really catch the eye. Robinson happily accepted second billing to Bogart – his adversary in several past Warners crime classics – to do the part of the gang boss at bay. 'Why not second billing?' he told his agent. 'At 53 most actors are lucky to get billing at all.' The result is short-fused dynamite, right up to the moments when the film bursts into action in its fogbound climax.

Keys of the Kingdom, The ○
1944, US, 137 mins, b/w
Dir: John M Stahl
Stars: Gregory Peck, Thomas Mitchell, Vincent Price, Edmund Gwenn, Cedric Hardwicke, Rosa Stradner
Rating: ★★★★

Long, elaborate, fairly faithful adaptation of A J Cronin's novel of a priest's adventures in China, which proved to be Gregory Peck's first major screen hit. The acting from a fine cast is solid and the story, which has some touching moments (and some exciting ones too), just about grips attention throughout.

Key to the City ○
1950, US, 101 mins, b/w
Dir: George Sidney
Stars: Clark Gable, Loretta Young, Frank Morgan, Marilyn Maxwell
Rating: ★★

A rather strained romantic comedy in which the two stars, Clark Gable and Loretta Young, are supported by a fine cast including Frank Morgan, Marilyn Maxwell, Raymond Burr and Lewis Stone, plus veteran James Gleason, who lends amusement to the edges of the film as a cop.

Khartoum ○
1966, UK, 134 mins, colour
Dir: Basil Dearden
Stars: Charlton Heston, Laurence Olivier, Richard Johnson, Ralph Richardson, Alexander Knox
Rating: ★★★★

Massive epic about General Gordon, with Charlton Heston lending tremendous presence to the role of the stubborn Gordon, and Laurence Olivier in frighteningly ferocious form as the 'mad' Mahdi. The electrically charged confrontation between the two is so well directed by Basil Dearden that one can forgive that it never actually happened. Sharp Technicolor photography and battle scenes round off one of the best pictures of its kind that the Sixties produced.

Kickboxer ● Ⓥ
1989, US, 105 mins, colour
Dir: Mark DiSalle
Stars: Jean-Claude Van Damme, Dennis Alexio, Rochelle Ashana
Rating: ★

This is *The Karate Kid* for sadistic adults. Very predictable too. Take a big, ugly villain, get him to beat up the meek hero's brother/friend, then set our hero on a trail of revenge. If your idea of entertainment is a barbaric fight where the protagonists tie cords round their fists and dip them in glue and broken glass, this is probably the film for you. Van Damme, world champ at kickboxing (though not acting), is the milksop who trains under an inscrutable oriental and soon proclaims, 'I'm in the best shape of my life', which we can see he always was. The bad guys do their best: they rape Jean-Claude's girl, poison his dog,

trap his trainer and kidnap his brother, the fighter that the villain crippled originally. What can poor Jean-Claude do? Don't strain yourself over the answer. It's all completely unconvincing, with previously invincible champions suddenly turning to jelly with one kick to the jaw.

Kid, The ⊙
1921, US, 52 mins, b/w
Dir: Charles Chaplin
Stars: Charlie Chaplin, Jackie Coogan
Rating: ★★★★

A Charlie Chaplin classic: a smash-hit dramatic comedy that mixes sentiment and slapstick with unerring accuracy in building up the touching relationship between Chaplin's fly-by-night and tiny Jackie Coogan's flop-haired kid, in a scene-stealing performance that set him up as a top child star for the ensuing decade. Especially well timed are the scenes in which Chaplin and Coogan 'operate' their window-fixing business, which involves the boy throwing a brick through a window which Chaplin subsequently offers to repair. A real winner, the film is genuinely charming throughout, with characters that tug at the heartstrings and tickle the funnybone in the next moment.

Kid ● Ⓥ
1990, US, 92 mins, colour
Dir: John Mark Robinson
Stars: C Thomas Howell, Sarah Trigger, Brian Austin Green, R Lee Ermey
Rating: ★

Presumably a kind of junior league spaghetti Western was the idea here. At least, somebody has obviously seen a few Clint Eastwood films, as even the flashbacks explaining the mysterious stranger's mission are thrown in. For the teen-fan trade it's C Thomas Howell in the long coat and short cigarette amid a ludicrous plot about redneck villains who'd gun down defenceless innocent people if they didn't want them around. The action needs to be special to make it all work, but it's no more than routine and John Mark Robinson's direction could, even at 92 minutes, do with a deal of tightening up. Howell's about the best actor around and he's lucky he doesn't have too much to say, especially with dialogue penned by the same guy who not only wrote the songs, but provides only basic comic-strip characters in his plot.

Kid Blue ◑
(aka: Dime Box)
1973, US, 100 mins, colour

Dir: James Frawley
Stars: Dennis Hopper, Warren Oates, Janice Rule, Ben Johnson, Peter Boyle, Lee Purcell
Rating: ★★★

A romantic Western in which Dennis Hopper gives one of his warmest performances as the outlaw who, tired of failure at robbing trains, tries life in a tiny Texas town. Here he fails too – to keep jobs, to avoid seduction by his best friend's wife, to steer clear of the sheriff (Mean John), to keep his past from becoming public and, finally, to resist the temptation to rob the firm where he stokes the boiler. But he meets some rich characters on the way, and eventually makes his exit in a flying machine invented by a dotty preacher. An old-fashioned film, swinging the cinematic pendulum back to the Fifties, and putting entertainment commendably before total authenticity.

Kid for Two Farthings, A ⊙
1954, UK, 96 mins, colour
Dir: Carol Reed
Stars: Celia Johnson, Diana Dors, David Kossoff, Brenda de Banzie, Jonathan Ashmore
Rating: ★★★

Director Carol Reed's thoroughly enjoyable fairy-tale, set in London's East End, brought all sorts of unexpected pleasures. Blond bombshells Diana Dors and Vera Day both showed their acting ability in softer roles; the market of Petticoat Lane, and its environs, sprang vividly to life; and the Eastman Color photography of Ted Scarfe was a delight. The best performance of all comes from David Kossoff as a kind of universal uncle.

Kid from Brooklyn, The ⊙
1946, US, 120 mins, colour
Dir: Norman Z McLeod
Stars: Danny Kaye, Virginia Mayo, Vera-Ellen, Steve Cochran, Eve Arden
Rating: ★★

One of Danny Kaye's Goldwyn films, casting him as a mild-mannered milkman credited with knocking out an unpleasant boxer. It's a remake of the 1936 Harold Lloyd comedy *The Milky Way*. Not too funny even in its day, it dates badly.

Kid from Spain, The ○
1932, US, 90 mins, b/w
Dir: Leo McCarey
Stars: Eddie Cantor, Lyda Roberti, Robert Young, Ruth Hall
Rating: ★★★

K

A big-budget musical extravaganza that has just about everything – romance, action, comedy, songs, Busby Berkeley dance routines and a galaxy of gorgeous Goldwyn Girls: not to mention the non-stop Eddie Cantor, singing another of his standards, 'What a Perfect Combination'. He plays a hapless college student who has to assume the identity of a bullfighter to escape the cops. The cops? Don't ask. Spot Betty Grable leading the girls in a chorus or two of 'The College Song'.

Kid from Texas, The O
(aka: Texas Kid – Outlaw)
1950, US, 78 mins, colour
Dir: Kurt Neumann
Stars: Audie Murphy, Gale Storm, Will Geer, Albert Dekker
Rating: ★★

Audie Murphy's third film, and first Western, giving him more of a character than usual to work on, based as it is on the early life of Billy the Kid. He gets good support from a host of good character actors, including Will Geer, Albert Dekker, Paul Ford, William Talman, and – inevitably as a sheriff – the moustachioed Ray Teal.

Kid Galahad O Ⓥ
1962, US, 95 mins, colour
Dir: Phil Karlson
Stars: Elvis Presley, Gig Young, Lola Albright, Charles Bronson
Rating: ★★

A remake of the 1937 Humphrey Bogart film of the same title, which exposed the seamy side of the fight game in America. This time Elvis Presley plays the fighter who only becomes dangerous when he's soaked up enough punishment to make his eyes look like two fried eggs. And, of course, in his spare time he sings.

Kid Galahad O Ⓥ
1937, US, 101 mins, b/w
Dir: Michael Curtiz
Stars: Edward G Robinson, Bette Davis, Humphrey Bogart
Rating: ★★★

Warner Brothers tough guys Edward G Robinson and Humphrey Bogart square off against each other as rival boxing promoters in this enjoyable fight film. Wayne Morris plays the title role – a bellhop with a sharp right hook whom Edward G thinks he can rum into a champ after Morris comes to the rescue of his girlfriend (Bette Davis). It's fast-moving and well-plotted, making you eager to watch the climactic fight between Morris and

nasty William Haade, even though you know this is Hollywood in its heyday and there can only be one outcome. Edward G snarls around his cigar, Bogie sneers menacingly and Morris is charming as the naive boxer. Only Davis seems uncomfortable and out of place.

Kid Millions O
1934, US, 90 mins, b/w
Dir: Roy Del Ruth
Stars: Eddie Cantor, Ann Sothern, Ethel Merman, George Murphy
Rating: ★★★

Eddie Cantor goes east and nearly loses his head, committing the unpardonable sin of tramofatch which, roughly translated, means kissing a sheik's daughter while riding a camel. It's that kind of film, splashily produced by Sam Goldwyn with 11 production numbers. Lucille Ball is easily spottable among The Goldwyn Girls and the pop-eyed star (then the highest-paid entertainer in America) is given a good run for his money in the energy stakes by the young Ethel Merman, from the time she belts out the film's opening number 'An Earful of Music', which should perhaps have become her signature tune. The adrenalin really flows in 'I Want To Be a Minstrel Man' (with Cantor, Merman, George Murphy, Ann Sothern and The Nicholas Brothers maintaining a tremendous pace), but even this is topped by the spectacular finale (the only sequence in Technicolor), set in a monumental ice-cream factory.

Kidnapped O
1938, US, 90 mins, b/w
Dir: Alfred Werker
Stars: Warner Baxter, Freddie Bartholomew, Arlene Whelan, John Carradine
Rating: ★★

Described by the New York *Times* as about as Scottish as a hot dog stand this is Darryl F Zanuck's version of Robert Louis Stevenson, which throws in a love interest called Jean MacDonald and jettisons Stevenson himself around the halfway mark. Freddie Bartholomew seems a little frail for the adventurous David Balfour but, if Warner Baxter is hardly ideal casting as Alan Breck, neither were Peter Finch and Michael Came who followed him. Still, if you can stand a little literary vandalism in the course of action and intrigue, this story certainly hits the mark.

Kidnapped ⊙
1960, UK, 100 mins, colour
Dir: Robert Stevenson
Stars: Peter Finch, James MacArthur, Bernard Lee, Peter O'Toole, John Laurie
Rating: ★★★

This Disney adaptation of Robert Louis Stevenson's tale (appropriately made by the studio's best director, who happened to be called Robert Stevenson!) is a little slow in the telling, mainly because of the stolid performance of James MacArthur in the leading role of David Balfour. But Peter Finch, though uneasily cast (as were Michael Caine and Warner Baxter in other versions) as Alan Breck, lends the part sufficient swashbuckling gusto to make it work. Director Stevenson gives the story a vivid atmosphere, and John Laurie, normally seen in comedy roles, turns in a fine study of evil to give the adventure a lift just when it needs it most. Technicolor photography is excellent.

Kidnapped O
1971, UK, 107 mins, colour
Dir: Delbert Mann
Stars: Michael Caine, Trevor Howard, Jack Hawkins, Donald Pleasence, Gordon Jackson
Rating: ★★

Film-makers do seem to choose the most unlikely actors to play Robert Louis Stevenson's adventurer Alan Breck. First American Warner Baxter, then Australian-raised Peter Finch, now Cockney Michael Caine. Still, Caine plays the role with dash and swagger, and the Scottish highlands are a treat in Technicolor.

Kidnappers, The ⊙
(aka: The Little Kidnappers)
1953, UK, 95 mins, b/w
Dir: Philip Leacock
Stars: Jon Whiteley, Vincent Winter, Duncan Macrae
Rating: ★★★★

Child actors Jon Whiteley and Vincent Winter won special Oscars for their roles in this wonderful Ealing Studios family film, set in Nova Scotia, as two orphaned boys ruled over with a rod of iron by their stern, bigoted grandfather (Duncan Macrae). The boys steer just the right side of cuteness and deliver delightfully natural performances.

Killer: A Journal of Murder
● Ⓥ
1995, US, 90 mins, colour
Dir: Tim Metcalfe
Stars: James Woods, Robert Sean

Leonard, Cara Buono, John Bedford
Lloyd, Ellen Greene, Steve Forrest
Rating: ★★★

Raw, grim and violent, this is nonetheless a quite compelling picture of a hardened criminal whose uncontrollable outbursts of violence made him want the law to end his own life – despite the efforts of a forward-thinking police officer to have him declared insane. James Woods is ideally cast as this nasty, frightening, irredeemable character, and it's a tribute to his performance that, for all his glints of evil, the man never quite loses all our sympathy: after all, he has been done down by life, not to mention unmercifully beaten by prison officers – on one of whom, in a scene of sickening violence, he eventually takes bloody revenge. Robert Sean Leonard does quite well as the young rookie warder who gradually wins the killer's grudging friendship and respect. The film however is rough-edged and unrelenting, and may be too much for many to take.

Killer ● ⓥ
(aka: Bulletproof Heart)
1994, US, 98 mins, colour
Dir: Mark Malone
Stars: Mimi Rogers, Anthony LaPaglia, Matt Craven, Peter Boyle
Rating: ★

A bit like an old avant-garde movie from the 50s or 60s that doesn't quite come off. This is a dull, dreary and frequently foolish film with twopence-worth of plot, about a hitman (Anthony LaPaglia) who falls in love with his victim (Mimi Rogers), a woman who appears to welcome the arrival of death. First-time director Mark Malone manages to spin this out to 98 minutes with the aid of one or two supporting scenes and characters, but the philosophical claptrap spouted along the way isn't likely to make your journey a happy one. Prentensions are all very well, but they need more substance than this to back them up, and you may wish LaPaglia had shot the director instead. Rogers is good with what she has, and heaven knows it's precious little.

Killer of Killers
See: The Mechanic

Killer on a Horse
See: Welcome to Hard Times

Killers, The ◑
1964, US, 95 mins, colour
Dir: Don Siegel

Stars: Lee Marvin, John Cassavetes, Angie Dickinson, Ronald Reagan, Clu Gulager
Rating: ★★★★

Based (very vaguely – but then so was the 1946 version) on a story by Ernest Hemingway, this is one of those 'how it really happened' stories, told in flashback. The clinically thrilling story revolves round two gunmen who are so puzzled as to why their victim calmly waits for his death that they decide to dig up his past. Lee Marvin gives a towering performance as the older hitman. Playing with great economy, he etches out a sharp character who is bad, but clearly understandable. Clu Gulager makes the younger gunman so repulsively likeable that you almost hope he won't get bumped off. All the more gripping for its sheer cold-bloodedness, *The Killers* is a fine film, directed in super-efficient style by Don Siegel. Oh yes, and Ronald Reagan is in there too, as a racketeer, in his final film role to date.

Killers, The ○
1946, US, 105 mins, b/w
Dir: Robert Siodmak
Stars: Burt Lancaster, Ava Gardner, Edmond O'Brien, Albert Dekker, Sam Levene, William Conrad
Rating: ★★★★★

First film version of Ernest Hemingway's thriller (remade 18 years later starring Lee Marvin), with its marvellously intricate plot, thundering drama throughout and a mighty punch in the final scene. A host of well-known players contribute to the film's success and there's an excellent performance from Edmond O'Brien in the pivotal role. Other noteworthy portrayals come from menacing Jack Lambert and from Burt Lancaster, shooting to stardom in his first film. Two then newish actors, William Conrad (later to find television fame as Cannon) and Charles McGraw, register solidly as the killers of the title. The plot reveals surprise after surprise, while director Robert Siodmak, a German exile then at the peak of his Hollywood career, ensures that the nervous tension never lets up from the first moment that the killers move on to the scene.

Killing, The ○
1956, US, 83 mins, b/w
Dir: Stanley Kubrick
Stars: Sterling Hayden, Coleen Gray, Vince Edwards
Rating: ★★★

Stanley Kubrick's breakthrough film. It's a hard-edged thriller along 'perfect robbery' lines, with a cluster of deeply etched performances from a tight-knit group of Hollywood's best character stars. Elisha Cook Jr is first among equals here with his portrait of a downtrodden racetrack employee who can barely control his terror of being caught; and Marie Windsor almost matches him as the avaricious wife whose duplicity ruins everything. A fascinating piece of filmmaking done in jigsaw style.

Killing Dad ○ ⓥ
1989, UK, 93 mins, colour
Dir: Michael Austin
Stars: Denholm Elliott, Julie Walters, Richard E Grant, Anna Massey
Rating: ★★

A strange black comedy – the sort that looks at life through a fish-eye lens. All of the characters are off kilter and one or two downright sinister. Definitely off his rocker – judging by the way he keeps thumping the side of his head and twitching – is Alistair (Richard E Grant), a failed hair-tonic salesman who reluctantly journeys to Southend to bring back the father he hasn't seen for 27 years. En route he resolves to kill him instead. Dad provides a prime part for the superbly rumpled Denholm Elliott, first encountered being sick into a plastic carrier (he hands it to Alistair), whose sole possessions seem to be a canary and a ventriloquist's dummy. Most of the laughs, though, come from Julie Walters as the glitzy but ageing seaside belle Dad currently has in tow. It's a bizarre brew and its pacing could do with a bit more frenzy. But relax a bit and you'll enjoy at least some of it.

Killing Fields, The ● ⓥ
1984, UK, 135 mins, colour
Dir: Roland Joffe
Stars: Sam Waterston, Dr Haing S Ngor, John Malkovich, Julian Sands, Craig T Nelson, Bill Patterson
Rating: ★★★

Almost two years in the making, this first major film about the Cambodian war is based on the true story of a friendship between an American war correspondent (Sam Waterston) and his Cambodian confederate. They are eventually separated at the time of the Khmer Rouge invasion of 1975, despite the guilt-ridden American's efforts to smuggle his friend out. A sad and angry plea for peace, and a successful attempt to engender revulsion at such

K

wars, the film is also an account of the survival of the human spirit against all the odds. The atrocities of war are, however, piled on rather too much, and the pace in places rather too leisurely to rivet our attention to the central story, despite the impassioned performances of Waterston and Haing S Ngor (who won an Oscar) in the leading roles. In the end, though, you can't help but be moved to tears at such a story, despite the shortcomings in its telling. That's only as it should be.

Killing of a Chinese Bookie, The ◐ Ⓥ

1976, US, 113 mins, colour
Dir: John Cassavetes
Stars: Ben Gazzara, Timothy Agoglia Carey, Seymour Cassel
Rating: ★★

You would expect a *film noir* by John Cassavetes to be a highly idiosyncratic addition to the genre, and here, at least, he does not disappoint. The moody, threatening atmosphere and the twists and turns of the convoluted plot have the unique Cassavetes stamp: powerful performances based partly on improvisation. Ben Gazzara dominates the film with his fine portrayal of the Los Angeles nightclub owner Cosmo Vitelli whose unsuccessful gambling spree leaves him with the obligation to despatch a troublesome Chinese bookie as payment in kind. There is a nice selection of gangsters and molls, with Timothy Agoglia Carey in danger of going over the top as the hit-man set on Gazzara's trail. Cassavetes fans will indulge the film's longueurs; others may not be so tolerant.

Killing of Sister George, The ● Ⓥ

1968, UK, 138 mins, colour
Dir: Robert Aldrich
Stars: Beryl Reid, Susannah York, Coral Browne, Ronald Fraser
Rating: ★★★★

Corrosive and powerful story about an ageing TV star (Beryl Reid brilliantly re-creating her stage role) whose affair with a younger woman is threatened by her own neurosis, the possible loss of her part in a long-running series, and finally by the intervention of a third party. If Lukas Heller's screenplay extracts some of the humanity from Frank Marcus's original play, it lacks nothing in impact; and the performances ensure that the drama remains both engrossing, entertaining and highly amusing.

Killing Zoe ● Ⓥ

1993, France/US, 96 mins, colour
Dir: Roger Avary
Stars: Eric Stoltz, Julie Delpy, Jean-Hugues Anglade
Rating: ★

Most people could probably do without another bloodsoaked bank robbery thriller in their lives, but if you really must, this example is at least efficiently done, once its robbery gets under way. Tedious up to then, though, with Eric Stoltz as the American safecracker in Paris to meet his old comrade-in-crime (Jean-Hugues Anglade). Hiring a hooker (Julie Delpy) who turns out to be a student moonlighting on her day job, he's more than a little disturbed when she turns up as a bank clerk at the place Anglade and his gang of fellow-junkies are robbing. Little of that matters, however, since the cops are quickly on the scene, and the climax soon develops into a regulation bloodbath, with psycho Anglade mowing down his hostages out of pique.

Kill Me Again ● Ⓥ

1989, US, 99 mins, colour
Dir: John Dahl
Stars: Val Kilmer, Joanne Whalley-Kilmer, Michael Madsen, Jonathan Gries
Rating: ★★★

Despite some iffy performances, the direction and story make this a pretty good imitation of an RKO Radio *film noir* from 40 years earlier. Private eye Jack Andrews (Val Kilmer, miscast but reasonably effective) in debt to gamblers who have just broken his finger, is confronted with $10,000 by white-suited, sloe-eyed Fay (Joanne Whalley-Kilmer) if he will arrange for her fake death to put a murderous boyfriend off her trail. Well, 'tecs have to agree to this kind of thing, or we wouldn't have any stories, but one of the things Jack doesn't know is that Fay has almost a million dollars in Mafia money stolen from her boyfriend, who killed a mobster to get it. Big trouble for Jack, as you can see, from the police, from the Mob, from the boyfriend and not least from the distinctly unreliable Fay. Whalley-Kilmer looks good in the Jane Greer tradition but occasionally overdoes her femme Fay-tale. But Madsen is a knockout as the ruthless boyfriend, and director John Dahl moves the story doomily along without too much wasted footage, and shows some nice touches with the inevitable cross and double-cross at the end.

Kill-Off, The ●

1989, US, 95 mins, colour
Dir: Maggie Greenwald
Stars: Loretta Gross, Andrew Lee Barrett, Jackson Sims
Rating: ★★★

This daring, grotesque murder thriller has a spartan, bleak look and feel which actually enhances its claustrophobic *film noir*-ish script. Director Maggie Greenwald, a former assistant sound effects editor, for Walter Hill among others, and film editor, proves to be happily at home in Thompson's regular milieu of bleak, corrupted lowlife. All the characters are emotionally dead with little hope for the future, and yet their story is compulsive viewing. Loretta Gross, as the acid-tongued town gossip-monger, whose murder leaves many suspects, gives a strong central performance.

Kill or Cure ○

1962, UK, 86 mins, b/w
Dir: George Pollock
Stars: Terry-Thomas, Eric Sykes, Dennis Price, Lionel Jeffries, David Lodge
Rating: ★★★

A plethora of British funny-men in a rib-tickling comedy-thriller set in a bizarre health resort. Produced in 1962 by the team that made the Miss Marple comedy-thrillers, this film also comes up with such familiar television faces as Ronnie Barker, Derren Nesbitt and Peter Butterworth.

Kim ☉

1950, US, 112 mins, colour
Dir: Victor Saville
Stars: Errol Flynn, Dean Stockwell, Paul Lukas, Robert Douglas
Rating: ★★★

A robust screen adaptation of Rudyard Kipling's famous Indian tale. It takes a few liberties with the original, but provides some intense excitement, '*Boy's Own*'-style, in the process. Stars Errol Flynn (the unlikeliest of Afghan horse dealers) and Paul Lukas actually got to film some of their scenes in India, but young Dean Stockwell, in the title role, never left California! The action, when it comes, is rousing enough, but there are too many stodgy patches for comfort.

Kindergarten Cop ◐ Ⓥ

1990, US, 111 mins, colour
Dir: Ivan Reitman
Stars: Arnold Schwarznegger, Penelope Ann Miller, Pamela Reed, Linda Hunt,

Carroll Baker
Rating: ★★★

Big Arnold ignores the advice about never acting with children or animals to form the centre piece of this artful concoction of a fistful of the elements most likely to make a box-office hit. How can you maximise Arnie's muscular, awkward appeal? Drop him, like a fish out of water, into a crowd of screaming, uncontrollable, pre-school kids. Aces. They probably thought of the title, then Arnie, then the story. Naturally, there's some action to go with this, as a killer hunts his small son who is somewhere at the school where Arnie has to go undercover as a teacher, after his partner (excellent Pamela Reed) falls ill. And romance appears in the shape of Penelope Ann Miller as another teacher whose son is in Arnie's class. Did we mention animals? Ah yes, Schwarzenegger has a pet ferret which helps him win over the kids after a nightmare first day in which he wishes he hadn't left his gun at home. It can't fail, can it? And it doesn't, even though the writer and director often use sentiment where charm and humour would have been better. Carroll Baker is chilling as the villain's domineering mother.

Kind Hearts and Coronets ○ Ⓥ

1949, UK, 106 mins, b/w
Dir: Robert Hamer
Stars: Alec Guinness, Dennis Price, Valerie Hobson, Joan Greenwood, Arthur Lowe
Rating: ★★★★★

A fiendishly funny satirical comedy from Ealing Studios. It treats murder as a joke, and gets away with it with elegant case. Every time a character is killed off, you'll rock with laughter. Affectionately regarded as the best of many good things to come from Ealing in the post-war years, the film is also a 'tour-de-farce' for Alec Guinness and made his name as a comedy star. He plays all eight heirs standing between murderous Dennis Price and a dukedom – and does it with mindboggling panache. Watch for Arthur Lowe in a small part at the end of the film as a reporter.

Kind of Loving, A ◑

1962, UK, 112 mins, b/w
Dir: John Schlesinger
Stars: Alan Bates, June Ritchie, Thora Hird, James Bolam, Leonard Rossiter
Rating: ★★★

A strong contender for box-office and critical acclaim in the bed-and-bosom environment of the British cinema of the early Sixties, this superbly acted downbeat romantic drama gave Alan Bates one of his biggest pushes towards stardom. His co-star, June Ritchie, alas, found herself subsequently in too many inferior imitations, and it was some time before she re-established herself as an actress of wide-ranging talent. Thora Hird gives the outstanding performance of her career as Ritchie's mother.

Kindred, The ● Ⓥ

1986, US, 92 mins, colour
Dir: Jeffrey Obrow, Stephen Carpenter
Stars: Rod Steiger, Kim Hunter, Amanda Pays, David Allen Brooks, Talia Balsam
Rating: ★★

This is a messy horror film with a monster that might be the derivation of the word slimebag. Quite what Professor Kim Hunter thought she was doing when she crossed a human skin graft with something like an octopus embryo one can't possibly imagine, but what she ended up with was something that has red eyes, hides in watermelons, lifts cars off the road and, not surprisingly, throttles people with its tentacles. Her son is understandably concerned by what he finds at his mother's home after she has been killed off by even madder scientist Rod Steiger. 'She must have started calling it Anthony,' he mutters, 'after her favourite saint.' Still, the film is scary at the right moments and boasts a cellar that looks like something out of the Spanish Inquisition.

King and I, The ○ Ⓥ

1956, US, 128 mins, colour
Dir: Walter Lang
Stars: Deborah Kerr, Yul Brynner, Rita Moreno, Martin Benson
Rating: ★★★★

Following hard on the heels of *Carousel*, and *Oklahoma!*, *The King and I* became the third Rodgers and Hammerstein musical within 12 months to break box-office records all over Britain and America. Yul Brynner (he won one of the film's five Academy Awards) and Deborah Kerr both recorded personal triumphs as the King of Siam and the governess whom he scorns at first but comes reluctantly to admire and respect. The score is Rodgers and Hammerstein at their most tuneful, including 'Getting to Know You' and 'Hello Young Lovers'.

King Arthur Was a Gentleman ⊙

1942, UK, 91 mins, b/w
Dir: Marcel Varnel
Stars: Arthur Askey, Evelyn Dall, Anne Shelton, Jack Train
Rating: ★★

A comedy with music that's a sort of very distant relative to *A Connecticut Yankee in King Arthur's Court*, with big-hearted Arthur Askey as a soldier in Africa (called Arthur King) who believes he has found King Arthur's magic sword. Some funny scenes and tuneful songs, but lots of missed opportunities as well.

King Creole ○ Ⓥ

1958, US, 116 mins, b/w
Dir: Michael Curtiz
Stars: Elvis Presley, Walter Matthau, Carolyn Jones
Rating: ★★★

Undoubtedly the best acting from Elvis Presley in a career in which most of his Hollywood efforts were purely mushy vehicles to sell record soundtracks. Much of the credit for this rests on the assured direction of Michael Curtiz who successfully put most of Hollywood's top male actors through their paces, including Humphrey Bogart, Errol Flynn (several times) and James Cagney. The plot is strong stuff for a musical, but there is a succession of now-familiar Elvis tracks for his fans. Both dynamic and dramatic by Elvis's later standards.

King David ◐ Ⓥ

1985, US, 114 mins, colour
Dir: Bruce Beresford
Stars: Richard Gere, Edward Woodward, Alice Krige, Cherie Lunghi
Rating: ★★

A good attempt to tell the Biblical story of David, with Richard Gere handsome and athletic in the title role. But director Bruce Beresford tries to cram too much of a colourful life into a film lasting less than two hours, which leads to some confusion if you haven't read the book! Edward Woodward comes out best of all as King Saul and the film also features Denis Quilley, Hurd Hatfield and Cherie Lunghi. She plays David's first wife in what could be termed a Second Division epic, unkindly known in Hollywood at the time as *An Israelite and a Gentleman*.

King in New York, A ○

1957, UK, 109 mins, b/w
Dir: Charles Chaplin
Stars: Charlie Chaplin, Dawn Addams
Rating: ★★

K

Charlie Chaplin's last starring film, a satire on America and its communist witchhunts. The film received only a limited release in its native Britain and wasn't seen at all in America until 1973. Yet it has many funny moments as the exiled European king, completely out of touch with the modern world, collides head-on with New York in the midst of the rock 'n' roll era. When the film goes serious towards the end, one longs for a return to these blissful interludes of slapstick, especially when the king chokes on an item he is advertising in front of the television cameras.

King Kong ◑
1933, US, 100 mins, b/w
Dir: Ernest B Schoedsack, Merian C Cooper
Stars: Fay Wray, Robert Armstrong, Bruce Cabot
Rating: ★★★★★

Very little one can add to the reams that have been written about this classic of the horror genre with its breathtaking trick work by Willis O'Brien. The story is about a giant gorilla brought to civilisation from a remote island: if you haven't seen it, don't miss the chance next time. Fay Wray is a genuinely touching heroine, and she and Kong himself combine to make this one of the few movies to induce real audience sympathy for its creature. The early part of the film, with the ship gliding through mists to Kong's island, is a splendidly atmospheric piece of cinema. It all still holds up well after more than 60 years.

King Kong ◑
1976, US, 136 mins, colour
Dir: John Guillermin
Stars: Jeff Bridges, Charles Grodin, Jessica Lange
Rating: ★★

Clodhopping remake of the imperishable original. Star Jessica Lange tried to shut it out of her mind: although it gave her a belated film debut at 27, she didn't film again for three years. The individual talents of Jeff Bridges and Charles Grodin are wasted, and the film's only major asset is the glittering Metrocolor photography by Richard H Kline, which won an Oscar nomination.

King Lear ○ ⓥ
1987, France/US/Switzerland, 90 mins, colour
Dir: Jean-Luc Godard
Stars: Peter Sellars, Burgess Meredith,

Molly Ringwald, Woody Allen, Norman Mailer, Jean-Luc Godard
Rating: **RB**

No doubt there was a four-page review in some highbrow magazine describing this Jean-Luc Godard film as a masterpiece. Fragments from Shakespeare's Lear are spoken – when there is anything at all going on up there on the screen – by characters wandering around a continental coastal resort. They make marginally more sense than the rest of the film, which we think portrays a young director looking for ideas for filming King Lear. Burgess Meredith blasts cantankerously through as Godard's version of Lear; Molly Ringwald sleepwalks Cordelia; Woody Allen speaks earnestly at the end. The rest is a meaningless shambles of bits and pieces assembled in haphazard fashion, as if from the cutting-room floor. But then again, this may be a masterpiece.

King of Alcatraz ○
(aka: King of the Alcatraz)
1938, US, 56 mins, b/w
Dir: Robert Florey
Stars: Gail Patrick, Lloyd Nolan, Harry Carey, Robert Preston
Rating: ★★★

Fast and furious, and ranging from comedy to dramatic action without a blink, this is one of the most star-studded minor films ever made. There's a cracking script by Irving Reis, later to become a top director (of such films as The Bachelor and the Bobby Soxer), masterful direction by Robert Florey (who made The Beast with Five Fingers) and dynamic performances from Lloyd Nolan, Robert Preston (making a great team as rival radio operators), Anthony Quinn, Gail Patrick, Richard Denning, Dennis Morgan, Tom Tyler and especially J Carrol Naish as the escaped convict of the title. Perennial screen drunk Jack Norton appears as the first officer on board the ship where the action is. It all feels a bit rushed, though, which isn't surprising.

King of Comedy, The ○
1982, US, 109 mins, colour
Dir: Martin Scorsese
Stars: Robert De Niro, Jerry Lewis
Rating: ★★

This much-feted comedy of sarcasm is about a desperate, distinctly unbalanced would-be stand-up comedian. Robert De Niro makes this character as obnoxious as he can, while Jerry Lewis is quite endearing more or less playing himself. Admirable in some ways, but

totally dislikeable and even quite annoying at times.

King of Jazz ○
1930, US, 93 mins, colour
Dir: John Murray Anderson
Stars: Paul Whiteman, John Boles, Laura la Plante, Bing Crosby
Rating: ★★★

Featured in this hugely entertaining early musical are roly-poly Paul Whiteman and his Orchestra and the singing trio The Rhythm Boys, one of whom, Bing Crosby, went on to bigger and better things. Very innovative: a veritable box of delights.

King of Kings ○
1961, US/Spain, 161 mins, colour
Dir: Nicholas Ray
Stars: Jeffrey Hunter, Hurd Hatfield, Harry Guardino, Rip Torn, Viveca Lindfors, Robert Ryan
Rating: ★★

It always seemed likely that the biggest weakness of Nicholas Ray's simply told and beautifully photographed Biblical epic would be the casting of the central role of Jesus. And so it proved to be, despite a dedicated effort at the role from Jeffrey Hunter. His performance had none of the nobility, subtlety and power that Max Von Sydow was to give the role four years later in The Greatest Story Ever Told. Far more memorable are Hurd Hatfield's Pilate, Siobhan McKenna's Virgin Mary and, surprisingly, Rita Gam as Herodias. Fine actor Robert Ryan seems too American (as did Charlton Heston) as John the Baptist, but Rip Torn is a splendidly shifty and furtive Judas. For once an actor accustomed to giving larger-than-life performances is cast in exactly the right role.

King of New York ● ⓥ
1989, US, 104 mins, colour
Dir: Abel Ferrara
Stars: Christopher Walken, David Caruso, Larry Fishburne, Wesley Snipes
Rating: ★★★

A gangster film, with all the modern violence, sex, drug trade and bad language you'd expect. This one, however, is made in the style of the Thirties: straight, with no sideline issues, as one man shoots his way to the top, gunning down all those who stand in the way of his becoming crime czar of the city. Christopher Walken's icy and unsettling charm is well-suited to this role, a criminal mastermind with dangerous double standards. He wants to be a do-gooder and build schools and hospitals: to do it he must gain control of all the city's illegal activity, excusing the wholesale slaughter that results on the grounds that the crime lords he kills are squeezing the poor or peddling in teenage prostitution. Cops are reduced to vigilante action in efforts to stop him. Whether he needs to go as far as he does is open to question: so is the ease with which he and a few confederates with tommy-guns take over the city. The story, however, is deliberately streamlined to eliminate all side issues, and stylised so that everybody in it is dressed in black.

King of the Grizzlies ⊙
1969, US, 93 mins, colour
Dir: Ron Kelly
Stars: John Yesno, Chris Wiggins
Rating: ★★★

A rousing Disney animal adventure based on Ernest Thompson Seton's *The Biography of a Grizzly*, with the usual musical comments and laconic Winston Hibler narration. Several bears seem to be used in the title role, but it hardly matters as children will love it anyway. Magnificently shot on location in the Canadian Rockies.

King of the Khyber Rifles ○
1953, US, 100 mins, colour
Dir: Henry King
Stars: Tyrone Power, Terry Moore, Guy Rolfe, Michael Rennie
Rating: ★★

One of Tyrone Power's later pictures, but still within his tradition of making adventure films which spanned the world. As the title indicates, the setting of this one is India in the turbulent late 19th century. It's rousing but rough-edged fare.

Kingpin ◑ ⓥ
1996, US, 107 mins, colour
Dir: The Farrelly Brothers
Stars: Woody Harrelson, Randy Quaid, Vanessa Angel, Bill Murray
Rating: ★★

Two films in one: the first half a sort of even grosser *Dumb and Dumber*, an at-times quite disgusting low comedy that will have even Jim Carrey fans reaching for the sick bag. In the second half, gross-out takes a back seat as the film develops into a comedic slant on a *Rocky* of the 10-pin bowling world. The characters get nicer too: weird but welcome. Harrelson is the kid who has the world in the palm of his bowling hand, which is shattered when he's suckered by former champ Murray into trying to hustle some

rednecks. Years later, appallingly down and out (and hairless), Woody puts in his rubber thumb and pulls out a plum in the shape of giant Amish idiot Quaid, who's also a bowling genius. They head for Nevada's million-dollar bowling challenge, where Quaid hurts his hand, Woody takes his place and his opponent in the final is none other than... but no, you guessed it. Stick with this and you may giggle instead of gag at the end.

King Ralph ○ ⓥ
1991, US, 97 mins, colour
Dir: David S Ward
Stars: John Goodman, Peter O'Toole, John Hurt, Camille Coduri
Rating: ★★

Big John Goodman is a second-rate Las Vegas lounge singer who is distantly related to our royal family. When a (hilarious) disaster at a photocall wipes out all those above him, Britain finds itself with a decidedly different new king. A nice comic idea that works well in patches. Unfortunately, those patches are a little too widely spaced for the film's own good. Goodman is engaging as the gauche Yank who creates his own Berk's Peerage, while Peter O'Toole does his 'actor laddie' bit as the new king's imperious private secretary and John Hurt enjoys himself as the sneaky Lord Graves: watch the scene where he visits the heroine's flat – the inside pages of his newspaper are blank! No, this may not be a terribly good film – but it's fun in spurts and jolly king Goodman makes the most of his starring role.

King Rat ◑
1965, UK, 134 mins, b/w
Dir: Bryan Forbes
Stars: George Segal, James Fox, Tom Courtenay, Denholm Elliott, John Mills
Rating: ★★★

PoW camp-film fans will find plenty to get their teeth into in writer-director Bryan Forbes' cleverly-framed story of a corporal who gets away with everything – even selling the officers in the camp rat-meat as venison. George Segal gives a razor-sharp portrayal of Cpl King, the biggest scrounger in the camp, who eats fried eggs for breakfast while others starve.

King Richard and the Crusaders ○
1954, US, 114 mins, colour
Dir: David Butler
Stars: Laurence Harvey, Rex Harrison,

Virginia Mayo, George Sanders
Rating: ★★★★

For once, the publicity says it all: 'A stirring saga of days of yore when bold knights rallied to the Christian cause'. This really is one of the best just-for-fun adventure stories Hollywood ever made. The storyline is so full of fights and thrills that there hardly seems time for noble hero Laurence Harvey to draw breath before the next battle. Never mind the script, just get an eyeful of that action.

Kings of the Sun ○
1963, US, 105 mins, colour
Dir: J Lee Thompson
Stars: Yul Brynner, George Chakiris, Shirley Anne Field, Richard Basehart, Brad Dexter
Rating: ★

Despite realistic location filming in Mexico, this historical drama about the ancient Mayan kingdom is sunk by uneasy casting, a superficial story and banal dialogue. Not even po-faced Yul Brynner, as chief of the local Indian tribe, can get away with lines as silly as 'And some day we will watch our babies lead buffaloes around by their noses'.

King Solomon's Mines ○
1937, UK, 80 mins, b/w
Dir: Robert Stevenson
Stars: Cedric Hardwicke, Paul Robeson, Roland Young, Anna Lee, John Loder
Rating: ★★★

Splendidly workmanlike version of Rider Haggard's famous jungle adventure yarn, full of action and with no time wasted. Paul Robeson gives a notable performance as Umbopa, the exiled native chief who guides the party of diamond-hunters, making the character so much more than just a noble savage.

King Solomon's Mines ○
1950, US, 102 mins, colour
Dir: Andrew Marton, Compton Bennett
Stars: Stewart Granger, Deborah Kerr, Richard Carlson, Hugo Haas
Rating: ★★★

This blockbuster jungle action yarn, based (though rather remotely) on Rider Haggard's famous story of a search for a missing man and the quest for the fabulous mines, was filmed in various parts of Africa. Its most striking feature is certainly the authentic location work of terrain, tribesmen and, above all, its spectacular animal footage, shot by co-director Andrew Marton.

K

King Solomon's Mines ○ Ⓥ
1985, US, 100 mins, colour
Dir: J Lee Thompson
Stars: Richard Chamberlain, Sharon
Stone, Herbert Lom, Ken Gampu
Rating: ★★★

Director J Lee Thompson has taken the
old, much-filmed adventure classic and
turned it into *Raiders of the Lost Mines*.
H Rider Haggard it isn't, but it is fast,
furious and fun, right down to the
music: every time hero Richard
Chamberlain swings into action, the
theme tune trumpets forth. And, in
Sharon Stone, whose previous roles
had been strictly decorative, it has a
heroine with a zany sense of humour
and a willingness to give it all she's got.
The plot moves rapidly from the incredible to the impossible, with poor
Bernard Archard whipped unmercifully for the secret of the mines by
Herbert Lom and John Rhys Davies
who have clearly slipped in from a
Pink Panther film and an Indiana Jones
adventure respectively. Ms Stone's
shorts shrink progressively along with
the plot. An underrated romp.

King's Pirate, The ○
1967, US, 100 mins, colour
Dir: Don Weis
Stars: Doug McClure, Guy Stockwell
Rating: ★★★

Universal Studios are obviously happy
on home ground with this agreeable
pantomime, set in Madagascar, in
1700, with Doug McClure baring his
chest obligingly in the sort of role once
reserved for Tony Curtis. Rewards on
the way include a former Miss
America, Mary Ann Mobley, as an
Indian with a Scots accent (!), and a
dazzling display of swordplay from Jill
St John in the finest Maureen O'Hara
traditions.

King's Rhapsody ○
1955, UK, 93 mins, colour
Dir: Herbert Wilcox
Stars: Errol Flynn, Anna Neagle
Rating: ★★

Errol Flynn, in one of the last roles of
his career, plays a European prince
who chooses to abdicate to be with his
mistress (Anna Neagle) but later takes
the throne and learns to love his wife
(played by Patrice Wymore, Flynn's
third wife at the time of writing).
Directed by Neagle's husband, Herbert
Wilcox, this British-made, rusty
Ruritanian romance with music (based
on Ivor Novello's operetta) is a fairly
threadbare affair with signs of a tight
budget. The same scenes and effects

are repeated again and again, the same
extras line the cathedral steps for successive marriages and coronations and
pasteboard is evident everywhere in
the sets. Neagle, however, rises above
the stilted script and pedestrian production with a sturdy assurance and great
grace.

King's Row ○
1941, US, 127 mins, b/w
Dir: Sam Wood
Stars: Ann Sheridan, Robert Cummings,
Ronald Reagan, Betty Field, Charles
Coburn, Claude Rains
Rating: ★★★★

The *Peyton Place* of its day and the reverse side of *Our Town* as Warners (in a
startling movie for its day) portrays (in
some cases for those who can read between the lines) sadism, incest,
homosexuality and murder behind the
neat-fronted Victorian houses of a
small American town. Ronald Reagan,
as a playboy, has never been better on
screen (although he was only sixth
choice for the role) and Ann Sheridan,
as his girlfriend, is superb. Even
Robert Cummings, as a brilliant medical student, managed acting beyond
his usual low-key range. The production design is also worthy of note, with
everything shot in the studio by master
cinematographer James Wong Howe,
even down to an orchard.

Kipps ○
(aka: The Remarkable Mr Kipps)
1941, UK, 112 mins, b/w
Dir: Carol Reed
Stars: Michael Redgrave, Phyllis Calvert,
Diana Wynyard, Arthur Riscoe
Rating: ★★★

Very respectable, detail-filled version of
H G Wells' novel, directed by Carol
Reed after a string of successes: *Bank
Holiday*, *A Girl Must Live*, *The Stars Look
Down* and *Night Train to Munich*. Many
years later Kipps would be made into
the musical, *Half a Sixpence*, with
Tommy Steele inheriting the role
played here diffidently but engagingly
by Michael Redgrave. Diana
Wynyard and Phyllis Calvert are fresh
and delightful as the girls.

Kismet ○
1944, US, 100 mins, colour
Dir: William Dieterle
Stars: Ronald Colman, Marlene Dietrich,
James Craig, Edward Arnold
Rating: ★★

Another 'king of the beggars' role for
Ronald Colman to follow that in *If I
Were King* in this songless version of the

yarn that later became more famous as
a musical. This one does have sumptuous Technicolor, plus a gold-painted
Marlene Dietrich in an exotic dance
routine.

Kiss, The ●
1988, US, 101 mins, colour
Dir: Pen Densham
Stars: Joanna Pacula, Meredith Salenger,
Mimi Kuzyk
Rating: ★★

Apart from a spectacular climax in a
swimming pool, nail-bitingly involving
the destruction of various monsters,
this Canadian opus is your average revolting horror film of today. It
features Joanna Pacula (rhymes with
Dracula?) as the African-born child afflicted by an aunt with the curse of the
undead and who must now pass it on
to her teenage niece, played by the nubile Salenger, whose figure the
director loses no chance to get into a
revealing bathing suit. Opposing
Pacula is one-time *Hill Street Blues* cop
Mimi Kuzyk as the nurse next door
with a yen for Meredith's dad, whose
late wife was Pacula's first victim.
Priests get devoured by fire, and various of Salenger's friends are cut away
by Pacula's familiar, a kind of critter-
cat, before the showdown at long last
looms. The three stars at least give
the rubbish no less than 100 per
cent, and special effects are suitably
repulsive.

Kiss Before Dying, A ◑
1956, US, 89 mins, colour
Dir: Gerd Oswald
Stars: Robert Wagner, Jeffrey Hunter,
Virginia Leith, Joanne Woodward
Rating: ★★★

Rather chilling thriller, with Robert
Wagner surprisingly good as a psychopathic killer and Joanne Woodward
and Virginia Leith as two of the girls
on his list. It's the plot that counts
here, rather than the acting, although
Wagner dominates the film and
George Macready and Mary Astor
offer stiff competition from the older
generation. The suspense is satisfactory, the climax exciting and the colour
excellent. An unusual and rewarding
film, still possibly the best thing
Wagner has turned out.

Kiss Before Dying, A ● Ⓥ
1991, US, 90 mins, colour
Dir: James Dearden
Stars: Matt Dillon, Sean Young, Max von
Sydow, Diane Ladd
Rating: ★★

A classy (if ultimately inferior) remake of the old Robert Wagner-Joanne Woodward thriller from Ira Levin's novel. Well-made, if not always well-acted, it features Dillon in the Wagner role, as Corliss, the baby-faced psycho determined to inherit the millions of one of the wealthiest rallies in America. Hooked up with one of its daughters (Sean Young), he murders her when she becomes pregnant and disinheritance looms. Her twin sister is his next target and, assuming a new identity (again by murder), he becomes a social worker and is soon shacked up with Ellen (also Young). Links with the past are ruthlessly eradicated as Corliss begins his climb to the top. Dillon does quite well in this kiss-me-kill-me role, but the murders themselves, though merciless, lack urgency. Young has her moments – and her lesser ones.

Kiss Me Deadly ◑
1955, US, 105 mins, b/w
Dir: Robert Aldrich
Stars: Ralph Meeker, Gaby Rodgers, Albert Dekker, Paul Stewart, Maxine Cooper, Jack Elam
Rating: ★★★

Mickey Spillane and Mike Hammer, the bull-at-a-gate detective he created, could have found no more apt screen interpreter than director Robert Aldrich, as pace, punch and violence, which saturate the Hammer novels, are present in almost all of Aldrich's film work, from *The Big Knife* to *The Choirboys*. Aggressive Ralph Meeker is perfectly cast as Hammer, adrift in the bleak streets and decaying buildings of the post-war New York and Los Angeles. Cloris Leachman makes her screen debut as a mystery girl.

Kiss Me Goodbye ●
1982, US, 101 mins, colour
Dir: Robert Mulligan
Stars: Sally Field, James Caan, Jeff Bridges, Paul Dooley, Claire Trevor, Mildred Natwick
Rating: ★

The Hollywood of the Eighties developed an absolute mania for remaking sexy comedies from countries abroad that made it big at the Englishspeaking box-offices of the world. This is a re-hash of the Brazilian smash *Dona Flor and Her Two Husbands*, but once again the recipe for success doesn't travel too well, in spite of an attractive cast. Director Robert Mulligan couldn't go altogether wrong with that collection, and there are indeed some nice mo-

ments, although the relaxed sexuality of the original isn't recaptured.

Kiss Me Kate ☉ ⓥ
1953, US, 111 mins, colour
Dir: George Sidney
Stars: Howard Keel, Kathryn Grayson, Ann Miller, Keenan Wynn
Rating: ★★★★

Brilliant, fast-moving musical based on Shakespeare's *The Taming of the Shrew*. Howard Keel has never been more virile and Kathryn Grayson never gutsier (she's a real surprise here) as the feuding singers, while Ann Miller dances up a storm in the 'Tom, Dick or Harry' number, with the help of talented MGM hoofers Bob Fosse, Tommy Rall and Bobby Van. Add James Whitmore and Keenan Wynn as gangsters giving a priceless rendition of 'Brush Up Your Shakespeare' and you have almost the perfect show.

Kiss of Death ○
1947, US, 98 mins, b/w
Dir: Henry Hathaway
Stars: Victor Mature, Brian Donlevy, Coleen Gray, Karl Malden, Richard Widmark
Rating: ★★★

Victor Mature, revealing himself a more sensitive actor than many suspected, gave one of his best performances in this brisk thriller as a petty thief turned stoolpigeon. Even so, the acting honours went straight to Richard Widmark. Making his film debut as a psychopathic killer called Tommy Udo, and cackling hysterically as he tips one of his victims in a wheelchair down a flight of stairs, Widmark earned himself an Academy Award nomination in best supporting actor category – his only Oscar 'nod' to date. Director Henry Hathaway makes excellent use of a variety of well-chosen New York locations to add verisimilitude to the story. Good support comes from Karl Malden, Taylor Holmes, Millard Mitchell, Coleen Gray and Mildred Dunnock.

Kiss of Death ● ⓥ
1994, US, 100 mins, colour
Dir: Barbet Schroeder
Stars: David Caruso, Nicolas Cage, Samuel L Jackson, Stanley Tucci, Ving Rhames, Helen Hunt
Rating: ★★

This laborious urban crime thriller is hardly tailor-made for red-haired David Caruso, ex-hero cop from TV's *NYPD Blue*. Caruso's at his best in control of things as an island of calm

fury. Here, looking like a babier-faced Alan Ladd, he's hardly in charge even of his own destiny as an ex-petty thief who, forced by a cousin to do one more run, is caught, jailed, loses his wife in a car crash, and suffers the final indignity of having to turn police informer to secure permanent freedom. Likewise, Nicolas Cage does his best to pump up the psycho-villain Caruso is asked to help catch, but the part as written is more silly than sinister. Director Barber Schroeder manages one jumpy moment in the otherwise routinely staged action, but not even Technicolor is at its best in a world of crime that seems at one remove from the real thing. The sharp-talking Samuel L Jackson though is close to his incisive best as the cop involved.

Kiss of Evil ●
(aka: Kiss of the Vampire)
1964, UK, 88 mins, colour
Dir: Don Sharp
Stars: Clifford Evans, Jennifer Daniel
Rating: ★★

It's business as usual for the men of Hammer here, in a story of a village of vampires. Director Don Sharp makes some of it pretty chilly (especially when Noel Willman first bites into Jennifer Daniel) with the help of some skilfully bleak colour camerawork.

Kiss of Fire ○
1955, US, 86 mins, colour
Dir: Joseph M Newman
Stars: Jack Palance, Barbara Rush
Rating: ★★

This unusual adventure story about a Spanish soldier-of-fortune escorting his country's princess through American Indian territory gave Jack Palance a rare romantic hero role, although he still endows the character of El Tigre with his customary ferocity. Nothing about this one, however, seems very relaxed or natural.

Kiss of the Spider Woman
● ⓥ -
1985, US, 119 mins, colour
Dir: Hector Babenco
Stars: William Hurt, Raul Julia, Sonia Braga
Rating: ★★★

No webs are woven by female fienas here. Not that horror of a subtler kind is not implicit in the sometimes harrowing story of the relationship between two men in a prison cell. Molina (William Hurt in a totally effective, Oscar-winning performance) is a flagrant homosexual who has

K

nothing common with cell-mate Valentin (Raul Julia), a morose revolutionary imprisoned for political beliefs and awaiting only the next torture session. But Molina spins a gossamer web made up from the surface glitter of bad old films (especially one made by the Nazis) as he acts out their absurdly melodramatic plots for Valentin's benefit – and perhaps his own sanity. The drawing-together of the two men is only occasionally embarrassing, often touching and always absorbing. It's a pity that the film inserts themselves are just too daft to capture the spirit of the original. At the end, though, everything is satisfyingly resolved, showing that the protagonists have found a kind of peace. A pretty unusual film, it's uncompromising but never unsavoury.

Kiss of the Vampire
See: Kiss of Evil

Kiss the Blood Off My Hands ○
(aka: Blood on My Hands)
1948, UK, 80 mins, b/w
Dir: Norman Foster
Stars: Burt Lancaster, Joan Fontaine, Robert Newton
Rating: ★★★

An early Burt Lancaster film, made two years after his sensational debut in *The Killers*. And that's what he plays in this turbulent thriller – a killer. It's a grim melodrama, with Lancaster as a man on the run. Good support comes from Joan Fontaine and Robert Newton. And there's wonderful black-and-white photography by Russell Metty, making the most of Lancaster's nocturnal flights from the law. The film has a similar doomy feel to Lancaster's *Criss Cross*.

Kiss Tomorrow Goodbye ○
1950, US, 102 mins, b/w
Dir: Gordon Douglas
Stars: James Cagney, Barbara Payton, Luther Adler, Helena Carter, Ward Bond, Steve Brodie
Rating: ★★

One more time for James Cagney as the mobster on the run in this thriller, almost a reprise of this classic *White Heat* the previous year. Director Gordon Douglas stages one or two good chase sequences, and a strong supporting cast includes Ward Bond, Steve Brodie, Luther Adler, Helena Carter, William Frawley and Barton MacLane.

Kitchen Toto, The ●
1987, UK, 97 mins, colour
Dir: Harry Hook
Stars: Edwin Mahinda, Bob Peck, Phyllis Logan
Rating: ★★★

This grim reconstruction of events during the emergence of the Mau Mau terrorists in Kenya between 1950 and 1952 reminds us that, whatever else, we can rely on our latest generation of British filmmakers for accuracy, especially in the depiction of the mutual lack of understanding between white and black at the time, which merely made the bloodshed worse. There are few likeable people here, save for the title character, a young African seconded into white colonial service after his clergyman father is slaughtered for preaching anti-terrorist sermons. All too soon the youth himself is inducted into Mau Mau ranks and events fall swiftly towards darkness and tragedy. More penetrating, if less entertaining than such films of 30 years back as *Simba* and *Something of Value*.

Kitty Foyle ○
1940, US, 100 mins, b/w
Dir: Sam Wood
Stars: Ginger Rogers, Dennis Morgan, James Craig
Rating: ★★★

No one could quite believe it when Ginger Rogers won the Best Actress Oscar, beating Bette Davis (for *The Letter*), Katharine Hepburn (*The Philadelphia Story*), Joan Fontaine (*Rebecca*) and Martha Scott (*Our Town*). This was Rogers' 40th film but her first starring dramatic role, playing a working girl who can't decide over rival suitors. Undeniably mushy in places, its success convinced Rogers that she didn't need to sing and dance to make hit movies.

Klute ● ⓥ
1971, US, 114 mins, colour
Dir: Alan J Pakula
Stars: Jane Fonda, Donald Sutherland, Charles Cioffi, Roy Scheider
Rating: ★★★

Part thriller, part character study, this film focuses on Jane Fonda who is compelling as a New York call girl. She gives the role an emotional and. dramatic depth not always apparent in the screenplay and deservedly took the Best Actress Academy Award for her performance. While Donald Sutherland is rather less lugubrious and mannered than usual (as the private detective involved in a somewhat

obsessive romance with Fonda), he is overshadowed by his co-star. Alan Pakula's often languorous direction tends to allow the narrative to slacken fatally at times, but there is no denying the overall impact of the movie or its more-adult-than-usual approach to its subject.

Knack . . . and How to Get It, The ⓞ
1965, UK, 84 mins, b/w
Dir: Richard Lester
Stars: Rita Tushingham, Ray Brooks, Michael Crawford, Donal Donnelly
Rating: ★★★

Hot on the heels of his first Beatles film, director Richard Lester made this way-out (or so it seemed at the time) modern farce. Quick-fire, sometimes Goonish, sometimes very satirical dialogue, lots of black-clothed players on white backgrounds, extensive use of rapid cross-cutting and the occasional burst into quick motion – these were the ingredients of Lester's art in 1965. The story is merely an excuse for a visual caper, involving Ray Brooks who has the Knack (of getting girls to the extent that he gives them Green Shield stamps) and Michael Crawford as a young teacher with two left feet, who most definitely has not got the Knack. Rita Tushingham has a delightful time sending up her own stock character of the wayside waif, as the girl who comes between them. Witty and inventive fun that gives sex its roughest, tongue-in-cheek handling on record.

Knickerbocker Holiday ○
1944, US, 85 mins, b/w
Dir: Harry Joe Brown
Stars: Nelson Eddy, Constance Towers, Charles Coburn, Shelley Winters
Rating: ★★

Pleasant musical, set in 17th century New Amsterdam (later New York), but uninspired in all but its Kurt Weill melodies, which include 'September Song' – sung in the stage version by Walter Huston but done here by Charles Coburn – and 'Indispensable Man'. Shelley Winters (billed as Winter) got her first big film chance as heroine Constance Dowling's sister.

Knight Moves ● ⓥ
1992, US, 115 mins, colour
Dir: Carl Schenken
Stars: Christopher Lambert, Diane Lane, Tom Skerritt, Daniel Baldwin
Rating: ★

Busty beauties are falling victim to a serial killer and it seems chess may have something to do with it. On an island where thunder and lightning seemingly occur every night, the police (Tom Skerritt, Daniel Baldwin) close in on Grandmaster Christopher Lambert, whose protests that the killer is playing a chess-type game with him seem to be substantiated by the murderer's phone calls. 'You have to face the things you feel,' psychiatrist Diane Lane tells Lambert before leaping into bed with him. Yes, well, there's no answer to that. But at least the police could have faced up to putting a tail on Lambert, which would have saved them grilling him after every murder. Never mind: we, the audience, have been let in on the key to the plot in the first scene, so it's only poor Lambert (very bad in the emotional scenes) who has to suffer. Though, when he howls about 'going somewhere where the pain will finally stop', you wonder whether it's a hint to leave the film early. Director Carl Schenken has a few routine ideas about action and suspense, but with this ludicrous script, it's nowhere near enough: even the colour is rotten.

Knights of the Round Table ○
1953, UK, 115 mins, colour
Dir: Richard Thorpe
Stars: Robert Taylor, Ava Gardner, Mel Ferrer, Stanley Baker, Anne Crawford
Rating: ★★★

MGM's spectacular version of the King Arthur romance, involving such characters as Sir Lancelot, Queen Guinevere and Merlin, may take liberties with the legend but does compensate with plenty of rollicking action. The supporting cast includes Felix Aylmer (surprisingly but imaginatively cast as Merlin) and Stanley Baker, who makes a first-rate villainous character out of Sir Modred.

Knight Without Armour ○
1937, UK, 108 mins, b/w
Dir: Jacques Feyder
Stars: Marlene Dietrich, Robert Donat
Rating: ★★★

Marlene Dietrich looks absolutely ravishing in an Alexander Korda adaptation of James Hilton's novel about an idealistic young Englishman at large in Russia during its last Czarist years. The great French film-maker Jacques Feyder came to England to direct this atmospheric and splendidly paced thriller.

K 9 ○ ⓥ
1989, US, 102 mins, colour
Dir: Rod Daniel

Stars: James Belushi, Mel Harris, Kevin Tighe, Ed O'Neill
Rating: ★★★

Recent times have brought us a new spate of doggy pictures, and this one has James Belushi as the cop saddled with a canine partner while on the trail of a drugs lord (the ubiquitous Kevin Tighe). Quite fun and certainly suitable for 10-year-olds and upwards, as the dog refuses to obey, messes up the hero's love life, comes to the rescue, helps Belushi make a getaway, falls for a poodle and finally makes us all cry by getting shot. Director Daniel trails the action in exciting style, but seems less sure of what to do when it comes to head to head conversations. The dog, of course, is the star, but Belushi, whether exasperated, grateful or desperate about his 'partner', runs him close.

Knock on Any Door ○
1949, US, 100 mins, b/w
Dir: Nicholas Ray
Stars: Humphrey Bogart, John Derek, George Macready
Rating: ★★★

One of Humphrey Bogart's first independent ventures away from the shelter of Warner Brothers, his studio for 14 years, this study of a young criminal was directed by Nicholas Ray. The following year, Ray and Bogart made *In a Lonely Place* together and both films show the same uncompromising treatment of inherent violence smouldering just below the surface of a seemingly calm personality. In this case, the dangerous element is not Bogart himself, but John Derek (in his first adult role) as the young hoodlum defended by lawyer Bogart on a charge of killing a policeman. The excitement and tension, both in and out of the courtroom, are crisply, cleanly captured in black-and-white.

Knock on Wood ⊙
1954, US, 103 mins, colour
Dir: Norman Panama, Melvin Frank
Stars: Danny Kaye, Mai Zetterling, David Burns, Torin Thatcher
Rating: ★★★★

Danny Kaye, the ideal mixture of zany hero and coward, is here a ventriloquist running unintentional rings . round a group of spies. And very funny it is, too. The highlights are Kaye's encounters with a gadget-ridden car and a super-twee ballet company.

Kotch ◐
1971, US, 114 mins, colour
Dir: Jack Lemmon

Stars: Walter Matthau, Deborah Winters, Felicia Farr
Rating: ★★★

Jack Lemmon's debut – and, to date, only effort – as a director won Oscar nominations for his old buddy Walter Matthau in the starring role and for the Marvin Hamlisch song 'Life Is What You Make It'. Through comedy, the film attempts to examine the plight of growing old in a society where it appears that only youth and beauty are treasured. Matthau has rarely been better cast or on better form as the too-alert 72-year-old man keen to baby-sit his grandchildren but whose daughter-in-law resents his interference. A noble first effort by Lemmon and a real mystery why he didn't continue.

Krakatoa – East of Java ○
1968, US, 138 mins, colour
Dir: Bernard I Kowalski
Stars: Maximilian Schell, Diane Baker
Rating: ★★

It's surprising that no one had previously spun an adventure film around the 1883 Krakatoa volcanic explosion, which proved the most spectacular natural disaster in history. Small wonder, then, that this epic action saga has an old-fashioned feel, with its elements of sunken treasure in ancient shipwrecks, deep-sea divers in difficulties, mutiny and fire. The action blazes across the screen, although at rather infrequent intervals, especially since the dialogue and characters are strictly skin-deep. Originally shot in Cinerama, which heightened the action but magnified the film's faults.

Kramer vs Kramer ○ ⓥ
1979, US, 104 mins, colour
Dir: Robert Benton
Stars: Dustin Hoffman, Meryl Streep, Justin Henry, Jane Alexander, Howard Duff, JoBeth Williams
Rating: ★★★★★

A soaringly affecting weepie about a tug-of-love situation which became one of the big money-spinners of its year and walked off with the Academy Award for best picture. There were Oscars, too, for Dustin Hoffman and Meryl Streep, as the warring parents and for director Benton. Streep and Hoffman both give heartfelt performances, with the aid of some mordant and perceptive dialogue; but spare a thought for Jane Alexander, who is simply faultless as the woman perhaps waiting in the wings. Full of scorching scenes, this is riveting, touching entertainment of the highest quality.

K

Krays, The ● ⓥ
1990, UK, 119 mins, colour
Dir: Peter Medak
Stars: Billie Whitelaw, Tom Bell, Gary Kemp, Martin Kemp, Susan Fleetwood
Rating: ★★★

For its first hour this is a strong, chronological, extremely well-set reconstruction of the bloody careers of twin ganglords who ruled London's crime from East End to West End in the Fifties. In the second hour, the film rather loses its grip, as if suddenly conscious of its length, by telescoping and merging events and jumping a yawning time gap at the end. Also, by giving too much screen time to fringe characters, the film fails to create an impression of the building of a criminal empire – more that of a couple of psychos on the loose in London's clubland and its backstreets. A pity, this, since real-life brothers Martin and Gary Kemp are startlingly good as the Krays, and Billie Whitelaw outstanding as their mother. Most of the other performances are good too (especially Jimmy Jewel as an inebriated uncle) and Susan Fleetwood has an excellent death scene as the twins' beloved Aunt Rose. Visually, the film has the right hard-as-ebony look and Michael Kamen's background score is one of the most musically inventive heard for some time in a British film.

Kremlin Letter, The ●
1969, US, 113 mins, colour
Dir: John Huston
Stars: Patrick O'Neal, Barbara Parkins, Orson Welles, George Sanders
Rating: ★

John Huston's vicious (and viciously complicated) espionage thriller in which few people are quite what they seem. An all-star cast includes Orson Welles, George Sanders, Richard Boone, Max Von Sydow, Barbara Parkins and Huston himself.

Krull ○ ⓥ
1983, US, 115 mins, colour
Dir: Peter Yates
Stars: Ken Marshall, Lysette Anthony, Freddie Jones, Francesca Annis, Bernard Bresslaw, Robbie Coltrane
Rating: ★★

The opening credits of this derivative British entry into the sci-fi genre promise a *Star Wars*-style space opera. But in the end the film settles for good old sword and sorcery in the Robin Hood tradition, too-knowing tongue-in-cheek humour and very little blood-letting. Everything in it has been done before, in many cases better, and the lead characters are bland in the extreme. But for all that, it's hard not to like *Krull*. Bernard Bresslaw's Rell, a friendly giant who can throw a mean javelin, makes most impact, and well down the cast there's room for Robbie Coltrane in an small early role.

Kuffs ① ⓥ
1991, US, 102 mins, colour
Dir: Bruce A Evans
Stars: Christian Slater, Milla Jovovich, Bruce Boxleitner, Tony Goldwyn
Rating: ★

Tolerant Christian Slater fans, of which there must be a good few, might get something out of this asinine action comedy, which has the hero addressing the camera in *Alfie* style. Slater's a ne'er-do-well layabout who's currently proposing to leave his pregnant girlfriend (Milla Jovovich) but finds his life changed when his older brother, a precinct cop, is gunned down. Due to a rather bizarre Los Angeles law, Slater finds himself in charge of his brother's beat and tangling with the crooks who want to take over the neighbourhood. Though the action scenes are efficiently shot, the film's comic side hardly works at all, being strenuously over-directed by first time helmer Bruce A Evans. Slater's charisma helps a little bit but not much. And there's another of those flatulent dogs who became a tiresome staple of the early Nineties Hollywood comedy.

L

La Bamba ① ⓥ
1986, US, 108 mins, colour
Dir: Luis Valdez
Stars: Lou Diamond Phillips, Rosana de Soto, Elizabeth Peña
Rating: ★★★★

The stuff of real life flows through this tribute to one of the youngest stars of the rock 'n' roll era, Ritchie Valens. The star's Mexican/Indian background promises to take this a little away from the run-of-the-mill and so it proves. Valens' meteoric rise to the top is perhaps taken in too low a key, but there's no doubting the emotional supercharge of his music, as launched from the screen by Phillips with the vocal assistance of Los Lobos. 'La Bamba' itself was quite unlike any other rock 'n' roll number and makes you wonder what someone of Valens' background might have achieved had his life run its full course. Phillips is pretty good as Valens, but the pick of a highly competent cast is Esai Morales as the handsome, glowering, misfit brother who proves an albatross around Ritchie's neck.

Labyrinth ○
1986, US, 97 mins, colour
Dir: Jim Henson
Stars: David Bowie, Jennifer Connelly
Rating: ★★

The Muppet version of *The Wizard of Oz*, with additional inspiration from the works of Lewis Carroll and Maurice Sendak. Teenager Sarah (Jennifer Connelly) accidentally says the words that will allow the King of the Goblins (David Bowie) to kidnap her baby brother. To get him back, she must find her way through the labyrinth that surrounds the goblin castle and face the king in his lair. The puppetry animation techniques impressively create a whole range of amusing characters, especially a jousting fox with Basil Brush voice, whose steed is an Old English sheepdog. But Bowie's songs are allowed to slow the film up badly and his speaking voice somehow doesn't fit the role of the goblin ruler. Connelly is, with her dark hair and eyes and the right aura of innocence, visually perfect as the heroine, even if her lipstick comes and goes from shot to shot! Too slow for young children and too fey for teenagers, the film's ideal appeal lies somewhere in a narrow band of nine-to 13-year-olds.

La Cage Aux Folles ● Ⓥ

1978, France/Italy, 91 mins, colour
Dir: Edouard Molinaro
Stars: Michel Serrault, Ugo Tognazzi
Rating: ★★★

This wildly successful French-Italian farce, which begat two sequels and gave a whole new lease of life to the play on which it was based, is really just the permissive cinema's variation on almost any cinematic frolic of misunderstandings, sexual and otherwise, from the 1930s onwards. A middle-aged gay couple, horrified when the son of one (no, don't ask) wants to marry a girl, get themselves into all sorts of trouble pending a confrontation with her parents. Funniest scene of all – when one of the couple miserably fails a crash course in heterosexual etiquette.

La Clociara

See: Two Women

L.A. Confidential ● Ⓥ

1997, US, 136 mins, colour
Dir: Curtis Hanson
Stars: Kim Basinger, Russell Crowe, Guy Pearce, Kevin Spacey, Danny DeVito, James Cromwell
Rating: ★★★★

Modern-day attemps at *film noir* always seem to work best when set in the post-war period of their heyday. This is a bit later than that (1935) although the settings, costumes and ambience seem to place it a few years earlier. Several characters interweave in one of those satisfying plots replete with darkness and violence, where all the pieces fall into place at the end. Three cops (Crowe, Pearce, Spacey) are set on separate paths as a mass murder in a diner proves to be a cover for something more sinister, involving a 'hush hush' gossip columnist (DeVito) and the smooth operator (David Strathairn) of a call-girl ring whose hookers have been redesigned to look like film stars – one of whom (Basinger) falls for bull-in-a-china-shop Crowe and convinces him to crack the case. How the cops fall out, band up, are almost coerced into killing one another and shoot it out with the bad guys forms the nub of an engrossing, constantly hard-as-nails story, conventional at heart, but crisp and atmospheric in the execution.

Ladies' Man, The ☉

1961, US, 106 mins, colour
Dir: Jerry Lewis
Stars: Jerry Lewis, Helen Traubel, Jack Kruschen, Gloria Jean
Rating: ★★★

That erratic comedy genius Jerry Lewis wrote, produced and directed this zany, often very funny comedy about a chicken-hearted mother's boy who gets goose-pimples on his goose-pimples at the sight of a pretty girl. Naturally, when he takes a job as a houseboy at a Hollywood hotel, it proves to be full of them. That splendid female fool Kathleen Freeman has a good chance to parade her comedy talents and guest spots are filled by Gloria Jean, George Raft and Harry James. There seemed no good reason to film it in colour but, that said, the Technicolor photography, especially of interiors, is first-rate.

Ladies Who Do ◯

1963, UK, 85 mins, b/w
Dir: C M Pennington Richards
Stars: Peggy Mount, Robert Morley, Harry H Corbett
Rating: ★

A comedy about a group of charwomen who find a bizarre way of making money on the Stock Exchange. Peggy Mount, Dandy Nichols, Avril Elgar and Miriam Karlin work hard as the chars. They have to – for the direction tends to lend leaden feet to what should be Ealing-style whimsy. Ron Moody and Nigel Davenport give great support.

Lady and the Tramp ☉ Ⓥ

1955, US, 76 mins, colour
Dir: Hamilton Luske, Clyde Geronimi, Wilfred Jackson
Rating: ★★★★

He's a tramp – but you'll love him. Sentimental it may be, but Disney's doggy romance is a wonderful cure for the blues for people of all ages. Amazing animation – especially in the deadly duo of Siamese cats, Si and Am – highly singable tunes (including the mega-hit 'Bella Notte') and a sunshine atmosphere. All the characters are likeable, especially the blowsy Peg of the Pound (brilliantly voiced and sung by Peggy Lee), and only the end seems to have been watered down to conform to popular appeal. See it in a 'letterboxed' Cinemascope version if you can.

Ladybird Ladybird ● Ⓥ

1994, UK, 102 mins, colour
Dir: Ken Loach
Stars: Crissy Rock, Vladimir Vega, Ray

Winstone
Rating: ★

A depressing story of a slum mum that you'd say was ridiculous if the makers didn't assure us it was based on fact. Even so, their account of it is so impossibly one-sided as to have the opposite effect to that they surely intended: the police are all pigs, and the social and welfare workers scruffy and uncaring 30-somethings who fail to display even the minimum standards of intelligence or understanding. But could you blame the real people behind these callous caricatures for taking children away from a foul-mouthed screech of a mother whose previous partners – four different men for four children – had beaten her up, and who had left her kids alone to almost burn to death? When she meets a gentle Paraguayan political refugee, she starts having more children, which police and social workers take by force before she's left hospital. True *maybe* – but unbelievable as depicted on screen, which is what counts for more. Crissy Rock rants and raves and effs and blinds without eliciting much sympathy. Tough to sit through.

Lady Eve, The ◯

1941, US, 93 mins, b/w
Dir: Preston Sturges
Stars: Henry Fonda, Barbara Stanwyck, Charles Coburn, William Demarest, Eugene Pailette
Rating: ★★★

Writer-director Preston Sturges, Hollywood's wonder boy of the wartime years, was at the top of his sparkling form with this romantic comedy in which 'clod' Henry Fonda ultimately turns the tables on cardsharps Barbara Stanwyck and Charles Coburn. Fonda's passion for reptiles ('Snakes are my life'), which probably explains his attraction to the sneaky Stanwyck, rivals, for sheer crazy fun, Cary Grant's obsession with bones in *Bringing Up Baby*. Sturges' breathless pacing steers the capers through to a riotous ending.

Lady from Shanghai, The ◯

1948, US, 87 mins, b/w
Dir: Orson Welles
Stars: Orson Welles, Rita Hayworth, Everett Sloane, Glenn Anders, Ted De Corsia
Rating: ★★★

Orson Welles cast his own wife, Rita Hayworth, as the beautiful *femme fatale* in this outrageously baroque *film noir*. But to the outrage of Columbia studio

L

boss, Harry Cohn, Welles cut off her famous trademark red hair and dyed it blonde, portraying the sex siren as a cold, heartless manipulator. And Welles rewrote much of the script on a daily basis, putting a tremendous strain on his actors. The film's plot, involving a naive Irish sailor with a murderous woman and her crippled, corrupt barrister husband, is virtually incomprehensible, but its visuals are memorable, in particular a shoot-out involving multiple mirror images.

Lady Hamilton ○ Ⓥ
(aka: That Hamilton Woman)
1940, US, 128 mins, b/w
Dir: Alexander Korda
Stars: Vivien Leigh, Laurence Olivier, Gladys Cooper, Alan Mowbray
Rating: ★★★

Sir Alexander Korda was more often producer than director, but this film, made in America and said to be Sir Winston Churchill's all-time favourite, was one he did direct himself. Starring Laurence Olivier as Nelson and Vivien Leigh as Lady Hamilton, it stands up remarkably well today, distinguished by some striking high-key photography by the Polish cinematographer Rudolph Maté, who later turned to directing. One large set – Hamilton's villa in Naples – was utilised as much as possible, naval battle sequences were kept to a minimum, and the film was completed in six weeks.

LadyHawke ○ Ⓥ
1985, US, 118 mins, colour
Dir: Richard Donner
Stars: Matthew Broderick, Rutger Hauer, Michelle Pfeiffer, Leo McKern, John Wood
Rating: ★★

A cross between sword-and-sorcery and *The Black Shield of Falworth*, this is a laborious adventure fantasy set in a mediaeval France where an evil bishop (John Wood) has cursed lovers Rutger Hauer and Michelle Pfeiffer – the blondest, bluest-eyed combo since Ladd and Lake – so that the one may turn into a wolf at night and the other into a hawk by day. Magnificent, imaginative set decoration and art direction, full of fires and torches against primaeval battlements, and amazing sewer systems, are wasted here on a fatuous script and foolish story. The playing is surprisingly indifferent considering the cast, save for another whiskey priest from Leo McKern, and the action too frenziedly edited to set the pulses racing.

Lady Ice ⓵
1973, US, 93 mins, colour
Dir: Tom Gries
Stars: Donald Sutherland, Jennifer O'Neill, Robert Duvall
Rating: ★★

An unusually straight role for Donald Sutherland, an actor who has specialised in the eccentric, as an insurance investigator who hijacks a priceless diamond necklace from a gang of jewel thieves. Perhaps it's not so surprising to find him in the part, however, as it followed directly on from his hugely successful detective in *Klute*. As to be expected from a film by the late Tom Gries, this thriller moves along in fine style, although the romantic comedy overtones refuse obstinately to blend with the rest of the film and nothing quite matches up to the slickly enjoyable opening sequence. Lucien Ballard's elegant Technicolor photography is a plus factor throughout, especially in the lushness of the scenes set in the Bahamas.

Lady In Cement ⓵
1968, US, 93 mins, colour
Dir: Gordon Douglas
Stars: Frank Sinatra, Raquel Welch, Richard Conte, Joe E Lewis
Rating: ★★

Frank Sinatra returns as the hard-boiled Miami private eye he created in the previous year's *Tony Rome* for more lively mystery, mayhem and murder, well crafted, but with little style, by director Gordon Douglas. The slick, fast-moving screenplay is spiced with tart wisecracks smartly delivered by Sinatra who displays his shaggy, somewhat dangerous, charm to good effect. The sex and violence was considered to be quite tough for its time.

Lady in the Dark ○
1944, US, 100 mins, colour
Dir: Mitchell Leisen
Stars: Ginger Rogers, Ray Milland, Jon Hall, Warner Baxter
Rating: ★★

Ginger Rogers, making her first all-colour film, had one of the juiciest parts of her career in this heady (and heavy) mixture of music, romance and psychiatry. Strangely, although many of them were filmed, not all the Kurt Weill-Ira Gershwin songs from the stage original by Moss Hart (which had starred Gertrude Lawrence) made it into the release print.

Lady in the Lake ○
1946, US, 103 mins, b/w
Dir: Robert Montgomery
Stars: Robert Montgomery, Audrey Totter, Lloyd Nolan, Tom Tully
Rating: ★★★

Perhaps the most unusual film adaptation on record of one of Raymond Chandler's tough and tortuous thrillers. Star/director Robert Montgomery employs the highly original, and brilliantly successful device of telling the story entirely in the first person, through the eyes of the principal character, Phillip Marlowe (spelt here with two Is), who is rarely seen except in reflection. Additionally, the subjective camera records Marlowe's impressions while he listens to a character speak. And, if you don't know the story, you'll be hard put to unravel its solution.

Lady in White ⓵
1988, US, 105 mins, colour
Dir: Frank LaLoggia
Stars: Lukas Haas, Len Cariou
Rating: ★★★

When young Frankie (Lukas Haas) is locked into his class cloakroom by his classmates as a Halloween joke, he sees the ghost of a young girl and a masked man. Are they connected to each other in some way? Frankie is determined to find out. Haas, the little Amish boy in *Witness*, is quite cute as the central character in this eerie supernatural thriller. The special effects are good and there's a nail-biting, if somewhat clichéd climax. All the elements here are familiar but writer/director Frank LaLoggia has mixed them well. Look out for Katherine (*Soap*) Helmond as a rather scary Miss Havisham-like eccentric.

Lady Jane ○ Ⓥ
1985, UK, 142 mins, colour
Dir: Trevor Nunn
Stars: Helena Bonham Carter, Cary Elwes, Michael Hordern, Jill Bennett, Jane Lapotaire
Rating: ★★★

This was former Royal Shakespeare Company director Trevor Nunn's second venture into movies (his first was the 1975 adaptation of Ibsen's *Hedda Gabler*, starring Glenda Jackson) and it's as wordy and weighty as you might expect. Playwright David Edgar has woven a story of political intrigue around Lady Jane Grey, who became queen in her teens but then was overthrown by Mary Tudor. His screenplay casts Jane in a new light, as a 16th-century social reformer who takes pity on the downtrodden peasantry and returns their land to them. The period detail and lavish sets, including 11 Tudor castles, give an air of grandeur, but the real interest lies in the relationship between religious, reclusive Lady Jane (Helena Bonham Carter) and her enforced husband, the wild wastrel Guilford Dudley (Cary Elwes), son of the scheming Duke of Northumberland.

Lady Killer ○
1934, US, 74 mins, b/w
Dir: Roy Del Ruth
Stars: James Cagney, Mae Clarke, Henry O'Neill, Margaret Lindsay
Rating: ★★★

James Cagney is every bit as pugnacious as ever in this Thirties' gangster drama and once again Mac Clarke (who got the famous grapefruit in the face from Cagney in *The Public Enemy*) is on the receiving end of the rough treatment. This time he drags her across a room by her hair and throws her out into the corridor. Elsewhere, the star struts his familiar way through a staccato tale of crooks, bullets and blackmail. The twist that makes the film different is that the leading character escapes his environment to become a film star – after sending himself fan letters. Director Roy Del Ruth's films all moved at a rare pace, and this one is no exception.

Ladykillers, The ○ ⓥ
1955, UK, 97 mins, colour
Dir: Alexander Mackendrick
Stars: Alec Guinness, Cecil Parker, Herbert Lom, Peter Sellers
Rating: ★★★★

Say 'Ealing Comedies' and this hilarious caper is one of the first films that springs to mind. Yet it isn't a typical Ealing offering, as it has a decidedly black edge. Alec Guinness is the seedy and sinister Professor Marcus who takes lodgings with the dithery Mrs Wilberforce in King's Cross. He is frequently visited by four equally shifty-looking friends, who, he says, are musicians. But they are really a gang of criminals planning a big robbery! The gang members (Peter Sellers, Herbert Lom, Cecil Parker and – seizing his best chance from a career of 'bit' parts – Danny Green) are perfectly cast and find a good balance between real villainy and farcical incompetence, while Guinness is at times genuinely menacing. But it is Katie Johnson as the delightfully dotty Mrs

Wilberforce who manages to steal every scene she is in.

Lady L ○
1966, US, 107 mins, colour
Dir: Peter Ustinov
Stars: Sophia Loren, Paul Newman, David Niven
Rating: ★★★

Peter Ustinov wrote and directed this richly entertaining *divertissement* about the memoirs of an outrageous peeress, played by Sophia Loren. Set pieces include gendarmes on bicycles chasing a horsless carriage, an army of umbrellas in pursuit of jewel thieves; and a dazzling party sequence, with dancers galloping through shadowed corridors like so many of Poe's revellers fleeing from the Red Death. An elegant film, with a devastating kick in the tail.

Lady Luck ○
1946, US, 97 mins, b/w
Dir: Edwin L Marin
Stars: Robert Young, Barbara Hale, Frank Morgan
Rating: ★★★

A divertingly dotty comedy with a Damon Runyon touch, as some of the character names (Happy Johnson, Little Joe, Sacramento Sam) would imply. Stars Robert Young and Barbara Hale are comfortably at home in this light romantic romp with a zany touch and confidently supply some pleasing entertainment with the help of a good few smart lines from Lynn Root and Frank Fenton's script.

Lady of Deceit ◐
(aka: Born to Kill)
1947, US, 95 mins, b/w
Dir: Robert Wise
Stars: Lawrence Tierney, Claire Trevor, Walter Slezak, Elisha Cook Jr
Rating: ★★★

A very dark, amoral thriller featuring Lawrence Tierney at his most psychopathic and full of characters whose hearts ruling their heads is the cause of their downfall. There are typical (but well-crafted) roles for Claire Trevor as the older woman furious with killer Tierney's fascination for her younger sister (Audrey Long), and Elisha Cook ir as Tierney's sycophantic but more level-headed sidekick. Robert Wise's spare, head-on direction brooks no frills either in storyline or production. Film buffs will spot star-to-be Martha Hyer as a snoopy maid.

Lady of the Boulevards
See: Nana

Lady of the Tropics ○
1939, US, 92 mins, b/w
Dir: Jack Conway
Stars: Robert Taylor, Hedy Lamarr, Joseph Schildkraut
Rating: ★★

The hot romantic combination of Robert Taylor and Hedy Lamarr proved dynamite at the box-office in this sad little MGM concoction about a tropic love affair between a carefree playboy and a girl of mixed race. Reliable director Jack Conway made as many box-office hits for the studio as anyone else and, despite backdrops which now seem phoney, he gives the tragic affair a timeless quality, even though it seems longer than it is.

Lady on a Train ○
1945, US, 84 mins, b/w
Dir: Charles David
Stars: Deanna Durbin, Ralph Bellamy, Dan Duryea, Patricia Morison, Edward Everett Horton
Rating: ★★★

This comedy-thriller with music gave Deanna Durbin one of her greatest hits – 'Night and Day'. In true Miss Marple style, Deanna sees a murder from a train and gets herself into lots of danger trying to get the police to believe her and track down the killer. Don't guess too soon at the guilty party – you could be wrong.

Lady Sings The Blues ●
1972, US, 144 mins, colour
Dir: Sidney J Furie
Stars: Diana Ross, Billy Dee Williams, Richard Pryor
Rating: ★

Never mind the lurid, strident treatment this film gives to the tormented life of entertainer Billie Holiday, just listen to the way the lady, as impersonated by Diana Ross, sings the blues. The dialogue pulls no punches, and the story careers along on peaks of hysteria that makes it hard to watch.

Lady Surrenders, A
See: Love Story [1944]

Lady Takes a Chance, A ○
(aka: The Cowboy and the Girl)
1943, US, 86 mins, b/w
Dir: William Seiter
Stars: Jean Arthur, John Wayne, Charles Winninger, Phil Silvers
Rating: ★★

The teaming of squeaky Jean Arthur and rumbling John Wayne in a romantic comedy works better than you expect, although not that much better. The stars do, however, extract some fun from the tall tale of a city girl who falls for a rodeo rider and uses all her wiles to rope him in.

Lady Vanishes, The ○ ⓥ

1938, UK, 98 mins, b/w
Dir: Alfred Hitchcock
Stars: Margaret Lockwood, Michael Redgrave, Dame May Whitty, Paul Lukas, Basil Radford, Naunton Wayne
Rating: ★★★★

A Hitchcock thriller which has become one of the few timeless classics from the British cinema of the Thirties, with its famous plot line of the little old lady who vanishes aboard the Transcontinental Express and full of distinctive touches – one remembers especially Catherine Lacey as the 'nun' who proves to be wearing high heels – that became a trademark of the master's work once he moved to Hollywood. It also had his favourite setting – a train. Made during what Hitchcock later called his 'adventurous period', it features, besides unlimited tension and excitement, Margaret Lockwood ('delightful, uninhibited girl' recalled Hitchcock once) as the heroine who almost comes to believe that she didn't meet the elderly lady (Dame May Whitty) who has now vanished.

Lady Vanishes, The ○

1979, UK, 99 mins, colour
Dir: Anthony Page
Stars: Elliott Gould, Cybill Shepherd, Angela Lansbury, Herbert Lom, Ian Carmichael, Arthur Lowe
Rating: ★★★

You can't recreate an original by taking a new set of paintbrushes and doing it all over again. But, with a few deft touches of its own to complement the wise preservation of the best of the old, this new version of Ethel Lina White's classic thriller (first made by Hitchcock in 1938) does very nicely under its own steam. Rattled along at a fine pace by director Anthony Page, with superb supporting performances from Angela Lansbury – as the lady who disappears aboard a transcontinental express train in 1939 – Arthur Lowe and Ian Carmichael, this lady also has some literately witty dialogue from American George Axelrod. It includes one classic line (said by hero Elliott Gould of madcap heroine Cybill Shepherd) that perhaps sums up the whole film: 'Maybe that beautiful girl with the wild body and no brassiere is right!' In fact, there are few signal fail-

ures in this loving remake of an old masterpiece.

Lady With a Lamp, The ○

1951, UK, 110 mins, b/w
Dir: Herbert Wilcox
Stars: Anna Neagle, Michael Wilding, Gladys Young, Felix Aylmer, Sybil Thorndike, Peter Graves
Rating: ★★★

The last of Anna Neagle's many portraits of famous ladies and one which her serenity and sincerity ideally qualified her to play. The film is not so much a biopic as episodes from the life of its subject, Florence Nightingale, and it tends to lack steel. But the period and its trappings are immaculate and Dame Anna's oft-time co-star Michael Wilding is there to provide elegant support.

Lady Without Passport, A ○

1950, US, 84 mins, b/w
Dir: Joseph H Lewis
Stars: Hedy Lamarr, John Hodiak, James Craig, George Macready
Rating: ★

A so-so thriller about illegal aliens trying to enter America, with Hedy Lamarr as a beautiful refugee. It was a brave attempt at a *film noir* thriller but didn't have enough *noir* to make it a film. Miss Lamarr needed better support than she received here, and the result was an unintended B-picture.

Lafayette Escadrille

See: Hell Bent For Glory

Lair of the White Worm, The ● ⓥ

1989, UK, 94 mins, colour
Dir: Ken Russell
Stars: Hugh Grant, Peter Capaldi, Amanda Donohoe, Sammi Davis, Catherine Oxenberg, Stratford Johns
Rating: ★

Ken Russell, that most mercurial of directors, managed to balance high camp and genuine horror modestly successfully in this, his own adaptation of Bram ('Dracula') Stoker's gothic novel. Amanda Donohoe is evilly seductive as the wicked and often scantily-clad Lady Sylvia Marsh and manages to dodge your laughter until near the end. By and large, though, the end-of-pier camp charade looks cheap and has acting to match. And its intentional jokes are feeble and fall pretty flat. It's certainly one of a kind though, with its streaks of humour, titillation and terror, coupled with some outrageous special effects. Stoker purists will be outraged.

Lamb ① ⓥ

1985, UK, 110 mins, colour
Dir: Colin Gregg
Stars: Liam Neeson, Hugh O'Conor, Ian Bannen, Frances Tomelty
Rating: ★★★

Grim though the story is in many ways, there are both a few attractive lighter moments and a true poignancy to this tale of the doomed journey of a young priest and the foul-mouthed yet endearing 10-year-old epileptic boy he rescues from the (slightly improbable) tyranny of a remand home, run with callous lack of compassion by his fellow-priests. Although the naiveté of the priest stretches the credulity, persuasive performances by Liam Neeson (his first major impression) as the priest and Hugh O'Conor as the boy win the day. And Dudley Sutton is convincingly repugnant as a clammy pervert with a military manner. *Lamb* may not cut deep enough to make you cry, but it will make you think.

Lancer Spy ○

1937, US, 84 mins, b/w
Dir: Gregory Ratoff
Stars: George Sanders, Dolores Del Rio, Joseph Schildkraut, Peter Lorre
Rating: ★★★

This exciting melodrama was Russian actor Gregory Ratoff's first try at directing a Hollywood film and a first-class job he made of it. The role of the young naval officer who undertakes a dangerous impersonation in Germany shot George Sanders, previously confined to supporting roles, to stardom. And Joseph Schildkraut, who won an Oscar in the same year as best supporting actor, in *The Life of Emile Zola*, is magnificent as a weakling prince. Ratoff's direction, always patient and at times inspired, leads to some thrilling moments, not least of which is the breathless final chase up to the Swiss border.

Land and Freedom ○ ⓥ

1995, UK, 109 mins, colour
Dir: Ken Loach
Stars: Ian Hart, Rosana Pastor
Rating: ★★★

This Cannes critics prizewinner is on the whole a well-realised film about one Briton's participation in the Spanish Civil War. The best bits are excellent. But a mid-section in which revolutionaries interminably discuss strategy seems to last about an hour. But director Ken Loach has the sense to right the ship in time to head unerringly for the ending which previous events have dictated shall have the maximum impact. David (Ian Hart), a Liverpudlian, enlists in a war that at first inspires a great and enduring spirit of camaraderie among its motley fighters. But it is also a war that becomes increasingly confused and David finds ideals frustratingly lost, culminating in foolish and tragic confrontations between 'friendly' forces. Loach's cries against injustice and oppression are effectively done, and less unsubtle than in some of his films. Hart is well in character as David, and Pastor totally convincing as the girl guerilla who fights and loves with equal ferocity and passion.

Land Before Time, The ⊙ Ⓥ

1988, US, 69 mins, colour
Dir: Don Bluth
Voice Stars: Pat Hingle, Gabriel Damon, Helen Shaver, Candice Houston
Rating: ★

Only the very youngest children will suffer this animated dinosaur feature gladly. From the same team as *An American Tail*, it is weighed down by a lack of imagination and an overwhelming sense of cuteness. The film sets out to preach the message that surviving in a changing environment depends on achieving unity among the species. But the idea isn't strong enough to carry the tale which, at just over an hour long, is one of the slowest cartoon hours ever to plod across a screen.

Landfall ○

1949, UK, 88 mins, b/w
Dir: Ken Annakin
Stars: Michael Denison, Patricia Plunkett, David Tomlinson
Rating: ★★★

Adapted from Nevil Shute's novel, this is the story of a British wartime pilot accused of sinking one of his own submarines – although he's convinced it was a German U-boat. Excellent characterisations of people ranging from air raid wardens to admirals make the plot entirely plausible, even if it's never in the class of the book. Liquid-lipped Patricia Plunkett is most attractive as hero Michael Denison's resourceful girlfriend.

Land of the Pharaohs ○

1955, US, 105 mins, colour
Dir: Howard Hawks
Stars: Jack Hawkins, Joan Collins
Rating: ★★

Spectacle and epic are blended well in this epic if raggedly-scripted story of life in Egypt 5,000 years ago. Jack Hawkins, in his first American film,

makes a statesmanlike Pharaoh, and Joan Collins' scheming princess could teach even Cleopatra a thing or two. This is a big film in every sense: director Howard Hawks used 9,000 extras to build a pyramid, the immensity of which makes them look like ants. Hawks also had 100 boats built for scenes on the Nile and hired Nobel prizewinner William Faulkner to work on the screenplay – which makes you wonder what the dialogue must have been like in the first place.

Land Raiders ◑

1969, US, 100 mins, colour
Dir: Nathan Juran
Stars: Telly Savalas, George Maharis, Arlene Dahl
Rating: ★

Blackly violent Western, with Telly Savalas in rampaging form as a merciless bully who runs the whole territory until his younger brother returns from exile to bring him to book. It was made in Spain, despite the dominance of English-speaking actors (Jocelyn Lane, George Coulouris and Guy Rolfe are also featured), and is listlessly directed.

Land That Time Forgot, The ○ Ⓥ

1974, UK, 91 mins, colour
Dir: Kevin Connor
Stars: Doug McClure, John McEnery, Susan Penhaligon, Keith Barron
Rating: ★★★

Although Doug McClure, Susan Penhaligon and John McEnery are its leading actors, the real stars of this prehistoric animal thriller are monster-maker Roger Dicken, editor John Ireland and director Kevin Connor. The pace is lively, the editing sharp and the story on the whole believable. Even the back-projection work is a cut above Hollywood efforts of the period. It's 1918 and German and English mariners, forced to band together, use a submarine to enter an underground river in Antarctica, discovering a land where hot springs bubble, allosauruses rear their ugly heads and pterodactyls patrol the skies. Some illogicalities in the plot and the inadequacy of McClure as leading man are more than compensated for with the excitement provided by Dicken's monsters, whether roaring menacingly towards the camera, shuddering against the impact of bullets or howling and weeping in defeat. And the backgrounds are futuristic, broodingly mysterious and brilliantly realised.

Larceny Inc ○

1941, US, 95 mins, b/w
Dir: Lloyd Bacon
Stars: Edward G Robinson, Jane Wyman, Broderick Crawford, Anthony Quinn, Jack Carson, Edward Brophy
Rating: ★★★

A broad but mostly delightful crime comedy about Edward G Robinson buying a shop next door to the bank he plans to rob, only to discover that he's making more of a profit from that than he ever did from crime. It's a pity that it's played as outright farce. Broderick Crawford's performance makes Jack Carson's look subtle, but watching Edward G wrap a suitcase in about 10 yards of brown paper for a customer is worth waiting for.

Larger Than Life ○ Ⓥ

1996, US, 93 mins, colour
Dir: Howard Franklin
Stars: Bill Murray, Tai the elephant, Janeane Garofalo, Matthew McConaughey, Linda Fiorentino, Harve Presnell
Rating: ★

This film is funny for about five minutes – the time taken up by Bill Murray's opening routine. Then an elephant comes into it. Unfortunately, the elephant proves to be the whole film, left to Murray by his circus clown father and now joining him on a trek to California. A really talented cast (Pat Hingle's also in it) tries hard to make what it can of this situation. But the task is hopeless, especially given Howard Franklin's stodgy direction and the laborious pace that makes the film's odyssey seem like a kind of *Plod Away Home*. Tai is probably charming if you like elephants, but pretty charmless to the rest of us; Murray shouts a lot; McConaughey may look back on this as his worst-ever film performance; Garofalo and Fiorentino barely have roles. The colour is as mucky as an elephant's poop. Not good.

Lassie ⊙ Ⓥ

1994, US, 92 mins, colour
Dir: Daniel Petrie
Stars: Helen Slater, Thomas Guiry, Jon Tenney, Frederic Forrest, Richard Farnsworth, Michelle Williams
Rating: ★★★

Spurred on no doubt by the spate of canine successes in the late Eighties and early Nineties, from *Turner & Hooch* to *Beethoven*, the oldest shaggy dog story of them all is back with us, given a new coat in this version, which owes very little, if anything, to Eric Knight's original best-selling novel of a collie's epic return to its master. In this story, the dog joins a city family en route to relocating in the country, and quickly proves its saviour. This isn't surprising as their new livelihood involves sheep ranching and the dog proves just about the best sheep wrangler outside of *Babe*. Frederick Forrest tries hard to be bullying as the rival sheep farmer who makes up most of what there is in the plot, and Helen Slater makes a bit more of the family stepmother's role than is really there. But hell, this is the dog's show, as usual, backed up by some fine colour photography of the Virginia countryside by Kenneth MacMillan.

Lassie Come Home ⊙

1943, US, 88 mins, colour
Dir: Fred M Wilcox
Stars: Roddy McDowall, Donald Crisp, Dame May Whitty, Elsa Lanchester
Rating: ★★★

The surprise box-office hit that spawned many sequels as well as a TV and radio series. Elizabeth Taylor had only seventh billing, but with the success of *National Velvet* was elevated to star status for a sequel, *Courage of Lassie*. Rising child star Roddy McDowall was loaned from Fox to MGM and he joined several other London-to-Hollywood actors, including Donald Crisp, Elsa Lanchester, Nigel Bruce, Dame May Whitty and Edmund Gwenn, to make this thoroughly enjoyable family entertainment that won't leave a dry eye in the sitting room.

Lassiter ◑

1983, US, 110 mins, colour
Dir: Roger Young
Stars: Tom Selleck, Jane Seymour, Lauren Hutton, Bob Hoskins
Rating: ★★★

Tom Selleck chose a good script for this cash-in on his *Magnum* success. It's engagingly set in 1939 where Lassiter, an American Raffles, is strong-armed into stealing millions in diamonds for the Nazis. Selleck is backed by good performances from both his leading ladies, Lauren Hutton, who enjoys herself in a Mata Hari role, and the underrated Jane Seymour. Warren Clarke and Bob Hoskins also register well as lethal influences in Lassiter's life, while Ed Lauter's engaging Cockney interpolations as Lassiter's chief cohort clearly owe a lot to Dick Van Dyke's interpretation of the chimney sweep in *Mary Poppins*. This thriller certainly is different, and Selleck's own performance in the title role is spot-on.

Last Action Hero ◐ ⓥ

1993, US, 130 mins, colour
Dir: John McTiernan
Stars: Arnold Schwarzenegger, F Murray Abraham, Austin O'Brien, Robert Prosky, Charles Dance, Anthony Quinn
Rating: ★★★

The idea of people jumping into films is hardly new, but this treatment is pretty inventive by the standards of the genre, and allows Arnold Schwarzenegger to play another amusing variant on his own image: no small achievement considering his limited range. Wide-eyed Austin O'Brien is the sub-teen film freak given a magic ticket (invented by Houdini!) to a preview of the latest film adventure of his favourite film character Jack Slater. No sooner have the first scenes unspooled than the kid finds himself catapulted into the film. Slater is baffled that the boy knows so much about him – not to mention his prior knowledge of the plot, which has villains Charles Dance and Anthony Quinn taking control of the LA underworld. Later, the movie neatly reverses everything when Slater comes back to real life in pursuit of his fictional enemies, and is puzzled to find he's longer invincible. The star pokes fun at himself – Slater can't remember the name of the actor who plays him and introduces himself as Arnold Braunschweiger – and some 'real life' stars contribute cameos, including Schwarzenegger himself, being nagged by his own wife for relentlessly plugging his own chain of restaurants. Underrated.

Last Boy Scout, The ● ⓥ

1991, US, 106 mins, colour
Dir: Tony Scott
Stars: Bruce Willis, Damon Wayans, Chelsea Field, Taylor Negron, Danielle Harris
Rating: ★★★

Bruce Willis returned to the *Die Hard* formula here with the kind of tough pulp fiction in which people will pay to see him. Full of sadistic violence, voluptuous undressed women and tough-talking Willis wisecracks. Bullets, blood and guts fly everywhere. Willis is a washed-up secret service man turned shabby, unshaven private eye. Handed a case by his partner, Willis drives home fast to find partner bedding Willis' wife. Partner exits in a car which promptly blows up, the first piece in the jigsaw of a multi-million dollar case involving legalising certain forms of gambling. Willis gets beaten up a lot, but (for once logically) never

rubbed out, as the villains suspect he has something they want. One civilised nasty offers to effect introductions. 'Who cares?' asks Willis. 'You're the bad guy, right?' It's the kind of weary humour Willis was beginning to make his own. Somewhere in there is Willis' foul-mouthed 13-year-old daughter, played with great confidence by Danielle Harris, who more than once pulls daddy out of a hole. The action is terrific and the bad guys are pretty horrible.

Last Dance ● ⓥ

1995, US, 103 mins, colour
Dir: Bruce Beresford
Stars: Sharon Stone, Rob Morrow, Randy Quaid, Rachel Glass, Peter Gallagher, Jack Thompson, Skeet Ulrich
Rating: ★

A grim variation on the *Dead Man Walking* theme, with Stone as the woman on Death Row awaiting execution by lethal injection. True, Stone doesn't do a bad job as the white trash murderess who has spent 12 years in prison and is now too jaded to let rookie lawyer Morrow, assigned to her case, plead for her life. But it's a bleak and depressing film with a disappointingly silly script, and the relationship between Stone and the lightweight Morrow just doesn't convince. If it's light entertainment you're seeking, then search elsewhere: this isn't even the best of its sombre kind.

Last Days of Pompeii, The ○

1935, US, 96 mins, b/w
Dir: Ernest B Schoedsack
Stars: Basil Rathbone, Preston Foster, Alan Hale, Louis Calhern
Rating: ★★

Despite special effects from Willis O'Brien and the team behind *King Kong*, this historical epic about the eruption of Mount Vesuvius lost $237,000 at the box office. The film actually bears no relation whatsoever to Sir Edward Bulwer-Lytton's novel, and much of the dialogue is of the wooden variety. Preston Foster is solid but uninspired in the lead role as an honest blacksmith caught up in the momentous events prior to eruption, but acting honours go to Basil Rathbone as Pilate, whose scenes were all shot in just seven days. Rathbone played the same role again 27 years later!

Last Detail, The ● ⓥ

1974, US, 105 mins, colour
Dir: Hal Ashby
Stars: Jack Nicholson, Randy Quaid,

Carol Kane, Otis Young, Michael Moriarty
Rating: ★★★

A raw, raucous, grainy and grim story about two hard-cursing US Navy petty officers (Jack Nicholson and Otis Young) escorting an 18-year-old prisoner (Randy Quaid) half-way across America to serve an eight-year prison sentence for stealing 40 dollars from a polio collection box (it was a favourite charity of the CO's wife). Jack Nicholson, who's in tremendous form as 'Bad Ass' Baddusky, and Randy Quaid were both nominated for Academy Awards.

Last Dragon, The ◐
1985, US, 109 mins, colour
Dir: Michael Schuitz
Stars: Taimak, Vanity
Rating: ★★

Billed as the first kung-fu musical, this is really a mishmash of several kinds of film all fighting against each other. Director Michael Schultz displays a good sense of visual wit but the characters are nothing more than cartoon cyphers. It's not difficult to see, though, why the film did so well in America. It's bright and loud, full of 'impossible' action and has a crunching disco score: a pantomime of violence populated by beautiful people. The female lead, Vanity, used to go by the name D D Winters.

Last Embrace ●
1979, US, 97 mins, colour
Dir: Jonathan Demme
Stars: Roy Scheider, Janet Margolin, Sam Levene, Christopher Walken
Rating: ★★★★

A strong and complex thriller with classic ingredients: a hero with a weakness battles mysterious forces that are out to get him. Someone certainly has it in for Roy Scheider, as a government agent barely recovered from nervous breakdown – after seeing his wife shot down by bullets meant for him. There's a mix-up over possession of his flat, someone tries to push him under a train – and he receives a mysterious death threat. Are his old colleagues (led by Christopher Walken) out to get him, or has he become involved in some deeper nightmare? Jonathan Demme's tribute to Hitchcock includes the bell-tower from *Vertigo*, the street scene (and more) from *Marnie* and the climax straight from *Saboteur*, breath-takingly transferred from the Statue of Liberty to Niagara Falls. A pounding score from Miklos Rosza makes its presence felt at all the right times. The

film was shunned by its British distributors for two years, perhaps because of the presence of the non-box office actress Janet Margolin as the anthropologist who unintentionally shares Scheider's flat. Ironically, Miss Margolin is tremendous.

Last Emperor, The ◐ ⓥ
1987, UK/Italy, 163 mins, colour
Dir: Bernardo Bertolucci
Stars: John Lone, Joan Chen, Peter O'Toole
Rating: ★★★★

Director Bernardo Bertolucci built this fascinating story of China's last emperor on an epic scale, but in essence it is the very intimate tale of a man raised in glorious isolation who struggles to come to terms with a rapidly changing world in which he is not equipped to live. Pu Yi became emperor of China at the age of three. Then, in 1912, China's new republic restricts him to the Forbidden City, the vast palace enclave, effectively creating the most opulent prison in history. His only connection with the outside world is his Scottish tutor, Reginald Johnson (Peter O'Toole). Although a long film, *The Last Emperor* never fails to fascinate, even when the pace seems decidedly leisurely. Four actors play the part of Pu Yi, but the move from one to the other as the character ages is seamless. Visually stunning, the picture's sheer scale is sometimes in danger of dwarfing the human tale it tells, but a strong cast and an intelligent script stop this happening. Maybe not the masterpiece Bertolucci hoped for, but a fine film not to be missed.

Last Exit to Brooklyn ● ⓥ
1989, US, 102 mins, colour
Dir: Ulrich Edel
Stars: Stephen Lang, Jennifer Jason Leigh, Burt Young, Jerry Orbach
Rating: ★★★

'Notorious' bestsellers don't normally make good movies, but this is a well-made, carefully composed film version of a prime piece of Fifties sleaze, the other side of the coin from such sentimental slices of Brooklyn life as *Wedding Breakfast* and *Marty*. Despite its blood, guts, four-letter words and fairly frank portrayal of a struggle for existence in Brooklyn's backstreets, this, too, is sentimental at heart, and even Jennifer Jason Leigh's raucous, breast-baring petty thief is looked on as a tart with a heart in search of a happy ending. German director Edel looks for, and sometimes finds, poetry in these

squalid surroundings, even in the strikers' riot which results in mashed bones and cracked skulls. The use of classical music is a trifle overdone, but undeniably effective.

Last Flight of Noah's Ark, The ☉
1980, US, 97 mins, colour
Dir: Charles Jarrott
Stars: Elliott Gould, Genevieve Bujold, Ricky Schroder
Rating: ★★

Charles Jarrott's direction largely keeps sentimentality at bay in this easy-going Disney offering, whose roster of performers includes two orphan children and a minor menagerie of goats, assorted poultry, pigs, sheep, bulls and a cow. Faced with this array of two and four-legged potential scene-stealers, adults Elliott Gould and Genevieve Bujold hold their own admirably.

Last Gangster, The ○
1937, US, 81 mins, b/w
Dir: Edward Ludwig
Stars: Edward G Robinson, James Stewart, Rosa Stradner, Lionel Stander
Rating: ★★★

Spitting and snarling, Edward G Robinson, who became the talkies first gangster in *Little Caesar*, carries on in the same vein as Joe Krozac, an underworld boss who finds things have changed after he comes out of prison. Robinson was delighted with the part, which he saw as a farewell to his time in crime. But the typecasting was to dog him on and off for the rest of his career. Co-star James Stewart took another stride towards stardom, though he isn't flattered by a moustache and almost never sported one in films again.

Last Giraffe, The
See: Raising Daisy Rothschild

Last Grenade, The ◐
(aka: Grigsby)
1969, UK, 94 mins, colour
Dir: Gordon Flemyng
Stars: Stanley Baker, Alex Cord, Honor Blackman, Richard Attenborough
Rating: ★★

The action's the thing in this jungle warfare thriller and there's plenty of it. A familiar crew of British actors, including John Thaw of *The Sweeney*, add substance to a tale of revenge, played out against the background of the adventures of a group of mercenaries led by Stanley Baker. There are chases and explosions galore, good colour

L

photography by Alan Hume and a forceful performance by Baker.

Last Hard Men, The ◑
1976, US, 103 mins, colour
Dir: Andrew V McLaglen
Stars: Charlton Heston, James Coburn, Barbara Hershey
Rating: ★★

Two big stars in a faintly unsavoury manhunt Western. Charlton Heston and James Coburn go through the paces that have served them well as the adversaries from way back who now engage in a final deadly duel, injecting much-needed personality into the catalogue of slow-motion violence that follows.

Last Holiday ◯
1950, UK, 88 mins, b/w
Dir: Henry Cass
Stars: Alec Guinness, Kay Walsh
Rating: ★★★

Although dating from a time when the famous Ealing comedies, with which Alec Guinness was then associated, were in full sway, this film is in an altogether gentler style. An affecting light drama with humorous insights, it comes from the pen of J B Priestley and features vivid supporting performances from Kay Walsh, Sidney James and Wilfrid Hyde White. But it's Guinness' quiet authority which lingers longest in the memory.

Last Hunt, The ◯
1955, US, 108 mins, colour
Dir: Richard Brooks
Stars: Robert Taytor, Stewart Granger, Debra Paget, Lloyd Nolan
Rating: ★★

This story about two men on a buffalo hunt is quite grim by MGM Western standards. Lots of buffalo and a fair few Indians get killed one way and another and the two stars, Robert Taylor and Stewart Granger, fall out over a young Indian girl rescued by Taylor. Having said that, it's a powerful Western drama which holds your interest right through to the icy climax (to say more would be to give the ending away!). Taylor and Granger are solid (if a bit stolid) as the hunter and the rancher who join forces, and Lloyd Nolan, playing a character called Woodfoot, looks as though he's thoroughly enjoying himself.

Last Hurrah, The ◯
1958, US, 121 mins, b/w
Dir: John Ford
Stars: Spencer Tracy, Jeffrey Hunter,

Dianne Foster, Pat O'Brien
Rating: ★★★

Based on the career of Boston's controversial Irish-American mayor Jim Curley, a role that enables Spencer Tracy to dominate this John Ford film, this is an overlong but still strong political saga. Tracy is surrounded by a veritable council of distinguished veteran stars, among them Basil Rathbone, Pat O'Brien, Donald Crisp, Ricardo Cortez, James Gleason and John Carradine.

Last Man Standing ● ⓥ
1996, US, 92 mins, colour
Dir: Walter Hill
Stars: Bruce Willis, Christopher Walken, Bruce Dern, Karina Lombard
Rating: ★★★

With one of the slimmest storylines put on screen, this Prohibition, blow-them-away gangster saga provides a rare old shoot-fest. Throaty Bruce Willis takes on whispering Christopher Walken in the story of a hired gun who drives into a small Texas town to find most of the locals fled, leaving two trigger-happy gangs to fight a private war over bootleg liquor. Willis takes first one side, then the other, until he's beaten to a pulp for his double-dealing pains. There's lots of body-blasting action and it's all well done, though more akin to the spirit of the spaghetti western than the Japanese samurai film on which it's actually based. The dialogue's difficult to hear, but the gun battles speak for themselves and the 1920s era costumes, especially bathed in brown filters, look just right. Nice supporting performance by Bruce Dern, whose character is less predictable than you might expect.

Last Married Couple in America, The ●
1980, US, 100 mins, colour
Dir: Gilbert Cates
Stars: George Segal, Natalie Wood, Richard Benjamin, Valerie Harper, Dom DeLuise
Rating: ★

A tiresome sex comedy about a couple who question their own relationship when all their friends start getting divorced. It might well have come from the Sixties apart from the ribald dialogue, manfully coped with by a personable cast, all of whom play comfortably within their most familiar screen images. Funniest of the supporting players is Bob Dishy as a womanising divorce lawyer, although Valerie Harper (from television's

Rhoda) and plumply likeable Dom DeLuise also provide good value.

Last Message from Saigon
See: Operation CIA

Last of England, The ●
1987, UK, 87 mins, colour
Dir: Derek Jarman
Stars: Tilda Swinton, Nigel Terry, Spencer Leigh, Derek Jarman, Spring
Rating: ★★

Told largely in subliminal flashes with a few grainy colour narrative sequences, this is a paean of despair for an England devastated by some nameless disaster. 'On every green hill,' intones narrator Nigel Terry (the film itself is virtually wordless) 'mourners stand and weep for the last of England.' On rubbish tips, waterfronts and in sewers too, according to director Derek Jarman, as the few contaminated survivors are guarded by masked SAS-type figures who represent what is left of authority. Told like this, the film perhaps sounds more accessible than it is. Most audiences, though, won't know what to make of it. The 'flashes' are too repetitive to grip the interest all the time and only towards the end does the film find some of the poetry it seems to seek. The poetry of the gutter maybe: but here the film is at its most challenging.

Last of Mrs Cheyney, The ◯
1937, US, 98 mins, b/w
Dir: Richard Boleslawski
Stars: Joan Crawford, William Powell
Rating: ★★★

Joan Crawford stars in this second version of Frederick Lonsdale's play. Although a moderate box office success, it's a cut below the original film (which starred Norma Shearer). A fake British aristocrat, Joan roams the parties of high-society London with her eyes on the jewelled necks and wrists of her so-called friends. Oozing charm, she and her trusted aide William Powell worm their way into a country mansion for a weekend party where her grace and charm have everyone fooled. Co-star Robert Montgomery has an unsympathetic role as a lord, but the comedy is well-handled and, Joan, who hadn't played for laughs much at the time, took to it with unexpected aplomb.

Last of Sheila, The ◑
1973, US, 123 mins, colour
Dir: Herbert Ross
Stars: Richard Benjamin, Dyan Cannon,

James Coburn, James Mason, Raquel Welch
Rating: ★★★★

As twisty thrillers go, this conundrum can show even *Sleuth* a thing or two and it's certainly a sight less stagey. The clues are all there, as the Ellery Queen books used to say. All you have to do is to sort the significant from the mass of insignificant. Not that one minds being told about the clues one missed – but it's rather humiliating to be actually shown them in flashback. So many things that one should have seen! The plot, written by Stephen Sondheim and actor Anthony Perkins, is as ingenious as any original cinematic work for years – and played to the hilt by a cast that also includes Joan Hackett and Ian McShane. Director Herbert Ross tends to explain things one too many times, but the sheer intricacy of it all is amazing.

Last of the Badmen ○
1957, US, 75 mins, colour
Dir: Paul Landres
Stars: George Montgomery, Keith Larsen
Rating: ★★

Unusually for a Western, this action drama adopts a semi-documentary approach as Pinkerton-style detective George Montgomery trails a particularly callous ring of outlaws that springs convicts, then kills them for the price on their heads. Nothing new apart from that, though the bounding music of Paul Sawtell provides spirited accompaniment to the proceedings.

Last of the Buccaneers ○
1950, US, 79 mins, colour
Dir: Lew Landers
Stars: Paul Henreid, Jack Oakie, Karin Booth, Mary Anderson
Rating: ★★

Another spectacular (but, apart from Mary Anderson, stiffly performed) story about pirate and adventurer Jean Lafitte, later to be given the epic treatment in De Mille's *The Buccaneer*. He's played by Paul Henreid, best remembered for his roles in such Warner Brothers films as *Casablanca*, *Now Voyager* and *Deception* before getting lost in an armada of 'easterns' like this one.

Last of the Comanches ○
(aka: The Sabre and the Arrow)
1953, US, 84 mins, colour
Dir: André De Toth
Stars: Broderick Crawford, Barbara Hale, Lloyd Bridges
Rating: ★★★★

Make a thousand double-bill Westerns, and you must come up with one gem. Thus runs an ancient Hollywood proverb, which is proved to the hilt by this moving, exciting film. Director André De Toth pulls every trick and Broderick Crawford's tough Cavalry sergeant leads a parade of performances that make the characters live. Sparkling Technicolor too.

Last of the Dogmen ○
1995, US, 117 mins, colour
Dir: Tab Murphy
Stars: Tom Berenger, Barbara Hershey, Kurtwood Smith
Rating: ★★★

If you've always had a weakness for *Lost Horizon*, you'll enjoy this native American version, while deploring the lack of depth and perception which prevents it from being a top-class film. A western in all but name, the film features Tom Berenger as a veteran tracker called back by the sheriff (Kurtwood Smith) who needs him for one last task – the finding of three escaped convicts, who've killed their guards and headed for the Canadian Rockies. 'There's only one thing standing in their way,' growls Smith, 'and that's 4,000 miles of the roughest country God ever put on a map.' Not the only thing though: the convicts are killed by unknown forces and only Berenger comes back alive. Back in town, with the help of anthropologist Barbara Hershey, he believes what he half-saw in the forest may be a forgotten tribe of Cheyenne Indians. Berenger and Hershey have to struggle to flesh out their characters, but great swelling music by David Arnold and bursts of action help to keep your attention. In spite of its faults, the film's heart is firmly in the right place.

Last of the Fast Guns ○
1958, US, 82 mins, colour
Dir: George Sherman
Stars: Jock Mahoney, Gilbert Roland, Linda Cristal, Lorne Greene
Rating: ★★

Veteran Western director George Sherman keeps the action going at a good clip in this story of a gunfighter searching south of the border for his employer's long-lost brother.

Last of the High Kings, The ○ ⓥ
1995, Ire, 104 mins, colour
Dir: David Keating
Stars: Jared Leto, Catherine O'Hara, Gabriel Byrne, Christina Ricci, Colm

Meaney
Rating: ★★

The rather grand title conceals a very slight and inconsequential film about leaving school, coping with girls and waiting for exam results to come. Nothing new here, then, in theme or treatment, only in the Irish setting: the teen hero (Leto) has a somewhat eccentric family, headed by an actor father (Byrne) who's hardly ever at home. This leaves Ma (O'Hara) with a free hand to browbeat the family into following her political and religious views. Although the tale that unfolds is pleasantly told, the flimsy storyline feels overstretched, despite a few mildly amusing incidents along the way: an American visitor (Ricci) develops an instant crush on our hero, and a notorious local politician (Meaney) finds his punch laced with lethal 'poteen' just as his attentions to Ma are becoming embarrassing.

Last of the Finest, The
See: Blue Heat

Last of the Mohicans, The ○
1936, US, 91 mins, b/w
Dir: George B Seitz
Stars: Randolph Scott, Bruce Cabot, Henry Wilcoxon, Binnie Barnes, Heather Angel
Rating: ★★★

James Fenimore Cooper's classic novel of the French and Indian war was brilliantly brought to the screen in this vintage but action-filled film directed by a veteran of early silent serials, George B Seitz. Two of Britain's brightest gifts to Hollywood in the Thirties, Binnie Barnes and Heather Angel, play the sisters who undertake a long and dangerous journey through hostile country.

Last of the Mohicans, The
① ⓥ
1992, US, 112 mins, colour
Dir: Michael Mann
Stars: Daniel Day-Lewis, Madeleine Stowe, Jodhi May, Russell Means, Eric Schweig, Steven Waddington
Rating: ★★★

James Fenimore Cooper's frontier Western, unfilmed for many years, gets a modern retelling, red in tooth and claw. Some stirring action scenes are the heart of the film's appeal, but director Michael Mann holds some of his carefully composed shots far too long, trying to infuse the tale with a resonance and importance it doesn't really have. Daniel Day-Lewis is a sort of

L

Irish-American Hawkeye, but all virility; and the fights are splendidly paced and edited, even if Day-Lewis and his Indian pals' idea of combat seems to be to run at their opponents from a distance. Like the negotiations with the Indians towards the end, this remains somewhat puzzling. In the supporting cast, Steven Waddington is well on target as the unpleasant English officer who becomes Hawkeye's rival for the love of Madeleine Stowe.

Last of the Redmen ○
(aka: Last of the Redskins)
1947, US, 77 mins, colour
Dir: George Sherman
Stars: Jon Hall, Evelyn Ankers, Michael O'Shea, Julie Bishop, Buster Crabbe
Rating: ★★

Also known as *Last of the Redskins*, this is in fact another version of James Fenimore Cooper's Western classic *The Last of the Mohicans*. Two of the stars were crack swimmers – Jon Hall was champion swimmer of Tahiti and Buster Crabbe was an Olympic ace. Virile, solid, if cut-budget version of the story, with the good action scenes you'd expect from director George Sherman.

Last of the Renegades ○
1964, West Germany, 93 mins, colour
Dir: Harald Reinl
Stars: Lex Barker, Pierre Brice, Anthony Steel, Karin Dor, Klaus Kinski, Mario Girotti (Terence Hill)
Rating: ★★

German-made Western about Karl May's famous characters Old Shatterhand and his Indian friend, Winnetou the Warrior. English actor Anthony Steel turns up as the villain of the piece, and there's a well-staged shootout finale, in the depths of a labyrinth of caves and the heat of the desert.

L.A. Story ◑ ⓥ
1990, US, 97 mins, colour
Dir: Mick Jackson
Stars: Steve Martin, Victoria Tennant, Richard E Grant, Marilu Henner, Sarah Jessica Parker
Rating: ★★

Pretty much a time-passer by Steve Martin's standards, this is partly Steve's equivalent of a Woody Allen film about Manhattan, and partly a reflection of his romance with his then real-life wife Victoria Tennant. There's a spot of parrot-juggling and skating in the art gallery but not quite as many zany moments as you'd expect in this sort of Martin movie. He's a TV

weatherman bored with his romance with LA hipster Marilu Henner. He goes off on a wild weekend with bounding shop assistant Sarah Jessica Parker, in spite of the fact that he's fallen wildly for seemingly unobtainable Tennant as an unlikely London *Times* correspondent. The path of true love is helped by a Los Angeles freeway sign, but this touch of lunacy isn't enough to save the film . from needing the big finish it doesn't get. Guest shots from Rick Moranis and Chevy Chase are more or less gratuitous and the funny moments get fewer as the film goes on.

Last Outlaw, The ● ⓥ
1993, US, 90 mins, colour
Dir: Geoff Murphy
Stars: Mickey Rourke, Dermot Mulroney, John C McGinley, Ted Levine
Rating: ★★★★

Mickey Rourke sits mean and moody in the saddle as Colonel Graff, the tyrannical leader of a gang of outlaws. After one too many bursts of brutality, Graff is shot by his own men and left for dead. But Graff is neither dead nor forgiving. The remainder of the film is a snarling, spitting cat-and-mouse chase, as the evil Graff teams up with the pursuing posse to wreak revenge on his rebel cohorts. An intelligent, even memorable (if also gory and sadistic) Western, well crafted by director Geoff Murphy.

Last Picture Show, The ◑ ⓥ
1971, US, 118 mins, b/w
Dir: Peter Bogdanovich
Stars: Jeff Bridges, Cybill Shepherd, Timothy Bottoms, Ben Johnson, Ellen Burstyn, Cloris Leachman, Randy Quaid
Rating: ★★★★

Seldom if ever was the atmosphere of desolation, decay and despair in a small American town that has had its day better caught than in this classic study of dust-blown Texas life in the 1950s. Not much happens, but the characters' lives intertwine and develop, the screenplay by Larry McMurtry (author of the original novel) and Peter Bogdanovich himself creating a field day for the ensemble cast. From four acting nominations, Oscars were won by Ben Johnson (unforgettable as fading Westerner Sam the Lion) and Cloris Leachman.

Last Remake of Beau Geste, The ◑
1977, US, 85 mins, colour
Dir: Marty Feldman

Stars: Marty Feldman, Ann-Margret, Michael York, Peter Ustinov
Rating: ★

There are a few chuckles in this expensive-looking comedy, written and directed by, as well as starring Marry Feldman as Digby Geste, twin brother of Michael York's Beau! Most of the best laughs come towards the beginning, many of them supplied by Spike Milligan as the Gestes' ancient retainer, a performance that may owe something to a study of that remarkable old actor Wilfrid Lawson's butler Peacock in *The Wrong Box*. A confrontation between Feldman and a mirage of Gary Cooper from the 1940 film almost comes off, Cooper providing an oasis of class in this comic desert.

Last Rites ●
1988, US, 99 mins, colour
Dir: Donald P Bellisario
Stars: Tom Berenger, Daphne Zuniga, Chick Vennera
Rating: ★★

Tom Berenger is sadly miscast as a confused priest in this steamy drama about the dilemma of being an Italian-American Catholic priest and son of a top Mafioso. Because of that fact, nothing else about the glossy production is very convincing. Daphne Zuniga, whose career at this time appeared to be on the ascendant, is an attractive femme fatale, but she delivers a highly suspect Spanish accent at times.

Last Seduction, The ● ⓥ
1993, US, 109 mins, colour
Dir: John Dahl
Stars; Linda Fiorentino, Peter Berg, Bill Pullman, J T Walsh
Rating: ★★★★

Opening on a shot of a great stone eagle (a heartless bird of prey like the central character), this is a jet-black *film noir* from *Red Rock West* director John Dahl. Although it could do with more charismatic leads than Linda Fiorentino and Peter Berg, the film compels your attention through the director's vigorous handling of a skilfully invented plot. Fiorentino is the hard-headed businesswoman who masterminds a one-off drugs heist with her pharmacist husband (Bill Pullman – different class to rest of the cast) that nets them $700,000. On the spur of the moment, after Pullman strikes her, Fiorentino makes off with the cash, pulling small-time claims adjuster Berg into bed with her and setting him up as the fall guy in her revenge plan against her husband.

You're almost certain not to get all of the twists in first-time screenwriter Steve Barancik's story, which will help keep you engrossed to the end.

Last Starfighter, The ○ ⓥ

1984, US, 100 mins, colour
Dir: Nick Castle
Stars: Lance Guest, Dan O'Herlihy, Robert Preston, Catherine Mary Stewart
Rating: ★★★

More star wars, eminently suitable for all ages. Adults can relax, while the action will get the kids cheering. Robert Preston is terrific in his last film as Centauri, the alien inventor of the galaxy-wide Starfighter game, who recruits Alex, earthling whizzkid at the game, to be a real starfighter, the last galactic hope against alien marauders. The action's pretty much cut to pattern, with the exception of the 'robot' Alex, left behind to fool his fellow earthmen, who gets involved in adventures of his own.

Last Summer ●

1969, US, 97 mins, colour
Dir: Frank Perry
Stars: Barbara Hershey, Richard Thomas, Bruce Davison, Cathy Burns
Rating: ★★★

Very highly-rated film about the violence that lurks beneath the skins of three holidaying teenagers, and the plain, teeth-braced girl who gets frighteningly caught up in their ever-darkening little circle. Compellingly spontaneous performances from the quartet of young actors – Barbara Hershey later changed her name to Barbara Seagull after the seagull her character kills in the film – and a terrifying ending.

Last Sunset, The ❶

1961, US, 112 mins, colour
Dir: Robert Aldrich
Stars: Kirk Douglas, Rock Hudson, Dorothy Malone, Joseph Cotten
Rating: ★★★

Director Robert Aldrich, the man who made *Whatever Happened to Baby Jane?* and *The Mean Machine*, goes down on the range and comes up with a typically weird Western. Rock Hudson and Kirk Douglas, who killed his brother-in-law, play a cat-and-mouse game on a cattle drive. But it's Joseph Cotten who picks up the cheese as an alcoholic rancher.

Last Supper, The ● ⓥ

1995, US, 92 mins, colour
Dir: Stacy Title

Stars: Cameron Diaz, Ron Eldard, Annabeth Gish, Bill Paxton, Mark Harmon, Ron Perlman
Rating: ★★

If you can imagine what it would be like if the friends of TV's *Friends* suddenly started going round killing people, then you'll have some idea of what goes on here. Diaz, Eldard, Gish, Jonathan Penner and Courtney B Vance are five graduate students who share a house where they sit around a table drinking wine and putting the world to rights. One night they give hospitality to a stranger (Paxton), a Desert Storm veteran who hates blacks and Jews, threatens one of our quintet with a knife and ends up being stabbed to death himself. This part of the film is blackly effective, an eye-opening nightmare of how things can get out of hand. But the film then spirals away into repetitive incidents, with one victim after another being dispatched by the grads until one 'guest' proves their undoing. Over-ambition kills this one.

Last Tango in Paris ● ⓥ

1972, France/Italy, 129 mins, colour
Dir: Bernardo Bertolucci
Stars: Marion Brando, Maria Schneider
Rating: ★★★

Director Bernardo Bertolucci's story of a vigorous (and sometimes violent) physical relationship between a middle-aged man and a young girl is a dark tale indeed, filled with sexual menace and foreboding. Paul, a middle-aged American, and Jeanne meet while viewing an empty apartment in Paris. They make love and from then on meet each day in the apartment to do the same. A powerful, mesmeric central performance by Marlon Brando holds the attention here, despite the fact that the film is gloomy and laden with Paul's confusion and despair. This pain and passion are painted in sombre colours by Bertolucci and the film's harsh and shocking ending is, on reflection, inevitable. Although there are no bright or uplifting moments to lighten its darkness, this is still a grimly fascinating film.

Last Train from Gun Hill ○ ⓥ

1959, US, 98 mins, colour
Dir: John Sturges
Stars: Kirk Douglas, Anthony Quinn, Carolyn Jones, Earl Holliman, Brad Dexter
Rating: ★★★

Kirk Douglas and Anthony Quinn, reunited from *Lust for Life*, are reluctant adversaries in this fiery Western di-

rected in steamroller style by John Sturges and blazingly shot in Technicolor by Charles B Lang. Brian Hutton, who plays one of the killers of Douglas' wife, later became a director, and you may also glimpse Ty Hardin in one of his earliest roles. The rousing climax, as Douglas fights to get a killer on the train of the title, is justly famous.

Last Tycoon, The ❶

1976, US, 120 mins, colour
Dir: Elia Kazan
Stars: Robert De Niro, Tony Curtis, Robert Mitchum, Jack Nicholson, Jeanne Moreau
Rating: ★

An amazing all-star cast provides support to Robert De Niro in a dreadfully protracted and dreary movie about Hollywood in the late Thirties. A few mock-Thirties film clips which one hopes are intentionally funny provide much-needed light relief from the gloomy central tale of a 'boy wonder' producer (modelled on Irving Thalberg) and his *amour fou* for some boring girl who happens to look like his late wife. De Niro delivers a rare lacklustre performance, but at least you can keep awake by spotting the stars here: Robert Mitchum, Dana Andrews, Jack Nicholson, Anjelica Huston, Tony Curtis, Donald Pleasance, Jeanne Moreau, Peter Strauss, Ray Milland and John Carradine among them. What a waste! You can only think studio boss Mitchum is describing this film at the studio preview when he says it 'needs about 20 minutes out of it. Otherwise, it just lies there and goes to sleep.'

Last Unicorn, The ☉

1982, US, 85 mins, colour
Dir: Jules Bass
Voice Stars: Angela Lansbury, Alan Arkin, Jeff Bridges, Mia Farrow
Rating: ★★★

A classy animated film based on the novel by Peter S Beagle about a unicorn's battle to save her kinfolk from an evil king. The pace is sprightly and animation highly colourful. The top-notch voice cast is headed by Angela Lansbury, Alan Arkin, Jeff Bridges and Mia Farrow.

Last Voyage, The ○

1960, US, 91 mins, colour
Dir: Andrew L Stone
Stars: Robert Stack, Dorothy Malone, George Sanders, Edmond O'Brien
Rating: ★★

L

One of the earliest examples of a true disaster movie, with the enterprising production team, Andrew L Stone and his then-wife Virginia, buying a real liner, the Ile de France, that was headed for the breaker's yard, and then sending it to the bottom. Everything in the film is geared to suspense, and quite a lot of it works.

Last Wagon, The ○
1956, US, 99 mins, colour
Dir: Delmer Daves
Stars: Richard Widmark, Felicia Farr, Susan Kohner, Tommy Rettig
Rating: ★★★

A red-blooded Western about the survivors of an Apache attack, and how they attempt to escape to freedom through rugged Indian territory. Richard Widmark is excellent as Commanche Todd, a primitive frontiersman whom the others believe to be a murderer but are forced to accept as leader. Directed by Delmer Daves in the middle of his best period – all Westerns – which included *Jubal* and *3.10 to Yuma*.

Last Wave, The ◐
1978, Australia, 106 mins, colour
Dir: Peter Weir
Stars: Richard Chamberlain, Olivia Hamnett, David Gulpilil
Rating: ★★★

A silly but stylish chiller by Australian director Peter Weir, who made *Picnic at Hanging Rock* and, more recently, *Witness*. Weir's confident direction of the bizarre material makes this a film to ponder upon. Richard Chamberlain is pretty good as the bemused lawyer, enmeshed in Aborigine tribal lore which seems to be connected with a series of 'natural' disasters, and who finds the chilly hand of fate leading him and his family in a direction he'd rather not go.

Late Edwina Black, The ○
(aka: Obsessed)
1951, UK, 78 mins, b/w
Dir: Maurice Elvey
Stars: Geraldine Fitzgerald, David Farrar, Roland Culver
Rating: ★★

Geraldine Fitzgerald and Roland Culver, just back from stays in Hollywood, co-star with David Farrar, who was just about to go there, in a film version of the classic stage play. Jean Cadell steals the film from all three of them, as the housekeeper whose love for the late Edwina amounted to an obsession.

Late for Dinner ○ ⓥ
1991, US, 93 mins, colour
Dir: W D Richter
Stars: Brian Wimmer, Peter Berg, Marcia Gay Harden, Colleen Flynn, Kyle Secor, Peter Gallagher
Rating: ★★★

An unusual idea that shouldn't come off but nearly does. Two Texans, on the run after one has shot a man in self-defence, are cryogenically frozen, waking up unchanged 29 years later. The surprise – and pleasure – is that developments in the story are played for charm rather than farce or horror. The leader (Brian Wimmer) just wants his glamorous wife back, hardly thinking about her being over 50. His slow-witted brother-in-law (Peter Berg) is simply baffled by 1991. 'There's money in that wall, Willie,' he gasps as they pass a bank. The real bouquet of the film, though, goes to Marcia Gay Harden, as the wife who manages to look both 23 and 52 without apparent use of excessive makeup.

Late George Apley, The ○
1947, US, 98 mins, b/w
Dir: Joseph L Mankiewicz
Stars: Ronald Colman, Peggy Cummins
Rating:★★★

One of those light, frothy portrayals of American family life (this one set in 1912) at which Hollywood proved so expert in the Forties. John P Marquand's satirical play about a stuffy Bostonian family had much of its sting removed in this Hollywoodised version, although it's enjoyable on its own merits. Percy Waram steals the show (as he had done on stage) as Apley's level-headed and cynical brother-in-law.

Laughing Policeman, The ●
(aka: An Investigation of Murder)
1973, US, 111 mins, colour
Dir: Stuart Rosenberg
Stars: Walter Matthau, Bruce Dern, Lou Gossett, Anthony Zerbe
Rating: ★★

Why does a man massacre a bus full of people? What connection does it have with the two-year-old murder of a kinky prostitute? Why was a policeman on the bus? Where does the stripper with the amazing figure fit in? Can Walter Matthau and Bruce Dern find the killer before the chief (Anthony Zerbe) takes them off the case? This laughing policeman is no joke, but at least the Matthau-Dern combination sets it from being a routine bloodsoaked urban thriller. You'll also like Lou Gossett as a hard

black cop who tells a suspect, 'Whatever you're reaching for had better be a sandwich 'cos you're gonna have to eat it.'

Laughterhouse
See: Singleton's Pluck

Laughter in Paradise ○
1951, UK, 93 mins, b/w
Dir: Mario Zampi
Stars: Alastair Sim, Joyce Grenfell, Hugh Griffith, Fay Compton
Rating: ★★★

A reminder that George Cole was already making us laugh more than 40 years ago. He and Alastair Sim are the best things in this surefire British comedy about four people who have to do things totally out of character in order to collect a fortune from the will of an eccentric relative. Director Mario Zampi's deft execution of this comedy of embarrassments doesn't leave many dull moments. But he has major help from Sim, richly larger than life as a penny-dreadful novelist who must become a petty thief, Cole as a meek cashier who must pretend to hold up his own bank and Joyce Grenfell as a gurglingly schoolgirlish ATS officer. Audrey Hepburn sparkles briefly as a cigarette girl in one of her earliest film appearances.

Laura ○ ⓥ
1944, US, 88 mins, b/w
Dir: Otto Preminger
Stars: Dana Andrews, Gene Tierney, Clifton Webb, Vincent Price
Rating: ★★★★

Superb dark thriller which made Otto Preminger's name as a director. It also clinched a sensational comeback for silent-screen actor Clifton Webb as the caustic radio star in love with the murdered Laura (Gene Tierney), and deservedly won an Academy Award for cameraman Joseph La Shelle, whose moody, ominously shadowed photography dominates the film.

Laurel and Hardy's Laughing Twenties ☉ ⓥ
1965, US, 90 mins, b/w
Dir: Various
Stars: Stan Laurel, Oliver Hardy
Rating: ★★★★★

One of the funniest films that is ever likely to come your way. Here are Stan Laurel and Oliver Hardy, wearing their angelic expressions, like small boys caught with catapults behind their backs. See them as musicians in 'You're Darn Tootin', waiters in

'From Soup to Nuts' and housebuilders in 'The Finishing Touch'. A scream.

Lavender Hill Mob, The ⊙ Ⓥ
1951, UK, 78 mins, b/w
Dir: Charles Crichton
Stars: Alec Guinness, Stanley Holloway, Sidney James, Alfie Bass
Rating: ★★★★★

Probably the zenith of the Ealing Studios comedies, never surpassed for sheer inventive meritment. Alec Guinness and Stanley Holloway revel in the witty script, bringing a featherlight comedy touch to the roles of the bank employee and his friend who plot a million-pound bullion robbery from their seedy boarding house. Even the small roles are immaculately played: one especially remembers Meredith Edwards (27th on the cast list!) as a harassed Welsh policeman. And there's a real bonus for star-spotters: the appearance of Audrey Hepburn (in her first year in British films) as a Brazilian señorita!

Law and Disorder ⊙ Ⓥ
1958, UK, 76 mins, b/w
Dir: Charles Crichton
Stars: Michael Redgrave, Robert Morley, Elizabeth Sellars
Rating: ★★★

It's unusual to find Michael Redgrave in a comedy this broad, but the script by 'Tibby' Clarke, Patrick Campbell and Vivienne Knight – ensures that there's a true Ealing flavour to this story of a confidence trickster who just can't stay out of trouble. Joan Hickson is a scream as the con-man's card-sharping sister.

Law and Order ○
1953, US, 80 mins, colour
Dir: Nathan Juran
Stars: Ronald Reagan, Dorothy Malone, Preston Foster
Rating: ★★

A rather free adaptation of *My Darling Clementine* (in which the real-life brothers Earp were the heroes), this vigorous Western has good performances from Ronald Reagan and Preston Foster who play the hero and the villain respectively. And Dennis 'McCloud' Weaver is a bad guy too.

Law and the Lady, The ○
1951, US, 104 mins, b/w
Dir: Edwin H Knopf
Stars: Greer Garson, Michael Wilding, Fernando Lamas
Rating: ★★

This comedy about two elegant tricksters (smoothly played by Greer Garson and Michael Wilding) who rob the rich to feed themselves is a remake of *The Last of Mrs Cheyney*. Majorie Main scores as a garrulous woman.

Lawless Street, A ○
1955, US, 78 mins, colour
Dir: Joseph H Lewis
Stars: Randolph Scott, Angela Lansbury, Warner Anderson, Jean Parker, Wallace Ford, Ruth Donnelly
Rating: ★★★

This Randolph Scott Western is another powerful drama from the hands of Joseph H Lewis, who directed *7th Cavalry* and *Gun Crazy*. It fits in well with Scott's Fifties gallery of men with things they must prove and things they must do. This time, he's a town marshal whose wife leaves him because he refuses to quit the job when an influx of dangerous outlaws makes his town a grim place to live in. Badly shot up by hired killers, the marshal can't throw away his principles even if it means his death. Better value than many bigger films, with biting performances from Scott, Angela Lansbury, Warner Anderson, Wallace Ford, Jean Parker and James Bell.

Lawman ●
1970, US, 99 mins, colour
Dir: Michael Winner
Stars: Burt Lancaster, Robert Ryan, Lee J Cobb, Sheree North, Robert Duvall
Rating: ★★

Michael Winner's first American picture saw him taking Horace Greeley's advice 'Go West, young man' and heading for New Mexico to make this tough and violent Western, which he directed with his usual vigour and rather too many zooms. A good cast work well with the British director, among them Burt Lancaster, Robert Ryan, Lee J Cobb (looking somewhat different without his usual toupee), Sheree North and one-time Bond villain Dr No, Joseph Wiseman. Too much blood and guts though.

Lawnmower Man, The ● Ⓥ
1992, US, 105 mins, colour
Dir: Brett Leonard
Stars: Jeff Fahey, Pierce Brosnan, Jenny Wright, Geoffrey Lewis, Austin O'Brien, Jeremy Slate
Rating: ★★★

Stunning computer-based graphic effects ('virtual reality') make you gasp while lines in the script make you giggle: pretty much a formula horror film then, but above par for a Stephen King adaptation. Men are dabbling once more in things Best Left Alone in a world where 'I have to run some tests' can have the most sinister implications. 'Goddam it Caroline,' snarls Pierce Brosnan at the start. 'Never unplug a programme while I'm engaged.' He's just ratty 'cos the chimp at the lab has gone berserk and bumped off a couple of scientists. Brosnan blames the mindblowing computer programmes he's subjected the chimp to: and he's right. But that doesn't stop him plucking a retarded man (Jeff Fahey) from lawnmowing duties to provide him with his first human subject. All pretty ludicrous, with interest kept alive by state-of-the-art effects rather than the actors.

Lawnmower Man 2 Beyond Cyberspace ○ Ⓥ
1995, US, 96 mins, colour
Dir: Farhad Mann
Stars: Patrick Bergin, Matt Frewer, Ely Pouget, Austin O'Brien
Rating: ★★

Expensive-looking and cheap-sounding, this is a cheeky B-movie sequel, with some awful dialogue, to the groundbreaking virtual reality thriller. This one has the ring of Hollywood science-fiction of decades earlier about it, as Jobe, the fallen simpleton turned-genius, is reconstituted by a clutch of alternately well-meaning and ambitious scientists. In no time at all, he's in charge of the whole computer network at their HQ and is not unnaturally plotting to take over the entire world. This is clearly time to recall gone-native ace scientist Trace (Patrick Bergin in ringlets) and the expected duel along cybernetic corridors soon materialises. There's a group of well-scrubbed street kids in Bergin's corner, as well as the ex-lady love scientist (Ely Pouget) who comes back to him. How can they lose? Bergin and Matt Frewer are quite good, whereas no one else is any good at all and the plot's serial-like developments are reminiscent of those Republic matinee cliffhangers of blackand-white days.

Law of the Lawless ○
1963, US, 88 mins, colour
Dir: William Claxton
Stars: Dale Robertson, Yvonne De Carlo, William Bendix, Bruce Cabot, Barton MacLane
Rating: ★★★

The first of a series of star Westerns made on tight budgets by producer A

L

C Lyles at Paramount in the Sixties. They featured many well-known Hollywood names from the Fifties who had seemed to be fading from the scene with the removal of the studio double-feature schedules. In its quiet, occasionally actionful way, this story of a frontier judge (Dale Robertson) was one of the best films Lyles did.

Lawrence of Arabia ○ ⓥ
1962, UK, 221 mins, colour
Dir: David Lean
Stars: Peter O'Toole, Alec Guinness, Anthony Quinn, Jack Hawkins, Omar Sharif, Anthony Quayle
Rating: ★★★★

David Lean's epic combination of physical deeds and mental agony. Peter O'Toole shot to first-rank stardom with his performance as T E Lawrence, the mystic, inscrutable young Army officer who started off by loving the desert and its way of life, and ended, two action-filled years later, half-demented and hating every grain of sand. O'Toole's strange, brooding portrait of Lawrence marked him out as an actor of the first magnitude. But there is also Anthony Quinn's very intelligently played Arab chief, I S Johar's marvellously human Gasim; Donald Wolfit's one-scene triumph as an army officer; and Alec Guinness' Feisal, almost as indefinable a character as Lawrence himself. Early scenes of the desert are especially moving, as is Lawrence's relationship with a Bedouin who is shortly to be killed by a tribal chief.

Lawyer, The ●
1968, US, 117 mins, colour
Dir: Sidney J Furie
Stars: Barry Newman, Diana Muldaur, Robert Colbert, Kathleen Crowley
Rating: ★★★

Barry Newman gives a high-pressure performance as the young lawyer who antagonises the legal profession and, it seems, an entire town, in the course of defending an unco-operative client. Director Sidney J Furie's restless cameras bob and weave their way through a mass of intrigue in this diverting thriller. Newman later revived his character to form the basis for his successful *Petrocelli* TV series.

Laxdale Hall ☉
1953, UK, 77 mins, b/w
Dir: John Eldridge
Stars: Raymond Huntley, Ronald Squire, Kathleen Ryan, Sebastian Shaw
Rating: ★★

Whimsical, refreshing comedy, much along the lines of *Whisky Galore!*. Ronald Squire is in fine blustering form as the leader of the rebel Hebridean islanders who refuse to pay their road fund licences until a new road and pier are provided by officialdom.

Leading Man, The ● ⓥ
1996, UK, 99 mins, colour
Dir: John Duigan
Stars: Jon Bon Jovi, Lambert Wilson, Thandie Newton, Anna Galiena, David Warner, Patricia Hodge
Rating: ★★

This slight romantic drama is a little on the slow side, but the ironies of its situations may keep you watching. Things are less clear-cut at the end than they were in the beginning, but then perhaps that's showbiz life. Playwright Felix (Wilson) is having an affair with starlet Hillary (Newton) to the dismay of his vivacious wife (Galiena). Salvation appears to come along in the shape of charismatic American leading man Robin (Bon Jovi) who, having slept his way through Hollywood, suggests seducing Felix's wife as a way of passing the time pleasurably while helping the harassed writer out of his marriage. On the sly, the amoral Robin plans to bed Hillary as well, but that, like most things in the story, doesn't *quite* work out. There's not much more than an hour's worth of drama here, but Bon Jovi is quite a charmer and steers it through. Supporting acting's a bit variable.

League of Gentlemen, The ○
1959, UK, 114 mins, b/w
Dir: Basil Dearden
Stars: Jack Hawkins, Nigel Patrick, Richard Attenborough, Roger Livesey, Bryan Forbes, Kieron Moore
Rating: ★★★

No better tribute to the acting style of British bulldog Jack Hawkins could be screened than this stylish crime film which paces its laughs and thrills in equal proportions. This was one of Bryan Forbes' first big film breakthroughs as a writer. He also plays one of the 'gentlemen' who plan a well-devised raid on an army camp.

League of Their Own, A ○ ⓥ
1992, US, 124 mins, colour
Dir: Penny Marshall
Stars: Geena Davis, Lori Petty, Madonna, Tom Hanks, Megan Cavanagh, Jon Lovitz
Rating: ★★★

Tom Hanks buries his clean-cut image to be suitably disgusting as the baccy-spitting, hard-drinking, unshaven ex-pro coach of one of the first all-girl baseball teams in this often entertaining comedy. The girls got their chance in 1943 because of the lack of wartime manpower and, although at first the public stayed away in droves, the women's game inevitably threw up front-page stars of its own. Tall Geena Davis is the team's ace catcher, Lori Singer as her kid sister is the pitcher, stand-up comedienne Megan Cavanagh the grim-looking star hitter and Madonna, of course, the team sex-bomb. Though the film seems forced and artificial in its earlier scenes, it gradually wins you over in the familiar progression of its story to the final game. There are enough poignant and funny moments – especially in the final come-uppance of the too-bad-to-be-true fat kid of one of the players – to make this league a winner on points.

Leap of Faith ○ ⓥ
1992, US, 107 mins, colour
Dir: Richard Pearce
Stars: Steve Martin, Debra Winger, Liam Neeson, Lolita Davidovich, Lukas Haas, Meat Loaf
Rating: ★★★★★

It's not often that a film hits every nail on the head but this is one. Steve Martin stars in his best non-comedy role to this time as Jonas Nightengale, con-man turned fake faith healer and razzmatazz preacher. A story of 'faith, hope and fraud', the film centres on Nightengale's visit to Rustwater, Kansas, where the glitz of his show – clairvoyancy and fake miracles are laid on by his faithful team, headed by master technician Debra Winger, who feeds him information through an earpiece – almost rivals a Las Vegas nightclub. Winger is wooed by the sheriff (Liam Neeson), who is nonetheless determined to expose Martin as a ne'er-do-well. But some strange things are destined to happen in Rustwater before Jonas' 'circus' leaves town. Martin, a mass of nervous energy, whose eyes are always open to the main chance, is right on the money as Jonas, never putting a strutting foot wrong, even when cavorting on the catwalk of Christ. He dominates even such good actors as Winger and Neeson in this totally diverting and fizzingly paced light-hearted version of *Elmer Gantry*.

Lease of Life ○
1954, UK, 94 mins, colour
Dir: Charles Frend

Stars: Robert Donat, Kay Walsh, Denholm Elliott, Adrienne Corn
Rating: ★★

Sincere if stilted melodrama with a sensitive performance by Robert Donat as the vicar with a year to live. In his impromptu sermon to a congregation of schoolboys, the performance of this remarkable actor, whose career was blighted by chronic asthma, bristles with emotion, excitement and truth.

Leather Boys, The ○ ⓥ
1964, UK, 108 mins, b/w
Dir: Sidney J Furie
Stars: Rita Tushingham, Colin Campbell, Dudley Sutton
Rating: ★★★

Sensitive acting from Colin Campbell as a ton-up boy who marries young and regrets it. Rita Tushingham has a rare unsympathetic role as a bride who all too soon yearns for the bright lights – motorcycle headlamps, that is.

Leather Saint, The ○
1956, US, 86 mins, b/w
Dir: Alvin Ganzer
Stars: John Derek, Paul Douglas, Jody Lawrance, Cesar Romero
Rating: ★★★

Hollywood boxing films are almost always good value for money. And this solid story about a priest with a knockout punch is no exception. John Derek is the KO curate and Paul Douglas puts in some good work as his adviser.

Leaving Las Vegas ● ⓥ
1995, US, 112 mins, colour
Dir: Mike Figgis
Stars: Nicolas Cage, Elisabeth Shue, Julian Sands, Valeria Golino, Richard Lewis
Rating: ★★★

A gruelling descent into the abyss of human despair, this brilliantly acted but terminally depressing film leaves a nasty aftertaste – and not just of booze. Ben (Nicolas Cage), inevitably fired from his job because of his alcoholism, heads for the world's gambling capital where he reckons he can drink himself to death inside a month. He pairs up with a prostitute (Elisabeth Shue), but few will expect a happy ending here and it duly fails to arrive. Cage is horrifyingly good and won the year's Oscar for best actor. Shue, Oscar-nominated, is a revelation. Hardly a light evening out, though; the whole thing's a sobering experience.

Leaving Normal ● ⓥ
1992, US, 110 mins, colour
Dir: Edward Zwick
Stars: Christine Lahti, Meg Tilly, Lenny Van Dohlen, Maury Chaykin, James Gammon
Rating: ★★★

Although its collection of adventures on the road don't give it the impetus of the contemporary *Thelma & Louise*, this is still a captivating female buddy road movie, starring Meg Tilly in one of her most beguiling turns as the sweet, innocent Marianne, running away from her unpleasant husband. She's partnered by Christine Lahti in an untypical role, subduing her natural warmnth to play the tough, cynical, dislikeable Darly, fleeing from all of her unhappy past. How these two sad souls leave Normal, Wyoming, and become pals on the road as they try to find their own paths to joy forms a bittersweet tale that's well-acted, well-observed, well-directed and certainly well worth watching.

Left Hand of God, The ○
1955, US, 87 mins, colour
Dir: Edward Dmytryk
Stars: Humphrey Bogart, Gene Tierney, Lee J Cobb, Agnes Moorehead, E G Marshall
Rating: ★★

Humphrey Bogart's second to last film provides him with the unusual role of an adventurer trying to escape, dressed as a priest, from the vengeance of a war lord – a role in which Lee J Cobb proves surprisingly effective. The hand of director Edward Dmytryk tends to weigh rather heavily on the proceedings, but Bogart sees it through, and Gene Tierney is as gorgeous as ever as the girl who believes she is falling in love with someone she can't marry.

Left, Right and Centre ○
1959, UK, 105 mins, b/w
Dir: Sidney Gilliat
Stars: Ian Carmichael, Patricia Bredin, Alastair Sim
Rating: ★★★

Frank Launder and Sidney Gilliat gleefully send up both British politics and the effect that television had on them in those dear distant days three decades ago when the swingometer wasn't even an electronic dot on the TV screen. Ian Carmichael and Alastair Sim combine to steal the show, while then TV luminaries Gilbert Harding, Eamonn Andrews and Josephine Douglas are on hand to add verisimilitude.

Legacy, The ●
1978, UK, 100 mins, colour
Dir: Richard Marquand
Stars: Katharine Ross, Sam Elliott, John Standing, Roger Daltrey
Rating: ★

Up at the old mansion they're dying off like flies. Bloodcurdling shrieks in the middle of the night and the like. And they do say the house is full of cats. This grisly story has more loose ends than poor Hildegarde Neil seems to have pints of blood. But if your tastes run to Hammer Horror meeting *Carrie* and *Ten Little Niggers*, it could be right up your *Nightmare Alley*.

Legal Eagles ● ⓥ
1986, US, 116 mins, colour
Dir: Ivan Reitman
Stars: Robert Redford, Debra Winger, Daryl Hannah, Brian Dennehy, Terence Stamp
Rating: ★★★

This legal caper thriller is a bit like a highly superior TV movie. Robert Redford's at the centre of it, but has to concede the acting honours to Debra Winger. She is outstanding as a gutsy lawyer determined to root out the truth about the 18-year-old blaze that killed the painter father of the tall blonde (Daryl Hannah) currently on a murder charge. Good entertaimnent, not too demanding, directed with polish by Ivan Reitman of *GhostBusters* fame. Although a shade light on credibility, the story's so craftily contrived around a few set-pieces that a lot of it works.

Legend ○ ⓥ
1985, US, 94 mins, colour
Dir: Ridley Scott
Stars: Tom Cruise, Mia Sara, Tim Curry
Rating: ★★

This is the film that Tom Cruise perhaps wishes he hadn't made. It took a whole year of his fife, and he was labelled an insipid hero by critics. A fairy tale on a grand scale, the film is everything we have come to expect from Ridley Scott (*Alien*, *Thelma & Louise*), with stunning visuals, epic sets and a battle between good and evil. However, its major problems are with the script, where it borrows heavily from *Jack and the Beanstalk*, *A Midsummer Night's Dream* and *Peter Pan*, but has little wit or wisdom of its own. Still, Tim Curry is the most memorable Devil for decades.

Legend of Billie Jean, The ●
1985, US, 95 mins, colour
Dir: Matthew Robbins

L

Stars: Helen Slater, Christian Slater, Peter Coyote
Rating: ★★

Helen Slater was unlucky with this follow-up to her starring debut in *Supergirl*. It wasn't as successful as it deserved to be, and co-star Christian Slater (no relation) not the major star he was soon to become. Both Slaters are good in a story of teens on the run from the law, but any message gets lost in the film's top-dressing and the adults, although played by good actors – Peter Coyote, Richard Bradford, Dean Stockwell – emerge as caricatures rather than characters.

Legend of the Lost ○
1957, US, 107 mins, colour
Dir: Henry Hathaway
Stars: John Wayne, Sophia Loren, Rossano Brazzi
Rating: ★★

Timbuktu is the background for this mostly dull action yarn about the search for a lost city in the desert and a fabulous treasure. John Wayne swaps his horse for a camel, but otherwise remains very much the same Big John (complete with stetson) as a desert adventurer with the unlikely name of Joe January. There's a very exciting last reel as the characters battle for the treasure, and their lives, in a sandstorm.

Legends of the Fall ● ⓥ
1994, US, 133 mins, colour
Dir: Edward Zwick
Stars: Anthony Hopkins, Brad Pitt, Aidan Quinn, Henry Thomas, Julia Ormond, Karina Lombard
Rating: ★★

An epic of the Far West as grim and miserable as it's long. No lasting happiness awaits any of the characters here, any more than it does the audience, save the joy of James Horner's sweeping music, which lifts many a sagging scene. Anthony Hopkins, progressively further over the top as the film goes on, is the horse rancher in the Montana wilds with three sons: the oldest, law-abiding Alfred (Aidan Quinn); the youngest, idealistic Samuel (Henry Thomas); and the middle son Tristan, a man of the earth (Brad Pitt). The catalyst for tragedy is Susannah (Julia Ormond), initially Samuel's fiancée but, this being a romantic epic, loved by all three brothers and drawn to Tristan, the most basic. Ormond, a British actress whose expressive face is not here matched by conviction of voice, sits uneasily at the heart of this manly tale, with its bursts of violent action – all three brothers enlist in World War One – and pretensions to grandeur which come across as ponderous. Still, there are one or two striking moments. Quinn gives the best performance by some way.

Le Mans ○
1971, US, 108 mins, colour
Dir: Lee H Katzin
Stars: Steve McQueen, Eiga Andersen, Siegfried Rauch
Rating: ★★

This is probably the most realistic film about motor racing ever made and also the most single-minded. Whereas most other racing films have had a sub-plot strong enough to keep the attention of those not interested in racing cars, the one here seems an afterthought. Race fans will find it an irritating gap in the action and it doesn't have enough meat for anyone else. Steve McQueen is Delaney, a driver on the Porsche team determined to win the Le Mans 24-hour endurance race and beat his main rival, Ferrari driver Erich Stahler. He also forms a hesitant relationship with Lisa, widow of a driver killed during the previous year's race. The race scenes (of which there are many) are exciting, noisy and atmospheric.

Lemon Drop Kid, The ○
1951, US, 91 mins, b/w
Dir: Sidney Lanfield
Stars: Bob Hope, Marilyn Maxwell, Lloyd Nolan, Jane Darwell
Rating: ★★★

Bob Hope works overtime at getting the gags in this racing comedy about a racetrack bookie, 'The Lemon Drop Kid', who gives a gangster a sure bet that loses. As the bad guys try to get the money back – or deliver Hope's head on a plate – the jokes come thick and fast. Based on a Damon Runyon and Edmund Beloin story, it has colourful characters with equally colourful names, such as Sam the Surgeon, No Thumbs Charlie and Gloomy Willie. Under Sidney Lanfield's zippy direction, it's anything but gloomy.

Lemon Sisters, The ◖
1989, US, 93 mins, colour
Dir: Joyce Chopra
Stars: Diane Keaton, Carol Kane, Kathryn Grody, Elliott Gould
Rating: ★★

Although it's decidedly quirky and has some purple patches, this rather wan comedy (about three friends who formed a singing group that's breaking up as the movie starts), which is also occasionally irritating and endearing in turn, is unlikely to make you laugh a lot. The script is very sub-*Beaches* and the one really funny scene comes when Keaton's cats fight to eat her dinner while she's trying to hold a conversation. The men, Gould, Ruben Blades and Aidan Quinn, give selfless, almost faceless support. And the bleakness of the Atlantic City coastline is flawlessly captured. Ultimately, though, this is a movie that promises much and never quite delivers. The actresses do their own singing, though the plot demands, unfortunately, that they don't do it very well.

Lenny ● ⓥ
1974, US, 111 mins, b/w
Dir: Bob Fosse
Stars: Dustin Hoffman, Valerie Perrine, Jan Miner
Rating: ★★★

This close-up of the 'dirty' American night-club comedian Lenny Bruce is a hard hitting film, but also one that proves difficult to watch. And too brief a glimpse is given of Lenny (edgily played by Dustin Hoffman) at his abrasive best on stage, giving the impression that, as a comedian, he was somewhat unfunny. Hoffman and the exquisite Valerie Perrine try their hardest as Lenny and his junkie-stripper wife: she is particularly heart-rending and shows, here at least, an impressive naturalistic acting style. Perhaps Lenny's environment, which gave birth to his humour, also did for him in the end. The thought is sad and depressing, rather like the film. Nominated for all four major Oscars (actor, actress, film, and director), it won none in the event.

Léon ● ⓥ
(aka: The Professional)
1994, France/US, 106 mins, colour
Dir: Luc Besson
Stars: Jean Reno, Gary Oldman, Natalie Portman, Danny Aiello
Rating: ★★

This is the one about the deadly hitman who's invulnerable as long as he works alone. But Léon (Jean Reno), a French assassin at large in America, is doomed from the moment he opens his door to a 12-year-old (Natalie Portman) whose family has just been massacred by a posse of corrupt policemen after the father has double-crossed them in a drugs heist. We know it and probably Léon knows it too. A streetwise waif playing truant from school, the girl latches herself onto Léon, who begins to teach her the rudiments of his trade. But her heart's desire for revenge on the cops is destined to make their relationship short but sweet. The story sometimes gets as silly and OTT as the performance of Gary Oldman as the psycho-cop villain (who seems to command men by the score), but there is no denying the efficiency of its action and the entertainment it provides. Portman is good, though she might have brought a little more toughness to the role. The hangdog Reno never quite rings true as the assassin.

Leon the Pig Farmer ❶ ⓥ
1992, UK, 104 mins, colour
Dir: Vadim Jean, Gary Sinyor
Stars: Mark Frankel, Janet Suzman, Brian Glover, Connie Booth, Maryam D'Abo, Gina Bellman
Rating: ★★

This home-grown comedy about Leon (Mark Frankel), a Jewish boy who discovers he is really the son of a Yorkshire pig farmer, is more or less a one-joke film. But the joke is sustained to a degree both by its offbeat characters and by the amusing performances of Connie Booth and Brian Glover as Leon's Yorkshire parents, taking down the pigs' heads that adorn their walls and adopting Jewish mannerisms to make Leon feel at home. Despite Frankel's rather one-note and permanently bemused portrayal of the title character, this is a charmingly offensive little comic number and certainly an original.

Leopard, The ◯
1963, Italy, 205 mins, colour
Dir: Luchino Visconti
Stars: Burt Lancaster, Alain Delon, Claudia Cardinale
Rating: ★★★

Historical fihn of great beauty, directed with care and superb understanding of the period and its people by Luchino Visconti. The period is 1860 in Sicily the time of the revolt of Garibaldi redshirts – which gives rise to spurts of action – and dynasties of noblemen dying out. In one superb scene, Visconti pans over one princely family sitting in church. Their days are numbered and they know it. Sitting in their pew, they already look enshrouded with dust. Avoid the shortened Hollywood version if possible.

Les Girls ◯ ⓥ
1957, US, 110 mins, colour
Dir: George Cukor
Stars: Gene Kelly, Mitzi Gaynor, Kay

Kendall, Taina Elg
Rating: ★★★

With a starry cast headed by Gene Kelly, Mitzi Gaynor and Kay Kendall, songs by Cole Porter and direction by George Cukor, this colourful musical had all the winning ingredients. If it doesn't quite live up to *Singin' in the Rain* or *An American in Paris*, it's still a delightful piece of escapism. Kendall, a former dancer, ends up in court after publishing her memoirs about her days with Barry Nichols and Les Girls (herself, Kelly, Gaynor and Taina Elg). All the musical interludes are in flashback as each member of the troupe recalls their days in showbiz.

Les Miserables ◯
1935, US, 109 mins, b/w
Dir: Richard Boleslawski
Stars: Fredric March, Charles Laughton, Cedric Hardwicke, Rochelle Hudson
Rating: ★★★

A typical Hollywood historical classic, made with meticulous attention to detail, and with commanding leading performances from Fredric March as the hounded Valjean and Charles Laughton as the relentless Javert. Fine direction by Richard Boleslawski ensures that not a second of the near two-hour actual running time is wasted.

Les Miserables ◯
1952, US, 106 mins, b/w
Dir: Lewis Milestone
Stars: Michael Rennie, Robert Newton, Edmund Gwenn, Debra Paget
Rating: ★★

Middling rendition with a star-studded cast doing little more than going through the motions. Would-be poignant scenes are emotionally unimpressive, while the focus of the story is shifted too often from the plight of Jean Valjean (Michael Rennie) to the revolutionary ideas of student Cameron Mitchell. Newton for once chooses (wrongly) not to give a full-blooded performance as the obsessed Javert. But atmosphere, production values and photography (by Joseph La Shelle) are all top-notch. A bit of a trudge.

Les Misérables ❶ ⓥ
1995, FR, 177 mins, colour
Dir: Claude Lelouch
Stars: Jean-Paul Belmondo, Michel Boujenah, Alessandra Martinés, Annie Girardot, Jean Marais
Rating: ★★★

Nothing comes easily in a Claude Lelouch film, and thank goodness

there's an upbeat ending here or, after three hours' hard slog, we'd all be trudging home like the 'misérables' of the title. This 50-year epic merely uses the famous Hugo story as a basis. Jean-Paul Belmondo is a chauffeur unjustly imprisoned for murder after the suicide of his employer, a fake count on the run from the law. From here on, everything moves in circles like the dancers at the beginning and end. Actions and events repeat themselves in different parts of the story. The main body of the film concerns Belmondo's middle-aged son (also Belmondo), now involved on the fringes of ctime, and his attempts to help a Jewish couple (Michel Boujenah, Alessandra Martinés) flee from the Nazis in 1939. Betrayed in flight, they and their daughter (enchantingly played by the director's daughter Salomé) undergo a three-way separation which leads to a typically Lelouchian resolution of triumph through hardship and adversity. Good performances throughout.

Less Than Zero ● ⓥ
1987, US, 98 mins, colour
Dir: Marek Kanievska
Stars: Andrew McCarthy, Jami Gertz, Robert Downey Jr, James Spader, Tony Bill, Nicholas Pryor
Rating: ★★

This drugs movie is well-meaning and, in parts, well-performed, but its one-note march to death makes it a bit of a drag to watch. Young college student Andrew McCarthy tries to help junkie ex-schoolfriend Robert Downey Jr, who stole the girlfriend (Jami Gertz) who finds getting back together with McCarthy easier than giving up cocaine. Downey himself is well and truly in the clutches of the local pusher (James Spader, whose oily crocodile is the best thing he does) for the tune of $50,000 and soon reduced to becoming a rent boy to stay even on the debt. A sad tale and one told without too much spark. McCarthy is overly mannered as the hero, Gertz offers the best display of cleavage since Raquel Welch quit the screen and Downey, acting them both out of sight, is effectively pathetic and drug-ridden as the elusive Julian.

Let 'Em Have It ◯
1935, US, 90 mins, b/w
Dir: Sam Wood
Stars: Richard Arlen, Virginia Bruce, Bruce Cabot, Alice Brady
Rating: ★★★

L

The title of this vintage gangster movie was too strong for its first issue outside America and it was changed to *False Faces*. Some of the scenes are strong stuff, too, and very effective, particularly the famous sequence in which mobster Bruce Cabot 'silences' the surgeon who has changed his face by plastic surgery, only to find, on removing the bandages, that the man has carved the gangster's own initials on his 'new' face.

Let George Do It ○
1940, UK, 82 mins, b/w
Dir: Marcel Varnel
Stars: George Formby, Phyllis Calvert
Rating: ★★★

A wartime Formby comedy, with our ukulele-toting hero getting mixed up with naval spies. There's time for a ditty or two in George's own inimitable style, including 'Mr Wu's a Window-Cleaner Now'. Bernard Lee, as a character called Slim, and Garry Marsh, as the villainous Mendez, provide poker-faced support.

Lethal Weapon ● ⓥ
1987, US, 110 mins, colour
Dir: Richard Donner
Stars: Mel Gibson, Danny Glover, Gary Busey, Mitchell Ryan
Rating: ★★★

Mel Gibson was never more lethal at the world's box-offices than in this typical Hollywood vigilante cop thriller with crackling dialogue, a protracted, exciting shoot-out climax, a few boring patches to pad it out and as many illogicalities in the plot as a James Bond film. He's a crackshot, loner cop still broodingly suicidal after the death of his wife in a road accident. Gibson's John Wayne-style American accent seems appropriate for the kind of shoot-out film that has these days replaced the Western while retaining many of its key elements. Danny Glover also does quite well as the near-ing-retirement cop who unwillingly takes Mad Mel as his partner, and Gary Busey, a chameleon actor one can only recognise by his teeth, is a solid albino villain.

Lethal Weapon 2 ● ⓥ
1989, US, 110 mins, colour
Dir: Richard Donner
Stars: Mel Gibson, Danny Glover, Joe Pesci, Joss Ackland, Patsy Kensit
Rating: ★★★★

An all-action sequel to the blockbuster original, with Mel Gibson and Glover back as the unlikely partners-against-

crime. This time they tangle with some evil South Africans running drugs under the shelter of diplomatic immunity. Thank goodness Mel goes berserk and flashes his smile at times: it adds a human element to the James Bond style thrills, staged in expert, polished fashion by director Donner, with more explosions than a gung-ho war film. Patsy Kensit is along to prove that all South Africans aren't bad, in what is marginally the best of the three *Lethal Weapon* movies to date.

Lethal Weapon 3 ● ⓥ
1992, US, 118 mins, colour
Dir: Richard Donner
Stars: Mel Gibson, Danny Glover, Joe Pesci, René Russo, Stuart Wilson
Rating: ★★

This long-serving police vehicle has distinct signs of 'Running down, please pass' stamped all over it here. There's good action at either end of the third Mel Gibson/Danny Glover police thriller in the series, but not much of a story in between, to say nothing of a distinctly soft centre and a frantically joky approach which betrays the film's lack of real ideas. Gibson and Glover have done better: the second film, in particular, was fun because they developed their relationship; but the third reveals they have nowhere left to go. Joe Pesci supplies a few good laughs in the film's rapid-fire style. But overall a quick tow to the pound is called for: this 'weapon' has had its day.

'Let Him Have It' ● ⓥ
1991, UK, 118 mins, colour
Dir: Peter Medak
Stars: Chris Eccleston, Paul Reynolds, Tom Courtenay, Tom Bell, Eileen Atkins
Rating: ★★★★

Britain's Craig/Bentley case of 1952 was an emotive issue at the time, and it still is today. It seemed then that everybody knew there had been a miscarriage of justice, even without the knowledge that the 19-year-old Bentley was an epileptic with a mental age of 11. This is largely a solid and careful reconstruction of Bentley's background and the events that led to his conviction. Bentley was much under the influence of 16-year-old tearaway Christopher Craig, and both were caught on the roof of a Croydon warehouse by police. Craig pulled a gun, the police told him to hand it over, Bentley allegedly shouted 'Let him have it, Chris', and a policeman was shot dead. The whole case for the murder charge against Bentley hinged

on those words, and to this day their meaning looks as 50/50 as it did then. The acting, especially from Eccleston and Reynolds as the teenagers, couldn't be bettered. See it for sure, and shake your head that it ever happened.

Let's Dance! ⊙
1950, US, 112 mins, colour
Dir: Norman Z McLeod
Stars: Betty Hutton, Fred Astaire, Roland Young, Ruth Warrick, Barton MacLane
Rating: ★★

No one should be surprised that Betty Hutton, at her peak when this musical was made, matches *Daddy Long Legs* Fred Astaire for vitality. She also proves adept at dogging his dance steps in their one full-scale routine together. And she provides the best piece of comedy in the film – getting herself, her son and two large suitcases trapped in a dog kennel with a Great Dane called Hamlet!

Let's Do It Again! ○
1953, US, 95 mins, colour
Dir: Alexander Hall
Stars: Jane Wyman, Ray Milland, Aldo Ray, Leon Ames
Rating: ★★★

One of the more successful remakes of the Fifties, a champagne musical re-modelling of the Cary Grant-Irene Dunne Oscar-winning 1937 comedy, *The Awful Truth*. Jane Wyman steps out in style after the gloom of *Johnny Belinda* and *The Blue Veil*, as a gay would-be divorcee off to Reno to sever all connections with her girlchasing, jazz-mad husband. Good Technicolor photography by Charles Lawton and smooth support for Ms Wyman from Ray Milland and Tom Helmore.

Let's Do It Again ○
1975, US, 110 mins, colour
Dir: Sidney Poitier
Stars: Sidney Poitier, Bill Cosby, Calvin Lockhart
Rating: ★★

Quite a lively all-black piece that just gets by as a likeable lark. It's about a couple of working men who make a mint by hypnotising a useless boxer into winning a world championship. Director Sidney Poitier keeps it bouncing along well for most of its running time, even though it sags at the beginning and slumps at the end. His acting forte, though, isn't comedy, and his own over-playing compares badly with the laid-back performances of such experienced comedy men as Bill Cosby and Jimmie Walker. The dialogue is pretty variable, but fast and nutty at its best; a pity this isn't a more consistent dose of laughter.

Let's Make Up
See: Lilacs in the Spring

Letter, The ○
1940, US, 95 mins, b/w
Dir: William Wyler
Stars: Bette Davis, Herbert Marshall, James Stephenson, Gale Sondergaard
Rating: ★★★★

Easily the best of several film versions of Somerset Maugham's story of murder in Malaya, Bette Davis winning yet another Oscar nomination (and really unlucky to lose to Ginger Rogers for *Kitty Foyle*) with a smouldering, predatory performance, absolutely hypnotic in her account of the murder that occurs at the start of the film. The plantation atmosphere, elaborately recreated in the Warner studio, is entirely convincing, and English actor James Stephenson rose to stardom with his performance as Davis' defending counsel. Alas, a year later he was dead after a heart attack. Censorship of the day demanded a changed ending, but the new one, underplayed by director William Wyler, is effective nonetheless.

Letter to Brezhnev ● Ⓥ
1985, UK, 94 mins, colour
Dir: Chris Bernard
Stars: Alexandra Pigg, Peter Firth, Margi Clarke, Neil Cunningham
Rating: ★★★

Forceful, lively, raunchy and full of imagination and creative energy. The backdrop of Liverpool and its clubs is gaudy but vital, just like the two central characters: short-skirted, wisecracking, street-smart dollies unashamedly out for a good time. The girls are soaringly well played in quite matter-of-fact fashion by Margi Clarke and Alexandra Pigg, neither of whom subsequently got the roles their talents deserved.

Letter to Three Wives, A ○
1949, US, 102 mins, b/w
Dir: Joseph L Mankiewicz
Stars: Jeanne Crain, Ann Sothern, Linda Darnell, Kirk Douglas, Jeffrey Lynn, Paul Douglas
Rating: ★★★★

Biting comedy-drama that won Joseph L Mankiewicz Oscars both for his direction and his script about three small-town wives who spend an agonising time trying to guess with which one of their husbands their mutual best

friend is running off. Fine ensemble acting too – not forgetting the acid voice of the malicious letter-writer, which belongs to Celeste Holm.

Leviathan ● Ⓥ
1989, US, 98 mins, colour
Dir: George P Cosmatos
Stars: Peter Weller, Richard Crenna, Amanda Pays, Daniel Stern, Ernie Hudson, Lisa Eilbacher
Rating: ★★★

If you've seen *Alien*, *The Blob* and *Deep Star Six*, you've seen just about all in this underwater horror film has to offer. But it's excitingly done under Cosmatos' fast-paced and intense direction, and the monsters are good enough for a scare or two. And with such lines as 'Oh my God, it got the blood supply', it's almost like being back on Hammer's home ground, in the days when they used to write dialogue just like that for Peter Cushing. No prizes for guessing which of the crew here survives at the end, although excitement not unpredictability is the name of the game and it's done well enough to send us home happy. Peter Weller plays cowboy of the deep as the geologist in charge of the doomed silver-mining mission, and Amanda Pays gets to show off a pretty collection of knickers, although they really shouldn't have given her such lines as 'My astronaut training starts in two days'. Never mind, it's all good, heart-thumping stuff for addicts.

Liar Liar ◐ Ⓥ
1997, US, 87 mins, colour
Dir: Tom Shadyac
Stars: Jim Carrey, Maura Tierney, Jennifer Tilly, Amanda Donohoe, Swoosie Kurtz
Rating: ★★★★

A goofy and generally funny comedy that gets wilder and less resistible as it goes on. Lecherous, lying lawyer Fletcher Reede (Carrey) is the despair of his ex-wife (Tierney) as he never arrives on time to see his adoring son Max, since he's always in bed with a client – well, one way or another. All this changes when Max makes a wish on his fifth birthday that his dad will be unable to lie for 24 hours. Not many of the comic possibilities of this are missed, especially when Carrey feels impelled to insult the entire board of directors at his firm, or has to represent a busty blonde (Tilly) seeking her husband's assets in a divorce case. The star has a field day; as a kind of lascivious Jerry Lewis he's all over the place,

notably when beating himself to a pulp to try to get out of a court appearance. Carrey-haters will quickly become irritated with it; but go with the flow and you could find *Liar Liar* funny funny.

Liar's Moon ◐
1982, US, 107 mins, colour
Dir: David Fisher
Stars: Matt Dillon, Cindy Fisher, Christopher Connelly, Yvonne De Carlo
Rating: ★★

A star-studded love story set in small-town America in 1949. Corny but endearing, it features a charismatic performance from teen idol Matt Dillon as a farm boy very much from the wrong side of the Texas tracks, who not only upsets some influential people, but rattles an old skeleton out of the cupboard by falling for the daughter of land-rich parents. The plot may be unbelievable, but there's nothing trite about the burnished Metrocolor photography of the Texas settings by John Hora, which helps make the period spring to life.

Libeled Lady ○
1936, US, 98 mins, b/w
Dir: Jack Conway
Stars: William Powell, Jean Harlow, Spencer Tracy, Myrna Loy
Rating: ★★★★

One of the wildest, fastest and funniest of the Thirties' screwball farces, with four top stars working at full throttle. Editor Spencer Tracy is being sued by wealthy Myrna Loy and gets fiancé Jean Harlow and old enemy William Powell (who needs money) to help concoct a plan and get him off the hook. The fact that Harlow is actually married to Powell is only one of the many complications in this witty frolic, which pretty well has laughs in every scene. Sit back and enjoy.

Licence to Kill ◐ Ⓥ
1989, UK, 133 mins, colour
Dir: John Glen
Stars: Timothy Dalton, Carey Lowell, Talisa Soto, Robert Davi, Anthony Zerbe, Wayne Newton
Rating: ★★★

A royal Dalton performance, as a tougher James Bond assumes a lone wolf role to pursue a personal vendetta against the drugs baron who has maimed Bond's old pal Felix Leiter. But the girls in the case still bring out the other kind of wolf in Britain's favourite agent for over 30 years. Carey Lowell is quite a looker and a decent actress too as an adventurous charter pilot and CIA agent, while

L

Talisa Soto provides somewhat less ability but stunningly exotic looks as the mistress of chief baddie Robert Davi. The ending provides 15 minutes of sustained excitement as Bond takes on the baddies aboard petrol tankers on a rocky roadway and the action throughout, although only spasmodic, is first-rate when it comes. Dalton and Davi both convince as dangerous men on opposite sides of the law and, if the villains miss their usual quota of chances to polish off Bond when they have him at their mercy, that's 007 showbiz for you.

License to Drive ◑ ⓥ
1988, US, 88 mins, colour
Dir: Greg Beeman
Stars: Corey Haim, Corey Feldman, Carol Kane, Richard Masur
Rating: ★★

You can slip your brain into neutral for this busy but highly unoriginal teen car-chase comedy. Youngster Les (Corey Haim) flunks his driving test which blows his chances of a date with dream girl Mercedes (Heather Graham) and disappoints his buddies. So he steals his grandfather's pristine '72 Cadillac and goes out on the town anyway. You don't need to be told that the Caddy suffers a number of indignities before the end of the film. A shame, because it acts the pants off the rest of the cast. To be fair, director Greg Beeman keeps things moving at a terrific pace, which injects the film with a certain juvenile vitality.

Liebestraum ● ⓥ
1991, US, 112 mins, colour
Dir: Mike Figgis
Stars: Kevin Anderson, Pamela Gidley, Bill Pullman, Catherine Hicks, Kim Novak
Rating: ★

Deliberately slow-paced, this has little to do with reality and everything to do with filming for effect. Part ghost story, part thriller, part erotic drama and all jigsaw, it starts with a decades-old murder in a deserted building. Now, fascinated by its iron structure, architect Kevin Anderson, in town to see his dying mother, becomes equally fascinated with the wife (Pamela Gidley) of the old friend (Bill Pullman) in charge of the demolition. Given the way ex-model Gidley looks, this isn't surprising. Alas, there follows some silly come-ons by women at parties, men pointlessly staring at each other, a ludicrous brothel scene, repeated lines and long shots of people sitting around: the kind of movie that seems in retro-

spect to have been shot in slowmotion. Anderson is dour, Pullman hangdog, Gidley just too available and Catherine Hicks just ridiculous. Old-timers Kim Novak (as Anderson's mother) and Taina Elg prove hazy figures in a plot which naturally interlocks all its elements and is much more than a romantic triangle. Stylish, though, to the point of sterility.

Life and Death of Colonel Blimp, The ○
(aka: Colonel Blimp)
1943, UK, 163 mins, colour
Dir: Michael Powell
Stars: Roger Livesey, Deborah Kerr, Anton Walbrook, Roland Culver
Rating: ★★★

This controversial portrait of a stuffy British officer was condemned by the British press as being 'disastrously bad propaganda' (because of the leading character's lifelong friendship with a Prussian officer). Believing the film undermined British confidence during WWII, Prime Minister Winston Churchill became enraged after a viewing and personally banned it from being exported. Because of this outrage, the film, completed in 1943, was not shown in the US until the war had ended and even then it was heavily edited to give the British a more favourable view. The central character, Colonel Blimp (played roisterously by Roger Livesey), stems from a cartoon strip which appeared in the London *Evening Standard*. Anton Walbrook is superb as his friend, and Deborah Kerr warmth itself as all of the several women in Blimp's life.

Life at the Top ◑
1965, UK, 117 mins, b/w
Dir: Ted Kotcheff
Stars: Laurence Harvey, Jean Simmons, Honor Blackman, Michael Craig
Rating: ★★

The blackly bitter drama that follows the career of Joe Lampton, 10 years after his ruthless ascent of the social ladder in *Room at the Top*. Jean Simmons takes over the Heather Sears part, as Susan, the girl Joe married, and catches exactly the right aura of disillusionment.

Life Begins at Eight Thirty ○
(aka: The Light of Heart)
1942, US, 85 mins, b/w
Dir: Irving Pichel
Stars: Monty Woolley, Ida Lupino, Cornel Wilde
Rating: ★★★

This sentimental comedy drama hands a plum role to irascible Monty Woolley as the has-been star saddled with a crippled daughter and drowning in a sea of alcohol. Woolley makes the most of the well-rounded insults that his character is afforded by Nunnally Johnson's dialogue, but Ida Lupino, who was giving some superlative performances at this stage of her career, is more than a match for him as his daughter, creating a flesh-and-blood character with compassion, simplicity and, evidently, a great deal of forethought, in a portrayal that really tugs at your emotions.

Life Begins for Andy Hardy ○
1941, US, 101 mins, b/w
Dir: George B Seitz
Stars: Mickey Rooney, Judy Garland, Lewis Stone, Fay Holden, Ann Rutherford
Rating: ★★★

Judy Garland makes her third and most telling contribution to the Andy Hardy films in this family drama, which is the sport in the litter as far as the series is concerned and, in retrospect, the best of the series. Andy becomes involved with a divorcee and even his 'chats' with his father, Lewis Stone, show a maturity missing elsewhere in the series. And there's a fairly sombre suicide scene, the impact of which isn't ducked by director George B Seitz. To add to Garland's sensitive performance, Rooney also does his best, and certainly most well-considered work in any Andy Hardy film.

Lifeboat ○
1943, US, 96 mins, b/w
Dir: Alfred Hitchcock
Stars: Tallulah Bankhead, Walter Slezak, John Hodiak, William Bendix, Hume Cronyn, Canada Lee
Rating: ★★★

Not many directors would have dared to make an entire suspense film set on board a lifeboat, but Alfred Hitchcock did it during World War Two, and it comes off pretty well. He even squeezes in his customary guest appearance – via an advertisement for a lose weight treatment on a newspaper floating past the boat. Forthright performances by Tallulah Bankhead, William Bendix and Walter Slezak (as the only German) keep the tension crackling.

LifeForce ● ⓥ
1985, US, 101 mins, colour
Dir: Tobe Hooper
Stars: Steve Railsback, Peter Firth, Frank

Finlay, Mathilda May
Rating: ★★★★

Say what you like about Tobe (*Poltergeist*) Hooper's films – and the script of this one is pretty uneven – but they all career along like a runaway train. So it is with this *Quatermass*-like tale, made on a grand scale. A crew of astronauts that obviously hasn't seen *Alien* unwittingly brings terror from outer space back to earth, and we're set for a plot that – unusually for this kind of film – actually makes sense and gives us such gigantic and impressive set-pieces as London reeling under a veritable plague of vampirism. There are special effects to relish (the electric-blue 'lifeforce' is especially effective) and dialogue to treasure: 'The other two bodies,' orders Professor Frank Finlay sternly. 'Collect the pieces and watch them!'

Life for Ruth ○
(aka: Walk in the Shadow)
1962, UK, 91 mins, b/w
Dir: Basil Dearden
Stars: Michael Craig, Patrick McGoohan, Janet Munro
Rating: ★★★

'Problem' thriller about a father who denies his injured daughter a vital blood transfusion because of religious convictions. Patrick McGoohan gives one of his most controlled performances as a doctor and the tension rises to an agonising climax.

Lifeguard ◐
1976, US, 96 mins, colour
Dir: Daniel Petrie
Stars: Sam Elliott, Anne Archer, Stephen Young, Kathleen Quinlan
Rating: ★★

Offbeat drama about a husky, 32-year-old lifeguard, played by beefy Sam Elliott, trying to decide whether the time has come to settle for a conventional life. Interesting performances from the ladies, especially Kathleen Quinlan and Anne Archer.

Life Is Sweet ◐ ⓥ
1990, UK, 103 mins, colour
Dir: Mike Leigh
Stars: Alison Steadman, Jim Broadbent, Claire Skinner, Jane Horrocks, Timothy Spall
Rating: ★★★★

Picking up awards at practically every film festival around the globe, this certainly ranks as one of independent British director Mike Leigh's biggest movie successes to date. Casting his

real-life wife Alison Steadman in the lead role, he also provides a wonderful showcase for rising star Jane Horrocks, as her confused, anorexic daughter. As a precise observation of the British at work and play, the film is a knockout. Wonderful ensemble acting is the icing on the cake: Stephen Rea and David Thewlis, both now major stars in British films, have supporting assignments here.

Life of Emile Zola, The ○
1937, US, 116 mins, b/w
Dir: William Dieterle
Stars: Paul Muni, Joseph Schildkraut, Gale Sondergaard, Gloria Holden
Rating: ★★★★

Less a biography of the celebrated French novelist than a dramatic reconstruction of the notorious Dreyfus affair when Zola took on the French Establishment to campaign on behalf of the wrongly-imprisoned army captain who was sentenced to be jailed in the hell-hole of Devil's Island. Muni, at his best in weighty roles, is an impressive Zola but the acting honours go to Joseph Schildkraut, whose performance won him the Oscar for Best Supporting Actor. The film, too, won an Oscar, as did the screenplay. Solid entertainment, solidly directed by William Dieterle.

Life of Her Own, A ◐
1950, US, 108 mins, b/w
Dir: George Cukor
Stars: Lana Turner, Ray Milland, Tom Ewell, Louis Calhern, Ann Dvorak
Rating: ★★

This dramatic epic, with Lana Turner as a ruthless model so hell-bent to get to the top that she can't see she is also careering down the path to self-destruction, contains fine performances from Ann Dvorak as a has-been model, riddled with drugs and alcohol, and Margaret Phillips as the disabled neurotic whose husband Miss Turner is out to steal. A glossy soap opera.

Life Stinks ◐ ⓥ
1991, US, 95 mins, colour
Dir: Mel Brooks
Stars: Mel Brooks, Lesley Ann Warren, Jeffrey Tambor, Howard Morris
Rating: ★★

Brooks in Frank Capra-land. He plays a billionaire businessman who makes a bet that he can live as a derelict for 30 days. Naturally he learns a lot more about life than from the top of his ivory tower, but the twist in the plot is that all his associates (he has no

friends) double-cross him, and it seems he must remain a derelict for the rest of his life. More of a piece (and just slightly more serious) than most Brooks films, this is an entertainment whose comedy often fails, but whose overall bitter-sweet mood is quite successfully sustained. We should all meet bag ladies as attractive as Lesley Ann Warren, but there are more credible sections of the film, involving Brooks' friendships with down-and-outs and his running rivalry with a man who thinks he's John Paul Getty.

Life With Father ☉
1947, US, 118 mins, colour
Dir: Michael Curtiz
Stars: William Powell, Irene Dunne, Elizabeth Taylor, Edmund Gwenn, ZaSu Pitts
Rating: ★★★

A tremendous box-office hit in its day, and the kind of film that Hollywood does so well. It's an amusing study, fun of warmth and lushly photographed in colour, of a Victorian-style household in New York, its joys, sorrows and family crises. The characters are delightful, but Donald Ogden Stewart's script for them lacks bite and rambles a bit, while director Michael Curtiz, more at home with Errol Flynn action films, often seems to dull the edges of the fun. Still it's a handsome production and boasts one of Max Steiner's best music scores, plus a larger-than-life, Oscar-nominated turn by William Powell as Father.

Light at the Edge of the World, The ○
1971, US/Spain, 119 mins, colour
Dir: Kevin Billington
Stars: Kirk Douglas, Yul Brynner, Samantha Eggar, Fernando Rey
Rating: ★

A lighthouse off Cape Horn is the spectacular setting for this Jules Verne adaptation, searingly well photographed in colour. Kirk Douglas has always seemed at home with basic schoolboy heroics, and here he has what should be a plum role as the mysterious American who takes on a whole crew of pirates (fiercely led by Yul Brynner) after they've taken over the lighthouse. The results, though, are alternately violent and laughable.

Lighthorsemen, The ○ ⓥ
1987, Australia, 115 mins, colour
Dir: Simon Wincer
Stars: Peter Phelps, Jon Blake, Tim

L

McKenzie
Rating: ★★

Spurred on perhaps by the international success of *Gallipoli*, Australian filmmakers turned their attention to this epic war film about Australian cavalry fighting in the Palestinian desert of 1917. Overlength spoils it, but there's a spectacular charging battle sequence at the end which fires the adrenalin and makes the whole wait for action worthwhile. Personable performances in the leading roles from Peter Phelps and John Waters do what they can to boost the rather insubstantial storyline.

Lightning Jack ◐ Ⓥ
1994, Australia, 93 mins, colour
Dir: Simon Wincer
Stars: Paul Hogan, Beverly D'Angelo, Cuba Gooding Jr, Pat Hingle, Roger Daltrey, L Q Jones
Rating: ★★

Lightning Jack Kane – bungling bank robber and the fastest gun alive – holds a young mute hostage and cries, 'One word – and you're dead!' setting the level of humour for this outdoor action comedy co-produced, written by and starring Paul Hogan as the aforementioned Jack. Pat Hingle and L Q Jones contribute tart cameos in this easygoing ramble, but Cuba Gooding is forced into some overripe reactions as the mute who becomes the ageing outlaw's sidekick as the plot sees them crossing the West in search of banks easy enough to rob. Amiable enough for undemanding Hogan fans who may turn a blind eye to the film's shortfalls on both the hilarity and action fronts.

Light of Heart, The
See: Life Begins at Eight Thirty

Lightship, The ◐ Ⓥ
1985, US, 89 mins, colour
Dir: Jerzy Skolimowski
Stars: Robert Duvall, Klaus Maria Brandauer, Tom Bower, Badja Djola, Arliss Howard, William Forsythe
Rating: ★

On paper, the combination of Hollywood's Oscar-winning Robert Duvall and Austria's international star Klaus Maria Brandauer seems an explosive one. In fact, their clash between good and evil hardly raises even a fizzle, the two men reacting to each other like negative poles and never raising any tension in dramatic terms. It's a ponderous, almost incident-less story of three fugitives boarding a 1955 lightship whose German-born captain is haunted by an incident in the war that echoes the dilemma of Jack Hawkins in *The Cruel Sea*. Jerzy Skolimowski's direction, however, is so slack that none of this hits home, nothing solidifies to bolster the plot, and the dialogue, although it has its pretensions, lurches perilously close to clichés of long ago. Duvall is mannered without being menacing and Brandauer merely enigmatic – his final act of heroism scarcely quickening the pulse.

Light Sleeper ● Ⓥ
1991, US, 103 mins, colour
Dir: Paul Schrader
Stars: Willem Dafoe, Susan Sarandon, Dana Delany, Mary Beth Hurt
Rating: ★

This story of a drug dealer suddenly reaching a crisis in his life doesn't amount to very much considering the talents involved. Film maker Paul Schrader offers a typically cold and atmospheric view of the city backstreets at night, but his writing of the story makes it seem hardly worth the effort. Willem Dafoe has the John Garfield role as the dealer. With his partners already considering changing their line of work, he runs into an old girlfriend and trouble. Dana Delany is a fresh new face in this role, but most of the other performances are no more than adequate, and Schrader almost tosses away what action there is.

Light that Failed, The ○
1939, US, 97 mins, b/w
Dir: William A Wellman
Stars: Ronald Colman, Walter Huston, Ida Lupino
Rating: ★★★

Sincere, moving and always gripping adaptation of the Rudyard Kipling novel about an artist going blind who hauls a girl from the gutters of London and makes her the subject of his last great masterpiece. Star Ronald Colman had wanted Vivien Leigh for the role of the guttersnipe, but it was grabbed (with both hands) by Ida Lupino who, fed up with a series of milk-and-water roles, ripped in with a corrosive performance that jetted her to stardom in similar hard-bitten roles.

Light Up the Sky ○
1960, UK, 90 mins, b/w
Dir: Lewis Gilbert
Stars: Ian Carmichael, Tommy Steele, Benny Hill
Rating: ★★

A mixture of high jinks and high drama with the members of a wartime searchlight unit. Experienced maker of war stories Lewis Gilbert directs. Such efficient 'types' as Victor Maddern, Sydney Tafler, Johnny Briggs and Harry Locke do him yeoman service in support, while Dick Emery, and Cardew Robinson make, with Benny Hill, a trio of comedians in character roles.

Like Father, Like Son ○ Ⓥ
1987, US, 98 mins, colour
Dir: Rod Daniel
Stars: Dudley Moore, Kirk Cameron, Margaret Colin
Rating: ★

Although made before *Big*, *Vice Versa* and *18 Again!*, this age-reversal comedy started, time-wise, from the back of the field in Britain and finished a distant fourth. Seen in isolation, this Dudley Moore comedy might not have looked too bad. As it was, three previous tellings of the tall tale only exposed its comic situations as merely embarrassing and its father-and-son characters more fun as themselves than when they switch bodies. Both Moore (as a famous surgeon) and Kirk Cameron (his truly average son) seem far too outspoken in their new identities; surely both would have been more cautious in the circumstances. Margaret Colin is on good form as a man-eater who can't believe Moore's new-found enthusiasm for women, but the film's tiresome and illogical developments soon drain our interest. And there have been few, if any, entries into the genre since.

Likely Lads, The ◐
1976, UK, 90 mins, colour
Dir: Michael Tuchner
Stars: Rodney Bewes, James Bolam, Brigit Forsyth
Rating: ★★

Yet another TV spin-off that fell apart on the hazardous journey to the big screen. Philosophical comedy is the vein aimed at, but the dialogue is unecessarily crude, and jars every time it steps out of key, which is often. It does best when indulging in quietly humorous nostalgia, or making the poker-faced Rodney Bewes the fall-guy for visual disasters. The uncertainty of much of the acting is no help, the only major success being Brigit Forsyth as Thelma.

L'il Abner ○
1959, US, 113 mins, colour
Dir: Melvin Frank
Stars: Peter Palmer, Leslie Parrish,

Stubby Kaye, Stella Stevens
Rating: ★★

Bright, loud, bouncy cartoon-like musical based on Al Capp's famous comic-strip characters, who ran for years in American newspapers. Stella Stevens is an amazing Appassionata Von Climax and Stubby Kaye terrific as Marryin' Sam, especially when singing the show's big hit 'Jubilation T Cornpone'. But the romance is a bit drippy, the corny comedy pales after a while and the whole just lacks that vital spark that would put it among the classic film musical comedies.

Lilacs in the Spring ○
(aka: Let's Make Up)
1954, UK, 94 mins, colour
Dir: Herbert Wilcox
Stars: Anna Neagle, Errol Flynn, David Farrar, Kathleen Harrison
Rating: ★★

This musical is bright and inconsequential, with Anna Neagle tripping vivaciously through a series of old favourites that include 'Keep the Home Fires Burning', 'We'll Gather Lilacs', Noel Coward's 'Dance Little Lady', 'Lily of Laguna', 'Tipperary' and 'Lilac Tango'. Much of the story is told in fantasies and flashbacks, which gives Dame Anna a chance to reprise her impressions of Nell Gwyn and Queen Victoria from earlier films, as well as fling herself with infectious abandon into some colourful period routines. A young Sean Connery is somewhere in the crowd of extras.

Lili ☉
1952, US, 81 mins, colour
Dir: Charles Walters
Stars: Leslie Caron, Mel Ferrer, Jean-Pierre Aumont, Zsa Zsa Gabor, Kurt Kasznar, Amanda Blake
Rating: ★★★★

A warm and winning MGM musical with Leslie Caron as a French orphan who joins a travelling carnival and meets self-pitying puppeteer Mel Ferrer and sophisticated magician Jean-Pierre Aumont. Caron is convincingly ingenuous, the puppets are real scene-stealers and the score so enchanting it won Bronislau Kaper an Academy Award. A real charmer.

Lilith ◑
1964, US, 126 mins, b/w
Dir: Robert Rossen
Stars: Warren Beatty, Jean Seberg, Peter Fonda, Kim Hunter, Jessica Walter, Gene Hackman
Rating: ★★

A rather fey psychological drama-romance whose star-studded cast was not enough to prevent it dying a thousand deaths at the box-office. The pace is slow and the actors seem to take a long time to deliver their lines. As an oddity it's worth a look, though certainly not up to the standards of Robert Rossen's previous film *The Hustler*.

Lillian Russell ○
1940, US, 127 mins, b/w
Dir: Irving Cummings
Stars: Alice Faye, Don Ameche, Henry Fonda, Warren William, Edward Arnold, Leo Carrillo
Rating: ★★

Whitewashed but very watchable biography of an American stage star of the Gay Nineties, giving star Alice Faye no fewer than four leading men in Don Ameche, Henry Fonda, Warren William and Edward Arnold, the latter being in especially good form, repeating his earlier film characterisation of 'Diamond Jim' Brady. Director Irving Cummings began his career as a stage actor, with a company headed by Lillian Russell.

Limelight ○ ⊙
1951, US, 144 mins, b/w
Dir: Charles Chaplin
Stars: Charlie Chaplin, Claire Bloom, Sydney Chaplin, Buster Keaton, Nigel Bruce
Rating: ★★★★

The best of Chaplin's post-war films, and too rarely seen on television. It has a Pagliacci theme – Chaplin is the fading clown who helps a young girl from the brink of suicide to success as a ballerina – set against the London music-hall in the early 20th century that Chaplin himself had known in his youth. Although its plot is melodramatic and dated, Chaplin demonstrates his ability once more to wring a tear as well as a smile. And there are moments of high hilarity, not least from the climactic stage routine in which Buster Keaton plays Chaplin's piano accompanist.

Line-Up, The ○
1958, US, 86 mins, b/w
Dir: Don Siegel
Stars: Eli Wallach, Robert Keith, Warner Anderson, Richard Jaeckel
Rating: ★★★

Classy Don Siegel-directed, Stirling Silliphant-scripted crime thriller with Eli Wallach outstanding as an assassin. Based on a highly successful TV series (which also featured Warner

Anderson), shown in Britain as *San Francisco Beat*. Forgettable stuff but sharply done with a taut climax.

Linguini Incident, The ● ⊙
1991, US, 99 mins, colour
Dir: Richard Shepherd
Stars: Rosanna Arquette, David Bowie, Eszter Balint, Marlee Matlin, Buck Henry
Rating: ★

What a difference a decent screenplay makes. The storyline to this foul-mouthed romantic comedy is pretty original and the settings delightfully gaudy. But the script is just so bad that the film never has a chance. Directorial mishandling doesn't help, while even the delectable Rosanna Arquette, as the cocktail waitress planning to be a female Houdini, comes across as irritating in this one. It does get a bit better towards the end: too little, too late.

Lion, The ○
1962, US, 96 mins, colour
Dir: Jack Cardiff
Stars: William Holden, Trevor Howard, Capucine, Pamela Franklin
Rating: ★★

Sentimental, cleverly acted drama, shot on location in East Africa. A young girl grows up there, and strikes up a friendship with a huge lion. Pamela Franklin, who plays the girl, later starred in such films as *The Prime of Miss Jean Brodie* and *David Copperfield*. Technicolor photography is as ravishing as one would expect from a film directed by former cameraman Jack Cardiff, who won an Oscar for his colour camerawork on the 1946 film, *Black Narcissus*.

Lionheart ●
(aka: AWOL)
1990, US, 110 mins, colour
Dir: Sheldon Lettich
Stars: Jean-Claude Van Damme, Harrison Page, Deborah Rennard, Lisa Pelikan
Rating: ★★★

Probably Jean-Claude Van Damme's best solo starring film to date, with more than a semblance of a decent story to go with kickboxing mayhem, in smoky backstreet rooms, or later, plusher joints. Van Damme's a French Legionnaire who deserts to come to America where his drug-dealing brother has been torched by competitors. Soon, realising that his fighting skills are the only way to help his brother's widow and young daughter, he reluctantly ties in with black street hustler

L

Harrison Page, and predatory, illegal-fight promoter Deborah Rennard, who turns against him when he fails to succumb to her advances. Although the story has its corny and woolly moments, first-time director Sheldon Lettich has an approach which now and again lends it freshness and shows he appreciates cinema. Rennard is just sufficiently over-the-top to be enjoyable without being silly and Van Damme shows his gentler side – wisely by sharing scenes with a kid who can't act.

Lion In Winter, The ○ Ⓥ

1968, UK, 135 mins, colour
Dir: Anthony Harvey
Stars: Peter O'Toole, Katharine Hepburn, Anthony Hopkins, Timothy Dalton, Jane Merrow
Rating: ★★★★★

There can have been few bigger certainties in Academy Award history than James Goldman's Oscar for his screenplay on this brilliantly written film, adapted from his own play. It's principally a game of verbal chess with a cutting edge, played out at Christmas 1183 between King Henry II and his estranged wife Eleanor of Aquitaine, whom he has shut away to stop her interference in affairs of state. In these plum roles, Peter O'Toole and Katharine Hepburn coat Goldman's coruscating dialogue in venom. The serious humour cuts deep as these two constantly hack away at each other, distant respect and attachment lurking behind years of bitterness as they amuse and stimulate us with the cut and thrust of it all. Add early appearances by Anthony Hopkins and Timothy Dalton and you have a rich pageant of entertainment for which Hepburn took her third Oscar.

Lion Is in the Streets, A ○

1953, US, 88 mins, colour
Dir: Raoul Walsh
Stars: James Cagney, Barbara Hale, Anne Francis, Warner Anderson
Rating: ★★

Although seemingly a change of pace for James Cagney – he plays a backwoods salesman who becomes a politician – this is still very much in the classic mould of the cocky little rebel. Very strikingly shot in Technicolor, with Cagney extremely effective in the 'young' scenes – even though he was 54 at the time!

Lion King, The ☉ Ⓥ

1994, US, 87 mins, colour
Dir: Roger Allers, Rob Minkoff

Voice Stars: Matthew Broderick, Jeremy Irons, James Earl Jones, Rowan Atkinson, Whoopi Goldberg, Robert Guillaume
Rating: ★★★

Disney's phenomenally successful cartoon cross between *Bambi*, *Hamlet* and *The Jungle Book*. Beautiful African vistas are as good as anything else in the story of a cub born to be king, who falls victim to the schemes of his evil Uncle Scar who, with the aid of a pack of hyenas, traps the cub in a wildebeest stampede that kills his father. Fleeing Pride Rock, the cub is befriended by a manic meerkat and a windy warthog (Disney's concession to modern film comedy) who teach him the bare necessities (or whatever) until he can grow up and return to confront his wicked uncle. Since George Sanders had died, Disney went for the voice of Jeremy Irons as Scar, and Irons rewards the faith with his best vocal performance in ages. Other peripheral characters are amusing, especially a pedantic hornbill (Rowan Atkinson), a baboon medicine man (Robert Guillaume), and a cackling hyena that looks like Whoopi Goldberg and actually is voiced by her. The songs are jolly without being in the same class as those for *The Little Mermaid* and *Beauty and the Beast*.

Lipstick ●

1976, US, 86 mins, colour
Dir: Lamont Johnson
Stars: Margaux Hemingway, Chris Sarandon, Anne Bancroft, Mariel Hemingway
Rating: ★

Out of 500,000 estimated cases of rape every year in California only 10,000 are reported and, of those cases brought to trial, just two per cent result in conviction. These shocking statistics are brought to light and then luridly expanded on in this notorious thriller. Margaux Hemingway plays the top model who brings just such a case after being raped by her psychotic teacher; and her younger (and more talented) sister Mariel plays the girl who introduces them without knowing the horrors around the corner. Strong stuff, this, but not good.

Lisa ○
(aka: The Inspector)

1962, US, 112 mins, colour
Dir: Philip Dunne
Stars: Stephen Boyd, Dolores Hart, Leo McKern, Hugh Griffith
Rating: ★★★

Sporadically interesting romantic melodrama based on Jan De Hartog's *The Inspector*. Handsomely photographed against authentic European backgrounds, the film flits from romance to action and mystery, with no one element dominating. Consequently, the final result is colourful, rambling and sometimes exciting. Leo ('Rumpole') McKern gives a sharp and bristling performance as a crotchety old sea dog. And Hugh Griffith is on form as a Dutchman who swats bats with a tennis racquet.

Lisbon ○

1956, US, 90 mins, colour
Dir: Ray Milland
Stars: Ray Milland, Maureen O'Hara, Claude Rains
Rating: ★★

Actor Ray Milland made some interesting films as director, but there wasn't very much he could do with this dullish tale of international intrigue. The Portuguese settings look attractive even in Republic Studios' awful Trucolor, and a good cast, including Milland himself, Maureen O'Hara, Francis Lederer, Yvonne Furneaux and that old smoothie Claude Rains, does what it can to spark the stock situations. There are one or two good twists in the plot.

Listen, Darling ○

1938, US, 70 mins, b/w
Dir: Edwin L Marin
Stars: Judy Garland, Walter Pidgeon, Mary Astor, Freddie Bartholomew
Rating: ★★★

This vehicle for the teenage Judy Garland is very similar to early Deanna Durbin films. Judy brings much the same quality of freshness to her innocent, yet polished performance as the matchmaking daughter of widow Mary Astor, who was to play Judy's mum again six years later in *Meet Me in St Louis*. The film's big musical hit was 'Zing! Went the Strings of My Heart', sung by you-know-who.

Listen to Me ●

1989, US, 110 mins, colour
Dir: Douglas Day Stewart
Stars: Kirk Cameron, Jami Gertz, Roy Scheider, Amanda Peterson, Tim Quill, Anthony Zerbe
Rating: ★★

It's a pretty hard assignment to make an entertaining 110-minute film about a college for debating societies, but Columbia almost pulls it off in this passionately well-acted film. By pretending that debating is a life-or-death occupation (and 'a road straight into law school and politics') and plucking relentlessly at the heartstrings, director Douglas Day Stewart, aided by patriotic music swelling vaguely in the background, will draw a tear from the easily moved as junior debaters Jami Gertz and Kirk Cameron take on the mighty Harvard in the final. *Rocky* with words instead of fists: Gertz doesn't miss out on her big chance towards the end and Roy Scheider goes over the top for the team as their professor.

List of Adrian Messenger, The O
1963, US, 98 mins, b/w
Dir: John Huston
Stars: George C Scott, Dana Wynter, Kirk Douglas, Clive Brook, Herbert Marshall, Gladys Cooper
Rating: ★★★

Under the watchful and inventive eye of director John Huston, this eventful and atmospheric thriller proves to be great fun. Not only is there a killer on the loose who proves to be a gleeful master of disguise, but a number of famous guest stars appear (not that you can tell) under mounds of make-up to strew red herrings across the trail. Suspenseful moments, classy black and white photography and a thrilling chase climax.

Little Big Man O Ⓥ
1970, US, 147 mins, colour
Dir: Arthur Penn
Stars: Dustin Hoffman, Faye Dunaway, Martin Balsam, Richard Mulligan
Rating: ★★★

A fascinating, rather odd Western, with Dustin Hoffman playing an unlikely (and occasionally very funny) hero. Raised by Indians, he has to learn to live in white society but goes back to the Indian tribe who brought him up. But then comes General Custer and the Battle of Little Big Horn. Amusing and shocking in turn, with a humanitarian message in the film somewhere.

Little Caesar O Ⓥ
1930, US, 80 mins, b/w
Dir: Mervyn Le Roy
Stars: Edward G Robinson, Douglas Fairbanks Jr, Ralph Ince, Glenda Farrell
Rating: ★★★★

This was the first talkie to glorify the gang wars of the Twenties and established Edward G Robinson as a star, pushing his minions around and spitting out dialogue like lead pellets in a

pheasant. Robinson dominates the entire film, which grips consistently, never misses with its action and has no wasted footage in its 80 minutes.

Little Colonel, The Ⓞ
1935, US, 80 mins, b/w
Dir: David Butler
Stars: Shirley Temple, Lionel Barrymore, John Lodge
Rating: ★★★

Shirley Temple in the Deep South, and at her most beguiling. Lionel Barrymore inevitably has his heart of stone melted by the end; the talented tot also does the famous dance up and down the wooden steps with Bill 'Bojangles' Robinson. One sequence in colour.

Little Darlings Ⓞ
1980, US, 92 mins, colour
Dir: Ronald F Maxwell
Stars: Tatum O'Neal, Kristy McNichol, Armand Assante, Matt Dillon
Rating: ★★

This is basically just another Hollywood 'summer camp' tale with a rather distasteful story about two girls involved in a bet about who will lose her virginity first. In this instance, however, the playing overcomes the formula development of Kimi Peck and Dalene Young's screenplay. In particular, Kristy McNichol as a tough teenager with a sleep-around divorcee mother, is so true, so natural in conveying of inner feelings as to leave you gasping for more. All the sadness and cynicism of 15 years of rootless existence is expressed in these brown eyes. It's a performance deserving of the Oscar nomination it didn't get.

Little Drummer Girl, The Ⓞ Ⓥ
1984, US, 130 mins, colour
Dir: George Roy Hill
Stars: Diane Keaton, Yorgo Voyagis, Klaus Kinski, David Suchet
Rating: ★★

Director George Roy Hill not only takes his time (well over two hours) with the film version of John Le Carré's best-seller, but doesn't do too well at getting us to believe that a pro-Palestinian American actress in England could be recruited to the Israeli cause to help root out the very people whose cause she has espoused. Diane Keaton certainly has her moments in the title role, Klaus Kinski is fine as an Israeli counter-intelligence officer and there's some suspense towards the end. Otherwise Hill's

treatment of a fine story lacks inspiration in too many departments.

Little Foxes, The Ⓞ Ⓥ
1941, US, 116 mins, b/w
Dir: William Wyler
Stars: Bette Davis, Herbert Marshall, Teresa Wright, Richard Carlson, Dan Duryea
Rating: ★★★★★

Lillian Hellman's own adaptation of her Broadway stage success, brilliantly directed by William Wyler and full of classic scenes and images. Bette Davis gives one of her most unforgettable performances as Regina Giddens, a scheming, ruthless woman who alienates all those about her. Dan Duryea makes a notable screen debut, while Teresa Wright and Herbert Marshall do fine, unselfish work in support of the star. Nominated for eight Oscars, the film shamefully came away empty-handed.

Little Girl Who Lives Down the Lane, The Ⓞ
1976, Canada, 90 mins, colour
Dir: Nicolas Gessner
Stars: Jodie Foster, Martin Sheen, Alexis Smith
Rating: ★★

With portraits of prostitutes and gangster's molls already behind her, the 13year-old Jodie Foster handled her role as a disturbed teenager with amazing confidence in this Canadian thriller that reminds you of Hammer chillers of the mid Sixties. She's the whole show, especially with a plot that telegraphs every shock a few shivers in advance.

Little Hut, The O
1957, US, 90 mins, colour
Dir: Mark Robson
Stars: Ava Gardner, Stewart Granger, David Niven, Walter Chiari, Finlay Currie
Rating: ★★

A pretty unrelaxed film version of a saucy stage farce, with Stewart Granger and Ava Gardner struggling in comedy this broad as two sides of a desert island triangle. David Niven is in raspingly good form as the rascally Brittingham-Brett, but there wasn't much else for MGM to celebrate from what must have looked a sure box-office hit. Granger and Gardner, who had done scarcely better together with *Bhowani Junction*, were doomed at the studio from here on.

Little Kidnappers, The
See: The Kidnappers

L

Little Man Tate ◑ ⓥ

1991, US, 99 mins, colour
Dir: Jodie Foster
Stars: Jodie Foster, Dianne Wiest, Adam
Hann-Byrd, Harry Connick Jr
Rating: ★★

'A Jodie Foster film' it says at the end,
just in case we've missed the point that
this simplistic fable (with its faint
echoes of *Pinocchio*) about a seven-year-
old genius is Jodie's directorial debut.
Jodie plays the kid's mother (the
Geppetto figure), a waitress-dancer
who's not as dim as she makes out.
But she provides no sort of environment, thinks pain-in-the-butt professor
Dianne Wiest (the Blue Fairy, sort of,
in which to bring the kid up. She
sweeps him off to bright kids' summer
college where he shows amazing aptitude at maths, but gains most from the
companionship of a human Lampwick
(singer Harry Connick Jr in his acting
debut) who teaches him how to play
pool. But, this not being *Pinocchio*, the
kids don't all turn into donkeys and,
starved of affection, the kid heads for
home and the life of a real little boy.
It's a low-key film with some good
laughs and the odd poignant moment.
B plus for Jodie this time.

Little Mermaid, The ⊙ ⓥ

1989, US, 87 mins, colour
Dir: John Musker
Voice Stars: Jodi Benson, Pat Carroll,
Samuel E Wright, Buddy Hackett
Rating: ★★★

A liltingly enjoyable cartoon feature in
the traditional Disney style. Though
based on the Hans Andersen fairy-tale,
it becomes, in Disney hands, a virtual
remake of *Sleeping Beauty*, even to the
final battle with the villainous sea-witch
Ursula. The heroine is a teenage mermaid, Ariel, with a fascination with all
things to do with humans. Rescuing a
prince from a shipwreck, she falls in
love with him and sells her voice to the
witch in return for three days as a
human. If she fails to get the prince to
give her a lover's kiss, she will turn
back into a mermaid and forfeit her
soul to Ursula as well. Ariel is quite a
feisty heroine by Disney standards and
her crab protector (a kind of West
Indian Jiminy Cricket) and seagull sage
are good characters too. Ursula is simply superb: an evil Mae West with
eight tentacles instead of feet. There
are three good songs – 'Part of This
World', 'Under the Sea' and 'Kiss the
Girl' – and children are certain to gasp,
laugh and snivel in all the right places.
It's too derivative to be a classic, but a

nice lightweight goodie to add to the
Disney hamper.

Little Miss Broadway ⊙

1938, US, 78 mins, b/w
Dir: Irving Cummings
Stars: Shirley Temple, George Murphy,
Jimmy Durante
Rating: ★★★

A Shirley Temple vehicle with more
music than usual, teaming her happily
with both Jimmy Durante and George
Murphy. Edna May Oliver also registers well as a crusty old landlady who
relents in the end. Temple and
Murphy both later went into politics
and here they duet appropriately on
'We Should Be Together!', one of half
a dozen tuneful songs that also include
'Be Optimistic', 'Hop, Skip and Jump'
and 'If All the World Were Paper'.
Nick Castle and Geneva Sawyer stage
the dance routines with their usual
flair, and Irving Cummings' direction
avoids any dull moments, in what,
helped by a snappy running time, is a
pretty lively package.

Little Miss Marker ○

1980, US, 103 mins, colour
Dir: Walter Bernstein
Stars: Walter Matthau, Julie Andrews,
Tony Curtis, Sara Stimson, Bob Newhart
Rating: ★★

Despite the fact that Damon Runyon's
story about a little girl left with a bookie as 'security' was definitively annexed
by Shirley Temple in 1934, producers
have felt compelled to have several
more tries at it since. Neither Mary
Jane Saunders (in Bob Hope's *Sorrowful
Jones*, 1949) nor Claire Wilcox (in
Tony Curtis' *40 Pounds of Trouble*, 1962)
laid a glove on the original and, in this
most recent version, it's Sara Stimson
struggling to make an impression as
'The Kid'. Walter Matthau makes a
dour Sorrowful and, strangely, it's
Tony Curtis who this time round takes
the role of the villain.

Little Nellie Kelly ○

1940, US, 100 mins, b/w
Dir: Norman Taurog
Stars: Judy Garland, George Murphy
Rating: ★★★

Judy Garland received her first solo
billing above the title of this little-seen
musical about a through-the-ages feud
between two stubborn Irish-American
families. Judy, stoutly supported by
George Murphy and Charles
Winninger, sings 'Nellie Kelly', 'It's a
Great Day for the Irish', 'Pretty Girl
Milking Her Cow' and – believe it or

not – 'Singin' in the Rain'. Her romantic interest is played by the promising
young singer Douglas McPhail, who
committed suicide a few years later.

Little Nikita

See: The Sleepers

Little Odessa ● ⓥ

1994, US, 98 mins, colour
Dir: James Gray
Stars: Tim Roth, Edward Furlong, Moira
Kelly, Maximilian Schell, Vanessa
Redgrave
Rating: ★

One of those grim, violent tragedies
that are darkly lit, have booming sound
and seem to be shot in corners of
rooms. Tim Roth is a hit-man who returns to the Russian-Jewish quarter of
an American city where his family still
lives in squalor. His father
(Maximilian Schell) runs a newstand
and keeps a mistress while his wife
(Vanessa Redgrave) lies dying. Roth's
young brother (Edward Furlong), although bright, hasn't been to school in
months. And there's a dumpling-pretty
girl (Moira Kelly) for Roth to come
back to and bed. They're all doomed,
of course, as if you couldn't tell from
the surly unsmiling performances.
These are cheerless people without any
real hope, and poor company indeed
after a tough day at the office. Russian
choirs drone mournfully in the background: all too much.

Little Prince, The ○

1974, UK, 88 mins, colour
Dir: Stanley Donen
Stars: Richard Kiley, Steven Warner, Bob
Fosse, Gene Wilder, Joss Ackland
Rating: ★

A musical treatment of Antoine de
Saint Exupéry's fabulous fairy-tale
about a little boy from outer space and
his quest for knowledge and understanding. Director Stanley Donen
plunges with both feet into a treacle
well of sentiment and it requires all the
efforts of Gene Wilder and Bob Fosse
to pull him out. Wilder's a wily fox all
in brown, but it's Fosse's snake,
dressed entirely in black, hissing and
bounding about, that steals the film.

Little Princess, The ⊙

1939, US, 91 mins, colour
Dir: Walter Lang
Stars: Shirley Temple, Ian Hunter,
Richard Greene, Cesar Romero
Rating: ★★

Shirley Temple's biggest (it cost $1.5
million) but by no means best film, this

turn-of-the-century story, which was also her first in colour, has her as a girl haunting hospitals in search of her father, believed a victim of the Boer War. Shirley is as forthright and winning as ever, while Mary Nash is splendidly vindictive as the headmistress who has it in for her. Skilfully made by Walter Lang, but he can't stop you cringing at the ending.

Little Princess, A ⊙ ⓥ

1995, US, 97 mins, colour
Dir: Alfonso Cuaron
Stars: Liesel Matthews, Eleanor Bron, Liam Cunningham, Rusty Schwimmer, Errol Sitahal, Arthur Malet
Rating: ★★★★★

Since pretty well every critic around the world agrees that this is a masterpiece of children's cinema, its almost total failure at the box-office is pretty mystifying. See it for yourself, though, and you will soon be caught up in its magical world. Far more delightful and impactful than the 1939 version with Shirley Temple, this has Temple lookalike Liesel Matthews as the small daughter of a British Army captain whose exotic upbringing in colonial India is brought to a grinding halt by the arrival of World War One. With her father posted away, Matthews finds herself billeted at the New York school of eagle-eyed Eleanor Bron, who is just dying to take the 'little princess' down a peg or two, and gets the chance when the girl's father is reported killed in action. Matthews is miraculous as the irrepressible Sara; Bron at her steely best as the hateful headmistress. And the treatment finds a perfect balance of fantasy and realism.

Little Rascals, The ○ ⓥ

1994, US, 82 mins, colour
Dir: Penelope Spheeris
Stars: Bug Hall, Travis Tedford, Brittany Ashton Holmes, Daryl Hannah
Rating: ★

Only the outtakes at the end reveal some of the agonies director Penelope Spheeris must have gone through to obtain any sort of performance from her tiny actors in this attempt to recreate the Hal Roach comedy series of the Twenties and Thirties about the scrapes of a gang of neighbourhood kids. And here they are again, complete with Petey, the dog with a circle drawn round his eye, who seems to have more talent here than most of the cast. Visually, this is almost a perfect colour replica of the times when Alfalfa, Darla, Buckwheat, Spanky and

their troop of toddlers ruled the kiddies' market roost around the world. But it's the spirit of innocence, the *joie de vivre*, that obstinately evades recapture. These camera conscious kids are going through the motions, and embarrassment, rather than simple fun, results. Juniors may get a squeal or two out of all this; adults are advised to take a stiff drink before (and during) the performance.

Little Romance, A ○

1979, US, 108 mins, colour
Dir: George Roy Hill
Stars: Diane Lane, Thelonius Bernard, Laurence Olivier, Sally Kellerman, Broderick Crawford
Rating: ★★★

An unlikely but fairly charming story about a 13-year-old French boy who lives in a world of films and a 13-yearold American girl who lives in a world (her mother's dizzy social whirl) from which her high IQ and sensible outlook leave her completely alienated. Their innocent affair culminates in a wild flight to Venice to kiss in a gondola under the Bridge of Sighs. The two youngsters (Diane Lane and Thelonius Bernard) are attractive but have their thunder stolen from them by the supporting cast. Broderick Crawford is splendid as himself, turning up at a party and growling, 'I figured what the hell, the booze is free and maybe I'll get laid.'

Little Shop of Horrors ① ⓥ

1986, US, 88 mins, colour
Dir: Frank Oz
Stars: Rick Moranis, Ellen Greene, Vincent Gardenia, Steve Martin, James Belushi, John Candy
Rating: ★★★

It's not often these days that producers gamble with a musical. So you can bet that when one does come along it has to be pretty special. This one is that – its central character is a man-eating plant. And it sings, displaying iris-shaped tonsils! Playgoers will find the ending changed from the stage original, but it's a move neither for better nor worse, simply providing the film with a climactic battle between man and plant. Rick Moranis is the weedy assistant in a (very) downtown flower shop whose discovery of a little plant that grows on blood makes the shop and its owner (Vincent Gardenia) famous, and may even help Rick win his Monroeish co-worker (Ellen Greene) away from hier sadistic dentist lover. This leading trio is so good that it's much to its credit

not to be overshadowed by the array of guest stars. Dentistry may never be the same after Steve Martin's driller-killer (once seen from inside a patient's mouth). Bill Murray is very droll as his masochistic patient, while plump John Candy pops up as the livewire of Skid Row Radio.

Littlest Rebel, The ⊙ ⓥ

1935, US, 70 mins, b/w
Dir: David Butler
Stars: Shirley Temple, John Boles, Jack Holt, Karen Morley
Rating: ★★★

This was the film (the setting is the American Civil War) in which talented tot Shirley Temple was first teamed with her black dancing partner Bill Robinson. Get the children to have a handkerchief handy, 'cos Shirley's mother gets killed and Daddy, John Boles, looks like getting shot by Unionist Jack Holt.

Little Women ○

1933, US, 115 mins, b/w
Dir: George Cukor
Stars: Katharine Hepburn, Joan Bennett, Paul Lukas
Rating: ★★★★

The definitive version of Louisa M Alcott's novel of four young women growing up is, in some ways, the other side of the coin from *Gone With the Wind*, in that it's set in New England at the time of the American Civil War. For one of the most successful adaptations of a difficult book ever brought to the screen, writers Victor Heerman and Sarah Mason were deservedly rewarded with Oscars. The production is as expensive as it is immaculate, and the four actresses flawless. Katharine Hepburn's bravura tendencies are beautifully kept in check by director George Cukor, enabling her to give a dominant but still sympathetic performance, and Frances Dee, Jean Parker (as the ailing Beth) and Joan Bennett are all appealing as her sisters. Spring Byington's marvellous 'Marmee' set her up for a whole run of engaging matrons and motherly types.

Little Women ○

1949, US, 122 mins, colour
Dir: Mervyn Le Roy
Stars: June Allyson, Elizabeth Taylor, Janet Leigh, Margaret O'Brien, Mary Astor, Rossano Brazzi
Rating: ★★★

A cosy, sentimental, but atmospheric version of the Louisa M Alcott classic, looking like a series of Christmas card

L

scenes in bright colours, but boasting sturdy performances from June Allyson as Jo, and Mary Astor as the beloved Marmee. MGM at its most family-minded. Director Mervyn Le Roy's simple, sincere appeal to basic emotions often works well.

Little Women ⊙ ⓥ

1994, US, 119 mins, colour
Dir: Gillian Armstrong
Stars: Winona Ryder, Trini Alvarado, Gabriel Byrne, Susan Sarandon, Kirsten Dunst, Samantha Mathis, Eric Stoltz
Rating: ★★

This third and latest film stab at Louisa May Alcott's autobiographical tale of four sisters growing up in straitened circumstances during the American Civil War lacks all the joy and brightness of the others. Sombre shades only track the Marches as they indulge in tedious play-acting, shot in cramped fashion by the director. What do the March girls do? Very little, it seems, although Jo (Winona Ryder) writes and Amy (Kirsten Dunst) briefly attends school, while others, you assume, await the arrival of husbands. Thus nothing much happens at some length against winter backgrounds. There are drippily written roles for the men in their lives, while Susan Sarandon has too little to do as Marmee, but does it well. Ryder's 'spirited' Jo is pretty grating, although she has her moments, notably in her delivery of the last line. Claire Danes has one very good scene as the ailing Beth. It picks up a bit towards the end, as indeed it needs to. But easily drawn tears here and there are not enough to leave a favourable impression overall. Reject slips all round.

Live and Let Die ○ ⓥ

1973, UK, 116 mins, colour
Dir: Guy Hamilton
Stars: Roger Moore, Yaphet Kotto, Jane Seymour, David Hedison
Rating: ★★★

The film that presented the world with its new James Bond. Roger Moore lacked Sean Connery's toughness, but made up for it in smoothness, dash and suavity. The plot is wildly improbable and nearly incomprehensible – all about voodoo and black power. But it's the usual imaginative, expensive production, in this case whisking us from London to New York to New Orleans; from a lengthy but admittedly exciting speedboat pursuit to a glider-car chase; each stunt sequence stretched to its limit. Jane Seymour is a cool heroine, while Julius W Harris's

sinister Tee Hee, whose right arm has been severed by an over-enthusiastic crocodile, is the best of the bad men.

Live It Up ⊙
(aka: Sing and Swing)

1963, UK, 78 mins, b/w
Dir: Lance Comfort
Stars: David Hemmings, Veronica Hurst, Heinz Burt, Patsy Ann Noble
Rating: ★★★

A British echo-chamber musical with plenty of teenage attraction in such contemporary pop stars as Gene Vincent, Heinz and Sounds Incorporated. The direction is smooth and the musical numbers on the whole are well staged. One of them, Vincent's 'Temptation Baby', is particularly good.

Live Now, Pay Later ❶

1962, UK, 104 mins, b/w
Dir: Jay Lewis
Stars: Ian Hendry, June Ritchie, John Gregson, Liz Fraser
Rating: ★★★

A blackly bitter satirical comedy which finds Ian Hendry in his element as the brash, fast-talking, womanising, salesman who blights everybody's life including (eventually) his own. Jack Trevor Story's screenplay creates a series of dislikeable characters which gives the morality tale real bite, and there are unusual (but excellent) contributions from John Gregson and Liz Fraser, both effectively cast against type. Like Hendry's character as far as his acquaintances are concerned, the film outstays its welcome before the end, but this is British realist drama of the early Sixties at its most acerbic.

Lives of a Bengal Lancer, The ○

1935, US, 107 mins, b/w
Dir: Henry Hathaway
Stars: Gary Cooper, Franchot Tone, Richard Cromwell
Rating: ★★★★

Rip-roaring, Oscar-winning adventure yarn set on India's North West frontier. Strong human values are not lost in director Henry Hathaway's successful search for great narrative drive and the vein of humour includes a marvellous snake-charming scene. Gary Cooper is in his element as the stalwart hero and there's a superbly sneaky minor performance by J. Carrol Naish as a grand vizier. Douglas Dumbrille and Akim Tamiroff complete a classic trio of Hollywood players you would rarely trust.

Living Daylights, The ○ ⓥ

1987, UK, 131 mins, colour
Dir: John Glen
Stars: Timothy Dalton, Maryam D'Abo, Joe Don Baker, Jeroen Krabbé, John Rhys-Davies, Art Malik
Rating: ★★

Timothy Dalton – the fourth actor to play 007 agent James Bond – is neatly introduced in a suitably tongue-in-cheek pre-credits sequence in which three double-O agents (the other two bearing a remarkable similarity to Roger Moore and George Lazenby) parachute on to Gibraltar to see if they can penetrate the Rock's radar installation. Although Dalton proves in this one to be a pale shadow of his predecessors, the film does see the return of Bond's trademark Aston Martin car, not the DB5 of the earlier films but a more recent model, the Volante, souped up by 'Q' to carry laser beams that can cut a car in half, automatic missiles, and skis so that it can travel on snow and ice. The formula was looking very dated when this one finally made it to cinemas – especially with its story of a Russian agent defecting to the West.

Living Desert, The ⊙

1953, US, 72 mins, colour
Dir: James Algar
Voice: Winston Hibler
Rating: ★★★★★

Although now often-shortened for television, this was originally the first feature-length entry in Walt Disney's True Life Adventure series. It won an Academy Award and became the first nature documentary in years to attract world-wide queues. Purists complained about the brilliant orchestration of the material to fit with some highly original musical accompaniment, but the move helped to make the film immensely entertaining. The 'square dance' of the scorpions, contrived as it is, remains a classic.

Living Free ○

1972, UK, 92 mins, colour
Dir: Jack Couffer
Stars: Nigel Davenport, Susan Hampshire
Rating: ★★

Pleasant, leisurely sequel to *Born Free* and *The Lions Are Free*, gorgeously photographed in colour by Wolfgang Suschitzky. Susan Hampshire and Nigel Davenport romp with their leonine friends as to the manner born, and children will love every sentimental moment of it.

Living In Oblivion ● Ⓥ
1994, US, 89 mins, colour
Dir: Tom DiCillo
Stars: Steve Buscemi, Catherine Keener, Dermot Mulroney, Danielle Von Zerneck, James LeGros
Rating: ★★

Writer/director Tom DiCillo, whose previous film, *Johnny Suede*, was also a 'cult' success, hasn't quite got the talent or imagination to make this lowbudget comedy worth more than a few chuckles. It takes place on the cramped set of a mini-budget movie where everything that could go wrong in one day's shooting proceeds to do so. Even in the dreams of the director (Steve Buscemi) and star (Catherine Keener), things are a mess. Given a really punchy treatment, this could have been a riot, but DiCillo's set-ups are too clumsy to make the real thing much better than the fictional fiasco he's portraying. Consequently, the film plays a one-note samba that soon becomes monotonous, with the actors doing little more than going through the motions on either side of the camera. Good for a few giggles here and there, but nowhere near as good as many critics thought it was.

Living It Up ○
1954, US, 95 mins, colour
Dir: Norman Taurog
Stars: Dean Martin, Jerry Lewis, Janet Leigh, Sheree North, Edward Arnold
Rating: ★★★

The Dean Martin-Jerry Lewis team adds its own way-out comedy touch to this remake of the Fredric March-Carole Lombard laughter classic, *Nothing Sacred*. Jerry Lewis plays the man who is treated to a last fling by his doctor and a pretty girl journalist when an incorrect diagnosis reveals that he is dying of radiation poisoning. The misadventures they run into, the pitfalls they have to avoid, and the eventual showdown, are fast, furious and in the best traditions of slapstick. Happily, the script also makes room for delicious Sheree North – who started as a dancer but proved a durable actress – and that apoplectic mountain of a supporting comedy star, Fred Clark.

Lizzie Ⓞ
1957, US, 81 mins, b/w
Dir: Hugo Haas
Stars: Eleanor Parker, Richard Boone
Rating: ★★

Although quite well written by Mel Dinelli, a veteran of RKO's *film noir* days, this story of a woman with three personalities ran a definite second-best

to *The Three Faces of Eve*, the classic psycho-drama released the same year. The most ambitious film of morose Czech-born actor-director Hugo Haas (who usually, as here, played roles in his own movies), the film is hard-put to keep hysteria and sleazy melodrama at arms' reach, especially in the uncharacteristically undisciplined performance of Eleanor Parker in the title role. Richard Boone and Joan Blondell offer lower-key, more believable portrayals. Johnny Mathis makes a rare screen appearance, as a nightclub singer.

Lloyds of London ○
1936, US, 115 mins, b/w
Dir: Henry King
Stars: Tyrone Power, Madeleine Carroll, George Sanders, Freddie Bartholomew
Rating: ★★★★

A good, solid piece of storytelling in the teemingly-detailed Hollywood style of the Thirties. Somehow the scriptwriters contrive to enliven the history of the famous English insurance and banking firm by pumping in romance, shipwrecks, conspiracies and even the Battle of Trafalgar. We watch little Freddie Bartholomew grow up to be Tyrone Power and they share the acting honours. Director Henry King keeps an impressive grip on his sprawling subject.

Local Hero ○ Ⓥ
1983, UK, 110 mins, colour
Dir: Bill Forsyth
Stars: Burt Lancaster, Peter Riegert, Fulton MacKay, Denis Lawson, Peter Capaldi, Jenny Seagrove
Rating: ★★★

A leisurely, Scottish-set comedy in the old Ealing tradition, with wonderful coastal scenery and some marvellous laughs, mostly along blithely silly lines as an American gas-oil company bids to buy up a whole slice of the Scottish coast. The locals are only too willing to drive a hard bargain, until it's discovered that the old beachcomber who owns a section of the coastline just won't budge. If this has the outward appearances of such Ealing comedies as *Whisky Galore!* and *The Maggie*, the souls of *Airplane!* and *Monty Python* lurk not far under the surface. The black vicar is called Murdo Macpherson, the boss of the American company (Burt Lancaster) enjoys a manic relationship with his analyst, and a girl marine biologist turns out to have webbed feet. Director Bill Forsyth gets it all right, especially at the end, and there are inch-perfect performances from

Lancaster, Peter Riegert (his young representative who falls under the spell of the place), and Fulton MacKay, the latter priceless as the beachcomber.

Loch Ness Ⓞ
1996, UK, 100 mins, colour
Dir: John Henderson
Stars: Ted Danson, Joely Richardson, Ian Holm, Kirsty Graham, Harris Yulin
Rating: ★★

This one laps by as quietly as the waters of the famous loch, and is liable to make barely a ripple in your memory. Ted Danson is pleasant enough as the American zoologist sent to roust out the monster of legend from the watery depths, but he's roundly out-acted by Joely Richardson, sporting a convincing Scots accent, and little Kirsty Graham, who's a real charmer. The photography of the Scottish highlands is gorgeous, but most of the drama is so low-key as to be unacceptably mild, with Scots stereotypes seemingly unchanged since the days when Ealing made such (much better) comedies as *Whisky Galore!* and *The Maggie*. Those going expecting a feast of special effects will come away disappointed, although Jim Henson's Creature Workshop supplies a little bit of magical trickery at the end.

Lock Up ● Ⓥ
1989, US, 106 mins, colour
Dir: John Flynn
Stars: Sylvester Stallone, Donald Sutherland, John Amos, Darianne Fluegel
Rating: ★★★

This is just the thing to see after a hard day at the office. Mindless, violent (but not that violent), well-made, professional entertainment: an entirely satisfactory vehicle for a star. Sylvester Stallone is the model prisoner with six months to serve who's suddenly and brutally transferred to a maximum security prison whose warden (Donald Sutherland) he once made a fool of in more ways than one. The plot's a joke, of course, but who cares? The mechanics of making a hard-hitting and effectively thrilling prison story, with all its stereotypes and clichés intact, are what matter here. Stallone does all that you could ask, and you can even understand some of his dialogue. Sutherland proves he's as effective as a psycho as in quieter roles. Forget your worries, sit back and let those brain cells not frazzled by the day just mop it up.

L

Lock Up Your Daughters! ◐

1969, UK, 102 mins, colour
Dir: Peter Coe
Stars: Christopher Plummer, Susannah York, Glynis Johns, Ian Bannen, Tom Bell, Jim Dale
Rating: ★★

Lusty comic entertainment along the lines of *Tom Jones*. Names such as Mr Squeezum, Lady Clumsey, Lusty, Hoyden and Lady Eager give an idea of the general tone, and the cast plunges in with a will. Jim Dale, Tom Bell and Ian Bannen are well contrasted as the three hot-blooded sailors desperate for wenches after months at sea; Susannah York is enchanting as the tomboy Hilaret; Fenella Fielding incredible as Lady Eager, uttering whispered cries for help when attacked by an attractive man; and Glynis Johns best of all in her lecherous observations on felons in the dock ('*Two* rapists? Indeed!').

Lolita ●

1962, US, 152 mins, b/w
Dir: Stanley Kubrick
Stars: James Mason, Sue Lyon, Peter Sellers, Shelley Winters
Rating: ★★

Director Stanley Kubrick was riding on the crest of a critical wave of applause, after *Paths of Glory* and *Spartacus*, when he persuaded Vladimir Nabokov to help make a film out of the novel – about a middle-aged man falling for a teenage temptress – that had delighted and scandalised the nation. He also got a formidable cast together, including Peter Sellers, who gives the best performance in what turned out to be a rather indigestible film, which did more for sunglasses (as worn by Sue Lyon's Lolita) than the cinema.

London Belongs to Me ○

(aka: Dulcimer Street)
1948, UK, 112 mins, b/w
Dir: Sidney Gilliat
Stars: Richard Attenborough, Alastair Sim, Fay Compton, Joyce Carey
Rating: ★★★★

Absorbing Launder and Gilliat film about the denizens of a south London boarding house in 1939. A touchingly human drama with fine London atmosphere. Richard Attenborough has a familiar early role as a cocky but panicky young man involved in crime. Such expert character stars as Fay Compton, Joyce Carey and Alastair Sim are less cast to type but just as good. The settings are convincingly drab and the dialogue is believably

written by Sidney Gilliat and J B Williams from a then-popular novel by Norman Collins.

London Kills Me ● ⓥ

1991, UK, 105 mins, colour
Dir: Hanif Kureishi
Stars: Justin Chadwick, Emer McCourt, Naveen Andrews, Steven Mackintosh, Brad Dourif, Eleanor David
Rating: ★★

For the most part, this is a bizarre and unlovely film about homeless teenage drug dealers/users on the streets of London. Gaunt and dishevelled, Clint (Justin Chadwick), basically a dishonest charmer, is beaten up by men to whom he owes money. He resolves to get a proper job and gets a promise of work in a diner – if he can get a pair of new shoes. As Clint steals constantly from his immediate boss Muffdiver (Steven Mackintosh), a pair of shoes would seem an easy option. But apparently not. Despite many unappealing aspects, the film does quite a fair job of dividing its time between a portrait of the drug generation and the story of Clint looking for shoes to steal. Sometimes the tale becomes tedious, especially when its women are involved, but the upbeat ending helps, and Chadwick and Mackintosh are fresh, newish faces who perform with enthusiasm and a degree of conviction.

London Town ○

(aka: My Heart Goes Crazy)
1946, UK, 126 mins, colour
Dir: Wesley Ruggles
Stars: Sid Field, Petula Clark, Greta Gynt, Kay Kendall, Claude Hulbert
Rating: ★

This big Technicolor film was made as Britain's answer to Hollywood musicals, and to showcase successful stage comedian Sid Field. In fact, it was not very effective as either, although it did give an early leading role to Kay Kendall; and the 14-year-old Petula Clark is delightful as Field's daughter. The director is a Hollywood expert, Wesley Ruggles. Alas, he lost the Rank Organisation a fortune on this one.

Loneliness of the Long Distance Runner, The ◐ ⓥ

1962, UK, 100 mins, b/w
Dir: Tony Richardson
Stars: Tom Courtenay, Julia Foster, Michael Redgrave, Alec McCowen
Rating: ★★★

A hard-edged drama filmed in stark black-and-white, this is the story of a

poor working-class youth sent to Borstal. Fine acting and a good script keep this early Sixties 'angry young man' drama fresh-looking today. The ending, although structurally sound, remains unsatisfying.

Lonely Are the Brave ○

1962, US, 107 mins, b/w
Dir: David Miller
Stars: Kirk Douglas, Gena Rowlands, Walter Matthau
Rating: ★★★

Kirk Douglas turns in another fine performance as the old-fashioned cowboy out of step with and resistant to the modern world. He starts a brawl in a bar just to get jailed so he can see an old friend, Michael Kane. He then breaks out of jail, pursued by sheriff Walter Matthau. Douglas is on horseback, Matthau drives a jeep. To say any more would be to hint at the film's ending. Douglas' personality dominates the picture, but Matthau is convincing as the lawman who feels empathy for Douglas' cowboy.

Lonelyhearts ○

1962, US, 101 mins, b/w
Dir: Vincent J Donehue
Stars: Montgomery Clift, Robert Ryan, Myrna Loy
Rating: ★★

Unusual film drama about a hard-up male reporter who becomes Miss Lonelyhearts of an agony column and gets involved with his readers' problems. Good portrayals from Montgomery Clift, Robert Ryan and Myrna Loy, and especially Broadway actress Maureen Stapleton, who, in one of her rare screen appearances, gives an outstanding performance as the wife of a bitter cripple.

Lonely Passion of Judith Hearne, The ● ⓥ

1987, UK, 116 mins, colour
Dir: Jack Clayton
Stars: Maggie Smith, Bob Hoskins, Wendy Hiller, Prunella Scales, Ian McNeice
Rating: ★★

One of those films that makes you admire the quality of its acting, but offers much less in the way of entertainment. Maggie Smith etches to the last detail a repressed Irish spinster with a sideline in piano teaching and a weakness for the whisky. Moving in with a mealy-mouthed landlady and her bloated post-graduate son who spends his nights with the 16-year-old maid, the spinster soon conceives a hopeless passion for the landlady's brother (Bob Hoskins), back from America after 30 years. Riddled with religious guilt, the story's also frequently dull, despite the razor-sharp acting of a cast that also includes Wendy Hiller and Prunella Scales. Another great performance from Maggie Smith, though, that certainly commands your attention.

Lone Ranger, The O
1956, US, 86 mins, colour
Dir: Stuart Heisler
Stars: Clayton Moore, Jay Silverheels
Rating: ★★

Feature-length version of the enormously popular television programme of the early Fifties, complete with the original stars. Husky voiced Lyle Bettger makes a stylish villain and former teenage star Bonita Granville is the heroine. Not great, but a lot better than the 1981 version.

Lone Ranger and the Lost City of Gold, The O
1958, US, 81 mins, colour
Dir: Lesley Selander
Stars: Clayton Moore, Jay Silverheels, Noreen Nash
Rating: ★★

Rousing action stuff for the children as the Lone Ranger and Tonto follow the trail of five medallions that lead to a fortune. Expert Western director Lesley Selander (a man, despite the spelling) keeps the rough-and-tumble brisk and uncomplicated. Noreen Nash, remembered as the freckled heroine from animal films of the Forties, gets a rare chance to play an all-out bad lot, and revels in the role.

Lone Star ◑ ⓥ
1995, US, 135 mins, colour
Dir: John Sayles
Stars: Chris Cooper, Elizabeth Pena, Kris Kristofferson, Matthew McConaughey, Ron Canada, Clifton James
Rating: ★★★

A mostly absorbing if finally overlong 'modern Western', whose token murder plot scarcely conceals its basic themes of relationships, reconciliation and coming to terms with the past. In the desert outside a Texas town, a set of bones and a sheriff's star sprout from the ground. It looks like the remains of much-hated Sheriff Charlie Wade (Kristofferson), a bribes-and-bullets lawman who vanished in 1957, rumoured to have been run out of town by his co-sheriff Buddy Deeds (McConaughey) whose son Sam (Cooper) is the present sheriff. Also

woven into the tapestry of the plot are Big O (Canada) and Hollis (James), a 1957 deputy who's Mayor (who were both in on a pivotal confrontation between Deeds and Wade) and Pilar (Pena) Sam's childhood sweetheart now back on the market. The intricate fabric of the story holds up quite well for most of the film, although the rekindled romance between Sam and Pilar punches holes in the pace that Sayles could have done without.

Lone Wolf McQuade ◑ ⓥ
1983, US, 107 mins, colour
Dir: Steve Carver
Stars: Chuck Norris, David Carradine, Barbara Carrera
Rating: ★

An orgy of carefully staged and edited violence. Chop-socky specialist Chuck Norris is the present-day Texas Ranger who's not certain to win until the bad guys hurt the things he loves: first the older Ranger he idolises, then his pet wolf, then his daughter. It's hard to know what the man of steel will run out of first: opponents or Achilles heels. Some well-known players, among them David Carradine, L Q Jones, R G Armstrong, Barbara Carrera and Leon Isaac Kennedy, are involved in the get-yourself-out-of-this situations that result. Action is heavily underlined by music in the Ennio Morricone mould.

Long and the Short and the Tall, The ◑
(aka: Jungle Fighters)
1960, UK, 110 mins, b/w
Dir: Leslie Norman
Stars: Richard Todd, Richard Harris, David McCallum, Laurence Harvey
Rating: ★★★

A British patrol in Burma sows the seeds of its own destruction in this tougher-than-tough war film. The script, by Wolf Mankowitz from Willis Hall's play, burns through the screen like vitriol.

Long Arm, The O
(aka: The Third Key)
1956, UK, 100 mins, b/w
Dir: Charles Frend
Stars: Jack Hawkins, John Stratton, Dorothy Alison
Rating: ★★★★

An excellent, intricately plotted story of police work from Ealing Studios, with Jack Hawkins in towering form as the inspector. He, Dorothy Alison and John Stratton build lifelike characters in the leading roles, while the exciting, well-knit plot has Hawkins and his

men trekking across half of England on the trail of a master cracksman – and killer. A bit like *Dragnet* with British accents, the film piles on its excitement in fine style, making it streets ahead of Hawkins' other Fifties police story *Gideon's Day*. Even the cameo roles are well done in this, the last Ealing film actually to be made at Ealing studios.

Long Duel, The O
1967, UK, 115 mins, colour
Dir: Ken Annakin
Stars: Yul Brynner, Trevor Howard, Harry Andrews, Andrew Keir, Charlotte Rampling
Rating: ★

A British attempt to match the American action spectacles of the mid-Sixties, with Brynner and Howard as adversaries in the India of the British Raj of the Twenties. Long and dull.

Long Kiss Goodnight, The ● ⓥ
1996, US, 120 mins, colour
Dir: Renny Harlin
Stars: Geena Davis, Samuel L Jackson, Patrick Malahide, Craig Bierko, Brian Cox, David Morse
Rating: ★★★

As ridiculously plotted as any James Bond film, this is nonetheless a real crowd-pleaser that equals any 007 film in the action stakes. Not surprisingly, Davis is cast as a sort of Jane Bond, a US government assassin who has made a new identity for herself these past years, following near-termination and amnesia. When Mitch, a private eye (Jackson), uncovers her past, a car accident triggers repressed memories and corrupt government agents discover a potential embarrassment who must be wiped out for good. Naturally Davis and Jackson bear charmed lives in the ensuing mayhem in which enough hardware is blown apart to justify at least most of the $70 million budget. Davis, escaping from death traps with the alacrity of a silent screen heroine, has her moments, but Jackson is the real scene-stealer here and has all the best lines.

Longest Day, The O ⓥ
1962, US/UK, 180 mins, b/w
Dir: Darryl F Zanuck, Ken Annakin, Andrew Marton, Gerd Oswald, Bernhard Wicki
Stars: John Wayne, Rod Steiger, Robert Ryan, Henry Fonda, Robert Mitchum, Richard Burton, Sean Connery
Rating: ★★★★

L

Just about the war film to end them all with the participation of more than 50 star names. This is Darryl F Zanuck's – he produced and was one of the five directors – massive reconstruction of the events leading to, and happening on, 6 June 1944, when the Allied forces invaded Nazi Europe. It sticks closely to the known facts, photographs its events in a semi-newsreel manner (it was one of the last major films made in black and white) and relates countless stories of individual heroism and tragedy in its three hours running time. When the action scenes do come, however, director Andrew Marton, deserves a large bouquet for his handling of them. How admirably he marshals his forces, taking our attention easily from one embattled group to another with apan of the camera, or via the path of an aeroplane skimming low over the beach battlegrounds. Any number of small cameo scenes are skilfully woven into the larger patchwork of the D-Day operation, allowing room for small-scale but excellent performances from Henry Fonda, Robert Mitchum, John Wayne, Eddie Albert, Red Buttons and Curt Jurgens. Sometimes shown on TV in an excellent (if less atmospheric) colourised version.

Longest Yard, The

See: The Mean Machine

Long Goodbye, The ● ⓥ

1973, US, 111 mins, colour
Dir: Robert Altman
Stars: Elliott Gould, Nina Van Pallandt, Sterling Hayden, Henry Gibson, Mark Rydell
Rating: ★

Raymond Chandler traditionalists who think private eve Philip Marlowe should wear a flap-down hat and look like Humphrey Bogart or Dick Powell won't take to director Robert Altman's Seventies version. More to the point, this is a tedious and sometimes confusing film. Elliott Gould's Marlowe is seedy and down-at-heel – and totally unconvincing. There is solid support from Sterling Hayden as a drunken writer and Henry Gibson as an evil doctor. And you can't miss a young Arnold Schwarzenegger, billed here as Arnold Strong! Watch out for the ending. For someone steeped in Chandler lore, it will be a culture shock – if you're still awake, that is.

Long Good Friday, The ● ⓥ

1979, UK, 114 mins, colour
Dir: John Mackenzie
Stars: Bob Hoskins, Helen Mirren, Dave King, Eddie Constantine
Rating: ★★★

In the early Sixties, there was *Hell is a City* and *The Criminal*, in the early Seventies *Villain* and *Get Carter*. Here the tough British crime film moves on another decade, revealing a yet blacker and more violent picture, as the over-complacent British gangster is ruthlessly brushed aside by interests from America and the new lawlessness from Ireland. As the Cockney kingpin of London crime, Bob Hoskins is best when roaring defiance at his enemies like a wounded, cornered animal. The scenes of violence are many, ugly and professional, and the film moves like a steamroller, heavy and relentless but ever onwards, greatly helped by the doomy background music of Francis Monkman. The acting does not always seem as relaxed as it might be, with the definite exception of Dave King's thoroughly bent policeman.

Long Gray Line, The ○

1955, US, 131 mins, colour
Dir: John Ford
Stars: Tyrone Power, Maureen O'Hara, Robert Francis, Ward Bond, Donald Crisp
Rating: ★★★★

Rolling along on a veritable flood of tears and nostalgia, this is John Ford's tribute to West Point, America's famous military academy, and to one Irishman who spent the greater part of his life there. Although the ending is protracted and over-sentimental (even by the film's own standards), most of it is a brilliant job of story construction by the director, who weaves many of his most personal themes into the piecemeal storyline, knitting it together and building a picture that packs a powerful emotional punch. If you're easily moved at the movies, keep a handkerchief or two safely by. Tyrone Power gives one of his better film performances as the central figure, but this is Maureen O'Hara's film. As the girl who becomes Power's wife, she has never been warmer or more winning.

Long Hot Summer, The ○

1958, US, 118 mins, colour
Dir: Martin Ritt
Stars: Paul Newman, Joanne Woodward, Orson Welles, Anthony Franciosa, Lee Remick, Angela Lansbury
Rating: ★★★

This fiery melodrama, based on two short stories and part of a novel by William Faulkner, shot Paul Newman, Joanne Woodward, Lee Remick and Anthony Franciosa to stardom. Newman is the young opportunist who arrives in town, bringing with him a reputation for burning people's barns if they cross him. On the basis that guts get you places, he makes an impression on his landlord (a boisterous performance by Orson Welles), the town bigwig, and meets his match in Joanne Woodward's sassy daughter. The scene is thus set for incident and passion and there's plenty of both. Newman and Woodward are first-class, and there's excellent support from Franciosa as Welles' wimpish son (who plans a dramatic revenge on his bully of a father), Lee Remick as his sweet-natured wife and Angela Lansbury as Welles' long-time mistress.

Long John Silver ○

1954, Australia, 109 mins, colour
Dir: Byron Haskin
Stars: Robert Newton, Kit Taylor, Grant Taylor, Rod Taylor, Connie Gilchrist
Rating: ★★

This was the second film that Robert Newton made in the character he created in *Treasure Island* – Long John Silver, the peg-legged scourge of the Caribbean. The film was produced in Australia, and many good Australian actors go miles over the top in a story that's simply crammed with incident action and colour. A fair dinkum kid called Kit Taylor takes over from Bobby Driscoll as Jim Hawkins, And its out with the telescopes, me hearties, to spot the actor lurking behind sightless eyes and a mass of stubble as bad old Israel Hands, waiting for Jim lad who blinded him. those many years before. Yes, it's a youngster called Rodney (later Rod) Taylor, who went to America the following year and launched a star career that lasted 20 years.

Long, Long Trailer, The ⊙

1954, US, 103 mins, colour
Dir: Vincente Minnelli
Stars: Lucille Ball, Desi Arnaz
Rating: ★★★★

A totally side-splitting comedy about the misadventures of a newly-married couple taking their honeymoon in a giant caravan. Full of funny little individual scenes, the film, boosted by Lucille Ball and Desi Arnaz's success on TV, proved an absolute goldmine at box-offices on both sides of the Atlantic. There are nice little 'bits' for Keenan Wynn and Marjorie Main, but really the stars are the whole show. Vincente Minnelli directs it all at 60 miles-an-hour speed and Robert Surtees' Ansco Color photography is simply stunning.

Long Riders, The ● ⓥ
1980, US, 95 mins, colour
Dir: Walter Hill
Stars: Stacy Keach, James Keach, David Carradine, Keith Carradine, Robert Carradine, Dennis Quaid, Randy Quaid, Connie Gilchrist
Rating: ★★

The James-Younger gang rides again in yet another re-telling of their infamous bank-robbing career from Missouri to Minnesota (and the fateful Northfield raid), each version bloodier and gutsier than the last. The trump card here is the casting of four sets of acting brothers as the Jameses, Youngers, Millers and treacherous Fords. This acting fraternity acquits itself well. The film tries not to make heroes of the boys; but they come out that way anyway.

Long Ships, The ○
1964, UK, 125 mins, colour
Dir: Jack Cardiff
Stars: Richard Widmark, Sidney Poitier, Russ Tamblyn, Rosanna Schiaffino
Rating: ★

Richard Widmark and Sidney Poitier never seem anything but Hollywood stars in costume in this colourful adventure story about a Viking odyssey, actually shot on and along the rocky coastline of Yugoslavia. Decades later, the film set village still existed – although a bit dilapidated – and was regularly shown to parties of tourists. It's not half as decrepit as the script, though, and even Christopher Challis' colour camerawork seems below par.

Longtime Companion ● ⓥ
1990, US, 99 mins, colour
Dir: Norman René
Stars: Bruce Davison, Campbell Scott, Mary-Louise Parker
Rating: ★★★

This was Hollywood's first film to tell the story of how AIDS devastated America's homosexual community during the 1980s. A big hit at the Cannes Film Festival, it tells the stories of a group of friends whose lives are all affected in different ways by the deaths of lovers. It skilfully weaves educational information with storyline and successfully avoids being at all mawkish during the more emotive scenes. Not without moments of great humour, the film does contain one truly outstanding performance from Bruce Davison who was deservedly nominat-

ed for a Best Supporting Actor Oscar for his role as the lover of a TV soap scriptwriter who allows his friend to die with as much dignity as possible. A brave landmark film.

Long Voyage Home, The ○
1940, US, 120 mins, b/w
Dir: John Ford
Stars: John Wayne, Thomas Mitchell, Ian Hunter, John Qualen, Barry Fitzgerald
Rating: ★★★★★

Great film that proves a major triumph for the John Ford/John Wayne partnership, then in its early days. In its story of seamen longing for a return home while going through hell and high water on the way, there are memorable performances from Thomas Mitchell and Ian Hunter, and the greasy, sweaty, smoky atmosphere of the tramp steamer in which the men live and toil is finely done. The story has a typical Eugene O'Neill air of futility about it (it's adapted from three of his one-act plays), but the tragedy-tinged ending, strongly reminiscent of a sequence in *Cavalcade*, only adds to the film's overall impact. There's great supporting acting from Ward Bond, Mildred Natwick and Arthur Shields, but all the cast sink themselves into the characters they play. A long, winding film, sometimes exciting, often touching, with some strongly descriptive black-and-white photography by Gregg Toland.

Look Back in Anger ① ⓥ
1959, UK, 99 mins, b/w
Dir: Tony Richardson
Stars: Richard Burton, Claire Bloom, Mary Ure, Gary Raymond, Edith Evans, Donald Pleasence
Rating: ★★★

This tough-talking film made an extraordinary impact on audiences in its day, and consolidated the arrival of the new-wave realism – termed 'kitchen sink' by some critics – begun by *Room at the Top*. The dialogue bristles with barbs – most of them from the lips of original angry young man Jimmy Porter, providing a prime role for Richard Burton.

Look for the Silver Lining ○
1949, US, 100 mins, colour
Dir: David Butler
Stars: June Haver, Ray Bolger, Gordon MacRae, Charlie Ruggles
Rating: ★★★

A typically cheerful Warner Bros. biopic – suitably fictionalised – with June Haver impersonating Twenties

Broadway musical comedy star Marilyn Miller. But it's Ray Bolger, playing Miller's mentor Jack Donohue, who steals the picture with some dazzling tap dancing, proving once again that he was one of the cinema's most shamefully underused dancers. Plenty of tuneful vintage songs (musical director Ray Heindorf received an Oscar nomination), LeRoy Prinz's smart choreography and David Buder's direction complete this lively package. The ending, very daring, actually hints at Miller's early death.

Looking Glass War, The ①
1969, UK, 108 mins, colour
Dir: Frank R Pierson
Stars: Christopher Jones, Pia Degermark, Ralph Richardson, Anthony Hopkins, Susan George, Paul Rogers
Rating: ★

This espionage yarn from the bitter pen of John Le Carré is both an adventure story and a clinical portrayal of British Cold War espionage as a world apart, almost outdated in its approach and ideals. Christopher Jones plays the young Polish refugee sent on a dangerous mission into East Germany. The long training he undergoes is the most entertaining section of the film. After that, uncharacteristic acting and a wordy script sink all concerned.

Look Who's Talking ① ⓥ
1989, US, 96 mins, colour
Dir: Amy Heckerling
Stars: John Travolta, Kirstie Alley, Olympia Dukakis, George Segal, Bruce Willis (voice)
Rating: ★★

One of the big money-spinners of its year, to the bafflement of many critics, this is a tolerable novelty romp if you care for cute comedies about babies. John Travolta's career certainly needed a break at this stage, but this was a mighty lucky one. An embarrassing beginning, giving an impression of a gang of sperms fertilising a human egg, is followed by a most unconvincing pregnancy in which unwed mum Kirstie Alley looks as though she is wearing a toilet seat under her dress. The tale is made partially palatable by the performance of the beautifully flat-faced Alley and by using the voice of Bruce Willis to give us the thoughts of the baby. You'll enjoy some of it though – also the continuity slip here our hero is 'driving' his cab, which is clearly being steered by a stuntman wearing dark glasses, while Travolta isn't wearing glasses at all!

L

Look Who's Talking Now
❶ ⓥ

1993, US, 97 mins, colour
Dir: Tom Ropelewski
Stars: John Travolta, Kirstie Alley,
Olympia Dukakis, Lysette Anthony,
Danny DeVito (voice), Diane Keaton
(voice)
Rating: ★

Here's a series that's gone to the dogs
in more ways than one. In this tired
second sequel, the familiar formula is
wearing pretty thin. Kirstie Alley and
John Travolta are mum and dad again,
this time saddled with a mangy mongrel (voiced by Danny DeVito) and a
pampered poodle (voiced by Diane
Keaton). A feeble subplot involves
Travolta's lady boss, the poodle owner
(Lysette Anthony) making a play for
him. It's left to the bickering dogs to
save the day and supply all the comedy
before the sugar-laden happy ending.
Come to think of it, why didn't they
leave the humans out of it altogether?

Look Who's Talking Too ❶ ⓥ
1990, US, 81 mins, colour
Dir: Amy Heckerling
Stars: John Travolta, Kirstie Alley, Bruce
Willis(voice), Roseanne Arnold (voice)
Rating: ★

Good sense and good taste are certainly not on the menu for this typically
crude Hollywood sequel to a wildly
successful original. Lavatory humour,
though, is well to the fore, emphasised
by the use of Mel Brooks' voice as Mr
Toilet Man, a loo-bowl come to life,
spitting blue water and threatening ir-
reparable damage to baby Mikey's
private parts. Bruce Willis is as laconic
as ever as the voice of Mikey, but
Roseanne Arnold's contribution as the
voice of his new baby sister is unexpectedly dull. Kirstie Alley and John
Travolta still play pleasingly as the parents, but the plotline is all too
obviously a rush job.

Loot ❶ ⓥ
1970, UK, 101 mins, colour
Dir: Silvio Narizzano
Stars: Richard Attenborough, Lee
Remick, Hwyel Bennett, Milo O'Shea
Rating: ★★★

A really dark-hued black comedy, well
adapted by *Hancock* and *Steptoe and Son*
writers Ray Galton and Alan Simpson
from Joe Orton's celebrated stage play.
Silvio Narizzano's stylish direction and
the neatly judged over-the-top performances perfectly complement the
writers' sardonic view of life and death.
Particularly effective are Lee Remick as

a blonde murderess and Richard
Attenborough as the kind of policeman
destined to give Scotland Yard a distinctly odd name.

Lord Jim ○
1965, US, 154 mins, colour
Dir: Richard Brooks
Stars: Peter O'Toole, James Mason, Curt
Jurgens, Jack Hawkins, Eli Wallach,
Daliah Lavi
Rating: ★★

Joseph Conrad's magnificent novel of
high adventure in the 19th-century Far
East is translated faithfully to the
screen in this film from the hands of
writer-director Richard Brooks. The
action is fierce and many of the characters are surely just as Conrad must
have seen them, particularly Jack
Hawkins as the narrator (Marlow) and
James Mason, almost unrecognisable
as the treacherous pirate Gentleman
Brown. But Peter O'Toole completely
misses the mystique of the central
character, which he seems to see as a
sort of Lawrence of Cambodia.

Lord Love a Duck ❶
1966, US, 104 mins, b/w
Dir: George Axelrod
Stars: Roddy McDowall, Tuesday Weld,
Lola Albright
Rating: ★★★

Wild and bitingly funny sex comedy
from George Axelrod, who wrote *The
Seven Year Itch* and *Breakfast at Tiffany's*.
Roddy (*Planet of the Apes*) McDowall
plays a collegiate who masterminds
his fellow students' lives through
hypnotism.

Lord of the Flies ❶ ⓥ
1963, UK, 90 mins, b/w
Dir: Peter Brook
Stars: James Aubrey, Tom Chapin, Hugh
Edwards
Rating: ★★★

What would happen if a party of
schoolboys were stranded on a desert
island? This horrifying parable gives
us the blackest possible answer. Their
brittle society shatters, rules are broken
and the boys become in turn arguers,
hunters, idolaters, cannibals and murderers. The impact of director Peter
Brook's film version of William
Golding's novel is considerable, even
though the acting of the minor roles is,
in many cases, little more than a mechanical repetition of lines. But James
Aubrey is solid as the sensible Ralph,
and Tom Chapin excellent as the
sullen, leering Jack, the head choirboy
with a hyena's sneer, laugh and man-

ners behind a public school veneer.
Though his pace is slow in parts,
Brook skilfully probes his way through
the mounting horror, just as the camera
weaves its grainy way through the undergrowth of the island. The 1990
version is not as good.

Lord of the Rings ○ ⓥ
1978, US, 133 mins, colour
Dir: Ralph Bakshi
Voice Stars: Christopher Guard, William
Squire, John Hurt, Michael Sholes
Rating: ★★★

Director Ralph Bakshi's attempt to set
down an animated version of J R R
Tolkien's massive saga of Middle Earth
(or at least the first half of it) must go
down as a jolly good try at an almost
impossible project. Certain sections –
the mines of Moria; the Ringwraiths in
the sky – are bitingly close to one's vi-
sualisation of the book. The voices of
the hobbits seem a little too light and
West Country at first but, like the rest
of the voices – John Hurt makes a
splendid Aragorn – they grow on you.
The action is at times a bit jerky where
so much has been telescoped into so little – don't miss the beginning or you'll
lose the thread of it; but we should be
grateful that Bakshi has tried so hard to
be faithful to the original that its spirit
and inspiration often shine through to
stir the blood. Gandalf, Saruman (the
good and evil wizards), Wormtongue
and Legolas are particularly well realised, and the flowing music theme is
of great assistance in lending the action
momentum when it needs it.

Lorenzo's Oil ❶ ⓥ
1992, US, 135 mins, colour
Dir: George Miller
Stars: Nick Nolte, Susan Sarandon, Peter
Ustinov, Zack O'Malley Greenburg,
Kathleen Wilholte
Rating: ★★★

If we pardon its occasional lapses, this
is a good, if very punishing account of
one couple's struggle to find a cure for
their son, stricken with ALD – a form
of dystrophy which affects male children – which no boy had previously
survived longer than 24 months. This
is an inspiring story but the problem
with the film, like so many modern
ones, is that it goes on too long. By
prolonging our agony as well as
Lorenzo's, director George Miller dissi-
pates the suspense and dissolves our
emotional involvement. Matters are
exacerbated near the end by a poorly-
acted English scientist who tells us he
has six months to retirement but looks

more like 90. That said, Nick Nolte and Susan Sarandon, as the parents, and Zack O'Malley Greenburg, as the boy, give performances that deserved to be jostling at the Oscar queues that year (though only Sarandon's did). A pity their story is too intense and too repetitious for too long, but the achievements of the real-life people involved are beyond praise and even belief.

Losing Isaiah ⦿ ⓥ
1995, US, 104 mins, colour
Dir: Stephen Gyllenhaal
Stars: Jessica Lange, Halle Berry, David Strathairn, Samuel L Jackson, Regina Taylor, Cuba Gooding Jr
Rating: ★★

It was perhaps predictable that there should be tedious patches in a tug-of-love story that wears its badges of political correctness so prominently on its sleeve. And the ending, too, is a trifle too convenient for us all. Although this is how America would like to think life and minds work in its black and white communities, the issues are probably less clear-cut than portrayed here. White forty-something Jessica Lange adopts the baby that black crack addict Halle Berry leaves in a cardboard box while looking for drugs. When she returns, dustmen have collected it and she assumes the baby is dead. Three years later, rehabilitated if little better housed, she finds the child is alive and launches a legal battle to get it back. Now as she comes to court looking not like a bag-lady but Halle Berry, there seems little doubt about the outcome. But the film-makers are more anxious to provide an emotive and upbeat ending than in showing us how (badly) things might have turned out.

Loss of Innocence
See: The Greengage Summer

Lost ○
(aka: Tears for Simon)
1955, UK, 89 mins, colour
Dir: Guy Green
Stars: David Farrar, David Knight, Julia Arnall
Rating: ★★★

Carefully-made British thriller with a fair share of tension and excitement. Screenplay writer Janet Green made some useful contributions to the British cinema (Sapphire, Life for Ruth and Victim were among her best) and here she fashions a tidy drama about a stolen toddler, which focuses both on the intricacies of the police hunt and the pressures faced by the distraught parents. As the mother, Austrian-born Julia Arnall, who was briefly under contract to Rank in the Fifties, gives her most effective screen performance.

Lost and Found ○
1979, US, 112 mins, colour
Dir: Melvin Frank
Stars: George Segal, Glenda Jackson, Maureen Stapleton, Paul Sorvino
Rating: ★★

If George Segal taught Glenda Jackson a thing or two about the art of screen comedy in A Touch of Class (for which she won an Oscar), then the lesson was well and truly learnt. For it's George who comes out the loser in their second film together, flapping around while Glenda piles up the points with her tart and acerbic delivery. Most of the best fun comes in the first two reels when Glenda, on the run from her ex-husband's mistress ('Mona – age 22, bust 38, IQ indiscernible') and George, on the run from his late wife's memory, keep bumping into each other with devastating effect at a Swiss resort.

Lost Boys, The ⦿ ⓥ
1987, US, 98 mins, colour
Dir: Joel Schumacher
Stars: Jason Patric, Corey Haim, Dianne Wiest, Edward Herrman, Kiefer Sutherland, Jami Gertz, Corey Feldman
Rating: ★★★

A lively horror film that also crams in as many amusing lines as possible, this ends up as a kind of Fangbusters. Two boys and their mother move into a town where, as their grandpa puts it, 'if all the corpses in the churchyards were to stand up, we'd have one hell of a population problem.' Lured on by the comely Star (Jami Gertz), older brother Michael (Jason Patric) is soon inducted into the society of The Lost Boys, led by the ghoulish David (Kiefer Sutherland). 'You're a vampire Michael,' squawks young Sam (Corey Haim). 'My own brother!' Enter Edgar and Allan, the real Fangbusters. 'We're almost certain,' says Edgar, 'that ghouls and werewolves are in high positions in City Hall.' So the scene is set for a special effects finale typical of today's cinema. The film drags a bit but it really gets motoring around the half-way mark.

Lost Command ⦿
1966, US, 130 mins, colour
Dir: Mark Robson
Stars: Anthony Quinn, Alain Delon, George Segal, Michelle Morgan, Claudia Cardinale
Rating: ★★

Scenes of incredibly tough paratroop training, and a sequence of bloodthirsty battles help to take your mind off thinking that the script of this blood-spattered story of France's war against Algeria is glorifying a messy war for the sake of entertainment. But, in more than two hours, surely some positive thinking on the whys and wherefores of this long and bitter affray could have replaced the devious side-track subjects which destroy any feeling of involvement with the characters. As it is, we have Anthony Quinn as a sort of Zorba the Sheep, who, after service in IndoChina, is deprived of his command, largely because he has no regard for higher authority, and is of peasant stock, a point the script loses no chance to ram home. 'I'd rather stand, sir,' Quinn tells a superior. 'It's a habit I developed as a shepherd boy.'

Lost Continent, The ⦿
1968, UK, 98 mins, colour
Dir: Michael Carreras
Stars: Eric Porter, Hildegarde Knef, Suzanna Leigh
Rating: ★★★

Eerie atmosphere and decent monsters boost this rather bizarre piece of science-fantasy about a tramp steamer wandering into uncharted seas and discovering a lost civilisation. Eric Porter keeps a straight face and stiff upper lip) Dana Gillespie offers statuesque support.

Lost Highway ● ⓥ
1997, US, 134 ins, colour
Dir: David Lynch
Stars: Bill Pullman, Patricia Arquette, Balthazar Getty
Rating: ★★★

Director David Lynch's baffling thriller unfolds with all the logic of a dream. It's a story that plays with parallel worlds, fused (and confused) identities and the occult. Briefly, jazz musician Bill Pullman finds himself, after a bewildering sequence of events, awaiting execution for the murder of his wife (Patricia Arquette). The next day, a stranger is found in his cell... It would be impressive if all this made sense at teh end, but this is not Lynch's game. The result is a surrealsitc, intriguing jigsaw, albeit one with much nudity, blood-letting and bad language, as Lynch shrewdly caters for the casual trade as well as the aficionados. The performances are suitably enigmatic.

L

Lost Horizon ○ ⓥ

1937, US, 130 mins, b/w
Dir: Frank Capra
Stars: Ronald Colman, Edward Everett Horton, H B Warner, Jane Wyatt, Sam Jaffe
Rating: ★★★★★

Now almost completely restored to its original running time, this is Frank Capra's totally engrossing film version of the famous James Hilton novel. The brilliant opening, catching all the turmoil and panic of confused flight from a revolution, pitches us straight into the action. Once in the lost valley of Shangri-La, the film depends more on its acting and dialogue, but still Capra rarely puts a foot wrong. Ronald Colman is perfectly cast as the idealistic Robert Conway, Jane Wyatt quietly effective as his girl in Shangri-La and Sam Jaffe magnificent in yet another extraordinary characterisation (to set beside his water-carrier in *Gunga Din*) as the ancient High Lama. Thomas Mitchell and Isabel Jewell are as solid and genuine as ever in supporting roles, and the climax is brilliantly realised. Only the most cynical will fail to be moved.

Lost Horizon ○

1972, US, 143 mins, colour
Dir: Charles Jarrott
Stars: Peter Finch, Liv Ullmann, Sally Kellerman, George Kennedy, Michael York, Olivia Hussey
Rating: ★★

Imagine how James Hilton's famous story of Shangri-La would be remade as a musical by the producer of the Doris Day/Rock Hudson comedies, and you'll have a pretty fair idea of how this frothy farrago turned out. Liv Ullmann, so brilliant in Ingmar Bergman films, has never been very lucky with her choice of international roles. Here, she and Peter Finch seem singularly ill at ease with a tuneful Burt Bacharach score that includes the catchy 'The World Is a Circle'. But the scene-setting is extremely well done, and veteran Charles Boyer is excellent as the wise and ancient High Lama.

Lost in a Harem ○

1944, US, 89 mins, b/w
Dir: Charles Riesner
Stars: Bud Abbott, Lou Costello, Marilyn Maxwell, John Conte
Rating: ★★

Abbott and Costello on one of their two visits to Metro-Goldwyn-Mayer, which means better production values

and a livelier overall drive. The boys have some nice scenes with wicked sultan Douglass Dumbrille whose idea of a hypnotising jewel was reprised by Crosby and Hope in *Road to Rio*.

Lost In America ⓓ

1985, US, 91 mins, colour
Dir: Albert Brooks
Stars: Albert Brooks, Julie Hagerty
Rating: ★★

A romantic road comedy directed by, co-written by and starring Albert Brooks who plays nervy, anxious Los Angeles advertising executive David Howard, in debt and mortgaged to the hilt but living a full and yuppie lifestyle with his successful personnel director wife (Julie Hagerty). When the big promotion he anticipates goes to an undeserving other, David persuades wife Linda to sell everything they own and invest in a motor home, the idea being to live a simple, carefree life on the road. Or so they think... The script is dotted with the occasional witty and insightful line and there are some sardonic sideswipes at 1980s materialism to lighten the hapless couple's clichéd voyage of discovery – although be warned, there is a cop-out ending. But if you can tolerate the manic overacting of both Brooks and *Airplane!*'s Hagerty as you watch misfortune upon catastrophe befall them, you could well enjoy this journey.

Lost Patrol, The ○

1934, US, 74 mins, b/w
Dir: John Ford
Stars: Victor McLaglen, Boris Karloff, Wallace Ford
Rating: ★★★★

One of John Ford's earliest classics, about a small group of soldiers trapped in the desert by marauding Arabs. Fierce, unrelenting tension, with ripe performances from Victor McLaglen as a tough soldier and Boris Karloff (memorably over the top) as a religious fanatic. Black and white photography by Harold Wenstrom catches exactly the oppressive combination of heat and fear that drives the men to the edge of insanity.

Lost Weekend, The ○

1945, US, 101 mins, b/w
Dir: Billy Wilder
Stars: Ray Milland, Jane Wyman, Howard da Silva
Rating: ★★★★★

This striking study of alcoholism not only changed Ray Milland's career from lounge lizard leading man to per-

sonable star in both heroic and villainous roles, but shook the film colony by taking four of the year's major Academy Awards. Besides the almost inevitable award for Milland – the competition that year wasn't strong but Milland's performance would probably have won against almost anything *The Lost Weekend* picked up statuettes for best film, best direction (Billy Wilder) and best screenplay (Wilder and Charles Brackett). And Frank Faylen should at least have been nominated in the best supporting actor category for his frightening study of a male nurse in the film's most nightmarish and memorable sequence, when Milland lands up in the alcoholic ward of a hospital. Wilder's direction conveys a fine sense of frenzy, especially when Milland is hunting for the bottles his brother has removed from their hiding places.

Lost World, The ○

1960, US, 98 mins, colour
Dir: Irwin Allen
Stars: Michael Rennie, Jill St John, Claude Rains
Rating: ★★

Amusingly entertaining remake of an old 1924 classic, based on the story by Sir Arthur Conan Doyle. This one has some good battles between prehistoric beasts, even if most of the human cast seems miscast. Not exactly *Jurassic Park*, perhaps, but children will still have a whale (or a dinosaur) of a time.

Lost World: Jurassic Park, The ⓓ ⓥ

1997, US, 134 mins, colour
Dir: Steven Spielberg
Stars: Jeff Goldblum, Julianne Moore, Richard Attenborough, Arliss Howard, Vince Vaughan, Pete Postlethwaite
Rating: ★★★★★

The dinos are back – and better than ever. And so's the story, which combines elements of the first film with *King Kong*, to provide sweeping and exciting entertainment. It seems there was a second island site, where the dinosaurs were allowed to breed and mix freely. And, once an expedition hits the island, the dinos quickly get the upper hand. in action scenes that blend creatures and humans more seamlessly than ever before. Both dialogue and action are humanised by typical Spielberg touches in a film that's more inventive and exciting than the first: shots of creature claws scrabbling to dig a hole to their prey are stunningly well matched to the human hands digging just as desperately to escape.

The best performance comes from Pete Postlethwaite as a hard-headed hunter out for the biggest fame of all.

Loudest Whisper, The
See: Children's Hour, The

Love and Bullets ◐
1978, UK, 103 mins, colour
Dir: Stuart Rosenberg
Stars: Charles Bronson, Rod Steiger, Jill Ireland, Strother Martin, Bradford Dillman
Rating: ★★

Charles Bronson does his worst, smearing blood over pretty locations as a cop who goes mob hunting for the FBI. Rod Steiger is wonderfully outrageous as a mobster nuts about MacDonald and Eddy. Henry Silva is as nasty as ever in a supporting role.

Love and Other Catastrophes ◐ ⓥ
1996, US, 80 mins, colour
Dir: Emma-Kate Coghlan
Stars: Alice Garner, Frances O'Connor, Matthew Dynarski
Rating: ★★★

Although perhaps not quite as good as its young director thinks it is, this is still a smart and spiky romantic comedy that's streets ahead of the contemporary (and more highly praised) She's the One. The leading characters have charm and personality to spare in Coghlan's tale of the interweaving destinies of five college students, headed by Alice Garner, a bright new face, who'll amuse you with her deadpan research on her long-delayed thesis 'Doris Day as Feminist Warrior'. It's familiar stuff, but on the whole fun to be with.

Love and Pain and the Whole Damn Thing ○
1972, US, 110 mins, colour
Dir: Alan J Pakula
Stars: Maggie Smith, Timothy Bottoms
Rating: ★★

Alan J Pakula, who directed All the President's Men and Klute, reveals himself as the romantic one always suspected in this sumptuously photographed weepie with humour trailing in not far behind the tears. It has a breathtakingly good performance by Maggie Smith as the dying spinster who finds unlikely romance with a 20-year-old American boy. Whether getting stuck in the loo, gloriously drunk as she attempts suicide, or getting bedded by the boy – 'Think of the generation gap!' she groans – Ms Smith is so good as to boggle the mind.

Love at First Bite ◐ ⓥ
1979, US, 96 mins, colour
Dir: Stan Dragoti
Stars: George Hamilton, Susan Saint James, Richard Benjamin, Dick Shawn
Rating: ★★★

'Here's blood in your eye,' says George Hamilton's Dracula in this fun-filled spoof of the old vampire legend. Evicted by authorities who plan to turn his castle into a gymnasium, the count emigrates to America, where he and devoted Renfield (irresistible Arte Johnson) are soon apologetically robbing a blood bank there, demanding, 'Give it to me in small bills – I mean bottles.' Dracula falls for a model (delightful Susan Saint James) whom he hopes will accept three bites and become his vampire bride. Hamilton happily plays it all dead straight. So, in a frenzied way, does Richard Benjamin, whom I can't ever remember laughing at before, as Saint James' on-off suitor who, confusing his monsters, tries to kill Dracula with silver bullets. But the real winner is the screenplay by Robert Kaufmann that keeps the witty cracks and situations constantly flowing.

Love at Large ◐
1990, US, 97 mins, colour
Dir: Alan Rudolph
Stars: Tom Berenger, Elizabeth Perkins, Anne Archer, Ted Levine, Kate Capshaw, Kevin J O'Connor
Rating: ★★

Trust director Alan Rudolph to make a detective story that isn't. Deliberately artificial, with oblique dialogue and story threads that turn to comic stylism, the film is really about people looking for love rather than people looking for people. Tom Berenger plays a detective, hired to follow a man, who picks the wrong man and finds himself in another case, followed by another detective (Elizabeth Perkins). The two eventually become partners in a story that never allows us the easy option, yet remains curiously unsatisfying. A cast of fine-looking women do unexpected things: the sophisticated Ms P plays a ragged embryo gumshoe; Anne Archer sings (well); Kate Capshaw subdues her usual bright glamour; Annette O'Toole takes off Meryl Streep; Ann Magnuson takes off Shirley MacLaine. There's even the occasional line of smart dialogue. 'Ever want kids?' asks Berenger. 'Kids?' queries Perkins. 'Yeah,' growls Berenger. 'Little people running around with your face.'

Maybe Bogart and Bacall could have made something of it all, though it might have baffled their fans as well.

Love Bug, The ⊙
1969, US, 107 mins, colour
Dir: Robert Stevenson
Stars: Dean Jones, Michele Lee, Buddy Hackett, David Tomlinson
Rating: ★★★★

This Walt Disney comedy about a Volkswagen with a mind – and life – of its own was an enormous box-office hit for the studio and gave rise to three sequels. None was as good as this extremely bright and funny romp, with breakneck direction from Robert Stevenson and personable degrees of heroism and villainy from Dean Jones, Michele Lee, Buddy Hackett and David Tomlinson.

Love Child, The ●
1987, UK, 96 mins, colour
Dir: Robert Smith
Stars: Sheila Hancock, Peter Capaldi, Percy Herbert, Alexei Sayle (voice), Lesley Sharp (voice)
Rating: ★

A sometimes amiable, sometimes objectionable comedy in typical British late Eighties manner. Its adult-certificate sitcom style will look better on a small screen, but stands exposed and awkward on anything bigger. Charm and subtlety are clearly elements absent from the armoury of writer Gordon Hann, whose head-on humour demands, like a Clint Eastwood action film, that you either go with it or take a running jump. Consequently, the dislikeable characters ensure just a few felicitous moments in what could have been an enjoyable dose of mildly anarchic humour. Veterans Sheila Hancock – as the gran offered a new life to the chagrin of dull accounts clerk grandson Peter Capaldi, trying to live down his hippie parents' memory – and Percy Herbert adapt themselves awkwardly to the new style, like dolphins gliding, uneasily, through shark-infested waters.

Love Crazy ○
1941, US, 99 mins, b/w
Dir: Jack Cummings
Stars: William Powell, Myrna Loy, Gail Patrick, Jack Carson
Rating: ★★★

A really wacky romantic comedy with the stars of the Thin Man series, William Powell and Myrna Loy, at the peak of their appeal. Catching his wife with a muscleman teaching her the

L

skills of a bow and arrow, Powell plans a divorce. In a flat spin when he realises his mistake, he launches all sorts of madcap schemes, including feigning madness and dressing up as his own sister, to set matters to rights. A bit too long, the film still has some very funny moments and a great supporting cast, including one of Florence Bates' famous grotesques. Contemporary audiences cheered when she gets pushed into a swimming pool.

Love Crimes ● Ⓥ

1991, US, 90 mins, colour
Dir: Lizzie Borden
Stars: Sean Young, Patrick Bergin, James Read, Arnetia Walker, Ron Orbach
Rating: ★

Although at times dull, weird and ludicrous by turns, there are times when this very off-centre thriller comes close to being very interesting indeed. Sean Young is the DA whose childhood sexual terrors remain lodged in the back of her mind. Small wonder that she becomes obsessed with the case of a fake photographer (Patrick Bergin), who preys on vulnerable women and gets them to make sexually provocative poses before having sex with them. When he begins beating them up as well, and is obviously nearing the edge of violence, Young offers herself as the bait, only to become involved in a game of sexual cat-and-mouse from which she and her career may not recover. Rather too low-key for its own cause, the film gets within striking distance of hitting some disturbing chords. In the end, though, not good, and seeming much longer than it is.

Love from a Stranger ○

(aka: A Stranger Walked In)
1947, US, 81 mins, b/w
Dir: Richard Whorf
Stars: John Hodiak, Sylvia Sidney
Rating: ★★

This was the fourth in a little group of comeback films made by Sylvia Sidney after an absence from the screen of five years. But, although quite tense in parts, it did not lead to a permanent renewal of her once glittering movie career. Based on Frank Vosper's stage adaptation of an Agatha Christie thriller, the film was a remake of the earlier version with Ann Harding and Basil Rathbone.

Love from a Stranger ○

1936, UK, 90 mins, b/w
Dir: Rowland V Lee

Stars: Ann Harding, Basil Rathbone
Rating: ★★★

After a slow beginning, suspense builds steadily as wealthy Ann Harding gradually, and only with anonymous help, cottons on to the fact that her sleek new husband (a menacingly plausible Basil Rathbone) may have married her with murder in mind. The film was made in Britain by a Hollywood director, Rowland V Lee: his inventive handling and skilful touches help tighten the tension to breaking point in the final cat-and-mouse game between the two protagonists.

Love Happy ☉

1949, US, 85 mins, b/w
Dir: David Miller
Stars: Groucho Marx, Chico Marx, Harpo Marx, Vera-Ellen, Marilyn Monroe, Raymond Burr
Rating: ★★★

By no means the dud that Marx Brothers purists would have you believe, this is a fast-moving comedy that showcases Harpo and Chico (far too little is seen of Groucho) close to their zaniest and best. Although the film is hampered by its slight story of a musical dancing troupe, it takes off every time the brothers are on screen. With the help of Vera-Ellen and an expert supporting cast, and especially a loony finish among the lights and signs high above the big city, the brothers bid a reasonably happy farewell to big-screen fame.

Love Hurts ●

1989, US, 115 mins, colour
Dir: Bud Yorkin
Stars: Jeff Daniels, John Mahoney, Cynthia Sikes, Cloris Leachman, Amy Wright
Rating: ★

This could have been called *A Wedding* if director Robert Altman hadn't already pinched the title as well as the theme. Bud Yorkin's comedy-drama is a much inferior version, full of morose, unpleasant characters and with far too few smartly funny lines. And it seems to go on for hours. The one bright spot is a nine-year-old actress called Mary Griffin, a relaxed child performer whose timing and natural delivery put some of her elders and betters here to shame. Jeff Daniels has the lead and the results don't say very much for his choice of scripts: he was playing far too many unsympathetic characters for his own good at this stage of his career.

Love Is a Many Splendored Thing ○

1955, US, 102 mins, colour
Dir: Henry King
Stars: William Holden, Jennifer Jones, Torin Thatcher
Rating: ★★

The chart-busting song is all that survives in most memories of this weepy love story set aginst some picturesque views of Hong Kong, ravishingly shot in colour by the Oscar-winning photographer Leon Shamroy. Jennifer Jones' exquisite portrayal of the real-life heroine, Han Suyin, rises above the basic stickiness of the situations. And the background of troubled times in the Orient – the film is set just before and during the Korean War – is handled well enough to make one realise what an intriguing and complex subject it was.

Love Letters ○

1945, US, 101 mins, b/w
Dir: William Dieterle
Stars: Jennifer Jones, Joseph Cotten, Ann Richards, Gladys Cooper
Rating: ★★

A rarely-seen romantic drama, a sort of suspense weepie in which Jennifer Jones plays an amnesiac who has been tried for the manslaughter of her husband. Victor Young's beautiful theme music and William Dieterle's persuasive direction help Miss Jones and co-star Joseph Cotten to keep the tears flowing.

Love Letters ● Ⓥ

1983, US, 98 mins, colour
Dir: Amy Jones
Stars: Jamie Lee Curtis, James Keach, Matt Clark, Amy Madigan
Rating: ★★★

A bit one-paced but touching at the end, this is, under the circumstances, a little miracle of a film from writer/director Amy Jones, made on the tiniest of budgets. Jamie Lee Curtis, working for next to nothing, throws herself wholeheartedly into some torrid love scenes, at the same time creating a movingly believable character who is an entirely true-life mixture of strengths and weaknesses. James Keach – brother of Stacy – is a bit of a bore as her paramour, but Amy Madigan and Matt Clark are useful supports in a slender but slightly offbeat drama that, thanks to the credible central performance, holds on to your interest to the end.

Love Lottery, The ○

1953, UK, 89 mins, colour
Dir: Charles Crichton

Stars: David Niven, Herbert Lom, Peggy Cummins

Rating: ★★

The film business laughs at itself in this joyous jibe at romantic star leads and their hysterical fans. David Niven smoothly plays the heart-throb actor who, after being half-killed by his admirers, suggests that he is put up for a lottery, in which he will marry the winner. Nonsense, of course, but light and frothy with it. Niven plays with the assurance that can come only from an actor equally at home in both comedy and drama. And Humphrey Bogart puts in an unexpected guest appearance.

Lovely Way to Go, A ○
(aka: A Lovely Way to Die)
1968, US, 103 mins, colour
Dir: David Lowell Rich
Stars: Kirk Douglas, Sylva Koscina, Eli Wallach, Sharon Farrell
Rating: ★★

This rather over-bright film, with its irritatingly cheerful score, is a mixture of high jinks, romantic comedy and private-eye thriller that could only have been made in the Sixties. Kirk Douglas plays up archly to the required mood, while Sylva Koscina is an extremely decorative heroine.

Love Match, The ○
1954, UK, 86 mins, b/w
Dir: David Paltenghi
Stars: Arthur Askey, Shirley Eaton, Glenn Melvyn, Thora Hird, James Kenney, Jill Adams
Rating: ★★★

Arthur Askey made a highly successful comeback to the cinema in this northcountry comedy with a soccer flavour. The film also provides a rare look at Robb Wilton, the famous music-hall comedian, here in his familiar role of Magistrate Muddlecombe; and at Glenn Melvyn, who also wrote the stage play on which this lark was based.

Love Me or Leave Me ○
1955, US, 122 mins, colour
Dir: Charles Vidor
Stars: Doris Day, James Cagney, Cameron Mitchell, Robert Keith
Rating: ★★★★

Doris Day stars in this spirited, acid-flavoured biopic of singer Ruth Etting, from a producer best known for glucose (Joe Pastemak). Etting's fraught life gave Day a chance to prove she was far more than a pretty face and

voice, though she has stiff competition from James Cagney (as Etting's gangster friend Marty the Gimp). Full of vintage songs.

Love Me Tender ○ Ⓥ
1956, US, 95 mins, b/w
Dir: Robert Webb
Stars: Richard Egan, Elvis Presley, Debra Paget, Neville Brand
Rating: ★★

Presley's debut is a civil war Western about a southern family's three feuding sons and their love for sultry Debra Paget. Elvis swings his hips to 'Let Me Be', 'Old Shep', 'Poor Boy' and the smoochy title ditty. Stiff Richard Egan is the nominal star. The fans liked it and made it a hit.

Love Me Tonight ○
1932, US, 96 mins, b/w
Dir: Rouben Mamoulian
Stars: Maurice Chevalier, Jeanette MacDonald, Charles Ruggles, Myrna Loy, Charles Butterworth, C Aubrey Smith
Rating: ★★★★

Among the most memorable of Hollywood's early musicals, this Rodgers and Hart song-feast is given added charm by the inventive cinematic treatment of director Rouben Mamoulian and the vivacious, almost mischievous performances of its two stars, Jeanette MacDonald and Maurice Chevalier. The score includes 'Mimi', 'Lover (When You're Near Me)', 'Isn't It Romantic?', 'Love Me Tonight' and 'The Son of a Gun is Nothing but a Tailor'.

Love on the Dole ○ Ⓥ
1941, UK, 100 mins, b/w
Dir: John Baxter
Stars: Deborah Kerr, Clifford Evans
Rating: ★★★

The 20-year-old Deborah Kerr gives a beautiful performance in this sombre but justly famous drama of life in Lancashire during the Depression of the Thirties.

Love on the Run ○ Ⓥ
1936, US, 80 mins, b/w
Dir: W S Van Dyke
Stars: Joan Crawford, Clark Gable, Franchot Tone
Rating: ★★★

Fast and furious globe-trotting romance involving rival foreign correspondents Clark Gable and Franchot Tone dodging continental spies as well as each other in the quest for a scoop, romancing runaway mad-

cap heiress Joan Crawford on the side. The plot's not much, but director 'Woody' Van Dyke wisely concentrates on the personalities of the stars, and there are good cameo roles for bristling William Demarest and incymincy Donald Meek. Tone gives the stars unselfish support, and Gable unbends with surprising style, especially in a daft sequence set in a castle.

Lover, The ● Ⓥ
1992, UK/France, 110 mins, colour
Dir: Jean-Jacques Annaud
Stars: Jane March, Tony Leung, Voice of Jeanne Moreau
Rating: ★★

Elaborately set, with some wonderful views of Saigon, this ambitious sex drama runs like a silent film with erotic inserts. Based on a vignette of her early life by writer Marguérite Duras, the slight narrative has Jane March as the 15-year-old Duras, restricted by her upbringing in France and Vietnam, being seduced by a handsome Chinaman (Tony Leung). March has presence, but not much acting ability at this stage of her career. Leung is well-cast, but the sex scenes are nothing special and quickly tedious, with March giving out with a few pouts too many before the end. Thank goodness for Saigon and for Jeanne Moreau's marvellous voice-over narration.

Lover Boy ◐ Ⓥ
1989, US, 98 mins, colour
Dir: Joan Micklin Silver
Stars: Patrick Dempsey, Nancy Valen, Kate Jackson, Carrie Fisher, Barbara Carrera, Kirstie Alley
Rating: ★★★

What Warren Beatty did for hairdressing in *Shampoo*, Patrick Dempsey does for pizza delivery here. This is a conventional but cute and often comic sex frolic, kept afloat by Dempsey's own brand of charm and clumsiness (he even dances!) as the pizza boy who finds himself sexually in demand by 30-something women customers, despite having the kind of frame that, in the old muscleman adverts would be guaranteed to have sand kicked all over it. Time and again, Dempsey's energy – and Joan Micklin Silver's stylish direction – overcomes the clichéd conventionality of the situations, though his producers help a lot by surrounding him with a very good cast that includes Kate Jackson, Carrie Fisher, Kirstie Alley, Barbara Carrera, Kim Miyori and Robert Ginty. Another winner from director Silver,

L

whose record of consistency is superior to that of most of her female contemporaries.

Lover Come Back ○
1961, US, 102 mins, colour
Dir: Delbert Mann
Stars: Doris Day, Rock Hudson
Rating: ★★★

Dialogue as bright as the colour, misunderstanding piled on misunderstanding and production values as high as the unlikelihood of the story: battle-of-the-sexes comedies never came glossier than in the Doris Day-Rock Hudson sparring matches in the late Fifties and early Sixties, and this is one of the best. Advertising exec Rock has to invent a non-existent product to cover up his chicanery and rival Doris goes after it without realising that it doesn't exist. Smoothly, confidently made by Delbert Mann, the film has delightful supporting performances from Tony Randall, giving his usual impression of a demented flywheel, Edie Adams, delicious as a brainless chorus-girl, and Jack Kruschen as a bumbling inventor called in to give substance to the mythical product. Sheer enjoyment, sophisticated in technique and execution, and marred only by the insertion of a soupy song from Ms Day at quite the wrong moment.

Lovers!, The ○
1972, UK, 90 mins, colour
Dir: Herbert Wise
Stars: Paula Wilcox, Richard Beckinsale
Rating: ★★★

One of the most successful of TV comedy spin-offs, shot in excellent colour, and owing most of its better qualities almost entirely to the warmth and spontaneity projected by the two young leads, Paula Wilcox and Richard Beckinsale. They provide a relationship that, thanks to their portrayals and the script by Jack Rosenthal (who also wrote the series), is likeable, warmhearted and funny.

Loves of Carmen, The ○
1948, US, 99 mins, colour
Dir: Charles Vidor
Stars: Rita Hayworth, Glenn Ford
Rating: ★★

Made by the same team responsible for the classic crime thriller *Gilda*, this romantic costume adventure – based on Mérimée's *Carmen* – strikes fewer sparks. Hayworth's tempestuous gipsy looks stunning but Ford's Spanish dragoon is merely silly. And Bizet's music might have helped a bit, rather than the tacky score that's provided by Mario Castelnuovo-Tedesco.

Loves of Joanna Godden, The ○
1947, UK, 85 mins, b/w
Dir: Charles Frend
Stars: Googie Withers, Jean Kent, John McCallum
Rating: ★★

A solid, well-acted rural drama with a human touch, the sort of thing you might have expected to find Barbara Stanwyck starring in on the other side of the Atlantic. In this Ealing Studios period saga, the strong-willed Joanna in a well-crafted film that doesn't quite tug at the emotions as it might have done. The film's leisurely pace irked one contemporary reviewer who said that it was 'like watching a village cricket match on a lovely summer's day, nodding off now and then and waking to find Googie still batting away'.

Love Stinks
See: Only You (1992)

Love Story ○
1970, US, 100 mins, colour
Dir: Arthur Hiller
Stars: Ryan O'Neal, Ali MacGraw, John Marley, Ray Milland, John Huston
Rating: ★★★

Totally resistible but phenomenally successful weepie about lovers from opposite ends of the social scale. Ali MacGraw expires as prettily (and from an unnamed disease) as any Hollywood star of the Thirties. But Ryan O'Neal will be okay since 'Love means never having to say you're sorry.' One way or another, you'll need a bucket.

Love Story ○
(aka: A Lady Surrenders)
1944, UK, 104 mins, b/w
Dir: Leslie Arliss
Stars: Margaret Lockwood, Stewart Granger, Patricia Roc, Tom Walls
Rating: ★★

The second of Margaret Lockwood's really big hits of the wartime years, reuniting her with Stewart Granger (her co-star from *The Man in Grey*). The story – dying lady pianist falling for engineer going blind – is pure schmaltz, but it was solid gold at the box-office in Britain, proving to be one of the biggest financial winners of its year from any country. And the theme music, 'Cornish Rhapsody', was also massively popular.

Love with the Proper Stranger ○
1964, US, 100 mins, b/w
Dir: Robert Mulligan
Stars: Natalie Wood, Steve McQueen, Edie Adams, Tom Bosley
Rating: ★★★

Romantic comedy, tinged with drama, set against the background of non-stop New York. Sometimes it seems as though Natalie Wood and Steve McQueen could do with rather more meaningful dialogue to get their teeth into, to help establish their growing relationship with each other. Nonetheless McQueen in particular still manages to give a performance that makes it easy to see why he was in the process of becoming a world box-office draw.

Loving You ○ ⓥ
1957, US, 101 mins, colour
Dir: Hal Kanter
Stars: Elvis Presley, Lizabeth Scott, Wendell Corey, Dolores Hart
Rating: ★★★

The second of Elvis Presley's 33 movies, nearly all of which were condemned by critics but profited at the box office. And it's always good to see the King in his pre-blobster days. This film is already the standard vehicle, tailor-made for his personality and talent. In this story Elvis the hillbilly singer is used as a gimmick to promote a waning cowboy band. Fame and romance await, but not before much heartache and singing have taken place. One of the better King-flicks.

L-Shaped Room, The ◐
1962, UK, 142 mins, b/w
Dir: Bryan Forbes
Stars: Leslie Caron, Tom Bell, Bernard Lee
Rating: ★★★

Moving, tenderly-observed portrait of a lonely, pregnant French girl and the people she encounters in her cramped, crammed London boarding house. Written and directed by Bryan Forbes, whose wife Nanette Newman appears in a tiny part right at the end. And there are penetrating performances from Cicely Courtneldge, Patricia Phoenix and Emlyn Williams.

Lt Robin Crusoe USN ☉
1966, US, 110 mins, colour
Dir: Byron Paul
Stars: Dick Van Dyke, Nancy Kwan
Rating: ★

This colourful comedy from the Walt Disney stable sounds a whole lot more fun than it is. The company had got some fine desert island action a few years earlier from their adaptation of *Swiss Family Robinson*, but here star Dick Van Dyke is given far too little to do, especially in the first half of the film. He tries valiantly to make us laugh and so does a talented chimpanzee called Floyd, but they get no help from the sluggish direction of Byron Paul. Very much later on, things liven up considerably, with Van Dyke's Crusoe leading a suffragette army of native girls against the big bad cannibal chief.

Lucky Jim ○ Ⓥ
1957, UK, 95 mins, b/w
Dir: John Boulting
Stars: Ian Carmichael, Terry-Thomas, Hugh Griffith, Sharon Acker
Rating: ★★★★

A Boulting Brothers' box-office blockbuster of its day, with Ian Carmichael scoring a big personal success as Jim Dixon, the accident-prone lecturer of the title. His final lecture on 'Merrie England' brings down the curtain on a riotous catalogue of disaster.

Lucky Nick Cain
See: I'll Get You for This

Lullaby of Broadway ○ Ⓥ
1951, US, 92 mins, colour
Dir: David Butler
Stars: Doris Day, Gene Nelson, Gladys George, S Z Sakall, Billy de Wolfe
Rating: ★★★

This was one of the earlier musical vehicles that Warner Brothers assembled for Doris Day in the days when she had just become their brightest new singing star. The story's not much, but who cares when Doris sings such standards as 'Somebody Loves Me', 'Lullaby of Broadway' and 'You're Getting to be a Habit with Me'? Gene Nelson weighs in with 'Zing! Went the Strings of My Heart', and veteran star Gladys George goes slightly over the top as Doris's mother, once a Broadway star but now singing in clubs. There are times when the film seems curiously lifeless – its comedy scenes aren't too funny – but the real revelation here is Day's dancing, gliding with almost the elegance of a Ginger Rogers and matching the leggy Nelson step for step.

Lured ○
1947, US, 102 mins, b/w
Dir: Douglas Sirk
Stars: Lucille Ball, George Sanders,

Charles Coburn, Boris Karloff
Rating: ★★★

Although it seems odd now to find Lucille Ball in a leading role as a lady in danger, this is an otherwise strongly-cast thriller, based on the 1939 French film *Pièges*, directed by Robert Siodmak just before he went to Hollywood. This version might have been creepier if Siodmak himself had directed it. Douglas Sirk, soon to make a name for himself with glossy weepies, gives it a handsome production and interesting London settings, but has trouble lending atmosphere to a routine script. There's no lack of suspects for policemen Charles Coburn (excellent, as usual), George Zucco and Alan Napier to sift through. George Sanders, Boris Karloff, Sir Cedric Hardwicke, Joseph Calleia and Alan Mowbray are all on hand to strew the plot with red herrings. Miss Ball's singing, incidentally, was dubbed by Annette Warren. Oddly, the British called both French and American versions of the story *Personal Column*.

Lure of the Wilderness ○
1952, US, 92 mins, colour
Dir: Jean Negulesco
Stars: Jean Peters, Jeffrey Hunter, Walter Brennan
Rating: ★★★

A really off-beat Western, which is about a man who strays into a swamp in 1910, and finds a man, living wild with his daughter, who has been hiding from the law for years. Good performances abound – and there's fine Technicolor photography on location in the Okefenokee Swamp Park by Edward Cronjager. His camerawork helps build up a fine sense of the claustrophobic menace conjured up by the oppressive green of the Everglades, and their sundry denizens, such as snakes and alligators.

Lust for a Vampire ● Ⓥ
1970, UK, 95 mins, colour
Dir: Jimmy Sangster
Stars: Ralph Bates, Yutte Stensgaard, Barbara Jefford
Rating: ★★★

Hammer horror films produced a number of hypnotic performances from vampire ladies, and Yutte Stensgaard, previously just a decorative actress, is extremely effective here as the finishing school girl who proves to be the reincarnation of the notorious Carmilla Karnstein from other Hammer blood feasts. It's easily Yutte's best film performance. Ralph Bates is also good as

one of the men who falls under her deadly spell.

Lust for Gold ○
1949, US, 90 mins, b/w
Dir: S Sylvan Simon
Stars: Glenn Ford, Ida Lupino, Gig Young, William Price, Edgar Buchanan
Rating: ★★★★

One often writes of underrated films, but surely *Lust for Gold* must now be one of the most neglected on record. A perfect little vignette about man's greed in the form of a Western, with the present-day story peripheral to the flash-back adventure yarn. It involves Glenn Ford in one of his best performances as a soulless émigré who discovers a fabulously wealthy mine, and is ruthless in his determination to keep sole possession. Very good performances also from Ida Lupino and Gig Young, and desperate suspense towards the end, make this a minor masterpiece.

Lust for Life ○ Ⓥ
1956, US, 122 mins, colour
Dir: Vincente Minnelli
Stars: Kirk Douglas, Anthony Quinn
Rating: ★★★

Kirk Douglas (cruelly denied an Oscar) is artist Vincent Van Gogh to the very life in this long, rambling, but brilliantly photographed (credited to Metrocolor, but actually made in Ansco Color) story of the painter's life. Great pains have obviously been taken by director Vincente Minnelli to get the look and flavour of the film right, and it's a pity that an at-times magnificent movie outstays its welcome by at least half an hour. Anthony Quinn's sketchy Gauguin won the film's only Academy Award, while the brilliant, tigerish Douglas had to be content with a mere nomination. There's no justice!

Lust in the Dust ●
1985, US, 87 mins, colour
Dir: Paul Bartel
Stars: Tab Hunter, Divine, Lainie Kazan
Rating: ★

Paul Bartel's follow-up to his decidedly different *Eating Raoul* is a spoof Western that's too wild-eyed and knowing by half. The accent is on the wildly farcical, and the film saves its best moments for the climactic showdown around a grave, with a barrage of bullets, bluffs and revelations.

Lydia ○
1941, US, 90 mins, b/w
Dir: Julien Duvivier

Stars: Merle Oberon, Edna May Oliver,
Alan Marshal, Joseph Cotten
Rating: ★★

Lush romantic trifle on the oft-tried
theme of an elderly lady looking back
on her love life. Director Julien
Duvivier based it on his French success
Un Carnet de Bal which he had made in
his native France four years earlier, before World War Two forced him to
take his talents to Hollywood. Merle
Oberon (in the title role) and Joseph
Cotten make a highly civilised romantic couple, and Miklos Rozsa earned an
Oscar nomination for his liltingly dramatic score.

Lydia Bailey ○
1952, US, 89 mins, colour
Dir: Jean Negulesco
Stars: Dale Roberton, Anne Francis,
William Marshall, Charles Korvin
Rating: ★★

Dale Robertson swaps his more usual
cowboy clothes for the garb of a native
field-hand in this romantic adventure
story set in the jungles and plantations
of Haiti in Napoleonic times. The studio, Fox, built up Robertson and Anne
Francis as a big young romantic team
at the time, though nothing further
came of it.

M

M ①
1931, Germany, 99 mins, b/w
Dir: Fritz Lang
Stars: Peter Lorre
Rating: ★★★★★

Long since firmly established as one of
the great classics of pre-war cinema (or
of any other era, for that matter), the
impact made by this film has hardly
lessened at all over the years. Loosely
based on the actual case of the
Düsseldorf child murderer of the
Twenties, it was Fritz Lang's first
sound film, and later in life Lang himself regarded it as the most satisfying
of all the films he had made. Its power
is certainly tremendous, with striking
imagery and visual qualities complemented by an often highly imaginative
use of sound (like Alfred Hitchcock before him in *Blackmail*, Lang clearly took
to the new medium like a duck to
water). The film is equally famous
now for marking the screen debut of
Peter Lorre, who in the central role of
the murderer gave a performance so
convincing and impressive that many
found it frightening: he was never to
get such a demanding role again.

Ma and Pa Kettle ○
1948, US, 75 mins, b/w
Dir: Charles Lamont
Stars: Marjorie Main, Percy Kilbride
Rating: ★★

Crow-voiced Marjorie Main, who was
nominated for an Oscar when she
played the harridan Ma Kettle in the
hit comedy *The Egg and I*, was persuaded to return for a comedy series based
on the hillbilly characters created by
herself and Percy Kilbride. None of
the nine Kettle films cost more than
half a million dollars to produce, yet
altogether they grossed close to $40
million for the studio, Universal, almost single-handedly saving it from
bankruptcy in the early 1950s. This
film got the series off to a rousing start.

Mac ● ⓥ
1992, US, 118 mins, colour
Dir: John Turturro
Stars: John Turturro, Michael Badalucco,
Katherine Borowitz, Ellen Barkin
Rating: ★★

This is a kind of building industry
equivalent of *The Godfather*. It must

also rate as a rare film whose language
is so bad it actually got it an 18 certificate from the British censor. Three
Italian-American brothers get cheesed
off working for a constructor building
houses his way and decide to do it
their way. Eventually they have some
success and split up. That's the story,
with star-director John Turturro as the
elder brother and driving force behind
their career, a man driven to fits of
anger and screaming (one of which
brings on an early heart attack), a trait
he must have inherited from his mother whose continual rants are mercifully
only heard off screen. It's earthy,
darkly photographed and its most
meaningful lines of dialogue are often
repeated – meaningfully. These people don't laugh a lot, but they do shout
and screech and behave violently towards each other most of the time.
Frankly their life, though like the film
not without merit, is mostly heavy
going.

Mac and Me ⊙
1988, US, 93 mins, colour
Dir: Stewart Raffill
Stars: Christine Ebersole, Jonathan
Ward
Rating: ★

Lovable extraterrestrial Mac finds himself stranded in suburban America but
survives on a diet of Coca-Cola and
the friendship of a disabled 10-year-old
boy. A squirm-inducing children's film
with more than a passing resemblance
to Spielberg's *E. T.* but with the
shameless product placement of the
MacDonalds hamburger chain. Young
children won't notice this, of course,
but it's a scandalous new form of advertising. Mercifully the film is so
awful it doesn't much matter.

**MacArthur the Rebel
General** ○
(aka: MacArthur)
1977, US, 130 mins, colour
Dir: Joseph Sargent
Stars: Gregory Peck, Dan O'Herlihy
Rating: ★★★

Although, even at 61, he looks absurdly
young for the role, Gregory Peck does
surprisingly well in this old-fashioned
war film with an authoritative tang.
Director Joseph Sargent wastes no time
in getting on with the action, from war
in the Philippines in 1942 to
MacArthur's final command in Korea
in 1951. The general's own speeches
are ringingly declaimed by Peck and the
Technicolor photography, by Mario
Tosi, is very good. The director's

fondness for tracking shots, which seems likely to hinder the film at first, actually helps to keep things moving in the later stages.

Macbeth ○
1948, US, 89 mins, b/w
Dir: Orson Welles
Stars: Orson Welles, Jeanette Nolan, Dan O'Herlihy
Rating: ★★★

Orson Welles played around with Shakespeare's Scottish play to such an extent that it must have had The Bard spinning furiously in his grave. Shot in a mere 23 days with papier-mâché rocks and sets so cardboard it's small wonder that the scenery-chewing antics of the cast didn't destroy them. Welles adopts similar oblique camera angles as in his masterful *Citizen Kane,* but here they are more of a distraction than anything else. For all this, the visuals do have a certain weird fascination.

MacDonald of the Canadian Mounties
See: Pony Soldier

Macho Callahan ◐
1970, US, 100 mins, b/w
Dir: Bernard L Kowalski
Stars: David Janssen, Jean Seberg, Lee J Cobb
Rating: ★★

David Janssen is as taciturn as ever in a rare Western role as a Civil War veteran, hunted by the widow of a man he has killed. The supporting cast is full of quality players, including Jean Seberg, Lee J Cobb and Britain's James Booth as a flashy gambler called 'King Harry' Wheeler. Watch also for David Carradine as a one-armed man who gets gunned down by the main character early in the picture – something of an in-joke, perhaps, in reference to Janssen's hunt for the one-armed man in the long-running television series *The Fugitive.* The action is bold and powerful, although spoiled at times by director Bernard Kowalski's insistence on too many angles.

MacKenna's Gold ○ ⓥ
1968, US, 136 mins, colour
Dir: J Lee Thompson
Stars: Gregory Peck, Omar Sharif, Telly Savalas, Keenan Wynn, Edward G Robinson, Julie Newmar
Rating: ★★

Another big adventure film from the same team – star Gregory Peck, writer/producer Carl Foreman and director J Lee Thompson – that made

The Guns of Navarone. The girls tend to get in the way a bit more here, and Foreman's script is not of as high a calibre. But Omar Sharif is unexpectedly mobile and spirited as the ruthless Colorado and Gregory Peck reliably staunch as Sheriff MacKenna, who comes by accident into possession of a map pointing the way to fabulous hidden treasure. The rugged desert terrain is also impressive, thanks to the fine Technicolor photography of Joseph MacDonald.

Mackintosh Man, The ◐
1973, US, 120 mins, colour
Dir: John Huston
Stars: Paul Newman, James Mason, Dominique Sanda, Harry Andrews, Ian Bannen, Michael Hordern
Rating: ★★

This thriller is not at all typical of its director John Huston or writer Walter Hill (who went on to direct hard action films like *The Streetfighter* and *Driver*). If it is reminiscent of anything, it's the stories of John Buchan, especially when Paul Newman's cover is blown and he flees from his enemies across the wilder parts of Ireland. A formidable battery of senior British actors – including Harry Andrews, Nigel Patrick, Niall MacGinnis, Roland Culver, Michael Hordern and Leo Genn contribute cameos if not always conviction in the midst of Hill's studiously intricate plot.

Mad About Men ○
1954, UK, 90 mins, colour
Dir: Ralph Thomas
Stars: Glynis Johns, Donald Sinden, Margaret Rutherford
Rating: ★★★

A sequel to 1948's *Miranda,* with Glynis Johns returning to her role as the man-mad mermaid. Despite the improbability of the plot (Miranda replaces her double with the aid of a wheelchair), this is a surprisingly amusing comedy, wittily scripted and played with fine relish, especially by Johns, Margaret Rutherford and Irene Handl, a formidable trio of female scene-stealers.

Mad About Music ○
1938, US, 98 mins, b/w
Dir: Norman Taurog
Stars: Deanna Durbin, Herbert Marshall, Arthur Treacher
Rating: ★★★

Deanna Durbin's natural charm edges everybody else off the screen in this story of an orphan who goes to a Swiss school and invents a fictitious father.

Deanna sings 'Ave Maria' (and more) and there's just about your only chance to see on screen Cappy Barra's Harmonica Band! They provide breezy backing for Durbin on another of her numbers, 'I Love to Whistle'.

Madame Bovary ○
1949, US, 115 mins, b/w
Dir: Vincente Minnelli
Stars: Jennifer Jones, James Mason, Van Heflin, Louis Jourdan
Rating: ★★★

With Vincente Minnelli directing and Louis Jourdan on the cast list you could almost be forgiven for expecting a Flaubert musical, and indeed the wonderfully well-organised ball sequence is one of the highlights of a film that, unlike many, has improved with age. There had been two earlier versions, but this one framed the novel within the author's trial on a charge of corrupting morals by writing his book. Jennifer Jones makes a sedate Madame, but James Mason is noble as Flaubert himself. It has rather more bite than the recent Claude Chabrol version with Isabelle Huppert, but the Renoir version is still the best of all.

Madame Curie ○
1943, US, 124 mins, b/w
Dir: Mervyn LeRoy
Stars: Greer Garson, Walter Pidgeon, Robert Walker, Van Johnson, Henry Travers
Rating: ★★★★

Film biographies had long been the province of Warner Brothers but Louis B Meyer wanted to change all that. His first attempt saw Spencer Tracy as Edison and despite the small box-office returns he decided to take a chance with a film based on Eve Curie's book about her scientist mother Marie – the Polish woman who discovered radium. The film itself stirred many hearts when it was released and stayed pretty close to the facts, something that many biographies failed to do in the Thirties and Forties.

Madame Sin ◐
1972, UK, 90 mins, colour
Dir: David Greene
Stars: Bette Davis, Robert Wagner, Denholm Elliott
Rating: ★★

Bette Davis in James Bond territory: her Madame Sin in this unlikely espionage adventure is as exotic a villainess as stalked the screen since Gale Sondergaard played Spider Woman in a couple of Forties'

M

thrillers. Co-star Robert Wagner also produced the film.

Madame Sousatzka ◑ ⓥ
1988, US, 122 mins, colour
Dir: John Schlesinger
Stars: Shirley MacLaine, Peggy Ashcroft, Navin Chowdhry, Twiggy, Leigh Lawson
Rating: ★★★

If you think they don't make 'em like they used to, this story of an eccentric piano tutor and her young star pupil will prove you wrong. Shirley MacLaine gives a fiery performance as Madame Sousatzka, living in a crumbling London house, obsessed with teaching her pupils good manners and good taste as well as the piano. Her young protegé, Manek, is played by Navin Chowdhry and their scenes together are well observed and directed by John Schlesinger. The film is, if anything a little long, but for fans of classical music, it's a delight. In the supporting cast, Twiggy rises above typecasting (she plays a model and would-be pop singer).

Madame X ○
1966, US, 100 mins, colour
Dir: David Lowell Rich
Stars: Lana Turner, Keir Dullea, John Forsythe, Ricardo Montalban, Constance Bennett, Burgess Meredith
Rating: ★★★★

Last but not least of the eight film versions of the story about that much-put-upon lady of the title, whose fortunes vary from rotten to worse. David Lowell Rich, here proving himself a strong and discerning director, holds it firmly and wisely to the spirit of the silent era, building up to an out-with-your-handkerchieves climax which is all the more effective for being handled in a strictly old-fashioned manner. Russell Metry's beautifully-keyed colour photography also plays its part in the impact of the film which, once it hits its stride after the first 20 minutes, never misses a trick – the juvenile saying his prayers, the wicked stepmother framed in a window during a storm, Madame X collapsing in snow and contracting pneumonia. Yet still, a lot depends on the star and one can rarely remember a more affecting portrayal from Lana Turner, especially in the latter half of the film when she is so much more impressive than one would have thought possible that we're held almost entirely captive to a last reel in which she is utterly deglamorised and says much with brown eyes that seem old and fathomless.

Mad Dog And Glory ● ⓥ
1993, US, 95 mins, colour
Dir: John McNaughton
Stars: Robert De Niro, Uma Thurman, Bill Murray, David Caruso, Kathy Baker
Rating: ★★

Robert De Niro and company just barely squeeze a feature-length film out of this slim dreams-come-true story. De Niro's a loner police photographer noticeably lacking in bravado. But when he saves the life of a big-shot gangster (Bill Murray), he's rewarded with a live-in girl (Uma Thurman) for a week. Paying the crook back her brother's debts, she has to do as she's told. So she's a good girl, natch, even though it's only a couple of days before they're in the sack, and De Niro finds there's a heavy price to pay if he wants to keep his new love. Murray is intriguing casting as the gang boss who's also a stand-up comic, but it's the only spark of interest in a story where the leads just don't coalesce and where developments are strictly make-believe. The talented Kathy Baker is criminally wasted in a bit-part here, but then De Niro had already won her in *Jacknife* – a much more convincing partner than Thurman for whom he's obviously too old. She's nothing much and neither are most of the cast in this kill-time film.

Made In America ◑ ⓥ
1993, US, 110 mins, colour
Dir: Richard Benjamin
Stars: Ted Danson, Whoopi Goldberg, Nia Long, Will Smith, Jennifer Tilly
Rating: ★★

A pretty broad romantic comedy with some laughs in the right places, plus giggles and grimaces in the wrong ones. Whoopi Goldberg is a widow who runs an African bookshop and has a daughter who's not only drop-dead gorgeous, but about to win a major science award. The girl, conceived by using a sperm bank after her father's death, resolves to find her 'donor' father and discovers to her horror he's a loud-mouthed white car salesman (Ted Danson) who pulls sick-making advertising stunts with bears, elephants and monkeys on TV. Naturally Ted reforms and falls for Whoopi, giving rise to the usual sit-com misunderstandings and allowing Jennifer Tilly to steal the film as Ted's squeaky live-in lover. The centrepiece is a funny sequence where Whoopi's bike-bell sends an elephant with Danson on it berserk through the town. Pretty long, though.

Made in Heaven ○
1952, UK, 78 mins, colour
Dir: John Paddy Carstairs
Stars: David Tomlinson, Petula Clark, Sonja Ziemann, A E Matthews
Rating: ★★

This soggy little romantic comedy, splendidly photographed in Technicolor by Geoffrey Unsworth, was typical of mainline British cinema in the early Fifties. The title has so many punning possibilities that is difficult to know where the real one lay, as a 'perfectly married' couple employ a Hungarian maid, whose statistics seem to be as much made in heaven as their marriage. Some fun, but it didn't make sparkling German actress Sonja Ziemann a star of the British cinema.

Made in Heaven ○ ⓥ
1987, US, 102 mins, colour
Dir: Alan Rudolph
Stars: Timothy Hutton, Kelly McGillis, Debra Winger, Maureen Stapleton, Don Murray, Mare Winningham
Rating: ★

This romantic fantasy is far from director Alan Rudolph's usual stamping ground of urban paranoia, which perhaps explains his failure to put any sort of personal stamp on the film. The story starts around 1946 when Mike (Timothy Hutton) is drowned and goes to Heaven where he falls in love with Annie (Kelly McGillis). She is an 'unborn soul' whom he marries but loses when she has to be 'born' to an earthling. Mike appeals to the heavenly supervisor – an unbilled Debra Winger completely stealing the film as the androgynous Emmett – who gives him 30 years to find Annie (now Ally) on Earth. Since the ending is always pretty obvious, the film depends heavily on the incidents that fill the lovers' journey along the way – but so little happens that it seems a very long and slow trip. The rest of the acting is forgettable, too, with the exception of a poignant performance by Ann Wedgeworth as Mike's mother. And the ending is anti-climactic, lacking all sense of joy.

Madeleine ○
1950, UK, 114 mins, b/w
Dir: David Lean
Stars: Ann Todd, Leslie Banks
Rating: ★★★

David Lean directed his then wife Ann Todd in this meticulous account of the events leading up to a famous murder trial in 19th-century Scotland. Miss Todd makes the enigmatic Madeleine such a cold fish that it's difficult to identify with her, but this is probably just what the situation orders here, and the case itself holds undeniable fascination. The final scene is handled in masterly style by both director and star.

Madhouse ① ⓥ
1974, UK, 92 mins, colour
Dir: Jim Clark
Stars: Vincent Price, Peter Cushing, Adrienne Corri, Robert Quarry
Rating: ★★

The only horror film of the Seventies to unite those masters of menace, Vincent Price, Peter Cushing and Robert *Count Yorga* Quarry. Despite the presence of the other two, however, the film is specifically devoted to the particular talents of Price. Cushing and Adrienne Corn (the latter as a demented and disfigured crone brooding over a colony of spiders in her basement) also have a splendid time in this vivid tale of an actor's revenge.

Madhouse ① ⓥ
1990, US, 90 mins, colour
Dir: Tom Ropelewski
Stars: John Larroquette, Kirstie Alley, John Diehl, Robert Ginty
Rating: ★★★

'If we have a nuclear war,' says Kirstie Alley, in the course of this not unfunny comedy, 'the only things to survive will be house guests.' Mack and Jessie (John Larroquette and Kirstie) have a cosy home that suits them fine until other people move into it. These include an old friend with a pregnant wife who talks non-stop and commandeers the bathroom; Jessie's spendthrift sister who moves in with her massive boyfriend after being kicked out by her rich Arab husband; a cat with nine lives; the man next door and his awful kids after his house burns down; an elephant; the sister's cocaine-dealing son. Mack has nightmares about zombies moving in, and soon he and Jessie are living in a tent on the lawn. It's not exactly frantically funny all the way through, but it does build to a fine pitch of madness towards the end. And there's always the nagging feeling that this could happen to you!

Madison Avenue ○
1961, US, 94 mins, b/w
Dir: Bruce Humberstone
Stars: Eleanor Parker, Dana Andrews, Jeanne Crain, Eddie Albert
Rating: ★★

A strange drama, which in cast and approach looks more like a film from the

early Fifties. A downbeat story of cross and double-cross in New York's big business jungle, it's directed by Bruce Humberstone, best known for Forties' musicals. Staid.

Mad Little Island
See: Rockets Galore

Mad Love ○
1935, US, 70 mins, b/w
Dir: Karl Freund
Stars: Peter Lorre, Frances Drake, Colin Clive
Rating: ★★★

Peter Lorre was never more striking, visually at least, than in this now seldom-seen version of *The Hands of Orlac* in which, shaven-headed (which makes his baby-faced looks more evil than ever), he plays a surgeon infatuated to the point of madness with a beautiful young actress, played by the gorgeous Frances Drake. His chilling presence smooths the film over passages which, in lesser hands, might seem absurdly melodramatic. Master cameraman Karl Freund, in one of his rare assignments as a director, crowds the film with low-key lighting, gloomy settings and bizarre camera angles which heighten Lorre's sidestep into madness. And May Beatty also scores as a drunken housekeeper (her cockatoo plays a memorable role in the climax) whose hobby is feeding flies to her carnivorous plant.

Mad Love ● ⓥ
1995, US, 95 mins, colour
Dir: Antonia Bird
Stars: Drew Barrymore, Chris O'Donnell, Joan Allen
Rating: ★★

Wild child Drew Barrymore attracts fellow student Chris O'Donnell, whose love blinds him to the fact that her flakiness hides real psychological problems, similar to those that plagued Mary Stuart Masterson in *Benny & Joon*. O'Donnell should perhaps have guessed when, thwarted in her attempts to pull him out of a vital exam for some extra-curricular nookie, Drew sets off the school fire alarm. Or when told she'd attempted suicide over a seemingly trivial spat with her parents. But no. It's only after he helps her escape from psychiatric care that he realises she will disintegrate without the drugs that control her mood swings. The leading actors here are good but not that good: we're not really drawn into their problems, even though their flight from authority is

rarely dull. And the script, like the performances, is adequate but never really penetrating.

Mad Magician, The ①
1954, US, 72 mins, b/w
Dir: John Brahm
Stars: Vincent Price, Mary Murphy, Eva Gabor
Rating: ★★

For his title role in this horror film about a vengeful illusionist, Vincent Price swotted up on a dozen real magician's tricks, and became quite accomplished at such things as making a stream of water run out of a sword, producing a girl from a flower pot, and making a man disappear through a wall. Patrick O'Neal makes his film debut as the goodie.

Mad Max ① ⓥ
1979, Australia, 93 mins, colour
Dir: George Miller
Stars: Mel Gibson, Joanne Samuel
Rating: ★★★

One of the most successful Australian films of all time, this is the first of the trilogy of *Mad Max* action movies starring Mel Gibson. All three were made in Australia, but this first one was dubbed with American accents for a wider audience. A weird, desolate, violent atmosphere prevails in all three, and this one tells us why Max became mad in the first place. There's plenty of exciting action on the road and some great stunts in this, director George Miller's impressive feature debut. Deservedly a cult favourite, although rough-edged compared with the others.

Mad Max 2 ● ⓥ
1981, Australia, 95 mins, colour
Dir: George Miller
Stars: Mel Gibson, Bruce Spence, Vernon Wells, Mike Preston
Rating: ★★

This is the movie to see if you like watching cars exploding or being blown to bits. The scene is the future in the Australian desert and the action reminiscent of American biker movies of the late Sixties in which Peter Fonda used to star. Max (Mel Gibson again) is a 'road warrior', a former pursuit cop embittered by the past who teams up, reluctantly, with a group of gasolene people protecting their wares against desert renegades. There are a lot of pretentious close-ups, rather like those begrimed Western faces Sergio Leone gave us in the 'Dollars' film. Nearly everyone gets blown up in the end, except a boy who kills people with steel

M

boomerangs, but is meant to be lovable and the symbolic future leader of his people. Utter rubbish this, done without style or polish (but carrying undoubted impact), a destructive millionaire's amateur dramatics piece.

Mad Max Beyond Thunderdome ❶ ⓥ

1985, Australia, 107 mins, colour
Dir: George Miller, George Ogilvie
Stars: Mel Gibson, Tina Turner, Angelo Rossitto, Helen Buday
Rating: ★★★★★

This third chunk of the adventures of an Australian desert warrior (still Mel Gibson) a few years after the nuclear apocalypse is a superior, well-crafted flight of the imagination. Bartertown, the centre of its action, is worthy of a Germanic science fiction film of the Twenties – a swarming, repulsive temple of thieves. And lording over this cesspit of humanity is Tina Turner as Aunty Entity, into whose voracious clutches Max falls. The dialogue, though sparse, always has something constructive or funny to say and the action is devastatingly well staged.

Mad Miss Manton, The ○

1938, US, 77 mins, b/w
Dir: Leigh Jason
Stars: Barbara Stanwyck, Henry Fonda, Sam Levene, Frances Mercer, Stanley Ridges
Rating: ★★

A tiresome screwball comedy-cum-murder mystery that wastes the talents of a great cast, headed by Barbara Stanwyck and Henry Fonda, and including Penny Singleton in one of a number of Thirties roles she played before becoming the screen's Blondie. Only those who like spotting a whole battery of character actors from the era are likely to sit through this one till the end. Stanwyck and Fonda give the professional performances you'd expect in this fast but flimsy frolic, though even here the strain shows at times.

Madness of King George, The ❶

1994, UK, 107 mins, colour
Dir: Nicholas Hytner
Stars: Nigel Hawthorne, Helen Mirren, Ian Holm, Rupert Everett, Amanda Donohoe, Rupert Graves
Rating: ★★★

All connections with our own royal family are, of course, coincidental in this well-acted if rather lengthy account of an illness that appeared to make George III lose his mind and encour-

aged the idle but scheming Prince of Wales to lay claim to the throne of England. Although Alan Bennett supplies some fruitily penetrating lines which Nigel Hawthorne, as the king, particularly relishes, there's rather too little in the way of court intrigue and too much concentration on bodily functions to keep a firm grip on the mind of the viewer, let alone the king. Looking for all the world like a taller version of Mel Brooks, Hawthorne rumblingly dominates proceedings as the king; he's a rattling old eccentric and recidivist to boot. Not entirely without lovability, though, and one look at the opposition will have you on his side. Rupert Everett is the prince to the dandified life, Helen Mirren effective as the queen, addressing her home-loving spouse as 'Mr King' and Amanda Donohoe miscast as a lady in waiting for her prey. The ending slightly lacks the bite we've been expecting but it's satisfying enough.

Madness of the Heart ○

1949, UK, 105 mins, b/w
Dir: Charles Bennett
Stars: Margaret Lockwood, Paul Dupuis, Maxwell Reed, Kathleen Byron
Rating: ★★

This unrestrained melodrama was Margaret Lockwood's last major success for the British cinema. She falls in love, goes blind, flees a convent and undergoes fierce romantic and acting competition from Kathleen Byron in her best *Black Narcissus* mood. It was pure gold-dust at the box-office.

Mad Room, The ●

1969, US, 92 mins, colour
Dir: Bernard Girard
Stars: Stella Stevens, Shelley Winters
Rating: ★★

A Grand Guignol shocker. Here, the delicious Stella Stevens is for once allowed some acting rope, and the audience's nerves are not the only thing that get hacked to pieces. A good performance also comes from the Queen of B pictures, Beverly Garland.

Mad Wednesday! ⊙

1946, US, 90 mins, b/w
Dir: Preston Sturges
Stars: Harold Lloyd, Frances Ramsden, Jimmy Conlin
Rating: ★★

Originally known as *The Sin of Harold Diddlebock*, this was the last film made by Harold Lloyd, renowned (especially in silent days) for his comedy capers on dizzy heights: almost everyone

knows the famous 'big clock' scene in his 1923 masterpiece *Safety Last*. High-ledge antics recur in the climax of *Mad Wednesday!*, which was written and directed by another great comedy talent, Preston Sturges. Unfortunately, by far the funniest part of this film is the beginning, which is lifted almost whole from Lloyd's 1925 classic *The Freshman*. It was a nice idea to look at what might have happened to the character from that film but here, like Sturges, Lloyd was past his prime and only a few mild smiles result as both men try too hard.

Maggie, The ⊙
(aka: High and Dry)

1953, UK, 93 mins, b/w
Dir: Alexander Mackendrick
Stars: Paul Douglas, Alex Mackenzie
Rating: ★★★

Ealing Studios comedy that's as refreshing as a dram of fresh air. Paul Douglas is a delight as the pushy American businessman who falls foul of an old puffer boat, The *Maggie*, and her crew of rascally Scottish seamen.

Magic ❶ ⓥ

1978, US, 106 mins, colour
Dir: Richard Attenborough
Stars: Anthony Hopkins, Ann-Margret, Burgess Meredith, Ed Lauter
Rating: ★★

Director Richard Attenborough's story of a ventriloquist taken over by his dummy, *Dead of Night*-style, aims to be a classic chiller. Anthony Hopkins conjures cleverly and sweats mightily as the possessed entertainer, also sporting a splendid backstreets American accent. But it's Ann-Margret, radiating warmth, who gives the best performance in the film. Burgess Meredith is also firmly in character as Hopkins' agent. Suspense, however, is a notably missing ingredient in the chilly proceedings.

Magic Bow, The ○

1947, UK, 106 mins, b/w
Dir: Bernard Knowles
Stars: Stewart Granger, Phyllis Calvert, Dennis Price, Jean Kent
Rating: ★★

Stewart Granger as the famous musician Paganini? Well, thanks to a lot of off-camera help, Granger at least looks convincing on the violin, while Yehudi Menuhin plays on the sound track. If you forget the story and enjoy the music, the film is a treat. The director is Bernard Knowles, whose second movie this was after a distinguished career as a film cameraman, much used in particular by Alfred Hitchcock.

Magic Box, The ○ ⓥ
1951, UK, 118 mins, colour
Dir: John Boulting
Stars: Robert Donat, Margaret Johnston, Maria Schell
Rating: ★★

Robert Donat oozes dignity as William Friese-Greene, inventor of the movie camera, whose life was, otherwise, full of hardships and disaster. The film, which was the industry's contribution to the Festival of Britain, has an appropriately stellar cast of actors who pop in for a few seconds in a well-mounted drama. Laurence Olivier, for example, has a highly amusing cameo as a policeman. Maria Schell and Margaret Johnston play Donat's two wives.

Magic of Lassie, The ○
1978, US, 100 mins, colour
Dir: Don Chaffey
Stars: Mickey Rooney, Stephanie Zimbalist, James Stewart, Alice Faye, Pernell Roberts
Rating: ★★

A game attempt to make a 1946 movie 32 years on. If only the pace weren't so slow, it might have come close to success. The colour photography mightn't be as lush as it was in the MGM days, but every possible ingredient to make the picture cute and lovable is thrown into the pot. The doggy star is immaculately trained, and, while the children are crying buckets over Lassie coming home after another incredible journey, for us adults there's always James Stewart, acting his heart out (and ridiculously losing star billing to Mickey Rooney) as if he thought he were in some other, better film. Mike Mazurki and Alice Faye are around to add to the nostalgia quotient, but it's Stewart's film: he even out-acts the dog and that's saying something.

Magnificent Ambersons, The ○
1942, US, 88 mins, b/w
Dir: Orson Welles
Stars: Joseph Cotten, Dolores Costello, Agnes Moorehead, Tim Holt, Anne Baxter, Ray Collins
Rating: ★★★★

Engrossing study by Orson Welles of a mid-western American family in terminal decay, set against a series of crowd scenes and backdrops that look like black and white etchings from an earlier era. Boasting imposing performances from Joseph Cotten, Tim

Holt and especially Agnes Moorehead, the film is full of scenes of thudding impact. To its undying shame, RKO tacked a new ending on to the film behind Welles' back and almost ruined it, leaving us with an unsatisfactory conclusion. In its original form, it could almost have been the equal of Welles' previous film *Citizen Kane*. The perfect narration is by Welles himself.

Magnificent Doll ○
1946, US, 95 mins, b/w
Dir: Frank Borzage
Stars: Ginger Rogers, David Niven, Burgess Meredith
Rating: ★★

Universal probably wasn't the best studio in the immediate post-war years for the mounting of this ambitious biography about Dolly Payne, a widow in Washington from 1796 on, who was wooed by several prominent politicians and eventually won by a man destined to become president. Ginger Rogers looks fabulous in gowns designed by Travis Banton and Vera West, but seems a little overawed by long speeches about democracy, which take her a step too far off the dance floor. David Niven, although miscast, at least performs with spirit. As usual with Hollywood at the time, any resemblance between the events of the plot and the accepted facts of American history is coincidental.

Magnificent Obsession ○
1954, US, 108 mins, colour
Dir: Douglas Sirk
Stars: Jane Wyman, Rock Hudson, Barbara Rush, Agnes Moorehead
Rating: ★★★

Douglas Sirk's glossy remake of the 1935 film of the same title, with Jane Wyman and Rock Hudson succeeding the original co-starring team of Irene Dunne and Robert Taylor. Basically the material is of the magazine-fiction school: playboy Hudson inadvertently causes Wyman to be knocked down by a car and blinded. Stricken with remorse, he takes the only way out: he becomes a brain surgeon and cures her. Simple really. Wyman takes it in her stride; Hudson looks a touch bewildered but toughs it out; Barbara Rush underplays effectively; and Agnes Moorehead steals the film. Lush colour, doleful glances, tasteful clothes, nothing nasty: another world.

Magnificent Seven, The ○ ⓥ
1960, US, 138 mins, colour
Dir: John Sturges

Stars: Yul Brynner, James Coburn, Steve McQueen, Horst Buchholz, Charles Bronson, Robert Vaughn, Brad Dexter
Rating: ★★★★★

A truly thunderous Western, with its wonderful ensemble cast and Elmer Bernstein's stirring music. The buildup is tremendous, the dialogue studded with memorably quotable lines, and director John Sturges' early action sequence in a graveyard as impressive and blood-surging as anything in the film. Charles Bronson, James Coburn, Steve McQueen and Robert Vaughn etch moving, unforgettable characters in a Hollywood remake (of the Japanese *Seven Samurai*) that for once doesn't disgrace the original.

Magnificent Showman, The ○ ⓥ
(aka: Circus World)
1964, US, 135 mins, colour
Dir: Henry Hathaway
Stars: John Wayne, Claudia Cardinale, Rita Hayworth, John Smith, Lloyd Nolan, Richard Conte
Rating: ★★

If you like circuses, John Wayne or Claudia Cardinale, then this merry, gaudy and faintly numbing panorama of circus life is the film for you. It's certainly a handsome piece with the accent on spectacle and sentiment, even if it tends to sit back and say, 'Aren't I a wonderful show?' and let the audience do the rest. Miss Cardinale, all bosom and sparkling teeth, has never used her native Italian charm to greater effect, and puts poor Rita Hayworth (at some disadvantage from the start in playing her mother) in the shade. But the film is really one big circus from start to finish. Wayne did much of his own stuntwork in the fire scenes and spent several days in bed for his trouble.

Magnificent Two, The ○
1967, UK, 96 mins, colour
Dir: Cliff Owen
Stars: Eric Morecambe, Ernie Wise
Rating: ★★

The Rank Organisation's third and last attempt to make film stars out of TV masterclowns Morecambe and Wise. The laughter measure is high in parts in this, the most successful of the three (Eric and Ernie get mixed up in a revolution), though there are vague and unsettling undercurrents of nastiness running through the story. And people get killed. In a Laurel and Hardy comedy, a lift could fall on a man from 60 feet and he got up. He got up as a dwarf, but he got up. Still, there's al-

M

ways Eric, bespectacled and bewildered and as deadpan as ever. 'I will always be the woman behind you,' Major Carla (Margit Saad) reminds him. Remarks Eric, looking perplexed: 'You'll come round the front now and again, won't you?'

Magnum Force ● Ⓥ
1973, US, 124 mins, colour
Dir: Ted Post
Stars: Clint Eastwood, Hal Holbrook, Mitchell Ryan, David Soul
Rating: ★★

Inspector Harry Callahan takes on a gang of hijackers, a band of store robbers, a mad bomber and even, in the storyline's main theme, a group of vigilantes who are conducting their own private massacre of the city's underworld. None of those characters is any match for tall, tough, taciturn Harry, as you can imagine, played with all the finesse of a Magnum .44 revolver by Clint Eastwood.

Mahler ◐ Ⓥ
1974, UK, 115 mins, colour
Dir: Ken Russell
Stars: Robert Powell, Georgina Hale, Richard Morant
Rating: ★★★★

Ken Russell's highly individual biography of the famous composer is an essay in style, image and effect. But what style! What eye-popping images! And what dazzling effect! Russell has virtually done no more than set Mahler's exciting music to his own visual interpretations, against a background of flashbacks on a train journey when the composer – strikingly well played by Robert Powell – has only a few days to live. A naked girl escapes from a crysalis; a child dies; a conversion to Catholicism turns into a cross between 'The Ride of the Valkyries' and a Busby Berkeley routine; a girl performs a striptease with SS men; and there's a ride on a white horse through moonlit woods. You can see that there's no lack of riches; that certainly it's outrageous; and that occasionally Russell overreaches himself. But Mahler's life story is there at the back of it all; and Robert Powell is exceptionally good at catching, besides the various ages, the man's uncertainties, determination, eccentricities and fear of death. Above all, the music makes you want to go out and buy the records!

Major and the Minor, The ○
1942, US, 100 mins, b/w
Dir: Billy Wilder

Stars: Ginger Rogers, Ray Milland, Rita Johnson, Robert Benchley
Rating: ★★★★

An enchantingly amusing comedy in which, posing as a 12-year-old schoolgirl, Ginger Rogers finds herself in the middle of a boys' military school. Diana Lynn is equally good as her impish sister. A big box-office and critical hit that sent the team of writer-director Billy Wilder and co-writer Charles Brackett on their way to a decade of success.

Major Barbara ○
1941, UK, 121 mins, b/w
Dir: Gabriel Pascal, Harold French, David Lean
Stars: Wendy Hiller, Rex Harrison, Robert Morley, Robert Newton, Emlyn Williams, Deborah Kerr
Rating: ★★★

An efficient and entertaining screen version of Bernard Shaw's satirical play about a wealthy girl who becomes a major in the Salvation Army. Wendy Hiller and Rex Harrison are the leading players, while Robert Newton's performance in support made him a star of the British cinema.

Major Dundee ○
1964, US, 120 mins, colour
Dir: Sam Peckinpah
Stars: Charlton Heston, Richard Harris, James Coburn, Senta Berger
Rating: ★★★★

A big Sam Peckinpah Western about a mixed bag of Unionists and Confederates hunting renegade Indians in the last months of the Civil War. The action is stirring, and the Metrocolor photography splendid in set pieces, particularly with one shot of Charlton Heston and Senta Berger on the outskirts of a small Mexican town. As a one-armed scout, James Coburn gives a portrayal which lifts an ordinary supporting role into one of compelling stature. Jim Hutton and Michael Anderson Jr show up well as younger soldiers, while R. G Armstrong also does well as a fire-eating, rifle-swinging priest. There's a glorious final battle sequence in which Dundee's rabble army not only ambushes and attacks a tribe of murderous Indians, but fights a splendid rearguard action against what seems to be the entire French Army.

Majority of One, A ○
1961, US, 156 mins, colour
Dir: Mervyn LeRoy
Stars: Alec Guinness, Rosalind Russell
Rating: ★★

A sentimental drama that fires on most tear ducts thanks to the moving performances of the two stars, Alec Guinness and Rosalind Russell, as a Japanese gentleman and a Jewish lady falling in love. Lushly photographed in Technicolor and less successful at the box-office than it deserved to be, it was the beginning of a gentle downswing in Guinness' phenomenally successful film career.

Major League ◐ Ⓥ
1989, US, 107 mins, colour
Dir: David S Ward
Stars: Tom Berenger, Charlie Sheen, Corbin Bernsen, Margaret Whitton, Rene Russo, Wesley Snipes
Rating: ★★

This okay baseball comedy is the usual Hollywood sporting stuff about the bunch of no-hopers who turn out to be world-beaters. Well put together,. it's not as funny as its publicity and reputation would have you believe. Plotwork is by the numbers and characters are stereotypes. But the acting from an all-star cast lends the enterprise an extra dimension, especially from Charlie Sheen as the short-sighted demon pitcher who becomes known as Wild Thing. A sequel followed five years later.

Make Mine Mink ○
1960, UK, 100 mins, b/w
Dir: Robert Asher
Stars: Terry-Thomas, Athene Seyler, Hattie Jacques, Billie Whitelaw
Rating: ★★★★

A rib-tickling comedy in which Terry-Thomas, Athene Seyler and Hattie Jacques ham it up delightfully as members of a genteel gang of fur thieves, while Billie Whitelaw's warm-hearted portrait of the maid with a police record almost steals the film. Lots of amusing sketch-like incidents carry the fun along in style, aided by a well above-par comedy cast that also includes Kenneth Williams, Ron Moody, Sydney Tafler, Raymond Huntley and Irene Handl.

Making Mr Right ◐ Ⓥ
1987, US, 98 mins, colour
Dir: Susan Seidelman
Stars: Ann Magnuson, John Malkovich, Glenne Headly, Ben Masters, Polly Bergen, Laurie Metcalf
Rating: ★★

A bright-looking misfire on the now-familiar theme of the android who develops human feelings. It's quite difficult to say why Susan Seidelman's film doesn't quite work, except that its leading performers do lack individuality. Ann Magnuson, for example, is nothing special and never quite hits the mark as the high-powered, highly sexed hype consultant hired to humanise a new space mission android, Ulysses (John Malkovich), for the benefit of the media. She looks like a supporting actress just slightly out of her depth. Malkovich also plays the robot's alter-ego scientist, who shows rather less in the way of emotions (surprisingly) than his creation. The fun and games that result from this situation are rather limited and not too inspired or involving. Okay for video, though, where attention is less demanding; and Glenne Headly is good as the heroine's dizzy friend.

Malaga

See: Moment of Danger

Malaya ○

(aka: East of the Rising Sun)
1949, US, 98 mins, b/w
Dir: Richard Thorpe
Stars: Spencer Tracy, James Stewart, Sydney Greenstreet, John Hodiak, Valentina Cortesa
Rating: ★★★

Big-scale, two-fisted adventure story set during World War Two. The film's action comes in frequent bursts once Spencer Tracy and James Stewart (playing an ex-jailbird and a newspaperman respectively) are put ashore behind enemy Japanese lines. The entire cast, in fact, is quite breathtakingly fomidable and, unsurprisingly, strike a good many sparks off one another, despite the inferior script and direction.

Malcolm X ● ⓥ

1992, US, 201 mins, colour
Dir: Spike Lee
Stars: Denzel Washington, Angela Bassett, Spike Lee, Al Freeman Jr, Theresa Randle, Lonette McKee
Rating: ★★★

Director Spike Lee's powerful portrait of the controversial black American leader gave Denzel Washington a great acting opportunity, and for his electrifying portrayal of Malcolm X's rise from teen thug to street preacher and political activist he was nominated for an Academy Award. Full of passionate ideas and inflammatory speeches, and with a powerful message, this is an extraordinary true story - but at over three hours it does take some watching, particularly since its most memorable moments are dotted in little bright

bursts throughout the film. Nelson Mandela makes a cameo appearance; the talented Angela Bassett is sadly underused.

Malice ● ⓥ

1993, US, 107 mins, colour
Dir: Harold Becker
Stars: Alec Baldwin, Nicole Kidman, Bill Pullman, Anne Bancroft, George C Scott
Rating: ★★★

If you're at home with the lights down and there's a storm raging outside, this might give you a creep or two. Set in an America where people leave doors, back and front, open (as you do) and an address like 36 Hedges Lane proves to be on the edge of a cliff, this is one of those plots where very little ends up being what it seemed in the first place. Without wishing to betray the plot... well, given that Nicole Kidman collects $20 million for surgeon Alec Baldwin cutting out a healthy ovary and walks out on husband Bill Pullman for letting Baldwin do it, and given that we're less than half way through the film, it won't take avid thriller fans long to figure that something is Going On. Nor are they likely to pause long before pouncing on the identity of the serial killer who just happens to be raping and murdering girls from Prof Pullman's college at the same time. Well-made and enjoyable rubbish, this, if a touch on the unpleasant side.

Malicious ● ⓥ

1995, US, 92 mins, colour
Dir: Ian Corson
Stars: Molly Ringwald, John Vernon, Patrick McGaw, Mimi Kuzyk, Sarah Lassez
Rating: ★

Where did Molly Ringwald's career go in the 1990s? As far down as this, is the answer: a *Fatal Attraction-in-a-College*-style thriller which features Ringwald in the Glenn Close-style role as the seductive but unbalanced Melissa. After a fling with college athlete Doug (Patrick McGaw), Melissa sets about making life hell for him, his family and his girlfriend (Sarah Lassez). There's nothing original here, and no surprises for those who've seen Close let rip in more spectacular style with the spurned woman emotions. Incidentally, the rabbit who, in *Fatal Attraction*, was the first victim of revenge, is here substituted by an unfortunate cat.

Malta Story ○

1953, UK, 103 mins, b/w
Dir: Brian Desmond Hurst

Stars: Alec Guinness, Jack Hawkins, Flora Robson
Rating: ★★★

The direction is sharper than the script in this sincere and clear-eyed story of the siege of Malta by the Germans and Italians in World War Two. Director Hurst brings the hot, rocky Malta scene brilliantly to life, and creates such moments to remember as close-ups of authentic Maltese faces, and shots of children at play during an air-raid. Muriel Pavlow is delicately touching as a young Maltese girl in love with part-time pilot Alec Guinness (slightly uncomfortable outside his normal comedy roles), and there are workmanlike service types from Jack Hawkins, Anthony Steel and - particularly good - Ralph Truman.

Maltese Falcon, The ○ ⓥ

1941, US, 101 mins, b/w
Dir: John Huston
Stars: Humphrey Bogart, Mary Astor, Peter Lorre, Sydney Greenstreet, Barton MacLane
Rating: ★★★★★

Humphrey Bogart's first major starring role, gripping from start to finish in its account of various eccentric criminals and their hunt for a fabulous statuette, in which detective Bogart becomes embroiled. Indelible performances from Bogart and especially from a perfumed Peter Lorre and the hulking Sydney Greenstreet as two of the oiliest and most treacherous conspirators in film history: the public loved them together and they co-starred in several more films thereafter. Original author Dashiell Hammett based the Greenstreet character on a real-life rogue, Maundy Gregory, a corpulent British detective who turned in his badge and became involved in numerous intrigues including a hunt for a lost treasure not unlike the plot for *The Maltese Falcon*.

Mambo Kings, The ◐ ⓥ

1992, US, 101 mins, colour
Dir: Arne Glimcher
Stars: Armand Assante, Antonio Banderas, Cathy Moriarty, Maruschka Detmers, J T Taylor, Desi Arnaz Jr
Rating: ★★★

Apart from the sex scenes, this is an old-fashioned film that reflects the Fifties in which it's set and catches well the cultural flavour of its central characters. Other characters and situations are pretty stereotyped, though, as Cuban musician brothers Armand Assante and Antonio Banderas flee

M

from gangsters in their native land and set out to become the mambo kings of the USA. Complications are provided by Banderas not being able to forget his true love in Cuba (now married to a gangster) and Assante falling heavily for the girl his brother marries on the rebound. The music is hot to begin with, but one mambo sounds much like another, and the film's key song, though lovely, is repeated rather too many times. As the older brother, Assante is excellent: this is probably the best performance of his career to date, in a film where everything else is pretty middling. Roscoe Lee Browne is the nasty villain who gets the brothers banned from his clubs.

Mame ○ ⓥ
1974, US, 131 mins, colour
Dir: Gene Saks
Stars: Lucille Ball, Robert Preston, Beatrice Arthur
Rating: ★

The hit Broadway musical transferred to the screen with Lucille Ball in Angela Lansbury's place (shot in close-up through a thousand gauze filters) as Auntie Mame, the eccentric socialite forced to take in her orphan nephew. There's a notable lack of singing talent involved. But Beatrice Arthur (later better known as Dorothy in TV's *The Golden Girls*) re-creates her stage success as Mame's actress friend Vera Charles. The best songs are Mame and Vera bitching at each other through 'Bosom Buddies' and 'The Man in the Moon is a Lady' sequence from Vera's latest stage success, which Mame manages to wreck in spectacular fashion. As a film musical it's a lumbering, static affair, but a must for lovers of high camp.

Man Alive ○
1945, US, 70 mins, b/w
Dir: Ray Enright
Stars: Pat O'Brien, Adolphe Menjou, Ellen Drew, Rudy Vallee, Fortunio Bonanova
Rating: ★★★

An amusing change of pace for tough guy Pat O'Brien as a man who, presumed dead, likes the idea until someone else makes a play for his wife. Then he becomes a 'ghost' to scare the suitor off. Entertaining comedy.

Man Alone, A ○
1955, US, 96 mins, colour
Dir: Ray Milland
Stars: Ray Milland, Mary Murphy, Ward Bond, Raymond Burr
Rating: ★★★

Ray Milland is a gunfighter on the run wrongly acused of murder in this well-plotted Western which was also Milland's directing debut. The sheriff's daughter (Mary Murphy) helps him prove his innocence and hides him from a lynch mob. Ward Bond gives good support as the town sheriff and there are two good baddies in Raymond Burr and a young, snake-eyed Lee Van Cleef. It's deliberate and humourless, but the tension is well concentrated.

Man and a Woman, A
See: Un Homme et une Femme

Man at the Top ○ ⓥ
1973, UK, 87 mins, colour
Dir: Mike Vardy
Stars: Kenneth Haigh, Nanette Newman, Harry Andrews
Rating: ★★

After starring in the long running television series of the same title, Kenneth Haigh gave a ruthless abrasiveness to the famous character of Joe Lampton, created in John Braine's best-seller and incarnated originally in the cinema by Laurence Harvey. In this okay spin-off from the TV series, Haigh is the new managing director of a pharmaceutical company: he finds out just why his predecessor killed himself and then uses the knowledge to blackmail his way to the top, showing that Lampton still has some nastiness left in him.

Man, a Woman and a Bank, A ○
(aka: A Very Big Withdrawal)
1979, Canada, 101 mins, colour
Dir: Noel Black
Stars: Donald Sutherland, Brooke Adams, Paul Mazursky
Rating: ★★★

This is better than most bank robbery capers, if only because of the determinedly light mood, skilfully maintained by director Noel Black, whose best-known film is *Pretty Poison*. Otherwise it's a routine job, involving a computerised heist executed by Donald Sutherland and Paul Mazursky. Little Mazursky shows as much talent here as a character actor as he does as the director of such films as *An Unmarried Woman*. Sutherland and Brooke Adams, reunited from *Invasion of the Body Snatchers*, work pleasingly well together and, although there are a few lulls, and a silly 10-minute interlude which serves little better purpose than the foreground for a song, this remains pleasing, undemanding entertainment

with a few clammy-handed thrills thrown in.

Man Between, The ○
1953, US, 100 mins, b/w
Dir: Carol Reed
Stars: James Mason, Claire Bloom, Hildegarde Neff
Rating: ★★

Carol Reed moved from the Vienna of *The Third Man* to Berlin, and from racketeers to refugees in this Cold-War thriller which has echoes of *The Spy Who Came In From the Cold*. Although the script is generally disappointing, Reed and his cameraman Desmond Dickinson conjure up some brilliant atmospheric moments and a tense climax.

Man Called Horse, A ① ⓥ
1970, US, 114 mins, colour
Dir: Elliot Silverstein
Stars: Richard Harris, Judith Anderson, Jean Gascon
Rating: ★★★

One of Richard Harris's mightiest box-office successes. He's in terrific form as the English aristocrat who falls into the clutches of a tribe of Sioux Indians. Fascinated by his fair skin and blond hair, they take him prisoner and proceed to inflict terrible torture by ritual (turn your eyes away at the 'Sun Vow' scene where our hero is suspended by horsehair ropes from bones inserted into holes made in his chest by eagle claws) before they will accept him. Obviously, this and other scenes make this far more brutal than Kevin Costner's *Dances With Wolves*, but it remains a fascinating, if slightly gauche, variation on the 'man living wild' theme, bluntly addressing both anthropological differences, and the inevitable contempt that ignorance of different cultures engenders.

Manchurian Candidate, The ① ⓥ
1962, US, 126 mins, b/w
Dir: John Frankenheimer
Stars: Frank Sinatra, Laurence Harvey, Janet Leigh, Angela Lansbury
Rating: ★★★★

Chilling, suspenseful, right-on-target adaptation of Richard Condon's novel about a soldier back from the Korean War who has been brainwashed and primed to kill at the release of a certain code. Electrifying direction by John Frankenheimer, good work from Frank Sinatra, Janet Leigh and Laurence Harvey (never better cast) and an outstanding performance by Angela Lansbury, far from her cosy Jessica

Fletcher image, as a woman ambitious for political power.

Mandy ⊙
(aka: The Crash of Silence)
1952, UK, 93 mins, b/w
Dir: Alexander Mackendrick
Stars: Phyllis Calvert, Jack Hawkins, Mandy Miller, Terence Morgan
Rating: ★★★

A dramatic, exciting film about the problems facing a young couple whose child is unable to speak or hear. Mandy Miller, as the little girl who lives in a silent world, gives an affecting performance which won the hearts of millions.

Man for All Seasons, A ○ ⓥ
1966, UK, 120 mins, colour
Dir: Fred Zinnemann
Stars: Paul Scofield, Wendy Hiller, Leo McKern, Robert Shaw, Orson Welles, Susannah York
Rating: ★★★★

Fred Zinnemann's handsome film of Sir Thomas More's trials under the whims of King Henry VIII scores in every department except its senior school history book dialogue. It won six Academy Awards, including Oscars for Paul Scofield as Sir Thomas, and for Ted Moore, whose colour photography would have won in almost any year. All the other performances are good, notably Orson Welles' plotting Cardinal Wolsey, Wendy Hiller's understanding, very human wife, and John Hurt's weak and waspish Richard Rich.

Man Friday ○
1975, UK, 115 mins, colour
Dir: Jack Gold
Stars: Peter O'Toole, Richard Roundtree
Rating: ★★

This colourful film plays a novel variation on Defoe's classic tale of life on a desert island. It supposes that Friday (Richard Roundtree), instead of being taught by Robinson Crusoe (Peter O'Toole), contrives, by craft and patience, to reverse the situation so that Crusoe learns a basic way of life from him, each assimilating the best of one another's culture. The setting is attractive, the performances appealing and the situations, particularly a sports day, are often amusing. Only in the last 10 minutes does it veer off line and go a bit to pieces.

Man from Bitter Ridge, The ○
1955, US, 80 mins, colour
Dir: Jack Arnold

Stars: Lex Barker, Stephen McNally, Mara Corday
Rating: ★★

Lex Barker, then still escaping from his Tarzan image, is the hero of this Western, as an undercover agent after stagecoach bandits. But all the acting class comes from Stephen McNally, who did such yeoman service in countless Universal Westeens.

Man from Colorado, The ○
1948, US, 99 mins, colour
Dir: Henry Levin
Stars: Glenn Ford, William Holden, Ellen Drew, Edgar Buchanan
Rating: ★★★

Lively Western in good Technicolor, with Glenn Ford in a very different role from his other co-starring Western with William Holden, *Texas*, in 1941. Here he plays an army officer with a streak of brutal violence, who is made a federal judge, and clashes with Holden, as his oldest friend. Ford does well as the totally dislikeable Devereaux, and the supporting cast is filmed with Columbia regulars.

Man from Dakota, The ○
(aka: Arouse and Beware)
1940, US, 75 mins, b/w
Dir: Leslie Fenton
Stars: Wallace Beery, John Howard, Dolores Del Rio
Rating: ★★

A tough-edged but rousing Western made as a vehicle for big, brawling Wallace Beery, here as a bullying sergeant contemptuous of the youthful officer (John Howard) with whom he escapes from a Confederate prison camp during the American Civil War. The plot doesn't develop quite as you might expect, thanks to its basis – a novel by Mackinlay Kantor – and makes room for the soulfully lovely Dolores Del Rio as a woman who helps the escapees.

Man from Del Rio, The ○
1956, US, 83 mins, b/w
Dir: Harry Horner
Stars: Anthony Quinn, Katy Jurado
Rating: ★★★

An unusual, thoughtful, and decidedly worthwhile Western. There's not a lot of action, apart from a fierce gunfight at the start and a tense climax. But the performances of the principals more than make up for it. Photographed by the great Stanley Cortez.

Man from Laramie, The ○ ⓥ
1955, US, 104 mins, colour
Dir: Anthony Mann
Stars: James Stewart, Arthur Kennedy, Donald Crisp, Cathy O'Donnell, Alex Nicol, Aline MacMahon
Rating: ★★★★

Superior Western with a famous theme tune, and James Stewart going through hell and high water to track down the man who sold Indians rifles that led to the death of Stewart's brother. There are two excellent performances from old-stagers Donald Crisp and Aline MacMahon, but delicate Cathy O'Donnell seems a little lost among the film's many fights. Jack Elam scores in a small but sinister role, and colour, music and action all hbit the mark well in this tautly strung outdoor whodunnit.

Man from Nevada, The
See: The Nevadan

Man from Snowy River, The ○ ⓥ
1982, Australia, 104 mins, colour
Dir: George Miller
Stars: Kirk Douglas, Jack Thompson
Rating: ★★

More like bargain basement Disney than a John Ford Western, this Australian saddle saga takes its cue from the successful *Wilderness Family* films. A growing pains melodrama, it suffers through the inexperience of its young leads – Tom Burlinson and Sigrid Thornton – and the cheap gimmick of casting Kirk Douglas as both a reclusive mountain man who helps the boy overcome his sudden state as an orphan and the girl's stubborn father. Even so, it was a huge hit Down Under. Incidentally, director George Miller is not the same as the George Miller who directed Mel Gibson's *Mad Max* trilogy.

Man from the Diners' Club, The ⊙
1963, US, 96 mins, b/w
Dir: Frank Tashlin
Stars: Danny Kaye, Martha Hyer, Telly Savalas, George Kennedy
Rating: ★★★

By 1963, Danny Kaye's best films and his peak of fame were certainly behind him, but this funny film didn't get its just deserts at the time. It's unusual to find a Kaye comedy in black-and-white (20 years earlier his films were already in colour). But the great man will soon get you laughing with impersonations of a dotty masseuse, or an unwittingly

M

brilliant gymnast, outmanoeuvring a gang of crooks led by a bewigged Telly Savalas. And the final half-hour includes a wild and wacky chase on the freeway.

Manhattan ○ ⓥ

1979, US, 96 mins, b/w
Dir: Woody Allen
Stars: Woody Allen, Diane Keaton, Michael Murphy, Mariel Hemingway, Meryl Streep
Rating: ★★★

Considered by many Woody Allen fans to be his best film, *Manhattan* is more thoughtful and less obviously funny than the similar but Oscar-laden *Annie Hall*. Allen is a successful television writer who wants to do something more worthwhile. He also feels guilty about his relationship with a teenage girl (Mariel Hemingway) who dotes on film. His ex-wife (Meryl Streep) is a lesbian and he hesitantly starts an affair with Diane Keaton. It all sounds more complicated than it is, and Allen's excellent script and deceptively simple direction make *Manhattan* a joy to watch. The fact that it is shot in black and white entirely on location in Allen's home town adds to its quirky appeal.

Manhattan Melodrama ○

1934, US, 93 mins, b/w
Dir: W S Van Dyke
Stars: Clark Gable, William Powell, Myrna Loy, Leo Carrillo, Mickey Rooney
Rating: ★★★

Clark Gable gained useful practice for the 1936 blockbuster *San Francisco* (in both cases he's a gambling house proprietor called Blackie) in this familiar but oh-so-well-done story of two orphaned kids, one of whom grows into an upright citizen, the other into a smooth-talking racketeer and gambler. Although he's uncredited on the MGM handout, you may notice that the boy playing Gable as a lad is Mickey Rooney. Arthur Caesar's screenplay won an Academy Award. *Manhattan Melodrama* was the film 'public enemy number one' John Dillinger had just seen when he was gunned down by federal agents.

Manhattan Murder Mystery ○ ⓥ

1993, US, 109 mins, colour
Dir: Woody Allen
Stars: Woody Allen, Diane Keaton, Alan Alda, Anjelica Huston
Rating: ★★★★

Something different from Woody with lots of smiles and rarely a neurosis in sight: a comedy-thriller that balances the comedy and thrills in the right ratio. A bit annoying at first (and its hand held camera wavers remain so), but increasingly enjoyable, it casts Woody Allen and Diane Keaton as a middle-aged couple indulging each other's pastimes of ice hockey (his) and opera (hers). 'Every time I hear Wagner,' he grumbles, 'I feel I should invade Poland.' Keaton is longing to do something with her life, and her curiosity runs wild when her fairly elderly neighbour drops dead. She feels sure the gossipy woman would have mentioned her heart condition. We share Woody's sceptical view of her suspicions, but amazingly it seems there *is* something going on – especially when the woman turns up alive. Stir in Alan Alda as Keaton's old flame who still has a yen for her, and publisher Allen's ace author Anjelica Huston, who fancies a mystery almost as much a man, and you have a feisty brew that actually has one or two exciting, stylish and creepy moments amidst the modish comedy.

Manhattan Project, The ◑ ⓥ

1986, US, 117 mins, colour
Dir: Marshall Brickman
Stars: John Lithgow, Christopher Collet, Jill Eikenberry, Cynthia Nixon, John Mahoney, Robert Sean Leonard
Rating: ★★

It's amazing what you can do while you're studying for your chemistry exam. Take young Paul, for example. Seeing his mother's getting pally with a nuclear scientist and recognising bottles of plutonium during a tour on which the scientist generously takes him, Paul decides to break into the lab, steal some and make his own atomic bomb. Well, this is America, so you can at least believe it if you take a heavy swallow. Although overlong, the film is a neat enough comedy-thriller offshoot of *WarGames*, with (thank goodness) a personable and accomplished quartet of leading portrayals from mighty John Lithgow (the scientist), Christopher Collet (the boy), Jill Eikenberry (his mother) and Cynthia Nixon (his rather mature girlfriend). Some tension is generated towards the end, although not about the bomb itself, which we know won't explode in a film of this timbre.

Manhunt

See: From Hell to Texas

Man Hunt ○

1941, US, 98 mins, b/w
Dir: Fritz Lang
Stars: Walter Pidgeon, Joan Bennett, George Sanders, John Carradine, Roddy McDowall
Rating: ★★★

This now little-known Fritz Lang film, about a man who almost kills Hitler, contains some of the most exciting chase sequences ever made. After years of minor films at MGM, Walter Pidgeon was loaned to 20th Century-Fox for two pictures, this and *How Green Was My Valley*. He returned to MGM a star. Another powerful performance is given by John Carradine, in frightening form as the man who hunts Pidgeon down.

Manhunter ● ⓥ

1986, US, 118 mins, colour
Dir: Michael Mann
Stars: William L Petersen, Kim Greist, Brian Cox, Joan Allen, Dennis Farina
Rating: ★★

The character of Hannibal the Cannibal makes its first film appearance in this blood-spattered but slow psychological thriller, with bursts of action including the inevitable confrontation between cop and killer at the climax. A full-moon killer (this one known as the Tooth Fairy) is on the loose again, and only an ex-FBI agent (William L Petersen), who is slightly deranged himself, seems likely to catch him. Quite a brooding performance from Petersen and some mildly interesting psychological overtones, but overall this thriller, though strong meat, is pretty routine.

Maniac ◑

1963, UK, 86 mins, b/w
Dir: Michael Carreras
Stars: Kerwin Mathews, Nadia Gray, Donald Houston
Rating: ★★

Kerwin Mathews is most commonly associated with the Dynamation films, but this time he's up to some very non U-certificate goings-on in this eerie Hammer suspense story, set in the Camargue marshlands of France. Liliane Brousse stirs up some genuine Gallic sex appeal in the steamy settings in a Jimmy Sangster-scripted story mostly shot at night – of a mad axe murderer on the loose.

Maniac Cop ● ⓥ

1988, US, 85 mins, colour
Dir: William Lustig
Stars: Tom Atkins, Bruce Campbell,

Laurene Landon, Richard Roundtree
Rating: ★

Even though he didn't direct it, the
hand of writer-director Larry Cohen
(*It's Alive!* was his biggest hit) puts its
dabs all over this horror film masquerading as a police thriller. A
vengeful brain-dead cop rises from the
grave, dons his uniform and initiates a
mass slaughter of the city's night-time
population. A detective smells a
(dead) rat and contacts a TV friend to
break the ban on the story. 'You gotta
make it bigger than AIDS,' he says.
The unfortunate consequence of his
action is that while the maniac cop
goes on killing innocent people, citizens start killing innocent cops. The
rest is pretty lively if rudimentary B-
movie stuff, sketchily acted with the
exception of Sheree North and sickeningly violent throughout. Most
unsuitable for children.

Maniac Cop 2 ● Ⓥ
1990, US, 85 mins, colour
Dir: William Lustig
Stars: Robert Davi, Claudia Christian,
Bruce Campbell, Laurene Landon, Leo
Rossi
Rating: ★

The psycho policeman is back on the
beat(ing), and this time he has a signature tune: 'You'd better watch out
when you hear that sound. It means
that the maniac cop's around.' Fun
huh? The first film was not without
interest, but this sequel is pure pulp.
The hero and heroine from *Maniac Cop*
(Campbell, Landon) are soon
despatched by Cordell, the disgraced
(and framed) cop risen from the dead,
as he teams up with a serial killer (Leo
Rossi) and kills the innocent to protect
the guilty. The trail eventually leads
back to Sing Sing prison where Cordell
was bumped off by three inmates, paid
with public money. Cynically cut to
the formula its public will expect, the
film also makes a miserable attempt to
forge a bond of friendship between the
cop and the killer along the lines of
Frankenstein's creature and the blind
hermit from *Bride of Frankenstein*. If
only this had a tenth of that film's flair
and style.

Maniacs on Wheels
See: Once a Jolly Swagman

Man in a Cocked Hat
See: Carlton-Browne of the FO

Man in Grey, The ○
1943, UK, 116 mins, b/w

Dir: Leslie Arliss
Stars: Margaret Lockwood, James
Mason, Phyllis Calvert, Stewart Granger
Rating: ★★★

This period adventure yarn was the
film that really started the box-office
clicking for Gainsborough Films, soon
to become Britain's most successful
company in the 1940s. All four stars –
Margaret Lockwood, Stewart Granger,
Phyllis Calvert and especially James
Mason, as the evil Marquis of Rohan –
gave fine performances which assured
their popularity for years to come.

Man in Love, A ● Ⓥ
1987, France, 110 mins, colour
Dir: Diane Kurys
Stars: Peter Coyote, Greta Scacchi, Peter
Riegert, Jamie Lee Curtis, Claudia
Cardinale
Rating: ★★★

I suppose it would take Greta Scacchi,
if anything, to drag one away from
Jamie Lee Curtis; but Peter Coyote certainly is a lucky man to have the two to
choose between in this moody romantic piece. A bit long, but with a nice
overall feel, the film has some really effective atmospheric shots of European
cities in summer and the affair between
movie star Coyote and starlet Scacchi is
accompanied by sweeping music from
Georges Delarue in the grand manner.
Claudia Cardinale looks magnificent as
Scacchi's mother and she, Coyote,
Peter Riegert and Curtis steal the acting honours, while Scacchi offers
frequent displays of skin that will have
her devotees drooling in the aisles.

Man In the Attic ○
1953, US, 82 mins, b/w
Dir: Hugo Fregonese
Stars: Jack Palance, Constance Smith
Rating: ★★★

Jack Palance adds a portrait of Jack the
Ripper to his gallery of screen
grotesques in this gripping and at times
quite frightening thriller. The
Victorian atmosphere rings true, and
there are two good supporting performances from Rhys Williams and
Frances Bavier as the parents of one of
the Ripper's would-be victims.

Man in the Dark ○
1953, US, 71 mins, b/w
Dir: Lew Landers
Stars: Edmond O'Brien, Audrey Totter,
Ted De Corsia
Rating: ★★

The credentials of this tense and sometimes frightening crime thriller make it

worth watching. The director, Lew
Landers, was responsible for some interesting horror films in the Thirties
and Forties. And the action is hair-rais-
ingly photographed, especially a chase
on a roller-coaster, by Hollywood veteran Floyd Crosby, who worked on all
of the Sixties' film adaptations of Edgar
Allan Poe stories.

Man in the Gray Flannel Suit, The ○
1956, US, 153 mins, colour
Dir: Nunnally Johnson
Stars: Gregory Peck, Jennifer Jones,
Fredric March, Marisa Pavan, Lee J Cobb
Rating: ★★★

Compelling, if overlong, account of a
man fighting to find hope in the future
and save his marriage. Dominated by
a brilliant performance from Fredric
March, although Marisa Pavan also
registers well as the girl in Gregory
Peck's past.

Man in the Iron Mask, The ○
1939, US, 110 mins, b/w
Dir: James Whale
Stars: Louis Hayward, Joan Bennett,
Joseph Schildkraut, Alan Hale
Rating: ★★★★

The amazing atmosphere in this
brooding version of Dumas' classic tale
of intrigue and derring-do is achieved
in masterly style by skilful lighting and
can chiefly be attributed to the di:rec-
tor, James Whale, whose last great film
this was, following a series of horror
classics that had included *The Invisible
Man* and *Bride of Frankenstein*. One cannot imagine an actor more able than
Louis Hayward to suggest the separate
natures – one foppish and treacherous,
the other straightforward and gallant –
of the twins who between them must
decide the fate of the throne of France.
Unfortunately, the role type-cast
Hayward in swashbucklers, and he
was unable to escape them. Watch for
a very young Peter Cushing in a walk-
on role.

Man in the Middle ○
1964, UK, 94 mins, b/w
Dir: Guy Hamilton
Stars: Robert Mitchum, Trevor Howard,
Keenan Wynn, Barry Sullivan, France
Nuyen
Rating: ★★

One thing stops this film from being
just another surprise witness courtroom
thriller: here, the last-minute surprise is
provided by the masterly Trevor
Howard. The climax is the last and
best of the three scenes in which

M

Howard appears. As he gives his vital evidence, chewing on every word, as if the rather ordinary script were something to be relished, one views the story subjectively for the first time, at last with the characters, rather than merely watching what is going on. Robert Mitchum goes through his sleepy paces willingly enough as the defending officer in an army court martial in India in 1944. He has to prove the defendant (an effectively ranting performance by Keenan Wynn) insane, if he is not to hang for the murder of a British soldier. In support, Alexander Knox and Sam Wanamaker are excellent as two doctors unwilling to give evidence.

Man in the Moon ○
1961, UK, 110 mins, b/w
Dir: Basil Dearden
Stars: Kenneth More, Shirley Ann Field, Michael Hordern, John Phillips
Rating: ★★

William Blood, human guinea-pig, was virtually the last of the cheerfully comic characters with which Kenneth More added colour and life to the British cinema of the Fifties and Sixties. This comedy from the Michael Relph-Basil Dearden team was co-written by Bryan Forbes and is given spice by the splendidly nasty, aristocratic performance of Charles Gray, as one of a snooty trio of astronauts with whom Blood becomes involved. Although the film's ideas are often superior to director Dearden's execution of them, the screenplay by Relph and Forbes keeps up a good quota of drily witty lines, from which More and Gray benefit in particular. Amusing cameos come from Danny Green and Jeremy Lloyd, as two motorists from opposite ends of the social scale.

Man in the Moon, The ◗ ⓥ
1991, US, 100 mins, colour
Dir: Robert Mulligan
Stars: Sam Waterston, Tess Harper, Gail Strickland, Reese Witherspoon, Jason London
Rating: ★

Well-meant and sincerely performed, this is nonetheless what some would call a real snoozeroo. The scripts of this kind of film have to be amazingly good for them to hold interest, and most of the dialogue here is moderate at best. It's packed with lines you've heard before – 'Maybe life's not supposed to make sense' – and lines that go too far — 'You're growing up like a weed' a 'kindly' neighbour tells the central character, a 14-year-old girl Dani

(Reese Witherspoon) living in rural Louisiana of the Fifties. Dani falls heavily for the new boy at the waterhole, but a promising friendship is blunted when he claps eyes on her ravishing 17-year-old sister. The resultant triangle is resolved in melodramatic rather than sympathetic fashion, resulting in scenes poised somewhere between *East Lynne* and *The Archers*. Director Robert Mulligan has proved expert at warming up slices of Americana, but he has too little to chew on here. 'Call me if anything happens,' says Dani at one point. Viewers might be justified in lodging a similar request.

Man in the Saddle ○
(aka: The Outcast)
1951, US, 87 mins, colour
Dir: Andre De Toth
Stars: Randolph Scott, Joan Leslie, Alexander Knox, Ellen Drew, Richard Rober, Cameron Mitchell
Rating: ★★★

This Randolph Scott Western is by no means run-of-the-mill, and includes such excellent actors as Alexander Knox, Richard Rober and Cameron Mitchell among the villains. The longer running time gives a clue that the script has more bite than most of Scott's Westerns of the early Fifties. Scott is a rancher caught between the love of two girls, and the jealousy of a rich cattleman who has married one of them. Fans needn't worry: there's still plenty of gunplay amid the romance.

Man in the White Suit, The ○ ⓥ
1951, UK, 81 mins, b/w
Dir: Alexander Mackendrick
Stars: Alec Guinness, Joan Greenwood, Cecil Parker, Michael Gough
Rating: ★★★★★

Highly original Ealing comedy about a young factory worker who invents a white fabric that won't wear out. Down the cast-list Mandy Miller makes her debut at the age of seven – a year before her tremendous success in *Mandy*. She was no problem – but the producers did have a snag. Guinness's white suit, supposedly dirt-resistant, became so easily soiled on set that 13 replicas had to be made to keep him looking whiter than white. The fun races along like the paraphernalia in Guinness' laboratory, with their unforgettable, symphonic gurgling. A classic.

Man is Ten Feet Tall, A
See: Edge of the City

Man Made Monster ●
(aka: The Electric Man)
1940, US, 59 mins, b/w
Dir: George Waggner
Stars: Lon Chaney Jr, Lionel Atwill, Anne Nagel, Frank Albertson
Rating: ★★

Lionel Atwill and Lon Chaney Jr slip easily into their familiar film personalities of mad scientist and genial, dumb, doomed ox in this story of an incredible hulk who develops a superimmunity to electricity but inevitably finds his 'gift' being used for evil ends. George Waggner, who directed Chaney to his triumph in *The Wolf Man*, is again in the director's chair.

Mannequin ○
1937, US, 95 mins, b/w
Dir: Frank Borzage
Stars: Joan Crawford, Spencer Tracy, Alan Curtis, Ralph Morgan
Rating: ★★

This rags-to-riches story was the sole screen coupling of MGM's top stars Spencer Tracy and Joan Crawford, so it's disappointing that their material is on the thin side. No matter how great her acting, nothing can convince you that Crawford's character comes from the downtrodden Hester Street area of New York, populated almost totally by East European and Jewish. However, Leo Gorcey, as her younger brother, is far more believable because he was actually born in that area. As Crawford's double-crossing husband, former male model Alan Curtis catches the eye, but his career was cut short when he died following a kidney operation at the age of 43.

Mannequin ○ ⓥ
1987, US, 90 mins, colour
Dir: Michael Gottlieb
Stars: Andrew McCarthy, Kim Cattrall, Estelle Getty, James Spader, G W Bailey
Rating: ★★★★

Extremely well performed, scripted, edited and directed, this batty comedy doesn't waste a second in telling its tall story. In other words, this department store romp offers you a real bargain. It's a fantasy-farce about a mannequin that, possessed by the wandering spirit of a wayward Egyptian princess (Kim Cattrall), comes to life and helps a loser (Andrew McCarthy) become an ace window-dresser. The script bulges with original comic characters: Carole Davis as McCarthy's fickle black girlfriend; James Spader as the smarmy store director ready to sell out to a rival from under the tiny feet of owner

Estelle Getty; G W Bailey from the *Police Academy* films, as the hawkish store cop whose bulldog Rambo has a yellow streak right down his brindle back; and, best of all, Meshach Taylor as a gay black window-dresser called Hollywood who's sympathetic to every crisis. 'You know what works best for me?' he tells McCarthy. 'Crying shamelessly.' You may find yourself laughing shamelessly at this cornball slice of fun that's never lost for a bright idea.

Mannequin on the Move ○ Ⓥ

1991, US, 95 mins, colour
Dir: Stewart Raffill
Stars: William Ragsdale, Kristy Swanson, Meshach Taylor, Terry Kiser
Rating: ★

The original *Mannequin* was a lively screwball romp. This stupefyingly unfunny follow-up has Kristy Swanson, a great looker who doesn't show much personality or acting talent here, as a medieval princess turned to wood by a cursed necklace. A thousand years later, she turns up in the same store where the original *Mannequin* took place. Dressed in bottom-hugging, bust-bulging minis, Swanson doesn't exactly cut a dewy-eyed or sympathetic figure, and the relentlessly overplayed 'fun' that follows will have you shaking your head in disbelief. Director Raffill has made some great *Wilderness Family*-style outdoors adventures, but his flat handling here proves comedy is definitely not his forte. And, with this script (by four people), the cast seems to be going through the motions; the store lights are on but, in this picture at least, there's no one at home.

Man of a Thousand Faces ○

1957, US, 122 mins, b/w
Dir: Joseph Pevney
Stars: James Cagney, Dorothy Malone, Jane Greer
Rating: ★★★

The 'Man of a Thousand Faces' was, of course, the gifted master of movie disguise Lon Chaney, here played energetically by James Cagney. Like most Hollywood biopics, facts are suitably coloured for dramatic purposes, but the film, a solid job if not especially inspired, provides much to admire. Chaney used to do his own make-up, but here the credit goes to Universal's Bud Westmore and Jack Kevan.

Man of La Mancha ○ Ⓥ

1972, US, 132 mins, colour
Dir: Arthur Hiller

Stars: Peter O'Toole, Sophia Loren, James Coco, Harry Andrews
Rating: ★★★★

The score here by Darion and Leigh is one of the all-time Broadway bests, and provides a super-emotive film musical based on *Don Quixote*, whose high spots all survive Arthur Hiller's flat direction. Peter O'Toole and Sophia Loren sing with fervour, although they have a little help on the high notes from other sources.

Man of No Importance, A ●Ⓥ

1994, UK, 98 mins, colour
Dir: Suri Krishnamma
Stars: Albert Finney, Tara Fitzgerald, Rufus Sewell, Brenda Fricker, Michael Gambon
Rating: ★★

Not a film of much importance either. It's a very slight anecdote about a Dublin bus conductor of the Sixties (Albert Finney), who entertains his passengers with poems by Oscar Wilde and others and plans to put on a slightly subversive production of Wilde's *Salome* performed by them at the local church hall. Living with his sister, he is also, of course, themes and trends being what they are, a closet homosexual. Finney is fine in the title role, apart from the accent which is the same as the one he used in *The Playboys*, a sort of Brummagem Dublin. When he 'comes out' in flowing cloak and green carnation, however, he cuts a swaggering figure that could almost be Wilde himself. Dublin locations are very nicely captured in Technicolor, but there's practically nothing to this, and debutant director Suri Krishnamma can only let it drift away at the end.

Man of the Moment ○

1955, UK, 88 mins, b/w
Dir: John Paddy Carstairs
Stars: Norman Wisdom, Lana Morris
Rating: ★★★★

This is possibly the best of Norman Wisdom's comedies of embarrassment which brought millions to British cinemas in the Fifties. The story for once is highly original and studded with inventive and hilarious moments. Lana Morris charms as the 'nice girl' in the story and Belinda Lee is every inch the foreign spy in a cast which includes such on-form character comics as Harold Kasket, Jerry Desmonde, Garry Marsh and Charles Hawtrey. Wisdom himself is in uproarious form as the hapless Foreign Office clerk who becomes an international figure;

contemporary audiences roared at the sequence in which a chase through the TV studios interrupts several well-known programmes.

Manon des Sources ○ Ⓥ

1986, France, 120 mins, colour
Dir: Claude Berri
Stars: Yves Montand, Daniel Auteuil, Emmanuelle Béart
Rating: ★★★

The sequel to *Jean de Florette*, which takes up the story of greed and deception in 1920s rural France. The action switches 10 years on and Manon (Emmanuelle Béart), daughter of Gérard Depardieu's hunchback farmer, seeks revenge for what happened to her father. Daniel Auteuil is once again superb as the rat-like nephew, Ugolin, but Hippolyte Girardot is unconvincing as the local schoolmaster. On the whole this is a rougher, less involving effort than its predecessor, but together they make up an imposing achievement.

Man on Fire ● Ⓥ

1957, US, 95 mins, b/w
Dir: Ranald Macdougall
Stars: Bing Crosby, Inger Stevens
Rating: ★★

One of the rare occasions Bing Crosby played a completely straight role. He gives a sincere performance as the father in a tug-of-love case. Inger Stevens made her film debut, and, for a while, the headlines, when she had a short-lived romance with the star.

Man on Fire ● Ⓥ

1987, US/Italy, 92 mins, colour
Dir: Elie Chouraqui
Stars: Scott Glenn, Jade Malle, Brooke Adams, Jonathan Pryce, Paul Steiner, Joe Pesci
Rating: ★★

Quite watchable for most of the time, this is all too often a ponderous and portentous thriller, with an exaggerated sense of its own weight, that looks like a Chuck Norris cast-off. Scott Glenn even assumes the Norris mien of bearded unkemptness as the soldier of fortune whose relationship with the 12-year-old daughter of a rich American family in Italy leads him into a crazed vendetta when she is kidnapped for a million-dollar ransom. Jade Malle (daughter of director Louis) is quite winning as the girl, but the film is weakly scripted and put together in such a way as to remind you that directors in films no longer have a studio at their shoulder to tactfully

M

suggest, at some stage in the rushes, that they might be making a hash of what is basically a quite workable concept. The opening and kidnap scenes are striking.

Manpower O
1941, US, 105 mins, b/w
Dir: Raoul Walsh
Stars: George Raft, Edward G Robinson, Marlene Dietrich, Alan Hale, Frank McHugh, Eve Arden
Rating: ★★★

In between turning down *High Sierra*, *The Maltese Falcon* and *Casablanca* (all inherited by Humphrey Bogart) because his character either died or didn't get the girl, George Raft did accept this highly charged account of two high-wire 'linemen' in love with the same woman. Raft may have missed out on the big ones, but this rip-roaring drama is pretty good for all that, with Edward G Robinson and Marlene Dietrich providing star wattage as the other two points of the triangle.

Man's Best Friend ● Ⓥ
1993, US, 87 mins, colour
Dir: John Lafia
Stars: Ally Sheedy, Lance Henriksen, Robert Costanzo, Fredric Lehne
Rating: ★

This demon doggie movie could almost be called *Mad Max 4*. And Max is mad all right, but then so would you be if you'd been made the subject of genetic experiments that gave you all the 'best' traits of other animals. When Max breaks loose so, consequently, does All Hell. Postmen have their throats ripped out and cats are swallowed whole. Not that Max ever kills without provocation – probably the reason he's so lovable to heroine Ally Sheedy, who hides him from the authorities. 'If I don't get him tonight,' grates chief scientist Lance Henriksen 'he's going to go through a psychotic episode.' Boldly treading in the footsteps of George Zucco and a whole string of Hollywood scientists and doomed medical ventures, Henriksen appears to be enjoying himself even more than Max. 'What about my dog,' he asks the head-scratching coppers. 'Any leads?' 'Ruff' stuff, this, an enjoyably bad movie in the good old style.

Man's Favourite Sport? ☉
1963, US, 120 mins, colour
Dir: Howard Hawks
Stars: Rock Hudson, Paula Prentiss
Rating: ★★★

Gangling, treacle-voiced comedienne Paula Prentiss came close (but alas not close enough) to stardom in this lazy-paced comedy about fishing which is, after all, a lazy-paced sport. Still, Prentiss and Rock Hudson keep us nicely amused for a couple of hours, which is not bad considering they spend most of their time falling in the lake. The plot is simple. Hudson plays an ace angling salesman who is forced to enter a big fishing competition, despite the fact that he has never fished before in his life. With the help of Paula, he lands some big fish – but in rather unorthodox ways. Pleasant entertainment, this is easy to take: you'll especially enjoy Prentiss trying to remove a plaster cast from Hudson's arm with the aid of a power saw, and a droll performance by Norman Alden as a very up-to-date native American called John Screaming Eagle.

Man Trouble ◐ Ⓥ
1992, US, 99 mins, colour
Dir: Bob Rafelson
Stars: Jack Nicholson, Ellen Barkin, Beverly D'Angelo, Harry Dean Stanton, Viveka Davis
Rating: ★★

There are some bright spots, if fewer than you'd expect from the star teaming, in this too-seldom-feisty romantic comedy (with some sinister undertones). It involves Jack Nicholson as a sort-of-detective who loans out alsatians to protect people, and Ellen Barkin as an opera star frightened of her own shadow, concerned about the Hillside Strangler, and absolutely *terrified* when her apartment is burgled. That's when Nicholson, the dog and unlikely romantic entanglement come in, with all the complications in the plot being provided by Barkin's sister Beverly D'Angelo's memoirs, which notably blacken the name of mega-rich crook Harry Dean Stanton (in for an overdone cameo near the end of the film). Nicholson delivers his dialogue in low, deliberate tones as if to reassure us that less is more. On this occasion, however, it would seem that less is less and Nicholson's approach only underlines the dull, low quality of director Bob Rafelson's treatment of the Doris Day-style caper. Barkin, though, whether sweetly sultry or scared stiff, is really quite good.

Man Who Came to Dinner, The O
1941, US, 112 mins, b/w
Dir: William Keighley
Stars: Bette Davis, Ann Sheridan, Monty

Woolley, Jimmy Durante, Reginald Gardiner
Rating: ★★★★

Despite a longish film career, big, bluff, bearded Monty Woolley scored his greatest success in this, his first major starring role, in which he repeated his pain-in-the-neck lecturer character from the equally funny stage play of the same title. The hilarious screenplay is by the talented Epstein brothers, Philip and Julius, who won an Oscar the following year for a very different kind of script: *Casablanca*. Beaky Mary Wickes made a notable comic debut as Woolley's nurse, and Bette Davis' role was especially expanded in accordance with her star status. To find out how four penguins and an octopus get into the plot, you'll just have to watch this priceless piece of fun.

Man Who Could Cheat Death, The ◐
1959, UK, 83 mins, colour
Dir: Terence Fisher
Stars: Anton Diffring, Christopher Lee, Hazel Court
Rating: ★★

Hammer horror at its grimmest – with a gruesome transformation scene for its climax. Anton Diffring breaks away from nasty Nazis, but keeps the sneer on his face, in the Dorian Gray-type role. Hazel Court is suitably terrified (and a treat in colour) as the girl who only just cheats death, while Christopher Lee, usually the source of screams, is for once a good sort.

Man Who Could Work Miracles, The O
1936, UK, 82 mins, b/w
Dir: Lothar Mendes
Stars: Roland Young, Ralph Richardson
Rating: ★★★

This hilarious comedy sees H G Wells in his most light-hearted fantasy vein, in a story of a man who suddenly finds all objects animate and inanimate, obey his command. The film contains some brilliant trick photography, genuine crackling wit and a riotous climax.

Man Who Fell to Earth, The ● Ⓥ
1976, UK, 135 mins, colour
Dir: Nicolas Roeg
Stars: David Bowie, Rip Torn, Candy Clark
Rating: ★★★

An alien comes to Earth, takes human form and, with his superior technical knowledge, soon amasses a fortune.

His aim is to find water for his and home planet. David Bowie's somewhat other-worldly and ambiguous persona means he's perfectly cast as the enigmatic alien in this curious and adult sci-fi fantasy and he is ably supported by Rip Torn, Candy Clark and Buck Henry. A little odd in places but always fascinating: director Nicolas Roeg created an unusual film which still has a strong cult following.

Man Who Haunted Himself, The ○
1970, UK, 90 mins, colour
Dir: Basil Dearden
Stars: Roger Moore, Anton Rodgers, Olga Georges-Picot, Hildegarde Neil
Rating: ★★★

Roger Moore gives perhaps his best screen performance in this interesting chiller-thriller about a man who finds that his life is being taken over by his 'double'. Director Basil Dearden mixes dull stretches with some palm-sweating suspense. Freddie Jones' twitching, pill-swallowing psychiatrist steals the supporting honours from a gallery of colourful minor characters.

Man Who Knew Too Much, The ○ Ⓥ
1956, US, 120 mins, colour
Dir: Alfred Hitchcock
Stars: James Stewart, Doris Day, Bernard Miles, Brenda de Banzie
Rating: ★★★★

This underrated suspense-builder is a remake by Alfred Hitchcock of his own 1934 film, whose brooding tension made it an instant classic. James Stewart and Doris Day play the American couple whose son's kidnap involves them unwittingly in an assassination plot. Miss Day's song 'Que Sera, Sera' won an Academy Award. The climax in the concert hall is as nail-biting as ever.

Man Who Loved Women, The ○
1983, US, 122 mins, colour
Dir: Blake Edwards
Stars: Burt Reynolds, Julie Andrews, Kim Basinger, Marilu Henner
Rating: ★★

This loose remake of the 1977 French film of the same title has some nice ideas of its own, even if central character Burt Reynolds spends rather too much screen time discussing his obsession about women with psychiatrist Julie Andrews. It's just as well the stars give subtle and appealing performances

in these roles, leaving the histrionics to co-star Kim Basinger as a voracious harpy who eats men for breakfast and spits out the pieces, then shoots her husband and jumps bail!

Man Who Never Was, The ○
1956, UK, 103 mins, colour
Dir: Ronald Neame
Stars: Clifton Webb, Gloria Grahame, Robert Flemyng, Stephen Boyd
Rating: ★★★

Ronald Neame's persuasive version of Ewen Montagu's book about the famous wartime deception. It involved planting fake documents on a corpse clothed in the uniform of a British officer, which was then 'washed ashore' at a spot which made it bound to come to the attention of the Nazis. Good work by Clifton Webb as Montagu, and some first-class colour photography as well.

Man Who Shot Liberty Valance, The ○
1962, US, 122 mins, b/w
Dir: John Ford
Stars: James Stewart, John Wayne, Vera Miles, Lee Marvin, Edmond O'Brien, Lee Van Cleef
Rating: ★★★

John Ford's last tribute to the values that he liked to remember both about the Old West and about America itself. The fact that it was shot in black and white and that John Wayne (taking second billing – a real rarity and a sign of his affection for the director) looks, with his huge white stetson, every inch the silent Western hero, are only two of the signs indicating a nostalgic tribute to times past. The film is beautifully structured – the key twist is cleverly concealed until the moment it happens – and the shoot-outs are thrillingly staged. The bad guys are Lee Marvin and Lee Van Cleef, both just before they became big box-office stars. This, incidentally, is the film in which the famous phrase 'When the legend becomes fact, print the legend' was heard for the first time.

Man Who Would Be King, The ○ Ⓥ
1975, UK, 129 mins, colour
Dir: John Huston
Stars: Sean Connery, Michael Caine, Christopher Plummer, Saeed Jaffrey, Shakira Caine
Rating: ★★★

This spirited yarn, set first in India and then in a country north of the North-

West Frontier, is based on a story by Rudyard Kipling and is generally regarded as among the best of director John Huston's latter-day films. And it gives splendid acting opportunities to Sean Connery and Michael Caine, who are compelling and amusing (though you may think the parts would have been better cast the other way round) as the roguish central characters of the story who get involved with warring tribesmen. The background gives rise to plenty of local colour and exotic settings, thanks to splendid location work in Morocco.

Man With a Cloak, The ○
1950, US, 81 mins, b/w
Dir: Fletcher Markle
Stars: Leslie Caron, Joseph Cotten, Barbara Stanwyck, Louis Calhern
Rating: ★★★

Canadian director Fletcher Markle builds up suspense and atmosphere in fascinating style in this mystery story set in the New York of the mid-1900s. Joseph Cotten is impressive as the mystery figure in the plot, which involves Leslie Caron in her first acting role, and blends its ingredients – such as a mysterious house, a poison ring and a missing will – with a fine sense of high drama. There's a devastating twist in the final few frames.

Man With a Million
See: The Million Pound Note

Man With Bogart's Face, The ○
(aka: Sam Marlow Private Eye)
1980, US, 106 mins, colour
Dir: Robert Day
Stars: Robert Sacchi, Franco Nero, Michelle Phillips, Olivia Hussey, Herbert Lom
Rating: ★★

This comedy-thriller is as star-studded as it's engagingly nutty. Robert Sacchi is an American actor who bears a remarkable resemblance to the great Humphrey Bogart and here the gimmick is happily milked for all it's worth, with Sacchi as a private eye who's forever relating incidents and personalities to films and stars of yesteryear. Franco Nero, Herbert Lom, Victor Buono and Jay Robinson are a splendid quartet of villains and there's one particularly funny sequence at the hall of mirrors in the Hollywood Wax Museum. Misty Rowe, who once played Marilyn Monroe, also scores as the hero's dumb blonde secretary.

M

Man with One Red Shoe, The
○ ⓥ
(aka: Mischief)
1985, US, 95 mins, colour
Dir: Stan Dragoti
Stars: Tom Hanks, Dabney Coleman, Lori
Singer, Charles Durning, Carrie Fisher,
Jim Belushi
Rating: ★★

Director Stan Dragoti's other comedies – Mr Mom, Love at First Bite, She's Out of Control – have all had their moments, but here he's working on a Hollywood remake of a French original that wasn't funny in the first place. A terrific cast works a bit too hard to make something of it, and even Hanks' fall-guy hero isn't as likeable as he should be. Some fun, though, from the odd good line and a couple of well-paced action sequences.

Man Without a Face, The
◑ ⓥ
1993, US, 110 mins, colour
Dir: Mel Gibson
Stars: Mel Gibson, Nick Stahl, Margaret
Whitton, Geoffrey Lewis, Richard Masur
Rating: ★★★★★

Mel Gibson's directorial debut is a tale of man's inhumanity to man and readiness to believe the worst. Gibson himself stars as a disfigured recluse shunned by the nearby townsfolk but reluctantly drawn into tutoring a troubled 12-year-old boy (Nick Stahl), who believes his only chance to escape the grasp of a mother about to embark on her fourth husband is to go to military academy like his dad. But there are secrets from their pasts that will threaten the relationship between man and boy that gradually grows into something special. Although at times the tutoring borders on the tedious, Gibson pushes his key plot developments through at just the right time, and ties everything together in an emotive ending that may have you punching the air. Young Stahl's dialogue is occasionally difficult to hear, yet he, like Gibson, still creates an unforgettable figure of alienation and isolation. A memorable movie from Mel.

Man Without a Star ○
1955, US, 89 mins, colour
Dir: King Vidor
Stars: Kirk Douglas, Jeanne Crain, Claire
Trevor, William Campbell
Rating: ★★

The plot of this range-war Western, prefaced by another of Frankie Laine's throbbing theme songs, is conventional enough. But the fierce performance of

Kirk Douglas as the drifter at its centre and the individual style of director King Vidor make it all very watchable. Jeanne Crain isn't too happy as a good/bad girl and loses out to Claire Trevor.

Man with the Golden Arm, The ◑ ⓥ
1955, US, 119 mins, b/w
Dir: Otto Preminger
Stars: Frank Sinatra, Kim Novak, Eleanor
Parker, Darren McGavin
Rating: ★★★★

A hot potato for the censor in its tinie, this is a savage indictment of drug-trafficking in which Frank Sinatra gives one of his most powerful performances as a junkie trying to 'kick the habit' – finally in a harrowing 'cold turkey' cure. In 1955 it was considered very daring for addiction and its resultant miseries to be so graphically portrayed. Eleanor Parker makes the most of her role as Sinatra's crippled wife and Kim Novak turns in one of her most dramatically effective performances as a sympathetic girl who stands by Sinatra when he's accused of killing a dope peddler.

Man With the Golden Gun, The ○ ⓥ
1974, UK, 125 mins, colour
Dir: Guy Hamilton
Stars: Roger Moore, Christopher Lee,
Britt Ekland, Maud Adams
Rating: ★★★

Film fans familiar with Christopher Lee only as the cinema's greatest Dracula may be surprised that the master of menace so effortlessly takes the acting honours in this James Bond thriller, prowling his island mansion like some suave but deadly lizard as arch-villain Scaramanga. Midget actor Herve Villechaize is personable as another of those out to exterminate Bond, while there are a couple of good shoot-out sequences in a hall of mirrors.

Man With the Gun, The ○
(aka: The Trouble Shooter)
1955, US, 88 mins, b/w
Dir: Richard Wilson
Stars: Robert Mitchum, Jan Sterling,
Angle Dickinson
Rating: ★★

Robert Mitchum in rough mood, as a westerner brought in to clear up a lawless town. The film was the first independent production venture of Sam Goldwyn Jr, son of the famous movie mogul. The younger Goldwyn was determined not to be outdone by

his famous father when it came to realism, and a huge fire was one of the scenes he staged. Watch out for Angie Dickinson in a tiny role as a saloon girl as well as this fire sequence: Mitchum started such a blaze that it got out of hand and nearly burned down the entire set.

Man With Two Brains, The ◑ ⓥ
1983, US, 93 mins, colour
Dir: Carl Reiner
Stars: Steve Martin, Kathleen Turner,
David Warner, Paul Benedict
Rating: ★★★

Feminists should be well pleased with the central premise of this hilarious comedy – Steve Martin falls not for a woman's body but for her mind or, rather, her brain (voiced by Sissy Spacek) which is conveniently portable in its glass jar. What could simply have been another horror movie spoof is turned by Martin and his director and co-writer Carl Reiner into a magnificently surreal movie which offers the star plenty of well-taken opportunities to display his unique brand of verbal and visual foolery. Mind you, while he steals the film, Kathleen Turner, in what appears to be a wicked send-up of her man-eating character from Body Heat, gives him a good run for his money and demonstrates that she is as skilled at comedy as she is at drama. As with the best comedy, good taste is largely kept at bay and the result is a genuine if rude treat.

Map of the Human Heart ◑ ⓥ
1992, Australia/Canada/France/UK, 121
mins, colour
Dir: Vincent Ward
Stars: Jason Scott Lee, Anne Parillaud,
Patrick Bergin, Annie Galipeau, Robert
Joamie, Jeanne Moreau, John Cusack
Rating: ★★★

Although it goes on too long, and sometimes falters towards the end, there are moments in this epic love story that are as good as anything the cinema had produced for some time. If you're looking for the unusual, you'll certainly find it here. A young Arctic boy, half-Eskimo, half-white, is befriended in 1931 by a young mapper/surveyor (Patrick Bergin) who, seeing the boy is suffering from tuberculosis, takes him to a sanitarium in the city. Here he becomes friends with another 'outcast', a half-white, half-Cree Indian girl. The close nature of their friendship is frowned on by the nuns there, who split them up. Years later the boy (now Jason Scott Lee) runs into Bergin again, and asks him to help find the girl. Later still, serving with other Canadians in the RAF, he meets her (Anne Parillaud) again, only to find she is romantically involved with Bergin himself... Subsequent developments don't entirely convince, but scenes of the children's friendship and, later, the wartime bombing of Dresden, are wonderfully well staged.

Maracaibo O
1958, US, 88 mins, colour
Dir: Cornel Wilde
Stars: Cornel Wilde, Jean Wallace, Francis Lederer, Abbe Lane, Michael Landon
Rating: ★★

Colourful drama of the lives and loves of oil fire-fighters in Venezuela. Cornel Wilde, whose wife, Jean Wallace, co-stars, also directed, a habit he was to pursue with some success (notably in *Lancelot and Guinevere*). Here, he gives us some exciting fire sequences that are masterpieces of stage management. The plot's not so hot.

Marathon Man ● Ⓥ
1976, US, 126 mins, colour
Dir: John Schlesinger
Stars: Dustin Hoffman, Laurence Olivier, Roy Scheider, William Devane, Marthe Keller
Rating: ★★★

Director John Schlesinger has tried with great intelligence to suggest that the plot of this thriller – Nazi war criminals after a fortune in diamonds – is more ingenious than it is, while William Goldman's elliptical screenplay, based on his own novel, also hints at depths not justified in the exposition. Dustin Hoffman is the marathon runner whose endurance stands him in good stead when he is caught up in the web of intrigue that his brother (Roy Scheider) is weaving on behalf of a CIA offshoot. The plot moves with a fair share of excitement along tried and true lines, to a carefully staged climax in which Hoffman and the arch-villain (Laurence Olivier) come face to face. By far the best performance comes from William Devane as a double-agent with a voice and a line that is all too plausible for the innocent fish to swallow.

March of the Wooden Soldiers
See: Babes in Toyland

March or Die Ⓓ
1977, US, 104 mins, colour
Dir: Dick Richards
Stars: Gene Hackman, Terence Hill, Catherine Deneuve, Max von Sydow, Ian Holm
Rating: ★

Aux armes, mes braves, those Arabs are revolting again. And our bold Legionnaires must try to defeat them in the desert, or perish in the attempt. Armed with a plot about Legionnaires defiling ancient Moroccan tombs and incurring the wrath of the Arabs in the post-World War One period, director Dick Richards tries to show the Foreign Legion warts and all, without completely destroying its myth. A pity, then, that the dialogue, clichéd from the start (a woman starts singing La Marseillaise as battered Legionnaires return from the war, and Major Gene Hackman grunts 'There are no heroes in war – only survivors'), gives him only rubber bullets for ammunition. Terence Hill, Max Von Sydow, Ian Holm (improbably blacked up as an Arab chief) and Catherine Deneuve (as the inevitable mystery woman) are among those making a last stand against the assaults of David Zelag Goodman's script.

Margaret's Museum ● Ⓥ
1995, UK/Can, 95 mins, colour
Dir: Mort Ransen
Stars: Helena Bonham Carter, Clive Russell, Kate Nelligan
Rating: ★★

A grim and finally grisly account of the toll exacted by the mines of Nova Scotia in the early 1950s – conditions that still claim lives today. In the ramshackle mining community of Glace Bay, the McNeil family has already lost its father and eldest son to the local pit. Upstairs, Grandpa lies dying from a lifetime of coal fumes, while embittered Ma (Nelligan) and her equally hard-cursing daughter Margaret (Bonham Carter) are clearly two lumps short of a scuttleful. Youngest brother Jimmy is dying too – to get down to the coal face, which shows he hasn't too much up top. Into this atmosphere comes the giant Neil (Russell) who hates the mines (where he used to work) but loves Margaret, marries her and builds a home by the sea. When he loses his menial job, however, the outlook is literally the pits. Not an easy film to be with, this goes downright peculiar at the end when tragedy strikes and Margaret falls apart in a truly horrifying way.

Bonham Carter and Nelligan are both unsettingly good.

Margie O
1946, US, 94 mins, colour
Dir: Henry King
Stars: Jeanne Crain, Glenn Langan, Alan Young, Lynn Bari
Rating: ★★★

This potent dose of Americana, glowingly evoking the late 1920s, was made by director Henry King, monarch of the genre. Bathed in Technicolor by Charles Clarke, the film contains Jeanne Crain's most charming performance as the brainbox who thinks herself unattractive to men. Since she's wrong, matters are easily resolved, but in a highly tuneful and entertaining way.

Maria's Lovers ● Ⓥ
1984, US, 100 mins, colour
Dir: Andrei Konchalovsky
Stars: Nastassja Kinski, John Savage, Robert Mitchum, Keith Carradine, Bud Cort
Rating: ★★★

John Savage keeps himself alive in a Japanese prisoner-of-war camp with the powerful mental image of his childhood sweetheart Maria (Nastassja Kinski). But when he returns to Pennsylvania and marries her, he finds that he cannot consummate the marriage with his idealised Maria. There's plenty to admire along the way as the subsequent drama is played out: there are good performances from the leads, with Savage in another of his offbeat choices of roles. Ms Kinski, glowingly photographed (by Juan Ruiz Anchia), is stunning to watch. Keith Carradine brings a weasely charm to the part of one of Maria's lovers and Robert Mitchum has a smaller, but telling role as Savage's lecherous father. Atmospheric, superior soap.

Marie Ⓓ Ⓥ
1985, US, 106 mins, colour
Dir: Roger Donaldson
Stars: Sissy Spacek, Jeff Daniels, Morgan Freeman
Rating: ★★★

The David and Goliath battle between the individual and the state/big business (take your pick) is now a familiar theme in films, so to make another variation on that well-worn theme takes courage. It also takes a good script if the film is to succeed. *Marie* succeeds thanks to a good script and good director (Roger Donaldson) and a strong cast in Sissy Spacek, Jeff

M

Daniels and Morgan Freeman. Spacek is a parole board chairman who, when asked to speed a few parolees through by an aide of the state governor, refuses. She is promptly sacked, but fights her case in court, opening up a big can of corrupt officialdom worms. Spacek as the parole chairman is excellent and Jeff Daniels makes a convincingly smooth aide. Based on a true story, and that adds to the drama, making it a very watchable piece.

Marie Antoinette ○
1938, US, 149 mins, b/w
Dir: W S Van Dyke II
Stars: Norma Shearer, Tyrone Power, John Barrymore, Robert Morley, Gladys George, Anita Louise
Rating: ★★★

Goodness knows what this sumptuous, near-three-hour spectacle would have cost if MGM had filmed it in colour. As it is, the budget still went close to the $2 million mark. Robert Morley, who was making his screen debut, hated all the opulence and razzmatazz and referred to the film as 'Marie and Toilette', but his performance as King Louis XVI still earned him an Oscar nomination, as did the work of Norma Shearer in the title role. Finally, though, all the cast is dwarfed by the stunning sets of Cedric Gibbons – halls, ballrooms and chambers simply dripping with period artefacts – and peopled by hundreds of cast and extras in authentic costumes of the period. This is Hollywood spectacle at its peak – and certainly at its most extravagant.

Marines, Let's Go ○
1961, US, 104 mins, colour
Dir: Raoul Walsh
Stars: Tom Tryon, David Hedison
Rating: ★★

Director Raoul Walsh attempts a difficult double: realistic war sequences coupled with the comic adventures of the Marines in, around and under the bars of Tokyo. The result: a sprawling, brawling, colourful adventure romp.

Marjorie Morningstar ○
1958, US, 121 mins, colour
Dir: Irving Rapper
Stars: Natalie Wood, Gene Kelly, Claire Trevor, Everett Sloane, Ed Wynn
Rating: ★★

In its day, this fairly faithful adaptation of Herman Wouk's huge novel was a major disappointment. Natalie Wood, at 19, proved not quite up to the de-

mands of the central role as the starstruck teenager, fleeing from a Jewish background she sees as claustrophobic, who becomes obsessed with a holiday resort entertainer twice her age (shades of *Dirty Dancing!*). As the self-centred showman, Gene Kelly is simply too classy to play a song-and-dance man whose ambitions to the highest class are torpedoed by his second-rate talent. The story, as somewhat restructured by Everett Freeman from Wouk's original, with the family background largely glossed over in favour of the show business angles, was described by one aggrieved critic as 'about as Jewish as *The Seven Samurai*'.

Marked for Death ● ⓥ
1990, US, 94 mins, colour
Dir: Dwight H Little
Stars: Steven Seagal, Basil Wallace, Keith David, Joanna Pacula
Rating: ★

'Try to find a gentle self inside you,' the priest tells a troubled Steven Seagal. No chance. Though an affable-looking chap with a pony-tail, Mr S is in the business of dealing out death and, when the bad guys shoot his niece, you can bet there's plenty of that to come. The trade-marks of Seagal action films are drugs, topless women, crunching bones and severed limbs, plentifully supplied and usually roughly in that order. This one adds a touch of voodoo, and about all you can say is that it isn't actually dull, though fearfully unimaginative. Director Dwight H Little does try to do something with it, not always going for the entirely expected, though Seagal fans are hardly likely to notice. Joanna Pacula is second-billed in the opening credits, but scarcely in the film at all.

Mark of the Vampire ◐
1935, US, 61 mins, b/w
Dir: Tod Browning
Stars: Lionel Barrymore, Elizabeth Allan, Bela Lugosi
Rating: ★★★

As much a teasing puzzle as a horror film – the atmosphere engendered by James Wong Howe's photography and Tod Browning's direction is even creepier than on Browning's original *Dracula*. This is a remake of another Browning picture *London After Midnight* (1927) which starred Lon Chaney Sr. Devotees of the genre say that Carol Borland's female vampire is the definitive interpretation. Nice twist ending.

Mark of Zorro, The ○
1940, US, 94 mins, b/w
Dir: Rouben Mamoulian
Stars: Tyrone Power, Linda Darnell, Basil Rathbone, Gale Sondergaard, Eugene Pallette
Rating: ★★★★

Dashing remake of the silent swashbuckling classic with Douglas Fairbanks, whose role of Zorro, a Western equivalent of *The Scarlet Pimpernel*, here goes to Tyrone Power, athletically setting female hearts a-flutter as the masked righter-of-wrongs in early California. Rhythmically directed by Rouben Mamoulian, it has a rousing music score by Alfred Newman, an early appearance by Linda Darnell at her loveliest, and the famous final duel between Power and Basil Rathbone.

Marlowe ◑ ⓥ
1969, US, 95 mins, colour
Dir: Paul Bogart
Stars: James Garner, Gayle Hunnicutt, Carroll O'Connor, Rita Moreno, Bruce Lee
Rating: ★★

It can't have been just coincidence that MGM hired a director called Bogart (Paul) for a story about the character made famous by another Bogart (Humphrey), and actually based on Raymond Chandler's novel *The Little Sister*. The result is the most muted Marlowe to appear on the screen. Its weakness is James Garner, miscast in the title role. For compensation there's a tortuous plot, and the first film appearance of Bruce Lee as an oriental bad guy who demolishes Marlowe's entire office by use of martial arts, as a grim warning. Lee, in fact, steals the film. It's strange his potential was ignored for so long.

Marnie ◑ ⓥ
1964, US, 130 mins, colour
Dir: Alfred Hitchcock
Stars: Tippi Hedren, Sean Connery
Rating: ★★★★

Alfred Hitchcock's sly psychological study of a compulsive thief – played by Tippi Hedren – marked a change of pace for her co-star Sean Connery, then solidly established as superspy James Bond. The film contains much for Hitchcock fans to admire, but one cannot help wondering why the director settled for so many poor process shots and some highly unconvincing backdrops. Even so, the efforts of writer and director persuade us to follow Marnie's adventures with sympathy and attention. And the moments when her past life starts to come to light are among the best in the film. Diane Baker gives excellent support as Connery's scheming, jealous sister-in-law.

Maroc 7 ◐

1967, UK, 91 mins, colour
Dir: Gerry O'Hara
Stars: Gene Barry, Cyd Charisse, Elsa Martinelli, Leslie Phillips, Denholm Elliott
Rating: RB

There's lots of high-fashion clothes and an attractive cast in this vaguely Bond-style thriller. The trouble is that too many of the cast are miscast, including co-producer Leslie Phillips, who obviously fancied a villainous role as a change from the comedy parts that had made him famous. Slowly directed by Gerry O'Hara (who was more at home with intimate drama), the film stars a languorous Gene Barry, in the wake of his *Burke's Law* fame, and proves that even exotic locations and a string of glamorous models can prove more of a hindrance to a film than an asset. A notable misfire.

Marriage on the Rocks ○

1965, US, 109 mins, colour
Dir: Jack Donohue
Stars: Frank Sinatra, Deborah Kerr, Dean Martin, Cesar Romero, Hermione Baddeley, Nancy Sinatra
Rating: ★★★

A scintillating light comedy that takes an hilarious look at the Great American Marriage gone sour. Dean Martin is very funny as the lifelong bachelor who suddenly finds himself married and doesn't like it, Hermione Baddeley a riot as Frank Sinatra's (later Martin's) ferocious Scottish mother-in-law. Beset for the umpteenth time by the bag-playing harridan, Martin says he'll take the dog out for a walk. But they don't have a dog, says his wife. That's all right, says Martin, he'll find one. Cy Howard's script is mostly delightful stuff. Martin is at his best when he wears his worried look, and the girls (Joi Lansing, Davey Davidson, Nancy Sinatra and Tara Ashton) all have acting talent.

Married to It ● Ⓥ

1991, US, 112 mins, colour
Dir: Arthur Hiller
Stars: Beau Bridges, Stockard Channing, Ron Silver, Cybill Shepherd, Mary Stuart Masterson, Robert Sean Leonard
Rating: ★★

A starry cast and a well-written script are the highlights of the entertaining enough slice-of-married-life that's not as black as most critics painted it, even though it sat on the shelf for two years before release. The story follows the complex relationships of three very different New York couples who become the unlikeliest of firm friends, and the dramatic events that unfold will hold great interest for fans of such 'old pals' movies as *The Big Chill* and *Grand Canyon*. Absorbing and involving thanks to its cast (especially Mary Stuart Masterson and Stockard Channing), but let down by characters that are often annoying, and by a cloying, too-good-to-be-true ending.

Married to the Mob ◐ Ⓥ

1988, US, 103 mins, colour
Dir: Jonathan Demme
Stars: Michelle Pfeiffer, Matthew Modine, Dean Stockwell, Mercedes Ruehl, Alec Baldwin, Joan Cusack, Nancy Travis
Rating: ★★★

An offbeat comedy about a Mafia widow attempting to sever her connections with the Mob after her husband is assassinated in the bathtub for dallying with a crime boss's girlfriend. Michelle Pfeiffer is a total delight in a very different portrait of a mobster's wife to the one she gave in *Scarface*. Director Jonathan Demme cooks up a manic stew so bright and exaggerated that it jumps cartoon-like out of the screen. Throughout the film he takes delight in creating as many unexpected oppositions and goofy juxtapositions as possible. Look out for singer Chris Isaak as a hitman disguised as a fast food restaurant clown.

Marrying Kind, The ○

1952, US, 93 mins, b/w
Dir: George Cukor
Stars: Judy Holliday, Aldo Ray
Rating: ★★★

Although there are plenty of good laughs in this, Judy Holliday's second film working with director George Cukor, there are also moments of sadness and drama. She and Aldo Ray are in the divorce court and the story of their marriage, the good and the bad times, is shown in flashback. The beefy Ray, in his first major role, makes a good foil for Holliday and the script is sharp and witty. Watch out for a young Charles Bronson (billed as Charles Buchinski) as a work buddy of Ray's.

Mars Attacks! ◐ Ⓥ

1996, US, 104 mins, colour
Dir: Tim Burton
Stars: Jack Nicholson, Glenn Close, Danny DeVito, Annette Bening. Pierce Brosnan, Michael J Fox, Sarah Jessica Parker
Rating: ★★★

And so it does, which makes the last reel of this sci-fi spoof a lot of fun, although for the most part it's a rambling, star-heavy caper about little green men who 'come in peace', but leave the earthly negotiators in pieces as soon as the opportunity presents itself. The tone set by the film is the cue for some hefty over-acting, by Nicholson and Close as the President and his wife, and others whose posturing makes you glad to see them exterminated. Exempt from all this are Annette Bening, veteran Sylvia Sidney and, amazingly, singer Tom Jones who, in his first acting role, is pretty nearly the hit of the show. Faultless special effects, loads of explosions and bodies flying all over the place – as the Martians are bested by a method likely to fall on uncomprehending ears in today's cinemagoers – keep this lively if not exactly lovely.

Marrying Man, The

See: Too Hot to Handle

Marty ○

1955, US, 91 mins, b/w
Dir: Delbert Mann
Stars: Ernest Borgnine, Betsy Blair
Rating: ★★★

Hollywood moguls were shocked by the critical and commercial success of this perceptive story about a lonely man in his mid-thirties who hesitantly finds love. With wide screen and Technicolor in full swing, a studio-bound black-and-white film based on an admittedly successful television play hadn't seemed such a great idea. But Ernest Borgnine showed an acting depth not hinted at in previous 'villain' roles, and his performance earned him an Oscar. The film also won for Best Director (Delbert Mann), Best Picture and Best Screenplay (Paddy Cheyefsky, adapting his own TV script). Borgnine makes the most of the part of his life and Esther Minciotti, as his mother, gives fine support. Betsy Blair, as the plain girl he falls in love with, is, although too attractive, delicately effective. The film looks decidedly dated now, as do many British 'kitchen sink' films of the same era, but Borgnine's affecting performance is not to be missed.

M

Marvin's Room ◐ ⓥ

1996, US, 98 mins, colour
Dir: Jerry Zaks
Stars: Meryl Streep. Diane Keaton,
Leonardo DiCaprio, Robert De Niro,
Hume Cronyn, Gwen Verdon
Rating: ★★★

This gut-wrenching tear-jerker is brilliantly acted by a fine cast. But the anguish of this story is simply too intense and too much for your aconstant attention. Bessie (Diane Keaton), a spinster dedicated to looking after her parents – he bedridden and near-catatonic, she dotty and TV soap-addicted – learns she is dying from leukaemia. Enter the sister (Meryl Streep) whom she barely knows, towing her delinquent son (Leonardo DiCaprio) who has just burnt their house down. At times horrifying and sickening, especially in a painful sequence where Keaton (who's amazing) collapses in Disneyland.

Maryland ⊙

1940, US, 92 mins, colour
Dir: Henry King
Stars: Walter Brennan, Fay Bainter,
Brenda Joyce, John Payne
Rating: ★★

Somewhere between *National Velvet* and *Now Voyager*, this was Darryl Zanuck's tribute to the Great American Outdoors and specifically its horses. Walter Brennan at his most endearing, but Fay Bainter also gets a look in as a tyrannical mother, with John Payne as her son. Early use of lush Technicolor by George Bames and Ray Rennahan celebrates the sumptuous natural landscapes, which are the real stars here, and not the script which, besides formula dialogue, provides such now-contentious issues as foxhunts and demeaning portraits of black servants.

Mary, Mary ○

1964, US, 126 mins, colour
Dir: Mervyn LeRoy
Stars: Debbie Reynolds, Barry Nelson,
Michael Rennie
Rating: ★★

An adaptation of the stage comedy success about a separated couple trying to get together again. Barry Nelson gives a magnificent, non-stop comic performance as the husband, the highlight being his efforts to keep awake with three sleeping pills inside him. Miss Reynolds copes well as the chain-smoking, wise-cracking wife, and still manages to look teenager-cute in pyjamas and an outsize overcoat. The only drawback is that it still looks like a stage play.

Mary of Scotland ○

1936, US, 123 mins, b/w
Dir: John Ford
Stars: Katharine Hepburn, Fredric March,
Donald Crisp, Florence Eldridge, John
Carradine
Rating: ★★

This historical drama proved that John Ford was more in his element with male orientated subjects. A financial dud despite its starry cast, including Katharine Hepburn (as Mary Stuart) Ford's direction of it was interesting and experimental with different lighting and camera angles for each character. A real curio.

Mary Poppins ⊙ ⓥ

1964, US, 139 mins, colour
Dir: Robert Stevenson
Stars: Julie Andrews, Dick Van Dyke,
David Tomlinson, Glynis Johns,
Hermione Baddeley, Ed Wynn
Rating: ★★★★★

Unjustly ignored for the film version of *My Fair Lady*, Julie Andrews bounced back to win an Oscar as the magical mystery nanny who changes the lives of the Banks family for the better. Perhaps the last great original Hollywood musical, with joyous dance routines – especially the chimney sweeps on rooftops – and a whole nursery full of hit songs. Andrews, Ed Wynn (as the uncle who floats when he laughs), Glynis Johns and David Tomlinson are delightful. And Dick Van Dyke, as Bert, pavement artist, sweep and one-man band, sang and danced his way to film stardom (in spite of a pawky cockney accent). Don't forget to stay tuned for the last line of the credits. It's definitely supercalifragilisticexpialidocious.

Mary, Queen of Scots ○

1971, UK, 128 mins, colour
Dir: Charles Jarrott
Stars: Vanessa Redgrave, Glenda
Jackson, Patrick McGoohan, Timothy
Dalton, Nigel Davenport, Trevor Howard
Rating: ★★★

Although it's not particularly accurate as a history lesson, this colourful period drama features something that similar films can't hope to boast – a dynamic acting battle between two of the foremost British female talents of the time, Vanessa Redgrave, as Mary, and Glenda Jackson, raspingly repeating her TV portrait of Elizabeth I. All credit, therefore, to Timothy Dalton, Patrick McGoohan and Nigel Davenport for bringing charisma and understanding to supporting roles.

Mary Reilly ● ⓥ

1996, UK, 108 mins, colour
Dir: Stephen Frears
Stars: Julia Roberts, John Malkovich,
Glenn Close, Michael Gambon, George
Cole, Bronagh Gallagher
Rating: ★

There must be some middle course between Hammer horror and the reverential to produce a dynamic new version of Stevenson's *Dr Jekyll and Mr Hyde*, but this grim and dimly-lit piece isn't it. Played out at a stately, suspense-stifling pace, the plot centres on Mary, a housemaid in the Jekyll employ, who sticks her pretty nose in where you and I would have left well alone, and gets involved in the whole can of worms when Jekyll, falling in love with her, leaves the murderous Hyde to conduct the more physical side of the relationship. There is some subsequent blood-letting and one sudden shock amidst the suffocating gloom. Julia Roberts' Mary attempts a Southern States Irish accent, while tending to an impossibly flourishing garden in the backyard and, in the house, to a metamorphosing John Malkovich, who isn't attempting an accent at all. Butler George Cole, cook Kathy Staff and the rest look suitably aghast as if sniffing some impending disaster... Not quite as bad as you may have heard – but not terribly successful either.

Mary Shelley's Frankenstein ● ⓥ

1994, UK, 123 mins, colour
Dir: Kenneth Branagh
Stars: Kenneth Branagh, Robert De Niro,
Helena Bonham Carter, Ian Holm, Aidan
Quinn, Tom Hulce
Rating: ★★★

Even though it predictably substitutes guts and gore for gothic darkness, this is probably as good a version of the man-made monster classic as you could find in the Nineties. Splendidly made and shot with some verve (if curiously structured), the film seems to stuff elements from several earlier films, while sticking fairly close to Shelley's book. De Niro, more restrained than usual, makes an imposing monster with only the occasional foolish line, and his friendship with the blind farmer (Richard Briers) is again touching. Branagh just hasn't the right facial structure to make Frankenstein quite the driven creature of one's mind's eye, but the birdlike Helena Bonham Carter is perfectly cast both as Elizabeth and a later reincarnation. There are minor quibbles – Frankenstein and the creature seem to zip to and from the Arctic with remarkable alacrity – but several stylish moments to compensate: a burning figure dashing along corridors is dazzlingly done.

M*A*S*H ◐ Ⓥ

1969, US, 116 mins, colour
Dir: Robert Altman
Stars: Donald Sutherland, Elliott Gould, Tom Skerritt, Sally Kellerman, Robert Duvall
Rating: ★★★

This blood-soaked black comedy gave new dimension to the word irreverence, and has perhaps been undeservedly eclipsed in memory by the outstanding TV series that stemmed from it. The film boosted several star careers, including those of Elliott Gould and Donald Sutherland, while Robert Altman's direction of their capers as surgeons in an ill-equipped mobile army service hospital (thus the title) in Korea brings home with full force the desperation behind the humour. The football match at the end is the funniest of its kind since the one enjoyed by the Marx Brothers in *Horse Feathers*. Screenwriter Ring Lardner Jr won an Academy Award.

Mask ◐ Ⓥ

1985, US, 120 mins, colour
Dir: Peter Bogdanovich
Stars: Cher, Eric Stoltz, Sam Elliott, Estelle Getty, Laura Dern
Rating: ★★★

After *The Elephant Man* comes the 'Elephant Boy'. Rocky (Eric Stoltz) was born with a kind of dysplasia – a one-in-22-million chance – which deformed his face to an alarming degree. His biker mother, nicely played by Cher, sent him to a nominal school, where he proved extremely bright. The story of Rocky's fight to live a normal life is told with a large amount of tender loving care by director Peter Bogdanovich, even though it's draped in an extremely tough exterior. Good performances, too, from Stoltz as the boy and Sam Elliott as his mother's charismatic on-off lover.

Mask, The ○ Ⓥ

1994, US, 101 mins, colour
Dir: Charles Russell
Stars: Jim Carrey, Cameron Diaz, Peter Riegert, Peter Greene, Amy Yasbeck
Rating: ★★★

Jim Carrey seems wisely to have ignored the motto about never acting with children or animals, since a talented Jack Russell terrier provides him with the ideal partner in this fun action fantasy about a nobody, Stanley Ipkiss, who becomes the amalgam of all his favourite cartoon characters when he dons an old mask he finds floating in the river of polluted Edge City, in whose bank he works. Once the mask has wound itself round his head, he becomes a man about town – no one seems concerned that he has a green face – with the power of cartoon character movement. Soon he's flexed his complexion on the bad guys of the city, while romancing their blonde moll (talented newcomer Cameron Diaz) and confounding the police. Pitched at a hectic pace, the film, though largely a vehicle for Carrey and the dog, is studded with funny moments. Told by the bad guys to do something terrible at the club that night, Carrey winces. 'Not,' he asks, 'the lambada?'

Mask of Dimitrios, The ○

1944, US, 95 mins, b/w
Dir: Jean Negulesco
Stars: Peter Lorre, Sydney Greenstreet, Zachary Scott, Faye Emerson
Rating: ★★★

Zachary Scott, one of Hollywood's best portrayers of sneering villainy, made his film debut as the mysterious international criminal Dimitrios in this shadow-strewn thriller gem. Acting honours, though, go almost inevitably to Sydney Greenstreet and little Peter Lorre, reunited from *The Maltese Falcon* and *Casablanca*. Their highly enjoyable teamwork established them as the Laurel and Hardy of the mystery movie world.

Mask of Fury

See: First Yank into Tokyo

Masque of the Red Death, The ● Ⓥ

1964, US, 89 mins, colour
Dir: Roger Corman
Stars: Vincent Price, Hazel Court, Jane Asher, David Weston, Patrick Magee
Rating: ★★★

Highly stylish, imaginative Roger Corman adaptation of the Edgar Allan Poe tale, although a touch disappointing compared with some of his earlier work in the same field. Gone are the cold, clammy sets Corman worked with in America. This one was made in England, against warm, rich tapestries. The horror is still ever-present,

but the icy finger up the spine is missing. We all know what these characters fear: it's the Red Death, a plague which has swept through villages and now menaces the castle of the rich Prince Propero (Vincent Price), a sort of medieval Faust who has sold his soul to the Devil. In the sub-plot (based on another Poe story, *Hop Frog*), a romance between two dwarfs is touchingly, tactfully done, and one of them, Skip Martin, reveals himself as rather a good actor in a little scene with Patrick Magee that's loaded with evil. But the final coming of the Red Death to the castle isn't as effective as it might have been, especially to those who have read Poe's story.

Masquerade ○

1965, UK, 101 mins, colour
Dir: Basil Dearden
Stars: Cliff Robertson, Jack Hawkins, Marisa Mell
Rating: ★★★

A good comedy-thriller full of twists and turns in a complicated plot which gives hero Cliff Robertson a headache in more ways than one. He's knocked on the head (twice), beaten up, thrown in a wine vat, lassoed and dragged along the ground, imprisoned in an animal cage, and nearly falls over a 100ft dam. About the only thing he temporarily gets the better of is a vulture called Charlie. Given that the film sets out to puzzle its audience from the word go, most of the twists are obviously, but one or two still spring quite a surprise. Jack Hawkins revels in a part that is tailor-made for him, and Robertson fits equally well into a role for which he does not seem naturally equipped.

Masquerade ● Ⓥ

1988, US, 87 mins, colour
Dir: Bob Swaim
Stars: Rob Lowe, Meg Tilly, Doug Savant, John Glover
Rating: ★★★

Film murder mysteries aren't exactly two-a-penny these days, so this throwback to the *film noir* is very welcome. Not that this film can stand comparison with the classics: although it's just about possible to work out at the end who is doing what to whom, far too many loose ends are left dangling elusively to fully satisfy fans of the genre. Yachtsman Rob Lowe, having a steamy romance with boss's wife Kim Cattrall, soon steers himself into the calmer waters of an equally sensual romance with heiress Meg Tilly. She's

M

loved from afar by local policeman Doug Savant, and hated by stepfather John Glover. You may think you can safely unravel the plot from here on, although you could find the final link in the chain of crime is a knot that writer Dick Wolf is not too willing to untie. Performances are adequate, especially from the dreamlike Tilly and the predatory Glover, and John Barry's music helps.

Masques ●

1987, France, 100 mins, colour
Dir: Claude Chabrol
Stars: Philippe Noiret, Robin Renucci, Monique Chaumette, Anne Brochet, Bernadette Lafont
Rating: ★★★

Thrillers in which no one is exactly what he seems are usually quite fun, and Claude Chabrol's country-house game of cat and mouse, although somewhat lacking in dramatic tension and variety of developments, proves, on the whole, no exception. Philippe Noiret is affable TV personality Christian who hosts a squirmy geriatric talent contest and has invited writer Wolf (Robin Renucci) to his country home to work on a ghosted autobiography. Such an avuncular figure can't be up to any good in a Chabrol film and, once in the lion's den, Wolf finds that Christian's granddaughter (Audrey Hepburn-lookalike Monique Chaumette) is bearing signs of undernourishment and has recently had treatment that accidentally (?) paralysed her legs. You'll probably have sorted out the goodies from the baddies by half-way, but personable performances by Noiret and Bernadette Lafont (as his in-house masseuse) keep the interest afloat and the tension pricking.

Massacre in Rome ◐

1973, Italy/France, 103 mins, colour
Dir: George Pan Cosmatos
Stars: Richard Burton, Marcello Mastroianni, Leo McKern
Rating: ★★

The story of a resistance action during World War Two that provoked a 10-for-one reprisal on the part of the Nazis. Richard Burton is the Nazi commanding officer and Marcello Mastroianni the priest who tries to prevent the reprisals. Both are very good in flashes; at other times each falls victim to a script that is 60 per cent literacy and 40 per cent platitudes, and sometimes huffs and puffs to little effect. Leo McKern gives one of his rare bad performances as the senior Fascist

officer, but it's interesting to see former British matinee idol Anthony Steel in a minor role. The film is a little too long, but it does have its moments of truth, especially towards the end.

Mass Appeal ●

1984, US, 100 mins, colour
Dir: Glenn Jordan
Stars: Jack Lemmon, Zeljko Ivanek, Charles Durning
Rating: ★★

The title is as contrived as everything else in this effectively emotive tear-jerker about a happy-go-lucky, wine-tippling priest (Jack Lemmon) with a touch of showbiz razzamatazz in his sermons. He finds himself taking on a young rebel deacon whose abrasive behaviour and admission of relations with both sexes threatens to have him thrown out on his ear. Naturally both men have a lot to learn from one another and they do. Most of the other characters, including Charles Durning's bigoted monseigneur, are too rigidly stereotyped to do much with, but the dialogue is truthful enough to make some of its lessons hit home. Young Zeljko Ivanek, as the deacon, probably learned a thing or two about acting, too, by watching yet another of Lemmon's expertly anguished performances.

Master of Ballantrae, The ○

1953, UK, 88 mins, colour
Dir: William Keighley
Stars: Errol Flynn, Roger Livesey, Anthony Steel, Beatrice Campbell, Felix Aylmer
Rating: ★★★

Master of swashbuckling, Errol Flynn could hardly have found a better vehicle for his talents than this colourful version of Robert Louis Stevenson's famous story of mystery and adventure. As the forceful Jacobite Jamie Durisdeer, his sword flashes as often as his smile and his winning ways win fair ladies.

Master of Lassie

See: The Hills of Home

Masters of the Universe ◐ ⓥ

1987, US, 106 mins, colour
Dir: Gary Goddard
Stars: Dolph Lundgren, Frank Langella, Meg Foster, Jon Cypher, Chelsea Field
Rating: ★★

Swedish muscle mountain Dolph Lundgren certainly looks the part of best-selling children's action toy He-

Man, in this would-be epic in the *Star Wars* mould. But he doesn't have enough charisma – or acting ability – to carry the film in which nothing less than the future of the universe is at stake. The evil Skeletor's 'Darth Vader' clones have no eyes – which explains their appalling aim with laser guns.

Mata Hari ○

1932, US, 95 mins, b/w
Dir: George Fitzmaurice
Stars: Greta Garbo, Ramon Novarro, Lionel Barrymore
Rating: ★★★

Not many actresses in screen history have had a stab at playing the infamous lady spy of World War One. Magda Sonja was a silent Mata, then along came Greta Garbo with her smouldering allure and exotic temple dance. More recently, Jeanne Moreau has done well in the part and there was a disastrous Eighties version with Sylvia Kristel once more baring her all. This Garbo version is a pictorial stunner under the elegant guidance of cultured director George Fitzmaurice.

Matchmaker, The ○

1959, US, 97 mins, b/w
Dir: Joseph Anthony
Stars: Shirley Booth, Paul Ford, Shirley MacLaine, Anthony Perkins
Rating: ★★★

Well-staged version of Thornton Wilder's famous comedy play, which was later made into the smash-hit Broadway and film musical *Hello Dolly!*. Shirley Booth is nearer the right age for the part than was Barbra Streisand, and Paul Ford is in fine, spluttering form in the part played by Walter Matthau in the later film. Rich in supporting talent, the film has many rewarding moments – not least of which is the sight of a very young Robert Morse masquerading as an elderly lady. This was Morse's first film and, surprisingly, his talent went unnoticed.

Matewan ◐ ⓥ

1988, US, 132 mins, colour
Dir: John Sayles
Stars: Chris Cooper, Mary McDonnell, Kevin Tighe, James Earl Jones
Rating: ★★

'Worthy' and 'admirable' are words that spring easily to mind to describe this account of the West Virginia miners' strike of the 1920s culminating in what became known as the Battle of Matewan. Compassion drips from every frame; yet the brutal truth is that

Matewan is a very slow film that, for all its brilliant re-creation of period and hardship, makes severe demands on our patience. Excellent performances by Chris Cooper, as the travelling union organiser, Mary McDonnell, as the widow with whom he rooms, Kevin Tighe, as the repugnant union-breaker hired by the mining company, David Strathairn as the down-the-line local sheriff, James Earl Jones as the leader of the black miners, and many more, can't paper over the fatal lack of pace that John Sayles brings to this slice of history sprung to life.

Matinee ○ ⓥ
1993, US, 98 mins, colour
Dir: Joe Dante
Stars: John Goodman, Cathy Moriarty, Simon Fenton, Jesse White, Dick Miller
Rating: ★

Dull, over-acted and very slow to start, this is a fun-sounding idea that in fact only livens up towards the end. The twin story threads – the Cuban missile crisis of 1962, and the visit of a film showman to Key West to plug his new horror film *Mant!* ('Half man, half ant, all terror!') – are obviously destined to intertwine, but John Goodman as the cigar-chomping movie mogul is kept out of the action far too long for the film's comfort. Drippy sub-teens dominate too much of the storyline, but the climax is just about worth hanging in there for. Pop out to the pub in the middle of this Matinee.

Mating Season, The ○
1951, US, 101 mins, b/w
Dir: Mitchell Leisen
Stars: Gene Tierney, John Lund, Miriam Hopkins, Thelma Ritter
Rating: ★★★

A comedy from one of Hollywood's more underrated directors, Mitchell Leisen, about a rich girl who falls in love with a man whose mother owns a hamburger shop. Thelma Ritter gives a show-stopping performance, as the mother and Gene Tierney's high-class society girl is exquisite and likeable.

Matter of Life and Death, A ○ ⓥ
(aka: Stairway to Heaven)
1946, UK, 104 mins, colour & b/w
Dir: Michael Powell, Emeric Pressburger
Stars: David Niven, Marius Goring, Roger Livesey, Kim Hunter, Raymond Massey, Richard Attenborough
Rating: ★★★★★

One of Britain's most famous movies: bizarre, beautiful, poignant and exciting, with a plot – about a pilot (David Niven) caught in limbo between Heaven and Earth – that is unique. Impressive portrayals from Niven, Kim Hunter (five years before her Oscar in *A Streetcar Named Desire*) and Roger Livesey, fresh from his triumph in *The Life and Death of Colonel Blimp*, giving a tremendous performance as a psychoanalyst involved in the strange affair, whose events are played out at a high pitch of tension. Partly in Technicolor, partly black and white.

Maurice ● ⓥ
1987, UK, 140 mins, colour
Dir: James Ivory
Stars: James Wilby, Denholm Elliott, Rupert Graves, Hugh Grant, Simon Callow, Billie Whitelaw
Rating: ★★

This poignant Merchant-Ivory film is a story of homosexuality in pre-war England based on the semi-autobiographical novel by E M Forster, not published until after the author's death because of its controversial nature. It has excellent, sustained portrayals by James Wilby and Hugh Grant, whose unconsummated university affair takes them ultimately in very different directions. Director James Ivory lets it run on for a bit too long, but the film is sumptuously well set in period and has some distinguished players acting to their strengths in supporting roles, if for once Ben Kingsley seems all at sea as an American quack psychiatrist trying to rid our hero of his 'affliction'. The script is carefully, literately composed, although you may giggle at the odd jarring line of dialogue, such as: 'Since I was here, I went wrong with the gatekeeper.'

Maverick ○ ⓥ
1994, US, 129 mins, colour
Dir: Richard Donner
Stars: Mel Gibson, Jodie Foster, James Coburn, James Garner, Alfred Molina, Graham Greene
Rating: ★★

The trouble with this spoof Western is that it's too improbable to be enjoyable. And, despite some amusing moments along the trail, it can't even come up with a decent finishing line after two hours plus. Basing its concept on the old TV series, the film has Mel Gibson in the title role: he's just faintly annoying as the beaming, master-bluffing gambler trying to get to a big riverboat game at which the pot is half a million. Aiming for the same table are Annabelle (Jodie Foster), a lady gambler and all-round sneak-thief, the bad guy, Angel (Alfred Molina) and upright marshal Zane Cooper (James Garner). Garner was of course the original Maverick on TV and even gets to use his trademark phrase 'A man could get killed doing that'. There are comic villains and comic Indians and Mel's *Lethal Weapon* partner Danny Glover is in it too, the pair making with the double-takes when Danny's robber is unmasked by Mel. Most of the witty and amusing bits are in the trailer: there aren't that many.

Maverick Queen, The ○
1956, US, 86 mins, colour
Dir: Joe Kane
Stars: Barbara Stanwyck, Barry Sullivan
Rating: ★★★

This Western has acquired something of a cult following along the lines of Joan Crawford's *Johnny Guitar*, perhaps because it comes from the same studio (Republic), has another Hollywood legend, Barbara Stanwyck, in a similar role, and Scott Brady again, as the Sundance Kid (he played the Dancin' Kid in the Crawford film). This isn't as good as *Guitar*, although it does have some rousing acting and a splendidly dominating performance from Stanwyck. Virtually the studio's last major production before it lurched towards extinction.

Maxie ○
1985, US, 90 mins, colour
Dir: Paul Aaron
Stars: Glenn Close, Mandy Patinkin, Ruth Gordon
Rating: ★★

One of the low points in the career of five-times Oscar-nominated Glenn Close. She has dual roles in this unashamedly old fashioned romantic comedy – a hard-working secretary and the ghost of a flamboyant jazz era flapper, who inhabits her body to grab one last chance of fame in films. The film contains Ruth Gordon's last screen appearance, as yet another in a long line of dotty neighbours. Production values look penny-pinching on screen, which doesn't help its B-movie feel. Only Glenn makes *Maxie* even a close call with success.

Maybe Baby ◖ ⓥ
(aka: For Keeps?)
1987, US, 98 mins, colour
Dir: John G Avildsen
Stars: Molly Ringwald, Randall Batinkoff, Kenneth Mars, Conchata Ferrell, Larry Drake
Rating: ★

M

Although technically very competent, this one really does prove a bit of a drag, It's hard to get involved in the problems of high school teenagers Molly Kingwald and Randall Batinkoff when they discover she's pregnant, especially with a script that runs the gamut of predictable situations – rejection of abortion, hasty marriage, struggles to make ends meet, money worries, constant bickering and moving in with mom – and fails to find anything penetrating or poignant about any of them. Ringwald looks as though she'd be happier in a comedy and indeed the film's best sequence is the Thanksgiving dinner at which she announces her pregnancy to the two families. Some tart dialogue winds its way through this scene, but the thread fails to reappear elsewhere and the film disappears up its own tear duct of gloom, doom and inevitable reconciliation.

Maytime O
1937, US, 132 mins, b/w
Dir: Robert Z Leonard
Stars: Jeanette MacDonald, Nelson Eddy, John Barrymore
Rating: ★★★

MGM began making this Jeanette MacDonald-Nelson Eddy musical in Technicolor. But, frightened by the cost, they got cold feet one-third of the way through and, abandoning all the colour footage, re-shot the entire film in black-and-white. Even so the film, with its stagey but uniquely emotive ending, remained MacDonald's favourite. No wonder: it glistens with fine music, and includes one of the peerless pair's finest duets: 'Will You Remember?'

Maytime in Mayfair O
1949, UK, 96 mins, colour
Dir: Herbert Wilcox
Stars: Anna Neagle, Michael Wilding, Peter Graves
Rating: ★★

Despite its coat of Technicolor, this post-war romp has worn less well than most of the box-office champions turned out by Anna Neagle and Michael Wilding. Perhaps it's because the romantic hijinks are set in a fashion house. Still, the stars play off one another as elegantly as ever.

McCabe and Mrs Miller ● Ⓥ
1972, US, 120 mins, colour
Dir: Robert Altman
Stars: Warren Beatty, Julie Christie, Rene Auberjonois, William Devane, Shelley

Duvall, Keith Carradine
Rating: ★★★

Director Robert Altman cast his usual idiosyncratic gaze upon the West and came up with this adult view where the men are men and the women are available. In this case the most available is Julie Christie as Mrs Miller, the ambitious English whore who goes into partnership with McCabe (Warren Beatty) to set up a lavish brothel for the sex-starved citizens of a frontier town called Presbyterian Church. Altman is determined to show the West as it really was. The bit part players contribute as much to the film as Beatty and Christie, who seem content to play within their screen images. William Devane has a small but flashy role as a lawyer.

McKenzie Break, The O
1970, UK, 106 mins, colour
Dir: Lamont Johnson
Stars: Brian Keith, Helmut Griem, Ian Hendry
Rating: ★★

A taut, well executed World War Two drama about a plan by Nazi PoWs to escape from a Scottish camp, and the efforts of an Irish intelligence officer to foil the attempt. It succeeds largely because of particularly strong characterisations by Brian Keith, as the special troubleshooter, and Helmut Griem is a hard-drinking U-boat captain suspected of being the mastermind behind the plot.

McMasters, The ●
1970, US, 90 mins, colour
Dir: Alf Kjellin
Stars: Burt Ives, Brock Peters, Nancy Kwan, David Carradine, Jack Palance
Rating: ★

A violent Western with Jack Palance as a bigoted Confederate determined to drive out an elderly rancher and his negro partner. The result is an orgy of murder, rape and sundry mayhem. There's a very good performance from David Carradine as a Red Indian supporter of the embattled duo, and a good one from Dane Clark (in a return to the screen after 10 years) as a liberal-minded rancher also sympathetic to their cause.

McQ ● Ⓥ
1974, US, 111 mins, colour
Dir: John Sturges
Stars: John Wayne, Eddie Albert, Clu Gulager
Rating: ★★

One of John Wayne's last films but a more workaday assignment than most. Stepping out of his Western togs and into the role of a Seattle police detective, big John goes in search of vengeance on the gangster who killed his friend. John Sturges directed this plain man's thriller with its ragbag of narcotics, corruption and shotguns. It rambles a bit, but then it does have plenty of plot.

McVicar ● Ⓥ
1980, UK, 112 mins, colour
Dir: Tom Clegg
Stars: Roger Daltrey, Adam Faith, Cheryl Campbell, Steven Berkoff, Ian Hendry
Rating: ★★

A muscular crime drama offering two pop stars-turned-actors for the price of one. Roger Daltrey takes the title role of the now rehabilitated and respectable criminal John McVicar, Adam Faith is his accomplice in a prison break-out, Walter Probyn. As one might expect, the film is somewhat sanitised but, despite that, the prison scenes carry conviction. Tom Clegg, more used to the confines of small screen series such as *The Sweeney,* provides efficient if anonymous direction.

Mean Machine, The ◗
(aka: The Longest Yard)
1974, US, 123 mins, colour
Dir: Robert Aldrich
Stars: Burt Reynolds, Eddie Albert, Ed Lauter, Michael Conrad
Rating: ★★★

A bit like a Laurel and Hardy film with an X certificate or the Marx Brothers' *Monkey Business* with brass knuckles. *It's Cool Hand Luke* prison fare all over again – except that the name of the game is not escaping but American football. It all works very happily indeed, mixing its modern violence with pleasant old-fashioned dialogue and some hard-nut humour.

Mean Season, The ◗
1985, US, 100 mins, colour
Dir: Phillip Borsos
Stars: Kurt Russell, Mariel Hemingway, Richard Jordan, Richard Masur, Joe Pantoliano
Rating: ★★

The spirit of Hollywood's old 'Poverty Row' studios lives in this B-movie plot about a Miami reporter (Kurt Russell) finding that his particular vice is getting hooked into a psycho-murderer (a weighty Richard Jordan) who sees the scribe as his private video screen to public exposure. Yes, you've guessed the plot: the police can't catch the killer as the body count mounts and the reporter's personal involvement increases. You won't be surprised either when the bad guy kidnaps the hero's girl (Mariel Hemingway). Russell is rather good as the reporter, but Hemingway proves ineffectually wimpish in a Grace Kelly kind of part of which she might have been expected to make more. Andy Garcia crops up in a small role. Technical credits are wobbly, with continuity slips, and newspapers having no date. But then what do you expect from a B-movie?

Mean Streets ● Ⓥ
1973, US, 110 mins, colour
Dir: Martin Scorsese
Stars: Harvey Keitel, Robert De Niro, Amy Robinson, Richard Romanus
Rating: ★★★★

New York's Little Italy district has never looked seedier or tougher than in this gripping slice-of-Mafia-life drama, the first of Martin Scorsese's many descents onto the grimier streets of the Big Apple. Shot on a shoestring budget of $600,000, it has been hailed as a masterpiece by Scorsese's most ardent fans, and gave Harvey Keitel an early leading role. All the other roles are astutely cast with special praise reserved for Robert De Niro in the difficult role of a mercurial loner constantly in debt to a slimy loan-shark (a bravura performance from Richard Romanus). The film also boasts a terrific rock score that actually heightens the effect of its dynamic images. Look out for the director in a cameo as Shorty – the killer in a car.

Mechanic, The ●
(aka: Killer of Killers)
1972, US, 100 mins, colour
Dir: Michael Winner
Stars: Charles Bronson, Jan-Michael Vincent, Jill Ireland, Keenan Wynn
Rating: ★

A thriller that's as cold, calculating and passionless as its central character – a hired assassin, philosophically played by Charles Bronson, teaming again with director Michael Winner who made the *Death Wish* films. The director's well-oiled techniques generate some explosive excitement as usual, although one cannot help but think the makers should have heeded the advice given by Bronson to protégé Jan-Michael Vincent when he tells him: 'You've been watching too many late-night movies.' No doubt, though,

Bronson and Winner could churn out these violent morality plays in their sleep.

Medicine Man ◑ Ⓥ
1992, US, 105 mins, colour
Dir: John McTiernan
Stars: Sean Connery, Lorraine Bracco, Jose Wilker, Rodolfo de Alexandre
Rating: ★★★★

A bit talky, but definitely different, this is an ecological adventure set deep in the Brazilian jungle. Lorraine Bracco is the Brooklyn girl whose brains have taken her to the top of the scientific tree. What she doesn't reckon on is swarming up to the top of the tallest tree in the Brazilian forest. Deep in the greenery works Dr Campbell, a scientist who has 'gone native', played bv a pigtailed Sean Connery. Already feeling responsible for the death of a village, he's now doubly shaken: having found a cure for cancer, he has been unable to duplicate it. As he searches desperately for the missing ingredient, the bulldozers clearing the jungle move closer. And now Bracco has arrived to tell him his time is running out. This is another super performance by Connery, giving us the whole man without portraying him as too much of a saint, or making him too unsympathetic. Plot-spotters will probably get the twist before Connery and Bracco stumble on it, but that won't detract from your enjoyment of a well-told story, where elements of fun, sadness, drama and action blend into good medicine.

Medusa Touch, The ◑
1978, UK, 109 mins, colour
Dir: Jack Gold
Stars: Richard Burton, Lee Remick, Lino Ventura, Harry Andrews
Rating: ★

'I am the man with the power to create catastrophe,' booms Richard Burton in this horror-style story. Burton's character has the power to move objects, to cause the death of anyone who stands in his way. Like his nanny, his parents, or all the passengers in a jumbo jet. When he turns his attention to cathedrals, atomic research establishments and moonshots, it's obvious the authorities have to step in. Fans of horrific hokum will enjoy themselves while cynics chuckle. Ironically, the film's most effective patches come with dialogue that is actually meant to be funny, especially Burton's scathingly vitriolic dissection of his faithless wife.

Meeting Venus ● Ⓥ
1991, Hungary/France, 119 mins, colour
Dir: Istvan Szabo
Stars: Glenn Close, Niels Arestrup
Rating: ★★

Films about opera and ballet have not been much at the box-office for the past 40 years, and this one hardly breaks through the 'culture barrier'. As a movie, it has its moments: a Hungarian conductor (Niels Arestrup) arrives in Paris to helm a polyglot production of Wagner's *Tannhauser*. Apart from walking into a Tower of Babel where not everyone understands a common language let alone each other's, he finds the inter-relations of the whole company akin to a TV soap. Affairs are rife, union demands disrupt every rehearsal as do tea and coffee breaks. Pretty soon, he himself is engulfed in a torrid affair with his leading lady (Glenn Close). Though Arestrup is good and Close lip-synchs superbly to Kiri Te Kanawa's singing, the film is too often not quite believable. But the ending is marvellous, and occasionally the passion of the performances – especially Close's – transcends the essentially cheapjack quality of the material.

Meet John Doe ○
1941, US. 123 mins, b/w
Dir: Frank Capra
Stars: Gary Cooper, Barbara Stanwyck, Edward Arnold, Walter Brennan
Rating: ★★★

A crowd-pleasing Frank Capra film that provides biting social comment and good entertainment at the same time. A bit slow in parts, with too many long speeches, but marvellously well cast and acted, with a sensational ending. Barbara Stanwyck is outstanding as the reporter who thinks up the idea of a made-up figure writing in to complain about injustice and finds that she has caught a tiger by the tail, as the 'complaints' take a nation by storm. Gary Cooper's natural sincerity lends quiet authority to the title role, although Walter Brennan as his sceptical friend steals all their scenes together.

Meet Me After the Show ○
1951, US, 88 mins, colour
Dir: Richard Sale
Stars: Betty Grable, Macdonald Carey, Rory Calhoun, Eddie Albert
Rating: ★★★

To compensate for the absence of regular partner Dan Dailey, Fox provided Betty Grable with three 'second league' leading men, Macdonald Carey, Rory Calhoun and Eddie

M

Albert, in this musical about a Broadway star who loses her memory. As well as those Million Dollar Legs, look for acid comedian Fred Clark as Tim and a couple of sizzling speciality dancers called Steve Condos and Jerry Brandow. Their routine benefits, as does the whole show, from scintillating choreography by the highly talented Gwen Verdon (who can also be seen on screen with Grable in the 'I Feel Like Dancing' number) and Jack Cole. This movie, with its vacuous plot and a waning star, had all the makings of a flop – but its dazzling dancing saved it.

Meet Me in St Louis ⊙ ○
1944, US, 113 mins, colour
Dir: Vincente Minnelli
Stars: Judy Garland, Margaret O'Brien, Mary Astor, Tom Drake, Leon Ames
Rating: ★★★★★

Vincente Minnelli directs his wife-to-be Judy Garland in one of the best and warmest period musicals ever filmed. It was his first colour film – and the Technicolor photography is Christmas card bright. The film follows a year in the lives of the Smith family. Nothing much happens, except that two of the daughters fall in love and the father faces a difficult job relocation decision. But the attention to ordinary detail made it a big success. Judy had to be persuaded against her will to star, but the finished film contains one of her best roles, her tear-jerking rendition of 'Have Yourself a Merry Little Christmas' and the show-stopping five-minute song and dance routine for 'The Trolley Song'. Child star Margaret O'Brien steals every scene she's in.

Meet Me Tonight ○
1952, UK, 85 mins, colour
Dir: Anthony Pelissier
Stars: Kay Walsh, Ted Ray, Stanley Holloway
Rating: ★★★

Alternately warmly witty and cuttingly cruel, this is typical Noel Coward fare, consisting of three short stories. Things get off to a rousing start with Kay Walsh and Ted Ray as the 'Red Peppers', supposedly a second-rate song-and-dance team but in fact just as enjoyable in harmony on stage as wrangling off it. The other tales have Stanley Holloway as a worm who takes rather too long to turn and (most dated but still quite funny) Valerie Hobson and Nigel Patrick as social butterflies living off rich Riviera friends.

Meet Mr Lucifer ○
1953, UK, 77 mins, b/w
Dir: Anthony Pelissier
Stars: Stanley Holloway, Peggy Cummins, Gordon Jackson
Rating: ★★★

Based on a play by Arnold Ridley, best remembered as one of the stars of *Dad's Army,* this amiable Ealing comedy takes some enjoyable sidewipes at television, and gives Stanley Holloway a good opportunity to flex his comic muscles in a dual role. Also on view: Ian Carmichael as Man Friday in a pantomime, Kay Kendall as a 'lonely hearts' singer and (briefly) star comic Norman Wisdom.

Meet the Applegates ◐ ⓥ
1990, US, 89 mins, colour
Dir: Michael Lehmann
Stars: Ed Begley Jr, Stockard Channing, Dabney Coleman, Bobby Jacoby
Rating: ★★

The Applegates are your average American family. They even look average. But their new neighbours think there's something weird about them and they're right: the A's are really mutated forms of six-foot high cockroaches from the rain forest of Brazil. They've come to America to destroy man's nuclear capacity – 'You must pronounce it nucular,' Pa (Ed Begley Jr) warns the kids – and millions of humans at the same time. Alas, the four Applegates soon fall victim to all the evils to which man has become heir. Ma (Stockard Channing) goes on a shopping spree with credit cards, junior (Bobby Jacoby) becomes a hophead, and the nubile girl Applegate (Cami Cooper) gets pregnant on her first date. Needless to say, this is a comedy, but one with an adult and sometimes stomach-churning content. Though high in the cinema's canon of mad movies, *Applegates* is just not mad enough, nor light enough, to make you laugh like a bug.

Melba ○ ⓥ
1953, UK, 120 mins, colour
Dir: Lewis Milestone
Stars: Patrice Munsel, John McCallum, Robert Morley, Sybil Thorndike
Rating: ★★★

Producer Sam Spiegel (under his alias of S P Eagle) and director Lewis Milestone, with lavish assistance from art director Andre Andrejew, make a spectacular job out of this highly coloured, immensely fictionalised biography of the famous Australian-born opera singer of Victorian times. Patrice

Munsel gives a sterling performance as the rancher's daughter who becomes a world star, and sings a good selection of arias quite beautifully. The men in the film fare less well, but there are memorable performances from two dowager duchesses of British acting: Sybil Thorndike, as Queen Victoria, and Martita Hunt, as the famous singing teacher who comes out of retirement to help the heroine attain her ambitions. In the story's hectic two-hour running time, Milestone's direction remains sensitive, dramatically effective, and full of imaginative little touches that raise the film out of the conventional class.

Melody ○
(aka: S.W.A.L.K.)
1971, UK, 103 mins, colour
Dir: Waris Hussein
Stars: Jack Wild, Mark Lester, Tracy Hyde
Rating: ★★★

A teenage comedy-drama reuniting Mark Lester and Jack Wild after their success as Oliver Twist and The Artful Dodger respectively in the musical *Oliver!* Despite its title, *Melody* is not a musical. Wild and Lester play school chums at a London comprehensive school whose friendship is threatened when Lester falls for a pretty girl in their class. Her name is Melody (Tracy Hyde). This film marks an early collaboration of David Puttnam (producer) and Alan Parker (screenplay) who were to become major forces in the cinema.

Melody Time ⊙
1948, US, 75 mins, colour
Dir: Hamilton Luske, Clyde Geronimi, Stars: Jack Kinney, Wilfred Jackson
Rating: ★★★★

A delightful Disney cartoon compilation. Children will be charmed by the sagas of Pecos Bill, Johnny Appleseed and Little Toot (a tugboat) and Donald Duck makes a guest appearance. The classical motifs of *Fantasia* are carried over into 'Trees' and, best of all, "Bumble Boogie", based on Rimsky Korsakov's 'Flight of the Bumble Bee', with a panic-stricken bee dodging various musical menaces. A real gem in which Disney's animators are allowed the full range of their creative abilities.

Melvin and Howard ◐ ⓥ
1980, US, 95 mins, colour
Dir: Jonathan Demme
Stars: Paul Le Mat, Jason Robards, Mary Steenburgen, Michael J Pollard, Dabney

Coleman, Gloria Grahame
Rating: ★★★

Episodic but extremely engaging escapade dealing with a true meeting between a milkman called Melvin and the film and business tycoon Howard Hughes. Like other films by director Jonathan Demme, it is full of fascinating characters; as Melvin's wife Lynda, Mary Steenburgen won an Oscar.

Memed My Hawk ○
1983, UK, 101 mins, colour
Dir: Peter Ustinov
Stars: Peter Ustinov, Herbert Lom, Denis Quilley, Michael Elphick
Rating: ★

Hard to tell whether star-writer-director Peter Ustinov intended this unlikely tale of Turkish bandits in 1923 as a whimsical action film or an outright satirical comedy. With its deliberately unreal performances, it tends to come across as the latter. Tedium and fits of giggles set in early in this adventure.

Memoirs of an Invisible Man ◐ ⓥ
1992, US, 99 mins, colour
Dir: John Carpenter
Stars: Chevy Chase, Daryl Hannah, Sam Neill, Michael McKean, Stephen Tobolowsky
Rating: ★

We always did find invisibility thrillers resistible stuff, and the lost art of the comedy-thriller is hardly revived by this thin script, hopefully written in invisible ink. Not fast enough, tight enough, or good enough, the slackly constructed story finds director John Carpenter struggling outside his usual horror genre. Chevy Chase is the indolent businessman who finds he has to move faster than for years when a laboratory accident renders him not only invisible, but the target for a nest of rogue CIA agents led by Sam Neill. Lots of tedious conversation between Chase and girlfriend Daryl Hannah follows, punctuated by special effects that are remarkably clumsy by modern standards and seem not to have moved on much since Claude Rains' day nearly 60 years earlier.

Memphis Belle ◐ ⓥ
1990, UK, 102 mins, colour
Dir: Michael Caton-Jones
Stars: Matthew Modine, Eric Stoltz, Tate Donovan, D B Sweeney, Billy Zane, Sean Astin, Jane Horrocks
Rating: ★★★

The story of the 25th and final mission of the Memphis Belle, the most celebrated of the US Air Force B-17 bombers, based in Britain. In the hands of director Michael Caton-Jones, who went on to make *Scandal*, it ends up a highly romanticised view of wartime heroics and just the sort of unashamedly commercial popcorn fodder that had Forties audiences cheering in the aisles for the likes of Errol Flynn and Jimmy Cagney. The plane is crewed by the freshest faces Hollywood could muster, with acting honours going to Eric Stoltz as the romantic Danny and Billy Zane's suave Val, whose bravado hides a guilty secret. The photography of sweeping landscapes is stunning and the model work in the aerial fight scenes is flawless. Film fans may notice original footage from the 1944 documentary *Memphis Belle*, used for tear-jerking effect with letters from parents of dead soldiers read over it by David Strathairn's commanding officer. A genuine crowd-pleaser of the old school of filmmaking.

Menace II Society ● ⓥ
1993, US, 97 mins, colour
Dir: The Hughes Brothers
Stars: Jada Pinkett, Tyrin Turner, Larenz Tate
Rating: ★★

If 23-year-old John Singleton made a stunning directorial debut with *Boyz N the Hood*, then what of this film from 20-year-old twin directors The Hughes Brothers? It's not as good as *Boyz*, but still a remarkable first feature, full of venom, passion and raw energy. Some of its directors' work lacks control, and their story is a series of scenes with predictable outcomes but, unlike Caine, their leading character, they surely have a bright future. Caine (Tyrin Turner) is a decent sort considering his upbringing with hopheaded parents, but still he sells drugs and runs with the local boyz. After he leaves school, his life soon enters a downward spiral: his running mate O-Dog (Larenz Tate) casually kills a Korean shopkeeper over some imagined insult, making Caine an accessory. When his cousin is killed by rival gangsters, Caine seeks and takes revenge. While O-Dog continues his rampage, Caine is offered a route out of the ghetto via his relationship with Ronnie (Jada Pinkett) and her young son ... Fluently told, not for the fainthearted or easily offended.

Men Are Not Gods ○
1936, UK, 92 mins, b/w
Dir: Walter Reisch
Stars: Miriam Hopkins, Rex Harrison,

Gertrude Lawrence, Sebastian Shaw
Rating: ★★★

Wittily contrived comedy-drama which plays an interesting variation on the *Othello* theme. Miriam Hopkins is a delight as the girl who makes an actor playing Othello want to murder his wife, and other bright contributions come from A E Matthews, as a drama critic, and Rex Harrison. The film also offers a rare opportunity to see the legendary Gertrude Lawrence, as the wife of the Othello actor, who's played by Sebastian Shaw.

Men at Work ◐ ⓥ
1990, US, 97 mins, colour
Dir: Emilio Estevez
Stars: Emilio Estevez, Charlie Sheen, Leslie Hope, John Getz
Rating: RB

Films like this shouldn't be allowed. A feckless farce from brothers Charlie Sheen and Emilio Estevez, this is a waste of (anybody's) money that wouldn't have got past first base in the old studio days. Way over the top playing and direction decorates a vapour-thin story about two garbage men who become involved with a murder and vital tape that incriminates those behind a scandal concerning the dumping of toxic waste. Sound promising? Forget it: Estevez wrote it as well and he didn't do a good job – the dialogue is more likely to send you to sleep than make you laugh. And what happened to the vital tape at the end? No-one seemed to care. Credit Leslie Hope with being the fastest movie mover in a short, tight skirt and you've said it all. Garbage is right.

Men Don't Leave ◐ ⓥ
1990, US, 115 mins, colour
Dir: Paul Brickman
Stars: Jessica Lange, Chris O'Donnell, Charlie Korsmo, Arliss Howard, Joan Cusack, Kathy Bates
Rating: ★★★

Yet another Hollywood movie based on a French original, this well-made weepie still has Gallic whiffs about its moods of melancholia. And, though it occasionally goes over the top, you will find yourself affected by the plight of Jessica Lange, suddenly widowed by a husband who leaves her with two sons, $63,000 in debts and insufficient insurance. Some of the editing seems a bit rough, doubtless in the effort to keep the film under two hours, but there's a multitude of incidents, well handled by director Paul Brickman, who creates a believable flat-dwellers' atmosphere

M

while his star acts her socks off having a nervous breakdown, coping with her older son's love affair with an older woman (superb Joan Cusack) and tackling her small son's traumas and petty thieving. Go, enjoy and have a good cry.

Men in Black ◐ Ⓥ

1997, US, 98 mins, colour
Dir: Barry Sonnenfeld
Stars: Tommy Lee Jones,. Will Smith, Linda Fiorentino, Vincent D'Onofrio, Rip Torn
Rating: ★★★

A combination of *Ghost Busters* and the SWAT Squad, this is the kind of entertainment only 1990s special effects could provide. Regulators of all things alien on earth, the Men in Black are a secret US government organisation, armed with torchlights that obliterate witnesses' memories of alien activity. Seconded to membership, New York cop J (Smith) joins veteran operative K (Jones) just in time to pursue a humanoid giant bug (Vincent D'Onofrio) out to steal a galaxy, while its own denizens, out there in space, threaten to terminate earth if it isn't rescued. Try if possible to avoid the trailer to this: all the best bits and most amazing effects are in it, with the exception of the head-on sight of the alien cockroach at the end. Good fun, though, especially the alienoid worms addicted to earthly nicotine, and a can of insect spray labelled 'Bug Off'.

Men in War ○

1956, US, 104 mins, b/w
Dir: Anthony Mann
Stars: Robert Ryan, Aldo Ray, Robert Keith, Vic Morrow
Rating: ★★

An ambitious film set in the Korean war. It was unusually realistic for its time, but finally found little new to offer. Rugged, uncompromising performances from Robert Ryan and Aldo Ray: in fact, all the cast come across as individuals in spite of a script that often requires them to do little but look miserable and unshaven.

Men of Boys Town ○

1941, US, 106 mins, b/w
Dir: Norman Taurog
Stars: Spencer Tracy, Mickey Rooney, Lee J Cobb, Mary Nash
Rating: ★★

Somehow, MGM managed to assemble pretty well all the original cast of *Boys' Town*, including Spencer Tracy and

Mickey Rooney, for this sentimental sequel. Such was the power of the studio contract system! The plot is more of the same, without the inspiration of the first film.

Men of Sherwood Forest, The ○

1954, UK, 77 mins, colour
Dir: Val Guest
Stars: Don Taylor, Eileen Moore
Rating: ★★

One of two lively, good-natured adventure films about Robin Hood to come from Hammer Films, mainly known for their horror products. This one has a genial American Robin, in the form of Don Taylor (who later met and married the British actress Hazel Court), and an excellent Friar Tuck in Reginald Beckwith. Attractive Eastman Colour photography by the experienced Jimmy Harvey adds the finishing gloss to the rousing yarn.

Men's Club, The ● Ⓥ

1986, US, 105 mins, colour
Dir: Peter Medak
Stars: Roy Scheider, David Dukes, Harvey Keitel, Stockard Channing, Jennifer Jason Leigh
Rating: **RB**

A thinking man's porno movie. Hard to believe, though, that voyeurs wouldn't be bored to tears by the first half, in which seven affluent men, at least three of them dangerously unbalanced, meet for their first 'club' meeting and end up gleefully wrecking their host's home (with his connivance), casually kicking the furniture around, smashing the kitchen door and shattering priceless ornaments in a wild knife-throwing competition. Even so, it's a little tough to credit that the host's wife (Stockard Channing, inevitably wasted) on arrival home would actually go so far as to fracture her husband's skull with a broiling pan. The remaining six 'boys' end up at an opulent brothel with just enough Playboy centrefolds to go round. A good cast, also including Craig Wasson, Frank Langella, Richard Jordan and Treat Williams, presumably saw something about the meaning of life in all this. Wrong, guys.

Mephisto Waltz, The ●

1971, US, 109 mins, colour
Dir: Paul Wendkos
Stars: Alan Alda, Jacqueline Bisset, Curt Jurgens, Barbara Parkins
Rating: ★★★

A highly effective devil-worship chiller directed by the underrated Paul

Wendkos. Here he makes the most of error that creeps up on one in luxurious surroundings, with some nerve-jangling use of Liszt's music.

Mermaids ◐ Ⓥ

1990, US, 110 mins, colour
Dir: Richard Benjamin
Stars: Cher, Bob Hoskins, Winona Ryder, Christina Ricci, Michael Schoeffling
Rating: ★★

A mother and daughter fable. And, this being the movies, these are no ordinary mother and daughter. Rachel Flax (Cher) is sexy, sassy, brassy and on the move from town to town, and man to man. Daughter Charlotte (Winona Ryder) thinks she wants to be a nun (no mean feat as they're Jewish) but finds she has too many of mother's hormones floating around and falls heavily for the hunky caretaker (Michael Schoeffling) out at the nunnery instead. There's also a younger daughter (Christina Ricci) who wants to be a swimming champ. The film revolves round Cher and Ryder and they keep it flowing warmly along in spite of the fact that deceptively little actually happens. Bob Hoskins is sweetly blue-collar as the man who may make momma settle down, but he's kept pretty much on the sidelines as the mermaids try to sort out a life together, via a rather contrived emotional climax.

Merrill's Marauders ○

1962, US, 98 mins, colour
Dir: Samuel Fuller
Stars: Jeff Chandler, Ty Hardin
Rating: ★★★

Jeff Chandler leads a band of US Marines through the Burmese jungle in this characteristically rugged World War Two action adventure directed and co-scripted by Samuel Fuller, an ebullient, cigar-chewing American who has become something of a cult figure in the film world. Shot in soft and very distinctive Technicolor the film has some striking and moving sequences, not least of which is a desperate pitched battle at a railhead, culminating in Stockton (Ty Hardin) walking desolately through piles of twisted bodies.

Merry Christmas Mr Lawrence ○

1982, UK, 124 mins, colour
Dir: Nagisa Oshima
Stars: Tom Conti, David Bowie, Ryuichi Sakamoto, Takeshi, Jack Thompson
Rating: ★★★

What happens, please, when Japanese director make international co-production about Allied prisoners in Jap World War Two prison camp? I tell you: you get very strange film. But, though *Mr Lawrence* has some slow and dreamy passages, it also possesses a fascination you can't deny. David Bowie is nicely cast as the enigmatic prisoner who arrives at the camp at the same time as the Japanese officer who seems hypnotised by his personality. Tom Conti gives a very civilised performance as the Japanese-speaking Allied officer who tries to keep the camp's atrocities within bounds, while Jack Thompson is excellent as the far less cerebral group captain in charge of the prisoners. Probably best of all is Takeshi as the master-sergeant only beginning to understand what human relationships are all about. For all its faults, this is a film you won't easily forget.

Merton of the Movies ○
1947, US, 82 mins, b/w
Dir: Robert Alton
Stars: Red Skelton, Virginia O'Brien, Gloria Grahame
Rating: ★★

This is the third film to be culled from the popular play. The eponymous hero here is played by Red Skelton, who rises from being a humble theatre usher to stardom. The premise of this version was to recapture the atmosphere of the early days of Hollywood and it does exude some of that good-time spirit, but not enough enthusiasm or *joie-de-vivre*. The producers employed Buster Keaton to give Skelton lessons in slapstick.

Message to Garcia, A ○
1936, US, 86 mins, b/w
Dir: George Marshall
Stars: Barbara Stanwyck, Wallace Beery, John Boles
Rating: ★★★

Barbara Stanwyck as a Cuban freedom fighter? Well, she's a feisty lady and, although the accent is distinctly strange, she goes at her role with gusto in this period adventure set in the last century during the Spanish-American war. Handsome, dependable John Boles plays Lieutenant Rowan, charged with getting a vital message from US President McKinley through to Cuban rebel leader General Garcia (Enrique Acosta). Needless to say, the terrain is tricky, and so is Wallace Beery as the maverick US marine Sgt Dory who is supposed to be aiding Rowan in his quest. Good traditional action fare.

Meteor ○
1979, US, 103 mins, colour
Dir: Ronald Nearne
Stars: Sean Connery, Natalie Wood, Karl Malden, Brian Keith, Martin Landau, Trevor Howard
Rating: ★★★

The ultimate in disaster movies. To pump up a rather slender story-line about a massive meteor headed for Earth, which must be deflected by a combination of Russian and American missiles, a tidal wave, an avalanche and the destruction of a city are thrown in, via convenient splinters from the meteor. Sean Connery has a few aptly acerbic lines as the scientist-in-chief, and the Russian spoken by Natalie Wood and Brian Keith is most impressive – perhaps partly the reason why they walk away with the film. Special effects, with the exception of the avalanche scenes, are acceptably done.

Metro ● ⓥ
1997, US, 117 mins, colour
Dir: Thomas Carter
Stars: Eddie Murphy, Michael Wincott, Carmen Ejogo, Denis Arndt, Michael Rapaport, Kim Miyori
Rating: ★★★

Eddie Murphy attempts something different again with a straight role in a violent police action thriller. The dialogue's a bit ordinary and the leading lady (Britain's Carmen Ejogo) painfully weak, but there are three or four world-class action sequences, including a sensational five-minute pursuit, ultimately involving a runaway San Francisco cable-car – and the plot has a viciously sardonic villain in Michael Wincott. A pity the film's allowed to drift on for several minutes after the action has come to a close, but that's typical of its stop-go structure. Really just a canter for Murphy, this, although his hostage negotiator does give Clint Eastwood's Dirty Harry a run for his money as Mr Cool when dealing with crazed gunmen.

Metropolis ①
1984, Germany, 87 mins, b/w
Dir: Fritz Lang
Stars: Brigitte Helm, Gustav Frolich
Rating: ★★★★

Composer and musician Giorgio Moroder is responsible for the re-editing, colourising and futuristic score of this version of Fritz Lang's silent sci-fi classic. At just over 80 minutes long, Moroder's 1984 version is 40 minutes shorter than the original cinema release, but it's not just a cutting job. He

has edited in footage from the original German 150-minute version to add clarity to the narrative. 'Colourising' simply means that many scenes are given an overall tint in different colours, presumably to heighten the mood of a particular sequence. It's a fascinating variation and tightens the rambling narrative of the original. Having said that, the ramblings are pretty good and add to what is still considered a masterpiece.

Metropolitan ① ⓥ
1989, US, 98 mins, colour
Dir: Whit Stillman
Stars: Edward Clements, Carolyn Farina, Christopher Eigeman
Rating: ★★★

Whit Stillman, a 37-year-old New Yorker sold his Manhattan apartment and persuaded friends to come up with the rest of the money to finance this low budget and engagingly quirky comedy of manners. The story centres on a group of East Side yuppies who dub themselves the Sally Fowler Rat Pack, after the girl whose sprawling Park Avenue flat is their meeting place, or the UHBS, short for Urban Haute Bourgeoise. Their self-deluding world, inspired by F Scott Fitzgerald's *This Side of Paradise*, is both attractive and repulsive to newcomer Tom (Edward Clements, giving the best performance). This talkative picture succeeds on many levels, offering intelligent arguments and dialogue, fully rounded characters and a welcome look behind the door of a seldom-seen milieu.

Miami Blues ● ⓥ
1989, US, 97 mins, colour
Dir: George Armitage
Stars: Fred Ward, Alec Baldwin, Jennifer Jason Leigh, Charles Napier
Rating: ★★★★

A consistently engrossing thriller whose extreme violence and quite funny dialogue blend unexpectedly well. Junior (Alec Baldwin) is a vicious and daring thief who steals from those who steal and is not above the odd murder to help him evade the law or change identifies. He sets up home with a little hotel hooker (Jennifer Jason Leigh) of whom he remains strangely fond, even when he decides to add her nest egg of $10,000 to his coffers. Hot on their trail is a veteran cop (Fred Ward) trying to cope with a massive workload as well as a new set of upper dentures. After a heavy interview, Junior decides said cop would be better in hospital for a while. Beating him up, he steals his

M

gun, badge and for added humiliation – his teeth. Baldwin creates a memorable portrait of this lethal Jack the Lad and, while Ward is a touch over the top as the grimacing cop, some of his exchanges with his partner (Charles Napier) are spot on target with their rough-edged but comradely banter. Leigh is perfect as the vulnerable call girl still chasing the American dream.

Michael O Ⓥ

1996, US, 105 mins, colour
Dir: Nora Ephron
Stars: John Travolta, Andie MacDowell, William Hurt, Bob Hoskins, Jean Stapleton, Robert Pastorelli
Rating: ★★★

About as light as an angel's wings, this pithy parable takes a while to warm to – and some explaining. Michael (Travolta) may be 'an angel but no saint' – although we thought the two were synonymous – but to enjoy the temptations of the flesh seems completely contrary to the angel's code. Never mind, at least he has been put on earth to help people. But his time is running out when reporters Hurt and Pastorelli get to hear of this evangelical expedition and are sent by editor Bob Hoskins to get the unlikeliest scoop of the century. Although the movie has some charm, it might have a bit more had Travolta's character been more mellow. Even so there are affecting moments, especially towards the end. Jean Stapleton scores as the elderly recipient of Michael's penultimate mission, and MacDowell does her own singing in an amusing and naïvely touching musical interlude.

Mickey's Christmas Carol ☉

1983, US, 26 mins, colour
Dir: Burny Mattinson
Rating: ★★★★

Disney's first pantomime is a delightful cartoon featurette version of Dickens' famous story. It brings together almost every well-known Disney character, including Mickey and Minnie Mouse as the Cratchits and Goofy as Marley's Ghost. Ratty and Mole collect for the poor, Toad appears as Mr Fezziwig and the three little pigs rush breathlessly along the sidelines. Only Pluto is sadly missing. A treat for Disney fans of all ages – although it's all too short, and could surely have used a song or two to prolong its welcome.

Micki + Maude ◑

1984, US, 118 mins, colour
Dir: Blake Edwards

Stars: Dudley Moore, Amy Irving, Ann Reinking, Richard Mulligan
Rating: ★★★

Cuddly Dudley Moore, whose Hollywood films have scaled the heights and plumbed the depths, is firing on all cylinders in this fast-moving farce. He is teamed up with director Blake Edwards, whose film 10 made Dud a star, and this is just the kind of broad, slightly wacky comedy that Edwards does so well. Dud plays Rob, who longs to be a dad. But wife Micki (Ann Reinking) is an ambitious lawyer, with no time for family life. Then he meets Maude (Amy Irving), a cellist, and they have an affair. When she tells him she is pregnant, Rob marries her, even though he's still married to Micki who also proves to be pregnant! This, as you can see, is a recipe for complete chaos, as Rob tries to keep his two lives separate. Not easy when both ladies have the same gynaecologist! A furiously paced comedy that's great fun, although it does peter out a bit towards the end.

Midas Run O
(aka: A Run on Gold)

1969, US, 106 mins, colour
Dir: Alf Kjellin
Stars: Richard Crenna, Anne Heywood, Fred Astaire, Ralph Richardson, Roddy McDowall
Rating: ★★

Caper film concerning a gang planning to hijack a bullion shipment. It's enlivened by some piquant vignettes, notably by Sir Ralph Richardson, and by Karl Alberty as a German ex-fighter pilot who, asked to force down an English plane, responds with relish; 'Gott in Himmel, I haven't done that for years!'

Middle of the Night O

1959, US, 118 mins, b/w
Dir: Delbert Mann
Stars: Fredric March, Kim Novak
Rating: ★★

A film for romantics, with Fredric March in fine form as the middle-aged widower who falls for a divorcee 20 years younger, played by Kim Novak in one of her finest performances. Talented supporting cast includes Albert Dekker, Lee Grant, Glenda Farrell and Martin Balsam which helps to guarantee quality. It's a hard-shelled film with a splendidly soft centre, and Paddy Chayefsky's observant, thoroughly believable script mounts a prodigious attack on the tear ducts. A pity it's so slow-moving.

Midnight O

1939, US, 90 mins, b/w
Dir: Mitchell Leisen
Stars: Claudette Colbert, Don Ameche, John Barrymore, Francis Lederer, Mary Astor
Rating: ★★★

Claudette Colbert and Don Ameche spar delightfully as director Mitchell Leisen demonstrates his stylish gift for sophisticated comedy to the full. Brilliantly scripted by Billy Wilder and Charles Brackett, it's marvellous entertainment, always lively and wittily funny. In its day, it was even considered somewhat 'naughty'.

Midnight Clear, A ● Ⓥ

1992, US, 108 mins, colour
Dir: Keith Gordon
Stars: Ethan Hawke, Kevin Dillon, Arye Gross, Frank Whaley, Gary Sinise
Rating: ★★

One more time for the futility of war, and at least the issues of World War Two are clearer in the snowbound Ardennes forest, than those of Vietnam. A patrol of six young Americans, holed up in December '44 at a chateau filled with art treasures, encounters seven Germans who, after snowball fights and singsongs round the Christmas tree, just want to surrender. A fake skirmish is arranged (for no seemingly viable reason except dramatic effect). This being the moralising, ironic kind of film it is, it all goes inevitably and messily wrong. Not much here, really, to keep you hanging around for nearly two hours. Decently acted and told, it would look better as an hour-long play on television. None of the cast is exactly charismatic, but then that was perhaps what the director wanted.

Midnight Cowboy ● Ⓥ

1969, US, 113. mins, colour
Dir: John Schlesinger
Stars: Jon Voight, Dustin Hoffman, Sylvia Miles, John McGiver
Rating: ★★★★

It was quite a shock when British director John Schlesinger's portrait of the grime and slime of New York's underbelly took the best film Oscar because it was the first to be honoured despite having an 'X' certificate. Today its subject matter looks pretty tame, but there was no denying its shock value more than 20 years ago. Jon Voight and Dustin Hoffman are both brilliant as the odd couple of drifters who try to eke out a meagre living as hustlers on the streets of the Big Apple. Sylvia

Miles is also memorable as one of gigolo Voight's many unsuccessful liaisons. Cinematographer Adam Holender wrings the last bit of atmosphere out of the locations, hitting a high spot with an absurd Andy Warholesque party scene.

Midnight Lace O
1960, US, 108 mins, colour
Dir: David Miller
Stars: Doris Day, Rex Harrison, John Gavin, Myrna Loy, Roddy McDowall, Herbert Marshall
Rating: ★★★

Based on Janet Green's stalwart seaside-rep murder mystery of the 1950s, *Matilda Shouted Fire*, which in itself was a modernised variant on *Gaslight*, this is a flossy Ross Hunter murder movie with Doris Day as the wife of wealthy Rex Harrison being terrified by eerie voices through the London fog. The special-effects boys went completely overboard with the pea-soup fog effects and Grosvenor Square is barely visible at all as rich American wife Doris (dressed in some of former top MGM designer Irene's most fabulous gowns) is pursued by the would-be killer.

Midnight Movie Massacre ●
1986, US, 86 mins, colour & b/w
Dir: Mark Stock
Stars: Robert Clarke, Ann Robinson
Rating: ★★

An affectionate spoof horror film about people in a mid-Fifties American cinema being devoured by a tentacled monster while they sit watching an opus called *Space Patrol*. The gory modern effects sit uneasily both with the sub *Carry On*-style comedy and with the affable recreation of an old-time science-fiction serial. But fantasy fans will be pleased with the presence of genre veterans Robert Clarke and Ann Robinson in an episode from the serial.

Midnight Run ● Ⓥ
1988, US, 122 mins, colour
Dir: Martin Brest
Stars: Robert De Niro, Charles Grodin, Yaphet Kotto, John Ashton, Joe Pantoliano
Rating: ★★★★

Looking leaner than in many of his recent films, Robert De Niro's in good form here as a modern-day bounty hunter intent on capturing his biggest prize in years – bail-jumping embezzler Charles Grodin – in New York and taking him across country to Los Angeles. It should be an easy job, a

'midnight run', but the accountant has robbed the Mafia. Soon enough the FBI, the Mob and a rival bounty hunter are all in pursuit. Subsequent developments run like a slightly darker *Planes, Trains and Automobiles*, with enough action to keep the plot in a state of perpetual motion. *Beverly Hills Cop* director Martin Brest handles the action with elan and the by-play between odd couple De Niro and Grodin produces genuine comic sparks. The film belongs firmly to the hangdog fugitive, a part in which Grodin gives his best performance in years, creating a funny/sad, canny/grumbling character who never sheds our sympathy.

Midnight Sting ●
(aka: Diggstown)
1992, US, 97 mins, colour
Dir: Michael Ritchie
Stars: James Woods, Louis Gossett Jr, Bruce Dern, Oliver Platt, Heather Graham, Randall 'Tex' Cobb
Rating: ★★★

The sting in this lively tale is the con set up by hustler James Woods to relieve a rich but evil businessman (Bruce Dern) of his wealth. And the method is to entice him to bet that ageing boxer 'Honey' Roy Palmer (Louis Gossett) can't knock out 10 men in successive bouts in a prize fight bonanza. The tournament is loaded with skulduggery, as Woods and Dern attempt to out-con each other, and the boxing action is first-class – although there's rather a lot of it for those of a more sensitive disposition. Sparkling entertainment, though, and not just for fans of the sport.

Midnight Story, The O
1957, US, 89 mins, b/w
Dir: Joseph Pevney
Stars: Tony Curtis, Marisa Pavan, Gilbert Roland, Ted de Corsia
Rating: ★★

Exciting, crisply-paced thriller, formerly known in Britain as *Appointment udth a Shadow*. Tony Curtis is a traffic cop who plays a lone hand in tracking down the murderer of a priest. The cast is good, but the production has a hand-me-down look.

Midsummer Night's Dream, A ☉
1935, US, 117 mins, b/w
Dir: William Dieterle, Max Reinhardt
Stars: James Cagney, Olivia de Havilland, Mickey Rooney, Dick Powell, Victor Jory
Rating: ★★★★

Quirkily fantastic Hollywood version of Shakespeare's play, with Mickey Rooney a quicksilver Puck, James Cagney a truculent Bottom, Victor Jory a splendidly sinister Oberon and Dick Powell a delightfully miscast Lysander. Anita Louise and Olivia de Havilland (as Titania and Hermia) were just about Hollywood's prettiest young actresses at the time, but the real star of the film is Hal Mohr's glistening, mystical black and white camerawork – a deserved Academy Award winner.

Midsummer Night's Sex Comedy, A O Ⓥ
1982, US, 88 mins, colour
Dir: Woody Allen
Stars: Woody Allen, Mia Farrow, Jose Ferrer, Julie Hagerty, Mary Steenburgen
Rating: ★★

This Woody Allen frolic is exactly what it says it is. There are a few laughs, much pictorial beauty in the photography of the New England countryside, and a fair attempt at catching the spirit of Shakespeare. Three couples pair off, re-pair, part, come together and air their neuroses within the comedy of anxiety familiar to Woody's fans, who will also be amused by his attempts to take to the air (the period is the early 1900s) in his newly-invented flying machine.

Midway
See: The Battle of Midway

Mighty Aphrodite ◑ Ⓥ
1995, US, 90 mins, colour
Dir: Woody Allen
Stars: Woody Allen, Helena Bonham Carter, Peter Weller, Mira Sorvino
Rating: ★★

Another of those talky, quirky Woody Allen films that will delight his fans and bore his detractors. Woody and gallery owner Helen Bonham Carter are married and adopt a baby boy. Six years later Woody, obsessed with the boy's brightness, hunts down his natural mother expecting a college professor, and finds instead a 5ft 10in. hooker (Mira Sorvino) with boobs as big as her permanent grin. Natch, Woody plans to reform the girl, sorts out a boxing farmer to court her, and buys off her pimp with tickets he can get through his sportswriting job. But, as the Greek chorus which accompanies the action warns, there's trouble in store. Helena is succumbing to the slimy charms of gallery partner Peter Weller and

M

Woody looks like missing out all round. Subsequent developments assume the kind of circular motif we saw in Woody's *Crimes and Misdemeanors*, before all the pieces of the jigsaw fall into place. Were it not for the increasingly potty chorus, this would run like a radio play: you could close your eyes and not miss a thing.

Mighty Barnum, The ○

1934, US, 95 mins, b/w
Dir: Waler Lang
Stars: Wallace Beery, Virginia Bruce, Adolphe Menjou
Rating: ★★

Wallace Beery (who had taken the role before in 1930's *A Lady's Morals*) plays the legendary American showman P T Barnum to the hilt (and often further) in this entertainingly fictionalised biopic. And there's a memorable slice of scene-stealing from Adolphe Menjou as the amiable drunk who eventually adds his name to Barnum's to form the celebrated Barnum and Bailey Circus.

Mighty Joe Young ○

1949, US, 94 mins, b/w
Dir: Ernest B Schoedsack
Stars: Terry Moore, Ben Johnson, Robert Armstrong, Frank McHugh
Rating: ★★★

This is the film on which the great Willis H *(King Kong)* O'Brien handed over the reins of monster magic to Ray (Dynamation) Harryhausen, who worked as his assistant on this enjoyable story about a giant but lovable gorilla. The orphanage fire scene, in which Joe rescues several children from certain death, was originally tinted.

Mighty Quinn, The ●

1989, US, 98 mins, colour
Dir: Carl Schenkel
Stars: Denzel Washington, James Fox, Mimi Rogers, M Emmet Walsh
Rating: ★

This ill-conceived affair tries to mix police mystery thriller elements with social comment about race relations in the Caribbean. On both scores it fails miserably. Denzel Washington is an island police chief under pressure to charge a childhood friend with the murder of a white businessman, who's been decapitated in a hotel jacuzzi. But his acting is all on the surface and the rest of the cast are criminally wasted, especially Mimi Rogers, who surely took the role because she fancied a holiday in a beautiful hot spot.

Milagro Beanfield War, The ○ ⓥ

1987, US, 118 mins, colour
Dir: Robert Redford
Stars: Ruben Blades, Richard Bradford, Sonia Braga, John Heard, Melanio Griffith
Rating: ★★★★★

Robert Redford's second film as director following *Ordinary People* is a suitably ecologically friendly story about the rights of citizens versus the might of the dollar and the preservation of a cultural heritage. The story of how one poor Mexican bean farmer's decision to cultivate land needed by outside developers leads to a stand-off between the downtrodden community and big business, it's a whimsical allegory that pits rich bad guys against poor good guys and never leaves any doubt about which side will win. Glowing location photography, a fistful of likeable characters and a lush score that won Dave Grusin an Oscar. Despite the draw of Redford's name and a cast that includes such familiar faces as Melanie Griffith and Christopher Walken, it was an undeserved box-office flop.

Mildred Pierce ○

1945, US, 109 mins, b/w
Dir: Michael Curtiz
Stars: Joan Crawford, Jack Carson, Zachary Scott, Eve Arden, Ann Blyth
Rating: ★★★★

Michael Curtiz, who made *Casablanca,* directed Joan Crawford to an Oscar as the tragic Mildred Pierce in another classic of what is now regarded as cinema's highest camp. Wonderfully well constructed, the film also has memorable portrayals from Zachary Scott as the worthless Monte, and Ann Blyth as the self-seeking Veda, both carving out repellent characters that equalled anything they subsequently did in the cinema.

Miles from Home ◑ ⓥ

1988, US, 120 mins, colour
Dir: Gary Sinise
Stars: Richard Gere, Kevin Anderson, Brian Dennehy, Penelope Ann Miller, John Malkovich, Laurie Metcalf
Rating: ★★

Richard Gere goes back to the farm for the first time since *Days of Heaven* for this think-piece about two brothers on the run, having burned down the farm whose fortunes have crumbled since they took it over from their father. The film reaches for pain and bitter irony but just misses them.

Milk Money ◑ ⓥ

1994, US, 109 mins, colour
Dir: Richard Benjamin
Stars: Melanie Griffith, Ed Harris, Malcolm McDowell, Michael Patrick Carter, Casey Siemaszko, Philip Bosco
Rating: ★

Pretty Woman with a teenage go-between. Would that this were half as successful. Melanie Griffith is the prostitute improbably (putting it kindly) hired by three pre-teens to show them her breasts for their $100 'milk money' savings. She subsequently flees from her pimp and his gangster boss and ends up staying in the treehouse at one of the boys' suburban home. Using her for a sex lesson at school (is this starting to sound unbelievable yet?), the boy introduces her to his widower father (Ed Harris) who falls for her on the spot. Malcolm McDowell gives another ludicrous performance as the gangster. Griffith's dialogue is largely unintelligible and even Harris seems ill-at-ease. They don't go well together. Don't pay good money for this, milk or otherwise.

Milky Way, The ⊙

1936, US, 88 mins, b/w
Dir: Leo McCarey
Stars: Harold Lloyd, Helen Mack, Adolphe Menjou
Rating: ★★★

Remade with Danny Kaye as *The Kid From Brooklyn*, this is the hilarious Harold Lloyd original, with Lloyd as the meek milman mistaken for a potential world boxing champion. Probably Lloyd's last classic comedy, it features great supporting performances from Adolphe Menjou and gravel-voiced Lionel Stander.

Millennium ○ ⓥ

1989, US, 108 mins, colour
Dir: Michael Anderson
Stars: Kris Kristofferson, Cheryl Ladd, Daniel J Travanti, Robert Jory
Rating: ★

Well dressed science-fiction claptrap about time travellers lifting deathbound passengers from crashing planes. There are some interesting ideas here but, with stiff performances, tatty effects, indifferent direction and a script full of such lines as 'It's incredible' that beg the viewer to agree, the whole thing runs like an uninspired TV miniseries. Kris Kristofferson looks too old and tired for the role of the crash investigator, Cheryl Ladd (as the time traveller) shows why she's never really broken out of television and poor

Daniel J Travanti hams in frenzied fashion in an impossible role as the professor who suspects not divine but alien intervention. At the predictably fiery climax, the time travellers open the gate for escape to safety. Audiences may rush for an earlier exit.

Miller's Crossing ● Ⓥ
1990, US, 115 mins, colour
Dir: Joel Coen
Stars: Gabriel Byrne, Albert Finney, Marcia Gay Harden, John Turturro, Jon Polito
Rating: ★★★★★

A perfect Twenties' gangster film beautifully written and scored and full of studied scenes. The flawlessly paced plot is crammed with darkness, menace and violence, but is faultlessly constructed and makes absolute sense. Tom Reagan (Gabriel Byrne) is the brains behind the throne of Irish ganglord Leo O'Bannon (Albert Finney): when they fall out, Reagan sets a complex plan in motion – and it's a joy to see the pieces of the jigsaw here fitting together towards the end. The dialogue is Bogart and Bacall crossed with a gangster relative of the Marx Brothers. 'Intimidatin'' helpless women is my business,' drawls Byrne to Harden. 'Then find one,' she snaps, 'and intimidate her.' Armed with this gem of a script, the actors give perfectly weighted performances. The expressions on their faces are never misjudged, shadow and angle adding emphasis to dilemma and resolution. The action blazes in bursts between the workings of the plot. And the violence is relentlessly real, earning a film without sex or any bad language an adult certificate on its own. Joel Coen's direction never puts a foot wrong.

Millionairess, The ○
1960, UK, 90 mins, colour
Dir: Anthony Asquith
Stars: Sophia Loren, Peter Sellers
Rating: ★★★★

No more delightful version of Shaw's play has been made than this. Sophia Loren and Peter Sellers are perfect foils for each other as the millionairess and the impoverished Indian doctor she sets out to enmesh.

Million Dollar Duck ☉
1971, US, 92 mins, colour
Dir: Vincent McEveety
Stars: Dean Jones, Sandy Duncan, Jack Kruschen
Rating: ★★★

Sandy Duncan is a smart little American actress-comedienne who never quite made it in the movies. Here's her best try, in a funny Disney comedy about a duck that lays eggs with solid gold yolks. It's hard not to be charmed by her bright-eyed, fizzy performance, especially when she is trying to deposit one of the eggs in her bank account. Personable support from a whole roster of Disney stalwarts, including Dean Jones, Edward Andrews, Joe Flynn, Jack Kruschen, Arthur Hunnicutt and Vaughn Taylor and a hectic chase that culminates in a rooftop rescue add to the winning brew.

Million Pound Note, The ○
(aka: Man With a Million)
1953, UK, 91 mins, colour
Dir: Ronald Neame
Stars: Gregory Peck, Jane Griffiths, Ronald Squire, Joyce Grenfell
Rating: ★★★

Witty, intelligent and charming, this film adds zest and zip to Mark Twain's famous story about a penniless seaman who finds himself living like a lord as a result of being in possession of a million pound note. Gregory Peck is in excellent form as the man lifted from the high seas to high society without spending a cent, and the appealing story is given an extremely attractive coat of Technicolor by cameraman Geoffrey Unsworth.

Mind Benders, The ❶
1962, UK, 101 mins, b/w
Dir: Basil Dearden
Stars: Dirk Bogarde, Mary Ure, John Clements
Rating: ★★★

One of director Basil Dearden's psychological thrillers, with Dirk Bogarde as the scientist who submits himself to the ultimate in mental stress, and a rare latter day appearance from John Clements as the government security officer who tracks Bogarde's gradual disintegration under pressure.

Mine Own Executioner ○
1947, UK, 108 mins, b/w
Dir: Anthony Kimmins
Stars: Burgess Meredith, Dulcie Gray, Kieron Moore
Rating: ★★★★

Tense, exciting and wholly absorbing, this psychological thriller was the best film of director Anthony Kimmins' career. Burgess Meredith's intense performance, given before his portrayals began to descend from character to

caricature, provides the film with a strong central pillar. And Kieron Moore's tortured portrait of the man being treated by Meredith's psychiatrist is a credit to actor and director alike.

Ministry of Fear ○
1943, US, 85 mins, b/w
Dir., Fritz Lang
Stars: Ray Milland, Marjorie Reynolds, Dan Duryea, Carl Esmond
Rating: ★★★★

Director Fritz Lang was still at his Hollywood peak when he made this suspense classic, bulging with sinister atmosphere (especially in the splendid opening sequences) and full of marvellous little touches worthy of Alfred Hitchcock. Ray Milland and Marjorie Reynolds have the leading roles, but most of the attention is taken by the performances of Carl Esmond – a handsomely menacing Austrian actor – and whining Dan Duryea, one of Lang's favourite villains. He takes part in one of the film's most gripping sequences, involving a stabbing with a pair of scissors.

Miniver Story, The ○
1950, US, 104 mins, b/w
Dir: H C Potter
Stars: Greer Garson, Walter Pidgeon, John Hodiak, Leo Genn, Cathy O'Donnell
Rating: ★★

Tragedy once again stalks the Miniver family in this stodgy sequel to the six-Oscar success *Mrs Miniver*. Greer Garson gives another sensitive performance as the mother of the family, and her young son, Toby, is played by William Fox, later to win adult acting fame as James Fox. Watch also for Peter Finch in a small role as a Polish army officer.

Miracle, The ○ Ⓥ
1959, US, 121 mins, colour
Dir: Irving Rapper
Stars: Carroll Baker, Roger Moore, Walter Slezak
Rating: ★★

Handsomely mounted if basically empty romance glossily set against the Napoleonic wars in 19th-century Spain. Director Irving Rapper moves it along so persuasively that he almost makes us believe its story of a nun (Carroll Baker) who falls in love with a handsome dragoon (Roger Moore) and runs away from her convent.

Miracle, The ❶ Ⓥ
1990, UK, 97 mins, colour
Dir: Neil Jordan

M

Stars: Beverly D'Angelo, Donal McCann, Niall Byrne, Lorraine Pilkington
Rating: ★★★

Irish filmmaker Neil Jordan returns to his home town of Bray on the coast of County Wicklow for this gentle, romantic fantasy-drama. A pair of 15-year-olds, Jimmy and Rose (charmingly played by Niall Byrne and Lorraine Pilkington), wander the streets (he to escape his drunken dad, she to avoid her uncommunicative parents), living in their own world, creating stories about the people they see. But the arrival of a smartly dressed American woman (Beverly D'Angelo) at the railway station is to send ripples across the waters of their fantasy life. No prizes for guessing that D'Angelo turns out to be closely connected to Jimmy in this variation on the Oedipal theme. It's a highly attractive, many-layered film which mixes fantasy, romance, dream and reality to tell its rites-of-passage story.

Miracle In the Rain ○
1956, US, 107 mins, b/w
Dir: Rudolph Maté
Stars: Jane Wyman, Van Johnson, Fred Clark, Peggie Castle, Josephine Hutchinson, Alan King
Rating: ★★

One of the last in the long line of 'Wyman weepies' which deluged audiences with tears in the Forties and Fifties. Beginning memorably with *Johnny Belinda* (which won Jane Wyman an Oscar), and including *Magnificent Obsession and All That Heaven Allows*, they progressed through to this story of a plain girl in love with a soldier in wartime, in which Heaven does indeed allow Jane a semi-happy ending. Her performance and the location filming on New York streets are big plus factors, and there's a bumper collection of the best Hollywood character people in the supporting cast.

Miracle of Fatima, The ⊙
(aka: The Miracle of Our Lady of Fatima)
1952, US, 102 mins, colour
Dir: John Brahm
Stars: Gilbert Roland, Frank Silvera, Angela Clarke, Sherry Jackson
Rating: ★★★

Gentle, unaffected film about three children who witness a miracle in a small Portuguese village in the early years of this century. The film has its share of action, too, as well as a sensitive performance by Gilbert Roland, and beautifully-toned Warnercolor photog-

raphy. It did rather better than expected at the box-office, where such subjects usually die the death, and it is well worth a look. Talented child actress Sherry Jackson shines in support.

Miracle of Morgan's Creek, The ⊙
1943, US, 99 mins, b/w
Dir: Preston Sturges
Stars: Betty Hutton, Eddie Bracken, Diana Lynn, William Demarest
Rating: ★★★★★

Frantic, fast-paced, outrageous comedy written and directed by Preston Sturges, with lunatic sub-plots going off everywhere. Betty Hutton was never funnier than as Trudy Kockenlocker, pregnant in wartime by a vanished soldier husband whose name she recalls vaguely as Ratzkiwatzki; the family of Kockenlockers discussing the unlikelihood of the name Ratzkiwatzki is itself hilarious. William Demarest is a tower of bewilderment as her father, Diana Lynn delightfully brattish as her kid sister and Eddie Bracken a riotously twitching rag doll as the idiot who loves her from afar (though not far enough for Trudy's liking). Riotous ending.

Miracle of the White Stallions ⊙
(aka: Flight of the White Stallions)
1962, US, 117 mins, colour
Dir: Arthur Hiller
Stars: Robert Taylor, Lilli Palmer, Eddie Albert, Curt Jurgens
Rating: ★★

Robert Taylor keeps a stiff upper lip as the director of the Spanish Riding School in Vienna, trying to smuggle his priceless white horses out of Austria in 1938 from under the noses of the Nazis. It's a little long and slow, but there's some fitful excitement and the colour is excellent. So, too, is the acting of Lilli Palmer.

Miracle on 34th Street ○ ⓥ
1994, US, 110 mins, colour
Dir: Les Mayfield
Stars: Richard Attenborough, Elizabeth Perkins, Dylan McDermott, J T Walsh, Mara Wilson, Joss Ackland
Rating: ★★★

Director Les Mayfield's previous credit, *California Man,* held out little hope of any subtlety in this remake of the story of an elderly man hired to be a Christmas store Santa Claus who, it transpires, really believes himself to be Claus. If finesse is predictably lacking in the treatment however, Richard

Attenborough turns out to be inspired casting as Kris Kringle, as perfect as Edmund Gwenn was almost 50 years before. Elizabeth Perkins is a down-to-earth heroine and Mara Wilson an uncute moppet and the courtroom scenes, although foolish, just about work. In other words the magic of the original material resists this heavyhanded re-stitching in some style.

Miracle on 34th Street ⊙
aka: The Big Heart)
1947, US, 93 mins, b/w
Dir: George Seaton
Stars: Maureen O'Hara, John Payne, Edmund Gwenn, Natalie Wood
Rating: ★★★★

Heartwarming piece of Hollywood comedy-fantasy which won three Academy Awards, one each for screenplay and original story and one for Edmund Gwenn's performance as the lovable old store Santa Claus who is all too convincing in the role. The child whose suspicious nature he has to conquer is played by an eight-year-old Natalie Wood – already a film veteran of some four years' experience. Scrape-voiced Thelma Ritter makes her screen debut as one of the mothers visiting the store; and Maureen O'Hara, as the store supervisor, takes a pleasant break from glamour and swashbuckling to prove herself an accomplished light comedienne, skilfully complementing Gwenn's eye-catching performance.

Miracles ○ ⓥ
1985, US, 88 mins, colour
Dir: Jim Kouf
Stars: Tom Conti, Teri Garr, Paul Rodriguez, Christopher Lloyd, Jorge Russek
Rating: RB

A pretty desperate comedy-adventure photographed in mucky colour that reminded us of those frantic Jean-Paul Belmondo capers of the mid-Sixties that took in several countries while putting hero and heroine through hell and high water. Here it's divorcees (from each other) Teri Garr and Tom Conti who lurch from a car crash in America through kidnap by Central American revolutionaries to crash-landing in the desert, storm at sea and capture by natives in the South American jungle. Ms Garr's makeup does gradually disappear but not her nail varnish, which sustains nary a chip to the bitter end. Everybody in the cast mugs like mad and Jim Kouf directs his own screenplay at breakneck pace but to no avail: it's still terrible.

Miracles for Sale O
1939, US, 71 mins, b/w
Dir: Tod Browning
Stars: Robert Young, Florence Rice, Henry Hull
Rating: ★★★

The last film directed by Tod Browning, who made *Dracula* (1931) and *Freaks*, is a strange thriller, in which magicians are murdered. Robert Young plays an illusionist who tries to protect Florence Rice after two of her friends have died while dabbling in the occult. Were their deaths magic or murder? Browning's well-paced direction keeps us guessing right up to the end.

Miracle Worker, The ◑
1962, US, 106 mins, b/w
Dir: Arthur Penn
Stars: Anne Bancroft, Patty Duke
Rating: ★★★

This powerful dramatic film about Helen Keller, the deaf, dumb and blind girl who triumphed over adversity, won Oscars for its two leading ladies, Anne Bancroft and Patty Duke. The director was Arthur Penn, later to make *Bonnie and Clyde*.

Mirage O
1965, US, 109 mins, b/w
Dir: Edward Dmytryk
Stars: Gregory Peck, Diane Baker, Walter Matthau, Kevin McCarthy, Jack Weston, George Kennedy
Rating: ★★★

A splendid star trio heads the cast of this intriguing thriller which, if it doesn't quite live up to the promise of its appetizing early sequences, nevertheless remains very entertaining and will keep you guessing. The plot (written by Peter Stone, who scripted *Charade*) has so many twists and turns that not even Edward Dmytryk's heavy-handed direction can muff everything; and he really lets his hair down in the film's best scene, when Gregory Peck finds an old acquaintance brutally done to death.

Miranda O
1947, UK, 80 mins, b/w
Dir: Ken Annakin
Stars: Glynis Johns, Googie Withers, Griffith Jones
Rating: ★★★

A superb comedy cast in the classic tale of Miranda the Mermaid. It's the film role, according to star Glynis Johns, for which people remember her most. Glynis plays to perfection as the

amorous mermaid who leaves a string of lovesick men floundering on dry land before returning to the briny. And there's a richly comic performance from Margaret Rutherford as Nurse Cary, who aids and abets Miranda in her intrigues.

Mirror Crack'd, The O Ⓥ
1980, UK, 105 mins, colour & b/w
Dir: Guy Hamilton
Stars: Elizabeth Taylor, Kim Novak, Angela Lansbury, Rock Hudson, Tony Curtis, Geraldine Chaplin
Rating: ★

Producers before John Brabourne have tried the theory that putting a cluster of veterans together creates a box-office success. Not here it didn't. Under Guy Hamilton's leaden direction, far too little is seen of Angela Lansbury as Miss Marple in this Agatha Christie mystery about a murder within the confines of an American film unit visiting Britain. For once, Ms Christie's elaborate plot scarcely holds water; neither do the performances, with the exception of Geraldine Chaplin's as the director's secretary. Don't blame the actors too much: directorial flair is sadly lacking. In fact, we preferred the mock-Fifties movie, *Murder at Midnight*, that begins the film. The storyline of the 'real' film is too subservient to stardom. Liz Taylor looks like a younger version of the Queen Mother.

Mirror Has Two Faces, The ◑ Ⓥ
1996, US, 126 mins, colour
Dir: Barbara Streisand
Stars: Streisand, Jeff Bridges, Pierce Brosnan, Lauren Bacall, George Segal, Mimi Rogers
Rating: ★★★

Another vanity project for La Streisand, who has no fewer than 12 mentions in the credits, this is the story of an ugly duckling who turns into a swan although, being Streisand, there doesn't seem to be much difference – save that the beautiful version combs her hair more. When Professor Jeff Bridges, impressed by her brain and her commitment to her work, suggests a sex-free marriage to Streisand, she accepts. The rest of the highly predictable story is culled strictly from the pages of the more rose-coloured women's fiction. What saves it is the witty and sometimes waspish quality of Richard la Gravenese's dialogue ('He asked me to some Alzheimer benefit – I told him to forget it'), the best of which is devoured voraciously by Lauren

Bacall in a show-stopping supporting performance that brims with relaxed confidence – not qualities one, sadly, could here attribute to the director-star.

Mischief
See: The Man With One Red Shoe

Misery ● Ⓥ
1990, US, 107 mins, colour
Dir: Rob Reiner
Stars: James Caan, Kathy Bates, Richard Farnsworth, Frances Sternhagen, Lauren Bacall
Rating: ★★★

Caught in a blizzard on the way back from the wilds of Colorado after finishing his new novel, Paul (James Caan) is rescued from certain death after his car crashes down a hill into the snow. Legs badly broken, Caan wakes in the warmth and comfort of a bed in a house in the countryside. But he still has a survival problem: his saviour (Kathy Bates) is as nutty as a fruitcake. Worse still, she turns into a fury when she reads his new novel and finds out that he has killed off Misery Chastain, the heroine of all the rest. This is a fine old two-hander in traditional shocker style, well played by Caan and particularly Bates, who won an Oscar: she's really frightening as the seemingly dowdy, frumpish spinster-sinister. None of it is exactly unpredictable, but director Rob Reiner does it well within its limitations, and gets well-observed supporting portraits from Richard Farnsworth and Frances Sternhagen as the local sheriff and his wife.

Miss Firecracker O Ⓥ
1989, US, 103 mins, colour
Dir: Thomas Schlamme
Stars: Holly Hunter, Mary Steenburgen, Tim Robbins, Alfre Woodard, Scott Glenn, Trey Wilson
Rating: ★★

Beth Henley's plays are southern states nostalgia pieces that haven't transferred too well to the screen. This one is about a magnolia-county beauty contest that the leading character's beautiful older cousin won a few years back. The younger sister (Holly Hunter), though plainer and less prepossessing, decides to try to emulate her cousin's achievement – but learns by the end how empty it was, and finds herself instead. Well, okay, I guess, but *Miss Firecracker* just barely justifies its existence as a film, with a screenplay that only occasionally rubs away its drabness to reveal the gleam of truth. There's one outstanding performance,

M

from Mary Steenburgen, as the spoiled older cousin..The rest of the acting is as humdrum as the movie and Hunter is harsh and unsympathetic.

Miss Grant Takes Richmond
See: Innocence is Bliss

Missing ●
1981, US, 117 mins, colour
Dir: Costa-Gavras
Stars: Jack Lemmon, Sissy Spacek
Rating: ★★★

An affecting and absorbing film. Jack Lemmon is the father, Sissy Spacek is the wife, searching for a missing American writer who has disappeared in Chile just after the 1973 coup. The Lemmon-Spacek relationship – he initially hostile but gradually sensing her worth – is what holds the film together and both give moving performances, Lemmon in particular blending his own persona with that of the character to produce a study of a not wholly admirable but thoroughly three-dimensional man.

Missing Pieces ○ Ⓥ
1991, US, 93 mins, colour
Dir: Leonard Stern
Stars: Eric Idle, Robert Wuhl, Lauren Hutton
Rating: ★

A comedy of ineptitudes featuring the one-off team of Robert Wuhl and Eric Idle, failed musician and failed poet respectively, who become involved with a mysterious inheritance which keeps threatening their lives. It's old-fashioned stuff where bodies keep turning up around open doors and in the boots of cars, and has a running gag about the name Hoo that dates back to Abbott and Costello. Lots of simple slapstick in the Three Stooges tradition, a bit of which is almost funny, including Idle's prolonged encounter with an electric mouthwash and a telephone in that order; and Idle's hiding in a vat of wine, a gag that dates back even further – to Laurel and Hardy. Wuhl, a Robert Preston lookalike, is notably less successful with a script that runs like a Gene Wilder-Richard Pryor reject. The film is bad, but not that bad: it will play better on video.

Mission, The ● ○ Ⓥ
1986, UK, 128 mins, colour
Dir: Roland Joffé
Stars: Robert De Niro, Jeremy Irons, Ray McAnally, Liam Neeson, Aidan Quinn,

Ronald Pickup
Rating: ★★★★★

Roland Joffe's film of Spanish and Portuguese oppression in 18th-century South America is all that the Cannes Festival thought it was when they awarded it the supreme Palme D'Or. It is brilliant, it is breathtakingly spectacular, it is packed with action and thought-provoking dialogue, it is heartbreaking at the end, and it is certainly one of the most unusual stories ever put on screen. At what cost, in both monetary and physical terms, one can only guess. Perhaps it's as well that such obviously Herculean labours have reaped their just rewards. As it is, thanks to the talents of Joffe and screenwriter Robert Bolt, the film remains a graphic monument of what madnesses and atrocities have been committed in the pursuit of 'progress' or, as in this case, religious persecution. The towering scenery is never allowed by Joffe to dwarf the drama; rather, he uses it to emphasise the issues at stake, as with impressive shots of the 'enemy' soldiers swarming up massive cliffs on their ropes, a little miracle of 'mise-en-scène'. The Mission is a rarity – a great film that entertains as well.

Mission Impossible ○ Ⓥ
1996, US, 110 mins, colour
Dir: Brian de Palma
Stars: Tom Cruise, Emmanuelle Béart, Jon Voight, Kristin Scott Thomas, Jean Reno, Vanessa Redgrave
Rating: ★★★

Fans of the TV series will love this elongated version, with dynamite special effects, an all-star cast and a spectacular climax atop a supercharged train in a tunnel. The downside is that you'll struggle to make sense of the plot (bits of which are just silly) and 40 per cent of the dialogue will fly by your ears in a buzz of jumbled sound. No matter, here's intrepid Tom Cruise as the agent whose colleagues, including Voight's Jim Phelps and guest star Emilio Estevez, are almost all blown away in a mission that proves all too impossible when someone betrays it. Are they all really dead? Who are the mysterious Max and Job? Are the guys Cruise hires to help him really on his side? Look sharp to spot some of the answers in a movie where dazzlingly exciting set pieces are spun round some stodgy dialogue. Did I mention that this is also a mission improbable? Chances are you won't notice when Lalo Schifrin's tremen-

dous original music is on hand to drive the action onwards.

Missionary, The ● Ⓥ
1981, UK, 90 mins, colour
Dir: Richard Loncraine
Stars: Michael Palin, Maggie Smith, Trevor Howard, Denholm Elliott, Michael Hordern
Rating: ★★

This kind of sideshoot from Michael Palin's Ripping Yarns is a black comedy about missionary Palin becoming (all too) involved with 'fallen women' in London's dockside. The film is quirkily entertaining, although fatally sentimental at its centre. It never quite seems to know where it's going. Michael Hordern's doddering butler is by far the most joyous thing in the film – forever losing his way in his employers' vast mansion and serving dinner in one of the bedrooms.

Mississippi Burning ● Ⓥ
1988, US, 125 mins, colour
Dir: Alan Parker
Stars: Gene Hackman, Willem Dafoe, Frances McDormand, Brad Dourif
Rating: ★★★★

British director Alan Parker always favours a sledgehammer to crack a nut and a lingering moment of agony rather than just the hint of violence. This horrifying study of racial violence allows him free rein to indulge in both practices, but not even his countless shots of burning crosses and frequent lynchings can detract from two powerful central performances from Willem Dafoe and Gene Hackman as FBI agents. Hackman should have won an Oscar for his portrait of a man who feels powerless to act to change things for blacks in America's Deep South but who knows how to wheedle information out of the locals. Frances McDormand also gives a standout performance as the wife of the local sheriff, who finds herself attracted to Hackman with terrifying consequences for herself. Peter Biziou's fabulous photography was a worthy Oscar winner.

Mississippi Masala ● Ⓥ
1991, US, 113 mins, colour
Dir: Mira Nair
Stars: Denzel Washington, Sarita Choudhury, Roshan Seth
Rating: ★★★

This is an attractive romantic drama with dashes of comedy on a familiar theme – racial prejudice – with a slightly different twist. Jay (Roshan Seth), a prosperous Asian lawyer, is forced to leave Idi Amin's Uganda with his wife Kinnu (Sharmila Tagore) and small daughter. In 1990, nearly 20 years later, in Mississippi, the family runs a liquor store and young Mina (Sarita Choudhury) has become thoroughly American. She also falls in love with a carpet cleaning operative, Demetrius (Denzel Washington). Not only is he black, but he comes from a distinctly humble background. The story is nicely told, with attractive performances from Choudhury and Washington as the illicit lovers, but examination of the real issues involved here remains rather superficial. More convincing is the depiction of Jay's loss of status in his adopted country and his inability, superbly conveyed by Seth, to let go of his old homeland.

Miss Mary ● ⓥ

1986, Argentina, 102 mins, colour
Dir: Maria Luisa Bemberg
Stars: Julie Christie, Nacha Guevara, Luisina Brando, Sofia Virnboff, Barbara Bunge
Rating: ★

A very slow, poorly constructed Argentinian film with all the elements of a continental sexploitation film of a decade earlier. The comely governess succumbs to her 15-year-old charge, while her employer helps to drive his family round the bend by laying a nubile widow across the snooker table. The film's pretensions to class lie in its setting – Argentina from 1938 to 1945 – and in the presence of Julie Christie as the governess. Christie, however, is not exactly ideally cast, and the rest of the acting is nowhere quite passable. Not even especially good to look at, it leans heavily on its attention to period – which its own fragmented structure works against – and on the performances of its younger players, of whom Sofia Virnboff and Barbara Bunge do show some aptitude, perkiness and individuality.

Missouri Breaks, The ● ⓥ

1976, US, 126 mins, colour
Dir: Arthur Penn
Stars: Marlon Brando, Jack Nicholson, Randy Quaid, Frederic Forrest, Harry Dean Stanton
Rating: ★★

Marlon Brando and Jack Nicholson add star power to this mud-strewn film about a bounty hunter after an obstinate rustler; but basically it's just another Western. Director Arthur Penn decks up the action with a few

new tricks, and Brando tries everything he knows to spark the role of the 'regulator', from a variety of accents to dressing up as a woman to shoot one of his victims.

Miss Robin Hood ☉

1952, UK, 78 mins, b/w
Dir: John Guillermin
Stars: Margaret Rutherford, Richard Hearne, James Robertson Justice, Sidney James, Michael Medwin
Rating: ★★

With Dame Margaret Rutherford at the helm, you can't go far wrong. *Miss Robin Hood* is a robust comedy of the Ealing school about an eccentric adventure story fan who becomes involved in a crazy plot to rescue a secret whisky formula. Dame Margaret is in fine form, especially when storming a newspaper office with a regiment of children. Watch for Reg Varney in a tiny role.

Miss Sadie Thompson ○

1954, US, 91 mins, colour
Dir: Curtis Bernhardt
Stars: Rita Hayworth, Jose Ferrer, Aldo Ray
Rating: ★★

Based (though rather remotely) on Somerset Maugham's *Rain*, this torrid drama features the gorgeous Rita Hayworth in the title role, following such stars as Joan Crawford and Gloria Swanson as Sadie Thompson, an 'entertainer' who finds herself on a tropical island, surrounded entirely by burly US marines. Among the soldiers crowding like moths around Miss Hayworth's flame-red hair, look out for the craggy features of Charles Bronson.

Mister Buddwing

See: Woman Without a Face

Mister Cory ○

1957, US, 92 mins, colour
Dir: Blake Edwards
Stars: Tony Curtis, Martha Hyer, Charles Bickford
Rating: ★★★

Universal were still grooming Tony Curtis as a big dramatic star when Blake (*Pink Panther*) Edwards directed him in this good, meaty story, with Curtis ideally cast as a crooked Chicago slum gambler. Charles Bickford donates his usual polished performance and there's forthright acting, too, from young Kathryn Grant, a sensitive and witty actress who later married Bing Crosby. Solid, underrated drama extremely well photographed

in Eastman Colour by Russell Metty.

Mister 880 ☉

1950, US, 90 mins, b/w
Dir: Edmund Goulding
Stars: Burt Lancaster, Dorothy McGuire, Edmund Gwenn, Millard Mitchell
Rating: ★★★

Wicked scene-stealer Edmund Gwenn is cast as an endearing old forger in this whimsical, winning comedy. The rest of the cast includes Burt Lancaster, Dorothy McGuire and some very good character players, but they just don't stand a chance. There's a good script by Robert Riskin and Edmund Goulding's discreet direction sews the package up nicely. Good for children too.

Mister Frost ● ⓥ

1990, France/UK, 103 mins, colour
Dir: Philip Setbon
Stars: Jeff Goldblum, Alan Bates, Kathy Baker, Jean-Pierre Cassel, Daniel Gelin
Rating: ★★

This very strange brew is an up-market chiller about a mass-murderer who may be the devil incarnate and can bend people and objects to his will. Jeff Goldblum (as the devil), Alan Bates (as his pursuer) and Kathy Baker (as the psychiatrist unwise enough to take him on) keep the story afloat with very little help from the largely wooden acting of their international supporting cast. Just so that you can tell when Frost has got to his victims, they have crosses in their eyes: just about the director's only concession to the conventional horror movie. His general approach, however, is far from sharp and it's left to hollow-eyed character actor Vincent Schiavelli to briefly enliven the proceedings as the cigar-chewing manager of a seedy boarding house.

Mister Johnson ◐ ⓥ

1990, UK, 102 mins, colour
Dir: Bruce Beresford
Stars: Maynard Eziashi, Pierce Brosnan, Edward Woodward, Beatie Edney, Denis Quilley
Rating: ★★★

This colonial tale of the 1920s finds director Bruce Beresford on sound ground. His central character is Johnson, a native wheeler dealer engagingly played (but not overdone) by stocky Nigerian actor Maynard Eziashi. Johnson wears a suit, tie and solar topi, thinks of himself as English and works for the district officer (Pierce Brosnan). Johnson's trouble is that, besides the deals and personal cuts that find their

M

way into his pocket, he is not above a little embezzlement (and eventually theft). It's these incursions across the thin line between chicanery and crime that eventually prove this likeable, always-in-debt rascal's undoing. Not, however, before he has helped with the seemingly impossible task of building a road that will connect his little outpost with the main highway and civilisation. Beresford establishes period and atmosphere immaculately, though his pacing is a shade too deliberate, if in keeping with the stumbling qualities of the natives' pidgin English. A nicely-made film that rewards the patient viewer.

Mister Moses ○
1965, UK, 103 mins, colour
Dir: Ronald Neame
Stars: Robert Mitchum, Carroll Baker, Ian Bannen
Rating: ★★

Robert Mitchum as a modern-day Moses – actually a gin-swigging adventurer who is lured on a strange pilgrimage by a missionary's daughter in an African-set action yarn which runs ingeniously parellel to the Biblical story, including a novel parting of the waves.

Mister Roberts ○
1955, US, 123 mins, colour
Dir: John Ford, Mervyn LeRoy
Stars: Henry Fonda, James Cagney, William Powell, Jack Lemmon, Ward Bond
Rating: ★★★

Henry Fonda recreates his Broadway role as a war-hungry officer aboard a cargo ship captained by a small-time Hitler (James Cagney, in his 44th movie for Warners). Jack Lemmon won the Best Supporting Actor Oscar as a sex-crazed ensign, but the film is an uneasy blend of slapstick and long boring passages. Despite its variable quality, the film was a big popular success.

Mitchell ●
1975, US, 96 mins, colour
Dir: Andrew V McLaglen
Stars: Joe Don Baker, Martin Balsam, Linda Evans, John Saxon
Rating: ★★

An ultra-tough thriller, one in a long line of hard-boiled detectives from Joe Don Baker. If the thought of seeing a maverick cop beating up the bad guys, slamming a crook's hand in a car door and bashing another repeatedly over the head with a rock is your cup of tea, then this by-the-numbers crime tale will fit the bill. But it has real problems

with a storyline that spends its first half on endless, uninteresting scene-setting. Mitchell is a cop with a nose for trouble. And he gets a deadly whiff of past-sell-by-date red herrings about a wealthy lawyer claiming self-defence over the savage murder of a burglar at his house. But before he can beat up his suspect, Mitchell is ordered off he case. Not that that stops him getting to the facts! *Dynasty* fans should look out for Linda Evans in an early role, cast against type as Greta, a $1,000-a-night call girl.

Mixed Nuts ◑ ⓥ
1994, US, 97 mins, colour
Dir: Nora Ephron
Stars: Steve Martin, Madeline Kahn, Robert Klein, Juliette Lewis, Anthony LaPaglia, Rob Reiner
Rating: ★★

This madcap Christmas comedy has a first-class pedigree, with Nora Ephron directing and Steve Martin as the star. Somewhere in the gestation period, however, an unlovable and at times unwatchable mongrel of a film emerged. Its comedy is very black and all extremely tasteless: Martin plays the head of Samaritan-style suicide helpline in the run-up to the festive season who faces not only personal failure and financial ruin, but every stereotypical oddball Hollywood can dream up. Martin hardly gives his best performance here; of more fascination is the casting of such 'heavy drama' players as Juliette Lewis and Anthony LaPaglia as a heavily pregnant couple with severe relationship problems, screaming at each other and running around with guns in cartoon style, and proving that comedy is best left to comedians. Always over the top, occasionally even funny – though you may not be around long enough for the laughs to start.

Mob, The ◑
(aka: Remember That Face)
1951, US, 90 mins, b/w
Dir: Robert Parrish
Stars: Broderick Crawford, Richard Kiley, Ernest Borgnine, Neville Brand, Charles Bronson
Rating: ★★★

A tough crime film, pretty violent for its day, filmed not only with sordid, fascinating characters but with early performances from soon to be well-known players, such as Neville Brand, Ernest Borgnine and Charles Bronson, here still acting under his real name, Charles Buchinsky. Broderick

Crawford is as hard as nails in the lead of this tale of waterfront corruption, in which it's sometimes hard to differentiate between the law and the lawless.

Mo' Better Blues ● ⓥ
1990, US, 127 mins, colour
Dir: Spike Lee
Stars: Denzel Washington, Spike Lee, Wesley Snipes, Robin Harris, John Turturro, Cynda Williams
Rating: ★★

Despite a big, glossy production, that diminutive dynamo Spike Lee doesn't quite do the right thing by the jazz world here. The film opens brilliantly, giving rise to hopes that it will open out into a gritty social drama in the *Bird* tradition, giving us insight into a jazz man's life. Instead, the film is soon marching to the beat of a different drum, with Denzel Washington providing star presence, but not enough depth, as the selfish New York horn player who freezes everyone out of his life. Even with prickingly individual supporting work from Lee himself, Wesley Snipes, Giancarlo Esposito (as the delightfully named Left Hand Lacey) and Ruben Blades (as Lee's Spanish-speaking bookie), plus some enticing love scenes and witty dialogue, this is a 'Bird' that never quite takes wing.

Mobsters ● ⓥ
(aka: Mobsters – The Evil Empire)
1991, US, 104 mins, colour
Dir: Michael Karbelnikoff
Stars: Christian Slater, Patrick Dempsey, Richard Grieco, Costas Mandylor, Anthony Quinn
Rating: ★★★

'It ain't enough Pop!' grates the young 'Lucky' Luciano (Christian Slater) in this moody portrait of the friendship of four of the gangland legends from America's prohibition era, setting the scene for their rise to the top in the world of crime. Nothing if not efficient, even though it rolls out most of the clichés in the gangsters' book, the film fiddles with the facts to create a sort *of Young Machine Guns*. Slater is first-rate as Luciano: dangerous and yet still sympathetic. Patrick Dempsey, Richard Grieco and Costas Mandylor are well in character as his cohorts Meyer Lansky, Bugsy Siegel and Frank Costello, while F Murray Abraham, Anthony Quinn and Michael Gambon are the gang bosses they must elbow past. Nicholas Sadler also makes a strong impression as the maniac killer 'Mad Dog' Coll. Despite the formula script, director Michael Karbelnikoff achieves a sense of imminent danger and death about almost every scene. Not a classic, but well-crafted.

Moby Dick ○ Ⓥ
1956, UK, 116 mins, colour
Dir: John Huston
Stars: Gregory Peck, Richard Basehart, Orson Welles
Rating: ★★★

The full power of Herman Melville's classic tale of Captain Ahab's obsessive hunt for the white whale that crippled and scarred him is brought vividly to the screen by director John Huston. The seemingly wayward casting of Gregory Peck as Ahab works well, although Huston had wanted to make the film 20 years earlier and star his father Walter. The mystery and romance of the sea is fully captured and the climactic battle with the whale is as epic a piece of cinema as you are likely to see. Huston, together with sci-fi writer Ray Bradbury, wrote a script that was pretty faithful to the book, stamping this film as one of the most enduring and exciting sea sagas ever made. Oswald Morris' unusual colour photography vividly conveys the bleaker qualities of the hunt.

Model Murder Case, The
See: Girl in the Headlines

Modern Miracle, The
See: The Story of Alexander Graham Bell

Modern Romance ◖
1981, US, 89 mins, colour
Dir., Albert Brooks
Stars: Albert Brooks, Kathryn Harrold, Bruno Kirby
Rating. ★★

Albert Brooks' fate in his film career has been a bit like that of the character he played in *Broadcast News*: talented but never quite making it on the big occasion. Alternately uncomfortable and very funny, this is a typically Brooksian view of an on-off romance, benefiting from the comedian's wry eye for the follies of modern life.

Moderns, The ● Ⓥ
1988, US, 121 mins, colour
Dir: Alan Rudolph
Stars: Keith Carradine, Linda Fiorentino, Genevieve Bujold, Geraldine Chaplin
Rating: ★★

Strong on atmosphere but less interesting in content, this is a skilful and

elaborate evocation of Paris in the 1920s, or more accurately its artists' quarter at that time. Although skilfully structured, the results still run more like a TV mini-series than a film. One admires director Alan Rudolph's beginning, with real-life Paris 1926 footage speeded up, to indicate people hurrying and scurrying about and getting nowhere, but, of the performances thereafter, only Keith Carradine's rises above the ordinary. Evocation can only go so far in itself, and these artistic butterflies and barnacles grow tiresome before the film is half-way through.

Modern Times ⊙ Ⓥ
1936, US, 87 mins, b/w
Dir: Charles Chaplin
Stars: Charlie Chaplin, Paulette Goddard, Chester Conklin
Rating: ★★★★

'Modern times' buffet Charlie Chaplin's tramp in this classic, much in the fashion that sound films offended his pantomimist's sensibilities. But the little man, moving from hapless factory worker to singing waiter, triumphs over adversity just as Chaplin the film-maker proved victorious over sound, his only dialogue being a song in gibberish Italian. There is, however, also Chaplin's own music, which includes the 'Smile' theme. His wife-to-be Paulette Goddard is charming in the feminine lead.

Modesty Blaise ○
1966, UK, 119 mins, colour
Dir: Joseph Losey
Stars: Monica Vitti, Dirk Bogarde, Terence Stamp, Harry Andrews
Rating: ★★

Director Joseph Losey makes no pretence at reality in his colourful adaptation of Peter O'Donnell's famous strip-cartoon thriller. Fantasy, or perhaps phantasmagoria, is the keynote of the proceedings. Monica Vitti is hardly ideal casting in the title role, and far from O'Donnell's (and Jim Holdaway's) original image. Terence Stamp is a dark-haired, brawny Willie Garvin. But the best of the characters is Dirk Bogarde's cool villain, with his endless collection of parasols – a man who only sheds his perfumed wig when the going gets hot. The best individual moment also belongs to Bogarde: staked out in the desert, he croaks 'Champagne, champagne. Also good are Clive Revill, as his twitching Scots assistant, and Rossella Falk as a villainess who kills her victims on the stoat and rabbit principle.

Mogambo ○
1953, US, 116 mins, colour
Dir: John Ford
Stars: Clark Gable, Ava Gardner, Grace Kelly, Donald Sinden, Eric Pohlmann
Rating: ★★

John Ford directed this jungle romance and Clark Gable, Ava Gardner and Grace Kelly star in it, which should guarantee a high quality entertainment. But it doesn't. Gable is a white hunter in Kenya, Ava Gardner is a wisecracking showgirl who falls for him. But along comes Grace Kelly, with husband Donald Sinden in tow and Gable goes for her. Yes, the old eternal triangle. If all this sounds a mite too familiar, it's because the film is merely a remake of the 1932 Gable/Jean Harlow vehicle *Red Dust*. Only the names and locations have been changed to fool the unwary. *Mogambo* looks better thanks to good location photography in Africa, but the original film had a sharper script and a steamier atmosphere.

Mohawk ○
1956, US, 79 mins, colour
Dir: Kurt Neumann
Stars: Scott Brady, Rita Gam, Neville Brand, Lori Nelson, John Hoyt, Allison Hayes
Rating: ★★

Take about 100 Western clichés all in the same film, superb Pathecolor photography, fine action scenes, pallid acting (with the notable exception of Rita Gam) and an unusually inventive music score and you have this bizarre mixture of good and bad, which is, in turn exciting and unintentionally hilarious. Most of the well-known cast (including Ted De Corsia and Mae Clarke as Red Indians!) seem to lack interest in the project. In view of the corny ending they knew they were coming to, you probably can't blame them.

Molly and Lawless John ○
1972, US, 97 mins, colour
Dir: Gary Nelson
Stars: Vera Miles, Sam Elliott, Clu Gulager, John Anderson
Rating: ★★

This rugged Western, which was described by one American reviewer as 'almost a love story', features a fine role for Vera Miles, one of Hitchcock's favourite actresses. She plays a much put-upon wife who forsakes her sheriff husband to flee to Mexico with a wanted outlaw. John Anderson has some powerful moments as the sheriff, and

M

so does the redoubtable Clu Gulager as his obnoxiously cocky sidekick.

Molly Maguires, The ○
1968, US, 123 mins, colour
Dir: Martin Ritt
Stars: Richard Harris, Sean Connery, Samantha Eggar, Frank Finlay, Anthony Zerbe
Rating: ★★★★

Probably Martin Ritt's most consistently underrated film – a grippingly dramatic story of unrest and sabotage in the grim Pennsylvania coal mines during the second half of the 19th century. The claustrophobic atmosphere of oppression and poverty is vividly caught, and the emotions of the major characters ripped gut-raw, with Richard Harris and Sean Connery each giving one of their strongest and most moving performances.

Mom and Dad Save the World ○ ⓥ
1992, US, 88 mins, colour
Dir: Greg Beeman
Stars: Teri Garr, Jeffrey Jones, Jon Lovitz, Eric Idle, Wallace Shawn, Kathy Ireland
Rating: ★★★

You'll have to be in a really silly mood to enjoy this one. Wholesome American couple Madge and Dick Nelson (Teri Garr, Jeffrey Jones) head for Santa Barbara for a rare romantic weekend. Some weekend! In no time at all, they find themselves whisked off to the planet Spengo by its evil emperor, who plans to make Madge his bride before he destroys the Earth with his all-consuming death ray! It's up to Madge and Dick to save the cosmos, and the whole cast has at least as much fun as the audience in this supremely daft but often captivating *Flash Gordon*-style space pantomime.

Moment By Moment ●
1978, US, 102 mins, colour
Dir: Jane Wagner
Stars: Lily Tomlin, John Travolta
Rating: ★

An unashamedly romantic film spun around the hopefully body beautiful of John Travolta. But the best performances in this beautifully coloured animated postcard from the beaches of California come from the women: comedienne Lily Tomlin, playing it straight as Travolta's toy-woman, and Debra Feuer, as the ex-Mrs Mickey Rourke, as Stacie. Not good, but perhaps not quite as bad as you've been led to believe.

Moment of Danger ○
(aka: Malaga)
1960, UK, 87 mins, b/w
Dir: Laslo Benedek
Stars: Trevor Howard, Dorothy Dandridge, Edmund Purdom, Michael Hordern
Rating: ★★

A chase thriller directed by Laslo Benedek, who made Marlon Brando's famous film *The Wild One*. The only assets of this sluggish drama, though, are a gritty portrayal by Trevor Howard and good location photography in Spain.

Mommie Dearest ◑
1981, US, 129 mins, colour
Dir: Frank Perry
Stars: Faye Dunaway, Diana Scarwid, Steve Forrest, Howard Da Silva
Rating: ★★

A fairly grim and unrelenting film about the relationship between Joan Crawford and her adopted daughter, Christina. The star is depicted as a vicious, self-serving monster who beat her child for petty reasons. Doubtless many of the actual events are true but, of course, we only see one side of the story – Christina's. Although one longs for the other point of view, the result is certainly a very efficient case history, with hard-driving Faye Dunaway at times looking uncannily like Crawford. Little Mara Hobel offers a very forthright and clearly delineated portrait of Christina as a child but Diana Scarwid's interpretation of the adult Christina is less certain.

Mo' Money ● ⓥ
1992, US, 91 mins, colour
Dir: Peter Macdonald
Stars: Damon Wayans, Marlon Wayans, Stacey Dash, John Diehl, Joe Santos
Rating: ★★★

Damon and Marlon Wayans, brothers in real life, play a pair of lovable rogues in this frantic, romantic action comedy. Damon not only stars but also wrote the screenplay and co-executive produced. So he gives himself lots of chances to show off his range of Eddie Murphy-style comic skills as Johnny, a sharp-talking, small-time conman who meets the girl of his dreams (Stacey Dash) and decides to go straight – with sometimes hilarious and often dangerous results. Fresh, fast and funny, but also unnecessarily violent in parts. An enormous public success, though, in its native land.

Mona Lisa ● ⓥ
1986, UK, 104 mins, colour
Dir: Neil Jordan
Stars: Bob Hoskins, Cathy Tyson, Michael Caine, Robbie Coltrane
Rating: ★★★★

It isn't just Bob Hoskins' terrific, Oscar-nominated performance that makes *Mona Lisa* one of the more memorable British films in recent years. His role of George, fresh out of prison and working as chauffeur for a gangland boss' prize call-girl, certainly dominates the film, but there's also much else to savour. Director Neil Jordan adopts a rich visual style that turns London's underbelly (including Soho sex dives and the Kings Cross red light district) into a garish and nightmarish hell-on-earth. Michael Caine, hair slicked back, turns up in a couple of key sequences as seedy crime czar Mortwell, oozing false bonhomie, while Cathy Tyson hypnotically combines slinky aloofness with bruised vulnerability as the up-market hooker, Simone. Still, it's Hoskins' touching portrayal of unrequited love that so splendidly fills the screen.

Money Mania ○ ⓥ
1987, US, 95 mins, colour
Dir: Richard Fleischer
Stars: Eddie Deezen, Wendy Sherman, Tom Bosley
Rating: ★

When a dying conman gives a cryptic clue to four separate hidden stashes, each of $1 million, the chase is on to find them. If you think the plot of this chase comedy sounds a lot like *It's a Mad, Mad, Mad, Mad World*, you're right. There's one fundamental difference, though: this one isn't funny. When you see that the two main characters are called Rollie and Lollie, warning bells should ring. *Variety* summed it up. 'The film has no momentum, no thrust, no continuity and, ultimately, nothing to recommend it.' Don't complain you weren't warned!

Money Pit, The ○ ⓥ
1985, US, 91 mins, colour
Dir: Richard Benjamin
Stars: Tom Hanks, Shelley Long, Alexander Godunov, Maureen Stapleton, Joe Mantegna, Philip Bosco
Rating: ★★★

This is a sort of yuppie version of Cary Grant's *Mr Blandings Builds His Dream House*. Tom Hanks and Shelley Long are the city couple who buy their dream house, but the restoration turns into a nightmare. Some of the horrors will strike familiar notes with anyone who has been at the mercy of builders and plumbers, and some scenes are genuinely funny. Where the whole thing parts company with reality is with the house itself. It looks about the size of Buckingham Palace and you keep asking: 'How can they afford it?' Still, Hanks and Long, both likeable personalities, work extra hard to keep things bubbling and, for the most part, they succeed.

Money Train ● Ⓥ

1995, US, 110 mins, colour
Dir: Joseph Ruben
Stars: Wesley Snipes, Woody Harrelson, Jennifer Lopez, Robert Blake, Chris Cooper
Rating: ★★

Wesley Snipes and Woody Harrelson are back together, but in an action story full of elements that don't belong in a movie that deserves any credibility. Even the beginning has a long chase through subway tunnels when it seemed easier (and more efficient) to arrest the miscreants quietly in the first place. And there's something underhand about Wesley and Woody's transit police spending all day setting themselves up as drunken decoys to tempt jobless youths to pick their pockets. The film rambles on in fits and starts for far too long until we get to an exciting last 20 minutes when the boys, oppressed to breaking point by sadistic boss Robert Blake, decide to take on his money train themselves. Jennifer Lopez is the statutory curvaceous ever-lipsticked cop who comes between our heroes who, in one of the film's few novel touches, play foster-brothers, with Woody the one whose gambling weakness puts them in need of money in the first place. Chris Cooper shows real menace as a sadist who likes torching booking clerks.

Monkey Business ☉ Ⓥ

1931, US, 81 mins, b/w
Dir: Norman Z McLeod
Stars: Groucho Marx, Chico Marx, Harpo Marx, Zeppo Marx, Ruth Hall
Rating ★★★★

The Marx Brothers stow away on board a ship, pour themselves tea and coffee while living in 'kippered herring' barrels and try to get through customs all disguised as Maurice Chevalier. The scene where Harpo joins a Punch and Judy show is a gem of sustained comic invention.

Monkey Business ☉ Ⓥ

1952, US, 97 mins, b/w
Dir: Howard Hawks
Stars: Cary Grant, Ginger Rogers, Marilyn Monroe, Charles Coburn
Rating: ★★★

This very funny comedy, directed by the incomparable Howard Hawks, is about a monkey that accidentally invents a chemical potion that makes everyone who takes it 20 years younger. Cary Grant and Ginger Rogers display a delightful sense of comic absurdity. And Marilyn Monroe is in sparkling form as a non-typing, non-shorthand secretary. 'Ah well,' says her boss (portly Charles Coburn). 'Anyone can type.'

Monkey on My Back ☉

1957, US, 93 mins, b/w
Dir: Andre De Toth
Stars: Cameron Mitcheil, Dianne Foster, Jack Albertson
Rating: ★★★

Cameron Mitchell gives one of his finest screen portrayals in this compelling story of a champion boxer (Barney Ross – 'the man with the million-dollar legs') whose greatest fight is against drug addiction. The fight scenes are excellent, and Mitchell's anguished, harrowing performance is complemented by those of Canadian actress Dianne Foster as his wife, and Jack Albertson – years later to win an Oscar in The Subject Was Roses (1968) – as his friend.

Monkeys, Go Home! ☉

1966, US, 101 mins, colour
Dir: Andrew V McLaglen
Stars: Maurice Chevalier, Dean Jones, Yvette Mimieux, Jules Munshin
Rating: ★

Disney whimsy, with Maurice Chevalier beaming benignly, Dean Jones looking harassed and Jules On the Town Munshin making a rare latter-day appearance. It's nice to see Marcel Hillaire (the village mayor) playing something other than a head-waiter, but Andrew V McLaglen, noted for his big action films, seems a strange choice as a director and, as a result, the enterprise lacks sparkle.

Monkey Shines ● Ⓥ

1988, US, 113 mins, colour
Dir: George A Romero
Stars: Jason Beghe, John Pankow, Kate McNeil
Rating: ★★★★

There's monkey business here all right, and it's no joke. A mad scientist (well, hopped-up on drugs) is injecting human brain serum into monkeys, but goes too far with Ella, one capuchin that he gives as helper to quadriplegic Alan (Jason Beghe), rendered near helpless in a road accident. All goes well at first, with the beast even learning to work the telephone. Trouble is, the scientist keeps upping the dosage and the monkey, forming some kind of mind bond with her wheelchaired master, acts out his deepest hate desires, like wanting to dispose of the girlfriend who left him for, of all people, the surgeon who operated after the accident. Murder and mayhem follow in a film that gets progressively more exciting towards the end, when nailbiters may be down to the quick.

Monkey's Uncle, The ☉

1964, US, 87 mins, colour
Dir: Robert Stevenson
Stars: Tommy Kirk, Annette Funicello
Rating. ★★

This Disney studio sequel to The Misadventures of Merlin Jones was made with an eye to television judging by the fact that it consists of two separate stories, both concerning the exploits of Merlin (Tommy Kirk) and his pet chimpanzee. The children will enjoy the special effects and flying machine of the second story. Annette Funicello – billed here as Annette – has co-star billing, though she does little more than hold the chimp.

Monkey Trouble ☉ Ⓥ

1994, US, 95 mins, colour
Dir: Franco Amurri
Stars: Thora Birch, Finster, Harvey Keitel, Mimi Rogers, Christopher McDonald
Rating: ★★★

One of the better animal pictures in recent years, this one centres on the exploits of an adorably talented Capuchin monkey, which has a line in party tricks unmatched since Cheta the chimp pounded the jungle in the days of vintage Tarzan films. Harvey Keitel makes a predictably extravagant bad guy, as the gypsy hustler who acts as the catalyst for the story, when the monkey he has trained to lift the wallets and jewels of people on a beach's boardwalk escapes its hated master and ends up with Thora Birch, whose parents had forbidden her to have a pet because they felt she wasn't mature enough to look after it. Suddenly the nine-year-old is cleaning up her room, getting on with her parents and even

M

being kind to her brother, while the monkey, a real charmer named Finster, improves its own lifestyle at the same time. Of course, Keitel wants the beast back, there's a hilarious chase scene and the monkey even ends up in a kite hovering over the beach. Only occasionally uninvolving, the story's a certain winner with schoolgirls.

Mon Oncle ⊙

1956, France, 126 mins, colour
Dir: Jacques Tati
Stars: Jacques Tati
Rating: ★★★

Jacques Tati's famous comic bungler Monsieur Hulot takes on the world of gadgetry and the results are gently hilarious; joke follows joke in miraculously timed sequences. A distant relative of Chaplin's *Modern Times* this, but with an engaging personality all its own – and a lasting remainder of a unique comic talent.

Monsieur Beaucaire ○

1946, US, 93 mins, b/w
Dir: George Marshall
Stars: Bob Hope, Joan Caulfield, Joseph Schildkraut, Patric Knowles
Rating: ★★★

The success of *The Princess and the Pirate*, made by Bob Hope on loan-out to Goldwyn, encouraged his home studio, Paramount, to go for period costume again in this Hope romp based very loosely on the Rudolph Valentino film of 1924. He's a bumbler sent on a suicidal masquerade to the court of Louis XV of France, but gags are strictly Forties Hollywood.

Monsieur Hulot's Holiday ⊙ ⓥ

1951, France, 114 mins, b/w
Dir: Jacques Tati
Stars: Jacques Tati
Rating: ★★★★

Delightful first appearance of Jacques Tati's pipe-smoking, disaster-prone blunderer whose well-meaning efforts constantly bring chaos to order, especially when that order involves modern contrivances. Here, the mood is delightfully all-of-a-piece and full of wordless gems of comedy. Who, for example, could forget the rocket flying in through the open window at the fireworks display?

Monsieur Verdoux ○ ⓥ

1947, US, 125 mins, b/w
Dir: Charles Chaplin
Stars: Charlie Chaplin, Martha Raye,

Isobel Elsom
Rating: ★★

Charlie Chaplin shocked some of his fans with this sinister black comedy about a mass murderer. By now shaken and disillusioned by the antagonism shown towards him in America which, in the panic waves emanating from the Communist witch hunts, seemed to want to be rid of him, Chaplin mingled his black humour with some rather bitter pacifist statements. 'Mass killing,' Verdoux remarks when arrested. 'Does the world not encourage it? I'm an amateur by comparison.' Scenes between Chaplin and wide-mouthed Martha Raye are the highlights of the film. Audiences, however, laughed nervously at such goings-on, and the film was not a great success.

Monsignor ◗

1982, US, 122 mins, colour
Dir: Frank Perry
Stars: Christopher Reeve, Genevieve Bujold, Fernando Rey, Jason Miller
Rating: ★

A change of pace for Christopher Reeve from his skyward swoopings as Superman sees him playing a Catholic priest with a past and a degree in finance charged with solving the Vatican's cash crisis. Genevieve Bujold is one of the more attractive temptations put in his way by the odd screenplay, co-written by once blacklisted Abraham Polonsky. Very hard going.

Monster of Terror

See: Die Monster Die

Monster Squad, The ◗ ⓥ

1987, US, 83 mins, colour
Dir: Fred Dekker
Stars: André Gower, Robby Kiger, Stephen Macht, Duncan Regehr, Tom Noonan
Rating: ★★★

Discarding modern film fiends, director Fred Dekker goes back to the traditional Hollywood gang of mon- sters for this junior league version of *Ghost Busters*, as Dracula and company stir from the depths to fight for possession of an amulet that controls the balance between good and evil. Once every century, the amulet becomes vulnerable to attack, and the moment for Drac and the gang, has arrived. As well as Frankentein's creature, the Wolf-Man and the Mummy, Old Fangface has also inherited the Gill-Man from the somewhat more recent *Creature from the*

Black Lagoon. Although their opponents are a gang of sub-teens who believe in monsters, time-honoured traditions are not neglected. Thus Frank's creature befriends the five-year-old junior girl member of the M Squad and is soon converted to its cause. The rest is average spoof hokum, apart from a spectacular ending as tots and grots battle to the death.

Monte Carlo or Bust ⊙ ⓥ

(aka: Those Daring Young Men In Their Jaunty Jalopies)
1969, UK, 120 mins, colour
Dir: Ken Annakin
Stars: Tony Curtis, Susan Hampshire, Peter Cook, Terry-Thomas, Dudley Moore, Eric Sykes
Rating: ★★★

As the American title would indicate, this is a sort of sequel to that flying machine comedy, with Terry-Thomas again in dastardly form as an English nobleman who plans to sabotage *all* his rivals in the Monte Carlo Rally. Ken Annakin's direction finds most fun in the sequences where the cars Terry-Thomas has sabotaged start coming apart here, there and everywhere.

Monte Walsh ◗

1970, US, 108 mins, colour
Dir: William A Fraker
Stars: Lee Marvin, Jack Palance, Jeanne Moreau
Rating: ★★

Melancholy, elegiac, dusty-looking Western with Lee Marvin as a veteran cowboy who finds himself a dinosaur in an old west that's dying out. First film as director for award-winning cinematographer William Fraker; his debut has a nice nostalgic feel, but the pace is too slow to keep a good grip on the interest. But there's a touching performance by Jack Palance in an unusual 'good guy' role.

Monty Python and the Holy Grail ◗ ⓥ

1974, UK, 90 mins, colour
Dir: Terry Gilliam, Terry Jones
Stars: Graham Chapman, John Cleese, Terry Gilliam, Terry Jones, Michael Palin, Eric Idle
Rating: ★★★

A grubby, muddy and vile picture of the Middle Ages, told in the inimitable, anarchic style of the Monty Python team. The funniest scenes involve a Trojan rabbit, Robin and his minstrels, a crazed bridgekeeper and a fight between King Arthur (Graham

Chapman) and the Black Knight (John Cleese) in which Arthur has to sever all his rival's limbs, leaving only a head that rants for him to come back and fight like a man. Made on a tight budget in a way that only adds to its lunatic charm, such as scenes where knights don't have horses but are followed around by servants knocking coconut shells together.

Monty Python's Life of Brian ◐ ⓥ

1979, UK, 93 mins, colour
Dir: Terry Jones
Stars: John Cleese, Michael Palin, Graham Chapman, Terry Gilliam, Eric Idle, Terry Jones
Rating: ★★★

Irreverent was for once the right word for this Monty Python pastiche of the New Testament, which provoked a furious outcry from religious organisations. Far be it for us to join the debate here: suffice to say the results are very funny. Director Terry Jones and his team confessed themselves baffled at the protests and petitions. 'We didn't have any quarrel with Christ himself,' he said at the time. 'My feelings towards Christ are that he was a bloody good bloke, even though he wasn't as funny as Margaret Thatcher.'

Monty Python's The Meaning of Life ○ ⓥ

1983, US, 91 mins, colour
Dir: Terry Jones
Stars: John Cleese, Terry Gilliam, Eric Idle, Michael Palin, Terry Jones, Graham Chapman
Rating: ★★

Touted by some as the film with something to offend everyone. Well, not in this day and age perhaps, although 90 per cent of the content is about sex and bodily functions and sometimes the film seems more intent on portraying taboos than being funny, which is a shame. Even so, some of the material undoubtedly achieves its intention of being offensively funny, especially in a sex lesson by teacher John Cleese to his boys. Cleese and his wife demonstrate the sexual act while at the same time ticking off the class for not paying attention. One gets the feeling that this is the film the Monty Python gang needed to make because the BBC would never have let them. One just wonders whether they're chiefly hoping you'll be shocked at what naughty boys they are – or be too busy laughing to care.

Monty's Double
See: I Was Monty's Double

Moonfleet ○

1955, US, 90 mins, colour
Dir: Fritz Lang
Stars: Stewart Granger, George Sanders, Joan Greenwood, Viveca Lindfors
Rating: ★★★★

One of director Fritz Lang's last films, this is a stylish adaptation of Meade Falkner's classic story of 18th-century smuggling and derring-do on and around the Dorset coast. Joan Greenwood is in fine, astringent form as the snooty Lady Ashwood; and young Jon Whiteley turns in a very real portrayal of the fatherless boy who forms an affectionate bond with a likeable rogue (Stewart Granger), the leader of an adventurous band of freebooters. The plot, in which man and boy chase after a fabulous lost diamond, is full of narrow escapes from revenue men, slashing sword duels and wild chases over fen and moor. And there's one terrific fight between Granger and a halberd-swinging smuggler. Mark this one down as splendid entertainment.

Moon Is Blue, The ◐

1953, US, 95 mins, b/w
Dir: Otto Preminger
Stars: William Holden, David Niven, Maggie McNamara
Rating: ★★

A really not very naughty sex comedy for which director Otto Preminger harvested enormous publicity by getting it refused a Seal of Decency in America rather than delete such words as 'virgin', 'mistress' and 'seduction'. It was some years before the film was released in Britain. It did, however, herald the first signs of crumbling in the bastions of the infamous Hollywood Production Code, and marked a major step forward (or backward, depending on your point of view) on what could be seen and heard on screen.

Moonlight and Valentino ◐ ⓥ

1995, US, 110 mins, colour
Dir: David Anspaugh
Stars: Elizabeth Perkins, Whoopi Goldberg, Gwyneth Paltrow, Kathleen Turner
Rating: ★★★

This film about bereavement is worth catching for its best moments. Chief among these are stepmother Kathleen Turner's attempts to reach out to her ex-husband's daughter. She's one of four women on whom the film focuses following the sudden death of the husband of one (Elizabeth Perkins), whose sister (Gwyneth Paltrow), friend (Whoopi Goldberg) and stepmother (Kathleen Turner) all rally round. Good performances, but a moderate, not-of-this-world script. There's a debut for Jon Bon Jovi as the painter who lays the winsome widow; and an unbilled appearance by Peter Coyote as Goldberg's husband.

Moonlighting ○ ⓥ

1982, UK, 97 mins, colour
Dir: Jerzy Skolimowski
Stars: Jeremy Irons, Eugene Lipinski
Rating: ★★★

Rather a nice little movie, ideally suited to the television screen in its intimate drama, about four Polish workmen sent to England to 'do up' a house for a quarter of what their boss would have to pay English workmen. Jeremy Irons plays their leader with an expression of permanent alarm on his face, trying desperately to make ends meet and keep papers (with news of the Solidarity suppression) away from his workmates, presumably on account of the pictures, as none of them speaks a word of English. Soon he is reduced to shoplifting, an occupation at which, although he develops a naive cunning, he bears a charmed life. These escapades, both tense and amusing, prove the most entertaining part of this interesting film.

Moon Over Miami ○ ⓥ

1941, US, 91 mins, colour
Dir: Walter Lang
Stars: Betty Grable, Don Ameche, Robert Cummings, Carole Landis
Rating: ★★★

A kind of forerunner of *On the Town*, with two gold-digging sisters on the loose on a millionaire-finding Miami holiday. Made with irresistible verve and energy by its stars (especially Betty Grable, Carole Landis and Charlotte Greenwood) and by director Walter Lang.

Moon Over Parador ◐ ⓥ

1988, US, 106 mins, colour
Dir: Paul Mazursky
Stars: Richard Dreyfuss, Raul Julia, Sonia Braga
Rating: ★★★

Richard Dreyfuss excels as a small-time actor who spends a deliciously dangerous year impersonating the newly killed president of the island re-

M

public of Parador. A bit over-the-top at times, but fun to be with and, thanks to his central performance, you really do care what happens to Dreyfuss in the end. Raul Julia is a little more restrained than usual as the power behind the throne and all the company takes the comedy seriously enough for you to enjoy it. Especially relishable is Dreyfuss' first speech to the nation when he calls on lines from *Man of La Mancha* in his hour of need. Only minus: a noisy music score by Maurice Jarre.

Moonraker O ⓥ

1979, UK, 126 mins, colour
Dir: Lewis Gilbert
Stars: Roger Moore, Lois Chiles, Michael Lonsdale, Richard Kiel, Bernard Lee
Rating: ★★

Each new James Bond film was a bit like an annual outing to a pantomime: comforting old characters and familiar situations where credibility and logic play second fiddle to the wonders that delight the eye. The plot relies alternately on the inconceivable and the impossible and all the proven ingredients are here, with the customary quota of mechanical marvels, including a jet-propelled gondola that converts into a hovercraft, plus an impressive outer-space battle at the end.

Moonshine War, The ◑

1970, US, 95 mins, colour
Dir: Richard Quine
Stars: Patrick McGoohan, Richard Widmark, Alan Alda
Rating: ★★

Deep in whiskey-still country (Kentucky, to be precise) for an action film fairly reminiscent of Mitchum's *Thunder Road,* and with echoes from *Bonnie and Clyde.* It's a pity that the leading character doesn't have a stronger actor than Alan Alda, and the music seems inapt considering the serious tenor of the plot. But Richard Widmark, Patrick McGoohan and singer Lee Hazlewood are first-rate portraying varying degrees of corruption and repulsiveness.

Moon Spinners, The O

1964, US/UK, 119 mins, colour
Dir: James Neilson
Stars: Hayley Mills, Eli Wallach, Peter McEnery, Joan Greenwood, John le Mesurier, Pola Negri
Rating: ★★★

Hayley Mills, Eli Wallach, Peter McEnery, Joan Greenwood and silent star Pola Negri. What are the odds against finding that line-up in one film? Walt Disney somehow got them all together for this Hitchcock-style caper about smuggling in Crete. The story's a little long for its weight, but there's lots of local colour, Hayley gets her first screen kiss and Wallach and Negri enjoy themselves.

Moonstruck O ⓥ

1987, US, 102 mins, colour
Dir: Norman Jewison
Stars: Cher, Nicolas Cage, Vincent Gardenia, Olympia Dukakis, Danny Aiello
Rating: ★★★

A romantic farce set in New York's Little Italy, crisscrossing several couples who all seem to be affected by a huge full moon. A young widow (Cher) accepts a proposal, but falls for her fiancé's estranged brother, the loving couple encountering her father and his mistress at the opera, while his wife finds herself dining with a man who has been jilted by his young student, just as he was before in an incident witnessed by the young widow ... a sort of *Il Rondo,* as you can see, although director Norman Jewison and the film's music rather overdo the amore and Italian openness. Still, there are winning performances from Cher (collecting an Oscar), Nicolas Cage as the hairy ape who sweeps her off her feet, and Olympia Dukakis and Vincent Gardenia as her parents. A little slow at times, the film becomes more amusing as it goes on and the personalities of the actors begin to make an impact on their roles.

Moonwalker O ⓥ

1988, US, 93 mins, colour
Dir: Colin Chilvers, Jerry Kramer
Stars: Michael Jackson, Joe Pesci
Rating: ★★

A spectacular fantasy film telling the story of Michael Jackson's phenomenal cotsuccess. It includes recent concert footage and a remake of his 'Bad' video, this time starring eight-year-olds. But the eye-popping highlight is the seduction based on his hit 'Smooth Criminal', directed by Colin Chilvers, who created the *Superman* effects and using Oscar-winning make-up guy Rick Baker (who transformed Michael into a werewolf in 'Thriller') who this time changes him into a gleaming silver robot. Unmissable if you're Jackson fan, with Oscar-winning Joe Pesci as a fiendish villain.

Morgan – A Suitable Case for Treatment O ⓥ

(aka: Morgan)
1965, UK, 97 mins, b/w
Dir: Karel Reisz
Stars: Vanessa Redgrave, David Warner, Robert Stevens, Irene Handl, Bernard Bresslaw
Rating: ★★★

Raw-boned actor David Warner made his first big impact in this with-it comedy about a young man with a passion for Trotsky, Marx (Karl, not the Brothers) and all furry animals. Not surprisingly, perhaps, he sees himself as an ape-man – the cue for some nostalgic footage of Tarzan (Weissmuller version) and the incomparable King Kong. These Tarzan/ape-man sequences, which include Morgan invading his ex-wife's remarriage reception dressed as a gorilla, are the best in the film. He's also the proud possessor of a stuffed gorilla, which gives rise to the film's biggest laugh when he tries, to save it from a fire. 'My God,' gasps his father-in-law, as Morgan staggers out of the smoke with an indistinct figure slung over his shoulder, 'he's got my wife.' A trio of believable eccentrics in the supporting cast comprises Irene Handl as Morgan's Stalinist mum, Bernard Bresslaw as a harassed, hopscotch-happy policeman and Arthur Mullard as a wrestler called Danny the Gorilla. No wonder Morgan has an affinity with him.

Morituri

See: Saboteur – Code Name Morituri

Morning After, The ◑ ⓥ

1986, US, 103 mins, colour
Dir: Sidney Lumet
Stars: Jane Fonda, Jeff Bridges, Raul Julia
Rating: ★★

Alcoholic Jane Fonda wakes up to find she's lying next to a brutally murdered soft-porn photographer. With a history of alcoholism and blackouts and an assault conviction, she decides that calling the police may not be a good idea. Luckily for her, she runs into Jeff Bridges an ex-cop who decides to help her solve the murder. Quite a tense thriller results from this beginning, although it loses steam a bit towards the end. Fonda and Bridges are very good, but increasingly the film focuses on their growing relationship rather than the murder, which is what slows it down. Still, the dialogue is good and you've got to keep watching to find out whodunnit.

Morning Departure O○

1949, UK, 115 mins, b/w
Dir: Roy Baker
Stars: John Mills, Helen Cherry, Richard Attenborough, Nigel Patrick
Rating: ★★★★

This British maritime drama has all the stiff-upper-lip characteristics typical of the period, with submarine commander John Mills giving a virtual repeat of his performance in the 1943 Gainsborough drama *We Dive at Dawn,* but fine for all that. Richard Attenborough, as the stoker who becomes hysterical, also gives a solid performance, in line with many of his weak, blustery characters of the period. There are lots of other British stalwarts here – Nigel Patrick, Lana Morris, James Hayter (providing some light relief to the intense, life-or-death proceedings), George Cole and Kenneth More.

Morocco O

1930, US, 92 mins, b/w
Dir: Joseph Von Sternberg
Stars: Gary Cooper, Marlene Dietrich, Adolphe Menjou
Rating: ★★★★

Marlene Dietrich's first American film cast her as the singer and adventuress Amy Jolly, ensnaring then being ensnared by legionnaire Gary Cooper. Brilliantly shot by Lee Garmes, whose work was nominated for an Oscar, *Morocco* is a film of shadows and shimmering heat, painstakingly directed for maximum effect by Dietrich's mentor Josef von Sternberg. Marlene never looked more alluring, and sings three songs, including 'What Am I Bid for My Apples?' A trail-blazing box-office success.

Morons from Outer Space ●

1985, UK, 91 mins, colour
Dir: Mike Hodges
Stars: Mel Smith, Griff Rhys Jones, Dinsdale Landen, James B Sikking, Joanne Pearce
Rating: ★

Alas indeed that wonderful Mel Smith and Griff Rhys Jones should have got involved in this fifth-form farce about four low-IQ aliens at large on earth. Fortunately, both they and Jimmy *(Spender)* Nail have moved on to more suitable fare since. Best gag has Mel rescued from spacedrift by a repulsive alien who gives him the galactic heave-ho after finding that he isn't the right

sex. Don't stay awake waiting for further laughs: there aren't any.

Mortal Thoughts ● ⊗

1991, US, 104 mins, colour
Dir: Alan Rudolph
Stars: Demi Moore, Glenne Headly, Bruce Willis, Harvey Keitel, John Pankow
Rating: ★★★

A slick, flashback-framed psychological thriller which the director can't resist making too complex, with surges of slow-motion and an ending that is not only loaded with a creel-full of red herrings but doesn't play fair with what's gone before. By and large, though, this is a slickly-produced thriller starring real-life husband-and-wife Bruce Willis and Demi Moore, he cast as the no-good husband of Glenn Headly playing Moore's best friend. When Willis is murdered, the two women weave a web of deceit – and dogged detectives Harvey Keitel and Co must root out the truth. Good performances in an offbeat, unsettling film.

Moscow on the Hudson ● ⊗

1984, US, 117 mins, colour
Dir: Paul Mazursky
Stars: Robin Williams, Maria Conchita Alonso, Cleavant Derricks, Alejandro Rey
Rating: ★★

This episodic account of the adventures of a Russian musician (Robin Williams) who defects to America in the middle of Bloomingdale's department store has some amusing moments, but rather lacks charm. And it seems (no doubt deliberately on the part of director Paul Mazursky) that none of the people Vladimir comes into contact with is actually American. His lawyer is Cuban, his doctor Indian, his girlfriend Italian and so forth. This is partly because he lives in a ghetto district, although there should be sufficient novelty value in a Russian saxophonist to get him showbiz dates. Mazursky himself helped to write the script, which is peppered with sardonically amusing lines and situations. Interesting fare, though you may find it hard to get involved.

Mosquito Coast, The ● ⊗

1986, US, 117 mins, colour
Dir: Peter Weir
Stars: Harrison Ford, Helen Mirren, River Phoenix
Rating: ★★

Fans of Harrison Ford's action films will be sorely disappointed by this wordy, downbeat ecological drama. He's a father who rants and raves

against prepackaged, mass consumed American culture, and packs his unquestioning family off to the Mosquito Coast of Central America in search of a Utopian lifestyle. But as Ford's character begins to unravel, so does this film, even though scriptwriter Paul Schrader makes the anti-hero more attractive and likeable than he was in Paul Theroux's original novel. Helen Mirren has little to do in the underwritten role of his wife, but River Phoenix successfully started to branch out from teen pictures as the eldest son who reflects his father's complex character and also acts as narrator. It's yet another brave attempt by Australian director Peter Weir to explore an unfriendly culture caught in a moment of decision, but in the end the miserable ending is the film's undoing.

Mosquito Squadron O

1968, UK, 90 mins, colour
Dir: Boris Sagal
Stars: David McCallum, Suzanne Neve, David Buck
Rating: ★★

It seems strange that anyone should still have wanted to make a standard World War Two action film in the late Sixties but, within the limited budget, experienced director Boris Sagal turns in a good job, with an exciting bombing raid at the end and sturdy performances.

Moss Rose O

1947, US, 83 mins, b/w
Dir: Gregory Ratoff
Stars: Peggy Cummins, Victor Mature, Ethel Barrymore, Vincent Price
Rating: ★★★

Absorbing and well-acted Edwardian thriller that will keep most viewers busily guessing until the final reel. Peggy Cummins' cockney accent has to be heard to be believed, but Ethel Barrymore gives a splendid, full-blooded performance as a domineering old dowager. Vincent Price is at his best and most restrained as the policeman on the case.

Most Dangerous Game, The O

(aka: The Hounds of Zaroff)
1932, US, 63 mins, b/w
Dir: Irving Pichel, Ernest B Schoedsack
Stars: Fay Wray, Joel McCrea, Leslie Banks, Robert Armstrong
Rating: ★★★

A classic, chilling chase story which has been remade and imitated many times

M

since. It provided a showy debut role in the cinema for British actor Leslie Banks as the sadistic count who hunts human quarry on his misty island. Badly wounded in World War One, Banks had bravely resumed his career that was to be dogged by illness in its later years. Among the stars he menaces here is the lustrous Fay Wray who was to fall into the clutches of an even bigger monster the following year when she starred in *King Kong*.

Mother ○ Ⓥ

1996, US, 101 mins, colour
Dir: Albert Brooks
Stars: Albert Brooks, Debbie Reynolds, Rob Morrow, Isabel Glasser, Lisa Kudrow
Rating: ★★

This is about as slight as movies get. Sci-fi author Albert Brooks is a failure at marriage and, blaming his poor relationship with his mother (Debbie Reynolds), decides to go back to live with her to find out what went wrong. That's the whole deal, but the film's problem is that, like Brooks' character, it's afraid to let go. Nothing that's riotous or penetrating or perceptive happens here and Brooks' brand of urban angst is several notches below Woody Allen's in its attempts to connect with our funny bone. It's left to Reynolds' rare latter-day appearance to preserve our interest, which she does with good grace if not much style. 'Never look back,' she wisely advises her son. 'They might be gaining on you.'

Mother, Jugs and Speed ○

1976, US, 95 mins, colour
Dir: Peter Yates
Stars: Bill Cosby, Raquel Welch, Harvey Keitel, Larry Hagman
Rating: ★★

One of those films that goes off in all directions. It's a case of love me, love my moods in this black comedy about rival ambulance services. And, while the funny bits are often very funny, the serious stuff works less well. Bill Cosby pulls the twin shafts of the plot with most success, and you have to admire a film that can make you fall about – Raquel Welch proves surprisingly adept with some of Tom Mankiewicz's wittier dialogue – after a couple of dramatic disasters.

Mother's Boys ● Ⓥ

1993, US, 95 mins, colour
Dir: Yves Simoneau
Stars: Jamie Lee Curtis, Peter Gallagher,

Joanne Whalley-Kilmer, Vanessa Redgrave, Joss Ackland
Rating: ★

A laughably ludicrous, if not entirely unenjoyable chiller starring Jamie Lee Curtis as an unbalanced woman who walked out on her husband and three boys a few years ago. Now that hubby (Peter Gallagher) has fallen in love with a teacher (Joanne Whalley-Kilmer), and sues for a divorce, his ex-wife decides she wants her family back. None of what follows is soundly enough based to have any impact beyond making you giggle, leading to a quite preposterous climax, with a car balanced on a tree overhanging a chasm. Jamie Lee tries hard in a blonde wig to be bad, and Joanne tries hard to be good, but both are wildly cast against type and arouse the wrong sort of reaction. Gallagher is just lost open-mouthed in the middle. Vanessa Redgrave is in for a few lines as granny and to give her stunt girl a chance to fall spectacularly down a flight of stairs.

Mother Night ◐ Ⓥ

1996, US/Can, 114 mins, colour
Dir: Keith Gordon
Stars: Nick Nolte, John Goodman, Sheryl Lee, Alan Arkin, David Strathairn
Rating: ★★

A fascinating central theme eventually gets lost here in a story that proves silly once too often. Nolte is an American playwright living in 1939 in Germany who is offered an intriguing deal by a mysterious US agent (Goodman): to be an apparent traitor, making weekly pro-Nazi, anti-Jewish broadcasts while working for the Allies through a secret radio code unknown even to him. Feeling he and his wife are on an island of their own making, he accepts. After she is killed, he's captured by US soldiers but returned to America in anonymity on Goodman's intervention. Why Nolte would hang on to his own name there, making him possible to trace, is only one of several foolish script contrivances that involve caricatured white supremists and an unconvincing last-minute change of heart by Nolte when it seems he's achieved his goal. A long slog, this, for meagre rewards.

Mother Wore Tights ○

1947, US, 107 mins, colour
Dir: Walter Lang
Betty Grable, Dan Dailey, Mona Freeman, Connie Marshall
Rating: ★★★

Probably the best of the post-war Betty Grable-Dan Dailey musicals at Fox, with superior direction by Walter Lang and dazzling colour camerawork by Harry Jackson. Alfred Newman won an Oscar for the best scoring of a musical and the film was a tremendous public success. The voice of the narrator is that of Oscar-winning actress Anne Baxter, who ironically co-starred with Dailey the following year in a not dissimilar musical called *You're My Everything*.

Moulin Rouge ○ Ⓥ

1952, UK, 120 mins, colour
Dir: John Huston
Stars: Jose Ferrer, Colette Marchand, Zsa Zsa Gabor, Christopher Lee
Rating: ★★★★

This stunningly beautiful film was director John Huston's triumph. He and Antony Veiller did a strong job of adapting Pierre La Mure's fictionalised biography of the famed French artist Toulouse-Lautrec for the screen. Jose Ferrer's extraordinary performance earned him an Academy Award nomination. The film, too, was nominated as Best Picture, Huston received an Oscar nomination as director and Colette Marchand, playing Marie, also received an Oscar nomination. The superb colour cinematography by Oswald Morris and Paul Sheriff's art direction created an impressive evocation of 19th-century Montmartre.

Mountain, The ○

1956, US, 105 mins, colour
Dir: Edward Dmytryk
Stars: Spencer Tracy, Robert Wagner, Claire Trevor, William Demarest
Rating: ★★

Beautifully photographed tale of selflessness and greed which maintains a fair degree of suspense. Spencer Tracy, as usual, displays a quiet dignity that take one's attention away from the plot's shortcomings. At times Tracy looks as imposing as the mountain with his crevasse-lined face capped by snowy hair, while Robert Wagner has winning but ruthless charm – although the disparity in their ages (they play brothers) is disconcerting.

Mountains of the Moon ● Ⓥ

1989, US, 135 mins, colour
Dir: Bob Rafelson
Stars: Patrick Bergin, Iain Glen, Richard E Grant, Fiona Shaw, Anna Massey
Rating: ★★★

The story of explorers Burton and Speke and their search for the Nile in the 1800s gains new life in this handsomely produced account. It has the added trimmings of some spicy sex scenes between Burton (Patrick Bergin) and his wife-to-be (the interesting Fiona Shaw) and red-blooded violence in which steel is quite often seen to penetrate flesh in one way or another – whether slowly, or with the speed of the spear that splits Burton (who survives) from cheekbone to cheekbone in one of the action's early skirmishes. Although the film's final segment telescopes a few years, director Bob Rafelson can certainly be excused such licence in view of the dramatic effect it achieves. Overall, the narrative is a little long, and contains a number of minor scenes which could have been trimmned more ruthlessly.

Mouse and his Child, The ☉
1977, US, 83 mins, colour
Dir Chuck Swenson
Rating: ★

Too much talk and not enough action sinks this dullish cartoon, which sets out to be a sort of *Pinocchio* of the mouse world. The film's dialogue and sentiments will be over the heads of most children, despite the efforts of a talented voice cast that includes Peter Ustinov, Cloris Leachman, Andy Devine (his last work in film, appropriately as the voice of a frog), Neville Brand and Sally Kellerman.

Mouse on the Moon, The ○
1963, UK, 85 mins, colour
Dir: Richard Lester
Stars: Margaret Rutherford, Bernard Cribbins, Ron Moody, June Ritchie
Rating: ★★★

A sequel to the Peter Sellers comedy hit, *The Mouse that Roared*. This time, the tiny Duchy of Great Fenwick joins the space race! Ron Moody's crafty prime minister and Margaret Rutherford's Grand Guignol-style Queen Gloriana make it well worth watching.

Mouse that Roared, The ○ ⓥ
1959, UK, 85 mins, colour
Dir: Jack Arnold
Stars: Peter Sellers, Jean Seberg
Rating: ★★★

Peter Sellers is at his sparkling, zany best in this comedy satire with a Richard Lester touch (in fact, Lester directed the sequel The *Mouse on the Moon)* about a tiny European Kingdom which declares war on the United States. Sellers plays Tully Bascombe, who leads his country's chain-mailed army in its invasion, launched so that Grand Fenwick won't have to go bankrupt. Besides Tully, Sellers also plays the Prime Minister of Grand Fenwick as well as its decaying queen, Gloriana. Director Jack Arnold puts the fun across in free and easy style, and the visual gags include one great belly-laugh built around the television series *Robin Hood*.

Move Over Darling ○ ⓥ
1963, US, 103 mins, colour
Dir: Michael Gordon
Stars: Doris Day, James Garner, Polly Bergen, Chuck Connors, Thelma Ritter
Rating: ★★★

This comedy about a wife who returns from the dead (actually a desert island) was the film on which Marilyn Monroe was working just before she died. It was re-modelled for Doris Day and right from the outset she seems determined to make the star part her own creation, attacking it with tremendous verve, and turning what could have been a routine sex comedy into a gay and amusing occasion. Thelma Ritter has too little to do, but 'nervous' comedian Don Knotts has a few acid moments as a shoe salesman; crusty Edgar Buchanan makes his mark as a divorce judge; and waspish comic actor Fred Clark is so good as a hotel manager that it's a pity we couldn't have seen more of him.

Movers and Shakers ◐
1985, US, 80 mins, colour
Dir: William Asher
Stars: Walter Matthau, Charles Grodin, Steve Martin, Gilda Radner, Tyne Daly
Rating: RB

Could you believe that a comedy film with the above cast could, even at 80 minutes, be a total waste of time? You wouldn't? Then you have a reason for seeing one of the few films we've ever watched in which almost nothing seems to happen. 'It looks very nice,' says one of the characters early on, about a stone dinosaur. 'But it just doesn't move.' Yes, well, there's no answer to that. The 'plot', written by Charles Grodin whose talent with the pen is usually much sharper than this, is about a film company that buys the title of a best-selling sex manual and tries to conjure a movie therefrom. They fail, and so does the film, which has powder-puff dialogue, rooted camerawork and performances in search of a director.

Moving Target, The
See: Harper

Mr & Mrs Bridge ◐ ⓥ
1990, US, 124 mins, colour
Dir: James Ivory
Stars: Paul Newman, Joanne Woodward, Robert Sean Leonard, Kyra Sedgwick, Blythe Danner, Simon Callow
Rating: ★★★

Both a pleasant study of upper-class American life 50 years ago and a scrutiny of repressed womanhood, this is an opportunity for Paul Newman and Joanne Woodward to shine, with performances that, though not always naturalistic, are carefully presented for our inspection, reflection and pleasure. The story spans roughly the years 1930 to 1945. Mrs Bridge, though secure in her family, remains a totally subjugated housewife whose consequently disturbed nature gives rise to occasional tearful outbursts. Husband Walter is a stuffy lawyer with rigid principles who is desirous of his wife, as he puts it, but not always as affectionate as he might be. Although rather heavily preoccupied with sexual relations, this is nonetheless rather a gentle and old-fashioned film by today's standards, with one or two particularly fine sequences, such as the scene in which the Bridges sit firm at their dinner table while a tornado howls outside and the rest of the restaurant customers cower in the cellar. The film is also a little dull at times.

Mr and Mrs North ○
1941, US, 67 mins, b/w
Dir: Robert B Sinclair
Stars: Gracie Allen, William Post Jr
Rating: ★★

Gracie Allen without George Burns seems pretty strange, and indeed it's difficult to see why George couldn't have played Mr North in this story of a couple of amateur sleuths. The results are sometimes funny, sometimes strained, but there's a good supporting cast, including Tom Conway, Virginia Grey, Rose Hobart, Porter Hall, Millard Mitchell, Jerome Cowan and Felix Bressart. William Post Jr is a rather nebulous Mr North, while Paul Kelly is the Norths' harassed police adversary. Also in there somewhere is Keye Luke, famous as Charlie Chan's meddlesome son.

Mr and Mrs Smith ○
1941, US, 95 mins, b/w
Dir: Alfred Hitchcock

M

Stars: Carole Lombard, Robert Montgomery, Gene Raymond, Jack Carson
Rating: ★★

Alfred Hitchcock's single stab at screwball comedy teams Carole Lombard and Robert Montgomery successfully as a couple discovering their marriage wasn't legal. Hitch makes his customary guest appearance, this time as a down-and-out cadging money for drink. Miss Lombard directed this scene, making the director do it over and over again, demanding more and more powder to cover his reddening face. It was her way of getting back at him for all the practical jokes he'd perpetrated.

Mr Arkadin
See: Confidential Report

Mr Ashton Was Indiscreet
See: The Senator Was Indiscreet

Mr Baseball ◐ ⓥ
1992, US, 113 mins, colour
Dir: Fred Schepisi
Stars: Tom Selleck, Ken Takakura, Dennis Haysbert, Aya Takanashi
Rating: ★★

Given that one nation can see as strengths the qualities that another nation sees as weaknesses, that America is as culturally different to Japan as chalk is to cheese, and that popular Tom Selleck barges bear-like through his role as a fading baseball player transferred from the US to Japan, we could have had the makings of a marvellously funny culture-clash comedy. Sadly, there is just not enough originality in this formula frolic, every development signposted from Selleck's initial smart Alec stance to his conversion to a human being thanks to the love of a Japanese girl. Selleck is engaging as the head-in-the-clouds hero, but it's not enough to make this any more than pleasant fun.

Mr Belvedere Rings the Bell ○
1951, US, 87 mins, b/w
Dir: Henry Koster
Stars: Clifton Webb, Joanne Dru, Hugh Marlowe, Zero Mostel
Rating: ★★

The last of the three Belvedere comedies which began with the character's unforgettable appearance in *Sitting Pretty*, when he poured a bowl of breakfast food over an errant baby's head. This time it is the other end of

the age scale: Belvedere, the self-styled genius, once again played by crusty Clifton Webb, is let loose on an old folks' home.

Mr Billion ○
1977, US, 93 mins, colour
Dir: Jonathan Kaplan
Stars: Terence Hill, Valerie Perrine, Jackie Gleason, Slim Pickens
Rating: ★★★

This light-hearted action romp is fast, furious and fun. Italian leading man Terence Hill, simply bursting with star quality (although previously best known in spaghetti Westerns) made a belated Hollywood debut as the garage mechanic who suddenly comes into a fortune and is immediately beset by homicidal vultures who will stop at nothing to get their hands on it. Hill and Valerie Perrine (she's the femme fatale who falls for her intended victim) do all that could be asked of them. But it's a writer's and director's film. Both script and treatment are full of quirky little touches that mark the film as above average of its kind. 'Wait,' pleads a rapist cornered by Hill, 'perverts are people too.' But Hill is undoubtedly the man to watch – and watch him you do, every incident-filled step of the way.

Mr Blandings Builds His Dream House ○
1948, US, 84 mins, b/w
Dir: H C Potter
Stars: Cary Grant, Myrna Loy, Melvyn Douglas, Jason Robards
Rating: ★★★★

Cary Grant and Myrna Loy delight, and H C Potter directs with immense good humour, in this lovable tale of two city people who have a house built in the country to their own special and somewhat extravagant specifications, and get taken for a ride by every country trickster in sight.

Mr Deeds Goes to Town ○
1936, US, 118 mins, b/w
Dir: Frank Capra
Stars: Gary Cooper, Jean Arthur, George Bancroft, Lionel Stander
Rating: ★★★★★

Country bumpkin Gary Cooper inherits $20 million and finds himself the centre of curious attention in sophisticated New York. Jean Arthur is the hard-nosed reporter sent by an equally hard-nosed editor to ridicule Cooper and his honest country ways. As you might expect, she falls in love with him.

Even in 1936, this plot wasn't exactly fresh, but the perfect casting and delightful playing of Cooper and Arthur, coupled with Frank Capra's light but observant directional touch, made this an instant hit and a lasting classic. The character of Deeds is not particularly real, but Capra's trick is making you want to believe people like him exist (a device he used in all his films) so sit and watch honesty and sincerity win the day against the smart guys and the cynics – you won't often see it happen in real life!

Mr Denning Drives North ○
1951, UK, 93 mins, b/w
Dir: Anthony Kimmins
Stars: John Mills, Phyllis Calvert, Sam Wanamaker
Rating: ★★★

This vehicle for John Mills at the height of his success as the most popular star of British cinema walks the tightrope between suspense and comedy with varying degrees of success. A difficult subject (Mills' character accidentally kills his daughter's blackmailing lover) to treat as a comedy-thriller and director Anthony Kimmins and writer Alec Coppel, even though working from Coppel's own novel, don't quite pull it off. There are some good performances, notably from Mills himself, and from Herbert Lom, as the crook he kills.

Mr Destiny ◐ ⓥ
1990, US, 105 mins, colour
Dir: James Orr
Stars: James Belushi, Michael Caine, Linda Hamilton, Jon Lovitz, Rene Russo, Courteney Cox
Rating: ★★

A disappointingly heavy-handed cross between *The Best of Times* and *It's a Wonderful Life,* this feelgood fantasy has a terrific basic idea, and it's just a shame that a director with a lighter touch than James Orr wasn't along to make us all cheer for its hero. That's Belushi, given a chance to turn his life around by angel (devil?) Michael Caine and marry the prom queen (Russo) he always wanted. The film's cutest notion is that Belushi finds he likes life the way it was – and attempts to get it back.

Mr Drake's Duck ⊙
1950, UK, 85 mins, b/w
Dir: Val Guest
Stars: Douglas Fairbanks Jr, Yolande Donlan, Wilfred Hyde White, A E

Matthews
Rating: ★★★

This fast-moving city-couple-down-on-the-farm comedy was a widespread favourite in its day and was pretty much along the successful furrows ploughed by *George Washington Slept Here* and *The Egg and I*. Yolande Donlan is a scatterbrained delight as the wife who (accidently) buys a duck that lays uranium eggs, and the situations come up fresh and funny. A good laugh.

Mr Hobbs Takes a Vacation ○
1962, US, 110 mins, colour
Dir: Henry Koster
Stars: James Stewart, Maureen O'Hara, Fabian, John Saxon, Reginald Gardiner, Marie Wilson
Rating: ★★

The first of James Stewart's three 'harassed father' comedies at 20th Century-Fox in the early Sixties. Here he tries to cope with a nightmare holiday home as well as a difficult family whose members include Lauri Peters, whose next role took her to Britain as Cliff Richard's leading lady in *Summer Holiday*. There are some amusing anecdotes involving plumbing and the like, but the enterprise is rather a long way from such previous Stewart comic glories as *The Jackpot*.

Mr Holland's Opus ○ ⓥ
1995, US, 143 mins, colour
Dir: Stephen Herek
Stars: Richard Dreyfuss, Glenne Headly, W H Macy, Olympia Dukakis, Jean Louisa Kelly
Rating: ★★★

There are some nice moments in this obscenely overlong film which proves that, though they can still make them (sort of) like they used to, they'd probably be best advised to leave well alone. Immmediately musician Richard Dreyfuss takes a teaching job to make ends meet for a few years, we know we're in for a sort of *Goodbye Mr Chords*. We'll see his initial failure with the class, his first successes, the birth of his deaf son, the temptation to leave his wife (Glenne Headly) for a beautiful singer-graduate (Jean Louisa Kelly), the achievement of teaching a sports major to play drums, the constant battles with the deputy head (Macy) – who actually says 'There are people in this community who think that rock 'n' roll is a message from the Devil himself' – and his final dismissal after 30 years. At last we get to the 'sur-

prise' farewell concert to hear that damned concerto Dreyfuss has been working on through the years. Shorn of half an hour or so, this could have been a terrific weepie in the old tradition. These days they just don't know when to cut and run.

Mr Jones ● ⓥ
1993, US, 114 mins, colour
Dir: Mike Figgis
Stars: Richard Gere, Lena Olin, Anne Bancroft, Bill Irwin, Lauren Tom, Bill Pullman
Rating: ★★

There are moments when this *amour fou* almost makes it. But it finally gets too silly too often. Richard Gere is the charming manic depressive who exists on an uncontrollable series of highs and lows. Lena Olin is the therapist who falls in love with him and tries to cure him. A doomed relationship, as you can well imagine, although director Mike Figgis contrives to give us a happy ending of sorts. Though the plot is predictable, Gere is not entirely unbelievable as the man full of suppressed rage, but Olin is a bit too glamorous as the shrink and her Swedish accent renders her dialogue unintelligible when her character gets excited. Some good moments include the scene where Gere attempts to rescue Olin from a berserk patient, but too often you're conscious of restlessly shifting in your seat, aware that the film has lost its grip, both on attention and credibility.

Mr Lucky ○
1943, US, 98 mins, b/w
Dir: H C Potter
Stars: Cary Grant, Laraine Day, Charles Bickford, Gladys Cooper
Rating: ★★★

An engaging comedy drama with lots of sharp little cameo performances, this story of a gambler reformed by love was later remade (very loosely) as *Gambling House*. Cary Grant's charisma in the title role ensured that the film, though nothing special, took more than $2 million at the box-office.

Mr Majestyk ◖
1974, US, 103 mins, colour
Dir: Richard Fleischer
Stars: Charles Bronson, Al Lettieri, Linda Cristal
Rating: ★★★

If you can actually believe in Charles Bronson as a simple watermelon farmer who won't bow down to the

local syndicate, you could find this more exciting than the average latter-day Bronson thriller. Nifty direction by Richard Fleischer makes the most of the action set-pieces. Good supporting work by Al Lettieri and Paul Koslo as two sneering bad guys, plus a script by Elmore Leonard that's surprisingly witty as well as hard-hitting.

Mr Music ○
1950, US, 108 mins, b/w
Dir: Richard Haydn
Stars: Bing Crosby, Nancy Olson, Charles Coburn, Ruth Hussey
Rating: ★★★

Tuneful Bing Crosby musical, additionally enlivened by the appearance of such guest stars as Peggy Lee, Dorothy Kirsten and, in particular, Groucho Marx. Bing plays a lazy songwriter whose friends hire a super-efficient secretary (the gorgeous Nancy Olson) to keep him on his toes. Richard Haydn, who plays a featured role, also directed.

Mr Nanny ○ ⓥ
(aka: Rough Stuff)
1993, US, 84 mins, colour
Dir: Michael Gottlieb
Stars: Terry 'Hulk' Hogan, Austin Pendleton, David Johansen
Rating: ★

After the modest success of *Suburban Commando*, wrestler Hulk Hogan crashes to the canvas with a resounding thump in this almost unbearable acdon-comedy about a wrestler hired as bodyguard to two hell-raising kids who have got rid of more nannies than Jane and Michael Banks in *Mary Poppins*. The plot, apart from the traps the kids set for the unwary Hulk, has them as offspring of a genius scientist (Austin Pendleton) who's invented a microchip that the bad guys, led by manic mastermind David Johansen, are dying to get their hands on. Johansen proves to be a madly mugging villain, whose OTT rants are allowed to stop the plot (such as it is) in its tracks far too often. And parents should be advised that many of the pranks the children play are potentially lethal. In fact, while dad is dozing off in this one, the kids may be taking notes for a surprise on his next trip downstairs.

Mr North ○ ⓥ
1988, US, 93 mins, colour
Dir: Danny Huston
Stars: Anthony Edwards, Lauren Bacall, Robert Mitchum, Angelica Huston, Mary Stuart Masterson, Harry Dean Stanton
Rating: ★★★

M

Danny Huston, son of John, made his debut with this gentle, inoffensive tale of a young traveller whose bedside manner and soothing, healing ways make him the toast of decadent Rhode Island society in 1926. Though the film meanders and occasionally falters, it's kept afloat by the class of the acting and the maintenance of an even pace and tenor, as Mr North brushes aside his detractors and paddles across the tricky waters of the *nouveau riche* with scarcely a ripple impeding his progress. The puppy-dog charm of Anthony Edwards is perfectly placed in the central role, and there's sympathetic support from players who hit exactly the note required, especially Robert Mitchum, Mary Stuart Masterson, Harry Dean Stanton (as a fake English butler!) and the delicious Virginia Madsen. The music (David McHugh) too never puts a note out of place in its tuneful elegance, even when Mr North is being pursued across town by dozens of would-be patients hoping for his healing touch.

Mr Peabody and the Mermaid ○
1948, US, 89 mins, b/w
Dir: Irving Pichel
Stars: William Powell, Ann Blyth, Irene Hervey
Rating: ★★

William Powell was well into his avuncular period when he made this mermaid comedy hot on the tail of the earlier British success with *Miranda*. This American copy isn't as effective, but Powell is always watchable and has one glorious scene when he buys the top half of a swimsuit and tries to explain its purpose to the mermaid coyly played by Ann Blyth. 'Prissy' comedy actor Clinton Sundberg also has a good role, as the press agent of the holiday resort where Powell encounters the finny charmer.

Mr Perrin and Mr Traill ○
1948, UK, 92 mins, b/w
Dir: Lawrence Huntington
Stars: David Farrar, Marius Goring, Greta Gynt
Rating: ★★★

Penetrating study of the way that resentment can eat away inside a man until it makes him do something quite out of character. Marius Goring is excellent as the middle-aged schoolmaster whose idiosyncratic but secure little world begins to crumble beneath his feet when a younger teacher chips away both at his authority and his aspi-

rations to romance. Absorbing, unusual and worthwhile drama.

Mr Reliable ● ⓥ
1996, Aus, 113 mins, colour
Dir: Nadia Tass
Stars: Colin Friels, Jacqueline McKenzie
Rating: ★★

Alternatively endearing and laboured, this Australian film examines with some humour the true events of 1998 when the attempted arrest of a petty criminal turned into a full-scale siege and, eventually, a public circus – with the media present in strength, fairy lights round the surrounding area and hot dogs and cold drink vendors having a field day. Even more bizarre was the marriage, by an imported chaplain, of the trapped man and his live-in girlfriend, who had at first been thought to be, with her baby, a hostage. Friels and McKenzie are personable performers as the besieged couple, but director Tass is so determined to milk every last drop from her cock-a-mamey story that she lets it go on far too long. Still, as one of the characters says (and you haven't heard the half of it), something like this could only happen in Australia.

Mr Saturday Night ① ⓥ
1992, US, US mins, colour
Dir: Billy Crystal
Stars: Billy Crystal, Julie Warner, David Paymer, Jerry Lewis, Jerry Orbach, Ron Silver
Rating: ★★

A curious mixture of good and not-so-good, this is the kind of film that looked better 30 years ago. Billy Crystal is the nightclub comedian who abuses those about him and whose nasty streak shows through everything he does. But he is funny: on and off. Only his wife (Julie Warner) and brother (David Paymer) stand by him for long and at the outset of the film we find him in his 60s, with a career that has long since gone down the toilet. 'You took every bad break you ever had – and made it worse,' Paymer tells him in a rare break from their jokey, but always master-and-servantlike relationship. Cue for a flashback, of which there should be more: the film carries too much of Crystal in unconvincing old-age makeup (Paymer ages much more gracefully and deserved his Oscar nomination) and too many downbeat scenes involving his vitriolic (if occasionally poisonously funny outbursts against those around him. Still, there are

funny moments here and there and moving ones, too.

Mrs Doubtfire ① ⓥ
1993, US, 125 mins, colour
Dir: Chris Columbus
Stars: Robin Williams, Sally Field, Pierce Brosnan, Harvey Fenstein
Rating: ★★★

Too much sentiment and not enough fun blemish this great idea which gives Robin Williams – an actor of enormous comic talent if limited charm – a dream role as the divorced husband who disguises himself as a Scottish housekeeper (who keeps saying she comes from England) to be near his three beloved kids. Whether the disguise is good enough to pull the wool over ex-wife Sally Field's eyes, especially as Williams slips and snarls his way out of character too often, is another matter. But there are a good many bright patches around here, especially when Williams, out of drag, demonstrates his mastery of a string of famous voices in a session with his social worker. Parents should note a sprinkling of bad language and suggestive dialogue: it underlines that subtlety is not one of this film's strengths. A field day, though, for fans of the star.

Mr Skeffington ○
1944, US, 127 mins, b/w
Dir: Vincent Sherman
Stars: Bette Davis, Claude Rains, Walter Abel, Richard Waring, George Coulouris
Rating: ★★★★

The inimitable Bette Davis was perfectly cast as the vain and selfish young woman who marries for money in this lavish melodrama which progresses from the turn of the century through to 1944. This was Davis's 53rd picture and she was nominated for an Oscar for the role, but lost to Ingrid Bergman (for *Gaslight*). A soap opera to end them all, it's heart-rending stuff and Davis is finely complemented by her distinguished co-star, Claude Rains, as the long-suffering Skeffington. The whole is deftly directed by Vincent Sherman, one of Warners' leading film-makers, who extracts one of Davis's most complex performances.

Mrs Winterbourne ① ⓥ
1996, US, 104 mins, colour
Dir: Richard Benjamin
Stars: Shirley MacLaine, Ricki Lake, Brendan Fraser, Miguel Sandoval, Loren

Dean, Susan Haskell

Rating: ★★

This unpredictable but appealing fairy-tale comedy (based on a 1950s' movie called *No Man of Her Own*) stars Ricki Lake as a young girl who, down on her luck, is mistaken (after an intricately plotted first 20 minutes, involving a train wreck) for the daughter-in-law of the very, very rich Mrs Winterbourne (Shirley MacLaine). There a few laughs as gauche Lake tries to fit in with her new upper-class family, but most of the fun and all of the acting quality, comes from MacLaine's performance as the loveable, ailing matriarch. Brendan Fraser doesn't have much to do as the suspicious, snobbish son, unaccountably easily won over by Lake, but Miguel Sandoval is hilarious as the family's loyal butler. Listlessly directed by Richard Benjamin, with a small, un-billed role for his real-life wife Paula Prentiss as a nurse.

Mrs Mike ○

1949, US, 98 mins, b/w

Dir: Louis King

Stars: Dick Powell, Evelyn Keyes

Rating: ★★

Tough stuff, this turn-of-the-century romantic drama set in the wilds of the Canadian northwest and based on a true story. Evelyn Keyes is Boston girl Kathy O'Fallon, who marries Canadian mounted policeman Dick Powell and swaps the comforts of urban life for the hardships of pioneering. Predictably, every imaginable hazard is encountered, with laughter and tears thrown in. Joseph Biroc's camera captures very effectively the great Canadian outdoors, Keyes and Powell are both sympathetic in their roles, and Powell even gets the chance to sing!

Mr Smith Goes to Washington ○ Ⓥ

1939, US, 129 mins, b/w

Dir: Frank Capra

Stars: James Stewart, Jean Arthur, Claude Rains, Edward Arnold, Thomas Mitchell, Guy Kibbee

Rating: ★★★★★

Nominated for eight Oscars, Frank Capra's magnificently corny epic of the 'little man' taking on corrupt politicians remains one of the cinema's enduring classics, with splendid performances all round. Young James Stewart, perfectly cast as the heartbreakingly sincere country boy, is delightfully teamed with lovely Jean Arthur, a city slicker secretary with a well concealed heart of gold. Edward Arnold and Claude Rains

make a formidable pair of villains, but Harry Carey's late appearance (as the Senate president) almost steals the whole show. Be prepared, though, for an over-hasty climax.

Mrs O'Malley and Mr Malone ○

1950, US, 69 mins, b/w

Dir: Norman Taurog

Stars: Marjorie Main, James Whitmore, Ann Dvorak, Fred Clark

Rating: ★★

Despite a tasty supporting cast, character stars Marjorie Main – she of the steely gaze and rasping voice – and James Whitmore are really the whole show in the energetic MGM programme-filler about a widow and a lawyer involved with murders on a train. No great shakes, but worth it just to hear Main singing 'Possum Up a Gum Stump'.

Mrs Parker and the Vicious Circle ● Ⓥ

1994, US, 123 mins, colour

Dir: Alan Rudolph

Stars: Jennifer Jason Leigh, Campbell Scott, Matthew Broderick, Andrew McCarthy, Martha Plimpton, Jennifer Beals

Rating: ★★★

Decidedly not everyone's cup of tea, but a fascinating recreation of its era, this is the story of the fabled humorist and writer Dorothy Parker and her round table of literary acquaintances whose lunchtime sessions at the Algonquin Hotel became legend in New York of the Twenties. The 'circle' included some of the most famous names of the day, including Robert Benchley, Scott Fitzgerald and Harold Ross. Jennifer Jason Leigh is the drawling Parker to the life, complete with a portfolio full of famous Parker lines, from 'I may die before a train of thought reaches the station' to 'One more drink and I'll be under the host', the second summarising her two failed marriages and numerous love affairs – as well as the one with the bottle. Although dull in spots, the film has a newsreel immediacy that makes it impossible to ditch. And Campbell Scott gives by far his finest film performance to date as Benchley, keeping a tightly-buttoned face as the film funny-man who was Parker's confidant, soulmate, but never quite lover.

Mrs Parkington ○

1944, US, 124 mins, b/w

Dir: Tay Garnett

Stars: Greer Garson, Walter Pidgeon, Edward Arnold, Dan Duryea, Agnes Moorehead, Cecil Kellaway

Rating: ★★★

Fifth teaming of Greer Garson and Walter Pidgeon in a typical grand-scale MGM vehicle for their popular talents, chronicling the fortunes over 60 years of a maid who becomes a great lady. Great supporting roles from pompous Edward Arnold and shifty Dan Duryea as two of the dowager Garson's grasping relations. The epic stature to which the film aspired is effortlessly reached by director Tay Garnett and a great production team, entirely overcoming an indifferent script to bring a lump to the throat at the end.

Mrs Soffel ① Ⓥ

1984, US, 110 mins, colour

Dir: Gillian Armstrong

Stars: Diane Keaton, Mel Gibson, Matthew Modine

Rating: ★★

In 1901, the wife of the warden of Pittsburgh Prison sneaked hacksaws to two convicted murderers she believed innocent and deserted hearth and home (and four children) to run off with them through snow-covered countryside towards Canada. This film examines at some length the all-consuming passion that led to such a hopeless action. In casting Diane Keaton as the 35-ish Bible-pushing wife and Mel Gibson as the main object of her obsession, it cheats to a degree, since the physical attraction of Miss Keaton at her most luminous and Mr Gibson at his most casually charming is all too obvious. Even so, one is drawn along to the story's inevitable end in fairly hypnotic fashion. The dingy backgrounds outside of the prison scenes fairly creak with Victorian trappings and indeed Kate Soffel's family life is sketched in with rather too much warmth for our ease in accepting her flight from it. But Keaton lightens this strain by skilfully steering Mrs Soffel from soberly loving mother to faintly zany fugitive.

Mr Wonderful ● Ⓥ

1993, US, 101 mins, colour

Dir: Anthony Minghella

Stars: Matt Dillon, Annabella Sciorra, William Hurt, Mary-Louise Parker, Vincent D'Onofrio, Jessica Harper

Rating: ★★★

Gus (Matt Dillon) needs money to open a bowling alley. The trouble is, all the cash he earns goes to maintaining his ex-wife (Annabella Sciorra). If

M

Sciorra re-marries, Dillon is financially free – so he hits on the idea of finding his ex-wife her 'Mr Wonderful'. Well, we can see where this is going, and there are no real surprises as the story builds. Still, it's a heartening tale for all romantics, and it's sweetly told by director Anthony Minghella, who works marvels considering the hackneyed quality of the material and the irritating characters it throws up. He's the real Mr Wonderful here.

Much Ado about Nothing
Ⓞ Ⓥ

1993, US/UK, 113 mins, colour
Dir: Kenneth Branagh
Stars: Kenneth Branagh, Emma Thompson, Michael Keaton, Denzel Washington, Keanu Reeves, Robert Sean Leonard
Rating: ★★★

Kenneth Branagh's second joust with the Bard is a bit of a mixed bag. Most successful in its comedy content, especially the dialogue shared by Branagh and Emma Thompson, it fares less well with the plot's heavier melodrama, while the musical interludes have much the same effect as one of Harpo Marx's solos or a Bing Crosby ballad in a *Road* film: yup, just time to get the popcorn. The main interest lies in seeing stars more familiar in other kinds of films: Denzel Washington (very good) as the noble Don Pedro – here depicted as a kind of John Wayne loner; Michael Keaton, rather too obnoxious as the constable, Dogberry; and Keanu Reeves, working hard on his sneer as the dastardly Don John. Branagh and Thompson invent some tasty bits of comic business (especially one involving Branagh's trying to erect a medieval deck chair) and it all runs along like a roistering and raunchy pantomime. On balance the best bits are worth waiting for.

Much Too Shy ○
1942, UK, 92 mins, b/w
Dir: Marcel Varnel
Stars: George Formby, Eileen Bennett, Jimmy Clitheroe
Rating: ★★

A George Formby wartime lark, notable for the appearance of diminutive Lancashire comedian Jimmy Clitheroe, then only 20 but later to become phenomenally popular as star of the radio comedy series *The Clitheroe Kid*. The cameraman is Arthur Crabtree, who successfully turned director two years later with *Madonna of the Seven Moons* and *They Were Sisters*. Formby's

ukulele-accompanied songs in this one include 'I'm Delivering the Morning Milk' and 'They Laughed When I Started to Play'.

Mudlark, The ○
1951, UK, 98 mins, b/w
Dir: Jean Negulesco
Stars: Irene Dunne, Alec Guinness, Andrew Ray, Anthony Steel, Finlay Currie, Wilfrid Hyde White
Rating: ★★★

Thank goodness Hollywood resisted what must have been an overwhelming desire to call this fascinating and charming piece of whimsy something like 'The Queen and the Kid'. Irene Dunne makes rather hard work of being Queen Victoria, and loses out along the line to Andrew Ray – son of Ted – in the title role, and to Alec Guinness' brilliant Disraeli.

Mulholland Falls ● Ⓥ
1995, US, 106 mins, colour
Dir: Lee Tamahori
Stars: Nick Nolte, Melanie Griffith, Chazz Palminteri, John Malkovich, Bruce Dern, Jennifer Connelly
Rating: ★★★

One to please *film noir* fans without actually having them drooling in the aisles. Impeccably set in the post-war years, with lovely music by David Grusin, the story centres on four burly cops who form an elite squad, none too fussy about the way they eliminate criminal elements in LA. Called to the scene of a crime, they find a voluptuous brunette (Connelly) virtually buried by some tremendous impact in a quarry. Disfigured as she is, the cops' leader (Nolte) recognises her as the girl with whom he recently had an affair. Then he gets a piece of film that shows that her most recent lover was the director (Malkovich) of an atomic energy research station. Things get down and dirty after that with the FBI, headed by Daniel Baldwin, stooping lowest of all. It's gruff, thick-ear, tolerably entertaining stuff with an amazing all-star cast. Great Technicolor photography in the grand manner is by veteran ace Haskell Wexler.

Multiplicity ◐ Ⓥ
1996, US, 117 mins, colour
Dir: Harold Ramis
Stars: Michael Keaton, Andie MacDowell, Harris Yulin, Richard Masur, Eugene Levy
Rating: ★★★

Michael Keaton turns to comedy again, and the results are a tonic for us all. It

may not be a riot of laughs, but this is fun to be with. Stressed-out Doug (Keaton) just can't keep up with the demands of his job, home, wife (MacDowell) and children. It's all getting too much. The answer comes along in the form of a geneticist (Yulin) who promises Doug a miracle – and provides three. Cloning's the name of the game and pretty soon Doug has triplet brothers. No 2's a slobby workaholic, No 3 a proper little kitchen devil and No 4, well, No 4 isn't Doug's idea and doesn't actually do anything but act the fool. These are conventional stereotypes that might give offence elsewhere. But in a special effects (and they are flawless) romp like this, too much subtlety might spoil the broth. and it's laughter we're after. Keaton provides a few miracles of his own keeping the four Dougs in character.

Mummy, The ◐
1932, US, 72 mins, b/w
Dir: Karl Freund
Stars: Boris Karloff, Zita Johann
Rating: ★★★

Boris Karloff's make-up as the mummy, layered on to his face filament by filament, is masterly in this vintage shocker – really giving the impression of having been hidden away for centuries; you can almost smell the must and dust. Bramwell Fletcher gives one of his best film portrayals as one of the men he frightens, and the visuals are most impressive under the direction of Karl Freund, an expert cinematographer who made too few appearances in the director's chair.

Mummy, The ◐
1959, UK, 88 mins, colour
Dir: Terence Fisher
Stars: Peter Cushing, Christopher Lee, Yvonne Furneaux
Rating: ★★

Director Terence Fisher's remake of *The Mummy's Hand* completed a Hammer/Fisher trilogy after their versions of the Frankenstein and Dracula stories. Christopher Lee is almost unrecognisable beneath layers of skilful make-up as the mummy who avenges himself on those who have defiled his tomb. Boris Karloff's original had first appeared in 1933. The trouble with it, and practically every other mummy film since, is that, although the initial appearance of the mummy, re-awakening after thousands of years, was suitably terrifying, writers rapidly ran out of ideas as to what to do with him once he was on the loose.

Munster Go Home! ○

1966, US, 90 mins, colour
Dir: Earl Bellamy
Stars: Fred Gwynne, Yvonne De Carlo, Al
Lewis, Hermione Gingold
Rating: ★★★

Remember the Munsters? They're a
whole family of movie monsters, headed by Frankenstein's little creation, and
here they are in their own film comedy.
Representing the less familiar English
branch of the family are Hermione
Gingold (as Lady Effigie!), Terry-
Thomas and Jeanne Arnold,
constituting a terrible trio much agin'
their American relatives. Watch, too,
for a cadaverous John Carradine in a
supporting role as Cruikshank.

Muppet Christmas Carol, The ☉ ⓥ

1992, US/UK, 86 mins, colour
Dir: Brian Henson
Stars: Michael Caine, The Muppets
Rating: ★★★

If you can imagine that Charles
Dickens was ever blue and furry and
hung around with a rat, you are
halfway to enjoying this irreverent
Muppet version of the author's classic
seasonal story. The Great Gonzo appears as Dickens, who narrates the tale
with his sidekick Rizzo the Rat, quip-
ping and wisecracking to keep both
kids and adults amused. Michael
Caine, the only human member of the
cast as the miserly Scrooge, blends so
well with the Muppet characters that
Muppet and human are indistinguish-
able. Paul Williams' songs are apt and
tuneful in a lively, colourful and witty
show which Caine may well remember
with affection as perhaps the highpoint
of the latter stages of his checkered career.

Muppet Movie, The ☉ ⓥ

1979, US, 97 mins, colour
Stars: Mel Brooks, Bob Hope, Telly
Savalas
Rating: ★★★

Make way for the Muppets! Jim
Henson and his personable puppet performers hit the big screen, with Kermit
at his rightful place at the centre of
things seeking his fame and fortune in
Hollywood, and proving a wistful and
appealing character in the process.
Even though there's much original
thought in the story, this remains a film
primarily for children and aficionados
although there are guest stars galore for
the unconverted, including Mel
Brooks, Bob Hope and James Coburn.

Muppets Take Manhattan, The ☉ ⓥ

1984, US, 94 mins, colour
Dir: Frank Oz
Stars: Dabney Coleman, Art Carney,
James Coco, Gregory Hines
Rating: ★★★★

Kermit and company really do turn
Manhattan into an isle of joy in this,
the best of the Muppet films. Good
story, witty script, inventive use of
New York locations, and some very
snappy verbal exchanges between
Kermit and Miss Piggy. Kermit loses
his memory and wanders the streets of
New York. Miss Piggy is mugged in
Central Park. Yes, all Muppet life is
here. And there's even the big finish to
end them all, with two of the main
characters getting married on stage. It
seemed that this might be the last of the
Muppets on film, but happily they re-
emerged years later with their version
of *A Christmas Carol*.

Muppet Treasure Island ☉ ⓥ

1996, UK, 99 mins, colour
Dir: Brian Henson
Stars: Kermit the Frog, Miss Piggy,
Gonzo the Great, Tim Curry, Jennifer
Saunders, Billy Connolly
Rating: ★★★★

Yo-ho-ho! After successfully putting
their own slant on Dickens' *A Christmas
Carol* the colourful, crazy Muppets send
up R L Stevenson's pirate classic as
only they can. The Great Gonzo and
Rizzo the rat take centre stage in a tale
of buried treasure and angry warthogs,
while Jennifer Saunders, Tim Curry
and Billy Connolly lead the human
cast. But they really can't compete
with 101 different kinds of cloth-head-
ed co-stars, with every Muppet
character from Kermit to the Swedish
chef getting a look-in. There are songs
too, with *Cabin Fever* a show-stopper
that would turn Busby Berkeley
Kermit-green with envy. And even
though many of the jokes are aimed at
an adult audience, the movie never
loses its all-round family appeal.
Especially funny is a running gag featuring a group of water-surfing,
marguerita-swilling rats who pay Rizzo
to join the ship on a world cruise. All
this and Miss Piggy as Benjamina
Gunn, in a hearty dose of high-seas fun.

Murder! ○

1930, UK, 100 mins, b/w
Dir: Alfred Hitchcock
Stars: Herbert Marshall, Norah Baring,
Edward Chapman, Miles Mander
Rating: ★★★

This Hitchcock film is the rarely-seen
follow-up to *Blackmail* and like that,
contains some brilliant composition of
scenes, as well as innovative devices
that soon became cinema clichés, such
as 'voice over' thoughts of a character
seen in tight-lipped close-up; Hitchcock
would still be working variations on
this as late as *Psycho*. Herbert Marshall
provides a reassuring star presence as
the juror determined to prove a convicted girl's innocence. Norah Baring
is sometimes quite touching as the girl,
and the story is full of well-cast character stars who may or may not be the
killer. Impressionistic sound is again
used (as in *Blackmail)* proving particularly effective in the jury sequences.

Murder Ahoy ○

1964, UK, 93 mins, b/w
Dir: George Pollock
Stars: Margaret Rutherford, Lionel
Jeffries
Rating: ★★★

The last of MGM's quartet of Miss
Marple thrillers, with Margaret
Rutherford tripping delightfully
through a series of murders with a
naval flavour. A number of familiar
television faces – Francis Matthews,
William Mervyn and Derek Nimmo
among them – decorate the mayhem,
but even Lionel Jeffries, as a snuff-tak-
ing seadog, is no match for Dame
Margaret, who deservedly dominates
the film. Her achievements here include a joyous sword-fight with the
villain that runs the length and breadth
of a ship. Her opening remark in this
sequence is delicious.

Murder at 1600 ● ⓥ

1997, US, 107 mins, colour
Dir: Dwight Little
Stars: Wesley Snipes, Diane Lane, Alan
Alda, Daniel Benzali, Stephen Lang,
Diane Baker
Rating: ★★

1600 is the address of the White House
and, following *Absolute Power*, here's another US president up to his neck in
murder. This is nowhere near as good
as the Clint Eastwood film. Although
that stepped beyong credibility towards the end, here the bounds of
belief are left behind almost from the
start. Once again, though, the presidential palace proves to be a nest of
conspirators. A voluptuous blonde
turns up dead in the White House loo
only an hour after being bonked by
the president's son in the Oval Office.
A cleaner is charged with the crime,
apparently to cover up for the young

M

stud. Detective Wesley Snipes sniffs something deeper going on, and enlists the help of curvy secret service agent Diane Lane before they both become targets for hit-men hired by whoever's behind it all. Slow, in between action that's a cut above Hollywood's most dynamic.

Murder at the Gallop ○
1963, UK, 81 mins, b/w
Dir: George Pollock
Stars: Margaret Rutherford, Robert Morley, Flora Robson
Rating: ★★★

Agatha Christie's spinster detective Miss Marple rides again, literally, in a jolly little murder mystery which, apart from being set at a riding stable, sticks closely to the established Christie who-dunnit formula: we open with one murder, witness another among the suspects, and finally see Miss Marple setting herself up as bait to catch the killer. Dame Margaret Rutherford's Miss Marple is at least twice as good as anything else in the film. Her double chin quivers with anticipation as she makes an important find or waits for the murderer to come into her room, and her extraordinarily mobile face ex-presses fiendish glee as she tells the hapless inspector (Charles Tingwell) that she has deduced who the murder-er is. And, if it had nothing else to offer, the film would still be worth a look to see Dame Margaret doing the twist.

Murder at the Vanities ○
1934, US, 95 mins, b/w
Dir: Mitchell Leisen
Stars: Victor McLaglen, Carl Brisson, Jack Oakie, Kitty Carlisle
Rating: ★★

Acceptable mixture of murder and music with detective Victor McLaglen suspecting everyone in sight and songs that include 'Cocktails for Two' and 'Sweet Marijuana'. See if you can spot future star Ann Sheridan in the chorus.

Murder by Death ○
1976, US, 94 mins, colour
Dir: Robert Moore
Stars: Eileen Brennan, Alec Guinness, David Niven, Peter Sellers, James Coco, Maggie Smith
Rating: ★★

Neil Simon took time off from writing his hard-shelled, soft-centred romantic comedies set in the big city to pen this popular charade in which a fistful of

well-known stars have the time of their lives playing famous detectives at large in a sinister country mansion. Although the script is not of Simon's highest quality, you'll enjoy the imper-sonations of legendary sleuths of fiction and the cinema. It's not too difficult to work out on which crime-solvers each of them is modelled.

Murder by Decree ●
1978, US, 112 mins, colour
Dir: Bob Clark
Stars: Christopher Plummer, James Mason, Genevieve Bujold, Donald Sutherland, David Hemmings
Rating: ★★★

Sherlock Holmes meets Jack the Ripper again. Despite a stellar cast, the real star of this gaslit chiller is production designer Harry Pottle, who creates nar-row, grimy streets, vaguely welcoming taverns, gaunt wharves and battered Victorian slums with all the flair of the old Hollywood. The film itself does its job well as a baffling thriller until the superfluous last half-hour.

Murderers' Row ○ ⓥ
1966, US, 108 mins, colour
Dir: Henry Levin
Stars: Dean Martin, Ann-Margret, Karl Malden
Rating: ★★

The second screen adventure of singing spy Matt Helm (Dean Martin at his most relaxed), pitting him against villain Karl Malden, who plays su-perbly tongue-in-cheek. Some of the gadgetry is outrageously ingenious, al-though you may find Helm's backward-firing gun a little too nasty for comfort.

Murder, He Says ○
1945, US, 93 mins, b/w
Dir: George Marshall
Stars: Fred MacMurray, Helen Walker, Marjorie Main
Rating: ★★★

Fred MacMurray encounters a family of hayseed murderers in a kind of hill-billy version of *The Old Dark House*. The plot is as daft as it's devious but the situations are often very funny under the direction of George Marshall.

Murder In Reverse ○
1945, UK, 88 mins, b/w
Dir: Montgomery Tully
Stars: William Hartnell, Chili Bouchier, Jimmy Hanley, Dinah Sheridan
Rating: ★★★

Age hasn't dulled the edge of this excel-lent British thriller about a man wno serves 15 years for a murder he didn't commit. Made on a low budget, it's full of atmosphere and tension.

Murder in the First ● ⓥ
1994, US, 122 mins, colour
Dir: Marc Rocco
Stars: Christian Slater, Kevin Bacon, Gary Oldman, Embeth Davidtz, R Lee Ermey, Brad Dourif
Rating: ★★★★★

American prison/courtroom dramas get more brutal and uncompromising by the year. But their emotive power is as great as ever: too bad for the history of America's penal system that the stories they tell are so often true. The treat-ment meted out at Alcatraz to escapee Henri Young (Kevin Bacon) is so inhu-mane as to be almost unwatchable. Beaten and degraded, he spent more than three years in filthy, windowless solitary – 'the hole' – before emerging to plunge a spoon into the neck of the convict who ratted on the escape. Even after his release from solitary, he was crippled for life with a razor by the sadistic associate warden (Gary Oldman). Such men as this officer then (in 1941) thought themselves above the law. But they reckon with-out a young attorney (Christian Slater) on his first case, who desperately tries to befriend a near-catatonic Young to save him from the gas chamber. This is first-rate, unflinching drama, ap-palling and sensational in every sense. Slater and Oldman are excellent, but Bacon is just amazing as the prisoner: a performance to die for.

Murder in the Private Car ○
(aka: Murder on the Runaway Train)
1934, US, 63 mins, b/w
Dir: Harry Beaumont
Stars: Mary Carlisle, Charlie Ruggles, Una Merkel
Rating: ★★★

Director Harry Beaumont made his name with Jazz Age romps featuring Joan Crawford and Clara Bow. This is an uncharacteristic mystery thriller about a threatened heiress. A thor-oughly enjoyable time-passer with some good character actors in the cast, among them Charlie Ruggles, Porter Hall, Una Merkel and Berton Churchill.

Murder in Thornton Square, The
See: Gaslight [1944]

Murder Man, The ○
1935, US, 70 mins, b/w
Dir: Tim Whelan
Stars: Spencer Tracy, Virginia Bruce,
Lionel Atwill, James Stewart
Rating: ★★★

A snappy little thriller with Spencer
Tracy at full throttle as a hard-drinking reporter who specialises in
homicide scoops. James Stewart
makes his film debut as another reporter, inaptly nicknamed Shorty.
Said Tracy later of the man who was
to become a lifelong friend: 'In his
very first scene on film he showed he
had all the good things.'

Murder Most Foul ○
1964, UK, 91 mins, b/w
Dir: George Pollock
Stars: Margaret Rutherford, Ron Moody,
Charles Tingwell, Andrew Cruickshank,
Dennis Price, Francesca Annis
Rating: ★★★

Agatha Christie's Miss Marple tackles
a series of murders in a travelling
repertory company. Charles Tingwell
is again the long-suffering inspector,
one of whose men is almost allowed to
beat Miss Marple in an hilarious game
of draughts. Margaret Rutherford, of
course, *is* the film. Her triumph here
includes a remarkable rendition of
'The Shooting of Dan McGrew' that
has to be seen and heard to be believed.

Murder, My Sweet
See Farewell, My Lovely [1945]

Murder on Monday
See Home at Seven

Murder on the Orient Express ○ ⓥ
1974, US, 131 mins, colour
Dir: Sidney Lumet
Stars: Albert Finney, Lauren Bacall,
Martin Balsam, Ingrid Bergman, Sean
Connery, Vanessa Redgrave
Rating: ★★

This star-studded, if laborious and deliberate thriller has Albert Finney as
Agatha Christie's detective Hercule
Poirot, trying to find out who murdered tycoon Richard Widmark on the
Orient Express in December 1935.
There is a glittering cast of suspects to
choose from and their performances
range from great to ghastly. Ingrid
Bergman won an Oscar for her missionary lady forever muttering about
'little brown babies'.

Murder She Said ○
1961, UK, 86 mins, b/w
Dir: George Pollock
Stars: Margaret Rutherford, Arthur
Kennedy, James Robertson Justice
Rating: ★★★

Dame Margaret Rutherford's first outing as Agatha Christie's spinster sleuth
Miss Marple is a workmanlike adaptation of the novel *4.50 to Paddington*.
The star has no trouble dominating her
motley cast of suspects, even though
they include Arthur Kennedy and
James Robertson Justice. For a Christie
mystery, the killer is fairly obvious.
The success of this film gave rise to
three more Miss Marple mysteries.

Murders in the Rue Morgue ◑
1932, US, 62 mins, b/w
Dir: Robert Florey
Stars: Bela Lugosi, Sidney Fox
Rating: ★★★

John Huston had a hand in the writing
of this expressionistic horror film, only
distantly related to the Edgar Allan Poe
story on which it's based. Bela
Lugosi's eyes glitter as he invites
prospective victims up for coffee.
Pretty, diminutive Sidney Fox is an
ideal frightened heroine. Silly but fun.

Murders in the Rue Morgue ●
1971, US/Spain, 87 mins, colour
Dir: Gordon Hessler
Stars: Jason Robards, Herbert Lom, Lilli
Palmer, Christine Kaufmann, Adolfo Celi
Rating: ★★★

Gordon Hessler's most stylish horror
film, baroque in effect, and reminiscent
of the work of another director, Roger
Corman, in its conception and execution. Poe addicts should be told right
away that the only connection with the
famous story of the same name is that
it is being the enacted by the travelling
company around whom the grisly plot
revolves. But Hessler's sole aim is to
shock and shock he does, by constantly
edgy direction and intelligent use of a
recurring dream sequence that fascinates, entertains and skilfully maintains
the theme. Ingeniously, the dream is
partly explained, partly made to come
true, before a down-beat ending which
it would be spoiling your post-midnight
shivers to reveal. But I think that Poe
would have approved of the climax
and of the film.

Murders in the Zoo
1933, US, 64 mins, b/w
Dir: Edward Sutherland

Stars: Charles Ruggles, Lionel Atwill,
Randolph Scott
Rating: ★★★

Strong stuff in its time, when short but
grisly horror films were giving censors
nightmares in more ways than one,
Murders in the Zoo opens with mad
Lionel Atwill sewing up the mouth of
one of his wife's lovers before feeding
him to one of the creatures in the zoo
and almost never lets up, save for
Charles Ruggles' comic relief. When
the wife asks if her friend left a message, Atwill replies grimly, 'He didn't
say anything.' A feast for horror fans
(as well as the pythons and crocodiles),
the film has a fine cast that also includes Randolph Scott and Gail
Patrick.

Muriel's Wedding ● ⓥ
1994, Australia, 110 mins, colour
Dir: P J Hogan
Stars: Toni Collette, Bill Hunter, Rachel
Griffiths, Jeanie Drynan, Matt Day,
Gennie Nevinson
Rating: ★★

Though you might think it sets itself
up as a fable in the tradition of *Strictly
Ballroom*, this Australian film is mostly
of a much darker hue. There are serious, even disturbing undertones to its
story of a frumpy girl from a family of
couch potatoes, looking for Mr Right.
Most of these characters are a few
steps away from being suicidal, and
one of them ends up that way. Muriel
herself is a compulsive liar and thief
kept out of the hands of the law by her
influential father, whose downtrodden
wife asks him for how much she
should make out a blank cheque.
Clearing out her father's account,
Muriel jets off for a dream holiday on
which she meets a high-living school
chum, with whom she flees to Sydney.
Alas, after a few heady flings, the
chum develops cancer of the spine and
Muriel finds herself pushing her
around in a wheelchair. Although the
ending is determinedly upbeat, you
may find yourself shifting uneasily at
this study of helplessness and hopelessness of life in the big city suburbs – as
well as questioning the actions of its
characters.

Murphy's Law ● ⓥ
1986, US, 100 mins, colour
Dir: J Lee Thompson
Stars: Charles Bronson, Kathleen
Wilhoite, Carrie Snodgress
Rating: ★★★

A not-so-bad latter-day Charles
Bronson thriller with lots of vivid ac-

M

tion and a plot that works through to a logical and well-staged climax. It also allows that good actress Carrie Snodgress to enjoy herself as the psycho who's bumping off all Bronson's friends because of a 10-year-old conviction. Bronson's whisky-cop, Jack Murphy, thinks it's the brother of a Mafia hood he's just gunned down who's framing him for the killings. And there's a fellow-cop who'd like nothing more than to see Murphy fry in the hot chair. All he's got to help him is a tough-talking street-criminal waif who keeps crossing his path. Newcomer Kathleen Wilhoite does what she can with this difficult and underwritten role, directory Lee Thompson's prowling camera sometimes makes a striking set-piece out of a molehill of violence that isn't unpalatable by today's standards. The dialogue is marginally the right side of risibility. Hardened Bronson fans will like it; it doesn't do them wrong.

Murphy's Romance ◐

1985, US, 102 mins, colour
Dir: Martin Ritt
Stars: Sally Field, James Garner, Brian Kerwin, Corey Haim
Rating: ★★★

There's an old-fashioned haze to this Arizona romance that provides James Garner with his most character-full leading role in a long while, and won him an Oscar nomination. Sally Field plays another of her now-familiar gutsy women of the outdoors as the divorcee who heads west to start a horse training ranch (and a new life) with her 12-year-old son. She's befriended by widower Garner and has trouble with her ex-husband. It all works well enough, with Garner's laidback charm making you wonder why the cinema always allowed him to slip back to the small screen. There's a nice running gag, too, about him refusing to reveal his age and the dialogue provides a few more warm chuckles along similar lines.

Murphy's War ◐

1970, UK, 108 mins, colour
Dir: Peter Yates
Stars: Peter O'Toole, Sian Phillips, Philippe Noiret, Horst Jansen
Rating: ★★★

Excellent colour photography on tropical locations and some stirring action scenes (especially in the last reel) put the fizz into this unusual war story. Peter O'Toole excels as the sole sur-

vivor of a German U-boat raid who carries on his own war from a settlement on the banks of the Orinoco River.

Music Box ◐ ⓥ

1989, US, 123 mins, colour
Dir: Costa-Gavras
Stars: Jessica Lange, Armin Mueller Stahl, Frederic Forrest
Rating: ★★

A lawyer defends her father on charges of being a Nazi war criminal in his native Hungary. As the case veers one way, then the other, the audience is asked to share her doubts as to his innocence or guilt. Despite the subject matter, and the excellence of Jessica Lange's acting as the lawyer, though, you'll find this only mildly involving, perhaps because of undynamic direction and the too-quiet performance of Armin Mueller-Stahl as the accused man. Most of the other portrayals are good, and Frederic Forrest gives one of his best performances as the prosecuting attorney. Although the story does remain interesting to the end, the outcome is never seriously in doubt, which perhaps accounts in part for the film's curiously muffled impact.

Music Lovers, The ● ⓥ

1971, UK, 122 mins, colour
Dir: Ken Russell
Stars: Richard Chamberlain, Glenda Jackson, Christopher Gable
Rating: ★

Controversial portrait of the life of Tchaikovsky, written by Melvyn Bragg and directed by the bad boy of British cinema, Ken Russell, who offers another full-frontal view of Glenda Jackson to follow the one in *Women in Love*: would that this film were anywhere near as good. Its scenes of sexual excess, however, at least ensured it of notoriety. The director really kicks over the traces in this lurid biography of the famous composer, who lived a short but gay life in Tsarist Russia before expiring of cholera (a scene in which Russell revels). Richard Chamberlain struggles gamely with the composer while Jackson nobly does her pieces as a nymphomaniac who can be relied on to go spectacularly mad in the end. Only the '1812' sequence works consistently well in a film that fails to endow its catalogue of depravities and deformities with any kind of depth. If only the composer's music had been allowed to speak for itself.

Music Man, The ☉ ⓥ

1961, US, 151 mins, colour
Dir: Morton Da Costa
Stars: Robert Preston, Shirley Jones, Buddy Hackett, Hermione Gingold
Rating: ★★★

A big, brassy, rumbustious musical packed with hummable tunes. Robert Preston repeats his Broadway triumph as the travelling swindler who breezes into River City, Iowa in 1912, and tells its citizens they 'have trouble with a capital T and that rhymes with P and that stands for Pool' – planning to woo the youngsters away from playing pool and sell the citizens a fortune's worth of musical instruments to form a boys' band. Hermione Gingold also excels as a mayor's wife with an astonishing collection of hats and a conviction that all literature is smut.

Music of Chance, The ◐ ⓥ

1993, US, 95 mins, colour
Dir: Philip Haas
Stars: James Spader, Mandy Patinkin, Charles Durning, M Emmet Walsh, Joel Grey
Rating: ★★

There's something strange going on here all right. But be warned: debut director Philip Haas is not about to let us in on the secret. Driver Mandy Patinkin picks up battered, bloodied roadside refugee James Spader (as you would) and gives him a ride. Spader proves to be a gambler, and Patinkin, whose inheritance appears to be on its last legs and who has mysteriously driven 97,000 miles in a year in his new car, has a proposition. Spader will take on two rich old pushovers at poker, and they'll share the proceeds. The Pushovers (Charles Durning, Joel Grey) naturally win, and their opponents find themselves landed with a strange forfeit: they must build a huge wall on the estate to pay for their debts. When these are 'cleared' in 50 days, they are handed a bill for food and other 'expenses' and must work on. There is no escape, either, over high walls and barbed wire. This has a 'circular' kind of feel to it, as in the best chillers: the men seem to be trapped in some kind of descending spiral – but the problem is that nothing is ever explained. The ending is a surprise all right, but not very likely the kind you'll welcome.

Mute Witness ● ⓥ

1994, US, 96 mins, colour
Dir: Anthony Waller

Stars: Marina Sudina, Fay Ripley, Evan Richards, Igor Volkov, Sergei Kachenkov, Alec Guinness
Rating: ★★★

Although the script and minor acting are poor, the direction, scoring and leading performance are all very good in this sustained terror story. The first 30 minutes are excellent and, though the film gradually falls apart after the initial pursuit is over, it never quite loses its grip. Three Americans are pretty much on their own in Russia making a low-budget slasher film with an all-girl crew. Makeup effects girl Billie (Marina Sudina) goes back to the studio at night for some reason (you'll soon forget what) and stumbles on the filming of a 'snuff movie in which the girl 'star', thinking she's acting in a porno film, is really killed. Billie, who can hear but not speak, spends the next half-hour fleeing the killers, who suspect there's someone there, but never quite see her: a descent down a liftshaft is particularly hair-raising. Once the film opens out to include menacing figures on both sides of the law, it becomes less convincing, even if you might at one point wonder if anyone is on poor Billie's side.

Mutiny on the Bounty ○
1935, US, 135 mins, b/w
Dir: Frank Lloyd
Stars: Charles Laughton, Clark Gable, Franchot Tone
Rating: ★★★★

In the days when there were so many films (especially from MGM) that attractions at London's Empire Cinema (Metro's English showcase) hardly ever ran longer than seven days, this great sea story packed them in for three weeks, and was sold out every night. Frank Lloyd's direction captures the feel of the sea, and the harshness of the times, putting the film well ahead of the (nonetheless underrated) Marlon Brando remake of 27 years afterwards. It won an Academy Award for best film. Its highlight of course, is Charles Laughton's rigid and inhuman Bligh, ruthless in his treatment of the seamen. Remembered, imitated, caricatured but never bettered, it stays indelibly in the mind long after the film is over.

Mutiny on the Bounty ○ ⓥ
1962, US, 185 mins, colour
Dir: Lewis Milestone
Stars: Marlon Brando, Trevor Howard, Richard Harris, Hugh Griffith, Richard Haydn
Rating: ★★★

Two of the screen's finest actors star in this giant-sized, stunningly-mounted remake of the 1935 classic, based on one of history's greatest true-life sea adventures. Marlon Brando and Trevor Howard each bring their own powerful individualism to contrasting roles in the spectacular drama of two men with opposing attitudes and opposite ideals whose inevitable clash is set against the barbaric cruelty of life aboard a Royal Navy Ship in the 18th century. Good action, spectacular colour photography, and many moving moments.

My Beautiful Laundrette ● ⓥ
1985, UK, 97 mins, colour
Dir: Stephen Frears
Stars: Gordon Warnecke, Daniel Day Lewis, Saeed Jaffrey, Roshan Seth, Shirley Anne Field
Rating: ★★★

An example of low-budget British filmmaking at its most abrasive. Hanif Kureishi's award-winning script is funny, sexy, violent and perceptive by turn and treats its central homosexual love story in an honest and low-key way. The gutsy pivotal performances of Daniel Day Lewis (remarkable as a blond punk) and Gordon Warnecke (as his business partner and lover) are complemented by Saeed Jaffrey's deliciously underhand uncle – a sort of Pakistani South London Arthur Daley – and by Shirley Anne Field as his white mistress.

My Best Friend's Wedding
1997, US 106 mins, colour
Dir: PJ Hogan
Stars: Julia Roberts, Dermot Mulroney, Cameron Diaz, Rupert Everett, M Emmet Walsh
Rating: ★★★★

Not quite consistently bright enough to be at the very top of its class, this screwball romantic comedy still has some delightful scenes and several very funny moments. When cookery writer Roberts gets a call from best friend (and ex-flame) Mulroney asking her to be maid of honour at his wedding, she realises she still loves him. She has just four days to win him back. Julia tries all she can think of, but the bride-to-be (Diaz) proves to be a real sweetie who just blunders her way past the obstacles her rival puts down. What is poor Julia to do? Enlist her gay editor (Everett) as a suitor to make Mulroney jealous, that's what! Unfortunately for Julia, Everett also steals the film with a nicely judged

performance that neatly steers clear of the over-camp. By today's comedy standards, it's a gem.

My Blue Heaven ● ⓥ
1990, US, 95 mins, colour
Dir: Herbert Ross
Stars: Steve Martin, Rick Moranis, Joan Cusack, Melanie Mayron, William Irwin
Rating: ★★★

It's good to see Steve Martin back in outright comedy and this one is a lot of fun. He's a laugh from the start as a Mafia gangster with loo-brush hair and sheer silk suits, transplanted by FBI agent Rick Moranis to Anytown America as part of the witness relocation programme. Naturally the Mafioso can't keep his fingers out of crime, not that he's fazed when DA Joan Cusack keeps arresting him: he knows Moranis will keep him out of jail and well protected from the hitmen who will try to bump him off. Dotty dialogue and a myriad of actionful incidents make this one of the snappiest and cleanest Martin comedies in years. The highspot is a wild dance sequence in the middle of the film, when Martin teaches Moranis the marenga.

My Bodyguard ○
1980, US, 96 mins, colour
Dir: Tony Bill
Stars: Chris Makepeace, Adam Baldwin, Matt Dillon, Ruth Gordon, John Houseman, Martin Mull
Rating: ★★★★

A heartwarming teen drama about school bullying that leads to a touching relationship between two boys. It's a modest film that never lets its message get in the way of the story. Among the cast of then-unknowns is Matt Dillon as the school bully, while Adam Baldwin is a true find as the silent brooding hulk who instils terror in every boy, but turns out to be a gentle giant. The screenplay is honest, the teens talk the way teens do, and first-time director Tony Bill (himself an actor) strikes not one false note. Dave Grusin's brooding score adds immeasurably to the atmosphere.

My Brother Jonathan ○
1947, UK, 107 mins, b/w
Dir: Harold French
Stars: Michael Denison, Dulcie Gray, Ronald Howard, Beatrice Campbell
Rating: ★★★★

An honest and entertaining piece of work about a doctor's life, this film made Michael Denison a British box-office star. The atmosphere of the

M

old-time slum areas of the Black country is very well sustained.

My Cousin Rachel ○

1952, US, 98 mins, b/w
Dir: Henry Koster
Stars: Olivia de Havilland, Richard Burton
Rating: ★★★

Atmospheric and compelling film of Daphne Du Maurier's best-seller, a perfect example of the way they just don't make 'em any more. It was Richard Burton's first film in Hollywood and although, understandably, he didn't register too well in a slightly weak role which is always subsidiary to Olivia de Havilland's splendid Rachel, his next two performances (in *The Robe and The Desert Rats*) established him as powerful actor of the widest range. The mood of *My Cousin Rachel* is magnificently all of a piece, achieved by the combined efforts of director Henry Koster, composer Franz Waxman and photographer Joseph La Shelle.

My Cousin Vinny ● ⓥ

1992, US, 119 mins, colour
Dir: Jonathan Lynn
Stars: Joe Pesci, Ralph Macchio, Marisa Tomei, Fred Gwynne
Rating: ★★

An enormously overlong comedy that runs like a 50-minute TV play expanded to two hours. Joe Pesci in a funny wig is Vinny, a forty-something Brooklyn boy, newly graduated from law school with amazingly little knowledge of legal procedure and absolutely no qualifications in social graces. Vinny's all at sea when called on to defend his nephew (Ralph Macchio) and a friend on a murder charge, and it looks like the boys are for the chair. Such fun as is to be had in the first hour stems from the constant flow of bad language from Vinny and his fiancée (the stunning Marisa Tomei in an Oscar-winning performance) and his fruitless efforts to find a hotel where he can actually get some sleep. Things liven up a bit when Vinny starts turning into a Columbo of the courtroom, but the meat of the film takes little more than 10 minutes to unfold. Big Fred Gwynne is drolly funny as the judge.

My Darling Clementine ○ ⓥ

1946, US, 100 mins, b/w
Dir: John Ford
Stars: Henry Fonda, Victor Mature, Linda Darnell, Walter Brennan, Ward Bond
Rating: ★★★★

Though by no means acclaimed in its day, this John Ford Western about Wyatt Earp and the gunfight at the OK Corral has now become accepted as a classic of the genre. 'This is not a film to rave about,' muttered the British *Monthly Film Bulletin* rebelliously. 'The story is not particularly good.' A true one, however, and good enough to form the axis of several other sturdy Western films. Decorated by the twin themes of camaraderie and action that were to dominate Ford films of the first post-war decade as never before, the film has black and white photography of amazing depth by Joe MacDonald and memorable portrayals by Henry Fonda (as Wyatt Earp), the underrated Victor Mature, coming up trumps as Doc Holliday, and Walter Brennan, the epitome of evil (even when not saying anything) as Old Man Clanton. John Ireland is again on the side of the Clantons, just as he was to be 10 years later in *Gunfight at the OK Corral*. But Ford's movie, studded with memorable individual scenes and shots, is the definitive version of the story.

My Fair Lady ○ ⓥ

1964, US, 175 mins, colour
Dir: George Cukor
Stars: Rex Harrison, Audrey Hepburn, Stanley Holloway, Wilfrid Hyde White, Gladys Cooper, Jeremy Brett
Rating: ★★★

With $17 million invested in transferring the monster stage musical to the screen, producer Jack L Warner was to rue the day he cast Audrey Hepburn over the stage actress Julie Andrews. Although she was yet to make it big as a household name, Andrews went on to stardom in *Mary Poppins* and *The Sound of Music* all within 12 months. Warner wanted Cary Grant to play Professor Higgins and James Cagney over Stanley Holloway as dustman Alfred Doolittle. But for all the casting disappointments, the film was a triumph and went on to win eight Oscars, including Best Film and for Cecil Beaton's amazing costumes, especially the stunning black and white Edwardian numbers as worn in the famous 'Ascot Gavotte' scene.

My Father the Hero ○ ⓥ

1994, US, 90 mins, colour
Dir: Steve Miner
Stars: Gérard Depardieu, Katharine Heigl, Dalton James, Lauren Hutton
Rating: ★

A one-joke comedy (the US version of a French frolic also starring Gérard

Depardieu) about a divorced father who takes his very advanced 14-year-old daughter (Katharine Heigl) for a holiday in the Bahamas. Fancying the nearest all-American hunk on the beach (Dalton James), the girl declares father Depardieu to be her lover (don't ask for logic) and some awkward and often embarrassing (not to mention boring) misunderstandings are set in motion for the next hour before the film livens up a bit towards the end as father and daughter gang up to net her the hunk. Highlight: Depardieu emptying the hotel restaurant (for more reasons than one) with a stirring rendition of 'Thank Heaven for Little Girls'. Lowpoint: a speedboat stunt sequence that goes on for ages.

My Favorite Blonde ○

1942, US, 78 mins, b/w
Dir: Sidney Lanfield
Stars: Bob Hope, Madeleine Carroll, Gale Sondergaard, George Zucco
Rating: ★★★★

Nearly all of Bob Hope's films in the comedy-thriller vein were successful, and this was one of the best. The presence of a gang of evil spies puts Hope into plenty of situations that expose the yellow streak running right down his character's back, especially when encountering dangers on a train with Madeleine Carroll as the blonde of the title. It also gives his writers (here including three of the best, Melvin Frank, Norman Panama and Don Hartman) the opportunity to provide 'Old Ski Nose' with the kind of 'cowardly wisecracks' his fans loved. Stony-faced Gale Sondergaard and oily George Zucco, who menaced Hope in his first great success, *The Cat and the Canary*, are on hand to lead the spies; but all concerned are upstaged in spectacular fashion by a talented penguin called Percy.

My Favorite Brunette ○

1947, US, 84 mins, b/w
Dir: Elliott Nugent
Stars: Bob Hope, Dorothy Lamour, Peter Lorre, Lon Chaney
Rating: ★★★★

A really well-sustained Bob Hope comedy that plays to all his strengths. There's an inventive story (baby photographer Hope gets mistaken for the detective in the office next door and is pitched headlong into a complex and dangerous adventure), lots of big laughs, Dorothy Lamour as the femme who almost proves fatale to Hope, an a wonderful cast of civilised and uncivilised heavies that includes Peter Lorre, Jack LaRue, Lon Chaney, Frank Puglia, Charles Dingle and John Hoyt. Alan Ladd's cameo as Hope's private eye pal is really good – played dead straight and right on the mark. And a certain 'old groaner' makes an inevitable and very amusing guest appearance almost at the end.

My Favorite Spy ○
1951, US, 93 mins, b/w
Dir: Norman Z McLeod
Stars: Bob Hope, Hedy Lamarr, Francis L Sullivan
Rating: ★★★

The third in Bob Hope's *Favorite* series of comedies gives him another delicious leading lady (Hedy Lamarr) to follow Madeleine Carroll and Dorothy Lamour. It casts him as a vaudeville comic compelled to impersonate the ruthless international spy who just happens to be his double, a trusty comedy situation on which Danny Kaye and Norman Wisdom, among others, would play variations in later years. Bob's wisecracks are in rattling good form. Asked to assume the spy's identity, he croaks: 'That ain't my line of work. I tell jokes. That's dangerous enough.'

My Favorite Wife ○
1940, US, 80 mins, b/w
Dir: Garson Kanin
Stars: Irene Dunne, Cary Grant, Randolph Scott, Gail Patrick
Rating: ★★★★

The original version of the famous comedy (since remade as *Three for the Show*, *Move Over Darling* and *Three's a Crowd*) about a wife who returns from being shipwrecked on a desert island to find that her husband is about to get married again. The direction was taken over by writer Garson Kanin after the original director, Leo McCarey, had been involved in a road accident. And a really slick, sophisticated, rib-tickling job Kanin turned in, with Cary Grant and Irene Dunne at the top of their form. Make yourself a pot of coffee and settle down for laughs galore.

My Favorite Year ○ Ⓥ
1982, US, 92 mins, colour
Dir: Richard Benjamin
Stars: Peter O'Toole, Mark Linn-Baker, Jessica Harper, Joseph Bologna
Rating: ★★★

A funny, nostalgic reminder of the days of live television, directed with warmth and affection by Richard Benjamin. Mark Linn-Baker makes an impressive feature debut as Benjy Stone, the eager young writer placed in charge of stylish, swashbuckling movie legend Alan Swann (Peter O'Toole), who is scheduled to guest star on the live TV show 'Comedy Cavalcade' – if he can stay sober for long enough. There is some cringingly hilarious mayhem, such as when Swann visits Benjy's Jewish Brooklyn family for dinner, and some inspired moments such as when Benjy tries to teach his girlfriend (Jessica Harper) the art of telling a good joke. The finale, with O'Toole swashing his buckle joyously, is truly heartwarming.

My Foolish Heart ○
1949, US, 98 mins, b/w
Dir: Mark Robson
Stars: Susan Hayward, Dana Andrews
Rating: ★★★

This was the big weepie of its year, boosted by the romantic musical theme by Victor Young, which was to become a world-wide best-seller. As the girl who is tempted to pass the responsibility for the pregnancy from a wartime romance on to a new admirer, Susan Hayward suffers nobly, as she was to do in a dozen films over the next decade, culminating in an Academy Award for her portrait of a condemned murderess in *I Want to Live!*.

My Friend Flicka ⊙
1943, US, 89 mins, colour
Dir: Harold Schuster
Stars: Roddy McDowall, Preston Foster, Rita Johnson
Rating: ★★★★

The teenage Roddy McDowall enjoyed one of his best Hollywood roles in this enormously popular story of a boy and his horse, stunningly shot in Technicolor on Utah locations by Dewey Wrigley. Director Harold Schuster, who made Britain's first Technicolor feature *Wings of the Morning* (also about a horse) shows a sure touch for this kind of outdoor adventure with a family background. The horse is the star, but Preston Foster and Rita Johnson skilfully and unobtrusively supply warmth and authority as McDowall's parents.

My Gal Sal ○
1942, US, 103 mins, colour
Dir: Irving Cummings
Stars: Rita Hayworth, Victor Mature,

Carole Landis, James Gleason
Rating: ★★★

The career of Paul Dreiser (brother of the novelist Theodore) forms the basis for this charming and beguiling musical set in the 1890s. Dreiser, who changed his name to Dresser, is played rather well by Victor Mature, but the real stars of the show are Rita Hayworth (although the singing voice she uses belongs to Nan Wynn) and a whole string of nostalgic song hits.

My Geisha ○
1962, US, 120 mins, colour
Dir: Jack Cardiff
Stars: Shirley MacLaine, Yves Montand, Edward G Robinson
Rating: ★★

This comedy about a director's wife (Shirley MacLaine) who whites up as a geisha girl to win the leading role in his next picture was produced by Miss MacLaine's real-life husband, Steve Parker, who lived in Japan for several years. Sadly it's a one-joke idea stretched out to two hours.

My Girl ○ Ⓥ
1991, US, 105 mins, colour
Dir: Howard Zieff
Stars: Dan Aykroyd, Jamie Lee Curtis, Macaulay Culkin, Anna Chlumsky, Richard Masur, Griffin Dunne
Rating: ★★

Rather pointlessly set in the Seventies, this is a merciless tear-jerker about the 12th summer of the daughter of an undertaker. A hypochondriac tomboy with a crush on her English teacher, her world comes crashing down when her widower father (Dan Aykroyd) takes on a beautician (Jamie Lee Curtis) to make up the corpses' faces and falls in love with her. The plot is slightly stiffened by the girl's aged grandma, who never says anything, but occasionally bursts vigorously into song, and by her friendship with a bespectacled fellow-student (Macaulay Culkin) who's very down-to-earth despite his fragile appearance. The film constantly strives not to be dull, but never quite succeeds, the dialogue needing to be sharper to make up for the lack of variety in the plot. But only the hardest of hearts will resist its massive attack on the tear-ducts in the last 20 minutes. Performances are OK.

My Girl 2 ○ Ⓥ
1994, US, 99 mins, colour
Dir: Howard Zieff
Stars: Anna Chlumsky, Dan Aykroyd, Jamie Lee Curtis, Austin O'Brien, Richard

M

Masur, Christine Ebersole
Rating: **RB**

The original *My Girl* was winning enough, apart from its mawkish ending But this sequal is a loser: a dull and pointless account of how 13-year-old Vada researches into the life of her mother, who died when she was born. Under Howard Zieff's direction, the acting is at best all-round modest as Vada goes to California and meets a seties of boringly colourful characters in her search for facts on mom. Efforts at romance between Anna Chlumsky and Austin O'Brien (as her teenage companion) are excruciatingly embarrassing – if you're still awake that is. Dan Aykroyd and Jamie Lee Curtis should be grateful that they're only in this supremely tedious exercise for the first 15 minutes. If you have to see this, watch for an early continuity slip when Vada's friend removes her glasses on the approach of a boy – the director blissfully unaware that she hadn't been wearing them in the scene in the first place.

My Girl Tisa ○

1948, US, 95 mins, b/w
Dir: Elliott Nugent
Stars: Lilli Palmer, Sam Wanamaker
Rating: ★★★

Lilli Palmer did rather better than her then husband Rex Harrison out of Hollywood during their stay there in the late 1940s, making some excellent films which also included *Cloak and Dagger* and *Body and Soul*. This charming period drama, with its strong romantic flavour, featured her appeal at its best. Allen Boretz's perceptive script takes some gentle but amusing sideswipes at politicians and red tape. Oddly, enough, the film's happy ending was changed on its British release to an unhappy one – a rare occurrence for the time.

My Heart Goes Crazy

See: London Town

My Hero

See: A Southem Yankee

My Left Foot ◐ ⓥ

1989, UK, 98 mins, colour
Dir: Jim Sheridan
Stars: Daniel Day-Lewis, Ray McAnally, Brenda Fricker
Rating: ★★★★

Don't miss Daniel Day-Lewis's Oscar-winning portrait of the Irish writer Christy Brown, afflicted from childhood with cerebral palsy. Quite apart from his crippling disability, Brown was also a witty, eccentric, difficult man, and Day-Lewis expresses the combination amazingly, sometimes frighteningly well, as does young Hugh O'Conor (from *Lamb*), playing Brown as a boy. Not an easy film from director Jim Sheridan but certainly a rewarding one.

My Life ◐ ⓥ

1993, US, 117 mins, colour
Dir: Bruce Joel Rubin
Stars: Michael Keaton, Nicole Kidman, Haing S Ngor
Rating: ★★

Skilfully sentimental, at least on the surface, this study of a man who, dying of cancer, decides to leave a video history of himself for his unborn child, is just about prevented from sinking into a sea of tears by the multi-faceted performance of Michael Keaton, who's allowed to show he can still be funny as well as dramatic – and just as well. Writer-director Bruce Joel Rubin seems to have no deeper objective than making his audience cry and his script, though competently written with some warmly amusing dialogue for the star, lacks the ambition to lend its story greater stature and contains too few surprises along the way. Nicole Kidman is competent in a quieter role than usual, but seems, like most of the cast, to be crying out for something more meaningful.

My Little Chickadee ○

1939, US, 83 mins, b/w
Dir: Edward Cline
Stars: Mae West, W C Fields
Rating: ★★★

'Is this a game of chance?' asks an innocent suckered by W C Fields into a card game. 'Not the way I play it, no,' replies Fields in this zany burlesque of Westerns which united his inmmoveable force with Mae West's irresistible object in a comedy battle that finally emerges as an entertaining draw. The two stars wrote the screenplay between them, delivering some of their most memorable lines. West, asked if she is trying to show contempt for the court, confides that she is trying to hide it. And Fields ends the film by inviting West to 'C'mon up and see me some time.' Not as funny as it might have been, the film's best sequences still make it a pleasure.

My Little Girl ● ⓥ

1986, US, 118 mins, colour
Dir: Connie Kaiserman

Stars: Mary Stuart Masterson, Geraldine Page, James Earl Jones, Anne Meara, Peter Gallagher, Page Hannah
Rating: ★★

This parable about a 16-year-old trainee social worker at a centre for homeless girls is almost as naive as its central character, a poor little rich girl played with some appeal by Mary Stuart Masterson. Overlong and with a script that doesn't cut deep enough, it's nonetheless sufficiently involving to make you want to learn a bit more about the ultimate fate of its characters. James Earl Jones gives a characteristically highly-charged performance as the centre's director – one of the few characters that isn't overdrawn – and Geraldine Page does what she can with the cameo role of the heroine's gran.

My Man Godfrey ○

1936, US, 90 mins, b/w
Dir: Gregory La Cava
Stars: William Powell, Carole Lombard
Rating: ★★★★

Sparkling screwball comedy, made during the Depression, about a tramp adopted as a butler by a millionaire's eccentric family. Peerless playing by William Powell (urbane even in rags) and the delightful Carole Lombard, both earning Oscar nominations.

My Man Godfrey ○

1957, US, 92 mins, colour
Dir: Henry Koster
Stars: David Niven, June Allyson
Rating: ★★★

A spirited remake of the classic original 1936 comedy film. Adroit playing from David Niven as Godfrey the butler complements clever direction by Henry Koster. Better than its reputation would have you think.

My Name is Julia Ross ○

1945, US, 70 mins, b/w
Dir: Joseph H Lewis
Stars: Nina Foch, George Macready, Dame May Whitty
Rating: ★★★

This moody little thriller about a girl who finds herself losing her identity is enthralling from beginning to end, and helped to make a cult figure of its director Joseph H Lewis. It looks less convincing today, with the villainy of George Macready and Dame May Whitty more amusing than chilling. Nina Foch, though (as Julia), was never better.

My New Gun ● Ⓥ

1992, US, 99 mins, colour
Dir: Stacy Cochran
Stars: Diane Lane, James LeGros, Stephen Collins, Tess Harper
Rating: ★★

A strange, semi-surrealist, almost *Twin Peaks*-like film about the bizarre consequences of a husband (Stephen Collins) believing his wife (Diane Lane) needs a gun for protection. He ends up in hospital, they part, and she ends up with the strange youth next door (James LeGros), whose pixilated mother (Tess Harper) is possibly a former country and western star in failing health ... who seems to be threatened by someone or something. It's one of those films with rather poor sound, lots of odd pauses and indecisive action and dialogue that sometimes sounds improvised. People move and act as if in a dream world. And you may not grasp what the film's about even when it's over. Downright peculiar.

My Own Private Idaho ● Ⓥ

1991, US, 104 mins, colour
Dir: Gus Van Sant
Stars: River Phoenix, Keanu Reeves, James Russo, William Richert
Rating: ★★★

This unusual and highly original road movie looks at the mixed fortunes or a couple of street hustlers: River Phoenix, as a sex-for-hire male prostitute, who suffers from narcolepsy – falling asleep at a second's notice – and Keanu Reeves as the wealthy son of Portland's mayor, and the object of Phoenix's unrequited love. It was a brave choice of role for Phoenix, and he brought to the role his trademark honesty and simplicity. The critical acclaim he received boded well for a long and fruitful career, but that was not to be. Actually, for a film about two gay hustlers, *Idaho* contains very little sex. Those who stick with it will discover a highly personal vision brimming over with passages of intriguing hallucinatory effects, and even a flirtation with Shakespeare's *Henry IV, Part 1* in the entertaining screenplay.

My Sister Eileen ○

1955, US, 108 mins, colour
Dir: Alexander Hall
Stars: Janet Leigh, Jack Lemmon, Betty Garrett, Bob Fosse
Rating: ★★★★

Columbia certainly pulled out a plum with this musical remake of their own comedy success of a dozen years earli-er. A bright, cheerful frolic full of vitality, the film is dominated by Janet Leigh – always surprisingly good when given the chance – and Betty Garrett (even better) as singing sisters. The comedy is joyously funny, the dancing scintillating and the singing delightful. All this and a singing Jack Lemmon too: no wonder this one leaves a warm glow behind.

My Six Convicts ○

1952, US, 104 mins, b/w
Dir: Hugo Fregonese
Stars: Millard Mitchell, Gilbert Roland, John Beal
Rating: ★★★★

Under a novel prison rehabilitation scheme, a group of six prisoners become 'trustys'. A first-rate and heartwarming semi-documentary produced by Stanley Kramer and featuring Swedish actor Alf Kjellin, Marshall Thompson and, lurking way down the cast-list under the anonymity of his real name, Charles Bronson, billed as Charles Buchinsky. The situations produce some very funny moments and a few tellingly dramatic ones, while the best performances come from veteran Millard Mitchell, and much-wasted actor John Beal.

My Stepmother is an Alien ○ Ⓥ

1988, US, 107 mins, colour
Dir: Richard Benjamin
Stars: Dan Aykroyd, Kim Basinger, Jon Lovitz
Rating: ★★★

Kim Basinger has never been sexier and Dan Aykroyd never funnier than in this Frankenscience comedy. Kim's alien is simply sensational, whether stripping for Aykroyd's pleasure, or doing an impression of Jimmy Durante learned from television. When widower Aykroyd first meets her, he's hooked: he hopes he isn't boring the pants off her. With an extra-terrestrial twist, Basinger checks it out and looks up her own skirt. No, she announces, they're still there. Actually, it's his secret she's after – an extra-galactic probe that can save her planet. Aykroyd has other probes in mind and, after Kim has learned about kissing and sex from her 'living' handbag, he's down on his knees proposing. 'Boy,' gasps Dan, 'I spend my whole career trying to find life on another planet and when I do I end up marrying it'. The situations bubble and the laughs come fairly thick and fast, with Basinger a dizzy delight.

Mysterious Island ○

1961, UK, 101 mins, colour
Dir: Cy Endfield
Stars: Michael Craig, Joan Greenwood, Herbert Lom
Rating: ★★★

This action-filled adventure film, based on a book by Jules Verne, provides a field day for the special effects boys, once again headed by the ubiquitous Ray Harryhausen. Here he provides a battery of giant beasts, birds, crabs and bees. Top composer Bernard Herrmann, one of Alfred Hitchcock's favourites for background music, weighs in with a characteristically full-blooded score. A good cast, which includes Gary Merrill, Nigel Green and Herbert Lom as the ever-present Captain Nemo, puts the hokum across with spirit.

Mystery of Edwin Drood, The ❶ Ⓥ

1993, UK, 100 mins, colour
Dir: Timothy Forder
Stars: Robert Powell, Finty Williams, Jonathan Phillips, Rupert Rainsford, Nanette Newman, Michelle Evans
Rating: ★

Various versions of Charles Dickens' last, unfinished story lead one only to conclude that the great CD had, by this time, lost it. The first hour of this story of foul deeds and unrequited passion is as dull as ditchwater. Photographed in black and brown, this section of the film is about as interesting as paint drying and has much the same pace. Only when writer-director Timothy Forder is able to break free of Dickens does he, in the words of Laurel and Hardy, start to get some place. If the last 40 minutes are more Victorian Gothic (with a touch of Hammer horror), they do seem to be closer to what Dickens' work was about than those parts of the story contributed by the novelist himself. Robert Powell isn't exactly right for John Jasper but does well when the script allows; but Finty Williams is poor as Rosa: an undistinguished film debut for Judi Dench's daughter.

Mystery of the Wax Museum, The ❶

1933, US, 77 mins, colour
Dir: Michael Curtiz
wvvill, Fay Wray, Glenda Farrell, Frank McHugh
Ratint: ★★★★

Director Michael Curtiz's macabre classic builds up an atmosphere of brooding evil that puts it several streets

M

ahead of the 1953 remake *House Wax.* Lionel Atwin is the disfigured and vengeful wax-modeller who captures the delicious Fay Wray in an alarming and disturbing climax. The film was thought to be totally lost until a perfect print turned up in a collection a few years ago. Now it can be shown in the original, and rare two-band Technicolor. Although the results here are remarkably successful, adding a strange, eerie quality to Anton Grot's spectacular art direction, the lighting involved during shooting produced such an intense heat that the wax figures used in the museum sequences were forever starting to melt, to say nothing of the poor actors. Glenda Farrell provides Miss Wray with some hot competition in the acting stakes with her intrepid, wisecracking reporter.

Mystery Street O
1950, US, 93 mins, b/w
Dir: John Sturges
Stars: Ricardo Montalban, Sally Forrest, Bruce Bennett, Jan Sterling
Rating: ★★★

A fascinating account of a criminal case solved almost entirely by science. Director John Sturges gives a wealth of detail about painstaking police work, employing semi-documentary techniques. Good acting from a cast that includes Ricardo Montalban, Bruce Bennett, Betsy Blair, Elsa Lanchester in viciously fine form as the victim's avaricious landlady – and Jan Sterling.

Mystery Submarine O
(aka: Decoy)
1962, UK, 92 mins, b/w
Dir: C M Pennington-Richards
Stars: Edward Judd, James Robertson Justice
Rating: ★★

A British war film that seems to have strayed into the 1960s from at least 10 years earlier. Resolute Edward Judd is fine as the commander of a wolf in sheep's clothing – a Nazi submarine with a British crew – and James Robertson justice is in typically fiery form as Rear-Admiral Rainbird.

Mystery Train ● Ⓥ
1989, US, 110 mins, colour
Dir: Jim Jarmusch
Stars: Screamin' Jay Hawkins, Nicoletta Braschi, Joe Strummer
Rating: ★★

The first colour film by the cult American director, Jim Jarmusch, composed of three tales featuring out-of-place foreigners who all end up in a seedy Memphis hotel on the same night. Certain details reappear, linking the three tales: a gunshot, a DJ's patter (the voice of Tom Waits) on the radio, the night clerk and bellhop at the hotel (played by veteran R&B singer Screamin' Jay Hawkins and Spike Lee's brother Cinque) who keep up a deadpan double act. The three sets of protagonists never meet and nothing much happens. Fans of Jarmusch's off-beat style of filmmaking, however, will relish his familiar trademarks, all present here – long takes, lots of lateral tracking shots, elliptical dialogue, and full of quirky details, like the plum the Japanese girl gives as a tip to the hotel bellhop. Newcomers to Jarmusch may find *Mystery Train* maddening but given half a chance it is oddly rewarding.

Mystic Pizza ❶ Ⓥ
1988, US, 104 mins, colour
Dir: Donald Petrie
Stars: Annabeth Gish, Julia Roberts, Lili Taylor, Vincent D'Onofrio
Rating: ★★

Another in the still-popular line of female buddy movies, this time about three waitresses working at a pizza house in the New England fishing town of Mystic. They're all part of the local Portuguese fishing community, which explains their restlessness at the all-too-real possibilities of becoming trapped for life in one small township. Lili Taylor, Annabeth Gish and Julia Roberts deliver knockout performances in these three roles and it's a shame their efforts aren't supported by a better script. Believable dialogue and logical plot and character developments are not, alas, on the menu at the Mystic Pizza, though there are some foolish sex scenes for those with a taste for them. Never mind, our dynamite girl trio serves up a feast of fine acting between courses to help you forget that the main meal has fallen flat.

My Teenage Daughter O
(aka: Teenage Bad Girl)
1956, UK, 100 mins, b/w
Dir: Herbert Wilcox
Stars: Anna Neagle, Sylvia Syms
Rating: ★★

Teenage dramas were all the rage when Sylvia Syms made her debut in this tearful but absorbing drama, which never fails to hold the attention. Kenneth Haigh also made an excellent debut as her boyfriend, but seemed afterwards to prefer the stage. Norman Wooland brings the right touch of masculine comfort as the suitor of harassed Dame Anna Neagle. But poor Wilfrid Hyde White, billed as co-star, gets so few lines that he might as well have stayed at home.

My Wife's Family O
1956, UK, 76 mins, colour
Dir: Gilbert Gunn
Stars: Ronald Shiner, Ted Ray, Diane Hart, Greta Gynt, Robertson Hare
Rating: ★★

Broad comedy, with Ronald Shiner and Ted Ray extracting the maximum number of laughs (not many) out of the mother-in-law-coming-to-stay situation. Fabia Drake gives a sharply observed portrait of the old battleaxe.

N

Nadine ○ Ⓥ
1987, US, 83 mins, colour
Dir: Robert Benton
Stars: Jeff Bridges, Kim Basinger, Rip Torn
Rating: ★★★

A lightweight, enjoyable comedy, entirely atypical of writer-director Robert Benton, and more like a TV movie with an above-average script. Though the plot doesn't have any situations that aren't familiar, Benton's script has enough life in it to make them seem, if not mint-new, at least acceptable. In the title role, Kim Basinger, radiant in Fifties costumes, and obviously in control of her material, has never looked better.

Nails ● Ⓥ
1992, US, 100 mins, colour
Dir: John Flynn
Stars: Dennis Hopper, Anne Archer, Tomas Milian, Keith David, Cliff De Young
Rating: ★★

Slam-bang action all the way, with Dennis Hopper as Detective Harry 'Nails' Niles, a good cop with a bad attitude (well, being Hopper he would have wouldn't he?). When his partner gets killed in an ambush while working on Something Big, dirty Harry sets out to foil the baddies and administer his own brand of vigilante-style justice. A well-plotted film whose endearing quirkiness is mainly down to Hopper's own offbeat personality. Director John Flynn, who made *The Outfit, Best Seller* and *Lock Up*, knows how to steamroll this sort of action crime thriller along and, like his leading character, doesn't allow too many sideline issues to get in his way. If you like Hopper the odds are on you liking this. Don't expect subtlety.

Naked ● Ⓥ
1993, UK, 126 mins, colour
Dir: Mike Leigh
Stars: David Thewlis, Katrin Cartlidge, Lesley Sharp
Rating: ★

Loved by 99 per cent of the world's critics, but not this one, nor I fancy quite a fair proportion of the video-watching public, this is appalling minimalist cinema from director Mike

Leigh which might well have shared the title of one of his previous films *Bleak Moments*. Shot to all intents and purposes in black and white (actually colour with the shades drained), this has little to do with entertainment or cinema. A drifter (David Thewlis) turns up at his ex-girlfriend's ramshackle flat and proceeds to couple with her gothic friend and anyone else who comes within range, all of whom are quite ready for instant sex. As a portrait of deadbeats, this is charmless, clumsy, cramped and only occasionally amusing. It could, in fact, be a cure for insomnia – but if you've had a hard day and feel like putting your head in the gas oven, these mannered manic depressives will give you a shove.

Naked Alibi ○
1954, US, 85 mins, b/w
Dir: Jerry Hopper
Stars: Sterling Hayden, Gloria Grahame
Rating: ★★★★

Described by *Picturegoer* as 'one of the best cop-crook thrillers of the year', this is a really tight melodrama about a policeman obsessed with proving an acquitted man guilty of murder. It starts off ordinarily, then gets better and better: every line of its sparse dialogue has a point, every spurt of action a punch. Sterling Hayden and Gloria Grahame both give gusty portrayals in this gripping drama – but Gene Barry, in the best performance of his career, is outstanding as the man the cop is after. Hair-raising climax.

Naked City, The ○
1948, US, 96 mins, b/w
Dir: Jules Dassin
Stars: Barry Fitzgerald, Howard Duff, Don Taylor
Rating: ★★★★★

Filmed almost entirely on location on the streets of New York City, this thrilling crime film deservedly took Oscars for editing and photography in its story of a hunt for a killer (one of the 'eight million stories in the naked city', according to its narrator). It also has a marvellously dry performance by Barry Fitzgerald, as the detective in charge of the investigation, some exciting action and chase sequences, and a famous climax on Brooklyn Bridge. One of the best films of its type ever made.

Naked Gun: From the Files of Police Squad!, The ◑ Ⓥ
1988, US, 85 mins, colour
Dir: David Zucker

Stars: Leslie Nielsen, Priscilla Presley, Ricardo Montalban, George Kennedy, O J Simpson
Rating: ★

David Zucker takes over from Jim Abrahams as director of the *Airplane!* team's comedy films, and the result is a laugh drought that may have fans screaming for half-an-hour of sitcom on the telly. The jokes are mostly elaborately telegraphed and clumsily executed; most of them will make you wince, grimace or pull any expression other than a smile. Leslie Nielsen heads an all-too-distinguished cast as a cop on the trail of a mob kingpin (Ricardo Montalban); he could have hit him over the head with a sledgehammer – it would have been well in keeping with the tenor of these disastrously unfunny proceedings. The Queen of England somehow gets dragged into the monumentally humourless affair that follows, but certainly to no-one's advantage. One funny scene: when the outline of a corpse is drawn on water at a murder scene; every cloud has a silver lining.

Naked Gun 2½: The Smell Of Fear, The ◑ Ⓥ
1991, US, 85 mins, colour
Dir: David Zucker
Stars: Leslie Nielsen, Priscilla Prestey, George Kennedy, O J Simpson, Robert Goulet
Rating: ★★★

Altogether more agreeable than its predecessor, this sequel to *The Naked Gun* is more akin to *Airplane!* in its humour. Sometimes there are so many gags going on in the background to a scene that it's hard to keep up, especially if you're trying to follow the plot about Lt Frank Drebin (Nielsen) uncovering a dastardly attempt to influence the energy policy of the US government. At the same time, he attempts to rekindle the fading embers of his affair with Jane (Presley) who just happens to be involved. Drebin's capacity for catastrophe is definitely rivalling that of Peter Sellers' Clouseau and is used to the full in a wildly successful running gag involving the misfortunes of then-First Lady Barbara Bush. Watch quickly for Zsa Zsa Gabor in a fleeting but funny guest appearance.

Naked Gun 33⅓: The Final Insult ◑ Ⓥ
1994, US, 81 mins, colour
Dir: David Zucker
Stars: Leslie Nielsen, Priscilla Presley, George Kennedy, O J Simpson, Fred

Ward, Kathleen Freeman
Rating: ★★

Quite good fun, this third helping of
Naked Goonery, if a little more
strained than before, and lacking the
spontaneous hilarity of the second segment. Jane (Priscilla Presley) leaves
Frank Drebin (Leslie Nielsen) who has
just retired, when he gets back on the
beat to thwart an Arab-controlled attempt to blow up the Academy
Awards. The jokes, as usual, are mostly below the belt, and some broad
swings are taken at other movies, the
most successful being *White Heat*, with
Fred Ward and a snarling Kathleen
Freeman filling in nicely for James
Cagney and Margaret Wycherly from
the original. Several guest stars also
submit to the Drebin treatment, notably Raquel Welch, as game as ever
in knockabout comedy, and still stunning at 54; and Pia Zadora, who
proves she can really belt out a song,
as well as run round with a tuba on
her head. Not for the easily offended.
Others will chuckle consistently.

Naked Jungle, The ○
1954, US, 90 mins, colour
Dir: Byron Haskin
Stars: Eleanor Parker, Charlton Heston,
William Conrad
Rating: ★★★

Ernest Laszlo's Technicolor photography makes the most of an unusual
setting – a turn-of-the-century cocoa
plantation in the South American jungle
– in this combination of romantic
drama and suspense thriller. Lots of
tension and excitement towards the end
as a massive army of soldier ants
marches towards plantation owner
Charlton Heston and his new bride.
The script is less effective, but this deficiency becomes insignificant once the
ants take charge of the story. Producer
George Pal and director Byron Haskin,
who also made *The War of the Worlds* together, conjure up some amazing special
effects involving ants that are guaranteed to make you itch, and imported
millions of the creatures for close-up
work actually filmed during production.

Naked Lunch ● Ⓥ
1991, US, 115 mins, colour
Dir: David Cronenberg
Stars: Peter Weller, Judy Davis, Ian
Holm, Julian Sands, Roy Scheider
Rating: ★

A film about drugs, hallucinations and
cockroaches, which sets out to disgust
us and succeeds admirably. Writer
William Lee moonlights as a bug ex-

terminator, but becomes hooked on his
own bug powder, shooting his wife (or
does he?) and hallucinating himself
into an 'inner zone', where he imagines
all the typewriters turn into cockroaches with talking orifices, or gooey
monsters with phallic appendages in
their heads. Sex and the drive to
write, together with the drugs, sends
the poor guy on the trip to end them
all, but might provide a cure for insomnia for the rest of us. Peter Weller
plays Lee morosely; Judy Davis as his
wife leers like Glenda Jackson on one
of her off days. On balance, Weller
could reflect that even *Robocop 3* might
have been better.

Naked Runner, The ○
1967, UK, 104 mins, colour
Dir: Sidney J Furie
Stars: Frank Sinatra, Peter Vaughan,
Nadia Gray
Rating: ★★

Frank Sinatra's only British film has
him cast as an ordinary businessman
caught up in international intrigue.
Sidney Furie directs tricksily, but the
action is explosively effective and there
are some good twists. In transferring
Francis Clifford's best-selling book to
the screen, Stanley Mann doesn't quite
manage to iron out the illogicalities
(how does a businessman happen to
have his gun with him on an apparently routine trip to a trade fair?) or the
confusions. But there's little doubt he
succeeds in keeping events coming at a
cracking pace.

Naked Spur, The ○
1953, US, 91 mins, colour
Dir: Anthony Mann
Stars: James Stewart, Janet Leigh,
Robert Ryan
Rating: ★★★★

Drawling James Stewart unhitches his
lower lip and hits the trail to capture
Robert Ryan, playing a picture of leering dishonesty called Ben
Vandergroat. The result is an excellent Western, with a brilliant, taut,
tense and exciting climax on a high
cliff, which was one of director
Anthony Mann's best. The classic dramatic framework – three men trying to
bring another back to justice – is superbly maintained, and Mann gets
excellent portrayals from each one of
his four men (Millard Mitchell and
Ralph Meeker are the others) as well
as from Janet Leigh, pretty much
deglamorised here and sporting a new
cropped haircut. The screenplay was
nominated for an Academy Award.

Naked Street, The ○
1955, US, 84 mins, b/w
Dir: Maxwell Shane
Stars: Anthony Quinn, Farley Granger,
Anne Bancroft
Rating: ★★

Tough thriller with Anthony Quinn as
a gangster resorting to desperate measures to save his sister's lover from the
death penalty. *The Naked Street* is one
of the films Anne Bancroft made in the
mid-Fifties, when struggling to establish herself as a dramatic actress
following a series of milk-and-water
roles at Fox. All of these films take on
new significance in the light of Miss
Bancroft's subsequent performances.

Naked Truth, The ⊙
(aka: Your Past is Showing)
1957, UK, 92 mins, b/w
Dir: Mario Zampi
Stars: Terry-Thomas, Peter Sellers,
Peggy Mount
Rating: ★★★

Terry-Thomas and Peter Sellers, fresh
from playing the robbers in *tom thumb*,
are both on top form in this zany comedy of errors about a scandal magazine
publisher (Dennis Price at his
smoothest) and the intended 'victims'
who turn on him in various hilarious
ways. The screenplay by Michael
Pertwee gives Sellers some delightfully
Goonish dialogue, and an opportunity
to demonstrate his mastery of disguises.

Name of the Rose, The ● Ⓥ
1986, US, 130 mins, colour
Dir: Jean-Jacques Annaud
Stars: Sean Connery, Christian Slater,
F Murray Abraham
Rating: ★★★

Too many grotesques almost spoil the
broth in this impressively well-made
film version of Umberto Eco's massive
best-seller. And the motivation and
resolution of the murders that plague
an isolated 14th-century Italian
monastery are never quite sharp
enough to focus our attention wholeheartedly on a story that struggles
manfully to pull its disparate elements
together. Sean Connery is admittedly
a great help as the investigator, a sort
of Franciscan Sherlock Holmes; and
production designer Dante Ferretti deserves high praise for his amazing
monastery with its clutter of mediaeval bric-a-brac and the labyrinth that
lies within its tower. Visually memorable then, if dramatically dense, the
film is on the whole an enjoyable experience.

Namu the Killer Whale ☉
1966, US, 88 mins, colour
Dir: Lasio Benedek
Stars: Robert Lansing, Lee Meriwether
Rating: ★★

An odd film to come from Laslo Benedek, who made Brando's *The Wild One*. But children will enjoy this beautifully photographed story of a killer whale which became a gentle pet long before *Free Willy*!

Nana ○
(aka: Lady of the Boulevards)
1934, US, 89 mins, b/w
Dir: Dorothy Arzner
Stars: Anna Sten, Phillips Holmes, Lionel Atwill
Rating: ★★

This adaptation of the Emile Zola classic was Samuel Goldwyn's attempt to make a new Garbo out of the beautiful Russian actress Anna Sten. She hadn't Garbo's mystique, though, and after a few more films was relegated to lesser roles.

Nana ◑
1955, France/Italy, 96 mins, colour
Dir: Christian-Jacque
Stars: Martine Carol, Charles Boyer
Rating: ★★

An opulent French-Italian version of Emile Zola's classic novel about a courtesan at the time of Napoleon III. Blonde sex symbol Martine Carol was well at home in such surroundings having also played Caroline Cherie, Lola Montes, Lucrezia Borgia and Madame DuBarry. Her gowns here are extraordinarily elaborate and, if the harsh realism and acute social observation of Zola's original goes largely by the board, the production design and evocative music by Georges van Parys provide some compensation.

Nancy Steele is Missing ○
1937, US, 86 mins, b/w
Dir: George Marshall
Stars: Victor McLaglen, Peter Lorre, June Lang, Walter Connolly
Rating: ★★★

Slightly unusual kidnap melodrama with an interesting cast. Censorship restrictions had meant very few such films since the real-life Lindbergh kidnapping case, and this one was particularly lucky to get through, in that it showed a kidnapper in a sympathetic light. Victor McLaglen's personality infuses this character with life, and there's distinctive support from June Lang, Jane Darwell, Walter

Connolly, John Carradine and especially Peter Lorre as McLaglen's devious cellmate.

Nanny, The ◑ ⓥ
1965, UK, 93 mins, b/w
Dir: Seth Holt,
Stars: Bette Davis, Wendy Craig
Rating: ★★★

The suspense is so well built up in this chilly drama that it's a pity the end is something of an anti-climax. No fault of the direction or actors: Jimmy Sangster's otherwise impeccable screenplay must shoulder the blame. Sitting perfectly poised on the suspense fence, the film asks the question: is Nanny (Bette Davis at her tightest-lipped) really the deranged and dangerous old woman that 10-year-old Joey (William Dix) alleges? Once or twice, the film descends to the ridiculous, but mostly the audience is kept well strung up awaiting the next development, to the accompaniment of some dramatic background music.

Narrow Margin, The ○
1952, US, 71 mins, b/w
Dir: Richard Fleischer
Stars: Charles McGraw, Marie Windsor
Rating: ★★★★

Tense, taut, sharply-acted low-budget thriller about a detective assigned to guard an important witness on a train journey. Charles McGraw, in one of a number of credibly tough performances he gave at this time, is first-rate as the witness's reluctant, hard-boiled protector who must save her from deadly strangers on a train. Marie Windsor is also strong as the gangster's widow he hates to have to keep alive. Richard Fleischer's fast-paced direction builds the suspense by the minute. A cracker.

Narrow Margin ◑ ⓥ
1990, US, 97 mins, colour
Dir: Peter Hyams
Stars: Gene Hackman, Anne Archer
Rating: ★★★

This thrilling chase thriller, set mostly aboard - and on top of - a speeding train hurtling through the stark Canadian wilderness, is a remake of one of the most successful B-movies in the history of RKO. This updated remake cost $21 million, and every cent of it is on the screen in the shape of spectacular stunts and breathtaking action set pieces. Gene Hackman turns in another reliable performance as a deputy district attorney charged with delivering key Mafia killing witness

Anne Archer to testify at a trial and having to keep them both safe from a gang of armed heavies in a pursuing helicopter and on the train. The two stars doing their own stuntwork adds to the tension.

National Health, The ◑
1973, UK, 97 mins, colour
Dir: Jack Gold
Stars: Lynn Redgrave, Donald Sinden, Jim Dale
Rating: ★★

Jim Dale gets all the best lines in Peter Nichols' skilful adaptation of his own hit play in which the scandalous conditions of a ramshackle national health hospital are contrasted with the comic cavortings in the medical soap opera being shown on the ward television. A beguiling, perceptive and sometimes funny black comedy.

National Lampoon's Animal House ● ⓥ
1978, US, 109 mins, colour
Dir: John Landis
Stars: John Belushi, Tim Matheson, John Vernon, Verna Bloom
Rating: ★

Several of the people associated with this hugely successful exercise in bad taste campus comedy - costing less than $3 million to make, it soon grossed more than $100 million - moved on to greater fame. For chubby star John Belushi, who plays the gross Bluto, however, there was no happy ending; he was found dead from a drug overdose in 1982.

National Lampoon's Christmas Vacation ◑ ⓥ
(aka: National Lampoon's Winter Holiday)
1989, US, 103 mins, colour
Dir: Jeremiah Chechik
Stars: Chevy Chase, Beverly D'Angelo, Randy Quaid, Diane Ladd, E G Marshall, Juliette Lewis
Rating: ★★★

A welcome return to form for the hapless Griswold family, back on native soil after the hapless *European Vacation*. Chase is superbly straight-faced as the father whose grandiose schemes for a 'Griswold family Christmas' inevitably lead to disaster, including the funniest rooftop antics since Laurel and Hardy tried to erect an aerial. The Christmas dinner scene, and the expression of those participating, is also a priceless piece of film farce. And keep an eye on the cat and the Christmas tree lights.

N

National Lampoon's European Vacation ◐ Ⓥ

1985, US, 94 mins, colour
Dir: Amy Heckerling
Stars: Chevy Chase, Beverly D'Angelo, Eric Idle
Rating: ★

With Chevy Chase's comedy *National Lampoon's Vacation* scoring a surprise $30 million hit, it was perhaps predictable that a second serving was on the cards. But this graceless affair – a sort of American *Carry On* farce – is a sorry sequel. Even Charles and Diana are dragged into the tiresome plot. The best thing in it, though, is the opening sequence. Director Amy Heckerling falls into the same trap as in her biggest hit to date, *Look Who's Talking*, by getting carried away with physical humour. But with the script providing just the sketchiest of character details, perhaps that was to be expected. Look out for fleeting cameos by British comedy stalwarts Mel Smith, Robbie Coltrane and Maureen Lipman.

National Lampoon's Loaded Weapon 1 ◐ Ⓥ

1993, US, 83 mins, colour
Dir: Gene Quintano
Stars: Emilio Estevez, Samuel L Jackson, Tim Curry, William Shatner, Whoopi Goldberg
Rating: ★★★

The hero rises from the heroine's bed andd walks off, ripplingly naked, down the corridor. 'What are you doing?' she asks. Emilio Estevez turns his head. 'Just taking one of those unmotivated butt-in-movie walks,' he replies. Yes, this is Hollywood in Lampoonland. This example is a very busy movie at 83 minutes, taking pot shots at *Lethal Weapon, Basic Instinct, The Silence of the Lambs, Star Trek* and even *Teenage Mutant Ninja Turtles*. Samuel L Jackson has the Danny Glover role while villains William Shatner and Tim Curry are not so far over the top that we don't enjoy them. Shatner's *Star Trek* engineer Scotty turns up trying to stop the police station coffee machine from blowing apart and there are amusing guest appearances from Whoopi Goldberg, Bruce Willis, F Murray Abraham (very good as Hannibal Lecher) and Erik Estrada, and a silly one from Charlie Sheen. Although it is often jolly rather than funny, at least this one doesn't tax your brain – or outstay its welcome.

National Lampoon's Vacation ◐ Ⓥ

1983, US, 95 mins, colour
Dir: Harold Ramis
Stars: Chevy Chase, Beverly D'Angelo, Randy Quaid
Rating: ★★★

Let's face it: any holiday where a maiden aunt *dies* in the back of your car has *got* to be a disaster. And catastrophe is virtually guaranteed with the hapless Griswold family, especially with Chevy Chase's know-it-all dad at the helm. He shows up well in this change-of-pace role as the father who drives his wife and kids thousands of miles to Walley World (a close relative of Walt Disney World) in Florida. En route they have the car stolen when they misroute into a ghetto district, enjoy a chaotic stay with poor country cousins ('Eddie says that after the baby comes I can quit one of my night jobs'), get lost in the desert and are thrown off a vibrating bed in a motel. That's just for starters! Beverly D'Angelo is a real little scene-stealer as Chase's wife, while the two kids, Anthony Michael Hall and Dana Barron, seem as natural and unspoilt as it's possible for movie kids to be.

National Lampoon's Winter Holiday

See: National Lampoon's Christmas Vacation

National Velvet ☉ Ⓥ

1944, US, 120 mins, colour
Dir: Clarence Brown
Stars: Elizabeth Taylor, Mickey Rooney, Donald Crisp, Angela Lansbury
Rating: ★★★★★

One of the greatest tearjerkers that MGM ever made: a warm-hearted piece of escapism about an 11-year-old girl and her horse, who take on the world's best steeplechasers in the Grand National. Elizabeth Taylor had already made a big impression in her first major film, *Lassie Come Home*, the previous year. Here her moving portrayal of Velvet, the girl determined to ride in the National, made millions reach for their handkerchieves, and shot her to stardom. Mickey Rooney gives her energetic support as the cynical jockey 'with a secret past' and Anne Revere won an Academy Award as her mother. It all adds up to an outsize dose of nostalgia for film fans, and a treat for children – and you'll notice Miss Taylor does much of her own horse-riding. During filming she took one particularly bad fall, injuring her

back to such an extent that she has suffered pain throughout her career.

Natural, The ◐ Ⓥ

1984, US, 137 mins, colour
Dir: Barry Levinson
Stars: Robert Redford, Robert Duvall, Glenn Close, Kim Basinger
Rating: ★★

A talented 19-year-old baseball player is shot in a hotel room by a mysterious woman. Fifteen years later Roy Hobbs, in his mid-thirties, tries out for an ailing major league team and impresses with his exceptional skills. With Roy, the team prospers, but not everybody is happy. Director Barry Levinson has given this baseball film an air of mystery and the supernatural that, although quite fun (every time there's a flash of lightning, you know Redford's going to hit the ball about two miles) doesn't sit comfortably in this framework. Set in the 1930s, the film has a good sense of period and the story is reminiscent of films of that time. There are times when everything seems to be moving rather slowly, but despite the long running time it's enjoyable enough.

Natural Born Killers ● Ⓥ

1994, US, 119 mins, colour
Dir: Oliver Stone
Stars: Woody Harrelson, Juliette Lewis, Robert Downey Jr, Tommy Lee Jones, Tom Sizemore, Rodney Dangerfield
Rating: ★★

A violent, blood-soaked nightmare. Woody Harrelson and Juliette Lewis star as a young couple who embark on a three-week killing spree which leaves 52 people dead. The first part of the film records each murder in horrific detail. The second half examines the intense media circus that surrounds their capture, imprisonment and subsequent escape during a riot. It's a brain-numbing experience which bombards the viewer with a multitude of images from nature and the killers' evil deeds, but all uniformly repellent. The film seeks to show how the vulture-like media's thirst for bloody and violent images actually encourages violent crime, but director Oliver Stone merely glorifies the very violence that he seeks to condemn. It is also exceedingly dull to watch after the first few shocking minutes. Expect it to be heavily cut for any video release.

Naughty Marietta ○

1935, US, 106 mins, b/w
Dir: W S Van Dyke II

Stars: Jeanette MacDonald, Nelson Eddy, Frank Morgan, Eisa Lanchester
Rating: ★★★

Ah, sweet mystery of life! It's the film that brought Nelson Eddy and Jeanette MacDonald together. She's a French princess running off to America. He's the Indian scout she falls in love with. Pleasing period operetta with a Victor Herbert score. It started a fabulous run of success for the stars.

Navigator, The ⊙ ⓥ
1924, US, 63 mins, b/w
Dir: Donald Crisp, Buster Keaton
Stars: Buster Keaton, Kathryn McGuire
Rating: ★★★★

One of Buster Keaton's most successful full-length films, which made $2 million on its initial release. The 'business' on board the good ship *Navigator* is often priceless.

Navy S.E.A.L.S. ● ⓥ
1990, US, 113 mins, colour
Dir: Lewis Teague
Stars: Charlie Sheen, Michael Biehn, Joanne Whalley-Kilmer, Bill Paxton
Rating: ★

This gung-ho American action film is just fine until any of its characters has to open his mouth. Outdated in attitudes by a good 40 years, it presents us with a US land/water squad in the SAS tradition that has to destroy stolen US missiles somewhere in Lebanon. No problem, of course. 'You're dealing with extremists,' the squad is told. 'You're dealing with the Navy Seals.' is the reply. Ha!! With men like this, we could be off on World War 3 at any moment, especially hothead Charlie Sheen, who shoots a man for speaking disrespectfully of his mother. Michael Biehn is the caring skipper ('Are you all right?' he asks an obviously dying man) and Joanne Whalley-Kilmer gives a career-worst performance as a half-Lebanese reporter in love with him. The action is competency staged and constant, making this an enjoyably awful movie.

Near Dark ● ⓥ
1987, US, 94 mins, colour
Dir: Kathryn Bigelow
Stars: Adrian Pasdar, Jenny Wright, Lance Henriksen, Bill Paxton, Tim Thomerson
Rating: ★★

In contrast to its contemporary, *The Lost Boys*, this represents the darker side of the vampire coin. Its vampires are made to expire in a painfully pro-

tracted way as opposed to a clean stake through the heart and the doomy theme music by Tangerine Dream indicates that director Kathryn Bigelow intends few smiles to be had in this one. 'They ain't normal,' growls hero Adrian Pasdar's father (Tim Thomerson), trying to rescue his son from their clutches after he has been seduced into the pack by a slinky lady vamp (Jenny Wright). 'Normal people don't spit out bullets when you shoot 'em.' Well, very true, but then normal people weren't around as far back as the American Civil War. There are times when the film's obsession with gore makes it hard to come to terms with, but the performances are solid and the director throws in a few genuine chills as well as liberally catering for more blood-hungry fans.

Nearest and Dearest ○
1972, UK, 93 mins, colour
Dir: John Robins
Stars: Hylda Baker, Jimmy Jewel
Rating: ★★★

Pledge's Purer Pickles ride again with Hylda Baker not only starring, but also singing the title song. The script is a kind of bumper bundle of seaside postcard jokes, with acting honours going to Jimmy Jewel, underrated as a character actor, and Yootha Joyce, who pops up as Mrs Rowbottom.

Nearly a Nasty Accident ○
1961, US, 94 mins, b/w
Dir: Don Chaffey
Stars: Jimmy Edwards, Kenneth Connor, Shirley Eaton, Richard Wattis
Rating: ★★

Frantic black-and-white farces proliferated in the British cinema of the 1958–1963 period, no doubt inspired by the box-office success of *Carry On Sergeant*. Not all of them were as funny as that, but they did give starring opportunities to such comedians as Bob Monkhouse, Alfred Marks, Spike Milligan and Jimmy Edwards. Here it's Edwards co-starring with diminutive, bumbling Kenneth Connor, who plays the 'erk' whose antics irk the Air Force.

Necessary Roughness ◐ ⓥ
1991, US, 105 mins, colour
Dir: Stan Dragoti
Stars: Scott Bakula, Harley Jane Kozak, Robert Loggia, Hector Elizondo, Jason Bateman, Kathy Ireland
Rating: ★

Who would want to make a movie especially about American football that

had nothing new to offer? Well, not quite. This one does have a girl goal kicker, although she barely gets a look in. Otherwise, this numskull sports comedy soon wastes whatever potential it had. The comic elements – especially the dean who hates football and will do anything to scupper the team – are pitifully over the top. The serious elements come close to making you laugh, especially the romance between 34-year-old Scott Bakula (brought back to the college education he never had, to make winning passes) and journalism teacher Harley Jane Kozak. Commiserations to them both: even Tom Cruise and Michelle Pfeiffer couldn't have done anything with these characters. 'Take 'em out,' says the coach to Bakula at the (anti) climactic game. 'It's your team, son.' Such dialogue might have worked 50 years ago. We only said might.

Necronomicon ● ⓥ
1993, US, 95 mins, colour
Dir: Brian Yuzna, Christophe Gans, Shu Kaneko
Stars: Richard Lynch, Bruce Payne, David Warner, Millie Perkins, Signy Coleman, Jeffrey Combs
Rating: ★★

A sensationally gory triple-decker horror story that blends modern horror techniques with memories of the way they used to make these things: swirling ground-mists, haunted noblemen and nubile maidens returned from the dead. Couple these with a variety of slimy tentacled, multi-jawed monsters that mostly seem to lurk beneath floorboards, and you have the formula to satisfy today's horror fiends. Jeffrey Combs plays author H P Lovecraft (on whose stories the film is based), who ventures into a monk-guarded library, where lurks the *Necronomicon*, or book of the dead. I seem to remember that the same volume caused a lot of trouble in Sam Raimi's *Evil Dead* films, but in this case it plays the role of storyteller. Too much guck and gore, though, and not enough of unseen horror. We enjoy being made to scream, but a shiver or two wouldn't do any harm.

Needful Things ● ⓥ
1993, US, 120 mins, colour
Dir: Fraser C Heston
Stars: Ed Harris, Bonnie Bedelia, Max Von Sydow, J T Walsh, Amanda Plummer
Rating: ★★

The Devil comes to the little American town of Castle Rock (coincidentally

N

the name of this film's distributors) and, considering all this is based on a Stephen King novel, the results are pretty much as you'd expect. In return for their heart's desire (from the depths of Satan's antique shop), the 'good' citizens of Castle Rock are only too keen to go about the Devil's bidding. In no time at all people are chopping each other up into little bits. All this is rather perplexing for Sheriff Ed Harris who thought he was in for the quiet country life when he quit the big-city force, but now finds himself in the middle of a holocaust. Subsequent developments allow that usually good character actor J T Walsh to go right over the top while Max Von Sydow's Satan abandons his antique shop owner guise and chuckles happily at the mayhem. Pretty silly but well-enough done and never dull.

Neighbors ❶ Ⓥ

1981, US, 94 mins, colour
Dir: John G Avildsen
Stars: John Belushi, Kathryn Walker, Dan Aykroyd, Cathy Moriarty
Rating: ★★

This follow-up comedy by John Belushi and Dan Aykroyd to their successful *The Blues Brothers* was never shown in Britain, despite the fact that it's often funny in an outrageous way, and both Belushi and Aykroyd give the best of their film portrayals together. If you like modern comedies of insult and embarrassment, in fact, you'll be in clover here.

Neither the Sea nor the Sand ●

1972, UK, 116 mins, colour
Dir: Fred Burnley
Stars: Susan Hampshire, Michael Petrovitch, Frank Finlay
Rating: ★★

Adapted from his own novel by TV newscaster Gordon Honeycombe, this is a most unusual combination of amour fou and horror story, with thoughtful performances from Susan Hampshire and Frank Finlay. If it doesn't quite capture the chilliness of the book, it's a brave try.

Nell ● Ⓥ

1994, US, 109 mins, colour
Dir: Michael Apted
Stars: Jodie Foster, Liam Neeson, Natasha Richardson
Rating: ★★★

Although beautifully shot on stunning locations and worthy in intent, this is quite often a long slog about a 'wild woman' found living alone in the North Carolina backwoods and speaking a language no one can understand. You may, however, find yourselves practising a few words of 'Nellish' after the film, a sign that the story has some charm, chiefly in the performance of Jodie Foster as Nell, the 30-year-old who has never met other humans but becomes the object of medical curiosity after her hermit mother dies. Despite a few irritations – would the woman really have such good teeth? – Foster's bewitching performance helps the film through some of its stickier patches and reaches a peak in one of those foolish but emotive courtroom scenes at the end with which Hollywood hardly ever fails.

Nell Gwyn ○

1934, UK, 85 mins, b/w
Dir: Herbert Wilcox
Stars: Anna Neagle, Cedric Hardwicke
Rating: ★★★

This well-produced slice of history proved a popular vehicle for Anna Neagle as the famous orange-seller who competes with the Duchess of Portsmouth (Jeanne de Casalis) for King Charles II (an unusually jovial Sir Cedric Hardwicke). It was one of the earliest of Neagle's historical heroines, providing a solid centre to Herbert Wilcox's rollicking costume romp which maintains a good sense of period. Written by chubbily jowled Miles Malleson, who gave himself a part as Chaffinch.

Neon Bible, The ● Ⓥ

1994, US, 92 mins, colour
Dir: Terence Davies
Stars: Jacob Tierney, Diana Scarwid, Gena Rowlands
Rating: ★★

Booed off the screen at the Cannes Festival, but not actually all that bad, this is British director Terence Davies' first American film – the story of a boy's traumatic upbringing in the US Bible Belt between the ages of eight and 15. His father dominates and occasionally beats his fragile mother, but the light of his life is charismatic Aunt Mae (Gena Rowlands), a faded dance-hall singer who comes into her own in the early Forties when the boy's father goes off to war. Unfortunately, his mother's tenuous grip on reality slips away completely when his father is killed on active service. Aunt Mae moves off to Nashville on a gig and events move to a tragic and violent conclusion. There are three good performances here – from Jacob Tierney as the boy, Diana Scarwid as his mother and especially Rowlands as Aunt Mac. But Davies takes it all at much too slow a pace and his habit of focusing on fabric seriously impairs the story. Still, it does have a certain haunting quality.

Neptune's Daughter ○

1949, US, 93 mins, colour
Dir: Edward Buzzell
Stars: Esther Williams, Red Skelton, Betty Garrett, Ricardo Montalban
Rating: ★★★

One of the most successful of MGM's Esther Williams aqua-musicals, with a handful of Frank Loesser songs spearheaded by the Oscar-winning 'Baby, It's Cold Outside', sung not only by Miss Williams and Ricardo Montalban, but also by Betty Garrett and Red Skelton, who steal the show with some anuable and enthusiastic fooling in their mistaken-identity romance. Director Edward Buzzell made sure that the production was full of Technicolor slickness and Xavier Cugat rhythm, plus the obligatory Willams water ballet.

Net, The ❶ Ⓥ

1995, US, 113 mins, colour
Dir: Irwin Winkler
Stars: Sandra Bullock, Jeremy Northam, Dennis Miller
Rating: ★★

'It only got going at the end', complained a teenager on the way out. Well yes I suppose, but this under-directed high-tech thriller hardly gets a real head of steam even then. Slackly handled by Irwin Winkler, who should be keeping it going like an express train from the start, the film is fashioned as a vehicle for sympathetic Sandra Bullock, a young computer expert who mends faults in systems, but unwillingly becomes party to a conspiracy to take over the government and soon finds herself a target for half the bad guys in America. Again the makers of a (supposedly) high voltage thriller get an unknown Brit to play the villain, in this case Jeremy Northam as the hit-man who chooses to catch Ms Bullock rather than dispatch her and spends the rest of the film trying to rectify his mistake. He effectively conveys menace, while Bullock does quite well with an underwritten part as the girl who finds her own identity snatched away from her as the villains try to finish her off.

Network ● ⓥ

1976, US, 121 mins, colour
Dir: Sidney Lumet
Stars: Faye Dunaway, Peter Finch,
William Holden, Robert Duvall
Rating: ★★★

Black satire with a vengeance, if ultimately a little wearing, taking a savage bite at American television and the ratings that rule the people who work in it. Peter Finch, winning an Oscar in his last film, is the ranting newscaster who flips his lid and announces that he is going to commit suicide on the air which boosts the ratings to such an extent that he finds his salary doubled for prophesying gloom and doom. Faye Dunaway's strident performance, though it threatens to overbalance the film, was also rewarded with an Oscar, as was Beatrice Straight's magnificent one-scene tour-de-force as William Holden's neglected wife. Sidney Lumet's direction is at times devastating, especially in a magnetic scene where people come to the windows of their block of flats in a thunderstorm.

Nevadan, The ○

(aka: The Man from Nevada)
1949, US, 81 mins, colour
Dir: Gordon Douglas
Stars: Randolph Scott, Dorothy Malone
Rating: ★★

Very much in the 'a-man's-gotta-do-what-a-man's-gotta-a-do' mould of Randolph Scott's later Westerns. Our grim-faced hero has to bring in both an outlaw (Forrest Tucker) and stolen gold to the value of $200,000. A rancher – expertly played by George Macready – and his disenchanted wife (Dorothy Malone) also become involved. Scott, who has to team up with Tucker at one point in one of the script's inventive little quirks, is sobriety itself as the hero, and Frank Faylen registers well in a supporting role.

Nevada Smith ○ ⓥ

1966, US, 135 mins, colour
Dir: Henry Hathaway
Stars: Steve McQueen, Karl Malden,
Suzanne Pleshette, Janet Margolin
Rating: ★★★

An epic Western that stems from the character created by Harold Robbins in The Carpetbaggers. John Michael Hayes wrote both films and this is how you would imagine he would tackle a Western – lengthy, packed with characters, blood, action and veiled moralising, with a dash of sex thrown in. Stir well and hope it turns out tasty. And, in fits and starts, it does:

the odds are that you'll enjoy watching Steve McQueen as a country boy on a long, long hunt for the trio of vicious killers who tortured and killed his parents. Star actors fill all the many main parts, although only Arthur Kennedy's convict on the run sticks for any length of time in the memory. The hunt is photographed in splendidly detailed colour by Lucien Ballard, who proves just as adept at following a night-time knife fight as portraying a lone rider in panoramic daytime view.

Never a Dull Moment ○

1967, US, 95 mins, colour
Dir: Jerry Paris
Stars: Dick Van Dyke, Edward G
Robinson, Dorothy Provine, Henry Silva
Rating: ★★

A frisky comedy crime caper that never quite adds up to the sum of the talents involved. With Dick Van Dyke and Dorothy Provine as leads, Edward G Robinson as a mob boss with a penchant for art (Robinson's sideline in real life) and such flavoursome character actors as Jack Elam, Henry Silva, Slim Pickens and Mickey Shaughnessy around, it could have been a comic chase classic. As it is, Jerry Paris' pacing doesn't always live up to the title of the film.

NeverEnding Story, The ○ ⓥ

1984, UK, 94 mins, colour
Dir: Wolfgang Petersen
Stars: Barret Oliver, Tami Stronach
Rating: ★★★

A combination of The Wizard of Oz and The Dark Crystal as a young bullied schoolboy discovers a fantasy world in which he can be a hero for once when he opens up a musty old book. Director Wolfgang Petersen, away from the claustrophobic underwater submarine world of Das Boot, displays a rare talent for children's storytelling. And the British special effects team of Brian Johnson (Alien) and Bruce Nicholson (The Empire Strikes Back) have created deadly swamplands and spooky woods and wondrous special effects. Two inferior sequels followed.

Never Give an Inch ◐

(aka: Sometimes a Great Notion)
1971, US, 130 mins, colour
Dir: Paul Newman
Stars: Paul Newman, Henry Fonda, Lee
Remick, Michael Sarrazin
Rating: ★★★

The title is the motto of a logging family in this formidably cast – Paul Newman, Henry Fonda, Lee Remick,

Michael Sarrazin – adaptation of a massive novel by Ken Kesey. But the outstanding performance, if a supporting one, is by long-time Hollywood character player Richard Jaeckel, who was nominated for an Academy Award.

Never Give a Sucker an Even Break ○

(aka: What a Man!)
1941, US, 71 mins, b/w
Dir: Edward Cline
Stars: W C Fields, Margaret Dumont,
Gloria Jean, Leon Errol
Rating: ★★★

W C Fields fans will be helpless with laughter at this, zany by even his standards – he wrote the story under the name Otis Criblecoblis – in which he plans to sell nutmegs to Russians in Mexico, but fans out of a plane and lands on a mountain-top where he meets Margaret Dumont. It all ends in a typically Fieldsian car chase.

Never Let Go ◐

1960, UK, 91 mins, b/w
Dir: John Guillermin
Stars: Richard Todd, Peter Sellers,
Elizabeth Sellars, Adam Faith, Carol
White, Mervyn Johns
Rating: ★★★

This nail-biting thriller has been all-too-rarely seen since its first release. Peter Sellers had his first truly unsympathetic part as the hard-cursing crook who imagines himself as England's answer to Little Caesar. Sellers is outgunned in more ways than one, however, by Richard Todd, who gives a tremendous performance as the down-at-heel salesman who, although beaten, battered and bruised by the gang who have stolen the car that is more important to him than life itself, won't give up. The director ensures that tension remains on a high level throughout, and the drama really packs a punch.

Never Let Me Go ○

1953, UK, 92 mins, b/w
Dir: Delmer Daves
Stars: Clark Gable, Gene Tierney
Rating: ★★

This drama of east-west romance was made entirely in Britain by an American director, Delmer Daves, mainly on location in Cornwall. Stalwart British-based cast includes former ice star Belita, Bernard Miles, Richard Haydn and Kenneth More (just before he shot to stardom in Genevieve) and such reliable Slavonic

N

types as Theodore Bikel and Karel Stepanek. Tense towards the end.

Never Say Die O
1939, US, 80 mins, b/w
Dir: Elliott Nugent
Stars: Bob Hope, Martha Raye
Rating: ★★★

The best of several late Thirties comedies Bob Hope made with chasm-mouthed Martha Raye, and something of a rarity. The wisecracks fly thick and fast as Hope (playing 'John Kidley the big bean man') goes for what he thinks are his dying days to Bad Gaswasser, a European health spa. Having nothing to lose, he proceeds to marry Martha, playing a Texas oil heiress called Mickey, to save her from a loveless marriage to a lecherous prince. A sequence in which the prince (Alan Mowbray) tries to insult Hope into fighting a duel is particularly funny. And the supporting cast is relishable, including stony Gale Sondergaard, who menaced Hope in several other films. This film contains the original inspiration for the famous 'Chalice from the Palace' routine from the Danny Kaye classic *The Court Jester*.

Never Say Goodbye O
1956, US, 96 mins, colour
Dir: Jerry Hopper
Stars: Rock Hudson, Cornell Borchers, George Sanders
Rating: ★★

Not to be confused with the Errol Flynn-Eleanor Parker film of the same title ten years earlier, this is a typically glossy Universal romantic melodrama of the mid-Fifties, with Hudson as man who tries to re-marry his long-estranged wife. Shelley Fabares, later to star several times with Elvis Presley, makes her screen debut as Hudson's daughter.

Never Say Never Again O Ⓥ
1983, UK, 137 mins, colour
Dir: Irvin Kershner
Stars: Sean Connery, Klaus Maria Brandauer, Kim Basinger, Barbara Carrera
Rating: ★★★

The original Bond returns, and it's quite a comeback. The lengthy exposition to this remake of *Thunderball*, in fact, merely detracts from the excellence of Sean Connery, purring lethally as 007, but given hot competition in the acting department by Klaus Maria Brandauer, who makes Largo a memorable smiling psychotic. Kim

Basinger and Barbara Carrera are extremely well cast as heroine and villainess, and respond wholeheartedly to the demands of their roles. The action is staged with all the mechanical efficiency of the Roger Moore Bond film, but with a bit more bite. The machines aren't quite allowed to take over from this Bond. Whether wearing a variety of brown and grey wigs, bedding a variety of pink and dusky girls, or outwitting rather than out-gunning the heavies, this monarch of mayhem strides easily back into his kingdom.

Never So Few O
1959, US, 124 mins, colour
Dir: John Sturges
Stars: Frank Sinatra, Gina Lollobrigida, Peter Lawford, Steve McQueen
Rating: ★★

There's a bit of everything in John Sturges' drama about wartime Burma: serious political talk, pretty scenery, and Gina Lollobrigida. The film proved once and for all that Frank Sinatra looks silly with a goatee, but it helped advance Steve McQueen's career: the following year he was one of the *Magnificent Seven*. This one, though, is pretty stolid stuff by Sturges' standards.

Never Take No for an Answer ⊙
1951, UK/Italy, 95 mins, b/w
Dir: Maurice Cloche
Stars: Vittorio Manunta, Denis O'Dea
Rating: ★★★★

This charming British-Italian co-producdon is a real heart-breaker; word of mouth made it an unexpected box-office hit in its day. Vittorio Manunta gives a totally winning performance as the little ragged scrap called Peppino, who stops at nothing to get his sick pet donkey to the crypt of St Francis of Assisi, where he is sure she will be cured.

Never Talk to Strangers ● Ⓥ
1995, US, 86 mins, colour
Dir: Peter Hall
Stars: Rebecca DeMornay, Antonio Banderas, Dennis Miller, Len Cariou, Harry Dean Stanton
Rating: ★

The icily sexy DeMornay gives another typically intense performance in this ludicrously overheated thriller. It's a case of physician heal thyself: criminal psychiatrist DeMornay, who looks severely in need of treatment, thrown off-kilter by her encounters with a serial killer (Stanton), becomes involved

with mysterious Antonio Banderas, whom she meets in the wine department of the local supermart. Before you can say Jacob's Creek, the diffident shrink is indulging in some heady wine-tasting followed by hot sex in Banderas' heavily stylised (and slightly sinister) loft, which looks like something out of a porno movie. Poor Banderas is saddled with pretty well every Latin lover cliché in the book here as the murder suspect who may turn out to be a red herring. Script and story alike lack sparkle. The end's a surprise all right and will have you shaking your heads in disbelief.

Never Too Late O
1965, US, 105 mins, colour
Dir: Bud Yorkin
Stars: Paul Ford, Connie Stevens, Maureen O'Sullivan, Jim Hutton
Rating: ★★★

Happy transference of the hit stage play to screen, with character actor Paul Ford wondrously well cast as the middle-aged businessman, who finds that his wife, played by old screen star Maureen O'Sullivan is expecting another baby, 20 years after the last. One of the funniest scenes is that in which Ford and his daughter's new husband (Jim Hutton) totter out together to get drunk after being given the brush-off by their respective wives. O'Sullivan and another Thirties' star, Jane Wyatt, are as pretty a pair of 50-year-olds as ever graced the screen, and even Connie Stevens has her moments as the buxom blonde bombshell who suddenly finds herself the family drudge.

New Adventures of Don Juan, The
See: The Adventures of Don Juan

New Age, The ● Ⓥ
1994, US, 107 mins, colour
Dir: Michael Tolkin
Stars: Judy Davis, Peter Weller, Samuel L Jackson, Adam West, Corbin Bernsen, John Diehl
Rating: ★★

Don't be deceived by the interesting cast here. Successful yuppies Davis and Weller lose their sources of income and launch a disastrous boutique venture in a trendy area of Hollywood. The dialogue is pretentious – 'Your inner child is driving us to bankruptcy,' yells Davis at one point – and the characters unsympathetic and dislikeable. Dragged down by their own shortcomings, Weller and Davis have nowhere to go but engage in an all-film whingeing contest with one another. Writer-director Michael Tolkin's screenplay lacks the bite and incident of his best work, although a sado-masochistic orgy in an exotic pool is highly amusing and provides a much-needed break from the dryness of the rest.

New Centurions, The ◑
(aka: Precinct 45: Los Angeles Police)
1972, US, 105 mins, colour
Dir: Richard Fleischer
Stars: George C Scott, Stacy Keach, Jane Alexander, Scott Wilson
Rating: ★★

'Laws change, people don't,' says one of the characters in this black thriller that takes another pretty gloomy look at the police – this time at the role they play in the violence-ridden America of the Seventies. Despite the customary excellence of George C Scott, it never really catches fire or makes us care about the characters who, Scott's apart, are indifferently acted. One can only blame director Richard Fleischer for not exercising tighter control. But he does raise the excitement in the chases.

New Face In Hell ◑
(aka: P J)
1969, US, 108 mins, colour
Dir: John Guillermin
Stars: George Peppard, Raymond Burr, Gayle Hunnicutt
Rating: ★★★

In America the title of this lively thick-ear thriller was the rather more sober *P J*, the initials of the sub-Philip Marlowe private detective played to the tough, laconic hilt by George Peppard. Sample dialogue: 'You know what I like about you? You're all armpit.' John Guillermin's first Hollywood movie shows him in splendid command of the requirements of this kind of hard-boiled action-cum-mystery movie.

New Interns, The ○
1964, US, 123 mins, b/w
Dir: John Rich
Stars: Michael Callan, Dean Jones, Barbara Eden, Stefanie Powers
Rating: ★

Sequel to *The Interns*, another hospital epic with sentiment unlimited, crises in the clinic and hysterics in the ward. Side-attractions include the tightest nurses' uniforms ever invented, a wild, party as-it-were below stairs and a surgeon who visits the children's ward with a funny face painted on his mask.

The girls, Stefanie Powers, Barbara Eden and Inger Stevens, are all very appealing.

New Jack City ● Ⓥ
1991, US, 97 mins, colour
Dir: Mario Van Peebles
Stars: Wesley Snipes, Ice T, Mario Van Peebles, Judd Nelson, Vanessa Williams
Rating: ★★★

The rise and fall of a black ganglord provides another very different central role for the versatile Wesley Snipes. This is a very violent, but crisp and cleanly made narcotics thriller, nicely put together in an old-fashioned style by director Van Peebles, who also plays (not very well, alas) one of its featured roles. Good playing all round otherwise, lots of action and dialogue you can hear. Nothing new here but incisively presented with punch and precision.

New Kind of Love, A ○
1963, US, 110 mins, color
Dir: Melville Shavelson
Stars: Joanne Woodward, Paul Newman, Thelma Ritter
Rating: ★★

This romantic romp, with its amusing dream sequences, made a pleasant change from heavy drama for Mr and Mrs Paul Newman (Joanne Woodward), and at its best is reminiscent of Hollywood's best light comedies of the Thirties and Forties. Unfortunately, that standard isn't often reached, although its husband-and-wife team play it impeccably, and the acid-tongued Thelma Ritter offers valuable support.

New Leaf, A ○
1971, US, 102 mins, colour
Dir: Elaine May
Stars: Walter Matthau, Elaine May
Rating: ★★★★★

Elaine May made Hollywood history with this wickedly funny throwback to the screwball comedies of the 1930s, as the first female star-writer-director. But Paramount were unhappy with her final version running to a weighty three hours and cut it by 78 minutes. Despite her understandable fury and (unsuccessful) attempt to have her name removed from the credits, the film was still a delight and went down well with critics and paying public alike. There are laughs-a-plenty from star Walter Matthau's attempts to stave off destitution by marrying a wealthy woman, and it makes several excellent observations on greed. Spare

a thought, however, for actor William Hickey, whose blackmailer character was deleted completely in the revised version of the film.

New Moon ○
1940, US, 105 mins, b/w
Dir: Robert Z Leonard
Stars: Jeanette MacDonald, Nelson Eddy, Mary Boland, George Zucco
Rating: ★★★

The rousing score keeps this creaky old operetta afloat, as Jeanette MacDonald and Nelson Eddy flee strife-torn France in 1788 and set sail for a new life in Louisiana USA. Never mind the acting, often pretty wooden, just feel the surge of adrenalin from such stirring numbers as 'Stout-Hearted Men', 'Lover Come Back to Me', 'Softly as in a Morning Sunrise', 'One Kiss' and 'Wanting You'. Good stuff, lovingly directed by Robert Z Leonard, and tightly edited down to a bare hour and three-quarters actual film, trimming that left several roles on the cutting-room floor, including Buster Keaton's cameo as a prisoner on the good ship *Lulu*. Shimmering photography and nicely orchestrated crowd scenes make this one of the most spirited of musical action films.

Newsfront ◑
1978, Australia, 110 mins, colour
Dir: Phillip Noyce
Stars: Bill Hunter, Wendy Hughes, Chris Haywood
Rating: ★★★★

Phillip Noyce's fascinating, fine look at the lives of newsreel cameramen in the Fifties. Gripping throughout, especially in its re-creation of a flood disaster. A most unusual and rewarding film which deservedly put its director on the map.

New York Confidential ◑
1955, US, 86 mins, b/w
Dir: Russell Rouse
Stars: Broderick Crawford, Richard Conte, Anne Bancroft, Marilyn Maxwell
Rating: ★★★

This allegedly fact-based gangster thriller, in which the police hardly get a look in, was black and violent enough in its day to get an 'X' certificate. Certainly the last reel contains enough bodies to decorate a production of *Hamlet*. Tough-guy actors Broderick Crawford and Richard Conte are completely at home in their mobster roles, but the best performance of all comes from a young

N

Anne Bancroft as Crawford's daughter, hopelessly trying to escape her father's gangland environment.

New York, New York O Ⓥ
1977, US, 164 mins, colour
Dir: Martin Scorsese
Stars: Robert De Niro, Liza Minnelli, Lionel Stander, Barry Primus, Mary Kay Place
Rating: ★★

Fitfully interesting colossus of a musical drama set in the Forties and Fifties. De Niro and Minnelli blaze a trail as the central characters – a glamorous 'big band' singer and a vain and selfish saxophonist – and the film portrays every bitter fight of their tempestuous, competitive marriage. Usually now shown with its 12-minute long climactic production number *Happy Endings*, originally cut from the film.

New York Stories ❶ Ⓥ
1989, US, 125 mins, colour
Dir: Woody Allen, Francis Coppola, Martin Scorsese
Stars: Nick Nolte, Rosanna Arquette, Woody Allen, Julie Kavner, Talia Shire
Rating: ★★

The good news about this view of New York life is that, in it, Woody Allen at last reaffirms his talent for wildly original comedy with a laugh around every other street corner. The bad news is that you have to sit through two really draggy episodes to get to the Allen part. They should release Woody's 40-minute wonder on its own and forget the other two stories altogether. In the first story, temperamental artist Nolte will go to any lengths to prevent untalented bimbo painter Arquette from leaving him; the second concerns a small girl whose personality and quick thinking helps reconcile her parents. Brother, forget it. These anecdotes, directed by Scorsese and Coppola, are much ado about nothing. In Woody's tale, *Oedipus Wrecks*, he's a lawyer beset by the Jewish mother to end them all. Imagine his joy when he takes her to a magic show and she disappears in the Chinese box. No-one sees her for days and he's a changed man. But retribution beckons. This segment is funny all the way through.

Next Man, The ❶
1976, US, 107 mins, colour
Dir: Richard C Sarafian
Stars: Sean Connery, Cornelia Sharpe
Rating: ★★★

Sean Connery triumphs over offbeat casting as an Arab politician who is the target of a glamorous assassin, played by attractive newcomer Cornelia Sharpe. Connery's authoritative performance dominates the film. Although the plot is rather confusing, director Richard C Sarafian stages much of it, especially the scenes at the United Nations, with considerable impact and conviction. Connery and Italian actor Adolfo Celi, old adversaries from *Thunderball* a decade earlier, clash again here.

Next of Kin ● Ⓥ
1989, US, 109 mins, colour
Dir: John Irvin
Stars: Patrick Swayze, Liam Neeson, Adam Baldwin, Helen Hunt, Bill Paxton
Rating: ★

As cut to formula as they come, this Patrick Swayze popcorn action yarn establishes his character as a hillbilly cop in Chicago in a prologue, then kills off his brother to set up the revenge plot. When it becomes apparent towards the end that he needs some help, his country cousins come storming in from the wilds of Kentucky, armed with snakes and bow-and-arrows, to take on the local branch of the Mafia. Guess who wins? Director Irvin is hard put to stop the audience giggling at all this, and settles for a bunch of vaguely comic crooks. The acting is, to say the least, rudimentary, although twitchy Michael J Pollard overacts most enjoyably as the owner of a shabby motel who surveys the arsenal imported by Swayze's brother with amusing calm.

Next to No Time! O
1958, UK, 93 mins, colour
Dir: Henry Cornelius
Stars: Kenneth More, Betsy Drake, Roland Culver
Rating: ★★

This whimsical comedy, beautifully shot in colour by the Oscar-winning cameraman Freddie Francis, was the last film to be made by the talented director Henry Cornelius before his early death at 45. Among Cornelius's greatest successes were *Passport to Pimlico*, *The Galloping Major* and *Genevieve*. Here the *Genevieve* star, Kenneth More, is caught up in a series of rib-tickling adventures on board the liner *Queen Elizabeth*, as he tries to pluck up the nerve to approach a millionaire in the hope of getting finance to help his engineering firm. Roland Culver, as the millionaire, and the delightful Betsy Drake play neatly in support of the star.

Niagara O Ⓥ
1952, US, 89 mins, colour
Dir: Henry Hathaway
Stars: Marilyn Monroe, Joseph Cotten, Jean Peters, Casey Adams
Rating: ★★★

The film that caused worldwide queues as the full impact of Marilyn Monroe's sexual appeal burst for the first time on the public. Looked at again through unsteamed glasses, *Niagara* can be seen to be a very moody, rather good thriller, extremely well directed by Henry Hathaway. Monroe's erotic charge and Jean Peters' simpler appeal make equally striking impacts.

Nice Girl? O
1941, US, 95 mins, b/w
Dir: William A Seiter,
Stars: Deanna Durbin, Franchot Tone, Robert Stack, Robert Benchley
Rating: ★★★

Deanna Durbin was just beginning to lose her unique freshness when she got an early kiss (from Robert Stack!) in this standard Hollywood frolic, with a plot predictably based almost entirely on misunderstandings. Franchot Tone and Robert Benchley supply polish and good humour and the star finds time to sing 'Thank You America' and 'Love At Last'.

Nice Girl Like Me, A ❶
1969, UK, 91 mins, colour
Dir: Desmond Davis
Stars: Barbara Ferris, Harry Andrews
Rating: ★★

Baby-faced blonde Barbara Ferris rocketed about the screen scene for several years from 1963 onwards, before concentrating on a stage career. In this quirky comedy, she's a warm-hearted (unmarried) girl who just can't stop having babies!

Nicholas and Alexandra O Ⓥ
1971, UK, 189 mins, colour
Dir: Franklin J Schaffner
Stars: Michael Jayston, Janet Suzman, Laurence Olivier, Jack Hawkins, Tom Baker
Rating: ★★

Even a film as long as this can only scratch the surface of its subject – the fall of Imperial Russia and the rise of the revolution. And this is perhaps its failing. It tries to cover too much historical ground, which means you get a little bit of everything but not enough to sink your teeth into. Having said that, the central tale, that of the last

Tsar, Nicholas, and his wife Alexandra, holds everything together. We are watching the fall of a dynasty and the pressures inside a family which you know is doomed. In the broad sweep of history, the problems of one family, even a Royal one, don't add up to much, so you find yourself wanting the film to concentrate more on what is happening outside the palace walls. Despite its faults, the film holds your interest thanks largely to Michael Jayston and Janet Suzman in the title roles, supported by a cast that looks like a British theatre roll call. Special mention must go to Tom Baker, gloriously evil as Rasputin.

Nicholas Nickleby O ⓥ
1947, UK, 108 mins, b/w
Dir: Alberto Cavalcanti
Stars: Derek Bond, Cedric Hardwicke, Sally Ann Howes, Bernard Miles
Rating: ★★★

Made when Dickens films were all the go in the British cinema – *Great Expectations*, *The Pickwick Papers*, *Scrooge* and *Oliver Twist* were all filmed between 1946 and 1952 – this Ealing Studios film is directed with great care and feel for the period by their distinguished Brazilian veteran, Alberto Cavalcanti. Despite the star-studded cast, the film doesn't exactly grab the attention throughout, although the Dotheboys Hall sequences spring vividly to life.

Nick Carter, Master Detective O
1939, US, 60 mins, b/w
Dir: Jacques Tourneur
Stars: Walter Pidgeon, Rita Johnson
Rating: ★★★

The stylish Jacques Tourneur cut his directing teeth on this, the first of three Carter thrillers made with Walter Pidgeon, battling against the villains, in the starring role. Loses momentum in its later stages.

Nickelodeon O ⓥ
1976, UK/US, 122 mins, colour
Dir: Peter Bogdanovich
Stars: Ryan O'Neal, Burt Reynolds, Tatum O'Neal, Brian Keith
Rating: ★

Throughout all its zany situations, this crazy comedy about early silent movies only rarely manages to raise a laugh. Director Peter Bogdanovich's pacing seems at fault and his actors might as well be in plastic bags as they thrash about trying to register as real live characters. Only Stella Stevens

breaks out of the clutches of the script to provide us with some genuine spark. Ryan O'Neal, Burt Reynolds, Brian Keith and Tatum O'Neal give sub-par performances; inexperienced leading lady Jane Hitchcock is a washout. Even photographer Laszlo Kovacs is less than his admirable self. At least it's a genuine family movie; if only it were a good one too.

Nick of Time ● ⓥ
1995, US, 89 mins, colour
Dir: John Badham
Stars: Johnny Depp, Christopher Walken, Charles S Dutton, Marsha Mason, Roma Maffia, Peter Strauss
Rating: ★★

Hitchcock would have made a real killer-diller of this one: shame that director John Badham can't quite make us believe it all. Accountant Johnny Depp arrives at the station with his six-year-old daughter, only to fall victim to two ne'er-do-wells (Christopher Walken, Roma Maffia) who kidnap Depp and daughter. Depp is told he has 90 minutes to assassinate a popular governor (Marsha Mason) – or the kid will die. One of the many weaknesses of the film is that there never seems any chance that Depp will actually bow to the kidnappers' demands. This considerably undercuts the suspense, even in the admittedly exciting shootout at the climax. Walken does his standard icy criminal act and Charles S Dutton has a good supporting role as a shoeshine man who pretends to be deaf to help Depp out. Always-getting-bumped-off Gloria Reuben once again fails to stay the course. This is a rare example of a film taking place in real time: it starts at noon and ends at 1.30. A few moments of tension do result, but they're aren't many surprises.

Nicky and Gino ● ⓥ
(aka: Dominick and Eugene)
1988, US, 109 mins, colour
Dir: Robert M Young
Stars: Tom Hulce, Ray Liotta, Jamie Lee Curtis, Todd Graft
Rating: ★★★

There's a lot of sincerity if not many laughs in this story of a 26-year-old aspiring doctor (Liotta) and his brain-damaged brother, played by Hulce with one silver tooth rather uneasily underlining the idiot image. But, though the story is gloomy and slow at the start, director Robert M Young has knitted a good pattern out of it by the finish, thanks to a subplot

that works wonders at bolstering the basic storyline, as Liotta battles with himself over the decision to leave Pittsburgh and Hulce (whose garbage-truck money has put him through college) and pass his finals in far-away California. Jamie Lee Curtis is her usual sterling self as Liotta's girlfriend and Todd Graff puts in a good job as Hulce's drug-dealing, hair-slicking workmate.

Nico
See: Above the Law

Night Ambush
See: Ill Met by Moonlight

Night and Day O ⓥ
1946, US, 132 mins, colour
Dir: Michael Curtiz
Stars: Cary Grant, Alexis Smith
Rating: ★★

Although this song-strewn tribute to the great composer Cole Porter obviously had to steer clear of his bisexuality, it does in other respects, and with the undervalued help of Cary Grant, capture something of the restrained, distant air which made Porter at the same time charismatic and sometimes difficult. Mary Martin is on hand to sing (brilliantly) 'My Heart Belongs to Daddy', and the film would have been better off handing this Broadway legend the leading singing role actually played by band vocalist Ginny Simms. Nice orchestrations by Ray Heindorf, however, can't disguise the fact that this film is, even just as a musical tribute, not the movie it might have been.

Night and the City O
1950, UK, 91 mins, b/w
Dir: Jules Dassin
Stars: Gene Tierney, Richard Widmark, Googie Withers, Francis L Sullivan
Rating: ★★★

Director Jules Dassin, whose previous three films had been *Brute Force*, *Naked City* and *Thieves' Highway*, continued his look at world-wide criminal life with this strongly atmospheric thriller set in London. The dark, sleazy, foggy Thameside setting is splendidly evocative and Richard Widmark's shifty, slippery weasel is one of his best early performances. The film opens as it means to continue, with Widmark's character hunted, fearful, out of breath and frantically trying to avoid being cornered. Past dark buildings and through alleyways, he is stalked by unseen feet, and by the insistent, frenetic

N

chords of a memorable score by Franz Waxman.

Night and the City ● ⓥ
1993, US, 105 mins, colour
Dir: Irwin Winkler
Stars: Robert De Niro, Jessica Lange, Cliff Gorman, Jack Warden, Eli Wallach
Rating: ★★

This low-life urban drama is a remake of the Hollywood-funded, British-based 1950 thriller with Richard Widmark. In the Nineties, the hustler, Harry Fabian, is played by Robert De Niro and has become a lawyer straight out of the Marx Brothers' Shyster, Flywheel and Shyster. Typical advice to a client is: 'If you want to walk in Central Park, leave the baseball bat at home.' Becoming involved with mobsters, an affair with his barman's wife (Jessica Lange) and the shadier end of the boxing world, Harry Fabian is clearly not destined for a dull, long or happy life. Despite De Niro's non-stop performance, however, and a veritable barrage of street language, this version of his downfall lacks dramatic weight and punch, and is further weakened by a softening of the original ending which was unusually bleak by Fifties' standards.

Night at the Opera, A ○ ⓥ
1935, US, 92 mins, b/w
Dir: Sam Wood
Stars: Groucho Marx, Chico Marx, Harpo Marx, Margaret Dumont, Allan Jones
Rating: ★★★★

Modestly described by its studio's publicists as 'A 30-ring circus of laughs, songs, girls, spectacle', this wild extravaganza of inspired lunacy is easily the best of the Marx Brothers' MGM movies, crammed with comic gems. See director Sam Wood cram more people into a tiny ship's cabin than British Rail manage to stuff into a commuter carriage! Marvel at the classic encounters between Groucho's irresistible force and Margaret Dumont's immoveable object! Watch and hear as Harpo introduces 'Take Me Out To The Ball Game' into Verdi's score for *Il Trovatore*'. And wonder at Jewish Chico's Italian accent! All this, and more, is on offer in a comedy that wears its age with great charm and effect. And remember: there ain't no sanity clause!

Night Boat to Dublin ○
1945, UK, 91 mins, b/w
Dir: Lawrence Huntington
Stars: Robert Newton, Raymond Lovell,

Guy Middleton, Muriel Pavlow
Rating: ★★★

Crisply photographed (by Otto Heller) spy thriller, developed by director Lawrence Huntington as a catalogue of breathless excitements. Several performers seized chances to establish themselves as stars of the post-war British cinema, among them Muriel Pavlow; and Robert Newton, quite unusually cast as the heroic secret agent thwarting Nazi plans, provides a sturdy central pillar around whom the film's tense action revolves.

Nightbreed ● ⓥ
1990, US, 101 mins, colour
Dir: Clive Barker
Stars: Craig Sheffer, David Cronenberg, Anne Bobby, Charles Haid
Rating: ★★★

Good fare for horror fans: noisy, full-blooded and slightly off the beaten track. A society of freaks and monsters (they're the heroes, by the way) lives beneath the Midian cemetery and Boone (Sheffer) finds himself drawn there, even after death – though to reveal quite why would be to unlock a key element in writer-director Clive Barker's plot. The first couple of reels are a bit wearisome, but the sheer expense and spectacle of the rest, even given the repulsive nature of some of the 'creatures', is quite overwhelming. The 'human' actors have an unenviable task in a film like this, but Sheffer, Bobby (his girl) and director Cronenberg (as Sheffer's psychiatrist) all infuse a creditable amount of personality into their characters under the circumstances. Barker's bizarre imagination and a pretty high budget provides some demented tableaux that even outdo Hieronymous Bosch. Non-horror fans may find it quite disgusting.

Night Creatures ❶
(aka: Captain Clegg)
1962, UK, 82 mins, b/w
Dir: Peter Graham Scott
Stars: Peter Cushing, Oliver Reed
Rating: ★★

A Hammer studios' mystery yarn, also known as *Captain Clegg*, in which the legendary 'phantoms' of Romney Marsh are used as cover for 18th-century smugglers. Based on Russell Thorndike's *Dr Syn*, with Oliver Reed leading the supporting cast.

Night Hair Child ●
1971, US, 89 mins, colour
Dir: James Kelly
Stars: Mark Lester, Britt Ekland, Hardy

Kruger, Lilli Palmer
Rating: ★★

Child star Mark Lester startled many of his fans from *Oliver!* with his performance in this shocker, as a psychotic 12-year-old, who preys on his new stepmother. Harry Andrews and Lilli Palmer contribute moments of cultured calm to the fevered proceedings that follow.

Night Has a Thousand Eyes ○
1948, US, 80 mins, b/w
Dir: John Farrow
Stars: Edward G Robinson, Gail Russell, John Lund
Rating: ★★★

One more time for the story of the mind-reader whose gift of foreseeing the future brings him nothing but torment and tragedy. This version certainly has the right fatalistic feel about it, plus a strong central performance from Edward G Robinson as the man who can flee the future but cannot escape his own destiny.

Nighthawks ● ⓥ
1981, US, 99 mins, colour
Dir: Bruce Malmuth
Stars: Sylvester Stallone, Billy Dee Williams, Lindsay Wagner, Rutger Hauer
Rating: ★★★

Sylvester Stallone took time out from his series of *Rocky* movies to play a tough New York policeman seconded to Interpol to join in the hunt for a ruthless terrorist. And he's rather good, well supported by Billy Dee Williams, as his partner, and Nigel Davenport, as the man who trains the cops in anti-terrorist tactics. But the film is dominated by Rutger Hauer as their quarry: his powerful performance took the blond Dutch actor into the big league of international screen actors.

Night Holds Terror, The ○
1955, US, 85 mins, b/w
Dir: Andrew Stone
Stars: Jack Kelly, Vince Edwards, John Cassavetes, Hildy Parks
Rating: ★★★

Hailed as an outstanding second-feature in its day, this hostage thriller keeps tension on high throughout, and was a boost to the careers of its stars, who include Jack Kelly, Vince Edwards and John Cassavetes. Director Andrew Stone, who specialised in fast moving, hard-hitting, location-shot thrillers, based his script on incidents from two real-life ransom cases.

Night in Casablanca, A ☉

1946, US, 85 mins, b/w
Dir: Archie Mayo
Stars: Groucho Marx, Harpo Marx, Chico Marx
Rating: ★★★

The film that brought The Marx Brothers and their zany magnificence back to the screen after a five-year absence. The humour is almost undiluted Marx lunacy, from the cork so huge that it leaves no room for wine, to the crashing collapse of a wall that Harpo has insisted he is holding up. Chico baffles his companions with double talk while Groucho lopes across the screen as the manager of the Hotel Casablanca. 'I'm Bea,' remarks a shapely guest. 'I stop at the hotel.' 'I'm the hotel manager,' Groucho leers. 'I stop at nothing.'

Nightingale Sang in Berkeley Square, A

See: The Biggest Bank Robbery

Night in Heaven, A ◖ Ⓥ

1983, US, 80 mins, colour
Dir: John G Avildsen
Stars: Christopher Atkins, Lesley Ann Warren, Robert Logan, Andy Garcia
Rating: ★★

Not an angelic comedy, as the title might suggest, but rather a sex romp through the world of Chippendale-style male exotic dancers. Christopher Atkins, the fresh-faced moppet from *The Blue Lagoon*, hardly looks old enough to be stripping to his assets as Rickey Rocket at the Heaven ladies-only night-club. Lesley Ann Warren is his college teacher who is dragged to the club by her thrill-seeking sister and ends up having the groin of the student she's just failed from her course thrust into her shocked face. You can guess the rest as student and teacher reawaken long-suppressed physical longings.

Night In the Life of Jimmy Reardon, A

See: Jimmy Reardon

Nightmare ◖

1963, UK, 82 mins, b/w
Dir: Freddie Francis
Stars: Jennie Linden, David Knight, Moira Redmond
Rating: ★★

An early Hammer chiller-thriller about a girl with a recurring nightmare, directed by Freddie Francis, an Oscar-winning cameraman (he photographed *The Innocents*). In common

with that film, this drama is creepily shot in black-and-white, and has Clytie Jessop again as a 'ghost woman'.

Nightmare ○

1956, US, 88 mins, b/w
Dir: Maxwell Shane
Stars: Edward G Robinson, Kevin McCarthy, Connie Russell
Rating: ★★

Clearly writer-director Maxwell Shane liked the plot of this ingenious thriller since he had filmed it before, in 1947, as *Fear in the Night*. Here, aided by Joseph Biroc's moody monochrome photography, he creates an effective atmosphere of mystery and menace and gets a good performance from Kevin McCarthy as the man who believes he's a murderer. But the acting honours go to Edward G Robinson's tough detective with a soft heart who discovers that all is not what it seems.

Nightmare Alley ○

1947, US, 111 mins, b/w
Dir: Edmund Goulding
Stars: Tyrone Power, Joan Blondell, Coleen Gray, Mike Mazurki
Rating: ★★★★

A strange and fascinating thriller-drama set against a background of carnival freaks and sideshows. It originally sprang from the equally strange mind of writer William Lindsay Gresham, who was obsessed by the darker corners of the entertainment world, and ended his days by committing suicide. Tyrone Power tackles, for him, a most unusual role as the fake spiritualist whose decline is as sudden as his success.

Nightmare Before Christmas, The ○ Ⓥ

1993, US, 76 mins, colour
Dir: Henry Selick
Voice Stars: Chris Sarandon, Danny Elfman, Catherine O'Hara, Paul Reubens (Pee-wee Herman), William Hickey, Glenn Shadix
Rating: ★★★

Although it boasts a Broadway-style score by Danny Elfman, who also sings the role of Jack Skellington, this stop-motion animation film is not exactly *Beauty and the Beast*. In Halloweentown, Jack is tired of the same old routine of making people scream every October 31 and, to the dismay of the fellow monsters who inhabit the town, sets out to find something better. What he stumbles on is Christmastown, whose goings-on so enchant him that he determines to

take over the work of the head honcho there, one Sandy Claws. Claws is not exactly overjoyed at being kidnapped by demon trick-or-treaters Lock, Stock and Barrel and delivered into the clutches of Halloweentown's Oogie Boogey Man – nor is Jack's idea of donning his scarlet robes and manning a crew of skeleton reindeer a raging success. This is ingenious stuff with some magic touches, but ponderously paced in keeping with the rather stately score, so it's hard to decide which age range will enjoy it. Adults, perhaps, with a sense of the bizarre.

Nightmare on Elm Street, A ● Ⓥ

1984, US, 91 mins, colour
Dir: Wes Craven
Stars: Robert Englund, Heather Langenkamp, Johnny Depp
Rating: ★★

'One, two, Freddy's comin' for you; three, four, better lock your door; five, six, grab your crucifix; seven, eight, gonna stay up late; nine, ten, never sleep again.' This haunting, twisted nursery rhyme launched one of the most successful horror film series since the Thirties. Six sequels have followed and a spin-off TV series, *Freddie's Nightmares*. The series proved to be a goldmine for Robert Englund – originally only ninth billed as the child-killer horrifically burned alive by his victims' parents, and who now wreaks revenge on their children through their dreams. There's a nice homage to Hitchcock's *Psycho*, in that Craven, like Hitchcock 30 years earlier, kills off in early scenes the person the audience is led to believe is the main character. Look out for rising star Johnny Depp in an early role as one of Freddy's victims.

'Night Mother ◖

1986, US, 96 mins, colour
Dir: Tom Moore
Stars: Sissy Spacek, Anne Bancroft, Ed Berke, Carol Robbins
Rating: ★★★

Director Tom Moore, whose only previous movie experience was the disastrous *Return to Boggy Creek* horror film in 1978, seems a strange choice to film this gruelling but ultimately stage-bound version of the Pulitzer Prize-winning play. But it is a small triumph on its own terms for Moore, who directed the original stage version. Sissy Spacek is intensely moving as the daughter who wants to end her own life and whose logic about that deci-

N

sion confounds her hysterical mother (Anne Bancroft).

Night Moves ●
1975, US, 95 mins, colour
Dir: Arthur Penn
Stars: Gene Hackman, Jennifer Warren, Edward Binns, James Woods, Melanie Griffith
Rating: ★★

Though it's highly rated in many circles, there are too many unanswered questions at the end of director Arthur Penn's detective story to make it a classic of the genre. Good though Gene Hackman is as the sleuth, you may not be prepared to work out his problems for him as the director seems to be asking. Complex it certainly is, though, with a bravura climax, and very early screen appearances from James Woods and Melanie Griffith. But this is the disillusioned detective syndrome taken to its ultimate extreme, and you may feel that it finally disappears up its own nightmare. See it and decide for yourself.

Night Must Fall ◑
1964, UK, 105 mins, b/w
Dir: Karel Reisz
Stars: Albert Finney, Susan Hampshire, Mona Washbourne, Sheila Hancock, Michael Medwin
Rating: ★★

A remake of the 1937 chiller about a mad young man (then Robert Montgomery, now Albert Finney) who kills a woman with an axe and pops her head in a hat-box. Montgomery whistled 'Danny Boy' to send shivers up our spines; Finney goes round the house in canvas shoes, a maniacal smile hovering at the corners of his lips. The suspense thus engendered, and grisly results, may well startle those who haven't seen the earlier version, although this one is more shocking than sinister. There's masterly black-and-white photography from Freddie Francis, and especially good acting from Mona Washbourne, who conveys well the pitiful vulnerability of old Mrs Bramson, who looks set fair to become Danny's next victim. But even so, it's not half as good as the rarely shown original.

Night My Number Came Up, The ○
1955, UK, 94 mins, b/w
Dir: Leslie Norman
Stars: Michael Redgrave, Sheila Sim, Alexander Knox
Rating: ★★★★

Ingenious thriller concerning a nightmare (about an air crash) which seems to be coming true. Within a few minutes of the opening, one knows exactly what is going to happen. The surprising thing is that the cast manages to sustain a high degree of suspense right up to the end. The whole thing is apt to send a shiver down your spine, Michael Redgrave, as an air marshal who scoffs at the dream at first, then finds himself enacting it, looks suitably perturbed.

Night of the Demon ◑
(aka: Curse of the Demon)
1957, UK, 82 mins, b/w
Dir: Jacques Tourneur
Stars: Dana Andrews, Peggy Cummins
Rating: ★★★★

This famous chiller opens with an attack on the nerves and sustains it right to the end. Evil, raised up by a professor of the occult, raises its head in such seemingly innocuous settings as the British Museum's library, the grounds of an English country home and in a railway carriage. The edgy direction by veteran Hollywood horror-man Jacques Tourneur makes the bizarre events seem spine-chillingly real.

Night of the Eagle ◑ Ⓥ
(aka: Burn, Witch, Burn)
1961, UK, 87 mins, b/w
Dir: Sidney Hayers
Stars: Janet Blair, Peter Wyngarde, Margaret Johnston
Rating: ★★★★

Director Sidney Hayers, one of the hardest-working British film-makers, who eventually went to Hollywood in the late Seventies, turned in one of his finest jobs in this genuinely frightening witchcraft thriller. Aided by menacing black and white photography from Reginald Wyer, director Hayers proves remarkably successful at suggesting an atmosphere of supernatural dangers, rather than relying simply on overt horror.

Night of the Following Day, The ◑ Ⓥ
1968, US, 93 mins, colour
Dir: Hubert Cornfield
Stars: Marlon Brando, Richard Boone
Rating: ★★

Brando has appeared in some strange films in his time, and this bizarre thriller is no exception. Its circular plot construction has more than a little in common with that classic of the macabre, *Dead of Night*.

Night of the Generals ◑ Ⓥ
1966, UK, 148 mins, colour
Dir: Anatole Litvak
Stars: Peter O'Toole, Omar Sharif, Joanna Pettet
Rating: ★★

A whodunnit of epic proportions, set in Nazi-occupied Paris during World War Two. Peter O'Toole and Omar Sharif are the big star guns, but Tom Courtenay contributes the most controlled performance in a formidable cast that also includes Donald Pleasence, Christopher Plummer, John Gregson and Joanna Pettet. A steamroller of a movie that falls between several stools.

Night of the Grizzly ○
1966, US, 102 mins, colour
Dir: Joseph Pevney
Stars: Clint Walker, Martha Hyer, Keenan Wynn
Rating: ★★★

A decidedly different action Western – Clint Walker plays an ex-lawman trying to forge a new life in wild country – in which normal human lives are intertwined skilfully with just that proportion of natural tragedy that must have haunted families in the old west. And the fights involving a marauding grizzly bear have a savage realism. The photography catches exactly the feel of the countryside, and swoops like a big cat on the odd object, such as a pumpkin head at Hallowe'en or, in a very funny scene, a drunken cockerel.

Night of the Hunter, The ● Ⓥ
1955, US, 93 mins, b/w
Dir: Charles Laughton
Stars: Robert Mitchum, Shelley Winters, Lillian Gish
Rating: ★★★★★

The only film directed by actor Charles Laughton – he called it 'a nightmarish sort of Mother Goose tale' – contains the performance of his life from lugubrious Robert Mitchum, as a psychopathic killer in search of hidden money. A *film noir* classic, *The Night of the Hunter* was, surprisingly, not a hit on original release and Laughton was never again offered the chance to get behind the cameras. Laughton's masterly direction drew heavily from German directors Fritz Lang and Josef von Sternberg in its use of shadows and darkness to create mood, apprehension and terror. But Stanley Cortez's camerawork also has its moments of bizarre beauty.

Night of the Iguana, The ◐
1964, US, 118 mins, b/w
Dir: John Huston
Stars: Richard Burton, Ava Gardner,
Deborah Kerr, Sue Lyon
Rating: ★★★

Typically overheated Tennessee
Williams melodrama, although with
rather more humour than one usually
associates with that playwright, co-directed with a full head of steam by
John Huston on location in the remote
Mexican fishing village of Mismaloya.
Richard Burton enjoys himself as a de-
frocked priest now reduced to working
as a courier to a party of American
teachers and finding himself locked
into a sexual square dance with Sue
Lyon (in her first role since her debut
as a pouting nymphet in *Lolita*), Ava
Gardner as a widow running the remote seaside hotel where he and his
party end up, and Deborah Kerr, superb as a spinster with hidden depths.
The performances match the ripeness
of the writing and the locations add to
the impact of an always watchable – if
rarely credible – star movie.

Night of the Living Dead ● ⓥ
1969, US, 96 mins, b/w
Dir: George A Romero
Stars: Duane Jones, Judith O'Dea, Karl
Hardman, Keith Wayne
Rating: ★★★★★

A genuinely frightening, edge-of-seat
suspense horror film, this made the
reputation of its director, George A
Romero, and led to two Romero-di-
rected sequels, *Zombies – Dawn of the
Dead* and *Day of the Dead*. All are
good, but this is the pick of the bunch,
uncomfortably made in black and
white. A plague of zombies in the
American countryside leads to some
truly terrifying scenes, with the main
protagonists trapped in a house. The
shock moments are very skilfully
done, and the horror presented head-
on, leaving the viewer with no escape.
Remade in 1993.

Night of the Living Dead ● ⓥ
1990, US, 96 mins, colour
Dir: Tom Savini
Stars: Patricia Tallman, Tony Todd, Tom
Towles, McKee Anderson
Rating: ★★

A pointless colour remake of the
George A Romero classic, which
gained immense power from being in
black and white. This one, scripted by
Romero but directed by Tom Savini, is
just your standard zombie movie, with
a few good moments and a lot of

chuckles. An excellent, hard-driving
performance by Patricia Tallman,
going from nervous wreck to intense,
knife-edge gun girl, is unfortunately
the only good one in the film. Tony
Todd, later much more effective in
Candyman, is particularly disappointing
as the hero, though he's by no means
the worst performer in the film. The
living dead themselves are always ludicrous rather than threatening.

Night of the Running Man ◐
1994, US, 93 mins, colour
Dir: Mark L Lester
Stars: Scott Glenn, Andrew McCarthy,
Janet Gunn, John Glover, Peter
Iacangelo
Rating: ★★★

Take a million dollars of Mafia
money, an opportunist cab driver and
a charming, ruthless Mafia hitman,
and you seem to have the ingredients
of a straightforward chase movie, a
sort of jokeless equivalent of *Dumb and
Dumber*. But *Commando* director Mark
L Lester's cat and mouse thriller is
more than that. From the start Lester
piles up the tension, with tons of action and some fairly offbeat touches,
plus a pace that never flags. Scott
Glenn is ice itself as the sadistic killer
on the trail of the stolen Mob money
and Andrew McCarthy, as the low-life
Las Vegas cabbie who becomes his
quarry, is believably edgy, as well he
might be. Faint hearts should be
warned that there's a nasty torture
scene that gives new meaning to the
expression 'hard boiled'.

Night on Earth ● ⓥ
1991, US, 120 mins, colour
Dir: Jim Jarmusch
Stars: Winona Ryder, Gena Rowlands,
Béatrice Dalle, Roberto Benigni
Rating: ★

Five cities, five stories, five dreary taxi
journeys. Jim Jarmusch's pointless cab
drive around the world does catch
some of the bleaker qualities of the
cities visited, and is briefly enlivened
by Robert Benigni's Roman scandals
when he confesses (to his priestly passenger) his sexual encounters with
pumpkins, sheep and his brother-in-
law's wife. Béatrice Dalle is quite
effective as a French blind girl, and
Winona Ryder and Gena Rowlands
act hard in one of the two American
sections. At two hours, though, this
ride has so little to say that's entertaining that it's hardly worth the fare.
Probably a cult movie in the making.

Night on the Town, A ◐ ⓥ
(aka: Adventures In Babysitting)
1987, US, 93 mins, colour
Dir: Chris Columbus
Stars: Elisabeth Shue, Maia Brewton,
Keith Coogan
Rating: ★★

Elisabeth Shue is the babysitter who
lurches into a kind of junior-grade *After
Hours* when her best friend calls up in
trouble and she's forced to take her
mother's car, her young charge and
two 15-year-olds in a ride into the big
city that turns into a nightmare of
often barefaced contrivance, with some
very annoying characters. The talented Shue, who's been unlucky with her
career, tries very hard to make something of it, and the film spurts into life
when she's forced to break into an impromptu 'Babysitting Blues' after
bursting on to a nightclub stage hotly
pursued by a couple of comic gangsters led by old sad-eyes John (Davis)
Chandler. Shue carries the sequence
through with delightful verve.
Otherwise you can only sympathise as
she yelps, 'This is not funny,' during
one of her misadventures. An old-
fashioned Disney night on the town,
then, but alas, with its four-letter
words, no longer one for the family.

Night Passage ○
1957, US, 88 mins, colour
Dir: James Neilson
Stars: James Stewart, Audie Murphy,
Dan Duryea, Dianne Foster
Rating: ★★

The mouth-watering Western combination of James Stewart, Audie
Murphy, Dan Duryea and Brandon de
Wilde doesn't quite produce the fireworks you'd expect in this railroad
Western, in spite of Murphy doing
well with his unusual casting as a
good-bad guy. The treatment sorely
misses the touch of Stewart's normal
Western director, Anthony Mann.
Even so, this remains a workmanlike
action picture, with Stewart contributing his usual double dose of sincerity,
and Duryea just walking away with
the film as the blink-eyed, double-dyed
Whitey Harbin.

Night People ○
1954, US, 93 mins, colour
Dir: Nunnally Johnson
Stars: Gregory Peck, Broderick
Crawford, Anita Bjork, Rita Gam
Rating: ★★★

Drama of espionage and counter-espionage in post-war Berlin. Broderick
Crawford is especially effective as the

N

man whose son has been kidnapped by the Communists. Attractive Rita Gam, usually seen in more sultry roles, appears as Colonel Gregory Peck's poker-faced secretary; and Swedish actress Anita Bjork plays an East German double-agent. For any suspense going Nunnally Johnson deserves all the praise. He not only produced the film, but wrote and directed it.

Night Shift ❶

1982, US, 105 mins, colour
Dir: Ron Howard
Stars: Henry Winkler, Michael Keaton, Shelley Long
Rating: ★★★

Delightfully macabre comedy which takes a series of tasteless elements and fashions them into a tasty romp about a wimpish type (Henry Winkler) who takes a job at the local morgue, where his sharpie assistant embroils him in a wild scheme involving a prostitution racket. The two leading roles are feistily played by Winkler and Michael Keaton. Shelley Long from *Cheers* is also in there somewhere.

Night Song ○

1947, US, 101 mins, b/w
Dir: John Cromwell
Stars: Dana Andrews, Merle Oberon
Rating: ★

A really drippy and unbelievable weepie about a pianist blinded in an accident, but given the will to compose by the love of a clever woman. Dana Andrews and Merle Oberon haven't the sympathetic personalities needed to make this work, even if the script gave them any help. Best moment: pianist Arthur Rubinstein performing with the New York Philharmonic.

Night They Raided Minsky's, The ○

(aka: The Night They Invented Striptease)
1967, US, 99 mins, colour
Dir: William Friedkin
Stars: Jason Robards, Britt Ekland, Norman Wisdom
Rating: ★★★★

The complicated plotline of this brilliant nostalgia piece culminates in Britt Ekland (improbably cast as a naive, stage-struck Amish girl) inventing striptease by accident and bringing the era of American burlesque to an end. But the story takes second place to the film's entertaining evocation of the old burlesque shows and Norman

Wisdom, in his only American film, shows his co-stars, notably Jason Robards, just how variety acts were done. Bert Lahr, best remembered for his Cowardly Lion in *The Wizard of Oz*, makes his final screen appearance: his role is truncated since he died during filming and a double had to be used in some scenes.

Night to Remember, A ○

1942, US, 91 mins, b/w
Dir: Richard Wallace
Stars: Loretta Young, Brian Aherne
Rating: ★★★

Nice little wartime frolic about a mystery writer and his wife who get a real-life murder puzzle to solve. Nothing new in this, for sure, but a vivid array of character players, including Gale Sondergaard, Sidney Toler, Lee Patrick and Blanche Yurka, ensures the right atmosphere for the not-too-serious thrills and chills.

Night to Remember, A ○ ⓥ

1958, US, 123 mins, b/w
Dir: Roy Baker
Stars: Kenneth More, Ronald Allen, Honor Blackman
Rating: ★★★

A tense, dramatic, watchable reconstruction of what happened on the disastrous night in 1912 when the liner *Titanic* sank. It has everything from stiff upper lips to panic, from high drama to low comedy, plus a first-rate performance from Kenneth More as the Second Officer, a role played in a 1953 Hollywood version (simply called *Titanic*) by Edmund Purdom.

Night Train to Munich ○

(aka: Night Train)
1940, UK, 95 mins, b/w
Dir: Carol Reed
Stars: Margaret Lockwood, Rex Harrison, Paul Henreid, Basil Radford, Naunton Wayne
Rating: ★★★★

The affinities of this lively spy thriller with Hitchcock's *The Lady Vanishes* are obvious. That's not surprising, however, since it was scripted by that film's writers, Frank Launder and Sidney Gilliat who also reintroduced the cricket enthusiasts Charters and Caldicott, played by Basil Radford and Naunton Wayne, and Margaret Lockwood once again stars. Carol Reed's direction is suitably tense and he stages excellent chase sequences. Notable among the set pieces is the cable-car shootout at the climax, much

imitated in later films, including 1969's *Where Eagles Dare*.

Night Walker, The ❶

1965, US, 86 mins, b/w
Dir: William Castle
Stars: Barbara Stanwyck, Robert Taylor
Rating: ★★

A strange film to reunite Barbara Stanwyck and Robert Taylor on screen after 20 years, this twisty, chilly thriller comes from the 'showman of shock', William Castle. It's a frightening tale he unfolds, at its creepiest and best in the first 20 minutes. Ms Stanwyck, who was married to Taylor from 1939 until 1952, proved she could still come out of a searching close-up with as many honours as actresses half her age.

Night Watch ❶

1973, UK, 98 mins, colour
Dir: Brian G Hutton
Stars: Elizabeth Taylor, Laurence Harvey, Billie Whitelaw
Rating: ★

Did Elizabeth Taylor really see a man with his throat cut in the window opposite her bedroom? Is she going mad after a nervous breakdown? Are her husband (Laurence Harvey in his last major film performance) and best friend (Billie Whitelaw) having an affair and plotting against her? By pitching his suspense at hysteria level throughout, director Brian G Hutton makes sure that no one dozes off in this film, even if we don't believe a word of it.

Night We Dropped a Clanger, The ○

1959, UK, 86 mins, b/w
Dir: Darcy Conyers
Stars: Brian Rix, Cecil Parker
Rating: ★

A fine cast of comedy performers all at sea in a typically rickety British farce of the late Fifties, a time when the *Carry On* films were gaining their first foothold. Brian Rix has a field day in a dual role and William Hartnell gives his comic all as a barking sergeant.

Night We Got the Bird, The ○

1960, UK, 82 mins, b/w
Dir: Darcy Conyers
Stars: Brian Rix, Ronald Shiner, Dora Bryan
Rating: ★★

A fast and furious farce about a man reincarnated as a parrot, with the regulars from the Brian Rix Theatre of

Laughter well to the fore. And there are some priceless cameo performances from the supporting cast, including Robertson Hare as a dithering doctor, John le Mesurier as a long-suffering court clerk and Kynaston Reeves, hillarious as a deaf magistrate.

Night We Never Met, The ● Ⓥ

1993, US, 99 mins, colour
Dir: Warren Light
Stars: Matthew Broderick, Annabella Sciorra, Kevin Anderson, Jeanne Tripplehorn, Louise Lasser, Justine Bateman
Rating: ★★

Matthew Broderick gives a bright, chirpy performance as New York bachelor Sam in this engaging if underwritten and highly predictable comedy of mistaken identity. Sam shares an apartment in the city with two other tenants, sensitive painter Ellen (Annabella Sciorra) and yuppie party animal Brian (Kevin Anderson). But as each uses the apartment on separate days, none of the tenants ever meets up. Before long, some farcical misunderstandings escalate to gigantic proportions. An old-fashioned sex comedy for cynical romantics, just about kept afloat to the end by its bright young cast.

Nine Days a Queen
See: Tudor Rose

Nine Hours to Rama ○

1962, US, 125 mins, colour
Dir: Mark Robson
Stars: Horst Buchholz, Jose Ferrer, Valerie Gearon
Rating: ★★★★★

So Indian, you can almost taste the curry, was how one critic described this tensely dramatic account of the events in Delhi, India, on the day of Mahatma Gandhi's assassination. Director Mark Robson's nationwide search to find an actor to play Gandhi was rewarded by the discovery of J S Casshyap, who bore such a striking resemblance as to make some of the film look almost like a newsreel. Horst Buchholz is suitably wide-eyed as the religious fanatic assigned the assassination, and there are good performances from Diane Baker and Don Borisenko. The whole thing is amazingly tense considering one is aware of the outcome, and the colour photography conveys exactly the heat, dust and dirt of the country.

Nine Months ● Ⓥ

1995, US, 101 mins, colour
Dir: Chris Columbus
Stars: Hugh Grant, Julianne Moore, Tom Arnold, Jeff Goldblum, Robin Williams
Rating: ★★

Fortunately there are a few funny moments, mostly towards the end, in this largely inane baby comedy. Grimacing like mad, Hugh Grant proves that he only has one role – Hugh Grant – as the expectant father for whom his girlfriend's pregnancy after five years' living together is all a little too much. Nothing subtle about what follows, epitomised by Tom Arnold's bull-in-a-china-shop friend whom Grant meets when Arnold's children spit food out into his lunch-box. The dialogue and situations, in fact, are unnecessarily crude in parts even by the standards of the Nineties. Robin Williams livens things up with his two appearances as a manic Russian doctor, but you could sleep through the more sentimental bits and not miss a thing. Joan Cusack and Jeff Goldblum are also in it, but they don't rise above the material. Grant and Julianne Moore are so wimpish here you want to jump into the screen and throttle them – but then perhaps that's the idea.

976 EVIL ● Ⓥ

1988, US, 100 mins, colour
Dir: Robert Englund
Stars: Stephen Geoffreys, Patrick O'Bryan, Jim Metzler, Sandy Dennis, Lezlie Deane
Rating: ★

Robert 'Freddy Krueger' Englund turns film director, but on the evidence of this one he was wise to return to Elm Street. A horror film in which almost nothing happens for 50 minutes, it eventually develops into a sort of *Little Phone of Horrors*, with a hero in direct descent from Rick Moranis' Seymour. Dial 976 EVIL and, before you know it, your mind has been consumed with evil thoughts and you start developing green toenails and looking like Dorian Gray's portrait in the attic. Clearly this state of affairs can't last, and towards the end Englund does stage some nice tableaux with visions of Hell breaking out all over the place. But it's too little evil and too late. Just about worth a look for horror fans, if only for Sandy Dennis' extraordinary performance as Aunt Lucy.

Nineteen Eighty Four ◐ Ⓥ

1984, UK, 115 mins, colour
Dir: Michael Radford

Stars: John Hurt, Richard Burton, Suzanna Hamilton
Rating: ★★★

John Hurt, the screen king of torture, torment, anguish and suffering, is at it again in this version of George Orwell's bleak vision of the future. And nobody does it better, whether the suffering is mental or, in the harrowing latter part of the film, physical, as interrogator Richard Burton (underplaying too much) sticks electricity through the thin-framed Hurt like a butcher skinning a carcass of meat. Hurt also has his hair chopped off again, and his fans must be wondering what it's like to see him smile. Cyril Cusack scoops up what acting scraps Hurt (and the film's ubiquitous rats) leaves around, as the treacherous junk dealer, but the ultimate result of Michael Radford's downbeat direction is a sombre and depressing film. After this one, you may not be able to look a rat in the eye for some time!

1969 ● Ⓥ

1988, US, 96 mins, colour
Dir: Ernest Thompson
Stars: Robert Downey Jr, Kiefer Sutherland, Bruce Dern, Mariette Hartley, Winona Ryder
Rating: ★

A whole crew of good actors is shipwrecked in a sea of precious dialogue in this look at 1969, flower power, Vietnam protests and all that. Mind you, Sutherland, Ryder and Mariette Hardey look good even when speaking these lines. Robert Downey has to tackle yet another bag-eyed loner pressing the self-destruct button, while Dern and Joanna Cassidy fare even less well trying to express an adulterous relationship the whole town knows about. The plot, alas, never flows with any fluency, and did anyone really say, especially back then: 'This is the last year of our innocence'? And would anyone have wanted to know them if they did?

Nine to Five ○ Ⓥ

1980, US, 110 mins, colour
Dir: Colin Higgins
Stars: Jane Fonda, Dolly Parton, Lily Tomlin, Dabney Coleman, Sterling Hayden
Rating: ★★★

Fast, furious and unusual comedy. For most of its running time, it proves to be fun to have around, tripping a zany fight fantastic round three lady office workers: the brains (Lily Tomlin), the

N

bust (Dolly Parton) and the bewildered (Jane Fonda) in an offbeat role – especially funny when trying to cope with a computer filing system). The main villain, however, is not the machine age but the girls' intolerable, grind-the-employees-into-the-ground sexiest employer. This is a thankless but well-played role for Dabney Coleman, who at least gets star billing for his pains. How the girls keep Coleman prisoner in his own home while proving fraudulent conversion against him is every henpecked clerk's dream. Wish-fulfilment to be sure but out of the happiest kind, with hallucination sequences, madcap encounters with a corpse on a trolley and even cartoon characters on the way. Lily Tomlin is delightful as Violet but subsequent suitable roles for both her and Dolly Parton have proved difficult for the cinema to provide.

99 44/100% Dead
See: Call Harry Crown

99 River Street O
1953, US, 83 mins, b/w
Dir: Phil Karlson
Stars: John Payne, Evelyn Keyes, Brad Dexter, Peggie Castle, Frank Faylen
Rating: ★★★

This was the first of a series of really good, fast-moving and extremely tough thrillers made by director Phil Karlson in the mid-Fifties. Here, former song-and-dance man John Payne plays a taxi-driver framed for murder.

Ninotchka O Ⓥ
1939, US, 110 mins, b/w
Dir: Ernst Lubitsch
Stars: Greta Garbo, Melvyn Douglas
Rating: ★★★★

Greta Garbo's first comedy role – the film was advertised as 'Garbo Laughs' and her penultimate film before self-imposed retirement. She brings out all the nuances of her role, and her stunning performance earned her a fourth Oscar nomination, but she was squeezed out by Vivien Leigh and *Gone With the Wind*, which swept the board that year. The film was quite daring for its day because of the fact that it made fun of Communism the first time in a major American film. The great star's scenes with Ina Claire were particularly electric, not surprising since Claire was the widow of John Gilbert, who had been Garbo's long-time lover on and off screen.

Ninth Configuration, The ●
(aka: Twinkle, Twinkle, Killer Kane)
1979, US, 118 mins, colour
Dir: William Peter Blatty
Stars: Stacy Keach, Scott Wilson
Rating: ★★

Psychological sideshow that runs like a play but strangely never was, its source being a novel by writer-director William Peter Blatty. Stacy Keach plays the slow-speaking psychiatrist colonel – it's apparent there's something odd about him from the start – caring for a group of demented 'Nam veterans at a grotesque castle in northwest America. Blatty tries in his usual fashion to grab his audience's attention any way he can, with violence and nudity thrown in at the end, but can't disguise the surface bag of tricks as anything but a pageant run by an entrepreneur who plays for effect rather than depth, show rather than substance. All the same, this rates highly in the canon of cinema curiosities and at least tries to be stimulating and thought provoking at the same time. There's a stupendous bar-room fight scene. Keach (a long way from Mike Hammer here) and Scott Wilson show sincerity, but the film's best performance comes from the ever-reliable Ed Flanders.

Nixon ● Ⓥ
1995, US, 192 mins, colour
Dir: Oliver Stone
Stars: Anthony Hopkins, Joan Allen, James Woods, Powers Boothe, Mary Steenburgen, Bob Hoskins
Rating: ★

Even Oliver Stone's most fervent fans would be hard put to deny that this is a tough one to sit through. Only in the last few minutes do we get a look at Nixon the man and what he felt, but the main body of the film is almost completely uninteresting. There must be a way to make the disgraced US ex-president's life watchable, but Stone hasn't found it here. Richard Nixon was never a loved man, even when he was winning elections and the film hints (while taking a broadly sympathetic view) at sundry unpleasant sides to his nature. 'When they look at you,' he tells a portrait of the dead John F Kennedy, 'they see what they want to be. When they look at me, they see what they are.' Still, he also said 'It's struggle that gives life meaning, not victory', a maxim that came back to haunt him when Congress voted to impeach him over Watergate and sundry other sins, most of which were probably on tape.

Anthony Hopkins impersonates Nixon with vigour if not much of an American accent.

No Blade of Grass O
1970, UK, 97 mins, colour
Dir: Cornel Wilde
Stars: Nigel Davenport, Jean Wallace
Rating: ★★★

Another of Cornel Wilde's primitive parables as director, to follow the success of *The Naked Prey* and *Beach Red*. For the first time here, Wilde wisely forewent the difficult double of acting and directing, leaving the leading role in the capable hands of Nigel Davenport as a man trying to take his family to safety through an English countryside devastated by a deadly virus. Wilde's real-life wife, Jean Wallace, co-stars.

Nobody Lives Forever O
1946, US, 95 mins, b/w
Dir: Jean Negulesco
Stars: John Garfield, Geraldine Fitzgerald, Walter Brennan, Faye Emerson
Rating: ★★★

You could almost sketch out the plot developments for this crime drama from films you'd seen before. But never mind, the acting glitters, especially from John Garfield with another of his embittered loners, and from Geraldine Fitzgerald as a widow whose fortune Garfield is after. Humphrey Bogart was originally slated to play the leading character, but it fits Garfield to a T.

Nobody Runs Forever O
(aka: The High Commissioner)
1968, UK, 101 mins, colour
Dir: Ralph Thomas
Stars: Rod Taylor, Christopher Plummer, Lilli Palmer
Rating: ★

After 12 years of Hollywood stardom, Rod Taylor reverted to his native Australian accent in this thriller about a detective trying to foil an assassination bid. You'll spot Franchot Tone in his last film and, maybe, Leo McKern (unbilled) as the Premier of New South Wales. The best performance comes from the ever-reliable Lilli Palmer, but somehow the whole tired enterprise lacks zest.

Nobody's Fool ◑ Ⓥ
1986, US, 105 mins, colour
Dir: Evelyn Purcell
Stars: Rosanna Arquette, Eric Roberts,

Mare Winningham
Rating: ★★

A kooky comedy that continued to prove that Rosanna Arquette is a poor picker of scripts. She hasn't had a sizeable hit since *Desperately Seeking Susan*, and it's not hard to see why. This flat romance fails to sparkle as small town waitress Arquette has to choose between a life of drudgery and regret or take a chance on a new Mr Wonderful in town played with craggy immobility by Eric Robot, sorry, Roberts. Nobody much fancied it, and they were no fools.

Nobody's Fool ● Ⓥ
1994, US, 110 mins, colour
Dir: Robert Benton
Stars: Paul Newman, Bruce Willis, Melanie Griffith, Jessica Tandy, Dylan Walsh, Pruitt Taylor Vance
Rating: ★★★

This small-town drama contains some pungent pieces of dialogue, mainly for Paul Newman as a 60-year-old construction worker currently failing to win damages for a gammy leg sustained while working for Carl (Bruce Willis). Having left his wife and child 30 years before, Newman lives with an elderly widow (Jessica Tandy), who depends on him not only to help her out but also to keep her out of the clutches of her banker son. But when the person who offers him a lift one day turns out to be his own son (Dylan Walsh) with his discontented wife and two small sons, a series of events take place in Newman's life that provide him with enough excitement, food for thought and insight into the future to occupy a normal five-year span. No big deal here, and with some rather unnecessary nudity, perhaps to emphasise the lightness of tone, but well-enough written by director Robert Benton to keep us cheerfully engaged throughout. Newman is right on the money here and Gene Saks also good as his one-legged lawyer, who provides drinking companionship but never seems to have won a case. 'I never knew you were a Jew,' Newman snarls. 'How come you ain't smart?'

Nocturne ○
1946, US, 88 mins, b/w
Dir: Edwin Marin
Stars: George Raft, Lynn Bari, Virginia Huston
Rating: ★★★

The detective fascinated by the lifestyle of someone in a murder case dates back to *Laura*, and has been seen as recently as 1987 in *Black Widow*.

Here it's George Raft as the loner envious of the libertine's life enjoyed by the murder victim. The result is a taut thriller, even if it never matches the brilliance of the opening sequence. Perhaps the best of Raft's post-war ventures.

No Deposit, No Return ☉
1976, US, 125 mins, colour
Dir: Norman Tokar
Stars: David Niven, Darren McGavin, Don Knotts
Rating: ★★

Although this Walt Disney comedy makes you wait a long time for a laugh it finally delivers the goods in a hectic wharfside chase. The story's about two children (personable Kim Richards and obnoxious Brad Savage) who, with their pet skunk, persuade two petty thieves to hold them to ransom so the crooks can pay their debts. The skunk is the best thing in the film, and David Niven is not noticeably stretched by his role as the kids' grandfather.

No Escape ● Ⓥ
(aka: The Penal Colony)
1994, US, 118 mins, colour
Dir: Martin Campbell
Stars: Ray Liotta, Lance Henriksen, Stuart Wilson, Kevin Dillon, Michael Lerner, Ernie Hudson
Rating: ★

Steely-eyed Ray Liotta, so memorably menacing in *Something Wild* and *Unlawful Entry*, gets to play the hard-nosed hero in this brainlessly plotted piece of futuristic action hokum. Liotta's a convict (innocent, naturally) sentenced to life imprisonment on a remote jungle island in 2022 where a gang of brutal savages rules and only the toughest survive. The spearings, beheadings, whackings and hackings are relentless. For those with weaker stomachs, there is indeed no escape here – unless, of course, you use that 'video eject' button, or want to hang on for yet another long shot of the ocean that seems to be as magnetic to cameraman Phil Meheux as the blue of Liotta's eyes.

No Highway in the Sky ○
1951, UK, 99 mins, b/w
Dir: Henry Koster
Stars: James Stewart, Marlene Dietrich, Glynis Johns, Jack Hawkins
Rating: ★★★

Mid-air suspense was always a good bet to bring the best out of cast-writer

and director, and here a fine cast miss few of the opportunities presented by the array of interesting characters in this tense and likeable adaptation of Nevil Shute's novel *No Highway* (the film's British title). James Stewart was still very much at his peak (which lasted from 1939–1958) when he played the mild-mannered professor who insists that a new plane will crack up after it has flown a specific number of hours. The plot uncannily predicted the cause of the comet crashes of the Fifties.

Noises Off ● Ⓥ
1992, US, 104 mins, colour
Dir: Peter Bogdanovich
Stars: Carol Burnett, Michael Caine, Denholm Elliott, Julie Hagerty, Christopher Reeve
Rating: ★★

A gallant but doomed attempt by director Peter Bogdanovich to film an unfilmable stage farce about a group of ham actors trying to put on a new British stage farce along traditional, trouser-dropping lines. Half a dozen irresistibly funny moments burst through the tedium of the rest, and remind you how hilarious the original was. Michael Caine and a distinguished company give frantic endeavour in their efforts to raise the few laughs going up to hysteria pitch. It certainly is fast but not, alas, too funny.

No Limit ○
1935, UK, 80 mins, b/w
Dir: Monty Banks
Stars: George Formby, Florence Desmond
Rating: ★★★

Just to see George Formby on his black-and-white checkered motorbike marked 'George Shuttleworth Speed Demon' is to start giggling, and audiences went for this sporty comedy in a big way. It was the lad from Lancashire's first big studio comedy, and he also sang one of his greatest hits, 'Riding at the TT Races'. The antics are directed at a fine pace by Monty Banks, himself a famous screen comedian who knew the art of comedy inside out, and are spiced up with footage from the actual 1935 TT event.

No Love for Johnnie ◑
1960, UK, 111 mins, b/w
Dir: Ralph Thomas
Stars: Peter Finch, Stanley Holloway, Mary Peach, Donald Pleasence
Rating: ★★★

N

A solid, downbeat drama based on a posthumous novel by MP Wilfred Fienburgh, who was killed in a car crash. Peter Finch is the MP who wrecks his private life to reach the top in politics; Mary Peach, Billie Whitelaw and Rosalie Crutchley are the unlucky ladies he discards on the way. And you'll catch a glimpse of Oliver Reed as a rowdy party guest. Donald Pleasence makes a rather more lasting impression as a shifty politico.

No Man of Her Own ○
1949, US, 98 mins, b/w
Dir: Mitchell Leisen
Stars: Barbara Stanwyck, John Lund
Rating: ★★

Strung out emotionally as usual, Barbara Stanwyck is well on form in this cross of weepie and *film noir*, based on a book by Cornel Woolrich, writing under the pseudonym of William Irish. Her blackmailing lover is very effectively played by Lyle Bettger, making his screen debut after a string of stage successes. The fair-haired actor with the evil grin was to fill his 25 film years with a whole gallery of bad men. Watch too for a brief appearance by Dooley Wilson, once Sam of 'play it again' fame, as a waiter in the dining-car of a train. Quite a comedown after taking the spotlight at Rick's Cafe Americain!

No Man's Land ● ⓥ
1987, US, 105 mins, colour
Dir: Peter Werner
Stars: Charlie Sheen, D B Sweeney, Lara Harris, Randy Quaid, Bill Duke, M Emmet Walsh
Rating: ★★★

This is the one about the policeman who goes undercover with a gang, is attracted to the leader's charm and falls in love with the bad guy's sister. As old as the hills then, right down to the ritual shoot-out climax. Still this version is quite well done, with the youth of D B Sweeney, as the cop, and Charlie Sheen, as the crook, lending an uncomfortable edge to the familiar tale. Sheen in particular catches the eye in a compelling portrayal of the mask of reckless boyishness which hides a deadly core. Randy Quaid takes a more mature role than hitherto as Sweeney's police chief contact. Car chase excitements punctuate the theme of cat and mouse and the story (souped up to hypertension by such tactics), though never memorable, entertains all the way.

No Mercy ● ⓥ
1986, US, 105 mins, colour
Dir: Richard Pearce
Stars: Richard Gere, Kim Basinger
Rating: ★★

For the most part darkly photographed and slow-moving, this New Orleans-set cop thriller does have a tremendous shoot-out climax, to which the whole film seems geared from the start. It's good that Richard Gere presents a more vulnerable character than, say, Stallone or Schwarzenegger would under similar circumstances, an element which lends a keener edge of tension to the fiery *High Noon*-type finish at a Western-style saloon in the centre of town. The villain (Jeroen Krabbé) has a pigtail, which makes him extra bad, but he's also extra foolish, killing one of his own men off at the end and shortening the odds against Gere's lone wolf hero. Gere and Kim Basinger do their best with the rest of the movie, but there's little chemistry between them, and it's the kind of film where you could pop out and make the coffee without missing a thing any time but the last 15 minutes.

Nora Prentiss ○
1947, US, 117 mins, b/w
Dir: Vincent Sherman
Stars: Ann Sheridan, Kent Smith, Bruce Bennett, Robert Alda
Rating: ★★

Although the twists and turns of this flashback melodrama take some swallowing, solid performances by Ann Sheridan and the underrated Kent Smith buoy up this glossy cross between a *film noir* and what was known then as a 'woman's picture'. The camerawork and direction neatly emphasises the plight of the two leading characters, trapped by circumstances and their own weaknesses.

Normal Life ● ⓥ
1995, US, 102 mins, colour
Dir: John McNaughton
Stars: Luke Perry, Ashley Judd
Rating: ★★★

Not one for the anti-gun lobby, this. Small town cop Luke Perry takes flaky, astronomy-loving new girl Ashley Judd for target practice on their first date. But beneath the blonde curls and ice-blue eyes lie rather clear hints of madness and anyone who's seen *Pretty Poison* will have a pretty good idea of developments from here on – especially as the film has inexplicably shown us the ending at the beginning. There's a brief attempt at domesticity after the couple get hitched, and a bit of psycho-babble about Judd being unable to reach orgasm. But this is basically *Gun Crazy* country, with Perry and Judd soon enjoying the thrill of life on the other side of the law. Interesting territory, this, but the excursion into it is too obvious by half, and Judd's accuracy in target practice seems to go to hell in a handbag when firing wildly at pursuing cops from a car. Apart from that, though, her portrayal is pretty interesting.

Norma Rae ⓞ
1979, US, 114 mins, colour
Dir: Martin Ritt
Stars: Sally Field, Beau Bridges, Ron Leibman, Pat Hingle
Rating: ★★★★★

Another triumph for Martin Ritt, surely one of the most consistent directors who ever worked in Hollywood. The performances of Sally Field (winning an Oscar), Beau Bridges – never better – and Ron Leibman are beyond reproach, but this is above all a director's film, so brilliantly organised and constructed that if the last 20 minutes don't bring a lump to your throat, nothing in the cinema ever will. The tiny, gritty Field has the title role as the best-looking gal in the mill factory: she has two children who live with her and her parents, one the daughter of her dead husband, the other illegitimate. The theme of the film, though, concerns the advent of a union man (Leibman) to the southern town where events are set, and the conversion of the bright but downtrodden Norma Rae to a fierce force 100 per cent behind the union cause. Ritt builds this activity to an enormous emotional impact by the climax.

North ○ ⓥ
1994, US, 91 mins, colour
Dir: Rob Reiner
Stars: Elijah Wood, Bruce Willis, Jon Lovitz, Dan Aykroyd, Kathy Bates, John Ritter
Rating: ★

A dumb comedy-fantasy about a boy, North (Elijah Wood), who, tired of his selfish parents, wins a court action against them and is given a limited period to circumnavigate the world in search of a new family. The school genius meanwhile uses North's fame and influence to establish his own power base whose Macchiavellian proportions will be ruined if North returns home.

Following this unpromising beginning, all the episodes of North's search are cut to the same formula: initial enthusiasm for prospective parents in Texas, Hawaii, Alaska, China, Zaire and France, then disillusionment, plus a homily on the values of life from Bruce Willis, who turns up as everything from an Easter bunny to a nightclub comedian called Joey Fingers. The name 'Bedford' crops up once or twice as a town, but any comparison with Frank Capra's *It's a Wonderful Life* (set in Bedford Falls) is wishful thinking on the part of the director.

North Avenue Irregulars, The

See: Hill's Angels

North by Northwest ○ Ⓥ

1959, US, 136 mins, colour
Dir: Alfred Hitchcock
Stars: Cary Grant, Eva Marie Saint, James Mason
Rating: ★★★★

There are strong echoes of *The 39 Steps* in this, perhaps Alfred Hitchcock's most famous suspense thriller on a chase theme. The attack on Cary Grant by the crop-duster plane in the middle of a desolate prairie has now passed into film folklore. But the film has many other fine moments, notably the tense scenes on board a train (one of Hitchcock's favourite locations), the assassination at the United Nations building, and the climax at Mount Rushmore.

North Dallas Forty ●

1979, US, 114 mins, colour
Dir: Ted Kotcheff
Stars: Nick Nolte, Mac Davis, Charles Durning, Dayle Haddon
Rating: ★★★

If this tough and funny film is a true picture of the way American football is run and played – most of its players must surely end physically damaged for life – then thank heavens for other varieties of the game. Its main weakness has dogged countless similar Hollywood movies: the star player is sent on at the end of the game to try win it for his side. It's the stuff of which dreams not dramas are made. But Nolte is extremely good as the player beginning to have doubts about it all, and he is almost matched by G D Spradlin as the fanatical coach, a portrayal that brilliantly skirts the pit of caricature into which several members of the cast plunge headlong.

North Sea Hijack ○
(aka: ffolkes)

1979, UK, 100 mins, colour
Dir: Andrew V McLaglen
Stars: Roger Moore, James Mason, Anthony Perkins
Rating: ★★

Rufus Excalibur ffolkes, the eccentric hero of this action-thriller, hates women, dresses in tweed suits, loves cats and has his own private underwater army of saboteurs. Not exactly James Bond, but he's just the man the government need when an oil drilling rig and platform is hijacked and a £25 million ransom demanded. The cast, with Roger Moore as the dotty ffolkes, James Mason as an admiral and Anthony Perkins as No 1 villain, have some fun with a formula story, but considering the calibre of the cast and the behind-the-scenes team, the film's a bit of a disappointment; it needed some of those spectacular Bond stunts to liven it up.

North Star, The ○

1943, US, 105 mins, b/w
Dir: Lewis Milestone
Stars: Anne Baxter, Farley Granger, Dana Andrews, Walter Huston
Rating: ★★

This is a decently made WWII propaganda film about a Soviet village resisting the Nazi onslaught. The credits are impeccable: Lewis Milestone (*All Quiet on the Western Front*) directed, Lillian Hellman wrote the script, James Wong Howe was the cinematographer and Aaron Copland supplied the score. In addition, there was a clutch of stars: Anne Baxter, Farley Granger (in his first starring role), Walter Huston as the village doctor and Erich von Stroheim as, inevitably, the Nazi doctor. Unfortunately, the film never rises above tub-thumping and Hellman made public her disappointment at what had happened to her script.

North to Alaska ○ Ⓥ

1960, US, 122 mins, colour
Dir: Henry Hathaway
Stars: John Wayne, Stewart Granger, Capucine, Fabian, Ernie Kovacs
Rating: ★★★

This rumbustious knockabout Western, with John Wayne and Stewart Granger as partners in Gold Rush days, seems in retrospect to be one long fist fight. It certainly does have the bar-room brawl to end them all, plus rich colour photography, a memorable theme song by Johnny Horton and stout support from a

whole saloon-full of Western character players.

North West Frontier ○ Ⓥ
(aka: Flame Over India)

1959, UK, 129 mins, colour
Dir: J Lee Thompson
Stars: Kenneth More, Lauren Bacall
Rating: ★★★

One of Kenneth More's best films: an exciting, old-fashioned action adventure set (mostly aboard a train) in 1905 India and blazingly shot in unusually rich Eastman Colour by Oscar-winning cameraman Geoffrey Unsworth. It's adventure all the way as More and cool governess Lauren Bacall try to get a young prince to safety through 300 miles of rebel-held country. The story races along and there are personable supporting performances from Herbert Lom, Wilfrid Hyde White, and especially I S Johar as a feisty engineer.

North West Mounted Police ○

1940, US, 125 mins, colour
Dir: Cecil B DeMille
Stars: Gary Cooper, Paulette Goddard, Madeleine Carroll, Preston Foster
Rating: ★★★

'Blood will run like water!' exclaims the villain, gleefully surveying his new Gatling gun. 'You won't notice it much,' grins his associate. 'The Mounted Police wear red coats.' Well, the Cecil B DeMille adventure spectacles never were noted for their dynamic dialogue, but the action and colour in this one more than make up for the winces in the script. Gary Cooper is perfect as the tall, taciturn Texas Ranger who helps the Mounties clear up the Riel Rebellion of 1885 and the film made Paramount a mint despite their penny-pinching on the cost, which included their refusing to allow DeMille to shoot in Canada, and planting 300 pine trees in the studio backlot instead.

Northwest Passage ○ Ⓥ

1940, US, 125 mins, colour
Dir: King Vidor
Stars: Spencer Tracy, Robert Young, Walter Brennan
Rating: ★★★★★

The Technicolor MGM classic (actually intended to be the first of a two-part epic) which paved the way for new standards of realism in open-air spectaculars. Horror and heroism, combined with action and battle scenes remarkable even by today's standards,

N

stamp the film with the hallmark of greatness. Urged on by King Vidor's uncompromising direction, Spencer Tracy gives a magnificent performances. Heartbreaking and blood-surging in turn, this is a winner all the way.

No Sex Please, We're British ◑ ⓥ
1973, UK, 91 mins, colour
Dir: Cliff Owen
Stars: Ronnie Corbett, Beryl Reid, Arthur Lowe, Ian Ogilvy
Rating: ★★

A film version of the epic-running British stage farce, with a cast of funsters more formidable than ever the theatre could muster. Ronnie Corbett – in fine dithering form – and Ian Ogilvy are the quiet bank clerks suddenly deluged with pornographic literature and other roles are filled by such familiar faces as Arthur Lowe (skilfully underplaying the moralising bank manager), Michael Bates, Robin Askwith, Michael Robbins, Deryck Guyler, Michael Ripper, Beryl Reid, Brian Wilde, Frank Thornton and Sydney Bromley. Cliff Owen directs at a helter-skelter pace throughout.

Nostradamus ● ⓥ
1993, UK/US/France/Spain, 122 mins, colour
Dir: Roger Christian
Stars: Tcheky Karyo, Julia Ormond, Rutger Hauer, F Murray Abraham, Amanda Plummer
Rating: ★★★

Though it wavers uneasily between the banal and the intriguing, the inherent interest in this story of the 16th-century prophet, who seems to have seen more of the future than anyone before or since, finally wins the day. If there is a way to present his life, this relatively sober account is probably as good as any. Tcheky Karyo is quite good (if uncharismatic) in the title role, a physician and scientist who miraculously escaped execution (although not persecution) at the hands of anti-heretics, most notably thanks to the intervention of the Queen of France (another offbeat performance by Amanda Plummer). As he becomes increasingly tormented by visions (presented often in lamentably facile fashion), the film studies his life story, from boyhood, through marriage to his first wife (Julia Ormond) who, with their two children, dies from the Plague. There's some impressive 'medieval' production design in all

this, and Rutger Hauer pops in for a cough-and-spit cameo as 'the mystic monk'.

Nothing But the Best ◑
1963, UK, 99 mins, colour
Dir: Clive Donner
Stars: Alan Bates, Denholm Elliott, Millicent Martin, Pauline Delany
Rating: ★★★★

Room at the Top played for laughs, as Jimmy Brewster, anti-hero and stop-at-nothing rogue, drags his way to the top of the firm by means strictly foul, and wins the boss's daughter. All the performances are attractive with Alan Bates superbly amoral as Jimmy, and Denholm Elliott establishing his latter-day seediness for the first time.

Nothing But the Night ●
1972, UK, 90 mins, colour
Dir: Peter Sasdy
Stars: Christopher Lee, Peter Cushing, Diana Dors
Rating: ★★

Christopher Lee here departs from the traditional style of horror film with which he has been most associated – and indeed, his traditional role, as he plays a Special Branch chief in this unsuccessful but occasionally unsettling mixture of mystery and the uncanny, with fantasy and even science-fiction overtones. The story, which concerns the strange deaths of various people who were all trustees of an orphanage, is adapted from an intriguing novel by John Blackburn.

Nothing But the Truth ☉
1941, US, 90 mins, b/w
Dir: Elliott Nugent
Stars: Bob Hope, Paulette Goddard, Edward Arnold, Leif Erickson
Rating: ★★★

Bob Hope wartime comedy, with Hope as a wimp who makes a foolish wager to tell nothing but the truth for 48 hours. Filmed twice before, the film provides surefire fun for Hope fans, centring on a lavish houseboat party in which the complications for Hope with his bet become increasingly not only precarious but hilarious. Seldom seen these days, this Hope rarity, which teams him with Paulette Goddard for the third time, remains timeless fun and well worth catching.

Nothing But Trouble ○ ⓥ
1991, US, 93 mins, colour
Dir: Dan Aykroyd
Stars: Chevy Chase, Dan Aykroyd, John

Candy, Demi Moore
Rating: ★

This may not be the laugh-a-minute comedy that you expect from director Dan Aykroyd and his fellow graduates from the *National Lampoon* school of lunacy, Chevy Chase and John Candy. 'An absolute failure as a comedy,' thundered one British critic. But it's an oddly satisfying film if only because it lets loose a real sense of the bizarre. Aykroyd plays a 106-year-old judge who dispenses mediaeval justice in an oddball corner of rural America. It's the sort of place where speeders are fed into a fairground device called 'Mr Bonestripper'. Chase plays the innocent New Yorker who gets trapped in the hell of Valkenavia and Candy plays, among other parts, the judge's deaf-mute granddaughter ...

Nothing in Common ◑ ⓥ
1986, US, 119 mins, colour
Dir: Garry Marshall
Stars: Tom Hanks, Jackie Gleason, Eva Marie Saint, Hector Elizondo, Bess Armstrong, Sela Ward
Rating: ★★

A generation gap comedy-drama that on the whole goes nowhere in particular, although it does have a few inspired moments of comedy, as you would expect from this director and these stars. In more dramatic moments, however, the script too often has that phoney ring – smart scripters writing lines for people who just wouldn't communicate like this, if they communicated at all. Chief non-communicators here are the parents (Jackie Gleason, Eva Marie Saint) of advertising whiz Tom Hanks, completely wrecking his hip, well laid-out (like his girls) life. Director Garry Marshall encourages the whole cast, Saint especially, to shout a lot, while the wry-faced Hanks is such a natural comedian that he's wasted on the poignant or emotional parts where the script is giving him so little help. Not bad, but you'd be hard put to find reasons to recommend people to actually see it.

Nothing Personal ● ⓥ
1995, UK, 85 mins, colour
Dir: Thaddeus O'Sullivan
Stars: John Lynch, Ian Hart, James Frain, Michael Gambon, Maria Doyle Kennedy, Jennifer Courtney
Rating: ★★★

Or: One night in the life of a Loyalist fighter in Northern Ireland. When Catholic John Lynch is unwise enough to venture out of his house to try to do something about street fighting between Catholics and Protestants, he is quickly swept up in a whirlwind of violence, specifically with the world of local enforcers James Frain and Ian Hart, the latter a psychopath to match Begbie in *Trainspotting*. Fuel both for those who plead for peace, and for those who would let the warring factions beat the Bejazus out of each other, director Thaddeus O'Sullivan's film is also a decent thriller in its own right, besides looking at the differing viewpoints of those caught in the violence; those who glory in it, those who condemn it, those who use it for political ends and those who, hero-worshipping the fighters on respective sides, are disillusioned by the unthinking reality. Both an impassioned and dispassionate view of the troubles, this is small-scale (the action takes place on a single night) but worth your attention.

Nothing Sacred O

1937, US, 77 mins, colour
Dir: William Wellman
Stars: Carole Lombard, Fredric March
Rating: ★★★★

A scathing satirical romp about a girl from the sticks who is given the time of her life in New York simply because a reporter there is mistakenly under the impression that she's dying from radiation poisoning. Carole Lombard, Fredric March and Walter Connolly (as the reporter's long-suffering publisher) work like demons to keep things moving at firecracker pace, Ben Hecht's inventive script not only bristles with wit, but its packed array of incidents enables director William Wellman to create some treasurable moments – especially the fist-fight between Lombard and March, and the scene where March ventures into a hostile small town and is attacked in a manner which has to be seen to be believed.

No Time to Die!

See: Tank Force

Notorious O Ⓥ

1946, US, 101 mins, b/w
Dir: Alfred Hitchcock
Stars: Cary Grant, Ingrid Bergman, Claude Rains, Louis Calhern
Rating: ★★★★

One of Alfred Hitchcock's most edge-of-seat films is this famous suspense thriller in which Cary Grant plays a US government agent after big and very dangerous fish in South America.

The camera angles which heighten the tension were not surpassed until *Psycho*. The photography is by Ted Tetzlaff, who is said to have got tired of Hitchcock's fussiness on getting shape and shadow exactly right – although Tetzlaff used both to great effect in *Riff Raff* and *The Window* when he himself turned director shortly afterwards. Ingrid Bergman lends her star presence as a refugee half-reluctantly in league with Grant, and Claude Rains is superb as the spy. Amazing finale.

Not Quite Jerusalem Ⓞ

1984, UK, 114 mins, colour
Dir: Lewis Gilbert
Stars: Joanna Pacula, Sam Robards
Rating: ★

It isn't too easy to see why anyone would want to make a film about life on an Israeli kibbutz, but at least director Lewis Gilbert strengthened this film's appeal by unearthing a new star in sultry Joanna Pacula. Otherwise Paul Kember's script straitjackets its characters into revue-sketch stereotypes, complete with an Australian girl who declares herself so hungry that 'Gosh, I could eat a dingo'. Small wonder, then, that the scenes without words are those that Gilbert makes work the best, especially in a well-staged fire sequence, and a couple of camp(us) romances, which include a touching Japanese-Jewish/American exchange of languages.

No Trees in the Street Ⓞ Ⓥ
(aka: No Tree in the Street)

1958, UK, 96 mins, b/w
Dir: J Lee-Thompson
Stars: Sylvia Syms, Herbert Lom, Stanley Holloway
Rating: ★★

Sylvia Syms' sensitive and poignant performance is the glittering prize in this otherwise stale, dreary and and unconvincing portrait of London slum life which falls rather heavily betwen the Ealing realism of post-war years and the 'kitchen sink' dramas which had started with *Room at the Top*. Stanley Holloway's classless sincerity is also much needed.

Not Without My Daughter
Ⓞ Ⓥ

1990, US, 115 mins, colour
Dir: Brian Gilbert
Stars: Sally Field, Alfred Molina, Sheila Rosenthal, Roshan Seth
Rating: ★★★★★

True stories about courage in the face of massive adversities are always guaranteed to tug at our emotions: this one has the edge on heart-on-sleeve pieces like *Born on the Fourth of July* in that it deliberately under-emphasises the horrors of the situation in which the central character finds herself. Betty (a typically pugnacious performance by Sally Field) is happily married to Moody (Molina), an Iranian-born doctor who has lived in America for 20 years. They have a five-year-old daughter. Very reluctantly, Betty agrees to a two-week holiday in Iran. Whether this is a ruse, or whether Moody very quickly reverts to the traditions of his native Islam, the film doesn't make clear, but the result is the same – a living nightmare for Betty and her daughter. Moody decides to stay in Iran and his wife finds herself watched day and night, confined to her quarters and beaten for disobedience. Field never overplays her hand as the terrorised wife and Molina, not batting an eyelid, achieves a seamless transfer from loving, gentle husband, to ranting, wife-beating tyrant.

Now and Then Ⓞ

1995, US, 102 mins, colour
Dir: Lesli Linka Glatter
Stars: Demi Moore, Melanie Griffith, Rita Wilson, Rosie O'Donnell, Lolita Davidovich
Rating: ★★★

Four of America's best teenage actresses play lifelong friends in this feminist sideshoot of *Stand By Me*. The story of their 13th summer, it involves them centrally holding seances in graveyards and believing they have raised a troubled spirit from the dead, in trying to solve the mysterious death of a 12-year-old boy and his mother 25 years before. Although it tells a few simple truths, the film has nothing of great perception to impart: the girls feud with boys, have problems with parents and hold wide-eyed discussions on sex and maturity. Gaby Hoffmann gives the most sensitive performance, which isn't to say that Christina Ricci, Thora Birch and Ashleigh Aston Moore aren't also good. Melanie Griffith, Rita Wilson, Demi Moore and Rosie O'Donnell rather less convincingly bookend the tale as their adult versions. It's a slightly more hard-edged version of the sentimental sort of small-town story that Hollywood was making long before this film is set.

No Way Home ● Ⓥ

1996, US, 93 mins, colour
Dir: Buddy Giovinazzo

N

Stars: Tim Roth, Deborah Kara Unger, James Russo
Rating: ★★

A low-budget grunge movie about life's losers, this blood-splattered tragedy might have been quite effective but for the most inept series of fight scenes seen on screen for years. Director Giovinazzo's complete failure to shoot these sequences with any conviction sabotages the entire film, but most notably a scene in which Tim Roth's backstreets brawl with a giant bouncer is edited together with his brother's bonking of a waitress in the rear of a sleazy strip-bar. Otherwise, the low-burning performances of Roth (as the slow-witted ex-con who took the rap for his brother) and Unger as the brother's stripper wife contrast quite well with the high intensity style of Russo as the brother himself, a small-time crook in debt to his hooded eyes to the local sharks. The ending neatly sidesteps total tragedy, but you're still never really absorbed by the lives of these sorry people.

No Way Out ● Ⓥ
1987, US, 116 mins, colour
Dir: Roger Donaldson
Stars: Kevin Costner, Gene Hackman, Sean Young, Will Patton, George Dzundza
Rating: ★★★

A very loose remake of the classic 1948 Ray Milland/Charles Laughton *film noir* thriller *The Big Clock*, with Kevin Costner as the Pentagon man investigating the death of his goodtime girlfriend Sean Young (who was also the lover of his boss, Gene Hackman). The thriller element comes in when Costner's character slowly realises that he has been set up as the fall guy and the men beneath him are on the verge of identifying him as the killer. The ending is a dramatic departure from the original film, and a little hard to swallow. But the rollercoaster journey to the final reel will leave you breathless.

No Way to Treat a Lady ◐
1968, US, 108 mins, colour
Dir: Jack Smight
Stars: Rod Steiger, Lee Remick, George Segal
Rating: ★★★★

This comedy about a serial killer who is a master of disguise is of the deepest black: in fact it's quite gruesome in places. Rod Steiger is a theatre owner who takes out his mother-hatred and

misogeny on a number of innocent victims. George Segal is the Jewish cop put on the case who has a typically Jewish mother. Steiger enjoys himself enormously going right over the top as the looney impresario. In one of his disguises he even plays a woman (Rod Steiger in drag? You'd better believe it). The yarn is rattled along at an exciting pace by director Jack Smight right up to the climactic showdown between killer and cop. A wicked sense of humour makes this film great fun – and watch out for Steiger getting the chance for a dry run at his W C Fields impression, which he would carry into a full-blown biopic a few years later.

Nowhere to Go ○
1958, UK, 87 mins, b/w
Dir: Seth Holt
Stars: George Nader, Maggie Smith
Rating: ★★

There's some interesting casting against type in this morose Ealing drama. Hollywood's mild-mannered George Nader, for example, is an escaped convict who had cheated a rich woman out of thousands, and Bernard Lee, who almost always played reliable coves, is an even more despicable crook who double-crosses him. Maggie Smith, in one of her earliest roles, plays a woman much milder and less flavoursome than those she depicted in coming years. The screenplay is intelligently written, but the interrelationship of characters, too few of whom are sympathetic, never really takes off.

Nowhere to Run ● Ⓥ
1993, US, 95 mins, colour
Dir: Robert Harmon
Stars: Jean-Claude Van Damme, Rosanna Arquette, Ted Levine, Joss Ackland
Rating: ★

Another attempted breakthrough into mainstream cinema from Jean-Claude Van Damme, this action-drama-romance gives us the Muscles from Brussels as a warm-hearted escaped convict who proves, among other things, a whiz with motorcycles. Alas, the vehicle that results here misfires on all cylinders except the action. Jean-Claude's acting style remains what you might call taciturn, while his heavy romance with Rosanna Arquette, a widow farmer (with two small children) menaced by land-grabbing Joss Ackland, founders on the rocks of such dialogue as (she)

'Would you like to sleep in my room tonight?' He: 'You're a very special woman. See you tomorrow', raising more giggles than sighs. The final fistfight with villain Ted Levine, however, really delivers, pitchforking us (literally) into the thick of things. Arquette, as usual, looks as though she could be good in a decent film, but Ackland is pretty ludicrous as the villain and the kids are not too hot by today's demanding standards.

Now, Voyager ○ Ⓥ
1942, US, 117 mins, b/w
Dir: Irving Rapper
Stars: Bette Davis, Paul Henreid, Claude Rains
Rating: ★★★★★

Bette Davis' portrayal of the repressed spinster Charlotte Vale in this magnificent weepie completed a remarkable run of seven Academy Award nominations for her in nine years. As full of memorable images and lines as any film in cinematic history: the farewell on the railway station, the lighting of two cigarettes at once, and 'Don't ask for the moon when we have the stars.' Some of the dialogue was inserted into the script by Davis herself using quotes from the original novel. Chock-full of successfully emotive moments and directed for maximum impact by Irving Rapper, with top-notch support from Gladys Cooper, Claude Rains and Bonita Granville, it's a classic that will have you furtively brushing away a tear at the end.

Now You See Him, Now You Don't ☉
1972, US, 88 mins, colour
Dir: Robert Butler
Stars: Kurt Russell, Cesar Romero
Rating: ★★★

This follow-up to the successful *The Computer Wore Tennis Shoes* has a young Kurt Russell again starring as smart student Dexter Riley. This time Dexter stumbles upon a serum that causes invisibility, which comes in very useful in the battles between his hard-up college and the baddies who want to take it over. Good fast-moving fun with nice comic performances from Russell, Jim Backus (the voice of Mr Magoo) and veteran star Cesar Romero, and well-realised special effects.

Number Seventeen ○
1932, UK, 64 mins, b/w
Dir: Alfred Hitchcock
Stars: Anne Grey, John Stuart, Garry

Marsh, Barry Jones
Rating: ★★★

This early Hitchcock thriller marked the real beginning of his obsession with trains as settings for suspense. There's a first-rate chase sequence dazzlingly photographed by Jack Cox, and skilfully edited, at the end of a story about jewel thieves hiding out in a deserted railwayside house.

Nuns on the Run ◗ Ⓥ
1990, UK, 89 mins, colour
Dir: Jonathan Lynn
Stars: Eric Idle, Robbie Coltrane, Camille Coduri, Janet Suzman, Doris Hare, Tom Hickey
Rating: ★★

Thin Eric Idle and plump Robbie Coltrane, though not in the Laurel and Hardy league, make an often amusing team in this romp about penny-ante gangsters who steal a million and seek sanctuary from rival gangs within the walls of a convent. The result is a comedy that's often mildly funny, with Camille Coduri refreshingly likeable as the short-sighted blonde in love with Idle. Donning nuns' habits, he and Coltrane become Sister Inviolata of the Annunciation and Sister Euphemia of the Five Winds as they hide away in Mother Janet Suzman's convent academy and ogle the nubile teenagers in the showers. Suzman has fun as the head nun trying to cope with her sisters' drinking and gambling habits, and veteran Doris Hare is in raspingly good form as the convent's oldest inhabitant.

Nun's Story, The ○ Ⓥ
1959, US, 151 mins, colour
Dir: Fred Zinnemann
Stars: Audrey Hepburn, Peter Finch
Rating: ★★★★

Luminous Audrey Hepburn chalked up another major success in this long but always absorbing story based on Kathryn Hulme's bestselling book. Director Fred Zinnemann struck a perfect balance of pace and sensitivity in the tale of a young Belgian girl who becomes a nun and is sent to the Belgian Congo to work in a hospital under the atheistic eye of surgeon Peter Finch. With an excellent script, fine performances and intelligent direction, it's amazing that the film didn't win any of the six Oscars for which it was nominated.

Nurse Edith Cavell ○
1939, US, 93 mins, b/w
Dir: Herbert Wilcox

Stars: Anna Neagle, Edna May Oliver, George Sanders
Rating: ★★★

The first of several real-life war-torn heroines Dame Anna Neagle would play in the later stages of her career. This film was made in America and cast her as the British nurse who helped thousands of World War One refugees to escape from Belgium to Holland.

Nurse on Wheels ○
1962, UK, 86 mins, b/w
Dir: Gerald Thomas
Stars: Juliet Mills, Ronald Lewis, Joan Sims, Ronald Howard
Rating: ★★

Thanks largely to Juliet Mills' chirpy performance in the leading role, this is an engaging comedy in sub-*Carry On* style, about the misadventures of a young and much mistrusted by veteran villagers, district nurse. Miss Mills' warm sense of fun, only really seen to its full advantage in Billy Wilder's *Avanti!* some years later, permeates the whole film, making the most farcical of developments seem amusingly possible. Veteran Irish character actor Noel Purcell enjoys himself as one of her more reluctant patients.

Nutcracker ●
1982, UK, 101 mins, colour
Dir: Anwar Kawadri
Stars: Joan Collins, Carol White, Paul Nicholas
Rating: ★

A mild little comedy-drama, glossed over with some soft-core sex, about a Russian ballerina defecting to the West. In other words, an archetypal Joan Collins vehicle of the Eighties – although one would have hardly thought that 'Russian ballerina breaks ankle' was worth a banner headline in the *Daily Mirror*. Finola Hughes is quite personable as the young dancer.

Nuts ● Ⓥ
1987, US, 115 mins, colour
Dir: Martin Ritt
Stars: Barbra Streisand, Richard Dreyfuss, Karl Malden, Eli Wallach, James Whitmore, Leslie Nielsen
Rating: ★★★★

A good, solid courtroom yarn, full of enough incidental humour to lighten the drama, and old-fashioned in all but the language. Streisand gives her best-balanced dramatic performance to date as the high-class, mid-thirties hooker

who has withdrawn to such an extent after killing one of her clients that the authorities are convinced she is mentally unfit to plead and should be put away. Enter her knight in shining armour (Richard Dreyfuss) in the shape of a pugnacious legal-aid lawyer (she has broken her previous lawyer's nose) who is determined to root out some causes. Before long, in traditional Hollywood style, skeletons are not only out of cupboards but cascading all over the courtroom floor. Director Ritt has a few problems keeping it going at a lively enough pace, but a veteran cast has seen this kind of thing on the *Perry Mason* show and has the know-how to bring it through to an emotional conclusion.

Nutty Professor, The ○
1963, US, 107 mins, colour
Dir: Jerry Lewis
Stars: Jerry Lewis, Stella Stevens, Kathleen Freeman
Rating: ★★★

Wild, spasmodic but mostly very funny comedy, produced by, directed by, and starring that wayward comic genius Jerry Lewis. It's a comic variation on the Jekyll and Hyde story (shades of Abbott and Costello!) with Jerry cleverly going through a series of highly coloured transformations that skilfully combine the fright with the fun, in his change from meek little professor to dashing debonair Hyde. In the supporting cast, watch for Stella Stevens, surely the most glamorous student any professor ever had. Jerry invents some side-splitting sight gags in this one, and even does a wicked impersonation of his old partner Dean Martin.

Nutty Professor, The ◗ Ⓥ
1996, US, 95 mins, colour
Dir: Tom Shadyac
Stars: Eddie Murphy, Jada Pinkett, James Coburn, Larry Miller, David Chappelle
Rating: ★

A comedy of corpulence and clumsiness, this is a pretty feeble (but popular) remake of the Jerry Lewis classic, with almost no laughs at all for those who dislike bodily function jokes. This is American low comedy at its lowest and it's a pity to see Murphy's talent largely wasted on it. Blown up to 400 pounds in a terrific make-up job by Rick Baker, Murphy is a waddly professor of science who falls heavily(!) for tiny Jada Pinkett and,

N

thanks to his secret formula, releases his glitzy, loud-mouthed slimline other self, Buddy Love (Murphy in more familiar mode) to court her in ways the professor could only have dreamed about. Most of the subsequent jokes centre on characters breaking wind and the only inventively funny scene is where thin Murphy gets his own back on the comedian (Chappelle) who insulted fat Murphy in a nightclub by verbally taking the man apart.

Objective, Burma ○ Ⓥ
1945, US, 142 mins, b/w
Dir: Raoul Walsh
Stars: Errol Flynn, James Brown, George Tobias
Rating: ★★★

Errol Flynn gives a performance all the stronger for its restraint in this much-maligned but actually very well made story of an American paratroop contingent struggling to get back to safety through the Burmese jungle after carrying out a sabotage mission behind enemy lines. Director Raoul Walsh offers a succession of fluid action scenes, especially early on, when the claustrophobic atmosphere of jungle warfare is skilfully built up, and he maintains suspense throughout the film's lengthy running time.

Object of Beauty ❶ Ⓥ
1991, UK, 103 mins, colour
Dir: Michael Lindsay-Hogg
Stars: John Malkovich, Andie MacDowell
Rating: ★★

Imported American leads John Malkovich and Andie MacDowell are rather miscast and find this lightweight romantic comedy material beyond their grasp. The plot revolves around a missing Henry Moore miniature, which Malkovich and MacDowell planned to use to make a false insurance claim to pay their extravagant London hotel bill and prop up his ailing business. A sub-plot about a deaf-mute chamber maid and her punk brother sits uneasily with the rest of the proceedings. *Object of Beauty* is a throwback to the escapist British cinema of the Sixties, but fails to recreate its frenetic energy.

Oblong Box, The ● Ⓥ
1968, UK, 95 mins, colour
Dir: Gordon Hessler
Stars: Vincent Price, Christopher Lee, Hilary Dwyer
Rating: ★★★

Another of director Gordon Hessler's very sinister essays on the theme of retribution claiming long-delayed victims, and reaching out even from beyond the grave. Lots of blood, though mostly spilled at night, not a little style and the eye-opening climax (just when one thought the evil was

over) that was to become a Hessler trademark.

Obsessed
See: The Late Edwina Black

Obsession ❶ Ⓥ
1976, US, 98 mins, colour
Dir: Brian De Palma
Stars: Cliff Robertson, Genevieve Bujold, John Lithgow
Rating: ★★

Hollywood's king of suspense in the Seventies and Eighties, director Brian De Palma strikes again with this basically silly but skilfully presented thriller. Cliff Robertson plays a businessman whose wife and daughter are killed in a blazing car after a police attempt to trap their kidnappers has backfired. The bodies are never recovered. Sixteen years later, Robertson goes to Italy with his partner, and meets a girl who looks exactly like his dead wife. But when he brings her back to America, she seems possessed by the wife's spirit. The partner calls in a psychiatrist, and if avid armchair detectives haven't got it after watching thus far, they should throw away their Crime Club memberships. De Palma gives the film a deliberately old-fashioned treatment – hazes, flashbacks, heavenly choirs and a tremendous, thundering background score by Bernard Herrmann. Robertson looks baffled throughout: but he should have guessed it, he really should.

Obsession ○ Ⓥ
(aka: The Hidden Room)
1948, UK, 95 mins, b/w
Dir: Edward Dmytryk
Stars: Robert Newton, Sally Gray, Naunton Wayne, Phil Brown
Rating: ★★★

A sombre drama about a man who keeps his wife's lover in an underground room, planning a grim death for him after prolonging his agony. Robert Newton is the 'jailer' bent on revenge, but acting honours in the are taken by Phil Brown as the lover and by Naunton Wayne as the policeman trying to trace the missing man. Solid suspense job.

Ocean's 11 ○
1960, US, 128 mins, colour
Dir: Lewis Milestone
Stars: Frank Sinatra, Dean Martin, Sammy Davis Jr, Peter Lawford, Angie Dickinson
Rating: ★★★

A glossy, sophisticated blend of comedy and thrills, this is the first and best of the Frank Sinatra 'Rat Pack' films, as he heads a gang of 11 ex-paratroopers planning to lift the entire Christmas takings from Las Vegas' five biggest casinos. The whole affair is a highly coloured chuckle from beginning to end, with a most satisfactory, if somewhat obvious climax. There are some bright guest appearances, especially that by Shirley MacLaine, and a galaxy of star names, with Sammy Davis Jr making the most impression, especially when standing idly by while gang members are blacking their faces in preparation for the raid, making reference to the fact that he has already been prepared by nature. Director Lewis Milestone gives us some poignant moments, too, supplied by Richard Conte in one of his most sympathetic performances.

October Man, The ○
1947, UK, 98 mins, b/w
Dir: Roy Baker
Stars: John Mills, Joan Greenwood
Rating: ★★★★

A first-class thriller. John Mills gives a memorable performance as a man haunted by his past and director Roy Baker, in his first major assignment, uses shape and shadow highly effectively. Direction, set design and photography combine very well to conjure up the interiors of the awful, seedy, middle-class hotel in which the pressures of the past catch up on the central character in violent fashion.

Octopussy ○ ⓥ
1983, UK, 130 mins, colour
Dir: John Glen
Stars: Roger Moore, Maud Adams, Louis Jourdan
Rating: ★★★

James Bond up to more of what his colleague 'Q' describes as 'adolescent antics' – although this Bond adventure has the edge on most other Roger Moore entries in the series and 007's battles with the baddies are meatier affairs than usual. Perhaps mindful of the competition offered by Sean Connery's *Never Say Never Again*, Moore looks more as though he means business, throwing himself energetically into an adventure that takes him to India and East Berlin. Bondian ripostes have multiplied, so that few situations are allowed to pass without witticisms of varying quality. But there are some good set-pieces too, among them a chase through an

Indian market area in which, to defend himself, Moore whips a sword from a sword-swallower, filches a flaming torch from a juggler and sees to it that beds of nails and hot coals are also put to use.

Odd Couple, The ○
1968, US, 105 mins, colour
Dir: Gene Saks
Stars: Jack Lemmon, Walter Matthau, Monica Evans, Carole Shelley
Rating: ★★★★

One of the rollicking situation comedies with which Neil Simon made his name. This is the one about two divorcée of contrasting character sharing a flat. Jack Lemmon and Walter Matthau play off each other to perfection in these roles, and Simon's clever screenplay is a constant source of amusement. Lemmon is fastidious Felix, who insists on cleaning up his friend Oscar's cluttered flat, much to the disgust of Oscar (Matthau) who says Felix is the kind of man who 'wears a seat belt at a drive-in movie' and is driven mad by his friend's myriad messages ('It took me two hours to work out that F U meant Felix Ungar'). A word for Monica Evans and Carole Shelley, also delightful as the giggly English girls who live upstairs.

Odd Job, The ◐ ⓥ
1978, UK, 83 mins, b/w
Dir: Peter Medak
Stars: David Jason, Graham Chapman, Diana Quick
Rating: ★

Refugee from Monty Pythonland Graham Chapman turns up in this dotty comedy as a man who hires an eccentric assassin to kill him – then changes his mind. David Jason features as the hapless assassin in this film adapted from a short television play. It's the sort of sketch granny used to laugh at on her visits to the pier.

Odd Man Out ○
1947, UK, 110 mins, b/w
Dir: Carol Reed
Stars: James Mason, Robert Newton, Kathleen Ryan
Rating: ★★★★

Carol Reed's haunting, suspenseful study of an IRA gunman on the run in the Twenties, through a Belfast permanently pelted by rain or coated with snow. James Mason broke right away from his run of regency cads in the title role, and there are memorable supporting performances from Kathleen Ryan,

as his tragic girlfriend, F J McCormick, as the little man who tries to sell him for money and Cyril Cusack as his hotheaded fellow-rebel. Fortunately, Robert Newton only appears in the last half-hour, as his extravagant performance almost unbalances the film. Robert Krasker's black-and-white photography adds greatly to the mounting tension, as events build up to an exciting and agonising finale.

Odds Against Tomorrow ○
1959, US, 96 mins, b/w
Dir: Robert Wise
Stars: Harry Belafonte, Robert Ryan, Shelley Winters, Ed Begley
Rating: ★★★

A carefully constructed thriller about a bank robbery, and the conflicting motives and ideals behind it. The least effective part of the story here is the sub-plot about the racial problem, although that does give us an early glimpse of Cicely Tyson, the remarkable black actress who was to win such praise 15 years later for her performances in *Sounder* and *The Autobiography of Miss Jane Pittman*. Based on a first-rate crime novel by William P McGivern, the corking climax to which is brilliantly recreated by Gidding and Wise in this film. Robert Ryan, excellent as always, runs away with the acting honours.

Odessa File, The ◐ ⓥ
1974, US/UK, 128 mins, colour
Dir: Ronald Neame
Stars: Jon Voight, Maria Schell, Maximilian Schell, Mary Tamm, Derek Jacobi
Rating: ★★

This was never the most vivid of Frederick Forsyth's novels and director Ronald Neame and his scriptwriters, Kenneth Ross and George Markstein, have worked hard to pep up the thinnish plot with bits of narrative addenda that bolster the action content, as well as a changed ending that reflects the same intention. Of the German accents with which the cast battle, the best is undoubtedly that of star Jon Voight, dourly playing against the baby-faced charm he displayed in his earlier roles.

Odette ○
1950, UK, 123 mins, b/w
Dir: Herbert Wilcox
Stars: Anna Neagle, Trevor Howard
Rating: ★★★

One of Anna Neagle's best performances, as the famous war heroine in

O

an otherwise fairly routine war film, based on the best-selling book by Jerrard Tickell. Once more Herbert Wilcox is in the director's chair, his best handling of the film coming in its big emotional scenes.

Off Beat ○
1986, US, 88 mins, colour
Dir: Michael Dinner
Stars: Judge Reinhold, Meg Tilly, Cleavant Derricks
Rating: ★★★

Silly but endearing, and pacily directed by Michael Dinner, this screwball comedy refreshingly has a beginning, middle and end, with the faintly ineffectual hero proving himself to the heroine. You won't believe the plot for a moment, but you can't help enjoying it for all that. The amiable Judge Reinhold is right on the money as the librarian forced to impersonate a cop friend when that worthy is drafted to take part in a police dance show. Not only does Reinhold get hooked on the dancing, but falls for a feisty lady cop (Meg Tilly) who's as likely to lay him out with a left hook as kiss him. It's a lightweight lark, but almost everything about it is fun and some of it funny as well – Harvey Keitel turns up as a bank robber and Austin Pendleton does a very amusing cameo as a gun shop salesman.

Offbeat ○
1960, UK, 72 mins, b/w
Dir: Cliff Owen
Stars: William Sylvester, Mai Zetterling
Rating: ★★★

Co-stars William Sylvester and Mai Zetterling impress, as does Australian actor John Meillon, in a tense story about a cleverly planned bank robbery. Much better than most of its kind.

Officer and a Gentleman, An ● ⓥ
1981, US, 125 mins, colour
Dir: Taylor Hackford
Stars: Richard Gere, Debra Winger, David Keith, Louis Gossett Jr, Robert Loggia, Lisa Eilbacher
Rating: ★★★★

One of the oldest plots in Hollywood's book – perhaps that's why it works so well. Officer recruits are taken to their limits on a training course, and a lot of it is pretty abrasive stuff. Yet we can cheerfully defy you not to be moved by the scene in which Richard Gere blows his chances of a record in the obstacle course to stay and shout the

only female recruit over the high wall that has always defeated her; or by the highly emotive ending. Strongly effective performances by Gere, Debra Winger, David Keith, Lisa Blount and – winning an Oscar as the tough sergeant – Louis Gossett Jr round off a cunningly wrapped package of commercial ingredients.

Off Limits
See: Saigon

Of Human Hearts ○
1938, US, 100 mins, b/w
Dir: Clarence Brown
Stars: Walter Huston, James Stewart, Beulah Bondi
Rating: ★★★

The direction, by Clarence Brown, of this poignant melodrama set in the Ohio Valleys before and during the American Civil War, is sensitive and pictorially very imaginative; and he extracts superb performances from Walter Huston, James Stewart and Beulah Bondi. The plot, about the resentful son of a martinet clergyman who becomes determined to make a go of his life as a doctor despite abject poverty, is often syrupy, but Brown overcomes the storyline faults with a lively eye and sprightly visuals.

Of Love and Desire ◑
1963, US, 97 mins, colour
Dir: Richard Rush
Stars: Merle Oberon, Curt Jurgens, Steve Cochran, John Agar
Rating: ★★

A good cast does its best to salvage something from this frantically overheated melodrama about a nymphomaniac's search for happiness. Merle Oberon swivels her eyeballs and looks distraught as the woman with a rack of male swimming trunks as trophies of past conquests. Steve Cochran, Curt Jurgens, John Agar and Steve Brodie are among the men who battle to put their wardrobe on a more permanent basis.

Of Mice and Men ○
1939, US, 107 mins, b/w
Dir: Lewis Milestone
Stars: Burgess Meredith, Lon Chaney Jr, Betty Field, Charles Bickford
Rating: ★★★★

Directed with taste and realism by Lewis Milestone, this excellent, moving film is still the best available version of John Steinbeck's play. The casting is without fault, with Burgess Meredith as the wily George, Betty

Field as the farmstead flirt and, in the performance of his career, Lon Chaney Jr as the simple, hulking Lennie. Streets ahead of the decent 1992 remake.

Of Mice and Men ◑ ⓥ
1992, US, 110 mins, colour
Dir: Gary Sinise
Stars: John Malkovich, Gary Sinise, Sherilyn Fenn, Alexis Arquette, Casey Siemaszko, Ray Walston
Rating: ★★★

A forthright new version of John Steinbeck's classic novel about the friendship between two men – one of them mentally backward and innocent (John Malkovich), and the other (Gary Sinise) his guardian. As they travel Depression-hit America in the 1930s working the land, their lives are changed forever by the arrival of a beautiful young woman (Sherilyn Fenn) in their unconventionally well-ordered lives. There's some stunning photography here, as well as first-rate performances from Malkovich and Sinise, who also directs. Not as good, though, as the classic 1939 version. Despite Kenneth MacMillian's splendid colour work on the heat-baked landscapes here, it's the black-and-white atmosphere of the original that sticks in the memory.

O'Hara's Wife ○
1982, US, 87 mins, colour
Dir: William S Bartman
Stars: Edward Asner, Mariette Hartley, Jodie Foster
Rating: ★★

The talented Mariette Hartley gets one of her rare leading roles in a cinema film in this sentimental romantic comedy drama. She plays a wife who returns from the dead in spectral form to help widower Edward (Lou Grant) Asner through the first few months without her.

O Henry's Full House ○
(aka: Full House)
1952, US, 117 mins, b/w
Dir: Howard Hawks
Stars: Marilyn Monroe, Richard Widmark, Anne Baxter, Farley Granger, Jeanne Crain
Rating: ★★★

A nap hand from the stories of O Henry. Comedy comes off best here, especially in *The Cop and the Anthem*, a delicious little sketch played with relish by Charles Laughton and David Wayne as a couple of tramps. Also funny is *The Ransom of Red Chief*, in which Fred Allen and Oscar Levant are suitably perplexed as two confidence tricksters hopelessly browbeaten and out-tricked by the small boy they are supposed to have kidnapped.

Oh! For a Man
See: Will Success Spoil Rock Hunter?

Oh, God! ○ ⓥ
1977, US, 104 mins, colour
Dir: Carl Reiner
Stars: George Burns, John Denver, Teri Garr, Donald Pleasence
Rating: ★★★

Overlong but generally amiable reversion to the supernatural farces of the Forties: its success seemed to show that people again needed this kind of comfort. George Burns's dry delivery and perfect timing boost this inoffensive comedy about a supermarket manager visited by God. His thoughts on ostriches, avocados and TV prove irresistible and undeniably funny.

Oh, God! Book II ○ ⓥ
1980, US, 90 mins, colour
Dir: Gilbert Cates
Stars: George Burns, Suzanne Pleshette
Rating: ★★

A mild follow-up to the enormous success of *Oh, God!*, with George Burns repeating his portrayal of a benign but salty God. There's too little of Burns and too much of child actress Louanne, but there's some strong talent in minor roles (including Howard Duff, Hans Conried and Wilfrid Hyde White) and a good sequence involving a motorcycle and sidecar.

Oh, God! You Devil ○ ⓥ
1984, US, 92 mins, colour
Dir: Paul Bogart
Stars: George Burns, Ron Silver
Rating: ★★

This light and often amusing canter through the Faust legend enabled George Burns to end his three-film stint as God on a relatively celestial note and play The Devil into the bargain. A bargain, of course, is just what hapless hero Ted Wass makes when he sells his soul (for a way out of financial ruin) to a Devil who drives around in a red sports car with the licence number HOT. Not, as Burns points out, that Satan needs the work, as Heaven is only half full and has had to close down its main dining hall. Good support from Ron Silver as a fast-talking executive with a record company.

Oh, Men! Oh, Women! ○
1957, US, 86 mins, colour
Dir: Nunnally Johnson
Stars: David Niven, Ginger Rogers
Rating: ★★★

Outstanding light comedy performances from David Niven, Dan Dailey, Barbara Rush and particularly Tony Randall (in his screen debut) illuminate this madcap, if inconsequential comedy with lush trimmings. Even the credit titles are presented in a novel way; it's a bright beginning the film lives up to. You've seen funnier farces, but this psychiatric caper scores high marks for originality and Charles G Clarke's colour photography is luscious.

Oh! Mr Porter ⊙
1937, UK, 84 mins, b/w
Dir: Marcel Varnel
Stars: Will Hay, Moore Marriott, Graham Moffatt
Rating: ★★★★

Blustering Will Hay finds himself the stationmaster of a railway station where no trains stop, in this classic British comedy. His staff, a doddery old clerk and a fat porter, are Moore Marriott and Graham Moffatt, who appeared to great comic effect in most of Hay's films. He spruces the station up and books a train to transport the local football team. But the train and its passengers disappear. There are foul deeds afoot and it's down to Will and his not terribly brave lads to save the day. Not very sophisticated by today's standards perhaps, with its music hall roots very much in evidence, but still great fun, and including Marriott's classic line: 'The next train's gone!' A chase at the climax of the film is, surprisingly, quite exciting.

O.H.M.S. ○
(aka: You're in the Army Now)
1936, US, 86 mins, b/w
Dir: Raoul Walsh
Stars: Wallace Ford, John Mills
Rating: ★★

This flag-waving action adventure is well up to all but the top Hollywood standards – not surprising as it was made in Britain by American director Raoul Walsh, who built a whole career out of such films, especially in vehicles for Errol Flynn, Humphrey Bogart and James Cagney. Here he has a somewhat lesser light in burly Wallace Ford, a Hollywood star who had been raised in a London orphanage and now made headlines when seeking and finding his real parents while in

England to make this film. The young John Mills gives him brisk support.

Oh! What a Lovely War ○
1969, UK, 144 mins, colour
Dir: Richard Attenborough
Stars: John Mills, Laurence Olivier, Susannah York, Maggie Smith
Rating: ★★★

The film that began Richard Attenborough's phenomenally successful new career as a director, following years of success as an acting star. Although he has difficulty in overcoming the unwieldy structure of Joan Littlewood's stage original, Attenborough conjures many vivid and poignant moments from this panoramic look at World War One from the end of Brighton Pier. Amid an enormous star cast, John Mills is outstanding as Sir Douglas Haig, and viewers will have fun spotting a multitude of stars in very tiny roles.

Oh, You Beautiful Doll ⊙
1949, US, 94 mins, colour
Dir: John M Stahl
Stars: June Haver, Mark Stevens
Rating: ★★★

June Haver and Mark Stevens, two of 20th Century-Fox's young talents of the time, received top billing in this bright and breezy musical, set in New York's Tin Pan Alley of 1910. Beautifully shot in Technicolor by Harry Jackson, the film has a gem of a part for 'Cuddles' Sakall as a striving but luckless 'serious' composer who everywhere lugs around with him the score of his monumental but unperformed opera. On top of this there's the delightful Charlotte Greenwood, here not only long-legged but long-suffering as the composer's wife.

O Kay for Sound ⊙
1937, UK, 85 mins, b/w
Dir: Marcel Varnel
Stars: Bud Flanagan, Chesney Allen
Rating: ★★★

One of the Crazy Gang's earliest film comedies. Not surprisingly, it contains most of their funniest stage routines (including slow motion wrestling, a TV commentary skit and a chaotic ballet) as the Gang turn a film studio upside down. The production is on the same lavish scale as the Gang's successful London Palladium show of the same name, but – horror of horrors! – the 'blue' jokes (well, they were blue then) and scantily clad chorus girls got the film an 'A' certificate!

O

Oklahoma! ○ ⓥ
1955, US, 145 mins, colour
Dir: Fred Zinnemann
Stars: Gordon MacRae, Shirley Jones,
Rod Steiger, Gloria Grahame
Rating: ★★★★

This sweeping Western musical contains probably the best score that Rodgers and Hammerstein ever wrote, from the breeziness of 'Kansas City' through the brashness of 'All 'Er Nuthin' and the sly humour of 'Poor Jud is Dead', to the dreamy lilt of 'Surrey with the Fringe on Top'. Talented director Fred Zinnemann's approach brought a joyous freshness to the genre, resulting in one of the cleanest, most enjoyable musicals ever to come out of Hollywood.

Oklahoma Crude ①
1973, US, 111 mins, colour
Dir: Stanley Kramer
Stars: George C Scott, Faye Dunaway,
John Mills, Jack Palance
Rating: ★★★

Stanley Kramer became a disappointing director since the late Sixties, but this is the best of his late films, a raw, rugged, amoral but oddly likeable story of conflict in the Oklahoma oilfield just before World War One. The plot is the one about the Cavalry and Indians besieging the fort, welded winningly to an account of a lone woman fighting to hang on to her wild-cat oil-rig against the 'heavy mob' employed by the state-wide oil trust to get her out. The stars all play very acceptably within their own images: George C Scott as the gruff, independent loner with a rough sense of humour; Faye Dunaway as the self-willed Lena, determined to give as good as any man; Jack Palance, back in *Shane* mood as the contemptuous, humourless heavy; and John Mills, almost stealing the film as Dunaway's dog-eared father, belatedly trying to help her make a mark on life.

Oklahoma Kid, The ○
1939, US, 85 mins, b/w
Dir: Lloyd Bacon
Stars: James Cagney, Humphrey Bogart,
Rosemary Lane
Rating: ★★★

In the same year that they made the classic crime picture *The Roaring Twenties*, Cagney and Bogart again played mortal enemies in this rousing Western. Neither looks at home in Western gear: Cagney's the Kid, Bogey the bad guy all-in-black. But their fans will love seeing them in such unfamiliar guise.

Oklahoman, The ○
1956, US, 76 mins, colour
Dir: Francis D Lyon
Stars: Joel McCrea, Barbara Hale
Rating: ★★

A Western full of wide vistas and clearcut issues, sparkhngly shot in colour by Carl Guthrie. Joel McCrea's shambling, too-old hero is the only hindrance to a fast-moving tale of racial prejudice and disputes over oil, with nicely judged performances from Barbara Hale, Brad Dexter and Gloria Talbott. More incisive action would have sparked the story more, but writer Daniel B Ullman's screenplay still gives us some telling moments. Saturnine Australian actor Michael Pate is once again cast as a Red Indian!

Old Acquaintance ○
1943, US, 110 mins, b/w
Dir: Vincent Sherman
Stars: Bette Davis, Miriam Hopkins
Rating: ★★★★

The film that reunited Bette Davis and Miriam Hopkins, the latter fast approaching the end of her major film days, after 1939's *The Old Maid*. Warners hoped that the off-screen friction and enmity between the two stars would help the plot about two childhood friends who become deadly rivals. And they were right. Davis, in particular, relished the scene in the film when Hopkins' character becomes hysterical and Bette has to slap her across the face. It would have been a great picture if director Vincent Sherman hadn't allowed it to run on too long towards the end; even so, the last scene makes up for a lot.

Old Dark House, The ①
1932, US, 75 mins, b/w
Dir: James Whale
Stars: Charles Laughton, Melvyn
Douglas, Boris Karloff, Gloria Stuart,
Raymond Massey
Rating: ★★★★★

Director James Whale's famous tongue-in-cheek horror film, alive with atmosphere, as travellers are stranded for the night at an old mansion which one almost expects to crumble to pieces at any moment. Based on J B Priestley's book *Benighted*, the film has a marvellous cast that, besides Boris Karloff as the great hulking butler, includes Charles Laughton, Gloria Stuart, Ernest Thesiger, Melvyn Douglas and Raymond Massey. Full of quotable lines and creepy moments, it's a must for fans of the genre.

Old Fashioned Way, The ○
1934, US, 74 mins, b/w
Dir: William Beaudine
Stars: W C Fields, Judith Allen
Rating: ★★★★

W C Fields in prime form, heading a Victorian acting troupe in performances of *The Drunkard*, doing his juggling act and having some classic encounters with Baby LeRoy. Fields' most underrated film and perhaps even his best.

Old Gringo ① ⓥ
1989, US, 119 mins, colour
Dir: Luis Puenzo
Stars: Jane Fonda, Gregory Peck, Jimmy Smits
Rating: ★★★★

Only the fact that the motivations of its characters are often obscure keeps this well-writen and extremely well-directed film from being among the best of the cinema's sprawling romantic adventures. But it will still bring a gasp and a tear to your throat. Fonda, looking amazingly young, is the spinster governess who breaks clear of her severe old mother at last, travelling to Mexico at Revolution time, where she becomes involved with the fortunes of a charismatic young general (Jimmy Smits) and an old writer (Gregory Peck) seeking an honourable death. Both the action and dialogue scenes are directed in such a way by Puenzo as to make characters and events spring to life and stir the emotions. Performances are not outstanding, but all good, making Old Gringo the cinematic equivalent of a good read.

Old Maid, The ○
1939, US, 95 mins, b/w
Dir: Edmund Goulding
Stars: Bette Davis, Miriam Hopkins,
George Brent
Rating: ★★★★★

By the time she made this incredibly powerful film, set during the American Civil War, Bette Davis had already won two Oscars, for *Dangerous* in 1935 and *Jezebel* in 1938, and she was coming into her prime as a Hollywood star. She showed herself capable of even greater emotional depth in the role of Charlotte, the sweet young woman who has an illegitimate child by her cousin's jilted fiancé and has to hide the fact by running an orphanage. It's a story that tugs at the heartstrings and one of Davis's great star turns. The ending won't leave a dry eye in the house.

Old Man and the Sea, The O

1958, US, 86 mins, colour
Dir: John Sturges
Stars: Spencer Tracy
Rating: ★★

Director John Sturges captures some of
the near Biblical simplicity of
Hemingway's classic story about an
old Cuban fisherman who vows to
make a great catch. In the lead, Tracy,
as ever, is superb. Dimitri Tiomkin's
music score won an Academy Award.
Tracy and cinematographer James
Wong Howe were both nominated.
For all their efforts, though, this is a
dull film that will have you looking at
your watch.

Old Yeller O Ⓥ

1957, US, 81 mins, colour
Dir: Robert Stevenson
Stars: Dorothy McGuire, Fess Parker,
Tommy Kirk, Chuck Connors
Rating: ★★★★

Both an exciting adventure and an effective tearjerker, this was the Disney
Studio's first film about a boy and his
dog, adapted from the novel by Fred
Gipson. It's photographed in warm,
clear Technicolor by Charles Boyle
and this, together with sturdy performances from Fess Parker and Dorothy
McGuire as the boy's ranching father
and his wife, and brisk, no-nonsense
direction by Robert Stevenson, builds
a convincing picture of life in the
Texas countryside in the mid-1850s.
The title dog is heartily well played by
an animal called Spike, who lives up
to the well-remembered song tribute
from the film as 'the best doggone dog
in the west'.

Oliver! O Ⓥ

1968, UK, 146 mins, colour
Dir: Carol Reed
Stars: Mark Lester, Ron Moody, Oliver
Reed, Jack Wild, Hugh Griffith
Rating: ★★★

Carol Reed's multiple Oscar-winner,
with claims to being one of the best
British film musicals ever made, still
comes up looking good thanks to Ron
Moody's wistful Fagin and Bart's one
totally successful score. Note Leonard
Rossiter as 'undertaker' and Harry
Secombe as the definitive Beadle.

Oliver Twist O Ⓥ

1948, UK, 116 mins, b/w
Dir: David Lean
Stars: Robert Newton, Alec Guinness,
John Howard Davies, Kay Walsh
Rating: ★★★★★

The definitive version of the Dickens
classic about an orphan boy struggling
to escape the underbelly of London in
the early 1800s. Made in the middle
of director David Lean's richest period, the film teems with detail and
imaginatively realised characters, particularly Alec Guinness's Fagin, piggy
eyes gleaming as his rat's-nest beard
dangles over some new plunder secured by his under-age army of
pickpockets. Robert Newton makes a
glowering, fearful Bill Sikes and Guy
Green's sharp photography of the
mainly dingy settings is a triumph of
the black-and-white cameraman's art,
bringing the London streets as alive
with atmosphere as they are with
predators.

Olly Olly Oxen Free
See: The Great Balloon Adventure

Omar Khayyam O

1957, US, 101 mins, colour
Dir: William Dieterle
Stars: Cornel Wilde, Michael Rennie,
Debra Paget, John Derek
Rating: ★★

They don't make them like this any
more. A typical Hollywood *Arabian
Nights* adventure, all action and colour
with a literate and faintly tongue-in-
cheek script by Barre Lyndon and a
good cast that also includes eight-oc-
tave Peruvian singer Yma Sumac in
one of her few film roles. Cornel
Wilde stars as the poet Omar, seeking
fame and fortune in 11th-century
Persia.

Omega Man, The ● Ⓥ

1971, US, 98 mins, colour
Dir: Boris Sagal
Stars: Charlton Heston, Anthony Zerbe,
Rosalind Cash
Rating: ★★★

This post-nuclear apocalypse sci-fi
drama has firm-jawed Charlton
Heston as one of the few survivors
who hasn't been turned into a pale-
skinned mutation. The mutants, led
by nasty, sneering Anthony Zerbe,
want to eradicate what is left of the culture they feel is responsible for the
nuclear disaster and this, of course, includes Chuck. Not a bad film, but
strangely dated now and seemingly
clichéd, although it wasn't at the time
it was made.

Omen, The ● Ⓥ

1976, US, 111 mins, colour
Dir: Richard Donner
Stars: Gregory Peck, Lee Remick, David

Warner, Billie Whitelaw
Rating: ★★★

During the Seventies, there were several key movies which brought an
individual slant and startling new concepts to horror-style films, completely
different from the familiar, traditional
idiom which had drawn enthusiastic
audiences for years. *The Exorcist* was a
notable example and, undoubtedly, so
was *The Omen*. Fundamentally, it centres on the rebirth of the anti-christ,
Damien. Several of the characters
come to a sticky end in scenes which
range from the bizarre to the genuinely
(and quite frighteningly) eerie, while
the most famous 'shock' scene is a
stunning and horrifying example of
first-rate special-effects work.

Omen II
See: Damien – Omen II

Omen III – The Final Conflict
● Ⓥ
(aka: The Final Conflict)
1981, US, 108 mins, colour
Dir: Graham Baker
Stars: Sam Neill, Rossano Brazzi, Don
Gordon, Lisa Harrow
Rating: ★

The final part of *The Omen* trilogy runs
a bit like a Macnee-Rigg episode of *The
Avengers*, but its predictability is redeemed in part by the charismatic
performance of Sam Neill, the New
Zealand-born actor, as Damien the
Antichrist. Poor old Damien is getting
like Dracula, with his stake, and the
werewolf, with his silver bullets, as he
can now only be killed by one of seven
ornate daggers, the significance of
which escaped us.

On an Island with You O

1948, US, 107 mins, colour
Dir: Richard Thorpe
Stars: Esther Williams, Peter Lawford,
Ricardo Montalban
Rating: ★★

Esther Williams was at her peak when
she made this aqua-musical, and
MGM had to look no further than the
box-office takings for the proof. This
one, though no great shakes in the
story department, is splashy in more
ways than one, and the studio sold it
with lots of moody shots of Esther in
slinky, shiny bathing suits. Peter
Lawford and Ricardo Montalban
mooned over her, Hawaiian backgrounds were lush and tropical, and
producer Joe Pasternak's budget even
allowed him to throw in Cyd Charisse,
Jimmy Durante and ever-beaming

O

Cuban-raised (Spanish-born) band-leader Xavier Cugat. Durante ripped into one of his speciality numbers, 'I Can Do Without Broadway', but even he couldn't upstage Esther. The story got itself unwaterlogged every time she hit the waves.

On Borrowed Time O
1939, US, 99 mins, b/w
Dir: Harold S Bucquet
Stars: Lionel Barrymore, Sir Cedric Hardwicke, Beulah Bondi
Rating: ★★★

Today it seems almost incredible that, when this film first appeared in Britain, it was given an 'H' (for horror) certificare. It's a fantasy and contains a vein of whimsy – an old man who isn't ready to die traps Death (who has come to collect him) up a tree! – but certainly not 'horror'. Lionel Barrymore and Cedric Hardwicke lead a fine cast of reliable character actors under the direction of Harold S Bucquet, a genial Londoner who worked for MGM in Hollywood. This is undoubtably Bucquet's most untypical work, worth seeing for the bizarre dream sequences alone.

Once a Jolly Swagman O
(aka: Maniacs on Wheels)
1948, UK, 100 mins, b/w
Dir: Jack Lee
Stars: Dirk Bogarde, Bill Owen, Renee Asherson, Bonar Colleano
Rating: ★★★

With a plot that rather rambles through its 13-year span, this is nonetheless a graphic and hard-edged portrait of the thrills and spills of a dangerous sport. Dirk Bogarde serves early notice of his promise of being more than just a matinee idol, giving depth and dimension to the speedway rider who starts as a cocky young ace and graduates to fighting for riders' rights through a union. The action scenes are, for their time, vividly done.

Once Around ◐ ⓥ
1990, US, 110 mins, colour
Dir: Lasse Hallstrom
Stars: Richard Dreyfuss, Holly Hunter, Danny Aiello, Laura San Giacomo, Gena Rowlands
Rating: ★

A romantic comedy of embarrassment that's almost unbearable to watch is bad news. This one is in-and-out for a little while, but completely falls apart in the last hour. One of its major problems is that you just can't see what's so wrong with the character

played by Dreyfuss, who's supposed to tear an Italian-American family apart when he marries its older daughter (Holly Hunter). He's alleged to be crass and arrogant, though he's certainly no more vulgar than the family he joins. And, as Dreyfuss is rather a charming actor, it's difficult to understand why Papa (Danny Aiello) would want to throw him out. Dreyfuss is good, as usual. The others try their best with what they've got. It isn't much.

Once in a Lifetime O
1932, US, 90 mins, b/w
Dir: Russell Mack
Stars: Jack Oakie, Sidney Fox, Aline MacMahon, ZaSu Pitts
Rating: ★★★

Another satire on Hollywood, this time angled on the panic that quickly envelops the film capital as it tries to convert to sound. Larger than life studio types are well delineated by Jack Oakie, Aline MacMahon, ZaSu Pitts, Louisa Fazenda and, best of all, Gregory Ratoff as Herman Glogauer.

Once Is Not Enough ●
1975, US, 121 mins, colour
Dir: Guy Green
Stars: Kirk Douglas, Deborah Raffin, David Janssen
Rating: ★

Based on Jacqueline Susann's brazen best-seller, this is a glossy saga of love and lust in the American millionaire belt. Tolerably well acted, especially by the gravel-voiced David Janssen and Brenda Vaccaro, with Deborah Raffin just about adequate as the sweet young thing who gets her heart broken several times over.

Once Upon a Crime O ⓥ
(aka: Criminals)
1992, US, 94 mins, colour
Dir: Eugene Levy
Stars: John Candy, James Belushi, Cybill Shepherd, Sean Young, Richard Lewis, Ornella Muti
Rating: ★

John Candy's co-star from *Armed and Dangerous* and *Speed Zone*, Eugene Levy, somehow managed to persuade the big guy (and a lot of other unfortunates) to star in this atrociously written, strenuously over-performed farce, directed by Levy in a unique, in-your-face fashion which may have you reaching for the earplugs. A furious farce involving a lost dog, a compulsive gambler, a jilted lover, an actor, a gigolo and a murder, it does at least

ensure you're not starved of familiar faces to recognise: besides the listed stars, there's George Hamilton, Joss Ackland, Elsa Martinelli and even Giancarlo Giannini, attempting a Herbert Lom-style police inspector amid the raucous comic chaos. Despite good intentions, it's a star-strangled bummer.

Once Upon a Forest ⊙ ⓥ
1993, US, 68 mins, colour
Dir: Charles Grosvenor
Voice Stars: Michael Crawford, Ben Vereen, Ellen Blain, Paige Gosney, Ben Gregory
Rating: ★★

Tinies will be enchanted by this eco-logically friendly cartoon, ideal for children of nursery school age. In similar fashion to *FernGully*, disaster overtakes the forest (here in the form of an overturned tanker full of poison gas) and it's up to three 'furlings' (animal children) to raise the medicine necessary to save a friend, after all other animals die or flee the forest. These prove to be a girl mouse (unusual to have a female lead character under these circumstances but it works rather well), a boy mole and a boy hedgehog, and their adventures form the core of the entertainment. Backgrounds are poor, but whizzy adventures of a home-made flying contraption almost make up for it. A fearsome one-eyed owl may frighten some of the smallest members of the family. Michael Crawford provides the voice of the victim's granddad and gets the chance to sing a song too.

Once Upon a Honeymoon O
1942, US, 116 mins, b/w
Dir: Leo McCarey
Stars: Cary Grant, Ginger Rogers, Walter Slezak
Rating: ★★★

Very entertaining movie from Leo McCarey and hard to categorise: perhaps thriller-cum-romantic comedy-melodrama would be about the nearest one could get. At any rate, Cary Grant and Ginger Rogers play delightfully against one another, and Walter Slezak is in fine form as the oily aristocrat who marries Ms Rogers, and then turns out to be a traitor to his country and a menace to her life. The ending is delightful.

Once Upon a Time in the West O ⓥ
1969, Italy, 165 mins, colour
Dir: Sergio Leone

Stars: Henry Fonda, Charles Bronson, Jason Robards, Claudia Cardinale
Rating: ★★★

The film that belatedly made a super-star of Charles Bronson after nearly 20 years of tough-guy roles. Ironically, he was actually billed fourth in the original cast (although his character is clearly the main one), the same as Alan Ladd when he made his breakthrough to stardom 26 years earlier as another cool killer in *This Gun for Hire*. The film is a typical Sergio Leone Western – long, languorous, punctuated with emphatic action, and full of close-ups of sweaty, grimy faces which go towards painting an atmospheric picture of a hot, desolate part of the west where life was hard, tempers could frequently explode and the weak were ruthlessly weeded out by the strong. Henry Fonda contributes a first-rate, fully rounded portrait of the villainous Frank, completing a trio of similar characters he had played in *Warlock* and *Firecreek*.

On Dangerous Ground ○

1951, US, 82 mins, b/w
Dir: Nicholas Ray
Stars: Ida Lupino, Robert Ryan, Ward Bond, Ed Begley
Rating: ★★★

Moody romantic thriller from director Nicholas Ray, with Robert Ryan well at home as the embittered cop who re-assesses his values when sent on a case that takes him away from the mean streets of his city environment. A good supporting cast is full of familiar Hollywood faces from the Fifties, and there's a tiny appearance by A I Bezzerides (he plays Gatos) who also wrote the script. Bernard Herrmann contributes an especially melodic background score, but it's Ryan – snarling 'Why do you punks make me do it?' as he smashes into a shady suspect – that you'll remember.

On Deadly Ground ● ⓥ

1994, US, 102 mins, colour
Dir: Steven Seagal
Stars: Steven Seagal, Michael Caine, Joan Chen, R Lee Ermey, John C McGinley
Rating: ★

An action movie that also has to be seen to be green, this breaks new ground all right – a new low even for Steven Seagal and Michael Caine, who have both made a fair number of turkeys in recent times, even if Seagal's have been comparatively successful. 'What does it take to change the soul

of a man?' asks Seagal, in one of the film's highly resistible bursts of pious philosophy. Broken bones, direst agony and long periods of unconsciousness will do the trick, judging by this film, in which Seagal casts himself as an oil rigger whose conscience is pricked by the plight of Eskimos in Alaska at the mercy of big business interests, headed up by Caine in a dark wig that makes him look like Robert Maxwell. The action scenes are nastily well done, but Seagal is on shaky ground here compared with the relative splendours of *Under Siege*.

One Born Every Minute

See: The Flim-Flam Man

One-Eyed Jacks ○ ⓥ

1961, US, 141 mins, colour
Dir: Marlon Brando
Stars: Marlon Brando, Karl Malden
Rating: ★★★

Marlon Brando's one-man-band film: he also produced and directed this lovely-to-look-at Western (it was shot along the California coastline) with himself as a bandit hunting down the former partner who betrayed him and netted him a stiff jail sentence. Look for a telling cameo portrayal from Elisha Cook Jr as a frightened bank cashier.

One False Move ● ⓥ

1990, US, 106 mins, colour
Dir: Carl Franklin
Stars: Bill Paxton, Cynda Williams, Billy Bob Thornton, Michael Beach
Rating: ★★

Aside from its language, the casual violence and black atmosphere of this modern *film noir* ties it to gangster films of the late 1950s when mid-west villains like Pretty Boy Floyd were shown in their unglamorous true colours. Two lethal criminals mercilessly slaughter two households, one of innocent partygoers, the other of drug holders that leads them to $15,000 in cash and a massive stash of narcotics. Their front girl is the impassive, drug-hyped Fantasia (Cynda Williams): on the run, the trio heads for her home ground, the territory of brash but efficient Arkansas sheriff Dale Dixon (Bill Paxton), who soon finds himself with two LA cops to deal with as well as the impending showdown with the criminals, and even darker revelations from his own past. *One False Move* works fine while its killers are on the run and the relationship between country and city cops is swaying to and fro. But di-

rector Carl Franklin's command of the pace falters when Dixon's past comes to the fore; Paxton, though, is right on the money as the small-town lawman with big ambitions.

One Fine Day ○ ⓥ

1996, US, 106 mins, colour
Dir: Michael Hoffman
Stars: Michelle Pfeiffer, George Clooney, Mae Whitman, Alex D Linz, Charles Durning, Eileen Greene
Rating: ★★★

This is the kind of film the French used to be so good at making. Two characters, strangers at the start of the story, are obviously destined to end up with each other from the first reel. The trick is to keep us watching through the fights and misadventures until they do it. Director Hoffman pretty much pulls it off here, throwing single mum Pfeiffer, an architect, and single dad-for-the-weekend Clooney, a reporter, together when they literally miss the boat for their respective offspring's 'field trip'. There's lots of pace, plenty of good humour and even a little genuine wit, amidst a welter of missed appointments, lost kids, near disasters and stand-up fights, before our protagonists fall exhausted into each other's arms in a neatly worked ending. Very lightweight fare, this, but nicely topped and tailed as all the apartment windows into which we've spied at the beginning of the film find their own happy endings.

One Flew over the Cuckoo's Nest ● ⓥ

1975, US, 134 mins, colour
Dir: Milos Forman
Stars: Jack Nicholson, Louise Fletcher, Christopher Lloyd, Danny DeVito
Rating: ★★★

A rare winner of all five major Oscars (actor, actress, film, direction and screenplay), this is an immensely skilful attempt to make a commercially enjoyable film out of life in a mental institution. The opening scenes – Hollywood-style shots of imbecilic inmates and the symbolic squirrel outside the wall (freedom) – signal the facile approach the film feels forced to adopt to get its message across. Fortunately, it has at its centre Jack Nicholson's brilliant performance as R P McMurphy, the sane patient who improbably brings a shaft of sunlight into the lives of his less sane fellows by holding a fateful all-night drinking spree and by taking them on a joyous fishing expedition. There are excellent supporting perfor-

O

mances by Louise Fletcher (another Oscar-winner), Brad Dourif (Oscar nominated) and the massive Will Sampson, and early appearances from Christopher Lloyd and Danny DeVito.

One Foot In Heaven ○
1941, US, 108 mins, b/w
Dir: Irving Rapper
Stars: Fredric March, Martha Scott
Rating: ★★★

The easily moved will cry a pulpit full of tears at this family drama about the life of an inspirational Methodist minister, constructed in Hollywood's finest heartwarming style. Fredric March and Martha Scott are at their most sincere as the minister and his wife in a film that looks a bit over-the-top today, but still works if you're in an indulgent mood. Directed by Irving Rapper who, used to directing Bette Davis weepies, extracts the maximum from your emotional reactions. Gene Lockhart and Laura Hope Crews supply two of several three-dimensional cameos in the supporting cast.

One Foot in Hell ○
1960, US, 90 mins, colour
Dir: James B Clark
Stars: Alan Ladd, Don Murray, Dan O'Herlihy
Rating: ★★

Alan Ladd plays an embittered man who resolves to take revenge on the townsfolk who refused to help him when his wife was dying in this rather offbeat Western. Feeling guilty, they offer him the job of deputy sheriff. Ladd kills the sheriff, takes his job and then gathers an unruly gang to help him rob the town bank and kill those who earlier didn't come to his aid. It's unusual and interesting to see Ladd as a baddie, and it's a shame the film itself turns out to be trite, implausible and hamstrung by the leaden direction of James B Clark.

One Good Cop ● ⓥ
1991, US, 105 mins, colour
Dir: Heywood Gould
Stars: Michael Keaton, Rene Russo, Anthony LaPaglia, Rachel Ticotin
Rating: ★★

You can sympathise with Keaton in the impossible attempt to find a follow-up to *Batman*, but he blew it here. Impossibly schmaltzy and of very dubious ethical value, it casts Keaton as a cop whose partner gets killed, leaving Keaton and his wife with the dead man's three small daughters. To

avoid losing the girls, and to buy a house for them, Keaton robs a drug dealer of his stake money. Generally, the film lacks strength in most departments, and Keaton's supporting cast is weak by the standards of modern cinema. Consequently, the film never whacks hard at the emotions, builds to a climax, or gives you the impression that it really knows where it's going. *One Good Cop* is one mediocre movie.

One Hour to Doomsday ○
(aka: City Beneath the Sea)
1971, US, 98 mins, colour
Dir: Irwin Allen
Stars: Stuart Whitman, Robert Wagner, Rosemary Forsyth
Rating: ★★★

A fast, exciting undersea comic-strip that resembles *Stingray* with real people. Stuart Whitman certainly has the eyebrows for the Troy Tempest part as the only man who can save the scientific city of Pacifica, beneath the ocean, from destruction by a huge, flaming meteorite headed straight for it. Told about the meteorite, with a density three million times that of earth, Whitman exclaims, with commendable understanding: 'Good God! Casualties could run into millions.' Robert Wagner enjoys himself immensely as Whitman's villainous brother, while the exquisite Rosemary Forsyth, so memorable in *The War Lord*, actually manages to contribute an acting performance that rivals the special effects (the meteorite, when it comes, is very convincing). Children, especially those between seven and 12, will love every minute of it.

One Hour with You ○
1932, US, 75 mins, b/w
Dir: Ernst Lubitsch, George Cukor
Stars: Maurice Chevalier, Jeanette MacDonald, Roland Young
Rating: ★★★★

Like *Love Me Tonight*, this is another scintillating vehicle for the delectable co-starring team of Maurice Chevalier and Jeanette MacDonald. Also similarly, it was notable at the time for its risqué elements which Hollywood could get away with in the early Thirties. It is not a musical as such, rather a dramatic comedy with music (largely written by the operetta composer Oscar Straus, noted particularly for *The Chocolate Soldier*). Unusual features included its use of rhyming dialogue and the device of having Chevalier address the audience direct-

ly to introduce characters and comment on situations. One way and another, it's a treat for vintage film fans.

One Hundred and One Dalmatians ⊙
1961, US, 79 mins, colour
Dir: Wolfgang Reitherman, Hamilton S Luske, Clyde Geronimi
Voice Stars: Rod Taylor, Lisa Davis, Cate Bauer, J Pat O'Malley, Betty Lou Gerson, Tom Conway, Mary Wickes
Rating: ★★★★

Innovative animation, an uncluttered storyline, a tremendous villainess and hilariously action-packed chase sequences all combined to make this a hugely popular feature cartoon from the Disney stable. Fifteen Dalmatian puppies are stolen from their home by the horrendous Cruella DeVil, or to be exact her henchmen Jasper and Horace Badun, who whisk the pups off to Cruella's home, Hell Hall, where they will go with dozens of other dogs to make Cruella an amazing black and white dreamcoat. She reckons, however, without the 'Twilight Bark', a series of cross-country messages that culminates in a rescue bid by the pups' parents, Pongo and Perdita, a crafty cat called Sergeant Tibs, a haughty sheepdog known as The Colonel and sundry allies. Delightful characters and an unrelenting pace make this a film that will enchant all children.

101 Dalmatians ○ ⓥ
1996, US, 103 mins, colour
Dir: Stephen Herek
Stars: Glenn Close, Jeff Daniels, Joely Richardson, Hugh Laurie, Joan Plowright, Mark Hopkins
Rating: ★★★★

Glenn Close is the epitome of evil as the fur-loving, fashion empire-owning Cruella DeVil in this rip-roaring live-action remake of the Disney classic. Real dogs as stars – 101, count them – only add to the appeal of this adventure from the producers of the *Home Alone* movies. Jeff Daniels and Joely Richardson are the couple who bring Dalmatian dogs Pongo and Purdy together, and all goes well until Cruella hears that Purdy is expecting puppies. Great fun for all the family results, especially in the performances of Hugh Laurie and Mark Hopkins as the kidnappers hired by Cruella. Some of the villainess' more awful antics may scare younger children.

100 Men and a Girl ☉
1937, US, 84 mins, b/w
Dir: Henry Koster
Stars: Deanna Durbin, Adolphe Menjou
Rating: ★★★★

The film in which Deanna Durbin's
freshness and spontaneity really burst
on the cinemagoing public like a breath
of spring. No doubt about it, Deanna
is delightful as the bouncy teenager
who charms a world-famous musician
into conducting a symphony played by
her father's orchestra of unemployed
musicians. Good support from Eugene
Pallette, Billy Gilbert and Mischa Auer,
but it's the little girl's show all the way.

One Man Mutiny
See: Court-Martial of Billy Mitchell

One Man's War ●
1990, UK, 87 mins, colour
Dir: Sergio Toledo
Stars: Anthony Hopkins, Norma
Aleandro, Ruben Blades
Rating: ★★

There's material for a grim and gripping film here. And, given Anthony
Hopkins as his leading man, director
Sergio Toledo really should have done
better. But, taking everything at a
snail's pace, he muffles much of the impact of this depressing tale of military
repression in 1976 Paraguay – then lets
the story slide into an abrupt and unsatisfying conclusion. Even with all its
faults, though, the film's to be com-
mended for opening a window on
little-known but no less horrifying violations of human rights. Tough talk
and details of torture mean it should be
kept away from sub 15-year-olds,
though older teenagers as well as adults
may find it food for thought and an education too. Slow and sombre stuff.

One Million Years BC ○ Ⓥ
1966, UK, 100 mins, colour
Dir: Don Chaffey
Stars: Raquel Welch, John Richardson
Rating: ★★★

With Raquel Welch in her famous fur-
trimmed bikini and special effects by
the legendary Ray Harryhausen,
Hammer could hardly fail with this,
their '100th film', and the movie duly
cleared up at the box-office. All the
monsters look superb, and special effects are first-rate, especially in the
final, earth-splitting volcanic eruption.
But it's Raquel you'll remember!

One More Train to Rob ○
1971, US, 108 mins, colour
Dir: Andrew V McLagien

Stars: George Peppard, Diana Muidaur,
John Vernon, France Nuyen
Rating: ★★

One is so used to seeing either John
Wayne or James Stewart as the star of
Andrew McLaglen's Westerns that it
comes as something of a surprise to
find George Peppard leading the cast
of One More Train to Rob. He plays an
ex-jailbird bent on revenge on the double-crossing partner who is now
wealthy. Sounds familiar? It should:
Brando used the same plot basis for his
One-Eyed Jacks. Keep an eye open for
former stars France Nuyen and Ben
Cooper down the cast as a Chinese girl
and a deputy sheriff.

One of Our Aircraft Is Missing ○
1941, UK, 102 mins, b/w
Dir: Michael Powell, Emeric Pressburger
Stars: Godfrey Tearle, Eric Portman,
Hugh Williams, Googie Withers
Rating: ★★★

Gripping war film from the Powell-
Pressburger team – later to make A
Matter of Life and Death and The Red
Shoes – about six airmen shot down
over Nazi-occupied Holland.

One of Our Dinosaurs Is Missing ☉
1975, US, 94 mins, colour
Dir: Robert Stevenson
Stars: Peter Ustinov, Helen Hayes, Clive
Revill, Derek Nimmo
Rating: ★★★★

There's this army of nannies being
pursued by fiendish Chinese spies because they've stolen a dinosaur. There
are also two boys with a snake, and
the police, and a microfilm, to say
nothing of a Mayfair sharpshooter
who's trying to bag the dinosaur. But
the nannies, driving a steam-engine on
and off a train, have stolen the wrong
dinosaur. Consequently, they have to
take on the Chinese kung-fu experts in
a free-for-all. It could only happen at
the Disney Studios in the Seventies,
and Dinosaurs was the merriest, most
madcap comedy to surface there in a
decade. The inspired lunatic who
thought it all up was Bill Walsh, who
wrote many Disney comedy hits.
Sadly, this was his last script.

One-Piece Bathing Suit, The ○
1952, US, 115 mins, colour
Dir: Mervyn LeRoy
Stars: Esther Williams, Victor Mature,
Walter Pidgeon, David Brian
Rating: ★★

That phenomenon of the Forties and
Fifties – the aqua-musical. This one is
far more tolerable than most, being
based on the inspiring life story of
Australian swimming star Annette
Kellerman. The original title, Million
Dollar Mermaid, was as appropriate for
Esther Williams – voted one of the 10
top box-office attractions in America in
the previous two years – as it was for
Annette. Victor Mature takes over
from Van Johnson and Ricardo
Montalban as Esther's leading man.
Pug-faced Jesse White is also featured.

One Step to Hell ○
1967, Spain/US, 94 mins, colour
Dir: Sandy Howard
Stars: Ty Hardin, Pier Angeli, Rossano
Brazzi, Helga Line, George Sanders
Rating: ★

Spanish-American co-production set in
Africa! Ty Hardin has the requisite
brawn as the policeman chasing a
group of escaped convicts through the
jungle, while Rossano Brazzi and
George Sanders have not much more
than walk-on roles, leaving the Spanish
supporting cast to do most of the donkey work.

One That Got Away, The ○
1957, UK, 110 mins, b/w
Dir: Roy Baker
Stars: Hardy Kruger
Rating: ★★★★

An interesting and unusual war story
with a nail-biting ending. It is, in fact,
the climax which lifts a goodish film
into another class altogether. It's a really fine sequence, staged against a
brilliantly photographed St Lawrence
Seaway in Canada. Hardy Kruger's
excellent performance as the German
PoW determined to escape his British
captors set him up for further international roles after 15 years journeyman
work in the German cinema. And
Terence Alexander registers well in a
small part. But the grip of this film is
almost entirely accounted for by its fascinating true story.

One-Trick Pony ◐
1980, US, 98 mins, colour
Dir: Robert M Young
Stars: Paul Simon, Blair Brown, Rip Torn
Rating: ★★

Paul Simon plays a past-it pop singer
trying to repair his career and his relationship with his ex-wife (Blair Brown)
in this interesting if not terribly good
rock drama. The story (scripted by
Simon) moves along familiar lines,
which is a minus, but the music is a

O

definite plus (especially if you're a fan of the man). You've got to admire Simon's guts because after amply demonstrating his profound lack of acting ability in *Annie Hall*, a lesser man than Simon would have gone back to what he is good at with his tail between his legs.

One, Two, Three ○
1961, US, 104 mins, b/w
Dir: Billy Wilder
Stars: James Cagney, Horst Buchholz, Pamela Tiffin, Lilo Pulver
Rating: ★

A raucous modern farce, played at breakneck pace by both star James Cagney and director Billy Wilder, although this is not such a happy visit to Berlin for Wilder as in his 1948 comedy, *A Foreign Affair*. There are some nice in-jokes, however, especially Cagney's threat to squash a grapefruit in Horst Buchholz's face.

One Way Passage ○
1932, US, 69 mins, b/w
Dir: Tay Garnett
Stars: William Powell, Kay Francis
Rating: ★★★

Said *Variety* on the first release of this weepie: 'Not a big box-office picture.' How wrong can you be? The film not only brought Warner Brothers some of its biggest returns of the year, but became one of the enduring classics of its genre. The romance between execution-bound criminal William Powell and ailing beauty Kay Francis, on board a ship bound from China to America, ensured that the cinema was a sea of handkerchiefs when the house lights went up at the end. Sharp supporting cameos by Frank McHugh, Aline MacMahon and Warren Hymer add the finishing touches. Robert Lord cocked a further snook at the poor unfortunate *Variety* reviewer by winning an Academy Award for the best original story of the year.

One Way Pendulum ○
1964, UK, 90 mins, b/w
Dir: Peter Yates
Stars: Eric Sykes, George Cole, Julia Foster, Jonathan Miller
Rating: ★★★

The Groomkirbys look like an ordinary family. But come into their home. They are all, if James Thurber will excuse the theft, as crazy as jay birds. Mr G reconstructs the Old Bailey in his living room, even to

knocking a hole in the ceiling to get the Statue of Justice in. Gran imagines she boarded a train at St Pancras and landed up in the Outer Hebrides. Mrs G pays a neighbour to eat up scraps of food left by the family. Daughter Sylvia has paid so many visits to the apes at the zoo she thinks her arms are too short. But the prize loon is son Kirby, teaching a choir of speak-your-weight machines to 'sing' by putting different weights on them. You need a Goonish (not to say ghoulish) sense of humour to appreciate the laughs in this film version of N F Simpson's madcap play. And the film slips in veiled acidities about human nature and racial prejudice that are still valid today. Jonathan Miller (Kirby) is really funniest without saying anything. Eric Sykes is delightfully bemused as Mr G. And the choir of weighing machines alone makes it worth seeing.

One Way Street ○
1950, US, 80 mins, b/w
Dir: Hugo Fregonese
Stars: James Mason, Marta Toren
Rating: ★★

Fairly routine action thriller with some exciting patches, but not really worthy of James Mason, then striving to establish himself in Hollywood after years as Britain's number one box office star. Here he plays a crooked physician on the run with some stolen loot. There's a first rate supporting quintet of bad guys – Dan Duryea, William Conrad, King Donovan, Jack Elam and Rudolfo Acosta – that adds character to the thrills. And you'll also spot Rock Hudson who, in one of his earliest roles, makes a small appearance as a truck driver.

One Woman's Story
See: The Passionate Friends

On Golden Pond ○ ⓥ
1981, US, 109 mins, colour
Dir: Mark Rydell
Stars: Katharine Hepburn, Henry Fonda, Jane Fonda
Rating: ★★★★★

A great Hollywood mogul used to say: 'If it makes you cry, it must be good.' It didn't necessarily follow, but he would have been proud of *On Golden Pond*. It does make you cry and it is superb. After a sticky beginning, both Katharine Hepburn and Henry Fonda relax into their roles of a crusty 79-year-old professor and his 10-years-younger wife, spending their

48th summer together at their holiday fishing lake. Jane Fonda, in a poignant piece of casting, has what amouts to little more than a cameo role as the daughter with whom the old man has failed to communicate for 40 years. Subsequent developments, involving the son she leaves with the old couple for a month could easily have been mawkish, but are very persuasively written by Ernest Thompson, on whose play the film is based. Billy Williams' colour photography of menacing skies and sun-flecked water is quite flawless and helps to catch the mood of the piece, a last fling, perhaps, for Hollywood's vintage years, in which Hepburn and Henry Fonda (both Oscar-winners for their roles) are finally unbearably touching. Critics, on the whole, hated it; the public responded with its feet.

On Her Majesty's Secret Service ○ ⓥ
1969, UK, 140 mins, colour
Dir: Peter Hunt
Stars: George Lazenby, Diana Rigg, Telly Savalas
Rating: ★★★

Sent to foil arch-villain Blofeld's plan for world domination by spreading a plague through ten beautiful women infected with a deadly virus, George Lazenby steps athletically into Sean Connery's 007 role. Director Peter Hunt, who edited earlier Bond fims, directs pacily, keeping the action moving and staging an exciting snow chase with one villain torn to pieces in a snow plough.

Onion Field, The ● ⓥ
1979, US, 126 mins, colour
Dir: Harold Becker
Stars: John Savage, James Woods, Ted Danson, Priscilla Pointer
Rating: ★★★

There are very few shafts of light in this black, bitter and violent true-life case study, involving the shooting of a young policeman and the gradual mental disintegration of his partner. Strong performances by John Savage, James Woods, Ronny Cox and Ted Danson help alleviate the fact that the film does go on a bit. But the central sequence – the nighttime killing in the onion field of the title – is chillingly well realised by director Harold Becker. Tough stuff.

Only Game in Town, The ○
1969, US, 113 mins, colour
Dir: George Stevens

Stars: Elizabeth Taylor, Warren Beatty
Rating: ★★★

Elizabeth Taylor is gorgeously gowned in this bitter-sweet story of the affair between a gambler and a chorus girl stranded in Las Vegas. Directed by double Oscar-winner George Stevens, it is the direction which lifts the rather old-fashioned story, based on a stage play, out of the ordinary. Stevens evokes the night-life of Las Vegas to perfection with the aid of only a few scenes – neon signs, coloured fountains, the dazzling brightness of the gambling casinos. And the persuasive performances of Warren Beatty and Ms Taylor makes us believe that the cattiness of their own private sex war could melt to the final realisation that marriage really is 'the only game in town'.

Only the Lonely ◐ ⓥ

1991, US, 104 mins, colour
Dir: Chris Columbus
Stars: John Candy, Maureen O'Hara, Ally Sheedy, Anthony Quinn, James Belushi
Rating: ★★★

The moral of this *Marty*-style romance is: never co-star with 70-year-old actresses making a come-back. They will wipe the floor with you. This should be Candy's film and, in a straight romantic role, the 20-stone comedian has probably never been better. But it's O'Hara as the overbearing Irish mother who has stifled his romantic chances, who walks away with the film. Candy is a plump cop who falls for mortician's plain daughter Sheedy. But his own concern for his mother (her opinion and her welfare) seemingly dooms the romance from the start. There's not much to the ensuing story, and some of it is pretty silly: but it does contain perhaps the best performance of O'Hara's career. Unlucky one, John.

Only the Strong ● ⓥ

1993, US, 96 mins, colour
Dir: Sheldon Lettich
Stars: Mark Dacascos, Stacey Travis, Paco Prieto, Tod Susman, Geoffrey Lewis, Richard Coca
Rating: ★★

Here's the answer, guys, to urban crime beginning in US ghetto schools. Teach 'em Brazilian kick-boxing. Ex-soldier Mark Dacascos (a sort of junior league Jean-Claude Van Damme) tries it out, and in no time at all has turned the worst seniors in the school into all-for-one boy scouts set to take on the

gangster element of the whole of Miami. Serviceable action is provided by director Sheldon Lettich on this simplistic theme and, although some of the supporting acting is hilarious, there have been worse chop-socky movies than this. At least it doesn't aim too high, and does try to promote, however naively, some decent values. Just as well the gangster kingpin is a martial arts expert himself, otherwise he might just blast our hero to kingdom come with a .45. But then that's action movies for you.

Only the Valiant ○ ⓥ

1951, US, 100 mins, b/w
Dir: Gordon Douglas
Stars: Gregory Peck, Barbara Payton, Gig Young, Ward Bond, Lon Chaney
Rating: ★★

Action galore but that's all for Western fans in this disappointingly written adaptation of Charles Marquis Warren's classic novel about a cavalry officer (stalwart Gregory Peck) who goes to hell and back to regain the respect of his men and his girl. Not the first classic Western novel Hollywood has messed up, nor the last. Only one of their mistakes here was not to make the film in colour.

Only Two Can Play ◐

1962, UK, 106 mins, b/w
Dir: Sidney Gilliat
Stars: Peter Sellers, Mai Zetterling, Virginia Maskell
Rating: ★★★

Peter Sellers' first real attempt to move outside the realm of straightforward farce. But it's still the farcical bits – mainly attempted seductions which end in disaster – that come off best, in this black comedy about a Welsh librarian and would-be lecher who is constantly frustrated in his attempts to get girls into bed. Sellers is admirably backed by Mai Zetterling, as the centre of his attentions, and by Richard Attenborough and Kenneth Griffith.

Only When I Larf ○

1968, UK, 103 mins, colour
Dir: Basil Dearden
Stars: Richard Attenborough, David Hemmings
Rating: ★★

David Hemmings, Richard Attenborough and Alexandra Stewart play confidence tricksters who cross and double-cross each other in a bewildering series of events, following an amusing opening sequence. Based on

a novel by Len Deighton, who wrote the Harry Palmer spy thrillers.

Only You ◐ ⓥ
(aka: Love Stinks)

1992, US, 88 mins, colour
Dir: Betty Thomas
Stars: Andrew McCarthy, Kelly Preston, Helen Hunt, Daniel Roebuck, Kid Creole, Reni Santoni
Rating: ★★

You'll be at least one step ahead of the hero all the way in this formula and totally predictable romantic frolic about a hot-blooded young man (Andrew McCarthy) trying to find the perfect mate. It's written to a well-tried Hollywood recipe: pretty airhead in a tropical paradise setting is the object of the male's desire, while his true love, the good-hearted, plain Jane type, lurks unnoticed in the background. Please! Despite the stereotyping, McCarthy carries it all quite well, whether fighting with feisty Helen Hunt (who has personality to spare) or swooning over brainless blonde Kelly Preston. Undemanding entertainment, but nicely stitched together by Betty Thomas.

Only You ○ ⓥ

1994, US 99 mins, colour
Dir: Norman Jewison
Stars: Marisa Tomei, Robert Downey Jr, Bonnie Hunt, Joaquim de Almeida, Billy Zane, Fisher Stevens
Rating: ★★

Annoying when it's supposed to be engaging, this is a cloying romantic comedy with principals so irritating that you want to get up and throw things at them. Marisa Tomei plays hopeless romantic Faith who lives up to her name in her belief that she'll find the perfect soulmate. This turns out to be a spaced-out-looking Robert Downey Jr in one of his less charming turns. Exotic locations in Venice and camerawork in bright, primary colours give the film the look of froth from an earlier era. Tomei does her best to be adorable in this one, but it's Bonnie Hunt and Billy Zane who give the vapid concoction what little kick it has. A few hilarious moments do brighten up the brew if you can stay the course.

On Moonlight Bay ○

1951, US, 95 mins, colour
Dir: Roy Del Ruth
Stars: Doris Day, Gordon MacRae
Rating: ★★★

Stuck for a musical vehicle for the fast-rising Doris Day, Warners took the *Penrod* stories that had been filmed before and (making the central character Day's younger brother) crossed them with *Meet Me in St Louis*, added period songs and set the whole thing in a small Indiana town around 1917. Day and Gordon MacRae are more than pleasant company, but it's the supporting cast (and colour photography) that really make this one glow: Leon Ames (especially good) as the father suspected of drunkenness; Rosemary DeCamp as mother; Ellen Corby as the schoolma'am; Mary Wickes as the acid family maid; and Billy Gray as the rumour-spreading brother.

On the Avenue O
1937, US, 86 mins, b/w
Dir: Roy Del Ruth
Stars: Dick Powell, Madeleine Carroll, Alice Faye, The Ritz Brothers
Rating: ★★★★

A smashing Irving Berlin score, three stars on top form and Roy Del Ruth's brisk direction make this one of the most enjoyable 20th Century-Fox musicals of the Thirties. Alice Faye sings 'This Year's Kisses' and duets with Dick Powell on 'I've got My Love to Keep Me Warm'. Top marks to her vocalising and to the zany antics of the Ritz Brothers, one of whom, Harry, appears in drag in an imitation of Faye in the novelty number 'O Chi Chornia'. And yes, musical buffs, Irving Berlin did write a title number called 'On the Avenue' for the film – but for some reason it was deleted before the movie's release. Very strange.

On the Beat ⊙ Ⓥ
1962, UK, 100 mins, b/w
Dir: Robert Asher
Stars: Norman Wisdom, Jennifer Jayne
Rating: ★★★

Norman Wisdom gets a chance to play a dual role. He's Norman Pitkin, who longs to join the police force but can't fill his father's size 12 boots, and Giulio Napolitani, Neapolitan king of London's underworld of crime. Best segment: Norman pursued over the fences of a long row of back gardens in a sequence which comes to resemble a human Grand National.

On the Black Hill ● Ⓥ
1987, UK, 117 mins, colour
Dir: Andrew Grieve
Stars: Mike Gwilym, Robert Gwilym, Bob Peck, Gemma Jones
Rating: ★★

Based on the award-winning novel of the same name by Bruce Chatwin, this is a dour diatribe, beautifully photographed in Welsh border country by Thaddeus O'Sullivan, that sets out to prove the old maxim that the answer lies in the soil. The land, in fact, is the silent but dominant character in this saga of twins (played by real-life brothers), their work, their loves, their quarrels and their makings-up over an 80-year period that proves a trifle too much for the film's structure. The episodes, though effective in their own right, fail to build up a single theme, but the performances are as dedicated as the twins themselves, especially from Bob Peck and Gemma Jones as their ill-matched parents.

On the Buses O
1971, UK, 88 mins, colour
Dir: Harry Booth
Stars: Reg Varney, Doris Hare, Michael Robbins
Rating: ★★

The popular TV series transferred to the cinema, complete with the original cast: Doris Hare as Mum, Michael Robbins as Arthur, Anna Karen as Olive, Bob Grant as Jack, Reg Varney as Stan and Stephen Lewis as Blakey. The story is about Blakey trying to introduce women drivers to the bus company.

On the Riviera ⊙
1951, US, 89 mins, colour
Dir: Walter Lang
Stars: Danny Kaye, Gene Tierney, Corinne Calvet
Rating: ★★

Brightish entertainment that will please Danny Kaye fans though probably not win any converts to his brand of fun. Like *Hans Christian Andersen*, the story isn't much, but the score is delightful, including 'Popo the Puppet', 'On the Riviera', 'Happy Ending' and 'Ballin' the Jack'. And there are lovely girls all over the place, including Gene Tierney, Corinne Calvet, Mari Blanchard and dancer Gwen Verdon.

On the Threshold of Space O
1955, US, 96 mins, colour
Dir: Robert D Webb
Stars: Guy Madison, Virginia Leith, John Hodiak, Dean Jagger
Rating: ★

This was one of Fox's big prestige movies at the time when CinemaScope was still all the rage. Guy Madison plays a young air force doctor who agrees to take part in a dangerous experiment involving a new ejector seat.

They should have tried the script on it instead.

On the Town ⊙ Ⓥ
1949, US, 98 mins, colour
Dir: Gene Kelly, Stanley Donen
Stars: Gene Kelly, Frank Sinatra, Vera-Ellen, Ann Miller, Betty Garrett, Jules Munshin
Rating: ★★★★★

The catchy songs and dazzling on-location dancing made this one of the best and most talked-about song-and-dance films ever to come out of Hollywood. With its scintillating rooftop routines and brilliant colour photography, this wonderfully paced tale of three sailors on brief leave in New York set new standards for musicals for years to come. And it still comes up fresh each time. Comedienne Alice Pearce, as Gene Kelly's adenoidal date-from-hell, deserved an Oscar nomination for best supporting actress which she sadly didn't get.

On the Waterfront O Ⓥ
1954, US, 108 mins, b/w
Dir: Elia Kazan
Stars: Marlon Brando, Karl Malden, Lee J Cobb, Eva Marie Saint
Rating: ★★★★★

Powerful drama set on New York's waterfront, where gangsters control the longshoremen's union and stevedore Terry Malloy (stunningly played by Marlon Brando) faces the terrible dilemma of whether or not to turn informer. Full of dynamic performances (Brando, Malden, Cobb, Saint, Rod Steiger), quotable, pungent lines and with a memorable climax, this, highly-charged throughout, is a winner all the way. The film won eight Oscars, including Best Picture, Director, Actor (Marlon Brando), Supporting Actress (Eva Marie Saint), Cinematography (Boris Kaufman) and Art Director (Richard Day).

Operation Amsterdam O
1958, UK, 104 mins, b/w
Dir: Michael McCarthy
Stars: Peter Finch, Eva Bartok, Tony Britton
Rating: ★★

Tony Britton, now best known as a smooth comedy actor from his work in TV series, turns to high dramatics in this true story of wartime derring-do in Holland. Another capable actor, Canadian-born Alexander Knox, gives a fine portrayal as a Dutch patriot, and Peter Finch is a solid lead.

Operation Bullshine O

1959, UK, 84 mins, colour
Dir: Gilbert Gunn
Stars: Donald Sinden, Barbara Murray,
Ronald Shiner
Rating: ★★

Well, they couldn't call this formula
army comedy anything stronger in the
late Fifties. Watch out for former
Olympic swimming champion Judy
Grinham as a PT instructress. She's
part of a formidable cast that also includes Barbara Murray, Carole Lesley,
Joan Rice, Ronald Shiner, Daniel
Massey and Naunton Wayne.

Operation CIA O
(aka: Last Message from Saigon)
1965, US, 90 mins, b/w
Dir: Christian Nyby
Stars: Burt Reynolds, Danielle Aubry
Rating: ★

Burt Reynolds as a CIA agent dispatched on a dangerous mission in the
Far East. Although it took him another four years to climb to the top, one
would have thought that his star quality was obvious, even in such minor
thrillers as this one.

Operation Daybreak O
1975, UK, 119 mins, colour
Dir: Lewis Gilbert
Stars: Timothy Bottoms, Martin Shaw,
Nicola Pagett, Anthony Andrews
Rating: ★★

Well-made and suspenseful, this war
film doesn't involve the emotions as
much as Lewis Gilbert's best work in
the genre, such as *Carve Her Name with
Pride* – and *Reach for the Sky*, although
the ending is undeniably moving.
Timothy Bottoms, Anthony Andrews
and Martin Shaw don't lend much personality to the three Czech saboteurs
out to kill Czech Nazi leader Heydrich,
a role in which Anton Diffring is as
hateful as ever. The action scenes are
all well-staged.

Operation Mad Ball O
1957, US, 105 mins, b/w
Dir: Richard Quine
Stars: Jack Lemmon, Ernie Kovacs,
Mickey Rooney, Kathryn Grant
Rating: ★★★

Lemmon is right at the top of his form
in this wild farce about an army private who breaks all the rules in order
to hold a 'mad ball'. Stores are
pinched, timetables tampered with,
and regiments re-routed. All these
happenings bring purple apoplexy to

the face of disciplinarian Captain Lock
– the cigar-chewing Kovacs, making a
big hit in his screen debut.

Operation Pacific O
1950, US, 109 mins, b/w
Dir: George Waggner
Stars: John Wayne, Patricia Neal, Philip
Carey, Ward Bond
Rating: ★★★

There are some roaring battle scenes,
well assembled by director George
Waggner (best known for such horror
films as *The Wolf Man*), in this large-
scale John Wayne war film. No doubt
Wayne was impressed by the production values the Warner Brothers were
able to inject into their action movies,
compared with those at Wayne's usual
studio (Republic), as he made several
more for them. Patricia Neal makes a
cool and believable love interest in this
story of the varied activities – attack,
interception and rescue – of a submarine in the Pearl Harbor area.

Operation Petticoat O
1959, US, 124 mins, colour
Dir: Blake Edwards
Stars: Cary Grant, Tony Curtis
Rating: ★★★

Those masters of comedy, Cary Grant
and Tony Curtis – Curtis always preferred playing comedy and Grant was
his hero in the genre – make the most
of their material in this World War
Two navy lark about the operation
mounted to rescue a sunken American
submarine. Grant is the sub's commander who experiences a certain
amount of confusion at the unconventional methods used by his first officer
(Tony Curtis), involving lots of lovely
ladies whose lingerie is put to some unusual uses. Although the humour
remains pretty obvious and the script
could have been snappier, Blake
Edwards directs with pace and the
whole is a happy and at times hilarious
vehicle for its stars' talents.

Opposite Sex, The O
1956, US, 117 mins, colour
Dir: David Miller
Stars: June Allyson, Ann Sheridan, Joan
Collins, Joan Blondell
Rating: ★★

Three great stars of MGM musicals,
June Allyson, Ann Miller and Dolores
Gray, are mixed with Joan Collins and
Ann Sheridan in a musical remake of
the Norma Shearer/Joan Crawford
comedy classic, *The Women*. Some
good numbers enliven the original

plot, which still retains much cattiness
in the in-fighting. Another change is
that men are this time seen, though not
to any great effect.

Optimists of Nine Elms, The
O Ⓥ
1973, UK, 110 mins, colour
Dir: Anthony Simmons
Stars: Peter Sellers, Donna Mullane
Rating: ★★★

This charming and touching story of
life by the slums of London's industrial
riverside represents Peter Sellers' best
work in the Seventies. He plays an old
busker with music-hall memories and a
sick dog for company. The two children who befriend him are played with
Cockney freshness by Donna Mullane
and John Chaffey. And the script by
Anthony Simmons (who also directed)
and Tudor Gates, based on Simmons'
novel, makes some perceptive observations about the futility and despair
involved in moving from a shabby
basement to a hardly more attractive
tower-block flat where the kids can't
even keep a dog.

Oracle, The O
(aka: The Horse's Mouth)
1952, UK, 84 mins, b/w
Dir: C M Pennington Richards
Stars: Robert Beatty, Mervyn Johns,
Michael Medwin, Virginia McKenna
Rating: ★★

A clever, enjoyable British comedy featuring Robert Beatty as a reporter who
goes on holiday to a little island off the
coast of Ireland. There he finds an
Oracle that lives at the bottom of the
well and can foretell any future event.
Persuading the Oracle to give him accurate weather forecasts, the reporter
cables the information to his boss –
and is promptly sacked for idiocy. But
when, with the Oracle's help, he starts
to forecast racing winners, matters
rapidly begin to escalate.

Orchestra Wives O
1942, US, 98 mins, b/w
Dir: Archie Mayo
Stars: George Montgomery, Glenn Miller,
Lynn Bari, Carole Landis
Rating: ★★

One of television's most-requested
films, with Glenn Miller and his band
(thinly disguised as Gene Morrison
and his band) giving out with a whole
string of Miller pearls, including 'At
Last', 'Serenade in Blue' and 'I've Got
a Gal in Kalamazoo'.

O

Ordeal by Innocence ◐

1984, UK, 87 mins, colour
Dir: Desmond Davis
Stars: Donald Sutherland, Faye
Dunaway, Sarah Miles, Christopher
Plummer, Ian MoShane
Rating: ★

Agatha Christie has continued down
the decades to be an irresistible magnet
for film-makers with star casts in mind,
even if the essence of the lady continues to elude many of them. Donald
Sutherland and Michael Elphick (although the latter is uncomfortable with
a Scottish accent) lend their distinctly
offbeat presences to this tale of murder
in Fifties' Devon. Faye Dunaway and
Sarah Miles are seen to less advantage,
but sex appeal is so piquantly provided
by Phoebe Nicholls and Cassie Stuart
that one is rather sorry to see one of
them get bumped off in the course of
the plot. Although Dave Brubeck's ob-
trusive jazz score seems to belong to
some other movie, Billy Williams conjures up some atmospheric Eastman
Colour photography on location in
Dartmouth. On the whole, though, ordeal is right.

Orders Are Orders ⊙

1954, UK, 78 mins, b/w
Dir: David Paltenghi
Stars: Margot Grahame, Brian Reece,
Sidney James, June Thorburn, Tony
Hancock, Donald Pleasence
Rating: ★★

Today the cast of this comedy looks
colossal, although in its time it wasn't
exactly a major film. But it did give a
first comedy character role to Peter
Sellers, who plays batman to Brian
Reece (whom vintage-radio fans will
remember in *The Adventures of PC 49*).
It proves to be a spasmodically side-
splitting army-based comedy that is
faintly reminiscent of *The Amorous
Prawn*. All its importance in retrospect,
however, lies in that first appearance of
Sellers in a character part.

Ordinary People ◐ Ⓥ

1980, US, 124 mins, colour
Dir: Robert Redford
Stars: Donald Sutherland, Mary Tyler
Moore, Timothy Hutton, Judd Hirsch
Rating: ★★★

Robert Redford's auspicious debut behind the camera earned him an
Academy Award as Best Director for
this overwrought study of a well-
heeled American family in crisis. The
picture took the Best Film Oscar and
young Timothy Hutton's passionate

performance as the teenage son eaten
up by guilt over his brother's death
earned him the Best Supporting Actor
statuette. Mary Tyler Moore also excels as the cold-hearted mother – a role
very much against type.

Oregon Trail, The ○

1959, US, 86 mins, colour
Dir: Gene Fowler Jr
Stars: Fred MacMurray, Gloria Talbott,
John Carradine
Rating: ★★

A Western that wanders as much as
the wagon train carrying ace reporter
Fred MacMurray from Missouri to
Oregon in 1846. A good cast, a much-
needed battle with the Indians at the
end, primitive colour photography
(don't adjust your sets) and a couple of
good singalong Western songs.
Typical late Fifties fare.

Orphans ●

1987, US, 120 mins, colour
Dir: Alan J Pakula
Stars: Albert Finney, Matthew Modine,
Kevin Anderson
Rating: ★★

This grim and unpalatable morsel was
once a successful stage play and still
looks like one. You may find it worth
wading through the boredom of the
first half-hour to reach the meat of the
performances by Matthew Modine and
Kevin Anderson as primevally reclusive brothers and especially by Albert
Finney as the gangster they kidnap.
How retribution catches up with them
all is unconvincingly contrived, but
there are some good individual scenes,
particularly the one in which Finney
tries to teach Modine to keep his explosive temper in check.

Oscar, The ◐

1966, US, 120 mins, colour
Dir: Russell Rouse
Stars: Stephen Boyd, Elke Sommer,
Eleanor Parker, Joseph Cotten,
Broderick Crawford, Walter Brennan
Rating: ★

Another knife in Hollywood's back, although the cast of this meretricious
melodrama boasts as many stars as the
script has reference to famous names.
Joseph Cotten wins out over all of
them – by cleverly underplaying his
role as a movie studio boss. Stephen
Boyd is the actor who will tread on
any friend to win the coveted
Academy Award. Five actors in the
cast have actually won Oscars:

Broderick Crawford, Ed Begley,
Walter Brennan (who won three times
as Best Supporting Actor), Ernest
Borgnine and James Dunn.

Oscar ○ Ⓥ

1991, US, 110 mins, colour
Dir: John Landis
Stars: Sylvester Stallone, Ornella Muti,
Kirk Douglas, Don Ameche, Peter
Riegert, Tim Curry, Marisa Tomei, Eddie
Bracken
Rating: RB

This is as stunningly bad an all-star
movie as you could find. Totally overplayed, and directed with cameras
seemingly riveted to the floor, it's
about a gangster (Sylvester Stallone),
who's promised his dying father (Kirk
Douglas!) that he'll go straight. His efforts to proceed in this direction and
become a banker are hampered by trying to marry off his daughter to several
different people in a single day. The
distinguished cast is encouraged to
move stiffly and mug gracelessly by director Landis, who deserves some kind
of onion for the worst direction of a
major film in ages. Stallone's wife and
daughter (Ornella Muti, Marisa
Tomei) look about the same age: the
least of the worries of a film that's so
awful you'll probably find the design
of the cinema (or living-room) ceiling
more interesting.

Oscar Wilde ◐

1960, UK, 96 mins, b/w
Dir: Gregory Ratoff
Stars: Robert Morley, Phyllis Calvert,
John Neville, Ralph Richardson
Rating: ★★

The first out (by a few days) of two
films both based on Oscar Wilde's last
few years, this one was the loser at the
box-office, chiefly through being made
in black-and-white, while its rival, *The
Trials of Oscar Wilde* (with Peter Finch)
was in splashy colour. More slowly
paced than the Finch version, this look
at Wilde's tragic obsession with the
young Lord Alfred Douglas benefits
from brilliant performances by Robert
Morley as Wilde and Ralph
Richardson as Sir Edward Carson.
The film really comes alive in the cut
and thrust of the courtroom scenes towards the end.

Osterman Weekend, The ● Ⓥ

1983, US, 102 mins, colour
Dir: Sam Peckinpah
Stars: Rutger Hauer, John Hurt, Burt
Lancaster, Meg Foster
Rating: ★★★

An everybody-is-corrupt thriller which involves a TV exposé man inviting three old friends for a reunion weekend knowing them all to be Russian agents. But beware: this plot is so fiendish it baffled even critics at the time. The film itself is a bit slow but quite fun when it gets going with its killing spree towards the end, although I wish the TV man's wife had been allowed to kill everyone with her bow and arrow. Rutger Hauer is adequate as the TV man, John Hurt good as the warped CIA agent, and Burt Lancaster familiar doing his corrupt older statesman bit as the CIA chief. Sam Peckinpah's last film.

Othello ○ Ⓥ
1965, UK, 166 mins, colour
Dir: Stuart Burge
Stars: Laurence Olivier, Maggie Smith, Frank Finlay, Derek Jacobi
Rating: ★★★

Laurence Olivier's towering stage portrayal of Shakespeare's Moor of Venice is sewn together for the screen by director Stuart Burge. The result is a remarkable experience. And, even if Maggie Smith doesn't seem quite right for Desdemona, she's a whole lot better than some previous interpreters of the role.

Othello ◑ Ⓥ
1995, UK, 124 mins, colour
Dir: Oliver Parker
Stars: Laurence Fishburne, Irène Jacob, Kenneth Branagh, Nathaniel Parker, Michael Maloney, Anna Patrick
Rating: ★★

More is less in this straightforward if much pared-down version of Shakespeare's story of scheming, jealousy and murder in 16th-century Venice. Kenneth Branagh's thin mouth and narrowed eyes make him ideal casting for the devious Iago – perhaps the Bard's sneakiest villain – but Laurence Fishburne and especially Irène Jacob are hard put to make the dialogue sound anything but stilted. Fishburne at least gets kudos for being the most striking screen Othello on record, alive with tattoos and dripping with jewellery, scalp shaved and beard trimmed to a provocative tuft. There are some strong moments in the subsequent action, but subtlety comes second-best in this plain man's guide to a literary classic.

Other People's Money ◑ Ⓥ
1991, US, 101 mins, colour
Dir: Norman Jewison

Stars: Danny DeVito, Gregory Peck, Penelope Ann Miller, Piper Laurie, Dean Jones
Rating: ★★

This has a beautiful idea, but it doesn't quite work. For that, blame the burgeoning romance between Danny DeVito and Penelope Ann Miller, as two opposing sharpsters. This not only hurts the film by being an unconvincing attraction but slows it up considerably. Things would have been much more entertainingly played here as a no-holds-barred fight to the finish between DeVito's side and Gregory Peck's. It's true that the central character, a piranha of the takeover world, is perfectly suited to DeVito's talents for abrasive blue-collar comedy. 'I like dogs, doughnuts and money,' he beams at the beginning. 'But best of all I like money. It doesn't make you fat and it doesn't poop on your carpet.' But he's fatally softened in the telling of the story, and even the result of the final confrontation is swept under the carpet in a cavalier climax. When Danny's being a shark, though, he's great. Peck is stiff but sincere. Miller seems miscast. The best performances come from Piper Laurie and Dean Jones, the latter especially good on his return to the screen as a small-time corporate chief losing sleep over deciding whether or not to sell out.

Otley ○
1968, UK, 91 mins, colour
Dir: Dick Clement
Stars: Tom Courtenay, Romy Schneider, Alan Badel, James Bolam
Rating: ★★★

Tremendously entertaining comedy-thriller from the talented team of Dick Clement (who also directed) and Ian La Frenais. Tom Courtenay, one of the cinema's great underrated actors, creates a sympathetic character out of the cowardly workshy 'hero'. The sardonic dialogue and brisk pace are spot on the mark throughout.

Our Betters ○
1933, US, 80 mins, b/w
Dir: George Cukor
Stars: Constance Bennett, Gilbert Roland, Anita Louise
Rating: ★★★

Spiky Constance Bennett (sister of Joan), in one of the best roles she ever had, sloughs off her philandering husband and gets by in London society of the Thirties with, in her own words, 'strength of character, wit and un-

scrupulousness'. Source material by Somerset Maugham, elegant production by David O Selznick, and sardonic direction by the masterly George Cukor: this is a film with pedigree, polish, pacing and pezazz, as Constance kicks over the traces and wears black to the ball. The only really dated note is struck by Tyrell Davis' mincing dance instructor.

Our Girl Friday ○ Ⓥ
(aka: The Adventures of Sadie)
1953, UK, 87 mins, colour
Dir: Noel Langley
Stars: Joan Collins, Kenneth More, George Cole, Robertson Hare
Rating: ★★

This fast and sometimes funny desert-island farce was the first film in Eastman Colour. Very attractive the settings look, too, though no more so than a very young Joan Collins as the girl shipwrecked with three men. Kenneth More scores as the ill-bred Irishman who bides his time while the other two (George Cole, Robertson Hare) make fools of themselves making passes at the girl; for More, it was one of the final steps upwards on the ladder to stardom.

Our Little Girl ○
1935, US, 64 mins, b/w
Dir: John Robertson
Stars: Shirley Temple, Joel McCrea
Rating: ★★

Almost songless (just the title number) Shirley Temple vehicle about a tug-of-love. On the set of this weepie in which Shirley plays a little girl whose parents' marriage seems headed for the rocks, co-star Joel McCrea earned the ultimate Temple accolade: 'I love you,' she told him.

Our Man Flint ○
1966, US, 107 mins, colour
Dir: Daniel Mann
Stars: James Coburn, Lee J Cobb, Gila Golan, Edward Mulhare
Rating: ★★★

Meet the computer spy. Derek Flint may be superbly entertaining, but he's also the most inhuman hero the spy wave has thrown up since Batman. The difference, though, is that no sex was allowed for poor old Batman, while Flint has a well-stocked harem and wins his battles by gadgetry as opposed to wizardry. However, the good old sock on the jaw – mostly with the hero's feet – is not entirely forgotten. As played by the cheetah-like Coburn,

O

Flint is certainly faster on those feet than any spy on celluloid, and a shade more invincible than Bond into the bargain. Visually, his adventures are lively, ingenious and amusing. And ridiculous, of course. But what marvellous, breath-taking stuff it is.

Our Man In Havana O
1959, UK, 112 mins, b/w
Dir: Carol Reed
Stars: Alec Guinness, Burt Ives, Maureen O'Hara, Ralph Richardson
Rating: ★★★★★

Graham Greene's cutting satire about the vacuum cleaner salesman who, in need of extra cash, joins the British Secret Service. The dialogue for Noel Coward as the suave spy chief might easily have been written by the Master himself. 'Have you got an electric kettle?' he asks an agent. 'You'll need it to steam open letters.' Possibly the last triumph of Alec Guinness's glittering screen career.

Our Mother's House ◐
1967, UK, 105 mins, colour
Dir: Jack Lachman
Stars: Dirk Bogarde
Rating: ★★

Sombre, sinister drama of seven children living together after their mother dies, but suddenly threatened by their long-missing father – a performance of great menace by Dirk Bogarde. The entire movie was shot on location at a real, rambling old house in Croydon, Surrey, the gloom of which is well captured by director Jack Clayton and adds much weight to the doomy atmosphere.

Our Relations ⊙ Ⓥ
1936, US, 65 mins, b/w
Dir: Harry Lachman
Stars: Stan Laurel, Oliver Hardy
Rating: ★★★

The feature film in which Stan and Ollie play not only respectable citizens much beset by nagging wives, but also their twin brothers, Alf and Bert, the black sheep of the families, who have become sailors. This is the cue for much mistaken identity, all building to a hilarious wharfside climax, with one pair of twins, having fallen foul of gangsters, rocking to and fro like Subbuteo figures, their feet encased in concrete, on the edge of a thirty-foot drop into the river. The film also contains the last of their escalating battles with their old enemy Jimmy

Finlayson, here cast as their ship's chief engineer.

Our Town O
1940, US, 90 mins, b/w
Dir: Sam Wood
Stars: William Holden, Martha Scott, Frank Craven, Thomas Mitchell
Rating: ★★★

A brilliant evocation of American small-town life over a 40-year period. This was always the kind of thing Hollywood did well, but few examples are better than this. The cast, headed by William Holden, sinks itself totally into the role of the two small-town families who are the subject of the film's all-pervading eye. Rich in detail, it is full of unexpected glimpses of everyday things that form a solid backcloth to the story. And it even has something extra: a mystical, timesliding last reel (as the heroine hovers between life and death in childbirth) that was far advanced for its time.

Our Very Own O
1950, US, 93 mins, b/w
Dir: David Miller
Stars: Ann Blyth, Farley Granger, Joan Evans, Jane Wyatt, Ann Dvorak
Rating: ★★

Ace producer Samuel Goldwyn almost always had his finger on the public pulse. So this was a rare miscalculation on his part. Even fresh, appealing performances from Ann Blyth, Joan Evans and Natalie Wood are no match for F Hugh Herbert's saccharine script, especially in Miss Blyth's squirm-making final speech extolling the virtues of the American family. And the story, set in an upper middle-class American suburb where the most important thing in the world seems to be the love problems of teenagers, found few sympathetic ears on this side of the Atlantic. For all that, there was a promising debut by pretty Phyllis Kirk as the girl who eventually sets Miss Blyth to rights.

Outback ●
1970, Australia, 109 mins, colour
Dir: Ted Kotcheff
Stars: Donald Pleasence, Gary Bond
Rating: ★★

An unpalatable, unpleasant but curiously hypnotic look at the underbelly of life in the outback Down Under, hardly likely to go down well with the Australian tourist board. Donald Pleasence is at his nastiest as the seedy

doctor who subjects the young hero to some of the numerous humiliations he undergoes on an alcohol-induced stay in bush country where life veers towards the primitive. Not for the squeamish.

Outbreak ● Ⓥ
1995, US, 122 mins, colour
Dir: Wolfgang Petersen
Stars: Dustin Hoffman, Rene Russo, Morgan Freeman, Donald Sutherland, Cuba Gooding Jr, Kevin Spacey
Rating: ★★★

Top military scientist Dustin Hoffman sniffs a disaster waiting to happen when he investigates an African village wiped out by a plague virus and he's right. We've been here before, though – and seen sinister superiors like Donald Sutherland. 'Do you know how much it costs to send out a special alert?' Hoffman is asked. 'You know the chances of such a virus turning up in the US are nil.' Hah! Pretty soon the residents of Cedar Creek, California are dying in their hundreds, and Sutherland, who 'eliminated' an infected African village 28 years before, and developed an antidote he plans to use as a biological weapon, now persuades the President to blast Cedar Creek off the face of the earth. Hoffman races against time to beat both Sutherland and the virus. 'It's one billionth our size,' he complains, 'and it's beating us.' The result of all this is a high-tech, high velocity if jingoistic thriller into which director Wolfgang Petersen even manages to inject (sorry!) a dogfight between helicopters.

Outcast, The O
(aka: The Fortune Hunter)
1954, US, 90 mins, colour
Dir: William Witney
Stars: John Derek, Joan Evans, Jim Davis, Ben Cooper
Rating: ★★

This was one of the last films made by director William Witney for Republic, the studio where he laboured for many years churning out a series of Westerns starring Roy Rogers. John Derek is a rancher who fights to win his rightful inheritance of his uncle's ranch, but is almost too macho for the role, constantly fingering his gun or battering his knuckles. The supporting cast features Jim Davis, later Jock Ewing in *Dallas*.

Outcast, The
See: Man in the Saddle

Outcast of the Islands ○ ⓥ

1951, UK, 102 mins, b/w
Dir: Carol Reed
Stars: Trevor Howard, Ralph Richardson, Kerima
Rating: ★★★★

The culmination of director Carol Reed's brilliant quartet of post-war films, following *Odd Man Out*, *The Fallen Idol* and *The Third Man*. It's based on a typical Joseph Conrad novel that has a lot in common with the also filmed Conrad story *Lord Jim*, in that it deals with a 'lost' man wandering the ports of Far Eastern seas – a role in which Trevor Howard gives a haunting performance, although most of the film's publicity headlines were won by Kerima as the sultry and highly desirable native girl who proves his downfall. Reed directs with great sympathy, and some outstanding location photography by John Wilcox adds immeasurably to the atmosphere. The climax, although different to the ending of the book (in which the story goes on quite a bit further) is admirably suited to Conrad's conception of the character.

Outcasts of Poker Flat, The ○

1952, US, 81 mins, b/w
Dir: Joseph M Newman
Stars: Anne Baxter, Dale Robertson, Miriam Hopkins, Cameron Mitchell
Rating: ★★

Absorbing, downbeat Western, about four assorted ne'er-do-wells, driven out of town by the local citizenry and subsequently marooned in an old cabin in a snowstorm. Adapted from a novel by Bret Harte, the suspenseful plot gains considerably from the tight acting performances, particularly from the three ladies. The black-and-white photography adds to the claustrophobic tension in and around the cabin.

Outfit, The ◐

1973, US, 103 mins, colour
Dir: John Flynn
Stars: Robert Duvall, Karen Black, Joe Don Baker, Robert Ryan
Rating: ★★★★★

In some respects, this crime thriller is like *Charley Varrick*, except that it's more basic, more excitingly directed, and cunningly fitted together with pieces, each of which piles on the tension. Here, as in *Varrick*, the central figure's crime lies in knocking over a bank belonging to the Outfit. Macklin (Robert Duvall) and his brother Ed get three years for the bank job, but the Outfit is still waiting for them when they come out. Ed is dispatched by an assassin, but Macklin turns the tables on his hit-man and determines to bleed the Outfit for all he can get. Enlisting the aid of another bank-raid confederate (Joe Don Baker), he embarks on a ruthless and skilful game of skinning the syndicate. The raids that follow are accomplished with staggering precision by director John Flynn, but the core of the film's appeal is that the non-action scenes are enthrallingly memorable. The cast is knee-deep in class, and the scenes between Duvall and Baker have an abrasive but close camaraderie that brings about an audience identification with the characters too often missing from today's impersonal thrillers.

Outland ● ⓥ

1981, US, 105 mins, colour
Dir: Peter Hyams
Stars: Sean Connery, Peter Boyle, Frances Sternhagen
Rating: ★★★

A version of *High Noon* set in outer space as marshal Sean Connery stands alone against a planet-wide drug ring. Connery is just right as the flawed hero and Frances Sternhagen first-rate as the doctor who ultimately risks death to give him a hand.

Outlaw Josey Wales, The ○ ⓥ

1976, US, 135 mins, colour
Dir: Clint Eastwood
Stars: Clint Eastwood, Chief Dan George, Sondra Locke
Rating: ★★★★

Parts of this tremendous and unusual Western, directed by as well as starring Clint Eastwood, are so good as to make one reluctant to admit that it actually goes off the boil towards the end. The script is almost all dry, laconic, amusing and literate, bolstering good performances by Paula Trueman as a dauntless octogenarian pioneer and Sam Bottoms as the boy soldier who is Josey's first trail partner. But the best lines go to Chief Dan George as an Indian as sardonic as he's ancient. The Chief, treating them all to the same deadpan delivery, just walks off with the film.

Out of Africa ○ ⓥ

1985, US, 162 mins, colour
Dir: Sydney Pollack
Stars: Meryl Streep, Robert Redford, Klaus Maria Brandauer
Rating: ★★★★

Overall a magnificent nostalgic romance about a Danish woman (Meryl Streep) who finds herself running a farm in Africa from 1913 after her husband (Klaus Maria Brandauer) decides to opt out for the life of a hunter. The first half is brilliantly paced and immaculately acted, but greatness rather drifts away from the film in the second half, somewhat aided by a misfit Robert Redford, who just doesn't seem to go with the rest of the film. Streep and her Danish accent are amazing, while Brandauer, Suzanna Hamilton, Michael Kitchen and Michael Gough offer really first-rate support. Intelligently scripted and beautifully shot on location by David Watkin, *Out of Africa* proves a moving, stimulating and entertaining experience. Winner of seven Oscars, including best film and best director.

Out of the Clouds ○

1954, UK, 88 mins, colour
Dir: Michael Relph, Basil Dearden
Stars: Anthony Steel, Robert Beatty, David Knight, Margo Lorenz
Rating: ★★★

This catalogue of crisis incidents in the lives of people stranded at a fogbound airport makes surprisingly good entertainment, with an array of second-line British stars all giving of their best, some nice cameos from such people as Sidney James and attractive Eastman Colour photography by Paul Beeson. Margo Lorenz not only looks beautiful, but gives her best screen performance.

Out of the Fog ○

1941, US, 86 mins, b/w
Dir: Anatole Litvak
Stars: Ida Lupino, John Garfield
Rating: ★★

Well thought of in its time, this now looks a very stage-bound version of Irwin Shaw's play *The Gentle People*, darkly photographed virtually on a single set, and with a broodingly charismatic performance by John Garfield as the gangster who's the terror of the Brooklyn waterfront. Good work in support by that consistent actress Aline MacMahon; and it's interesting to see little tough guy Leo Gorcey outside his normal Dead End Kids/Bowery Boys milieu.

Out-of-Towners, The ○

1969, US, 97 mins, colour
Dir: Arthur Hiller
Stars: Jack Lemmon, Sandy Dennis
Rating: ★★

O

More of Jack Lemmon's urban angst, with he and Sandy Dennis staggering from bad to worse in Neil Simon's very black comedy about a small-town couple getting torn to pieces in the big city. But these are dislikeable characters, and their catastrophes accumulate rather than develop, robbing the tale of some of its momentum. Simon's script though, is consistently witty and portrays the couple's trials and tribulations with acid humour.

Outpost in Malaya
See: The Planter's Wife

Outrageous Fortune ❶ ⓥ
1987, US, 100 mins, colour
Dir: Arthur Hiller
Stars: Shelley Long, Bette Midler, Peter Coyote
Rating: ★★★

A hard-cursing but outrageously funny comedy-thriller with Shelley Long and Bette Midler working wonderfully well together as aspiring actresses duped by Romeo teacher Peter Coyote who turns out to be an international double-agent. Savour some very funny dialogue mostly delivered by Midler as a bit-part film player who has just appeared in a movie called *Ninja Vixens*.

Outriders, The ○
1950, US, 93 mins, colour
Dir: Roy Rowland
Stars: Joel McCrea, Arlene Dahl, Barry Sullivan, Claude Jarman Jr
Rating: ★★★

Rousing Western about a trio of Civil War Confederates on the run. The colour photography is excellent throughout: seldom have horses on the move been so excitingly pictured, and shots of a wagon train moving through Indian territory are also exceptional. Barry Sullivan steals the acting honours as bad Jesse Wallace.

Out West With the Hardys ○
1938, US, 90 mins, b/w
Dir: George B Seitz
Stars: Lewis Stone, Mickey Rooney
Rating: ★★

Another episode in the money-spinning Hardy series, chiefly notable for the duel of wit and muscle between Mickey Rooney's teenage Andy, who fancies himself as the 'terror of the plains', and 10-year-old cowgirl Virginia Weidler, a tiny terror who not unexpectedly wipes the floor with him. Weidler played many other juvenile roles in the late Thirties and early

Forties, usually as a homely-looking kid told to scram because she bothered the adults.

Overboard ○ ⓥ
1987, US, 112 mins, colour
Dir: Garry Marshall
Stars: Goldie Hawn, Kurt Russell, Edward Herrmann
Rating: ★★★

Here's a romantic comedy that's both romantic and a comedy without being sticky about either. Rich bitch Goldie Hawn, married to boring Edward Herrmann, falls off her luxury yacht and surfaces in the home of handyman Kurt Russell suffering from amnesia. Having endured her overbearing manner while working on the yacht, Russell claims her as his missing wife and sets her to work raising his four unruly sons. Needless to say, Goldie, initially repelled by the squalor around her, eventually makes herself indispensable in these five male lives. That all this doesn't make you squirm owes a lot to a script by Leslie Dixon that's clear-eyed and buzzing with incident and inbuilt pace. Good for Goldie: this is something a bit different for her and she brings it off.

Over Her Dead Body ❶ ⓥ
(aka: Enid is Sleeping)
1991, US, 101 mins, colour
Dir: Maurice Phillips
Stars: Judge Reinhold, Elizabeth Perkins, Jeffrey Jones, Rhea Perlman, Maureen Mueller
Rating: ★

This is the familiar black comedy about the couple who have to dispose of a dead body but find fate conspiring against them. Under this treatment by Maurice Phillips, almost none of it works, despite strenuous (at times too strenuous) efforts by Elizabeth Perkins and Judge Reinhold. The sheer accumulation of events does achieve a certain wild grandeur towards the end, but by then we're looking at a lost cause, thanks to directorial handling that's as leaden as the corpse that just won't lie down. Such extravagant character players as Michael J Pollard, Brion James, Henry Jones and Charles Tyner are also on hand, but the cameos they supply are, like the film, largely tedious and heavy-handed.

Overlanders, The ○
1946, UK/Australia, 91 mins, b/w
Dir: Harry Watt
Stars: Chips Rafferty, Daphne Campbell
Rating: ★★★

The first of the highly successful series of Ealing Studios action and adventure film set in Australia. The outstanding score is by John Ireland – the only music the great composer wrote directly for the cinema. Tremendous scenes of cattle on the move complete a dust-rousing package.

Over the Edge
1979, US, 95 mins, colour
Dir: Jonathan Kaplan
Stars: Michael Kramer, Matt Dillon, Pamela Ludwig, Vincent Spano
Rating: ★★★

A disturbing American classic about alienated teenagers, in the tradition of *Blackboard Jungle* and *Rebel Without a Cause*. Not seen outside America (and only given a minor showing there) until 1984, the film eventually reached the wider audience it deserved thanks to the increasing popularity of one of its 14-year-old stars, Matt Dillon. A strong, violent and pretty bleak chronicle of the criminal lives of kids with nowhere to go, it's directed by Jonathan Kaplan with a surprisingly keen sense of the American pre-teen's eye-view of modern suburban life.

Over the Top ○ ⓥ
1987, US, 93 mins, colour
Dir: Menahem Golan
Stars: Sylvester Stallone, Robert Loggia, David Mendenhall, Susan Blakely, Rick Zurnwalt
Rating: ★★

A pretty cunning departure from style from Sly Stallone, this offers his fans the action they'll expect while allowing the star the chance to play slight variations on the working-class characters that have made his name. Armwrestling (whatever next?) is the name of the game here, but the Rocky-style build-up is given an interesting twist by Stallone's bicep-bulging trucker's battle for the heart and custody of his 10-year-old son, played with old-fashioned charm by David Mendenhall. The relationship that springs up between them ensures that even though the film lays everything on a bit thickly, you'll be cheering for Sly on both custody and arm-wrestling fronts at the finale. David Garfinkel's photography is ever alert to bright clear composition and his remarkably good use of Metrocolor gives the film a crisp, natural look.

Oxford Blues ❶
1984, US, 97 mins, colour
Dir: Robert Boris

Stars: Rob Lowe, Ally Sheedy, Amanda Pays, Julian Sands
Rating: ★★

A thinly veiled remake of the 1938 film *A Yank in Oxford*, with Rob Lowe in the Robert Taylor role as the up-start American who tries to use his rowing prowess to impress the aristocratic English beauty on whom he's set his heart. There's a nice college atmosphere, and some engaging performances, notably from Ally Sheedy (as the American lady cox Lowe seems destined to end up with) and Julian Sands. Otherwise the conventions of the Hollywood teen movie are strictly adhered to in spite of the picturesque English settings.

P

Pacific Heights ● Ⓥ
1990, US, 104 mins, colour
Dir: John Schlesinger
Stars: Melanie Griffith, Matthew Modine, Michael Keaton, Laurie Metcalf
Rating: ★★★★

A good thriller that could have been called *The Tenant* if someone hadn't already used the title. Keaton and Griffith both deliver spot-on performances in the offbeat, unsettling tale of a couple (Griffith, Matthew Modine), who spend every cent to rent an apartment building (with the intention of leasing two of its three flats), then fall foul of a sitting tenant (Keaton) who stalls on paying the rent. They soon find out that, as the lease has been signed by both parties, the law is on the squatter's side. But this is no ordinary tenant; and this aspect of the plot makes for some suspenseful and exciting later developments. The fact that almost none of this holds water, but still grips our attention, is a tribute to John Schlesinger's direction of it, and to the performances of the stars, although Modine is a little bland in the least interesting of the three main roles. Griffith's mother Tippi Hedren is in for a cameo.

Package, The ◐
1989, US, 108 mins, colour
Dir: Andrew Davis
Stars: Gene Hackman, Joanna Cassidy, Tommy Lee Jones, Dennis Franz
Rating: ★★★

Although its tale of cold warfare and secret police in East Berlin was overtaken by events, this is a very efficient thriller of its type. There's a plot to assassinate both the American president and the Soviet general secretary and only Gene Hackman can stop it. Yes, we've been here before, but scenes between high-up conspirators are mercifully sidelined in favour of the thriller aspects of the plot, its interlocking pieces falling nicely into place before the end. Tommy Lee Jones is fine as the assassin, and director Davis keeps it moving to a predictable but briskly staged finale. Above all, it's Hackman's grit and integrity as an actor and a personality that keep it marginally believable as well as exciting.

Pack Up Your Troubles ☉ Ⓥ
1932, US, 65 mins, b/w
Dir: George Marshall, Raymond McCarey
Stars: Stan Laurel, Oliver Hardy
Rating: ★★★

This early Laurel and Hardy feature film is now best remembered for the scene in which Stan reads a small girl a story to send her to sleep and succeeds in sending himself to sleep instead. Oliver Hardy was actually to have played this scene, but generously decided it would be funnier with Stan. Watch for the film's co-director George Marshall, playing a homicidal chef.

Pagan Love Song ○
1950, US, 76 mins, colour
Dir: Robert Alton
Stars: Esther Williams, Howard Keel, Rita Moreno
Rating: ★

Despite the title, don't expect anything more exotic than the MGM backlot in this musical vehicle for swim star Esther Williams, then tops at the box-office. Director Robert Alton, better known as a choreographer, only really scores here in the inevitable Williams water ballets. Producer Arthur Freed also wrote some of the songs, and did his best to suggest an atmosphere with the titles: 'Tahiti', 'The Sea of the Moon', 'Pagan Love Song' and 'The House of Singing Bamboo'. At least you can't accuse it of going on too long.

Pagemaster, The ☉ Ⓥ
1994, US, 83 mins, colour
Dir: (animation) Maurice Hunt, (live-action) Joe Johnston
Stars: Macaulay Culkin, Christopher Lloyd
Voices: Whoopi Goldberg, Patrick Stewart, Leonard Nimoy
Rating: ★★

A highly resistible, flatly animated mixture of cartoon and live-action, as bespectacled wimp Macaulay Culkin learns the noble art of self-respect when a library comes to life and his animated self has to reach the exit, with the help of talking books, through a Jekyll and Hyde mansion, past a fire-breathing dragon, pirates and Moby Dick. Sounds good, and it could have been too, if Disney's animators had got their hands on it. But this Saturday morning TV-style animation just won't do, reducing the adventures to something that's one-dimensional, without character and sometimes even tedious.

O

Paid in Full ○
1950, US, 105 mins, b/w
Dir: William Dieterle
Stars: Lizabeth Scott, Diana Lynn,
Robert Cummings
Rating: ★★

Familiar story about two sisters, one of them nice, the other unscrupulous, who fall in love with the same man. Tragedy, unrequited love, honeymoons, death and insanity are dealt with in that order. It's left to that brilliant comedienne Eve Arden, as the hard-boiled Tommy Thompson, to inject some much-needed comic relief into this triple-handkerchief weepie.

Paint Your Wagon ○ ⓥ
1969, US, 164 mins, colour
Dir: Joshua Logan
Stars: Lee Marvin, Clint Eastwood, Jean Seberg, Harve Presnell
Rating: ★★★

The film that put Lee Marvin's gravel voice at the top of the charts, with the million-selling 'Wandrin' Star'. The setting for this hard-shelled musical Western is the California Gold Rush, rendered very pretty to look at by director Joshua Logan's picture-postcard approach to history. The story concerns a lady pioneer (Jean Seberg) who takes two husbands, but its quality scarcely matters, given that the husbands are played by Marvin and Clint Eastwood, and that there's a supremely tuneful score. The other vocal highlight: Harve Presnell's spectacular rendition of 'They Call the Wind Maria'.

Pajama Game, The ○ ⓥ
1957, US, 101 mins, colour
Dir: Stanley Donen
Stars: Doris Day, John Raitt
Rating: ★★★★

One of the most exhilarating of all Hollywood musicals, with a clutch of performances as nearly perfect as one could wish to see. Doris Day – who else more fitted to the part of Babe Williams? – gives a more extrovert performance than one would have thought possible. The score includes such hits as 'Hey There', 'The Pajama Game', 'Once a Year Day', 'I'm Not at All in Love' and the spirited Day-John Raitt duet 'There Once Was a Man', one of the best performed musical numbers of all time. Like the film, it's enormous fun.

Paleface, The ○
1948, US, 90 mins, colour
Dir: Norman Z McLeod

Stars: Bob Hope, Jane Russell
Rating: ★★★★

This glorious romp was the first of Bob Hope's four spoof Westerns, and also a much-needed hit for his co-star Jane Russell, who joins him in the Academy Award-winning song 'Buttons and Bows'. One of the film's best comedy routines harks back to Hope's duel scene in *Never Say Die* (and forward to Danny Kaye's in *The Court Jester*) as Hope faces a feared gunman in the main street while attempting to remember advice like 'He moves to the right, so shoot to the left' and trying to calculate the direction of the wind. Richly enjoyable stuff, fun to the final scene.

Pale Rider ◑ ⓥ
1985, US, 115 mins, colour
Dir: Clint Eastwood
Stars: Clint Eastwood, Michael Moriarty, Carrie Snodgress
Rating: ★★

A virtual remake of *Shane,* that classic Western from the Fifties in which a mysterious stranger (then Alan Ladd, now Eastwood) helps a band of farmers (now gold prospectors) against the ruthless land grabbers (and their hired gunman) who threaten to blow them off the face of the earth. Michael Moriarty is very good in the part originally played by Van Heflin, Carrie Snodgress is his 'fiancée' and Sydney Penny the teenager who storms on to do the 'Come back, Shane' bit at the end. *Pale Rider* works well as a kind of latter-day Dollars-style adventure, with a blazing action showdown at the end, but it can't quite fill *Shane's* boots, partly because the writing isn't strong enough and partly because the Eastwood character is so invincible there is no chance of him losing, and only the vaguest of hints about his past.

Pal Joey ○ ⓥ
1957, US, 111 mins, colour
Dir: George Sidney
Stars: Frank Sinatra, Rita Hayworth, Kim Novak
Rating: ★★★★

Splashy, garishly entertaining, perfectly cast musical, with Frank Sinatra ideal as the singing con-man who finds hell hath no fury like a rich mistress scorned when true love comes along. One of Rodgers and Hart's best scores includes 'Bewitched, Bothered and Bewildered', 'The Lady Is a Tramp', 'Small Hotel', 'I Didn't Know What Time It Was' and 'Funny Valentine'. Rita Hayworth and Kim Novak both

have some good moments as the contrasting women in Joey's life, but the songs are the thing.

Palm Beach Story, The ○
1942, US, 90 mins, b/w
Dir: Preston Sturges
Stars: Claudette Colbert, Joel McCrea, Mary Astor, Rudy Vallee
Rating: ★★★

Romantic comedy crossed with moments of sheerest lunacy as straw-brained wife Claudette Colbert deserts husband Joel McCrea in order to find someone who will give her 99 thousand dollars – to finance McCrea's daft invention. Decorated with pleasing idiocies as only director Preston Sturges knows how, plus the treasurable Ale and Quail Club, and one of the earliest of one-time singing idol Rudy Vallee's appearances as a wistfully comic character star. Here, as the world's wealthiest bachelor, he's allowed to give vent to his famous complaint about 'one of the tragedies of this life is that the men most in need of a beating-up are always enormous.'

Palmy Days ○
1931, US, 80 mins, b/w
Dir: A Edward Sutherland
Stars: Eddie Cantor, Charlotte Greenwood, George Raft
Rating: ★★★

This farcical musical, a cute follow-up to Samuel Goldwyn's production of *Whoopee!,* had the benefit of Busby Berkeley's choreography just as the master was beginning to develop his inimitable style. The storyline is fairly ordinary, but lots of pretty girls, plenty of songs and the incredible energy of Eddie Cantor make it well worthwhile. Look hard at the Goldwyn Girls and you will spot Betty Grable, legs 'n' all, in her seventh film appearance. George Raft is also on board, but he adds little to the picture.

Palooka ○
1934, US, 86 mins, b/w
Dir: Benjamin Stoloff
Stars: Jimmy Durante, Lupe Velez, Stuart Erwin, Robert Armstrong
Rating: ★★★

In the long-running American comic strip, Joe Palooka was a big, gormless, hopeful boxer who somehow succeeded every time in spite of his own lack of pugilistic ability. The role of his scheming manager, Knobby Walsh, was a gift for Jimmy Durante in his first real starring role and 'The Great Schnozzle' (coincidentally that was the

British title of the film) even gets to sing his famous novelty number 'Inka Dinka Doo'. A good time is had by all in this fast-moving romp, not least by the viewer!

Pancho Villa ◐

1972, Spain, 93 mins, colour
Dir: Gene Martin
Stars: Telly Savalas, Clint Walker, Anne Francis, Chuck Connors
Rating: ★★

Telly Savalas as the infamous Mexican bandit chief takes some swallowing, but director Eugenio (Gene) Martin, who also directed the actor in *Horror Express*, has it that his head is shaven by the authorities 'to make him look like the convict he is'. The film itself is a routine Western, but full of noise and fury and with a head-on train crash for a spectacular climax.

Pandora and the Flying Dutchman ○

1951, UK, 120 mins, colour
Dir: Albert Lewin
Stars: James Mason, Ava Gardner
Rating: ★★

A rum kettle of fish and no mistake. A long, ornate, dry, lovely-to-look-at Technicolor fantasy that split the critics and died at the box-office. Ava Gardner never looked more ravishing than as Pandora, James Mason never more agonised as the Dutchman doomed to roam the seas for ever. Gardner also sings two songs, including 'How Am I to Know?' Strange is the word.

Panic in the Parlor

See: Sailor Beware!

Panic in the Streets ○

1950, US, 96 mins, b/w
Dir: Elia Kazan
Stars: Richard Widmark, Paul Douglas, Barbara Bel Geddes, Jack Palance
Rating: ★★★★

Elia Kazan's extremely exciting and splendidly paced (in recollection it seems like one long chase) thriller about two killers on the run in New Orleans, carrying with them pneumonic plague. Edna and Edward Anhalt won an Oscar for best original story, and there are powerful performances from Jack Palance and Zero Mostel, both getting their first big film chances. The film deserved one Academy Award it didn't win: for Joe MacDonald's great location photography of the back alleys, low bars and wharfs of New Orleans.

Papa's Delicate Condition ☉

1963, US, 98 mins, colour
Dir: George Marshall
Stars: Glynis Johns, Jackie Gleason
Rating: ★★★

Gentle, sometimes very funny comedy, lushly shot in Technicolor, about a man living in Texas at the turn of the century, whose 'delicate condition' is almost perpetual inebriation. Jackie Gleason revels in his role as portly Papa.

Paper, The ● Ⓥ

1994, US, 112 mins, colour
Dir: Ron Howard
Stars: Michael Keaton, Glenn Close, Marisa Tomei, Robert Duvall, Randy Quaid, Jason Robards
Rating: ★★★★

Apart from the salty modern language, this is a solid, comfortingly familiar story of hard-pressed newspapermen and the traditional 24-hour sweat to produce a front page. Sweat, in fact, is something people do a lot in this film, from Michael Keaton as the 'metro editor' (No. 3) through Glenn Close as the managing editor (No. 2) to Robert Duvall (No. 1) as the chain-smoking editor who's just been told he's got prostate cancer. There's lots of shouting and hard-boiled humour, plus, of course, the inevitable story to be chased: two black youths arrested for a double murder they didn't commit. Director Ron Howard hardly lets the pace drop, so you won't have too much time to ponder the near-impossibility of Keaton's achievements on the trail of the truth. Drily humorous lines, or remarks that the audience finds funnier than the characters, take the place of jokes in David and Stephen Koepp's script, and keep you willing the right story to land on the town's doorsteps in the morning.

Paperhouse ◐ Ⓥ

1988, UK, 92 mins, colour
Dir: Bernard Rose
Stars: Charlotte Burke, Jane Bertish, Ben Cross, Glenne Headly
Rating: ★★★

The heroine of this film is in a lot of danger in a house of her worst nightmares. And she's only 11. An original chiller with not a drop of blood, *Paperhouse* is about a schoolgirl who draws a house and finds herself going to it in her dreams. When she draws a face at a window, it becomes a boy, trapped in the house and unable to walk, whom the girl realises is taken to bed with glandular fever, is

just like the boy her doctor is treating for muscular dystrophy. But there is more danger around, from a figure familiar in her life, than just the fight for the boy's survival. Fascinating stuff, directed with many a frisson by Bernard Rose, who conjures up just the kind of world one might imagine in a fever, and grips our attention almost throughout. Rose employs the interesting device of giving the story two or three false endings before finishing on an unexpected upbeat note.

Paper Mask ● Ⓥ

1990, UK, 105 mins, colour
Dir: Christopher Morahan
Stars: Paul McGann, Amanda Donohoe, Tim Wilkinson
Rating: ★★★

Thriller fans will be familiar with the situation: you can't see the expression on the face behind the surgeon's mask as he reaches for the scalpel. But what if he were not even a doctor? Even though some of its developments – especially a man falling hundreds of feet down Cheddar Gorge and surviving – take a lot of believing, this remains a suspenseful thriller about a bogus doctor who gets away with murder. Close enough to reality to be pretty chilling, the film stars Paul McGann as the hospital porter who longs to escape his mundane existence. McGann is stickily palmed plausible as the man always on the edge of being found out, Wilkinson excellent as a suspicious superior and Donohoe effective, if not at her best as the gullible nurse who mistakes incompetence for inexperience. Recommended to all except those with a mortal fear of hypodermic needles.

Paper Moon ◐

1973, US, 100 mins, b/w
Dir: Peter Bogdanovich
Stars: Ryan O'Neal, Tatum O'Neal, Madeline Kahn, John Hillerman
Rating: ★★★

Tatum O'Neal became the youngest ever winner of a best supporting actress Oscar (she was 10 when the film was made) in this winning fable. She proves more than a match for father Ryan O'Neal, who's a bible-selling con-man at large in the American midwest of the mid-Thirties. Jut-jawed comedienne Madeline Kahn was also nominated for an Oscar for her portrayal of fading floozie Trixie Delight.

Paper Tiger ○ Ⓥ

1975, US, 99 mins, colour
Dir: Ken Annakin

P

Stars: David Niven, Toshiro Mifune
Rating: ★

A rather awkwardly contrived parable about an English tutor (David Niven) whose title of major, and tales of military heroism, are equally fraudulent. Niven is persuasive in the title role (which has echoes of his Oscar-winning character in *Separate Tables*). He offers a performance far superior to the script, which fatally compromises itself between comedy, adventure and socio-political statement.

Papillon ◑ ⓥ

1973, US, 150 mins, colour
Dir: Franklin J Schaffner
Stars: Steve McQueen, Dustin Hoffman, Victor Jory
Rating: ★★

This could have been the film of a lifetime. As it is, it just seems to last that long. Tiring, rather than inspiring, is this story of Papillon (Steve McQueen), the French prisoner sent in the Thirties to a horrendous prison establishment in French Guiana, from which his attempts to escape land him with various periods of solitary confinement. But he never gives up. The dialogue between McQueen and Dustin Hoffman, as his fellow prisoner, is a shade too joky, though, for such desperate situations, and the film's doses of philosophy are somehow hard to swallow. McQueen works tremendously hard, but the situations are so banal – there's even an idyllic interlude with a native girl – that all but a few of them defeat him. If only this had settled for being harrowing drama, or high adventure, it might have been a more powerful document against the monstrous – and now departed – system it indicts.

Paradine Case, The ○ ⓥ

1947, US, 115 mins, b/w
Dir: Alfred Hitchcock
Stars: Gregory Peck, Ann Todd, Charles Laughton, Valli, Louis Jourdan
Rating: ★★★

Another Alfred Hitchcock-David O Selznick production to follow *Rebecca* and *Spellbound*. Riveting stuff, underrated in its time, when everything Hitchcock made was being judged by an impossibly high standard. Valli plays the beautiful adventuress who is accused of the murder of her wealthy husband. Gregory Peck is the lawyer who defends her and falls under her hypnotic spell.

Paradise ○ ⓥ

1992, US, 110 mins, colour
Dir: Mary Agnes Donoghue
Stars: Melanie Griffith, Don Johnson, Elijah Wood, Thora Birch
Rating: ★★

A Hollywood retread of a much better French film, *Le Grand Chemin*. A 10-year-old boy (Elijah Wood) is shunted by his heavily pregnant mother (whose husband may have deserted her) to stay the summer with friends in the country. The friends (Melanie Griffith, Don Johnson) have problems of their own: they're hardly on speaking, let alone touching terms since the death of their three-year-old son in an accident four years before. At first the boy spends much of his time up trees with his nine-year-old neighbour (Thora Birch). But then Ben (Johnson) takes an interest and takes the boy shrimp fishing: the prelude to a summer both idyllic and traumatic. Writer/director Mary Agnes Donoghue also wrote *Beaches*, but her treatment of this story makes it hard to care about any of the people, and the narrative, despite its emotive elements, proves dull and boring.

Paradise Alley ◑

1978, US, 104 mins, colour
Dir: Sylvester Stallone
Stars: Sylvester Stallone, Lee Canalito, Armand Assante
Rating: ★★★

The phrase 'sensitive and intelligent film-maker' and the name Sylvester Stallone don't mix in most people's minds, but this story proves the two *can* go together to produce an entertaining and well-made film. Stallone wrote, directed and starred in this story about three slum brothers who try to make some money by encouraging the youngest (and by far the biggest) brother (Lee Canalito) to become a wrestler. For a change Stallone isn't the monosyllabic brute; he's the fast-talking sharp guy. Canalito is endearing as the slow but powerful Victor and Armand Assante is effective as the bitter, war-wounded elder brother. With an intelligent story and some well-staged action, supported by a solid cast, this is a film that was undeservedly overlooked.

Paradise – Hawaiian Style ○ ⓥ

1966, US, 91 mins, colour
Dir: Michael Moore
Stars: Elvis Presley, Suzanna Leigh, James Shigeta, Donna Butterworth,

Marianna Hill
Rating: ★

Elvis's off-screen high living was beginning to show when he made this rather sad and fey attempt to recapture the feeling of his earlier *Blue Hawaii*. Here he's overweight and puffy rather like the storyline – and it's numbing to see the 'King' reduced to singing such ineffectual numbers as 'A Dog's Life' and 'Bill Bailey, Won't You Please Come Home?' 'I've changed,' he says at one point in the 'action' here. But he hasn't: it's still the same tired old stuff that was soon to see him get out of movies.

Paradise Lagoon

See: The Admirable Crichton

Parallax View, The ◑

1974, US, 102 mins, colour
Dir: Alan J Pakula
Stars: Warren Beatty, Paula Prentiss, Hume Cronyn
Rating: ★★★★

The Manchurian Candidate taken a stage further: this black thriller from director Alan J Pakula opens with the assassination of a presidential candidate and proceeds along familiar, if nightmare roads – the 'assassin' is swiftly dispatched and material witnesses disappear faster than a tub of butter under the grill. Can crusading reporter Warren Beatty penetrate the 'Parallax Corporation' and bring them to book? Stylish and persuasive, this is a much more consistent film than Pakula's earlier *Klute* and infinitely more complex than it first appears. Hume Cronyn almost steals Beatty's acting thunder as an editor who seems to produce his paper single-handed.

Paranoiac ◑

1963, UK, 80 mins, b/w
Dir: Freddie Francis
Stars: Janette Scott, Oliver Reed, Liliane Brousse, Alexander Davion, Maurice Denham
Rating: ★★

Hammer chilling and thrilling, with melodrama given full rein in the story of a girl whose dead brother 'returns' from the past. Reed enjoys himself as the heroine's brutal second brother, and there's a suitable holocaust to tidy things up at the end.

Pardners ⊙

1956, US, 88 mins, colour
Dir: Norman Taurog
Stars: Dean Martin, Jerry Lewis, Lon Chaney Jr, Lori Nelson
Rating: ★★

That excellent comedy craftsman Norman Taurog directed this spoof Western. Jerry Lewis as the simple-minded son of a rich mother is the centre of the film and his fans will enjoy some bouts of inspired clowning. 'Young' cowhand Dean Martin croons away in a splendid parody of back-woods music, Lori Nelson is a charming heroine and Agnes Moorehead is in fine fettle as the formidable Mrs Kingsley. A terrific cast of heavies, including Lon Chaney Jr, Jack Elam, Jeff Morrow and Lee Van Cleef, wildly exaggerates the villainy.

Pardon Mon Affaire ◐
1977, France, 105 mins, colour
Dir: Yves Robert
Stars: Jean Rochefort, Claude Brasseur, Victor Lanoux, Danièle Delorme
Rating: ★★★

Several of French director Yves Robert's Gallic farces have travelled well abroad. This one was one of his biggest international successes (and was remade badly in Hollywood by Gene Wilder as *The Woman in Red*). Jean Rochefort has some nice moments as the middle-aged man with a roving eye, while the lovely Danièle Delorme (a star of French films 20 years earlier) is still so attractive that it makes Rochefort's amorous excursion just a little hard to believe.

Pardon My Sarong ☉
1942, US, 85 mins, b/w
Dir: Erle C Kenton
Stars: Bud Abbott, Lou Costello, Virginia Bruce, Robert Paige
Rating: ★★★

This Abbott and Costello South Seas romp makes a nice change from their taking on city crooks or military might, and there are good supporting turns from Lionel Atwill as a jewel thief-cum-pirate, William Demarest as a flat-footed detective and Leif Erickson as the big-headed islander Whaba ('I biggest stinker of them all'). There's a volcano, an island, a yacht race, hidden treasure, a jungle pursuit, a performing seal, musical numbers and native girls by the lagoon-full, including a rare on-camera appearance by Nan Wynn, best known in films as the singing voice of Rita Hayworth.

Pardon Us ☉
(aka: Jailbirds)
1931, US, 55 mins, b/w
Dir: James Parrott
Stars: Stan Laurel, Oliver Hardy
Rating: ★★★

Stan and Ollie fall foul of Prohibition and are sent to prison where their bumbling protests about a pending hunger-strike foil an escape plot. Originally intended as a two-reeler, it was expanded for economic reasons when the prison set proved too expensive to build.

Parenthood ◐ ○
1989, US, 124 mins, colour
Dir: Ron Howard
Stars: Steve Martin, Mary Steenburgen, Dianne Wiest, Jason Robards
Rating: ★★★

Only a quasi-comedy, this Steve Martin film examines a uniquely American upbringing of angst and pain that people elsewhere can only barely comprehend. A nine-year-old in therapy is obviously a fairly normal experience there, while the three sets of parents involved, and those around them, insist on making a crisis out of every drama. At the end, the film settles for an unconvincing reconciliation to basic values: it's a cop-out and the makers clearly know it. Only comfortably middle-class American parents could get into messes like these and the implications of it all fill you with unease. One doesn't give a cent for the future chances of any of these people and it's kind of frightening that we should be asked to care. Martin fortunately supplies a few characteristic laughs along the way.

Parent Trap, The ☉
1961, US, 124 mins, colour
Dir: David Swift
Stars: Hayley Mills, Maureen O'Hara, Brian Keith
Rating: ★★★

'Hayley Mills and Hayley Mills' boasted the posters for this Disney frolic, in which the Sixties' most popular child star plays twin sisters intent on reuniting their parents, a story filmed before (but far less successfully) 10 years previously in Britain as *Twice Upon a Time*, with real-life twins playing the girls. This version gave the Disney boys the chance to show their expertise at trick photography by putting the two Hayleys in one scene at the same time. And Hayley's personality and popularity was such that, despite being no great singer, she took the film's song hit, 'Let's Get Together', high into the charts. Three TV movie sequels, all pretty average (and all with Haley), followed nearly 30 years later.

Paris, Texas ◐ ⓥ
1984, US, 150 mins, colour
Dir: Wim Wenders
Stars: Harry Dean Stanton, Nastassja Kinski, Dean Stockwell
Rating: ★★★

Ry Cooder's haunting guitar music sets the mood and the pace of a film that is fascinating, dramatic, amusing and touching by turns. As the man found wandering in the Mojave Desert, refusing to say a word, the laconic Harry Dean Stanton shows how well he could have handled leading roles long before this if he had been given the chance. The film is very well made, terrifically acted, flawlessly photographed and... well... a bit boring, especially towards the end.

Paris Trout ● ⓥ
1991, US, 110 mins, colour
Dir: Stephen Gyllenhaal
Stars: Ed Harris, Barbara Hershey, Dennis Hopper
Rating: ★★

Dennis Hopper creates a monster more frightening than anything in *The Silence of the Lambs* as Paris Trout, a psychotic white bigot making a living as a storekeeper in the Georgia of 1949. When he feels gypped by a black sharecropper who's pranged the dud car Paris sold him and wants to claim the insurance (on which Paris intends to welch), Trout storms out to his home with a friend, both armed. There Trout goes berserk, shooting the man's kid sister dead and severely wounding his mother. When his wife (Barbara Hershey) expresses her horror, he attacks and humiliates her sexually, in a revoltingly graphic scene. She flees to the arms of his lawyer (Ed Harris) who is already becoming uneasy at defending Paris. Unrelentingly grim, the film is full of dingy, dust-filled rooms that make you wonder if the sun ever shone in this part of the post-war American South.

Paris When it Sizzles ○
1964, US, 110 mins, colour
Dir: Richard Quine
Stars: William Holden, Audrey Hepburn
Rating: ★★

Some nice moments in this comedy about a screenplay writer and his secretary acting out the weird and wonderful ideas they dream up for a film script, with diversions into *Dracula,* spy stories and jungle epics on the way. Although the film, scripted by George Axelrod, who wrote *The Seven Year Itch,* tends to be an hour of

P

unadulterated fun and 50 minutes of rather tiresome talk, it's well worth a look for its high quota of madcap moments. Hepburn is a delight, too: what a shame the script had to lace its champagne with flat beer.

Party, The ○ ⓥ

1968, US, 94 mins, colour
Dir: Blake Edwards
Stars: Peter Sellers, Claudine Longet, Marge Champion, Steve Franken, Fay McKenzie
Rating: ★★★

Consistently funny comedy from the team responsible for the *Pink Panther* series star Peter Sellers and director Blake Edwards. Sellers plays an Indian actor who is an absolute walking disaster. Sight gags abound.

Party Girl ○

1958, US, 98 mins, colour
Dir: Nicholas Ray
Stars: Robert Taylor, Cyd Charisse, Lee J Cobb, John Ireland
Rating: ★★★

The best of Robert Taylor's later films, this crime drama comes across like a black-and-white movie suddenly converted into CinemaScope and colour. Pushily, vividly directed by Nicholas Ray, it makes a few salient points about the morals of the law and the underworld having a lot in common, before settling for a formula action finale. Co-star Cyd Charisse has a couple of well-staged dances.

Pascali's Island ❶ ⓥ

1988, UK, 104 mins, colour
Dir: James Dearden
Stars: Ben Kingsley, Charles Dance, Helen Mirren
Rating: ★★

This good-looking, but slow-moving drama, set in the early years of the 20th century and based on Barry Unsworth's novel, was James Dearden's first screenplay following *Fatal Attraction*. Here he directs as well, though he keeps the drama too much at a distance for the audience to get very involved. Ben Kingsley gives an eye-catching, if mannered central performance as a small-time spy operating from an Aegean island, Charles Dance repeats his *White Mischief* portrayal of the bronzed, womanising adventurer and Helen Mirren brings some much-needed warmth to the story as the object of both their desires.

Passage, The ❶

1978, US, 98 mins, colour
Dir: J Lee Thompson
Stars: Anthony Quinn, James Mason, Malcolm McDowell, Patricia Neal
Rating: ★

An intended tribute to the strength of the human spirit in adversity during World War Two. Stuck in France, James Mason and his family need to escape the Nazis and the only way out, as for the von Trapps before them, is over the mountains. Selected by the underground to guide them is a big, gruff, sheep-loving man of the mountains. It has to be Anthony Quinn and it is. Malcolm McDowell, eyes gleaming madly, gives an extraordinary performance as the Nazi pursuing them.

Passage Home ○

1955, UK, 102 mins, b/w
Dir: Roy Baker
Stars: Peter Finch, Diane Cilento, Anthony Steel, Cyril Cusack
Rating: ★★★

Director Roy Baker creates an exciting action film here – no mean feat considering he has a basic plot that has seen service in a dozen other previous films. Diane Cilento sparkles as the hub of the yarn – one girl among a shipload of seamen on a perilous 30-day voyage. The sea scenes have an authentic ring, the story moves along not only rapidly but even plausibly, and the acting, especially from Peter Finch as the captain and Geoffrey Keen as the bosun, has a lusty, gritty feel.

Passage to India, A ○ ⓥ

1984, UK, 163 mins, colour
Dir: David Lean
Stars: Judy Davis, Victor Banerjee, Peggy Ashcroft, James Fox, Alec Guinness, Nigel Havers
Rating: ★★★

David Lean's pleasing if typically over-long account of E M Forster's novel set in India in the 1920s. Judy Davis gives an intriguingly enigmatic performance as the young English woman who goes to India with her fiancé's mother (Peggy Ashcroft). Dazed by the heat, the erotic influence of a love temple and the more immediate impact of a bizarre echo cave, she brings a charge of rape against the hapless Dr Aziz (Victor Banerjee), a friendly if oversubservient young doctor who has accompanied Davis and Ashcroft on a somewhat ambitious and costly trip to the mountains. Dame Peggy is excellent and deservedly won an Oscar,

although Lean's old ally Alec Guinness never quite escapes caricature as the Brahmin mystic professor who believes that fate decides all. Still, all in all this is a worthwhile passage, distinguished by the fascination of the story and the richness of its flavour.

Passage to Marseille ○ ⓥ

1943, US, 110 mins, b/w
Dir: Michael Curtiz
Stars: Humphrey Bogart, Michele Morgan, Claude Rains, Sydney Greenstreet, Peter Lorre
Rating: ★★★★

What seems like half the cast of *Casablanca* is reunited in this rugged wartime adventure story that has won rather undeserved notoriety as the only film with flashbacks within flashbacks within flashbacks to the main story. If you feel confused already, don't worry. Director Michael Curtiz (also from *Casablanca*) packs the complex scenario with tense action scenes, from an escape from Devil's Island, through a mutiny on board an Atlantic freighter, to a night-time raid of Free French bombers over Germany. Michele Morgan isn't quite Ingrid Bergman, but comes creditably close; and there are the flavour-filled performances you'd expect from Humphrey Bogart (intelligently shedding his semi-toupee in later scenes to make himself look older), Claude Rains, Sydney Greenstreet, Peter Lorre, and practically Hollywood's entire collection of European emigrés. Fluid camerawork by James Wong Howe often ups the tempo of the action.

Passed Away ❶ ⓥ

1992, US, 96 mins, colour
Dir: Charlie Peters
Stars: Bob Hoskins, Maureen Stapleton, William Petersen, Nancy Travis, Jack Warden, Pamela Reed, Tim Curry, Blair Brown
Rating: ★★

A talented cast is largely sold down the river by director Charlie Peters' script here. 'We'll give Dad a wake he'll never forget,' declares doting son Bob Hoskins (whose American accent is not quite so on-the-ball as usual) at the start of this quirky, lightweight black farce set over one weekend in the lives of a distinctly oddball Irish-American family. Besides Maureen Stapleton giving good value to the role of the new widow, and Nancy Travis playing commendably straight as a mysterious stranger at the funeral, the cast also includes Peter Riegert, Teri Polo and

Frances McDormand. All of them capture well their characters' eccentricities. Expect gently humorous, but not side-splitting entertainment from this offbeat caper.

Passenger 57 ● Ⓥ
1992, US, 84 mins, colour
Dir: Kevin Hooks
Stars: Wesley Snipes, Bruce Payne, Alex Datcher, Tom Sizemore, Marc Macaulay, Elizabeth Hurley
Rating: ★★

This brief but very violent action film is, in all but name, Die Hard, Sky High, with Wesley Snipes nearly but not quite a match for Bruce Willis. Wesley plays a security chief who, still haunted by the death of his wife in a supermarket robbery, finds himself on the same plane as the world's most wanted hijack terrorist, now a captive, but whose men are planted aboard ready to extract him from FBI custody (a bullet between the eyes is the preferred method) and take over the plane. Snipes, trapped in the john just like Willis, or as Steven Seagal in the freezer in Under Siege, soon starts cutting down the odds, together with a very curvy stewardess (Alex Datcher) who is obviously going to help him get over his wife's death in the course of time. Although the pace of the film varies, a lot of incident is packed into its 84 minutes, which even throws in action in a fairground when the plane is forced to land and the terrorists attempt getaway on foot. The dialogue has moments of high lunacy: 'It's Charles Rane: the sophisticated British aristocrat known as the Rane of Terror', but action fans won't find much to complain about.

Passion ○
1954, US, 84 mins, colour
Dir: Allan Dwan
Stars: Cornel Wilde, Yvonne De Carlo, Raymond Burr
Rating: ★

Not a love story but a poorly-written Western vendetta thriller into which co-stars Cornel Wilde and Yvonne De Carlo put plenty of spirit. The action scenes whip up some excitement and the supporting cast includes Raymond Burr, Lon Chaney Jr and veteran John Qualen.

Passionate Friends, The ○
(aka: One Woman's Story)
1949, UK, 95 mins, b/w
Dir: David Lean
Stars: Ann Todd, Claude Rains, Trevor

Howard
Rating: ★★★

Pitched somewhere between Brief Encounter and Ryan's Daughter, this romantic drama, enormously popular in its day, gives further evidence of director David Lean's fascination with women caught up in circumstances over which they seem to have no control, and which alter the lives of those around them. Here, it's Ann Todd as the married woman whose innocent day out with a former lover leads to a complex sequence of events. Claude Rains is masterly as the husband, while the story itself develops swiftly and incisively in a way that Lean's films failed to do in later times.

Passionate Summer ○
1958 UK, 104 mins, colour
Dir: Rudolph Cartier
Stars: Virginia McKenna, Bill Travers, Yvonne Mitchell
Rating: ★★

Tangled love tale which should prove especially satisfying to all women who like a good-going romance with tons of complications. Bill Travers really makes one feel for him as the man caught in the middle of it all. And it seems only natural that of the three ladies vying for his affections he should plump for Virginia McKenna – after all, in real life, they had just been married.

Passion Fish ● Ⓥ
1992, US, 135 mins, colour
Dir: John Sayles
Stars: Mary McDonnell, Alfre Woodard, David Strathairn, Vondie Curtis-Hall, Angela Bassett, Sheila Kelley
Rating: ★★★★

Handed the role of a lifetime, the underrated Mary McDonnell deservedly notched up an Oscar nomination for her portrayal of the sour soap star who, paralysed in a car crash, returns to her childhood home in Louisiana. Various nurses desert her because of her bitchiness, until Chantelle (Alfre Woodard) appears, with problems of her own, but more than able to stand up to her new employer. Writer-director John Sayles has come up with a touching and gently funny story of the unlikely friendship that springs up between two people who feel they deserve better out of life. The supporting cast gleams with class and, if the piece drifts on just too long in the final reckoning, its visual qualities and emotional appeal more than make up for that.

Passport to Fame
See: The Whole Town's Talking

Passport to Pimlico ⊙ Ⓥ
1949, UK, 84 mins, b/w
Dir: Henry Cornelius
Stars: Margaret Rutherford, Stanley Holloway, Basil Radford, Hermione Baddeley
Rating: ★★★★★

Possibly the best film Ealing Studios made, a delightfully inventive comedy, brilliantly executed by director Henry Cornelius and a dazzling cast headed by Margaret Rutherford and Stanley Holloway. Pimlico's inhabitants find documents saying they belong to Burgundy, and promptly secede from the UK. Subsequent developments bring a chuckle a minute.

Pat and Mike ○
1952, US, 95 mins, b/w
Dir: George Cukor
Stars: Spencer Tracy, Katharine Hepburn, William Ching
Rating: ★★★★

Spencer Tracy and Katharine Hepburn play off against each other with immense pleasure in this constantly entertaining comedy about a lady who's a whiz at several sports (a role tailor-made for Hepburn) but who seizes up when her boyfriend's around. Several well-known sports stars of the day appear as themselves, one of the highlights of the action being a tennis match between Hepburn (quite a tennis enthusiast in real life) and 'Gorgeous' Gussie Moran. Possibly the most enjoyable of all the Tracy-Hepburn films.

Patch of Blue, A ◑
1965, US, 105 mins, b/w
Dir: Guy Green
Stars: Sidney Poitier, Shelley Winters, Elizabeth Hartman
Rating: ★★★★

Blindness in films tends to be a subject on which most directors fail to avoid dipping their fingers into the sticky jar of over-sentiment. Guy Green is an exception to the rule, as he proves in this touching story of an 18-year-old girl who falls in love with a black reporter without knowing the colour of his skin. Shelley Winters won an Oscar as the sluttish mother who still knocks the girl around despite the fact that it was she who accidentally blinded her daughter at the age of five with acid (in a brilliantly handled flashback scene). Elizabeth Hartman is excellent as the girl, giving the kind of intense

P

performance often given by a young actress at the beginning of her career, and often never repeated. But perhaps best of all is the Ol' Pa of Wallace Ford. His last role, it also proved his meatiest for many years. The director tops it all off by not skipping any detail of the girl's everyday life, so that her joys really do seem joyous.

Paternity ❶ ⓥ
1981, US, 90 mins, colour
Dir: David Steinberg
Stars: Burt Reynolds, Elizabeth Ashley
Rating: ★★★

There was much conjecture that this romantic comedy echoed star Burt Reynolds' real life in that he plays a man called Buddy (his own nickname) who wants to father a baby though he isn't married. Easy enough? Not the way Burt goes about it in a fun film which steers clear of the rocks of reality and contains some witty exchanges between Reynolds and Juanita Moore as his sardonic housekeeper. 'What does the name Erasmus mean?' he asks her. 'That means your child won't have friends,' she answers.

Pat Garrett and Billy the Kid ❶ ⓥ
1973, US, 106 mins, colour
Dir: Sam Peckinpah
Stars: James Coburn, Kris Kristofferson, Bob Dylan, Jason Robards, Rita Coolidge
Rating: ★★

Director Sam Peckinpah's version of the Billy the Kid legend is a moody and atmospheric Western which, despite the wide open spaces, is almost claustrophobic. There's enough action to keep things moving, though, although it's not as overtly violent as some of Peckinpah's other films. The friendship between Billy and Sheriff Pat Garrett is really only hinted at, which reduces the drama of the final scenes. There are strong central performances from James Coburn as Garrett and Kris Kristofferson as Billy.

Paths of Glory ◯
1957, US, 86 mins, b/w
Dir: Stanley Kubrick
Stars: Kirk Douglas, Wayne Morris, Adolphe Menjou, Ralph Meeker
Rating: ★★★

Staffley Kubrick's prize-winning film about man's folly in World War One, when three young soldiers are picked at random to be tried and shot for cowardice. The idea is to instil fear into their comrades. Kirk Douglas, as

the young colonel who tries to defend the three men, gives one of his best performances in a sad and angry film that puts its message across without compromise.

Patriot Games ❶ ⓥ
1992, US, 116 mins, colour
Dir: Phillip Noyce
Stars: Harrison Ford, Patrick Bergin, Anne Archer, James Fox, Thora Birch, Sean Bean
Rating: ★★★

This thriller, exciting stuff towards the end, imagines that a rogue faction of the IRA (led by Patrick Bergin) might try to kill members of the British royal family, and that ex-CIA analyst Jack Ryan (Harrison Ford) might find himself caught up in one such attempt. 'Having a go' in the midst of the mayhem, Jack shoots dead the brother of fanatical Sean Miller (Sean Bean), who subsequently escapes to make life a living nightmare for Jack and his family. There are holes galore in a plot that grows progressively less pacy until it gets down to business in the last 15 minutes, as Ryan and a visiting royal (James Fox) are besieged in a house (guarded by only three security men!) in a thrilling game of cat and mouse that ends up in speeding boats. Don't get too logical about this thriller and you'll enjoy most of it.

Patsy, The ☉ ⓥ
1964, US, 101 mins, colour
Dir: Jerry Lewis
Stars: Jerry Lewis, Ina Balin
Rating: ★★

Another of star Jerry Lewis' inspired ideas half-ruined by director Lewis' own laborious treatment. A group of Hollywood technicians, all experts in their fields, take a goofy bellboy under their wing and vow to mould him into a famous comedy star. Fecklessly and sometimes embarrassingly, he wrecks all their efforts to do so. How funny this might have been. But always there is too much 'space' on screen. Too long with nothing doing. When director Lewis gives comic Lewis a chance, the picture bursts with fun – as with the superbly staged scene where the music teacher (Hans Conried) finds both himself and his apartment gradually torn apart when he tries to teach Lewis how to sing.

Patterns ◯
(aka: Patterns of Power)
1956, US, 83 mins, b/w
Dir: Fielder Cook

Stars: Van Heflin, Everett Sloane, Ed Begley, Beatrice Straight
Rating: ★★★

Based on a television hit play by Rod Serling, this film takes a candid and unusually discerning peep into the executive suites of the world of big business in America. The cut and thrust of the business giants' tactics is thrilling and the dialogue diamond-hard and brilliant. The film was praised to the skies by critics, but thrown away by distributors and practically ignored by the public. One of its best scenes comes when Van Heflin and Everett Sloane slug it out together in a verbal battle about the film's central theme. Is big business, they argue, a good or an evil thing. Finding the answer poses a lot of problems for the characters.

Patton: Lust for Glory ❶ ⓥ
(aka: Patton)
1969, US, 171 mins, colour
Dir: Franklin J Schaffner
Stars: George C Scott, Karl Malden
Rating: ★★★

Now mainly remembered as the film for which George C Scott was awarded, and refused, an Oscar, this is an intimate war film, in the sense that it concentrates on the complex character of Patton himself, with the help of some tremendous work by Scott. The battle scenes themselves are exciting enough, but it's the character conflicts you'll remember.

Patty Hearst ● ⓥ
1988, US, 108 mins, colour
Dir: Paul Schrader
Stars: Natasha Richardson, William Forsythe, Ving Rhames, Dana Delany, Frances Fisher
Rating: ★

Patty's is one of the most fascinating and extraordinary stories of our violent times. A pity it's made such a boring film. Hard to see what director Paul Schrader could have done about it, apart from not stylising the bank robberies involved, presumably to eliminate vicarious excitement. Well, we could have done with some vicarious excitement to liven up the retelling of the story of rich girl Patty's kidnap and brainwashing by an obscure liberation army who seem to do little apart from indoctrinate their members, think about robberies to raise money, and have sex with each other. Natasha Richardson, looking exactly like mum Vanessa Redgrave, puts heart and soul into Patty and is the only thing that comes close to holding the movie together. Great American accent too, Natasha; shame about the film.

Paula
See: Framed

Pay Day ⊙ ⓥ
1922, US, 21 mins, b/w
Dir: Charles Chaplin
Stars: Charlie Chaplin
Rating: ★★★

Charlie Chaplin's last short film, this contains a marvellous sequence of comic events that begins when workman Charlie staggers home drunk in the pouring rain.

Pay Or Die! ○
1960, US, 111 mins, b/w
Dir: Richard Wilson
Stars: Ernest Borgnine, Zohra Lampert, Alan Austin, Murvyn Vye
Rating: ★★★

Ernest Borgnine's best post-*Marty* role, as a detective who wages a one-man war against the Mafia, in this interesting, exciting and forceful crime thriller set in the early 1900s. Borgnine's honest-to-goodness performance gives the drama just the grittiness it needs, and Zohra Lampert makes a pleasing debut as his wife. Other good performances come from Alan Austin and Murvyn Vye, as two characters very much on different sides of the law.

Payroll ○
1961, UK, 105 mins, b/w
Dir: Sidney Hayers
Stars: Michael Craig, Françoise Prevost, Billie Whitelaw, William Lucas
Rating: ★★★

For more than 20 years, filmgoers have been familiar with the type of crime thriller on the 'caper' theme. The idea had been used in the cinema before, certainly, but it is hard to escape the feeling that it was Jules Dassin's famous French film *Rififi*, with its celebrated, virtually soundless robbery sequence, which really set the fashion for so many films of this ilk – a fashion which has continued almost ever since. The 'robbery which goes wrong' is a favourite theme and *Payroll* is a British variation which makes a well-knit thriller tale.

Pearl of the South Pacific ⊙
1955, US, 85 mins, colour
Dir: Allan Dwan
Stars: Virginia Mayo, Dennis Morgan, David Farrar
Rating: ★

Technicolor tales of the South Seas really got under way with Dorothy Lamour and her sarong in the mid-Thirties. This tiresome yarn limped in right at the end of the cycle, but contains all the familiar elements: beautiful girl, dashing hero, hot-headed tribal chief and even the octopus that guards the sunken treasure. No treasure here, though.

Peeping Tom ●
1959, UK, 109 mins, colour
Dir: Michael Powell
Stars: Carl Boehm, Moira Shearer
Rating: ★★★★

Producer-director Michael Powell, usually associated with get-away-from-it-all films, here made one of the most horrifying contributions to the cinema of the macabre since World War Two. Written by Leo Marks, who co-scripted *Twisted Nerve*, it tells of a psychopathic young cameraman who photographs his victims' terrified death agonies. The murders themselves are horrifyingly tense, and Carl Boehm couldn't be bettered as the psychopath. It makes gripping, adult entertainment: not recommended for the nervous.

Pee-wee's Big Adventure ○ ⓥ
1985, US, 91 mins, colour
Dir: Tim Burton
Stars: Paul Reubens, Elizabeth Daily
Rating: ★★★

The feature debut of Pee-wee Herman, the on-screen persona of cult comedian Paul Reubens, is a most stylish affair. From the start, when the childlike Pee-wee awakens in a room filled with Heath Robinson-style contraptions on the traumatic day his beloved red bicycle is stolen, we know we're in for a visual treat. There's not really much of a story. But Pee-wee, with his comical white pan-sticked face, rosy cheeks and red painted lips, offers us the perfect opportunity to re-experience our own innocent wonder as we see things through his eyes. Director Tim Burton, paints a colourful canvas, and the overall effect is rather like a huge box of brightly coloured toys being spilled onto the screen. Don't be fooled into thinking that this film is just for kids – adults will find it inventive, imaginative and totally engaging.

Peggy Sue Got Married ◑ ⓥ
1986, US, 104 mins, colour
Dir: Francis Coppola
Stars: Kathleen Turner, Nicolas Cage
Rating: ★★

Although its cast has strength in depth, this is a tedious and inexplicably overrated fantasy which comes across as a romance-orientated version of *Back to the Future*. Middle-aged Kathleen Turner (unconvincing as a teenager) magically returns to high school and gets a second chance with her boyfriend (Nicolas Cage, over-acting) and future husband. There are plenty of faces to look out for in the supporting cast, including such personable veterans as Maureen O'Sullivan, Don Murray, Barbara Harris, John Carradine and Leon Ames. A pity Coppola couldn't conjure up something more worthy of such a starry gathering.

Pelican Brief, The ◐ ⓥ
1993, US, 141 mins, colour
Dir: Alan J Pakula
Stars: Julia Roberts, Denzel Washington, Tony Goldwyn, John Heard, Sam Shepard, John Lithgow
Rating: ★★

Dodging killers while bodies are dropping all about her, Julia Roberts plays the young law student whose intelligence and nose for suspicious detail get her into all sorts of trouble. Based on John Grisham's best-seller (reputedly written with Roberts in mind), it's a little too similar in flavour to Grisham's other blockbuster *The Firm;* the plot is even more complex and assured, leaving you no time to go out and make the coffee unless you stop the film. Denzel Washington is competent in the co-starring role as the determined reporter who proves to be Roberts' only reliable ally in her flight from powerful and deadly forces, but like hers, his role is underwritten so that these people, like their opponents, remain little more than cyphers, albeit of good against evil. Action scenes keep the pulse racing; but don't bank on remembering the plot if anyone asks you.

Penal Colony, The
See: No Escape

Pendulum ◐
1968, US, 106 mins, colour
Dir: George Schaefer
Stars: George Peppard, Jean Seberg
Rating: ★★

Routine tough American detective thriller, somewhat after the style of Don Siegel, but here integrating the various aspects of its plot together without the same panache. Good performances from Charles McGraw, as a

P

rugged chief of detectives, and Robert F Lyons, as a psychopathic killer. Razor-sharp colour photography by Lionel Linden is another asset to the violent parable.

Penny Princess O
1952, UK, 92 mins, colour
Dir: Val Guest
Stars: Yolande Donlan, Dirk Bogarde
Rating: ★★★

Given a storyline that is not so much slim as positively anorexic, this romantic froth has to rely on the charm of the actors and the pace of their playing and, in this respect, Yolande Donlan comes through with flying colours, putting over her lines with genuine fizz. Dirk Bogarde supports nobly and spent most of the film in his pyjamas but, since it had a 'U' certificate, everything was naturally proper and above board. Donlan's husband Val Guest wrote and directed breezily.

Penny Serenade O
1941, US, 120 mins, b/w
Dir: George Stevens
Stars: Cary Grant, Irene Dunne, Beulah Bondi, Edgar Buchanan
Rating: ★★

Well thought of in many quarters, George Stevens' over-extended weepie about a will-they-won't-they-part? couple looks rather stiff and maudlin today: only stars like Irene Dunne and Cary Grant could see material like this through, but even they are unlikely to stop you drifting off to make the coffee half-way through.

People That Time Forgot, The O
1977, UK, 96 mins, colour
Dir: Kevin Connor
Stars: Patrick Wayne, Sarah Douglas, Doug McClure, Dana Gillespie
Rating: ★★★

This sequel to *The Land That Time Forgot* is a funny (sometimes intentionally) and altogether rather smashing pantomime adventure which the kids will swallow whole while adults sit convulsed in an adjoining armchair. The beginning of the picture, with Captain Tony Britton – apparently strayed in from a British war film of the Fifties piloting his icebreaker into the wilder Antarctic regions through which Doug McClure was seen plodding at the end of the previous film – is definitely weak. But, once away from exteriors, director Kevin Connor finds his touch. Among the more spectacular of his visuals are: a party of

scarlet-pennoned horsemen riding out from Skull Mountain across the horizon; and a deeply shrouded cavern, walled with tiny skulls, where the explorers are kept captured. A little tableau compromising a grotesque executioner and his grubby dwarf familiar is also splendidly imaginative.

People Vs Dr Kildare, The O
1941, US, 78 mins, b/w
Dir: Harold S Bucquet
Stars: Lew Ayres, Lionel Barrymore
Rating:★★

More of the action takes place in the courtroom than in the hospital in this Kildare drama which has the good doctor defending himself against a malpractice suit. The supporting cast is fairly extraordinary, with the former child star Bonita Granville as the girl whose skating career seems to have ended under Kildare's knife and comic Red Skelton as a hospital janitor.

People Vs Larry Flynt, The ● Ⓥ
1996, US, 127 mins, colour
Dir: Milos Forman
Stars: Woody Harrelson, Courtney Love, Edward Norton, Larry Flynt, James Cromwell, Brett Harrelson
Rating: ★★★

Woody Harrelson gives an Oscar-nominated performance as porn magazine king Larry Flynt in this forcefully directed film whose skilfully written screenplay provides an eye-opening and sometimes painful insight into the life of a man who told his heavily employed lawyer (Edward Norton): 'I'm your ideal client. I'm the most fun. I'm rich. And I'm always in trouble.' From backwoods beginnings and ownership of a strip club, Flynt founded *Hustler*, a magazine that made *Playboy* look like *Good Housekeeping*. This is an even-handed and sometimes humorous account of his trials, incarcerations, paralysis by shooting and drug dependency. The material is controversial; the performances rightly leave the viewer nowhere to hide.

People Will Talk O
1951, US, 110 mins, b/w
Dir: Joseph L Mankiewicz
Stars: Cary Grant, Jeanne Crain, Hume Cronyn, Walter Slezak
Rating:★★

Joseph L Mankiewicz's follow-up to the Oscar-winning successes of his *All About Eve* lacks the venom that so distinguished the previous film. Cary

Grant smoothly plays the eccentric medico whom all the 'talk' is about, but Mankiewicz did not get on with leading lady Jeanne Crain, thrust upon him by the studio after his original choice Anne Baxter had to withdraw because she was expecting a baby. At least the film is hard to categorise. It belongs in the cinema's bulging vaults of one-off near misses.

Pepe O
1960, US, 157 mins, colour
Dir: George Sidney
Stars: Cantinflas, Shirley Jones, Dan Dailey, Ernie Kovacs
Rating: ★★

Colourful musical trip around Hollywood, with many stars appearing as themselves. The song-and-dance numbers are sparklingly shot in colour and well worth watching. The slim storyline revolves around Cantinflas – the Mexican comic actor who made such a name for himself as Passepartout in *Around the World in 80 Days* – as a simple peasant whose horse is bought by a film director. Seems to go on forever though.

Percy ● Ⓥ
1971, UK, 103 mins, colour
Dir: Ralph.Thomas
Stars: Hywel Bennett, Denholm Elliott, Elke Sommer, Britt Ekland
Rating: ★

This is a one-joke film and the joke isn't that funny. Hywel Bennett is the recipient of the world's first penis transplant after a freak accident. He spends most of the film trying to discover the identity of Percy's (his pet name for his new organ) owner. It's not simply that this is all in rather bad taste, it's not very good either. Positively limp, in fact. You're not shocked by the humour or the naff music hall phallic references, but you are embarrassed for all the talented people who obviously spent so much time producing so little. Unbelievably, they made a sequel, *Percy's Progress*. Believably, it was worse.

Perez Family, The ◑ Ⓥ
1995, US, 112 mins, colour
Dir: Mira Nair
Stars: Marisa Tomei, Alfred Molina, Anjelica Huston, Chazz Palminteri, Trini Alvarado
Rating:★★

This film about love and loss is archly stylised at the beginning and it's the quality of the performances rather than script and direction that finally see it hit its stride two-thirds of the way through. Alfred Molina is Juan, a Cuban dissident who, released from prison after 15 years, heads for America and Carmela (Anjelica Huston), the wife who, with their daughter (Trini Alvarado), got out of the country. On the way he encounters ex-hooker Dottie (Marisa Tomei), also a Perez. Accidentally labelled husband and wife, Juan and Dottie take on other family members, forming a unit that enables them to pick up sponsorship and stay. While Juan is hunting for Carmela, he is, of course, falling for Dottie, while Carmela is flattered by the attentions of local cop Chazz Palminteri. These four central performances are well considered (especially Huston's), but rather undercut by a sometimes over-light, almost farcical treatment, and by an ending that's too pat and abrupt to convince.

Perfect ● ⓥ
1985, US, 119 mins, colour
Dir: James Bridges
Stars: John Travolta, Jamie Lee Curtis, Laraine Newman, Marilu Henner, Anne de Salvo
Rating: ★★★

The cast of this drama (with yet another pre-sold disco soundtrack), about an investigative reporter doing a story on aerobic clubs being the singles bars of the Eighties, is so charismatic as to make you quite like a story of which you can hardly believe a word. John Travolta as the journalist does his best to carve a likeable centrepoint to the drama, although the screenplay hardly helps. And, if the whipcord Jamie Lee Curtis is on her best form, she is certainly given very tough competition by all three of the other *femmes* in the cast – Laraine Newman and Marilu Henner as ladies of the club and Anne de Salvo as Travolta's sometime photographer colleague. All three catch the exact essence of the characters they play – and Newman and Henner both convey the vulnerability of the banter and pushiness of the man-mad swingers they portray.

Perfect Couple, A ◐
1979, US, 110 mins, colour
Dir: Robert Altman
Stars: Paul Dooley, Marta Heflin
Rating: ★★

A well-crafted, engagingly acted but basically silly story about a romance (by computer dating) between two people from weird and absurdly exaggerated family units. If you think her

'pop' commune is offbeat, wait until you see his martinet Greek family, ruled over with a rod of iron by a father who conducts gramophone records while a family of all ages sits and watches. If the story fails by and large to take off, its music is most attractive. In fact, the soundtrack may be a better bargain than the film itself, despite the gauche charm with which it is endowed by stars Paul Dooley and Marta Heflin.

Perfect Friday ◐
1970, UK, 94 mins, colour
Dir: Peter Hall
Stars: Ursula Andress, Stanley Baker, David Warner
Rating: ★★★

Bank robbery thriller, given light-hearted treatment by director Peter Hall and especially by John Dankworth's racy music score. Ursula Andress is always worth watching, in and out of clothes, the robbery itself is quite tensely staged, and the whole caper never outstays its welcome. The sugar-coated spoof is delightfully easy to swallow and makes for thoroughly diverting entertainment.

Perfect Furlough, The ○
(aka: Strictly for Pleasure)
1958, US, 93 mins, colour
Dir: Blake Edwards
Stars: Tony Curtis, Janet Leigh, Keenan Wynn
Rating: ★★

Comedy written round the talents of Tony Curtis and Janet Leigh when they were still Hollywood's ideal young couple. Talented supporting cast includes television superstar Elaine Stritch. Curtis, though, was never as good in comedy as he liked to think, with the honourable exception of *Some Like It Hot*.

Perfectly Normal ● ⓥ
1990, Canada, 107 mins, colour
Dir: Yves Simoneau
Stars: Michael Riley, Robbie Coltrane, Deborah Duchene, Kristina Nicholl
Rating: ★

Although slow-moving and over-long, this comedy piece has a certain slight charm. Renzo (Michael Riley) is an Italianate Canadian who inherits his mother's spacious home, but carries on working at a drink factory, secretly singing opera in the shower and keeping goal for the local ice hockey team. Renzo's life begins to change when he meets Alonzo Lafayette Turner (Robbie Coltrane), a porky failed

restaurateur, who moves in. Riley is too low-key for words as the shy, harassed and uncommunicative Renzo. You can believe the works foreman who tells him: 'This is some new territory you've entered here. You've gone past dull.' Too many of Renzo's qualities rub off on the film too, although the climactic fight in Alonzo's operatic diner has a certain nutty grandeur.

Perfect Woman, The ○
1949, UK, 89 mins, b/w
Dir: Bernard Knowles
Stars: Patricia Roc, Stanley Holloway, Nigel Patrick
Rating: ★★

A scatterbrained comedy about a professor who invents a robot woman. That delicious ditherer Miles Malleson plays the inventor and Patricia Roc, though miscast, enters into the spirit of the thing as his daughter who takes the robot's place.

Perfect World, A ◐ ⓥ
1993, US, 138 mins, colour
Dir: Clint Eastwood
Stars: Kevin Costner, Clint Eastwood, Laura Dern, T J Lowther
Rating: ★★

This manhunt thriller has some of the best performances in a Hollywood action drama for some little time past, but suffers from severe credibility problems at crucial stages of its plot. Kevin Costner is the man on the run with a boy (T J Lowther) as hostage – even the circumstances of the initial kidnapping themselves are somewhat unconvincing – Clint Eastwood the pursuing Texas Ranger and Laura Dern a criminologist assigned to the case. All four of these performances are first-class, and the ending, when it comes, is quite emotive, but drags on far too long and, like much of the plot, is bedevilled by a failure to dodge any contrivance or cliché you might expect (and hope to avoid) in this kind of film.

Performance ● ⓥ
1970, UK, 105 mins, colour
Dir: Donald Cammell, Nicolas Roeg
Stars: James Fox, Mick Jagger, Anita Pallenberg
Rating: ★★★

Nicolas Roeg, up till then a distinguished cinematographer, advanced his career by co-directing this ugly but compelling mood piece about a gangster on the run who finds a hideout in the mansion of a reclusive pop star. Glowingly photographed by Roeg

P

himself, the film is tough and sometimes violent, with personable performances from James Fox and Mick Jagger in the two leading roles.

Perils of Pauline, The ○

1947, US, 96 mins, colour
Dir: George Marshall
Stars: Betty Hutton, John Lund, Billy de Wolfe, William Demarest
Rating: ★★★

It's laughter, tears and songs again with Betty Hutton, and another of her larger-than-life heroines (she also played Annie Oakley, Texas Guinan and Blossom Seeley). This time around, it's Pearl White, queen of the silent serial world, getting the Hutton treatment. Doyenne screen actress Constance Collier heads the supporting cast, which also includes William Demarest, Frank Faylen and Billy de Wolfe. Pretty colourful.

Personal Services ● Ⓥ

1987, UK, 105 mins, colour
Dir: Terry Jones
Stars: Julie Walters, Alec McCowen, Danny Schiller, Shirley Stelfox
Rating: ★★

The story of London 'madam' Cynthia Payne. Alternately bright and grim and occasionally amusing in its desperate way, the result is about what you'd expect: lots of earthy language and 'late-night' wit, with a salty if rather variable performance by Julie Walters which, like the story, gets wearing after a while. Generally, the film falls between vulgar low-life humour and St Trinian's titillation but, if you like that sort of thing, it's all good clean dirty fun, both the film and its characters being in the good old British tradition. Indeed, the last two reels could have come straight out of *Carry On Whoring*. 'You'll go down for this,' scowls the police sergeant after the final raid on Christine's suburban brothel. 'I only go down for a price dear,' retorts Walters, 'and I doubt whether you can afford it.' You can just see Barbara Windsor saying the same thing to Kenneth Williams.

Pete Kelly's Blues ○

1955, US, 95 mins, colour
Dir: Jack Webb
Stars: Jack Webb, Janet Leigh, Edmond O'Brien, Lee Marvin, Peggy Lee, Ella Fitzgerald
Rating: ★★★★

Only a contrived ending mars Jack Webb's forceful drama of gangsters and musicians in the Jazz Age of the

Twenties. The jazz is brassy and basic, and the story has a cutting edge of realism that gives it a gritty feel. There's good support from Andy Devine and Lee Marvin (cast for once as the hero's wisecracking friend) and a solid story, plus a few unconventional directorial tricks from Webb, who also has the sense to surround himself with such real jazz people as singers Peggy Lee (her striking performance got her nominated for an Oscar) and Ella Fitzgerald. And you can't miss Jayne Mansfield as a cigarette girl! It's hard-hitting and well on the beat.

Peter Ibbetson ○

1935, US, 91 mins, b/w
Dir: Henry Hathaway
Stars: Gary Cooper, Ann Harding, John Halliday, Ida Lupino
Rating: ★★

This fey, not to say bizarre romantic fantasy baffled most critics of the mid-Thirties, who were accustomed to a cinema that went in for realism. Gary Cooper struggles with a role to which he seems not entirely suited, but Ann Harding is fine as the childhood sweetheart with whom he is reunited in dreams, and that sharp character star John Halliday excels in the rather too small role of Miss Harding's screen husband.

Peter No-Tail ☉

1981, Sweden, 75 mins, colour
Dir: Stig Lasseby
Rating: ★★★

This Swedish feature cartoon was so successful internationally that a sequel, *Peter No-Tail in America*, appeared two years later. Its hero, a cat born without a tail, has been a favourite of Scandinavian children since stories about him (written first by Gosta Knutsson, later by Leif Krantz) first appeared in the Thirties. Almost three million books have since been sold relating the adventures of Peter, who was based on a cat that Knutsson had encountered as a child: that animal, however, Knutsson learned, had had its tail bitten off by a rat! This first film's good entertainment, with vivid animation, a resourceful hero and an eventful story.

Peter Pan ☉ Ⓥ

1952, US, 77 mins, colour
Dir: Hamilton Luske, Clyde Geronimi
Voice stars: Bobby Driscoll, Kathryn Beaumont, Hans Conried, Bill Thompson, Heather Angel, Tom Conway
Rating: ★★★★

Cruelly underrated in its day, this sees the Disney studio close to its best in a cleverly detailed fairy-tale adventure of great charm, spun round J M Barrie's play about the boy who never grew up, lives in a faraway island with The Lost Boys and engages in duels of wits and sword-play with the dastardly Captain Hook. There are memorable songs – 'I Can Fly', 'The Second Star to the Right' – although they take second place to the action. You might be surprised to find that one of the most popular songs from the film, 'Never Smile at a Crocodile', was actually cut from the film and only survives as a musical theme when the crocodile appears to menace his old enemy Hook. Younger children will be enthralled and excited at this one, and rightly so.

Peter's Friends ● Ⓥ

1992, UK, 103 mins, colour
Dir: Kenneth Branagh
Stars: Kenneth Branagh, Emma Thompson, Stephen Fry, Hugh Laurie, Rita Rudner, Imelda Staunton
Rating: ★★

The kind of modish ensemble piece that may look woefully dated in years to come, enabling a group of Britain's ageing bright young things to portray university friends 10 years on. The story of their reunion has moments of wit and perception but, after a delightful and often funny first 40 minutes, becomes increasingly heavy going, dominated by a torrent of four-letter words and unlikely sexual shenanigans, and going right over the top with Kenneth Branagh's drunken rant at the end. A credibility problem exists here right from the start (could any university footlights revuers really have performed for an audience that sat with their backs to them, ignored them, or went to sleep?) and continues right through the film. The Branagh and Emma Thompson characters – she's initially delightful as a bookish spinster worried about the welfare of her cat – are especially inconsistent and hard to take, and only Stephen Fry achieves the right blend of wit and melancholy the piece requires.

Pete's Dragon ☉ Ⓥ

1977, US, 134 mins, colour
Dir: Don Chaffey
Stars: Helen Reddy, Jim Dale, Mickey Rooney, Shelley Winters
Rating: ★★

This Disney musical fantasy combines live action and animation and very young children will love it. Purists will notice that foregrounds do occasionally wobble, and the songs are largely undistinguished. But the cast has its moments, especially in a vertigo-inducing trio sung by Helen Reddy, Mickey Rooney and youngster Sean Marshall at the top of a lighthouse. And it really is them hauling themselves up and dancing round the top. At such times, *Pete's Dragon* almost spreads its wings.

Pet Sematary ● Ⓥ
1989, US, 103 mins, colour
Dir: Mary Lambert
Stars: Dale Midkiff, Fred Gwynne, Brad Greenquist
Rating: ★

Screen adaptations of Stephen King's best sellers have been mainly disappointing, but for this atrocity the author has only himself to blame. He wrote the screenplay, as well as appearing in a rather incongruous bit part. Even to begin with, it's hard to sympathise with a family who, with two kids and a cat, move to a home about six yards away from a dangerous, unguarded motorway. But they do, or we wouldn't have a story, such as it is. which involves an Indian burial ground (actually beyond the 'pet sematary') which brings the dead back to life in fiendish form. King could never be accused of good taste, but here logic deserts him as well. People behave in impossibly idiotic fashion in order to sustain the horror, and the dialogue all too often matches the plot developments for sheer lunacy. The sequel *Pet Sematary Two*, is marginally better, but displays no more common sense.

Petticoat Pirates ○ Ⓥ
1961, UK, 87 mins, colour
Dir: David MacDonald
Stars: Charlie Drake, Anne Heywood, Cecil Parker, John Turner
Rating: ★★

A laugh on the ocean wave with Charlie Drake among the Wrens. Charlie's antics include dressing up as a girl and – in the funniest sequence – taking part with the Wrens in a chaotic exercise at sea. By no means great, but offbeat. bright and breezy.

Petulia ◐ Ⓥ
1967, UK, 105 mins, colour
Dir: Richard Lester
Stars: Julie Christie, George C Scott, Richard Chamberlain, Joseph Cotten
Rating: ★★★★

Richard Lester directed this highly individual and thoroughly entertaining film after making those delightfully in-

consequential Beatles pictures and the different but equally amusing *The Knack*. Julie Christie plays Petulia, the unorthodox heroine, one of whose actions is to steal a tuba at night from a pawnshop. The film drew mixed reactions from critics on its release, but in our book it is classified only fractionally below the top class. It is certainly Lester's best performance as director.

Peyton Place ◐ Ⓥ
1957, US, 157 mins, colour
Dir: Mark Robson
Stars: Lana Turner, Lee Philips, Arthur Kennedy, Hope Lange, Lloyd Nolan, Diane Varsi
Rating: ★★★★

The original film version of Grace Metalious's best-selling book about the sores that lurk beneath the respectable facade of a small American town. William Mellor's brilliant colour photography – especially notable in the passing of the seasons – complements Mark Robson's deft direction of this lusty slice of Americana. The cast also includes Lee Philips, Terry Moore and Russ Tamblyn; but it's the more experienced hands – Lana Turner, Leon Ames and Mildred Dunnock – who take the acting honours.

Phantasm ● Ⓥ
1978, US, 89 mins, colour
Dir: Don Coscarelli
Stars: Michael Baldwin, Bill Thornbury, Reggie Bannister, Kathy Lester, Angus Scrimm
Rating: ★★

A horror film about strange goings-on in and around a mortuary that purposely draws no line between nightmare and reality. You are left wondering where one ends and the other begins. This deliberately confusing approach eventually works against the film, however, as it gets sillier and sillier and ends desperately needing a punchy climax that would bring everything together with a sickening crunch. All it gets is a renewal of the nightmare cycle, leaving too many loose ends and non-sequiturs floating in mid-air. Nevertheless it does have its shock moments, carried off with considerable style and editing skill by director Don Coscarelli, who fortunately survived to frighten us another day. Angus Scrimm has a genuinely frightening screen presence as The Tall Man.

Phantasm II ● Ⓥ
1988, US, 97 mins, colour
Dir: Don Coscarelli

Stars: James LeGros, Reggie Bannister, Angus Scrimm, Paul Irvine, Kenneth Tigar
Rating: ★★★

A drive-in movie that gets sillier and sillier as it goes along or more and more fun, according to your inclinations. Spot the name 'Sam Raimi' (another horror film-maker) on a dead man in the mortuary, and you know that Don Coscarelli, who made the first *Phantasm*, is only playing fun and games. There'll be an ending in which the forces of evil are vanquished, but then a tailpiece paving the way for yet another sequel. Angus Scrimm is back as the Tall Man, a thinking man's Freddie Krueger, along with his deadly flying spheres and.demon dwarfs. Lots of blood, both red and yellow, is spilt, but sufficient pace, imagination and lightness of tone ensure that we don't take it all too seriously. Horror fans can confidently swallow the grisly dose in one gulp: just watch out for the flying spheres.

Phantom, The ○ Ⓥ
1996, US, 100 mins, colour
Dir: Simon Wincer
Stars: Billy Zane, Kristy Swanson, Treat Williams, Catherine Zeta Jones
Rating: ★★★

Arm yourself with a six-pack, a mountain of crisps and a barrel of popcorn for this lightest of light entertainment adventures that runs like a cross between an Indiana Jones caper and an old Forties serial. Full of get-up-and-go and feistily directed by Simon Wincer, the story, set in 1938/39, is about a masked phantom of the jungle who becomes caught up in a plot by a crooked New York businessman to gain possession of three jewel-eyed skulls that will enable him to control the world, or at least that part of it not about to be ravaged by impending world war. Zane, Swanson and Zeta Jones are well up to the demands of the hero, heroine and villainess and the action is as tightly shot as in any Forties 'chapter play'. It's rather lacking in witty dialogue, but still enjoyable enough as a faithful record of a long-running comic-strip hero.

Phantom Lady ○
1944, US, 87 mins, b/w
Dir: Robert Siodmak
Stars: Elia Raines, Franchot Tone, Alan Curtis, Thomas Gomez
Rating: ★★★★

This top-flight *film noir* about a missing witness in a murder case was directed

P

by Robert Siodmak, second only in the Forties to Alfred Hitchcock as a purveyor of suspense and claustrophobic terror. His use of camera angles, sound effects and sequences without dialogue is remarkably effective and moody monochrome cinematography by Woody Bredell serves to underline the growing atmosphere of tension and unease. There's a fine performance by Elisha Cook Jr as a frightened little man (amazing in his final scene) and Aurora Miranda, the sister of Brazilian Bombshell Carmen Miranda, appears briefly as the star of a musical show and sings 'Chick-Ee-Chick'.

Phantom of the Opera, The ○ ⓥ

1925, US, 94 mins, b/w & colour
Dir: Rupert Julian
Stars: Lon Chaney, Mary Philbin
Rating: ★★★★

The first and still most famous screen version of Gaston Leroux's lurid tale of the mad music master who haunts the secret corridors of the Paris Opera House. Lon Chaney, the 'man of a thousand faces', took the title role and achieved another triumph in make-up when the face beneath the mask was finally revealed (heightened by the film's bursting into colour), to the horror of the heroine, played by the bewitching, birdlike Mary Philbin. Amazing sets, splendid atmosphere.

Phantom of the Opera, The ○ ⓥ

1943, US, 92 mins, colour
Dir: Arthur Lubin
Stars: Nelson Eddy, Claude Rains, Susanna Foster
Rating: ★★★

Despite some critics' cynical reservations about any version of *The Phantom of the Opera* in which the actor playing the Phantom was billed beneath Nelson Eddy, this was a huge moneyspinner for Universal Films – in spite of its nine million dollar budget, a big outlay for the studio at the time. Claude Rains gives a fine, sympathetic performance as the man behind the mask. This was one of a great actor's most memorable hours. The stunning Technicolor photography of Hal Mohr and W Howard Greene won an Academy Award, as did the opulent art direction by John B Goodman and Alexander Golitzen.

Phantom of the Opera ● ⓥ

1989, US, 92 mins, colour
Dir: Dwight H Little

Stars: Robert Englund, Jill Schoelen, Alex Hyde White, Bill Nighy, Stephanie Lawrence
Rating: ★★

It's a nightmare at the opera house! Yes, Robert Englund, alias Freddy Krueger, takes his turn as the masked master of murder and music, and the results make the good Hammer rendition of 1962 look a model of restraint. This isn't a modernised version, simply the old chestnut with a silly modern framing story which makes no sort of sense, in which the heroine discovers Freddy's – sorry, Erik's – old manuscripts and history and gasps, 'Gee, isn't that weird – composer by day and serial killer by night!' The script, in fact, is a bigger villain than the Phantom, although the settings are opulently, painstakingly stylish. Englund is actually all right as the Phantom, when he's allowed to do more than skin his victims alive and peel layers of bloody guck off his face. But Schoelen seems all wrong as a flat-chested opera singer with little sense of dramatic timing. The last two reels do contain some bravura moments and the enterprise, though disappointingly trite and silly, is by no means a bore.

Phantom of the Paradise ●

1974, US, 91 mins, colour
Dir: Brian De Palma
Stars: Paul Williams, William Finley, Jessica Harper
Rating: ★★

This film, which started director Brian De Palma on an eye-catching orgy of violence and suspense, is a cheeky rock music remake of *Phantom of the Opera*. That diminutive dynamo of the pop world, Paul Williams, not only stars as the megalomaniac impresario Swan, who callously steals the hero's songs, but also wrote the music and lyrics for the film himself. Among the minor credits, you'll notice the name of Sissy Spacek, taking time out from acting, as set decorator. Her real-life husband Jack Fisk was production designer on the film.

Phantom of the Rue Morgue ◐

1954, US, 84 mins, colour
Dir: Roy Del Ruth
Stars: Karl Malden, Claude Dauphin, Patricia Medina, Steve Forrest
Rating: ★★

One of the few big scale adaptations of stories by Edgar Allan Poe not to star Vincent Price. This time it's Karl Malden dispensing the sneers in the

story of a grisly series of murders in turn-of-the-century Paris. Poe's storyline is followed quite faithfully, sombre Warnercolor photography plays up the creepy scenes, and there are good performances from Malden, Claude Dauphin and Allyn McLerie, plus an appealing one from blonde stage star Dolores Dorn, who sadly ends up as one of the killer's victims.

Phantom Tollbooth, The ⓥ

1970, US, 90 mins, colour
Dir: Chuck Jones, Abe Levitow, David Monahan
Stars: Butch Patrick
Rating: ★★★

A charming, part-live action but mostly animated version of Norton Justin's children's book which marked the debut as a feature film director of Chuck Jones. Jones was the Warners animator who helped create such classic cartoon characters as Bugs Bunny, Porky Pig, Daffy Duck, Tweetie Pie and Road Runner, and his early work was notable for speed, violent action and side-splitting sight gags. This film combines some fairly sophisticated ideas, such as demons from the 'Mountains of Ignorance' with cute and likeable characters that will grab a young child's attention. The principal voice talent is the late and much lamented Mel Blanc, the 'voice' of Bugs, Porky and Daffy.

Phar Lap ○ ⓥ

1984, Australia, 118 mins, colour
Dir: Simon Wincer
Stars: Tom Burlinson, Martin Vaughan
Rating: ★★★

It's 1928. Struggling Australian racehorse trainer Harry Telford (Martin Vaughan) buys a horse, sight unseen, from New Zealand. Mockingly called Phar Lap (Siamese for Lightning), the horse comes last in his first five races. But an inspired change of diet and an intense training programme turns Phar Lap into a winner. The true story of Phar Lap has now become part of Australian folk history and this film captures the spirit of the time and the sport. There are engaging performances from Vaughan, Leibman and Tom Burlinson and the whole thing is a kind of cross between *Chariots of Fire and National Velvet*. If that sounds like a put-down, it's not meant to – *Phar Lap* is a thoroughly enjoyable film.

Phase IV ●

1973, US, 86 mins, colour
Dir: Saul Bass

Stars: Nigel Davenport, Lynne Frederick, Michael Murphy
Rating: ★★

If you're a victim of formication – someone who suffers a prickly sensation, as of ants crawling over the skin – you're not likely to enjoy this visually brilliant – courtesy of director Saul Bass and photographer Dick Bush – but tricky-to-follow story of scientists trying to discover why colonies of normally antagonistic ants are banding together and attacking as a collective force. Nigel Davenport, Lynne Frederick and Michael Murphy are the humans in danger. Bush's colour camerawork is the best thing in the film.

Phenomenon ○ ⓥ
1996, US, 124 mins, colour
Dir: Jon Turteltaub
Stars: John Travolta, Kyra Sedgwick, Forest Whitaker, Robert Duvall
Rating: ★★★

John Travolta lands a plum role in this potentially intriguing drama, but even his down-to-earth charm can't keep sentimentality at bay. It begins well, a bit like a Capra fantasy, as small-town, simple Iowa car mechanic George Malley finds himself knocked out by a white light in the sky, and suddenly comes into possession of remarkable powers that enable him to move objects without touching them, predict earthquakes and learn a new language in a matter of minutes. So far, we're hooked. Is it magic? Is it aliens? But no, there's a dark shock ahead, and you'll end up feeling not only cheated out of a good mystery but also wishing you'd bought more tissues.

Phfft! ○
1954, US, 91 mins, b/w
Dir: Mark Robson
Stars: Judy Holliday, Jack Lemmon, Kim Novak, Jack Carson
Rating: ★★★

Columbia got much publicity mileage from the title of this (then) saucy comedy romp, one of a series of very bright comedies from the studio made throughout the Fifties and early Sixties, starring any or all of the formidable trio of Judy Holliday, Jack Lemmon and Kim Novak. All three are in this story of a marriage breaking apart (giving rise to the sound in the title). Add Jack Carson as Holliday's new beau and a sparkling script by George Axelrod, and you had the formula for a surefire laughter success.

Philadelphia ● ⓥ
1993, US, 122 mins, colour
Dir: Jonathan Demme
Stars: Tom Hanks, Denzel Washington, Mary Steenburgen, Jason Robards, Antonio Banderas, Joanne Woodward
Rating: ★★★★

A real tear jerker this, and professionally done, with a strong directorial focus on emotive performances from the leading actors. Gay lawyer Tom Hanks believes he has been sacked by his plush leather firm because they found out he has AIDS, and gets wheeler-dealer counsel Denzel Washington to bring suit against them. Director Jonathan Demme makes sure sympathies are not weighted too blatantly by making Washington a man who dislikes homosexuals, but whose love of the law impels him to take the case. Jason Robards and Mary Steenburgen (she going for the Anthony Hopkins school of understatement) get a chance to show their sharper side as the bigoted head of the law firm and his chief counsel – although one might question a man of Robards' perspicacity sacking Hanks when it's obvious from the timespan of the scenario that he would have had to resign in a matter of weeks. But the principle is the thing here; our support is solicited and indeed assured as Hanks – whose Oscar-winning performance rises to a carefully choreographed crescendo when he describes his love of opera – rivets our attention to his dying countenance.

Philadelphia Story, The ○ ⓥ
1940, US, 112 mins, b/w
Dir: George Cukor
Stars: Cary Grant, Katharine Hepburn, James Stewart
Rating: ★★★★★

Pungently witty classic which was remade 15 years later as High Society. The original is still the best. Stewarts scooped two Oscars for this superb piece of escapism: James Stewart, then only 31, was acclaimed 1940's best actor for his performance as Mac; Donald Ogden Stewart deservedly took the writer's award for the best screenplay of the year. Katharine Hepburn, too, was nominated for an Academy Award in her role as Tracy Lord, the poor little rich girl dissatisfied with the men in her life. This film belongs to a now extinct highly polished and sophisticated, light Hollywood comedy style in which a thin story was made to race along beautifully on the wings of excellent dialogue and talented stars.

Phobia ●
1980, US, 90 mins, colour
Dir: John Huston
Stars: Paul Michael Glaser, John Colicos, Susan Hogan
Rating: ★

John Huston playing with his audience within a whodunit framework as in The List of Adrian Messenger, although not as effectively. The plot isn't really believable, and takes too long unwinding to the (expected) unexpected ending. But Huston's enjoyable professional juggling of his narrative just about keeps you watching to find out just how unlikely the ending is going to be.

Physical Evidence ●
1988, US, 99 mins, colour
Dir: Michael Crichton
Stars: Burt Reynolds, Theresa Russell, Ned Beatty, Kay Lenz
Rating: ★★

The latter half of the 1980s wasn't a particularly good time for Burt Reynolds. He increasingly found himself in tough cop roles, most of which weren't very good. This film, in which Burt plays an ex-cop accused of murder, is better than most. Even so, the film is rather slow and disjointed and doesn't come across as very credible, although Burt turns in a creditable performance, given the run-of-the-mill script. Theresa Russell, not convincingly prim and efficient, is badly miscast as his lawyer – she's much more fun when she's bad. A lady lawyer defends a discredited cop on a murder charge? Sounds familiar and it is, just like the film, routine and truly average right down the line. There's a bit of action and some decent stalking through city streets, with Toronto standing in for the States, but all concerned, especially director Michael Crichton, should have done better.

Piano, The ● ⓥ
1993, New Zealand/UK/US, 120 mins, colour
Dir: Jane Campion
Stars: Holly Hunter, Sam Neill, Harvey Keitel, Anna Paquin
Rating: ★★★

An unusual erotic drama with some striking visual moments (but rather too little story and dramatic movement) about a strong-willed but mute Scottish widow (Holly Hunter) who travels to 19th-century New Zealand to fulfil an arranged marriage with a landowner (Sam Neill). He refuses to bring her beloved piano up from the beach and

P

it falls into the hands of Baines (Harvey Keitel), his construction manager who has 'gone native'. Neill proves a cold husband who can't bring himself to touch his wife, while Keitel can't wait to get his hands on her, exacting progressive sexual favours in return for her earning back the piano key by key. All this is pretty weird and only marginally convincing. After a slow start, the film picks up and unreels like a silent drama, producing some stunning images towards the end when the murky Eastman Color process work permits. Oscar-winning Hunter is wonderfully expressive and does her own piano playing, which is just fine. Sexually direct, the film has some very explicit scenes. Young Anna Paquin, as Hunter's daughter, also received an Oscar.

Piccadilly Jim O
1936, US, 100 mins, b/w
Dir: Robert Z Leonard
Stars: Robert Montgomery, Frank Morgan, Madge Evans, Billie Burke
Rating: ★★★

P G Wodehouse's book filmed as elegantly as only MGM knew how. Robert Montgomery and Madge Evans provide the appropriate light comedy touch, while Frank Morgan and Billie Burke bumble and dither in the expected manner. But the film is stolen from all of them by Eric Blore as Bayliss the butler who seems – mercifully for the slightly overlength screenplay – to be everywhere at once.

Piccadilly Third Stop O
1960, UK, 90 mins, b/w
Dir: Wolf Rilla
Stars: Terence Morgan, Yoko Tani, Mai Zetterling, Dennis Price
Rating: ★★★

No one can accuse Leigh Vance's screenplay of being devoid of incident, including as it does theft, blackmail, smuggling and adultery. It's all directed with pace and polish by Wolf Rilla, and the climactic chase in the underground sizzles with excitement. The cast, too, is not without interest and there's some good support from Mai Zetterling, Yoko Tani and, in particular, William Hartnell, who gives one of his excellent portrayals of smarmy villainy.

Pickup Alley
See: Interpol

Pick-Up Artist, The ☾ ⓥ
1987, US, 79 mins, colour
Dir: James Toback

Stars: Molly Ringwald, Robert Downey, Dennis Hopper, Harvey Keitel
Rating: ★

Molly Ringwald, who was *Pretty in Pink*, proves pesky in purple in this dialogue-heavy romantic comedy. Robert Downey is the girl-chaser who is more than somewhat surprised when his seasoned approaches are so successful with Ringwald that she jumps him as soon as his car has ground to a halt. Unfortunately, Downey has leapt straight into bed with a nest of vipers, as her alcoholic father (it has to be Dennis Hopper and it is) is heavily in debt to a cabal of dangerous gamblers led by a scowling Harvey Keitel. The odds are that you won't care how the plot's confusions sort themselves out, since the script never touches the right emotions. Hopper does his familiar wild-eyed, unshaven act and veteran Mildren Dunnock crops up in a rare role as Downey's diabetic gran.

Pickwick Papers, The O
1952, UK, 115 mins, b/w
Dir: Noel Langley
Stars: James Hayter, James Donald, Alexander Gauge, Kathleen Harrison, Joyce Grenfell, Hermione Gingold
Rating: ★★★

Director Noel Langley scripted this effective adaptation of Charles Dickens' comic novel and filled it with plenty of entertaining incident. He filled it, too, with an excellent cast headed by James Hayter as a splendidly jovial Pickwick. Lively playing all round, especially from Nigel Patrick and Donald Wolfit.

Picnic O
1955, US, 113 mins, colour
Dir: Joshua Logan
Stars: William Holden, Kim Novak
Rating: ★★★★

Superb colour photography by James Wong Howe and splendid acting highlight this striking and unusual film, which is something between a comedy-drama and a love story. Full marks to the writer, Daniel Taradash (adapting William Inge's play to the screen), and congratulations to the players, particularly Rosalind Russell as the town's spinster teacher and William Holden as the drifter who sets everyone's emotions on edge. Also good though are Kim Novak, Susan Strasberg and Cliff Robertson. The ending may take you (happily) by surprise, and even the music (notably the 'Moonglow' theme) is great in this memorable and delightful film.

Picnic at Hanging Rock ☾
1975, Australia, 110 mins, colour
Dir: Peter Weir
Stars: Rachel Roberts, Dominic Guard, Helen Morse
Rating: ★★★★

After a rather ordinary beginning, in which events are somewhat overly staged, this richly textured piece develops into a haunting, extremely good ghost-horror story played out in broad daylight. A group of Australian schoolgirls and teachers in 1900 go for a picnic to the towering, primeval Hanging Rock deep in the desert – an excursion from which three of them are never to return. It's only after things start to happen, which is rather a long time, that Weir's film really hits its stride, with the director always keeping the explanation of the horrors tantalisingly out of reach.

Picture Mommy Dead ☾
1966, US, 88 mins, colour
Dir: Bert I Gordon
Stars: Don Ameche, Martha Hyer, Susan Gordon
Rating: ★★

Fascinating cast-from-the-past (it also includes Wendell Corey, Zsa Zsa Gabor, Maxwell Reed and Signe Hasso) in a lurid shocker only weakened by the central casting of Susan Gordon as the young girl still suffering from hallucinations in dead mummy's mansion. Superb Pathecolor photography makes the most of the shocks.

Picture Bride ☾
1993, US, 90 mins, colour
Dir: Kayo Hatta
Stars: Youki Kudoh, Tamlyn Tomita, Akira Takayama, Cary-Hiroyuki Tagawa, Toshiro Mifune
Rating: ★★

The plight of teenage Japanese girls shipped off to Hawaii as 'picture brides' (they and their husbands selected by photograph) before the practice was stopped in the 1920s is examined in the well-meant and good-looking but slightly uninteresting film. Director Kayo Hatta tries to spice the subject up a bit by making the heroine a 16-year-old city girl (Youki Kudoh) and the bridegroom a 43-year-old man who has lied about his age. Naturally she'll have nothing to do with him and hates her new life on a sugar cane plantation – in a worker's shack. Still the city girl proves, in only one of the film's many predictable moves, to be made of tougher stuff. The best performance comes from Tamlyn Tomita as the strong-willed worker who becomes Kudoh's best friend – and her salvation. The film ends abruptly, leaving many of its plot threads dangling in the air.

Picture of Dorian Gray, The ○
1945, US, 110 mins, b/w & colour
Dir: Albert Lewin
Stars: George Sanders, Hurd Hatfield, Donna Reed, Angela Lansbury
Rating: ★★★

Elaborately produced version of Oscar Wilde's famous story of the bizarre, elegantly shot in black and white, with a startling burst into vivid Technicolor at the climax. Harry Stradling won the Oscar for his cinematography. Hurd Hatfield made a tremendous impression in this, being admirably suited to his role as the coldly sardonic Victorian gentlemen whose portrait in the attic grows hideous with age and sin while he himself alters not a whit. Hatfield's subsequent film career, however, was less successful.

Picture Snatcher ◐
1933, US, 73 mins, b/w
Dir: Lloyd Bacon
Stars: James Cagney, Ralph Bellamy, Patricia Ellis
Rating: ★★

James Cagney is perpetual motion in this typically fast-paced Warners action film based rather uneasily on real-life events. His occupation – snapping sensational pictures of unsavoury events – paralleled the real-life activities of a New York Daily News photographer who captured a death-cell execution on film. Two well-rehearsed fight sequences that went wrong left Alice White (at the hands of Cagney) and Cagney himself (at the hands of Ralph Bellamy) nursing sore jaws. 'I sure was sorry,' said Cagney of the White accident, 'to hit that cute little kisser.'

Pied Piper, The ○
1942, US, 86 mins, b/w
Dir: Irving Pichel
Stars: Monty Woolley, Roddy McDowall, Peggy Ann Garner
Rating: ★★★

A winning Hollywood version of Nevil Shute's novel, which provides a tailor-made role for Monty Woolley as the child-hating Englishman forced to shepherd a handful of kids through occupied France during the Nazi occupation. The film catches the story's delicately tender feel and holds

it well. Suspense is built-in, but the movie also has warmth and jollity – and keeps strictly within the fragile mood it creates. Roddy McDowall and Peggy Ann Garner head the youngsters.

Pied Piper, The ○
1972, UK, 90 mins, colour
Dir: Jacques Demy
Stars: Donovan, Donald Pleasence, Jack Wild
Rating: ★★★

The title character of this quaint musical fantasy, based on Browning's famous poem and set in 14th-century Germany, gave popular folk singer Donovan his only film role. Frenchman Jacques Demy directed, bringing a picture-book prettiness to the olde-worlde settings.

Pie in the Sky ● ⓥ
1995, US, 94 mins, colour
Dir: Bryan Gordon
Stars: Josh Charles, Anne Heche, Peter Riegert, Christine Ebersole
Rating: ★★

A gentle, romantic coming-of-age comedy with a host of good stars – among them John Goodman and Christine Lahti – in small roles. The story sees traffic-obsessed Charlie (Josh Charles), conceived on a highway during rush-hour gridlock, discovering the joy and pain of love with oddball Amy (interesting newcomer Anne Heche). John Goodman, only on screen for a few minutes, steals the limelight as Charlie's hero, a traffic radio deejay. Muddled and uneven in tone, the film is still charmingly played, especially by Charles and by Lahti as his much older lover.

Pigeon That Took Rome, The ○
1962, US, 101 mins, b/w
Dir: Melville Shavelson
Stars: Charlton Heston, Elsa Martinelli
Rating: ★★

Charlton Heston got a chance to break away from his 'Mr Epic' image, and exercise his considerable talent for light-comedy in this amiable romp about two American agents getting messages out of wartime Italy by pigeon post. Plump Italian comedy actor Salvatore Baccaloni adds to the fun.

Pigskin Parade ○
1936, US, 93 mins, b/w
Dir: David Butler
Stars: Stuart Erwin, Patsy Kelly, Jack

Haley, Betty Grable, Judy Garland
Rating: ★★★

Judy Garland fans will really appreciate this rarely seen college football musical. It was the 14-year-old Judy's feature film debut. She's billed ninth down the cast, playing the kid sister of hunky young quarterback Amos Dodd (Stuart Erwin, Oscar-nominated for his performance), who, based on his reputation for hurling melons, leads a Texan hillbilly team invited to play against Yale up in snooty New England. It's all jolly college stuff and you can forget the plot and concentrate on an interesting cast: snappy Patsy Kelly as the coach's wife, cheery Jack Haley as the coach (he would go on to be the Tin Man in *The Wizard of Oz*), Betty Grable (the million-dollar legs had not yet reached the top rung of stardom) and, would you believe, toughie Alan Ladd as a student, singing with The Yacht Club Boys! The pigskin, of course, refers to the football itself.

Pilgrim, The ○
1922, US, 48 mins, b/w
Dir: Charles Chaplin
Stars: Charlie Chaplin, Edna Purviance, Mack Swain
Rating: ★★★

Charlie Chaplin's films, once so plentiful, were beginning to become few and far between in comparison by the time *The Pilgrim* came out in January 1923, five months after its completion. It opens in similar style to *The Adventurer*, with Chaplin as a convict on the run, and ends with the classic image of the fugitive with a foot in each country, an ironic pointer to the wanderer he would later become.

Pillow Talk ○ ⓥ
1959, US, 100 mins, colour
Dir: Michael Gordon
Stars: Doris Day, Rock Hudson, Tony Randall, Thelma Ritter, Nick Adams
Rating: ★★★★

Doris Day and Rock Hudson's first comedy together, this battle-of-the-sexes romp was one of the box-office blockbusters of its day. The film marked quite a change of style for director Michael Gordon, who was then better known for well-made thrillers and such meaty dramas as *An Act Of Murder*. It also enabled Day to lose a little of her virginal girl-next-door image and Hudson to prove that he was more than just a handsome hunk. Directed with verve, it's dotty, witty and highly entertaining. Writers Stanley Shapiro and Maurice Richlin

P

won that year's Oscar for Best Screenplay.

Pillow Book, The ● ⓥ

1995, UK, 126 mins, colour
Dir: Peter Greenaway
Stars: Vivian Wu, Ewan McGregor, Yoshi Oida, Ken Ogata
Rating: **RB**

This 'story' about a woman who paints books on men's bodies is a film for pseudo intellectuals who believe the director has something meaningful to say. It is, however, unutterable nonsense whose split-screen techniques add nothing to the *mise-en-scène* (such as it is) and which frequently follows an aphorism with a clattering banality. Britain's Ewan McGregor, who spends most of the time looking awkward in the nude, somehow got mixed up in this as the bisexual lover of heroine Vivian Wu. Most of her inkwork goes down the plughole before the end, much like the film. Unlike most Peter Greenaway pictures, this one, shot in Cinecolor, doesn't even *look* good.

Pimpernel Smith ○

1941, UK, 121 mins, b/w
Dir: Leslie Howard
Stars: Leslie Howard, Francis L Sullivan, Mary Morris
Rating: ★★★★

Known in America as *Mister V,* which rather defeated the object of the exercise, this was an updating of Baroness Orczy's French Revolution hero to World War Two. Leslie Howard (who had starred in the original version of *The Scarlet Pimpernel* seven years earlier) directed and also gave one of his best ever performances as the archaeology professor helping Jewish refugees escape from Hitler in the period just before the outbreak of war.

Pink Panther, The ○ ⓥ

1963, US, 113 mins, colour
Dir: Blake Edwards
Stars: David Niven, Peter Sellers, Claudia Cardinale, Robert Wagner
Rating: ★★★★

Gay, warm and amusing comedie-desriches that introduced the bungling French detective Clouseau, as personified by Peter Sellers. Everything Clouseau touches turns to dust. He can't even get his wife sleeping pills without spilling them all over the floor. The screen is filled with his wife's disgusted expression, and the sound of crunching as Clouseau treads a bedward path. Naturally, when such a man comes to grips with a master

criminal known as The Phantom, it's long odds on him coming to grief and on our doubling up with mirth watching him. After a while, of course, one knows what is going to happen. It becomes no longer necessary to show Sellers falling to the floor, dropping things, or draping a blanket over his head while trying to put it on the bed. A noise, a crash, a clatter, together with the lugubrious face of Sellers, is sufficient to convince us that disaster has struck again.

Pink Panther Strikes Again, The ○ ⓥ

1976, UK, 103 mins, colour
Dir: Blake Edwards
Stars: Peter Sellers, Herbert Lom, Leonard Rossiter, Lesley-Anne Down
Rating: ★★

Sellers' bungling Inspector Clouseau encounters (as he would put it) more hurmps and burmps, plus Herbert Lom's marvellous ex-Inspector Dreyfuss, who has escaped from his asylum and laid hands on a doomsday machine with which he threatens to extinguish the whole world unless it gives him Clouseau. Brilliantly inventive titles by Richard Williams Animation are followed by the usual spasmodically funny Sellers shenanigans, with the peripheral characters coming off better as laughter-raisers than Clouseau himself. Particularly good is a running joke about then-President Ford falling over things, plus Lom's relishable pop-eyed maniac who sets up his new headquarters in a Dracula-style castle.

Pink String and Sealing Wax ○

1945, UK, 89 mins, b/w
Dir: Robert Hamer
Stars: Googie Withers, John Carol, Mervyn Johns, Gordon Jackson
Rating: ★★★★

Love, murder and blackmail are the ingredients of this classic British thriller – one of several fine films directed by Robert Hamer at Ealing Studios in the mid-Forties. Others were *Kind Hearts and Coronets, Dead of Night* and *It Always Rains on Sunday.* Here he has Googie Withers (Britain had no one better at being bad) as the evil-hearted landlady of a seaside pub, who blackens all the lives she touches. A young Gordon Jackson has a co-starring role.

Pinocchio ⊙

1940, US, 88 mins, colour
Dir: Ben Sharpsteen, Hamilton Luske
Rating: ★★★★★

Still perhaps Disney's best single-story cartoon, this tale of a little wooden boy is vividly related and crammed with adventures (some a little frightening for the very young). Memorable characters abound: Geppetto the woodcarver; Jiminy Cricket; Figaro and Cleo (a cat and a goldfish); and the villains J Worthington Foulfellow (a fox), Gideon (an alleycat), Stromboli the showman, and the terrifying coachman. Teeming with detail, it even had an Oscar-winning song: 'When You Wish Upon A Star'.

Pin Up Girl ○ ⓥ

1944, US, 85 mins, colour
Dir: Bruce Humberstone
Stars: Betty Grable, John Harvey, Martha Raye, Joe E Brown
Rating: ★★

A pretty obvious title for a pretty obvious Betty Grable wartime vehicle which makes up in zest and high spirits for what it lacks in the way of plot. Martha Raye and Joe E Brown provide the comedy, Hermes Pan provides some lively choreography. The flagwaving finale seems to go on forever.

P.I. Private Investigations ○

1987, US, 91 mins, colour
Dir: Nigel Dick
Stars: Clayton Rohner, Talia Balsam
Rating: ★★★

Writer-director Nigel Dick has come up with a cheerful, love-and-bullets caper that rushes forward at a tremendous pace. It's from the 'Yuppie-almost-gets-it-but-learns-to-be-a-regular-guy-in-time' school of movies, but is packed with zest. There are nice performances from newcomers Clayton Rohner and Talia Balsam (daughter of Martin, who also appears).

Piranha ●

1978, US, 92 mins, colour
Dir: Joe Dante
Stars: Bradford Dillman, Heather Menzies, Kevin McCarthy
Rating: ★★★

Swimming in on the tail of *Jaws,* but with teeth firmly in cheek, this is both an enjoyable story in its own right and an amusing take-off of fishy disaster stories. The horrific parts are all very well done, and the dialogue often scores too. Our favourite line: 'But sir, they're eating the guests.' Former horror star Barbara Steele also appears, almost as disturbing as ever.

Pirates ◑

1986, France, 124 mins, colour
Dir: Roman Polanski
Stars: Walter Matthau, Cris Campion
Rating: ★★

Pirate adventures, are, by their very nature, over the top, so it's pretty difficult to overplay your hand when making one. Roman Polanski managed it, though, in this colourful buccaneering romp. Walter Matthau is notorious sea-dog Captain Red, cast adrift on a raft with only a treasure chest and 'The Frog' (Cris Campion) for company. They are rescued when a Spanish ship picks them up, but the treasure is lost in the rescue. Still, never mind, there's a priceless golden Inca throne on board, but how can the wily Captain steal it? Matthau obviously enjoyed himself as Captain Red, but all the other players seem merely caricatures. Nevertheless, it's an enjoyable, if occasionally vulgar yarn. It's not in the same class as Burt Lancaster's *The Crimson Pirate* as a pirate parody, but lightweight fun.

Pirates of Blood River, The ○

1961, UK, 87 mins, colour
Dir: John Gilling
Stars: Kerwin Mathews, Glenn Corbett
Rating: ★★

An interesting attempt by Hammer films in the early Sixties to widen their range beyond the horror film. In this story of piracy in the Caribbean, they tried, with considerable success, to match the pace and technical standards of the best Hollywood action films. Although two American stars were imported to boost the film's chances in the US, all the acting quality comes from Christopher Lee and Oliver Reed, who have a high old time as two really villainous buccaneers.

Pirates of Tortuga ○

1961, US, 97 mins, colour
Dir: Robert D Webb
Stars: Ken Scott, Leticia Roman, Dave King, John Richardson
Rating: ★★

Two Britons – comedian Dave King and husky John Richardson – share the fencing honours with American hero Ken Scott in this sparky pirate thriller. Another British actor, Robert Stephens, turns up as the famous buccaneer, Sir Henry Morgan. Action abounds, and it's a sure bet to keep the children quiet if it's a wet day.

Pirates of Tripoli ○

1955, US, 72 mins, colour
Dir: Felix Feist

Stars: Paul Henreid, Patricia Medina
Rating: ★★

A bright and lively swashbuckler. Henry Freulich's admirable Technicolor photography is effective particularly in an exciting naval battle scene. Paul Henreid maintains the immobile expression he also used for such trifles as *Thief of Damascus, Siren Of Baghdad* and *Last of the Buccaneers,* but Patricia Medina is given the opportunity to show both spirit and a handsome wardrobe.

Pistolero of Red River, The ○

1967, US, 90 mins, colour
Dir: Richard Thorpe
Stars: Glenn Ford, Angie Dickinson, Chad Everett, Gary Merrill
Rating: ★★

One more time for one of the oldest Western stories in the book: it's the yarn about the young gunslinger who has to prove himself against the older man. But a good cast all turn in fine performances, and veteran director Richard Thorpe brings it in with a fresh lick of paint, and just a suspicion of a surprise about the ending. Glenn Ford endows the lawman with an air of rugged authority; there's a peach of a performance from Jack Elam, as a hired, but tired assassin who just isn't quite good enough.

Pit and the Pendulum, The ● ⓥ

1961, US, 82 mins, colour
Dir: Roger Corman
Stars: Vincent Price, John Kerr, Barbara Steele
Rating: ★★★★

Directed by Roger Corman, master of the cut-price horror saga, this chiller is more Price than Poe, but our Vincent is in great form showing off his Spanish Inquisition torture chamber –'This room was my father's life...' Barbara Steele is typically fierce, proving an ideal foil for Price's very slightly tongue-in-cheek performance, and the sets are wonderful. Pretty spooky, too, as its characters creep along cobwebbed corridors clutching flickering candles, and, with stunning shock moments, this is altogether the best of the earlier Corman horror films made in America.

Pitfall ○

1948, US, 85 mins, b/w
Dir: André De Toth
Stars: Dick Powell, Lizabeth Scott, Raymond Burr, Jane Wyatt
Rating: ★★★

More than just a thriller, *Pitfall* is also a far-seeing film in that it takes an early look at a man's disillusionment with the American dream of secure job, home and family, none of which prevent insurance agent Dick Powell from falling into the clutches of predatory Lizabeth Scott and a world of violence, suspicion and death. An exciting film that also makes you think.

Pit of Darkness ○

1961, UK, 76 mins, b/w
Dir: Lance Comfort
Stars: William Franklyn, Moira Redmond
Rating: ★★★

William Franklyn had one of his best film roles (as an amnesia victim) in this black little thriller. You'll recognise many of the supporting cast, including Anthony Booth, Nanette Newman in a rare bad-girl role, Nigel Green, Leonard Sachs and veteran actor John Stuart.

Pittsburgh ○

1942, US, 90 mins, b/w
Dir: Lewis Seiler
Stars: Marlene Dietrich, Randolph Scott, John Wayne
Rating: ★★★

This lusty mixture of romance and melodrama, seasoned with flag waving World War Two propaganda, reunited the stars of the same year's *The Spoilers* and once again found John Wayne and Randolph Scott as rivals for the favours of Marlene Dietrich. Scott may get the girl, but Wayne has the more substantial role and does well as a man who is ready to ride roughshod over everyone to get to the top but finally comes to see the folly of his ways. The director, Lewis Seiler, stages some vigorous action scenes but tends to take much of the film at rather too sedate a pace. The stars, however, carry all before them.

PJ

See: New Face in Hell

Place in the Sun, A ○

1951, US, 122 mins, b/w
Dir: George Stevens
Stars: Montgomery Clift, Elizabeth Taylor, Shelley Winters
Rating: ★★★

A powerful version of Theodore Dreiser's story *An American Tragedy*, filmed 20 years previously under its original title in a now-forgotten version. Director George Stevens made sure his would be the film everyone would remember, by getting vivid per-

P

formances from a cast headed by Montgomery Clift as the poor-born young man anxious to climb the social ladder. The film was made in the same year (1951) as *A Streetcar Named Desire* and *An American in Paris*, and there was hot competition for Oscars. But it came away with six, including one for Stevens as best director. It hasn't worn too well by today's standards, but isolated moments still catch the breath.

Place of One's Own, A ○
1945, UK, 92 mins, b/w
Dir: Bernard Knowles
Stars: Margaret Lockwood, James Mason, Barbara Mullen, Dennis Price
Rating: ★★★

'A fine piece of work... gripping, marvellous, outstanding, eerie, perky, beautiful, lovely and different.' Thus was how the film was described on its first appearance by no less a critic than C A Lejeune. It's an elegant ghost story that will raise the hackles on your neck, but without any of today's obligatory trimmings of sex and gore. James Mason is first-rate in the leading role.

Places in the Heart ◐ ⓥ
1984, US, 111 mins, colour
Dir: Robert Benton
Stars: Sally Field, Lindsay Crouse, Ed Harris, John Malkovich, Danny Glover
Rating: ★★

Nice to see Sally Field in her best form, in this rather meandering rural drama, set in 1935 Texas, which won her a second Oscar. She's a widow who has somehow to fend for herself and ward off the bank whose first thought is to foreclose on the mortgage. With a few companions – the black handyman who she saves from the law when he steals from her, the sister whose husband is having an affair with his best friend's wife, the blind man foisted on her by his conniving banker relative – she plants fields of cotton and scrapes up a living while learning the hard facts of commercial life through the black man's seasoned eyes. All these elements are entertaining in themselves, as is the tornado scene in their midst, but they never quite pull together. And the ending, though 'different', just doesn't work: the structure of the film demands a big emotional climax which it doesn't get.

Plague Dogs, The ◐
1982, US, 103 mins, colour
Dir: Martin Rosen
Voice stars: John Hurt, James Bolam,

Judy Geeson
Rating: ★★★

Don't expect a cheerful or light-hearted time from this animated feature. It's a good but gloomy story with a real tearjerker ending (changed from the one in Richard Adams' book) that will leave you needing a bucket to cry in. The central characters are two dogs who, neither of them fully fit in mind and body, escape from a horrendous experimental station in England's Lake District. But the film is entirely stolen, probably at the intention of the filmmakers, by The Tod, the fell-wise fox they meet out on the moors. The dogs have scant regard for the self-serving fox, yet he twice saves their hides and finally... but that would be telling. Suffice to say that, in a world where, in contrast to Disney, total realism is demanded of the animations, The Tod survives such a personality draining approach to become a definitive character in his own right. Not suitable for younger children.

Plague of the Zombies, The ● ⓥ
1966, UK, 91 mins, colour
Dir: John Gilling
Stars: André Morell, John Carson, Diane Clare, Jacqueline Pearce
Rating: ★★★

An enjoyable Hammer horror film for late night fiends. It strives to be a little different and shows some original thought in Peter Bryan's screenplay, which has some interesting new ideas. There's one excellent nightmare sequence when the dead rise from their graves and for comic relief, the irreplacable Michael Ripper as the village policeman. 'It doesn't need me to tell you,' huffs Ripper at the start of the mayhem (you can almost see his hands on his braces), 'that there's something strange going on in the village.' Chief assets of the suspense are André Morell's very human, strong and identifiable sexagenarian hero, and John Carson's villainous squire, with a James Mason voice full of silky menace. Jacqueline Pearce is also good as the dying girl who turns into one of the zombies of the title.

Plainsman, The ○
1936, US, 92 mins, b/w
Dir: Cecil B DeMille
Stars: Gary Cooper, Jean Arthur, James Ellison
Rating: ★★★

As big as you would expect a Western from Cecil B DeMille to be, *The*

Plainsman's spectacle is balanced by the astringent, off-beat relationship between Gary Cooper, playing Wild Bill Hickok, and the delightfully squeaky-voiced Jean Arthur as Calamity Jane. The supporting cast includes those stalwart Western 'sidekicks' of the Forties and Fifties, George 'Gabby' Hayes and Fuzzy Knight, and you'll also spot Anthony Quinn as a Cheyenne Indian. Lots of action, too.

Planes, Trains and Automobiles ◐ ⓥ
1987, US, 92 mins, colour
Dir: John Hughes
Stars: Steve Martin, John Candy, Michael McKean
Rating: ★★★

A rollercoaster ride of accidents and disasters. Frazzled ad executive Steve Martin finds he's stuck with slobby salesman John Candy when his flight is cancelled and he tries to get home to his family in time for Christmas. An outrageously funny film in which Martin is the straight man to Candy's loudmouthed and uncouth buffoon. Whatever can go wrong, does, and the film is a catalogue of comic chaos., Martin is marvellous and Candy also very funny (and, at the end, quite touching) in what is arguably his best film to that time. Nice ending too.

Planet of the Apes ○ ⓥ
1967, US, 112 mins, colour
Dir: Franklin J Schaffner
Stars: Charlton Heston, Roddy McDowall, Kim Hunter
Rating: ★★★

Although its impact has perhaps been lessened by four sequels, *Planet of the Apes* was at the time of its release regarded as the most outstanding science-fiction film in years. Its director, Franklin Schaffner, succeeded in making a powerful allegory out of a book which even original author Pierre Boulle had thought unfilmable. Leon Shamroy, a veteran cinematographer who had won three Oscars, assisted him greatly, taking his cameras on location to desolate areas of Utah and Arizona to create superbly the cold, unfriendly, barren atmosphere of the planet on which Charlton Heston and his doomed fellow space-travellers crash-land at the beginning.

Plan 9 from Outer Space ○ ⓥ
1958, US, 79 mins, b/w
Dir: Edward D Wood Jr
Stars: Bela Lugosi, Tor Johnson,

Vampira, Lyle Talbot
Rating: **RB**

This ultra-cheap, ultra-ridiculous science-fiction 'shocker' won a nationwide poll in America as the worst film of all time. A bold claim you may think: but then you haven't seen the paper plates which stand in for flying saucers; or the director's wife's friend who stood in for star Bela Lugosi who died after three days of shooting; or heard director Edward D Wood's unique screenplay. Probably funniest of all is the commentator who asks the audience at the end: 'My friends, you have seen this incident based on sworn testimony. Can you prove it didn't happen?' No answers, please.

Planter's Wife, The ○
(aka: Outpost in Malaya)
1952, UK, 91 mins, b/w
Dir: Ken Annakin
Stars: Claudette Colbert, Jack Hawkins, Anthony Steel
Rating: ★★

Unusual drama about a plantation owner and his wife in Malaya of the early Fifties, facing up to the probability of a terrorist attack on their home. Although the plot lacks dramatic cohesion, the treacherous jungle atmosphere is well conjured up. Jack Hawkins is forthright and virile as the planter and Claudette Colbert competent as his wavering wife, while Ram Gopal's native servant is a skilfully drawn portrait.

Platinum Blonde ○
1931, US, 92 mins, b/w
Dir: Frank Capra
Stars: Loretta Young, Robert Williams, Jean Harlow, Reginald Owen
Rating: ★★★

Director Frank Capra's comedy about a culture clash between newspapers and high society. Loretta Young is top-billed but, as one contemporary critic put it 'runs third on footage', leaving the show to be stolen by Jean Harlow, as the 'blonde' of the title, and Robert Williams, whose bumbling, laconic personality is well-suited to the reporter who marries in haste and repents at (too much) leisure. Both Harlow and Williams were destined to die tragically young. The screenplay creates lots of likeable characters, and bluff character star Halliwell Hobbes is delightful as a snooty butler, a role in which he tended to find himself typecast.

Platoon ● ⓥ
1986, US, 120 mins, colour
Dir: Oliver Stone
Stars: Tom Berenger, Willem Dafoe, Charlie Sheen
Rating: ★★★

The first part of director Oliver Stone's Vietnam War trilogy is a bloody, brutal vision of the conflict as witnessed first hand by the ordinary foot soldiers, or 'grunts'. Forget all previous, blindly patriotic Hollywood Vietnam films such as John Wayne's *The Green Berets*: this is the reality of the conflict with no-one shown as right or wrong. It made a star out of Charlie Sheen, as the central figure through whose shell-shocked eyes we see the atrocities, and Stone cast him in his follow-up film *Wall Street*. Well down the cast you'll spot stars-in-waiting Johnny Depp and Kevin (brother of Matt) Dillon. It won Oscars for Best Picture and Best Director. Graphically violent.

Playboys, The ◑ ⓥ
1992, US, 108 mins, colour
Dir: Gillies MacKinnon
Stars: Albert Finney, Aidan Quinn, Robin Wright, Milo O'Shea, Niamh Cusack
Rating: ★★

A drop o' the Oirish – old-fashioned style. Credit director Gillies MacKinnon for wanting to get away from a) the IRA and b) an avalanche of swearing in this tinker's tale of a nubile unmarried mum who falls for a travelling carnival man while the local police sergeant, who lusts after her, threatens to ensure everything ends in tragedy. Aidan Quinn's Irish accent passes muster as the carny; rather shakier on the old brogue are Robin Wright as the girl and Albert Finney as the ruddy-cheeked sergeant. Still at least they don't stick out like sore thumbs from an otherwise genuinely Irish cast, and their film is okay in a meandering, TV drama-ish sort of way. It has a real feel of country life, and appealing performances from Milo O'Shea as the chief of the travelling 'Playboys' and Niamh Cusack as Wright's sister.

Play Dirty ◑
1968, UK, 115 mins, colour
Dir: André De Toth
Stars: Michael Caine, Nigel Davenport
Rating: ★★

Serviceable war adventure along the lines of *The Dirty Dozen*, with Michael Caine leading a unit of ex-convicts on an 'impossible' mission in World War Two North Africa. Strong performances from Nigel Green and Nigel Davenport in this rugged offering.

Player, The ● ⓥ
1992, US, 123 mins, colour
Dir: Robert Altman
Stars: Tim Robbins, Greta Scacchi, Fred Ward, Whoopi Goldberg, Richard E Grant, Peter Gallagher
Rating: ★★

Long, rambling, critically applauded black comedy which, like most Robert Altman films, starts very well and has the enticing main setting of a Hollywood studio and its surrounds. When the film sticks to the plot, it's an intriguing little number in *noir* style, but interest gradually drains away and you may even get tired before the end of trying to spot all the 65 famous guest stars who flit in and out of the real scenario (only Patrick Swayze actually ended up on the cutting-room floor). Tim Robbins is a pretty irritating lead and the original offbeat casting of Chevy Chase might have worked better. Lots of amusing in-jokes about the Hollywood scene, but most of these will undoubtedly fly right over the head of the average viewer. There's a corker of a 65-minute thriller battling to get out here, but Altman smothers it in top-dressing before the end.

Playing for Time ◑
1980, US, 130 mins, colour
Dir: Daniel Mann
Stars: Vanessa Redgrave, Jane Alexander, Maud Adams
Rating: ★★★

This grim but compelling true-life story of a woman's orchestra in Auschwitz, whose members played literally to keep themselves alive, was scripted by famous author Arthur Miller, who won a Pulitzer Prize for his fine play *Death of a Salesman*. Despite all the controversy which surrounded the selection of Vanessa Redgrave to play the central character, Jewish cabaret singer Fania Fenelon on whose memoirs the film is based, there was no dispute that her performance was a remarkable one. And Jane Alexander's account of the orchestra's leader, a niece of the great composer Mahler, also attracted much praise. In a generally admirable cast, there is a forceful performance, too, from Shirley Knight as the Nazi in charge of the women.

Play it Again, Sam ○ ⓥ
1973, US, 86 mins, colour
Dir: Herbert Ross

P

Stars: Woody Allen, Diane Keaton, Tony Roberts, Jerry Lacy
Rating: ★★★★

This Woody Allen comedy, adapted from his stage hit but directed for once not by Woody but by Herbert Ross, is a very funny, very endearing film on Allen's recurring theme, the lifelong failure. His wife has walked out and his two best friends Dick and Linda try to encourage him to score with somebody else. But Allen, nervous and weedy, is mostly at home watching old Bogart movies, and the only advice he heeds is from a fantasised Bogey. played to the hilt by Jerry Lacy. 'Don't you cook anything but those frozen TV dinners?' asks Dick. 'Who cooks 'em?' replies a despondent Allen, I suck 'em.' Falling for Linda only leads to another attack of nerves about telling Dick. 'If you want me.' he tells Linda, as they go to do the deed, 'I'll be home on the floor, having an anxiety attack.' Telling the plot isn't likely to spoil your enjoyment of a film whose incidental touches – and they are numerous – mark it out as one of the most unusual as well as one of the funniest of its year. The ending restages *Casablanca* with great panache.

Play Misty for Me ● ⓥ
1971, US, 100 mins, colour
Dir: Clint Eastwood
Stars: Clint Eastwood, Jessica Walter, Donna Mills
Rating: ★★★★

Hold tight to the edge of the armchair for as jumpy and chilling a thriller as there's been since *Psycho*. Indeed, there are many comparisons between that film and Clint Eastwood's impressive directorial debut, although it would be unfair to the plot to go into detail. Eastwood the actor unselfishly hands the spotlight to Jessica Walter, an actress much underused by the cinema, who turns in a frightening, virtuoso performance as the unbalanced young girl who starts the chills rolling by ringing up disc jockey Eastwood insistently with her requests for 'Misty'. Eastwood's regular cameraman Bruce Surtees handles the night-time photography especially well, combining with the director to extract maximum impact from the spine-jolting scenes towards the end.

Plaza Suite ○
1971, US, 110 mins, colour
Dir: Arthur Hiller
Stars: Walter Matthau, Maureen

Stapleton, Barbara Harris
Rating: ★★

That lovable grouch Walter Matthau and his famous lived-in face crop up not once but three times in this mildly amusing romp (from Neil Simon's play) with three different segments. He's very good (even though miscast) in the first episode, about a middle-aged wife (marvellous Maureen Stapleton) whose wisecracks hide her insecurities. 'Everyone cheats with their secretaries,' she chides Matthau. 'I expected something better from my husband.'

Please Sir! ○
1971, UK, 101 mins, colour
Dir: Mark Stewart
Stars: John Alderton, Deryck Guyler, Joan Sanderson
Rating: ★★★

More warm-hearted high jinks at Fenn Street Secondary School, with John Alderton, Deryck Guyler and the unruly pupils of 5C. To one who thought the TV series of this title the funniest and most original show in years, this film version was more than welcome. The performances of Alderton, Guyler and Joan Sanderson are models of comic timing.

Please Turn Over ○
1959, UK, 87 mins, b/w
Dir: Gerald Thomas
Stars: Julia Lockwood, Ted Ray, Jean Kent, Lionel Jeffries
Rating: ★★

A kind of *Return to Peyton Place* played for laughs, *Carry On* style. A young girl writes a book in which – so her fellow-townspeople believe – their intimate secrets are exposed in scandalsheet fashion. Fair fun.

Pleasure of His Company, The ○
1961, US, 114 mins, colour
Dir: George Seaton
Stars: Fred Astaire, Debbie Reynolds, Lilli Palmer, Tab Hunter
Rating: ★★★

Underrated comedy film which gives Fred Astaire full play for his dazzling dancing and sophisticated humour. Reminiscent of the British film *Quiet Wedding* with Astaire as the black sheep of the family, whose daughter (Debbie Reynolds) is about to get married. Astaire worked out his dance routines in collaboration with Hermes Pan, the dance director who masterminded almost all of Astaire's classic

film dances of the Thirties with his most famous partner, Ginger Rogers.

Plenty ● ⓥ
1985, UK, 124 mins, colour
Dir: Fred Schepisi
Stars: Meryl Streep, Charles Dance, Tracey Ullman, John Gielgud, Sting, Sam Neill
Rating: ★★★

This ambitious film, scripted by David Hare from his hit play, charts the growing social malaise in Britain in the years following World War Two. Meryl Streep gives a tour de force performance as the central character, a neurotic young woman who moves from idealism to frustration and madness in her passage through a succession of bleak political and personal events. Director Fred Schepisi, who reteamed with Streep for *A Cry in the Dark*, about the dingo baby case, here coaxed a dazzling if cold performance from her. Top marks too for another of her brilliant accent jobs. The rest of the (mostly British) cast are well up to their roles. All it lacks is passion.

Ploughman's Lunch, The ● ⓥ
1983, UK, 100 mins, colour
Dir: Richard Eyre
Stars: Jonathan Pryce, Tim Curry, Rosemary Harris, Frank Finlay
Rating: ★★★

Hailed in some quarters as a *Room at the Top* for the Eighties, this renews the collaboration between writer Ian McEwan and director Richard Eyre who had earlier worked together on *The Imitation Game* for television. It features a stunning leading performance from Jonathan Pryce as the central character, a self-seeking, hardly laudable writer who is prepared if need be to rewrite history.

Pocahontas ⊙ ⓥ
1995, US, 81 mins, colour
Dir: Mike Gabriel, Eric Goldberg
Voice Stars: Mel Gibson, Irene Bedard, Russell Means, Linda Hunt, Billy Connolly
Rating: ★★★

Only barely suitable for younger children, this is an adult-slanted cartoon that looks like an animated dry run for a Broadway musical. Not so much *Miss Saigon*, here though, as *Miss Wigwam*. For the period is 1607 when British adventurers who set sail for the New World included John Smith, a sort of English equivalent of a fearless frontiersman. Rather bizarrely voiced by Australian-raised Mel Gibson, Smith soon encounters Pocahontas, the equally intrepid daughter of an Indian chief. She introduces Smith to such strange notions as peace, harmony and love of the land. Lovingly made and breathtakingly drawn, the film has heart and emotive appeal, but rather too many human characters; animals are really marginalised here, and tinies will grow restless accordingly. And, just as we're all geared up for a mighty final battle, that pesky Pocahontas sticks her oar in again in the cause of peace. 'Too slushy and too much snogging,' said my daughter. Disney Studios, please note.

Pocketful of Miracles ○
1961, US, 130 mins, colour
Dir: Frank Capra
Stars: Glenn Ford, Bette Davis
Rating: ★★

Frank Capra's swansong was a re-working of his earlier *Lady for a Day*. Based on a Damon Runyon story, its gangsters, as always, talk tough but underneath are real pussycats. Helen Hayes was first choice to play 'Apple Annie', a drunken fruit salesperson who tries to convince her long lost daughter that she's a grand, moneyed lady. But she was on a State department tour of Russia, so Bette Davis stepped in. But the real star of the film is Peter Falk, stealing every scene he lurches through as 'Joy Boy', the chauffeur of a New York gangster. The role changed Falk's career, taking him away from the world of hoodlums and into the exalted ranks of film stardom.

Point Blank ● Ⓥ
1967, US, 92 mins, colour
Dir: John Boorman
Stars: Lee Marvin, Angie Dickinson, Keenan Wynn
Rating: ★★★

Fresh from his debut success, *Catch Us If You Can*, British director John Boorman was grabbed by Hollywood to direct two thrillers starring Lee Marvin, of which *Point Blank* was the first. In this first film, Boorman appears obsessed with vertical lines, with much of the film being shot through Venetian blinds, prison bars, concrete slats and metal grids. The picture opens with crook Marvin shot and left for dead in the deserted Alcatraz island prison. Just how he manages to swim ashore while injured – a feat that defeated fit and active characters in Clint Eastwood's *Escape from Alcatraz* – is just one of the more bizarre plot twists that

will either intrigue or leave you cold, although Boorman keeps it coming at a cracking pace.

Point Break ○ Ⓥ
1991, US, 125 mins, colour
Dir: Kathryn Bigelow
Stars: Patrick Swayze, Keanu Reeves, Gary Busey, Lori Petty, John C McGinley
Rating: ★★

Full of philosophizing in between its action scenes, this is the surfers' guide to high crime. Four surfin' 'nuts spend their spare time robbing banks as the 'Ex-Presidents Gang', wearing Carter, Reagan, Johnson and Nixon masks. The reason? Says their leader Patrick Swayze, blue eyes misting over: 'It's about the human spirit... we show them that the human spirit is still alive.' But they never shoot anyone, and never go into the banks' vaults. Enter sharp young FBI man Johnny Utah (Keanu Reeves), fresh off the shooting-range. He's hot on the trail, but sucked into the cool mysticism of the surfin' guru. Best not to ask such questions as what Reeves is doing in the FBI with a gammy leg, or why he goes back to the beach when his cover is blown, or why Swayze chooses to go for the vault on his ultimate raid. Director Kathryn Bigelow patches over script and story deficiencies here by giving us action on land, sea and in the air, including the screen's first freefall fistfight!

Point of No Return
See: The Assassin

Poison Ivy ● Ⓥ
1992, US, 90 mins, colour
Dir: Katt Shea Rubin
Stars: Drew Barrymore, Tom Skerritt, Sara Gilbert, Cheryl Ladd
Rating: ★★

A polished, adult performance by Drew Barrymore as the poisonous Ivy – a sleazy, sexy teenager who wheedles her destructive way into the lives of lonely Cooper (*Roseanne*'s Sara Gilbert), Cooper's ailing mother (an uneasily cast Cheryl Ladd) and rich alcoholic father – will be the main reason for watching this rather nasty thriller. Gilbert does well in her Bohemian misfit role, in a sometimes gripping tale of obsession, manipulation and murder, which would work better if its characters were more clearly fleshed out and without the sledgehammer direction of Katt Shea Ruben. Barrymore's quite a number in this one, though: the right role for

this talented gal must be out there somewhere.

Police Academy ● Ⓥ
1984, US, 95 mins, colour
Dir: Hugh Wilson
Stars: Steve Guttenberg, Kim Cattrall, G W Bailey, Bubba Smith
Rating: ★★★

As a cross between *Animal House* and *Airplane!*, this comedy along *Carry on Copper* lines has one big advantage over most of its kind: it's funny. Especially good is George Gaynes as the vague, even slightly touched commandant of a police academy which receives more than its fair share of misfit recruits. Director Hugh Wilson probably knows you could write the script and character developments for him, but that doesn't stop him doing the best he can with his material. His knack of getting the most out of characters and situations without ever going over the top makes for some very big laughs. You'll enjoy Bubba Smith as the tree-like black recruit who used to be a florist, G W Bailey as the sneering sergeant and, of course, the ever-beaming Steve Guttenberg at the centre of things. But Gaynes is the icing on this comic cake. Followed by five sequels, all markedly inferior.

Police Academy 2: Their First Assignment ○ Ⓥ
1985, US, 87 mins, colour
Dir: Jerry Paris
Stars: Steve Guttenberg, Colleen Camp
Rating: ★★

A predictable sequel to the first film in the series, with the accent on sight gags – a store manager has a cardboard cutout of Clint Eastwood on show to deter robbers – and humour that stems from the characters established in the first film. Cheap-looking but very, very cheerful, the film also has some nice by-play in its script, especially between the laid-back police captain and his power-hungry lieutenant.

Police Academy 3: Back In Training ○ Ⓥ
1986, US, 82 mins, colour
Dir: Jerry Paris
Stars: Steve Guttenberg, Bubba Smith
Rating: ★★

Anyone who does not know what to expect when the motley band of misfits strap on their truncheons for another madcap adventure has been walking the Himalayas for years. The team that makes the *Carry Ons* seem as subtle and sophisticated as Noel Coward are

P

back again making the streets safe to walk. The jokes come as thick and fast, hit and miss as usual and it is all done in good spirit if not always in good taste. An improvement on *Police Academy 2*, if not as good as the original.

Police Academy 4: Citizens on Patrol ○ Ⓥ

1987, US, 87 mins, colour
Dir: Jim Drake
Stars: Steve Guttenberg, Sharon Stone
Rating: ★

Predictable lunacy from the boys in blue of Washington Police Academy. The main failing of this, and in fact all six sequels, is that they neither expand upon nor exploit the characters established in the original. Instead, they offer more of the same Keystone Kops style chaos which, while avoiding all Academy Awards for excellence, nevertheless managed, as a series, to take over a billion dollars at box-offices worldwide. Steve Guttenberg's last appearance in the series, though the principal interest for Nineties' filmgoers is that superstar Sharon Stone's in it too.

Police Academy 5: Assignment Miami Beach ○ Ⓥ

1988, US, 90 mins, colour
Dir: Alan Myerson
Stars: Bubba Smith, David Graf
Rating: ★

Without Steve Guttenberg, star of the four previous *Police Academy* movies, who had wisely decided that enough was enough, the charm level in this story of the blunderers in blue manages to fall even lower. Locating the action in Miami provides a pretty picture postcard setting, but a serious lack of decent script and plot substance means that the law and order goofballs have to rely more than ever on tasteless sight gags. One funny moment when someone's hat is set alight is about the high spot; other routines make The Three Stooges look like The Marx Brothers.

Police Academy 6: City Under Siege ◐ Ⓥ

1989, US, 83 mins, colour
Dir: Peter Bonerz
Stars: Bubba Smith, David Graf
Rating: ★

More law and disorder with the asinine antics of those Police Academy underachievers. And it's more of the same with this their sixth outing. Same situations, same gags – well you

get the picture. The formula is looking decidedly tired now and you may find yourself nodding off, too. You might get a couple of laughs out of it, but none you haven't had before. Still, number seven followed.

Pollyanna ⊙

1960, US, 134 mins, colour
Dir: David Swift
Stars: Hayley Mills, Richard Egan, Nancy Olson, Karl Malden, Adolphe Menjou
Rating: ★★★

Somewhere in a small American town that never was, we encounter Hayley Mills as one of the do-gooders of all time, melting hearts of stone and winning a special Oscar in this massive money-spinner from the Disney studio. David Swift's easy-going direction and well-written script coat the old-fashioned exercise with a lot of charm. Jane Wyman and Nancy Olson resolutely refuse to let Hayley's urchin appeal hog the limelight, dispensing laughter and tears with a practised grace. Despite the thick sugar coating, the story is at times very entertaining.

Polly Fulton

See: B F's Daughter

Poltergeist ● Ⓥ

1982, US, 114 mins, colour
Dir: Tobe Hooper
Stars: Craig T Nelson, JoBeth Williams, Heather O'Rourke, Beatrice Straight
Rating: ★★★★★

If this film doesn't scare you, nothing ever will. Somewhere in the middle of a night of terror for a suburban American family, their cute little daughter seems to have been sucked into the TV, which has been left on by dozing (and dozy) Dad. This is only the beginning of the most sensational ghost story since *The Haunting*. If your nerves can stand the pounding director Tobe Hooper and producer-co-writer Steven Spielberg give them in the last hour of this, they're up to anything. And JoBeth Williams, as Mum, braving monsters, corpses, poltergeists and even the jaws of hell with shrieks of 'Take your hands off my babies!' will tear you right apart. The film is one superbly engineered shock upon another; from writhing wraiths to gaping ghouls and sinister spectres, the story is an orgy of horrific action that never lets up for a moment. Truly frightening, even if it ends with a delightful chilly smile. The moral: never leave your TV on at night.

Poltergeist II: The Other Side ● Ⓥ

1986, US, 86 mins, colour
Dir: Brian Gibson
Stars: JoBeth Williams, Craig T Nelson, Heather O'Rourke
Rating: ★★★

A sequel was inevitable to Tobe Hooper's film about possession in suburbia, which scared up terrific box office takings. If you've seen that, you'll understand that it's just another of those nights for the Freeling family. So please be understanding when father is possessed by a caterpillar in his tequila, mother sees armies of 19th-century religious fanatics and daughter talks to her dead granny on a toy phone. To the Freelings, it's just one of those Things – even if it is after their daughter. After all, they can simply enlist the aid of a passing Indian medicine man and battle it out with Satan's lot between the underground caverns of the dead and the jaws of hell. I mean, you'd do the same yourself. All the original cast are back in harness, although Craig T Nelson, as Dad, unfortunately gets most screen time as a soppy drunk and ghoulie-spewing monster. The denouement is a bit of a let down, but the special effects and shocks up to that point are top-notch.

Poltergeist III ● Ⓥ

1988, US, 97 mins, colour
Dir: Gary Sherman
Stars: Tom Skerritt, Nancy Allen, Heather O'Rourke, Zelda Rubinstein
Rating: ★★

This third entry in the popular but increasingly derivative horror series carries a tribute to its young star, Heather O'Rourke, who died soon after filming was completed. When Craig T Nelson and JoBeth Williams (sensibly) called a halt to playing the exasperated parents of poltergeist-prone Carol Anne (O'Rourke) after episode two, the writers came up with the wheeze of sending her to plague the living daylights out of other relatives. And sure enough, as soon as she moves into the spanking new Chicago high-rise home of Nancy Allen and Tom Skerritt, mirrors crack, smoke follows her down corridors and she can hear noises in her bedroom – not to mention the ice in the swimming pool (one of the best of a bad, cheap group of special effects). Various friends and lovers get bumped off and there's a lot of mumbo-jumbo spouted by mystics and psychics, but director

Gary Sherman has no interest in supplying any meaning or motivation for what occurs in his own screenplay. Disappointing.

Pony Express ○
1953, US, 101 mins, colour
Dir: Jerry Hopper
Stars: Charlton Heston, Rhonda Fleming, Jan Sterling, Forrest Tucker
Rating: ★★

Charlton Heston, in his pre-Moses days, sits massively in the saddle in this big-scale frontier Western as Buffalo Bill Cody. Vigorous performances from Heston, Forrest Tucker and Jan Sterling and a neat study in hawk-cruel villainy from mean-featured Henry Brandon. Sturdy action fare, just short of the top class.

Pony Soldier ○
(aka: MacDonald of the Canadian Mounties)
1952, US, 82 mins, colour
Dir: Joseph M Newman
Stars: Tyrone Power, Cameron Mitchell, Thomas Gomez, Penny Edwards
Rating: ★★

Attractively photographed in pale but pretty Technicolor by Harry Jackson, this is a story of the early days of the Mounties and their relationships with the Indians. Penny Edwards, who spent many years languishing in Roy Rogers Westerns, is the heroine. Very minor stuff by Tyrone Power's standards.

Pool of London ○
1950, UK, 85 mins, b/w
Dir: Basil Dearden
Stars: Bonar Colleano, Susan Shaw, Earl Cameron
Rating: ★★★

Another of the thrillers – started by the success of It Always Rains on Sunday – that Ealing Studios made against natural backgrounds, in this case London's dockland. The theme of a friendship between black man and white girl is boldly treated for the time (and honestly acted by Earl Cameron and Susan Shaw) and leads to a moving and suspenseful twist ending. Leslie Phillips has a featured role.

Poor Cow ●
1967, UK, 104 mins, colour
Dir: Kenneth Loach
Stars: Carol White, Terence Stamp, John Bindon, Kate Williams
Rating: ★★★

Director Kenneth Loach made his name with a series of socially committed plays for television, making his feature film debut with this production in the same style: aggressively realistic but with a soft centre that ultimately tends to diffuse the drama. Poor Cow – whose principal characters happily accept lying, thieving and sexual promiscuity as a way of survival – seems very much a period piece now, but a fascinating one, with a script (Loach and Nell Dunn, from Dunn's novel) and direction that veer between small-screen compromises and big screen lyricism. What still holds the attention is Carol White's vital and beautifully conceived performance as the much put-upon heroine.

Poor Little Rich Girl ⊙
1936, US, 79 mins, b/w
Dir: Irving Cummings
Stars: Shirley Temple, Alice Faye, Jack Haley
Rating: ★★★★

Little Miss Hollywood, in one of her biggest successes, with such co-stars as Jack Haley (Tin Man in The Wizard of Oz) and Alice Faye and big production numbers. Shirley plays a millionaire's runaway daughter who teams up with two vaudevillians – giving her the chance to sing 'But Definitely', 'Oh My Goodness' and 'When I'm with You'.

Pope Must Die, The ◑ ⓥ
(aka: The Pope Must Diet)
1991, UK, 97 mins, colour
Dir: Peter Richardson
Stars: Robbie Coltrane, Beverly D'Angelo, Herbert Lom, Peter Richardson
Rating: ★★

In all but name, another 'Comic Strip' film. The boys are on uneasy territory here, and there's an amateurish edge to their crude satire of Catholicism. Except from this the 20-stone Robbie Coltrane who achieves pretty well the only real character in the film as the ex-mechanic priest who, through a clerical (!) error, finds himself elevated to the Papacy. The subsequent farce needed to carry a sharper cutting edge and a shade more seriousness to hit the mark. Lom plays a twitching Godfather to follow his twitching Dreyfuss in the Pink Panther films; like the other characters, he's drawn strictly in one dimension. The film's cardinal sin is that it has something to offend most people, but not enough laughs to convert them to its cause.

Pope Must Diet, The
See: The Pope Must Die

Popeye ⊙
1980, US, 114 mins, colour
Dir: Robert Altman
Stars: Robin Williams, Shelley Duvall, Ray Walston
Rating: ★★★

Out with the videotape, parents, for this is simple, spring-heeled fun for tiny tots, much along the lines of the famous cartoons. It's very well cast – Robin Williams looks and sounds like Popeye, Shelley Duvall is enchanting as Olive Oyl, Paul Dooley and Paul Smith are visually perfect as Wimpey and Bluto – but there are drawbacks for adults: the score is poor and there are dull patches, especially when Williams and Duvall sing two mawkish songs in a row. But the settings are charming and, although the film tends to substitute noise for pace, most children of six and under will love it. It's exuberant, ebullient and ingenuous enough to appeal to all tinies – and the young at heart.

Pork Chop Hill ○
1959, US, 97 mins, b/w
Dir: Lewis Milestone
Stars: Gregory Peck, Rip Torn, George Peppard, Harry Guardino
Rating: ★★

Bitter story of the last days of the Korean War, brought to the screen with harrowing and uncompromising clarity by Lewis Milestone who directed All Quiet on the Western Front. This was his seventh essay in the field and to it Milestone brought his characteristic striving for realism. 'One scene alone must have cost twice as much as the actual combat,' he commented. Unlike war, Hollywood demands retakes.' Gregory Peck leads a cast which includes George Peppard, Rip Torn, Robert Blake, Woody Strode, Harry Guardino and Martin Landau.

Porky's ● ⓥ
1982, US, 98 mins, colour
Dir: Bob Clark
Stars: Dan Monahan, Mark Herrier, Wyatt Knight, Roger Wilson
Rating: ★

A raucous, rowdy, bawdy college comedy with randy collegiates as its heroes and redneck night-clubbers as its villains. Although crude in its sentiments, dialogue and 'story' content (complete with the famous shower scene), it certainly isn't dull – thanks to the pacily crafted direction of Bob Clark. A huge success at box-offices worldwide. Two

P

inferior sequels with much the same cast followed.

Port Afrique O
1956, UK, 91 mins, colour
Dir: Rudolph Maté
Stars: Pier Angeli, Phil Carey
Rating: ★★

An unusual role for the late Pier Angeli as a woman of mystery, in this modern-day adventure story set in Morocco. Partly made on location, partly in Britain, where Ms Angeli made one of her best-ever films, *The Angry Silence*. In the supporting cast here: a jaunty Anthony Newley and a suave Christopher Lee, for whom fame and *Frankenstein* were still four films away. This sounds good, but proves plodding in the telling.

Portrait of a Lady, The ❶ ⓥ
1996, US/It/UK, 142 mins, colour
Dir: Jane Campion
Stars: Nicole Kidman, John Malkovich, Barbara Hershey, Viggo Mortenson, Martin Donovan, Mary-Louise Parker
Rating: ★★

Awash with artifice and artificiality, this is a well-acted but boring period piece abut two evil American dilettantes (Malkovich, Hershey) in Italy who determine to break the spirit of an innocent, single-minded heiress (Kidman), at the same time providing funds and a mother for Malkovich's facelessly obedient daughter (Sofia Coppola). Close to *Dangerous Liaisons* territory, as you can see, but director Campion takes Henry James' story and, picking up her cue from Malkovich's malevolent Macchiavelli, squeezes the life from it, keeping its emotions cramped and confined. Kidman – hard to see why she falls for such an obvious nasty – seems to be forever in tears, reflective no doubt of the character's inner pain, but trying to us, the audience, long before an open-ended climax in which she seems to love one man, then be drawn to another. A long day's journey it is, into this particular night.

Portrait of Alison
See: Postmark for Danger

Portrait of Jennie O
(aka: Jennie)
1948, US, 86 mins, b/w
Dir: William Dieterle
Stars: Jennifer Jones, Joseph Cotten, Ethel Barrymore
Rating: ★★★★

A haunting, compelling fantasy about an artist who meets a young girl off

and on through the years and begins, chillingly, to realise that she is an apparition. Excellent acting, especially from Joseph Cotten and veterans Ethel Barrymore and Lillian Gish; breathtaking black and white photography by Joseph August.

Poseidon Adventure, The O ⓥ
1972, US, 117 mins, colour
Dir: Ronald Neame
Stars: Gene Hackman, Ernest Borgnine, Roddy McDowall, Shelley Winters, Red Buttons
Rating: ★★★★

The film that started a whole wave of disaster movies in the 1970s and one of the best, though you may find it hard to take it seriously with Leslie Nielsen as the ship's captain. Nevertheless, it's one of the most human and believable of its kind, once you accept the idea that an ocean liner could flip over quickly enough to trap a huge reservoir of air under its upturned hull. Another point in its favour is that there are no Hollywood heroes, although the central characters are heroic. Gene Hackman is a Catholic priest who leads the survivors to the bottom of the ship (upturned = top, remember) hoping to break through to a rescue team. Good tense action keeps things moving, without letting you know if rescue is at hand.

Posse ❶
1975, US, 94 mins, colour
Dir: Kirk Douglas
Stars: Kirk Douglas, Bruce Dern
Rating: ★★

A Western that reverses all the traditions. Audience sympathy is invited for the outlaw (Bruce Dern), although he has shot a sheriff. And the marshal (Kirk Douglas) who heads the posse in pursuit is seen as a man consumed by ambition for high office. The killer ultimately buys all the posse men but one, by offering them money they have robbed a town to get, thinking it was to save the marshal. It's an unusual action film that nearly works. One never quite believes it all, but Kirk Douglas's direction, coupled with tight editing, almost suspends our disbelief, even if Douglas is bested in the acting stakes by Dern's steely scoundrel.

Posse ● ⓥ
1993, US, 111 mins, colour
Dir: Mario Van Peebles
Stars: Mario Van Peebles, Stephen Baldwin, Salli Richardson, Billy Zane,

Pam Grier, Richard Jordan, Blair Underwood
Rating: ★

A thoroughly pretentious black spaghetti Western, complete with old-timer Woody Strode topping and tailing the film. It has swirling camera angles, filters to make the old west look golden, an embarrassing would-be erotic love scene, and a story that's deadly dull in between the admittedly frequent bursts of violent, savage but heavily stylised action. The whole thing does end in a good old-fashioned shootout, by which time the tale has taken nearly two hours to unfold. As a document on the black experience in the old West, the film isn't nearly as interesting as it might be, thanks to the tiresome treatment. That needs to be told in a less angry and more considered way.

Posse from Hell O
1961, US, 85 mins, colour
Dir: Herbert Coleman
Stars: Audie Murphy, John Saxon, Vic Morrow
Rating: ★★★

A high quality Audie Murphy Western, distinguished by the playing of Murphy and John Saxon, as leaders of a posse chasing four killers. Their characters strike up a credible and likeable association of opposites to track the killers down. Clair Huffaker's adaptation of his own novel is sharp and literate for a Western, and the bad-guy department is also good value, comprising Vic Morrow, Rudolfo Acosta, James Bell and Lee Van Cleef.

Possessed O
1947, US, 108 mins, b/w
Dir: Curtis Bernhardt
Stars: Joan Crawford, Van Heflin, Raymond Massey, Geraldine Brooks
Rating: ★★★

Highly watchable melodrama that earned Joan Crawford an Oscar nomination, two years after she won the award for *Mildred Pierce*. The director, Curtis Bernhardt, had a penchant for psychological dramas, notably in *Conflict* and *The High Wall*, and he skilfully evokes the events and surroundings which chip away at the Crawford character's mental control. The result, right from the dreamlike opening sequences, is absorbing from start to finish.

Postcards from the Edge
❶ ⓥ
1990, US, 101 mins, colour
Dir: Mike Nichols

Stars: Meryl Streep, Shirley MacLaine, Dennis Quaid, Gene Hackman, Richard Dreyfuss
Rating: ★★★★★

It's a pity that Carrie Fisher's real talent – for writing, which far outshines her acting abilities – had to come to light in such a cathartic and traumatic way. For, despite the usual disclaimers in these *romans à clef*, this is essentially the story of her relationship with her mother, musical superstar Debbie Reynolds. Fortunately, their shouting matches are punctuated with stretches of wickedly funny humour that makes you relish the thought of Fisher writing an out-and-out comedy. Streep, a little too old but great anyway, is the daughter whose wisecracks for every occasion thinly veil an inner bitterness and confusion. MacLaine matches her as the mother who tells her 'Sing me one of your old numbers from my act.' She gets the very best of a script that drips with gems of wit and pearls of wisdom. And who's that singing for Streep in the musical numbers? Ha! Who would dare dub Meryl? It's her, of course – and terrific too.

Postman Always Rings Twice, The ○
1946, US, 113 mins, b/w
Dir: Tay Garnett
Stars: Lana Turner, John Garfield
Rating: ★★★★

A hard-hitting *film noir* smouldering with sexual sparks in an era when Hollywood could hardly film James M Caine's steamy novel in its original form. Lana Turner in white is the angel from hell who seduces John Garfield's grubby drifter into a nightmare world of attempted murder, as he strives to get rid of Turner's unwanted husband (a performance of pathetic brilliance by Cecil Kellaway). Turner was rarely better and Hume Cronyn gives superb support in the film's later stages. A classic, stylishly, purposefully directed by Tay Garnett, and simply streets ahead of the sweaty, oversexed remake with Jack Nicholson and Jessica Lange many years later.

Postman Always Rings Twice, The ● ⓥ
1981, US, 123 mins, colour
Dir: Rob Rafelson
Stars: Jack Nicholson, Jessica Lange
Rating: ★★

A no-holds-barred, steamy remake of the classic 1946 MGM film, based on the controversial and once-banned novel by James M Cain. Jack Nicholson

is nothing less than his typically audacious best, but the film's real find is Jessica Lange (in the role made famous by Lana Turner). Nothing in the remake of *King Kong* or Bob Fosse's *All That Jazz* prepared us for her amazing acting range, which director Bob Rafelson skilfully exploits. However, David Mamet's script piles on the twists and ends up too plot-heavy for its own good. But the power and passion of the central performances just about bring this deeply unpleasant film home.

Postmark for Danger ○
(aka: Portrait of Alison)
1955, UK, 84 mins, b/w
Dir: Guy Green
Stars: Robert Beatty, Terry Moore, William Sylvester
Rating: ★★

As with so many British co-features of the Fifties, the producers of this neat thriller imported an American star – in this case Terry Moore – to give their film appeal at the box-office in the United States. Moore acquits herself well in this screen version of a television serial by the prolific Francis Durbridge, creator of detective Paul Temple. Cinematographer-turned-director Guy Green handles the twists and red herrings effectively.

Powder ● ⓘ ⓥ
1996, US, 112 mins, colour
Dir: Victor Salva
Stars: Sean Patrick Flanery, Mary Steenburgen, Jeff Goldblum, Lance Henriksen
Rating: ★★

An intriguing idea is allowed to go for very little here, thanks to inept writing and direction that nullifies the actors' efforts. Powder is a freak of nature. His mother hit by lightning when she was pregnant, he has a hairless, all-white appearance which alienates him from his fellows (and the people of the town). He also has remarkable powers, including the ability to act as an electricity conductor, telekinesis and an insight into the human condition akin to genius. An over-use of religious symbolism disables the film towards the end, but Flanery, as Powder, and Henriksen, as the local sheriff trying to make peace with his dying mother, still manage to touch the heart in spite of the inferior material with which they're working.

Powder River ○
1953, US, 78 mins, colour
Dir: Louis King

Stars: Rory Calhoun, Cameron Mitchell, Corinne Calvet, Penny Edwards
Rating: ★★★

Cameron Mitchell walks away with the acting honours in this rousing Western from the 20th Century-Fox stable. It's full of all the best ingredients, including gunfights that shatter the mirror behind the bar, and fist fights that threaten to shatter the jaws of the participants. But characterisation is not ignored in Louis King's fresh and vigorous direction and Edward Cronjager's bright Technicolor photography brings the small mining town of the title to vivid life.

Power ● ⓘ ⓥ
1985, US, 111 mins, colour
Dir: Sidney Lumet
Stars: Richard Gere, Julie Christie, Gene Hackman, Denzel Washington
Rating: ★

This trite and often downright embarrassing tale of politics and media manipulation marked a real low point in the career of Richard Gere. He's an amoral image-maker whose services, packaging politicians for a TV-orientated society, guarantee success. His offices, wardrobe, and fee of $25,000 a month are witness to his ability. But things go wrong when he takes on a new client. All the plot twists are well telegraphed in a script that doesn't come anywhere near director Sidney Lumet's corrosive exposé of television in *Network*. Julie Christie and Kate Capshaw add love interest, but their characters are bland cyphers.

Powwow Highway ●
1988, US, 87 mins, colour
Dir: Jonathan Wacks
Stars: A Martinez, Gary Farmer, Amanda Wyss, Graham Greene
Rating: ★★

Americans do love their road movies – long-held shots of cars travelling along the highway to twangy musical accompaniment. This story of modern Indians trying to fight for their rights is not too bad once it gets going, but it does take a long time for its events to gain momentum. A Martinez is the political activist whose sister is jailed on a trumped-up charge in far-away Santa Fe, as soon as he shows signs of throwing a spanner in the works of unscrupulous whites seeking to do the native Americans down over the riches of their lands. The bad guys reckon without his man-mountain friend (Gary Farmer), who buys a clapped-out Buick and sets out with Martinez for Santa Fe, discovering himself as a

P

spirited warrior on the way. Once the Indians hit town the film takes wing, but that's in the last half-hour and it's a heap long trek, my braves, till then.

Prayer for the Dying, A ● Ⓥ
1987, UK, 108 mins, colour
Dir: Mike Figgis
Stars: Mickey Rourke, Bob Hoskins, Alan Bates, Sammi Davis, Liam Neeson, Alison Doody
Rating: ★★

Streaks of reverence and sentimentality, plus uncertainties of casting, fatally flaw this often interesting, well paced and rarely boring thriller about an IRA hit-man on the run. Fallon (Mickey Rourke), sickened by the killing of innocent people in Northern Ireland, has come to England where he is sought by the IRA, the police and an underworld kingpin (Alan Bates), who wants a killing from Fallon in return for a passport and money. It seems strange that a man with nowhere to run should go for such a deal, but the execution is duly carried out, triggering off the rest of the plot in which a priest (Bob Hoskins) witnesses the murder, only to be silenced by Fallon's admissions in the Confessional. Rourke, sporting a decent Irish brogue, makes a good job of the lonely Fallon, while it's sad to see Bates so over-the-top in an unworthy role. Action scenes are toughly, sharply staged and the film rarely seems its length.

Precinct 45: Los Angeles Police
See: The New Centurions

Predator ● Ⓥ
1987, US, 107 mins, colour
Dir: John McTiernan
Stars: Arnold Schwarzenegger, Carl Weathers, Elpidia Carrillo
Rating: ★★★

A semi-remake of *Alien*, told in terms of jungle warfare, this is a violent, brutal and exciting science-fiction thriller that scales new heights of savagery even by the standards of previous Arnold Schwarzenegger films. It would be nice not to be able to forecast the ending of one of these crescendoes of death, but we all know that Big Arnie will triumph in the end, even over an eight-foot-tall, nearly invisible alien with an armoury of sophisticated weapons that tear you apart. So we must sit through the dispatch of his comrades one by one before the final showdown comes, leaving the sheer mechanics of the thing to keep our in-terest buzzing, which they do, especially the semi-invisibility which is very well realised.

Predator 2 ● Ⓥ
1990, US, 107 mins, colour
Dir: Stephen Hopkins
Stars: Danny Glover, Kevin Peter Hall, Gary Busey, Ruben Blades, Maria Conchita Alonso, Robert Davi
Rating: ★★★

What with Colombian and Jamaican drug dealers ruling the streets, and police getting mown down by the precinct-full, the last thing the city's finest of the near future needs is an alien predator on the loose. Yet that's just what it gets and street cop Glover is out to nail his hide, even if it means getting in the way of a special unit led by Busey, who knows the alien's on the rampage but wants him alive. The result is a thoroughly unpleasant but undeniably thrilling action film, with a strong cast giving sweatily good value to their abrasive roles. The last 15 minutes, with a just-one-thing-after-another structure, is particularly exciting stuff even though it makes no great sense.

Prelude to a Kiss ○ Ⓥ
1992, US, 106 mins, colour
Dir: Norman René
Stars: Meg Ryan, Alec Baldwin, Kathy Bates, Ned Beatty, Patty Duke, Stanley Tucci
Rating: ★★

After a whirlwind romance, Meg Ryan and Alec Baldwin get hitched. But things start to go seriously wrong at the wedding when the bride is kissed by a mysterious old man. Suddenly, she isn't herself any more. A neat twist makes this amusing story that little bit different, with Baldwin trying to figure out what on earth (or elsewhere?) has happened. An enjoyable romp, this, although it does leave a lot of questions unanswered. Since Ryan is as enchanting as ever, it's just a pity they couldn't have done more with such a highly original idea.

Preacher's Wife, The ⊙ Ⓥ
1996, US, 124 mins, colour
Dir: Penny Marshall
Stars: Denzel Washington, Whitney Houston, Courtney B Vance, Gregory Hines, Jennifer Lewis, Loretta Devine
Rating: ★★

Some of the old magic still clings to this hectoring, squeaky-clean remake of the old Cary Grant/Loretta Young hit *The Bishop's Wife*. But its re-shaping into a vanity project for Whitney Houston, who sings nicely but far too often, only underlines the narrative's more tedious and sentimental stretches. Denzel Washington, as the angel sent down to earth to deal with the problems of a Baptist minister and his wife, glides through the film with surprisingly little charm – and no rapport with his co-stars, the best of whom by far is Courtney B Vance, who offers a strikingly sincere portrait of the minister, whose humanity the rest of the cast would have done well to copy.

Preaching to the Perverted ● Ⓥ
1997, UK, 99 mins, colour
Dir: Stuart Urban
Stars: Guinevere Turner, Christien Anholt, Tom Bell, Georgina Hale, Julie Graham
Rating: RB

More European Script Fund money down the drain. This is a very rude (and very bad) fetishist farce in *Confessions* vein about an MP (Bell) and his lackey (Anholt) attempting to prove immoral and unlawful acts charges against an S & M club with whose dominatrix owner (Turner) the lackey inevitably falls in love. The club itself is rather well done, although there's far too much of it. And Graham is quite sexy as the owner's lesbian henchperson. But nothing else is remotely titillating (or funny) in this repulsive, unpleasant and almost unwatchable farrago. Tom Bell, once an actor of integrity, hits rock bottom (no pun intended) in this one.

Presenting Lily Mars ○
1943, US, 104 mins, b/w
Dir: Norman Taurog
Stars: Judy Garland, Van Heflin
Rating: ★★★

Joe Pastemak's second vehicle as producer for MGM is a budget-conscious black-and-white musical with a good crop of songs and the ineffable advantage of Judy Garland as star. The legendary Judy was not yet 21 when she made the film, but her name now sold tickets on its own and, when she sang, a film came alive. As Lily Mars, a small-town girl who makes it to the big time on Broadway, Judy sings a lot. But one song is special – a duet sung by Judy with veteran character actor Connie Gilchrist. Beautifully staged by director Norman Taurog, the number, 'Every Little Movement', is a combination of acting, singing and choreographed movement that brings a tear to the eye. There's a big finish too, in the MGM style – but only because studio boss Louis B Mayer insisted on it. They called in dance director Charles Walters, threw what they had in the dustbin, and re-shot the last few minutes from top to bottom.

President's Analyst, The ○
1967, US, 107 mins, colour
Dir: Theodore J Flicker
Stars: James Coburn, Joan Delaney
Rating: ★★★★★

This brilliantly funny and inventive satire was ahead of its time (and therefore failed to find an audience) and remains by far and away the best film that director Theodore J Flicker ever made. The script (also by Flicker) is sharp and witty and the film, with the panther-like James Coburn at the centre of its action, rollicks along from one outrageous incident to another with a never-slackening pace. Stay tuned for the glorious finale involving the Telephone Company. The whole enterprise is an unexpected treat.

Presidio, The ● ⓥ
1988, US, 98 mins, colour
Dir: Peter Hyams
Stars: Sean Connery, Mark Harmon, Meg Ryan, Jack Warden
Rating: ★★

The well-worn cop thriller theme of two opposites having to work together despite not liking each other is given a military/civilian twist in this well-paced film. A military policeman is shot checking out a break-in at the officers' club and civilian cop Jay Austin (Mark Harmon) is called in to investigate. An ex-soldier, he has to team up with his old commanding officer (Sean Connery). Austin was discharged from the service for trying to arrest an officer, who (surprise, surprise) is a suspect in the murder case. Strong performances from Connery and Meg Ryan as his daughter Donna almost lift this film above the average. Harmon, on the other hand, is a little bland and doesn't quite carry conviction.

Press for Time ⊙
1966, UK, 102 mins, colour
Dir: Robert Asher
Stars: Norman Wisdom, Derek Bond, Angela Browne
Rating: ★

The last in Norman Wisdom's long string of madcap comedies for the Rank Organisation, this one casts him

as a hapless reporter and gives him the chance to do a mini Alec Guinness by playing four different parts. Pretty nearly laughless: the star and studio called it a day after this one.

Presumed Innocent ● ⓥ
1990, US, 126 mins, colour
Dir: Alan J Pakula
Stars: Harrison Ford, Greta Scacchi, Brian Dennehy, Raul Julia, Bonnie Bedelia
Rating: ★★★★

While other genres come and go in cycles, the courtroom drama marches on. Every couple of years, Hollywood throws up a lengthy, well-scripted legal labyrinth that engrosses everyone, right up to the twist surprise ending. This was the 1990 offering, given additional clout as the guy presumed innocent until proven guilty is played by harassed-looking Harrison Ford. Twist number one is that Ford is a top prosecuting attorney himself and his alleged murder victim a beautiful, self-serving attorney in his own department. That's the trigger for the plot and, if red herrings are rather strenuously spread across our path in the cause of one suspect, the identity of the killer will baffle almost everyone until at best a couple of minutes before it's revealed. Occasional dull patches, loose ends and improbabilities can't prevent the thing from exercising a grip and a fascination to the very end. Good performances from Ford, Julia (his lawyer), Bedelia (his wife), Scacchi (the mistress) and others.

Pretty Baby ○
1950, US, 92 mins, b/w
Dir: Bretaigne Windust
Stars: Betsy Drake, Dennis Morgan, Zachary Scott, Edmund Gwenn
Rating: ★★★★

Delightful romantic comedy with the enchanting Betsy Drake as the girl whose blanket-wrapped doll brings her a whole new life. Edmund Gwenn is his engaging self as the crusty old tycoon who takes a shine to her, unaware that her 'baby' is a doll she uses to get her a seat on the subway. The screenplay by Everett Freeman and Harry Kurnitz has lots of laughs and funny situations.

Pretty in Pink ◐ ⓥ
1986, US, 99 mins, colour
Dir: Howard Deutch
Stars: Motly Ringwald, Harry Dean Stanton, Andrew McCarthy, Jon Cryer,

James Spader
Rating: ★★

A pretty weird (but hugely successful) movie from the John Hughes factory, in that it's odd anyone would still want to make a poor-girl-being-asked-to-the-prom-by-rich-boy film that didn't amount to any more than that. Given that its elements have been used in countless other films, though, there's a lot of Acting going on here with a capital A, especially from Molly Ringwald and Andrew McCarthy as the couple concerned, both shifting and twitching away like mad, but failing to avoid being upstaged both by Jon Cryer as her unrequited Teddy-Boy-style love, and by Harry Dean Stanton as the heroine's disarming father, his five o'-clock shadow as permanent as his unemployment.

Pretty Maids All in a Row ●
1971, US, 95 mins, colour
Dir: Roger Vadim
Stars: Rock Hudson, Angie Dickinson, Telly Savalas
Rating: ★

It's not surprising that Angie Dickinson seems sexier than ever before in this campus murder thriller – the director is Frenchman Roger Vadim, who moulded the careers of Brigitte Bardot ,Catherine Deneuve and other French femmes fatales. The film itself is the usual Vadim jumble, effective only in flashes. But Ms Dickinson's the girl to watch: she almost sets the screen on fire. The casting of Telly Savalas as the policeman on the case seems all too inevitable in the height of his fame as Kojak. But, when this film was made, the part of police captain Surcher got him away from a run of psychopathic villains.

Pretty Poison ◑
1968, US, 89 mins, colour
Dir: Noel Black
Stars: Anthony Perkins, Tuesday Weld
Rating: ★★★★

A very chilly psycho-drama with Anthony Perkins as an arsonist who joins forces with a young blonde thrillseeker (Tuesday Weld) on his latest sabotage mission, only to find that her fluffy exterior conceals an unbalanced mind of pure evil. Very soon she has spiralled out of control. A one-of-a-kind movie with a very effective performance by Perkins and a simply amazing one by Weld, who rarely got the parts she deserved in the movies, but really rose to the occasion when

P

she did. A very disturbing movie in which things keep going from bad to worse, especially for Perkins. The best film of director Noel Black, who never made anything half as good again. Here he rounds the story off with a beautifully conceived and highly satisfactory tailpiece.

Pretty Woman ❶ Ⓥ

1990, US, 117 mins, colour
Dir: Garry Marshall
Stars: Richard Gere, Julia Roberts, Ralph Bellamy, Laura San Giacomo, Hector Elizondo
Rating: ★★★★★

Romantic comedy makes a comeback in style – even with a few tears at the end. Hollywood hooker meets millionaire wheeler-dealer. At first he's just amused, she's bemused. But then wham! It is, as a character reminds us at the end, only the stuff that dreams are made of. But here it's wrapped round a script, by J F Lawton that, 30 years ago, Rock Hudson and Paula Prentiss would have killed to lay hands on immaculately tailored to be funny, dramatic or touching as to the moment. Roberts is just adorable as the hooker: a star-making performance in the old tradition. Opposite her, Gere unexpectedly blossoms as a light romantic comedian of the very deftest touch. And there are wonderful supporting roles: Elizondo as the manager of the hotel where the action is, Patrick Richwood as the ogling night elevator boy who can't believe it all, and Jason Alexander, a real slimebag as Gere's oily lawyer. Okay, so the sex is a little raunchier than the genre's used to, the language a bit saltier and the ending a tiny bit muffed. But the whole thing's so warm and funny you'll cry.

Prick Up Your Ears ● Ⓥ

1987, UK, 108 mins, colour
Dir: Stephen Frears
Stars: Gary Oldman, Alfred Molina, Vanessa Redgrave, Julie Walters
Rating: ★★★

One feels that this scabrous comedy-drama is the kind of biography that grinning satyr Joe Orton would have liked. A rampant homosexual and diamond-sharp literary talent, he lived, despite the wealth his brilliant plays brought him, in a cramped bedsit with his one-time lover, failed actor-writer Kenneth Halliwell – a relationship that inevitably led to tragedy. Alan Bennett's script, which intersperses their crises with the kind of cruel humour in which Orton revelled, keeps the story from becoming too tawdry and grim. If anything, the film underplays the natural vulgarity that gave the waspish Orton so much pleasure and provided the acid edge to his all-too-few plays.

Pride and Prejudice ○

1940, US, 118 mins, b/w
Dir: Robert Z Leonard
Stars: Greer Garson, Laurence Olivier, Mary Boland, Edmund Gwenn
Rating: ★★★★

An elegant, marvellously well-produced version of Jane Austen's book, liberally laced with charm, humour and style. Delightfully acted by a very strong cast, it's full of good things. Clark Gable, Robert Donat, Norma Shearer and Vivien Leigh were all in the running at one time for Elizabeth Bennet and Mr Darcy, the roles played eventually by Greer Garson and Laurence Olivier. But Garson and Olivier make a first-class team.

Pride and the Passion, The ○

1957, US, 131 mins, colour
Dir: Stanley Kramer
Stars: Cary Grant, Frank Sinatra, Sophia Loren
Rating: ★★

Stanley Kramer's version of C S Forester's Napoleonic adventure *The Gun* is packed with action and spectacle and gave Sophia Loren her first English-speaking role. But Cary Grant and Frank Sinatra are uncomfortably cast and Edna and Edward Anhalt's script is below par.

Pride of the Yankees, The ○ Ⓥ

1942, US, 128 mins, b/w
Dir: Sam Wood
Stars: Gary Cooper, Teresa Wright, Walter Brennan
Rating: ★★★★

Gary Cooper stars as the doomed baseball star Lou Gehrig, struck down by illness at the peak of his notable career. There's a beautifully understated performance by Cooper himself, given shortly after he had won his first Academy Award, for Sergeant York. Many baseball 'greats' of the era, including the famous Babe Ruth, appear as themselves in what, tactfully and intelligently directed by Sam Wood, remains one of the best tributes to a sporting hero ever made. Keep a very large handkerchief ready for the ending.

Primal Fear ● Ⓥ

1996, US, 130 mins, colour
Dir: Gregory Hoblit
Stars: Richard Gere, Laura Linney, Edward Norton, John Mahoney, Alfre Woodard, Frances McDormand, Terry O'Quinn
Rating: ★★★

Familiar elements. A gruesome murder. A seemingly innocent but dead-to-rights suspect. A hotshot lawyer more interested in winning than in his client's guilt or innocence. Corruption in high places revealed along the way. This would be a mediocre example of its type, but for its desire to blind you to the truth. Just as Richard Gere manipulates the jury, so writers Steve Shagan and Ann Biderman juggle with us, the audience, in an effort to conceal the real facts. The film's inevitable final twist is cleverly thought out, if rather clumsily disclosed in the final reckoning. An archbishop is murdered and disfigured and stammering altar boy Aaron (Edward Norton) is held after fleeing the scene ... but naturally this isn't the whole story. Gregory Hoblit's direction grips in bits and pieces: Gere and Norton are superior to anything else in the film. Fair fare for fans, although the title is a mystery of another kind.

Prime Cut ● Ⓥ

1972, US, 91 mins, colour
Dir: Michael Ritchie
Stars: Lee Marvin, Gene Hackman, Sissy Spacek, Angel Tompkins
Rating: ★★

A strange kettle of fish and no mistake. A gangster thriller with a Seventies touch or two, it has a poor script and variable performances but is very well directed (by Michael Ritchie) and photographed in colour at Oscar-winning level by Gene Polito. Lee Marvin plays a cool Chicago gunman sent to collect half a milllion dollars in unpaid rakeoff money from Kansas big shot Gene Hackman. Previous messengers have come back in parcels as sausage meat. There's a sleazy sub-plot involving Sissy Spacek in her major film debut, and everything builds, of course, to the final shoot-out. This is superbly realised, as Marvin battles his way through the bad guy's gunmen, in a vast field of sunflowers, under thunder-filled skies.

Prime of Miss Jean Brodie, The ❶ Ⓥ

1968, UK, 116 mins, colour
Dir: Ronald Neame

Stars: Maggie Smith, Gordon Jackson, Robert Stephens, Pamela Franklin, Celia Johnson
Rating: ★★★

A remarkable encapsulation of character by Maggie Smith as an eccentric schoolteacher in the Edinburgh of the Thirties earned her an Academy Award for this film version of the famous stage success. It's Smith you'll remember long after the fadeout, despite doughty support from Celia Johnson (excellent as her headmistress), Robert Stephens and real-life husband-and-wife Gordon Jackson and Rona Anderson.

Prince and the Pauper, The ☉
1962, UK, 89 mins, colour
Dir: Don Chaffey
Stars: Guy Williams, Sean Scully, Donald Houston, Jane Asher
Rating: ★★★

A zestful, well-staged and unjustly neglected Walt Disney version of the Mark Twain classic. Photographed in excellent colour by Paul Beeson, this is certainly the equal of the Errol Flynn film of 1937 and one way ahead of the Reed version. Director Don Chaffey has always done well at the Disney studio with adventure films aimed at younger audiences and he grips the attention throughout here, even with the old familiar story of the beggar boy who swaps places with his double, who happens to be Edward Tudor, the future king of England. Vigorous performances from the predominantly British cast, notably Donald Houston as the pauper's scurrilous father. Jane Asher makes a fetching Lady Jane Grey and Guy Williams (then a big star for Disney on TV in the *Zorro* series) acquits himself pretty well as the boys' dashing and unlikely protector.

Prince and the Pauper, The ○ Ⓥ
(aka: Crossed Swords)
1977, UK, 121 mins, colour
Dir: Richard Fleischer
Stars: Oliver Reed, Raquel Welch, Mark Lester, George C Scott
Rating: ★★

Mark Twain's classic story of twin boys, one a prince, the other a pauper, in the time of King Henry VIII, is a rattling good yarn, and has been filmed several times before. Sumptuously staged, this version really does look magnificent. George MacDonald Fraser's screenplay, however, is somewhat less splendid, and

the star cast meets its coy and often awkward phraseology with varying degrees of success. Oliver Reed, in the part once played by Errol Flynn, fares quite well as the pauper's mentor, a nobleman usurped of his castle and his woman (Raquel Welch) by his treacherous brother. George C Scott gives an extraordinary account of the King of the Beggars in a scene in which one expects the assembled cast at any moment to burst into a chorus of 'Gotta Pick a Pocket or Two'. The film's best performance is given by a little lady called Lalla Ward, all fire and steel as Young Bess.

Prince and the Showgirl, The ○ Ⓥ
1957, US, 117 mins, colour
Dir: Laurence Olivier
Stars: Laurence Olivier, Marilyn Monroe, Sybil Thorndike, Jeremy Spenser
Rating: ★★

Playwright Terence Rattigan wrings a few laughs and a tear or two from this screen version of his stage success *The Sleeping Prince*. The performances are delightful, especially Marilyn Monroe's sophisticated innocent and Sybil Thorndike's dotty dowager. Laurence Olivier provides an unselfish foil to Monroe's breathy charm, but his heavy direction puts too many brakes on the film's pace.

Prince of Darkness ● Ⓥ
1987, US, 101 mins, colour
Dir: John Carpenter
Stars: Donald Pleasence, Jameson Parker, Lisa Blount
Rating: ★★★

Slightly above average of its type, John Carpenter's onrush of horrors is a quite successful grafting together of several genres – the youngsters-in-peril film, the AntiChrist film and the *10 Little Niggers* thriller. Carpenter's own, doomy, basso profundo music sets the tone for the story of a group of scientists and graduate students who gather together in an abandoned church surrounded by zombie-like tramps, to learn the secret of a mysterious, centuries-old canister whose whirling green contents seem to be generating new life from within. Not a pretty can of worms (creatures which, along with others, swarm across the screen from time to time) but quite well realised, with an unusually understated performance from Donald Pleasence. The graduates aren't much on the whole, but then most of them are turned into zombies anyway.

Prince of Foxes ○
1949, US, 107 mins, b/w
Dir: Henry King
Stars: Tyrone Power, Orson Welles, Wanda Hendrix, Katina Paxinou, Marina Berti, Everett Sloane
Rating: ★★

Tyrone Power pageantry, in a fictional episode from the life of the Italian Renaissance despot, Cesare Borgia. Hold on tight for the scene in which Power has his eyes gouged out by Everett Sloane. But be prepared for a surprise. Pretty fiery stuff, this, with not too many dull moments and amazingly detailed photography by the awesome Leon Shamroy.

Prince of Pennsylvania, The ● Ⓥ
1988, US, 87 mins, colour
Dir: Ron Nyswaner
Stars: Keanu Reeves, Fred Ward, Bonnie Bedelia, Amy Madigan
Rating: ★★★

A cross between a rites of passage film and a black comedy – and even that doesn't quite get it. Keanu Reeves plays an angry young man who should have walked out months before on macho father Fred Ward, unfaithful mum Bonnie Bedelia and faceless younger brother. It takes an affair with cafe owner Amy Madigan and a lunatic kidnap scheme to help him see the attraction of the broad white highway. Slow to start, the film does get to you later on with its mixture of oddball characters, funny one-liners and emotional pull. Ward reveals a talent for dry comedy with his portrait of a man whose outlook is as limited as his word power. 'Sometimes', yells his wife, 'I feel I married Jimi Hendrix and woke up with Oliver North'.

Prince of Pirates ○
1953, US, 81 mins, colour
Dir: Sidney Salkow
Stars: Barbara Rush, John Derek
Rating: ★★

Spectacular action picture, with battles on sea and land, as Spain and Holland get all tangled up during the 17th century. Pretty Barbara Rush joins in the sword fights with welcome vigour. She and John Derek share the action honours as a spirited pair of Dutch patriots, and help give pace and point to the energetic pantomime.

Prince of Shadows ● Ⓥ
1991, Spain, 114 mins, colour
Dir: Pilar Miru
Stars: Terence Stamp, Patsy Kensit,

P

Geraldine James
Rating: **RB**

Drained of both colour and interest, this is no horror film (well, not in that sense) but a tired espionage thriller briefly enlivened by Patsy Kensit's quite passable impression of Rita Hayworth doing 'Put the Blame on Mame' in a nightclub scene. Terence Stamp toplines as a former hitman drawn back into the world of subterfuge to eliminate another 'traitor' (to an unnamed cause) somewhere in Spain. The story, such as it is, unfolds slowly (revealing Stamp's past assassination of an innocent man for whose wife he had fallen), but at least avoids being silly until a quite ludicrous climax which will leave you falling around the sitting-room. Poor acting and stilted, vaguely pretentious dialogue torpedo the ship beyond repair: director Pilar Miru even manages to get a rare bad performance from Geraldine James. Scarcely in colour to speak of, the film hardly even engages the interest, although it will tax your patience.

Prince of the City ●

1981, US, 167 mins, colour
Dir: Sidney Lumet
Stars: Treat Williams, Jerry Orbach, Richard Foronjy
Rating: ★★★

Director Sidney Lumet's epic treatise on police corruption makes his earlier film on a similar subject, *Serpico*, seem like a flyweight fantasy. Realist drama at its most compelling, this is the true story of NYPD detective Bob Leuci (played with intense sincerity by Treat Williams), who acceded to pressure and informed for the notorious King Commission into corruption on the force. Falling into a classic trap, Leuci (rechristened Danny Ciello in the movie) tangles with powerful forces believing that he can manipulate and control them. The results are catastrophic: from a body of 70 men Leuci considered to be his friends and compatriots, 52 are indicted, two commit suicide and one goes insane. But there's no doubt that Lumet views Leuci/Ciello not only as a victim but also as a hero. It's just a pity his film goes on so damned long, diluting its own power in progressive fashion.

Prince of Tides, The ● ⓥ

1991, US, 132 mins, colour
Dir: Barbra Streisand
Stars: Barbra Streisand, Nick Nolte,

Blythe Danner, Kate Nelligan, Jeroen Krabbé, Melinda Dillon
Rating: ★★★

A much more impressive turn in the director's chair from Barbra Streisand compared with her first, *Yentl*. This is a finely crafted, beautifully shot voyage of self-discovery. Streisand hands the spotlight to Nick Nolte's excellent, Oscar-nominated performance in the difficult role of Southern boy Tom Wingo who, when summoned to New York by his sister's psychiatrist (Streisand) after the sister has attempted suicide, must learn to reveal his repressed emotions and face the horrors in his past. You may find the only problem with this film is Streisand's own performance; she continues to impress less in straight drama than in musicals or comedies, and perhaps should have limited herself to the director's chair here. Otherwise, it's a high class weepie.

Princess and the Pirate, The ○

1944, US, 94 mins, colour
Dir: David Butler
Stars: Bob Hope, Virginia Mayo, Walter Brennan, Victor McLaglen
Rating: ★★★

One of Bob Hope's early Technicolor outings, this one made on loan from Paramount to Samuel Goldwyn. Hope plays Sylvester the Great, a conceited actor with the familiar yellow streak running right down the middle of his back, trying to save a princess (Virginia Mayo) from being kidnapped. Guess which famous guest star whisks the girl from under Hope's ski-nose at the end of the film.

Princess Bride, The ○ ⓥ

1987, US, 98 mins, colour
Dir: Rob Reiner
Stars: Cary Elwes, Mandy Patinkin, Chris Sarandon, Peter Falk
Rating: ★★

'Not just your average ho-hum fairy tale' promised the publicity for this movie. The problem is that all too often, despite some Pythonesque shafts of humour, it *is* your average ho-hum fairy tale, and sometimes its only interest lies in trying to recognise well-known stars beneath mounds of makeup: Billy Crystal and Carol Kane, for example, will surely defeat all but those in the know. The playing, though, is on the whole extremely good, especially from Chris Sarandon's James Mason-like villain. 'I've got my country's 500th anniver-

sary to arrange,' he complains, 'my wife to murder and Guilder (a neighbouring kingdom) to blame it for it. I'm swamped.' Peter Falk's storyteller does Grandpa Columbo. But Rob Reiner's direction and William Goldman's screenplay finally fall fatally between fairy tale, Flynn fantasy and outright satirical comedy.

Prince Valiant ○

1954, US, 100 mins, colour
Dir: Henry Hathaway
Stars: Robert Wagner, James Mason, Janet Leigh, Debra Paget, Sterling Hayden, Victor McLaglen, Brian Aherne
Rating: ★★

This period adventure was based on a famous comic strip. James Mason easily steals the acting honours as the villainous Sir Brack, leaving Janet Leigh with little to do but look chastely desirable as usual. It took *Psycho* to prove what a good actress she really is. Robert Wagner (with a page-boy bob) plays the spirited young Valiant, and the whole cast is far too distinguished to be appearing in this sort of nonsense. In any case, the real heroes are director Henry Hathaway and his cameraman Lucien Ballard: they make the jousting scenes and the burning of a Viking stronghold colourful and vividly exciting.

Prince Who Was a Thief, The ○

1950, US, 88 mins, colour
Dir: Rudolph Maté
Stars: Tony Curtis, Piper Laurie, Everett Sloane
Rating: ★★

The totally unexpected box-office success of this slight romantic *Arabian Nights* adventure shot Bernie Schwartz, alias Mr Curtis, and Rosetta Jacobs, alias Ms Laurie, to stardom. Another look at *The Prince Who Was a Thief* today reveals it to be a bit short on action, but Piper really was a pretty package, and it was worth the price of admission to see her slithering through a maze of iron bars. Former cameraman Rudolph Maté directs it all in stylish Technicolor.

Prison ● ⓥ

1987, US, 102 mins, colour
Dir: Renny Harlin
Stars: Lane Smith, Viggo Mortensen, Chelsea Field, Lincoln Kilpatrick
Rating: ★★★★

There can't be too many horror films set inside a prison. Director Renny

Harlin and writer C Courtney Joiner give both styles of film full value here, combining the toughest possible elements from both genres. The sadistic warden (Lane Smith, a Richard Nixon lookalike hidden for years in character roles) is the villain of the piece, a man who had an innocent prisoner sent to the chair for an 'inside' killing he didn't commit. The hero is his victim, returning supernaturally from the grave when the prison in which they clashed is reopened years later. The inevitable deaths that start to happen once the avenging force is released are ingeniouly contrived and staged with considerable panache. Horror fans can look forward to a thoroughly grisly night out on the town, while prison film aficionados will find that this film contains all the fondly remembered clichés tightly wrapped within some (literally) electrifying special effects. Performances are appropriately full throttle in this vivid dose of horrific hokum.

Prisoner, The ○
1955, UK, 91 mins, b/w
Dir: Peter Glenville
Stars: Alec Guinness, Jack Hawkins
Rating: ★★★★

This gripping drama was inspired by the real-life case of Hungarian Cardinal Mindszenty who was jailed by the Nazis in 1944 for not allowing his Catholic parishioners to say a mass and sing a Nazi-ordered 'Te Deum' for 'the liberation of Budapest from the Jews'. Then, in 1948, he rebelled against Communist domination and was put in solitary confinement, an act that led to the action shown in this film. Although it remains very much a filmed stage play, Alec Guinness as the Cardinal and Jack Hawkins as a police state psychologist, are never less than compulsively watchable. It ranks as one of the finest films in both actors' distinguished careers.

Prisoner of Second Avenue, The ○
1975, US, 98 mins, colour
Dir: Melvin Frank
Stars: Jack Lemmon, Anne Bancroft, Gene Saks
Rating: ★★

Jack Lemmon plays an advertising executive who has a nervous breakdown after losing his job and Anne Bancroft his supportive wife in this Neil Simon comedy. Replete with typical Simon one-liners and sharp dialogue, this is still only slightly better than the

strangely similar (in tone, anyway) *The Out-of-Towners,* which also starred Lemmon. Nevertheless, there's plenty to enjoy, with Lemmon and Bancroft on top form. Sharp eyes will spot Sylvester Stallone in a scene set in Central Park.

Prisoner of Zenda, The ○ Ⓥ
1979, UK, 105 mins, colour
Dir: Richard Quine
Stars: Peter Sellers, Lynne Frederick, Lionel Jeffries, Eike Sommer
Rating: ★★★

A spoof by Dick Clement and Ian La Frenais of the famous old swashbuckler by Anthony Hope about the commoner forced to impersonate a weak and beleaguered king. Here it's Peter Sellers in the dual role, but Hope who has the last laugh, for the thrills work better than the comedy. Sellers is not too funny as the foppish king, but good as the London cabby who steps into his shoes. Stuart Wilson, whose Rupert of Hentzau is a very well-modulated parody of Douglas Fairbanks Jr, and Jeremy Kemp are stylishly over the top as the villains, while Lynne Frederick, Elke Sommer and Catherine Schell (even though the latter two roles could have been telescoped into one) are as pretty a trio of doll-faced, well-bosomed but animated ladies fayre as you could wish to collect. Pleasant entertainment then: just don't expect to laugh too much.

Prisoner of Zenda, The ○
1937, US, 101 mins, b/w
Dir: John Cromwell
Stars: Ronald Colman, Madeleine Carroll, Douglas Fairbanks Jr, Mary Astor
Rating: ★★★★

This Selznick production, a blockbuster of its day, is vastly superior to the MGM remake of 1953, even though the final duel in that (between Stewart Granger and James Mason) was almost as good as the one here between Ronald Colman and Douglas Fairbanks Junior. Colman plays the commoner forced to impersonate a king in a mythical European country, a situation that gives rise to some moments from which director John Cromwell manages to extract the maximum of tension. There had been two silent versions of Anthony Hope's famous novel of swordplay, intrigue and derring-do, but this justly eclipsed them both. And, in Fairbanks as Rupert of Hentzau, and Raymond

Massey as Black Michael, it produced two of the outstanding villains of Thirties' action film. The rest of the casting is exemplary and with good reason the film has never lost its reputation of being one of the most outstanding adventure-romances ever made.

Prisoner of Zenda, The ○ Ⓥ
1952, US, 100 mins, colour
Dir: Richard Thorpe
Stars: Stewart Granger, Deborah Kerr, James Mason, Louis Calhern
Rating: ★★★

The fifth of six film versions of Anthony Hope's famous adventure story of royal impersonation is more swish-buckler than swashbuckler. James Mason is miscast as Granger's adversary, Rupert of Hentzau, with a Rommel haircut and a penchant for heel-clicking. Nonetheless, the story still carries its own excitement, and the final duel scene is almost as good as the original. Lewis Stone, who played the dual leading role in a silent version made in 1922, has a small cameo here as the Cardinal.

Prisoners of the Sun
See: Blood Oath

Private Benjamin ◐ Ⓥ
1980, US, 110 mins, colour
Dir: Howard Zieff
Stars: Goldie Hawn, Eileen Brennan, Armand Assante, Sam Wanamaker
Rating: ★★★

A comedy-drama-romance that packs all its fun in the first half, with Goldie Hawn as a fairly scatterbrained Jewish girl who enlists in the army. The basic training she undergoes provides good fun in the Abbott and Costello tradition, and Goldie's triumph against the odds is both funny and uplifting. The second half of this film is rather a different kettle of fish. From the moment Colonel Robert Webber tries to force himself on our heroine in an aircraft after she has (somewhat unconvincingly) chickened out of jumping, the film dips into a romantic nosedive. With Goldie's involvement with a French doctor, the story, suddenly shot in pastel colours, loses the spirit of adventure that has sustained it so well. Still, for the fun of the first 50 minutes, it remains well worth watching, and won Goldie an Oscar nomination.

Private Function, A ◐ Ⓥ
1984, UK, 94 mins, colour
Dir: Malcolm Mowbray

P

Stars: Michael Palin, Maggie Smith,
Denholm Elliott, Richard Griffiths
Rating: ★★★

Only the best ingredients are used in
this feast of a film. There is the
prizewinning screenplay by Alan
Bennett, Malcolm Mowbray's sharply
observant direction and, tastiest of all,
a hand-picked cast headed by the delicious Maggie Smith and spiced with
the talents of such character stars as
Denholm Elliott, Richard Griffiths, Liz
Smith and Alison Steadman. The result is a comedy in the tradition of
Ealing at its prime in which the quirks
and eccentricities of the English mid-
dle-classes are gently, always
affectionately but nevertheless sharply
lampooned. The easily offended may
not like the messier aspects of this
shaggy Pig story.

Private Hell ○
1954, US, 81 mins, b/w
Dir: Don Siegel
Stars: Ida Lupino, Steve Cochran,
Howard Duff, Dorothy Malone
Rating: ★★

Despite an excellent cast, director
(Don Siegel) and director of photography (Burnett Guffey), this
independent production (looking as if
it cost no more than a handful of dollars) comes through as just an average
crime drama. Ida Lupino is good, as
usual. She also helped to write the
script.

Private Life of Henry VIII, The ○ ⓥ
1933, UK, 97 mins, b/w
Dir: Alexander Korda
Stars: Charles Laughton, Robert Donat,
Merle Oberon, Binnie Barnes, Eisa
Lanchester, Wendy Barrie
Rating: ★★★★

Classic Alexander Korda-directed
satirical dissection of Tudor court life.
Laughton gives probably his finest
performance on screen as the lusty
king, particularly in the section concerning the marriage to Anne of
Cleves. Perhaps the reason for success was that Anne was played by
Elsa Lanchester, Laughton's wife in
real life.

Private Life of Sherfock Holmes, The ○ ⓥ
1969, UK, 125 mins, colour
Dir: Billy Wilder
Stars: Robert Stephens, Colin Blakely,
Genevieve Page, Christopher Lee
Rating: ★★★

Director Billy Wilder's personal and
rather melancholy look at the Baker
Street sleuth comes at you in sections
and indeed was originally a much
longer film running close to three and
a half hours. Robert Stephens is
whimsical as Holmes, Irene Handl
priceless as Mrs Hudson. Lyrical interludes don't work as well as the parts
that owe most to Conan Doyle, but
the enterprise sparkles with wit and
polish and the ending is as exciting as
it is preposterous.

Private Lives of Elizabeth and Essex, The ○ ⓥ
1939, US, 100 mins, colour
Dir: Michael Curtiz
Stars: Bette Davis, Errol Flynn, Olivia de
Havilland, Vincent Price
Rating; ★★★

A talky slice of history with Bette
Davis, in her first Technicolor film, as
the Virgin Queen, Elizabeth I, whose
love affair with the Earl of Essex led
to his downfall and execution. Davis,
the reigning queen of the Warners studio with no less than three films on
release in 1939, wanted Laurence
Olivier to play her suitor, but was
overruled by boss Jack L Warner in
favour of the studio's swashbuckling
champ Errol Flynn. Seeking the ut-
most authenticity, Davis shaved the
front of her head and her eyebrows
and insisted on ugly bags under her
eyes. In the final analysis, Davis stole
the acting honours with one contemporary critic noting, 'Bette Davis's
Elizabeth is a strong, resolute, glam-
our-skimping characterisation against
which Mr Flynn's Essex has about as
much chance as a beanshooter against
a tank.'

Privates on Parade ◑
1982, UK, 100 mins, colour
Dir: Michael Blakemore
Stars: John Cleese, Denis Quilley, Nicola
Pagett
Rating: ★★

An *Oh! What a Lovely War* of the
Malayan jungle in 1948 that despite
enjoyable individual performances,
snappy choreography and a good
many bright moments, never quite
works. Being an Eighties' product, it
tries to be all things to all filmgoers, injecting real drama, real sex and real
blood into the central theme of a camp
(in more ways than one) concert. But
there are great compensations, notably
John Cleese, presenting Basil Fawlty in
uniform as the God-fearing, high-step-
ping major, and Denis Quilley, richly

pleasurable as the perfumed Queen of
the Boards – a really expert performance that never puts a crooked finger
wrong. Perhaps the most unexpected
hit of the show is Nicola Pagett, absolutely bursting with talent as the
Welsh-Indian (difficult accent but she
just about gets it) 'black velvet' girl
who keeps the camp's few heterosexual boys in line (waiting). The
interludes from the unit's show are so
good that the fringe drama could be
better than it is and still not stand up
to them!

Private Parts ● ⓥ
1997, US, 109 mins, colour
Dir: Betty Thomas
Stars: Howard Stern, Mary McCormack,
Robin Quivers, Fred Norris, Richard
Portnow, Mia Farrow
Rating: ★

American shock jock Howard Stern's
idea of a good time on radio is to have
big-breasted girls stripping off and having orgasms or giving him massages in
the studio. Or, he'll make jokes offending every minority in sight (there's
one really amusing one about getting
one adult point for killing 100 children
in Vietnam) or bodily function gags –
mostly about sex. Oh, and he plays
records. His rise to the top says a lot
about the American sense of humour
in the 1990s. The saddest thing about
the film of his meteoric career is that
it's almost totally unfunny, although
the odd moment – Stern is so ugly at
college even a blind girl rejects him –
does raise a chuckle. Mostly, though
this rough-and-ready number is much
like a sexploitation romp of the 1970s,
with a larger-than-life hero who alienates everybody in his life but his
audience. One's instinct is that anyone
could be this offensive if he tried – and
on this showing it could be a smart career move.

Private's Progress ○
1955, UK, 97 mins, b/w
Dir: John Boulting
Stars: Richard Attenborough, Dennis
Price, Ian Carmichael
Rating: ★★

The unexpected success of this army
comedy started – and set the pattern
for – a whole rush of popular Boulting
Brothers capers – a run that included
Brothers-in-Law and *Lucky Jim*. Ian
Carmichael, playing the first of his several dithering heroes, and
Terry-Thomas, getting the opportunity
to call his men 'an absolute shower',
both established distinct comic person-

alities that saw them through several years of crowd-pulling comedy films. It's not actually all that funny – but nearly all of the Boulting comedies that followed it were.

Private War of Major Benson, The ⊙

1955, US, 105 mins, colour
Dir: Jerry Hopper
Stars: Charlton Heston, Julie Adams
Rating: ★★★★

Credit Charlton Heston with a largely successful attempt to do something different here as the martinet commander of a military school, guying his own tough image and allowing tiny Tim Hovey to steal scenes from him left, right and centre. You'll enjoy the scene where Heston, thundering at the mite, asks him how tall he thinks he (Heston) is, and Hovey quavers about 10 feet. A film whose bright ideas all come off, this will give a lot of pleasure to family audiences. Heston makes it seem as though he were made for the part of the gruff Major Benson, Julie Adams is a capable heroine, and Hovey does admirably as the boy in a role that thrust him into the public eye for a short while as a new child star. Heartwarming laughter all the way.

Prize of Arms, A ○

1961, UK, 105 mins, b/w
Dir: Cliff Owen
Stars: Stanley Baker, Helmut Schmid, Tom Bell
Rating: ★★★

One of a long line of tough thrillers made by Stanley Baker in the Sixties. All of them had good casts and here, in small roles, you'll spot Fulton Mackay, Glynn Edwards, Patrick Magee, Roddy McMillan, Rodney Bewes and two familiar faces from the *On the Buses* TV series and films, Michael Robbins and Stephen Lewis.

Prize of Gold, A ○

1954, UK, 98 mins, colour
Dir: Mark Robson
Stars: Richard Widmark, Mai Zetterling, Nigel Patrick, George Cole
Rating: ★★

The plot of this film may be none too convincing but, under the direction of Mark Robson, it provides both entertainment and excitement in generous proportions. George Cole is very good as the British sergeant involved with tough-guy Widmark in a plan to steal a fortune in gold bullion from occupied Berlin.

Prizzi's Honor ● Ⓥ

1985, US, 129 mins, colour
Dir: John Huston
Stars: Jack Nicholson, Kathleen Turner, Robert Loggia, Anjelica Huston
Rating: ★★★★

An outrageous black comedy about two very different hitmen for the Mafia. Jack Nicholson's street-tough assassin for the Prizzi family is not the brightest of men. When his girlfriend (Anjelica Huston, deservedly winning an Oscar) tells him about Art Deco, he responds 'Art who?' Kathleen Turner's svelte blonde hired killer, on the other hand, is as different as chalk from cheese. But the mixture is pure dynamite. The air fairly crackles with sexual tension whenever Turner and Nicholson spar verbally, but the best scenes were claimed by Huston, daughter of the film's director, John Huston. Film fans will relish an appearance by B-movie actor of old, Lawrence Tierney (who took the title role in *Dillinger in* 1945) as a bald-headed (and predictably tough) cop on the take. The script credits its audience with intelligence.

Problem Child ◑ Ⓥ

1990, US, 80 mins, colour
Dir: Dennis Dugan
Stars: John Ritter, Michael Oliver, Jack Warden, Amy Yasbeck
Rating: ★

Or how not to make a comic variation on *The Bad Seed*. This repulsive comedy will turn your stomach over rather than tickle your ribs. Michael Oliver is obscenely awful as the monstrous kid Ritter and Yasbeck are unwise enough to adopt. It begins quite well, but subsequent scenes are so crude as to make the *Carry On*-films seem a tower of good taste. But then, if you like seeing cats tortured, this could be for you. Amazingly, practically the entire cast signed on for a sequel.

Problem Child 2 ◑ Ⓥ

1991, US, 88 mins, colour
Dir: Brian Levant
Stars: John Ritter, Michael Oliver, Jack Warden, Laraine Newman, Amy Yasbeck, Ivyann Schwann
Rating: RB

If you have a fondness for 'adult' comedies that delight in the disgusting, there could be something here for you. For most tastes, though, this is an unbelievably bad sequel to a gruesome original, a flatulent farce about an awful child who blows up his teacher in the toilet, accelerates a merry-go-

round to a crazy rate and makes everybody sick, and swaps medical cards on a woman he doesn't like so that she'll have plastic surgery to make her nose bigger. You may say that all this is surreal, but this is a nasty, thoroughly ill-natured film that makes *Porky's* look like a comedy classic. There are jokes about the bowel movements of dogs, and any other bodily function the writers can think of. One step forward has been made, though: instead of a custard pie fight, the characters have a pizza fight. Boy actor Michael Oliver gives another dreadful, camera-hogging performance.

Prodigal, The ○

1955, US, 114 mins, colour
Dir: Richard Thorpe
Stars: Lana Turner, Edmund Purdom
Rating: ★★

Another lavish but empty Hollywood excursion into the stories of the Bible, this was Edmund Purdom's second film venture into the realms of ancient history. And it has similar virtues to the first, *The Egyptian*. The sets and costumes are magnificent, and the supporting cast is full of interesting faces. Notable among them is that of Francis L Sullivan, one of filmland's finest fat men, as a villain, Bosra.

Producers, The ○ Ⓥ

1967, US, 88 mins, colour
Dir: Mel Brooks
Stars: Zero Mostel, Gene Wilder
Rating: ★★★

Down-and-out theatrical producer Zero Mostel and his naive accountant Gene Wilder plan to make a fortune by finding rich backers for a flop show and running off with the money. The result is *Springtime for Hitler*, a rabid musical written by a fanatical Nazi! The show is so bad, it's a roaring success. This cult classic was director Mel Brooks' first film. A vulgar and broad farce, it has something to offend everyone – and it's outrageously funny, with Mostel on top eyeball-rolling form. The scenes from the musical – goosestepping Nazis singing the show's title song – are displays of gross bad taste that will either offend or have you helpless with laughter.

Professional, The

See: Léon

Professionals, The ○

1966, US, 117 mins, colour
Dir: Richard Brooks

P

Stars: Burt Lancaster, Lee Marvin, Robert Ryan, Jack Palance, Claudia Cardinale, Ralph Bellamy
Rating: ★★★★

One of the best action-adventure films of the Sixties, epitomised, perhaps, by Burt Lancaster, biting on a cigar butt and wriggling through enemy lines with a fistful of explosive and a fuse timed to burn to the exact second. Gunfights, train ambushes and night-time raids are equally well handled as the action thunders on its way. Lancaster's deadly charm impresses – like an iron fist in a velvet glove. And director Richard Brooks' adaptation of a Frank O'Rourke novel pares the dialogue to a terse minimum, letting action and the fierce Nevada desert locations speak eloquently of the dangers facing the quartet of adventurers.

Professor Beware ○
1938, US, 87 mins, b/w
Dir: Elliott Nugent
Stars: Harold Lloyd, Phyllis Welch, Raymond Walburn
Rating: ★★

Harold Lloyd, in one of his last major pictures, as the archaeologist in search of the rare tablet which will explain the mystery of a 3,000-year-old romance; the classic top-of-the-train encounter is here, and a great deal of this sequence was for real.

Projectionist, The
See: The Inner Circle

Project X ◐ ⓥ
1987, US, 103 mins, colour
Dir: Jonathan Kaplan
Stars: Matthew Broderick, Helen Hunt
Rating: ★★★

Cunningly contrived to make the maximum appeal to the emotions in its last 30 minutes, this is an escape story with a difference. An intelligent chimp, trained for three years by a university researcher (Helen Hunt), somehow ends up with a dozen other chimps at a USAF secret project base where, under the tutelage of Jimmy (Matthew Broderick), he learns to fly a simulated aircraft. It wouldn't be fair to the plot to reveal more; suffice to say that the time comes when, with the chimps' lives at stake, Broderick and Hunt meet up and resolve to do something about it. Slow in parts, this picks up a good deal in the last three reels, the emotive charge of James Horner's music cleverly reinforcing the impact of the escalating action.

Promised Land ● ⓥ
1987, US, 102 mins, colour
Dir: Michael Hoffman
Stars: Jason Gedrick, Kiefer Sutherland, Meg Ryan, Tracy Pollan
Rating: ★

Slow motion. Dark photography. Flashbacks to the big game and golden days. Yes folks, the great American masterpiece bites the dust again – especially with a tragic ending plain from the first few moments of its scene. Disillusionment runs riot: can the American Dream be as nightmarish as this? Depressing and predictable throughout, the film fails to enliven familiar characters and shows no subtlety. Meg Ryan's personality, though, shines through, even in a ridiculously obvious role. This would be an attractive performance in a good film; in a bad one, it's outstanding. And Kiefer Sutherland is also convincing in a poorly written role.

Promise Her Anything ○
1966, US, 97 mins, colour
Dir: Arthur Hiller
Stars: Warren Beatty, Leslie Caron, Bob Cummings, Hermione Gingold
Rating: ★★

Zany, freewheeling comedy about a blue-movie maker (Warren Beatty) with a French widow in his room in the shape of Leslie Caron. It's pleasant, lightweight and occasionally gratifyingly lunatic. Spot Warren Mitchell, silent star Bessie Love and Donald Sutherland in small roles; bemoan the waste of comediennes Hermione Gingold and Libby Morris; and applaud Keenan Wynn, who deservedly gets all the best lines as a super-salesman.

Promoter, The
See: The Card

Prospero's Books ● ⓥ
1991, Netherlands/France/Italy/UK, 120 mins, colour
Dir: Peter Greenaway
Star: John Gielgud
Rating: ★★

Prospero's Books is difficult to assess because it is a visually bold film, filled with stunning images that live long in the memory – images often as powerful and persuasive as the words of the Bard that accompany them. Director Peter Greenaway deserves much credit for the courage to bring Shakespeare's *The Tempest* to the screen in his own

uncompromising fashion. So it's a pity to say that it is ultimately a deeply unsatisfying film. John Gielgud's central performance as Prospero dominates to such a degree that all the other players seem mere cyphers. This feeling is heightened by the fact that Sir John speaks the majority of the dialogue, which, even if you know the play, causes no small amount of confusion. Almost every scene contains some nudity (although no sex), often simply there as background. As this neither helps the story nor provides any kind of worthwhile titillation, the question arises: 'what's the point?' That question could be used to sum up the whole film, were it not for the rich photography and the vivid visual invention Greenaway shows in almost every scene.

Protocol ○ ⓥ
1984, US, 95 mins, colour
Dir: Herbert Ross
Stars: Goldie Hawn, Chris Sarandon
Rating: ★★

A movie specifically designed for its star, in this case Goldie Hawn. It plays to all her strong points – daffiness, endearing vulnerability and resilience under pressure. Not surprisingly its executive producer is one Goldie Hawn and the plot structure bears a passing resemblance to that of a previous Hawn success, *Private Benjamin*. Starting off as a sort of lunatic comedy of the Sixties (with a few sharply funny lines), it ends up more as *Miss Smith Goes to Washington,* with Goldie telling a Congressional hearing that to which it is not accustomed – the truth (including her age). She's a cocktail waitress pitched into the public eye when foiling an assassination attempt. on an eastern emir, and subsequently winning the hearts of TV millions with her slightly scatterbrained frankness. Subsequent developments provide rich pastures for Goldie Hawn fans, though others may regret that the more biting wit drifts out of the film in favour of patriotic sentiment.

Proud Ones, The ○
1956, US, 94 mins, colour
Dir: Robert D Webb
Stars: Robert Ryan, Virginia Mayo, Jeffrey Hunter, Walter Brennan
Rating: ★★★

A first-rate Western of the kind that was already close to hitting the dust in the then-changing climate of Hollywood. Robert Ryan and Jeffrey Hunter both give honest-to-goodness, hard-biting performances in the two leading roles of this suspenseful piece, although Virginia Mayo, more used to working her way through college in Warners musicals, seems miscast as the girl. The climax of the film, expertly staged by director Robert D Webb, may stay with you for some while, as could the whistled theme tune.

Proud Rebel, The ○
1958, US, 103 mins, colour
Dir: Michael Curtiz
Stars: Alan Ladd, Olivia de Havilland
Rating: ★★★

Alan Ladd's last film of any stature: a well-made (by Michael Curtiz) Western about a Southerner and his mute son roaming the countryside after the Civil War. Olivia de Havilland submerges her natural beauty to play a tough spinster farmer.

Providence ●
1977, France/Switzerland, 107 mins, colour
Dir: Alain Resnais
Stars: Dirk Bogarde, Ellen Burstyn, David Warner, John Gielgud
Rating: ★

This bizarre, one-of-a-kind film from Alain Resnais is a kind of obscene sideshoot from *Citizen Kane,* only with John Gielgud as the dislikeable, dying old man, effing and blinding away to himself in his lonely mansion as the pain gets worse. We see his offspring as he sees them in fantasy, crude daydreams that reflect his bitterness. David Mercer's script is a flamboyant, if crass criss-cross of role-play and Freudian puzzles, with Gielgud as both tormentor and victim. The director's treatment of all this is pretty unsubtle, but Mercer finds worthier allies in photographer Ricardo Aronovitch and composer Miklos Rosza, who both make major contributions to the film.

Prudence and the Pill ◐
1968, UK, 98 mins, colour
Dir: Fielder Cook
Stars: Deborah Kerr, David Niven, Judy Geeson
Rating: ★

The much-teamed David Niven and Deborah Kerr – this was their fourth film together – are backed by Joyce Redman, Judy Geeson, Keith Michell, Robert Coote, Vickery Turner, Edith Evans and Irina Demick in this comedy about contraceptives, in which doors open and close in true Feydeau

fashion. There's one incredible scene in which Edith Evans (actually a stunt woman, of course) walks across the track at Brands Hatch while a race is on, with Formula 3 cars doing 100mph missing her by inches. No trick photography took place here – the scene took place exactly as shot.

Psyche 59 ◐
1964, UK, 94 mins, b/w
Dir: Alexander Singer
Stars: Patricia Neal, Curt Jurgens, Samantha Eggar, Ian Bannen
Rating: ★

Ever since this psychological sex drama came out, we have been trying to fathom the significance of the title. The plot concerns a nymphomaniac who sets her cap at her blind sister's husband, doing her tempting in front of her sister's sightless eyes. Patricia Neal and Samantha Eggar deserve credit for acting it so well. Walter Lassally's black and white photography also gives it some style.

Psycho ● ⓥ
1960, US, 109 mins, b/w
Dir: Alfred Hitchcock
Stars: Anthony Perkins, Janet Leigh, Vera Miles, John Gavin
Rating: ★★★★★

Psycho is now rightly regarded as a masterpiece and probably Alfred Hitchcock's most accomplished and consistently sustained film, filled with delicious black humour that was even more concentrated than in Hitchcock's equally misunderstood *The Trouble With Harry* a few years previously. There's a great deal more to the movie than simply the justly celebrated set pieces, most memorably the legendary murder in the shower, shot by Saul Bass. For a start, there is the inventive and superbly constructed screenplay by Joseph Stefano, based on Robert Bloch's novel; and Bernard Herrmann's sinister and screeching score. Add to that Hitchcock's impeccable control of every scene, casting and performances that could hardly be bettered and you have a not-to-be-missed cinema experience to be savoured time and time again. Some parts are still hard to watch. Leigh's Oscar nomination was the only one of her career.

Psycho II ● ⓥ
1983, US, 125 mins, colour
Dir: Richard Franklin
Stars: Anthony Perkins, Vera Miles,

Meg Tilly
Rating: ★★★

Just when you thought it was safe to go back into the shower, Anthony Perkins returned as Norman Bates, 23 years after he first operated the Bates Motel under Alfred Hitchcock's management. Unlike most sequels, this one comes off remarkably well. Perkins is in fine, twitchy form, developing the character with some sly touches of black humour rather than simply reprising it. Nice to see Vera Miles back too, still pursuing Norman over her sister's death.

Psycho III ● ⓥ
1986, US, 93 mins, colour
Dir: Anthony Perkins
Stars: Anthony Perkins, Diana Scarwid, Jeff Fahey
Rating: ★★★

Good news for horror fans. The Bates Motel is back in business. 'Could you tell me – is there an inexpensive place to spend the night around here?' asks runaway nun Diana Scarwid, fleeing from the desires of the flesh right into the arms of Hollywood's favourite psychopath (still Anthony Perkins) until Freddy Krueger came along. Scarwid is even made up to look like Janet Leigh (complete with the same character initials) – but 'momma' don't allow... and, as the Perkins features assume the familiar twitch, the corpse count soon piles up. 'Can't have that sort of thing happening in my motel,' Perkins chides Scarwid, after finding her, wrists slashed, in the bath, rather pre-empting his 'mother's' intention of murdering her. 'I guess I did leave the bathroom in a mess,' she apologises. Perkins smiles. 'I've seen it worse, he says. Such black irony sits well with Perkins' own direction, which piles on the gore with a tactful hand of which even Hitchcock might not have disapproved.

Psychomania ●
(aka: The Death Wheelers)
1972, UK, 95 mins, colour
Dir: Don Sharp
Stars: George Sanders, Beryl Reid, Nicky Henson
Rating: ★★

Considering Don Sharp's reputation as a fine director of action scenes and horror films, it's not surprising that the scenes without dialogue work best in this black horror comedy about a gang of Hell's Angels motorcyclists. They make a pact with the Devil in return for the secret of immortality, then com-

P

mit suicide and return from the grave. Sounds silly and it is, but Sharp ensures that you'll jump out of your armchair on at least one occasion and maybe more.

P'tang, Yang, Kipperbang ○
1982, UK, 93 mins, colour
Dir: Michael Apted
Stars: Alison Steadman, Robert Urquhart, John Albasiny
Rating: ★★★

This touching, gently comic account of a schoolboy's obsession with a girl in his class, skilfully drawn by Jack Rosenthal, centres on Alan, perfectly played by John Albasiny, whose secret torment is as pure as the idyllic postwar setting. Young Alan's seething mass of schoolboy desire is, in fact, as chaste as the private life of his teacher (Alison Steadman) is unchaste. As the elusive heroine, Abigail Cruttenden, in the role of the prettiest girl in the class, expresses all the boredom and smugness that third form girls tend to adopt in such circumstances. As Alan's cohorts, Mark Brelsford and Chris Caballis commendably display the more unsavoury nature of rampant schoolboys (short of hair but long on curiosity), leaving their more sensitive friend to suffer alone those first steps along the rocky road from word games to women.

Public Enemy, The ○ ⓥ
1931, US, 84 mins, b/w
Dir: William A Wellman
Stars: James Cagney, Jean Harlow, Edward Woods, Joan Blondell
Rating: ★★★★

James Cagney's blazing performance in this classic Warner Bros gangster film confirmed him as a major star and endeared him to all the grapefruit growers of America when he found a new use for their product by pushing one into Mae Clarke's face. The story of the rise and fall of a crime czar may have been something of a cliché through over-use but here, under William A Wellman's pacy direction, it fizzes across the screen with excitement, and Cagney's death, wrapped like a mummy and delivered, bullet-ridden to his mother's door, still retains its power.

Public Enemy's Wife ○
(aka: G-Man's Wife)
1935, US, 69 mins, b/w
Dir: Nick Grindé
Stars: Pat O'Brien, Margaret Lindsay,

Cesar Romero, Dick Foran
Rating: ★★★

Pat O'Brien and Robert *King Kong* Armstrong are G-Men and Margaret Lindsay takes the title role of the much put-upon heroine who is saddled not only with gangster Cesar Romero as a husband, but also a fake marriage that turns out to be the real thing, plus the kind of merry melodrama typical of Warner Bros co-features of the period. Slick direction by Nick Grindé covers up the less credible moments.

G-Man's Wife
See: Public Enemy's Wife

Public Eye, The ● ⓥ
1992, US, 98 mins, colour
Dir: Howard Franklin
Stars: Joe Pesci, Barbara Hershey, Stanley Tucci, Jerry Adler, Jared Harris
Rating: ★★★★

An unusual film for crime connoisseurs, appropriately set in 1942. There hasn't been a film about a sensation-hungry photographer in many a year: this darkly shaded example spotlights Joe Pesci as the shutterbug with pretensions to recognition, a sad little whippet of a man who's always first on the scene at fires, killings, car crashes and other tragedies. Human suffering is stamped on all his work but no one will publish his portfolio of front-page sensations. Depressed, Pesci is putty in the hands of femme fatale Kay (Barbara Hershey) who runs her late husband's nightclub, but is worried about his Mob connections. When one of them turns up dead when Pesci knocks on his door on Kay's behest, the little man opens up a whole well of worms that looks as if it might suck him right down inside. Pesci catches exactly the vulnerability beneath the camera hotshot's cockiness. Hershey is particularly good as the flame to his moth, no better than she ought to be but no worse. It's an impressive piece of work on an offbeat but constantly absorbing theme.

Pulp ❶
1972, US, 95 mins, colour
Dir: Mike Hodges
Stars: Michael Caine, Mickey Rooney, Lizabeth Scott
Rating: ★★

Second-rate crime writer Michael Caine finds himself involved in murder and political intrigue when he is invited to write the biography of a has-been Hollywood movie gangster

(Mickey Rooney) in this spoof thriller. Director Mike Hodges obviously enjoyed making this fun but uneven film; having said that, his scattergun tactics mean that many of his targets are missed. Michael Caine seems somewhat detached from all the goings-on, but Mickey Rooney gets his teeth into what was one of his best roles for years. Any sideswipe at gangster films and thrillers is somewhat obscured by the script and the sunny Mediterranean setting.

Pulp Fiction ● ⓥ
1994, US, 150 mins, colour
Dir: Quentin Tarantino
Stars: John Travolta, Uma Thurman, Bruce Willis, Samuel L Jackson, Tim Roth, Harvey Keitel
Rating: ★★★

Or: *Tales from the Darkside* – of life, that is. This could only be Quentin Tarantino's idea of a comedy, though with all the adult elements that spatter his more dramatic offerings. It's in the manner of a circular jigsaw, although not all the pieces appear in the right order, it seems, even if some are more entertaining than others. An almost hairless Bruce Willis appears in the best of them as a pug boxer who plans a spectacular double-cross against the meanest ganglord in town. Also involved in the patchwork quilt that surrounds Willis' efforts to avoid a sticky end are John Travolta and Samuel L Jackson as the mobster's hitmen. You'll find some of the blood and guts involved – especially if you're nervous of needles – take some watching, but a lot of the sequences are inventively sewn together. Very odd, though, about the non-chronological order: see it and be puzzled.

Pumping Iron ○
1976, US, 85 mins, colour
Dir: George Butler, Robert Fiore
Stars: Arnold Schwarzenegger, Lou Ferrigno
Rating: ★★★

This beautifully made documentary on the unique world of bodybuilders presaged, in its way, the new interest in 'muscle-man' films. Once populated by Steve Reeves and Gordon Scott in the late Fifties and early Sixties, they were given a fresh lease of life in the Eighties by the popularity of Lou Ferrigno as the green half of *The Incredible Hulk* and of Arnold Schwarzenegger in a host of macho roles. Both men are on show here, Schwarzenegger proving particularly personable in his articulate and humorous approach to his 'art', in this unexpectedly winning and agreeable film.

Pumpkin Eater, The ◐
1964, UK, 110 mins, b/w
Dir: Jack Clayton
Stars: Anne Bancroft, Peter Finch, James Mason
Rating: ★★★

'Perceptive' and 'lacerating' are among the adjectives which have been used to describe this powerful drama dealing with the disintegration of a marriage. The three stars all give excellent performances, and Anne Bancroft won a British Oscar for her interpretation of the role of the inward-looking wife. The film was a landmark in the British cinema of the Sixties. Its excellent supporting cast includes Sir Cedric Hardwicke (superb in his last role), Richard Johnson, Maggie Smith and Yootha Joyce, who has a small but telling role as a woman in a hairdressing salon. Still, it remains emotionally distant.

Pump Up the Volume ● ⓥ
1990, US, 100 mins, colour
Dir: Allan Moyle
Stars: Christian Slater, Scott Paulin, Ellen Greene, Samantha Mathis, Annie Ross
Rating: ★★★

It's obvious from the outset of this story of a teenage radio pirate that the star has to be something special to make it work. Well, the brooding Slater is something special here and, after a fairly tedious couple of reels, this film gets a grip on you. The purpose of Slater's 10 o'clock broadcasts, which somehow remains a mystery to his parents (he makes them from home) is to expose the corruption at his own school; and this he eventually does. It's always nice to see injustice stood on its head and there's a special irony here in that Slater's father is the school commissioner who needs his eyes opened by his own son. Slater is fine, and he's virtually the whole show, although there's a nice turn from singer Ellen Greene in a straight role as a conscientious teacher. Annie Ross is slightly over the top as the corrupt headmistress of the school.

Punch and Judy Man, The ○
1962, UK, 90 mins, b/w
Dir: Jeremy Summers
Stars: Tony Hancock, Sylvia Syms
Rating: ★★

Tony Hancock should have stuck with his TV writers Ray Galton and Alan Simpson, even though their first movie script for him, *The Rebel,* had proved less than a total success. Slow, self-indulgent and far too lugubrious to be a hit with the millions who had switched on to 'the lad 'imself' on TV, this second effort flattened Hancock's movie career at a swoop. Yet it has some incidental pleasures, not least in the opening sequence of Hancock dressing and morosely eating breakfast, and in the performances of Hancock himself and John le Mesurier as the melancholy Sandman who instructs him obliquely about the obligations of marriage.

Punchline ◐ ⓥ
1988, US, 128 mins, colour
Dir: David Seltzer
Stars: Sally Field, Tom Hanks, John Goodman
Rating: ★★

They say that by and large comedians are rather sad people. You can well believe it after watching this cuttingly well acted, out-of-the-ordinary but rather dislikeable picture about the stand-up comics of a downtown American nightclub. Naturally, they all long to leap from the part-time to the big time, and this story focuses on two particular cases: the brilliant but unstable Steven (Tom Hanks) and the housewife (Sally Field) who just likes making people laugh, but whose husband (John Goodman) doesn't understand. No prizes for guessing that a contest at the club for a TV spot will come down to a battle between them. Hanks is at times brilliant, even memorable, and Field tries hard for sympathy in her familiar puppy-dog fashion. But it's difficult to get close to these people, or to root for them at the end. The film does catch some of the roar of the greasepaint and the smell of the crowd, though you can't see any of these melancholy funny-people enjoying it for long.

Punisher, The ● ⓥ
1990, US, 89 mins, colour
Dir: Mark Goldblatt
Stars: Dolph Lundgren, Louis Gossett Jr, Jeroen Krabbé, Kim Miyori
Rating: ★

There are surely too many martial arts avengers with vaguely foreign accents around for the genre to last. You feel it's only a matter of time before Lundgren, Van Damme and Co are joining forces to meet Dracula and the Werewolf. In the meantime, here's Dolph as a *Marvel* comic-strip hero, an ex-cop who knocks off a few dozen gangsters a year and lurks in the sewers with only an arsenal of weapons for company, brooding over the death of his wife and children these five years before. It's a pretty unpleasant exercise in which the main object seems to be to impale those parts of the body that haven't already been sliced off. Nancy Everhard has a fresh appeal as one of the cops pursuing The Punisher and the action scenes are well-edited and directed with ruthless efficiency. Pretty nasty.

Punk and the Princess, The ◐ ⓥ
1992, UK, 96 mins, colour
Dir: Mike Sarne
Stars: Charlie Creed-Miles, Vanessa Hadaway, Jess Conrad, David Shawyer, Alex Mollo, Yolanda Mason
Rating: **RB**

This is a dispiritingly bad street-level update of amateurish British looks-at-teenagers in the Sixties, not surprising perhaps as director Mike Same's own acting roles were much along these 'lost soul' lines. Charlie Creed-Miles is the punk Romeo whose idea of foreplay with Vanessa Hadaway's American heiress is to exclaim 'Jump on to my willie', an invitation she accepts with some alacrity. Supporting acting falls somewhat short of basic requirements, especially Vanessa's stepmother, who deservedly gets the worst of a wretched script. 'I mean,' she protests. 'Fancy going out with a murderer!'

Puppet on a Chain ○
1970, UK, 98 mins, colour
Dir: Geoffrey Reeve
Stars: Sven-Bertil Taube, Barbara Parkins, Alexander Knox
Rating: ★

A breathtaking speedboat chase through the canals of Amsterdam is the highlight of this Alistair MacLean thriller about a gang of heroin smugglers. The acting and the action are formula Seventies' style, but that waterbound sequence – made, incidentally, not by director, Geoffrey Reeve, but by another director Don Sharp – will jolt you right out of your seats.

Pure Hell of St Trinian's, The ○
1960, UK, 94 mins, b/w
Dir: Frank Launder
Stars: Cecil Parker, George Cole, Joyce

Grenfell
Rating: ★★

The *St Trinian's* cycle was beginning to run down a little, but while George Cole (as Flash Harry) and Joyce Grenfell (as Sgt Ruby Gates) are around, there are still some laughs to be squeezed out of the little horrors, who are discovered at the outset busy at their usual occupation of burning down the school.

Pure Luck ○ ⓥ

1991, US, 96 mins, colour
Dir: Nadia Tass
Stars: Martin Short, Danny Glover, Sheila Kelley, Sam Wanamaker, Scott Wilson
Rating: ★

Another French success, *Le Chèvre*, gets the Hollywood treatment, and the result is pure disaster. Some guys have all the luck. Eugene Proctor (the manic Martin Short) isn't one of them. When an accident-prone heiress goes missing in Mexico, disaster-magnet Eugene is chosen to find her: the theory apparently is that, as his fatal attraction for mishaps mirrors hers, so he will retrace her steps. Hmm. Sent to search with him is a humourless detective (Danny Glover), rapidly to realise how lethal a weapon his new partner can be. Slapstick pure and simple with Short at his most resistible. A long 96 minutes.

Purple Mask, The ○

1955, US, 83 mins, colour
Dir: Bruce Humberstone
Stars: Tony Curtis, Colleen Miller, Gene Barry, Angela Lansbury
Rating: ★★★

Tony Curtis enjoys himself as a kind of Napoleonic Scarlet Pimpernel, in an adventure story with a polish and literacy that places it several grades above such early Curtis swashbucklers as *Son of Ali Baba*. Here he has some sizzling duels, notably with Dan O'Herlihy.

Purple Plain, The ○

1954, UK, 100 mins, colour
Dir: Robert Parrish
Stars: Gregory Peck, Win Min Than, Bernard Lee, Brenda de Banzie
Rating: ★★★

Harrowing, exciting war film, set largely in the Burmese jungle, with Peck as a nerve-shot pilot trying to get himself and his wounded navigator back to safety after their plane has been

downed in a dogfight. Eric Ambler's screenplay agonisingly recreates the novel by H E Bates, and Maurice Denham gives an awesomely good account of an out-and-out coward. Excellent photography in Technicolor by Geoffrey Unsworth includes a first-rate crash sequence.

Purple Rain ● ⓥ

1984, US, 111 mins, colour
Dir: Albert Magnoli
Stars: Prince, Apollonia Kotero, Morris Day, Olga Kariatos, Clarence Williams III, Jerome Benton
Rating: ★★

In his first major movie, the purple popinjay of pop, Prince, comes across as a kind of coffee-coloured Elvis Presley for the Eighties, complete with a story that might have been ripped from one of The King's earlier films. Short of stature, but with an eager contempt for his audience and an obvious confidence in his own entertaining ability, Prince dominates the show. Subtlety, as you might expect, is hardly the keynote of a film that is crude in every sense of the word, overdrawn and archly written in such time-honoured movie phrases as (Prince's mother to his father) 'You don't let me have any fun.' A strange and violent film this, but true to its own lights and shamelessly aimed at a teenage disco-dancing public. Prince has a nice casual way with the odd humorous line – the very few, that is, that don't contain four-letter words.

Purple Rose of Cairo, The ● ⓥ

1985, US, 82 mins, colour
Dir: Woody Allen
Stars: Mia Farrow, Jeff Daniels, Danny Aiello, Dianne Wiest
Rating: ★★★

Woody Allen's fascination with technical wizardry continued with this delightful comedy about a 1930s waitress (Mia Farrow) who falls in love with a fictional hero (Jeff Daniels) in the latest attraction, *The Purple Rose of Cairo*, at her local cinema. One day he steps out of the movie screen and into reality and literally sweeps her off her feet. 'I just met a wonderful man,' she confides to a friend. 'He's fictional but you can't have everything.' It's the kind of inventive, ingenious, romantic, endearingly silly fantasy that scriptwriters once turned out for Hollywood at regular intervals. This one bears the imprint of Allen's own wistful, sense-of-loss comedy. Farrow

is quite outstanding as the amazed Cecilia and Daniels more mobile and personable that any movie star of his type would have been (or allowed to be) in the mid-Thirties.

Pursuit of the Graf Spee

See: The Battle of the River Plate

Pushover ○

1954, US, 88 mins, b/w
Dir: Richard Quine
Stars: Fred MacMurray, Kim Novak, Phil Carey, Dorothy Malone
Rating: ★★★

The cynical detective in this thriller, which shot Kim Novak to stardom, might well be Fred MacMurray's character from *Double Indemnity* 10 years on. A decade older and wearier, but no wiser than his earlier character, MacMurray falls for the ample charms of Novak and turns against his own kind to get the girl and the proceeds of the robbery with which she was involved. The script comes up with some nice ironies, and MacMurray is perfect in the kind of shallow but not dislikeable character he always played wonderfully well.

Pygmalion ○

1938, UK, 96 mins, b/w
Dir: Leslie Howard, Anthony Asquith
Stars: Leslie Howard, Wendy Hiller, Wilfrid Lawson
Rating: ★★★★

The original, now classic 'straight' version of Bernard Shaw's play, long before it was set to music to emerge as *My Fair Lady*. It's a well-known fact that Shaw himself didn't care at all for the casting of Leslie Howard as Professor Higgins, though in the event Howard's account of the role won acclaim. Nonetheless, the show was stolen by Wendy Hiller, who scored a major triumph in the part of Eliza Doolittle and as a result soared to film stardom. Even today, many regard her performance as the yardstick by which successive Elizas are judged. Enjoyable, too, is Wilfrid Lawson as Eliza's father, Doolittle the dustman. Those who like a story to be neatly rounded off could well feel that in his play Shaw somewhat evaded resolving the problem he'd set himself. The film opts for a different, more conclusive if not altogether convincing ending. Witty, entertaining and thoroughly delightful, this remains one of the great British films of the late Thirties.

Pyrates ● Ⓥ
1991, US, 95 mins, colour
Dir: Noah Stern
Stars: Kevin Bacon, Kyra Sedgwick, Bruce Payne, Deborah Falconer
Rating: ★

A very rude sex comedy about a couple who set things alight when they make love. It's also a very bad sex comedy. The script runs like a Woody Allen throw-out, with such lines as 'You realise that memories are not your own but shared by someone else.' There's the spark (!) of a fun idea here, but Kevin Bacon can't play comedy this broad and his real-life wife Kyra Sedgwick is way over the top as his fiery friend. The best things in this film are the impressive clips of cities on fire from such vintage movies as *In Old Chicago*.

Q & A ● Ⓥ
1990, US, 132 mins, colour
Dir: Sidney Lumet
Stars: Nick Nolte, Timothy Hutton, Armand Assante, Patrick O'Neal
Rating: ★★

A good formula detective story on everybody's corrupt lines, its impact muffled in the telling. Director Lumet has only himself to blame: he wrote it as well. A cop called Brennan (Nolte) as maverick as he's crooked, takes it on himself to gun down an underworld figure. The DA (who, being played by Patrick O'Neal, you wouldn't trust as far as the next room) hires assistant DA Al Reilly (Hutton) to investigate. Reilly's green, inexperienced: and that's the idea. He'll wrap the case up neatly and quickly. We've seen too many of these movies, of course, to think it will turn out like that. But it takes Lumet a long time to reach his expected conclusion: minor bad guys are expendable, but you never get the ones at the top.

Q Planes ○
1939, UK, 80 mins, b/w
Dir: Tim Whelan
Stars: Laurence Olivier, Valerie Hobson, Ralph Richardson
Rating: ★★★

Exciting film about British bomber planes disappearing on test flights. The story was written by American writer Brock Williams (although four people worked on the eventual screenplay). Williams was called into Alexander Korda's office and told of a newspaper article about a plane that went up but never came down. Williams asked what happened, and Korda said: 'How should I know? It's for you to write the rest of the story!' This he did, capturing both thrills and the mood of the period.

Q – The Winged Serpent ●
1982, US, 100 mins, colour
Dir: Larry Cohen
Stars: Michael Moriarty, David Carradine, Candy Clark
Rating: ★★

Older cinemagoers who have seen *The Giant Claw* or *The Feathered Serpent* will know what to expect from this piece of mumbo jumbo about a pterodactyl-type monster. Brought to life by an ancient Aztec prayer, it lays an egg in a feathery-looking tower and proceeds to pluck nubile maidens from every rooftop swimming pool and lilo in New York. All this is coupled with the story of a smalltime crook (a busy, eye-catching performance by Michael Moriarty) who finds the creature's lair and feeds it the two associates menacing him for the gems he has lost after a robbery.

Quackser Fortune Has a Cousin in the Bronx ○
1970, US, 90 mins, colour
Dir: Waris Hussein
Stars: Gene Wilder, Margot Kidder
Rating: ★★★

American stars Gene Wilder and Margot Kidder, both at the beginning of distinguished careers, head an otherwise Irish cast in this pleasing regional comedy, with Wilder ideally cast (and sporting a fruity Irish accent) as the happy-go-lucky horse-manure salesman whose life is changed by an American girl he meets in Dublin. A good script by Gabriel Walsh and sensitive direction by Waris Hussein bring out both the fun and the embarrassment of the hero's futile attempts to become part of student society.

Quadrophenia ● Ⓥ
1979, UK, 120 mins, colour
Dir: Franc Roddam
Stars: Phil Daniels, Sting, Leslie Ash, Toyah Wilcox
Rating: ★★★

An adrenalin-high film which successfully explores the Sixties Mod culture. Its source material is the rock album by The Who, whose film company produced *Quadrophenia*. The violent centrepiece is a well-staged Bank Holiday seaside riot. Director Franc Roddam brings it all down to human terms through the emotional and social conflicts of the central character Jimmy (a meaty role for Phil Daniels). Stylish, angry, loud – just like the era it recreates – the film also features the acting debut of singer Sting.

Quality Street ○
1937, US, 80 mins, b/w
Dir: George Stevens
Stars: Katharine Hepburn, Franchot Tone, Fay Bainter
Rating: ★★

Flimsy 19th-century whimsy from Hollywood. It has a typical Katharine Hepburn performance of the Thirties, and you'll find her radiant or annoying according to your tastes. Fay Bainter, soon to move on to mother roles (and an Oscar for *Jezebel*) is excellent as Hepburn's level-headed older sister and Joan Fontaine has a minor role.

Quantez ○
1958, US, 80 mins, colour
Dir: Harry Keller
Stars: Fred MacMurray, Dorothy Malone, Sydney Chaplin, John Gavin
Rating: ★★★

Tough and gripping Western about a group of fugitives from justice, holed up in a ghost town near the Mexican border. Fine performances, especially from John Gavin and Doroth Malone. Ms Malone had won an Oscar two years previously for *Written on the Wind*, and she shows clearly here that that was no flash in the pan. The ending packs a powerful impact. The pace is a bit stodgy, but the strength of the acting sees it through.

Quantrill's Raiders ○
1958, US, 68 mins, colour
Dir: Edward Bernds
Stars: Steve Cochran, Leo Gordon, Diane Brewster, Gale Robbins
Rating: ★

Westcott, a Confederate spy, enlists the help of Quantrill, a lawless raider, in a poor, unsubtle (but action-packed) Western adventure with Steve Cochran sitting comfortably in the saddle as the hero. In the proverbial black hat is Leo Gordon as Quantrill, an effective baddie. Colour and music are good but the script isn't: every ragged cliché in the Western hall of fame is trotted out here.

Quatermass and the Pit ● Ⓥ
(aka: Five Million Miles to Earth)
1967, UK, 100 mins, colour
Dir: Roy Ward Baker
Stars: James Donald, Barbara Shelley
Rating: ★★

Despite muddy colour and occasionally laughable effects, the air of foreboding and evil that hangs over this third of the *Quatermass* films gives it an atmosphere that makes it a worthy addition to the series. Although not as suspenseful as the TV original, this film version contains forthright performances from James Donald, Andrew Keir (as Quatermass) and Barbara Shelley, offering the last in her long line of Hammer heroines.

Quatermass Experiment, The ◑
(aka: The Creeping Unknown)
1955, UK, 82 mins, b/w

Dir: Val Guest
Stars: Brian Donlevy, Jack Warner, Margia Dean, Gordon Jackson
Rating: ★★★

A nail-biting chiller based on the television serial that kept millions glued to their screens. As a film it owes a lot to the tremendously powerful performance of Richard Wordsworth as the former space pilot now possessed by he knows not what. He brings horror, loneliness and helpessness to the role. Special effects are as good as one could possibly expect and the film encouraged its studio, Hanmer, to go on to become Britain's foremost purveyor of horror.

Quatermass 2 ❶ Ⓥ
(aka: Enemy from Space)
1957, UK, 85 mins, b/w
Dir: Val Guest
Stars: Brian Donlevy, John Longden, Sidney James
Rating: ★★

The sequel to the legendary *The Quatermass Experiment* doesn't recapture the bleakness, originality and excitement generated by the original. Still, it has a fascinating cast, including Brian Donlevy, Bryan Forbes, Sidney James and John Longden.

Queen Bee ○ Ⓥ
1955, US, 95 mins, b/w
Dir: Ranald MacDougall
Stars: Joan Crawford, Barry Sullivan, Betsy Palmer, John Ireland, Fay Wray, Lucy Marlow
Rating: ★★★

Totally tailored to the talents of Joan Crawford, Hollywood's queen of postwar melodrama, this gives her a chance to dominate her supporting cast as a villainess you'll love to hate. One American critic wrote when the film came out that 'Miss Crawford plays her role with such silky villainy that we long to see her dispatched'. Writer-director Ranald MacDougall turns in a thoroughly adept slice of lush film melodrama, and Crawford's vicious, neurotic Eva is magnificently gowned throughout by Jean Louis.

Queen Kelly ○ Ⓥ
1928, US, 96 mins, b/w
Dir: Erich Von Stroheim
Stars: Gloria Swanson, Seena Owen, Walter Byron, Wilhelm von Brincken, Madge Hunt, Wilson Benge
Rating: ★★★

This much troubled film was undertaken by Gloria Swanson against all

advice, especially when she hired profligate director Erich Von Stroheim to direct the screen version of his own story. A typical Von Stroheim yarn about debauched royalty and aristocracy (with a degenerate prince that he must have created with himself in mind), it received the usual Von Stroheim extravagance. There are some striking sequences, but others (such as Kelly's marriage in Africa) are prolonged to ridiculous lengths. Swanson's a little old and sophisticated for the adorable orphan, as her plentiful close-ups emphasise. Still, she makes a fair stab at the role. Seena Owen, who later became a respected screenwriter, is particularly effective as the possessive monarch who blights Kelly's chances of romance with the prince, and Tully Marshall absolutely odious as the dissolute ruffian who enters Kelly's life late in the story.

Queen of Destiny
See: Sixty Glorious Years

Queen of Spades, The ○
1948, UK, 96 mins, b/w
Dir: Thorold Dickinson
Stars: Anton Walbrook, Edith Evans, Yvonne Mitchell
Rating: ★★★★

An outstanding film from a particularly productive period in British cinema, *The Queen of Spades* is a macabre fantasy set in Russia in 1806. The leading role is played by Austrian-born Anton Walbrook, who had earlier made another British success, *Gaslight,* for the same director, Thorold Dickinson. As the old Countess, Edith Evans gives one of her most memorable screen portrayals in a baroque chiller that remains one of a kind.

Quentin Durward
See: The Adventures of Quentin Durward

Quest, The ● Ⓥ
1996, US, 95 mins, colour
Dir: Jean-Claude Van Damme
Stars: Jean-Claude Van Damme, Roger Moore, Janet Gunn, James Remar, Jack McGee
Rating: RB

Van Damme goes back to his roots and to call the results really bad are damning them with faint praise. Time has passed Jean-Claude by here, and the story of kick-boxing championships in far-off lands (Thailand masquerading as Tibet) is no longer even faintly believable. A pity in a way, because the backgrounds are teeming with detail in a manner that recalls the Far Eastern tales of Joseph Conrad. As soon as the dialogue begins in this up-market version of *Bloodsport*, however, you'll soon be helpless with laughter, as Jean-Claude, aided and abetted by Roger Moore at his most arch, proceeds to demolish the kick-boxing titans of the world (again). Van Damme's old-age makeup in the opening scenes is not the best recorded in a film for 50 years, either. 'It was long ago,' he mutters, as the screen dissolves to 'Tibet 1925' and the audience dissolves altogether. Much funnier than a real comedy.

Quest for Love O
(aka: Quest)
1971, UK, 90 mins, colour
Dir: Ralph Thomas
Stars: Joan Collins, Tom Bell, Denholm Elliott
Rating: ★★★

One of the narrowest near-misses in the realm of highly original science fiction to be recorded in recent years. There's a lot to admire, not least in the performances of Tom Bell and Joan Collins, in this Ralph Thomas-directed version of a strange little short story by John Wyndham, who wrote *The Midwich Cuckoos* and *Day of the Triffids*. The initial stages of the film are chillingly well realised and the final chase comes off heart-warmingly well. Only in the middle stages does it all not quite work. But give this unusual film a try: you could find that you like it a lot.

Quick and the Dead, The ● Ⓥ
1995, US, 107 mins, colour
Dir: Sam Raimi
Stars: Sharon Stone, Gene Hackman, Russell Crowe, Leonardo DiCaprio, Lance Henriksen, Gary Sinise
Rating: ★★

The spaghetti western is back – 30 years too late. With Sharon Stone as The Woman With No Name – complete with poncho and cheroot – this is probably not that different to early Clint Eastwood 'Dollars' film, although the terse, stylised dialogue and slow motion action that excited Sixties audiences are now likely to provoke more giggles than gasps. Ditto the over-emphatic acting, as director Sam Raimi grinds out a homage to decades gone by, complete with flashbacks to the nameless leading character's past to emphasise her motivation. Pausing

only to pack several outfits into her saddlebag, Stone rides into the outlaw-ruled town of Redemption to take part in a 16-gunfighter shootout in which the last man standing wins. The gunfights pack some excitement and Stone fans will be glad to know she sheds her duds for a hot love scene with fellow combatant Russell Crowe, before taking on big green meanie Gene Hackman in an extra-time shootout where the only penalty is death.

Quick Before it Melts O
1965, US, 98 mins, colour
Dir: Delbert Mann
Stars: George Maharis, Robert Morse, Anjanette Corner, Yvonne Craig
Rating: ★★★

Bright, if sporadic comedy, with rubber-faced Robert Morse mugging gamely as the reporter from *Sage* – 'the magazine that thinks for you' – sent out to cover life at the South Pole, although he and George Maharis are rather hampered by having their faces covered by huge beards most of the time. Pretty Yvonne Craig keeps the feminine flag flying bravely and the script does come up with one gem. While Morse is flirting with Ms Craig (his fiancée and the boss's daughter), the boss rings up. 'What are you doing?' he barks. 'Well,' replies Morse happily, 'I'm trying to seduce your daughter.' 'How're you making out?' demands the boss. (Pause) 'Oh, yeah, I know. I had the same trouble with her mother.' Better comedies would have given their right arm for less.

Quick Change ◑ Ⓥ
1990, US, 88 mins, colour
Dir: Bill Murray
Stars: Bill Murray, Geena Davis, Randy Quaid, Jason Robards, Bob Elliott, Philip Bosco
Rating: ★★

Canadian Bill Murray of *Groundhog Day* fame is a comic worth crossing the street for – and the best thing about this frantic, fragmented bank robbery comedy-thriller, which he co-directed with Howard Franklin. Franklin also wrote the screenplay and that's where the fault lies – the plot is littered with far more inconsistencies than jokes, and takes to meandering as it goes on. It works in fits and starts though, and the stars are fun to be with. Murray as the robber who disguises himself as a clown is a joy to watch: the man is a master of the deadpan.

Quiet American, The O
1957, US, 120 mins, b/w
Dir: Joseph L Mankiewicz
Stars: Audie Murphy, Michael Redgrave, Claude Dauphin
Rating: ★★

Graham Greene's *The Quiet American* is elegant and also scrupulously faithful until the end. Greene's story is basically anti-American, but the climax here – as the naive American seeks an end to the war in Saigon – shifts all the blame onto the Communists. Audie Murphy is audaciously cast as the (unnamed) American, but the acting honours are shared by Michael Redgrave's memorably cynical journalist and Claude Dauphin's wary police chief. Perhaps not surprisingly, disappointingly little is made of the few bursts of action. Mankiewicz was very much a man of words.

Quiet Man, The O Ⓥ
1952, US, 129 mins, colour
Dir: John Ford
Stars: John Wayne, Maureen O'Hara, Barry Fitzgerald
Rating: ★★★★

Director John Ford and his favourite leading man John Wayne transfer the fisticuffs of the Old West to the West of Ireland in this love story with bloody knuckles. It is one of Ford's finest hours, painstakingly constructed as if he were at work on an oil painting, and highlighted by a terrific knock-down fight between Wayne and Victor McLaglen. The whole thing has a wonderful fresh-air feel.

Quiet Please Murder O
1942, US, 70 mins, b/w
Dir: John Larkin
Stars: George Sanders, Gail Patrick, Richard Denning, Lynne Roberts
Rating: ★★★

A most unusual little crime drama, with an excellent study in sardonic degeneracy from George Sanders as Fleg – one of his admirable gallery of villains from Hollywood's early Forties. Sanders is just the man to give full value to some of the amazingly deep (for the time) psychological dialogue here and, even though the Nazis are inevitably dragged into what is basically an art forgery caper, the film still works well as a crime thriller, with lots of shoot-outs and knifings in the dark. Good supporting performances from Gail Patrick, Lynne Roberts (as bad and good girls respectively), fussy Byron Foulger and droop-lipped Kurt Katch (as a mute assassin).

Q

Quiet Wedding ○

1941, UK, 80 mins, b/w
Dir: Anthony Asquith
Stars: Margaret Lockwood, Derek Farr,
A E Matthews, Peggy Ashcroft
Rating: ★★★★

Classic farce of pre-nuptial chaos,
much imitated but rarely bettered, not
even by the lively remake *Happy is the
Bride!* 16 years later. This version, full
of kindly caricature and spiky wit, allows room for splendid cameo
performances by, among others, Peggy
Ashcroft, David Tomlinson, Bernard
Miles and Margaret Rutherford.

Quiet Weekend ○

1946, UK, 93 mins, b/w
Dir: Harold French
Stars: Derek Farr, Marjorie Fielding,
George Thorpe
Rating: ★★

A sequel to *Quiet Wedding,* this comedy
is based on a hit play by Esther
McCracken, and again has the Royd
family well to the fore, this time (unsuccessfully) seeking peace and quiet in
country cottage. Some fun is had, and
the weekend cottage is a beautiful piece
of the production designer's art, with its
antique plumbing and 'Mind your
head' signs beside low doorways. Only
in comparison with the original, in fact,
does the material here look a bit thin.

Quigley Down Under ○ Ⓥ

1990, Australia, 116 mins, colour
Dir: Simon Wincer
Stars: Tom Selleck, Alan Rickman, Laura
San Giacomo, Chris Haywood, Ben
Mendelsohn
Rating: ★★★

Or: *A Fistful of Dingos,* as Selleck's
Australian Western proves to have a
distinct flavour of spaghetti. Although
the music is sub-Elmer Bernstein, the
pacing and treatment of this long film
is strictly Sergio Leone, with a nod to
the horses on the march and towering
outback mountainscapes that always
feature strongly in director Wincer's
film. Selleck is a 19th-century Yank
adventurer who travels hundreds of
miles in response to rancher Rickman's
ad for a crack long shot, only to find
that all Rickman wants him to do is
shoot Aborigines from a distance.
Selleck throws Rickman out of his
ranch-house window, which earns him
and the 'crazy woman' (San Giacomo)
who has attached herself to him a one-
way ticket to the middle of the desert.
Or, at least, it should be one way. But
this being a Western where the hero
never misses and the villain has ex-

pendable henchmen by the ranchful,
you can guess the rest, down to the
final shoot-out when the bad guys
have Selleck at their mercy, but decide
to give him a gun. San Giacomo, overshadowed by Julia Roberts in *Pretty
Woman,* is terrific.

Quiller Memorandum, The ◐

1966, UK, 100 mins, colour
Dir: Michael Anderson
Stars: George Segal, Alec Guinness,
Max Von Sydow, Senta Berger
Rating: ★★★★

George Segal had one of his best parts
in this taut, sometimes very exciting
spy thriller set in present-day Berlin.
Segal, hunted by low-key camerawork
on the one hand, and a neo-Nazi group
of killers on the other, is perfectly cast
as the dogged special agent, humorous
as the hunter, defiant in defeat as the
hunted. To this chilly and compelling
spy thriller, writer Harold Pinter contributed a faintly mocking, faintly
menacing collection of words that gives
the characters identities all their own,
and raises the stealthy, nervy prowl-
ings-around to a high level of suspense.
Alec Guinness has all the most acid
lines, but Segal does particularly well.

Quintet ◐

1979, US, 110 mins, colour
Dir: Robert Altman
Stars: Paul Newman, Vittorio Gassman,
Bibi Andersson, Brigitte Fossey
Rating: ★★★★

Director Robert Altman's best work
since *Images* eight years earlier. A sort
of science-fiction Western, with hints
of *10 Little Niggers,* it's ingenious, imaginative and, rare for an Altman film, at
times even exciting. The time is the
future, and the setting is a remote
colony near one of the poles, where
mankind seems to be in the painful
process of dying out. The only game
in town is Quintet, deadly offshoots of
which have developed into 'tourna-
ments', in which the players really try
to kill one another. And it is in just
such a tournament that 'hero' Paul
Newman becomes involved.
Absolute hocus-pocus, this, of course,
but carried off with some style. The
sub-Arctic settings are splendidly
realised, and Jean Boffety's icy camerawork does these imaginatively bleak
surrounds full justice.

Quiz Show ◐ Ⓥ

1994, US, 143 mins, colour
Dir: Robert Redford
Stars: Ralph Fiennes, Rob Morrow,

John Turturro, Griffin Dunne, Paul
Scofield
Rating: ★★

One of the problems with this Robert
Redford-directed film is that it just isn't
interesting enough. A long and wordy
explanation of a scandal that blew up
when a US TV quiz show was found
to be rigged, it's likely to provoke a reaction of 'So what?' from many
quarters. John Turturro plays the contestant whose Jewish face doesn't fit.
He's ordered to take a dive on the sim-
plest of questions, so that the baton
can be handed on to WASP English
lecturer Charles Van Doren (Ralph
Fiennes), who is fed the questions to
keep him going (in a sop to integrity
he chooses that rather than get the answers direct) and whose popularity
increases the programme's ratings by
mega-proportions. The subsequent investigation by a Congressional
committee marginally holds the interest, but Fiennes' high-flown statement
at the end does little to provide the
film with a proper climax.

Quo Vadis

1951, US, 171 mins, colour
Dir: Mervyn LeRoy
Stars: Robert Taylor, Deborah Kerr, Leo
Genn, Peter Ustinov
Rating: ★★★

The famous film with dramatic scenes
of combat between Christians and
lions in the arena, and many other
spectacular sequences that include the
burning of Rome. Deborah Kerr became the first Christian martyr to go
to the stake in diaphanous blue chif-
fon. Peter Ustinov scene-steals as
Nero while Rome burns: they should
have thrown the sermonising script in
as well.

R

Race for Your Life, Charlie Brown ⊙
1977, US, 75 mins, colour
Dir: Bill Melendez
Rating: ★★

A brainless cartoon feature which does little justice to the *Peanuts* gang of comic strip fame. It chronicles their adventures, together with Snoopy the dog and Woodstock the canary, on a raft race during a summer camp. No story, no characterisation, zero. And the humour of the newspaper strip remains obstinately on the other side of the screen. Harmless enough for kids, but a major disappointment for Snoopy fans.

Racers, The ○
(aka: Such Men Are Dangerous)
1955, US, 112 mins, colour
Dir: Henry Hathaway
Stars: Kirk Douglas, Bella Darvi, Gilbert Roland
Rating: ★★

A motor-racing drama made by Henry Hathaway, a master of action and adventure since the mid-Thirties when he made *The Lives of a Bengal Lancer*. The main character, well played by Kirk Douglas, who revels in such casting, is as unpleasant a 'hero' as one could hope to find before the days of angry young men. And the hair-raising routine of the dedicated driver's life, always wondering whether the next race will be his last, is perfectly captured. Gilbert Roland and Cesar Romero, two 'Latin lovers' from Hollywood's golden days of the Thirties, are both impressive as two drivers who are almost over the hill. Even so, it's Katy Jurado, so good in a small role as a driver's wife, who steals the show from the stars.

Race to the Yankee Zephyr ◑
(aka: Treasure of the Yankee Zephyr)
1981, Australia/New Zealand, 108 mins, colour
Dir: David Hemmings
Stars: Ken Wahl, Lesley Ann Warren, Donald Pleasence, George Peppard
Rating: ★★

It's non-stop action all the way in actor David Hemmings' fifth film as director. Shot on location in the rugged terrain of New Zealand's South Island, it puts mean and moody Ken Wahl (later to hit the big time as star of the *Wiseguy* TV series) and Donald Pleasence (just moody) as the good guys chasing a $50 million payroll hidden since 1944 in the wreck of the 'Yankee Zephyr' plane. George Peppard is the snarling villain on their tails. There's no denying the energy in the frantically paced production, but it remains unfocussed, and the helicopter chases seemingly go on forever.

Rachel Papers, The ● ⓥ
1989, UK, 95 mins, colour
Dir: Damian Harris
Stars: Dexter Fletcher, Ione Skye, Jonathan Pryce, James Spader
Rating: ★★

This film of the bestselling Martin Amis novel will annoy anyone who read and loved the original and confuse newcomers to it, who will only be mystified by the novel's cult status. Dexter Fletcher treads water as the film's hero, Charles Highway, a precocious 19-year-old who embarks on a steamy affair with a beautiful American girl (Ione Skye), tires of her and ends up single again. End of story. End of film. In the end Fletcher is too self-conscious in the role (especially given his endless monologues to camera). Skye, on the other hand, gives such a sensual, glowing performance that you can't understand why Charles grows bored with her. *The Rachel Papers* is a lost opportunity in more ways than one.

Racing with the Moon ●
1984, US, 108 mins, colour
Dir: Richard Benjamin
Stars: Sean Penn, Elizabeth McGovern, Nicolas Cage
Rating: ★★

This teen film about two boys about to be drafted into World War Two is a nostalgia picture but nothing special. Although competently and occasionally amusingly written, it doesn't make us care about its characters and, however hard the cast tries, the movie remains superficial. Sean Penn and Nicolas Cage certainly look the parts, but Cage's accent jars, as it would when he went on to star in *Peggy Sue Got Married*, and only Elizabeth McGovern seems really of the period. An onion too to director Richard Benjamin for not spotting that the 'contemporary' Paramount newsreel logo he uses bears a copyright date of 1927!

Racket, The ○
1951, US, 88 mins, b/w
Dir: John Cromwell
Stars: Robert Mitchum, Lizabeth Scott, Robert Ryan
Rating: ★★★

An exciting crime thriller that's decidedly different from the usual run. It features Robert Mitchum as a city cop, and Robert Ryan as a mobster, both dinosaurs in their respective worlds, doing things the old way and refusing to listen to superiors. In their way, both are pawns of modern-style corruption above them. Although Samuel Fuller and Nicholas Ray also worked on the film, John Cromwell directed the vast majority of the footage, and a hard-hitting job he made of it, even if the lack of background music does it no favours. A star-studded cast all get a fair share of the acting cake, and down-the-cast Robert Hutton actually gets to walk off with heroine Lizabeth Scott!

Radio Days ○ ⓥ
1987, US, 85 mins, colour
Dir: Woody Allen
Stars: Julie Kavner, Seth Green, Dianne Wiest, Mia Farrow, Michael Tucker, Danny Aiello, Jeff Daniels
Rating: ★★★★★

The Woody Allen film that hits the nostalgia jackpot. This is everything that an evocation of childhood should be but rarely is. It has warmth, many shafts of humour, a setting perfect in look and feel and a title that is no cover of convenience, the theme of radio running richly through an immensely enjoyable story about a childhood in a central American town around the years 1939 to 1944. Allen's own anecdotes (he narrates but doesn't appear) enliven and enrich the narrative, which runs separate stories of a poorish Jewish family from the backstreets, and a cigarette girl (Mia Farrow) who narrowly avoids being shot by a gangster, gains a precarious living as a radio 'chantoose' and ends up becoming a lioness among Hollywood gossip columnists. Farrow, whether squeaking bronchial Bronx or clambering over rounded vowels when she takes elocution lessons, has never been better.

Radio Flyer ◑ ⓥ
1992, US, 120 mins, colour
Dir: Richard Donner
Stars: Lorraine Bracco, Adam Baldwin, Elijah Wood, John Heard, Joseph Mazzello, Ben Johnson
Rating: ★★

R

Much re-filmed in a checkered production, this is a disturbing drama with strong performances from intelligent young actors Elijah Wood and Joseph Mazzello as two brothers forced to retreat into a world of fantasy to escape their living nightmare. When their mother (Lorraine Bracco) remarries, young Mike and Bobby find themselves at the mercy of a brutal and unpredictable new stepfather (Adam Baldwin, a decade on from his more friendly hulk in *My Bodyguard*). Seeking refuge in a world of their imagination, they dream of building a flying machine. There are some pretty simplistic, uneasy, sub-Spielberg views afloat in all this, and it remains hard for the viewer to accept its concepts, in spite of the thoroughly engaging portrayals of the two boys. Tom Hanks is the unbilled narrator.

Rage in Harlem, A ● Ⓥ
1991, US, 110 mins, colour
Dir: Bill Duke
Stars: Forest Whitaker, Gregory Hines, Robin Givens, Zakes Mokae, Danny Glover, Badja Djola
Rating: ★★

Today's black romantic comedy crime-thriller: that is to say, laced with extreme violence and language, with most of the dialogue pitched at top decibel level. The action starts in the sticks, with a black-white shootout that ends with sweet trick Givens hotfooting it out of a charnel-house full of bodies clutching a suitcase full of crude gold. Once in town, she latches on to plump, religious, virginal Whitaker as a prospective meal-ticket, falls in love with him and involves him with various literally cutthroat factions out to get the gold. Whitaker is quite sympathetic, and Givens seductive enough to kill for all right, but Glover has the only interesting role as a gangster who trusts only his beloved Pomeranian dog.

Raggedy Man ○
1981, US, 94 mins, colour
Dir: Jack Fisk
Stars: Sissy Spacek, Eric Roberts, Sam Shepard
Rating: ★★

A well-made, low-key drama which ends, not unexpectedly, in violence. Its most charismatic performance is given by Sissy Spacek as a divorcee with two sons who works as sole telephone operator at a small American town almost as forsaken as the one in *The Last Picture Show*.

Raggedy Rawney, The ◗ Ⓥ
1988, UK, 102 mins, colour
Dir: Bob Hoskins
Stars: Bob Hoskins, Dexter Fletcher, Zoe Nathenson, Ian MacNeice
Rating: ★★★

A good film, unusual too – but downbeat and quite unpleasant to sit through: aspects of Bob Hoskins' debut as director/star which harmed its prospects at the box-office. The rawney of the title is a deserter from an unnamed war in an unknown country. He stumbles, dressed as a woman, into an encampment of gypsies also on the run from the war, and is sheltered by a girl, who knows he's a man and subsequently has his baby. To the gypsies, he remains a rawney, a mad woman, and brings them magical luck before turning into a jinx. Though Hoskins himself never really convinces as a gypsy, the film is full of super performances, especially Ian MacNeice as a friendly farmer and Zoe Nathenson as the girl. The ending is smashing, just right and, unlike some of the film, not over-protracted.

Raging Bull ● Ⓥ
1980, US, 119 mins, b/w
Dir: Martin Scorsese
Stars: Robert De Niro, Cathy Moriarty, Joe Pesci, Burt Young
Rating: ★★★★

The boxing sequences occupy only some 12 minutes, but they rank among the most realistic and painful ever put on film: one thanks the fact that director Martin Scorsese chose to film this searing account of life and times of world middleweight champion Jake La Motta in black and white. The dramatic scenes are no less searing, carrying an emotional power and impact far in excess of the usual conventions of the Hollywood biopic. The movie is adult, both in its frank language and its characterization and narrative and, like its central character, pulls few punches. It is also completely compelling. Robert De Niro, who went as far for his art as to gain 50 pounds for the scenes where La Motta is on the way down, gives a commanding performance that more than deserved the Oscar it won. And Cathy Moriarty, as his wife, is no less impressive. You'll rock with every punch in the boxing scenes.

Raiders of the Lost Ark ○ Ⓥ
1981, US, 115 mins, colour
Dir: Steven Spielberg
Stars: Harrison Ford, Karen Allen,

Denholm Elliott, Paul Freeman, Alfred Molina, Ronald Lacey
Rating: ★★★★

A 1941-style high adventure made in the James Bond manner and driven along with tremendous panache by director Steven Spielberg. It's the kind of film where the hero can say 'Meet me at Oscar's' while parting from a friend in the middle of the desert and no one seems to think it matters. Harrison Ford is the intrepid archaeologist transformed into a man of action at the drop of his spectacles; Karen Allen more than matches him as the feisty heroine who follows him through fire, water and – in one especially hackle-raising sequence – a pit of writhing snakes.

Raid on Entebbe ○
1976, US, 144 mins, colour
Dir: Irvin Kershner
Stars: Charles Bronson, Peter Finch, Horst Buchholz
Rating: ★★★

Considering the haste with which it was made – a rival version of the famous attack by Israeli forces to rescue hostages held at Uganda's Entebbe Airport, *Victory at Entebbe,* was in production at the same time – the quality of this film surprised many critics. Cool, detached, exciting and well directed by Irvin Kershner, the film recreates the whole nightmare situation with chilling conviction. Nothing is overstated, people are drawn as real characters with no false heroics and the suspense builds remorselessly up to the raid itself.

Raid on Rommel ○ Ⓥ
1971, US, 99 mins, colour
Dir: Henry Hathaway
Stars: Richard Burton, John Colicos, Clinton Greyn, Wolfgang Preiss
Rating: ★★

A war adventure, made in Mexico, aimed at boys of all ages. As in The *Desert Rats,* almost 20 years before, Richard Burton plays a British Army captain who crosses swords with the legendary Rommel in the North African desert. That talented German actor Wolfgang Preiss sensitively matches James Mason's classic portrayal of Rommel from earlier films, but the rest of the acting, from an assorted crew of British and Continental players, simply isn't in the same class. The action is plentiful and explosive but – a common Hollywood ploy – extensive sections of it are taken from an earlier Universal desert warfare epic, *Tobruk.*

Rails into Laramie ○
1954, US, 81 mins, colour
Dir: Jesse Hibbs
Stars: John Payne, Mari Blanchard, Dan Duryea, Lee Van Cleef
Rating: ★★★

Rousing Western action, in one of the many genre pictures made at Universal during the Fifties, with a neat line in sneering villainy from Dan Duryea. The brisk direction is by Jesse Hibbs, who made 11 films in the Fifties before moving to television and working on series such as *Wagon Train, Rawhide, Laramie* and *Perry Mason*.

Railway Children, The ○ ⓥ
1970, UK, 108 mins, colour
Dir: Lionel Jeffries
Stars: Dinah Sheridan, Jenny Agutter, Bernard Cribbins, William Mervyn, Iain Cuthbertson, Salty Thomsett
Rating: ★★★★

The wife and three children of a Foreign Office employee falsely accused of treason have to start a new life in Yorkshire. The girls soon get used to their new home and befriend a neighbour who says he will try to clear their father's name. A well-acted and scripted film from E Nesbit's much read book, with lots of warmth and lovingly accurate attention to period detail (it's set in Edwardian times). Comic actor Lionel Jeffries directs effectively to produce a drama that holds attention right to the end. Acting kudos go to a young Jenny Agutter as the older daughter, and Bernard Cribbins as Perks, the porter at the local railway station.

Rainbow ○ ⓥ
1995, Can/UK, 97 mins, colour
Dir: Bob Hoskins
Stars: Bob Hoskins, Dan Aykroyd, Terry Finn, Jacob Tierney, Saul Rubinek
Rating: ★

This is the kind of film that makes you wonder if they've forgotten how to make films. It's a Saturday-morning-cinema sort of story about kids who find the end of the rainbow and are sucked into it. The special effects involved in this are so basic that a laugh rather than excitement is the only emotion you'll muster. Nothing interesting happens while they're there, except that the oldest of the kids steal some of the bow's suspended gold rhomboids, as a result of which the world goes to pot. Deprived of colour and therefore oxygen, its atmosphere provokes depression and rioting, effects achieved without finesse or flair: you could get

the same pictorial effect by turning down the colour on your TV. The kids are poor, or annoying, or both, while Hoskins' direction lacks any pace or imagination. Childish wonderment in all this is almost entirely missed: childlike boredom is the likely result.

Rainbow, The ● ⓥ
1988, UK, 104 mins, colour
Dir: Ken Russell
Stars: Sammi Davis, Paul McGann, Amanda Donohoe, Glenda Jackson
Rating: ★★★

Russell returns to the works of D H Lawrence with this prequel to *Women in Love* and, at least in fits and starts, to his best form. The film does, though, suffer from typical Russellian excesses, especially in the nude scenes, and from a rather strained central performance by Sammi Davis as Ursula. More relaxed portrayals come from Amanda Donohoe, as her lesbian seducer, and inevitably from Glenda Jackson as her mother, not given quite sufficient screen time to walk off with the film. The most successful sequences are those set in junior teacher Davis's first school, a veritable workhouse of a place presided over with Dickensian intensity by Jim Carter. Particularly effective is the scene where Davis's worm turns and literally gets up off the floor to thrash a recalcitrant troublemaker within an inch of his life.

Raining Stones ● ⓥ
1993, UK, 90 mins, colour
Dir: Ken Loach
Stars: Bruce Jones, Julie Brown
Rating: ★★

Director Ken Loach returns to showing life as it is, and this is a depressing look at the workless (though not work-shy) working-class of Oldham. Bob (Bruce Jones) will turn his hand to anything from sheep-stealing to drain-cleaning to make a few bob for his family. Of course, he gets into trouble after going to the local loan shark. But it's hard to feel as much sympathy for the guy as Loach wants us to. While resorting stubbornly to illegal activities to pay £100 for his daughter's Confirmation outfit, Bob still finds plenty for a profuse amount of smoking and drinking, plus an occasional flutter on the nags. Character inconsistencies and poor continuity, coupled with inadequate acting in minor roles (although Julie Brown is excellent as the long-suffering wife), all conspire to

drain your interest in this one, however commendable its intentions.

Rain Man ● ⓥ
1988, US, 140 mins, colour
Dir: Barry Levinson
Stars: Dustin Hoffman, Tom Cruise, Valeria Golino, Jerry Molen
Rating: ★★★★

When a film goes through four directors and the same number of possible stars in as many years, it's usually a sign that something is badly wrong. But director Barry Levinson struck box office gold with the finished film, winning Oscars for both Best Actor and Best Original Screenplay. On the surface, the idea of a young hustler (Tom Cruise) kidnapping his autistic savant (a person extremely limited in some mental areas and extremely gifted in others) brother (Hoffman) because he's been left a bigger share of their father's inheritance, doesn't sound like blockbuster material. But it was. The scenes where the relationship between the brothers changes are raw and touching. Cruise displays a new maturity as an actor but is simply outclassed by Hoffman in a more sympathetic and showy role.

Raintree County ○
1958, US, 166 mins, colour
Dir: Edward Dmytryk
Stars: Elizabeth Taylor, Montgomery Clift, Eva Marie Saint, Lee Marvin
Rating: ★★

A sweeping romance with Elizabeth Taylor and Montgomery Clift, set against the backcloth of the American Civil War, and on a similar grandiose scale to *Gone With the Wind*. It was MGM's costliest film when originally made – small wonder, with such crowd scenes, and a cast that also includes Eva Marie Saint, Lee Marvin, Nigel Patrick, Rod Taylor, Tom Drake, Agnes Moorehead and DeForest Kelley. The burning of Atlanta, Sherman's march through Georgia and the lavish scenes of life in the Deep South are all impressively spectacular. Yet, strangely, the most memorable scene is a small one: an hilarious sequence in which Clift defeats Marvin in a foot race, despite a plot to get him drunk.

Raise the Titanic! ○
1980, US, 112 mins, colour
Dir: Jerry Jameson
Stars: Jason Robards, Anne Archer, Alec Guinness
Rating: ★★

R

An adaptation of Clive Cussler's best-selling novel about the greatest salvage operation of all time. The final scenes are exhilaratingly exciting, although it takes rather long time to get to them. Alec Guinness is along for the splash to provide a touch of acting class.

Raising a Riot ○
1955, UK, 91 mins, colour
Dir: Wendy Toye
Stars: Kenneth More, Shelagh Fraser, Mandy Miller, Jan Miller
Rating: ★★★

Sunny, fun-filled comedy that soon happily settles down into a series of domestic mishaps as Kenneth More tries to cope with his three kids (while the wife's away) at his father's ramshackle country home. A refreshing romp, carefree and uninhibited. Jan Miller is a bright leading lady, while sister Mandy plays one of the children.

Raising Arizona ◐ Ⓥ
1987, US, 92 mins, colour
Dir: Joel Coen
Stars: Nicolas Cage, Holly Hunter, Trey Wilson, John Goodman
Rating: ★★

Romantic action farce from the *Blood Simple* and *Miller's Crossing* director Joel Coen. The criminal of *Raising Arizona*, however – a role in which Nicolas Cage is perfectly cast – is strictly second-rate. A habitual cornerstore hold-up man, he falls in love with the lady cop (Holly Hunter) who takes his picture each time he goes to jail. When she finds she can't have children, the solution seems easy: steal one of the quins recently born nearby. Now is that a dumb idea or what? It's a fiercely flaky film with charmless characters but lots of inspiration: the notion of a bounty hunter (called in by the distraught father of the kidnapped child) called the Lone Biker of the Apocalypse is very funny, and an extended chase scene involving a rapid tracking camera and pack of dogs is also worth a smile or two.

Raising Cain ● Ⓥ
1992, US, 91 mins, colour
Dir: Brian De Palma
Stars: John Lithgow, Lolita Davidovich, Steven Bauer
Rating: ★★★

Big husky men dressing as women; bodies in cars disappearing into lakes; multiple personalities; dreams; people returning from the dead; the sudden shock at the end; yes, this is Brian De Palma's version of a black comedy.

And, as De Palma's films are always at a remove from reality, it proves quite successful. John Lithgow is the child psychologist sorely in need of psychiatric help, and seemingly collecting babies (after killing their mothers) to satisfy some whim of his dead father. All the De Palma trademarks are here: tracking camera, slow-motion, over-prolonged suspense, set pieces. The over-the-top performances of the three stars sit nicely within the film once you gauge the mood. It's De Palma at his least visceral and most playful.

Raising the Wind ○ Ⓥ
1961, UK, 91 mins, colour
Dir: Gerald Thomas
Stars: Paul Massie, Jennifer Jayne, Leslie Phillips, Kenneth Williams, James Robertson Justice
Rating: ★★

A *Carry On* film in all but name, this is a farcical comedy set in a music academy, where six young students run through the gamut of musical jokes under the baton of Sir Benjamin Boyd, world famous conductor. Sir Benjamin is played by James Robertson Justice, in an extension of his Sir Lancelot Spratt creation for the *Doctor* series. Among the music students, watch out for a young Jim Dale in a very small role playing a very large musical instrument.

Rally 'Round the Flag, Boys ○ Ⓥ
1958, US, 106 mins, colour
Dir: Leo McCarey
Stars: Paul Newman, Joanne Woodward, Joan Collins
Rating: ★★

Its surprising to find Paul Newman and Joanne Woodward in a bedroom farce this broad, and Newman's strenuous over-playing in it gave such contemporaries as Cary Grant and David Niven little to worry about. Joanne Woodward takes a game shot at a role that needed a Carole Lombard, and Joan Collins is cast to type as a man-hungry neighbour with designs on Newman. Two of Hollywood's most talented men, Leo McCarey and Claude Binyon, wrote the script; that only suggests that this romp about a small American town menaced by military installations was never a good idea in the first place.

Rambling Rose ● Ⓥ
1991, US, 113 mins, colour
Dir: Martha Coolidge
Stars: Laura Dern, Robert Duvall, Diane

Ladd, Lukas Haas
Rating: ★★

Passion drums in the Deep South, and beats in the hearts of all men who meet Rose (Laura Dern). Quite happy to open up her petals to anyone who catches a whiff of her scent, this little nymphomaniac of the magnolia belt is devastating to the small community into which she's taken as a maid by the Hillyer family during the Depression. Before a few weeks are out, she's thrown herself at Daddy (Robert Duvall), popped into bed with the family's 13-year-old son (Lukas Haas) who helps himself to an impromptu sex lesson, and teeters around town in a dress that reveals more than it covers. Surprisingly, the film of Rose's misadventures aims at charm and atmosphere rather than titillation. Laura Dern is quite good as Rose, but Diane Ladd and Duvall are rather mannered and artificial as her long-suffering employers.

Rambo: First Blood Part II ● Ⓥ
1985, US, 96 mins, colour
Dir: George P Cosmatos
Stars: Sylvester Stallone, Richard Crenna, Julia Nickson, Charles Napier, Steven Berkoff
Rating: ★★★

Again played by Sylvester Stallone, by now assuming the proportions of a mini Schwarzenegger, war veteran John Rambo is extracted from prison and sent back to Vietnam to locate missing American PoWs in this dazzling dose of jungle mayhem. When Rambo realises he has been set up as a sacrificial goat to appease a complaining American public, to be shot down in search of non-existent (the opposite of the truth) prisoners, the mission becomes one of revenge as well as rescue. The resultant hell-let-loose is breathtaking rubbish that entertains every foot of the way. For adventure fans, Rambo's trek provides action on a first-class ticket: never mind reality, feel the speed and power, and the skill of the editing.

Rambo III ● Ⓥ
1987, US, 101 mins, colour
Dir: Peter MacDonald
Stars: Sylvester Stallone, Richard Crenna
Rating: ★★

Spectacularly topping its predecessors with a magnitude of panoramic action pyrotechnics, here are the further adventures of Rambo (Sylvester Stallone), the muscular monosyllabic warrior, and his mission into Soviet-occupied Afghanistan. The battle scenes are explosive and terrifying with Rambo, as usual, gloriously and inhumanly impervious to fear and danger (who else could outrun a bullet-spitting helicopter?). Stallone, to his credit, makes the insane singlemindedness of Rambo believable in its fantastical context, but not surprisingly, the screenplay gives short shrift to the complexities of the Afghan war.

Rampage O
1963, UK, 98 mins, colour
Dir: Phil Karlson
Stars: Robert Mitchum, Jack Hawkins, Elsa Martinelli
Rating: ★

Fine colour photography, a foot-tapping musical score by Elmer Bernstein and the sense of pace about Phil Karlson's direction, all contribute towards compensating for the holes in the script of this tawdry jungle adventure yarn. The object of the safari is to catch the 'enchantress' – 'half tiger, half-leopard' boasts the film – but when she does appear, it's rather a disenchantment, as she proves to be a sad-looking leopard with her coat partially dyed pink. Far more exciting are scenes of a tiger hunt, when two of the animals are caught in nets at the same time. Robert Mitchum and, particularly, Jack Hawkins, struggle manfully to extract some sense from their cardboard characters.

Ramrod O
1947, US, 94 mins, b/w
Dir: André De Toth
Stars: Veronica Lake, Joel McCrea
Rating: ★★★

A somewhat underrated Western that looks rather more interesting now than when it first appeared – and vanished quickly, partly because of the declining box-office fortunes of its star, Veronica Lake. She's actually quite well cast as a headstrong spitfire in Barbara Stanwyck mould who takes the law into her own hands when her spineless rancher father knuckles under to a bigshot cattleman, nastily well played by Preston Foster. Strongly cast (Joel McCrea, Charles Ruggles, Arlene Whelan, Lloyd Bridges, Don DeFore and Donald Crisp are also in it), the film fairly gallops along under André de Toth's hard-driving direction.

Rancho Notorious O
1952, US, 89 mins, colour
Dir: Fritz Lang

Stars: Marlene Dietrich, Arthur Kennedy, Mel Ferrer
Rating: ★★★★

For all those who love moody, singing-commentary Westerns, there's only one better than this, and that's *High Noon*. Arthur Kennedy wears his 'twisted' expression to great effect as the embittered cowboy hunting the man who killed his fiancée, following the trail to an outlaws' roost run by Marlene Dietrich at her slinkiest – triggering off a story, in the words of the song, 'of hate, murder and revenge'. Tightly, seethingly directed by the great Fritz Lang.

Random Harvest O
1942, US, 126 mins, b/w
Dir: Mervyn LeRoy
Stars: Ronald Colman, Greer Garson
Rating: ★★★★★

Charles Rainer (Ronald Colman), a British officer in the First World War, loses his memory and is being cared for in a sanatorium. Eluding the staff he wanders off and starts a new life for himself and becomes a successful businessman, with the help of his devoted secretary. A delightful period piece that is lifted above mere soap opera by the performances of Colman and Greer Garson. A weepie with a happy ending, it was a Best Picture Oscar nomination. They don't make sentimental dramas like this anymore (not successfully anyway), which is a shame. A major triumph of treatment over content.

Randy Rides Alone O Ⓥ
1934, US, 54 mins, b/w
Dir: Harry Frazer
Stars: John Wayne, Alberta Vaughan, George 'Gabby' Hayes
Rating: ★★

Here's a real rarity – an early John Wayne film with George 'Gabby' Hayes as the villain! Gabby's as nasty as he can manage as a character appropriately called Matt Black, but doubtless he was glad to get back to playing sidekicks who made up in whiskers for what they lacked in the way of teeth.

Ransom O
1955, US, 109 mins, b/w
Dir: Alex Segal
Stars: Glenn Ford, Donna Reed, Juano Hernandez
Rating: ★★★★

Following on *Blackboard Jungle* and *Trial*, this was the third of Glenn Ford's famous 'anguished' roles all within the same year, in which he revealed his new 'Method' style of acting after a spell with the Actors' Studio. Here, he is cast as a rich industrialist who incurs public wrath when he decides not to pay a massive ransom demand after his small son has been kidnapped. Good though Ford is, he has the acting honours stolen from under his nose by veteran black actor Juano Hemandez. The movie itself, fraught with tension, is streets ahead of the usual Hollywood kidnap thriller. As Ford's hysterical wife, Donna Reed had her best film role since winning an Academy Award for *From Here to Eternity*.

Ransom O
1977, UK, 97 mins, colour
Dir: Richard Compton
Stars: Oliver Reed, Deborah Raffin, Stuart Whitman, John Ireland
Rating: ★★

Cat-and-mouse Oliver Reed-Stuart Whitman thriller also known as *Assault on Paradise* and *Maniac*. Paradise is the name of the Arizona town subjected to a ransom demand as unusual as it is terrifying. Some serviceable suspense from the efforts to trap the fiend who is responsible.

Ransom ● Ⓥ
1996, US, 120 mins, colour
Dir: Ron Howard
Stars: Mel Gibson, René Russo, Gary Sinise, Lili Taylor, Brawley Nolte
Rating: ★★

The law in Nineties' Hollywood seemed to be: Never shoot 90 minutes where 120 will do. Some of their directors are skilful enough to get away with it. But not this time. Ron Howard simply hasn't enough plot to spin this kidnap thriller beyond the clutches of our boredom. What he has got often defies the laws of logic too. Aviation tycoon Gibson has his son whisked from under his nose and cop/kidnapper Sinise and his gang demand two million dollars. Gibson decides to cough up and, though you may ask why the FBI choose to challenge the villain's henchmen at the drop, it goes messily wrong. The plot's only twist lies in Gibson then refusing to pay and putting the money on the kidnapper's head instead. All Howard can do after this is get our (flawed) hero to refuse to pay again, and pad out the time with people's opinions of what he's

R

done. Gibson, Russo (as his wife) and Sinise give it their best shots and create a few telling moments.

Rapid Fire ● ⓥ

1992, US, 95 mins, colour
Dir: Dwight H Little
Stars: Brandon Lee, Powers Boothe, Nick Mancuso, Kate Hodge
Rating: ★★

Enter the baby dragon: Brandon Lee, son of Bruce, is the Chinese American with a short fuse who demolishes people and objects alike if they come within three feet of him. After displaying the quieter side of his character – he draws a detailed likeness of a killer after a fleeting glimpse through a doorway – he gets down to the wisp of a plot and destroying the drug barons of east and west who are still operating through the same Chinese laundry such ne'er-do-wells ran in films of the Thirties. The film is almost nothing but action – well choreographed by Lee, director Dwight H Little and Jeff Imada – and nearly everyone gets killed but the star. Powers Boothe has some charisma, but delivers dialogue harshly as the lawman who becomes Lee's father figure; Kate Hodge is the obligatory curvy cop with the hots for our hero. 'Jake,' says Boothe, in an in-joke that may draw a groan or two, 'why don't you take those fists of fury of yours outside?' Fists of fury, flashing feet: Lee fans will love it.

Rare Breed, The ○

1966, US, 97 mins, colour
Dir: Andrew V McLaglen
Stars: James Stewart, Maureen O'Hara
Rating: ★★★

Fresh from his triumph with *Shenandoah*, director Andrew V McLaglen strengthens his reputation for creating warm, human characters and genuine wide-open-spaces atmosphere, in this engaging, richly-coloured yarn. His star, as in *Shenandoah*, is James Stewart, here as an ageing cowhand still looking for a dream. Gradually, unwillingly at first, Stewart acquires a fanatical belief in the potential of one Hereford breed bull, brought to America by prissy Englishwoman Maureen O'Hara. Stewart, blue eyes blazing with determination, especially when searching for the Hereford in a blizzard – is ideally matched by Brian Keith's red-bearded, extravagantly Scots-accented rancher, who has a whisky bottle in his bath instead of a cake of soap. And Jack Elam's bit-part villain

sticks in the mind long after he is rather precipitously killed off.

Rashomon ● ⓥ

1950, Japan, 88 mins, b/w
Dir: Akira Kurosawa
Stars: Toshiro Mifune, Machiko Kyo, Masayuki Mori
Rating: ★★★★★

Deservedly taking the Oscar for Best Foreign Language Film, this compelling drama ranks among director Akira Kurosawa's finest works. Using the story of the rape of a woman and the murder of her samurai husband, recounted in various versions by different eye witnesses, Kurosawa came up with a haunting, poetic and totally riveting study of the nature of truth and experience. His grouping and fluid visuals make the film a feast for the eye and superb performances – particularly by Toshiro Mifune as the violator and Machiko Kyo as the wife – engage the imagination. A masterpiece.

Rasputin and the Empress ○

1933, US, 123 mins, b/w
Dir: Richard Boleslawski
Stars: John Barrymore, Ethel Barrymore, Lionel Barrymore
Rating: ★★★

The only screen teaming of the three famous Barrymores. Strangely, although John Barrymore had already starred in *Svengali* and *The Mad Genius*, it's Lionel, the character actor of the family, who plays the flamboyant Rasputin in this film, with Ethel as the Empress fascinated by his evil charm. Treatment is tense, lavish and exciting, but the real treat for film fans is the three Barrymores on screen together.

Rasputin – The Mad Monk ●

1965, UK, 92 mins, colour
Dir: Don Sharp
Stars: Christopher Lee, Barbara Shelley
Rating: ★★

The legend of Rasputin, the monk who exerted a powerful and mysterious influence on the Russian royal family during the last days before the revolution, is a good basis for a thrilling drama. This Hammer offering doesn't quite make the most of its opportunities, though, despite a powerful and pretty frightening central performance from Christopher Lee as Rasputin. As you might expect from Hammer, the film is highly coloured and quite bloody at times. Unfortunately, apart from the tense

final scenes, director Don Sharp doesn't give the film the pace to make it truly gripping.

Rat Race, The ○

1960, US, 105 mins, colour
Dir: Robert Mulligan
Stars: Tony Curtis, Debbie Reynolds
Rating: ★★★★

One of the few films to make the proper demands on Debbie Reynolds' undervalued acting ability, this is a heartwarming and thoroughly entertaining study of struggling showbusiness hopefuls in the garrets of New York. Tony Curtis and Ms Reynolds succeed in striking up a relationship of real warmth, involving us in all their ups and downs – mostly downs. And Jack Oakie gives them splendid support in his part as the barman-confidant. This was director Robert Mulligan's second film. Here, in addition to the performances of his cast, he's helped by a screenplay by Garson Kanin that is warmly rich in its observation of human behaviour.

Rattle of a Simple Man ◑ ⓥ

1964, UK, 95 mins, b/w
Dir: Muriel Box
Stars: Harry H Corbett, Diane Cilento, Michael Medwin, Thora Hird
Rating: ★★★

A rather touching and at times richly amusing extended playlet about an 'innocent' football fan from the north, and the night he spends talking to a London prostitute in her flat. Not very plausible, perhaps, but winningly done. As Cyrenne, the streetwalker, Diane Cilento is persuasive and just right. And Harry H Corbett was able to break away completely from his *Steptoe* image. Michael Medwin is also very good as Corbett's big-talking friend. It was the last film directed by Muriel Box, wife of producer Sydney.

Raven, The ◑

1935, US, 61 mins, b/w
Dir: Lewis Friedlander
Stars: Boris Karloff, Bela Lugosi
Rating: ★★★

Director Lew Landers was a specialist in quickfire films that rarely ran longer than 70 minutes. This was his first feature (made under his real name, Lewis Friedlander) and among his fastest and most forceful, thanks mainly to a fortuitous teaming of horror kings Boris Karloff and Bela Lugosi. The plot has very little to do with Edgar Allan Poe, although the writers do manage to squeeze in his pendulum torture from *The Pit and the Pendulum*.

Raven, The O
1963, US, 86 mins, colour
Dir: Roger Corman
Stars: Vincent Price, Peter Lorre, Boris Karloff, Hazel Court, Jack Nicholson
Rating: ★★★★

Horror has rarely been more skilfully spoofed than in this delightful Roger Corman-directed spree. Vincent Price excels as a retired magician who needs to change a raven into human (Peter Lorre) form by a mixture of dead man's hair, jellied spiders and bat's blood – 'Dried or dehydrated?' Price asks the bird. But the cauldronful is not enough – Lorre still has his wings and Price has run out of dead man's bait. So down they trot to the family vault. 'I'm sure Dad wouldn't mind,' smiles Price. It gets funnier, too, ending up with our two friends pitting their magical wits against the wickedest wizard of all (dear old Boris Karloff) in a storm-surrounded castle. Despite the original 'X' certificate, most children will enjoy this hugely. Jack Nicholson's in it too, though you'd never guess he'd end up a superstar from his performance here.

Raw Deal O
1948, US, 85 mins, b/w
Dir: Anthony Mann
Stars: Dennis O'Keefe, Claire Trevor, Marsha Hunt, Raymond Burr
Rating: ★★★

The last (and probably best) of an excellent quartet of tough, medium-budget thrillers made by director Anthony Mann before he moved on to a memorable series of Westerns with James Stewart. There are few likeable characters in this story of a framed gangster's ruthless revenge. Claire Trevor scores heavily as his moll (as well as providing the laconic narration), Dennis O'Keefe makes a good job of the 'hero' who cynically uses people for his own ends, and Raymond Burr is an excellent, sadistic heavy. The excitement of the climax is underlined by the skilful, shadow-laden photography.

Raw Deal ● Ⓥ
1986, US, 105 mins, colour
Dir: John Irvin
Stars: Arnold Schwarzenegger, Kathryn Harrold, Sam Wanamaker, Darren McGavin, Robert Davi
Rating: ★★

The problem with Schwarzenegger, Norris and Stallone's Eighties' movies like this is that, however polished and persuasive the build-up of the plot, we know that our heroes will eventually take a machine-gun and mow down the entire syndicate of bad guys just like shelling peas. Pieces of furniture to hide behind? Forget it. Only the hero does that. A pity, for much of *Raw Deal* is held firmly in the *film noir* tradition by John Irvin even if the hero is not quite the alienated loner the genre customarily demands. The theme of the undercover man being trapped into doing things he doesn't want to do to keep his cover intact has been around for more than half a century, and it works well enough here on a pulp fiction level, with a burnished performance by Harrold as the gangster's moll with whom good ol' Arnold won't sleep 'cos he's married – even though his wife thinks he's dead. But then you know he can get out of the tightest corner just because he's Arnold. No vulnerability, you see. That's what made you grip your chairs for the safety of the agents of yore.

Raw Edge O
1956, US, 76 mins, colour
Dir: John Sherwood
Stars: Yvonne De Carlo, Rory Calhoun, Mara Corday, Rex Reason
Rating: ★★

A very unusual Western, set in the wilds of Oregon. For a principal ingredient in its action-packed story, it makes use of an old pioneer custom which decreed that a widow goes to the first man who claims her. The central character is played by the glamorous Yvonne De Carlo, so it's understandable that competition is pretty fierce. Ms De Carlo herself gets plenty of competition in the spitfire stakes from sultry Mara Corday.

Rawhide O
(aka: Desperate Siege)
1950, US, 86 mins, b/w
Dir: Henry Hathaway
Stars: Tyrone Power, Susan Hayward
Rating: ★★

Rawhide is the name of the trail station at which Tyrone Power and Susan Hayward are trapped by outlaws in this Henry Hathaway-directed Western which gave a first sizeable role to Jack Elam as one of the bandits. Hathaway sustains the claustrophobic tension well and stages a couple of exciting gunfights.

Rawhide Years, The O
1955, US, 84 mins, colour
Dir: Rudolph Maté
Stars: Tony Curtis, Arthur Kennedy
Rating: ★★★

Western fans shouldn't miss this well plotted, firmly characterised but little seen action film. Arthur Kennedy gives another of his nicely done, double-shaded portrayals as a genial ruffian who helps a riverboat gambler clear himself of a murder charge. Earl Felton's screenplay, from an excellent novel by Norman A Fox, gives Kennedy and Tony Curtis (as the gambler) many opportunities to score off one another, as well as keeping the story going at a lively pace.

Razor's Edge, The O Ⓥ
1946, US, 146 mins, b/w
Dir: Edmund Goulding
Stars: Tyrone Power, Gene Tierney, John Payne, Anne Baxter, Clifton Webb
Rating: ★★★

Hollywood had a brave stab here at filming Somerset Maugham's famous philosophical novel, and the results ran well over the two-hour mark. It did, however, win an Oscar for Anne Baxter, cast against type as the dipsomaniac Sophie. Tyrone Power is the restless aviator searching for meaning in his life; Herbert Marshall plays Maugham himself, and there are sparkling supporting performances from Clifton Webb and Elsa Lanchester.

Razor's Edge, The ◐
1984, US, 128 mins, colour
Dir: John Byrum
Stars: Bill Murray, Theresa Russell, Denholm Elliott
Rating: ★★

Remaking a classic film is a dangerous business usually doomed to failure and so it proved here. It's doubly difficult when the original film is based on an equally classic novel. Bill Murray, good though he is, can't fill Tyrone Power's shoes as the tormented man who doesn't want to settle down. He becomes involved in the First World War then travels to India to 'find himself. Murray's persona makes Somerset Maugham's central character something of a lightweight, robbing it of a lot of credibility. On the plus side, Theresa Russell, as the girl Murray tries to rescue from a life of sin and degradation, gives a very strong performance, as does the ever-reliable Denholm Elliott. But the film is stuffed to the gills with stilted dialogue that seems to belong to another era.

R

Reach for the Sky ○
1957, UK, 135 mins, b/w
Dir: Lewis Gilbert
Stars: Kenneth More, Muriel Pavlow
Rating: ★★★★

Written and directed by Lewis Gilbert, this is based on Paul Brickhill's book about Douglas Bader, the air ace who lost both legs but was determined to overcome his disability and fly again. Kenneth More's legs were encased in aluminium and he spent hours with Bader himself – an adviser to the film – perfecting the stiff-legged gait of a man with artificial legs. More inevitably dominates and takes a lion's share of the limelight, although Dorothy Alison sneaks it from him for a while with her sympathetic portrayal of Nurse Brace. The film stays the course smoothly and seems but half its length.

Real Genius ●
1985, US, 106 mins, colour
Dir: Martha Coolidge
Stars: Val Kilmer, Michelle Meyrink
Rating: ★

This attempted satirical comedy about scientists being corrupted in the search for *Star Wars*-type weapons misfires in all directions. After *Top Secret!* and *Top Gun*, this was distinctly bottom-drawer for star Val Kilmer, and relies on below-the-belt humour for what impact it can muster. Best of the cast is Michelle Meyrink as a curvaceous, non-stop engineering student.

Real Glory, The ○ ⓥ
1939, US, 95 mins, b/w
Dir: Henry Hathaway
Stars: Gary Cooper, Andrea Leeds, David Niven
Rating: ★★★

Unjustly neglected Hollywood action film, directed with dash by Henry Hathaway, staging some excellent action scenes as Doctor Gary Cooper tries to save Philippine patriots from murderous insurgents just after the Spanish-American war. 'Coop', David Niven and Broderick Crawford form a *Soldiers Three*-style triumvirate and battle scenes explode all over the screen. Even if you saw the film long ago, you'd be hard put to remember the name of the actress who shares top billing with the star: it was Andrea Leeds. Far more interesting though is Vladimir Sokoloff, playing the sneaky, treacherous Datu, with the skin and eyes of a reptile.

Reality Bites ① ⓥ
1994, US, 99 mins, colour
Dir: Ben Stiller

Stars: Winona Ryder, Ethan Hawke, Ben Stiller
Rating: **RB**

Director Ben Stiller chooses to give us quite a chunk of this dose of post-graduate blues on home videos shot by the characters – trying to the eyes and hardly cinema either. Not that you'll want to trouble yourself with the unconvincing problems of a dishevelled quartet of wannabes, who share a cluttered bedsit. Two of them, Winona Ryder and Ethan Hawke, are obviously destined to end up together and it seems an eternity before they realise what the rest of us could have told them during the opening credits. These are tiresome 20-somethings from the start and they don't get any better. See it for the stars if you must, but you could pack your bags and go home 10 minutes from the end when the dialogue reaches an all-time low as Hawke declares he has 'a planet of regret sitting on my shoulders'. We know what he means.

Real McCoy, The ① ⓥ
1993, US, 100 mins, colour
Dir: Russell Mulcahy
Stars: Kim Basinger, Val Kilmer, Terence Stamp
Rating: ★★

One more time for the caper thriller about the robbery of the impregnable bank. There's nothing new here and the only twist is that the gang is led by a woman, fresh out of prison and blackmailed into the job by the kidnap of her son. Kim Basinger is pretty good in the role and she's about all the dullish film has going for it. Val Kilmer is not much of anything as the guy who helps her double-cross the raiders, and Terence Stamp attempts an American accent as the gang boss that just doesn't pass muster by today's high standards. Even the robbery itself is pretty routine: there are one or two tense moments, but not enough to keep the eyelids from drooping before the end.

Real Men ①
1987, US, 93 mins, colour
Dir: Dennis Feldman
Stars: James Belushi, John Ritter, Barbara Barrie
Rating: ★

A distinctly unfunny spy spoof comedy about aliens battling with the CIA over some kind of big gun that can blow up an entire planet. Scenes fail to hang together as a cohesive whole and James Belushi and John Ritter mug

their embarrassed way through it by the skin of their teeth, no doubt justifiably thinking that their talents deserved better.

Rear Window ○ ⓥ
1954, US, 112 mins, colour
Dir: Alfred Hitchcock
Stars: James Stewart, Grace Kelly, Raymond Burr
Rating: ★★★★

Hitchcock suspense classic about a press photographer who, housebound with his leg in plaster, becomes obsessed with the notion that his neighbour across the way (a white-haired Raymond Burr in pre-*Perry Mason* and *Ironside* days) has done away with his wife. Besides the mounting suspense (especially of the 'will they or won't they get away with investigations before the 'murderer' comes back to catch them?' variety), there's the famous love scene where Hitch's camera circles hero James Stewart and girlfriend Grace Kelly as they kiss. All this plus prime performances from Stewart (no mean feat to achieve such emotion and conviction in such an immobile role) and from sandpaper-voiced Thelma Ritter as his nurse. John Michael Hayes and Hitchcock were Oscar-nominated for screenplay and direction.

Rebecca ○ ⓥ
1940, US, 130 mins, b/w
Dir: Alfred Hitchcock
Stars: Joan Fontaine, Laurence Olivier, Judith Anderson, George Sanders
Rating: ★★★★★

Hitchcock's first work in Hollywood, a brilliantly realised and atmospheric adaptation of Daphne du Maurier's enduring novel, won Oscars for Best Film and for George Barnes' fine camerawork. Joan Fontaine made her breakthrough to stardom as the (nameless) young bride haunted by the memory of husband Laurence Olivier's first wife, the enigmatic Rebecca of the title, who died in mysterious circumstances. In later years, Hitchcock rather mischievously dismissed Rebecca as a novelette, 'a woman's picture' lacking in humour. But its virtues are simplicity, superb performances and a richly textured visual style that compels attention. And just one of the many typical touches by the Master is his representation of Manderley's creepy housekeeper Mrs Danvers: in her unforgettable portrayal of this key role, Judith Anderson is almost never shown in motion but seems to materialise in rooms and doorways, standing still, as if from nowhere.

Rebel ◑ ⓥ
1985, Australia, 91 mins, colour
Dir: Michael Jenkins
Stars: Matt Dillon, Debbie Byrne, Bryan Brown
Rating: ★★

Matt Dillon has a character name to match his screen persona, even if he's badly miscast in this Australian musical romance. As Rebel, a US marine who has gone AWOL in Sydney in 1942, Dillon hasn't the dramatic depth to carry off a character whose motives are ambiguous to say the least. Craggy Bryan Brown, who went on to leading man status in Hollywood is a sharp profiteer, while there is a startling cameo from Ray Barrett as a flamboyant club pianist. But it is left to pretty Debbie Byrne, as the married singer in an all-girl showband, to sweep all before her as she belts out a clutch of songs written specially for the film.

Rebel, The ○ ⓥ
(aka: Call Me Genius)
1960, UK, 105 mins, colour
Dir: Robert Day
Stars: Tony Hancock, Paul Massie, Irene Handl, George Sanders
Rating: ★★★

Despite being attacked by the British critics at the time, Tony Hancock's first starring venture is a minor comedy classic. Admittedly, Hancock's gloomily truculent persona was stretched wider by the big sceen, but his shabby splendour, his conviction of unrecognised grandeur and his whole down-at-heel veneer of respectability, all shine through to make his frustrated insurance clerk with visions of artistic excellence a thoroughly sympathetic and loveable figure. *The Rebel* is scripted by the creators of the pompous denizen of 23 Railway Cuttings, Alan Simpson and Ray Galton, and although one misses Tony's streetwise anchor-man Sidney James, doughty support is given by Irene Handl, as the awful landlady Mrs Crevette. A treat for all lovers of this fine British funnyman.

Rebel Without a Cause ◑ ⓥ
1955, US, 111 mins, colour
Dir: Nicholas Ray
Stars: James Dean, Natalie Wood, Sal Mineo, Dennis Hopper
Rating: ★★★★

James Dean, the legendary idol of the 1950s, starred in just three feature films. This powerful work gave him the role with which he is most associated – the troubled and delinquent youth misunderstood by his parents and society. His highly charged, very personal portrayal of Jim helped create the cult which has persisted around his name ever since. Natalie Wood (in one of her best performances) and Sal Mineo are fellow rebels; action and colour photography are excellent, and the script full of well-remembered lines. The only weakness is the ending, which doesn't seem to prove very much at all.

Reckless ○
1935, US, 92 mins, colour
Dir: Victor Fleming
Stars: Jean Harlow, Franchot Tone, William Powell
Rating: ★★

Producer David O Selznick severely and unnecessarily dented Jean Harlow's confidence here by casting her in the completely unsuitable role of a song-and-dance star. Joan Crawford, who could at least dance, had originally been slated for the role of a showgirl who marries the wrong man, but the plot probably carried too many echoes of her own *Dancing Lady* two years earlier (complete with Franchot Tone as the wrong man). So Harlow was uncomfortably straitjacketed into a role where her singing had to be dubbed and her dancing heavily edited. A good supporting cast, including Tone, William Powell, Rosalind Russell, Allan Jones and Henry Stephenson (and, in much smaller roles, Mickey Rooney and Akim Tamiroff) provides consolation for film buffs, along with a score that includes 'Trocadero', 'Cyclone', and the Kern-Hammerstein title number.

Reckless Moment, The ○
1949, US, 82 mins, b/w
Dir: Max Ophuls
Stars: Joan Bennett, James Mason, Geraldine Brooks
Rating: ★★★

James Mason scored his first major Hollywood success as a reluctant blackmailer in this tautly made melodrama about a woman who falls into the clutches of ne'er-do-wells while trying to protect her errant daughter. Good local detail, sadly ironic ending. Joan Bennett co-stars as the woman in a thriller/drama that still looks good.

Reckoning, The ◑
1969, UK, 111 mins, colour
Dir: Jack Gold
Stars: Nicol Williamson, Rachel Roberts
Rating: ★★

Nicol Williamson's sexual bull on the rampage was much in vogue in the late Sixties and early Seventies but, somehow, he couldn't extend the characterisation into fully fledged stardom. Here, he's in typical stop-at-nothing mood as a rough diamond, climbing to the top of London's social ladder. The film is distinguished by Rachel Roberts' very erotic account of a sensual northern landlady, and by Ann Bell, a constantly underrated actress, who is also good as Williamson's much put-upon wife.

Red
See: Three Colours Red

Red Badge of Courage, The ○ ⓥ
1951, US, 69 mins, b/w
Dir: John Huston
Stars: Audie Murphy, Bill Mauldin
Rating: ★★★

Huston shot Stephen Crane's novel about a young soldier's baptism of fire in the American Civil War in painstaking, poetic style. The film, made in black and white, is full of swirling mists and smoke of battle, but Huston's fast-moving cameras, tracking the action and charging with the soldiers, ensure that there's plenty of excitement as well. MGM saw the finished product, got cold feet about the meaning and impact of its anti-war sentiments and hacked it down to a mere 69 minutes of cinema running time. The original was probably a masterpiece; even these tattered remnants are full of striking moments, with actors chosen for the characters they can express rather than their abilities. Audie Murphy plays the youth, Bill Mauldin (later a Pulitzer Prize-winning cartoonist) is his friend.

Red Beret, The ○
1953, UK, 88 mins, colour
Dir: Terence Young
Stars: Alan Ladd, Leo Genn, Susan Stephen
Rating: ★★

There was much alarm when Ladd came to Britain to make this film about the Paratroopers, for fear it should show him winning the war for the Americans in the same way as did Errol Flynn eight years earlier in *Objective Burma*. But it's a straightfor-

R

ward and exciting war film, with fine colour photography, and Ladd backed by a strong British cast.

Red Dust ○

1932, US, 89 mins, b/w
Dir: Victor Fleming
Stars: Clark Gable, Jean Harlow, Mary Astor
Rating: ★★★

A sturdy and enjoyable romantic melodrama set in Indo-China where Clark Gable romances sexy floozie Jean Harlow and meanwhile married Mary Astor falls for him. The triangular relationship reappeared in 1940 as *Congo Maisie* and again in 1954 as *Mogambo*, in which Gable – now in Africa – repeated his original role. This one is still the best version, with all three stars in top form.

Red Fury, The ○

1985, US, 90 mins, colour
Stars: Katherine Cannon, William Jordan
Rating: ★★

Hardly an original story – boy loves horse and, naturally, makes good in the final reel. But, given the somewhat old-fashioned plot, which also delves into the realms of racial intolerance, the drama makes its way pleasantly to its upbeat conclusion. Familiar faces in the cast include Alan Hale Jr – the son of the great Hollywood character actor Alan Hale in one of his last screen roles – and Diane McBain. Hardly another *Black Stallion*, although horse-loving children and teenagers will doubtless be enthralled by the vivid tracking shots of horses on the move.

Redhead from Wyoming, The ○

1953, US, 80 mins, colour
Dir: Lee Sholem
Stars: Maureen O'Hara, Alex Nicol, Alexander Scourby, William Bishop
Rating: ★★

Alex Nicol, fair-haired contract player from several Universal-International films of the Fifties, landed his biggest role in this Grade A Western, opposite fiery Maureen O'Hara as Kate (the redhead of the title) who runs a gambling casino that's also a hideaway tor wanted men.

Red Heat ○ ⓥ

1988, US, 106 mins, colour
Dir: Walter Hill
Stars: Arnold Schwarzenegger, James Belushi, Peter Boyle
Rating: ★★

Poor old Arnold Schwarzenegger. No matter how different the plot they give him, it still comes out the same. Arnie walks in, demolishes the bad guys and walks out again. No sweat. Just the odd bruise or two for effect. He almost smiles in this one. But not quite. The smiles came later, in *Twins* and *Kindergarten Cop*. Here the thud of fist on bone is much the same in any language, even when big Arnie is a Soviet policeman come to Chicago to bring home the Russian drugs dealer who shot his comrade cop. 'I now vork undercover,' growls Arnie, which presumably means he takes his shirt off less in this one. At any rate, multiple mayhem in the States, with local lawman James Belushi in tow, results. There is a lot of shouting, swearing, killing and knocking over cars and other convenient obstacles. It's all fair video entertainment and Belushi even gets the odd good line: 'I'd like to break this up,' he tells the incredible hulk, 'but we're parked in a red zone – no offence.'

Red Mountain ○

1951, US, 84 mins, colour
Dir: William Dieterle
Stars: Alan Ladd, Lizabeth Scott, Arthur Kennedy
Rating: ★★

This fast-paced, if dramatically stodgy, Western was made on the Paramount lot by veteran Hollywood director William Dieterle and blazingly photographed in Technicolor by colour specialist Charles B Lang. Alan Ladd and Lizabeth Scott make a fine fair-haired, blue-eyed partnership, but the film is stolen by John Ireland, fresh from the Oscar-winning *All the King's Men*, contributing a full-blooded portrayal of the rebel General Quantrell.

Red Pony, The ⊙

1949, US, 90 mins, colour
Dir: Lewis Milestone
Stars: Myrna Loy, Robert Mitchum
Rating: ★★★

Outdoor adventure stories about boys and horses held great appeal in Hollywood in the Forties, so John Steinbeck's short novel about a chestnut colt seemed a natural for fans. All credit to Republic Studios who hired a good cast, top photographer Tony Gaudio (whose Technicolor camerawork is wonderful) and noted composer Aaron Copland to provide the score. The results are poignant

and winning; Peter Miles, who plays the boy, later became a screenwriter and author.

Red River ○ ⓥ

1948, US, 133 mins, b/w
Dir: Howard Hawks
Stars: John Wayne, Montgomery Clift, Joanne Dru
Rating: ★★★★

Howard Hawks was at his pinnacle when he directed this grand-scale movie which stars John Wayne, has a first-rate screenplay and dazzling black-and-white photography, and features Montgomery Clift giving one of his most attractive and least complicated performances. The sprawling story, about the epic first cattle drive from Texas to Abilene, along the Chisholm Trail, first appeared as a *Saturday Evening Post* serial. Wayne's towering performance as Thomas Dunson foreshadowed many of the larger-than-life Westerners he would in fact be playing two decades later. And he dominates even a cast of this quality, including as it does John Ireland, Joanne Dru, three-time Academy Award winner Walter Brennan and Western veteran Harry Carey Senior, whose last film this was, and to whom it is dedicated. Music composer Dmitri Tiomkin's rousing score underlines the width and depth of a drama that frequently raises the dust without ever becoming dusty, and no more so than in the magnificent final flat-out scrap between the two stars at the end of the trail.

Red Rock West ● ⓥ

1992, US, 98 mins, colour
Dir: John Dahl
Stars: Nicolas Cage, Dennis Hopper, Lara Flynn Boyle, J T Walsh
Rating: ★★★★

Another journey into director John Dahl's world of *noir* duplicity: hired killers, lovers trapped by circumstance and women you can't trust. Nicolas Cage is the Texas drifter whose gammy leg costs him a job in Wyoming and forces him to drive on to the town of Red Rock, where he's almost immediately mistaken by Wayne (J T Walsh) as the killer he's hired to dispatch his faithless wife (Lara Flynn Boyle). Taking the money, Cage hotfoots it to warn the wife who immediately gives him more money to kill her husband. Stocking up with provisions, Cage goes for the sensible course and drives off with all the money. Circumstances in these films being what they are, however, he soon finds himself driving in and out of Red Rock like a yo-yo, always on the run from someone, most notably the real hitman (Dennis Hopper). Doomy, tightly shot and with a suitably desperate hero, *Red Rock* is all that this kind of film should be, down to the bitter climax. The characters are cold and passionless, oblivious till the last moment that fate is closing in on them all.

Reds O ⓥ
1981, US, 200 mins, colour
Dir: Warren Beatty
Stars: Warren Beatty, Diane Keaton, Jack Nicholson, Maureen Stapleton
Rating: ★★★

A story of epic proportions, set in America and Russia in the 1915-1921 period. And it is also a love story – on scale to match *Doctor Zhivago* and *Gone With the Wind*. Warren Beatty plays an idealistic Communist in America, Diane Keaton the free-thinking writer who joins his semi-underground movement. Together, they are caught up in momentous events in world history which culminate in her trekking across frozen wastes to find him in Finland, after he has fled the Bolsheviks. When it concentrates on people and not politics, in fact, this film is a winner. Diane Keaton is superb – a tribute to the direction of Beatty, for which he won an Academy Award.

Red Shoes, The O ⓥ
1948, UK, 136 mins, colour
Dir: Michael Powell, Emeric Pressburger
Stars: Moira Shearer, Anton Walbrook
Rating: ★★★★

One of the very few successful films about ballet, this movie was helped by striking design and ravishing Technicolor, with the result that it was a delight to the eye. Many a ballet-mad schoolgirl went crazy about the film in general and the 20-year-old red-haired Ms Shearer in particular. The highlight of it all was The Red Shoes Ballet, perhaps the most effective and entertaining thing of its kind ever put on film, the music for which was especially composed by Brian Easdale. The drama is less successful.

Red Skies of Montana O
1952, US, 90 mins, colour
Dir: Joseph M Newman
Stars: Richard Widmark, Jeffrey Hunt Constance Smith
Rating: ★★

An action-filled account of the work of the parachute firefighters of the US

Forest Rescue service. A cast of some of America's most rugged actors, including Richard Widmark, Jeffrey Hunter, Richard Boone, Richard Crenna and Charles Bronson, does sterling work under the direction of Joseph M Newman, whose film career petered out sooner than it should have, despite constant accolades from certain critical quarters. The script of this one is pretty average, but Newman splices in some superb action sequences involving forest fires, some of them doubtless inspired by his own documentary film, *Smokejumpers*.

Red Sonja ◑ ⓥ
1985, US, 89 mins, colour
Dir: Richard Fleischer
Stars: Brigitte Nielsen, Arnold Schwarzenegger
Rating: ★

Although the statuesque Brigitte Nielsen gets top billing in this sword and sorcery epic, it is pumped-up Arnold Schwarzenegger who steals the attention. As a mythical warrior who declares 'Danger is my trade', he certainly looks the part, but his big problem is that he has to talk too much. About every 15 minutes or so! Arnie fights to get his thick Austrian accent around the most banal dialogue (written by Clive Exton and George MacDonald Fraser, both of whom obviously had an off day) and mispronounces Red Sonja's name as 'Sony-uh' at every rum. To her credit, Nielsen never seems to listen to a word he says. But despite the presence of such testosterone giants of the cinema and Arnie's earlier success as *Conan the Barbarian*, the film flopped.

Red Sun ◑
1971, Italy, 112 mins, colour
Dir: Terence Young
Stars: Charles Bronson, Toshiro Mifune, Alain Delon, Ursula Andress
Rating: ★★

A blood-and-guts adventure film that's not so much a spaghetti Western (actually a Franco-Italian-Spanish-American co-production) as a Samurai Western, as Japanese warrior Toshiro Mifune stalks the Wild West with unlikely partner Charles Bronson in search of a fabulous jewel-encrusted sword. The sword has been stolen by Bronson's treacherous ex-partner, a New Orleans gambler played by Alain Delon (sporting one silver tooth amid the white). The heroine is Ursula Andress who, with her habit of stripping to the waist in every film, reminds me of those

beefcake heroes who couldn't appear without taking off their shirts at least once. In the acting stakes, though, Ursula loses out to Capucine, who makes the most of an almost non-existent part. The action will satisfy the most bloodthirsty Western fan.

Red Sundown O
1955, US, 82 mins, colour
Dir: Jack Arnold
Stars: Rory Calhoun, Martha Hyer, Robert Middleton, Dean Jagger
Rating: ★★★ .

In pace and uncompromising toughness, this blood-spattered Western was years ahead of its time. Not surprising, as its director, Jack Arnold, was at the peak of his form, and was to combine a year later with one of the stars, Grant Williams, to make the outstanding science-fiction thriller *The Incredible Shrinking Man*. Here, he has Rory Calhoun as the gunfighter who discovers the life of a deputy sheriff is not all patrolling the streets and throwing drunks in jail, when fat and influential Rufus Henshaw (Robert Middleton) tries taking over the town. Martha Hyer is remarkably successful as the nice girl, there are good performances from Williams and Dean Jagger, and sandy-haired James Millican is outstanding as Bud Purvis. Tragically he died later the same year, at the age of 45.

Red Tent, The O
1969, UK, 121 mins, colour
Dir: Mikhail K Kalatozov
Stars: Peter Finch, Sean Connery, Claudia Cardinale, Hardy Kruger
Rating: ★★

In between his last two assignments as James Bond, Sean Connery gave some fine performances for the cinema, and this portrait of the Norwegian explorer Amundsen is one of them. This is not an account of his race with Scott to reach the South Pole, but a later episode in his exciting career, dealing with his bid to rescue the survivors of an airship which crashed in a blizzard near the North Pole. The pictorial qualities of the film are strong, but the cast, which includes British, German, Italian and Russian players, has to struggle hard to come to terms with the inconsistencies in the dialogue.

Red Tomahawk O
1966, US, 82 mins, colour
Dir: R G Springstein
Stars: Howard Keel, Broderick Crawford, Scott Brady, Joan Crawford
Rating: ★★

R

This Western about the aftermath of the Custer massacre provided a nostalgic return to Dodge City for its star Howard Keel, who had first ridden through the town in the Doris Day musical *Calamity Jane*. Betty Hutton was slated to make a comeback in this film, but quit soon after shooting began. Another Paramount star of the Forties, Joan Caulfield, replaced her.

Ref, The
See: Hostile Hostages

Reflections in a Golden Eye ● Ⓥ
1967, US, 105 mins, colour
Dir: John Huston
Stars: Marlon Brando, Elizabeth Taylor, Brian Keith, Julie Harris
Rating: ★★

One of John Huston's most bizarre ventures. Brando gives one of the more interesting of his latter performances as the repressed homosexual soldier whose wife has to turn to another officer (Brian Keith) for affection. Elizabeth Taylor is beautifully cast as Brando's desirable but insensitive wife. Huston confessed himself angered by the studio's refusal to carry out his original plan to desaturate the print to a duo-tone of pinks and golds – but he did use severely under-exposed stock, giving the picture the dull sepiatone look of an old photograph.

Regarding Henry Ⓞ Ⓥ
1990, US, 116 mins, colour
Dir: Mike Nichols
Stars: Harrison Ford, Annette Bening, Bill Nunn, Mikki Allen
Rating: ★★★

Excellent performances by Ford and Bening help keep sentimentality largely at bay in this manipulative but successful movie about a hard-nosed lawyer who changes for the better after being brain-damaged by a bullet in a liquor-store raid. Slowly recovering the powers of speech and movement, he returns to his wife and family, unaware that his daughter lives in fear of him, and that he and his wife had drifted apart and were both having affairs. His wife finds herself with a new man and likes what she finds, even if Henry has become simple, slow-witted and methodical rather than his sharp, soulless and sharklike former self. His former associates can offer him only pity, and precious little of that. 'One minute you're an attorney, the next an imbecile,' they joke at a party. You'll

be able to find plenty of sympathy for Henry, however, and enjoy his redemption and rehabilitation, not to mention righting a few wrongs along the way.

Reivers, The Ⓞ
1969, US, 107 mins, colour
Dir: Mark Rydell
Stars: Steve McQueen, Sharon Farrell, Rupert Crosse, Mitch Vogel, Clifton James
Rating: ★★★★★

A gentle, rambling tale of a young boy's adventures in the Deep South, which start when his grandfather's hired hand Boon (Steve McQueen) 'borrows' his boss's new 1905 Winton car and takes the lad to Memphis. There they visit a bordello, lose the car and try to win a horse-race. The episodic tale is taken from the book by William Faulkner (his last and probably most difficult to read) and given rhythm by Burgess Meredith's narration. It's beautifully photographed, has a strong sense of period, and the rite-of-passage elements of the story avoid the usual mawkish pitfalls. McQueen is excellent, as is young Mitch Vogel as the boy. Having said that, they have strong competition from Rupert Crosse as McQueen's black workmate who tags along for the ride: he manages to steal many of the scenes he's in. A delightful film, full of the fun of being alive.

Relic, The ● Ⓥ
1996, US, 110 mins, colour
Dir: Peter Hyams
Stars: Penelope Ann Miller, Tom Sizemore, James Whitmore
Rating: ★★

A big-budget horror movie with all the tired old trappings of the genre. The monster, supposedly a combination of man-eating man, galloping gecko and rampaging rhinoceros, looks like that angry old alien to us, complete with slobbery tombstone teeth and a craving for those parts of the human brain it needs to keep it healthy. Unwary explorers in the Brazilian rainforest only have to drink certain jungle juices to be consumed with a craving for those leaves and berries that turn them into a decapitating monster that wreaks havoc in Dr Penelope Ann Miller's museum. Never fear, Dr Penny, changing into a little black number for the opening of her superstition exhibition, is sure to find a way to put paid to this megagodzilla before half of Chicago is scrunched in its

jaws. As usual, people creep around in the dark and get gobbled up, but director Hyams can be relied on to keep the old formula brisk enough to ensure we clutch our partner even as we chuckle.

Reluctant Debutante, The Ⓞ
1958, UK, 94 mins, colour
Dir: Vincente Minnelli
Stars: Rex Harrison, Kay Kendall, Sandra Dee
Rating: ★★★★

A sparkling romantic romp that shows Rex Harrison at his elegant and witty best. Both he and his wife Kay Kendall supply accurate but offhand comedy timing to a diamond-sharp script by William Douglas-Home that also brings a career-best performance from Sandra Dee as the deb of the title. Polished, accomplished, relaxed yet fast-moving, the whole enterprise is a delight. Angela Lansbury supplies the icing on the cake as a designing society mother.

Reluctant Dragon, The ☉
1941, US, 72 mins, colour
Dir: Alfred Werker, Jim Handley, Ford Beebe, Erwin Verity, Jasper Blystone
Stars: Robert Benchley
Rating: ★★★

This film mixes live action and animation, using the arrival of the popular humorist Robert Benchley at the Disney Studio (watch for Alan Ladd as an animator) as the excuse for a behind-the-scenes look at the magic of animation. Disney fans will enjoy glimpses of some of their favourite characters as well as some fascinating footage of how artists drew an elephant from life for *Dumbo*, the recording of a duet for Donald Duck and Clara Cluck, and sound men creating thunder and talking railway trains. The dragon of the title is of course a delight, but, as a peaceable fellow who thinks jaw is better than war, he was out of step with the public mood at the time.

Remains of the Day, The Ⓞ Ⓥ
1993, UK, 135 mins, colour
Dir: James Ivory
Stars: Anthony Hopkins, Emma Thompson, James Fox, Christopher Reeve, Peter Vaughan, Hugh Grant, Tim Pigott-Smith
Rating: ★★★★★

This beautifully crafted film is a very English piece, full of unspoken emotions. Anthony Hopkins is perfectly cast as Stevens, the butler in a stately home of the 1930s whose noble owner

(James Fox) talks appeasement with the Germans and who will, with the coming of war, be reviled as a traitor. Also among his ancestral home's many servants is the housekeeper, Miss Kenton (Emma Thompson), whose relationship with Stevens develops into one of mutual respect and affection, if the butler ever permitted himself such an emotion. The fact that he does not, and despises relationships among servants, is a fatal flaw in his makeup, and one that is to cost him dear. Ruth Prawer Jhabvala's screenplay, pretty faithful to the book by Kazuo Ishiguro, arrows unerringly to a heartrending conclusion. Brilliant performances by the principals; good support from Fox, Tim Pigott-Smith and Christopher Reeve. Peter Vaughan is a touch over the top but still memorable as Stevens' father, whom he employs as an under-butler even though he knows the old man is past it.

Remarkable Mr Kipps, The
See: Kipps

Rembrandt O
1936, UK, 85 mins, b/w
Dir: Alexander Korda
Stars: Charles Laughton, Gertrude Lawrence, Elsa Lanchester
Rating: ★★★★

This biography of the 17th-century Dutch painter has been described as Alexander Korda's greatest film, and through it he won over some of his most severe critics. Korda, who produced and directed the film, concentrates on the later, poverty-stricken years of Rembrandt, when his work was no longer appreciated. The sets (by Korda's brother Vincent) and costumes were based on Dutch paintings of the period. Korda's ambition was to interpret, by camera and film, the scenes which Rembrandt had captured with paint and canvas. The critics felt he had succeeded, and praised film and performances – especially Charles Laughton and his wife Elsa Lanchester – highly.

Remember? O
1939, US, 83 mins, b/w
Dir: Norman Z McLeod
Stars: Robert Taylor, Greer Garson, Lew Ayres
Rating: ★★

A loss-of-memory comedy from director Norman Z McLeod, whose zany sense of fun contributed largely to some of the best efforts in the genre, from W C Fields to Bob Hope. This

offering, however, is not in the *Paleface* class. Great dramatic actors do not necessarily make very deft comics and perhaps the starry cast of Robert Taylor, Greer Garson and Lew Ayres is a bit overpowering for such a slight vehicle: like putting a Formula 1 engine in a go-kart.

Remember My Name ◑
1978, US, 96 mins, colour
Dir: Alan Rudolph
Stars: Anthony Perkins, Geraldine Chaplin
Rating: ★★★

A kind of avant-garde *film noir*, with Geraldine Chaplin perfectly cast as the enigmatic ex-convict clearly determined on vengeance for some past miscarriage of justice. Anthony Perkins proves almost equally well-suited to the role of the man whose life she bedevils, which gives him the opportunity to offer another of his expert studies in personal torment.

Remember the Day O
1941, UK, 85 mins, b/w
Dir: Henry King
Stars: Claudette Colbert, John Payne
Rating: ★★★

This weepie isn't much remembered today, although it's actually compulsive viewing. It's very well directed by Henry King, who was a master at pulling the tear strings from the silent days right up to the late Fifties and impeccably structured throughout. It also gave John Payne a chance to break away from musicals, and Claudette Colbert the opportunity to escape from glamour into character, as an elderly schoolteacher journeying to see one of her former pupils.

Remo – Unarmed and Dangerous O ⓥ
(aka: Remo Williams – The Adventure Begins)
1985, US, 110 mins, colour
Dir: Guy Hamilton
Stars: Fred Ward, Joel Grey, Wilford Brimley
Rating: ★★

Typical mid-Eighties Hollywood hokum, with a streetsmart cop (Fred Ward) being 'killed off' so that he can start life afresh as Remo Williams, supreme righter of wrongs for a secret syndicate. Director Guy Hamilton's job is to dress this up so that it doesn't seem too preposterous, at least while we're watching, and he doesn't do a bad job of it. Remo is trained in martial arts by an ancient Korean, then

pitted against a corrupt armaments manufacturer whose weapons, great and small, are not quite what they're cracked up to be. There's a fair-enough dice with death around the Statue of Liberty and an amazing encounter with three lethal and intelligent Doberman dogs in the film's serial-like developments on the way to the bad guys meeting a demise that seems tame by the Eighties' exacting standards of violence. Most of the cast seem to be in need of acting rather than combat lessons, although Joel Grey enjoys himself as Ward's Korean mentor.

Remo Williams – The Adventure Begins
See: Remo – Unarmed and Dangerous

Renaissance Man ◑ ⓥ
1994, US, 129 mins, colour
Dir: Penny Marshall
Stars: Danny DeVito, Gregory Hines, Cliff Robertson, James Remar, Stacey Dash, Kadeem Hardison
Rating: ★★★

An overlong bittersweet comedy with some feel-good highlights, starring Danny DeVito as Bill Rago, an out-of-work advertising executive hired by the army to teach English to a bunch of illiterate recruits. Bill has never taught before, and there are lessons to be learned by all about discipline, self-esteem and achievement while Bill strives to get his backward pupils over the intellectual hill. DeVito as usual is excellent, and he's given plenty of witty lines if not too much in the way of support. Director Penny Marshall tries to keep track of rather too many subplots, and DeVito's relationship with a female officer is so underplayed as to make you wonder why they bothered. Gregory Hines plays a tough drill sergeant and top rapper Marky Mark – billed as Mark Wahlberg – makes his film debut as one of the recruits.

Renegades O
1946, US, 88 mins, colour
Dir: George Sherman
Stars: Evelyn Keyes, Willard Parker, Larry Parks
Rating: ★★★

Although Larry Parks (he later fell foul of the Un-American Activities Committee) is best remembered for his film portrayals of Al Jolson, he never gave a better performance than in this rousing, unexpectedly good Western. Nominally, Parks, as a bad guy trying

R

to go straight, gets third billing on the cast list. But the film is his from the moment he appears on the screen. This was his last film before *The Jolson Story* and his acting here probably helped him win the part. Those he outplays include such seasoned Western heroes as Willard Parker, Jim (Red Ryder) Bannon, Forrest Tucker and Edgar Buchanan. Director George Sherman manoeuvres the action with a fine grasp of dramatic impact and the Technicolor photography is sheer delight.

Renegades ● Ⓥ
1989, US, 102 mins, colour
Dir: Jack Sholder
Stars: Kiefer Sutherland, Lou Diamond Phillips, Jami Gertz
Rating: ★★★

Hollywood was running out of variations for its cycle of buddy action films around this time, but this one has a thread that at least gives a slightly different slant to its parade of icy killers, undercover cops, car chases and violent action set pieces. The title might suggest it's a modern Western and indeed Lou Diamond Phillips' impassive native American might have ridden straight out of the past as, in pursuit of a stolen sacred spear, he time and again rescues faintly inefficient maverick cop Sutherland from his own poor judgment. You couldn't really give a nickel for the chances of the duo surviving in this world of corruption and instant death, but as usual the killers and their henchmen are bad shots and our heroes make it through to the well-staged climax involving a blazing barn, a handy motorcycle, a cat-and-mouse hunt through woods and, of course, the Final Vengeance of the spear. Leave your thinking caps in the hall and enjoy.

Repo Man ● Ⓥ
1984, US, 92 mins, colour
Dir: Alex Cox
Stars: Emilio Estevez, Harry Dean Stanton, Tracy Walter
Rating: ★★★

Unemployed Emilio Estevez learns to steal cars from Harry Dean Stanton, but it's all legal: Stanton is a finance company repossession man. Then they pick up a car with a dangerous 'box of tricks' in the boot. The film, set in the urban sprawl of Los Angeles, looks great and the ending, coming as it does after a long chase sequence, is unexpected and dazzling. Estevez and Stanton obviously had great fun in

this, British director Alex Cox's debut film. It has now become a cult film and not without reason, although bits of it do drag.

Repossessed ● Ⓥ
1990, US, 93 mins, colour
Dir: Bob Logan
Stars: Linda Blair, Leslie Nielsen, Ned Beatty, Anthony Starke
Rating: ★

Blair has had a chequered film career since she first sprang to public attention as the possessed pre-teen in *The Exorcist*. But whatever 'possessed' her to make this simply appalling comedy can only be guessed at. That the public would briefly flock to see it has to be the answer, as script and treatment are so fourth-formish that anyone could tell at a glance that the results would be deadeningly unfunny. Director Bob Logan's sense of comic timing is non-existent, his idea of an amusing scene being to expose girls with big breasts or have people be sick a lot. Blair, by now a chubby 30-year-old, at least performs with puppy-dog enthusiasm as the housewife possessed anew by her childhood demon. Nielsen's exorcist is even more arch and camera-nudging that his character in the *Naked Gun* films. And everything else is so far over the top as to have every drop of humour squeezed from it.

Repulsion ● Ⓥ
1965, UK, 105 mins, b/w
Dir: Roman Polanski
Stars: Catherine Deneuve, Ian Hendry, John Fraser, Patrick Wymark
Rating: ★★★★

This disturbing horror film was such a critical and public success that it quickly established itself as a classic in its field. The chilling feeling of incipient madness has seldom been realised with such skill and imagination, although many of its more famous hallucinatory scenes have been imitated since. Roman Polanski's direction is slow but deliberate, never missing a chance of jolting the audience with a sudden shock. Catherine Deneuve, as Carol, the girl whose revulsion for men leads her along the corridors of lunacy to the cashpoint of violence that is the light at the end of her nightmare visions, shows all the agony of a tormented mind in her eyes. Also very good are Ian Hendry and Helen Fraser as Carol's chatty friend at the beauty salon where they work, who occasionally brings her into a reality that

doesn't frighten her. A compelling film that's a must for connoisseurs of the cinema's darker corners.

Requiem for a Heavyweight
See: Blood Money

Rescue, The ○
1988, US, 98 mins, colour
Dir: Ferdinand Fairfax
Stars: Kevin Dillon, Christina Harnos, Marc Price
Rating: ★

This action adventure film about a group of teenagers who go to rescue their Navy fathers captured by the North Koreans doesn't lack excitement but does fall short in almost every other department. It seems to be an attempt to combine those wholesome Disney adventures and their cute young heroes with a Chuck Norris movie. In a plot of spiralling improbability we have our teen team getting halfway across Korea undetected and then blowing away all the slant-eyed 'Commies' with a high-tech arsenal they just happened to take with them. Come back Chuck, all is forgiven.

Rescuers, The ☉ Ⓥ
1977, US, 77 mins, colour
Dir: Wolfgang Reitherman, John Lounsbery, Art Stevens
Voice stars: Bob Newhart, Eva Gabor, Geraldine Page, Joe Flynn, Jim Jordan, John Mcintire, Michelle Stacy
Rating: ★★★

Although a little short on excitement, pace and comedy, this Disney cartoon feature creates the best set of characters from the studio for a decade: Orville, the albatross who runs his own airline, with whom each take-off brings a new nightmare; Evinrude, a dragonfly who ferries the mice heroes through the swamps on leaves when he's not on the run from a gang of bats; the monstrous Madam Medusa, Disney's best villainess since Cruella de Vil; two knowing alligators named Brutus and Nero; a bespectacled cat called Rufus; and two charming mice, of whom Eva Gabor's Bianca, the sexpot from Hungary, is undoubtedly the hit of the whole show in terms of vocalising.

Rescuers Down Under, The
☉ Ⓥ
1990, US, 74 mins, colour
Dir: Hendel Butoy
Voice stars: Bob Newhart, Eva Gabor, John Candy, George C Scott, Tristan Rogers
Rating: ★★

A passable Disney follow-up to *The Rescuers*, nicely animated in most of its scenes, with the Disney draughtsmen getting a chance to draw Australian flora and fauna when 'rescue mice' Bianca and Bernard are called across continents to save a young Australian boy at the mercy of an evil trapper who wants to capture the boy's friend, an eagle. There are not so many good characters here as in the first film – Joanna, the slimy salamander, is the pick of the bunch – but the story moves swiftly enough, and there's a typically Disneyesque exciting climax, with the boy about to be dropped into the mouths of snapping crocodiles while Bianca and Bernard battle to save him.

Reservoir Dogs ● ⊙
1991, US, 100 mins, colour
Dir: Quentin Tarantino
Stars: Harvey Keitel, Tim Roth, Michael Madsen, Lawrence Tierney
Rating: ★

A silly, very violent and stagy account of bank robbers falling out, this never makes up its mind what kind of movie it wants to be. The actors strike poses and stand in their assigned positions as often as they leak blood as they argue amongst each other as to what went wrong with their planned jewellery heist. Nice, though, to see veteran actor Lawrence Tierney, knocking spots off the rest of this over-intense cast. Tierney, who contributed a memorable portrayal of the gangster almost 50 years earlier, is here given a chance to quip, on being asked if a confederate has snuffed it, that he's 'as dead as Dillinger'! A cult success.

Restless Natives ○ ⊙
1985, UK, 89 mins, colour
Dir: Michael Hoffman
Stars: Vincent Friell, Joe Mullaney, Teri Laily, Ned Beatty
Rating: ★★

Innovative Scottish comedy in the style (though not with the style) of Bill Forsyth, who made *Gregory's Girl* and *Local Hero*. Director Michael Hoffman's local heroes are two work-shy Edinburgh youths who dress up as a clown and a wolfman and proceed to hold up tourist coaches travelling through the Scottish countryside. There's a sugar coating of whimsical larkiness to the screenplay.

Restoration ● ⊙
1995, UK/US, 118 mins, colour
Dir: Michael Hoffman

Stars: Robert Downey Jr, Meg Ryan, Sam Neill, Ian McKellen, David Thewlis, Hugh Grant
Rating: ★★★

The amazing sets and production design all but dwarf the drama in this story of London life in the 1660s. Robert Downey Jr's position as the court physician who eventually sees the error of the ways of debauchery gives the makers of the film the opportunity to run the whole gamut of this turbulent decade, from Downey's sham marriage to one of the king's mistresses, to his (unlikely) rehabilitation through madhouse, plague and fire. Deliberately evocative of old paintings, the film is finely detailed, both in its depiction of London's riverside life and the ornate splendour of the king's palace. Downey, English accent firmly in place, is well in character throughout as the man who travels from physician to fop to fool and back again. Emotive moments towards the end when Downey battles the plague give the film an extra lift. Sam Neill, David Thewlis, Hugh Grant, Ian McKellen and Meg Ryan all make effective contributions to a film that remains consistently impressive until tailing off a little disappointingly at the end.

Resurrection ◐
1980, US, 103 mins, colour
Dir: Daniel Petrie
Stars: Ellen Burstyn, Sam Shepard
Rating: ★★★

Lewis John Carlino's screenplay is rather too soft-centred for its potentially tough subject, but it does provide fine roles for Ellen Burstyn (an Oscar winner for *Alice Doesn't Live Here Any More*) and Sam Shepard. While the two stars are on the screen, the movie, carefully directed by Daniel Petrie, catches fire dramatically, while Mario Tosi's cinematography adds an attractive sheen.

Return from the River Kwai ◐ ⊙
1988, US, 100 mins, colour
Dir: Andrew V McLaglen
Stars: Edward Fox, Denholm Elliott, Christopher Penn, George Takei
Rating: ★★

The original *Bridge on the River Kwai*, however spurious, was a classic war film. This much belated follow-up attempts to tell a true story from the same period but, sadly lacking charismatic players, comes over as no more than a routine war saga. Edward Fox

and George Takei are both so stilted as the humane English and Japanese commanders that you long to stick a pin in them to make them behave naturally. Christopher Penn looks mighty overweight for an American pilot going through hell and high water, and it's left to Denhohn Elliott (killed too soon) and Nick Tate (as the Australian PoW commander) to inject the briskness, conviction and down-to-earth life the film needs. And, though handed a routine character, Tatsuya Nakadai is also good as the tightly fanatical Japanese camp supervisor. The action scenes carry some excitement, but lack a certain edge and vitality.

Return from Witch Mountain ○
1978, US, 95 mins, colour
Dir: John Hough
Stars: Kim Richards, Ike Eisenmann, Bette Davis, Christopher Lee
Rating: ★★

Undemanding fun from the Disney Studio, with Christopher Lee and Bette Davis as villains who might have stepped straight out of a silent serial, and a plot pitched on the level of an *Our Gang* comedy. Endearing young heroes Kim Richards and Ike Eisenmann return from the first film.

Return of Frank James, The ○
1940, US, 92 mins, colour
Dir: Fritz Lang
Stars: Henry Fonda, Gene Tierney
Rating: ★★★

One of the rare occasions in the cinema when a sequel is as good as the original. The reason lies mostly in the direction – by master craftsman Fritz Lang. The action is fast and fierce and the colour photography first-rate. Henry Fonda provides an authoritative and intensely sympathetic portrayal of Frank James, and proves no slouch at the gunplay game either. The opening sequence shows Jesse's death from the end of the previous film, *Jesse James*, made in 1939. The actor playing Jesse is Tyrone Power.

Return of Swamp Thing, The ◐ ⊙
1989, US, 89 mins, colour
Dir: Jim Wynorski
Stars: Louis Jourdan, Heather Locklear, Sarah Douglas, Dick Durock
Rating: ★★

This is a literal transplantation of a horror comic to the screen with the accent on the comic – but it's hard to

R

know whether to laugh at it or with it. 'Where do you come from?' gasps one of two very tiresome children. 'From the bog,' chortles the jolly green giant of the title, though he turns serious when romanced by healthily curvy Heather Locklear. 'Please don't,' he admonishes. 'This will never work.' That's OK, she reassures him: she's a vegetarian. Well folks, there's also a plot about mad scientist Louis Jourdan (originally responsible for the hero's state of vegetation) who plays the organ in between creating horrific mutants in his search for eternal life. 'You sold your soul to the Devil,' Locklear accuses him. He smiles: 'Let's just say he has a lease with an option to buy.' DC comics have a lot to answer for, but at least their monstrous offspring, though badly acted, is never dull.

Return of the Fly ◖ ⓥ
1959, US, 80 mins, colour
Dir: Edward L Bernds
Stars: Vincent Price, Brett Halsey, David Frankham, Danielle De Metz
Rating: ★★

The second of three horror films about the Delambre family and their obsession with 'teleporting' human beings through space, from one country to another. In the first film, *The Fly*, André Delambre became half-man, half-fly. This sequel has Vincent Price back in his original role as André's brother François, with his now grown-up nephew Philippe (Brett Halsey) undergoing some nasty but predictable disasters in the teleportation chamber. Scowling Dan Seymour, one of the most memorable of the cinema's fat, ugly and menacing villains, plays Max Berthold.

Return of the Jedi ○ ⓥ
1983, US, 133 mins, colour
Dir: Richard Marquand
Stars: Mark Hamill, Harrison Ford, Carrie Fisher, Billy Dee Williams, Anthony Daniels
Rating: ★★★★

Delightful finish to the trilogy that George Lucas always said was intended for children but ended up, because of its scale, style and imagination, as fabulous entertainment for all. Some marvellous new creations, especially Jabba and the Ewoks, and the unbeatable special effects more than make up for a slightly tired storyline. Though it is more sentimental than its predecessors, it's no less enjoyable or uplifting, and the fireworks at the end restore it

to the realm of super-pantomime to which it belongs.

Return of the Living Dead Part II ● ⓥ
1988, US, 89 mins, colour
Dir: Ken Wiederhorn
Stars: James Karen, Thorn Mathews, Dana Ashbrook, Michael Kenwortky
Rating: ★★

Another one of those radiation waste disposal canisters has fallen off the back of a lorry and before you can say 'Aargh!' zombies by the thousand are scissoring up through the earth and advancing on the local population. 'Symptoms,' says the boozy doctor (Phillip Bruns) inspecting an infected patient, 'suggest chronic intractable rigor mortis!' 'My God,' says his cohort, 'is it serious?' Yes, this is a (very gruesome) horror comedy, quite hilarious in spots, specially the zombie who, pranged by the heroes, complains: 'Get this goddam screwdriver out of my head.' The zombies advance with cries of 'Fresh brains!' but never fear: the heroine is 'Junior state sharpshooter champion' and her younger brother grabs a hefty pistol, crying: 'Make my night!' Excessive it's true, the film runs out of steam before the end, but you can forgive it a lot for its sense of humour.

Return of the Musketeers, The ○ ⓥ
1989, UK, 100 mins, colour
Dir: Richard Lester
Stars: Michael York, Oliver Reed, Frank Finlay, C Thomas Howell, Kim Cattrall
Rating: ★★

Michael York, Oliver Reed, Richard Chamberlain and Frank Finlay all return for more swash and buckle in this sequel to the *Musketeers* stories, an adaptation of Dumas's *Twenty Years After*. As an action yarn it works quite well. As a comedy, though, it doesn't work at all, which is a pity, as the vein of humour is clearly meant to be its trump card. The problem is that director Lester doesn't treat this as a comedy of character, making fun of the heroes' ageing bones, rather as one of incidental (and very heavy-handed) humour, with peripheral characters rhubarbing away to themselves as they comment on the action. Never mind, Kim Cattrall enjoys herself lustily as the villainous Justine, snapping, fighting and leaping with an energy unparalleled since the days of Maureen O'Hara. And Geraldine Chaplin is delightful as a feather-headed, flibbertigibbet Anne

of Austria. The best acting performance, though, is Alan Howard's cool and calculating Cromwell. Although Finlay appears to be killed in the final fight, he is magically resurrected for the triumphant brotherly fadeout!

Return of the Pink Panther, The ○ ⓥ
1974, UK, 113 mins, colour
Dir: Blake Edwards
Stars: Peter Sellers, Christopher Plummer, Catherine Schell, Herbert Lom
Rating: ★★★

He is defeated by a door-bell, tricked by a telephone, routed by a radio, beset by a bath and vanquished by a vacuum cleaner. Mechanical contrivances confound him; 'apparati' assail him. In short, Inspector Clouseau is back, as, for a third time, Peter Sellers assumes his most famous role. Again the famous diamond known as the Pink Panther has been stolen. Ostensibly, the thief is once more The Phantom (formerly David Niven, now Christopher Plummer, who registers well). Clouseau, first encountered haranguing an organ-grinder in a Paris street while a bank robbery takes place in the window behind them, is assigned to break the case, much to the chagrin of his superior (Herbert Lom) whose mental control of the Clouseau situation is rapidly slipping. Some of the comedy is a little crude, especially at first, and slow-motion gags generally don't work. But the film is awash with inventive comic touches.

Return of the Scarlet Pimpernel, The ○
1937, UK, 94 mins, b/w
Dir: Hans Schwartz
Stars: Barry K Barnes, Sophie Stewart, Margaretta Scott, James Mason
Rating: ★★

Fair swashbuckler based on Baroness Orczy's *The Elusive Pimpernel*. Barry K Barnes made his film debut in this film, in the role previously played by Leslie Howard. Barnes' elegant performance made him a star. But ill-health curtailed his later career and he died in 1965 at the age of 58. Another actor whose acting span was brief was David Tree, who can be seen as Lord Harry Denning. From a famous acting family, Tree seemed set for a bright future, but lost an arm in war service, and left the profession.

Return of the Seven ○
1966, US, 95 mins, colour
Dir: Burt Kennedy

Stars: Yul Brynner, Robert Fuller, Warren Oates

Rating: ★★

A sequel to *The Magnificent Seven,* with Yul Brynner again, as the leader of a new septet of crusading gunmen. The theme – defence of a village against marauding outlaws – is similar to that in the original film. Here the cast includes Claude Akins and Warren Oates, and the director is Burt Kennedy, one of Hollywood's best-respected makers of Westerns. The screenplay is written by Larry Cohen, who later wrote and directed his own distinctive films, often in horror vein. This is very ordinary fare compared to the first film, and shot in muddy colour to boot.

Return to Oz ○

1985, US, 110 mins, colour
Dir: Walter Murch
Stars: Nicol Williamson, Jean Marsh, Piper Laurie, Fairuza Balk, Matt Clark
Rating: ★★★

More tales of derring-do along the yellow brick road as the Disney people mix up incidents and characters from L Frank Baum's second and third Oz books in an adventure that has good special effects (notably the rock-men who provide little Dorothy Gale's principal opposition), looks expensive and shows lots of imagination. Some early bits may prove a little scary for nervous toddlers.

Return to Paradise ○

1953, US, 85 mins, colour
Dir: Mark Robson
Stars: Gary Cooper, Roberta Haynes, Barry Jones, Moira MacDonald, John Hudson
Rating: ★★

Gary Cooper moves from the Wild West to the South Seas, but remains as much the man of action as ever, in this adaptation of a James *(Hawaii)* Michener story, in which a beachcomber has to pit himself against a firebreathing missionary for control of an island in the South Pacific. Leading lady Roberta Haynes, a sultry beauty of her day, later became a film producer.

Return to Peyton Place ○

1961, US, 135 mins, colour
Dir: Jose Ferrer
Stars: Jeff Chandler, Carol Lynley, Eleanor Parker, Mary Astor
Rating: ★★

The second Peyton Place film shares one virtue with the original – fine

colour photography. Actor Jose Ferrer, who directed, was not auspiciously successful on the other side of the camera – *The Great Man* was perhaps his best. Here veteran actresses Eleanor Parker and Mary Astor offer him stout support. Carol Lynley plays Allison, who has now written a scandalous book about her home town, turning the wheel full circle.

Return to the Blue Lagoon ◐ ⓥ

1991, US, 105 mins, colour
Dir: William A Graham
Stars: Milla Jovovich, Brian Krause, Lisa Pelikan
Rating: ★

A truly unnecessary sequel to the Brooke Shields remake of the old classic. All the old plot lines are trotted out and, after a fair beginning – with two new children shipwrecked on a desert isle with a guardian who'll conveniently die when they are old enough to fend for themselves – the movie becomes completely expendable as soon as the kids grow up. The teenagers – Brian Krause, who looks like a tennis pro, and Milla Jovovich, a genuine, sun-kissed Californian maid – simply aren't up to it. Monsoon rains, a few tame natives, underwater kissing scenes and a mangy-looking shark. That's about it, and it'll bore you stiff.

Reunion ◐ ⓥ

1988, US, 101 mins, colour
Dir: Jerry Schatzberg
Stars: Jason Robards, Christien Anholt, Samuel West, François Fabian
Rating: ★★

There were a number of films about the Nazi rise in Germany around in the late Eighties, but this one, though over-leisurely, is off the beaten track. In 1932, an unlikely friendship springs up between two 16-year-old boys: Konradin, a member of the German aristocracy and Hans, the son of a Jewish doctor. Much welcomed by both youths, neither gregarious by nature, their time together can only be numbered in months, as Hitler rises to power and the oppression of the Jews begins. But, though they part in bitterness, each has opened the other's eyes. The film opens as Hans (Jason Robards) prepares to return to Germany after 55 years to discover what happened to his friend. The film is competently acted by Anholt and West as the boys and more than competently by Robards, though the physical disparity between himself and

Anholt, as his younger self, is rather disturbing. The ironic twist ending is well-worked and works well.

Revenge ● ⓥ

1989, US, 123 mins, colour
Dir: Tony Scott
Stars: Kevin Costner, Anthony Quinn, Madeleine Stowe, Sally Kirkland, Miguel Ferrer
Rating: ★

Given that rugged Costner is a divorced flier who's just quit the US armed forces and gone to see his aged friend Quinn, a ruthless Mexican power broker and man of violence, with a beautiful, unhappy wife (Stowe), would you need over two hours to tell the ensuing story? The biggest mystery, though, is not that the film got made, but that the two lead characters ever thought they could get away with a love affair under the nose of such a man. It needs a special chemistry, giving off heatwaves of passion, to overcome these improbabilities, but every time Costner and Stowe are together on screen, the film goes to sleep. The violence and sleaze that vein the film are more successful than the eroticism, though, with good support work from Ferrer (son of Jose), Kirkland, James Gammon and Joe Santos. Be warned: after more than two hours, the film still doesn't have much of an ending.

Revenge of Frankenstein, The ●

1958, UK, 89 mins, colour
Dir: Terence Fisher
Stars: Peter Cushing, Francis Matthews, Eunice Gayson
Rating: ★★

Another Jimmy Sangster-written, Terence Fisher-directed film with excellent colour photography that distinguished their earlier entries into the genre. The police inspector in the case (another Frankenstein creature has gone berserk) is played by former matinee idol John Stuart whose debut in films was as long ago as 1920, and who went on to star in such Hitchcock films as *Number Seventeen.*

Return of the Pink Panther ○ ⓥ

1978, UK, 98 mins, colour
Dir: Blake Edwards
Stars: Peter Sellers, Herbert Lom, Dyan Cannon, Robert Webber, Robert Loggia
Rating: ★★★

But for the untimely death of Peter Sellers, one imagines that the *Pink*

R

Panther film series would have gone on for years with him at the helm, very much like the James Bond films. Here Clouseau is believed dead, which prompts his now-mad ex superior Dreyfuss (marvellous Herbert Lom) to leave his mental home and rejoin the force, and his houseboy Cato to turn their apartment into what Clouseau terms in 'Chinese nookie factory'. The usual inept disguises, fights with Cato and triumph over self-inflicted disasters follow in this, the last fully fledged Panther film.

Revengers, The ◑
1972, US, 108 mins, colour
Dir: Daniel Mann
Stars: William Holden, Susan Hayward
Rating: ★

The Western was in decline by the early Seventies, but the producers of this one decided there was still some mileage to be gained in re-teaming William Holden and Ernest Borgnine, co-stars in one of the genre's great successes, *The Wild Bunch*. Susan Hayward is wasted as an unlikely Irish frontier nurse, though her ravishing looks totally belie her 55 years at the time. The film itself is formula stuff for tiring stars, redeemed in part by a set of nicely varied locations.

Reversal of Fortune ● ⓥ
1990, US, 110 mins, colour
Dir: Barbet Schroeder
Stars: Glenn Close, Jeremy Irons, Ron Silver, Annabella Sciorra, Fisher Stevens
Rating: ★★

Some fine acting can't stop this being a fairly comprehensively tedious reconstruction of the Claus Von Bulow trial and subsequent appeal. Von Bulow was accused of the attempted murder of his wife Sunny to gain possession of her fortune. The defence counsel (Ron Silver), a professor, was helped by a gaggle of associates and students who found serious holes in the prosecution's case. Director Schroeder elects not to show the trial itself, a serious miscalculation since it involves far too many static conversations between Silver and Jeremy Irons (winning an Oscar) as Claus (who although clearly no Santa, may well have been innocent), as well as slow and lengthy reconstructions of various crises in the Von Bulows' lives. Glenn Close's Sunny delivers a deadpan narration from the hospital bed, assuring the viewer they should be in no hurry to find out the truth. By the end, she preaching to the converted.

Revolution ◑ ⓥ
1985, UK, 123 mins,
Dir: Hugh Hudson
Stars: Al Pacino, Donald Sutherland, Nastassja Kinski, Joan Plowright
Rating: ★

Condemned by the critics and shunned by the paying public, this American Independence film helped to sink the British production company Goldcrest that backed it. Not even the presence of Al Pacino, then at a career low point, could create enough box-office interest. Director Hugh Hudson certainly has a great visual style but a ludicrous script with huge moments of incoherence delivers the death-blow here.

Rhapsody ○
1954, US, 116 mins, colour
Dir: Charles Vidor
Stars: Elizabeth Taylor, Vittorio Gassman, John Ericson
Rating: ★★

If you have tears, prepare to shed them as poor little rich girl Elizabeth Taylor (MGM gowned and groomed) vacillates between violinist Vittorio Gassman and pianist John Ericson with appropriate musical passion. Charles Vidor had a way of dressing up clichés as though they were eternal truths and this triangular love story takes strength from him.

Rhapsody In August ◑ ⓥ
1990, Japan, 104 mins, colour
Dir: Akira Kurosawa
Stars: Sachiko Murase, Hisashi Agawa, Richard Gere
Rating: ★★

This is not the greatest film you ever saw by Japanese master director Akira Kurosawa – far from it. It allows an obsession with the Nagasaki A-bomb to get fatally in the way of a delicate observation of four children staying with their grandmother for the summer holidays. There are some nicely composed shots, and winning performances from the children and granny. But it's very slow (more of a drawback here than in some Japanese films) and some of its attitudes may be less acceptable to western eyes.

Rhapsody In Blue ○
1945, US, 139 mins, b/w
Dir: Irving Rapper
Stars: Robert Alda, Joan Leslie, Charles Coburn, Alexis Smith, Oscar Levant
Rating: ★★★

The usual tuppence-coloured Hollywood version of a famous composer's life, in this case that of George Gershwin, and almost wholly redeemed by the quality of the music involved. Robert Alda, father of Alan, made his screen debut as Gershwin, but the film didn't make him into the superstar it might have done. Joan Leslie is very appealing as the early love of his life and the treatment, however fast-and-loose it may play with the facts, does capture some of Gershwin's genius and the conflicts he faced within his own world of music.

Rhinestone ○
1984, US, 111 mins, colour
Dir: Bob Clark
Stars: Dolly Parton, Sylvester Stallone
Rating: ★★

Although the corn is as high as an elephant's eye in the script of this comedy-musical with a country and western flavour, Dolly Parton proves again her facility for mocking her own image, and her songs (15 of them) make the film much more lively musically than *The Best Little Whorehouse in Texas*. Sylvester Stallone also sings acceptably as the loudmouthed Bronx cab driver whom Dolly tries to turn into a singing star for a bet. Still, it's Dolly's show, whether deflating the male macho image by the lift of an eyebrow, or moving into more positive action by flooring an antagonist with a single punch. 'Who are you?' Stallone gasps. 'Jane Wayne?'

Rhino! ○
1964, US, 91 mins, colour
Dir: Ivan Tors
Stars: Harry Guardino, Robert Cuip, Shirley Eaton
Rating: ★

Another colourful animal film from the hands of Ivan Tors, creator of *Flipper* and *Daktari*. The film, which was made entirely on location in Zululand, features within its fictional plot a whole cross-section of African wild life, but concentrates on the white rhino, perhaps the most remarkable of all animals remaining on Earth. Its massive horn is capable of smashing a truck. Its hoof can crush a man to pulp. It's certainly more interesting than the human cast here, who battle to no avail with a formula jungle plot.

Rhodes of Africa ○
1936, UK, 92 mins, b/w
Dir: Berthold Viertel
Stars: Walter Huston, Oscar Homolka
Rating: ★★★

A major British film of its time, for which the famous American actor, Walter Huston, then a major screen personality, was invited to come to Britain to play the 19th-century pioneer Cecil Rhodes. Oscar Homolka plays Rhodes' dangerous adversary, President Paul Kruger of South Africa. Peggy Ashcroft makes a rare and welcome appearance and there's also an early screen role for Bernard Lee, later to become famous as James Bond's boss M.

Rhubarb O
1951, US, 95 mins, b/w
Dir: Arthur Lubin
Stars: Ray Milland, Jan Sterling
Rating: ★★★★

Riotous comedy that may well make the children fall out of their armchairs. A dotty millionaire leaves his entire fortune to a ferocious ginger cat who inherits a baseball team and proves its indispensable mascot. The cat out-acts everyone in sight, no mean feat considering the cast, which includes Ray Milland, Jan Sterling, Gene Lockhart and William Frawley. In an hysterically comic climax, it looks as though all is lost. But the cat deservedly has the last miaow! In a cast packed with Damon Runyon-style character actors, watch quickly for Paul Douglas (husband of Sterling) as a man in the park, and a young Leonard Nimoy as one of the baseball players.

Richard III O ⓥ
1955, UK, 161 mins, colour
Dir: Laurence Olivier
Stars: Laurence Olivier, Ralph Richardson, Claire Bloom, John Gielgud
Rating: ★★★★★

Not even in the same actor-director's *Henry V* has Shakespeare ever made such dazzling, hypnotic screen entertainment as in Laurence Olivier's *Richard III*. And Olivier's power-hungry Richard Crookback is unforgettable – a ruthless, dominant, unstoppable, gross black spider of a figure that devours or possesses everything in its path. Tremendous colour photography and stunning dramatic impact in one of the most successful Shakespeare films ever made. Named best film at the British Oscars of 1956, with Olivier honoured as best actor.

Richard III ● ⓥ
1995, UK, 96 mins, colour
Dir: Richard Loncraine
Stars: Ian McKellen, Annette Bening,

Robert Downey Jr, Kristin Scott Thomas, Nigel Hawthorne, Maggie Smith
Rating: ★★

This so-so updating of Shakespeare's play to the Thirties fairly races through the Bard's text, but still only just succeeds in keeping the tedium at bay. And Richard himself, played by McKellen as a camera-addressing jack-booted fascist, seems far too easily bested at the end. The best performance comes from Nigel Hawthorne, but unfortunately his character doesn't last very long. Give it high marks for originality and admire one or two striking set pieces, but hand the real crown to Olivier's 1956 classic.

Richest Cat in the World, The O
1986, US, 92 mins, colour
Dir: Gregg Beeman
Stars: Ramon Bieri, Steven Kampmann, Caroline McWilliams, George Wyner
Rating: ★★★★

Above average on all counts, this is a refreshing dose of lunacy from the Disney studio, very much along the lines of *The Cat from Outer Space,* with a talking feline called Palmer who may well rank towards the top of the all-time great cat actors. Fun all the way.

Richie Rich ☉ ⓥ
1994, US, 95 mins, colour
Dir: Donald Petrie
Stars: Macaulay Culkin, John Larroquette, Edward Herrmann, Jonathan Hyde, Christine Ebersole, Michael McShane
Rating: ★★

This comedy about the world's richest 12-year-old is actually quite faithful to the spirit of the comic books and cartoons on which it is based. But that doesn't stop it from being quite charmless. Macaulay Culkin is Richie, so rich that he has supermodel Claudia Schiffer as his personal trainer and sporting legend Reggie Jackson to coach him at baseball. But Culkin is clearly too mature for the role. He is surrounded by extra-tall adult actors, but nothing could disguise the fact that he was moving from cute childhood into gawky teenage years, or that his acting range here seems strictly limited. The plot, with nasty underling John Larroquette attempting to bump off Richie's billionaire parents, then the brat himself, is a hit-and-miss affair, with several good gags and one-liners, but long periods in which very little happens.

Rich in Love O ⓥ
1992, US, 106 mins, colour
Dir: Bruce Beresford
Stars: Albert Finney, Jill Clayburgh, Kyle MacLachlan, Suzy Amis, Piper Laurie, Kathryn Erbe, Ethan Hawke
Rating: ★★

One of those lovingly photographed films drenched in nostalgia, warmth and the scent of magnolias, this is also a portrait of a time when life changes irrevocably for one South Carolina family. Mother (Jill Clayburgh) takes off for a second life and 17-year-old daughter Lucille (Kathryn Erbe) is left not only to cope with leaving school, drifting away from her boyfriend and trying to get her father (Albert Finney) to survive the blow, but face the arrival of her pregnant, newly married sister (Suzy Amis) and a husband (Kyle MacLachlan) whom Lucille soon begins to fancy. For its first hour, this film is nearly as beguiling as its teenage heroine, although the film runs out of steam towards the end and is of little account after Clayburgh returns to hearth and home, upsetting Finney who has taken up with widder-woman Piper Laurie. Laurie's appropriately sassy in this role, but some of the other acting isn't up to much.

Rich Kids O
1979, US, 101 mins, colour
Dir: Robert M Young
Stars: Trini Alvarado, Jeremy Levy
Rating: ★★★

The name of Robert Altman on this film's credits, albeit only as executive producer, leads us to expect something out of the ordinary. The film, directed by Robert M Young, is certainly that, for its leading characters are only 12 years old. Through their eyes, the film takes a perceptive look at the effect on young teenage children of that frequent occurrence in American upper-middle-bracket life – the marriage break-up. It develops ultimately into a mixture of astringent observation and more routine situation comedy, with bright performances by Trini Alvarado and Jeremy Levy as the 'rich kids' involved.

Ricochet ● ⓥ
1991, US, 110 mins, colour
Dir: Russell Mulcahy
Stars: Denzel Washington, John Lithgow, Ice T, Kevin Pollak, Lindsay Wagner
Rating: ★★

A familiar sort of action thriller, this Denzel Washington vehicle begins savagely but well. It gets increasingly

R

fatuous after half-way, though, ending on a note of James Bond spoof. Washington is the hotshot cop who brings down hit-man John Lithgow on the verge of his breakthrough to big-time crime. Lithgow nurses an insane desire for revenge while behind bars. By the time he escapes seven years later, Washington has risen to assistant DA. But it's seven years' bad luck when Lithgow's evil plotting turns his life upside down and makes him the wanted man. Russell Mulcahy tries hard to make us credit that no-one would believe Washington's story of a madman bent on framing him, but he never quite succeeds, nor convinces us that Washington's underworld childhood friends (led by Ice T) would come to his rescue at the end. Lithgow's an excellent menace when the script doesn't make him look silly; Washington has his moments and seemingly does much of his own stuntwork.

Riddle of the Sands, The ○ ⓥ
1978, UK, 102 mins, colour
Dir: Tony Maylam
Stars: Michael York, Jenny Agutter, Simon MacCorkindale
Rating: ★★

When Erskine Childers' classic novel was first published in 1903, its theme was to underline the vulnerability of England's eastern coast to foreign invasion – and this handsomely mounted film retains the theme to good effect. Its two well-bred heroes, Michael York and Simon MacCorkindale, are in the best tradition of the gifted amateur caught up in mystery and intrigue and coming up trumps against sinister foreign villains, in this case led by urbane Alan Badel, who gives the film's most stylish and enjoyable performance. Director (and co-writer) Tony Maylam admirably captures the timeless attraction of small-boat sailing that provides the backcloth to the clean-cut heroics.

Ride a Crooked Trail ○
1959, US, 87 mins, colour
Dir: Jesse Hibbs
Stars: Audie Murphy, Gia Scala, Walter Matthau, Henry Silva
Rating: ★★

Man-sized Audie Murphy Western, casting him for once as a bad guy, directed with great punch by Jesse Hibbs, and featuring one of the early screen performances of Walter Matthau, here as the judge of a frontier town, who was already stealing scenes

even at this stage of his career. Cold-eyed Henry Silva also adds quality to the supporting cast.

Ride Clear of Diablo ○
1954, US, 80 mins, colour
Dir: Jesse Hibbs
Stars: Audie Murphy, Dan Duryea, Susan Cabot
Rating: ★★★

Audie Murphy Western, with a strong humorous content and a *Destry*-like plot. Murphy gives a mild, but finely timed performance as the railroad surveyor who brings in a notorious outlaw, and Dan Duryea is a laconic knock-out as the not-so-bad villain. Fine Technicolor location photography by Irving Glassberg.

Ride 'em Cowboy ⊙
1941, US, 82 mins, b/w
Dir: Arthur Lubin
Stars: Bud Abbott, Lou Costello, Anne Gwynne, Dick Foran
Rating: ★★

One of the earliest and most energetic of the Abbott and Costello comedies, made in a year when they had four big box-office hits. It's also one of Ella Fitzgerald's rare film appearances (she sings 'A Tisket, A Tasket'); and another bonus comes in the friendly shape of Johnny Mack Brown, who once starred with Garbo before becoming one of America's favourite film cowboys.

Ride In the Whirlwind ◐
1966, US, 85 mins, colour
Dir: Monte Hellman
Stars: Jack Nicholson, Cameron Mitchell, Millie Perkins
Rating: ★★

Jack Nicholson was a busy man in this somewhat offbeat Western. Not only did he star in it, he also co-produced it and wrote the screenplay. He and Cameron Mitchell are two cowboys wrongly pursued as outlaws by a relentless posse. Slammed by the critics when it was first released in America it has now become a minor cult film. Different to, but not nearly as good as the Western filmed back-to-back with this, *The Shooting*.

Rider on the Rain ●
1969, France, 119 mins, colour
Dir: René Clément
Stars: Marlène Jobert, Charles Bronson
Rating: ★

The highlights of distinguished French director René Clément's career were

far behind him when he turned his hand to this extraordinary melodrama, one of whose many oddities is the habit of the leading character (Charles Bronson) of throwing walnuts at windows, and breaking the nuts but not the glass. Ms Jobert is delicious, but faint hearts should be warned that the beginning is rather nasty. Everything else about this leaden melodrama is highly resistible.

Riders of the Storm
See: The American Way

Ride the High Country
See: Guns in the Afternoon

Riding High ○
1950, US, 112 mins, b/w
Dir: Frank Capra
Stars: Bing Crosby, Coleen Gray, Charles Bickford, Frances Gifford
Rating: ★★★★

Much underrated remake by Frank Capra of his 1934 hit *Broadway Bill* full of skilful character players (nine of them repeating their roles from the earlier film) and with a real lump-in-the-throat finale. Particularly memorable are Harry Davenport as a drunken butler, Oliver Hardy as the betting man taken for a ride by con-men and William Demarest as Happy, perfectly countering Bing Crosby's 'How's your wallet?' with 'I don't know. I ate it yesterday.' Songs include the Oscar nominated 'Sunshine Cake'. Richly enjoyable.

Riff-Raff ○
1935, US, 90 mins, b/w
Dir: J Walter Ruben
Stars: Jean Harlow, Spencer Tracy, Joseph Calleia
Rating: ★★

Platinum-blonde bombshell Jean Harlow is pretty unrecognisable here in a brown wig as a tuna cannery worker who falls in love with big-headed fisherman Spencer Tracy, leading to tragedy. While not the pair's most memorable film, it does contain snappy, hard-boiled dialogue from one of Hollywood's top female writers: Frances Marion.

Riff-Raff ● ⓥ
1990, UK, 95 mins, colour
Dir: Ken Loach
Stars: Robert Carlyle, Emer McCourt, Ricky Tomlinson
Rating: ★★★

Director Ken Loach pushes his politics right into the background for this gritty comedy very much based on real life on a building site. Writer Bill Jesse was himself a building worker and his colourful, wisecracking script is a joy. Loach insisted that all the actors should have had building site experience, and this pays off in some strong performances, particularly from Robert Carlyle as Stevie, Willie Ross as the hard-bitten foreman Gus, and Derek Young as the black guy keen to search for his roots in Africa. Comedy and real life at the bottom of the heap mix well in this entertaining film but you will have to concentrate hard to understand some of the richer regional accents.

Right Stuff, The ❶ Ⓥ
1983, US, 193 mins, colour
Dir: Philip Kaufman
Stars: Sam Shepard, Scott Glenn, Ed Harris, Barbara Hershey, Lance Henriksen, Dennis Quaid, Fred Ward
Rating: ★★★

There are some great moments in this story of the first American astronauts and let that not be forgotten. The special effects work and aerial photography, for example, could hardly be bettered. And the film tries hard to tell the story of human beings as well as hardware. But, at more than three hours, you long for the excision of unnecessary material and an earlier splashdown. The film attempts to tell parallel stories, although it never quite successfully integrates them. Yeager (perhaps Sam Shepard's best film performance) is a test pilot of the old breed, breaking the sound barrier and scorching his plane though Mach 2. He wants nothing to do with the 'suicide squadron' who volunteer for astronaut training, although he stares a little wistfully at their trail of glory in the sky. He remains, you feel, what the film's makers really consider the 'right stuff?. Creditable performances from a long star cast bolster a film of enough inspired sequences to make it linger in the memory.

Ring of Bright Water ☉ Ⓥ
1969, UK, 107 mins, colour
Dir: Jack Couffer
Stars: Bill Travers, Virginia McKenna
Rating: ★★★

A fair British attempt to emulate the success of Walt Disney's family-orientated animal films. Bill Travers is the London gent who starts a new life with a loveable but destructive otter in the Scottish Highlands. His real-life wife and *Born Free* co-star Virginia

McKenna is on hand. The film is perfect family entertainment, and only contains one brief incident of violence that may upset very small children.

Rio Bravo ☉ Ⓥ
1961, US, 140 mins, colour
Dir: Howard Hawks
Stars: John Wayne, Dean Martin, Ricky Nelson, Angle Dickinson, Walter Brennan, John Russell
Rating: ★★★

Director Howard Hawks made several good Westerns with John Wayne and here's one of the best-regarded, on Hawks' favourite theme of a tightlyknit group of goodies, beset by their own failings as much as anything else, taking on a whole nest of baddies. Long but involving, with an unexpectedly good performance from Dean Martin.

Rio Conchos ☉
1964, US, 107 mins, colour
Dir: Gordon Douglas
Stars: Richard Boone, Stuart Whitman, Tony Franciosa
Rating: ★★★

A Western in the old 20th Century-Fox tradition, with towering scenery, truly De Luxe colour, and men who are as tough and hard-hitting as the action that frequently punctuates the story. Richard Boone, a favourite actor of mine from his pre-television days when he played nasty villains very well, is a bitter ex-Rebel army major whose wife and children have been killed by the Apache (it beats me how these desert wanderers always get the money to survive). He agrees to lead a hazardous expedition through Apache territory. The object is to find another ex-Confederate (splendid Edmond O'Brien) who is about to sell hundreds of stolen guns to the Indians.

Rio Grande ☉ Ⓥ
1950, US, 107 mins, b/w
Dir: John Ford
Stars: John Wayne, Maureen O'Hara, Ben Johnson
Rating: ★★★

The third in director John Ford's Cavalry trilogy (following *Fort Apache* and *She Wore a Yellow Ribbon*) and the first of John Wayne and Maureen O'Hara's five films together. Wayne is larger than life in his role as an embattled fort commander and he did all his own riding and stunts as usual. He even persuaded Ford to cast his son Patrick in a cameo role. It's a power-

ful portrait of the wild and far southwest during the Indian wars.

Rio Lobo ☉ Ⓥ
1970, US, 110 mins, colour
Dir: Howard Hawks
Stars: John Wayne, Jennifer O'Neill, Jack Elam
Rating: ★★★

Both star John Wayne and director Howard Hawks – whose last film this was – were getting a bit long in the tooth and saddlesore when they churned out this enjoyable but derivative Western. It's a virtual retread of their previous two horse operas, *Rio Bravo* and *El Dorado,* with wronged soldier Wayne ending up in a showdown in a dusty town. Events run like a door-slamming Feydeau farce ensuring plenty of laughs between the bullets. The Technicolor camerawork is top drawer and the film is finally lifted out of the rut by veteran Jack Elam's marvellously Gothic performance as a half-crazed old rancher, whose finger itches demonically on the trigger every rime he gets a bad guy in his sights.

Rio Rita ☉
1942, US, 91 mins, b/w
Dir: S Sylvan Simon
Stars: Bud Abbott, Lou Costello, Kathryn Grayson, John Carroll, Tom Conway
Rating: ★★

For Abbott and Costello's first visit to MGM, the studio decided to revamp the hit stage musical that had provided a successful feature debut for another comedy team, Wheeler and Woolsey, in 1929. The plot is almost entirely changed, to make room for a gang of Nazi agents. And only a few of the songs were retained, although enough for young singer Kathryn Grayson to make an impression on the critics: she would go on to become one of Metro's biggest stars in the next decade. The Abbott and Costello bits are much as their fans will expect – the applechanging routine, the 'mirage' that turns out to be real, the talking dog, the spinning car at the garage and the tequila stew scene, most of them borrowed from old radio and vaudeville routines.

Riot in Cell Block 11 ☉
1954, US, 80 mins, b/w
Dir: Don Siegel
Stars: Neville Brand, Emile Meyer
Rating: ★★★★

A gritty, harsh and forceful thriller, which, under the pin-point direction of

R

double Oscar-winner Don Siegel, broke new grounds in realism, and looked at the root of trouble from both sides. It also opened up a whole new career for Neville Brand as the leader of the rioters, a tough but thinking man who keeps the convicts just sufficiently under control to ensure that the better conditions they are fighting for are not threatened by their own behaviour.

Riptide O
1934, US, 90 mins, b/w
Dir: Edmund Goulding
Stars: Norma Shearer, Herbert Marshall, Robert Montgomery
Rating: ★★

Norma Shearer, she of the flawless complexion, and debonair Robert Montgomery, so successful together in the film version of Noel Coward's *Private Lives*, were paired again in this piece of frou-frou in which their performances are far superior to director Edmund Goulding's screenplay. The charm and elegant playing of the stars pulls it through, although there must have been times when they didn't know whether to play scenes for laughs, tears or dramatic effect.

Rising Damp O
1980, UK, 96 mins, colour
Dir: Joe McGrath
Stars: Leonard Rossiter, Frances de la Tour, Don Warrington, Christopher Strauli, Denholm Elliott
Rating: ★★★

The film version of the television success about the lecherous landlord (a role which rightly made a star of Leonard Rossiter) and his incredibly seedy boarding-house wisely sticks to the 'sketch' formula. If it succeeds only in fits and starts, that's because Joe McGrath's direction seems to be working against the efforts of the excellent Rossiter and the adorable Frances de la Tour, as the wallflower tenant who finally succumbs to the advances of the wolfish lodger (Denholm Elliott at the top of his form) who really covets her Post Office Saving Books. One could have done with a little more fun at the expense of the conditions which Rossiter's tenants suffer; even so, there are some very funny lines, and Ms de la Tour's description of her father's death remains the laugh of a lifetime.

Rising Sun ● Ⓥ
1993, US, 129 mins, colour
Dir: Philip Kaufman
Stars: Sean Connery, Wesley Snipes,

Cary-Hiroyuki Tagawa, Tia Carrere, Harvey Keitel, Ray Wise
Rating: ★★★

Despite the backdrop of Japanese-American business competition in LA, this is really a mystery thriller about a videotape recording of a murder: what it it tells detectives, what it doesn't tell them, and what it conceals from them. A high-priced mistress is strangled on a boardroom table (it seems) while having sex with her lover (it seems), but the identity of the killer is hidden on the missing disk taken by a security camera (or is it?). Sean Connery is the cop with the know-how to penetrate the Japanese community; Wesley Snipes is the cop who's officially on the case. Together they have to wade through layers of deceit that conceal – what? More deceit? With the help of a beautiful video expert (Tia Carrere), they soon discover that even the truth can lie. Parts of this are intriguing, parts exciting and parts drag a bit. Connery's cool authority and the intrigue of video-trickery keep you watching this complex whodunit to the end.

Risk, The
See: Suspect

Risky Business ● Ⓥ
1983, US, 95 mins, colour
Dir: Paul Brickman
Stars: Tom Cruise, Rebecca DeMornay, Richard Masur
Rating: ★★

It's the old, old story of a teenage boy's initiation into manhood, but in this case given a whole new and potentially hilarious slant – besides providing Tom Cruise with his initiation into stardom. Joel (Cruise) is cornered into calling a call girl while his parents are away. After the inevitable night of bliss, he gets involved in her running away from a pimp, then incurs thousands of dollars worth of damage when he plunges his father's car into Lake Michigan. The girl (Rebecca DeMornay) turns out to have quite a head for business, and suggests that he can make a mint by inviting all her 'friends' over for a night if he'll invite his fellow students. This isn't quite the end of a story which has some beautifully funny moments, but doesn't carry its basic idea through with enough conviction. Still, you'll be glad about the upbeat ending the scriptwriters have managed to devise to round it off.

Rita, Sue and Bob Too ● Ⓥ
1986, UK, 95 mins, colour
Dir: Alan Clarke
Stars: Siobhan Finneran, Michelle Holmes, George Costigan, Lesley Sharp
Rating: ★

An ugly, sad, tedious four-letter farrago about life as it is lived in the backstreets of Bradford. Rita and Sue are two 16-year-old tarts well on their way to becoming slum mums, even though their school days are not quite over. They babysit for Bob who drives them home over the moors. The girls casually comply with his leering request for a double lay and a permanent liaison is soon forged. 'He certainly knows how to give a girl a good time,' remarks Rita, pathetically, after 30 seconds in the reclining seat of Bob's car. When Bob's frayed wife throws him out, he takes in pregnant Rita, and Sue's forced to move in with a Pakistani boyfriend. The film's idea of twists in the plot is pretty well limited to Bob's failure to 'make it' on one occasion and the song 'Gang Bang' is well in keeping with its spirit.

River, The O
1951, UK, 87 mins, colour
Dir: Jean Renoir
Stars: Nora Swinburne, Esmond Knight
Rating: ★★★

Jean Renoir's touching film about adolescent love among the English community in India is simply ablaze with vivid, contrasting colours. Its storyline encompassing death, birth and a girl's journey into womanhood is devoid of any emotional highpoints and flows gently along as seamlessly as the river Ganges, on whose banks the action is set. Thomas Breen is well cast as the ex-US soldier to whom three girls lose their hearts, but the standout performance is by Radha, who dances enchantingly and plays the part of a girl of mixed race with memorable intensity.

River, The ◑
1984, US, 122 mins, colour
Dir: Mark Rydell
Stars: Mel Gibson, Sissy Spacek, Scott Glenn
Rating: ★★★

Mel Gibson is living dangerously again, although the evils that face him in this back-to-the-land drama are drought, flooding and the efforts of bad guy Scott Glenn to drive him off his farm. Sissy Spacek follows along the trail blazed by Sally Field and Jessica Lange as the wife who tends the farm (and nearly loses her life in a tractor accident which provides the film's most agonising scene) when her man is forced to go away to earn money – as a 'scab' at a striking steel works. The combination of Gibson and Spacek should have been dynamite but, though both are good, a unifying element between them seems to be missing, so that the scene-stealers are little Becky Jo Lynch as their daughter, and Glenn, coming on like a younger James Coburn as Spacek's high-school beau, now bent on flooding the valley he grew up in.

River of No Return ○ Ⓥ
1954, US, 91 mins, colour
Dir: Otto Preminger
Stars: Robert Mitchum, Marilyn Monroe, Rory Calhoun
Rating: ★★★

Almost a classic, as Marilyn Monroe and Robert Mitchum fight the rapids, greasy villain Rory Calhoun and themselves in a spectacular Western that also gives Marilyn time to sing 'One Silver Dollar', 'River of No Return' and 'I'm Gonna File My Claim'. Even if they're in the studio tank, the stars' ride on the raft looks pretty hairy, and the second half of the film, brightly shot in colour by Joseph LaShelle, is terrific all through.

River Runs Through It, A ◐
1992, US, 123 mins, colour
Dir: Robert Redford
Stars: Craig Sheffer, Brad Pitt, Tom Skerritt, Emily Lloyd, Brenda Blethyn
Rating: ★★★★

Robert Redford's third film as director is a poetic tale of a Montana childhood. Mention that it's also about fly-fishing and you might run a mile. But you would be mistaken. For, although this film never savages the emotions, it certainly stirs them through its tale of the sons of a fishing preacher. One is destined for an academic life and, on a return to Montana, tries to look after the life of his wilder, charismatic and clearly doomed younger brother. Brad Pitt not unnaturally steals the film in this latter role, with his flashing smile and star personality, though one hoped (to no avail) that there might be an Oscar nod for the long-serving Tom Skerritt for his deeply-etched and never overstated portrait of their father.

River Wild, The ◐ Ⓥ
1994, US, 112 mins, colour
Dir: Curtis Hanson

Stars: Meryl Streep, Kevin Bacon, David Strathairn, Joseph Mazzello, John C Reilly
Rating: ★★★

A real old-fashioned crowd-pleaser with a crunchingly exciting last 20 minutes after a sometimes slow progression of the plot. Seeing a holiday on the whitewater river, with its cumulative rapids, as a last chance to save her crumbling marriage, Gail (Meryl Streep), who was once a guide on the river, hires a raft for the trip of a lifetime for her 10-year-old son (Joseph Mazzello) and bespectacled husband Tom (David Strathaim), who turns up at the last minute. Dangers afloat turn into the two-legged variety when they encounter Wade (Kevin Bacon) and Terry (John C Reilly), escaped armed robbers who subsequently take the family hostage and force Gail to negotiate a stretch of churning, swirling treacherous whitewater considered too dangerous to survive. A river of no return indeed, but shot not in a studio tank but on actual locations with the stars doing 90 per cent of the tough work on board. Streep is every inch the woman of the river and looks good enough to row in the Olympics.

Roadgames ◐
1981, Australia, 100 mins, colour
Dir: Richard Franklin
Stars: Stacy Keach, Jamie Lee Curtis
Rating: ★★★★★

Director Richard Franklin, who also made *Psycho II*, is a self-confessed Hitchcock fanatic, and this scary thriller is full of references to the Master. Truck driver Stacy Keach has in his cab a magazine called *Hitchcock*, and the leading female character is not only called Hitch but is played by Jamie Lee Curtis, daughter of Janet *Psycho* Leigh. The resulting mix of murder and mystery, is faultlessly done and the two leading performances perfectly balanced. The audience is continually kept guessing, but Franklin finds time for one or two demonstrations of flair; such as the flashing lightning that suddenly reveals the 'killer' van and its owner, as if from nowhere, or a suspicious Keach, training binoculars on the van-driver, only to turn away again just as the man looks up and straight at him. The climax is a nerve-grinding affair and includes a glorious twist when everyone who suspects Keach closes in on him while the actual killer begins to recede into the crowd.

Road House ○
1948, US, 105 mins, b/w
Dir: Jean Negulesco
Stars: Ida Lupino, Cornel Wilde, Richard Widmark, Celeste Holm
Rating: ★★★

Smokily atmospheric triangle melodrama, with a typically hard-boiled performance from Ida Lupino as the roadhouse chanteuse whose cigarettes burn grooves in her piano, and about whom one character says: 'She does more without a voice than anyone I've ever heard.' Richard Widmark is chillingly effective as the roadhouse owner whose obsession with Lupino turns him into a psychotic villain. Outdoor scenes are too stagy.

Road House ● Ⓥ
1988, US, 114 mins, colour
Dir: Rowdy Herrington
Stars: Patrick Swayze, Kelly Lynch, Ben Gazzara, Sam Elliott
Rating: ★

A beefcake vehicle for Patrick Swayze, this is a modern version of the spaghetti Western, full of heavy sex and even heavier violence, as Swayze takes on the job of marshal – sorry I mean 'cooler' (head bouncer) – at a rowdy midwest road house. 'It's the kind of place,' explains owner Kevin Tighe, 'where they sweep the eyeballs up after closing.' 'It's my way or the highway,' growls Swayze in response, although he doesn't say that to the local medico, played by tanned, long-legged Kelly Lynch, who's no match for harum-scarum Kathleen Wilhoite in the personality stakes. Soon, Swayze finds he has to take on the whole lawless town, especially local big shot Gazzara and his formidable gang of heavies. No problem. Blood, sweat and tears are here in plenty, but originality is nowhere in sight.

Road to Bali ○
1952, US, 90 mins, colour
Dir: Hal Walker
Stars: Bing Crosby, Bob Hope, Dorothy Lamour
Rating: ★★

The only *Road* comedy in colour, this hasn't the joie-de-vivre of some of Hope, Crosby and Lamour's earlier efforts, although there are funny guest spots from Jane Russell (right at the end), Dean Martin and Jerry Lewis and (on film) Katharine Hepburn and Humphrey Bogart. The most popular song was Bing and Bob's duet 'Chicago Style'. The humour here seems more forced than before and

R

Hope and Crosby (though not Lamour) too old to be cavorting in such capers any more.

Road to Denver, The ○
1955, US, 90 mins, colour
Dir: Joseph Kane
Stars: John Payne, Mona Freeman, Lee J Cobb, Lee Van Cleef
Rating: ★★★

A vigorous, satisfying Western, well adapted from Bill Gulick's good novel *Man from Texas*, and with as strong a cast as Republic Studios could muster on the budget. The leading roles are well played by John Payne and Mona Freeman while, in support, glowering Lee J Cobb, leering Skip Homeier, snarling Lee Van Cleef and grizzled Andy Clyde all catch the eye. The studio's colour process, Trucolor, had greatly improved since it was first introduced some years earlier, and cameraman Reggie Lanning was able to achieve some rich photography with it. Although the film is set in Texas and Colorado, a lot of the location shooting was done in Utah! Sturdy stuff.

Road to Hong Kong, The ⊙
1961, UK, 100 mins, b/w
Dir: Norman Panama
Stars: Bing Crosby, Bob Hope, Joan Collins, Dorothy Lamour
Rating: ★★

The last of the *Road* comedy films, and the formula's now looking as tired as veteran stars Bing Crosby and Bob Hope as they chase a drug to cure amnesia and end up on another planet. The plot's enlivened by some funny guest appearances (from Frank Sinatra, Dean Martin, David Niven, Jerry Colonna and especially Peter Sellers) and zingy songs that include 'Warmer Than a Whisper'. Joan Collins is the leading lady, but it should really have been Dorothy Lamour, here shame-fully relegated to a guest appearance.

Road to Morocco ⊙
1942, US, 83 mins, b/w
Dir: Victor Schertzinger
Stars: Bing Crosby, Bob Hope, Dorothy Lamour, Anthony Quinn
Rating: ★★★

The third of the *Road* comedies that were as sure-fire box-office bets in the war years as a *Rambo*, *Rocky* or *Dirty Harry* film would be later. As usual Hope loses Lamour to Crosby, who also sings ('Time to get the popcorn folks,' laments Hope) 'Moonlight

Becomes You', the film's big hit, although nowadays it's the title duet that people seem to remember. This is also the one with the camel who complains that this is 'the screwiest picture I was ever in.'

Road to Rio ⊙
1947, US, 100 mins, b/w
Dir: Norman Z McLeod
Stars: Bing Crosby, Bob Hope, Dorothy Lamour
Rating: ★★★

The last of the really funny *Road* comedies with Bing Crosby, Bob Hope and Dorothy Lamour. The Wiere Brothers, a zany musical comedy trio, are a big hit as Brazilian musicians hired by Bing and Bob to make up a quintet of Americans and given the briefest of crash courses in American slang; villainess Gale Sondergaard hypnotises Dorothy Lamour into hating Bing and Bob at inconvenient moments; and Crosby and the Andrews Sisters had a big hit with 'You Don't Have to Know the Language'. And how come Hope manages to land Lamour at the end instead of Crosby getting her? You'll have to watch the last few feet of the film to find out the answer to that.

Road to Singapore ⊙
1940, US, 84 mins, b/w
Dir: Victor Schertzinger
Stars: Bing Crosby, Bob Hope, Dorothy Lamour, Charles Coburn
Rating: ★★★

Who could have guessed that this modest Paramount comedy-musical could have ignited the world with laughter under the complementary talents of Bing Crosby and Bob Hope and lead to nationwide queues for the most successful comedy series of its time? In this one, the 'patty-cake' routine is invented and songs include 'Sweet Potato Piper', 'Captain Custard' and 'The Moon and the Willow Tree'. Easy-going fun.

Road to Utopia ⊙
1945, US, 90 mins, b/w
Dir: Hal Walker
Stars: Bing Crosby, Bob Hope, Dorothy Lamour, Robert Benchley
Rating: ★★★★

Or, more properly, *Road to Alaska*. Drily narrated by that ineffable wit Robert Benchley, it has Bing Crosby, Bob Hope and Dorothy Lamour skating all over the Klondike in search of a lost gold mine. All this and dancing bears, talking fish and a very funny

twist-ending. An absolute riot of wit and invention. Best of the series.

Road to Wellville, The ● Ⓥ
1994, US, 120 mins, colour
Dir: Alan Parker
Stars: Anthony Hopkins, Bridget Fonda, Matthew Broderick, John Cusack, Dana Carvey, Lara Flynn Boyle
Rating: ★★

Appropriately accompanied by Edwardian oompah music, this satirical comedy about sex and other bodily functions is the 'adult' cinema's equivalent of a Restoration romp. Lewd, crude and rude, its fun centres on the Battle Creek Sanatorium, where bogus Dr Kellogg presides over a health farm where, as he puts it, 'the spirit soars, the mind is educated and the bowels are born again'. The action is mainly about sexual frustration and stimulation, involving a young husband and wife (Matthew Broderick, Bridget Fonda) who are out of sorts in the loo and in bed. Everything that you could imagine emerging from any part of the body is dwelt on at some length, while Anthony Hopkins, buck teeth jammed into the top of his mouth, wrestles with an American accent and a script that's often as flatulent as several of the characters. The beautifully observed period detail would grace a much more elegant (and better) film.

Road to Zanzibar ⊙
1941, US, 92 mins, b/w
Dir: Victor Schertzinger
Stars: Bing Crosby, Bob Hope, Dorothy Lamour
Rating: ★★★

The second *Road* film, a bungle through the jungle that's possibly the wildest of the lot. Said the publicity: '152 more laughs (count 'em) than *Road to Singapore*'. Bob Hope's Fearless Frazier has some terrific one-line gags, while Bing Crosby and Dorothy Lamour parody their romantic duets in 'You're Dangerous'. Burly Charles Gemora gets inside a gorilla suit, as he did in Laurel and Hardy's *Swiss Miss*.

Roaring Twenties, The ○ Ⓥ
1939, US, 106 mins, b/w
Dir: Raoul Walsh
Stars: James Cagney, Humphrey Bogart, Priscilla Lane, Jeffrey Lynn
Rating: ★★★★

Spinning madly through a plot that would take today's directors twice the time to tell, Raoul Walsh vividly sets out a panorama not only of the violent decade under survey, but of the whole gangster-film product of his studio (Warner Brothers) throughout the Thirties. James Cagney, Humphrey Bogart, Priscilla Lane and Gladys George all give, in their different veins, what the American press of the time might have dubbed 'socko' performances. The final scene is a classic of Hollywood cinema.

Robbers of the Sacred Mountain ◖
1983, US, 90 mins, colour
Dir: Olaf Pooley
Stars: John Marley, Simon MacCorkindale
Rating: ★★

Clearly inspired by the success of *Raiders of the Lost Ark,* this is an effective low-budget update of traditional serials, spliced with frequent action sequences, treachery and twists. Britain's Simon MacCorkindale is the Indy-type lead; Blanca Guerra and Louise Vallance provide him with striking female company.

Robbery ◖
1967, UK, 114 mins, colour
Dir: Peter Yates
Stars: Stanley Baker, Joanna Pettet, James Booth, Frank Finlay
Rating: ★★★

Thriller that follows up a successful raid on a night train from Glasgow, loaded with millions of banknotes. The film caused quite a stir on its initial release, particularly as its theme had an obvious parallel in real life. And Hollywood star Steve McQueen was so taken by Peter Yates' snappy direction that he insisted on having the Englishman helm *Bullitt.*

Robe, The ○ ⓥ
1953, US, 135 mins, colour
Dir: Henry Koster
Stars: Richard Burton, Jean Simmons, Victor Mature, Michael Rennie, Dean Jagger
Rating: ★★★

This dignified pageant of Ancient Rome, dealing with the events following the Crucifixion, has the appropriate cast of thousands and a literate script by Philip Dunne, from the mammoth novel by Lloyd C Douglas. Richard Burton and Jean Simmons are both good but the best performance for my money – and, indeed, the best portrayal of his career – comes, surprisingly, from Victor Mature as Demetrius. The 'beefcake' star gives a sensitive performance which adds more to the reality of the story than

anything else. The exciting photography of Leon Shamroy – particularly in the action sequences – makes a brilliant backcloth to a story that reaches a moving peak.

Roberta ○
1935, US, 105 mins, b/w
Dir: William A Seiter
Stars: Irene Dunne, Fred Astaire, Ginger Rogers, Randolph Scott
Rating: ★★★

In their third film together, Fred Astaire and Ginger Rogers played second fiddle to Irene Dunne, as a Russian princess, sparring in and out of love with American footballer Randolph Scott, and get to perform four inspired dance routines. Look out for new RKO girl Lucille Ball in the lineup of mannequins in the extended fashion show sequence. Swathed in ostrich feathers, she descended a staircase onto the runway, making the most of what she later called 'halfway between an extra and a bit.' Leisurely but enjoyable.

Robin and Marian ○ ⓥ
1976, UK, 106 mins, colour
Dir: Richard Lester
Stars: Sean Connery, Audrey Hepburn, Robert Shaw, Nicol Williamson
Rating: ★★

Sherwood Forest 20 years after, and it's hardly the Nottingham of Errol Flynn's day that we are in here. It's a land of mud and grime, but the wicked sheriff (Robert Shaw) is still in there oppressing the peasants, as Robin Hood (Sean Connery) and Little John return from the Crusades. Director Richard Lester's how-it-really-was style, coupled with typical surrealist comic touches, somehow leaves the film struggling to find a rhythm. The only performance which suggests Lester's theme while proving attractive in its own right is Nicol Williamson's Little John. But the final battle between Connery and Shaw is gruelling, pulsating and bloody stuff.

Robin Hood ⊙ ⓥ
1973, US, 83 mins, colour
Dir: Wolfgang Reitherman
Voice stars: Peter Ustinov, Terry-Thomas, Brian Bedford
Rating: ★★

Coloured in pastel shades, this is a pleasant if unexceptional (by Disney standards) cartoon version of the story made live by the studio 20 years earlier. The voices of Peter Ustinov and Terry-Thomas are amusingly em-

ployed as cowardly lion and sneaky snake, but the music of the Sherman Brothers *(Mary Poppins* etc) is much missed.

Robin Hood ○ ⓥ
1991, US, 104 mins, colour
Dir: John Irvin
Stars: Patrick Bergin, Jeroen Krabbé, Edward Fox, Uma Thurman, Jurgen Prochnow
Rating: ★★

This is the kind of film that looks absolutely marvellous until the actors have to open their mouths. The credit sequence of lights on a hillside, followed by a thrillingly shot and cunningly edited manhunt sequence, promises a stylish slice of Sherwood until the dialogue begins, a strange mixture of vulgarity and Richard Greenery. Bergin and Thurman as Robin and Marian show enough spirit to get the better of it at times, but Prochnow and Krabbé are bludgeoned into ludicrous over-acting, only half trying to make sense of such lines as 'Sometimes, you're so wet one could shoot snipe off you', and even conceding the laurels for worst supporting actor to Edward Fox's Prince John, who bags the honour in one short appearance.

Robin Hood: Men in Tights ◖ ⓥ
1993, US, 102 mins, colour
Dir: Mel Brooks
Stars: Cary Elwes, Amy Yasbeck, Richard Lewis, Roger Rees, Tracey Ullman, Dom DeLuise, Mel Brooks
Rating: ★★

Mel Brooks runs wild in a Sherwood Forest that's more blue than green. Subtlety dies a thousand deaths, as Brooks' lavatorial arrows find the mark time and again in this skit (satire is definitely too strong a word here) on the Hood legend. Cary Elwes and Amy Yasbeck wisely play this straight as Robin and Marian, letting Brooks have his head as Rabbi Tuckman, who's given a good run for his money by Roger Rees' snivelling Sheriff of Rottingham and Tracey Ullman's cackling hag Latrine. Brooks, never a man to let good taste stand in his way, steals shamelessly from past successes in what resembles an English countryside version of *Blazing Saddles.*

Robin Hood: Prince of Thieves ◖ ⓥ
1991, US, 128 mins, colour
Dir: Kevin Reynolds

R

Stars: Kevin Costner, Morgan Freeman, Mary Elizabeth Mastrantonio, Christian Slater, Alan Rickman, Sean Connery
Rating: ★★★

Credit this version of the Sherwood legend with trying to be something different, then ask what it is that it's trying to be. There's a tongue-in-cheek Robin (Kevin Costner) with an American accent. A thoroughly modern Marian, played by Hollywood's Mastrantonio with an English accent. A comic Sheriff of Nottingham (Alan Rickman) who gets lines like, 'Cancel the kitchen scraps for lepers and orphans. And cancel Christmas!' And a collection of English yokels as the merrie men, mustering as much cursing and crudity as they think a PG-13 (or in the UK, 12) certificate will take. The end product looks as though the cast read the script and decided the best thing to do was have a good time and enjoy themselves. And it unexpectedly comes up with one memorable character in the form of Morgan Freeman as a Moor, brought back by Robin from the Crusades. The action is reasonably well-staged, though some of it is so unlikely as not to be thrilling.

Robinson Crusoe on Mars ○
1964, US, 110 mins, colour
Dir: Byron Haskin
Stars: Paul Mantee, Adam West
Rating: ★★★★

Remarkably successful transition of Daniel Defoe's classic castaway novel to a futuristic setting. While sticking quite close to the incidents in the original, it transports its hero to outer space, as the first American astronaut to land on Mars – albeit unwillingly. The oppressively desolate Martian landscapes are well conceived in splendid Technicolor and Byron Haskin's direction is impressively imaginative, making this fine fun for boys from five to 85.

RoboCop ● ⓥ
1987, US, 103 mins, colour
Dir: Paul Verhoeven
Stars: Peter Weller, Nancy Allen, Dan O'Herlihy, Ronny Cox, Ray Wise
Rating: ★★★★

Looking like a vehicle tailor-made for Arnold Sch-you know who, this is a technician's dream of a film, set in the near future with crime rampant on the streets of 'old' Detroit. Robot policemen are a fledgling idea, but inclined to go haywire at the drop of a connection. So when cop Murphy (Peter

Weller) is drilled to bits by the local mob, Morton (Miguel Ferrer), a brain-box as obsequious as he is obnoxious, reassembles him electronically to become the world's first RoboCop. After preliminary skirmishes, in which RoboCop cleans up a few local hoodlums, the nub of the plot comes into play. He starts to have recollections of the gang who obliterated him, who are in turn the henchmen of Jones (Ronny Cox) who controls the city's crime as well as being second-in-command of the company which built RoboCop, and now runs the local police. Although scarcely plausible at several key junctures, and aimed at producing the maximum grievous bodily damage, this is an entertaining adult romp with the villains, Ronny Cox and Kurtwood Smith, coolly stealing the show. The firepower around here is tremendous – the blood and gore (one villain disintegrates in toxic waste) splatters all over the screen. But there are one or two subtler comic moments too, such as the futuristic family playing a game of Nukem (together with fake explosion) in their sitting room.

Robocop 2 ● ⓥ
1990, US, 116 mins, colour
Dir: Irwin Kershner
Stars: Peter Weller, Nancy Allen, Daniel O'Herlihy, Tom Noonan
Rating: ★★

Number Two certainly delivers the action, even if its plot is impossible to follow. The city is wide open to criminals and looters, the police are on strike and unscrupulous private interests plan to take over. The chief criminal having been hospitalised by Robocop, his henchmen plan to make a deal with the mayor: they'll deliver a crime-free city in return for a 'nuke' (Futuristic drug) market at lower cost and safer substances. Private interests cannot allow such a devil's contract. And that's where *Robocop 2* comes in. Although the way is left clear for *Robocop 3*, this sequel lacks the humour and originality of the first film, often running like an old-time serial. Peter Weller and Nancy Allen, though both looking a bit long in the tooth, resume their roles with straight-faced gusto. Weller also gets the only line of any real wit, but unfortunately it's the last one in the film. The beginning, too, with a guest shot from John Glover, is quite amusing.

RoboCop 3 ◑ ⓥ
1993, US, 104 mins, colour
Dir: Fred Dekker

Stars: Robert Burke, Nancy Allen, Rip Torn, John Castle, Mako, Robert DoQui
Rating: ★★

The saga rumbles on: the Japanese have taken over the Omni Consumer Corporation and plan to demolish Detroit to build a Manhattan-style Metropolis. When the inhabitants fight back, RoboCop (now played by Robert Burke, even more facelessly than Peter Weller) sides with the resistance and faces battle with a Japanese 'terminator'. Plenty of action, if less violent than the previous two films, but with some strenuous overplaying in the supporting cast, where Rip Torn and Mako fight a well-earned draw for the worst performance in the film. Excellent music by Basil Poledouris deserves something with more depth to go with it.

Rob Roy ⓥ
1995, UK, 139 mins, colour
Dir: Michael Caton-Jones
Stars: Liam Neeson, Jessica Lange, Tim Roth, John Hurt, Eric Stoltz
Rating: ★★★

This is assuredly not Scotland of Disney's day, but a land red in the guts and gore, stench and sweat of the poor crofters who struggle to survive while the perfumed English gentry control their destinies from the cold comfort of castle cloisters. But, although the plot throws in a gratuitously graphic rape, hiding inside a dead animal and other visceral details, some elements have a ring as familiar as the clash of claymores. A little long in the telling considering it's so low on the legend, the film is bolstered by some spirited action scenes and a splendidly hateful villain in Tim Roth, whose curling lips indicate his relish at his role. Despite the odd dull bits, this is good action fare for those of strong stomach.

Rob Roy – The Highland Rogue ☉
1953, UK, 85 mins, colour
Dir: Harold French
Stars: Richard Todd, Glynis Johns, James Robertson Justice, Jean Taylor-Smith
Rating: ★★★

Adventure has fine old fling in these Highland fun and games from the Disney studio. It may merit a dunce's cap as a history lesson, but as a lively, colourful, action-filled yarn with something of a 'Western' feel, it belongs near the top of the class.

Rock, The ● Ⓥ

1996, US, 136 mins, colour
Dir: Michael Bay
Stars: Nicolas Cage, Sean Connery,
Michael Biehn, Ed Harris, William
Forsythe, John Spencer
Rating: ★★★★

Small wonder Connery chose this
heavy-duty action film. It hands him a
role tailor-made to his own brand of
lethal charm. Incensed by the government's refusal to compensate families
of those of his men killed in covert actions, Gen Hammond (Harris) leads
an elite band of Marine mercenaries to
heist rockets armed with VX gas. The
gas will wipe out a large proportion of
the American population unless a million dollars for each family, plus a
million for each mercenary, is paid.
Enter Goodspeed (Cage), an FBI
chemical weapons ace entirely unused
to any other kind of warfare; and
Mason (Connery), a long-term prisoner who has done many years (and
escaped from) the island where the
rockets, along with 81 hostages, now
nestle: Alcatraz. Stand well back from
this combustible formula and let the
action blast. It's a pretty well non-stop
and well-varied too, from a San
Francisco car chase, through a hectic
monorail car ride, to the more conventional shoot-up stuff. Nice ending too.

Rock-a-Doodie ⊙

1990, US, 74 mins, colour
Dir: Don Bluth
Voice Stars: Phil Harris, Glen Campbell,
Christopher Plummer, Sandy Duncan
Rating: ★

Children's entertainment is always to be
welcomed but, though teenies will surely love it, accompanying adults are
likely to give a thumbs down to this
dumb, dim cartoon feature based on the
story of Chanticleer. Cock of the roost
on his farm, he's forced to leave when
the animals discover that his crow does-
n't actually make the sun rise. This is
all the work of the owls (led by the
Duke of Owl) who love the dark and
don't want the sun to come up any
more at all. The animals, flooded out
by storms, decide to make for the city
and bring Chanticleer back from his career there as a rock star. Despite a good
voice cast, director Bluth has failed to
create any interesting characters here,
with the possible exception of a magpie
who seems to think he's a woodpecker.

Rock Around the Clock ○

1956, US, 74 mins, b/w
Dir: Fred F Sears

Stars: Bill Haley and the Comets,
Johnnie Johnston, The Platters
Rating: ★★

This was the one that really set the
Rock movement alight. As Bill Haley
and his saxophone descended slowly
to the floor, teenagers of all shapes and
sizes on both sides of the Atlantic left
their cinema seats and bopped it up in
the aisles. Oldies: look in on this and
remember what it was like when you
were misunderstood teenagers. You'll
find that the slight story looks even
slighter today and that now, as then,
it's only the music that matters.

Rock Around the World

See: The Tommy Steele Story

Rocketeer, The ⊙ Ⓥ

1991, US, 108 mins, colour
Dir: Joe Johnston
Stars: Bill Campbell, Jennifer Connelly,
Alan Arkin, Timothy Dalton
Rating: ★★★

Pretty stylish by strip-comic-epic standards and with something a little
different to offer, this is an adventure
(set in 1938) about a revolutionary
rocket pack that, when strapped to
man's back, can jet him around the
skies. We seem to remember that
Sylvester the Cat went awfully wrong
with one of these in a Warner Brothers
cartoon, but hero Bill Campbell can
just about steer the damn thing well
enough to effect a daring aerial rescue
when a pal gets into trouble.
Unfortunately, this attracts the attention not only of the FBI, and of
aviation pioneer Howard Hughes, but
also a group of Nazi infiltrators led (in
a sly dig at Errol Flynn) by a swashbuckling movie star, expertly played
by Timothy Dalton. For good measure, there's an almost-too-voluptuous
heroine (Jennifer Connelly), a lovable
old inventor sidekick (Alan Arkin) and
a hulking assassin made up to look like
Forties' film villain Rondo Hatton.
Director Johnston, who made *Honey, I
Shrunk the Kids*, pitches us straight into
the action from the start and there's no
lack of it. Acting, apart from Dalton
who's on a subtler level, is fairly rudimentary.

Rockets Galore ⊙

(aka: Mad Little Island)
1958, UK, 94 mins, colour
Dir: Michael Relph
Stars: Donald Sinden, Jeannie Carson
Rating: ★★

Ealing Studios first turned their attention to Sir Compton Mackenzie's

whimsical tales of the Scottish highlands and islands in the memorable
Whisky Galore!. This sequel brings the
island of Todday into the nuclear age
and proves a spotty successor to the
original, with the islanders fighting to
stop a rocket base being built there.
Gordon Jackson and Ian Hunter have
featured roles, and you'll also spot
Ronnie Corbett.

Rocking Horse Winner, The ○

1949, UK, 90 mins, b/w
Dir: Anthony Pelissier
Stars: Valerie Hobson, John Howard
Davies, John Mills, Hugh Sinclair, Ronald
Squire, Susan Richards
Rating: ★★★★

John Howard Davies, later the producer of TV's *Fawlty Towers*, plays the
sinister child who, once aboard his
rocking horse, can predict the winner
in any given race. As might be expected from the star of *Oliver Twist*, Master
Davies brings this version of a D H
Lawrence novella to chilling, disturbing, but fascinating life.

Rocky ○ Ⓥ

1976, US, 119 mins, colour
Dir: John G Avildsen
Stars: Sylvester Stallone, Talia Shire,
Burt Young, Carl Weathers, Burgess
Meredith
Rating: ★★★★★

Sylvester Stallone's career-making film
is a cross between *Marty* and *Somebody
Up There Likes Me*. Rocky, a boxer, is
30 and, although a winner of 44 of his
64 fights, is already considered a bum
by his local gym manager (Burgess
Meredith) who hates him 'because he
had the talent to become a good fighter' but has let his chance slip away and
now fights for two-bit purses in smoky
halls. Out of the blue, the world
champion decides to offer a chance to
an unknown home town boy. Of
course, the choice is Rocky. The nice
thing about the film from then on –
that allows it to build cleanly to the
grandstand finish – is, of course, that
no one will try to nobble the challenger, or get him to take a dive, since
they don't think he has a chance. The
fight itself is quite superbly done, all
thud and blood, and pace, adrenalin
and noise. Like the movie, it never relaxes its grip.

Rocky II ○ Ⓥ

1979, US, 119 mins, colour
Dir: Sylvester Stallone

R

Stars: Sylvester Stallone, Talia Shire,
Burt Young, Burgess Meredith
Rating: ★★★

Stallone does it again. Against all the
odds, he brings home his *Rocky* sequel
as another winner – even if it's a notch
below its predecessor in every respect.
Even so, if your knees aren't trembling
at the end of the inevitable re-match
for the World Heavyweight
Championship, then your adrenalin
must have dried up and gone away.
The early scenes of Rocky hitting the
skids after blowing his money are
sticky and predictable, and only the luminous performance of Talia Shire as
his wife keeps it going at this stage.
Rocky's dry, throwaway, semi-dim humour improves things still further, and
the music, photography and boxing
'choreography' really come into their
own in the build-up to the big fight.
But Ms Shire's conversion to wanting
Stallone to fight again (despite the risk
to his eyesight) is hardly more convincing than the result of the fight
itself.

Rocky III ○ ⓥ

1982, US, 99 mins, colour
Dir: Sylvester Stallone
Stars: Sylvester Stallone, Talia Shire,
Burt Young, Burgess Meredith, Carl
Weathers, Mr T
Rating: ★★★

Sylvester Stallone's boxing saga rolls
on in this predictable but effective
third segment. Rocky is now world
champ. His manager (Burgess
Meredith) has set him up with 10
hand-picked opponents in a row – only
Rocky doesn't know it. What we need
to psych us (and Rocky) up is a defeat
that has to be avenged. Conveniently,
it comes along in the shape of Clubber
Lang (Mr T), a fearsome and hungry
black fighter who wants Rocky's guts
in a sling. After Rocky bites the inevitable dust, his old opponent Apollo
Creed (Carl Weathers) comes back
into the picture ... as his new trainer.
The fights here don't measure up to
those from the two previous films, but
the series retains its likeability and
stays afloat on the personalities of its
performers: Stallone is again the grunting Rocky to the life; Talia Shire as his
wife only has one big scene this time
and she doesn't muff it.

Rocky IV ◑ ⓥ

1985, US, 110 mins, colour
Dir: Sylvester Stallone
Stars: Sylvester Stallone, Talia Shire
Rating: ★★

The spiralling improbabilities of the
Rocky saga reached their pinnacle
with this moronically jingoistic
episode. The Russians have biologically engineered a huge fighting
machine, Ivan Drago (Dolph
Lundgren), and former world heavyweight champ Apollo Creed
challenges him to an exhibition bout
in Las Vegas. Drago fells him with
his left hook and he dies. Rocky
Balboa (Sylvester Stallone) gives up
his title to fight the Russian in an
unauthorised bout in the Soviet
Union. What we get here is Rocky
(looking decidedly pebble-like compared with the giant Lundgren)
defending the American way against
the dark evils of communism. The
odd thing is, although you know this
is all rubbish, you still find yourself
rooting for the good guy. There's a
lesson there somewhere, and
Stallone's astute enough to have
learned it.

Rocky Horror Picture Show, The ◑

1974, UK, 95 mins, colour
Dir: Jim Sharman
Stars: Tim Curry, Susan Sarandon, Barry
Bostwick, Richard O'Brien, Jonathan
Adams, Little Nell
Rating: ★★

After the comedy horror film came this
hugely successful musical comedy horror, which is pretty far out even for the
mid-Seventies. An all-American couple, unwise enough to stop at a castle
to use the phone, are both seduced by
its occupant, a transsexual transvestite
Transylvanian intent on creating a superman for his own pleasures. The
best performance comes from Richard
O'Brien (who also wrote it) as the
obligatory hunchback; his first appearance at a window is a sensationally
striking moment that the rest of the
film never quite matches.

Roger and Me ●

1989, US, 91 mins, colour
Dir: Michael Moore
Rating: ★★★★

A bitingly funny documentary on the
collapse of an American town – Flint,
Michigan – following the decision of
General Motors and its chairman
Roger Smith to throw 23 per cent of its
people out of work by closing the auto
factory there. Director Moore describes not only his own battle to
interview Smith, but also the descent
of Flint into a living hell where half the
population are on general welfare.

Many of the car workers are in the
new huge prison there, many others
are guards in the same grim structure.
The film has scenes that some viewers
may find upsetting; the story is not a
downbeat one, though, thanks to
Moore's telling it with bitter sarcasm
and a prowling camera that catches the
funny side as well as the tragic. He
also reveals that America has some
spooky people. Some of them even
live in Flint ...

Rogues of Sherwood Forest ⊙

1950, US, 75 mins, colour
Dir: Gordon Douglas
Stars: John Derek, Diana Lynn, George
Macready
Rating: ★★

John Derek as the son of Robin Hood
in a typical Columbia action film of its
time in which reality is kept at arm's
length. Diana Lynn, former child actress, who was one of the sweetest
Hollywood heroines, makes a beautiful
lady fair, George Macready is as sleek
a villain as you could wish for, and
old-time silent comedian Billy Bevan
pops up as Will Scarlett. The action,
ravishingly photographed in
Technicolor by ace cameraman
Charles Lawton Jr, provides a new
slant on why King John signed the
Magna Carta.

Rogues' Regiment ○

1948, US, 86 mins, b/w
Dir: Robert Florey
Stars: Dick Powell, Marta Toren, Vincent
Price, Stephen McNally
Rating: ★★

Typically tough Dick Powell post-war
thriller with Powell as an American intelligence officer at large in the Foreign
Legion trying to ferret out a Nazi war
criminal. Not very exciting.

Rollerball ● ⓥ

1975, US, 129 mins, colour
Dir: Norman Jewison
Stars: James Caan, John Houseman,
Maud Adams, Ralph Richardson
Rating: ★★

The futuristic society of 2018 is rather
vaguely realised but there's no doubting the ferocious power of the actual
Rollerball sequences. This savage
spectator sport is brought to life in a
powerful series of brutally exciting
scenes. james Caan and John Beck are
well teamed as Rollerball stars while
John Houseman scores as the seemingly benign Bartholomew.

Rollercoaster ○

1977, US, 115 mins, colour
Dir: James Goldstone
Stars: George Segal, Richard Widmark
Rating: ★★★★

Fancy a ride on a scenic railway? The chances are that you'll be off them for some time after you've seen this good old-fashioned entertainment thriller about a cool young bomber (Timothy Bottoms) who blew one up, and threatens to do it again unless America's amusement park chiefs come up with a million dollars. Bottoms contributes his best film work for some time as the icy assassin, but it's George Segal who dominates the film by making the leading role (that of the safety inspector after the saboteur) seem tailor-made for his own attractive blend of cynicism and sincerity. Despite the massacre at the beginning, this is one the children could safely watch as well.

Rollover ●

1981, US, 118 mins, colour
Dir: Alan J Pakula
Stars: Jane Fonda, Kris Kristofferson
Rating: ★

From director Alan J Pakula, who made All the President's Men and The Parallax View, comes another convoluted study of the underside of American public life. This time, the subject is its financial world. Although you may not understand all the ins and outs of the plot, you're still likely to be hooked on its enticing mystery element which has banking wizard Kris Kristofferson and heiress widow Jane Fonda uncovering each other and a plot to undermine the world money market. Far too pretentious, though.

Romance in the High Seas

See: It's Magic

Romancing the Stone ○ ⓥ

1984, US, 105 mins, colour
Dir: Robert Zemeckis
Stars: Michael Douglas, Kathleen Turner, Danny DeVito
Rating: ★★★

A colourful slice of escapism that's so likeable and fast-moving that you often forget how silly it all is. Kathleen Turner, Michael Douglas and Danny DeVito all boosted their careers with larger-than-life performances. These days, all pretences towards reality and conviction have been tossed away in this kind of romp, but Turner's sympathetic performance as the beleaguered authoress helps a lot as she is hauled out to a sea of mud and the tropical storms in the Colombian outback to rescue a kidnapped sister, by yielding up the treasure map sent to her by her sister's dead husband. In South America, she's rescued by Jack Colton (Michael Douglas) who, while having an eye on the treasure map, is the amalgam of all the romantic heroes of her own fiction. Their subsequent hunt for the treasure might be even more fun if the villains weren't so intentionally comic, but we should still be grateful for such non-stop action entertainment.

Roman Holiday ○ ⓥ

1953, US, 118 mins, b/w
Dir: William Wyler
Stars: Gregory Peck, Audrey Hepburn, Eddie Albert
Rating: ★★★★

This is William Wyler's enchanting romantic comedy (in which Audrey Hepburn won an Oscar) about a princess who spends 24 hours incognito in Rome, squired by a reporter and photographer, who are well aware of her real identity, and out for a scoop for their paper. A series of small, but delightful incidents subtly builds up our identification with the characters, lending a great charm and making the climax a truly moving movie moment. Eddie Albert offers a richly humorous account of the photographer, and Gregory Peck's casual romantic style is ideally suited to the role of the reporter. As the princess, Hepburn brought a unique blend of naive charm, refinement and elegance to the part that justly made her Hollywood's newest star.

Roman Scandals ○

1933, US, 92 mins, b/w
Dir: Frank Tuttle
Stars: Eddie Cantor, Ruth Etting
Rating: ★★★

Quite a few funny things happen to pop-eyed Eddie Cantor on his way to the forum in this lavish Goldwyn musical comedy. Cantor's co-star is torch singer Ruth Etting, whose life story was later told in Doris Day's Love Me or Leave Me. There are some wild dance numbers organised by the ubiquitous Busby Berkeley and director Frank Tuttle gives it lots of joie de vivre. The hit of the show is undoubtedly 'Keep Young and Beautiful'. Fast-moving fun.

Roman Spring of Mrs Stone, The ○

1961, US, 104 mins, colour
Dir: José Quintero
Stars: Vivien Leigh, Warren Beatty
Rating: ★★★

This adaptation of a Tennessee Williams novel about a middle-aged actress falling for a young Italian gigolo has a bizarre, rather chilling charm. Vivien Leigh and Warren Beatty give interesting performances in these roles, but the film is stolen from both of them by Lotte Lenya as the widow's wasp-tongued friend.

Romantic Comedy ◑

1983, US, 103 mins, colour
Dir: Arthur Hiller
Stars: Dudley Moore, Mary Steenburgen
Rating: ★★

Cuddly Dudley Moore tried to reverse his fortunes after two box office bombs (Six Weeks and Lovesick) with this film version of Bernard Slade's Broadway play. With this tale of two playwrights who team up with varying personal and professional success he unfortunately scored a hat-trick, as the end product, although enjoyable in parts, and with a good performance by Mary Steenburgen, ends up being neither very romantic nor very funny. Steenburgen plays the other writer and she and Moore battle hard against a script and pacing that lack the snap and crackle this type of comedy needs.

Romantic Englishwoman, The ● ⓥ

1975, UK, 116 mins, colour
Dir: Joseph Losey
Stars: Glenda Jackson, Michael Caine, Helmut Berger, Kate Nelligan
Rating: ★

Director Joseph Losey's answer to Last Year in Marienbad; it's only his direction that makes this puzzle picture an occasionally fascinating, if too often ludicrous cinematic exercise. Certainly, he has little help from the screenplay. In fact, it's hard to tell which is more trite – the film's script, or the pulp books written in the attic by author Michael Caine while downstairs he is losing his wife (Glenda Jackson) to narcotics-smuggling gigolo Helmut Berger. Or is he? That's just one of the riddles you have to tackle.

Romeo and Juliet ○

1936, US, 126 mins, b/w
Dir: George Cukor
Stars: Leslie Howard, Norma Shearer
Rating: ★★★

R

Although it sports a pair of over-age lovers in Norma Shearer and Leslie Howard, this is in all other respects a perfectly splendid version of Shakespeare's classic, still the best available on film. Sensitive direction by George Cukor brings out all the passion of the play, with a last great flamboyant performance by John Barrymore as Mercutio. Howard at first insisted that he was too old for Romeo but, after the part had been turned down by Fredric March, Clark Gable, Errol Flynn and Robert Donat, the studio went back to its original choice and persuaded him to play the role.

Romeo and Juliet ○ Ⓥ
1968, UK/Italy, 138 mins, colour
Dir: Franco Zeffirelli
Stars: Olivia Hussey, Leonard Whiting, Michael York
Rating: ★★★

The brilliance of the supporting cast and the haunting music by Nino Rota more than compensate for the inexpedence of the young leading players in Franco Zeffirelli's version of Shakespeare's tragic romance. It's a delight to the eye if not always to the ear.

Romeo is Bleeding ● Ⓥ
1993, US, 112 mins, colour
Dir: Peter Medak
Stars: Gary Oldman, Lena Olin, Annabella Sciorra, Juliette Lewis
Rating: ★

Gary Oldman lurches through the grunge once again for the sake of his art in this bloodsoaked story that's described as a black comedy, but isn't much like any comedy you ever saw, and a sight more difficult to follow. Oldman's a cop on the make who hoards his Mob bribes in a hole in his yard, is fond of his wife (Annabella Sciorra, good in a thankless role) and his mistress (Juliette Lewis), but comes unstuck when he becomes involved with a ruthless hit-girl (Lena Olin). There's also the matter of the Mob don (Roy Scheider) cutting off one of his toes, when one of his tip-offs goes wrong. Yes, Oldman's in a mess. And it gets worse. Unlike the film, which actually gets a bit better (though not much) towards the end. Olin does her best to be bad, Lewis does her mindless bimbo act, and Oldman, looking like Dick Powell, kills or nearly gets killed by everyone. Very slow.

Romero ● Ⓥ
1989, US, 106 mins, colour
Dir: John Duigan

Stars: Raul Julia, Richard Jordan, Ana Alicia, Eddie Velez, Alejandro Bracho, Tony Plana
Rating: ★★★

Sickeningly, the most remarkable thing about Archbishop Oscar Romero's time as the head of the church in turbulent, tortured El Salvador from 1977 to 1980 is that he actually lasted three years. 'He's a good compromise choice,' it was said at his inauguration. 'He'll make no waves. He's a bookworm'. 'His health is delicate. He won't last.' This proves partly true at first. However, faced with the massacres of his people, assassinations of priests and desecration of churches, Romero really has little alternative but to speak out against the atrocities perpetrated by the repressive, army-based government. Raul Julia is much less flamboyant than usual as Romero, but Richard Jordan's charismatic priest catches the eye before he's despatched early on in this sad, solid, sincere film, entirely untypical of its director, that leaves you with a sense of despair.

Rommel – Desert Fox ○ Ⓥ
(aka: The Desert Fox)
1951, US, 88 mins, b/w
Dir: Henry Hathaway
Stars: James Mason, Cedric Hardwicke, Jessica Tandy
Rating: ★★★

James Mason's performance as the famous World War Two German field-marshal established him as a star in Hollywood after a tentative start to his career on the other side of the Atlantic. This story involves not so much Rommel's North Africa campaign as his involvement in a plot to assassinate Hitler (played by Luther Adler who took on the role again a year later in The Magic Face). Under Henry Hathaway's cool, detached direction, the plot grips throughout.

Rookie, The ● Ⓥ
1990, US, 121 mins, colour
Dir: Clint Eastwood
Stars: Clint Eastwood, Charlie Sheen, Sonia Braga, Raul Julia
Rating: ★

Tough cop Clint Eastwood and his new partner Charlie Sheen (the rookie of the title) go on an orgy of destruction to catch baddie Raul Julia in this crash bang wallop cop thriller. Lots of action rattled along at a rapid pace but Eastwood wearing his director's hat doesn't cover the fact that The Rookie is formula stuff poorly served by an in-

different script. It's as if Eastwood got fed up with everyone else making second-rate Dirty Harry rip-offs, so made one himself. Eastwood's cop is the grim avenger you would expect, but Sheen is pretty unconvincing and the usually excellent Julia is a dreadfully clichéd baddie, complete with indefinable (and bad) foreign accent. Slip your brain into neutral and you may enjoy this mindless slice of mayhem.

Rookie of the Year ○ Ⓥ
1993, US, 100 mins, colour
Dir: Daniel Stern
Stars: Thomas Ian Nicholas, Gary Busey, Daniel Stern, John Candy
Rating: ★

Actor Daniel Stern positively does not seem set for a shining career as a director after this fairly agonising debut behind the cameras. It's a sporting fantasy about a 12-year-old kid (Thomas Ian Nicholas) who becomes a dynamite baseball pitcher after a broken arm accident 'fuses his tendons with his humerus'. Subsequent developments are quite ingeniously worked out, but director Stern encourages all the cast to mug shamelessly, setting them an example himself with some painfully rampant over-acting in an all-too-high-profile cameo role. Gary Busey, looking just like Nick Nolte in this one, does his best to calm things down a bit as the veteran pitcher who takes the kid under his wing. Pretty bad.

Rookies
See: Buck Privates

Room at the Top ⓒ
1958, UK, 117 mins, b/w
Dir: Jack Clayton
Stars: Laurence Harvey, Simone Signoret, Heather Sears, Donald Wolfit
Rating: ★★★★

The powerful drama that brought a new freedom to the British cinema. It also introduced audiences to Joe Lampton who later became the anti-hero of the television series Man at the Top. Simone Signoret won an Academy Award for her performance in this film, as did Neil Paterson for his biting screenplay, adapted from John Braine's original novel.

Room Service ○ Ⓥ
1938, US, 78 mins, b/w
Dir: William A Seiter
Stars: Groucho Marx, Chico Marx, Harpo Marx
Rating: ★★

RKO paid a then-record $225,000 for the film rights to the hit Broadway play *Room Service* and lured The Marx Brothers from MGM as stars, then sat back and expected a box-office smash. But it was almost devoid of the usual Marx Brothers lunacy and verbal jousting. Groucho is a theatrical con man trying to stage a hit Broadway play while hanging on to his hotel room, which he hasn't the money to pay for. RKO contract players Lucille Ball and Ann Miller – the hoofer with the million-dollar legs – are woefully underused with only a walk-on role for Lucy and little chance allowed for Ann to display her wonderful singing and dancing talents.

Room With a View, A ○ ⓥ

1985, UK, 115 mins, colour
Dir: James Ivory
Stars: Maggie Smith, Helena Bonham Carter, Denholm Elliott, Julian Sands, Daniel Day Lewis, Simon Callow
Rating: ★★★

A film which pleases the eye, if not the soul, *A Room With a View* is reminiscent of a Claude Monet painting – beautiful to look at, but hardly passionately afire – in this triple Oscar-winning adaptation of E M Forster's rather fey novel. It is a soporifically gentle film about manners but the viewer clamours for some outrageous behaviour and it takes a street fight from some unruly Italians to convince young Lucy (Helena Bonham Carter) that there is more to life than poetry, decorum and cucumber sandwiches. When a headstrong Englishman (Julian Sands) plants a kiss on her unsullied lips it's regarded as an apocalyptic scandal. Subsequently, more and more social restraints are subtly breached by a superb British cast.

Rooney ○

1958, UK, 88 mins, b/w
Dir: George Pollock
Stars: John Gregson, Muriel Pavlow, Barry Fitzgerald
Rating: ★★★

It's not often that a dustman is the central character in a film, but here is an exception – rejoicing in the delightful name of James Ignatius Rooney. It's an enjoyable if relatively little known British comedy film, based on a book by that highly popular novelist Catherine Cookson.

Rooster Cogburn ○ ⓥ

1975, US, 108 mins, colour
Dir: Stuart Millar

Stars: John Wayne, Katharine Hepburn
Rating: ★★

There are echoes of *The African Queen* in this Western adventure, what with Katharine Hepburn as a fire-breathing (and sharpshooting) missionary, and John Wayne as the crusty old lawman who's forced to take her along on a manhunt – not to mention the river setting which dominates most of the film. Worth a look for the way in which Wayne and Hepburn deliver their dialogue, for the superb scenery and for a good cruel villain from Richard Jordan. Wayne reprises the character that won him an Oscar in *True Grit*, but the script here is not in the same class.

Rope ○ ⓥ

1948, US, 80 mins, colour
Dir: Alfred Hitchcock
Stars: James Stewart, Farley Granger, Sir Cedric Hardwicke, John Dall
Rating: ★★

It's a plot right up Alfred Hitchcock's macabre street: two college boys murder a friend, just for kicks, and hide his body in a trunk which they then use as a drinks table for a party attended by the dead man's parents and fiancée. James Stewart is the school-teacher who begins to smell a rat. For this, his first film in colour, Hitchcock used a technique of long takes to give a smooth feel to the story, which is all set in one claustrophobic room. But it often seems all too static.

Rope of Sand ○

1949, US, 105 mins, b/w
Dir: William Dieterle
Stars: Burt Lancaster, Paul Henreid, Peter Lorre, Claude Rains, Corinne Calvet
Rating: ★★★

This rugged adventure yarn, set in South Africa, is a replica of the kind of Bogart thriller that held audiences to their seats throughout the Forties and early Fifties. The Bogart-style supporting cast is headed by Claude Rains, Paul Henreid and Peter Lorre, and the only change is Burt Lancaster for Bogey in the leading role. The plot concerns a search for a cache of diamonds and the action is enough to satisfy fans of the toughest thriller.

Rosalie Goes Shopping ○ ⓥ

1989, US, 95 mins, colour
Dir: Percy Adlon
Stars: Marianne Sägebrecht, Brad Davis, Judge Reinhold, William Harlander
Rating: ★★★

Rosalie is a Bavarian hausfrau transplanted to Arkansas by the simple-minded, crop-dusting husband she calls Liebling. Rosalie has seven children and a nifty line in shoplifting and major credit card fraud that keeps her family in the style to which she has accustomed them. That means gourmet dinner materials for her trainee chef son, wardrobes of clothes for herself and the kids, trampolines and slides in the garden and the latest gadgets which she throws away if they show the slightest signs of not working. Financial problems with the bank or cheque card companies? Rosalie just reports her card stolen and goes out on a spree with it. But a $11,000 computer almost proves her undoing. This is basically a half-hour anecdote stretched out to 95 minutes and so only amusing every now and again. But plump Sägebrecht is winning as Rosalie and Reinhold on the mark as the priest bewildered by the extent of her confessions.

Rose, The ● ⓥ

1979, US, 134 mins, colour
Dir: Mark Rydell
Stars: Bette Midler, Alan Bates, Frederic Forrest
Rating: ★★★★

The initial impact of singer Bette Midler as a performer and actress is undoubtedly sensational in the opening sequences of *The Rose*. It must be added that, at well over two hours of film, you may find Ms Midler at full throttle a trifle wearing, as with the film, a powerful no-holds-barred portrait of a rock star of the Sixties (supposedly modelled on Janis Joplin). She's on the run from drink and drugs and vainly seeking either stability in her life or respite from the constant strain. Little concession is made to the period, particularly in the star's frothy hairdo, yet the film remains an unforgettable experience, thanks to its supercharged (and Oscar-nominated) star.

Roseanna McCoy ○ ⓥ

1949, US, 100 mins, b/w
Dir: Irving Reis
Stars: Farley Granger, Joan Evans, Charles Bickford, Raymond Massey
Rating: ★★

A sort of *Romeo and Juliet* of the hillbilly world, with young lovers from the Hatfields and McCoys sparking up embers from the legendary family feud of the 1880s. Charles Bickford and Raymond Massey are the unlikely leaders of the two clans, with the title role going to Joan Evans, a striking young actress Goldwyn hoped to turn into a big star. That never quite happened, though she worked steadily in the industry for another 12 years.

Rosebud O
1974, US, 126 mins, colour
Dir: Otto Preminger
Stars: Peter O'Toole, Richard Attenborough, Isabelle Huppert, Cliff Gorman, Kim Catrall
Rating: ★

'Topical' suspense tale of wealthy girls kidnapped by Arabs, best regarded as an outrageous attempt at smart entertainment. A dramatic exposition with a curious mixture of panache and laughable heavy-handedness, making it look increasingly like a cut-price Frederick Forsyth thriller.

Rose-Marie O
1936, US, 113 mins, b/w
Dir: W S Van Dyke II
Stars: Jeanette MacDonald, Nelson Eddy
Rating: ★★★

Despite the occasional artificial back drop, location filming at Lake Tahoe lends a fresh, breezy feel to the old story about the backwoods singer (in this version a Canadian opera star) and the Mountie who gets his woman. Jeanette MacDonald and Nelson Eddy, then the screen's hottest romantic singing team, were surefire box-office in these roles. But there's additional interest for film buffs today in early appearances by James Stewart (as the heroine's villainous brother!), singer Allan Jones (who would rise to fully fledged co-star with Ms MacDonald in *The Firefly*) and a very young-looking David Niven (billed as Nivens). It couldn't miss and it didn't: MGM made a mint. Remade (without the same zest) in 1954.

Rosemary's Baby ● ⓥ
1968, US, 137 mins, colour
Dir: Roman Polanski
Stars: Mia Farrow, John Cassavetes, Ruth Gordon, Ralph Bellamy
Rating: ★★★★

Roman Polanski's famous film about modern witchcraft on the loose in an ordinary-looking New York apartment budding, where new tenant Rosemary (Mia Farrow) plunges deeply, giddily into a nightmare world which enfolds her in evil. Polanski uses every throat-clutching trick in the book to compel his audience into total belief of

what is basically a rather preposterous tale. At times he is so persuasively nasty that it needs strong nerves to see him out as he opts for a (then smart) open-ended climax. Mia Farrow grips your sympathy every inch of the way as the beleaguered Rosemary, in spite of occasionally banal snatches of script: 'I've been to Vidal Sassoon,' she tells her jobless husband (another thankless role for John Cassavetes) after she must have already spent a fortune on clothes. As the witch who ensnares her, veteran Hollywood writer and actress Ruth Gordon took an Oscar.

Rosencrantz and Guildenstern are Dead O ⓥ
1990, US, 117 mins, colour
Dir: Tom Stoppard
Stars: Gary Oldman, Tim Roth, Richard Dreyfuss, Iain Glen, Ian Richardson
Rating: ★

Playwright (and here writer-director) Stoppard has taken two never-seen characters from *Hamlet*, and given them a story of their own. However, the results, on screen at least, are such that we venture to suggest a run round the block would be more entertaining. Oldman and Roth, exchanging dialogue like a medieval Abbott and Costello, are the hapless pair recalled to Denmark where they become involved in a plot as potty as it's soporific, in which a group of strolling minstrels (led by Richard Dreyfuss, in the role illness prevented Sean Connery playing) depict the events in *Hamlet* before they happen. Photographed in atrocious colour, this is about as much fun as it sounds (although it worked much better on stage), the proceedings dragging on for nearly two hours. 'I've had enough,' says Oldman (who gives the film's only watchable performance) at one stage, and he's right. Connery was lucky.

Rose of Washington Square O
1939, US, 86 mins, b/w
Dir: Gregory Ratoff
Stars: Tyrone Power, Al Jolson, Alice Faye
Rating: ★★★

Or, the original *Funny Girl*. This vintage 20th Century-Fox musical is loosely based on the life of Fanny Brice, with Alice Faye and Tyrone Power in the roles later filmed by Barbra Streisand and Omar Sharif.

The songs include 'My Man' and 'Toot, Toot, Tootsie'.

Rose Tattoo, The O
1955, US, 117 mins, b/w
Dir: Daniel Mann
Stars: Anna Magnani, Burt Lancaster, Marisa Pavan, Ben Cooper
Rating: ★★★★

Although the story isn't very strong, the sheer weight and quality of the acting pull it through in style in this screen version of the play by Tennessee Williams. It's headed by a deservedly Oscar-winning performance by Anna Magnani as the Sicilian peasant woman transported by her (now dead) husband to the gulf coast of America. Burt Lancaster, as the man who comes physically into her life, and Jo Van Fleet are excellent in support, while Marisa Pavan (also Oscar nominated) Virginia Grey, Ben Cooper and Sandro Giglio all give career-best performances under Daniel Mann's direction. Despite its characters' fits of bad temper, this is, in fact, for the most part a happy, friendly, intimate film, well-made, well-photographed (James Wong Howe won another of the movie's Oscars) and superbly acted.

Rough Company
See: The Violent Men

Rough Magic ◑
1995, US, 106 mins, colour
Dir: Clare Peploe
Stars: Bridget Fonda, Russell Crowe, Jim Broadbent, Andy Romano, Kenneth Mars, D W Moffett
Rating: ★★

After starting out, promisingly, as a thriller with disarming touches of magic, this ditches the thriller aspect in favour of magic, mysticism and not a little all-round silliness. Bridget Fonda plays a magician's assistant in immediate post-war times who agrees, for social gain, to marry a wealthy aspiring politician (D W Moffett) much to the chagrin of her fatherly boss. After getting trapped in a fake guillotine machine, the slimy politico accidentally shoots the magician dead, an action photographed by Fonda, who goes on the run with the film. Husband-to-be, escaping, hires disreputable war vet Russell Crowe to track her down as she flees through Mexico. This section of the film is the most entertaining, full of pseudo-smart dialogue, with Crowe and Fonda looking like Alan Ladd and Veronica Lake in their period gear.

Once Fonda travels to a mysterious island to obtain some kind of native magic potion, though, the whole thing goes haywire, developing into a screwball comedy of the wildest (and crudest) kind.

Rough Shoot ○
(aka: Shoot First)
1952, UK, 87 mins, b/w
Dir: Robert Parrish
Stars: Joel McCrea, Evelyn Keyes, Herbert Lom
Rating: ★★★

Hollywood stars Joel McCrea and Evelyn Keyes made a worthwhile trip across the Atlantic to make this polished British thriller. Eric Ambler's highly professional script provides some comedy amidst the excitement and clever plot developments. Herbert Lom and Roland Culver excel as two rather quirky secret agents.

Rounders, The ○
1965, US, 85 mins, colour
Dir: Burt Kennedy
Stars: Glenn Ford, Henry Fonda
Rating: ★★

Pleasing comedy Western about two veteran cowhands, played by Henry Fonda and Glenn Ford, forever trying to tame the same bucking bronco.

Round Midnight ◐ ⓥ
1986, France/US, 131 mins, colour
Dir: Bertrand Tavernier
Stars: Dexter Gordon, François Cluzet, Christine Pascal
Rating: ★★

A loving homage to jazz musicians and their world from French director Bertrand Tavernier. The story of an ageing and burned-out American jazz musician and a passionate French admirer is very loosely based on the real-life relationship between Bud Powell and Francis Paudras in the Paris of the late 1950s : Paris of that era was a haven for many jazz musicians because the interest in jazz didn't fade in France as it did in America. Tavernier cast a real jazz musician – tenor sax great Dexter Gordon – rather than an actor in the central role and Gordon fills the part well, perhaps giving it an authenticity an actor would have struggled to achieve. Jazz fans will have a good time listening to the music (of which there is plenty) and spotting Herbie Hancock, Ron Carter, Freddie Hubbard and Wayne Shorter. All the music was recorded live while filming, not dubbed over afterwards, as is usual.

Roustabout ○ ⓥ
1964, US, 101 mins, colour
Dir: John Rich
Stars: Elvis Presley, Barbara Stanwyck, Joan Freeman, Leif Erickson
Rating: ★

With Barbara Stanwyck as co-star, there were high hopes for this Elvis Presley film. Alas, the King hit a new low instead, saddled with the oldest story in showbusiness – and some of the oldest dialogue to go with it. The story can be cut to a few words: wild motorcycle youth rides into carnival, and is tamed by lovely young girl (Joan Blackman). Girl: 'Everyone needs somebody to worry about them.' Driven away by the girl's oafish father, the youth returns when the carnival cannot do without him. Oafish father: 'Let's go on with the show.' That's all folks, and, this time round, even the songs, apart from 'Little Egypt', are unmemorable.

Rover Dangerfield ⊙ ⓥ
1991, US, 74 mins, colour
Dir: Jim George, Jim Seeley
Voice stars: Rodney Dangerfield, Susan Boyd, Ronnie Schell, Ned Luke, Dana Hill
Rating: ★★

A cute-for-a-while cartoon comedy written by twitchy US comic Rodney Dangerfield, who also provides the voice of the canine star. Streetwise Rover is snatched from his big city life and dumped on a backwater farm. But this wisecracking hound's bone idle, and soon Rover's in the doghouse. Lively animation – just watch that opening sequence – lovable characters and lavish songs (listen to the instant classic love song 'I'd Give Up a Bone for You') make this fun for the whole family, although adults may tire of it after the half-way mark. Dangerfield is, however, funnier when you don't have to look at him!

Roxanne ○ ⓥ
1987, US, 107 mins, colour
Dir: Fred Schepisi
Stars: Steve Martin, Daryl Hannah, Rick Rossovich, Shelley Duvall
Rating: ★★★

Steve Martin always said he had a nose for comedy. But this is carrying the notion rather too far! Steve's had a nose job all right, and the result is on the whole a delightful reworking of the classic Cyrano de Bergerac – although this version is never quite as funny or touching as it might be. Steve plays a fire chief who's the most

easy-going of chaps unless someone insults his pronounced proboscis. Then he tends to take them to pieces. But when leggy astronomer Daryl Hannah sashays into town, Steve's eyes pop out of his head – well, at least as far as the end of his nose. The boy's in love. Alas, Daryl has a yen for the latest recruit to Steve's Keystone Kops fire brigade. And pretty soon the fire chief finds himself standing in on literacy for the boneheaded Romeo. 'I guess I mistook sex for love,' moans Daryl, wise after the event. 'I did that once,' confidante Shelley Duvall tells her. 'It was great.' Sadly, such gems in Martin's own script aren't as many as you'd like. This, though, is a film that's almost always fun to be with.

Roxie Hart ○
1942, US, 75 mins, b/w
Dir: William A Wellman
Stars: Ginger Rogers, Adolphe Menjou, George Montgomery
Rating: ★★★

Ginger Rogers' second great success from 1942 following The Major and the Minor, this was much later made into a hit stage musical called Chicago. Ginger portrays a showgirl who agrees to go on trial for murder for the publicity she'll reap (naturally she didn't do it). The trial itself turns into something of a carnival, with the photographers crying, 'The knees, Roxie, the knees.' Rogers and Adolphe Menjou are well matched as defendant and shyster lawyer, and play it to the hilt.

Royal Wedding ⊙ ⓥ
(aka: Wedding Bells)
1951, US, 93 mins, colour
Dir: Stanley Donen
Stars: Fred Astaire, Jane Powell, Peter Lawford, Sarah Churchill
Rating: ★★★

This slim musical is decorated by two classic Fred Astaire numbers – his brilliant solo dance with a hat-stand as a partner and his mind-boggling routine in which he dances not just on the floor but on the walls and ceiling as well. Also contains a dynamic Astaire-Powell duet with one of the longest song titles in history: 'How Could You Believe Me When I Said I Loved You When You Know I've Been a Liar All My Life?'

Ruby ● ⓥ
1992, US, 110 mins, colour
Dir: John Mackenzie

Stars: Danny Aiello, Sherilyn Fenn, Arliss Howard, David Duchovny, Marc Lawrence
Rating: ★★★

Jack Ruby, of course, was the small-time Dallas nightclub owner who earned his place in history by shooting Kennedy's alleged assassin Lee Harvey Oswald. Vaguely clinging to connections with both the Mafia and the CIA, Ruby (Danny Aiello) is close to closure when he runs into Candy Cane (Sherilyn Fenn) who becomes his premier stripper and goes with him to Cuba when he travels to help free a Mafia boss. Told to hit the man instead, Ruby turns on the assassin. It seems loyal, but is probably a big mistake, as he becomes embroiled at the edges of a Mafia/CIA conspiracy which he thinks is to assassinate Castro, but realises too late is to assassinate Kennedy instead. It's the relationship between Ruby and Candy, though, solidly done by Aiello and Fenn who come alive as people, that saves the enterprise from going stale before it starts. Though the story sags in the middle, its fascinating to see its bits and pieces falling together.

Ruby Cairo ● Ⓥ
1992, US, US mins, colour
Dir: Graeme Clifford
Stars: Andie MacDowell, Liam Neeson, Viggo Mortensen
Rating: ★★

A pretty intriguing plot (at least to begin with) is set adrift here by wishy-washy treatment that turns it into something of an extended travelogue. Andie MacDowell is the mother-of-three seemingly left with nothing but a crateful of bills when her chauvinistic husband, struggling to keep his airplane salvage business afloat, is killed in a Mexican air crash. However, in this kind of film, as soon as the local authorities tell her that he was 'burned from head to toe', you can smell a live rat. When Andie finds a pack of baseball cards and cracks the codes on the backs of them (only one of the film's unlikely premises), the trail leads her to a cache of secret bank accounts across the world. MacDowell is appealing and keeps her credibility intact; but a lighter, more skilful directorial hand was needed to lend impact to this flight of fancy.

Ruby Gentry ○ Ⓥ
1952, US, 82 mins, b/w
Dir: King Vidor
Stars: Jennifer Jones, Chariton Heston,

Karl Malden
Rating: ★★

Down in the Carolina swamplands, where they have names like Boake, Jud, Jewel (a man) and Cullen, springs yet another overheated Hollywood melodrama about a doomed damsel from the wrong side of the swamp. Jennifer Jones tosses her hair tempestuously, making the sultry most of a thoroughly artificial role, even if it sometimes looks like a re-run from her earlier *Duel in the Sun*.

Rude Awakening ◐ Ⓥ
1989, US, 101 mins, colour
Dir: Aaron Russo, David Greenwalt
Stars: Eric Roberts, Cheech Marin, Robert Carradine, Julie Hagerty
Rating: ★

Supposing two hippies had lived wild in the jungles of Central America for 20 years, growing and smoking marijuana and eating fish, only to suddenly re-emerge into the world when they stumble across a CIA plot to start a war in their new-found paradise. The possibilities for fun are practically endless; alas, directors Russo and Greenwalt have missed almost all of them in this tiresome film whose budget seems barely to extend beyond the sparsely furnished interiors of people's flats. Its people, too, are no fun to be with: stolid Roberts, whining Hagerty, bland Carradine and irksome Marin, once of the equally resistible Cheech and Chong.

Rudyard Kipling's The Jungle Book ○ Ⓥ
1994, US, 108 mins, colour
Dir: Stephen Sommers
Stars: Jason Scott Lee, Lena Headey, Sam Neill, Cary Elwes, John Cleese
Rating: ★★★

If you can get through a really boring first half-hour, this is a pretty enjoyable live-action version of the Kipling yarn, concentrating on Mowgli's adventures as a young man and the quest for the fabulous lost treasure beneath the Ape City. Jason Scott Lee gives an intelligent performance as the boy raised by wolves, really contriving to look facially like an animal in many of his scenes. And Cary Elwes (as the villain), John Cleese and Sam Neill all give their roles a light treatment which adds amusement and personality to the thrills. Amazing stuff with panthers, tigers, monkeys, bears and elephants must have taken much ingenuity and patience to shoot and remains true to the spirit, if perhaps

not the letter of R Kipling's classic. Cleese even gets to mention 'the bare necessities', presumably a reference to the Disney cartoon version, of which this can't quite eclipse the memory – although it does get better as it goes on.

Ruggles of Red Gap ○
1935, US, 92 mins, b/w
Dir: Leo McCarey
Stars: Charles Laughton, Mary Boland
Rating: ★★★

Heartwarming comedy about an English butler taken to Red Gap in America where he becomes a celebrity. Charles Laughton, in very spritely form, never puts a foot wrong as the manservant who becomes his own master, and shares the film's best sequence with Charlie Ruggles and James Burke when the three go out on a boozy binge together.

Rumble Fish ● Ⓥ
1983, US, 100 mins, b/w
Dir: Francis Ford Coppola
Stars: Matt Dillon, Mickey Rourke, Diane Lane, Dennis Hopper
Rating: ★★

This bizarre and visually arresting film was shot back-to-back with director Francis Ford Coppola's other S E Hinton novel adaptation about teen alienation, *The Outsiders*, with much the same cast and crew. It's a case of a youth (Matt Dillon) living under the shadow of his older, idolised brother (Mickey Rourke). But don't go looking for Freudian messages in the screenplay which answers few questions. *Rumble Fish* is an exercise in style over content. Moody black-and-white photography (with Technicolor sequences) is matched with a pounding, impressionistic score by Stewart Copeland of The Police. But for all that it looks good, it leaves the viewer cold and uninvolved.

Rumble in the Bronx ● Ⓥ
1995, US/Hong Kong, 90 mins, colour
Dir: Stanley Tong
Stars: Jackie Chan, Anita Mui, Bill Tung
Rating: ★★★

That most self-deprecating of bone-crunching action stars, Jackie Chan, is making increasing bids for mainstream recognition while retaining the balletic and sometimes comic action qualities that made him a star in his native Hong Kong. Crude but effective gags spice the action in this thunderously paced, incredibly energetic slugfest in which Chan first protects a supermarket from a band of thugs, them takes on a rather more evil enemy with the almost inevitable array of muscle-bound henchmen. As usual with Chan films, there are what-went-wrong outtakes at the end.

Runaway ◐

1984, US, 100 mins, colour
Dir: Michael Crichton
Stars: Tom Selleck, Cynthia Rhodes, Gene Simmons
Rating: ★★★

Specialist policeman Tom Selleck is the man they call when there's a rogue robot on the loose in this well-made and exciting sci-fi thriller. A criminal genius is reprogramming robots to use for his own illegal ends and it's Selleck and his new partner Cynthia Rhodes' job to catch him. Despite the sci-fi theme, the film keeps its feet firmly on the ground, making it completely believable. This is thanks both to the underrated Selleck, who gives a thoughtful and intelligent performance, and director Michael Crichton, who wrote *Westworld* and *Coma*. This is perhaps less thought-provoking than those, but it's a well-rounded story with an exciting, vertigo-inducing climax.

Runaway Bus, The ○

1954, UK, 80 mins, b/w
Dir: Val Guest ·
Stars: Frankie Howerd, Petula Clark, Belinda Lee
Rating: ★★

Frankie Howerd's thunder is rather stolen by his female co-stars in this, his first starring vehicle (if you'll pardon the pun). He plays a coach driver lost in the fog, with a fortune in stolen bullion in the boot. Dame Margaret Rutherford steals the film as surely as she stole Norman Wisdom's first starring comedy film, *Trouble in Store*. Belinda Lee runs her a very close second as a dumb-belle who reads thrillers ad infinitum and is genuinely funny in the process.

Runaway Train ● Ⓥ

1985, US, 111 mins, colour
Dir: Andrei Konchalovksy
Stars: Jon Voight, Eric Roberts, Rebecca DeMornay, John P Ryan
Rating: ★★★

Visually, this is a dynamite action film, with a driverless train thundering across the snow-covered Alaskan wastes. The engineer has died from a heart attack and the only people on board, unbeknown to the authorities, are two long-term escaped convicts (Jon Voight, Oscar-nominated) and an unlikely female railway worker played by Rebecca DeMornay. The action is hammer-hard and never less than gripping, while all the train scenes are brilliantly handled by director Andrei Konchalovsky, and his actors and stuntmen. The dialogue, unsurprisingly, isn't in the same class; it never quite rings true, and occasionally ascends to the highly fanciful considering the semi-literate nature of the characters. In the end the film matches Voight's description of Roberts: 'more guts than brains.' But those guts make it worth watching.

Run for Cover ○

1954, US, 92 mins, colour
Dir: Nicholas Ray
Stars: James Cagney, Viveca Lindfors, John Derek
Rating: ★★★

Good, solid Western with ultra-sharp Technicolor photography by Daniel Fapp. John Derek is excellent as the embittered young man who provides the axis for the action, and James Cagney, although clearly ageing, is his usual tough self as the youth's ex-jailbird friend, now a sheriff. Fight scenes are effectively done and, if the denouement seems rather improbable, there's compensation in the vigorous playing of the bad guys, notably Grant Withers and Ernest Borgnine.

Run for the Sun ○

1956, US, 95 mins, colour
Dir: Roy Boulting
Stars: Richard Widmark, Jane Greer, Trevor Howard
Rating: ★★★★

This re-working of *The Hounds of Zaroff* makes exciting popular entertainment. Richard Widmark and jane Greer (both on good form) are the intrepid hero and game heroine being pursued through various arduous trials by nasty villains who, in this kind of action thriller, are reassuringly bound to come to a sticky end. It's a go-ey, gory adventure, directed at a rare pace by Britain's Roy Boulting, and with a brilliant performance by Peter van Eyck as chief villain Trevor Howard's co-hort. There are more than enough thrills along the way and the ending is quite startling. The odds are you'll enjoy every moment of this adventurous hokum.

Run for Your Money, A ○

1949, UK, 83 mins, b/w
Dir: Charles Frend
Stars: Alec Guinness, Moira Lister, Donald Houston, Joyce Grenfell, Hugh Griffith
Rating: ★★★★

Another fast and funny comedy from the Ealing Studios stable. Released in their peak year, 1949, it's about two Welsh miners who win a trip to London to see the Wales v England rugby match. Alec Guinness uses a rapier-like wit to keep the laughs coming, leaving Donald Houston and Meredith Edwards as the miners to raise the broad guffaws. The final chase through the streets of London rates as one of the most hilarious and best edited since Keystone days.

Running Brave ○

1983, US, 106 mins, colour
Dir: D S Everett
Stars: Robby Benson, Pat Hingle, Claudia Cron
Rating: ★★

The punning title (it's about an American Indian athlete) heralds a sort of *Wigwams of Fire* with Robby Benson as Billy Mills, the half-Sioux who unexpectedly qualified to run the 10,000 metres for the United States at the 1964 Japan Olympics. The reconstruction of Mills' road to Tokyo doesn't entirely escape soap-opera conventions – the script sees to that – but it scores points for being true. Benson – becoming another blue-eyed Hollywood Indian – does the running stuff well, and his fellow-Indians are mostly made out to be the pitiable figures they were. Denis Lacroix is excellent here as one of Billy's most tragic comrades.

Running Man, The ○

1963, UK, 100 mins, colour
Dir: Carol Reed
Stars: Laurence Harvey, Lee Remick, Alan Bates
Rating: ★★★

The late Carol Reed's underrated film about a couple (Laurence Harvey and Lee Remick) who try to bring off a giant insurance fraud, and the mysterious man who appears to be dogging their footsteps. A good story well told, with a high proportion of suspenseful moments, thanks partly to John Mortimer's edgy script.

Running Man, The ● Ⓥ

1987, US, 101 mins, colour
Dir: Paul Michael Glaser

R

Stars: Arnold Schwarzenegger, Maria Conchita Alonso, Yaphet Kotto, Jim Brown, Richard Dawson
Rating: ★★★

Another extended comic-strip adventure with Big Arnie, perhaps the most literal translation of comic image from page to screen since the 1966 *Batman*. You can see the pictures come alive and visualise Schwarzenegger's shameless sub-Bond puns in 'balloons', as each villain is dispatched in turn. Earlier in this futuristic frolic there are signs of seriousness, in Schwarzenegger's escape from prison, following his arrest on trumped-up charges after failing, in his time as a helicopter cop, to massacre unarmed civilians when ordered to do so. The overall view of an American police-state city of 2019 is quite imaginative but, once the game show of the title starts – criminals run for their lives on video before a live audience – we're on familiar Schwarzenegger ground, with our hero (and a few friends) taking on a series of massive opponents armed with flame throwers, spiked scythes, chain-saws and anything else the scriptwriter can lay hands on.

Running on Empty ◐
1988, US, 117 mins, colour
Dir: Sidney Lumet
Stars: Christine Lahti, River Phoenix, Judd Hirsch, Martha Plimpton
Rating: ★★

Whatever the qualities of his movie, at least director Lumet has a new idea here. A family of activists, forever on the run since bombing a napalm lab many years before (a man who shouldn't have been there was blinded and paralysed), meets its inevitable crisis of conscience when the elder of its two sons reaches 17 and feels other tugs of loyalty. These come for the boy (snub-nosed, slight River Phoenix, a most unlikely offspring of hook-nosed Hirsch and steeple-tall Lahti) in the form of a girlfriend (the Jodie Fosterish Martha Plimpton) and the chance of a scholarship to improve his already impressive talents on the piano. It's a film of effective moments which just about outweigh the patches of tedium. Lahti is excellent as the mother, especially when meeting her father for the first time in 14 years and telling him she's 'sorry for having caused you so much pain'.

Running Scared ◐ Ⓥ
1986, US, 106 mins, colour
Dir: Peter Hyams

Stars: Billy Crystal, Gregory Hines, Darlanne Fluegel, Steven Bauer, Joe Pantoliano, Jimmy Smits
Rating: ★★

A totally typical Hollywood buddy-buddy cop movie, but so well made by photographer-director Peter Hyams that, for all its routineness, it does keep you watching, albeit in a slightly detached way, right through to the end. Billy Crystal and Gregory Hines (no reason, I suppose why you shouldn't pick a comic and a dancer to play policemen) are the partners who joke their way through the pursuit of a king drug dealer (Jimmy Smits) who always seem to be slipping away from justice, if for no other reason than to allow further developments, chases and shoot-outs in the plot. You couldn't describe this as a bad movie, nor say you didn't get your money's worth in the way of action and excitement. But any episode of such classic US cop shows as *Hill Street Blues* or *NYPD Blue* would supply more humanity, wit and delicacy of touch in the acting.

Run of the Country, The ● Ⓥ
1995, UK, 110 mins, colour
Dir: Peter Yates
Stars: Albert Finney, Matt Keeslar, Victoria Smurfit, Anthony Brophy, David Kelly
Rating: ★

The countryside of Ireland proved a favourite location for films of the 1990s, but this really is a bog too far. With nothing new to offer, it speaks in platitudes from beginning to end. Its characters lack genuine humanity and, although Albert Finney gives his red-cheeked Irishman yet another try, his is a thankless role that would reward no-one who tried to play it. Once again he's a police sergeant in a small village but the action, such as it is, revolves round his son (America's Matt Keeslar) who justifiably can't stand the sight of him. Emma Thompson lookalike Victoria Smurfit is quite good as the well-to-do girl who improbably falls for the son's naive approach and gets pregnant in less time than it takes to down a pint of Guinness. There's a bit of cockfighting and peripheral references to Border Guards and the IRA, but the sum total is a monumental bore. Even the 'emerald' countryside looks unappetising in this one.

Run Wild, Run Free ○ Ⓥ
1969, UK, 98 mins, colour
Dir: Richard C Sarafian

Stars: John Mills, Sylvia Syms, Mark Lester, Gordon Jackson
Rating: ★★★

Children will enjoy this fairly charming tale of a mute boy and a white colt, picturesquely set on Dartmoor. The fog-bound climax is highly effective.

Rush ● Ⓥ
1991, US, 120 mins, colour
Dir: Lili Fini Zanuck
Stars: Jason Patric, Jennifer Jason Leigh, Sam Elliott, Max Perlich, Gregg Allman, William Sadler
Rating: ★

Whoever thought the idea of two narcotics cops becoming addicts themselves in pursuit of their prey was surefire reckoned without this treatment of the theme. Decked out with mournful music by Eric Clapton, the story is slow to the point of abstraction. Leading man Jason Patric mumbles unattractively even when not on drugs, while Jennifer Jason Leigh, in a rare below-par performance, sounds as though she has a stone in her mouth in her efforts to effect a Texas accent. Unbelievable, poorly written and filled with extraneous stretches of repetitive and meaningless dialogue to pad out some slow action scenes, the film is difficult to watch in more ways than one.

Russia House, The ● Ⓥ
1990, US, 117 mins, colour
Dir: Fred Schepisi
Stars: Sean Connery, Michelle Pfeiffer, Roy Scheider, James Fox, Klaus Maria Brandauer
Rating: ★★

Very slow to get going, but mercifully sparked by the performances of Connery and Pfeiffer, this is hopefully about the last we'll see of cold-war thrillers full of tired CIA, MI5 and KGB men trying to outwit each other, while others undergo the physical danger. Connery, as reliable as ever as the jazz-playing publisher caught up in the espionage game, and Pfeiffer, with a convincing-sounding Russian accent, create characters that evolve into the only believable or interesting people in the film. A strong cast otherwise does not acquit itself with distinction, director Schepisi spends far too long touring the sights of his locations, and Tom Stoppard's script (from John Le Carré's novel) is routine even by the standards of this genre. Trust Connery to find the few gems in it and polish them up bright enough to bring tears to our eyes.

Russian Roulette ○

1975, Canada, 93 mins, colour
Dir: Lou Lombardo
Stars: George Segal, Christina Raines
Rating: ★★★

The Falcon lives! At least in spirit. For those who remember that suave Forties' screen sleuth, this is just the kind of exciting espionage nonsense that Hollywood was turning out with such success in the period, but doesn't seem to make any more. The story, about a plot to kill Russian premier Kosygin, is pure moonshine. But director Lou Lombardo keeps it careering crazily along and throws in a nerve-grinding climax on the acutely-slanting roof of the Royal Canadian Mounted Police headquarters in Vancouver. George Segal and Christina Raines play it with gusto while the villains are just as badly acted as in Tom Conway's day.

Russians Are Coming, the Russians Are Coming, The ⊙

1966, US, 126 mins, colour
Dir: Norman Jewison
Stars: Carl Reiner, Eva Marie Saint, Alan Arkin, Brian Keith
Rating: ★★★★★

You'll find many extraordinarily funny moments in this gem of a comedy about a Russian submarine that runs aground off America. It's in the Russians' panic that the fun chiefly lies. Lots of face-twitching, grunting and the Russians' broken English helps build a mountain of laughter. Seldom has a comic jigsaw had so many perfectly fitting pieces. There's a magnificent little cameo involving a garrulous old woman captured by the Russians. Her husband, old, doddery and deaf, comes down and eats his breakfast, blissfully unaware that the old harridan is making frantic efforts to free herself from a position on top of the wardrobe just over his right shoulder. One feels it's probably the first morning's peace the old man's ever had in his life.

Rustler's Rhapsody ◐

1985, US, 88 mins, colour
Dir: Hugh Wilson
Stars: Tom Berenger, Marilu Henner, G W Bailey
Rating: ★★

Good guys in white hats and bad guys in black hats are what this comedy Western is all about. *Rustler's Rhapsody* is an affectionate parody of those adorably dreadful Saturday morning Western serials. Unfortunately, the parody is too well done and the film itself outstays its welcome and becomes the victim of its own joke. Tom Berenger, in a rare comic role, is our firm-jawed hero, while Marilu Henner is a feisty heroine. The advantage of the original serials is that although they were embarrassingly bad, they at least only lasted 20 minutes an episode.

Ruthless ○

1948, US, 104 mins, b/w
Dir: Edgar G Ulmer
Stars: Zachary Scott, Louis Hayward, Diana Lynn, Sydney Greenstreet
Rating: ★★★

A stylish *film noir* that hardly deserved its famous one-line dismissal by British film critic C A Lejeune, who wrote, 'I'd find *Ruthless* far more winning if it could end at the beginning.' Time has brought a well-merited re-assessment, with Zachary Scott playing the archetype of all his roles as sharks in wolf's clothing: you'll love to hate him as he steps on everyone as if they were bothersome bugs on the rungs of his ladder to the top. Sydney Greenstreet is excellent as a Southern tycoon, and the girls – Diana Lynn (in a dual role), Martha Vickers and Lucille Bremer – are no mere ciphers. Directed by cult favourite Edgar G Ulmer, who had slightly more than his usual shoestring budget to work on, but had to put up with a contrived 'tidy' ending imposed by the studio. At least he made this look unconvincing.

Ruthless People ● ⓥ

1986, US, 93 mins, colour
Dir: Jim Abrahams, David Zucker, Jerry Zucker
Stars: Danny DeVito, Bette Midler, Judge Reinhold, Helen Slater
Rating: ★★

A broad blue-collar farce about a kidnapped wife who is so gross her husband is only too pleased not to pay the ransom, especially as he was planning to bump her off anyway. The film gets funnier as it goes on, due mostly to the increasing role played by Bette Midler as the wife. For her, it's a triumph.

Ryan's Daughter ◐ ⓥ

1970, UK, 206 mins, colour
Dir: David Lean
Stars: Sarah Mites, Robert Mitchum, Trevor Howard
Rating: ★★★

David Lean's epic story of a self-willed Irish girl at the time of World War One, her unsuccessful marriage to a quiet teacher, and the consequences of her passionate affair with a shell-shocked English army officer. The film won two Academy Awards, one for its photography and one for John Mills who moved totally out of character as the misshapen village idiot. It also has outstanding performances by Robert Mitchum and Trevor Howard as teacher and priest, respectively, but its love scenes are so picturesque they look more like TV commercials.

R

S

Saadia ○
1953, US, 85 mins, colour
Dir: Albert Lewin
Stars: Cornel Wilde, Rita Gam
Rating: ★★★

Underrated in its time, this is an extremely exciting story set in Morocco, about a girl, smoulderingly played by Rita Gam, who believes she brings bad luck to those who know her. Good stuff for children, who won't notice the vague literary pretensions of maverick director Albert Lewin. Gam and Mel Ferrer share acting honours: Cornel Wilde seems less happy as the French-educated nobleman who battles the local witch doctor and native superstition. Burningly photographed in ultra-rich Technicolor by Christopher Challis.

Sabotage ○ ⓥ
(aka: The Woman Alone)
1937, UK, 76 mins, b/w
Dir: Alfred Hitchcock
Stars: Sylvia Sidney, Oscar Homolka
Rating: ★★★★

In view of the bomb attacks that these days punctuate life in major cities around the world, this Hitchcock thriller about an anarchist plotting to blow up Piccadilly Circus has acquired fresh topicality. It's based on Joseph Conrad's novel *The Secret Agent* and has splendidly seedy locales, a brooding, doom-laden atmosphere and the usual crop of memorable sequences, including the meeting of spies in an aquarium.

Saboteur ○ ⓥ
1942, US, 108 mins, b/w
Dir: Alfred Hitchcock
Stars: Robert Cummings, Priscilla Lane, Otto Kruger
Rating: ★★★★

Hitchcock's story of wartime sabotage, beginning and ending memorably, with the factory fire and the scenes in and on the Statue of Liberty. The trek in between, as hero Robert Cummings flees from the web of circumstantial evidence threatening to entrap him, is sometimes a bit wearing, but Priscilla Lane, as always, is a personable heroine, and Hitchcock 'touches' constantly boost the suspense.

Saboteur – Code Name Morituri, The ○
(aka: Morituri)
1965, US, 122 mins, b/w
Dir: Bernhard Wicki
Stars: Marlon Brando, Yul Brynner, Janet Margolin, Trevor Howard
Rating: ★★★

A tense spy thriller, set at sea during World War Two. Marlon Brando is a saboteur sent to steer a vital cargo of rubber into Allied hands, while at the same time preventing the captain (Yul Brynner) from scuttling the ship. For Brynner, it was the best role he'd had in years. With plenty to get his teeth into – he plays an anti-Nazi German who takes to drink when he hears of his once-gentle son sinking a hospital ship – and no worries about his dialogue, he's a more relaxed and therefore more effective actor. Bernhard Wicki directs always to a purpose, and keeps the high tension smouldering in a film that we fancy will have stood the test of time better than most – despite the cumbersome title.

Sabre and the Arrow, The
See: Last of the Comanches

Sabrina ○
1995, US, 130 mins, colour
Dir: Sydney Pollack
Stars: Harrison Ford, Julia Ormond, Greg Kinnear, Richard Crenna, John Wood, Nancy Marchand, Angie Dickinson, Lauren Holly
Rating: ★★★

A silky-smooth Nineties version of the old Audrey Hepburn/Humphrey Bogart romantic comedy, pleasingly and intelligently written to give us lots of smiles, rich supporting characters and even a sniffle at the end. Julia Ormond gives her best screen performance to date as the ugly duckling who blossoms into a swan after a two-year stay in Paris. A chauffeur's daughter who covets David (Greg Kinnear), the playboy son of her employer's millionaire family, Sabrina throws a spanner in the works of a profitable merger when David is attracted to the new 'her' and away from his fiancée (Lauren Holly), daughter of one of his mother's potential business partners. Enter older brother Linus (Harrison Ford) who proposes to entice Sabrina away from David, take her back to Paris and dump her. Ah, but of course. You've guessed the rest, even if you haven't seen the original, so it's not the destination but the getting there

that's the pleasure. And Ford as Linus doesn't put a foot wrong.

Sabrina Fair ○
(aka: Sabrina)
1954, US, 113 mins, b/w
Dir: Billy Wilder
Stars: Humphrey Bogart, Audrey Hepburn, William Holden
Rating: ★★★★

A slick, witty and immensely charming Billy Wilder comedy, set among the Long Island homes of some of America's wealthiest families. Audrey Hepburn, in a Cinderella-type role, is at her most impish and even William Holden seems more relaxed and dashing than usual. But the hit of the show is undoubtedly Humphrey Bogart as Holden's grumpy older brother who tries to arrange a marriage for him. The kind of film where you know what's coming but, because of the treatment, enjoy it all the same. Remade in 1995.

Saddle the Wind ○
1958, US, 84 mins, colour
Dir: Robert Parrish
Stars: Robert Taylor, John Cassavetes, Julie London, Donald Crisp
Rating: ★★★

This thoughtfully written Western, the best film of Robert Taylor's later work, hardly received its fair due when it first appeared, both the star and genre being past their peak of populadty. As well as making plenty of sense, Rod Serling's screenplay provides an abundance of action and colour, setting itself against the magnificent backdrop of the Colorado Rockies. John Cassavetes catches the eye as gunfighter Taylor's reckless young brother, a mannered but imaginative performance. And the ending is dynamically and poignantly unexpected.

Saddle Tramp ○
1950, US, 77 mins, colour
Dir: Hugo Fregonese
Stars: Joel McCrea, Wanda Hendrix, John Russell
Rating: ★★

Veteran film cowboy Joel McCrea offers one of his most likeable characterisations as the hobo on horseback in this well-made Western about a drifter reluctantly involved with a large family of children and their problems. Character-full supporting cast includes John Russell, John McIntire, Jeanette Nolan, Ed Begley and former silent screen idol Antonio Moreno.

Safari O
1956, UK, 91 mins, colour
Dir: Terence Young
Stars: Victor Mature, Janet Leigh, Roland Culver
Rating: ★★

One of several lively, all-action colour adventure films produced by Britain's Warwick Films – usually with Victor Mature or Robert Taylor as star – in the late Fifties. It's rich, robust, hell-for-leather stuff, with the animals out-acting the cast.

Safety Last ⊙
1923, US, 70 mins, b/w
Dir: Fred Newmeyer
Stars: Harold Lloyd, Mildred Davis
Rating: ★★★★★

The Harold Lloyd comedy that everyone seems to remember, with Harold hanging on to the hands of a clock in an attempt to carry out a daredevil stunt. Lloyd did nearly all the dangerous climbing scenes himself, no mean feat considering that, earlier in the picture, he had lost the thumb and half a finger from his right hand, after a 'fake' bomb he had been holding exploded. He was forced to go through the rest of his films wearing a special glove. Lloyd did work above a platform – though it was three storeys below – and made good use of camera angles and careful editing. Even so the climbing sequence, which occupies half an hour of the film, still remains the greatest – and funniest – of its kind ever put on film. But the whole film is beautifully made and fun of cleverly funny moments. Said one contemporary critic: 'Even Lloyd's worst enemy will have to laugh.'

Sahara O
1943, US, 97 mins, b/w
Dir: Zoltan Korda
Stars: Humphrey Bogart, Dan Duryea, Bruce Bennett
Rating: ★★★

This exciting war yarn was originally seen as a Russian film, *The Thirteen*. Britain also made a variation on the story, called *Nine Men*. But this version – thanks largely to a dominating performance by Humphrey Bogart at his taciturn best – became the most famous. Directed by Zoltan Korda, it transfers the action of the story, with great effect, to the Western desert, and throws in some of Hollywood's most penetrating performers, including Dan Duryea, Lloyd Bridges, Rex Ingram and J Carrol Naish.

Sahara O
1984, US, 104 mins, colour
Dir: Andrew V McLaglen
Stars: Brooke Shields, Lambert Wilson, Horst Buchholz, John Mills
Rating: ★

A sort of modern-day version of *The Perils of Pauline*, with Brooke Shields as the girl posing as a man, competing in a no-holds barred cross-country car race in the Sahara Desert and getting herself kidnapped by a desert sheik. John Mills turns up in the cast, but not even action-man director Andrew V McLaglen can rescue this one from the quicksands.

Sahara O ⓥ
1995, Aus/US, 105 mins, colour
Dir: Brian Trenchard-Smith
Stars: James Belushi, Mark Lee, Jerome Ehlers, Ian David Lee, William Upjohn
Rating: ★★

Boring at the beginning, but exciting at the end, this exceptionally dusty-looking remake of the Bogart classic has too many silly moments to qualify as quality entertainment. A group of Allied stragglers from all nations rides a tank across the Sahara during World War Two in search of water. They find it among desert ruins, only to realise that 500 German soldiers converging on them need it even more. Contrived heroic deaths and tedious duologues – normally giving one of our heroes a speech just before he's killed – drag this one down, although the excitement comes fast and fierce in the last reel.

Saigon ● ⓥ
(aka: Off Limits)
1987, US, 102 mins, colour
Dir: Christopher Crowe
Stars: Willem Dafoe, Gregory Hines, Fred Ward, Scott Glenn, Amanda Pays
Rating: ★

Remember the crime thriller where the suspects keep getting bumped off as they're about to talk? Someone had the bright idea of transferring the locale to 1968 Vietnam in the middle of *that* war. Prostitutes are being murdered by someone who is evidently a high-ranking officer and US Army CI (criminal investigation) men Willem Dafoe and Gregory Hines are given the case which gradually becomes an obsession. The resolution of the plot doesn't make any sense, but the screenplay is the real killer to this film's chances and even Dafoe and Hines' efforts to weld a buddy-buddy relationship are destroyed by lines de-

void of literacy, humour or even sense. The sanest person here is probably Scott Glenn, who jumps out of a plane without a parachute. Perhaps he, at least, read the script.

Sailor Beware! O
(aka: Panic in the Parlor)
1956, UK, 80 mins, b/w
Dir: Gordon Parry
Stars: Peggy Mount, Cyril Smith, Shirley Eaton, Ronald Lewis
Rating: ★★

In this screen version of the wildly successful stage farce, Peggy Mount shot to stardom by repeating her characterisation of Emma Hornett, the world's most formidable mother-in-law. Most of her co-players seem not surprisingly over-awed, but look out for some amusing cameos from Thora Hird, Geoffrey Keen (as a vicar), Gordon Jackson and Henry McGee (as a milk-man).

Sailor Beware ⊙
1952, US, 108 mins, b/w
Dir: Hal Walker
Stars: Jerry Lewis, Dean Martin
Rating: ★

Dean Martin and Jerry Lewis's enlistment in the Navy proves even less funny than their army manoeuvres. The plot is a predictable series of skits, with a running gag of Jerry Lewis taking up a bet to kiss real-life actress Corinne Calvet. A boxing sequence provides the only real laughs.

Sailor of the King O
(aka: Single-Handed)
1953, UK, 84 mins, b/w
Dir: Roy Boulting
Stars: Jeffrey Hunter, Michael Rennie, Wendy Hiller
Rating: ★★★

A remake of the famous C S Forester story, *Brown on Resolution*, the 1935 version of which (first shown under that title but reissued as *For Ever England*) gave John Mills his first big critical film success. Here, it's Jeffrey Hunter as the young seaman whose bravery and resourcefulness keep a German battleship pinned down. Stirring, sturdy stuff.

Sailors Three O
(aka: Three Cockeyed Sailors)
1940, US, 86 mins, b/w
Dir: Walter Forde
Stars: Tommy Trinder, Claude Hulbert, Michael Wilding
Rating: ★★

S

Tommy 'You lucky people' Trinder is the fulcrum of this Ealing wartime propaganda comedy about three drunken sailors who stumble on to a German ship and capture it. Slow to get under way, but pretty funny in the end. Star-spotters might like to decide whether or not there's a fleeting glimpse of a young Anton Diffring in this one.

Saint in New York, The ○
1938, US, 71 mins, b/w
Dir: Ben Holmes
Stars: Louis Hayward, Kay Sutton, Jack Carson
Rating: ★★★

A real treat for lovers of Thirties' detective fiction: the original *Saint* film, based on the character created by Leslie Charteris, in turn immortalised by Roger Moore on television. Louis Hayward handed the role over to George Sanders in the late Thirties, but played the Saint again 15 years later. He brought a certain mocking humour to the role that none of his successors could match.

Saint Jack ❶
1979, US, 112 mins, colour
Dir: Peter Bogdanovich
Stars: Ben Gazzara, Denholm Elliott, James Villiers
Rating: ★★

Director Peter Bogdanovich finds himself deep in Graham Greene country in this study of disillusionment and moral disintegration, qualities which the stars, Ben Gazzara and Denholm Elliott, have proved themselves expert in projecting over the years. Robby Muller, a West German cinematographer who has worked on several of the films of Wim Wenders, really brings the teeming streets of Singapore to colourful life.

Saint's Girl Friday, The ○
(aka: The Saint's Return)
1953, UK, 73 mins, b/w
Dir: Seymour Friedman
Stars: Louis Hayward, Naomi Chance, Sydney Tafler
Rating: ★★

Louis Hayward, the screen's best Simon Templar, returned to the role in this fair British thriller. Charles Victor is perfectly cast as the long-suffering Inspector Claude Eustace Teal and steals even Hayward's thunder. Thomas Gallagher is an acceptable Hoppy Uniatz and Diana Dors makes a brief appearance. The film's low budget cramps its style, but the plot

and Hayward's charm just about see it through.

Saint, The ❶ ⓥ
1997, US, 116 mins, colour
Dir: Phillip Noyce
Stars: Val Kilmer, Elisabeth Shue, Alun Armstrong
Rating: ★

Original 'Saint' author Leslie Charteris would be spinning in his grave at this film version of his dashing adventurer in crime. Charteris' books were always page-turners: this is okay when it gets going but that isn't often, and most of the time it's a yawn. Star Val Kilmer has about as much saintly charisma as a bucket of wet cement, while the plot, despite its portentous (and pretentious) scene-setting, is as featherweight as the most light-hearted of the Saint's written adventures. Anyone who's read the books knows that the Saint's nickname comes from his initials – S.T. for Simon Templar. But no. The film has to invent some poppycock about a repressive orphanage where all the children have names of saints. That's just the first mistake in a screenplay that rarely strikes the right mood – but does supply some standard excitements with scarred Russian agents.

Salaam Bombay! ● ⓥ
1988, UK/India, 113 mins, colour
Dir: Mira Nair
Stars: Shafiq Syed, Aneeta Kanwar
Rating: ★★

A poignantly made and vividly drawn (if consistently depressing) tale of the life of an urchin on the streets of Bombay. Its continuity is not too hot, but the terrific, sun-soaked colour photography reflects both the climate and the burnt-out quality of the characters' lives. And the immediacy is such that we cannot help but be drawn into parts of the story. Overall, an impressive debut feature film from director Mira Nair, even if the portrait it paints of homelessness in India is such a very miserable one.

Salem's Lot ● ⓥ
1979, US, 112 mins, colour
Dir: Tobe Hooper
Stars: David Soul, James Mason, Bonnie Bedelia, Lance Kerwin
Rating: ★★★

Tobe Hooper's scary version of the Stephen King bestseller retains its visceral power – and even has a few extra frames of added gore for good measure in the video version. David Soul

is not ideally cast as a writer but James Mason displays creepy authority as a sinister antiques dealer who is actually the ruthless watchdog for one of the most frightening vampires on film – Reggie Nalder's haunting appearance terrifyingly recalls the original *Nosferatu.*

Salome ○
1953, US, 104 mins, colour
Dir: William Dieterle
Stars: Rita Hayworth, Stewart Granger, Charles Laughton
Rating: ★★

Spectacular, certainly, if far from faithful, the Bible according to Columbia Pictures finds Rita Hayworth sinuously shedding her Seven Veils while Alan Badel (giving the film's best performance as John the Baptist) loses his head. Director William Dieterle stages some vivid large-scale scenes, Charles Laughton makes a memorable meal of a licentious King Herod, well supported by Judith Anderson as his Queen.

Salome's Last Dance ● ⓥ
1988, UK, 88 mins, colour
Dir: Ken Russell
Stars: Glenda Jackson, Stratford Johns, Nickolas Grace, Imogen Millais-Scott
Rating: ★

Decadence there certainly is, in this version of Oscar Wilde's banned *Salome.* But director Ken Russell has stretched Wilde's playlet interminably to 88 minutes when it should charitably run no more than 45, a slot admittedly destined for late-night TV. Glenda Jackson and Stratford Johns play up, play the game and keep their clothes on. Elsewhere, beautiful boys and bounteous boobs abound in the traditional Russell manner, as Wilde lounges around a brothel watching a production of his work. Once again, Russell, the old reprobate, has produced something here to offend everyone. Unfortunately, this time, he has offended our powers of endurance as well.

Salsa ❶ ⓥ
1988, US, 97 mins, colour
Dir: Boaz Davidson
Stars: Robby Rosa, Magali Alvarado, Rodney Harvey, Miranda Garrison
Rating: RB

In decades gone by, when turkeys were turkeys, a really bad film could make you laugh until you couldn't stop. Most bad films today are merely boring. But not *Salsa,* a kind of Puerto Rican *Saturday Night Fever.* The music is hot, the dancing's dynamic and the rest of the film is wonderfully, gloriously awful. The dialogue, ludicrous throughout, tries to run through the standard musical clichés but can't even string those together. Unintentionally funny lines drop, rat-a-tat-tat, like dud grenades, from the mouths of the youthful and unskilled players. 'Rico has a lot of problems,' observes one character, omitting to point out that one of them is that Bobby Rosa, as Rico, can only pose and not act. Even so, he's a Brando compared to Rodney Harvey as his pal, whose declaration of blood brotherhood towards the end almost had the audience on the floor.

Saludos Amigos ⊙
1943, US, 42 mins, colour
Dir: Jack Kinney, Hamilton Luske, Wilfred Jackson
Rating: ★★★

Don't let the children miss this little seen short animated feature from Walt Disney which shook away the wartime blues on a cartoon-strewn tour of South America. Something of a dry run for *The Three Caballeros*, live-action footage leads into four main cartoon sequences, mingling such established favourites as Donald Duck and Goofy with such popular newcomers as the cigar-puffing, samba-dancing parrot José 'Joe' Carioca and, in one of the best novelty cartoons Disney ever made, Pedro the little mail plane. Pedro's adventures feature some vivid and inspired animation, as he makes his first solo flight across the Andes, braving freak air currents and thunderstorms to get the mail through.

Salute of the Jugger ● Ⓥ
1990, Australia, 92 mins, colour
Dir: David Peoples
Stars: Rutger Hauer, Joan Chen, Vincent Phillip D'Onofrio, Anna Katarina
Rating: ★★

Or: *Mad Max Meets Rollerball*. It's year two-thousand-and-something in the South Australian outback where teams of wandering 'juggers' engage in a kind of gladiatorial version of American football played with a dog's skull that has to be stuck on a post. Broken bones and scar tissue are the orders of the day but, although it's all pretty idiotic, the Australians are good at this kind of movie, especially when it comes to the underground city at the end, where spectators are 'caged' and the combatants play in leagues. Hauer and his men are just another bunch of nomadic bonecrushers until they ac-

quire a new 'quick' in the form of oriental Joan Chen. The film is slow in between games, but then it has nowhere to go except the final bloodfeast. Chen gives her all in the arena, with some great individual somersaults: she really does impress as a likely league player.

Salute to the Marines ○
1943, US, 101 mins, colour
Dir: S Sylvan Simon
Stars: Wallace Beery, Fay Bainter, Reginald Owen
Rating: ★★★

MGM crossed a typical rumbustious Wallace Beery vehicle with a flag-waving war film and came up with this rip-snorting rough diamond of a film about a retired sergeant major who organises a peace settlement force on a Pacific island, then finds himself heading his rag-tag army to delay the Japanese advance. Keye Luke, familiar as Charlie Chan's number one son, has a rather different role here as a character called Flashy.

Salvador ● Ⓥ
1986, US, 123 mins, colour
Dir: Oliver Stone
Stars: James Woods, James Belushi, John Savage, Michael Murphy, Elpedia Carrillo
Rating: ★★

A rather determinedly grim exposé of the atrocities of the El Salvador civil war of the early Sixties, and the part played by America in the reinstatement of an allegedly oppressive regime. The body count piles up, mass open graves are graphically portrayed and the blood flows through mouth and limb. But the film never really grips us in a narrative, despite the (perhaps over) committed performances of James Woods, John Savage and Michael Murphy, leaving James Belushi to linger longest in the mind as a hard-cursing American abroad floating bewildered on a sea of booze and blood. Unpleasant, depressing and angry, the film finally falls victim to its own viscera-thumping rhetoric in failing to convert us to a probably worthy cause.

Salvation! ● Ⓥ
1987, US, 80 mins, colour
Dir: Beth B
Stars: Stephen McHattie, Dominique Davalos, Rockets Redglare, Viggo Mortensen, Exene Cervenka
Rating: RB

These pointless pyrotechnics from underworld darling director Beth B

seemed unlikely to inject her into the mainstream of film-making, and so it proved. Her splashy style unnecessarily maroons Stephen McHattie's quite compelling central performance as the TV Bible-thumper invaded by a demonic group of people which, with the help of the sister (Dominique Davalos) of one, he eventually rejects. Underneath all the glitz and flashy editing, something very trite is being said here. What happened to plots?

Sam Marlow Private Eye
See: The Man With Bogart's Face

Sammy and Rosie Get Laid ●
1987, UK, 100 mins, colour
Dir: Stephen Frears
Stars: Shashi Kapoor, Frances Barber, Claire Bloom, Ayub Khan Din, Roland Gift
Rating: ★

Not a sex film (though there's plenty of that) but a fiercely political diatribe about the evils of racial hatred at large in Britain today, to which writer Hanif Kureishi offers no solutions. What he presents us with (within the framework of an Indian returning, horrified, to the London he once knew) is the Brixton riots, police brutality, oppression of squatters and street and tube muggings laid end to end, as if this were everyday life in urban Britain. Authority and government are, without exception, uncaring fiends. 'Buy yourself a house in a part of England that is not twinned with Beirut,' remarks Sammy's father (Shashi Kapoor), in one of the film's best black comedy lines. Whether haunted by the past, or squashing the latest Pinteresque harangue of his deserted love (Claire Bloom) with earthy realism, Kapoor is excellent throughout.

Sammy Going South ○
(aka: A Boy 10 Feet Tall)
1963, US, 118 mins, colour
Dir: Alexander Mackendrick
Stars: Edward G Robinson, Fergus McClelland
Rating: ★★★★

In that it's a Michael Balcon production directed by Alexander Mackendrick, this colourful, absorbing and engaging picture is an Ealing film in all but name. You'll be gripped throughout to the adventures of 10-year-old Sammy (Fergus McClelland) as he journeys down the length of Africa to find his only surviving relation. Edward G Robinson steals the

S

film as a rascally but friendly diamond smuggler.

Sammy the Way-out Seal ○
1962, US, 92 mins, colour
Dir: Norman Tokar
Stars: Jack Carson, Robert Culp, Patricia Barry
Rating: ★★★

Charming, amusing, light-hearted comedy, brightly photographed in Technicolor by Gordon Avil, and featuring the last screen appearance of Jack Carson, in heartily blustering form as the small-town entrepreneur who wants to turn a pet seal into the local attraction, much to the chagrin of his two small owners. Sammy causing chaos in a supermarket with the help of a pack of dogs is a genuinely funny sequence and the fun never outstays its welcome. It should be pointed out that Sammy is actually played by a sea-lion!

Samson and Delilah ○ ⓥ
1949, US, 128 mins, colour
Dir: Cecil B DeMille
Stars: Victor Mature, Hedy Lamarr, George Sanders, Angela Lansbury
Rating: ★★

This Cecil B DeMille epic was described by one waspish critic as 'the most expensive haircut in history.' But the showman/director had the last laugh when the film grossed more than $12 million, becoming the then biggest money-making film in Paramount's 34 years. The temple pulled down by Samson at the end actually took five months to build and eight days to demolish. Victor Mature and Hedy Lamarr (a slightly mature Delilah!) provide the brawn and the beauty, but the acid acting of George Sanders and Angela Lansbury outshines the stars.

Sam Whiskey ◑
1969, US, 96 mins, colour
Dir: Arnold Laven
Stars: Burt Reynolds, Angie Dickinson, Clint Walker
Rating: ★★

This lightweight but amusing comedy Western has our hero Burt Reynolds breaking into a bank to put back a gold consignment stolen by someone else. Widow Angie Dickinson hires Burt to do the job as she doesn't want her husband's crime to be discovered, thereby soiling the family name. The lively plot has Burt, with help from Clint Walker and Ossie Davis, scheming to get into the bank while trying to avoid outlaw Rick Davis, who wants the bullion for himself. It's all good

fun, although lacklustre direction from Arnold Laven fails occasionally to keep the humour on the boil. Still, Burt is on good form and good fun to be with.

San Antonio ○ ⓥ
1945, US, 111 mins, colour
Dir: David Butler
Stars: Errol Flynn, Alexis Smith
Rating: ★★★

This was Errol Flynn trying to pick up where he left off in 1941, when a series of war films succeeded the superbly organised Westerns and swashbucklers that had made his name. The production is elaborate, and there's a splendid battle between Flynn and villain Paul Kelly at the finish. Nonetheless, the hand of director Michael Curtiz, who made almost all of Flynn's best action films before their wrangling grew too much for either man to take, is sorely missed; and Flynn's subsequent vehicles at Warners confirmed the beginning of his decline. Glowingly good Technicolor photography makes this always a handsome film.

San Demetrio, London ○
1943, UK, 105 mins, b/w
Dir: Charles Frend
Stars: Walter Fitzgerald, Robert Beatty
Rating: ★★★★★

Classic, unforgettable Ealing Studios war film guaranteed to bring a lump to your throat. A petrol tanker's crew are forced to abandon ship, drift for two days, then sight the still-burning, still-floating remains of their own ship. Totally inspiring, uplifting, exciting epic of the sea. A whole crew of then less than well-known film faces helps to prove that truth can indeed be stranger – and stronger – than fiction. Don't miss this rarity if it comes your way.

Sandlot Kids, The ○ ⓥ
(aka: The Sandlot)
1993, US, 101 mins, colour
Dir: David Mickey Evans
Stars: Mike Vitar, Tom Guiry, Dennis Leary, Karen Allen, James Earl Jones
Rating: ★

Rarely has 101 minutes seemed longer than in this Hollywood nostalgia piece about an idyllic summer in the life of nine baseball-mad kids who play on a vacant lot near their homes. Almost nothing of interest happens in the first 70 minutes of the film but, if you've paid good money to see this, stay tuned for a last two reels of Sylvester and Tweety Pie-style slapstick, as the

kids resort to various home-made mechanical contraptions in their efforts to retrieve a valuable baseball from a junkyard guarded by a legendary ferocious dog.

Sand Pebbles, The ○
1966, US, 193 mins, colour
Dir: Robert Wise
Stars: Steve McQueen, Richard Attenborough, Candice Bergen, Richard Crenna
Rating: ★★

A three-hour action epic, set in China 50 years ago, that Robert Wise made hard on the heels of the two musicals for which he won Academy Awards, *West Side Story* and *The Sound of Music*. Steve McQueen plays Jake, a seaman who is a newcomer to the crew of an old gunboat now doing duty on the Yangtze River; and Richard Attenborough is the only other member of the crew with whom Jake, essentially a 'loner', forms any real attachment. Also featured are Richard Crenna as the Captain, and Candice Bergen as an American girl who has arrived in China to teach at a mission. It has its moments.

Sands of Iwo Jima ○ ⓥ
1949, US, 109 mins, b/w
Dir: Allan Dwan
Stars: John Wayne, John Agar, Forrest Tucker, Adele Mara
Rating: ★★★★

'Before I'm through with you, you're gonna move like one man and think like one man,' growls Sergeant John Wayne to the new recruits in this flag-waving but strong and believable war film. When an old hand tells the newcomers that Wayne 'knows his business', the recruit retorts: 'So did Jack the Ripper.' Full of this kind of mildly tough humour, and very decent action scenes that convey well the confusion of war, the film brought Wayne his only Oscar nomination before his triumph in *True Grit* 20 years later.

Sands of the Desert ☉ ⓥ
1961, UK, 92 mins, colour
Dir: John Paddy Carstairs
Stars: Charlie Drake, Sarah Branch
Rating: ★★

That tiny bundle of energy, Charlie Drake, capers across the desert wastes in a quick-fire series of comic escapades. He plays a shy little clerk in a travel agency who finds himself involved in foreign intrigues once he's transferred to the desert. Valentino himself would have shed glycerine tears at Peter Arne's amusing portrait of a woman-chasing sheik.

Sands of the Kalahari ◐
1964, UK, 119 mins, colour
Dir: Cy Endfield
Stars: Stanley Baker, Stuart Whitman, Susannah York
Rating: ★★★

A really bloodthirsty picture on a survival-in-the-desert theme, with some brilliant desert cinematography by Erwin Hillier. The camerawork reaches an early highpoint with a view of the co-pilot's grave (the action starts with a plane crash) against the background of a giant arrow, fashioned from the fragments of the wrecked aircraft, and pointing the way the survivors have gone. Susannah York copes bravely with a character that is unexplainedly puzzling and takes a shower without getting her hair wet. Scenes of apparent animal cruelty are terrifyingly done.

San Francisco ○
1936, US, 110 mins, b/w
Dir: W S Van Dyke
Stars: Clark Gable, Jeanette MacDonald, Spencer Tracy
Rating: ★★★

Nostalgia sweetens one's memories of this, the film with the famous, extremely impressive and really magnificently edited reconstruction of the San Francisco earthquake of 1906. In fact, the earthquake is tacked on to a rather trite story about a selfish gambling-house proprietor, his infatuation with a poor but lovely singer, and his lifelong friendship with the local priest. In other words, an excuse for the stars to go through their familiar paces but pulled through in style by the sheer professionalism of Woody Van Dyke's direction, and the slickness and sincerity, respectively, of the performances by Clark Gable and Spencer Tracy.

San Quentin ○
1946, US, 66 mins, b/w
Dir: Gordon M Douglas
Stars: Lawrence Tierney, Barton MacLane, Marian Carr
Rating: ★★

Inmates in San Quentin prison organise an Inmates Welfare League to help order in the prison and prepare prisoners for life back on the outside. But when Nick (Barton MacLane) breaks out and goes on a crime spree, the scheme is in danger of being scrapped. The prisoners send a former founding member (Lawrence Tierney), already

out, to track Nick down. Although this all sounds a little far-fetched (which it is), there's enough action in this short sharp RKO drama to make you forget the fact. Some way down the cast list there's a prisoner who became a solid cornerstone of the law as Perry Mason and Ironside – Raymond Burr.

Santa and the Three Bears ⊙
1970, US, 60 mins, colour
Dir: Tony Benedict
Rating: ★★★

Enchanting little American feature, mainly animated, with a live-action framework, combining two folk legends in one. The principal part of the story concerns two baby bears who put off their hibernation so that they can stay awake and see Father Christmas. Their mother's plans to make sure they're not disappointed go somewhat awry. Highly original entertainment with children in mind.

Santa Claus ⊙ ⓥ
1985, US, 105 mins, colour
Dir: Jeannot Szwarc
Stars: Dudley Moore, John Lithgow, David Huddleston
Rating: ★★

After convincing the world that they could make a man fly in the *Superman* series, producers Alexander and Ilya Salkind poured $50 million into this (unintentional) Christmas turkey. David Huddleston comes across as a department store Santa, while Dudley Moore chases around manically as Santa's go-ahead elf helper Patch. Nothing quite lives up to the magical opening scenes, and it's not surprising that the film was less successful than expected at the box office. Called *Santa Claus: The Movie* (as opposed to what?) on all publicity, although those last words don't appear on screen.

Santa Clause, The ⊙ ⓥ
1994, US, 98 mins, colour
Dir: John Pasquin
Stars: Tim Allen, Judge Reinhold, Wendy Crewson, Eric Lloyd
Rating: ★★

Looks like those Disney folk have developed a conscience making all those violent adult movies in recent years, 'cos here's one in the old style. Divorcé Scott Calvin (Tim Allen) has his little son Charlie (Eric Lloyd) back for Christmas Eve and tries to bolster the kid's belief in Santa, which is rapidly being destroyed by his stepfather (Judge Reinhold) a man who majors in

gaudy sweaters. What Scott isn't prepared for is the real Santa making a pancake landing on his roof, being startled by Scott and falling to his death. By entering the sleigh, Scott unwittingly becomes the next Santa and, after a whirlwind tour of chimneytops, is whisked off to the North Pole. One might ask why the elves here are busy on colourful toys rather than Nintendo games, but no matter. As Allen spreads in girth and whiskers, the script occasionally shows flashes of wit above its station before succumbing to sticky sentiment in a far-from-snappy ending. This may be the only film where you ever see a credit to 'Elf Wrangler' at the end.

Santa Fe Trail ○
1940, US, 110 mins, b/w
Dir: Michael Curtiz
Stars: Errol Flynn, Olivia de Havilland, Raymond Massey, Van Heflin
Rating: ★★

Another blockbuster action film from the team of star Errol Flynn and director Michael Curtiz, who also made *Captain Blood*. This one is a minor *Gone With the Wind* with the obligatory cast of thousands, some splendidly-staged battle scenes, and Ronald Reagan as the young Custer, whose last years would ironically be portrayed by Flynn himself the following year in, *They Died With Their Boots On*.

Santiago
See: The Gun Runner

Saphead, The ○
1920, US, 70 mins, b/w
Dir: Herbert Blaché
Stars: Buster Keaton
Rating: ★★★

Buster Keaton's first feature film is a fascinating example of his unique talent in embryo. There's too much plot for Keaton really to break out, but he gives a memorable display of vaudeville acrobatics in the Stock Exchange and the movie's rarity value makes it unmissable.

Saps at Sea ⊙
1940, US, 60 mins, b/w
Dir: Gordon Douglas
Stars: Stan Laurel, Oliver Hardy
Rating: ★★★

The last feature comedy that Stan and Ollie made for the Hal Roach studio. Here, they're off on an ocean cruise, with an escaped convict stowed away on board. Some good sight gags include several during a medical

S

inspection of Mr Hardy by Dr James Finlayson; and the famous sequence where they make a feast for the convict without using anything that's actually edible... see it to believe it.

Saraband for Dead Lovers ○
(aka: Saraband)
1948, UK, 96 mins, colour
Dir: Michael Relph
Stars: Stewart Granger, Joan Greenwood, Flora Robson
Rating: ★★★★

Stewart Granger and Anthony Quayle have to concede the acting honours to Flora Robson in this splendidly mounted costume adventure-tragedy set in 17th-century Germany. Dame Flora is superb, especially in a horrifying scene where she burns Granger's face with a curling iron. He and Quayle do at least have a splendid sword duel, all flashing blades and dancing shadows.

Saracen Blade, The ○
1954, US, 78 mins, colour
Dir: William Castle
Stars: Ricardo Montalban, Betta St John, Rick Jason, Carolyn Jones
Rating: ★★★★

A sprawling novel by the prolific Frank Yerby is condensed into a full-blooded costume action film, typical of Hollywood's sword and sandal sagas of the early Fifties, full of clichéd but effective dialogue and stirring action scenes. Enthusiastic performances by Ricardo Montalban, Betta St John, Michael Ansara, Rick Jason and especially Carolyn Jones, whose minxish portrayal steals the film, ensure you'll be cheering the hero on through a slew of improbable adventures. An underrated film: very entertaining.

Sarafina! ◑ Ⓥ
1992, US/South Africa, 118 mins, colour
Dir: Darrell James Roodt
Stars: Leleti Khumalo, Whoopi Goldberg, Mariam Makeba, John Kani
Rating: ★★★

Most people will find this semi-musical about South Africa's apartheid years deeply disturbing. And, because it is a passionately committed enterprise, its dramas are more affecting than those of such better-acted African stories as *Cry Freedom* and *A Dry White Season*. Sarafina (Leleti Khumalo) is a teenage pupil at a Soweto school where rebellious talk costs lives and oppression by the military is the order of the day. Her teacher Mary (Whoopi Goldberg) teaches national pride mixed with history which is too heady a brew for the

authorities who soon have her in their sights. What follows is an all too familiar story of massacre, beating, kidnap and torture, only slightly relieved by the surging songs that drive the story along. Well-shot and edited and just well enough acted to get by, this is a harrowing, moving and entertaining history lesson.

Sarah ☉
(aka: The Seventh Match)
1981, US, 71 mins, colour
Dir: Yoram Gross
Rating: ★★★

An unusual, inventive cartoon feature from the prolific Australian animator Yoram Gross, whose best-known work to date is probably *Dot and the Kangaroo*. This is more serious than most of his films, concerning a small girl befriended by the animals of the forest while on the run from the Nazis in World War Two. Mia Farrow gives Sarah a suitably delicate yet determined voice.

Satanic Rites of Dracula, The ● Ⓥ
1973, UK, 88 mins, colour
Dir: Alan Gibson
Stars: Christopher Lee, Peter Cushing, Freddie Jones, Joanna Lumley
Rating: ★★

A modern-dress entry into the Dracula series, which gives a new, if rather improbable method of disposing of vampires and presents the bad count as a property speculator with a cellar full of nubile girl vampires. Peter Cushing and Christopher Lee play with their usual aplomb.

Satan's Skin
See: Blood on Satan's Claw

Saturday Night and Sunday Morning ◑ Ⓥ
1960, UK, 90 mins, b/w
Dir: Karel Reisz
Stars: Albert Finney, Rachel Roberts, Shirley Anne Field
Rating: ★★★★

This was a significant milestone in British cinema since the film not only took a highly (for the time) adult attitude towards sex, but also treated working class people without any attempt either to patronise or to mock them. Much of its still considerable power derives from Allan Stilltoe's honest and abrasive screenplay – based on his own novel – and Karel Reisz's impressive direction in his first film in this capacity. He succeeded in getting quite superb performances

from Finney as an archetypal angry young man forced to face up to his responsibilities, Rachel Roberts as his married mistress, and from music hall comedienne Hylda Baker whose portrayal of a working class woman gave her career a major boost. And the fine use of locations marvellously photographed by Freddie Francis – gives an almost documentary view of an English industrial town.

Saturday Night Fever ◑ Ⓥ
1977, US, 119 mins, colour
Dir: John Badham
Stars: John Travolta, Karen Lynn Gorney
Rating: ★★★

Never mind the quality of the script, feel the vibrations that made John Travolta a star in this famous and really rather bitter story of life in the slums of Brooklyn. The teenagers slave away in thankless jobs, and only come to life on Saturday nights at the spectacular local disco. Brilliant photography by Ralph D Bode makes the most of the sequences in which Travolta proves he's the dancing king.

Saturn 3 ○ Ⓥ
1980, US, 87 mins, colour
Dir: Stanley Donen
Stars: Kirk Douglas, Farrah Fawcett
Rating: ★★★

A not unexciting variant on a formula science-fiction theme, as a space station (manned by Kirk Douglas and Farrah Fawcett) is invaded by a killer and the robot he constructs. Director Stanley Donen gives it a gutsy pace, lots of pounding chases up and down the station and a spectacular climax. The film is good to look at, its effects as competent as anything in *Star Wars*. The editing wisely relies as little as possible on the dialogue to provide the thrills. Harvey Keitel co-stars.

Savage Innocents, The ○
1959, UK, 107 mins, colour
Dir: Baccio Bandini, Nicholas Ray
Stars: Anthony Quinn, Yoko Tani, Peter O'Toole
Rating: ★★★

A bizarre offering from cult director Nicholas Ray. Anthony Quinn and Yoko Tani star as Eskimos battling to survive against nature – and the onset of civilisation, in the shape of white traders, Christianity and rock 'n' roll! Not surprisingly, it ends in tears. The film does contain some striking location photography (as well as dodgy back projection at Pinewood studios). Animal lovers should be prepared for the savagery of the Eskimo lifestyle, with close-up scenes of caribou eyes and crawling maggots as food and the ripping open of a dog's belly so that frozen hands can be thawed in the entrails.

Savage Islands ○
1983, US, 100 mins, colour
Dir: Ferdinand Fairfax
Stars: Tommy Lee Jones, Michael O'Keefe, Jenny Seagrove
Rating: ★★

Like *The Scarlet Buccaneer*, this is a doomed attempt to duplicate the Hollywood pirate picture of the Fifties. It starts well, but becomes progressively less spirited and well-organised as the story progresses. Made in New Zealand with an American, British and Australasian cast.

Save the Tiger ●
1972, US, 100 mins, colour
Dir: John G Avildsen
Stars: Jack Lemmon, Jack Gilford
Rating: ★★

Although this is rather an unpalatable film, it has a typical Jack Lemmon performance of full-throttled intensity, revelling in another portrait of modern angst, chewing the role voraciously before swallowing it whole. For his performance as the snarlingly harassed Harry, Lemmon was rewarded with an Oscar.

Saving Grace ○
1986, UK, 112 mins, colour
Dir: Robert M Young
Stars: Tom Conti, Fernando Rey
Rating: ★

A gentler affair than Robbie Coltrane's irreverent *The Pope Must Die*, although paced nowhere near as well. This comedy casts Tom Conti as a Pope who runs away from office to live among ordinary people for a while to re-learn his trade. Actually, he not so much runs away as locks himself out of the Vatican garden while dressed in civvies, and just takes his time in getting back in! Scriptwriter David S Ward captures well the naive spirit of Italian English (in spite of the plot taking place in Italy) while Conti uses a heavy Italian accent! He makes an owlishly smiling Pope in a role he would probably have lost to Peter Sellers had the latter lived, while sawn-off Angelo Evans is excellent as the sub-teen wide boy who becomes his first convert. Pretty dull though.

Say Anything ◑ ⊙
1989, US, 104 mins, colour
Dir: Cameron Crowe
Stars: John Cusack, Ione Skye, John Mahoney
Rating: ★★★

A teenage drama with a difference. The excellent John Cusack is the average Joe graduating from college who falls in love with the lovely school brainbox (Ione Skye) who has an incredibly close relationship with her adoring father. But all is not quite what it seems, and this is what strikes the spark that sets the movie apart from the average teenage romance. That, plus excellent performances – the film is all but stolen by John Mahoney as Skye's dad – and the fact that the story's about people with feet of clay. An uplifting film for teenagers to see, it proves that you can do anything if you think clearly and keep the major relationships in your life intact at the same time.

Say It With Flowers ○
1933, UK, 71 mins, b/w
Dir: John Baxter
Stars: Mary Clare, Ben Field, George Carney
Rating: ★★

Many 'greats' of the old-time music-hall appear in this affectionately made film about two street traders who fall on hard times. Directed by John Baxter, portrayer par excellence of the British working classes through three decades of the cinema.

Sayonara ○ ⊙
1957, US, 147 mins, colour
Dir: Joshua Logan
Stars: Marlon Brando, Miiko Taka, Patricia Owens
Rating: ★★★★

Marathon tear-jerker about American servicemen in love with Japanese girls at the time of the Korean War, and the sometimes tragic consequences. Brando puts on a convincing Southern States accent, and develops his character nicely. But acting honours went to Red Buttons, previously known only as a comic actor, and Miyoshi Umeki as the Japanese girl he marries. Both players deservedly won Oscars. The atmosphere is authentic and the story absorbing.

Scalawag ⊙
1973, US, 93 mins, colour
Dir: Kirk Douglas
Stars: Kirk Douglas, Mark Lester
Rating: ★

As well as being the star, Kirk Douglas made his debut as a director on this pirate yarn based on a story by Robert Louis Stevenson. Douglas became an enthusiastic balloonist – a balloon figures prominently in the action – when he filmed the story on locations along the Yugoslavian coast. In the film, Douglas, like everyone else, strenuously over-plays, as a one-legged rogue called Peg, in a story whose strongest asset is Jack Cardiff's sunny Technicolor photography. Children will enjoy the simple blood-and-thunder Douglas provides. Adults may just stay awake long enough to spot Danny DeVito in one of his earliest roles.

Scalphunters, The ◐
1968, US, 102 mins, colour
Dir: Sydney Pollack
Stars: Burt Lancaster, Shelley Winters, Telly Savalas, Ossie Davis
Rating: ★★★★

An uncharacteristic film for both Burt Lancaster (in his later years, at any rate) and director Sydney Pollack. This is a rip-roaring adventure story about a tough fur trapper 'landed' with a runaway slave for company, during a dangerous few days in which they get involved with a gang of scalphunters, and a tribe of Kiowa Indians. Shelley Winters is splendidly fiery and surprisingly glamorous in a throwback to the kind of role she was playing 15 years earlier.

Scam ● ⊙
1992, US, 102 mins, colour
Dir: John Flynn
Stars: Christopher Walken, Lorraine Bracco, Miguel Ferrer
Rating: ★

Something that has more twists than a corkscrew ought to grip all right, but this 'scam' doesn't even bite into the cork. The plot dodges this way and that and changes course several times in the last few minutes, but all to no avail; the odds are that you won't care too much about who's doing what to whom. Lorraine Bracco's a con-girl in cahoots with Miguel Ferrer, coming on to rich pick-ups, drugging their drinks and relieving them of their bankrolls and Rolexes. Along comes Christopher Walken, who abducts her, may or may not be an FBI man and enlists her in a scheme to rob the bad guys of computer disk information – or maybe a few million in banknotes. Jamaican backgrounds supply some colourful padding as director John Flynn allows the plot to ramble on in its tired and outmoded way. Walken and Bracco give pat performances that

S

smack of insufficient enthusiasm for the project: you won't care much what happens to either of them at the end.

Scandal ● Ⓥ
1989, UK, 106 mins, colour
Dir: Michael Caton-Jones
Stars: Joanne Whalley-Kilmer, John Hurt, Bridget Fonda, Ian McKellen
Rating: ★★

Despite a script culled from no less than five books on the subject, this film of the notorious Profumo case 'The Minister, the Model, and the Russian Spy' – is a sadly whitewashed affair. Joanne Whalley-Kilmer certainly looks the part of 'showgirl' Christine Keeler, whose affairs with a Russian official and British Cabinet minister helped bring down the Conservative government of the day. But the film's revelation is American actress Bridget Fonda (daughter of Peter and niece of Jane) who perfectly captures the capricious nature and British accent of fellow goodtime girl Mandy Rice-Davies, famous for her 'Well, he would say that' line during the famous court case. John Hurt is excellent as the sad establishment fall guy, Dr Stephen Ward. But this scandal resembles nothing more than a storm in a china teacup.

Scandal at Scourie ○
1952, US, 91 mins, colour
Dir: Jean Negulesco
Stars: Greer Garson, Walter Pidgeon
Rating: ★★★

Scandal at Scourie was the end of an era: it was the last film the famous Greer Garson-Walter Pidgeon team made together in 12 years which included such colossal hits as *Mrs Miniver* and *Madame Curie*. This is a typical Garson-Pidgeon mixture of laughter and tears, with cute and clever Donna Corcoran as a little orphan girl who causes no end of trouble to her foster-parents. An irresistible and highly enjoyable piece of sheer sentiment, with Canadian backgrounds richly photographed in Technicolor.

Scandal Sheet ○
(aka: The Dark Page)
1951, US, 82 mins, b/w
Dir: Phil Karlson
Stars: Broderick Crawford, John Derek, Donna Reed, Henry Morgan
Rating: ★★★

Broderick Crawford is in typical scowling, hard-hitting form as the ruthless editor of a gutter newspaper, who finds himself pursued by his own re-

porters when he accidentally puts an end to his ex-wife. This last scene is the best in the film, filled with an atmosphere of doom. There are fine performances from Crawford and from Rosemary DeCamp, usually cast in cosy mother roles, but here in splendidly vengeful form as the long-deserted wife. Director Phil Karlson ensures that the pace is fast and the action crackles.

Scanners ● Ⓥ
1981, Canada, 103 mins, colour
Dir: David Cronenberg
Stars: Jennifer O'Neill, Patrick McGoohan
Rating: ★★★

This was director David Cronenberg's best film to date and deservedly put him on the international map. Scanners are superior if tormented beings who can kill by thought transference. Literally, they blow your mind. Consequently, Cronenberg is predictably interested not so much in the story as in the opportunity it provides for special effects. These are exceptionally good, especially the scene of a head blowing apart, and in the final duel between two master scanners. The ending is cryptic in the way the best of Roger Corman's films were and, if the acting is not too hot, the subject matter remains fascinating to the end.

Scapegoat, The ○
1958, UK, 92 mins, b/w
Dir: Robert Hamer
Stars: Alec Guinness, Bette Davis, Nicole Maurey
Rating: ★★★★

Brilliant thriller – based on the novel by Daphne du Maurier – in which an English schoolmaster (Alec Guinness) finds himself in desperate trouble after meeting his 'double' in France. The nerve-wracking closing scenes in which Guinness once more confronts his lookalike will keep you guessing up to the last moment.

Scar, The
See: Hollow Triumph

Scaramouche ○
1952, US, 110 mins, colour
Dir: George Sidney
Stars: Stewart Granger, Eleanor Parker, Mel Ferrer, Janet Leigh
Rating: ★★★★

One of Stewart Granger's best films at MGM: a remake of the famous Rafael Sabatini swashbuckler set in 18th-cen-

tury France, with Granger as the rake who turns avenger when his best friend is murdered. The climax is one of the most dazzling and longest duel scenes ever filmed, between Granger and Mel Ferrer, that bettered even the one Granger was to have with James Mason in another spectacular MGM remake, *The Prisoner of Zenda*.

Scared Stiff ○
1953, US, 108 mins, b/w
Dir: George Marshall
Stars: Dean Martin, Jerry Lewis, Lizabeth Scott, Carmen Miranda
Rating: ★★★

A remake – and a pretty funny one of the old Bob Hope classic *The Ghost Breakers*, with Dean Martin and Jerry Lewis jointly taking the Hope role of a cowardly entertainer dodging zombies on a mist-enshrouded island. Lewis pulls some incredible faces and gives a passable impression of Brazilian bombshell Carmen Miranda, whose last film appearance this was.

Scarface ○ Ⓥ
1932, US, 90 mins, b/w
Dir: Howard Hawks
Stars: Paul Muni, Ann Dvorak, Karen Morley, Boris Karloff, George Raft
Rating: ★★★★

This landmark gangster movie is strong stuff, indeed too strong for America in 1932, where it had to be subtitled *The Shame of a Nation*. The film is dominated by the tenacious performance of Paul Muni as the gangster of the title, who shoots his way venomously to the top. The film is drivingly well directed by Howard Hawks, although it took later critics to pick out the 'cross' motif which accompanies most of the deaths in the film – a parallel to the crosslike scar on Muni's face.

Scarface Mob, The ○
1959, US, 102 mins, colour
Dir: Phil Karlson
Stars: Robert Stack, Neville Brand, Pat Crowley, Keenan Wynn
Rating: ★★

This fast-moving gangster story hearkened back to the vintage years of tommy-gun thrillers at Warner Brothers and triggered off the long-running television series *The Untouchables*. Neville Brand plays famous gangster Al Capone for the first of several times for film and television. Pretty Pat Crowley makes an appealing heroine, providing a welcome gentle touch amid the 'macho' machine-gun mayhem of the rest of the movie.

Scarlet Angel ○
1952, US, 80 mins, colour
Dir: Sidney Salkow
Stars: Yvonne De Carlo, Rock Hudson
Rating: ★★

This colourful romantic adventure was Rock Hudson's last step up the ladder before becoming a fully fledged star. He was billed above the title, in type almost as big as the lead, Yvonne De Carlo, who plays an adventuress called Roxy, at large in New Orleans waterfront saloons – and later high society – in the early 1800s. Television fans with long memories will recognise the actress playing Susan Caldwell. She's Amanda Blake, later Miss Kitty in the *Gunsmoke* series.

Scarlet Buccaneer, The ○
(aka: Swashbuckler)
1976, US, 100 mins, colour
Dir: James Goldstone
Stars: Robert Shaw, James Earl Jones, Peter Boyle, Genevieve Bujold
Rating: ★★

Pirate films seek no logic. Therefore, it's not surprising that, with a mild nod to modern times in the form of the villain's bisexuality, director James Goldstone has chosen to make a swashbuckler in the truest Errol Flynn – well, at any rate, Burt Lancaster – tradition. Unfortunately, Goldstone is no Michael Curtiz when it comes to marshalling crowded action scenes and the dialogue plays the whole thing a shade too tongue-in-cheek. Robert Shaw's brighter buccaneer of the title is really the only good performance, but if Genevieve Bujold is a mite short on acting strength, she shows herself handy with a sword and pitches into her fiery heroine with genuine Maureen O'Hara spirit. The whole thing is noisy, violent and, especially in the early stages, moves at a rare old clip.

Scarlet Empress, The ○
1934, US, 110 mins, b/w
Dir: Josef von Sternberg
Stars: Marlene Dietrich, John Lodge
Rating: ★★★

The story almost drowns in a sea of lushness and exoticism in this version of the rise to power in Russia of Catherine the Great – very different to that being made in Britain at the same time with Elisabeth Bergner as Catherine. There, the emphasis was on character creation; here, it is wholly on costume, spectacle and camerawork, Bert Glennon excelling in this last department with his ultra-mobile

black and white cameras (later he would become an acknowledged expert in colour as well). Marlene Dietrich is fine as the shy young princess, but less effective when a figure of power. The film itself, which nowadays would be described as high camp is, under Josef von Sternberg's dedicated direction, a treat to the eye. And there's an amazing performance by Sam Jaffe.

Scarlet Letter, The ● ⓥ
1995, US, 135 mins, colour
Dir: Roland Joffé
Stars: Demi Moore, Gary Oldman, Robert Duvall, Robert Prosky, Edward Hardwicke, Joan Plowright
Rating: ★

Roland Joffé, who made such fine films as *The Killing Fields*, *The Mission* and *City of Joy*, blots his copybook in no uncertain fashion with this ludicrous Nineties-style take on a 19th-century classic that would have original author Nathaniel Hawthorne spinning in his grave. Hawthorne's story of guilt and redemption has become a glisteningly set bodice-ripper entirely fashioned to the buxom charms of Demi Moore as the lusty 16th-century wife who defrocks the local priest, gets herself pregnant and is forced to wear a scarlet 'A' (for adulteress) on her apparel for the rest of her days. Those days seem long indeed in this solemn, foolish chestheaver which sees Gary Oldman making a bigger fool of himself than the leading lady as the cleric who finds her irresistible and Robert Duvall playing with uncharacteristic flatness as the husband whose absence causes her to go off the rails. A miserable misfire: the Lillian Gish 1926 silent version is better.

Scarlet Pimpernel, The ○
1934, UK, 98 mins, b/w
Dir: Harold Young
Stars: Leslie Howard, Merle Oberon, Raymond Massey
Rating: ★★★★★

Best-remembered of the many films about the adventures of Baroness Orczy's famous chameleon Sir Percy Blakeney, the soldier of fortune who confounds the French revolutionaries who seek him here, there and everywhere. Originally, Charles Laughton had been chosen for the title role, but the public protested that he didn't match up to the popular conception of the Pimpernel – and Leslie Howard was chosen. His Pimpernel remains

the archetypal performance, catching exactly the false foppishness and underlying steel, as well as the mythical qualities which make the character seem so invincible.

Scarlet Pimpernel, The ○
1982, UK, 144 mins, colour
Dir: Clive Donner
Stars: Anthony Andrews, Jane Seymour, Ian McKellen
Rating: ★★★★

It took London Films 48 years to repeat the ideal casting of their 1934 version of this swashbuckling classic (which starred Leslie Howard as Sir Percy and Merle Oberon as his wife), but they did it to perfection: Anthony Andrews and Jane Seymour fit the roles like elegant gloves. The production design, too, is superb.

Scarlet Street ○
1945, US, 103 mins, b/w
Dir: Fritz Lang
Stars: Edward G Robinson, Joan Bennett, Dan Duryea
Rating: ★★★★

Fine seedy thriller, with a perfect performance by Edward G Robinson as the meek cashier ensnared by trollop Joan Bennett into providing her with the luxuries she craves. Dan Duryea's sleek straw-hatted con-boy completes the same trio of stars from director Fritz Lang's other great Forties' crime drama, *The Woman in the Window*. An amazingly intense *film noir*.

Scars of Dracula, The ● ⓥ
1970, UK, 96 mins, colour
Dir: Roy Ward Baker
Stars: Christopher Lee, Dennis Waterman
Rating: ★★

Dennis Waterman is less at home here battling the vampire count (Christopher Lee) than he was soon to become in TV's *The Sweeney* and *Minder* series. Roger Dicken's special effects are excellent, but there's too little of Lee in this one.

Scenes from a Mall ◑ ⓥ
1991, US, 85 mins, colour
Dir: Paul Mazursky
Stars: Bette Midler, Woody Allen, Bill Irwin
Rating: ★

Bette Midler and Woody Allen together. It's an idea good enough to start you laughing while you're still in the queue. And, for a while, it works. The trouble is that the scripters have no idea what to do with the terrible two once they get them inside a massive shopping mall. It was certainly not a great notion, either, to cast them as long-term husband and wife who, after they've told each other about their recent affairs, just make up and bicker, make up and bicker, through the rest of the film. There are occasional good moments (but not many) in the last hour of a film that mercifully is at least short. What a waste of these two tiny titans of talent to have them go even semi-serious on us under circumstances like these.

Scenes from the Class Struggle in Beverly Hills ● ⓥ
1989, US, 104 mins, colour
Dir: Paul Bartel
Stars: Jacqueline Bisset, Ray Sharkey, Mary Woronov, Ed Begley Jr
Rating: ★★

Director Bartel made *Eating Raoul* and lots of similarly outrageous stuff. So you can guarantee that his idea of a sexploitation comedy is not going to be quite like anyone else's. Lunatic? You got it. And, even though Barrel himself said at the time that 'if this doesn't offend anybody, it isn't working', it isn't actually as rude and crass as its reputation would have you believe. In a Hollywood mansion couples couple compulsively and without compunction. It's light, lusty and luxuriously lewd; and occasionally funny too.

Scent of a Woman ● ⓥ
1992, US, 157 mins, colour
Dir: Martin Brest
Stars: Al Pacino, Chris O'Donnell, Gabrielle Anwar, James Rebhorn
Rating: ★★

You know the one about opposites having something to learn from each other and forging the unlikeliest of friendships. *Beaches* somehow made it work; here writer Bo Goldman and director Martin Brest show us how to go right over the top with the idea. Chris O'Donnell (not half firm enough) is a 17-year-old prep student saddled for the weekend with irascible, unreasonable, unmanageable, blind, retired Lt Col Slade (a notably mannered performance from Al Pacino which took an Oscar). The kid finds himself whisked off to New York, where the colonel has in mind spending his disability pension on one hell of a time, followed by blowing his brains out. The adventures of this unlikely if somewhat unlovable couple have a certain charm, and sequences involving a dance and a madcap car drive work winningly. But it's 92 minutes'

worth spread out to more than 150. The climax piles our disbelief into a sandwich of sentiment, and opportunities for meaningful dialogue between the two protagonists are all wasted.

Schindler's List ● ⓥ
1993, US, 195 mins, b/w
Dir: Steven Spielberg
Stars: Liam Neeson, Ben Kingsley, Ralph Fiennes, Caroline Goodall, Embeth Davidtz
Rating: ★★★★

Steven Spielberg's very worthy (although *very* long) and sometimes moving Oscar-winning account of the wartime exploits of Oskar Schindler, an Austro-German businessman and profiteer who made a fortune from a Polish pots-and-pans factory using Jewish labour he didn't have to pay except in kind. To those Jews in the Krakow ghetto, work for Schindler was infinitely preferable to anything else. Concerned only with making money, he was basically a kind of sharp wheeler-dealer who treated his staff fairly. Hobnobbing with the Germans, he bought Nazi friendship with money and black market goods, even beguiling their psychotic local commandant (Ralph Fiennes) whose hobby was taking pot shots at passing Jews. But the high-living, womanising Schindler inevitably became drawn to the deprivations of his workforce. As the man who became an unlikely hero and the saviour of a race not his own, Liam Neeson is excellent all the way through, only faltering in an out-of-character breakdown at the end.

School for Scoundrels ☉
1959, UK, 95 mins, b/w
Dir: Robert Hamer
Stars: Ian Carmichael, Terry-Thomas, Alastair Sim, Janette Scott
Rating: ★★★

A fitting and hilarious tribute to the late Stephen Potter, on whose incomparable books *Gamesmanship, Lifemanship* and *Oneupmanship* this comedy film was based. One remembers with particular pleasure the snooker and tennis confrontations between Ian Carmichael and Terry-Thomas, and Alastair Sim is perfect casting as the author himself. The supporting cast includes Janette Scott, Dennis Price, Peter Jones – especially funny as a car salesman – and Hattie Jacques.

School Ties ◑ ⓥ
1992, US, 107 mins, colour
Dir: Robert Mandel

Stars: Brendan Fraser, Chris O'Donnell, Andrew Lowery, Amy Locane, Zeljko Ivanek
Rating: ★★

This drama of racial prejudice at a senior college for the sons of rich men lies somewhere between so-so and quite good. Though not without merit or food for thought, it's by no means as gripping as landmark films in the genre. David (Brendan Fraser) comes from a working-class Jewish family and is at the college on a football scholarship. On his father's (and coach's) advice, he doesn't tell his roommates he's a Jew, which with hindsight proves a grave mistake, and one which is to have serious repercussions. As with many of these dramas, this is simplistic in treatment and its issues are fairly black and white, with characters either basically sympathetic to David or total bigots. Nonethless, it doesn't always opt for the obvious, as in David's attitude to authority, which is barely respectful and although prepared to talk frankly to his seniors, rarely having anything really telling to say. Fraser has a difficult role in this not entirely sympathetic part, but does it well.

Scorchers ● ⓥ
1991, US, 88 mins, colour
Dir: David Beaird
Stars: Faye Dunaway, Denholm Elliott, Emily Lloyd, James Wilder, Jennifer Tilly
Rating: RB

This strange kettle of catfish down in the Bayou is one of those films that makes it glaringly obvious that it started life as a play. It seems to be about young brides losing their inhibitions through a) imagined contact with a dead mother and b) positive contact with the town whore. 'I'm scared, daddy,' wails Emily Lloyd. 'I'm not woman enough to please my man,' pouts Jennifer Tilly. Both are better actresses than you could possibly guess from this very badly directed (by its writer) film that has an all-too-distinguished cast embarrassingly and stiltedly over-acting to the extent that it simply turns an audience off. You get the feeling that here and there the film is meant to be affecting and amusing, but it isn't either. Son of a gun, it's just no fun on this Bayou.

Scorpio ◑
1972, UK, 114 mins, colour
Dir: Michael Winner
Stars: Burt Lancaster, Alain Delon, Paul Scofield, Gayle Hunnicutt
Rating: ★★

Tough espionage thriller awash with unsympathetic characters, good action scenes, sharp dialogue and a pretty confusing plot. Burt Lancaster is at his most taciturn as the hit-man who wants to turn it in, but inevitably cannot shake himself free of the spider's web cast by his organisation, and finds another hit-man (played by Alain Delon) on his heels.

Scott of the Antarctic O Ⓥ

1948, UK, 111 mins, colour
Dir: Charles Frend
Stars: John Mills, Derek Bond, James Robertson Justice, Kenneth More, Harold Warrender, Reginald Beckwith
Rating: ★★★

John Mills has the lead role in this moving screen monument to the men of the ill-fated trek to the South Pole. Much of the shooting was done on arduous locations in Switzerland and Norway, where packed lunches froze solid, and several crewmen were sent back to base with frostbite. Of the other actors doing yeoman work under such conditions, Harold Warrender is Wilson, Reginald Beckwith plays 'Birdie' Bowers and James Robertson Justice is the ill-fated Evans, the first to die. An honest account, but still inspiring, with fantastic Technicolor camerawork from three of Britain's finest carneramen – Jack Cardiff, Osmond Borrodaile and Geoffrey Unsworth.

Scream ● Ⓥ

1996, US, 109 mins, colour
Dir: Wes Craven
Stars: Neve Campbell, Skeet Ulrich, Courteney Cox, Henry Winkler, Drew Barrymore
Rating: ★★★

Formerly known as *Scary Movie* (a much better title), this is Craven's slightly (but only slightly) joky version of a *Halloween*-style horror film. Full of in-references to horror movies, the story gives Drew Barrymore a juicy 10 minutes to steal the picture at the start before she becomes the latest victim of a maniac slasher wearing a 'Father Death' costume, her dying cries heard on the cellular phone to which she has clung instead of the kitchen knife with which she was defending herself! As the gutted body count mounts, it becomes apparent that the chief stalkee is Sidney (Neve Campbell) whose mother was stabbed to death a year before by a killer Sid identified, now languishing on Death Row. It's pretty slow in between the murders, but

there are enough of those to keep things thumping along most of the time, even if the plot has more holes than the poor victims...

Screamers ● Ⓥ

1995, US/Can/Jap, 109 mins, colour
Dir: Christian Duguay
Stars: Peter Weller, Jennifer Rubin, Roy Dupois, Andy Lauer, Charles Powell
Rating: ★★

Recognisably from the fertile imagination of Philip K Dick, who wrote the original of *Blade Runner*, this too is about replicants, things not of flesh and bone who only appear to be human. It's 2078AD and, on a distant planet turned into a battered shell by hostilities, rival groups who fought long for the rare mineral contained on the planet must seek peace when news comes that the mineral has been discovered elsewhere. Self-maintaining killing devices called screamers, which can appear in human form, and 'Davids', sophisticated weapons disguised as small boys clutching teddy bears, are only two of the obstacles weary commander Peter Weller must overcome to get off the planet. Boasting superb production design and special effects, the film's bright ideas are fatally negated by its lack of pace. The morose Weller is fast becoming the Stephen Rea of Hollywood films.

Scrooge O

1935, UK, 79 mins, b/w
Dir: Henry Edwards
Stars: Seymour Hicks, Donald Calthrop, Athene Seyler, Oscar Asche, Barbara Everest, Maurice Evans
Rating: ★★★

A good early version of the cast-iron Dickens classic *A Christmas Carol*, with convincing Victorian atmosphere and settings. The famous actor-manager and comedy character star Sir Seymour Hicks is in topnotch form in the title role. This remained the best film account of the story until eclipsed by the Alastair Sim version of 1951.

Scrooge O Ⓥ
(aka: A Christmas Carol)

1951, UK, 86 mins, b/w
Dir: Brian Desmond Hurst
Stars: Alastair Sim, Kathleen Harrison, Jack Warner, Michael Hordern
Rating: ★★★★★

Alastair Sim was born to play Charles Dickens' supernaturally reformed miser from *A Christmas Carol* and he relishes every moment of his time on screen to provide a performance to

treasure. Kathleen Harrison, Mervyn Johns and a splendidly sepulchral Michael Hordem, as the ghost of Jacob Marley, offer sterling support and Brian Desmond Hurst's solid direction is complemented by the work of two directors-to-be, cinematographer C Pennington Richards and editor Clive Donner. The definitive screen version of the story.

Scrooge O

1970, UK, 113 mins, colour
Dir: Ronald Neame
Stars: Albert Finney, Alec Guinness, Edith Evans, Kenneth More
Rating: ★★★

A great victory over poor material is enjoyed by Albert Finney as Scrooge, in this lively and lavish version. Alec Guinness and Edith Evans enjoy themselves as, respectively, Jacob Marley and the spirit of Christmas Past, but the screenplay is only middling and the music and lyrics by Leslie Bricusse fairly forgettable. It's left to Finney, whether scowling behind iced-up windows, or jigging for joy when converted by the Spirits, to bring this Christmas treat home in triumph.

Scrooged ◑ Ⓥ

1988, US, 101 mins, colour
Dir: Richard Donner
Stars: Bill Murray, Karen Allen, John Forsythe
Rating: ★★★

Bill Murray's first star comedy in four years following *Ghost Busters* is an updating of *A Christmas Carol* with him cast in the Scrooge role as an utterly venal TV chief whose taste lies well and truly in the gutter. Attacked in some quarters for its questionable humour – a Richard Pryor flambé joke is particularly tasteless – it remains a top drawer production, with sumptuous sets and costumes, and some impressive special effects. Its comic highlight is unquestionably Carol Kane's appearance as the Ghost of Christmas Present. She looks like the Good Witch of the North from *The Wizard of Oz*, but dispenses verbal and physical punishment with sadistic glee.

Sea Chase, The O

1955, US, 117 mins, colour
Dir: John Farrow
Stars: John Wayne, Lana Turner, David Farrar, Lyle Bettger
Rating: ★★

John Wayne takes an unusual role in this vigorous war drama, as a skipper determined to steer his ship back to

S

Germany despite a British blockade. The Wayne-Lana Turner combination doesn't quite ignite the sparks you'd expect, but there's a colourful supporting cast that includes Tab Hunter, James Arness, John Qualen, Paul Fix and Claude Akins.

Sea Devils O
1937, US, 88 mins, b/w
Dir: Ben Stoloff
Stars: Victor McLaglen, Preston Foster, Ida Lupino
Rating: ★★

Only Victor McLaglen or Wallace Beery could have played a character called Medals Malone and here it's McLaglen in a typically rough-and-ready vehicle about coastguards who seem to spend more time feuding with each other than carrying out their duties. The idea of ice patrols and daring sea rescues should make a good film story, but here the originality is all but stifled by the treatment. The performances, even from such experienced campaigners as McLaglen, Preston Foster and Ida Lupino, are rather too spirited for comfort.

Sea Devils O
1953, UK, 91 mins, colour
Dir: Raoul Walsh
Stars: Yvonne de Carlo, Rock Hudson, Bryan Forbes
Rating: ★★

British-made action film about smuggling and espionage in the Napoleonic era, directed by American Raoul Walsh. One can only admire the untroubled.gusto with which stars Rock Hudson and Yvonne de Carlo enter the fray. Events move at such a cracking pace it hardly seems to matter that so many of them are inexplicable. As the much-in-evidence friend of the hero, Britain's Bryan Forbes gets all the best lines and makes the most of them.

Sea Hawk, The O ⓥ
1940, US, 127 mins, b/w
Dir: Michael Curtiz
Stars: Errol Flynn, Brenda Marshall, Claude Rains, Flora Robson
Rating: ★★★★★

This is Errol Flynn swashing his buckle as only he knows how. Although every bit as good as *The Adventures of Robin Hood*, *The Sea Hawk* hasn't achieved the same classic status. One possible explanation for this is that it isn't in colour. This doesn't stop the film being one of the most exciting adventure yarns ever made. Flynn is a

privateer, robbing and sinking Spanish ships during the reign of Elizabeth I. Flora Robson is regal as Elizabeth, while Claude Rains is rascally as the cunning Spanish ambassador to the English court. Brenda Marshall is his beautiful daughter, for whom Flynn falls. Directed by Michael Curtiz, an action specialist who had already directed most of Flynn's other adventures, the film is fast-moving and thrilling right up to the almost balletic climactic duel between Flynn and traitor Henry Daniell. Wonderful stuff.

Sea of Grass, The O
1947, US, 131 mins, b/w
Dir: Elia Kazan
Stars: Spencer Tracy, Katharine Hepburn, Robert Walker, Melvyn Douglas
Rating: ★★

The great Spencer Tracy-Katharine Hepburn team has the acting honours whisked from under its nose in this rather talky piece, and the culprit is that distinctive actor Robert Walker. Elia Kazan directs with his customary force. Robert Armstrong of *King Kong* fame is effective in support.

Sea of Love ● ⓥ
1989, US, 108 mins, colour
Dir: Harold Becker
Stars: Al Pacino, Ellen Barkin, John Goodman
Rating: ★★★★

This tightly scripted thriller about a killer who places romantic rhyming ads in newspaper personal columns and the Fitfies' hit *Sea of Love* on the record player at the scenes of the crimes, marked a triumphant return to movies by Al Pacino four years after his disastrous flop, *Revolution*. His riveting performance as a burned-out New York cop clutching at a second chance at love with chief suspect Ellen Barkin is the highlight of this glossy *film noir* that will have you guessing right up to the final double twist ending. The sexual chemistry between the two leads is a big plus, as is the atmospheric photography of British cinematographer Ronnie Taylor. Patricia Barry also scores as a much older woman who heartbreakingly picks up the wrong vibes from Pacino over lunch after answering one of his own phony ads to catch the killer. Strong, adult and good.

Sea of Sand O
(aka: Desert Patrol)
1958, UK, 97 mins, b/w

Dir: Guy Green
Stars: Richard Attenborough, John Gregson, Michael Craig
Rating: ★★★

Gruelling location filming in Libya paid off handsomely here, giving this gritty World War Two drama a compelling sense of the heat and desolation of the desert. The story is a moving and exciting one of a dangerous mission by the Long Range Desert Group to destroy a vital German petrol dump behind enemy lines in North Africa, strongly acted by the all-male cast. Director Guy Green stages tank battles, machine-gun duels and desperate crossings of minefields with great realism.

Searchers, The O ⓥ
1956, US, 119 mins, colour
Dir: John Ford
Stars: John Wayne, Jeffrey Hunter, Natalie Wood, Vera Miles
Rating: ★★★★

Ethan (John Wayne) spends five years searching for his two nieces, abducted by Indians, in this lengthy Western, with Wayne sort of playing himself and Vera Miles being a bit disappointing. Jeffrey Hunter, though, is excellent and Ward Bond solid, while a great featured-role performance by veteran Antonio Moreno leads some eye-catching supporting acting, which includes a surprisingly small, if key role for the star-billed Natalie Wood. Action is pretty good, story first-rate and powerfully told too. You'll find the ending haunting, or over-melodramatic according to your tastes, although it's lovingly composed by director John Ford, who really picks up the pace towards the end. Full of wide open spaces and interesting characters, this may not be Ford or Wayne's best Western, as many would claim, but it's still head and shoulders above most big-scale adventure films.

Sea Shall Not Have Them, The O
1954, UK, 91 mins, b/w
Dir: Lewis Gilbert
Stars: Michael Redgrave, Dirk Bogarde, Anthony Steel
Rating: ★★

One of the most star-studded of all films, this harrowing tale of air-sea rescue was made by former boy actor Lewis Gilbert, soon to have a smash success on his hands with *Reach for the Sky*. Unfortunately, the scriptwriters set the film itself adrift in a sea of repetitious situations - but the cast itself brings redemption, from such megastars of the time as Michael Redgrave, Dirk Bogarde and Anthony Steel to a crew of familiar faces that includes Bonar Colleano, Nigel Patrick, Jack Watling, Anton Diffring, Guy Middleton, Griffith Jones, Paul Carpenter and Joan Sims.

Season of Passion
See: Summer of the Seventeenth Doll

Sea Wife ○ ⓥ
1957, UK, 82 mins, colour
Dir: Bob McNaught
Stars: Richard Burton, Joan Collins, Basil Sydney, Cy Grant
Rating: ★★★

Four assorted shipwreck survivors one of them a nun – are thrown together in an open boat in this sturdy adaptation of J M Scott's novel, *Sea Wyf and Biscuit*, which boasted explosive star power in Richard Burton and Joan Collins. Director Bob McNaught, who took over after Italian film-maker Roberto Rossellini had resigned from the production, shot the film in and around Jamaica. Commented Joan Collins at the time: 'When I made my first island picture (*Our Girl Friday*), I could hardly swim at all. Now I'm almost a second Esther Williams.'

Sea Wolf, The ○ ⓥ
1940, US, 90 mins, b/w
Dir: Michael Curtiz
Stars: Edward G Robinson, Ida Lupino, John Garfield, Alexander Knox
Rating: ★★★

The studio's fog machines work overtime on this dark and moody adaptation of Jack London's famous story. Edward G Robinson again demonstrates his versatility, this time playing the tyrannical captain of the bad ship *Ghost*. It obviously wasn't too much for supporting cast members Barry Fitzgerald and Howard da Silva. They switched studios a few years later and signed up for *Two Years Before the Mast*.

Sea Wolves, The ○ ⓥ
1980, UK, 120 mins, colour
Dir: Andrew V McLaglen
Stars: Gregory Peck, David Niven, Roger Moore, Trevor Howard
Rating: ★★★

A spectacular war film about a crew of veteran saboteurs recruited to blow up a ship. The chief fascination about the film, as far as hardened film fans are concerned, some of them with no more than a line or two to say, of such stalwarts of post-

war British cinema as Patrick Allen, Patrick Holt, Percy Herbert, Donald Houston, Michael Medwin, Kenneth Griffith and several more besides. Most of them play members of the semi-retired group of saboteurs – they're not the 'Sea Wolves' of the title, by the way: that refers to the German U-boats that are doing the damage. Gregory Peck, Roger Moore, David Niven and Trevor Howard are the actual stars of the film and they all offer professionally competent performances, as does director Andrew V McLaglen on the action sequences.

Sebastian ○
1967, UK, 95 mins, colour
Dir: David Greene
Stars: Dirk Bogarde, Susannah York, Lilli Palmer, John Gielgud
Rating: ★★★

Stylish, inventive comedy-thriller, with Dirk Bogarde as a super-brain, involved in code-breaking and dodging double-agents. Director David Greene sets the right note from the beginning, spicing the thrills with sophisticated laughs – notably in Sebastian's army of girl secretaries, all with pencils poised to put down his thoughts – and setting it all in motion at a cracking pace.

Second Best Secret Agent in the Whole Wide World, The
See: Licensed to Kill

Second Chance ○
1953, US, 82 mins, colour
Dir: Rudolph Maté
Stars: Robert Mitchum, Jack Palance, Linda Darnell
Rating: ★★★

Vividly shot thriller, with a climactic fight in a cable car, hundreds of feet above the ground, between those two big men of the screen – Robert Mitchum, as a prizefighter on the run from killing a man, and Jack Palance as a gangster. The ending must have been even more hair-raising in the 3-D for which the film was originally made.

Seconds ◐
1966, US, 110 mins, b/w
Dir: John Frankenheimer
Stars: Rock Hudson, Salome Jens, John Randolph
Rating: ★★★

An exciting piece of science-fiction that only just failed to make the grade. The storyline bulges with originality. A middle-aged man, convinced that he has nothing left to live for, is offered a

new life by a strange firm, employing bright-eyed plastic surgeons. A body, he is told, will be found; a death certificate will be issued. So far, so very good. John Randolph comes incredibly close to the life of the hollow man who is offered substance of a sort. And director John Frankenheimer holds a Hitchcock-like grip on the opening scenes, which leave one's mouth dry with suspense. The macabre underthoughts, too, are subtly implanted. The offer seems unbelievable if wondrous. But where do the bodies come from, for certification of death? Later, when Randolph has been transformed into Rock Hudson, the dialogue becomes less persuasive, the pace less positive. But the blood-chilling ending fully restores the film to its former high plane.

Second Time Around, The ○
1961, US, 99 mins, colour
Dir: Vincent Sherman
Stars: Debbie Reynolds, Andy Griffith, Steve Forrest
Rating: ★★

In spite of a really strong supporting cast, this rambunctious romp soon turns into another one-woman show by Debbie Reynolds, who's all over the scenery as the winsome widow out west in 1912 who foils a bank raid and gets herself elected sheriff. A good-natured film with likeable characters (including one of the last of Thelma Ritter's treasurable cameos, almost inevitably as a character called Aggie), energetic fight scenes and smartly paced direction by Vincent Sherman. Mild fun.

Secret Admirer ◑ ⓥ
1985, US, 98 mins, colour
Dir: David Greenwalt
Stars: C Thomas Howell, Lori Loughlin, Kelly Preston, Fred Ward, Dee Wallace Stone, Casey Siemaszko
Rating: ★★

Above the average in ideas and general good humour for the high-school comedy of the mid-Eighties, this film's *raison d'être* lies in the letters a lovestruck girl pens to the boy next door. In turn, she decides to rewrite the letters he's written to the nubile 17-year-old of his dreams. Certain letters get into certain other hands and in no time at all the boy's mother is on the verge of an affair with the sexbomb's father while the boy's father is responding to the overtures of the sexbomb's mother. There are generic improbabilities in all this (a blonde

S

daughter of parents with raven-dark hair for openers) but some funny lines too. 'What'd you think I should wear?' asks the sexbomb. 'Oh,' says her friend, the letter-writing cause of all the trouble, 'something demure'. 'Oh,' says the sexbomb. 'Christian Demure. I got tons of her stuff.'

Secret Agent ○
1936, UK, 83 mins, b/w
Dir: Alfred Hitchcock
Stars: John Gielgud, Madeleine Carroll, Peter Lorre
Rating: ★★★

Following the previous year's *The 39 Steps*, Hitchcock again cast Madeleine Carroll as a feisty leading lady with considerably more get-up-and-go than the hero – here, the young John Gielgud as a spectacularly languorous spy reluctantly recruited to kill a foreign agent. Some fine set pieces including a climactic chase through a Swiss chocolate factory – and a scene-stealing performance from Peter Lorre.

Secret Agent Club, The ⊙ ⓥ
1996, US, 87 mins, colour
Dir: John Murlowski
Stars: Hulk Hogan, Lesley-Anne Down, Barry Bostwick, Richard Moll, Edward Albert, James Hong
Rating: ★

A poor man's version of *True Lies*, crossed with *The Little Rascals*, this is about the standard of children's teatime TV. Hulk Hogan has the Schwarzenegger role as the toy salesman who moonlights as a Shadow agent by night. His adventures, though, are straight out of comic books, as he pinches a secret laser gun from a group of spies who, as led by Leslie-Anne Down, are even less threatening than the bad guys from an old spoof series like *The Man from UNCLE*. Hulk's son and his racially friendly pals soon rout the villains with some ease with a collection of toy weapons, after daddy has been kidnapped and tortured by a mad scientist. For gullible five-year-olds with an old-fashioned outlook on life, it could be just the job.

Secret Beyond the Door, The ○
1948, US, 98 mins, b/w
Dir: Fritz Lang
Stars: Joan Bennett, Michael Redgrave
Rating: ★★★

Weird and wonderful movie from director Fritz Lang and star Joan Bennett, not as strong as their previous films together, *Man Hunt, The Women in the Window* and *Scarlet Street*, but definitely not your run-of-the-mill thriller. Bennett at her most beautiful and Michael Redgrave at his most tormented just manage to suspend our disbelief through a mind-boggling tale of murder, jealousy, hallucination and mental disorder, set in a mansion of rooms that are replicas of famous murder sites, and mistily photographed in black and white by the great Stanley Cortez. If it had all worked, and had a stronger script, this might even have been a masterpiece of the macabre.

Secret Four, The ○
(aka: Kansas City Confidential)
1954, US, 98 mins, b/w
Dir: Phil Karlson
Stars: John Payne, Coleen Gray
Rating: ★★★★

This tough, tense study of a robbery is directed with fine ruthlessness of purpose by Phil Karlson. The 'four' all give good portrayals, not surprising when the actors are Preston Foster, Lee Van Cleef, Jack Elam and Neville Brand. Karlson was just hitting his stride at about this time, into a five-year period in which he made a series of films that are still considered his best work. Tough, hard-hitting action films, sometimes exposing actual scandals and criminal activities, they remain a slice of American cinema to be remembered.

Secret Friends ● ⓥ
1992, UK, 98 mins, colour
Dir: Dennis Potter
Stars: Alan Bates, Gina Bellman, Tony Doyle, Frances Barber
Rating: RB

If you manage to make head or tail of Dennis Potter's enormously self-indulgent study of imaginary friends, fantasies and a disordered mind you'll be a lot wiser than we were after seeing the whole film. Flower-painter Alan Bates, haunted by a repressed past, is going off his rocker. Ex high-class hooker Gina Bellman has been unwise enough to marry him. Well, probably not. This is more likely to be one of the many manifestations of a fevered brain shown in the film. You keep waiting for something coherent to happen: but this is not Potter's plan, which appears to be to bore the hide off his audience rather than let them get any sort of grasp on anything approaching a plot. Bates is annoying; Bellman looks like Ava Gardner but hasn't the talent; Frances Barber hovers lasciviously on the fringes of the film waiting for something to do.

Secret Garden, The ⊙
1949, US, 92 mins, b/w & colour
Dir: Fred M Wilcox
Stars: Margaret O'Brien, Herbert Marshall, Dean Stockwell, Gladys Cooper
Rating: ★★★

The awesomely talented Margaret O'Brien steals the acting honours in this well-made film of Frances Hodgson Burnett's suspenseful novel. It proves to be richly atmospheric under the direction of Fred M Wilcox. Here he elicits a sensitive, attractive performance from O'Brien (not difficult, admittedly), who is joined by another child star of the Forties, Dean Stockwell. Don't adjust your set when the screen suddenly blazes into Technicolor.

Secret Garden, The ⊙
1987, UK, 96 mins, colour
Dir: Alan Grint
Stars: Gennie James, Michael Hordern, Billie Whitelaw
Rating: ★★★

Visually handsome adaptation of Frances Hodgson Burnett's popular children's novel, turned by MGM into a charming vehicle for Margaret O'Brien in 1949. This remake remains steadfastly faithful to the book, and is similarly disinclined to shy away from the serious subject of bereavement. It also benefits from some top-notch character acting by Michael Hordern (as the curmudgeonly gardener Ben) and Billie Whitelaw (perfectly cast as the Dickensian housekeeper Mrs Medlock). An engrossing couple of hours for adults and youngsters alike.

Secret Garden, The ○ ⓥ
1993, UK, 100 mins, colour
Dir: Agnieszka Holland
Stars: Kate Maberly, Maggie Smith
Rating: ★★

A competent new version of the novel about a spoiled (but unloved) 10-year-old girl, Mary, whose parents live in India and get killed in an earthquake there. Brought to the forbidding and loveless mansion of her widowed uncle and his hidebound housekeeper and servant, Mary soon proves more than a match for the lot, discovering hidden passageways, her sickly cousin Colin (who has never walked) and, of course, the secret garden of the title, where her uncle's wife died, giving premature birth to Colin, after falling off a swing. A lot depends on the central performance and Kate Maberly, although no great actress, is just right for the role. It's a bit halting in pace, though, and the ending is on the weak side.

Secret Life of Walter Mitty, The ○ ⓥ
1947, US, 104 mins, colour
Dir: Norrnan Z McLeod
Stars: Danny Kaye, Virginia Mayo, Boris Karloff
Rating: ★★★

An extension of James Thurber's famous story of a man who lives in a world of daydreams, this is a custom-built vehicle for Danny Kaye's much-admired talents in the field of comedy and mimicry. The villains' roles are rather disappointingly ordinary, especially that given to old horror master Boris Karloff, leaving Kaye as the whole show. His impressions of fearless gunman, air ace, miracle surgeon, riverboat gambler (and many more) are topped off with his virtuoso rendition of 'Anatole of Paris'.

Secret of My Success, The ○
1965, UK, 112 mins, colour
Dir: Andrew L Stone
Stars: James Booth, Lionel Jeffries, Shirley Jones, Honor Blackman
Rating: ★★

Pleasing comedy about an inept policeman who unwittingly helps three lovely but lethal ladies of crime. Lionel Jeffries does a mini-Alec Guinness by playing four parts.

Secret of My Success, The ○ ⓥ
1987, US, 110 mins, colour
Dir: Herbert Ross
Stars: Michael J Fox, Helen Slater, Richard Jordan
Rating: ★★

Hick from the sticks Michael J Fox wants the ultimate yuppie dream – a penthouse in New York, jacuzzi, a beautiful girlfriend and a private jet to go home in. Setting up in an abandoned office, his life becomes ever more complicated by the attentions of his uncle's neglected wife and the fact that the girl of his dreams is his uncle's mistress. A nice twist on the classic screwball farces of the 1930s, but given a leaden treatment and suffering from the lightweight central performance and the Eighties' vogue for a loud pop soundtrack to replace dialogue and speed up the action. The film does

capture well New York as a city of gleaming steel and concrete – but too often the characters seem to be made of the same stuff.

Secret of NIMH, The ⊙
1982, US, 82 mins, colour
Dir: Don Bluth
Voice stars: Derek Jacobi, Dom DeLuise, Shannen Doherty, Wil Wheaton
Rating: ★★★

This was the first film from Don Blurb and fellow Disney animators who tired of the way the American studio was penny pinching on their feature length films and set up in exile in Ireland. The story of a mother mouse desperately trying to save her family from a farmer's plans to plough over their home, is beautifully animated but strangely uninvolving because of a weak script. The assembled voice cast is outstanding.

Secret of Roan Inish, The ○ ⓥ
1993, US, 103 mins, colour
Dir: John Sayles
Stars: Mick Lally, Eileen Colgan, John Lynch, Jeni Courtney, Richard Sheridan
Rating: ★★★★

This gentle drama, full of Irish whimsy, makes a change for writer-director John Sayles after so much serious drama in his career. Beautifully set in a picturesque Donegal fishing village in the 1940s, it tells the story of the search by a 10-year-old girl (Jeni Courtney) for her long-lost baby brother who, local legend has it, was carried off by a mythical half-woman, half-seal creature. A charming foray into the world of Celtic mythology, this makes delightful old-fashioned entertainment which gradually draws you into its spell. The shimmeringly moody camerawork is by the great Haskell Wexler.

Secret of the Incas, The ○
1954, US, 103 mins, colour
Dir: Jerry Hopper
Stars: Charlton Heston, Nicole Maurey, Robert Young, Thomas Mitchell
Rating: ★★

Rugged, if unsubtle, jungle thriller, the kind of stuff that Steven Spielberg nowadays turns into an extravaganza. Charlton Heston is very good as the ruthless adventurer hunting a priceless Inca jewel. And he gets good support from veteran Hollywood character actor Thomas Mitchell. Colour and scenery are excellent and the plot has a neat twist at the end.

Secret Partner, The ○
1961, UK, 91 mins, b/w
Dir: Basil Dearden
Stars: Stewart Granger, Haya Harareet, Bernard Lee
Rating: ★★★

A tightly written thriller starring Stewart Granger which keeps the suspense going until the last reel. Norman Bird is excellent as a seedy, blackmailing dentist. Another unheralded, low-key winner from the consistent Basil Dearden.

Secret Rapture, The ● ⓥ
1993, UK, 96 mins, colour
Dir: Howard Davies
Stars: Juliet Stevenson, Neil Pearson, Joanne Whalley-Kilmer, Penelope Wilton
Rating: ★

Heavy drama, cheerless people: this is a doleful piece from the Film on Four stable which has an interesting performance from Juliet Stevenson (though she takes her clothes off too often) but little else to bring a smile in any sense. Not least of its deficiencies is a budget apparently so low that no-one ever wants to turn the light on. As bleak as the stone cottage whose elderly owner's death triggers the drama, the story concerns his young alcoholic widow (Joanne Whalley-Kilmer) and the foisting of her, via embittered sister Penelope Wilton and husband Alan Howard, on to Stevenson and her lover Neil Pearson, whose *volte-face* in agreeing to sell the business to Wilton for expansion is only one of the things insufficiently validated by David Hare's screenplay. The ending is at least in character with the rest, although those in a depressed mood are advised to stay clear.

Secrets & Lies ● ⓥ
1996, UK, 142 mins, colour
Dir: Mike Leigh
Stars: Timothy Spall, Brenda Blethyn, Phyllis Logan, Claire Rushbrook
Rating: ★★★

Although it starts off looking just like a long film about glum women, this tale of secret shames unnecessarily withheld from nearest and dearest is really rather good: too long overall but with one or two excellent scenes that stick in the memory. A young black businesswoman (Marianne Jean-Baptiste), still grieving for her late foster-mother, decides to seek out her birth mother. To her surprise (and everyone else's) it turns out to be frumpy, cotton-headed (white) factory worker Brenda Blethyn, whose other daughter (Claire

S

Rushbrook) is a roadsweeper. Meanwhile, the other half of this family, Blethyn's brother (Timothy Spall) and his barren wife (Phyllis Logan) live in luxury thanks to his photographic and her interior design talents. Blethyn recovers from the initial shock and gets friendly with Jean-Baptiste, resulting in both going to the 21st birthday party Spall throws for his long-unseen niece. Not surprisingly, skeletons fairly tumble from cupboards at the party, and every actor gets a big emotional scene.

Seekers, The ○
1954, UK, 90 mins, colour
Dir: Ken Annakin
Stars: Jack Hawkins, Glynis Johns
Rating: ★★

Rip-roaring saga of pioneers trying to forge new frontiers in 19th-century New Zealand against all the odds. An uncertain attempt to match the power and sweep of the American covered-wagon epics, with Maoris doing the marauding Injuns bit and the British settlers standing in for the cowboys. It has its exciting moments.

See No Evil
See: Blind Terror

See No Evil, Hear No Evil
● ⓥ
1989, US, 107 mins, colour
Dir: Arthur Hiller
Stars: Richard Pryor, Gene Wilder, Joan Severance
Rating: ★

Getting a blind man and a deaf man to be each other's eyes and ears against a gang of crooks sounds like a great comic idea. But with Wilder and Pryor offering overpitched performances (especially when giving painful impersonations of foreign doctors), the results are pretty feeble – except for a couple of bright sequences here and there. The female lead, Joan Severance, must have been hired for her stunning looks rather than acting ability and the only highspots are blind Pryor being asked to help another blind man across the road, and two blind men stalking each other with revolvers. Parents might also note that this has an amazingly high ration of four-letter words for a comedy. Still, if you want a comedy-adventure that's frantic if not funny, this could pass a couple of hours without too much pain.

See You in Hell, Darling ●
1966, US, 103 mins, colour
Dir: Robert Gist

Stars: Stuart Whitman, Janet Leigh, Eleanor Parker
Rating: ★★

A harsh, amoral gangster yarn, adapted from Norman Mailer's novel *An American Dream*. The theme and its treatment are reminiscent of Hollywood thrillers of the Forties, with Whitman as an anti-gangster television crusader who falls into the clutches of the underworld through the death of his wife. In a small part as a maid, who, clad only in towel and shower-water, tries to seduce the hero, Austrian actress Susan Denberg, with sulky stare, flaxen tresses and eyes like opaque green marble, quite walks away with the film.

See You in the Morning ● ⓥ
1988, US, 119 mins, colour
Dir: Alan J Pakula
Stars: Jeff Bridges, Alice Krige, Farrah Fawcett, Drew Barrymore, Macaulay Culkin
Rating: ★

It's hard to know what to say about a film as dull as this. Of two marriages in 1984, one breaks up, the other leaves the wife a widow. The husband of the first (Jeff Bridges) marries the widow (Alice Krige), misses his two children and has a few minor problems with his two stepchildren. This all takes two hours to unfold and the best the film can do in the way of a spanner in the works is having the husband sleeping with his ex-wife (Farrah Fawcett) the night after his mother dies. The script never gives the players a chance to pluck the heartstrings and even gets mawkish at times. You can see that director Pakula was trying to make a valid human document here, but his writers have let him down by the sheer ordinariness of their script.

Sellout, The ●
1975, UK/Italy, 102 mins, colour
Dir: Peter Collinson
Stars: Richard Widmark, Oliver Reed, Gayle Hunnicutt
Rating: ★

This espionage thriller must have seemed an attractively downbeat drama during its conception although, as it turns out, the screenplay gives it very little character. Oliver Reed plays an ex-CIA agent who defected to Moscow, and is now lured to Israel where he is the target for both CIA and KGB killers. The stunt driving is by Remy Julienne, so effective on *The Italian Job*, although here the object seems only to

be for the cars to knock down as many unnecessary obstacles as possible.

Semi-Tough ●
1977, US, 103 mins, colour
Dir: Michael Ritchie
Stars: Burt Reynolds, Kris Kristofferson, Jill Clayburgh
Rating: ★★

Jill Clayburgh, the delightful Hollywood actress who sounds as though she gargles honey, makes a silk purse out of a sow's ear in this free-wheeling comedy. The film, mainly about the relationship between Ms Clayburgh, Burt Reynolds and a miscast Kris Kristofferson, tries very, very hard to be outrageous. That it succeeds in being merely quite funny is to our advantage. Reynolds' natural charm supplies most of the laughs – more, in fact, than the aimless script has any right to expect.

Senator Was Indiscreet, The ○
(aka: Mr Ashton Was Indiscreet)
1947, US, 81 mins, b/w
Dir: George S Kaufman
Stars: William Powell, Ella Raines, Peter Lind Hayes
Rating: ★★★

Don't miss the chance to see this rare screwball comedy, written by Charles MacArthur (husband of Helen Hayes and father of James MacArthur) whose Hollywood career was harmed by the McCarthy blacklist. His witty script is anarchic without being too satirical, pitching William Powell's asinine senator, up for President, into a series of splendidly ridiculous situations. Especially funny is the sequence where Powell takes on a bunch of kids in an IQ test – and loses.

Send Me No Flowers ○
1964, US, 1964 mins, colour
Dir: Norman Jewison
Stars: Rock Hudson, Doris Day
Rating: ★★★★

You'll get a good quota of laughs from this grey comedy (it isn't really sinister enough to be called black) about a hypochondriac (Rock Hudson) who believes, through a misunderstanding with his long-suffering doctor, that he is dying from a heart condition. Doris Day was probably the only Hollywood actress of the time who could have handled this brand of light, bright comedy-with-kinks in such expert fashion. Tony Randall is even better than usual as the inevitable sidekick of the hero, and toothsome Paul Lynde also scores as a funeral director with a lugubrious leer, giving away green stamps with his plot reservations. But the real winner is Julius Epstein's screenplay, full of funny lines and situations which enable the actors to make the most of themselves.

Sense and Sensibility ○ Ⓥ
1995, UK, 135 mins, colour
Dir: Ang Lee
Stars: Emma Thompson, Kate Winslet, Alan Rickman, Hugh Grant, Greg Rowe, Imogen Stubbs
Rating: ★★★

Elegant, literate and rather long in the telling, this is one of those Jane Austen pieces that makes sharp observations on society and relationships while steering its heroines through some rocky romances to the inevitable double-wedding at the end. Leading lady Emma Thompson also wrote the screenplay, unselfishly giving the best lines to supporting actor Hugh Laurie, who snaps them up like a hungry shark. Emma and her two sisters are left penniless (well, by the standards of the landed gentry) when their dead father's money goes to his son by another marriage. Left with a small income but nowhere to live, the girls are gifted a Devon country cottage on the estate of a crass cousin. Emma and middle sister Kate Winslet become the subject of various amorous entanglements, but, just when an engagement seems on the horizon, their suitors gallop mysteriously over it, not to reappear until Ms Austen's plot has unravelled. All this is only marginally intriguing, although it's nice to see Alan Rickman, so often the bad guy, in a more kindly light.

Separate Tables ○
1958, US, 98 mins, b/w
Dir: Delbert Mann
Stars: Deborah Kerr, Rita Hayworth, David Niven, Burt Lancaster
Rating: ★★★★

This fine, enjoyable film about the hidden weaknesses of the guests at an English seaside hotel (adapted from his own play by Terence Rattigan) provides absorbing entertainment and a feast of fine acting. For their sensitive portrayals, David Niven, as the fake major, and Wendy Hiller, as the hotel proprietress, both won deserved Academy Awards. Niven's last few scenes in the film are especially moving.

September ○ Ⓥ
1987, US, 83 mins, colour
Dir: Woody Allen

Stars: Mia Farrow, Denholm Elliott, Sam Waterston, Elaine Stritch, Dianne Wiest, Jack Warden
Rating: ★

Woody Allen shot this script with one set of actors, then decided to scrap the results and do it all over again with a completely different cast. He should have quit while he was ahead. Boring is the word and only Britain's Denholm Elliott in an elegant, low-key performance, can handle Allen's overwrought romantic dialogue with the appropriate kid gloves. The lives of these artificial characters of fiction, and of Mia Farrow's mother and stepfather (Elaine Stritch, Jack Warden), whose past is clearly copied from Lana Turner's, are only of the vaguest interest and, if your attention is gripped at all by this sexual merry-go-round, it will be by how the actors handle their key emotional scenes: Farrow best, Dianne Wiest whiningly worst and so on. The film is largely photographed in brown and yellow except for scenes involving a pool table for which such filters would clearly be inappropriate.

September Affair ○
1950, US, 104 mins, b/w
Dir: William Dieterle
Stars: Joan Fontaine, Joseph Cotten, Françoise Rosay
Rating: ★★★

Exceptionally well-made weepie about a couple who decide to seize their chance for love late in life, when they are reported killed in an air crash. Director William Dieterle steers it on its romantic way with tremendous pictorial flair. Although many of his films took Academy Awards, Dieterle himself never won one.

Sergeant, The ●
1968, US, 107 mins, colour
Dir: John Flynn
Stars: Rod Steiger, John Phillip Law, Ludmila Mikael
Rating: ★★★

John Flynn's first feature film – he later directed *The Jerusalem File* and the brilliant crime thriller *The Outfit* – is one of the most powerful portrayals of a man destroyed by his own homosexuality to be put on screen. Rod Steiger pours everything into his portrait of Master-Sergeant Callan and it hurts to watch the man's disintegration. It isn't a likeable film, nor exactly an enjoyable one. If it were a book, however, you would find it hard to put it down.

Sergeant Bilko ○
1996, US, 99 mins, colour
Dir: Jonathan Lynn
Stars: Steve Martin, Dan Aykroyd, Glenne Headly, Phil Hartman
Rating: ★★★

A jolly if perhaps not riotously amusing reprise of the famous Fifties TV series. With Martin and Aykroyd as acceptable substitutes for Phil Silvers and Paul Ford, director Lynn keeps the fun simple and the characters the caricatures they were in the original. Master-Sgt Ernie Bilko is the real power behind the throne at the Fort Baxter US Army base. In charge of any gambling racket going, Bilko's motorpool misfits live a life of Riley – until an old enemy, Col Thorn (Phil Hartman) comes on the scene. Thorn is determined to hang Bilko from the yardarm but the sergeant is as adept at slipping his neck from the noose, as leaving his ever-loving girlfriend (Headly) at the altar. Things come to a head over a hovertank that hovers but never hits its target... The results run much like an elongated episode of the TV show: fast, noisy, easy on the eye, and occasionally even funny.

Sergeant Rutledge ◐
1960, US, 111 mins, colour
Dir: John Ford
Stars: Jeffrey Hunter, Woody Strode, Constance Towers
Rating: ★★★★

This was truly a landmark film, as it marked a rare occasion when a movie from a major studio (Warner Brothers) depicted a black actor as the central heroic figure. Woody Strode gives a moving performance as a sergeant accused of the murder of his commanding officer and rape and murder of the dead man's daughter. While the film's stance on tackling racism is laudable, the courtroom setting proves too claustrophobic for director John Ford, and the master of the unspoken emotion has to rely on long speeches to get his points across. Still first-class entertainment, though, intriguing to the end.

Sergeant York ○ Ⓥ
1941, US, 134 mins, b/w
Dir: Howard Hawks
Stars: Gary Cooper, Walter Brennan
Rating: ★★★★

One of Gary Cooper's finest roles, as a true-life peace-loving farmer who becomes a hero of World War One. The film's patriotic sentiments were immensely popular in the dark early

S

days of World War Two and Cooper's sensitive and caring performance was rightly rewarded with an Oscar. There's a nice balance between rural and combat sequences and simply superb black-and-white photography by Arthur Edeson. Too long, perhaps, but that's partially justified by the atmosphere the movie builds.

Serial Mom ● ⓥ
1994, US, 93 mins, colour
Dir: John Waters
Stars: Kathleen Turner, Sam Waterston, Ricki Lake, Matthew Lilliard, Mary Jo Catiett
Rating: ★★★

Housewife Beverly Sutphin (Kathleen Turner) is a perfect, all-American mum with one major drawback – she's a serial killer too. Turner gives a perfectly honed performance, whether protecting daughter Misty (Ricki Lake) by running her two-timing boyfriend through with a fire poker, clubbing to death with a leg of lamb a woman who won't rewind her videotapes or, perhaps most memorable, lavishing obscene phone calls on a selfish neighbour. Arrested for six murders, Beverly soon becomes a media favourite in this dark satire from John (*Hairspray*) Waters at somewhere near his best. Not for the easily offended.

Serpico ●
1973, US, 129 mins, colour
Dir: Sidney Lumet
Stars: Al Pacino, John Randolph, Cornelia Sharpe
Rating: ★★★

Al Pacino gives a very edgy and intelligent performance as Frank Serpico, the honest and idealistic cop who sees corruption all around him. Based on a true story, director Sidney Lumet's intense and hard-hitting thriller hits all the right notes and maintains its dramatic tension from beginning to end. Although Pacino's portrayal dominates the film, all the supporting roles are finely cast, particularly Tony Roberts, who plays an officer close to the mayor's investigating committee.

Servant, The ● ⓥ
1964, UK, 110 mins, b/w
Dir: Joseph Losey
Stars: Dirk Bogarde, James Fox, Sarah Miles, Wendy Craig
Rating: ★★★★

An illogical ending is the one sin committed by Joseph Losey's otherwise splendid black-and-white investigation into the treachery and power of evil. Dirk Bogarde does brilliantly as the calculating servant, especially in the lighter scenes after Tony (James Fox) has re-engaged him, when for a few moments he becomes more akin to a nagging housewife. For the most part, however, the performance is more likely to make your flesh creep than to tickle your funnybone.

Set It Off ● ⓥ
1996, US, 122 mins, colour
Dir: F Gary Gray
Stars: Jada Pinkett, Queen Latifah, Vivica A Fox, Kimberley Elise, John C McGinley
Rating: ★★

Done down by life, four young black women from the 'hood take to the streets as bank robbers. At its adrenalin-surging best, this is an action blast, but the plot is, unlike the girls, old and tired and its downbeat ending obvious always. The girls themselves, though, put body and soul into their roles, particularly Latifah, emoting fiercely as the gun-wielding, foul-mouthed, lesbian hardman of the group. The film has attitude to spare – too much, perhaps, for the good of the characters, who fail to win as much of our sympathy as they should. And, at 122 minutes, it does go on a bit.

Set Up, The ○
1949, US, 72 mins, b/w
Dir: Robert Wise
Stars: Robert Ryan, Audrey Totter
Rating: ★★★★

Powerful, thrilling and very moving in turn, this fine film is now universally recognised as one of the two or three best boxing movies ever made. It was directed by Robert Wise long before he won Oscars for *West Side Story* and *The Sound of Music,* and contains one of the screen's great performances from Robert Ryan as an ageing boxer whose manager hasn't bothered to tell him that he is supposed to take a dive. Cleverly, the action takes place within the same time span as the movie, which underlines the tension.

Se7en ● ⓥ
1995, US, 127 mins, colour
Dir: David Fincher
Stars: Morgan Freeman, Brad Pitt, Gwyneth Paltrow, Kevin Spacey, Richard Roundtree
Rating: ★★★

Grim and grisly serial killer thrillers often make gripping and exciting adult entertainment, but here's one that's just too much. Evisceration runs riot as a maniac murderer picks out victims who exemplify one of the seven deadly sins and puts them to death in the most gruesome and revolting ways possible, often forcing the victims to carve themselves up as part of the slow-death punishment. If you think *this* is a turnoff, wait (or don't) for the quite disgusting climax which will send few away happy. Morgan Freeman is outstanding as the near-retirement detective, forced to take on a young, eager partner (Brad Pitt) in his last days, and even counsel the man's newly pregnant wife (Gwyneth Paltrow, weepy as usual). There's an excitingly shot chase sequence towards the end, when the cops corner the killer, but the intense horror of it all ultimately leaves you not stunned but simply wanting to go away and watch some other film.

Seven Chances ☉
1925, US, 69 mins, b/w
Dir: Buster Keaton
Stars: Buster Keaton
Rating: ★★★

Lovely, cleanly made Buster Keaton comedy, directed by the star. It's the one in which Buster has but a few hours to find a bride and ends up getting pursued by a veritable army of ferocious women. He is also pursued, in another scene, by an avalanche of rocks – yet another sequence that reflects Keaton's unshowy mastery of comic timing.

Seven Cities of Gold ○
1955, US, 103 mins, colour
Dir: Robert D Webb
Stars: Richard Egan, Anthony Quinn, Michael Rennie, Rita Moreno
Rating: ★

This is a turgid action and adventure yarn about Spanish explorers in 18th-century Mexico and California. A sincere religious theme fails to lift this history book Western from the routine class, although it provides Michael Rennie with a plum role, as the priest along on the expedition. Acting with great feeling, he's streets ahead even of such spirited company as Rita Moreno and Anthony Quinn.

Seven Days in May ○
1964, US, 120 mins, b/w
Dir: John Frankenheimer
Stars: Burt Lancaster, Kirk Douglas, Fredric March, Ava Gardner
Rating: ★★★

John Frankenheimer's powerful thriller about a coup d'etat in the United

States. Burt Lancaster plays the grim-faced leader of the military conspirators, Fredric March the President who uses advance warning of the take-over to try and prevent it. The film is admirable for its brisk efficiency. March is particularly good as the President, but it's in Edmond O'Brien's senator and Martin Balsam's presidential aide and life-long friend that one sees the breath of life. Ava Gardner is better here than for years past. For Lancaster and Kirk Douglas, it seems too often an exercise in acting technique – but Rod Serling's crackling screenplay keeps their performances rooted in reality.

Seven Days to Noon ○
1950, UK, 93 mins, b/w
Dir: John Boulting
Stars: Barry Jones, Olive Sloane, André Morell, Joan Hickson
Rating: ★★★★

A classic thriller from the Boulting Brothers in the days before they turned their talents to comedy. Barry Jones has the best part of his career as the unbalanced scientist who threatens to blow up the Houses of Parliament unless his demands are met. The suspense grows almost unbearable in the subsequent search for the scientist and the bomb he has planted.

7 Faces of Dr Lao ○
1964, US, 95 mins, colour
Dir: George Pal
Stars: Tony Randall, Barbara Eden, Arthur O'Connell, John Ericson
Rating: ★★★

That expert light comedian Tony Randall enjoys himself hugely in a very different characterisation as a Chinese magician – at large in a turn-of-the-century America – who can turn himself into anything. The story is slyly engaging and the special effects – when the magician changes himself into all kinds of creatures, natural and mythical – are admirable.

Seven Hills of Rome ○
1957, US/Italy, 104 mins, colour
Dir: Roy Rowland
Stars: Mario Lanza, Marisa Allasio, Peggie Castle
Rating: ★★

Made a year before Lanza's death, this musical might well have been titled *An American in Rome*. But, in keeping with the trends of the time, the waif-like Continental girl, as personified by Leslie Caron, was replaced by a busty Italian charmer, in this case Marisa

Allasio, who had already built up a reputation in some torrid melodramas. Lanza, cast as a successful singer revisiting the land of his fathers, offers a liberal display of tonsils and interesting impressions of Dean Martin, Perry Como, Frankie Laine and even Louis Armstrong! Ms Allasio offers a liberal helping of daring decolletage hardly in keeping with her role as a sweet Italian working girl. But the film is stolen from both of them by impish Italian comedian Renato Rascel.

Seven Little Foys, The ○
1955, US, 95 mins, colour
Dir: Melville Shavelson
Stars: Bob Hope, Milly Vitale
Rating: ★★★

Based on a true story, this musical whimsical-sentimental look at the life of renowned vaudeville performer Eddie Foy cramps Bob Hope's style by casting him in an unsympathetic and uncomic role. It's left to James Cagney, recreating his Oscar-winning role from *Yankee Doodle Dandy* of song-and-dance man George M Cohan, to steal the show. Together he and Hope hoof their way through 'Mary's a Grand Old Name'and 'Yankee Doodle Dandy' and momentarily the screen lights up.

Seven Nights in Japan ○
1976, UK, 104 mins, colour
Dir: Lewis Gilbert
Stars: Michael York, Hidemi Aoki, James Villiers
Rating: ★

A truly sticky romance about an English prince who falls for a Japanese geisha girl who doubles as a tour-bus conductress. It does have one very funny line, when tourist Yolande Donlan (in for a brief cameo) asks her husband, with regard to a statue: 'How many concubines did he have?' Replies hubby, with some logic: 'I guess he had 'em all.'

Seven Samurai ◐ ⓥ
1954, Japan, 208 mins, b/w
Dir: Akira Kurosawa
Stars: Takashi Shimura, Toshiro Mifune
Rating: ★★★★★

Akira Kurosawa took an elemental Western 'good guys versus bad guys' plot and turned it into a classic epic which is still probably the best-known – and one of the best – films to come from Japan where, at the time of its making, it was that country's most expensive picture ever. Kurosawa's pacing is immaculate and allows for

periods of calm in which to establish character, punctuated by viscerally exciting bursts of action. These culminate in the extraordinary climactic battle between the samurai and the bandits which ranks among the very finest combat sequences ever put on film. Unlike John Sturges' remake, *The Magnificent Seven*, the characters grow originally from the action and are not conveniently established by star-castings. And the performances – even those of the bit players – are superb, with Toshiro Mifune's portrait of the harebrained but courageous young warrior dominating.

Seven Sinners ○
(aka: Doomed Cargo)
1936, UK, 70 mins, b/w
Dir: Albert De Courville
Stars: Edmund Lowe, Constance Cummings
Rating: ★★★

A vintage thriller with a clever plot, likeable characters and an express train as one of its settings (as in Hitchcock's *The Lady Vanishes* two years later). Both films were written by that distinguished duo, Frank Launder and Sidney Gilliat. Their plot developments here may well have you struggling to identify the guilty party.

Seven Sinners ○
1940, US, 86 mins, b/w
Dir: Tay Garnett
Stars: Marlene Dietrich, John Wayne
Rating: ★★★

'We don't need her around,' someone complains, 'the Navy already has plenty of destroyers.' The reference is to Marlene Dietrich, singing siren of the South Seas, who takes John Wayne's mind away from ships. Sprawling, brawling entertainment, made in the wake of *Destry Rides Again*, with three songs and some vigorous action. A bit rough-hewn.

7th Cavalry ○
1956, US, 75 mins, colour
Dir: Joseph H Lewis
Stars: Randolph Scott, Barbara Hale
Rating: ★★★

This Western is just a shade different, thanks to Peter Packer's screenplay, and especially to the direction of Joseph H Lewis. He never really rose above the second feature, but turned in some fine work within the genre. The story is about a cavalry officer accused of cowardice who is placed in charge of misfits and 'ne'er-do-wells' detailed to bury the dead after the massacre of

S

the Little Big Horn. Good cast of 'misfits' includes Jay C Flippen and Denver Pyle.

7th Dawn, The ◐

1964, US, 123 mins, colour
Dir: Lewis Gilbert
Stars: William Holden, Susannah York, Capucine, Tetsuro Tamba, Sydney Tafler
Rating: ★

A colourful adventure-romance set in the terrorist-torn Malaya of the 1950s. The story is the old reliable of two men, friends in the war against the Japanese who, years later, find themselves on opposite sides. It's all quite exciting, although the ending is a disappointing anti-climax. Of the four stars, Capucine is the only one who gives her role any real feeling, as the other three – William Holden, Susannah York and Tetsuro Tamba go through absolute hell in rain, mud and undergrowth to save her from hanging for a crime she did not commit. Sydney Tafler is very good in support as a sympathetic police chief. Director Lewis Gilbert drives his players hard, although his efforts are often stunted by Karl Tunberg's clichéd script. Sample: Ms York (discovered swimming in the nude): 'I'm in excellent condition.' Holden: 'Yes, you look in good shape.'

Seventh Heaven ○

1937, US, 102 mins, b/w
Dir: Henry King
Stars: Simone Simon, James Stewart, Jean Hersholt, Gale Sondergaard
Rating: ★★

This wartime romance is a tear-strewn remake of the 1927 classic, with James Stewart and Simone Simon in the roles created by Charles Farrell and Janet Gaynor. This time, however, acting honours are secured by screen schemer Gale Sondergaard as the cruelly dominant Nana. She was unlucky not to be nominated for an Oscar, the year after she actually won the award, for *Anthony Adverse*.

Seventh Match, The

See: Sarah

Seventh Seal, The ◐ ⓥ

1957, Sweden, 96 mins, b/w
Dir: Ingmar Bergman
Stars: Max Von Sydow, Bengt Ekerot
Rating: ★★★★★

One of Ingmar Bergman's most brilliant and approachable films, as a knight returning from the Crusades plays chess with Death for the lives of his companions while the plague rages all around. Full of images that stay in the mind (especially in the final sequence), *The Seventh Seal* ranks with *The Silence* and *Wild Strawberries* as the best of Bergman's films, but is probably the one you should see above all others. As the knight, Max Von Sydow made his first major impact on international audiences.

Seventh Sign, The ● ⓥ

1988, US, 97 mins, colour
Dir: Carl Schultz
Stars: Demi Moore, Michael Biehn, Jurgen Prochnow, Lee Garlington, John Heard
Rating: ★★

This preposterous poppycock, mumbo-jumbo in the *Omen* mould, is stylishly and emotively made and benefits from an impassioned performance by Demi Moore in the leading role. She's a pregnant American wife who alone can prevent the Apocalypse, the destruction of the world. You see, we've already had the rivers of blood, the desert village frozen in ice, an eclipse, the death of the oceans and all that. The birth of the first baby without a soul (Demi's), due to the emptying of the celestial Guf (no comment) is the final sign – and that's what she has to prevent. It's to the credit of the actors and technicians that this arrant nonsense keeps our attention if not our belief. Michael Biehn is sincere as Moore's husband, Peter Friedman fun as the priest who turns out to be Pilate's gatekeeper (yes he does) and Manny Jacobs amusing as a knowledgable young Jew who has trouble helping Demi with the New Testament because it's 'not my book'.

Seven Thunders ○

(aka: The Beasts of Marseilles)
1957, UK, 100 mins, b/w
Dir: Hugo Fregonese
Stars: Stephen Boyd, Tony Wright, Anna Gaylor
Rating: ★★★

A good Marseilles setting lifts this prisoner-of-war escape film out of the rut. The tensions of the occupied town, outwardly unruffled, inwardly seething with intrigue, are effectively suggested. James Robertson Justice is colourfully improbable as a Frenchman who offers freedom but deals in double-cross. Anna Gaylor, a French actress with looks, charm and style, and Kathleen Harrison (miscast but great fun as Madame Abou) add body to a supporting cast in which

Rosalie Crutchley, Marcel Pagliero and Eugene Deckers give the settings a believable smack of wartime Marseilles life. Director Hugo Fregonese's skilful handling of the suspense reaches a nail-biting peak when the two English heroes are forced to make a desperate bid for freedom after the Germans begin a systematic destruction of their quarter of the city. Steely-eyed Anton Diffring is inevitably cast as a Nazi officer.

7th Voyage of Sinbad, The ○ ⓥ

1958, US, 87 mins, colour
Dir: Nathan Juran
Stars: Kerwin Mathews, Kathryn Grant
Rating: ★★★

The film that started the DynaMation craze and made the reputation of the system's creator, Ray Harryhausen, who provides monsters galore to thrill children and adults alike. A snakewoman, a dragon, a man-eating Cyclops, two-headed rocs and living skeletons (to become Harryhausen's favourite 'characters' in later films) are all impressive.

Seven-ups, The ◐

1973, US, 103 mins, colour
Dir: Philip D'Antoni
Stars: Roy Scheider, Tony Lo Bianco
Rating: ★★★★

Philip D'Antoni, who produced *The French Connection,* turned director himself with this even-darker, hard-driving detective yarn, with spectacularly successful results. The set-pieces, especially the nerve-grinding mid-film sequence in a carwash which becomes a chamber of doom, are hard, uncompromising and right on target. Roy Scheider contributes a performance of almost frightening power in the pivotal role of the senior detective hunting down a group of loan-sharks: no soft-centred detective this. The sharp, low-key colour photography of Urs Furrer is absolutely right, and the final dialogue between Scheider and Tony Lo Bianco forms a devasting and brilliantly fashioned coda to a very cinematic crime thriller.

Seven Waves Away

See: Abandon Ship

Seven Ways from Sundown ○

1960, US, 87 mins, colour
Dir: Harry Keller
Stars: Audie Murphy, Barry Sullivan, John McIntire
Rating: ★★★

Better-than-average Audie Murphy Western, with an excellent performance from Barry Sullivan as a wily outlaw whom a young lawman – his name is Seven-Ways-from-Sundown Jones and thus the title – has to escort back to justice. Clair Huffaker's inventive screenplay has the vein of humour that keeps this sort of film going well: the continual element of surprise and turning-of-the-tables, deft acting from all concerned and of course, the shootout – here with a subtle difference. Exciting stuff.

7 Women ◐

1964, US, 80 mins, colour
Dir: John Ford
Stars: Anne Bancroft, Eddie Albert, Mike Mazurki, Flora Robson, Margaret Leighton, Sue Lyon, Anna Lee
Rating: ★★★

John Ford forsook Westerns, but stayed with action, to make this absorbing adventure film about a mission on the violent Chinese-Mongolian border in 1935. Anne Bancroft has the John Wayne role as a cigarette-smoking, jackbooted, stetsoned doctor, and plays it superbly, while the Metrocolor photography is absolutely splendid. Eddie Albert and Mike Mazurki lead the men.

Seven Year Itch, The ◯ ⓥ

1955, US, 105 mins, colour
Dir: Billy Wilder
Stars: Marilyn Monroe, Tom Ewell
Rating: ★★★★

Always entertaining, at times vastly amusing, this famous comedy has Tom Ewell at the top of his form as a fortyish husband left alone while his wife and son go off on holiday. Soon, he forms the famous but abortive liaison with the blonde upstairs (Marilyn Monroe), his wolfish dreams coming to nothing in the face of her brick-solid ingenuousness and his own ineptitude. Clever performances by the stars, with the funniest sequences of all being those in which Ewell dreams of himself as the great lover.

Severed Head, A ●

1970, UK, 96 mins, colour
Dir: Dick Clement
Stars: Lee Remick, Richard Attenborough, Ian Holm, Claire Bloom
Rating: ★

Determinedly smart and sophisticated comedy about partner-swapping in the supertax belt. Adapted by Frederic Raphael from the hit play, which was in turn taken by J B Priestley and Iris

Murdoch from Ms Murdoch's blackly funny novel of the early Sixties. Director Dick Clement accentuates the glossiness a shade too much, but the ladies in the cast, Lee Remick, Claire Bloom, Jennie Linden and Ann Firbank, all acquit themselves admirably. Pretty arid, though.

Sex and the Single Girl ◯

1964, US, 114 mins, colour
Dir: Richard Quine
Stars: Tony Curtis, Natalie Wood, Henry Fonda, Lauren Bacall
Rating: ★★

A sex comedy that's as crisp and, polished as the thin ice over which it go skilfully skates. In an hilarious last 20 minutes, the starry cast are all outshone by Larry Storch as a hatchet-faced motor-cycle cop with cars stamped on his machine. At other times, Henry Fonda and Lauren Bacall show their experience in coolly outpointing Tony Curtis and Natalie Wood. Mel Ferrer, Edward Everett Horton and even Count Basie and his Orchestra are all in there somewhere as Helen Gurley Brown's book (allegedly the source material) is pushed aside in favour of sex 'n' slapstick capers.

sex, lies, and videotape ● ⓥ

1989, US, 100 mins, colour
Dir: Steven Soderbergh
Stars: James Spader, Andie MacDowell, Peter Gallagher, Laura San Giacomo
Rating: ★★★

Although this piece is not exactly ideal cinema material,. its deliberate pace, carefully considered acting and doomy background music do sneak under your guard after a while. The catalyst to the action, such as it is, is James Spader as a drifter majoring in weirdness who looks up an old friend (Peter Gallagher) whose affair with his wife's sister (Laura San Giacomo) is on the verge of writing finis to his crumbling yuppie marriage to Andie MacDowell. Spader's occupation is interviewing women about their sex lives, and in the course of the next few days, some 'trapped' people are freed and 'free' people deservedly trapped. Despite its foul language and sombre approach to the eponymous items, this is a film which champions, in the end, all the traditional values of love and happiness. Spader is perfectly cast as the alienated soul who can only 'get on' with his tapes, and MacDowell gives a glowing account of the wronged wife who, clearly going round the bend at the start of the film, is accidentally and

miraculously gifted with a chance to repair her life.

SFW ● ⓥ

1994, US, 96 mins, colour
Dir: Jefery Levy
Stars: Stephen Dorff, Reese Witherspoon, Jake Busey, Joey Lauren Adams, Pamela Gidley, Richard Portnow
Rating: ★★★★

A strange, interesting and probably seminal film: not so much the hostage situation as the situation of hostage as celebrity – a concept nobody's explored before. After 36 days of being held by an obscure terrorist group – an epic siege that ends in a shootout with every minute being shown on national TV at the insistence of the terrorists, Cliff Spab (Stephen Dorff) finds himself trapped in the limelight. Everybody wants a piece of the man worshipped by millions for his don't-care attitudes. Dorff is excellent, but Reece Witherspoon is not entirely well cast as his vis-à-vis, the girl from the better side of the tracks who's the five-week siege's only other survivor.

Shadow, The ◐ ⓥ

1994, US, 107 mins, colour
Dir: Russell Mulcahy
Stars: Alec Baldwin, Penelope Ann Miller, John Lone, Alan Arkin, Tim Curry, Ian McKellen
Rating: ★★

Comic-book rubbish with very watchable special effects (and lots of them), this runs like an old Republic serial of the Fifties on a multi-million dollar budget. When Alec Baldwin's caped crusader is trapped in rising water inside a locked chamber, you almost expect 'Next Week: Episode 16 –The Cyclotrode Ray' to flash across the screen. Paying little attention to logic – the hero and villain (John Lone) have equal powers yet the heroine (Penelope Arm Miller) can be hypnotised by one and not the other – the film charges into a story of a man who turned from evil in Tibet and re-emerged tö fight it 'in that most wretched lair of iniquity we know as New York City'. Much of the dialogue springs as if balloons from the printed page, and the acting is appropriately rudimentary – rather more so, perhaps, in the cases of Ian McKellen and Tim Curry, as the heroine's father and villain's smarmy ally.

Shadowlands ◯ ⓥ

1993, UK, 131 mins, colour
Dir: Richard Attenborough

Stars: Anthony Hopkins, Debra Winger, Edward Hardwicke, Michael Denison, Joseph Mazzello, John Wood
Rating: ★★

Impeccable performances by Anthony Hopkins, Debra Winger and especially Edward Hardwicke (as Hopkins' brother) illuminate this story of the initially unspoken love affair between the academic and children's author C S Lewis and the Jewish Communist American poet Joy Gresham. It's their efforts that touch the heart in this otherwise dusty account of a dying woman that might almost be called *A Stately Way to Go*. Director Richard Attenborough has not so much filmed William Nicholson's fine play as embalmed it. But the dialogue, as literate as Lewis himself, and with a welcome sense of gallows humour, proves a sturdy ally to the actors' efforts. A film that will bore children, though patient adults will find the dialogue and acting enough to sustain them.

Shadow Conspiracy ◐ ⓥ

1996, US, 112 mins, colour
Dir: George P Cosmatos
Stars: Charlie Sheen, Donald Sutherland, Linda Hamilton, Ben Gazzara, Stephen Lang, Sam Waterston
Rating: ★★

There are the makings of a good thriller here if only the characters had other lines to say. There's a plot to assassinate the US president and the members of the think tank who've latched on to it are wiped out – leaving only one member, who runs straight to his former pupil Bobby Bishop (Sheen), now a presidential adviser. Soon the survivor (Theodore Bikel) becomes the hitman's latest victim, leaving Sheen to go on the run for the rest of the picture. For a top man, Sheen's not too bright: it takes two calls and two near misses from death for him to realise his mobile's being monitored. But then whom can he trust? Back at the White House, chief of staff Sutherland and vice-president Gazzara are only two of those looking foxy enough to earn our suspicions. Joined by reporter Hamilton, Sheen has only his wits and a sloppy script to combat the bad guy's armoury of technology. Action scenes are well orchestrated by the director and the piece is thunderingly well scored by Bruce Broughton and has excitement a-plenty, including a careering subway chase. Sheen runs and runs, but he just can't get away from that damned screenplay.

Shadow Makers ◐ ⓥ
(aka: Fat Man and Little Boy)

1989, US, 127 mins, colour
Dir: Roland Joffé
Stars: Paul Newman, Dwight Schultz, Bonnie Bedelia, John Cusack
Rating: ★

Immaculately set in its period, this film about the making of the first atomic bomb by the Americans is not a bad movie, merely a dull one. But, at 127 minutes, that's almost as grievous a sin. Almost nothing happens until near the end, when one of the main characters gets burned by radiation, and there's very little that Newman (as the military head of the project), Schultz (as Oppenheimer, the brains behind it), Bedelia, Cusack, Laura Dern, Natasha Richardson and the rest of a very distinguished cast can do to enliven it. A film that talks itself out of being any good.

Shadow of a Doubt ○ ⓥ

1943, US, 108 mins, b/w
Dir: Alfred Hitchcock
Stars: Teresa Wright, Joseph Cotten, MacDonald Carey
Rating: ★★★★★

Perceptive as well as suspenseful, this is one of Alfred Hitchcock's best all-round films. The thread of unease is skilfully woven into the narrative, gradually becoming stronger as Young Charlie (Teresa Wright) begins to suspect that her beloved Uncle Charlie (Joseph Cotten) may not be the sunny, uncomplicated figure she always thought. Further developments ensure engrossing viewing and a chilling climax.

Shadow of the Thin Man ○

1941, US, 95 mins, b/w
Dir: W S Van Dyke 11
Stars: William Powell, Myrna Loy
Rating: ★★

The fourth *Thin Man* film and pretty thin it is too, even if the teaming of William Powell and Myrna Loy is still a joy to behold. This time the sleuthing socialites are visiting a race-track when a jockey is murdered. MGM used the occasion to show off its latest contract players, in this case Donna Reed and Barry Nelson.

Shadows and Fog ◐ ⓥ

1991, US, 86 mins, b/w
Dir: Woody Allen
Stars: Woody Allen, John Malkovich, Mia Farrow, John Cusack
Rating: ★★

Woody Allen's black-and-white pastiche offers expressionistic frolics with a few light laughs for those in the mood. In a mittel-European town of the 1920s, a killer lurches through the fog strangling his victims. Woody's Kleinmann (little man, get it?) staggers in bewilderment between vigilante factions while seeking to evade the long arm of the law and the clutches of the killer. Waiting for guest appearances by Madonna, Lily Tomlin, Jodie Foster, Kate Nelligan and others helps to stave off tedium from time to time, though authentic Allen one-liners are as thin on the ground as the dry ice is thick. The best line goes to Jodie Foster. 'I've never paid for sex in my life,' Woody protests. But she is much wiser. 'Oh,' she says lightly, 'you just think you haven't.'

Shag ◐ ⓥ

1988, US, 100 mins, colour
Dir: Zelda Barron
Stars: Phoebe Cates, Annabeth Gish, Bridget Fonda, Page Hannah, Scott Coffey, Shirley Anne Field
Rating: ★

Shag is a drag. It's difficult to understand what made director Zelda Barron, who specialises in stories of close-knit girl friendships, actually want to re-create a 1963 beach film, unless she discerned some qualities in the script that don't make themselves apparent on screen. The story follows pretty much familiar lines – four teenage girls escape parental control to set up a fun weekend on the beach – except that, unlike the similarly coiffed Phoebe Cates here, Annette Funicello would never have gone 'all the way'! The girls show about as much talent as the strictly one-dimensional script will allow, although Annabeth Gish does invest her role – the pudgy wallflower – with a special glow that the others (even Bridget Fonda, at this early stage of her career) don't have. Shag, by the way, is the name of a dance supposedly all the rage at the time.

Shaggy DA, The ☉

1976, US, 91 mins, colour
Dir: Robert Stevenson
Stars: Dean Jones, Tim Conway, Suzanne Pleshette
Rating: ★★★

This Disney canine caper is based on a book by Felix Salten, the author of *Bambi*, and is a follow-up to the studio's riotous 1959 film *The Shaggy Dog*. Dean Jones has the role originally played by Tommy Kirk as a young lawyer running for the office of District Attorney, but whose past catches up with him in the shape of an ancient curse that turns him into a dog at the most unfortunate moments. Especially funny are scenes in a dog-pound that hark back to those in *Lady and the Tramp*. Fun.

Shakedown
See: Blue Jean Cop

Shakiest Gun In the West, The ⊙
1967, US, 101 mins, colour
Dir: Alan Rafkin
Stars: Don Knotts, Barbara Rhoades, Jackie Coogan, Don Barry
Rating: ★★

Knotts, a humbling, 'nervous' American comedian who shot to fame on television, was so good in his early films that Universal decided to build a whole series of big colour comedies around him in the late Sixties. This one is a remake of the Bob Hope/Jane Russell classic *The Paleface*, with Knotts as Jesse Heywood (Painless Potter in the original) and the personable Barbara Rhoades rather good value in the Calamity Jane part, here called Bad Penny Cushings. Movie veterans Don 'Red' Barry, who has a fine time as a fake vicar, and Jackie Coogan, the former child star, fill the villains' shoes with easy skill.

Shaking the Tree ❶ ⓥ
1990, US, 107 mins, colour
Dir: Duane Clark
Stars: Arye Gross, Doug Savant, Courteney Cox, Steven Wilde, Gail Hansen
Rating: ★

Director Duane Clark has related how he and co-writer Steven Wilde had trouble interesting studios in this script; on seeing the film, that causes no surprise. A second-rate story of four guys (who have been friends since college 10 years ago and now rally round when one has problems), it needs a much stronger screenplay to give it any chance of working. Though their story is brightly shot in Astro Color, these are dull, unattractive characters and their problems don't seem to amount to a hill of beans in terms of entertainment.

Shalako ❶
1968, UK, 118 mins, colour
Dir: Edward Dmytryk
Stars: Sean Connery, Brigitte Bardot, Stephen Boyd, Jack Hawkins
Rating: ★★

Sean Connery turned his back on James Bond for this so-so big budget British Western. Henry Fonda was first choice of the producers here for the lead character, a wandering cowboy whose Indian name means 'he who brings rain'. But no-one could have pumped much life into the arid script. It is left to the picturesque location filming of Spain, standing in for New Mexico, to stay in the mind long after the plot has faded to grey.

Shallow Grave ● ⓥ
1994, UK, 91 mins, colour
Dir: Danny Boyle
Stars: Kerry Fox, Christopher Eccleston, Ewan McGregor
Rating: ★★★

A grisly and violent thriller, made with some flair by debutant director Danny Boyle. Flatmates Juliet, David and Alex, a doctor, accountant and journalist, delight in taking the rise out of prospective flatmates and humiliating them. These are dislikeable people and obviously ripe for a fall. The descent begins when they rather unbelievably let the fourth room to faintly menacing Hugo, who says he's been 'away for a while'. Hugo's away for longer, though, when he dies from a drug overdose, leaving a suitcase of money behind him. After much wrangling, our 'heroes' decide to keep the cash and make Hugo a thing to dismember, burying the bits in a forest. Despite a few blackly comic fines, the plot soon boils down to the old thieves-fall-out syndrome, hurtling to three-way violence at the finish. Performances are competent, and Boyle does everything possible to enliven the gruesome morality tale.

Shall We Dance ○ ⓥ
1937, US, 116 mins, b/w
Dir: Mark Sandrich
Stars: Fred Astaire, Ginger Rogers
Rating: ★★★

Ginger Rogers accepted Fred Astaire's invitation to trip the light fantastic for the seventh time in four years. But this time they were just rehashing old plots and the film got a thumbs down from critics. Just as well that George and Ira Gershwin delivered the goods in their second film as composers (the first was *Delicious*, six years earlier) and only collaboration with Rogers and Astaire. The highlight is the roller-skating sequence, 'Let's Call the Whole Thing Off', against a Central Park setting.

Shampoo ● ⓥ
1975, US, 110 mins, colour
Dir: Hal Ashby
Stars: Warren Beatty, Julie Christie, Goldie Hawn, Lee Grant, Jack Warden
Rating: ★★★★

An immensely successful film in which the vein of strong black humour disguises criticisms of American morals and society. Warren Beatty is the hairdresser, determined to set up his own business, who preys on those wealthy female clients whom he knows won't upset his diet of shampoo and sex with wails about marriage and divorce. But it is that formidable actress Lee Grant, as Beatty's first big catch, who won an Academy Award.

Shamus ❶
1972, US, 106 mins, colour
Dir: Buzz Kulik
Stars: Burt Reynolds, Dyan Cannon
Rating: ★★

Private-eye thriller that promises rather more than it delivers, especially given Burt Reynolds, as a 'gumshoe' who sleeps on a pool table, showing early signs of the Reynolds comedy touch, and doing most of his own, bone-crunching stuntwork. It was this film, in fact, that brought the star's long-standing feud with Hollywood insurance men to a head, when he injured his back in one flying leap, and production was held up while he recovered. One other coup: the casting of opera singer Giorgio Tozzi as a gourmet gangster who 'snitches' on his fellow criminals over a four-course lunch. The film takes some sly digs at *The Big Sleep* on the way, and its plot is every bit as complicated.

Shane ○ ⓥ
1953, US, 118 mins, colour
Dir: George Stevens
Stars: Alan Ladd, Jean Arthur, Van Heflin, Jack Palance
Rating: ★★★★

Even though it's about as slow as you'd expect of a two-hour film adapted from a novelette, George Stevens' Western caught the public imagination in no uncertain fashion. Its gunplay is magnetically powerful and the camerawork superb. The only surprise was that Loyal Griggs' award for Technicolor photography was the only Oscar the film received. Alan Ladd found that *Shane* revived a faltering career, in a role similar in some respects to the one that originally shot him to stardom in *This Gun for Hire*, and provided Jean Arthur with a suitable swan

S

song to her career, as the rancher's wife half in love with the gunman. There's tremendous support from a mightily sinister Jack Palance as a sadistic gunslinger.

Shanghai Express O
1932, US, 81 mins, b/w
Dir: Josef von Sternberg
Stars: Marlene Dietrich, Clive Brook, Anna May Wong, Eugene Pallette
Rating: ★★★★★

'It took more than one man to change my name to Shanghai Lily,' drawls Marlene Dietrich in one of cinema's classic lines, and the scene is set for a visually stunning melodrama that was the third film she made in Hollywood with director Josef von Sternberg. It's one of his finest films, a kind of *Grand Hotel* on wheels. Lee Garmes' amazing photography won an Academy Award and Dietrich's sultry siren is enough to make even Clive Brook's stiff upper lip quiver.

Shanghai Surprise ◑ Ⓥ
1986, US, 97 mins, colour
Dir: Jim Goddard
Stars: Sean Penn, Madonna
Rating: ★

Watching Madonna trying (unsuccessfully) to play a Thirties' missionary lady called Gloria is one of the few reasons to bother with this adventure film that never fulfils its eastern promise. Her then-husband Sean Penn portrays too sleazy a character for him to fill Indiana Jones's boots, and the film moves along at the pace of a waterlogged rat negotiating a paddy-field.

Shark! ◑
1967, US, 92 mins, colour
Dir: Samuel Fuller
Stars: Burt Reynolds, Barry Sullivan
Rating: ★★

In making this underwater adventure yarn a stuntman was killed by a shark. Freak weather conditions drove hundreds of the huge fish down the California coast into the Mexican eaters, where star Burt Reynolds and director Samuel Fuller were filming. Famous underwater explorer Jacques Cousteau commented that despite its name, he had never before known a white killer shark attack a man in so vicious a manner which was little consolation for the relatives of José Marco. The film itself is so-so.

Sharkfighters, The O
1956, US, 76 mins, colour
Dir: Jerry Hopper

Stars: Victor Mature, Karen Steele, James Olsen
Rating: ★★

Mighty Mature is given every opportunity to flex his muscles in this story of a team of scientists in World War Two, struggling to perfect a shark-repellent in the Pacific. The underwater photography is splendid, and James Olsen, since a star in *Rachel, Rachel,* makes his film debut in a featured role.

Sharky's Machine ● Ⓥ
1981, US, 117 mins, colour
Dir: Burt Reynolds
Stars: Burt Reynolds, Vittorio Gassman, Rachel Ward
Rating: ★★★

A very, very tough Burt Reynolds thriller about crime, cops, corruption and all that. Blood runs down the walls and people get blown away, but Reynolds, who also directed the film, still finds time for an intelligently presented obsessive affair with a high-class hooker, played by the British actress Rachel Ward. She's used to better advantage and clearly given more help by her director than in any previous film. As a director, in fact, Reynolds is full of ideas, even if, like his character (who also loses a couple of fingers in a close-your-eyes torture scene), he occasionally loses his cool. But it's good to see Henry Silva back in the role he does best – a cold-blooded killer. The action goes on and on: no fan of blood-soaked cop thrillers could ask for more.

Shattered ● Ⓥ
1991, US, 106 mins, colour
Dir: Wolfgang Petersen
Stars: Tom Berenger, Bob Hoskins, Greta Scacchi, Joanne Whalley-Kilmer, Corbin Bernsen
Rating: ★★

Sometimes amnesia thrillers can still be good, but here's one that's not as good as it thinks it is. The makings are here, but neither the execution, nor the twists that should make you gasp with surprise. Given that things are not what they appear to be for car crash victim Tom Berenger, there's only one other likely explanation, and most viewers are likely to get it early on. Some of the performances are good (Greta Scacchi as Berenger's wife, Bob Hoskins as the part-time detective he hires), but most are ordinary, and one or two poor. Berenger looks as though he can't make up his mind what to do with his role: fatal vacillation at the centre of a well-scored,

stylish thriller that's just not intricate enough.

Shawshank Redemption, The ● Ⓥ
1994, US, 143 mins, colour
Dir: Frank Darabont
Stars: Tim Robbins, Morgan Freeman, Clancy Brown, James Whitmore, William Sadler
Rating: ★★★★

US prison films have been making solid fare for more than 50 years and, apart from slowness of pace in the second half, this one is well up to standards. You know the scene: corrupt warden, sadistic head guard, prison 'fixer', gang oppression, hardnut camaraderie and the central character – likely to be innocent of his 'crime'. He's Andy (Tim Robbins), a bright young banker convicted of the slayings of his wife and her lover. The twist here is that Andy is *exceptionally* bright. Despite rebellious lapses that land him in solitary, his ability with accountancy leads to his handling the finances of everyone from the humblest guard to the warden. But when the proof of Andy's innocence is ripped away by those who need his services, we learn that all is not quite what it seems at Shawshank Prison, provoking a few surprises in the last two reels. Prison fans will find lots of incidents to relish, along with Robbins' best screen performance and Oscar-worthy supporting shows by Morgan Freeman as the 'fixer' and James Whitmore as the crow-keeping librarian.

She O
1935, US, 95 mins, b/w
Dir: Lansing C Holden, Irving Pichel
Stars: Helen Gahagan, Randolph Scott, Helen Mack, Nigel Bruce
Rating: ★★★

Thought at one time to be a lost film, this is an impressively set first sound version (there had been several silents) of Rider Haggard's yarn about a legendary, ageless female ruler of a city, situated in Africa in the book but here transferred to the Arctic. Excellent photography by J Roy Hunt and music by Max Steiner help stir up atmosphere you can almost grasp. The title role is played by Helen Gahagan, who later married Melvyn Douglas, and became a Congresswoman. This was her only film.

She ◑
1965, US, 105 mins, colour
Dir: Robert Day

Stars: Ursula Andress, Peter Cushing, Bernard Cribbins, John Richardson, Christopher Lee, Rosenda Monteros
Rating: ★★

Hammer version of H Rider Haggard's oft-filmed novel, with Ursula Andress (more magnificent than when she rose out of the sea and into stardom in *Dr No*) as 'She Who Must Be Obeyed'. It's all done with tongue-in-cheek zest by director Robert Day and Hammer's stalwarts, Peter Cushing and Christopher Lee, are on hand to support Ms Andress. But the most striking performances come from Bernard Cribbins (who has all the best lines) and Rosenda Monteros as a native girl.

She-Devil ◑ Ⓥ
1989, US, 99 mins, colour
Dir: Susan Seidelman
Stars: Meryl Streep, Roseanne Barr, Ed Begley, Linda Hunt
Rating: ★★

TV's scorching trilogy by Fay Weldon is well and truly revamped by Hollywood into a scatty romantic comedy which serves as a vehicle for Barr to expand her popular TV image and Streep to let her hair down. Ed Begley Jr is nicely cast, being equally believable as a desirable man and a figure of fun, as the husband Barr loses to romantic novelist Streep. Deserted, the frumpy housewife turns she-devil to exact a tortured (and tortuous) revenge. Streep and Barr have fun and so, to a degree, do we, even if the enterprise lacks a certain vital spark. As a wet weather time passer, it does the job. Lovers of the TV serial, though, may be advised to stay away.

She Didn't Say No! ○
1958, UK, 97 mins, colour
Dir: Cyril Frankel
Stars: Eileen Herlie, Niall MacGinnis, Ian Bannen
Rating: ★★

The dangers of playing alongside scene-stealing child actors have rarely been more evident than in this charming comedy about an unmarried mother with six children. Little Raymond Manthorpe, as Toughy, manages to steal every scene in which he appears.

She Done Him Wrong ○
1933, US, 66 mins, b/w
Dir: Lowell Sherman
Stars: Mae West, Cary Grant, Gilbert Roland, Owen Moore
Rating: ★★★★

Mae West proving for the first time the truth of her famous maxim that 'When women go wrong, men go right after them.' She also has the benefit of Cary Grant as leading man, plus such songs as 'Frankie and Johnny', 'Easy Rider' and 'I Like a Man Who Takes His Time'. Slyly salty dialogue makes Mae sexy and side-splitting at the same time. It was her first big film hit, short and very sharp and based on her self-written stage success *Diamond Lil*. The film contains some of Mae's finest gems of dialogue, including 'I was once so poor I didn't know where my next husband was coming from' and 'Why don't you come up sometime, see me?', plus the famous no-claws-barred fight between Mae and dagger-eyed Rafaela Ottiano.

She's the One ● Ⓥ
1996, US, 97 mins,
Dir: Edward Burns
Stars: Jennifer Aniston, Maxine Bahns, Edward Burns, Cameron Diaz, John Mahoney, Mike McGlone
Rating: ★

This one-man film (star Edward Burns also wrote and directed) may think it's a smart, outspoken comedy of manners set in Brooklyn. In truth, however, it does little more than set some personable performers adrift in a slight story of sexual shenanigans among unpleasant and tiresome characters who spend half the film sniping at each other. These touchy people major in sarcasm and it doesn't take much to set them bitching. When one says 'I gotta get some air' you may feel the same way. Jennifer Aniston is the best of a cast whose younger members, Burns included, look in need of a few stiff acting lessons.

Sheena – Queen of the Jungle ○
1984, US, 117 mins, colour
Dir: John Guillermin
Stars: Tanya Roberts, Ted Wass, Donovan Scott
Rating: ★

Shades of *Tarzan* in a spectacular jungle adventure which, with a script straight out of the early Forties, may remind older viewers of a Saturday morning serial. Tanya Roberts, with her bleached blonde hair, spectacular figure, coral-pink lipstick, eye makeup and shaved armpits, is every curvy inch Hollywood's idea of the title role. John Guillermin and his second unit director Jack Couffer do a great job in capturing the breathtaking Kenyan lo-

cations, so that the highly coloured yarn is alternately good for a gasp and a giggle.

Sheepman, The ○
1958, US, 86 mins, colour
Dir: George Marshall
Stars: Glenn Ford, Shirley MacLaine, Leslie Nielsen
Rating: ★★★★

A charmingly natural Western, photographed in glowing Metrocolor by Robert Bronner. It has laughs, action and a lot of attractive characters, not least Shirley MacLaine's copper-haired tomboy heroine and Mickey Shaughnessy's Jumbo McCall. Glenn Ford has the title role as the sheepman fenced in by cattle ranchers but determined to stay put, and *Naked Gun* fans will be surprised to find a young Leslie Nielsen turning up as the treacherous villain. Good stuff this, genial, fresh and likeable, with a little gentle satire on the conventional Western thrown in for good measure.

She'll Be Wearing Pink Pyjamas ◑
1984, UK, 90 mins, colour
Dir: John Goldschmidt
Stars: Julie Walters, Anthony Higgins
Rating: ★★★★

An excellent emotive outdoor drama about eight very varied women tackling an adventure course. Naturally it's their souls as well as their soles that get bared. Julie Walters, as the brassy northerner whose feelings as well as feet are really the most vulnerable in the octet, is the only star name and indeed comes over as the most clearly defined character. But several of her fellows acquit themselves more than adequately in roles that, like the course, stretch women far more than the average film. A lot of the dialogue is very frank, but the relaxed delivery of the players keeps it from being offensive. And the ending brings a lump to the throat without resorting to high draimatics. An unusual film that is, by its own standards, right on target.

Shenandoah ○
1965, US, 101 mins, colour
Dir: Andrew V McLaglen
Stars: James Stewart, Doug McClure, Katharine Ross, Rosemary Forsyth, Glenn Corbett, Patrick Wayne
Rating: ★★★★★

This is director Andrew V McLaglen's best film by a country mile. The story of a farming family that tries to keep out of the American Civil War, it's unpretentious, very much to do with real life and absolutely beautifully made. And it gives James Stewart, as the father of the family, the kind of role that actors of his potential and maturity must dream about. He plays it so well that the performance has to be seen to appreciate its closeness to life. Every inch of the way, the film, while punctuated with imaginative action scenes, has something to say that is sensible, thought-provoking or humorous. At the birth of his eldest son's first child, Stewart's youngest son asks for a glass of celebration liquor. 'I only want a taste,' he pleads. 'Boy,' says Stewart, 'some men have drunk it all their lives and never tasted it.'

She Played with Fire
See: Fortune is a Woman

Sheriff of Fractured Jaw, The ○
1958, UK, 103 mins, colour
Dir: Raoul Walsh
Stars: Kenneth More, Jayne Mansfield
Rating: ★★★

The unlikely combination of Kenneth More and Jayne Mansfield shouldn't really have worked, but under Raoul Walsh's rousing direction, most of the difficulties were ironed out. The result is a sunny and fun-filled spoof Western, with More as the tweedy English gunsmith who finds himself the most feared gunman in the Wild West. Such familiar Hollywood faces as Henry Hull, William Campbell and Bruce Cabot are on hand to lend a touch of authenticity to the atmosphere. Sid James totters in and out as the town drunkard. Mansfield's singing voice comes courtesy of Connie Francis.

Sherlock and Me
See: Without a Clue

Sherlock Holmes and the Spider Woman ○ ⓥ
1944, US, 63 mins, b/w
Dir: Roy William Neill
Stars: Basil Rathbone, Nigel Bruce
Rating: ★★★

Basil Rathbone is in cracking form as Sherlock Holmes in this adaptation of a Conan Doyle short story, as he adopts his usual disguise and undergoes some pretty harrowing experiences to solve the case. He is finely matched in a battle of wits and wills by that mistress of menace, Gale Sondergaard, whose character survived to make a sequel (without Rathbone), *Spider Woman Strikes Back*.

Sherlock Holmes in New York ○
1976, US, 94 mins, colour
Dir: Boris Sagal
Stars: Roger Moore, John Huston, Patrick Macnee
Rating: ★★★

Bond-man Roger Moore joins the illustrious ranks of actors who have assumed deerstalker and violin as Conan Doyle's famous Victorian sleuth. But this classy romp has Holmes far from his usual haunts and chasing the evil Professor Moriarty (a dastardly John Huston) through the streets of turn-of-the-century New York. For once Moore gets material that requires a little more than the customary raised eyebrows!

Sherlock Junior ⊙
1924, US, 46 mins, b/w
Dir: Buster Keaton
Stars: Buster Keaton
Rating: ★★★★

One of the most enjoyable of Buster Keaton's silent feature films. He ends up outwitting the crooks in a marvellous sequence involving a falling sword, poison and an exploding pool ball.

She's Gotta Have It ● ⓥ
1986, US, 84 mins, b/w
Dir: Spike Lee
Stars: Tracy Camila Johns, Tommy Redmond Hicks, John Canada Terrell, Spike Lee
Rating: ★★★

Spike Lee, the driving force behind this off-the-wall sexual sparring match with jokes, is a kind of babbling black Woody Allen in this one. He wrote, directed, edited and ultimately had the good sense to cast himself as the 'funny one' of the three lovers of the girl to whom the provocative ride refers. The script is sharp and witty, but Lee's pacing is not all it might be, and the film only comes to life when he and his ideas are around. Tracy Camila Johns has a certain sexuality as the girl with three men in tow, none of them surely a permanent prospect, even though the film tries to sustain itself on the possibility that she might end up with one of them.

She's Out of Control ◐ ⓥ
1990, US, 95 mins, colour
Dir: Stan Dragoti
Stars: Tony Danza, Catherine Hicks, Wallace Shawn, Ami Dolenz
Rating: ★

A dated but occasionally amusing farce about the pains of a father with a teenage daughter. There was a rash of these about 20 years before, with such veteran stars as James Stewart and David Niven. At least here Tony Danza is the right age, making a very young-looking 37-year-old, as daughter Dolenz does all the things that teenage girls with pretty faces and curvy figures are wont to do in these films. The best sequence comes in the middle, when Danza attempts to fit in with his daughter's lifestyle and befriend her associates. Otherwise it's pretty tired and painful – and not too well performed either, with some strenuous 'reacting' from most of the cast. Its contrived charm is easily resistible.

She's Working Her Way Through College ○
1952, US, 101 mins, colour
Dir: Bruce Humberstone
Stars: Virginia Mayo, Ronald Reagan, Gene Nelson, Phyllis Thaxter
Rating: ★★

This is quite a bright, snappy Technicolor musical. Here the plum role goes to Mayo as a burlesque queen who aspires to a writing career, re-enrols (incognito) at her old college and soon replaces the annual Shakespeare play with a musical written by herself, which, as usual, proves a more elaborate show than any educational establishment could afford to stage. If this sounds zany, it certainly is, and the 'plot' is just a peg on which to hang a series of zippy song-and-dance numbers with room for a witty cameo by Roland Winters, fresh from being Hollywood's last Charlie Chan, as a college governor with a murky past. As the stuffy English teacher, Ronald Reagan looks suitably discomfited at such goings-on (as might befit a future US president) and Gene Nelson again steals the film from everyone with his acrobatic dancing.

She Wore a Yellow Ribbon ○ ⓥ
1949, US, 103 mins, colour
Dir: John Ford
Stars: John Wayne, Joanne Dru, John Agar, Ben Johnson, Victor McLaglen
Rating: ★★★★★

One of John Wayne's best performances, as an ageing cavalry officer trying to drive Indians off lands they regard as their own. This is the second of what has now come to be regarded as John Ford's unofficial cavalry trilogy, completed by *Fort Apache* and *Rio Grande*. What particularly distinguishes it is its feel for those early pioneer days of wide open spaces, especially well captured in Ford's sensitive direction, and in Winton C Hoch's breathtaking colour photography, which deservedly won an Oscar. The film's quiet power – only the comedy scenes involving Victor McLaglen seem out of key – makes it an unchallenged classic.

Shinbone Alley ⊙
1971, US, 86 mins, colour
Dir: David Detiege
Voice stars: Eddie Bracken, Carol Channing, John Carradine
Rating: ★★

A full-length cartoon, not shown in Britain's cinemas, based on the famous *Archy and Mehitabel* stories by Don Marquis, about a cat and a cockroach.. Voices to be heard behind the characters include those of Carol Charming, Eddle Bracken and John Carradine. Second-class animation, maybe, compared to that from the Disney studio, but top-class tunes and colourful characters make this a pleasure to be with.

Shine ◑ ⓥ
1996, Aus, 106 mins, colour
Dir: Scott Hicks
Stars: Armin Mueller-Stahl, Noah Taylor, Geoffrey Rush, Lynn Redgrave, Googie Withers, John Gielgud
Rating: ★★★★

A true story about a classical pianist who suffers a mental breakdown may not sound the stuff of fine commercial cinema, but the quality of the music and acting, plus the careful and imaginative direction of Scott Hicks, carry this one far above its seeming limitations. Driven on by an obsessive (and oppressive) father (Stahl), the young David Helfgott (Taylor) wins a scholarship to study music in London. But the stresses in him run deep and, despite some brilliant accomplishments, he breaks down during a performance of a Rachmaninov concerto and seems doomed to spend his adult life (now played by Rush) in and out of psychiatric hospitals. But the intervention of a caring woman gives him unexpected hope... and gives us a sweeping, uplifting last reel. Excellent performances; inspiring stuff: Rush won an Oscar.

Shining, The ● ⓥ
1980, US, 119 mins, colour
Dir: Stanley Kubrick
Stars: Jack Nicholson, Shelley Duvall,

Danny Lloyd
Rating: ★★★★

Stanley Kubrick's underrated chiller is one of those films that makes you check under the bed to see there's no-one there after you've finished watching it – especially if you imagine Jack Nicholson and his axe could soon be after you. This is grim and grisly ghost story telling with a vengeance, as Nicholson, his wife (Shelley Duvall) and son (Danny Lloyd), who is endowed with extra-sensory perception (the 'shining' of the title) and can see the horrors in store for them, take on the caretakership of a Rocky Mountain hotel for the winter. Somewhere in the past a previous caretaker has gone berserk and axed his wife and daughters to death, and it isn't long before the house is exercising an evil influence on Nicholson. Kubrick paces the symphony of horror with masterly precision, using tracking cameras a lot to heighten the fright and emphasise the terror of a pursued victim. Nicholson has a wonderful time, while Shelley Duvall registers a fine line in hysteria. You shouldn't really see it alone.

Shining Through ◑ ⓥ
1991, US, 133 mins, colour
Dir: David Seltzer
Stars: Michael Douglas, Melanie Griffith, Liam Neeson, Joely Richardson, John Gielgud
Rating: ★

A real Mills and Boon of a film about a World War Two heroine. The preposterous cock-and-bull story has Melanie Griffith as one of the more inept wartime agents. She's recruited chiefly, it seems, for her ability to speak German (badly) and her knowledge of Hollywood films, which isn't up to much since she thinks Cary Grant and Brenda Marshall were in *The Fighting 69th* (they weren't). The film itself, indeed, could come from the Forties, were it not for the fact that Griffith is required to bare her breasts in the course of her affair with equally incompetent spymaster Michael Douglas, who sends her off on a mission that requires her to cook for a Nazi. The story that follows has lots of silliness, but no dramatic tension and very little subtlety. A ludicrous framing interview by 'the BBC' is even more embarrassing than the story it surrounds.

Ship Ahoy ○
1942, US, 91 mins, b/w
Dir: Edward Buzzell

Stars: Eleanor Powell, Red Skelton, Bert Lahr, Virginia O'Brien
Rating: ★★

Lots of talented people decorate this very silly MGM musical, whose ragged editing makes it look like a patchwork quilt. Even though it was obviously cobbled together in a hurry to provide patriotic war fare, there's plenty of entertainment value: Tommy Dorsey's trombone work, Eleanor Powell's dancing, Frank Sinatra's singing and Buddy Rich's devastating drumming. Red Skelton's addled fooling is put in the shade by vaudeville veteran Bert Lahr, here making one of his too-rare movie appearances outside of his immortal Cowardly Lion in *The Wizard of Oz*.

Ship of Fools ○
1965, US, 149 mins, b/w
Dir: Stanley Kramer
Stars: Vivien Leigh, Simone Signoret, Lee Marvin, Oskar Werner
Rating: ★★★

Stanley Kramer's allegorical drama of passengers aboard a transatlantic ship in 1933. Noteworthy for the doomed love affair memorably carved out by Simone Signoret and Oskar Werner, for Vivien Leigh's bored divorcee, breaking indecorously into a solo Charleston below decks when no-one is looking, and for Lee Marvin's retired baseball player who could never hit 'a curving ball on the outside corner.' Although the voyage is a long one, a lot of its drama is good, meaty stuff. You'll also like Michael Dunn's dwarf, moralising though he is, while Jose Greco's acting surprisingly shows the same snap and fire as his flamenco dancing.

Ship Was Loaded, The
See: Carry On Admiral

Shipwreck! ⊙
1978, US, 98 mins, colour
Dir: Stewart Raffill
Stars: Robert Logan, Mikki Jamison-Olsen
Rating: ★★★

Another of the man-against-nature films made by director Stewart Raffill and likeable star Robert Logan, best known for their *Wilderness Family* series and for the splendid *Across the Great Divide*. The title tells you all you need to know about the story, although the site of the shipwreck may be a surprise: it's not a desert island but the coast of Alaska. Cuteness threatens, but is skilfully kept at bay, and the

S

scenes involving animals are exceedingly well done.

Shirley Valentine ◐ ⓥ
1989, UK, 108 mins, colour
Dir: Lewis Gilbert
Stars: Pauline Collins, Tom Conti, Alison Steadman, Julia McKenzie, Joanna Lumley, Bernard Hill
Rating: ★★★

This delightful romantic comedy started life as a one-woman stage show, but you'd never know it, as it took to the big screen like a duck to water. Following their success with *Educating Rita*, director Lewis Gilbert and writer Willy Russell teamed up again for this film. Pauline Collins reprised the role she filled so successfully on stage and, inevitably, dominates the film. She plays a bored housewife who dreams of drinking 'a glass of wine in a country where the grape is grown' and eventually takes off for a Greek island, leaving a note to her husband in the kitchen! The fine supporting cast includes Tom Conti, Bernard Hill, Julia McKenzie and Joanna Lumley, but it's Pauline's show. It's something a little different and fun too.

Shock! ◐
1945, US, 70 mins, b/w
Dir: Alfred Werker
Stars: Vincent Price, Lynn Bari
Rating: ★★

When he made this film, Vincent Price's screen career had been in a variety of roles, and he had not yet become a specialist in horror films which were later to make him so famous. Here, he enjoys himself as a lethal psychiatrist.

Shock to the System, A ◐ ⓥ
1990, US, 87 mins, colour
Dir: Jan Egleson
Stars: Michael Caine, Peter Riegert, Elizabeth McGovern, Will Patton
Rating: ★★

This is a minor black comedy, but the art of Michael Caine turns it into an enjoyable if forgettable lark. Caine is the good-natured, efficient, henpecked businessman tipped over the edge by his failure to clinch a long-expected promotion within his firm. After accidentally pushing a tramp under a subway train without recrimination, he does what 90 per cent of the world's population dream about. He murders the ruthless, obnoxious and ambitious yuppie who has leap-frogged him at the firm. Then, of course, there's the nagging wife. She'll have to go too.

And there's the detective on his trail (Patton, with apologies to Peter Falk). And the managing director. And even the mistress who could betray him. Caine keeps it all jogging nicely along, with only token help from his script and director. Just watch his face as his wife's ashes blow back over him at her funeral. And Riegert proves he can play a nasty blowhard as well as unassuming nice guy.

Shoes of the Fisherman, The ◯
1968, US, 157 mins, colour
Dir: Michael Anderson
Stars: Anthony Quinn, Laurence Olivier, Oskar Werner, David Janssen
Rating: ★★★

Impressive, strikingly coloured epic about a fighting Russian bishop. This was not popular with the critics when it first appeared, even though Quinn was tipped at the time for an Oscar. But it has several moving scenes, beautiful photography by Erwin Hillier and an eye-catching performance by Leo McKernn. It also uncannily predicted the emergence of a Pope from Eastern Europe.

Shoot First
See: Rough Shoot

Shooting, The ◯
1966, US, 82 mins, colour
Dir: Monte Hellman
Stars: Warren Oates, Millie Perkins, Jack Nicholson
Rating: ★★★

A cult Western, set against the parched backdrop of the desert, that will fascinate some viewers and severely try the patience of others. A few people play out destinies from which none of them seems fated to escape. Enigmatic to the last, the film will certainly keep you guessing as to who is doing what to whom and why. Co-produced by Jack Nicholson, who also plays a featured role as the hired gunman on the trail of bounty hunter Warren Oates.

Shootist, The ◯ ⓥ
1976, US, 99 mins, colour
Dir: Don Siegel
Stars: John Wayne, Lauren Bacall, Ron Howard, James Stewart, Richard Boone
Rating: ★★★★★

Well may this finely crafted film use clips of John Wayne shoot-outs through the years under its credits. For it is both a summation of the Wayne legend and an ending to it – a tying, if you like, of all the ends in one knot.

Wayne plays a gunfighter – the name is unimportant, he is Wayne – who comes to an elderly doctor friend to be told he has cancer: there is no escape. Spending his dying days in the embryo Carson City, he is surrounded – as Wayne is surrounded in the film by star acting friends – by those who come to sponge on him, those who come to mock or pity him, and those who come to kill him. Around all this, director Don Siegel has delivered a beautiful job of work. If the pace leaves a little to be desired, never mind: it may be argued that is the pace of an old man making the most of his winter years. And, in a notable achievement, Siegel has elicited fine performances from people who might have been considered past giving them, especially Wayne (quieter and more effective than in the Oscar-winning *True Grit*) Stewart and Lauren Bacall. This concise, caring and lovingly photographed (by Bruce Surtees) film makes a not inconsiderable headstone beneath which to bury the Wayne Western legend.

Shooting Fish ◐ ⓥ
1997, UK, 113 mins, colour
Dir: Stefan Schwartz
Stars: Kate Beckinsale, Dan Futterman, Stuart Townsend
Rating: ★★★

A pleasant, zesty, if not too believable comedy about two orphans turned con-men, this runs like several episodes of an above-par TV sitcom. Happy-go-lucky swindlers, Jez (Townsend) and Dylan (Futterman) are joined on one 'sting' by upper-crust English girl Georgie (Beckinsale), who's temping for extra money while training as a doctor. With one thing leading to another, Georgie's need to save a foundation for Down's Syndrome children and the boys' scheme to net a million and a mansion are pretty well bound to collide. A g ood deal of sub-Ealing fun is had before and after they do, although the film moves in fits and starts and seems to have several endings. The three leads are enthusiastic (and the lads' Battersea Power Station home splendidly inventive), but all the best performances come from the people they gyp along the way.

Shoot to Kill
See: Deadly Pursuit

Shopping ● ⓥ
1993, UK, 107 mins, colour
Dir: Paul Anderson

Stars: Jude Law, Sadie Frost, Sean Pertwee, Jonathan Pryce
Rating: ★★

The British 'B' crime movie of long ago updates itself here to the near future. It begins well: in a *noir*-lit backstreets world of gleaming grime, anarchy rules and teenage gangs roam unchecked. Crime of the month is ram raiding: the smashing through shop windows by cars which load up with goods and flee into the night. The police are an endangered species. Billy (Jude Law), released from prison, and greeted by his Irish girl (Sadie Frost, with a mostly credible accent) in a stolen car, is resolved to re-establish himself as a joy-riding, ram-raiding kingpin. Tommy (Sean Pertwee), current black market boss, is set on defending his territory. On the fringes, Inspector Conway (Jonathan Pryce) waits like a patient wolf for one to dump the other into his jaws. Looking good, the film's poorly paced in between its bursts of action: the only thing that's constantly on the move is the camera which doesn't help a lot.

Shopworn Angel O
1938, US, 82 mins, b/w
Dir: H C Potter
Stars: Margaret Sullavan, James Stewart, Walter Pidgeon
Rating: ★★★

This dated but still touching vehicle for Margaret Sullavan and James Stewart (the second of their four films together) is a remake of an even older weepie that starred Nancy Carroll and Gary Cooper as the showgirl and the soldier who enjoy a mad fling in New York the night before he is due to be shipped overseas for wartime service. In keeping with the sweetness of her image, Sullavan's angel isn't quite as shopworn as Carroll's was in 1928, but Stewart's gangly charm is every inch the equal of Cooper's and there will be few dry eyes in the house as Sullavan goes on stage to sing 'Pack Up Your Troubles in Your Old Kit Bag' at the end.

Short Circuit O Ⓥ
1986, US, 98 mins, colour
Dir: John Badham
Stars: Ally Sheedy, Steve Guttenberg, Fisher Stevens, Austin Pendleton, G W Bailey, Brian McNamara
Rating: ★★★

A pleasant and occasionally very funny caper about a runaway robot that, having been struck by lightning,

reprogrammes itself to believe it's alive. And, assimilating all the knowledge it can find and imitating any human function it can cope with, Number Five does become alive – as near as dammit. Unfortunately, it's also armed with an annihilating laser weapon. So the authorities want the escapee back and, with the help of an animal-hoarding girl (Ally Sheedy), Number Five must hide, run dodge and fight with all the capacity it can find in its brainbox. The robot is really the whole show and most of the fun stems from the information it 'gathers' from watching TV, especially when it reprogrammes three enemy robots to behave like The Three Stooges. Excellent for children, who will enjoy the odd rude word, Sheedy's house of animals and Number Five making mincemeat of the opposition.

Short Circuit 2 O Ⓥ
1988, US, 110 mins, colour
Dir: Kenneth Johnson
Stars: Fisher Stevens, Cynthia Gibb
Rating: ★★

So often follow-ups are doomed to failure, if only because they are merely warmed-over copies of the original. Unfortunately, this is true of *Short Circuit 2*. The stars of the original film, Steve Guttenberg and Ally Sheedy, obviously saw it coming, as they ducked the sequel, leaving their co-star Fisher Stevens to take the lead (and the can!). The robot, Number Five, insists on being called Johnny Five and, mysteriously, Stevens' character's name has changed from Ben Jabituya to Ben Jahrvi. Stevens' Indian accent is so awful it's embarrassing. The kids will love it, though.

Short Cuts ● Ⓥ
1993, US, 188 mins, colour
Dir: Robert Altman
Stars: Anne Archer, Tim Robbins, Jennifer Jason Leigh, Madeleine Stowe, Andie MacDowell
Rating: ★★

Rather a long cut at more than three hours, this proves, after an excellent beginning – as pesticide-dropping helicopters drone over the city – to be a pretty aimless amble through the substrata of Los Angeles by director Robert Altman, as a score or more lives crisscross and sometimes come to climaxes or watersheds. These are mostly deeply unpleasant people who often have no patience with one another and to stay in their company for this length of time certainly demands

stamina to savour the occasional rewarding moment. An all-star cast appears willingly in various stages of undress; for Altman is a master, is he not, and so it is all in the cause of art.

Short Time ◑ Ⓥ
1990, US, 97 mins, colour
Dir: Gregg Champion
Stars: Dabney Coleman, Matt Frewer, Teri Garr, Joe Pantoliano, Xander Berkeley
Rating: ★★

For the first half-hour, it seems that this tale of a long-serving cop (Dabney Coleman) who thinks he's about to die is going to strike out. It's frenetic, over-played and awkward too. As soon as Coleman starts trying to get himself killed, though, the film moves into another gear. Never wildly funny, but consistently chucklesome, the main body of the film is packed with chases and mindlessly enjoyable. Divorced and depressed, Coleman is saddled with a partner who looks like Clint Eastwood and sounds like Kermit the Frog and a career that has eight days to run before retirement. Then there's a mix-up at the hospital and Coleman's told he has Wexler's Curtain: his retirement will be permanent in about 20 days. The only thing he can do is die in the line of duty and net $300,000 insurance for his young son. He doffs his gun and bullet-proof vest and becomes a fearless vigilante cop, only to find himself bearing a charmed life.

Shot in the Dark, A O Ⓥ
1964, US, 101 mins, colour
Dir: Blake Edwards
Stars: Peter Sellers, Elke Sommer, Herbert Lom, Burt Kwouk, Graham Stark
Rating: ★★★

Like the Mounties, Inspector Clouseau (alias Peter Sellers) always gets his man. He just has a little more trouble than they do. Take his problem here. A murder has been committed at a millionaire's mansion. Clouseau is assigned. No sooner has he picked himself out of the lake in the grounds than he falls head over heels for the chief suspect (Elke Sommer). He determines to prove her innocence. But, alas, in addition to being accident-prone, the defective detective becomes corpse-prone. Three more murders turn up at the mansion. And 10 more people are killed (accidentally) as an unseen hand goes after Clouseau himself. Sellers is supremely funny as Clouseau. And Herbert Lom proves

S

superbly comic as the superior whom Sellers gradually reduces to a nervous wreck.

Shoulder Arms ☉
1918, US, 35 mins, b/w
Dir: Charles Chaplin
Stars: Charlie Chaplin
Rating: ★★★

Charlie Chaplin took so long to make this three-reel comedy – his longest to that date – that it finally premiered only three weeks before the end of the World War One. Still, the public loved it, especially the scenes where Charlie kicks the Kaiser in the seat of his pants, disguises himself as a tree – he still looks like a tramp – or eats the cheese from a mousetrap.

Shout at the Devil ○
1976, UK, 119 mins, colour
Dir: Peter Hunt
Stars: Lee Marvin, Roger Moore, Barbara Parkins
Rating: ★★

As with the previous collaboration between star Roger Moore and director Peter Hunt, the action is everything in this explosive account of two Zanzibar-based mercenaries in 1913 making ivory-poaching forays against what seems to be half the German armed forces. The technical skill with which the set-pieces are filmed – a biplane going down in flames, a David-and-Goliath duel between contrasting boats, an exploding battleship, and a free-for-all fist fight between Moore and Lee Marvin – is of a high order. Only the love interest, between Moore and Barbara Parkins, as Marvin's daughter, is dull and redundant. Otherwise, extravagant and enjoyable adventures for all ages.

Show Boat ○
1936, US, 113 mins, b/w
Dir: James Whale
Stars: Irene Dunne, Allan Jones, Paul Robeson, Helen Morgan
Rating: ★★★★

Possibly the most famous version of the Kern-Hammerstein musical about life and love on a Mississippi show boat in the early 1900s. Skilful direction by James Whale, best known for his Universal horror films, milks the story for every emotional moment, while Irene Dunne's vivacious performance – she's an absolute delight singing 'Can't Help Loving That Man' – should have alerted producers to her possibilities long before they were fully realised. The songs, all beautifully

staged, also include the Dunne-Allan Jones duet 'Only Make Believe', Paul Robeson's famous rendition of 'Ol' Man River', sung while the camera sweeps a circle around him, and Helen Morgan's 'My Bill'.

Show Boat ○ ⓥ
1951, US, 107 mins, colour
Dir: George Sidney
Stars: Kathryn Grayson, Ava Gardner, Howard Keel, William Warfield, Marge & Gower Champion, Joe E Brown
Rating: ★★★★

Most critics will tell you that this marvellous musical doesn't compare with James Whale's 1936 version: but don't believe a word of it. Certainly the earlier film is smashing too. But this MGM remake, with all their technical departments working at full throttle and George Sidney in the director's chair, is much underrated. And how the stars shine. Howard Keel, especially, acts and sings well as the gambling Gaylord; Kathryn Grayson, in one of her best performances, is charming (and very pretty) as Magnolia and more vivacious than one could credit from some of her other roles. Old-time comic Joe E Brown deserves special mention for his superb playing as her father, while Ava Gardner and Agnes Moorehead also tug skilfully at the emotions in their big scenes.

Showdown ○
1963, US, 79 mins, b/w
Dir: R G Springsteen
Stars: Audie Murphy, Kathleen Crowley, Charles Drake, Harold J Stone
Rating: ★★

Slowdown might be a better title for this Audie Murphy Western, made at a time when Murphy's fortunes at Universal were on the wane and the studio were no longer even prepared to splash out colour on his vehicles. But his old (real-life) friend Charles Drake is there to support him. Together the two conjure up some action and one or two moments that touch the emotions.

Showdown ○
1972, US, 99 mins, colour
Dir: George Seaton
Stars: Rock Hudson, Dean Martin, Susan Clark
Rating: ★★★

A pity Hudson and Martin were past their box-office peak when this film was issued in 1973, for it's above-average of its kind, thanks to thoroughly professional direction by George

Seaton and an intelligent script by Theodore Taylor that's full of drily witty dialogue exchanges. You feel that if the two stars had intended it as their cinematic swan-song they could not have chosen much better: you may be reminded at times of another Western, *Guns in the Afternoon*, in which Randolph Scott and Joel McCrea virtually said goodbye to the cinema. The two films also share remarkably good colour photography of the Western countryside among their assets, in this case by the ever-excellent Ernest Laszlo.

Showdown at Abliene ○
1956, US, 80 mins, colour
Dir: Charles Haas
Stars: Jock Mahoney, Martha Hyer, Lyle Bettger
Rating: ★★

This story of a gun-shy sheriff was a favourite Western plot at Universal, who filmed it several times up to 1967, when Bobby Darin featured in *Gunfight in Abilene*. This version features Jock Mahoney who, a couple of years later, became one of the screen's many Tarzans. The splendid, husky-voiced Lyle Bettger is the villain, heading a supporting cast which also includes Martha Hyer, Grant Williams, David Janssen and Ted de Corsia.

Showgirls ● ⓥ
1995, US, 131 mins, colour
Dir: Paul Verhoeven
Stars: Elizabeth Berkley, Kyle MacLachlan, Gina Gershon, Glenn Plummer, Robert Davi, Alan Rachins
Rating: ★

The most talked-about flop of 1995, this is the tackiest and sleaziest of movie travesties. Topless girls abound in this strip club version of *All About Eve*, but its plot and dialogue are so bad that you'll be hard-pressed not to laugh out loud. The central character is Nomi (Elizabeth Berkley), a brattish girl with a mystery past. She eats dog food (we kid you not) and acts like a bitch on permanent heat when there are any men around. Hitching a lift to Las Vegas, she quickly gets a job at the seedy Cheetahs 'lap-dancing' strip joint. But she is desperate to land the starring role at the glitzy Stardust Hotel, a topless, volcano-erupting homage to *Staying Alive*. There's a lesbian seduction, a brutal gang rape and sleaze everywhere. The film, like Vegas itself, is about the big sell. The trouble is that *Showgirls* is bankrupt.

Show Goes On, The ○
1937, UK, 93 mins, b/w
Dir: Basil Dean
Stars: Gracie Fields, Owen Nares
Rating: ★★

Gracie was well established as one of Britain's top box-office stars when this tearful musical was made. She was cast opposite silent screen matinee idol, Owen Nares, a young Patrick Barr, and that hearty actor, Cyril Ritchard. Helping to lighten the gloom of the story are Olsen's Sea Lions and, of course, Our Gracie, who stands on the topmost deck of the Queen Mary, and sings 'Smile When You Wave Goodbye' to a troopship.

Shuttered Room, The ●
1966, UK, 110 mins, colour
Dir: David Greene
Stars: Gig Young, Carol Lynley, Oliver Reed, Flora Robson
Rating: ★★

'Things' locked away in shuttered rooms, villagers frightened by goings-on at the old mill, and strange webbed footprints. A sound horror formula and, with a screenplay based on a story by that master of the macabre H P Lovecraft, a chilly one at that. Oliver Reed is splendidly menacing in a glowering key role.

Shy People ● Ⓥ
1987, US, 119 mins, colour
Dir: Andrei Konchalovsky
Stars: Jill Clayburgh, Barbara Hershey, Martha Plimpton, Mare Winningham, Merritt Butrick, Don Swayze
Rating: ★

Every so often, film-makers suffer a mental aberration which causes them to go down to the American swamplands. Few of the resulting movies have proved less than ludicrous and most, as here, are about people who seem to be as potty as the films themselves. Shy's hardly the word, for sure, Barbara Hershey and her sons, a less civilised version of Ma Barker and her killer brood. Mentally deranged from too much time in the swamps, perhaps, but hardly shy. The catalyst that turns their bizarre lives into a series of violent confrontations is a visit from civilised cousin Jill Clayburgh and her nymphet daughter Martha Plimpton. What can have attracted Hershey and Clayburgh to two equally unsuitable roles in this frenzied farrago is a matter for them and their agents to ponder. The scenes in the swamps have a predictably weird beauty, though, even if they add layers of lethargy to an already slow-moving film.

Sibling Rivalry ◑ Ⓥ
1990, US, 88 mins, colour
Dir: Carl Reiner
Stars: Kirstie Alley, Bill Pullman, Carrie Fisher, Jami Gertz, Scott Bakula, Sam Elliott
Rating: ★★

The modern equivalent of a Feydeau farce, this is mostly a limp affair in spite of its top-flight cast. Alley is unhappily married to granite-jawed Bakula, one of a family of doctors who treat her as something the pathologist dragged in. A casual hot affair with a man (Sam Elliott) who dies at the end of an epic love-making session triggers off one of those games of consequences that only happen under the covers of fiction. Kirstie's lover was her husband's long-lost brother, but he's discovered by an inept salesman (Bill Pullman) who thinks he's killed him. Pullman's brother (Ed O'Neill), a top cop, calls on Kirstie because she made a panic phone call about the dead man, and falls for Alley's sister Jami Gertz. This goes on (and on) but, despite a few nice moments, is directed without verve by Carl Reiner, who could definitely do with some kind of wild climax to round it off.

Sicilian Cross ◑
1976, Italy, 102 mins, colour
Dir: Maurizio Lucidi
Stars: Roger Moore, Stacy Keach
Rating: ★★

Unquenchable British nonchalance marks Roger Moore's characterisation of a Sicilian peasant somehow transformed by an English education into a crooked American lawyer, in this loosely constructed Mafia thriller. A scenic tour of Sicily, ominous statements about family honour, and the vulture-like presence of an ageing godfather would seem to underline the film's ancestry. But the oddball pairing of Moore and Stacy Keach suggests that director Maurizio Lucidi was thinking more along the lines of a crooked *Starsky and Hutch*.

Sid and Nancy ● Ⓥ
1986, UK, 107 mins, colour
Dir: Alex Cox
Stars: Gary Oldman, Chloe Webb, Drew Schofield, David Hayman, Debby Bishop
Rating: ★★

This exceptionally well-made film about the rise and fall of punk rocker Sid Vicious and his groupie love Nancy Spungen is about as comfortable an evening as spending an hour and three-quarters sitting on barbed wire. Hardly entertainment and that's a fact but not to be thrust aside either. The performances of Gary Oldman and Chloe Webb, who live their roles to a frightening degree, are just amazing; and at least a small feeling of obsessive romance, even beneath layers of drug-induced stupor, does filter through.

Sidewalks of London
See: St Martin's Lane

Siege at Red River, The ○
1954, US, 81 mins, colour
Dir: Rudolph Maté
Stars: Van Johnson, Joanne Dru, Richard Boone, Milburn Stone
Rating: ★★

Well-photographed Western from the short-lived Panoramic Productions. The story is set at the time of the American Civil War, and concerns the battle for the first Gatling gun. It's a good plot, well unfolded, with action all the way, and plenty of suspense for good measure. Richard Boone and Jeff Morrow are strong villains; but Edward Cronjager's Technicolor photography is the real star.

Siege of Pinchgut, The ○
(aka: Four Desperate Men)
1959, UK, 104 mins, b/w
Dir: Harry Watt
Stars: Aldo Ray, Heather Sears
Rating: ★★★

This cliff-hanging thriller was the last film to come out of Ealing Studios, which produced many of Britain's most famous films. Gravel-voiced American giant Aldo Ray glowers and Heather Sears cowers as the bullets whiz around them. Director Harry Watt makes good use of an unusual location – Australia's Sydney Harbour, long before the Opera House.

Siege of the Saxons ○
1963, UK, 85 mins, colour
Dir: Nathan Juran
Stars: Ronald Lewis, Janette Scott
Rating: ★★★

Broadswords flash and arrows whistle in a busy slice of Arthurian history, made by an American company on location in Britain, with an all-British cast. Showing scant respect for legend, the film kills Arthur off at an early stage, leaving a Robin Hood-style woodsman (Ronald Lewis) and Arthur's hoyden daughter (Janette

S

Scott's best role in ages) to ward off the claims of the treacherous Duke of Cornwall (Ronald Howard) to the throne. Certainly it has an unintentional laugh or two – as when Scott, bouncing up and down on the throne, declares, 'I'll be a good queen, I know I will' – but such quibbles are largely irrelevant when the end product is well-acted, colourful, exciting and whose constant tongue-in-cheek aim is to entertain. Lewis obviously enjoys every moment of his role as the dashing hero in this rip-roaring stuff.

Sierra O
1950, US, 83 mins, colour
Dir: Alfred E Green
Stars: Wanda Hendrix, Audie Murphy, Dean Jagger, Buri Ives
Rating: ★★

One of Murphy's first Westerns, casting him as a young cowboy whose father has been in hiding for years from the law and the one on which he met and married the star, Wanda Hendrix. It was up-and-coming Tony Curtis's fourth movie role. A big break, too, for fast-rising villain actor, Richard Rober. But Rober didn't have the luck of the others. Two years later, he was killed in a car crash.

Siesta ● Ⓥ
1987, US, 104 mins, colour
Dir: Mary Lambert
Stars: Ellen Barkin, Gabriel Byrne, Jodie Foster, Julian Sands, Martin Sheen, Isabella Rossellini
Rating: RB

Poor Ellen Barkin: this irredeemably potty farrago looks like a Brigitte Bardot reject from 30 years before. And it's filled with people of striking talent who have often proved bad choosers of scripts; all of them are adrift here in a ludicrous screenplay that provides quotable bad lines by the pageful. Barkin plays a skydiver who, fearful of her latest stunt and hungry for former lover Gabriel Byrne, flees hubby Martin Sheen and flies to Spain, where she throws herself at her ex-paramour. 'Do you remember,' she gasps, 'at the circus, when we crept into the cage and made love with the lions still inside?' Byrne remembers: 'We didn't even know they were there.' Julian Sands is so awful that he deserves such lines as: 'To me, the only falling that doesn't mean failing is falling in love.' At least Jodie Foster contributes a grand English aristocratic accent and isn't quite as wasted as the rest. The plot structure has a poten-

tially intriguing puzzle framework, but the dialogue and treatment by the director sink it without trace.

Sign of Four, The ◑
1983, UK, 103 mins, colour
Dir: Desmond Davis
Stars: Ian Richardson, David Healy, Cherie Lunghi, Thorley Walters
Rating: ★★

The excellent Ian Richardson emphasises Sherlock Holmes' haughty intellect and steely arrogance in this accomplished adaptation of the Arthur Conan Doyle story. Good support too, from blustering Thorley Walters, sinister Joe Melia and waspish Clive Merrison, while Cherie Lunghi makes a most fetching damsel in distress.

Sign of the Pagan O
1954, US, 92 mins, colour
Dir: Douglas Sirk
Stars: Jeff Chandler, Jack Palance
Rating: ★★

Having learned something, perhaps, from Anthony Quinn's portrayal of Attila the Hun the previous year, Jack Palance ferociously dominates this 5th-century adventure yarn about the Hun chieftain and his (fictitious) battle of wits and wills with a Roman centurion, grumpily played by Jeff Chandler. Scenes of the Huns on the move are impressively done but, as you'd expect from Universal-International at the time, the film just lacks that extra something. Rita Gam, Eduard Franz and Alexander Scourby provide some solid support.

Silence of the Lambs, The ● Ⓥ
1990, US, 119 mins, colour
Dir: Jonathan Demme
Stars: Jodie Foster, Anthony Hopkins, Scott Glenn, Ted Levine, Diane Baker
Rating: ★★★★

The particular brand of gore and psychiatry on offer here is highly effective in its best scenes, even though it does go on a bit. And what better method of mayhem could you devise than a serial killer who skins his victims alive? And what better help than from America's most feared prisoner, a psychiatrist turned mass murderer called Hannibal the Cannibal from his habit of eating parts of his victims? Anthony Hopkins makes Hannibal at once a frightening and almost sympathetic character, locked away from the world until interviewed by fledgling agent Jodie Foster, looking for a clue to the Buffalo Bill murders. Writer Ted

Tally inserts another key element into the plot by having 'Bill' kidnap each of his victims for three days before killing and skinning them, for a foul purpose that becomes clear later – this giving brainy Foster time to work out Hopkins' enigmatic clues to the killer. Director Jonathan Demme can now sit back and let the story unwind to a scary confrontation climax in the cellars of a house which seem to have endless doors and patches of darkness. Hopkins and Foster won Oscars, as did the film.

Silencers, The O
1966, US, 103 mins, colour
Dir: Phil Karlson
Stars: Dean Martin, Stella Stevens
Rating: ★★★

Dean Martin became the screen's first singing super-spy in this splendidly entertaining action film. Victor Buono hams it up gloriously as the oriental villain. And a Martin crack about Sinatra brings back memories of the Crosby-Hope screen 'feud'. With Cyd Charisse and Nancy Kovack out of the way in the first half-hour, Dean is torn between the rosebud lips of Stella Stevens and the escalating eyebrows of Daliah Lavi as to who is the double-agent. Ms Stevens wins the acting battle from her rivals – but she does have the best lines.

Silent Enemy, The O
1958, UK, 112 mins, b/w
Dir: William Fairchild
Stars: Laurence Harvey, Dawn Addams, Michael Craig, John Clements
Rating: ★★

An exciting war film based freely on the adventures of Britain's most famous frogman, 'Buster' Crabb. Filled with action, suspense and deeds of derring-do, it also has a vein of humour and a thread of wartime romance, provided by Dawn Addams.

Silent Movie O Ⓥ
1976, US, 87 mins, colour
Dir: Mel Brooks
Stars: Mel Brooks, Marty Feldman, Dom DeLuise
Rating: ★★

One of those comedies that's fun without being very funny. Made almost entirely without words, it tells of three lunatic film-makers who save a major studio by making a silent movie in 1976. Several big stars come on and play themselves, and most of them show a much more precise sense of comedy than the central trio of Mel

Brooks, Marry Feldman and Dom DeLuise, whose frantic mugging is entirely alien to the style of comedy to which the film is presumably taking a bow. The jokes are mainly telegraphed so far in advance that you can forecast a punchline (on silent credit cards, that is) about five seconds before it comes. Pleasant, lightweight and good for a giggle, the film falls some way short of the standards you feel it's setting itself.

Silent Running ○

1971, US, 90 mins, colour
Dir: Douglas Trumball
Stars: Bruce Dern, Cliff Potts
Rating: ★★★★★

A beautiful, gentle, constantly entertaining science-fiction film, ahead of its time as far as ecology is concerned. Bruce Dern gives perhaps his best screen performance as the outer-space gardener who refuses to terminate his floating greenhouse and goes to any lengths, including the murder of his colleagues, to ensure its continuance. Not even two delightful robots called Huey and Dewey can steal Dern's show here. One of a kind, with lovely, crystal-clear colour photography by Charles F Wheeler.

Silk Stockings ○ ⓥ

1957, US, 111 mins, colour
Dir: Rouben Mamoulian
Stars: Fred Astaire, Cyd Charisse, Peter Lorre
Rating: ★★★★

Elegant, long-legged Cyd Charisse was cast opposite Fred Astaire in this delightful Cole Porter musical set in Paris. It was a remake of *Ninotchka*, the glittering dour-communist-East-meets-decadent-West comedy of 1939 that starred Greta Garbo as the Soviet ice-maiden melted by romance. Charisse may be no match for Garbo in the acting department, but no matter: in the dance numbers she is stunning. Hermes Pan and Eugene Loring provided some fine choreography to match Porter's toe-tapping score and witty lyrics, all briskly directed by Rouben Mamoulian.

Silkwood ● ⓥ

1983, US, 131 mins, colour
Dir: Mike Nichols
Stars: Meryl Streep, Kurt Russell, Cher
Rating: ★★

Long and slow, but interesting and well-acted, this film revolves around the real-life Karen Silkwood, the plutonium worker who set out to expose contami-

nation risks and other irregularities at her plant. This would make a fascinating subject for an hour-long TV documentary and, despite Streep's charismatic performance (which brought another deserved Oscar nomination), re-creating the flyaway character Karen must have been as well, as her rather goofy lifestyle, there are times when you long to jump up with a huge pair of scissors and cut great chunks out of the film, as director Mike Nichols drifts dream-like through the story. Streep's performance, though, is something else: see it for that alone.

Sliverado ① ⓥ

1985, US, 132 mins, colour
Dir: Lawrence Kasdan
Stars: Kevin Kline, Kevin Costner, Scott Glenn, Jeff Goldblum, Danny Glover, John Cleese
Rating: ★★★

Although the Western was later given the kiss of life by Kevin Costner's *Dances With Wolves* and Clint Eastwood's *Unforgiven*, it was little more than a sad corpse when brothers Lawrence and Mark Kasdan penned this entertaining homage to the best in the west (and ironically co-starring Costner). All the classical Western themes, including loyalty and friendship and the need of social misfits to find their niche in the great landscape, are explored, and there's an all-star cast that any Hollywood producer today would give his right arm for if he had the budget. John Cleese has a scene-stealing cameo as an English sheriff who knows when not to cross state boundaries and Brian Dennehy is a pugnacious villain.

Silver Bears ○ ⓥ

1977, US, 113 mins, colour
Dir: Ivan Passer
Stars: Michael Caine, Cybill Shepherd, Louis Jourdan
Rating: ★★

A light-hearted caper thriller that makes adequate entertainment but hardly comes up to the standard of the same writer's *Charade*. The story is something about crooks involved with banking and silver mines, but the film's approach is scarcely calculated to make you want to keep track of it. There are a few double-crosses, Cybill Shepherd does her kooky act (which is amusing at first but wears thin) and there are familiar characterisations from Michael Came, Louis Jourdan and David Warner. It is, above all, a rather mechanical exercise in the art of

making an international movie in the Seventies: local charm, a 'money' theme, ingratiating characters, colourful backrounds – the kind of film that has become increasingly less commercial in recent times.

Silver Chalice, The ○

1954, US, 144 mins, colour
Dir: Victor Saville
Stars: Paul Newman, Pier Angeli, Virginia Mayo, Jack Palance
Rating: ★★

Paul Newman made his film debut in this spectacular slice of Biblical Hollywoodiana about the silver chalice used at the Last Supper. In its way, it was Warner Brothers' answer to *The Robe*. The supporting cast also includes Joseph Wiseman, Albert Dekker, Lorne Greene and a 15-year-old Natalie Wood, who plays Mayo's character when younger. Only flashes of the brilliance to come emerge from Newman's performance.

Silver City ○
(aka: High Vermilion)

1951, US, 90 mins, colour
Dir: Byron Haskin
Stars: Yvonne De Carlo, Barry Fitzgerald, Edmond O'Brien, Lyle Bettger
Rating: ★★★

Three fine film old-timers, Barry Fitzgerald, Richard Arlen and Gladys George, give solid supporting performances in this Western about a mine-owner trying to trick a girl out of her ownership of a rich vein of silver. Director Byron Haskin injects a lot of fierce action which keeps the plot moving along like a racing stagecoach, and there's an exciting chase sequence along the top of a moving train.

Silver Dream Racer ○

1980, UK, 111 mins, colour
Dir: David Wickes
Stars: David Essex, Beau Bridges, Cristina Raines
Rating: ★

Pop star David Essex's third foray into film stardom (after *That'll Be the Day* and *Stardust*) is the type of adolescent motorbike racing yarn that almost writes itself. Fighting the script's clichés and David Wickes' determinely flashy direction are such reliable British performers as Lee Montague, Diane Keen and Harry H Corbett, and the American actor Beau Bridges.

Silver Lode ○

1954, US, 80 mins, colour
Dir: Allan Dwan

S

Stars: John Payne, Lizabeth Scott, Dan Duryea
Rating: ★★★

The impact of this crackerjack Western was totally unexpected. The story has echoes of *High Noon:* John Payne is very good as the man against whom the whole town gradually turns when an alleged posse shows up to arrest him for murder. The direction by veteran Allan Dwan, colour photography by John Alton and art direction by Van Nest Polglase all go towards making the most of the action and tension that result. The final scenes – following an agonisingly exciting shoot-out in a bell tower – are extremely moving. Dan Duryea, excellent as always, and Lizabeth Scott contribute strong support.

Silver Streak ○ ⓥ
1976, US, 130 mins, colour
Dir: Arthur Hiller
Stars: Gene Wilder, Jill Clayburgh, Richard Pryor, Scatman Crothers, Ned Beatty, Patrick McGoohan
Rating: ★★★

A train full of crooks, a bemused hero and a heroine in distress. It's a surefire formula for a successful comedy thriller, and one used all too seldom in recent years. Gene Wilder's wide-eyed and unbelieving George is just right and Jill Clayburgh makes the most of her too-few chances as a smouldering blonde. Only Arthur Hiller's rather sluggish direction lags behind the other elements in the film, but he doesn't muff much of Colin Higgins' sparkling script, and Wilder's delivery of some of its comic gems would have even had Cary Grant's nod of approval. Staring at a newspaper headline with himself as a murder suspect he cries: 'That's my driving licence picture. I hate that picture!'

Simba ○
1955, UK, 99 mins, colour
Dir: Brian Desmond Hurst
Stars: Dirk Bogarde, Donald Sinden, Virginia McKenna
Rating: ★★★

Pretty nearly the full force of the Mau Mau terror in the Kenya of the Fifties is brought vividly to the screen in this intelligent, moving and at times terrifying film. Although not all the characters interest us as they might, the action builds up to a terrific climax and the film wisely offers no solution to what was a horrifying situation in its time. Geoffrey Unsworth's photography is a model lesson in how to make

the most of the not always brilliant Eastman Colour process.

Simple Twist of Fate, A ○ ⓥ
1994, US, 112 mins, colour
Dir: Gillies Mackinnon
Stars: Steve Martin, Gabriel Byrne, Laura Linney, Stephen Baldwin
Rating: ★

More than one twist of fate is involved in this dreary modern adaptation of *Silas Marner,* in which Steve Martin joins the ranks of comedians wanting to play Hamlet. Reclusive after his wife reveals her baby isn't his, Martin is robbed of his collection of gold coins by Stephen Baldwin, ne'er-do-well younger brother of equally ne'er-do-well local politician Gabriel Byrne, but inherits Byrne's bastard daughter when her mother dies in the snow near Martin's humble dwelling. This might all be marginally better without the miscast Martin himself, whose individuality remains infuriatingly elusive throughout. At least, writing the screenplay himself, he describes his character accurately by having a local remark that 'I heard he had a personality. He must have hocked it at Mrs Simon's store, 'cos he sure hasn't got one now.' The ensuing tug-of-love is never as gripping or emotive as it might have been with another actor.

Sinbad and the Eye of the Tiger ○ ⓥ
1977, US, 113 mins, colour
Dir: Sam Wanamaker
Stars: Patrick Wayne, Taryn Power, Jane Seymour
Rating: ★★

More magical adventures from the fertile imagination and painstaking creativity of special-effects genius Ray Harryhausen. This time, however, Sinbad's escapades are more padded out than usual, so you may find the children shifting restlessly in their armchairs waiting for the good parts. And Harryhausen's colleagues let him down a little with their back-projection work on the enchanted country Sinbad visits at the North Pole, which might well have been called the Land of the Wobbly Lines. Harryhausen's own work is well up to standard, especially in the swarm of flying devils.

Sinbad the Sailor ⊙
1947, US, 117 mins, colour
Dir: Richard Wallace
Stars: Douglas Fairbanks Jr, Maureen O'Hara, Walter Slezak, Jane Greer
Rating: ★★★

Colourful extravaganza which has Douglas Fairbanks Junior flying in the footsteps of his fabulous father in the title role. Maureen O'Hara is a spirited heroine, and Walter Slezak contributes another of his famous studies in leering villainy as the conniving barber aboard Sinbad's ship. Amazing art direction is the last word in Hollywood 'eastern' taste.

Since You Went Away ○
1944, US, 172 mins, b/w
Dir: John Cromwell
Stars: Claudette Colbert, Jennifer Jones, Joseph Cotten, Shirley Temple
Rating: ★★★

Tremendously professional three-hour epic of the American way of life, as patriotic film-makers liked to see it, during World War Two. Memorable scenes include family gatherings; an instant nostalgia dance held in a deserted aircraft hangar, before the men go off to fight; and a lovers' farewell at a railway station.

Sing ○
1989, US, 98 mins, colour
Dir: Richard Baskin
Stars: Lorraine Bracco, Peter Dobson, Patti LaBelle
Rating: ★★★

Somewhere between *Dirty Dancing, Fame, Blackboard Jungle* and *42nd Street* lies *Sing,* as good a bad film as you'll see. The kids are putting on a show, but the adults are closing down the school. Nice Jewish Hannah is pitched in with Italianate delinquent Dominic as co-organisers of the Brooklyn school's last-ever 'sing' and guess what happens? No kidding! Hannah's hard-hearted mamma won't come to the concert, but will she relent at the last moment? Is the Pope still a Catholic? The clichés are deeper than the songsheets in this one, but it's richly enjoyable, pumped full of *joie-de-vivre* with tuneful music and brilliantly executed production numbers. The New York critics who thought it was performed without enthusiasm must have rocks for brains. Lorraine Bracco top stars as the dynamo teacher who puts on the show, and she can dance as well as act. And the emotive surge of the musical climax will bring a tear to the eye in this glitzy, supercharged package.

Sing and Swing
See: Live It Up

Singapore ○
1947, US, 79 mins, colour
Dir: John Brahm
Stars: Fred MacMurray, Ava Gardner
Rating: ★★

One of the films that helped Ms
Gardner's rise to stardom, this well-
mounted but lifeless thriller features
MacMurray as an adventurer searching for a priceless pearl, and English
actor Roland Culver, in one of the
parts he played during a prolonged
stay in Hollywood – as a Dutchman!

Sing As We Go ○
1934, UK, 80 mins, b/w
Dir: Basil Dean
Stars: Gracie Fields, John Loder
Rating: ★★★

Gracie Fields' most famous comedy-
musical (also the title of her
autobiography). It was especially written for her by J B Priestley. Gracie
seems to be enjoying herself more than
in any other film, Stanley Holloway
scores as a policeman, and you'll have
to look fast and hard to spot 13-year-
old Muriel Pavlow in the van of a
crowd of cheering schoolgirls.

Singin' in the Rain ☉ Ⓥ
1952, US, 102 mins, colour
Dir: Stanley Donen
Stars: Gene Kelly, Donald O'Connor,
Debbie Reynolds, Jean Hagen
Rating: ★★★★★

This famous MGM musical about the
adventures of a matinee idol (Gene
Kelly) in the early days of sound films
is perhaps the most enduring ever to
roll off the Hollywood production line.
And while nothing in it can top the
brilliant foot-tapping sequence to the
title song, with Kelly joyously dancing
in a California downpour – 'an irrepressible ode to optimism' according to
the screenwriters – every other number was still head and shoulders above
most musicals of the 1950s. Jean
Hagen gives the best performance as a
dim star who has endless difficulties
with concealed microphones but
knows the value of a contract. And a
sequence where Cyd Charisse dances
in a veil taxed Kelly's abilities as a
choreographer and required no less
than three aircraft engines to give the
veil the right flow. The whole thing
probably runs neck and neck with
Kelly's *On the Town* for the most joyous
musical of all time.

Single-Handed
See: Sailor of the King

Singles ◖ Ⓥ
1992, US, 100 mins, colour
Dir: Cameron Crowe
Stars: Bridget Fonda, Campbell Scott,
Kyra Sedgwick, Matt Dillon, Bill Pullman,
Jim True
Rating: ★

This modish film about the single life
in Seattle has no good characters and
is practically devoid of interest. Boring
is the word, and you might find yourself sleepy in Seattle long before the
end. Little warmth is generated by the
people played by Bridget Fonda, Kyra
Sedgwick, Campbell Scott and Matt
Dillon (not that the script gives them
much chance) and their future as couples doesn't seem to hold too much
promise. Sheila Kelley (taking time
out from her *LA Law* duties on TV) is
a little more interesting as the 'single'
looking for her opposite number via a
videotape date agency.

Singleton's Pluck ○
(aka: Laughterhouse)
1984, UK, 93 mins, colour
Dir: Richard Eyre
Stars: Ian Holm, Penelope Wilton, Bill
Owen
Rating: ★★★★

Red River with geese. All this laughter
and tears film needs in fact, is a stampede. But, with geese, that would be
difficult. The story and its execution,
however, would not disgrace Ealing
Studios at their best. Faced with transport and union problems, after one of
his men loses a finger in the plucking
machine, farmer Singleton (Ian Holm)
sets out to drive his flock of several
hundred geese all the way from
Norfolk to London in time for the
Christmas market. He is pursued not
only by TV crews – who at one stage
let the geese loose simply to provide a
story – but by a goose-loving fox
whom Singleton calls Basil, but whose
feathery prey lies forever just beyond
his dripping jaws. The human element
in this chronicle struggles to make itself felt but gradually rises triumphant
against a background of Constable-like
landscapes lovingly photographed by
Clive Tickner. Holm, Penelope
Wilton and Stephanie Tague as their
(too tall?) daughter are excellent in
their roles, but the picture is stolen by
Bill Owen as the rustic-type goosehand
who gets all the juiciest lines.

Single White Female ● Ⓥ
1992, US, 107 mins, colour
Dir: Barbet Schroeder
Stars: Bridget Fonda, Jennifer Jason

Leigh, Stephen Tobolowsky, Steven
Weber
Rating: ★★

This is the one about the unsuspecting
hero/heroine who hires a psycho as
servant/housekeeper/babysitter/flat-
mate. Perm heroine and flatmate from
these possibilities and you have
Bridget Fonda and Jennifer Jason
Leigh as the protagonists in a tale of
terror. The story's nicely set up, the
last 15 minutes superbly edited and
very exciting with a final duel to the
death, predictably in the spooky underbelly of the apartment block we've
been shown at the beginning. In between, though, it goes on a bit and gets
tedious, moving in fits and starts when
it should be tightening the tension.
Tiny Jason Leigh is tough to take as a
ferocious fiend, but she really does
give it her best shot, as does Fonda in
one of the most effective roles of her
career.

Sink the Bismarck! ○ Ⓥ
1959, UK, 97 mins, b/w
Dir: Lewis Gilbert
Stars: Kenneth More, Dana Wynter, Carl
Mohner
Rating: ★★★

Although this World War Two action
film is based on fact, there have been
complaints that it is most inaccurate.
Be that as it may, this – one of the last
great British films about wartime naval
action – is a most exciting account of
the quest for the formidable German
battleship *Bismarck*. As the withdrawn
officer directing operations, Kenneth
More has one of his most interesting
roles and is well supported by a fleet of
the best British character actors.

Sins of Rachel Cade, The ○
1960, US, 123 mins, colour
Dir: Gordon Douglas
Stars: Angie Dickinson, Peter Finch,
Roger Moore
Rating: ★★

A poor man's version of *The Nun's
Story*, with Angie Dickinson delivering
one of her best performances as the
medical missionary who finds the call
of the flesh stronger than the call of
duty. Peter Finch, left over from *The
Nun's Story*, provides quiet authority,
and Roger Moore handsome egotism
as the pilot who leads Ms Dickinson
astray during this episodic drama set in
the then Belgian Congo.

Sirens ● Ⓥ
1994, Australia, 94 mins, colour
Dir: John Duigan

S

Stars: Hugh Grant, Tara Fitzgerald, Sam Neill, Elle MacPherson
Rating: ★

A silly Australian sex frolic that could have come from West Germany 25 years ago and ended up in porno cinemas. Coming from Australia rather than Austria, perhaps this kind of thing now qualifies as art. At any rate Hugh Grant and Tara Fitzgerald amusingly and skilfully do what they can as the cleric and wife who come to interview painter Sam Neill (underused) about his crude nude pictures. She is soon seduced by the exotic atmosphere of this household of nude models, not to mention the convenient and muscular blind handyman. Titillating garbage, derivative and completely unbelievable.

Sister Act O Ⓥ

1992, US, 102 mins, colour
Dir: Emile Ardolino
Stars: Whoopi Goldberg, Maggie Smith, Harvey Keitel, Mary Wickes, Kathy Najimy
Rating: ★★★

Hollywood's been making films like this ever since they put gangster James Cagney in charge of the reformatory in *The Mayor of Hell* nearly 60 years before. Not that Whoopi Goldberg is actually a bad guy here. She's Deloris, a Reno lounge singer who's forced into the witness protection programme after accidentally barging in on a hit by her gangster boyfriend (Harvey Keitel). Her hideout proves to be a convent and her 'cover' is just that. 'Look at me,' she wails. 'I'm a nun. I'm a penguin.' Inevitably, Deloris comes to be affected by her surroundings, notably in organising the convent choir into an enlargement of Diana Ross and the Supremes. So, when her cover is blown, with a concert before the Pope by the now-famous choir just hours away, she doesn't want to leave. This all gets a bit over-the-top towards the end, even for a farce, but very enjoyable for all that. Whoopi is pretty well the whole show, with the eminent Dame Maggie Smith a little lost as the waspish Mother Superior who disapproves of modern methods.

Sister Act 2: Back in the Habit O Ⓥ

1994, US, 107 mins, colour
Dir: Bill Duke
Stars: Whoopi Goldberg, Maggie Smith, James Coburn, Kathy Najimy, Mary Wickes, Barnard Hughes
Rating: ★★

Soul sister Whoopi Goldberg is back in wimple and designer sunspecs, but fails to make quite as much Whoopi on her second visit to the convent. This time the action switches from a rundown parish church to a rundown high school, where motormouth Whoopi is soon transforming the local tearaways into a choir to save the place from closure. Kathy Najimy as Sister Mary Patrick and veteran Mary Wickes as sourpuss Sister Mary Lazarus steal the best laughs again, with Maggie Smith more peripheral this time as the 'mother of all mother superiors'. But the film strikes a bum note with its hardly magical choreography and several confusing, stodgy sub-plots to the main action. Overall, it's a case of sequelitis with limited mass appeal. The trailer's great, though: don't let it make you expect too much.

Sister My Sister ● Ⓥ

1995, UK, 89 mins, colour
Dir: Nancy Meckler
Stars: Joely Richardson, Julie Walters, Jodhi May
Rating: ★★

'These two are different – you mark my words,' says Julie Walters as a French bourgeoise of the early 1930s, on the two sisters she has employed as maids. She doesn't know how right she is. Within the intense confinement of the shuttered house, the girls soon progress from being 'blood sisters' to something more. Their obsession with each other inevitably leads to the neglect of duties, which in turn gives rise to the violent ending of this shocking true story. Despite an excellent performance by Walters, however, the slow-moving piece rarely packs the impact it carried on stage and the story itself seems more suited to a 50-minute adult documentary on TV. Joely Richardson and Jodhi May are a little too stilted as the sisters, although both do extremely well with their big scene at the end. Annoying continuity slips further damage the film's credibility: if you want an effective cinematic treatment of a similar theme, rather try *Heavenly Creatures*.

Sisters ●

(aka: Some Girls)
1988, US, 94 mins, colour
Dir: Michael Hoffman
Stars: Patrick Dempsey, Jennifer Connelly, Lila Kedrova
Rating ★

A boring film with human dynamo Patrick Dempsey would seem a contradiction in terms, but here it is. A downright peculiar Gothic comedy romance, it exists principally for one more virtuoso performance by veteran European star Lila Kedrova as the grandmother whose dying spirit dominates a weird family whose three daughters all enjoy an on/off romantic entanglement with Dempsey when he comes to stay with the youngest (Jennifer Connelly) for Christmas. As things develop (or fail to), you may soon feel like donning Dempsey's nightshirt and nightcap and joining this latter-day Eddie Bracken in slumber.

Sitting Bull O

1954, US, 106 mins, colour
Dir: Sidney Salkow
Stars: Dale Robertson, Mary Murphy
Rating: ★

Custer's Last Stand gets another airing in this big action film originally made as one of the early CinemaScope spectacles. J Carrol Naish plays Sitting Bull for the second time on film. Shot in blurred colour, the results are overlong, melodramatic, unconvincing and at times even boring. Dull and uninspired then, adjectives which can certainly also be applied to Naish as the great Indian warrior, although Dale Robertson shows up well as the hero. Only real bright spot: an excellent, dignified song, 'Great Spirit'.

Sitting Pretty O

1948, US, 84 mins, b/w
Dir: Walter Lang
Stars: Robert Young, Maureen O'Hara, Clifton Webb
Rating: ★★★

It's probably fair to say that Clifton Webb was a shooting star in the Hollywood of the late Forties. He had been a film actor (and a dancer) since the silent days, but it wasn't until he was about 50 and had gone to 20th Century-Fox as a character actor that he quite suddenly became famous. He attracted attention in films such as *Laura* and *The Razor's Edge*, but it was this comedy, *Sitting Pretty*, that really launched him into popularity. For here he essayed what has rightly been called his 'waspish' speciality, playing for the first time the role of Lynn Belvedere, the testy but unconventional babysitter who stolidly maintains he's a genius. The film is great fun throughout and includes the classic scene in which Belvedere fulfils the wishful thinking of thousands of frustrated parents by pouring a bowl of porridge over a fractious toddler's head, leaving the bowl stuck on top.

6 Degrees of Separation ● ⓥ

1994, US, 111 mins, colour
Dir: Fred Schepisi
Stars: Donald Sutherland, Stockard Channing, Will Smith, Ian McKellen, Mary Beth Hurt, Bruce Davison, Eric Thal
Rating: ★★★

John Guare adapted this elegant screen version of his own witty play about a charismatic black youth, who disrupts the routine lives of New York's upper class. Donald Sutherland and Stockard Channing play a wealthy couple from the Big Apple who encounter a boy (Will Smith) one night when he drops in to their luxurious apartment claiming to be the schoolfriend of their Harvard student children. At first charmed by the excitement he offers, they later learn that he is a con man, which leads them to question the superficiality of their existence. A lot more entertaining than this framework suggests, this is an inventive circular tale, talky but totally absorbing.

633 Squadron ○ ⓥ

1964, UK, 94 mins, colour
Dir: Walter E Grauman
Stars: Cliff Robertson, George Chakiris
Rating: ★★

The rousing music composed by Ron Goodwin is the thing most people remember about this sporadically exciting but ultimately indifferent war film. It centres on a plan to bomb and destroy a Nazi V2 rocket factory in Norway, with the aid of the Norwegian Resistance. Cliff Robertson is firm-jawed as the American leader of the British squadron assigned to the task and George Chakiris is the resistance leader involved. Those with memories long enough objected to the idea of a Yank showing us how to win the war in this one, but in any event, the story was ill-served by a poor script and the film only comes to life during the well-realised battle scenes.

Sixty Glorious Years ○

(aka: Queen of Destiny)
1938, UK, 95 mins, colour
Dir: Herbert Wilcox
Stars: Anna Neagle, Anton Walbrook, C Aubrey Smith
Rating: ★★★

A companion film to *Victoria the Great*. This time, the whole film is in

Technicolor. Producer-director Herbert Wilcox, who five years later married the star, Anna Neagle, obtained special permission to film much of it at Windsor Castle. The result was an immense popular success.

Skin Deep ● ⓥ

1989, US, 101 mins, colour
Dir: Blake Edwards
Stars: John Ritter, Vincent Gardenia, Alyson Reed, Chelsea Field
Rating: ★

A few years before this, the prolific Edwards made a movie called *The Man Who Loved Women*. It would have exactly fitted this one, too, with Ritter as a compulsive womaniser and all-round pain in the butt. The film's overall tedium is lightened by a couple of very funny scenes, including one outrageous sequence involving luminous condoms, and another in which Ritter accidentally sits on his hated mother-in-law's pet dog. Alas, his character plays too much of a one-note samba to appeal to audience sympathy for long. And Alyson Reed is dull as the wife he's trying to win back.

Skin Game ○

1971, US, 102 mins, colour
Dir: Paul Bogart
Stars: James Garner, Lou Gossett, Susan Clark
Rating: ★

An overrated, squirmingly unfunny Western comedy with James *Maverick* Garner shamelessly over the top as a con-man travelling the American south 'selling' his black partner (Lou Gossett) as a slave. The latter subsequently escapes and the men share the spoils. Gossett supplies what few smiles are going, while Andrew Duggan at least tries to play it straight as a cruel plantation owner. Subtlety is not in the script's vocabulary, however, allowing us to have little feeling for any of the characters, as the plot limps laughlessly along. The underlying message about the evils of slavery and human greed is, of course, serious, and enhances the film – a little.

Skull, The ◑

1965, UK, 83 mins, colour
Dir: Freddie Francis
Stars: Peter Cushing, Patrick Wymark, Christopher Lee, Jill Bennett
Rating: ★★★

A fine cast of horror-mongers adds gloss to this beautifully mounted horror film, directed with a nerve-jangling edge by Freddie Francis, who endows

everything with a chilly sense of menace, even though the special effects occasionally wobble. Black candles smoke evilly; browns and yellows give flickering light to moments of horror; and Peter Cushing gives a fine study in bewildered terror as the ultimate owner of the skull. Other moments to remember include an eerily effective dream sequence; and an aged doctor, marked for doom, seen through the eyes of... the skull.

Skullduggery ○

1969, US, 101 mins, colour
Dir: Gordon Douglas
Stars: Burt Reynolds, Susan Clark, Edward Fox
Rating: ★

Reynolds brings his own tongue-in-cheek approach to this unlikely but attractively photographed tale of an archaeological expedition to New Guinea that ends up finding what might be the missing link, that unexpected gap in evolution between anthropoid apes and man. Engaging performances also from Susan Clark as a sniffy lady scientist, Roger C Carmel, Edward Fox and, in almost his last film, Australian veteran Chips Rafferty.

Skyjacked ○

1972, US, 100 mins, colour
Dir: John Guillermin
Stars: Charlton Heston, Yvette Mimieux, James Brolin
Rating: ★★

Skyjackings were particularly rife at the time this mid-air suspense epic was rushed out by the capable hands of John Guillermin, later to make *The Towering Inferno* and *King Kong*. Given that there's a maniac with a bomb aboard Charlton Heston's airliner, characters, situations and developments are highly predictable, and the main interest lies in guessing Who Planted It. Guillermin ensures that what suspense he can muster is capped by a suitably explosive ending.

Sky Murder ○

1940, US, 72 mins, b/w
Dir: George B Seitz
Stars: Walter Pidgeon, Kaaren Verne
Rating: ★★

Urbane Walter Pidgeon possessed many good qualities as an actor, but dynamism wasn't one of them. Thus he was somewhat uneasily cast as Nick Carter, the 'dime novel' detective whose exploits had been thrilling Americans since his first appearance in print in 1886. In this, the third of

S

Pidgeon's three stabs at the role, Carter is inevitably involved with Axis spies, out to perpetrate dastardly deeds against poor Uncle Sam. What acting honours there are in this film go to sparky Joyce Compton, and to smooth Tom Conway (real-life brother of George Sanders), who was to make a bigger mark than Pidgeon in screen detective fiction by playing The Falcon in several adventures.

Sky West and Crooked ○
(aka: Gypsy Girl)
1965, UK, 102 mins, colour
Dir: John Mills
Stars: Hayley Mills, Ian McShane, Laurence Naismith, Geoffrey Bayldon
Rating: ★★

This rather fey attempt to broaden Hayley Mills' image toward adult roles was directed by her father, John Mills, and co-written by her mother, Mary Hayley Bell. It's the kind of film where everyone speaks in Mummerset, but Hayley gives a spirited performance as the retarded 17-year-old daughter of a gin-sodden mother and the English countryside is prettily photographed in Eastmancolor by Arthur Ibbetson.

Slab Boys, The ◐
1997, UK, 97 mins, colour
Dir: John Byrne
Stars: Robin Laing, Russell Barr, Bill Gardiner, Louise Berry, Anna Massey
Rating: ★★

Scotland, the late 1950s. Stuck in hopeless jobs at a carpet factory, three Paisely teenagers (Robin Laing, Russell Barr, Bill Gardiner) live for the firm's upcoming dance, and the chance to move in on secretary Lucille. Two have other dreams: Phil (Laing) has the talent to go to art college, while Spanky (Barr) thinks about emigration. Disappointment awaits them both, although all three, in their own way, get to make it with the lovely Lucille. As a slice of life it never quite catches fire, despite some good moments. the performances are fine.

Slamdance ◐
1987, US, 101 mins, colour
Dir: Wayne Wang
Stars: Tom Hulce, Mary Elizabeth Mastrantonio, Virginia Madsen, Adam Ant, Harry Dean Stanton
Rating: ★

With a weak script to start with, director Wayne Wang obviously decided to take the 'style over content' route with this thriller. Unfortunately, that didn't

work either. Tom Hulce (who played Mozart in *Amadeus)* is a cartoonist who has an affair but then finds the lady murdered and that he is the prime suspect. Hulce is wild-eyed and slightly psychotic as usual, which is irritating, while Mary Elizabeth Mastrantonio is given little to do but look lovely. Harry Dean Stanton is wasted as a shady detective and Adam Ant once again proves that he couldn't act startled if you set his trousers alight. A deeply unsatisfying film.

Slap Shot ● ⓥ
1977, US, 122 mins, colour
Dir: George Hill
Stars: Paul Newman, Michael Ontkean, Lindsay Crouse
Rating: ★★

A blood-and-guts action drama that takes us into a world of low-grade, free-for-all ice hockey, where brawls are more frequent than goals and the really bad mauler-with-a-stick 'has been known to carve a man's eye out with a flick of his wrist.' You can believe it, too, when Paul Newman and his team of no-hopers become the Bad News Boars as they fight and claw their way up to the top of their game by playing dirty. Like their game, the film is sometimes a bit too abrasive to take. But it does have its moments of apocalyptic joy, notably when three backward, bespectacled colts turn into fighting furies as Newman sends them out on the ice; or when one player decides that a solo spotlight is better than a mass punch-up and does a mildly successful striptease to the delight of the crowd and the chagrin of the fighting players.

Slattery's Hurricane ○
1951, US, 83 mins, b/w
Dir: André De Toth
Stars: Richard Widmark, Veronica Lake, Linda Darnell
Rating: ★★

One of the earliest of Richard Widmark's part-good-part-bad roles: here he plays a war hero and smuggler. Good storm sequences, but the film did little at the box-office and signalled a sadly early end to Veronica Lake's career in mainline films. Director De Toth was her husband at the time.

Slaughter on 10th Avenue ○
1957, US, 103 mins, b/w
Dir: Arnold Laven
Stars: Richard Egan, Julie Adams, Walter Matthau, Jan Sterling
Rating: ★★

A cast that's only a little short of terrific, in a grimly told crime thriller that's only a little better than routine. A sort of *On the Waterfront* seen from the police point of view, it features Walter Matthau in one of his earliest cinema roles, giving a memorable portrayal of a pig-mannered, odiously self-assured union chief. Dan Duryea has a disappointingly small role towards the end, but there are good performances from Julie Adams, Jan Sterling, Mickey Shaughnessy, Charles McGraw and Sam Levene. Director Arnold Laven does manage one brilliantly jumpy moment that may jerk you from the armchair.

Slaughter Trail ○
1952, US, 78 mins, colour
Dir: Irving Allen
Stars: Brian Donlevy, Gig Young, Virginia Grey, Robert Hutton
Rating: ★★

A singing commentary is the principal attraction of this Western in woozy Cinecolor, but, as a device, it doesn't work as well as in, say, *Cat Ballou* or *Rancho Notorious*. Brian Donlevy boosted the cast when he replaced blacklisted Howard Da Silva, but the interiors have a cramped look, and the whole project could have had more style with an injection of funds from stingy RKO boss Howard Hughes. The occasional bursts of 'Injun' action are more than welcome.

Slaves of Babylon ○
1953, US, 82 mins, colour
Dir: William Castle
Stars: Richard Conte, Linda Christian
Rating: ★

Surprising to find Richard Conte in this, one of a series of 'easterns' made by Columbia in the early Fifties. This one tells the story of Cyrus, a young shepherd who turns out to be the rightful heir to the throne of Persia. Cyrus is played by Terence Kilburn, a Hollywood child star of a decade before. The story of Daniel in the Lions' Den is also thrown in by director William Castle, to accentuate the Biblical flavour.

Slaves of New York ◐
1988, US, 126 mins, colour
Dir: James Ivory
Stars: Bernadette Peters, Mary Beth Hurt, Chris Sarandon, Mercedes Ruehl
Rating: ★★

There's more than a touch of eccentricity in this film about the struggling denizens of the artists' quarter in downtown Manhattan. Bernadette Peters is excellent in the pivotal role (and thank God there is one) of the near-normal 'working girl' hat designer who can't get over her crush on her live-in lover, a batty artist whose petty jealousies are hardly compatible with his own double standards in matters of the heart. She's a much better person than him, but her grasshopper mind can't take the concept. Offered drugs at a party, she parries with 'No thanks, I have enough trouble with regular reality.' A bit of a jumble, the resultant trip through the artistic jungle, but with Ms Peters to guide us, the safari is at least rarely dull.

Sleeper ○ Ⓥ
1973, US, 88 mins, colour
Dir: Woody Allen
Stars: Woody Allen, Diane Keaton, John Beck
Rating: ★★★★

No Woody Allen comedy is funny all the way through, but this one comes closer than most. Woody's been frozen alive and awoken by scientists 200 years later, only to find that nothing has changed except clothes, buildings and sex (it's automatised). He also has a robot dog, which disturbs him. 'Is he housebroken?' he asks, 'or will he leave little batteries all over the floor?' Diane Keaton was never funnier as a female clown than here, and she and Woody go together like Laurel and Hardy. Ultimately, they join the revolution, which makes Woody remember another female acquaintance. 'Yes,' he sighs, 'she was arrested for selling pornographic join-the-dots books.'

Sleepers ● Ⓥ
1996, US, 147 mins, colour
Dir: Barry Levinson
Stars: Jason Patric, Robert De Niro, Brad Pitt, Dustin Hoffman, Kevin Bacon, Minnie Driver
Rating: ★★★

Excellent for its first hour, this tough backstreets epic rather falls away once its teenage protagonists grow into men. Everything seems cut up rather too neatly for their revenge on four guards who beat, tortured, abused and raped them in juvenile detention centre. And part of their final triumph turns (unconvincingly) on the old chestnut of a villain breaking down and confessing in the witness box. Unnecessary footage towards the end spins the story out too far, although it remains a powerful one with a deliciously repellent

turn by Bacon as the leader of the guards, and strong showings from all the boys. As the grown men, Patric, Pitt, Ron Eldard and Billy Crudup are slightly less memorable. But this is still a compelling (and, horrifyingly, largely true) document with impressive support from Vittorio Gassman, never overdoing the menace as the local Don.

Sleepers, The ○
(aka: Little Nikita)
1988, US, 77 mins, colour
Dir: Richard Benjamin
Stars: Sidney Poitier, River Phoenix, Richard Jenkins, Caroline Kava, Richard Bradford, Richard Lynch
Rating: ★★

This much foreshortened version of a film known in its native America as *Little Nikita* adds further staccato impetus to an already fast-paced if formula thriller. The idea is clever and the story starts strongly. But, even in the full version, implausibilities and disjointed events soon overwhelmed our sympathy with the leading characters. Sidney Poitier and River Phoenix bond together quite well as the FBI agent and prospective Air Force trainee who become involved in a dangerous situation as society spies, but acting honours are stolen from both of them by Richard Bradford as a dangerous KGB agent. Like Poitier's, his performance is loaded with controlled intensity.

Sleeping Beauty ☉ Ⓥ
1958, US, 75 mins, colour
Dir: Clyde Geronimi
Rating: ★★★

It is hard to believe with recent Disney feature-length films *Aladdin* and *The Lion King* earning more than $400 million each worldwide that it wasn't always so for the studio. This adaptation of the classic fairy story was a financial flop at the box-office. It is not without its delights, however, especially the heart-stopping finale in which the effects animators excel themselves as the evil fairy Maleficent is transformed into a towering, firebreathing dragon for a fight to the death with the gallant Prince Phillip.

Sleeping Car to Trieste ○
1948, UK, 95 mins, b/w
Dir: John Paddy Carstairs
Stars: Jean Kent, Albert Lieven
Rating: ★★★

In this skilful remake of the Thirties suspense classic *Rome Express*, Albert Lieven takes the part originally played

by Conrad Veidt – Zurta, the criminal mastermind tracking down the petty crook who's double-crossed him. The familiar faces of Finlay Currie, Alan Wheatley and Hugh Burden appear in a strong supporting cast. Lively thriller from the confident British cinema of the post-war years.

Sleeping Tiger, The ○
1954, UK, 89 mins, b/w
Dir: Joseph Losey
Stars: Dirk Bogarde, Alexis Smith, Alexander Knox
Rating: ★★★

Foolish but full-blooded stuff in the highest Warner Brothers melodramatic style. But this is a British film made by blacklisted Hollywood talents. Screenwriter Derek Frye is really Carl Foreman, and director Joseph Losey lurks under the pseudonym of Victor Hanbury, who actually produced the film. Alexis Smith revels in the kind of part she could never have won at Warners where Bette Davis had first choice of such red meat.

Sleeping With the Enemy ● Ⓥ
1991, US, 100 mins, colour
Dir: Joseph Ruben
Stars: Julia Roberts, Patrick Bergin, Kevin Anderson
Rating: ★★★

This vehicle for the talents of Julia Roberts is a suspense chiller that does its job pretty well. The action starts off by establishing Roberts as a wife beaten by her affluent but unbalanced husband (Patrick Bergin) and continues with a very effective midnight storm at sea, in which she escapes to a new life. The rest of the film is a slow build-up to the last reel, as Bergin finds out she's alive and tracks her down. The climax is chock full of false shocks as director Ruben shamelessly plays on his audience's nerves. Where will Bergin jump out from, to make us, and Roberts, collapse with fright? The middle-section romance between Roberts and small-town drama teacher Anderson is predictably soppy but, nonetheless, this is a seat-gripper from which fans of the genre will not come away disappointed.

Sleepless In Seattle ○ Ⓥ
1993, US, 105 mins, colour
Dir: Nora Ephron
Stars: Tom Hanks, Meg Ryan, Bill Pullman, Ross Malinger, Victor Garber, Rosie O'Donnell
Rating: ★★★

S

It's amazing that a film can sustain a theme of two people not destined to meet until its final scenes. French director Claude Lelouch used to help this mixture go down with a tablespoonful of sugar, but this sweet and funny movie just about makes it on its own – aided by romantic songs from unlikely sources Louis Armstrong and Jimmy Durante. And it has Tom Hanks and Meg Ryan. Especially Ryan, more appealing than ever as a journalist about to marry snuffly suitor Bill Pullman (also very good) – until, on the car radio, she hears Hanks pouring out his heart (to the agony aunt his young son Jonah has rung) over the death of his beloved wife 18 months before. Like women all over America, Ryan is hooked. But, as we know, this one is different. Jonah (Ross Malinger) knows it too: he picks out Annie's letter from the rest, because of a simpatico reference to baseball. So will they ever meet? It doesn't seem like it, but director/co-writer Nora Ephron knows she can't string us this far without a happy ending. One for a smile and a furtive tear, rather than a good cry.

Sleep My Love ○
1948, US, 96 mins, b/w
Dir: Douglas Sirk
Stars: Claudette Colbert, Robert Cummings, Don Ameche
Rating: ★★★

When she made this film, Claudette Colbert had been a top star for over 20 years and was now approaching the end of the main, uninterrupted part of her career. Here she plays a woman who is a victim of amnesia, unable to remember why she left New York on a train to Boston. The film, which includes an early appearance by Raymond Burr, was directed by the long-neglected, now esteemed, Douglas Sirk.

Sleepwalkers ● Ⓥ
1992, US, 89 mins, colour
Dir: Mick Garrick
Stars: Mädchen Amick, Brian Krause, Alice Krige
Rating: ★★

An unintentionally funny but still lively Stephen King horror film about a family of furless werecats that can change their shape to look like human beings. They also possess superhuman powers and, so that the horror content of the story is not neglected, have to drain the lifeforce from virgins to survive, though you would have

thought a good fat steak would do them more good. Somehow the nearest local virgin (Mädchen Amick) manages to survive the attempts of the werecat son (Brian Krause) to deprive her of said force so as to feed mum (Alice Krige), while all about her are meeting grisly deaths. The werecats' only natural enemies are real cats, which converge on their house in hordes, although even some of these turn out to have less than nine lives, and it's left to a police cat called Clovis to keep Amick's lifeforce intact. In fairness, King's script occasionally goes for real gallows humour, but never settles for one brand of horror and emerges as an uneasy if action-packed mix for fans of the genre.

Sleep With Me ● Ⓥ
1994, US, 94 mins, colour
Dir: Rory Kelly
Stars: Meg Tilly, Eric Stoltz, Craig Sheffer, Todd Field
Rating: RB

A pretentious, rather *avant-garde*, somewhat improvisational and wholly boring love triangle involving a man with the hots for his best friend's wife. She led him on unforgivably the night before the wedding and is obviously dying to sleep with him throughout the film. Poor stream-of-consciousness performances by Meg Tilly, Craig Sheffer and Eric Stoltz reflect badly on director Rory Kelly and do little to alleviate the tedium. Once again the talented Adrienne Shelly is completely wasted in a minor role: another backward step for a distinctive actress seemingly unable to get the right breaks. *Molto* bad language in this one, by the way, for those who object to that sort of thing.

Slender Thread, The ○
1965, US, 98 mins, b/w
Dir: Sydney Pollack
Stars: Sidney Poitier, Anne Bancroft, Telly Savalas
Rating: ★★

Director Sydney Pollack made his big screen bow with this essay in suspense, about the fight to locate a woman (Anne Bancroft) who is threatening to commit suicide. Pollack and Oscar-winning writer Stirling Silliphant (he won it for *In the Heat of the Night*) cast the star of the film, Sidney Poitier, as the young worker at a 'crisis clinic' (an American equivalent of The Samaritans), and he responds with a performance that radiates sincerity and fervour. Silliphant

based the story of the film on real-life characters and incidents.

Sleuth ① Ⓥ
1972, US, 133 mins, colour
Dir: Joseph L Mankiewicz
Stars: Laurence Olivier, Michael Caine
Rating: ★★★

Multi-Oscar-winning director Joseph L Mankiewicz ended his cinema career on a high note with this virtuoso version of the famous stage play. The two central roles have provided prime acting material for a number of actors down the years, and Laurence Olivier (in particular) and Michael Caine enjoy themselves enormously with them here. The only problem with a cinema version of the play's famous puzzle plot is that the film camera has a penetrating and enquiring eye, so that some of the story's deceptions, disguises, decoys and detours appear more transparent than when viewed from the safer distance of the theatre stalls. But the film is richly enjoyable for all that, and Ken Adam's inventive production design is a marvel.

Slight Case of Murder, A ○
1938, US, 85 mins, b/w
Dir: Lloyd Bacon
Stars: Edward G Robinson, Jane Bryan
Rating: ★★★

Of all the great gangster stars who rose to fame at Warner Brothers in the Thirties, none was better at guying his own image than Edward G Robinson. This rollicking Damon Runyon comedy stands alongside *Brother Orchid* as one of the most joyously successful parodies of the genre. Beer baron Robinson tries to go straight as Prohibition wanes, but suddenly starts to find dead bodies all over his swish country mansion. This needs to be seen after seeing a 'straight' Warner crime film to appreciate how funny it really is.

Slipper and the Rose, The ○ Ⓥ
1976, UK, 146 mins, colour
Dir: Bryan Forbes
Stars: Richard Chamberlain, Gemma Craven, Annette Crosbie, Edith Evans, Michael Hordern
Rating: ★★★

'There's someone in the room!' booms Edith Evans' vague and deaf Dowager Queen in this sumptuous if ultimately empty reworking of the *Cinderella* story. The joy in Evans' performance comes from the fact that director Bryan Forbes has tailored each role perfectly to the stock company of the cream of British acting talent he has assembled. Richard Chamberlain is a suave prince and Gemma Craven the servant girl he falls for. The opening snowbound shots were filmed in Austria and add to the atmosphere. Bright and bouncy.

Slipstream ○ Ⓥ

1989, UK, 101 mins, colour
Dir: Steven Lisberger
Stars: Bill Paxton, Mark Hamill, Bob Peck, Kitty Aldridge, Ben Kingsley, F Murray Abraham
Rating: ★

The producer of this science-fantasy about a planet dominated by its 'slipstream' is Gary *Star Wars* Kurtz. But lightning doesn't strike twice in these weird waters and this loop-the-loopy aerial 'trip' is no mega-hit. It took me a while to work out the difference between Ben Kingsley and F Murray Abraham in two cameos that amount to no more than a cough and a spit. And even longer to figure out that Mark Hamill was the villain. But that's the least of the film's problems since, although it possesses some bizarre notions that might prove absorbing on the printed page, there's almost no action or incident to back them up, with the dialogue gradually falling away to the point where it produces titters from the audience. Bob Peck's oddball reading of the android-on-the-run doesn't really work; Hamill has little to do; and hero (or so, in the end, it proves) Bill Paxton can't quite fill Harrison Ford's boots.

Slither ◑

1973, US, 96 mins, colour
Dir: Howard Zieff
Stars: James Caan, Peter Boyle, Sally Kellerman.
Rating: ★★★★

Written by W D Richter, creator of some thoroughly off-beat entertainments down the years, this crime comedy-thriller proves conclusively that an ingeniously constructed story, with carefully made individual scenes and twist after twist, can be as strong a winner as it ever was – and perhaps still the most entertaining genre of all. The plot is like a Bogart film gone haywire. James Caan plays an ex-convict on the trail of an embezzled $300,000, with the help (and hindrance) of kooky Sally Kellerman, who holds up restaurants when she needs money. Soon Dick and his contact are being pursued by two sinister black Dormobiles half-

way across California. Who is doing what to whom? It's all lovely jigsaw-puzzle stuff, with one masterly scene from director Howard Zieff, as Caan tries desperately to escape four would-be assassins in a bingo tent.

Sliver ● Ⓥ

1993, US, 106 mins, colour
Dir: Phillip Noyce
Stars: Sharon Stone, William Baldwin, Tom Berenger, Martin Landau, Polly Walker
Rating: ★

A poor, slow thriller, its impoverished plot overwhelmed by its erotic content. Sharon Stone is the new tenant in a high-rise block whose denizens have a habit of falling to their deaths from a great height. Very soon she's involved with William Baldwin, the young owner of the building, whose control-room houses myriads of screens that enable him to spy on all the occupants. Also in the frame for Sharon's affections as well as a murder rap is poor Tom Berenger (what a comedown) as a dried-up author. There's about 30 minutes of plot here, but time enough to completely waste Martin Landau, Nina Foch, Colleen Camp and other talented players in peripheral roles. Don't hang around for the 'climax': it isn't worth it.

Slow Dancing in the Big City ○

1978, US, 101 mins, colour
Dir: John G Avildsen
Stars: Paul Sorvino, Anne Ditchburn
Rating: ★

'Dancing she's a star – talking she ain't.' Let's paraphrase the famous comment on Esther Williams and apply it to Anne Ditchburn, the brilliant Canadian dancer who made her film debut in this rocky (if director John G Avildsen will excuse the in-pun) weepie about a reporter with a heart condition who falls in love with a ballet dancer who learns she will never dance again. Unlikely it is and yet it almost works towards the end, thanks to Paul Sorvino's hard-grafting performance as the reporter. And, though Ms Ditchburn is patently no actress, her dancing's a delight. No marks, though, for the scene where she arrives covered in sweat from rehearsal and changes into her clothes without so much as a shower. Pooh!

Small Back Room, The ○

(aka: Hour of Glory)
1948, UK, 106 mins, b/w

Dir: Emeric Pressburger, Michael Powell
Stars: David Farrar, Kathleen Byron, Jack Hawkins
Rating: ★★★

Tight, tense and fascinating drama about a crippled scientist battling both with his own problems and a new kind of German bomb which he and his fellow boffins are studying. A star-studded cast includes Sidney James and Bryan Forbes (his first film) in minor roles. The direction of Michael Powell and the black and white camerawork of Christopher Challis heighten the claustrophobically compelling scenes of the difficult conditions under which boffins worked in wartime London.

Smallest Show On Earth, The ☉

1957, UK, 80 mins, b/w
Dir: Basil Dearden
Stars: Virginia McKenna, Bill Travers, Peter Sellers, Margaret Rutherford
Rating: ★★★

All too short, this is a quite delightful comedy about a young couple who inherit a ramshackle old cinema together with its equally ramshackle staff. With Margaret Rutherford as the cashier, Bernard Miles as the commissionaire, Peter Sellers as the drunken projectionist who gets hilariously entangled in thousands of feet of film, Leslie Phillips and Sidney James to support stars McKenna and Travers, it just can't miss.

Small Faces ●

1995, UK, 108 mins, colour
Dir: Gillies Mackinnon
Stars: Iain Robertson, Joseph McFadden, J S Duffy, Laura Fraser, Clare Higgins, Ian McElhinney
Rating: ★★

Growing up in Glasgow in the late Sixties two brothers from a single-parent tenement family are both talented artists. The third, less literate, runs with the slum gangs. But all three are drawn into a world of teen warfare that can only end in death. Mild compared with *Trainspotting* and none too riveting, this is presumably director Gillies Mackinnon's account of his own childhood. Well performed and shot, it fails to grip the attention over a two-hour period, seeming as dated as the time in which it is set.

Smashing Time ○

1967, UK, 96 mins, colour
Dir: Desmond Davis
Stars: Rita Tushingham, Lynn Redgrave,

S

Michael York
Rating: ★★

Although there are many chuckles in this custard pie comedy about two northern lasses on the loose in swinging London, the film has one fault: it tries too hard to be funny. With such a cast – Anna Quayle and Irene Handl contribute invaluable cameos – a screenplay by George Melly and direction by Desmond Davis, it is hard not to expect too much. Incidentally, the names of many of the characters are taken from poems by Lewis Carroll, principally *Jabberwocky*.

Smoke ● Ⓥ
1995, US, 108 mins, colour
Dir: Wayne Wang
Stars: Harvey Keitel, William Hurt, Stockard Channing, Forest Whitaker, Harold Perrineau, Ashley Judd
Rating: ★★★★

Quiet and sweet-natured, but penetrating in its view of the human character, this is a minor gem. Fate deals most of its characters unexpected blows, but they remain fascinating, vulnerable and likeable – in contrast to some gangsters who make a brief appearance, but fail to disturb the tranquillity of the neighbourhood for long. The stories revolve round Auggie (Harvey Keitel), who runs a small Brooklyn cigar store. He lends comfort and help to friends – things he needs himself when his ex-lover (Stockard Channing) returns to tell him their daughter has become a drug addict. A low-key drama about roots, friendship and the inevitability of change, it's a real slice of life. An offshoot, *Blue in the Face* (qv) has almost as much rough charm.

Smokey and the Bandit ○ Ⓥ
1977, US, 96 mins, colour
Dir: Hal Needham
Stars: Burt Reynolds, Sally Field
Rating: ★★★

Another smash-'em-up chase movie, set in America's Deep South. But this one shows enough humour in the dialogue to make one wish there had been a few more words and a little less crashing of cars. The action is Road Runner-style stuff. Bandit (Burt Reynolds), the hero, is brilliant, and the 'smokeys' (cops), led by Jackie Gleason, are all clods. Their cars are forever landing in streams, canals or bridges or the backs of other vehicles, as they hurtle in fruitless pursuit of Bandit's car. Followed by several increasingly resistible sequels.

Smokey and the Bandit II ○
1980, US, 104 mins, colour
Dir: Hal Needham
Stars: Burt Reynolds, Jackie Gleason, Sally Field
Rating: ★★

There are some nice comic moments in this sequel to *Smokey and the Bandit*. Notably the 'It'll Be All Right on the Night' section right at the end, when things that went wrong during filming of this hell-for-leather comedy can be seen between the end credits. Jackie Gleason is again the Sheriff, forever pursuing The Bandit in hair-raising car chases, although he is rather outpointed by ex-Tarzan Mike Henry, playing his son. Emptying his own gun and grabbing his son's, Gleason is told by his giant-sized son: 'When I put bullets in it, Daddy, it gets too heavy.' The film's British title was *Smokey and the Bandit Ride Again*.

Smokey and the Bandit III ○
1983, US, 88 mins, colour
Dir: Dick Lowry
Stars: Jackie Gleason, Jerry Reed, Colleen Camp, Mike Henry
Rating: ★

Although the sense of fun that so distinguished the first entry in this series of comedy chase films is less in evidence, director Dick Lowry decided to return to the non-stop car-to-car destruction derby of the original. Jackie Gleason and Mike Henry are still around as the sheriff and his son, Jerry Reed takes over as the Bandit, and Burt Reynolds puts in a brief guest appearance as 'the Real Bandit'. Gleason remains as funny as ever at the centre of this patchwork of arbitrary mayhem. Brothel sequences makes it unsuitable for younger kids.

Smoky ○
1946, US, 87 mins, colour
Dir: Louis King
Stars: Fred MacMurray, Anne Baxter, Burt Ives
Rating: ★★★

A cowboy captures and trains a wild horse which he calls Smoky. A special bond is formed between the two, but Smoky is lost during a cattle raid. This blatantly sentimental film was quite a hit in its day and is the best of the three versions of the story made. Luckily it manages to avoid wallowing in the mire of mawkishness it could so easily have slipped into even though it occasionally brings a lump to the throat. This is thanks to fine playing by Fred MacMurray, Anne Baxter and (in his first film) Burt Ives, and to director Louis King's firm grip on the story. You'll cheer for Smoky and hiss bad old Bruce Cabot as he ill-treats the horse in a scene that may upset some younger children.

Smooth Talk ◐
1985, US, 92 mins, colour
Dir: Joyce Chopra
Stars: Treat Williams, Laura Dern
Rating: ★★

The relationship Mary Kay Place has with teenage daughter Laura Dern in this bizarre film will gladden the hearts of mothers and daughters who believe theirs couldn't be worse. Both living their lives on a hair-trigger, they fling insults at each other for little apparent reason, in the manner of long-lost enemies. Virgin-on-the-verge Dern simmers in the summer of a small American town, beset by Mom, indecisive Dad and the goody-goody older sister she used to love. Well, something's gotta happen, right? And it does, in the form of smooth-talking stranger Treat Williams, who lures Laura out of the house and into a ride in his car, after which everything in her life seems okay. There should be some kind of prize to anyone who can guess what the last two reels of the film are all about, although you won't find us taking part: we hadn't a clue. This is sumptuously photographed by James Glennon and contains a very promising performance by Dern.

Smuggler's Island ○
1951, US, 74 mins, colour
Dir: Edward Ludwig
Stars: Jeff Chandler, Evelyn Keyes, Philip Friend
Rating: ★★

Jeff Chandler and Evelyn Keyes star in this exotic adventure yarn about gold-running and deep-sea diving off the coast of China. One of several colourful films that British star Philip Friend – who perhaps looked a little too much like Richard Greene – made in Hollywood at the time, other examples being *Panther's Moon*, *Buccaneer's Girl*, *Sword in the Desert* and The *Highwayman*. Mild stuff.

Snake Pit, The ○
1948, US, 108 mins, b/w
Dir: Anatole Litvak
Stars: Olivia de Havilland, Mark Stevens, Celeste Holm, Leo Genn, Glenn Langan, Leif Erickson
Rating: ★★★

Gruelling film about life in an outdated mental asylum. Olivia de Havilland came close to winning her second Oscar in three years (she made up for it a year later in *The Heiress*) with her portrayal of the gentle but tormented woman pitched into a horrifying and barbaric environment.

Sneakers ❶ Ⓥ

1992, US, 125 mins, colour
Dir: Phil Alden Robinson
Stars: Robert Redford, Dan Aykroyd, Sidney Poitier, River Phoenix, Ben Kingsley, Mary McDonnell
Rating: ★★

The title characters in this star-heavy film are code-crackers or, as the script has it, 'People you hire to break into their places to make sure no one can break into their places.' The more intriguing possibilities of such a set-up are largely ignored by writer-director Phil Alden Robinson in favour of a straightforward jokey 'caper' film, as the sneakers mount a plan to break into the mega-security building run by leader Robert Redford's old college partner Ben Kingsley. Kingsley has a master code-breaking device that the sneakers stole, gave to the 'government' and now want back. It's all quite good fun, although it gets very silly at the end, as a group of agents bargain with the sneakers when they could just as easily gun them down. An ageing Redford looks ill-at-ease; Sidney Poitier is better on both counts as his ex-FBI aide, and Dan Aykroyd has a few good lines as their comrade, 'Mother'.

Sniper ● Ⓥ

1992, US, 97 mins, colour
Dir: Luis Llosa
Stars: Tom Berenger, Billy Zane, J T Walsh
Rating: ★★★

Inconsequential but exciting, this 'hit'-strewn movie is about two US soldiers on a covert mission in the South American jungle. Their orders: to kill a rebel general and a drugs overlord with simultaneous shots. It's a sort of hard man's buddy-buddy movie, except that the two snipers are at war with each other more often than they engage the enemy. Tom Berenger, in yet another jungle picture, is the kill-hardened veteran taking on a new partner in superior-ranked Billy Zane, who has never even killed a man. They reach a kind of understanding by the end, but only after thoughts of killing each other have been interrupt-

ed by more immediate danger. The dialogue, blunt and to the point, has little new to say, but does introduce action audiences to a new phrase: 'just a click away'. Shots of bullets coming towards you are nastily effective, though oddly reminiscent of 3D effects that never were. On target, though, this one, as far as action fans are concerned.

Snowball Express ☉

1972, US, 99 mins, colour
Dir: Norman Tokar
Stars: Dean Jones, Nancy Olson, Harry Morgan, Keenan Wynn
Rating: ★★★★

The Baxters escape the New York rat race when they inherit a dilapidated hotel in the Rockies – but their plans to create a ski resort go dreadfully wrong in this often very funny Disney family film. Dean Jones is particularly good as the harassed father and there are some very amusing sequences (especially the final chase scene) and valuable comedy contributions from Harry Morgan, Keenan Wynn and Mary Wickes.

Snowbound ○

1948, UK, 87 mins, b/w
Dir: David Macdonald
Stars: Robert Newton, Dennis Price, Stanley Holloway
Rating: ★★★

Director David Macdonald sustains the claustrophobic menace well in this story of a group of men gathered in an isolated ski-hut, ostensibly to make a film but in fact for some much darker purpose, which is revealed only in the last reel. Guy Middleton is splendid as Gilbert Mayne, cleverly allying his usual blue characterisation with a hint of real steely evil. An exciting thriller, it should keep you guessing.

Snows of Kilimanjaro, The ○ Ⓥ

1952, US, 117 mins, colour
Dir: Henry King
Stars: Gregory Peck, Susan Hayward, Ava Gardner
Rating: ★★

20th Century-Fox had several attempts at the works of Ernest Hemingway in the Fifties, and despite high technical standards – Leon Shamroy's colour photography here is particularly fine – never really came to grips with the great man. It's not so much the studio's insistence on altering the original ending that's at fault

here, more the screenplay of Casey Robinson, which expands Hemingway's story so much as to blur its impact. But there are some solid performances, plus excellent music by Bernard Herrmann.

Snow White and the Seven Dwarfs ☉ Ⓥ

1937, US, 82 mins, colour
Supervising dir: David Hand
Rating: ★★★★

Walt Disney took the world by storm with this first full-length animated feature, creating seven memorably different characters in the dwarfs and filling a colourful, detailed screen with comic highlights and dramatic moments that had children of the day scurrying for their parents' protection. The evil queen and her disguised alter ego, the wicked witch, set the pattern for memorable Disney villainesses that continues to this day, but it's the scenes involving the dwarfs that retain huge charm and remain the core of the film's appeal. And the depth of colour on display here has never been equalled. It's a pity it's a bit scary for younger children and not quite robust enough for older ones because so many of its elements still work just as well as the day it was first shown.

Soapdish ❶ Ⓥ

1991, US, 97 mins, colour
Dir: Michael Hoffman
Stars: Sally Field, Kevin Kline, Robert Downey Jr, Whoopi Goldberg, Carrie Fisher
Rating: ★★

If only it had been more consistent, this broad comic satire on US day-time soap TV could have been a riot. Field throws herself wholeheartedly into the role of the veteran soap queen who finds younger wolves snapping at her heels, and skeletons from the cupboard of her past tumbling out on set. 'This place is crawling with sub-plots', grumbles one executive, while the head of programming (director Garry Marshall in a rare acting role) is more concerned with the content of the studio's top soap *The Sun Never Sets*. 'That's cute,' he snaps at chief writer Goldberg, 'but when are we gonna put someone in a coma?'

S.O.B. ● Ⓥ

1981, US, 121 mins, colour
Dir: Blake Edwards
Stars: Julie Andrews, Richard Mulligan, William Holden
Rating: ★

S

Director Blake Edwards' rudely satirical bite at the Hollywood hand that fed him. Richard Mulligan, alias Burt from the *Soap* series, plays the director who tries to retrieve a disastrous film by turning it into a sex saga. Crude, rude and most unforgivable of all – squirmingly unfunny.

So Dark the Night O
1946, US, 71 mins, b/w
Dir: Joseph H Lewis
Stars: Steven Geray, Micheline Cheirel
Rating: ★★★★

An intelligently made psychological thriller, outstanding by 'B-feature' standards. In almost his only leading role, the Russian-Czech actor Steven Geray delivers the performance of a lifetime as the Simenon-like detective who becomes involved in murder while on holiday in the country. It's a pity the rest of the cast is weak by comparison. Even so, the film is justly renowned for Burnett Guffey's photography, 'trapping' characters by shooting through windows, using 'framing' devices and making astoundingly effective use of light, shadow, rain and darkness.

So Evil, My Love O
1948, UK, 109 mins, b/w
Dir: Lewis Allen
Stars: Ann Todd, Ray Milland, Geraldine Fitzgerald, Leo G Carroll
Rating: ★★

Hollywood director Lewis Allen, who made those fine Forties' chillers *The Uninvited* and *The Unseen,* came back to his native England to make this intricately detailed portrait of evil, with Ann Todd giving a perfectly judged performance that's more effective than her portrayal of the maybe murderess in *Madeleine.* Although well acted and set, the film lacks a sympathetic centre.

So Fine ●
1981, US, 91 mins, colour
Di: Andrew Bergman
Stars: Ryan O'Neal, Jack Warden
Rating: ★★★

A splendidly silly farce which gives Ryan O'Neal his happiest role in years, repeating his *What's Up Doc?* persona as a bespectacled college professor forced to help out with the family clothing business when his father (Jack Warden) falls in debt to a seven-foot gangster (who else but Richard Kiel?). When Ryan falls in bed with the gangster's wife (sexy Italian star Mariangela Melato), every-

thing is set for a sublimely scatty operatic finale. The stars perform heroically, with Andrew Bergman directing at a pace faster than Ms Melato can get her clothes off, or Warden can cut the million pairs of see-through jeans that save his bacon. Even so, cavern-voiced Fred Gwynne, once Herman Munster of TV fame, steals it from all of them with a wickedly funny impersonation of the self-centred state university chairman.

Soft Beds, Hard Battles ●
(aka: Undercovers Hero)
1973, UK, 94 mins, colour
Dir: Roy Boulting
Stars: Peter Sellers, Lila Kedrova
Rating: ★

Peter Sellers plays seven roles in this Roy Boulting comedy about a wartime brothel. There are a couple of good jokes, but most of the capers are crashingly leaden. A good cast (including Rula Lenska and Windsor Davies in the minor roles) gives its all, but it is as if each had a ball and chain around his leg. Not exactly one of Sellers' best films.

Soft Top Hard Shoulder ◑ ⓥ
1992, UK, 90 mins, colour
Dir: Stefan Schwartz
Stars: Peter Capaldi, Elaine Collins, Simon Callow, Frances Barber, Phyllis Logan
Rating: ★★

Shafts of wry Scottish wit brighten this meandering road movie, as a failed graphic artist (Peter Capaldi, who also wrote the screenplay) attempts to drive from London to Glasgow in his clapped-out car in a bid to claim a share of the family inheritance. Along the way, he picks up Wendy (Elaine Collins, the real-life Mrs Capaldi), who clearly has some dark secret by the way she hides from the police. The film's major problem is that it's too full of 'just as if' situations, especially a silly interlude where the couple tries to buy bus tickets, which seems inserted for the sake of some rather arch humour. The ending's nice, though, even if it's the one you expect from such a gently humorous film. Capaldi goes at his self-penned hero full throttle; Collins is a bit mature but refreshingly unglamorous as the girl; Simon Callow does a nice guest shot.

So I Married an Axe Murderer ◑ ⓥ
1993, US, 92 mins, colour
Dir: Thomas Schlamme

Stars: Mike Myers, Nancy Travis, Anthony LaPaglia, Amanda Plummer, Brenda Fricker, Charles Grodin
Rating: ★★★

This anarchic comedy, an uneasy mixture of Monty Python, Grand Guignol horror and the deadpan humour of someone like Bill *(Gregory's Girl)* Forsyth, was Mike Myers' eagerly awaited follow-up to the comedy hit *Wayne's World.* And, despite rumours of frantic re-editing before the film was released, it's a laughter winner. Myers' puppydog eagerness and naive charm are perfect ingredients for the man with a fear of commitment who soon comes to suspect his new bride (Nancy Travis) is a husband killer. Wry-faced Amanda Plummer enjoys herself in yet another oddball role as Travis' sister.

Solarbabies ◑
(aka: Solarwarriors)
1986, US, 94 mins, colour
Dir: Alan Johnson
Stars: Richard Jordan, Jami Gertz, Jason Patric, Lukas Haas, Charles Durning, Adrian Pasdar
Rating: ★

On a futuristic planet earth where every drop of water is precious, heroine Gertz and her roller-skating 'solarwarrior' cohorts battle a tyrannical enemy with the aid of an ancient mystical force. Filmed on location in a drought-stricken Spain, and using the country's national roller hockey players, by (Mel) Brooks Films. Too violent for younger children.

Soldier In the Rain O
1963, US, 88 mins, b/w
Dir: Ralph Nelson
Stars: Steve McQueen, Jackie Gleason, Tuesday Weld, Tony Bill, Ed Nelson
Rating: ★★

A rare comedy film for both Steve McQueen and director Ralph Nelson, who made *Soldier Blue.* McQueen plays the arch scrounger in an army camp, and Jackie Gleason contributes a gem of a performance as the master-sergeant who reaps the benefit of McQueen's labours.

Soldier of Fortune O
1955, US, 96 mins, colour
Dir: Edward Dmytryk
Stars: Clark Gable, Susan Hayward, Michael Rennie, Gene Barry
Rating: ★★

Director Edward Dmytryk's later films tended to be on the sluggish side. This one looks like being no exception until it finds its feet about half-way through when Clark Gable, as a smuggler hunting a missing man in Hong Kong, becomes involved with an impressive collection of unsavoury underworld figures. There's an exciting escape climax, but Susan Hayward has a role less dynamic than those she was used to at the time, and it's a surprise to find Thirties' glamour star Anna Sten in a small role of a middle-aged woman. The story bristles with clichés, but there's plenty of action to keep adventure fans happy. And Leo Tover's probing colour camera really makes the teeming streets and waterways of Hong Kong spring to life.

Soldier's Story, A ● ⓥ
1984, US, 101 mins, colour
Dir: Norman Jewison
Stars: Howard E Rollins Jr, Adolph Caesar, Denzel Washington
Rating: ★★★★

This electrifyng and totally absorbing whodunit/social drama runs like an off-shoot of *In the Heat of the Night*, as a black millitary attorney from the north arrives to investigate the murder of a black master-sergeant stationed in Louisiana. The mystery element grips throughout, while your brain cells will be exercised in different directions by the screenplay's incisive probe into racism within black ranks. Solid performances from a (then) little-known cast that includes Denzel Washington (who went on to win an Oscar for *Glory*) as one of the suspects.

Soldiers Three ○
1951, US, 87 mins, b/w
Dir: Tay Garnett
Stars: Stewart Granger, Walter Pidgeon, David Niven, Greta Gynt
Rating: ★★

Boisterous Indian Army romp, reminiscent of *Gunga Din*, and featuring Stewart Granger, Robert Newton and Cyril Cusack as the three brawling privates forever in hot water. Their broad comedy playing just about keeps the antediluvian antics afloat.

Solid Gold Cadillac ○ ⓥ
1956, US, 99 mins, b/w
Dir: Richard Quine
Stars: Judy Holliday, Paul Douglas, Fred Clark, Arthur O'Connell
Rating: ★★★★

One of a series of delightful comedies made by Judy Holliday in the Fifties, offering her the kind of material that

Goldie Hawn would love to get her hands on today. Here, in a reworking of a hit Broadway play, she's the small stockholder who makes life deservedly miserable for the crooked board of directors of a vast company eventually forced to employ her to try and hush her up. This hapless bunch of crooks is beautifully drawn by Fred Clark, Ray Collins, Ralph Dumke and John Williams, insincerity dripping delightfully from their jaws. It's a hilarious plot, smartly developed and propelled along by a gorgeously witty script. You'll recognise the voice of the narrator: it's George Burns.

Solitaire for 2 ● ⓥ
1995, UK, 107 mins, colour
Dir: Gary Sinyor
Stars: Mark Frankel, Amanda Pays, Roshan Seth
Rating: ★

Intensely annoying, one-joke romantic comedy whose good ideas are all spent inside the first six minutes. Palaeontologist Amanda Pays can read people's minds through ESP, which explains why she keeps bashing suitors on the boko or in the breadbasket. But muscly yuppie Mark Frankel teaches self-belief and refuses to quit after three knockdowns in the first two rounds. Before long she's in the sack with a blindfold on, but misunderstandings have their usual way before true love triumphs. Frankel leans heavily on his puppy-dog charm; Pays is okay but lacking in real emotional appeal. Thirty years ago Rock Hudson and Doris Day might just have made it work, unencumbered as they would have been by director Gary Sinyor's ponderous cameras and bludgeoning scriptwork.

Solomon and Sheba ○
1959, US, 142 mins, colour
Dir: King Vidor
Stars: Gina Lollobrigida, Yul Brynner
Rating: ★★

This is the epic that Tyrone Power was making when he collapsed on set with a heart attack. Soon afterwards he was dead, at the age of 44. Yul Brynner took over the part of Solomon, opposite Gina Lollobrigida's fiery Sheba. It was the first Hollywood epic to be made away from America. Director King Vidor chose Spain to stand in for the plains of the Middle East in Israel's battle against the Egyptian hordes; and several Spanish actors take prominent roles. Harry Andrews and David Farrar are included in the British contingent.

So Long at the Fair ○
1950, UK, 86 mins, b/w
Dir: Terence Fisher, Antony Darnborough
Stars: Jean Simmons, Dirk Bogarde, Honor Blackman, David Tomlinson
Rating: ★★★

A good old film plot stand-by that hardly ever fails: someone disappears, and everyone denies all knowledge of the missing party, while their friend/wife/lover spends the rest of the film trying to trace them. All a diabolical plot, of course, but at least this time there's a nice young artist on hand to help pretty Jean Simmons when her brother mysteriously disappears at the Paris Exhibition of 1889. Directors Terence Fisher – later to do the initial Hammer horror films – and Anthony Darnborough don't miss many tricks, and keep the suspense mounting.

Somebody Killed Her Husband ○ ⓥ
1978, US, 97 mins, colour
Dir: Lamont Johnson
Stars: Farrah Fawcett-Majors, Jeff Bridges, John Wood, John Glover
Rating: ★★

Romance, mystery and murder, with Farrah Fawcett-Majors (as she was then) and Jeff Bridges uneasily cast together in Reginald Rose's rather zany comedy-thriller. The final fight amid the giant toys of Macy's store works better than anything else in the film.

Somebody Loves Me ○
1952, US, 97 mins, colour
Dir: Irving Brecher
Stars: Betty Hutton, Ralph Meeker, Adele Jergens, Robert Keith
Rating: ★★

Colourful (and highly coloured!) account of the life of singer Blossom Seeley makes a typical Betty Hutton helping of songs, laughter and tears. As well as Blossom's career and love life, the movie throws in the San Francisco earthquake – and happily makes room for a guest spot from master comedian Jack Benny. Could have been better though.

Somebody Up There Likes Me ○
1956, US, 112 mins, b/w
Dir: Robert Wise
Stars: Paul Newman, Pier Angeli
Rating: ★★★★

After a disastrous start to his film career as a Greek sculptor in *The Silver Chalice*, Paul Newman quickly recov-

S

ered. His first step up the ladder to star status was here as boxer Rocky Graziano, a role originally written for James Dean, before his car-crash death. Newman adopted a range of Brando-style mannerisms as the rebellious East Side delinquent, who rose through reform school, jail and army detention to become middleweight boxing champion of the world. The film proved a knockout with both the public and the annual Oscars voters, who awarded it two statuettes, for Best Cinematography and Best Art Direction. Look closely among the supporting players and you'll spot Steve McQueen making his film debut, as well as a young Robert Loggia.

Some Came Running O
1959, US, 136 mins, colour
Dir: Vincente Minnelli
Stars: Frank Sinatra, Dean Martin, Shirley MacLaine, Arthur Kennedy
Rating: ★★★

Madison, Indiana, 73 miles from Cincinnati, suddenly found itself elevated to more than just an insignificant spot on the American map, when Frank Sinatra, Dean Martin and 80 actors and location workers moved in overnight to make the film of James Jones' massive novel about snobbishness in smalltown America. Madison bore a fine resemblance to Jones' description of the fictional town of Parkman, where returning serviceman Dave Hirsh (Frank Sinatra) meets all sorts of problems and prejudices. The best performance, in the sprawling, brawling film that results, comes surprisingly from Dean Martin as a gambler. But it was durable blonde Martha Hyer who grabbed the film's Oscar nomination.

Some Girls
See: Sisters

Some Girls Do ◗
1968, UK, 93 mins, colour
Dir: Ralph Thomas
Stars: Richard Johnson, Sydne Rome
Rating: ★

Here come the bikini assassins again in the sequel to Johnson's first Bulldog Drummond film, *Deadlier Than the Male*. Robert Morley makes an all-too-brief excursion into the mayhem as a cookery expert with one earring, and the girls – Daliah Lavi, Beba Loncar, Adrienne Posta, Virginia North, Vanessa Howard, and especially heroine Sydne Rome – are almost enough

to take one's mind off the absurdities of the plot.

Some Kind of Wonderful ◗ ⓥ
1987, US, 93 mins, colour
Dir: Howard Deutch
Stars: Eric Stoltz, Mary Stuart Masterson, Lea Thompson
Rating: ★★

Writer/director John Hughes has enjoyed a prolific Hollywood career spanning angst-ridden teen-dramas *Pretty in Pink, The Breakfast Club, 16 Candles* – and screwball comedies. *Some Kind of Wonderful* falls into the first category, and confirm Hughes' standing as one of the most insightful writers around on contemporary American youth. Eric Stoltz is the focus of attention here. He's a rather fey youth chasing the most popular girl in school, unaware that his tomboy best friend also has the hots for him. The bond between him and Mary Stuart Masterson (in her most assured performance to that date) as the tongue-tied best friend is nicely etched out, and for once the adult characters have shape and depth.

Some Like It Hot O ⓥ
1959, US, 122 mins, b/w
Dir: Billy Wilder
Stars: Marilyn Monroe, Tony Curtis, Jack Lemmon, George Raft, Joe E Brown, Pat O'Brien
Rating: ★★★★★

The legendary comic masterpiece from director Billy Wilder. Marilyn Monroe parades sexily in her role as singer Sugar Kane, object of pursuit by musicians Tony Curtis and Jack Lemmon (who cannot reveal their lust for her because they are dressed as women in order to escape from murderous mobsters). The performances by Lemmon and Curtis are sensational, and the script, by Wilder and I A L Diamond, simply sizzles with wit – listen for Joe E Brown's now-classic closing line. A milestone comedy to see and see again.

Some Mother's Son ● ⓥ
1996, UK, 112 mins, colour
Dir: Terry George
Stars: Helen Mirren, John Lynch, Fionnula Flanagan, Aidan Gillen, David O'Hara
Rating: ★★

IRA films on the whole have been tense and hard-hitting, but the freshness of the genre is beginning to drain away in this one. Set at the time of the 1981 Maze hunger strikes, the

story focuses on the plight of the two mothers (Mirren, Flanagan) who must decide whether to acquiesce in their son's starving to death for the cause, or to fight for their lives. Mirren (reunited with Lynch for the first time in 12 years, when they co-starred in another IRA drama, *Cal*) is the film's lynchpin and its strongest asset, with an impassioned performance that may touch your heart inspite of the ordinariness of the screenplay and most of the supporting acting. Mirren apart, the characters here simply aren't interesting enough to sustain you through the film's lengthy (and often slow) running time.

Someone to Watch Over Me ● ⓥ
1987, US, 102 mins, colour
Dir: Ridley Scott
Stars: Tom Berenger, Mimi Rogers, Lorraine Bracco, Jerry Orbach, John Rubinstein
Rating: ★★

Good to look at but lethargic in development, this is yet another thriller about a cop who falls for the witness he's trying to protect. And there's not much logic to its sketchy story about a murderer who corners the witness in a powder room but threatens her with disfigurement rather than bumping her off. Tom Berenger is suitably dewy-eyed as the besotted cop, and strong when he should be. The abrasive Lorraine Bracco as his wife wins the personality battle hands down over Kathleen Turner-lookalike Mimi Rogers who has about as much charisma in this role as a slab of marble. It's all nicely shot and beautifully dressed but, despite its explosive showdown, this is, on the whole, too slow to set our pulses racing.

Something Big O
1971, US, 108 mins, colour
Dir: Andrew V McLaglen
Stars: Dean Martin, Brian Keith, Honor Blackman
Rating: ★★★

A spirited spoof Western with some inspired patches of dialogue. Dean Martin's lazy charm makes him a disarming rogue, and there's even room for two British actresses, Honor Blackman and Carol White, in this slice of the wild west. Character actors from the world of McLaglen's mentor, John Ford, abound in the supporting cast, and Barrett gives them some richly comic lines to deliver. Particularly good is the character who, asked if he intends to bury a recently deceased comrade, replies: 'Naw. Perhaps somethin'll come down out of the hills tonight and drag him off.'

Something of Value ◐
1956, US, 113 mins, b/w
Dir: Richard Brooks
Stars: Rock Hudson, Dana Wynter
Rating: ★★★★

Richard Brooks' strong drama about the Mau Mau terror, well-acted and not for the squeamish. Wendy Hiller is excellent as a doomed wife. The suspense plot maintains a strong grip throughout.

Something to Talk About ⓥ
1995, US, 106 mins, colour
Dir: Lasse Hallstrom
Stars: Julia Roberts, Dennis Quaid, Robert Duvall, Gena Rowlands, Kyra Sedgwick
Rating: ★★

Yawny romantic comedy vehicle for fading stars. Work-obsessed wife (Julia Roberts, overworking the charm) catches skirt-obsessed husband Dennis Quaid in one of his seemingly frequent affairs. With daughter in tow (a rare event, since she's always forgetting the child) she flees to her parents (Robert Duvall and Gena Rowlands) at whose stable she works. In the course of attempting to get Quaid out of her system (obviously a lost cause), she blows the gaffe on the affairs of all those around her including her parents. There's a show jumping background to all this, but the chances are you won't care about the very obviously fabricated problems of these people, and the film peppers its screenplay with obscenities, perhaps to shove us into staying awake. Kyra Sedgwick as the heroine's earthy sister deservedly gets all the best lines. There aren't many.

Something Wicked This Way Comes ◐
1983, US, 94 mins, colour
Dir: Jack Clayton
Stars: Jason Robards, Jonathan Pryce
Rating: ★★

Or: A nostalgic nightmare. Ray Bradbury's story of a boy's dream of evil in early 20th-century America is quite well realised in this rare film from Jack Clayton, whose previous movie had been *The Great Gatsby* in 1974. Although somewhat slow at times, this is a work of much imagination that at least deserves a minor place in the hall of fame of film fantas-

tique. To music that surely owes something to *A Night on Bare Mountain*, a carnival and freak show rolls into a small American town, two small boys soon sniff out the supernatural behind the razzmatazz as Mr Dark and his cohorts grant the dearest wishes of those who come – at a heavy price. The fact that the film leaves a lot to the imagination adds to its shivery air of mystery. And Britain's Jonathan Pryce is a formidable Mr Dark indeed.

Something Wild ● ⓥ
1986, US, 113 mins, colour
Dir: Jonathan Demme
Stars: Jeff Daniels, Melanie Griffith, Ray Liotta
Rating: ★★★

This nightmare comedy became the cult success of the year, and deservedly so. Its theme of a clean-cut yuppie hero being dragged kicking and screaming into dark and dangerous terrain by a woman and the lure of dangerous sex, and the fear of the unknown, was a popular one at the time, surfacing again in *After Hours and Blue Velvet*. Director Jonathan Demme never allows his audience to relax for a minute as he constantly shifts style and throws in more twists than a corkscrew. Melanie Griffith boosted her own career as the kinky Lulu, who starts events moving by handcuffing hapless Jeff Daniels to her motel bed; so did *Goodfellas* star Ray Liotta, in his first major film, as her menacing, psychotic husband. But the greater fun in early Demme films can be found in the incidental characters and details – the soundtrack music ending when Lulu switches off the radio in her car, a dog in a crash helmet riding motorcycle pillion and the owners of 'Mom and Dad's' restaurant answering phone enquiries with 'Mom and Dad's: 'Dad here'.

Sometimes a Great Notion
See: Never Give an Inch

Somewhere I'll Find You ○
1942, US, 108 mins, b/w
Dir: Wesley Ruggles
Stars: Clark Gable, Lana Turner, Robert Sterling
Rating: ★★★

The Clark Gable/Lana Turner partnership set up in 1941 for *Honky Tonk* was such a box-office hit that MGM just had to bring them together again, striking while the iron was hot, so to speak – and they certainly knock sparks off each other in this romance-

cum-war story. Gable is at his commanding best as a fast-talking newsman, but Lana doesn't have any trouble at all getting a word in edgeways. Predictable but effective.

Somewhere in France
See: The Foreman Went to France

Somewhere in the Night ○
1946, US, 108 mins, b/w
Dir: Joseph L Mankiewicz
Stars: John Hodiak, Nancy Guild, Lloyd Nolan, Richard Conte
Rating: ★★★

Joseph L Mankiewicz's second film as director provides John Hodiak with one of his best roles in a fascinating thriller about an amnesia victim's attempts to uncover his true identity... a search that brings him into contact with gangsters, a beautiful night-club singer – and sudden death. A well-worn theme, perhaps. But at least Mankiewicz concentrates on the mystery angle of the plot – part-written by him – and doesn't digress into any phoney psychological prattle. Lloyd Nolan, best known at the time for his portrait of screen private eye Michael Shayne, steps over to the official side of the law as a tough police lieutenant, and, in a supporting role, Richard Conte took another pace towards stardom.

Somewhere in Time ○ ⓥ
1980, US, 103 mins, colour
Dir: Jeannot Szwarc
Stars: Christopher Reeve, Jane Seymour, Christopher Plummer
Rating: ★★★★

This delicately crafted movie offers us a chance, rare in modern cinema, to have a good cry. The story – about time-travel and a great love affair – doesn't quite hang together under close inspection, but the immense fondness with which director, Jeannot Szwarc (with a little help from music by Rachmaninov) treats it, sees it through. Jane Seymour gets a real acting chance and proves herself a player of no mean ability. But the real triumph belongs to Christopher Reeve, who not only dominates the film, but shows great power to reach out and affect the emotions of an audience. A pity that the otherwise excellent ending goes too far: you may have to suppress a giggle through the tears.

Some Will, Some Won't ◐
1969, UK, 90 mins, colour
Dir: Duncan Wood
Stars: Ronnie Corbett, Thora Hird,

S

Michael Hordern, Leslie Phillips
Rating: ★

A host of faces famliar from TV,
splashy use of colour and a nudging
title mark this remake of the classic
1951 comedy *Laughter in Paradise*. The
foolproof plot – an eccentric practical
joker places embarrassing obstacles in
the way of relatives grasping for his
will – provides a steady stream of
amusing situations, but the tone (like
the title) is rather strained compared to
the original.

Sommersby ◐ ⓥ

1993, US, 112 mins, colour
Dir: Jon Amiel
Stars: Richard Gere, Jodie Foster, Bill
Pullman, James Earl Jones
Rating: ★★

After the American Civil War, Jack
Sommersby (Richard Gere) returns to
his wife (Jodie Foster) and son a
changed man, following six years
away. He is, says his wife, 'so much
better it scares me.' But is he really
Sommersby at all? All might be well
under these circumstances, with Foster
happy to love her greatly improved
husband whether he be Jack or no.
But in films there is always a spanner
in the works. It duly arrives in the
form of Orin (Bill Pulman), a flop-
haired farmer embittered by the
disablement of his foot, who figures
that he smells a rat and that the rat is
the 'new' Sommersby. Gere, Foster
and director Jon Amiel only seem to be
operating a seven-eighths throttle here
and that's not quite enough to convince us of the validity of a resolution
that doesn't hold up for reasons you
couldn't go into without spoiling the
story. But the writers must hope we
won't question the options obviously
open to Foster and Gere without taking the course they do. There are lots
of good moments in *Sommersby* but, perhaps because it tries so hard to touch
the heart, it doesn't quite succeed.

Song Is Born, A ○ ⓥ

1948, US, 113 mins, colour
Dir: Howard Hawks
Stars: Danny Kaye, Virginia Mayo,
Benny Goodman, Steve Cochran
Rating: ★★

An almost scene-for-scene musical remake of *Ball of Fire*. Danny Kaye (in
the Gary Cooper part) is more restrained than usual, and there's no
room even for one of his tongue-twisting songs. But there is lots of music
from a gaggle of jazz greats, including
Louis Armstrong, Benny Goodman,

Lionel Hampton and Charlie Barnet.
Tommy Dorsey and His Orchestra
also pitch in with 'I'm Getting
Sentimental Over You'. Virginia
Mayo plays the Barbara Stanwyck
part, her last role for Goldwyn, the
man who raised her from chorus girl
to star.

Song of Bernadette, The ○ ⓥ

1943, US, 156 mins, b/w
Dir: Henry King
Stars: Jennifer Jones, William Eythe,
Charles Bickford, Vincent Price
Rating: ★★★

Although it's overlong and cries out
for a more colourful treatment, this
reverently made story of the simple
French girl who saw visions at
Lourdes is at times very moving, and
won four Academy Awards: for
Jennifer Jones, rocketing to stardom as
Bernadette, and for its photography,
art direction and music. It lost out on
the best film competition, though – to
Casablanca, which was only justice.

Song of Norway ⊙

1970, US, 142 mins, colour
Dir: Andrew L Stone
Stars: Toralv Maurstad, Florence
Henderson, Harry Secombe, Robert
Morley, Edward G Robinson
Rating: ★★

The fjords are alive with the sound of
music... as producer-director Andrew
L Stone forsook the action thrillers that
made him famous and went for a big-
scale musical biopic of Edvard Greig.
The scenery is magnificent, the music
too, the script a rather distant third.
Harry Secombe, Robert Morley,
Edward G Robinson and Oscar
Homolka are in there somewhere, although even they cannot compete with
the film's pictorial values.

Song of the Islands ○

1942, US, 75 mins, colour
Dir: Walter Lang
Stars: Betty Grable, Victor Mature, Jack
Oakie, Thomas Mitchell
Rating: ★★

Lavish and colourful dose of musical
escapism for fun-starved wartime audiences, even if it did cause *Variety* to
complain that it had taken four writers
to create a 'semblance of a plot' which
their reviewer was 'practically unable
to find'. Most of the film seems to
have been staged by dance director
Hermes Pan, in fact, with Betty Grable
no doubt increasing her GI fan mail
after twitching through her grass-skirt
dance routines.

Song of the South ⊙

1946, US, 94 mins, colour
Dir: Wilfred Jackson, Harve Foster
Stars: Bobby Driscoll, James Baskett
Rating: ★★★★

An almost wholly delightful Disney
combination of cartoon and live-action
which won two Oscars and pulled
post-war audiences into cinemas in
droves. James Baskett, as the tale-
telling Uncle Remus (he won a special
Oscar), and Bobby Driscoll and Luana
Patten as the children all give winning
performances, the cartoon segments involving the crafty Brer Rabbit are
among Disney's sharpest and the
songs (of which 'Zip-a-Dee-Doo-Dah'
took another Academy Award) caught
the imagination of millions.

Song to Remember, A ○

1945, US, 113 mins, colour
Dir: Charles Vidor
Stars: Cornel Wilde, Paul Muni, Merle
Oberon
Rating: ★★★

And how could we forget Cornel Wilde
coughing photogenic blood on the
piano keys, Paul Muni acting his head
off as the old music master, or Merle
Oberon's glacially seductive George
Sand, all in this memorable Hollywood
biopic of Chopin? Of course, Sidney
Buchman's script has more than its
share of unintentionally funny lines, but
Jose Iturbi's playing (and Wilde's first-
class finger-matching) of Chopin's
music has a glorious sweep.

Song Without End ○

1960, US, 141 mins, colour
Dir: Charles Vidor
Stars: Dirk Bogarde, Capucine,
Genevieve Page
Rating: ★★

Having prettied up Chopin's life in *A
Song to Remember,* Columbia decided to
do some further tampering with history and gloss up the Franz Liszt story.
Patricia Morison makes a viperish
George Sand and the music (the scoring won an Oscar) is lovely. Star Dirk
Bogarde, confronted with a script of
awesome banality, must have wished
he had stayed at home. Director
Charles Vidor died during the making
of the film, which was completed by
George Cukor.

Son of a Gunfighter ○

1965, Spain, 93 mins, colour
Dir: Paul Landres
Stars: Russ Tamblyn, Kieron Moore
Rating: ★

Ex-dancer Russ Tamblyn finds little time for fancy footwork in this lively 'vendetta' Western made in Spain. The cast is nothing if not cosmopolitan and Britain's Kieron Moore turns up as a Mexican-Texan half-breed. Maria Granada is a pretty heroine who looks exactly like American actress Annette Funicello, and James Philbrook is good enough as the hero's outlaw father to make one wonder why the role wasn't built up a little more. The climax raises the dust effectively, and there's the bonus of attractive Metrocolor photography.

Son of Ali Baba ⊙

1952, US, 75 mins, colour
Dir: Kurt Neumann
Stars: Tony Curtis, Piper Laurie
Rating: ★★

Action and spectacle, Arabian Nights-style, with Tony Curtis and Piper Laude a photogenic pair in one of four popular films they made together in the Fifties. This film followed their initial impact in *The Prince Who Was a Thief* two years earlier.

Son of Dracula ◑

1943, US, 80 mins, b/w
Dir: Robert Siodmak
Stars: Lon Chaney Jr, Louise Allbritton
Rating: ★★

Hollywood's third entry into the Dracula syndrome certainly whips up some chilling moments, and a well-staged climax. The eerie effectiveness of its more sinister scenes isn't surprising: the director was Robert Siodmak, who, two years later, was to direct a notable essay in claustrophobic suspense called *The Spiral Staircase*.

Son of Frankenstein ◑

1939, US, 99 mins, b/w
Dir: Rowland V Lee
Stars: Boris Karloff, Basil Rathbone, Bela Lugosi
Rating: ★★★

Third in the Frankenstein series keeps up a good standard, with imposing sets, steamroller direction by Rowland V Lee and the introduction of Bela Lugosi's best film character, Ygor the mad shepherd. For Boris Karloff, this was also the third – and last – time he stomped in his asphalt spreader's boots for Universal as the Creature: he should have stayed away from pits of boiling sulphur. Watch for an amusingly different performance by Lionel Atwill as a police inspector.

Son of Fury ○

1942, US, 110 mins, b/w
Dir: John Cromwell
Stars: Tyrone Power, Gene Tierney, George Sanders, Frances Farmer
Rating: ★★

Adapted from one of Edison Marshall's huge swashbuckling romantic novels, this gave Tyrone Power one of the last of his dashing early roles before he enlisted in war service. Set in the late 18th century, it provides solid escapist fare. The central section in the Polynesian islands sags a bit, but there's Gene Tierney's glamorous native charmer for compensation.

Son of Kong ○

1934, US, 70 mins, b/w
Dir: Ernest B Schoedsack
Stars: Robert Armstrong, Helen Mack
Rating: ★★

A semi-comic sequel to the great *King Kong* with a rather endearing, if somewhat smaller 'son' of Kong, good creatures by Willis O'Brien on a very limited budget and the return of several characters (headed by Robert Armstrong as Denham) from the original. Helen Mack is a feisty and interesting heroine and, though the film takes a long while to get going, it has some touching, tense and amusing moments.

Son of Lassie ⊙

1945, US, 100 mins, colour
Dir: S Sylvan Simon
Stars: Peter Lawford, Donald Crisp
Rating: ★★★

Laddie, son of Lassie, the collie that made MGM millions, goes to war in this enormously popular entry to the Lassie series, blazingly shot in Technicolor by Charles Schoenbaum. The dog almost seems to be more hindrance than help to master Peter Lawford, attracting Nazis like some dogs attract fleas while trying to reach safety after being shot down over Norway. No matter: it makes for a tense and exciting film.

Son of Monte Cristo, The ○

1940, US, 102 mins, b/w
Dir: Rowland V Lee
Stars: Louis Hayward, Joan Bennett, George Sanders
Rating: ★★★

Lively swashbuckler whose stylish presentation can be chiefly attributed to its director, Rowland V Lee, who also made the original *The Count of Monte*

Cristo with Robert Donat a few years earlier. Here, he got Louis Hayward away from a run of smiling detectives and into a run of swashbucklers that was to last for 15 years. Hayward has the title role, as a masked avenger who fights to free his country from the shackles of a dictator's rule.

Son of Paleface ⊙

1952, US, 95 mins, colour
Dir: Frank Tashlin
Stars: Bob Hope, Jane Russell, Roy Rogers, Bill Williams
Rating: ★★★

All three of Bob Hope's comic Westerns were among his funniest films, and this one is a sequel to his first *The Paleface*. Hope's gags perhaps lack the snap and crackle of 10 years earlier, but even so most of the material is bright. Told that co-star Jane Russell is 'tops in California', Hope retorts that she's not so bad in North and South Dakota either. And, as the director is the cartoon-trained Frank Tashlin, sight gags abound, including the one where Hope shoots a stuffed moose, which consequently pours out coins like a jackpot. There are one or two guest stars to spot too. Shivering as a photographer takes a picture of him in a towel, Hope snaps, 'Hurry up! Who do you think you are – Cecil B DeMille?' It *is* Cecil B DeMille.

Son of Robin Hood ⊙

1958, UK, 77 mins, colour
Dir: George Sherman
Stars: June Laverick, Al Hedison, David Farrar, Marius Goring
Rating: ★★

Not so much Son as Daughter of, with trim British blonde June Laverick swashing many a buckle as the offspring of the famous Sherwood outlaw. The Hollywood influence is pronounced in the presence of veteran Western director George Sherman and of American star Al Hedison, fresh from playing *The Fly*, ensuring that 20th Century-Fox financing reaped the rewards on both sides of the Atlantic. David Farrar (as the Black Duke!) and Philip Friend had also spent some years in Hollywood. The hearty features of George Woodbridge make a robust Little John, although staring-eyed villain George Coulouris is somewhat rum casting as Alan A'Dale. Otherwise characterisation is in the best, full-blooded, comic-strip tradition, as is the action, handled in highly professional style by the director.

S

Son of Sinbad ○

1955, US, 88 mins, colour
Dir: Ted Tetzlaff
Stars: Dale Robertson, Sally Forrest, Lili
St Cyr, Vincent Price
Rating: ★★

This wittily scripted *Arabian Nights*
spoof proffers a scene-stealing part to
that most suave master of menace
Vincent Price. He really relishes his
role here as Omar Khayyam, composing love poems for Dale Robertson's
Sinbad as they stroll through this burlesque 'eastern', and in which sharp
eyes may pick out Kim Novak as one
of the Khalif's harem girls. Novak
can't have been much amused;
Pushover, which she made subsequently, had already been released, making
her a star.

Son of the Pink Panther ○ ⓥ

1993, UK/Italy/US, 93 mins, colour
Dir: Blake Edwards
Stars: Roberto Benigni, Herbert Lom,
Claudia Cardinale, Jennifer Edwards,
Robert Davi, Burt Kwouk
Rating: ★★

Blake Edwards, who directed all of
those spasmodically hilarious Peter
Sellers 'Pink Panther' comedies, takes
the reins again for a new Clouseau adventure with the look and feel of the
Sixties originals. Despite the best grimacing efforts of sometimes funny
Italian comic Roberto Benigni in the
leading role, Sellers is sadly missed,
and the capers all too often have the
leaden feel sometimes apparent in
Panther films made towards the end of
the Sellers series. Still, Benigni is a
competent clown as Clouseau's illegitimate son – who, like his father, leaves
a trail of comic chaos in his wake.
Herbert Lom is once again the long-
suffering Commissioner Dreyfus,
although his role has long since disappeared into caricature; and the plot,
for those who need one, involves a
kidnapping.

Sons and Lovers ◐

1960, UK, 103 mins, b/w
Dir: Jack Cardiff
Stars: Trevor Howard, Wendy Hiller,
Dean Stockwell, Mary Ure
Rating: ★★★★

One of the most successful attempts to
translate a work by D H Lawrence to
the screen, with Trevor Howard (nominated for an Oscar) and Dean
Stockwell (the finest English accent
ever done by an American actor at that
time) in conflict as father and son, over
whether the latter shall go into the pits

or become a painter. Wendy Hiller is
also fine as the mother; while Freddie
Francis did win an Academy Award
for his black-and-white photography in
this absorbing, entertaining film.

Sons of Katie Elder, The ○

1965, US, 122 mins, colour
Dir: Henry Hathaway
Stars: John Wayne, Dean Martin, Martha
Hyer, George Kennedy
Rating: ★★★

Films about brothers or heroes banded
together in a common cause have always been among the cinema's most
successful and usually work very well
especially if some of the heroes get
killed, putting subtle pressure on our
emotions. Nowhere does this apply
more than in the Western, and this
John Wayne film is well in the tradition of *My Darling Clementine* and *The
Magnificent Seven*, with the story about
about four brothers out to avenge their
father's death. Background music by
Elmer Bernstein and the cultured direction of Henry Hathaway both help
to shunt the story along in cracking
style. The action is dashingly violent,
giving a foretaste of the spaghetti
Westerns to follow, with gunman
George Kennedy falling victim to one
of the most devastating blows ever
struck on the cinema screen.

Sons of the Desert ○ ⓥ
(aka: Fraternally Yours)

1933, US, 69 mins, b/w
Dir: William A Seiter
Stars: Stan Laurel, Oliver Hardy, Charley
Chase, Mae Busch
Rating: ★★★★

Stan Laurel and Oliver Hardy in one
of their finest feature films, the one in
which they deceive the dreaded wives
in order to attend a riotous fraternal
convention. Many laughs, wonderful
ending and Ollie singing 'Honolulu
Baby!' Bliss.

Sons of the Musketeers ○
(aka: At Sword's Point)

1952, US, 75 mins, colour
Dir: Lewis Allen
Stars: Maureen O'Hara, Cornel Wilde,
Robert Douglas
Rating: ★★

This entertaining if hardly inspired
costume drama set in medieval France
pits the children of the original Three
Musketeers (who are now too old and
doddery) against the sinister Duke
Lavalle. Fiery Maureen O'Hara, who
does her own stuntwork, steals the acting honours as a female swordsman

who proves herself just as deadly with
a rapier as her male counterparts.
Moroni Olsen, who played Porthos in
RKO's original *Three Musketeers* in
1935, plays Elderly Porthos here.
Good swashbuckling fun if occasionally a trifle clumsy.

Sophie's Choice ● ⓥ

1982, US, 145 mins, colour
Dir: Alan J Pakula
Stars: Meryl Streep, Kevin Kline, Peter
MacNicol
Rating: ★★★

Meryl Streep learned Polish and
German in order to speak authentically, and her English accent is impeccable
in this grim but gripping post-
Holocaust drama. Her gut-wrenching
performance was duly rewarded with a
Best Actress Oscar – her second statuette following *Kramer Vs Kramer*. For a
full three-quarters of the film's running
time, it appears that the choice facing
Streep's character is between the two
love rivals (Broadway musical star
Kevin Kline, in his film debut, and
young Peter MacNicol) in the boarding
house where they live. But the truth is
far more horrifying. Some of the war
footage is hard to watch and the language is fairly abrasive. Marvin
Hamlisch took an Oscar for the score.

Sophie's Place

See: Crooks and Coronets

Sorcerer

See: The Wages of Fear

Sorry, Wrong Number ◐

1948, US, 90 mins, b/w
Dir: Anatole Litvak
Stars: Barbara Stanwyck, Burt
Lancaster, Ann Richards, Wendell
Corey, Ed Begley
Rating: ★★★

A vintage suspense thriller about a
bedridden wife who overhears phone
conversations which gradually convince her that there is a plot against
her life. Barbara Stanwyck's fine study
in mounting hysteria was rightly nominated for an Best Actress Academy
Award and Burt Lancaster is glower-
ingly menacing as the husband who
may be planning her demise. Stand by
to chew a few fingernails as the killer
closes in on the frantic heroine: even
by today's standards this is probably a
bit too intense for younger children.

SOS Titanic ○

1979, US, 140 mins, colour
Dir: William Hale

Stars: David Janssen, Cloris Leachman, Susan Saint James, Helen Mirren
Rating: ★★

Epic TV movie on a favourite screen theme. Like *Mayerling*, the *Titanic* story seems to offer everything – great wealth, tragic death, the end of an era, plus the added thrill of its having actually happened. Stylish, good performances; a bit long.

So This Is New York ○

1948, US, 79 mins, b/w
Dir: Richard Fleischer
Stars: Henry Morgan, Rudy Vallee, Bill Goodwin, Virginia Grey, Leo Gorcey
Rating: ★★★

A smartly written comedy about country bumpkins 'at the mercy' of city slickers. It was one of the films that helped establish director Richard Fleischer's reputation as a young filmmaker capable of handling all types of story. The funny screenplay by Carl Foreman and Herbert Baker is based on Ring Lardner's Runyonesque novel *The Big Town*.

So This Is Paris ○

1954, US, 96 mins, colour
Dir: Richard Quine
Stars: Tony Curtis, Gloria de Haven, Gene Nelson, Corinne Calvet, Paul Gilbert, Mara Corday
Rating: ★★★

A slick, lively musical in On *the Town* style, this tuneful trifle gave Tony Curtis the chance to prove he could be a song-and-dance man. The songs are hummable, and the dance routines acrobatically excellent. Paul Gilbert is especially impressive in his one solo number, 'I Can't Do a Single, But I'll Try'. But it's teamwork and verve that pulls this one up high in the entertainment ratings.

Soul Man ◐ ⓥ

1986, US, 104 mins, colour
Dir: Steve Miner
Stars: C Thomas Howell, Arye Gross, Rae Dawn Chong, James Earl Jones
Rating: ★★

Too trite by half to be anything like the classic of satirical comedy for which half the American critics took it, this attempt to make fun out of a white man posing as black still has some ingratiating moments, especially in the relationship between the central protagonist (C Thomas Howell), the black girl (Rae Dawn Chong) whose scholarship he has inadvertently usurped and her four-year-old son, very winningly

played by little Jonathan 'Fudge' Leonard. But its straighter scenes tend to be embarrassing rather than effective, with the consequence that the film has laughs in the wrong as well as the right places. Most successful funny scene comes when the tall Howell reveals himself as the world's most inept black basketball player.

Souls at Sea ○

1937, US, 92 mins, b/w
Dir: Henry Hathaway
Stars: Gary Cooper, George Raft, Frances Dee, Robert Cummings
Rating: ★★★

Rousing 19th-century seafaring tale made on a fairly lavish scale, and given plenty of guts by action specialist Henry Hathaway. Gary Cooper is the ex-slaver who finds himself wielding the power of life and death in a maritime disaster with not enough lifeboats to go round. He's more than matched, unexpectedly, by George Raft, who offers one of his best performances as his fellow adventurer. Some vivid minor scenes round out this colourful and seldom-seen film.

Sound and the Fury, The ◑

1958, US, 115 mins, colour
Dir: Martin Ritt
Stars: Yul Brynner, Joanne Woodward, Margaret Leighton
Rating: ★★

Rather dreary drama from the foetid pen of William Faulkner, who takes yet another look at an old-established family in the southern states of America. A tremendous cast, led by Yul Brynner in a toupee, works very hard to extract some life from the tale and Joanne Woodward and Margaret Leighton really give acting enthusiasts value for money.

Sound Barrier, The ○

(aka: Breaking the Sound Barrier)
1952, UK, 109 mins, b/w
Dir: David Lean
Stars: Ralph Richardson, Ann Todd, Nigel Patrick
Rating: ★★★★

A dynamic British film about the air pioneers who tried to break the sound barrier in the post-war years. Director David Lean conjures up not only tremendous tension in the flying scenes, but forceful performances, especially from Ralph Richardson, John Justin, Nigel Patrick, Dinah Sheridan and Denholm Elliott, that really make their characters spring to life. Lean's approach to his subject is unmelodra-

matic and, at times, likely to make the viewer miss a heartbeat or two. The technical side of the picture is dealt with swiftly and with enlightening simplicity, making the purpose and ultimate achievement of the project to beat the 'barrier' lucid to the layman. Among its most effective dramatic moments is the scene where a test pilot's pregnant wife tries to persuade her husband not to risk his life in a dangerous experimental flight.

Sounder ○

1972, US, 105 mins, colour
Dir: Martin Ritt
Stars: Cicely Tyson, Paul Winfield, Kevin Hooks
Rating: ★★★★

A beautiful, throat-gripping film that deserves to be seen much more often than it is. Its story of black sharecroppers' struggles during the American depression gets its blend of hope and tragedy exactly right, as you would expect from the caring direction of Martin Ritt, a firm confronter of oppression and injustice in such films as as *A Man is 10 Feet Tall*, *The Molly Maguires*, *The Front* and *Norma Rae*. Cicely Tyson gives a flawless, completely natural portrayal of the mother of the family.

Sound of Music, The ○ ⓥ

1965, US, 174 mins, colour
Dir: Robert Wise
Stars: Julie Andrews, Christopher Plummer, Eleanor Parker
Rating: ★★★★

Although it fails to avoid sentimentality (unlike the stage show) and even abbreviates the original score, this epic musical, about a postulant nun who comes as governess to seven Austrian children in the late Thirties, is saved time and again by Julie Andrews' own special brand of sincerity. She's really the only genuine character in sight, even if, when she sings 'Confidence in Me' (one of two songs written specially for the film), like some mischievous vagabond, it's so *Poppins*-ish that you almost expect her to jump on her brolly and sail back to the Abbey. For the rest, the children are well-drilled and sing pleasantly (though their acting is pretty appalling) and the scenery is, apart from one obvious backcloth, beautifully caught in Technicolor by Boris Leven. At the end, it's the overwhelming impact of those magnificent tunes that sweeps aside your resistance to the closing sentiment, even though not a treacly trick is missed.

S

The film won the Academy Award for Best Picture.

Soursweet ◐
1988, UK, 107 mins, colour
Dir: Mike Newell
Stars: Sylvia Chang, Danny Dun, Jodi Long
Rating: ★★★

In days gone by, Hollywood stars would have given their matchsticks and makeup to play the role here taken by Hong Kong megastar Sylvia Chang in the saga of an oriental couple struggling to make a go of life in England. She, the daughter of an ace martial artist, wants to run their own restaurant; he (Danny Dun) is happy to work in a Chinatown kitchen. The upshot is a kind of Chinese *This Happy Breed,* dominated by Chang and interrupted slightly implausibly by a story-thread of gang warfare in Central London's Chinese community. This whole side of the plot, in fact, hangs on the hero's inability to stop gambling after obtaining the money to clear his father's Hong Kong debts. Frankly it's out of character, and only underlines what would have been the wisdom of sticking to the central theme. Chang's sister's pregnancy by a passing truck-driver and the eccentricities of Grandpa are handled tenderly, build nicely and have sufficient dramatic weight to stand by themselves. Chang is faultless and, even though a lot of the acting is only serviceable (including another overbalanced performance from Hollywood's Soon Teck-Oh), a sense of community and lifetime struggle is caught. Recommended with regretful reservations.

Southern Comfort ● ⓥ
1981, US, 100 mins, colour
Dir: Walter Hill
Stars: Keith Carradine, Powers Boothe
Rating: ★

A tough but foolish action thriller on a *Ten Little Niggers* theme, in which the characters stupidly go and do all the things most likely to get them killed. A squad of nine National Guardsmen goes on exercise in the Louisiana swamps and so stirs up the local trappers that those worthies kill the Guardsmen one by one. The initial incident – the soldiers steal three canoes to get across the swamp – is believable enough. But the trigger to the subsequent violence (a soldier 'machineguns' the shorebound trappers with blanks) is far less likely, and the film gets more unpleasant and incredible by the minute. Keith Carradine and Powers Boothe give personable performances as the ultimate leaders of the beleaguered group.

Southern Star, The ○
1968, US/UK, 105 mins, colour
Dir: Sidney Hayers
Stars: George Segal, Ursula Andress, Orson Welles, Ian Hendry
Rating: ★★★★

Set in French West Africa just prior to World War One, this lively film, based on a story by Jules Verne, is a combination of action and adventure, blood and thunder, animal interest (ranging from snakes to stampeding elephants) and tongue-in-cheek humour. The title refers to a large diamond. The gem is found by George Segal, as a geologist who has a taste for teach-yourself banjo-playing. The diamond is, nevertheless, the property of a big business magnate, played by Harry Andrews, with whose daughter (Ursula Andress) the geologist is in love. Ian Hendry, as the head of the tycoon's private army, would like to get his hands on both the diamond and Ursula, and he tries to effect a frame-up with Segal as his victim. Meanwhile, Orson Welles has a whale of a time as Hendry's confederate, drilling his native troops to a record of a bugle. Another vital character in the drama is, of all things, a kleptomaniac ostrich! One way and another, it's great stuff for schoolboys – of all ages.

Southern Yankee, A ⊙
(aka: My Hero)
1948, US, 90 mins, b/w
Dir: Edward Sedgwick
Stars: Red Skelton, Arlene Dahl, Brian Donlevy, John Ireland
Rating: ★★★

This is probably Red Skelton's funniest film outing. That's hardly surprising, as it was directed by Edward Sedgwick, and many of its visual gags were devised by Buster Keaton. Sedgwick and Keaton combined on two of Buster's best comedies, *The Cameraman* and *Spite Marriage* in the last days of the silent era, and *A Southern Yankee* would have made a wonderful Keaton vehicle in itself. As it is the rubber-faced Skelton does well enough in this Civil War spoof, especially in Keaton-inspired routines when, in one instance, he escapes through a forest of legs and, in another, where he rides between Confederate and Unionist lines wearing a uniform dark blue on one side and grey on the other.

South of Pago Pago ○
1940, US, 96 mins, b/w
Dir: Alfred E Green
Stars: Victor McLaglen, Jon Hall, Frances Farmer
Rating: ★★★

This rip-roaring South Seas adventure is unjustly more famous today for the beginning of the downswing of the career of the tragic Frances Farmer, as she was forced to play roles unworthy of her talent. In its own right, though, this is a hard-hitting adventure movie with a swaggering performance from Victor McLaglen as the improbably named Bucko Larson, and first-class black-and-white photography by John Mescall.

South of St Louis ○
1949, US, 88 mins, colour
Dir: Ray Enright
Stars: Joel McCrea, Alexis Smith, Zachary Scott, Dorothy Malone
Rating: ★★

A good cast, fast-paced direction by Ray Enright (who had just finished a spate of eight good Westerns with Randolph Scott) and classy colour camerawork by Karl Freund all help strengthen this routine Western about three Texans (Joel McCrea, Zachary Scott, Douglas Kennedy) who get tangled up with gun-runners and Civil War renegades. The plot is pretty complicated, and most of it, despite the title, takes place *west* of St Louis! Victor Jory and Bob Steele (once himself a Western hero) make a thoroughly unpleasant pair of bad guys and Alan Hale, in one of his last film roles, etches a vivid portrait of the local bartender.

South Pacific ○ ⓥ
1958, UK, 151 mins, colour
Dir: Joshua Logan
Stars: Mitzi Gaynor, Rossano Brazzi, John Kerr, Juanita Hall
Rating: ★★

Successful on stage but less on screen, even with a score that includes 'Some Enchanted Evening', 'Happy Talk', 'Younger Than Springtime' ' 'There is Nothing Like a Dame', 'I'm Gonna Wash That Man Right Outa My Hair and 'Bali Ha'i'. The stage show was a smash success, but the film, with its tremendous colour photography (including the use of colour filters) and dazzling musical scenes actually shot on location amid sea and sand, was potentially even better: the performances, though, from Mitzi Gaynor, Rossano Brazzi and John Kerr, are by and large disappointing.

Souvenir ●

1987, UK, 93 mins, colour
Dir: Geoffrey Reeve
Stars: Christopher Plummer, Catherine Hicks, Michael Lonsdale, Christopher Cazenove
Rating: ★

This flashback drama has an absorbing and initially fascinating idea, but proves boring in its progressive exposition and over-melodramatic towards the end. Touching early scenes – between Christopher Plummer as an ex-German soldier just retired from his Canadian butcher's shop, and Susannah York-lookalike Catherine Hicks as his daughter – go for nothing once the action reaches the French rural community where Plummer fell in love with a young French housewife in World War Two. The village, however, has a subsequent history of which he is unaware. Michael Lonsdale's English-speaking mayor, who knows 'ambush' and 'skirmish' but not the English for 'chest', is, with Christopher Cazenove's stereotype English reporter abroad, the most flawed character and a sideline romance between Cazenove and Hicks is risibly handled. Amélie Pick is very attractive as Plummer's lost love, and Tony Kinsey's music has that haunting quality that so much of *Souvenir* lacks.

Soylent Green ◐

1973, US, 97 mins, colour
Dir: Richard Fleischer
Stars: Charlton Heston, Edward G Robinson, Leigh Taylor-Young
Rating: ★★★★

This ecological science-fiction thriller, set in the year 2022, bulges with originality and imagination. Charlton Heston gives his usual sincere and impassioned performance as the detective who investigates assassination in high places and stumbles across a horrendous secret. And Edward G Robinson is tremendous in his last film as the aged researcher with whom Heston shares a precious flat while the vast majority of New Yorkers live on the green-befogged streets or on the filthy stairways of grossly overcrowded tenement buildings. In the background, there are one or two gratifyingly large sets that take one back to the Hollywood of 15 years ago; and director Richard Fleischer uses them well.

And 20th-century buildings that stand in for 21st-century ones are as skilfully used by Fleischer as by Lang or Godard before him. The extermination centre, probably some ordinary New York skyscraper by day, becomes a forbidding tomb of light with a gaping mouth at its base, that dominates the wide, dusty, waste-ravaged avenue before it.

Spaceballs ◐ Ⓥ

1987, US, 96 mins, colour
Dir: Mel Brooks
Stars: Mel Brooks, John Candy, Rick Moranis, Bill Pullman
Rating: ★★

There are half-a-dozen brilliant comic ideas in this Mel Brooks parody of a space movie: e.g. John Hurt repeating his chest-expanding bit from *Alien*. The sad thing is that they're lost in a downpour of puerile jokes, feeble puns and idiotic gags – 'Beam me down, Snotty'! is a fair example.

SpaceCamp ○ Ⓥ

1986, US, 108 mins, colour
Dir: Harry Winer
Stars: Lea Thompson, Kate Capshaw, Leaf Phoenix, Kelly Preston, Tom Skerritt, Terry O'Quinn, Tate Donovan
Rating: ★★

Let's give a hoot and a holler for good old-fashioned teamwork. Because that's what this Disneyish teenage adventure is all about. Initially believable, but finally ridiculous, especially with some bargain-basement special effects, the film still has bits that work on the emotions in the way that was obviously intended, especially with a stirring and well-thought out performance by Lea Thompson. She plays the girl who eventually has to fly a space shuttle after the only professional pilot on board is badly injured. The first third of the film is really a non-event as four teenagers and a space-mad sub-teen assemble for holiday 'training' to be astronauts at NASA's SpaceCamp. Once aloft, the film gains both momentum and emotional tug, although the tatty effects badly undercut scenes of the tiro astronauts making a life or death mission to get more oxygen from a floating space station.

Spaced Invaders ☉

1990, US, 100 mins, colour
Dir: Patrick Read Johnson
Stars: Douglas Barr, Royal Dano, Ariana Richards, J J Anderson
Rating: ★★

'Well, Jim, says the old-timer to his dog. 'It looks like you and me is the Earth's only hope. Kinda sad, isn't it?' Kinda sad, too, that poor delivery spoils most of the funny lines in this overlong space-age pantomime in which little green men from Mars storm down to Earth after hearing an anniversary broadcast of Orson Welles' famous radio programme about the landing of Martians. A granny and grandpa are recalling how he put a bucket on his head when the original *The War of the Worlds* was broadcast, when a spaceship hurtles past the house. 'I'll get the bucket,' she says.

Spacehunter: Adventures In the Forbidden Zone ◐ Ⓥ

1983, US, 85 mins, colour
Dir: Lamont Johnson
Stars: Peter Strauss, Molly Ringwald, Ernie Hudson, Michael Ironside
Rating: ★★★

Originally in 3D, this comic strip sci-fi *Star Wars* clone has lots of action, large, complex and very impressive sets, a good monster or two, and dislikable performances from the leading players. Ingenuity, however, wins the day, as Spacehunter (Peter Strauss) searches for three simpering maidens kidnapped by an aged megalomaniac (Michael Ironside) kept alive by artificial means on a distant and inhospitable planet. 'Are they missing any limbs?' grumbles Ironside, in one of the script's few flashes of genuine humour. 'I hate it when they're missing limbs.' Fair enough.

Space Jam ☉ ○

1996, US, 88 mins, colour
Dir: Joe Pytka
Stars: Bugs Bunny, Michael Johnson, Bill Murray, Theresa Randle, Wayne Randle, Wayne Knight, voice of Danny DeVito
Rating: ★★

Cartoon superstar Bugs Bunny deserves better than this moth-eaten mishmash of animation and live action, in which mangy monsters from space invade Looney Tunes Land and agree to play Bugs and fellow cartoon stars at basketball – the losers to spend forever on Moron Mountain's funfair. Alas the monsters, teeny to begin with, swell themselves to giant size to play the game. Cue Michael Johnson, real-life basketball great (but no great actor) as the star of the film and the Looneys' secret weapon. This is real Saturday morning stuff, the cartoon characters' three-dimensional images don't work,

S

and real invention is in scarce supply – the selection of 'injuries' sustained in the game against the bad guys is about the best bit and musters a rare chuckle. Who framed Bugs Bunny? Warner Brothers – that's who folks!

Space Truckers ◐ ⓥ

1996, US/UK, 97 mins, colour
Dir: Stuart Gordon
Stars: Stephen Dorff, Dennis Hopper, Debi Mazar, Charles Dance, George Wendt, Shane Rimmer
Rating: ★★★★

Good-natured and easily director Gordon's best film, this is very good fun: a non-stop, all-action sci-fi comedy with awesome special effects that goes along like a runaway train. Unpolished, though – a rough diamond, in fact, just like John Canyon (Hopper), a galactic trucker who tows cargoes around in space in his creaky old ship *Pachyderm*, without asking too many questions. Currently, he's delivering a load of square pigs, but his next load is dodgy – and we can guess what it is from having seen the precredits sequence about an army of invincible killing machines. Taking off with fellow trucker Dorff and waitress Mazar, who's agreed to his proposal of marriage as a ticket back to Earth, Hopper's hijacked by space pirates led by sneering Charles Dance as a kind of android Long John Silver of the skies. Sometimes near the knuckle, even for 12-year-olds, the whole film is still a blast – a rocky but rewarding ride.

Spaceman and King Arthur, The ☉

(aka: Unidentified Flying Oddball)
1979, UK, 93 mins, colour
Dir: Russ Mayberry
Stars: Dennis Dugan, Jim Dale, Ron Moody, Kenneth More
Rating: ★★★

A jolly shenanigan from the Disney people, which transposes Mark Twain's tale of the *Connecticut Yankee at King Arthur's Court* into the space age, with an astronaut jetting back through time and landing in Camelot. Dennis Dugan differentiates nicely between the astronaut and his robot twin and there are some ingenious laughs from the timewarp situation. Kenneth More and John le Mesurier are both treasurable as King Arthur and Sir Gawain, each in turn more fey and fuddled than the other. 'Can I have a word with you after the burning?' enquires Dugan, as he goes to the stake. 'Very

well,' sighs More to le Mesurier. 'If he feels up to it.'

Spaceways ○

1953, UK, 76 mins, b/w
Dir: Terence Fisher
Stars: Howard Duff, Eva Bartok
Rating: ★

Adapted from a radio play, this British entry into the major league of science-fiction films fails to stir the blood in spite of having Terence Fisher in the director's chair, a Hollywood star (Howard Duff) in the lead, and smart photography by Reginald Wyer. A lame script is the chief culprit, although the actors do their best.

Spanish Gardener, The ○

1956, UK, 97 mins, colour
Dir: Philip Leacock
Stars: Dirk Bogarde, Jon Whiteley, Michael Hordern
Rating: ★★★

Rank didn't purchase many class properties for Dirk Bogarde when he was their most popular star, but this was definitely one of them. Adapted from the novel by A J Cronin, it reunites Bogarde with Jon Whiteley, the talented boy actor who had previously starred with him in *Hunted*. And the director Philip Leacock was renowned for eliciting brilliant portrayals from child players; he also directed Whiteley (and Vincent Winter) in the classic Ealing success *The Kidnappers*. The result of all this talent is not surprisingly a fresh and entertaining film.

Spanish Main, The ☉

1945, US, 100 mins, colour
Dir: Frank Borzage
Stars: Paul Henreid, Maureen O'Hara, Walter Slezak, Binnie Barnes
Rating: ★★★

A really big pirate adventure story from RKO-Radio, clips from which turned up in the studio's action pictures for years afterwards. Chiefly notable for Binnie Barnes' spirited contribution as the lady pirate Ann Bonny (the character later reappeared in Cecil B DeMille's *The Buccaneer*) and for getting Henreid away from a series of women's pictures at Warners. He subsequently became equally typed in swashbucklers!

Spanking the Monkey ●

1994, US, 103 mins, colour
Dir: David 0 Russell
Stars: Jeremy Davies, Alberta Watson, Carla Gallo, Benjamin Hendrickson
Rating: ★

The subject is incest: and this is a tedious, grungy film with a soft soundtrack: low-budget stuff that will send you to sleep swifter than a Sominex. Jeremy Davies (son) and Alberta Watson (mum) look worried, as well they might. Meanwhile, Davies' father (Benjamin Hendrickson) is a salesman who beds more curvy cuties on the road than seems possible. Don't hire this expecting titillation, though: it will bore the average video viewer silly.

Spare a Copper ○

1941, UK, 75 mins, b/w
Dir: John Paddy Carstairs
Stars: George Formby
Rating: ★★★

George as a gormless war reserve policeman, in a comedy formula that couldn't miss with British wartime audiences. Some inimitable Formby songs including 'I'm Shy' and 'On the Beat'.

Spare the Rod ○

1961, UK, 93 mins, b/w
Dir: Leslie Norman
Stars: Max Bygraves, Donald Pleasence, Betty McDowall
Rating: ★★★

Max Bygraves, who plays an idealistic schoolmaster in this story of life in a tough London school, staked nearly £50,000 of his own money to bring Michael Croft's controversial novel to the screen, determined to bring this angry swipe at corporal punishment before a viewing public. No punches are pulled, even though the school's problems may look minor compared with some of those today. There are savage thrashings, administered mainly by hardliner Geoffrey Keen, and a riot in which pupils wreck furniture and windows and scream slogans of hate. The children's problems are studied more closely than is usual in this kind of film and the direction at crucial points is very telling. The results ring true right to the final scene, helped by good performances from all the youngsters.

Spartacus

1960, US, 184 mins, colour
Dir: Stanley Kubrick
Stars: Kirk Douglas, Laurence Olivier, Jean Simmons, Tony Curtis, Charles Laughton, Peter Ustinov
Rating: ★★★★★

The sole surprise about Stanley Kubrick's marvellous epic is that it only won four Oscars. They included awards for Peter Ustinov's clever and finally greatly moving performance as Batiatus and for Russell Metty's breathtaking colour photography, at its very best in the final tableau of a sea of crosses silhouetted against a sunset. Kubrick's control of the massive battle scenes is commendable. But it is in the observation of human detail, and in many memorable little scenes that the film scores most heavily over other epics, and in which it finds an inner strength. It has at least half a dozen flawless portrayals. Ustinov, Kirk Douglas, Jean Simmons, Tony Curtis and John Ireland all do commendably craftsmanlike work. Topping them all is Charles Laughton as the wily old senator Gracchus. With a flicker of the corner of his mouth, or the raising of an eyelid, Laughton conveys more in an instant than others might in an hour.

Special Delivery O
1955, US, 86 mins, b/w
Dir: John Brahm
Stars: Joseph Cotten, Eva Bartok, Niall MacGinnis
Rating: ★★★

Here's a novel angle on an old plot. The suspense and thrills take place behind the Iron Curtain of the Fifties, but it isn't the theft of confidential plans or a swap of double-agents that sparks off the excitement – it's a baby. Filmed in Germany, the impressive settings give the sentimental story some stylish weight. Eva Bartok makes a charming and touching heroine.

Special Delivery ①
1976, US, 99 mins, colour
Dir: Paul Wendkos
Stars: Bo Svenson, Cybill Shepherd
Rating: ★★★

An action caper that skilfully steers its way between thriller, romance and black comedy. A breathless opening, when four ex-marines rob a bank posing as toy salesmen, gives way to some nice dark jokes and acceptable romantic comedy, building to a suspenseful climax in which all interested parties close in warily on a mailbox containing the proceeds of the robbery. Sleekly directed by the talented Paul Wendkos, it's perhaps the best film of granite-jawed Bo Svenson's prolific career.

Specialist, The ● ⓥ
1994, US, 110 mins, colour
Dir: Luis Llosa
Stars: Sylvester Stallone, Sharon Stone, James Woods, Rod Steiger, Eric Roberts
Rating: ★

This abysmal action thriller is a film for those who like seeing people and things blown to pieces. Sylvester Stallone and Woods are CIA blast men – 'the rigger and the trigger' – who fall out and become enemies for the rest of the movie. The main body (an operative word here) of the plot concerns Sharon Stone's attempts (through Stallone) to take revenge on the Miami mobsters for whom Woods just happens to be working. Director Luis Llosa takes most of the discredit here. Stallone, as difficult to hear as ever, is encouraged to do his vein-bulging fitness training; Stone is encouraged to take her clothes off (often); Steiger's Italianate Mafioso is encouraged to say 'chew' (for 'you') a lot, which is what he does to the scenery; and John Barry is encouraged to supply a sub-Bondian score which plumbs ludicrous depths in a nude love scene choreographed as carefully as any of Stallone's *Rocky* battles in the ring. Woods, who gets the few good lines in the film, should perhaps have tried dynamiting the script instead of Stallone.

Species ● ⓥ
1995, US, 108 mins. colour
Dir: Roger Donaldson
Stars: Ben Kingsley, Michael Madsen, Marg Helgenberger, Forest Whitaker, Alfred Molina, Natasha Henstridge
Rating: ★★★

The Applegates have a lot to answer for. Another one of those slavering aliens disguised as a human is on the loose, pursued desperately by Prof Ben Kingsley and his colleagues. Having created the thing, they have only themselves to blame. Just to spice things up for the adult rating, this particular species comes in the shape of a gorgeous if deadly female who has to hunt down especially nubile male prey to procreate her alien race. You get the idea: naked nibblings that turn into flesh feasts. 'I'd say she fits the classic pattern of the psychopath,' mutters anthropologist Alfred Molina just before the creature seduces him into mating with her to produce the baby that seems to be her *raison d'être*. Good if predictably unpleasant fun for fans of the modern horror genre, with a distinct whiff of the Fifties about it. The aliens at the end are a bit disappointing, but the climax itself is cliffhanging stuff of which serial heroes like Flash Gordon would have been proud

Speed ● ⓥ
1994, US, 112 mins
Dir: Jan de Bont

Stars: Keanu Reeves, Sandra Bullock, Dennis Hopper, Jeff Daniels
Rating: ★★★★

This one is fast and furious all the way down the line, as mad bomber Dennis Hopper makes three attempts to collect several million dollars by placing hostages in a life-threatening situation. The film concentrates mainly on the second, as Hopper wires a bus to explode if it goes slower than 50 mph. The driver is accidentally shot while at the wheel when a passenger panics and, with special cop Keanu Reeves at her side, the driving is taken over by Annie (Sandra Bullock) who has appropriately just lost her licence for speeding. Reeves and back-at-base partner Jeff Daniels try to figure a way out of this impossible situation, pretty difficult as Hopper always seems be one hop ahead. Framing this breakneck dice with disaster are two equally hair-raising episodes in a lift-shaft and on a runaway subway train. Reeves is tougher than you'd expect from his previous roles and helps keep the tension coiled tighter than a fuse wire. More frenzied editing might have made the last few minutes even more suspenseful: all in all, though, this goes like a bomb.

Speed II: Cruise Control O ⓥ
1997, US, 125 mins, colour
Dir: Jan de Bont
Stars: Sandra Bullock, Jason Patric, Willem Dafoe, Temuera Morrison, Bo Svenson
Rating: ★★

Sandra Bullock is back, alas without Keanu Reeves, in this waterborne addition to the panic button series, as dying, rejected computer genius Dafoe masterminds a solo takeover of a cruise liner from which he plans to remove a fortune in diamonds before blowing it up. Unfortunately for him, not all the pasengers and crew manage to abandon ship on schedule, including Sandra and her new boyfriend, a speed-happy LA cop (Patric). Desperate editing and thumping music try to crank up the ensuing suspence as the liner ploughs onward. Bullock's 'endearing' mannerisms, however, prove very annoying here and Patric, though he throws himself into the action stuff in terrific style, has all the charisma and range of expression of a beached whale. The result is a grind rather than a ride and, despite some big-money action scenees, you'll probably be glad when it's over. Supporting acting is, like the film, generally under-powered.

S

Spellbinder ●

1988, US, 94 mins, colour
Dir: Janet Greek
Stars: Timothy Daly, Kelly Preston, Rick Rossovich
Rating: ★

When young lawyer Jett Mills (Timothy Daly) rescues a young girl from a savage beating he suddenly gains a girlfriend and a whole load of supernatural trouble. The girl (Kelly Preston) is the intended victim of a coven of diabolists and you know how these types hate to let a good victim slip through their fingers. If this all sounds pretty daft, it's because it is. Even by second-division horror standards, this film doesn't make much sense and was a poor choice for debut director Janet Greek. Special effects are good and the film has pace, but plot and dialogue leave a lot to be desired.

Spellbound ○ Ⓥ

1945, US, 111 mins, b/w
Dir: Alfred Hitchcock
Stars: Gregory Peck, Ingrid Bergman
Rating: ★★★★

Dazzling Hitchcock suspense film about an amnesiac, brilliantly written and directed, with a shock revelation around every corner. There's also a breathtaking – and very relevant dream sequence designed by Salvador Dali. During the Forties, Ingrid Bergman was a favourite actress for the heroine of Hitchcock films. Here she plays a psychiatrist trying to help a man who is suffering from amnesia – and who might be a murderer too.

Spencer's Mountain ⊙

1963, US, 110 mins, colour
Dir: Delmer Daves
Stars: Henry Fonda, Maureen O'Hara, James MacArthur
Ratng: ★★

This rose-tinted American rural drama, about a talented farm boy desperate to get a college education, proved too twee for British critics. But the homespun wisdom and hillbilly memories of its source novel, by Earl Hamner Jr, struck gold almost a decade later when the location was changed from Spencer's Mountain to Walton's Mountain for the long-running TV series *The Waltons.*

Sphinx ○

1980, US, 117 mins, colour
Dir: Franklin J Schaffner
Stars: Lesley Anne-Down, Frank

Langella, Maurice Ronet
Rating: ★

Easy-on-the-eye, easier-on-the-mind adventure hokum with Lesley-Anne Down facing more perils than Pauline as she searches for the long-lost tomb of an ancient Pharaoh. The direction, by Franklin J Schaffner, is lively enough to cover most of the holes in the story-line; Frank Langelia is a suitably ambivalent hero, and John Gielgud turns up, rather surprisingly, as the Egyptian owner of an antique shop – probably the same one where the script was purchased. Ernest Day's attractive cinematography makes the most of the seductive locations.

Spider Woman Strikes Back, The ○

1946, US, 59 mins, b/w
Dir: Arthur Lubin
Stars: Gale Sondergaard, Brenda Joyce, Kirby Grant, Rondo Hatton
Rating: ★★

Fresh from her encounter with Sherlock Holmes, the Spider Woman (formidable Gale Sondergaard) is now slaughtering cattle with a poison distilled from carnivorous plants which she feeds with blood and spiders. Rather a devious way of doing it, but it makes for a suitably shuddery shocker. 'You're going to die, Jean, like the others,' she tells heroine Brenda Joyce. 'But it won't be really dying, because you'll live on in this beautiful plant.' Ace!

Spies Like Us ○ Ⓥ

1985, US, 109 mins, colour
Dir: John Landis
Stars: Dan Aykroyd, Chevy Chase, Donna Dixon
Rating: ★★

A comedy of funny moments rather than consistent achievement, this update of the Hope and Crosby *Road* films has Chevy Chase and Dan Aykroyd off on the road to Afghanistan and bound for trouble. Many filmic in-jokes and guest appearances by famous directors will probably fly over the head of the average cinema-goer who will, however, recognise Ronald Reagan, Steve Forrest, Terry Gilliam and Bob Hope. But the plot and script – both co-written by Aykroyd – are endearingly silly enough to keep viewers chuckling happily most of the way.

Spin of a Coin ○

(aka: The George Raft Story)
1961, US, 106 mins, b/w

Dir: Joseph M Newman
Stars: Ray Danton, Jayne Mansfield, Julie London, Neville Brand
Rating: ★★

A field day for Hollywood's gangster-type character actors in this incident-packed film biography of George Raft, the famous tough-guy star. Ray Danton endows Raft with cool charm, Neville Brand plays Al Capone for the second time, and the whole thing is fascinating for those who know little of how Raft started his career, as a dancer. The film spotlights Raft's continual fight against criticism of his underworld associations. Curiously cold, though.

Spinout

See: California Holiday

Spiral Staircase, The ◐

1945, US, 83 mins, b/w
Dir: Robert Siodmak
Stars: Dorothy McGuire, George Brent, Ethel Barrymore
Rating: ★★★★★

Under Robert Siodmak's expert direction the potentially creaky plot – defenceless mute girl in mortal danger in an old dark house during a thunderstorm – is genuinely gripping, the suspense piled on to chilling effect. As the put-upon heroine unable to scream, Dorothy McGuire suffers gracefully, with telling support from Ethel Barrymore, Elsa Lanchester and Sara Allgood. The men are less effective (Kent Smith is an unusually stiff hero), but in any case the real stars are that magnificently malevolent house and the utterly relentless thunderstorm. Vastly superior to the 1975 remake starring Jacqueline Bisset.

Spirit of St Louis, The ◐ Ⓥ

1957, US, 138 mins, colour
Dir: Billy Wilder
Stars: James Stewart, Patricia Smith, Murray Hamilton
Rating: ★★★

A gripping, if rather long, reconstruction of Charles Lindbergh's epic solo flight from New York to Paris in 1927. Honest and sincere and intelligently acted, especially by James Stewart (as Lindbergh) and Patricia Smith (an actress who unaccountably missed top stardom), there are times when true inspiration is lacking. But the climax is wonderfully emotive and the account of Lindbergh's early exploits as stunt pilot and mail flyer fascinatingly provides the film with an extra dimension.

Splash O Ⓥ

1984, US, 110 mins, colour
Dir: Ron Howard
Stars: Tom Hanks, Daryl Hannah, John Candy
Rating: ★★★

It was certainly about time we had another mermaid film (it being nearly 30 years since Glynis Johns splashed her way through the sequel to *Miranda*). That might help explain the huge success of this comedy, which heralded a profitable new era for Disney's Touchstone Pictures unit, now one of the most successful in the world. This romp takes a while to get going (until the appearance of the mermaid, in fact), but when it does it has some funny lines, amusing characters and an engagingly funny heroine in Daryl Hannah as the amorous Madison. Though insufficient thought is given to technical details, the film is never less than fun to be with. These days you can't ask for much more than that.

Splash, Too O

1988, US, 96 mins, colour
Dir: Greg Antonacci
Stars: Todd Waring, Amy Yasbeck
Rating: ★★

Another fishy comedy-adventure for Madison the mermaid, with Amy Yasbeck as the girl whose legs turn into a fishtail at the touch of water. Humour is laid on thick but, despite the familiar treatment, the story stays afloat and the family audience at whom it's aimed should enjoy it.

Splendor O

1935, US, 77 mins, b/w
Dir: Elliott Nugent
Stars: Miriam Hopkins, Joel McCrea, Paul Cavanagh, David Niven
Rating: ★★

Miriam Hopkins, best known for her bitchy roles, was not ideally cast in this quiet romantic tearjerker, routinely adapted by Rachel Crothers from her own play. A notable supporting cast includes comedienne Billie Burke, 'the perfect butler' Arthur Treacher and a dashing young David Niven. Dated but interesting.

Splendor in the Grass ◑

1961, US, 124 mins, colour
Dir: Elia Kazan
Stars: Natalie Wood, Warren Beatty
Rating: ★★★★

Warren Beatty made his film debut in this heated drama of teenage sexuality, which was specially written for him by playwright William Inge after the actor had appeared in Inge's stage play *A Loss of Roses*. Inge, who has a small role in the film as a minister, won a Best Screenplay Oscar. And Natalie Wood has seldom involved us more with one of her performances.

Spitfire Grill, The O

1996, US, 116 mins, colour
Dir: Lee David Zlotoff
Stars: Alison Elliott, Ellen Burstyn, Kieran Mulroney, Will Patton, Marcia Gay Harden
Rating: ★★★★★

Get the handkerchieves out for this brilliant weepie. Released convict Perchance, known as Percy (Elliott) arrives in the small Maine town of Gilead to work in the Spitfire Grill under crusty old Hannah (Burstyn). Apart from disasters in cooking, Percy gradually proves herself a pearl in the eyes of everyone except Hannah's son-in-law Nahum (Patton) whose seething resentment at the hiring of an ex-con represent s very real threat to her survival. There's also a strange hermit in the woods who gradually finds in Percy a kindred spirit. No one will be surprised at his eventual identity, but the script shies away from a conventional happy ending in such a fashion as to leave you needing a bucket to weep in. Well acted by all concerned, but the real winners are the story construction, three-dimensional characters, a plethora of interesting incident, and the direction by writer Zlotoff. An unqualified winner.

Split, The O

1968, US, 91 mins, colour
Dir: Gordon Flemyng
Stars: Jim Brown, Ernest Borgnine, Diahann Carroll, Julie Harris, Gene Hackman, Donald Sutherland
Rating: ★★★

Director Gordon Flemyng may not have known it, but he had a star-studded cast of the future on his hands when he made this brutal robbery thriller, based on a novel by Richard Stark, who also wrote *Point Blank*. Photographer Burnett Guffey, who won an Oscar the previous year on *Bonnie and Clyde*, again dazzles us with the splendour of his colour camera-work – from sunny scenes of Southern California, through a shattering car-smashing 'initiation test', to a night-time shoot-out on the cargo-crammed wharfside.

Split Second O

1953, US, 85 mins, b/w
Dir: Dick Powell
Stars: Stephen McNally, Alexis Smith, Jan Sterling, Keith Andes
Rating: ★★★

A high-tension suspense movie from first-time director Dick Powell, former crooner and tough guy actor. Stephen McNally is rough and mean as the escaped convict holding hostages in an atomic testing area.

Split Second ● Ⓥ

1991, UK, 90 mins, colour
Dir: Tony Maylam
Stars: Rutger Hauer, Kim Cattrall, Neil Duncan, Michael J Pollard, Ian Dury
Rating: ★★

A silly but watchable horror thriller starring Rutger Hauer in his familiar garb of long topcoat and shotgun. This time Rutger's a cop in water-logged, rat-infested London of 2008. A mutant monster is going around ripping out people's hearts (as monsters do) and Rutger's after its alien guts. It's already dispatched his partner, causing Rutger, who was having an affair with said partner's wife (Kim Cattrall), to go on the sauce. By 2008 the only black stuff he's on is constant coffee, but he's still one step behind the monster, who's taunting him by leaving him messages and ripping out a fresh heart every full moon. Saddled with bespectacled partner Neil Duncan, Rutger marches masterfully through murky mush in a bid to end the reign of terror of the fiend, which has the familiar breathing difficulties beloved of the screen's sound effects boys. Lots of unintentionally funny lines – 'It looks like an astrological symbol,' gasps Duncan, looking at an incomprehensible mass of blood on the ceiling – and gruesome, well-edited, well-shot action.

Spoilers, The ◑

1942, US, 87 mins, b/w
Dir: Ray Enright
Stars: Marlene Dietrich, John Wayne, Randolph Scott
Rating: ★★★

Rex Beach's famous adventure yarn set in Alaska of the Gold Rush era has been filmed several times and, despite the presence of Marlene Dietrich in this version, is most famous for the tremendous fist fight at the end between its two male rotagonists. The one here, between John Wayne and

S

Randolph Scott, is perhaps the daddy of them all. A very strong supporting cast includes Margaret Lindsay, Harry Carey and, as The Bronco Kid, that romantic idol of the silent screen Richard Barthelmess.

Spoilers, The ○
1955, US, 84 mins, colour
Dir: Jesse Hibbs
Stars: Jeff Chandler, Anne Baxter, Rory Calhoun, Barbara Britton
Rating: ★★

Fifth screen version of Rex Beach's classic action story, set in the Yukon. A terrific fist fight between Jeff Chandler and Rory Calhoun leaves both participants needing a bath or two. The old chestnut was showing its age, though (so was Anne Baxter), and hasn't been remade to date.

Spooks Run Wild ○
1941, US, 69 mins, b/w
Dir: Phil Rosen
Stars: Bela Lugosi, Leo Gorcey, Huntz Hall
Rating: ★★

Once *The Cat and the Canary* had proved that you could successfully mix chuckles with chills, there was no lack of takers jumping on the band wagon. The original sound Dracula, Bela Lugosi, was roped in for this East Side Kids (later The Bowery Boys) romp, and he has rather too much class for the Kids to handle. Pity about the tame ending, otherwise it's good fun.

Spot Marks the X ○
1986, US, 90 mins, colour
Dir: Mark Rosman
Stars: Barret Oliver, Natalie Gregory, David Huddleston, Geoffrey Lewis
Rating: ★★

Mike the dog, who all but stole the hit movie *Down and Out in Beverly Hills*, as tramp Nick Nolte's pooch, dognaps the limelight again in this Disney TV movie which casts him as a gangsters' mutt who becomes the pet of some youngsters who help him 'go straight'. Barret Oliver, the boy from *The NeverEnding Story*, is his young master, and expert character actors Geoffrey Lewis and David Huddleston bolster the supporting cast. Mike goes himself through his paces in fine style, helping to eradicate his criminal past by bringing a gang of bank-robbers to book.

Spotswood ○ Ⓥ
1991, Australia, 93 mins, colour
Dir: Mark Joffe

Stars: Anthony Hopkins, Russell Crowe, Ben Mendelsohn, Rebecca Rigg, Toni Collette
Rating: ★★★★

Anthony Hopkins took time off from the big league in 1991 to star in this small-scale, pleasing Australian film as an English time-and-motion expert in the late 1960s, faced with the difficult task of estimating possible redundancies at a moccasin factory in a small Melbourne suburb. What makes this film spring to life though, is the variety of characters flitting in and out of Hopkins's life. Ball, the boss, played with immense sympathy by Alwyn Kurtz; Carey, the nerdish dispatch clerk (Ben Mendelsohn), lovelorn for the boss's daughter (Rebecca Rigg); Wendy, Carey's unglamorous friend (an exceptionally honest performance by Toni Collette); Kim (Russell Crowe), the smart-ass opposite side of the coin to Carey; and the workmen and women at Ball's, the men indulging in a passion for slot-car racing (toy-car stuff on a grand scale) in which Hopkins finds himself beguilingly embroiled. A wise choice by Hopkins, this choice being the operative word for a quietly effective film that wears its heart on its sleeve in the old-fashioned way.

Spring and Port Wine ○
1970, UK, 101 mins, colour
Dir: Peter Hammond
Stars: James Mason, Diana Coupland, Susan George, Rodney Bewes
Rating: ★★★

Phlegmatic, rather patronising, story of a Bolton family dominated by the patriarchal James Mason (himself a northerner, but from the White Rose county). The fulcrum of the tale is the reluctance of his younger daughter (a pert, teenaged Susan George) to eat a herring for supper and the subsequent plot centres on the tortuous ritual imposed by her father of serving up the hapless fish at every meal until she devours it.

Springfield Rifle ○ Ⓥ
1952, US, 92 mins, colour
Dir: André De Toth
Stars: Gary Cooper, Phyllis Thaxter, David Brian, Lon Chaney Jr, Paul Kelly, Phil Carey
Rating: ★★

Filmed on location at altitudes of up to 9,500 feet on the slopes of California's Mount Whitney, and breathtakingly shot in WarnerColor by Edwin DuPar, this is a spasmodically exciting

account of espionage and counter-espionage during the American Civil War. Gary Cooper makes an impassive hero. Good supporting cast largely hangs around waiting for something decent to do.

Spring in Park Lane ○
1948, UK, 92 mins, b/w
Dir: Herbert Wilcox
Stars: Michael Wilding, Anna Neagle
Rating: ★★★★

This brightest and wittiest of all the Anna Neagle-Michael Wilding films which boosted British box-office takings in post-war years. A brilliant script by Nicholas Phipps embellishes a lightweight plot about a footman in a high-society household who is not quite what he pretends to be. In this role, Wilding steals this particular film from under Dame Anna's delightful nose.

Springtime in the Rockies ⊙ Ⓥ
1942, US, 85 mins, colour
Dir: Irving Cummings
Stars: Betty Grable, John Payne, Carmen Miranda, Cesar Romero
Rating: ★★★

The Fox musical stock company moved from Cuba and *A Week-End in Havana* to the Canadian rockies for this zingy song-and-dance feast. John Payne, Carmen Miranda – weighing in with 'Chattanooga Choo-Choo' as well as her usual South American tongue-twister – and Cesar Romero, displaying a nifty line in dancing, were along for the ride, and, as the icing on the cake, Fox top-billed their newest musical sensation, Betty Grable, for the first time. For vitality and vivacity, it's one of Betty's brightest performances. Ace trumpeter Harry James made a guest appearance in the film and, a year later, he and Grable were man and wife. Charlotte Greenwood and Edward Everett Horton add their own brands of vitality and waspish wit and even get to dance a step or two at the finale.

Spy in Black, The ○
1939, UK, 82 mins, b/w
Dir: Michael Powell
Stars: Conrad Veidt, Sebastian Shaw, Valerie Hobson
Rating: ★★★

Alexander Korda's participation in this tense, romantic melodrama is tenuous and uncredited. His name does not appear on the titles, but, according to one biographer, Korda 'couldn't keep his fingers out of it.' The American title was *U-Boat 29* and has under-water sequences directed by Vernon Sewell, who was to direct over 200 films himself. Vivien Leigh was originally scheduled to play the schoolteacher spy eventually portrayed by Valerie Hobson.

Spy Hard ○ ⓥ

1996, US, 81 mins, colour
Dir: Rick Friedberg
Stars: Leslie Nielsen, Nicollette Sheridan, Charles Durning, Marcia Gay Harden, Barry Bostwick, Andy Griffith
Rating: ★

Strenuously overplayed by its entire cast, this is a spy comedy that should never have come in out of the cold. Outside of the work of the Zucker brothers, Leslie Nielsen has had about as much luck as Rodney Dangerfield in the veteran funny-man stakes, and the jokes are as feeble as they come; any episode of television's *Get Smart* would be sharper and funnier. The opening sequence is bright: Weird Al Yankovic directs his own parody of a James Bond film's credit titles complete with swimming silhouettes and 007-style song. And there are a couple of good gags to follow. The rest, alas, is all downhill, as Nielsen limps from one damp skit to another, as agent Dick Steele (ho ho), called out of retirement (just like Frank Drebin) to foil the plans of his former nemesis (Andy Griffith) who's still out to control the world. Would that Andy had turned his missiles on this heavy-handed farce instead.

Spy Who Came in From the Cold, The ○

1965, UK, 112 mins, b/w
Dir: Martin Ritt
Stars: Richard Burton, Claire Bloom
Rating: ★★★

The first film to show the dirty, squalid side of spying, as opposed to the luxury world of James Bond. Twist piles upon twist as a British agent Alec Leamas (Richard Burton at his most world weary) becomes involved in a fiendishly complicated plot to get an ex-Nazi spy chief, a plot that's more monstrously twisted than he imagines it to be. The script by Guy Trosper and Paul Dehn, from the novel by John Le Carré, is razor sharp and especially acute in its observations of human nature. Claire Bloom gives a stand-out performance in a film as ingenious as it is bitter.

Spy Who Loved Me, The ○ ⓥ

1977, UK, 125 mins, colour
Dir: Lewis Gilbert
Stars: Roger Moore, Barbara Bach, Curt Jurgens, Richard Kiel, Caroline Munro
Rating: ★★★

Roger Moore's third and best outing as James Bond is an enjoyable mixture of hectic action, big set-pieces and tongue-in-cheek humour. Richard Kiel makes his first appearance as the monstrous 'Jaws' and Carly Simon sings one of the more memorable Bond themes, 'Nobody Does it Better'. A ski sequence (culminating in a good visual joke) gets the action off to a fine start and tense underwater scenes have a vital bearing on the plot.

Square Dance ❶ ⓥ

1986, US, 112 mins, colour
Dir: Daniel Petrie
Stars: Jason Robards, Jane Alexander, Rob Lowe, Winona Ryder, Deborah Richter
Rating: ★★

A moderate script is lit from within by the performances of its four leading players in this story of a 13-year-old girl who leaves her elderly father's egg farm to live with her gadabout mother in the bright lights of Texas's Fort Worth. Rob Lowe, in a showy but difficult role, is better than one could have ever expected as the retarded boy who becomes the object of her affection and Winona Ryder (as the girl), Jane Alexander and Jason Robards all play far above the level of the lines they are asked to read.

Square Peg, The ☉ ⓥ

1958, US, 89 mins, b/w
Dir: John Paddy Carstairs
Stars: Norman Wisdom, Honor Blackman, Edward Chapman
Rating: ★★

A slapdash romp made by Norman Wisdom, the little big man of British comedy of the Fifties and Sixties. As Norman the road-mender, he is accidentally parachuted behind enemy lines in 1943 with his tetchy boss, Mr Grimsdale. Fortunately, he turns out to be the double of a German general, whom he impersonates and, after singing an operatic aria with Hattie Jacques in the funniest scene in the film, manages to circumvent a firing squad, rescue his friends and become a war hero. The film gave Oliver Reed one of his earliest screen opportunities.

Sssssnake ●
(aka: Sssss)

1973, US, 99 mins, colour
Dir: Bernard L Kowalski
Stars: Strother Martin, Dirk Benedict
Rating: ★★★

An archetypal mad scientist movie that cheerfully recalls the heyday of such films in the Fifties with Strother Martin giving a zestful performance as the man who decides to turn luckless Dirk Benedict into a reptile. Great grisly fun but not for snake lovers!

Stagecoach ○

1966, US, 114 mins, colour
Dir: Gordon Douglas
Stars: Ann-Margret, Alex Cord, Bing Crosby, Van Heflin, Red Buttons
Rating: ★★

Not the John Wayne/John Ford classic, nor even the Kris Kristofferson TV movie, but the 20th Century-Fox remake, too long for its content, but still good for some thrills as the stagecoach load of passengers, mostly fleeing from their own pasts, rattles its way through Indian territory, bringing each to his own destiny. Some roles are miscast, but Bing Crosby does well as the drunken Doc Boone, the role originally played by Thomas Mitchell. Overall, though, it underlines the motto: 'If it ain't broke, don't fix it.'

Stagecoach ○ ⓥ

1939, US, 99 mins, b/w
Dir: John Ford
Stars: Claire Trevor, John Wayne, George Bancroft, John Carradine, Thomas Mitchell
Rating: ★★★★★

John Ford's supreme triumph and perhaps even the greatest Western of all time. John Wayne, then languishing on the tiny backlots of Poverty Row studios, became a major star as an escaped prisoner who joins a stagecoach packed with an odd assortment of individuals for a journey through Apache territory that none of them will ever forget. It was the first 'adult' Western to portray in-depth characters with allegorical themes running just beneath the surface plot of their life and death stuggles. Ford had a tough job persuading any major studio to cast Wayne, and Claire Trevor received top billing. But the film's $392,000 budget looked money well spent when *Stagecoach* earned more than one million dollars on first release.

S

Stage Door ○

1937, US, 92 mins, b/w
Dir: Gregory La Cava
Stars: Katharine Hepburn, Ginger
Rogers, Adolphe Menjou, Lucille Ball
Rating: ★★★★★

This has to be one of the best films about show business ever made, and was, in fact, nominated for several Oscars, including Best Film, Best Screenplay and Best Director for Gregory La Cava. Katharine Hepburn is a society debutante who defies her father by becoming a Broadway hopeful. The luck of the draw sees her sharing a room in a New York boarding house with Ginger Rogers, a tough cookie who heckles everyone. The feuding actresses are equally determined to make it to the top. Hepburn had been in several costume epics and was beginning to be typecast, but this outing showed her as someone who could play comedy and pathos equally convincingly. The film is a totally absorbing treat to the eyes and the ears, especially seeing such stars-to-be as Lucille Ball, Jack Carson, Eve Arden and Ann Miller all grabbing early chances.

Stage Fright ○

1949, UK, 106 mins, b/w
Dir: Alfred Hitchcock
Stars: Jane Wyman, Richard Todd,
Marlene Dietrich, Michael Wilding
Rating: ★★★

A Hitchcock thriller in which the murderer of a famous actress's husband remains unidentified until the final, hectic moments. It's based on a novel by Selwyn Jepson – the Special Operations major who recruited many wartime agents including Violette Szabo GC – with Jane Wyman uneasily cast as a student actress who helps Richard Todd, the man on the run from a murder rap. Alastair Sim's own special brand of humour (as Ms Wyman's father) is given fair play as he begins to diagnose the cause of foul play. The rest of the cast, though, could have easily been better chosen. It also includes Marlene Dietrich (singing 'The Laziest Gal in Town') and Sybil Thorndike, each apparently determined to act the other off the screen.

Staggered ● ⓥ

1994, UK, 94 mins, colour
Dir: Martin Clunes
Stars: Martin Clunes, Michael Praed,
Anna Chancellor, Sylvia Syms, Griff
Rhys Jones, Virginia McKenna
Rating: ★★

Lively, if patchily paced British farce, both starring and directed by the vacant-looking Martin Clunes, star of the TV sitcom *Men Behaving Badly*. The man with a behavioural problem here is Gary (Michael Praed). What a best friend: he organises a stag night that leaves groom-to-be Neil (Clunes) stranded, naked and alone, on a remote Scottish isle just three days before his wedding. The laughs come thick and fairly fast along Neil's journey back to London before he discovers (as we know all along) that Gary's not such a great mate after all. Although it runs out of steam before arrival at a weak finale, the film makes way for some interesting cameos along Neil's own version of the yellow-brick road: Virginia McKenna is winsome and winning as a Scots hermit-woman, Griff Rhys Jones enjoyably over the top as a Welsh sales rep into S & M.

Staircase ❶

1969, UK, 101 mins, colour
Dir: Stanley Donen
Stars: Richard Burton, Rex Harrison,
Cathleen Nesbitt, Beatrix Lehmann
Rating: ★★

An opening-out by playwright Charles Dyer of his own hit play about two middle-aged homosexuals living above a barber's shop. This film version is tailored to the acting talents of its two leading players, although it seems almost wilfully perverse to cast two of filmland's most married actors, Richard Burton and Rex Harrison, in these roles. The music score for this curio is by Dudley Moore.

Stairway to Heaven

See: A Matter of Life and Death

StakeOut ❶ ⓥ

1987, US, 115 mins, colour
Dir: John Badham
Stars: Richard Dreyfuss, Emilio Estevez,
Aidan Quinn, Madeleine Stowe
Rating: ★★★★

The plot for this film is both improbable and unoriginal – a cop on a surveillance job falls in love with the woman he is spying on – but that doesn't stop *StakeOut* being a thoroughly enjoyable picture. This is principally thanks to Richard Dreyfuss and Emilio Estevez as the two cops on surveillance and some sharp dialogue. They make such a good double act, you're left hoping they'll make more films together.

Stalag 17 ○ ⓥ

1953, US, 120 mins, b/w
Dir: Billy Wilder
Stars: William Holden, Don Taylor, Otto
Preminger
Rating: ★★★★

William Holden in his Oscar-winning performance as a World War Two PoW camp scrounger, whose rackets include a peep-show by telescope into the women's barracks, horse races with mice competitors and distilling homebrewed gin. Naturally, he's number one on his fellow-prisoners' list of suspects when deaths of would-be escapers make it plain than an informer is at work. Billy Wilder's film strikes several different notes – it's comic, dramatic, suspenseful and touching in turn. But most notable is the comedy vein, in which character actor Robert Strauss had his biggest film success as Animal, a neolithic type who shuffles around in underwear that no washday mum could be proud of.

Stalking Moon, The ○

1968, US, 109 mins, colour
Dir: Robert Mulligan
Stars: Gregory Peck, Eva Marie Saint
Rating: ★★

Off-beat Western, ravishingly photographed in colour by Charles Lang (who won an Academy Award as long ago as 1933 for his photography on *A Farewell to Arms*). Peck plays a veteran cavalry scout trying to protect a young widow and her son from a marauding Indian who sees himself as the boy's rightful father. It's an unusual film to come from director Robert Mulligan, more a specialist in human drama. His sure touch in the interior scenes is very much in evidence, especially in a charming sequence where Peck's half-breed friend teaches the boy to count by initiating him into the rules of poker. There's also a quota of excitement when Peck and his friends try to kill the Indian before he kills them, and look like losing.

Stamboul Quest ○

1934, US, 88 mins, b/w
Dir: Sam Wood
Stars: Myrna Loy, George Brent, Lionel
Atwill, C Henry Gordon
Rating: ★★★

An early Hollywood stab at a fact-based World War One story much later filmed in Britain as *Fraulein Doktor*. In this stylish and exciting version, scripted by Herman J Mankiewicz, it's Myrna Loy as the conscience-torn German spy falling in love with an enemy in Turkey. Sam Wood, one of MGM's top directors, keeps the heady combination of romance and intrigue moving well.

Stampeded!
See: The Big Land

Stand and Deliver ◐ Ⓥ
1988, US, 107 mins, colour
Dir: Ramon Menendez
Stars: Edward James Olmos, Lou Diamond Phillips, Vanessa Marquez, Andy Garcia, Rosana De Soto
Rating: ★★★★★

A totally inspirational film whose cumulative emotional impact is such that it may have you weeping like a child in the last few minutes. In fact, the only criticism you could level against it, that it stretches credulity to the limit, is totally invalidated by the fact that it's a true story. Oscar-nominated James Edward Olmos lives the role of the sly, humorous, seemingly laid-back maths teacher at a Los Angeles ghetto school, who takes a class of ragged, rebellious, tough Mexican-American girls and boys on the verge of juvenile delinquency or lives of drudgery and turns them into dedicated students. Ace performances, cleverly written screenplay: don't miss it.

Stand by for Action
See: Cargo of Innocents

Stand by Me ◐ Ⓥ
1986, US, 89 mins, colour
Dir: Rob Reiner
Stars: Wil Wheaton, River Phoenix, Corey Feldman, Kiefer Sutherland, Richard Dreyfuss
Rating: ★★★

A group of young friends search for the body of a missing teenager after one of them overhears his older brother, who claims to have seen it. A simple plot, but there's a lot more to the film than the basic storyline. The search for the body becomes something of an odyssey for the boys and more of an adventure than even they expected. Unusually, the tale is narrated by one of the boys, now in middle age. Not always a device that works, it succeeds here, as it doesn't interfere with or slow down the story. It's also a very nostalgic film, which is heightened by the late Fifties songs used in the soundtrack.

Stand-in ○
1937, US, 90 mins, b/w
Dir: Tay Garnett

Stars: Leslie Howard, Joan Blondell, Humphrey Bogart
Rating: ★★★

A high-grade comedy on Hollywood low-life and an absolute treat for fans of Leslie Howard and Humphrey Bogart to see them step outside their normal genres and play such an intelligently-made blend of satire, sentiment and farce. Howard is delicious as the head-in-the-books accountant sent to save Colossal Studios from financial ruin and Bogart quite amazing as a drunken director.

Stanley & Iris ◐ Ⓥ
1989, US, 102 mins, colour
Dir: Martin Ritt
Stars: Jane Fonda, Robert De Niro, Swoosie Kurtz, Martha Plimpton
Rating: ★★★

It sounds unkind to say it in these harsh times, but the characters in *Stanley & Iris* are really too nice for words. Fonda is a widow with a pregnant daughter, scraping up a living in a bakery. De Niro is a cook with the same firm. He helps her when she gets mugged, but gets fired because he can't read or write. Yes, we know, you can tell us the rest (given that De Niro's an inventor, too), but it's pleasantly done, without too much incident or bite, but rarely boring to be with and leisurely rather than slow, as the two characters tentatively and uncertainly build their relationship.

Stanley and Livingstone ○
1939, US, 101 mins, b/w
Dir: Henry King
Stars: Spencer Tracy, Nancy Kelly, Richard Greene
Rating: ★★★

Always absorbing account of newspaperman Henry Stanley's endeavours to find the missionary doctor David Livingstone in the depths of then-darkest Africa of 1869. Spencer Tracy and Walter Brennan both foreshadow the roles they played in the following year's *Northwest Passage*, with the locale changed from Africa to the Canadian wilderness. The ending is stirring stuff.

Star! ○
1968, US, 175 mins, colour
Dir: Robert Wise
Stars: Julie Andrews, Richard Crenna, Michael Craig
Rating: ★★

A feast of brilliantly recreated Twenties' and Thirties' songs is the

main attraction of this mammoth musical biopic about Gertrude Lawrence, with Julie Andrews in the title role. On stage the film's a hit; off-stage it never quite catches fire, in spite of Daniel Massey's delightful impersonation of Noel Coward, which was rightly rewarded with an Academy Award nomination.

Star Chamber, The ● Ⓥ
1983, US, 109 mins, colour
Dir: Peter Hyams
Stars: Michael Douglas, Hal Holbrook, Yaphet Kotto, Sharon Gless
Rating: ★★

Vicious criminals are getting off on technicalities thanks to the smartness of their lawyers. Under these circumstances, talented writer-director Peter Hyams would have us believe, a group of high court judges might set up their own court of no appeal, where sentences are carried out by a hit-man. It sounds reasonable enough and the only dubious part of the plot is why newest judicial recruit Michael Douglas would really want to do anything about it when he finds that two homicidal crooks 'sentenced' to death didn't commit the actual murders of which they have been accused. Hyams craftily hypes up the action, but pat performances make this an occasionally routine urban thriller.

Stardust ● Ⓥ
1974, US, 105 mins, colour
Dir: Michael Apted
Stars: David Essex, Adam Faith, Larry Hagman
Rating: ★★

It's surprising that the weak link in this powerful and provocative follow up to *That'll Be The Day* should prove to be the music. It wouldn't have lifted the Beatles to stardom, let alone Jim MacLaine (David Essex), the subject of this bitter and harrowing morality play about the sorrows and solitude of stardom. Limply acted by Essex and by Ines de Longchamps as his mom, the film is rescued and dominated by Adam Faith as the star's manager. Even given that Essex meekly hands him centre stage, Faith takes it like a lion, giving a magnetic portrayal of seemingly innocuous evil that creates a memorable movie character.

Stardust Memories ○
1980, US, 88 mins, b/w
Dir: Woody Allen
Stars: Woody Allen, Charlotte Rampling,

S

Jessica Harper
Rating: ★★

Or: Woody Allen strikes back. Setting out all the things of which his detractors have accused him, he creates an entire film (of fragments) around them. Allen is Sandy, a movie-maker accused of 'trying to document his private suffering and fob it off as art'. The resulting film has its good moments, mostly in the too-few scenes from the comedy films Sandy has made in the past, but is sometimes equally likely to send you to sleep. It also doesn't have Diane Keaton or Mia Farrow, and Charlotte Rampling (although quite effective), Jessica Harper and the charmless Marie-Christine Barrault are simply no substitute. Viewers may find that, as people keep telling Woody in the film, they 'prefer his earlier, funny comedies' to this. The background score, though, is a vintage-jazz enthusiast's delight.

Starflight One ○

1982, US, 155 mins, colour
Dir: Jerry Jameson
Stars: Lee Majors, Hal Linden
Rating: ★

They really should have called this one *Airplane III*. Hypersonic Starflight One, piloted by iron-jawed Cody Briggs (Lee Majors) goes into orbit trying to avoid a rogue rocket. Some good players are caught up in the events that follow; Ray Milland grits his teeth and wades through the dialogue like a man eating chalk. One-time rising star Michael Sacks has a supporting role as the navigator (at least he takes the quick way out as guinea-pig for a failed rescue bid) and even lower in the cast is Robert Englund, now enshrined in the minds of a whole generation of horror film fans for his portrayal of evil Freddie Krueger in the *Nightmare On Elm Street* shockers.

Stargate ○ ⓥ

1994, US, 121 mins, colour
Dir: Roland Emmerich
Stars: James Spader, Kurt Russell, Jaye Davidson, Viveca Lindfors, Alexis Cruz, Mili Avital
Rating: ★★★

This science-fiction fantasy, a cross between Rider Haggard, Indiana Jones and *Star Wars*, was panned by most critics, but struck a chord with ordinary filmgoers who flocked to it in their millions. Meek-mannered James Spader got a rare mainstream film role as the boffinish scientist who solves the

missing link to open up a teleportation gate to a distant world. This is ruled by a tyrannical alien called Ra (a role tailor-made for Jaye Davidson's androgynous looks) who poses a threat to destroy Earth. Kurt Russell is every inch the square-jawed military team leader who has his own secret agenda for the mission through the Stargate. Major production values, seamless special effects, huge sets and armies of extras – even a human-alien love story – are thrown into the melting pot by director and co-writer Roland Emmerich, who proved himself an action expert with *Universal Soldier*. The plot may be on the creaky side, but Emmerich always has a dazzling action scene up his sleeve to power the story on.

Star Is Born, A ○ ⓥ

1937, US, 111 mins, colour
Dir: William A Wellman
Stars: Janet Gaynor, Fredric March, Adolphe Menjou, Andy Devine
Rating: ★★★★

First of three versions of the classic Hollywood drama about the tempestuous star couple whose show careers are going in opposite directions: hers up, his down. Janet Gaynor and Fredric March shine in the parts later played by Judy Garland and James Mason, and by Barbra Streisand and Kris Kristofferson. Written by Dorothy Parker, Alan Campbell and Robert Carson, from a story by Wellman and Carson, but based in part on the 1932 film *What Price Hollywood?* Splendidly filmed in early Technicolor, *A Star Is Born* won Oscars for W Howard Green's cinematography and for Best Original Story. On the film's release the *New York Times* described it as the 'the most accurate mirror ever held before the glittering, tinselled, trivial, generous, cruel and ecstatic world that is Hollywood.'

Star Is Born, A ○ ⓥ

1954, US, 154 mins, colour
Dir: George Cukor
Stars: Judy Garland, James Mason, Charles Bickford
Rating: ★★★★

The best of three versions of the story about a rising actress (Judy Garland never better) and her sinking, alcoholic fading star husband (James Mason). An artistic and personal triumph for Garland, who took her character through an emotional gamut, pulling a heartrending performance from the depths of her own life. And Mason is magnificent: thank goodness Cary

Grant, Humphrey Bogart and Frank Sinatra failed to win the part. The show stopping 'Born in a Trunk' sequence was only added at a later date to show how the character became a star. Garland was nominated for a Best Actress Oscar. A later, 'restored' version runs 170 minutes.

Star Is Born, A ● ⓥ

1976, US, 140 mins, colour
Dir: Frank Pierson
Stars: Barbra Streisand, Kris Kristofferson, Gary Busey
Rating: ★

Modern remake of the famous musical about love, fame and tragedy – as you can tell by the proliferation of four-letter words, which tend to distract your attention from the story of a rock idol on the way down who marries a pop singer on the way up to international stardom. In the Fredric March/James Mason role, Kris Kristofferson does best with the quieter moments, seeming sometimes too intense; too often director Frank Pierson appears to be allowing his players to act the scene as they think fit rather than under his guidance. Barbra Streisand sings a good variety of showy songs which her fans should enjoy. Even so, the film trails in a dismal third of the three versions, causing some carpers to call it *A Bore is Starred*.

Starman ◑ ⓥ

1984, US, 115 mins, colour
Dir: John Carpenter
Stars: Jeff Bridges, Karen Allen, Charles Martin Smith, Richard Jaeckel
Rating: ★★★

This story about a human *E. T.* – or at least an alien in human form – is a built-in success for a director who can pull the right emotional chords at the right time. John Carpenter isn't the sort to miss easy opportunities, and the result is a fairly old-fashioned mix of emotion, excitement and enjoyment although we could have done with a little more extra-terrestrial activity and a little less earthly romance, even if Starman's miracles seem limited to the number of 'magic marbles' he carries on his person. Jeff Bridges gives a clever performance as the alien who learns about human emotions through the young widow (appealing Karen Allen) whose dead husband he has fashioned himself to resemble. No big surprises about this film, but, despite one or two script lapses that provide unintentional smiles, it offers solid entertainment along reassuring lines.

Star of India ☉

1953, UK, 97 mins, colour
Dir: Arthur Lubin
Stars: Cornel Wilde, Jean Wallace,
Herbert Lom
Rating: ★★★

Cornel Wilde and his wife, Jean
Wallace, came to Britain to make this
cheerfully ingenuous swashbuckler, as
did their Hollywood director, Arthur
Lubin. The best performance comes
from Herbert Lom as the villain of the
piece and C Pennington Richards,
later to turn to direction, provides
some attractive colour photography.

Stars and Bars ◐ ⓥ

1988, US, 94 mins, colour
Dir: Pat O'Connor
Stars: Daniel Day-Lewis, Harry Dean
Stanton, Martha Plimpton, Joan Cusack,
Will Patton, Glenne Headly
Rating: RB

Superstardom was around the corner
for Daniel Day-Lewis, but you could
never have guessed it from this atrocious hillbilly comedy with a
misbegotten central idea. It features
Day-Lewis as an Englishman in
America given the task of buying a
newly discovered Renoir from an eccentric Southerner, played by Harry
Dean Stanton. All of the performances
are bad (quite a feat with this cast) but
script and direction are worse. Day-
Lewis's dedication in dragging his
bag-of-bones body through the rain in
the altogether is painful to behold and
probably led to him beefing up his
physique for subsequent roles. A complete shambles.

Stars Are Singing, The ○

1953, US, 99 mins, colour
Dir: Norman Taurog
Stars: Rosemary Clooney, Anna Maria
Alberghetti, Lauritz Melchior
Rating: ★★★★

Bright, tuneful musical about a teenage
refugee with a glorious soprano voice.
It introduced filmgoers to Rosemary
Clooney and, in the role of the
refugee, gave a big singing chance to
Anna Maria Alberghetti, for whom
suitable subsequent roles proved hard
to find ' But the show is stolen by a
droll comedian called Bob Williams,
and his even funnier 'trick' dog, Red
Dust, who makes a hilarious hash of
every command he receives.

Stars Look Down, The ○

1939, UK, 110 mins, b/w
Dir: Carol Reed
Stars: Michael Redgrave, Margaret

Lockwood, Emlyn Williams
Rating: ★★★★

This solidly crafted film of A J Cronin's
pre-war best-seller set in a mining community in the North of England placed
director Carol Reed in the forefront of
young British directors. Co-written by
Cronin, it's finely acted by a strong cast
headed by Michael Redgrave,
Margaret Lockwood and Emlyn
Williams. Ms Lockwood is shrewishly
effective in the first of her many famous film bad girls.

Star-Spangled Rhythm ○

1942, US, 99 mins, b/w
Dir: George Marshall
Stars: Eddie Bracken, Betty Hutton, Bob
Hope, Dorothy Lamour, Bing Crosby
Rating: ★★★

One of five films that Betty Hutton
and Eddie Bracken made together at
Paramount in the war years, the best
remembered of which is *The Miracle of
Morgan's Creek*. In post-war times, their
stars exploded, and both were out of
Hollywood by the early Fifties. Their
roles here are as nominal stars to one
of those marvellous wartime studio extravaganzas in which pretty well every
contractee was bound to turn up; in
this case that meant Bob Hope, Bing
Crosby, Dorothy Lamour, Alan Ladd,
Veronica Lake, William Bendix, Fred
MacMurray, Ray Milland, Susan
Hayward, Paulette Goddard, Dick
Powell and many more. Betty Hutton
plays the studio's scatterbrained telephone operator involved in putting on
a show for her sailor boyfriend
(Bracken) and his pals, and the songs
include 'That Old Black Magic'.

Starting Over ◐

1979, US, 93 mins, colour
Dir: Alan J Pakula
Stars: Burt Reynolds, Jill Clayburgh,
Candice Bergen, Charles Durning
Rating: ★★★

A funny-sad comedy-romance that has
Burt Reynolds trying to decide between the respective attractions of
ex-wife Candice Bergen and new lady
Jill Clayburgh. As Bergen is no match
for Clayburgh in both acting and
charm departments, you can guess the
outcome, but, though there are a few
dead patches on the way, the script offers some nice laughs and a sniffle or
two as well. The wry-faced Reynolds
gives a peerless performance, again be-
lying his muscleman image and even
stealing the film from the luminous
Clayburgh. Austin Pendleton also
does a very nice job as Reynolds' be-

spectacled friend at the almost convincing men's divorce circle. Director
Alan Pakula's efforts at making a
charming film seem a little calculated,
but they work quite a lot of the time.

Star Trek: The Motion Picture ○ ⓥ

1979, US, 132 mins, colour
Dir: Robert Wise
Stars: William Shatner, Leonard Nimoy,
DeForest Kelley, James Doohan
Rating: ★★

Robert Wise, who made such science
fiction classics as *The Day the Earth
Stood Still* and *The Andromeda Strain*, returned to the genre for this film.
Glamorous Persis Khambatta joins the
Star Trek regulars, as a bald-headed
Deltan beauty who forms part of a desperate Earth bid to reunite the original
crew of the Starship *Enterprise* and stop
an irresistible force travelling towards
our planet. Special effects are good, as
well they might be in the hands of
Douglas Trumbull of *2001* and *Silent
Running* fame. So are the set designs
and Jerry Goldsmith's music. But the
cast often seems undecided as to
whether the venture should be played
straight or tongue-in-cheek. 'Dammit,
Bones,' growls William Shatner at one
stage to DeForest Kelley, 'I need you –
badly.' Not as badly, Admiral Kirk, as
you needed some better lines.

Star Trek II: The Wrath of Khan ○ ⓥ

1982, US, 113 mins, colour
Dir: Nicholas Meyer
Stars: William Shatner, Leonard Nimoy,
DeForest Kelley, Kirstie Alley
Rating: ★★★★

Trekkies will not be disappointed with
this second feature film from the famous TV series, even though it seems
to deprive them of one of their
favourite characters. Kirk (William
Shatner) once again says, 'Don't mince
words, Bones, what do you really
mean?' and the whole legend is cleverly camped up by the actors (and
director Nicholas Meyer) with many
an arched eyebrow and amused twitch
of the corner of the mouth. Kirk's adversary is Khan (played by Ricardo
Montalban as the Demon King of
Space: so much so that you almost expect him to appear in a puff of smoke),
a renegade out for revenge for his casting away on a desert planet these 15
years before. But the plot concentrates
on character rather than action, although there's enough of that too.
Effects are limited but well done and

James Horner's Tchaikovsky-style music captures the spirit of the thing with tongue-in-cheek panache.

Star Trek III: The Search for Spock ○ ⓥ

1984, US, 105 mins, colour
Dir: Leonard Nimoy
Stars: William Shatner, Leonard Nimoy, DeForest Kelley
Rating: ★★

There's a glorious innocence about the continuing adventures of the Starship Enterprise, though this one is more routine than its theme promises. Spock 'died' in the last adventure, but you can bet your last Klingon coin that Captain Kirk (still William Shatner) and his trusty crew will not allow him to rest in peace for long. Add a Klingon warlord out to wrest the secret of 'Genesis' (the regeneration of a dead planet) from its inventor (Kirk's son) and you have a simple mixture which goes down at a rather leisurely pace for the next hour and three-quarters. Shatner continues to grow younger while all about him look ready to draw their old-age pensions: an offshoot from the 'Genesis' project perhaps. A giggle a minute for the rest of us while Trekkies remain spell-bound.

Star Trek IV

See: The Voyage Home – Star Trek IV

Star Trek V: The Final Frontier ○ ⓥ

1989, US, 100 mins, colour
Dir: William Shatner
Stars: William Shatner, Leonard Nimoy, DeForest Kelley, James Doohan, David Warner, Nichelle Nichols
Rating: ★★

This fifth attempt to boldly venture where no man has gone before is an improvement on one or two of the others, even though it sags in the middle when batty Vulcan Lawrence Luckinbill holds forth on the state of God, pain and the Galaxy. Just as well there's a ship full of hostile Klingons to contend with as well, so, at the beginnning and end at least, the sci-fi pot is kept bubbling with a good deal of action. The direction (by star William Shatner) is serviceable enough and, if things sometimes get too deliberately silly, there's still a deal of amusement to be gained from the banter between the old comrades. 'Please, Captain,' chides Spock (Leonard Nimoy), as Kirk is about to embrace him, 'not in front of the Klingons.'

Star Trek VI: The Undiscovered Country ○ ⓥ

1991, US, 109 mins, colour
Dir: Nicholas Meyer
Stars: William Shatner, Leonard Nimoy, DeForest Kelley, James Doohan, Nichelle Nichols
Rating: ★★★

Sentiment over what's the last of the original Star Trek films, nicely rounded off with the signatures of the cast, can't cloak the fact that it isn't actually the finest entry in the captain's log. Kirk's old enemies the Klingons are faced with extinction and agree to attend a world conference relevant to their survival. Faced with the unthinkable – peace and retirement – Kirk and his men are perhaps more relieved than they'd care to admit that certain elements are determined to destroy the conference and ensure the continuation of war. The film's centrepiece is the imprisonment of Kirk and Dr McCoy (William Shatner, DeForest Kelley) in the mines beneath a planet of icy wastes. Here as elsewhere, though, the pace is pretty lethargic, and a sense of urgency only grows towards the end.

Star Trek Generations ○ ⓥ

1994, US, 118 mins, colour
Dir: David Carson
Stars: William Shatner, Patrick Stewart, Malcolm McDowell, Whoopi Goldberg, James Doohan, Walter Koenig
Rating: ★★

Trekkers whooped with glee at the preview of this meeting of the old and new captains of the Starship Enterprise. But their enthusiasm can't hide the fact that this is a slow trek through time in between the bursts of action on land and in space. Most of the acting, in fact, is pretty shaky, apart from Patrick Stewart's solid (if slightly stolid) Jean Luc Picard, leaving Shatner's Kirk to subtly scoop up the honours with his appearances in the first and last 15 minutes of the film. 'I was out saving the galaxy when your grandfather was in diapers,' he reminds Stewart: it's the kind of line the new boys may never grow into. Here they have enough trouble on their hands, aside from some very OTT Klingon villains, skimming over the gaping holes in logic in a tale of a madman (Malcolm McDowell) trying to reach a state of perpetual joy, an ambition that causes him to destroy planets to alter the course of the 'Nexus' that can take him there. At least Scotty gets to say, one last time: 'I don't know how much

longer I can hold it together' although here he might have been referring to the plot.

Star Trek: First Contact ◐ ⓥ

1996, US, 110 mins, colour
Dir: Jonathan Frakes
Stars: Patrick Stewart, Alice Krige, Alfre Woodard, Jonathan Frakes, Brent Spiner, Michael Dorn
Rating: ★★★★★

Sensationally good of its kind, this is the best Star Trek film of the series so far. Exchanges between *Enterprise* captain Stewart and earthling Woodard have a vital, human quality missing from the dry dialogue of previous entries. And co-star Frakes' handling of the intelligent, not-too-complex plot should ensure he lives long and prospers as a film director. Tension and excitement are rhythmically controlled through a whole series of seat-gripping sequences, as the half-machine, half-organic Borg threaten to destroy history – and with it the Starfleet itself. Tackled head on by the *Enterprise*, whose captain was once 'assimilated' by the Borg but rescued, the bad guys head through a time warp to Earth 2063 to prevent 'first contact' between Earthmen and Vulcans. Stewart proves himself a first-rate actor in a demandingly written role and there's a strong showing by Krige as the reptilian Borg queen.

Start the Revolution Without Me ◐

1969, US, 95 mins, colour
Dir: Bud Yorkin
Stars: Gene Wilder, Donald Sutherland
Rating: ★★★★

Lively, underrated swashbuckling spoof. Fred Freeman and Lawrence J Cohen's screenplay gives the French Revolution the runaround and casts Gene Wilder and Donald Sutherland as two sets of twins – The Corsican Brothers (master swordsmen) and a couple of feckless peasants, who, of course, get mistaken for them. The fun lies chiefly in the by-play between Wilder and Sutherland ('I'll run him through.' 'You'd be lucky to run the girl through.'). But the giant ballroom scene is also a hysterical success, with a surfeit of notes, most of them hinting at assassination plots, passing bewilderingly from dancer to dancer, until Wilder receives one (from a man) saying 'Hello, handsome'. The scene ends in masterly fashion, as the comic king (Hugh Griffith), dressed as a cockerel under the mistaken impression that the ball was fancy dress, weaves his way slowly back through the revellers to the royal chamber.

Star Wars ○ Ⓥ
1977, US, 116 mins, colour
Dir: George Lucas
Stars: Mark Hamill, Harrison Ford, Carrie Fisher, Alec Guinness
Rating: ★★★★

This super-colossal science-fiction pantomime smashed box-office records all over the world. And, like most pantomimes, it's a lot of fun. There are monsters, robots and battles galore, and an endearing pair of androids, C-3P0 and R2-D2, that accompany the hero (Mark Hamill) on his exploits. Alec Guinness and Peter Cushing are there to provide the class, and Carrie Fisher makes a practical heroine, even if her ancestry seems closer to Brooklyn than outer space. The film's adrenalin-raising drive makes it well-nigh irresistible.

State Fair ○
1962, US, 113 mins, colour
Dir: Jose Ferrer
Stars: Pat Boone, Ann-Margret, Bobby Darin, Alice Faye, Tom Ewell
Rating: ★★★

Jose Ferrer directed this re-make of the famous Rodgers and Hammerstein musical about a country family who all come up for the huge state fair. Sultry Ann-Margret offsets the pure charm of Mr Boone, but it is the older generation which steals the honours – Tom Ewell and Alice Faye, herself making a comeback as the mother and looking just as trim and lovely as in the days when she starred in such musicals as *Alexander's Ragtime Band*. Not as good as the Forties' version, but the score is still enchanting.

State Fair ⊙ Ⓥ
1945, US, 100 mins, colour
Dir: Walter Lang
Stars: Jeanne Crain, Dana Andrews, Dick Haymes, Vivian Blaine
Rating: ★★★★

Warm-hearted musical in marvellous colour made by that unsung hero of film musicals, Walter Lang. Lilting Rodgers and Hammerstein score includes, as well as the title number, 'That's for Me', 'It's a Grand Night for Singing' and 'It Might As Well Be Spring', the latter winning an Oscar as the year's best song. Louanna Hogan 'ghost' sings for Jeanne Crain, who makes a charming heroine. Vivian Blaine and Dick Haymes contribute

their own tonsil work. The songs put it ahead of the 1933 original with Will Rogers and Janet Gaynor.

State of Grace ● Ⓥ
1990, US, 134 mins, colour
Dir: Phil Joanou
Stars: Sean Penn, Ed Harris, Gary Oldman, Robin Wright, John Turturro, Burgess Meredith
Rating: ★★

A long and gruelling film about the Irish gangsters of New York's *Hell's Kitchen*. The script is only marginally compelling and all of the performances have moments when melodrama takes over from conviction. Penn is a young man who escaped the Kitchen and now, it seems, has returned. He renews acquaintance with Jackie (Gary Oldman) and his brother Frankie (Ed Harris), now the neighbourhood protection boss – and rekindles his steamy affair with their sister (Robin Wright). The Irish gangsters are dinosaurs at the mercy of the modern technology of the Mafia, but they still kill people. And, street warfare being what it is, most of the cops' work is done for them in the end, more effectively than they could do it themselves. It's a harsh and familiar tale of executions and betrayals, somewhat hampered in the telling by the fact that the characters, even the girl, are cold and unsympathetic throughout.

State of the Union ○
(aka: The World and His Wife)
1948, US, 110 mins, b/w
Dir: Frank Capra
Stars: Spencer Tracy, Katharine Hepburn, Van Johnson, Angela Lansbury
Rating: ★★★

Another Spencer Tracy/Katharine Hepburn vehicle, this Frank Capra-directed dissection of political chicanery has an excellent script by Anthony Veiller and Myles Connolly. Although basically an emotive drama, the screenplay is veined with marvellous wisecracks and the moral brought home strongly in the approved Capra style. Angela Lansbury has an excellent 'bitch' role which she plays icily and to the hilt, while Tracy's outburst at the end reminds one of the speech he was to make nearly 20 years later, at the end of his last film *Guess Who's Coming to Dinner*.

State Secret ○
(aka: The Great Manhunt)
1950, UK, 104 mins, b/w
Dir: Sidney Gilliat

Stars: Douglas Fairbanks Jr, Glynis Johns, Jack Hawkins, Herbert Lom
Rating: ★★★★

A superior, stylish, fast paced thriller, absolutely alive with atmosphere, as a surgeon played by Douglas Fairbanks Jr goes on the run from the state police of an East European country after he has failed to save their dictator on the operating table. Its sheer panache and excitement, together with excellent performances from all four principals, made this film a classic.

Static ● Ⓥ
1985, US, 93 mins, colour
Dir: Mark Romanek
Stars: Keith Gordon, Amanda Plummer, Bob Gunton, Barton Heyman
Rating: ★★

Now Ernie Blick is what you and I would call a weirdo. With his parents dead in a car crash, this mechanical maniac has invented a machine that will show him a picture of Heaven so that he can find and talk to them. Director Mark Romanek, whose first film this was, and who wrote the script with star Keith Gordon, gets marks for originality here, but the film is played out at a halting, deliberate pace that renders it much too slow for the average viewer, stop-starting to an ending that just isn't believable. Gordon is every inch the nut who may just have something, but Amanda Plummer is too downbeat to make an impact as the girl who comes back into his life after time away.

Station West ○
1948, US, 92 mins, b/w
Dir: Sidney Lanfield
Stars: Dick Powell, Jane Greer, Agnes Moorehead
Rating: ★★★★

A very sharply written sort of Western *film noir*, with tough guy Dick Powell donning cowboy duds and going undercover in pursuit of a gang of gold robbers. Powell shares some smart exchanges of dialogue with a blonde (but still dangerous) Jane Greer as a casino owner who may or may not be involved with it all. 'Have you ever made love to a woman?' she asks, in a scene worthy of Mae West. 'Only from the doorway,' replies Powell cryptically. 'You haven't made love to me,' purrs Jane, to which Powell's response is, 'Come over to the doorway.' Crisp, confident stuff from RKO Radio in the purple patch of its immediate post-war years. A superior supporting cast includes Agnes

S

Moorehead, Burt Ives, Steve Brodie and Raymond Burr.

Staying Alive ○ Ⓥ
1983, US, 96 mins, colour
Dir: Sylvester Stallone
Stars: John Travolta, Cynthia Rhodes, Finola Hughes
Rating: ★★

John Travolta's second appearance as dancer Tony Manero is, under Sylvester Stallone's direction, actually better than his first in *Saturday Night Fever* – though not all of this sequel matches up to the original so well. Manero's now a dance instructor in Manhattan but, like Dustin Hoffman in *Tootsie*, he fails auditions for Broadway shows. The Bee Gees' driving music and the sweat gland-bursting dances should get teenagers clapping everywhere. Travolta is first-rate and Cynthia Rhodes as his long-suffering girl (doing all her own singing and dancing as well as proving a definite personality) also has lots of talent.

Stay Tuned ○ Ⓥ
1992, US, US mins, colour
Dir: Peter Hyams
Stars: John Ritter, Pam Dawber, Jeffrey Jones
Rating: ★★

This comedy, that gets A for invention and B for execution, shows what might happen to *you* if you watch too much television. Sold a massive set with a garden dish the size of a tennis wheel, compulsive goggler Roy Knabel (John Ritter) is sucked into the dish with his wife (Pam Dawber) who was about to leave him, and lands in Hellvision, a multi-channel nightmare in which the Knables are zapped from programme to programme by Mr Spike (Jeffrey Jones), a Be'elzebub of the box, who sold Roy the set in the first place. Thus Roy finds himself in many of the things he has watched most: a gameshow, a Western, a swashbuckler, a black-and-white detective movie, a cartoon – entertainingly done by the legendary Chuck Jones – an Arctic adventure, a *Star Trek* episode and others. These are sketched in with varying degrees of success, but don't miss the brief clip from Hellvision's *Three Men and Rosemary's Baby*.

Steal Big, Steal Little ◑ Ⓥ
1995, US, 134 mins, colour
Dir: Andrew Davis
Stars: Andy Garcia, Alan Arkin, Rachel Ticotin, Joe Pantoliano, Ally Walker,

Kevin McCarthy
Rating: ★

Andrew Davis, a director of action films from Chuck Norris days, later raised his profile with the success of *Under Siege* and *The Fugitive*. But he takes a good few paces back with this muddled, tedious and almost interminable comedy-drama with a plotline more familiar in Hindi popular cinema – two orphaned twins are raised by a millionaire – and just as abundant in bristling moustaches, the characters here being Mexican or Mexican-American. Andy Garcia unwisely attempts this dual role, but hasn't the range to delineate the twins, one of whom naturally goes bad while the other is upright and identifies with the people and the land. To underline the Hindi connection, there are corrupt policemen and judges – and that marathon running time. You'll battle to keep up with the plot, but the chances are that, like a motor-racing champion, it'll zoom right away from you before the end.

Stealing Beauty ● Ⓥ
1995, Ita, 119 mins, colour
Dir: Bernardo Bertolucci
Stars: Liv Tyler, Jeremy Irons, Sinead Cusack, Jean Marais, D W Moffett, Rachel Weisz, Jason Flemyng, Stefania Sandrelli
Rating: ★★

It may well be, of course, that 19-year-old American girls go on summer hols to Italy to lose their virginity. Director Bertolucci and star Liv Tyler almost make us believe the tall tale before we sink into a heat-induced tedium. Tyler has an additional motive, however: to find her real father. So it's highly possible, the director supposes, that she might do both, as well as befriend a dying poet (Irons) and be pursued by several separate swains, all within the confines of a stone cottage. Thanks to well-signposted plot developments, there isn't a single thing here that you could call a surprise. Its actors pose modishly about the Italian countryside and there is much fornication which, under Bertolucci's cultured hands, almost passes for art. Tall Tyler has a certain Caron-like gamine appeal.

Steamboat Bill Jr ☉
1928, US, 71 mins, b/w
Dir: Charles F Reisner
Stars: Buster Keaton, Ernest Torrence
Rating: ★★★★

One of Buster Keaton's last great silent comedies, memorable particularly for the hilarious scene in which Keaton

tries to smuggle a file to his father in jail, and for the climactic cyclone which sweeps Keaton along the streets of the town in his hospital bed. The antics are crisply directed by Charles F 'Chuck' Reisner, a Hollywood comedy expert who later made vehicles for W C Fields, Abbott and Costello and The Marx Brothers.

Steaming ●
1985, UK, 95 mins, colour
Dir: Joseph Losey
Stars: Vanessa Redgrave, Sarah Miles, Diana Dors, Patti Love, Brenda Bruce
Rating: ★★

Steaming was a highly successful play on both sides of the Atlantic, but it loses something in its translation to the big screen. Director Joseph Losey's reverential treatment of playwright Nell *(Up The Junction)* Dunn's play as sapped the original's wit and pace. It does have its lighter moments, though, thanks to a strong cast headed by Vanessa Redgrave, Sarah Miles and especially Diana Dors. It's set in a bath house, where Violet (Diana Dors) has to deal with both the emotional ups and downs of her customers and the threat of closure from the local council. A sad footnote to the film was that both Losey and Diana Dors died soon after it was made.

Steel ◑
1979, US, 101 mins, colour
Dir: Steve Carver
Stars: Lee Majors, Jennifer O'Neill, Art Carney, Harris Yulin
Rating: ★★★

This is cheerfully old-fashioned Hollywood hokum in Universal-International 1950 style, with Jennifer O'Neill in the Ann Sheridan role as the lady thrust into heading a race against time to erect a gigantic building and Lee Majors as the ramrod she hires despite his having lost his nerve for heights. The credibility barrier is nearly breached at times, but Michel Colombier's rousing music drives it along. Majors has said that it was a most dangerous film to work on and one can quite see his point. Back projection hadn't been invented as far as this unit was concerned, and it adds bags to the realism of an enterprise on which one stuntman was killed.

Steel Magnolias ○ Ⓥ
1989, US, 115 mins, colour
Dir: Herbert Ross
Stars: Sally Field, Dolly Parton, Shirley MacLaine, Daryl Hannah, Olympia

Dukakis, Julia Roberts
Rating: ★★★

A really big all-girl weepie for which you'll require a bucket rather than a handkerchief. Fortunately, its tears and tragedy are deliberately leavened with some funny dialogue, mainly stemming from the relationship of the six main characters within the confines of a hairdressing salon. Sally Field is the loving mother whose only daughter (Julia Roberts) is trying to get married while their father (Tom Skerritt) shoots at birds in the trees and local granny-grump Ouiser (Shirley MacLaine) is upsetting everyone. It transpires that Roberts is a diabetic and despite all medical advice, decides to have a baby. You won't need a diagram of the rest of the plot, but the film stays afloat on its sea of tears through a series of treasurable one-liners. You'll sympathise with MacLaine at Christmas, when she asks Field (whose character's frankly a bit of a pain): 'What's wrong with you these days? You got a reindeer up your butt?' Some excellent performances, especially from MacLaine, Skerritt and, surprisingly, Daryl Hannah. You may find the characters a shade too nice, but it's this quality that gives the film some backbone and helps see it through.

Stella ● Ⓥ
1990, US, 114 mins, colour
Dir: John Erman
Stars: Bette Midler, Trini Alvarado, John Goodman, Marsha Mason, Stephen Collins
Rating: ★

This 'classic' weepie was creaky even in Barbara Stanwyck's day. So there was little chance that even Bette Midler could pull a new version of this old chestnut out of the fire. And so it proves, although the new *Stella* (Dallas, that is) is actually worse than you might fear. Collins, as the man who makes Stella pregnant, actually achieves the unwelcome distinction of being as bad as John Boles in the original, although, required to keep telling Alvarado, 'I don't know about you, but I need you to put your head right here' (on his shoulder), he can be partially excused the glazed look and slack-jawed disbelief. There remain a few Midler whiplash wisecracks but, over 114 minutes, they fade like drops of water in a desert.

Stella Dallas ○
1937, US, 106 mins, b/w
Dir: King Vidor

Stars: Barbara Stanwyck, John Boles, Anne Shirley
Rating: ★★★

One of the great weepies of the screen, filmed before in 1925, but here in a definitive version directed by King Vidor. Barbara Stanwyck suffers memorably (she was nominated for an Academy Award) as the woman dedicated to her daughter's happiness at her own expense. Wonderfully well made; keep a couple of handkerchiefs at the ready for the end.

St Elmo's Fire ● Ⓥ
1985, US, 108 mins, colour
Dir: Joel Schumacher
Stars: Emilio Estevez, Rob Lowe, Andrew McCarthy, Demi Moore, Judd Nelson, Ally Sheedy
Rating: ★★

This is one of those films, like *Silverado* which, years after its heyday, proves to be knee-deep in stars. A nostalgic look at school friendships thrown into the big wide world, it has so many good points that you wish you could say they amounted to more. The framework of intertwining relationships among the seven contrasting 22-year-olds who congregate in the noisy St Elmo's Bar, filled with music and smoke, is handled with warmth, compassion and skill by director Joel Schumacher and his cast. Without the players and the music, it's doubtful if the story would involve us enough: they're the elements which set St Elmo's if not on fire then at least constantly glowing with their talents.

Stepfather, The ● Ⓥ
1986, US, 93 mins, colour
Dir: Joseph Ruben
Stars: Terry O'Quinn, Shelley Hack, Jill Schoelen, Stephen Shellen, Charles Lanyer
Rating: ★★★

Good for a giggle and a grip of the arm of your seat is this chiller that doesn't take itself seriously for a second longer than it takes to make an audience jump. Terry O'Quinn is splendidly nutty as the schizo killer who sets up home with fatherless families, then slaughters the lot when his authority is challenged. Shelley Hack and Jill Schoelen, the latter particularly natural, are the latest hapless stones onto which this lethal barnacle has battened itself. It's to the film's credit that it keeps the interest mounting in spite of the foregone conclusion the plot rolls inexorably towards from then on. First-class editing – not a scene is held

too long – has a lot to do with it. Two inferior sequels followed.

Stepford Wives, The ◐
1974, US, 115 mins, colour
Dir: Bryan Forbes
Stars: Katharine Ross, Paula Prentiss
Rating: ★★

Walter and Joanna (Peter Masterson and Katharine Ross) tire of the rat race and move to the sleepy Connecticut town of Stepford. Joanna meets the local wives, but finds them rather odd – they seem to delight in moronic conversation and are cheerfully subservient to their husbands. But the truth about the wives is more shocking than their lives... A nice idea given a light touch, with a neat twist at the end. It's just a shame that the first hour or so of this film is so slow. The little girl in the film is a seven-year-old Mary Stuart Masterson (son of star Peter) in her first film role. Not a bad film, but not one that does justice to Ira Levin's enjoyable book.

Stepkids ○ Ⓥ
(aka: Big Girls Don't Cry... They Get Even)
1992, US, 104 mins, colour
Dir: Joan Micklin Silver
Stars: Hillary Wolf, Griffin Dunne, David Strathairn, Patricia Kalember, Adrienne Shelly, Margaret Whitton, Dan Futterman
Rating: ★

An interminable tale about a 13-year-old misfit girl lost in a sea of stepfathers, stepbrothers and stepsisters. By running away from home, she brings everyone back together again. Harmless but pointless, the film is a wry comedy that hardly makes you laugh at all. Hillary Wolf is so annoying as the girl that it's no wonder everyone else finds her such a drag.

Step Lively ○
1944, US, 88 mins, b/w
Dir: Tim Whelan
Stars: Frank Sinatra, George Murphy, Gloria DeHaven
Rating: ★★★

Frank Sinatra, the biggest vocal star in showbusiness in the year this film was made, took top billing and did quite well as a country yokel from upstate New York who has written a play and sends it, along with his savings, to Miller (George Murphy), a New York producer. Twists abound when his money is used to stage a different production, which Miller offers him a part in. The romantic interest is added when Sinatra meets showgirl Gloria

S

DeHaven – with whom he has his first screen kiss! The songs, which include 'Other Time', 'As Long As There's Music' and 'Where Does Love Begin?', add a great deal to an otherwise slim story, even if they do interfere with its flow.

Stepping Out ○ ⓥ

1991, US, 110 mins, colour
Dir: Lewis Gilbert
Stars: Liza Minnelli, Shelley Winters, Bill Irwin, Ellen Greene, Julie Walters
Rating: ★★★★

Cynics may scoff, but there are some good bad films you just can't help enjoying and this one is pretty near the top of the list. Failed hoofer Mavis Turner (Liza Minnelli) runs a dance class downtown in a church hall and has a motley class of no-hopers and a pianist (Shelley Winters) who looks like a bag lady. Mavis has her own problems, as do her pupils whose ages range from 20 to 40; not half of them, however, measure up to those on the dance floor, and these are given a new edge with the 'opportunity' to perform in a charity show. Thanks to Liza, one of the great wasted talents of our generation, and her perfectly cast oddball chorus line, this proves to be a movie with heart. Even a poor script and clumsy direction can't kill it; and the chances are you'll cry your eyes out on the night of the big show. It's a triumph of talent and personality over everything else.

Steptoe and Son ◐

1972, UK, 98 mins, colour
Dir: Cliff Owen
Stars: Wilfred Brambell, Harry H Corbett
Rating: ★★

TV comedy spinoffs proliferated in the early Seventies; this example is brighter than most, thanks to the basic strength of Galton and Simpson's original series. Directed by Cliff Owen, a neglected talent.

Steptoe & Son Ride Again ◐

1973, UK, 98 mins, colour
Dir: Peter Sykes
Stars: Wilfrid Brambell, Harry H Corbett
Rating: ★

The tone of this big screen version of the hit TV series about the sparring rag-and-bone father and son is firmly set by buxom co-star Diana Dors. Bending over a drinks cabinet to reveal her knickers, she purrs, as only she can, 'Can you see anything you like?' It's strictly below the belt material, with plenty of references to

lavatories, booze, breasts and the hilarity of death. Sadly, the sharply observed class distinctions and the perfect turn of phrase of the small screen series are sacrificed in preference for a crude and lewd series of loosely linked sketches.

Stevie ○ ⓥ

1978, UK, 102 mins, colour
Dir: Robert Enders
Stars: Glenda Jackson, Mona Washbourne, Trevor Howard
Rating: ★★★★★

'Who or what is Stevie Smith? Is she woman or is she myth?' wrote Ogden Nash. Robert Enders' beautifully balanced film about the spinster English poet who shocked many with her work shatters the mirror of the myth and shows us the woman standing behind it. Initially, you may resist the treatment of one-room action and addressing the camera. But soon, very soon, you'll be drawn into the web of poor Stevie Smith (Glenda Jackson) and her sad, determinedly lonely existence in suburban London, initially with her 'lion aunt' (superb Mona Washbourne) and later alone. 'I was too far out for most of my life, and not waving but drowning': thus Stevie on that existence and her preoccupation with death, whom she called Black March, even when he promised her, in her visions, 'a breath of fresh air' and she attempted suicide. But the film can be funny and knowing as well as sad and bitter, and one anecdote where Stevie meets the Queen to receive an award is rich in dry and deadly wit. Ms Jackson's delivery here, as everywhere, is perfection. As the narrator and her latter-day friend, Trevor Howard offers his best portrayal in ages. And Ms Washbourne, cruelly denied even an Oscar nomination (although she did win a British Oscar), is brilliant in her last great performance.

Stiff Upper Lips ● ⓥ

1996, UK, 95 mins, colour
Dir: Gary Sinyor
Stars: Peter Ustinov, Georgina Cates, Sean Pertwee, Prunella Scales, Samuel West, Robert Portal, Frank Finlay
Rating: ★

Another awfully big adventure for comely Georgina Cates, this time as the heroine of a well-dressed but heavy-handed spoof of *A Passage to India*, *Chariots of Fire* and almost everything Merchant-Ivory ever made (or E M Forster ever wrote). Unfortunately, the TV-style comedy sketches that re-

sult prove rather a long stretch at 95 minutes. And, despite the efforts of a game cast, the emphasis on phallic and physical humour becomes tiresome quite quickly, in spite of some felicities in the performances of West and Portal as two improbable upper-class twits at large in 1908 England, Italy and India. Lovely to look at, you'll find this rather less delightful to know unless your sense of humour is as broad as Ustinov's beam.

Sting, The ◐ ⓥ

1973, US, 129 mins, colour
Dir: George Roy Hill
Stars: Paul Newman, Robert Redford, Robert Shaw
Rating: ★★★★

This fortuitous re-teaming of Paul Newman and Robert Redford (from *Butch Cassidy and The Sundance Kid*) drew seven Oscars and worldwide queues. The Thirties' settings, in the hands of cameraman Robert Surtees, costume designer Edith Head and art director Henry Bumstead, veterans all, vividly recreate conditions of the period, and the humorous playing of the stars is immensely winning. The film also revived the ragtime music of Scott Joplin, arranged here by Marvin Hamlisch. Amusing, exciting, ingeniously plotted and very entertaining.

Sting II, The ◐

1983, US, 102 mins, colour
Dir: Jeremy Paul Kagan
Stars: Jackie Gleason, Mac Davis, Teri Garr, Oliver Reed
Rating: ★★

Ten years after Paul Newman and Robert Redford fleeced Robert Shaw in *The Sting*, for which screenwriter David M Walsh won an Oscar, Walsh struck back with the inevitable sequel. But now Shaw was dead and, presumably, Newman and Redford passed up the opportunity to return to the scene of their former triumph. Given the unenviable task of following on are Jackie Gleason and Mac Davis as the conmen and Oliver Reed as their victim. Teri Garr scoops the acting honours under Jeremy Paul Kagan's direction.

Stir Crazy ● ⓥ

1980, US, 110 mins, colour
Dir: Sidney Poitier
Stars: Gene Wilder, Richard Pryor
Rating: ★★

This salty, offbeat comedy has a few nice ideas rattling around in its story of two drifters wrongly imprisoned on bank robbery charges – such as Gene

Wilder coming up trumps after each new torture, more horrendous than the last, to make him ride in the annual inter-prison rodeo. Co-star Richard Pryor mugs dreadfully, but Wilder's natural off-centre charm is proof even against director Sidney Poitier's crowd-the-screen technique and the uneven quality of the script. Make sure you see the movie from the start and don't miss the pre-credits scene where a woman gets her shoe caught in a grating.

St Ives ●
1976, US, 93 mins, colour
Dir: J Lee Thompson
Stars: Charles Bronson, John Houseman, Jacqueline Bisset, Maximilian Schell
Rating: ★

'Every time we find a stiff, you're around.' This snatch of Forties-style dialogue gives you an idea of what to expect from this confusing and poorly acted cloak-and-dagger story. It starts off well enough as a routine tough thriller, but long before the end you're left wondering just what's going on, and why they keep showing the same clip of film at the drive-in movie where a 'drop' is being made. Mark this down as for hardened Charles Bronson fans only.

St Louis Blues ○
1958, US, 90 mins, b/w
Dir: Allen Reisner
Stars: Nat 'King' Cole, Eartha Kitt, Pearl Bailey
Rating: ★★

Suitable film roles for the great Nat 'King' Cole proved sadly few and far between. However, half the jazz greats in the Hollywood vicinity were in this all-black musical about the famous blues composer W C Handy, and Cole has the star role, although it arrived too late, at 39, to set him up for a film career. Even so, his singing and piano playing are, as always, a delight. Of the 'real' actors, Juano Hernandez (as Handy's father) and Ruby Dee put in sterling work, while a string of blues standards includes 'Yellow Dog Blues', 'Careless Love', 'St Louis Blues', 'Chantez Les Bas' and 'Morning Star'.

St Martin's Lane ○
(aka: Sidewalks of London)
1938, UK, 85 mins, b/w
Dir: Tim Whelan
Stars: Charles Laughton, Vivien Leigh, Rex Harrison
Rating: ★★★★

One of Charles Laughton's most likeable and at the same time moving performances: he plays a busker entertaining on the streets of London. Vivien Leigh's vivacious performance as the guttersnipe pickpocket, who becomes part of Laughton's grubby little group is said to be the one that first attracted the attention of Hollywood producers. American director Tim Whelan really does capture some of the atmosphere of London's West End streets of the time, one of the few filmmakers of his era to do so.

Stockade ● ⓥ
1990, US, 98 mins, colour
Dir: Martin Sheen
Stars: Martin Sheen, Charlie Sheen, F Murray Abraham, Larry Fishburne, Michael Beach
Rating: ★★

This combined effort from the ubiquitous Sheen family – Charlie's brother Ramon Estevez is also in it – is almost, but not quite a good film. This is about as pleasant a tale of life in a military stockade as you're ever likely to see, and you'll undoubtedly warm to the growing friendship of hardcase Charlie Sheen and his five even-harder-case black fellow prisoners. At heart, though, you've got to admit that Charlie's character is a whinger steeped in self-pity and you can't quite side with him when he tells psychotic sergeant-major Martin Sheen that 'You're on me' or 'You're a bully and I hate everything you stand for' any more than you could believe Sheen Sr wouldn't have had him on treble duties for a week for insubordination.

Stolen Face ○
1952, UK, 72 mins, b/w
Dir: Terence Fisher
Stars: Lizabeth Scott, Paul Henreid, Andre Morell, Susan Stephen
Rating: ★★

Paul Henreid and Lizabeth Scott came to Britain to make this thriller which proves to be a melodramatic variation on Bogart's Dark Passage. Henreid is the surgeon who operates on lady criminals to improve their looks and he gets grim-faced support from Ms Scott, Mary Mackenzie and Andre Morell. Pretty Susan Stephen shows up well in a supporting role. The fevered plot developments are handled by the experienced Terence Fisher.

Stolen Hours ○
1963, UK, 100 mins, colour
Dir: Daniel Petrie

Stars: Susan Hayward, Michael Craig, Diane Baker
Rating: ★★★

This is a real tear-jerker, although there is often great charm about its story (a remake of 1939's Dark Victory, for which Bette Davis nearly won a third Oscar) of a rich socialite who, with a year to live and a wasted life behind her, grabs her chance of happiness while she may. And one cannot imagine anyone being better than Ms Hayward in the leading role.

Stolen Life, A ○
1946, US, 107 mins, b/w
Dir: Curtis Bernhardt
Stars: Bette Davis, Glenn Ford, Dane Clark
Rating: ★★★

A stolen idea, too, as eight years previously this story of twin sisters falling for the same fellow, with the nasty one initially getting him, had been filmed with Elisabeth Bergner playing the two sisters. Admittedly, this version, with Bette Davis as the sisters, is better. Glenn Ford is the chap they both fall for and there's solid support from Walter Brennan, Dane Clark and Charles Ruggles. Bette, obviously, dominates the film with two fine and distinct characterisations. It's pure melodrama and deservedly popular in its day. A double (or even triple) success for Bette, as she was also the film's producer.

Stone Killer, The ●
1973, US, 96 mins, colour
Dir: Michael Winner
Stars: Charles Bronson, Martin Balsam
Rating: ★★

Formula tough-cop stuff in the Dirty Harry mould. Under Michael Winner's professional but passionless direction, the film emerges as a series of violent set-pieces, each perfectly executed and as cold and clinical as a gun-barrel. The best of these is saved until last – an exciting multiple shoot-out staged in a remote desert fortress. Charles Bronson is the star, and sharp eyes may pick out John Ritter in a minor role.

Stooge, The ⊙
1951, US, 100 mins, b/w
Dir: Norman Taurog
Stars: Dean Martin, Jerry Lewis
Rating: ★★★★

A song-and-dance man finds his act a success when he acquires a seemingly moronic stooge. This often funny and

S

strangely affecting film is a real must for connoisseurs of Martin and Lewis, and rightly considered about the best thing they ever did as a team. The situations may be old, but under the skilled direction of Norman Taurog, both comedy and pathos prove effective. You'll be cheering for the guys to do the right thing at the end.

Stop! or My Mom Will Shoot
○ ⓥ
1992, US, 92 mins, colour
Dir: Roger Spottiswoode
Stars: Sylvester Stallone, Estelle Getty, JoBeth Williams, Roger Rees
Rating: RB

Even after the debacle of *Oscar*, Sylvester Stallone still had the idea he could play comedy. This deplorable caper clearly proves him wrong – even if the script gives him no help at all. Stallone's a cop whose 4ft 11in mother (Estelle Getty – terrible) sets his career in reverse gear from the moment of her arrival at his apartment. Overplayed by everyone, the ensuing plot is trying in the extreme. 'This whole thing is just ridiculous,' laments Stallone at one point, and you truly just have to agree. Even *Rocky 6* or *Rambo 4* would be better than this, and the star wisely returned to well choreographed action with *Cliffhanger*.

Stopover Tokyo ○ ⓥ
1957, US, 95 mins, colour
Dir: Richard L Breen
Stars: Robert Wagner, Joan Collins, Edmund O'Brien
Rating: ★★

Director Richard L Breen's adaptation of John P Marquand's espionage story is attractively photographed against some picturesque backgrounds and Robert Wagner is, as always, likable and efficient. However, the tale fails to deliver much eastern promise in the way of real suspense or excitement. Only stop over here if you've nothing better to do.

Storm Boy ☉
1976, Australia, 89 mins, colour
Dir: Henri Safran
Stars: Greg Rowe, Peter Cummins, David Guipilil
Rating: ★★★

This Australian film, winner of the Aussie Academy Award as Best Picture, is the sort of wholesome family entertainment at which Disney excels. You'll need the tissues handy for the tear-jerking story of a boy and his relationship with a baby pelican.

Ten-year-old non-professional Greg Rowe is a natural in the title role, while first-time Paris-born director Henri Safran captures perfectly the bleak, grim environment of the rugged South Australian coastline with beautiful, atmospheric photography.

Storm Over the Nile ○
1955, UK, 107 mins, colour
Dir: Zoltan Korda, Terence Young
Stars: Anthony Steel, Laurence Harvey, Mary Ure, Jan Carmichael
Rating: ★★★

A remake of *The Four Feathers*, with its vivid action scenes and breathtaking Technicolor locations intact. Although the story is jingoistic and full of *Boy's Own* heroics, the treatment teems with detail that puts it not too far behind the original. And there are fine supporting performances from James Robertson Justice and Christopher Lee. It was the fourth screen version of A E W Mason's famous full-blooded adventure novel. A fifth version appeared with Robert Powell more than 20 years later, and the story still wore well.

Stormy Monday ● ⓥ
1988, UK, 93 mins, colour
Dir: Mike Figgis
Stars: Melanie Griffith, Tommy Lee Jones, Sting, Sean Bean
Rating: ★★★★

A sturdy little *film noir* from Film Four International that takes full advantage of its Newcastle and jazz backgrounds, using both to give a smoky local edge to its story of a crooked American wheeler-dealer (Tommy Lee Jones) moving in on Tyneside. Sean Bean makes an impressive star debut as the young drifter who becomes involved in all this when he both strikes up a relationship with the part-time hooker (Melanie Griffith) who works for the big shot, and obtains employment at the jazz club the American hopes to take over, presumably as a front for his nefarious activities. Sting is more effective than for several films past, reverting to his native Geordie accent as the club owner whose friendship proves useful to the hero – even though it's always slanted towards his own interests.

Stormy Weather ○
1943, US, 77 mins, b/w
Dir: Andrew Stone
Stars: Lena Horne, Bill Robinson
Rating: ★★★★

Dazzling, all-black musical that purports to tell the life story of Bill

'Bojangles' Robinson, whom most people associate with Shirley Temple in those wonderfully intricate dances of the Thirties. Robinson stars as himself, and star supporting turns include Lena Horne singing the title number, brilliant dancing by The Nicholas Brothers, and Fats Waller playing and singing 'Ain't Misbehavin'. Can't be bad.

Story of Alexander Graham Bell, The ○
(aka: The Modern Miracle)
1939, US, 97 mins, b/w
Dir: Irving Cummings
Stars: Don Ameche, Loretta Young, Henry Fonda, Charles Coburn
Rating: ★★★

A typically professional Hollywood biopic of the late Thirties, this was the film that dogged its star, Don Ameche, for years to come. In later years, he would complain that many people thought that Don Ameche had invented the telephone and not Mr Bell! Henry Fonda surprisingly takes a subordinate role as Bell's co-worker.

Story of Dr Wassell, The ○
1944, US, 140 mins, colour
Dir: Cecil B DeMille
Stars: Gary Cooper, Laraine Day, Signe Hasso, Dennis O'Keefe
Rating: ★★

A Cecil B DeMille war epic with a cast of thousands and a budget of millions. It also contains just about every war film cliché in the book, but the patriotic wartime public didn't seem to mind, and swallowed the familiar mixture whole. Gary Cooper's solid sincerity gives the lengthy adventure the bulwark it needs, and Dennis O'Keefe, as one of the wounded men he treats on Java, soared finally to stardom after years of patient extra work.

Story of Esther Costello, The ❶
(aka: Golden Virgin)
1957, UK, 103 mins, b/w
Dir: David Miller
Stars: Joan Crawford, Rossano Brazzi, Heather Sears
Rating: ★★

The film that shot the talented and sensitive Heather Sears to stardom, although subsequent roles (such as *Room at the Top* and *Sons and Lovers*) proved rather too similar for her career's good. She plays a beautiful mute girl, all too soon the victim of ruthless promoters who exploit her as the front for what seems charitable work, but is in fact a scurrilous swindle. Joan Crawford emotes in mournfully melodramatic style as her 'benefactor'.

Story of Gilbert and Sullivan, The ○
1953, UK, 109 mins, colour
Dir: Sidney Gilliat
Stars: Robert Morley, Maurice Evans, Eileen Herlie, Dinah Sheridan
Rating: ★★★

There's some glowing Technicolor camerawork by Christopher Challis in this biopic, plus a generous ration of the famous G and S operettas. A feast for fans of their music, with Robert Morley in particularly good form as the irascible Gilbert.

Story of Louis Pasteur, The ○
1935, US, 85 mins, b/w
Dir: William Dieterle
Stars: Paul Muni, Josephine Hutchinson, Anita Louise, Donald Woods
Rating: ★★★★

The film that made biography box-office in the Hollywood of the Thirties. Paul Muni won an Academy Award as the distinguished French chemist of the title, director William Dieterle wastes not a second in racing through the more interesting aspects of his career battling infection and disease, and writers Pierre Collings and Sheridan Gibney also took an Oscar for their screenplay.

Story of Mankind, The ○
1957, US, 100 mins, colour
Dir: Irwin Allen
Stars: Ronald Colman, Vincent Price, Peter Lorre, Virginia Mayo
Rating: ★

Human history served up in about an hour and a half. Such is the scope of this quite extraordinary star-studded film. Indicative of its quality and conviction is the casting of Hedy Lamarr as Joan of Arc, Peter Lorre as Nero and Harpo Marx as Isaac Newton.

Story of Robin Hood and His Merrie Men, The ⊙
1952, UK, 83 mins, colour
Dir: Ken Annakin
Stars: Richard Todd, Joan Rice, Peter Finch, James Hayter
Rating: ★★★

Another cheerful romp through Sherwood Forest in the company of Robin and his band of outlaws, made in England by Walt Disney. Attractively photographed by director-to-be Guy Green, it was directed by

Ken Annakin who staged the action set pieces with verve, if little originality. Richard Todd as Robin Hood and Joan Rice as Maid Marion are serviceable rather than inspired and the most enjoyable performances come from James Hayter as Friar Tuck, Hubert Gregg as a sly Prince John and Elton Hayes who is in pleasant voice as Allan-a-Dale. Peter Finch also catches the eye as the Sheriff of Nottingham.

Story of Vernon and Irene Castle, The ○ ⓥ
1939, US, 93 mins, b/w
Dir: H C Potter
Stars: Fred Astaire, Ginger Rogers
Rating: ★★★★

Fred Astaire and Ginger Rogers were the perfect pair to portray Vernon and Irene Castle, the vaudeville entertainer and the doctor's daughter whose care-free glamour had captivated Europe and America in those magic years just before World War One. They created a complete dance revolution, making the new syncopated dances stylish and socially acceptable to all. This film, directed by H C Potter, is full of delightful pastiches (choreographed by Hermes Pan) of the dances that the Castles made popular and packed with favourite songs of the period, but underplays the social and personal history. Even if Astaire and Rogers were ever so slightly past their peak, this final picture that they made with RKO is a must for dance fans. Watch out in particular for that famous montage when they dance their way across a huge map of America. And stand by to shed a tear at the end. The film undeservedly lost money and signalled the end of the Astaire-Rogers partnership for 10 years.

Stowaway ⊙ ⓥ
1936, US, 86 mins, b/w
Dir: William A Seiter
Stars: Shirley Temple, Robert Young, Alice Faye
Rating: ★★★★

One of Shirley Temple's most charming movies. As a little girl brought up in China, she gets a chance to speak some bewildering pidgin Chinese, and sing a rickshaw-full of hits. She also impersonates (with great confidence) Al Jolson and Eddie Cantor and does a Ginger Rogers routine with a Fred Astaire doll. Okay Shirley, we're convinced you have talent! Luminous black-and-white photography by Arthur Miller, and self-effacing back-up for the star from Alice Faye (who

also sings a couple of numbers), Robert Young, Eugene Pallette, Helen Westley and Arthur Treacher. Definitely a stowaway to get on board with.

Straight On Till Morning ●
1972, UK, 96 mins, colour
Dir: Peter Collinson
Stars: Rita Tushingham, Shane Briant, Tom Bell
Rating: ★★

Made hard on the heels of his other tale of terror, *Fright,* director Peter Collinson's second Seventies' chiller is again pitched on one sustained note: hysteria. Rita Tushingham, in a rare latter-day film role, is again cast as an ugly duckling from the north of England, but this time one in love with a psychotic killer. Subsequent plot developments are hardly credible, but at least Collinson gallops through the mayhem with singular aplomb.

Straight Talk ○ ⓥ
1992, US, 91 mins, colour
Dir: Barnett Kellman
Stars: Dolly Parton, James Woods, Griffin Dunne, Michael Madsen, Teri Hatcher, Jerry Orbach
Rating: ★★

Soft-hearted comedies needed to be way sharper than this to succeed in the early Nineties. Even Doris Day might have blinked at taking on this Dolly Parton vehicle in which the star is allowed to pour southern treacle all over a story about a dance instructress who, fired for discussing too many of her customers' problems with them, accidentally ends up as 'Dr Shirlee', an agony aunt on a Chicago radio station. This brings her to the attention of a scoop-hungry reporter (James Woods) who worms his way into her life, then, natch, falls in love with her. Dolly squeaks unconvincingly through a role that Doris or Judy Holliday would at least have made you believe. Woods tries not to look embarrassed and squirms around doing it. There are a few funny lines from Griffin Dunne, a sort of chain-store Dudley Moore, but no-one seems at ease with the star.

Straight to Hell ● ⓥ
1987, US/UK, 86 mins, colour
Dir: Alex Cox
Stars: Sy Richardson, Joe Strummer, Dick Rude, Dennis Hopper, Elvis Costello, Grace Jones
Rating: RB

They said that director Alex Cox could write his own ticket after *Repo Man* and

S

Sid and Nancy. The trouble is, they let him do it. And this is the result. Three bandits bungle a killing, somehow reap a suitcase full of money and hide out in a Mexican desert town where they are fired upon by a group of British and American actors and actresses wearing false beards and corselettes. Presumably intended to be surrealistic, this never grips the interest for a moment. Appallingly self-indulgent, it's a waste of everybody's time and money.

Straitjacket ◐

1964, US, 89 mins, b/w
Dir: William Castle
Stars: Joan Crawford, Diane Baker, Leif Erickson, George Kennedy
Rating: ★★★

Vivid, gruesome melodrama, with Joan Crawford as a woman jailed for two particularly grisly axe murders – a type of killing that begins all over again when she is released from jail 15 years later. Down go the lights, bang goes the door on the victim, up screams the music and there, sure enough, is that shadowy figure on the wall, axe aloft. Appropriately the screenplay was written by Robert Bloch, who wrote *Psycho*. Much of the time, director William Castle tips the suspense over into melodrama and doesn't keep in touch with reality; but at least it can never be accused of not being lively. Whether you die giggling or of fright is a matter between you and your nerves.

Strange Cargo ○

1940, US, 113 mins, b/w
Dir: Frank Borzage
Stars: Clark Gable, Joan Crawford, Ian Hunter, Peter Lorre
Rating: ★★★

This unusual, exciting and even mystical film about a group of prisoners escaping from a South American penal colony featured the then-explosive box-office team of Joan Crawford and Clark Gable. But it is in the supporting acting that the real riches lie – particularly from Peter Lorre as a creepy character called M'Sieu Pig. One of the film's highlights is a terrific fight between the characters played by Gable and Albert Dekker. It takes place in the surf beside a boat and, although it lasts only two minutes on screen, it look two days to film, divided up into rounds because the action proved so exhausting to the two actors.

Strange Days ● Ⓥ

1995, US, 145 mins, colour
Dir: Kathryn Bigelow

Stars: Ralph Fiennes, Angela Bassett, Juliette Lewis, Tom Sizemore, Brigitte Bako
Rating: ★★★

Something to blow your mind here all right, which is what happens to several of the characters in this noisy, nasty, violent but very watchable cross of science-fantasy and whodunnit, set in Los Angeles at the turn of the millennium. Lenny Nero (Ralph Fiennes), an ex-cop, is a dishevelled hustler selling digital tapes of real-life sex and violence which the buyers play on head-sets that make them the participant. 'I'm your main connection to the switchboard of your soul,' he tells prospective punters. He has an ex (Juliette Lewis) who is now the mistress of a promotions mogul, and another (Angela Bassett), who's a tough security driver for important clients. When the mogul's own top client, a black militant leader, has his brains blown out and a girl on the run (Brigitte Bako) throws a tape into Lenny's soon-towed-away car, the worlds of these people collide with nation-impacting violence. Though its brutality is sometimes hard to bear, the film works well enough, both as an action thriller and a chilling portrait of a nightmare near-future.

Strange Invaders ○ Ⓥ

1983, US, 94 mins, colour
Dir: Michael Laughlin
Stars: Paul LeMat, Nancy Allen, Diana Scarwid
Rating: ★★★

Striking special effects and scary scenes when the bug-like aliens return to their proper shape made one blink at the British censor's decision to let this well-made pastiche of Fifties horror films off with a 'PG' certificate. By and large, though, director and co-writer Michael Laughlin succeeds in his aim of 'recapturing a sense of fun characteristic of Hollywood in the Fifties', though the separate elements of light comedy and heavy horror don't always mix readily, even with the engagingly offbeat performances of stars Paul LeMat and Nancy Allen. But the whole thing is made with such pace and affection that one can't really complain.

Strange Love of Martha Ivers, The ○

1946, US, 117 mins, b/w
Dir: Lewis Milestone
Stars: Barbara Stanwyck, Van Heflin, Kirk Douglas, Lizabeth Scott
Rating: ★★★

A pity that – mainly because of war service – Kirk Douglas didn't make his film debut until he was 28, in this typical Forties black drama, directed in this case by the veteran director Lewis Milestone, who skilfully handles a flashback tale of blackmail and murder. Barbara Stanwyck is in her element as the poisonous Miss Ivers, but critics quite rightly picked out Douglas's magnetic performance as the beginning of a long star career.

Stranger Among Us, A

See: Close to Eden

Stranger In Between, The

See: Hunted

Stranger on the Third Floor ◐

1940, US, 64 mins, b/w
Dir: Boris Ingster
Stars: Peter Lorre, John McGuire, Margaret Tallichet, Elisha Cook Jr
Rating: ★★★★

Classic RKO thriller where menace lurks in every shadow and staircase. Sets, photography, an amazing dream sequence and Peter Lorre all contribute to the bizarre Germanic atmosphere. A brief but most rewarding oddity.

Strangers Kiss ●

1983, US, 94 mins, colour
Dir: Matthew Chapman
Stars: Peter Coyote, Victoria Tennant, Richard Romanus
Rating: ★★★

There are some interesting bits and pieces about this story, and they just need one or two more elements integrated into them to make a really fascinating movie. Presumably based on director Stanley Kubrick's early career, it's about the making of a film in 1955, in which a shady character puts up the money so that his mistress can play the lead. Peter Coyote displays an attractive personality as the director and has happily been seen more often since. But Blaine Novak is surely nobody's idea of a leading man, although his co-scripting does show talent.

Strangers on a Train ○ Ⓥ

1951, US, 101 mins, b/w
Dir: Alfred Hitchcock
Stars: Robert Walker, Farley Granger, Ruth Roman
Rating: ★★★★

Co-scripted by Raymond Chandler, *Strangers on a Train* is a roller-coaster ride of suspense with actor Robert Walker gleefully creating an extravagant killer who hatches a bizarre, psychopathic scheme to 'swap' murder victims with an understandably bemused Farley Granger. The locations are chosen with Hitchcock's customary care in this taut adaptation of Patricia Highsmith's novel and the climactic chase through a fairground is a triumph of photography, editing and direction.

Strangers When We Meet ○
1960, US, 117 mins, colour
Dir: Richard Quine
Stars: Kirk Douglas, Kim Novak, Ernie Kovacs, Barbara Rush
Rating: ★★

A searching look at love and life in an upper-class American suburb. Adapted by Evan Hunter from his own bestseller, it finds Kirk Douglas understandably torn between Kim Novak and Barbara Rush while trying to find himself as an architect. Douglas looks pained, Novak expresses pent-up desire quite well, Rush is poignantly pretty and Ernie Kovacs has a few waspishly funny lines though not enough. Walter Matthau, not unexpectedly, steals it from them all with his skilful portrait of a callous neighbour. Charles Lang's lush Technicolor photography expertly complements the characters' high-flying lifestyle.

Stranger Wore a Gun, The ○
1953, US, 83 mins, colour
Dir: André De Toth
Stars: Randolph Scott, Joan Weldon
Rating: ★★

A hard-riding, fast-shooting, grim-faced hombre (Randolph Scott, of course) helps the pretty owner of a stagecoach line to beat off bandits. But not before some well-staged gunfights and a splendid fire. The Academy Award-winning actress Claire Trevor completes a formidable supporting cast, in which the three villains are played by George Macready, Lee Marvin and Ernest Borgnine.

Strangler, The
See: East of Piccadilly

Strapless ● ⓥ
1988, UK, 97 mins, colour
Dir: David Hare
Stars: Blair Brown, Bruno Ganz, Bridget Fonda
Rating: RB

Endless in both senses, David Hare's trying film gives us dialogue that exists only on the printed page for people who surely never were. The central

character is an American nurse working in Britain who finds herself swept off her feet by the persistence of a West German 'businessman' who, it turns out, believes only in the ideal of romantic love, and disappears over the horizon as soon as a woman indicates she'd like to settle down. There's a message in there somewhere about taking responsibility for your feelings, but it gets lost in the welter of Hare's strange, unbelievable script that only exists two paces away from reality. Blair Brown tries hard as the nurse, Bruno Ganz looks puzzled as the eternal lover. Bridget Fonda is hardly in it as the heroine's sloppy sister, but the chances are that you'll lose patience with these shadow people long before the end.

Strategic Air Command ○
1955, US, 114 mins, colour
Dir: Anthony Mann
Stars: James Stewart, June Allyson
Rating: ★★

James Stewart and June Allyson had already had one smash-hit at Universal with *The Glenn Miller Story*. Here the human drama they provide is intermingled with an engrossing study of men in their magnificent flying machines, in this case the B-36 bomber and its postwar development. Scorching colour photography both on the ground and in the wild blue yonder.

Stratton Story, The ○
1949, US, 106 mins, b/w
Dir: Sam Wood
Stars: James Stewart, June Allyson, Agnes Moorehead
Rating: ★★★

This sports biography, well directed by Sam Wood, was strengthened by the fact that it stuck more closely to the facts than was usual for its time. Athletic James Stewart was well cast in the role of baseball pitcher Monty Stratton, as was archetypal dutiful wife June Allyson as the girl Stratton marries. As Stratton's mother, Agnes Moorehead contributes a calm and restrained performance. Even if you know nothing about baseball, the film tells an inspiring human story, with Stratton battling against incredible odds after a tragic accident. The picture won an Oscar for screenplay writer Douglas Morrow.

Streetcar Named Desire, A ①
1951, US, 122 mins, b/w
Dir: Elia Kazan
Stars: Vivien Leigh, Marlon Brando, Kim

Hunter, Karl Malden
Rating: ★★★★

Brilliant ensemble performances won Academy Awards for Vivien Leigh, Kim Hunter and Karl Malden, plus a nomination for Marlon Brando in this explosive film version of Tennessee Williams' uncomfortably powerful play. Leigh is unforgettable as a fading southern belle who is forced to stay with her sister (Kim Hunter) and her heavy-drinking husband (Marlon Brando) in their rattrap New Orleans apartment (really too grand a word for it). Although sordid and gloomy throughout, Elia Kazan's film fascinates rather than alienates the viewer, thanks to the unpredictabihty of the plot, the hypnotic qualities in the acting, and art direction and set decoration (you can almost feel the damp and hear the cockroaches) that were both also rewarded with Oscars. Brando's sweaty, animalistic Stanley Kowalski shot him to superstardom and brought forth a million imitators of his earthy, vaguely slurred delivery. Only reservation: all the characters with the exception of Hunter are just fairly unbelievable.

Street Corner ○
(aka: Both Sides of the Law)
1953, UK, 93 mins, b/w
Dir: Muriel Box
Stars: Peggy Cummins, Terence Morgan, Anne Crawford, Rosamund John,
Rating: ★★

Director Muriel Box offers one excellent chase sequence in this faintly unreal tribute to the work of women police. And there are fine character roles for Thora Hird and Dora Bryan.

Streetfighter, The ○ ⓥ
(aka: Hard Times)
1975, US, 97 mins, colour
Dir: Walter Hill
Stars: Charles Bronson, James Coburn, Jill Ireland, Strother Martin
Rating: ★★★★★

Although the plot of this gritty film follows a well-worn theme, it is carefully and economically made, and distinguished by some of the best colour photography in a very long while. Charles Bronson has the title role, a man who drifts into New Orleans in 1936 with six dollars and the knowledge that he can fight. Not for him the small purses of the boxing ring. He has trained himself hard while still unknown, and seeks a nest-egg from the richest game of all: bareknuckle street-fighting. Philip Lathrop's photography shows masterly composition in catching the dingy darkness of the era and its back streets, keying his scenes perfectly without ever sacrificing clarity or true colours. The warehouses in which the fights are held, in a netted arena where tiers of yelling gallery fans clamour for blood, seem cold and clammy, or bright and oppressive; and one can almost smell the night air at the stockyards in the perfect final scene. Under Walter Hill's firm and assured direction, both Bronson and Jill Ireland give their best performances in ages. Nothing is over-emphasised, and the thud of fist on bone speaks for itself.

Street Fighter ◐ ⓥ

1994, Australia/US, 100 mins, colour
Dir: Steven E de Souza
Stars: Jean-Claude Van Damme, Raul Julia, Ming Na-Wen, Damian Chapa, Kylie Minogue, Simon Callow, Wes Studi
Rating: ★★

A combination of James Bond film, martial arts thriller and Nintendo game. You know the scene: thousands of the villain's men get punched out, shot down and blown to smithereens while the 'Allied Nations', led by Jean-Claude Van Damme with the Stars and Stripes tattooed on his arm muscle just like Popeye, sustain nary a casualty. Maniac warlord Raul Julia (a nice, wild-eyed performance in his last film) has a laboratory and torture chamber that, for those old enough to remember, look like leftovers from an UNCLE film. Never mind, Raul still gives getting a $20 million ransom for a few relief-worker hostages the old college try, makes a monster or two, and gets to give out such lines as 'Take him to the laboratory!' before being despatched to oblivion without even smudging Kylie Minogue's lipstick. As comic book action brought to life, this slugfest does the job.

Streets of Fire ○

1984, US, 94 mins, colour
Dir: Walter Hill
Stars: Michael Paré, Diane Lane, Rick Moranis, Willem Dafoe
Rating: ★★★

A 'rock 'n' roll fable', say the credits, and that's what Walter Hill's film is – its action is there merely to entertain and not convince. And entertain it does, in this kind of spaghetti street film with Diane Lane as the singer kidnapped by bikers, Michael Paré as the ex-lover/ex-soldier called in to get her back, and husky-voiced Amy

Madigan, given a part that enables her to walk off with the film, as another ex-soldier who becomes Paré's strong right arm. Rick Moranis and Willem Dafoe complete a striking cast.

Streets of Gold ◐ ⓥ

1986, US, 95 mins, colour
Dir: Joe Roth
Stars: Klaus Maria Brandauer, Adrian Pasdar, Wesley Snipes
Rating: ★★

The great Klaus Maria Brandauer hasn't quite had the roles he deserves in Hollywood; here he plays a Russian emigré ex-boxer who was denied a chance of world glory in the Soviet Union because he was Jewish. Now, in America, he trains boxers for a Golden Gloves side to fight a Russian team managed by his own ex-manager. There are no surprises in this film, but it will please *Rocky* fans, if not dialogue purists, who will moan about the number of clichéd fines and situations. The boxing sequences are smartly staged, and Brandauer is always worth watching, as he bobs and weaves around the worst the script can throw at him.

Streets of Laredo ○

1949, US, 92 mins, colour
Dir: Leslie Fenton
Stars: William Holden, William Bendix, Macdonald Carey, Mona Freeman
Rating: ★★★

A solid remake of the 1936 version of *The Texas Rangers*, with William Holden, William Bendix and Macdonald Carey this time around as the three bandits who end up on different sides of the law. Carey, handsomely moustachioed, steals every scene he's in as the really bad apple of the three (it's his best screen performance) and Mona Freeman is a most attractive spitfire heroine. The action could have done with a more sparkling script to back it up, but the film's burnishingly shot in Technicolor by Ray Rennahan and a hit theme song did it no harm at the box-office.

Street With No Name, The ◉

1948, US, 100 mins, b/w
Dir: William Keighley
Stars: Mark Stevens, Richard Widmark, Lloyd Nolan, Barbara Lawrence, Ed Begley
Rating: ★★★

Although taciturn Mark Stevens is the nominal star of this hard-hitting crime drama, based on a real case, the film belongs to Richard Widmark who plays the gang leader with a fine collec-

tion of neuroses and hinted perversions. Actual FBI personnel were used in supporting roles.

Strictly Ballroom ○ ⓥ

1992, Australia, 94 mins, colour
Dir: Baz Luhrmann
Stars: Paul Mercurio, Tara Morice, Bill Hunter, Barry Otto, Gia Carides, Pat Thompson
Rating: ★★★

This sweet-natured, lively, colourful, stylised Australian comedy musical about the brittle world of ballroom dancing was a hit around the world, and it's not hard to see why. Innovative young dancer Paul Mercurio dreams of winning the Australian ballroom championship, even after his flighty partner leaves him when he refuses to conform to tradition. Along comes dance school wallflower Tara Morice who persuades him to take her on as a partner and (no, really?) takes off her glasses and transforms an ugly duckling into a swinging swan. Although the often funny comedy-romance that results soon ditches credibility in favour of caricature and coincidence, the film remains winning throughout; low in budget but high in returns, thanks to the talent and enthusiasm of all concerned.

Strictly for Pleasure

See: The Perfect Furlough

Strike Me Pink ○ ⓥ

1936, US, 100 mins, b/w
Dir: Norman Taurog
Stars: Eddie Cantor, Ethel Merman
Rating: ★★

The last of the five comedy-musicals that pop-eyed Eddie Cantor made in the Thirties for Samuel Goldwyn, although he rarely had a co-star as dynamic as Ethel Merman, who's involved in three of the movie's four big song numbers. Not quite in the same class as *Kid Millions* or *Roman Scandals*, the film still has some snappy dialogue (supplied by four writers) and plenty of zest. Making one of her earliest appearances is peppy brunette Rita Rio who led her all-girl band in several shorts and features of the time.

Striking Distance ● ⓥ

1993, US, 101 mins, colour
Dir: Rowdy Herrington
Stars: Bruce Willis, Sarah Jessica Parker, Dennis Farina, Tom Sizemore, Brion James
Rating: ★★

Stripping him of much of his laconically humorous dialogue, this routine thriller hardly showcases Bruce Willis at his best. A 'B' movie in flimsy 'A' feature coating, it has Willis as a cop whose life has gone down the tubes since he denounced his own partner (who jumped off a bridge) and challenged police conclusions over the identity of a serial killer who also murdered Willis's cop father. Now, two years on, Willis works for the river police, and it seems that the serial murders have started again, bumping off women Willis has known. To use the film's own background, none of this holds water for a minute: how on earth could the killer track down so many of Willis's old flames in so short a time? A decent leading lady might help, but Sarah Jessica Parker, admittedly miscast as Willis's river partner, is limp and unconvincing. Rowdy Herrington's direction offers efficient action, but no more. Careless, too: don't look too closely at the first body being dumped in the river, or you might identify the killer.

Stripes ◑ ⓥ
1981, US, 102 mins, colour
Dir: Ivan Reitman
Stars: Bill Murray, Harold Ramis, Warren Oates, John Candy
Rating: ★★

This army comedy from the *Ghost Busters* team has a few modern trimmings and original laughs, but it is otherwise pretty much like every other army comedy from Abbott and Costello and Bob Hope to Goldie Hawn's *Private Benjamin*. The laconic Bill Murray is in his element as the wise guy who joins up just for something to do, riles the sergeant, gets double-duty, finds himself in a misfit platoon, flops all over the obstacle course and wins comic glory in the last reel. Most of the visual jokes are telegraphed in advance, but it really doesn't matter – the film remains mildly amusing throughout, apart from one genuine belly laugh early on involving a football.

Striptease ● ⓥ
1996, US, 127 mins, colour
Dir: Andrew Bergman
Stars: Demi Moore, Armand Assante, Burt Reynolds, Ving Rhames, Robert Patrick
Rating: ★

Demi Moore's much-vaunted unveiling session turns out to be a cross between *film noir* and the Keystone Kops. The film starts to make like a thriller, with two dead bodies and a

whiff of blackmail. But, since its plot isn't worth a plugged nickel, it soon disintegrates into comic capers of the crassest kind. Moore at least gives it a go and keeps her face straight; the rest of the cast just strenuously overacts, especially Burt Reynolds as the girl-chasing senator at the centre of the affair. Finally, though, the movie's downfall is its own refusal to take itself seriously. The decision to play for laughs clashes uncomfortably with Demi's relationship with her small daughter (her own real-life daughter Rumer Willis) and proves never less than irritating.

Stroker Ace ○
1983, US, 91 mins, colour
Dir: Hal Needham
Stars: Burt Reynolds, Ned Beatty
Rating: ★

Never shown in the UK's cinemas, this is one of the more recent offerings from crash-'em-up race-and-chase specialist director Hal Needham who made the *Cannonball Run* and *Smokey and the Bandit* films, Burt Reynolds is again on hand with his laid-back charm, this time as a stock-car driver who at one time turns up in a chicken suit – well in context with the film's cartoon-like structure and standard 'good ol' boy' hijinks.

Stronger than Fear
See: Edge of Doom

Strongest Man In the World, The ⊙
1975, US, 92 mins, colour
Dir: Vincent McEveety
Stars: Kurt Russell, Joe Flynn, Eve Arden
Rating: ★★★

The third film in Disney's college comedy trilogy, and pretty nearly as funny as the first two, *The Computer Wore Tennis Shoes* and *Now You See Him, Now You Don't*. Kurt Russell (though by now 24) is still the accident-prone student Dexter Riley, Joe Flynn is back as the opportunistic Dean Higgins and bizarre mishaps are still occurring in the science labs of Medfield College. This time Dexter accidentally invents a cereal that gives the eater superhuman strength. Phil Silvers is in there too, providing his own brand of humour, but it's Flynn who steals many of the laughs.

Strong Man, The ◑
1926, US, 75 mins, b/w
Dir: Frank Capra

Stars: Harry Langdon, Priscilla Bonner, Gertrude Astor, William V Mong
Rating: ★★★★

Harry Langdon was at his butter-innocent, baby-faced best when directed by the young Frank Capra. Delights of this enchanting comedy include Langdon trying to carry a golddigger up a long flight of stairs and trying to make a reputation as a weightlifter when his strongman friend gets drunk.

Stud, The ● ⓥ
1978, UK, 90 mins, colour
Dir: Quentin Masters
Stars: Joan Collins, Oliver Tobias, Sue Lloyd
Rating: ★

Solidly backed with a pre-sold pop soundtrack, this dislikeable version of Jackie Collins' lurid bestselling novel proved to be just what the public wanted in the late Seventies and revived Joan Collins' star career. The best thing in it, however, is the performance of Doug Fisher as the best friend of Oliver Tobias, playing the title role. The girls are pretty and they and their sex scenes are attractively photographed. The rest, apart from some flashes of native wit, is preposterous, pretentious and very pseudo-sophisticated.

Student Prince, The ⊙
1954, US/UK, 107 mins, colour
Dir: Richard Thorpe
Stars: Ann Blyth, Edmund Purdom, Mario Lanza (voice)
Rating: ★★★

A joyous musical featuring the throbbing tenor of Mario Lanza – but not his acting! Feuding with his studio, MGM, Lanza recorded the songs for this remake of Sigmund Romberg's famous operetta, but there were arguments over the interpretation of the role and he walked out. English actor Edmund Purdom, who played a supporting role in the studio's *Julius Caesar*, was called in to act the title role and mime the songs to Lanza's voice. Purdom's excellent performance made him an MGM star, but his popularity only lasted a few years. Ann Blyth, who had co-starred with Lanza in *The Great Caruso*, is in excellent form (and voice) as the love of the prince's life, and Lanza songs include 'The Drinking Song', 'Deep in My Heart' and 'Serenade', as well has his very popular renditions of two new songs written for the film, 'I'll Walk with God' and 'Beloved'.

S

Study In Terror, A ●
(aka: Fog)
1965, UK, 94 mins, colour
Dir: James Hill
Stars: John Neville, Donald Houston, John Fraser
Rating: ★★★

Sherlock Holmes gets to grips with Jack the Ripper as he was to do 14 years later in *Murder by Decree*. Director James Hill's all-stops-out style ensures that the results here are both thrilling and frightening, with lurid killings, sparkling photography and some nail-biting suspense. The last murder in particular is improbably, but successfully, drawn out to set one's teeth right on edge.

Stunt Man, The ● ⓥ
1979, US, 129 mins, colour
Dir: Richard Rush
Stars: Peter O'Toole, Barbara Hershey, Steve Railsback, Sharon Farrell
Rating: ★★★

Director Richard Rush cut his teeth on low-budget exploitation films and then worked for a reported nine years on this extraordinary project, an outrageous black comedy that brought Oscar nominations both for Rush and for his leading man Peter O'Toole as a dictatorial film director who hires a man on the run as a stuntman on his latest picture. Packed with first-rate action and sly wit, the film demands close attention from its viewer – but proves worth the effort in the end.

Stupids, The ⊙ ⓥ
1995, US, 94 mins, colour
Director: John Landis
Stars: Tom Arnold, Jessica Lundy, Bug Hall, Matt Keeslar, Christopher Lee
Rating: RB

This may well be the most stupid film you ever saw, yet the problem is that it's just too stupid to be funny. This family isn't just stupid: nothing they do makes any sense, even in a cockeyed way. What's lacking here is a clever treatment of the stupid theme, following through some kind of idiotic logic. But there's none of that, merely a very tiresome, uninspired and entirely laughless comedy about a family who sleep upside-down in their clothes and think their garbage is stolen because they left it out at night. Anyone this stupid, in fact, would have been locked away years ago. Pa Stupid (Arnold), who thinks the car won't start because he can't open the glove compartment, believes he's on the trail of a massive conspiracy, which he is,

although it doesn't involve the theft of garbage but that of advance government weapons. Things get no better. An hour and a half stuck in a traffic jam would probably be preferable.

St Valentine's Day Massacre, The ①
1966, US, 100 mins, colour
Dir: Roger Corman
Stars: Jason Robards, George Segal, Ralph Meeker
Rating: ★★

Director Roger Corman's body-strewn look at the feud between gangsters Al Capone and Bugs Moran is as coldly clinical as a gun barrel. The supporting cast is a mine of Brooklyn-type menaces and film fans can have fun picking out such familiar faces as Bruce Dern, Jack Nicholson, John Agar, Ralph Meeker, Joseph Campanella and Richard Bakalyan.

Submarine X-1 ○
1968, US, 89 mins, colour
Dir: William Graham
Stars: James Caan, Norman Bowler
Rating: ★★

A brisk, if routine World War Two action film with American star James Caan heading a cast of British performers under the competent direction of fellow-American William Graham. The underwater climax is well staged and the film always succeeds in holding one's interest.

Substitute, The ● ⓥ
1996, US, 114 mins, colour
Dir: Robert Mandel
Stars: Tom Berenger, Ernie Hudson, Diane Venora, Marc Anthony, Glenn Plummer
Rating: ★

After his teacher girlfriend is beaten up by a school gang, mercenary Berenger takes her place in the classroom to get the inside track on a huge drugs trade that seems to be funnelled through the school. Since he lectures only on Vietnam and how the kids should stick to the straight and narrow, it's obvious he wouldn't last five minutes. However, as this is strictly an action movie, the principal (Hudson), secretly in the drugs ring, has good cause to fire this Dangerous Mind anyway. He has to give him two weeks' notice though, which, as Berenger (who has already sussed him) smiles, 'is all I need'. Too silly to be more than mindlessly entertaining, the film's occasionally good for a giggle, as when heroine Venora tells Berenger to 'Be

straight with me. Guess that's kinda hard,' she adds, 'when your whole life's a covert operation.'

Suburban Commando ○ ⓥ
1991, US, 91 mins, colour
Dir: Burt Kennedy
Stars: Hulk Hogan, Christopher Lloyd, Shelley Duvall, Larry Miller
Rating: ★★★

Wrestler Hulk Hogan takes on a new guise as a space warrior in a science-fiction action comedy that shows his wrestling days to have taught him the full range of facial expressions, especially anguished looks. It's a comment on Hogan's way-out presence and appearance that the wild-haired, wild-eyed Christopher Lloyd is allowed to represent the essence of normality as the head of the suburban family upon whom Hogan descends. Lloyd's character can't quite grasp the concept of alien bounty hunters being out to get the incredible Hulk. 'A couple of leeches,' growls Hogan by way of explanation, 'they make their living off the blood of others.' 'You mean,' gasps Lloyd, 'investment bankers?' It's in keeping with this kind of humour that not many things in this film turn out the way you'd expect, in a comedy that, though by no means great, is more fun than most.

Subway ① ⓥ
1985, France, 104 mins, colour
Dir: Luc Besson
Stars: Christopher Lambert, Isabelle Adjani
Rating: ★★

Modernised French fatalism. In fact, substitute the Quai des Brumes or some top-floor hideout for the subway here and we might almost (apart from the language of course) be back in prewar days. Star Christopher Lambert, looking here more like Jean-Paul Belmondo than Tarzan of the Apes, is the safeblower who escapes via a street-ripping car chase to the subway. Below the underground system he meets a weird mob of subterranean denizens who protect him from police and pursuers while bored rich wife Isabelle Adjani is falling in love with him. But, just as with Jean Gabin and Michelle Morgan in *Quai des Brumes*, you know it can't last. The film's sense of the idiotic sits ill-at-ease with its gutter language, but it's definitely different, and welcome for that alone.

Such Men Are Dangerous
See: The Racers

Sudden Death ● Ⓥ

1995, US, 108 mins, colour
Dir: Peter Hyams
Stars: Jean-Claude Van Damme, Powers Boothe, Raymond J Barry, Whittni Wright, Dorian Harewood, Ross Malinger
Rating: ★★★★

This may be complete rubbish, but it doesn't half go. With Jean-Claude Van Damme at the helm, director Peter Hyams thunders this *Die Hard at the Ice Rink* along to the beat of a pounding background score that, like the action, never lets up. The bad guys, with a little help from US Secret Service renegades, have sewn up the giant ice stadium tighter than the fuse wire that's attached to the bombs set to go off all over the arena. That's their insurance, as, led by suave Powers Boothe, they quickly infiltrate the US vice-president's box and hold his guests hostage, killing one or two to speed government responses to their demands for money. Van Damme comes into the story as an ex-fireman whose small daughter joins the hostages after accidentally witnessing a killing. Naturally, when official forces seem to be getting nowhere, he takes the bad guys on by himself. Hyams' staging of the subsequent action is absolutely tremendous. Credibility's an early casualty, but you'll be too busy clenching your fists with excitement to care.

Sudden Fear ○

1952, US, 111 mins, b/w
Dir: David Miller
Stars: Joan Crawford, Jack Palance
Rating: ★★★★

Engrossing all the way is this story of a woman marrying a man she gradually begins to suspect may be planning to murder her. Spot-on performances by Crawford, Palance and Gloria Grahame. Good control of the mounting suspense by director David Miller. This is one film that's much better than its reputation.

Suddenly It's Spring ○

1946, US, 87 mins, b/w
Dir: Mitchell Leisen
Stars: Fred MacMurray, Paulette Goddard, Macdonald Carey
Rating: ★★

A lightly comic variation on the British film *Perfect Strangers,* in that it deals with the problems faced by husbands and wives separated for months, even years, by war. Realistic characters and some, if not enough, amusing dialogue. Competent performances by leading players Paulette Goddard and Fred MacMurray.

Suddenly Last Summer ● Ⓥ

1959, UK, 114 mins, b/w
Dir: Joseph L Mankiewicz
Stars: Elizabeth Taylor, Katharine Hepburn, Montgomery Clift
Rating: ★★★★

Three Oscar-winning ladies (Elizabeth Taylor, Katharine Hepburn and Mercedes McCambridge) compete for the acting honours in this headily absorbing suspense drama, based on Tennessee Williams' strong play about a girl committed to an institution after witnessing the violent death of her cousin. Hepburn wins the acting battle, while the film is so powerfully written by Gore Vidal and Williams himself that it's almost frightening.

Sudden Terror

See: Eyewitness

Suez ○

1938, US, 104 mins, b/w
Dir: Allan Dwan
Stars: Tyrone Power, Loretta Young, Annabella, Henry Stephenson
Rating: ★★★

How the Suez Canal was built, according to Hollywood. Lavishly mounted, the film's best sequence is a thrilling game of real tennis between Tyrone Power and Joseph Schildkraut. The story is so well structured and full of action that it is a pity it has so little to do with the truth.

Sugarfoot ○

1951, US, 80 mins, colour
Dir: Edwin L Marin
Stars: Randolph Scott, Raymond Massey, Adele Jergens
Rating: ★★

Very much a formula Randolph Scott Western of the period, slightly enhanced by the presence of Raymond Massey as the villain, and by some sparkling Technicolor photography by Wilfrid M Cline. Massey came back for more in a second Scott Western, *Carson City,* the following year. Pretty ordinary.

Sugarland Express, The ◑

1974, US, 110 mins, colour
Dir: Steven Spielberg
Stars: Goldie Hawn, Ben Johnson, Michael Sacks, William Atherton
Rating: ★★

Chase films shouldn't really last as long as this. And given that the me-chanics of the thing are devilishly well achieved, this one really does ramble on a bit. The story is supposed to be true and could probably only happen in America: a young wife (Goldie Hawn) springs her husband from jail because their baby son is being fostered out. They capture a patrolman and are tracked across the length of the state by about 100 police cars. You may find Hawn's performance here rather annoying: it's all show and no heart. But Ben Johnson is excellent as the head of the pursuing cops,. There's a well-wrought screenplay and on-the-ball direction by Steven Spielberg: it's just too darned long though!

Suicide Squadron

See: Dangerous Moonlight

Sullivan's Travels ○

1941, 91 mins, b/w
Dir: Preston Sturges
Stars: Joel McCrea, Veronica Lake
Rating: ★★★★

Brilliant picaresque comedy about a film director tired of making comedies and looking for a meaning in life. Some might see it as a portrait of director Preston Sturges' own state at the time. Whatever the conclusions to be drawn from the plot, the end results are delightfully amusing, with Veronica Lake at her most bewitching as 'The Girl' and Joel McCrea as the director who becomes a tramp in his quest for the truth. Sturges was over time and over budget on this one, but its tricky blend of slapstick and sadness never jars and the studio forgave him when it made a mint.

Summer and Smoke ◑

1961, US, 118 mins, colour
Dir: Peter Glenville
Stars: Laurence Harvey, Geraldine Page, Una Merkel, John Mcintire, Rita Moreno, Thomas Gomez
Rating: ★★★★

One of the least violent of all Tennessee Williams' stories, although, in this story of a spinster and a gambler, some of the dialogue is explosive enough. The British director, Peter Glenville, gets fine performances from Geraldine Page as the spinster and from Una Merkel: both were Academy Award nominees.

Summer Holiday ☉

1962, UK, 105 mins, colour
Dir: Peter Yates
Stars: Cliff Richard, Lauri Peters, The

S

Shadows
Rating: ★★

With the title song proving a massive number one hit for star Cliff Richard, the distributors of this tuneful, if slightly wishy-washy musical could start counting the takings even before it opened. They also had the fortune to have a dynamic young director, Peter Yates, and an inventive choreographer, Herbert Ross, both of whom would go on to become major directors in international cinema. Another plus is the engagingly chirpy personality of the young Una Stubbs.

Summer Madness ○
(aka: Summertime)
1955, UK, 99 mins, colour
Dir: David Lean
Stars: Katharine Hepburn, Rossano Brazzi, Isa Miranda, Darren McGavin
Rating: ★★★★

Memorable, bitter-sweet love affair, directed by David Lean. He coaxes a fine performance from Katharine Hepburn, endearingly vulnerable as the plain, middle-ageing secretary who goes to Venice on holiday and finds herself improbably caught up in an idyllic romance with a (married) antiques dealer. Jack Hildyard's majestic Eastman Colour photography of Venice and its environs adds immeasuringly to the flavour. There's an endearing waif who follows Hepburn everywhere, and her famous tumble into the canal. It's a film that has in abundance what most of Lean's bigger-scale films, however excellent, lack: charm.

Summer of the Seventeenth Doll ◐
(aka: Season of Passion)
1960, Australia, 94 mins, b/w
Dir: Leslie Norman
Stars: John Mills, Ernest Borgnine, Anne Baxter, Angela Lansbury
Rating: ★★★

Super title for the film version of a fine Australian play about the sweet life of two cane cutters turning sour. The script was written by John Dighton, author of the celebrated Ealing comedy *Kind Hearts and Coronets*. Full-blooded performances.

Summer Stock ○
1950, US, 109 mins, colour
Dir: Charles Walters
Stars: Judy Garland, Gene Kelly, Eddie

Bracken, Gloria DeHaven
Rating: ★★★

This farmyard frolic was Judy Garland's last big musical for MGM, and her on-off weight problems can clearly be spotted from scene to scene. But she puts plenty of bounce into a film that reunites her with Gene Kelly from *The Pirate* and gives her a chance to sing two of her best-known numbers, 'If You Feel Like Singing, Sing' and 'Get Happy'.

Summertime
See: Summer Madness

Sun Also Rises, The ○
1957, US, 129 mins, colour
Dir: Henry King
Stars: Tyrone Power, Ava Gardner, Mel Ferrer, Errol Flynn
Rating: ★★

Ernest Hemingway's paean of hope and disillusionment to the lost generation in the wake of World War One may be the most faithful of all his transcriptions to the screen. While the film has many flaws, producer Darryl F Zanuck was determined to follow the novel as closely as possible. Tyrone Power is in the lead as Jake Barnes, a man rendered impotent by a war wound. At 43, many thought Power was too old for the part, but the criticisms seemed somewhat churlish in light of the fact that this proved to be his second-to-last film. He died the following year of a heart attack. This was also Errol Flynn's penultimate picture, but his self-parodying performance is the best thing in the film which also stars Mel Ferrer and Juliette Greco, who was making her American movie debut.

Sunburn ○
1979, US, 94 mins, colour
Dir: Richard C Sarafian
Stars: Farrah Fawcett, Charles Grodin, Art Carney, Joan Collins
Rating: ★★

Identikit movie stitches together dozens of familiar film elements in a blandly exciting story of a $5 million insurance fraud. Farrah Fawcett Majors (who later dropped the Majors and proved herself a capable actress) acts with her teeth, and a mighty supporting cast includes Charles Grodin, Eleanor Parker, Art Carney, Keenan Wynn – and Joan Collins! The action is drenched in sunshine and there's a zingy pop soundtrack.

Sunchaser ● ⓥ
1996, US, 122 mins, colour
Dir: Michael Cimino
Stars: Woody Harrelson, Jon Seda, Anne Bancroft, Talisa Soto, Alexandra Tydings, Harry Carey Jr
Rating: ★★

Although its locations are stunning, this is a long, long journey to go nowhere in particular. Director Cimino has over-inflated a simple story until it balloons past two hours, then pops the balloon by opting for pat solutions to some plot threads and no solutions at all to others. Deflation, both for the audience and the film, is the result. That said, Harrelson and Seda give pretty fair performances as the ambitious, self-seeking doctor and the patient who kidnaps him – a convicted teenage killer suffering from a rare tumour that leaves him only weeks to live. The teenager believes that the powers of a healing lake at the top of an Arizona mountain are the only things that can cure him. Gradually, the doctor himself becomes caught up in the quest. The women – Bancroft, Soto and Tydings – all have silly supporting roles.

Sunday Bloody Sunday ● ⓥ
1971, UK, 110 mins, colour
Dir: John Schlesinger
Stars: Glenda Jackson, Peter Finch, Murray Head, Peggy Ashcroft
Rating: ★★

This film really shows its age now, through no fault of its own. In the AIDS aware 1990s no-one would make this story of a slightly unusual menage à trois, with Glenda Jackson and Peter Finch sharing the same lover, Murray Head. It was critically acclaimed for its low-key approach to its subject. Jackson and Finch were nominated for Oscars, as were director John Schlesinger and screenplay writer Penelope Gilliatt. The three main characters are terribly modern and civilized about the situation which is perhaps the film's biggest downfall as none of them displays any great amount of emotion. With such a strong cast (and Peggy Ashcroft, Tony Britton, Maurice Denham and Frank Windsor give sterling support) and a director of Schlesinger's calibre the result could and should have been better.

Sunday Too Far Away ●
1975, Australia, 94 mins, colour
Dir: Ken Hannam

Stars: Jack Thompson, Phyllis Ophel
Rating: ★★★

This thoroughly enjoyable visit to the hard-drinking, hard-working world of Australian sheep shearers heralded international recognition for the Australian film industry and garnered great critical acclaim. Star Jack Thompson won a Best Actor prize at the Australian Film Awards for his portrayal of a shearer who leads a strike while managing to hold onto his own job. If there are shades of Fred Zimmerman's *The Sundowners*, that's no bad thing and, in fact, the shearing scenes were shot in the same shed!

Sundowners, The ○
1960, Australia, 133 mins, colour
Dir: Fred Zinnemann
Stars: Deborah Kerr, Robert Mitchum
Rating: ★★★★★

Tender story of the travels of a happy-go-lucky Australian sheep farmer, with a wife who desperately wants to settle down. Director Fred Zinnemann captures a whole panorama of Australian outdoor life, and his commonplace tapestry is enriched by a whole series of wonderful character studies from Ronald Fraser, Mervyn Johns, and especially Glynis Johns as a faintly blowzy widow with sights firmly set on Peter Ustinov's rascally Venneker. Robert Mitchum's Australian accent is impeccable and his portrayal one of his finest achievements. It's a film that really makes one feel for the characters it presents.

Sunflower ○
1969, Italy, 101 mins, colour
Di: Vittorio De Sica
Stars: Sophia Loren, Marcello Mastroianni
Rating: ★★

One of the more effective of director Vittorio De Sica's later films, this epic romantic melodrama, described by one contemporary critic as 'gloriously batty' gives Sophia Loren full rein for some unrestrained emotional acting in a story positively soaked in one of Henry Mancini's lushest scores. The Technicolor photography of Giuseppe Rotunno and David Vinitsi is truly ravishing, helping more than anything else to approach realisation of the director's obvious ambition: to make a classic love story.

Sunset ❶ ⓥ
1988, US, 107 mins, colour
Dir: Blake Edwards
Stars: Bruce Willis, James Garner, Mariel

Hemingway, Kathleen Quinlan, Malcolm McDowell
Rating: ★★

Cowboy star Tom Mix meets Western legend Wyatt Earp in Hollywood and they solve a murder together. Very much fiction, very much a concoction: if only they'd set it 15 years earlier than 1929, everything would have been right, not least the ages of the two men as portrayed here by Bruce Willis and James Garner (Earp died in 1928). As it is, not much of it is believable, especially with the casting of a Charlie Chaplin-type comedian (Malcolm McDowell) as the villain. And, although Willis and Garner carry the TV-style plot comfortably enough, what the film needs is dynamism, pace and a sense of period. Not only does the director not supply these in sufficient quantities, but he has to cope with a corny musical score by Henry Mancini that intrudes on the action rather than underlining it. At least Willis and Garner give the venture a sense of grace.

Sunset Boulevard ○ ⓥ
1950, US, 110 mins, b/w
Dir: Billy Wilder
Stars: William Holden, Gloria Swanson, Erich von Stroheim, Nancy Olson
Rating: ★★★★

There's a superbly doom-laden atmosphere about this abrasively distinctive portrait of a reclusive Hollywood star and the writer enmeshed in her web, which clinched a sensational comeback to film for the silent superstar Gloria Swanson and won Oscar nominations for all four stars. William Holden, Nancy Olson and Erich von Stroheim were the three others. Holden and Ms Olson give impressive performances, but cannot help but be overshadowed by the magnetic, powerful portrayal of the faded actress by Ms Swanson.

Sun Valley Serenade ○
1941, US, 86 mins, b/w
Dir: H Bruce Humberstone
Stars: Sonja Henie, John Payne, Glenn Miller, Milton Berle
Rating: ★★★

This toe-tapping musical was one of Glenn Miller's rare acting roles in a short Hollywood career before his ill-fated flight across the English Channel. World champion ice skater Sonja Henie gets to smile more than skate, and her final showstopping number, skated on ice sprayed black, dissolves into a rendition of 'Chattanooga Choo Choo' because she fell during shooting

and Zanuck refused to pay for an extra day's filming. The Glenn Miller Band have too little to do, but the film does include such killer Miller standards as 'In the Mood'. The cinematography and music were nominated for Oscars.

Supergirl ○ ⓥ
1984, US, 124 mins, colour
Dir: Jeannot Szwarc
Stars: Helen Slater, Faye Dunaway, Peter O'Toole, Peter Cook, Mia Farrow
Rating: ★★

The lifeblood, or whatever it is that flows through the veins of super-people, is clearly thinning in this episode from the 'super' series and, although Helen Slater and Faye Dunaway give their all to Supergirl and her sorceress adversary, the plot and situations that surround them are strictly one-dimensional. Slater is actually more fun in her schoolgirl disguise than as Supergirl herself and it would have been nice to see more of the film spun round this side of her life. However, the demands for bigger-and-better decree that she shall combat the forces of evil, the Phantom Zone, the Alien Storm, the Fearful Fireball and all that sort of thing. Ms Dunaway and especially Brenda Vaccaro as her cigarette puffing confidante, plotting nothing less than world domination from a room in a funfair ghost house, make the most of their roles.

Superman ○ ⓥ
1978, US, 143 mins, colour
Dir: Richard Donner
Stars: Christopher Reeve, Margot Kidder, Gene Hackman, Marlon Brando, Trevor Howard, Terence Stamp
Rating: ★★★

After a very impressive first 20 minutes, this develops into predictable comic-strip action. But in those stunning opening scenes, there are enough brilliant special effects to satisfy the most avid science-fiction fan. Christopher Reeve is actually rather good as Superman, getting away nicely with being both bespectacled newspaperman and wrong-righting wonder, without making you ask why no one spotted the similarity.

Superman II ○ ⓥ
1980, US, 127 mins, colour
Dir: Richard Lester
Stars: Christopher Reeve, Gene Hackman, Margot Kidder
Rating: ★★★★

The best and certainly the most refreshing of the three *Superman* films,

S

given a witty approach by director Richard Lester, another clever dual-identity characterisation by Christopher Reeve and slam-band action that boasts both a joyous zing and a wicked sense of humour. The script has a good sprinkling of funny lines: 'When will these dummies learn to use a doorknob?' mutters one character watching the bad guys break down walls to get at hapless Jackie Cooper (once again as the editor-employer of Superman in his Clark Kent guise). Sparkling Technicolor photography lends the top-dressing to a fast-moving (apart from the expendable romantic interludes when Superman – horrors! actually gets to go to bed with Lois Lane) piece of first-class entertainment.

Superman III ○ Ⓥ

1983, US, 123 mins, colour
Dir: Richard Lester
Stars: Christopher Reeve, Richard Pryor, Jackie Cooper, Pamela Stephenson
Rating: ★★★

Superman falls temporarily from grace in this inventive third film in the high-flying series. Poisoned by synthetic Kryptonite containing nicotine tar, he blows out the Olympic torch, straightens up the Tower of Pisa and pollutes the oceans with oil, just for starters. Christopher Reeve gives the whole thing a human element some actors wouldn't manage, and excels in the battle between good and bad Supermen. The start is riotously good, the main plotline rather less so with Richard Pryor not at his best as a crooked computer genius. Special effects are well up to the mark, especially when Superman uses a frozen lake to put out a raging fire.

Superman IV – The Quest for Peace ○ Ⓥ

1987, US, 90 mins, colour
Dir: Sidney J Furie
Stars: Christopher Reeve, Gene Hackman, Margot Kidder, Jackie Cooper
Rating: ★★

This fourth and last outing for Christopher Reeve as the Man of Steel has him ridding the world of nuclear armaments and battling against Nuclear Man, a super-baddie created by Superman's arch-enemy Lex Luthor (Gene Hackman). The special effects look decidedly cut-rate, the direction is flaccid and the script (based on a story by Reeve) is pretty poor, too. Hackman gets most of the best lines and he has to work hard for those. Still, the scene where Superman

disposes of all the world's nuclear weapons by tossing them into the sun and the final battle on the moon with Nuclear Man are both enjoyable. The undemanding will probably enjoy this, but if you really liked *Superman* and *Superman II*, you'll be disappointed with this.

Super Mario Brothers ○ Ⓥ

1993, US, 104 mins, colour
Dir: Rocky Morton, Annabel Jankel
Stars: Bob Hoskins, John Leguizamo, Dennis Hopper, Samantha Mathis, Fisher Stevens, Fiona Shaw, Lance Henriksen
Rating: ★★

Take a few dinosaurs. Add state-of-the-art special effects. Stir in an old-fashioned 'save the world from evil' story in a modern computer-game setting, and you have a recipe for success – at least with kids who love the game and its characters, while their parents sit bewildered in adjoining armchairs. Bob Hoskins and John Leguizamo play a pair of intrepid plumbers who answer a call from a maiden in distress and enter a nether world full of slimy monsters. Dennis Hopper has a field day as the monsters' tyrannical leader in a fantasy-adventure for teens and under that entertains, but could have been so much better. We yield to no one in our admiration for the directors' critically panned version of *DOA*, but they have pretty well blown a promising premise here with this over-charged, OTT ear-blaster.

Support Your Local Gunfighter ○ Ⓥ

1971, US, 92 mins, colour
Dir: Burt Kennedy
Stars: James Garner, Suzanne Pleshette, Jack Elam, Chuck Connors, Joan Blondell, Harry Morgan
Rating: ★★★

A surprisingly successful follow-up to *Support Your Local Sheriff!*, in which James Garner's rogue gambler jumps train at a small gold-mining town of Purgatory and is immediately taken to be the feared gunman Swifty Morgan. Garner's determined to take the town for everything he can get, but naturally the real Swifty turns up towards the end and there's a fast and furious finale. Excellent support from Suzanne Pleshette, as a feisty dame whose aggression belies her intentions of running a ladies' finishing school, from a whole Main Street full of colourful Hollywood characters, and best of all

from scowling Jack Elam as the town drunk who becomes Garner's sidekick. His on-train monologue at the end just grabs the film its third star.

Support Your Local Sheriff! ○ Ⓥ

1968, US, 89 mins, colour
Dir: Burt Kennedy
Stars: James Garner, Joan Hackett, Walter Brennan, Harry Morgan, Bruce Dern, Jack Elam
Rating: ★★★★

Wonderfully funny and likeable spoof Western, with James Garner guying his Maverick image as the tall dark stranger who prefers the use of brains to brawn, and cleans up a lawless town in his own highly individual way. William Bowers' screenplay, besides having more than its fair share of amusing lines, throws up any number of rich characters. There's Joan Hackett as the accident-prone heroine, forever falling on her bustle; Jack Elam as the drunken brawler whom Garner makes deputy sheriff, and Walter Brennan, clearly relishing his comic villain.

Sure Thing, The ◑ Ⓥ

1985, US, 94 mins, colour
Dir: Rob Reiner
Stars: John Cusack, Daphne Zuniga, Boyd Gaines, Anthony Edwards, Tim Robbins, Viveca Lindfors
Rating: ★★★

A sharp comedy from the director of *Misery, When Harry Met Sally* and *Stand by Me*. A pleasant mix of road movie and teen drama, it stars John Cusack as the fast-food junkie youth ready to clear the last hurdle in coming-of-age and Daphne Zuniga as a prim and proper fellow student who thinks that spontaneity is a social disease. Thrown together on a car journey to California, the couple start out as sparring opposites, but gradually come to see that their oil and water mix could be complementary. It's a familiar theme but Reiner casts a refreshing eye at the clichéd goings-on and gives events a nice twist.

Surrender ◑ Ⓥ

1987, US, 110 mins, colour
Dir: Jerry Belson
Stars: Sally Field, Michael Caine, Steve Guttenberg, Peter Boyle
Rating: ★★★

As battle-of-the-sexes comedies go, this is only a little above the average at base, but writer/director Jerry Belson gets such crackerjack performances from Michael Caine, Sally Field, Steve Guttenberg and Peter Boyle that his film is a constant pleasure to be with. Caine plays a successful writer with a weakness for women who systematically take him to the cleaners. Once the despair of his lawyer (Boyle), Caine now has a sign on the gates of his mansion banning women. Then along comes failed painter Sally Field and, tied up to her during a robbery, Caine soon gets that mating urge again. The film is full of chuckles, and a few big laughs too, such as when Caine tells Boyle that he's 'getting rid of all the parasites in my life.' 'You mean,' gasps Boyle, 'that you're firing me?'

Susannah of the Mounties ○
1939, US, 78 mins, b/w
Dir: William A Seiter
Stars: Shirley Temple, Randolph Scott, Margaret Lockwood
Rating: ★★

One of Shirley Temple's last big films. Two years later she finished as a child star, and her mother sent her to a full-time school for two years before she resumed her career (less successfully) as a teenager. One of her co-stars in this spectacular action film about Mounties and Indians was a full-blooded Blackfoot Indian boy called Martin Good Rider.

Susan Slept Here ○
1954, US, 98 mins, colour
Dir: Frank Tashlin
Stars: Dick Powell, Debbie Reynolds
Rating: ★★★

Just about the madcap blend of musical and wacky comedy you'd expect from ex-cartoonist Frank Tashlin, this bright, light-hearted frolic has real perfect performances from a smooth Dick Powell and a sparky Debbie Reynolds, excellent colour and even flashes of genuine wit. Anne Francis is excellent as Powell's cold-hearted fiancée and wisecracking Glenda Farrell superb as the secretary who knows all the answers.

Suspect, The ○
1944, US, 84 mins, b/w
Dir: Robert Siodmak
Stars: Charles Laughton, Ella Raines, Henry Daniell, Rosalind Ivan
Rating: ★★★★

Superbly directed by Robert Siodmak, who made *Phantom Lady*, this is the ab-

sorbing story of a vaguely Crippen-like murder (although Charles Laughton's reluctant killer is really quite a sympathetic character) committed in the gaslit London just after the turn of the century. Siodmak tightens the tension much in the manner of Hitchcock and extracts a string of first-rate performances from his cast. Laughton is memorable as the henpecked worm who finally turns, but he is extremely well supported by Ella Raines as the lonely girl who impels him to strive for a divorce, Stanley Ridges as the dogged inspector determined to nail the killer, Rosalind Ivan (never better) as Laughton's vicious wife and Henry Daniell, supremely smarmy as his drunken, blackmailing, thoroughly unpleasant neighbour. A beautifully made thriller, one of the best from the war years.

Suspect ○
(aka: The Risk)
1960, UK, 81 mins, b/w
Dir: Roy Boulting
Stars: Tony Britton, Peter Cushing, Virginia Maskell
Rating: ★★★

A gripping comedy-thriller that's as full of twists as the Boulting Brothers can make it. Good performances from Tony Britton, Ian Bannen and Virginia Maskell in a story of research chemists tempted to betray their country to get their findings on a plague serum published.

Suspect ● Ⓥ
1987, US, 101 mins, colour
Dir: Peter Yates
Stars: Cher, Dennis Quaid, Liam Neeson, John Mahoney, Joe Mantegna, Philip Bosco
Rating: ★★★★

As this is a nicely made courtroom whodunnit, it would be a kindness not to dwell too deeply on its plot. Suffice to say that, despite a central performance by Cher that's only adequate, and a screenplay that definitely does not bear close inspection, director Peter Yates, helped a great deal by Michael Kamen's tense music score, hooks us on to the action throughout. A supreme court justice hands a package to a female court official. Soon after, both are dead, he a suicide, she murdered. A deaf-and-dumb vagrant (well played by Liam Neeson) is brought to trial on strong circumstantial evidence. Of course, there's more to it, as his floundering defence counsel discovers, especially when helped

out by an inquisitive juror (Dennis Quaid). Just as well, too, for, as written and played, the lady doesn't seem able to prove her way out of a paper bag. Never mind, the continuation of the suspense is the thing. That's where Yates and his lieutenants do a fine job out of making a silk purse out of a sow's ear.

Suspicion ○
1941, US, 99 mins, b/w
Dir: Alfred Hitchcock
Stars: Cary Grant, Joan Fontaine
Rating: ★★★★

This second American film from Alfred Hitchcock has an all-British cast except for Joan Fontaine, who was born in the Far East to British parents, and who won an Oscar for her role here. Cary Grant is the fortune hunting cad who woos a spinster into marriage. She then begins to suspect that he is a murderer who wants to kill her next. The film's denouement isn't worthy of the moody build-up, but that can be blamed on the studio, RKO, who demanded an upbeat ending in the days before Hitchcock had absolute control of his material.

Suture ●
1993, US, 96 mins, b/w
Dir: Scott McGehee, David Siegel
Stars: Dennis Haysbert, Mel Harris, Sab Shimono, Michael Harris, Dina Merrill
Rating: RB

How anyone gets the money these days to make a film as bizarre and crazy as this is quite beyond us. Shot in black and white and CinemaScope, it tells the story of two half-brothers. One, suspected of murdering their father, plants his identity (and car) on the other and blows him up. Only, he survives and is accepted as the 'dead man', no longer suspected of the crime. Sounds okay, doesn't it? But here's the thing: one brother is white, the other black. But no one seems to notice. Ready to quit now? You're the lucky ones: we had to sit through the whole dreamlike, deadly thing. Not likely to suit ya.

Svengali ○
1931, US, 83 mins, b/w
Dir: Archie Mayo
Stars: John Barrymore, Marion Marsh, Bramwell Fletcher
Rating: ★★★

This classic melodrama is dominated by an extraordinary performance from John Barrymore as the mesmerist of the title. The expressionistic sets by Anton Grot add to the film's considerable atmosphere, and the photography by Barney McGill, especially a tight shot that begins on Barrymore's face, then tracks across the roofs of Paris to end on a close-up of his hypnotised victim, is a tour-de-force.

Svengali ○
1954, UK, 82 mins, colour
Dir: Noel Langley
Stars: Donald Wolfit, Hildegarde Neff, Terence Morgan, Derek Bond
Rating: ★★

A lavish, if rather bizarrely coloured version of George du Maurier's hoary old yarn about the singer and the hypnotist in old-time Paris. It seemed somewhat unwise of the producers to hire a German actress (Hildegarde Neff) who has to attempt an Irish accent – it's a brave try, even so – but the film is dominated by Donald Wolfit's Svengali, at once horrifying and pathetic. The production is handsomely and authentically dressed, but the script fails to give the yarn the lift it needs, and it's left to Wolfit to provide the film's strength single-handed.

Svengali ○
1983, US, 93 mins, colour
Dir: Anthony Harvey
Stars: Peter O'Toole, Jodie Foster
Rating: ★★

John Barrymore and David Wolfit, *outré* performers both, have each had their wicked way with George du Maurier's famous creation, the mad artist-teacher who completely dominates his youthful pupil. Now the story is updated, none too convincingly, to allow Peter O'Toole's haughty imperiousness full range as a voice teacher training a young rock singer (Jodie Foster retaining her puppy fat in the Trilby role). Clearly relishing the script's ample opportunities for overplaying, O'Toole gleefully describes Ms Foster's voice as being 'like raw meat'. He hasn't been as enjoyably excessive as this since his marvellous portrayal of the dictatorial film director in *The Stunt Man* four years before.

S.W.A.L.K.
See: Melody

Swallows and Amazons ⊙
1974, UK, 92 mins, colour
Dir: Claude Whatham
Stars: Virginia McKenna, Ronald Fraser
Rating: ★★★

The Lake District looks lovely in this delightful, traditional children's adventure tale adapted from Arthur Ransome's novel and involving boats, an island, a cross uncle and a burglary. There's rather a lot of obvious scene-setting, but the island sequences are great fun and the film is attractively acted by all the children involved. There are also personable performances from Virginia McKenna, Ronald Fraser and Brenda Bruce as the adults.

Swamp Thing ① ⓥ
1982, US, 90 mins, colour
Dir: Wes Craven
Stars: Louis Jourdan, Adrienne Barbeau, Ray Wise
Rating: ★★

Is it a man? Is it a compost heap? No, it's Swamp Thing! This pretty well sums up director Wes *(Nightmare on Elm Street)* Craven's monster movie parody of Fifties creature 'B' films. At least this green giant is jollier than the Incredible Hulk, and the script has a sense of humour too, even if it's more knowing than its counterparts from the Fifties.

Swanee River ○
1939, US, 84 mins, colour
Dir: Sidney Lanfield
Stars: Don Ameche, Andrea Leeds, Al Jolson
Rating: ★★★

Lavish biography of the famous American composer Stephen Foster, resplendent in early Technicolor and bursting with drama, sentiment and such famous ditties as 'Oh! Susanna', 'Jeannie with the Light Brown Hair', 'Camptown Paces' and 'The Old Folks at Home'. Director Sidney Lanfield keeps a firm hold on the thread of the story (and even on the histrionics of Al Jolson, playing the famous minstrel man E P Christy). The photographer who brings such warmth and atmosphere to the Deep South setting is Bert Glennon, a distinguished cameraman who started in the early silent days.

Swashbuckler
See: The Scarlet Buccaneer

Sweeney! ①
1976, UK, 89 mins, colour
Dir: David Wickes
Stars: John Thaw, Dennis Waterman, Barry Foster
Rating: ★★

The first spin-off film from the TV series that brought a whole new

toughness to the police genre. It established a gritty and amusing camaraderie between its two major characters (played by John Thaw and Dennis Waterman) which, coupled with a *Z Cars* pattern of small scenes, made it among the most fluid and hard-hitting thrillers seen on television. The action still packs a punch here, even though it serves up a B-feature plot about oil sheiks and blackmail in high places. Michael Coles, as the leader of an unlikely squad of assassins, is the best of the supporting cast.

Sweeney 2 ①
1978, UK, 108 mins, colour
Dir: Tom Clegg
Stars: John Thaw, Dennis Waterman
Rating: ★★

Action, tough, rugged and plentiful, is the order of the day in this second film to stem from the famous TV crime series. The story – Regan and Carter pursuing the perpetrators of a long and clever series of armed bank robberies from London to Malta – works very well apart from one episode involving a bomb scare which is not only poorly done but superfluous. John Thaw and Dennis Waterman make their farewell appearances as Regan and Carter, roles that fitted them like gloves.

Sweet Charity ○
1969, US, 149 mins, colour
Dir: Bob Fosse
Stars: Shirley MacLaine, Sammy Davis Jr, Ricardo Montalban
Rating: ★★★★

Shirley MacLaine is the tart with the heart of gold who falls in love with a naive young man who doesn't know about her 'profession' in this lively adaptation of the successful stage musical. Directed by choreographer Bob Fosse, there are some great routines and some memorable songs – 'Big Spender', 'If My Friends Could See Me Now'and 'The Rhythm of Life'. Peter Stone wrote the script, based on Neil Simon's play, which itself is an adaptation of Fellini's film *Notte di Cabiria*. If the third-hand story doesn't quite hold up in places, it really doesn't matter, Ms MacLaine's exuberance and a fine supporting cast – Sammy Davis Jr, Stubby Kaye, dancers Chita Rivera and Paula Kelly – keep things moving along in style.

Sweethearts ○
1938, US, 114 mins, colour
Dir: W S Van Dyke II
Stars: Jeanette MacDonald, Nelson

Eddy, Frank Morgan, Ray Bolger
Rating: ★★★

One of the longest of the Jeanette
MacDonald-Nelson Eddy musicals,
which is good news for their fans –
and in Technicolor, too. The Victor
Herbert melodies are really the whole
show, especially the lilting title number. The script is certainly above
average for a MacDonald-Eddy musical, and the songs also include
'Wooden Shoes', 'Every Lover Must
Meet His Fate' and 'Little Gray Home
in the West'.

Sweet Liberty ◑
1986, US, 107 mins, colour
Dir: Alan Alda
Stars: Alan Alda, Michael Caine, Michelle
Pfeiffer, Bob Hoskins
Rating: ★★★

Alan Alda wrote, directed and stars in
this swipe at films and film-making.
He's the writer of a serious book about
the American Revolution, which is to
be filmed. Screenwriter Bob Hoskins
wants to liven it up; and temperamental stars Michael Caine and Michelle
Pfeiffer cause their own problems.
The plot meanders a bit but the stars
hold the film together and it remains a
witty tale with some genuinely funny
moments.

Sweet November ○
1968, US, 114 mins, colour
Dir: Robert Ellis Miller
Stars: Sandy Dennis, Anthony Newley
Rating: ★★

Sandy Dennis is one of those mannered but unusual actresses whom one
either finds hard to take or likes very
much. She has a good part here as a
Brooklyn girl with advanced ideas, in a
bitter-sweet romance. There are some
witty lines in Herman Raucher's script,
mostly for Anthony Newley – who also
sings the title song – as a prosperous
young tycoon who moves in with Ms
Dennis, the girl who takes on a different lover each month. Like all Miller's
films, the crisp black edges conceal a
soft centre, but it would be unfair to
the storyline to reveal just what.

Sweet Rosie O'Grady ○
1943, US, 74 mins, colour
Dir: Irving Cummings
Stars: Betty Grable, Robert Young,
Adolphe Menjou
Rating: ★★

Described by the New York *Times* as
'pretty as a bowl of wax fruit... in luscious Technicolor... with Betty Grable

in some low-necked ensembles that resemble an Italian wedding cake', this
musical, although rather on the short
side for such a classy item, was just the
ticket for wartime audiences gasping
for escapism. Ms Grable is the songbird who moves from high-kicks in a
Brooklyn beer garden to high society
in London. Nice period feel, as always
in these Fox 'Gay Nineties' type musical marshmallows.

Sweet Smell of Success ○
1957, US, 96 mins, b/w
Dir: Alexander Mackendrick
Stars: Burt Lancaster, Tony Curtis
Rating: ★★★★

A fine American film, directed by
Britain's Alexander Mackendrick, who
learned his trade in Ealing comedies.
Burt Lancaster, wearing a pair of
owlish spectacles for his role, is frighteningly sinister as the newspaperman
who glories in the cringing servility of
those who seek his favours; and Tony
Curtis gives a magnificent performance
as the crawling press agent, Sidney
Falco, who would – and does – sell his
soul for a paragraph in Lancaster's column. Susan Harrison plays
Lancaster's sister, in a permanent state
of white-faced fear, and Marty Milner
is her upright, incorruptible boyfriend.
Clifford Odets and Ernest Lehman
dipped their pens in acid to write the
screenplay; the black (and blacker)
photography is superb and the whole
package is backed up by the haunting
jazz of Chico Hamilton.

Sweet William ●
1979, UK, 90 mins, colour
Dir: Claude Whatham
Stars: Sam Waterston, Jenny Agutter,
Anna Massey
Rating: ★★

A loveable rogue who loves them and
leaves them, 'Sweet' William speeds
around on his bike from conquest to
conquest without his live-in girlfriend
Ann knowing much about it – until its
too late and she's pregnant. It's basically a sex comedy-drama of the old
school, but handled with delicacy and
sensitivity by director Claude
Whatham. The best sequence is an
episode involving Ann's visit to her father (superb Arthur Lowe) and awful
mother by the seaside, which says
more in a few glances than the rest of
the script in its entirety. Sam
Waterston is quite nicely cast as the
freewheeling William and Jenny
Agutter pretty good as the bedded,
bothered and bewildered Ann.

Swimmer, The ○
1968, US, 94 mins, colour
Dir: Frank Perry
Stars: Burt Lancaster, Janet Landgard,
Janice Rule
Rating: ★★

Fascinating evocation of schizophrenia,
with Burt Lancaster offering a thoughtful performance as the man who
attempts a swim across the county via
his friends' pools, encountering increasing hostility on the way.
Location filming in Connecticut perfectly recaptures the mood of the
interesting John Cheever short story
on which the film is based. Watch for
chat show hostess Joan Rivers in a
minor role.

Swimming With Sharks ● ⓥ
1994, US, 90 mins, colour
Dir: George Huang
Stars: Kevin Spacey, Frank Whaley,
Michelle Forbes, Benicio Del Toro
Rating: ★★

A very intense look at the bootlicking
Hollywood requires to stay alive.
Frank Whaley is Guy, a tenderfoot
film school graduate who has somehow landed a job as assistant to the
vice-president of a big Hollywood studio. The mogul, Buddy (Kevin
Spacey), proves to be a total tyrant of
whose shouted insults Guy finds himself the constant butt – but who can
switch to a wheedling charm at the
mere swish of a starlet's skirt. While
Guy must duck even for putting the
wrong sweetener in Buddy's coffee, his
sanity is temporarily saved by his affair with Dawn (Michelle Forbes), a
fledgling producer who has slept her
way to the top, and whose film Guy
gets Buddy to make. When Buddy decides he wants Dawn (an ex-flame,
natch) back, the worm finally turns.
The film, though often very entertaining and bitingly witty, does wear out
its welcome after an hour or so, and
there's a twist ending we didn't begin
to understand. Even so, Spacey is a
delight as the movie-maker who taunts
his staff even as he toys with the opposition.

Swing Kids ◑ ⓥ
1993, US, 112 mins, colour
Dir: Thomas Carter
Stars: Robert Sean Leonard, Christian
Bale, Frank Whaley, Barbara Hershey,
Kenneth Branagh
Rating: ★★★

Quite well done but awfully familiar,
and we're once again with the rise of
Nazism in Germany in the Thirties.

S

Based on real events, it's the spirited story of a group of rebellious German teenagers. By embracing the American swing music and dancing, forbidden by their Führer, the Swing Kids openly demonstrate their dedication to freedom of expression. But before long the propaganda machines of the Hitler Youth are in motion and some of the youngsters prove to be more dedicated to their ideals than others. It starts stickily, but builds in character and atmosphere as it goes along. A moving eye-opener in some ways, it will certainly make you cheer for the Swing Kids as they spit dangerously in the eye of authority. Okay performances really needed to be, special though, to lift this film to excellence.

Swing Shift ❶ Ⓥ

1984, US, 100 mins, colour
Dir: Jonathan Demme
Stars: Goldie Hawn, Kurt Russell, Christine Lahti, Fred Ward
Rating: ★★

Surprisingly anti-feminist for a Goldie Hawn film, and much-troubled in the making (three reels were apparently reshot at the star's insistence), this wartime drama is much better than you might expect from all its production problems. There are sterling performances from a very strong cast, but what really gives the film its credibility is the work of its production designer, costume designer and photographer. Together they create an evocative period (the early 1940s) that brims with patriotism and feeling for a lifestyle and values worth defending. It's just a pity that the actual characters and their actions are not more likeable.

Swing Shift Maisie ◯

1943, US, 87 mins, b/w
Dir: Norman Z McLeod
Stars: Ann Sothern, James Craig, Jean Rogers
Rating: ★★

An experienced comedy director, Norman Z McLeod, adds some brighter moments than usual to this *Maisie* romp, in which, it being wartime, our girl takes a job at the local defence factory, and works the anti-social hours of the swing shift. That would have meant little to British audiences, so the title was changed to *The Girl In Overalls*, hardly more of an invitation to view. In the supporting cast, there's a good role for little, huffly-snuffly character player John Qualen, as the owner of a troupe of

performing dogs who looks a bit like one of his own charges.

Swing Time ◯ Ⓥ

1936, US, 103 mins, b/w
Dir: George Stevens
Stars: Fred Astaire, Ginger Rogers
Rating: ★★★★

The sixth pairing of Fred Astaire and Ginger Rogers. He blacks up for 'Bojangles of Harlem' in tribute to Bill Robinson and she croons 'Pick Yourself Up'. There are only six songs and the first isn't heard for almost 30 minutes (a big mistake) but 'The Way You Look Tonight' won the Oscar. A smart, hip movie that recreates the nightclub era of the 'Roaring Twenties' with superb sets.

Swiss Family Robinson ⊙

1959, US, 128 mins, colour
Dir: Ken Annakin
Stars: John Mills, Dorothy McGuire, James MacArthur, Janet Munro
Rating: ★★★

This roistering Disney version of the Johann Wyss novel, filmed on location in Tobago, is all action and colour. John Mills enthusiastically leads the Robinsons in their adventures on a desert island, where they battle giant snakes and dispatch a gang of cutthroats in splendidly entertaining style.

Swiss Miss ⊙

1938, US, 73 mins, b/w
Dir: Hal Roach
Stars: Stan Laurel, Oliver Hardy, Della Lind, Walter Woolf King
Rating: ★★★

A Laurel and Hardy 'comic opera' which is particularly notable for two famous sequences. One of these is Stan's hilarious attempts to rob a Saint Bernard dog of the barrel of brandy round its neck. The other is a scene in which the boys try to move a piano across a suspension bridge high above the ground, encountering a gorilla halfway across. The gorilla makes another appearance in the riotously funny climax.

Switch ❶ Ⓥ

1991, US, 114 mins, colour
Dir: Blake Edwards
Stars: Ellen Barkin, Jimmy Smits, Lorraine Bracco, JoBeth Williams, Perry King, Tony Roberts
Rating: ★

Shades of *Goodbye Charlie!* In this case, it's goodbye Steve, as a sleazy sexist of that name is murdered by a trio of

angry lovers. His womanising life, however, ensures that Heaven's gates remain firmly closed. He's sent back to earth to mend his wicked ways, but there's a twist: Steve now has the body of a beautiful blonde female (Ellen Barkin). Much of the humour is deadeningly heavy-handed, in typical latter-day Blake Edwards style, with the only real entertainment provided by Barkin's slinky sexiness – voted 'Sexiest Man Alive' by *U. S. Magazine*. Not for the first time she's the only good thing in a film, which doesn't say a lot for her choice of scripts.

Switching Channels ◯ Ⓥ

1987, US, 97 mins, colour
Dir: Ted Kotcheff
Stars: Kathleen Turner, Burt Reynolds, Christopher Reeve, Ned Beatty
Rating: ★

Look out, here comes *The Front Page* again. One of the cinema's most-filmed plots switches its leading reporter role from male to female, and its setting from a newspaper to a TV newsroom. But no amount of switching can crank the hoary old vehicle into life, especially with a script that almost totally lacks wit and sparkle. Kathleen Turner, Burt Reynolds and Christopher Reeve play over-brightly; Ted Kotcheff's direction is faceless if occasionally frenzied.

Sword and the Rose, The ⊙

1953, UK, 93 mins, colour
Dir: Ken Annakin
Stars: Glynis Johns, Richard Todd
Rating: ★★★

Colourful, fast-moving, if thoroughly inaccurate slice of Disney history with Glynis Johns a first-rate spitfire Mary Tudor and James Robertson Justice a witty, athletic Henry VIII. Polished sword-and-cloak stuff, it has the expert touch.

Sword and the Sorcerer, The ❶ Ⓥ

1982, US, 100 mins, colour
Dir: Albert Pyun
Stars: Lee Horsley, Kathleen Beller, Simon MacCorkindale, Richard Lynch
Rating: ★★★

Lee Horsley is the prince out to reclaim his rightful position and Kathleen Beller the spitfire princess who has rather rashly promised him a night of love for rescuing her brother. 'Buccaneer! Slave! Rogue! General!' raves the script about its hero. Unfortunately, Horsley's rather negative personality allows us to believe little of this buildup and the film is entirely stolen by its villains – gimlet-eyed Richard Lynch, impassive George Maharis (dead sneaky) and Richard Moll as the sorcerer, a gentleman who seems to have trouble preventing his face from liquefying. Kathleen Beller is allowed to do little more than heave a heroic bosom which is rather a pity, as we know from other films that she can act as well. Special effects are often shimmeringly good, and nowhere more so than the opening scene when a creature rises from the dead and plucks out a witch's heart; definitely not for the squeamish. This, like most of the action, is photographed through a permanent brown haze which, we think, is intended to give a medieval feel.

Sword In the Stone, The ⊙
1963, US, 80 mins, colour
Dir: Wolfgang Reitherman
Voice stars: Rickie Sorenson, Sebastian Cabot
Rating: ★★★★

Much underrated on first release, this delightful Disney feature was described as 'whiz-bang wizard of whimsy!'. It's about the young days of King Arthur, although the story is just an excuse for a series of extraordinarily ingenious situations. Children will delight in a whole range of inventive characters: Archimedes, the wizard's owl; a ferociously funny pike which chases 'Wart' when Merlin changes him into a fish; and the self-described 'marvellous, mad, mad, mad Madame Mim', a Gingold-like witch with pink hair. Our personal favourite is a beautifully drawn scraggy wolf who lurks around in the forest for the titbit that always seems to just evade his rat-trap jaws. Despite the somewhat ineffectual songs by the Sherman brothers, it's a dazzling show, with one scene that really stands out – the marvellous wizards' duel between Merlin and the evil Madame Mim, who transform themselves into a variety of animals as they seek to gain the upper hand.

Sword of Monte Cristo, The ⊙
1951, US, 80 mins, colour
Dir: Maurice Geraghty
Stars: George Montgomery, Paula Corday, Betty Kroeger, William Conrad
Rating: ★★

Set in early 19th-century France, this is a swashbuckler with a slight difference. The masked avenger and righter of

wrongs who is by day a member of Napoleon III's court is a woman. It is she who has the valuable sword which once belonged to the Count of Monte Cristo and holds the key to his hidden fortune. Despite this variation, this is a formula adventure with stereotyped characters, which hardly does justice to Alexandre Dumas' novel. Still, it rattles along at a fair pace and Paula Corday is an attractive heroine, although George Montgomery is a rather stiff hero. Lurid colour photography helps to take your mind off the plot deficiencies.

Sword of Sherwood Forest
○ ⓥ
1961, UK, 80 mins, colour
Dir: Terence Fisher
Stars: Richard Greene, Peter Cushing
Rating: ★★

This was the film that sprang from the long-running television series, with Richard Greene following in the footsteps of such famous Hoods as Douglas Fairbanks Sr, Errol Flynn and Richard Todd. Faces to watch out for include that of Oliver Reed (fresh from playing a werewolf for the same studio, Hammer) as a vicious villain called Melton, who takes part in a smashing sword battle in the last reel.

Swordsman, The ○
1947, US, 81 mins, colour
Dir: Joseph H Lewis
Stars: Larry Parks, Ellen Drew, George Macready
Rating: ★★★★

First-rate action film about a blood feud in the Scottish highlands, that owes a lot to the spirit of the Western. Rarely, too, was CineColor ever better used, and there are superb chase sequences through forests and across streams. Director Joseph H Lewis has, in fact, done a fine job, which has been compared by some writers to the style of the best of the Japanese action films. Larry Parks and George Macready are as personable as you could wish as hero and villain.

Sylvia ◑
1964, US, 115 mins, b/w
Dir: Gordon Douglas
Stars: Carroll Baker, George Maharis, Edmond O'Brien
Rating: ★★★

A suspicious millionaire can't resist asking Maharis' private eye to investigate the background of his seemingly perfect fiancée. Sylvia – prize rosegrower, poetess and bookworm –

is revealed through a series of jigsaw flashbacks to have had a tough time in her younger days, turned on to prostitution by a brutal rape. Sydney Boehm's screenplay shades in the scarlet past without too much purple prose. Though melodrama is really rampant, Boehm steers a careful course on the right side of bathos. Even when Sylvia goes joylessly back on the game to pay for her best friend's hospital bills, credibility is maintained. Much is owed to Carroll Baker's spirited rendering of the title role, emerging finally from the years of Harlow-like promotion. There is uncommonly strong support from Joanne Dru as Sylvia's best friend; Viveca Lindfors, as a guardian angel librarian; and Nancy Kovack as a tall, myopic showgirl.

S

T

Table for Five O
1983, US, 122 mins, colour
Dir: Robert Lieberman
Stars: Jon Voight, Richard Crenna
Rating: ★★★

The Royal Performance Film of its year, this is a calculated (and calculating) tear-jerker that ultimately does its job with clinical efficiency. Jon Voight has a lot of speeches to make as the absentee father and lifelong failure whose decision to take the children he deserted on a once-in-a-lifetime cruise to Egypt has far-reaching consequences. This rose-coloured look at the 'Ideal' solution to his problems obviously expects us to swallow the glutinous dose in one gulp.

Take a Girl Like You ◐
1970, UK, 101 mins, colour
Dir: Jonathan Miller
Stars: Hayley Mills, Oliver Reed
Rating: ★★

Ms Mills again cast as a virgin-on the-verge in a sex comedy directed by Jonathan Miller. Oliver Reed does very well in an unusual (for him) light comedy role. He imagines he's irresistible to women (and isn't too far out). George Melly wrote the screenplay from the novel by Kingsley Amis, and in a supporting part you'll spot Penelope Keith, who later proved her worth in star roles.

Take Her, She's Mine O
1963, US, 98 mins, colour
Dir: Henry Koster
Stars: James Stewart, Sandra Dee, Audrey Meadows, Robert Morley
Rating: ★★

This generation-gap comedy is cheerfully recommended to all fans of James Stewart. Whether fuming over the courting of his blossoming daughters, or accidentally getting arrested at a students' sit-in, Stewart's deceptively funny performance gives the shenanigans a lift they barely deserve. Stewart himself deserves much better, and would mercifully receive it with *Shenandoah*. In the featured cast, Charla Docherty's fresh approach outshines the limited talent of Sandra Dee as her sister.

Take It Easy
See: American Anthem

Take Me High O
(aka: Hot Property)
1973, UK, 90 mins, colour
Dir: David Askey
Stars: Cliff Richard, Debbie Watling, George Cole, Anthony Andrews
Rating: ★

Cliff Richard makes an unlikely merchant banker in this breezy romantic comedy, his last screen musical to date. Hugh Griffith provides some welcome light relief as a rumbustious eccentric and the remarkable cast also includes the delicious Debbie Watling and Madeline Smith, George Cole, Richard Wattis and a very young Anthony Andrews as Richard's chief competitor.

Take Me Out to the Ball Game O Ⓥ
(aka: Everybody's Cheering)
1948, US, 93 mins, colour
Dir: Busby Berkeley
Stars: Gene Kelly, Frank Sinatra, Esther Williams, Betty Garrett
Rating: ★★★★

This Busby Berkeley musical is a period baseball romp that finds Sinatra and Kelly in dynamic form and even Esther Williams (as the team manager) much livelier than usual. There's a tremendous fun finale, while two novelty songs, 'O'Brien to Ryan to Goldberg'. and 'The Hat My Father Wore on St Patrick's Day', provide the musical highspots.

Take One False Step O
1949, US, 94 mins, b/w
Dir: Chester Erskine
Stars: William Powell, Shelley Winters, Marsha Hunt
Rating: ★★★

Although writer-producer-director Chester Erskine specialised in tightly-knit thrillers like this one, his biggest hit (two years earlier) was, oddly, a comedy, *The Egg and I*. William Powell excels here as a college professor unwittingly involved in murder, while a strong supporting cast includes Marsha Hunt, James Gleason, Dorothy Hart and Sheldon Leonard.

Take the Money and Run O Ⓥ
1969, US, 90 mins, colour
Dir: Woody Allen
Stars: Woody Allen, Janet Margolin
Rating: ★★★★

Woody Allen's first film as his own director is a hotchpotch comedy about a bungling criminal who spends more time behind bars than on the outside. But forget the uneven storyline and

enjoy it for what it is: a non-stop cavalcade of sight gags and inspired oneliners. Especially good is the sequence where Woody tries to break out of jail with a gun made of soap.

Take the Stage
See: Curtain Call at Cactus Creek

Taking Care of Business
See: Filofax

Taking of Pelham One Two Three, The ●
1974, US, 104 mins, colour
Dir: Joseph Sargent
Stars: Walter Matthau, Robert Shaw, Martin Balsam
Rating: ★★★

A fast and stylish, if slightly mechanical thriller about a gang that hijacks a subway car and its passengers with a juicy million dollar ransom in mind. Walter Matthau is invaluable as the railway security chief, and Peter Stone's snappy screenplay hardly needs to resort to the tough language it sometimes uses. Best of the rest: Tony Roberts as a straight-talking deputy mayor determined to pay the money and get things over.

Taking the Heat ◐ Ⓥ
1993, US, 91 mins, colour
Dir: Tom Mankiewicz
Stars: Tony Goldwyn, Lynn Whitfield, Alan Arkin, George Segal, Will Patton, Peter Boyle
Rating: ★

This one must have dropped on a few stars' doorsteps before they finally found any takers. Tony Goldwyn and Lynn Whitfield ended up playing the lead roles in an action comedy where only the action scenes show any sign of working at all. It's the kind of thing that was considered high fashion in the Seventies, where the hero (a material witness) and heroine (a feisty cop) go by truck, taxi, speedboat and car, running, swimming and riding their way to a vital court hearing in between dodging the villain's sextet of hit-men (well, you would need six assassins to bump off one man, wouldn't you?). The dated antics are padded out to feature length with deejays on the soundtrack and panoramic views of New York City.

Tale of Two Cities, A O
1935, US, 128 mins, b/w
Dir: Jack Conway
Stars: Ronald Colman, Elizabeth Allan
Rating: ★★★★

The definitive version of Charles Dickens' classic story. Made by David O Selznick in 1935, the film superbly captures the period atmosphere and is splendidly held together by Colman's dominating performance as Sydney Carton. The Revolutionary sequences were 'arranged' – and seldom have crowd scenes been better staged – by Val Lewton and Jacques Tourneur. Six years later, they became producer and director on one of the very best sequences of horror films in film history, including *Cat People* and *I Walked with a Zombie*.

Tale of Two Cities, A ○ Ⓥ
1958, UK, 117 mins, b/w
Dir: Ralph Thomas
Stars: Dirk Bogarde, Dorothy Tutin, Cecil Parker, Athene Seyler
Rating: ★★★

Steady, interesting British version of Dickens' novel. There are no crowd scenes to compare with the Hollywood 1935 film, but the story is forthrightly acted and simply told. Dirk Bogarde gives one of the best performances of his career as Sidney Carton, and there's a beautiful, gentle performance by Marie Versini, who unfortunately only appears towards the end of the film. Christopher Lee also makes a vivid impression as the evil Marquis St Evremonde. Character roles are ably filled by such reliable British stalwarts as Athene Seyler, Donald Pleasence and Leo McKern.

Tales from the Crypt ●
1972, UK, 92 mins, colour
Dir: Freddie Francis
Stars: Ralph Richardson, Joan Collins, Ian Hendry, Peter Cushing
Rating: ★★

Another of the Amicus Films horror compilations, taking in five tales of terror for the price of one. As usual, it roves to be a mixture of good and bad, with the best episode – nerve-janglingly directed by Freddie Francis – rightly reserved until last.

Tales from the Crypt: Demon Knight ● Ⓥ
1995, US, 93 mins, colour
Dir: Ernest Dickerson
Stars: Billy Zane, Jada Pinkett, William Sadler, Brenda Bakke, Dick Miller
Rating: ★★

Quite a jolly little horror film for gore fans, as 'Collector' Billy Zane and his gang of slimy demons try to pick up the last of the seven galactic keys that will enable them to take control of the

universe. Unfortunately, the blood it contains can seal entrances off from them, and it is currently in the possession of William Sadler who, after decades of fleeing from the demons, is about to hand the burden on to another. The rest of the action soon settles into a predictable siege format, with heroine Jada Pinkett's costumes shrinking progressively along with the characters and their chances of survival – Zane is a persuasive devil who can take over their souls. Lots of gore, decapitation, slime and big-breasted nudity for those who like relish as well as ketchup with their meals.

Tales of Beatrix Potter ⊙
1971, UK, 90 mins, colour
Dir: Reginald Mills
Rating: ★★★

Brilliantly costumed ballet film based on such Beatrix Potter characters as Mrs Tiggy-Winkle, Peter Rabbit and Jeremy Fisher. Fine dancing, imaginative choreography (recognisably by Sir Frederic Ashton) and some super animal masks. Fun for all the family, even if you dislike ballet: endearing and entertaining, this is one of the most successful films of its kind ever made.

Talk of a Million ○
1951, UK, 78 mins, b/w
Dir: John Paddy Carstairs
Stars: Jack Warner, Barbara Mullen
Rating: ★★

A typical British comedy film from the late Forties/early Fifties period, a time which produced such gems as *Whisky Galore!, A Run for Your Money* and *Another Shore,* all finding fun from England's neighbours in the United Kingdom. This time it's the Emerald Isle, with Jack Warner improbably cast as a carefree hobo who will do anything to avoid work. Besides Milo O'Shea as a signwriter, other familiar faces in the supporting cast belong to Alfie Bass, as a townsman, and Sidney James as an American lawyer. Both were to appear together three years later in another vintage comedy – *The Lavender Hill Mob*.

Talk of the Town, The ○ Ⓥ
1942, US, 118 mins, b/w
Dir: George Stevens
Stars: Cary Grant, Jean Arthur, Ronald Colman
Rating: ★★★

It's unusual to find two stars of the magnitude of Cary Grant and Ronald Colman in the same film (especially

with the delightful Jean Arthur sandwiched between them) and indeed the script only just manages to give all three leading players a fair crack of the whip in this enjoyable manic comedy leavened with a tablespoonful of social satire. Grant is a treat in the urbanely bewildered mood he also displayed in *Arsenic and Old Lace,* and his timing is as immaculate as ever.

Talk Radio ● Ⓥ
1988, US, 108 mins, colour
Dir: Oliver Stone
Stars: Eric Bogosian, Alec Baldwin, Ellen Greene, Leslie Hope
Rating: ★★

Barry Champlain is that new phenomenon – a 'shock jock'. A master of talk-insult on air whom most people hate but find compulsive. A user, never a giver, he feeds off people's fears, hatreds and prejudices. An expert on the callous putdown and the cutoff button alike, he lets callers vent their spleen and then flushes them down the radio waves and out of his system. 'Why do you hurt so many people?' asks an angry caller. The answer is that it gives him a charge and earns him a living. 'We reap what we sow,' Barry patly tells a listener, and so the ending of *Talk Radio* will surprise no-one (it's partly based on a real-life personality). Although the movie sometimes comes close to talking itself to death, moments to admire in the script (co-written by Bogosian) come thick and fast, making it often compulsive stuff. Just don't expect to like anyone in this story.

Tall Guy, The ● Ⓥ
1989, UK, 94 mins, colour
Dir: Mel Smith
Stars: Jeff Goldblum, Emma Thompson, Rowan Atkinson
Rating: ★★

Although there aren't too many outright laughs in comedian Mel Smith's debut as film director, it's a jolly and lively romp with some highly original ideas. Directionally, it's a bit of a mess, sloppily edited and shapeless. But there are compensations. A musical monstrosity based on *The Elephant Man,* for example, is such a hoot that you'd like to see the whole show! Hollywood's Jeff Goldblum is suitably laconic in the title role, as a 'bit' actor desperate for a break, Emma Thompson shows off her offbeat personality (and a lot else) as the uninhibited heroine and Rowan Atkinson is wonderfully obnoxious as

T

the comedian for whom Goldblum has to stooge at the beginning of the story. The director himself makes a rather predictable guest appearance as a belching drunk.

Tall in the Saddle ○
1944, US, 87 mins, b/w
Dir: Edwin L Marin
Stars: John Wayne, Ella Raines
Rating: ★★

This hard-hitting but overly plotted oater was a labour of love for star John Wayne, who tried unsuccessfully to persuade John Ford to direct. It was written by Paul Fix, a personal friend of the Duke, and a frequent acting co-star (he also had a bit part here). Wayne starts out in the film as a virtual misogynist, but is tamed by frisky Ella Raines, who not only shoots at him but also flings a knife in his direction. There's sterling support from Wayne's regular sidekick, George 'Gabby' Hayes, as a stagecoach driver.

Tall Man Riding ○
1955, US, 83 mins, colour
Dir: Lesley Selander
Stars: Randolph Scott, Dorothy Malone, Peggie Castle, John Dehner
Rating: ★★

The tall man is sharp shooting Randolph Scott, involved in a vendetta with cattle baron Robert Barrat, whose daughter Dorothy Malone he has set his sights on. Sturdy cowboy fare, lifted slightly out of the rut by its theme of greed during the land-granting to the Montana settlers.

Tall Men, The ○
1955, US, 122 mins, colour
Dir: Raoul Walsh
Stars: Clark Gable, Jane Russell, Robert Ryan, Cameron Mitchell
Rating: ★★★

Rugged, enjoyable Western which furnished meaty roles for Clark Gable and Jane Russell when both had been going through a patch of bad films. Their initial meeting provides some rich dialogue: 'I want a man with great, big dreams,' pouts Jane (coming on like Mae West), 'who's goin' places an' has room for a passenger.' Replies Gable: 'Help me pull off this boot.' Good photography, tough action and a real feel for the wide open spaces of the west, for which veteran director Raoul Walsh must take most of the credit. Gable seems to enjoy himself a lot, whether picking off Indians, bandying words with Jane, rushing barricades or, in one especially hand-

some sequence, stampeding a herd of cattle.

Tall T, The ○
1957, US, 78 mins, colour
Dir: Budd Boetticher
Stars: Randolph Scott, Maureen O'Sullivan, Richard Boone
Rating: ★★

A very tough, adult and bloody Western for its time, about a rancher and a newly married couple held captive by outlaws at a stagecoach relay station. The ending, a crescendo of violence, foreshadowed Italian Westerns to come. One of a series of Westerns made by Scott with director Budd Boetticher, now rated in many critical circles as among their best work. This one, though, is not as good as some people think it is.

Tall Target ○
1951, US, 78 mins, b/w
Dir: Anthony Mann
Stars: Dick Powell, Paula Raymond, Adolphe Menjou
Rating: ★★★

Hyper-tense suspense thriller set in 1861, and centring on an attempted presidential assassination on board a train. For director Anthony Mann. it bridged the gap between his tough thrillers of the Forties (such as *T-Men*) and his brilliant series of James Stewart Westerns in the Fifties. Here, Dick Powell is the star.

Tamahine ○
1963, UK, 95 mins, colour
Dir: Philip Leacock
Stars: Nancy Kwan, John Fraser, Dennis Price
Rating: ★★

Fast-paced frolic, rather similar in style to the Boulting Brothers' *A French Mistress* a couple of years earlier, featuring Nancy Kwan as the nut-brown Polynesian maiden who not only disrupts life at a boy's public school, but beats them out of sight at the school sports. Ms Kwan bounds around with suitable abandon, and smiles and undresses attractively; while a small crowd of unbelievably 18-year-old sixth-formers, led by John Fraser and James Fox, slaver suitably in return.

Tamarind Seed, The ○
1974, UK, 125 mins, colour
Dir: Blake Edwards
Stars: Julie Andrews, Omar Sharif, Anthony Quayle, Daniel O'Herlihy, Sylvia Syms, Oscar Homolka
Rating: ★★

There's an interesting idea in this romantic drama which would have been more effective if someone like Alfred Hitchcock could have got to work on it. Omar Sharif turns on the famous charm to some effect as the Russian diplomat who falls in love with cool Julie Andrews, playing a girl who can somehow afford a Dior wardrobe on a Home Office salary. She provides an additional motive for him to defect when his liberal views make him a target for KGB suspicions. All very promising, though the dialogue makes the stars labour mightily to make anything of the situations. There are one or two moments of high suspense, especially towards the end, but not enough to keep tedium at bay throughout.

Taming of the Shrew, The ○ Ⓥ
1967, US/Italy, 126 mins, colour
Dir: Franco Zeffirelli
Stars: Elizabeth Taylor, Richard Burton, Michael York, Cyril Cusack, Michael Hordern
Rating: ★★★

This really spectacular version of Shakespeare's comedy owed much of its impact to Franco Zeffirelli's fizzing direction and the dazzling colour camerawork of Oswald Morris. Elizabeth Taylor's shrew and Richard Burton's tamer are at their best in the extraordinarily funny wedding scene.

Tanganyika ○
1954, US, 81 mins, colour
Dir: Andre De Toth
Stars: Van Heflin, Ruth Roman, Howard Duff, Jeff Morrow
Rating: ★★

One of the colourful all-action features that Universal-International trotted out with such regularity and polish in the Fifties. This jungle thriller features Van Heflin as a white hunter battling against a mercenary army in the forests of British East Africa. Alas, it's relentlessly routine.

Tango & Cash ● Ⓥ
1989, US, 106 mins, colour
Dir: Andrei Konchalovsky
Stars: Sylvester Stallone, Kurt Russell, Jack Palance, Teri Hatcher
Rating: ★

Times were when Konchalovsky made acclaimed movies in his native Russia. His Hollywood career slipped into pulp fiction, and heaven knows what attracted him to this sloppily scripted variation on Sixties' superspy movies like *Our Man Flint*. There are two heroes for the price of one. Stallone (the best thing in the film) is the pinstriped, market-playing Tango. Kurt Russell is the T-shirted Cash. Both are supercops, rapidly getting under the skin of super drugs baron Palance who, with the help of henchman Brion James (with a misbegotten 'British' accent that will afford considerable amusement in the UK), railroads our heroes most unconvincingly into prison, from where they escape and blast the bad guys out of existence. End of story. Despite quite imaginative sets and bursts of action – the prison scenes are particularly vividly staged – this is a fitfully boring film with perished elastic in its would-be whiplash dialogue.

Tank Force O
(aka: No Time to Die!)
1958, UK, 102 mins, colour
Dir: Terence Young
Stars: Victor Mature, Leo Genn, Anthony Newley, Luciana Paluzzi
Rating: ★

'C'mon, let's hit the road,' says Victor Mature at one stage in this exciting, if implausible, *Boy's Own*-style World War Two adventure. But you really can't blame Sergeant Mature for his idiomatic choice of command to his fellow escapees from an Italian prison camp in the Libyan desert. Because he is playing that almost inevitable character in British movies of the Fifties, the token Yank. Director Terence Young and his cast and crew of 88 were filming in the Libyan desert for eight weeks. The film was released in Britain as *No Time To Die!* By the time the plentiful action and incident get under way, there's not much time to relax either.

Tank Girl ● ⓥ
1995, US, 104 mins, colour
Dir: Rachel Talalay
Stars: Lori Petty, Malcolm McDowell, Ice T, Naomi Watts, Don Harvey
Rating: ★★

Pop art comic strip meets science-fiction meets *The Girl from UNCLE*, in a sort of *Mad Maxine*. Unfortunately, the story is slimmer than a supermodel in this live-action adventure comedy with Lori Petty virtually perfect as the title character, and fast with the hip banter too. Naomi Watts is too pretty and talented for the heroine's own good, though, as her cohort Jet Girl and Malcolm McDowell surprisingly a touch less OTT than usual as the villain intent on taking over a

comet-devastated world's water supply, while desert warrior Tank Girl, who, naturally, bears a charmed life, attempts to stop him. Her army of kangaroo-men is funny rather than threatening, but the music is good, including a wickedly choreographed version of Cole Porter's *Let's Do It* set in a futuristic brothel. It's noisy throughout, but that doesn't prevent tedium sometimes raising a head uglier than the kangaroo men in this TV-style hokum.

Tap ●
1988, US, 110 mins, colour
Dir: Nick Castle
Stars: Gregory Hines, Suzzanne Douglas, Sammy Davis Jr
Rating: ★★

You've got to hand it to Gregory Hines for single-handedly forwarding the cause of dancing – and tap, in particular – in the face of indifference from the Hollywood studios and public alike. Undeterred by the lack of success of his earlier *White Nights* and *The Cotton Club*, he puts his heart and soul into this rich blend mixing dance and a tale of urban struggle. The story is certainly no great shakes but the dancing is sensational (Hines is credited for 'improvography'). This ranges from a 'challenge' contest between tap greats Sandman Sims, Bunny Briggs, Jimmy Slyde, Steve Condos, Pat Rico, Arthur Duncan and Harold Nicholas to Hines' own 'Tap-Tronics' finale, in which his taps are connected with synthesizers to make rhythmic and melodic music.

Taps O ⓥ
1981, US, 126 mins, colour
Dir: Harold Becker
Stars: George C Scott, Timothy Hutton, Sean Penn, Tom Cruise
Rating: ★★

Tom Cruise was originally signed to just a small cameo role as one of the recruits at a military academy taken over by its students in this gripping siege drama. But director Harold Becker spotted his potential and on the second day of filming elevated him to play the third lead, as the gung-ho right-hand lieutenant of Timothy Hutton's maverick gun-toting lead recruit. Fellow Brat Pack star Sean Penn adds his menacing presence, but a central fault lies in the fact that, despite a military crew cut and serious swagger, Hutton is just too nice to be believable as the ruthless renegade who leads the students in armed revolt at plans to

close their academy and sell off the land for land development. George C Scott scores in a brief cameo as a slightly deranged academy principal.

Tarantula! O
1955, US, 80 mins, b/w
Dir: Jack Arnold
Stars: John Agar, Mara Corday, Leo G Carroll, Nestor Paiva
Rating: ★★★★

A pulsating thriller and technically superb horror film, which is probably the best 'giant creature' film since *King Kong*. The director is Jack Arnold, who made a whole parcel of quality chilers in the mid-Fifties including *The Incredible Shrinking Man*. This one is about a giant spider that escapes from a laboratory in Arizona. Watch out for Clint Eastwood as the leader of the bomber pilots who try to put paid to the hairy horror.

Taras Bulba O
1962, US, 124 mins, colour
Dir: J Lee Thompson
Stars: Tony Curtis, Yul Brynner
Rating: ★★

Tony Curtis among the Cossacks in J Lee Thompson's spectacular epic set in the 16th century. He's every inch the all-American boy, leaving the film to be entirely stolen by Yul Brynner's dynamic account of the title character. The action is exciting and occasionally even stylish. But scenes of Cossack home life seem phony and there's too much singing and dancing hereabouts to pad out the running time. Only in its scenes of plague in a besieged city and in the battle scenes towards the end does the film come to life and approach the achievement of its own ambitions. Time and again, though, Curtis' indifferent showing as Brynner's son drags it down.

Target ● ⓥ
1985, US, 118 mins, colour
Dir: Arthur Penn
Stars: Gene Hackman, Matt Dillon, Gayle Hunnicutt
Rating: ★★

Surprise! Surprise! – for young Chris (Matt Dillon) when his mother is kidnapped in Paris. It turns out that years ago Daddy (Gene Hackman) was a CIA agent. Now someone is out to settle an old score. Actually, it's only the father-and-son relationship – as they dodge bullets, glamorous spies and double-agents in their hunt for Mama (Gayle Hunnicutt) – that sets this film above any run-of-the-mill spy

T

thriller of the Sixties. Even here, though, it doesn't dig deep enough, a shame as the theme is especially well handled in Hackman's thoughtful performance. Disappointing to find a director of Arthur Penn's standing associated with a film that manages its routine chases, shoot-outs and explosions well enough, but is otherwise strictly for fans of the stars.

Targets ◐

1967, US, 90 mins, colour
Dir: Peter Bogdanovich
Stars: Boris Karloff, Tim O'Kelly, Nancy Hsueh
Rating: ★★★

A very unsettling film which not only put Peter Bogdanovich right on the map as a director but gave ageing horror star Boris Karloff a welcome meaty role as – an ageing horror star. But its concern over American gun laws, voiced through the story of a sniper who has already killed his own family, went largely unheeded. Ingeniously constructed, hard-hitting stuff.

Tarka the Otter ○ ⓥ

1978, UK, 90 mins, colour
Dir: David Cobham
Stars: Peter Bennett, Edward Underdown
Rating: ★★★

Enormous care has been taken to keep this film version faithful to spirit of Henry Williamson's fine novel. The visuals are as evocative as they are brilliant. The wild-life photography is phenomenal. The film is full of memorable images – none more so than the owl's feather drifting down on to the nose of the mother otter in the old oak they share at the start of the film. Wildlife documentary-maker David Cobham handles the material with skill and respect. Filmed in Devon.

Tartu

See: The Adventures of Tartu

Tarzan the Ape Man ⊙

1932, US, 95 mins, b/w
Dir: W S Van Dyke
Stars: Johnny Weissmuller, Maureen O'Sullivan
Rating: ★★★

The 'Garbo speaks!' headline could have been followed by 'Tarzan talks!' when this first sound Tarzan film hit the screens. Ex-Olympic swimmer Johnny Weissmuller, longer-haired and slimmer than in later efforts, became the definitive screen ape man in this, the first and arguably the best of

his jungle adventures. This pre-Hays Office picture also had Weissmuller and Maureen O'Sullivan (as Jane) more scantily-clad than in subsequent outings. Despite production values that make the film look almost as primitive as its central character, this 1932 film is still an exciting and adventurous yarn. Even the 'Me Tarzan, you Jane' line doesn't sound bad when heard in context! Fresh, fast fun, and very much in the spirit (if not the letter) of the original Edgar Rice Burroughs books.

Tarzan the Ape Man ○

1959, US, 82 mins, colour
Dir: Joseph Newman
Stars: Denny Miller, Joanna Barnes
Rating: ★★

This colourful Tarzan jungle remake gave muscular blond basketball star Denny Miller his finest hour as an actor. The 12th screen incarnation of the ape man, Miller went on to play small bit parts in films as diverse as *The Vikings* and *The Party*. His Jane, who is attacked by cannibals, angry elephants, a rhinoceros and a tarantula, is played by Californian blonde Joanna Barnes, who as well as acting, wrote several steamy novels based on life in Hollywood. The film is a rehash of every previous Tarzan effort, with predictable incidents, colour tinting of stock black and white footage, and even the placing of fake large ears on the smaller ears of Asiatic elephants.

Tarzan, the Ape Man ● ⓥ

1981, US, 112 mins, colour
Dir: John Derek
Stars: Bo Derek, Richard Harris, Miles O'Keeffe
Rating: ★

Over the years many cinematic liberties have been taken with Edgar Rice Burroughs' jungle hero, but none were more flagrant than this shoddy excuse to get Bo Derek frolicking naked at every opportunity. In fact Burroughs' estate filed a lawsuit against John Derek, Bo's mentor, husband and director of this dreadful film. The ape man himself is relegated to third billing behind the nubile Bo and Richard Harris, who rises to the occasion here and produces a ham performance stunning in both its vigour and ineptitude. Bo, for her part, also managed a unique distinction. Admittedly very attractive, she's also bland and boring. To walk around naked and yet be uninteresting

is a curious achievement, but one Bo achieves with charmlessness to spare.

Task Force ○

1949, US, 116 mins, colour & b/w
Dir: Delmer Daves
Stars: Gary Cooper, Jane Wyatt, Wayne Morris, Walter Brennan
Rating: ★★★

A typically splashy Warner biopic from the Forties, made in black and white, but with some Technicolor newsreel footage added in to spice up the impact. Gary Cooper gives his usual solid and sincere performance, even if he has difficulty in looking in his late twenties when the story begins. Jane Wyatt is delightful (and acts well too) as the widow he eventually marries. Very well produced by Jerry Wald, the film looks terrific and went down like a bomb with the public.

Taste of Fear ◐

1961, UK, 81 mins, b/w
Dir: Seth Holt
Stars: Susan Strasberg, Ronald Lewis, Ann Todd, Christopher Lee
Rating: ★★★★

A lonely house with creaking shutters. Flickering candles. A piano playing in an empty room – apparently of its own accord. A disappearing corpse. A girl scared to the point of hysteria. The archetypal formula for a Hammer nightmare thriller and this is one of the best, full of red herrings and unexpected twists. Definitely not for the nervous, it's like a masquerade where the players only take off their masks at the end.

Taste of Honey, A ◐ ⓥ

1961, UK, 100 mins, b/w
Dir: Tony Richardson
Stars: Rita Tushingham, Dora Bryan, Robert Stephens
Rating: ★★★★

Fashioned from Shelagh Delaney's successful play, this poignant film about an unloved, ugly duckling teenage girl brought Rita Tushingham to stardom, and marked Dora Bryan's breakaway from comic character roles. She's first-rate as the heartless, tartish mother heedlessly setting her daughter up for a lifetime of misery. Murray Melvin gives his finest screen performance as the homosexual who proves to be the girl's only real friend.

Taste the Blood of Dracula ● ⓥ

1969, UK, 95 mins, colour
Dir: Peter Sasdy

Stars: Christopher Lee, Geoffrey Keen, Gwen Watford, Linda Hayden
Rating: ★★

In this addition to Hammer Films' celebrated *Dracula* cycle, the action takes place in England instead of Europe. The reactivating process for the dreaded vampire is a quantity of red powder contained in a phial. Innocent enough looking in itself, but once mixed with human blood – up pops the dreaded Drac. The film differs from its predecessors in that Dracula himself, here in a vengeful frame of mind, remains substantially an onlooker while others accomplish the death and destruction. Director Peter Sasdy stages some effective shock moments, particularly in scenes shot inside a church.

Tatie Danielle ❶ ⓥ
1990, France, 112 mins, colour
Dir: Etienne Chatiliez
Stars: Tsilla Chelton, Catherine Jacob, Eric Prat, Isabelle Nanty
Rating: ★★★★

Tatie Danielle is a horrible old woman who makes life hell for those she despises and who pussy-foot to her every demand – most notably her great-nephew and his well-meaning wife. Only when her family goes on holiday and a strong-willed teenager is assigned to care for her does Tatie Danielle meet her match. Blackly funny, if not for all tastes, this French film is a dire warning to all those planning to bring granny home to live. Stage star Tsilla Chelton is splendidly appalling and malevolent in the title role.

Taxi Driver ● ⓥ
1976, US, 110 mins, colour
Dir: Martin Scorsese
Stars: Robert De Niro, Cybill Shepherd, Jodie Foster, Harvey Keitel
Rating: ★★★★

This brilliant film is enough to put you off New York for life. This is strong, strong meat and no mistake, its jetblack theme underlined by Bernard Herrmann's tremendous music. The film is both a damning indictment of the conditions that so easily beget violence in so many ways and from so many different directions, and a tremendous conjuring-up of the nighttime atmosphere of downtown New York. All the night scenes are powerful, sombre, affecting stuff. There are one or two passages that are near-dull, or don't fit the general tenor, but the ending is brilliant, restoring the film to the black plane to

which it so often soars. If there are any reservations with the acting, they have to rest with the central performance of Robert De Niro, as the psychotic taxi driver whose environment and insomnia combine to drive him berserk. It is a splendid performance on the surface, but there doesn't seem to be too much going on behind the eyes. Jodie Foster is quite amazing as a 12-year-old prostitute, and just saunters away with the film.

Taza, Son of Cochise ○
1954, US, 79 mins, colour
Dir: Douglas Sirk
Stars: Rock Hudson, Barbara Rush
Rating: ★★

The last of Jeff Chandler's three appearances as the Apache chief Cochise. He's briefly glimpsed as a dying man at the beginning of this action saga, handing over the reins of power to Rock Hudson. The director is Douglas Sirk, later to make the most successful of Hudson's Fifties' films, including *Magnificent Obsession* and *Written on the Wind*.

Tchin Tchin
See: A Fine Romance

Teachers ●
1984, US, 106 mins, colour
Dir: Arthur Hiller
Stars: Nick Nolte, JoBeth Williams, Judd Hirsch, Ralph Macchio
Rating: ★

Low grades for this story of a horrendous American ghetto school – the old story of one honest man bucking the whole rotten system. The execution of it here is often embarrassing, especially in the screenplay. But its simple, emotional appeal almost works towards the end.

Teacher's Pet ○
1958, US, 120 mins, b/w
Dir: George Seaton
Stars: Clark Gable, Doris Day, Gig Young
Rating: ★★★

A slickly funny comedy that enables both Clark Gable and Doris Day to show a sure sense of tongue-in-cheek humour. Gig Young is a bonus as the rival for Ms Day's hand, whom Gable continually outwits. Funniest scene: when the two men try to slip each other knock-out drops at a nightclub. Young and the script (by Fay and Michael Kanin) were both nominated for Academy Awards.

Tea for Two ○
1950, US, 97 mins, colour
Dir: David Butler
Stars: Doris Day, Gordon MacRae, Gene Nelson, Eve Arden
Rating: ★★★

More than any other, this musical set Doris Day up for her run of success at Warners in the Fifties. It's a bright, lively and tuneful version of *No, No, Nanette* (first filmed with Anna Neagle in 1940) in which Doris, as the girl who has to say 'No' to everything for 24 hours, danced on screen for the first time. She also duetted so well with Gordon MacRae on the title number that they made two further films together. Other songs include 'Crazy Rhythm', 'I Only Have Eyes for You' and 'I Want to Be Happy'.

Tears for Simon
See: Lost

Teenage Bad Girl
See: My Teenage Daughter

Teenage Mutant Ninja Turtles ○ ⓥ
1990, US, 93 mins, colour
Dir: Steve Barron
Stars: Judith Hoag, Elias Koteas, Michael Turney, Raymond Serra, James Saito, Jay Patterson
Rating: ★★

Darkly photographed fantasy adventure that created four new high-kicking heroes and blitzed box offices everywhere. What's afoot? The Foot Clan, that's what, terrorising the New York streets (as if they weren't terrorised enough) and incurring the wrath of the sewer-dwelling, pizza-eating, giant-sized (mutated by radioactive waste) turtles, who swing into action, demolishing scores of Oriental extras with a degree of violence that alarmed guardians of the children at whom the film is aimed. The headbanded amphibians also prove better actors than most of the human cast, although that's not too difficult. Their constant stream of in-lingo wisecracks amuses or annoys according to taste in this hardly awesome, but passably bodacious slice of tongue-in-cheek, half-shelled action.

Teenage Mutant Ninja Turtles II: The Secret of the Ooze ○ ⓥ
1991, US, 87 mins, colour
Dir: Michael Pressman
Stars: Paige Turco, David Warner, Ernie Reyes Jr
Rating: ★

T

For turtle fans only is this rather tired first sequel to the hit original, which runs like a Three Stooges feature with violent action scenes added on. Not many people will be frightened by the monster-villains and you keep expecting the turtles to take their heads off and show that they're really human after all. David Warner comes on as the mad scientist in charge of the dreaded Ooze. Unfortunately, he makes off with it again at the end, probably paving the way for a future Oozy farrago with the fearsome four, who here have lost whatever personality they might once have possessed. *Turtles I* and *III*, it must be said, are both a little better than this.

Teenage Mutant Ninja Turtles III ○ ⓥ
1992, US, 92 mins, colour
Dir: Stuart Gillard
Stars: Paige Turco, Stuart Wilson, Elias Koteas, Sab Shimono, Vivian Wu
Rating: ★★

The combative amphibians travel back in time to 1603 Japan where, not surprisingly, they are regarded as demons. They intervene in a battle between feudal lords and village warriors who all covet the very magic sceptre that has whisked the Turtles and their reporter friend April (still Paige Turco, now looking too mature for the part) nearly 400 years back in time. Their efforts to save the day at least score more success than teaching the 17th-century Orientals to make pizza. Stuart Wilson's villain has style and swagger in the manner of Captain Hook (motto: 'Places to go, people to kill'). But the adventure never really takes off in a way that might excite any but the youngest children. There are isolated moments of satirical fun, though, as when Samurai warriors, whisked forward in exchange to New York, watch ice hockey on TV. Invited to have the kind of game they've just seen, they simply start to fight each other.

Teen Wolf ○ ⓥ
1985, US, 90 mins, colour
Dir: Rod Daniel
Stars: Michael J Fox, James Hampton, Susan Ursitti
Rating: ★★★

It had been a decade or so since we'd had a werewolf comedy, when this simple but effective vehicle for the appropriately named Michael J Fox arrived to surprise us pleasantly as a follow-up (actually shot earlier) to his

smash-hit *Back To The Future*. He's almost the whole show in this romp as a college kid who starts growling when annoyed, gets an itchy feeling round the neck and arms and hears high pitched whistles no-one else can. He goes for advice to his basketball coach (Fox playing basketball? Never mind, somehow they make it work). The coach, however, has only three rules to follow: never miss 12 hours' sleep, never play cards with a man whose first name is a state, and never go near a woman with a dagger tattoo. Werewolves? No problem. The tail, sorry, tale, climaxes with a very well choreographed basketball game as the ghoul-in-school fights to go straight and avoid a lifetime of biting the mailman and dodging silver bullets.

Teen Wolf Too ⊙ ⓥ
1987, US, 93 mins, colour
Dir: Christopher Leitch
Stars: Jason Bateman, Kim Darby, John Astin, Paul Sand, Kathleen Freeman
Rating: ★

Nice title, shame about the film. Sequels to comedy successes are always a problem, but this one gives itself unnecessary feet of lead by substituting the charmless Jason Bateman for the Michael J Fox of the original. Otherwise the elements are much as before, with special effects on the meagre side, emphasis shifted to college stereotype and the 'wolf's' sport changed from basketball to boxing. John Astin overdoes it (as usual) as the dean, Kim Darby is wasted (again) as the wolf's biology teacher, and veteran Kathleen Freeman turns in a nice little job as an unrelenting admissions clerk. Even with all the film's familiarity, the final boxing match carries some excitement. Sure makes the original look good though.

Telefon ◐ ⓥ
1977, US, 103 mins, colour
Dir: Don Siegel
Stars: Charles Bronson, Lee Remick, Tyne Daly, Donald Pleasence, Patrick Magee
Rating: ★★

Something rather out of the ordinary run of spy thrillers, this film also covers a lot of territory so far as locations are concerned. The story moves with pace from Russia (actually shot in Finland) to a wide variety of places in the US. Charles Bronson stars as a KGB agent named Borzov assigned to stop the nefarious activities in America of a hardline Stalinist agent (played by

Donald Pleasence) who has practical – and very sinister – plans of his own to reinstigate the Cold War. The star is partnered by attractive Lee Remick, another double agent; Patrick Magee and Alan Badel are effective as high officials in the Russian secret police; and the dynamic Tyne Daly almost steals the show as a CIA computer analyst.

Tempest ○
1959, Italy, 123 mins, colour
Dir: Alberto Lattuada
Stars: Van Heflin, Silvana Mangano, Viveca Lindfors
Rating: ★★

Van Heflin as the Russian rebel Pugachev, taking on Catherine the Great (Viveca Lindfors). Based on stories by Pushkin, this impressively mounted epic has some of the biggest battle scenes ever filmed. It also has Agnes Moorehead, in superb form as a pipe-smoking wife of the Steppes.

10 ◐ ⓥ
1979, US, 122 mins, colour
Dir: Blake Edwards
Stars: Dudley Moore, Julie Andrews, Bo Derek
Rating: ★

Julie Andrews in an 'X' certificate film? It certainly seemed a surprise at the time, but then poor Julie is hardly ever in this wish fulfilment sex frolic which made hot box-office properties of her co-stars, Dudley Moore and Bo Derek. The plot is the kind of thing director Blake Edwards might have done, a little less outspokenly, perhaps, with his favourite star Peter Sellers some years before. But here it's cuddly Dudley as the fortyish bachelor who finds his perfect girl (the '10' of the title) and follows her everywhere only to discover in the end that looks can be all too deceptive. Edwards finds a few funny situations in all this, mostly in his familiar Clouseau vein, such as the doddery old maidservant who tries to serve drinks to a chimney in a very amusing sequence.

Ten Commandments, The ○
1956, US, 219 mins, colour
Dir: Cecil B DeMille
Stars: Charlton Heston, Yul Brynner, Anne Baxter, Yvonne De Carlo, Edward G Robinson, John Derek
Rating: ★★★★

Cecil B DeMille's last film (he made his first in 1913) is a remake of the Biblical epic he first directed in 1923. Even then the parting of the Red Sea (in early colour) was impressive, but, with the benefit of more modern special effects, DeMille was able to turn in a really spectacular job, and the sequence won the film an Oscar. The writing of the tablets in the wilderness is also a highlight of a film that remains a supreme example of vivid Hollywood story-telling at its best, with Charlton Heston in towering form as Moses.

Tender Comrade ○
1943, US, 101 mins, b/w
Dir: Edward Dymtryk
Stars: Ginger Rogers, Robert Ryan
Rating: ★★

When the McCarthy anti-Communist witch-hunts were in full flow, Senator McCarthy branded this Ginger Rogers film as red-tinged throughout. Its story of four women during wartime setting up in a commune-style home was not surprising, considering the film's director (Edward Dmytryk) and scriptwriter (Dalton Trumbo) would later be jailed for a year as two of the 'Hollywood Ten'. But none of that could detract from the fact that *Tender Comrade* was a weak affair, with Ms Rogers offering a stagey performance. RKO tried to spice things up with a new ending, but then ditched that in favour of re-editing the original final shots.

Tender Is the Night ○
1961, US, 146 mins, colour
Dir: Henry King
Stars: Jennifer Jones, Jason Robards Jr, Joan Fontaine, Tom Ewell
Rating: ★★

Although the film lacks pace and atmosphere the polished performances of Jennifer Jones and Joan Fontaine see this disappointing version of Scott Fitzgerald's novel through. But spectacular locations and a feel for the period can't compensate for director Henry King and writer Ivan Moffat failing to get to grips with Fitzgerald's coruscating (and corrosive) characters.

Tender Mercies ◐ ⓥ
1982, US, 90 mins, colour
Dir: Bruce Beresford
Stars: Robert Duvall, Tess Harper, Wiford Brimley, Ellen Barkin
Rating: ★★★

Robert Duvall won an Oscar for his portrayal of a down-on-his-luck country singer in this low-key domestic drama. After the break-up of his marriage, Mac Sledge (Duvall) takes a job working for Rosa Lee (Tess Harper), a religious widow who owns a motel and

gas station. They fall in love and Sledge tries to make a comeback as a singer. Although Duvall plays his part well, this is a very talky film with no action to spice it up and give it tension. Australian director Bruce Beresford perhaps should have let an American direct this quintessentially American story.

Tender Trap, The ○
1955, US, 111 mins, colour
Dir: Charles Walters
Stars: Frank Sinatra, Debbie Reynolds
Rating: ★★★★

This thoroughly enjoyable Frank Sinatra comedy has him as the swinging New York bachelor on the trail of winsome Debbie Reynolds, though the very best things here are the title song and the more acid support of Celeste Holm (a year later to partner Sinatra herself in *High Society*) and David Wayne.

Ten Gentlemen from West Point ○
1942, US, 104 mins, b/w
Dir: Henry Hathaway
Stars: George Montgomery, Maureen O'Hara, Laird Cregar
Rating: ★★

Though not too close to the real facts, this spirited film about the establishment of West Point as a military academy in the early 1800s is, under Henry Hathaway's direction, an exciting adventure story in its own right. George Montgomery – who had started in films four years earlier as a stuntman – stars as the backwoodsman who doesn't fit in with his fellow cadets. But the film is stolen by burly Laird Cregar, in commanding form as the major in charge of the raw recruits. Two years later Cregar was dead at 28, killed by a heart condition following a crash diet.

Ten Little Niggers
See: And Then There Were None

Tennessee's Partner ○
1955, US, 87 mins, colour
Dir: Allan Dwan
Stars: John Payne, Ronald Reagan
Rating: ★★★

Although it was nearing the end of its life, RKO Radio produced some remarkably good action pictures in its last few years – mainly directed, as here, by the veteran Allan Dwan. It's a lavishly produced version of Bret Harte's Western novel, with surprisingly effective performances from

Ronald Reagan and Rhonda Fleming. The climax is extremely moving and, overall, the film reaches and maintains a very high entertainment value.

10 Rillington Place ●
1970, UK, 106 mins, colour
Dir: Richard Fleischer
Stars: Richard Attenborough, Judy Geeson, John Hurt, Pat Heywood
Rating: ★★★

Director Richard Fleischer's occasional preoccupation with bizarre murder cases (one remembers *Compulsion*, about the Leopold-Loeb murders, and *The Boston Strangler*), brought him to England in 1970 to make this grim reconstruction of the case of John Reginald Christie, who murdered seven people between 1944 and 1952 in his dingy North London home. Richard Attenborough sinks himself frighteningly well into this role. Even so, he is more than matched by the splendid John Hurt, whose pathetic Timothy Evans, convicted of two of the murders committed by Christie, compels total sympathy. The case itself is brought to life with harrowing authenticity, sparing little of the horrifying and gruesome detail involved, and never sensationalising its subject.

Ten Seconds to Hell ○
1960, US, 93 mins, b/w
Dir: Robert Aldrich
Stars: Jeff Chandler, Jack Palance, Martine Carol
Rating: ★★

A strange and sometimes exciting film of mixed origins, dealing with German demolition workers in Berlin after World War Two. It was made by the English Hammer company, directed by American Robert Aldrich, shot on location in Berlin, and with English, French and American actors in the cast. Jeff Chandler enjoys himself thoroughly in a rare villain role, in a film where character development plays second fiddle to inbuilt suspense.

Tension ○
1949, US, 91 mins, b/w
Dir: John Berry
Stars: Richard Basehart, Audrey Totter
Rating: ★★★

A downbeat, curiously unrelaxed *film noir* with a typically alienated hero in Richard Basehart's unassuming chemist, pushed over the edge when his virago of a wife (a splendidly spiteful performance by diminutive but curvy Audrey Totter) decides to leave him for another man. Being an MGM

T

film, this is treated rather less darkly than similar stuff being made across the road at RKO and Columbia, but writer Allen Rivkin's sharpish script doesn't allow John Berry to fudge the issues involved. The inane narration, though you get used to it, does do some harm to the film, but there's an unexpectedly good performance by Cyd Charisse who makes the most out of a dull role as the girl who steers Basehart away from his murder plan.

Tension at Table Rock O
1956, US, 89 mins, colour
Dir: Charles Marquis Warren
Stars: Richard Egan, Dorothy Malone, Cameron Mitchell, Billy Chapin
Rating: ★★★

Another Western with a theme song (what Western hadn't in those days?), as well as echoes of *High Noon* and *Shane*. It's adapted from Frank Gruber's novel *Bitter Sage* and directed by Charles Marquis Warren, himself a distinguished author of wild west yarns. Richard Egan is impassive as the friendless gunman, Edward Andrews impressive as a sneaky villain. Dorothy Malone is a bit too good to believe in a pokey town like Table Rock, but she should worry; her next film, *Written on the Wind,* would bring her an Oscar. The colour photography by Joseph Biroc is extremely fine and the credits nicely done. *Star Trek's* DeForest Kelley is first-class in a cameo as another gunman.

Ten Tall Men O
1951, US, 97 mins, colour
Dir: Willis Goldbeck
Stars: Burt Lancaster, Gilbert Roland, Kieron Moore, Jody Lawrance
Rating: ★★

Burt Lancaster was still in his all-action mould when he turned out this superficially exciting Foreign Legion story, in between making *The Flame and the Arrow* and *The Crimson Pirate*. The formidable features of Mike Mazurki loom large in support, and you can spot up-and-coming star Mari Blanchard in a small role. A good sandstorm sequence and some frisky editing can't really disguise the fact that this is typical Columbia oriental mutton dressed up as lamb.

10.30pm Summer ◐
1966, US/Spain, 85 mins, colour
Dir: Jules Dassin
Stars: Melina Mercouri, Peter Finch, Romy Schneider
Rating: ★★

Three international stars form the points of this torrid emotional triangle: Greek-born Melina Mercouri, Britain's Peter Finch, who initially made his name in Australian films, and Austrian actress Romy Schneider. It's a tangled web their characters weave in the sun-baked square of a small Spanish town in which they have been stranded, ironically by floods. When night falls, Dassin captures the heat and tension with camerawork that sears the screen in reds, yellows and dark browns. And there's a wild flamenco dancing scene towards the end which plays its part in releasing the pent-up feelings the characters have towards each other.

10 to Midnight ●
1983, US, 95 mins, colour
Dir: J Lee Thompson
Stars: Charles Bronson, Lisa Eilbacher, Andrew Stevens
Rating: ★★★

Don't ask us to explain the title, but, as blood-soaked vigilante cop thrillers go, this is a fairly good example. Not very believable perhaps, but thrashed along by veteran director Lee Thompson (and well edited by his son Peter) with plenty of emphasis on the characters involved, and on the pace of the action. Feminists may complain that the story exploits women since the killer seems to aim his knife at some of the most nubile girls in town! To add to the film's sensational aspect, the killer (disturbing newcomer Gene Davis) also does his bloody work in the altogether (save for gloves). This is logical in the sense that he avoids bloodstains on his clothes, but does raise the query about how he manages to both get his clothes off and sneak into buildings without anyone seeing him. Still, the treatment bears a very professional stamp, the scenes of menace are skilfully exploited for suspense and excitement and individual people are clearly drawn in three dimensions.

Ten Wanted Men O
1955, US, 80 mins, colour
Dir: Bruce Humberstone
Stars: Randolph Scott, Jocelyn Brando, Richard Boone
Rating: ★

Though the situations move slowly through well-trodden pastures, there's plenty of fire-power in this gritty Western about a peacable rancher – Randolph Scott, forced to protect his woman and property against hired killers imported by a jealous rancher.

In the role of Corinne, Marlon Brando's sister Jocelyn makes one of her rare screen appearances. And the bad guys include a whole crop of faces you love to see bite the dust, including Lee Van Cleef's.

Tequila Sunrise ● Ⓥ
1988, US, 108 mins, colour
Dir: Robert Towne
Stars: Mel Gibson, Michelle Pfeiffer, Kurt Russell, Raul Julia
Rating: ★★

This flashy thriller is a strange kettle of tequila and no mistake. You'll have as hard a time following the plot as figuring out when it's meant to be taken seriously. Robert Towne, who scripted *Chinatown*, wrote and directed this multi-mooded drug-bust drama set near the California-Mexico border. Mel Gibson is the ex-cocaine king whom the script tries hard to convince us should be allowed to go free after getting out of the business and falling for a good woman (Michelle Pfeiffer in an interesting portrayal). It's Kurt Russell, though, who gives the film's best performance, as the cop who also beds Pfeiffer and has a long-term friendship with Gibson, although he too has problems with the screenplay's declarations of love, clumsily directed by Towne. Raul Julia, playing a devious Mexican 'coke king', gives an extraordinarily misjudged performance that bears comparison with some of Orson Welles' less restrained cameos. There's some good smart dialogue in all this, but the film's constant switches of mood and pace do it no good at all.

Terminator, The ● Ⓥ
1984, US, 108 mins, colour
Dir: James Cameron
Stars: Arnold Schwarzenegger, Linda Hamilton, Michael Biehn, Paul Winfield, Lance Henriksen
Rating: ★★★★

Good for a laugh and a thrill and pounded along in typical style by director James Cameron, who gets an 'A' for cinema-craft from the opening scene. Schwarzenegger and Michael Biehn come back from the future: Arnie's an android who starts killing women called Sarah Connor. The one he wants, of course, is bound to be last on the list, or we wouldn't have any suspense, and Cameron makes sure there's plenty of that, as well as electrifying action – as Biehn, who's returned from the future to save the relevant Sarah, has to find a way to stop The Terminator – and that's not easy.

Schwarzenegger dominates the film as Mr T, and his famous line 'I'll be back' has passed into film legend. The prolonged climactic sequence is one of the most nail-biting and brilliantly edited of the Eighties. There are a few dull patches and poor supporting performances; however, Cameron made sure there were none of either in the sequel seven years later.

Terminator 2: Judgment Day ● ⓥ
1991, US, 136 mins, colour
Dir: James Cameron
Stars: Arnold Schwarzenegger, Linda Hamilton. Edward Furlong, Robert Patrick
Rating: ★★★★★

If big Arnold was well cast as the bad Terminator sent back to the future to kill the mother of the future world leader, then he's perfectly cast as the good Terminator sent back to protect the now 10-year-old boy against bad Terminator 2. The twists and turns of logic and time will amaze you almost as much as the 'liquid metal' effects and the highway chases of this 10-years-later sequel, as Arnie develops sufficient human traits and command of slang to bring additional veins of humour to the almost non-stop action. If he was paid around $15 million, then Hamilton, appropriately beefed up as befits the world's toughest lady, is worth every cent of the one million she is said to have got to repeat her role. Notable assists come from Edward Furlong as her son and Robert Patrick as T2, who has the edge on Arnie as he's a more advanced model. There's a welcome sprinkling of deadpan humour to give you relief from the bludgeoning action, too. 'Were you gonna kill him?' the boy asks Arnie of one victim. 'Of course I was,' snaps the big man. 'I'm a Terminator.'

Term of Trial ◐
1962, UK, 113 mins, b/w
Dir: Peter Glenville
Stars: Laurence Olivier, Simone Signoret, Sarah Miles, Terence Stamp
Rating: ★★

Controversial drama about a school-teacher accused of assaulting a teenage pupil. Laurence Olivier is sternly superb as the teacher, while Sarah Miles, in her film debut, oozes sex appeal as the precocious girl.

Terms of Endearment ● ⓥ
1983, US, 132 mins, colour
Dir: James L Brooks

Stars: Shirley MacLaine, Debra Winger, Jack Nicholson, Jeff Daniels
Rating: ★★★★

What starts out as a finely balanced mixture of comedy and drama, about a mother-daughter relationship and its ups and downs over the years, slips uncomfortably at the midpoint into unadulterated soap-opera as the daughter contracts cancer. Even so, there wasn't a dry eye as the film topped the box-office the world over and then cleaned up at the Oscars, taking statuettes for Best Film, Director (James L Brooks), Actress (Shirley MacLaine), Supporting Actor (Jack Nicholson) and Screenplay (Brooks, again). Only Nicholson could get away with playing an ex-astronaut called Garrett Breedlove, and he almost steals the film from under the noses of MacLaine and Debra Winger, as her daughter. The supporting cast includes Danny DeVito (who worked with the director on *Taxi*) and Jeff Daniels – and there's a wealth of foot-tapping hit songs on the soundtrack.

Terry Fox Story, The ○
1983, Canada, 97 mins, colour
Dir: Ralph L Thomas
Stars: Robert Duvall, Eric Fryer, Christopher Makepeace, Rosalind Chao
Rating: ★★★

A modern-day, true-life story of real heroism. Director Ralph L Thomas presents a heartwarming biography of a young man with cancer who, after having his leg amputated, finds enough of the right stuff to undertake a one-man marathon across Canada to raise money to help other cancer sufferers. This film follows the marathon of hope undertaken by Terry (played by real amputee Eric Fryer). The scenes where Terry courageously runs into Toronto, and is met by thousands of adoring admirers, are handled with much inspiration. It's an altogether uplifting experience.

Tex and the Lord of the Deep ○
1985, US, 90 mins, colour
Dir: Duccio Tessari
Stars: Giuliano Gemma, William Berger, Isabel Russinova
Poating: ★★

One of the greatest of comic-book heroes on the continent, Tex was created in 1948 by Giovanni Luigi Bonelli, who makes a cameo appearance in this fantasy Western adventure as an old witch-doctor. The action is fast and furious, but curiously uinvolving, as our

three heroes escape from one impossible situation after another with the regularity of an old-fashioned serial. But Riccardo Petrazzi is a colourful villain, a hooded alchemist who manufactures a deadly, glowing-green rock from the depths of his headquarters in a volcano.

Texas Kid – Outlaw
See: The Kid from Texas

Texas Rangers, The ○
1951, US, 74 mins, colour
Dir: Phil Karlson
Stars: George Montgomery, Gale Storm, Jerome Courtland, Noah Beery
Rating: ★★★

Rudimentary but rousing Western, ferociously paced by director Phil Karlson, who gives us battles on land, horseback and train as well as grouping together several famous Western outlaws who have to be corralled by upright rangers George Montgomery and Jerome Courtland. Rather uncertainly shot in SuperCinecolor and very routinely scripted, the film has a feisty heroine in Gale Storm and a good cast of outlaws that includes William Bishop, Douglas Kennedy, John Dehner and Ian MacDonald. Action fans won't complain either: there are more fights and gun battles here than in many a longer Western.

Texas Rangers, The ○
1936, US, 95 mins, b/w
Dir: King Vidor
Stars: Fred MacMurray, Jack Oakie, Jean Parker, Lloyd Nolan
Rating: ★★

Strongly-mounted Western about three outlaws, two of whom join the Texas rangers and eventually, inevitably, have to bring in the third. Fred MacMurray, Jack Oakie and Lloyd Nolan are quite well contrasted as the three guys, with Nolan stealing the acting honours just as Macdonald Carey did in the same role in the rather more memorable 1949 remake *Streets of Laredo*.

Texasville ○ ⓥ
1990, US, 126 mins, colour
Dir: Peter Bogdanovich
Stars: Jeff Bridges, Cybill Shepherd, Cloris Leachman, Timothy Bottoms, Eileen Brennan, Randy Quaid
Rating: ★

Although it has a few good moments and a touching ending, this is a largely pointless sequel to the Oscar-winning *The Last Picture Show* from the same di-

T

rector and with much the same cast, now 20 years older. Alas, these are characters who no longer have anywhere to go. Duane (Jeff Bridges) has seen his oil-wells run as dry as his marriage to Karla (Annie Potts). Lester (Randy Quaid) is the town barber, in financial trouble of his own, Sonny (Timothy Bottoms) retreats into the movie shows of the past and towards a gentle madness, his affair with Ruth (Cloris Leachman), now Duane's ageing secretary, almost forgotten. Lusty waitress Genevieve (Eileen Brennan) is now disabled on the sidelines. Jacy (Cybill Shepherd), Duane's high school crush, returns to the town for its centenary celebration after the collapse of her marriage and death of her son. With all these elements of tragedy running through, it's surprising that *Texasville* tries so hard to be a comedy. The strain shows in over-acting by the players, Quaid especially, in scenes that stretch for humour. It's a long, slow and boring prowl over fields of past glory.

Texican, The ○

1966, US/Spain, 91 mins, colour
Dir: Lesley Selander
Stars: Audie Murphy, Diana Lorys, Broderick Crawford
Rating: ★★

A gritty Western, made in Spain, with American director Lesley Selander (a man, despite the spelling) making sure the action stays fast and lively Audie Murphy is his poker-faced self as the man hunting the murderer of his brother, after escaping from a chain gang. Red-haired Diana Lorys decorated several such Westerns in the Sixties.

Thank God It's Friday ○

1978, US, 90 mins, colour
Dir: Robert Klane
Stars: Donna Summer, Chick Vennera, Jeff Goldblum, Debra Winger
Rating: ★

A piledriving beat infuses this disco movie that follows the events in a Hollywood disco-cum-nightclub over a single evening. Director Robert Klane gives the episodic structure pace and visual excitement, abetted by a splendid score which includes the Oscar-winning song 'Last Dance', performed by star Donna Summer. The Commodores appear as themselves, and there's a neat performance by Chick Vennera who was to score the following year in *Yanks*.

Thanks a Million ○

1937, US, 87 mins, b/w
Dir: Roy Del Ruth
Stars: Dick Powell, Ann Dvorak, Fred Allen, Patsy Kelly
Rating: ★★★

A satirical musical romp that still looks smart today. Dick Powell has one of the breeziest and brightest of his early roles as the singer who finds himself running for governor because his personality is such a hit with the public. But there's one big snag: he's honest. Powell gets plenty of help with the musical numbers (sometimes from such unexpected quarters as Ann Dvorak and Patsy Kelly) and the script by Nunnally Johnson has more wit, bite and insight (not to mention good laughs) than any musical has a right to deserve.

Thank You All Very Much

See: A Touch of Love

Thank You, Mr Moto ○

1937, US, 68 mins, b/w
Dir: Norman Foster
Stars: Peter Lorre, Pauline Frederick, Sidney Blackmer, John Carradine
Rating: ★★★

The oriental sleuth, (played by Peter Lorre) as cunning as he is courteous, first appeared in serial stories in the popular *Saturday Evening Post,* and very quickly became a cult hero. Unfortunately, the series was terminated with the emergence of the Japanese as American enemies in World War Two. Buried treasure is on the menu here, with silent star Pauline Frederick in her penultimate film, as the villainess.

That Certain Age ○

1938, US, 100 mins, b/w
Dir: Edward Ludwig
Stars: Deanna Durbin, Melvyn Douglas, Jackie Cooper, Irene Rich
Rating: ★★

Deanna Durbin, allowed by Universal to grow up (but not too much), develops a teenage crush on sophisticated older man Melvyn Douglas, to the understandable annoyance of her young screen boyfriend, Jackie Cooper. Despite this daring romantic innovation, the film is the same cheerfully innocent mixture of sentiment and comedy as before, decorated by Durbin's attractive singing. She and Douglas give light and charming performances that give the frothy tale the lift it needs.

That Certain Feeling ○

1956, US, 103 mins, colour
Dir: Melvin Frank, Norman Panama
Stars: Bob Hope, Eva Marie Saint, George Sanders, Pearl Bailey
Rating: ★★

There are some delightful moments in this bright Bob Hope comedy from the experienced team of Melvin Frank and Norman Panama, which a year earlier had been responsible for Danny Kaye's classic *The Court Jester*. Hope gets a chance to build a genuine character, Pearl Bailey enhances every scene in which she appears, and Eva Marie Saint exploits an unsuspected comedy talent to good effect in the film's best musical sequence, a drunken dance romp. Songs include the title number, 'Zing Went the Strings of My Heart' and 'Time to Hit the Road to Dreamland'.

That Darn Cat! ⊙

1965, US, 116 mins, colour
Dir: Robert Stevenson
Stars: Dean Jones, Hayley Mills, Roddy McDowall
Rating: ★★★★

This stylish comedy-thriller is the best of all the films Hayley Mills made for the Disney studio. She's the owner of DC (Darn Cat, supposedly the Siamese from *The Incredible Journey*) who, in-between stealing duck dinners and outwitting bulldogs, stumbles, through his nose for fish, across the hideout of two bank-robbers holding hostage a woman teller from the bank they've just robbed. The teller substitutes her watch for DC's collar and, in no time at all, Hayley has grabbed the best-looking FBI agent she can lay hands on, and a tail (!) is put on DC, in the hope that he will lead the law to the lair. The cast, ankle-deep in star names, all give perfectly judged performances. Ed Wynn, fresh from *Mary Poppins*, has a hilarious few minutes as a querulous clockmaker, petrified by the FBI saying they 'won't forget him'.

That Forsyte Woman ○

(aka: The Forsyte Saga)
1948, US, 114 mins, colour
Dir: Compton Bennett
Stars: Greer Garson, Walter Pidgeon, Errol Flynn, Janet Leigh
Rating: ★★★

Metro-Goldwyn-Mayer's lavish, colourful version of the first part of Galsworthy's Forsyte odyssey, concentrating on the fortunes of Irene. This is not surprising, as Greer Garson, who plays her, was one of the studio's biggest stars of the time.

That Hamilton Woman
See: Lady Hamilton

That Jane from Maine
See: It Happened to Jane

That'll Be the Day ◑ Ⓥ
1973, UK, 91 mins, colour
Dir: Claude Whatham
Stars: David Essex, Ringo Starr, James Booth
Rating: ★★

A curiously flat rendition of the Fifties, with David Essex manfully shouldering a lead role that isn't always sympathetic. Good cameo work from Ringo Starr and Keith Moon, both hinting at the excesses which were to feature in the sequel, *Stardust*.

That Lucky Touch ○
1975, UK, 90 mins, colour
Dir: Christopher Miles
Stars: Roger Moore, Susannah York, Shelley Winters, Lee J Cobb
Rating: ★

Director Christopher Miles' location scenes in Brussels here recall his earlier work in *Time for Loving*. That was a film with great feel for romantic atmosphere, and indeed it is the romantic moments that work best in this silly comedy about an arms dealer and a crusading journalist. It really needs Cary Grant and Katharine Hepburn to make it work properly (here the leads are Roger Moore and Susannah York) and the plot is so thin that the dialogue needs to be as slick, smart and steely as possible to make it stand up. Shelley Winters has the best lines, but it's Raf Vallone who gets the closest to hitting the right note with his performance as an amorous Italian brass-hat.

That Man from Rio ○
(aka: L'Homme de Rio)
1964, France, 120 mins, colour
Dir: Phillippe De Broca
Stars: Jean-Paul Belmondo, Françoise Dorleac
Rating: ★★★

This hectic French comedy-thriller was one of the first, and best, spoofs of the James Bond films. Hero Jean-Paul Belmondo is pitched from crisis to crisis in a style of which Pearl White would have been proud.

That Midnight Kiss ○
1949, US, 96 mins, colour
Dir: Norman Taurog

Stars: Mario Lanza, Kathryn Grayson, Jose Iturbi, Ethel Barrymore
Rating: ★★

Mario Lanza made his starring screen debut in this sugary MGM musical produced by Joe Pasternak, the man behind Deanna Durbin's successes at Universal in the Thirties. The plot is the standard one of an unknown making good, well used as a showcase for Lanza's singing talents, solo and with his co-star Kathryn Grayson, offering a musical feast for his fans. Even Keenan Wynn gets in on the act, leading a quartet with 'Down Among the Sheltering Palms'.

That Old Feeling ◑ Ⓥ
1996, US, 102 mins, colour
Dir: Carl Reiner
Stars: Bette Midler, Dennis Farina, Paula Marshall, Danny Nucci, Gail O'Grady, David Rasche
Rating: ★★

A change-your-partners romantic comedy with an equal share of good lines and slack scenes. Every meeting of bride-to-be Marshall's divorced parents (Midler, Farina) is like a nuclear war. Until, that is, Paula's marriage to stuffed shirt senatorial candidate Jamie Denton. After the usual massive rows, the amorous spark between Midler and Farina re-ignites. Awash with that old feeling, they run off together, to the consternation of *his* wife (O'Grady), who beds the bridegroom, and *her* husband (Rasche), a therapist who blames the whole thing on the purchase of his third dog. Daughter Paula pursues the errant pair, together with the paparazzi photographer Nucci, for whom she gradually gets that old feeling... When it's showing warmth and wit, the film is good to be with, but too much of it is taken up with raucous and unfunny quarrels. Midler is marvellous, and even sings a mellow, jazzy version of *Somewhere Along the Way*.

That Riviera Touch ○ Ⓥ
1966, UK, 98 mins, colour
Dir: Cliff Owen
Stars: Eric Morecambe, Ernie Wise
Rating: ★★

Eric Morecambe and Ernie Wise never seemed to hit it off on the big screen, where producers unsuccessfully tried to open out their intimate style of humour. Much the same sort of thing happened to Laurel and Hardy in the early Forties. This is the best of the three Morecambe and Wise films, with a comic cliffhanger climax in finest

Harold Lloyd traditions. Fired from their humdrum jobs in a chocolate-making factory, Eric and Ernie decide to splash their (well, actually Eric's) savings on a glorious spree on the French Riviera.

That Thing You Do! ○ Ⓥ
1996, US, 106 mins, colour
Dir: Tom Hanks
Stars: Tom Everett Scott, Johnathan Schaech, Liv Tyler, Steve Zahn, Ethan Embry, Tom Hanks
Rating: ★★

A pleasant little film for most of the time, though it tails away at the end, Hanks' debut as a movie director – he also (mistakenly) plays a featured role – has the same fault as Alan Parker's superior *The Commitments*. The break-up of the band at such an early stage – in this case even before their first record has reached number one – just isn't believable. Neither is the break-up of the lead singer (Schaech) and his girlfriend (Tyler) so that she can conveniently fall into the arms of the drummer (Scott) who's become the central character in the story. The music, though, is toe-tappingly good, the recreation of the 1960s more or less authentic and, if the title number is flogged to death, well that's the way it would have been. As the boy's manager, Hanks lacks the requisite snarl that an actor like James Woods might have brought to the role. Best thing in the film is ironically Hanks' wife Rita Wilson as a sultry hostess in a bar.

That's Entertainment ⊙ Ⓥ
1974, US, 122 mins, colour & b/w
Dir: Jack Haley Jr
Stars: Fred Astaire, Bing Crosby, Gene Kelly, Peter Lawford
Rating: ★★★★

The history of MGM musicals gives us rather too much of its commentators and rather too little of the actual films, but it's a small quibble at a magnificent spectrum of musical entertainment, with such inevitable gems as Gene Kelly 'Singin' in the Rain' being balanced by such amusing oddities as Cary Grant, James Stewart and Clark Gable exercising their tonsils in rare bursts of song. The film is also a feast for Judy Garland fans. It seems to take in something from almost every MGM film she made.

That's Entertainment – Part II ⊙ Ⓥ
1976, US, 121 mins, colour, b/w
Dir: Gene Kelly

T

Stars: Doris Day, Gene Kelly, Fred Astaire
Rating: ★★★★

Criticised at the time it came out for not being quite as good as *That's Entertainment* (how could it be? – that was *la crème de la crème*), this sequel is still a glorious wallow in mainly musical nostalgia, featuring literally scores of clips from MGM films spanning the years 1929 to 1958. Our personal favourites from a good crop of musical numbers include Leslie Caron singing 'Hi Lili Hi Lo', 'Now You Has Jazz' by Bing Crosby and Louis Armstrong from *High Society* and Fred Astaire and Judy Garland dressed as tramps singing 'A Couple of Swells' from *Easter Parade*. Comedy gets its fair share of the limelight, too, with Laurel and Hardy sinking into roadworks in their car from *Leave 'Em Laughing*, the cabin sequence from the Marx Brothers' *A Night at the Opera*, and W C Fields letting David Copperfield in on the perils of high finance.

That's Entertainment! III ⊙ ⓥ
1994, US, 113 mins, colour & b/w
Dir: Various
Stars: June Allyson, Ann Miller, Debbie Reynolds, Cyd Charisse, Mickey Rooney, Gene Kelly
Rating: ★★★★

The attraction of this addition to previous collections of MGM musical highlights from 1930 to 1960 is the amount of discarded numbers that have been retrieved from the vaults. Thus, for the first time, we can see the torchlit 'March of the Dogies' from *The Harvey Girls*, a Judy Garland solo called 'Mr Monotony', take away the opening credits under which Astaire and Rogers were forced to dance in *The Barkleys of Broadway* and hear Ava Gardner's real singing voice (dubbed at the last minute) from *Show Boat*. The narration by nine ageing luminaries is pretty hammy (June Allyson and Lena Horne are the best of a poor bunch), but no matter – the excerpts speak for themselves. The accent here is on novelty, from Gene Kelly and Donald O'Connor as fiddling fools in *Singin' in the Rain*, through Joan Crawford in blackface and Lena Horne in a bubble bath (another outtake) to Betty Hutton and Howard Keel in *Anything You Can Do* from *Annie Get your Gun*.

That Sinking Feeling ○ ⓥ
1979, UK, 92 mins, colour
Dir: Bill Forsyth

Stars: Robert Buchanan, John Hughes, Janette Rankin
Rating: ★★★

A delightful early comedy from director Bill Forsyth (who subsequently made *Gregory's Girl* and *Local Hero*) about a group of young Glaswegians on the dole who come to the conclusion that there must be something more to life than contemplating suicide and decide to do something (a trifle illegal) about it. Fresh and funny.

That's Life! ◑ ⓥ
1986, US, 102 mins, colour
Dir: Blake Edwards
Stars: Jack Lemmon, Julie Andrews, Sally Kellerman, Robert Loggia
Rating: ★★★

The character of Harvey Fairchild could have been written for Jack Lemmon. Harvey's acute hypochondria begets the kind of comedy of desperation in which Lemmon's expertise has become a byword. Approaching his 60th birthday, Harvey thinks he has blood pressure, heart trouble, impotency and allergies galore and his doctor can't find a thing wrong with him. Harvey doesn't exactly seem a true-life character but, if he were, Lemmon wouldn't be able to get so much anguished fun out of him. What he doesn't know is that his wife (Julie Andrews) really does have something to worry about – a throat tumour that may be malignant or benign. If all this sounds less than a barrel of laughs, there are times when that's true. But, in between, the script is peppered with enough amusing one-liners to pull it through.

That's My Boy ⊙
1951, US, 98 mins, b/w
Dir: Hal Walker
Stars: Jerry Lewis, Dean Martin
Rating: ★★

This football-flavoured comedy was the second major film vehicle for Martin and his then-partner Jerry Lewis. The film isn't terribly good, but the public totally ignored critical opinion and had made the team America's top film attractions by the following year. Much of their thunder is stolen here by raucous Eddie Mayehoff, as Lewis' domineering father, but the comedy routines drop to earth with a dull thud and, as with the boys' *The Stooge* a year later, it's the sentimental aspects of the plot which work best.

That Was Then, This Is Now ● ⓥ
1985, US, 100 mins, colour
Dir: Christopher Cain
Stars: Emilio Estevez, Craig Sheffer, Kim Delaney, Jill Schoelen, Barbara Babcock, Morgan Freeman
Rating: ★

The appeal of American teenage angst, a popular subject in the early Eighties, was noticeably wearing thin here, as it became apparent that the novels of S E Hinton, once the hottest properties around, were played out as acceptable film material. Although there are moments when you feel for the characters and want their story to go on, there are rather more when you just want to close your eyes and forget about them. Emilio Estevez wrote it as well as starring as the maybe-psychotic, maybe homosexual, but for sure confused friend of hero Craig Sheffer, whose acquiring of a girlfriend is something he can't accept. Estevez even gives off some reverberations of a young Kirk Douglas in this role, but the film is stolen from everybody by that earthy actress Barbara Babcock as Sheffer's mother.

Thelma & Louise ● ⓥ
1991, US, 130 mins, colour
Dir: Ridley Scott
Stars: Susan Sarandon, Geena Davis, Harvey Keitel, Michael Madsen, Brad Pitt
Rating: ★★★★

A road movie with female companions is quite unusual. Quite how Thelma and Louise go off on a fishing holiday and end up cornered by dozens of police cars in the Grand Canyon takes some explaining and some hard-to-swallow turns of the plot. Fortunately, the performances of Sarandon and Davis (both Oscar-nominated) keep this vehicle, as well as their '66 Cadillac, on the road, despite a sight too many 'travelling' shots and little scenes that could have been lost altogether. But if you can believe in: the girls taking a gun (not too difficult), Davis encountering a rapist at their first motel (a bit less easy), Sarandon shooting the man (for a motive explained later), their happening to encounter a travelling bandit, and Davis robbing a store and disarming a policeman, to say nothing of Sarandon phoning the pursuing police chief (Harvey Keitel) to discuss the case, then you're in for a fine time. 'Thelma,' says Sarandon, 'You are disturbed.' 'Yes,' beams Davis, 'I believe I am.'

Thelma Jordon
See: The File on Thelma Jordon

Them! ●
1954, US, 95 mins, b/w
Dir: Gordon Douglas
Stars: James Whitmore, Edmund Gwenn, Joan Weldon, James Arness, Onslow Stevens, Fess Parker
Rating: ★★★

This famous science-fiction thriller was so good (and popular) that it started a whole new syndrome of giant-animal horror films. Even the performances are solid down the line: James Whitmore, as a heroically tough policeman, takes most of the honours, but little Sandy Descher is excellent as the terrified little girl who appears at the beginning and big James Arness, as an FBI agent, as much the man of action as in his TV days as Matt Dillon. Excellent trick photography and ingenious special effects add to the excitement. The tableau of the 'monsters' in their collective lair at the end is unpleasant but unforgettable. Starspotters will notice Leonard Nimoy in a very minor role.

There's a Girl In My Soup ○ Ⓥ
1970, UK, 95 mins, colour
Dir: Roy Boulting
Stars: Peter Sellers, Goldie Hawn
Rating: ★★

Terence Frisby's long-running comedy play was obviously a must for a film with two big stars, and eventually Peter Sellers and Goldie Hawn landed the roles. Hawn is in especially good form as the dumb blonde who confounds Sellers' bon-viveur with a unique blend of corruption and innocence.

There's No Business Like Show Business ○ Ⓥ
1954, US, 117 mins, colour
Dir: Walter Lang
Stars: Ethel Merman, Donald O'Connor, Marilyn Monroe, Dan Dailey, Mitzi Gaynor, Johnnie Ray
Rating: ★★★

Big, gaudy Irving Berlin musical, awash with clichés and saving the biggest of all for a tearful reunion scene at the end. Of its six major stars, Mitzi Gaynor shows up best; she gives her role any amount of bounce and vitality. Dan Dailey's also good while Marilyn Monroe weighs in with two of her best-remembered songs, 'Heatwave' and 'After You Get What You Want You Don't Want It'. Ethel Merman is, as usual, larger than life as

the mother hen with greasepaint in her veins, and there's also 'crying' crooner Johnnie Ray in one of his very rare film roles.

There Was a Crooked Man ... ○
1970, US, 125 mins, colour
Dir: Joseph L Mankiewicz
Stars: Kirk Douglas, Henry Fonda, Hume Cronyn
Rating: ★★★★

Kirk Douglas playing one of the smiling rogues that he did so well. He dominates this Western film as Paris Pitman Junior, a scurrilous but immensely likeable master thief making plans to escape from an impregnable territorial prison and collect his buried loot. It's a richly entertaining tale.

These Thousand Hills ○
960, US, 96 mins, colour
Dir: Richard Fleischer
Stars: Don Murray, Richard Egan, Lee Remick
Rating: ★★

Firmly directed by Richard Fleischer, this well characterised Western is about two cowboys who antagonise a flashy rancher/gambler, and pay a heavy price. Richard Egan enjoys himself in a rare villain role. Don Murray and Lee Remick also take advantage of a satisfying and well-structured script by Alfred Hayes.

These Three ○
1936, US, 93 mins, b/w
Dir: William Wyler
Stars: Miriam Hopkins, Merle Oberon
Rating: ★★★★

As controversial themes were strictly taboo in the Hollywood of the Thirties, it was plain that there would have to be some changes made to *The Children's Hour*, Lillian Hellman's successful play about a latently lesbian affair, and the consequences when a vicious schoolgirl spills the beans. Fortunately, as so often happened in those studio-dominated days, the revised version that appeared on screen made just as strong, if different, entertainment. Hellman herself brilliantly adapted her play into a straightforward romantic triangle, and there's a scene-stealing performance from Bonita Granville as the nasty teenager. Director William Wyler got unusually low-key performances from both his highly-strung female stars, Miriam Hopkins and Merle Oberon, that heightened one's sympathy for their characters.

They All Died Laughing
(See: A Jolly Bad Fellow)

They Call Me MISTER Tibbs! ◐
1970, US, 108 mins, colour
Dir: Gordon Douglas
Stars: Sidney Poitier, Martin Landau, Barbara McNair, Anthony Zerbe
Rating: ★★

The second of three films featuring Sidney Poitier as tough city cop Virgil Tibbs, this time investigating the violent murder of a prostitute. The prime suspect is Tibbs' close friend, an activist priest, played by Martin Landau. While the character of Tibbs is hardly fleshed out at all, Landau does a magnificent job at creating a well-rounded figure of a guilt-ridden cleric. Poitier was allowed to direct several scenes that he didn't appear in, but it's hardly a distinguished affair in the same class as the earlier Tibbs outing, *In the Heat of the Night*.

They Came to Cordura ○
1959, US, 123 mins, colour
Dir: Robert Rossen
Stars: Gary Cooper, Rita Hayworth, Van Heflin, Tab Hunter, Richard Conte
Rating: ★★★

Rugged and punishing action film about seven people on an arduous Mexican desert trek in 1916. Bursts of action and bags of hot atmosphere.

They Died With Their Boots On ○ Ⓥ
1941, US, 140 mins, b/w
Dir: Raoul Walsh
Stars: Errol Flynn, Olivia de Havilland, Arthur Kennedy, Anthony Quinn
Rating: ★★★

Rousing if historically inaccurate picture of General George Armstrong's career – culminating in a thrilling portrayal of the battle of Little Big Horn. As a long-haired, hippie-type Custer, fighting Indians and red tape with equal dash, Errol Flynn was the embodiment of every boy's idea of a Western hero, and every girl's dream. Expertly directed by Raoul Walsh, and packed with splendidly staged battles, it remains one of the screen's more impressive epic Westerns.

They Drive By Night ○
1938, UK, 84 mins, b/w
Dir: Arthur Woods
Stars: Emlyn Williams, Anna Konstam, Ernest Thesiger
Rating: ★★★

T

Not to be confused with the George Raft/Humphrey Bogart film of the same name, this is an excellent atmospheric black thriller directed by Arthur Woods, a promising British director killed during World War Two. Emlyn Williams gives a dominant performance as the man just released from prison who finds himself in desperate straits when he comes under suspicion of murders committed by a psychotic strangler. Racy direction from Woods makes the film's 80-odd minutes fly by; good photography, too, from Basil Emmott, most of it at night.

They Drive By Night ○
1940, US, 93 mins, b/w
Dir: Raoul Walsh
Stars: George Raft, Ann Sheridan, Humphrey Bogart, Ida Lupino
Rating: ★★★★

This trucking drama (later developing into a courtroom thriller) has a formidable Warners star quartet in George Raft, Ann Sheridan, Humphrey Bogart (his last film before stardom at last overtook him in *High Sierra*) and Ida Lupino. Lupino's unforgettable performance as a psychotic wife puts the other stars well in the shade, and established the British-born actress as one of Hollywood's most powerful portrayers of neurotic women.

They Got Me Covered ○ Ⓥ
1943, US, 95 mins, b/w
Dir: David Butler
Stars: Bob Hope, Dorothy Lamour, Otto Preminger
Rating: ★★★

Hailed at the time of its release as Bob Hope's best film, this comedy has Hope as the Moscow correspondent of an American agency who achieves journalism's greatest reverse scoop by missing the German invasion of Russia. Muscling in on the act are a sarong-less Dorothy Lamour plus Otto Preminger, Edward (Eduardo) Cianelli and Philip Ahn, who give neat burlesques of enemy agents as Hollywood used to see them.

They Live! ● Ⓥ
1988, US, 95 mins, colour
Dir: John Carpenter
Stars: Roddy Piper, Keith David, Meg Foster
Rating: ★★

A lively science-fiction adventure somewhat along the lines of *Invasion of the Body Snatchers*. Aliens have taken over, but the man in the street doesn't know it – until he puts his dark glasses

on. How the freedom fighters could have found out that a certain kind of glass revealed an alien to them is only one of the many holes in the plot – but the tale is fun while it lasts. Roddy Piper is a hero far too dozy to ever expose the aliens nationwide – he can't twig one enemy agent even after she throws him out of a window when he offers her the dark glasses – then convinces him she didn't realise he was 'in the know'. Lots of stuntmen fling themselves around as Piper closes in on the alien transmission: mindless but enjoyable.

They Made Me a Criminal ○ Ⓥ
1939, US, 92 mins, b/w
Dir: Busby Berkeley
Stars: John Garfield, Claude Rains
Rating: ★★★

This, John Garfield's third starring film, confirmed his status as Warner Brothers' new tough guy. He plays a boxer who, believing he has killed a reporter in a drunken brawl, goes on the run. He ends up in Arizona, working on a farm which is also a rehabilitation centre for New York slum kids. As you might expect, helping the kids reforms the boozy, womanising, selfish Garfield. He is on good form as the central character, but is given a run for his money by the Dead End Kids as the young offenders. Although miscast, Claude Rains is enjoyable as the police detective on Garfield's trail. The director, perhaps surprisingly, is Busby Berkeley, more famous for his extravagantly staged musicals. Berkeley pleaded with Warners to give him something other than a musical to direct and this was the result. His skills as a choreographer are still evident in the well-staged and (for the time) realistic boxing scenes.

They Met in Bombay ○
1941, US, 100 mins, b/w
Dir: Clarence Brown
Stars: Clark Gable, Rosalind Russell, Peter Lorre
Rating: ★★★

An opulent adventure story set in the troubled Far East shortly before Pearl Harbor. And thousands of splendidly dressed extras swarm through the streets of Bombay, from which jewel thieves Clark Gable and Rosalind Russell flee when the going gets too hot – straight into the arms of rascally Peter Lorre, who not only threatens to turn them in, but steals the film as well. It's no great movie, but the stars

are fun to be with, and you'll spot Alan Ladd in a minor role.

They Might Be Giants ○
1971, US, 98 mins, colour
Dir: Anthony Harvey
Stars: Joanne Woodward, George C Scott, Jack Gifford
Rating: ★★★

Fiction's most famous detective, the Baker Street sleuth Sherlock Holmes, has figured in many a motion picture but never before in quite the way he's involved in this film. In James Goldman's adaptation of his own stage play, the central figure (George C Scott) is a man who, facing an emotional crisis, retreats into a private fantasy world, becoming a replica in outlook and behaviour of the immortal Holmes. He finds his Dr Watson in a psychiatrist of that name (played by Joanne Woodward in one of her best, superbly controlled performances) whom he persuades to help him in his quest for Holmes's dreaded archenemy Moriarty.

They Rode West ○
1954, US, 97 mins, colour
Dir: Phil Karlson
Stars: Robert Francis, Donna Reed, Phil Carey, May Wynn
Rating: ★★★

A thinking man's Western, directed in the John Ford manner by Phil Karlson. Richly photographed in Technicolor by the experienced Charles Lawton, it has strong performances from Robert Francis, as the caring young doctor out west, Donna Reed and Phil Carey. Francis, a most promising leading man, was killed in 1955 in a plane crash.

They Shoot Horses, Don't They? ◑ Ⓥ
1969, US, 129 mins, colour
Dir: Sydney Pollack
Stars: Jane Fonda, Michael Sarrazin, Susannah York, Gig Young, Bruce Dern, Red Buttons
Rating: ★★★

Gig Young got his Oscar for playing the promoter of a Thirties dance marathon. We are given a depressing view of humanity, but it's fascinating.

They Were Expendable ○
1945, US, 135 mins, b/w
Dir: John Ford
Stars: Robert Montgomery, John Wayne, Donna Reed
Rating: ★★★

John Ford's moving salute to the American torpedo crews in the Pacific during World War Two is an episodic but passionate drama that shows the pain, loneliness and sacrifice of war. Ford packed one poignant and powerful scene after another into this film and got so carried away that he fell from scaffolding and broke a leg. Star Robert Montgomery, who also gives the best performance, took over the directing chores for the last two weeks of filming. The movie's battle scenes are particularly impressive, but it's now a little dated in places and generally difficult to follow.

They Who Dare ○
1953, UK, 107 mins, colour
Dir: Lewis Milestone
Stars: Dirk Bogarde, Denholm Elliott, Akim Tamiroff, Kay Callard
Rating: ★★

A distant wartime ancestor of *Who Dares Wins*, as men of the special Boat Service launch a daring expedition to blow up German-held Aegean airfields. Dirk Bogarde, Denholm Elhott and Akim Tamiroff provide plenty of personality behind the sweat and grime, and the too-sparse action is brilliantly photographed in Technicolor by Wilkie Cooper.

They Won't Believe Me ○
1947, US, 95 mins, b/w
Dir: Irving Pichel
Stars: Robert Young, Susan Hayward, Jane Greer, Rita Johnson
Rating: ★★★

And you won't believe the ending, either, to this otherwise fine dark thriller about a man involved with three women. It was essentially a cop-out to skirt around the then severe censorial requirements. Jane Greer, Susan Hayward and Rita Johnson give vivid portrayals which unfortunately put a somewhat miscast Robert Young rather in the shade.

Thief
See: Violent Streets

Thief of Bagdad, The ⊙ ⓥ
1924, US, 155 mins, b/w
Dir: Raoul Walsh
Stars: Douglas Fairbanks
Rating: ★★★

Acclaimed at the time as 'the furthest and most sudden advance films have made', this was Douglas Fairbanks' most ambitious production, wildly and wonderfully extravagant, and filled

with magical special effects far ahead of their time.

Thief of Bagdad, The ⊙
1940, US/UK, 109 mins, colour
Dir: Michael Powell, Tim Whelan
Stars: Conrad Veidt, Sabu, June Duprez, John Justin
Rating: ★★★★

This spectacular *Arabian Nights* fantasy provided plum parts for Conrad Veidt, as the wicked Grand Vizier, and black actor Rex Ingram, as the giant djinn. John Justin and June Duprez make a striking romantic team in this magical adventure whose special effects look amateurish now, but were then sensational. Some scenes just bulge with imagination.

Thief of Baghdad, The ⊙
1961, Italy, 90 mins, colour
Dir: Arthur Lubin
Stars: Steve Reeves
Rating: ★★

Third screen version of the famous *Arabian Nights* tale of a thief who falls in love with a princess, and has to brave all sorts of dangers to win her. It was Reeves' attempt at a breakaway from pure musclemen roles. And although it's not as good as the Douglas Fairbanks Sr (1924) or Sabu (1940) versions, the trick photography is clever, and the children will enjoy every minute of the fun.

Thief of Baghdad, The ○
1978, UK, 100 mins, colour
Dir: Clive Donner
Stars: Roddy McDowall, Terence Stamp
Rating: ★★

The most recent film version of the famous *Arabian Nights* story, complete with such ingredients as the magic carpet, the wicked wazir, the All-Seeing Eye and the Temple of Truth. Peter Ustinov does a variation on his baffled panda act as the cuddly caliph. Terence Stamp's wazir, flapping in on his black cloak like a living corpse, is clearly a dry run for his villains in the Superman movies and the stage version of *Dracula*. French actor Daniel Emilfork also scores with his mischievously grinning genie. The juvenile leads, as in previous versions, are good looking but negligible.

Thief Who Came to Dinner, The ○
1973, US, 105 mins, colour
Dir: Bud Yorkin
Stars: Ryan O'Neal, Jacqueline Bisset
Rating: ★★★

With one of her most delicious performances, Jill Clayburgh entirely steals this entertaining comedy-thriller about a computer analyst turned jewel thief whose plot might itself have rolled out of a computer. Clayburgh makes the most of some nice throwaway lines in a film whose disparate elements are all permitted by director Bud Yorkin to pursue their own course at their own pace. Ryan O'Neal is the thief. Superficial but pleasing entertainment.

Thieves' Highway ○
1949, US, 94 mins, b/w
Dir: Jules Dassin
Stars: Richard Conte, Valentina Cortesa, Lee J Cobb
Rating: ★★★★

Rough, tough, no-holds-barred story of California truckers battling against corrupt wholesalers quite happy to stoop to murder to get things done their way. This was shot against genuine locations, in this case arterial roads in and around San Francisco. The sense of imminent threat is well-maintained by director Jules Dassin throughout the film, and there's a wagonload of tension and excitement on the roads.

Thieves Like Us ⓒ
1973, US, 123 mins, colour
Dir: Robert Altman
Stars: Keith Carradine, Shelley Duvall, John Schuck
Rating: ★

A long and very protracted film from Robert Altman (about three bank robbers in the Thirties) whose very length robs it of much of its intended impact. Keith Carradine is too impersonal as the youngest robber, Shelley Duvall better as his backwoods moll and John Schuck horrifyingly homicidal as the drinker of the three. It has its excitements and the Thirties radio programmes used as background are fascinating.

Thin Line Between Love and Hate, A ● ⓥ
1996, US, 108 mins, colour
Dir: Martin Lawrence
Stars: Lawrence, Lynn Whitfield, Regina King, Bobby Brown, Della Reese, Roger E Mosley
Rating: ★

Eddie Murphy look-alike Lawrence comes as big a cropper here as Murphy himself did with *Harlem Nights*. Like Murphy, Lawrence wears too many hats (as director, star, exec producer, co-writer and story supplier) and never looks like getting to grips

T

with a *Fatal Attraction*-style story. He's Darnell, a cruising Casanova who, remembers Carmen Jones' cry of 'If you're hard to get I go for you' by ditching a string of chicks and making a beeline for chic Brandi (Whitfield) who at first rebuffs his advance. Once bedded, this bawd proves a scorned fury when Darnell opts to go back to his 'safer' childhood sweetheart (King). The ending is lively, but not that much less feeble than the rest of the story. Lawrence's performance is incredibly self-indulgent, Whitfield okay and King below her usual par. Forgettable.

Thing, The ● Ⓥ
1982, US, 108 mins, colour
Dir: John Carpenter
Stars: Kurt Russell, A Wilford Brimley
Rating: ★★

John Carpenter's visceral remake of the famous 1951 horror film, about an alien at large in the Antarctic that takes the form of those it destroys. Carpenter's aim is to make you jump out of your seat and maybe hide behind it as well. Watch out!

Thing Called Love, The ◐ Ⓥ
1993, US, 114 mins, colour
Dir: Peter Bogdanovich
Stars: River Phoenix, Samantha Mathis, Dermot Mulroney, Sandra Bullock
Rating: ★★

Once upon a time, there would have been a rush to release the final film of a newly deceased teen idol star. After River Phoenix's death, though, this was barely released in America and went straight to video elsewhere, an odd decision, since Peter Bogdanovich's Country and Western romance, though not without flaws, has a good deal of charm. The story's plain but sweet: four aspiring young Country singer-songwriters descend on Nashville's famous Bluebird Cafe for auditions – but get bogged down by the thing called love. A cast of rising Hollywood stars does quite well with this innocuous but charmingly played romance.

Thing (From Another World), The ◐
1951, US, 95 mins, b/w
Dir: Christian Nyby
Stars: Margaret Sheridan, Kenneth Tobey, James Arness
Rating: ★★★

The great Howard Hawks supervised production (and, it is said, direction)

on this classic science-fiction thriller. The film is so well made, in fact, that even its more absurd implausibilities carry some measure of conviction under the guidance of Hawks, director Christian Nyby and screenplay writer Charles Lederer. And Dimitri Tiomkin contributes a notable music score. The 'Thing' itself is played by 6ft 8in James Arness, later to win fame as Marshal Dillon in TV's *Gunsmoke*.

Things Change ○ Ⓥ
1988, US, 96 mins, colour
Dir: David Mamet
Stars: Don Ameche, Joe Mantegna, Robert Prosky
Rating: ★★

A gentle, amusing, well-played but slow gangster comedy. The games in this film begin when Gino (Don Ameche), a shoe repairer who happens to resemble a notorious Mafia hit-man, is persuaded to confess to a gangland killing in return for money, security on release and the fulfilment of his dream – a boat. Now the bad guys don't exactly intend to stick to their end of the bargain, but Gino doesn't know this, and neither does Jerry, a gangster (Joe Mantegna) whose 'probationary' assignment after a bungled job is to look after Gino for a few days before the trial. Fed up, and taking pity on the shoeshop 'Mafioso', Jerry sweeps him off to Lake Tahoe for a couple of days, where things change... and dramatically alter what would otherwise have been the logical ending of the film. Ameche and Mantegna are excellent, but the treatment of their story is too low-key and far too leisurely to make this outstanding entertainment.

Things to Come ○
1936, UK, 97 mins, b/w
Dir: William Cameron Menzies
Stars: Raymond Massey, Cedric Hardwicke, Edward Chapman, Ralph Richardson
Rating: ★★★

H G Wells' classic science-fiction saga translated to the screen with superb sets and great imagination by director William Cameron Menzies' team. Cedric Hardwicke, brought in to replace another British actor, as Theotocopulos, is reported to have said: 'My work in *Things to Come* was completed with such speed and lack of ceremony, that the actor I had replaced had no idea that his entire performance lay on the cutting room floor... until he went to the premiere with a party of expectant friends.'

Things to Do in Denver When You're Dead ●
1995, US, 120 mins, colour
Dir: Gary Fleder
Stars: Andy Garcia, Christopher Walken, Gabrielle Anwar, Treat Williams, Fairuza Balk, Jack Warden, Christopher Lloyd
Rating: ★

Grim, harrowing, unrelenting and ultra-violent – all of which might be acceptable if it were in any way believable – this is not the film to rent for a relaxing evening. Andy Garcia plays an ex-gangster called back for one last job by his ex-boss. This turns out to be Christopher Walken as another of his stupid sub-Bondian villains, blowing a tube to move his wheelchair and getting stroked in the sauna by his ridiculously curvy nurse. Walken just wants his simpleton son's ex-girl's new beau frightened off. Quite why seasoned pro Garcia (now running an afterlife service where dying relatives tape advice to their loved ones) should be called in for this, or why he needs four obviously unreliable associates to help him, isn't clear; there are signs here and there that this might have started out as a black comedy, but debutant director Gary Fleder can't get a handle on that, or much else. Suffice to say, the job goes wrong, the boy and girl are killed and Garcia & Co are doomed. Nobody wins – least of all the viewer.

Thin Ice ○
1937, US, 78 mins, b/w
Dir: Sidney Lanfield
Stars: Sonja Henie, Tyrone Power
Rating: ★★

With this, her second (and best) film, skating champion Sonja Henie briefly became Hollywood's highest-paid female star, with earnings in excess of $200,000 for the year. The fun-filled romantic musical (based on a Viennese operetta) contains an excellent role for rubber-faced comedienne Joan Davis. Here she makes a big hit with the film's great novelty number 'I'm Olga from the Volga'. The movie was first shown in Britain as *Lovely to Look At*.

Think Dirty
See: Every Home Should Have One

Thin Man, The ○
1934, US, 93 mins, b/w
Dir: W S Van Dyke
Stars: William Powell, Myrna Loy
Rating: ★★★★

Nick Charles and his wife Nora (personified by William Powell and Myrna

Loy) were the most sophisticated sleuths the screen had seen – a clue in one hand and a champagne cocktail in the other. Nick, in fact, seemed to be in a permanent state of semi-inebriation, but that didn't stop him from bringing a number of murderers to book between 1934 and 1947, the dates of the first and last of the *Thin Man* films. The Thin Man himself is a character from this snappy first adventure, but the soubriquet gradually became attached to Powell himself, who was hardly slim enough to warrant it. Myrna Loy, however, was pencil-slim, and the role of Nora Charles got her away from a string of oriental temptresses and well up the ladder towards becoming the Queen of Hollywood, a title she won in a nation-wide poll.

Thin Man Goes Home, The ○
1944, US, 100 mins, b/w
Dir: Richard Thorpe
Stars: William Powell, Myrna Loy
Rating: ★★★

This later adventure of sophisticated sleuths Nick and Nora Charles suffers from the demands of wartime on the plot, and from the fact that Woody Van Dyke, who had directed previous films in the series, had just died. And the dialogue for Myrna Loy as Nora is flat champagne compared with previous scripts. But William Powell is in his usual smooth form as Nick, and a whole gallery of familiar character actors from the period enjoy themselves immensely as the various suspects in the case of the murdered painter.

Third Key, The
See: The Long Arm

Third Man, The ○ ⓥ
1949, UK, 104 mins, b/w
Dir: Carol Reed
Stars: Joseph Cotten, Alida Valli, Orson Welles, Trevor Howard, Wilfrid Hyde White
Rating: ★★★★★

Welles' last great Forties' role, as Harry Lime, master-criminal at large in a post-war Vienna of fairs and ruins, shapes and shadows. They seek him here, they seek him there. Harry Lime is presumed dead, but there can be few filmgoers now who don't know that he turns out to be alive, and ultimately pursued through the sewers of the city by Joseph Cotten, Trevor Howard, Bernard Lee, and Anton Karas' insistent zither music, which hooked itself into the minds of the world. There's

devastating photography by Robert Krasker (deservedly winning an Oscar), and inspired direction by Carol Reed. Not to be missed.

Thirty-Nine Steps, The ○ ⓥ
1935, UK, 87 mins, b/w
Dir: Alfred Hitchcock
Stars: Robert Donat, Madeleine Carroll, Godfrey Tearle, Peggy Ashcroft
Rating: ★★★★★

Outstanding Alfred Hitchcock version of the John Buchan thriller which subsequent remakes have struggled in vain to emulate. Excitement and suspense are skilfully maintained by the director, whose stitching together of a pattern of telling individual scenes makes for a memorable film. Atmospheric black-and-white photography by Bernard Knowles provides a compelling backcloth to alert, witty performances by Robert Donat and Madeleine Carroll with vivid supporting contributions from Godfrey Tearle, Wylie Watson (as Mr Memory), Peggy Ashcroft and Lucie Mannheim.

39 Steps, The ○
1959, UK, 93 mins, colour
Dir: Ralph Thomas
Stars: Kenneth More, Taina Elg
Rating: ★★

When John Buchan wrote *The 39 Steps* at the outbreak of World War One, he could hardly foresee that it would eventually lead to a peerage (although he showed his gratitude by knighting his hero, Richard Hannay, in a subsequent book). Hannay's unintentional forays into the world of espionage first attracted the attention of suspense master Alfred Hitchcock in 1935 and the resultant film was acclaimed as a classic. This later production, starring Kenneth More as Hannay, is an ambitious if doomed attempt to improve it still further. Wonderful Scottish scenery complements exciting sequences showing the first aerial manhunt – in fiction at any rate.

Thirty Nine Steps, The ○
1978, UK, 102 mins, colour
Dir: Don Sharp
Stars: Robert Powell, Karen Dotrice, John Mills
Rating: ★★★

This exciting version of the famous thriller is closer to John Buchan's original novel than any other, even if the Hitchcock 1935 film remains the best. Robert Powell again advanced his star career with his portrayal of Richard

Hannay, and there's some lovely colour photography of the Scottish countryside. The action set-pieces, if sometimes a little preposterous, are excitingly done by director Don Sharp, especially the climax on the face of Big Ben. There's a nice supporting performance from John Mills.

Thirty Seconds Over Tokyo ○
1944, US, 138 mins, b/w
Dir: Mervyn Leroy
Stars: Spencer Tracy, Van Johnson, Robert Walker, Phyllis Thaxter
Rating: ★★★

Quasi-documentary re-creation of the events which took place 131 days after the Japanese bombing of Pearl Harbor, the incident which brought the USA into World War Two in December 1941. The story is based on the account of one of the survivors of the retaliatory American bombing raid on the Japanese cities of Tokyo and Yokohama – Captain Ted W Lawson. He is played here by Van Johnson. Spencer Tracy gives his usual exemplary performance as the leader of the mission and look out for a young Robert Mitchum and, well down the cast, Blake Edwards, director of the *Pink Panther* films.

37.2° le Matin
See: Betty Blue

36 Hours ○
1964, US, 104 mins, b/w
Dir: George Seaton
Stars: James Garner, Eva Marie Saint, Rod Taylor
Rating: ★★★

Unusual war thriller about an American officer who is made to believe that the war is over so that he will talk of the Normandy invasion plans to his Nazi captors. James Garner and Eva Marie Saint turn in solid performances under George Seaton's workmanlike direction. But the really great performance in the film comes from Rod Taylor, unusually cast but memorable as an American-speaking dedicated German doctor.

This Above All ○
1942, US, 110 mins, b/w
Dir: Anatole Litvak
Stars: Tyrone Power, Joan Fontaine, Thomas Mitchell
Rating: ★★★

This stylish World War Two morale-booster has Tyrone Power as a lower-middle-class Englishman who

T

deserts from the army because he does not believe in fighting for a country dominated by the upper class. But, naturally, he turns out to be a hero in the end, redeemed by his romance with Joan Fontaine. The screenplay was by English playwright R C Sherriff. Anatole Litvak directed in a studio-bound Hollywood version of Britain which won an Oscar for art directors Richard Day and Joseph Wright; another went to set decorator Thomas Little..

This Boy's Life ● Ⓥ
1993, US, 115 mins, colour
Dir: Michael Caton-Jones
Stars: Robert De Niro, Ellen Barkin, Leonardo DiCaprio
Rating: ★★

Thank goodness there's an upbeat ending to what is mostly a deeply unpleasant and depressing film about the teenage years of the writer Tobias Wolff. Toby (Leonardo DiCaprio) and his mother Caroline (Ellen Barkin) are discovered at the outset of the film on the run from her latest ill-chosen lover. Once in Seattle, Toby is soon on the verge of juvenile delinquency and, to provide a stable background, Caroline marries rough but seemingly benevolent and courteous Dwight Larsen (Robert De Niro). The wedding ring on, Dwight proves to be a ranting, bullying tyrant, determined to bestow Caroline no more favours and to knock her son into shape. The rest of the movie is a catalogue of oppression, repression and suppression, punctuated by Toby's exploits on the streets and at school. Barkin gives the best performance in this film by some little way, and the scene where she outshoots her new husband at a target contest, summing up her basic superiority, is one of the few moments of subtlety.

This Gun for Hire ○ Ⓥ
1942, US, 125 mins, b/w
Dir: Frank Tuttle
Stars: Veronica Lake, Robert Preston, Laird Cregar, Alan Ladd
Rating: ★★★★

Although clearly having the central role, Alan Ladd was actually billed fourth, after Veronica Lake, Laird Cregar and Robert Preston, in this adaptation of a Graham Greene thriller. However, the role of the expressionless killer of the title made the fair-haired, pint-sized Ladd a big star. A whole series of larger-than-life characters help director Frank Tuttle move

the story along in gripping style, although the photographer John Seitz can take all the credit for one of the film's most atmospheric sequences – a chase through freight yards.

This Happy Breed ○
1944, UK, 114 mins, colour
Dir: David Lean
Stars: Robert Newton, Celia Johnson, John Mills, Kay Walsh, Stanley Holloway
Rating: ★★★★

This sentimental and nostalgic look at the lives of an average British working-class family between the two world wars was David Lean's debut as a solo director and his first in Technicolor. Although not his greatest critical success, the film was hugely popular with the public; by toning down the more patronising aspects of Noel Coward's original play, Lean really captured the spirit of the people. And, to his great credit, he obtained one of Robert Newton's rare understated performances as the father of the family. The much-praised photography by Ronald Neame (himself later to become a noted director) actually lent warmth to the subject, and really showed Hollywood a thing or two about the subtler uses of Technicolor.

This Happy Feeling ⊙
1958, US, 92 mins, colour
Dir: Blake Edwards
Stars: Curt Jurgens, Debbie Reynolds, Alexis Smith, John Saxon
Rating: ★★★

An engaging cast is in good form in this zippy romantic comedy, one of the earliest films directed by Blake Edwards. Veteran actress Estelle Winwood is particularly noteworthy as an eccentric housekeeper. The chirpy title song is by three-time Oscar-winners Ray Livingston and Jay Evans.

This Island Earth ○
1955, US, 86 mins, colour
Dir: Joseph M Newman
Stars: Jeff Morrow, Faith Domergue, Rex Reason
Rating: ★★

A rare piece of imaginative, genuine science-fiction that's gradually allowed to slide into juvenile space opera. Something for everyone in this, though, the only Technicolor sci-fi film Universal-International ever made. There's some intricate gadgetry, a gorgeous heroine menaced by forces unknown, special effects ahead of their time and a super mutant monster. Rex

Reason is quite good, but Faith Domergue is given little to do but scream lustily and look gorgeous. Technical details are presented in convincing enough fashion.

This Is My Affair ◐
(aka: His Affair)
1937, US, 101 mins, b/w
Dir: William A Seiter
Stars: Robert Taylor, Barbara Stanwyck, Victor McLaglen
Rating: ★★

Not the full-blown romance the title would suggest (especially as stars Robert Taylor and Barbara Stanwyck were a steady twosome in real life and would marry two years later), but more of a melodrama with elements of excitement, suspense, romance and ingenious plot twists. Well set (at the turn of the century) and skilfully directed by the always workmanlike William A Seiter, it deals with an undercover agent on a presidential mission to root out a gang of bank robbers.

This Is My Life ◐ Ⓥ
1992, US, 95 mins, colour
Dir: Nora Ephron
Stars: Julie Kavner, Samantha Mathis, Dan Aykroyd, Carrie Fisher, Gaby Hoffmann
Rating: ★★

Nice performances, good one-liners, shame about the film: the story of a Jewish mother who, after years of looking after two daughters, comes into some money and becomes famous as a stand-up comic. Despite the wisecracks – mom (Julie Kavner) tells the girls she only had one detour into folly 'but we'll leave your father out of this' – the tale just isn't particularly interesting. Kavner is on the mark, if somewhat uncharismatic, as the mom who is always 'on'. Dan Aykroyd lends considered support as the impresario – 'the Moss' – for whom she falls and Samantha Mathis is quite superb as the older daughter – emotions conveyed in the clenching of a fist or the tightening of a lip. Gaby Hoffman is mercifully uncute as her sister. But you just can't imagine anyone actually paying a cent to share an hour and a half with these people.

This Is My Love ◐
1954, US, 91 mins, colour
Dir: Stuart Heisler
Stars: Linda Darnell, Rick Jason, Dan Duryea, Faith Domergue
Rating: ★★★★

The best of the later films of director Stuart Heisler, who made his name with the Alan Ladd version of *The Glass Key*. This is a powerful, tragic drama with haunting theme music by Franz Waxman, a throbbingly true performance from Linda Darnell which carries great impact, and a pathetically brilliant portrayal of an embittered cripple by Dan Duryea. The film is also richly photographed in Pathecolor by Ray June.

This Is My Street ❶
1963, UK, 94 mins, b/w
Dir: Sidney Hayers
Stars: Ian Hendry, June Ritchie
Rating: ★★

Although this film does cash in on the backstreets bedroom drama popular in Sixties' British cinema, director Sidney Hayers has at the same time contrived a very interesting drama from a rather middling English *Peyton Place-type* novel by Nan Maynard. A strong, magnetic story, and genuinely sympathetic characters are the best things about a film that sees Ian Hendry giving a performance of compelling brilliance as an alley-cat charmer, turning laughter to menace and back in the flicker of an eyelid. As the working wife he seduces, June Ritchie's vocal delivery is somewhat short of her range of facial emotions.

This Is Spinal Tap ● Ⓥ
1984, US, 82 mins, colour
Dir: Rob Reiner
Stars: Christopher Guest, Michael McKean
Rating: ★★★

A spoof 'rockumentary' chronicling the adventures of an English rock band while on tour in America. Director Rob Reiner amusingly takes a subsidiary role as a 'movie-brat'-type filmmaker and you'll also spot Anjelica Huston, who two years later was the deserved winner of a best supporting actress Oscar for her role in *Prizzi's Honour*. The flat, South London accents of the group members (who are actually American and Canadian actors) are uncannily and hilariously accurate. Bruno Kirby, Ed Begley Jr and Billy Crystal also contribute cameos in the supporting cast.

This Land Is Mine ○
1943, US, 103 mins, b/w
Dir: Jean Renoir
Stars: Charles Laughton, Maureen O'Hara, George Sanders
Rating: ★★

A forceful, poignant war drama marred by a script that takes some be-

lieving, even in the midst of Hollywood's most flag-waving years. The camera-hogging Charles Laughton plays a seemingly mild teacher who becomes a local hero when the occupying Nazis arrest him for murder. But then there are so many eye-catching performances in this movie, passionately well directed by wartime refugee Jean Renoir, that one contemporary critic thought it should have been called *This Film Is Mine!*

This Man's Navy ○
1945, US, 100 mins, b/w
Dir: William A Wellman
Stars: Wallace Beery, Tom Drake
Rating: ★★

And this is a man-sized World War Two action film from the MGM stable, with overwhelming Wallace Beery making life difficult for Tom Drake as a rookie sailor Beery treats as a son. The combat scenes are sturdy and noisy, as to be expected from enthusiastic war-film director William A Wellman.

This Property Is Condemned ❶
1966, US, 110 mins, colour
Dir: Sydney Pollack
Stars: Natalie Wood, Robert Redford, Charles Bronson
Rating: ★★★

There's a formidable trio of stars in this turbulent love story (adapted from a play by Tennessee Williams) which is played out against a background of violence and industrial strife. Robert Redford and Natalie Wood give impressive portrayals; but the really great performance comes from Mary Badham, as an ugly 12-year-old, worldly-wise beyond her years. Director Sydney Pollack keeps a tight grip on the sentimentality until towards the end, and James Wong Howe's colour camerawork is superb, capturing a hot Southern-states night, or making a breathtaking pan over the muddy, sun-flecked Mississippi River.

This Sporting Life ❶ Ⓥ
1963, UK, 134 mins, b/w
Dir: Lindsay Anderson
Stars: Richard Harris, Rachel Roberts, Alan Badel
Rating: ★★★

Richard Harris broke through to bigtime stardom in this gritty study of a coal-miner who becomes a professional rugby player. In many ways the highpoint of the British 'kitchen sink'

movement that had begun five years earlier, it gave Rachel Roberts an eye-catching 'good-hearted tart' type of role that she was to play, with variations, for the rest of her career. Unflinching direction (and dissection) of the characters by Lindsay Anderson draws us right into their high-pressure world. Watch out for Glenda Jackson (her screen debut) in a miniscule role as one of a group of people singing around a piano.

Thomas Crown Affair, The ❶ Ⓥ
1968, US, 102 mins, colour
Dir: Norman Jewison
Stars: Steve McQueen, Faye Dunaway
Rating: ★★★

Thirty years before, this would have starred Kay Francis and been called *Undercover Girl*. In 1968, with the stars making psychedelic love, it seemed a glitzy fuss about not very much. The plot is too slight to allow Steve McQueen and Faye Dunaway to expand their roles enough for us to identify fully with them, although the bank raid scenes are tautly effective and there's a nice chess/seduction scene reminiscent of the eating orgy in *Tom Jones*.

Thoroughly Modern Millie ○
1967, US, 138 mins, colour
Dir: George Roy Hill
Stars: Julie Andrews, Mary Tyler Moore, James Fox
Rating: ★★★★

One of Julie Andrews' most successful vehicles; the star gives one of her sprightliest performances in the title role of this Twenties' musical spoof and there's a delicious turn by Beatrice Lillie as the white-slaving Mrs Meers. A bit long, but the score is tuneful (Elmer Bernstein won an Oscar for it) and director George Roy Hill keeps the idiotic plot going at a nice pace.

Those Daring Young Men In Their Jaunty Jalopies
See: Monte Carlo or Bust

Those Magnificent Men In Their Flying Machines ⊙ Ⓥ
1965, US/UK, 133 mins, colour
Dir: Ken Annakin
Stars: Sarah Miles, James Fox, Terry-Thomas, Robert Morley, Eric Sykes, Benny Hill
Rating: ★★★

It's a sure-fire bet that, sooner or later, one of the 1910 aviators in this crazy all-star comedy will crash into the local

T

sewage farm. These gigantic splashes provide the most side-splitting moments in a film whose greatest assets are the animated Ronald Searle cartoons at the beginning, middle and end. There's rather too much romance and too little of Terry-Thomas, as a dastardly Victorian villain, and Eric Sykes – his downtrodden manservant. Hilarious compensations include a Keystone Kops fire brigade bossed by Benny Hill.

Thousands Cheer O
1943, US, 126 mins, colour
Dir: George Sidney
Stars: Gene Kelly, Kathryn Grayson, Mary Astor
Rating: ★★★

Probably the biggest of all wartime musical extravaganzas. Being made at MGM, it was in Technicolor and had a cast no other studio could match, with Gene Kelly (doing his famous 'mop' dance) and Kathryn Grayson singing 'The Joint is Really Jumpin' at Carnegie Hall', Red Skelton and little Margaret O'Brien competing to see who can eat the most ice-cream, Virginia O'Brien's famous deadpan rendition of 'In a Little Spanish Town' and Lena Horne's showstopping 'Honeysuckle Rose'. Thousands cheered all right: the film was a massive box-office hit.

Three Amigos! O ⓥ
1986, US, 105 mins, colour
Dir: John Landis
Stars: Chevy Chase, Steve Martin, Martin Short
Rating: ★

This comedy Western spoof is like a plate of Mexican refried beans in bad need of a dose of red hot chillis to spice it up. The idea of having three wimpy silent cowboy movie heroes coming to the aid of downtrodden Mexicans in a sort of affectionate spoof of *The Magnificent Seven* is a great one, especially with Steve Martin, Chevy Chase and Martin Short in the title roles. But the execution by director John Landis is unexpectedly ham-fisted, and the script weak and illogical. Why is there a medieval dungeon beneath one of the houses? But a funny scene where the Three Amigos sit singing a corny cowboy bedtime song in front of a matte painting of Monument Valley, where they are joined by a mountain lion, a turtle, a coyote, an owl and other desert creatures, shows the film's potential in the hands of better writers.

Three Caballeros, The ❶
1944, US, 71 mins, colour
Dir: Norman Ferguson
Stars: Aurora Miranda, Carmen Molina
Rating: ★★★★

Donald Duck sings! If Mickey Mouse had soared to a career peak as The Sorcerer's Apprentice, then the spluttering duck enjoys his finest hour vocalising with Joe Carioca the parrot and Panchito the rooster, and dancing with Aurora Miranda in this brilliant Disney cartoon/live-action compilation that ends with a whizzbang tour of Mexico. Earlier cartoon sequences introduce such memorable characters as Pablo the Cold-Blooded Penguin and The Flying Donkey! And, just as you are starting to yawn at the antics of the live actors, Disney peps you up again with such brilliant cartoon images as a little train chugging through gardens of flowers against a background of black. Altogether, it's a quacker.

Three Cockeyed Sailors
See: Sailors Three

Three Coins In the Fountain
O ⓥ
1954, US, 102 mins, colour
Dir: Jean Negulesco
Stars: Clifton Webb, Dorothy McGuire, Jean Peters, Louis Jourdan, Rossano Brazzi
Rating: ★★

Famous romantic weepie about the love affairs of three American girls in Rome whose storyline follows very much the same path as Jean Negulesco's earlier *How to Marry a Millionaire*. Remembered now chiefly for the theme song and for its lyrical colour photography which won an Oscar, although the travelogue elements almost swamp the story. The actresses concerned, Dorothy McGuire, Jean Peters and Maggie McNamara, give the formula material rather more than it deserves.

Three Colours Red ● ⓥ
(aka: Trois Couleurs Rouge)
1993, France/Poland, 96 mins, colour
Dir: Krzysztof Kieslowski
Stars: Irène Jacob, Jean-Louis Trintignant, Jean-Pierre Lorit, Frédérique Féder
Rating: ★★★★★

Similar in structure to Claude Lelouch's romantic films about *un homme* finally meeting *une femme*, after just missing each other throughout the story, but vastly superior in the writing and in the central theme. Model Irène

Jacob, whose current boyfriend seems like a bad investment, runs over a dog belonging to retired judge Jean-Louis Trintignant, who appears scarcely to care whether the animal lives or dies. Drawn to his house when the dog survives and flees back to its owner she begins to uncover some strange facts about her elderly and reclusive acquaintance. Gradually, the wheels begin to grind towards a preordained fate, but we never have the sense of being manipulated. Jacob and Trintignant give two quite exceptional, amazingly focused performances: she is gravely sincere and wholly sympathetic (but never dull); his embittered old man is one of the best things he has ever done. And the scene where she rescues the dog after running it over is astoundingly well realised, with the dog a great scene-stealer. Flawless filmmaking of a very high order.

Three Days of the Condor ❶
1975, US, 118 mins, colour
Dir: Sydney Pollack
Stars: Robert Redford, Faye Dunaway, Cliff Robertson
Rating: ★★★

A *39 Steps*-type spy thriller in which bookish Robert Redford finds himself the only survivor when his CIA section is massacred. But this bookworm is a clever man. He wriggles off the hook of further assassination attempts and noses his way towards the rotten core of an organisation where sides change constantly and one's friend may be forced to become one's enemy in the space of a phone call. Will Redford survive? The suspense is killing. Apart from its fashionably enigmatic ending, this is a film with much to recommend it, with its atmospheric nighttime sequences, Redford's own edgy performance (peering nervously from behind gold-rimmed spectacles and putting his brain to dreadful tortures to try to stay alive) and Owen Roizman's clever but subtle colour photography.

Three Faces of Eve, The ❶
1957, US, 95 mins, b/w
Dir: Nunnally Johnson
Stars: Joanne Woodward, David Wayne, Lee J Cobb
Rating: ★★★

This was the early highpoint of Joanne Woodward's distinguished acting career, in a portrait of a split personality woman said to be based on a real-life case. The actress's clever differentiation between the three faces of Eve

(and then some) marked her out as a dramatic star of most skilful talents. She was nominated for an Oscar alongside Deborah Kerr, Anna Magnani, Elizabeth Taylor and (rather unexpectedly) Lana Turner and, when it came to awards night, Joanne was announced as the winner. The voice of the narrator in *The Three Faces of Eve* will be familiar to radio listeners: it belongs to Alastair Cooke.
Writer-director Nunnally Johnson makes this story a compelling casebook history.

Three Fugitives ① ⓥ

1989, US, 93 mins, colour
Dir: Francis Veber
Stars: Nick Nolte, Martin Short, James Earl Jones
Rating: ★★★

Lord knows why weedy bank robber Martin Short chooses hulking Nick Nolte as a hostage during his one-man bank raid. I mean, you'd pick a little old lady, wouldn't you? Never mind, we wouldn't have a film otherwise, so we must allow writer-director Francis Veber this little quirk in an otherwise feisty comedy that almost seamlessly blends fun, action and sentiment. Nolte, you see, is a man just out of jail after committing 14 armed robberies himself. And he's determined to go straight – until Short skitters on to the scene, a bundle of nerves but determined to hijack the bank for enough money to keep his six-year-old daughter (who hasn't spoken since her mother died) in her special school. You won't need to be told that, despite his best intentions, Nolte becomes hopelessly embroiled with Short and his problems. There are few dead patches in the ensuing flight of the ill-matched duo (later with little girl in tow) and some quite funny interludes. Nolte's tough guy is the best thing in the film.

3 Godfathers ○

1948, US, 106 mins, colour
Dir: John Ford
Stars: John Wayne, Pedro Armendariz, Harry Carey Jr, Ward Bond
Rating: ★★★★★

If you're prepared to let its liberal doses of sentiment get to you, this is a brilliant John Wayne-John Ford Western, their first together in colour, about three bank raiders (Wayne, Pedro Armendariz, Harry Carey Jr) who become saddled with a baby when its mother dies in the desert. From then on the film maintains a

wonderful balance between suspense, sentiment and some grim humour. 'The best and surest way of feeding the baby,' Carey reads from a manual, 'is the one which nature has provided.' 'Well,' growls Wayne, 'that's out!' Ford took pleasure in goading young Carey (to whose father, early Western star Harry Carey, the film is dedicated) to a fine, moving performance, by telling him every time he did something wrong that he wished he had hired Audie Murphy for the part. Breathtakingly shot in Technicolor by Winton C Hoch, this underrated film deserves to stand with the best of the Ford-Wayne Westerns from the Forties and Fifties.

Three Lives of Thomasina, The ⊙

1964, UK, 97 mins, colour
Dir: Don Chaffey
Stars: Patrick McGoohan, Susan Hampshire, Karen Dotrice
Rating: ★★★

The Scots have always been easy prey for animal sob-stories and the Disney studio wrings the tears from this one with practised ease. The children, Karen Dotrice and Matthew Garber (the pair from Disney's *Mary Poppins)* have a natural appeal which puts them among the better grade of screen tots, while Susan Hampshire scores a big personal success as the 'witch' who tends to sick animals. The storyline itself is strong, although there's one amusing howler early on when Thomasina (the ginger cat of the title) says her family called her Thomas at first until they 'got to know her better'. And her master a vet? Pull the other one, Disney.

3 Men and a Baby ○ ⓥ

1987, US, 98 mins, colour
Dir Leonard Nimoy
Stars: Tom Selleck, Steve Guttenberg, Ted Danson, Nancy Travis
Rating: ★★

The old film maxim 'Never act with children or animals' seems not to have scared Tom Selleck, Ted Danson and Steve Guttenberg. Otherwise, none of them would have taken on this airy romp about three macho bachelors in their 30s who get landed with a baby girl by Danson's decamping ex-mistress. Selleck and Guttenberg look after the infant while Danson's away and soon become doting foster-fathers, handling more nappies than women. Fortunately, this somewhat gooey narrative is injected with a subplot

involving drugs which supplies some much-needed action and variation in theme. The three stars all have their moments in a tolerable toddle through triteness that turned into a bundle of box-office joy for its producers.

Three Men and a Cradle
(aka: Trois Hommes et un Couffin)

1985, France, 106 mins, colour
Dir: Coline Serreau
Stars: Roland Giraud, Michel Boujenah, Andre Dussollier
Rating: ★★

Charm, amusement and tedium mingle in equal parts in this very Gallic comedy, subsequently remade into Hollywood into a smash-hit called *3 Men and a Baby.* Three macho bachelors in their thirties are suddenly burdened with the illegitimate infant daughter of one. Their instant devotion does take some swallowing especially when, on the very first day, their landlady offers to change the baby and is met with a refusal! Nice performances, particularly by Michel Boujenah (who won a French Oscar) and Roland Giraud; the overrated remake robbed it of what charm it possessed in the first place.

3 Men and a Little Lady ○ ⓥ

1990, US, 103 mins, colour
Dir: Emile Ardolino
Stars: Tom Selleck, Steve Guttenberg, Ted Danson, Nancy Travis
Rating: ★★★

It's five years on and the bachelor guys from *3 Men and a Baby* are still living together in harmony with baby Mary (now Robin Weisman) whose actress mother Sylvia (Nancy Travis) returned several years back, and is secretly adored by Selleck, who can't find the words to tell her. You know what we mean: silly characters and situations, but fun anyway. Even when the trio pursues Sylvia to England, where she plans to marry, there's still some merriment to be had, although most of it seems to stem from a study of British comedies of the Fifties. Danson has the showiest role, and carries it off with great confidence and panache: he's the real laughter-getter here, and a 'rap' lullaby the three men do to send Mary to sleep is a genuine show-stopper. By and large, this is more fun than the original.

Three Musketeers, The ○ ⓥ

1948, US, 125 mins, colour
Dir: George Sidney
Stars: Gene Kelly, June Allyson, Lana

T

Turner, Vincent Price
Rating: ★★★

MGM spared no expense in this spectacular Technicolor version of Dumas' classic tale of intrigue, romance, derring-do, and treachery in 17th-century France. It's every bit as star-studded as the two Seventies' films made from Dumas' novels. A fine cast is headed by Gene Kelly, taking a rest from his dancing duties, and turning D'Artagnan into a balletic athlete; Vincent Price, as evil as ever, as Cardinal Richelieu; and Lana Turner, contributing one of her best screen portrayals as the poisonous Milady de Winter. Angela Lansbury, Lana's rival for the part at MGM, eventually lost out, and had to be content with portraying Queen Anne. Suave Gig Young plays Porthos, and portly Robert Coote is Aramis. Strange: one would have thought these two parts better cast the other way round.

Three Musketeers, The ○ ⓥ
1938, US, 73 mins, colour
Dir: Allan Dwan
Stars: Don Ameche, The Ritz Brothers, Binnie Barnes, Gloria Stuart
Rating: ★★★

A film comedy based – more or less – on Dumas' famous story! The Ritzes – zany nightclub comedians of the Thirties whose stature at one time rivalled that of the brothers Marx – collide head-on with Alexandre Dumas in this pastiche of the famous swashbuckling tale. Villainy is in the capable hands of Binnie Barnes, Lionel Atwill, John Carradine, and Douglas Dumbrille, and the Oscar-winning Joseph Schildkraut completes an excellent supporting cast.

Three Musketeers, The ○ ⓥ
1993, US, 106 mins, colour
Dir: Stephen Herek
Stars: Chris O'Donnell, Charlie Sheen, Kiefer Sutherland, Rebecca DeMornay, Tim Curry, Oliver Platt
Rating: ★★

Almost inevitably dubbed *Young Swords*, this fiercely paced version of the Dumas classic, full of crashing, clangorous action, suffers from its players, with Charlie Sheen and Kiefer Sutherland equalling MGM's old pairing of Van Heflin and Robert Coote in making the 1973 Athos and Aramis, Oliver Reed and Richard Chamberlain, seem positive gems of casting. As in the latter film, a vein of humour is evident here and the blame for its falling flat can be levelled at

some pretty stolid performances. Never mind, there are compensations: Rebecca DeMornay is well cast as the icy Milady de Winter, and Oliver Platt cheerfully steals the show as a brawling, sprawling, carousing young Porthos. For the film itself, though, colourful and energetic are about the best adjectives you could think of to describe its attractions.

Three Musketeers: The Queen's Diamonds, The ○
1973, UK, 107 mins, colour
Dir: Richard Lester
Stars: Michael York, Oliver Reed, Raquel Welch, Faye Dunaway, Charlton Heston, Richard Chamberlain
Rating: ★★★★

Inuneasurably the better of Richard Lester's two *Musketeers* films, this actually seems funnier on a second viewing. So if you've seen it in the cinema, take another look. Although the cutting and editing might have been tighter, the director's visual style provides comedy and drama in equal proportions. The stars are largely left to their own devices, and those who play the straightest succeed the most, notably Raquel Welch and Simon Ward. Michael York's D'Artagnan is rather wetter than I suspect even Lester intended and although Richard Chamberlain is elegantly cast as Aramis, Oliver Reed's rapidly increasing proportions reveal him as more suitable to Porthos (actually played by Frank Finlay) than to the stalwart Athos.

Three of Hearts ● ⓥ
1992, US, 110 mins, colour
Dir: Yurek Bogayevicz
Stars: William Baldwin, Sherilyn Fenn, Kelly Lynch, Joe Pantoliano, Gail Strickland
Rating: ★★

'Any woman, any time, any place. Guaranteed.' That's the motto of Joe (William Baldwin), an up-market male prostitute or, as he prefers to be called, escort for hire. So who more suitable for getting back the girlfriend (a brunette Sherilyn Fenn) of Connie, a lesbian (Kelly Lynch), and sending her running back to Connie. Now you don't need a crystal ball to see that Baldwin and Fenn are going to fall in love, but there's a bit more to the story than that, although not enough to stretch the film to 110 minutes without a few lulls. Lynch has some endearingly goofy moments as Connie who, perhaps unfortunately for the film's

emotional centre, turns out to be the most likeable character in the film. Baldwin exercises his charismatic grin to good effect, but overall the film doesn't quite engage the emotions.

Three Ring Circus ⊙
1954, US, 103 mins, colour
Dir: Joseph Pevney
Stars: Dean Martin, Jerry Lewis, Joanne Dru, Zsa Zsa Gabor
Rating: ★★★

Although not as side-splittingly funny as some of their films together, this is about as colourful and entertaining a show as Dean Martin and Jerry Lewis ever put on screen. Jerry is a natural for the assistant lion tamer who wants to be a clown and Dean's lazy charm and melodious warble hit it big with a song called 'It's a Big, Wide, Wonderful World'. A rare Martin-Lewis duet, 'Hey, Punchinello', is also a highlight of the film.

Three Smart Girls ○
1936, US, 84 mins, b/w
Dir: Henry Koster
Stars: Deanna Durbin, Charles Winninger, Binnie Barnes, Ray Milland
Rating: ★★★

Deanna Durbin was never more delightful than this, her feature debut, as a matchmaking teenager out to keep her (divorced) errant father on the straight and narrow path back to mother. Songs include 'My Heart is Singing' and 'Someone to Care for Me'. As always in her pre-war films, the Durbin kid is like a breath of fresh air.

Three Smart Girls Grow Up ○
1939, US, 90 mins, b/w
Dir: Henry Koster
Stars: Deanna Durbin, Charles Winninger, Nan Grey
Rating: ★★★

The sequel to 1937's *Three Smart Girls*, again directed by Henry Koster. Little Deanna matchmakes for her sisters, sings 'Because' and wins over every crusty heart in sight. Very refreshing.

Threesome ● ⓥ
1994, US, 93 mins, colour
Dir: Andrew Fleming
Stars: Lara Flynn Boyle, Josh Charles, Stephen Baldwin, Alexis Arquette
Rating: ★

This crude and coarse college drama certainly does redraw the boundaries of sex and language in its tale of three in a bed, but alas it is all too often dull in the attempt. Betrayed by her male name, Alex (Lara Flynn Boyle) finds herself dormed with Stuart (Stephen Baldwin) and Eddy (Josh Charles). Stuart fancies Alex who fancies Eddy who fancies Stuart, convinced he's a closet gay. 'On top of everything else,' he asserts, in one of the film's few funny lines, 'he knows all the lyrics to *Oklahoma* and *The Music Man.*' The sexual game of musical chairs that results is hampered by the unsympathetic personalities of the actors concerned and seems much longer than its 93 minutes.

3.10 to Yuma ○ Ⓥ
1957, US, 92 mins, b/w
Dir: Delmer Daves
Stars: Glenn Ford, Van Heflin
Rating: ★★★★

Very high-quality suspense Western which will have you biting your nails right up to the memorable climax. It seemed that every other Western in the Fifties had a theme song by Frankie Laine and this is no exception. Other bonuses are tight performances by Ford as the outlaw and Van Heflin as the poor farmer who tries to bring him in against all the odds, and Charles Lawton's crisp black and white photography. Of the supporting cast, Henry Jones and Richard Jaeckel both etch sharp portrayals of gentlemen on opposite sides of the law, but the finest performance in the film is given by Leora Dana as Heflin's wife.

3 Women ●
1977, US, 125 mins, colour
Dir: Robert Altman
Stars: Sissy Spacek, Shelley Duvall, Janice Rule .
Rating: ★

Downright peculiar film from Robert Altman that you will find totally compelling or heavy going according to taste. The 'plot' is about three women who metamorphose into identities other than their original ones. There is certainly more to its events than meets the eye, although quite what is sometimes hard to fathom. And everything is so stylised that the characters simple aren't believable – although Altman devotees aren't likely to find that a hindrance to fascination or enjoyment.

Three Worlds of Gulliver, The ○ Ⓥ
1960, UK, 100 mins, colour
Dir: Jack Sher
Stars: Kerwin Mathews, Jo Morrow, June

Thorburn
Rating: ★★★

Master of DynaMation Ray Harryhausen allows that perennial hero of mythical magic, Kerwin Mathews, to wander among Lilliputians and giants. There's no sign of Gulliver's other two voyages or Swift's satire but it's all very entertaining and pleasant.

Three Young Texans ○
1954, US, 78 mins, colour
Dir: Henry Levin
Stars: Mitzi Gaynor, Keefe Brasselle, Jeffrey Hunter
Rating: ★★

An exuberant Western which gave the sparkling Mitzi Gaynor her only outdoors role. Director Henry Levin makes the most of a good train robbery sequence, and the Technicolor photography is first-rate throughout.

Thrill of a Romance ○
1945, US, 105 mins, colour
Dir: Richard Thorpe
Stars: Van Johnson, Esther Williams, Frances Gifford
Rating: ★★

MGM obviously figured in this plush musical-comedy that with Esther Williams swimming, Van Johnson smiling, opera star Lauritz Melchior singing and Tommy Dorsey, Xavier Cugat and their orchestras playing away like billy-o, they didn't need to bother too much about story or script. How right they were. The film proved to be one of the big money-spinners of its year. And it had two huge song hits: 'I Should Care' and 'Don't Say No, Say Maybe'.

Thrill of It All, The ○
1963, US, 108 mins, colour
Dir: Norman Jewison
Stars: Doris Day, James Garner
Rating: ★★★

Producer Ross Hunter's luxurious world of make-believe receives another comic twist in this story of housewife Beverley Boyer (Doris Day) who becomes a national celebrity through selling soap on TV. All this upsets her husband (James Garner) not a little, especially when he becomes known as 'Mr Beverley' and finds himself driving into the swimming pool the TV sponsors have made out of his wife's garage. Day, as genuinely nice as ever, and Garner make a perfect team together in this pleasant entertainment with a good few laughs.

Throne of Blood ① Ⓥ
1957, Japan, 108 mins, b/w
Dir: Akira Kurosawa
Stars: Toshiro Mifune, Isuzu Yamada
Rating: ★★★★★

Japanese master Akira Kurosawa's version of Shakespeare's *Macbeth*, impressively transferred to a Samurai setting. As with *Ran*, Kurosawa's more recent version of *King Lear*, the film's most powerful performance is provided by the leading lady, in this case Isuzu Yamada, in fierce and frightening form as the film's equivalent of the Lady Macbeth character. The redoubtable Toshiro Mifune, Kurosawa's usual protagonist, has the leading role in this graphic film, bulging with imagination and with a brilliant, unforgettable finale.

Throw Momma from the Train ① Ⓥ
1987, US, 88 mins, colour
Dir: Danny DeVito
Stars: Danny DeVito, Billy Crystal, Anne Ramsey, Kim Greist
Rating: ★★

Directors seem to have developed a fine art in today's comedy cinema of making films that are fun without actually being funny. A fine line, perhaps, but one that can make the difference between staggering off holding your sides or having been mildly amused. That gripe apart, this black romp, nicely performed and well produced, has a lovely basic idea. Failed writer-teacher Billy Crystal hates the wife who stole his only publishable novel. Danny DeVito, who also directed, is his dimwit pupil (with an ogre of a mother) who conceives the idea of a 'swap' murder after watching Hitchcock's *Strangers on a Train*. The film has too many semi-climaxes thereafter, but both DeVito and Crystal give it their all and a bit more, and Anne Ramsey cuts a horrendous figure as the fiend who yells and cuffs her middle-aged son into frequent cowering submission.

Thumbelina ⊙ Ⓥ
1994, US, 86 mins, colour
Dir: Don Bluth, Gary Goldman
Voice stars: Jodi Benson, John Hurt, Gino Conforti, Carol Channing, Barbara Cook, Will Ryan
Rating: ★★

Not so much a cartoon feature, more an animated musical. Don Bluth's version of the Andersen tale of a tiny girl found in an opening flower (good job a bee didn't get there first) has songs by Barry Manilow (some of them pretty,

T

some pretty nondescript) but is very slow to get going into any sort of story and seriously lacks charm. Derivative of *The Little Mermaid,* the film becomes more interesting in the second half, dazzlingly coloured and detailed, when Thumbelina loses her fairy prince, and is coveted in turn by a vaudevillian toad, a bebop beetle and a wealthy mole. The animation, though skilfully done, especially in the animal characters, is reminiscent of cartoons of many years ago, even before *Snow White,* with lots of indefinable bugs and woodland creatures outlandishly dressed and jumping up and down on the edges of the frame; if anything, the screen here's too busy. Small children will enjoy it.

Thunderball ○ ⓥ
1965, UK, 140 mins, colour
Dir: Terence Young
Stars: Sean Connery, Claudine Auger, Adolfo Celi, Luciana Paluzzi
Rating: ★★

Regular Bond devotees won't be disappointed with this, his fourth film adventure, although it's the weakest of his early capers and underwater battles don't somehow carry the same charge as adventures on terra firma. There's the usual preliminary fencing with the main adversary (splendid Italian actor Adolfo Celi), a welter of fantastic gadgets – plus the famous Aston Martin again – and a plentiful array of Bond beauties. In this department, the two girls with lesser roles – flashing-eyed Martine Beswick as an agent, and sultry Molly Peters as a physiotherapist – rather outshine the leading ladies, Claudine Auger and Luciana Paluzzi.

Thunder Bay ○
1953, US, 102 mins, colour
Dir: Anthony Mann
Stars: James Stewart, Joanne Dru, Dan Duryea
Rating: ★★★

James Stewart and Anthony Mann took a break from their great series of rugged Westerns to make this equally action-filled, ahead-of-its-time story of wildcatters drilling for oil under the sea. There's much of the spirit of the Western here, though, especially in a rich supporting cast which includes old reliables Gilbert Roland, Dan Duryea, Jay C Flippen and Henry Morgan. Joanne Dru and Marcia Henderson are less effective as the girls. There's a hurricane, a killing, a near-lynching and plenty of free-for-alls. Does Stewart complete the winning formula

by getting covered in oil at the end? See the picture to find out.

Thunderbolt and Lightfoot ● ⓥ
1974, US, 114 mins, colour
Dir: Michael Cimino
Stars: Clint Eastwood, Jeff Bridges, George Kennedy, Gary Busey
Rating: ★★★

This fast-moving crime caper starts off in high spirits but ends in a black mood. Clint Eastwood is a bank robber who is trying to keep one step ahead of two former cronies who believe he cheated them out of their share of a robbery. Jeff Bridges is a young drifter who latches onto Eastwood. The cronies (George Kennedy and Geoffrey Lewis) eventually catch up with Eastwood and are persuaded to pull another caper. Although Eastwood is the central character, Bridges, Kennedy and Lewis all fill their roles impressively, collectively overshadowing the star. The film picks up momentum as it goes along and the robbery and getaway scenes are well done and exciting. The grim turn towards the end of the film gives it a somewhat downbeat ending, and leaves you wishing director Cimino hadn't changed horses in midstream.

Thunderhead – Son of Flicka ⊙
1945, US, 78 mins, colour
Dir: Louis King
Stars: Preston Foster, Roddy McDowall
Rating: ★★★

Dog-fever in the Hollywood of the Forties, after MGM struck it rich with Lassie, was quickly followed by horse-fever. A colt called Flicka, the creation of author Mary O'Hara, spearheaded a whole host of vigorous, colourful outdoor adventures, guaranteed to thrill animal-lovers and wring a tear from the most hardened animal-hater around. This is the sequel to the original Flicka film *(My Friend Flicka),* with Preston Foster and Roddy McDowall again as the McLaughlins, ranch folk of America's mid-west.

Thunderheart ❶ ⓥ
1992, US, 119 mins, colour
Dir: Michael Apted
Stars: Val Kilmer, Sam Shepard, Graham Greene, Fred Ward, Ted Thin Elk
Rating: ★★

You'll have reservations about this modern American Indian murder thriller – one of which will probably

be that it's overlong. When it comes together in the last half-hour, though, the film becomes engrossing and enjoyable, topped with a stunning overhead shot at the action climax and one of those emotive endings you thought Hollywood had forgotten how to make. A young FBI agent (Val Kilmer) of Indian ancestry is uprooted from his Washington DC patch and dispatched to the South Dakota badlands, where murders of native Americans there need to be solved and, as usual in these films, cloak some far more sinister goings-on. The film builds up some interesting characters along its rather plodding course. And, like the film, the script gets more interesting towards the end. But you'll need patience to extract heap good medicine from this one.

Thunder In the Valley ⊙
(aka: Bob, Son of Battle)
1947, US, 103 mins, colour
Dir: Louis King
Stars: Peggy Ann Garner, Lon McCallister, Edmund Gwenn
Rating: ★★★

An American film, set in the Scottish Highlands, from a book by an Englishman, Alfred Ollivant; *Owd Bob* is one of the best famous animal stories in the English language. And Hollywood gave it the full treatment. Edmund Gwenn is at his crusty best as the embittered old shepherd who owns one of the two dogs suspected of being a sheep-killer; and the exhilarating scenery is handsomely photographed in Technicolor. Two of filmland's brightest stars of the Forties, Lon McCallister and Peggy Ann Garner, give sympathetic performances in the lead roles. The dogs, of course, are magnificent. The children should keep a handkerchief ready for the scenes in which the dogs come close to getting killed; and when McCallister's treasured violin is broken by the ill-tempered Edmund Gwenn.

Thunder of Drums, A ○
1961, US, 97 mins, colour
Dir: Joseph M Newman
Stars: Richard Boone, George Hamilton, Luana Patten, Charles Bronson
Rating: ★★★

This tough Western will please all fans of Cavalry-versus-Indians adventures, and gives the commendable Richard Boone a role he can sink his teeth into. He's the battle- and memory-scarred commander of a grossly under-manned desert garrison, who gets saddled with three young and inexperienced lieutenants with whom to fight the Indians. The most aggressive of them is played by George Hamilton, in one of his more mobile and thoughtful portrayals. In addition to its tough action and rich colour camerawork, the film is a real bonanza for star-spotters. Besides Richard Chamberlain in his first major role as another of the lieutenants, there are pop guitarist Duane Eddy (his only straight part) and that granite-faced man of action Charles Bronson, who later moved on to star roles.

Thunder Over Arizona ○
1956, US, 72 mins, colour
Dir: Joe Kane
Stars: Skip Homeier, Kristine Miller
Rating: ★★

A minor Western from Republic that is instantly forgettable, but proves to be a pleasant enough time filler, thanks mainly to its attractive landscapes captured in the studio's Naturama and Trucolor processes. The directing chores are in the capable hands of Joe Kane who churned out dozens of low budget action pictures for Republic, including many starring John Wayne, Gene Autry and Roy Rogers.

THX 2138 ● ⓥ
1970, US, 95 mins, colour
Dir: George Lucas
Stars: Robert Duvall, Donald Pleasence, Maggie McOmie
Rating: ★★★

Director George Lucas' first film, and just as good as either of his two subsequent hits, *American Graffiti* and *Star Wars*. This is a more serious, very 1984-like science-fiction thriller, although the director shows the same schoolboy relish at unveiling the special effects in his cinematic box of tricks, the same enthusiasm for entertaining his audience, that made his later features so enjoyable. And the final flight from robot police is as exciting as anything in *Star Wars*.

Tiara Tahiti ○
1962, UK, 100 mins, colour
Dir: William T Kotcheff
Stars: John Mills, James Mason, Claude Dauphin, Herbert Lom
Rating: ★★

Engaging battle of wits between the two stars, as an ex-officer and a beachcomber, against the magnificent backdrop of Tahiti. James Mason is a raking beachcomber, crossing wits with John Mills, who offers an amus-

ing variation on his pompous, vulnerable officer from *Tunes of Glory*.

Ticket to Tomahawk, A ☉
1950, US, 90 mins, colour
Dir: Richard Sale
Stars: Dan Dailey, Anne Baxter, Rory Calhoun, Walter Brennan
Rating: ★★★★

A riotous comedy-musical, directed at a brisk pace by Richard Sale, and set aboard a train in the Old Wild West, where passengers are besieged by bad guys and Indians. Down among Les Girls in the theatrical troupe involved, watch out for Marilyn Monroe in one of her early film parts. In the same chorus line are Marion Marshall and Joyce Mackenzie who, while not in the Monroe bracket, also became stars. In another small role, wall-eyed Jack Elam was just starting out on a very profitable career in film villainy. See if you can figure out who Dailey has named his daughters after in the final scene.

Tie That Binds, The ● ⓥ
1995, US, 98 mins, colour
Dir: Wesley Strick
Stars: Daryl Hannah, Keith Carradine, Moira Kelly, Vincent Spano
Rating: ★

A nasty, unpleasant and quite unnecessary film about a couple of homicidal robbers whose daughter is captured by police and put up for adoption. Naturally the bad guys come to reclaim the child when she's adopted by unsuspecting foster-parents. Daryl Hannah, Keith Carradine, Moira Kelly and Vincent Spano are the unfortunate quartet caught up in this; heaven knows what effect the events of the film would have on the poor, traumatised child. Avoid.

Tiger Bay ○ ⓥ
1959, UK, 105 mins, b/w
Dir: J Lee Thompson
Stars: Hayley Mills, Horst Buchholz, John Mills, Yvonne Mitchell
Rating: ★★★★★

The brilliant thriller, both tense and touching, in which Hayley Mills burst on the film world with her superb portrayal of a hoydenish nine-year-old Welsh girl who becomes involved with a murderer. Hayley and her co-star, Horst Buchholz, both give tremendously human performances. John Mills is a steady foil as the determined police inspector. Atmosphere is excellent, and the suspense generated is tremendous. You'll be held to every second.

Tigers Don't Cry ○
(aka: African Rage)
1976, South Africa, 102 mins, colour
Dir: Peter Collinson
Stars: Anthony Quinn, John Phillip Law
Rating: ★

An eventful story of attempted assassination, told in the helter-skelter grasshopper style that director Peter Collinson stamped on all his films before his early death at 44 in 1980. Although one could have done without most of the intrusive music score, Anthony Quinn gives a typically gutsy performance as the kidnapper looking for a big ransom to assure his daughter's future, and Simon Sabela has an interesting if clumsily developed role as Quinn's target – an educated black president given to quoting Shakespeare alongside *The Wind in the Willows*.

Tiger's Tale, A ◑ ⓥ
1992, US, 97 mins, colour
Dir: Peter Douglas
Stars: Ann-Margret, C Thomas Howell, Charles Durning, Kelly Preston
Rating: ★★

Common sense tells me that this story of a spring-autumn affair isn't a terribly good film, basically because its screenplay (by the director, Peter Douglas) doesn't cut deep enough to affect the emotions. But it's hard to be objective about any film that gives that neglected talent Ann-Margret as many chances as this. Lucky C Thomas Howell. Every 19-year-old should have an affair with a lady in her forties who looks this good. Typical Hollywood wish-fulfilment, of course, and with spots of tedium along the way; but the animals in the movie – Howell's father (Charles Durning) is a retired vet – are an unusual added attraction, and Howell, while his acting lacks depth, romps most courageously with the two tigers who double the role of his pet. Pardon me while I don my teenager disguise and book a flight to California.

Tiger Warsaw ◑ ⓥ
1987, US, 92 mins, colour
Dir: Amin Q Chaudhri
Stars: Patrick Swayze, Barbara Williams, Lee Richardson, Piper Laurie
Rating: ★

All-American angst, dull and depressing and scripted in such a way that the actors' big emotional scenes are liable to make you laugh rather than cry. Tiger (Patrick Swayze) is the prodigal son, the black sheep of the Warsaw family exiled these many years since

T

he shot daddy following a row when he was discovered spaced out on drugs and peeping on sister. Now Tiger's back, unaware that his sister cancelled her marriage plans and is about to marry again, or that his father is a mental and physical shell. 'Is it really true you can't go home again?' wails Tiger, a sentiment which a suffering audience may well endorse. Under the circumstances, Piper Laurie is pretty good, even when having to hide Tiger in the closet. Everyone else stinks.

Tight Little Island
See: Whisky Galore!

Tightrope ● Ⓥ
1984, US, 114 mins, colour
Dir: Richard Tuggle
Stars: Clint Eastwood, Genevieve Bujold
Rating: ★★★

A tough, exploitative Clint Eastwood crime film that looks like a latter-day vehicle for Charles Bronson. Prostitutes were surely never as dishy as the crew who make up the hit-list in this urban thriller which casts Eastwood as Dirty Harry with problems, alias Wes Block, a cop who finds himself under suspicion and his family and friends in danger as a result of his consorting with hookers after his wife has left him. Eastwood's own daughter Alison is the 12-year-old who waits at home while her father first goes out on his midnight prowls, then hunts a killer who seems to be playing cat and mouse with him. The thrills and kills are efficiently stage-managed by debutant director Richard Tuggle who steers clear of gore until the final scene.

Tight Spot ○
1955, US, 97 mins, b/w
Dir: Phil Karlson
Stars: Ginger Rogers, Edward G Robinson, Brian Keith, Lorne Greene
Rating: ★★★★

A thriller that will have you rooted to your armchair for nearly two hours. Ginger Rogers is in dynamic form as the woman convict pressured to testify against a gangland czar and Brian Keith's terrific (the best performance of an undervalued career) as the detective assigned to protect her. Katherine Anderson is also very good in a supporting role. Terse dialogue, interspersed at just the right intervals with bursts of action by director Phil Karlson, ensures that the claustrophobic suspense engendered by the film becomes almost unbearable towards

the end. Thrilling and moving at once, this was one of the best crime films of its year.

Till the Clouds Roll By ○
1946 , US, 137 mins, colour
Dir: Richard Whorf
Stars: Robert Walker, Judy Garland, Van Heflin, Lucille Bremer
Rating: ★★

Never mind the quality of the script, feel the width of these Jerome Kern songs, more than 20 of them, in this potted MGM biography of the composer's life, awash with guest stars (of whom June Allyson is the liveliest), plus Judy Garland as Marilyn Miller and an earnest performance from Robert Walker as Kern himself. And just get a look at the young Frank Sinatra in that pink dinner suit.

'Til There Was You ◑ Ⓥ
1996, US, 114 mins, colour
Dir: Scott Winant
Stars: Jeanne Tripplehorn, Dylan McDermott, Sarah Jessica Parker, Patrick Malahide, Jennifer Aniston, Nina Foch, Michael Tucker
Rating: RB

Two hours of tedium masquerading as a movie, this a Lelouch-type romance that's not even a quarter good as those old French films in which the hero and heroine are destined for each other but never meet before the last reel. With a script this pretentious, it would take players far better than Jeanne Tripplehorn and Dylan McDermott to make any emotional impact with this story of two people emotionally stunted since childhood. And, because you know Tripplehorn and McDermott are going to end up with each other, you can't summon up enthusiasm for any other relationships in the film. The courtyard setting of 'La Fortuna', where ghost writer Tripplehorn moves in the second half of the film, is enough of a star by itself to have been awarded a whole movie; here it enters proceedings too late for us to maintain any interest in the outcome.

Tim ◑ Ⓥ
1978, Australia, 108 mins, colour
Dir: Michael Pate
Stars: Mel Gibson, Piper Laurie
Rating: ★★★

The talents of a youthful Mel Gibson and a Piper Laurie slimmed down from her comeback in *Carrie* two years earlier are just enough to make us care about the outcome of the slow-building romance between a retarded man in

his twenties and the fortysomething woman who teaches him to read and opens his eyes to the world. A thoughtful romantic drama based on a book by Colleen McCullough, who wrote *The Thorn Birds*, and directed by Michael Pate, an Australian actor who spent many years in Hollywood.

Timberjack ○
1954, US, 94 mins, colour
Dir: Joseph Kane
Stars: Sterling Hayden, Vera Ralston, David Brian, Adolphe Menjou, Chill Wills, Jim Davis
Rating: ★

A trite script and acting as wooden as the lumber that's felled during the action sequences sink this tiresome story of inter-family rivalry in the woods of western Montana. The only diversion comes from laconic jazzman Hoagy Carmichael, who tinkles the ivories as the local saloon pianist. An unusually generous Republic poured money down the drain on this one with good production values and better-than-usual Trucolor.

Time After Time ◑ Ⓥ
1979, US, 112 mins, colour
Dir: Nicholas Meyer
Stars: Malcolm McDowell, David Warner, Mary Steenburgen
Rating: ★★★★

The clever premise of this fantasy thriller is that H G Wells builds the time machine of his stories and that Jack the Ripper, being one of Wells' associates, escapes in it to the future. As he hasn't the retainer key, the machine returns (without him) to its Victorian resting-place. Wells, anguished that he has loosed the Ripper on what he has always imagined to be a Utopian future, determines to pursue. Writer-director Nicholas Meyer has constructed an ingenious and highly original thriller on this basic theme, whose every piece falls into its proper place before the end, leaving no loose ends. The raging music of Miklos Rosza is a fine asset to the atmosphere; and the performances, especially that of Mary Steenbergen, create the believable characters so vital to this kind of science-fiction.

Time Bandits ◑ Ⓥ
1980, UK, 110 mins, b/w
Dir: Terry Gilliam
Stars: Craig Warnock, David Rappaport, John Cleese, Sean Connery, David Warner, Ralph Richardson
Rating: ★★

For most of its length a cross between a sword and sorcery adventure and *Monty Python and the Holy Grail,* this fantasy from director Terry Gilliam (later to make *Brazil)* becomes exciting and really imaginative in cinematic terms only when our six dwarf heroes reach the fortress of Ultimate Darkness; otherwise it's a comic-strip trip through time and space. Devotees of Python humour, however, will undoubtedly savour John Cleese's Robin Hood.

Timecop ● ⓥ
1994, US, 98 mins, colour
Dir: Peter Hyams
Stars: Jean-Claude Van Damme, Leon Silver, Mia Sara, Gloria Reuben
Rating: ★★★

Routine Jean-Claude Van Damme mayhem given a lift by its time-travel plot, even if the comings and goings are not always easy to follow. Travelling back into the past from 2004 to prevent power-hungry elements from altering the course of history, timecop Van Damme finds he has a chance not only to end the plans of a corrupt senator (must have been tough weeding that one out) but reverse the death of his own wife in 1994. So many things seem to depend on others that may depend on the first things that it's best not trying to get your head round the plot. But it makes for some interesting variations on a theme, while Van Damme fans can just enjoy their hero strutting his stuff, as he bears a charmed life in the path of the bad guys' bullets. There's a completely gratuitous nude love scene for those not just along for the action, and director Peter Hyams sets a blastingly fast pace throughout.

Time Flies ☉
1944, UK, 88 mins, b/w
Dir: Walter Forde
Stars: Tommy Handley, Evelyn Dall, George Moon
Rating: ★★

One of the great radio comedian Tommy Handley's few feature films, this sends him to Elizabethan London in a time machine. Unseen now for many years, the film features guest appearances (as a soothsayer and his nephew) by those stalwarts of Will Hay comedies, plump Graham Moffatt and wheezy Moore Marriott. Despite the subject and the cast, the treatment lacks vivacity.

Time for Giving, A ◐
(aka: Generation)
1969, US, 104 mins, colour

Dir: George Schaefer
Stars: David Janssen, Kim Darby, Pete Duel
Rating: ★★★

Tenderly observed, often amusing and ultimately moving human drama about a young couple who want to deliver their own baby and resent the well-meaning interference of the girl's father. It's far from being as cloying as it sounds, and David Janssen, who didn't have much luck with his film roles, delivers a fine performance as the father. Making his screen debut in a supporting role is Sam Waterston.

Time Gentlemen Please! ○
1952, UK, 83 mins, b/w
Dir: Lewis Gilbert
Stars: Eddie Byrne, Jane Barrett, Sidney James, Hermione Baddeley, Dora Bryan, Edie Martin
Rating: ★★

This is a charming little comedy from the all-too-short-lived Group 3 Productions (formed to boost British independent film-making). Its story, which involves the village drunk-cum-layabout coming into a fortune, clearly shows the influence of the Ealing Studios school of fun, and gives Irish character star Eddie Byrne an opportunity for a richly comic characterisation as the idler. The best of any number of amusing performances in support (Ian Carmichael has a tiny role as a public relations man), comes from little Edie Martin as a blood-and-thunder prophetess.

Time Lock ○
1957, UK, 73 mins, b/w
Dir: Gerald Thomas
Stars: Robert Beatty, Betty McDowall
Rating: ★★

That talented child star Vincent Winter, who first came to prominence in *The Kidnappers,* is at the heart of this tense thriller made by Peter Rogers and Gerald Thomas before they turned their attention to making *Carry On* comedies. Vincent plays a little boy who gets accidentally locked in a bank vault; and the suspense mounts steadily as attempts to rescue him become increasingly desperate. Spot the young Sean Connery in a brief role as a welder.

Time Machine, The ○ ⓥ
1960, US, 103 mins, colour
Dir: George Pal
Stars: Rod Taylor, Yvette Mimieux
Rating: ★★★

Special effects wizards Gene Warren and Tim Baar took an Academy Award for their visual trickery in this adaptation of the H G Wells fantasy classic. Comic-strip action, but some eerily effective moments too.

Time of Destiny, A ◐
1988, US, 117 mins, colour
Dir: Gregory Nava
Stars: William Hurt, Timothy Hutton, Melissa Leo, Francisco Rabal, Stockard Channing
Rating: ★★

This very slow war-romance-family vendetta epic offered the first evidence that not even the Oscar-winning William Hurt was director-proof. Very old-fashioned in its execution (and set in the 1943-45 period), the plot hands Hurt a rare villainous role as the GI who has vowed to kill his sister's new husband, whom he holds responsible for the death of the family father who tried to prevent the marriage. Gregory Nava's direction is top-heavy with symbolism and has no pace, hampered a bit perhaps by the film's complex flashback and flash-forward structure. The script isn't bad, although it has one or two laughable lines even Hurt can't cope with. The best thing in the film is Melissa Leo's utterly sincere portrayal of the beleaguered but strongly-characterised heroine. The climax in a bell-tower is enjoyably badly staged and at least gives the movie a lively final reel.

Timescape ◑ ⓥ
(aka: Grand Tour: Disaster in Time)
1991, Canada, 98 mins, colour
Dir: David N Twohy
Stars: Jeff Daniels, Ariana Richards, Jim Haynie, Emilia Crow
Rating: ★★

An intriguing idea is never quite carried out with sufficient urgency by writer-director David Twohy to put this in the top flight of fantasy. Innkeeper Jeff Daniels, battling the booze and the memory of leaving his wife to die, finds his hotel housing a group of strange tourists who turn out to be time travellers visiting earthly disasters. Can he prevent one happening in 1991 and rescue a child from her vengeful grandfather at the same time? Watch this space!

Timeslip ○
1955, UK, 93 mins, b/w
Dir: Ken Hughes
Stars: Gene Nelson, Faith Domergue
Rating: ★★★

T

The plot of this thriller takes some believing. But director Ken Hughes makes it so fast and exciting that you won't have time to work out the deficiencies. Hollywood players Gene Nelson and Faith Domergue head the cast, but Britain's Peter Arne steals the film in the dual role that provides the key to the story.

Timetable O
1955, US, 79 mins, colour
Dir: Mark Stevens
Stars: Mark Stevens, Felicia Farr
Rating: ★★★

Star Mark Stevens also directed this taut, fast-moving thriller about a big train robbery. As a director, he was much sharper than as an actor, as he showed in such other films as *Cry Vengeance!* Here, he keeps the action going like the train that is robbed in a well-planned and brilliantly executed raid. Jack Klugman makes his screen debut as a frightened witness, and it's a notable first film performance.

Time to Kill, A ● Ⓥ
1996, US, 149 mins, colour
Dir: Joel Schumacher
Stars: Sandra Bullock, Matthew McConaughey, Samuel L Jackson, Kevin Spacey, Ashley Judd
Rating: ★★★

Black Southerner Jackson sees liberal white lawyer McConaughey as the right man to defend him on charges of gunning down the two rednecks who raped and almost killed his 10-year-old daughter. Jackson wants a white defender the same way McConaughey wants a jury of caring fathers: hotshot prosecutor Spacey see to it that he doesn't get them. From here on, McConaughey, his family and associates come under increasing mental and physical pressure as he fights to keep Jackson out of the gas chamber. Ah yes, and we almost forgot Sandra Bullock (top-billed but a distant third in screen time) as the sharp legal student who declares herself McConaughey's researcher and nearly has an affair with him while his wife Ashley Judd flees town just before her house is burned to the ground. Inflammatory stuff then, in more ways than one: morally dubious, slow to start and overlong, but well performed and persuasively done.

Time Travellers, The O
1964, US, 82 mins, colour
Dir: Ib Melchior
Stars: Preston Foster, Philip Carey,

Merry Anders
Rating: ★★★

An interesting piece of science-fiction which had a limited release in British cinemas. An uneven film, it has good performances from Merry Anders – one of those great unsung Hollywood actresses who work steadily for 20 years without really becoming stars – and John Hoyt. The ending is unexpected and rather chilling.

Tina – What's Love Got to Do with It ● Ⓥ
1993, US, 118 mins, colour
Dir: Brian Gibson
Stars: Angela Bassett, Lawrence Fishburne
Rating: ★★★★

River deep and mountain high, sang Tina Turner in one of her greatest hits. That was about how low she sank and how high she had to climb to survive and escape a marriage to her stage partner Ike Turner from which her music was the only relief. Subjected to a savage 15-year campaign of beating, Tina only divorced him as late as 1977, making a sensational solo comeback three years later. In two Oscar-nominated performances, Angela Bassett mimes superbly to Turner's songs and Lawrence Fishburne is excellent as Ike, moving convincingly from smooth Romeo with deep bass singing voice into a drug-sniffing, short-fused monster and ageing believably at the same time. Yet the strength of the performance is that he never quite loses all our sympathy. Bassett conveys well the transformation in Tina when she takes to the stage, and it was possibly a mistake for Turner to come on as herself on stage at the end; this is rightly Bassett's show (audiences cheered when she hits back for the first time in 15 years) and it's wrong to deprive her shining performance of its final bow.

Tin Drum, The ◑ Ⓥ
1979, West Germany/France, 142 mins, colour
Dir: Volker Schlondorff
Stars: David Bennent, Mario Adorf, Angela Winkler
Rating: ★★★★

Disturbing West German movie which deservedly won an Oscar as the best foreign film of its year. Director Volker Schlondorff races through a complex but coherent narrative at a good rhythm, and the film never sags in its look at 20th-century German his-

tory through the rather scary gaze of a boy who has stunted his own growth because he has decided not to grow up. Some scenes are memorably unsettling; semi-surrealistic details may be too much for the squeamish.

Tin Cup ◑ Ⓥ
1996, US, 133 mins, colour
Dir: Ron Shelton
Stars: Kevin Costner, René Russo, Don Johnson, Cheech Marin
Rating: ★★★

Even if you don't fancy a golfing film, here's one that's below par in the nicest way, presenting golf for beginners, Hollywood style. A washed-up golf pro now running a desert driving range gets his act together, enters the American Open and breaks the course record. In your dreams. Never mind, with Costner at his most relaxed in ages and looking more like Gary Cooper than ever, the getting to this cup of moonshine is pretty enjoyable. Marginally less believable than *Rocky*, it has a decent share of funny lines, and nicely drawn supporting characters from Marin (Latino caddie) and Johnson (smarmy rival); René Russo's the gal. And the film's message – 'Go for it!' – isn't such bad advice in life.

Tin Men ● Ⓥ
1987, US, 112 mins, colour
Dir: Barry Levinson
Stars: Richard Dreyfuss, Danny DeVito, Barbara Hershey, John Mahoney
Rating: ★★★

A sad, oddly touching and well-acted slice-of-life story which would be even more effective if you didn't have the feeling that it's meant to be a comedy. Richard Dreyfuss and Danny DeVito are 'aluminium siding' salesmen, door-to-door hustlers who find their livelihoods under threat from the Home Improvement Commission. As if this weren't enough, the two men are involved in a collision in their new cars which very rapidly escalates into a tit-for-tat war of ridiculously ugly proportions. As the coup de grace, Dreyfuss beds DeVito's wife (Barbara Hershey). But – you've guessed it – he falls in love with her. Nice, lived-in dialogue by director Barry Levinson, with the occasional acidly amusing line cloaking the wretchedness in the lives of these smooth-moving losers. Hershey is exceptionally good as the wasted wife, Dreyfuss spot-on as the rustproof Romeo. DeVito fits round his oily, four-letter character like a well-worn glove. These are bad-tempered, sweaty people, but they have the whiff of life.

Tin Pan Alley ⊙
1940, US, 94 mins, b/w
Dir: Walter Lang
Stars: Alice Faye, Betty Grable, John Payne, Jack Oakie
Rating: ★★

The only major teaming of Fox's two big musical blondes of the early Forties, Alice Faye and Betty Grable, is a bright, bustling musical set in the early years of the 20th century, against America's music publishing business. Director Walter Lang fizzes the story along, the teeming streets of 'Tin Pan Alley' are vividly captured, and there's a tuneful score. The highlight is probably 'The Sheik of Araby', danced and sung by Grable and Faye, with plump Billy Gilbert as the sheik. One of the few big Fox musicals of the time not to be shot in colour – a pity, as. the story cries out for the Technicolor treatment.

Tin Star, The ○
1957, US, 93 mins, b/w
Dir: Anthony Mann
Stars: Henry Fonda, Anthony Perkins, Betsy Palmer, Neville Brand
Rating: ★★★★

Despite the absence of his usual star, James Stewart, this is probably Anthony Mann's best Western. It's a classic re-telling of the one about the inexperienced lawman helped by an older, embittered gunman. It provided Henry Fonda with one of a series of meaty Western roles in the Fifties and Sixties. In this film, there's one stand-out scene, superbly caught in black-and-white, as the doctor's black carriage rattles back into town after he has gone ' missing. And the showdown climax is in the best tradition of the Western, while Anthony Perkins gives an especially sensitive performance as Fonda's very agreeable foil.

Titanic ○
1953, US, 97 mins, b/w
Dir: Jean Negulesco
Stars: Clifton Webb, Barbara Stanwyck, Robert Wagner
Rating: ★★★

One of two Fifties' films on the great 1912 maritime disaster that are superior to any other film on the subject before or since. Clifton Webb and Barbara Stanwyck provide more depth to their roles than the script really deserves while Richard Basehart gives a quietly striking performance as a drunken, unfrocked priest. Edmund

Purdom makes one of his earliest screen appearances as Lightoller, the role played by Kenneth More in the other famous 'Titanic' film *A Night to Remember*.

Titfield Thunderbolt, The ⊙ ⓥ
1953, UK, 84 mins, colour
Dir: Charles Crichton
Stars: Stanley Holloway, George Relph, Naunton Wayne
Rating: ★★★

Sunny, enjoyable Ealing Studios fun about the fight to preserve a 'one-horse' railway. The first Ealing comedy in colour, and the gorgeous Technicolor photography of darkest Surrey is quite splendid. It's in similar vein to *Passport to Pimlico* and *The Lavender Hill Mob*, with the usual stock Ealing characters tilting at local windmills. George Relph stands out as an engine-loving cleric and Stanley Holloway offers another of those amiable drunks who are always littered around Ealing pictures.

T-Men ○
1947, US, 87 mins, b/w
Dir: Anthony Mann
Stars: Dennis O'Keefe, Mary Meade, Charles McGraw
Rating: ★★★★

Dynamic, documentary-style thriller about US Treasury agents in great danger while tracking down a gang of counterfeiters. Its hard-hitting style made the reputations of director Anthony Mann and cinematographer John Alton, who close in on the action like hired assassins stalking their victim and create an urgent atmosphere of high tension throughout. Star Dennis O'Keefe, whose previous star career had been mainly in comedy, found himself with a new image as a screen tough guy and, as a new member of the T-Men, a little-known actor called Alfred Ryder makes an especially strong impression.

Toast of New Orleans, The ○
1950, US, 97 mins, colour
Dir: Norman Taurog
Stars: Mario Lanza, David Niven
Rating: ★★★

Mario Lanza's second film was one of the biggest musicals that even MGM had ever mounted. A cast of thousands swarms across 35 sets – including complicated construction jobs for the fishing village and the opera house. Magnificent Technicolor

photography makes the most of it all, the supporting cast is full of character and Lanza (with Kathryn Grayson) sings perhaps his biggest film hit – 'Be My Love'.

Tobacco Road ○
1941, US, 84 mins, b/w
Dir: John Ford
Stars: Charley Grapewin, Marjorie Rambeau, Gene Tierney, Dana Andrews
Rating: ★★

Charley Grapewin added another to his gallery of wheezy old codgers with the idle Jeeter Lester in this somewhat bowdlerised version of a notorious novel and play, one of the earliest about steamy goings-on in the American deep South. John Ford's direction and Arthur Miller's photography lend the film poetic touches which help balance its portrait of degradation and despair.

To Be or Not to Be ○
1942, US, 99 mins, b/w
Dir: Ernst Lubitsch
Stars: Carole Lombard, Jack Benny, Robert Stack
Rating: ★★★★

A fairly close remake of the Lubitsch black comedy classic – now in colour and well over the top, for those who like it that way. Not aided b y laan Johnson's clodhopping direction, Mel Brooks comes nowhere near capturing the part of Bronski, so beautifully played in the original by Jack Benny. Anne Bancroft wers some gorgeous gowns and has a game stab at the Carole Lombard role, while Charles Durning raises a few smiles as 'Concentration Camp' Erhardt, the loudly inefficient German officer. Like most of the roles, however, his is wildly exaggerated as in any early silent comedy – although the actors may feel forced to 'mug' so vigorously by the director's insistence on placing the cameras so close to their faces.

Tobruk ○
1966, US, 110 mins, colour
Dir: Arthur Hiller
Stars: Rock Hudson, George Peppard
Rating: ★★

A straightforward World War Two action film, with an exciting beginning (a night raid by frogmen), an explosive ending and a pretty routine middle. Rock Hudson is surprisingly effective as the British major who does everything from conversing in the vernacular with a passing Tuareg tribesman to destroying the German

T

fuel installations at Tobruk. The screenplay is by veteran Hollywood 'heavy' Leo Gordon, who also plays a supporting role. George Peppard plays a German-born Jew working for the Allies.

To Catch a Thief ○ Ⓥ
1955, US, 106 mins, colour
Dir: Alfred Hitchcock
Stars: Cary Grant, Grace Kelly, Jessie Royce Landis, John Williams
Rating: ★★★★

Like any work by the master of suspense, Alfred Hitchcock, this thriller – about a jewel thief trying to track down his impersonator – has its fair share of mystery. But it is also the one in which Hitchcock plays some jokes (some of them at the expense of the audience), with plentiful red herrings and dead-end trails. Distinctive Hitchcockian touches are here too, in plenty: one remembers especially Jessie Royce Landis stubbing out her cigarette in an egg, and a bizarre costume ball with policemen awkwardly masquerading in fancy dress. And there's a splendid car chase along the Grand Corniche (a Riviera hilltop road), filmed from a helicopter. Cary Grant is smooth, if improbable, as the jewel thief while Grace Kelly is icily effective as the high society girl whose reserve is gradually melted.

To Die For ● Ⓥ
1995, US, 107 mins, colour
Dir: Gus Van Sant
Stars: Nicole Kidman, Matt Dillon, Joaquin Phoenix, Illeana Douglas, Kurtwood Smith, George Segal
Rating: ★★★★

Beware the airhead with ambition. Nicole Kidman, in her best performance for several years, is beautiful but deadly in this blackest of comedies. Suzanne (Nicole Kidman) spots handsome Larry (Matt Dillon) playing drums at a disco, and sets her cap at him. No dowdy housewife our Suzanne, though. The grey matter may not work too well on the subtleties of life, but she knows how to use her good looks – and settles on getting a job as a local TV weathergirl as a step towards becoming a national small-screen personality. When Dillon decides she should stay at home and have babies, the emotionless Kidman sees a student (Joaquin Phoenix) with a crush on her as the answer to a maiden's prayer for hubby's removal. Phoenix is excellent as the teen who takes it as a compliment when his best

friend tells him his dick is bigger than his brain, Kidman frighteningly icy as the Barbie doll from Hell. A few sags in the middle contribute to the film's slight overlength, but overall this is a work of no small achievement with a terrific ending.

To Each His Own ○
1946, US, 122 mins, b/w
Dir: Mitchell Leisen
Stars: Olivia de Havilland, John Lund, Mary Anderson, Roland Culver
Rating: ★★★★

Olivia de Havilland finally achieved the recognition she craved as an actress with her fine performance in this very classy weepie, notable for its well-constructed script and remarkably unstarry cast. The star's leading man was an unknown from Broadway, John Lund, who does well here, but never achieved true front-rank stardom in the cinema. But Olivia went on to greater glories. She won her first Oscar here, for her performance as the embittered spinster, and it was not long before she would win another, for *The Heiress*.

To Have and Have Not ○ Ⓥ
1944, US, 100 mins, b/w
Dir: Howard Hawks
Stars: Humphrey Bogart, Walter Brennan, Lauren Bacall
Rating: ★★★★★

An absolute screen classic, brimming over with razor-sharp dialogue, first-rate direction and acting as good as it comes. Warners wanted another *Casablanca* from this tale of WWII intrigue in exotic Martinique – and found the perfect foil to Humphrey Bogart in 18-year-old New York model Betty Bacall. Her name was changed to Lauren, she was whisked off her feet in real life by her co-star and the rest, as they say, is movie history. Bacall was so nervous during the early days of filming that she had to keep her trembling chin down almost to her chest and flick her eyes upwards to look at Bogey. In an instant 'The Look' was born and it launched her smouldering beauty into a succession of hit films.

To Hell and Back ○ Ⓥ
1955, US, 106 mins, colour
Dir: Jesse Hibbs
Stars: Audie Murphy, Marshall Thompson, Charles Drake
Rating: ★★★★

Remarkably successful film of Audie Murphy's book about his early life,

and the wartime heroics which made him the most decorated American soldier of World War Two. Very exciting, too. Murphy gives a commendably modest portrayal without being too self-effacing.

To Kill a Mockingbird ◑ Ⓥ
962, US, 129 mins, b/w
Dir: Robert Mulligan
Stars: Gregory Peck, Mary Badham, Philip Alford, Robert Duvall
Rating: ★★★★

Gregory Peck finally won a coveted Best Actor Oscar at the fifth time of being nominated for his compassionate performance in this classic race-hate drama. Peck gives a fine character reading of the lawyer and widowed father of two children who has to defend a black man accused of raping a white girl in a Deep South town in the 1930s. But it's the child actors who steal every scene in which they appear. Mary Badham, a nine-year-old who had never acted before, is truly charming as the tough little sister who tries to keep pace with her brother, but ends up having to wear a dress, however embarrassing it is to her. Still Peck's favourite film from a varied career.

To Kill a Priest ● Ⓥ
1988, UK, 119 mins, colour
Dir: Agnieszka Holland
Stars: Christopher Lambert, Ed Harris, Joanne Whalley-Kilmer, Cherie Lunghi, Peter Postlethwaite
Rating: ★

Something went dramatically wrong with this film about the young Solidarity priest murdered by Polish secret agents in 1984. Too great an attempt has been made, for one thing, to *dramatise* the story, causing a bevy of good British actors to overact like mad. And Agnieszka Holland has, in her sincerity as a Polish patriot, allowed the enterprise to go on for far too long. Christopher Lambert is adequate if not terribly charismatic as the priest. Hollywood's Ed Harris strives mightily to pull it all together as the tortured secret policeman who yearns to kill him and spare him at the same time, but Tim Roth and Timothy Spall as his associates give garish performances more suited to a *Carry On* film. The sad thing about the whole sorry business is that it's such a limp tribute to a genuine martyr.

To Live and Die In L.A. ● Ⓥ
1985, US, 116 mins, colour
Dir: William Friedkin

Stars: William L Petersen, Willem Dafoe, John Pankow, Debra Feuer
Rating: ★

This violent police thriller with all the ingredients you'd expect from an adults-only Eighties film was described in its publicity as 'sophisticated'. But believe me there is *nothing* in the least sophisticated in this story about a cop (William L Petersen) who swears to break all the rules to avenge the death of his partner at the hands of a killer. Despite a great cast (including Willem Dafoe, John Turturro, Dean Stockwell and Robert Downey Jr), the film is hard to follow and harder still to get involved in when its characters on both sides of the law are so dislikeable. Stockwell gives easily the best performance as a lawyer with one money-grabbing foot on either side of the legal fence.

Tomahawk ◌
(aka: Battle of Powder River)
1950, US, 82 mins, colour
Dir: George Sherman
Stars: Van Heflin, Yvonne De Carlo, Jack Oakie
Rating: ★★

A colourful saga about Cavalrymen and Indians. This was one of the earliest of the vivid 80-minute co-features for which Universal-International was to become famous in the Fifties. Several of the actors in this adventure – Alex Nicol, Yvonne De Carlo, Rock Hudson and Susan Cabot among them – were to become staple elements of these action films, while the cast here is considerably boosted by the presence of such experienced Hollywood stars as Van Heflin, Jack Oakie and Preston Foster.

Tom and Jerry: The Movie
◉ Ⓥ
1992, US, 84 mins, colour
Dir: Phil Roman
Voice stars: Richard Kind, Dana Hill, Henry Gibson, Charlotte Rae
Rating: ★★

The famous cat and mouse's first feature film is a lively enough caper which can't begin to compare with the classic MGM cartoons, but might please modern tots who have somehow missed these on TV. The story – in which Tom and Jerry save a young orphan from her evil guardians (a wellworn cartoon theme) – works well enough, but there are a few shocks for vintage T & J fans. The first is that they speak! This makes their normal rough-and-tumble antics seem merely gratuitously violent. The second is that they become pals! Still, the cat-and-mouse slapstick that results will please simple minds, although younger viewers may find the darker side, which includes kidnap and death threats, slightly upsetting. Although it has more low spots than highpoints, the caper will still give rise to the occasional guffaw. There's life in the old cat and mouse yet.

Tom & Viv ◑ Ⓥ
1994, UK/US, 125 mins, colour
Dir: Brian Gilbert
Stars: Willem Dafoe, Miranda Richardson, Rosemary Harris, Tim Dutton, Nickolas Grace, Philip Locke
Rating: ★★★

This is the tragic true tale of the troubled love between a high-spirited but unstable Englishwoman, Vivienne Haigh-Wood (Miranda Richardson, Oscar-nominated) and the American poet T S Eliot (Willem Dafoe). It's impeccably acted, especially by Richardson as the woman who really loved Eliot, but whose mood swings sent her spiralling into what appeared to be insanity, although there's too little chemistry between her and an unusually subdued Dafoe. Rosemary Harris, as her snooty mother, was also nominated for an Academy Award in an absorbing and rather shocking drama that lets rip with emotion in the last reel.

Tomb of Ligeia, The ◑
1964, US, 81 mins, colour
Dir: Roger Corman
Stars: Vincent Price, Elizabeth Shepherd, John Westbrook
Rating: ★★★★

Director Roger Corman's second film in Britain, and the last and best of his series of horror tales based on the works of Edgar Allan Poe. Corman hardly puts a foot wrong in this one, which is not only quite faithful to the Poe original (a short story), but adds its own conclusion to Poe's unfinished scenario. It's very literate, frightening in parts and very well acted, particularly by Vincent Price and by Oliver Johnston as his manservant. And the plot has as many twists and turns as the black cat which plays such a vital part in its disentanglement. Some of the earlier scenes – notably one in which the heroine is lured by the cat into a bell-tower – are especially well-staged. A minor classic of its genre.

Tom Brown's Schooldays ◉
1951, UK, 95 mins, b/w
Dir: Gordon Parry
Stars: John Howard Davies, Robert Newton, Diana Wynyard, Hermione Baddeley
Rating: ★★★

Less well-paced than the 1940 Hollywood version of Thomas Hughes' famous school story, but more solidly acted, this British version was directed by Gordon Parry and proved an immense success at the box-office. A young Max Bygraves makes an early film appearance aboard a coach, and John Howard Davies, reunited with his *Oliver Twist* co-star Robert Newton (who plays the headmaster) is ideal as Tom Brown.

Tombstone ◑ Ⓥ
1993, US, 129 mins, colour
Dir: George P Cosmatos
Stars: Kurt Russell, Val Kilmer, Powers Boothe, Michael Biehn, Charlton Heston, Dana Delany
Rating: ★★★

A colourful and vigorous retelling of a familiar tale. What may be seen by some as clichéd and unoriginal, is also a very old-fashioned but thoroughly enjoyable Western. Unlike *My Darling Clementine* and *Gunfight at the OK Corral*, the fabled showdown, seen about two-thirds of the way through this film, isn't the climax to the story, but the start of a small war between the avenging Wyatt Earp and the baddies, led by Curly Bill (Powers Boothe – very effective). Kurt Russell looks and sounds the part more than any other Earp, helped in no small measure by costuming and by his courage in growing a magnificent Earp-like moustache. There's also vigorous 'tache-wearing from Sam Elliott and Bill Paxton as brothers Virgil and Morgan. Val Kilmer makes Doc Holliday the fine Southern gent he probably was and coughs with consumptive conviction, giving an impressive portrayal of the doomed dentist. Wonderful photography and a fine sense of period both help make this an entertaining action film.

Tom, Dick and Harry ◌
1941, US, 86 mins, b/w
Dir: Garson Kanin
Stars: Ginger Rogers, George Murphy, Alan Marshal, Burgess Meredith
Rating: ★★★

A deliciously scatty comedy about a girl who has three suitors on the go at one time, but tends to get them and their financial status mixed up. Director Garson Kanin shot the ending three ways, so that none of the actors

T

concerned would know who got the girl. Highly original stuff, much less pretentious than star Ginger Rogers' faintly similar film called *Lady in the Dark*, three years later.

Tom Horn ○ Ⓥ

1980, US, 98 mins, colour
Dir: William Wiard
Stars: Steve McQueen, Linda Evans, Richard Farnsworth, Slim Pickens
Rating: ★★★

There's certainly a touch of the genuine old west about Steve McQueen's second-last film, picturesquely set and lovingly photographed. The first half is packed with rugged action, the second brings us down to earth as frontiersman Horn is laid low. One would have liked to have seen more of the character's colourful early life, especially his involvement in the Indian wars. That said, it must be added that John Alonzo's colour cinematography is not only beyound fault, but also imaginative and the work of a real stylist.

Tom Jones ◑ Ⓥ

1963, UK, 129 mins, colour
Dir Tony Richardson
Stars: Albert Finney, Susannah York, Hugh Griffith, Edith Evans, Diane Cilento
Rating: ★★★★★

A deserved Academy Award winner. Director Tony Richardson (who never equalled his achievements here), takes Henry Fielding's famous story of a foundling's amorous adventures and, with incredibly cheeky sleight-of-hand, including quick motion, freeze-frame, and characters addressing the audience, enriches the screen with earthy entertainment played for laughs at breakneck speed. Five members of the cast were Oscar nominees, including Albert Finney, endowing Tom with a drive and a lust for life that is irresistible, and Hugh Griffith as the squire. Red-cheeked, debauched, leering at his farmgirls, or angrily pushing away his farm animals while he is trying to think, his is a richly comic performance. Best of all, though, is Edith Evans, as the haughty Miss Western. 'Stand and deliver!' cries a highwayman. 'Sir,' retorts Dame Edith. 'I am no travelling midwife. Coachman, drive on!' But Oscars *were* won by Richardson, by John Osborne for his script, and by John Addison for his devastatingly witty 18th-century-style music.

Tommy ◑ Ⓥ

1975, UK, 111 mins, colour
Dir: Ken Russell

Stars: Ann-Margret, Oliver Reed, Roger Daltrey, Elton John, Tina Turner
Rating., ★★★

A bizarre, full-blooded and drivingly powerful version of the rock opera by The Who. The story is of a boy struck deaf, dumb and blind by seeing his father killed by his stepfather – who becomes the king of the pinball wizards and, on recovery of his full faculties, a Messiah-like figure for the young. Director Ken Russell's typically pile-driving approach ensures that you'll be swept away in the film's title of dazzlingly entertaining obscenities. And you must admire the tremendous singing and uninhibited verve of Ann Margret and the sardonic subtlety of Oliver Reed's hilarious teddy boy. Tina Turner is something else as the Acid Queen.

Tommy Steele Story, The ○ Ⓥ

(aka: Rock Around the World)
1957, UK, 82 mins, b/w
Dir: Gerard Bryant
Stars: Tommy Steele, Lisa Daniely
Rating: ★★★

There can't be many film biopics that were made when their subject (and star) was still only 21. Even Keaton and Jolson had to wait until they were well into middle age. But already Tommy Steele had packed enough incident into his young life to make the conception of a tune-filled life story well worthwhile. Tommy himself sings a wide variety of songs, the best of which is 'Butterfingers'. An engaging entertainment, dominated by the star's own chirpy personality.

Tommy the Toreador ○ Ⓥ

1959, UK, 86 mins, colour
Dir: John Paddy Carstairs
Stars: Tommy Steele, Janet Munro, Sidney James
Rating: ★★★

No time at all for a siesta in this enjoyably lightweight comedy with music, a British version of the type of family fare Elvis Presley turned out in the early Sixties. Tommy Steele's energetic performance is nicely offset by comedy cameos from a host of familiar funny men (including Sidney James, Eric Sykes, Bernard Cribbins, Kenneth Williams and Warren Mitchell) and by Janet Munro's attractive presence.

Tomorrow Is Forever ○

1945, US, 105 mins, b/w
Dir: Irving Pichel
Stars: Claudette Colbert, Orson Welles,

George Brent
Rating: ★★★

Natalie Wood appears here in her first major film, at the age of six. It's a big weepie about a man (Orson Welles) returned from the dead to find his wife has re-married. The director is Irving Pichel, a former actor who brought considerable bulky presence to such horror films as *Dracula's Daughter*.

Tomorrow We Live ○

(aka: At Dawn We Die)
1942, UK, 82 mins, b/w
Dir: George King
Stars: John Clements, Godfrey Tearle, Hugh Sinclair, Greta Gynt
Rating: ★★★

An eventful war film about French freedom fighters, 'made with the official co-operation of General de Gaulle'. Good performances from Greta Gynt, Judy Kelly, Yvonne Arnaud and Karel Stepanek, all of whom outshine the nominal stars of the film headed by John Clements. It may look a bit stiff by today's standards, but it was food and drink to the British wartime box-office and didn't do badly in America either, the February 1943 première being treated as an important social event.

tom thumb ⊙

1958, US, 98 mins, colour
Dir: George Pal
Stars: Russ Tamblyn, Peter Sellers, Terry-Thomas
Rating: ★★★★

A delightful children's entertainment, with Russ Tamblyn a sprightly inch-high hero and Peter Sellers and Terry-Thomas stealing all their scenes as the roguishly comic villains. The scene where they count and share out their ill-gotten gains is hilarious. Hummable tunes (especially 'The Yawning Song'), good puppet animation and notable contributions from Jessie Matthews and Bernard Miles as Tom's foster-parents complete a delightful entertainment.

Tonight's the Night

See: Happy Ever After

Tony Rome ○

1967, US, 110 mins, colour
Dir: Gordon Douglas
Stars: Frank Sinatra, Jill St John, Richard Conte, Gena Rowlands
Rating: ★★

Tired-eye private eye Tony Rome, who tackles his cases from a houseboat, was Frank Sinatra's first stab at playing detective in a career stretching back 25 years. He promptly proceeded to make two more films in the same vein, *Lady in Cement* and *The Detective*. All three were directed by Sinatra's old friend Gordon Douglas and all feature the maximum feminine distraction and a collection of weird characters in the finest Bogart tradition. This one, set in Miami, was highly thought-of in some critical circles and involves our weary hero in a rather nasty mystery concerning drugs and, of course, murder.

Too Hot to Handle ◖ ⓥ
(aka: The Marrying Man)
1991, US, 117 mins, colour
Dir: Jerry Rees
Stars: Kim Basinger, Alec Baldwin, Robert Loggia, Elisabeth Shue, Armand Assante
Rating: ★★

On the face of it (and everywhere else), Basinger would seem to have everything: looks, talent, sex appeal and even singing ability, as she proves here. But most of it doesn't come across in this one. And the problems of Kim and the equally charmless Alec Baldwin just don't seem to amount to a hill of beans, when they should be carrying us through two hours of on-off-love/hate-love. Neil Simon has fashioned a very corny over-the-years romance which starts in 1948 when playboy Baldwin, about to marry a film magnate's daughter, becomes a heap of quivering lust at one sighting of sultry songbird Basinger, who just happens to be the mistress of gangster Bugsy Siegel. Strangely, this situation doesn't qualify the duo for concrete overcoats, but instead triggers a plot in which Baldwin marries Basinger four times over. If only he'd left it at one!

Too Late for Tears ○
1949, US, 99 mins, b/w
Dir: Byron Haskin
Stars: Lizabeth Scott, Don DeFore, Dan Duryea, Arthur Kennedy
Rating: ★★★

Lizabeth Scott excels as a particularly deadly femme fatale in this dark thriller that casts her as a hard-bitten blonde only too ready to stoop to murder to keep her hands on $60,000 in cash that has accidentally come her way, in her anxiety to 'move out of the ranks of the middle-class poor'. Even Dan Duryea's slimy, corrupt detective pales besides the pure evil of the Scott character. Good, unsettling use of Los Angeles locations by director Byron

Haskin adds the finishing touch to an efficient, if slightly unpleasant thriller.

Too Late the Hero ◖ ⓥ
1969, US, 144 mins, colour
Dir: Robert Aldrich
Stars: Michael Caine, Cliff Robertson, Ian Bannen, Denholm Elliott
Rating: ★★★

A tense and exciting war drama set in the Pacific, with Michael Caine and Cliff Robertson sent behind enemy lines to destroy a Japanese observation post which monitors allied shipping. Almost as violent but nowhere near as gung-ho as director Robert Aldrich's earlier war adventure *The Dirty Dozen*. Perhaps this has something to do with the fact that it has a largely British cast, although there is nothing stiff-upper-lipped about Caine's performance as Cockney tough Tosh Hearne. Robertson gives good value, as usual, and there are also strong portrayals by Ian Bannen and Denholm Elliott. Thrilling stuff, with a few twists and turns before the end.

Too Many Crooks ⊙
1958, UK, 87 mins, b/w
Dir: Mario Zampi
Stars: Terry-Thomas, George Cole, Brenda De Banzie
Rating: ★★

British film comedy, so often in the doldrums, was going through one of its richest periods when director Mario Zampi made this very funny farce about a bunch of bungling burglars. Zampi's previous comedies included *Laughter in Paradise*, *Happy Ever After* and *The Naked Truth* – all winners. His early death in 1963 was a great loss to the British cinema.

Tootsie ◖ ⓥ
1982, US, 116 mins, colour
Dir: Sydney Pollack
Stars: Dustin Hoffman, Jessica Lange, Teri Garr, Dabney Coleman, Bill Murray
Rating: ★★★★

Dustin Hoffman acts both his male and female co-stars off the screen as an out-of-work actor who 'drags' up as a woman he names Dorothy Michaels to land a job on a daytime soap opera. And he was so convincing as a woman that industry wags suggest that Hoffman should have been nominated for a Best Actress Oscar as well as the Best Actor statuette. He himself wasn't convinced that he could pull off the deception and spent a year and thousands of dollars on screen tests. He even fooled actor friend Jon Voight by

making a pass at him in a lift at the studio! But he was sad that although he was believable, he didn't make an attractive woman. On Oscars night, it was Jessica Lange who scooped the Best Supporting Actress Award as the girl Hoffman fancies and who Hoffman as 'Dorothy' gets to sleep with as best girlfriends, causing no end of comic complications.

Topaz ○
1969, US, 127 mins, colour
Dir: Alfred Hitchcock
Stars: Frederick Stafford, John Forsythe, Karin Dor
Rating: ★★★★

Underrated Hitchcock thriller based on the best-selling book by Leon Uris, author of the (also filmed) *Exodus*. Keep your thinking caps on for the incredibly complicated plot and you'll be gripped throughout.

Top Gun ◖ ⓥ
1986, US, 110 mins, colour
Dir: Tony Scott
Stars: Tom Cruise, Kelly McGillis, Val Kilmer, Anthony Edwards, Tom Skerritt, Meg Ryan
Rating: ★★

The searing aerial action in this thunderous action film took the filmgoing world and especially younger filmgoers by storm on its first appearance, pushing Tom Cruise and Kelly McGillis into the megastar bracket at a single step. Movie buffs from way back, though, will have seen its like before. It's the one about the maverick fighter pilot who bucks authority, proves he's the best, cracks up on the death of a friend, but comes good in the end to claim the glory and the girl. Here it's Cruise, flashing his teeth a lot and oozing charisma, and McGillis, with multiple under-lid looks, who keep us watching, with the aid of lots of noisy action and a synthesised pop score. The rest of the characters are such cardboard cut-outs that they could be wheeled on and off the set without affecting the plot. And, this being the computer age, that thing on Cruise's shoulder is presumably a microchip!

Top Hat ○ ⓥ
1935, US, 100 mins, b/w
Dir: Mark Sandrich
Stars: Fred Astaire, Ginger Rogers
Rating: ★★★★★

This effervescent Fred Astaire and Ginger Rogers musical was the perfect panacea for Depression-era audiences. Every one of Irving Berlin's five songs

T

from the film was a hit and the movie was the second highest grossing of the year after *Mutiny on the Bounty*, and proved to be RKO's biggest moneymaker of the decade. Astaire and Berlin were on a percentage, so they were happy men. Look out for the scenes where Astaire flies off to Venice – they're outtakes from *Flying Down to Rio*!

Topkapi ○ ⓥ

1964, US, 120 mins, colour
Dir: Jules Dassin
Stars: Melina Mercouri, Maximilian Schell, Peter Ustinov, Robert Morley
Rating: ★★★

Thieves as ingenious as those in this thriller really do deserve to get away with it. Unfortunately, in films at least, they rarely do. Their target here is the Topkapi jewels, four fabulous emeralds in an Istanbul museum. Husky-voiced Melina Mercouri is the boss of the gang. But it's Peter Ustinov's film as the seedy, down-at-heel Englishman, Arthur Simpson, who makes a living selling blue postcards to tourists. He stumbles into the plot by mistake, and soon becomes a conscript. A sequence where he tries to drive a grenade-loaded car into Istanbul, and falls foul of the Customs and the police, is one of the funniest in the film. Ustinov won an Oscar for the performance. Robert Morley is bewitching too, as the craftsman of the gang, whose home is crammed with toys and gadgets that make it look like something out of James Bond. The film really whips up the suspense when three of the crooks clamber dizzily across Istanbul rooftops to reach the museum.

Top of the Form ⊙

1952, UK, 75 mins, b/w
Dir: John Paddy Carstairs
Stars: Ronald Shiner, Anthony Newley, Harry Fowler
Rating: ★★

Ronald Shiner was at the peak of his popularity when he made this broad remake of the Will Hay comedy film *Good Morning, Boys* – casting him as a bogus professor (in reality a horse tipster) who finds himself working as a real teacher. Anthony Newley, Harry Fowler and Gerald Campion are among the overgrown schoolboys in his bizarre classroom, and you may spot Ronnie Corbett (at the age of 22) as the 'titch' of the form.

Topper ○

1937, US, 97 mins, b/w
Dir: Norman Z McLeod
Stars: Constance Bennett, Roland Young
Rating: ★★★

Another of Thorne Smith's novels about mischievous ghosts (he also wrote *I Married a Witch*) is turned into a film comedy classic. Constance Bennett not only revived her entire career as the vivacious (if ethereal) Marion Kerby, but also starred in a sequel, *Topper Returns*. She and Cary Grant make a totally delightful duo, but great credit must also be given to Roy Seawright's special effects, which allow them to materialise at will in their efforts to help a harassed bank president overcome the malevolent machinations of his shrewish wife – two memorable performances by Roland Young (as Topper) and Billie Burke.

Topper Returns ○

1941, US, 88 mins, b/w
Dir: Roy del Ruth
Stars: Joan Blondell, Roland Young, Billie Burke, Dennis O'Keefe
Rating: ★★★

In the famous series of fantasy comedies which began with *Topper* in 1937, full of humorous ghostly adventures, this was the third and last. It's seldom that a sequel or follow-up measures up to the original, but here is an exception. And, despite the success of the first two, it had a different director – Roy Del Ruth instead of Norman Z McLeod. Absolutely scatty, delightful comedy entertainment.

Topper Takes a Trip ○

1939, US, 85 mins, b/w
Dir: Norman Z McLeod
Stars: Constance Bennett, Roland Young, Billie Burke
Rating: ★★★

The second of the three original highly successful *Topper* films about two ghosts interfering in the life of Cosmo Topper, the timid, henpecked little banker hero of Thorne Smith's novels. Throughout the short-lived series, the ghosts changed, but the central character was always played by Roland Young, adding yet another whimsical, bemused character to his collection. He was actually nominated for an Oscar for the original film, which co-starred Cary Grant.

Top Secret! ◑ ⓥ

1984, US, 90 mins, colour
Dir: David and Jerry Zucker
Stars: Val Kilmer, Lucy Gutteridge, Jeremy Kemp, Christopher Villiers
Rating: ★★

Not so many outright guffaws this time around from the *Airplane!* team, but it's fun identifying all the old movies parodied in this spoof on spy/espionage films, set in the rock 'n' roll (well, surfin') era. Aficionados will assuredly recognise *The Conspirators* (a whole sequence), *The Blue Lagoon, Gidget, Jailhouse Rock, The Great Escape* and *The Wizard of Oz*, but there are countless more besides. There's a briskly confident performance from Val Kilmer as the rock star on the run.

Tora! Tora! Tora! ○ ⓥ

1970, US/Japan, 144 mins, colour
Dir: Ray Kellogg, Toshio Masuda, Kinji Fukasaku
Stars: Martin Balsam, Soh Yamamura, Joseph Cotten, Jason Robards
Rating: ★★★

Long, lavish and meticulous re-creation of the Japanese invasion of Pearl Harbor, which attempts to tell the true story from both sides. It proves to be an impressively impartial account of the events, and the special effects are superb, but the film as a whole turns out to be one-paced and worthy rather than inspired. Best performances in the piece, however, come from James Whitmore, as America's Admiral Halsey, Soh Yamamura, as a conscience-stricken Japanese admiral, and Takahiro Tamura, as the man who led the actual attack.

Torch Song ○

1953, US, 90 mins, colour
Dir: Charles Walters
Stars: Joan Crawford, Michael Wilding, Gig Young
Rating: ★★

Near-laughable in parts, but pretty enjoyable as a whole, this all-out melodrama casts Joan Crawford as a bitchy Broadway star who unexpectedly meets her match in the form of a blind pianist, played by Britain's Michael Wilding in the best of his not-very-impressive bunch of Hollywood roles. Strangely, Crawford's singing is dubbed in all but one number 'Tenderly'. The 'clumsy' dancer with her in the film's opening sequence is in fact the director of the movie, Charles Walters, a musical expert who also made *Easter Parade, Lili* and *High Society*. Amazingly, it was Crawford's first starring role in a colour film. Her appearance in 'blackface' has to be seen to be believed.

Torch Song Trilogy● ⓥ

1988, US, 120 mins, colour
Dir: Paul Bogart

Stars: Harvey Fierstein, Anne Bancroft, Matthew Broderick, Karen Young
Rating: ★★

As full of smart Jewish humour as it is, this film version of Harvey Fierstein's stage hit, complete with the author as star (ludicrous to bill himself third in the credits), still makes pretty heavy going as a film. In spite of the humour, tragedy is perhaps kept too much to the fore in this story of a gay drag queen and his life from 10 to 40. The central character, who seemed so touchingly human in Antony Sher's London stage interpretation, comes across on screen as harsh, unsympathetic and self-centred. Worth sitting through, though, if only to watch Arnold's hefty black transvestite friend hold up a gold ladies' shoe in a dress shop and ask the assistant if she has it in a 16.

Torn Curtain ◑

1966, US, 128 mins, colour
Dir: Alfred Hitchcock
Stars: Paul Newman, Julie Andrews, Lila Kedrova, David Opatoshu
Rating: ★★

This was the most un-Hitchcock-like Hitchcock in a decade. Despite a nail-bitingly grisly murder scene, in which Hitchcock demonstrates how difficult it really is to kill someone, there are no twists, shocks or surprises to speak of in this conventional spy thriller with some arch dialogue. 'We're sending you out,' whispers an underground worker, 'in the costume bags of a Czech ballet company.' A subdued Paul Newman is the scientist who, apparently detecting to East Berlin, couldn't act more suspiciously if he tried. Small wonder the secret police are soon on his trail, or that fiancée/secretary Julie Andrews treats him like Jane and Michael Banks rolled into one. The film picks up once the couple go on the run from Iron Curtain police and encounter Lila Kedrov a as a refugee Polish countess. Her extravagant portrayal is in a completely different world – a Hitchcock world in fact – from the rest of the film.

Torrid Zone ◯

1940, US, 88 mins, b/w
Dir: William Keighley
Stars: James Cagney, Ann Sheridan, Pat O'Brien
Rating: ★★★

Robust action and ready wisecracks are the order of the day in another typical Warners vehicle of the early war years, although the setting – a plantation in Central America – is quite unusual for the time. Ann Sheridan steals the show with her honest-to-goodness torch singer, James Cagney and Pat O'Brien exchange banter and double-cross each other with practised ease.

To Sir, With Love ◯ Ⓥ

1966, UK, 105 mins, colour
Dir: James Clavell
Stars: Sidney Poitier, Suzy Kendall, Judy Geeson
Rating: ★★

This brightly coloured look (through rose-tinted glasses) at the trials and tribulations of an idealistic black teacher at a tough London school made a mint in its day. If it looks more than a little dated and simplistic today, there are good performances from Sidney Poitier, Suzy Kendall, Faith Brook and Adrienne Posta to carry it through its stickier patches. Pop star Lulu seems happier performing the film's hit song than in acting tough with the classroom rebels.

Total Eclipse ● Ⓥ

1995, Fr/UK/US, 118 mins, colour
Dir: Agnieszka Holland
Stars: Leonardo DiCaprio, David Thewlis, Romane Bohringer
Rating: ★★

Modern language, replete with four-letter words, proves an uneasy bedfellow for the admirably atmospheric detail in this incompletely realised but not inconsiderable account of the relationship between the 19th-century French poets Rimbaud and Verlaine. Like Mozart, Rimbaud (DiCaprio) was a flamboyant vulgarian; like Mozart he was also a genius. The volatile, alcoholic, bisexual Verlaine (Thewlis) experiences a fatal attraction for the equally bisexual teenager when he comes to stay in Paris, and has soon left his voluptuous but brainless wife (Bohringer) for Rimbauld's boyish charms. The rest of the film concerns their tempestuous on-off relationship through several countries and degrees of poverty and, though there are times when things get OTT and you wish these fairly charmless people would put themselves and us out of their misery, director Holland's treatment wields a morbid fascination that urges us to see things through to the end.

Total Recall ● Ⓥ

1990, US, 109 mins, colour
Dir: Paul Verhoeven

Stars: Arnold Schwarzenegger, Rachel Ticotin, Sharon Stone, Ronny Cox, Michael Ironside
Rating: ★★★

Though perhaps not quite 'the ride of your life' promised by its posters, this action yarn is still a lively sci-fi thriller about a man who has had his memory erased for a purpose other than that which he imagines. It's the distant future. Mars is colonised and Schwarzenegger's Doug Quaid is haunted by nightmares about life there. This is somewhat surprising as he's a building worker who lives on Earth. But Quaid soon becomes convinced he must get back to Mars and end the despotic reign of the men in charge there. From here on, the action hardly stops, with space machine-guns chattering, Schwarzenegger and heroine Rachel Ticotin diving everywhere and special effects running riot, especially in the creation of a colony of mutants who prove to be the hero's allies rather than his enemies. Ironside and Cox are excellent tight-lipped villains, one snapping to the other: 'You should have killed Quaid on Mars!' Well, yes, but they all say that. Actually, there's a special reason why they didn't, but that would be giving too much away of a plot that's above-average in complexirty for this kind of film.

To the Devil a Daughter ● Ⓥ

1976, UK/Germany, 95 mins, colour
Dir: Peter Sykes
Stars: Richard Widmark, Christopher Lee, Denholm Elliott, Nastassja Kinski
Rating: ★★

Not the first time that the house of Hammer had dabbled in Dennis Wheatley's diabolic books, but fortunately the last, in this resistible mix of revulsion and laughter. Devil's child Nastassja Kinski arrives in London coutesy of head satanist Christopher Lee, and is soon causing no end of trouble for her friends. Honor Blackman gets it in the neck (with a steel comb) for not looking after her, and Anthony Valentine gets all burnt up about her. Only trusty old Richard Widmark, displaying commendable conviction, is left to save the girl from being baptised in blood and becoming the devil herself, although why Widmark thought her worth saving we can't say. Director Peter Sykes achieves one or two nice images of monks boating mysteriously across the lake, but it all seems a bit daft. Kinski is well cast in the pivotal role, though –

T

a beguiling mix of innocence and malevolence.

To the Ends of the Earth ○
1948, US, 109 mins, b/w
Dir: Robert Stevenson
Stars: Dick Powell, Signe Hasso
Rating: ★★★★

A great thriller from the Forties: suspenseful, brilliantly lit and photographed, grittily acted and with a splendid twist at the end. Dick Powell holds the whole thing together with strength and great skill as the agent who pursues a narcotics ring halfway around the world. But don't go out to make the tea or you may lose the thread of the cleverly plotted story.

To the Shores of Tripoli ○
1943, US, 86 mins, colour
Dir: Bruce Humberstone
Stars: John Payne, Randolph Scott, Maureen O'Hara
Rating: ★★

It's almost bizarre to see Randolph Scott's face not beneath a stetson. This was one of his last non-Western roles as a rival for the hand of the delicious Maureen O'Hara in a story of life in a Marine training camp in wartime. Shot in vivid Technicolor, and giving Henry Morgan his first screen role, it's not to be confused with *Tripoli*, a period adventure made eight years later, which also starred John Payne and O'Hara. Pretty Nancy Kelly provides additional decoration.

Touch of Adultery, A
See: A Fine Romance

Touch of Class, A ○
1972, US, 106 mins, colour
Dir: Melvin Frank
Stars: George Segal, Glenda Jackson
Rating: ★★★★

For the first half of its running time, this delightful comedy is quite the best of its kind since the heyday of such witty cat-and-dog forays into sexual sparring, some 30 years earlier. Although Glenda Jackson doesn't seem entirely happy in comedy at first, she reacts superbly to the brilliant timing and deft underplaying of her co-star, making their early scenes together comparable with similar Tracy-Hepburn encounters in the past. Things do run down a bit towards the end, when the script forgoes wit for sarcasm and abrasiveness for sentimentality. Still, there is much that is memorable and much to enjoy in this story of a love affair that turns alter-

nately sweet and sour. For it, Jackson won her second Oscar.

Touch of Evil ○
1958, US, 114 mins, b/w
Dir: Orson Welles
Stars: Charlton Heston, Orson Welles, Janet Leigh, Joseph Calleia
Rating: ★★★★

Now generally recognised as one of Orson Welles' masterpieces, this broodingly menacing film was originally intended to feature Welles just as an actor. But when megastar Charlton Heston became involved under the (then-mistaken) impression that Welles was to direct, the seeds were sown for the creation of an unforgettable cinema classic film of warped, tormented, unpleasant characters who litter the paths of Heston and his screen wife Janet Leigh as they become dangerously involved on honeymoon with narcotics and murder down Mexico way. A little too wayward to be an outright classic, this is still a film to haunt your dreams. Despite being recut by a studio that didn't understand its structure, it still picked up international awards, accepted by a somewhat bemused Welles who was convinced Universal had almost ruined his film.

Touch of Larceny, A ○
1959, UK, 93 mins, b/w
Dir: Guy Hamilton
Stars: James Mason, Vera Miles, George Sanders
Rating: ★★★

James Mason is cast as a naval officer in this entertaining and enjoyable comedy a role vastly different from the types he played in his earlier days in such films as *The Seventh Veil* and *Odd Man Out* when perhaps only the more perspicacious could foresee what a wide-ranging actor he would soon become. He demonstrates how deftly he can handle comedy as he organises a scheme to get libel damages.

Touch of Love, A ○ ⊙
(aka: Thank You All Very Much)
1969, UK, 102 mins, colour
Dir: Waris Hussein
Stars: Sandy Dennis, Ian McKellen
Rating: ★

Four talents who venture all too rarely into the cinema – actors Sandy Dennis and Ian McKellen, writer Margaret Drabble (here adapting her own novel *The Millstone*) and director Waris Hussein – are involved in this story of a young graduate and the decisions she has to make on finding herself preg-

nant. The characters remain strangely unsympathetic and don't involve one despite Sandy Dennis' delicate portrayal.

Tough Guys ○
1986, US, 120 mins, colour
Dir: Jeff Kanew
Stars: Burt Lancaster, Kirk Douglas, Charles Durning, Alexis Smith
Rating: ★★★

It was a sweet idea, teaming Kirk Douglas and Burt Lancaster as two elderly bank robbers returning to life on the outside after 30 years in jail. And, by and large, it works. The action-comedy that results is hardly a blockbuster and its laughs and thrills are amiable rather than dynamic, but it's made with affection – their probation officer is 40 years younger than they are – and its veteran performers do at least come across as real people, halfway between snarling gangsters and Hope and Crosby in a *Road* film. These tough guys may be small-time in terms of today's megamovies, but their act has class and style.

Towering Inferno, The ○ ⊙
1974, US, 165 mins, colour
Dir: Irwin Allen
Stars: Steve McQueen, Paul Newman, William Holden, Faye Dunaway
Rating: ★★★★

Amazingly suspenseful disaster epic, given that British director John Guillermin was presented with a cast top-heavy with major stars. It was such a major undertaking, it took two rival studios, 20th Century-Fox and Warners, to finance the project and the script was culled from two weighty books. In fact, the setting-up of the disaster – a fire that traps civic dignitaries near the top of a new 138-storey skyscraper – is far more interesting than later rescue attempts. An Oscar winner for cinematography, editing and theme song, 'We May Never Love Like This Again', sung by Maureen McGovern.

Tower of London ○
1939, US, 92 mins, b/w
Dir: Rowland V Lee
Stars: Basil Rathbone, Boris Karloff, Vincent Price
Rating: ★★★

Extremely well-produced and atmospheric film about Richard III, which gave Boris Karloff one of his best roles as the shaven-headed executioner who looks like a forerunner of Fester in *The Addams Family* films. Basil Rathbone provides an incisive Richard III, a role taken over in the 1962 remake by Vincent Price, who coincidentally appears here as the doomed Duke of Clarence. Disappointing battle scenes.

Town Like Alice, A ○
1956, UK, 107 mins, b/w
Dir: Jack Lee
Stars: Virginia McKenna, Peter Finch
Rating: ★★★★

Grim, moving, mud-bespattered account of a group of refugee Englishwomen in World War Two Malaya who cannot find a place to stay. They trek hundreds of miles through jungle and swamp simply because no Japanese officer will take responsibility for their welfare. Virginia McKenna and Peter Finch (as an Australian soldier-prisoner who tries to help the women) reach near-brilliance in their harrowing portrayals. No effort is spared to make the story ring true to life, and only the contrived ending is off-key.

Town on Trial! ◑
1956, UK, 96 mins, b/w
Dir: John Guillermin
Stars: John Mills, Charles Coburn
Rating: ★★★

A formidable list of suspects for Supt Halloran (John Mills) to sort through in this sinister adaptation of Francis Durbridge's story *The Nylon Murders*. Mills digs deeper into the character than the script has any right to expect, and director John Guillermin conjures up some genuine excitement, particularly in the initial murder sequence where poor Magda Miller 'gets hers', as the killer and the camera stalk through a shadowy wood. The ending – a pursuit up a church steeple – is equally nail-biting.

To Wong Foo Thanks For Everything, Julie Newmar ◑ ⓥ
1995, US, 107 mins, colour
Dir: Beeban Kidron
Stars: Patrick Swayze, Wesley Snipes, John Leguizamo, Stockard Channing, Robin Williams
Rating: ★★★

Three drag queens head for Hollywood and end up in the sticks – with a vengeful cop pursuing them. How they put the lives of the Stixville citizens to rights while maintaining their queenly dignity is pure Tinseltown moonshine. But there are some nice ideas here and several of them are hard to resist. Of the magnif-

icently befrocked trio, Patrick Swayze looks like Jack Lemmon in *Some Like It Hot*, Wesley Snipes looks like Wesley Snipes with a wig on, and John Leguizamo really looks like a girl who might be known as Chi Chi. Often betraying its stage origins, the film has some magic moments that compensate for its more embarrassing ones. And Chris Penn is treasurable as the cop bent on revenge for having been out-manoeuvred by the besequined trio. Even by its own standards, though, the film is OTT at the climactic picnic, when the assembled company looks ready to burst into a chorus of *Oklahoma!*

Toxic Avenger, The ● ⓥ
1985, US, 100 mins, colour
Dir: Michael Herz
Stars: Andree Maranda, Mitchell Cohen, Jennifer Baptist, Cindy Manion, Robert Pritchard, Mark Torgi
Rating: ★★

A madcap spoof on *The Incredible Hulk* that launched the low budget Troma company on the road to schlock horror riches. It's an outlandish mix of gory violence (fingers poked through eyeballs, dismemberment, a seeing-eye dog shot by nasty villains) and a sadistic, silly story about a wimp turned into a toxic superhero. The effects are actually quite good; the girls minimally dressed in the style of Benny Hill. It's instantly forgettable and yet manages to raise many a non politically-correct chuckle along the way. Three sequels to date.

Toys ◑ ⓥ
1993, US, 121 mins, colour
Dir: Barry Levinson
Stars: Robin Williams, Michael Gambon, Joan Cusack, Robin Wright, LL Cool J, Donald O'Connor
Rating: ★★

Coming to life in its last 20 minutes with a pitched battle between wind-up toys and modern war toys for control of the factory, this is a fey fantasy with elements of coarse language, a sex scene, and a slow pace that all mark it out as unsuitable for younger children. Robin Williams toplines as the son his dying father (Donald O'Connor) considers too immature to leave in charge, though O'Connor himself scarcely seems to live in the adult world. Enter, as the new boss, O'Connor's megalomaniac military brother (Michael Gambon) who sees real-life possibilities for miniature tanks and helicopters and shuts off most of the

factory for his own nefarious purposes. Sounds like a great idea, and indeed brightness and invention are everywhere, but the film is nowhere near fleet enough of foot, light enough of hand or innocent enough of mind to succeed on almost any level.

Toys in the Attic ◑
1963, US, 90 mins, b/w
Dir: George Roy Hill
Stars: Geraldine Page, Wendy Hiller, Dean Martin, Yvette Mimieux
Rating: ★★★★

George Roy Hill (he went on to direct *Butch Cassidy and the Sundance Kid* and *The Sting*) brought a deftness of touch to Lillian Hellman's adaptation of her own play. Dean Martin is on top form as the gadabout who comes home to spinster sisters Geraldine Page and Wendy Hiller with a child bride.

Toy Soldiers ● ⓥ
1991, US, 112 mins, colour
Dir: Daniel Petrie
Stars: Lou Gossett, Sean Astin, Wil Wheaton, Keith Coogan, Denholm Elliott, Jerry Orbach
Rating: ★

Gung-ho Americana of the lowest kind as, to stirring music, prep school boys soften up the Colombian drug runners holding them hostage before the military move in to mop up. These, one must add in fairness, are teenagers with behavioural problems, all from rich families, which accounts for the Colombians moving in to try to get their leader released in exchange for the boys' lives. There's some suspense along the way as the boys' rebel leader (Sean Astin) attempts various acts of escape and sabotage without being found out; it's a measure of the film's failure to appeal that your sympathies remain largely with the Colombians. Dean Lou Gossett takes a bullet through the heart, but survives to wave cheerily to his boys: in flag-waving, rose-coloured Hollywood corners like this, some things never change.

Toy Story ☉ ⓥ
1995, US, 80 mins, colour
Dir: John Lasseter
Voice Stars: Tom Hanks, Tim Allen, Don Rickles, Jim Varney, Wallace Shawn, Annie Potts
Rating: ★★★★

Excellent though this first computer-produced cartoon feature is, you hope it's not the complete view of the future in Toontown. The system is peculiarly well suited to the tale of toys that come

T

to life when their owner is away, creating three-dimensional images that exactly match the scenario: conventional animation wouldn't have done this so well. Even so, Tom Hanks and Tim Allen have to work harder than most voice-over men to bring life to their toys: Hanks is Woody, the cowboy king of the nursery, who falls from favour when his master, young Andy, gets spaceman Buzz Lightyear for his birthday. Strutting Buzz, who believes himself to be a real astronaut, soon takes over Woody's territory. Their feud almost ends tragically until they find themselves with a common enemy – the demon boy next door who destroys toys when he is not dismembering them to create toy freaks. Well-paced and winning, the ensuing action is a treat for tots and adults alike.

Traces of Red ● Ⓥ
1992, US, 104 mins, colour
Dir: Andy Wolk
Stars: James Belushi, Lorraine Bracco, Tony Goldwyn, William Russ
Rating: ★

Nubile corpses, hard-boiled cops ever-ready to be seduced, a plot in which little is what it seems: *Traces of Red* runs like a Hank Janson pulp novel. Yet, despite a generally inept script and a poor performance by (an admittedly miscast) Lorraine Bracco, there's a good little thriller struggling to get out here. James Belushi's performance in the lead might be quite acceptable, for example, if other events in the movie were in working order. His laconic narration, begun over his own dead body, tells us he and those around him all seem to be involved in the case of the psycho who murders girls, smears their faces with lipstick and leaves not a trace of their clothing behind. Andy Wolk's direction of the subsequent twists is often very competent, although even he can't convince us about the climax which, although inventively done, simply isn't believable. The music, though, bluesy and *noir*ish, is just the kind of accompaniment this kind of soft-porn, soft-cover fiction demands.

Track 29 ● Ⓥ
1987, UK, 90 mins, colour
Dir: Nicolas Roeg
Stars: Theresa Russell, Gary Oldman, Christopher Lloyd, Colleen Camp
Rating: ★★★

Director Nicolas Roeg in playful mood, toying with his audience as he de-

scribes the hallucinations of a mind in breakdown. Linda (Theresa Russell) contemplates suicide, but demons torment her, chiefly the vision of her son (Gary Oldman, doing a satanic variation on Norman Wisdom) returned from her past to give her some fleeting happiness. Oldman is the dynamo that galvanises this bizarre comedy into life. See it, be manipulated and enjoy it: this is Roeg at his most Roegish.

Track of the Cat ○
1954, US, 102 mins, colour
Dir: William A Wellman
Stars: Robert Mitchum, Teresa Wright, Tab Hunter, Diana Lynn
Rating: ★★★★

Sadly neglected in its time, this is one of the most important location-shot films of the Fifties. Director William A Wellman experimented with colour photography in striking fashion in this story of a ranch menaced by a giant mountain lion. The snowbound ranch and its environs are confined almost entirely to sharp, crisp black-and-white, the only splashes of colour being the bright clothes and the green of the trees. William Clothier's photography is complemented by Roy Webb's distinctive music and some striking directorial set pieces, including a mother guarding her son's body like a vulture and a burial scene from inside the open grave. The screenplay is given full value by the players, especially Robert Mitchum, and Beulah Bondi and Philip Tonge as his mother and father.

Trade Winds ○
1938, US, 95 mins, b/w
Dir: Tay Garnett
Stars: Fredric March, Joan Bennett, Ralph Bellamy, Ann Sothern
Rating: ★★★

Not quite the South Seas idyll you might imagine from the title, this rarely seen Hollywood movie is a crisply scripted mystery-romance whose stars, despite the varying Far Eastern backgrounds, never left the studio! Fredric March takes himself a little less seriously than usual as the cynical sleuth tracking murder suspect Joan Bennett on a round-the-world hunt.

Trading Hearts ○
1988, US, 88 mins, colour
Dir: Neil Leifer
Stars: Raul Julia, Beverly D'Angelo
Rating: ★★

This is one of those would-be romantic charmers where a child tries to find a new father/mother for its single parent.

In this case, 11-year-old Jenny Lewis is such a sassy charmer that she does manage to bring a little extra fun to the tired old formula, which here involves her trying to net over-the-hill baseball star Raul Julia for her divorced mum (Beverly D'Angelo) who is having an uphill struggle making ends meet. D'Angelo also sings nicely on a couple of songs (remember her as singer Patsy Cline in *Coal Miner's Daughter?*) but the whole thing makes you wonder why the stars and filmmakers bothered.

Trading Places ● Ⓥ
1983, US, 116 mins, colour
Dir: John Landis
Stars: Dan Aykroyd, Eddie Murphy, Ralph Bellamy, Don Ameche, Jamie Lee Curtis, Denholm Elliott
Rating: ★★★★

Reminiscent at times of a Preston Sturges film, this bright comedy is director John Landis' best (and most popular) film to date. And when the good guys hit back at the bad guys who have been doing them down all evening, it stands to reason that the audience is in for some fun. Dan Aykroyd is the stuck-up white blueblood who wheels and deals in stocks and shares for the aged Duke brothers, Eddie Murphy (shooting to stardom) the failed black conman whose wheelings are confined to his efforts to convince the populace he's a legless veteran and whose dealings are mainly with the police. On a bet, the (crooked) Dukes swop them round, and everything goes to plan – until the two men understand what's happened. Then the fun really begins. Jamie Lee Curtis weighs in as a tart with a nest egg of gold and Denholm Elliott's butler gets the best lines in the film, delivered with just the right bite.

Traffic ○
1970, France, 96 mins, colour
Dir: Jacques Tati
Stars: Jacques Tati
Rating: ★★

Jacques Tati's famous comic creation Monsieur Hulot let loose on the French motorway system. Much of the fun in this particular catalogue of hilarious disasters stems from Tati's treatment of cars as creatures with wills of their own, liable to seize up, or even turn on their masters, if they feel they are being treated badly.

Trail of the Pink Panther
○ Ⓥ
1982, UK, 97 mins, colour
Dir: Blake Edwards

Stars: Peter Sellers, David Niven, Herbert Lom, Joanna Lumley
Rating: ★★

The first half of this Blake Edwards venture is a coy, affectionate look at the late Peter Sellers' famous creation Inspector Clouseau, with the help of footage not previously used in *Pink Panther* films. Later developments are less interesting, but the film is briefly enlivened by the performance of Richard Mulligan (helped by a talented dog) as Clouseau's father, the original stumbling block from which the chip was fashioned.

Trail of the Vigilantes ○
1940, US, 78 mins, b/w
Dir: Allan Dwan
Stars: Franchot Tone, Warren William, Broderick Crawford
Rating: ★★★

Wild and wacky comedy-Western that moves along like a stagecoach pursued by Indians. Matinee idol Franchot Tone, a lounge-suit actor if ever there was one, had never made a Western before. But the script of this one – written by Harold Shumate, a Texas-born writer who contributed over 100 movie screenplays – lured him into the wide open spaces for the first time.

Trail Street ○
1947, US, 84 mins, b/w
Dir: Ray Enright
Stars: Randolph Scott, Robert Ryan
Rating: ★★

This modest little Western plays out the familiar tale about the conflict between ranchers and crop farmers but is lifted by its two stars – Randolph Scott and Robert Ryan. Scott plays Western legend Bat Masterson who rides into town to help land agent Ryan sort out the bad guys. The script's as bit clichéd but the action's good and the film sets a fair pace. There's also Roy Rogers' long-time sidekick George 'Gabby' Hayes around for a bit of light relief.

Train, The ○ ⓥ
1964, US, 140 mins, b/w
Dir: John Frankenheimer
Stars: Burt Lancaster, Paul Scofield, Jeanne Moreau
Rating: ★★★★

Gripping action film concerning the attempts of the French Resistance movement to save art treasures from the Nazis. Burt Lancaster, who also collaborated with director John Frankenheimer on *Bird Man of Alcatraz*,

The Young Savages and *Seven Days in May*, got his first all-action part for almost a decade when he was cast as Resistance leader Labiche. Lancaster captures the spirit of this fighting man with relish and feeling. The three German officers involved bring outstanding performances from Paul Scofield (in one of his rare film roles), Wolfgang Preiss and Howard Vernon.

Train of Events ○
1949, UK, 85 mins, b/w
Dir: Charles Crichton
Stars: Jack Warner, Valerie Hobson, John Clements, Irina Baronova
Rating: ★★

Trains are always good for an hour-and-a-half of meaty drama and this film holds our attention throughout by offering us several train stories for the price of one. Various people on board the train of the title have their problems resolved in one way or another by the end of their journey, with the story switching from humour to icy drama as different characters appear. Don't blink too much while you're watching: you might miss someone like Leslie Phillips or John Gregson in a minor role. Jack Warner is the train driver, and there's a youthful Peter Finch as an actor who has strangled his wife.

Train Robbers, The ○ ⓥ
1973, US, 92 mins, colour
Dir: Burt Kennedy
Stars: John Wayne, Ann-Margret, Rod Taylor, Ricardo Montalban
Rating: ★★

The characters in this Western will be old friends to those familar with Wayne's work in the last 20 years. The hardened gunfighter (Wayne), the kid (usually a pop star, and in this case Bobby Vinton), the co-star (here Rod Taylor) and the veteran (Ben Johnson) against a mob of gunmen who far outnumber them. Burt Kennedy's script contains some amusing exchanges of dialogue. But his direction, although pitching one nicely into the core of the action, asks little more of the star than that he be John Wayne, which is rather a pity.

Trainspotting ● ⓥ
1995, UK, 97 mins, colour
Dir: Danny Boyle
Stars: Ewan McGregor, Ewen Bremner, Jonny Lee Miller, Robert Carlyle
Rating: ★★★

A fashionable film for the mid-1990s. Director Danny Boyle, who made

Shallow Grave, turns over life to show us an underbelly of society we'd probably rather leave untouched. Workless Scottish teens do drugs, have sex and get violent in between discussing Sean Connery and soccer. They live (and sometimes die) in squalor: an unappetising lifestyle that the film, despite its graphic depiction of it, comes close to glorifying, with its gallows wit and savage sophistication. It's well made, but tough to watch, especially if you can't stand needles going into flesh – the sort of film that will go down well in the very trendy areas its characters would hold in the greatest contempt, and less well in the suburbs, where the problems it depicts may be closer to home. Ferociously well acted, particularly by Ewan McGregor and by Robert Carlyle as Begbie, the short-fused psycho you'd least like to bump into in the public bar.

Trancers ❶ ⓥ
(aka: Future Cop)
1984, US, 85 mins, colour
Dir: Charles Band
Stars: Tim Thomerson, Helen Hunt, Michael Stefani
Rating: ★★★

Inspired by those classics of the futuristic genre *Blade Runner* and *The Terminator*, Charles Band – once dubbed the Eighties' answer to Roger Corman – produced and directed this clever science fiction thriller. Comedian Tim Thomerson is well cast as a low-budget version of Harrison Ford who is sent back in time some 300 years to 1985 Los Angeles. He has to inhabit the body of one of his ancestors and change history to prevent a totalitarian state from coming to power. The satire is well observed and the film is visually arresting. Four sequels followed, all starring Thomerson.

Trap, The ○
1966, UK, 106 mins, colour
Dir: Sidney Hayers
Stars: Oliver Reed, Rita Tushingham
Rating: ★★★★

In the depths of some of the most beautiful rugged scenery in the world, director Sidney Hayers creates a tough-but-tender love story that often keeps you on the very edge of the seat and riveted to the characters of the black-bearded trapper who survives in the heart of the wilds, and the mute bond maiden whom he buys as a bride, for two bags of gold dust. The

T

very best of the film is its mid-section when, following a hair-raising fight with wolves, with the girl racing to save the trapper from ending as fox in the grip of hounds, she has to call on all her courage and strength of character to keep him alive. As the trapper, Oliver Reed has never been better.

Trapeze O
1956, US, 105 mins, colour
Dir: Carol Reed
Stars: Burt Lancaster, Gina Lollobrigida, Tony Curtis, Katy Jurado, Thomas Gomez
Rating: ★★

You can almost smell the elephant droppings in this popular film that captures the fun, danger and excitement of life under the Big Top. The script is actually a lacklustre affair, but that didn't seem to bother audiences of the day who flocked to see former acrobat Burt Lancaster in a milieu he loved as a famous circus trapeze artist. The high wire work, as Lancaster and Curtis train to perform the impossible, a triple somersault in mid-air off the trapeze, is very exciting to watch, compensating for script shortcomings once the action returns to the ground.

Travelling North O
1986, Australia, 98 mins, colour
Dir: Carl Schultz
Stars: Leo McKern, Julia Blake, Graham Kennedy
Rating: ★★★

This well-written, occasionally funny but ultimately sad Australian film about old age gives Leo McKern a powerful central role which he lives up to by giving a remarkable performance. He plays Frank, a widower who retires at 70 and plans to move from Melbourne to Northern Queensland where he has bought a spectacular clifftop house. The well observed script was based by David Williamson on his own successful stage play. Sharp dialogue and fine acting all round make this an absorbing and affecting drama and director Carl Schultz has created a film that belies its stage origins.

Travels With My Aunt ◐
1972, US, 109 mins, colour
Dir: George Cukor
Stars: Maggie Smith, Alec McCowen, Lou Gossett Jr, Robert Stephens
Rating: ★★

Graham Greene's novel, brought to the screen with Maggie Smith in the role originally intended for Katharine Hepburn – the eccentric lady adventurer who introduces her staid nephew, a bank manager, to a world of intrigue and chicanery. George Cukor directs briskly and divertingly without ever quite drawing us into Aunt Augusta's own bizarre lifestyle, despite admirable support from John Box's stylised settings and Douglas Slocombe's garish but attractive (and suited to the subject) photography.

Treasure Island O Ⓥ
1934, US, 105 mins, b/w
Dir: Victor Fleming
Stars: Wallace Beery, Jackie Cooper
Rating: ★★★

A solid version of Robert Louis Stevenson's tale of high seas adventure, and, of the many movies made from it, a respectable second-best after the classic Robert Newton version. Long John Silver is played by a relatively subdued Wallace Beery, and the whole piece teems with action, atmosphere and period detail. Cultured Douglass Dumbrille is a strange choice to play the murderous Israel Hands, though.

Treasure Island O
1950, UK, 96 mins, colour
Dir: Byron Haskin
Stars: Robert Newton, Bobby Driscoll, Basil Sydney
Rating: ★★★★

Full-blooded Disney version of the classic story, with the definitive portrait of Long John Silver from an eyeball-rolling Robert Newton and an appealing performance as Jim Hawkins from rosy-cheeked Bobby Driscoll: you'll be on the edges of your seats as he flees up the mast from kill-crazed Israel Hands.

Treasure of Lost Canyon, The ☉
1952, US, 82 mins, colour
Dir: Ted Tetzlaff
Stars: William Powell, Julie Adams, Rosemary DeCamp, Tommy Ivo
Rating: ★★

William Powell returned to movies after a three-year break for this family Western, but although pleasant, sunny fare, it lacks bite. Based on a story by Robert Louis Stevenson, but hardly the high adventure that might promise, its finest asset is the customary high-quality photography by Russell Metty, an Oscar-winning master of his trade. Powell's co-star is rising child actor Tommy Ivo, whose career didn't go much further.

Treasure of Pancho Villa, The O
1955, US, 96 mins, colour
Dir: George Sherman
Stars: Rory Calhoun, Shelley Winters, Gilbert Roland, Joseph Calleia
Rating: ★★★

Mexican revolutions often bring out the best in Hollywood's 'soldier of fortune' action heroes. Come to think of it, they're apt to give quite a lift, too, to a routine Western yarn. And so it proves in this sizzling adventure drama with a magnificently exciting climax. The colour photography is highly commendable (the great William Snyder), as is the acting of Rory Calhoun, as the freelance fighter, and Gilbert Roland, as a fiery, dedicated rebel. Atmosphere and excitement surge along with the story under the hand of director George Sherman, who is clearly more at home with the action scenes than with Niven Busch's somewhat wordy script. There's some gold around too, not to mention a girl – Shelley Winters as a high-thinking American allied to the revolutionaries.

Treasure of the Golden Condor O
1953, US, 93 mins, colour
Dir: Delmer Daves
Stars: Cornel Wilde, Constance Smith, Finlay Currie, Anne Bancroft
Rating: ★★

Some rugged scenery, magnificently photographed in Technicolor by Edward Cronjager, on location in Guatemala, highlights this period action film from Delmer Daves. Cornel Wilde portrays the young Frenchman hunting treasure in the Central American forests, but all the acting class comes from the suppporting cast, which includes Anne Bancroft, George Macready, Fay Wray and Leo G Carroll.

Treasure of the Sierra Madre, The O Ⓥ
1948, US, 126 mins, b/w
Dir: John Huston
Stars: Humphrey Bogart, Walter Huston, Tim Holt, Bruce Bennett
Rating: ★★★★★

Thought by many to be John Huston's finest film, this is a tale of greed, fear and murder in Mexico as three men fall out over the gold they have clawed out of the inhospitable and bandit-ridden mountains. Humphrey Bogart gives a riveting portrait of an increasingly unhinged prospector, but the kudos went to the Huston clan, with

John receiving Oscars for screenplay and direction and his father Walter best supporting actor. The first post-war film to be shot entirely on location, its budget spiralled crazily out of control to $3 million. Studio boss Jack Warner, who had been conned into believing it was just a cheap Western, went berserk, but it was a huge hit with the public and made its costs back several times over.

Treasure of the Yankee Zephyr

See: Race to the Yankee Zephyr

Tree Grows In Brooklyn, A ○

1945, US, 128 mins, b/w
Dir: Elia Kazan
Stars: Dorothy McGuire, James Dunn, Joan Blondell, Lloyd Nolan
Rating: ★★★★

Touching Hollywood adaptation of Betty Smith's novel about life in the slums of an American city in the early 1900s. The film is beautifully scripted and photographed and tellingly observed in its loving depiction of a little girl's joys and sadnesses growing up in this environment. It has extremely attractive performances from Dorothy McGuire, Joan Blondell, James Dunn (a marvellous comeback performance as the drunken father) and wistful Peggy Ann Garner as the child. Dunn and Garner won Oscars.

Trees Lounge ● ⓥ

1996, US, 95 mins, colour
Dir: Steve Buscemi
Stars: Buscemi, Anthony La Paglia, Chloe Sevigny, Elizabeth Bracco, Seymour Cassel, Carol Kane
Rating: ★★★

A personal project for that suspicious-looking character actor Buscemi, this is a flavoursome, wryly humoured slice of grunge-style life spun round the losers and layabouts who drown their sorrows in the seediest bar in town. Buscemi alternates between playing likeable lowlifes and loathable lowlifes; here he's in the former mould as an unemployed mechanic (fired by his best friend), ditched by his wife and by his pregnant girlfriend, who uses the environment of Trees Lounge to try to make some senses out of the mess he seems to have made of his life. Fans will find Buscemi nice 'n' sleazy as usual, but it's difficult to get close to these characters, even with cameos from the likes of Samuel L Jackson and Daniel Baldwin, or to care about their destinies.

Tremors ● ⓥ

1990, US, 96 mins, colour
Dir: Ron Underwood
Stars: Kevin Bacon, Fred Ward, Finn Carter, Reba McEntire
Rating: ★★★★

Another creature feature that's pretty exciting once it hits its stride. Its monsters, sort of underground alien slugs 10 times the size of humans, are far more intelligent than your average slug – the beasties even dig a trap for our human heroes when they try to escape in a bulldozer. It's all set in a remote part of the Nevada desert, although you're still inclined to ask why creatures that have presumably been around for zillions of years have only just started gobbling people up. There's no shortage of excitement, though and heroes Kevin Bacon and Fred Ward give 100 per cent to their unlikely exploits in blowing the sons o' bitches to pieces.

Trent's Last Case ○

1952, UK, 90 mins, b/w
Dir: Herbert Wilcox
Stars: Margaret Lockwood, Michael Wilding, Orson Welles, John McCallum
Rating: ★★

The famous novel by E C Bentley gets the full Herbert Wilcox polish in this adaptation, co-produced by the director's wife, Anna Neagle. Her producing chores presumably meant that she was unable to take on the leading role, of a woman suspected of complicity in the murder of her husband. But it's one that Margaret Lockwood handles coolly and capably, even if the screenplay gives her few highspots to hit. Despite the efforts of Michael Wilding (as Trent, the detective), John McCallum and such experienced scene stealers as Miles Malleson, it's Orson Welles who dominates proceedings with a sinister flashback account of the murdered man. Kenneth Williams makes his debut as the gardener.

Trespass ● ⓥ

1992, US, 101 mins, colour
Dir: Walter Hill
Stars: Bill Paxton, William Sadler, Ice T, Ice Cube, Art Evans
Rating: ★★★

'A billion dollars in gold just laying there waitin' for us.' Famous last cinematic words, and so it proves once again in Walter Hill's all-go action thriller. Bill Paxton and William Sadler are two Arkansas firemen who have undiscovered treasure apparently

handed to them on a plate when they attend a fire and receive a map and solid gold cross from a demented old man who staggers off into the flames. Seems like it's the key to the where-abouts of the loot from a fabled 50-year-old robbery. But, once arrived on the scene, the pair soon become in-volved with the local underworld kingpin (Ice T) and his gang, who corner them in the abandoned building that the treasure's hiding-place has now become. Hill doesn't waste any footage in the subsequent game of vio-lent cat-and-mouse, although he misses a chance to put a kick in the tail after the principal protagonists have bitten the dust. Action fans won't complain though: they get a full ration here as rival factions and splinter groups from all sides blast the daylights out of one another.

Trial ○

1955, US, 105 mins, b/w
Dir: Mark Robson
Stars: Glenn Ford, Dorothy McGuire, Arthur Kennedy, John Hodiak
Rating: ★★★

Fine, tense courtroom thriller about a university instructor in criminal law who undertakes to defend a young Mexican on a charge of murder, but finds himself made the dupe of political factions. Glenn Ford plays the instructor in suitably tormented fashion.

Trial by Combat ○

(aka: Dirty Knight's Work)
1976, UK, 90 mins, colour
Dir: Kevin Connor
Stars: John Mills, Donald Pleasence, Barbara Hershey, Peter Cushing
Rating: ★

A wildly eccentric comedy-thriller that fails on some levels and succeeds on others. The plot, completely potty, concerns a group of titled Englishmen who dress up as knights and do to death wrongdoers who have escaped the police. Some of the action that follows is genuinely exciting, some plain silly. None of it, however, is even re-motely credible. John Mills even seems to play on two levels, sometimes straight, sometimes for obvious comic effect. At one time, Mills is chained to the cellar wall, Barbara Hershey is driving a car pursued by men on horseback, the new police commission-er is turning out to be a homicidal maniac, David Birney is fighting with the gamekeeper and Donald Pleasence, dressed in full armour, is pursuing an East End crook through a castle green-

T

house. Whatever else, this film certainly is extraordinary.

Trials of Oscar Wilde, The ○
1960, UK, 123 mins, colour
Dir: Ken Hughes
Stars: Peter Finch, Yvonne Mitchell, John Fraser, Lionel Jeffries
Rating: ★★★★

Gripping historical drama portraying the downfall of the great dramatist and wit Oscar Wilde following his unsuccessful libel action against the Marquis of Queensberry. Peter Finch, in what was seen at the time as a curious casting decision, plays the writer. Written and directed by Ken Hughes, the film was shot at the same time as another film treating the same events, *Oscar Wilde*, starring Robert Morley.

Trigger Happy ● Ⓥ
(aka: Mad Dog Time)
1996, US, 93 mins, colour
Dir: Larry Bishop
Stars: Richard Dreyfuss, Jeff Goldblum, Ellen Barkin, Gabriel Byrne, Diane Lane, Burt Reynolds, Gregory Hines
Rating: ★★

We think this gangster comedy spoof is set in an 'alternative universe' – and certainly one that can't afford many sets or extras. The main setting is a crime-oriented nightclub bracing itself for the return of Mafia boss Vic (Richard Dreyfuss) from the 'loony bin'. Vic's main man, Ben (Gabriel Byrne) has already been charged with bumping off Vic's rivals in preparation. This sounds like fun, but it plays like drivel. The amazing cast simply can't mend director Bishop's broken-backed script that strives for laughs so hard that it rarely gets them. Nicely photographed, though, the film looks good for its low budget. Byrne is the only one of the starry line-up to hit the right tone, and his duet with Paul Anka on 'My Way' definitely has its moments.

Trio ○
1950, UK, 88 mins, b/w
Dir: Harold French
Stars: James Hayter, Nigel Patrick, Jean Simmons, Michael Rennie
Rating: ★★★

Three stories, each very different, from the work of W Somerset Maugham. Although they seem a little more stretched, understandably, than the tales in *Quartet* (the first of the Maugham films, made two years earlier), each remains a fine example of the author's craftsmanship and observa-

tion of life. Character star James Hayter, just entering his most profitable period in the British cinema (he was soon to play Mr Pickwick) revels in his leading role as the illiterate verger who makes a mint.

Triple Cross ○
1966, UK/France, 126 mins, colour
Dir: Terence Young
Stars: Christopher Plummer, Romy Schneider, Yul Brynner, Trevor Howard
Rating: ★★

World War Two spy yarn based on fact, with Christopher Plummer as the cunning safecracker who works for both sides. Gert *(Goldfinger)* Frobe gives the best performance as a disillusioned German officer. Tense at times.

Triple Echo, The ●
1972, UK, 100 mins, colour
Dir: Michael Apted
Stars: Glenda Jackson, Oliver Reed
Rating: ★

Although Michael Apted is best known as a director of television plays, the few films that he has made have all been powerful, striking and unusual. This is another of H E Bates' rural tragedies, a companion to the previous year's *Dulcima*, although considerably less successful and progressively more turgid and unlikely.

Trip to Bountiful, The ○ Ⓥ
1985, US, 105 mins, colour
Dir: Peter Masterson
Stars: Geraldine Page, John Heard, Rebecca DeMornay
Rating: ★★★

For those who fancy a good, old-fashioned howl, this tear-jerker will fit the bill nicely. In her Oscar-winning performance (following eight unsuccessful nominations), Geraldine Page plays a feisty, sentimental, hymn-singing old southern lady with a slightly dicky heart and a grasping sourpuss of a daughter-in-law who makes her life hell and has the Indian sign on the old girl's submissive son. After one bitter row, Page packs up and makes one of her occasional attempts to get back to her home town of Bountiful, now all but deserted. Somehow, this time she evades pursuit, with a small assist from a friendly fellow traveller, and begins the long bus journey to the nearest town. That's really the whole story, although incidentals, dialogue and the central performance all count for a lot, even if they don't quite prevent a yawn sometimes sneaking in between

the tears: the truth behind the basic situations sometimes cuts too deep for comfort.

Triumph of the Spirit ● Ⓥ
1989, US, 120 mins, colour
Dir: Robert M Young
Stars: Willem Dafoe, Robert Loggia, Edward James Olmos, Costas Mandylor
Rating: ★★

Or: *A Boxer in Auschwitz*. Decently made, this is the true story of a Greek boxing champion who, being Jewish, was shipped off to a German concentration camp in World War Two. Here, while all his fellows gradually dropped away, he kept alive by undergoing 200 bouts and winning every one. Though somewhat sanitised, this is still horrific enough for most tastes, with heartfelt performances from Willem Dafoe (the boxer), Robert Loggia (his father) and Edward James Olmos, that Gary Merrill lookalike, as their 'gypsy' guard. The Jenny Agutter-like Wendy Gazelle is a poignant heroine who makes the most of her few scenes.

Trojan Eddie ● Ⓥ
1996, UK/Ire, 105 mins, colour
Dir: Gillies MacKinnon
Stars: Stephen Rea, Richard Harris, Brendan Gleeson, Aislin McGluckin, Stuart Townsend, Sean McGinley, Angeline Ball
Rating: ★★

The hangdog Stephen Rea was born to play life's losers, and they don't come much more downtrodden than Irish Eddie. A small-time salesman reduced to muddy fetching and carrying for the local tinker godfather (Richard Harris), Eddie would like his own business: but it's a distant dream. When Harris marries a feisty teenage bride only to see her run off with his own nephew (and the dowry), who was Eddie's business assistant, extinction looks likelier than distinction for our dog-eared hero. This is a slow film considering it has a lot of plot, and a dismal one too – but at least it has an upbeat ending.

Trois Couleurs Rouge
See: Three Colours Red

Trois Hommes et un Couffin
See: Three Men and a Cradle

Troll ● Ⓥ
1985, US, 83 mins, colour
Dir: John Carl Buechler
Stars: Michael Moriarty, Shelley Hack, Noah Hathaway, Sonny Bono, June

Lockhart
Rating: ★★

Gremlins, ghoulies and other beastly offspring of modern special effects were bound to give birth to all manner of evil creatures of mythology and here it's the turn of the troll. Like most of the rest, he's small and smart, drips with saliva, has teeth that would keep a dentist in bridgework for life and is out to rule the world by a combined action of transmogrification and extermination. The best lines in this stop-start catalogue of his attempts to take over a modern apartment building all go to June Lockhart as the witch assigned to stop him. When youthful hero Noah Hathaway, out to save his 'taken over' younger sister, pays her a visit, he asks her how she knew it was him. 'I recognise the knock,' she tells him. 'It's pre-pubescent.'

Tron ○ Ⓥ
1982, US, 96 mins, colour
Dir: Stephen Lisberger
Stars: Jeff Bridges, Bruce Boxleitner, David Warner
Rating: ★★★

The Disney Studio comes up with a new way to play cops and robbers in this innovative thriller about a man who finds himself inside a computer game fighting for his life. David Warner is a splendidly hateful villain who could hold you, adding, in the same breath: 'Bring in the laser probe!'

Troopship
See: Farewell Again

Trouble Bound ● Ⓥ
1993, US, 89 mins, colour
Dir: Jeffrey Reiner
Stars: Michael Madsen, Patricia Arquette, Seymour Cassel, Florence Stanley
Rating: ★★

There's a bad guy lurking around every corner in this clone of the far better *Something Wild*. Michael Madsen, a student of the Bruce Willis school of charm in this one, plays Harry, an ex-convict who wins a car in a poker game little realising that its trunk contains a dead body, the victim of a Mafia assassination. And when he meets wacky Kit (Patricia Arquette), out for revenge on the Mob for the murder of her father, Harry's troubles double. Madsen still looks more powerful as a top supporting bad guy than a leading man, but at least he and the spunky Arquette manage to lift these black frolics out of the rut from time to

time, although there are far too many chases when the director's lack of imagination is all too evident.

Trouble Brewing ○
1939, UK, 90 mins, b/w
Dir: Anthony Kimmins
Stars: George Formby, Googie Withers
Rating: ★★★

Toothy George Formby was Britain's top box-office star when this comedy film was made. He plays a compositor involved with a gang of counterfeiters. The Formby vocal chords work overtime on such ditties as 'Fanlight Fanny' and 'Hitting the Highspots Now', and the climax is a hectic pursuit through a brewery.

Trouble in Mind ● Ⓥ
1985, US, 111 mins, colour
Dir: Alan Rudolph
Stars: Kris Kristofferson, Keith Carradine, Lori Singer, Genevieve Bujold, Divine
Rating: ★★

Love them or loathe them, most of director Alan Rudolph's films are unlike those by anyone else, and this science fiction thriller/comedy/philsophical drama is certainly no exception. Kris Kristofferson is perfectly cast as the loner ex-cop trying to prevent a drifter and his wife from falling in with the underworld of Rain City. Stylish it certainly is and some scenes have a wonderfully bleak feel, but Rudolph's computer mind finally overloads (and explodes) in a semi-slapstick finale.

Trouble in Paradise ○
1932, US, 83 mins, b/w
Dir: Ernst Lubitsch
Stars: Miriam Hopkins, Herbert Marshall, Kay Francis, Charlie Ruggles, C Aubrey Smith, Edward Everett Horton
Rating: ★★★

Feather-light, delightfully naughty Ernst Lubitsch comedy classic about cross and double cross among international jewel thieves, as they move from Venice to Paris and other European society spots with rich pickings. It's among the most cultured and sophisticated films ever made, although Lubitsch does leave room for a very funny running gag involving Kay Francis and that delightful ditherer, Edward Everett Horton. The first voice you hear while watching the scene in Venice is that of the famous tenor Enrico Caruso.

Trouble in Store ⊙ Ⓥ
1953, UK, 85 mins, b/w
Dir: John Paddy Carstairs

Stars: Norman Wisdom, Margaret Rutherford, Lana Morris
Rating: ★★★

Norman Wisdom's first starring comedy, a side-splitting romp which has him falling over his own feet all over a large department store. Margaret Rutherford is at her hilariously imperious best as a shoplifter, whose top coat seems to be able to hold more goods than that of Harpo Marx.

Trouble in the Glen ○
1953, UK, 91 mins, colour
Dir: Herbert Wilcox
Stars: Margaret Lockwood, Orson Welles
Rating: ★

Trouble here all right: Herbert Wilcox's tartan turkey trots out Orson Welles as a monstrously bewigged Highland laird being unpleasant to local tinkers and incurring the wrath of a little girl crippled with polio. So, predictable comedy about Scots and treacly sentimentality are guaranteed. Margaret Lockwood, Forrest Tucker, Victor McLaglen and John McCallum are wasted. Even the heather looks unreal in Trucolor.

Trouble in the Sky
See: Cone of Silence

Trouble Shooter, The
See: The Man With the Gun

Trouble with Angels, The ⊙
1966, US, 112 mins, colour
Dir: Ida Lupino
Stars: Rosalind Russell, Hayley Mills
Rating: ★★★

A most effective dose of funnery in the nunnery, persuasively directed by Ida Lupino, with a delightful collection of individual nuns gracing a story of two high-spirited teenagers at a convent school. There's the elderly nun, always asleep; the shy one, having to go out with girls to choose bras; the ungainly games nun, forced to dive in to save non-swimmers who have got out of swimming lessons for three years. And the death of a nun one has come to know is a genuinely moving moment. Hayley Mills produces one of her best performances while Rosalind Russell is gloriously in control of her dialogue as the Mother Superior, and has classic moments when operating on a student unable to get her head out of a plaster cast.

Trouble with Harry, The ○ Ⓥ
1955, US, 99 mins, colour
Dir: Alfred Hitchcock

T

Stars: Shirley MacLaine, John Forsythe, Edmund Gwenn, Mildred Natwick
Rating: ★★★★

This is Alfred Hitchcock's zany, off-beat suspense comedy about a corpse that very definitely won't lie down. Endearing portrayals by John Forsythe, Shirley MacLaine, Edmund Gwenn and Mildred Natwick, filled both with impishness and dramatic sense, key in perfectly with the black hijinks. And Robert Burks' colour photography of autumnal settings is some of the best ever seen. The dialogue is surprisingly risqué for a Fifties' film, but Hitchcock's brilliant handling of a corpse being buried and dug up six times in all makes the film a triumphant and very unusual laughter-raiser. A winner and no trouble.

True Confessions ● Ⓥ
1981, US, 108 mins, colour
Dir: Ulu Grosbard
Stars: Robert De Niro, Robert Duvall, Charles Durning
Rating: ★★★★

The cinematic equivalent of a good read, a rarity in modern cinema. De Niro is very good as a wheeler-dealer priest and Duvall even better as his blunt and bitter policeman brother. Together they become involved in a grisly murder hunt that leaves scars on them both – and on several of those around them.

True Glory, The ○
1945, US/UK, 90 mins, b/w
Dir: Garson Kanin, Carol Reed
Rating: ★★★

Breathtakingly good wartime documentary, made by Britain's Carol Reed and America's Garson Kanin, who assembled a vividly personal picture of the last 18 months of World War Two from newsreel records shot by more than 1,400 cameramen. The commentary, spoken by men from different advancing armies, is outstanding in the way it clarifies situations but at the same time provides them with an intensely human realism.

True Grit ○ Ⓥ
1969, US, 128 mins, colour
Dir: Henry Hathaway
Stars: John Wayne, Glen Campbell, Kim Darby
Rating: ★★★★

Taking on a gang of badmen who include Dennis Hopper and Robert Duvall, John Wayne roared into Western history with an Oscar under

his belt. More than any other of his postwar films, this and his last film *The Shootist* summed up the man and his career. 'It was the first really decent role I'd had in 20 years,' he growled, clutching his Academy Award – a reference to his only previous Oscar nomination, for *The Sands of Iwo Jima* in 1949. The film deserved one other Oscar it didn't get – for Lucien Ballard's Technicolor photography.

True Identity ● Ⓥ
1991, US, 93 mins, colour
Dir: Charles Lane
Stars: Lenny Henry, Frank Langella, Andreas Katsulas, Charles Lane, James Earl Jones
Rating: ★★

Comedy star Lenny Henry literally changes his face for this, his Hollywood debut. He plays Miles, a budding actor who hears the confession of a Mafia hitman on an out-of-control plane, then has to use the help of a friend who's a movie makeup genius to disguise himself as a white man to stay alive when the plane lands safely. A fair showcase for Henry which does at least allow him full scope for his talent for mimicry and impersonation. The humour is pretty obvious, and it's uncomfortable in parts; even so, you'll find it hard not to chuckle on several occasions.

True Lies ◗ Ⓥ
1994, US, 142 mins, colour
Dir: James Cameron
Stars: Arnold Schwarzenegger, Jamie Lee Curtis, Tom Arnold, Tia Carrere, Art Malik, Charlton Heston, Bill Paxton
Rating: ★★★

Or: how a James Bond movie might be with a Mrs Bond at home. Harry (Arnie) has been a secret agent, bumping off foreign bad guys, for 15 years without wifey (Jamie Lee Curtis) suspecting. Each night he comes home from his 'job' as a computer salesman, late only if there were extra buildings to blow up or bad guys to kill. But when Curtis becomes involved with a salesman who *pretends* to be a spy, Harry's two worlds lock onto a collision course. Actually, this whole film is like a Bond movie – with even more sensational effects. There's the 10-minute adventure at the beginning, the lengthy running time, the sag in the middle – usually where Bond spars with the villain, here where Harry suspects his wife of an affair – and the explosive last reel where double-O Sch-you-know-who blasts hundreds of

baddies to oblivion. Curtis is sensationally good and the airborne action effects in the last reel had preview audiences whooping with glee. Earlier stages, though, are marred by poor continuity and obvious use of stunt doubles.

True Love ● Ⓥ
1989, US, 104 mins, colour
Dir: Nancy Savoca
Stars: Annabella Sciorra, Ron Eldard, Aida Turturro, Roger Rignack, Star Jasper
Rating: ★

Think it would be tedious, eavesdropping on stag and hen parties and the dogfights in the 48-hour run-up to an Italian-American wedding? Think right! A colleague thought the piece well-observed and that may well be true: the film is certainly well thought of in some quarters. But a well-observed portrait of a boring lifestyle and klutzy characters still makes for a boring film. The bridegroom (Ron Eldard) is a deli assistant who even wants to party with the boys on his honeymoon night. It's the height of his ambition. The bride (Annabella Sciorra, in her first big leading role) is a foul-mouthed, angel-faced sweetie understandably having doubts about the whole thing. The ending is obvious right from the beginning but, even so, I still hoped someone might get shot and liven things up a bit.

True Romance ● Ⓥ
1993, US, 118 mins, colour
Dir: Tony Scott
Stars: Christian Slater, Patricia Arquette, Dennis Hopper, Christopher Walken, Gary Oldman, Brad Pitt
Rating: ★

To be stuffed with extreme violence and still be boring takes some doing, but this offbeat action farce-thriller does it in style. A star-studded cast, including cameos from Brad Pitt, Val Kilmer, Dennis Hopper, Gary Oldman, Chris Penn and Christopher Walken, all presumably saw something in the raucous and sometimes embarrassing script that doesn't manifest itself on the screen. 'To this day,' drones heroine Patricia Arquette, 'the events that followed seemed like a distant dream. They changed our lives forever.' When new hubby Christian Slater comes back from blasting her pimp to hell and stealing millions in cocaine, she tells him, 'I think what you did was so romantic.' It gets less romantic when the Mafia gets on the trail, headed by Walken (who disappears after one scene) while the happy couple has dreams of selling their booty to a hophead Hollywood producer. The orgy of sadism and violence that follows is like an old-fashioned Disney comedy with an adult certificate. The characters are all dislikeable and their performances are pitched at high-decibel level.

True Story of Jesse James, The ○
1956, US, 92 mins, colour
Dir: Nicholas Ray
Stars: Robert Wagner, Jeffrey Hunter, Hope Lange
Rating: ★★

Hollywood has filmed the Jesse James saga at least half-a-dozen times, each time trying to analyse why the James Brothers turned outlaw. Some have claimed they were victims of circumstance; others have painted their characters black. This film, which professes to have the facts, shows them to be a bit of both. Robert Wagner as Jesse and Jeffrey Hunter as Frank – they really do look like brothers – handle their roles with veteran-like authority.

Truly Madly Deeply ○ ⓥ
1990, UK, 107 mins, colour
Dir: Anthony Minghella
Stars: Juliet Stevenson, Alan Rickman, Bill Paterson
Rating: ★★★

This romantic – and funny – ghost story received huge critical acclaim for Minghella on his movie debut. Early on, you suspect that you are in for some heavy stuff about the psychology of grief, but when Rickman appears in ghost form, the tone of the film lightens. Stevenson gives a performance of great charm and is well complemented by Rickman, so that you can happily forget that the joke – how does one actually live day-to-day with a ghost? – is a little overworked, especially when Rickman invites a number of his friends. 'Are you telling me,' asks an incredulous Stevenson, 'that there are dead people in my living-room watching videos?' A strong support cast includes Bill Paterson as Stevenson's sympathetic boss and David Ryall in a delightful cameo as a philosophical pest control officer.

Trust ● ⓥ
1990, UK/US, 106 mins, colour
Dir: Hal Hartley

Stars: Adrienne Shelly, Martin Donovan
Rating: ★★

Based firmly on unreality, this is silly low-budget nonsense and the only surprise is that the actors and director actually manage to make something of it. Director Hal Hartley, who made the critically-successful *The Unbelievable Truth* with much the same cast, has only himself to blame for the material he has to work with here: he wrote it. And while such phrases as 'A family's like a gun – you point in the wrong direction, you're going to kill somebody' sound as if they have something to say, they're actually pretty daft. If one warms to the film as it goes on, this is due to the affecting performances of Adrienne Shelly and Martin Donovan as the two losers, seemingly set for a lifetime of unhappiness, who touch each other's lives and make them better.

Truth About Cats & Dogs, The ● ⓥ
1996, US, 97 mins, colour
Dir: Michael Lehmann
Stars: Uma Thurman, Janeane Garofolo, Ben Chaplin, Hank the dog
Rating: ★★

The first 10 minutes of this film are hilarious, with Janeane Garofolo in her element as a radio vet dispensing witty and uproarious advice to pet-obsessed (and distressed) callers. All too soon, though, this potentially smart, warm and funny number loses its way, descending through misunderstandings and embarrassments into sloppy romantic comedy. As the vet who falls for one of her (human) radio patients, stand-up comic Garofolo shows great promise as an offbeat leading lady. And Uma Thurman could also hardly be better as the dizzy blonde neighbour forced to assume Garofolo's identity after the latter has had a panic attack about her looks. Thurman finds herself hard-put to avoid falling for Garofolo's knight in shining armour (rather stickily played by British actor Ben Chaplin) although you'll know complications like these were made to be straightened out in a conventional girl-gets-boy finale.

Truth About Spring, The ☉
1965, UK, 102 mins, colour
Dir: Richard Thorpe
Stars: Hayley Mills, John Mills, James MacArthur
Rating: ★★

A tolerably enjoyable adventure romp which casts Hayley Mills as the tomboy daughter of a roguish old sea-

dog, played by father John Mills. Such British film stalwarts as Lionel Jeffries, Harry Andrews and Niall MacGinnis have a high old time rolling their eyes and pretending to be piratical. This was shot on location in the Costa Brava, providing the stars with a working holiday in the sun.

Truth About Women, The ○
1957, UK, 98 mins, colour
Dir: Muriel Box
Stars: Laurence Harvey, Julie Harris, Derek Farr
Rating: ★★★

Rather rambling and slapdash but very enjoyable period drama in which an aristocrat (Laurence Harvey) relates sundry romantic adventures from his past. The cinematic equivalent of a good book, the film is very attractively photographed in Eastman Colour by Otto Heller, and its ladies stunningly costumed by Cecil Beaton: they include Julie Harris, Jackie (later Jocelyn) Lane, Elina Labourdette, Mai Zetterling, Diane Cilento, Eva Gabor and Catherine (later Katie) Boyle. The art direction by George Provis is also striking – often opulent, it presents the period most convincingly.

Tucker – The Man and His Dreams ○ ⓥ
1988, US, 107 mins, colour
Dir: Francis Ford Coppola
Stars: Jeff Bridges, Joan Allen, Frederic Forrest, Martin Landau, Dean Stockwell, Christian Slater
Rating: ★★★

As beautifully crafted as one of the revolutionary cars of its title, *Tucker* is like a Frank Capra film in an age when America finally recognises that the good guys rarely won in real life. Jeff Bridges is the ever-smiling post-war inventor whose affable exterior envelops a nervous system as tightly wound as a clockwork coil. Capra would have let him win, but this is the real world where big business interests crush private initiative with the ruthlessness of a bulldozer, and you'll clench your fists in frustration at the realisation that Tucker stood no chance against them. Though its pace is sometimes on the stately side, Coppola's film comes alive in the final courtroom scenes when Bridges' performance rivals that of James Stewart in *Mr Smith Goes to Washington*. The dialogue is well-written if a shade cautious, and gives its best line to Martin Landau's elderly adviser: 'Don't get too close to people – you'll catch their dreams.'

T

Tudor Rose ○
(aka: Nine Days a Queen)
1936, UK, 79 mins, b/w
Dir: Robert Stevenson
Stars: Sir Cedric Hardwicke, Nova
Pilbeam, John Mills, Sybil Thorndike
Rating: ★★★

A forcefully impressive and affecting
piece of history, rich in period detail
and photographed with great skill by
Mutz Greenbaum. There are biting
performances from Sir Cedric
Hardwicke and Felix Aylmer in this
story of Lady Jane Grey (played with
touching vulnerability by teenage star
Nova Pilbeam). The juvenile lead is a
fresh-looking young chap called John
Mills.

Tugboat Annie ⊙
1933, US, 87 mins, b/w
Dir: Mervyn LeRoy
Stars: Marie Dressler, Wallace Beery
Rating: ★★★

Marie Dressler and Wallace Beery, reunited from *Min and Bill*, in which she
took an Oscar (he won an Academy
Award that same year – 1931 – for *The
Champ*), climb all over the scenery as
feuding river-dwellers in this immensely popular MGM comedy. It must
have been a relaxing chore for director
Mervyn LeRoy, following on his work
on the much grimmer *Five Star Final*,
Two Seconds and *I Am a Fugitive from a
Chain Gang*.

Tumbleweed ○
1953, US, 79 mins, colour
Dir: Nathan Juran
Stars: Audie Murphy, Lori Nelson, Chill
Wills, Lee Van Cleef
Rating: ★★★

Nice-looking Western with Audie
Murphy as a wagon train guard unust-
ly (of course) accused of desertion. A
warm and sometimes wryly humorous
script makes the film a pleasure to listen to as well as watch, although
Murphy's thunder is well stolen by K
T Stevens (actress daughter of director
Sam Wood) and a personable white
horse. The mean features of Lee Van
Cleef make an early appearance as one
of the bad guys.

Tune In Tomorrow
See: Aunt Julia and the Scriptwriter

Tunes of Glory ◐
1960, UK, 106 mins, colour
Dir: Ronald Neame
Stars: Alec Guinness, John Mills, Dennis

Price, Kay Walsh
Rating: ★★★

Scathingly memorable drama about
two contrasting army officers who
drive each other to the brink of madness. Ronald Neame directs the
powerful clash of wills in uncompromisingly frank fashion, and Susannah
York makes her film debut. Alec
Guinness gives a fine character reading
of the hard-drinking Scots officer replaced by a British martinet. But John
Mills, playing from deep within and
giving the performance of a lifetime,
wins this acting duel by a whisker.

Tunnel of Love, The ○
1958, US, 98 mins, b/w
Dir: Gene Kelly
Stars: Doris Day, Richard Widmark, Gig
Young
Rating: ★★

A rare comedy role for Richard
Widmark in this Gene Kelly-directed
frolic about a couple trying to adopt a
baby. Complications ensue, with
Widmark getting involved with a
glamorous 'other woman' from the
adoption agency, played by the smouldering Gia Scala. Giving Widmark
and Doris Day stalwart backing is Gig
Young, who played the hero's friend
dozens of times before his adept acting
was rewarded by a 1970 Oscar for
They Shoot Horses, Don't They?

Turbulence ● ⓥ
1997, US, 101 mins, colour
Dir: Robert Butler
Stars: Ray Liotta, Rachel Holly, Ben
Cross, Rachel Ticotin, Catherine Hicks
Rating: ★★

It's rare indeed these days to see a film
that's so bad it's good. But here's a
dilly that runs like a cross between a
disaster movie, a serial killer thriller
and a panto. Murderer Ray Liotta,
full of pretty-boy charm, is being flown
back to justice. Soon the escorting
marshals are killed, Liotta's on the
loose and Cinderella stewardess
Lauren Holly – the pilot's also dead –
is flying the plane. But Liotta, revealed in his true colours as the
Demon King, is on to her and, over-
acting like fury, lures her out of the
cabin time and again even while Prince
Charming Ben Cross, at ground control, is trying to talk her down. 'This
is bad! This is bad!' groans Liotta at
the advent of another crisis. He's
right, too, but the film has a compulsive, hysterical awfulness that will keep
you watching.

Turk 182! ◐
1985, US, 98 mins, colour
Dir: Bob Clark
Stars: Timothy Hutton, Robert Urich, Kim
Cattrall
Rating: ★★★

Everybody likes to see injustice be
made to stand on its head, so there
should be a lot of people cheering for
this unlikely but vigorous and mildly
enjoyable spot of escapism. Timothy
Hutton is the 20-year-old who heeds
the famous advice 'Go fight City Hall'
after his older brother, a fireman (a
role that gives Robert Urich rather
more acting opportunities than the
star), is badly injured when, off-duty
and slightly the worse for drink, he
rescues a child from a tenement blaze.
After Urich is denied private treatment, and then a disability pension,
because he'd been drinking, Hutton
goes to work as a kind of plain-clothes
caped crusader, humiliating the vaguely corrupt New York mayor (a
sharkishly smiling Robert Culp) at
every opportunity. If the thrills are
cheap and the lines occasionally cheaper, the enterprise still has the surefire
appeal of a non-league side taking on
Liverpool in the Cup. The American
dream lives!

Turkey Time ⊙
1933, UK, 73 mins, b/w
Dir: Tom Walls
Stars: Tom Walls, Ralph Lynn, Mary
Brough
Rating: ★★★

The Aldwych farces kept audiences of
the late Twenties and early Thirties
laughing. The Tom Walls-Ralph
Lynn-Robertson Hare trio are supported here by such stalwarts as Mary
Brough and Norma Varden and there
are Christmas carols for good measure.

Turner & Hooch ○ ⓥ
1989, US, 97 mins, colour
Dir: Roger Spottiswoode
Stars: Tom Hanks, Mare Winningham,
Craig T Nelson
Rating: ★★★

This affable movie is hardly likely to
rate highly in Tom Hanks' career, yet
Hanks' inventive comedy sense and, an
incredibly ugly (and talented) dog give
it enough extra life to make it worthwhile. Hanks is a police officer in a
quiet coastal town who's acquainted
with the local derelict (John McIntire)
and his fearsome dog. Pinned down
by the pooch, Hanks is reassured by
McIntire that 'He didn't even break the
skin. He loves you boy.' And so he

does, after McIntire has been murdered and Hooch has reduced Hanks' house to rubble before knuckling down to crack the case. Hanks is beautiful as the house-proud snooper who hoovers his new partner's shirtfront in the car as he's eating a muffin; the dog is almost (but not quite) too slobby to be lovable and, like all canine heroes, does what a dog has to do in the end. The rest of the cast isn't much, but then this gruesome twosome would probably show them up anyway.

Turning Point, The ○
1977, US, 119 mins, colour
Dir: Herbert Ross
Stars: Shirley MacLaine, Anne Bancroft, Mikhail Baryshnikov
Rating: ★★★

An interesting, although not wholly successful film about careers, regrets, love, applause and envy, set against the unusual backcloth of ballet. The story is treated with great delicacy by director Herbert Ross, as are its two stars: Shirley MacLaine as the ballerina who married and gave it all up, and Anne Bancroft as the one who went on, and must now face the inevitability of getting too old. There are several good performances in support of their histrionics, notably from Tom Skerritt as MacLaine's husband and Mikhail Baryshnikov who, besides being a brilliant dancer, projects a pleasing personality. The first hour is exceptionally good, but leaves too little room for expansion of the plot.

Turn the Key Softly ○
1953, UK, 83 mins, b/w
Dir: Jack Lee
Stars: Yvonne Mitchell, Joan Collins, Terence Morgan
Rating: ★★

Unusual melodrama about three women convicts and their attempts to come to terms with freedom. Although realism scarcely gets a look in, the plot rattles along with all the self-confidence of a driver making speed along a familiar road. Joan Collins draws the tart to the life, tight of skirt and loose of eye. Kathleen Harrison's pathetic little shoplifter offers a fresh slant on old age and poverty. But the best performance is given by Yvonne Mitchell, giving a sensitive lift to the classy lady unable to break away from her criminal lover.

Turtle Beach ● ⓥ
1992, Australia, 88 mins, colour
Dir: Stephen Wallace

Stars: Greta Scacchi, Joan Chen, Art Malik, Jack Thompson, Norman Kaye
Rating: ★★

Beginning with vivid violence, including an amazing shot of a head being sliced off, this story of unrest in Malaysia has moments of poignancy, but at the same time seems designed as an exercise to allow Greta Scacchi and Joan Chen to take their clothes off. Not very well acted – Scacchi is about the best of a mediocre bunch – the film examines the plight of Vietnamese and other boat people, trying to land in a Malaysia where they are hated, and where, on Turtle Beach, an army of extras waving knives emerges on cue, like some kind of demon chorus, every time a refugee boat heaves into view. Lots of local colour here, but not much story.

Turtle Diary ○ ⓥ
1985, UK, 97 mins, colour
Dir: John Irvin
Stars: Glenda Jackson, Ben Kingsley, Richard Johnson
Rating: ★★★★★

Ben Kingsley creates one of the most fully rounded everyday men you're ever likely to meet in this excellent film, full of sudden changes of expression and nervous smiles that could spring from real emotions. It's an amazing performance that even develops as the character careers through a basically crazy adventure. In fact, if we told you that the film was about two cranks who steal three turtles from the zoo and let them loose in the sea, you'd probably turn the other way. But the everyday, incident-filled world that writer Harold Pinter creates around these two rush-of-blood-to-the-heads conservationists will make you cry a little and laugh a lot. Pinter's ear for commonplace dialogue, full of embarrassing pauses, has never been better, especially when used to create the seedy milieu of the boarding house where divorced bookshop assistant Kingsley lodges with people as lonely as himself. There's not a false note in this eccentric slice of everyday life.

12 Angy Men ○ ⓥ
1957, US, 95 mins, b/w
Dir: Sidney Lumet
Stars: Henry Fonda, Lee J Cobb, Ed Begley, E G Marshall, Jack Warden, Martin Balsam
Rating: ★★★★★

Surely the finest ensemble picture ever made, as 12 jurors sweat it out to decide the guilt or innocence of a

teenager accused of murdering his father. It was director Sidney Lumet's first film – and what a debut. Virtually the entire film is set in one room, as the doughty dozen play cat and mouse with a man's life. It seems to be an open and shut case, as 11 jurors give the metaphoric thumbs down to the accused. His only hope lies with the sole holdout – liberal Henry Fonda, who was also co-producer of this ambitious but brilliant work. Meticulously analysing the facts as he heard them in court, Fonda tries to convince his colleagues that there might be room for reasonable doubt. But he's working against deeply-ingrained prejudices and dubious priorities. Creating an excruciatingly stifling atmosphere, Lumet delivers as powerful a drama as you're likely to see on screen.

Twelfth Night ○ ⓥ
1996, UK, 135 mins, colour
Dir: Trevor Nunn
Stars: Imogen Stubbs, Helena Bonham Carter, Ben Kingsley, Nigel Hawthorne, Mel Smith, Richard E Grant
Rating: ★

Despite the all-star cast, and Stubbs' most appealing performance as Viola, this is by no means another *Much Ado About Nothing*. Director Nunn stages an exciting beginning and a sweeping ending but in between, like the characters at the start, he's all at sea. Kingsley is striking as Feste the Jester, yet another example of this actor's versatility, but the rest – although Bonham Carter is competent enough as Olivia – seem to be able to do little but go through Shakespearian motions under Nunn's unimaginative direction, a stage director in search of cinematic style he never looks likely to achieve. Slow and boring all too often, the film sparks to life every time the delectable Stubbs is on screen as the girl posing as a boy. Stubbs may be few people's idea of a man, but she makes you care about the character more than anyone else does here. When Kingsley say' I would that we were well rid of this knavery', you may echo the sentiments.

Twelve Chairs, The ○
1969, US, 94 mins, colour
Dir: Mel Brooks
Stars: Ron Moody, Dom DeLuise, Mel Brooks
Rating: ★★

Another zany comedy from Mel Brooks (who also makes an acting appearance), made between *The Producers* and *Blazing Saddles*. Based on the same Russian story from which Jack Benny and Fred Allen derived their famous Forties' hit *It's in the Bag!*, about a fortune hidden away in a presumably worthless old armchair. Some typical Brooks bursts of lunacy liven up a basically rather soggy story.

Twelve Monkeys ● ⓥ
1995, US, 132 mins, colour
Dir: Terry Gilliam
Stars: Bruce Willis, Madeleine Stowe, Brad Pitt, Christopher Plummer
Rating: ★★★

It's certainly a cute title for an inventive piece of science-fantasy which presupposes that most people have been wiped out by a virus and that, in 2035, scientists living underground might send a reluctant volunteer back, via time travel, to 1996 when the plague began. A shaven-headed Bruce Willis as the guinea pig misses the target first time and ends up in a mental asylum in 1990. Here he meets two of the protagonists of the apocalypse-to-come: psychiatrist Madeleine Stowe and raving loony Brad Pitt, who turns out to be the son of unbalanced generic scientist (you've met 'em) Christopher Plummer. Subsequent developments, as Willis is recalled to 2035 but manages each time to talk his way back, are never less than intriguing, even if they lack dramatic force in the second half of the film, as Stowe gradually comes to believe that Willis isn't barking mad and can see her 'future'. And those little red monkeys? They may or may not be red herrings: you'll have to see the film to find out.

Twelve O'Clock High ○ ⓥ
1949, US, 132 mins, b/w
Dir: Henry King
Stars: Gregory Peck, Hugh Marlowe, Gary Merrill
Rating: ★★★★★

This memorable study of men in war and under stress won an Academy Award for Dean Jagger as best supporting actor of the year, and produced deserved queues at box offices all round the world. It combines action and penetrating dialogue with a long line of well-rounded characters in its story of an American air unit based in Britain during World War Two.

Twentieth Century ○
1934, US, 91 mins, b/w
Dir: Howard Hawks

Stars: John Barrymore, Carole Lombard
Rating: ★★★★

Matinee idol John Barrymore said of his sassy co-star Carole Lombard after completing this screwball comedy: 'She is perhaps the greatest actress I ever worked with.' And Barrymore plus Lombard equals dynamite in this fast-paced, frantic entertainment about a harum-scarum impresario trying to talk his ex-mistress into acting in one of his plays. There are fights, histrionics, and even a fake suicide in a film that thunders along like the train of the title.

Twenty Mule Team ○
1940, US, 84 mins, b/w
Dir: Richard Thorpe
Stars: Wallace Beery, Leo Carrillo Marjorie Rambeau, Anne Baxter
Rating: ★★★

A typical Wallace Beery vehicle of its time, when he had ceased to be one of the studio's major stars, but still had a solid fan following. Often in these action comedies, he was teamed with horse-faced Marjorie Main; but here brisk Marjorie Rambeau is his vis-à-vis (with Anne Baxter making her film debut as her daughter) in a lively tale of borax bandits. Borax? It was a kind of salt crystal much mined in old California. The vigorous melodramatics are directed by MGM stalwart Richard Thorpe.

Twenty One ● ⓥ
1990, UK, 100 mins, colour
Dir: Don Boyd
Stars: Patsy Kensit, Jack Shepherd, Patrick Ryecart
Rating: ★★

This sleazy little number is one of those fashionable British films still swimming in the wake of the swinging Sixties. Patsy Kensit tries to crack her milk-and-water image as the girl involved with a junkie and a married man and her loser father, but she still emerges as a sweet young suburban thing, talking dirty but enraged by her own mother's infidelity. Kensit has her moments – especially when, after bereavement, singing along to a Nina Simone record – but there isn't much enjoyment to the film: if this is the life of the average secretary, you think, then Heaven help her.

20,000 Leagues Under the Sea ⊙ ⓥ
1954, US, 125 mins, colour
Dir: Richard Fleischer
Stars: Kirk Douglas, James Mason, Paul

Lukas, Peter Lorre
Rating: ★★★

James Mason is a memorably brooding Captain Nemo in Disney's handsomely produced film of the Jules Verne classic. There were Oscars for art direction and special effects, the latter featuring an exciting underwater fight with a huge octopus. There aren't many films, either, in which you can hear Kirk Douglas sing, but this is one of them! His song, like the film, is 'A Whale Of Tale'.

20,000 Years In Sing Sing ○
1932, US, 77 mins, b/w
Dir: Michael Curtiz
Stars: Spencer Tracy, Bette Davis
Rating: ★★★

A rare unsympathetic role for Spencer Tracy in a role that looks hand-tailored for James Cagney and was: Cagney priced himself out of the running and Tracy's career got a big boost from his skilful handling of the cocky criminal sent 'up the river'. The first of several films based on accounts of prison life by real-life Sing Sing warden Lewis Lawes, who acted as technical adviser on this film. Bette Davis' rather flashy portrayal of Tracy's moll is not one of her best.

Twice in a Lifetime ◑
1985, US, 117 mins, colour
Dir: Bud Yorkin
Stars: Gene Hackman, Ann-Margret, Ellen Burstyn
Rating: ★★★

I suppose that if there's one thing that might make a man leave the super Ellen Burstyn, it could be the delicious Ann-Margret. On those grounds, this family drama about an extreme case of the 30-year itch could at least be said to be well cast. And none of the players could be bettered: Burstyn, Margret, Ally Sheedy, Amy Madigan, Brian Dennehy and Gene Hackman as the father at the centre of it all. They combine to bring warmth and understanding to a film that could have gone home laden with Oscars with a better script. Madigan gives an outstanding performance as the daughter who simply can't forgive dad his desertion. The ending doesn't make it clear which woman Hackman's going back to: but we should all have such a choice.

Twice Round the Daffodils ○
1962, UK, 89 mins, b/w
Dir: Gerald Thomas
Stars: Juliet Mills, Donald Sinden,

Ronald Lewis, Donald Houston
Rating: ★★

An unlikely setting for a comedy – a TB sanatorium – in this film from the *Carry On* team. It's in slightly more serious vein and the title refers to the ritual in which patients do a double turn round the flower bed before being discharged. Juliet Mills is charming as an efficient, selfless nurse nicknamed Catty and Donald Sinden, a busy screen star of the Fifties and Sixties, scores as a patient with frustrated sex urges. Also in the cast are *Carry On* stalwarts Kenneth Williams and Joan Sims.

Twilight for the Gods ○
1958, US, 120 mins, colour
Dir: Joseph Pevney
Stars: Rock Hudson, Cyd Charisse
Rating: ★★

Writer Ernest K Gann (who also penned *The High and the Mighty*) had only himself to blame for this messy and sluggish version of his great bestselling novel, since he did the screenplay. Gann and director Joseph Pevney (an ex-actor who directed numerous big-budget films for Universal without making much of any of them) flagrantly waste exotic South Seas settings, a decent storyline and an excellent cast that includes Rock Hudson, Cyd Charisse and Arthur Kennedy. A shame.

Twilight of Honor
See: The Charge is Murder

Twilight's Last Gleaming ◐
1977, US/Germany, 146 mins, colour
Dir: Robert Aldrich
Stars: Burt Lancaster, Richard Widmark, Charles Durning
Rating: ★★

Nothing wrong from a directorial point of view with this action thriller, even though its story of a thinking madman who holds America to ransom by 'kidnapping' atomic missiles is familiar to the point of contempt. Robert Aldrich's direction keeps the action sharp, tense and exciting, his extended use of split screens working to a large degree in tightening the suspense. The film's weakest point is the script. 'Perhaps it might be a midget,' suggests saboteur Paul Winfield as an enemy sniper scuttles behind a tank. Head saboteur Burt Lancaster thinks for a moment. 'There are no midgets,' he snaps, 'in the United States Air Force!'

Twilight Zone – The Movie ◐ ⓥ
1983, US, 102 mins, colour
Dir: Steven Spielberg, Joe Dante, George Miller, John Landis
Stars: Vic Morrow, Scatman Crothers, Dan Aykroyd, Selma Diamond
Rating: ★★★

This series of bizarre journeys into an unknown dimension is very much a curate's egg. Its four stories are all made by different directors, the best effort being a gentle little tale from Steven Spielberg about a group of old folk made young again by a roguish old black man. But the last episode is the most exciting, with John Lithgow going splendidly to pieces as the only passenger who can see a malign and destructive gremlin on the wing of his plane in mid flight. Despite the original '15' certificate, the highly coloured trip could cheerfully be recommended for all sturdier children of secondary school age. Just be prepared for the odd monster or two.

Twin Beds ○
1942, US, 85 mins, b/w
Dir: Tim Whelan
Stars: George Brent, Joan Bennett, Mischa Auer
Rating: ★★

This rather faded farce wouldn't amount to much without the participation of that pop-eyed, Russian-born Hollywood character star Mischa Auer. Auer chose this film to give one of his most memorable performances, especially when heavily involved in the comic pandemonium at the end of the film. He's quite irresistible, playing an eccentric slavic musician called Cherubin who's infatuated with heroine Joan Bennett.

Twinkle, Twinkle, Killer Kane
See: The Ninth Configuration

Twinky ●
(aka: Lola)
1969, UK, 98 mins, colour
Dir: Richard Donner
Stars: Charles Bronson, Susan George, Trevor Howard
Rating: ★

This story of a middle-aged author in love with a nubile nymphet was also titled *Lola*, presumably to cash in on the Lolita image. The combination of rugged Charles Bronson and prettily pouting Susan George would, I suspect, be irresistible in an action film,. but seems faintly bizarre in this early

offering from director Richard Donner, who, not long after, hit the big time with such hits as *The Omen* and *Superman*. Here Donner resorts to a full bag of cinematic tricks – freeze frames, a clangorous pop score, slow-motion action and speeded-up bicycle rides to pep up his picture of London at the end of the allegedly swinging Sixties. Trevor Howard plays all stops out as the grandpa with a roving eye and a penchant for potting foreigners with his shotgun.

Twin Peaks: Fire Walk with Me ● ⓥ
1992, US, 135 mins, colour
Dir: David Lynch
Stars: Sheryl Lee, Kyle MacLachlan, Moira Kelly, David Bowie, Harry Dean Stanton, Kiefer Sutherland
Rating: ★

A surrealistic comment on a prequel to the cult TV series, this seems, at two and a quarter hours, a long indulgence. The wanton Laura Palmer (Sheryl Lee) is duly bumped off by her possibly incestuous father (Ray Wise) but who cares? David Bowie appears and says nothing, while other stars appear and may wish they had said nothing. Subliminal shots, strobe lights, half-seen things, pictures coming to life and not much sense: just the film, I'm sure, that David Lynch wanted to make – not forgetting the sex and titillation that are high on his agenda. Somewhere, we're certain, there are people waiting to see this.

Twins ◐ ⓥ
1988, US, 112 mins, colour
Dir: Ivan Reitman
Stars: Arnold Schwarzenegger, Danny DeVito, Chloe Webb, Kelly Preston
Rating: ★★★

Inspirational casting is the basis for success in this unlikely action comedy. You couldn't imagine two actors less alike than hairy, strapping Arnold Scwarzenegger and little, barrel-shaped Danny DeVito. Casting them as twins is so ridiculous it just has to pay off in terms of laughs. And so it proves, even if they seem to be having slightly more fun than the audience. 'I hate violence,' groans Arnie, throwing the bad guys 'through' a lift. 'But you're so good at it,' beams Danny, amazed to have a protective twin whose back 'looks like a map of North Dakota.' There's a bit of a plot too, but it's only an excuse for Arnie and Danny to fool around to some effect in identical costumes, whether wooing Chloe Webb

T

and Kelly Preston or dancing with each other.

Twisted Nerve ●

1968, UK, 115 mins, colour
Dir: Roy Boulting
Stars: Hywel Bennett, Billie Whitelaw
Rating: ★★★

There hadn't been a film as jumpy as this in quite a while. Is that the killer's shadow on the door as Hayley Mills tries to call up her boyfriend? The Boulting Brothers prove that most of the old suspense tricks are still the best, in this story of a psychotic youth who kills his stepfather and landlady on his way to mental disintegration. Barry Foster scores as a bawdy lodger with an eye on landlady Billie Whitelaw.

Twister ○ Ⓥ

1996, US, 114 mins, colour
Dir: Jan De Bont
Stars: Helen Hunt, Bill Paxton, Jami Gertz, Cary Elwes
Rating: ★★★

In Herefordshire, Hertfordshire and Hampshire, so we're told, hurricanes hardly ever happen. Tornados in Texas, Oklahoma and Kansas, though, seem to be hourly events. This improbable action adventure, with devastatingly effective 'twister' sequences, follows the efforts of two rival groups of hurricane hunters to race to the root of the tornado and, by launching a scientific equipment pack into its eye, record valuable data concerning its structure. Paxton and Hunt look to be having a tough time doing their own stuntwork, but acting honours are clearly stolen by Jami Gertz as the 'other woman' who comes between them. Shots of cows and tractors flying through the air are delightfully well done, even if the plot is never remotely credible. 'Maybe we should get off this road,' suggests Hunt to Paxton as an entire house crashes down in front of them. People whose favourite TV programme is the weather will love it.

Two-faced Woman ○

1941, US, 94 mins, b/w
Dir: George Cukor
Stars: Greta Garbo, Melvyn Douglas, Constance Bennett, Roland Young
Rating: ★★★

Notorious as the film which caused Greta Garbo to leave MGM and end her screen career, this romantic comedy turns out to be an entertaining and frothy confection. Perhaps it was because the star deliberately abandoned

her image of aloofness and mystery that the film was reviled by contemporary critics. Garbo proves in fact to be a dab hand at light comedy as a woman who poses as her own sister in order to win back her philandering husband, played by her *Ninotchka* partner Melvyn Douglas. She has a classic tipsy scene, dances a lively variation of the rumba, the 'chica-choca', and even, more surprisingly, gets to appear in a one-piece bathing suit.

2 Days in the Valley ● Ⓥ

1996, US, 100 mins, colour
Dir: John Herzfeld
Stars: Teri Hatcher, James Spader, Jeff Daniels, Danny Aiello, Eric Stoltz, Glenne Headly, Keith Carradine
Rating: ★★★★

A quirky black-thriller much along the lines of work by the Coen brothers, this is the kind of thing that either works like a charm or falls flat on its face. Thanks to a constantly well-written script that cunningly makes you care about the characters this one's a winner all the way. There's death in the air in LA's San Fernando Valley. Hotshot skier Hatcher has a visit from her ex (Peter Horton) and, later, two hit-men (Spader and Aiello) who sedate the girl and despatch the man. Nearby, failed director Paul Mazursky contemplates suicide, but is saved by nurse Marsha Mason, who takes him to her half-brother (Greg Crutwell) and his browbeaten secretary (Headly) to find them being held up by Aiello, who has survived a double-cross by Spader. Cops Stoltz and Daniels also find their destinies intertwining... All the performances are good here, with a notable debut from Crutwell, a combination of Tim Roth and Dirk Bogarde, as a repulsively self-pitying yuppie upstart.

Two Faces of Dr Jekyll, The ◐

(aka: House of Fright)
1960, UK, 88 mins, colour
Dir: Terence Fisher
Stars: Paul Massie, Dawn Addams, Christopher Lee
Rating: ★★

Hammer horror meets Robert Louis Stevenson. In this generous adaptation of R L S's classic tale of double identity and murder, the colour photography gives a good impression of bright Victorian decadence. Christopher Lee looks distinctly uncomfortable at having to play a straightforward 'good guy' in a horror film, Paul Massie plays the hapless

Jekyll and, in a small part, you can spot a young Oliver Reed as a bully.

Two Flags West ○

1950, US, 92 mins, b/w
Dir: Robert Wise
Stars: Joseph Cotten, Linda Darnell, Cornel Wilde, Dale Robertson
Rating: ★★

Director Robert Wise had just left RKO where he had made his name and started up at Fox, where his career would reach its high point 15 years later with *The Sound of Music*. In *Two Flags West,* Wise augmented a formidable cast with some spectacular battles between cavalry and Indians. Dramatically, though, the film is much less exciting.

Two for the Road ○

1967, UK, 112 mins, colour
Dir: Stanley Donen
Stars: Audrey Hepburn, Albert Finney, Eleanor Bron, William Daniels
Rating: ★★★

Centred on one particular car journey through France, but mixed with numerous scenes set in various times in the past, this comedy concerns the superficial changes that come over a young married couple. The dialogue is incisively accurate on the moods, manners and morals of modern life but, despite the problems of the couple involved, it's very much a 'pro-marriage' story. Author Frederic Raphael admitted that he first hit on the idea while on a drive through France with his wife, but resisted the suggestion that it might be any more autobiographical than any of his other writing. Fine acting by Albert Finney and Audrey Hepburn, with some scene-stealing by Eleanor Bron and the ineffably fussy William Daniels.

Two Girls and a Sailor ○

1944, US, 124 mins, b/w
Dir: Richard Thorpe
Stars: Van Johnson, June Allyson
Rating★★★

A really swinging musical packed full of songs and speciality numbers which deservedly swamp a typically weak June Allyson-Van Johnson MGM plot about... well, two girls and a sailor. Tom Drake and Gloria De Haven are in there to ensure misunderstandings are sorted out by a double happy ending, but the music's the thing. Jimmy Durante reprises one of his greatest numbers, 'Inka Dinka Doo', Lena Horne gives a classic rendition of 'Paper Doll', and Allyson, De Haven and Helen Forrest help Harry James and His Music Makers swing into 'Sweet and Lovely'.

Two Jakes, The ● Ⓥ

1990, US, 137 mins, colour
Dir: Jack Nicholson
Stars: Jack Nicholson, Harvey Keitel, Meg Tilly, Madeleine Stowe, Eli Wallach, Frederic Forrest
Rating: ★★

The problem with this lacklustre sequel to *Chinatown* is that it never really goes anywhere. There are no great revelations at the end of a story that is immensely difficult to follow and way too long in the telling. As director as well as star, Jack Nicholson, repeating his role as Jake Gittes, is obviously responsible for the stately and rather suffocating feel of the piece. It is, however, marvellously well set in period and written with great literary bite by Robert Towne, who also penned the original. Alas, even Nicholson, now roly-poly and flat-footed, no longer seems ideal casting for the private eye fallen on better times, who finds ghosts from the past rising to haunt him during a seemingly straightforward case of revenge killing. There are some good moments here, but they just don't fuse together; and the acting, considering the strength of the cast, is not that great.

Two Minute Warning ○

1976, US, 115 mins, colour
Dir: Larry Peerce
Stars: Charlton Heston, John Cassavetes, Martin Balsam, Beau Bridges, David Janssen
Rating: ★★

The all-star disaster movie was nearing the end of its useful life when Universal put Charlton Heston at the head of the cast, and a sniper on a tower overlooking a football stadium and hoped that that would be enough to shore up a shaky plot. Full of sound and fury, but signifying very little, the film provides good actors like Gena Rowland, John Cassavetes, Jack Klugman, David Janssen and Brock Peters with hackneyed characters they do their best to enliven. Walter Pidgeon makes one of his last film appearances as an aged pickpocket.

Two Much ◐ Ⓥ

1995, US/Spain, 117 mins, colour
Dir: Fernando Trueba
Stars: Melanie Griffith, Antonio Banderas, Daryl Hannah, Danny Aiello, Eil Wallach, Joan Cusack
Rating: ★

This Spanish-American mishmash attempts to be a romantic comedy in the style of long ago. Mostly, however, it falls flatter than a tortilla. Banderas is a faded painter turned art dealer who specialises in selling pictures to families of the recently bereaved (no, don't ask). At one funeral, he runs into shapely, twice-divorced heiress Griffith and it's lust at first sight. Melanie plans marriage in a week or so, but Antonio has already fallen in love with her art-loving sister Daryl Hannah. Banderas invents a twin brother to court Daryl on the sly, and matters are further complicated by Griffith's ex, Aiello, who just happens to be the son of a man to whom Banderas pretends to have sold a pre-funeral painting. Poor Griffith is hardly in it after this, which is perhaps lucky for her, as things get progressively more tedious from here on. Banderas gives it his best shot, but, heaven knows, Cary Grant he isn't. Cusack (his secretary) and Wallach (his roving-eye dad) mop up the few good lines going.

Two Mules for Sister Sara ◐ Ⓥ

1969, US, 105 mins, colour
Dir: Don Siegel
Stars: Shirley MacLaine, Clint Eastwood
Rating: ★★★

Set in Mexico, this is an American-made film but one which resembles in some of its content and most of its style – the so-called 'spaghetti' Westerns which were being turned out in Italy at the time, achieving such popularity over here. Despite its quite lengthy running time, the film is a lively one with considerable outbursts of action, a story which has more than one surprise up its sleeve and magnetic performances by its stars, Clint Eastwood and Shirley MacLaine.

Two of a Kind ◐ Ⓥ

1983, US, 87 mins, colour
Dir: John Herzfeld
Stars: John Travolta, Olivia Newton-John, Oliver Reed, Charles Durning
Rating: ★

It might have seemed like a bright idea to reunite John Travolta and Olivia Newton-John after the huge success of *Grease,* but whoever dreamt up this load of nonsense must have had an oil slick on the brain. God is so angry at the human race that he's about to destroy the Earth until four angels persuade him to give humanity one more chance. Salvation is in the hands of inventor-turned-robber Travolta and bank teller Newton-John. If they

can be nice to each other ... Sharp eyes may spot Kathy Bates way down the cast list, long before her Oscar-winning success in *Misery.*

2001: A Space Odyssey ○ Ⓥ

1968, UK, 141 mins, colour
Dir: Stanley Kubrick
Stars: Keir Dullea, Gary Lockwood
Rating: ★★★

Stanley Kubrick's visually stunning sci-fi epic is something of a space oddity and one that has confused and confounded almost everyone who has seen it. Arguments about what it all means still continue, 25 years after the film was released. The story starts four million years ago when a group of cavemen discover a mysterious monolith. The moment they touch it, they turn from peaceful vegetarians into war-like carnivores. Four million years later the monolith is discovered on the moon and a spaceship is on a mysterious mission to Jupiter. Things become curiouser and curiouser and if you manage to keep up with it, you'll be doing better than most. It all looks fantastic, even though special effects have improved greatly since the film was made. Very much a curate's egg, *2001*'s delights compensate for its confusions.

2010 ◐

1984, US, 111 mins, colour
Dir: Peter Hyams
Stars: Roy Scheider, John Lithgow, Helen Mirren
Rating: ★★★

Boldly going where few men would have dared to tread, writer-director Peter Hyams has fashioned an entirely respectful sequel to Stanley Kubrick's influential science-fiction classic *2001: A Space Odyssey.* Overcoming the slight hiccup of its wordy scene-setting opening, 2010 develops into a fascinating space saga in its own right as American Roy Scheider (inheriting William Sylvester's role from Kubrick's film) joins a Russian team to solve the mystery of *Discovery*'s disappearance. The tension between these reluctant colleagues is keenly felt, and the state-of-the-art effects culminate in a climactic revelation that's as eerie as it is wonderful.

Two-Way Stretch ⊙ Ⓥ

1960, US, 87 mins, b/w
Dir: Robert Day
Stars: Peter Sellers, Wilfrid Hyde White, Lionel Jeffries, Beryl Reid, David Lodge
Rating: ★★★★

T

Probably the funniest and most consistently riotous of all Peter Sellers' British comedies, a short head in front of *The Wrong Arm of the Law*. Sellers, David Lodge and Bernard Cribbins are a trio of unholy jailbirds, but Lionel Jeffries steals the show as a would-be vicious warder called Sidney Crout. Jeffries tries to prevent Sellers and Co from carrying out a million pound robbery (while technically still in prison) but succeeds only in falling hilariously foul of their nefarious schemes. Maurice Denham, Wilfrid Hyde White (in his element as an educated, plausible, ever-smiling con-man), Irene Handl, Liz Fraser and Beryl Reid round out a hand-picked supporting cast.

Two Women ◑
(aka: La Ciociara)
1961, Italy, 110 mins, b/w
Dir: Vittorio De Sica
Stars: Sophia Loren, Eleanora Brown
Rating: ★★★★

Sophia Loren's Oscar-winning tour-de-force in an Anna Magnani-type role that few believed she was capable of playing. But Sophia was superbly moving as a wartime widow with a teenage daughter. Their survival after horrendous rape at the hands of Moroccan soldiers makes for an involving and emotional story. The desolate atmosphere of war-torn Italy is superbly captured by director Vittorio de Sica.

Two Years Before the Mast ○
1946, US, 98 mins, b/w
Dir: John Farrow
Stars: Alan Ladd, Howard Da Silva, Brian Donlevy, William Bendix
Rating: ★★

Round the Horn, me hearties, in the days of wooden ships and iron men. Some of the acting is a little wooden, too, in this catalogue of maritime brutality based on a rather more literate book by Richard Henry Dana. Used to the night-time world of Paramount's crime dramas, Alan Ladd, Howard da Silva, Brian Donlevy and William Bendix look a little pale around the gills, or maybe it was just the rocking of the ship in the studio tank. Da Silva has a high old time as a martinet captain who makes Captain Bligh and Ahab seem positively avuncular by comparison. Several of the cast are lashed to the mast and mercilessly flogged – a treatment that should have been reserved for the writers.

Tycoon ○
1947, US, 129 mins, colour
Dir: Richard Wallace
Stars: John Wayne, Laraine Day, Cedric Hardwicke, Anthony Quinn
Rating: ★★

A relatively lesser-known John Wayne film from the Forties, although there's no reason why it should be, apart from having been made by a studio in difficulties (R-KO Radio). It's no stodgy boardroom drama, either, but a spectacular action adventure story with some hair-raising storm scenes, brilliantly photographed in Technicolor. Wayne and co-star Laraine Day reputedly didn't get on together, and it shows in the stiffness of their romantic scenes.

U

Ugly Dachshund, The ⊙
1965, US, 93 mins, colour
Dir: Norman Tokar
Stars: Dean Jones, Suzanne Pleshette, Charlie Ruggles
Rating: ★

Flimsy Disney whimsy about a filthy rich young couple who adopt a Great Dane puppy as a brother for their four dachshund bitches. 'You've got a boy puppy,' he tells his wife. 'That's what you always wanted.' Dean Jones and Suzanne Pleshette coat the treacle with their winning brands of charm.

Ulysses ○
1954, Italy, 104 mins, colour
Dir: Mario Camerini
Stars: Kirk Douglas, Silvana Mangano, Anthony Quinn, Rossana Podesta
Rating: ★★

No fewer than seven writers, including Irwin (*The Young Lions*) Shaw, worked on creating a film script from Homer's *Odyssey*. They managed to condense the epic poem into four main incidents: the clash between Ulysses and the Cyclops, and his encounters with Circe, the Sirens and Nausicaa. This telescoping of events enabled Mario Camerini to gradually increase the pace until the hectic climax in which Ulysses takes on his wife's suitors. The mistily beautiful photography of the sea scenes greatly enhances the film.

Ulzana's Raid ●
1972, US, 103 mins, colour
Dir: Robert Aldrich
Stars: Burt Lancaster, Bruce Davison, Torge Luke, Richard Jaeckel
Rating: ★★★

World-weary but wise scout Burt Lancaster helps callow and naive cavalry officer Bruce Davison track down a renegade Apache in this violent Western from director Robert Aldrich. Exciting though it is, the film isn't without its thoughtful side. Lancaster, while not justifying Ulzana's actions, has sympathy for the Indians, and indeed has an Indian wife. Davison believes them all to be savages, little more than animals, until he sees the savagery of his own men. Lancaster gives a fine performance as the scout and Davison is also very good as the young lieutenant fresh from an Eastern military academy. Well-scripted by Alan Sharp, this powerful Western has drama and action in equal measure.

Umbrella Woman, The
See: The Good Wife

Uncanny, The ●
1977, UK/Canada, 85 mins, colour
Dir: Denis Heroux
Stars: Peter Cushing, Ray Milland, Donald Pleasence
Rating: ★

Three horror stories about cats very much in the style established by the British outfit Amicus Films in.the Sixties. This picture, however, was made in Canada with a star-studded cast. Special effects are rather below par and the light-heartedness of the last episode (somewhat after the humour of *The Raven*) comes as a welcome relief.

Uncle Buck ○ Ⓥ
1989, US, 94 mins, colour
Dir: John Hughes
Stars: John Candy, Jean Louisa Kelly, Gaby Hoffman, Macaulay Culkin, Amy Madigan
Rating: ★★★

For Buck, read schmuck. That's how bulbous John Candy's cast in this simplistic but rather enjoyable comedy. Fat, out-of-work and 40, and forever evading marriage to his long-suffering girlfriend (Amy Madigan), Buck suddenly finds himself temporarily in charge of his brother's kids, two wild juves and Tia, a teenager who shows all the signs of getting herself pregnant at an early age. Buck is a sausage-fingers who breaks everything and cooks enormous breakfasts consisting of eggs on onions, but the kids' problems appeal in no time to his innate sense of adulthood and, in a few weeks, he proves himself a better parent than his brother ever was. It all sounds too predictable to be much fun, but in fact it works pretty well, giving Candy a chance to show what he can do, playing a variant on the slob who comes good that he played in *Planes, Trains and Automobiles*. Not a great film, but one that makes you feel better for having seen it.

Uncle Silas ○
1947, UK, 103 mins, b/w
Dir: Charles Frank
Stars: Jean Simmons, Katina Paxinou
Rating: ★★★

This creepy thriller was the film that consolidated Jean Simmons' position as a new young star of the British cinema.

Here, she plays a plucky Victorian miss who refuses to knuckle under to the sinister uncle and strange governess into whose chilly care she has been placed following the death of her father. The combination of screenplay writer Ben Travers (more famous for his Aldwych stage farces) and J Sheridan Le Fanu, the Victorian master of the chiller on whose story Travers based his script, couldn't have seemed too promising. But in the hands of Simmons and her cohorts, plus the edgy direction of Charles Frank, the time-honoured old plot generates fresh suspense around every shadowy corner and down each dark stairway.

Uncommon Valor ◑ Ⓥ
1983, US, 105 mins, colour
Dir: Ted Kotcheff
Stars: Gene Hackman, Robert Stack, Fred Ward, Patrick Swayze
Rating: ★★★

Searching for its battered self-esteem after Vietnam, America welcomed a rash of 'let's rescue our boys' action films. This one, starring Gene Hackman, was one of the better ones (Hackman also made another *Bat*21*). He stars as a colonel whose son is missing in action. Despairing of the slow-moving 'usual' channels, he gathers together a group of hardened veterans and goes to find him. The politics behind this (and similar films) may be a bit questionable, but it's exciting and fast-moving. Hackman gives his character a bit more emotional depth and motivation than is usually found in such films and director Ted Kotcheff moves it at a pace that maintains the tension.

Unconquered ○
1947, US, 146 mins, colour
Dir: Cecil B DeMille
Stars: Gary Cooper, Paulette Goddard, Howard Da Silva, Boris Karloff
Rating: ★★

Cecil B DeMille spent a reported $4 million to bring this epic story of colonial America to the screen. Most of it shows up on the screen, although, to judge from some of the contemporary reviews, only a small part of the budget went to the screenplay. This combines melodrama with improbability and garnishes it with enough hokum to fill three regulation-size films. Not that it matters because DeMille's speciality was spectacle and he certainly provides a full measure here – splendidly staged Indian attacks and an edge-of-the-seat escape by Gary Cooper and Paulette

Goddard over treacherous rapids are most notable among the set pieces. The heroic derring-do of Cooper is in the best tradition of the genre, Howard Da Silva is an eminently hissable villain and Boris Karloff makes a rather surprising appearance as an Indian chief.

Undefeated, The ○ Ⓥ
1969, US, 119 mins, colour
Dir: Andrew V McLaglen
Stars: John Wayne, Rock Hudson, Tony Aguilar, Bruce Cabot
Rating.

Director Andrew V McLaglen carried his interest in the American Civil War a stage further on from *Shenandoah*, in which a peace-loving family was drawn into the conflict, to look at the first days following the war. After a moving opening, the theme of bitterness lingering on gradually disappears beneath the action and the spectacle for which McLaglen later became famous. John Wayne is the Unionist and Rock Hudson the Confederate, compelled to join forces against bandits, Emperor Maximilian's agents and a troop of French cavalry, across 2,000 miles of adventure to the wilds of Mexico.

Under Capricorn ○
1948, UK, 117 mins, colour
Dir: Alfred Hitchcock
Stars: Ingrid Bergman, Joseph Cotten, Michael Wilding, Margaret Leighton
Rating:

After *Spellbound and Notorious*, Alfred Hitchcock cast around in vain for another major hit until his dazzling run of success in the Fifties. For *Under Capricorn*, he even had the star of those two great Forties hits, Ingrid Bergman, working with him again. And the plot included such surefire Hitchcock elements as the dominant housekeeper, the skeleton in the cupboard and the confession of guilt towards the end. But, as he admitted himself, basic mistakes were made in the preparation of the movie. There was the ludicrous miscasting of the principals, Bergman (as an aristocratic Irish girl!) and Joseph Cotten, plus the expensive decision to shoot the film in (unnecessary) Technicolor. 'If I'd been thinking clearly,' said Hitchcock ruefully afterwards, 'I'd have never tackled a costume picture at all.' Still, the film was ineffably romantic, and Jack Cardiff's colour photography did make it beautiful to look at. Margaret Leighton took the acting honours.
Undercover Blues yy zz
1993, US, 90 mins, colour

U

Dir: Herbert Ross
Stars: Kathleen Turner, Dennis Quaid, Fiona Shaw
Rating: **RB**

Whatever happened to Kathleen Turner and Dennis Quaid? Two of the brightest stars of the mid-Eighties, their careers slid downwards and downwards until they ended up in this stunningly inept farce, played so far over the top by its cast as to be an embarrassment. The only hint of subtlety in the whole enterprise is the title: Quaid and Turner are Mr and Mrs Blue, undercover FBI (or something, who cares?) agents working on a case to deport a continental mastermind. The villains are quite ludicrously comic, and you can't help puzzle why, even at this low point in their careers, Turner and Quaid ever became involved in it.

Undercovers Hero

See: Soft Beds, Hard Battles

Undercurrent O

1946, US, 116 mins, b/w
Dir: Vincente Minnelli
Stars: Katharine Hepburn, Robert Taylor, Robert Mitchum, Edmund Gwenn
Rating: ★★★

This was the first film which Robert Taylor made after his return to Hollywood from three years' wartime service in the US Navy. And his choice of role surprised many fans who were used to seeing him play heroes of unblemished character. Here he takes the part of a man who outrageously swindles own brother, then sweeps a scientist's daughter off her feet, marries her and takes her off to an isolated home in Virginia Woods. Katharine Hepburn is cast as the bride who finds that behind her husband's pleasant facade is a seething mass of fears and hatreds. Worse, she realises that he is a psychopath with her in mind as his victim. Strong dramatic entertainment.

Under Fire ● Ⓥ

1983, US, 128 mins, colour
Dir: Roger Spottiswoode
Stars: Gene Hackman, Nick Nolte, Joanna Cassidy, Ed Harris, Jean-Louis Trintignant
Rating: ★★★★

This fine, raw film features Nick Nolte, Gene Hackman and Joanna Cassidy as roving war correspondents found at the start in the process of moving from Chad to Nicaragua in 1979. In the Central American melting-pot, the three newshounds – Nolte is a photo-journal-ist, the others news reporters – become all too personally involved as the revolution boils over into fighting in the streets. Few of the horrors of such a situation are spared us. Besides the leading trio, all giving soild portrayals, Jean-Louis Trintignant as a mysterious French 'spy', Ed Harris as a grinning mercenary killer and Alma Martinez as a girl guerilla all make their marks. Some rather trite points about exchanging one set of tyrants for another – so that the film can wave its white flag of impartiality cannot obscure the tension dripping from every frame of such reconstructed immediacy.

Under Milk Wood O

1971, UK, 90 mins, colour
Dir: Andrew Sinclair
Stars: Richard Burton, Elizabeth Taylor, Peter O'Toole, Glynis Johns
Rating: ★★

A star-heavy film version of Dylan Thomas' famous 'radio play for voices'. But the big names, Elizabeth Taylor, Richard Burton, Peter O'Toole and Glynis Johns, have to yield best to Rachel Thomas, a joy as Mary Ann Sailors, and Talfryn Thomas, quietly hilarious as Pugh the Poisoner. Most of the other players (and director Andrew Sinclair) seem to approach Thomas' material with too much respect, leaving it on the fringes of some picturesque rural images.

Under Siege ● Ⓥ

1992, US, 98 mins, colour
Dir: Andrew Davis
Stars: Steven Seagal, Tommy Lee Jones, Gary Busey, Erika Eleniak, Patrick O'Neal, Nick Mancuso
Rating: ★★★

A team of trained saboteurs has taken over a US nuclear warship. The outlook for mankind looks bleak. 'Wake up the President,' growls the admiral. But when master cook Steven Seagal sums up the situation and swallows hard, you know the bad guys have had. it. Armed only with a chopping knife and accompanied by busty centrefold playmate Erika Eleniak, he sets about decimating the opposition in the most painful possible way. It gets progressively more ludicrous, but remains thoroughly entertaining, apart from going right over the top at the end when villain Tommy Lee Jones, in finest movie tradition, gets the drop on Seagal, but chooses not to finish him off. Seagal actually gets to make a joke or two and, thanks to J F (*Pretty Woman*) Lawton's script, shows up bet-ter as an actor than on previous assignments. Gary Busey enjoys himself hugely as Jones' 'inside man' on the ship, an extravagant performance (including a wild drag act) that almost steals the show.

Under Siege 2 ● Ⓥ

1995, US, 99 mins, colour
Dir: Geoff Murphy
Stars: Steven Seagal, Eric Bogosian, Katherine Heigl, Everett McGill
Rating: ★★★

This is just what you'd expect from a Steven Seagal sequel to a hit original: well-made, but exactly like the first. Once again, Seagal, just like Bruce Willis in the *Die Hard* films, is the wrong guy in the wrong place at the right time. This time a trainload of passengers is held hostage by a computer/weapons genius (Eric Bogosian) keen to seek revenge for his dismissal by the US government by taking control of the super-weapon satellite he invented and demanding a billion dollars. Seagal, lethally talented agent-turned-cook, evades the initial heist and starts picking off Bogosian's men one by one. Sound familiar? Of course it does, and it's just an excuse for limb-cracking, head-bashing mayhem, but fast-paced and enjoyable too. Bogosian does what he can with the maniac mastermind ('Good evening, ladies and gentlemen, this is your captor speaking'). The fiery ending is sublimely silly but pretty sensational all the same. Hard to see that Steve can keep recycling the same story, but then if it ain't broke, why fix it?

Under Suspicion ● Ⓥ

1991, US/UK, 100 mins, colour
Dir: Simon Moore
Stars: Liam Neeson, Laura San Giacomo, Kenneth Cranham
Rating: ★★

A fufi-blooded British attempt at a *film noir* thriller, complete with a seemingly watertight murder case with a detective (disgraced cop Liam Neeson) as number one suspect, who just happens to be having an affair with the number two suspect. Is one of them setting the other up to take the rap? Is neither of them guilty? They certainly both look and act as if they are, but that's just two of the possible red herrings floating around. Kenneth Cranham is the detective on the case and looks as if he doesn't believe a word he, has to say. The illusion of sinful Brighton in the 1950s is ruined by a modern telephone box in one scene. By the final prison gallows scene, you'll either be on the edge of your seat with excitement or rolling around the floor in uncontrolled mirth.

Under 10 Flags ○
1960, US/Italy, 92 mins, b/w
Dir: Duilio Coletti, Silvio Narizzano
Stars: Van Heflin, Charles Laughton, Mylene Demongeot
Rating: ★★

Producer Dino de Laurendis was really aiming for the international market when he made this war film in four different languages. The cast includes American, British, French, German and Italian players!

Under the Clock ○
(aka: The Clock)
1945, US, 90 mins, b/w
Dir: Vincente Minnelli
Stars: Judy Garland, Robert Walker
Rating: ★★★

In a rare and successful non-singing role, Judy Garland re-teamed with director Vincente Minnelli for their second box-office smash in a row after *Meet Me In St Louis*. But while audiences flocked to see Garland and co-star Robert Walker portray one of Hollywood's best-matched young-screen couples, presenting an image of pure and innocent first-love, both stars were well on the road to personal tragedy.

Under the Volcano ●
1984, US, 111 mins, colour
Dir: John Huston
Stars: Albert Finney, Jacqueline Bisset, Anthony Andrews
Rating: ★★

Director John Huston's sombre, ultra-gloomy, but well-acted piece about a British ex-consul in Mexico who cannot live with or without the wife who has had an affair with his half-brother. Albert Finney's highly mannered performance as the permanently stoned-into-oblivion diplomat takes a while to get attuned to, but Huston extracts the best performance from Jacqueline Bisset in quite a while as the wife. James Villiers contributes an amusing few minutes as an 'Englishman abroad' who almost runs over a Finney finally felled by alcohol. The tragic ending is rather too contrived to compel total belief, and emotionally the film remains at a distance.

Under the Yum Yum Tree ○
1963, US, 110 mins, colour
Dir: David Swift

Stars: Jack Lemmon, Carol Lynley, Dean Jones
Rating: ★★★

Jack Lemmon in top comedy form as a lothario landlord who lives in an apartment that might have been designed by Edgar Allan Poe, and whose tenants are all female. One of them (Carol Lynley) is living platonically with her fiancé, and Lemmon tries all sorts of spying tricks to see how the battle of the bedroom is getting on. But an enchanting ginger cat – the one from *Breakfast at Tiffany's* – keeps upsetting his applecart as he climbs on to the roof/patio balustrade, and Lemmon somehow always ends up in the bushes below. This is that modern-day rarity: a good adult comedy. Lynley wins us over with a charming portrayal, while Dean Jones is excellent as the fiancé. In support, Paul Lynde and Imogene Coca grab what chances are going with eager hands. Even so, Lemmon is almost the whole show on his own.

Under Two Flags ○
1936, US, 111 mins, b/w
Dir: Frank Lloyd
Stars: Ronald Colman, Claudette Colbert, Victor McLaglen, Rosalind Russell
Rating: ★★★

Rousing *Boy's Own* stuit here, with handsome Ronald Colman joining the Foreign Legion after being accused of a crime his brother committed. Camp follower Claudette Colbert takes a shine to him in a big way which arouses the jealousy of Legion commander Victor McLaglen, who proceeds to make Colman's life a misery. Unfair, really, as Colman has fallen for Rosalind Russell. It all comes to a head when Colman is captured by Arabs and only Colbert, now feeling the anger of a woman scorned, can save him. If not quite up to *Beau Geste*, this fast moving adventure yarn isn't far behind. All the ingredients are mixed thoroughly and baked to perfection in the classic Hollywood recipe. Colman is a firm-jawed hero and McLaglen plays the nasty to the hilt.

Underwater ○
1955, US, 99 mins, colour
Dir: John Sturges
Stars: Jane Russell, Richard Egan
Rating: ★★

Howard Hughes and RKO Radio poured $3 million into this adventure story, made mainly as a vehicle for Jane Russell, and it shows, particularly in the technical excellence of the underwater scenes. Russell fans will ask no

more than the sight of their idol in a swimsuit, although Lori Nelson comes across as the more likeable of the two girls involved in a fast-moving sunken treasure yarn.

Unfaithfully Yours ○ Ⓥ
1948, US, 105 mins, b/w
Dir: Preston Sturges
Stars: Rex Harrison, Linda Darnell, Rudy Vallee, Lionel Stander
Rating: ★★★

A classic black comedy from Hollywood's fun king of the Forties, writer-director Preston Sturges. Rex Harrison is the orchestra conductor who visualises various fiendish demises for his wife (gorgeous Linda Darnell) while he is in the middle of a concert. Very good support from bandleader Rudy Vallee who proved himself an admirable comedy foil when his days as a musical star were over.

Unfaithfully Yours ❶
1983, US, 105 mins, colour
Dir: Howard Zieff
Stars: Dudley Moore, Nastassja Kinski, Armand Assante, Albert Brooks
Rating: ★★★

A likeable remake of the classic 1948 Preston Sturges comedy, with Dudley Moore inheriting the role played by Rex Harrison in the original. Like Harrison before film, Moore ably captures the main character's dual personality: a world-famous conductor who's both obnoxiously arrogant and insecure enough to doubt his beautiful wife's fidelity. As the wife in question, Nastassja Kinski pouts prettily, but the laughs belong to Moore (who envisages an elaborate murder plot to do away with his wife and her mysterious lover) and a gallery of comic turns in support: Albert Brooks as Moore's manager, Richard Libertini as the devoted valet and Richard B Shull as the excessively eager detective who sets in motion the chaos that ensues.

Unforgettable ● Ⓥ
1996, US, 116 mins, colour
Dir: John Dahl
Stars: Ray Liotta, Linda Fiorentino, Peter Coyote, Christopher McDonald, David Paymer, Kim Cattrall
Rating: ★★

All-too-unfortunately titled, this is something of a glitch in director['s] Dahl's meteoric career following the glories of *Red Rock West* and *The Last Seduction*. Things start strongly: brilliant forensic psychologist Liotta has found his only friend is the bottle since

U

he was acquitted of his wife's murder on a technicality. Most people still believe he did it. And maybe he did... This is where the sci-fi content of the plot comes into play, though: Liotta injects himself with some of his dead wife's brain fluid, and relives her killing – trying to see the face of the murderer. Around this point, the plot strains and then snaps. The count mounts of things that just don't add up. Echoes of *The Fugitive* are carried through into some good chase sequences, but they can't stop the film's grip from slipping dramatically in the second half – not helped by a cast that seems to be playing on different levels. Liotta's interesting, but Fiorentino struggles badly with an unsuitable role.

Unforgiven, The ○
1960, US, 125 mins, colour
Dir: John Huston
Stars: Burt Lancaster, Audrey Hepburn, Audie Murphy, John Saxon
Rating: ★★★★

Magnificent John Huston Western that compares in tension to *High Noon* or *Shane*. The claustrophobic atmosphere of the tiny ranch under siege by the Kiowa Indians is splendidly conveyed by director and cameraman. And there are excellent performances from Burt Lancaster, Audrey Hepburn, Audie Murphy and veteran screen queen Lillian Gish.

Unforgiven ● Ⓥ
1992, US, 130 mins, colour
Dir: Clint Eastwood
Stars: Clint Eastwood, Gene Hackman, Morgan Freeman, Richard Harris, Frances Fisher, Jaimz Woolvett
Rating: ★★★★

In what may be his swan song to the Western, Clint Eastwood plays a character who could be 'The Man With No Name' 20 years on. An infamous gunslinger tamed by the love of a woman who has since died, he now farms pigs with his two children. Hatred of his new life, coupled with a need for money, impels him to ride out in search of a reward offered by a brothel, one of whose girls was cut up by two cowhands who got off with little more than a fine. The sadistic sheriff, Gene Hackman (who handed out the 'penalty'), deals more summarily with bounty hunters, but all might still have been straightforward were it not for an event that finally makes Eastwood reach for both bottle and gun and turns him back into 'The Man With No Name' for the last 15 minutes of the film. Too slow at

times, the film is redeemed not by its realistic view of the old west (what else is new?), but by its rich array of characters. Appropriately, the survivor of the final shootout rides not into the sunset, but through mud and a night-time rainstorm. The film won a saddle film of Oscars at the 1993 Academy Awards.

Unholy, The ● Ⓥ
1988, Spain/US, 104 mins, colour
Dir: Camilo Avila
Stars: Ben Cross, Jill Carroll, William Russ, Trevor Howard, Hal Holbrook, Ned Beatty
Rating: ★★

A routine horror tale of demonology and a priestly temptation, this chiller has all the expected ingredients of the genre: passable special effects, oodles of gore, nubile maidens in flimsies and bags of dry ice floating up from the ground. Very sub-John Carpenter, but quite good fun for fans of this sort of thing, if a bit nasty for the average cinemagoer. Ben Cross is the priest who must do battle with a demon from Hell and makes rather a meal of it (all he has to do, for God's sake, is call it by name) and Trevor Howard, Hal Holbrook and Ned Beatty do their bit as the usual grim-faced priests and detectives. Only William Russ, as the sub-Brando owner of a devil-worship club, is a character away from the ordinary in this kind of thing.

Unholy Partners ○
1941, US, 95 mins, b/w
Dir: Mervyn LeRoy
Stars: Edward G Robinson, Edward Arnold, Laraine Day, Marsha Hunt, Marcel Dalio, Frank Faylen
Rating: ★★

Another little-known goodir from the Edward G Robinson collection. Vaguely based on the exploits of a real-life pressman who worked for the *New York Mirror*, it's an entertaining newspaper melodrama which takes Robinson and director Mervyn LeRoy back to their *Five Star Final* setting. But, being made at MGM, rather lacks the sinew that Robinson's home studio, Warner Brothers, might have brought to the story. Still, Robinson and Edward Arnold are both rock-solid as the newspaperman and the underworld Czar who become the unholy partners of the title.

Unholy Wife, The ○
1957, US, 94 mins, colour
Dir: John Farrow
Stars: Rod Steiger, Diana Dors, Tom

Tryon, Beulah Bondi, Marie Windsor, Arthur Franz
Rating: ★★

This was Diana Dors' first Hollywood picture and she plays a typical man-hungry woman who plots no good to get what she wants. Justice, of course, prevails, but no matter how good a film, it hardly lives up to its own advertising fine, 'Half Angel, Half Devil, She Made Him Half a Man'. It was actually a rather insipid remake of the 1940 film *They Knew What They Wanted*. Rod Steiger, as Dors' long-suffering husband, is hampered by a bad dose of Method-actingitis, and it is left to Tom Tryon, as her no-good seducer, to bring any conviction to the proceedings. But it looks better today than it did then.

Unhook the Stars ● Ⓥ
1996, US, 104 mins, colour
Dir: Nick Cassavetes
Stars: Gena Rowlands, Gérard Depardieu, Marisa Tomei, Moira Kelly, David Sherrill, Bridgette Anderson
Rating: ★★

A sometimes tedious, but sometimes warm and comforting film. Rowlands is a widow whose mixed-up daughter (Kelly) flees the coop, her adored son (Sherrill) already living in San Francisco with his new wife. Then her battered neighbour (Tomei) throws out her abusive husband and, for a while, Rowlands becomes surrogate mother to her bright six-year-old son. A grateful Tomei introduces Rowlands to the local bar where she meets a French-Canadian trucker (Depardieu), with whom she strikes up a tentative romance. After an idyllic while, Tomei's contrite spouse returns and Rowlands' son asks her to move in with him – as a baby sitter for his pregnant wife: he turns nasty when she refuses. Just after she's sold the house, her daughter wants to come back: it's too late for Rowlands, who looks to have fallen between stools – or has she? We'll never know because the film doesn't have an ending. Despite its torrent of four-letter words, this is a kind-hearted movie. It's crafted as a vehicle for Rowlands and, unlike the picture, she's perfect.

Un Homme et une Femme ● Ⓥ
(aka: A Man and a Woman)
1966, France, 102 mins, colour
Dir: Claude Lelouch
Stars: Jean-Louis Trintignant, Anouk Aimee
Rating: ★★★★

This is a stylish bitter-sweet romance between a racing driver and a film script girl. Her husband died in a stunt accident, his wife committed suicide and they meet because their children go to the same boarding school. Like all those Sixties British films set in swinging London, the film is set very firmly in its own time and therefore looks rather dated now. Unlike those British films, it's not a squirming embarrassment to watch, although the theme song gets on your nerves after a while. The performances of Anouk Aimee and Jean-Louis Trintignant are strong, if not entirely convincing, and hold the film together.

Uninvited, The ◐
1944, US, 98 mins, b/w
Dir: Lewis Smith
Stars: Ray Milland, Ruth Hussey, Donald Crisp, Gail Russell
Rating: ★★★★

A real surprise in its day, this is one of Hollywood's best ghost stories, which should send some genuine shivers up your spine. Hauntingly beautiful Gail Russell is just right on her screen debut for the role of the girl who holds the key to the mystery of the haunted house that brother and sister Ray Milland and Ruth Hussey have bought on the English coast. British-born director Lewis Allen keeps you guessing every step of the way and the ending is a real chiller.

Union Pacific ○
1939, US, 135 mins, b/w
Dir: Cecil B DeMille
Stars: Barbara Stanwyck, Joel McCrea
Rating: ★★★

Cecil B DeMille's epic Western is one of his most enjoyable film, full of sprawling, brawling adventure, the highlight of which is a spectacular train crash. Barbara Stanwyck's gutsy daughter of a railroad engineer (she has a becoming Irish Brogue), more than holds her own with a virtually all-male cast, and there's one of the screen's great fist fights for good measure – between Joel McCrea and Robert Barrat. All this and Indians too.

Union Station ○
1950, US, 80 mins, b/w
Dir: Rudolph Mate
Stars: William Holden, Nancy Olson, Barry Fitzgerald
Rating: ★★★★

Tight, hard-hitting thriller about the kidnap of a blind girl by a vicious gang. William Holden and Barry Fitzgerald create likeable and contrasting characters as the policemen on the case; Nancy Olson is a pretty and resourceful heroine who enlists our sympathies from the outset; Allene Roberts is touchingly true as the hapless kidnap victim; and Lyle Bettger and Jan Sterling carve memorably nasty portraits of those on the wrong side of the law. Rudolph Mate's taut and skilful direction doesn't miss a thrill. The suspense builds irresistibly to a nail-biting underground climax.

Universal Soldier ● Ⓥ
1992, US, 104 mins, colour
Dir: Roland Emmerich
Stars: Jean-Claude Van Damme, Dolph Lundgren, Ally Walker, Ed O'Ross, Jerry Orbach
Rating: ★★

Just about the ultimate in muscular violence, this overrated, futuristic saga gives us two invincible icons of the screen for the price of one. Dolph Lundgren (who at least gets to enjoy himself playing a thoroughly bad lot) and Jean-Claude Van Damme are a couple of military corpses revived to become perfect fighting machines (just *like RoboCop*), devoid of memory (just like *Robocop*) but one of whom accidentally starts recalling pieces of the past (yes, just like *RoboCop*) which sets them off on a collision course an eventual battle to the death. Don't let the plot (and certainly not the weak leading lady) detract from the real thing – the non-stop, muscle-ripping action. And remember: Lundgren is 'all ears' . . .

Unlawful Entry ● Ⓥ
1992, US, 111 mins, colour
Dir: Jonathan Kaplan
Stars: Kurt Russell, Madeleine Stowe, Ray Liotta
Rating: ★

Developments are heavily signalled in this thriller of menace, in which psychotic policeman Ray Liotta develops a fixation on the beautiful wife (Madeleine Stowe) of businessman Kurt Russell, and determines to ruin Russell's life and take her away from him. From here on in, you'd better be prey to the easy thrill as the plot goes strictly by the numbers. Showers are on while phones ring; the family cat is good for several attempts to make us jump; and people do the usual silly things they do in such films. Liotta's partner tells him he'll turn him in if he doesn't get help: no prizes for guessing his fate. Stowe's friend goes straight to the door and dismantles the burglar alarm after she's persuaded Liotta, who threatens her, to leave his 'groceries' outside the door. Curtains again! And Russell, framed by Liotta on a drugs charge, can't get bail because of some mysterious long-past misdemeanour. Deprived of any touch of originality or surprise, director Jonathan Kaplan does the best he can with what's left, giving us lots of violent action and a modicum of suspense.

Unmarried Woman, An ◐
1978, US, 124 mins, colour
Dir: Paul Mazursky
Stars: Jill Clayburgh, Alan Bates
Rating: ★★★★

It was high time in 1978 that someone dedicated a film to the wide-ranging talents of Jill Clayburgh – and director Paul Mazursky did just that in this perceptive and penetrating study of a woman in her mid-thirties whose husband suddenly and her unexpectedly leaves her and her 15-year-old daughter. Oscar-nominated Clayburgh is flawless in the title role and Michael Murphy also offers a well-considered account of the husband. Alan Bates seems less at case as the artist who offers the heroine a somewhat unlikely second chance at happiness, but it's 'an underwritten part and he makes the most of what's there. It is what once might have been termed a 'woman's picture' – but this one plays fair with both sexes, gently but firmly.

Unseen, The ◐
1945, US, 81 mins, b/w
Dir: Lewis Allen
Stars: Joel McCrea, Gail Russell
Rating: ★★★

A follow-up by star Gail Russell and director Lewis Allen to their previous chiller success *The Uninvited*. The plot, even though you may guess the solution of its mystery early on, remains interesting, as Russell's limpid beauty comes under threat from strange goings-on in a mysterious boarded-up house that's next door to the one owned by her employer (Joel McCrea), a withdrawn figure still under suspicion himself following the death of his wife two years before. John F Seitz's black-and-white cameras skilfully cloak the mystery in shape and shadow and provide some effectively jumpy moments.

Unsuspected, The ○
1947, US, 103 mins, b/w
Dir: Michael Curtiz
Stars: Claude Rains, Joan Caulfield, Audrey Totter, Constance Bennett, Hurd

U

Hatfield, Michael North
Rating: ★★★

One of the best of Hollywood's black Forties' thrillers, with Claude Rains in superb form as the deadly sophisticate whose lust for a fortune leads him into a feverish dance with murder as his partner. Writer Ranald MacDougall and director Michael Curtiz, who collaborated on the Oscar-winning *Mildred Pierce*, spin a beguiling web of dark streets, shrieking trains and black-mirrored mansions. Especially memorable is the glimpse of an intended poison victim, seen through the bubbles in a glass of champagne.

Untamed ○

1955, US, 111 mins, colour
Dir: Henry King
Stars: Tyrone Power, Susan Hayward, Agnes Moorehead, Richard Egan
Rating: ★★

A spectacular period adventure, with wagon train travellers fighting to establish the Dutch Free State in 19th-century South Africa. Tyrone Power plays the leader of a commando group, while Susan Hayward, who excelled herself in all kinds of melodrama, is outrageously superb as what one critic called 'a kind of Scarlett O'Hara of the veldt'. In a way, the picture is similar in vein to a Western, but transplanted to an African setting. It was directed by Henry King, a reliable and versatile director of general entertainment movies, and for many years associated with 20th Century-Fox. My favourite line comes when Power tells Hayward: 'You, here in South Africa, fighting Zulus? I can't believe it.'

Untamed Heart ◑ ⓥ

1993, US, 102 mins, colour
Dir: Tony Bill
Stars: Christian Slater, Marisa Tomei, Rosie Perez, Kyle Secor, Willie Garson
Rating: ★★★

This is a boy-meets-girl story with a difference, though not one for the cynical or hardhearted. Waitress Marisa Tomei is a loser in love. Loner busboy Christian Slater is a loser in life: an orphan convinced by convent custodians that his diseased heart is that of a baboon. It's inevitable, of course,.that they should end up together, even though Slater is, by most people's standards, a bit of a weirdo. His habit of following Tomei home (and, it turns out, sometimes getting into her house and watching her sleep) pays off when he saves her from rape

on a wintry night. It's obvious from developments that their subsequent relationship can't have too happy an ending, but director Tony Bill lets us down easy on the tears and, if the story will be too silly and simplistic for some, at least Slater and Tomei, two of the most talented of Hollywood's younger stars in the early Nineties, give it 101 per cent.

Until the End of the World ● ⓥ

1991, Germany/France/Australia, 158 mins, colour
Dir: Wim Wenders
Stars: William Hurt, Solveig Dommartin, Sam Neill, Max Von Sydow, Jeanne Moreau
Rating: ★

Originally over three hours long, Wim Wenders' trip around the world is still a hard slog at its present length, and with Sam Neill narrating to help you follow the plot. Did we say plot? Well, there's about enough to fill the back of an envelope. The first half of the film consists of a 'road' movie in which heroine Solveig Dommartin (not destined to become an international star) follows William Hurt from France on to China, America and Australia in pursuit of some money he's stolen, which she in turn was holding for the bank robbers who caused her to crash her car into them in the middle of nowhere. The second half is set in South Australia, where Hurt's father (Max Von Sydow) is conducting experiments in an underground laboratory that will help his blind wife (Jeanne Moreau) see. All this seems to go on for more than four hours let alone nearly three; Hurt and Von Sydow offer unattractive, occasionally overwrought performances.

Until They Sail ◑

1957, US, 95 mins, b/w
Dir: Robert Wise
Stars: Jean Simmons, Joan Fontaine, Paul Newman
Rating: ★★

Robert Wise's observant portrait of women in war – four sisters in New Zealand during World War Two. Watch for a startling performance by Piper Laurie, previously seen in 'sweet spitfire' roles, but here pretty good as a pretty bad lot. Laurie did nothing else of great note until another excellent portrayal as Paul Newman's girlfriend in *The Hustler*. The other sister is played by Sandra Dee.

Untouchables, The ● ⓥ

1987, US, 119 mins, colour
Dir: Brian De Palma
Stars: Kevin Costner, Sean Connery, Robert De Niro, Andy Garcia, Charles Martin Smith
Rating: ★★★

Whatever you might have expected from director Brian De Palma's account of the 1931 battle of wills between clean-cut law enforcer Eliot Ness (Kevin Costner) and gangland czar Al Capone (played by Robert De Niro), it couldn't have been a re-run of the old Robert Stack TV series. Yet that's more or less what you get only done with some style, and the addition of blood (lots of it) and expletives. And there's a further dimension in the welcome shape of Sean Connery's veteran cop who joins and mentors the Untouchables; this fully-rounded portrait deservedly won Connery an Academy Award. Otherwise, there's the same vacuum feeling about the periods between the action, and the same slow build-up to the action set-pieces themselves, which are hard-hitting, but only rarely anything but predictable. Only once does De Palma use the element of surprise, turning a suspense scene involving a mother and her baby into a tribute to Hitchcock and Eisenstein. Otherwise, this bumper bundle of guns and gangsters (gals hardly get a look in) doesn't quite punch its weight.

Up Close & Personal ● ⓥ

1996, US, 119 mins, colour
Dir: Jon Avnet
Stars: Robert Redford, Michelle Pfeiffer, Joe Mantegna, Stockard Channing, Kate Nelligan, James Rebhorn
Rating: ★★★

This glossy romantic combination of *Broadcast News* and *A Star is Born* gives us the impossibly glamorous pairing of Michelle Pfeiffer and Robert Redford, as the small-town girl who makes good as a TV reporter and the seen-it-all newsroom veteran who helps her do it. Fairly resistible for most of the way, the film just flows by you until it moves up a gear towards the end, with Pfeiffer trapped in a prison riot but, thanks to Redford's help on the phone, turning it into a sensational scoop, and Redford inevitably deciding to be his own man and not hang on to Pfeiffer's impeccably styled coat-tails. Roughly edited, with a couple of abrupt cuts, the movie contains a gem of a supporting performance by Kate Nelligan as Redford's ex-wife. Stockard Channing and James

Rebhorn are more stereotyped (and faintly unlikely) types who help and hinder pilgrim Pfeiffer's progress along the way.

Up in Arms ☉ ⓥ
1944, UK, 83 mins, colour
Dir: Elliott Nugent
Stars: Danny Kaye, Dinah Shore
Rating: ★★★

After years of struggle in vaudeville, Danny Kaye enjoyed a career surge engineered by his talented wife, Sylvia Fine, who wrote most of the tongue-twisting songs that helped to make him such a success. This was his feature film debut and, if a story about a hypochondriac who joins the US Army in World War Two and is captured and tortured doesn't sound a likely basis for comedy, you just haven't got the Goldwyn spirit. The whole troopship, for example, is festooned with sunbathing Goldwyn Girls, who include Virginia Mayo, soon to become Danny's leading lady.

Up in Central Park ○
1948, US, 88 mins, b/W
Dir: William A Seiter
Stars: Deanna Durbin, Dick Haymes, Vincent Price
Rating: ★★

This lavishly produced but otherwise routine musical was Deanna Durbin's penultimate picture. Durbin is in fine voice and there's an attractively staged skating routine performed by William Skipper and Nelle Fisher. Albert Sharpe hams happily as Durbin's dad.

Up in the World ☉
1956, US, 106 mins, b/w
Dir: John Paddy Carstairs
Stars: Norman Wisdom
Rating: ★★★

In his seventh film, Norman Wisdom the window cleaner breaks many panes, falls off ladders, goes to jail, sings songs, and keeps a hamster called Harold. The laughter quotient is roughly one belly laugh for each of the three writers involved. Even so, this film is a vast improvement on some Wisdom comedies, and this one has just enough chuckles to keep it going.

Up Periscope ○
1958, US, 111 mins, colour
Dir: Gordon Douglas
Stars: James Garner, Edmond O'Brien
Rating: ★★

A routine submarine drama with rebellious demolition expert James Garner

assigned to serve on Edmond O'Brien's by-the-book ship. There's plenty of suspense in the final action scenes, and keep your eyes peeled for a very young Warren Oates as a sailor always to be found in the mess hall eating.

Up Pompeii ◑ ⓥ
1971, UK, 90 mins, colour
Dir: Bob Kellett
Stars: Frankie Howerd, Michael Hordern
Rating: ★★

The first of three big screen spin-offs from Frankie Howerd's Roman TV comedy. The jokes are not only similar to those in the sitcom penned by Talbot Rothwell, many are exactly the same – although this script is credited to Sid Colin! But the cast has more star quality, with the addition of Michael Hordern, Roy Hudd and Adrienne Posta. Howerd runs his usual gamut of grunts, exclamations and wheezes, but his thunder is somewhat stolen by Patrick Cargill's accomplished portrayal of boredom as Emperor Nero. All but ardent fans of these Roman scandals will be in complete agreement.

Upstairs and Downstairs ○
1959, UK, 101 mins, colour
Dir: Ralph Thomas
Stars: Michael Craig, Anne Heywood, Mylene Demongeot
Rating: ★★

This lightweight domestic comedy about a young middle-class couple who have trouble finding suitable servants manages to misfire on all cylinders. Such problems were outdated and outmoded even when it was made and certainly look unreal today. A witty script would have offset these problems, but one wasn't forthcoming. Michael Craig and Anne Heywood can't find reliable servants. Ahh, ain't life tough! Mylene Demongeot as a Swedish maid and Daniel Massey as the man who falls in love with her are bright points.

Up the Chastity Belt ◑ ⓥ
1971, UK, 94 mins, colour
Dir: Bob Kellett
Stars: Frankie Howerd, Graham Crowden, Bill Fraser
Rating: ★★

Frankie Howerd as a serf called Lurkalot? It must be funny, surely? Alas, it's not so much a case of lurkalot as laugh a little. And, considering Alan Galton and Ray Simpson were two of the writers on this Crusades charade,

it's all the sadder that it proves that all great comics are at the mercy of their writers. Even in such a relentless essay in sexual innuendo, though, Howerd's Lurkalot still contrives some delicious moments, notably in his confrontation with Rita Webb's amazingly gross Maid Marian. 'Who is this fragile wood nymph?' he gasps.

Up the Creek ◑
1958, UK, 83 mins, b/w
Dir: Val Guest
Stars: David Tomlinson, Peter Sellers
Rating: ★★★

This Val Guest romp is firmly in the tradition of British naval farces, but given a big boost by the presence of Peter Sellers as the wily Irish bo'sun who operates a black-market laundry, grocery, bakery and general stores to the nearest village from the depths of his mothballed ship.

Up the Down Staircase ◑
1967, US, 124 mins, colour
Dir: Robert Mulligan
Stars: Sandy Dennis, Eileen Heckart
Rating: ★★★

Sandy Dennis and Eileen Heckart, Oscar-winners both, in Robert Mulligan's penetrating school story of a young teacher's struggle to help her tough pupils to realise their potential and, if possible, escape their ghetto environment. A sort of *Blackboard Jungle* 12 years on, with welcome nods to the humour of *Please, Sir!*

Up the Junction ●
1967, UK, 119 mins, colour
Dir: Peter Collinson
Stars: Suzy Kendall, Dennis Waterman, Adrienne Posta, Susan George
Rating: ★★

It was hard to imagine anyone bettering the biting television original of this look at Battersea life with all its warts and sores. But director Peter Collinson decided to have a try, and turned out a colour film which slants its story towards the adventures of an upperclass girl in a working-class district of London. Screen writer Roger Smith has fashioned a script which holds the episodic structure of Nell Dunn's original together with some skill, thanks to the central relationship between the girl and her cockney boyfriend, which benefits from the understated performances of Suzy Kendall and Dennis Waterman. These two emerge as real characters, as opposed to the rest of the cast, which verge on caricature and include a young Susan George

U

as one of the girls in the sweet factory where the heroine goes to work.

Uptown Saturday Night ◐

1974, US, 104 mins, colour
Dir: Sidney Poitier
Stars: Sidney Poitier, Bill Cosby, Harry Belafonte
Rating: ★★

Sidney Poitier and Bill Cosby hit a profitable vein of broad, black-slanted comedy with this farcical tale of two innocents entering the lion's den of crooks and Godfathers. As director, Poitier showed more control in the sequels *Let's Do It Again* and *A Piece of the Action*, but the film's silliness is engaging.

Urban Cowboy ◐

1980, US, 135 mins, colour
Dir: James Bridges
Stars: John Travolta, Debra Winger, Scott Glenn
Rating: ★★

John Travolta plays a saloon-bar rodeo rider on an automated bucking bronco here – but both he and the film bite the dust. Travolta's acting in this one is as over-melodramatic as John Gilbert's seemed with the coming of sound. Far more watchable are Debra Winger as his barroom bride and Scott Glenn as the bad guy. But their story, crazily overlong at two and a quarter hours, takes a lot of swallowing.

Used Cars ◐

1980, US, 115 mins, colour
Dir: Robert Zemeckis
Stars: Kurt Russell, Jack Warden
Rating: ★★

A fascination with cars has certainly been profitable for Hollywood writers Bob Gale and Robert Zemeckis (who also directed this comedy about the used car business). Kurt Russell and Jack Warden (in a dual role) give feisty, energetic performances, and Al Lewis (Grandpa in *The Munsters*) has a nice stand-out cameo as an imposing judge. But the ropy script lets the proceedings down, choosing to find humour in the various characters' humiliation, embarrassment and even death. 'Tasteless' humour, brief nudity and bad language make this one unsuitable for most younger children.

Used People ◐ Ⓥ

1992, US, 126 mins, colour
Dir: Beeban Kidron
Stars: Shirley MacLaine, Marcello Mastroianni, Kathy Bates, Marcia Gay Harden, Jessica Tandy
Rating: ★★

The winning, sweetness-and-light ending to this story of love the second time around tends to obscure the fact that parts of the tale are quite tediously told. The Bermans, mother Pearl (Shirley MacLaine) and daughters Nora (Marcia Gay Harden) and Bibby (Kathy Bates), are angry, ill-tempered, ahnost tragic figures always shouting at each other in public. Joe (Marcello Mastroianni), a long-time admirer of Pearl's, must certainly be an ardent suitor not only to ask her out for dinner at her husband's funeral (exceptionally unlikely!) but to want to jump in with this nest of vipers. Joe, however, a widower, is a true Italian and even snakebites, though they may annoy him, can't deter his passion. Jessica Tandy and Sylvia Sidney do good work as MacLaine's mother and her equally aged confidante – the scene where they visit a nursing home straight out of *Metropolis* is one of the best in the film – but these used people are not likeable people and it's hard to share their joys and (mostly) sorrows.

Usual Suspects, The ● Ⓥ

1995, US, 105 mins, colour
Dir: Bryan Singer
Stars: Gabriel Byrne, Chazz Palminteri, Stephen Baldwin, Kevin Spacey, Kevin Pollak, Suzy Amis
Rating: ★★★

This cleverly constructed crime thriller will catch you napping if you're not very careful. Not that you have much time to doze as you follow the trail of five middle-range crooks (Gabriel Byrne, Stephen Baldwin, Kevin Spacey, Kevin Pollak, Benecio del Toro) who meet in a police lineup and plan a major heist together. The film opens, though, on their last desperate enterprise, when it appears that all but one have been killed on a drugs-and-money raid on a foreign ship. The survivor is the runt of the fitter, a humping con-man (Spacey); he's ruthlessly grilled by determined cop Chazz Palminteri, who's convinced that crooked ex-cop Byrne, whom he's been after for years, is still alive and may even be the mystery figure behind it all. All this gets a bit drawn-out towards the end; the fact that you know roughly what's going to happen detracts from the suspense. And it isn't clear why Spacey, even with his gammy leg, would have been taken by police who had no idea he was in on the raid. Set-piece action scenes, though, are performed with ruthless efficiency, and the denouement really is a cracker.

Utu ◐ Ⓥ

1983, New Zealand, 100 mins, colour
Dir: Geoff Murphy
Stars: Bruno Lawrence, Anzac Wallace, Kelly Johnson, Kuki Kaa
Rating: ★★★

This epic drama, about British colonial presence in New Zealand in the 1870s, was at the time the most expensive film in New Zealand's history. Bruno Lawrence is totally believable as a man driven to seek revenge against the Brits. The film's title actually transiates from the Maori word for 'retribution' and action fans will not be disappointed by director Geoff Murphy's slambang style of delivery.

U2 – Rattle and Hum ◐ Ⓥ

1988, US, 99 mins, colour
Dir: Phil Joanou
Stars: Bono, The Edge, Adam Clayton, Larry Mullen, B B King
Rating: ★★★

At a cost of $5 million, this concert film of Irish rock group U2 ranks as the most expensive music documentary ever. It captures the group during a period when lead singer Bono and the lads explored American music and culture following the blockbuster commercial and critical success of their seventh album, 'The Joshua Tree'. Director Phil Joanou pulls off his task thanks to the use of black-and-white footage, using grainy blow-ups of 16mm film to create a gritty 'street' feel. But the film's momentum drops when it switches to colour and scenes of the group visiting Elvis's Graceland mansion are as awkward as the band appear to be at mugging in front of the camera. But, on the whole, *Rattle and Hum* emerges as an exhilarating celebration of one of the greatest rock bands still on the go.

V

Vagabond King, The ○
1956, US, 86 mins, colour
Dir: Michael Curtiz
Stars: Kathryn Grayson, Oreste, Rita Moreno
Rating: ★★

This bright and colourful version of Friml's famous stage musical was supposed to have made a star of Oreste (Kirkop), when he stepped into one of the many singing roles vacated by an overweight Mario Lanza. Although Oreste projected an attractive personality and warm tenor voice, the public didn't take to him as a cinema personality. And the film itself lacks sparkle, apart, that is, from Rita Moreno's flashing-eyed portrait of Huguette.

Valachi Papers, The ● ⓥ
1972, France/Italy, 125 mins, colour
Dir: Terence Young
Stars: Charles Bronson, Jill Ireland
Rating: ★★

This crime thriller, based on a best-selling book by Peter Maas, gives Charles Bronson an unusual role in that he's an elderly gangster looking back on the time he started as a young petty thief. The film could use some humour and individuality, but there's no lack of action. The feeling of the underworld is well caught in this treatment, which is annoyingly inattentive to detail and seems most interested in letting blood flow all over the screen.

Valdez Is Coming ○
1970, US, 86 mins, colour
Dir: Edwin Sherin
Stars: Burt Lancaster, Susan Clark
Rating: ★★

Murkily shot in the dreaded Colour by De Luxe, this is a revenge Western in which Burt Lancaster's stoical Valdez takes a mighty long time in arriving to get his own back on those who humiliated him. The cast includes early roles for Jon Cypher, Hector Elizondo and Richard Jordan. In a minor part you may spot Roberta Haynes, who 18 years earlier had been Gary Cooper's leading lady in *Return to Paradise*.

Valentino ● ⓥ
1977, US, 127 mins, colour
Dir: Ken Russell
Stars: Rudolf Nureyev, Leslie Caron,

Michelle Phillips
Rating: ★

Ken Russell's 'pop' version of the career of the unique silent film idol is colourful, outrageous and keeps on tne move and, even if we never really get to know the man himself, presents us with a vivid picture of the free-for-all life of New York and Hollywood in the Twenties. Nureyev is not actually asked to do much beyond look and seem like Valentino on the surface, re-enact scenes from some of his most famous films, but there is a wealth of striking acting in support, especially from Leslie Caron (as Nazimova), Huntz Hall (as Jesse Lasky) and Felicity Kendal as Valentino's agent June Mathis.

Valley of Fury
See: Chief Crazy Horse

Valley of Gwangi, The ○
1968, US, 95 mins, colour
Dir: James O'Connolly
Stars: James Franciscus, Gila Golan, Richard Carlson
Rating: ★★

More magic from Ray Harryhausen's box of monsters, which here include a tiny prehistoric horse, a styrocosaurus and an allosaurus (the giant Gwangi of the title) in a story of early 20th-century cowboys exploring a forbidden valley in Mexico.

Valley of the Dolls ●
1967, US, 123 mins, colour
Dir: Mark Robson
Stars: Barbara Parkins, Patty Duke, Sharon Tate, Susan Hayward
Rating: ★★

The film version of Jacqueline Susann's notorious novel about drug abuse on the showbiz scene was a built-in success, thanks in part to Susann's own constant publicity campaigning. Susan Hayward took over the role of Helen Lawson from an ailing Judy Garland (after it had been rejected by Ginger Rogers as 'too smutty') and stormed away with the picture.

Valley of the Kings ○
1954, US, 86 mins, colour
Dir: Robert Pirosh
Stars: Robert Taylor, Eleanor Parker
Rating: ★★

The first Hollywood film ever shot on location in Egypt proves to be a workmanlike and sometimes exciting story that just lacks the surges of real excitement that might have turned it into an adventure classic. The natural backdrops are fascinating, and look mighty hot, leaving Eleanor Parker's cool beauty to add a refreshing touch to those parched desert sands. On the whole it's pretty good fun, and a scene where hero Robert Taylor shows a Bedouin swordsman that a blade and buckler are no match for a good American right hook may well have influenced Steven Spielberg when he came to film a similar scene for *Raiders of the Lost Ark*.

Valmont ● ⓥ
1989, UK/France/US, 140 mins, colour
Dir: Milos Forman
Stars: Annette Bening, Colin Firth, Meg Tilly, Fairuza Balk, Sian Phillips, Jeffrey Jones, Henry Thomas
Rating: ★★

Another version of *Dangerous Liaisons*. While quite an effective satirical look at the sexual mores of the 18th-century French upper class, it doesn't have the same impact as the Glenn Close-John Malkovich starrer which had already pinched all the kudos. Bening and Meg Tilly are exceptionally good, it's true, but the film, stretched out to 140 minutes, doesn't exactly grip you all the way through. Nor is Colin Firth quite as rakish and amoral as you might expect as the corrupt seducer Valmont; and Fairuza Balk, although actually the right age, seems a little young for the all-too-easily-deflowered convent maid. Veteran actress Fabia Drake, though, is tremendous in her last film role. The dread Eastman Color makes the look of the film pretty drained in comparison with its competitor.

Value for Money ○
1955, UK, 89 mins, colour
Dir: Ken Annakin
Stars: John Gregson, Susan Stephen, Diana Dors, Derek Farr
Rating: ★★

Robust, regional comedy along traditional British lines, but made with tremendous confidence by director Ken Annakin for the Rank Organisation at a time when they were prepared to splash out on Technicolor and VistaVision for their brighter products. Diana Dors is at her best as a brass-digging blond who sets her cap at Yorkshire millionaire

V

John Gregson, there's some music thrown in and you may catch glimpses of Leslie Phillips, Donald Pleasence, Ferdy Mayne, Joan Hickson, Molly Weir and a teenage Oliver Reed.

Vamp ● Ⓥ
1986, US, 94 mins, colour
Dir: Richard Wenk
Stars: Grace Jones, Chris Makepeace
Rating: ★★★

'You get the feeling we're not in Kansas any more' trembles one of three out-of-town, wet-behind-the-ears college kids as they first stumble on the neon-lit lair of disco vampire Grace Jones. First time writer-director Richard Wenk has taken a tired horror genre and injected new blood, ensuring this contemporary bloodsucking black comedy carries plenty of bite. It's also the perfect vehicle for disco diva Jones and her wide-eyed dangerous persona. Just as it suggests it is going to jump on the teen sexploitation comedy bandwagon, *Vamp* does a swift U-turn and ends up being a camp, wisecracking chase.

Vampire Circus ●
1971, UK, 87 mins, colour
Dir: Robert Young
Stars: Adrienne Corri, Laurence Payne, Thorley Walters
Rating: ★★

Another creep in the crypt from Hammer who took two scripts, one about vampire depredations and the other about a sinister circus – and cobbled them together quite successfully. There are some good sequences in a hall of mirrors, and film buffs will no doubt recognise the village of Schtettel from *Twins of Evil*.

Vampire in Brooklyn ● Ⓥ
1995, US, 101 mins, colour
Dir: Wes Craven
Stars: Eddie Murphy, Angela Bassett, Kadeem Hardison, Allen Payne, Zakes Mokae
Rating: ★★

A bloodthirsty, heart-ripping comedy chiller in which the comedy all too rarely bubbles to the surface. Nightmare horror, in fact, is the order of the day as Caribbean vampire Eddie Murphy descends on America via another ship full of dead men, to find the only surviving female half-vampire to convert to his cause. She turns out to be a cop (Angela Bassett), who's none too willing to turn on to her heritage. Kadeem Hardison has a little fun with Murphy's rotting acolyte, bits of whom

drop off as the film progresses. Special effects, though, are not only below par but almost non-existent, especially when it comes to a traditional vampire transformation scene. Murphy dons a few disguises and gets a chuckle or two, but he's really wasted in such genuinely ghoulish surroundings.

Vampire's Kiss ● Ⓥ
1989, US, 103 mins, colour
Dir: Robert Bierman
Stars: Nicolas Cage, Maria Conchita Alonso, Jennifer Seals, Elizabeth Ashley
Rating: RB

Not content with being one of the most foul-mouthed movies of even these modern times, this is an amazingly miscalculated spoof horror/black comedy, with a wildly miscast Nicolas Cage (looking like British TV host Jonathan Ross) as a young executive who compulsively bites bar-girls and goes completely round the bend when one of them bites him in the neck. The fire of madness in his diminished marbles is further fuelled by the appearance of a bat in his flat. Before you can say Nosferatu, Cage is lurching around the New York streets eating insects and pigeons, biting people in the neck, and inviting passers-by to kill him with a stake through the heart. Viewers will find it hard to tell when the film *is* trying to be funny and the repulsive and violent nature of Cage's affliction will, in any case, make laughter hard to summon. Cage is grotesque: come to think of it, Jonathan Ross could probably have done it better.

Vampires of Venice ●
1988, US, 92 mins, colour
Dir: Augusto Caminito
Stars: Klaus Kinski, Barbara De Rossi, Donald Pleasence
Rating: ★★

A follow-up to *Nosferatu the Vampire*, this has the same kind of eerie atmosphere, but less credibility. Klaus Kinski is back as the man with the miniature tusks, while Christopher Plummer and Donald Pleasance lend additional star value as ineffectual vampire hunters. The ending is annoyingly inconclusive, but Kinski's performance and a screeching score by Vangelis and Luigi Ceccarelli do their best to bolster the chills.

Vanishing, The ● Ⓥ
1993, US, 110 mins, colour
Dir: George Sluizer
Stars: Jeff Bridges, Kiefer Sutherland, Nancy Travis, Sandra Bullock, Lisa

Eichhorn
Rating: ★★★

If you haven't seen the even more chilling Dutch original, you should enjoy this suspense yarn about a girl who mysteriously disappears – and her lover's obsessive search for her over a three-year period. It becomes apparent rather earlier this time that the girl has been kidnapped (during a service station stop) by professional nutcase Jeff Bridges, who has just saved a girl from drowning and is now anxious to prove to his beloved daughter that he is as capable of evil as of heroism (!) But is the victim (Sandra Bullock) alive or dead? Bridges just keeps the right side of idiocy as the learned madman and Kiefer Sutherland's role tends to dwindle as the film goes on, though he's already getting hot competition from the strong performance of Nancy Travis (as his new girlfriend) before she rises admirably to the challenge of ferocity and a battle of wits with Bridges at the end. A bit long and dawdling at times, but director George Sluizer (who made the original) has a baited hook to keep us snapping to the end of the film.

Vanishing Point ◐
1971, US, 107 mins, colour
Dir: Richard C Sarafian
Stars: Barry Newman, Cleavon Little, Dean Jagger
Rating: ★★★

Perhaps more so even than *Bullitt*, this was the film that started a craze for car chase movies. Richard C Sarafian takes his carefully plotted story (an embittered ex-war hero driving all out from Colorado to California for the sheer hell and exhilaration of it) and endows it with a crude raw energy that sustains it throughout its fast-moving running time. The film is very much an *Easy Rider* of the four-wheel world. Its theme of individuality in a uniform society is vividly put across with the help of a powerful performance from the rugged Barry Newman.

Variety Girl ○
1947, US, 83 mins, b/w
Dir: George Marshall
Stars: Bing Crosby, Bob Hope, Dorothy Lamour, Alan Ladd
Rating: ★★★

One of those marvellous all-star cocktails that are no longer possible into s cimena, this one offering the entire 1947 roster of Paramount players with the exception of Betty Hutton who was pregnant at the time. Highlights are a couple of duets – 'Friendship' by Bing Crosby and Bob Hope and 'Tallahassee' by the less likely combination of Alan Ladd and Dorothy Lamour. The juvenile lead proves to be DeForest Kelley, years later to become Doc McCoy of the *Star Trek* series.

Vault of Horror ●
1973, UK, 87 mins, colour
Dir: Roy Ward Baker
Stars: Dawn Addams, Tom Baker, Michael Craig, Denholm Elliott
Rating: ★★

Another melange of five horror stories from the gore-minded lads at Amicus Films. The better episodes involve firstly Glynis Johns and Terry-Thomas, and then Curt Jurgens and Dawn Addams in the story of a rope with a mind of its own. The rest of the cast is no less impressive, including Michael Craig, Denholm Elliott, Anna Massey, Edward Judd, Daniel Massey and Mike Pratt.

Venetian Bird ○
(aka: The Assassin)
1952, UK, 95 mins, b/w
Dir: Ralph Thomas
Stars: Richard Todd, Eva Bartok, John Gregson, George Coulouris
Rating: ★★

Written by Victor Canning from his own novel, this thriller is something of a reworking of *The Third Man*, with Richard Todd caught up in mystery and intrigue as he tries to find an Italian partisan in Venice. John Gregson scores as a sly but engaging villain, Sidney James is a somewhat improbable Italian (although, why not, since this archetypal British movie cockney was actually a South African?) and Eva Bartok is decorative. Nice cinematography from Ernest Steward, who makes some dazzling use of the Venetian locations.

Vengeance ●
1962, UK, 82 mins, b/w
Dir: Freddie Francis
Stars: Anne Heywood, Peter Van Eyck, Cecil Parker
Rating: ★★

Third screen version of Curt Siodmak's classic science-fiction shocker *Donovan's Brain*. This time round (it was Erich von Stroheim in 1944 and Lew Ayres in 1953), it's Peter Van Eyck as the scientist convinced that a dead man's brain can be kept alive.

But the brain has a strange effect on him. This was one of the earliest shockers directed by Freddie Francis, who has won Oscars for his work as a cameraman.

Vengeance of She, The ○
1967, UK, 101 mins, colour
Dir: Cliff Owen
Stars: John Richardson, Olinka Berova, Edward Judd, Colin Blakely
Rating: ★

Czech actress Olinka Berova takes over from Ursula Andress as 'She Who Must Be Obeyed' in this sequel by Hammer Films to their own 1964 version of H Rider Haggard's famous fantasy yarn. For those ready to jump up and point out that Andress died at the end of the previous adventure, let us hasten to point out that it's her spirit that possesses the busty Berova in this risibly scripted romp, played with enthusiasm by a largely British cast that includes Colin Blakeley, George Sewell, Andre Morelli and Noel Willman.

Vengeance Valley ○
1951, US, 83 mins, colour
Dir: Richard Thorpe
Stars: Burt Lancaster, Robert Walker, Joanne Dru
Rating: ★★

A sombre, very serious and gripping Western on the theme of the good and the bad brother. Burt Lancaster puts on a more sober face than his fans were used to seeing in such films as *The Flame and the Arrow*, although he still gets plenty of chances to show his athleticism, but Robert Walker steals the film as his slimy brother. The compact plot, based on a novel by Luke Short, could do with some more action, but gets by with the help of ravishing colour camerawork by George Folsey.

Venom ●
1981, UK, 98 mins, colour
Dir: Piers Haggard
Stars: Klaus Kinski, Oliver Reed, Nicol Williamson, Sarah Miles
Rating: ★★

A startlingly good cast should perhaps have heeded the famous film maxim about never appearing with children and animals in this chiller about a kidnapped boy (engaging Lance Holcomb) and an elusive black mamba. Klaus Kinski, Sarah Miles and Susan George

are among those fleeing its fangs, and you'll long treasure the expression on Oliver Reed's face as the snake crawls up his trouser leg.

Venus Peter ○
1989, UK, 100 mins, colour
Dir: Ian Sellar
Stars: Ray McAnally, David Hayman, Sinead Cusack
Rating: ★★

In many ways, this tangy tale can be seen as a companion piece to *When the Males Came*. This one is set in the Orkney Islands, again concerns children growing up in a fishing community and, yes, there's a stranded whale to heighten the comparison. Mostly, the smack of salt is almost tangible enough to taste, nowhere more so than in Ray McAnally's measured portrayal of the boy's grandfather. To spice up the plot, there's the island mad woman, the awakening of the boy's interest in poetry by his new teacher (Sinead Cusack), the return of the boy's prodigal father and the war over the family boat. But the script shies away from too close an inspection of the complex issues involved.

Vera Cruz ○
1954, US, 94 mins, colour
Dir: Robert Aldrich
Stars: Gary Cooper, Burt Lancaster, George Macready, Ernest Borgnine, Charles Bronson
Rating: ★★★

Riotous, big-scale Gary Cooper Western that never lacks excitement, and gives Burt Lancaster (of the flashing teeth and villainous smile) one of his most colourful characters. It is reputed to have cost $3 million to make (in 1954) – a figure that looks from the stars and the sets to be no exaggeration. The bad guys in this vivid and virile yarn of old Mexico include Jack Elam, Ernest Borgnine, Charles Bronson (billed as Charles Buchinsky) and George Macready.

Verdict, The ❶ Ⓥ
1982, US, 129 mins, colour
Dir: Sidney Lumet
Stars: Paul Newman, Charlotte Rampling, Jack Warden, James Mason
Rating: ★★★★

It's an old Hollywood chestnut, of course – the drunken lawyer winning back his self-respect in a case that proves not as straightforward as everyone thought. But with the help of an immaculately structured screenplay by

V

David Mamet, this film plays fair and square with its audience and emerges as gripping, old-style entertainment. James Mason is as smoothly persuasive as ever as Newman's courtroom opponent, but what really gives the film a lift is Newman's grip on the central character. This piece of exemplary filmcraft, rather than *The Color of Money*, is surely the movie for which he should have won an Oscar.

Vertigo ○ ⓥ
1958, US, 128 mins, colour
Dir: Alfred Hitchcock
Stars: James Stewart, Kim Novak, Barbara Bel Geddes
Rating: ★★★★

A classic in suspense from Alfred Hitchcock, pitching us right into the action from the start, and baffling most of us to the finish. There is much for The Master's fans to savour in his smooth and atmospheric handling of the complex tale (based on a story by the authors of *The Fiends*). James Stewart is as assured as ever as the obsessed hero battling against his fear of heights, and Kim Novak's lack of expression in a difficult role strangely adds depth to her performance. The tense key scenes in a bell-tower are brilliantly staged.

Very Big Withdrawal, A
See: A Man, a Woman and a Bank

Very Brady Sequel, A ❶ ⓥ
1996, US, 89 mins, colour
Dir: Arlene Sanford
Stars: Shelley Long, Gary Cole, Christine Taylor, Adam Sandler, RuPaul
Rating: ★★★

Considerably more fun than the original Brady Bunch Movie, thanks in part to a better story that involves a priceless ancient statue of a horse sought by the world's collectors and currently sitting in the Bradys' lounge; the return of Carol Brady's first husband, long believed dead; and the two older Brady children falling in love (with each other). Better elements from the first film are retained – the parent Bradys' risqué relationship, for example – but the screenplay is quite different in tone, and treats the Bradys' home as a base rather than a set. The Bradys themselves emerge as people as well as posers. Comic timing under Arlene Sanford's direction is much improved, and guest appearances from

old and new TV and movie stars will delight nostalgia buffs.

Very Important Person ○
1961, UK, 100 mins, b/w
Dir: Ken Annakin
Stars: James Robertson Justice, Leslie Phillips, Stanley Baxter
Rating: ★★★

First and best of the four comedies made by its star trio of James Robertson Justice, Leslie Phillips and Stanley Baxter, set in a PoW camp. Funniest of a talented supporting cast is Eric Sykes, as an escape fanatic nicknamed The Mole.

Vibes ❶ ⓥ
1988, US, 99 mins, colour
Dir: Ken Kwapis
Stars: Cyndi Lauper, Jeff Goldblum, Peter Falk, Julian Sands, Elizabeth Pena, Michael Lerner
Rating: ★

There are some endearingly goofy moments in this comedy about psychics hired to find a world-changing 'McGuffin' high in the Ecuador mountains. In the end, though, they don't add up to much without solid direction, decent special effects or a script that needs to back its barbs with some character and story development. You couldn't get a much more unorthodox hero and heroine than bug-eyed Jeff Goldblum and squeaky rock star Cyndi Lauper, but neither of them wins our sympathy and it's left to Peter Falk's unscrupulous rogue to give the affair some heart. Elizabeth Pena also scores briefly as a local *femme fatale who* strips oltand asks Goldblum, 'You like?' 'Parts of me,' he pants, 'are already applauding.' Scraps of gold, these, though, from a film that muffs pretty well all its chances.

Vice Squad ○
(aka: The Girl In Room 17)
1953, US, 88 mins, b/w
Dir: Arnold Laven
Stars: Edward G Robinson, Paulette Goddard
Rating: ★★★

A good solid little thriller, the kind that would probably these days be labelled with the overworked 'gritty'. No real suprises here, but Edward G Robinson gives it a boost as the hard-pressed police captain, and there are good supporting performances from Lee Van Cleef, Paulette Goddard, Porter Hall and, especially, Mary Ellen Kay as a frightened hostage.

Vice Versa ☉
1947, UK, 111 mins, b/w
Dir: Peter Ustinov
Stars: Roger Livesey, Kay Walsh, Anthony Newley, Petula Clark
Rating: ★★

Peter Ustinov wrote and directed this tale of an Edwardian identity switch between father and son. Fascinating to see Petula Clark and Anthony Newley (who both have leading roles) as teenagers.

Vice Versa ○ ⓥ
1988, US, 100 mins, colour
Dir: Brian Gilbert
Stars: Judge Reinhold, Fred Savage, Corinne Bohrer, Swoosie Kurtz
Rating: ★★★

Another of the late Eighties' 'role reversal' comedies in a period that could have been called the invasion of the body switchers. Judge Reinhold holds centre stage in this one (a loose remake of the 1947 British film of the same title). In this version the fun is a little less naive and sex rears its head along with other foreseeable complications. Reinhold clowns around like mad, but its young Fred Savage from *The Wonder Years*, stuck in school as a 35-year-old, who gets the best stuff to do. Corinne Bohrer is a sweet love interest, and the film is pleasant to have around if pretty forgettable – sometimes amusing, occasionally embarrassing.

Vicki ○
1953, US, 85 mins, b/w
Dir: Harry Homer
Stars: Jeanne Crain, Elliott Reid, Richard Boone, Jean Peters
Rating: ★★

Suspense thriller, centred on the murder of a model (played by Jean Peters), with plenty of red herrings along the way. In its way, it's quite an ingenious whodunnit, told in flashback, and with a good characterisation from Richard Boone as a vindictive detective with a grudge against one of the suspects. A web of suspense is intriguingly spun, and it's comparable to the Berry Grable-Victor Mature *I Wake Up Screaming*, from which its plot is derived. If it had a stronger leading man than benign Elliott Reid, this might have been a winner.

Victim ❶
1961, UK, 100 mins, b/w
Dir: Basil Dearden
Stars: Dirk Bogarde, Sylvia Syms,

Dennis Price
Rating: ★★★

Forthright and fascinating British film on the hitherto taboo subject of homosexuality, which also turns out to be a good thriller in its own right. Dirk Bogarde is fine as the successful and now-married barrister threatened by spectres from the past. And Norman Bird is especially good as a frightened small-time bookseller.

Victoria the Great ○
1937, UK, 118 mins, b/w & colour
Dir: Herbert Wilcox
Stars: Anna Neagle, Anton Walbrook
Rating: ★★★

Anna Neagle's performance in this film about Queen Victoria won such tremendous popular acclaim that it was followed by a companion story – *Sixty Glorious Years*, made in the following year. *Victoria the Great*, which was made in black and white, with a burst into colour in the climactic Diamond Jubilee scenes, and led to a whole series of Neagle-portrayed great ladies, such as *The Lady With a Lamp* (Florence Nightingale) and *They Flew Alone* (Amy Johnson).

Victory Through Air Power ○
1943, US, 65 mins, colour
Dir: Jack Kinney, James Algar
Rating: ★★★

A unique cartoon combination of humour, deadly seriousness, detailed maps and highly imaginative animation, that treads a fine line between entertainment and realism. The humorous 'History of Aviation' animation sequence gives way to a rather wooden major going into detail about bombing. But do wait for the extraordinary animated climax as the American eagle dive-bombs the Japanese octopus in the South Pacific!

View to a Kill, A ○ ⓥ
1985, UK, 121 mins, colour
Dir: John Glen
Stars: Roger Moore, Christopher Walken, Tanya Roberts, Grace Jones
Rating: ★★

Roger Moore, selected 12 years earlier to take over Sean Connery's position in the 007 shirt (George Lazenby had popped up for one appearance in 1969), makes his seventh and last showing as everyone's favourite hitman in this extravagant Bondian escapade packed with 'he'll-never-get-out-of-this, surely' situations. The gamut of apocalyptic

scenarios is run (the denouement involves an airship hitched up to the Golden Gate Bridge); there's a stylish villain (Christopher Walken); and the beauties are really beautiful (Tanya Roberts, Grace Jones, Alison Doody and Fiona Fullerton). But for all these typically glossy ingredients, Moore looks a tired old warhorse, resorting to double entendres, which might have been cast-offs from a *Carry* On script.

Vigil ◑ ⓥ
1984, New Zealand, 90 mins, colour
Dir: Vincent Ward
Stars: Bill Kerr, Fiona Kay, Gordon Shields, Penelope Stewart, Frank Whitten
Rating: ★★

Life for a family on a remote sheep farm is dramatically changed when the farmer is killed in a hunting accident and his body is brought home to his wife and daughter by a mysterious stranger. This strange story is told from the pubescent daughter's viewpoint as she watches the stranger's influence on her mother and eccentric grandfather. New Zealand director Vincent Ward has created a visually arresting and stylish film, but the poor script and obscure storyline don't live up to the way it looks.

Viking Queen, The ○
1966, UK, 91 mins, colour
Dir: Don Chaffey
Stars: Don Murray, Carita, Donald Houston, Adrienne Corri
Rating: ★

'See: Bladed chariots of death! Men roasted alive in the cage of hell! Mighty legions of Rome! Barbarism of the mad emperor! Savage rites of the Iceni!' blazed the original publicity. If you're careful, you'll also see a watch on the wrist of one of the actors in this Roman Britain epic. Finnish beauty Carita plays the title role.

Vikings, The ○
1958, US, 116 mins, colour
Dir: Richard Fleischer
Stars: Kirk Douglas, Tony Curtis, Janet Leigh, Ernest Borgnine
Rating: ★★★

Kirk Douglas and Tony Curtis have the times of their acting lives in Richard Fleischer's Norse opera about the battle-loving Vikings of the 10th century, spectacularly shot by Jack Cardiff on locations in Brittany and Norway (Hardangerford). Eileen Way makes a distinct Agnes Moorehead-

style impression as an old crone, and some fierce hand-to-hand combat scenes will have you on the edge of your armchair. Britain's James Donald is also good as a treacherous informer.

Village of Daughters ○
1961, UK, 86 mins, b/w
Dir: George Pollock
Stars: Eric Sykes, Scilia Gabel
Rating: ★★

Sparky comedy about a salesman asked to judge an Italian beauty contest with a difference. In a rare leading role, lucky Eric Sykes is surrounded by some of Britain's loveliest young starlets of the time.

Village of the Damned ◑
1960, UK, 79 mins, b/w
Dir: Wolf Rilla
Stars: George Sanders, Barbara Shelley
Rating: ★★★

Edgy, eerie and effective, this is a fine screen adaptation of John Wyndham's classic science-fiction novel *The Midwich Cuckoos*, about demon children born during a short period when life in an English village appears to have come to a stop. Director Wolf Rilla's discreetly incisive handling of the mounting suspense evokes some quite frightening moments.

Villain ● ⓥ
1971, UK, 98 mins, colour
Dir: Michael Tuchner
Stars: Richard Burton, Ian McShane, Nigel Davenport, Fiona Lewis
Rating: ★★★

Richard Burton's choice of roles in his last years was not always the happiest, but this is one of his most striking and intense portrayals: a homosexual East End gang leader who treads people down like insects. A thriller as tough as its central character. Ian La Frenais and Dick Clement – more usually associated with comedy series – contribute a script that drips venom.

Villain, The
See: Cactus Jack

Villa Rides! ○
1968, US, 125 mins, colour
Dir: Buzz Kulik
Stars: Yul Brynner, Robert Mitchum, Charles Bronson, Grazia Buccella
Rating: ★★

There's not much to test the brain cells but a feast of action for the eyes in this story about the Mexican patriot-bandit

V

who flourished in the early part of this century. Jack Hildyard's Technicolor photography helps director Buzz Kulik to milk the maximum impact from a succession of battles, explosions, raids, duels and chases. Charles Bronson, giving one of the last of his sadistic tough-guy portrayals before being promoted to stone-faced superstar, breathes life into his role.

Violent Men, The ○
1955, US, 96 mins, colour
Dir: Rudolph Maté
Stars: Glenn Ford, Barbara Stanwyck, Edward G Robinson
Rating: ★★

Columbia's much-trumpeted first film in CinemaScope is a Western that sets out to be another *Shane* with its 'greed for land' theme, but misses the mark. Polish-born director Rudolph Maté produces several thrillng action shots but is less sure-footed when marshalling his actors. In fact, Edward G Robinson picked out *The Violent Men* in his autobiography as one of the movies that marked his decline from stardom. In Britain, it was released as *Rough Company*, the title of the novel by Donald Hamilton on which the film is based.

Violent Playground ○
1957, UK, 108 mins, b/w
Dir: Basil Dearden
Stars: Stanley Baker, Anne Heywood, David McCallum, Peter Cushing
Rating: ★★

A tough-minded British thriller about a detective's hunt for an arsonist. Its semi-documentary style and good location shots of the Liverpool slums lend authority to a polished script. It's a well-paced film which builds up to a tension-filled climax.

Violent Saturday ○
1955, US, 91 mins, colour
Dir: Richard Fleischer
Stars: Victor Mature, Richard Egan, Stephen McNally, Virginia Leith
Rating: ★★★

Richard Fleischer's forceful thriller about three bank-raiders who indirectly bring to the surface all the sores, weaknesses and suspicions of the small town whose bank they are about to rob. The bank robbers are exceptionally well played by Stephen McNally, Lee Marvin and, particularly, J Carrol Naish.

Violent Streets ●
(aka: Thief)
1981, US, 126 mins, colour
Dir: Michael Mann
Stars: James Caan, Tuesday Weld, Willie Nelson
Rating: ★★★

An uncompromising thriller about a professional robber who makes one of the few mistakes in his meticulous career when he allies himself with organised crime for what he thinks is one job. Tuesday Weld is, as usual, wasted as his wife, and James Belushi makes a notable debut as Caan's skilful associate. The ending splatters bodies all over the pavement, somewhat compensating for the snail-like pace of much of the film.

Virgin and the Gypsy, The ●
1970, UK, 95 mins, colour
Dir: Christopher Miles
Stars: Joanna Shimkus, Franco Nero, Honor Blackman, Mark Burns
Rating: ★★

Direction (by Christopher Miles) and photography (by Robert Huke) come very close to capturing the brooding atmosphere of the original in this adaptation of an earthy short novel by D H Lawrence. Joanna Shimkus shines as the gentle Yvette who is emancipated from her surroundings through her friendship with, and love for, a gypsy who calls, selling his wares, at the north of England rectory which is her home. The gypsy is played by Franco Nero, but generally the acting honours go to the ladies in the cast.

Virginia City ○
1940, US, 121 mins, b/w
Dir: Michael Curtiz
Stars: Errol Flynn, Randolph Scott, Humphrey Bogart, Miriam Hopkins
Rating: ★★★

They couldn't afford stars such as Errol Flynn, Humphrey Bogart and Randolph Scott in the same film today – not unless the producers had millions in the bank. Not unexpectedly the resulting movie, directed by Michael Curtiz is a Western par excellence. Nor will action fans be disappointed: the film is packed with battles of one kind or another. As a Rebel spy, the acerbic Miriam Hopkins steals the acting honours from under the noses of the eminent trio.

Virgin Island ○
1958, UK, 94 mins, colour
Dir: Pat Jackson

Stars: John Cassavetes, Virginia Maskell, Sidney Poitier
Rating: ★★

The stars of *A Man is 10 Feet Tall* reunited in a far gender film about a young couple starring a new life on a far-from-civilised island. Directed by Pat Jackson, who distinguished himself on the wartime documentary *Western Approaches,* and later, in contrast, proved best at 'women's pictures'.

Virgin Queen, The ○ ⓥ
1955, US, 92 mins, colour
Dir: Henry Koster
Stars: Bette Davis, Richard Todd, Joan Collins
Rating: ★★

Bette Davis' second interpretation of the role of Elizabeth I, and considered by many critics to be even better than her first essay in *The Private Lives of Elizabeth and Essex*. Richard Todd plays Sir Walter Raleigh, and Joan Collins gives a spirited performance as the lady-in-waiting with whom he falls in love.

Virgin Soldiers, The ● ⓥ
1969, UK, 96 mins, colour
Dir: John Dexter
Stars: Lynn Redgrave, Hywel Bennett, Nigel Davenport, Nigel Patrick
Rating: ★★

Popular film version of Leslie Thomas' best-seller with raw recruits learning about the birds and battles in the Far East. A good performance from Lynn Redgrave, as usual, but the message about the uselessness of war and National Service is largely submerged by the *Carry On* style. However, this does make the best shock moments all the more telling.

Virtuosity ● ⓥ
1995, US, 100 mins, colour
Dir: Brett Leonard
Stars: Denzel Washington, Kelly Lynch, Russell Crowe
Rating: ★★★★

One of those mad professors beloved of old horror movies re-creates his virtual reality personification as an android, Sid 6.7 (Russell Crowe), who proceeds to a self-glorifying orgy of killing. Cue hero Denzel Washington, a cop jailed for slaughtering innocent bystanders in his revenge killing of the evil hostage terrorist whose DNA now forms part of the computer chip that makes Sid 6.7's time-bomb tick. Deemed the only man who can stop the rampage of killing, Washington is implanted with a tracker device that can (unknown to him) be set to kill him – and let loose. Cue the heroine: Kelly Lynch as the criminal psychologist who designates herself as Washington's partner. The ensuing, virtual reality-enhanced carnage makes for an exciting thriller, even if the makers hardly play fair with helping the viewer keep up with the plot towards the end. Very snappily directed by Brett Leonard, who made *The Lawmower Man*, the film is an expensive-looking ride to Hell and back that you might call *Devil in a Blue Chip*.

Vivacious Lady ○
1938, US, 90 mins, b/w
Dir: George Stevens
Stars: Ginger Rogers, James Stewart
Rating: ★★★

Here's another dancing lady – in the shape of Ginger Rogers as the nightclub entertainer whom mild professor James Stewart falls for in this one-joke but still fairly sparkling romantic comedy. Penny-pinching RKO allowed Ginger only one dance, but the personalities of the stars save the day.

Viva Villa! ○
1934, France/Italy, 125 mins, b/w
Dir: Jack Conway
Stars: Wallace Beery, Leo Carrillo, Fay Wray
Rating: ★★★

Rowdy, roistering, well-scripted account of the famous Mexican bandit's exploits. Its episodic quality might be partly due to the fact that director Howard Hawks left half-way through, and was replaced by Jack Conway, who is credited with the final version of the film. But it was assistant director John Waters who took the film's only Academy Award, although Ben Hecht's script contains some pungent exchanges, particularly the final dialogue between Wallace Beery (as Villa) and Stuart Erwin as the reporter who chronicles his career.

Viva Zapata! ○ ⓥ
1952, US, 113 mins, b/w
Dir: Elia Kazan
Stars: Marlon Brando, Jean Peters, Anthony Quinn
Rating: ★★★★

One of Marlon Brando's earliest screen roles, as the famous bandit of Mexican history. Although his brooding portrait proved him capable of a wide range of roles, he is outgunned both by Jean Peters as his fiersly ambi-

tious wife, and by Anthony Quinn as his roistering brother, the latter winning an Oscar which established him as a serious actor after 17 years' hard labour on the Hollywood scene – and also setting the pattern for the remainder of his career. Under Elia Kazan's direction, the action and treatment are fierce and uncompromising.

V.I. Warshawski ● ⓥ
1991, US, 89 mins, colour
Dir: Jeff Kanew
Stars: Kathleen Turner, Jay O Sanders, Charles Durning, Angela Goethals
Rating: ★★★

This female private-eye film runs like tough pulp fiction from another era. The heroine always has a ready wisecrack (with a literacy rather above her station in life), the mystery she has to solve is mighty murky and, of course, it involves a woman. 'I've just told you everything I know,' gasps VI's sometime lover/reporter friend. Tut, rut,' she chides, 'you always did suffer from premature articulation.' When a villain boasts of having had 500 women, she has an answer for that too. 'Can't get the hang of it, huh?' Yes, this Warshawski is tough all right. An aikido expert, she's inclined to beat up on thugs sent to work her over and almost always has the last word. Kathleen Turner plays her about right: the story she's involved with has something to do with three brothers feuding over selling their shipping concern. Despite its awful background music, this film was underrated by public and critics alike.

Vogues ○
1937, US, 108 mins, colour
Dir: Irving Cummings
Stars: Warner Baxter, Joan Bennett, Helen Vinson, Mischa Auer
Rating: ★★

Amazing fashions, a smooth script and pretty indifferent musical numbers make up the mix for this archetypal slice of lavish late-Thirties entertainment, Hollywood-style, chiefly remarkable for its innovative use of early Technicolor under the skilled camera of Ray Rennahan. Experienced smoothie Warner Baxter, used to putting on shows since *42nd Street,* here mounts a fashion show to remember, while The Wiere Brothers, underused by films, steal the comedy honours. And just cast an eye over Miss Chesterfield, Miss Pepsodent, Miss Lux Soap and Miss Lucky Strike!

Voice In the Night, A
See: Freedom Radio

Volcano ◑ ⓥ
1997, US, 103 mins, colour
Dir: Mick Jackson
Stars: Tommy Lee Jones, Anne Heche, Gaby Hoffmann, Don Cheadle
Rating: ★★★

The publicity's correct: the coast is toast all right, and it's headed your way. This is a rousing erupter that wastes little time in setting up its action. The Los Angeles tar pits explode in fireballs, spitting out an advancing tide of magma, while an even greater horror waits below. 'Hold on, baby, you'll be safe here,' says emergencies chief Tommy Lee Jones, leaving daughter Gaby Hoffmann in the car and adding to the lines of classic film remarks no one but the speaker believes. Special effects do pretty well all you could expect here, apart from a few chesy fireball moments when it looks as though the film's been run backwards. Otherwise moments of sacrifice and heroism are well mixed into the general panic in a film that proves a real goer from start to finish.

Volunteers ◑ ⓥ
1985, US, 107 mins, colour
Dir: Nicholas Meyer
Stars: Tom Hanks, John Candy
Rating: ★★

Hollywood's Mr Nice Guy, Tom Hanks, and Tinseltown's tub of fun, John Candy, teamed up only a year after they played brothers in the hugely successful *Splash* for this lightweight comedy. The premise – compulsive gambler (Hanks) escapes from his creditors and inadvertently ends up on a Peace Corps mission to Thailand – is promising but considering the combined talents of Hanks and Candy, the end product is largely disappointing. However, in their distinctly different ways, both leads prove worth watching here, and went on to greater glories.

VI
See: Battle of the VI

Von Ryan's Express ○ ⓥ
1965, US, 117 mins, colour
Dir: Mark Robson
Stars: Frank Sinatra, Trevor Howard, Brad Dexter
Rating: ★★★★

A very successful mixture of *The Train* and *The Great Escape*, dealing with a

V

group of Allied prisoners-of-war who capture the train taking them to Berlin, and set off full steam for Switzerland. And, incorporating the tenser situations from each film it has the edge on both for sheer excitement. Frank Sinatra and Trevor Howard turn in thoroughly workmanlike performances, and in support Italian actors Sergio Fantoni and Adolfo Celi, as Allied-sympathiser and Nazi-sympathiser respectively, are outstanding. And Edward Mulhare gives a delicately wry portrayal of the padre forced to pose as a German officer – because he is the only one of the prisoners who can speak the language fluently. But the action is everything. And nowhere more so than in the edge-of-seat ending.

Vote for Huggett ○

1949, UK, 95 mins, b/w
Dir: Ken Annakin
Stars: Jack Warner, Kathleen Harrison, Susan Shaw, David Tomlinson
Rating: ★★

The third in the series about the adventures of a Cockney family. All were directed by Ken Annakin, and were a kind of throwback to the hearty humour purveyed in the British cinema of the Thirties by such comedians as Leslie Fuller. The cast, too, was constant: Jack Warner as Dad, Kathleen Harrison (with an epithet for every occasion) as Mum, Susan Shaw as daughter Sue, Petula Clark as daughter Pet, and Peter Hammond as the perennial boyfriend. Here the cast also includes David Tomlinson, Diana Dors and Anthony Newley.

Voyage Home – Star Trek IV, The ○ ⓥ

1986, US, 119 mins, colour
Dir: Leonard Nimoy
Stars: William Shatner, Leonard Nimoy, DeForest Kelley, Catherine Hicks
Rating: ★★★

Half a science-fiction adventure and half a timely plea for whale conservation, this adventure of the Starship *Enterprise* shows the formula wearing pretty thin despite four credited writers. Returning to earth to face court martial, Kirk and Co find the planet in a state of panic thanks to the presence high above of a paralysing probe trying to communicate with a species of whale that's extinct. Kirk and his crew travel back in time (conveniently to 1986) when the whales still existed and find a pair in a San Francisco aquarium that are about to be booted off to Alaska where whale-hunters

abound. This makes for a reasonably tense, if slightly over-extended climax and, if not much is made of the invaders' bemusement in 20th-century America, the camaraderie of the cast does produce some nice lines and reactions.

Voyage of the Damned ○

1976, UK, 155 mins, colour
Dir: Stuart Rosenberg
Stars: Faye Dunaway, Max Von Sydow, Oskar Werner, Malcolm McDowell, Orson Welles
Rating: ★★

The movie equivalent of a good, long read, this is an epic drama, based on fact. The all-star cast includes Orson Welles as a wily Cuban industrialist, Faye Dunaway, Max Von Sydow (whose sterling performance holds the disparate dramas together), Oskar Werner, James Mason, Malcolm McDowell and Ben Gazzara. Director Stuart Rosenberg keeps his huge cast and sprawling narrative steadily in control.

Voyager ● ⓥ

1991, Germany/France, 117 mins, colour
Dir: Volker Schlondorff
Stars: Sam Shepard, Julie Delpy, Barbara Sukowa
Rating: ★

Gloom and doom are draped all over this journey into grace, especially as we can guess very well what hero Sam Shepard doesn't know – that the pert teenager (Julie Delpy) he plans to bed is his own daughter. 'Do you believe in chance?' asks Shepard. And you'd better. Because Max Frisch's bestseller, on which this glum number is based, depends entirely on it. Solemn Sam is ideally . cast in this sort of thing, as the man without belief in life, or a future. You just have to feel sorry for his character, even though it's hard to sympathise with a man who comes out with things like 'Three or four days with a woman is my maximum. After that, I start to dissimilate.' Even the few moments of humour seem forced and unreal.

Voyage to the Bottom of the Sea ○ ⓥ

1961, US, 105 mins, colour
Dir: Irwin Allen
Stars: Walter Pidgeon, Joan Fontaine, Peter Lorre
Rating: ★★

Special effects are top-notch in this exciting, colourful and fluid piece of

science fiction, on which the TV series was based. Here, it's Walter Pidgeon leading the star-studded cast as Admiral Nelson battling against giant octopi and melting Polar ice-caps in his huge submarine, *Seaview*. Older film fans may recognise Regis Toomey (as Dr Jameson). Toomey was in scores of films in the Thirties and Forties, as pugnacious policemen, wisecracking reporters, or 'squealers' who inevitably 'bought it' in the final reel.

W

Wabash Avenue ◉
1950, US, 92 mins, colour
Dir: Henry Koster
Stars: Betty Grable, Victor Mature, Phil Harris
Rating: ★★★

If you have a feeling of déjà vu, don't be surprised – this bright and brash musical is a remake of 1943's *Coney Island*, with the same producer (William Perlberg) and the same star, Betty Grable. This time Victor Mature (all teeth and bogus charm) and Phil Harris are the two men with Grable on their minds when they are not trying to swindle each other, but the film belongs firmly to its leading lady, million-dollar legs enjoyably in evidence as she performs a series of lively musical numbers. Easy on the eye (20th Century-Fox's Technicolor was never lovelier) and on the mind, with engaging support from James Barton as an Irish drunk and Margaret Hamilton as a crusading reformer. A good show.

Wackiest Ship in the Army, The ◉
1960, US, 99 mins, colour
Dir: Richard Murphy
Stars: Jack Lemmon, Ricky Nelson, John Lurid, Chips Rafferty
Rating: ★★

Jack Lemmon as a yachtsman with a crew of novices on a dangerous wartime mission. It is one of his sunniest although not funniest comedies. Patricia Driscoll, one-time Maid Marian in the *Robin Hood* TV series, has the main female role.

Wages of Fear, The ◑
(aka: Sorcerer)
1977, US, 122 mins, colour
Dir: William Friedkin
Stars: Roy Scheider, Bruno Cremer
Rating: ★★

A $21 million remake of the famous suspense movie, the first version of which starred Yves Montand in the role now played by Roy Scheider. The remainder of the characters remain less well developed than in the original, which so entrapped us in following the fortunes of the four men desperate enough to undertake a suicidal journey with a cargo of nitroglycerine along the dangerous jungle and cliffside roads.

Wagonmaster ○
1950, US, 86 mins, b/w
Dir: John Ford
Stars: Ben Johnson, Joanne Dru, Harry Carey Jr, Ward Bond
Rating: ★★★

Brimming with atmosphere, this John Ford Western is resplendent with all the Ford trademarks: breathtaking scenery, dancing, songs and a warm sense of humour. Ben Johnson takes over as star from Ford's ever-present John Wayne, though in fairness Wayne is too big a personality to fit into this small, intimate story about two drifter cowhands joining a Mormon wagon train. Ford's son, Patrick, co-wrote the screenplay, and it remained a personal favourite throughout Ford Sr's career. *Wagonmaster* is pure poetry, eschewing plot twists and rugged action for a bird's eye view of ordinary people going about their ordinary lives. In short, it's an uplifting film about life which affirms that anyone can achieve the ultimate dream.

Wagons East ◑ ⓥ
1994, US, 107 mins, colour
Dir: Peter Markle
Stars: John Candy, Ellen Greene, Richard Lewis, John C McGinley, Ed Lauter
Rating: RB

Comic Westerns have pretty much bitten the dust since the distant days of *Support Your Local Sheriff* and *Blazing Saddles*, but here's one that hardly even deserves a critic's arrow in the back. How sad that big John Candy should have succumbed to a heart attack on the torrid location of this heavily overperformed turkey about a group of settlers who reckon enough is enough in the Wild West and decide to head back east. There are offensive gay jokes, bodily function jokes, cartoonstyle jokes and comic Indians, but absolutely nothing that raises a laugh. Actually the big fella's not bad in his last film, although everyone else is, relentlessly driven over the precipice of unsubtlety by director Peter Markle. Photography and music are good enough for a real movie.

Waiting for the Light ○ ⓥ
1990, US, 102 mins, colour
Dir: Christopher Monger
Stars: Shirley MacLaine, Teri Garr, Clancy Brown, Vincent Schiavelli, Hillary Wolf
Rating: ★★

A family film of lightweight charm with Shirley MacLaine as an eccentric aunt

whose magic first gets her niece's children into trouble, then proves their salvation when she provides the 'miracle' that brings people to their little cafe in the middle of nowhere. Not much to stir the blood here, but MacLaine deservedly assumes centre stage and there are good, pleasant performances from Teri Garr, Clancy Brown, Vincent Schiavelli, John Bedford Lloyd and especially Hillary Wolf as Garr's daughter. Some amusingly staged special eeects make MacLaine's miracle magic seem real enough for the gullible.

Waiting to Exhale ○ ⓥ
1995, US, 128 mins, colour
Dir: Forest Whitaker
Stars: Whitney Housten, Angela Bassett, Loretta Devine, Lela Rochon, Gregory Hines
Rating: ★

A soundtrack album in search of a film, this saga of sex and soap, through the man-strewn lives of four black girls in America, seems to go on all evening. Sex is had at the drop of a hat and seems to last about 25 seconds, although to be fair a couple of the girls do complain about their lovers not taking their time. Monotonous is the word as our ever immaculately made-up quartet lurches from one sexual crisis to another. The same studio (Fox) used to make movies like this 30 years before, although with an all-white cast, of course, and a touch more finesse. Like then, though, nothing seems for real here, and even the magnificent Angela Bassett over-emotes at times, which at least makes her stand out from the anodyne performances of the other three. The men for the most part stand around awkwardly, while dialogue is pitched at gutter-level throughout. Watch, though, for the scene where Lela Rochon throws her knickers out of the bed. In the next shot she clearly has them on. That's what we *call* a foxy lady!

Wait 'Til the Sun Shines, Nellie' ○
1952, US, 108 mins, colour
Dir: Henry King
Stars: David Wayne, Jean Peters, Hugh Marlowe, Albert Dekker
Rating: ★★★★★

One of director Henry King's warmest pieces of nostalgia. In fact, if this had starred a high-profile star like Spencer Tracy in the leading role it might now be regarded as a classic – not that David Wayne is anything but excellent as the small-town barber looking back over half a century of his life. It rambles a

W

bit, but the acting, direction and glowing colour photography of Leon Shamroy more than make up for that. Not to be missed.

Wait Until Dark ◐
1967, US, 108 mins, colour
Dir: Terence Young
Stars: Audrey Hepburn, Alan Arkin, Richard Crenna
Rating: ★★★★

Don't be put off: sit through the first hour or so of stagey, confined melodrama to see the petrifying last 40 minutes of this jolting thriller, as blind girl Audrey Hepburn (one character describes her as the World's Champion Blind Lady and he's right) smashes all the lights and takes on two baddies and one very evil psycho who are after a doll stuffed with heroin, which is in her basement flat. One moment of fright in particular, near the end, is terrifyingly sudden.

Wake Island ○
1942, US, 88 mins, colour
Dir: John Farrow
Stars: Brian Donlevy, Robert Preston, MacDonald Carey
Rating: ★★★

Exciting and typically flag-waving American film of the early war years. In this case, there really was something to wave the flag about – the heroic defence of a Pacific island by a few hundred Marines against 10,000 Japanese that lasted for 15 days. Brian Donlevy is very good as the island commander.

Wake of the Red Witch ○ ⓥ
1948, US, 106 mins, b/w
Dir: Edward Ludwig
Stars: John Wayne, Gail Russell, Gig Young
Rating: ★★★

High adventure with a richly detailed story (made rather too complicated by flashbacks) that's vaguely reminiscent of the work of Joseph Conrad, though actually based on a novel by Garland Roark. It kicked off a three-year period for star John Wayne in which he made some of his best films. This one gives him a chance to play a more complex character than usual and Wayne responds with one of his most haunting performances. It's an East Indies seafaring yarn that takes in fist-fights, storms, romance, friendship, treachery and the pursuit of sunken treasure, and has a climax that should have you gripping the armchair. Wayne was so fond of the film that he

took the name of his production company, Batjac, from its shipping line. Hawaiian sporting star Duke Kahanamoku appears in a minor role.

Wake Up and Live ○
1937, US, 91 mins, b/w
Dir: Sidney Lanfield
Stars: Walter Winchell, Ben Bernie and His Band, Alice Faye, Jack Haley
Rating: ★★★

An excellent satire on the world of radio which was big time showbusiness when this was made. Newspaper columnist Walter Winchell and bandleader Ben Bernie, as themselves, play 'feuding' radio show hosts (not unlike the real-life Jack Benny-Fred Allen 'feud' which was a complete fabrication) in this slap-happy comedy musical which fairly bounces along. Alice Faye also stars as a kind of radio agony aunt. Winchell was a powerful character and allegedly the model for Burt Lancaster's J J Hunsecker in *Sweet Smell of Success*. As anyone who has seen that film will recall, this was hardly a man overflowing with the milk of human kindness: so see how convincing you find Winchell's performance here!

Walkabout ◐
1970, Australia, 100 mins, colour
Dir: Nicolas Roeg
Stars: Jenny Agutter, David Gumpilil
Rating: ★★★★

Cameraman Nicolas Roeg made a new reputation as an innovative director with this exciting and sad moral tale about two children marooned in Australia's alien outback, strikingly captured in burnished colour.

Walk, Don't Run ◐
1966, US, 114 mins, colour
Dir: Charles Walters
Stars: Cary Grant, Samantha Eggar, Jim Hutton
Rating: ★★★★

This story was originally used in the 1943 Charles Coburn-Jean Arthur hit *The More the Merrier*. But the setting is here transferred from wartime Washington to Tokyo's 1964 Olympics. Grant is on top comedy form as a match-making diplomat, raising laughs often without saying a word. Watch his face and listen to his Bluto-like grunts as he potters around Samantha Eggar's kitchen (he has become her flat-mate through sheer gift of the gab) trying to find things.

Walking My Baby Back Home ⊙
1953, US, 95 mins, colour
Dir: Lloyd Bacon
Stars: Donald O'Connor, Janet Leigh, Buddy Hackett
Rating: ★★★

A bright, colourful musical that didn't quite come off as a star vehicle. Probably it's because Donald O'Connor was better playing second fiddle to people like Gene Kelly and Bing Crosby, and because Janet Leigh, although she dances gracefully, sings pleasantly and looks gorgeous, isn't really a musical star. 'Scatman' Crothers scores in a support as a jazz-loving pianist, the dance numbers are expertly, if slightly mechanically, staged and the music takes in everything from a hot version of Liszt's 'Liebestraum' to some good old New Orleans blues. Secondgrade, but undemandingly enjoyable, even though Universal couldn't make this sort of musical like MGM, or even 20th Century-Fox.

Walk in the Clouds, A ○ ⓥ
1995, US, 98 mins, colour
Dir: Alfonso Arau
Stars: Keanu Reeves, Aitana Sanche-Gijon, Giancarlo Giannini, Anthony Quinn
Rating: ★

This grape-growing saga looks good, but by golly it tastes bad. Dialogue that's been too long on the vine sticks in the throat, providing a choke and a giggle, as GI Keanu Reeves returns from World War 2 to a wife who doesn't love him. On a bus he encounters Victoria (Aitana Sanchez-Gijon) who is promptly sick on him. The daughter of a prominent vine-growing family in California, she's pregnant and returning in shame. The gallant Reeves, after getting into a fight over her on a bus, agrees to return with her and pose as her husband. Papa (Giancarlo Giannini) is hostile, perhaps not surprising as his side has just lost the war. 'Don't think because I speak with an accent I think with an accent,' he snarls. Hmm. Grandpa, though, is willing to give Reeves a try at being a grapie. 'You have to have the permissions of the four winds,' he mutters, 'to harvest what the earth gives.' Yes, folks, it has to be Anthony Quinn and it is, as a sort of Zorba the Grape. Reeves looks lost. So, despite ravishing photography and a brilliantly staged fire, does the cause of the film.

Walk in the Shadow
See: Life for Ruth

Walk in the Spring Rain, A ○

1969, US, 100 mins, colour
Dir: Guy Green
Stars: Anthony Quinn, Ingrid Bergman,
Fritz Weaver
Rating: ★★

Spring romance in their Autumn years
for middle-agers Anthony Quinn and
Ingrid Bergman, who had previously
appeared together in the starkly contrasted *The Visit*. Bergman's husband is
played by Fritz Weaver, the authodta-
tive American actor who first sprang to
prominence as the colonel who cracked
up in Sidney Lumet's *Fail Safe*. Set in
the mountainous but attractive countryside of Tennessee, *A Walk in the
Spring Rain* is exquisitely shot in colour
by the distinguished cameraman
Charles B Lang.

Walk In the Sun, A ○

1945, US, 117 mins, b/w
Dir: Lewis Milestone
Stars: Dana Andrews, Richard Conte,
Sterling Holloway, John Ireland
Rating: ★★★

One of the most highly regarded
World War Two movies, with an un-
sentimental screenplay by Robert
Rossen Gater to turn director with
such films as *All the King's Men* and *The
Hustler*) plus concentrated direction by
Lewis Milestone, who made the classic
World War One pacifist movie *All
Quiet on the Western Front*.

Walk the Proud Land ○

1956, US, 88 mins, colour
Dir: Jesse Hibbs
Stars: Audie Murphy, Pat Crowley, Anne
Bancroft, Charles Drake
Rating: ★★★

This excellent true-life story of the first
Apache agent was Audie Murphy's follow-up to the great success of the
autobiographical *To Hell and Back*.
Murphy dominates the film, with the
usually sparky Pat Crowley rather subdued, leaving Anne Bancroft free to
take the feminine acting honours as an
Apache widow woman. Supporting
acting is sturdy, especially from
Charles Drake, as a friendly sergeant,
and Robert Warwick, as the resigned
and noble old Apache chief.

Wall Street ○ ⓥ

1987, US, 124 mins, colour
Dir: Oliver Stone
Stars: Michael Douglas, Charlie Sheen,
Martin Sheen, Daryl Hannah, Terence
Stamp, Sean Young
Rating: ★★★

Director Oliver Stone's swift follow-up
to the Oscar-winning *Platoon* takes him
from the battlefields of Vietnam to the
battlefields of the New York financial
markets. Charlie Sheen, who played
the central character in *Platoon*, is again
the youngster through whose eyes
Stone shows the ugly underbelly of life.
As an ambitious young broker, he
achieves the ultimate yuppie dream of
a huge salary, high-powered car, glamorous girlfriend and luxury penthouse.
But there's a terrible personal cost to
him as he crosses the line of legality in
providing his corporate raider idol
Gordon Gekko with illegal insider information on Sheen's father's airline
business. There is a nice touch in the
casting of real-life father Martin Sheen
as Charlie's screen dad, but it was
Michael Douglas, as the monstrous
Gekko – motto: 'Greed is good' – who
scooped the Best Actor Oscar.

Waltz of the Toreadors ○

1962, UK, 105 mins, colour
Dir: John Guillermin
Stars: Peter Sellers, Margaret Leighton,
Dany Robin, John Fraser
Rating: ★★★★

Peter Sellers excels as an ageing general with an eye for the ladies in this
happy and successful, sometimes
touching, adaptation of Jean Anouilh's
famous play. And the excellent
Technicolor photography fairly
sparkles, especially in a scene of lovers
meeting in a cornfield.

Wanted Dead or Alive ○ ⓥ

1987, US, 104 mins, colour
Dir: Gary Sherman
Stars: Rutger Hauer, Gene Simmons, Mel
Harris, Robert Guillaume
Rating: ★★

Massive blows, explosions and assassinations are the order of the day in this
assembly-line vehicle about a modern-
day bounty hunter, supposedly the
grandson of the character played by
Steve McQueen in the TV Western series of the same title. Dutch actor
Rutger Hauer, already sporting a near-
perfect American accent, plays the
ex-CIA agent recruited by his old bosses to stop an Arab terrorist who plans
to blow up half of Los Angeles.
Remaining developments are cut to formula, with bludgeoning sentiment,
corny situations and a brave attempt
by Robert Guillaume to make something out of his cornball dialogue. But
like his character, nothing in this film
ever quite comes to life.

War and Peace ○ ⓥ

1956, US, 208 mins, colour
Dir: King Vidor
Stars: Henry Fonda, Audrey Hepburn,
Mel Ferrer
Rating: ★★★

This impressive – and a little overwhelming – Hollywood version of Leo
Tolstoy's Napoleonic saga suffers from
too much peace and too little war, especially given that the battle scenes are
tremendously staged by Mario Soldati,
helping out credited director King
Vidor. Henry Fonda, though miscast
and too old, is still amazingly good as
Pierre, and there are excellent contributions from Mel Ferrer, Herbert Lom,
Anita Ekberg and especially Oscar
Homolka. Although developments in
the drama are signalled heavily, this is
still a commendable stab at a mammoth undertaking.

WarGames ○ ⓥ

1983, US, 113 mins, colour
Dir: John Badham
Stars: Matthew Broderick, Dabney
Coleman, Ally Sheedy, Barry Corbin,
John Wood
Rating: ★★★★

Another computer-age thriller, though a
pretty exciting one about a teenage computer freak who accidentally plugs into
America's nuclear defence system and
finds the computer playing a war game
with him that may very well be for real.
Though you may not understand the
ending, you'll appreciate the tension that
leads up to it, as the boy and his girlfriend fight desperately to a) convince
the authorities and b) find the thought-
dead scientist who may be able to stop it
all. Matthew Broderick, Dabney
Coleman, John Wood and Juanin Clay
are convincingly disraught: but then it's
only a game. Or is it? From January
1979 to June 1980, some 147 such full-
scale alerts had their grim scenarios
played out in earnest before America
and Russia pulled back from the brink.

Warlock ○

1959, US, 123 mins, colour
Dir: Edward Dmytryk
Stars: Richard Widmark, Henry Fonda,
Anthony Quinn, Dorothy Malone
Rating: ★★

Over 200,000 rounds of blank ammunition – the script calls for 47 people to
bite the dust – were fired during the
making of this epic Western. Director
Edward Dmytryk initially wanted
Henry Fonda to play the hero, and
Richard Widmark the villain. But after
they had read the screenplay, each

W

actor wanted to play the other's role. And that's the way it ended up, setting Fonda on a course that culminated memorably in his bad guy in *Once Upon a Time in the West*.

Warlock ●
1988, US, 102 mins, colour
Dir: Steve Miner
Stars: Richard E Grant, Julian Sands, Lori Singer
Rating: ★★

There's a laugh and a thrill to be had in this witch's brew which has Julian Sands as a 17th-century warlock who escapes to avoid being hanged and burned. But he's pursued by the spirit of his sworn enemy (Richard E Grant) who rises from the grave to protect the heroine (Lori Singer) which is just as well as Sands has put a spell on her which ages her at the rate of 20 years a day. 'Nothing can be worse than this,' she howls, presumably referring to her 60-year-old makeup. So she sets out to trek with Grant to prevent Sands putting three parts of a book together (the Grand Grimoire), find out God's real name and reverse the Creation. There's the inevitable race to get to the third part of the book, which lies in a tomb with a hex-mark on it. Hex, you see, marks the spot. All this, plus good 'hex' music by Jerry Goldsmith, some good lines, pretty variable special effects and enjoyable unintentional humour.

War Lord, The ○
1965, US, 122 mins, colour
Dir: Franklin Schaffner
Stars: Charlton Heston, Richard Boone, Rosemary Forsyth, Maurice Evans, Guy Stockwell
Rating: ★★★★★

Moody and magnificent (even after studio interference), this is one of the most impressive pieces of medieval drama that Hollywood ever made. Charlton Heston heightens the sense of period by his skilful handling of the dialogue as an embittered, war-hardened Norman noble who invokes his feudal right and steals a bride in his Belgian territory on her wedding night. He's matched by Rosemary Forsyth, who never bettered her blazingly sincere portrait of the girl. But the film's aces in the hole are Jerome Moross's melodic, mood-invoking music, and Russell Metty's amazing colour photography. He gives us beautiful portraits of all kinds of skies, outdoor scenes like old prints and interiors that use and blend colour – gold, turquoise and blood-red against sullen backgrounds – in masterly style.

Warlords of Atlantis ○
1978, US, 96 mins, colour
Dir: Kevin Connor
Stars: Doug McClure, Peter Gilmore
Rating: ★★

The fourth, least likely and probably most colourful adventure film from the John Dark/Kevin Connor team (who made the *Time Forgot* movies). Again, its chief attribute is the monsters created by Roger Dicken. The story is laughable, but the effects better than ever and the film, crammed with action, should appeal both to the young and the young at heart.

Warning Shot ○
1967, US, 95 mins, colour
Dir: Buzz Kulik
Stars: David Janssen, Eleanor Parker, George Sanders, Joan Collins
Rating: ★★★

This big police thriller was David Janssen's reward for doing so well on *The Fugitive*. It casts him as a dedicated law officer accused of murder. Good supporting performances from Eleanor Parker and Lillian Gish, in a corker of a plot. Janssen and Keenan Wynn play off well against each other as police partners. A few years later, they repeated the partnership, this time as truckers, in an excellent TV movie, *Hijack*.

War of the Roses, The ● ⓥ
1989, US, 111 mins, colour
Dir: Danny DeVito
Stars: Michael Douglas, Kathleen Turner, Danny DeVito, Marianne Sagebrecht
Rating: ★★★★

A truly vicious black comedy about a divorce that escalates into a war. The story of the Roses (Michael Douglas and Kathleen Turner) is told as a cautionary tale by a megabuck lawyer (Danny DeVito) to a divorce-bent client. As DeVito points out: 'When a $450-an-hour lawyer advises you for nothing, you'd better listen.' The problem with the Roses is that they really have nothing in common but sex. The cracks soon star to appear, aggravated by the husband's stifling of his wife's individuality and undermining her confidence. What follows, although perhaps over the top, is a horrifying lesson to us all and pretty good entertainment as well. Turner, Douglas and DeVito are all good, DeVito especially, and the later action, as the Roses go for the jugular in a house of horrors, is staged with the appropriate touch of *Grand Guignol* by DeVito himself, doubling as director.

War of the Wildcats ○
(aka: In Old Oklahoma)
1943, US, 102 mins, b/w
Dir: Albert S Rogell
Stars: John Wayne, Martha Scott, Albert Dekker
Rating: ★★

The wildcats of the title are oil-drilling pioneers, with John Wayne and Albert Dekker as rivals in the oilfields of old Oklahoma. Songthrush Dale Evans, soon to marry cowboy star Roy Rogers and appear exclusively in his films, plays a character called Cuddles and gets to sing 'Put Your Arms Around Me, Honey'. Red-headed glamour star Rhonda Fleming is supposed to have made her debut in this film, but little if any of her role seems to have been left in the finished version. Lots of vigour, little subtlety.

War of the Worlds, The ① ⓥ
1953, US, 85 mins, colour
Dir: Byron Haskin
Stars: Gene Barry, Ann Robinson, Les Tremayne, Henry Bromdon, Jack Kruschen
Rating: ★★★

This film version of H G Wells' science fiction classic won an Academy Award for its special effects, and was justly acclaimed by the critics. The imaginative treatment by producer George Pal and director Byron Haskin does full justice to Wells' nightmare vision of an interplanetary war, and is full of telling little touches. If you are struggling to recognise the voice of the narrator – it belongs to Cedric Hardwicke. Vivid Technicolor is intelligently used at all times by camera chief George Barnes. The script is the only routine thing about this sci-fi sizzler.

Warpath ○
1951, US, 95 mins, colour
Dir: Byron Haskin
Stars: Edmond O'Brien, Dean Jagger, Forrest Tucker, Polly Bergen
Rating: ★★

A rousing Western on the revenge theme. The opening reel is, in fact, reminiscent of another Western, *Rancho Notorious*: the hero's fiancée is murdered by outlaws and he sets out to hunt them down. Edmond O'Brien is just fine in the central role, and there's lots of action against the Indians, after O'Brien joins the Cavalry in pursuit of his prey. Ray Rennahan's Technicolor photography paints an attractive background to the drama.

Warriors, The
See: Dark Avenger

War Wagon, The ○
1967, US, 101 mins, colour
Dir: Burt Kennedy
Stars: John Wayne, Kirk Douglas
Rating: ★★★

Here come John Wayne and Kirk Douglas as the fastest guns in the territory in a Western that sits well with such other big hits of the Sixties for Wayne as *The Comancheros* and *El Dorado*. Douglas is hired to kill Wayne, but you know he won't and soon the two are happily in harness against the hired guns. 'Mine hit the ground first!' claims Douglas as two of their enemies bite the dust. 'Huh,' grunts Wayne. 'Mine was taller.' Add Howard Keel, bizarrely cast as a renegade Redskin who calls his brethren 'dumb Indians' and a succulent cast of villains that includes Bruce Cabot, Bruce Dern and Gene Evans and you have a Western with humour that director Burt Kennedy keeps solidly and comfortably in the best traditions.

War Zone ● ⊙
1988, West Germany/Israel, 100 mins, colour
Dir: Nathaniel Gutman
Stars: Christopher Walken, Hywel Bennett
Rating: ★★★

War-torn cities infested with rival factions have always been popular locations for movie-makers and Beirut in the late 1980s was an obvious candidate. Taking advantage of its setting, this is quite a good little movie, fun of the sense of imminent danger. Christopher Walken contributes a thoughtful performance as the opportunistic American journalist dragged from the fireside comfort of 'reporting' with the help of old cassettes to a real-life interview with a Palestinian leader who wants to advocate diplomacy instead of violence. Or, is he being made a gullible dupe? In the end, Walken's Steven, forced by circumstance to become a real reporter, is as bewildered as he is involved. As an English reporter (Hywel Bennett) tells him: 'Here you don't kill who you want. You kill who you can.'

Watch It, Sailor! ○
1961, UK, 81 mins, b/w
Dir: Wolf Rilla
Stars: Dennis Price, Liz Fraser, Irene Handl, Frankie Howerd
Rating: ★★

Broad comedy about the world's most fearsome mother-in-law – no, not Peggy Mount but that similarly formidable lady, Marjorie Rhodes. John Meillon, now a distinguished and frequent performer in Australian film, is the lad who has to put up with Ma Rhodes if he wants to marry pretty Vera Day.

Watch Your Stem ○
1960, UK, 100 mins, b/w
Dir: Gerald Thomas
Stars: Kenneth Connor, Joan Sims
Rating: ★★

A broad but fairly rollicking British comedy produced by the *Carry On* team. Kenneth Connor stars as an Ordinary Seaman who is called upon to impersonate a scientist, summoned to help correct a top secret torpedo called The Creeper which has a disconcerting habit of returning to base when fired. Hectically involved are such other *Carry On* stalwarts as Sid James, Hattie Jacques and Joan Sims.

Water ◐
1985, UK, 95 mins, colour
Dir: Dick Clement
Stars: Michael Caine, Valerie Perrine, Brenda Vacarro, Leonard Rossiter, Billy Connolly, Maureen Lipman
Rating: ★★★

Although it has its share of embarrassing moments when things go over the top, this throwback to Ealing comedies has more funny lines than most British comedies of the previous decade put together. The setting is Cascara, a very small British island in the Caribbean (its features include Desolation Bay, Point Peril and Calamity Cove and it has no beaches) where the local industry is largely confined to the governor's (Michael Caine) cultivation of marijuana. The British government, led by Leonard Rossiter as a ministerial buffoon under the lash of a superb impersonation of Margaret Thatcher by Maureen Lipman, decides to evacuate Cascara and turn it into the rubbish-tip of the Empire. Meanwhile an oil company has struck mineral water, exciting the local rebels led by Billy Connolly wielding a guitar. Pretty dotty all round, but with some very good one-liners, including a scandalous put-down of Mahatma Gandhi by Lipman's Thatcher.

Water Babies, The ⊙
1978, UK, 92 mins, colour
Dir: Lionel Jeffries
Stars: James Mason, Billie Whitelaw,

Tommy Pender
Rating: ★★

Not as successful as *The Railway Children*, which was actor Lionel Jefffies' first stab at directing, this charming story is part-animated. The Polish animation is not particularly inspired but the performances of James Mason, Bernard Cribbins and Billie Whitelaw are some compensation. Young children will be entertained, but anyone over eight years may be less than gripped.

Waterdance, The ● ⊙
1991, US, 106 mins, colour
Dir: Neal Jimenez, Michael Steinberg
Stars: Eric Stoltz, Wesley Snipes, Helen Hunt, William Forsythe, Elizabeth Pena
Rating: ★★

'Good thing we're already paralysed,' gasps one of the escaping paraplegics, as they break out of their 'rehab' hospital in an ambulance, and narrowly avoid an accident. The film could do with even more of this black humour, as it follows the forging friendships and sexual problems of the rather deliberately disparate residents of one particular ward. Eric Stoltz, portraying wheelchaired writer-director Neal Jimenez's alter ego (the film is partially autobiographical) isn't the strongest of leads, and one grows rather tired of him, but there are compensations in Helen Hunt, as his confused (and married) girlfriend, Wesley Snipes as the black philanderer whose wife refuses to stand by him and William Forsythe as the biker whose aggression hides a desire for macho friendship with his fellows. On the whole, a worthy addition to the cinema's studies of the disabled and their attempts to come to terms with what life now holds.

Waterland ● ⊙
1992, UK, 93 mins, colour
Dir: Stephen Gyllenhaal
Stars: Jeremy Irons, Sinead Cusack, Ethan Hawke, John Heard, Grant Warnock
Rating: ★

A sad tale in more ways than one. This picturesquely set nostalgia piece is tedious when it should be poignant and, though it has some original ideas, doesn't weld them together in such a way as to glue us to its story. Jeremy Irons play a professor of history with a wife whose mind is cracking under the strain of the memories of their collective past. As bored as his American pupils with the routine of the classroom, Irons begins telling them about his own past life in the East Anglian

W

fenlands of England. Unfortunately, this is almost entirely concerned with sex and incest and has so little story content that it would surely send most American children to sleep.

Waterloo ○ ⓥ
1970, Italy/Russia, 132 mins, colour
Dir: Sergei Bondarchuk
Stars: Rod Steiger, Christopher Plummer, Orson Welles, Virginia McKenna, Jack Hawkins
Rating: ★★

An enormously expensive epic, culminating in an hour-long battle scene. Unexpectedly, it's Christopher Plummer's Wellington who steals the attention, and the acting honours, from Rod Steiger's Napoleon, the one an understatement in suavity and wit, always cool and collected, the other all exaggeration, never stating anything simply where a whisper or a shout will do.

Watership Down ○ ⓥ
1978, UK, 92 mins, colour
Dir: Martin Rosen
Voice stars: John Hunt, Richard Briers, Ralph Richardson, Zero Mostel, Roy Kinnear, Denholm Elliott
Rating: ★★★

Red in tooth and claw (but not unsuitable for family viewing) this is an appropriately dark adaptation of Richard Adams' novel about an itinerant rabbit colony, tailored to the talents of an impressive voice cast whose characters tend to take on the identities of such familiar actors as John Hunt, Richard Briers, Ralph Richardson and Zero Mostel, whose seagull proves the liveliest character in the film. Older kids may get restless in the dull bits, but the action towards the end is genuinely nail-biting stuff and the animation of the rabbits amazing in its accuracy.

Waterworld ◑ ⓥ
1995, US, 135 mins, colour
Dir: Kevin Reynolds
Stars: Kevin Costner, Dennis Hopper, Jeanne Tripplehorn, Tina Majorino
Rating: ★★★

Mad Max afloat. It's all here – the hardware, the eccentric, often shaven villains, the frenzied chases on (sea) bikes and clapped-together planes and the hero, in this case the Mad Mariner (Kevin Costner). A loner with gills behind his ears and webbed feet, the Mariner sails a water-covered planet after its northern ice-cap has melted, in a craft whose gadgets would have taken an entire special effects unit to build, let alone the Mad Mariner. The

credibility problem of all this wouldn't matter too much if the film had kept up the blazing action of its first half hour, a ferocious siege of an atoll (floating town) by smokers – high-tech pirates led by a grinning Dennis Hopper who lends some personality to the film and deserves its few bright lines. 'Don't just stand there,' he exhorts his henchman, 'Kill something.' This hardly looks like a $200 million production, but its action above and below water continues at just frequent enough bursts to keep action fans happy.

Watusi ○
1958, US, 85 mins, colour
Dir: Kurt Neumann
Stars: George Montgomery, David Farrar
Rating: ★★

MGM go back to their old hunting grounds in this sequel to *King Solomon's Mines* but don't quite strike the same riches. George Montgomery, David Farrar and Taina Elg see the thrills along in fair enough fashion, but some of the dialogue seems a little tarnished and the stampede of wild animals had already begun to outlive its function as a useful plot element. Against this, James Clavell's screenplay rightly brooks no interruption from side issues and Harold E Wellman's lush Technicolor photography is well above average for jungle melodrama.

Wayne's World ○ ⓥ
1992, US, 95 mins, colour
Dir: Penelope Spheeris
Stars: Mike Myers, Dana Carvey, Rob Lowe, Tia Carrere
Rating: ★★★

Or: Wayne and Garth's Excellent Adventures. The shades of *Bill and Ted* ride again in this endearingly silly tale of two all-American goofballs who broadcast a weekly cable TV show from the basement of a private house. Major networks reach out for them in the shape of all-American slimebag Rob Lowe, but – surprise, dudes! Wayne and Garth not only refuse to conform, but even tack their own ending on the film when it looks as though Lowe is going to snatch Wayne's singer girlfriend (Tia Carrere). Carrere is a stunning-looking Eurasian girl who can really sing and darned nearly steals this idiot's delight of a show. The fun could have been more sustained, but party-on-ers will find it quite excellent anyway.

Wayne's World 2 ○ ⓥ
1993, US, 95 mins, colour
Dir: Stephen Sudik

Stars: Mike Myers, Dana Carvey, Tia Carrere, Christopher Walken
Rating: ★★

Partied out, guys: *Wayne's World 2* has little of the freshness which made the original so endearingly amusing, and only one really funny scene – when Wayne and his friends break into an impromptu version of 'YMCA' when trapped in a gay club by bad guy Christopher Walken. Mike Myers mugs madly as Wayne. Dana Carvey's Garth comes on as a wizened Norman Wisdom and is forced to act out a coy sex comedy with Kim Basinger in scenes which embarrass both of them. Spotting guest stars like Basinger, Drew Barrymore and Charlton Heston is, though, more fun than most of the script, which involves Wayne trying to organise a vast pop concert called Waynestock in which everyone proves supremely disinterested. It's all harmless fun, but here's a cult that was definitely on the Wayne.

Way Out, The
See: Dial 999

Way Out West ⊙ ⓥ
1937, US, 65 mins, b/w
Dir: James Horne
Stars: Stan Laurel, Oliver Hardy
Rating: ★★★★★

Laurel and Hardy classic that is probably most people's favourite. Stan and Ollie go to Brushwood Gulch to deliver the deed to a goldmine, do the most famous of their dances, sing 'Trail of the Lonesome Pine' and have riotous encounters with a mudhole, Jimmy Finlayson and a mule, in that order. Packed with comic gems and splendidly idiotic Laurel one-liners. 'What did he die of?' he's asked. 'I think he died of a Tuesday,' says Stan.

Way to the Stars, The ○
(aka: Johnny in the Clouds)
1945, UK, 109 mins, b/w
Dir: Anthony Asquith
Stars: Michael Redgrave, John Mills, Rosamund John
Rating: ★★★★★

Crafted with typical British understatement, and exquisitely structured, this is one of the greatest war films from any country. As well as a string of fine performances from such familiar names as Michael Redgrave, Trevor Howard and John Mills, and a sensitive one from the American Douglass Montgomery (whose film career was over before the decade was out), the film contains early appearances by Jean

Simmons and Bill Owen (here billed under his real name, Bill Rowbotham). Anthony Asquith's direction is inspired, and the story is greatly enhanced by the poetry of John Pudney and the uplifting music by Nicholas Brodzsky.

Way West, The O
1967, US, 122 mins, colour
Dir: Andrew V McLaglen
Stars: Kirk Douglas, Robert Mitchum, Richard Widmark, Sally Field
Rating: ★★

Epic Western about a wagon train of pioneers bound from Missouri to Oregon. Robert Mitchum plays Dick, the taciturn scout who leads them over hazard after hazard, including one massive cliff. 'D'you think we could maybe go round, Dick?' asks one of the emigrants. They don't, of course, which results in some breathtaking excitement. Good performances by the trio of masculine stars are supplemented by those of leading lady Lola Albright and well-known featured players including William Lundigan, Jack Elam and Harry Carey Jr. Adding lustre is the breathtaking sweep of William Clothier's glorious photography.

Way We Were, The O ⓥ
1973, US, 118 mins, colour
Dir: Sydney Pollack
Stars: Barbra Streisand, Robert Redford, Bradford Dillman, Viveca Lindfors
Rating: ★★

This superstar tearjerker chronicles the romance – from the late Thirties to the early Fifties – between two irreconcilable opposites. She is Barbra Streisand, outspoken, aggressive Jewish activist; he is Robert Redford, the all-American, golden-haired college boy who becomes a successful novelist and then goes to Hollywood as a screenwriter. The movie equivalent of a good read, it's fascinating to see how expertly director Sydney Pollack succeeds in making the stars' very different acting styles – Streisand's vigour and Redford's shallow reliance on his good looks – work so well together. The title song took one of the film's two Oscars.

Web, The O
1947, US, 87 mins, b/w
Dir: Michael Gordon
Stars: Edmond O'Brien, William Bendix, Vincent Price
Rating: ★★★

Typical *film noir* of the post-war years, more shadow and style than substance, but given strength by the powerful ensemble playing of a personable cast.

Edmond O'Brien, Vincent Price, Ella Raines and William Bendix have the leads. But shifty John Abbott and dependable Fritz Leiber also enjoy two of their juiciest roles. It's thanks to the personalities involved that this is a satisfying thriller.

Wedding Bells
See: Royal Wedding

Wedding Breakfast
See: The Catered Affair

We Dive at Dawn O ⓥ
1943, UK, 92 mins, b/w
Dir: Anthony Asquith
Stars: Eric Portman, John Mills
Rating: ★★★★

Not quite as well-known as some classic British war films, this is a clever and claustrophobic study in mounting excitement, focusing first on the shore-leave lives of the crew of a submarine, then on their secret mission to torpedo a Nazi battleship before she can reach the Kiel Canal. John Mills and Eric Portman are excellent and the original script was re-tailored (very tightly) by Frank Launder. Launder remembered in more recent times that the Royal Navy had decided the screenplay 'lacked authenticity'and he found himself despatched to a submarine base to gather first-hand knowledge. Here Launder was lucky enough to meet a submarine officer with writing talent, who wrote a rough draft of the final attack sequence 'most authentically with a lot of human touches'. In the end, neither Launder nor the officer received official screen credit!

Weekend at Bernie's ◐ ⓥ
1989, US, 97 mins, colour
Dir: Ted Kotcheff
Stars: Andrew McCarthy, Jonathan Silverman, Catherine Mary Stewart
Rating: ★★★

It's party time at Bernie's beach house, but the host is late. Murdered that is. But the world refuses to admit that Bernie has passed away, and life goes on as before. Naturally his first guests (Andrew McCarthy, Jonathan Silverman) should report the corpse to the cops, but when they cop a look at Bernie's weekend lifestyle, they decide to delay matters just a wee while. The problem is that, in creating the impression that Bernie's alive, they fool the departing killer (a sort of demented Ken Dodd) as well. All this makes for a jolly, occasionally over-energetic jape with some fast and furious fun towards

the end, and a staggering performance as Bernie by Terry Kiser who, through thick and thin, never bats an eyelid. They should strike a special Oscar for best supporting stiff. A disappointing sequel followed in 1994.

Weekend with Lulu, A O
1961, UK, 91 mins, b/w
Dir: John Paddy Carstairs
Stars: Bob Monkhouse, Leslie Phillips, Shirley Eaton, Alfred Marks
Rating: ★★

Bob Monkhouse, Leslie Phillips and Alfred Marks mug furiously in the cause of comic entertainment in this breezy farce spiced with salty wisecracks and additionally decorated with such members of the *Carry On* team as Kenneth Connor and Sidney James. Irene Handl is wonderful as the interfering busybody who accompanies her daughter (Shirley Eaton) on what was supposed to be a romantic weekend, and then-popular Russ Conway pops up as a French pianist.

Weird Science ◐ ⓥ
1985, US, 94 mins, colour
Dir: John Hughes
Stars: Kelly LeBrock, Anthony Michael Hall, Ilan Mitchell-Smith, Robert Downey Jr, Bill Paxton
Rating: ★

Two high school no-hopers are unable to attract girls, so they decide to create one, with the help of a home computer, a Barbie doll and a fistful of centrefolds. What they end up with is Kelly LeBrock. Not bad for two physically unattractive and intellectually underdeveloped 15-year-olds. As is usual with such high-school high jinks, they then go on a series of adventures which involve getting drunk, driving fast cars and having wild and destructive parties. They also chase girls, despite having the sultry LeBrock in tow. Throw in some mutant bikers and LeBrock's unexplained magical powers and you end up with a confusing hotchpotch of asinine American schoolboy sex humour.

Welcome Home ◐ ⓥ
1989, US, 94 mins, colour
Dir: Franklin J Schaffner
Stars: Kris Kristofferson, JoBeth Williams, Sam Waterson, Trey Wilson, Brian Keith, Thomas Wilson Brown
Rating: ★★

Pretty well every complication you could imagine about a 'missing' serviceman returning home after 17 years in Vietnam and Cambodia is tossed into this script. Kris Kristofferson has every reason to look troubled as he's first parted from his Cambodian wife and child (later learning she's died), then in hot water with the US government, and finally finds that his wife at home gave birth to his son before remarrying. Of course, he has to see them, and of course everything isn't explained to anyone before they meet the man returned from the dead. Rather than adding anything to the drama, this tends to make it slow and ponderous. But the sheer nature of the story occasionally helps director Franklin J Schaffner achieve some affecting moments from what was his last film. Teenager Thomas Wilson Brown, quite apart from not being very good, is a generically unlikely result of Kristofferson and JoBeth Williams' union.

Welcome to Hard Times ◐
(aka: Killer on a Horse)
1966, US, 105 mins, colour
Dir: Burt Kennedy
Stars: Henry Fonda, Janice Rule, Keenan Wynn, Janis Page
Rating: ★★

Welcome indeed to this fascinating mixture of the psychological, symbol-laden Western and the basic cowboy action yarn. Henry Fonda (aged 62) is exactly right as a leading citizen of the rundown town of Hard Times who at first doesn't stand up to crazed gunman Aldo Ray (wonderfully wicked). Written and directed by Burt Kennedy from a novel by E L Doctorow (author of *Ragtime*). And just look at that support cast: Warren Oates, Edgar Buchanan, Lon Chaney, Elisha Cook.

Welcome To L.A. ●
1976, US, 106 mins, colour
Dir: Alan Rudolph
Stars: Keith Carradine, Sally Kellerman, Geraldine Chaplin, Harvey Keitel
Rating: ★★

A cinema curiosity made by Alan Rudolph, a disciple of Robert Altman. It turns out to be a kind of tragi-comic *La Ronde*, set against the free-living music business of Los Angeles. Keith Carradine has the central role of the composer back in LA for the recording of a pop cantata he has composed. Despite (or perhaps) because of a goatee beard and a deerstalker hat, he hardly displays the charisma one would have thought necessary to attract such personable ladies as Sally Kellerman, Sissy Spacek, Geraldine Chaplin, Diahann Abbott, Viveca Lindfors and Lauren Hutton into his bed.

Went the Day Well ○ ⓥ
(aka: 48 Hours)
1942, UK, 92 mins, b/w
Dir: Alberto Cavalcanti
Stars: Leslie Banks, Basil Sydney, Frank Lawton, Elizabeth Allan
Rating: ★★★

Intriguing Ealing Studios wartime film, somewhat akin to the later *It Happened Here*. The theme – not surprisingly the subject of a few outcries in its time – was the infiltration of an English village by a group of Nazis. Thora Hird plays a land-girl and briefly glimpsed is her real-life toddler daughter Janette Scott.

We're No Angels ○
1954, US, 106 mins, colour
Dir: Michael Curtiz
Stars: Humphrey Bogart, Aldo Ray, Peter Ustinov, Joan Bennett
Rating: ★★★★

A really exquisite comedy which gives Humphrey Bogart a rare chance to lean to the lighter side, as one of three French convicts on the run from Devil's Island, who choose to sort out the problems of some friends in their own way. Most of the screenplay's gems go to Peter Ustinov, as a rolypoly convict who pretends to be straitlaced, but covets secret memories of the flesh-pots of Marseilles. There's also a pearl of a performance from Basil Rathbone as the ruthless cousin of the nice family with whom the jailbirds are hiding.

We're No Angels ◐ ⓥ
1989, US, 106 mins, colour
Dir: Neil Jordan
Stars: Robert De Niro, Sean Penn, Demi Moore, Hoyt Axton, Bruno Kirby, Ray McAnally
Rating: ★★

Based – but only in theme – on the Bogart film of 1954, this romp gives Robert De Niro and Sean Penn a chance to play for laughs as two (unwillingly) escaped convicts in 1935 who, in the course of attempting to flee to Canada, disguise themselves as priests and gradually become involved in affairs at the Sanctuary of the Weeping Virgin. De Niro mugs ferociously in his worst film performance to date, but Penn is better and Demi Moore excellent as a rough-tongued single mum. The film itself is not too bad when not straining for laughs, though the violence at the beginning is a bit excessive for a comedy. The last 20 minutes, though, do score with a good blend of laughs, sentiment and thrills, and show the virtue of playing comedy straight, as opposed to the strenuous facial contor-

tions employed by De Niro and Penn for much of the film.

WereWolf of London ◐
1935, US, 75 mins, b/w
Dir: Stuart Walker
Stars: Henry Hull, Valerie Hobson, Warner Oland
Rating: ★★★

The first Hollywood film centred totally round the idea of a man who became a werewolf at the time of the full moon, this predated the famous wolf man series by six years. Although the first transmogrification of man into werewolf is achieved by having the character pass behind a series of heavy pillars, the acting by Henry Hull fills one with sympathy for the plight of the good doctor afflicted with the curse of the werewolf . The photography, especiafly in the moonlit sequences, is reminiscent of the best of the great pre-war German films, and altogether this little-known horror film is one to catch if you can.

Wes Craven's New Nightmare ● ⓥ
1994, US, 112 mins, colour
Dir: Wes Craven
Stars: Robert Englund, Heather Langenkamp, Miko Hughes, David Newsom, John Saxon, Wes Craven
Rating: ★★★★

Round seven: and Freddy Krueger, the nightmare-dwelling child-killer, invades the lives and dreams of the actors who made the first film (even Robert Englund's) in an ingenious variation on the original theme. There are lots of good in-jokes, a dire warning against letting children watch video nasties, and a sterling performance by Heather Langenkamp, as her Freddy-based self, that ought to win her a wider range of roles. Trust Wes Craven (who also plays himself, along with John Saxon and others) to make something more inventive and applaudable than any of the other five sequels. Heather's husband is killed and Freddy attempts to return via the sleep of her son, until he is unwise enough to take Heather on in a dreamworld finale. Mothers protecting their offspring, as anyone who has seen *Poltergeist* will testify, are fearsome opponents. It's pulsating stuff with good intentional giggles, all the way.

Westbound ○
1959, US, 72 mins, colour
Dir: Budd Boetticher
Stars: Randolph Scott, Virginia Mayo
Rating: ★★★

Director Budd Boetticher has a rather overinflated cult reputation, but his Westerns with Randolph Scott were always better than their second-feature status. This is one of the best of the bunch, pacy and attractively photographed by J Peverell Marley and with a commanding performance by the star as a Northern captain trying to keep gold deliveries running by stage from California during the Civil War. Look out for Australian actor Michael Pate, who, after a sturdy career in Hollywood, often playing Indians, returned Down Under to become a surprisingly good producer and director.

Westerner, The O
1940, US, 100 mins, b/w
Dir: William Wyler
Stars: Gary Cooper, Walter Brennan, Doris Davenport
Rating: ★★★

This outdoor epic about a range war gave Gary Cooper one of the best of his strong, laconic roles as the drifter caught between opposing factions. A shrewd piece of villainy as judge Roy Bean brought Walter Brennan's total of 'best supporting actor' Oscars up to three.

West of Zanzibar O
1954, UK, 94 mins, colour
Dir: Harry Watt
Stars: Anthony Steel, Sheila Sim
Rating: ★★

Sequel to the 1951 Royal Film Performance movie *Where No Vultures Fly*, retaining the same director and producer, Harry Watts and Leslie Norman, and having Anthony Steel once again as the game warden Bob Payton. He shares the Hollywood hero's ability to come through the most vicious fight with no more than a spotless handkerchief tied around one bulging bicep.

West Point Story, The O
(aka: Fine and Dandy)
1950, US, 107 mins, b/w
Dir: Roy Del Ruth
Stars: James Cagney, Virginia Mayo, Gordon MacRae, Doris Day, Gene Nelson, Alan Hale Jr
Rating: ★★

Bright, breezy backstage musical which gave James Cagney his first song-and-dance role since his great success in *Yankee Doodle Dandy*. The plot is the old stand-by about the two partners who come together again. But a star-studded cast, including Doris Day in

one of her very early musical roles, does it more than justice. A pity it's in black and white.

West Side Story O ⓥ
1961, US, 151 mins, colour
Dir: Robert Wise, Jerome Robbins
Stars: Natalie Wood, Richard Beymer, George Chakiris, Rita Moreno, Russ Tamblyn
Rating: ★★★★

The dazzling and devastating dancing set new standards for the film musical in this wildly successful transition of Leonard Bernstein's stage musical to the screen. George Chakiris and Rita Moreno were never sharper and their performances won them two of the film's 10 Oscars, which also included best film and best director for Robert Wise. As the star-crossed lovers, Natalie Wood and Richard Beymer do touching work in this New York ghetto update of *Romeo and Juliet*, even if their singing voices belonged to other people. And the tragic finale will leave few eyes dry: such emotive moments in musicals are rare indeed. Prepare to be both moved and exhilarated.

Westward Ho, the Wagons O
1956, US, 90 mins, colour
Dir: William Beaudine
Stars: Fess Parker, Kathleen Crowley, Jeff York
Rating: ★★

This lightweight Western looks great, thanks to impressive Technicolor photography, but generates very little tension and excitement. Fess *(Davy Crockett)* Parker is our firm-jawed hero, but this Walt Disney view of the West is sanitised even by the standards of the 1950s. Doc Grayson (Parker) is a scout helping a wagon train on its way to Oregon which meets both hostile and friendly Indians en route. Even the well staged action scenes, created by second-unit director Yakima Canutt, aren't enough to lift this bland pioneer saga.

Westward Passage O
1932, US, 73 mins, b/w
Dir: Robert Milton
Stars: Ann Harding, Laurence Olivier
Rating: ★★

A lightweight romance with Ann Harding and Laurence Olivier as the two young lovebirds. Olivier is a poverty-stricken, struggling author, but his love for Harding sustains him through the hard times. They marry, have a child and get on with life. But as time goes by, his patience wears thin

and the marriage breaks up. Harding marries again on the rebound... but that's not the last twist in a story that, although prone to be overly theatrical at times, does manage to engage and entertain the whole way through.

Westward the Women O
1951, US, 118 mins, b/w
Dir: William Wellman
Stars: Robert Taylor, Denise Darcel, Henry Nakamura
Rating: ★★★

This story of 140 women bound for California through Indian country is vintage MGM action. And they had the ideal director in William Wellman, a devoted chronicler of the west who already had two classic Westerns, The *Ox-Bow Incident*, from 1942, and *Yellow Sky*, from 1948, to his name.

Westworld O ⓥ
1973, US, 89 mins, colour
Dir: Michael Crichton
Stars: Yul Brynner, Richard Benjamin, James Brolin
Rating: ★★★★

Director Michael *(Jurassic Park)* Crichton's sci-fi thriller about robots in a futuristic theme park running out of control comes across as suprisingly fresh considering the basic idea of the tale wasn't new even then. The robot-turning-on-its-master theme goes right back to Fritz Lang's *Metropolis*. With *Westworld*, though, Crichton has created an entirely believable scenario which makes the whole thing pretty frightening. Yul Brynner is chilling as the android gunslinger who can't be gunned down and who inexorably pursues resort guests Richard Benjamin and James Brolin. Fast-moving and exciting – and you get the feeling that it all so easily could happen.

Wetherby ●
1985, UK, 97 mins, colour
Dir: David Hare
Stars: Vanessa Redgrave, Ian Holm, Judi Dench
Rating: ★

What really happened in a Yorkshire town to cause a young man to blow his brains out? Director David Hare's screenplay will certainly keep you guessing in all the wrong ways, its elliptical dialogue has the characters uttering disconnected phrases like unrelated sections of a Pinter play. There's a touching performance by Joely Richardson, daughter of the film's star, Vanessa Redgrave.

W

Whales of August, The ○ Ⓥ
1987, US, 90 mins, colour
Dir: Lindsay Anderson
Stars: Bette Davis, Lillian Gish, Vincent Price
Rating: ★★★★★

This is a little gem about two elderly sisters living on an island off the coast of New England. Not only is Lindsay Anderson to be congratulated on directing his best film in quite a while, but in achieving the almost impossible in getting legends Gish and Davis to play the sisters. Gish edges out her rival by a whisker with her intuitive warmth, but that isn't to say Davis doesn't have some striking, subtle and emotive moments. Also good are Ann Sothern, as the well-meaning lifelong friend of the sisters and Vincent Price as the Russian emigré who tries to batten on to the sisters before confessing that 'I have spent my life visiting friends.' Full of poignant moments, the film has an ending that is certain to have you on the verge of tears. Gish is simply a marvel, Davis as cantankerously indomitable as ever. Together, they carve out a memorable movie memorial in roles for once worthy of their own greatness.

What About Bob? ○ Ⓥ
1991, US, 99 mins, colour
Dir: Frank Oz
Stars: Bill Murray, Richard Dreyfuss, Julie Hagerty, Charlie Korsmo
Rating: ★★★★

This is the one about the psychiatric patient who proves so persistent that he finally drives the psychiatrist nuts. Bob (Bill Murray) is a walking nightmare who has a phobia about touching things and going places, and thinks his bladder is about to explode. Leo (Richard Dreyfuss) is a shrink wallowing in self-control, self-satisfaction and self-glory who sees all three gradually disintegrate when Bob pursues him to his holiday home by a New Hampshire lake. The trouble with Bob is not that he's dangerous, just that he won't go away. Delightfully manic performances from Murray and Dreyfuss help us forget that this is little more than an anecdote, and keep us happily chuckling towards the climax, and Leo's last desperate attempt to send Bob where he feels he belongs – eternity.

What a Carve-Up! ○ Ⓥ
(aka: Home Sweet Homicide)
1961, UK, 88 mins, b/w

Dir: Pat Jackson
Stars: Kenneth Connor, Sidney James
Rating: ★★★

Although it begins and ends weakly, this comedy-chiller is great fun as long as it's going at full throttle, which is most of the time once Kenneth Connor and Sidney James have arrived at spooky Blackshaw Towers for the reading of Connor's uncle's will. Supposedly based on *The Ghoul* (filmed straight in the Thirties with Boris Karloff, but owing more to another Karloff starrer, *The Old Dark House*), this is fast and furious fun, thanks to Pat Jackson's inventive direction and the straight-faced playing of a supporting cast that includes Shirley Eaton, Dennis Price, Michael Gough and Donald Pleasence. Any subtlety in British comedy in the early Sixties was as unexpected as it was welcome.

What a Man!
See: Never Give a Sucker an Even Break

What a Way to Go! ○
1964, US, 145 mins, colour
Dir: J Lee-Thompson
Stars: Shirley MacLaine, Paul Newman, Dean Martin, Robert Mitchum
Rating: ★★

Shirley MacLaine stars in this frivolity as Louisa, an unwittingly lethal lady. Much of the fun in this colourful, star-studded romp lies in waiting to see how Louisa's various husbands meet their doom. Funniest of all is probably Gene Kelly, as a dancer who gets trampled to death by his own fans. There's also Dean Martin, Robert Mitchum, Bob Cummings, Dick Van Dyke and Reginald Gardiner to watch for, not to mention the Marx Brothers' great foil Margaret Dumont.

What Ever Happened to Baby Jane? ◑ Ⓥ
1962, US, 132 mins, b/w
Dir: Robert Aldrich
Stars: Bette Davis, Joan Crawford
Rating: ★★★★

Robert Aldrich's classic of the chilly grotesque, with Bette Davis and Joan Crawford a convincingly gruesome twosome as ex-silent stars living together – and hating each other – in a gloomy mansion.

What Price Glory? ○ Ⓥ
1952, US, 111 mins, colour
Dir: John Ford
Stars: James Cagney, Dan Dailey
Rating: ★★

John Ford's remake of the raucous army comedy about a feuding officer and sergeant, previously filmed by Victor McLaglen and Edmund Lowe (who made a whole series out of it) but here with James Cagney and Dan Dailey. The honours are quietly sneaked from them, though, by Robert Wagner and Marisa Pavan as young lovers.

What's Eating Gilbert Grape ◑ Ⓥ
1993, US, 117 mins, colour
Dir: Lasse Hallstrom
Stars: Johnny Depp, Juliette Lewis, Leonardo Di Caprio, Mary Steenburgen, Kevin Tighe
Rating: ★★★

Johnny Depp continues to make the oddest films. Hollywood's Mr Solemn followed *Edward Scissorhands* and *Benny & Joon* with this sweet-natured but rather slow goofball of a film that casts him as the senior son in a decidedly different rural household. Father hanged himself and mother has ballooned to 35 stone. There are two sisters but it's Gilbert (Depp) who's responsible for the safe keeping of his 17-year-old mentally handicapped brother Arnie (a miraculous performance by Leonardo Di Caprio that was Oscar nominated). Gilbert is also having an affair with a housewife (Mary Steenburgen) that is until strange new girl Becky (Juliette Lewis) blows into town in her granny's trailer. Yes, this is odd all right, but so haltingly paced that your attention wanders. Yet its heart's in the right place, and you may remember these characters longer than those from your average mainline movie. Though you may have trouble digesting it all, in fact, there are no sour grapes here.

What's New Pussycat? ◑ Ⓥ
1965, US, 108 mins, colour
Dir: Clive Donner
Stars: Peter Sellers, Peter O'Toole, Romy Schneider, Woody Allen
Rating: ★★★

Definitely the kinkiest comedy of its year, *Pussycat* has a screenplay by Woody Allen that varies from sheer smut to sheer genius and casts Peter O'Toole as a playboy journalist who's irresistible to women – whose clothes come apart at his touch. As he, too, is coming apart at the seams, he consults Peter Sellers – a long-haired Viennese psychiatrist who's more of a couch case than he is. Sellers' trouble is the reverse of O'Toole's, in that he attacks women on sight – and they scream in terror. (Funny? Well, it is the way Sellers plays it.) All, that is, except his mountainous wife. 'Pretty?' he asks her. 'I am prettier than you!' Sellers is highly comical, so is Paula Prentiss when given the chance. Edra Gale does Sellers' Wagner-spouting wife to a hilarious T.

What's the Matter with Helen? ●
1971, US, 101 mins, colour
Dir: Curtis Harrington
Stars: Debbie Reynolds, Shelley Winters, Dennis Weaver
Rating: ★★★

Another expert chiller from Curtis Harrington. This one, with its echoes of *Whatever Happened to Baby Jane?* is (very well) set in the Thirties and lavishly photographed in colour by Lucien Ballard. Debbie Reynolds (very good) and Shelley Winters (somewhat over the top) play two middle-aged ladies on the run from their past which, naturally, catches up with them, preying on their sanity as Harrington steers the story skilfully to a bravura climax.

What's UP Doc? ○ ⓥ
1972, US, 94 mins, colour
Dir: Peter Bogdanovich
Stars: Barbra Streisand, Ryan O'Neal
Rating: ★★★

Director Peter Bogdanovich's tribute to those great screwball comedies of the Thirties - a sort-of remake of the Katharine Hepburn-Cary Grant classic *Bringing Up Baby*. And pretty funny it is, too, with Barbara Streisand doing what she does best - being funny in a loveable, uncomplicated way, and singing too - and some hilarious chase sequences involving split-second timing such as we haven't seen since Mack Sennett's days.

What's Up, Tiger Lily? ○
1966, US, 80 mins, colour
Dir: Senkichi Taniguchi
Stars: Tatsua Mihashi, Mie Hama, Akiko Wakabayashi, Tadeo Nakamuru, Susumu Kurobe, Woody Allen
Rating: ★★

Woody Allen has taken a disastrous Japanese comedy-thriller in the James Bond vein and spoofed it up with dubbed American dialogue that bears no relation to what the oriental actors are saying. Thus fights are punctuated by cries of 'Roman cow!', 'Russian snake!', 'Spartan dog!', 'Spanish fly!' or 'Turkish taffy!' There are a dozen good chuckles here, but one is left with a sneaking suspicion that the original might have been (unintentionally) even funnier.

When a Man Loves a Woman ● ⓥ
1994, US, 126 mins, colour
Dir: Luis Mandoki
Stars: Meg Ryan, Andy Garcia, Lauren Tom, Ellen Burstyn, Tina Majorino
Rating: ★★

This gruelling romantic drama about an alcoholic wife certainly does go on a bit at 126 minutes - with the aid of far too many pop songs on the soundtrack. Even so, it still barely manages to scratch the surface of its subject: Meg Ryan does quite well with her big speeches, but Andy Garcia struggles as much with his role as his character does to come to temis with his wife's problem. They both annoy you that they're making their own paths so difficult - but then, if they didn't, we certainly wouldn't have a two-hour film. For an alcohol drama that really cuts deep, though, *Clean and Sober* is a better bet.

When a Stranger Calls ● ⓥ
1979, US, 97 mins, colour
Dir: Fred Walton
Stars: Charles Durning, Carol Kane, Tony Beckley, Rachel Roberts
Rating: ★★

After carefully building up a palpable sense of claustrophobic tension in its lengthy opening sequence, this babysitter-in-peril thriller goes somewhat off the rails by concentrating on the psychopath's inconclusive relationships with a psychiatrist and a female barfly. Good to see that valuable character actor Charles Durning centre stage for once, even if his role of a vengeance-driven detective isn't particularly rewarding.

When Dinosaurs Ruled the Earth ◐
1969, UK, 100 mins, colour
Dir: Val Guest
Stars: Victoria Vetri, Robin Hawdon
Rating: ★

The visual effects are predictably the best things in this prehistoric potboiler. The bronzed Victoria Vetri, once better-known under her real name, Angela Dodan, is an excellent physical successor to Raquel Welch, star of Hammer's previous extravaganza *One Million Years BC*. The men behind the monsters include Roger Dicken, who subsequently created those in The *Land That Time Forgot*.

When Eight Bells Toll ○ ⓥ
1971, UK, 94 mins, colour
Dir: Etienne Perier

Stars: Anthony Hopkins, Jack Hawkins, Robert Morley
Rating: ★★★

As usual with Alistair MacLean's thrillers, there are no unnecessary embellishments to this rousing story of bullion robbers off the coast of Scotland. It's just scenery and action and plenty of both. However, there's a good role for Robert Morley, who's in splendid form as an Intelligence boss whose major worry lies in the fact that the chief suspect may be on his club's wine committee. The character of Philip Calvert gives Anthony Hopkins a rare straightforward leading man role.

When Harry Met Sally. . . ● ⓥ
1989, US, 95 mins, colour
Dir: Rob Reiner
Stars: Billy Crystal, Meg Ryan, Carrie Fisher, Bruno Kirby
Rating: ★★★

This offbeat romantic comedy is rather protracted but kept afloat by some very good individual lines. Billy Crystal and Meg Ryan play the couple for whom (at college) it's indifference at first sight. This mutual non-attraction is followed by an on-off 12-year period as friends despite his assertion that 'Men and women can't be merely friends, because sex always gets in the way.' He's right in this case, of course, and we know it too, but Nora Ephron's script makes it worthwhile staying the course to see the maxim proved. Crystal, Ryan, Bruno Kirby and especially Carrie Fisher are all fine, and Ryan's famous 'fake orgasm' scene in a restaurant remains the funniest thing in the film.

When I Fall In Love ●
(aka: Everybody's All American)
1989, US, 127 mins, colour
Dir: Taylor Hackford
Stars: Jessica Lange, Dennis Quaid, Timothy Hutton, John Goodman
Rating: ★

Despite solid (if not great) performances from a good cast, practically everything else is wrong with this down-the-years story of embattlement and disillusionment. Direction, script and treatment (including too-dark camera work) all make the narrative far too fragmentary and never dig below the surface to stir our emotions - or those of the characters. Dennis Quaid is the star footballer whose life and career gradually but surely go down the tubes. He's the best thing in the film, although somewhat mysteriously sec-

W

ond-billed below Jessica Lange, who doesn't give much to the role of the cheer-leader who becomes his wife. Quaid's appearance at the end – bloated, thick-limbed and near alcoholic is brilliant, but, even with his enthusiasm for the role, the storyline never holds your attention for more than a minute or two.

When Knights Were Bold O
1936, UK, 75 mins, b/w
Dir: Jack Raymond
Stars: Jack Buchanan, Fay Wray, Garry Marsh, Moore Marriott
Rating: ★★

Thirties tomfoolery along the lines of a British *A Yankee at King Arthur's Court* with Jack Buchanan as the man who imagines himself back in the Middle Ages after a suit of armour fails on him. Buchanan is allowed his usual polished tap-dance and warbles a tune or two, and the film is fun to be with, especially when Moore Marriott, as a trombone-playing tramp, is around. Hollywood's Fay Wray is a classy leading lady and there, are funny supporting turns by Garry Marsh as a blusterer called Brian, and Kate Cutler and Martita Hunt as the hero's maiden aunts.

When Saturday Comes ● Ⓥ
1995, UK, 105 mins, colour
Dir: Maria Giese
Stars: Sean Bean, Emily Lloyd, Pete Postlethwaite, John McEnery, Ann Bell
Rating: ★★

Three-quarters of a gritty north-country drama, this goes doolally in the last two reels, with Sean Bean going on as substitute for Sheffield United in the cup semi-final (shouldn't this be on a neutral ground?) and scoring two goals against Manchester United to win the tie: just a touch of wish fulfillment here. Now, if Bean had come on and scored to reduce a losing margin, we might just have believed it. You have to have some knowledge of English football to realise how far-fetched this all is, but the majority of the movie speaks for itself, about wasted lives and missed chances. Bean is a twentysomething brewery worker who has always wanted to make soccer his career but has been held back by uncaring teachers and a shiftless father. When he meets feisty accounts clerk Emily Lloyd, his life begins to take shape, though it's a pity Lloyd never does once she gets pregnant. Neither are we convinced by Bean blowing his big football trial by bedding a stripper the night before. For all that, he and

Lloyd are both very good before the script deserts them.

When Strangers Marry
See: Betrayed [1944]

When the Daltons Rode O
1940, US, 80 mins, b/w
Dir: George Marshall
Stars: Randolph Scott, Kay Francis, Brian Donlevy, George Bancroft
Rating: ★★★

This was a more straightforward Western for director George Marshall, coming, as it did, hard on the heels of his famous *Destry Rides Again*. More than any other film, it can be said to have set the pattern for the majority of Randolph Scott's later roles. Like most of those latter Scott Westerns this has fast-moving, convincing action and a splendid supporting cast, including Brian Donlevy, Frank Albertson, Broderick Crawford and Andy Devine.

When the Legends Die O
1972, US, 105 mins, colour
Dir: Stuart Millar
Stars: Richard Widmark, Frederic Forrest
Rating: ★★★

Although it didn't do well at the box-office, director Stuart Millar had the satisfaction of hearing resounding critical applause for his film about a young American Indian in modern times who becomes, in his search for 'the new ways', a great rodeo star. Richard Widmark gives a dominating, unforgettable performance as the ex-rodeo rider, sinking into an alcoholic haze, who becomes the hero's guardian and friend.

When the Whales Came O Ⓥ
1989, UK, 100 mins, colour
Dir: Clive Rees
Stars: Helen Mirren, David Suchet, Paul Scofield, David Threlfall
Rating: ★★

This prestigious British film is picturesquely set in the Scilly Isles, 1914, and tells of the effect of war on the islanders (they hide driftwood from the authorities, à la *Whisky Galore*), the growing-up of two friendly children and the expiation of a curse relating to narwhals (horned aquatic mammals). The film's emotive ending works well and the children are charming. Elsewhere, Paul Scofield's old man of the sea is King Lear with weatherbeaten cheeks; Helen Mirren tries hard to look unglamorous as a fisher-wife and John Hallam's lascivious child-beater might have stepped from the pages of a Scilly *Mallens*. Costumes are carefully

ragged and dirty, and the animatronic narwhal is brilliant.

When Time Ran Out. . . O
1980, US, 121 mins, colour
Dir: James Goldstone
Stars: Paul Newman, Jacqueline Bisset, William Holden, Veronica Hamel, Red Buttons, Ernest Borgnine
Rating: ★

The disaster movie reaches new heights of lunacy (despite a script penned by Oscar-winners Carl Foreman and Stirling Siliphant) in this old pals' reunion from *The Towering Inferno* as producer Irwin Allen and stars Paul Newman and William Holden from that film face fresh catastrophe. Here, it's crisis time on that volcanic island again – a new towering inferno indeed that produces the biggest bang since Krakatoa exploded east of Java.

When Worlds Collide O
1951, US, 82 mins, colour
Dir: Rudolph Maté
Stars: Richard Derr, Barbara Rush, John Hoyt
Rating: ★★★

Producer George Pal won the second of five Academy Awards for the special effects in this particular piece of science fiction about a planet on a collision course with the Earth. It's also a very exciting film in its own right. It set pretty Barbara Rush up for a long screen career in which she was able to prove herself a capable actress in such films as *Magnificent Obsession* and *Bigger Than Life*.

Where Angels Fear to Tread ● Ⓥ
1991, UK, 118 mins, colour
Dir: Charles Sturridge
Stars: Helena Bonham Carter, Rupert Graves, Judy Davis, Helen Mirren
Rating: ★★

Beautifully staged, set and costumed, as destinies flit between England and Italy, this is a typical product of early Nineties, prestige, TV-backed cinema in Britain. Yet another adaptation of the work of E M Forster, it's acted with bare competence by such familiar faces in these period dramas as Helena Bonham Carter, Rupert Graves and Judy Davis, and written with tact and some literacy but no inspiration. The pace is stately for, after all, the piece must run towards the two-hour mark, even though the novella on which it's based is slim indeed. Only Helen Mirren of the cast (and she disappears all too soon) commands our attention in a film which above all lacks any excitement, physical or cerebral.

Where Angels Go... Trouble Follows ⊙
1968, US, 95 mins, colour
Dir: James Neilson
Stars: Rosalind Russell, Stella Stevens
Rating: ★★

Well, well, it's television's Sally McMillan, alias Susan Saint James, taking over from Hayley Mills as the chief mischief-maker at St Francis Convent School, in the sequel to *The Trouble with Angels*. Rosalind Russell carries on as the Mother Superior.

Where Does It Hurt? ◑
1971, US, 88 mins, colour
Dir: Rod Amateau
Stars: Peter Sellers, Jo Ann Pflug, Rick Lenz
Rating: ★

The medical profession takes another torpedo amidships in this rudely irreverent comedy. A treasured memory is of Peter Sellers, as the money-mad, nurse-mad head of the hospital, inspecting the coke machine, which doesn't actually give out coke but vomits the money into his private office. 'A dollar twenty-five' he muses, looking at the 'take'... 'I'll have to put more salt in the water.'

Where Do We Go From Here? ○
1945, US, 77 mins, colour
Dir: Gregory Ratoff
Stars: Fred MacMurray, June Haver, Joan Leslie, Gene Sheldon
Rating: ★★

One of Hollywood's more extraordinary ventures, a piece of wartime escapism in which Fred MacMurray's efforts to get into the army with the help of a genie only result in him visiting various episodes of American history. The score by Kurt Weill and Ira Gershwin includes 'Christopher Columbus' and 'The Nina, the Pinta and the Santa Maria', both of which come from the film's best section – an operatic version of Columbus's adventures. June Haver and Joan Leslie are sweetly decorative; Anthony Quinn looks bewildered as a comic Indian chief.

Where Eagles Dare ○ ⓥ
1968, US, 158 mins, colour
Dir: Brian G Hutton
Stars: Richard Burton, Clint Eastwood, Mary Ure, Michael Hordern, Patrick Wymark
Rating: ★★★★

A great piece of *Boys' Own* derring-do, this World War Two adventure is immensely enjoyable. Its star Richard Burton, after a series of intense roles, was seeking a starring role in a more popular genre. Ace thriller writer Alistair MacLean obviously had fun with this one: what with a nasty Nazi enclave in a medieval castle perched high on a mountain, devious double agents and all manner of extraordinary exploits. Burton is fine, Clint Eastwood is suitably gritty as his second-in-command, Allied agent Mary Ure remains impeccably groomed, a host of British stalwarts do their bits for their countries and Anton Diffring does what is expected of him. But the real stars are the special effects directed by the legendary stuntman Yakima Canutt.

Where No Vultures Fly ⊙
(aka: Ivory Hunter)
1951, UK, 107 mins, colour
Dir: Harry Watt
Stars: Anthony Steel, Dinah Sheridan, Harold Warrender
Rating: ★★★

A colourful African adventure, full of fights with lions and leopards, chosen for the 1951 Royal Film Performance. As with most such choices, the film took a greater mauling from the critics than any big cat could provide. But the public adored the picture, and turned it into Britain's biggest box-office smash of the year, at the same time establishing Dinah Sheridan and Anthony Steel as major British stars.

Where's Charley? ○
1952, UK, 97 mins, colour
Dir: David Butler
Stars: Ray Bolger, Allyn McLerie, Mary Germaine
Rating: ★★★★

This sunny musical version of *Charley's Aunt* resulted in a tour-de-force for visiting American star Ray Bolger in the title role. Bolger's dazzling dancing, combined with his deceptively casual handling of the tuneful score (which includes 'Once in Love with Amy') makes his performance a joy to watch. And he throws himself into the slapstick situations with unbridled enthusiasm, creating the most convincing 48-year-old undergraduate ever seen! Allyn McLerie is delightful as Charley's girlfriend Amy, and the whole thing makes for relaxing, and sometimes very funny entertainment for the whole family.

Where's Jack? ○
1968, UK, 119 mins, colour
Dir: James Clavell
Stars: Tommy Steele, Stanley Baker
Rating: ★★★

Tommy Steele's first non-musical in a curiously sporadic cinema career. He plays a young lad, forced into a life of crime by an unscrupulous 'thief-taker', who becomes a legend in his own lifetime through his ability to escape from prison, bring off daring thefts and elude the law. Crowd scenes, particularly the one at the climactic hanging, are brilliantly handled by director James Clavell, while John Wilcox's fluorescent colour photography has a quality all its own. Two thoroughly enjoyable supporting performances are contributed by Dudley Foster and Noel Purcell, as scurrilous a pair of rogues as stalked the screen.

Where's That Fire? ○
1939, UK, 73 mins, b/w
Dir: Marcel Varnel
Stars: Will Hay, Moore Marriott, Graham Moffatt
Rating: ★★★

This Will Hay comedy is ideal for children as, although not among his best films, it relies more than usual on slapstick for its laughs. Hay's cohorts, whiskery Moore Marriott and tubby, belligerent Graham Moffatt, are on hand to help with the frolics, which are all (just about) under the control of Hay's best director, the French-born Marcel Varnel.

Where There's a Will ⊙
1936, UK, 81 mins, b/w
Dir: William Beaudine
Stars: Will Hay, Hartley Power, Gina Malo, Graham Moffatt
Rating: ★★★

This lesser-known Will Hay comedy treasure, with the star as an incompetent lawyer, was made between *Good Morning, Boys* and *Windbag the Sailor*. The great man is as delightful as ever and there are plenty of complications with a policeman's carol party forming part of the wild climactic chase. Famous fat boy Graham Moffatt adds to the fun, playing the office boy.

Where the River Bends ○
(aka: Bend of the River)
1952, US, 90 mins, colour
Dir: Anthony Mann
Stars: James Stewart, Arthur Kennedy, Julia Adams, Rock Hudson
Rating: ★★★★

W

This excellent Western has top grade written all over it. One of a series made by star James Stewart with director Anthony Mann, it features stunning Western vistas, fierce fist fights, impressively busy crowd scenes and a show-stealing performance by Arthur Kennedy as the good-bad guy who must be bested in the end. And it provided almost the final step up the ladder to stardom for Rock Hudson, here as a gambler.

Where the Spies Are O
1965, UK, 113 mins, colour
Dir: Val Guest
Stars: David Niven, Françoise Dorleac, Nigel Davenport
Rating: ★

A spy comedy thriller about Dr Jason Love, the reluctant agent created by novelist James Leasor, on whose novel *Passport to Oblivion* this film was based. Deep in trouble from the word go, Jason fumbles his way through the case: the film includes a wide-eyed blond, a foiled assassination and a high-flying climax aboard a Soviet plane. Françoise Dorleac, brunette sister of Catherine Deneuve, was headed for a big star career at this time. But two years later, she was killed in a car crash at only 25.

Where Were You When the Lights Went Out? O
1968, US, 94 mins, colour
Dir: Martin Melcher
Stars: Doris Day, Robert Morse, Terry-Thomas
Rating: ★★★★

Manic comedy of the misadventures that befall various people in the famous New York blackout a few years ago. Doris Day guys her own image and displays superb comic timing, especially in a drunk scene. Terry-Thomas and Robert Morse have some splendidly lunatic moments, but no one tops veteran vaudeville comic Ben Blue as a man continually trying to finish a shave.

While the City Sleeps O ⓥ
1956, US, 100 mins, b/w
Dir: Fritz Lang
Stars: Dana Andrews, Vincent Price, Ida Lupino
Rating: ★★★

With this film, German director Fritz Lang completed 20 memorable years in Hollywood after a distinguished early career in the German cinema that included such classics as *Metropolis*. The film is both a jaded look at the morals of big-city newspapermen and a slick, smooth crime yarn, which has a memo-

rable subway chase climax, and suffers only from having too many characters, which throws meat to a hungry all-star cast but also lends the film a certain disjointedness in its storytelling. Good work from Dana Andrews, Sally Forrest, Thomas Mitchell, Vincent Price and John Barrymore Jr.

While You Were Sleeping
O ⓥ
1995, US, 104 mins, colour
Dir: Jon Turteltaub
Stars: Sandra Bullock, Bill Pullman, Peter Gallagher, Jack Warden, Glynis Johns
Rating: ★★★

Although its heroine is rather determinedly cute, this is quite a winning, good-feel romantic comedy based on the old plot of someone being assumed to be something they're not and finding it difficult to extricate themselves. In this case, the someone is Lucy (Sandra Bullock), who is just too sweet and good to be true: so it is natural that, this being Hollywood wish-fulfilment-land, we should find her alone, lonely, stuck in a dead-end job, with no company for Christmas and only able to cast doe eyes at the man (Peter Gallagher) who passes her ticket window every morning at the subway station where she works. When he's mugged on the platform and falls on the line, Lucy storms to the rescue, only to inherit his entire family (while he lies in a coma at the hospital). When they believe through a misunderstanding, that she's his fiancée, Bullock tries hard to be adorable and with some success. Bill Pullman, as Gallagher's brother for whom she falls, looks confused at getting a role where he wins the girl.

Whipsaw O
1935, US, 83 mins, b/w
Dir: Sam Wood
Stars: Spencer Tracy, Myrna Loy
Rating: ★★★

Crisp romantic crime thriller which gave Myrna Loy just about the last of her screen 'bad girl' roles, unsuspectingly Leading G-man Spencer Tracy to the lair of the gang of criminals with whom she's associated. A routine plot but, under the direction of Sam Wood, one of MGM's finest – it thrills, amuses and entertains all the way. The pace is kept up right through to the punchy fade-out.

Whirlpool O
1949, US, 97 mins, b/w
Dir: Otto Preminger
Stars: Gene Tierney, Richard Conte,

Jose Ferrer, Charles Bickford
Rating: ★★★

This tense thriller dates from a time when Otto Preminger was really coming to the fore as a major director. Jose Ferrer delivers a fine portrayal as the evil Korvo in what was his third film. Beautiful Gene Tierney plays the woman who falls foul of Ferrer's Svengaliesque villain.

Whisky Galore! O ⓥ
(aka: Tight Little Island)
1948, UK, 82 mins, b/w
Dir: Alexander Mackendrick
Stars: Basil Radford, Joan Greenwood, James Robertson Justice
Rating: ★★★★★

The Ealing Studios comedy masterpiece that took the world by storm. The joyous story concerns a Hebridean island whose inhabitants confiscate a cargo of whisky which founders on the rocks, and find the most unlikely places to hide it.

Whisperers, The O
1966, UK, 106 mins, b/w
Dir: Bryan Forbes
Stars: Edith Evans, Eric Portman
Rating: ★★★

One of the few films to study closely the problem of old age, this Bryan Forbes film gained immensely in stature from the performance of Dame Edith Evans, which deservedly won a British Academy Award. She plays old Mrs Ross, whose only friends are the 'whisperers' – the voices that she insists she hears in her dank and dingy old flat. There's good support from Eric Portman as her errant husband, and especially Gerald Sim as a friendly Assistance Board man who tries to help her.

Whispering Ghosts O
1942, US, 75 mins, b/w
Dir: Alfred Werker
Stars: Milton Berle, Brenda Joyce, John Carradine
Rating: ★★

Popular television comedian Milton Berle played one of his earliest film roles in this comedy-thriller about a menaced heiress and missing diamonds.

Whispering Smith O
1948, US, 88 mins, colour
Dir: Leslie Fenton
Stars: Alan Ladd, Robert Preston, Brenda Marshall
Rating: ★★★

A blazing railroad Western that provides an ideal companion piece for

Alan Ladd's other classic Western, *Shane*. Brilliantly shot in Technicolor by Ray Rennahan, this constantly exciting film has Ladd, Robert Preston and Frank Faylen playing characters loosely based on real-life Westerners Joe Lefors, Butch Cassidy and Harvey Logan. Good performances from all three charge the film with emotional tension, creating fine entertainment for Western fans.

Whispers In the Dark ● ⓥ

1992, US, 102 mins, colour
Dir: Christopher Crowe
Stars: Annabella Sciorra, Alan Alda, Anthony LaPaglia, Jamey Sheridan, Jill Clayburgh, Deborah Unger
Rating: ★★★

The whispers are the shocking secrets told to psychiatrist Ann Hecker (Annabella Sciorra). And the dark, you might say, is the trouble she gets into when, after she has an affair with a man who turns out to be the lover of one of her patients, the patient is murdered. Plagued by erotic dreams and hounded by a dogged detective (Anthony LaPaglia), Dr Ann runs to her old friend and mentor Alan Alda. But is even he to be trusted? Everyone's a suspect in this intelligently written, strongly cast, *Jagged Edge*-style adult thriller. Unfortunately, Christopher Crowe's direction of it is characteristically sluggish and tends to take the edge off the suspense. Sciorra, LaPaglia and Alda are all spot-on.

Whistle Blower, The ◑ ⓥ

1986, UK, 107 mins, colour
Dir: Simon Langton
Stars: Michael Caine, James Fox, Nigel Havers
Rating: ★★

Skilfully handled but slightly tired British spy thriller full of character stars playing grim-faced government/security types who know that the hero's investigation is doomed to fail. Familiar territory this, since the beginning of John le Carré's popularity as a writer, yet with excellent performances by Michael Caine and Nigel Havers that score by understatement.

Whistle Down the Wind ○ ⓥ

1961, UK, 99 mins, b/w
Dir: Bryan Forbes
Stars: Hayley Mills, Alan Bates, Bernard Lee
Rating: ★★★★★

This brilliant, totally convincing British film was the first directed by Bryan Forbes. It's about three young farm children who find a man on the run in their barn, and believe him to be Jesus Christ. Hayley Mills follows up solidly her success in *Tiger Bay*, and little Alan Barnes is unbelievably good. The last five minutes remain among the most moving ever seen.

Whistling in Brooklyn ○

1943, US, 87 mins, b/w
Dir: S Sylvan Simon
Stars: Red Skelton, Ann Rutherford, Jean Rogers
Rating: ★★

The third in the series of scatterbrained comedies featuring Red Skelton as the radio sleuth 'The Fox' who turns to jelly when confronted by a real mystery. The character is clearly inspired by those that made Bob Hope a star, but nonetheless effective. Co-star Annn Rutherford and director S Sylvan Simon carry on from the first two films.

Whistling in Dixie ○

1942, US, 74 mins, b/w
Dir: S Sylvan Simon
Stars: Red Skelton, Ann Rutherford
Rating: ★★

This fairly bright comedy is one of three wartime MGM capers revolving round the adventures of a radio detective' called 'The Fox', embodied by the rubber-faced Red Skelton, who finds himself mixed up in real-life crime capers. Here he's in deep trouble in the Deep South.

Whistling in the Dark ○

1941, US, 77 mins, b/w
Dir: S Sylvan Simon
Stars: Red Skelton, Conrad Veidt, Ann Rutherford
Rating: ★★

Red Skelton – here in his first starring role – was compared by contemporary critics with Bob Hope, which was not too surprising since MGM had provided him with a plot for this lively comedy-thriller very much in the vein of Hope's *The Cat and the Canary*, complete with a creepy mansion replete with sliding panels and hidden passages. The film was the first of Skelton's three outings as radio criminologist 'The Fox' and packs in plenty of good gags under S Sylvan Simon's brisk direction.

White Cargo ○

1942, US, 90 mins, b/w
Dir: Richard Thorpe
Stars: Hedy Lamarr, Walter Pidgeon, Frank Morgan
Rating: ★★

First made as an early British sound film, this Hollywood version of a hoary old classic, which silent vamps would surely have given their eye teeth to star in, features a suitably tall and taciturn Walter Pidgeon – a top box-office star thanks to his screen partnership with Greer Garson. He is the plantation owner trying to fend off the advances of a (literally) poisonous native charmer who seems to have vamped half the white men within 50 miles of the Equator. The delicious Hedy Lamarr was never more exotic and effective than as Tondelayo, luring men to destruction from under her dusky lids.

White Christmas ○ ⓥ

1954, US, 120 mins, colour
Dir: Michael Curtiz
Stars: Bing Crosby, Danny Kaye, Rosemary Clooney, Dean Jagger, Vera-Ellen
Rating: ★★

A slam-bang Christmas classic that grossed $12 million on its first release. Its combination of Bing Crosby and Danny Kaye – the latter a last-minute replacement for Donald O'Connor, who broke his leg – and an enchanting score by Irving Berlin proved irresistible. The boys are a song and dance team who organise a Christmas benefit concert for their ex-army general, whose ski resort is going bankrupt due to the lack of snow. Of the songs, 'Sisters', sung by both Rosemary Clooney and Vera-Ellen and then mimed to the girls' voices by Crosby and Kaye, stands out above the rest save the title song, of course.

White Feather ○

1955, US, 104 mins, colour
Dir: Robert Webb
Stars: Robert Wagner, John Lurid, Debra Paget, Jeffrey Hunter
Rating: ★★★

Spectacular Western with Robert Wagner in good form as a peace-maker between cavalry and Indians. And it has some superb scenery, beautifully shot in colour by Lucien Ballard. Debra Paget, Wagner and Jeffrey Hunter all do well in a film which, although filled with action, is notable as an early example of Hollywood's more sympathetic and respectful attitude to what we would soon come to call native Americans.

White Heat ○ ⓥ

1949, US, 114 mins, b/w
Dir: Raoul Walsh

W

Stars: James Cagney, Edmond O'Brien,
Virginia Mayo, Steve Cochran
Rating: ★★★★

The last fling of the Warners gangster
film and of James Cagney's roles there-
in. Raoul Walsh, who made Cagney's
famous *The Roaring Twenties* 10 years
earlier, is again in charge of the
snarling mayhem and few ardent film
fans can be unaware that it all ends in
an explosive gun battle with Cagney
making his famous 'Made it, Ma – top
of the world' speech from high up on
the gasholder. Margaret Wycherly's
brooding portrait of his obsessed mother also makes an indelible impression
on the film. Walsh's zestful direction
reaches its peak in the scene in the
prison dining-hall where his cameras
track feverishly along the prisoners as
events conspire to send Cagney
berserk.

White Hunter, Black Heart
◑ ⓥ
1990, US, 112 mins, colour
Dir: Clint Eastwood
Stars: Clint Eastwood, Jeff Fahey,
George Dzundza, Marisa Berenson
Rating: ★★

Clint Eastwood's account of the traumas undergone in trying to get
director John Huston to make *The
African Queen* in 1951 makes interesting,
if hardly stimulating screen fare, shimmeringly shot on location in
Zimbabwe. You imagine that the
Peter Viertel book on which it's based
is rather more engrossing. Viertel,
screenwriter on the film, is played as a
narrator figure by the arrestingly good-
looking Jeff Fahey as a cross between
James Mason and Audie Murphy.
Eastwood does a kind of Burt
Lancaster impersonation as the Huston
character, here called John Wilson:
like Eastwood's direction of this one,
it's on the stodgy side. Timothy Spall
and Mel Martin make bright supporting appearances as a bush pilot and a
white bigot, and the impersonations of
Bogart, Hepburn and Co are close
enough to provoke a smile.

White Lions, The ⊙
1981, US, 110 mins, colour
Dir: Mel Stuart
Stars: Michael York, Glynnis O'Connor
Rating: ★★

Michael York stars in this pretty well-
worn story of a naturalist in the African
bush who fights to preserve the wildlife
there. The African locations make this
enjoyable viewing, despite the familiar
simplicity of the story. York didn't win

any awards for this one, you won't be
surprised to hear, but the animals are
the stars, and its fair to assume he realised that.

White Man's Burden ● ⓥ
1995, US, 88 mins, colour
Dir: Desmond Nakano
Stars: John Travolta, Harry Belafonte,
Kelly Lynch, Margaret Avery
Rating: ★★

First-time director Nakano has such a
fascinating idea here that it's sad to see
it become so tedious in the exposition.
In the neighbourhood where the black
guys are rich and the white guys are
blue-collar workers living in shacks,
white guy Travolta finds himself out of
a job when he delivers a package to
black boss Belafonte and accidentally
spots the latter's wife nude at a window. The company manager takes
Belafonte's mild complaint as an order
to fire Travolta on the spot. In no time
at all, Travolta finds himself jobless,
homeless and separated from his wife
(Lynch) and children. Belafonte refuses to listen to his pleas for a hearing.
Desperate, Travolta kidnaps his ex-
boss at the point of a gun – and the
film spirals downward into darker
tragedy, culminating in a deeply contrived and violent ending. Perhaps
Nakano should get someone else to
shape and direct his ideas. Thanks to
him, you'll soon lose interest in what
should be a riveting drama.

White Men Can't Jump ● ⓥ
1992, US, 114 mins, colour
Dir: Ron Shelton
Stars: Wesley Snipes, Woody Harrelson,
Rosie Perez, Tyra Ferrell
Rating: ★★

A shouting-and-screaming film about
hustling in the backstreets basketball
courts of Venice, California. Moulded
along the lines of a buddy-buddy comedy film, it features Wesley Snipes
and Woody Harrelson as a
black/white combination that will lull
the opposition into a false sense of security, then take all their money in the
subsequent game. Director Ron
Shelton leaves nothing to chance here:
there are gangsters, four-letter words
and steamy sex scenes galore.
Wesley's sensuous spouse wants to get
away from the ghetto. Woody's
voluptuous Puerto Rican girlfriend –
hey, let's get another ethnic group in,
guys – has a different ambition: she's
stuffing her head full of knowledge for
the day she gets on to the TV quiz
show *Jeopardy*. That's the whole plot,

and it has a few streetwise smiles
along the way, although, like its characters, it gets a bit tiresome towards
the end and you, too, may grow
weary at making the effort to keep up
with its screeching, squeaking, high-
velocity dialogue.

White Mischief ● ⓥ
1987, UK, 107 mins, colour
Dir: Michael Radford
Stars: Greta Scacchi, Charles Dance,
Joss Ackland, Sarah Miles
Rating: ★★★

A beautifully shot tale of lust and murder among a hedonistic group of
expatriate Britons living in Nairobi,
Kenya, during World War Two.
Stylishness, elegance and decadence
ooze from the very pores of Michael
Radford's interesting if leisurely treatment of the cause célèbre that resulted
from the murder of one of the 'Happy
Valley' sophisticates, whose high society resembles nothing more than
Berlin at the time of *Cabaret*. Greta
Scacchi, in and out of period costume,
certainly does look well worth dying
for, as a couple of characters do before
the end. And her Forties' 'look', as
with everything else in the film, is impeccable. The murder suspects line up
as if in an Agatha Christie tale, and
though the real killer was never
brought to book, the filmmakers leave
the viewer in no doubt as to their own
solution of the crime. The film gets
slower as it goes, but it never quite
loses its overall fascination.

White Palace ● ⓥ
1990, US, 110 mins, colour
Dir: Luis Mandoki
Stars: Susan Sarandon, James Spader,
Jason Alexander, Kathy Bates, Eileen
Brennan
Rating: ★★★★

If you've been saving up your tears for
a really sloshy romance, this is it – an
ace love story where you really get to
know the characters. Widower James
Spader is a 27-year-old high flyer of
immaculate (Jewish) breeding. Susan
Sarandon is a 43-year-old, foul-
mouthed, sloppy, failed Catholic
('Confession made me jumpy') waitress. They get the hots for each other
and if you can't guess subsequent developments, or the final outcome, then
you haven't seen too many romantic
movies. Sarandon and Spader (she especially) are great; as for the film itself,
apart from the frankness of its dialogue, it could have been made 20, 30,
even 40 years ago. Some things, in-

cluding Hollywood wish-fulfilment, thankfully never change!

White Sands ● Ⓥ
1992, US, 101 mins, colour
Dir: Roger Donaldson
Stars: Willem Dafoe, Mickey Rourke, Mary Elizabeth Mastrantonio, M Emmet Walsh
Rating: ★★★

Such a nicely-made thriller that it's a shame that, from start to finish, you haven't a clue what's going on. Sheriff Willem Dafoe discovers a body, a gun and a suitcase full of banknotes in remote New Mexico ruins and from here on in you're on your own. The FBI, the CIA and a couple of arms dealers are in there somewhere, but the thrill of the chase is the thing. You can see director Roger Donaldson's mind ticking as he gives us a mobile shot of Dafoe taking a gun from the glove compartment of his car, a time-saving, pace-setting device that sums up the tempo of the whole plot. Dafoe is particularly good as the resourceful, likeable, laid-back lawman. Not far behind are Mary Elizabeth Mastrantonio, Mickey Rourke, M Emmet Walsh, J E Freeman and (uncredited) Mimi Rogers, John Ryan and Fred Dalton Thompson. Royce Applegate is also noteworthy in a one-scene role as a motel owner. Never mind the plot, feel the quality: It's the real stuff.

White Squall ◑ Ⓥ
1996, US, 128 mins, colour
Dir: Ridley Scott
Stars: Jeff Bridges, Caroline Goodall, Scott Wolf, John Savage, Balthazar Getty, Ethan Embry
Rating: ★★★

Rent a wide screen version of this one if you can, to catch the full flavour of Ridley Scott's sea story, and especially the pulsating excitement of its last 40 minutes, when the inexperienced crew of teenage boys aboard with Captain Jeff Bridges is caught in a violent whitewater whirlwind – the white squall of the title. These scenes are sensational stuff, but unfortunately the near 90 minutes that precedes them is rather less so, as the boys undergo their rites of passage both afloat and ashore. Routine at best away from that white squall, it has a script awash with all the clichés of the genre. Terrific on-board camerawork, though, really makes us experience the voyage – and there are one or two emotionally draining moments towards the end. Bridges is both forthright and sensitive as the skipper.

White Tie and Tails ○
1946, US, 81.mins, b/w
Dir: Charles Barton
Stars: Dan Duryea, Elia Raines, William Bendix
Rating: ★★★

This breezy comedy of embarrassment gives those film tough guys Dan Duryea and William Bendix a chance to lean to the lighter side. The plot, an old standby, is about menials taking over a household while their employers are away.

White Witch Doctor ○
1953, US, 96 mins, colour
Dir: Henry Hathaway
Stars: Susan Hayward, Robert Mitchum, Walter Slezak
Rating: ★★

African missionary nurse meets rugged white hunter in one of 20th Century-Fox's wilder excursions into the jungle, not dissimilar from another Robert Mitchum film, *Mister Moses,* made 12 years later. Susan Hayward offers sensitive acting above and beyond the call of duty as the inhibited Ellen, but not enough happens to sustain the film through its running time, although the Technicolor photography of Leon Shanzoy, including some exciting animal shots, is masterly. Oily villainy is in the hands of Walter Slezak and Timothy Carey.

White Zombie ◑
1932, US, 74 mins, b/w
Dir: Victor Halperin
Stars: Bela Lugosi, Madge Bellamy
Rating: ★★★

This cult movie has an eerie atmosphere all its own. Bela Lugosi gives one of his best performances as Murder, the Haitian sorcerer who commands an army of zombies. The film's out-of-this-world quality makes it seem dated even by Thirties' standards, but this somehow only adds to its fascination. And director Victor Halperin achieves some remarkable tableaux that could be removed from the film and hung in art galleries alongside the work of Hieronymous Bosch. The film, too, is bosh, but bosh with sinister style.

Who Dares Wins ◑ Ⓥ
1982, UK, 140 mins, colour
Dir: Ian Sharp
Stars: Lewis Collins, Judy Davis, Richard Widmark
Rating: ★★

The exploits of the SAS, with their masks, machine guns and deadly effi-

ciency, here gave British filmmakers the chance to reply in kind to the increasingly tough thrillers from Hollywood. On TV, *The Sweeney and The Professionals* had shown the way and it can be no coincidence that Lewis Collins, a star from the second of these, features here as the SAS man who goes undercover to undermine a terrorist organisation planning to hold top politicians hostage. The action is a long time coming, but is brilliantly staged in an explosive last 20 minutes when it does. Something about it remains intractably British: after all, it's dining-room windows the bullets are spraying through here, not ghetto slums.

Who Done It? ☉
1942, US, 75 mins, b/w
Dir: Eric C Kenton
Stars: Bud Abbott, Lou Costello, William Bendix, William Gargan, Thomas Gomez
Rating: ★★★

This tongue-in-cheek thriller, about a murder committed on a mystery show broadcast, has one of the best casts of any Abbott and Costello film. It's full of such experienced Hollywood heavies as William Bendix, William Gargan and Thomas Gomez. Vintage film fans may also spot Jerome Cowan (Humphrey Bogart's partner in *The Maltese Falcon),* Don Porter and horse-faced Mary Wickes. The fun comes fast and furious. One of Bud and Lou's snappiest numbers; funny finish too.

Who Done It? ☉
1955, UK, 85 mins, b/w
Dir: Basil Dearden
Stars: Benny Hill, Belinda Lee, David Kossoff, Garry Marsh
Rating: ★★★

Although something of a rough diamond, this Ealing Studios comedy vehicle for Benny Hill is so funny as to make one wonder why the star didn't make more such films. A bloodhound called Fabian and Belinda Lee, as a strong-arm showgirl, both give Benny (who gives a likeable performance) a run for his money in the laughter-raising stakes.

Who Framed Roger Rabbit ○ Ⓥ
1988, US, 103 mins, colour
Dir: Robert Zemeckis
Stars: Bob Hoskins, Christopher Lloyd, Joanna Cassidy
Rating: ★★★★★

Humans and cartoon characters have been intermixed before, but never so

W

noisily, inventively or abrasively as in this raucous romp which casts Bob Hoskins as a drunken Californian gumshoe hired to dig the dirt on the seductive human-toon wife of a cartoon rabbit. It all runs deeper than that, of course, and Hoskins' Eddie Valiant soon finds himself reluctantly drawn back towards Toontown to help Roger Rabbit beat a murder rap, and the toons from being wiped off the face of the earth. Besides playing fair by the rules of its own game, the film allows room for pretty well all the Disney and Warners cartoon characters. Daffy and Donald Duck appear for positively the only time together in a piano duet, Mickey Mouse and Bugs Bunny team up to baffle Hoskins with cartoon logic, Betty Boop regrets being in black and white and Frank Sinatra provides the voice of the Singing Sword.

Whole Town's Talking, The ○
(aka: Passport to Fame)
1934, US, 95 mins, b/w
Dir: John Ford
Stars: Edward G Robinson, Jean Arthur, Wallace Ford
Rating: ★★★★

Director John Ford gave Jean Arthur her big break in 1923 in *Cameo Kirby*, but her career failed to take off. Twelve years later, he finally made her a star with this excellent combination of farce and melodrama that was a huge box-office hit. Edward G Robinson has great fun playing dual roles, as a timid white collar clerk and his 'double', 'Killer Mannion', a notorious gangster. And as the girlfriend with a smart lip, Arthur (who dyed her hair blond for the role) firmly established her screen persona as a wisecracking, cynical woman who would usually start taking advantage of an idealist, eventually fall in love with him, and then use her wordly knowledge to help him beat the bad guys by the end of the picture.

Wholly Moses! ◑
1979, US, 109 mins, colour
Dir: Gary Weis
Stars: Dudley Moore, Laraine Newman, James Coco, Richard Pryor
Rating: ★★

A sort of unholy sideshoot to Monty Python's *Life of Brian*, this Hollywood comedy has Dudley Moore as Herschel, who fondly imagines that it was he, and not Moses, who was chosen to lead his people out of bondage. Guy Thomas's script is peppered with

amusing puns and clever situations, although director Gary Weis's pacing is too often slow to take advantage of them all. Laraine Newman has a nicely offbeat personality as the heroine, and James Coco is a delight as Herschel's father.

Whoopee! ○
1930, US, 93 mins, colour
Dir: Thornton Freeland
Stars: Eddie Cantor, Eleanor Hunt
Rating: ★★★

This early two-colour Technicolor musical has Eddie Cantor singing such hits as 'Makin' Whoopee' and 'My Baby just Cares for Me' and established him as a star of screen as well as stage. It also provided a foothold in films for the young Broadway dance director Busby Berkeley, who would go on to become the foremost man in his field in Thirties' musical films. The Goldwyn Girls include an allegedly 14-year-old Betty Grable leading the chorus in the opening cowboy number. But it's Cantor's clowning that holds centre stage in this early musical treat.

Whoops Apocalypse ● ⓥ
1986, UK, 91 mins, colour
Dir: Tom Bussmann
Stars: Loretta Swit, Peter Cook, Michael Richards, Rik Mayall
Rating: R B

Whoops – a laugh eclipse. British satire hits rock bottom with a cavernous clang in this awful attempted comedy whose sex, nudity, gore and four-letter words are possibly marginally more entertaining than the – er – jokes. Loretta Swit as the US president, is, under impossible circumstances, one of the few performers not highly over the top in this story of Britain taking back a Central American colony by force, then threatening a nuclear strike when the invaders kidnap a British princess in retaliation. More suffering might have been pre-empted by a nuclear strike on the whole idea. The sequence depicting the SAS is probably the most overextended film joke since Pinocchio's nose.

Whore ● ⓥ
1991, US, 80 mins, colour
Dir: Ken Russell
Stars: Theresa Russell, Antonio Fargas, Benjamin Mouton
Rating: ★

Ken Russell's idea of a docudrama on prostitution runs like a lurid but old-fashioned sexploitation film, with

raunchy Nineties dialogue and a theme song called 'I Want to Bang Her'. Theresa Russell (no relation) tries hard, but isn't very good, in the title role; Antonio Fargas is rather more effective as the black hobo who eventually proves that a friend in need is a friend in deed. Penny dreadful and tuppence coloured, the gaudy parable is calculated only to titillate, not to be informative or teach a moral lesson.

Who's Afraid of Virginia Woolf? ◑ ⓥ
1966, US, 129 mins, b/w
Dir: Mike Nichols
Stars: Elizabeth Taylor, Richard Burton, George Segal, Sandy Dennis
Rating: ★★★★

Elizabeth Taylor won her second Oscar for this abrasive four-hander about an embattled middle-ageing couple, living on a college campus. 'You are cordially invited to George and Martha's for an evening of fun and games,' said the publicity at the time. But George and Martha's idea of fun and games is a marathon, macabre shouting match, in which the young couple who are their guests for the evening become semi-willing participants. The film depends almost entirely for its effect on its very powerful dialogue, the creation of playwright Edward Albee, admirably translated for the screen in Ernest Lehman's screenplay. As Martha and George, Taylor and Richard Burton never quite get away from being Elizabeth Taylor and Richard Burton, although Taylor, deglamourised at least about the face, and looking most unlike her usual self, is every bit as good as we have any right to expect.

Who's Been Sleeping in My Bed? ○
1963, US, 103 mins, colour
Dir: Daniel Mann
Stars: Dean Martin, Elizabeth Montgomery
Rating: ★★

Dean Martin is surrounded by lovely girls in this comedy about a television personality forced to live up to his own amorous image. But the honours are entirely stolen by a performance of non-stop verve from comedienne Carol Burnett.

Who's Got the Action? ○
1962, US, 93 mins, colour
Dir: Daniel Mann
Stars: Dean Martin, Lana Turner
Rating: ★★★

A talented cast make the most of Jack Rose's consistently funny script and Daniel Mann's direction moves the fun along at an irresistible pace, in this comedy about a wife who becomes her own husband's bookie in order to try and cure him of the betting craze. Of course, his horses begin to win ... and win... and...

Who's Harry Crumb? ◐ Ⓥ
1989, US, 98 mins, colour
Dir: Paul Flaherty
Stars: John Candy, Jeffrey Jones, Annie Potts, Shawnee Smith
Rating: ★

You wanna hear a joke? Here it is. 'I am from Budapest.' 'Ah, Hungary.' 'No, filled up before I got here.' Yes folks, alas for poor John Candy, this is the kind of script every comedian has nightmares about getting for his first solo vehicle. The plot, which runs like a Norman Wisdom reject from 1966, casts Candy as an inept private eye called in to investigate a kidnapping because his boss has masterminded the crime himself and needs the worst operative in the country. Ham-fisted Harry knocks over every priceless object and wall in slight and is called on not to apologise, just look pained. Director Paul Flaherty's execution is as clumsy as Harry, but then this script must have given him migraines from the start. Don't call us Harry – we certainly won't call you.

Who's Minding the Store? ☉
1963, US, 90 mins, colour
Dir: Frank Tashlin
Stars: Jerry Lewis, Jill St John, Agnes Moorehead, John McGiver, Ray Walston
Rating: ★★★

Under Frank Tashlin's skilful direction, Jerry Lewis gives one of his zaniest performances in this very entertaining comedy. Watch him trying to paint the tip of a flagpole, selling shoes to a female wrestler, and demonstrating a vacuum cleaner that sucks up everything, including a customer's chihuahua dog. And Jill St John as the amorous Barbara is everyone's idea of a dream lift-girl.

Who's That Girl ○ Ⓥ
1987, US, 94 mins, colour
Dir: James Foley
Stars: Madonna, Griffin Dunne, John Mills
Rating: ★

Madonna's first mainline solo starring vehicle is, alas for the lass, a wretchedly unfunny, woefully mistimed

comedy with one of those plots you thought had gone out in the Sixties. Comic heroes flee comic crooks who are in turn pursued by comic police. Everybody's in on the joke except the audience. Madonna's okay as the squeaky streetgirl jailbird, out to clear herself of the frame that gave her four years inside. But Griffin Dunne is highly resistible as her hapless hero, waylaid from marrying the inevitable rich girl. And what is John Mills doing in all this? Very little, mercifully. But not, he might have thought on seeing the results, little enough.

Why Bother to Knock?
See: Don't Bother to Knock

Why Me? ◐ Ⓥ
1989, US, 87 mins, colour
Dir: Gene Quintano
Stars: Christopher Lambert, Christopher Lloyd, Kim Griest
Rating: ★

On top of everything else, this feebly written and directed caper comedy is saddled with a completely meaningless title! The stars, as a trio of safecrackers, show a little, but not much enthusiasm for a story about one of those fabulous *Pink Panther*-style jewels that passes from hand to hand as several factions strive to gain possession of it. J T Walsh has one or two funny moments as the local police chief, but most of the acting has the desperate air of players going resolutely over the top. Old-timers Michael J Pollard and Lawrence Tierney make nominal appearances in the supporting cast of this ill-fated enterprise.

Wichita ○
1955, US, 81 mins, colour
Dir: Jacques Tourneur
Stars: Joel McCrea, Vera Miles
Rating: ★★

Joel McCrea pins on a tin star to play legendary lawman Wyatt Earp in this surprisingly stylish Western. He's hired to clean up the town and starts by banning firearms – not a popular decision. But when the wife of the town banker is killed it's down to Earp to track down the outlaw responsible. An all-too familiar plot and an indirect script could have condemned this horse opera to oblivion, but director Jacques Tourneur created a fast-moving action-filled tale whose pace gallops over any plot deficiencies. And, yes – there's a theme song, too, sung by the *High Noon* man Tex Ritter.

Wicked As They Come ○
1956, UK, 94 mins, colour
Dir: Ken Hughes
Stars: Arlene Dahl, Phil Carey, Herbert Marshall
Rating: ★★

A British attempt to catch up on the American *film noir* of the late Forties. Arlene Dahl is the girl who will stop at nothing to get what she wants out of life. Men fall at her feet, and soon she's covered in diamonds and mink, to say nothing of dirt. Retribution is just around the corner ... but wait, there's a twist in the tail. Very professionally directed by Ken Hughes.

Wicked Lady, The ○
1945, UK, 104 mins, b/w
Dir: Leslie Artiss
Stars: Margaret Lockwood, James Mason
Rating: ★★★

The definitive Margaret Lockwood vehicle, this Lime Grove-shot film scandalised wartime London when it first appeared. Plunging necklines (which had to be re-shot for American audiences) and a racy story about a 17th-century married lady who carries on with a highwayman combined to spell pure box-office. And something else pulled them in: the sheer star quality of Lockwood and James Mason. In all honesty, it's little more than lurid melodrama, but still streets ahead of the ill-advised Eighties' remake with Faye Dunaway.

Wicked Lady, The ○
1983, UK, 99 mins, colour
Dir: Michael Winner
Stars: Faye Dunaway, Alan Bates, John Gielgud, Denholm Elliott
Rating: ★

Mighty are the depths to which the wicked Lady Barbara sinks in this hoary old period tale of a woman with a thirst for danger and adventure, revamped for the modern cinema by director Michael Winner, with Faye Dunaway in the old Margaret Lockwood role. Some of photographer Jack Cardiff's colour compositions are so good, catching the period flavour in their crowd scenes especially, that they might grace a masterpiece.

Wicker Man, The ● Ⓥ
1973, UK, 110 mins, colour
Dir: Robin Hardy
Stars: Edward Woodward, Christopher Lee, Britt Ekland
Rating: ★★★★

W

One of the most unusual British horror films since Hammer pumped new blood into the genre in the mid-Fifties. *The Wicker Man* was treated somewhat unfairly by its distributors, being sent out as a second-feature to *Don't Look Now*, which meant that it was hardly noticed, and, indeed, half-missed by many. It turns out to be a chilling relative of *The Dark Secret of Harvest Home*, all about pagan worship on a Scottish offshore island, and very persuasively written by Anthony Schaffer, author of *Sleuth* and other big stage-into-film hits. A very good, unsettling performance from Edward Woodward is far removed from his famous portrait of Callan in the long-running TV series.

Wide Sargasso Sea ● ⑰
1992, UK/Jamaica, 98 mins, colour
Dir: John Duigan
Stars: Karina Lombard, Nathaniel Parker, Rachel Ward, Casey Robinson
Rating: ★★

An erotic prequel to *Jane Eyre:* whatever next? The idea is inspired, the tropical Jamaican settings lush and colourful. But the (attempted) eroticism overwhelms it, to the extent that there seems to be virtually no story, especially as John Duigan's direction is so slow. And it would take better actors than Karina Lombard and Nathaniel Parker (as Rochester) to survive this script as written. She at least emerges with pride intact, but he is made to look a little foolish by what must be the foreshortenings of plot in Jean Rhys's acclaimed last novel. Still, it all has a certain touch of the bizarre, that's for sure. Rachel Ward is quite good as the heroine's mad mother and there are moments of poetry – the parrot consumed by flames is a gruesome masterpiece of special effects – that sparkle like jewels in the paste of the rest.

Widows' Peak ○ ⑰
1993, UK, 101 mins, colour
Dir: John Irvin
Stars: Mia Farrow, Joan Plowright, Natasha Richardson, Adrian Dunbar, Jim Broadbent
Rating: ★★★

Here's one film it's difficult to discuss without giving too much of the plot away. A sparkling comedy with undertones of mystery, it's set in a 1920s Irish community ruled by a formidable colony of widows that might have even put the fear of God into the witch from *The Wizard of Oz*. Witchcraft of a sort seems to be somewhere on the

menu, especially with the arrival of Edwina Broom (Natasha Richardson), a war widow whom Peak residents, led by Joan Plowright, see as a most suitable asset to the community, even with her American accent (not clear why English Richardson has to be an American, but no matter) and glamorous appearance. All, that is, save Miss O'Hare (Mia Farrow), a spinster whose quiet existence and deference to other residents may owe something to a scarlet past. Thus begins a feud that, via dance hall brawls, regatta shunts, acts of mutual revenge and mysterious letters, spirals rapidly out of control ... We can say no more in deference to Hugh Leonard's plot, which is of a higher calibre than the Irish accents attempted by those members of the cast who aren't. Entertaining.

Wife Vs Secretary ○
1936, US, 88 mins, b/w
Dir: Clarence Brown
Stars: Clark Gable, Jean Harlow, Myrna Loy, James Stewart
Rating: ★★★★

Never mind the plot, a frothy trifle of marital misunderstandings, just savour the teaming of Clark Gable, Jean Harlow, Myrna Loy and James Stewart, the intelligent direction by Clarence Brown and the witty dialogue exchanges supplied by Norman Krasna, Alice Duer Miller and John Lee Mahin. Gable's a publisher and Harlow his firecracker assistant, with both Loy (Gable's wife) and Stewart (Harlow's boyfriend) wrongly suspicious of the relationship. Stewart, in his fourth feature film, revelled in his scenes with Harlow. 'Clarence,' he recalled, 'wasn't too pleased by the way I did the smooching. He made us go over it several times. I botched it up on purpose, of course. That Jean Harlow sure was a good kisser!'

Wild and the Innocent, The ○
1959, US, 84 mins, colour
Dir: Jack Sher
Stars: Audie Murphy, Joanne Dru, Gilbert Roland, Sandra Dee
Rating: ★★★★

Something of a departure for Audie Murphy, and almost a throwback to his first Western, *Sierra*. It's a well-made adventure story, which creates instantly sympathetic characters. Down the cast, Strother Martin, typed even then as the uncouth villain, a mould which took him to good parts in *Cool Hand Luke* and *Butch Cassidy and the*

Sundance Kid. Probably Murphy's best Western.

Wild at Heart ● ⑰
1990, US, 127 mins, colour
Dir: David Lynch
Stars: Nicolas Cage, Laura Dern, Diane Ladd, Willem Dafoe, Isabella Rossellini, Harry Dean Stanton
Rating: ★★★★

Imagine a combination of *Twin Peaks* and *Bonnie and Clyde*, with touches of *Rambo* and *The Wizard of Oz*, and you're perhaps half-way to catching the flavour of this love-it-or-leave-it 'on the road' movie. It's a jet-black comedy that's unmistakably the work of maverick Hollywood director David Lynch (*Blue Velvet*, *The Elephant Man*). Nicolas Cage, released from jail after serving time for manslaughter, is reunited with tearaway sweetheart Laura Dern. Her vengeful mother (Diane Ladd), who once fancied Cage herself, is determined to separate them. Cage is 'wild at heart', wears a snakeskin jacket to demonstrate his individuality, sings Elvis Presley songs – and kills people. Brace yourself for the ensuing journey. Violent, adult, alienating and compelling all at the same time.

Wild Bunch, The ◐ ⑰
1969, US, 134 mins, colour
Dir: Sam Peckinpah
Stars: William Holden, Ernest Borgnine, Robert Ryan, Warren Oates, Ben Johnson
Rating: ★★★

This famous Western epic was one of a group of much-imitated movies (*Bonnie and Clyde* and *Easy Rider* were others) which changed the face and concept of their particular genre, each bent on disproving a popular myth, yet tinged with the sadness of an impending and inevitable tragic ending. And, although the Clint Eastwood spaghetti Westerns were visually violent, only *The Wild Bunch* truly brought home the horrors of a violent death. Its climactic orgy of annihilation is justly famous, writing *finis* both to its characters and to the old-style Western. It also proved that William Holden, in his best performance since winning an Academy Award for *Stalag 17*, was a much stronger actor when being something darker than a straightforward hero.

Wildcats ◐ ⑰
1986, US, 107 mins, colour
Dir: Michael Ritchie
Stars: Goldie Hawn, James Keach,

Swoosie Kurtz, M Emmet Walsh
Rating: ★★★

Goldie Hawn has a happy facility of choosing scripts that showcase her particular brand of charm, feistiness and vulnerability, and once again she's virtually the whole show in this predictable but enjoyable tale of a teacher who becomes coach to a football team at an unspeakable Chicago ghetto school. Nothing unexpected happens, but there are a few good laughs and you'll be rooting for the school team at the climax. There are some interesting names down the cast, too, notably Woody Harrelson and Wesley Snipes (later co-stars in another sports romp, *White Men Can't Jump*), L L Cool J, M Emmet Walsh and, for fans of old late-night movies, Ann Doran and Gloria Stuart.

Wild Country, The ☉

1970, US, 100 mins, colour
Dir: Robert Totten
Stars: Steve Forrest, Vera Miles, Jack Elam, Ron Howard
Rating: ★★★

A warm-hearted, incident-filled combination of Western and pioneering drama from the Disney studio, based on the conventional opposition between might and right. The mountain locations are stunning, and veteran character star Jack Elam gets a chance to create a real character instead of being a mean villain or a figure of farce. Ron Howard, who plays the son of the family trying to make a go of farming in the wilds of Wyoming in the 1880s, is the same Howard who later turned director with such effect on *Splash*, *Cocoon* and *Backdraft*.

Wilde ● ⓥ

1997, UK, 117 mins, colour
Dir: Brian Gilbert
Stars: Stephen Fry, Jude Law, Jennifer Ehle
Rating: ★★★

An elegant and sparklingly well written account of the playwright Oscar Wilde's fall from grace, following his scandal-defying affair with Bosie, a young aristocrat (Jude Law) which led to a court case and Wilde's imprisonment for two years. Wilde's own children's story *The Selfish Giant*, is woven through the narrative, standing in many ways for the man himself, not least in his stature – as reflected in the gentle hulk of Stephen Fry, who is excellent throughout in a beautiful but complex and difficult role. Fry's Wilde is a bit like the *Titanic*, – huge, glittering

and doomed. Along the way, the film rambles a bit, sometimes seeming longer than it is. But it gathers momentum and emotive impact again towards the end. Full of civilised and finely judged performances, as well as Wildean wit, it's the sharpest look yet at one of our greatest writers.

Wild Geese, The ○ ⓥ

1978, UK, 134 mins, colour
Dir: Andrew V McLaglen
Stars: Richard Burton, Roger Moore, Richard Harris
Rating: ★★

This explosive adventure film produced huge queues at the box office. Its plot is as predictable as the coming of Christmas and doesn't contain half as many surprises. However, it is also crammed with incident, noise, movement and action. Richard Burton, Roger Moore and Richard Harris play the leaders of a group of hand-picked mercenaries flown to Africa to rescue an African politician from the clutches of his enemies. Burton, as the hard-drinking mercenary-in-chief, gives one of his better performances. You'll have fun (but not much difficulty) keeping one jump ahead of the scriptwriter and in identifying a whole parade of stalwart supporting players.

Wild Geese II ◑ ⓥ

1985, UK, 125 mins, colour
Dir: Peter Hunt
Stars: Scott Glenn, Barbara Carrera, Laurence Olivier, Edward Fox
Rating: ★★

Although dedicated to Richard Burton, this is only a sequel to *The Wild Geese* in the loosest possible way. Dealing with a much darker kind of espionage (with its attendant element of betrayal), the story is closer to Harry Palmer territory than it is to the Burton film. Scott Glenn provides a muscular and laconic performance in the lead, but co-star Barbara Carrera is understandably defeated by such dialogue as 'With a man like you, surely nothing is impossible?'

Wild Heart, The ○
(aka: Gone to Earth)

1950, UK, 82 mins, colour
Dir: Emeric Pressburger
Stars: Jennifer Jones, David Farrar, Cyril Cusack
Rating: ★★

Jennifer Jones as one of those tempestuous country girls – this one is a kind of English equivalent to Ruby Gentry and a forerunner of *Ryan's Daughter* that she played in between portraying saints

and martyrs. Jones tries to save her beloved fox cub from pursuing hunters, and herself from pursuing men, notably the local squire, brutishly played by David Farrar.

Wild in the Country ○ ⓥ

1961, US, 114 mins, colour
Dir: Philip Dunne
Stars: Elvis Presley, Hope Lange, Tuesday Weld
Rating: ★★

A curiosity among Elvis Presley films, portraying him as a rebellious country boy with the talent to become a legendary giant. A strong cast does doughty battle with an overblown Clifford Odets screenplay, Elvis sings five songs, and there's a glimpse of Joan Crawford's daughter Christina in a small acting role.

Wild North, The ○

1951, US, 97 mins, colour
Dir: Andrew Marton
Stars: Stewart Granger, Wendell Corey, Cyd Charisse
Rating: ★★

Hardly distinguished in itself, *The Wild North* is nonetheless a noteworthy film in several respects. It was MGM's first film in AnscoColor – an attractive process which they developed themselves. The new colour coped particularly well with the snowbound scenery. It was also Stewart Granger's first Western, the fore-runner of many in the later stages of his career. The director was Andrew Marton, the Budapest-born filmmaker who came to Hollywood with the great Ernst Lubitsch in 1923. Marton was noted for the quality of his action scenes in such films as *The Longest Day*.

Wild One, The ○ ⓥ

1953, US, 80 mins, b/w
Dir: Laslo Benedek
Stars: Marlon Brando, Lee Marvin, Mary Murphy
Rating: ★★★

This shatteringly forceful film about mob-rule (produced by noted filmmaker Stanley Kramer) was banned by the British Board of Censors on its initial appearance, in 1953, because its smouldering atmosphere was considered too conducive to teenage violence. In today's climate, when such films as *Quadrophenia* paint an even more graphic picture of teenage gang violence, *The Wild One* seems a less frightening, if no less powerful film.

W

Wild Orchid ● ⓥ

1989, US, 112 mins, colour
Dir: Zalman King
Stars: Mickey Rourke, Carre Otis, Jacqueline Bisset, Bruce Greenwood
Rating: ★

Welcome to Brazil, where they party all day and party all night. Or so director Zalman King, master of well-dressed erotic claptrap, would have us believe. Leggy young lawyer Carre Otis is overwhelmed by the eroticism of the place, what with voluptuous couples having sex around every corner and even in the back seat of a car next to her. Small wonder that when she can't get frigid wheeler-dealer Mickey Rourke to respond to her, the virginal Otis, breathing heavily, goes off for a steamy session with an American who thinks she's a hooker. He subsequently proves to be her opponent in a land deal being negotiated by her decadent boss (Jacqueline Bisset). All this is probably giving the film credit for more plot than it has, especially when you consider it runs 112 minutes. Rourke, underplaying, and Otis, wide-eyed, do what they can to play the Rio sex-and-soap opera straight. Bisset over-acts with relish, probably just as well with dialogue that has Dallas licked all the way. It's like an old Warners melodrama, only feverishly overheated and running completely out of control.

Wild River ○

1960, US, 110 mins, colour
Dir: Elia Kazan
Stars: Montgomery Clift, Lee Remick, Jo Van Fleet, Albert Salmi
Rating: ★★★

Apart from the fact that it comes across in a curiously cool way, this Elia Kazan film is one of the finest examples in films of an evocation of a particular time and place, in this case the Tennessee Valley area of the early Thirties. Brilliantly controlled performances from Montgomery Clift, nicely edgy as the water authority agent sent to deal with a difficult situation; Lee Remick, creating touching moments as the widow who falls for him; Albert Salmi, making a superb smiling sadist of the local bully; and consummate character actress Jo Van Fleet, as usual playing a woman years beyond her own age, as the matriarch who refuses to budge from her property so that the land might be flooded. A rare example of a film adapted from two novels: William Bradford Huie's *Mud on the Stars*, and Borden Deal's *Dunbar's Cove*.

Wild Strawberries ◐ ⓥ

1957, Sweden, 93 mins, b/w
Dir: Ingmar Bergman
Stars: Victor Sjöström, Bibi Andersson
Rating: ★★★★

Bergman put one of his own recurring dreams (the coffin falling from the hearse) into this rich tapestry of memories and fears. Film director Victor Sjöström – Swedish cinema's best-known pioneer (best known for his silent work) – gives an astonishingly moving performance as the aged scientist who embarks on a sentimental journey; he died three years later, aged 81. Beautifully paced and acted, it's an occasionally over-symbolic work, but is riddled with richly observed characters and a real feeling for the joys of nature and youth; one of Bergman's warmest, and therefore finest, films.

Wild Target ● ⓥ

1992, France, 87 mins, colour
Dir: Pierre Salvadori
Stars: Jean Rochefort, Marie Trintignant, Guillaume Depardieu
Rating: ★★★

This black comedy about a hired assassin (lugubrious Jean Rochefort) starts in hilariously funny style and ends brightly too. In between some nicely timed shoot-outs, though, it sags more than a bit when the plot involves Marie Trintignant as a forgery fence whom Rochefort is ordered to hit but ends up protecting. The beginning, though, when he almost silences a parrot which he subsequently gives to his mother (a retired assassin who does silence the bird) is just the funniest few moments in ages.

Wild West ◐ ⓥ

1992, UK, 85 mins, colour
Dir: David Attwood
Stars: Naveen Andrews, Sarita Choudhury, Ronny Jhutti, Ravi Kapoor
Rating: ★★★

This engaging if rough-hewn film about a Pakistani Country-and-Western band is a kind of low-key Asian equivalent of *The Commitments*. Despite the rough language, casual violence and smattering of sex, it's at heart a gentle sort of film in which three brothers from Southall led by Zaf (Naveen Andrews) try to get away from their suburban semi as the Honky Tonk Cowboys. Zaf seems to find it impossible to hold down a job for longer than a day, and is in trouble with a local gang of white toughs after taking a shine to the battered wife (Sarita Choudhury) of their leader.

When she proves to be the kind of vocalist Zaf is dreaming of, hope burns anew for the Honky Tonk Cowboys. Unfortunately Mother, whose house is their haven, wants to move back to Pakistan. The ending is upbeat and downbeat at the same time, but the film is more interested in capturing the spirit of people than anything else: that and the cosmopolitan atmosphere of Southall, with its attendant dangers, is flavourfully caught.

Will Any Gentleman. . .? ☉

1953, UK, 84 mins, colour
Dir: Michael Anderson
Stars: George Cole, Veronica Hurst, Jon Pertwee
Rating: ★★★

Madcap comedy about a meek little man who is transformed into a tiger by a hypnotist. Typical of George Cole's film roles of the time, with a nicely dotty script, good colour photography and contributions from such jesters as Sid James, Jon Pertwee and Lionel Jeffries.

Willard ●

1971, US, 95 mins, colour
Dir: Daniel Mann
Stars: Bruce Davison, Ernest Borgnine, Elsa Lanchester
Rating: ★★★

This scary film was a runaway success when it first came out. Bruce Davison, whose subsequent career has not quite fired on all cylinders, plays the lonely young man of the title who makes friends with a pack of rats, one of whom proves particularly devious and intelligent, rather like Napoleon the pig in *Animal Farm*. The results of this alliance moved publicists to advise that 'this is the one movie you should not see alone'. A sequel, *Ben*, followed.

William at the Circus ☉

(aka: William Comes to Town)
1948, UK, 90 mins, colour
Dir: Val Guest
Stars: William Graham, Brian Roper
Rating: ★★

He's back! Richmal Crompton's ragged rascal springs to tousled life again in the third and last of his three screen adventures. The supporting cast has Brian Roper as an excellent Ginger, and Marquis the chimpanzee, who steals every scene he's in.

William Comes to Town

See: William at the Circus

William Shakespeare's Romeo and Juliet ◐ Ⓥ

1996, US, 117 mins, colour
Dir: Baz Luhrmann
Stars: Leonardo DiCaprio, Claire Danes, John Leguizamo, Harold Perrineau, Pete Postlethwaite, Paul Sorvino
Rating: ★★★

Updated Shakespeare is usually unsatisfactory in one way or another, but this really is a nice try. Family gang warfare is an ongoing thing at Verona Beach and its surrounds, as the local police try to keep a lid on the feud between the Montagues and the Capulets. Dreamy poet Romeo (DiCaprio) is the non-violent Montague who meets Juliet (Danes), seemingly the sole Capulet daughter, at a fancy dress ball. Pretty soon the star-crossed lovers are married, a union still unconsummated when Romeo is drawn into the families' world of violence and shoots Capulet son Tybalt to avenge the death of a friend. Director Luhrmann just about gets away with slapping the Bard's original dialogue into a world of lethal weapons and fast cars. DiCaprio and Danes both have their moments as the lovers, although she should watch pushing the winsomeness. Bravura action moments, though, just carry this one through.

Willie & Phil ○

1980, US, 116 mins, colour
Dir: Paul Mazursky
Stars: Michael Ontkean, Margot Kidder, Ray Sharkey
Rating: ★★

On paper, the concept of a homage to François Truffaut's *Jules et Jim* must have seemed a non-starter, with Michael Ontkean and Ray Sharkey so in love with the French film that they model their personal relationships on its two male characters. On the screen,however, it works surprisingly well, thanks to charming and unforced performances by Ontkean and Sharkey and by Margot Kidder as the third person in their decade-long *ménage à trois*. Writer-director Paul Mazursky infuses the film with a nice line of humour, with the occasional satirical bite and Sven Nykvist's colour photography gives the whole affair an attractive gloss.

Willow ○ Ⓥ

1988, US, 125 mins, colour
Dir: Ron Howard
Stars: Val Kilmer, Joanne Whalley-Kilmer, Warwick Davis, Jean Marsh
Rating: ★★★

This epic fantasy has more than a few elements in common with *Lord of the Rings*, in that it's about little people (played by dwarf actors) who set out, in a time long ago, to destroy the power of evil, by shepherding an abandoned baby on a journey to fulfil its destiny as a saviour for good. The trek's sometimes a bit slow, but the screen is alive with adventure most of the time and the final duel of magic and muscle provides an exciting climax. Not recommended for very young children, who might find a fear some two-headed monster the stuff which nightmares are made.

Will Penny ◐

1967, US, 109 mins, colour
Dir: Tom Gries
Stars: Charlton Heston, Joan Hackett, Donald Pleasence, Quentin Dean
Rating: ★★★★

There is a magnificent cast in this elegiac Western that was the best thing writer-director Tom Gries ever made. Charlton Heston is a middle-ageing cowboy offered a rewarding but dangerous new life with a frontier widow and her son. Joan Hackett as the widow forms a strong axis for the action in a touching and warm relationship with Heston. Donald Pleasence is memorably over-the-top as the psychotic preacher who menaces their happiness. The fight scenes are red-blooded and raw, and the ending will leave all but the hardest pretty misty-eyed.

Will Success Spoil Rock Hunter? ○

(aka: Oh! For a Man)
1957, US, 94 mins, colour
Dir: Frank Tashlin
Stars: Tony Randall, Jayne Mansfield
Rating: ★★★★

Zany, good-natured and packed with inventive gags, writer-director Frank Tashlin's adaptation of George Axelrod's Broadway hit provided Jayne Mansfield with her best film. From the opening sequence, combining credits with a skit on TV commercials, the fun hardly ever lets up, and there are delightful contributions from Tony Randall, Betsy Drake and Henry Jones, plus a 'surprise' appearance from Groucho Marx. Two stars of comedy films from a much earlier era, Minta Durfee and Benny Rubin, appear in cameo roles.

Willy Wonka and the Chocolate Factory ☉

1971, US, 100 mins, colour
Dir: Mel Stuart

Stars: Gene Wilder, Jack Albertson, Peter Ostrum
Rating: ★★★★★

Pure magic: the only filmed version of a Roald Dahl story written by Dahl himself and the most successful by a mile. Foot-tapping songs, especially 'Oompa Loompa Doompadee Doo', amazing Heath Robinson-type settings in the chocolate factory and, enjoying his finest hour, Gene Wilder as the charmingly devious Wonka himself. Julie Dawn Cole is wonderfully horrid as the most obnoxious of the five children who go on a tour of the factory, several of them destined for appallingly appropriate fates.

Wilt ◐ Ⓥ

1989, UK, 91 mins, colour
Dir: Michael Tuchner
Stars: Griff Rhys Jones, Mel Smith, Alison Steadman, Diana Quick
Rating: ★★

An adult comedy only in the sense that there's a lot of coarse comic business with an inflatable doll, this vehicle for Mel Smith and Griff Rhys Jones leans more towards the world of a lewder *Carry On* humour than that of *Lucky Jim*, out of which its leading character, Henry Wilt (Rhys Jones), seems to have stepped. Murder and mayhem ensue, but mirth is largely absent, notably in a bungled ending which should have been hilarious. Smith and Jones do their things, Alison Steadman is gorgeous. Bright and breezy, and the team's best film work to date, *Wilt* still seriously lacks the roots in reality that all quality comedy needs.

Winchester 73 ○

1950, US, 92 mins, b/w
Dir: Anthony Mann
Stars: James Stewart, Shelley Winters, Dan Duryea, Stephen McNally
Rating: ★★★★★

First-rate picturesque Western which was a major springboard for the revival of the genre in the Fifties, with a fine leading performance from James Stewart, taut direction by Anthony Mann and superb photography by Greta Garbo's favourite cameraman, William Daniels. Rock Hudson and Tony Curtis, both then-newcomers, have small featured roles (Hudson plays a Red Indian) and there are sharply etched portraits of Western characters on either sides of the law from such reliable players as Dan Duryea, Shelley Winters, Stephen McNally, Millard Mitchell, Jay C Flippen, Will Geer and John McIntire.

W

Wind ◐ Ⓥ

1992, US, 125 mins, colour
Dir: Carroll Ballard
Stars: Matthew Modine, Jennifer Grey,
Cliff Robertson, Jack Thompson, Rebba
Miller
Rating: ★★

'Winning is everything,' is the message in this often exhilarating, always superbly shot (by John Toll) yachting drama, which sometimes hits the doldrums away from its action scenes. The prize at stake here is the America's Cup, for which American sailor Matthew Modine and his girlfriend (Jennifer Grey) have to take on the forces of nature as well as an arrogant Australian (but of course) rival. The plot is a bit clichéd and the emotional elements are bland, but the stars seem to be giving it all they've got on board the yacht, and the spectacular racing action, particularly at the breathtaking climax of this patriotic tale, will keep you near the edges of your seats. Another outdoors action drama from Carroll Ballard: a specialist in the genre, he also made *Never Cry Wolf* and *The Black Stallion*.

Wind and the Lion, The ○

1975, US, 119 mins, colour
Dir: John Milius
Stars: Sean Connery, Candice Bergen,
Brian Keith, John Huston
Rating: ★★★★★

Seldom has a story been so stylishly, colourfully, excitingly and movingly captured as in John Milius' saga of action in Morocco in 1904. The pace, the action and the spirit of pre-war adventure rush across the screen in a never-slackening surge. At the centre of it sits the formidable figure of Sean Connery, wildly miscast as a sort of whimsical Scottish Berber, but giving a brilliantly understated performance that overcomes all and will leave you cheering for him before the end; and Candice Bergen could not be bettered as the cool and gutsy American widow he kidnaps from Tangier, with her two children, aiming to exchange them for money, rifles and his rightful place in the country's aristocracy. President Teddy Roosevelt (Brian Keith's best performance in ages) agrees to the bargain, but plans to assert his authority with force if necessary. Add German intervention and Moroccan intrigue and it is thrillingly inevitable that the pot should boil over in the last reel. The participation of the two children will

have watching youngsters living the saga with them.

Windbag the Sailor ☉

1936, UK, 85 mins, b/w
Dir: William Beaudine
Stars: Will Hay, Moore Marriott
Rating: ★★★

Will Hay himself helped to write this priceless comedy about a bogus sea captain shipwrecked on a cannibal isle. Hay, bewhiskered Moore Marriott and tubby Graham Moffatt enjoy some hilarious scenes, especially those revolving around the compass.

Wind Cannot Read, The ○

1958, UK, 115 mins, colour
Dir: Ralph Thomas
Stars: Dirk Bogarde, Yoko Tani, Ronald
Lewis
Rating: ★★★★

Simple, touching story of a doomed romance between an RAF officer and a delicately lovely Japanese girl during World War Two. Sensitive acting from Dirk Bogarde and Yoko Tani ensures that you'll need a handkerchief long before the end. Author Richard Mason provided a perceptive screenplay from his own novel, a far superior piece to that other east-west romance *The World of Suzie Wong* which Mason also wrote. And there's some beautiful photography by Ernest Steward – the Eastmancolour process has surely never looked better.

Wind in the Willows, The ☉ Ⓥ

1996, UK, 88 mins, colour
Dir: Terry Jones
Stars: Terry Jones, Eric Idle, Nicol
Williamson, John Cleese, Antony Sher,
Steve Coogan
Rating: ★★

They keep trying to make Kenneth Grahame's classic with live actors, but it just doesn't work. The whole secret of the appeal of children's stories like these are the characters as animals with recognisable human traits. This is a game and ambitious attempt to capture its magic but when the most interesting characters in an adaptation of *The Wind in the Willows* prove to be the villainous weasels, you know you're in trouble. Director Terry Jones' own charmless performance robs Toad of much of his lovability and renders him simply a scoundrel – effective only in the courtroom scene with Stephen Fry as the defence counsel, John Cleese as the judge and chief weasel Antony Sher disguised as a rab-

bit on the jury. Here alone is the inanely likeable spirit of the original recaptured; otherwise sparkle and wit are in short supply and the songs are wincingly indifferent.

Window in London, A ○

1939, UK, 76 mins, b/w
Dir: Herbert Mason
Stars: Michael Redgrave, Sally Gray,
Paul Lukas, Patricia Roc
Rating: ★★★

This absorbing film, translated from the original French, has a real sting in the tail. It was also the last British film made by Paul Lukas before he went back to Hollywood where, four years later, he won an Academy Award in *Watch on the Rhine*.

Wings ○

1927, US, 143 mins, b/w
Dir: William Wellman
Stars: Clara Bow, Richard Arlen, Jobyna
Ralston, Gary Cooper
Rating: ★★★

The flying sequences in the first winner of Hollywood's best film Oscar are still among the most breathtaking ever put on screen, with the infantry battle scenes not far behind. Despite some extremely poignant moments, however, the story is really too slight for this sort of running time. It's a pity, as the action stuff is unmissable: all that you see on screen was actually shot by dedicated daredevil director William Wellman for the film, with scores of photographers positioned in planes and cameras largely positioned on gun mounts. Clara Bow, Buddy Rogers and Richard Arlen head the cast (with a young Gary Cooper getting a moving cameo – and lots of fan mail): but the planes are still the stars.

Wings of Eagles, The ○

1957, US, 110 mins, colour
Dir: John Ford
Stars: John Wayne, Maureen O'Hara
Rating: ★★

Epic John Ford film, beautifully constructed and with its fair share of action. It's based on the life of one of America's greatest air heroes, Frank 'Spig' Wead, a kind of American equivalent to Douglas Bader. The real-life Wead, despite being crippled by a fall after some spectacular Twenties' exploits in the Schneider Cup air races, made a substantial contribution to America's war effort in the Pacific in World War Two. He also wrote plays about the war. And one of them *They Were Expendable* – was filmed by Ford in 1945, ironically with Wayne in the starring role. Ward Bond, another of Ford's favourite actors, does sterling, unobtrusive work as Wead's right-hand man and Maureen O'Hara gets well into the character of Mrs Wead and grows old, as always, beautifully.

Wings of Fame ❶ ⓥ

1990, Holland, 109 mins, colour
Dir: Otakar Volocek
Stars: Peter O'Toole, Colin Firth, Marie Trintignant
Rating: ★★

Films about people who die and find themselves in some kind of staging post for the dead have enjoyed sporadic popularity with film-makers since the success of *Outward Bound* more than 60 years ago. *Wings of Fame* is not destined to join the greats of the genre, although it does get better – a lot better – towards the end. For the most part, although the idea is nice, the execution is poor, full of clumsily staged scenes and actors talking at the tops of their voices. And the notion of blending real famous dead people with fictitious ones in the vast hotel on a fog-shrouded.island, is one that works against the film rather than in its favour. Towards the end, director Otakar Volocek seems to get the hang of it, and things come together to rather better effect. Peter O'Toole and Colin Firth star as the matinee idol actor and his youthful murderer and the idea of it all, I think, is that fame is fleeting.

Wings of the Apache ❶ ⓥ

(aka: Fire Birds)
1990, US, 89 mins, colour
Dir: David Green
Stars: Nicolas Cage, Tommy Lee Jones, Sean Young
Rating: ★★★

Down-the-line Hollywood combat film of the old school, with American Apache helicopters in aerial action against new foes: Colombian drug dealers and the ace pilot who protects them. Nicolas Cage is the young hotshot US pilot, Tommy Lee Jones the older instructor who wishes he were back in the action. And, in these days of equality, Sean Young is no wilting violet waiting back at the base, but a scout pilot who helps the boys out of trouble at the end. Shortish, noisy and incident-filled, the film has a serviceable script and keeps you hopping, if hardly guessing. Cliffhanging stuff for action fans and an unusually straightforward role for Cage that his fans will like.

Winnie the Pooh and a Day for Eeyore ☉ ⓥ

1983, US, 26 mins, colour
Dir: Wolfgang Reitherman
Rating: ★★★

If anything, the Disney series of adaptations from the stories of A A Milne gained in charm as it went along. There's a definite woodland feel as well as a nostalgic tug as the stories of Poohsticks and Eeyore's holiday interweave and unravel deep in the Hundred Acre Wood. Eeyore has a wonderful laconic voice and his tribulations are always pleasing and sometimes amusing.

Winnie the Pooh and the Blustery Day ☉ ⓥ

1968, US, 26 mins, colour
Dir: Wolfgang Reitherman
Rating: ★★★

Chronologically the second of the charming Disney featurettes from the works of A A Milne, in which Tigger arrives in the forest and Owl's house is blown down in a storm. A nightmare ballet involving pink and blue elephants seems to have strayed in from *Fantasia* via *Dumbo!*

Winnie the Pooh and the Honey Tree ☉ ⓥ

1965, US, 26 mins, colour
Dir: Wolfgang Reitherman
Rating: ★★★

Apart from the intrusion of a character called Gopher (who hastens to tell us that he isn't in the books), this is a delightful Disney featurette from stories by A A Milne. The drawing, for example, is quite beautiful and faithful to a rare stage of delicacy to Ernest Shepard's original illustrations. Much of the stories' text, too, has been retained. The catchy songs are by the Mary Poppins men, Oscar-winners Richard and Robert Sherman.

Winnie the Pooh and Tigger Too ☉ ⓥ

1974, US, 26 mins, colour
Dir: John Lounsbery
Rating: ★★★

The third in the series of Walt Disney cartoon featurettes from the books of A A Milne. Charming, amusing and refreshingly close to the spirit of the original.

Winslow Boy, The ○ ⓥ

1948, UK, 117 mins, b/w
Dir: Anthony Asquith

Stars: Robert Donat, Margaret Leighton, Cedric Hardwicke
Rating: ★★★★

Terence Rattigan's stage success, based on a real-life *cause célèbre*, is the very stuff that drama, suspense and audience appeal are made of. After it proved equally effective as a radio play, the playwright himself helped translate the piece into a film, the screen version getting a boost from the powerful portrayal of Robert Donat, as the QC who defends a young naval cadet accused of a theft which, although minor, could ruin his career. The plot is brilliantly constructed, with a highly satisfying climax, and directed with a keen insight into English character by Anthony Asquith, who keeps tension on high throughout, especially in the climactic courtroom scenes. A highly superior cast includes fully-rounded characterisations from Margaret Leighton, Cedric Hardwicke, Frank Lawton, Basil Radford, Kathleen Harrison, Francis L Sullivan and Stanley Holloway.

Winter Kills ●

1979, US, 97 mins, colour
Dir: William Richert
Stars: Jeff Bridges, John Huston, Anthony Perkins, Dorothy Malone
Rating: ★

Very complex film about a presidential assassination mystery that makes the John F Kennedy killing, as one critic put it 'look like a connect-the-dots puzzle'. Jeff Bridges achieves a believable characterisation of a man caught up in a situation he can't grasp, a situation with which the audience might well sympathise. 'It's a conundrum,' growls Richard Boone. 'A riddle within a riddle.' He can say that again. Elizabeth Taylor pops in for a brief wordless cameo role as a former movie star who served as procuress for the late president.

Winter People ○ ⓥ

1988, US, 111 mins, colour
Dir: Ted Kotcheff
Stars: Kurt Russell, Kelly McGillis, Lloyd Bridges
Rating: ★

Another of those backwoods/hillbilly feuding families dramas where a good beginning and better intentions are soon submerged beneath a morass of rampant melodrama. John Ehle's book may well have the 'beauty and depth of feeling' that screenwriter Carol Fobieski described in interviews, but if it does then she has made a hash of it.

W

Kelly McGillis acts her socks off as the unwed mother who lives alone and nurses a guilty secret (pretty obvious that her baby's father is one of the rival clan), but she's fighting a losing battle against this script and the miscasting of Kurt Russell as the wandering clock-maker for whom she falls after he and his eight-year-old daughter stumble on her cottage. The daughter (Amelia Burnette) is a real charmer, but has too little to do in further proceedings, which are strictly along East Lynne lines and become progressively more ludicrous.

Wired ● ⓥ
1989, US, 108 mins, colour
Dir: Larry Peerce
Stars: Michael Chiklis, Patti D'Arbanville, J T Walsh
Rating: ★★

Tubby, high-living John Belushi was a film star, comedian and drug addict and in the end his habit killed him. Ultimately, this is all that director Larry Peerce's biopic (based on Bob Woodward's best-selling biography) can say, despite a bright beginning, and adopting the unusual approach of having the dead Belushi rise from the morgue and relive parts of his past with the help of his guardian angel. A wonderful life it's not, and the film doesn't paint it that way. But it's too one-note to grip and fascinate, despite the excellent impersonation of Belushi by 25-year-old Michael Chiklis, and the entertainingly accurate recreation of some of Belushi and Dan Aykroyd's *Blues Brothers* routines.

Wisdom ● ⓥ
1987, US, 109 mins, colour
Dir: Emilio Estevez
Stars: Emilio Estevez, Demi Moore, Tom Skerritt, Veronica Cartwright
Rating: ★★

A distinctly quirky latter-day *Bonnie and Clyde*, with Clyde coming in the form of John Wisdom, played rather glumly by Emilio Estevez. Wisdom has a record – he stole a car in a drunken spree when 19. Now that conviction disqualifies him from all but the most menial jobs. Inspired by a TV programme about banks foreclosing on farmers and small businessmen unable to maintain their mortgage payments, Wisdom decides to do something positive with his life. He buys a powerful automatic rifle with the money he has saved for a car, and starts to hold up banks – not to steal money, but to burn their mortgage records. His girlfriend (Demi Moore), at first his un-

suspecting getaway driver, soon begins to believe in his cause while, to half the population of America, Wisdom becomes some kind of folk hero.

Wise Blood ⓞ
1979, US/Germany, 108 mins, colour
Dir: John Huston
Stars: Brad Dourif, Ned Beatty, Amy Wright, John Huston
Rating: ★★★

John Huston's very black comedy about the exploits of the atheist son of a hellfire preacher in America's southern states' 'Bible belt', a character whom Brad Dourif makes both funny and frightening. It's a disturbing sermon on gullibility and greed, sometimes quite horrifying, but at its funniest in the sequences where a fake gorilla visits the town to promote a film.

Wish You Were Here ● ⓥ
1987, UK, 92 mins, colour
Dir: David Leland
Stars: Emily Lloyd, Tom Bell
Rating: ★★★

This famous film hid elements from every avant-garde British film you've seen in the past 25 years. And, like his central character, a 'difficult' teenager, writer-director David Leland is out to impress. His work, though, pales by comparison with sassy, delightful newcomer Emily Lloyd as the girl, whose top-notch performance made her Britain's youngest international star at 16. Her character, Lynda, is cocky, rude, sexually aware and can't wait to get on with life. As played by the piquant Lloyd, she's also quite delightful, even if enough to make all fathers of teenage daughters wince. And she's also got a ready quip for every occasion. 'Your mother would have shown you the door,' her father grates. 'I've seen it,' she replies. The film, set in the early Fifties, is, although not credited as such, based on the early life of Cynthia *(Personal Services)* Payne. Stanley Myers' music to accompany Lynda's high and low jinks is as quirkily individual as ever.

Wistful Widow of Wagon Gap, The ⓞ
1947, US, 78 mins, b/w
Dir: Charles Barton
Stars: Bud Abbott, Lou Costello, Marjorie Main
Rating: ★★★

Bud and Lou go west, and get saddled with a fearsome widow (Marjorie Main, later famous as Ma Kettle) and numerous children. One of the bad

guys is played by 6ft 4in Glenn Strange, who also appeared in the following Abbott and Costello film comedy – as the Frankenstein monster! The screenplay is by Robert Lees, Fred Rinaldo and John Grant who did so much of Abbott and Costello's best work in the Forties.

Witchcraft ⓞ
1964, UK, 79 mins, b/w
Dir: Don Sharp
Stars: Lon Chaney Jr, Jack Hedley, Jill Dixon
Rating: ★★★

A witch rises from the dead and strange and fatal things begin to happen to the descendants of those who had buried her alive. Director Don Sharp (who made *Rasputin* and *Kiss of the Vampire*) is an old hand at this sort of thing and conjures up bags of creepy atmosphere with the aid of good black and white photography.

Witches, The ⓞ ⓥ
1989, UK, 90 mins, colour
Dir: Nicolas Roeg
Stars: Anjelica Huston, Mai Zetterling, Rowan Atkinson, Jasen Fisher
Rating: ★★★★★

There's a witches' convention going on in Newquay and it's the decision of the Grand High Witch to use an evil potion (via sweet shops) to turn the children of Britain into mice. Nothing can stop the cackling fiends and their evil plans – except perhaps a cigar-smoking Swedish granny and the grandson the High Witch has turned into a mouse. What is it about Roald Dahl's stories that makes such excellent cinema? Who can say, but this is a truly delightful children's film in which real mice and 'mice' from Jim Henson's Creature Workshop blend almost seamlessly as the battle between good and evil maintains a fevered pace. Huston is magnificently malevolent as a witch as fearsome as anything from Disney, and Zetterling excellent as the fearful but determined grandma. There's loads of green and purple smoke and action galore. Tinies, though, should have a parent standing by.

Witches of Eastwick, The ● ⓥ
1987, US, 118 mins, colour
Dir: George Miller
Stars: Jack Nicholson, Cher, Susan Sarandon, Michelle Pfeiffer
Rating: ★★★

Fast-moving and fun (once the scene is set), this black erotic fantasy has 'witches' Cher, Susan Sarandon and Michefle Pfeiffer trying to conjure up their perfect man. Enter Jack Nicholson who with the right blend of charm, bravado and promises manages to seduce all three. Director George *(Mad Max)* Miller is a master of pace and keeps the ball rolling here, which disguises the fact that the plot is a bit thin in places. In addition to this, Jack Nicholson goes wildly over the top in a demonic role that is perfect for his kind of histrionics. His manically gleeful portrait of Daryl Van Horne, the lover unwisely and mystically summoned by the three ladies, dominates the whole film, almost eclipsing his female co-stars.

Witchfinder-General ● Ⓥ
(aka: The Conqueror Worm)
1967, UK, 98 mins, colour
Dir: Michael Reeves
Stars: Vincent Price, Ian Ogilvy, Patrick Wymark
Rating: ★★★

The third and last horror film made by the talented young director Michael Reeves, who died soon after at the age of 25. This one deals with religious persecution in England at the time of Cromwell. Reeves made his first film, *Revenge of the Blood Beast*, with Barbara Steele, in Italy. But he returned to his native Britain in 1967 to direct veteran horror star Boris Karloff in *The Sorcerers*. *Witchfinder-General* has been accused of painting too bloody and violent a picture of the times, but its power is undeniable.

With a Song in My Heart ○
1952, US, 117 mins, colour
Dir: Walter Lang
Stars: Susan Hayward, Rory Calhoun, David Wayne, Thelma Ritter
Rating: ★★

Susan Hayward, who seemed to be forever being nominated for an Oscar until she finally won it in 1958 for *I Want to Live!*, contributes another attention-grabbing performance in this musical blopic about singer Jane Froman, who lost the use of both legs after a wartime plane crash. Hayward is really the whole show, although the young Robert Wagner has a few effective moments as a GI, and Froman herself makes a notable contribution by supplying the rich, melodic singing voice to which Hayward mimes so well.

With Honors ○ Ⓥ
1994, US, 100 mins, colour
Dir: Alek Keshishian
Stars: Joe Pesci, Brendan Fraser, Moira

Kelly, Patrick Dempsey, Josh Hamilton, Gore Vidal
Rating: ★★★

If you can get past the very silly initial premise, this is an ultimately winning parable that develops into a real tearjerker towards the end. Joe Pesci plays a bum, a homeless hobo squatting in the boiler-room beneath a university library. Monty (Brendan Fraser), a graduate whose thesis is threatened by computer failure, is on his way to copy what he's printed of it when he trips, the thesis falling through a grating into Pesci's hands. Down in the boiler room Fraser finds Pesci beginning to incinerate his beloved work because he doesn't approve of its sentiments. Now you and I would have thrown ourselves on the tramp and wrested away the thesis. But not Fraser. He strikes up a deal with Pesci, offering daily favours in return for the pages, one by one. Naturally, the hobo proves to be wiser than the students and helps them on the road to citizenship, although he also proves to be dying of asbestosis. The film's simple virtues and direct sentiments prove quite effective at times, and Pesci never overplays. In the end the story passes perhaps not with honours, but at least with credit.

Withnail & I ● Ⓥ
1986, UK, 107 mins, colour
Dir: Bruce Robinson
Stars: Richard E Grant, Paul McGann, Richard Griffiths, Michael Elphick
Rating: ★★★

This comic chronicle of the hazardous times of two out-of-work actors holidaying at a farm in Penrith, the one pursued by the 25-stone gay uncle of the other, is a successor in its comedy of desperation to such TV series as *Hancock* and *The Likely Lads*. Despite well-drawn characters, though, the film remains as bogged in tedium as the actors' flat is in dirty dishes until the boys hit the road to the country. Here their efforts to keep body and soul together are often more than mildly amusing, especially when suffering the attentions of Richard Griffiths as the puffing billy gourmet uncle, and Michael Elphick as the local poacher with a chicken in his coat and eels down his trousers.

Without a Clue ○ ● Ⓥ
(aka: Sherlock and Me)
1988, UK, 106 mins, colour
Dir: Thorn Eberhardt
Stars: Michael Caine, Ben Kingsley, Jeffrey Jones
Rating: ★

It's a lovely idea, to spin a Sherlock Holmes adventure around the notion that the real crime-solver was Dr Watson but, at least in this treatment, it doesn't work. The simple-minded script supposes that Holmes is in fact a ham actor whom Watson is forced to employ in order to hide his own activities from the medical profession. But the vein struck is *Carry On Holmes*, with Michael Caine as Holmes given the thankless task of incarnating a character who's just too idiotic to be true. It's impossible to identify with such a farcical blunderer and so, in spite of Ben Kingsley's cerebral medical mastermind and Lysette Anthony's spirited lady in distress, who has an amusing role to play in the finale, the charade never holds our interest until the setpiece of the final 20 minutes, a showdown in and below a deserted theatre.

Without a Trace ◑
1983, US, 120 mins, colour
Dir: Stanley R Jaffe
Stars: Kate Nelligan, Judd Hirsch, David Dukes, Stockard Channing
Rating: ★★★

Kate Nelligan was fast bidding to become the queen of screen anguish when she made this heartrending film. She's out on her own again in this three-handkerchief drama as a mother whose six-year-old son disappears without trace on a short journey to school one morning. The subsequent drama is too strung-out, especially in the closing stages, when director Stanley Jaffe's treatment of the story robs it of some of its inherent tension. Still, Nelligan, looking very Lilli Palmer-ish in this role, holds it together, intelligently conveying a literate woman holding hard to her sanity and only giving way to pity when it doesn't matter. And the ending will make most viewers reach for at least one tissue to wipe away a tear.

Without Love ○
1945, US, 111 mins, b/w
Dir: Harold S Bucquet
Stars: Spencer Tracy, Katharine Hepburn, Lucille Ball
Rating: ★★★

Philip Barry's plays had made successful films twice before for Katharine Hepburn (in *Holiday* and *The Philadelphia Story*) so, especially selecting Spencer Tracy as her leading man, she was obviously on to another winner here in a comedy about a 'platonic' marriage. The stars, though, have

W

scenes stolen from under their noses by Lucille Ball and Keenan Wynn. But Tracy, too, has his comic moments, especially in the scenes where he walks in his sleep and encounters a dog that has been trained to stop him.

With Six You Get Eggroll ○

1968, US, 95 mins, colour
Dir: Howard Morris
Stars: Doris Day, Bhan Keith
Rating: ★★

A wholesome if rather obviously-plotted comedy about the disaster-prone romance of a widow (with three sons and an enormous Old English sheepdog) and a widower with a teenage daughter and a French poodle. Their numerous troubles seem largely of their own making, but nonetheless it's fun, with a good chase sequence, and some nice comic 'bits' from Alice Ghostley (as a nutty housekeeper), Pat Caroll (as heroine Doris Day's wisecracking sister) and George Carlin as a smart-Alec hamburger stand operator.

Witness ◐ Ⓥ

1985, US, 112 mins, colour
Dir: Peter Weir
Stars: Harrison Ford, Kelly McGillis, Lukas Haas, Danny Glover, Alexander Godunov, Josef Sommer
Rating: ★★★★

A high-tension thriller that won an Oscar for its editing, and was unlucky not to take several more. Remarkably sensitive performances from Harrison Ford and Kelly McGillis, still among the best either has done, and wide-eyed boy actor Lukas Haas, plus a thrilling *High Noon*-style shootout at the climax. One of the villains is played by Danny Glover before he became part of the *Lethal Weapon* team.

Witness for the Prosecution ○ Ⓥ

1957, US, 114 mins, b/w
Dir: Billy Wilder
Stars: Tyrone Power, Marlene Dietrich, Charles Laughton
Rating: ★★★★

Now you think you've solved it, now you haven't, is the theme of this Agatha Christie-inspired suspense classic directed by Billy Wilder, with Charles Laughton giving his last great screen performance as the eccentric barrister who uses a monocle to reflect sunlight into the eye of a hostile witness. Based on Christie's hit play, the story, of a man on trial for murder, is vastly entertaining with many twists and blind turnings. But Laughton's

real-life wife, Elsa Lanchester, almost steals his thunder as nurse Miss Plimsoll – always ready to administer yet another injection or pop another series of pills down his throat – and her delightful performance earned her an Oscar nomination.

Wiz, The ⊙ Ⓥ

1978, US, 133 mins, colour
Dir: Sidney Lumet
Stars: Diana Ross, Michael Jackson, Richard Pryor
Rating: ★★★

A hip, black, Motown *Wizard of Oz*. Diana Ross couldn't have seemed further from the concept of Dorothy: but, apart from being entirely the wrong age, she is unexpectedly excellent. So is the choreography and especially Tony Walton's production design. The first sight of the Emerald City and scenes of Dorothy and friends dancing away down the yellow-brick road are all eye-catchingly successful. The ensemble scenes are mostly good too especially 'Brand New Day' – and the make-up for Tin Man and Lion quite superb. The script, alas, is the film's weak link and there is too much of it, though. Nonetheless, this trip up the yellow-brick road has something to please almost everyone.

Wizard of Oz, The ⊙ Ⓥ

1939, US, 101 mins, colour
Dir: Victor Fleming
Stars: Judy Garland, Frank Morgan, Ray Bolger, Bert Lahr
Rating: ★★★★★

Pure, vintage magic. The most fabulous fairy-story ever filmed – and a triumph for MGM's decision to make L Frank Baum's story as a live-action musical and not a cartoon. And, when Shirley Temple proved unavailable, Judy Garland was an inspired choice as Dorothy, breaking everyone's hearts with her simple rendition of 'Over the Rainbow', which nearly got cut out of the finished film. Over the years, the film has lost none of its original charm, and several of its actors – Margaret Hamilton (Wicked Witch), Ray Bolger (Scarecrow), Jack Haley (Tin Man) and Bert Lahr (Cowardly Lion) achieved immortality in a single performance.

Wolf ● Ⓥ

1994, US, 125 mins, colour
Dir: Mike Nichols
Stars: Jack Nicholson, Michelle Pfeiffer, James Spader, Kate Nelligan, Om Puri, Prunella Scales
Rating: ★★★

Given that Dracula and Frankenstein had succumbed to the all-star treatment in the early Nineties, the Wolf Man was the obvious classic horror candidate to complete the trilogy. Surprise to find such stars as Jack Nicholson and Michefle Pfeiffer in such goings-on, but then this is a slightly offbeat treatment of the legend, and one that wastes no time getting under way. Nicholson hits a wolf on a snowbound road at a time when the full moon is at its closest to earth. Bitten by the injured beast, he is soon feeling the first twitches of possession. The twist here is that his lupine elements give him heightened senses of smell, sight, hearing and perception, enabling him to fight back against the slimebag (James Spader, up to his old tricks again) who has nicked his secure job as editor-in-chief at a publishing firm. To say more would spoil the plot, which rises to a fine crescendo, only to lope off slightly disappointingly over the horizon. This cast gives the hairy old piece better value than it's had in years.

Wolfen ●

1981, US, 110 mins, colour
Dir: Michael Wadleigh
Stars: Albert Finney, Diane Venora, Gregory Hines, Edward James Olmos
Rating: ★★

A horror film with pretensions. People are getting their throats torn out in New York City, and Michael Wadleigh's prowling cameras, plus killings 'seen' in negative give you a pretty good idea of what's going on. Albert Finney, with a ragged American accent left over from *Annie*, is the detective hauled off suspension to investigate, running into a lot of mumbo-jumbo about hunting grounds, families and killing to survive. With all its creeping around, frank dialogue and bits of people flying through the air when the 'wolfen' attack, it's not a film for the nervous or easily shocked. Director Wadleigh tries hard to cover the film with an other-wordly quality and a feeling of something outside our understanding, and Gregory Hines scores nicely on his film debut as a hip coroner with a disarming sense of humour.

Wolf Man, The ◐

1941, US, 70 mins, b/w
Dir: George Waggner
Stars: Lon Chaney Jr, Claude Rains, Bela Lugosi, Evelyn Ankers
Rating: ★★★

Werewolves, unlike Dracula and Frankenstein, have no literary origin.

So, for Universal's second stab at lycanthropy, writer Curt Siodmak concocted a slice of instant mythology in the form of the old Romany rhyme: 'Even a man who is pure at heart and says his prayers by night, can become a wolf when the wolfbane blooms and the moon is full and bright.' The movie, set in an improbable Hollywood version of Wales, gave Lon Chaney Jr his chance – excellently taken – to join the pantheon of movie monsters as the reluctant victim of the bite of the werewolf. Helped by make-up wizard Jack Pierce and his painfully applied yak hairs and by splendid special effects from John P Fulton, Chaney gives a memorable and quite moving performance which was to typecast him in horror movies for much of his subsequent career.

Wolves of Willoughby Chase, The ① ⓥ
1988, UK, 93 mins, colour
Dir: Stuart Orme
Stars: Stephanie Beacham, Mel Smith, Geraldine James, Richard O'Brien
Rating: ★★

Stephanie Beacham took time out from crossing verbal swords with Joan Collins in *Dynasty* to jet to Prague to play monstrous Victorian governess, Letitia Slighcarp, whose twisted schemes put Disney's Cruella DeVil to shame. She and Mel Smith, as rotund Dickensian sidekick, Mr Grimshaw, are the best things in this very dark children's fantasy from the superb Joan Aiken novel. It's a familiar story of two adventurous girls from different social backgrounds who are abandoned into a nightmare world of the workhouse and poverty. All the elements are in place for a classic children's film along the lines of *The Railway Children;* but somewhere down the line they refused to gel, even though the settings are brilliant. As to the wolves of the title, they look more like Alsatian pets and never likely to devour our young heroines.

Woman Alone, The
See: Sabotage

Woman In a Dressing Gown ○
1957, UK, 93 mins, b/w
Dir: J Lee Thompson
Stars: Yvonne Mitchell, Anthony Quayle, Sylvia Syms
Rating: ★★★

An adult and unsentimental drama, one of a wave of British realist dramas

of its time. Putting a marriage on the rocks under a magnifying glass, it brings into focus the faults on both sides. Anthony Quayle and Yvonne Mitchell are magnificent as the couple under scrutiny, Mitchell especially deserving praise for allowing the make-up department to turn her into such a spectacular drab.

Woman in Question, The ○
(aka: Five Angles on Murder)
1949, UK, 88 mins, b/w
Dir: Anthony Asquith
Stars: Jean Kent, Dirk Bogarde
Rating: ★★★

Absorbing whodunnit with the accent on character. The victim, a fairground fortune teller, is viewed in different lights by each of five acquaintances; their recollections make up the thread of the story – but which, if any, shows her in the true light? An interesting experiment which doesn't quite work, but Anthony Asquith's clever handling of the mounting suspense ensures that you'll stay watching to the end to discover the answer.

Woman in Red, The ① ⓥ
1984, US, 87 mins, colour
Dir: Gene Wilder
Stars: Gene Wilder, Kelly LeBrock, Gina Radner, Joseph Bologna, Charles Grodin
Rating: ★

Hollywood has had considerable success with remakes of such French successes as *3 Men and a Baby*. But Gene Wilder came a coinsiderable cropper with this revised version of *Pardon Mon Affaire,* which flattens the delicate Gallic naughtiness and fails to come up with anything funny by way of compensation. Wilder does bring some warmth and his own zany charm to the minor executive obsessed with a girl in red (Kelly LeBrock, a great looker of limited acting ability) but the talents of Joseph Bologna and Charles Grodin as his friends are wasted.

Woman in the Window, The ○ ⓥ
1944, US, 99 mins, b/w
Dir: Fritz Lang
Stars: Edward G Robinson, Joan Bennett, Raymond Massey, Dan Duryea
Rating: ★★★★

Tremendous thriller made by the German director Fritz Lang at the end of a very profitable decade in Hollywood. Edward G Robinson gives a fine study in increasingly anguished desperation as the mild professor who becomes enmeshed in

violence, murder and blackmail after a little innocent flirtation with a woman who resembles a portrait that has fascinated him. Robinson and co-stars Joan Bennett and Dan Duryea, here at his silkily treacherous best as the blackmailer, teamed again the following year with Lang for the equally remarkable *Scarlet Street.*

Woman Obsessed, A ○
1959, US, 102 mins, colour
Dir: Henry Hathaway
Stars: Susan Hayward, Stephen Boyd
Rating: ★★

Triple-handkerchief weepie, with Susan Hayward as the courageous widow carving out a new life for herself and her seven-year-old son. Beautiful colour photography of the Canadian Rockies. One time leading man Arthur Franz can be seen in a small role as Hayward's husband, killed in a forest fire early on.

Woman of Straw ○
1964, UK, 117 mins, colour
Dir: Basil Dearden
Stars: Gina Lollobrigida, Sean Connery, Ralph Richardson
Rating: ★★★

This electrifying thriller with a fistful of twists provided a respite from 007 for Sean Connery. He plays the ne'er-do-well nephew of a wheelchair-bound millionaire and talks the old man's nurse (Gina Lollobrigida) into a marriage of convenience. The question of inheritance is greedily anticipated until the poor man's untimely death complicates matters. La Lollo and Connery play the situations crisp and tight, in direct contrast to the flamboyant cackle of Ralph Richardson's millionaire. Director Basil Dearden sometimes shows a tendency to pull Hammer horror tricks to enliven the suspense, but the acting keeps things going smoothly, the colour photography is nicely in tune with the surroundings, and the love scenes have genuine passion. Only the ending is weak and flaws the film's impact.

Woman of the Year ○
1941, US, 115 mins, b/w
Dir: George Stevens
Stars: Spencer Tracy, Katharine Hepburn
Rating: ★★★★

A great start to the Spencer Tracy-Katharine Hepburn screen partnership. It's a real pleasure to see two big stars indulging in barbed-wire banter in such a relaxed way, as Tracy's down-to-earth sports reporter tames Hepburn's

W

current affairs hotshot. Watching her trying to cope with his pugilistic friends and her first game of baseball are only two of the delights in this sophisticated, witty, highly enjoyable film. Ring Lardner Jr and Michael Kanin deservedly won an Oscar for Best Original Screenplay. William Bendix makes his screen debut.

Woman's Face, A ○
1941, US, 105 mins, b/w
Dir: George Cukor
Stars: Joan Crawford
Rating: ★★★

The film that set the pattern for Joan Crawford's decade of suffering. She plays a badly scarred woman set for a life of crime until a skilful surgeon restores her looks and changes her attitudes to the world. This is a trace tougher than director George Cukor's usual elegant film fare, but he makes it a most exciting thriller with a human touch and some striking visual moments. Conrad Veidt is especially good as Crawford's former partner in blackmail who is naturally reluctant to let her go.

Woman's Secret, A ○
1949, US, 85 mins, b/w
Dir: Nicholas Ray
Stars: Maureen O'Hara, Melvyn Douglas, Gloria Grahame
Rating: ★

A half-baked *film noir* written by Herman J Mankiewicz, who co-authored *Citizen Kane* with Orson Welles. A series of crisscross flashbacks jolt rather than help the story along, and (a miscast) Maureen O'Hara's confession to murder in the opening scenes is a mystery. Just why did she confess at all? We will never know... All very peculiar.

Woman Times Seven ●
1967, US, 99 mins, colour
Dir: Vittorio De Sica
Stars: Shirley MacLaine, Peter Sellers, Rossano Brazzi
Rating: ★★

Very ambitious seven-part comedy that's almost inevitably hit-and-miss, the best episodes involving Shirley MacLaine as (a) a plain, neglected housewife who resolves to turn herself into husband Lex Barker's Super Girl fictional character and (b) with Alan Arkin in a double-suicide pact that backfires at every turn.

Woman Without a Face ○
(aka: Mister Buddwing)
1965, US, 100 mins, b/w

Dir: Delbert Mann
Stars: James Garner, Jean Simmons, Suzanne Pleshette, Katharine Ross
Rating: ★★

James Garner gets a rare old going over in the acting stakes as his four female co-stars all turn in eye-catching performances in this variation on one of Hollywood's most durable plots: the man who has lost his memory. His encounters with four women bring back fragments of the past, of past women or just one woman. The plot is so satisfying that it's a pity the solution to it all isn't more of a climax. Delbert Mann directs in an efficient, if old-fashioned way, and there's some splendid black and white photography of New York by Ellsworth Fredericks. Suzanne Pleshette is as warmly real as she always is – whenever she has a character to work on – while Angela Lansbury and Jean Simmons play to the gallery to great effect as floozies from opposite ends of the social scale.

Women, The ○
1939, US, 132 mins, b/w
Dir: George Cukor
Stars: Norma Shearer, Joan Crawford, Rosalind Russell, Paulette Goddard
Rating: ★★★

George Cukor, almost every Hollywood actress's favourite director in the Thirties, was the ideal man to direct this all-woman show about a wife coerced by her catty circle of friends into seeking a divorce she doesn't really want. A starry cast takes full advantage of the bitchy dialogue, adapted by Anita Loos and Jane Murfin from Clare Boothe's original play. The all-claws-out approach is led by Norma Shearer, Joan Crawford, Rosalind Russell, Paulette Goddard, Mary Boland and Hedda Hopper.

Women In Love ● ⓥ
1969, UK, 130 mins, colour
Dir: Ken Russell
Stars: Alan Bates, Oliver Reed, Glenda Jackson, Jennie Linden
Rating: ★★★★★

Ken Russell's most disciplined film, a clever and atmospheric adaptation of D H Lawrence's classic novel of two turbulent love affairs in a small Midlands colliery town in the Twenties. Glenda Jackson won her first Oscar and there are fine performances, too, from Alan Bates, Jenny Linden and a perfectly cast Oliver Reed. Only Eleanor Bron seems ill-at-ease. Evocative colour photography by Billy Williams decorates this almost perfect film.

Women on the Verge of a Nervous Breakdown ● ⓥ
1988, Spain, 89 mins, colour
Dir: Pedro Almodovar
Stars: Carmen Maura, Antonio Banderas, Julieta Serrano
Rating: ★★

Mysteriously Oscar-nominated as best foreign film, this much over-praised film is an innocuous, if foul-mouthed, comedy that looks like a stage adaptation. Fairly tedious for most of its exposition, it does come together a bit (like its characters) at the end. Carmen Maura is a lively and interesting leading lady, and there are one or two amusing, if irreverent touches, such as the soap powder ad on TV in which a murderer's mother shows pride in getting the bloodstains out of his clothes. Fashionable Spanish director Almodovar sees to it that doors open and close at the requisite moments in the best of farcical traditions. But an Oscar nomination? That's a bigger laugh than anything on display here.

Wonder Bar ○
1934, US, 84 mins, b/w
Dir: Lloyd Bacon
Stars: Al Jolson, Kay Francis
Rating: ★★★

A rare treat for fans of Hollywood musicals of the Thirties in this Busby Berkeley-staged musical with numbers including the eye-popping 'Goin' to Heaven on a Mule'. Directed by Lloyd Bacon, who was especially good at comedy (although he could turn his talents to anything) and whose contribution to such other Berkeley-choreographed musicals *42nd Street*, *In Caliente* and *Gold Diggers of 1933* has been unjustly neglected.

Wonderful Life ⊙
1964, UK, 108 mins, colour
Dir: Sidney J Furie
Stars: Cliff Richard, Walter Slezak, Susan Hampshire
Rating: ★★

In the desert, Cliff slows down. This Cliff Richard musical is pleasant, sunny entertainment, but a bit yawn-inducing at times. There's too much preplanning here and too little of the youthful exuberance that the same star and director (Sidney J Furie) showed in *The Young Ones*. Cliff and Susan Hampshire compete with each other in upturned noses, but not in the acting stakes (she wins hands down). One or two of the dance routines are lively, particularly those featuring Una Stubbs, and other points to note include Cliff being dragged 200 yards by a runaway camel and getting up without a grain of sand on him, and a rather sharp take-off of The Marx Brothers.

Wonderful Things ○
1958, UK, 85 mins, b/w
Dir: Herbert Wilcox
Stars: Frankie Vaughan, Jeremy Spenser, Jackie Lane, Wilfrid Hyde White
Rating: ★★★

If you can believe in Frankie Vaughan and Jeremy Spenser as Gibraltar fishermen you'll enjoy this Anna Neagle-produced trifle about love and life, Lane-style. Fiery Jackie Lane eclipses model Jean Dawnay's screen debut.

Wonderful World of the Brothers Grimm ⊙
1962, US, 134 mins, colour
Dir: Henry Levin
Stars: Laurence Harvey, Karl Boehm, Claire Bloom
Rating: ★★

With Laurence Harvey and Karl Boehm miscast as the Grimms (too cool and charmless), all the best moments in this fanciful biopic come from Oscar-winning George Pal's presentation of the fairy-tales themselves: Russ Tamblyn's bounding woodsman and Jim Backus's Magoo-voiced king in *The Dancing Princess;* Buddy Hackett , battle with a cleverly animated dragon in *The Singing Bone;* and the brilliant 'Puppetoon' sequence in *The Cobbler and the Elves*. Originally a long-runner in Cinerama, the rest of its drama looks pretty faded today.

Wonder Man ⊙
1945, US, 98 mins, colour
Dir: Bruce Humberstone
Stars: Danny Kaye, Virginia Mayo, VeraEllen
Rating: ★★

Danny Kaye gets plenty of scope for his own individual brand of fooling in this Goldwyn comedy which very successfully blends elements of a musical, a gangster spoof and ghost-comedy thriller to provide lavishly zany entertainment. The film won an Academy Award for its special effects (photographic and sound) and remains one of Kaye's most satisfying and colourful vehicles. Songs include the famous tongue-twister 'Ochitchorna'.

Won Ton Ton, the Dog who Saved Hollywood ⊙
1975, US, 92 mins, colour
Dir: Michael Winner

Stars: Bruce Dern, Madeline Kahn, Art Carney
Rating: ★★★

With some 75 former Hollywood stars making cameo appearances, this is an affectionate satire on *Rin Tin Tin*. Bruce Dern and Madeline Kahn are pleasant leads, and the canine is talented enough to have been given more of the film. Certainly the funniest sequence is when the dog, down on his luck and taken to drink, tries to commit suicide. It only remains to say that Ann Miller, Cyd Charisse, Gloria De Haven and Rhonda Fleming still look quite dazzling.

Wooden Horse, The ○ ⓥ
1950, UK, 101 mins, b/w
Dir: Jack Lee
Stars: Leo Genn, Anthony Steel, David Tomlinson
Rating: ★★★

An exciting ingenious prisoner-of-war camp story that set the pattern for several such films to come. It also made Anthony Steel a major star of the British cinema while, in a small supporting role, Peter Finch was soon to attain similar status.

Woodstock ◐ ⓥ
1969, US, 184 mins, colour
Dir: Michael Wadleigh
Rating: ★★★

There has never been a pop music festival to compare with (to give it its full title) The Woodstock Music and Art Fair, held over 72 tumultuous hours in some fields outside the tiny township of Bethel in up-state New York. The music itself is now legendary, and the film treatment of it set new standards for the filming of pop concerts. Outstanding contributions come especially from Joan Baez, Jimi Hendrix, The Who, Sly and the Family Stone and Country Joe MacDonald. The nudity, from spectators removing wet and muddy clothes (the torrential rain quickly turned the concert grounds into a quagmire) is almost completely inoffensive. Altogether, a remarkable record of a unique occasion.

Woo Woo Kid, The ◐ ⓥ
1987, US, 100 mins, colour
Dir: Phil Alden Robinson
Stars: Patrick Dempey, Beverly D'Angelo, Talia Balsam, Michael Constantine
Rating: ★★

A fetching little comedy about a teenager, Sonny 'Woo Woo' Wisecarver, who grabbed headline notoriety in wartime

America by running off with a couple of married women. His ingenuous odyssey needed a Preston Sturges or Woody Allen, though, to turn it into a rollicking oddity. It has a good star in the Eddie Bracken-like Patrick Dempsey, but what it lacks is outright laughs. Dempsey's one-liners mainly consist of repeat lines like 'It'll be great' or 'That's the saddest thing I've ever heard'. They don't quite give the picture the sweep of madness it needs. But Talia Balsam is particularly appealing as Sonny's first love, and there are good cameos from raucous Kathleen Freeman as the kid's landlady and mournful Michael Constantine as his father. Glenn Miller tunes give the piece a familiar period feel. The real Sonny Wisecarver appears as a mailman.

Words and Music ○
1948, US, 120 mins, colour
Dir: Norman Taurog
Stars: Mickey Rooney, Tom Drake, Janet Leigh, Judy Garland
Rating: ★★★

Known as *The Works* when it first came out, this ludicrously fictionalised biography of Rodgers and Hart cost MGM one of its biggest-ever salary bills. Mickey Rooney, who could hardly have portrayed Hart as the homosexual he was, at least had a good stab at the mercurial nature of the man, and sometimes seems to be asking his audience to be reading between the lines. But you can forget about the story (pure Hollywood schmaltz, expertly produced and melodramatic to the last reel) and wallow instead in the glorious music of the composers. Almost every song, every dance routine is a highspot in the film. But watch out especially for Lena Horne, scorching the screen with 'Where or When'; Cyd Charisse's dazzling dancing dexterity in 'On Your Toes'; Judy Garland – surely the only singer who could be heard above the brass on 'Johnny One Note'; and the razor-slick version of 'Slaughter on 10th Avenue' from Gene Kelly and Vera-Ellen.

Working Girl ◐ ⓥ
1988, US, 125 mins, colour
Dir: Mike Nichols
Stars: Harrison Ford, Melanie Griffith, Sigourney Weaver, Alec Baldwin, Joan Cusack
Rating: ★★★★

A solid entertainment picture from director Mike Nichols with a plum role for Melanie Griffith as the breathy but brainy secretary who has a business de-

W

gree but not the right background for success. Escaping the clutches of one lecherous boss after another, she goes to work for a woman (Sigourney Weaver), an outwardly friendly broker but a treacherous piranha of a woman who swallows competitors whole and ruthlessly steals the first bright idea Griffith sets in front of her. Griffith finds out about the deception and determines to put through the deal involved herself. This being a warmhearted sort of film, with few lapses into bad taste, you can guess subsequent developments; but the cast handle their roles with panache and skill, especially Griffith, Weaver (a vivacious villainess), Harrison Ford (an unexpectedly subtle comedian), and Philip Bosco as the big fish Griffith hopes to hook. Griffith is terrific, whether determined, dampened, drunk, dejected or radiant.

World According to Garp, The ● ⓥ

1982, US, 136 mins, colour
Dir: George Roy Hill
Stars: Robin Williams, Mary Beth Hurt, Glenn Close, John Lithgow
Rating: ★★

A very serious film about life, masquerading as a black comedy, this is a very weird kettle of fish. Robin Williams' Garp, the son of a woman who chose a dying serviceman as his father because she wanted to owe no allegiance to a man, lives a life riddled with pain, both mental and physical; his story is far-fetched in the manner of the blackest farce, with all the crises in his life revolving round sex in one way or another. Williams and Mary Beth Hurt as his wife often look puzzled, as well they might, and are outshone by Glenn Close, in her major film debut, bringing an inner glow even to such an unlikely person as Garp's mother, and by John Lithgow, who gently brings real character to the sex-change lady who becomes Garp's confidante. Both these performances received Oscar nominations.

World and His Wife, The

See: State of the Union

World Apart, A ○ ⓥ

1988, US, 113 mins, colour
Dir: Chris Menges
Stars: Jeroen Krabbé, Barbara Hershey, Jodhi May, David Suchet, Tim Roth
Rating: ★★

This horrendous portrait of the beginnings of repression in South Africa in

1961, when the 90-day custody law was introduced, is well-meant and extremely well-acted and occasionally even heartbreaking. Director Chris Menges' sympathy with his actors is obvious, but otherwise his treatment is unnecessarily laborious, unable to resist stretching the true story out and driving every anti-Apartheid point home. A script that paid more attention to literary persuasion and wore its heart less obviously on its sleeve would also have helped the film's impact. Still, there are great performances from Barbara Hershey and young Jodhi May (as his daughter) and from Nadine Chambers as Hershey's friend, not strong enough to leap the gulf of ostracism. Worth seeing then for the acting and for its vitally important and tragic theme.

World in His Arms, The ○

1952, US, 104 mins, colour
Dir: Raoul Walsh
Stars: Gregory Peck, Ann Blyth, Anthony Quinn, John Mcintire
Rating: ★★★

Gregory Peck isn't the sort one naturally associates with high adventure, although this boisterous period yarn about a 19th-century adventurer who wants to buy Alaska was a natural follow-up for him to the naval heroics of *Captain Horatio Hornblower RN*. The rousing action scenes are in the capable hands of veteran director Raoul Walsh. A race between the hero's ship and that of the rascally Portugee (Anthony Quinn) is especially well done.

World's Greatest Athlete, The ⊙

1973, US, 93 mins, colour
Dir: Robert Scheerer
Stars: Jan-Michael Vincent, Tim Conway, Roscoe Lee Browne, Dayle Haddon
Rating:

Some decent trick photography and a scene where the Tarzan-like hero's myopic landlady fails to see that his roommate is a tiger enliven this otherwise standard Disney comedy with a lively pace but a dismally unfunny supporting comedy team in Tim Conway and John Amos.

World's Greatest Lover, The ○

1977, US, 89 mins, colour
Dir: Gene Wilder
Stars: Gene Wilder, Carol Kane, Dom DeLuise
Rating: ★★

For his second foray into direction Gene Wilder, who also scripted, sends

up Hollywood in the Twenties, although his satirical barbs take second place to wild slapstick in the style of his mentor Mel Brooks. Carol Kane is excellent as Wilder's wife, who goes off with Rudolph Valentino while her husband attempts to win a contest to find a screen star to outshine The Great Lover. Dom DeLuise is entertainingly over the top as an explosive studio head.

Wrecking Crew, The ○

1969, US, 105 mins, colour
Dir: Phil Karlson
Stars: Dean Martin, Eike Sommer
Rating: ★★

The last of the four films about Donald Hamilton's super-agent Matt Helm, and better than the second and third, if not quite up to the first of the series, *The Silencers*. The director is Phil Karlson, which at least guarantees that the screen will be busy 100 per cent of the time. The action, as a result, fairly buzzes along. Once more Helm proclaims he's through with ICE, the super-secret organisation out to conquer an enemy organisation known as Big O; but soon he's involved in a hunt for a billion dollars in gold which has been hi-jacked in Denmark.

Wrestling Ernest Hemingway ① ⓥ

1993, US, 123 mins, colour
Dir: Randa Haines
Stars: Robert Duvall, Richard Harris, Shirley MacLaine, Piper Laurie, Sandra Bullock, Micole Mercurio
Rating: ★★★

A distinguished cast of over-60s give their all in this thoughtful coming-of-old-age drama. The central characters are Frank (Richard Harris), a raucous Irish ex-sailor, and Wait (Robert Duvall), a dignified retired Cuban barber. The story tells in bittersweet tones the tale of their unlikely friendship. Piper Laurie is piquant as the unwilling focus of Frank's romantic intentions, while Shirley MacLaine brings her customary world-weariness as his embittered landlady. Of the younger cast, *Speed's* Sandra Bullock has little to do as a local waitress who's the object of Walt's immaculate respect. Nothing much happens in the two-hour running time, yet this is still a leisurely and increasingly absorbing study of loneliness and old age, with Harris notably impressive as the former hellraiser whose spirit is very much alive but whose body is failing.

Written on the Wind ○
1956, US, 99 mins, colour
Dir: Douglas Sirk
Stars: Lauren Bacall, Rock Hudson
Rating: ★★★

Incest, alcoholism, blackmail, murder, sexual promiscuity and dark secrets. This scathing indictment of the state of the family in Fifties America throws ill of this – and more – into its vibrant Technicolor pot and gives the mixture a good stir. Although not perhaps director Douglas Sirk's best film, this was the one that caught the critics' eye, and won Dorothy Malone an Oscar for her portrayal of a nymphomaniac Texan. This is melodrama on a grand scale with enough scandal and double-dealing to fill an entire series of *Dynasty* or *Dallas*. The men (Rock Hudson, Robert Keith) are strong, the women (Malone, Lauren Bacall) are sexy, the family black sheep (Robert Stack as an alcoholic playboy) is as nasty as a cornered rattlesnake.

Wrong Arm of the Law, The ○
1962, UK, 94 mins, b/w
Dir: Cliff Owen
Stars: Peter Sellers, Lionel Jeffries, Bernard Cribbins, Bill Kerr
Rating: ★★★

Irresistibly funny comedy, thanks to a screenplay that simply never lets up for a minute. The fun and games are full of moments to treasure: Bill Kerr as the leader of the Australian gang who pose as policemen in order to 'confiscate' the loot from robberies committed by other crooks; Lionel Jeffries as the impossibly inept Inspector 'Nosey' Parker; Bernard Cribbins as a nervous crook who wears a seat belt in the back seat of his car and Peter Sellers as 'Pearly' Gates, whose suave French accent slips deliciously into snarling Cockney when the Law appears on the scene.

Wrong Box, The ○
1966, UK, 105 mins, colour
Dir: Bryan Forbes
Stars: Michael Caine, Nanette Newman, Peter Cook, Dudley Moore
Rating: ★★★

A rich black comedy, set in London just before the turn of the century, and concerning the last two (elderly) survivors of a bizarre lottery. The fun gets increasingly wilder, as Grandpa John Mills, superbly made up, and rushing about in a nightshirt like an aged imp, makes frenzied attempts to assassinate Grandpa Ralph Richardson and collect the money. Also very

funny are Peter Sellers, as a doctor who has cats around his house the way some people have mice; and Wilfrid Lawson, in his last film, as the family's decrepit butler. ·

Wrong Man, The ○ ⓥ
1957, US, 105 mins, b/w
Dir: Alfred Hitchcock
Stars: Henry Fonda, Vera Miles, Anthony Quayle
Rating: ★★★★

A taut, moving Hitchcock suspense film, much underrated in its day, told in semi-documentary style and based on a true story. Henry Fonda is just right as the sensitive musician bewildered by the way circumstantial evidence piles up against him on a robbery count. Vera Miles gives the finest performance of her career as his mentally fragile wife. The film was also one of the first to employ the talents of British actor Anthony Quayle in a major role; but he quickly established himself on the international scene.

Wrong Man, The ● ⓥ
1993, US, 110 mins, colour
Dir: Jim McBride
Stars: Rosanna Arquette, John Lithgow, Kevin Anderson, Jorge Cervera Jr
Rating: ★★★

Shades of *Detour* here. On shore leave (and on the run from a broken heart), sailor Kevin Anderson – who even looks like Tom Neal in the Forties' classic – is robbed by a drunk, rushes back to find the man shot and dying, flees the scene and, with the police at his heels, hitches a lift with the couple from hell, bad-tempered tubercular Mills (Lithgow) and his tempting floozy of a wife (Arquette). Too much (very) bad language and nudity will put some people off this, but the whole idea of a man trapped both by circumstance and sexual allure is a fascinating one and carried to the limit by director McBride, down to a real *noir* ending. Required to be totally uninhibited, Arquette does her best work in ages.

WUSA ◐
1970, US, 117 mins, colour
Dir: Stuart Rosenberg
Stars: Paul Newman, Joanne Woodward, Anthony Perkins, Laurence Harvey
Rating: ★★

WUSA, taking its name from the ultra-right wing New Orleans radio station where drunkard Newman talks his way into a job, is a political satire, but a dire and pretentious one at that. At times it

looks like a travelogue as Newman and real-life wife Joanne Woodward, as the girl he picks up, exchange predictable dialogue while walking hand in hand through the city streets. Anthony Perkins is the redeeming factor, delivering a twitching, nervous performance as a trendy liberal/revolutionary.

Wuthering Heights ○ ⓥ
1939, US, 104 mins, b/w
Dir: William Wyler
Stars: Laurence Olivier, Merle Oberon, David Niven
Rating: ★★★★

Easily the most memorable version of Emily Brontë's romantic novel, with haunting characterisations by Laurence Olivier and Merle Oberon as Heathcliff and Cathy. Olivier had wanted Vivien Leigh for the role, but, under William Wyler's persuasive direction, Oberon gave the best performance of her career. The film was nominated for numerous Academy Awards, but on the night won only one: it went, however, to the most deserving of all nominees – Gregg Toland, whose evocative black-and-white photography in this film has been seldom equalled.

Wuthering Heights ○
1970, UK, 105 mins, colour
Dir: Robert Fuest
Stars: Timothy Dalton, Anna Calder-Marshall, Harry Andrews
Rating: ★★

Remake of the story of the famous doomed love affair between Catherine and Heathcliff on their beloved Yorkshire moors. Director Robert Fuest and his talented cameraman John Coquillin capture the ghastly bleak beauty of Emily Brontë's powerful novel. But the script is much less spirited than in the famous 1939 Olivier film, and only Anna Calder-Marshall (as Catherine) and the ever excellent Judy Cornwell remain for long in the memory.

Wuthering Heights ○ ⓥ
1992, US, 106 mins, colour
Dir: Peter Kosminsky
Stars: Ralph Fiennes, Juliette Binoche, Janet McTeer, Sophie Ward, Simon Ward, Jennifer Daniel
Rating: ★

This stickily cast, TV-style version of Emily Brontë's passionate novel of obsessive love in the 18th century runs more like a Gothic horror story than a romance. Ralph Fiennes, through unorthodox casting, at least looks and sounds the part as the wild-eyed,

W

rugged Heathcliff, descending into madness at the loss of his love. But Juliette Binoche's Cathy is a total disaster and she tries in vain to conceal her French accent, or makes risible attempts at a sort of Parisian Yorkshire. The windswept, barren Yorkshire moors are the only stars of this dark and doomy costume piece, directed in TV commercial style by debutant director Peter Kosminsky and scored for a thoroughly annoying collection or screeching violins by Ryuichi Sakamoto. Alas, poor 'Eathcleef, we knew 'eem well.

W W and the Dixie Dancekings ◑

1975, US, 94 mins, colour
Dir: John G Avildsen
Stars: Burt Reynolds, Art Carney, Connie Van Dyke, Ned Beatty
Rating: ★★★

Little known off-beat Burt Reynolds comedy in which he plays W W Bright, an ex-garage hold-up artist who accidentally takes charge of a sleazy band known as Dixie and the Dancekings. John G Avildsen's film is marvellously light handed, using Fifties Presley hits by Lelber and Stoller to recapture a lost world of 1950s Country and Western.

Wyatt Earp ◑ Ⓥ

1994, US, 191 mins, colour
Dir: Lawrence Kasdan
Stars: Kevin Costner, Dennis Quaid, Gene Hackman, Joanna Going, Jeff Fahey, Bill Pullman, Mark Harmon, Isabella Rossellini
Rating: ★★

This is a serious (a very serious) film about the life of Wyatt Earp. Disgustingly overlong, it will have you reaching for your watches rather than your six-guns when things seem to be coming to some kind of climax and you realise there's still 90 minutes to go. The early scenes have promise: Wyatt grows up on a grain ranch and marries the girl he always fancied played by Annabeth Gish with possibly the best performance in the film. Of course, she dies young and, after long spells as a drunkard, buffalo hunter and croupier, Wyatt ends up (as do most of his brothers) as a lawman. There's much unnecessary fiddling around in Tombstone as the brothers try to settle down to prospecting, the gunfight at the OK Corral is more of a skirmish, and the film then drifts on, as the Earps and the Clantons try to exact mutual revenge. No classic.

Wyoming Mail ○

1950, US, 87 mins, colour
Dir: Reginald Leborg
Stars: Stephen McNally, Alexis Smith, Ed Begley
Rating: ★★

A rough, tough Western, dazzlingly photographed in Technicolor by Oscar-winning cameraman Russell Metty. Stephen McNally is suitably forceful as the boxer on a dangerous undercover mission for the government, and a fine supporting cast includes Ed Begley, Alexis Smith, Howard Da Silva, Richard Jaeckel, Gene Evans, James Arness and Richard Egan.

Wyoming Renegades ○

1955, US, 73 mins, colour
Dir: Fred F Sears
Stars: Phil Carey, Martha Hyer
Rating: ★★

Butch Cassidy and the Sundance Kid ride again – but here as in so many westerns before Newman and Redford made the characters folk heroes, they're the villains of the piece. This is a vigorous Western in good Technicolor, one of innumerable colour horse-operas turned out at Columbia in the Fifties, all of them moving alon at a rattling pace, and hardly one over 80 minutes. Here Phil Carey's the hero, but burly Gene Evans as Butch Cassidy has no trouble acting the rest of the cast clear off the screen.

Xanadu ○ Ⓥ

1980, US, 96 mins, colour
Dir: Robert Greenwald
Stars: Olivia Newton-John, Gene Kelly, Michael Beck, James Sloyan
Rating: ★★★

Vivid musical fantasy remake of *Down to Earth* (the old Rita Hayworth musical) which has one drawback – its leading lady, Olivia Newton-John, as a goddess helping to put on an earthly show. Fortunately production designer John Corso and director Robert Greenwold demonstrate great flair for colour, composition and movement, with the result that *Xanadu* is as dazzling to the eye as any of the vintage Hollywood musicals. Story? Well, hardly any, but it's engagingly surrealistic in a pop glitter way, and Gene Kelly's there to help Newton-John shine in her most successful scene when they dance together in his memories of the Forties. Expect a super deluxe version of *Top Of The Pops* and you won't be disappointed.

X the Unknown ◑

1956, UK, 80 mins, b/w
Dir: Leslie Norman
Stars: Dean Jagger, Edward Chapman
Rating: ★★

Pretty nasty and effective by 1956 standards, this early Hammer horror film has the benefits of sinister black and white photography by Gerald Gibbs and such sterling players as Dean Jagger, Edward Chapman, Leo McKern and William Lucas. There is also an interesting performance from the less well known John Harvey and the familiar faces of Michael Ripper and Anthony Newley crop up as two of the soldiers battling a mysterious 'something' that creeps up from a bottomless fissure created by an atomic explosion on the Scottish moors. Leslie Norman's direction misses few chances to point up the shock moments – and there are plenty.

X, Y and Zee ●

1971, UK, 110 mins, colour
Dir: Brian G Hutton
Stars: Elizabeth Taylor, Michael Caine, Susannah York
Rating: ★

A strident and sometimes effective dissection of a marriage on the rocks, of mutual dislike and the eternal triangle. It certainly has star value, with Elizabeth Taylor, Michael Caine and Susannah York as the embattled trio. The film is often abrasive and occasionally funny, although you may find it, like the raucous Zee (a super professional performance by Elizabeth Taylor), just a little wearing.

Yakuza, The ●
1975, US, 112 mins, colour
Dir: Sydney Pollack
Stars: Robert Mitchum, Takakura Ken, Brian Keith
Rating: ★★★

Those with no stomach for blood are advised to steer clear of this well-made gangster film in which limbs are sliced off (sometimes by their owners) here, there and everywhere, while other parts of the body are slit open or blasted apart. Robert Mitchum and Takakum Ken give excellent performances as two men who hate each other (it's a woman, of course) but come to deep mutual respect through a body-strewn battle against a common enemy. The action with swords is sometimes hard to watch, but the code of honour, and its burden of obligation, in the world of the yakuza (Japanese mobster) comes across strongly under the sensitive direction of Sydney Pollack. Recommended for those with constitutions strong enough to take it.

Yangtse Incident ○
1956, UK, 110 mins, b/w
Dir: Michael Anderson
Stars: Richard Todd, William Hartnell
Rating: ★★★

Stirring account of the real-life suspense saga of HMS *Amethyst*, held virtual prisoner by the Chinese on the Yangtse River in 1949 until a sensational and daring escape plan was devised. Richard Todd is in his element as the forthright captain; below decks, Bernard Cribbins plays one of his earliest screen roles.

Yank at Oxford, A ○
1937, US/UK, 100 mins, b/w
Dir: Jack Conway
Stars: Robert Taylor, Lionel Barrymore, Maureen O'Sullivan, Vivien Leigh
Rating: ★★★

Considering that it underwent almost a year of writing and re-writing, this was and is – a remarkably entertaining and successful story about English university life knocking the rough edges off of a brash American and teaching him some real values. Robert Taylor studies with Maureen O'Sullivan, dallies with Vivien Leigh (one of her best performances) and (in a marvellous scene) bandies words with an old English gent (Morton Selten) on a train. When Taylor boasts that the whole of Britain could be put into the state of Nebraska, his companion replies: 'Doubtless – but with what object?' The exchange was contributed by Sidney Gilliat, one of eight writers credited.

Yankee Buccaneer ○
1952, US, 86 mins, colour
Dir: Frederick De Cordova
Stars: Jeff Chandler, Scott Brady, David Janssen
Rating: ★★

One of those colourful action-packed 90-minute adventure stories which Universal-International rolled out with such regularity and expertise in the Fifties. The story moves along in aggressive style, and the Technicolor photography of Russell Metty makes the film a constant pleasure to look at. In the supporting cast, you can spot a very young David Janssen.

Yankee Doodle Dandy ○
1942, US, 126 mins, b/w
Dir: Michael Curtiz
Stars: James Cagney, Joan Leslie, Walter Huston
Rating: ★★★★

Even James Cagney was rarely as dominant as he is in this musical biography of George M Cohan, awash with music, sentiment and patriotic fervour. Cagney swept triumphantly to an Academy Award, and the film took two other Oscars, including one for the best scoring of a musical. It remained the star's favourite, throughout the remainder of his career. The songs include 'Over There', 'Yankee Doodle Boy' and 'Give My Regards to Broadway'. Its highlight remains Cagney's dazzling cross-stage strutting dance, involving 'climbs' on either side.

Yankee Pasha ○
1953, US, 84 mins, colour
Dir: Joseph Pevney
Stars: Jeff Chandler, Rhonda Fleming, Lee J Cobb
Rating: ★★

One of the major wonders of Fifties' cinema is how Universal-International managed to take Edison Marshall's enormous novel *Yankee Pasha*, and compress it into 84 minutes without actually losing much of the plot. Not surprisingly, there's incident and excitement a-plenty in their version of Marshall's extravagant yarn about an

American fur-trapper in the 1800s (played by Jeff Chandler), who sets out to recover his lost love from Moroccan pirates and ends up as arms adviser to the Sultan of Morocco. No film that casts Lee J Cobb as an eastern sultan can be taking itself entirely seriously and proceedings are very much on the light-hearted side.

Yank in the RAF, A ○
1941, US, 98 mins, b/w
Dir: Henry King
Stars: Tyrone Power, Betty Grable
Rating: ★★★

Tyrone Power winning the Battle of Britain in a Hollywood war film that strangely raised fewer hackles than Errol Flynn's subsequent (and lower-key) exploits in *Objective, Burma*. The British are in there somewhere, though, and there are some fine aerial combat scenes.

Yanks ◑ ⓥ
1979, US, 141 mins, colour
Dir: John Schlesinger
Stars: Vanessa Redgrave, Richard Gere, William Devane, Lisa Eichhorn, Tony Melody, Rachel Roberts
Rating: ★★★

There are many pleasurable things in this long John Schlesinger film, not least the way in which it flawlessly rereates the life of an English town in 1943. Schlesinger directs with great affection for the time and place (the north of England) and a keen eye and ear for the right sights and sounds. And he gets well-sustained performances from his principal players, Richard Gere, Lisa Eichhorn, William Devane , and Tony Melody. Vanessa Redgrave and Rachel Roberts are less consistent, though they have their affecting moments, Rachel Roberts really looking painfully close to death when she is supposed to be. Scenes of a ballroom dance, a children's party and a mass farewell on a station (could one small town boast quite so many girls?) are reminiscent of such American films of that time as *Since You Went Away:* in this respect at least, and greatly helped by the thoughtful colour photography of Dick Bush, the director has preserved the moment in time to perfection.

Yearling, The ⊙
1946, US, 134 mins, colour
Dir: Clarence Brown
Stars: Gregory Peck, Jane Wyman, Claude Jarman Jr
Rating: ★★★★

Based on a book by Marjorie Kinnan Rawlings (whose own story was told in *Cross Creek),* this is a lovingly made, glowingly photographed (Technicolor was never richer than in Charles Rosher and Leonard Smith's hands) and completely unforced study of a backwoods boy and his love for a tame fawn that must eventually inevitably be returned to the wild. Gregory Peck and Jane Wyman exude sympathy and understanding as the boy's parents, and the story is compellingly told through a series of small but enthralling incidents. Oscars for photography and art direction, plus a special award to Claude Jarman Jr (the boy) as outstanding child actor of the year.

Year of Living Dangerously, The ◑ ⓥ
1983, Australia, 115 mins, colour
Dir: Peter Weir
Stars: Mel Gibson, Sigourney Weaver, Linda Hunt, Michael Murphy, Bill Kerr
Rating: ★★★

Director Peter Weir catches all the tension and turmoil of an impoverished and oppressed country (in this case 1965 Indonesia under Sukarno) as it overheats and boils over into revolution. The atmosphere and seething background to this is captured down to the last bead of sweat; but what Weir has largely failed to do is tell an exciting story to go with it. Mel Gibson is too cool and dispassionate here as the Australian correspondent coming to prominence in the last days of Sukarno's regime. Other casting is weird, but more successful, especially Linda Hunt as the native photographer Billy: as a woman playing a man she adds to the enigmatic qualities of the character, and the performance won her an Oscar. Even so, the richness of all the film's teeming detail pales after a while and you long for something more: involvement.

Year of the Gun ● ⓥ
1991, US/Italy, 111 mins, colour
Dir: John Frankenheimer
Stars: Andrew McCarthy, Valeria Golino, Sharon Stone, John Pankow
Rating: ★

These days, an international co-production like this seems dated before it hits the screen. The players act loudly and strenuously, the director focuses on them with lenses that pick out every pock-mark, characters look grim or compliant according to the tenor of their role, and the colour has those washed-out shades that make greenery take on tinges of blue. The acting by Andrew McCarthy, Sharon Stone and Valeria Golino is hardly top-notch, either, in this tedious story of undercover saboteurs in Italy's Red Brigade of the late Seventies, but then the dialogue and this treatment would make Streep and Hoffman look silly. The city of Rome, too, is hardly made the most of. Ah, for the days when Carol Reed turned Vienna into a character by itself in *The Third Man.*

Years Without Days
See: Castle on the Hudson

Yellow Balloon, The ◑
1952, UK, 80 mins, b/w
Dir: J Lee-Thompson
Stars: Andrew Ray, Kenneth More, Kathleen Ryan
Rating: ★★★

A suspense thriller about a little boy involved with a murderer. Andrew Ray (son of Ted) was, at the age of 12, already an established star when he made this,'and his role as Frankie Palmer endeared him further to the critics. There is a frighteningly effective climax, as a killer lures him into a disused tube stadon, planning to throw him down a lift shaft. The silence is broken only by the panting of hunter and hunted, and the eerie clatter of trains. The star gets lots of quality support in this one, from a cast that includes Kenneth More, Kathleen Ryan, William Sylvester, Sandra Dome, Sidney James, Bernard Lee, Veronica Hurst and Hy Hazell.

Yellowbeard ◑ ⓥ
1983, US, 101 mins, colour
Dir: Mel Damski
Stars: Graham Chapman, Peter Boyle, Peter Cook, Marty Feldman
Rating: ★

Pirate spoofs got a bad name in the 1980s, what with Roman Polanski's *Pirates* and this directionless jumble of comic sketches. The film was actually the brainchild of Keith Moon, drummer with The Who; hence one of the main characters, an evil bosun, being called Moon.

Yellow Rolls Royce, The ○
1964, UK, 122 mins, colour
Dir: Anthony Asquith
Stars: Ingrid Bergman, Rex Harrison, Omar Sharif, Shirley MacLaine
Rating: ★★

Multi-story film about the love affairs – and adventures – that start in the back seat of a vintage car. With a sizzling international cast, the team of Anthony Asquith (director), Anatole de Grunwald (producer) and Terence Rattigan (writer) have produced a sleek bit of entertainment.

Yellow Sky ○
1948, US, 98 mins, b/w
Dir: William Wellman
Stars: Gregory Peck, Anne Baxter, Richard Widmark
Rating: ★★★

Set in an Arizona ghost town, director William Wellman, expert purveyor of man-sized action, makes this Western of confrontation a gritty, suspenseful and exciting affair. There are sharp-edged portraits from Gregory Peck (always best when cast against his seemingly natural gentle type), Anne Baxter (also enjoying a change of pace as a rifle-toting tomboy) and John Russell. But no one out-acts Richard Widmark, offering another of the smiling psychopaths that decorated his early years in film.

Yellow Submarine ⊙
1968, UK, 87 mins, colour
Dir: George Dunning
Stars: The Beatles
Rating: ★★★

Moving from live-action comic-strip in *Help!*, The Beatles became even more animated in this lively 'day-glo' feature-length animation film with a storyline full of such bizarre characters as the Blue Meanies (who want to rid the world of music and happiness), a sea of monsters and a super-intellectual pendant called Boob (voice courtesy of Dick Emery). Its hippie theme that L-O-V-E conquers all may be a bit too twee in this day and age, but there's no denying the fihn's stunning animation, in particular the weird and wonderful 'kinky boot beasts'.

Yentl ○ ⓥ
1983, US, 134 mins, colour
Dir: Barbra Streisand
Stars: Barbra Streisand, Mandy Patinkin, Amy Irving
Rating: ★★

Barbra Streisand's first film as star and director is a bizarre cross-dressing story of a Jewish girl who disguises herself as a man to beat limitations her society imposes on her. Songs have been added to bolster the doubts that soon begin to creep in, but nothing can shore up the crumbling structure of the central situation: few actresses would be believable as a man and Streisand

isn't one of them. Even ignoring the stature, the feminine gestures and the tiny feet, there's the voice... 'How could I have been so blind?' asks Avigdor (Mandy Patinkin) when she finally tells him. And we can but agree. Its major achievement in the middle of the expected razzle-dazzle of a Streisand musical is that moments of quiet observation and reflective wisdom are given their due, and that Streisand manages to play the scenes requiring her to be discreetly demure with surprising success.

Yol ◑ ⓥ
1982, Switzerland, 111 mins, colour
Dir: Serif Goren
Stars: Tarik Akan
Rating: ★★★

This harrowing and unrelenting portrait of the hard life endured by Kurds, and others, in Turkey in the Eighties had to be smuggled into western Europe, where it took practically every prize going at the 1982 Cannes Film Festival. It will make many wince, not only at the grim lives of the main characters – prisoners allowed a brief period of freedom, spelling doom to most but also at the treatment of women who stray from the law.

You Can't Sleep Here
See: I Was a Male War Bride

You Can't Take It with You ⊙ ⓥ
1938, US, 127 mins, b/w
Dir: Frank Capra
Stars: Jean Arthur, James Stewart, Lionel Barrymore
Rating: jj zz

Although it's worn less well than some Frank Capra classics, this is still a charming and amusing study of a care-free, eccentric family and their tangles with the authorities. It gave Capra his third Academy Award for best director and his second for best picture. Lionel Barrymore, who plays the head of the family, was suddenly crippled at the outset of the film by the arthritis that had been troubling him for years. Capra put a plaster cast on Barrymore's foot, had him hop around on crutches and explained it by having Vanderhof say that he has sprained his ankle after his granddaughter dared him to slide down the banisters – wholly in keeping with the character! Capra added Jean Arthur and James Stewart for the romantic leads, plus one character who hadn't been in the original play, a Mr Poppins, who

makes ingenious toys for fun, and is delightfully portrayed by gnomish Donald Meek. The results are wonderful and warm, or faintly irritating, according to your tastes!

You Can't Win 'Em All ⊙ ⓥ
1970, US, 95 Mins, colour
Dir: Peter Collinson
Stars: Charles Bronson, Tony Curtis, Michele Mercier
Rating: ★★★

There can't be many films set against the Turkish Civil War in 1922, but it crops up here as the backcloth to a rousing comedy adventure story set mainly on board a train carrying a shipment of treasure from Turkey to Egypt. Charles Bronson and Tony Curtis are the two American adventurers hired to guard the train, and the treasure, against the constant attacks of a band of determined hijackers. Pretty Michele Mercier is the governor's daughter who's also under their care. Veteran Hollywood heavy Leo Gordon brings his familiar mean features to a supporting role – and reveals an unexpected side to his talent. He also wrote the screenplay for the film.

You'll Never Get Rich ○
1941, US, 88 mins, b/w
Dir: Sidney Lanfield
Stars: Fred Astaire, Rita Hayworth
Rating: ★★★

A brisk, good-humoured combination of backstage musical and wartime romance, with Rita Hayworth proving a delightful (and likeable) new partner for Fred Astaire after Ginger Rogers had quit the team for high drama. Cole Porter's score, hamstrung by patriotic necessities, isn't exactly his best, but the stars dance impressively together and Astaire goes solo on the memorable 'A-Stairable Rag'.

Young Americans, The ● ⓥ
1993, UK, 104 mins, colour
Dir: Danny Cannon
Stars: Harvey Keitel, Iain Glen, Thandie Newton, Viggo Mortensen, Craig Kelly
Rating: ★★

A New York cop comes to Britain and soon gets in the British law's hair: a familiar movie theme from time immemorial. Seeing that it's Harvey Keitel as the cop, we get a performance of typical clamped-down intensity – a man doing his job despite the weight of the world (and a broken marriage) on his shoulders. No bad lieutenant this, though: he's even willing to go out on a limb for the young informer (Craig

Y

Kelly) who's resolved to trap criminals he grew up with after they become involved with the death of his father. Thandie Newton is appealing as Kelly's girl, while Terence Rigby, Keith Allen and others give traditional British portrayals of nightclub crooks. Iain Glen and John Wood are the men in macs who soon come to respect Keitel's ability to crack crimes it normally takes British bobbies months to bring to book.

Young and Innocent ○ Ⓥ
1937, UK, 80 mins, b/w
Dir: Alfred Hitchcock
Stars: Nova Pilbeam, Derrick De Marney
Rating: ★★★

This rarely-seen Alfred Hitchcock suspense thriller was adapted from Josephine Tey's novel *A Shilling for Candles*. It was made at the newly opened Pinewood Studios, which had stages big enough to allow Hitchcock to indulge in some spectacular crane shots in a story of two young people on the run trying to clear the man of murder, as in *The 39 Steps*. Hitchcock himself makes his usual cameo appearance: watch out for him in the crowd outside a courthouse. A scene in which fugitives try to get away from a party is priceless.

Young at Heart ○ Ⓥ
1954, US, 117 mins, colour
Dir: Gordon Douglas
Stars: Doris Day, Frank Sinatra
Rating: ★★★

Frank Sinatra lends his own touch of moody melancholy to a musical remake of the 1938 John Garfield film *Four Daughters*. Playing a loner who thinks he's a loser, his character's grudge against the world isn't settled even when he falls for a homely girl from a small Connecticut town. Some good songs include 'Someone to Watch Over Me', 'Just One of Those Things', 'One for My Baby' and 'Young at Heart'.

Young Bess ○
1953, US, 112 mins, colour
Dir: George Sidney
Stars: Jean Simmons, Stewart Granger, Charles Laughton
Rating: ★★★

Close that history book and settle back for Hollywood's version of the childhood and first great romance of Queen Elizabeth I. Never mind the facts, there's a feast of good acting on show here, from Jean Simmons as the rebellious Bess, Charles Laughton repeating

his Oscar-winning triumph of 20 years before as Henry VIII, Deborah Kerr as a dignified and kindly Catherine Parr, Guy Rolfe and Kathleen Byron as nasty as you could wish as Bess's enemies and young Rex Thompson, endearingly first-class as Edward VI, the boy king. Thanks to Charles Rosher's rich Technicolor camerawork, one of the earliest examples of photography making scenes look like old paintings, it's also one of the best-looking films even MGM ever made.

Young Billy Young ○
1969, US, 89 mins, colour
Dir: Burt Kennedy
Stars: Robert Mitchum, Angie Dickinson, Robert Walker, David Carradine
Rating: ★★

Sheriff Robert Mitchum and killer Robert Walker team up to find the murderer of Mitchum's son. They become lawmen in the town of Lordsburg, as Mitchum hopes to track down the killer there. There's really nothing new in this Western, but it's a good yarn told with style by director Burt Kennedy. There are also good performances from Mitchum, Walker, David Carradine and Angie Dickinson as the dance hall girl who falls for the sheriff.

Youngblood ● Ⓥ
1986, US, 110 mins, colour
Dir: Peter Markle
Stars: Rob Lowe, Cynthia Gibb, Patrick Swayze
Rating: ★

A truly dreadful ice hockey film depicting the Canadian variety of the sport as a cross between hockey, boxing and unlawful wounding. The entertainment value of the sporting scenes is zero and the film is naively scripted and badly acted into the bargain. Brat Pack frontrunner Rob Lowe leans heavily on his shyly cocky smile, but apart from the maelstrom of four-letter words, this would look more at home as a TV movie. Sin-bin penalties all round.

Youngblood Hawke ○
1964, US, 137 mins, b/w
Dir: Delmer Daves
Stars: James Franciscus, Suzanne Pleshette, Genevieve Page
Rating: ★

James Franciscus plays a young author who loses his ideals in the high society jungle. Adapted from a huge novel by Herman Wouk, with a good supporting

role for Don Porter, this is another slice of romantic melodrama from the hands of Delmer Daves, who made all those Troy Donahue films in the Fifties. The supporting cast – Suzanne Pleshette, Mary Astor, Lee Bowman, Eva Gabor – work hard to cover up a non-performance by Franciscus in the lead.

Young Cassidy ○
1964, UK, 110 mins, colour
Dir: Jack Cardiff, John Ford
Stars: Rod Taylor, Flora Robson, Maggie Smith, Julie Christie
Rating: ★★

Begun by John Ford and completed by cameraman-turned-director Jack Cardiff, this atmospheric drama recounts the early struggles of the Irish playwright Sean O'Casey, here known as Johnny Cassidy. Rod Taylor is hardly ideally cast in the title role, but he has stout support from the distinguished ladies in the cast, among them Maggie Smith, Julie Christie, Flora Robson, Edith Evans and Sian Phillips.

Young Dr Kildare ○
1938, US, 81 mins, b/w
Dir: Harold S Bucquet
Stars: Lew Ayres, Lionel Barrymore
Rating: ★★

This is the first 'official' entry of MGM's *Dr Kildare* series, although the first film adaptation of author Max Brand's characters came a year earlier with *Interns Can't Take Money*. Lew Ayres stars as the idealistic medic.

Young Einstein ○ Ⓥ
1988, Australia, 90 mins, colour
Dir: Yahoo Serious
Stars: Yahoo Serious
Rating: ★★★

The wacky, wild-haired Yahoo Serious was already something of an Australian phenomenon when he made this startlingly successful screen debut at 26. Writer, director, singer, comedian and dancer: how's that for a start? As an actor, he's not much yet, but as a filmmaker he proves full of way-out comedy ideas. Indeed, the biggest laughs in this amiable romp stem from its incidental scenes: Einstein's mother contentedly knitting wool unravelling from an unconcerned (talking) sheep, or the cook in the lunatic asylum making a pie with several live kittens in it (not as awful as it sounds!) Serious also takes some inspired pratfalls, and if there aren't many more outright laughs around, the lark remains good-natured and watchable throughout.

Young Frankenstein ❶ ⓥ

1974, US, 105 mins, b/w
Dir: Mel Brooks
Stars: Gene Wilder, Peter Boyle, Marty
Feldman, Madeline Kahn
Rating: ★★

It's a pity that Mel Brooks' film always
sound much funnier than they turn
out. This black-and-white monster mix
is one of the better ones. It is, of
course, a pastiche on the Frankenstein
legend. Or, to be more precise, the
first few Universal films on that subject
in the Thirties. The most successful
scene is a masterpiece of comic business between the Monster (Peter Boyle)
and the blind hermit (an unbilled Gene
Hackman). Gene Wilder has the
thankless task of carrying the lion's
share of both the less funny bits – apart
from a glorious song-and-dance with
the Monster – and the film's slightly
more serious side. A pity that this
misses so many opportunities, if by a
narrow margin, because it still has
enough laughs to keep you entertained.

Young Guns ● ⓥ

1988, US, 107 mins, colour
Dir: Christopher Cain
Stars: Emilio Estevez, Kiefer Sutherland,
Lou Diamond Phillips, Charlie Sheen
Rating: ★★★

Some people thought the Hollywood
Western was in trouble – until the Brat
Pack rode to the rescue. And a pretty
reasonable job, too, they made of these
early adventures of Billy the Kid.
Personable performances by Emilio
Estevez as the kid and Kiefer
Sutherland as his poetic sidekick Doc
help offset a slight overlength in the
telling, and inevitable 'Wild Bunch'
slow-motion at the climactic shootout.
Not that slow motion plays any part in
the rest of the action, of which there's
a lot. Terence Stamp is the
Englishman who harbours young fugitives and helps civilise them while they
work on his ranch, but old Jack
Palance sets the young guns on a
killing spree when he becomes jealous
of Stamp's growing influence and has
him eliminated. The rest of it is tough
and bloody, but varied in content and
rarely dull.

Young Guns II ❶ ⓥ

1990, US, 104 mins, colour
Dir: Geoff Murphy
Stars: Emilio Estevez, Kiefer Sutherland,
Lou Diamond Phillips, Christian Slater
Rating: ★★★★

This gunfire-packed sequel turns its
back on what we learned at the end of

Young Guns about the fates of its characters and tells another, darker, maybe
truer story of Billy the Kid and his
merry men. Director Geoff Murphy, a
New Zealander, gives us vividly
rounded portraits of the characters involved: Emilio Estevez, cackling
maniacally as Billy – still very much
the kid: 'I aim to play the game,' he
says, meaning only partly to see things
through. Kiefer Sutherland's Doc, reluctantly dragged back to outlawry by
a federal dragnet, Lou Diamond
Phillips' superstitious Mexican Indian,
William Peterson's tortured turncoat
Pat Garrett and Viggo Mortensen's
nasty, sardonic Irish John Poe are all
sharply sketched. James Coburn is in
it too, as land boss John Chisum: only
a 'bit', but as authoritatively Coburn
as ever. And Christian Slater's headstrong, self-centred Arkansas Dave
Rudabaugh lends a cutting edge to the
gang's constant flight from the law. A
major new Western that's pretty much
in the old style, with a strikingly rousing score by Alan Silvestri.

Young Guns of Texas ○

1962, US, 84 mins, colour
Dir: Maury Dexter
Stars: James Mitchum, Alana Ladd, Jody
McCrea
Rating: ★★

Boisterous Western about four young
people forced to go on the run after
one of them has killed a man in a gunfight. Its chief attraction lies in the fact
that the offspring of three famous
Hollywood stars play the leading roles.
Director Maury Dexter, who made a
couple of good horror films in the
early Sixties, throws in a mixed bag of
ingredients, including marauding
Apaches, renegade Confederates,
buried gold and even Calamity Jane
(played by Barbara Mansell) to keep
the going lively, and has Western veterans Chill Wills and Robert Lowery
to help him along.

Young in Heart, The ○

1938, US, 95 mins, b/w
Dir: Richard Wallace
Stars: Janet Gaynor, Douglas Fairbanks
Jr, Paulette Goddard, Roland Young
Rating: ★★★★

A delightful romantic comedy about a
family of confidence tricksters who are
reformed by a rich old lady. At the
heart of its success is a witty script by
Paul Osborn and Charles Bennett
from the story *The Gay Banditti* by I A
R Wylie. The banditti in question are
headed by Roland Young and Billie

Burke as the parents, with Janet
Gaynor and Douglas Fairbanks Jr as
their children. Richard Carlson made
his screen debut as Gaynor's suitor.
Sharp and funny, expertly handled by
director Richard Wallace.

Young Lions, The ○ ⓥ

1958, US, 167 mins, b/w
Dir: Edward Dmytryk
Stars: Marlon Brando, Montgomery Clift,
Dean Martin
Rating: ★★★★

Edward Dmytryk's powerful film from
Irwin Shaw's novel of three young soldiers – two American, one German
during World War Two. Marlon
Brando and screenwriter Edward
Anhalt remoulded the central character
of the young Nazi, Christian. The
brute of the book was changed to a
dedicated but humane officer whose
conscience troubles him more and
more until he can no longer shut his
eyes to atrocities committed in the
name of the Reich. Three more outstanding performances – by
Maximilian Schell as the officer whose
wife becomes Christian's mistress,
Parley Baer, as Christian's friend and,
surprisingly, Dean Martin, as the
brasher of the Americans – make this a
film to stay in the memory.

Young Lovers, The ○
(aka: Chance Meeting)

1954, UK, 96 mins, b/w
Dir: Anthony Asquith
Stars: Odile Versois, David Knight
Rating: ★★★★

American boy falls for Russian girl in
London in this fine, moving film, delicately handled by director Anthony
Asquith. Towards the end it becomes
both a love story and a tense thriller in
its own right, as the couple battle to
stay together.

Young Man of Music ○
(aka: Young Man with a Horn)

1949, US, 112 mins, b/w
Dir: Michael Curtiz
Stars: Kirk Douglas, Lauren Bacall, Doris
Day, Hoagy Carmichael
Rating: ★★

Adapted from the Dorothy Baker
book *Young Man with a Horn*, this musical biopic was inspired by the life of
trumpet player Bix Beiderbecke. Kirk
Douglas gives a typically fierce and intense performance as the young man
of the title, but Hoagy Carmichael almost steals the film as his laconic
sidekick Smoke. Although written by
the formidable team of Carl Foreman

Y

and Edmund H North, the screenplay, which is rather a long way from the real facts, tends to be overwrought and contains the classic line: 'Put down your trumpet, jazz man, I'm in the mood for love.'

Young Man with a Horn
See: Young Man of Music

Young Mr Lincoln ○
1939, US, 100 mins, b/w
Dir: John Ford
Stars: Henry Fonda, Alice Brady, Marjorie Weaver, Arleen Whelan
Rating: ★★★

A finely detailed piece of Americana from director John Ford with a sterling performance by Henry Fonda, playing the young Abraham Lincoln as a travelling lawyer of the 1880s. There's a fine supporting performance by Alice Brady (an appealing leading lady of silent times), who had won an Academy Award the previous year for her moving performance in *In Old Chicago*. Unfortunately *Young Mr Lincoln* was to be her last film, before her early death from cancer.

Young Ones, The ⊙ ⓥ
1960, UK, 104 mins, colour
Dir: Sidney J Furie
Stars: Cliff Richard, Carole Gray, Robert Morley
Rating: ★★★★

Music, comedy and drama are combined with an unquenchable get-up-and-go zippy story which raised the level of the British musical to a new high. The song-and-dance routines are brilliantly staged within the framework of a story about a group of teenagers fighting to save their youth club.

Young Poisoner's Handbook, The ● ⓥ
1994, UK, 99 mins, colour
Dir: Benjamin Ross
Stars: Hugh O'Conor, Antony Sher, Charlotte Coleman
Rating: ★★

An ultra-black comedy based on true events, whose Ealing-style treatment doesn't always sustain your interest in its rather unvarying developements. Occasional zany moments in the dialogue – a doctor recommends 'plenty of fluid and no staring into the fire' attempt to counter the horror of the schoolboy scientist (Hugh O'Conor) who undertakes the poisoning of those who oppress him as his life's work. O'Conor does well with this bleak-

eyed role at first, but you do tire of this bizarre film some time before the end. Really a bit sick.

Young Scarface
See: Brighton Rock

Young Sherlock Holmes ○ ⓥ
(aka: Young Sherlock Holmes and the Pyramid of Fear)
1985, US, 109 mins, colour
Dir: Barry Levinson
Stars: Nicholas Rowe, Alan Cox, Sophie Ward
Rating: ★★★

A fun adventure with a schoolboy Sherlock hot on the trail of a strange Egyptian cult who kill anyone who gets in their way. Lively performances from Nicholas Rowe as Holmes and Alan Cox as Watson go a long way towards making up for the silliness of the plot, which kicks off like an old episode of *The Avengers*. Its adventurous spirit is certainly more in keeping with a schoolboy romp than the adult Holmes' more cerebral investigations. The only jarring notes in the narrative are some hallucination scenes, which don't add anything to the story. Stay tuned to the end of the credits – there is an extra scene!

Young Sherlock Holmes and the Pyramid of Fear
See: Young Sherlock Holmes

Young Soul Rebels ● ⓥ
1991, UK, 105 mins, colour
Dir: Isaac Julien
Stars: Valentine Nonyela, Mo Sesau, Dorian Healy
Rating: ★★

You have to hand it to Britain's BFI and Film Four International. There can't be any other companies who would make a film about the black homosexual experience set against the Queen's silver jubilee in 1977. Not only that, but the film also portrays the racial prejudice that prevents even black Djs from making progress in the London of the late Seventies, and tries (not very successfully) to be a murder thriller as well. Performances are rough-edged but good, and the characters have an infectious energy that doesn't let your attention drop. This is no great movie but, given its elements (and its budget), this is probably about as good as it could get. Just don't try fathoming the thriller elements of the plot. You'll guess 'who done it' but still wonder why.

Young Tom Edison ○
1939, US, 82 mins, b/w
Dir: Norman Taurog
Stars: Mickey Rooney, Fay Bainter, George Bancroft
Rating: ★★★

Mickey Rooney was America's top box-office star, ahead of even Clark Gable, when this biography of the inventor's youth was made. It's a surprisingly effective and entertaining picture, relying less on Rooney's personality and mannerisms than almost any other of his star vehicles.

Young Winston ○ ⓥ
1971, UK, 157 mins, colour
Dir: Richard Attenborough
Stars: Robert Shaw, Anne Bancroft, Simon Ward, Anthony Hopkins
Rating: ★★★★

Don't be deceived into thinking that this is a political drama unworthy of your attention. From the opening battle scenes, in strife-torn India before the turn of the century, to Winston Churchill's hair-raising adventures as a correspondent caught up in the Boer War, the exploits of the great man's youth are rousingly recalled by director Richard Attenborough and a stalwart British cast. Simon Ward's portrayal of the young Winston is quite faultless, even if it lacked the magnetism to make him a superstar. But there are colouful characterisations from Anne Bancroft (as Jennie, Lady Churchill), Robert Shaw (as Randolph Churchill), Anthony Hopkins (as David Lloyd George) and especially Pat Heywood as Winston's loving nanny – while the spectacularly shot scenes of desert warfare offer John Mills the chance of a sharp little cameo as Kitchener.

Young Wives' Tale ○
1951, UK, 78 mins, b/w
Dir: Henry Cass
Stars: Joan Greenwood, Nigel Patrick, Derek Farr, Helen Cherry
Rating: ★★

Fast-paced, incident-filled and very British comedy about two young couples who share a home to beat the housing shortage. Some households seem made for mishaps. In this one baths overflow, kettles vainly whistle and the neighbour's dog steals the Sunday joint. The house's three bedrooms. are occupied by the two married couples and a man-hungry girl lodger, played by Audrey Hepburn in one of her earliest film roles, before she went to Hollywood. Anne

Burnaby puts plenty of comic business into her adaptation of Ronald Jeans' stage hit and director Henry Cass keeps the plot bowling along through an endless senes of compromising situations, giving a new twist to the 'not in front of the servants' theme. There are fine comic performances from Joan Greenwood, Nigel Patrick and the moustache-twirling Guy Middleton.

You Only Live Once ○
1937, US, 85 mins, b/w
Dir: Fritz Lang
Stars: Henry Fonda, Sylvia Sidney, William Gargan, Barton MacLane
Rating: ★★★★

A superb early variation on a *Bonnie and Clyde* theme, this consolidated Gemian director Fritz Lang's Hollywood career following his shattering debut with *Fury*. The feeling of the inevitability of doom was never more poignantly captured than in the story of Henry Fonda's ex-convict trying black and white photography is by Leon Shamroy, later to become master of the colour camera. Especially memorable here is a masterly shot of a rain-drenched street in front of a bank, where pedestrians scurry by beneath a canopy of black umbrellas.

You Only Live Twice ○ ⓥ
1967, UK, 117 mins, colour
Dir: Lewis Gilbert
Stars: Sean Connery, Donald Pleasence
Rating: ★★★

James Bond goes east, anticipating future film trends as usual: five years later, martial arts thrillers would be all the rage. Lewis Gilbert directs the plentiful action in fme style, it's definitely the mechanical marvels that hold sway in this adventure. They include a deadly rocket that uses a cigarette as its firing tube, and a speedy one-seat autogiro in which Bond does battle with a fleet of SPECTRE helicopters. The most amusing item though, is a helicopter equipped with an electromagnet - for removing unwanted cars from the highway.

You're a Big Boy Now ◑
1966, US, 96 mins, colour
Dir: Francis Ford Coppola
Stars: Elizabeth Hartman, Geraldine Page, Peter Kastner
Rating: ★★★

This adult comedy about a youth's induction to manhood was a huge critical success at the time. Only one of its stars has progressed notably in the film world since, however: young

Karen Black, who was nominated for an Oscar in *Five Easy Pieces*. But the director did go places. His name was Francis Ford Coppola, and he subsequently made *The Godfather*.

You're In the Army Now
See: O.H.M.S.

You're My Everything ○
1949, US, 94 mins, colour
Dir: Walter Lang
Stars: Dan Dailey, Anne Baxter
Rating: ★★★

Tuneful and sharply scripted variation on the backstage marriage theme, this Dan Dailey movie also takes an amusing look at the Hollywood scene of the Twenties and Thirties. Oscar-winning actress Anne Baxter shows she can go through a dance routine with the best of them, Shad Robinson is a sweet tot in the best Shirley Temple tradition and Buster Keaton has a few wildly funny moments as a delightfully improbable butler.

You're Never Too Young ⊙
1955, US, 102 mins, colour
Dir: Norman Taurog
Stars: Dean Martin, Jerry Lewis
Rating: ★★★

Another remake, as were many of the Dean Martin-Jerry Lewis comedies, this time of *The Minor and the Major*, a 1942 hit, in which Ginger Rogers played the Jerry Lewis role of the woman/man who dresses as a child on a train to avoid a murderer. This time round, it's Raymond Burr, now thoroughly moulded as a television goodie, who plays the villain.

You're Telling Me ⊙
1934, US, 67 mins, b/w
Dir: Eric C Kenton
Stars: W C Fields, Larry Buster Crabbe
Rating: ★★★

Vintage comedy classic with henpecked Fields' friendship with a visiting princess enabling the worm to turn. The great golfing sequence is probably the best of his many old routines.

Z

Zandalee ● ⓥ
1990, US, 104 mins, colour
Dir: Sam Pillsbury
Stars: Nicolas Cage, Judge Reinhold, Erika Anderson, Viveca Lindfors, Joe Pantoliano, Marisa Tomei
Rating: ★

Nicolas Cage has made some pretty loony movies in his time, and this sex-filled Southern States steamer is so off kilter as to be almost round the bend. It's not so much *Wild Orchid* as *Wild Magnolia*, as Cage's painter drifts into New Orleans, and into the life of leggy Zandalee (the seldom-clad Erika Anderson) whose mind rarely strays off sex and whose husband Judge Reinhold), a poet turned enforced businessman, just happens not to be giving her any. This is the kind of sleazy subject European soft-porn filmmakers were flooding the market with in the Seventies, dressed up here with some ragin' Cajun music and vapidly coloured Louisiana locations which executive producer Reinhold presumably afforded by saving on Anderson's wardrobe. It seems amazing that a couple of fairly major stars could find nothing better to do than make this overcooked kettle of catfish pie.

Zarak ○
1956, UK, 99 mins, colour
Dir: Terence Young
Stars: Victor Mature, Michael Wilding, Anita Ekberg
Rating: ★★

Although never quite credible, this is a colourful adventure yarn, set in old India, but in fact shot on location in Spanish Morocco! The realism of the battle scenes was such that the first-aid unit was kept as busy as the crew and cast. In the charging mêlées, dozens of extras came a cropper, Michael Wildin cracked three ribs and Victor Mature suffered concussion from an ill-timed blow. The film was a hit with the public although not kindly received by the critics. The writer, producers and director had the last laugh, though, six years later, when they made an even more successful film - *Dr No*.

Zardoz ●
1973, UK, 105 mins, colour
Dir: John Boorman
Stars: Sean Connery, Charlotte

Z

Rampling
Rating: ★★

A sort of *2001: A Space Odyssey*. But the basic concept of this adult fable, set in the 23rd century, is *The Wizard of Oz* – as the title indicates. Some critics thought the resultant work (directed by John Boorman) was tinged with genius, while others condemned it as pretentious drivel. Whatever your verdict, you'll agree that Sean Connery compels attention as the 'Brutal' who finds himself betrayed by his masters and vows vengeance – especially on the 'Eternals' who live for ever.

Zebra In the Kitchen ⊙
1965, US, 93 mins, colour
Dir: Ivan Tors
Stars: Jay North, Martin Milner, Andy Devine
Rating: ★★

Animal film directed by Ivan Tors, creator of the television series *Flipper* and *Daktari*. It's a riotous comedy set in the city, about a boy who lets all the animals out of his local zoo.

Zelig ◑ Ⓥ
1983, US, 79 mins, b/w
Dir: Woody Allen
Stars: Woody Allen, Mia Farrow
Rating: ★★★★

A highly original comedy that restored Woody Allen's stature in the genre after some early Eighties' lapses. He plays a mysterious figure from the past, traced by contemporary' newsreel, whose longing for friendship and companionship gave him the power to turn himself into likenesses of those whom he was with. More clever than funny but marvellously hypnotic to watch, and with a few typically goofy Allen asides. As well as marrying several wives in various identities, his character is accused of 'performing unnecessary dental extraction'! His story is related (in a dig at *Reds*) by 'witnesses', including a couple of aged reporters. 'You just told the truth,' says one, 'and it sold papers. It never happened before!'

Zeppelin ◯
1971, UK, 101 mins, colour
Dir: Etienne Perier
Stars: Michael York, Elke Sommer, Peter Carsten, Marius Goring
Rating: ★

World War One adventure fiasco with Michael York as an Allied spy trying to pinch the Zeppelin plans from the Germans. The glamorous Elke

Sommer is an unlikely aviatrix, and Marius Goring pops up as her professor husband. The rest of the cast includes such reliable German 'types' as Anton Diffring and Peter Carsten.

Ziegfeld Follies ◯ Ⓥ
1944, US, 110 mins, colour
Dir: Vincente Minnelli
Stars: Fred Astaire, Lucille Ball, Judy Garland, Kathryn Grayson, William Powell, Gene Kelly
Rating: ★★★

The third and last of MGM's Ziegfeld musicals is a straightforward revue directed by Vincente Minnelli who had worked on some of the Great Flo's stage extravaganzas.

Zigzag
See: False Witness

Zorba the Greek ◯ Ⓥ
1964, US, 131 mins, b/w
Dir: Michael Cacoyannis
Stars: Anthony Quinn, Alan Bates
Rating: ★★★★

A long and patiently made picture with a twofold aim. It tells both of the rites and customs of a small Cretan Village, and of a young Englishman (Alan Bates) who comes to the village to reopen the disused mine that belonged to his late father. His major domo is Zorba, a real character, played with careful relish by Anthony Quinn, who has his own madcap schemes for reworking the mine. Full of long, lingering pans from the artistic camera of Walter Lassally, who took one of the film's three Academy Awards, *Zorba* is, at its best, both human and amusing. It also has its horrifying moments, such as a throat-slitting, and the looting of a dead woman's house by old crones who look like so many black cockroaches. The performances are topped by that of Lila Kedrova (another Academy Award winner) with her brilliant, almost gruesome portrait of the fading countess.

Zorro, the Gay Blade ◑
1981, US, 93 mins, colour
Dir: Peter Medak
Stars: George Hamilton, Lauren Hutton, Brenda Vaccaro
Rating: ★

Spoof variation on the Zorro legend, but the pacing is all wrong for high voltage laughter. George Hamilton mugs frantically as the foppish son of the fimous swordsrnan and his lookalike gay brother Bunny.

Zulu ◯ Ⓥ
1963, UK, 138 mins, colour
Dir: Cy Endfield
Stars: Stanley Baker, Jack Hawkins, James Booth, Michael Caine
Rating: ★★★★

This is that rarity in film – an all-action, no-frills, straightforward recreation of an heroic moment in history. On this occasion, the action concerns the Zulu wars in South Africa and, in particular, the electrifying Battle of Rorke's Drift in 1879, where little more than 100 men of the South Wales Borderers made a staggeringly brave stand against 4,000 yelling Zulu warriors, who had just massacred a force of over 1,000 British troops. It is in the supporting roles that the film finds its own strength. James Booth, as the malingering Private Hook, Nigel Green, as the colour-sergeant, Ivor Emmanuel (in his only film appearance) and Kelly Jordan (the camp cook) all give exemplary service. And then-newcomer Michael Caine is so impressive it's amazing he wasn't snapped up for more star roles long before *The Ipcress File*. The last scenes of *Zulu*, as rank after rank of the last defenders pour leaden defiance at the Zulus from a few yards' range, are pulsatingly thrilling.

Zulu Dawn ◯
1979, US, 121 mins, colour
Dir: Douglas Hickox
Stars: Burt Lancaster, Peter O'Toole, Simon Ward
Rating: ★★★

This spectacular account of the events leading up to those shown in the famous film *Zulu* is an outstanding piece of movie-making craftsmanship, especially in its deployment of the vast forces used in its epic battle scenes. Burt Lancaster has a key role as Colonel Durnford, a one-armed veteran of numerous African campaigns, and Peter O'Toole plays General Lord Chelmsford in command of the British forces.